PICTURE INDUSTRY

A Provisional History of the Technical Image 1844–2018

Edited, with an introduction by
Walead Beshty

Foreword by
Maja Hoffmann
Tom Eccles

LUMA CCS BARD

Table of contents

Foreword 17
Maja Hoffmann and Tom Eccles

Acknowledgments 19

Introduction: The Commons in the Age of Its Technological Reproducibility 20
Walead Beshty

TAKEN FROM HERE TO WHERE IT CAME FROM AND TAKEN TO A PLACE AND USED IN SUCH A MANNER THAT IT CAN ONLY REMAIN AS A REPRESENTATION OF WHAT IT WAS WHERE IT CAME FROM 34
Lawrence Weiner
1980

Introductory Remarks and Selected Plates from *Pencil of Nature* 36
William Henry Fox Talbot
1844–46

A Scene in a Library: The First Photographically Illustrated Book 41
Carol Armstrong
1998

The Stereoscope and Stereograph 54
Oliver Wendell Holmes
1859

Selections from *Mechanisms of Human Facial Expression* 62
Guillaume-Amant Duchenne de Boulogne
1862

Photographs of the High Rockies in *Harper's New Monthly Magazine*, Vol. CCXXXII, No. 39, September 1869 68
John Samson [likely a pseudonym of Timothy H. O'Sullivan]

Photography's Discursive Spaces 80
Rosalind E. Krauss
1986

Naming the View 89
Alan Trachtenberg
1990

United States Geological Exploration of the Fortieth Parallel, Volume III: Mining Industry 106
James D. Hague and Clarence King
1870

Report on the United States and Mexican Boundary Survey, Vol. I 110
William H. Emory
1857

Prefatory Note and Preface to *United States Geological Survey of the Territories, Descriptive Catalogue of Photographs of North American Indians* 112
Ferdinand Vandeveer Hayden and William Henry Jackson
1877

Colorchromes from the Detroit Photographic Company 114
William Henry Jackson
1892–1903

Carte de visite 118
Sojourner Truth
1864

Introduction to *Enduring Truths: Sojourner's Shadows and Substance* 119
Darcy Grimaldo Grigsby
2015

The Golden Caribbean, Vol. II, No. 1, January 1904 125
United Fruit Company

The Evidence of Things Not Photographed: Slavery and Historical Memory in the British West Indies 135
Krista Thompson
2011

The Other Half and How They Live: Story in Pictures [Reconstruction of a Magic Lantern Slide Lecture Presented at the Sixth Annual Convention of Christian Workers] 146
Jacob Riis
1891

How the Other Half Lives: Studies Among the Tenements in *Scribner's* Magazine, Vol. VI, No. 6, December 1889 162
Jacob Riis

Inquiries into Human Faculty and Its Development 167
Francis Galton
1883

Physiological Study of Normal Walking 170
Georges Gilles de la Tourette
1885

Notes on Gesture 175
Giorgio Agamben
2000

Selections from *Theoretical Study of Signalment* 179
Alphonse Bertillon
1896

Bertillon System of Criminal Identification [Selected by Cameron Rowland] 194
National Law Enforcement Museum Website
2018

TABLE OF CONTENTS

Selection from *Attitudes of Animals in Motion* 195
Eadweard Muybridge
1882

Selections from *Animal Locomotion* 196
Eadweard Muybridge
1887

Iron Horses: Leland Stanford, Eadweard Muybridge, and the Industrialized Eye 200
John Ott
2005

Physiologie du mouvement: le vol des oiseaux 209
Étienne-Jules Marey
1890

Chronophotography 212
Étienne-Jules Marey
1899

Marey and the Organization of Work 222
Marta Braun
1994

Selections of X-Ray Photographs from *Journal of Electrochemistry* 231
Wilhelm Röntgen
1896–97

On a New Kind of Rays 233
Wilhelm Röntgen
1896

Injured Right Hand of Workman in *The Röntgen Rays in Medical Work* 235
David Walsh
1897

Still from *Workers Leaving the Lumière Factory* 236
Louis and Auguste Lumière
1895

Still from *Employees Leaving Williamson's Factory, Lancaster* 237
Still from *Employees Leaving Messrs Vickers & Maxim's in Barrow*
Sagar Mitchell and James Kenyon
1901

Preface to *Motion Study: A Method for Increasing the Efficiency of the Workman* 238
Frank B. Gilbreth
1911

Motion Study Photographs 239
Frank B. Gilbreth
1913–1917

Radiography, Cinematography and the Decline of the Lens 240
Lisa Cartwright and Brian Goldfarb
1992

Selections from: *Charities and The Commons,* and *The Survey,* 1908–1913 246
Lewis Hine

The Homestead Plant: Carnegie Steel Company in *Homestead: The Households of a Mill Town,* Vol. 4 250
Lewis Hine
1910

Production – Reproduction 252
László Moholy-Nagy
1922

War Against War! 254
Ernst Friedrich
1924

Ernst Friedrich's Pacifistic Anarchism 260
Douglas Kellner
1987

Der Mensch als Industriepalast 264
Fritz Kahn
1926

Selections from *Das Leben des Menschen, Eine volkstümliche Anatomie, Biologie, Physiologie und Entwicklungeschichte des Menschen* 265
Fritz Kahn
1926–1931

Photography 266
Siegfried Kracauer
1927

Perspective as Symbolic Form 274
Erwin Panofsky
1927

(Not) In Place: The Grid, or, Cultural Techniques of Ruling Spaces 282
Bernhard Siegert
2015

Dictionary: Man in *Documents 4* 294
Georges Bataille
1929

Type 89 Moving-image Machine-gun Camera, Kai 2, Serial No. 7967 295
Manufactured by Rokuoh-sha [currently Konica Minolta Electronics Co., Ltd.]
Produced from 1933–44

Selections from *Arbeiter-Illustrierte Zeitung* 296
John Heartfield
1930–32

The Work of Art in the Age of Its Technological Reproducibility (Second Version) 300
Walter Benjamin
1935–36

TABLE OF CONTENTS

There Are No Mass Media
Bernhard Siegert
2003 312

Julian Sander, Great-Grandson of August Sander, as Recounted to Walead Beshty
2017 316

Student of Philosophy [Erich Sander], 1926
Political Prisoner [Erich Sander], 1943
Death Mask of Erich Sander, 1944
August Sander 317

Images in Spite of All
Georges Didi-Huberman
2008 320

A Mathematical Theory of Communication
Claude Shannon
1948 328

Woman Operating a Hollerith Pantographic Card-Punching Machine
Harris and Ewing Studio [George W. Harris and Martha Ewing]
ca. 1915 336

Computing Machinery and Intelligence
Alan Turing
1950 337

Labor Anonymous in *Fortune* Magazine, November 1946
Selections from *Fortune* Magazine, 1941–1962
Homes of Americans in *Fortune* Magazine, 1946
Walker Evans 340

Walker Evans: The Magazine Work
David Campany
2014 358

Nation Horrified by Murder of Kidnapped Chicago Youth in *Jet* Magazine, Vol. XIII, No. 19, September 15, 1955 362

Emmett Till Ever After
Darby English
2013 364

The Restraints: Open and Hidden in *LIFE* Magazine, September 24, 1956
Selections from *Ebony* and *LIFE* Magazine, 1947–1968
Gordon Parks 372

They Fight a Fire That Won't Go Out in *LIFE* Magazine, May 17, 1963
Charles Moore 388

Mechanical ("The Dogs' Attack is Negroes' Reward," from LIFE Magazine, May 17, 1963)
Andy Warhol
1964 390

Race Riot 391
Andy Warhol
1964

Roentgenizdat [bootleg audio recording on X-ray film] 392
Unknown makers
ca. 1960s

The Medium Is the Message 397
Marshall McLuhan
1964

Poem, March 1966 in *Aspen* Magazine, No. 5+6, 1967 400
Dan Graham

My Works for Magazine Pages: A History of Conceptual Art, 1965–1969 403
Dan Graham
1985

Homes for America [photo offset reproduction of layout for magazine article] 406
Dan Graham
1972

Selections from *House Beautiful: Bringing the War Home* 408
Martha Rosler
ca. 1967–72

Tron (Amputee) in *Goodbye to All That*, No. 3, October 13, 1970 410
Martha Rosler

Amarillo—Tall in Texas 412
Stephen Shore
1971

Still from *Phi Phenomenon* 414
Morgan Fisher
1968

Phi Phenomenon 415
Morgan Fisher
1976

Preparation Plants from Coal Mines 418
Bernd and Hilla Becher
1966–78

[Untitled] in *January 5–13, 1969* 422
Douglas Huebler

Projects Class 424
David Askevold
1969

Advertisements in *Artforum* Magazine, 1968–69 426
Stephen Kaltenbach

TABLE OF CONTENTS

Misunderstandings (A Theory of Photography) 430
Mel Bochner
1970

Still from *Finally Got the News* 432
Stewart Bird, Rene Lichtman, and Peter Gessner
1970

Still from *Hour of the Furnaces* 433
Fernando Solanas and Octavio Getino
1968

Towards a Third Cinema: Notes and Experiences for the Development of a Cinema of Liberation in the Third World 434
Fernando Solanas and Octavio Getino
1969

Photograph and Screen 439
Stanley Cavell
1971

Ideological Effects of the Basic Cinematographic Apparatus 441
Jean-Louis Baudry
1974

Cover and Preface to *How To Read Donald Duck: Imperialist Ideology in the Disney Comic* 448
Ariel Dorfman and Armand Mattelart
1975

A Declaration of Dependence 450
Sarah Charlesworth
1975

Washing/Tracks/Maintenance: Outside 455
Mierle Laderman Ukeles
1973

Advertisement in *Artforum* Magazine, November 1974 458
Lydia Benglis

Magazine Actions in *Fiesta* Magazine, Vol. 10, No. 7, 1976 460
Cosey Fanni Tutti

Still from *Eadweard Muybridge, Zoopraxographer* 462
Thom Andersen
1976

Five Notes for a Phenomenology of the Photographic Image 463
Hubert Damisch
1963

Mapplethorped: Art, Photography, and the Pornographic Imagination 465
Richard Meyer
2016

X Portfolio
Robert Mapplethorpe
1977–78 467

Photography *en abyme*
Craig Owens
1978 470

Young Workers
Jeff Wall
1978/1983 478

Artist Statement from *Horror Pleni: Pictures in New York Today*
Ericka Beckman
1980 480

Selections from *Camera Lucida: Reflections on Photography*
Roland Barthes
1982 481

Allegorical Procedures: Appropriation and Montage in Contemporary Art
Benjamin H. D. Buchloh
1982 489

Selections from *Travel Posters*
Barbara Bloom
1981/2009 498

After Walker Evans: 1–22
Sherrie Levine
1981 500

Collection of Ten Plaster Surrogates
Allan McCollum
1982/1990 504

Arrangements of Pictures in *October*, Vol. 26, 1983
Louise Lawler 506

Still from *Sans Soleil*
Chris Marker
1983 510

Wild Dead
Gretchen Bender
1984 511

Towards a Philosophy of Photography
Vilém Flusser
1983 512

Still from *Standard Gauge*
Morgan Fisher
1984 518

TABLE OF CONTENTS

Standard Gauge 519
Morgan Fisher
1984

Introduction to *Gramophone, Film, Typewriter* 523
Friedrich A. Kittler
1986

Still from *Handsworth Songs* 532
Black Audio Film Collective
1986

Black Audio Film Collective: John Akomfrah, Reece Auguiste, Lina Gopaul, and Avril Johnson 533
Coco Fusco
1987

Selections from *Cray at Chippewa Falls: Photographs by Lee Friedlander* 542
Lee Friedlander
1987

Ektachrome Archive 546
Lyle Ashton Harris
1986–96

Lyle Ashton Harris on Ektachrome Archive (1986–1996), as told to Alpesh Kantilal Patel 548
2015

Scripts from *Monodramas* 549
Stan Douglas
1987–1991

News Hour Viewer Call-in Segment Regarding Original Broadcast of Stan Douglas's *Monodramas* 555
BCTV
1992

Herald Tribune, January 18–February 28, 1991 556
Sarah Charlesworth
1991

The Gesture of Video 558
Vilém Flusser
1991

Red Portfolio 560
Glenn Ligon
1993

Self Portrait (James Dean) 565
Jack Pierson
1993

Hiatus: Work in Progress Lecture 566
Ericka Beckman
1993

Video and Resistance: Against Documentaries 568
Critical Art Ensemble
1994

'Can you be BLACK and Look at This?': Reading the Rodney King Videos 574
Elizabeth Alexander
1994

Being the Subject of Art 583
bell hooks
1995

Still From *Workers Leaving the Factory* 586
Harun Farocki
1995

Workers Leaving the Factory 587
Harun Farocki
2004

Automation of Sight: From Photography to Computer Vision 591
Lev Manovich
1996

Selections from *Case History* 598
Boris Mikhailov
1997–1998

Case History 601
Boris Mikhailov
1999

Selections from *Venezia Marghera Series* 604
Lewis Baltz
1999/2011

Strike Objects 606
Jean-Luc Moulène
1999

Selections from *Inflight* Magazine, 2000 626
Johan Grimonprez

Post-Documentary, Post-Photography? 634
Martha Rosler
2001

schema; Aquafresh plus Crest with whitener 644
schema; Aquafresh plus Crest with Scope
Kelley Walker
2003

Civilian (adjusted to fit) 647
Louise Lawler
2010/2011

TABLE OF CONTENTS

Black Mo'nin' 648
Fred Moten
2003

Orange 657
de Rijke/de Rooij
2004

Stills from *Eye/Machine I, II, and III* 658
Harun Farocki
2001–2003

Phantom Images 659
Harun Farocki
2004

Live Evil (Kuala Lumpur) 663
Paul Pfeiffer
2003

Digital Video Effect: "Holes" 664
Seth Price
2003

The Full Edition of Smoke and Mirrors 24A 666
Eileen Quinlan
2006

Protocol 668
Alexander R. Galloway
2006

Documentary Uncertainty 671
Hito Steyerl
2007

Supplement '14 (Mixed Typologies) #6 676
Christopher Williams
2014

Christopher Williams in Conversation with Mark Godfrey 678
2007

Declassification 683
United States Department of Defense Website
2018

From the Redaction Paintings Series 684
Jenny Holzer
2007

The Civil Contract of Photography 686
Ariella Azoulay
2008

Still from *Episode III: Enjoy Poverty* 706
Renzo Martens
2008

Toward a New Institutional Critique: A Conversation with Renzo Martens 707
T. J. Demos
2012

Still from *Exit (Bath Iron Works, July 7–11, 2008, Bath, Maine)* 712
Sharon Lockhart
2008

On Compression 713
Cory Arcangel
2008

Repression and the Information Boom 717
Zuhair al-Jezairy
2005

Redistribution (video transcript) 720
Seth Price
2010

Dailies from Rythm Mastr 726
Kerry James Marshall
2010

Still from *In Free Fall* 728
Hito Steyerl
2010

In Free Fall: A Thought Experiment on Vertical Perspective 729
Hito Steyerl
2011

Photography and the Law: Five Groundbreaking Cases of Photography in Litigation 735
Daniel McClean
2011

Still from *The Unstable Object* 739
Daniel Eisenberg
2011

Still from *Workers Leaving the Googleplex* 740
Andrew Norman Wilson
2011

Still from *Touching Reality* 742
Thomas Hirschhorn
2012

Why Is It Important—Today—to Show and Look at Images of Destroyed Human Bodies? 743
Thomas Hirschhorn
2012

TABLE OF CONTENTS

You've Lost That Loving Feeling: Rineke Dijkstra After Empathy 746
Johanna Burton
2012

Diane Arbus: A Printed Retrospective, 1960–1971 751
Pierre Leguillon
2012

Anonymous Needs and Desires (Various Castoffs: Ceramic Tile, Potato Chips, Garlic, Men's Socks, Blackberry, iPod, Baby Food, Perfume, Chocolate, and Cigarettes) 752
Liz Glynn
2012

Truth Study Center 754
Wolfgang Tillmans
2016

The Tower 757
Hito Steyerl
2015

In Defense of Representation 758
Tristan Garcia
2015

Great Things Never Come from Comfort Zones in *i-D* Magazine, No. 336, 2015 762
Wolfgang Tillmans

Infrastructuralism 768
John Durham Peters
2015

The Distributed Image 772
Peter Osborne
2015

Untitled 776
Isa Genzken
2016

Parasagittal Brain 777
Yngve Holen
2013

Flint is Family in *Elle* Magazine, September 2016 778
LaToya Ruby Frazier

The Phantasmagoric Dispositif: An Assembly of Bodies and Images in Real Time and Space 788
Noam M. Elcott
2016

Handpunch 801
Cameron Rowland
2014–2015

Love Is the Message, the Message Is Death 804
Arthur Jafa
2016

Love is the Message, The Plan is Death 805
Arthur Jafa and Tina Campt
2017

Martha Rosler in Conversation with Walead Beshty 812
2017

Stephen Shore in Conversation with Walead Beshty 814
2017

Stan Douglas in Conversation with Walead Beshty 816
2016

Hito Steyerl in Conversation with Walead Beshty 827
2017

James Merle Thomas in Conversation with Walead Beshty 834
2018

Contributors 842

Index 852

Thanks 858

Credits 859

Colophon 863

Citation style, idiosyncratic spelling, and unusual capitalization have been modernized following *The Chicago Manual of Style*, 17th edition (2017). Any alterations to original texts are designated by the use of an editorial bracket and ellipses ([...]). Complete bibliographic and copyright information for all texts can be found in the "Contributors" section of this volume.

Foreword
Maja Hoffmann and Tom Eccles

Picture Industry: A Provisional History of the Technical Image (1844–2018) offers a poignant reflection both from the formative moments of photographic history and also contemporary responses to that history (and those texts) from our current condition of one that refutes universalization whether through race, gender, or class. But Beshty's argument goes further to suggest that the photographic medium is also affirmative, providing the means to counter dominant narratives in highly responsive ways.

In this, *Picture Industry* aims to complicate traditional accounts of photography, drawing from its role within science, the humanities and contemporary art. As media that derive their potency from the ability to circulate—in a sense, the ability to easily *reproduce*—Walead Beshty argues that photography and film are not reflections of the world and its inequities, but rather constitutive in processes of colonization, class repression, criminalization, racism. This is particularly so with regards to modes of circulation. The texts included here offer a poignant reflection from the formative moments of photographic history and also contemporary responses to that history from a current perspective that refutes universalization whether through race, gender or class. But Beshty's argument goes further to suggest that the photographic medium is also affirmative, providing the means to counter dominant narratives in highly responsive ways.

For this publication, Beshty has also drawn from the artists and artworks featured in the exhibition, *Picture Industry*, presented at the Parc des Ateliers, Luma Arles (2016[1] and 2018) and at the Center for Curatorial Studies, Bard College (2017). The wide variety of materials that constituted the three exhibitions (including collections of photographs, slide projections, periodicals, wallpaper, films and recent video installations, sculptures, and printed works on paper) created numerous situations within which to consider not only the materiality of images and the technologies that form their reception, but also the conflicted social history that lies under their surfaces and is inextricable from their origins.

Art historian Noam Elcott, in his *Artforum* review of the exhibition states: "*Picture Industry* has quietly thrown down the gauntlet, not only for exhibitions that address the history of photography, but for all future surveys of twentieth-century art and political imagery broadly....Stated polemically, the argument is that photography does not exist—only photographic platforms do; the photograph does not exist—only its circulation does."[2]

For the Luma Foundation (and on this occasion our partners at the Center for Curatorial Studies, Bard College), *Picture Industry* represents an ongoing research project into image production and its distribution—a component part of an archipelago of programs that broadly address the artistic, environmental and human rights urgencies of our time.[3]

Picture Industry is the result of a multi-year investigation and curatorial project that has benefitted from the efforts of many collaborators. Our thanks first and foremost to Walead Beshty for his original vision, tireless research and ongoing commitment to a project that at times seemed without bounds. The challenges presented by Beshty's ambitiously broad-ranging vision for *Picture Industry* were equally matched by our various teams of collaborators, registrars, exhibition organizers, editors and

1 *Picture Industry* was commissioned and produced by the Luma Foundation for the Parc des Ateliers in Arles, France as part of *Systematically Open? New Forms for Contemporary Image Production* (July–December 2016).
2 Noam Elcott, *Picture Industry*, CCS Bard Hessel Museum, *Artforum* magazine, December 2017
3 See *The Human Snapshot*, edited by Thomas Keenan and Tirdad Zolghadr, 2013, and *The Flood of Rights*, edited by Thomas Keenan, Tirdad Zolghadr and Suhail Malick, 2017, Luma Foundation, Center for Curatorial Studies, Sternberg Press.

designers. We would like to extend a special thanks to Bryne Rasmussen and John Ryan Moore at Walead Beshty Studios, Luz Gyalui at Luma Arles, and Marcia Acita and Amy Linker at CCS Bard, without whom this project could not have been accomplished. The early development of this publication benefitted greatly from the extensive research and editorial efforts of Molly Everett and Andrew Blackley. We are particularly grateful for the dedicated work of editor James Merle Thomas and designer Ria Roberts, both of whom embraced the task of producing such an extensive publication within a limited timespan. And finally, our thanks to all our colleagues who together made this project possible.

Maja Hoffmann
Founder and Executive President
Luma Foundation

Tom Eccles
Executive Director
CCS Bard

Acknowledgments

Walead Beshty

Individuals who find themselves responsible for projects of this scale, duration and complexity invariably owe a great many debts, and what follows is only a partial accounting. Firstly, my sincere thanks to the artists, scholars, writers, and the respective estates and foundations who placed their trust in me and the conception of this project. To Maja Hoffmann and the Luma Foundation for support throughout, from the initial invitation to organize a small group show, to the project's rapid expansion into the complex exhibitions and the weighty volume that resulted, I owe my greatest thanks.

My gratitude to Liam Gillick who initially invited me to take part in *Systematically Open?*, where this project first began to take on its current shape, and to Luz Gyalui who toiled to execute what became its increasingly ambitious scope. They were both central to the project's early development, and continued to enrich it at each stage. I would like to thank Tom Eccles not only for seeing the potential in that exhibition, extending the invitation to expand it to several times its original scale for CCS Bard, and to bring that richer exhibition back to Arles, but also for encouraging my conviction in the value of what at the time seemed an unrealizably ambitious publication; I owe him a major debt for his unrelenting faith, support, and enthusiasm for the project, and most of all, his friendship and unflagging generosity with his time and thoughts throughout.

The teams at Luma Arles and at CCS Bard who worked on that exhibition, especially Marcia Acita and Amy Linker, were dedicated colleagues. I owe a debt of thanks to Molly Everett and Andrew Blackley who worked on this volume in its earliest phases, and the team who took over under the direction of James Merle Thomas. I could not have hoped for a more thoughtful, invested, resourceful, or generous collaborator, and he along with Ria Roberts's intelligence and flexibility as a designer were core to this volume's realization; their patience, fortitude, and dedication, is everywhere present in what follows. I also owe a huge debt of thanks to my studio who collectively logged innumerable hours on this project, while keeping everything else running smoothly: to John Ryan Moore, my studio manager for more than a decade, and to my staff Robert Acklen-Brečko, Thomas Lucero, Suzanna Zak, and especially to Bryne Rasmussen, who for the past three and a half years was instrumental in all the phases of this exhibition and the accompanying volume, from conception to conclusion it bears the marks of her tireless efforts, the project and my sanity would not have survived without her.

In particular I would like to single out the following people who provided personal support and encouragement, generously offering their time and consideration to the realization of this project: Hans Ulrich Obrist, Julian Sander, LaToya Ruby Frazier, Martha Rosler, Stephen Shore, Hito Steyerl, Stan Douglas, Sharon Lockhart, Jeff Wall, Louise Lawler, Cameron Rowland, Morgan Fisher, Kelley Walker, Thomas Hirschhorn, Liz Deschenes, Miljohn Ruperto, Wolfgang Tillmans, Paul Pfeiffer, Eileen Quinlan, Johan Grimonprez, Armelle Pradalier, Johanna Burton, Noam M. Elcott, Daniel McClean, Michal Raz-Russo, Robbie Myers, Peter W. Kunhardt, Jr. and the Gordon Parks Foundation, George Baker, Russell Ferguson, Hamza Walker, Matthew S. Witkovsky, Shaun Caley Regen, Jennifer Loh, Friedrich Petzel, Jane Park, Eva Presenhuber, Rodolphe Janssen, Thomas Dane, François Chantala, and finally Kristen Carpenter, who put up with me at my most insufferable, and never wavered in her loving support.

Finally, this project is dedicated to the memory of my father, Bahjat Sadek Beshty, whose passionate and rigorous pursuit of knowledge, and belief in the boundless potential of ideas to bring a richer world into being, instilled in me a set of values which this volume, and the project it describes, aspires to.

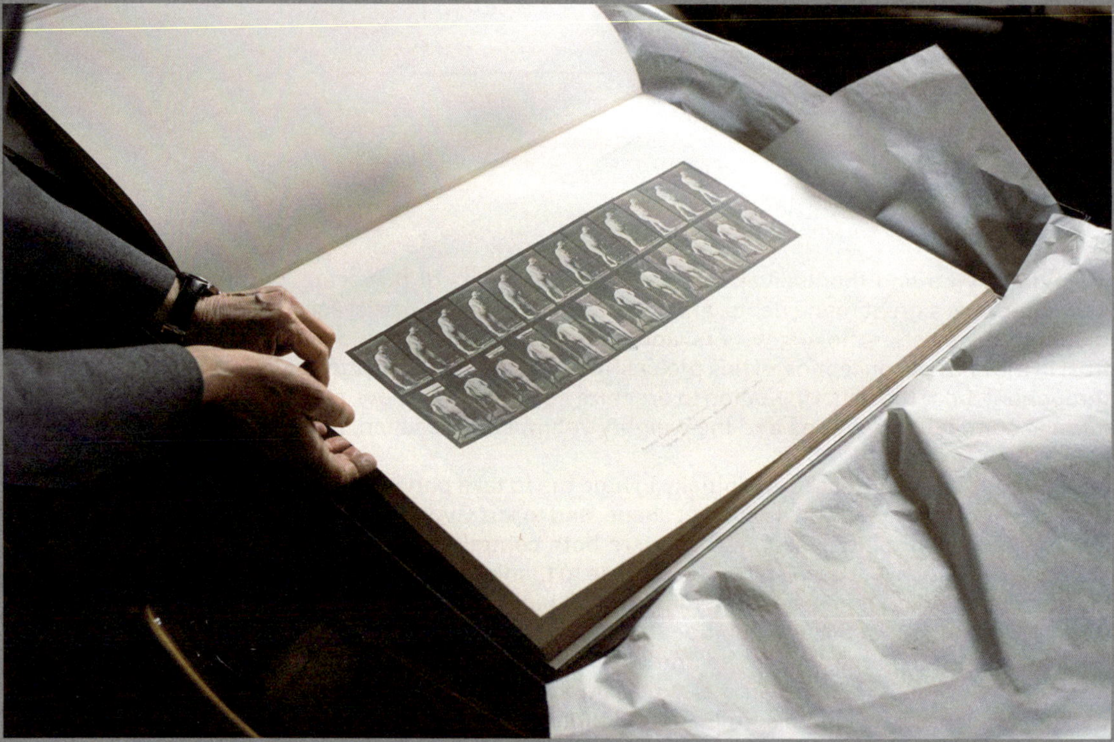

Walead Beshty, *Scene in a Library (Galerie de Morphologie, École Nationale Supérieure des Beaux-Arts, Paris, France, March 12, 2013; Roll 4: Frame No. 31)*, 2014.

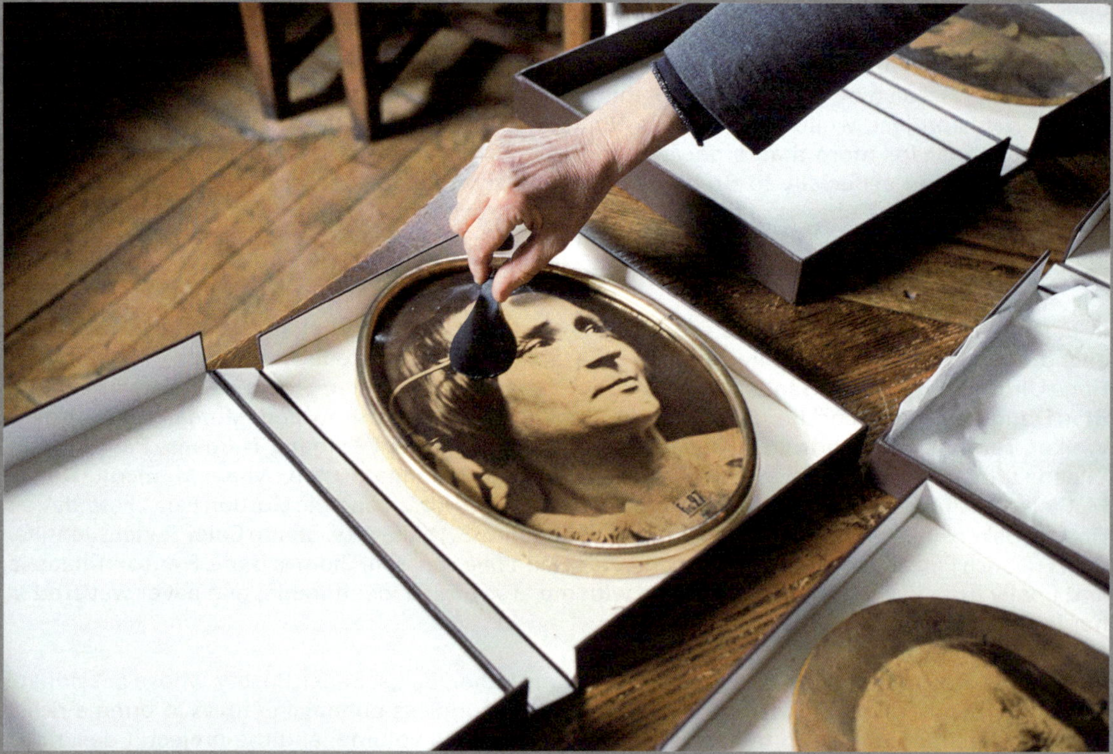

Walead Beshty, *Scene in a Library (Galerie de Morphologie, École Nationale Supérieure des Beaux-Arts, Paris, France, March 12, 2013; Roll 3: Frame No. 7)*, 2014.

The Commons in the Age of Its Technological Reproducibility

Walead Beshty

Woe to those who, to the very end, insist on regulating the movement that exceeds them with the narrow mind of the mechanic who changes a tire.
—Georges Bataille

1. ON ~~PHOTOGRAPHY~~

I am going to begin with a note about an exclusion. The exclusion of a term, both tenacious and hollow, that has loomed over the majority of my professional activities. A term that, in the vernacular, can be used to describe (and misdescribe) much of what comprises this book and the exhibition that it accompanies; a term that may very well appear in this volume with greater frequency than any other. While it has codified a number of significant debates in the twentieth century, inspiring some of the most ambitious and seminal writing on aesthetics—many examples of which are included here—its relevance now appears deeply limited. It is a term whose seeming matter-of-factness is no longer precise or provocative, that is, it neither accurately describes a set of practices we might call a discipline (for it is too archaic and arbitrary in its inclusions and exclusions, too dispersed in its methods), nor is it conceptually useful. For it offers neither a stable developmental trajectory, nor does it provide a *frame*—a device within which one may gather objects and ideas, and regard them with the complexity or specificity that our contemporary world demands. Instead it arbitrarily links together disparate objects with radically different conditions of production and reception, while producing distinctions between things that are intertwined historically and technologically. In short, the term fails us both practically and epistemologically. For more than a decade I have been drawn back to it over and again in attempts to understand its persistence in scholarship and in art; I have written numerous times on the organizational predispositions that perpetuate it, the intellectual problems it fosters, and the aesthetic practices it obscures or renders illegible. It is a term that I hope this volume allows me to leave behind as a minor category to be absorbed into a broader, more urgent historical trajectory, satisfied that the rich complexity it suffocates has been, at least in part, addressed.

Despite long feeling discomfort at its use, my first formal and focused responses began in the mid-2000s, culminating in a text that dismissed it (and the field it purported to describe) as an anachronism:

> Despite being vaguely nostalgic, and at worst retrograde, the impulse to revive categorical boundaries signals a deeper critical dilemma facing devotees of the medium, for the drive to reconstitute a stable and practicable definition of photography is inextricable from the very real sense that the prominence of photographic discourse in contemporary art has receded.[1]

I later came to see its persistence as an institutional symptom, an expression of the arbitrariness of bureaucratic disciplinary management:

> When we ask the value of a term beyond its provisional utility, and moreover, when we ask these questions from the perspective of the [art] institution... we are implicating the categorical system applied to all art objects, questioning the way medium specificity is applied on an institutional level. "Photography" becomes, in this instance, a way to name this institutional anxiety ... when medium specificity is staged from within academia or museums, it is really a question of paying the bills, of funding lines, departmental autonomy, curriculum, intellectual fiefdoms, library tabs, allotted real estate, and canons wrapped in the guise of a

1 Walead Beshty, "Abstracting Photography," in Charlotte Cotton and Alex Klein (eds.), *Words Without Pictures* (Los Angeles: LACMA Books, 2008).

> broad philosophical conundrum. When these debates are realized on the level of abstraction, such as "what is photography?" or "is photography over?" the details of this bureaucratic topography are glossed over [and] we are reduced to the intellectual equivalent of theorizing empty filing cabinets [...][2]

This thread then shifted to a broad assessment of differential media for which the term seemed exemplary—an indication of an intractable methodological problem for academic art criticism that has permeated the institutional and discursive foundations of art:

> Returning to the subject of photography now is both a matter of things left unsaid and things not worth saying. Like arguing over old wounds with an ex-lover, one is inclined toward the remedial and the personal, to impotent summaries and well-worn frustrations. Flipping through the dog-eared volumes that introduced me to theories of the medium, or, more precisely, to the very idea of theorizing media, I find little relevant to the problems of the present. So different was the world at the time of their writing, so distinct and urgent were the stakes, that the only thing made evident by revisiting them is distance. And distance is where one might want to start, where so much writing on photography starts, with what is unknowable and mysterious about a depiction, what lies beyond or behind or between it and us. A medium is simply this, a separation, a marker of distance and difference. It is an untraversable boundary; that which conveys but also obscures, that which places things in the past as it draws them near. It is a boundary invented to explain the differences between things and their representations, to delineate what of a thing persists in its representation, if anything persists at all. These distinctions are aggregated into a spectral entity and lent solidity through naming. The act of naming christens the theoretical object that exists only so that the mind can hold it steady, make it discrete, and move on to less unruly things. The ontology of a medium is never more than the search for a static and stable boundary whose contours in truth only exist when in action, a thing that we assume must have solidity because convention necessitates it. [...]
>
> Photography is exemplary of this instability; the sheer range of the photographic object's sites of reception, not to mention the technological diversity of photographs themselves (the term being inclusive of a multitude of objects and attendant conditions of production), makes nailing the term down the equivalent of herding cats. Despite the column inches devoted to its discussion, a sense of imprecision remains when "photography" is used to designate something discrete, separate, categorical; that is, when it is theorized in and of itself. [...] Perhaps what is most interesting about these arguments over medium identity lies not in their substance but in their presence as a symptom of larger methodological issues. As Peter Bürger noted in his *Theory of the Avant-Garde,* the critical issue is not whether the autonomy of art is true or not, but rather why such a drive exists at all, what it satisfies, and why it emerges at a particular time in relation to a particular set of conditions. We have seen these impulses before: Sculpture, for example, was granted an expanded field when it ceased being capable of keeping up with the practices it had once so comfortably corralled; painting as a category became the object of scrutiny when it became apparent that it was a tragically outmoded means by which to achieve a mass audience, rendering certain formulations of its political stakes tenuous; and photography became the theoretical object of choice for the academy when it was adopted by the institutions of contemporary art and thus cordoned off from the din of mass culture that had, until then, given it explicit purpose. That these discussions arose in a relatively narrow time period should give us some indication that what was at stake was, in fact, a broader methodological issue, and that the actual object of debate was expertise and discipline, i.e., the role of those who were meant to bring systematic order to their chosen field, who were meant to divide one thing from another, who were meant to judge. This is, in short, a juridical crisis glossed over by terminology. When medium-based distinctions are called into question, eliciting anxious recovery from the threat of dissolution, one must ask, *What is actually being rescued?* [...].[3]

Each of these writings were chiefly concerned with the form of categorical medium distinctions native to the contexts for which they were commissioned (a critical anthology, a museum conference, and an academic art journal, respectively). Yet, in their dissection of methodology and institutional practice, they did little more than outline the presence of an array of practices whose core qualities escape the awkward parsing of aesthetics into canons and medium-specific categories, qualities that were fundamentally distorted or rendered invisible by those treatments. In retrospect, their focus on usurping

2 Walead Beshty, contribution to the panel "Is Photography Over?" organized by the San Francisco Museum of Modern Art, April 2010.

3 Walead Beshty, "Against Distinction: Photography and Legendary Psychasthenia," *October* 158 (Fall 2016), 67–88.

medium-specific categories is relatively pointless, as traditional medium classifications do not seem likely to have much of an impact on our future as they strain in the early decades of the twenty-first century to be even nominally applicable. Spread out over the years, the above excerpts paraphrase an extended argument that was preoccupied with the confinements and restrictions of terminology—and by doing so, could not fully exceed them, for, as I concluded in the most recent of these texts:

> We should return to the specificities of things, rather than the unending reparation of organizational structures. A logical conclusion of this system of medium-based distinctions—painting, performance, photography, sculpture, etc.—is the claim that objects, not observers, produce distinctions; or that somehow these tidy categories preexist the objects they order, rather than the understanding that every categorical delimiter is a contract to be rewritten in each and every moment of communion with an object and then retroactively applied. This logic makes it seem that, rather than allowing objects, by our own imaginations, to act or perform an idea of medium, a concept of medium is somehow contained within the object itself, such that objects "represent" or "refer" to something outside of themselves on their own, without interpretation. A rather vulgar anthropomorphism lies at the heart of this conundrum. The claim that it is objects that "play" as something else is offered in place of an acknowledgement that it is we who are playing. We project our fantasies onto our objects, and by doing so we pretend that we are ghosts who rely on objects to provide us bodies to inhabit [...] investing our objects with personalities while we become things. This is the horror inscribed in the taxonomic, that life, by escaping its ledgers, is alienable from the world, and that we can see the world while turning a blind eye to that which animates it. This is how the taxonomist imagines death inscribed in all things. But if we embrace indistinction and interconnectivity [...] disease becomes a freedom from obstruction. For what is a disease but a running wild of life through the boundaries meant to contain it? Infection, reproduction, and infestation are the means by which life always prevails over the inertia of divisive stricture.[4]

Such critical dismantling can go on indefinitely, never achieving satisfactory completion, and this last entry expresses my own exhaustion at the airing of these grievances. What persists throughout those texts is the notion of an unbounded and unnamed remainder, a life realized through the things of our making, a life obscured when we look at a particular object in isolation. It is a life expressed in how we animate the things around us, and are in turn transformed, extended, and animated through those things. This project—which encompasses this book and the exhibitions it accompanies—aims to draw an argument that began with terminological discontent to a close, and while concerned primarily with images and their permutations, is not limited to the conventional notion of images *as such*. It attempts to answer the negatively-posed questions above with an affirmation of aesthetic practice—how *aesthetics*, as a discourse staged through material appearances, evades the restrictions that have been applied to it. To that end, this is not a volume organized against some term or ideological position. It is not chiefly concerned with correcting absences in the historical record, however urgent that need may seem, nor do its omissions equate to unspoken dismissals. Instead its concern is positing the industrialization of the image as a primary force behind the transformation of aesthetics through the period that can be called the long twentieth century. Hence the real drive behind my extended preoccupation with terminology, for the restrictions the term "photography" imposes upon our understanding of the materials it purports to describe inhibit our observation of the explosive plurality of a period defined by the exponential expansion of the automatization of daily life, a process that is dynamic, ever-growing, and continuing to increase in intensity through to the present day.

Despite the dynamism of the aesthetic field, the terms associated with differential media are meant to hold things static, like specimens in a vitrine; they do not cope well with objects for whom circulation is a core quality, oftentimes proving incapable of addressing this aspect at all. This is not a problem related to newly emergent characteristics of images, a chaos brought on by the ubiquity of smart phones, social media, and the like, but a quality inherent even in the earliest phases of the industrialization of the image. As Darcy Grimaldo Grigsby observes in her movingly eloquent treatment of the cartes de visite of Sojourner Truth, in the mid-nineteenth century:

> ...the borders between different forms of representation were not fixed. Photography and photographic processes everywhere coexisted with far older technologies such as engraving and printing. Improvisation and expediency were essential, and different media served inconsistent, overlapping purposes.[5]

4 Beshty, "Against Distinction: Photography and Legendary Psychasthenia," 88.

Such is the context for works created several years later, like Jacob Riis's *The Other Half and How They Live*, its title variously describing a photographic magic lantern slide lecture, a group of etchings, a mass market book, and a series of magazine essays; or Eadweard Muybridge's motion studies, which were tipped into massive bound volumes, or animated in zoopraxiscopes.[6] Despite this variety of formatting (and similar to many of their nineteenth-century counterparts), such images are frequently presented as antiseptically framed works on the wall, a presentational mode rarely (if ever) adopted during the lives of their makers—and one that perpetuates their misinterpretation in the present.

By extension, many of the objects under consideration here do not fit neatly into art history, nor does their arrangement comport with the predispositions of cultural studies, and its analysis of material culture as a coded expression of dominant cultural values. Of the objects collected here (be they aesthetic, textual, or both), some have met with repeated dissection in the name of revealing the repressive powers they supposedly conceal; others have been claimed, by their very existence, to be a form of critique or counter-discourse—an opposition to the dominant order (when, in truth, none are wholly one or the other). To deal with this disorderly topography, all of these entries are given uniform treatment. Too many exhibitions unwittingly reproduce a hierarchy of objects based on their availability to connoisseurship; others fall into the trap of rushing to construct new categories for the disenfranchised or the unconventional, or attempt to bracket out influential historical precedents for their suspect politics. The latter is especially common for those projects that present themselves as politically oriented, calling out allies and enemies, organizing themselves methodologically against some approach or another, setting out to expose or reveal, revise or rewrite some master text. While this can be successful when pointed and specific, such prescriptions would have done a disservice to the reader in this instance, impeding the historical imagining the project hopes to inspire. Far too often we opt to sanitize history, creating new ghettos and new exclusions, all of which reinforce an implied, albeit absented, dominant canon which is granted sublime ubiquity in the process.

Instead the anthology that follows is a constellation of relations premised on formal morphologies, distributional systems, overlapping subject matter, and intersecting methodologies. Each contribution is posited as a thing put into circulation at a particular time, from a particular place, by particular individuals, and while these contexts are incomplete, the hope is that a fair indication of the broad field from which they emerge is made apparent. Aesthetic objects, depictive or otherwise, are fundamentally things in the world; they accrue meanings, zoom from body to body along myriad pathways, and they are always in motion, giving rise to a constantly evolving set of implications. The focus here, and in this volume, is the active work of the image, its movement, its building up, extending, and thickening of social ties. In understanding *how* each particular entry approaches doing that, we are given a clearer view of our past, and a set of possibilities for the comprehension and establishment of new modes of connectivity. Toward that end, this project avoids the rehearsal of various disciplinary organizational systems to better understand how images, in all their manifestations, work, and to attempt to incorporate their dispersal across various platforms of reception into their contemporary display and analysis.

2. THE TECHNICS OF THE IMAGE

In place of more conventional medium designations, the term this project relies upon is *technical image (technisches Bild)*, coined in the early 1980s by the Czech-born philosopher Vilém Flusser.[7] While chiefly descriptive of the industrialization of images, it is a term whose roots reach back into the Renaissance, to the lenticular experiments of Brunelleschi, the writings of Alberti, and the camera obscura, while giving a strong conceptual ground for the discussion of various digital platforms, implying a nascent form of post-industrial society through its sensitivity to the networks of production and reception of images. It incorporates images arising from science, journalism, and art alike.

5 Darcy Grimaldo Grigsby, "Introduction" in *Enduring Truths: Sojourner's Shadows and Substance* (Chicago: University of Chicago Press, 2015), 17. Excerpted in this volume, 119–124.

6 For more on Riis and Muybridge, see elsewhere in this anthology. Several variations of Riis's essay, including an illustrated lecture (1891) and a version that includes his etchings published in *Scribner's Magazine* (1889), are reproduced in this volume, Riis 146–166. Several of Muybridge's motion studies are reproduced on pages 195–199; see also John Ott, "Iron Horses: Leland Stanford, Eadweard Muybridge, and the Industrialized Eye," 200–208.

It accepts the optical and the diagrammatic as viable forms, and as I will show, immediately brings forward the political as central to the understanding of images and their implications. Primarily, it addresses a shared quality of certain images, their automaticism, their internalization of a set of rules to which they must dutifully adhere as they merge seamlessly into our experience.

Flusser defines the technical image simply enough as "...an image produced by apparatuses," (14) and apparatuses as inventions made to "simulate specific thought processes," (31) much the way tools are simulations and extensions of body parts—the hammer focusing the force of the hand, the saw the cutting of the teeth, and so on. Unlike tools, apparatuses automate decision-making and the execution of material and symbolic work simultaneously: they arrange symbols and inscribe them in objects. These simulations have grown more complex over time. Flusser, likening the work of apparatuses to the functioning of a game, asserts that apparatuses have become "so complex that those playing with [them] are not able to get to the bottom of [them]." (31). Unlike tools, apparatuses can be either "hard," or "soft," or some combination of both. As Flusser notes, "A camera is constructed out of metal, glass, plastic, etc. But it is not this hardness that makes it capable of being played with, nor is it the wood of the chessboard and the chess-pieces that make the game possible, but the rules of the game, the chess program [...]" (30)

Already, we are provided a pathway from the concrete production of a specific thing, into a much larger world via the complex socio-technical functioning of the "apparatus." It catapults us into the realm of the polis and politics—a sphere that the term "photograph," despite being the impetus for Flusser's book, neither implies nor requires. For Flusser's apparatus describes a network of relations, of human and mechanical actors, within which the technical image is situated and constituted. It sets the stage for an expanded set of discussions of both the production and reception of aesthetics, which is curtailed neither by what might constitute an art world (although much in this book and the accompanying exhibition is properly art), nor the world of instrumental images, whether they arise from governmental agencies, news organizations, or scientific research, each with their own agendas and disciplinary conditions, and each allowing for some degree of improvisational freedom for the individuals who serve as their functionaries. In particular, the implied hierarchy between art contexts and other spheres of aesthetics has greatly limited the reception of many significant contributions, a prohibition dissolved in Flusser's formulation. It is here where Flusser reorganizes the task at hand for cultural critique, particularly that informed by the Frankfurt School tradition, for such criticism:

> ...misses the essential thing about apparatuses, i.e. their automaticity. And this is precisely what needs to be criticized. Apparatuses were invented in order to function automatically, in other words independently of future human involvement. This is the intention with which they were created: that the human being would be ruled out. And this intention has been successful without a doubt. While the human being is being more and more sidelined, the programs of apparatuses, these rigid combination games, are increasingly rich in elements: they make combinations more and more quickly and are going beyond the ability of the human being to see what they are up to and to control them. Anyone who is involved with apparatuses is involved with black boxes where one is unable to see what they are up to.[8]

Apparatuses, for Flusser, formalize and externalize our actions into a set of automatic procedures; they do not come from mustache twirling charlatans or fat cat capitalists, nor do they lend themselves to such revelation. They are not top-down ("As apparatuses function automatically and do not obey any human decision, they cannot be owned by anybody"), but arise innocently enough from the simple impulse to efficiency and productivity, from automation, intended to conserve our efforts by outsourcing rote operations (73). They carry with them the biases of the times and places of their formulation, and as such, perpetuate and expand based upon them, but their transformations are automatic, they improve themselves through the incorporation of new technologies and component parts from disparate locations, and this process exceeds the control of any singular group or entity.

---

7 Flusser's key exposition of the technical image, *Für eine Philosophie der Fotografie,* was first published in 1983. Subsequent references, designated by parentheses, refer to Vilém Flusser, *Towards a Philosophy of Photography,* translated by Anthony Mathews (London: Reaktion, 2000). See "The Photographic Universe," and "Why a Philosophy of Photography Is Necessary," (both reprinted in this anthology, 512–517 and 558–559); and elsewhere, Vilém Flusser, *Into the Universe of Technical Images* (Minneapolis: University of Minnesota Press, 2011).

8 Flusser, 73.

They do this on their own, according to their internal logic. As Flusser describes, "Human beings create tools and in so doing take themselves as the model for this creation—until the situation is reversed and human beings take their tools as the model of themselves, of the world and society." (78). This insight emphasizes both our integration with the technological, and the transformative effects it has on every facet of human experience. Although their speed and complexity are alien to us, they nonetheless inform our most fundamental self-conceptions.

The operations of the technical image are the classical compositional strategies—montage, cropping, flattening, decontextualization, sequencing, juxtaposition, and most of all, monocular vision—and these operations have become wholly natural to our comprehension of the world. It is fitting that *history*, that other form of self-reflection, is constructed from a similar set of compositional automata, a similar drawing together in the face of the present through the propagation of unthought convention, condensing knowledge into a naturalized form, and a similar circularity, informing us as we formulate it. The unique strength of Flusser's terminology is that it extends a logic not only through to the origins of the mechanically-aided picture, or from the single object into the expansive system that is required to produce it, but also across disciplines, into the practical fields of communication theory, psychology, cognitive science, and engineering. In this way, not only are troublesome distinctions within aesthetics dissolved, but the very boundaries of aesthetics are rendered intellectually porous, its penetration into all facets of daily life given a model through which its far-reaching effects can be productively thought.

One such insight this opening up allows is an accounting of the implications of the digital, which is possible through the compatibility of Flusser's model with communication theory, where the foundations of computer-aided communication were established. To the reader of classical texts in the humanities, a fundamental concept within Flusser's argument is counterintuitive and bears some explanation. Chiefly, he organizes the world of images into the redundant and informative. Redundant images "carry no new information," and are "similar to those we have seen before." (26). Technical images are the result of a combination game (apparatuses and their programs), and as such, this game has a finite (even if unthinkably massive) set of possible outcomes (i.e. potential images). The evaluation of these images is based on their being "informative." Here Flusser's definition of *information*—"an improbable combination of elements"—is significant, both for its allusion to probability, and thus statistical analysis, and for its invocation of the combinatory, suggesting a finite set of preexisting elements.[9] It is only when we turn to communication theory that this terminology gains meaningful context. As Norbert Wiener, a founder of communication theory and the field of cybernetics, wrote in 1950:

> Messages are themselves a form of pattern and organization. Indeed, it is possible to treat sets of messages as having an entropy like sets of states of the external world. Just as entropy is a measure of disorganization, the information carried by a set of messages is a measure of organization. In fact, it is possible to interpret the information carried by a message as essentially the negative of its entropy, and the negative logarithm of its probability. That is, the more probable the message, the less information it gives. Clichés, for example, are less illuminating than great poems.[10]

Wiener's concept of improbability is the implicit metaphor for Flusser's characterization of the informational: the more information-rich, the less probable, or (otherwise put) the more uniquely organized a particular thing is, the more informational and improbable it is. It is important to note that in this model, information is never immaterial; it is always imbedded into objects. Mechanical and electronic systems of communication always require some transformation into a material state, whether by electro-static charges on a magnetic tape, or the mechanical imprinting of sound waves into the grooves of a vinyl record, and so on. But Flusser goes further, designating the informational image as an image that deserves and demands attention. What one is left with is essentially a Kantian notion of aesthetic

---

9 Flusser, 84.

10 Norbert Wiener, *The Human Use of Human Beings* (Boston: Houghton Mifflin, 1950), 21. The absence of Wiener within this volume is the first of what I imagine will turn out to be many glaring omissions in this anthology, but thankfully his writings are fully in print, and easily accessible on the internet. I would point readers to the opening chapter of *The Human Use of Human Beings*, "Cybernetics in History," as a useful introduction to his work.

judgment (disinterested, universal, necessary, and 'purposive without purpose') filtered through communication theory. It describes in quantitative terms the notion of appreciation, or aesthetic value, albeit only hypothetically calculable; more exactly, it is a construct of contemplative pleasure, of influence, engagement, and significance produced through the functioning of automated systems of production and distribution.

A central condition of the real-world transmission of messages poses a significant problem to communication theory, a loss or variability in the message between the point of emission and the point of reception due to the resistances of the materials used to convey that message, i.e. "noise." As Wiener describes the problem:

> The commands through which we exercise our control over our environment are a kind of information which we impart to it. Like any form of information, these commands are subject to disorganization in transit. They generally come through in less coherent fashion and certainly not more coherently than they were sent. In control and communication we are always fighting nature's tendency to degrade the organized and to destroy the meaningful [...][11]

For Wiener, according to the second law of thermodynamics, nature's "overwhelming tendency" is toward entropy, manifesting itself in "a message contaminated by extraneous disturbances," which he rephrases as "*background noise.*"[12] We can then conceptualize noise as a system's inherent resistance to communication, or more exactly, to being *informed* within objects; a message's propensity toward degradation, that is caused by the behavior of the material through which a message is conveyed. For Wiener, noise is an obstruction to humanity as a whole: "[t]o live effectively is to live with adequate information. Thus, communication and control belong to the essence of man's inner life, even as they belong to his life in society."[13] Noise is combatted in closed communication systems through redundancy. The more copies of a message sent, the more likely, through statistical analysis of the messages, that the original message might accurately be conveyed. In social systems, Weiner posits, the problem is combatted in a similar way, by issuing the command over and again until there is proper "compliance," in such a way that noise, that innate natural resistance to order, is aggregated away through the message's inscription into multiple redundant forms.[14]

But this prohibition on noise has its own implications, for noise can be understood as unintelligibility. What was originally thought to be noise arising from technical problems in their radio telescopes (bird droppings, or flaws in the arrangement of receivers) led astrophysicists Arno Penzias and Robert Wilson to their discovery of the Cosmic Microwave Background (CMB) in the mid-1960s, an act that earned them the 1978 Nobel Prize in Physics. Within what amounted to a persistent "noise," Penzias and Wilson discovered the residual energy of the Big Bang, whose study gave us the earliest known images of the universe itself mere moments after its inception. This background noise, rather than being evidence of the entropic degradation of our means of reception, was the first concrete evidence that the universe was expanding, and the source of the persistent static on television and radio. That these images of the early Universe were as available to those at the forefront of scientific research as they were to millions of television viewers is remarkable; for both, what was seen was an informational image that did not adhere to any of the conventional parameters of images they had come to expect from their devices. That these transmissions were present for decades and similarly dismissed by all as unintelligible (save the two scientists who received a Nobel Prize as a result) is enough to give us some reservations about our ability to accurately identify the informational significance of novel or information-rich images when the source is unfamiliar to us.

For Wiener, the prohibition on noise—and the need to combat it—approaches a moral argument: the resistance of things to the proper and socially necessary circulation of information, the constant threat of entropic dissolution and chaos, the intolerance to aberrations within communication systems,

11 Wiener, *The Human Use of Human Beings*, 17.

12 Norbert Wiener, *Cybernetics: or Control and Communication in the Animal and the Machine*, (Mansfield Centre: Martino Publishing, 2013), 10.

13 Wiener, *The Human Use of Human Beings*, 18.

14 Wiener, *The Human Use of Human Beings*, 16.

is clearly a value extended from the command and control structure implicit to the military conditions under which he conducted his research. The military depends on the transmission of crisp directives and notifications of compliance but social systems necessitate more flexible, interjective communication; still, computer networks are ingrained with the command and control structures, and similarly are designed to discount and eliminate the expression of noise. We too are similarly inclined, yet, through their deepening influence on our experience of the world, we run the risk of compounding the effects of our respective blindnesses. By drawing analogies to the social sphere (analogies Wiener was uniquely predisposed to make), "noise" can be conceived as an emergent social factor, unnamable and hiding in plain sight. As with the example above regarding the CMB, noise can indicate a meaningful, cogent, and coherent alterity; something as yet unnamed or unintelligible to the system it arises through. Grassroots revolutionary responses to, in Louis Althusser's terminology, the Repressive State Apparatus, could, from the perspective of command and control, be similarly construed as uncategorizable noise, as defects or contaminations in the political apparatus, an externality arising from a degrading and dysfunctional social fabric. The Civil Rights movement, Vietnam War protests, the activities of May '68, in the form of sit-ins, walkouts, violent and non-violent modes of resistance, are similarly indicative of systemic failures, where entropy threatens the smooth operations of the state. In retrospect, the social "noise" of the sixties and seventies within the state apparatus is indicative of the first emergence of a socio-political formation whose genesis was anti-militarist, anti-racist, anti-corporate in nature. What came with it was a new state of political affairs that was integrated into the functioning of our institutions, and similarly subject to disruption by forces it was unable to identify. The shock of the United States Presidential Election of 2016 can be considered from this perspective, as the seemingly fringe "alt-right" contingents within the country's fabric emerged as the first indication of a new political organization—a development which many found wholly inconsistent with the widely held self-conception of the United States as an exemplar of humanist social values formulated in the countercultural movements of the sixties and seventies. Amid a process that curiously resonates with both the moralizing dimensions of Wiener's text, and the apparatus-like nature of contemporary electoral politics, the shock of this contingent seizing a majority in a popular election was the direct result of relegating certain improbably arranged (i.e. informational) elements within the public discourse to mere "noise."

3. BROWSING HISTORIES

All histories are provisional, a corralling together of bits and pieces into a pastiche that is then formulated into an order as fragile as the recollections and ephemera which are its raw material. Viewed from above, histories are in a similar war with entropy as they combat the dissolution of the past. Despite their compositional nature, we look to them for abstractions, guidelines and schemas, but what they mostly express is how ideas are made solid, given form, made to obey some set of operational parameters often dictated by the innocuous and mundane. A history is governed by the form it takes, it is never spectral or ubiquitous—it is always embodied, that is to say *incorporated*; it is constituted in real things, in films, in books, in historical archives and web pages, and it always obeys the logic of those forms. It can never escape real world conditions. It is we who set them in motion, who circulate them beyond the boundaries of their material confines. They give us purchase on our existence and common ground to tread upon. We interface with them, pass them along, and as we do so, we physically imbed their attributes in ourselves, carrying them with us in the way we commune with others; in this sense, we reproduce them in our performances with one another, and through the distortions we create in their transmission; they reproduce us, or at least, disseminate our effects on them. For example, when we adopt a historical understanding from a book, or newspaper, internalize it, and then pass it on, our acts of dissemination integrate the logic of the original *informed* object within our activities. Our dissemination of information that is garnered from other forms and passed on in new forms, whether in speech acts, further writing, or our performances of that understanding, contain the traces of the original object and its receptivity to encoding; i.e., how each of these materials lend themselves to being *informed* is passed on, along with the types and forms of information it registers.

These types of activities, those imparted over and again from one to another which integrate us with our devices, are what the German media theorist Bernhard Siegert describes when he speaks of "cultural techniques" (*Kulturtechniken*)—of the ways our bodies are trained and extended through the technologies among us.[15] Even when they are absent, their material conditions continue to formulate our existence in the world in the form of the habitual. But this is not the whole story, for we not only carry them, but they contain us, give us existence and a shared sense of the past, as he writes:

> Humans *as such* do not exist independently of cultural techniques of hominization, time *as such* does not exist independently of cultural techniques of time measurement, and space *as such* does not exist independently of cultural techniques of spatial control [...] As a historically given micronetwork of technologies and techniques, cultural techniques are the "exteriority and/or materiality of the signifier." An abacus allows for different calculations than ten fingers; a computer, in turn, allows for different calculations than an abacus. When we speak of cultural techniques, therefore, we envisage a more or less complex actor network that comprises technological objects as well as the operative chains they are part of and that configure or constitute them.[16]

We would do well to remember that these cultural techniques are not simply trafficked through a particular culture or society but hold that society together. They insert the transformations, or noise, produced by individuals into the matrix of their dispersal, and as such, provide a comprehension of degradations within transmission as a significant, and meaningful aspect of our circulation of objects and practices through the world. We not only carry these acts or habits with us; they comprise the very "us" that they move through, for we are not only destined to push these messages through the world, but are defined by the behaviors they engender, and this indistinction, our inseparability from them and each other is what in fact makes us human beings; it is—in the words of Giorgio Agamben—the being-in-language of human beings.[17]

This can seem quite overwhelming: our bodies distributed and dispersed through the world by experiential prosthetics, our sense of self, our boundaries, constantly evolving and changing shape, defined by often competing agendas and technologies, subject to the ebb and flow of myriad expansions and contractions. And so we revert to cognitive abstractions, we invent standards and practices and build them into our habits as maps for structuring the rampant pulsations we are subjected to, and we lock these into objects, and gestures, which are conservative in the true sense of the term, for these are literally means to conserve what has transpired. Incident is made concrete and stable through our ritual repetitions, inscribing and reinscribing them in our objects and the performances they engender. As we reach out into the world through them, we formulate the world available to us. We cut a path through the interconnectedness of things, of bodies, by enacting the lessons of our abstractions—such as gender, race, or class—organizational systems that must be endlessly performed to remain solid. That is not to say they are fictions, or that they are immaterial, nor are they easily banished through simple acknowledgement; they are abstractions derived from earlier, anachronistic arrangements of capital and sovereign power, they are automated effects of our reliance on apparatuses, recirculated and made solid through our material acts, extended through movements which reinforce and distribute them. They are inextricable from our world at the micro level, and the violence and suffering they justify must be rooted out at their bases, like an infestation of rats. The sin is to pretend to their stability even as we continually mold and reinforce them, masking their contingent, collaged nature, their attendant improvisations, and the localized personal agendas that are expressed through them. They refuse general address, but require an investigation of the specificities of things; that is to say, they are immune to critiques of their ideologies. As Althusser reminds us, "an ideology always exists in an apparatus, and its practice, or practices. This existence is material."[18]

15 Bernhard Siegert, *Cultural Techniques, Grids, Filters, Doors, and Other Articulations of the Real*, translated by Geoffrey Winthrop-Young (New York: Fordham University Press, 2015). See "(Not) In Place: The Grid, or, Cultural Techniques of Ruling Spaces," reprinted in this volume, 282–293.

16 Siegert, 9–11. See in particular notes 30 and 31.

17 Giorgio Agamben, "Notes on Gesture," in *Means without End: Notes on Politics*, translated by Vincenzo Binetti and Cesare Casarino (Minneapolis & London: University of Minnesota Press, 2000), 60, and reprinted elsewhere in this volume, 175–178.

18 Louis Althusser, *Lenin and Philosophy and Other Essays*, translated by Ben Brewster (New York: Monthly Review Press, 2001), 112.

4. AESTHETICS AS POLITICS IN-FORMATION

Aesthetics establish what is held in common among individuals, what Jacques Rancière has described as the "distribution of the sensible," of what is knowable and held in common by the group. In Rancière's words, "a distribution of the sensible" is:

> the system of self-evident facts of sense perception that simultaneously discloses the existence of something in common and the delimitations that define the respective parts and positions within it. A distribution of the sensible therefore establishes at one and the same time something common that is shared, and exclusive parts. This apportionment of parts and positions is based on a distribution of spaces, times, and forms of activity that determines the very manner in which something in common lends itself to participation and in what way various individuals have a part in this distribution [...] aesthetics can be understood in a Kantian sense—re-examined perhaps by Foucault—as the system of *a priori* forms determining what presents itself to sense experience. It is a delimitation of spaces and times, of the visible and invisible, of speech and noise, that simultaneously determines the place and the stakes of politics as a form of experience. Politics revolves around what is seen and what can be said about it, around who has the ability to see and the talent to speak, around the properties of spaces and the possibilities of time.[19]

The significance of this commentary is twofold. It both outlines that one of the most urgent questions facing the political pertains to the boundaries that produce inclusion and exclusion—of who is counted among the polis and who is not—and secondly, that aesthetics, in the Greek sense of the word, by its very nature of making things knowable to the senses [αισθητικές], is at the base of the political—that there is no sense of the term aesthetics which can be addressed without tending to its political implications. Rancière continues that "[a]rtistic practices are 'ways of doing and making' that intervene in the general distribution of ways of doing and making as well as in the relationships they maintain to modes of being and forms of visibility."[20] This "intervention" is a mode by which the "distribution of the sensible" is transformed and expanded, a concept which is immediately compatible with the privileged position Flusser reserves for informative images: each exceed the *a priori* conditions within which they were formulated.

This model posits a politics freed from the management of the state, for it has the capacity to exceed regulation, disperse its parts, and operate close to the ground amongst the rabble. It includes and excludes without recourse to the sovereign; the sovereign mandate may be replicated there, but aesthetics is not contained by it, for aesthetics originates in the senses and is received there, in our base existence as bodies among bodies. The location of aesthetics, then, is the field of politics as constituted by bodies, in the parameters of what is knowable and sensate, and in the production of a body politic [πολιτεία] who shares in this knowledge, i.e. in the members of this community who are, by extension, acknowledged as participants in that community through their address. The nefarious flip side to the establishment of a commons is that it necessarily creates exclusion, and however provisional those exclusions may be, or elusive they seem for their symbolic nature, the suffering that exclusions create far exceed the merely metaphorical or symbolic. They are expressly a matter of life and death, a matter of lives that are given value, and those that are not (again, the concreteness of Flusser's model helps conceptualize this in a manner that conventional ideology critique cannot). Thus, aesthetics is an equally potent tool for establishing connectivity and reinforcing the relations among those it acknowledges as subjects, as much as it is an agent of repression for those it condemns to objectification, or worse, invisibility.

What has been lacking in the critical appraisal of images, and aesthetics more broadly, is how aesthetics can be harnessed to intervene in economies of power, not simply reflect and reify them. Aesthetic activity is constantly at war with exclusion, an endless battle which pushes on the boundaries of who can speak and what can be expressed. But this activity invariably creates newly apparent exclusions in the margins of its expansion. Thus, it makes sense that the bulk of politically minded scholarship on aesthetics focuses on these exclusions, in the spirit of expanding the field of aesthetics, even though doing so threatens to turn the history of aesthetic activity into a relentless march of dominance. We've

19 Jacques Rancière, *The Politics of Aesthetics: The Distribution of the Sensible* (London & New York: Continuum, 2004), 12–13.
20 Rancière, 13.

seen as much in the body of aesthetic theory of the twentieth century. This is not only a lie of omission, it manufactures an even more elusive and powerful form of exclusion by reifying and sublimating (i.e. making sublime) dominance, giving it newly elusive, omniscient, and omnipotent form by assuming classical narratives of class, race, and gender as an explanation, not an effect.

Perhaps one symptom of the overemphasis on dominance is at the core of the term which is most often applied to the discussion of the political implications of aesthetic practices, the *politics of representation*, that old chestnut of seventies and eighties critical theory. The issue is that as this term has been tidied up, anthologized, and summarized, condensed into the disciplinary prescriptions of cultural critique, it has also been caricatured, and reduced—the particular nuances of the work of various contributors to this discussion reveal a much more complex, nuanced, and revealing understanding of the ethics of aesthetics. While there are a great many important authors and practitioners that have been corralled within this heading (some of whom are anthologized here), most exceed this sphere of cultural studies as it is most readily cast about. This limitation in large part rests with the term *representation*, which hides within it the assumption that aesthetics is always backward-looking, that all that is possible is to restate what *is so*, to *re-present*. This is of course a portion of what aesthetics does, for convention, redundancy, that basis of all modes of communication, is undeniably at work here, each and every expression straddling the gulf between the necessity of comprehensibility—which is by nature conservative as comprehension relies on recognizing patterns established previously—but also includes the urgent work of pushing the boundaries of what can be said. The same applies to language, of course, and is at the core of democracy, the struggle between the *demos*, those who are counted, and those who are not (a status Agamben importantly described as *homo sacer*, "those that can be killed but not sacrificed," life reduced to the status of a body); but to argue that aesthetics is limited to the reiteration of the beliefs of those "who are counted" as a purely repressive force is akin to arguing that history is a steady state of affairs.[21] Our world clearly shows this to be not only cynical but absurd, and the contributions to this volume stand as evidence of practices that have, in some form or another, escaped convention, making some unaccounted for quotient knowable to the senses in a way that had not been before.

5. THE POST-INDUSTRIALIZATION OF AESTHETICS

In the trajectory of aesthetic communication, the long twentieth century has been a period during which communities of shared knowledge have both grown exponentially and radically transformed. While it has expanded the reach of convention, propagating its norms, it has also radically democratized the production and reception of aesthetics, putting large audiences within reach of individual producers in ways that had been impossible, and in doing so, ushered in a period of radical experimentation with not only what can be "said" but how it can be said; to whom it can speak, and by extension who it allows to speak. At the heart of technological advancements in the conveyance of images lies a catalyst for the transformation of human relations through the means by which those relations are communicated (as those relations are inextricable from their means of communication), which presents a crisis for conservatives and progressives alike. It is a non-ideological crisis; it is a crisis pertaining to our existence integrated within the technological, or as Allan Sekula put it, "at the heart of this crisis lies the question of the survival and deformation of human creative energies under the impact of mechanization."[22]

We appear to have arrived at a moment where such a crisis seems all the more pervasive: the saturation of our contemporary lives with aesthetic platforms that actively present themselves as portals to communities, which are themselves privatized (a fundamental contradiction of the very notion of the commons). We are confronted here with the fantasy of the right to formulate a body politic [πολιτεία] through a commons, which is in fact not one—spheres of communion which are the intellectual property of the corporations that maintain them, corporations which actively monetize our

21 Giorgio Agamben, *Homo Sacer: Sovereign Power and Bare Life* (Stanford, CA: Stanford University Press, 1998), 12.
22 Allan Sekula, "Reading an Archive: Photography Between Labour and Capital," in Benjamin H. D. Buchloh and Robert Willkie (eds.), *Mining Photographs and Other Pictures 1948–1968*. (Halifax, Nova Scotia: The Press of the Nova Scotia College of Art and Design), 201.

unpaid participation, like feudal landlords reaping the profit of the fields their peons are graciously allowed to farm, all the while literally "mining" our lives for saleable data, like ore from the earth. The cost of entry is our absorption into their data sets, the delivery of our attentions to ad buyers, and in exchange, we are allowed to be participants in a collective that spans continents and demographics. Refusal is a form of self-exile, an unbearably bleak option for those who are the most isolated, geographically dispersed, or otherwise unaccounted for. Just as mineral rights, air space, and water supplies were once exclusively part of the commons—until, that is, their value was understood and capitalist innovators ingeniously brought them under private control—so too are the investments we make in the production of internet-based communities. Yet, as they attract us away from truly public forums, we are presented another potential tragedy of the commons, a disinvestment in other forms of civic participation. Perhaps, as the entrepreneur often argues, private interests are best able to make these public resources productive, and the forums for exchange these corporations provide are impossible for any other entity to supply. This may prove to be the case, but to assume that there are no ramifications would be to ignore the lessons the history of transitions from public to private control have taught us. The private capitalization of public resources always brings along costs which are borne by those who are least likely to profit from their monetization in the first place.

From this perspective, the frantic early twentieth-century bell ringing about the ubiquity of industrial images in daily experience, whether in the form of the corporate picture magazine, the movie industry and its attendant celebrity culture, their use within newspapers and advertising, or the fascination of the masses with producing endless amounts of snapshots, can seem rather quaint. But it reveals the impact that these voices of discontent and resistance have made on the contemporary image world, how critiques of centralized privately controlled modes of communication, and how arenas originally constructed to evade commercial interest—the days of early bulletin board systems (BBS), of open source software, and peer to peer sharing—gave private interests a playbook for new territories to exploit. The radicality of Napster became the corporate profits reaped by iTunes, Spotify, and Pandora. What can the personalization of data streams into a single platform algorithmically derived from the expression of our tastes be but a direct response to the standardization and centralization of media witnessed in the mid-twentieth century? The mistrust of midcentury corporate media oligopolies, such as television networks, record companies, news magazines, and so on, provided the raw materials for the new era of megacorporations. Facebook, Google, and Amazon all monetized fields of human activity that had been free and public prior to their ascension—all of which were specifically designed to evade overt commercialization and corporate consolidation. The brilliance of these corporations was their ability to capture and monetize an uncommodified resource, our very drive to connect with one another, and relocate it within the field of private ownership. As Luc Boltanski and Eve Chiapello described in "The New Spirit of Capitalism," our current moment was borne from the countercultural revolutions of the sixties and seventies when:

> [t]he critique of the 'consumer society' brought out onto the streets, as it were, the denunciation of a world given over to the series, mass production, standardized opinion [...] Capitalism's response to the intense demand for differentiation and demassification that marked the end of the 1960's and 1970's was to internalize it. This recuperation took the form of a commodification—that is to say, the transformation into 'products', allocated at a price and hence exchangeable on a market, of goods and practices *that in a different state of affairs remained outside the commodity sphere.*[23]

They continue:

> It proceeded in tandem with a commodification of goods *that had hitherto remained outside the commodity sphere* [...] capitalism was to penetrate domains [...] which had hitherto remained comparatively external to mass commodity circulation. Developments in the direction of an *increased commodification of certain qualities of human beings* also started [...][24]

23 Luc Boltanski and Eve Chiapello, *The New Spirit of Capitalism* (New York & London: Verso, 2005), 441. Original emphasis.
24 Boltanski and Chiapello, 442–43. Original emphasis.

From the capitalist logic of tapping untapped resources, to the increased commodification of human beings, the through line is the circulatory system of technical images, the very currency traded within online forums, which compose new class stratifications and untold revenue streams for the corporations that facilitate them. This is a transformation that has a direct impact on the status of human beings; it forms conceptions of human rights, our rights to privacy, and our very ability to construct and maintain viable and ethical communities. To better be able to recognize and combat these constructions and encroachments—to realize the significance of net neutrality or guarantees of how personal data may be used; or to address the cloistering of online communities, each of whom subscribe to radically incompatible notions of reality—an important lesson can be learned from the history of technical images. Through them we not only are given tools to analyze their current concrete arrangements, but are provided the understanding that none of these systems for the distribution and receptions of images have been stable *as such*, and that innovation, improvisation, and participation under sometimes daunting constraint— i.e., the invention of new pathways for communion and resistance to command and control networks—are neither peripheral nor marginal aspects of our history. They are, in fact, its primary catalyst.

TAKEN FROM HERE TO WHERE IT CAME FROM AND TAKEN TO A PLACE AND USED IN SUCH A MANNER THAT IT CAN ONLY REMAIN AS A REPRESENTATION OF WHAT IT WAS WHERE IT CAME FROM

Lawrence Weiner

1980

TAKEN FROM HERE TO WHER

AND TAKEN TO A PLACE

AND USED IN SUCH A MANNE

A REPRESENTATION OF WHAT

T CAME FROM

HAT IT CAN ONLY REMAIN AS
WAS WHERE IT CAME FROM

Introductory Remarks and Selected Plates from *Pencil of Nature*
William Henry Fox Talbot
1844–46

"INTRODUCTORY REMARKS"

The little work now presented to the Public is the first attempt to publish a series of plates or pictures wholly executed by the new art of Photogenic Drawing, without any aid whatever from the artist's pencil. The term "Photography" is now so well known, that an explanation of it is perhaps superfluous; yet, as some persons may still be unacquainted with the art, even by name, its discovery being still of very recent date, a few words may be looked for of general explanation.

It may suffice, then, to say, that the plates of this work have been obtained by the mere action of Light upon sensitive paper. They have been formed or depicted by optical and chemical means alone, and without the aid of any one acquainted with the art of drawing. It is needless, therefore, to say that they differ in all respects, and as widely as possible, in their origin, from plates of the ordinary kind, which owe their existence to the united skill of the Artist and the Engraver.

They are impressed by Nature's hand; and what they want as yet of delicacy and finish of execution arises chiefly from our want of sufficient knowledge of her laws. When we have learnt more, by experience, respecting the formation of such pictures, they will doubtless be brought much nearer to perfection; and though we may not be able to conjecture with any certainty what rank they may hereafter attain to as pictorial productions, they will surely find their own sphere of utility, both for completeness of detail and correctness of perspective.

The Author of the present work having been so fortunate as to discover, about ten years ago, the principles and practice of Photogenic Drawing, is desirous that the first specimen of an Art, likely in all probability to be much employed in future, should be published in the country where it was first discovered. And he makes no doubt that his countrymen will deem such an intention sufficiently laudable to induce them to excuse the imperfections necessarily incident to a first attempt to exhibit an Art of so great singularity which employs processes entirely new and having no analogy to anything in use before. That such imperfections will occur in a first essay, must indeed be expected. At present the Art can hardly be said to have advanced beyond its infancy—at any rate, it is yet in a very early stage—and its practice is often impeded by doubts and difficulties, which, with increasing knowledge, will diminish and disappear. Its progress will be more rapid when more minds are devoted to its improvement, and when more of skillful manual assistance is employed in the manipulation of its delicate processes; the paucity of which skilled assistance at the present moment the Author finds one of the chief difficulties in his way. [...]

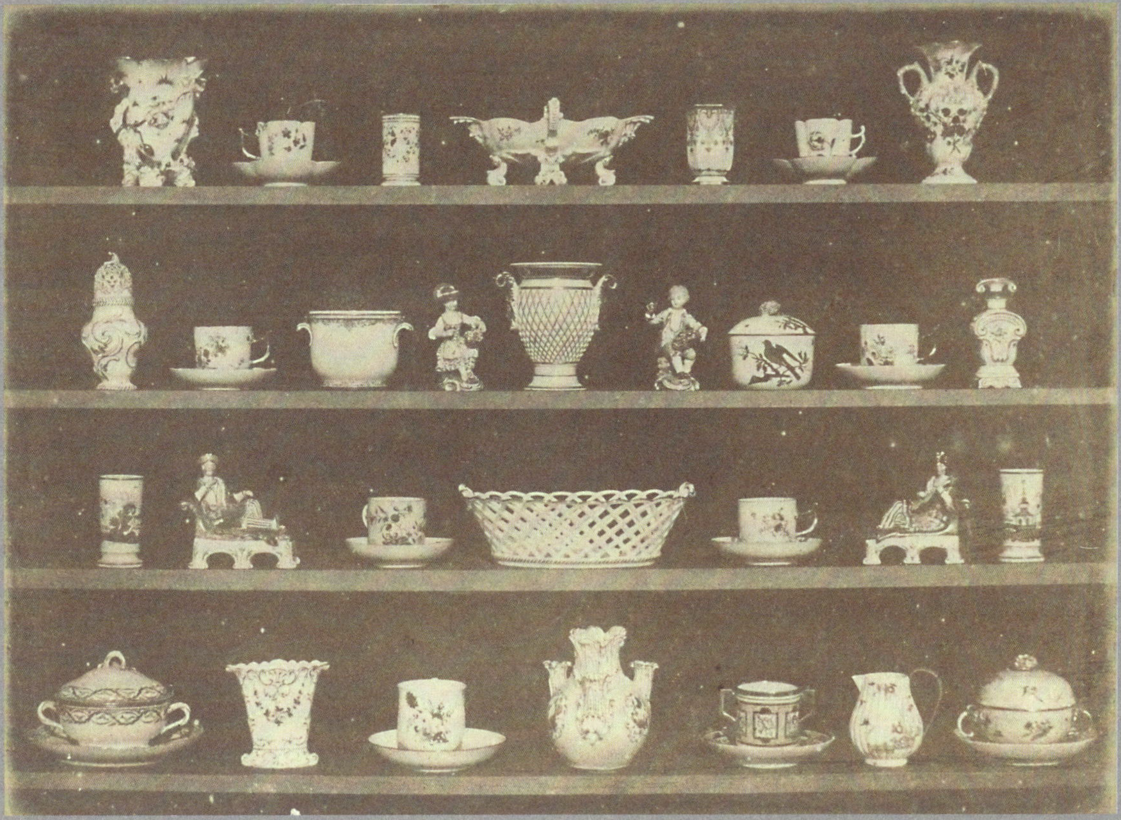

"PLATE III. ARTICLES OF CHINA."

From the specimen here given it is sufficiently manifest, that the whole cabinet of a Virtuoso and collector of old China might be depicted on paper in little more time than it would take him to make a written inventory describing it in the usual way. The more strange and fantastic the forms of his old teapots, the more advantage in having their pictures given instead of their descriptions.

And should a thief afterwards purloin the treasures—if the mute testimony of the picture were to be produced against him in court—it would certainly be evidence of a novel kind; but what the judge and jury might say to it, is a matter which I leave to the speculation of those who possess legal acumen.

The articles represented on this plate are numerous: but, however numerous the objects—however complicated the arrangement—the Camera depicts them all at once. It may be said to make a picture of whatever *it sees.* The object glass is the *eye* of the instrument—the sensitive paper may be compared to the *retina*. And, the eye should not have too large a *pupil*: that is to say, the glass should be diminished by placing a screen or diaphragm before it, having a small circular hole, through which alone the rays of light may pass. When the eye of the instrument is made to look at the objects through this contracted aperture, the resulting image is much more sharp and correct. But it takes a longer time to impress itself upon the paper, because, in proportion as the aperture is contracted, fewer rays enter the instrument from the surrounding objects, and consequently fewer fall upon each part of the paper.

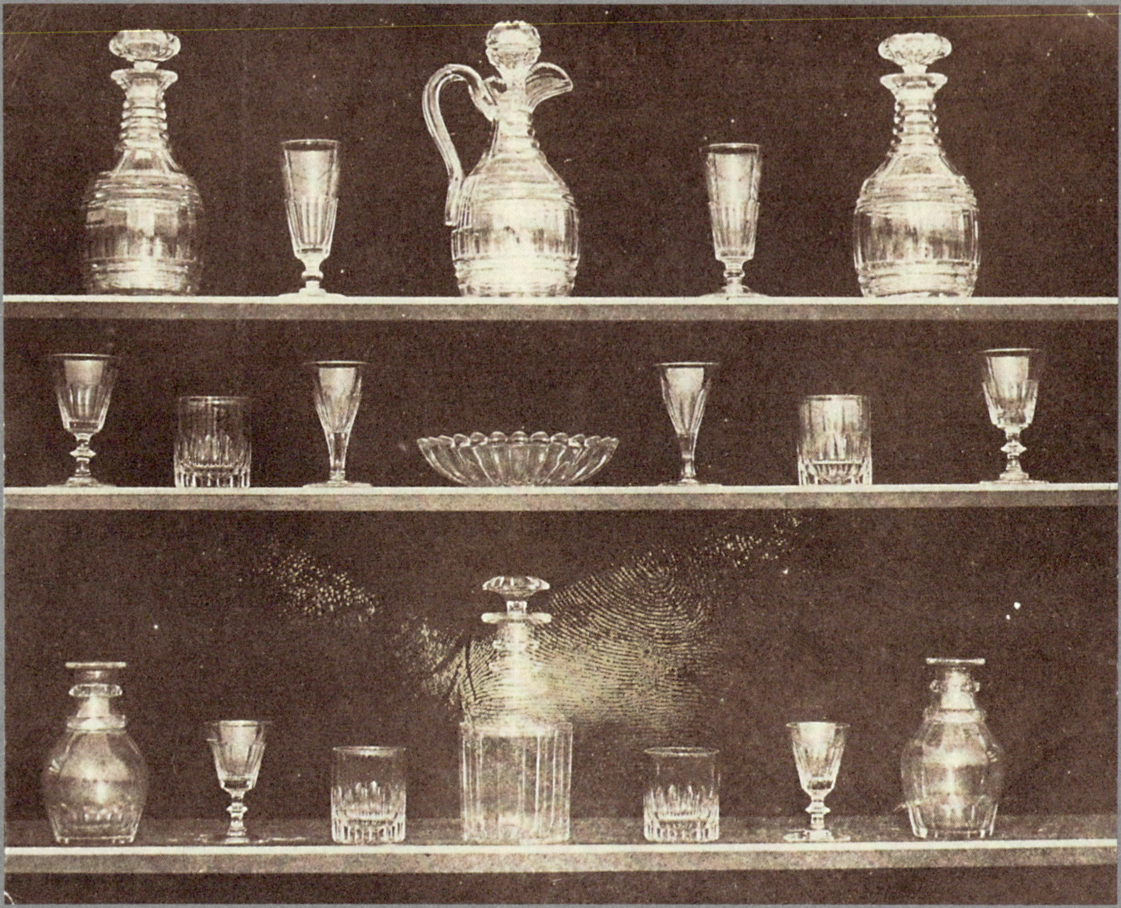

"PLATE IV. ARTICLES OF GLASS."

The photogenic images of glass articles impress the sensitive paper with a very peculiar touch, which is quite different from that of the China in Plate III. And it may be remarked that white china and glass do not succeed well when represented together, because the picture of the china, from its superior brightness, is completed before that of the glass is well begun. But colored china may be introduced along with glass in the same picture, provided the colour is not a pure blue: since blue objects affect the sensitive paper almost as rapidly as white ones do. On the contrary, green rays act very feebly—an inconvenient circumstance, whenever green trees are to be represented in the same picture with buildings of a light hue, or with any other light coloured objects. [...]

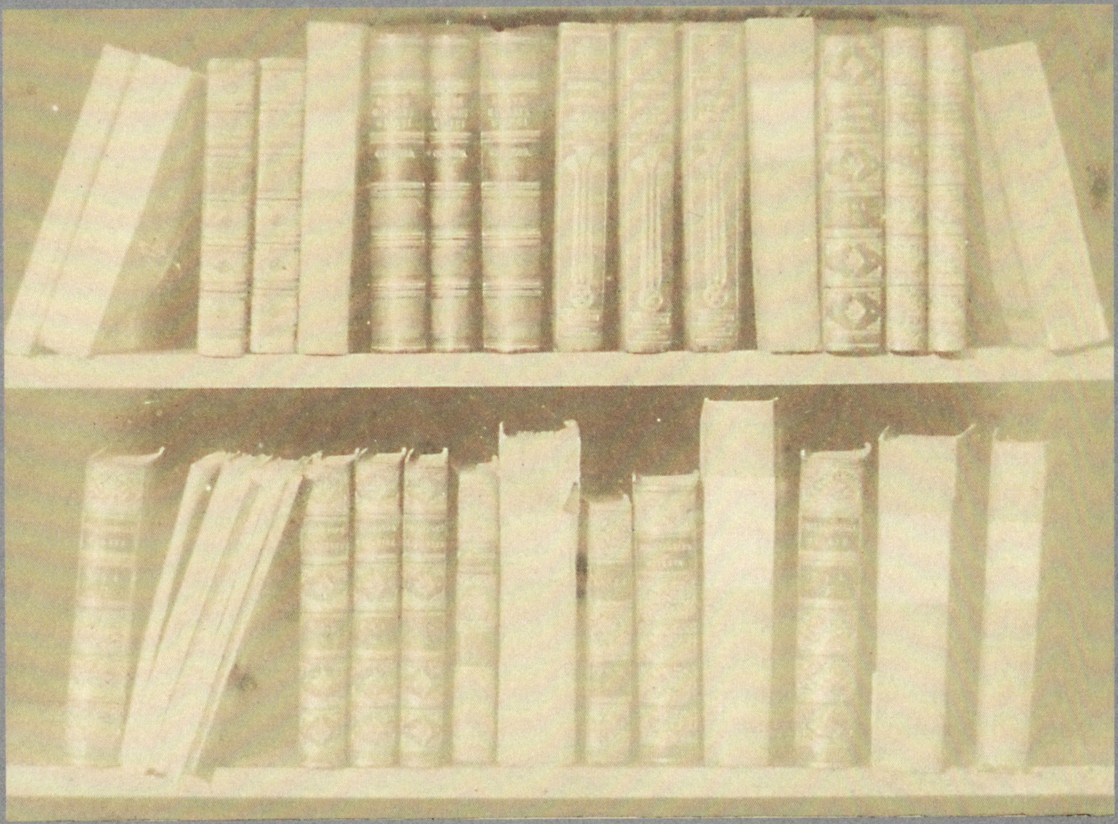

"PLATE VIII. A SCENE IN A LIBRARY."

Among the many novel ideas which the discovery of Photography has suggested, is the following rather curious experiment or speculation. I have never tried it, indeed, nor am I aware that any one else has either tried or proposed it, yet I think it is one which, if properly managed, must inevitably succeed.

When a ray of solar light is refracted by a prism and thrown upon a screen, it forms there the very beautiful coloured band known by the name of the solar spectrum.

Experimenters have found that if this spectrum is thrown upon a sheet of sensitive paper, the violet end of it produces the principal effect: and, what is truly remarkable, a similar effect is produced by certain *invisible rays* which lie beyond the violet, and beyond the limits of the spectrum, and whose existence is only revealed to us by this action which they exert.

Now, I would propose to separate these invisible rays from the rest, by suffering them to pass into an adjoining apartment through an aperture in a wall or screen of partition. This apartment would thus become filled (we must not call it *illuminated*) with invisible rays, which might be scattered in all directions by a convex lens placed behind the aperture. If there were a number of persons in the room, no one would see the other: and yet nevertheless if a *camera* were so placed as to point in the direction in which any one were standing, it would take his portrait, and reveal his actions.

For to use a metaphor we have already employed, the eye of the camera would see plainly where the human eye would find nothing but darkness.

Alas! that this speculation is somewhat too refined to be introduced with effect into a modern novel or romance; for what a *dénouement* we should have, if we could suppose the secrets of the darkened chamber to be revealed by the testimony of the imprinted paper.

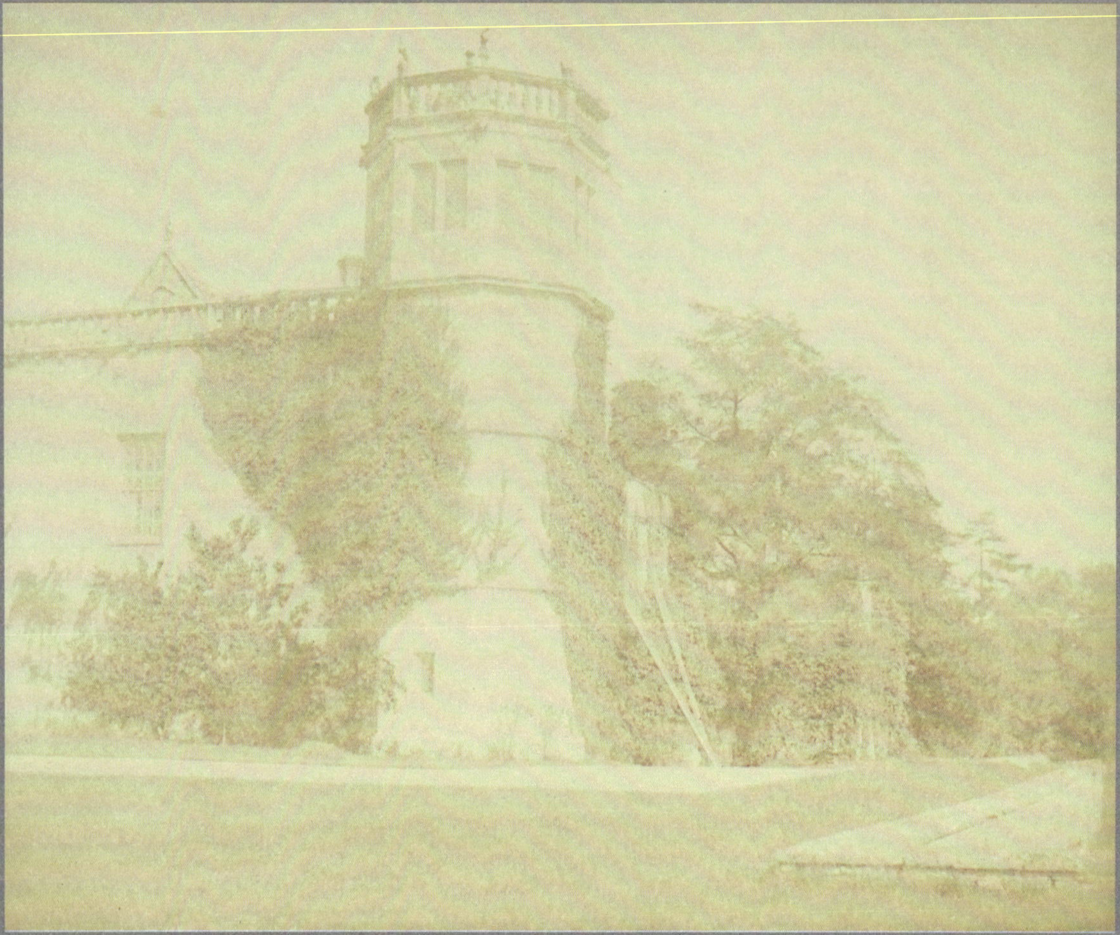

"PLATE XIX:
THE TOWER OF LACOCK ABBEY."

The upper part of the tower is believed to be of Queen Elizabeth's time, but the lower part is probably coeval with the first foundation of the abbey, in the reign of Henry III.

The tower contains three apartments, one in each story. In the central one, which Is used as a muniment room, there is preserved an invaluable curiosity, an original copy of the Magna Charta of King Henry III. It appears that a copy of this Great Charter was sent to the sheriffs of all the counties in England. The illustrious Ela, Countess of Salisbury, was at that time sheriff of Wiltshire (at least so the tradition confidently avers), and this was the copy transmitted to her, and carefully preserved ever since her days in the abbey which she founded about four years after the date of this Great Charter. [...]

From the parapet wall of this building, three centuries ago, Olive Sherington, the heiress of Lacock, threw herself into the arms of her lover, a gallant gentleman of Worcestershire, John Talbot, a kinsman of the Earl of Shrewsbury. He was felled to the earth by the blow, and for a time lay lifeless, while the lady only wounded or broke her finger. Upon this, Sir Henry Sherington, her father, relented, and shortly after consented to their marriage, giving as a reason *"the step which his daughter had taken."*

Unwritten tradition in many families has preserved ancient stories which border on the marvellous, and it may have embellished the tale of this lover's leap by an incident belonging to another age. For I doubt the story of the broken finger, or at least that Olive was its rightful owner. Who can tell what tragic scenes may not have passed within these walls during the thirteenth and fourteenth centuries? The spectre of a nun with a bleeding finger long haunted the precincts of the abbey, and has been seen by many in former times, though I believe that her unquiet spirit is at length at rest. And I think the tale of Olive has borrowed this incident from that of a frail sister of earlier days.

A Scene in a Library: The First Photographically Illustrated Book

Carol Armstrong

1998

A Preliminary Discourse on the Study of Natural History was published eight years before the invention of photography was announced to the public on both sides of the Channel. In it, Herschel gave an image of the printing press as an example of the unforeseen benefits of experimentation and inductive reasoning backward from effects to causes: "... we see regular and beautiful results brought about in human works by means which nobody would, at first sight, think could have any thing to do with them. A sheet of blank paper is placed upon a frame, and shoved forwards, and after winding its way successively over and under half a dozen rollers, and performing many other strange evolutions, comes out printed on both sides ... which *sets the whole apparatus in motion* ... (*A Preliminary Discourse,* p. 145).

Herschel supplies an emblem of the industry to which the photograph would soon be joined. Printing and reversing and stamping, so the great machine turns and winds in Herschel's image, squeezing through its frame and its rollers a figuration of science as a Nature-imprinted mechanism, and of photography to be, by extension, as a matter of the Nature-based apparatus of the printed book. Except that, until much later, photographs were hand-glued intrusions into this technological framework, more stoppages within it than smoothly functioning extensions of it, "natural" but not yet assimilated to the industrial naturalism of the book machine, their presence within it contested, not assumed.

Talbot, the author of the "first" photographically illustrated book, was a friend of Herschel's, and just as committed to the inductive methods of natural philosophy, to which he tied the new medium.[1] He announced his invention of the calotype, the first paper negative-positive photographic process (and hence the first to be potentially assimilable to the page), to his peers at the Royal Society on January 31, 1839:

> This remarkable *phenomenon,* of whatever value it may turn out in its application to the arts, will at least be accepted as *a new proof of the value of the inductive methods of modern science,* which by noticing the occurrence of unusual circumstances (which *accident* perhaps first manifests itself in some small degree), and by following them up with *experiments,* and varying the conditions of these until *the true law of nature* which they express is apprehended, conducts us at length to consequences altogether unexpected, remote from the usual experience, and contrary to almost universal belief.[2]

Thus, photography was not only allied to the natural philosophy of positivism, it was also "a new proof" of its value, proceeding through experiments to arrive at "the true law of nature." This was to underline the proof-function of the photograph and highlight the inductive nature of the medium. It also suggested Talbot's conception of himself as an amateur natural philosopher.[3]

Talbot was a Cambridge-educated member of the landed gentry who had been interested since childhood in amateur chemistry and botany, later adding

1 Just as Daguerre may be said to have stolen the credit for the invention of the eponymous daguerreotype from the Niépce brothers, so Talbot received credit for a process that was being experimented with simultaneously in France by Hippolyte Bayard. The early history of photography is full of proper names all vying for the position of "first": it is not my aim, however, to sort this out.

2 William Henry Fox Talbot, *Some Account of the Art of Photogenic Drawing, of the Process by which Natural Objects may be made to Delineate Themselves without the Aid of the Artist's Pencil* (London: R. and J.E. Taylor, 1939); *emphasis mine.* Cited in Larry J. Schaaf, *Out of the Shadows: Herschel, Talbot, and the Invention of Photography* (New Haven: Yale University Press, 1992), 6. Most of the information regarding Talbot and Herschel contained here derives from Schaaf's account. I depart, however, from its unproblematically positivist investment in the topos of the progressive advancement of photography, and its understanding of Talbot's description of the calotype as art. See also Helmut Gernsheim, "Talbot's and Herschel's Photographic Experiments in 1839," *Image*, vol. 8, no. 3 (September 1959), 133–37; Schaaf, *Tracings of Light: Sir John Herschel and the Camera Lucida*, San Francisco, Friends of Photography, 1989, and "The First Fifty Years of British Photography: 1794–1855," in Michael Pritchard, ed., *Technology and Art, The Birth and Early Years of Photography* (Bath: Royal Photographic Society, 1990), 9-18.

3 To be an amateur at this moment was not necessarily a derogated position, nor did it undermine one's scientific credentials; quite the contrary. Talbot's amateur is an *amateur* in the sense of lover in the old French usage: a passionate, but disinterested devotée, whose amateurism confirms his privilege and classes his endeavor as distinct from entrepreneurial self-interest and tradesmanly practice. Science itself was not sufficiently specialized and professionalized at this point, nor were the values of bourgeois culture hegemonic enough, for the distinction between the professional and the dilettante to be operative as we know it now. See M. Berman, "'Hegemony' and the Amateur Tradition in British Science," *Journal of Social History*, vol. 8 (1974–1975), 30-50. On the role of amateurism in early English photography, see Grace Seiberling, *Amateurs, Photography and the Victorian Imagination*, International Museum of Photography at George Eastman House, Chicago and London, University of Chicago Press, 1986.

optics (microscopy, in particular), antiquities, and philology to the list.[4] He also had a (failed) desire to reproduce in drawing what he saw on his various grand tours around Europe, on an early one of which he met Herschel in Munich, in 1824. He published articles in mathematical journals; wrote on classical mythology, Egyptology, etymology, and British folklore; translated Assyrian cuneiform inscriptions; worked on the polarization of light; and invented an internal combustion machine: he was, in other words, an all-around man of science and letters. As such, in 1831 he was elected a Fellow of the Royal Society, the body to which he would announce his invention of the calotype in 1839.[5] In this he was supported by other important men of science of the day besides Herschel, most notable among them Michael Faraday, who nudged Talbot forward to present his invention.

Faraday is now known for having helped systematize the experimental procedures of modern science, breaking them down into two moments, a private one of trial and error and a rehearsed public one of proof by demonstration.[6] This breaking down of the experimental process had a social aspect. That it began in private meant that the experimentation was still in great part an extension of the social sphere of the private gentleman.[7] That it had to be proved in public signaled a connection to lawyerly procedures and legal demonstrations in the form of public trials,[8] as well as a fairly strict social division between the gentility of laboratory work and the public apparatus of proof, with its showmanship, hiding of its devices, overtones of charlatanism and magician's tricks, and tradesmanly efforts to persuade the public to "buy" the evidence put before it. Talbot associated his invention with the first of the two aspects of experimental science.

In France, Daguerre would attach his invention to the public side of science, taking full advantage of his connections to its apparatus of professional practice and civic presentation, not to mention his ties to show business, to publicize his invention.[9] Talbot himself would indicate this contrast in *The Pencil of Nature.* It is well known that Talbot hesitated to patent his invention, wishing to keep it to himself rather than ceding it to the public sphere. In *The Pencil of Nature,* he distinguished that kind of hesitation from Daguerre's rush to announce the daguerreotype to an uninformed public. He was also fairly clear that the social ideology of private experimentation underwrote both his photographic investigations and his limited publication of his discovery in the form of a book by and for gentlemen, in which he narrated his private investigations much in the manner that Faraday recorded his experimental efforts in his *Diaries*, semipublicly endowing photography with the stamp of private science.

Instead of patenting the calotype right away, Talbot set up his own private photograph-printing establishment in Reading, placing it under the direction of an indentured servant, one Nicolaas Henneman.

There Talbot worked on preparing the deluxe, limited edition *The Pencil of Nature*, in which he told the story of his invention and illustrated its various uses with a set of twenty-four tipped-in calotypes. The book came out in six installments between June 1844 and April 1846 at a total cost of three guineas.[10] In its

---

4 On Cambridge, see M. M. Garland, *Cambridge before Darwin: The Ideal of a Liberal Education, 1800–1860* (Cambridge: Cambridge University Press, 1980).

5 On the Royal Society, see A. B. Granville, *Science without a Head; or the Royal Society Dissected*, London, T. Ridgway, 1830; and M. B. Hall, *All Scientists Now: The Royal Society in the Nineteenth Century* (Cambridge: Cambridge University Press, 1984). On the Royal Institution and other scientific associations, see D. S. L. Cardwell, *The Organization of Science in England*, London, Heinemann, 1972; M. Berman, *Social Change and Scientific Organization: The Royal Institution, 1799–1844*, London, Heinemann, 1978; and J. Morrell and A. Thackray, *Gentlemen of Science: Early Years of the British Association for the Advancement of Science* (Oxford: Claredon Press, 1981).

6 See David Gooding, "'In Nature's School': Faraday as an Experimentalist," in David Gooding and Frank A. J. L. James, eds., *Faraday Rediscovered: Essays on the Life and Work of Michael Faraday 1791–1867*, New York, Stockton Press, 1985, pp. 105–135. See also Sydney Ross, "John Herschel on Faraday and on Science," *Notes and Records of the Royal Society of London*, vol. 33 no. 1 (August 1978), 72-82. Jed Buchwald, *The Rise of Wave Theory of Light, Optical Theory and Experiment in the Early Nineteenth Century*, Chicago, Chicago University Press, 1989; David Gooding, Trevor Pinch, and Simon Schaffer, eds., *The Uses of Experiment: Studies in the Natural Sciences*, Cambridge, Cambridge University Press, 1989; and Steven Shapin, *A Social History of Truth: Civility and Science in Seventeenth Century England* (Chicago: University of Chicago Press, 1994).

7 Whereas Gooding ("In Nature's School") stresses the public aspect of Faraday's system of experimentation, I want to emphasize its private side. Talbot's formation as a landed gentleman given to a variety of amateur scientific pursuits, his own account of his process of experimentation, and even paradoxically, the publication venture of *The Pencil of Nature*, all privilege the private aspect of the experiment. (To speak about private science in this classed way is to put a particular social spin on Crary's notion, articulated in *Techniques of the Observer*, of the camera obscura as the epistemological space of the private individual.)

8 See Nicholas Wade, "Method and Madness: Trials and Errors," *New York Times Magazine*, July 24, 1994, for a popularized modern-day account of the relationship between science and the law and their procedures for arriving at the truth. For Wade, the law, because it relies on "the contest between tenacious advocates and their credibility to a jury," rather than on "cross-examining nature through rigorously objective trials," falls short of the "objectivity" of science. Nonetheless, it is evident that science and the law are now, as they were in the nineteenth century, thoroughly interpenetrated with one another and frequently modeled on each other's examples. This relationship was announced already in 1844, in sections of *The Pencil of Nature*.

9 On the other side of the Channel, photography's beginnings were in fact tied much more closely to the smoke-and-mirrors side of experimental demonstration. This is evident not only in the early public presentation of Daguerre's invention, but also in Daguerre's own background in dioramic light shows and other kinds of theatrical illusionism. See Helmut and Alison Gernsheim, *L. J. M. Daguerre: The History of the Diorama and the Daguerreotype* (New York: Dover Publications, 1968) (2nd ed.).

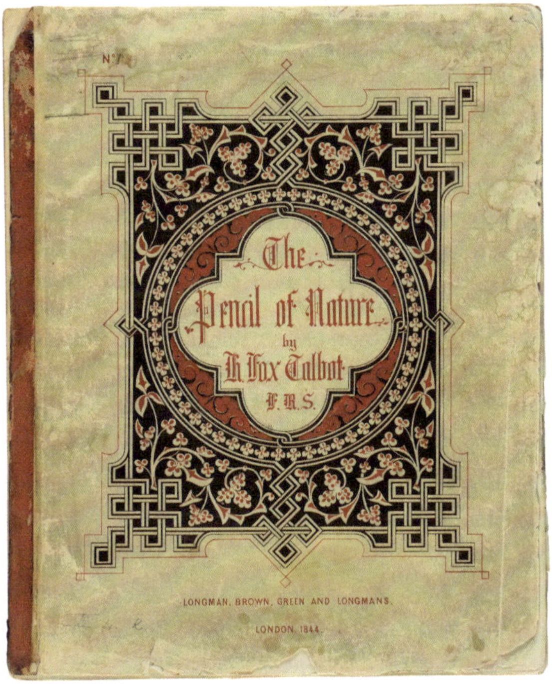

Figure 1. William Henry Fox Talbot, title page from *The Pencil of Nature*, 1844, 12 × 9.5 in.

expensive presentation—each of the installments of *The Pencil of Nature* came replete with an elaborately decorated black and terracotta cover designed by the well-known architect and ornament designer, Owen Jones (Fig. 1)—, the book was an elite production, disregarding Talbot's own involvement in its limited mass production and commercialization.[11] Although the darkroom efforts of Talbot and Henneman were tremendous by the as yet nonexistent standards of this early moment in photographic printing, the number of copies was small (and ever smaller) by publishing standards: fewer than three hundred sets were printed of the first installment, which included five illustrations, diminishing to half the number of copies for the second installment, which contained seven photographs and so on.[12]

The series of experiments that led up to *The Pencil of Nature* have been investigated in full; because of its claim to be a first and its contribution to the progress of the science of photography, it has long been viewed as a classic. Moreover, this initial endeavor to multiply the photographic print has been treated as the origin of the mass media incarnation of the photograph, with the Reading establishment described as "the first mass production photofinishing laboratory in the world."[13] Thus my interest in *The Pencil of Nature* is not new; however, in the most of these regards, it runs contrary to the usual way of understanding this "first" book.

Rather than treating it as a transparent record of an invention and the steps that led to it, I wish to give it a close reading as a new discursive entity. Rather than treating the experimentation that led up to the calotype, I want to read the narrative for the way in which it constructs itself as experimental, not merely as the end product of experimentation, but itself as the experiment. My aim is to denaturalize it; rather than a familiar kind of contribution to the progress of science, I wish to regard it as an experiment in putting the photograph together with text and, as such, as a kind of owner's manual or reader's guide providing instructions on how to read the unfamiliar entity of the photographically illustrated book. Finally, rather than a point of origin in the teleological development of the photograph toward its manifest destiny as a mass medium, I wish to understand it again as an experiment, but by no means a foregone conclusion, in the "massification" of the photograph and the photographically illustrated book, sewn with its author's gentlemanly ambivalence

10 See Schaaf, *Out of the Shadows*. See also Gail Buckland, *Fox Talbot and the Invention of Photography* (Boston: David Godine, 1980); H. J. P. Arnold, *William Henry Fox Talbot, Pioneer of Photography and Man of Science*, (London: Hutchinson Benham, 1977); and the introduction by Beaumont Newhall to the 1961 facsimile edition of *The Pencil of Nature* published by Da Capo Press in New York. The best and most recent of the facsimiles is Larry Schaaf's *H. Fox Talbot's The Pencil of Nature: Anniversary Facsimile*, (New York: Hans P. Kraus, Jr., 1989). Most of my reproductions are taken from this facsimile edition.

11 Talbot named the book's London publishers (Longman, Brown, Green, and Longmans) and printers (J. and H. Cox Brothers, "Printers to the Honourable East-India Company") on the recto and verso of his title page, but made no mention at all of the Reading Talbotype Establishment. Significantly, Longman was one of those to support protectionism in the bookselling trade when it was brought before the court in 1852. See Paul Goldman, *Victorian Illustrated Books 1850–1870* (London: British Museum Press, 1994), 39.

12 Talbot's book was published just before the beginning of a publishing boom in nineteenth-century England and the efflorescence of the (wood-engraved) illustrated publication in the form both of books and of periodicals. This boom responded to a number of factors, including the spread of wood engraving, invention of electrotyping (in 1839), replacement of the hand press by the power platen and cylinder press (virtually complete by the 1850s), encouragement of literacy by both church and state, abolition of the compulsory newspaper stamp duty in 1855 and of the paper duty in 1861, and the growth of bookstall distributors. The last responded in turn to the expansion of railway travel, examples of which include Routledge, whose "Railway Library" started up in 1848, and W. H. Smith, who had over five hundred railway bookstalls throughout Britain by the end of the 1860s. The advent of free trade in bookselling, with the dissolution of the protectionist Bookseller's Association in 1852, was also a factor. Consequently, book and periodical prices went down and circulation numbers rose rapidly, with *Cornhill* magazine garnering an audience of 120,000 a month, and by 1864 *Good Words* 160,000 a month. (This information comes from Goldman, *Victorian Illustrated Books*.) See also Louis Dudek, *Literature and the Press: A History of Printing, Printed Media, and Their Relation to Literature*, (Toronto: Ryerson Press, 1960).

13 See Newhall introduction, *The Pencil of Nature* facsimile, p. 5 (unnumbered). See also Schaaf, *Out of the Shadows*, 137. on Talbot's reluctance to release his invention for others' use, particularly before he had published his book.

on that score, with the marks of his contrarian desire to preserve its privacy and its preindustrial nature, and with the unfamiliarity of another era besides our own whose values were other than ours. No matter how self-explanatory the form and obvious the content of *The Pencil of Nature* might seem to us now, it is worth the labor to make it strange.

"INTRODUCTORY REMARKS" AND "BRIEF HISTORICAL SKETCH OF THE INVENTION OF THE ART"

The Pencil of Nature unfolds according to the procedures of positive science, its opening account of the invention of the calotype and the various experiments that led to it verified by its calotype illustrations. These are on the order of scientific demonstrations, following the self-reflexive logic of both positivism and photography, in which photographs demonstrate the powers of photography. And the experimental nature of Talbot's matching of photographs to text is striking.

The "Introductory Remarks" to *The Pencil of Nature* declare Talbot's invention to be a matter of the book: "The little work now presented to the Public is *the first attempt to publish a series of plates* or pictures wholly executed by the new art of Photogenic Drawing, without any aid whatever from the artist's pencil" (*The Pencil of Nature,* p.1).[14] Rather than announce the calotype as the first photograph per se, Talbot defines it as the first photograph publishable in book form. He proceeds to distinguish photography from other methods of producing book plates: the "*plates of this work* have been obtained by the mere action of Light upon sensitive paper. They have been formed or depicted by optical and chemical means alone, and without the aid of any one acquainted with the art of drawing. It is needless, therefore, to say that they *differ in all respects, and as widely as possible, in their origin, from plates of the ordinary kind,* which owe their existence to the united skill of the Artist and the Engraver" (p. 2). Again and again Talbot refers to his photographs as plates, comparing them not merely with other graphic arts, but with other arts of illustration. Photography, in short, is Nature's paper art, Nature's method of producing book illustrations. In other words, *The Pencil of Nature* is the "first specimen" of a bookish as well as a scientific art. Its function as a book is self-reflexive: to exhibit itself as a first example of the experimental phenomenon of photographs in a book.

Talbot's "Brief Historical Sketch of the Invention of the Art" is, among other things, a narrative of the private privilege of his endeavor. [. . .]

He thus describes himself as an amateur amusing himself at his leisure, and foregrounds the grand tour several times as the enabling condition of his first steps in the direction of his invention. His narrative is immediately insinuated within the discourse of scientific investigation. Carefully he logs in the place and date of his experimental trial runs, as befits a scientific diarist. Repeatedly he emphasizes his failures and flops. Throughout the "Brief Historical Sketch," he continues to do so. But his is clearly not meant as a narrative of ineptitude. Instead, his aborted attempts are inscribed within the "natural method" of the experiment and within the logic of inductive science. Of course, the reader does know one thing in advance, that Talbot is finally going to get it right. The very fact of the publication of the book is proof of his ultimate success. (Indeed, publication of the book as such, with its plates, stands in place of a conventional narrative climax, of which there really is none.)

In the course of his narrative, Talbot defines the photograph as Nature's imprint:

> And this led me to reflect on the inimitable beauty of the pictures of *nature's painting* which the glass lens of the Camera throws *upon the paper* in its focus—*fairy pictures, creations of a moment, and destined as rapidly to fade away.*
>
> It was during these thoughts that the idea occurred to me . . . how charming it would be if it were possible to cause these *natural images* to imprint themselves durably, and remain fixed *upon the paper!*
>
> And why should it not be possible? I asked myself.
>
> The picture, divested of the ideas which accompany it, and considered only in its ultimate nature, is but *a succession or variety of stronger lights thrown upon one part of the paper, and of deeper shadows on another.* Now Light, where it exists, can exert an action, and, in certain circumstances, does exert one sufficient to *cause changes in material bodies.* Suppose, then, such an action could be exerted *on the paper;* and suppose *the paper* could be visibly changed by it. *In that case surely some effect must result having a general resemblance to the cause which produced it:* so that *the variegated scene of light and shade might leave its image or impression behind,* stronger or weaker on different parts *of the paper* according to the strength or weakness of the light which had acted there. . . . lest the thought should again escape me between that time and my return to England, I made a careful note of it in writing, and also of such experiments as I thought would be most likely to realize it, if it were possible. (pp. 3–5)

Talbot proceeds to insert his delight in "nature's painting" into the flow of note taking and future experimentation, inscribing his "fairy pictures" in a discussion of causation, of Nature's action of "caus[ing] changes

14 The text is unpaginated; all page indications are mine.

in material bodies." That is, he defines the photograph as an index, a tonally variegated trace of Nature's variations in light and shade. When Talbot uses the word "impression," he speaks of the index in the language of print making, reiterating the fact that the photograph is an image imprinted on paper that accommodates the illustrated book to the causes and effects of Nature.

As befits his indexical definition of the photograph, Talbot's narrative of experimentation is preoccupied with the chemistry of photography. It is in the domain of chemistry that he speaks most insistently of putting his "theories and speculations to the test of experiment." It is with chemistry that observations recorded in "chemical books" must be submitted to "trial" (pp. 5–6). [. . .]

Chemistry, in Comte's account, is particularly susceptible to prescientific modes of explanation such as are implied in Talbot's alchemical notion of the "fairy picture." Yet chemistry also figures positivism's naturalization of Mind. "All the means employed are subject, especially, but not solely in chemistry,—to a verification by the precise collation of the two procedures of analysis and synthesis;—or, (as these terms have been corrupted by metaphysical uses) composition and decomposition" (p. 255). Then there is Comte's emphasis on the "artificial circumstances" (or experimental induction) of chemical composition and decomposition. It is worth remembering, indeed, that Comte's definition of the experiment was to be found in his discussion of the science of chemistry.

> As for *Experiment*, it is enough to say that the greater number of chemical phenomena, and especially the most instructive, are of artificial production. Still, *we must remember that the essential character of experimentation consists in the institution, or the choice of the circumstances of the phenomena, in order to a more evident and decisive investigation. . . .* From the early days of the science, the immortal series of Priestley's experiments, and yet more, those of Lavoisier, have offered admirable models, almost comparable to the most perfect researches in physics, and quite enough to prove that there is nothing in the nature of chemical phenomena to prevent the extended and luminous employment of the experimental methods. (p. 249)

Talbot (like Barthes, much later) clearly takes photography to be chemical "art" in all these regards.

In *The Pencil of Nature* the experimental method of chemistry and the narrative mode are synonymous: to conduct a series of experiments *is* to conduct a narrative process (in the first person) whose denouement is putatively open and unknown. Along the way, one of Talbot's chemical experiments involves some botanical specimens:

> This process, of the formation of a subchloride by the use of a very weak solution of salt, having been discovered in the spring of 1834, no difficulty was found in obtaining distinct and very pleasing *images of such things as leaves, lace, and other flat objects of complicated forms and outlines,* by exposing them to the light of the sun.
>
> *The paper being well dried, the leaves, &c. were spread upon it*, and covered with a glass pressed down tightly, and then placed in sunshine; and when the paper grew dark, the whole was carried into the shade, and *the objects being removed from off the paper, were found to have left their images very perfectly and beautifully impressed or delineated upon it.* ("Brief Historical Sketch of the Invention of the Art," p. 10)

For Talbot the photogram is a primitive experimental moment. Primitive though it may be, however, it is also an example of perfect delineation, so that it is a photographic illustration of one of the central paradoxes of positivism—the inverse proportion of the perfection of a science to its modernity.

More important, the photogram is at once consummately artificial and quintessentially natural. This makes it the embodiment of the experiment with its combination of artifice and Nature. At the same time Talbot describes the photogram as at once the quintessence of the index—"the objects being removed from off the paper, were found to have left their images very perfectly and beautifully impressed or delineated upon it"—and the epitomy of the chemical idea of photography, and thus emblematic of *The Pencil of Nature*'s definition of the photograph. (I will come back to the photogram in the discussion of Talbot's plates, which instance the leaves and lace mentioned above; this is the first occasion of Talbot's tying the "Brief Historical Sketch" directly to his plates, as both illustrations and culminations of the narrative.) [. . .]

At this point in the "Brief Historical Sketch" the rhythm of the narrative begins to suggest the spurts and lags that characterize experimental progress, and Talbot steps up his dramatization of the competitive pattern of the first-person narrative of positive science. Increasingly, he plays the role of the experimental protagonist, digging into the theme of self-evidence, contrasting the observations of others and "the statements of chemical writers" to his own experimentation, the surprised evidence of his own eyes, and the drawing of his own conclusions (pp. 11–12). Of course, this is also to make the written assertion compete with the visual impression, the text with the photograph, as kinds of scientific claim, and to establish them as separate steps—the hypothetical and the evidentiary—in the scientific process. [. . .]

Immediately after Talbot's delay, we are told of a major setback in the scientific fortunes of our hero:

> Such was the progress which I had made in this inquiry at the close of the year 1838, when *an event occurred in the scientific world, which in some degree frustrated the*

> *hope with which I had pursued, during nearly five years, this long and complicated, but interesting series of experiments*—the hope, namely, of being the first to announce to the world the existence of the New Art—which has been since named Photography.
>
> *I allude, of course, to the publication in the month of January 1839, of the great discovery of M. Daguerre,* of the photographic process which he has called the Daguerreotype. I need not speak of the sensation created in all parts of the world by the first announcement of this splendid discovery, or rather, of the fact of its having been made, (for the actual method made use of was kept secret for many months longer). This great and sudden celebrity was due to two causes: first, to the beauty of the discovery itself: secondly, to the zeal and enthusiasm of Arago, whose eloquence, animated by private friendship, delighted in extolling the inventor of this new art, sometimes to the assembled science of the French Academy, at other rimes to the less scientific judgement, but not less eager patriotism, of the Chamber of Deputies. ("Brief Historical Sketch of the Invention of the Art," pp. 7–9)

It is as if, precisely in his stopping to admire and puzzle over a strange new phenomenon (and in his hesitation to publish), that Talbot, interested only in experimental advancement, had lost the race. Moreover, in Talbot's account of him, Daguerre is a bit of a vulgar self-publicist, and the theme of national and personal competition so integral to the progress of science is enframed within the interlinked questions of disinterested private experimentation and publication. This in turn is enframed within the difference of Talbot's form of announcement—printed (rather than hawked), private (relative to Daguerre's promotional activities), and scientific.

At the end of the narrative, this is a bit of an anticlimax. Talbot doesn't even bother to narrate the culmination of his experimental process. What he does instead, however, is significant. All along he had been proposing, in one way and another, that the publication of *The Pencil of Nature* is proof of the final success and resolution of his experiments: it is a see-it-for-yourself demonstration of his discovery. Thus the book obviates the need for narrating the end of his investigation, as its illustrations stand in for his final experiments. So rather than bring his story to a narrative close, in the final two pages of the "Brief Historical Sketch" Talbot speaks to the quality of his publication as a publication:

> *There is a point to which I wish to advert, which respects the execution of the following specimens. As far as respects the design, the copies are almost facsimiles of each other, but there is some variety in the tint which they present.* This arises from a twofold cause. In the first place, each picture is separately formed by the light of the sun, and in our climate the strength of the sun's rays is exceedingly variable even in serene weather. When clouds intervene, a longer time is of course allowed for the impression of a picture, but it is not possible to reduce this to a matter of strict and accurate calculation.
>
> The other cause is the variable quality *of the paper* employed, even when furnished by the same manufacturers—some differences in the fabrication and in the *sizing of the paper*, known only to themselves, and perhaps secrets of the trade, have a considerable influence on the tone of colour which the picture ultimately assumes.
>
> *These tints, however, might undoubtedly be brought nearer to uniformity, if any great advantage appeared likely to result: but, several persons of taste having been consulted on the point, viz. which tint on the whole deserved a preference, it was found that their opinions offered nothing approaching unanimity, and therefore, as the process presents us spontaneously with a variety of shades of colour, it was thought best to admit whichever appeared pleasing to the eye, without aiming at an uniformity which is hardly attainable.* And with these brief observations I commend the pictures to the indulgence of the Gentle Reader. (pp. 20–21)

This is a curious way to conclude. What it accomplishes is the following: stressing the particular boon of Talbot's (as opposed to Daguerre's) invention, it asserts that the Talbotype, or calotype, is a printable, reproducible paper photograph; it is a photograph that can appear, as it does here, in a book.[15]

It has that advantage over the one-of-a-kind, metal plate daguerreotype, which cannot be incorporated into the book, which cannot be published in that sense. The contrast to the daguerreotype is implicit but telling. Talbot's definition of the photograph predicts our modern mass media definition of it: a photograph is a reproducible image that is printable, publishable, and at least potentially assimilable to the page, to the printing press, to mechanically reproduced text.

Talbot's celebration of the reproducibility of his photographic process also involves a paradox, however, which distinguishes his sense of the reproducible photograph from ours. For Talbot speaks in praise of the

15 In his concluding chapter, "Photography Becomes an Art," Schaaf cites several reviewers of Talbot's book who were quite clear on this point, that the calotype was specifically a book-ready image, and *The Pencil of Nature* a book about photographs in books: "these illustrations are not simple imitative transcripts, but book pictures executed by nature herself" ("The Talbotype, Daguerreotype Engraving, &c.," *Morning Herald*, no. 19, 339, November 6, 1844, 5); "The experiment of photographically illustrated books is now before the world . . ." (Athenaeum, n. 904, February 22, 1845, 202; Schaaf, *Out of the Shadows*, 147, 151). Schaaf makes little of this, concentrating instead on the reviewers' remarks about the success of the new "art," but it is clear that Talbot's nineteenth-century audience was alive to the specific question of the book utility of the calotype and to the fact that the experiment in *The Pencil of Nature* was an experiment in book illustration and book publication.

variability of the print, and with it of the reproducible photograph's escape from absolute control. More than that, he commends the singularity of the duplicate. Contradictory as this is, it speaks to the particular nineteenth-century culture of the book to which *The Pencil of Nature* belongs. For the oxymoron that Talbot is recommending is a one-of-a-kind reproduction that helps to individuate the book in which it is placed, to ensure both its rarity and its personality—its status as the property of this person as distinguished from that person. For decades to come, the photographically illustrated book would continue to belong to the upper crust of the book trade, its very mode guaranteeing the personal distinction of its owners and readers. It is this that Talbot announces and celebrates when he conducts a poll of his own, made up of "persons of taste," from whom he discovers the limited value of uniformity, the lack of unanimity of opinion as the best print, and the desirability of leaving the choice of print color up to the pleasure of the individual eye. In so doing, he underscores *The Pencil of Nature*'s difference from the massification of the photograph that it predicts, and from the values of the mass publication as we know them.

Evidently, neither books nor photographs were produced according to anything near our present criteria of uniformity. And, that the manufacturing standards of the darkroom were not yet up to those of the book-printing trade goes without saying. That it also constituted a glitch in the apparatus of the book needs some highlighting, however, for it tells us something of the nineteenth-century view of the nature of the photograph and of its place within industrial culture. In this regard, it is important that Talbot factors two variables into the production of his "facsimiles": weather and paper manufacture. With the weather variable Talbot emphasizes the natural production of the single print. His prints are made one by one according to the whimsy of sun and cloud, rather than according to the "strict and accurate calculation" of the industrial printmaker. With his industrial variable, that of the manufacture of paper, Talbot insists on separating the domains of Nature and industry; he also suggests that the manufacturing side of his "Art" is out of his hands, distinct from what he and his servant Henneman contributed to *The Pencil of Nature.*

Thus in his book the full industrialization of the photograph is evaded by stressing Nature's individuated mode of production. Refusing to include mechanical reproduction within the naturalness of the "pencil of nature," Talbot treats his singularized "facsimiles" as indexes of Nature's resistance to being made over utterly in the image of industry. Echoing the episode of the colored rings, Talbot's differently colored prints stand for the amateur's private pleasure in phenomena for the sake of phenomena outside of all industrial or scientific use. And they also underline their own experimental status as replicated book illustrations.

So ends the "Brief Historical Sketch," with an advertisement about the bookishness of Talbot's invention, and emphasis on the "gentle" status of *The Pencil of Nature* as an individuated private publication, on the tension between the nature and the industry of the photographic book illustration, and on its implied difference from the singular daguerreotype. Now, says Talbot, "I commend the pictures to the indulgence of the Gentle Reader." A conventional address, this nonetheless admonishes the reader to read the pictures that come next, to read them within a book and as a book, and in relation to the narrative not quite concluded.

PLATES: A SCENE IN A LIBRARY

Each of Talbot's plates is accompanied by numbered and captioned passages of explanatory text, and in each case it is the text the "illustrates" the image, rather more than the other way around. As a book that inaugurates the text-image ratio of photography, *The Pencil of Nature* addresses the question of illustration per se. In some instances, it begins the process of naturalizing that relationship, so that the text right away appears to inhabit the images and the images to visualize the text, as if we see that process happen before our eyes. In other cases, it leaves the relationship so open that the reader is forced to confront his or her readerly activity of moving between text and plates. In these cases, there appears to be nothing natural or inherent about the relationship between the two: the reader is made to understand the artifice of wedding the semiologically distinct spaces of the photograph and the printed page to one another, and the fundamentally hybrid quality, not to mention oddity, of the photographically illustrated book.

That is the case of the plate that Talbot entitles "A Scene in a Library" (fig. 2.2), which although it is not the first in the book's series (it is the eighth plate), can be taken as emblematic of *The Pencil of Nature*'s construction of the scenario of photographic illustration. For that reason I begin out of order, with "A Scene in a Library." (For the same reason I chose it as my title image.) It depicts two shelves of books arrayed in a mixture of orderliness and disorder, as countable sets grouped by their height, thickness, and gilt-embossed bindings, with odd single, unembossed books of different heights intervening here and there, some neatly upright, each flush with the other, some tilted at angles, opening up gaps between books, including a set of seven thin pamphlets on the bottom shelf. One well-worn book is roughly in the middle of the lower shelf, its spine torn and peeling away to reveal the sewing of pages in series. The inscriptions on the spines of these books are almost but not quite legible. Here the camera counts the books, distinguishes one kind from another according to binding, and also suggests its own shortcomings (pointed out in an earlier piece of text) in registering a wide range of tones, from the near-white of certain book labels to the dark into which the books appear to recede. Above all "A Scene in a Library" is an inventorial photograph, and the object of its inventory is the author's library, the same library in which *The Pencil of Nature* itself surely would be included. Self-reflexively, "A Scene in a Library" images the world of books into which the photograph would be inserted, as well as the relationship between printed text and the photograph's capacities that would structure such books, and even the manner in which those books are put together.

But as emblematic as it is, it is also an anomalous photograph, primarily because of its accompanying text, a little piece of sci-fi fantasy that seems to have very little to do with the plate [...]

This curious passage, picking up the experimental thread of the "Brief Historical Sketch" and speaking directly to the experimental inclination of photography, describes a scene involving ultraviolet rays all but predicts infrared photography and the X-ray image. Given that such forms of photography were not yet in existence, and given the imaginary cast of this passage and its thematics of invisibility, no photographic image could possibly illustrate it. But why is this text next to this photograph? What does the *text* "illustrate"?

The link between this passage and other passages of text in *The Pencil of Nature* is more evident than its connection to the plate "A Scene in a Library." For instance, the passage's stated connection to the camera-as-eye metaphor, familiar from the treatise on natural philosophy by Herschel, is found in the discussion of plate III, "Articles of China," one of two other explicitly inventorial photographs, to which I will return.

Talbot places us imaginatively in the camera obscura, a dark room or "apartment" with "an aperture in a wall or screen of partition" through which rays of light pass. He shifts between the photographic camera and the interior of the apartment that both metaphorizes and includes the camera. Talbot's ultraviolet dream shuttles between one model of vision and another, collapsing the one into the other, and suggesting an inverted version of the positivist notion of the subject blind to itself. As it does so, it also figures self-reflexivity as such, both as a theme of the text and, indirectly, of the photograph (which depicts the contents of a "darkened chamber," too).

The text to "A Scene in a Library" ties together the camera-as-eye with the evidentiary status of the photograph—"the testimony of the imprinted paper." But although it suggests the fundamentally evidentiary nature of the relationship between text and photograph, the connection between the ultraviolet scenario hypothesized by the text and the "testimony of the imprinted paper" found next to it remains difficult to determine. Perhaps that is the point, for this particular conjunction of text and image stands as an assertion of the openness of the relationship between text and photograph, and of the difference that divides them. That is, the mismatch of image and text is an instantiation of the speculative rather than bespoke nature of the relationship between text and photographic plate. It suggests the inversion of the logic of the illustration described by Barthes, that in the case of photography it is the illustration that is prior to the text that adjoins it and the text that is after the fact—the text that historiates the image, rather than the other way around.[16]

The (mis)joining of text and image also insists on the gap between reading and viewing, suggesting the change of cognitive and semiological focus between one and other, and proposing that it is the reader who imaginatively fills in the missing link. In that way the play of meaning is displaced from the text, photograph, and the author, and assigned to the reader of the book. Perhaps "A Scene in a Library" and its text together suggest that this transfer of signifying power and interpretive action from the author and his objects to the subjectivity of the reader is definitive of photographs and of books illustrated with photographs.[17] After all, the text thematizes subjectivity—the subjectivity of the "darkened chamber" described by the camera and attached to photography, whereas the photograph, exchanging places with the text, thematizes the library and with it, readership.

Attaching *The Pencil of Nature* to Talbot's library—a private gentlemen's library—the image of the shelved volumes figures an old world of the text into which a new kind of image intrudes to make a new, scarcely imaginable world of the book. "A Scene in a Library" is "the testimony of the imprinted paper," which, with its authenticating yet barely readable trace of two shelves of books, verifies in advance the future possibilities of that new world, its new set of speculative

16 The term "historiate," properly used (as in historiated capital or initial), suggests the use of a visual narrative as decoration, the transformation of the decorative register of architectural space or of the verbal sign into a narrative, pictorial one. I use it in an invested sense to suggest the verbal decoration of the photograph, in particular its supplementation by history, by legends and anecdotes, historical stories and narratives.

17 In this regard as well, *The Pencil of Nature* is in harmony with Barthes's *Camera Lucida* and its development of a theory of photographic reception as subjectively variable by nature, not to mention its attaching photography to the spectator over and above the operator. It is, moreover, in line with Barthes's more general theory of reading, and his replacement of the author with the reader as the site and source of the meaning of a text. See Barthes, "The Death of the Author," in *Image, Music, Text*, trans., Stephen Heath (New York: Hill and Wang, 1977). See as well Michel Foucault, "What Is an Author?," in *Language, Counter-Memory, Practice*, trans., Donald Bourchard and Sherry Simon (Ithaca: Cornell University Press, 1977). But although this is a critical feature of deconstructionist reading, Talbot's articulation of it is specific to the phenomenon of the photographically illustrated book, and for that reason the important resonance is with *Camera Lucida*'s theory of photographic readership.

relations between text and image, and its new relay of visibility and invisibility. The last paragraph of the passage accompanying "A Scene in a Library" makes an experimental case for this new world of the book and its new space of imagination: "Alas! that this speculation is somewhat too refined to be introduced with effect into a modern novel or romance; for what a *dénouement* we should have, if we could suppose the secrets of the darkened chamber to be revealed by the testimony of the imprinted paper." Is this the missing (and future) dénouement of the anticlimactic "Brief Historical Sketch"? Perhaps: the printing press is clattering and clanging away, and out of it will come something strange, a new breed of "romance" in which yet to be determined evidentiary material intervenes to produce new solutions and narrative conclusions. The "testimony of the imprinted paper" that is photography breeds a whole new library with a new kind of publication in it, a yet unrealized apparatus of the printed book. That, if anything, is the concerted statement, discoverable by the reader of the text and the image captioned "A Scene in a Library."

PLATES, I: TWO VIEWS THROUGH THE CAMERA OBSCURA

Neither the plates nor their related passages are ordered in the linear manner of Talbot's opening narrative. Nor are they really grouped according to any readily apparent order. The only logic that their sequencing suggests is one of instantiation, a pattern of this and that. Out of Talbot's series of plates, then, we will have to determine our own categories and construct our own sequence and groupings of photographs. (Such flipping back and forth is intrinsic to perusal of the book with photographic plates. Certainly it was solicited by the publication of books like *The Pencil of Nature* in serial parts, which could be taken apart and bound in different orders.)

At the beginning of the plates portion of his book Talbot places two pairs of photographs that are the only exceptions to the rule of complete randomness.

First there are two architectural views taken with the camera obscura; after them are two photographs of objects on shelves (figs. 2.3, 2.4, 2.6, and 2.7). It is significant that Talbot begins with perspectival views that are exemplars of the culmination of his voyage of discovery: the successful putting together of the camera obscura and chemistry-on-paper. With the first of his plates, in fact, he comes home from the travels abroad recounted in the "Brief Historical Sketch," not to his residence Lacock Abbey, which figures prominently among the later plates, but to Oxford University, which is also conspicuous in later plates. (Talbot took a trip there in 1843. Oxford, which fortuitously would be the university site of the English spread of Comtean

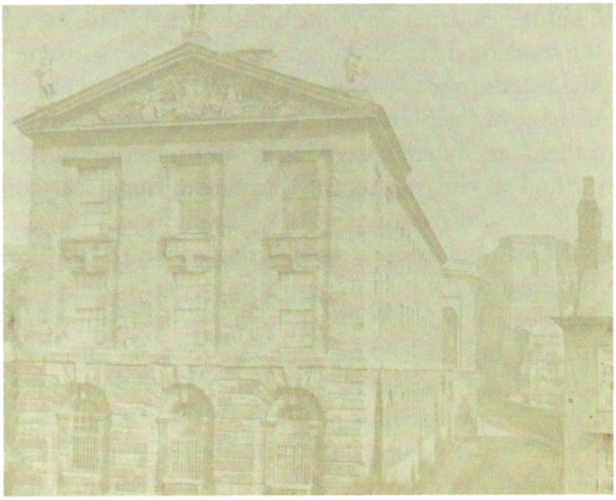

Figure 2. William Henry Fox Talbot, *Plate I. Part of Queen's College, Oxford*, 1844, salted paper print, 6.5 × 8 in.

positivism, serves well enough to stand for Talbot's status as an educated gentleman.)

Under the caption of plate I, "Part of Queen's College, Oxford" (Fig. 2), Talbot tells us what to look for:

> *This building presents on its surface the most evident marks of the injuries of time and weather,* in the abraded state of the stone, which probably was of a bad quality originally.
>
> The view is taken from the other side of the High Street—looking North. The time is morning.
>
> In the distance is seen at the end of a narrow street the Church of St. Peter's in the East, said to be the most ancient church in Oxford, and built during the Saxon era. This street, shortly after passing the church, turns to the left, and leads to New College. (*The Pencil of Nature,* plate I)

The photograph so described and situated presents us with an eroded, much roughened façade that is lined up flush with the surface plane of the photograph, taking up over half of its space and almost but not quite abutting its left edge. On the right side of the photograph is a small fragment of another façade, marked by a chimney, cropped by the right edge, also aligned with the surface plane. Between one façade and the other, a little shadowed street angles up and slightly to the left, disappearing behind the perspectivally seen side of the part of Queen's College whose front façade dominates the photograph. At the point where that street angles around, two towers on either side of it mark its disappearance from view. In the right middle distance a mottled massing of dark gray behind the rectangular tower suggests some trees.

Talbot has us read from left to right. He asks that we look first at the surface of the façade on the left, where we are to notice "on its surface the most evident marks of the injuries of time and weather, in the abraded state of the stone." This is primarily what they photograph is a picture of; namely, a surface marked with the indexical traces of time and weather. This is, of course, also what a photograph is. So Talbot's instructions ask us to read the photograph self-reflexively, as an image of the photography, defined as a surface full of the imaged detail, deriving from the action of Nature and serving as a temporal index of the history of the material it records.

From a first encounter with its surface, the instructions turn to the photograph's function as a view. In telling us where the view was taken from and in what direction he was looking when he took it, Talbot directs us as to where to imagine ourselves standing and looking, converting his position in front of the scene into our position in front of the photograph. Telling us what time it was, Talbot then directs us to the back, right-hand portion of the image. From surface to depth, from the trace to the view, Talbot also moves us from the present to the past—from the present condition of Queen's College to the "Saxon era" and "the most ancient church in Oxford." Increasingly we move from what is visible in the photograph to what is either invisible or not a matter of visibility at all, to the history of the place, which must be given in words. Thus Talbot directs us to a point of conjunction between image and text, where each is grafted onto the other to make an indivisible whole, such that the traces of "time and weather" in and on the photograph have added to them spatial and temporal indications that describe the photograph's parameters, and text-provided historical information that comes to seem as if given by the photograph itself, by the indexical marks on its surface.

In the next and final sentence Talbot leads us to the vanishing point of the photograph and out of the bounds of invisibility altogether, completing the circuit from surface description to perspectival reading, and from the photograph's contents to its enframing edges. Thus he ties the photograph to the world by mapping out its coordinates and connecting the landmarks within it to those without it. If at the borders of the photograph we find history and geography, it is there that we find text as well, enframing the image and securing it again to the world from which it was taken, strengthening its indexical links to time and space, and reinforcing its evidentiary ties to what lies outside of its visual scope. [...]

Having provided two examples of the culmination of his "art" as narrated in the "Brief Historical Sketch," having structured his text as a frame, a set of viewing directions, and an explanation from effect back to cause, and having constituted the reader as a vicarious spectator and as a subject both unfixed and fixed, both standing in front of pictures and scanning paper surfaces for the punctal details that happen to catch the glancing light and snag the drifting, alighting gaze, he proceeds to other illustrative functions of the photograph.

PLATES, II: TWO INVENTORIES

Talbot's next two plates, "Articles of China" and "Articles of Glass," make another pair. Each presents the viewer with objects arrayed symmetrically on horizontal shelves, parallel with the top and bottom edges of the image, as if the photographs were two matching glass cases enclosing and displaying precious possessions, china and glassware owned by Talbot and housed at Lacock Abbey. Talbot's descriptions of these plates are even sparser than his descriptions of the first two views. Indeed, instead of describing, orienting, and directing our viewing, he begins to imagine the potential uses and values of photography.

Talbot commences by comparing this photograph to a written inventory, telling the reader that the camera can record "the whole cabinet of a Virtuoso and collector of old China" (here he is both the photographer and the collector) "in little more time that it would take him to make a written inventory describing it in the usual way." Thus he treats the photograph as a paper record much like the inventory, thereby stressing the relationship between the photograph and information given in writing.[18]

In fact, the photographic document is *better* than either an inventory or a written description. Talbot's inclusion of a variety of differently worked china—teacups and saucers, sugarbowls, pitchers, compotiers, figurines, vases of various descriptions, what appear to be candlestick and stem holders, and so on—works to prove the point. For any such effort to inventory this collection and describe its contents verbally merely shows it laboriousness. And so Talbot doesn't bother describing "Articles of China"—the demonstration of the photograph is that it obviates verbal description. At the center of the collection is a china basket with an open-weave design that emblematizes the difficulty of verbal description in the face of intricate detail. Lined up above and below are items of a similar high degree of decorative intricacy, delineating a vertical axis that is at once the spine of the composition's symmetry and the marker of the beginnings of a grid formation, which serves as the visual counterpart of the written

18 In his shorter remarks about plate IV, "Articles of Glass," Talbot picks up the comparative thread of the positivist means of "observation, experiment, and comparison," and contrasts the photographic rendering of glass to that of china: "The photogenic images of glass articles impress the sensitive paper with a very peculiar touch, which is quite different from that of the China in Plate III. And it may be remarked that white china and glass do not succeed well when represented together, because the picture of the china, from its superior brightness, is completed before that of the glass is well begun" (plate IV). Because of Nature's working, in other words, different kinds of objects must be taken down separately, categorized under different headings, and entered in different lists, as it were.

list. If description is the enumeration of detail, then these objects center the gaze on the hopelessness of the verbal task and on the immediacy and thoroughness, the all-at-once-ness of the photograph's descriptive accomplishments.

Thus Talbot takes up the matter that is perhaps most fundamental to *The Pencil of Nature*, namely, that of writing and the photograph. Throughout he inscribes photography within the space of writing. In this case, however, the photograph not only inhabits the space of writing, it also is defined as something given in place of writing. If *The Pencil of Nature* can be taken as a study of different text-image relations suggested by the photograph in the book, that is the one proposed here: the photograph instead of text. [...]

Talbot also draws the link between the photograph and the legal document, proposing that it could provide testimony in court, should one's possessions be stolen, and that it would be "evidence of a novel kind." But he qualifies his assertion: "what the judge and jury might say to it, is a matter which I leave to the speculation of those who possess legal acumen." This is an admission that he is not a legal professional. (Here he represents himself as a man with possessions rather than a profession, a man whose objects and ownings, and amateur preoccupations define his identity.) But more important, it is an inductive statement about the unknown future application of this kind of testimony, positivist in its experimental disposition and its open-ended futurism. Perhaps most suggestive, it is an admission of the difficulty of knowing how to read the testimony provided by the photographic document, which once more suggested the opposition between the functions of authentication and legibility that Barthes sees as integral to the photograph.

Difficult to interpret or not, the photograph is irrefutable evidence, of that much Talbot is sure. This claim rests on a particular determination as to what kind of "specimen" a photograph is. Putting the photograph in place of the written document, it detaches the photograph's evidentiary status from any pregiven system of signification or interpretation. The photograph is evidence just because it is a photograph, and not because it is governed by a body of law or by the rules of the legal game. Certainly, Talbot's claim as to its future legal status as a document is an example of the overlapping and mutual inflection of the discourses of science and law, which join and shape each other most significantly where the question of evidence is involved.[19] But although legal discourse must be in place for the photograph to be used, even before it is so used, all by itself and by its very nature, it constitutes a new (if indeterminate) evidentiary entity; indeed, it constitutes the modern notion of evidence per se. [...]

It is then that Talbot characterizes the instrument that produces that form of evidence physiologically, as an eye with a retina and pupil; whose contraction generates "sharp and correct" images. This metaphor is servant to the instructions he wishes to give as to how to produce a sharp, clear photograph with the greatest depth of field. Here the reader is in do-it-yourself terrain: the instructions are from one amateur scientific practitioner to another. From a spectator, the viewer has become more of a reader again, and the photographic plates are beginning to serve less as pictures to be viewed than as examples of the kinds of images that can be produced by a certain manner of using the instrument. The plates are part of the instructions now.

If Talbot began with plates demonstrating the coincidence of the camera obscura photograph with the old perspectival picture, with the plates III and IV and the instructions in which they take part, he turns to a rather different conception of the instrument and the images it produces. He moves the reader imaginatively inside the camera obscura to consider its functioning parts according to the same physiological conception of vision propounded by Herschel in *A Preliminary Discourse.* In this conception vision is to be understood less as proceeding from and belonging to a subject (as it is in the text accompanying plates I and II) than as a technology, which, pulling the subject inside its mechanical spaces, stands in place of subjectivity as much as of writing.

With Talbot's soliciting the reader's imaginative diminution and displacement into the machine, he carves out a space in which both the subject and its objects are to be found together. The objects that are being recorded are described as surrounding the lens through which they are seen; the camera, the reader-viewer, and the pieces of china are all objects together in the same dark room, which is the virtuoso collector's cabinet. (This is the same collapse of spaces described in the enigmatic passage accompanying "A Scene in a Library.") In other words, the space of china objects and that of the box-camera interior described

19 See John Tagg, "Power and Photography—Part I, A Means of Surveillance: The Photograph as Evidence in Law," Screen Education, no. 6, Autumn 1980. See also Tagg, The Burden of Representation, "Introduction" (pp. 103–116), on the question of the "evidential force" of the photograph as institutionally framed rather than an ontological condition of the photographic image. Talbot's remarks on the future legal uses of the photograph indicate both, I think: both that he does not know how it will be institutionally framed (it will be, and that is what Tagg is concerned with), and that the evidentiary function is inherent in the photograph (which is what Barthes is concerned with in taking up the semiologics of photography). What this suggest is that there is something about the photograph (its semiological status as an index) that qualifies it to be used in the ways that it will be within the discursive practices of the institutions of law and science. And before those institutions solidified, a broader epistemological structure was coming into place (concurrently with the photograph itself) within which the evidentiary function of the photograph could be conceived, namely, the structure of positivist thought, which embraces a variety of institutions and discursive practices, including those of law and science.

in quick succession are one and the same, and the old dark room of the interiorized individual subject has been stopped down to a sharp, correct point where it is conflated with its objects. Or to put it less absolutely, the reader-viewer is asked to imagine himself in turn within the interior of the camera-as-room and within the inner works of the camera-as-machine, and to shuttle constantly between the two. Thus, Talbot's camera is both an old metaphor and a new one, both the dark room of old, the house of the autonomous subject, and the much tighter, more complex, and intertwined space of the objective apparatus.

This contraction of the subjective space of the camera is responsible, in Talbot's view, for the production of court-worthy documents and the substitution of those documents for the old written kind. The stopping down of the machine yields the all-at-once specificity that in turn qualifies the photographic record, as evidence of a superior sort to that of the subjectivity selective written description, and makes it so much more efficient than the painstaking owner's inventory. In Talbot's Herschelian, natural-philosophical view, the camera obscura in its mechanical aspect is Nature's instrument. In being like the eye it approximates Nature's handiwork and transcribes Nature's vision on its "object glass." [...]

PLATES, THE END: VARIABLE PRINTS

The Pencil of Nature ends with another anomaly, a still life. Plate XXIV, "A Fruit Piece" (Fig. 3), is another of Talbot's painting-like photographs in the realist tradition. Depicting two furit-laden baskets on a table top covered with a plaid blanket, it mimicks the dark backgrounds and shallow table-top spaces of Dutch still life painting, as well as the Chardinesque strewing of isolated pieces of fruit to contrast with the massing of edibles in containers. To the familiar apples and plums and peaches of the still life tradition, Talbot adds a spiky-topped pineapple to give his arrangement a slight, exotically tinged diagonal twist, more or less predicting the more opulent still lifes of photographers such as Roger Fenton and John Thomson. One might expect the matching text to delve into the photographic capacity for rendering texture and for numbering, differentiating, and identifying different items. One might expect it to announce photography's suitedness to the still life genre, indeed its potential ability to take over the reins from painting, but it does none of that. [...]

The visuality of "A Fruit Piece" seems mainly decorative—a good picture, a nice flourish to end with, a piece of out-and-out embellishment: the photograph can do that too. At the same time, it emphasizes the book's logic of random instantiation, and its lack of closure; a still life comes after a facsimile of a drawing, which comes after a view of Westminster Abbey, and

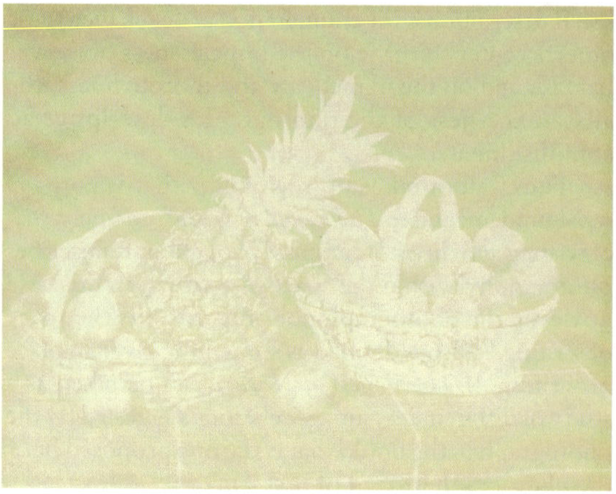

Figure 3. William Henry Fox Talbot, *Plate XXIV. A Fruit Piece*, 1844, salted paper print, 6.5 × 7.8 in.

so on. What will come next in the experimental installments that follow? As well, like "A Scene in a Library," "A Fruit Piece" stands as a contradictory indicator of the incommensurability of image and text, of the necessary disjunction between the photograph's visuality and the book's textuality, condensed in the meeting between the illusionist space of the still life and the printed page next to it.

One may like to imagine that there is more to it than that. An image of an object world, "A Fruit Piece" thematizes the one and the many, the numbered mass and the isolated item that falls out of the set, the slight distinctions between such similar objects as apples and peaches and plums and the larger distinction between the pineapple and the other fruit, as well as the variations within one species of object. No one specimen of the apple is exactly like every other specimen. Without adding the still life's traditional function of preserving perishables into the equation (and the connection to the perishability of the photograph suggested in the text), there is, it turns out, something about the contents of the plate's visual field that matches the closing themes of the last piece of text. Photographs, that is to say, are like the fruit in that they constitute a natural series, subject to change and injury and decay, in which specimens of the same species vary. To our understanding, there is an important difference: the photograph is of the order not of biological but of mechanical reproduction. Thus "A Fruit Piece" provides one more measure of the distance between Talbot's world of the photograph and our own: his focus on the incomplete assimilation of the photograph to the published book; his stress on the preindustrial individuality of the photographic copy and his straining against its massification; finally, his emphasis on the similarity between the natural and the photographic series. This is to understand the photograph and its place within the book and other mass media in a way that is foreign to us now.

As readers-cum-viewers, we close Talbot's book on the last plate's note of resistance to mass production, and its lack of assimilation to the adjacent text. It is best, perhaps, to leave it there, ending with the anomalousness of the plate, at the point of contact and distance between it and the page. It is also best, perhaps, not to put too firm a full stop at the end of *The Pencil of Nature*, whose narrative of experimentation is never quite concluded, although as in the "Brief Historical Sketch," it happens to come to a halt just there. It is as good a place as any to finish—with the book's difference from the "age of mechanical reproduction" that it helped inaugurate, with its attention to the strangeness of the meeting between text and photograph, its celebration of Nature's fabrication of the photographically illustrated book, and its early ties to the private spaces of the book production and consumption, of experimental science and equally experimental readership.

The Stereoscope and Stereograph

Oliver Wendell Holmes

1859

Democritius of Abdera, commonly known as the Laughing Philosopher, probably because he did not consider the study of truth inconsistent with a cheerful countenance, believed and taught that all bodies were continually throwing off certain images like themselves, which subtile emanations, striking on our bodily organs, gave rise to our sensations. Epicurus borrowed the idea from him, and incorporated it into the famous system, of which Lucretius has given us the most popular version. Those who are curious on the matter will find the poet's description at the beginning of his fourth book. Forms, effigies, membranes, or films, are the nearest representatives of the terms applied to these effluences. They are perpetually shed from the surfaces of solids, as bark is shed by trees. Cortex is, indeed, one of the names applied to them by Lucretius.

These evanescent films may be seen in one of their aspects in any clear, calm sheet of water, in a mirror, in the eye of an animal by one who looks at it in front, but better still by the consciousness behind the eye in the ordinary act of vision. They must be packed like the leaves of a closed book; for suppose a mirror to give an image of an object a mile off, it will give one at every point less than a mile, though this were subdivided into a million parts. Yet the images will not be the same; for the one taken a mile off will be very small, at half a mile as large again, at a hundred feet fifty times as large, and so on, as long as the mirror can contain the image.

Under the action of light, then, a body makes its superficial aspect potentially present at a distance, becoming appreciable as a shadow or as a picture. But remove the cause,—the body itself—and the effect is removed. The man beholdeth himself in the glass and goeth his way, and straightway both the mirror and the mirrored forget what manner of man he was. These visible films or membranous excurse of objects, which the old philosophers talked about, have no real existence, separable from their illuminated source, and perish instantly when it is withdrawn.

If a man had handed a metallic speculum to Democritus of Abdera, and told him to look at his face in it while his heart was beating thirty or forty times, promising that one of the films his face was shedding should stick there, so that neither he, nor it, nor anybody should forget what manner of man he was, the Laughing Philosopher would probably have vindicated his claim to his title by an explosion that would have astonished the speaker.

This is just what the Daguerreotype has done. It has fixed the most fleeting of our illusions, that which the apostle and the philosopher and the poet have alike used as the type of instability and unreality. The photograph has completed the triumph, by making a sheet of paper reflect images like a mirror and hold them as a picture.

This triumph of human ingenuity is the most audacious, remote, improbable, incredible,—the one that would seem least likely to be regained, if all traces of it were lost, of all the discoveries man has made. It has become such an everyday matter with us, that we forget its miraculous nature, as we forget that of the sun itself, to which we owe the creations of our new art. Yet in all the prophecies of dreaming enthusiasts, in all the random guesses of the future conquests over matter, we do not remember any prediction of such an inconceivable wonder, as our neighbor round the corner, or the proprietor of the small house on wheels, standing on the village common, will furnish any of us for the most painfully slender remuneration. No Century of Inventions includes this among its possibilities. Nothing but the vision of a Laputan, who passed his days in extracting sunbeams out of cucumbers, Could have reached such a height of delirium as to rave about the time when a man should paint his miniature by looking at a blank tablet, and a multitudinous wilderness of forest foliage or an endless Babel of roofs and spires stamp itself, in a moment, so faithfully and so minutely, that one may creep over the surface of the picture with his microscope and find every leaf perfect, or read the letters of distant signs, and see what was the play at the "Variétés" or the "Victoria," on the evening of the day when it was taken, just as he would sweep the real view with a spy-glass to explore all that it contains.

Some years ago, we sent a page or two to one of the magazines,—the "Knickerbocker," if we remember aright,—in which the story was told from the "Arabian Nights," of the three kings' sons, who each wished to obtain the hand of a lovely princess, and received for answer, that he who brought home the most wonderful object should obtain the lady's hand as his reward. Our readers, doubtless, remember the original tale, with the flying carpet, the tube which showed what a distant friend was doing by looking into it, and the apple which gave relief to the most desperate sufferings only by inhalation of its fragrance. The railroad-car, the telegraph, and the apple-flavored chloroform could and do realize, every day,—as was stated in the passage referred to, with a certain rhetorical amplitude not doubtfully suggestive of the lecture-room,—all that was fabled to have been done by the carpet, the tube, and the fruit of the Arabian story.

All these inventions force themselves upon us to the full extent of their significance. It is therefore hardly necessary to waste any considerable amount of rhetoric upon wonders that are so thoroughly appreciated. When human art says to each one of us, I will give you ears that can hear a whisper in New Orleans, and legs that can walk six hundred miles in a day, and if, in consequence of any defect of rail or carriage, you should be so injured that your own very insignificant walking members must be taken off, I can make the surgeon's visit a pleasant dream for you, on awaking from which you will ask when he is coming to do that which he has done already,—what is the use of poetical or rhetorical amplification? But this other invention of the mirror with a memory, and especially that application of it which has given us the wonders of the stereoscope, is not so easily, completely, universally recognized in all the immensity of its applications and suggestions. The stereoscope, and the pictures it gives, are, however, common enough to be in the hands of many of our readers; and as many of those who are not acquainted with it must before long become as familiar with it as they are now with friction-matches, we feel sure that a few pages relating to it will not be unacceptable.

Our readers may like to know the outlines of the process of making daguerreotypes and photographs, as just furnished us by Mr. Whipple, one of the most successful operators in this country. We omit many of those details which are everything to the practical artist, but nothing to the general reader. We must premise, that certain substances undergo chemical alterations, when exposed to the light, which produce a change of color. Some of the compounds of silver possess this faculty to a remarkable degree,—as the common indelible marking-ink, (a solution of nitrate of silver,) which soon darkens in the light, shows us every day. This is only one of the innumerable illustrations of the varied effects of light on color. A living plant owes its brilliant hues to the sunshine; but a dead one, or the tints extracted from it, will fade in the same rays which clothe the tulip in crimson and gold,—as our lady-readers who have rich curtains in their drawing rooms know full well. The sun, then, is a master of chiaroscuro, and, if he has a living petal for his pallet, is the first of colorists.—Let us walk into his studio, and examine some of his painting machinery.

1. THE DAGUERREOTYPE

A silver-plated sheet of copper is resilvered by electro-plating, and perfectly polished. It is then exposed in a glass box to the vapor of iodine until its surface turns to a golden yellow. Then it is exposed in another box to the fumes of the bromide of lime until it becomes of a blood-red tint. Then it is exposed once more, for a few seconds, to the vapor of iodine. The plate is now sensitive to light, and is of course kept from it, until, having been placed in the darkened camera, the screen is withdrawn and the camera-picture falls upon it. In strong light, and with the best instruments, three seconds' exposure is enough,—but the time varies with circumstances. The plate is now withdrawn and exposed to the vapor of mercury at 212 degrees. Where the daylight was strongest, the sensitive coating of the plate has undergone such a chemical change, that the mercury penetrates readily to the silver, producing a minute white granular deposit upon it, like a very thin fall of snow, drifted by the wind. The strong lights are little heaps of these granules, the middle lights thinner sheets of them; the shades are formed by the dark silver itself thinly sprinkled only, as the earth shows with a few scattered snow-flakes on its surface. The precise chemical nature of these granules we care less for than their palpable presence, which may be perfectly made out by a microscope magnifying fifty diameters or even less.

The picture thus formed would soon fade under the action of light, in consequence of further changes in the chemical elements of the film of which it consists. Some of these elements are therefore removed by washing it with a solution of hyposulphite of soda, after which it is rinsed with pure water. It is now permanent in the light, but a touch wipes off the picture as it does the bloom from a plum. To fix it, a solution of hyposulphite of soda containing chloride of gold is poured on the plate while this is held over a spirit-lamp. It is then again rinsed with pure water, and is ready for its frame.

2. THE PHOTOGRAPH

Just as we must have a mould before we can make a cast, we must get a negative or reversed picture on glass before we can get our positive or natural picture. The first thing, then, is to lay a sensitive coating on a piece of glass,—crown-glass, which has a natural surface, being preferable to plate-glass. *Collodion*, which is a solution of gun-cotton in alcohol and ether, mingled with a solution of iodide and bromide of potassium, is used to form a thin coating over the glass. Before the plate is dry, it is dipped into a solution of nitrate of silver, where it remains from one to three or four minutes. Here, then, we have essentially the same chemical elements that we have seen employed in the daguerreotype,—namely, iodine, bromine, and silver; and by their mutual reactions in the last process we have formed the sensitive iodide and bromide of silver.

The glass is now placed, still wet, in the camera, and there remains from three seconds to one or two minutes, according to circumstances. It is then washed with a solution of sulphate of iron. Every light spot in the camera-picture becomes dark on the sensitive coating of the glass-plate. But where the shadows or dark parts of the camera-picture fall, the sensitive coating is less darkened, or not at all, if the shadows are very deep, and so these shadows of the camera-picture become the lights of the glass-picture, as the lights become the shadows. Again, the picture is reversed, just as in every camera-obscura where the image is received on a screen direct from the lens. Thus the glass plate has the right part of the object on the left side of its picture, and the left part on its right side; its light is darkness, and its darkness is light. Everything is just as wrong as it can be, except that the relations of each wrong to the other wrongs are like the relations of the corresponding rights to each other in the original natural image. This is a negative picture.

Extremes meet. Every given point of the picture is as far from truth as a lie can be. But in travelling away from the pattern it has gone round a complete circle, and is at once as remote from Nature and as near it as possible. "How far is it to Taunton?" said a countryman, who was walking exactly the wrong way to reach that commercial and piscatory centre. "'Baout twenty-five thaousan' mild,"—said the boy he asked,—"'f y' go 'z y' 'r' goin' naow, 'n' 'baout haaf a mild 'f y' turn right raoun' 'n' go t'other way."

The negative picture being formed, it is washed with a solution of hyposulphite of soda, to remove the soluble principles which are liable to decomposition, and then coated with shellac varnish to protect it.

This *negative* is now to give birth to a *positive*,—this mass of contradictions to assert its hidden truth in a perfect harmonious affirmation of the realities of Nature. Behold the process!

A sheet of the vest linen paper is dipped in salt water and suffered to dry. Then a solution of nitrate of silver is poured over it and it is dried in a dark place. This paper is now sensitive; it has a conscience, and is afraid of daylight. Press it against the glass negative and lay them in the sun, the glass uppermost leaving them so for from three to ten minutes. The paper, having the picture formed on it, is then washed with the solution of hyposulphite of soda, rinsed in pure water, soaked again in a solution of hyposulphite of soda, to which, however, the chloride of gold has been added, and again rinsed. It is then sized or varnished.

Out of the perverse and totally depraved negative,—where it might almost seem as if some magic and diabolic power had wrenched all things from their proprieties, where the light of the eye was darkness, and the deepest blackness was gilded with the brightest glare,—is to come the true end of all this series of operations, a copy of Nature in all her sweet gradations and harmonies and contrasts.

We owe the suggestion to a great wit, who overflowed our small intellectual home-lot with a rushing freshet of fertilizing talk the other day,—one of our friends, who quarries thought on his own premises, but does not care to build his blocks into hooks and essays,—that perhaps this world is only the negative of that better one in which lights will be turned to shadows and shadows into light, but all harmonized, so that we shall see why these ugly patches, these misplaced gleams and blots, were wrought into the temporary arrangements of our planetary life.

For, ho! when the sensitive paper is laid in the sun under the negative glass, every dark spot on the glass arrests a sunbeam, and so the spot of the paper lying beneath remains unchanged; but every light space of the negative lets the sunlight through, and the sensitive paper beneath confesses its weakness, and betrays it by growing dark just in proportion to the glare that strikes upon it. So, too, we have only to turn the glass before laying it on the paper, and we bring all the natural relations of the object delineated back again,—its right to the right of the picture, its left to the picture's left.

On examining the glass negative by transmitted light with a power of a hundred diameters, we observe minute granules, whether crystalline or not we cannot say, very similar to those described in the account of the daguerreotype. But now their effect is reversed. Being opaque, they darken the glass wherever they are accumulated, just as the snow darkens our skylights. Where these particles are drifted, therefore, we have our shadows, and where they are thinly scattered, our lights. On examining the paper photographs, we have found no distinct granules, but diffused stains of deeper or lighter shades.

Such is the sun-picture, in the form in which we now most commonly meet it,—for the daguerreotype, perfect and cheap as it is, and admirably adapted for miniatures, has almost disappeared from the field of landscape, still life, architecture, and genre painting, to make room for the photograph. Mr. Whipple tells us that even now he takes a much greater number of miniature portraits on metal than on paper; and yet, except occasionally a statue, it is rare to see anything besides a portrait shown in a daguerreotype. But the greatest number of sun-pictures we see are the photographs which are intended to be looked at with the aid of the instrument we are next to describe, and to the stimulus of which the recent vast extension of photographic copies of Nature and Art is mainly owing.

3. THE STEREOSCOPE

This instrument was invented by Professor Wheatstone, and first described by him in 1838. It was only a year after this that M. Daguerre made known his discovery in Paris; and almost at the same time Mr. Fox Talbot sent his communication to the Royal Society, giving an account of his method of obtaining pictures on paper by the action of light. Iodine was discovered in 1811, bromine in 1826, chloroform in 1831, gun-cotton, from which coilodion is made, in 1846, the electro-plating process about the same time with photography; "all things, great and small, working together to produce what seemed at first as delightful, but as fabulous, as Aladdin's ring, which is now as little suggestive of surprise as our daily bread."

A stereoscope is an instrument which makes surfaces look solid. All pictures in which perspective and light and shade are properly managed, have more or less of the effect of solidity; but by this instrument that effect is so heightened as to produce an appearance of reality which cheats the senses with its seeming truth.

There is good reason to believe that the appreciation of solidity by the eye is purely a matter of education. The famous case of a young man who underwent the operation of couching for cataract, related by Cheselden, and a similar one reported in the Appendix to Miiller's Physiology, go to prove that everything is seen only as a superficial extension, until the other senses have taught the eye to recognize depth, or the third dimension, which gives solidity, by converging outlines, distribution of light and shade, change of size, and of the texture of surfaces. Cheselden's patient thought "all objects whatever touched his eyes, as what he felt did his skin." The patient whose case is reported by Muller could not tell the form of a cube held obliquely before his eye from that of a flat piece of pasteboard presenting the same outline. Each of these patients saw only with one eye,—the other being destroyed, in one case, and not restored to sight until long after the first, in the other case. In two months' time Cheselden's patient had learned to know solids; in fact, he argued so logically from light and shade and perspective that he felt of pictures, expecting to find reliefs and depressions, and was surprised to discover that they were flat surfaces. If these patients had suddenly recovered the sight of both eyes, they would probably have learned to recognize solids more easily and speedily.

We can commonly tell whether an object is solid, readily enough with one eye, but still better with two eyes, and sometimes only by using both. If we look at a square piece of ivory with one eye alone, we cannot tell whether it is a scale of veneer, or the side of a cube, or the base of a pyramid, or the end of a prism. But if we now open the other eye, we shall see one or more of its sides, if it have any, and then know it to be a solid, and what kind of a solid. We see something with the second eye which we did not see with the first; in other words, the two eyes see different pictures of the same thing, for the obvious reason that they look from points two or three inches apart. By means of these two different views of an object, the mind, as it were, feels round it and gets an idea of its solidity. We clasp an object with our eyes, as with our arms, or with our hands, or with our thumb and finger, and then we know it to be something more than a surface. This, of course, is an illustration of the fact, rather than an explanation of its mechanism.

Though, as we have seen, the two eyes look on two different pictures, we perceive but one picture. The two have run together and become blended in a third, which shows us everything we see in each. But, in order that they should so run together, both the eye and the brain must be in a natural state. Push one eye a little inward with the forefinger, and the image is doubled, or at least confused. Only certain parts of the two retina work harmoniously together, and you have disturbed their natural relations. Again, take two or three glasses more than temperance permits, and you see double; the eyes are right enough, probably, but the brain is in trouble, and does not report their telegraphic messages correctly. These exceptions illustrate the every-day truth, that, when we are in right condition, our two eyes see two somewhat different pictures, which our perception combines to form one picture, representing objects in all their dimensions, and not merely as surfaces.

Now, if we can get two artificial pictures of any given object, one as we should see it with the right eye, the other as we should see it with the left eye, and then, looking at the right picture, and that only, with the right eye, and at the left picture, and that only, with the left eye, contrive some way of making these pictures run together as we have seen our two views of a natural object do, we shall get the sense of solidity that natural objects give us. The arrangement which effects it will be a stereoscope, according to our definition of that instrument. How shall we attain these two ends?

1. An artist can draw an object as he sees it, looking at it only with his right eye. Then be can draw a second view of the same object as he sees it with his left eye. It will not be hard to draw a cube or an octahedron in this way; indeed, the first stereoscopic figures were pairs of outlines, right and left, of solid bodies, thus drawn. But the minute details of a portrait, a group, or a landscape, all so nearly alike to the two eyes, yet not identical in each picture of our natural double view, would defy any human skill to reproduce them exactly. And just here comes in the photograph to meet the difficulty. A first picture of an object is taken,—then the instrument is moved a couple of inches or a little more, the distance between the human eyes, and a second picture is taken. Better than this, two pictures are taken at once in a double camera.

We were just now stereographed, ourselves, at a moment's warning, as if we were fugitives from justice.

A skeleton shape, of about a man's height, its head covered with a black veil, glided across the floor, faced us, lifted its veil, and took a preliminary look. When we had grown sufficiently rigid in our attitude of studied ease, and got our umbrella into a position of thoughtful carelessness, and put our features with much effort into an unconstrained aspect of cheerfulness tempered with dignity, of manly firmness blended with womanly sensibility, of courtesy, as much as to imply, — "You honor me, Sir," toned or sized, as one may say, with something of the self-assertion of a human soul which reflects proudly, "I am superior to all this," — when, I say, we were all right, the spectral Mokanna dropped his long veil, and his waiting-slave put a sensitive tablet under its folds. The veil was then again lifted, and the two great glassy eyes stared at us once more for some thirty seconds. The veil then dropped again; but in the mean time, the shrouded sorcerer had stolen our double image; we were immortal. Posterity might thenceforth inspect us, (if not otherwise engaged,) not as a surface only, but in all our dimensions as an undisputed solid man of Boston.

2. We have now obtained the doubleeyed or twin pictures, or stereograph, if we may coin a name. But the pictures are two, and we want to slide them into each other, so to speak, as in natural vision, that we may see them as one. How shall we make one picture out of two, the corresponding parts of which are separated by a distance of two or three inches?

We can do this in two ways. First, by squinting as we look at them. But this is tedious, painful, and to some impossible, or at least very difficult. We shall find it much easier to look through a couple of glasses that squint for us. If at the same time they magnify the two pictures, we gain just so much in the distinctness of the picture, which, if the figures on the slide are small, is a great advantage. One of the easiest ways of accomplishing this double purpose is to cut a convex lens through the middle, grind the curves of the two halves down to straight lines, and join them by their thin edges. This is a squinting magnifier, and if arranged so that with its right half we see the right picture on the slide, and with its left half the left picture, it squints them both inward so that they run together and form a single picture.

Such are the stereoscope and the photograph, by the aid of which form is henceforth to make itself seen through the world of intelligence, as thought has long made itself heard by means of the art of printing. The morphotype, or form-print, must hereafter take its place by the side of the logotype or word-print. The stereograph, as we have called the double picture designed for the stereoscope, is to be the card of introduction to make all mankind acquaintances.

The first effect of looking at a good photograph through the stereoscope is a surprise such as no painting ever produced. The mind feels its way into the very depths of the picture. The scraggy branches of a tree in the foreground run out at us as if they would scratch our eyes out. The elbow of a figure stands forth so as to make us almost uncomfortable. Then there is such a frightful amount of detail, that we have the same sense of infinite complexity which Nature gives us. A painter shows us masses; the stereoscopic figure spares us nothing — all must be there, every stick, straw, scratch, as faithfully as the dome of St. Peter's, or the summit of Mont Blanc, or the ever-moving stillness of Niagara. The sun is no respecter of persons or of things.

This is one infinite charm of the photographic delineation. Theoretically, a perfect photograph is absolutely inexhaustible. In a picture you can find nothing which the artist has not seen before you; but in a perfect photograph there will be as many beauties lurking, unobserved, as there are flowers that blush unseen in forests and meadows. It is a mistake to suppose one knows a stereoscopic picture when he has studied it a hundred times by the aid of the best of our common instruments. Do we know all that there is in a landscape by looking out at it from our parlor-windows? In one of the glass stereoscopic views of Table Rock, two figures, so minute as to be mere objects of comparison with the surrounding vastness, may be seen standing side by side. Look at the two faces with a strong magnifier, and you could identify their owners, if you met them in a court of law.

Many persons suppose that they are looking on miniatures of the objects represented, when they see them in the stereoscope. They will be surprised to be told that they see most objects as large as they appear in Nature. A few simple experiments will show how what we see in ordinary vision is modified in our perceptions by what we think we see. We made a sham stereoscope, the other day, with no glasses, and an opening in the place where the pictures belong, about the size of one of the common stereoscopic pictures. Through this we got a very ample view of the town of Cambridge, including Mount Auburn and the Colleges, in a single field of vision. We do not recognize how minute distant objects really look to us, without something to bring the fact home to our conceptions. A man does not deceive us as to his real size when we see him at the distance of the length of Cambridge Bridge. But hold a common black pin before the eyes at the distance of distinct vision, and one-twentieth of its length, nearest the point, is enough to cover him so that he cannot be seen. The head of the same pin will cover one of the Cambridge horse-cars at the same distance, and conceal the tower of Mount Auburn, as seen from Boston.

We are near enough to an edifice to see it well, when we can easily read an inscription upon it. The stereoscopic views of the arches of Constantine and of Titus give not only every letter of the old inscriptions, but render the grain of the stone itself. On the pediment of the Pantheon may be read, not only the words traced by Agrippa, but a rough inscription above it, scratched or hacked into the stone by some wanton hand during an insurrectionary tumult.

This distinctness of the lesser details of a building or a landscape often gives us incidental truths which interest us more than the central object of the picture. Here is Alloway Kirk, in the churchyard of which you may read a real story by the side of the ruin that tells of more romantic fiction. There stands the stone "Erected by James Russell, seedsman, Ayr, in memory of his children,"—three little boys, James, and Thomas, and John, all snatched away from him in the space of three successive summer-days, and lying under the matted grass in the shadow of the old witch-haunted walls. It was Burns's Alloway Kirk we paid for, and we find we have bought a share in the griefs of James Russell, seedsman; for is not the stone that tells this blinding sorrow of real life the true centre of the picture, and not the roofless pile which reminds us of an idle legend?

We have often found these incidental glimpses of life and death running away with us from the main object the picture was meant to delineate. The more evidently accidental their introduction, the more trivial they are in themselves, the more they take hold of the imagination. It is common to find an object in one of the twin pictures which we miss in the other; the person or the vehicle having moved in the interval of taking the two photographs. There is before us a view of the Pool of David at Hebron, in which a shadowy figure appears at the water's edge, in the right-hand farther corner of the right-hand picture only. This muffled shape stealing silently into the solemn scene has already written a hundred biographies in our imagination. In the lovely glass stereograph of the Lake of Brienz, on the left-hand side, a vaguely hinted female figure stands by the margin of the fair water; on the other side of the picture she is not seen. This is life; we seem to see her come and go. All the longings, passions, experiences, possibilities of womanhood animate that gliding shadow which has flitted through our consciousness, nameless, dateless, featureless, yet more profoundly real than the sharpest of portraits traced by a human hand. Here is the Fountain of the Ogre, at Berne. In the right picture two women are chatting, with arms akimbo, over its basin; before the plate for the left picture is got ready, "one shall be taken and the other left"; look! on the left side there is but one woman, and you may see the blur where the other is melting into thin air as she fades forever from your eyes.

Oh, infinite volumes of poems that I treasure in this small library of glass and pasteboard! I creep over the vast features of Rameses, on the face of his rock-hewn Nubian temple; I scale the huge mountain-crystal that calls itself the Pyramid of Cheops. I pace the length of the three Titanic stones of the wall of Baalbec,—mightiest masses of quarried rock that man has lifted into the air; and then I dive into some mass of foliage with my microscope, and trace the veinings of a leaf so delicately wrought in the painting not made with hands, that I can almost see its down and the green aphis that sucks its juices. I look into the eyes of the caged tiger, and on the scaly train of the crocodile, stretched on the sands of the river that has mirrored a hundred dynasties. I stroll through Rhenish vineyards, I sit under Roman arches, I walk the streets of once buried cities, I look into the chasms of Alpine glaciers, and on the rush of wasteful cataracts. I pass, in a moment, from the banks of the Charles to the ford of the Jordan, and leave my outward frame in the armchair at my table, while in spirit I am looking down upon Jerusalem from the Mount of Olives.

"Give me the full tide of life at Charing Cross," said Dr. Johnson. here is Charing Cross, but without the full tide of life. A perpetual stream of figures leaves no definite shapes upon the picture. But on one side of this stereoscopic doublet a little London "gent" is leaning pensively against a post; on the other side he is seen sitting at the foot of the next post;—what is the matter with the little "gent"?

The very things which an artist would leave out, or render imperfectly, the photograph takes infinite care with, and so makes its illusions perfect. What is the picture of a drum without the marks on its head where the beating of the sticks has darkened the parchment? In three pictures of the Ann Hathaway Cottage, before us,—the most perfect, perhaps, of all the paper stereographs we have seen,—the door at the farther end of the cottage is open, and we see the marks left by the rubbing of hands and shoulders as the good people came through the entry, or leaned against it, or felt for the latch. It is not impossible that scales from the epidermis of the trembling hand of Ann Hathaway's young suitor, Will Shakespeare, are still adherent about the old latch and door, and that they contribute to the stains we see in our picture.

Among the accidents of life, as delineated in the stereograph, there is one that rarely fails in any extended view which shows us the details of streets and buildings. There may be neither man nor beast nor vehicle to be seen. You may be looking down on a place in such a way that none of the ordinary marks of its being actually inhabited show themselves. But in the rawest Western settlement and the oldest Eastern city, in the midst of the shanties at Pike's Peak and stretching across the court-yards as you look into them from above the clay-plastered roofs of Damascus, wherever man lives with any of the decencies of civilization, you will find the clothes-line. It may be a fence, (in Ireland,)—it may be a tree, (if the Irish license is still allowed us,)—but clothes-drying, or a place to dry clothes on, the stereoscopic photograph insists on finding, wherever it gives us a group of houses. This is the city of Berne. How it brings the people who sleep under that roof before us to see their sheets drying on that fence! and how real it makes the men in that house to look at their shirts hanging, arms down, from yonder line!

The reader will, perhaps, thank us for a few hints as to the choice of stereoscopes and stereoscopic pictures. The only way to be sure of getting a good instrument is to try a number of them, but it may be well to know which are worth trying. Those made with achromatic glasses may be as much better as they are dearer, but we have not been able to satisfy ourselves of the fact. We do not commonly find any trouble from chromatic aberration (or false color in the image). It is an excellent thing to have the glasses adjust by pulling out and pushing in, either by the hand, or, more conveniently, by a screw. The large instruments, holding twenty-five slides, are best adapted to the use of those who wish to show their views often to friends; the owner is a little apt to get tired of the unvarying round in which they present themselves. Perhaps we relish them more for having a little trouble in placing them, as we do nuts that we crack better than those we buy cracked. In optical effect, there is not much difference between them and the best ordinary instruments. We employ one stereoscope with adjusting glasses for the hand, and another common one upon a broad rosewood stand. The stand may be added to any instrument, and is a great convenience.

Some will have none but glass stereoscopic pictures; paper ones are not good enough for them. Wisdom dwells not with such. It is true that there is a brilliancy in a glass picture, with a flood of light pouring through it, which no paper one, with the light necessarily falling on it, can approach. But this brilliancy fatigues the eye much more than the quiet reflected light of the paper stereograph. Twenty-five glass slides, well inspected in a strong light, are good for one headache, if a person is disposed to that trouble.

Again, a good paper photograph is infinitely better than a bad glass one. We have a glass stereograph of Bethlehem, which looks as if the ground were covered with snow-and-paper ones of Jerusalem, colored and uncolored, much superior to it both in effect and detail. The Oriental pictures, we think, are apt to have this white, patchy look; possibly we do not get the best in this country.

A good view on glass or paper is, as a rule, best uncolored. But some of the American views of Niagara on glass are greatly improved by being colored; the water being rendered vastly more suggestive of the reality by the deep green tinge. Per contra, we have seen some American views so carelessly colored that they were all the worse for having been meddled with. The views of the Hathaway Cottage, before referred to, are not only admirable in themselves, but some of them are admirably colored also. Few glass stereographs compare with them as real representatives of Nature.

In choosing stereoscopic pictures, beware of investing largely in groups. The owner soon gets tired to death of them. Two or three of the most striking among them are worth having, but mostly they are detestable,—vulgar repetitions of vulgar models, shamming grace, gentility, and emotion, by the aid of costumes, attitudes, expressions, and accessories worthy only of a Thespian society of candlesnuffers. In buying brides under veils, and such figures, look at the lady's hands. You will very probably find the young countess is a maid-of-all-work. The presence of a human figure adds greatly to the interest of all architectural views, by giving us a standard of size, and should often decide our choice out of a variety of such pictures. No view pleases the eye which has glaring patches in it,—a perfectly white-looking river, for instance,—or trees and shrubs in full leaf, but looking as if they were covered with snow,—or glaring roads, or frosted-looking stones and pebbles. As for composition in landscape, each person must consult his own taste. All have agreed in admiring many of the Irish views, as those about the Lakes of Killarney, for instance, which are beautiful alike in general effect and in nicety of detail. The glass views on the Rhine, and of the Pyrenees in Spain, are of consummate beauty. As a specimen of the most perfect, in its truth and union of harmony and contrast, the view of the Circus of Gavarni, with the female figure on horseback in the front ground, is not surpassed by any we remember to have seen.

What is to come of the stereoscope and the photograph we are almost afraid to guess, lest we should seem extravagant. But, premising that we are to give a colored stereoscopic mental view of their prospects, we will venture on a few glimpses at a conceivable, if not a possible future.

Form is henceforth divorced from matter. In fact, matter as a visible object is of no great use any longer, except as the mould on which form is shaped. Give us a few negatives of a thing worth seeing, taken from different points of view, and that is all we want of it. Pull it down or burn it up, if you please. We must, perhaps, sacrifice some luxury in the loss of color; but form and light and shade are the great things, and even color can be added, and perhaps by and by may be got direct from Nature.

There is only one Coliseum or Pantheon; but how many millions of potential negatives have they shed,—representatives of billions of pictures,—since they were erected! Matter in large masses must always be fixed and dear; form is cheap and transportable. We have got the fruit of creation now, and need not trouble ourselves with the core. Every conceivable object of Nature and Art will soon scale off its surface for us. Men will hunt all curious, beautiful, grand objects, as they hunt the cattle in South America, for their skins, and leave the carcasses as of little worth.

The consequence of this will soon be such an enormous collection of forms that they will have to be classified and arranged in vast libraries, as books are now. The time will come when a man who wishes to see any object, natural or artificial, will go to the Imperial, National, or City Stereographic Library and call for its skin or form, as he would for a book at any common library. We do now distinctly propose the creation of a comprehensive and systematic stereographic library, where all men can find the special forms they particularly desire to see as artists, or as scholars, or as mechanics, or in any other capacity. Already a workman has been travelling about the country with stereographic views of furniture, showing his employer's patterns in this way, and taking orders for them. This is a mere hint of what is coming before long.

Again, we must have special stereographic collections, just as we have professional and other special libraries. And as a means of facilitating the formation of public and private stereographic collections, there must be arranged a comprehensive system of exchanges, so that there may grow up something like a universal currency of these bank-notes, or promises to pay in solid substance, which the sun has engraved for the great Bank of Nature. To render comparison of similar objects, or of any that we may wish to see side by side, easy, there should be a stereographic metre or fixed standard of focal length for the camera lens, to furnish by its multiples or fractions, if necessary, the scale of distances, and the standard of power in the stereoscope-lens. In this way the eye can make the most rapid and exact comparisons. If the "great elm" and the Cowthorpe oak, if the State-House and St. Peter's, were taken on the same scale, and looked at with the same magnifying power, we should compare them without the possibility of being misled by those partialities which might tend to make us overrate the indigenous vegetable and the dome of our native Michel Angelo.

The next European war will send us stereographs of battles. It is asserted that a bursting shell can be photographed. The time is perhaps at hand when a flash of light, as sudden and brief as that of the lightning which shows a whirling wheel standing stock still, shall preserve the very instant of the shock of contact of the mighty armies that are even now gathering. The lightning from heaven does actually photograph natural objects on the bodies of those it has just blasted,—so we are told by many witnesses. The lightning of clashing sabres and bayonets may be forced to stereotype itself in a stillness as complete as that of the tumbling tide of Niagara as we see it self-pictured.

We should be led on too far, if we developed our belief as to the transformations to be wrought by this greatest of human triumph over earthly conditions, the divorce of form and substance. Let our readers fill out a blank check on the future as they like,—we give our indorsement to their imaginations beforehand. We are looking into stereoscopes as pretty toys, and wondering over the photograph as a charming novelty; but before another generation has passed away, it will be recognized that a new epoch in the history of human progress dates from the time when He who

> never but in uncreated light
> Dwelt from eternity—

took a pencil of fire from the hand of the "angel standing in the sun," and placed it in the hands of a mortal.

Selections from *Mechanisms of Human Facial Expression*
Guillaume-Amant Duchenne de Boulogne
1862

III. THE BACKGROUND TO MY ELECTROPHYSIOLOGICAL RESEARCH ON FACIAL EXPRESSION IN MOVEMENT

All movements, both voluntary and instinctive, result from simultaneous (synergistic) contraction of a more or less large number of muscles. Nature has not given man the ability to localize the action of the nervous fluid to an individual muscle to provoke an isolated contraction. This ability, functionally useless, would have exposed man to accidents and deformities, as I have already demonstrated elsewhere.[1] As we cannot break down the movements and thus analyze the individual actions of muscles, how may we study them? How are we to arrive at a precise knowledge of the true action of these muscles? If we were able to master the electrical current, an agent so analogous to the nervous fluid, and could limit its effect to individual muscles, we could certainly shed some light on their localized actions. In the face in particular, one could determine the isolated actions of the muscles with ease! Armed with electrodes, one would be able, like nature herself, to paint the expressive lines of the emotions of the soul on the face of man. What a source of new observations!

For a dozen years, this has been the fundamental idea of my electrophysiological research, an idea with a rich future that inflamed my imagination.

This is not the place to report the long series of physical and anatomical experiments through which I had to pass, and the difficulties I have had to surmount before proving my idea. After several years of experimentation, I can apply electrical power to the surface of the body, in a controlled manner and then make it traverse the skin without burning or cutting it and concentrate its action in one muscle or in a muscle bundle, in a nerve trunk in a nerve branch. The first application of the method of electrization that I invented was in the study of the face. "Localized electrization" has helped me resolve the problem, both so difficult and so interesting, stated in the previous paragraph; it permitted me to see the tiny radiations of the muscles occurring under the influence of the instrument. The muscular contraction revealed their direction and their anatomical situation more clearly than the scalpel of the anatomist. At least this is true in face where one inevitably sacrifices, in anatomical dissections, the terminal portions of the muscle fibers that have their crucial insertion into the skin.

This is then a new sort of anatomy, to which one can apply the two words by which Haller described physiology: it is *animated anatomy—anatome animata;* Soemmerring would have without doubt called it *contemplatio musculi vivi.*

By 1850, I had enough new facts for me to present a series of papers entitled "Functions of the muscles of the face demonstrated by localized electrization" to the Academies of Science and of Medicine of Paris, based on my electrophysiological experiments. This work provoked the brilliant discussion of Professor Bérard, member of the Academy of Medicine, in 1851.[2] I take the liberty of affirming that this electromuscular method had not been used before my experiments.

No one thought that the study of myology could benefit from gross experiments by a physician who provoked convulsions on the faces of his tortured subjects using electrical currents. [...]

It will be recognized, I hope, that the honor of revealing the mechanism of human facial expression, this anatomical analysis of the emotions, was reserved for the method of electrization, which alone permitted the exact determination of the isolation action of the muscles and the dissection of their movements.

My initial research was not and could not be anything but a rough sketch. The electrophysiological facts I originally observed did not give me a complete idea of the physiological movements of the faces. And which actions should one give to each of the muscle of the face to see how they act in the play of facial expression? I was far from answering these complex and difficult questions, whose surface I had barely scratched.

Today, based on long and continuing experimentation, I believe that I can reveal my research to the public. I hope it will shed great light on these questions.

1 De l'electrisation localisée et de son application à la physiologie, à la pathologie et à la thérapeutique. Paris, 1855; 2nd edition, 1861.
2 This includes a note at the bottom: Meeting of 18 March 1851, *Bulletin de l'Académie de médecine*, t. XVI, 609.

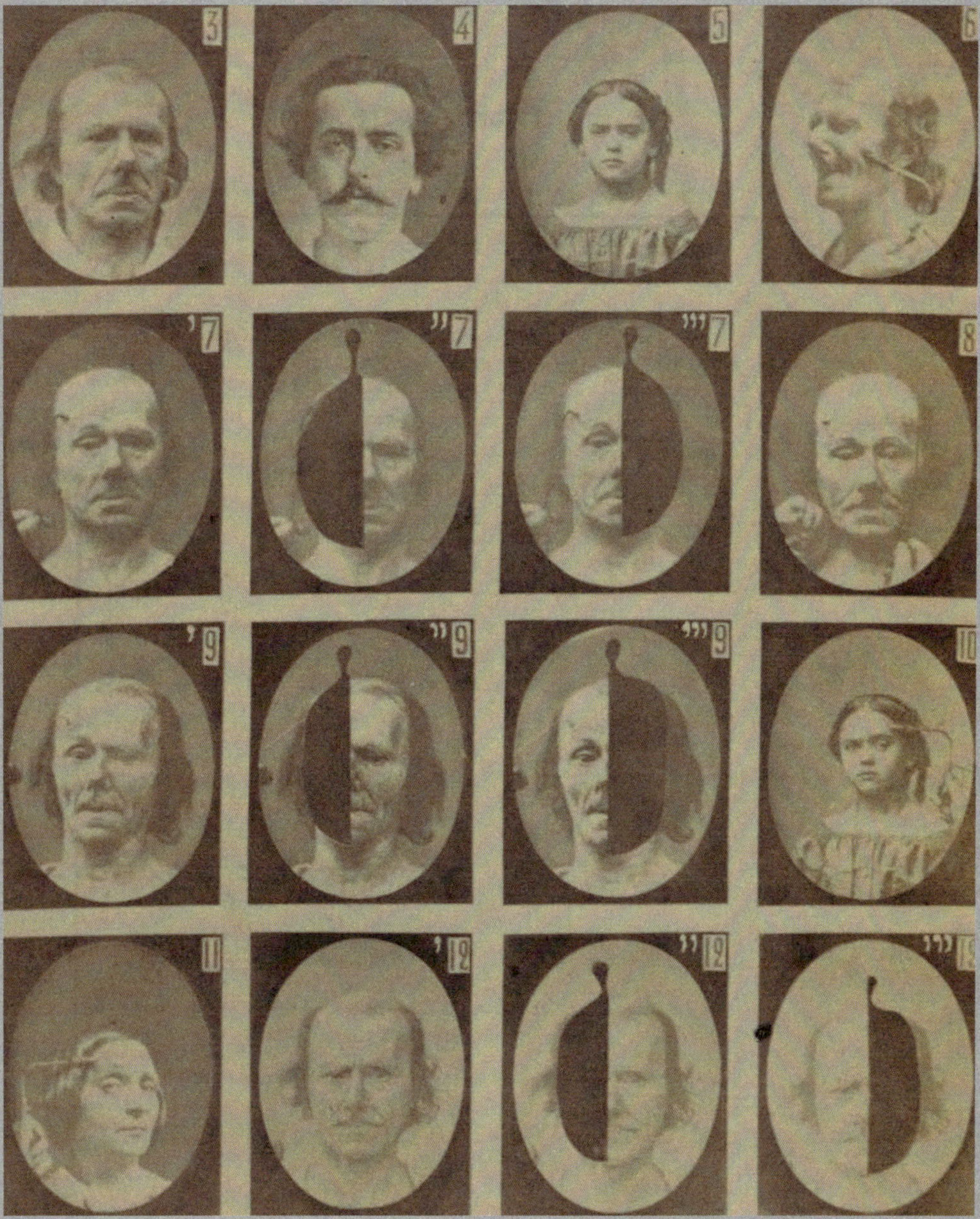

ÉLECTRO-PHYSIOLOGIE PHOTOGRAPHIQUE, PLATE 1

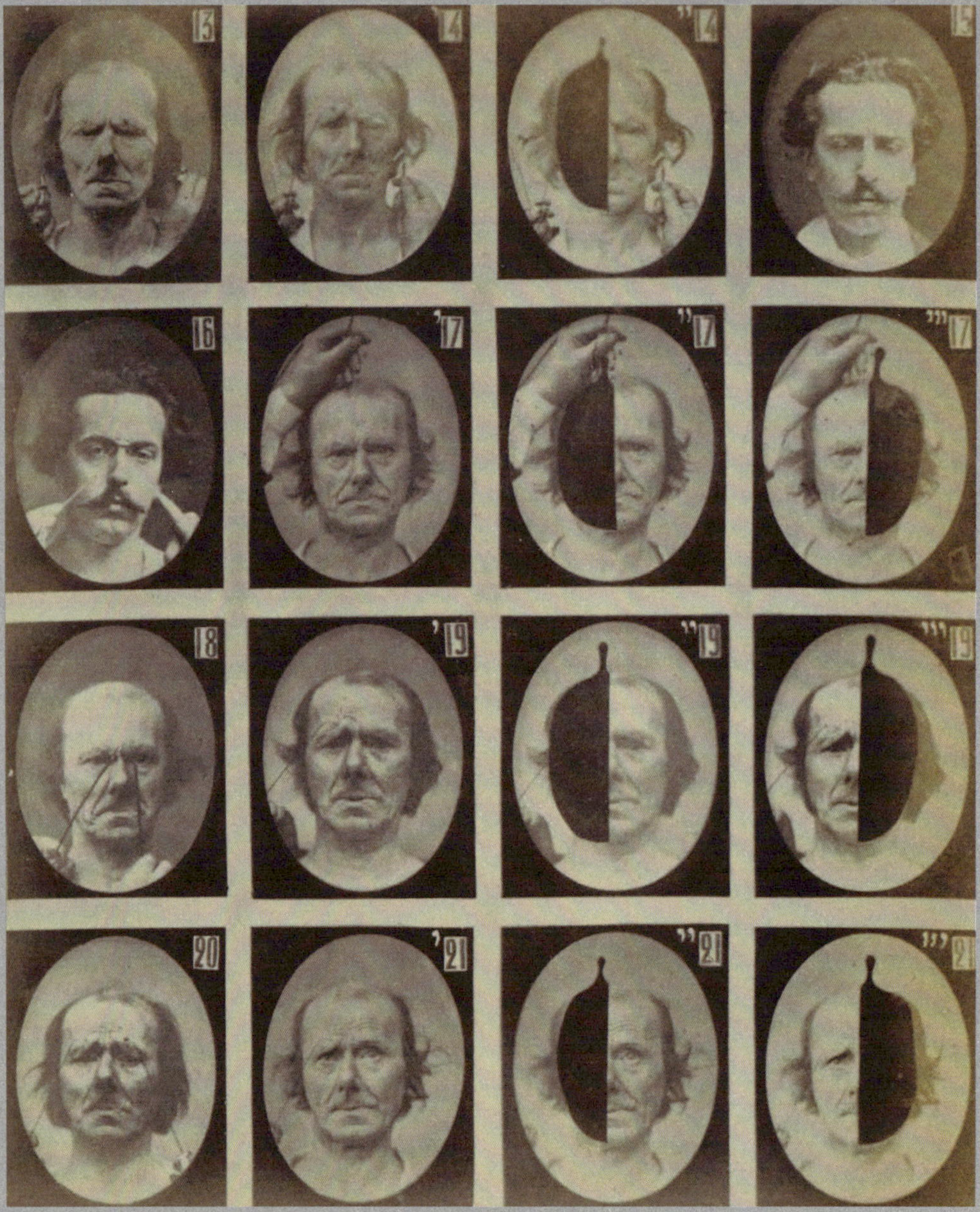

ÉLECTRO-PHYSIOLOGIE PHOTOGRAPHIQUE, PLATE 2

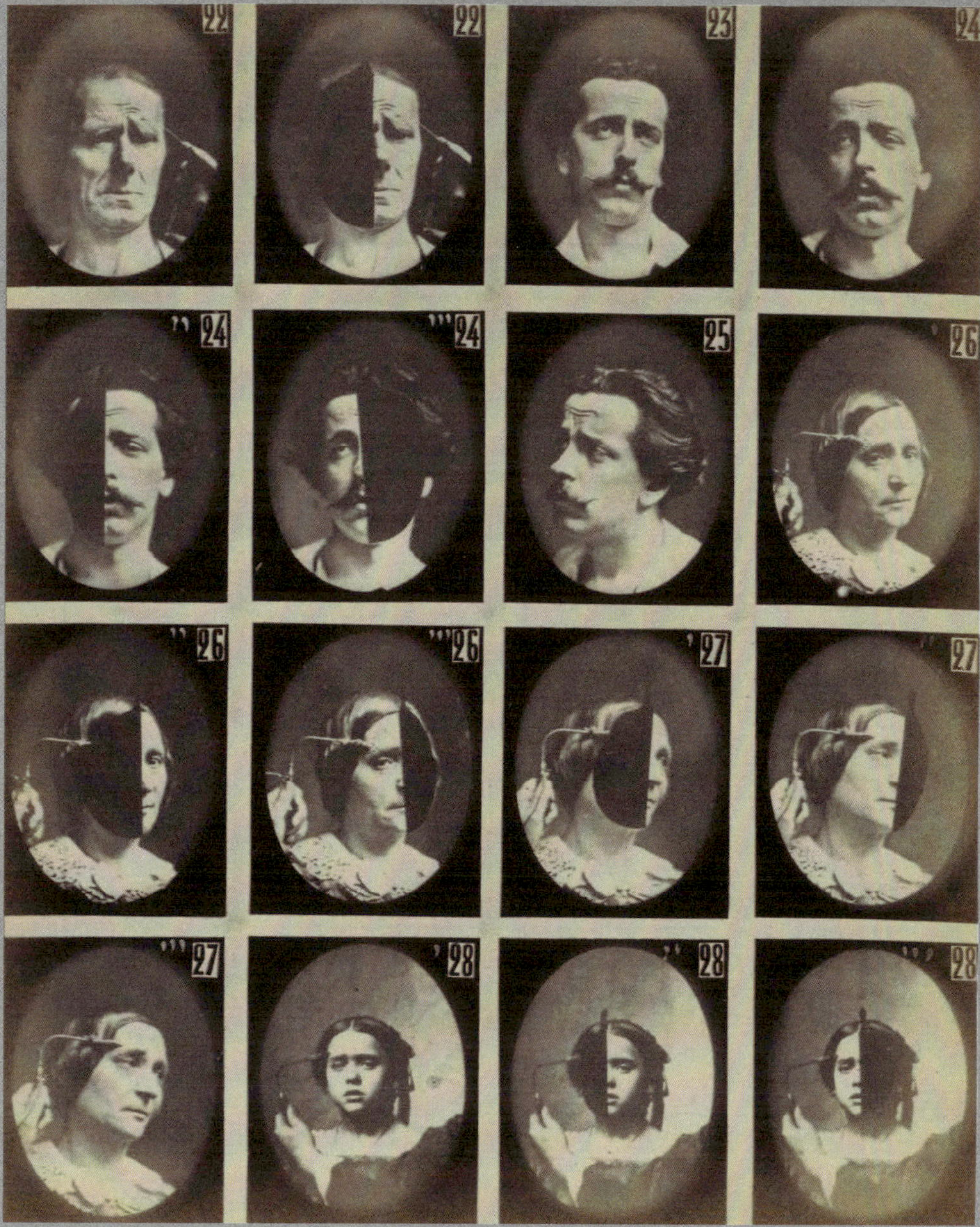

ÉLECTRO-PHYSIOLOGIE PHOTOGRAPHIQUE, PLATE 3

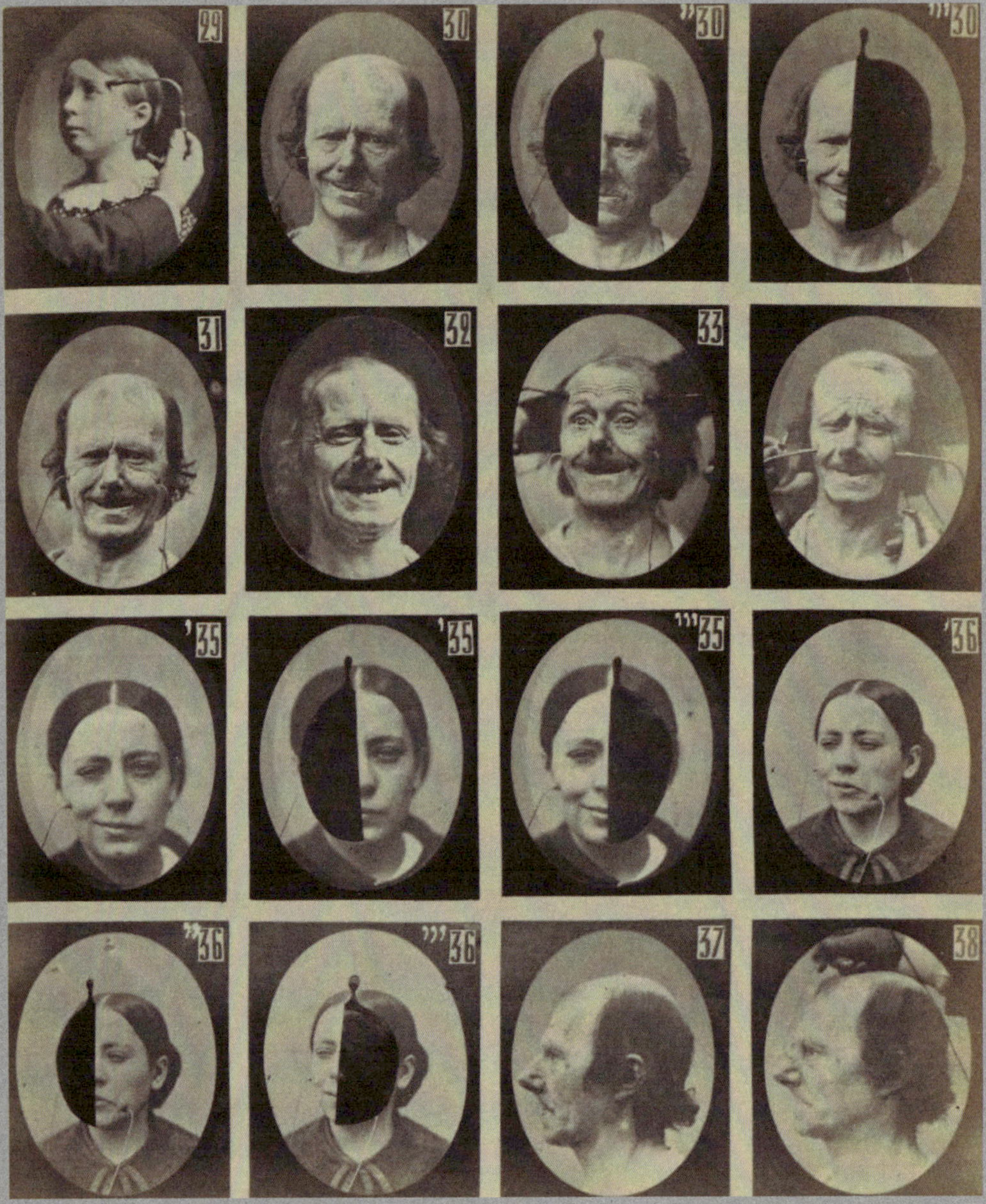

ÉLECTRO-PHYSIOLOGIE PHOTOGRAPHIQUE, PLATE 4

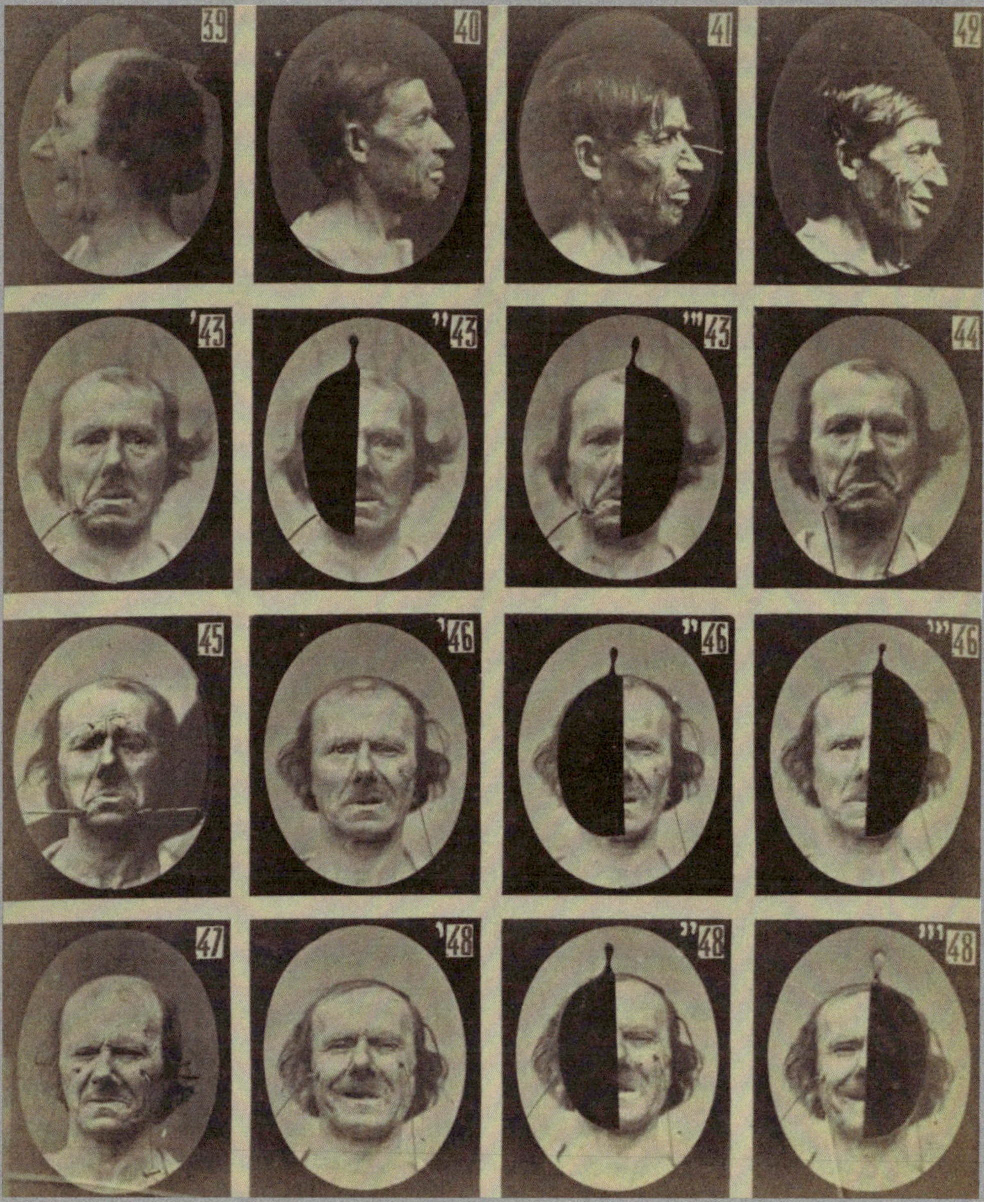

ÉLECTRO-PHYSIOLOGIE PHOTOGRAPHIQUE, PLATE 5

Photographs of the High Rockies in *Harper's New Monthly Magazine*, September 1869

John Samson [likely a pseudonym of Timothy H. O'Sullivan]

VOLUME 39. NUMBER 232. HARPER'S MAGAZINE. NEW YORK, SEPTEMBER, 1869.

PHOTOGRAPHS FROM THE HIGH ROCKIES 465
ILLUSTRATIONS.—Traveling above the Snow-Line.—The Photographer's Outfit.—Gold Hill and Silver City.—The Nettie.—Pyramid Lake.—Strange Tufa.—The Carson Sink.—High Water.—The Ruby Range.—Cañon in the Ruby Range.—Shifting Sand-Mounds.—Above the Shoshone Falls.—Natural Bridge.

THE EYE AND THE CAMERA 476
ILLUSTRATIONS.—The Photographic Camera.—Photographic Operating Room.—The Inverted Image.—The Eyeball.—The Dark Chamber.—Section of the Eye.—Reversed Image in the Dark Chamber.—The Three Aspects of the Hand.—Taking Stereoscopic Picture of near Objects.—Stereoscopic Camera.—Sliding Stereoscope.

OUT IN THE STREETS 482

BORDER REMINISCENCES 483
ILLUSTRATIONS.—Dismounted Cavalry.—A Demoralized Negro.—"Look-a-yere, Mister!"—A Scene in Court.

A SUMMER FRIEND 488

A HEALTH TRIP TO BRAZIL 489
ILLUSTRATIONS.—Street Scene, Pernambuco.—Charlotte Amalie, St. Thomas.—Hauling in a Dolphin.—Para, from the River.—The Environs of Para.—Snake Merchant.—Monkeys for sale.—Pernambuco.—Street in Pernambuco.—Ox-Cart.—Pack Horses.—Fleet of Jagandas.—Suburbs of Pernambuco.—Bahia, from the Bay.—Avenue of Palms.—Market Scene, Bahia.

BOB WHITE 505
ILLUSTRATIONS.—Hunting Bob White.—The True Quail.—Head of Bob White, Life Size.—Covey Alarmed.—Head of California Valley Quail, Life Size.—Head of California Mountain Quail, Life Size.

IN QUIET DAYS 512

A BRAVE LADY. By the Author of "JOHN HALIFAX, GENTLEMAN." 513
ILLUSTRATIONS.—"Mamma, you bring Good News."—"Marriage is a Great Mystery."

CHANGE 526

AN AUTHOR'S MEMORIES OF AUTHORS 527
ILLUSTRATIONS.—S. C. Hall.—Mrs. S. C. Hall.

THE FOSTER-BROTHERS 535

TOO CLEVER BY HALF 544

THE PROGRESS OF ELECTRICITY 548

LEANDER DOOLITTLE 560

MY ENEMY'S DAUGHTER. By JUSTIN M'CARTHY 570
CHAPTER XXVI. Lilla gone.
CHAPTER XXVII. The Conspirator.
CHAPTER XXVIII. "Ah, bear in Mind that Garden was Enchanted."
ILLUSTRATION.—Salaris and I.

GOING OVER TO THE ENEMY 582

THE PURITAN CAPTAIN 589

THE NEW TIMOTHY. PART X 596

EDITOR'S EASY CHAIR 605
The Amherst Commencement.—D.D., LL.D., and the like.—Senator Patterson and the Press.—Patent Leather.—Public Men and the Press.—Domestic Service.—Co-operative Housekeeping.—Mrs. Peirce's Statement.—The Rochdale Experiment.—Some Talk with Glen's Falls.—Champagne Charlie of Great Britain.—Plantagenets, Tudors, and Napoleons.—Edmund Burke and British Royalty.—Champagne Charlie and Gentleman George.—What is the Use of Champagne Charlie?

EDITOR'S BOOK TABLE 610
Dr. Anderson's Foreign Missions.—Smith's Old Testament History.—Clark's Primary Truths in Religion.—Angus's Bible Hand-Book.—Life and Epistles of St. Paul.—Moore's Views of Life.—Wood's Gates Wide Open.—Cowles on Jeremiah.—Bowles's Our New West.—Brace's The New West.—Foster's Mississippi Valley.—Coffin's Our New Way Round the World.—The Cruise of Admiral Farragut.—Buffum's Sights and Sensations in France, Germany, and Switzerland.—Flagg's European Vineyards.—Taine's Italy.—Whitney's Yosemite Guide-Book.—Life of Audubon.—Neal's Recollections.—Anecdotes of the Wesleys.—Famous London Merchants.

MONTHLY RECORD OF CURRENT EVENTS 615
The Virginia Election.—Cuban Expedition frustrated.—Members arrested and discharged.—The French Atlantic Cable.—The Cuban Insurrection.—Paraguay.—South American Republics.—The Alabama Question in England.—The Irish Church Bill finally passed.—Spain.—France.

EDITOR'S DRAWER 618
Two-Bucket Business played out.—A miserable Shot.—Things go Wrong.—A clean Plate.—Ridiculous.—Lively but not Solemn.—A legal Prayer.—American and British "Yatches."—Don't want to Sponge.—The Heavenly Banker.—Shylock's Deeds upon his Head.—Don't take Medals for Drinks.—Against Life Insurance.—Saxe within One of being Governor.—The Child brought forth.—Duces Tecum missing.—Sweetened Wind.—Keep thy Lips, etc.—Eat and Ate.—The Creator pleased with Fun.—Within the Line of Forty-tude.—Brigham Young's Tithes.—Too many Wives better than none.—Fermenting on the Skin.—Mr. Flagg on Wines, etc.—Abraham and the Ark.—Milk a Bear.—Poem "To the Mune."—A Fire-Insurance Policy.—A desirable Pew.—A cold Chair wanted.—A Marriage License.—Here she goes.—Lincoln and Douglas.—Lager in Battle.—A bad Baptist Minister.—To Omaha.—Epitaphs.—The Fourth of July on the Twenty-second of February.—Preaching extempore.—Five Cats.—Unfit for a Cartman.—Balancing Books.—Alexander Stephens's white Pants.

HARPER'S
NEW MONTHLY MAGAZINE.

No. CCXXXII.—SEPTEMBER, 1869.—Vol. XXXIX.

PHOTOGRAPHS FROM THE HIGH ROCKIES.

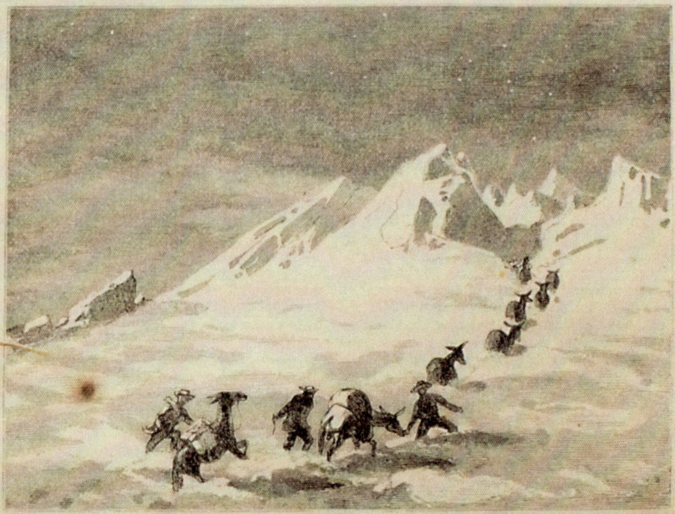

TRAVELING ABOVE THE SNOW-LINE.

PLACES and people are made familiar to us by means of the camera in the hands of skillful operators, who, vying with each other in the artistic excellence of their productions, avail themselves of every opportunity to visit interesting points, and take care to lose no good chance to scour the country in search of new fields for photographic labor.

During our late war we had photographic representations of battle-fields, which are now valuable as historical material, both for present and for future use.

The battle of Bull Run would have been photographed "close up" but for the fact that a shell from one of the rebel field-pieces took away the photographer's camera. In 1863, while photographing Fort Sumter and the Confederate batteries in the vicinity of Charleston, a courageous operator saw his camera twice knocked over by fragments of shell, his camera-cloth torn, and the loose white sand of Morris Island scattered over plates and chemicals. The veteran artillerists who manned the battery from which the views were made wisely sought refuge in the bomb-proofs to secure themselves from the heavy shell fire which was opened upon their fortification; but the photographer stuck to his work, and the pictures made on that memorable occasion are among the most interesting of the war. Many of the best photographs of events that occurred during the war were made by the adventurous artist who now furnishes pictures of scenes among the High Rockies, and narrates the adventures incident of the long journey during which the photographs were made.

Early in the summer of 1867 a surveying party of about forty persons left California to

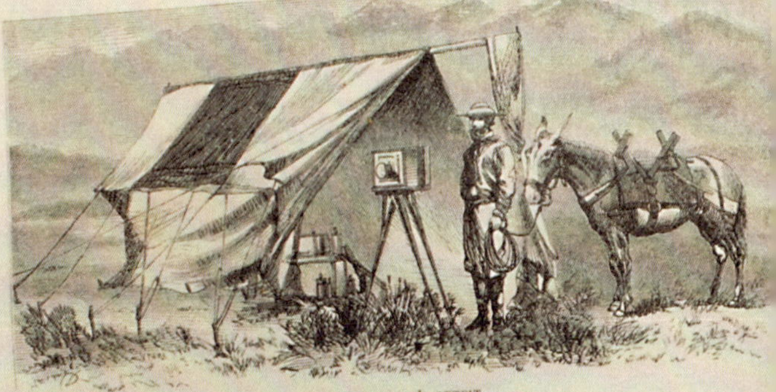

THE PHOTOGRAPHER'S OUTFIT.

proceed eastward directly across the different ranges of the Rocky Mountains as far as the Great Salt Lake, and traveled most of the distance in the vicinity of the proposed route of the Central Pacific Railroad. The company comprised scientific gentlemen and other civilians, such as cooks and packers, to the number of seventeen. An escort of twenty men from the Eighth United States Cavalry, under the command of a sergeant, was considered a force quite adequate to guard against any danger from the Piutes and other tribes of mountain Indians who might be attracted by the stock,

rations, or *hair* of the party. Two mules an
an experienced packer were assigned to th
photographing artist, and were by him duly a
cepted as a satisfactory outfit for the propos
expedition.

Traveling for some days in California, throu
fair mountain country, the mules became us
to their packs, and the party sufficiently fam
iar with each other to realize the fact that
know a man well you must campaign with hi

A tarry at Nevada City, long enough to r
the stock, gave the Artist time to explore
mines along the great Comstock Lode, situa

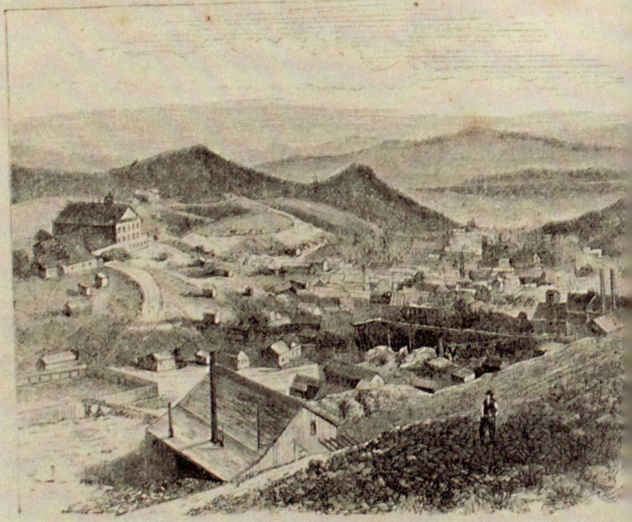

GOLD HILL AND SILVER CITY.

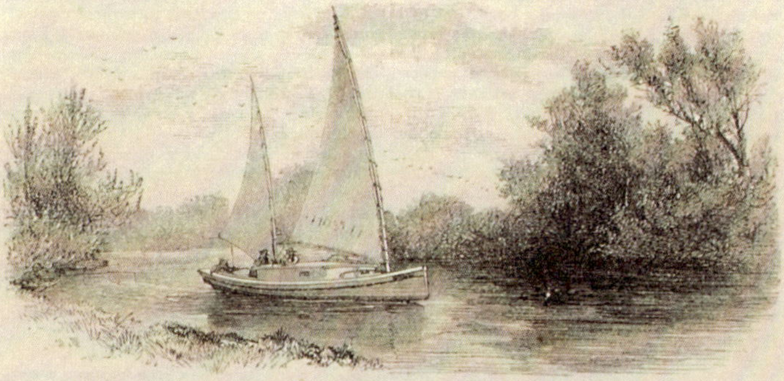

THE NETTIE.

in Gold Hill and Silver City. This locality was a few months since visited by one of the direst calamities that ever befell the inhabitants of the mining regions of our country. I refer to the fires on the different levels of the Crown Point, Kentuck, and Yellow Jacket mines.

By means of magnesium light interesting views were taken of places located several hundred feet below daylight; but as this is not an article relating to gold mining, we will come up out of that profitable hole in the ground from which something like ninety million dollars in gold have been taken, and proceed northward to the banks of the Truckee, a swiftly flowing stream which empties its alkaline waters into the southern portion of Pyramid Lake.

The Truckee has its source in the Wabash Mountains, from the cañon and gorges of which flow brooks that may be traced to living springs of almost any mineral property that one may desire. These brooks combining form the Truckee. On this river the *Nettie*, a boat at which a single glance was all that was necessary to convince a man reared on the rugged coast of New England that the craft was the handiwork of an artisan who had built boats for New London fishermen. She was a perfect model of her class.

The pack animals were left in charge of the men who were not desirous to visit Pyramid Lake, while into the *Nettie* were stowed provisions and articles of actual necessity, among which may be mentioned the instruments and chemicals necessary for our photographer to "work up his views."

To sail or float down the rapids of the Truckee in a boat of the *Nettie's* build was an undertaking that, prior to this time, had not been accomplished. Between the rapids of the stream lay stretches of deep still water, through which the boat glided, impelled either by sail or sweeps. Presently the great rapids are reached; the stream is wider and shallower. Danger is near. The location of the rock, that is hidden beneath the rushing water, is discovered by the whirling eddy. In some places the foaming torrent dashes against a projecting spur of rock that breaks the current in showers of spray, of which the larger drops fall in the form of tiny crystal spheres that dance and sparkle for an instant ere they disappear below in the swift stream that has, in places, worn its course through, and exposed to view singular rock formations that tell of volcanic action.

The trunk of a tree comes floating swiftly down the tide, and is plunged into the whirling rapids. The stout stem that has stood for years, a landmark for the Piutes, is in a moment splintered by the rushing water as if riven by lightning. It is through these rapids that the *Nettie* must be navigated, if she can be released from the strong hold which the current has of her, as she lies jammed by the mad velocity of the stream against two projecting rocks. The strong oars are swept away and caught by the rocks below. In a twinkling the tough ash is bent into a shape more like the bow of an ox yoke than that of the tried oar.

Our photographic friend, being a swimmer of no ordinary power, succeeded in reaching the shore, not opposite the *Nettie*, though it was but forty yards from the shore, for he was carried a hundred yards down the rapids. A rope was thrown to him from the boat, and thus he rescued the little craft with her crew from their perilous situation. The sharp rocks had torn the little clothing of which he had not divested himself, and had so cut and bruised his body that he was glad to crawl into the brier tangle that fringed the river's brink. When at last he gained the point nearest to the boat his excited friends threw shoreward his pocket-book, freighted with three hundred dollars in twenty-dollar gold pieces. "That was rough," said he; "for I never found that 'dust' again, though I prospected a long time, barefooted, for it." The line which had been thrown was quickly made fast to a convenient spur of rock, and the

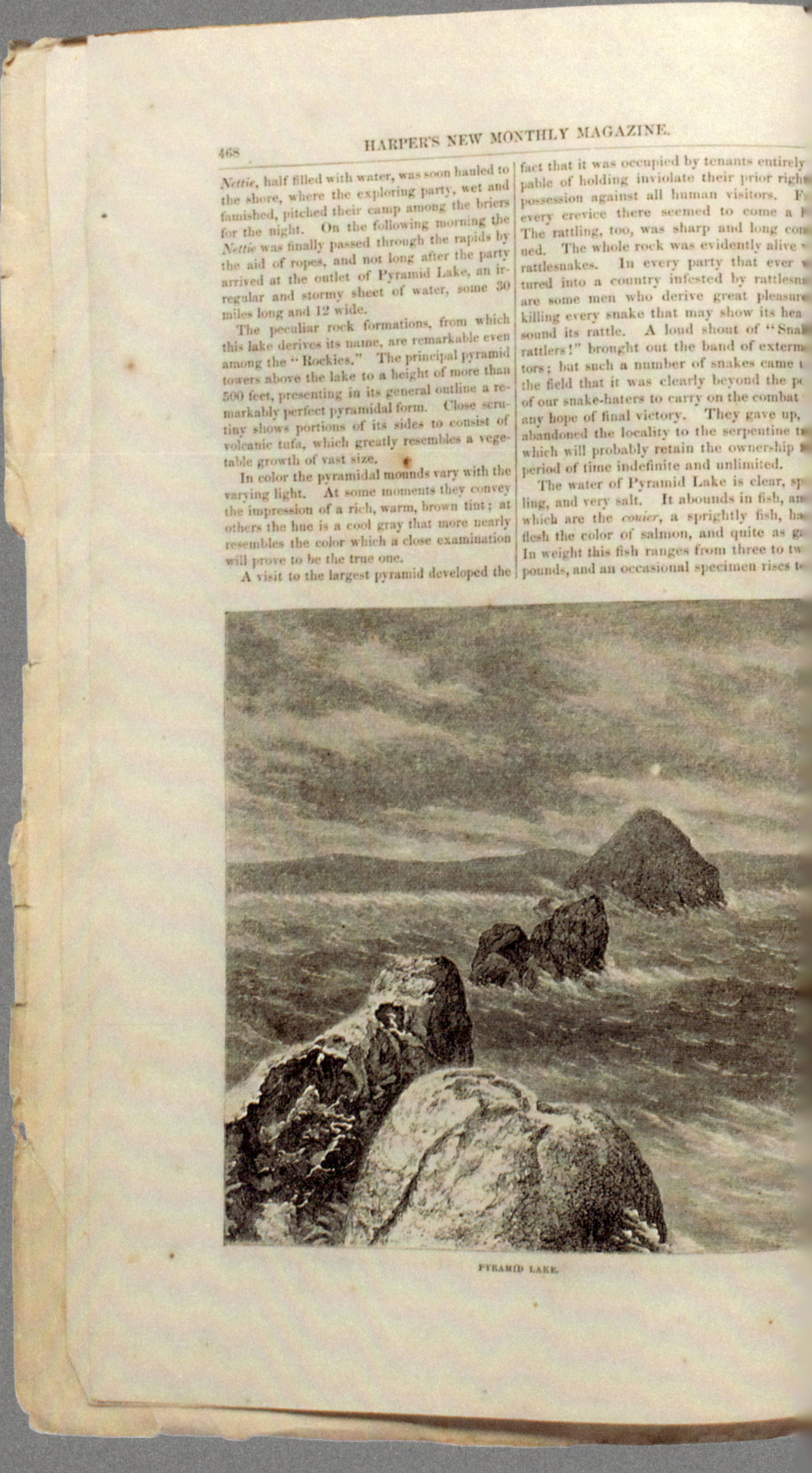

Nettie, half filled with water, was soon hauled to the shore, where the exploring party, wet and famished, pitched their camp among the briers for the night. On the following morning the *Nettie* was finally passed through the rapids by the aid of ropes, and not long after the party arrived at the outlet of Pyramid Lake, an irregular and stormy sheet of water, some 30 miles long and 12 wide.

The peculiar rock formations, from which this lake derives its name, are remarkable even among the "Rockies." The principal pyramid towers above the lake to a height of more than 500 feet, presenting in its general outline a remarkably perfect pyramidal form. Close scrutiny shows portions of its sides to consist of volcanic tufa, which greatly resembles a vegetable growth of vast size.

In color the pyramidal mounds vary with the varying light. At some moments they convey the impression of a rich, warm, brown tint; at others the hue is a cool gray that more nearly resembles the color which a close examination will prove to be the true one.

A visit to the largest pyramid developed the fact that it was occupied by tenants entirely
pable of holding inviolate their prior righ
possession against all human visitors. F
every crevice there seemed to come a
The rattling, too, was sharp and long con
ued. The whole rock was evidently alive
rattlesnakes. In every party that ever
tured into a country infested by rattlesn
are some men who derive great pleasur
killing every snake that may show its hea
sound its rattle. A loud shout of "Sna
rattlers!" brought out the band of exterm
tors; but such a number of snakes came
the field that it was clearly beyond the p
of our snake-haters to carry on the combat
any hope of final victory. They gave up,
abandoned the locality to the serpentine t
which will probably retain the ownership
period of time indefinite and unlimited.

The water of Pyramid Lake is clear, sp
ling, and very salt. It abounds in fish, an
which are the *couier*, a sprightly fish, ha
flesh the color of salmon, and quite as g
In weight this fish ranges from three to tw
pounds, and an occasional specimen rises t

PYRAMID LAKE.

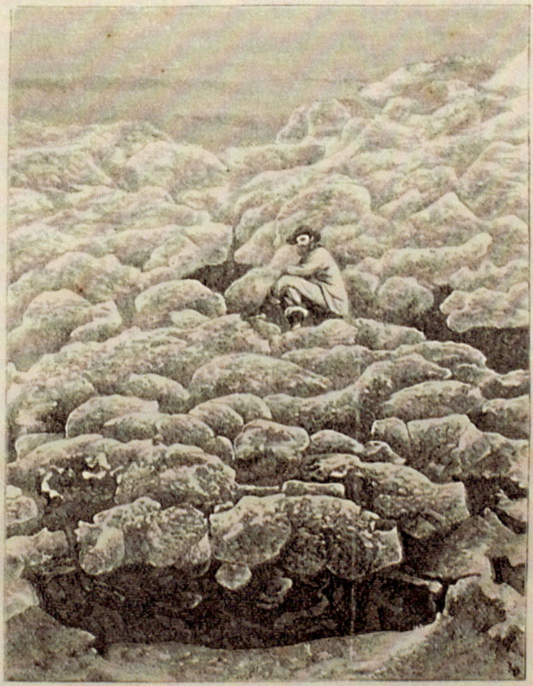

STRANGE TUFA.

fly that will scale quite twenty-five pounds. Besides the *couier* there is an abundance of trout, not precisely the speckled beauties of the Lake Superior region; neither do they bear a very close resemblance to the sluggish, black, spotted trout of our more Southern States. It is a trout, nevertheless, which rises readily to the artificial fly, and is a pleasing morsel for the epicurean palate. Cooked in the various styles known to the campers, this fish will compare favorably with its eastern brethren. Other varieties of the finny tribe abound in Pyramid Lake; but these are the ones which will be most sought after by any courageous disciple of Izaak Walton, who leaves the cars of the Central Pacific Railroad where it strikes the Truckee, and who ventures down to its outlet in this curious lake.

From Pyramid Lake the exploring party journeyed back by land to a point on the overland stage route, where the animals and extra camp equipage were in waiting for them. The Central Pacific Railroad has now its iron bands beside this road, and, in this vicinity, passes through a valley picturesque, and, for this section, tolerably fertile.

The next point of interest was the Humboldt Valley and Sink, on the way to which the party passed through a country where, besides the Indians, were occasionally found white inhabitants who had come from the Eastern States and traveled thus far on their long journey to California, and here they had squatted. These people seem to be peculiar to this portion of the Union. They have, ordinarily, left the States many years before, and migrating toward the famed Eldorado of the Pacific coast, have, from some reasons best known to themselves, here shortened their trail and come to a full stop. Possibly, and even quite probably, the Indians have "cleaned them out," to use the Plains' phraseology; that is, have stampeded their stock, and appropriated whatever was of any value in the "outfit" to their own use and behoof, leaving the emigrant to settle down, squat, where he was, and obtain such subsistence as he might be able to secure by cutting and preparing wild hay for the use of the great mining

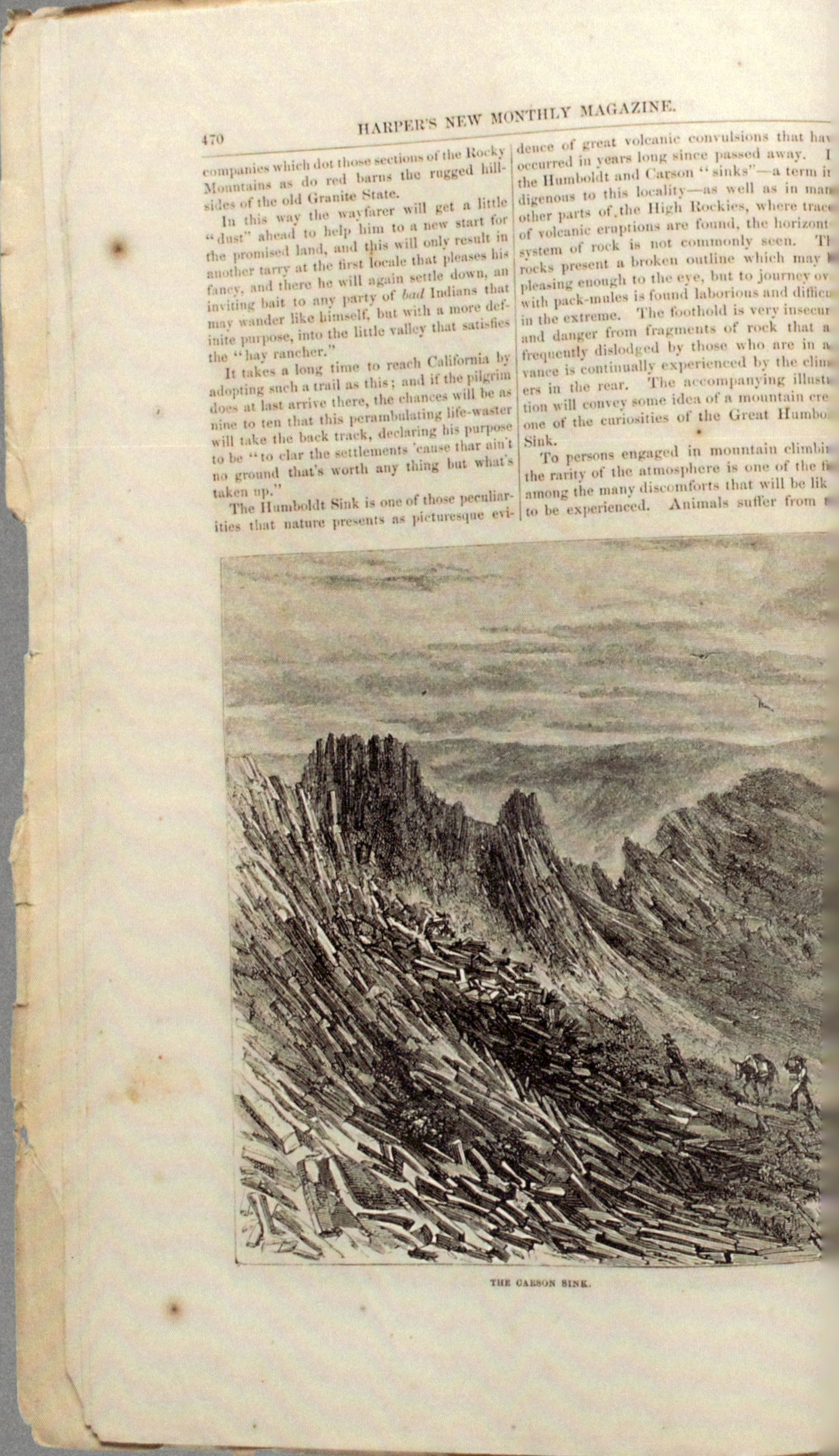

companies which dot those sections of the Rocky Mountains as do red barns the rugged hill-sides of the old Granite State.

In this way the wayfarer will get a little "dust" ahead to help him to a new start for the promised land, and this will only result in another tarry at the first locale that pleases his fancy, and there he will again settle down, an inviting bait to any party of *bad* Indians that may wander like himself, but with a more definite purpose, into the little valley that satisfies the "hay rancher."

It takes a long time to reach California by adopting such a trail as this; and if the pilgrim does at last arrive there, the chances will be as nine to ten that this perambulating life-waster will take the back track, declaring his purpose to be "to clar the settlements 'cause thar ain't no ground that's worth any thing but what's taken up."

The Humboldt Sink is one of those peculiarities that nature presents as picturesque evi-
dence of great volcanic convulsions that hav
occurred in years long since passed away. I
the Humboldt and Carson "sinks"—a term ir
digenous to this locality—as well as in man
other parts of the High Rockies, where trace
of volcanic eruptions are found, the horizont
system of rock is not commonly seen. Th
rocks present a broken outline which may b
pleasing enough to the eye, but to journey ov
with pack-mules is found laborious and difficu
in the extreme. The foothold is very insecur
and danger from fragments of rock that a
frequently dislodged by those who are in a
vance is continually experienced by the clim
ers in the rear. The accompanying illustr
tion will convey some idea of a mountain cre
one of the curiosities of the Great Humbo
Sink.

To persons engaged in mountain climbin
the rarity of the atmosphere is one of the fi
among the many discomforts that will be lik
to be experienced. Animals suffer from t

THE CARSON SINK.

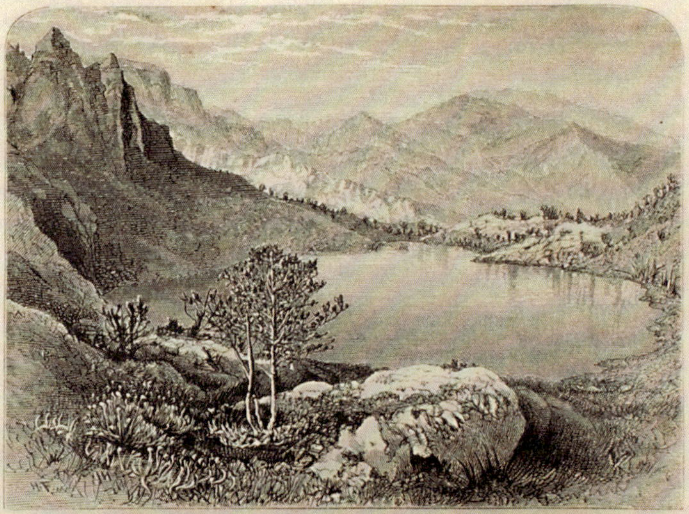

HIGH WATER.

thin, depreciated atmosphere quite as much as men, and it was not difficult to learn that the mule which made an easy burden of a pack at the altitude of 2000 feet above the Pacific could not bear the same load over any long trail at the height of 10,000 or 11,000. It will be noticed, too, that birds seldom make long flights when in the rarer atmosphere of the higher peaks of the Rockies.

In speaking of the Humboldt and Carson sinks our photographer remarks: "It was a pretty location to work in, and *viewing* there was as pleasant work as could be desired; the only drawback was an unlimited number of the most voracious and particularly poisonous mosquitoes that we met with during our entire trip. Add to this the entire impossibility to save one's precious body from frequent attacks of that most enervating of all fevers, known as the 'mountain ail,' and you will see why we did not work up more of that country. We were, in fact, driven out by the mosquitoes and fever. Which of the two should be considered as the more unbearable it is impossible to state."

Some portions of the trail next followed were over a traveled route; but the greater portion of the distance was through or over a country absolutely wild and unexplored, except what the Indians and fur-trappers who frequent the mountains may have accomplished in the way of exploitation.

In moving from the Pacific coast toward the foot-hills, which form the eastern limit of the great mountain range of our continent, the traveler will find it necessary to cross range after range, all having a general direction from north to south. Many of these ranges are only separated by little valleys. The usual distance from range to range is not more than 25 or 30 miles, and frequently the distance is not even so great.

In crossing these ranges or "divides," as these irregularities are designated in the language of the country, our exploring party found it necessary to travel during the midnight hours. The reason for this being the condition of the snow-crust, which in the summer season is not sufficiently thick, even on the highest ranges, during the day, to sustain the weight of either man or beast. In crossing some of these snow-covered crests the party endured indescribable hardships, for the crust was in some cases too thin, even at two or three o'clock in the morning, to bear up the sharp hoofed mules, burdened with their heavy packs. In one instance not less than thirteen hours were consumed in crossing a divide, and the whole distance traveled did not exceed 2½ miles. On this occasion snow-drifts from 30 to 40 feet in depth were crossed. The men and animals were frequently lost from sight.

When, during the day, they arrived at the snow-line, they camped until midnight, or even later, to wait till the surface snow which had thawed during the day should become frozen or crusted by the frosty air of night—this crust, as a general rule, being sufficiently strong to bear up men and animals, and make it pos-

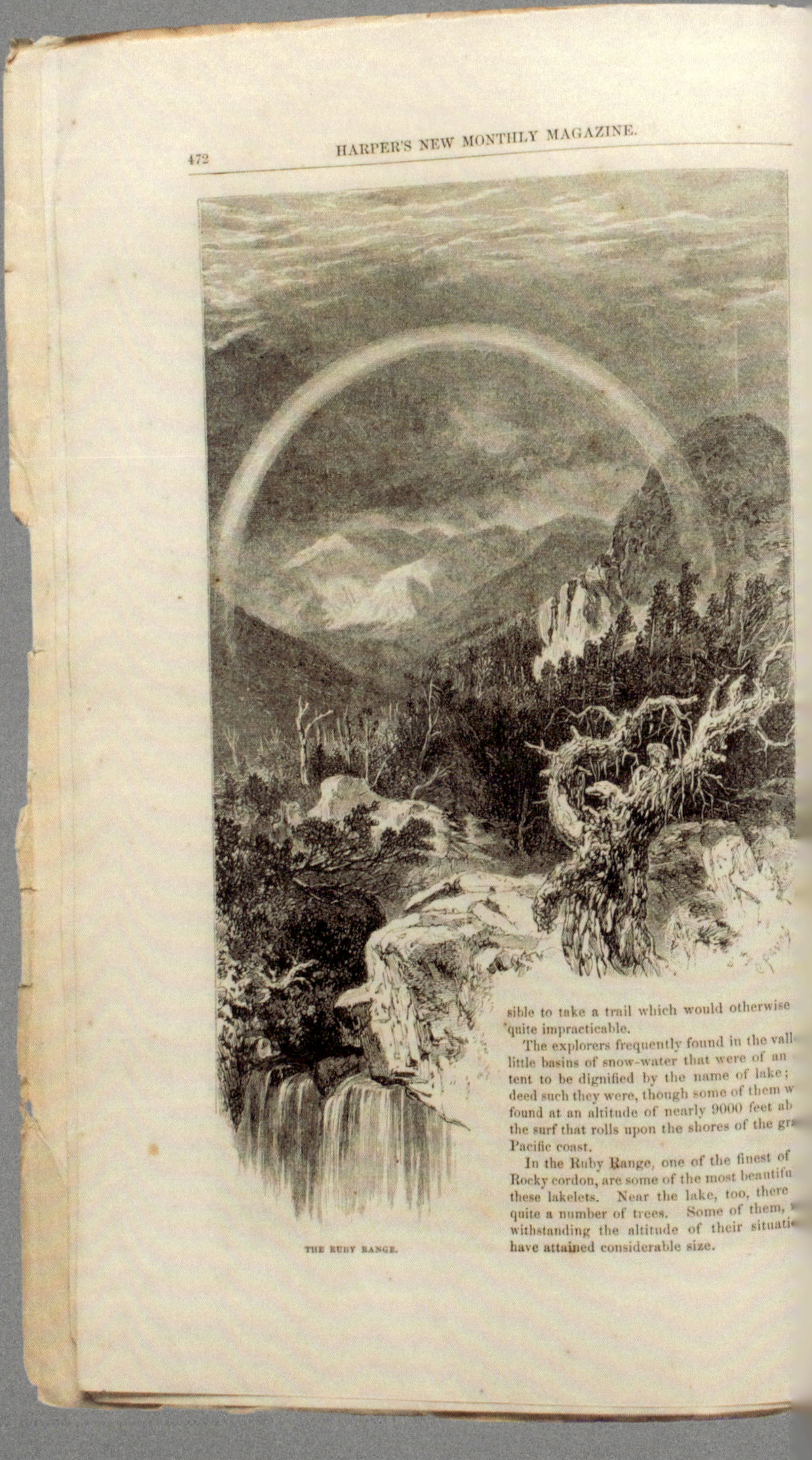

THE RUBY RANGE.

sible to take a trail which would otherwise quite impracticable.

The explorers frequently found in the vall little basins of snow-water that were of an tent to be dignified by the name of lake; deed such they were, though some of them w found at an altitude of nearly 9000 feet ab the surf that rolls upon the shores of the gr Pacific coast.

In the Ruby Range, one of the finest of Rocky cordon, are some of the most beautifu these lakelets. Near the lake, too, there quite a number of trees. Some of them, withstanding the altitude of their situati have attained considerable size.

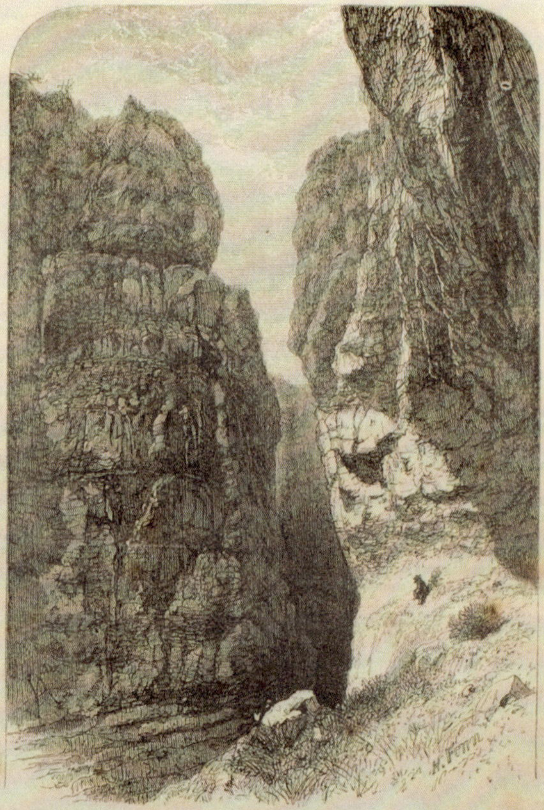

CAÑON IN THE RUBY RANGE.

This particular locality has been for years a favorite resort for some few Indians of the Piute tribe, attracted, maybe, by the excellence of the pine-nut which grows in the vicinity, and by springs of which the waters are said to possess great curative properties in certain cases of physical malady. The pine-nut is one of the principal articles used as food by these Piutes and other mountain tribes. The general appearance of the tree is not unlike our pine of the Eastern States; the branches are more gnarled and the leaf somewhat longer; the cone or bur is much larger, and affords the little wedge-shaped nut, which the Indians secure late in the fall by throwing the burs into a fire, from which they are taken when charred and the nuts shaken out. From some of these burs the number of nuts obtained would quite fill an ordinary tea-cup. This nut, when dried, is sometimes pounded into a coarse meal, which is made into cakes and baked in the ashes, in much the same manner as the hoe-cake is by the negroes of the South. In taste the nut is resinous, and to the palate unaccustomed to the food not extremely agreeable.

The cañons in the Ruby Range were among the most interesting places met with during the entire trip. Standing just within the entrance of the one here shown it was possible to realize the immense power which could force this vast passage through a rock that would seem quite too hard to suffer greatly from the pigmy strength of man. The strata of the rocks are quite regular, and no marked appearance that

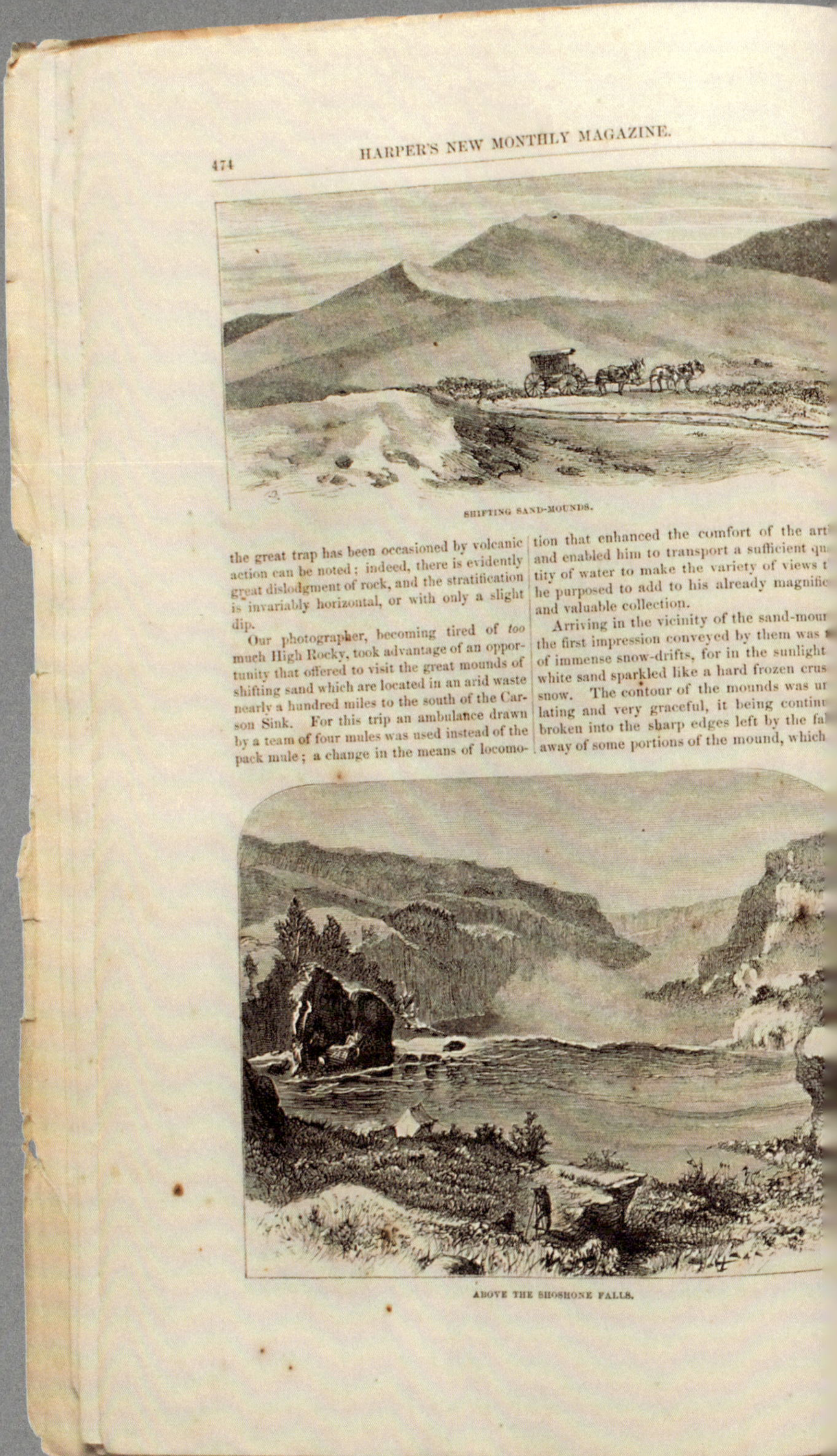

SHIFTING SAND-MOUNDS.

the great trap has been occasioned by volcanic action can be noted; indeed, there is evidently great dislodgment of rock, and the stratification is invariably horizontal, or with only a slight dip.

Our photographer, becoming tired of *too* much High Rocky, took advantage of an opportunity that offered to visit the great mounds of shifting sand which are located in an arid waste nearly a hundred miles to the south of the Carson Sink. For this trip an ambulance drawn by a team of four mules was used instead of the pack mule; a change in the means of locomotion that enhanced the comfort of the art
and enabled him to transport a sufficient qu
tity of water to make the variety of views t
he purposed to add to his already magnific
and valuable collection.

Arriving in the vicinity of the sand-mou
the first impression conveyed by them was
of immense snow-drifts, for in the sunlight
white sand sparkled like a hard frozen crus
snow. The contour of the mounds was u
lating and very graceful, it being contin
broken into the sharp edges left by the fa
away of some portions of the mound, which

ABOVE THE SHOSHONE FALLS.

been undermined by the keen winds that spring up during the last hours of daylight and continue throughout the night.

Frequently, while traversing this waste, a light breeze would catch the sand, loosened by a footstep, and carry the sparkling crystals up the mound in the form of a whirlwind. This circling cloud of sand appeared each moment to increase in size and strength until the crest of the mound was attained, when, as if ambitious of continuing its flight, the dancing sand took one whirl more, then broke, and its dismembered fragments were added to the other side of the mound. It is by the whirlwinds that these great mounds of sand—some of them reaching to the height of 500 feet—are shifted from place to place.

The photographer returned from the shifting sand-mounds and joined the party, which had already advanced some distance along the trail to the eastward, taking for their route the overland stage road. Then leaving this they moved northward toward the falls of the Snake River, designated, in the vicinity of Salt Lake, as the Great Shoshone Falls. The volume of water pouring over the Shoshone Falls is small compared with the great flood which gives grandeur to Niagara. Neither is the width of the river greater than that portion of Niagara known as the American Fall. In the Shoshone we have fall after fall to view as a preliminary exhibition. Each cascade is a splendid fall of itself, and the vast walls of rock are worn into weird forms by the constant action of rushing water.

The surroundings of the main fall are such that any number of views may be had of the scene. Standing upon the craggy rocks that jut out from and form the walls of the table-land below the falls, one may obtain a bird's-eye view of one of the most sublime of Rocky Mountain scenes. Even in this location, which is many feet above the falls, the air is heavy with moisture, which is attributable to the mist into which the river's great leap shivers the water. From the position on the crags you have also a grand sight of the different falls, of which the main one seems but the culmination. Each small fall is in itself a perfect gem with a setting of grandeur in the glorious masses of rock. On one great wall can be traced a tolerably perfect outline of a vast figure of a man. The whole form is not less than 160 feet in height.

There is in the entire region of the falls such wildness of beauty that a feeling pervades the mind almost unconsciously that you are, if not the *first* white man who has ever trod that trail, certainly one of the very few who have ventured so far. From the island above the falls you may not see the great leap that the water takes, but you will certainly feel sensible of the fact that you are in the presence of one of Nature's greatest spectacles as you listen to the roar of the falling water and gaze down the stream over the fall at the wild scene beyond.

Our photographic glimpses of Rocky Mountain scenery end with the picturesque little natural bridge which serves for a crossing over a deep gorge in the neighborhood of the falls.

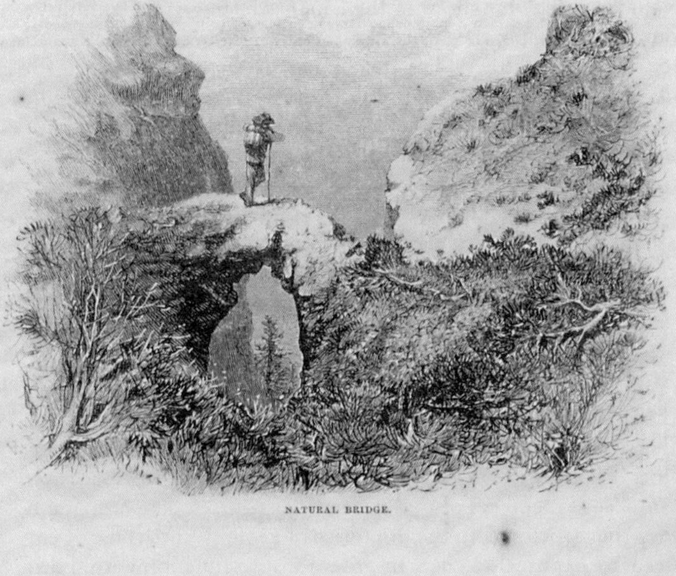

NATURAL BRIDGE.

Photography's Discursive Spaces
Rosalind E. Krauss
1986

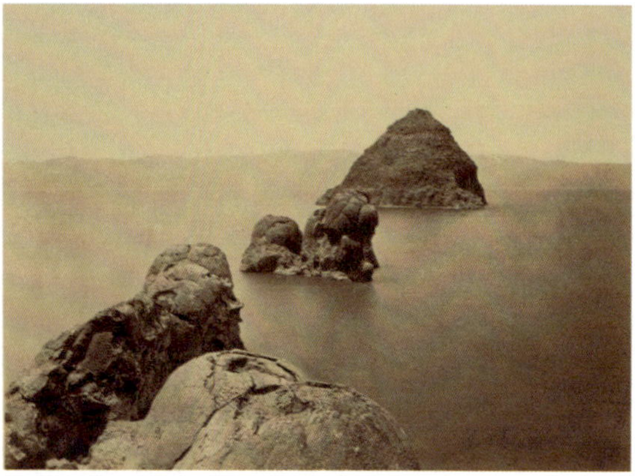

Figure 1. Timothy O'Sullivan, *The Pyramid and Domes, Pyramid Lake, Nevada*, 1867.

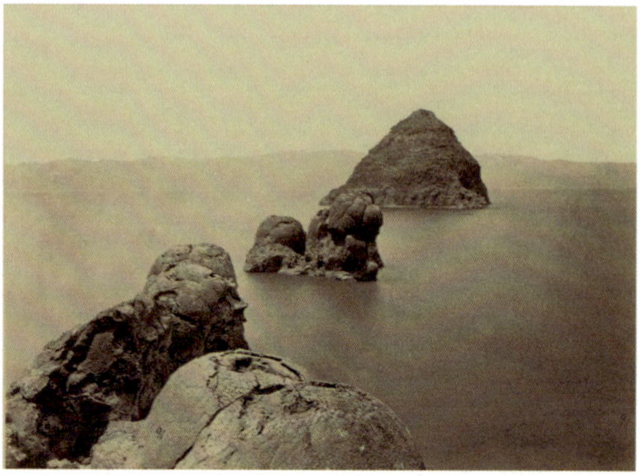

Figure 2. Photolithograph after O'Sullivan, *Tufa Domes, Pyramid Lake*, published in King Survey Report, 1875.

Let us start with two images, identically titled *Tufa Domes, Pyramid Lake, Nevada.* The first (Fig. 1) is a (recently) celebrated photograph made by Timothy O'Sullivan in 1868 that functions with special insistence within the art historical construction of nineteenth-century landscape photography. The second (Fig. 2) is a lithographic copy of the first, produced for the publication of Clarence King's *Systematic Geology* in 1878.[1]

Twentieth-century sensibility welcomes the original O'Sullivan as a model of the mysterious, silent beauty to which landscape photography had access during the early decades of the medium. In the photograph, three bulky masses of rock are seen as if deployed on a kind of abstract, transparent chessboard, marking by their separate positions a retreating trajectory into depth. A fanatical descriptive clarity has bestowed on the bodies of these rocks a hallucinatory wealth of detail, so that each crevice, each granular trace of the original volcanic heat finds its record. Yet the rocks seem unreal and the space dreamlike, the tufa domes appear as if suspended in a luminous ether, unbounded and directionless. The brilliance of this undifferentiated ground, in which water and sky connect in an almost seamless continuum, overpowers the material objects within it, so that if the rocks seem to float, to hover, they do so as shape merely. The luminous ground overmasters their bulk, making them instead, the functions of design. The mysterious beauty of the image is in this opulent flattening of its space.

By comparison, the lithograph is an object of insistent visual banality. Everything that is mysterious in the photograph has been explained with supplemental, chatty detail. Clouds have been massed in the sky. The far shore of the lake has been given a definitive shape; the surface of the lake has been characterized by little eddies and ripples. And most important for the demotion of this image from strange to commonplace, the reflections of the rocks in the water have been carefully re-created, so that gravity and direction are now restored to this space formerly awash with the vague luminosity of too rapidly exposed collodion.

But it is clear, of course, that the difference between the two images—the photograph and its translation—is not a function of the inspiration of the photographer and the insipidity of the lithographer. They belong to two separate domains of culture, they assume different expectations in the user of the image, they convey two distinct kinds of knowledge. In a more recent vocabulary, one would say that they operate as representations within two separate discursive spaces, as members of two different discourses. The lithograph belongs to the discourse of geology and, thus, of empirical science. In order for it to function within this discourse, the ordinary elements of topographical description had to be restored to the image produced by

1 Clarence King, Systematic Geology, 1878, is Vol. 1 of *Professional Papers of the Engineer Department U.S. Army*, 7 vols. & atlas, (Washington, D.C.: US Government Printing Office, 1877–78).

O'Sullivan. The coordinates of a continuous homogeneous space, mapped not so much by perspective as by the cartographic grid, had to be reconstructed in terms of a coherent recession along an intelligibly horizontal plane retreating towards a definite horizon. The geological data of the tufa domes had to be grounded, coordinated, mapped. As shapes afloat on a continuous, vertical plane, they would have been useless.[2]

And the photograph? Within what discursive space does it operate?

Aesthetic discourse as it developed in the nineteenth century organized itself increasingly around what could be called the space of exhibition. Whether public museum, official salon, world's fair, or private showing, the space of exhibition was constituted in part by the continuous surface of wall—a wall increasingly unstructured for any purpose other than the display of art. The space of exhibition had other features besides the gallery wall. It was also the ground of criticism, which is to say, on the one hand, the ground of a written response to the works' appearance in that special context, and, on the other, the implicit ground of choice (of either inclusion or exclusion) with everything excluded from the space of exhibition becoming marginalized with regard to its status as Art.[3] Given its function as the physical vehicle of exhibition, the gallery wall became the signifier of inclusion and, thus, can be seen as constituting in itself a representation of what could be called *exhibitionality*, or that which was developing as the crucial medium of exchange between patrons and artists within the changing structure of art in the nineteenth century. And in the last half of the century painting—particularly landscape painting—responded with its own corresponding set of depictions. It began to internalize the space of exhibition—the wall—and to represent it.

The transformation of landscape after 1860 into a flattened and compressed experience of space spreading laterally across the surface was extremely rapid. It began with the insistent voiding of perspective, as landscape painting counteracted perspectival recession with a variety of devices, among them sharp value contrast, which had the effect of converting the orthogonal penetration of depth—effected, for example, by a lane of trees—into a diagonal ordering of the surface. No sooner had this compression occurred, constituting within the single easel painting a representation of the very space of exhibition, than other means of composing this representation were employed: serial landscapes, hung in succession, mimed the horizontal extension of the wall, as in Monet's Rouen Cathedral paintings; or landscapes, compressed and horizonless, expanded to become the absolute size of the wall. The synonymy of landscape and wall (the one a representation of the other) of Monet's late waterlilies is thus an advanced moment in a series of operations in which aesthetic discourse resolves itself around a representation of the very space that grounds it institutionally.

This constitution of the work of art as a representation of its own space of exhibition is in fact what we know as the history of modernism. It is now fascinating to watch historians of photography assimilating their medium to the logic of that history. For if we ask, once again, within what discursive space does the original O'Sullivan—as I described it at the outset—function, we have to answer: that of the aesthetic discourse. And if we ask, then, what it is a representation *of*, the answer must be that within this space it is constituted as a representation of the plane of exhibition, the surface of the museum, the capacity of the gallery to constitute the objects it selects for inclusion as Art.

But did O'Sullivan in his own day, the 1860s and 1870s, construct his work for the aesthetic discourse and the space of exhibition? Or did he create it for the scientific/topographical discourse which it more or less efficiently serves? Is the interpretation of O'Sullivan's work as a representation of aesthetic values—flatness, graphic design, ambiguity, and, behind these, certain intentions towards aesthetic significations: sublimity, transcendence—not a retrospective construction designed to secure it as art?[4] And is this projection not illegitimate, the composition of a false history?

This question has a special methodological thrust from the vantage of the present, as a newly organized and energized history of photography is at work constructing an account of the early years of the medium. Central to this account is that type of photography, most of it topographical in character, originally undertaken for the purposes of exploration, expedition, and survey. Matted, framed, labeled, these images now

---

2 The cartographic grid onto which this information is reconstructed has other purposes besides the collation of scientific information. As Alan Trachtenberg argues, the government-sponsored Western surveys were intended to gain access to the mineral resources needed for industrialization. It was an industrial as well as a scientific program that generated this photography, which "when viewed outside the context of the reports it accompanied seems to perpetuate the landscape tradition." And Trachtenberg continues: "The photographs represent an essential aspect of the enterprise, a form of record keeping; they contributed to the federal government's policy of supplying fundamental needs of industrialization, needs for reliable data concerning raw materials, and promoted a public willingness to support government policy of conquest, settlement, and exploitation." Alan Trachtenberg, *The Incorporation of America* (New York: Hill and Wang, 1982), 20.

3 In his important essay "L'espace de l'art," Jean-Claude Lebensztejn discusses the museum's function, since its relatively recent inception, in determining what will count as Art: "The museum has a double but complementary function: to exclude everything else, and through this exclusion to constitute what we mean by the word art. It does not overstate the case to say that the concept of art underwent a profound transformation when a space, fashioned for its very definition, was opened to contain it." In Lebensztejn, *Zigzag* (Paris: Flammarion), 41.

enter the space of historical reconstruction through the museum. Decorously isolated on the wall of exhibition, the objects can now be read according to a certain logic, a logic that insists on their representational character within the discursive space of art, in an attempt to "legitimate" them. The term is Peter Galassi's, and the issue of legitimacy was the focus of the Museum of Modern Art exhibition *Before Photography*, which he organized. In a sentence that has been repeated by every reviewer of his argument, Galassi sets up this question of photography's position with respect to the aesthetic discourse: "The object here is to show that photography was not a bastard left by science on the doorstep of art, but a legitimate child of the Western pictorial tradition."[5]

The legitimation that follows depends on something far more ambitious than proving that certain nineteenth-century photographers had pretensions to being artists, or theorizing that photographs were as good as, or even superior to, paintings, or showing that photographic societies organized exhibitions on the model of Establishment salons. Legitimations depend on going beyond the presentation of apparent membership in a given family; they demand, instead, the demonstration of the internal, genetic necessity of such membership. Galassi wants, therefore, to address internal, formal structures rather than external, circumstantial details. To this end he wishes to prove that the perspective so prominent in nineteenth-century outdoor photography—a perspective that tends to flatten, to fragment, to generate ambiguous overlap; a perspective to which Galassi gives the name "analytic," as opposed to the "synthetic" constructive perspective of the Renaissance—was fully developed by the late eighteenth century within the discipline of painting. The force of this proof, Galassi maintains, will be to rebut the notion that photography is essentially a "child of technical rather than aesthetic traditions" and an outsider to the internal issues of aesthetic debate and to show, instead, that it is a product of that very same spirit of inquiry *within the arts* that welcomed and developed both "analytic" perspective and an empiricist vision. The radically fore-shortened and elliptical sketches by Constable (and even Degas) can then be used as models for a subsequent photographic practice, which in Galassi's exhibition turns out overwhelmingly to be that of topography: Samuel Bourne, Felice Beato, August Salzmann, Charles Marville, and, of course, Timothy O'Sullivan. [...]

When viewing the evidence on the walls of the museum, we have no doubt that Art has not only been intended, but has also been represented—in the flattened, decoratively unifying drawing of "analytic" perspective.

But here is where the demonstration runs into difficulty. For Timothy O'Sullivan's photographs were not published in the nineteenth century and the only real public distribution they can be shown to have had was through the medium of stereography. Most of the famous O'Sullivans—the Canyon de Chelly ruins from the Wheeler Expedition, for example—exist as stereographic views, and it was to these that, in O'Sullivan's case, as in William Henry Jackson's, the wider public had access.[6] Thus, if we began with a comparison between two images—the photograph and the lithographic translation—we can continue with a comparison between two cameras: a 9 × 12 plate camera and a camera for stereoscopic views. And these two pieces of equipment mark distinct domains of experience.

Stereographic space is perspectival space raised to a higher power. Organized as a kind of tunnel vision, the experience of deep recession is insistent and inescapable. This experience is all the more heightened by the fact that the viewer's own ambient space is masked out by the optical instrument he must hold before his eyes. As he views the image in an ideal isolation, his own surrounds, with their walls and floors, are banished from sight. The apparatus of the stereoscope mechanically focuses all attention on the matter at hand and precludes the visual meandering experienced in the museum gallery as one's eyes wander from picture

4 The treatment of Western survey photography as continuous with painterly depictions of nature is everywhere in the literature. Barbara Novak, Weston Naef, and Elisabeth Lindquist-Cock are three specialists who see this work as an extension of those landscape sensibilities operative in American nineteenth-century painting, with transcendentalist fervor constantly conditioning the way nature is seen. Thus, the by-now standard argument about the King/O'Sullivan collaboration is that this visual material amounts to a proof-by-photography of creationism and the presence of God. King, it is argued, resisted both Lyell's geological uniformitarianism and Darwin's evolutionism. A catastrophist, King read the geological records of the Utah and Nevada landscape as a series of acts of creation in which all species were given their permanent shape by a divine creator. The great upheavals and escarpments, the dramatic basalt formations were, it is argued, all produced by nature and photographed by O'Sullivan as proof of King's catastrophist doctrine. With this mission to perform, the Western photography of O'Sullivan becomes continuous with the landscape vision of Bierstadt or Church.

There is some support for this argument, there is an equal amount of support for its opposite: King was a serious scientist, who made great efforts to publish as part of the findings of his survey Marsh's palaeontological finds, which he knew full well provided one of the important "missing links" needed to give empirical support to Darwin's theory. Furthermore, as we have seen, O'Sullivan's photographs in their lithographic form function as neutralized, scientific testimony in the context of King's report; the transcendentalists' God does not inhabit the visual field of *Systematic Geology.* See, Barbara Novak, *Nature and Culture* (New York: Oxford University Press, 1980). Weston Naef, *Era of Exploration* (New York: The Metropolitan Museum of Art, 1975); and Elisabeth Lindquist-Cock, *Influence of Photography on American Landscape Painting*, New York, Garland Press, 1977.

5 Peter Galassi, *Before Photography* Before Photography (New York: The Museum of Modern Art, 1981), 12.

6 See the chapter "Landscape and the Published Photograph," in Naef, *Era of Exploration*. In 1871 the Government Printing Office published a catalogue of Jackson's work as, *Catalogue of Stereoscopic, 6 × 8 and 8 × 10 Photographs by Wm. H. Jackson.*

to picture and to surrounding space. Instead, the refocusing of attention can occur only within the spectator's channel of vision constructed by the optical machine.

The stereographic image appears multilayered, a steep gradient of different planes stretching away from the nearby space into depth. The operation of viewing this space involves scanning the field of the image, moving from its lower left corner, say, to its upper right. That much is like looking at a painting. But the actual experience of this scan is something wholly different. As one moves, visually, through the stereoscopic tunnel from inspecting the nearest ground to attending to an object in the middle distance, one has the sensation of refocusing one's eyes. And then again, into the farthest plane, another effort is made, and felt, to refocus.[7]

These micromuscular efforts are the kinesthetic counterpart to the sheerly optical illusion of the stereograph. They are a kind of enactment, only on a very reduced scale, of what happens when a deep channel of space is opened before one. The actual readjustment of the eyes from plane to plane within the stereoscopic field is the representation by one part of the body of what another part of the body, the feet, would do in passing through real space. And it goes without saying that from this physio-optical traversal of the stereo field, another difference between it and pictorial space derives. This is a difference that concerns the dimension of time.

The contemporary accounts of what it was like to look at stereographs all dilate on the length of time spent examining the contents of the image. For Oliver Wendell Holmes, Sr., a passionate advocate of stereography, this perusal was the response appropriate to the "inexhaustible" wealth of detail provided by the image. As he picks his way over this detail in his writing on stereography—in describing, for example, his experience of an E. & H. T. Anthony view up Broadway—Holmes enacts for his readers the protracted engagement with the spectacle demanded by stereo viewing. By contrast, paintings do not require (and as they become more modernist, certainly do not support) this temporal dilation of attention, this minute-by-minute examining of every inch of the ground.

When Holmes characterizes this special modality of viewing, where "the mind feels its way into the very depths of the picture," he has recourse to extreme mental states—like hypnotism, "half-magnetic effects," and dream. "At least the shutting out of surrounding objects, and the concentration of the whole attention which is a consequence of this, produce a dream-like exaltation," he writes, "in which we seem to leave the body behind us and sail away into one strange scene after another, like disembodied spirits."[8]

The phenomenology of the stereoscope produces a situation that is not unlike that of looking at cinema. Both involve the isolation of the viewer with an image from which surrounding interference is masked out. In both, the image transports the viewer optically, while his body remains immobile. In both, the pleasure derives from the experience of the simulacrum: the appearance of reality from which any testing of the real-effect by actually, physically, moving through the scene is denied. And in both, the real-effect of the simulacrum is heightened by a temporal dilation. What has been called the *apparatus* of cinematic process had, then, a certain proto-history in the institution of stereography, just as stereography's own proto-history is to be found in the similarly darkened and isolating but spectacularly illusionistic space of the diorama.[9] And in the case of the stereograph, as would later be the case for film, the specific pleasures that seem to be released by that apparatus—the desires that it seems to gratify—led to the instantly wild popularity of the instrument.

The diffusion of stereography as a truly mass medium was made possible by mechanized printing techniques. Beginning in the 1850s but continuing almost unabated into the 1880s, the figures for stereo sales are dizzying. As early as 1857 the London Stereoscopic Company had sold 500,000 stereoscopes and, in 1859, was able to claim a catalogue listing more than 100,000 different stereo views.[10]

It is in this very term—*view*—by which the practice of stereoscopy identified its object, that we can locate the particularity of that experience. First of all, *view* speaks to the dramatic insistence of the perspectivally organized depth that I have been describing. This was often heightened, or acknowledged, by the makers of stereo views by structuring the image around a vertical marker in fore- or middle-ground that works to *center* the space, forming a representation within the visual field of the eyes' convergence at a vanishing point. Many of Timothy O'Sullivan's images organize

7 The eye is not actually refocusing, of course. Rather, given the nearness of the image to the eyes and the fixity of the head in relation to it, in order to scan the space of the image a viewer must readjust and recoordinate the two eyeballs from point to point as vision moves over the surface.

8 Oliver Wendell Holmes, "Sun-Painting and Sun-Sculpture," *Atlantic Monthly*, VIII (July 1861), 14–15. The discussion of the view of Broadway occurs on Page 17. Holmes's other two essays appeared as "The Stereoscope and the Stereograph," *Atlantic Monthly*, III (June 1859), 738–48; and "Doings of the Sunbeam," *Atlantic Monthly*, XII (July 1863), 1–15.

9 See, Jean-Louis Baudry, "The Apparatus," *Camera Obscura*, no. 1 (1976), 104–26, originally published as "Le Dispositif," *Communications*, No. 23 (1975), 56–72; and Baudry, "Cinéma: Effets idéologiques produits par l'appareil de base," *Cinéthique*, No. 7–8 (1979), 1–8.

10 Edward W. Earle, ed., *Points of View: The Stereograph in America: A Cultural History* A Cultural History (Rochester, NY: The Visual Studies Workshop Press, 1979), 12. In 1856 Robert Hunt in the *Art Journal* reported, "The stereoscope is now seen in every drawing-room; philosophers talk learnedly upon it, ladies are delighted with its magic representation, and children play with it." Baudry, p. 28.

themselves around such a center—the staff of a bare tree-trunk, the sheer edge of a rock formation—whose compositional sense derives from the special sensations of the *view*. Given O'Sullivan's tendency to compose around the diagonal recession and centering of the *view*, it is not surprising to find that in his one published account of his work as a Western photographer he consistently speaks of what he makes as "views" and what he does when making them as "viewing." Writing of the expedition to Pyramid Lake, he describes the provisions, "among which may be mentioned the instruments and chemicals necessary for our photographer to 'work up his view.'" Of the Humboldt Sink, he says, "It was a pretty location to work in, and viewing there was as pleasant work as could be desired."[11] *View* was the term consistently used in the photographic journals, as it was overwhelmingly the appellation photographers gave to their entries in photographic salons in the 1860s. Thus, even when consciously entering the space of exhibition, they tended to choose *view* rather than *landscape* as their descriptive category.

Further, *view* addresses a notion of authorship in which the natural phenomenon, the point of interest, rises up to confront the viewer, seemingly without the mediation of an individual recorder or artist, leaving "authorship" of the views to their publishers, rather than to the operators (as they were called) who took the pictures. Thus, authorship is characteristically made a function of publication, with copyright held by the various companies, e.g., ©Keystone Views, while the photographers remain anonymous. In this sense the phenomenological character of the view, its exaggerated depth and focus, opens onto a second feature, which is the isolating of the object of that view. Indeed, it is a "point of interest," a natural wonder, a singular phenomenon that comes to occupy this centering of attention. This experience of the *singular* is, as Barbara Stafford has shown in an examination of singularity as a special category associated with travel accounts beginning in the late eighteenth century, founded on the transfer of authorship from the subjectivity of the artist to the objective manifestations of nature.[12] For this reason, the institution of the view does not claim the imaginative projection of an author so much as the legal protection of property in the form of the copyright.

Finally, *view* registers this singularity, this focal point, as one moment in a complex representation of the world, a kind of complete topographical atlas. For the physical space within which the "views" were kept was invariably a cabinet in whose drawers were catalogued and stored a whole geographical system. The file cabinet is very different as an object from the wall or the easel. It holds out the possibility of storing and cross-referencing bits of information and of collating them through the particular grid of a system of knowledge. The elaborate cabinets of stereo views that were part of the furnishing of nineteenth-century middle-class homes as well as of the equipment of public libraries comprise a compound representation of geographic space. The spatiality of the view, its insistent penetration, functions, then, as the sensory model for a more abstract system whose subject is also space. View and land survey are interdetermined and interrelated.

What can be seen to emerge from this analysis, then, is a system of historically specific requirements that were satisfied by the view and in relation to which *view* formed a coherent discourse. That this discourse is disjunct from what aesthetic discourse intends by the term "landscape" is also, I hope, apparent. Just as the view's construction of space cannot be assimilated, phenomenologically, to the compressed and fragmented space of what *Before Photography* calls analytic perspective,[13] so the representation formed by the collectivity of these views cannot be likened to the representation organized by the space of exhibition. The one composes an image of geographic order; the other represents the space of an autonomous Art and its idealized, specialized History, which is constituted by aesthetic discourse. The complex collective representations of that quality called style—period style, personal style—are dependent

11 "Photographs from the High Rockies," *Harper's Magazine*, XXXIX (September 1869), 465–75. In this article *Tufa Domes, Pyramid Lake* finds yet one more place of publication, in a crude translation of the photograph, this time as an illustration to the author's adventure narrative. Thus one more imaginative space is projected onto the blank, collodion screen. This time, in response to the account of the near capsize of the exploration party's boat, the engraver whips the waters into a darkened frenzy and the sky into banks of lowering storm clouds.

12 Thus Stafford writes, "The concept that true history is natural history emancipates the objects of nature from the government of man. For the idea of singularity it is significant . . . that geological phenomena—taken in their widest sense to include specimens from the mineral kingdom—constitute landscape forms in which natural history finds aesthetic expression. . . . The final stage in the historicizing of nature sees the products of history naturalized. In 1789, the German *savant* Samuel Witte—basing his conclusions on the writings of Desmarets, Duluc and Faujas de Saint-Fond—annexed the pyramids of Egypt for nature, declaring that they were basalt eruptions; he also identified the ruins of Persepolis, Baalbek, Palmyra, as well as the Temple of Jupiter at Agrigento and the Palace of the Incas in Peru, as lithic outcroppings." Barbara M. Stafford, "Toward Romantic Landscape Perception: Illustrated Travels and the Rise of 'Singularity' as an Aesthetic Category," *Art Quarterly*, n.s. I (1977), 108–9. She concludes her study of "the cultivation of taste for the natural phenomenon as singularity," by insisting that "the lone natural object . . . need not be interpreted as human surrogates; on the contrary, [the 19th century Romantic landscape painter's] isolated, detached monoliths should be placed within the vitalist aesthetic tradition—emerging from the illustrated voyage—that valued the natural singular. One might refer to this tradition as that of a 'neue Sachlichkeit' in which the regard for the specifics of nature produces a repertory of animate particulars." 117–18.

13 For another discussion of Galassi's argument with relation to the roots of "analytic perspective" in seventeenth-century optics and the *camera obscura*, see, Svetlana Alpers, *The Art of Describing: Dutch Art in the Seventeenth Century*, University of Chicago Press, 1983, Chapter 2.

upon the space of exhibition; one could say they are a function of it. Modern art history is in that sense a product of the most rigorously organized nineteenth-century space of exhibition: the museum.[14]

It is André Malraux who has explained to us how, in its turn, the museum, with its succession of (representations of) styles, collectively organizes the master representation of Art. Having updated themselves through the institution of the modern art book, Malraux's museums are now "without walls," the galleries' contents collectivized by means of photographic reproduction. But this serves only to intensify the picture:

> Thus it is that, thanks to the rather specious unity imposed by the photographic reproduction on a multiplicity of objects, ranging from the statue to the bas-relief, from bas-reliefs to seal-impressions, and from these to the plaques of the nomads, a "Babylonian style" seems to emerge as a real entity, not a mere classification—as something resembling, rather the life-story of a great creator. Nothing conveys more vividly and compellingly the notion of a destiny shaping human ends than do the great styles, whose evolutions and transformations seem like long scars that Fate has left, in passing, on the face of the earth.[15]

Having decided that nineteenth-century photography belongs in a museum, having decided that the genres of aesthetic discourse are applicable to it, having decided that the art historical model will map nicely onto this material, recent scholars of photography have decided (ahead of time) quite a lot. For one thing, they have concluded that given images are *landscapes* (rather than *views*) and they are thus certain about the discourse these images belong to and what they are representations of. For another (but it is a conclusion that is reached simultaneously with the first), they have determined that other fundamental concepts of aesthetic discourse will be applicable to this visual archive. One of these is the concept *artist* with its correlative notion of sustained and intentional progress, to which we give the term *career*. The other is the possibility of coherence and meaning that will unfold through the collective body of work so produced, this constituting the unity of an *oeuvre*. But, it can be argued, these are terms that nineteenth-century topographic photography tends not only not to support, but also to open to question.

The concept *artist* implies more than the mere fact of authorship; it also suggests that one must go through certain steps to earn the right to claim the condition of being an author, the word *artist* somehow semantically being connected with the notion of vocation. Generally, "vocation" implies an apprenticeship, a juvenilia, a learning of the tradition of one's craft, the gaining of an individuated view of that tradition through a process that includes both success and failure. If this, or at least some part of it, is what is necessarily included in the term *artist*, can we then imagine someone being an artist for just one year? Would this not be a logical (some would say, grammatical) contradiction, like the example adduced by Stanley Cavell in relation to aesthetic judgments, where he repeats Wittgenstein's question: "Could someone have a feeling of ardent love or hope for the space of one second—*no matter what* preceded or followed this second?"[16]

But this is the case with August Salzmann, whose career as a photographer began in 1853 and was over in less than a year. Little else on the horizon of nineteenth-century photography appeared only to vanish quite so meteorically. But other major figures within this history enter this métier and then leave it in less than a decade. This is true of the careers of Roger Fenton, Gustave LeGray, and Henri LeSecq, all of them acknowledged "masters" of the art. Some of these desertions involved a return to the more traditional arts; others, like Fenton's, meant taking up a totally different field such as the law. What do the span and nature of these engagements with the medium mean for the concept of *career*? Can we study these "careers" with the same methodological presuppositions, the same assumptions of personal style and its continuity, that we bring to the careers of another sort of artist?[17]

And what of the other great aesthetic unity: *oeuvre*? Once again we encounter practices that seem difficult to bring into conformity with what the term comprises, with its assumptions that the oeuvre is the result of sustained intention and that it is organically

14 Michel Foucault opens a discussion of the museum in "Fantasia of the Library," in *Language, Counter-Memory, Practice*, trans. D. F. Bouchard and S. Simon, Simon (Ithaca, NY: Cornell University Press, 1977), 87–109. See, also, Eugenio Donato, "The Museum's Furnace: Notes toward a Contextual Reading of *Bouvard and Pécuchet*," *Textual Strategies: Perspectives in Post-Structuralist Criticism*, ed. Josue V. Harari (Ithaca, NY: Cornell University Press, 1979); and Douglas Crimp, "On the Museum's Ruins," *October*, No. 13 (Summer 1980), 41–57.

15 André Malraux, "Museum without Walls," *The Voices of Silence*, Princeton, Princeton University Press, Bollingen Series XXIV, 1978, p. 46.

16 Stanley Cavell, *Must We Mean What We Say?*, New York, Scribners, 1969, 91, n. 9.

17 Students of photography's history are not encouraged to question whether art historical models might (or might not) apply. The session on the history of photography at the 1982 College Art Association meeting (a session proudly introduced as the fruits of real scholarly research at last applied to this formerly unsystematically studied field) was a display of what can go wrong. In the paper "Charles Marville, Popular Illustrator: Origins of a Photographic Aesthetic," presented by Constance Kane Hungerford, the model of the necessary internal consistency of an oeuvre encouraged the idea that there had to be a stylistic connection between Marville's early practice as an engraver and his later work as a photographer. The characterizations of style this promoted with regard to Marville's photographic work (e.g., sharp contrasts of light and dark, hard, crisp contours) were not only hard to see, consistently, but when these did apply they did not distinguish him in any way from his fellows on the Mission Héliographique. For every "graphic" Marville, it is possible to find an equally graphic LeSecq.

related to the effort of its maker: that it is coherent. One practice already mentioned was the imperious assumption of copyright, so that certain oeuvres, like Matthew Brady's and Francis Frith's, are largely a function of the work of their employees. Another practice, related to the nature of photographic commissions, left large bodies of the "oeuvre" unachieved. An example is the Heliographic Mission of 1851 in which LeSecq, LeGray, Baldus, Bayard, and Mestral (which is to say some of the greatest figures in early photographic history in France) did survey work for the Commission des Monuments Historiques. Their results, some 300 negatives in which were recorded medieval architecture about to submit to restoration, not only were never published or exhibited by the Commission, but were never even printed. This is analogous to a director shooting a film but never having the footage developed, hence never seeing the rushes. How would the result fit into the oeuvre of this director?[18]

There are other practices, other exhibits, in the archive that also test the applicability of the concept *oeuvre*. One of these is the body of work that is too meager for this notion; the other is the body that is too large. Can we imagine an oeuvre consisting of one work? The history of photography tries to do this with the single photographic effort ever produced by August Salzmann, a lone volume of archaeological photographs (of great formal beauty), some portion of which are known to have been taken by his assistant.[19] And, at the opposite extreme, can we imagine an oeuvre consisting of 10,000 works?

Eugène Atget's labors produced a vast body of work which he sold over the years of its production, roughly 1895–1927, to various historical collections, such as the Bibliothèque de la Ville de Paris, the Musée de la Ville de Paris (Musée Carnavalet), the Bibliothèque Nationale, the Monuments Historiques, as well as to commercial builders and artists. The assimilation of this work of documentation into a specifically aesthetic discourse began in 1925 with its notice and publication by the Surrealists and was followed, in 1929, by its placement within the photographic sensibility of the German New Vision.[20] Thus began the various partial viewings of the 10,000-piece archive; each view the result of a selection intended to make a given aesthetic or formal point.

The repetitive rhythm of accumulation that interested the *Neue Sachlichkeit* could be found and illustrated within this material, as could the collage sensibility of the Surrealists, who were particularly drawn to the Atget shopfronts, which they made famous. Other selections sustain other interpretations of the material. The frequent visual superimpositions of object and agent, as when Atget himself is captured as a reflection in the glazed entrance of the café he is photographing, permit a reading of the work as reflexive, picturing its own conditions of making. Other readings of the images are more architectonically formal. They see Atget managing to locate a point around which the complex spatial trajectories of the site will unfold with an especially clarifying symmetry. Most often images of parks and rural scenes are used for such analyses.

But each of these readings is partial, like tiny core samples that are extracted from a vast geological field, each displaying the presence of a different ore. Or like the blindmen's elephant. Ten thousand pieces are a lot to collate. Yet, if Atget's work is to be considered art, and he an artist, this collation must be made; we must acknowledge ourselves to be in the presence of an oeuvre. The Museum of Modern Art's four-part exhibition of Atget, assembled under the already loaded title *Atget and the Art of Photography*, moves briskly towards the solution of this problem, always assuming that the model that will serve to ensure the unity for this archive is the concept of an *artist's oeuvre*. For what else could it be?

John Szarkowski, after recognizing that, from the point of view of formal invention, the work is extremely uneven, speculates on why this should be so:

> There are a number of ways to interpret this apparent incoherence. We could assume that it was Atget's goal to make glorious pictures that would delight and thrill us, and that in this ambition he failed as often as not. Or we could assume that he began photographing as a novice and gradually, through the pedagogical device of work,

---

18 An example of this is the nearly four miles of footage shot by Eisenstein in Mexico for his project *Que Viva Mexico*. Sent to California where it was developed, this footage was never seen by Eisenstein, who was forced to leave the U.S. immediately upon his return from Mexico. The footage was then cannibalized by two American editors to compose *Thunder over Mexico* and *Time in the Sun*. Neither of these is supposed to be part of Eisenstein's oeuvre. Only a "shooting chronology" assembled by Jay Leyda in the Museum of Modern Art now exists. Its status in relation to Eisenstein's oeuvre is obviously peculiar. But given Eisenstein's nearly ten years of filmmaking experience at the time of the shooting, given also the state of the art of cinema in terms of the body of material that existed by 1930 and the extent to which this had been theorized, it is probable that Eisenstein had a more complete sense, from the script and his working conception of the film, of what he had made as a "work"—even though he never saw it—than the photographers of the Mission Héliographique could have had of theirs. The history of Eisenstein's project is documented in full detail in Sergei Eisenstein and Upton Sinclair, *The Making and Unmaking of "Que Viva Mexico,"* ed. Harry M. Geduld and Ronald Gottesman (Bloomington: Indiana University Press, 1970).

19 See, Abigail Solomon-Godeau, "A Photographer in Jerusalem, 1855: Auguste Salzmann and His Times," *October*, No. 18 (fall 1981), 95. This essay raises some of the issues about the problematic nature of Salzmann's work considered as oeuvre that are engaged above.

20 Man Ray arranged for publication of four photographs by Atget in *La Révolution Surréaliste*, three in the June 1926 issue, and one in the December 1926 issue. The exhibition *Film und Foto* Foto-Auge (Stuttgart: Wedekind Verlag, 1929), included Atget, whose work was also reproduced in *Foto-Auge*, Stuttgart, Wedekind Verlag, 1929.

learned to use his peculiar, recalcitrant medium with economy and sureness, so that his work became better and better as he grew older. Or we could point out that he worked both for others and for himself and that the work he did for himself was better, because it served a more demanding master. Or we could say that it was Atget's goal to explain in visual terms an issue of great richness and complexity—the spirit of his own culture—and that in service to this goal he was willing to accept the results of his own best efforts, even when they did not rise above the role of simple records.

I believe that all of these explanations are in some degree true, but the last is especially interesting to us, since it is so foreign to our understanding of artistic ambition. It is not easy for us to be comfortable with the idea that an artist might work as a servant to an idea larger than he. We have been educated to believe, or rather, to assume, that no value transcends the value of the creative individual. A logical corollary of this assumption is that no subject matter except the artist's own sensibility is quite worthy of his best attention.[21]

This inching forward from the normal categories of description of aesthetic production—formal success/formal failure; apprenticeship/maturity; public commission/personal statement—towards a position that he acknowledges as "foreign to our understanding of artistic ambition," namely, work "in the service of an issue larger than self-expression," evidently troubles Szarkowski. So that just before breaking off this train of thought he meditates on why Atget revisited sites (sometimes after several years) to choose different aspects of, say, a given building to photograph. Szarkowski's answer resolves itself in terms of formal success/formal failure and the categories of artistic maturation that are consistent with the notion of oeuvre. His own persistence in thinking about the work in relation to this aesthetic model surfaces in his decision to continue to treat it in terms of stylistic evolution: "The earlier pictures show the tree as complete and discrete, as an object against a ground; as centrally positioned within the frame; as frontally lighted, from behind the photographer's shoulder. The later pictures show the tree radically cut by the frame, asymmetrically positioned, and more obviously inflected by the quality of light that falls upon it."[22] This is what produces the "elegiac" mood of some of the late work.

But this whole matter of artistic intention and stylistic evolution must be integrated with the "idea larger than he" that Atget can be thought to have served. If the 10,000 images form *Atget's* picture of the larger idea, then that idea can inform us of Atget's aesthetic intentions, for there will be a reciprocal relation between the two, one inside, the other outside the artist.

To get hold, simultaneously, of this larger idea and of Atget's elusive intentions in making this vast archive ("It is difficult," Szarkowski writes, "to name an important artist of the modern period whose life and intention have been so perfectly withheld from us as those of Eugène Atget"), it was long believed to be necessary to decipher the code provided by Atget's negative numbers. Each of the 10,000 plates is numbered. Yet the numbers are not strictly successive; they do not organize the work chronologically; they sometimes double back on each other.[23]

For researchers into the problem of Atget's oeuvre, the numbers were seen as providing the all-important code to the artist's intentions and the work's meaning. Maria Morris Hambourg has finally and most definitively deciphered this code, to find in it the systematization of a catalogue of topographic subjects, divided into five major series and many smaller sub-series and groups.[24] The names given to the various series and groupings, names like Landscape-Documents, Picturesque Paris, Environs, Old-France, etc., establish as the master, larger idea for the work a collective picture of the spirit of French culture—not unlike, we could say, the undertaking of Balzac in the *Comédie Humaine*. In relation to this master subject, Atget's vision can then be organized around a set of intentions that are socio-aesthetic, so to speak; he becomes photography's great visual anthropologist. The unifying intention of the oeuvre can then be understood as a continuing search for the representation of the moment of interface between nature and culture [...] But this analysis, interesting and often brilliant as it is, is once again only partial. The desire to represent the paradigm nature/culture can be traced in only a small fraction of the images and then, like the trail of an elusive animal, it dies out, leaving the intentions as mute and mysterious as ever.

What is interesting in this case is that the Museum of Modem Art and Maria Morris Hambourg hold in their hands the solution to this mystery, a key that will not so much unlock the system of Atget's aesthetic intentions as dispel them. And this example seems all the more informative as it demonstrates the resistance

21 Maria Morris Hambourg and John Szarkowski, *The Work of Atget: Volume 1,* Old France (New York: The Museum of Modern Art, and Boston, New York Graphic Society, 1981), 18–19.

22 Hambourg and Szrakowski, 21.

23 The first published discussion of this problem characterizes it as follows: "Atget's numbering system is puzzling. His pictures are not numbered in a simple serial system, but in a confusing manner. In many cases, low-numbered photographs are dated later than high-numbered photographs, and in many cases numbers are duplicated." See, Barbara Michaels, "An Introduction to the Dating and Organization of Eugène Atget's Photographs" *The Art Bulletin*, LXI (September 1979), 461.

24 Maria Morris Hambourg, "Eugène Atget, 1857–1927: The Structure of the Work," unpublished Ph.D. dissertation (New York: Columbia University, 1980).

of the museological and art historical disciplines to using that key.

The coding system Atget applied to his images derives from the card files of the libraries and topographic collections for which Atget worked. His subjects are often standardized, dictated by the established categories of survey and historical documentation. The reason many of Atget's street images uncannily resemble the photographs by Marville taken a half century earlier is that both are functions of the same documentary master-plan.[25] A catalogue is not so much an idea as it is a mathesis, a system of organization. It submits not so much to intellectual as to institutional analysis. And it seems very clear that Atget's work is the *function* of a catalogue that he had no hand in inventing and for which *authorship* is an irrelevant term.

The normal conditions of authorship that the Museum wishes to maintain tend to collapse under this observation, leading us to a rather startling reflection. The Museum undertook to crack the code of Atget's negative numbers in order to discover an aesthetic anima. What they found, instead, was a card catalogue.

With this in mind we get a very different answer to various earlier questions, like the problem of why Atget photographed certain subjects piecemeal, the image of a façade separated by months or even years from the view of the same building's doorway or window mullions or wrought-iron work. The answer, it would seem, lies less in the conditions of aesthetic success or failure than in the requirements of the catalogue and its categorical spaces.

Subject is the fulcrum in all of this. Are the doorways and the ironwork balconies Atget's subjects, his choices, the manifest expression of him as active *subject*, thinking, willing, intending, creating? Or are they simply (although there is nothing simple in this) *subjects*, the functions of the catalogue, to which Atget himself is *subject*? What possible price of historical clarity are we willing to pay in order to maintain the former interpretation over the latter?

Everything that has been put forward about the need to abandon or at least to submit to a serious critique the aesthetically derived categories of authorship, oeuvre, and genre (as in *landscape*) obviously amounts to an attempt to maintain early photography as an archive and to call for the sort of archaeological examination of this archive that Michel Foucault both theorizes and provides a model for. Describing the analysis to which archaeology submits the archive in order to reveal the conditions of its discursive formations, Foucault writes that

> [They] must not be understood as a set of determinations imposed from the outside on the thought of individuals, or inhabiting it from the inside, in advance as it were; they constitute rather the set of conditions in accordance with which a practice is exercised, in accordance with which that practice gives rise to partially or totally new statements, and in accordance with which it can be modified. [The relations established by archaeology] are not so much limitations imposed on the initiative of subjects as the field in which that initiative is articulated (without however constituting its center), rules that it puts into operation (without it having invented or formulated them), relations that provide it with a support (without it being either their final result or their point of convergence). [Archaeology] is an attempt to reveal discursive practices in their complexity and density; to show that to speak is to do something—something other than to express what one thinks.[26]

Everywhere at present there is an attempt to dismantle the photographic archive—the set of practices, institutions, and relationships to which nineteenth-century photography originally belonged—and to reassemble it within the categories previously constituted by art and its history.[27] It is not hard to conceive of what the inducements for doing so are, but it is more difficult to understand the tolerance for the kind of incoherence it produces.

---

25 See, *Charles Marville, Photographs of Paris 1852–1878*, (New York: The French Institute/Alliance Française, 1981). This contains an essay, "Charles Marville's Old Paris," by Maria Morris Hambourg.

26 Michel Foucault, *The Archaeology of Knowledge*, trans. A. M. Sheridan Smith, (New York: Harper and Row, 1976), 208–9.

27 Thus far the work of Alan Sekula has been the one consistent analysis of the history of photography to attack this effort. See, Alan Sekula, "The Traffic in Photographs," *Art Journal*, XLI (Spring 1981), 15–25; and "The Instrumental Image: Steichen at War," *Artforum*, XIII (December 1975). A discussion of the rearrangement of the archive in relation to the need to protect the values of modernism is mounted by Douglas Crimp's "The Museum's Old/The Library's New Subject," *Parachute* (Spring 1981).

Naming the View
Alan Trachtenberg
1990

Beneath our America lies buried another distinct continent—an archaean America.
—Clarence King, *Systematic Geology* (1878)

I

Sometime in 1870 Clarence King, the brilliant young geologist then at the head of a government survey in the deserts and mountains of the Southwest, paused from his labors to fashion a charming Christmas gift for his half sister Marian and two of her friends. A small, ornamented volume of twenty-two pages, the gift book includes two poems set in type, two letters in his own hand reproduced by lithography, and twelve mounted albumen photographs (including the frontispiece). The photographs appear anonymously, though they were made by Timothy O'Sullivan, official photographer with King's survey party. [...] *The Three Lakes: Marian, Lall, Jan, and how they were named* casts King as a romantic explorer, not as a scientist at the head of a complex expedition seeking specific knowledge of a rugged and difficult terrain. Apparently an idle whimsy, the little book makes no mention of the survey.[1]

King's official project at the time represented one of the most significant mobilizations of energy and intellect in postwar America. At the astonishing youthful age of twenty-six, he was appointed in 1867 the first civilian head of a government survey (earlier surveys had been led by military officers). A graduate of the Yale Sheffield School in 1863, he had worked for the California Geological Survey, won admiration for his skills in the field, his innovative mind, his wit, cultivation, love of risk, and remarkable self-confidence. With the support of well-placed friends, King was able to persuade the Department of War to put him in charge of the most meticulously planned survey of continental lands yet undertaken in the United States—the forerunner of three other surveys funded in the following years in contiguous regions of the Far West and the Southwest. Together the four projects launched in the late 1860s comprised the "great surveys" of the postwar era. In 1879 the separate undertakings were disbanded, their activities incorporated in the United States Geological Survey, and King appointed its first director.[2]

In the authorizing letter of March 21, 1867, addressed to King, Brigadier General A. A. Humphreys, Chief of Engineers, Department of War, gave King his charge "to direct a geological and topographical exploration of the territory between the Rocky Mountains and the Sierra Nevada mountains, including the route or routes of the Pacific railroad." The object, he wrote, "is to examine and describe the geological structure, geographical condition and natural resources of a belt of country extending from the 120th meridian eastward to the 105th meridian, along the 40th parallel of latitude, with sufficient expansion north and south to include the lines of the 'Central' and 'Union Pacific' railroads." Known as the "40th Parallel Survey," the project included study of "all rock formations, mountain ranges, detrital plains, mines, coal deposits, soils, minerals, ores, saline and alkaline deposits"—in addition to the preparation of "detailed maps of the chief mining districts" and a topographical map of the entire region, barometric and thermometric observations of atmospheric conditions "bearing upon the subject of refraction and evaporation." Collections in botany and geology—and the publication of detailed studies of all these matters—rounded out Humphreys's charge. After specific instruction about the

1 I have consulted the copy in the Beinecke Library, Yale University. Other copies are at the New York Public Library and the Bancroft Library, University of California at Berkeley. See Francis P. Farquhar, "An Introduction to Clarence King's 'The Three Lakes,'" in *Sierra Club Bulletin* 24 (June 1939), 109–20 (including text). Also, Thurman Wilkins, *Clarence King* (New York: Macmillan, 1958), 120. While the photographs are not attributed in the book, most are unmistakably by O'Sullivan. One, however, is sometimes attributed to A. J. Russell—the picture of King mimicking a mountain climber, "Taking Breath" (No. 5 in the book). Russell had briefly joined the King party in the Uinta Mountains in August 1869, and another photograph which appears on a mount with his name is of the very same site. It is a scene showing the rigors of mountain photography: a group of men carrying equipment up a steep rock. One of the men is King; another is very likely O'Sullivan. King is dressed in the same attire as in "Taking Breath"—strong evidence that both pictures were made on the same occasion. The scene recorded in this picture suggests the kind of playfulness and improvisation evident in several of the *Three Lakes* photographs. See Weston Naef and James N. Wood, *Era of Exploration: The Rise of Landscape Photography in the American West, 1860–1885* (Buffalo/Boston: Albright-Knox Art Gallery, 1975), 67, 204.

2 See William H. Goetzmann, *Exploration and Empire: The Explorer and the Scientist in the Winning of the American West* (New York: Knopf, 1966), 430–66; and Richard A. Bartlett, *Great Surveys of the American West* (Norman, Okla.: University of Oklahoma Press, 1962), 123–215.

disbursement of funds, the letter closed with the requirement that King post a bond for twenty thousand dollars as surety "for the faithful expenditure of such funds."[3]

Each of the four surveys included photographers in their parties—O'Sullivan and Carleton Watkins (briefly) with the King survey, William Bell and O'Sullivan with the Wheeler survey of the 100th meridian, William Henry Jackson with the Hayden survey, Jack Hillers and E. O. Beaman with the Powell survey of the Colorado River. The photographs were used in a variety of ways—published with official reports as mounted prints, heliotype reproductions, or engraved lithographs; bound in small-edition albums for government officials and congressmen; provided to publishers for use as engravings in newspapers, periodicals, and books; sold directly to the public as stereographic views. Their importance may have seemed at the time secondary to the central tasks of exploration and scientific investigation, but their public impact and their continuing power in registering the meaning of the survey enterprises suggest in retrospect that they played an integral role in redefining the geological survey as a modern activity.

Hardly a lark, the project was a complex bureaucratic undertaking for which the young King bore full responsibility. Along with the transcontinental railroad system whose route it followed, King's survey was part of a concerted program of economic expansion implemented by the triumphant government immediately after the Civil War. Under a policy of stimulating private enterprise with public money and resources, the Republican-led Congress appropriated vast sums of money and land to fund a privately owned national railroad system. Surveys of mineral-rich regions along the railroad routes were part of the same economic program, in this case providing indirect subsidies to developers, miners, timbermen, and settlers in the form of free information and maps. Centrally funded, planned, and supervised by scientist-administrators, the surveys were direct government aid to science and indirect aid to the private sphere. This support by Congress was, in Henry Adams's words, "almost its first modern act of legislation."[4] The "40th Parallel" topographers and geologists, Adams noted, "held under their hammers a thousand miles of mineral country with all its riddles to solve, and its stores of possible wealth to mark. They felt the future in their hands."[5]

The aim was not just to discover what lay beneath the surface but to describe the surface—to analyze and to map. The King survey, Adams wrote in 1872 in a review of its reports, not only provided "the first trustworthy representation of a highly important portion of our vast territory" but its accurate maps "give some meaning to the geological results."[6] A map is, of course, a kind of symbolic picture. It is one way of "seeing" the land, and as part of the enterprise it helps clarify the role of photographers in the "great surveys." For one of the major goals implicit in King's charge was to produce a body of visual documents—traverse sections and charts for geological knowledge, maps and pictures for topographical knowledge. And the conjunction of maps and photographs within the same project suggests that *The Three Lakes* may prove more pertinent than it might at first seem, for a map consists not only of symbolic shapes and markers but of *names*.[7] The fairy tale tells indirectly of the making of a map, the filling in of names. And the role of the photographs which bear the fictional names—Marian, Jan, Lall—is to put an image to a name and a place.[8]

King describes several acts of naming in *Mountaineering in the Sierra Nevada*, acts of exhilarated triumph. "I rang my hammer on the topmost rock; we grasped hands, and I reverently named the grand peak MOUNT TYNDALL."[9] At the peak of Mount Shasta, waving the flag serves as the equivalent of ringing the hammer.

> Fred Clark and I climbed together out upon the highest pinnacle, a trachyte needle rising a few feet above the rest, and so small we could barely balance there together, but we stood a moment and waved the American flag, looking down over our shoulders eleven thousand feet.[10]

The name lays claim to the view. By the same token, a photographic view attaches a possessable image to a place name. A named view is one that has been seen, known, and thereby already possessed. Of course there was, in a sense, no question of ownership of the lands traversed by the surveys and the railroads—they belonged under the flag and laws of the nation. King

---

3 A. A. Humphreys to Clarence King, 21 March 1867, Record Group 57, Geological Survey of the 40th Parallel, National Archives.

4 Henry Adams, *The Education of Henry Adams* (Boston, 1918), 312.

5 Adams, 309; Goetzmann, 437–38, 593–94; George M. Wheeler, *Address before the American Geographical Society* (Washington, D.C., 1874), 18.

6 Henry Adams, "King's Fortieth Parallel Survey," *North American Review*, July 1871, 205; George P. Merrill, *The First Hundred Years of American Geology* (New Haven: Yale University Press, 1924), 530.

7 See George Stewart, *Names on the Land: A Historical Account of Place-Naming in the United States* (New York: Random House, 1945), 6–10, 333, 341, 353.

8 From his camp in the Wasatch Mountains in July 1869, King transmitted to Humphreys a map of the United States "with errors marked in red ink." He suggests revising a number of names and retaining others. King to Humphreys, 15 July 1869, Record Group 57, Geological Survey of the 40th Parallel, National Archives.

9 Clarence King, *Mountaineering in the Sierra Nevada* (Lincoln: University of Nebraska Press, 1970; original edition Boston, MA, 1872), 75.

10 King, 239.

had at his command a squadron of United States troops to enforce that fact, a protective shield against hostile Indians who had not yet succumbed to the logic of that flag and its laws. In their eyes the land belonged to them by virtue of another and earlier body of principles, tradition, and common use.

The conflict of law and interest between the expanding American nation and the defensive Indian nations arose from cultural antagonisms as well as economic interest. John Wesley Powell, director of one of the surveys, observed that native peoples viewed the land in a manner much different from that embodied in the survey: land was not an exploitable resource available for private ownership; it was collective property, the medium of communal life. Powell notes:

> Among all the North American Indians, when in a primitive condition, personal property was almost unknown. ... The right to the soil as landed property, the right to the products of the chase, etc., was inherent in the gens, or clan, a body of consanguinii [sic], a group of relatives. ... No other crime was so great, no other vice so abnormal, as the attempt of an individual to use for himself that which belonged to his gens in common; hence the personal rights to property recognized in civilization are intensely obnoxious to the Indian. He looks upon our whole system of property rights as an enormous evil and an unpardonable sin, for which the gods will eventually punish the wicked and blasphemous white man.[11]

The act of mapping and naming was, in the eyes of Indians, an act of trespass, not upon property but on religion, upon the sacred itself. The white man's maps threatened a whole way of life.[12]

Although King's poems in *The Three Lakes* evoke Indian legend and myth [...] it is not clear whether he knew the aboriginal names (if any existed). But do these hints of Indian lore suggest an unconscious recognition that the new Anglo-Saxon names violate the original identity of the lakes? In *Mountaineering in the Sierra Nevada*, King confesses to uncertainty in his attitudes toward Native Americans. He confesses that his "convictions concerning Indians" had been "tinged with the most sanguinary Caucasian prejudice." But watching a man's grief at the funeral pyre of his wife, King realizes that "not a stoical savage, but a despairing husband, stood before us. I felt him to be human." When he learns the next day that the same husband had gotten drunk that night, "I went back to camp an enlightened but disillusioned man."

> Since then I guardedly avoid all discussion of the 'Indian question.' When interrogated, I dodge, or protest ignorance; when pressed, I have been known to turn the subject; or, if driven to the wall, I usually confess my opinion that the Quakers will have to work a great reformation in the Indian before he is really fit to be exterminated.[13]

In the peaceful setting of a village, he can "find them picturesque: low conical huts, opening upon small smoking fires attended by squaws." Close up to a woman "engaged in maternal duties," he writes: "I am almost afraid to describe the squalor and grotesque hideousness of her person." Her husband, "the 'buck,'" on the other hand, caught in the act of spearing a salmon, reminds King of a statue cast in bronze.[14] The term "savage," then, holds mixed meanings for King, as in the "savage elements of sky, ice and rock" at the "lifeless" top of mountains, which make the descent into softer air and the presence of trees seem "a strange renewal of life."[15] "Savage" means for him something in nature impossible to resist and impossible to accept—a term which inflicts the consequences of a white man's dilemma upon native dwellers.

A similar ambivalence appears in the account by Josiah Dwight Whitney of the state-based California Geological Survey that tells how Yosemite Valley was renamed. In *The Yosemite Book* (1868)—which includes a sequence of twenty-four photographs by Carleton Watkins—Whitney notes that Indians of the region "had a name for every meadow, cliff and waterfall in and about the Valley." "It were much desired," he writes, "that these names could have been retained, but that is impossible; they have already almost passed into oblivion," "entirely replaced" by "names given by the early white visitors to the region." Still, "it is well known that the present Indian name of

11 John Wesley Powell, *Report on the Methods of Surveying the Public Domain to the Secretary of the Interior* (Washington, D.C., 1878), 15. Powell's jeremiad tone suggests he may be projecting some of his own contempt—he was a leading advocate of public planning for industrial development of the West—for the Gilded Age spectacle of private property riding roughshod over American communal values. Yet Indians remain "savages," and Powell wanted only a more effective system of instilling European culture, respect for work and law, than the government's military and "reservation" policy implied: "Savagery is not inchoate civilization; it is a distinct status of society, with its own institutions, customs, philosophy, and religion; and all these must necessarily be overthrown before new institutions, customs, philosophy, and religion can be introduced. The failure to recognize this fact has wrought inconceivable mischief in our management of the Indians." See Francis P. Prucha, *American Indian Policy in Crisis: Christian Reformers and the Indians, 1865–1900* (Norman: University of Oklahoma Press, 1976). Also relevant is Henry Nash Smith, "Clarence King, John Wesley Powell, and the Establishment of the United States Geological Survey," *Mississippi Valley Historical Review* 24 (June 1947), 37–58.

12 See Alexander B. Adams, *The Disputed Lands* (New York: Putnam, 1981).

13 King, *Mountaineering*, 37–40.

14 King, 226–27.

15 King, 245.

the Valley is not Yosemite, but Ahwahnee." As a sign of his lament—although he describes the remaining "digger" Indians (not native to Yosemite, incidentally) as "a miserable, degraded and fast disappearing set of beings, who must die out before the progress of the white man's civilization, and for whom there is neither hope or chance"—Whitney includes two pages of original Indian names in Yosemite and regions nearby. We learn, for example, that the original of El Capitan was Tolokonula—an imitation of the cry of the crane; that certain rocks were once called Ummo, meaning "lost arrow"; that the North Dome was once known as Tokoya, meaning "basket," from the rounded shape of the rock. Waijau ("pine mountains") was the Indian name for Mount Whitney itself—a name bestowed a few years earlier by a party which included King.

Whitney exonerates his survey team from responsibility for the regrettable loss of native names; they simply adopted nomenclature already "in well-established use" by white settlers and visitors. The surveyors, he conceded, did attach names to High Sierra peaks "previously unnamed," though he does not say how it could be known that a site was "without appellation." "We have . . . a full and ample right," he added defensively, "as the first explorers, describers and mappers of the High Sierra, to give such names as we please to the previously unnamed peaks which we locate." He passes over Waijau, the original of Mount Whitney, without comment.[16]

The new names brought the alien and unfamiliar into a familiar system of knowledge. Just as the photographs in *Three Lakes* depict the terrain as at once mythical (in the poems) and historical (in the letters), the survey photographs provide a visual parallel to the symbolic forms of the map—what historian Martin Rudwick calls a "conceptual bridge" between an abstract and a concrete visual mode. Naming and viewing complement each other. As a work of fiction illustrated with photographs, *The Three Lakes* thus clarifies one of the purposes of survey photographs: to provide visual means of following the work of the survey, particularly by giving place names a visual aspect. [...]

As King's little book shows, with a change of title or caption the survey photographs were freely adopted to sundry uses. This flexibility founds the question of their precise role within the surveys. The fact is that they probably did not have a precise scientific role. They served purposes as varied as the subjects they depict—geological formations, topographical vistas, views of Indian villages and artifacts, scenes in mining towns and in the mines themselves, waterfalls, and alkaline deserts. Of what practical use were the pictures? For decades they lay more or less unnoticed in archives and volumes of official reports or scattered in private collections. Recently these Western photographs have enjoyed a renaissance of interest [...] As a body of work the pictures by Timothy O'Sullivan, Carleton Watkins, William Henry Jackson, A.J. Russell, and others have been described as comprising "a golden age of landscape photography" in America.[17] [...] Attempts to define and interpret a distinctive style have been most prominent in the case of Timothy O'Sullivan, [whose] Western pictures have been described, for example, as "a sustained meditation on nature and on man's relationship with it.[18] His view of "nature" and of "man" has been seen as harsh, foreboding, desperate—not unlike Herman Melville's. While other photographers depict the West as "essentially picturesque," O'Sullivan's landscapes are seen as threatening, inhospitable either to habitation or conventional pictorial landscape formulas.[19] This may or may not be the case. Like poems (and everything else), photographs are open to interpretation. But to read his pictures as if they are indistinguishable from paintings is to ignore the medium in which they were made. [...]

Trained in [Matthew] Brady's New York and Washington galleries before the Civil War, O'Sullivan belonged to a generation which still thought of photography as an artisanal craft. An unsigned essay in *Harper's New Monthly Magazine* in 1869 on "Photographs in the High Rockies"—it may have been written by O'Sullivan himself—puts the credo of the cameraman-artisan in the opening paragraph:

> Places and people are made familiar to us by means of the camera in the hands of skillful operators, who, vying with each other in the artistic excellence of their productions avail themselves of every opportunity to visit interesting points, and take care to lose no good chance to scour the country in search of new fields for photographic labor.[20]

"Vying with each other in the artistic excellence of their

---

16 Josiah Dwight Whitney, *The Yosemite Book* (New York, 1868), 15–18. Whitney also wrote a brief treatise on place names: *Names and Places: Studies in Geographical and Topographical Nomenclature* (Cambridge, MA: The University Press, 1888).

17 Naef and Wood, *Era of Exploration*, 12.

18 Rick Dingus, *The Photographic Artifacts of Timothy O'Sullivan* (Albuquerque: University of New Mexico Press, 1982), xiv.

19 A view argued vigorously in Joel Snyder, *American Frontiers: The Photographs of Timothy H. O'Sullivan, 1867-1874* (Millerton, NY: Aperture, 1981). See also Naef and Wood, *Era of Exploration*, 125-36; and Amy R. Weinstein Meyers, *Sketches from the Wilderness: Changing Conceptions of Nature in American Natural History Illustration, 1680-1880* (Yale University dissertation, 1985), 259-319.

20 "Photographs from the High Rockies," *Harper's New Monthly Magazine* 39 (September 1869), 465, reproduced as facsimile in this volume on pages 68–79. The article is indexed under John Samson–perhaps a pseudonym for O'Sullivan. [As Trachtenberg notes, it is likely that O'Sullivan assumed the pseudonym John Samson when writing for *Harper's*. See "Naming the View," in *Reading American Photographs: Images as History, Mathew Brady to Walker Evans* (New York: Hill and Wang, 1990), 127–132.]

productions" was taken for granted in the guild of wet-plate operators […] O'Sullivan was known as one of the best—known for his skill, not his sensibility, style, or unique vision. He and his colleagues never doubted that their purpose was to make clear reports of things visible in the world. Even if their work displayed conventional aspects—what is more conventional, more imitative of painting, than the conventional studio portrait?—the real interest of the work lies in its social use as photograph. There also lay its aesthetic effects. While certain pictures may have made their appeal as landscape art, the category proves limiting, if we wish to see how such pictures as O'Sullivan made for the King survey played a role in the survey itself.

It seems unlikely that King would have asked O'Sullivan to make his own interpretations of the terrain, or that O'Sullivan would have conceived of doing so. It is true that O'Sullivan's pictures are often distinctive in their flattening of objects, their rendering of horizon lines, their glaringly bright unclouded skies. But more important as a mark of distinction, particularly in pictures produced for King, is their presentation of the survey project itself. Rather than "a boundless place of isolation," a landscape "unmarked, unmeasured, O'Sullivan's views often show survey teams at work, taking measurements, making their marks.[21]

Often the same pictures will include pieces of photographic apparatus: dark cloths, plate holders, portable darkrooms, even cameras—deliberate signs of the Industrial Age invading nature's domain. One purpose of including cameras or survey equipment may be to suggest the scale of things in vistas without other human measurements. But the effect is more complex and occurs with such frequency in O'Sullivan's 40th Parallel pictures as to suggest a deliberate practice. […] the photographer shows that the picture is indeed a picture and not the real thing or a scene itself, and at the same time says that the photographer was really there placing the terrain within a context of actuality. […]

III

At the end of their first season in the field, the King party returned to Washington in the winter of 1868–69, and among their labors was the preparation of photographs to be presented to various important and influential people, military leaders, and congressmen. Someone—perhaps King, perhaps O'Sullivan—assembled eighty photographs into two bound volumes, forty pictures in each, covering O'Sullivan's work in 1867–68.[22] The volumes were bound but not published, not produced for public sale, and seem to be unique—at least, no duplication of these particular pictures in this particular order exists among the several other volumes of King survey photographs. On the spine of each of the volumes prepared in 1868–69 is printed: *Photographs, Geological Explorations, 40th Parallel, Clarence King, Geologist in Charge, 1868*, the separate volumes identified as *Volume I, No. 1–40*, and *Volume II, No. 41–80*. Each individual photograph is mounted on a board which reads: "U.S. Engineer Department, Geological Exploration, Fortieth Parallel, T. H. O'Sullivan, Photographer." Unlike *The Three Lakes*, or the books published by Whitney and Hayden, the two volumes do not relate their images to a written text. Each image is numbered on its mount, and this key refers to a separate list of printed titles.

The pictures are arranged in clusters focused on regions and subjects. Volume One includes pictures of Shoshone Falls in the Snake River Canyon in Idaho, mining activities in and around Virginia City, Nevada, and desert phenomena such as silica mounds, alkali lakes, fissure vents, hot springs and geysers, in the vicinity of Steamboat Springs, Ragtown, Truckee Desert, Humboldt Desert, Ruby Valley, and Carson Desert. Volume Two contains pictures mainly of geological formations—volcanic columns, limestone outcroppings, rhyolite hills, canyons, and lakes—in the Humboldt Mountain ranges in California, Nevada, and Utah. Survey crews appear in many of the photographs. Volume One opens with two pictures of the "explorers" in camp, and similar pictures are scattered through Volume Two.

The two volumes may have been intended as a catalogue, an inventory or archive of images to be drawn upon for reproduction as lithographs in the reports. We can guess that they were made to be seen by a limited number of people—other members of the survey party, very likely General Humphreys, and others. Still, because the volumes represent, as far as we can tell, the first attempt to put O'Sullivan's survey photographs into a coherent form, we can ask whether there is more to that form than the record of a reconnaissance through a particular terrain, the clustering of images taken at particular places and times. Is there a controlling idea, a deliberate ordering of images to express a coherent point of view?

Volume One shows a thematic grouping by location and, as we shall see, a careful placement of images within each group to suggest the development of a point of view. Volume Two is less systematic, less varied in its regions, its sequence less coherent. Volume One is the more interesting, for the point of view reflects on the activity of surveying and the role of photography within it. If *The Three Lakes* can be taken as an essay on viewing and naming, Volume One can be read as a

21 Snyder, 7.

22 See "O'Sullivan Albumen Prints in Official Publications," compiled by Jonathan Heller, in Snyder, *American Frontiers*, 117.

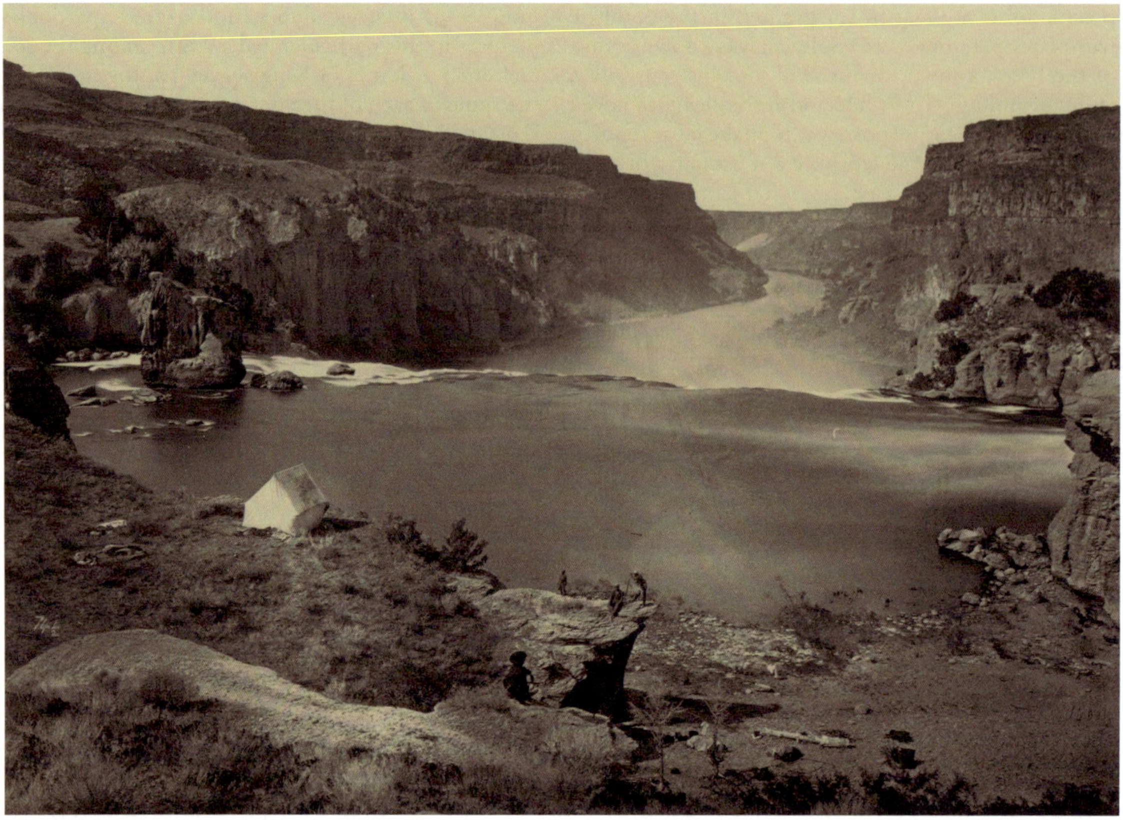

Figure 1. Timothy H. O'Sullivan, *Shoshone Falls, Snake River* (Plate 9), 1867, albumen silver print.

more expansive and complex reflection upon the survey enterprise itself in a region King called an American "*terra incognita*," "a labyrinth of intricate changes."[23] The survey writings of King and other scientists, along with the remarks attributed to O'Sullivan in a 1869 *Harper's* article, help us piece together a point of view.[24] It is the pictures themselves as they are arranged which disclose an intention. We are concerned, of course, not with why O'Sullivan made these pictures but with why they appear in this particular order.

The first impression is of diversity. There is a wide range of views, beginning with the opening two pictures of the explorers in camp, followed by a series showing Shoshone Falls from several perspectives; then there are views of mining in Nevada, followed by desert views. The pictures are as varied as their subjects: panoramic views with a number of prominent features; closer views of singular features; scenes from different perspectives. The mining pictures introduce another range of differences: pictures made above and below ground—mining settlements viewed as part of the natural setting, and miners at work in the cramped spaces of the mines, illuminated by magnesium flares. Diversity of camera angles, of subjects, and of geographical locations conveys the idea that the camera itself, the instrument of picture making, can produce various visual results, from close-ups to panoramas. While it makes us aware, through the photographer's control, of natural scenes, it also makes us aware of the photographer's own creativity in choosing what to depict—the human and mechanical activity of camera operator. By their diversity, which calls attention to our dependency for what we see upon the photographer's choices and the camera's position, the pictures raise a question about cognition, the relation between seeing, investigating, and knowing—the question which lies at the base of the survey as a whole.

Consider the Shoshone Falls sequence. These eight pictures form the first distinctly unified group in the album. It is followed by seventeen mining pictures in and around Virginia City, hundreds of miles away from the falls. Though the captions provide no specific dates, we know from other sources that some of the mining pictures were made in the spring of 1867 and most in the winter of 1867–68, many months before the visit to Shoshone Falls in October 1868.[25] The order of the photographs deviates from the actual sequence of

23 Clarence King, *Systematic Geology* (Washington, D.C., 1878), 2–4.
24 *Harper's*, 470.

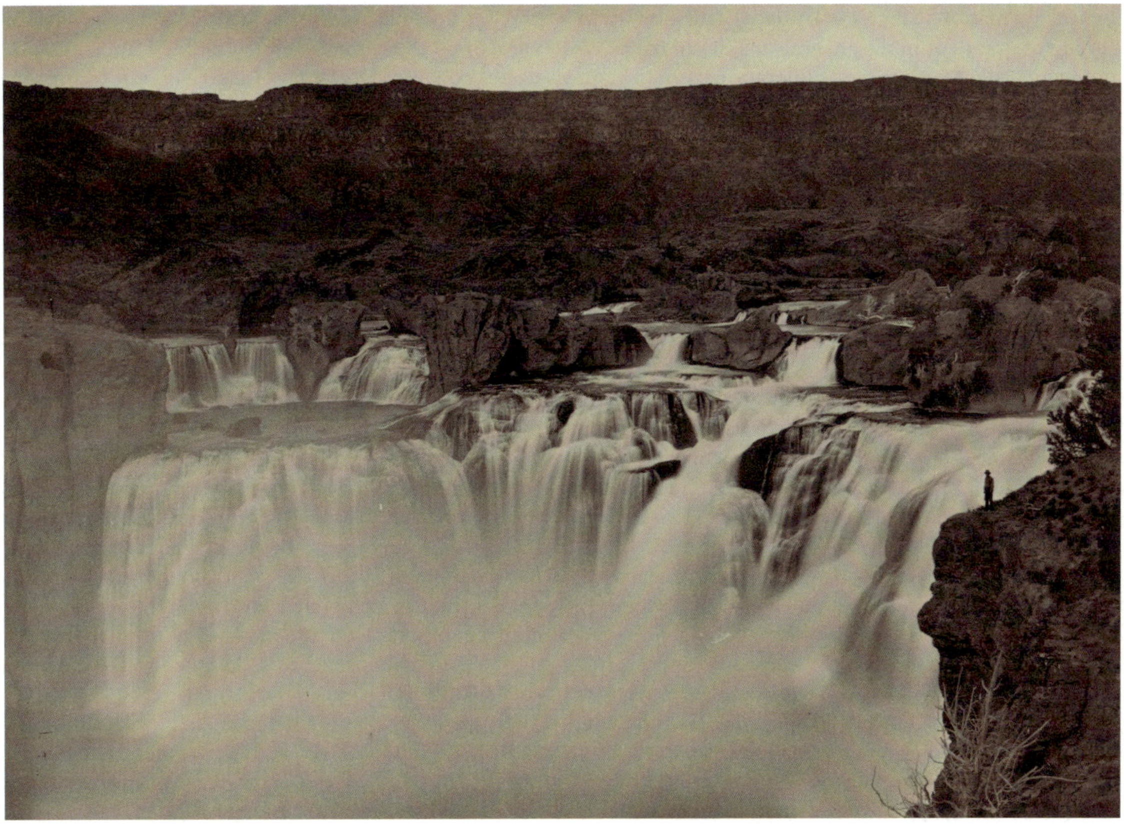

Figure 2. Timothy H. O'Sullivan, *Shoshone Falls, Snake River* (Plate 6), 1867, albumen silver print.

exploration. The governing principle, clearly, is not to represent a strict chronology of the survey.

The Shoshone sequence includes pictures of the cataract from a number of perspectives: from above, at water level, from the side, from behind. Images of the falls, of course, predominate, the powerful cascade rushing over the upper terraces to gather into a single immensity of falling water, blurred by the slowness of the film into a crashing wall of whiteness. The group begins with a long view of the entire falls and the Snake River Canyon. "In the Shoshone we have fall after fall to view as a preliminary exhibition," O'Sullivan explained in the *Harper's* article.[26] His use of the present tense raises the possibility that he is writing directly from the actual sequence of pictures, for the first picture is precisely such a "preliminary exhibition" with a comfortably seated spectator. The figure seems to be King's black attendant, Jim, in the rather incongruously formal attire (like King's) in the picture, No. 2, which precedes the Shoshone group. "The surroundings of the main fall are such that any number of views may be had of the scene," the *Harper's* article continues, in the vein of a working photographer assigned to survey a scene. The author speaks of the "bird's-eye view" one can have by "standing upon the craggy rocks that jut out from and form the walls of the table-land above the falls," of the "grand sight of the different falls" from the same position.

The group might be taken as the photographic composite view of a spectacle, a way of making the awesome scene available to mere viewing, to the sensations of majesty and sublimity of the sort long associated with Niagara Falls. Indeed, the *Harper's* essay reinforces this idea: "From the island above the falls you may not see the great leap that the water takes, but you will certainly feel sensible of the fact that you are in the presence of one of Nature's greatest spectacles as you listen to the roar of the falling water and gaze down the stream at the wild scene below."[27] But while sublimity may well be a part of these pictures, it is clear, especially from their place within the structure of the album, that these are survey pictures.

Several of them show the men at their tasks, No. 9 (Fig. 1) with camera equipment in the foreground. As a group, the pictures take the viewer around a natural phenomenon in order better to see its site and its geo-

25 Snyder, "Chronology," in *American Frontiers*, 114–15.
26 *Harper's New Monthly Magazine*, 475.
27 *Harper's New Monthly Magazine*, 470.

logical formations (Fig. 2). To depict the site as "a setting of grandeur in the glorious masses of rocks" is not inconsistent with survey illustrations. On the contrary, as we will see, King shows in an intense essay on the Shoshone Falls exploration how a powerful affective response might coexist with objective observation. [...]

By the late 1860s, spectacular viewing already threatened to become a leading recreation at the site. Writing in *Mountaineering* about his exploration of Yosemite in 1864 with the Whitney California survey party, King remarks about the already well-visited Inspiration Point: "I always go swiftly by this famous point of view now, feeling somehow that I don't belong to that army of literary travelers who have planted themselves and burst into rhetoric."[28] He may have had in mind something like this passage by Samuel Bowles, editor of the Springfield, Massachusetts, *Republican*, who stood at Inspiration Point sometime in 1868:

> The overpowering sense of the sublime, of awful desolation, of transcending marvelousness and unexpectedness, that swept over us, as we reined our horses sharply out of green fields, and stood upon the high jutting rock that overlooked this rolling, upheaving sea of granite mountains, holding far down its rough lap this vale of beauty of meadow and grove and river,—such tide of feeling, such stoppage of ordinary emotions comes at rare intervals in any life. It was the confrontal of God face to face.[29]

[...] King's solution to the problem of representing at once the place and himself within it is to make dramatic an issue that runs through *Mountaineering*: the issue of perception, of the dependence of knowing upon different modes of seeing. Its simplest form appears in the effects of atmosphere on aspects of the scene—for example, in the differences between June and October. [...] The ever-changing aspect of the scene corresponds with King's constant mobility, his fluid shifts from one observation point to another: "Lying upon a sharp neatly fractured edge, I was able to look down and study..." He takes scrupulous care to say where he is while looking and studying, to specify his point of view, the physical ground of his perceptions.[30]

A third element or filter that colors the view arises from a different source: "It was impossible for me, as I sat perched upon this jutting rock mass, in full view of all the canyons which had led into this wonderful converging system of ice-river, not to imagine a picture of the glacier period."[31] Geological knowledge permits, indeed insists upon, the superimposition of one picture upon another—the invisible past upon the fluctuating image of the present. King reads the scene before him as evidence of cataclysmic natural forces and vast reaches of time, "legibly traced with the history of the past." [...] This additional factor in perception—let us call it geological imagination—results in a doubled vision: not just past and present, visible and invisible, but a vanished order of cataclysm (or, in the more common term used by geologists, catastrophe) and a visible order of tranquility. The fusion of the two perspectives— "wonderfully opposite," as King puts it, without being contradictory—results in the complexly layered texture of *Mountaineering*, its ease of movement between beauty and terror. King's apparent shifts between enchantment and disenchantment register his modern awareness of the contingent character of knowledge, its dependence upon necessarily partial acts of perception—and upon the metaphoric properties of language.

"What sentiment, what idea," King asks of his Yosemite ramblings, "does this wonder-valley leave upon the earnest observer? what impression does it leave upon his heart?"[32] In a passage that serves as a bridge to an extraordinary account of the expedition to Shoshone Falls which resulted in O'Sullivan's pictures, his answer puts the divided perspective into the succinct form of "two leading ideas": "First, the titanic power, the awful stress, which has rent this solid tableland of granite in twain; secondly, the magical faculty displayed by vegetation in redeeming the aspect of wreck and masking a vast geological tragedy behind the draperies of fresh and living green." Titan, magic, mask, tragedy, draperies: these more prominent of the figures of speech in the passage reveal the underlying metaphor of drama and stagecraft through which King views natural process in all his writing, from *The Three Lakes* to *Mountaineering* to *Systematic Geology*, and his most sustained exercise in the application of metaphor to science, the lecture "Catastrophism and Evolution."[33] King employs dramatic language in order to hold both perceptions in the mind at once, the granite with its inscriptions of an awesome history, the "fresh

28 King, *Mountaineering*, 149.

29 Samuel Bowles, *Our New West* (Hartford, CT, 1869), 374. See Dimock on how idealizations obscured the natural and economic effects of more rapacious uses of natural resources in Mariposa. Interestingly, Bowles traveled in the summer of 1868 in the company of A. J. Russell, who the following year briefly joined the King party and O'Sullivan in the Uinta Mountains. See Susan Danly, in *The Railroad in American Art: Representations of Technological Change*, ed. Leo Marx and Susan Danly (Cambridge, MA: MIT Press, 1988), 98; and Russell, "On the Mountains with Tripod and Camera," *Anthony's Photographic Bulletin*, Vol. 1 (1870), 33–34. It was on this occasion that Russell must have made (or participated in the making of) the picture discussed in note 1, and perhaps the picture of King "taking breath" in *Three Lakes*.

30 King, *Mountaineering*, 133–34, 143.

31 King, 152.

32 King, 184.

and living green" with its enchantment and pastoral delight, without giving way (as Bowles most egregiously does) to an exclusive emotion, a single, fixed perspective. And his formulation of these "two leading ideas" opens the appropriate space for an account of an experience several years after his explorations of Yosemite: "I can never cease marvelling how all this terrible crush and sundering is made fair, even lovely, by meadow, by wandering grove . . . ; nor can I ever banish from memory another gorge and fall, that of the Shoshone in Idaho."

What follows in King's essay is an extraordinary narrative of exploration of the Snake River Valley in October 1868. Across a sage desert, the monotony of which is "overpowering," the survey party seeks "a good outlook" upon the falls they know only by rumor and sketchy report. A "dull, throbbing" roar and the first sight of the falls shatter the monotony, as King watches "a broad river, smooth and unruffled, flowing quietly into the middle of the scene, and then plunging into a labyrinth of rocks." "A strange, savage scene," with its "circling wall" and "battlemented . . . fortress-like masses," a "forbidding gloom" heightened by "the mere suggestion of trees clinging here and there along the walls": King portrays the view as if he were gazing at a Gothic landscape by Salvator Rosa. He speaks of "the abyss of foam," of the "fatal fascination" apt to overcome the viewer, of "black precipices," and "strange, wild sounds" that rise from within the monotone of "a slow, measured beat." At night, "gleams of pale moonlight" through drifting clouds create "intervals of light and blank darkness," the lower river "veiled and unveiled again and again." The effect is of a "Dantean gulf": "A moment of this strange picture, and then a rush of black shadow, when nothing could be seen but the breaks in the clouds, the rim of the basin, and a vague, white centre in the general darkness." At the same time, King's highly pictorial language coexists without the least discomfort with a language of close observation and study: "Wherever large fields of basalt have overflowed an earlier rock, and erosion has afterward laid it bare, there is found a strong tendency to fracture in vertical lines." The purpose of "studying the falls and rocks" never disappears from the account. The morning after "sleeping on the nightmarish brink of the falls," he is abroad on "an old Indian trail" exploring the terrain with an eye to its structure and composition, the character of its basalt and the "underlying porphyritic trachyte."[34]

As assembled in the 1868–69 album, O'Sullivan's Shoshone pictures might well serve as a visual supplement to King's narrative. Both describe a spatial pattern, toward and away from the central visual emblem: "in the centre a dazzling sheet of foam." Certainly, as in the case of *The Three Lakes*, King's affective figures transfer themselves to the pictures—not as definitive meanings, however, but simply as metaphors inspired by the views. In a key passage King writes that "the eye constantly wanders" away from the "white front of the cataract" up to "the black, frowning parapet of lava," noting "bastions" and rocks that "strikingly recall barbette batteries." Possibly recalling the inflated rhetoric of Inspiration Point, he adds: "To goad one's imagination up to the point of perpetually seeing resemblances of every thing else in the forms of rocks, is the most vulgar vice of travellers. To refuse to see the architectural suggestions upon the Snake Canyon, however, is to administer a snub to one's fancy." King confesses that the Gothic and Dantean figures are indulgences of fancy—necessary to convey his feelings, but as an admitted indulgence, not to be taken as the same kind of description as "basalt" or "trachyte," though no less true to actual experience.

King's acknowledgment of the vulgar but excusable vice of seeing resemblances everywhere brings us once more to the cognitive issue at the heart of the survey: how to picture place and object in this strange, uncharted terrain where "intervals of light and blank darkness hurriedly followed each other," and where exploration follows the route of an old Indian trail. The Dantean metaphor of the abyss served as one kind of picture, the findings about vertical fractures in basalt another, and the photographs by Timothy O'Sullivan, enacting the movement toward and around the falls even while showing the surveyors at their work of taking observations, yet another. To imagine the photographs as a supplement to King's essay is also to recover a relation—not of image to factual reality but of visual picture to verbal picture, of the visual as a "conceptual bridge" to both kinds of metaphors King employs: the geological and the Dantean.

King closes the Shoshone episode with a reprise of the entire experience:

> You ride upon a waste—the pale earth stretched in desolation. Suddenly you stand upon a brink, as if the earth had yawned. Black walls flank the abyss. Deep in the bed a great river fights its way through labyrinths of blackened ruins, and plunges in foaming whiteness over a cliff of lava. You turn from the brink as from a frightful glimpse of the Inferno, and when you have gone a mile the earth seems to have closed again; every trace of canyon has vanished, and the stillness of the desert reigns.[35]

The compacted narrative resonates with the album sequence, which closes with a beautifully transitional image of the river below the falls, settled into tranquility and turning a bend beyond the horizon—toward

33 Clarence King, "Catastrophism and Evolution," *American Naturalist* 11 (Aug. 1877), 339–470.

34 Clarence King, "The Falls of Shoshone," *Overland Monthly* 5 (Oct. 1870), 381–85.

the desert, we presume—through a canyon of fantastical trachyte forms. But if we are following the pictures with King's words as a parallel text, the next image proves an astonishment.

IV

We find ourselves not in desert stillness but in another shrieking landscape of power: in this case, the industrial power represented by factories, smokestacks, smelting works, mining shafts, and miners at work underground. This jolting turn in the album thrusts us toward yet another Dantean Inferno. The next sequence, which postpones the desert for a tour among the dark Satanic mills of the hard-rock mining industry in western Nevada, plunges us at once into an actual history, both of the mining industry at the celebrated Comstock Lode centered at Virginia City and of the survey itself.

With these pictures we find ourselves at the epicenter of the survey's purpose and task. To see why, we need first to describe the context. King had won his prestigious assignment in 1867 partly by arguing that the economic value of the transcontinental railroad would be immeasurably enhanced by an accurate topographical map of the Great Basin as well as detailed information about mineral deposits.[36] The unexplored mountains contiguous to the railroad route, King explained, were not as barren and worthless as commonly thought, "but full of wealth...All that is needed is to explore and declare the nature of the national domain."[37] In such a survey, his argument implied, science could prove its legitimacy as an instrument of social policy by demonstrating its practical value to capitalist enterprise. With all his enthusiasm for theoretical science, for converting the history of upheavals and cataclysms inscribed in rocks into theories of "systematic geology," King accepted the priority of information convertible to "wealth." There is no indication that he felt any contradiction or tension between the "pure" and the applied aspects of science, that they were anything other than two faces of the same enterprise, just as exploration and naming were one seamless activity. Later he would make a career (strangely unsuccessful) as a private consultant for mining companies and as a speculative investor. *Mining Industry* (1870), the first of the written reports published by the survey (unlike the volumes of photographs, this and other official survey reports were available for sale), was "first prepared and published," King explained, "because its subject . . . is most directly applicable to the material development of that great extent of mountain territory opened up by the Pacific Railroad."[38]

Only one photograph appears in *Mining Industry*—the lithographed frontispiece of six miners standing either patiently or glumly at the "Shaft Landing of Savage Mine" (No. 13 in the 1868 album, "Shaft Mouth, Mining Works, Virginia City, Nevada"). The report includes thirty-seven plates of precise drawings, sectional views of shaft timbering and ventilation systems, the mechanical parts of hoisting apparatus and milling equipment, along with a separate atlas of fourteen maps and geological sections in coded colors relevant to mining activities chiefly at the celebrated Comstock Lode and at other locations in Nevada and Colorado. In light of this flood of abstract visual models, the frontispiece plays an especially interesting role as a sign of what is missing: the absent literalness of the photographs, especially as assembled and arranged in the 1868 volume. Very much like King's Shoshone essay, *Mining Industry* provides, nonetheless, an implied text. O'Sullivan's mining photographs come to life when viewed alongside the treatment of hard-rock mining in the report, the geological, technological, and economic facts represented in word and drawing—a visual investigation parallel to, and interestingly divergent from, the report.

Why did King's survey concern itself with this subject, and what was his attitude toward it? The 1870 report and O'Sullivan's mining pictures together make it clear that King's interest lay not merely in general reconnaissance of mineral deposits but in a functioning industry comprised of a large number of competing private companies. The report includes contributions by King on the "geological distribution" of the region, and on the chemistry of the Washoe process of amalgamation by Arnold Hague and S. F. Emmons. The main sections of the report, written by James D. Hague, deal with "engineering and economy," which King calls in his covering letter to General Humphreys "this grave task" in the study of "those mining districts in Nevada and Colorado which afford the most instructive results, and produce the largest yield of precious metals." Three-fifths of the volume concerns the richest, most productive district of all, the famed Comstock Lode centered at Virginia City and Gold Hill, where several large corporations and countless smaller claim holders had been extracting the wondrous silver from the bowels of the mountains since 1859.[39] The silver strike gave enormous impetus to plans for a Pacific railroad through what Henry Adams described as "the interminable, uninhabited,

35 King, "The Falls of Shoshone," 196.
36 Goetzmann, 437; Wilkins, *King*, 94–96.
37 Wilkins, 95.
38 James D. Hague, *Mining Industry* (Washington D.C., 1870), n.p.

hideous region of the Great Basin." Reviewing *Mining Industry* in 1871, Adams noted that the discovery of silver ore led to "a feverish, or even furious, spasm of speculative excitement, during which roads and stage lines traversed the region in every direction, while mining camps, towns, and even cities shot up like mushrooms."[40] Local trade as well as the mining industry cried out for the railroad, silver now doing for rail transport what California gold had earlier done for steamboat travel across the Isthmus of Panama. In short, Comstock created the very conditions which invited the railroad, speculators, corporations, and, in their wake, the 40th Parallel Survey.

By 1870 Comstock seemed to be in trouble, its annual yield declining; there were suspicions that the vein would soon be exhausted. While the 1870 report seems at first glance an uncomplicated act of applied research describing how the silver, gold, quartz, and other minerals got to be where they are, and how the companies go about extracting and refining the ore, closer examination shows that their fears of a crisis guide the authors' research. They treat the mines not only as a geological fact but as a distinct economic community, and while they omit the information that the industry was controlled chiefly by San Francisco financial interests, absentee landlords who sought the quickest returns on their investments, that Virginia City had burgeoned into an industrial city with a predominantly foreign-born work force and a militant union movement, the dubious future of the industry is much on their minds. Moreover, by the issues addressed and by those omitted, the report speaks from the point of view of an evolving government policy. It does not refer to the "mining industry," which in the broadest definition includes the labor force, but to the ownership and management of the largest corporations. Accidents and threats to life underground, for example, are not a category, nor are working conditions: labor appears as a "cost," with no mention of the unions organized in Virginia City as early as 1863.

The practical issues understandably concern profitability. The report turns on two questions: what can be done to increase the yield of bullion from ore, and how much longer can the corporations assume that the mines will continue to yield enough ore and profit to keep them going? Henry Adams observed that the commercial importance of the Comstock Lode alone endowed these questions with more than an abstract scientific interest: by 1870, over $100 million had been produced by the mines, and one speculator had requested of Congress funds to drill a deep tunnel to replace the shafts widely in use, in order to mine the vein at a deeper level. As a result of deeper mining and greater yield, as Adams summarized the argument, "the amount of our national debt thus [would] be indirectly decreased." We can see why King speaks of a study of the "engineering and economy" of the mines as a "grave" matter. Proponents of the tunnel assumed that richer veins lay at greater depth. One of King's purposes was to provide geological evidence pro or con. The report's specific findings—that the value of a lode is indeed likely to increase at a greater depth, though deep shafts are adequate for now to determine the issue—matter less than the focus provided for scientific research by marketplace economics, through a social policy advocating the use of public revenue to provide indirect subsidy of private enterprise.

The *Mining Industry* report to Congress delivered by the Department of War was specifically concerned with the oversight or regulation of the mining industry. It is not an overtly political document, yet a political meaning is unequivocal, for, by its focus on management and profitability, the report evokes the postwar subsidies of land and revenues to private capitalists, to railroad and mining interests, and indirect subsidies such as official and free information on potential resources and their accessibility. The mining report makes plain King's conception of the role of the survey in transferring at least the mineral resources of the public domain to private or corporate ownership. Thus, while it is not a proposal for government action or new legislation, the report on "engineering and economy" cannot be taken as dispassionate description.[41] The authors sprinkle their science with observations of direct interest to speculators, claim holders (many of whom desired only to sell out to the large companies), and managers of the mines, and speaks directly to their fears about the future of their investments.

"The Comstock Lode," Hague notes, "judged by present appearances, would hold out but doubtful promise for the future, if there were no hope of greatly reducing the present costs of mining and milling." He proposes, in the report's most blunt suggestion, a cut in wages, adding without further explanation that such a reduction "seems unavoidable, for the high wages at present are quite out of proportion to costs of living."[42] Apparently Hague did not seek to learn the views of the miners themselves, for $4 a day had been the rallying cry in several strikes since 1863.[43] His oversight is consistent, moreover, with the report's most glaring omission: an account of working conditions in the mines. We have to read between the lines—or consult O'Sullivan's underground photographs—for any inkling of the labors which brought the Comstock treasures to market. Writing about "thermal conditions," King points out that the temperature of waters below 700 feet rise to 108 degrees Fahrenheit;

39 See Rodman W. Paul, *Mining Frontiers of the Far West, 1848–1880* (New York: Rinehart and Winston, 1963), 56–86.
40 Adams, "King's Fortieth Parallel Survey," 206.

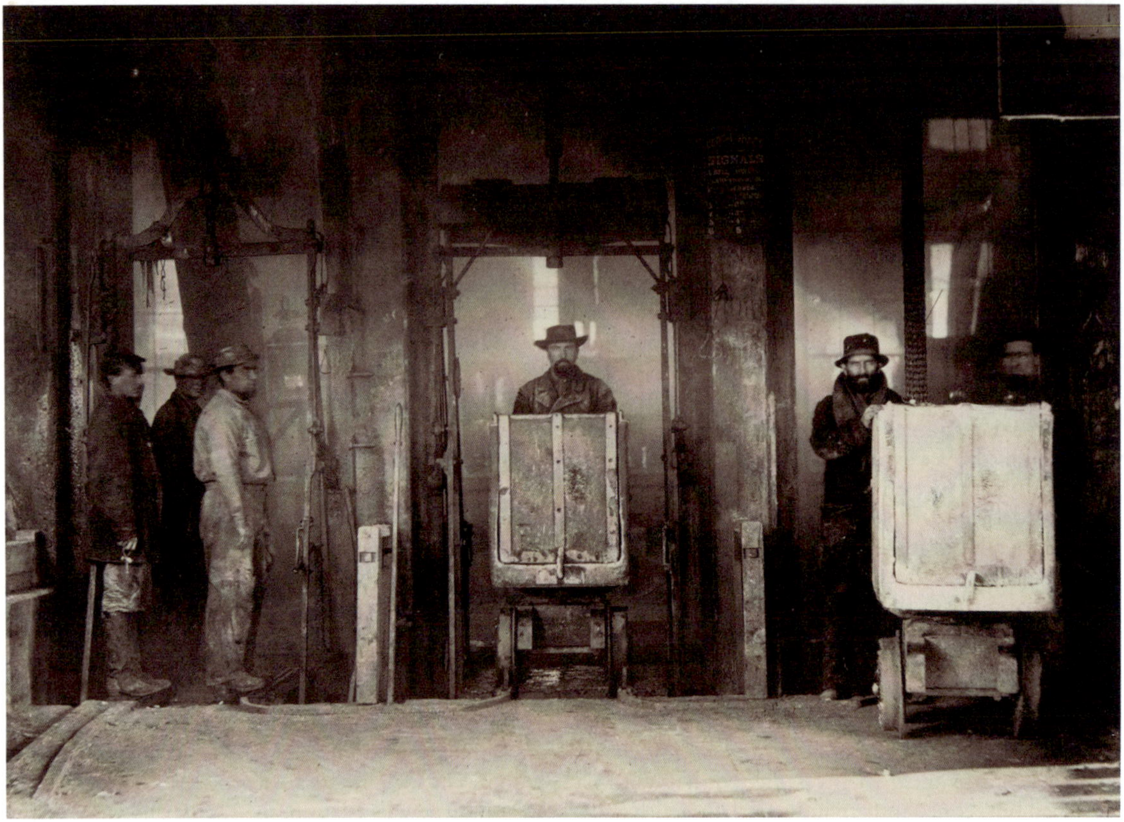

Figure 3. Timothy H. O'Sullivan, *Savage Mine, Curtis Shaft, Virginia City, Nevada*, 1868, albumen silver print.

that "the vapors from these hot waters fill the lower chambers of these mines, penetrating every crevice and fissure-line of the vein-material, and have converted the whole lower zone into a moist, steaming region"; that once, after a cut, "such volumes of heated water" poured in that "the miners were barely able to jump upon the cage and escape to the surface."[44] This is one of the very few mentions of miners in the entire report, other than brief mention of the "costs of labor." The numerous instances when trapped workers did not reach the cage in time, when the hoisting mechanism failed, when sudden cave-ins occurred or fires such as the major blaze that converted much of the town into an inferno in 1866: the dangers of deep mining were actually increased by the installation of untested mechanical devices during the feverish capitalization of the early 1860s. All these facts were beyond the scope of the surveyors' investigation of the "engineering and economy" of the mining district.[45]

How, then, are we to understand the choice of "Shaft Landing of Savage Mine" as the frontispiece of the official report? Allan Sekula's suggestion cannot be discounted, that in its "neatly symmetrical view . . . [of] a disciplined work crew about to descend into the depths," the picture is "full of industrial promise"—a symbol of the social order envisioned by the report.[46] This view does accord with the managerial point of view evident in the text, and indeed the lithographed

41 One motive was to encourage rationalization of the industry, of its system of ownership as well as its technical processes. James Hague says (100): "The subdivision of the workable portions of the lode among so many independent owners, has not only given rise to much expensive litigation, but has doubtless increased the cost of development, multiplying the expenses of administration, the outlays for machinery, and other requisite equipment of the mines, and in various ways involving expenditures that would be avoided under more comprehensive or consolidated management." In a similar vein, consistent with the reformist outlook developing among upper-class Eastern intellectuals, King remarked (457–58) that development of the "practically inexhaustible supply of coal" in the Green River Basin was hindered by a land-ownership policy confused by Mormon land claims of ambiguous legality on one hand and, on the other, by the habit of the Pacific Railroad Company, an "already overloaded monopoly," to claim whatever it desired of the public domain. "Until a survey is made defining clearly the possessions of the Pacific Railroad Company, or else an act is passed by Congress declaring the whole belt open to preemptions, no thorough development can be applied to the coal system."

42 King, 160.

43 Richard E. Lingenfelter, *The Hard-Rock Miners: A History of the Mining Labor Movement in the American West, 1863–1893* (Berkeley: University of California Press, 1974), 31–65.

44 King, *Mining Industry*, 87.

version does make the figures seem more limp, more acquiescent, less individual, than the print, in which it is evident that the figures are standing in a pose, aware of the camera, even smiling slightly as if mildly amused by the situation. The transposition of print to lithograph to frontispiece reflects the process whereby the photograph comes to represent the "mining industry." (Fig. 3) They are about to descend into, or have just returned from, a region everyone acknowledged was a living hell. "View their work," writes a visitor to Comstock a decade later:

> Descending from the surface in the shaft-cages, they enter narrow galleries where the air is scarce respirable. By the dim light of their lanterns a dingy rock surface, braced by rotting props, is visible. The stenches of decaying vegetable matter, hot foul water, and human excretions intensify the effect of the heat.[47]

The report on mining gives only an inkling, and the array of charts and engineering drawings indicates nothing at all, of human experience deep in the mines. Yet the frontispiece invites us to imagine where these men are going, and where they have been. The report answers such a question in its own terms—at once "scientific" and ideological. However, O'Sullivan's photographs assembled in the 1868 volume, the views of Virginia City on its hillside, of shafts, mills, smokestacks, and men at work deep within the mines, offer another. Thus, if the photographs in the 1868–69 album can be taken as supplements to the report, a "conceptual bridge" to its abstract drawings of shafts, timberings, hoists, milling plants, and geological maps and cross sections, then we have to say that the photographs exceed the bounds of the report, of its "engineering and economy" categories and its explicit ideology. They present "mining industry" as a social fact, a matter of buildings in a certain setting, and men at work.

Considering how freely King used lithographed photographs in his strictly geological reports, we must wonder: does the use of only one photograph in *Mining Industry* imply suppression, particularly of the underground images, which include a collapsed section of timbering? Did the photographs provide the wrong information that the report itself failed to acknowledge? Are the photographs in the volume, then, a kind of countertext to the report, too literal, too concrete to be accommodated by the text, as similarly detailed images of waterfalls and rock formations and desert lakes and sand dunes were obviously not deemed to be? Unanswerable, these questions suggest at least that the notion of the photograph as "conceptual bridge" entails not simply a visual literalness but a social act of seeing and defining.

In the 1868 volume the mining photographs appear as a self-contained group of seventeen images between the images of Shoshone and the desert: probably the first arrangement of industrial pictures before the work of Lewis Hine early in the twentieth century in an order that describes (albeit sketchily) an industrial community.[48] What is their effect here? We see in the first seven images of the sequence a steady, systematic narrowing of focus, from a distant, inclusive view of Virginia City to sharply detailed close-up images underground. Following the natural power of Shoshone, the opening shot shows a scene of social power: a city with roads and streets, houses with fences, church steeples competing with smokestacks, a view corresponding to a visitor's description of what appears to be "a great village perched upon the side of a high mountain" but actually is "a cosmopolitan city, with the diversified interests and varied social features of a large and important centre."[49] The sequence then takes us closer to the industrial city, to the shaft mouth, into the mine. There, we catch ourselves mesmerized observing laborers, so close to the shovel, pick, hammer, wheelbarrow, and precious candle (they were distributed stingily, and each miner was responsible for rationing his own limited source of light) that we can hardly avoid identifying with the miners in their cramped positions—filling in the other sensory experiences as best we can imagine (or endure) them. The last of the underground images, "Crash of timbers in cave-in, Gould & Curry Mine" (No. 17), stands as grim parallel to the imagined extinction of self-provoked by Shoshone; here, the image of a leg severed from its body seems (at least this is its effect) a camera-made equivalent to the absent vision of bodies

45 See Lingenfelter, 3–30; Mark Wyman, *Hard Rock Epic: Western Miners and the Industrial Revolution, 1860–1910* (Berkeley: University of California Press, 1979), especially chap. 4, "Betrayed by the New Technology," 84–117. Also Ronald C. Brown, *Hard-Rock Miners: The Intermountain West, 1860–1920* (College Station: Texas A&M University Press, 1979), especially Appendix B, "Accidents and Injuries Typical in Hard-Rock Mining," 173–76.

46 Allan Sekula, "Photography Between Labor and Capital," in Benjamin H. D. Buchloh and Robert Wilkie, eds., *Mining Photographs and Other Pictures, 1948–1968* (Halifax: Press of the Nova Scotia College of Art and Design, 1983), 230–31.

47 Quoted in Lingenfelter, 13.

48 O'Sullivan's mining pictures are not, however, the first made in the American West. Though only a handful remain, Carleton Watkins made photographs in the California gold fields and mining towns in the early 1860s; and even earlier, the San Francisco daguerreotypist Robert H. Vance assembled three hundred images, including some of gold mining, which were exhibited in New York in 1851. A contemporary description of Vance's pictures, long lost, mentions working miners along with topographical and city views of the gold-mining region. "Mr. Vance's California Views," *Photographic Art-Journal* 2 (Oct. 1851), 252–53. See also Peter E. Palmquist, *Carleton E. Watkins, Photographer of the American West* (Albuquerque: University of New Mexico Press, 1983), 8–11, Plates 19–20, and especially Martha A. Sandweiss's "Foreword," xii-xiii. I am indebted to Ms. Sandweiss for calling these details to my attention.

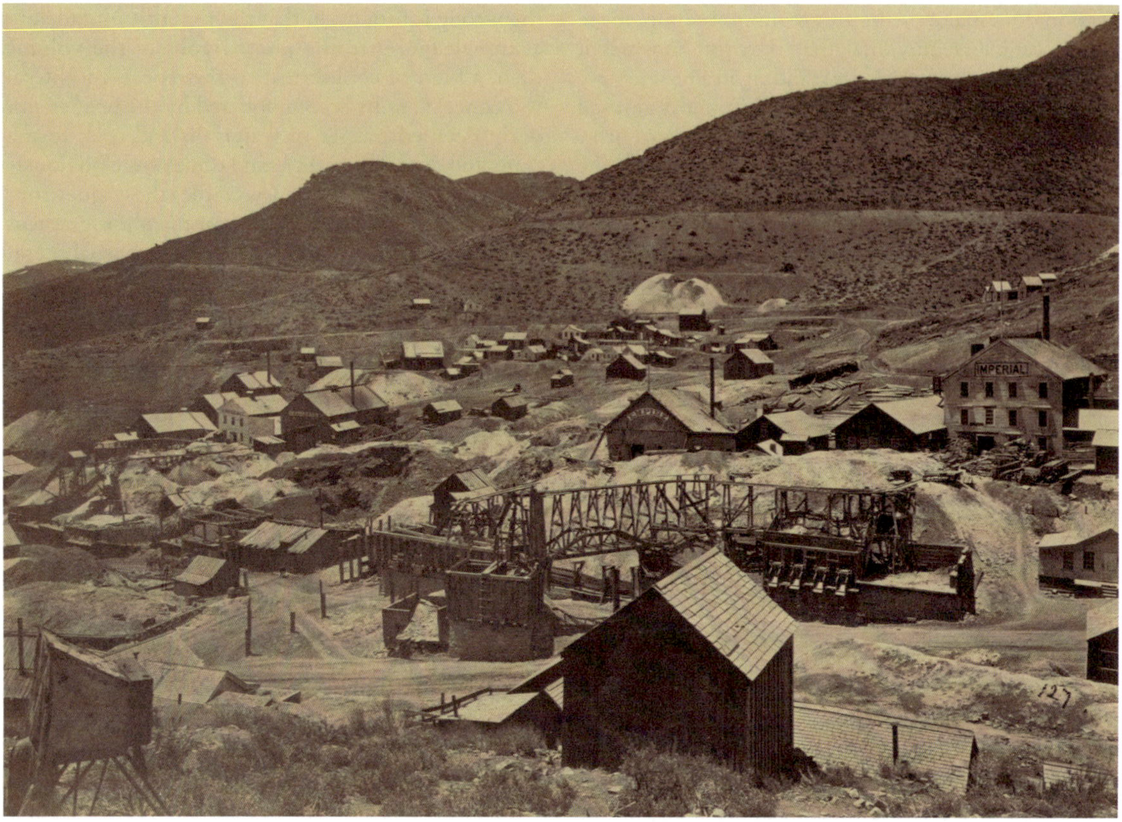

Figure 4. Timothy H. O'Sullivan, *Gold Hill Mining Camp, Nevada*, (Plate 21), 1867, albumen silver print.

actually dismembered by such accidents. It is not surprising that King found no space for such an image in the report, for it is difficult to view these underground pictures except by taking for the moment the point of view of the laboring miner.

Emerging from the pit, the photographer takes in buildings housing the ore-reduction process, and then moves out to other communities: Gold Hill, Washoe, and, farther away, Oreana and Austin. Indeed, O'Sullivan calls attention to his camera by its swiftly changing perspectives, and in "Gold Hill Mining Camp" (No. 21), (Fig. 4) the camera itself appears, at least its surrogate, the portable darkroom situated in profile at the lower left, which resembles a camera with its bellows aimed at the view below. Whatever O'Sullivan had in mind, the effect is strong and assertive: the medium has transformed random industrial elements into a picture which brings them together in a meaningful form. The picture focuses on the sharp, straight lines of the shed in the foreground, against the airy tracery of the trusswork just behind it, static mechanical shapes set against the jagged patterns made by distant hills. Within this play of industrial against natural forms, O'Sullivan has aligned a broken arc of buildings across the middle belt of the picture, in which our eye picks out a line of words, an array of painted signs declaring Confidence, Challenge, Empire, Imperial. The names declare both private ownership (each a legally sanctioned corporation) and its self-justifying ideology, competition and expansion. Like the names of scientist-heroes King and others bestowed upon "unnamed" peaks and lakes, these more nakedly aggressive names superimpose a sophisticated social system upon an alien terrain: outward signs of the act of appropriation represented by the "mining industry," if not by the "survey" itself.

The photograph depicts a landscape in which "nature" has already been worked over, converted to "culture"—culture not as an abstract category but as the product of a specific history—and depicts itself as something made by human labor, as much a technological act as the reduction of ore to silver bullion. The photograph shows that the oppositions within which the survey performed its tasks—nature and culture, alien and familiar, nameless and named—are themselves the product of an already established and expanding cultural power, an imperial energy of which both the mining industry and the survey which serves it are leading forces. A countertext to the 1870 report from which they are (deliberately?) excluded, O'Sul-

49 Paul, *Mining Frontiers*, 72.

livan's mining photographs play a complex role in the album. They represent history and society directly within the sequence, between the "natural" power of Shoshone and what we shall see as the peculiar power of the desert to deceive and baffle perception. The mining pictures force us to recognize that even Shoshone, even Carson Desert, cannot be understood simply as "nature" existing prior to and apart from the social activity of survey, but as the product of a distinct mode of seeing, knowing, and possessing. They disclose not only the "landscape" of the 40th Parallel as already within the domain of history and force, but the work of survey as precisely to confirm that fact, to make it real by making it graphic: by putting a view to the name.

V

[...] In *Systematic Geology* (1878) Clarence King stated that by deciphering rocks he hoped to learn about their origins and chart their history, to "construct a continuous piece of geological history." His scheme, he explains, "is chronological," starting in Archaean time at the bottom of "the geological column," "and proceeding without break through the Quaternary."[50] The column, a conventional image among geologists, defines time as linear, and King tells the story of the rocks of the Cordilleras (Rocky Mountain) region as just such a continuous narrative occurring in the vertical dimension. The story he tells in the language of science resembles a creation myth: how things came to be as they appear to the eye and its instruments. The mythic element is sometimes explicit in King's use of commonplace metaphors: canyons are "gateways," ridges "mural escarpments," sand and marl formations are "innumerable turrets, isolated towers, and citadel-like masses, which, when seen at a little distance, present the aspect of a great walled city, with outlying bastions and buttresses."[51] Masonry, architecture, and sculpture provide the most frequent metaphors, endowing the natural terrain with an aesthetic structure.

Metaphors are names, a way of bringing the unfamiliar into familiarity. A discourse in words rather than number, King's geology necessarily had recourse to metaphor. His "purest" science, in *Systematic Geology*, coexists with a poetic method of naming by figure of speech. King's love of Ruskin is well known: "Ruskin alone, among prose writers on the Alps, re-echoes the dim past, in ever-recurring myth-making, over cloud and peak and glacier."[52] It takes nothing away from King's science to see it fused with aesthetic inclinations, a fusion encouraged by Ruskin's view of the mutuality of beauty and truthfulness (topographical exactitude) in landscape painting. Nor is it surprising that a geologist be drawn to thoughts of "the dim past" and of myth making. It is in this light that his preference for the theory of "catastrophism" should be seen, for the language in which he espoused the theory, one of two great principles of explanation then current in the earth sciences (he uses it to account for the history of the Cordilleras), indicates a powerful attraction to metaphor and myth.

Catastrophists argued that geological change did not take place at a uniform rate, as Lyell had theorized and the British Uniformitarians believed, but alternately between steady change and violent upheaval. The catastrophic view has been wrongfully thought of as no more than an excuse for reinstating divinely ordained floods and earthquakes within the evolutionary process. As Stephen Jay Gould points out, while the theory did provide an aura of science for some "theological apologists," catastrophism had its legitimate side and respectable scientific defenders.[53] King has been described as one of the apologists, and indeed, in his commencement lecture at the Yale Sheffield School in June 1877, "Catastrophism and Evolution," he makes a reference to "He who brought to bear that mysterious energy we call life." Otherwise, his citations are wholly within the secular field, to Darwin, Huxley, and the American paleontologist Marsh. But he concedes that the argument for catastrophism draws on sources other than scientific induction. "That the rate of physical change progressing today . . . is inadequate to produce the grander features of American geological history" is a deduction King makes from atavistic fears, from the "ancient belief" of "primeval man" in "terrestrial catastrophe"—surely the result of witnessing "certain terrible and destructive exhibi-

50 King, *Systematic Geology*, 2-3.

51 King, *Systematic Geology*, 6–9.

52 Quoted in Wilkins, *King*, 44. See 44–45 for King's love of Ruskin and his participation, before leaving for California in April 1863, in the Society for the Advancement of Truth in Art, a group of aesthetic Ruskinites led by art critics Clarence Cook and Russell Sturgis. For more about the influence of Ruskin in these years, particularly among scientists, see Roger Stein, *John Ruskin and Aesthetic Thought in America, 1840–1900* (Cambridge, MA, 1967). The place of aestheticism in the social thought and attitudes, especially during the Civil War, of Eastern upper-class intellectuals is touched upon in a number of studies—Frederickson's *Inner Civil War*, for example—and deserves a full-scale study.

53 Stephen Jay Gould, *Ever Since Darwin: Reflections in Natural History* (New York: Norton, 1977), 147–52; and *Time's Arrow, Time's Cycle: Myth and Metaphor on the Discovery of Geological Time* (Cambridge, MA: Harvard University Press, 1987), especially 115–32. See also recent critiques of uniformitarianism in Claude C. Albritton, Jr., et al., eds., *Uniformity and Simplicity: A Symposium of the Principle of the Uniformity of Nature* (New York, 1967).

tions of sudden, unusual telluric energy" (earthquakes and volcanic eruptions). "Catastrophism is therefore the survival of a terrible impression burned in upon the very substance of human memory" of "the destructive in nature." A poetic doctrine, in short, "most powerful in its effect on the imagination."[54]

The intent of King's argument is not to reject Darwin's theory of natural selection but to modify it. In periods of uniform environmental change, "the war of competitive extermination become[s] the dominant engine of change and development." But in the circumstances of catastrophe, "struggle for existence" waged among species and individuals loses its power to a struggle with the physical environment. Catastrophe changes the game. "When catastrophic change burst in upon the ages of uniformity, and sounded in the ear of every living thing the words 'change or die,' plasticity becomes the sole principle of salvation." King proposes "survival of the plastic" as the catastrophic equivalent to "survival of the fittest." The Darwinian notion of a "struggle for existence" is a "gospel of chance" which holds that "we are what we are because this brain and this body form the most effective fighting-machine the dice-box of the ages has thrown." Survival of the plastic, the same struggle redirected to the environment, converts chance to destiny:

> He who brought to bear that mysterious energy we call life upon primeval matter bestowed at the same time a power of development by change, arranging that the interaction of energy and matter which make up environment should, from time to time, burst in upon the current of life and sweep it onward and upward to ever higher and better manifestations. Moments of great catastrophes, thus translated into the language of life, become moments of creation when out of plastic organisms something newer and nobler is called into being.[55]

Catastrophism clarifies a linear process: from the fears of primeval man to the inevitable transcendence of superior organisms.

"Men are born either catastrophists or uniformitarians. You may divide the race into imaginative people who believe in all sorts of impending crises—physical, social, political—and others who anchor their very souls *in status quo*." But more than a quirk of temperament is involved in how King presents the theory, for his figures of speech intimate that society rather than nature is the real threat to "serenity." King delivered the lecture just weeks before a sudden upheaval—it was likened in the press to an erupting volcano, the worst bloodshed since the Civil War: what seemed a spontaneous and an unrelated series of strikes along the Eastern and Midwestern railroad systems. Violence erupted, troops were called in, pitched battles fought, and in St. Louis an entire city fell briefly under control of a socialist commune. The specter of Communism loomed in the immigrant-dominated cities—a fear of anarchy and chaos King's friend John Hay would later re-create in his novel *The Breadwinners* (1884). Lecturing just before the upheaval but in the tense atmosphere of an unsettled moment, King speaks of "the battle-field of life," the "heat of the strife," of "upheaval," "revolution," and the "terrible catastrophic engine." He describes catastrophism in language drawn from current events—for example, a railroad that "dashes against a bridge and is utterly wrecked." The imagery of Spencer's "social Darwinism" intrudes into his geological discourse—imagery of relentless struggle between men defined as strong or weak (degrees of plasticity rather than of wealth or power) and a violent environment.

Did King ten years earlier imbue Timothy O'Sullivan with his Ruskinian doctrine of nature as a spiritual presence, interlaced with the theory of catastrophism?[56] Another beguiling thought, and not implausible. But the photographs have a more complex relation to King's ideas and his literary imagination. Names and metaphors must also be counted among the instruments of measuring, mapping, and picturing at the command of the surveyors. O'Sullivan's photographs cannot be taken simply as illustrations either of facts or of ideas. The representational activities of the survey are as much their subject as nature itself—indeed, as deliberate acts of framing a view, even views devoid of human signs, the photographs themselves represent human inscription upon the blankness of nature, an equivalent to a place name. The photographs seem to say that there are no views without names—no nature except what can be seen through the lenses of culture. The paradox represented in "Sand Dunes, Carson Desert" suggests ambiguities in the enterprise of natural science that had not yet risen to the surface of scientific discourse. The labor of survey, its daily encounter with recalcitrance, can be taken as O'Sullivan's chief subject in this album: not nature as something given but as something simultaneously made and known in the act of perception, something as contingent as the name of a view.

It is the 1868 sequence which releases, or creates, these meanings, and King himself may have been the author of that provocative album. In any case, the pictures partake of the contradictions in King's own situation, his uneasy joining of aggressive commercial-imperial motives with what his outlook defined as disinterested science and autonomous art. Arranged as a journey from natural power at Shoshone to urban-technical power in the silver mines to the desert investigations

54 King, "Catastrophism and Evolution," 450–51.
55 King, "Catastrophism and Evolution," 468–70.

of the power of survey itself—the representational power of its measuring, mapping, and picturing instruments—the sequence reads very much like a text by King. Yet, in a way, by its desert reflections upon its own means of representation, its own resources as a technical medium of cognition, it surpasses King's own self-reflections. Even apart from the particular order of this sequence, O'Sullivan's survey photographs for Clarence King and, later, George Wheeler, introduce a new element in American photographs: a pictorial self-consciousness about the relation of aesthetic and cognitive aspects of the image. Whether or not King organized O'Sullivan's 1868 pictures, O'Sullivan was responsible at least for the pictures themselves and their extraordinary self-awareness as *survey* photographs.

The self-reflexive aspect of particular pictures is echoed in the sequential placement of the mining images of capitalist-industrial enterprise at the center of the album. Even if the intention may have been to wheedle more funds out of a development-minded Congress, the strategic location of these pictures makes a more acute statement than does King's prose about the cultural work of the survey, its role in the conversion of the "nature" Peale rearranged for the sake of classified knowledge, into a "resource" for commercial profit. O'Sullivan placed his camera at the scene of American contradiction, the place where Peale's Enlightenment quest for disinterested knowledge through science and art turns into its opposite: a quest for instrumental knowledge for the sake of private gain and imperial power, at the expense of the illustrious community about which Peale and Brady, in their separate ways, dreamed. While O'Sullivan's fame as an artist of landscape has flourished, the album has been buried in an archive for more than a hundred years, an ironic fate for a key document in the emergence of a critical art of American photographs.

56 The congruence of vision in King and O'Sullivan is ably argued in Richard Wilson, *American Vision and Landscape: The Western Images of Clarence King and Timothy O'Sullivan* (University of New Mexico dissertation, 1979).

United States Geological Exploration of the Fortieth Parallel, Volume III: Mining Industry

James D. Hague and Clarence King

1870

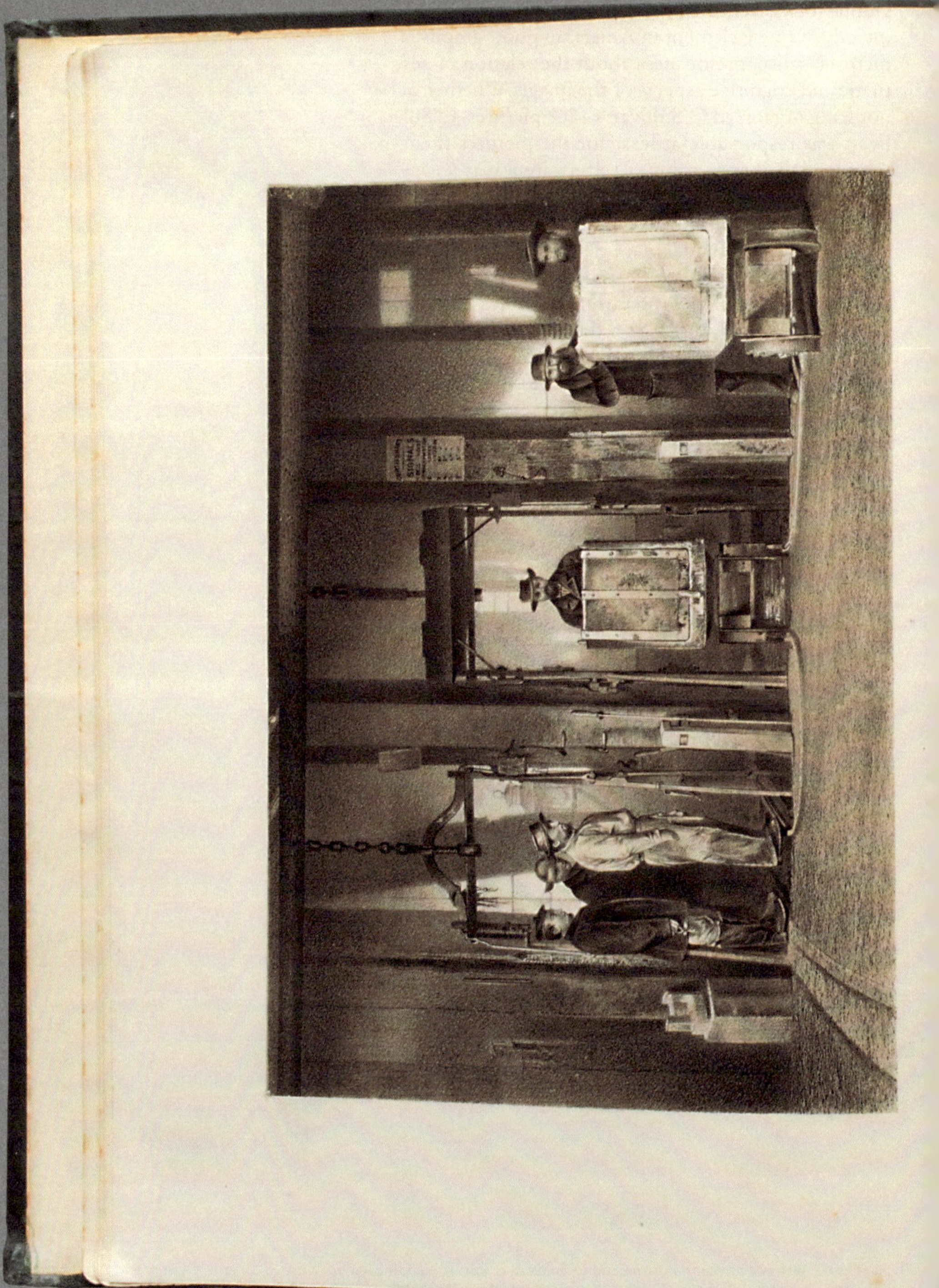

UNITED STATES GEOLOGICAL EXPLORATION OF THE FORTIETH PARALLEL.
CLARENCE KING, GEOLOGIST-IN-CHARGE.

MINING INDUSTRY

BY

JAMES D. HAGUE

WITH GEOLOGICAL CONTRIBUTIONS

BY

CLARENCE KING.

SUBMITTED TO THE CHIEF OF ENGINEERS AND PUBLISHED BY ORDER OF THE SECRETARY OF WAR UNDER AUTHORITY OF CONGRESS.

ILLUSTRATED BY XXXVII PLATES AND ACCOMPANYING ATLAS.

WASHINGTON.
GOVERNMENT PRINTING OFFICE.
1870.

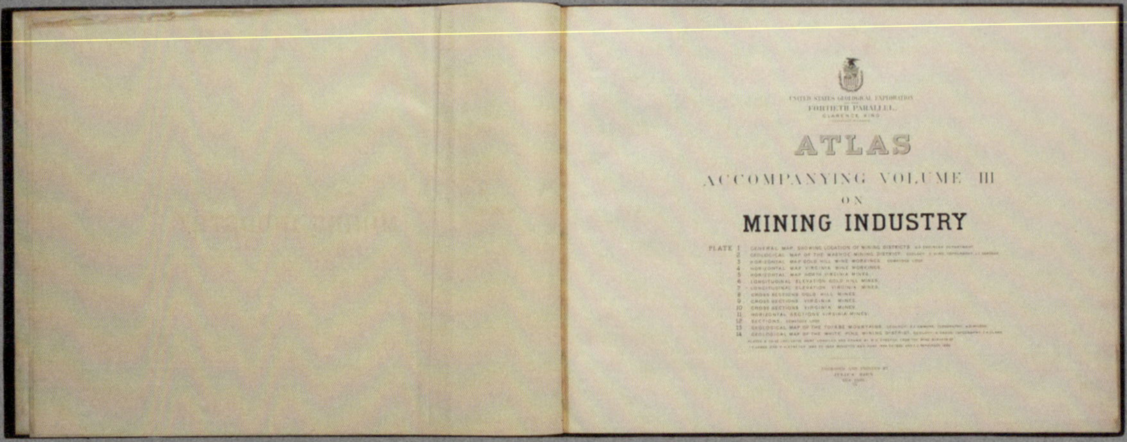
UNITED STATES GEOLOGICAL EXPLORATION
FORTIETH PARALLEL.
CLARENCE KING
ATLAS
ACCOMPANYING VOLUME III
ON
MINING INDUSTRY
PLATE

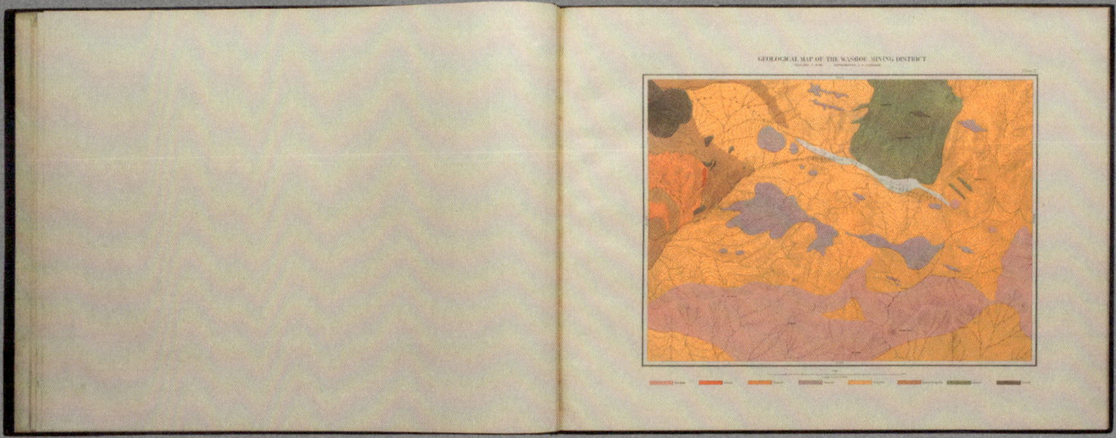
GEOLOGICAL MAP OF THE WASHOE MINING DISTRICT

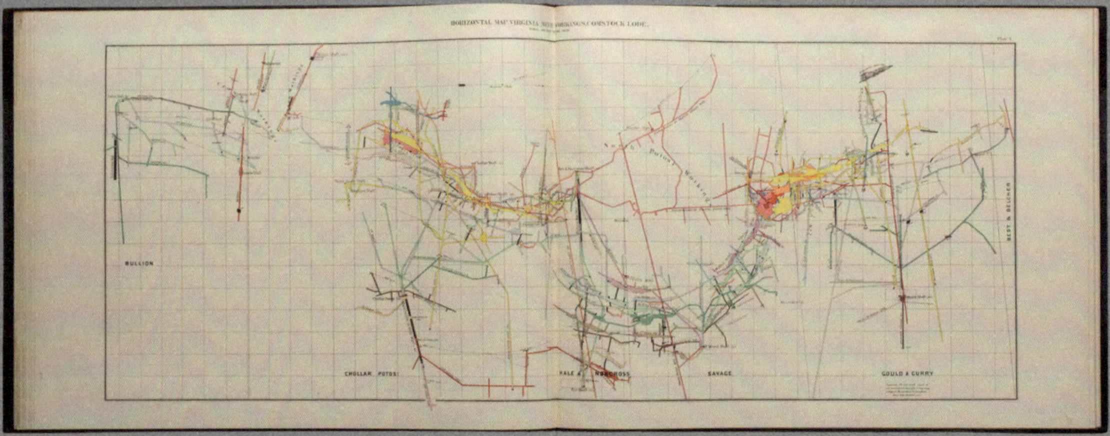
HORIZONTAL MAP VIRGINIA MINE WORKINGS COMSTOCK LODE.
BULLION
CHOLLAR POTOSI
HALE & NORCROSS
SAVAGE
GOULD & CURRY
BEST & BELCHER

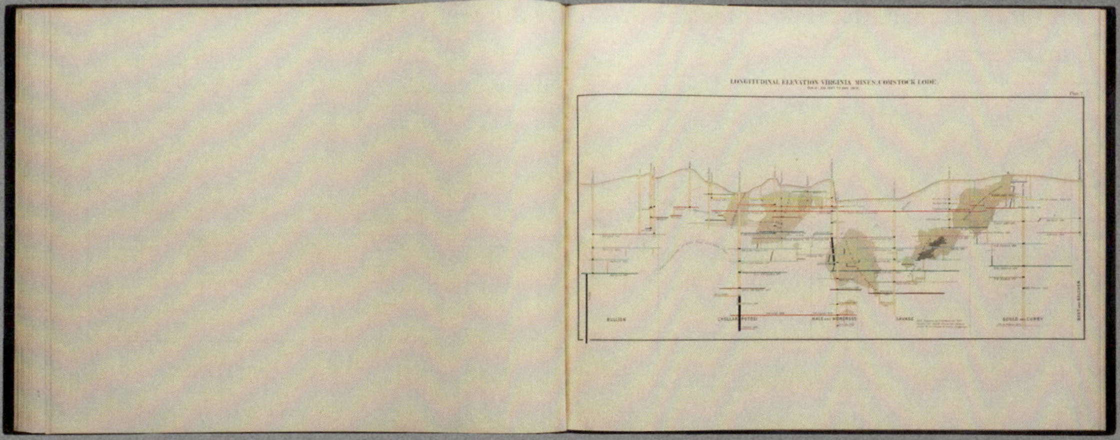
LONGITUDINAL ELEVATION VIRGINIA MINES, COMSTOCK LODE.

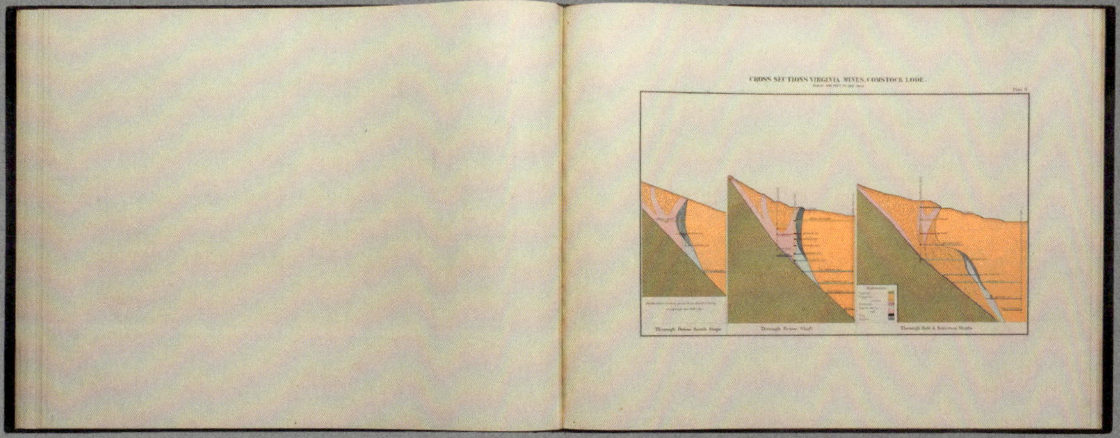
CROSS SECTIONS VIRGINIA MINES, COMSTOCK LODE.

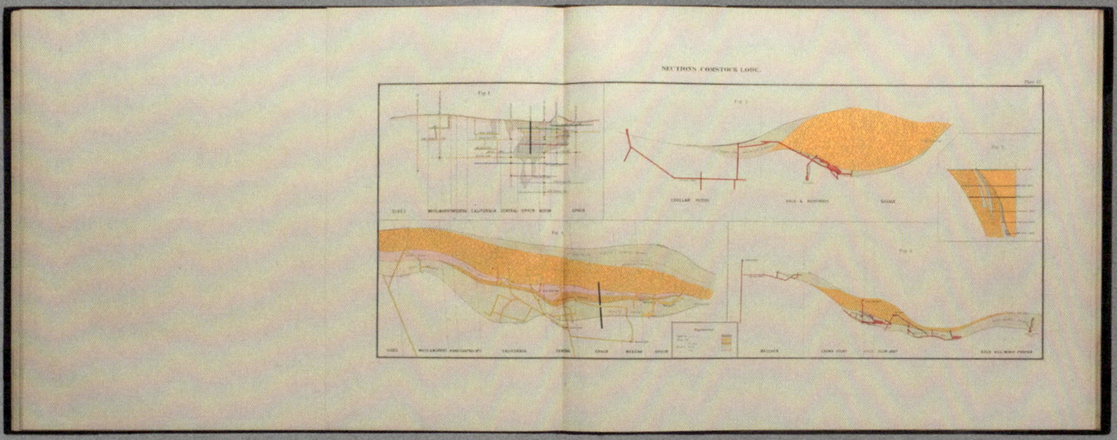
SECTIONS COMSTOCK LODE.

Report on the United States and Mexican Boundary Survey, Vol. I

William H. Emory

1857

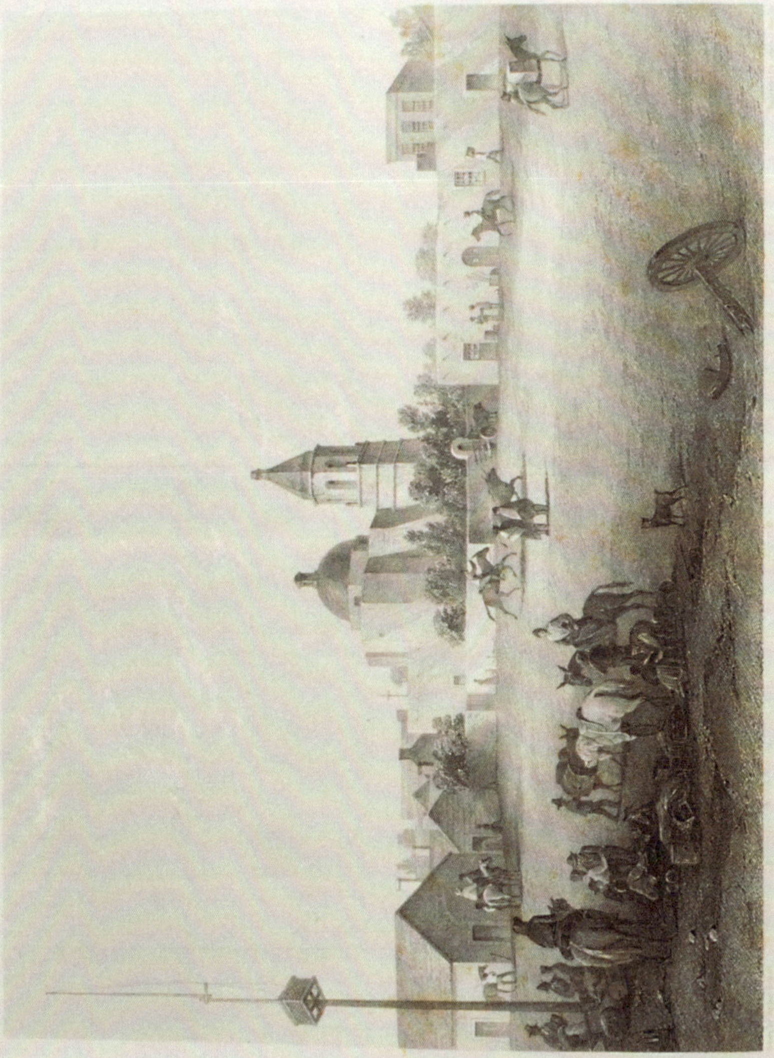

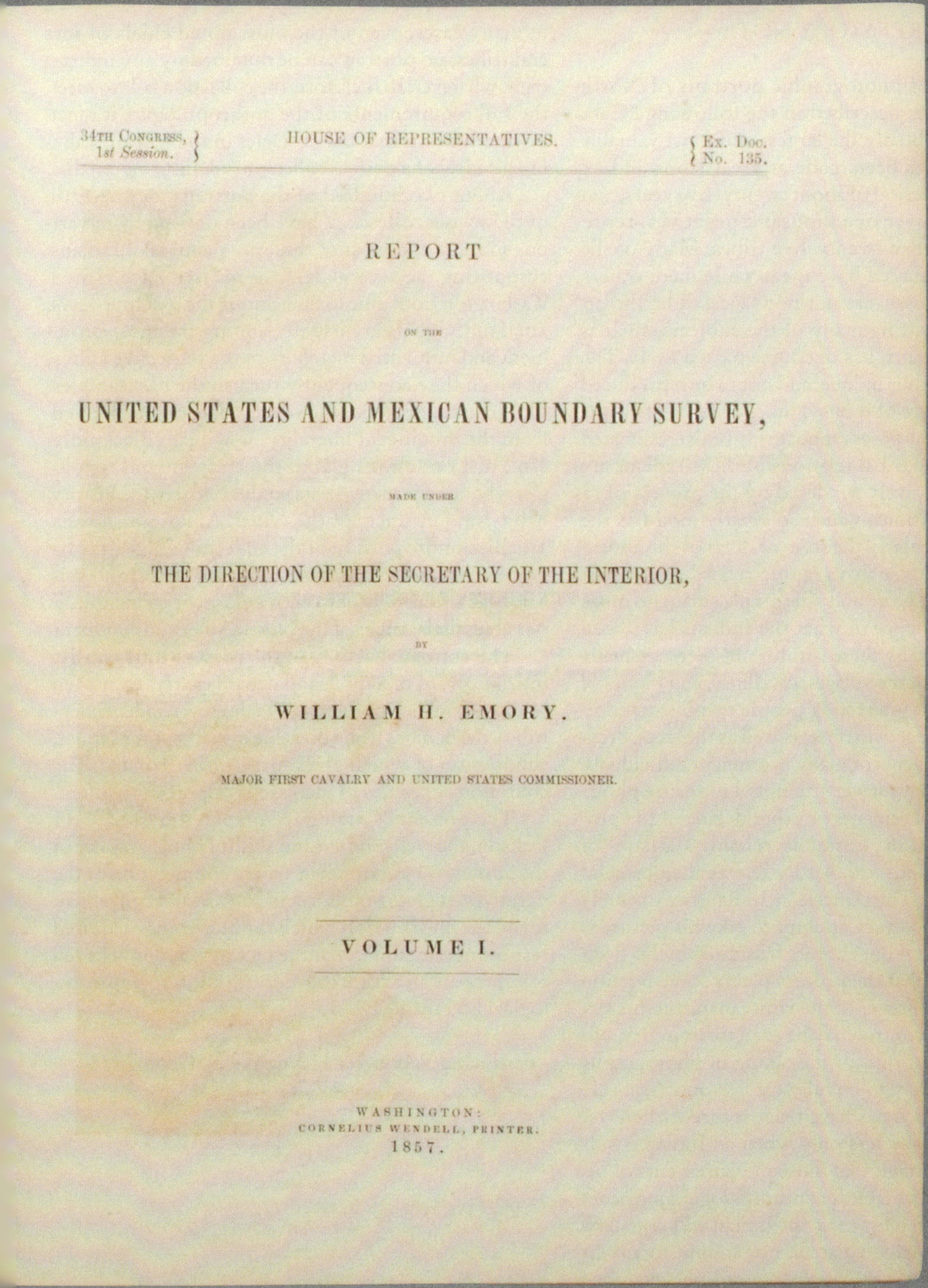

34TH CONGRESS, 1st Session. | HOUSE OF REPRESENTATIVES. | Ex. Doc. No. 135.

REPORT

ON THE

UNITED STATES AND MEXICAN BOUNDARY SURVEY,

MADE UNDER

THE DIRECTION OF THE SECRETARY OF THE INTERIOR,

BY

WILLIAM H. EMORY.

MAJOR FIRST CAVALRY AND UNITED STATES COMMISSIONER.

VOLUME I.

WASHINGTON:
CORNELIUS WENDELL, PRINTER.
1857.

Prefatory Note and Preface to *United States Geological Survey of the Territories, Descriptive Catalogue of Photographs of North American Indians*

Ferdinand Vandeveer Hayden and William Henry Jackson

1877

PREFATORY NOTE

The collection of photographic portraits of North American Indians described in the following "Catalogue" is undoubtedly the largest and most valuable one extant. It has been made at great labor and expense, during a period of about twenty-five years, and now embraces over one thousand negatives, representing no less than twenty-five tribes. Many of the individuals portrayed have meanwhile died; others, from various causes, are not now accessible; the opportunity of securing many of the subjects, such as scenes and incidents, has of course passed away. The collection being thus unique, and not to be reproduced at any expenditure of money, time, or labor, its value for ethnological purposes cannot easily be overestimated.

Now that the tribal relations of these Indians are fast being successively sundered by the process of removal to reservations, which so greatly modifies the habits and particularly the style of dress of the aborigines, the value of such a graphic record of the past increases year by year; and there will remain no more trustworthy evidence of what the Indians have been than that afforded by these faithful sun-pictures, many of which represent the villages, dwellings, and modes of life of these most interesting people and historical incidents of the respective tribes, as well as the faces, dresses, and accoutrements of many prominent individuals.

Those who have never attempted to secure photographs and measurements or other details of the physique of Indians, in short, any reliable statistics of individuals or bands, can hardly realize the obstacles to be overcome. The American Indian is extremely superstitious, and every attempt to take his picture is rendered difficult if not entirely frustrated by his deeply-rooted belief that the process places some portion of himself in the power of the white man, and his suspicion that such control may be used to his injury. No prescribed regulations for the taking of photographs, therefore, are likely to be fully carried out. As a rule, front and profile views have been secured whenever practicable. Usually it is only when an Indian is subjected to confinement that those measurements of his person which are suitable for anthropological purposes can be secured. In most cases the Indian will not allow his person to be handled at all, nor submit to any inconvenience whatever. Much tact and perseverance are required to overcome his superstitious notions, and in many cases, even of the most noted chiefs of several tribes, no portrait can be obtained by any inducement whatever. If, therefore, the collection fails to meet the full requirements of the anthropologist, it must be remembered that the obstacles in the way of realizing his ideal of a perfect collection are insurmountable.

About two hundred of the portraits, or one-fifth of the whole collection, have been derived from various sources, and most of these are pictures of Indians composing the several delegations that have visited Washington from time to time during the past four years. Such individuals are usually among the most prominent and influential members of the respective tribes, of which they consequently furnish the best samples. The greater portion of the whole collection is derived from the munificent liberality of William Blackmore, esq., of London, England, the eminent anthropologist who has for many years studied closely the history, habits, and manners of the North American Indians. The Blackmore portion of the collections consists of a number of smaller lots from various sources; and it is Mr. Blackmore's intention to enlarge it to include, if possible, all the tribes of the North American continent.

The entire collection, at the present time consisting of upward of a thousand negatives, represents ten leading "families" of Indians, besides seven independent tribes, the families being divisible into fifty-four "tribes," subdivision of which gives forty-three "bands." The collection continues to increase as opportunity offers.

The present "Catalogue" prepared by Mr. W.H. Jackson, the well-known and skillful photographer of the Survey, is far more than a mere enumeration of the negatives. It gives in full, yet in concise and convenient form, the information which the Survey has acquired respecting the subjects of the pictures, and is believed to represent an acceptable contribution to anthropological literature.

—Ferdinand Vandeveer Hayden, U.S. Geologist

PREFACE

The following Descriptive Catalogue is intended to systematize the collection of Photographic Portraits of Indians now in the possession of the United States Geological Survey of the Territories, and to place on record all the information we have been able to obtain of the various individuals and scenes represented. It is of course far from complete; but it is a beginning, and every new fact that comes to light will be added to what has already been secured. This information has been gathered from many resources, principally from Indian delegates visiting Washington, and by correspondence with agents and others living in the Indian country.

Particular attention has been paid to proving the authenticity of the portraits of the various individuals represented, and it is believed that few, if any, mistakes occur in that respect.

The historical notices are mainly compilations from standard works on the subject. All of the following portraits and views are photographed direct from nature and are in nearly every case from the original plates, the exceptions being good copies from original daguerreotypes or photographs that are not now accessible. The portraits made under the supervision of the Survey are generally accompanied by measurements that are as nearly accurate as it has been possible to make them. The pictures vary in size from the ordinary small card to groups on plates 16 by 20 inches square. The majority, however, are on plates 6 ½ by 8 ½ inches square; these are usually trimmed to 4 by 5 ½ inches and mounted on cabinet cards. All the photographs are numbered upon their faces, and as these numbers do not occur in regular order in the text a Numerical index is appended, by means of which the name of any picture, and the page on which the subject is treated, may be readily found.

—W. H. Jackson

Colorchromes from the Detroit Photographic Company

William Henry Jackson

1892–1903

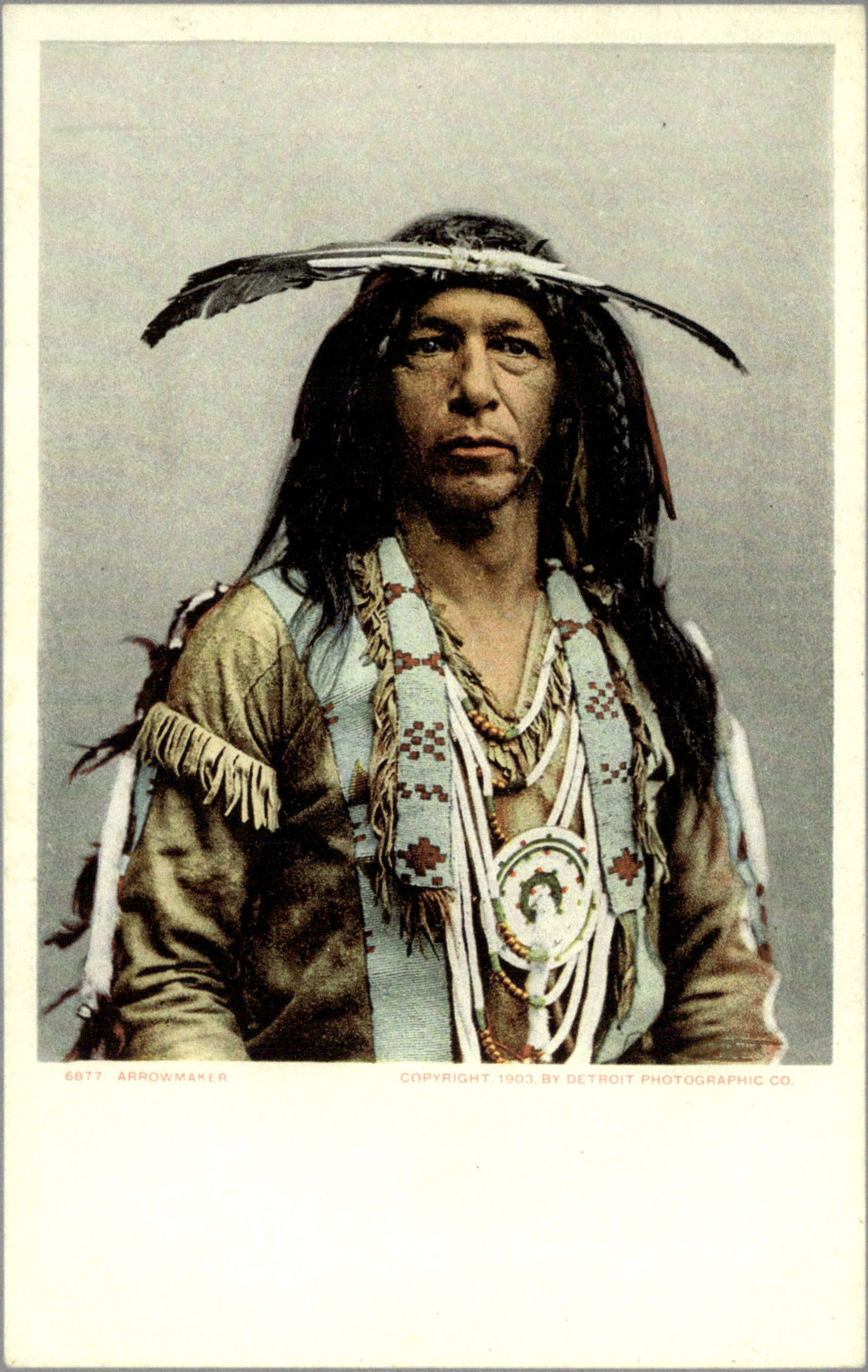

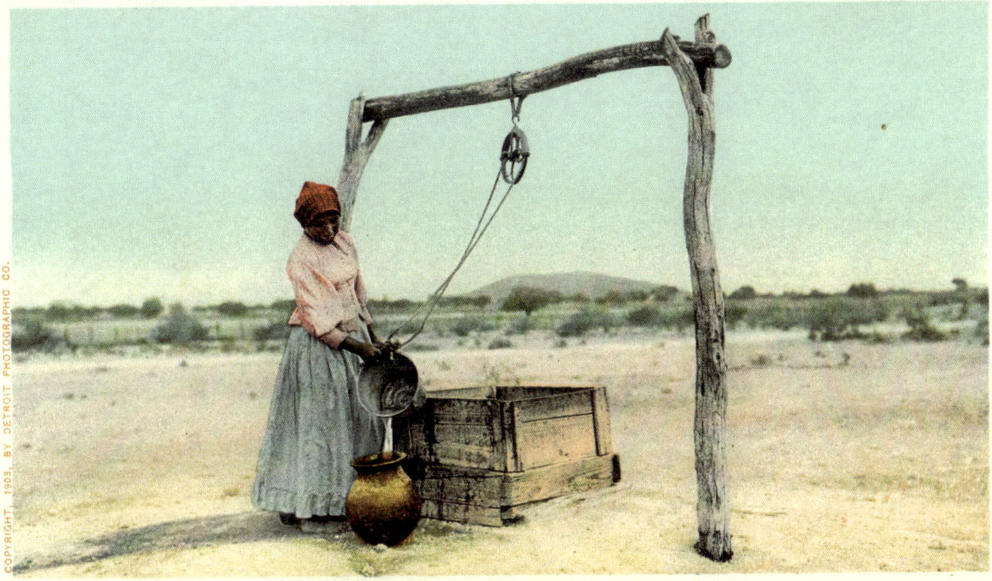

6506. PAPAGO INDIAN FILLING THE OLLA.

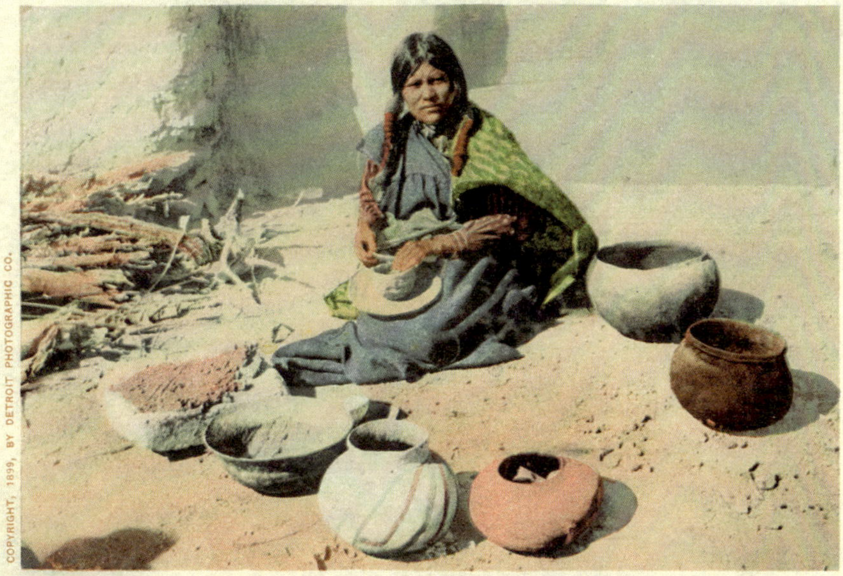

5511. MOKI INDIAN WOMAN MAKING POTTERY.

COPYRIGHT, 1898, BY DETROIT PHOTOGRAPHIC CO.

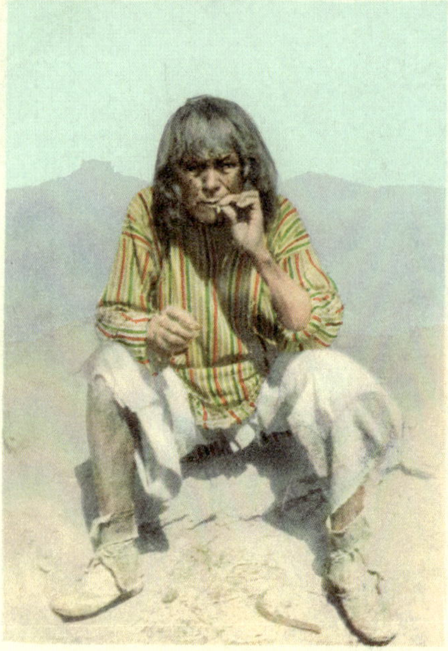

5244. MOKI INDIAN CIGARETTE SMOKER.

COPYRIGHT, 1903, BY DETROIT PHOTOGRAPHIC CO.

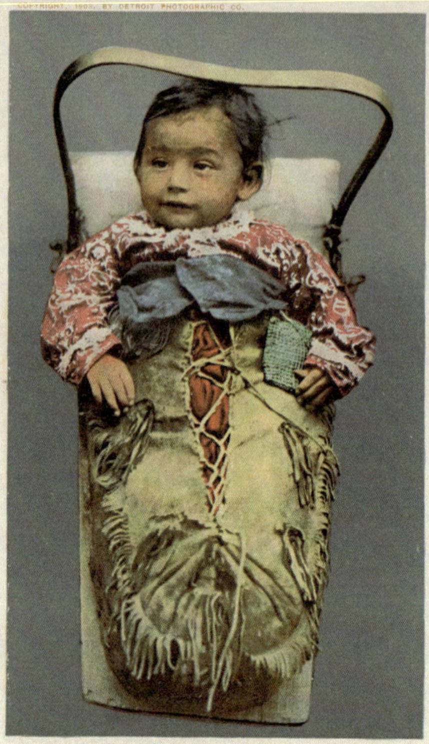

6885. ANTICIPATION.

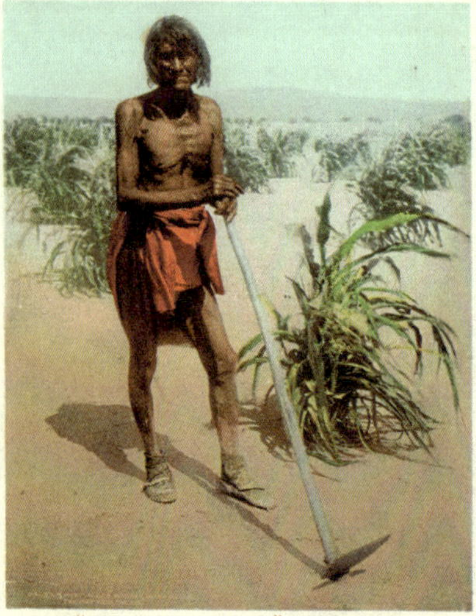

"THE MAN WITH THE HOE," MOKI PUEBLO.

5890. COPYRIGHT. 1902, BY DETROIT PHOTOGRAPHIC CO.

COPYRIGHT, 1902, BY DETROIT PHOTOGRAPHIC CO.

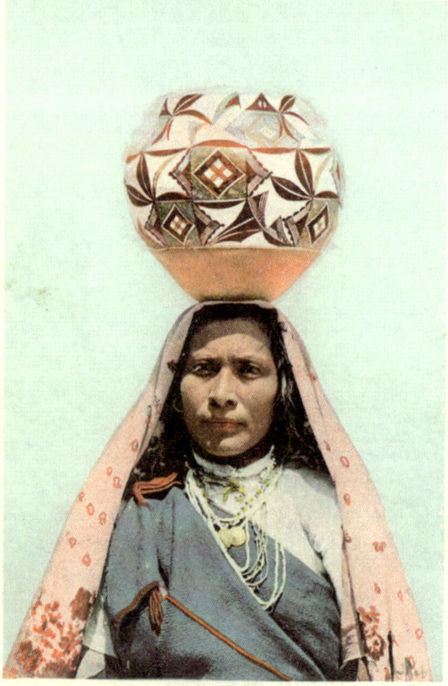

6503. A PUEBLO WOMAN WITH OLLA.

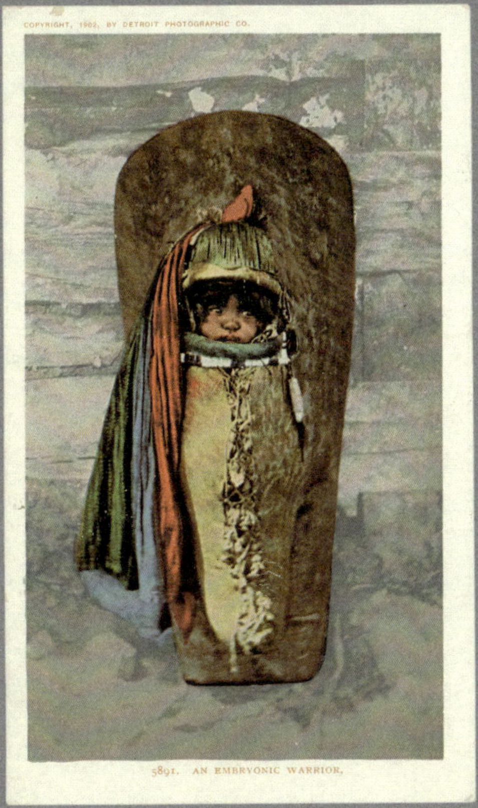
COPYRIGHT, 1902, BY DETROIT PHOTOGRAPHIC CO.
5891. AN EMBRYONIC WARRIOR.

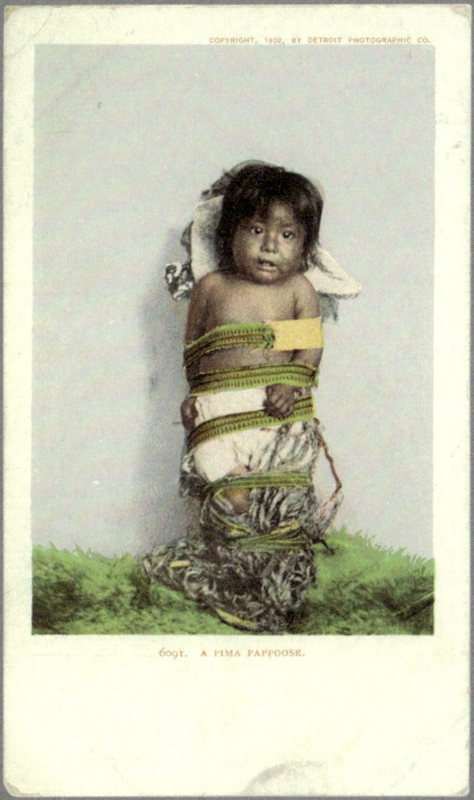
COPYRIGHT, 1902, BY DETROIT PHOTOGRAPHIC CO.
6091. A PIMA PAPPOOSE.

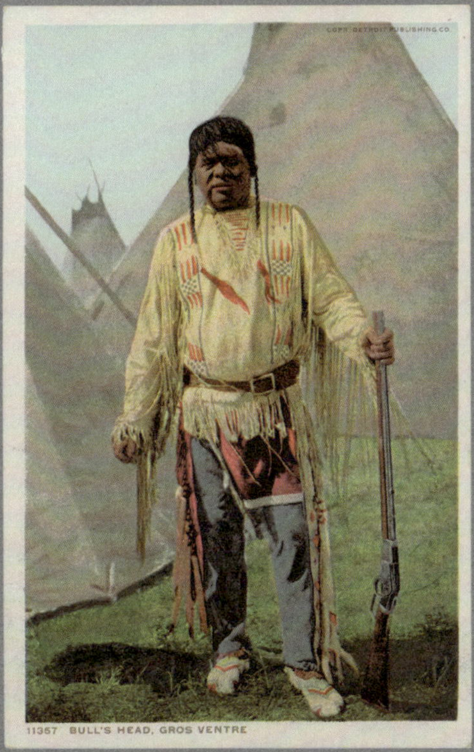
COPR DETROIT PUBLISHING CO.
11357 BULL'S HEAD, GROS VENTRE

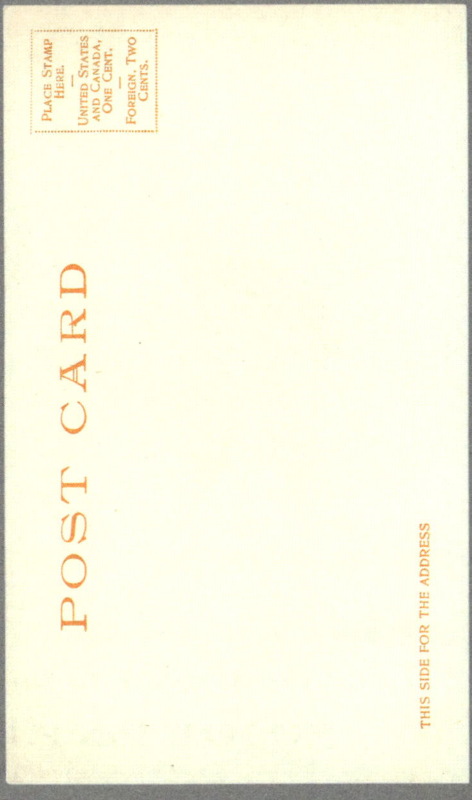
PLACE STAMP HERE.
UNITED STATES AND CANADA, ONE CENT.
FOREIGN, TWO CENTS.
POST CARD
THIS SIDE FOR THE ADDRESS

Carte de visite

Sojourner Truth

1864

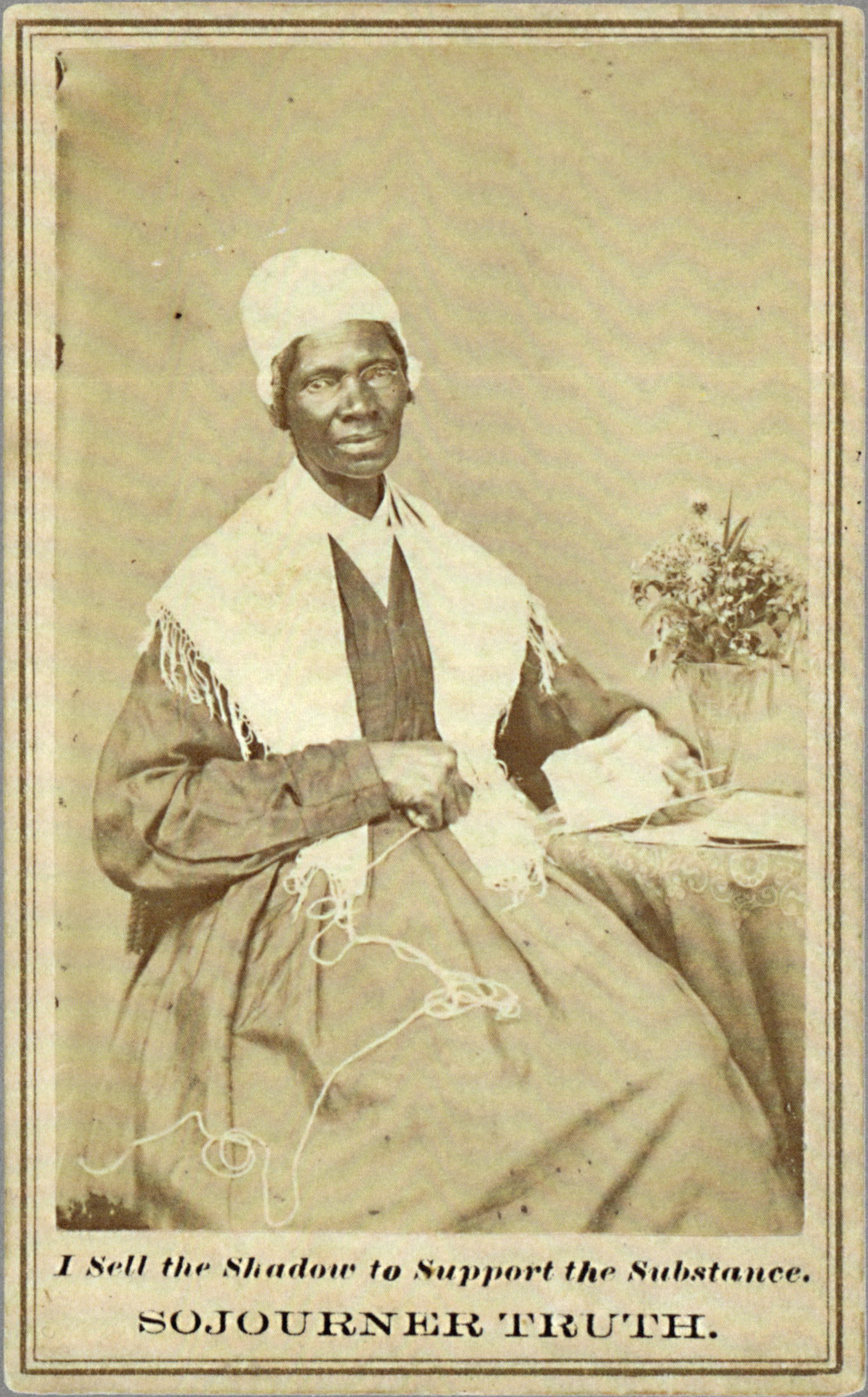

Introduction to *Enduring Truths: Sojourner's Shadows and Substance*

Darcy Grimaldo Grigsby

2015

Sojourner Truth was one of the many sitters for cartes de visite who would not have been able to afford a painted portrait, although she may have had a daguerreotype taken in 1850 to be reproduced as the engraving facing her *Narrative's* title page. The woman Sojourner Truth is elusive and the archival evidence contradictory, but we do know salient facts about her life, some of which I list here:

She was born a slave named Isabella Baumfree, perhaps in 1797.[1]

She spoke Dutch as her first language in an Upstate New York community.

She was separated from her parents in 1810, when she was sold by her first owner for a hundred dollars; she was probably thirteen years old.

She had three different slave owners the first year she was separated from her parents.[2]

She was beaten as a slave; she also lost a portion of her right hand's index finger in a field accident in 1826.[3]

She bore five children between 1815 and 1826, one of whom died.

She expressed affection toward her last owner, but in 1826 at the age of thirty, she ran away after completing the spinning of some one hundred pounds of wool, work that she felt she owed him. [...]

She renamed herself Sojourner Truth in 1843 at the age of forty-six.

She wrote a book with the help of two different women friends and paid for its first printing in 1850 on credit; she later recovered the printing plates and reissued the book in three further editions in 1875, 1878, and 1881. The last posthumous edition of 1884 was entitled *Narrative of Sojourner Truth: A Bondswoman of Olden Time, with a History of Her Labors and Correspondence Drawn from Her "Book of Life"; Also, a Memorial Chapter, Giving the Particulars of Her Last Illness and Death.*[4] [...]

She posed for photographic portraits, primarily cartes de visite, over a dozen different times—mostly during the years of the Civil War, when she was in her late sixties, but also in the years immediately before her death in 1883.

She had a copyright filed in her name for her cartes de visite in 1864; the copyright in her name appeared on the backs of her portraits. At the same time, she added her printed name and a caption to the fronts.[5]

She could neither read nor write. When she made out her will in 1881, she was purportedly unable to sign her name. She signed her "mark" to petitions.[6] [...]

We have no moving pictures to help us imagine the way Sojourner Truth carried her angular frame, almost six feet in height. Nor do we have audio recordings of her voice, described so often as powerful and idiosyncratic. She had a Dutch accent, but how that sounded when she sang or spoke is uncertain. Writers ascribed numerous accents to her, even a southern dialect that we know she did not have. We read her speech and her letters sometimes in the first person and sometimes in the third. We cannot assume that the transcriber who preferred to shift her first-person statements into the

1 On Sojourner Truth there is a vast bibliography, but the key books are as follows, listed in chronological order: Carleton Mabee, *Sojourner Truth—Slave, Prophet, Legend* (New York: New York University Press, 1993); Carla Peterson, *Doers of the Word: African-American Women Speakers and Writers in the North (1830-1880)* (New York: Oxford University Press, 1995); Nell Irvin Painter, *Sojourner Truth: A Life, A Symbol* (New York: W.W. Norton, 1996); Suzanne Pullon Fitch and Roseann M. Mandziuk, *Sojourner Truth as Orator: Wit, Story and Song* (Westport, CT: Greenwood Press, 1997); Margaret Washington, *Sojourner Truth's America* (Urbana: University of Illinois Press, 2009).

2 Washington, *Sojourner Truth's America*, 32-35.

3 Washington, 55; *Narrative of Sojourner Truth, a Bondswoman of Olden Time, with a History of Her Labors and Correspondence Drawn from Her "Book of Life": Also a Memorial Chapter, Giving the Particulars of Her Last Illness and Death*, comp. Olive Gilbert and Frances Titus (Battle Creek, Ml, 1884; reprint, ed. Nell lrvin Painter, New York: Penguin, 1998), p. 26; *New York Times*, September 7, 1853. According to Painter, *Sojourner Truth*, pp. 14-15, Sojourner had been badly beaten at the age of nine by John Neely, and also by John Dumont, to whom she was very attached; she may also have been sexually abused by Dumont's wife. Painter describes her as "an abused child." Matthias also treated her brutally; Painter, 59-60.

4 On the publishing and reprinting of her Narrative, see Painter, *Sojourner Truth*, pp.110-11; Mabee, *Sojourner Truth*, pp. 52, 203, 212; Washington, *Sojourner Truth's America*, pp. 206, 232, 250, 251, 258, 369, 374, 378.

third person was any less accurate than the writer who wrote in the first. "She sends her love" or "I send my love": either could accurately convey what Sojourner herself had said as she dictated her letters, her life story, or her political appeals. Either might not.

Illiteracy makes the interpretation of textual sources challenging, but it does not mean there were few such traces. Sojourner Truth's life left behind many substances: among them, an inordinate number of texts written down by her friends and grandsons. Given her illiteracy, she was a stunningly prolific producer of writing: an autobiography, personal letters, letters intended for publication in the press, speeches, petitions, announcements, and songs.

In addition, Sojourner Truth left us a visual archive [...] this corpus of at least twenty-eight different photographs, mostly cartes de visite, deriving from perhaps fourteen different sessions with a half dozen or so photographers. Here are portraits that she chose to have made again and again throughout the Civil War, and once more at the end of her life in the early 1880s. After 1864, she appended texts: a caption followed by her proper name, "I Sell the Shadow to Support the Substance. Sojourner Truth," and also a copyright in her name. Truth repeatedly advertised the sale of these pictures in newspapers and letters, and she sold them at lectures and by mail. Some were reprinted and attached to different mounts, each with her caption and name. At the end of her life, she commissioned a few cabinet cards with the same inscriptions. Many of her photographic portraits exist in multiple copies scattered across the country in different collections. I believe there may be yet others in regional historical societies, libraries, museums, and, perhaps most intriguingly, personal albums: I have found only four of the latter, all outside official archives.

War inspired Sojourner Truth 's embrace of photography. Like Frederick Douglass, she knew how important its invention was for a society attempting to redefine the status of black men and women.[7] Both former slaves believed in the liberatory power of modernization. According to Truth's friend Eliza Seaman Leggett in a letter to Walt Whitman, Truth "doesn't see anything useful in the new translation of the New Testament—says that the history belongs to past ages, we have outgrown the history...[She] thinks there ought to be scriptures written of what God has done ever since the times of the early creation and Moses, scriptures telling of Railroads and Telephones and the Atlantic Cable. She sees God in a steam engine and electricity."[8] Frederick Douglass went so far as to credit technology with the power to end slavery: "In every bar of rail road iron a missionary—In every locomotive a herald of progress—the startling scream of the Engine—and the small ticking sound of the telegraph are alike prophecies of hope to the philanthropist, and warnings to the system of slavery, superstition and oppression."[9]

Douglass was certain that of all modern inventions, photography had the most far-reaching impact. He devoted public lectures in 1861 and 1865 to ruminate on its power. Not known for art, the nineteenth century, he admitted, could be "condemned" for its "utilitarianism." Douglass's wording connotes the press and the very process of creating photographs, picture-making of the machine age, but he quickly shifts from condemnation to celebration of this new invention:

> Our age gets very little credit either for poetry or song. It is generally condemned to wear the cold metalic [sic] stamp of a passionless utilitarianism. It certainly is remarkable for many achievements, small and great, which accord with this popular description—and yet, for nothing is it more remarkable, than for the multitude, variety and cheapness of its pictures...Daguerre by the simple but all abounding sunlight has converted the planet into

5 On Sojourner Truth's use of photography, see, in chronological order: Kathleen Collins, "Shadow and Substance: Sojourner Truth," *History of Photography* 7, no. 3 (July–September 1983): 183–205; Painter, *Sojourner Truth*, 185–99; Peterson, *Doers of the Word*, 40-44; Nicholas Mirzoeff, "The Shadow and the Substance: Race, Photography, and the Index," in *Only Skin Deep: Changing Visions of the American Self*, ed. Coco Fusco and Brian Wallis (New York: International Center of Photography, 2003), 111-28; Teresa Zackodnik, "The 'Green-Backs of Civilization': Sojourner Truth and Portrait Photography," *American Studies* 46, no. 2 (Summer 2005): 117–43; Mandy Reid, "Selling Shadows and Substance: Photographing Race in the United States, 1850s–1870s," *Early Popular Visual Culture* 4, no. 3 (November 2006): 285–305; Gwendolyn DuBois Shaw, *Portraits of a People: Picturing African Americans in the Nineteenth Century* (Seattle: University of Washington Press, 2006), pp. 48, 168–69; Darcy Grimaldo Grigsby, "Negative-Positive Truths," *Representations* 113 (Winter 2011): 16–38; Augusta Rohrbach, "Shadow and Substance: Sojourner Truth in Black and White," in *Pictures and Progress: Early Photography and the Making of African American Identity*, ed. Maurice O. Wallace and Shawn Michelle Smith (Durham, NC: Duke University Press, 2012), 83–100.
Regarding her marketing strategies more generally, see Augusta Rohrbach, "Profits of Protest: The Market Strategies of Sojourner Truth and Louisa May Alcott," in *Prophets of Protest: Reconsidering the History of American Abolitionism*, ed. Timothy Patrick McCarthy and John Stauffer (New York: New Press, 2006), 235–55.

6 Chicago Tribune, December 22, 1881; cited in Mabee, *Sojourner Truth*, p. 68.

7 A number of recent books attend to the technological skills of slaves, often, however, overlooking photography; see, for example, Carroll Pursell, ed., *A Hammer in Their Hands: A Documentary History of Technology and the African-American Experience* (Cambridge, MA: MIT Press, 2005)

8 Eliza Seaman Leggett, letter to Walt Whitman, June 22, 1881; cited in Donaldson, *Walt Whitman*, p. 244.

9 Laura Wexler, "'A More Perfect Likeness': Frederick Douglass and the Image of the Nation," in Wallace and Smith, *Pictures and Progress*, 18–40; quotation is from p. 24.

> a picture gallery… Men of all conditions may see themselves as others see them. What was once the exclusive luxury of the rich and great is now within reach of all.[10]

Douglass had entitled his lecture "Pictures and Progress," and he imagined progress as the conversion of the "planet" into a "picture gallery." Portraits were now "within reach of all," and they permitted people of all conditions to "see themselves as others see them." As Ginger Hill has observed, Douglass's lectures underscore "not solely self-possession but a possession of and by others. To be self-possessed is not just to present one's own image but to be intruded upon, aware of how one is perceived by others. [Self-possession] requires recognition from others. To achieve such recognition, one must participate in a self-objectification, become one's own object of scrutiny."[11] Hill asks us to entertain the possibility that former slaves, persons treated as fungible things, paradoxically needed to objectify themselves—to see themselves as they were seen by others—in order to attain full self-possession. And former slaves were also inclined to turn their newly obtained private right to property in themselves into their right to publicize that achievement, that personhood. Jane Gaines has alerted us to the contradiction in law "between personhood that is thought to be constituted as a private entity and personhood that is constituted as public and commercial." "The right of privacy," she asserts, is repeatedly "used to secure the right of publicity."[12] After all, to claim only the right to personhood as private property would be to "threaten to remove [one's] image from the public domain of history."[13] Truth was negotiating precisely this tension between self-possession and self-publicity. […]

Sojourner Truth, like Douglass, seems to have believed that self-possession hinged on a form of self-objectification. In 1867, for instance, she chose to have her skull read, even when it meant subjecting her body to analysis by an ostensibly expert white examiner. She took the risk of being subjected to racism masquerading as science—four years earlier in 1863, the firm's Phrenological Journal had attributed "negro"features to "uncultured whites."[14] But Truth's examiner, Nelson Sizer, was an abolitionist who had denounced the Fugitive Slave Bill "as the roughest bill that a legal Turkey buzzard ever held a piece of human carrion in."[15] What is remarkable about Sizer's reading of Truth is the utter absence of physiognomic description or racial reference. The report is entirely unmoored from her physical body. There are no references to the shape of her skull. Nothing indicates whether Sojourner Truth is white or black; she is unmarked as a woman, and nothing tells us about the hills and valleys of her skull. Instead, Truth received a flattering and altogether generalized portrait of her character that begins:

> You have a moral firmness of character, a kind of endurance that lasts forever: you never give up. You have Conscientiousness, and the love of justice. You believe that truth is a jewel.

Sizer proceeded to describe Truth as courageous, self-reliant, persevering, steadfast, ingenious, upright, good with numbers, endowed with parental (not maternal) affection, and liked by pets and children. He concluded:

> You are a good reader of character—you understand strangers and are not easily deceived. You are ingenious-could learn to use tools, and be a good mechanic.
> You are upright by nature.[16]

---

10 Frederick Douglass, "Pictures and Progress," a public lecture in Boston, December 3, 1861 in The Frederick Douglass Papers, ed. John W. Blassingame, ser. 1 (New Haven, CT: Yale University Press, 1985), 3:452-73. On Frederick Douglass's speech, see Ginger Hill, "'Rightly Viewed': Theorizations of Self in Frederick Douglass's Lectures on Pictures," in Wallace and Smith, *Pictures and Progress*, 41–82; and Wexler, "'A More Perfect Likeness.'" See also Jessica Morgan-Owens, "Black and White: Photographic Writing in the Literature of Abolition" (PhD diss., New York University, 2009), chap. 4, 173–232.

11 Hill, "Rightly Viewed," 53.

12 Jane M. Gaines, "The Absurdity of Property in the Person," *Yale Journal of Law & the Humanities* 10, no. 2 (1998): 537–48; quotation is from p. 545.

13 Gaines, 547.

14 *Phrenological Journal* 38, no. 2 (August 1863): 54, cited in Madeline B. Stern, *Heads and Headlines: The Phrenological Fowlers* (Norman: University of Oklahoma Press, 1971), 204.

15 Nelson Sizer, letter to John Brown Jr., New York, October 1850; cited in Stern, *Heads and Headlines*, 176.

16 The report is held at the Kimball House Museum, Battle Creek, Michigan. The rest reads:
You are cautious: always on your guard. You are hopeful: always expecting something favorable in the future.
You have the love of praise, a strong desire to be approved.
Your self-reliance enables you to do your own thinking and planning: gives you confidence in your own judgment. Hence whatever you have to do, you take hold with confidence; and do not feel the necessity of asking advice or help from others.
You have very strong parental affection—you have the motherly feeling, and children and pets like you.
You have strong friendship and naturally very strong love.
You have courage, but you are not quarrelsome. You are more persistent, persevering and steadfast; more thorough, than noisy, or quarrelsome, or disagreeable.
You have an excellent memory of faces; and you remember places well; and facts; you seldom forget anything that is important.
You have a naturally good talent for figures—can reckon money and do it very straight and correctly.

Sizer credits Truth with his own professional skill as a "reader of character." And he attributes qualities to her—courage, self-reliance, and perseverance—resembling those of John Brown, the early radical abolitionist willing to kill to end slavery, whom Sizer had analyzed almost a decade earlier in 1858, the year before he was executed. Corning into his office from the outdoors' bright glare, the phrenologist had barely discerned the "man's dim outline" seen from the back, yet without even seeing his face, he put his "hands on the other" and offered a phrenological reading.[17] Hardly able to see the man, Sizer was analyzing form, not the barely visible appearance of a man approached from the back. Phrenology presumes character is registered on the body, that the body betrays its interiority, but its analysis hinges not on appearance but on small protuberances and convexities often beneath the hair and purportedly uniquely configured for each individual. The 1863 *Phrenological Journal*'s reference to "negro" features betrays an offensively racializing propensity, but Sizer's ostensibly expert, tactile probing and reading of the skulls of John Brown and Sojourner Truth do not. Indeed, they do not describe. Personhood in this phrenological cabinet is paradoxically independent of the appearance of the body.

Unlike phrenological examinations, cameras offer optical surfaces visible to the sight of one and all, the literate and illiterate. Relative to the blind, manual probing of a skull's landscape, photographs are superficial, simplified condensations of information about a sitter's unique embodiment. Photographs are also visible; one does not need to read a report summarizing the expert's observations in looping script. The photographic portrait is democratically available to all who can see and compare and examine the self in relation to others.

Sojourner Truth chose to have one phrenological reading, but she did not publish her report. Instead, she repeatedly sat before the camera. Her recurrent decision to be photographed betrays her impulse, like Douglass's, to scrutinize herself but also to be recognized by others. And she intended to disseminate and profit from her multiples. The information registered by a photograph was not solely for her purview. Once again, Truth took a risk. If nineteenth-century phrenology could be deployed as a racist tool, so too could photography. Over twenty-five years ago, Allan Sekula alerted us to the ways photography's democratic promise was shadowed by its role as a mechanism for surveillance and the construction of racial and class typologies.[18] The decade before Truth's decision to sit for cartes de visite, Harvard racial scientist Louis Agassiz commissioned daguerreotypes of slaves by J.T. Zealy, devastating photographs showing black men and women stripped bare in frontal and profile poses.[19] But Sojourner Truth was nothing if not brave. She, like Douglass, embraced the opportunity to enter photographic portraiture. She wished to present herself to others. And unlike the slaves subjected by Agassiz to unwelcome scrutiny and violence, she made the choice to be photographed, and she decided how she would appear.

[*Enduring Truths*] insists that Sojourner Truth was the author of her representation and its circulation during and after the Civil War. Audiences and readers have alerted me to a pervasive resistance to recognize her agency. Again and again, people assume that Sojourner Truth was constructed by others both during her lifetime and since. In marked contrast to the scholarly attribution of agency (and complexity) to Douglass, I have learned in the process of writing this book that there is a marked hesitation to credit Truth for her savvy production and circulation of her image.[20] Against such skepticism, I argue that Sojourner Truth was the strategic author of her public self and her photographic portrait. I agree therefore with Maurice O. Wallace and Shawn Michelle Smith, who argue that many famous African Americans, including Truth, Frederick Douglass, Harriet Jacobs, and W. E. B. DuBois, were "theorists and *practitioners* of photography...although they might never have focused the lens or released the shutter on a camera."[21]

By exploiting newly affordable photographic portraits, Sojourner Truth created a new community, another form of political persuasion, and also a way financially to support her activism on behalf of former slaves and women. She relied not only on her many friends but on the new "photographic intimacy between persons who never saw each other's faces." Truth was making a vital argument out of exceedingly humble and fragile artifacts. She was also turning paper into value. Always fighting poverty, Truth made a portrait of herself worth money. None of this comes as a surprise: the socially marginal turned into value by art is a very old story in-deed. In *Camera Lucida* (1981), Roland Barthes introduced Richard Avedon's photograph captioned as "William Casby, born a slave" immediately after stating: "In an initial period, Photography

17 Nelson Sizer, *Forty Years in Phrenology, Embracing Recollections of History, Anecdote, and Experience* (New York: Fowler and Wells, 1882), 309; cited in Stern, Heads and Headlines, 134.

18 Allan Sekula, "The Body and the Archive," *October* 39 (Winter 1986): 3–64.

19 Brian Wallis, "Black Bodies, White Science: Louis Agassiz's Slave Daguerreotypes," *American Art* 9, no. 2 (Summer 1995): 38–61.

20 Of course, this resistance has not been shared by the major scholars of her life, Carleton Mabee, Nell lrvin Painter, and Margaret Washington; exceptional too is Rohrbach, "Profits of Protest."

21 Wallace and Smith, introduction to *Pictures and Progress*, 4.

in order to surprise, photographs the notable; but soon, by a familiar reversal, it decrees notable whatever it photographs. The 'anything whatever' then becomes the sophisticated acme of value."[22] Like Avedon, Barthes uses the former slave to prove that "anything whatever" can accrue value if photographed. In this proposition, he who was once property is now a thing turned by photography into another form of property of higher worth.

The transformation of the impoverished into substances of elevated value is not specific to photography; painters have long performed such metamorphoses, making valuable illusions of humble things with inexpensive pigments applied to modest supports, whether canvas, wood, or paper. But Barthes emphasizes the unique evidentiary power of photography: "The man I see here *has been* a slave: he certifies that slavery has existed, not so far from us; and he certifies this . . . by a new, somehow experienced order of proof."[23] Still, Barthes fails to acknowledge his utter reliance on the supplement of the caption: only the picture's accompanying text proclaims that Casby was a slave. The photograph alone cannot make visible the man's legal and social status. Looking at the photograph, we believe William Casby "has been," but we cannot perceive whether he was born a slave or a free man.

The French theorist's surprise that he shares a temporal continuity with slavery derives not from the photograph's legibility as a testament to that institution but from how modern he apprehends the medium to be. I think many viewers may share that response to the dissonance between a far-removed past and a medium so fully part of modern life. Photography also heightens our awareness of representation's inequities. Avedon turns the "anything whatever," in this case a man, into a thing—an artwork—whose value enriches Avedon, not William Casby. The man Casby flickers in and out of value here. Eclipsed between this man's birth as a slave and his capture as an object before Avedon's lens is the length of a life gone unremarked; for us, as viewers, the man's life matters only insomuch as it signifies the physical continuity of the present with the past. That life as a self-determined free man is not valued here; it is merely the interim, the means by which Casby's present is bound to his birth as a slave. Casby accrues value (and visibility) only once image and caption define him as a slave turned into an art object by a famous photographer. The slave made into light, then paper—another form of property—productive of wealth.

The power of Sojourner Truth's photographic portraits partly resides in the dissonance between her origins as a slave and the modernity of the medium of photography. Truth spent the first thirty years of her life as a slave, and her photographic image, like Casby's, has accrued value. But during her free life, Truth, *not the photographer*, profited from the sale of her photographic portrait. As a free woman, she supported herself by the sale of her likeness. William Casby's life as a free man was eclipsed by Avedon's captioned photograph. Truth, by contrast, made her photograph and wrote her caption, and she turned both into a sign of her own freedom and rights. Like Douglass, she believed that photography mattered. Like him, she was determined to author and profit from her representation of self. [...]

When Oliver Wendell Holmes Sr. called cartes de visite "the social *currency*, the sentimental 'green-backs' of civilization," he likened photographs to paper money, the new bills whose backs were often printed in green ink that had been invented to support the Union cause, and also to *currency* more generally. Derived from the Middle English *curraunt*, meaning "in circulation," currency refers not solely to money or a medium of exchange but to the transmission from person to person of such tokens as well as their wider circulation. *Currency* signifies both prevalence—a general acceptance or use—and being up-to-date or "current."

Holmes's word, especially when modified by the adjective *social*, thus offers a nexus of overlapping ideas: representation as constitutive of value; transmission of representation among persons; wide circulation dependent on collective consensus; and cutting-edge contemporaneity. All these meanings pertain to this book, and to Sojourner Truth's prescient use of a relatively new mechanical medium and its inexpensive paper manifestations both to sustain herself and to construct communities of supporters across vast spaces. Like the federal government that resorted to the printing of paper currency to finance the war, Truth was improvising new ways of creating value in order to finance

22 Barthes, *Camera Lucida*, refers to Avedon's photograph twice: 34, 79. On p. 34: "Since every photograph is contingent (and therefore outside meaning), Photography cannot signify (aim at generality) except by assuming a mask. It is this word which Calvino correctly uses to designate what makes a face into the product of a society and of its history. As in the portraits of William Casby, photographed by Avedon: the essence of slavery is laid bare; the mask is the meaning, insofar as it is absolutely pure (as it was in the ancient theater). This is why the great portrait photographers are great mythologists (the French bourgeoisie); Sander (the Germans of pre-Nazi Germany), Avedon (New York's 'upper crust')."

Barthes's recourse to Avedon's photograph of William Casby has been discussed by Carol Mavor, "Black and Blue: The Shadows of Camera Lucida," in *Photography Degree Zero: Reflections on Roland Barthes's "Camera Lucida,"* ed. Geoffrey Batchen (Cambridge, MA: MIT Press, 2009), 211–42; Shawn Michelle Smith, "Race and Reproduction in Camera Lucida," in Batchen, *Photography Degree Zero*, 243–58; and in J.J. Long, Andrea Noble, and Edward Welch, eds., *Photography: Theoretical Snapshots* (London: Routledge, 2009), 98–111, and also my "Negative-Positive Truths." On Barthes's misremembering of James Van der Zee's portrait of an African American family (1926), see Margaret Olin," Touching Photographs: Roland Barthes's 'Mistaken' Identification," *Representations* 80 (Fall 2002): 99–188.

23 Barthes, *Camera Lucida*, 79–80. Barthes describes Casby's face alternately as "a mask" and as a demonstration of photography's power as proof, as a generality, and as a record of a reality "that has been."

her activism and a war that she believed was being fought on behalf of slaves. Throughout the Civil War, paper—printed, engraved, and developed as photographs—was being made into value.

The process was homely, improvised, and subject to fits and starts—like so much nineteenth-century technology betwixt and between the artisanal workshop and the factory, between the unique object and the mass-produced multiple. Midcentury, the borders between different forms of representation were not fixed. Photography and photographic processes everywhere coexisted with far older technologies such as engraving and printing. Improvisation and expediency were essential, and different media served inconsistent, overlapping purposes. Newly invented federal monetary notes, for example, were merely slightly enlarged pieces of engraved paper with postal stamp portraits at their center. Signatures were initially handwritten in ink on the Treasury notes, and for a brief period, precious metal was overlaid onto paper bills. Cartes de visite and tintypes also combined materials, even postal stamps. During the Civil War, stamps were glued to their backs as a federal tax on behalf of the Union cause. [...]

Invisible to us, postage stamps were portraits, a fact highlighted on the back of a carte de visite where such a portrait is inadvertently glorified by a preprinted frame (intended to function as the carte's recto, not its verso). Photography, as Douglass and Truth well appreciated, delivered formerly disenfranchised persons into the portraiture heretofore reserved for the nation's elite. Such an achievement was especially notable for African Americans during the Civil War. If slavery defined black men and women as fungible commodities, anonymous and exchangeable things, [cartes de visite and small tintype portraits] made claims for the uniqueness of the black individual. [...]

Like early monetary bills, [...] tintypes are complex, aggregate objects, combining multiple materials, media, and registers of address. During the Civil War, such private mementos were inscribed by public uses and legal requirements; chemically developed photographs were joined to small rectangles of government-issued, printed paper onto which ink had been applied by hand. Cartes de visite were also modest, rudimentary, often aggregate objects; they were mechanically made but not entirely; they existed as multiples that were not identical; they bore the marks of their makers which were sometimes printed, sometimes hand-drawn, sometimes stylistic; they betrayed the peculiarities of their often hasty production; and later their worn surfaces registered their circulation by countless users. Sojourner Truth's cartes de visite were (and are) complex, multilayered things.

Because Sojourner Truth went to court three times, won each case, authored and signed petitions with her "mark," and copyrighted her photographs, we need to examine the legal ramifications of her textual additions to her portrait. Throughout the Civil War era, the legal status of circulating, inscribed pieces of paper was vigorously debated. The arguments were heated because currency itself was interpreted as an expression of pro-slavery and anti-slavery commitments.

During the conflict, avalanches of paper—bills, notes, stamps, prints, petitions, autographs, newspapers, and photographs—were put to new uses and subjected to new laws, raising questions not only about representation but about value itself [... and] the anxieties engendered by the currency—or wide circulation—of representations on paper: Could inscribed paper really function as a substitute for precious metal? Could paper sustain its value? Who would profit from the exchange of newly issued federal bills? Could value be counterfeited? Was a photograph a shadow capable of supporting substance? Who legally owned a photographic portrait—the sitter or the photographer, or were photographs in fact public property?

The Golden Caribbean, Vol. II, No. 1, January 1904

United Fruit Company

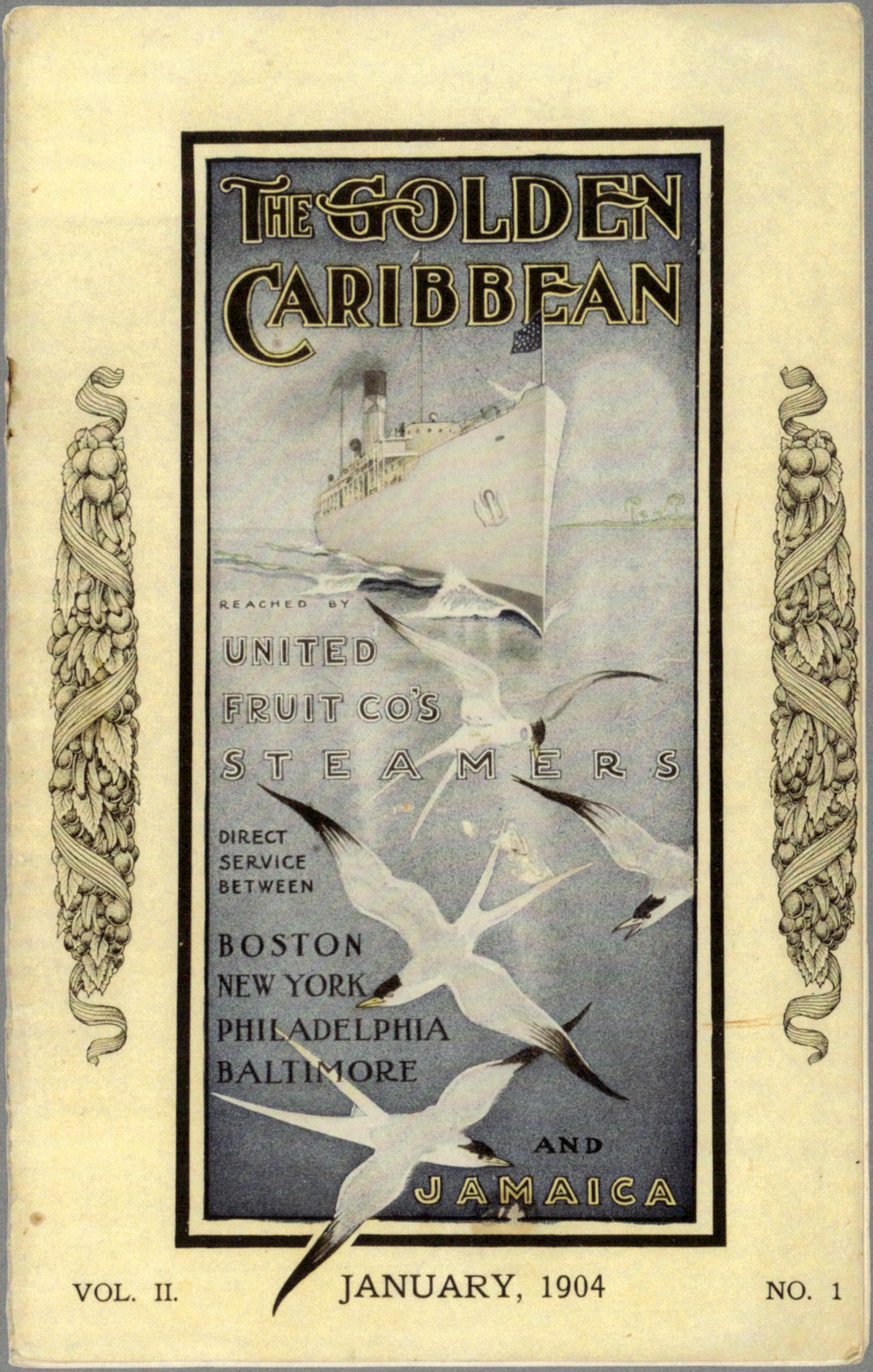

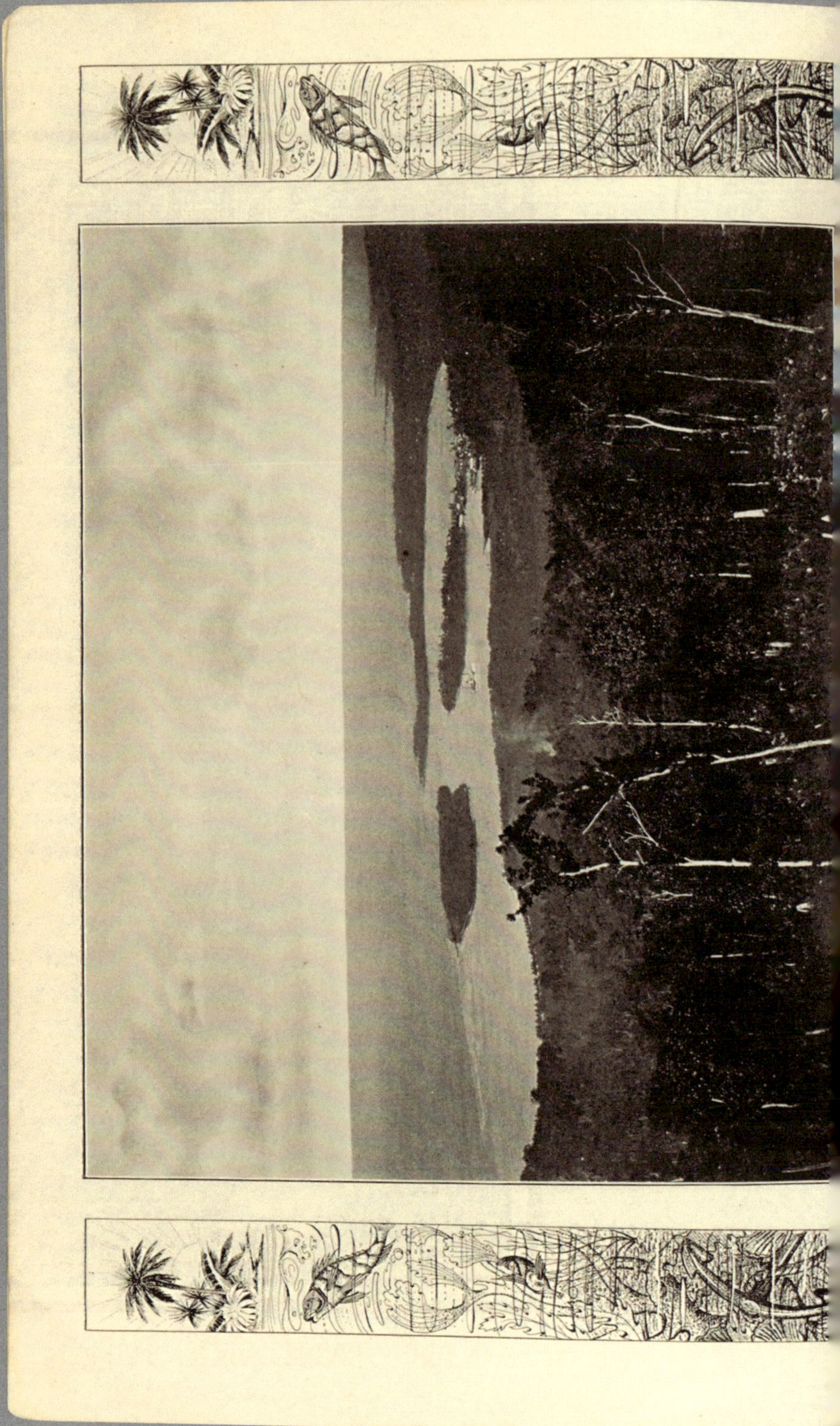

The GOLDEN CARIBBEAN
PUBLISHED MONTHLY BY THE UNITED FRUIT COMPANY LONG WHARF, BOSTON, MASS.
VOL. 2 JANUARY, 1904 NO. 1

IMPRESSIONS OF JAMAICA.

BY A. M. KELLOGG.

IT was a raw, cold day near the close of October when I took passage from Boston on the "Admiral Farragut" for Jamaica. There is a certain unexplained halo aroused by the mention of any of the West India Islands, and a thought of Jamaica had conjured up in me a thousand figures derived from Bernard's "Days of the Freebooters," read long ago. The scenes of those fascinating times was now really to be visited. I was agreeably surprised at the arrangements on the steamer for the comfort of the travelers. The "Farragut" is one of a fleet of new vessels built for the United Fruit Company. The staterooms were found to be large and well appointed — the construction strong and commodious — so that we started off from Long Wharf in a proper state of mind for those who venture on the sea.

I had been exceedingly interested for many years in Florida as a resort for people in broken health, and one of the objects of my visit to Jamaica was to ascertain its fitness in this respect. There are a hundred thousand of those engaged in teaching, or connected therewith, who would be benefited in health by a milder climate, and this only is the medicine they need.

A voyage to Jamaica will furnish indelible remembrances, the entrance into the Gulf stream giving a foretaste of the wonderful tropical region to be visited; the change into indigo blue of the green waves of the North Atlantic; the rising above those waves of San Salvador islands; the appearance next of Castle Island and Bird Island lights successively; the massive rocks of Cuba, long in view; the movements of the flying fish; the rise in the temperature; the sudden coming on of the darkness when the sun disappears; the splendor of the sunrise and sunset, and finally, the wholly different landscape and vegetation. These and a thousand others will remain with the tourist.

We landed after a voyage of four and a half days on the north side of the island of Jamaica at Port Antonio. The visitor is at once struck by the tropical scenery and

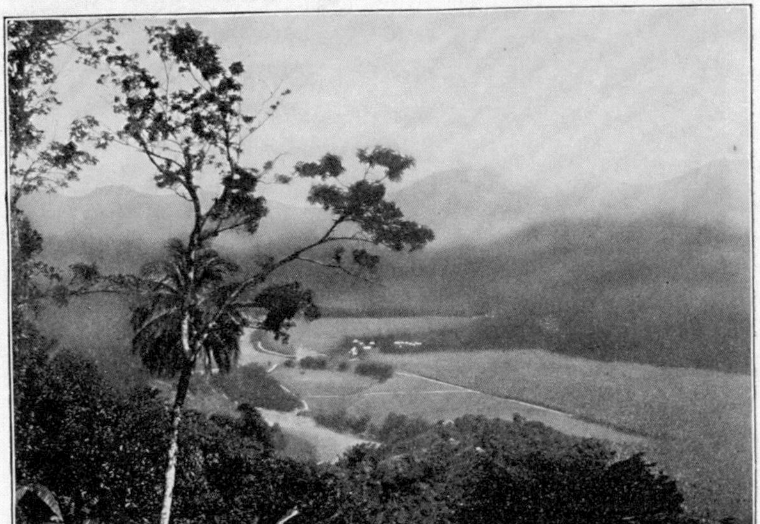

Golden Vale, Blue Mountains in Distance.

vegetation, and quite as much by the stationary civilization of the black population. They are no longer slaves, but they remain much as they were at the time of their emancipation in 1834.

No matter how long one stays in the island the condition and characteristics of the blacks will attract his attention. They are vastly in the majority, numbering 683,000 out of a total of 700,000. Upon them falls the manual labor needed, but it is done slowly and clumsily. The truth is that the languor that seizes at once on us when we land has permanently affected them, and they have become constitutionally lazy. Some own little donkeys and load them with oranges, yams, wood or

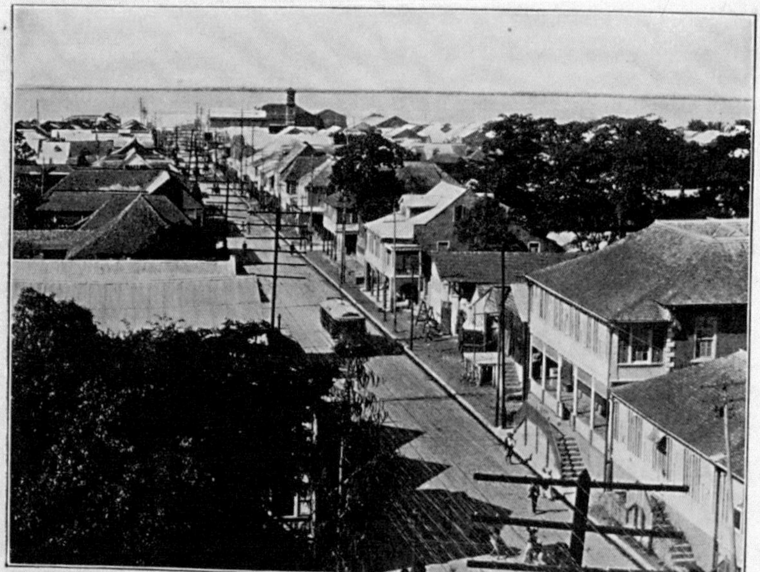

View of King Street, Kingston, Jamaica.

coal, and trudge after them for five, ten or fifteen miles to reach a market.

A railroad extends to Kingston, and we took passage. The surface of the island, it must constantly be borne in mind, is tossed up in high waves. There are no large plains. In the eastern part there is a range of mountains whose highest peak is 7,360 feet above sea level. Hills abound everywhere. The railroad winds among these hills through many tunnels and gives the traveler a fine view of many most picturesque points and an idea of the way the various products are cultivated.

Leaving Port Antonio we skirted along the north coast and reached Annotta Bay, a village which had a special interest for us, because it is close to the point where Columbus arrived in 1502 on his fifth voyage. But he came not as a glorious discoverer. His crew had tired of this mode of life; they bored holes in the bottom of his ships; they mutinied and refused to obey. He could only ground his now useless vessels and take to the shore and live on the charity of the natives. Over a year was thus spent at a cove that bears the name of Don Christopher still, though 400 years have passed. We look at the desolate spot and try to fancy his feelings. Columbus makes a pathetic figure for the imagination. He returned to Spain, history saying of him, "showing an appearance of great sorrow of heart." He lived but two years after his return. In 1509 the Spaniards placed a colony on the islands named Santiago by Columbus, but the Indian name Xaymaca was too firmly fixed to be displaced. They brought captive Africans here and sold them as slaves. Jamaica became the source from whence America obtained her slaves. The present black population are the descendants of those imported Africans.

Passing numerous plantations of bananas, oranges and cocoanuts, we find a crevice in the high hills and cross to the southern side and descend into Kingston. This is a city of 50,000 inhabitants, and there are several intersecting streets. The bay is one of the best in the world as a harbor for ships. There are electric cars, but the carriage charge is only twelve cents, and these are extensively employed. The great bay is southward. Northward is a semi-circle of high wooded hills—those to the west become mountains. On the side of these soldiers are sent on arrival to become acclimated. The encampment can be seen from the city. It is nine miles distant and at an elevation of 4,000 feet.

Life in Kingston is fitted to the climate. You are awakened at six in the morning by the servant with coffee. The dining room is usually separate from the house, or is a piazza with a stone or brick floor. The kitchen and servants' quarters are

Water is furnished the city from a mountain stream in great abundance. In some streets it runs constantly. This island is famous for making rum. All the street cars had as their most conspicuous advertisement in bold letters in front, "Fine Old Jamaica Rum," as though they had it on tap within. It would seem that the good women of the Christian Temperance Union must decline to ride on the Kingston street cars. But drunkenness is not the special vice of the Jamaicans.

As a winter resort Jamaica has probably the most attractions of any of the tropical regions. The steamers of the United Fruit Company afford such ready and comfortable means of reaching the island that it is

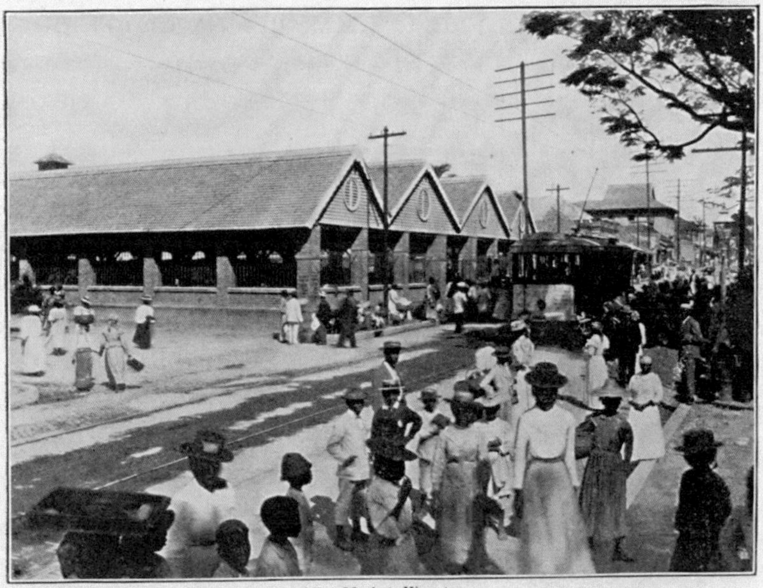

Jubilee Market, Kingston.

separated from this. Everywhere, except in the streets, there are trees growing and profuse shrubbery.

The food follows the climate. In the morning the delicious grape fruit begins the repast—here cut into halves with the seeds taken out fill a generous dish. The visitor sifts sugar into the hollow, but not so the Jamaican—oranges, bananas, alligator pears, cocoanuts and other fruits are reserved to finish the repast. A cup of Jamaican coffee, said to be equal to any in the world, is placed before you; or you may have cocoa, which abounds here. While meats are served, one comes to follow the custom of the inhabitants of preferring fish, which are abundant.

almost as accessible as Florida, which requires three days' sail against four and one-half to the other. The operations of this company cannot but be of the highest benefit to Jamaica. Not only does it transport fruit from the island; it purchases plantations and aids in its production.

The economic development of Jamaica is quite probable. The first step has been taken by this company. It is plain that it is admirably fitted as a winter resort as far as climate is concerned. The first problem will be to induce people from New England to settle on the hills accessible to the railroads and conduct family hotels or boarding houses. The need of such is already seriously felt. Were such to be

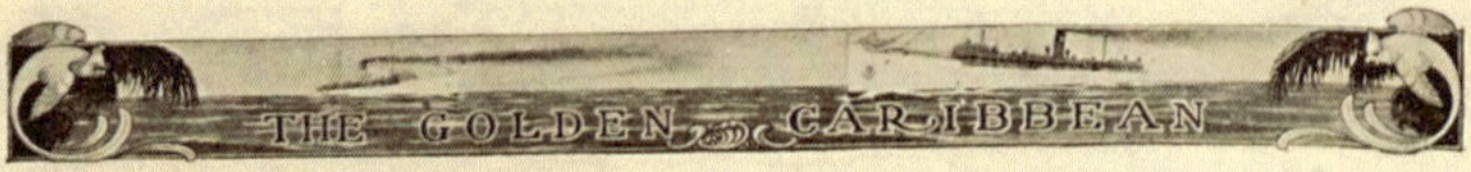

opened, and I think the northern coast the preferable part, I could recommend Jamaica as a winter resort to the educational public.

The traveler is constantly surprised at the luxuriance of the vegetation in Jamaica. It is a shock to him for many days. A planter at Port Antonio stated the matter thus: "Nature here is in supreme power. Our effort is not to make things grow. We have a constant conflict with nature to overcome her abundance."

One who leaves the north in the winter months is peculiarly and powerfully affected by the balmy, delightful atmosphere as the steamer reaches Port Antonio. No matter how well he has prepared his mind beforehand, there is a great surprise in store for him. Longfellow's poem was continually running through my mind:

> "The night shall be filled with music,
> And the cares which infest the day
> Shall fold their tents like the Arabs,
> And as silently steal away."

For in this delightful corner of God's universe all cares, worries, aches and tribulations seem to fly away, and one only longs to inhale the delicious, dreamy air and simply rest — and how we did dread returning north to our frosts, chills and blizzards.

EXTRACTS FROM "JIMMY JOHN" LETTERS

THIS is the 19th day of blustering February, and attired in the thinnest of garments, gossamer hats and within easy reaching distance of the life-saving palm leaf, we have turned Christian Scientists and are trying the absent treatment on snow that flies and winds that blow.

laden, if you ever have been, or think that you ever may be, shut down your desk and start for Jamaica, and nature will do the rest.

You may have to turn Episcopalian, and believe with them that there is a Purgatory before there is a Paradise. For a couple of days life on the boat will not be

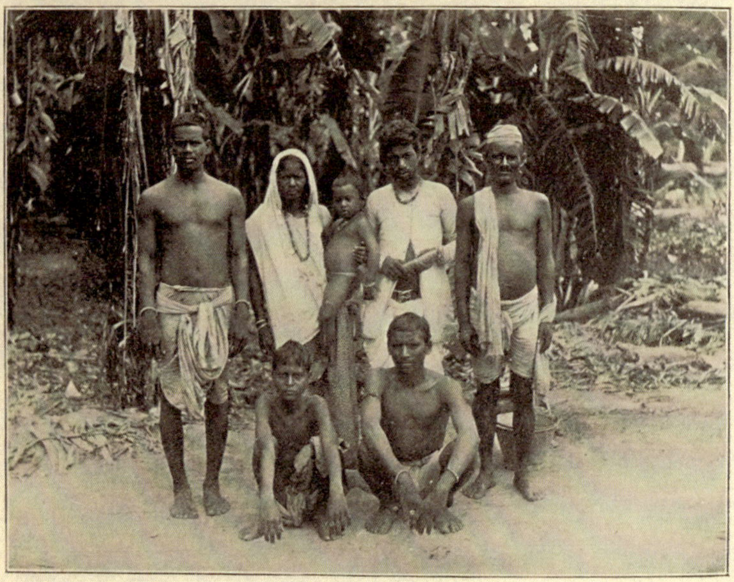

A Group of Coolies.

Here is a prescription which we cheerfully give without money and without price and without being registered pharmacists. If you are weary and heavy-

one long, sweet song. The Gulf Stream is acrobatic in its temperament and habits, and tosses ships as a Sandow does cannon balls. For the winds they blow and do an

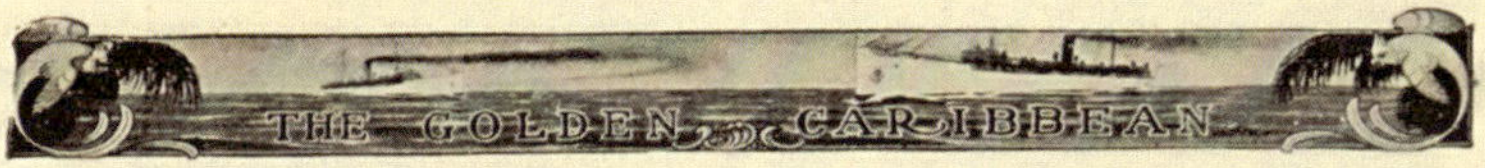

amount of churning to the waves that would make the fortune of a dairy. And your boat will develop a sudden streak of Methodism, and act out the good old

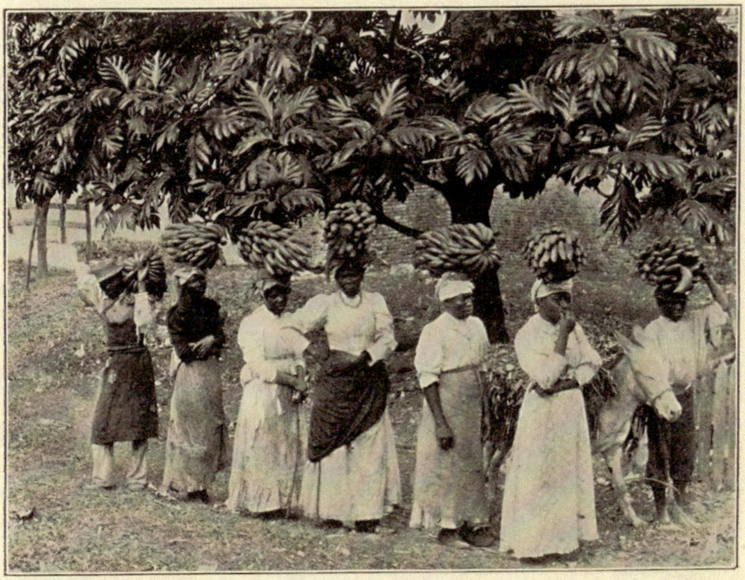

Banana Carriers in Jamaica.

chorus of "Roll, Jordan, Roll" with all the fervor of a camp-meeting convert.

And you have other troubles, in the passenger line. There is the lady who gets up at break of day and goes out on deck and talks to the deckhands, and tells them how she is never, never sick at sea; and has a nose like unto a Lawson pink, and cheeks like a sunset on the Rhine; and wears a huge Tam-O'Shanter cap that makes her look like an unfinished church spire. And you call her Miss O'Shanter and dodge her as you would some Ancient Mariner who "holds you with his glittering eye," and wonder at the splendid taste shown by sea-sickness in selecting victims for its embrace, and also sigh over its cruelty in leaving some monuments unscathed.

Then there is the lady whom you call the Madonna, because she looks so little like one, and never brushes her hair. She has the voice of a marked-down phonograph and insists upon reading aloud novels of the Laura Jean Libbey stamp, where the hero is always clasping his lady love in his strong arms and the heroine insisting upon an encore.

Then there is another. She is dressed in furs, with fur cap, fur coat, fur gloves and fur shoes. You christen her Mrs. Peary, because she looks so much like an Arctic explorer. Then the hot weather comes, she puts aside her furs, and henceforth she is known as Mrs. Disappeary.

But finally clouds go way back, the winds cease from troubling and the wild waves are at rest. You get out your coolest suit, and begin to feel like last summer. You sit out on the deck as a shirt-waist man from morning until night, and wonder if anywhere there is such a thing as snow, and look at flying-fish and water-spouts, and the deep blue water all around, as blue as a Bryan Democrat after the last Presidential election. And moonlight comes, and the tropical moon looks down so straight that you have the delightful sensation of stepping on the shadow of your own head on the deck.

And you glide by the island that so excited Columbus that he got off there and neglected to get a transfer for the mainland, now ornamented with a lighthouse; and you learn that lighthouses are wearing black and white stripes this season. And Cuba appears, and the part that reaches out to shake hands with you looks like a deserted farm in Massachusetts. And you strain your eyes to see Santiago, and San Juan hill, and it all looks so much alike that you marvel that Cervera's fleet was ever discovered.

Then you are at Jamaica. Geography will tell you that a certain English gentleman with a past, by the name of Edward, is ruler of the island. But geography is an Ananias of the deepest dye. The banana is king of Jamaica. It is a government for, by and of—not the people, but the banana. Bananas first, everything else afterwards. Ships bear them hence to all the world. Even the ship of state is filled with them. Even the climate is made for them; here where it is eleven months summer and one month late in the spring.

There is only one rival to the banana as a part of the scenery, the cocoanut palm, the most ridiculous looking thing in all the bright lexicon of trees. When Mark Twain described it as a giant feather duster, struck by lightning, he made the bell of the bull's-eye ring loud and long. During the day it looks like a man with a wilted collar and an unlaced shoe trying to appear dignified. At night in the moonlight it makes you feel like seeing the chariot race in "Ben Hur" and betting on the wrong chariot.

Then you remember that it is Lent and you give up meat, but, candidly, the weather has fully as much to do with it as religious scruple; and you give up everything else in the eating line, but fruit, and in that you revel for days. You meet real grape fruit, not high-priced imitations; you put your teeth into the little brown neesberry, sweet as love's young dream; the star apple, that looks like a rainbow and tastes like a touch of the life beyond; the cho-cho, first cousin to the cucumber and sister-in-law to the summer squash; the pineapple that here smiles sweetly between your lips, not frowns sourly; the paw paw, a watermelon painted yellow on the inside; and so through all the list. If it is true that by their fruits ye shall know them, Jamaica should have a place near the head of the procession.

You will find our text this morning in the chapter of Jamaica, the Port Antonio verse. Port Antonio is a town that is trying to serve two masters—the United Fruit Company and Grosset. One is a trust, the other a man whom you instinctively trust. The company is like unto others, the man is unique. Any state with an easy running corporation sewing-machine could produce the company, only Jamaica could produce Grosset.

Grosset started with a small bar and a cocoanut tree. To-day forty thousand cocoanut trees call him master and a bank that knew its business and him would cash his check for a million and ask for more. His plantations stretch away for miles, his country house bows to none on the island. His son is a physician, with diplomas and honors from the best medical schools of Europe. And, Grosset himself sits in a dingy corner of a dingy store, where the sun never enters, his shrewd eyes blinking through the railing, his mouth full of smiles and his mind of stories. What the Waldorf is to New York, "Grosset's" is to this part of Jamaica.

In the matter of dispensing liquids he not only separates the sheep from the goats, but makes two divisions of goats as well. He has a first, second and third class bar, and woe unto the thirsty individual who tries to get out of his class. And to mention Grosset without mentioning "Rum and Kola" is Hamlet without the character of the thin and thinky Dane. There is a tradition that this concoction is the lineal descendent of the ambrosia, with which thirsty gods and goddesses were wont to make life on Olympus worth living. Certain it is that

"To those who know it not no words can paint,
And to those who know it, know all words are faint."

And, to descend from the sublime to the ridiculous, there is the Jamaica pony. There is no Society for the Prevention of Cruelty to Animals here. It would fail in a week for lack of business. What is needed is a Society for the Prevention of Cruelty to Pleasure Drivers. The Jamaica pony is a dainty thing with a distinctively reflective mind, which compels him to stop and think when you are most anxious to rush. After riding for an afternoon behind such conservative animals you are strongly reminded of Ned Sibley's proud boast that he had a four-in-hand at his house, a saw-horse, a clothes-horse, horse-radish and the nightmare. And the Jamaica horse lives to a ripe old age. They are sweet young things at twenty, middle-aged at thirty, and are expected to draw breath and carriages until they are at least forty-two. At least such is the testimony of the native driver; but, as he has no idea of his own age, no knowledge whatever of the date of his birth, there may be an element of fiction in his horse statements.

And the languor that pervades the horse is contagious. Never do to-day what you can do at any other time, is the motto that should be inscribed upon the Jamaica coat-of-arms, and a very thin coat it must be, too, in this atmosphere. And the Jamaica crest should be a darkey restant upon a field of green bananas. Anything rampant in the crest would be a libel on the land.

There is one exception, one person who has life. It is the tailor. You land in this country impressed with the idea that you have in your possession clothes that are thin. A couple of hours pass and you are convinced that they are made of lead, with sheetiron trimmings, so heavy do they hang. You rush for linen of the lightest weave. At ten A.M. you select the cloth and get measured; at noon you try on; at four o'clock you are proudly and coolly wearing a new suit. And its total cost to you is $4.49. If you are of a tremendously extravagant nature you can spend $4.70 on a suit, but that is the highest you can pay unless you line the coat with gold leaf and use real diamonds for buttons.

Everywhere else there is languor. Think thrice before you move, is the regular rule, and then think it over again after that. Nothing happens, nothing can happen. Even nothing is too lazy to do such an active thing as happen. Such a thing as a Strout activity is as unknown as the Sanskrit language. You even hate to have money, it is such a job to carry it. The Jamaica coins were invented by some one who wished to throw bricks at the future of the island. In the first place they all look alike and feel alike, and it takes several minutes to find out whether you are giving a half penny, or a half crown. Then they are twice as large and thick as they should be, and weigh in the pocket as murder does on the soul. To carry ten dollars in your trousers' pockets makes your limbs look like the before taking picture of a spavin advertisement in a farmers' almanac.

The moonlight is also larger here. Take the finest moonlight night you ever saw, multiply it by four, add eighteen, throw in a dash of rose color, add three ounces of pousse café, and you have about a 12-karat imitation of a tropical moonlight.

As in days of old all roads led to Rome, so in Jamaica all thoughts lead to fruit. And you learn how to eat it as it should be eaten; how to split the banana lengthwise and eat it out of the skin with a fork, and how to balance a peeled orange upon a fork in mystic fashion while you eat around. Then there is the yam, a mugwump potato, —with no flavor and no apparent reason for its existence. But its colleague, the yampie, is a different matter. That has that splendid flavor of the potatoes that you used to steal when young and take away into the woods and cook in a fire that you built yourself. They have that splendid thick black skin, and reminiscent interior, and altogether a friend to be cultivated.

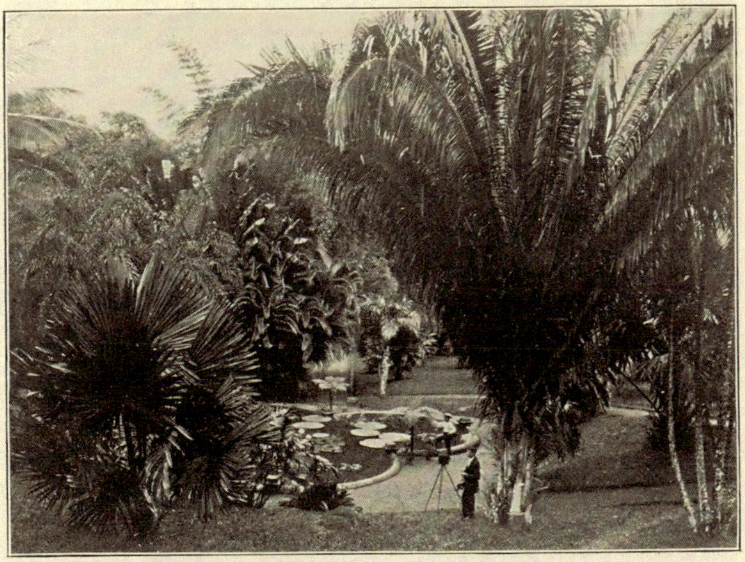

Botanical Gardens at Castleton.

ONE SUNDAY MORNING IN JAMAICA.

By FRANCIS DODSWORTH.

THE church stood in the midst of the hills, resting on an eminence, as on a pillow, in the cradle of the valley. All around the kindly sides of the mountains reared themselves.

As we rode along the winding hill paths, with every fibre capable of appreciating beauty lulled into semi-slumber by pleasant satiety, yet ever gaining fresh vigor and strength from the cool breeze

IMPORTANT CHANGE OF SCHEDULE.

New American Twin-Screw Steamships

"Admiral Dewey" & "Admiral Farragut"

AND STEAMSHIP PRESTON.

United States Mail Service.

BOSTON TO

JAMAICA, WEST INDIES

... AND ...

PORT LIMON, COSTA RICA.

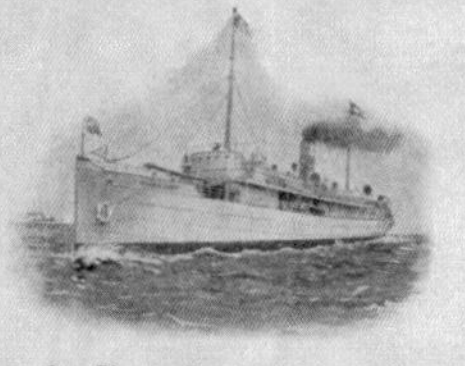

Commencing with Saturday, December 26th at 10 a.m., the Steamships Admiral Dewey, Admiral Farragut and Preston will leave respectively every Saturday at 10 a.m. from Long Wharf, Boston, instead of Wednesday as formerly, direct for Port Antonio, Jamaica, thence to Port Limon, Costa Rica.

This arrangement offers a superb opportunity for those desiring a longer sea voyage in tropical waters than our former schedule permitted.

Passengers to or from Port Limon, Costa Rica are allowed the privilege of stop-over at Jamaica.

Connections at Port Limon with steamers for Colon, Carthagena, Savanilla, Santa Marta and South American Coast Points. With Costa Rica Railway Company for San Jose and interior.

The United Fruit Company operates the only line of Passenger Steamers between Boston and Central American Ports.

FOR FURTHER INFORMATION ADDRESS

F. S. JOPP, - Division Passenger Agent,

UNITED FRUIT COMPANY, LONG WHARF, BOSTON.

RATES OF FARE:

JAMAICA, - - - - - One Way, $40. Round Trip, $75.

PORT LIMON, COSTA RICA, - One Way, $75. Round Trip, $135.

For return sailings and connections see page D.

IMPORTANT CHANGE OF SCHEDULE.

New American Twin-Screw Steamships

"Admiral Schley" & "Admiral Sampson"

AND STEAMSHIP BEVERLY.

United States Mail Service.

PHILADELPHIA TO

JAMAICA, WEST INDIES

... AND ...

BOCAS DEL TORO, R. P.

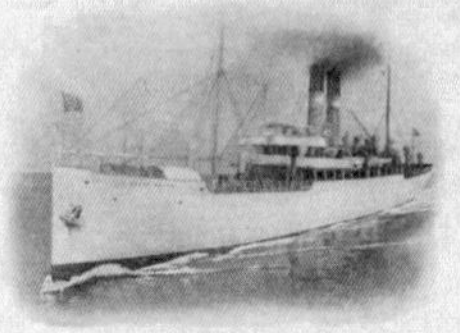

Commencing with Monday, December 28th at 10 a.m. the Steamships Admiral Schley, Admiral Sampson and Beverly will leave respectively every Monday at 10 a.m. from Pier 5, No. Wharves, Philadelphia, Pa., instead of Thursdays as formerly, direct for Port Antonio, Jamaica, thence to Bocas del Toro.

This change in schedule offers additional opportunities to tourists of continuing on to Bocas del Toro, stopping off at Jamaica in either direction.

FOR FURTHER INFORMATION ADDRESS

S. B. WILLS, Division Passenger Agent,

UNITED FRUIT COMPANY, PIER 5, NO. WHARVES, PHILA.

RATES OF FARE:

PORT ANTONIO, JAMAICA, One Way, $40. Round Trip, $75.

BOCAS DEL TORO, R. P., - One Way, $60. Round Trip, $110.

For return sailings and connections see page D.

CONNECTIONS.

AT PORT ANTONIO, JA. With Jamaica Railway for Kingston, Spanishtown, Montego Bay, Mandeville and all railroad towns on north coast. Also with steamers of the "Royal Mail" and "Imperial Direct" coastal service for ports on north and south coasts of Jamaica.

Boston outward passengers desiring to return via Philadelphia will transfer here.

AT KINGSTON, JA. With steamers of the "Hamburg American Line" to Central and South American ports and for New York.

With "Elder Dempster & Co.'s Direct Line" to Bristol, Eng.

With the "Royal Mail Steam Packet Co.'s" steamers for San Juan, Porto Rico, and all Windward Islands; also Colon, Limon, Savanilla and Carthagena, and Southampton, Eng.

With the "Halifax & West Indies Steamship Co." to Halifax via Turks Island and Bermuda.

CONNECTIONS AT PORT LIMON. With steamers for Colon, Carthagena, Savanilla, Santa Marta and South American coast points. With Costa Rica Railway Co. for San Jose and interior, and with steamers of the "Hamburg American Line" to New York. And also with "United Fruit Company Fast Mail Line," leaving Port Limon every Thursday; arriving at New Orleans every Tuesday.

SPECIAL NOTE.

In regard to sailings from Boston or Philadelphia and return sailings from Jamaica. Steamers will leave Long Wharf, Boston, promptly at 10 A. M. every Saturday, for Port Limon, Costa Rica, calling at Port Antonio, Jamaica, en route. They are due to arrive at Port Antonio the following Thursday morning at daybreak. All Jamaica passengers will disembark at Port Antonio. Outward steamers will remain at Port Antonio about 24 hours, thus giving passengers for Port Limon a short break in the voyage at this Port. Passengers for Kingston or other points in Jamaica will transfer at Port Antonio. A train by steam railway for Kingston leaves at 6 A. M., arriving at Kingston at 11 A. M. See Railroad time table. Those desiring to go to Kingston by sea will find vessels leaving Port Antonio nearly every week-day for either Kingston or various ports around the island. Accommodations good and fares very reasonable. It will be observed that the steamers leave Philadelphia on Mondays, their arrivals will consequently be 18 hours later than the Boston arrivals.

Return sailings from Port Antonio for Boston every Friday A. M. Arriving Boston each Wednesday morning. Return sailings from Port Antonio for Philadelphia every Saturday A. M. Arriving Philadelphia each Wednesday afternoon.

Passengers will save themselves much delay and annoyance if on arrival at Port Antonio they will call at the United Fruit Company's office and arrange day, date and stateroom bookings for return passage, or at least as soon as your date of returning is decided upon. The company's agents at Port Antonio will be pleased to give any information desired in regard to trips or outings about the island, foreign money, date of sailings, etc.

ADDITIONAL SCHEDULES.

STEAMERS LEAVE

NEW YORK & BALTIMORE, MD.

FOR

Banes, Cuba,
Bluefields, Nic.,
Ceiba, B. H.,
Santa Marta, Col.

For Sailing dates, address Managers at either point.

I. CADMUS, - - - - Manager,
NEW YORK.

C. C. BUCKMAN, - - Manager,
BALTIMORE, MD.

From MOBILE, ALA.

To Puerto Cortes and Spanish Honduras Coast Points, Weekly.

To Bocas del Toro, Republic of Panama, Weekly.

From NEW ORLEANS, LA.

To Bluefields, Nicaragua, Weekly.

To Ceiba, Puerto Cortes and Spanish Honduras Coast Points, Weekly.

To Port Limon, Costa Rica, Weekly.

For further information address

M. J. DEMPSEY, - Traffic Manager,
321 St. Charles St., NEW ORLEANS, LA.

The Evidence of Things Not Photographed: Slavery and Historical Memory in the British West Indies
Krista Thompson
2011

Slavery and the period of apprenticeship came to an end in the British West Indies in 1838, the year photography was developed.[1] The twilight of slavery occurred as the new medium literally came to light. Superficially, the two moments would seem unrelated: they would seem to be two events falling in separate historical forests. Slavery's occurrence outside the purview of photography would, however, profoundly inform how the pre-emancipation era in the British Empire was reproduced, remembered, or willfully forgotten. If, as photography historian Alan Trachtenberg postulates, "historical knowledge declares its true value by its photographability," what impact would photography's development at the end of slavery have on the production of history in the African diaspora within the British West Indies specifically?[2] How would the fact of slavery in Britain's colonies accrue its historical valence without photography as firsthand witness?

Despite this absence of photographs dating from the pre-emancipation era, and perhaps because of the intimate relationship between the camera and the production of modern forms of historical knowledge, some historians of the Anglophone Caribbean have drawn on photographs—albeit images from the late nineteenth century—to give slavery historical form in their accounts. It is this use of photographic archives to represent slavery in the West Indies in popular and scholarly accounts that I investigate in this essay. How does the employment of photographs that date from almost a century after emancipation dramatically transform the visual imagination of slavery in the Anglophone Caribbean? How does photography cloud or bring into focus the memory of slavery? While the use of late nineteenth-century photographs may obstruct from view aspects of the history of slavery, this occlusion may in fact be revelatory. The reproduction of these photographic images may bring to the fore ways of remembering and ways of reconfiguring photographic representation, memory, and history in the African diaspora. Indeed, the transposition of accounts of slavery and photographs from the late nineteenth century in some historical accounts may aptly capture what Toni Morrison characterizes as "rememory" among enslaved Africans and their descendants—the ruptures in space and time and the ever-presentness of the past that are intrinsic to the memory of slavery and to the formation of the African diaspora more generally.[3] The presentation of late nineteenth-century photographs as the pictorial face of slavery might precisely visualize the continuities between the period of slavery and post-emancipation, the ghostly and all too real reappearance of forms of unfreedom past. As such the reproduction of photographs in contemporary historical accounts may highlight new ways of reading photographic archives from the perspective of African diasporic subjects and alternate ways of bringing to light the histories of the enslaved and their descendants.

The complexities of creating histories of slavery in the Anglophone Caribbean through the lens of photography can be seen in the volume *Slavery, Abolition, and Emancipation: Black Slaves and the British Empire*, a book that is symptomatic of the problem of the photographic in studies of slavery in the British West Indies.[4] Three eminent and prolific historians of the Anglophone Caribbean, Michael Craton, James Walvin, and David Wright, produced the collection of essays and primary documents in 1976. In it, they set out to present what they describe as a reexamination of slavery in the face of the unbalanced focus on the abolitionist movement in historical scholarship. [...] The period of apprenticeship in 1838 bookends the publication's historical coverage, and photographs appear as illustrations throughout the book. Coincidentally, 1838 is the same year that the Frenchman Louis Jacques Mandé Daguerre announced the invention of a photographic process he called the daguerreotype, which fixed the impressions of light as created in the camera obscura on a metal plate, creating a nonduplicatable, laterally reversed, monochrome picture. [...] by the early 1840s, a photographer in Jamaica, Adolphe Duperly, opened the first daguerreotype studio in Kingston, but this came after the period of apprenticeship. It is the presence of photographs in the

1 Apprenticeship was the four-year transitional period following slavery during which ex-slaves trained, without pay, with their former masters.
2 Alan Trachtenberg, "Albums of War: On Reading Civil War Photographs," *Representations* 9 (Winter 1985): 1.
3 Toni Morrison, *Beloved: A Novel* (New York: Alfred A. Knopf, 1987), 35.
4 Michael Craton, James Walvin, and David Wright, *Slavery, Abolition, and Emancipation: Black Slaves and the British Empire: A Thematic Documentary* (London: Addison-Wesley Longman Ltd, 1976).

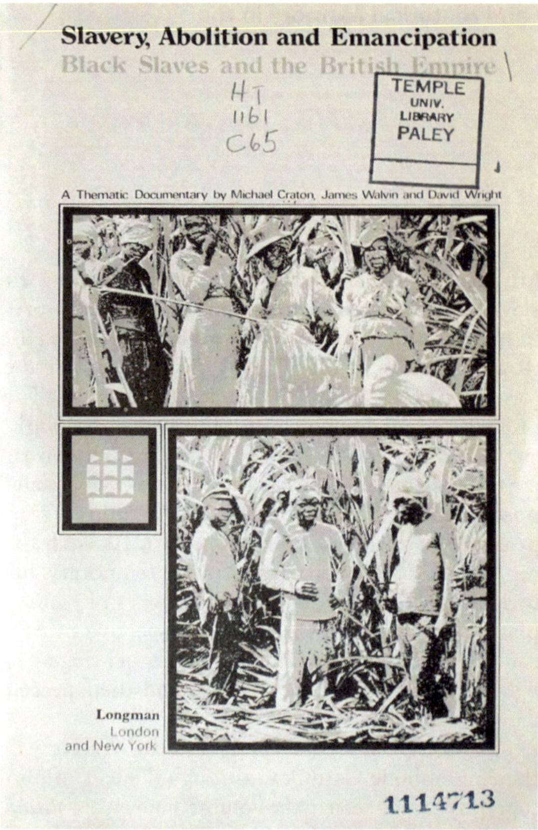

Figure 1. Frontispiece to Michael Craton, James Walvin, and David Wright, *Slavery, Abolition, and Emancipation: Black Slaves and the British Empire*, 1976.

Craton, Walvin, and Wright text on the slavery and the immediate post-emancipation period—an era that predates the earliest uses of photography in Jamaica—that will serve as a point of departure in this consideration.

The frontispiece of *Slavery, Abolition, and Emancipation* reproduces two photographs of black laborers standing amid sharp blades of sugarcane (Fig. 1). In the bottom image, four male figures (and one cut off by the frame) turn toward the camera. The two central figures hold up machetes, proffering the tools as photographic props. Just above the image of the men, in a shape oddly incongruous with that of its neighbor, another photograph pictures several women, all of whom also address the camera. Two of them appear to chew on the fruits of their labor, while the central figure rests her head in her hand in a gesture that seems to suggest both tired repose and self-aware pose. Not only do the figures appear in their dual group portraits in the frontispiece, but their individually framed countenances also stare out from the book jacket and at the beginning of each chapter. Since the photographs appear with no information about their producer, without titles or dates, they come to bear the representational weight of the chapters they introduce. As the subjects of the only images in the book, the bodies of these laborers, shown at work and at photographic rest, serve as visual proxies for the black experience of slavery in the British Empire.

The images, although enlisted in a certain historical recounting of slavery, however, do not date from the era of enforced labor at all, but from the end of the nineteenth century. They were also not created as two separate representations, but as a single photograph entitled *Cane Cutters, Jamaica*, taken on the island by an agent of the Scottish photo-publishing firm James Valentine and Sons in the early 1890s (Fig. 2). The company, which advertised itself as "photographers to the Queen," came to the British crown colony on the invitation of the governor in 1891.[5] If the photograph can be seen as representative of transitions of labor at all (as suggested by the placement of the images at the opening of each period-focused chapter), it is Jamaica's transition to a tourism economy and its closely related fruit trade in the late nineteenth century that informs the photograph's production. [...]

Starting in 1889, Jamaica's British crown government, the white mercantile elite, and their British and American corporate bedfellows aimed to promote a new ideal of the colony for the purposes of promoting tourism and a new fruit trade, particularly in bananas. Toward this end, tourism and fruit industry advocates in Jamaica organized an international exhibition in 1891 that they hoped would bring new visibility to what they deemed "the New Jamaica" as an "unequal health resort and as a profitable field of settlement for would-be British Colonists or United States citizens."[6] The American United Fruit Company and the British Elder, Dempster, and Company—both of which transported tourists and bananas on their steamships—were doubly invested in refashioning the island. After the rapid decline of the colony's once crowning sugar industry in the early nineteenth century, the island's ruling classes complained that Jamaica could "hang only on the skirts of modern civilization."[7] Through tourism and new commerce, however, they prophesied that

5 As art historian David Boxer notes, "The photographers were in Jamaica at the invitation of the Governor to prepare a series of photographs for exhibition at the Chicago Columbian Exhibition in 1892"; Boxer, 20. For newspaper articles on the photography of Valentine and Sons in Jamaica, see *Daily Gleaner*, May 2, 1891; February 15, 1893; April 12, 1900, January 10, 1903.

6 C. J. Ward, *World's Fair: Jamaica at Chicago: An Account Descriptive of the Colony of Jamaica with Historical and Other Appendices* (New York, 1893), preface; Edgar Mayhew Bacon and Eugene Murray-Aaron, *The New Jamaica; Describing the Island, Explaining Its Conditions of Life and Growth and Discussing Its Mercantile Relations and Potential Importance; Adding Somewhat in Relation to Those Matters Which Directly Interest the Tourist and the Health Seeker* (New York: Walbridge; Kingston, A. W. Gardner, 1890).

7 *Daily Gleaner*, September 28, 1889.

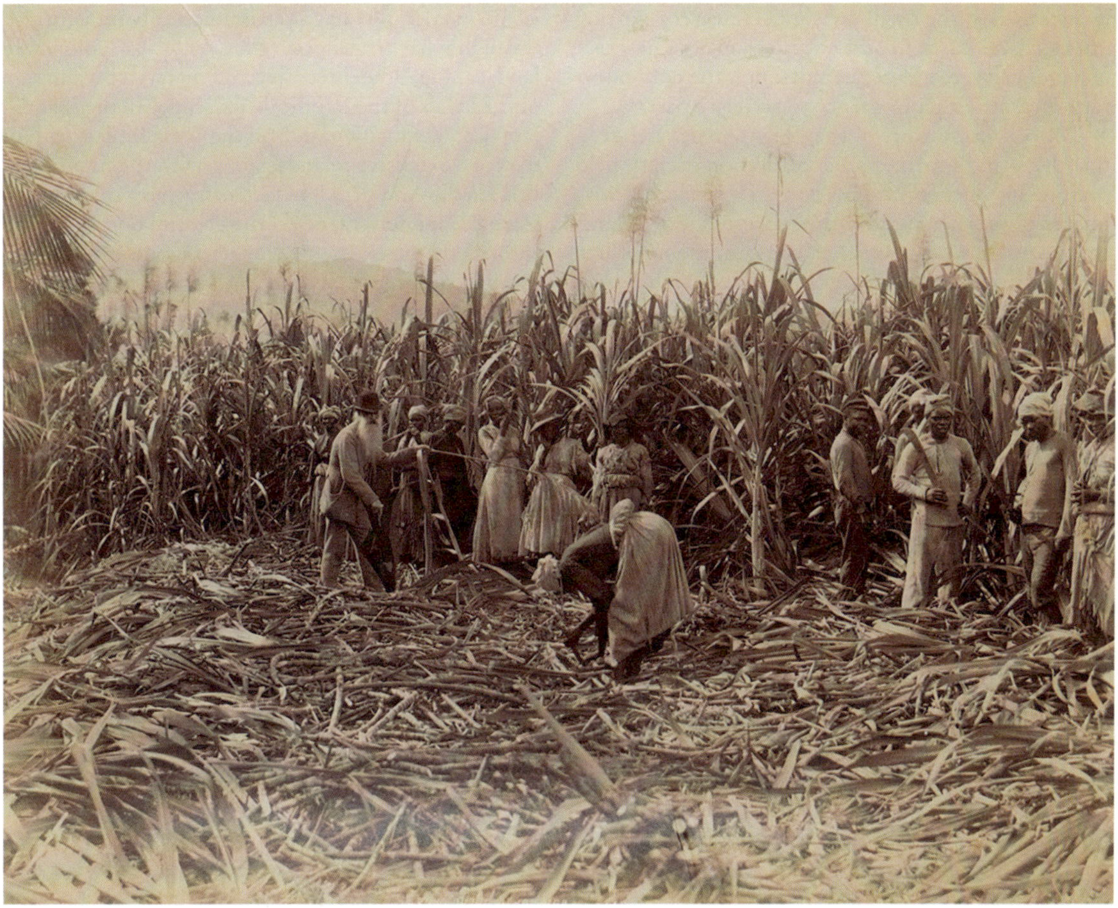

Figure 2. James Valentine and Sons, *Cane Cutters*, Jamaica, 1891

the New Jamaica, in the words of one hopeful resident, would "be 'discovered' in the modern sense, and if we succeed in pleasing the fastidious taste of the class [of tourists] . . . we may also in the modern sense be 'made.'"[8] Photographs, like the one Valentine and Sons created, were central to the formation and propagation of these ideals.

To bring about "the New Jamaica," promoters discerned that they had to create images to dispel widespread fears of the tropics as a place of death and disease, and, more specifically, they had to debunk concerns that Jamaica had been "ruined" by emancipation. As a contemporaneous newspaper editor put it in 1892, "The popular idea of Jamaica at home [in Britain] is of an island ruined by emancipation, a region of derelict estates with a scattered population of negro squatters, paying no rent, living in squalid huts, supporting life on yams and bananas."[9] Crafters of Jamaica's new image enlisted British, American, and local photographers to produce, perpetuate, and project a new vision of the post-emancipation era in the British colony. Their images often circulated as lantern slides, illuminating the faces of audiences; as photographs at colonial exhibitions, offering inhabitable vistas for international audiences; as representations in illustrated guides, providing visual testimony in texts; as stereographs, presenting privately experienced three-dimensional views of the island and its inhabitants; and as postcards, providing miniature and portable souvenirs of the colony. [...]

What is particularly pertinent here is that modern progress in the New Jamaica also entailed a return to the slave past, a desire for the former glory and prosperity that existed under slavery. A local visitor to one pavilion of Jamaica's international exhibition, for instance, lauded the perceived parallels between representations of cultivated lands from the "palmy days" of slavery and those of the New Jamaica, and encouraged exposition viewers to do the same. "When the public look at the diagram exhibited by the Jamaica Institute, showing the cane lands cultivated in 1790, the chief of the so-called 'palmy days' of old, and turn to the companion diagram showing the cane-fields cul-

8 *Daily Gleaner*, January 9, 1893.
9 *Daily Gleaner*, February 2, 1892.

tivated to-day, they will see some reason for writing of a *new* Jamaica."[10] In other words, Jamaica's newness, its modernity, could be seen through the contemporary landscape's acquiescence to slavery's past.

Moreover, crafters of the New Jamaica believed that the island's former slave plantation society held prestige in tourists' imaginations. This is likely why images of workers within the representational landscape of cane would remain a constant theme of late nineteenth-century photographs like *Cane Cutters*, although sugar production had declined to 11 percent of the agricultural product by this period. In an effort to support the notion that the islands had not declined since emancipation, some tourism promoters suggested in promotional literature that the landscape and those that labored on the land had not changed since the days of slavery. American promoters in particular propagated this view. In the United Fruit Company magazine, *The Golden Caribbean*, published in 1904, for instance, writer A. M. Kellogg remarked on "the stationary civilization of the black population" in Jamaica.[11] He maintained, "They [the black population] are no longer slaves, but they remain much as they were at the time of their emancipation in 1834… The truth is that the languor that seizes at once on us when we land has permanently affected them, and they have become constitutionally lazy."[12] The same periodical reproduced a text from 1790 from the planter William Beckford and assured readers that "this charming island has not changed in the least in over one hundred years."[13] The United Fruit Company also reproduced photographs of their own plantations in the same *Golden Caribbean* publication and in contemporaneous promotional literature.[14] In such images they replace the sugar crops of old with newly transplanted banana plants. In other words, tourism promoters framed the period of slavery as an ideal era in Jamaica's history—a time when the potential of the land and its inhabitants were realized—and quite literally framed, through photographs, their own plantations as continuing the slave-owners' legacy.

This return to the slave past as a development scheme in the New Jamaica performed two historical erasures at once. First, it presented the island's slave-maintained plantations as naturally occurring and aesthetically ideal landscapes, even though much of the island's geography had been dramatically transformed through what art historian Jill Casid calls "colonial relandscaping," the discursive and material production of the ideals of the "tropical landscape" in the island.[15] Jamaica, like many islands in the West Indies, had undergone extensive relandscaping with the first plantations in the Americas.[16] In fact, many parts of the island were completely razed to the ground and recreated through the introduction of botanical grafts from around the British Empire. Second, the literal late nineteenth-century focus on the slave-maintained sugar plantation also effectively erased and idealized the subsequent dramatic transformations of the landscape inaugurated by the new fruit industry. The United Fruit Company dramatically transformed both the landscape and labor relations on the island through its transnational conglomeration of their fruit plantations. By claiming that nothing had changed since slavery, the United Fruit Company erased, naturalized, and aestheticized their recent transplantation of the island, encouraging visitors and locals alike to see these transformations not as changes at all but as somehow a naturally occurring, seamless extension of and return to slavery's natural order.

The fruit companies and other authors of the New Jamaica, while promoting the immutable nature of Jamaica's landscape, did help to inaugurate a change in the way visitors viewed the island: they encouraged travelers to recognize value in the colony's picturesque scenery and its inhabitants. As an editorial entitled "The New Jamaica" outlined, "There is another new thing connected with Jamaica. The character of its scenery is not new. So far from that, it is as old as the hills. But the recognition of it and of the character of the climate is new."[17] Through the efforts of promoters, gazing at and photographing the island's scenery became a new form of commodity in the island. Tourism industry supporters encouraged visitors to travel to its contemporary plantations, in particular to view the landscape and those who labored on it. The United Fruit Company indeed installed railcars on their plantations that they used for this purpose. A rare stereograph, dating from 1890 and taken by the photographer C. H. Graves pictures one such observation car bearing well-dressed white male and female passengers in the process of sightseeing on the plantation (Fig. 3).[18] "Everyone who goes to Jamaica wants to see bananas

---

10 *Daily Gleaner*, January 29, 1891.
11 Kellogg's article from *The Golden Caribbean* was reprinted in *Daily Gleaner*, January 26, 1904.
12 *Daily Gleaner*, January 26, 1904.
13 The editors of *The Golden Caribbean* framed William Beckford's statements with this quote: "We accidentally picked up an old volume published in England, about 1790, by William Bickford [sic], an old time English painter"; *The Golden Caribbean* 1, no. 1 (Nov. 1903): 4.
14 *The Golden Caribbean 1*, no. 1 (Nov.1903): 3, 5.
15 Jill H. Casid, *Sowing Empire: Landscape and Colonization* (Minneapolis, 2005), 1–14.
16 Casid, 14–24.
17 *Daily Gleaner*, January 29, 1891.
18 The stereograph is rare in that it makes the tourists, the consumers of Jamaica's newly recognized scenery and laborers, the subject of the photograph, in a reversal of the typical scenarios in which tourists observed and photographed local laborers.

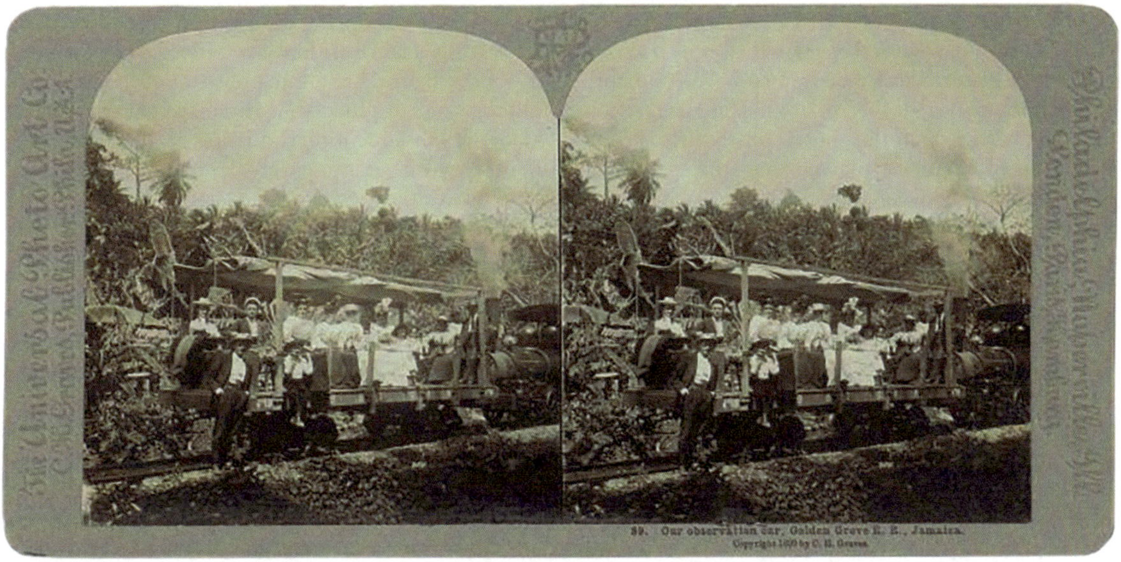

Figure 3. Carleton H. Graves, *Our Observation Car, Golden Grove R. R.*, Jamaica, 1899. Stereograph, 3.5 × 7 in.

growing, and guests are always welcome at the immense plantation of the United Fruit Company at Golden Vale," one early guidebook crowed.[19] The Graves and Valentine and Sons photographs capture this particular and peculiar moment when the plantation and black laborers became objects of touristic leisure; when, as photography historian Peter Osborne puts it, the "overseeing stare of the planter with time and space in his hands" metamorphosed into "the ludic, pleasuring gaze of the tourists with time and space *on* their hands."[20]

It is precisely this image pool, filled with photographs produced precisely when the needs of the agricultural industry intersected with the demands of touristic leisure in the late nineteenth century, that some late twentieth-century historians—like Craton, Walvin, and Wright—dip into to reflect on slavery. Given that tourism and fruit industry promoters created images like the *Cane Cutters* that picture laboring and lounging black workers to reframe the new fruit plantations through the lens of slavery, to both bring about and disguise modernity, what view of slavery in the British Empire can they offer? And how is slavery reconfigured in the process? I do not want to dwell on the obvious historical incongruities and temporal warps produced when a late nineteenth-century image is presented as representative of slavery—on the way the details of the image, such as the figures' dress, if understood as set in the era of slavery, would be a misrepresentation of the period. Indeed, the very engagement with the camera evident in the image captures a particular historically specific understanding of what it means to be represented as a photographic subject.

Rather, what I find more pertinent epistemologically is the publication's recasting of the late nineteenth-century image as representative of the slave era, which inadvertently replays precisely the narrative of the New Jamaica that the fruit companies and ruling classes were projecting through photographs in the last decade of the nineteenth century: the narrative that nothing had changed since the end of slavery, that the landscape and ethnoscape remained unchanged since the sun set on that peculiar institution. Perhaps to enhance the case that the late nineteenth-century image represents the slave past, in *Slavery, Abolition, and Emancipation*, the book's designers appear to have altered the photograph to seem older, more antique, and to bear the visual traces of age. In the process, the image becomes a mirage, representing any desired time or place through its shadowy new form. The presentation of the image in *Slavery, Abolition, and Emancipation* threatens to enact in the register of the visual precisely the forms of historical erasure that became central to the production of certain touristic narratives of the New Jamaica. In a book purporting to offer a temporally accurate textual account of slavery, the image erases a certain temporal passage by reproducing a photograph that was designed precisely to occlude a sense of history and historicity. Post-production manipulation of the photograph further creates the sense of temporal erasure. The reproduction of *Cane Cutters* in the Craton, Walvin, and Wright volume conjures the dreamwork of tourism, which is itself based on a creative reimagining of slavery, on giving the slave past visual substance.

19 Mortimer C. DeSouza, *A Tourist's Guide to the Parishes of Jamaica: Together with an Account Descriptive of the Jamaica Exhibition, 1891, Being a Supplement to Desouza's...Jamaica Commercial Almanack* (Kingston, Jamaica: James Valentine & Sons, 1891).

20 Peter D. Osborne, *Travelling Light: Photography, Travel, and Visual Culture* (Manchester, England: Manchester University Press, 2000), 113.

The use of a photograph that aimed to aestheticize black labor to represent slavery in the book also runs the risk of historicizing a benign and even romantic sense of the period of forced labor. The image of picturesque blacks cannot begin to convey the daily negotiations of life on the plantation or the spectacular forms of bodily violence that governed black labor in the pre-emancipation period. As Saidiya Hartman reminds us, it is difficult to recover the experience of slavery through any image, photographic or literary, since attempts to empathize with or figure the slave often result in the occlusion or displacement of his or her subjectivity.[21] The representational slippery allusiveness of slavery through photographic representation in the Anglophone Caribbean seems especially evident in *Slavery, Abolition, and Emancipation*. Indeed, in a publication about black slave labor, it is notable that the only figure in the *Cane Cutters* photograph who explicitly appears engaged in agricultural work is erased. The black woman, who bends over with axe in hand, is removed from the frontispiece. The odd shape of the top photograph seems to stem from efforts to crop the figure out of the image altogether. Like the post-development manipulation of nineteenth-century photographs, the book's creators engage in their own form of visual excision. Only the barest traces of the figure, a crescent moon–shaped sliver of her back, remain visible in the image. In the process, the photograph originally enlisted to signify slavery in the end resists showing black subjects performing agricultural work, presenting instead figures who participate in a form of labor new to the late nineteenth century: working as a photographic subject.

The absented figure is revealing not only for the labor she performs, but for what her image refuses. She does not appear to offer her body readily as a visual commodity. Her "*Gleaner*esque" pose does not yield to the camera, as do those of her counterparts, who uniformly turn their eyes, faces, and bodies toward the photographer. Indeed, her steadfast attention to her labor and stooping position result in the least camera-friendly position one can imagine. This is not to attribute intentionality to the figure, since her appearance in the same position in two photographs makes it clear that she posed at the urging of the photographer, holding the posture for the time required to secure the photographic images and retaining it perhaps as the photographer reorganized the other figures. Irrespective of the conditions and purposes of the image's creation, the resulting posture of the woman denies visual consumption. Indeed, the very opacity of the figure, her anomalous presence within the photograph's production, is visualized in her exclusion from the subsequent reproduction of the photograph. In other words, it is precisely because she is not made available to the viewer in the typical ways that photographers required black subjects to address the camera in Jamaican tourism-oriented photographs that she is likely excised from the subsequent reproduction. The woman's erasure, I want to suggest, highlights how we might and should read absences in images for what they make present, how we might read photographs against the grain to assess certain histories and historiographies of African diasporic subjects. What does the exclusion of the figure render legible about possibilities and the impossibilities of certain forms of knowledge through the photographic archive? What does the figure's disqualification from the production of history reveal about visual ideals of slavery specifically? What ways of remembering slavery does the photographic archive of tourism conveniently offer and occlude?

Although I have concentrated primarily on Craton, Walvin, and Wright's book, their use of photography is not unique. Their book simply provides a catalyst for a conversation about a widespread practice.[22] [...] I suspect that many authors of books pertaining to slavery, as well as their publishers and designers, use photographs to render slavery more legible, the unrepresentable more imaginable, the unrecorded more truthful, the past more present. They lay claim to the ontology of the photographic image and its indexicality to substantiate their narrative accounting of slavery. For a historical period that has often been shrouded by what Marcus Wood refers to as "blind memory," photographs may appear to offer an unblinking witness to the institutional practices of slavery.[23] Photography historian Jens Ruchatz points out that photographs are intrinsic to the externalization of memory for many social groups.[24] Photography is a technology through which memory can be materialized and stored outside the body, and in the process transmitted across generations over time. The books' creators may use the photographs to give slavery material form, substantiating and consolidating memory and history in the process.

By using photographs to represent slavery, book producers and authors also place the experience of slavery within a genealogy of other traumatic world events

21 Saidiya V. Hartman, *Scenes of Subjection: Terror, Slavery, and Self-Making in Nineteenth-Century America* New York: Oxford UP, 1997).
22 [Ed. While acknowledging the complex responsibilities for determining the inclusion of the photographs in academic publishing, Thompson cites a number of recent academic volumes in order to acknowledge the "broader use of the photographic archive to cast historical light on slavery, and that, regardless of how and why these photographs came to be in these accounts, they inform and frame the presentation of historical knowledge about the region." For a list of related publications, see Thompson, 2011, 55.]
23 Wood, *Blind Memory: Visual Representations of Slavery in England and America* (New York: Routledge, 2000).
24 Jens Ruchatz, "The Photograph as Externalization and Trace," in *Cultural Memory Studies: An International and Interdisciplinary Handbook*, ed. Astrid Erll (Berlin/New York: de Gruyter, 2008).

that have become ingrained in popular memory through photography. Alan Trachtenberg suggests that the impact of photography on the production of historical knowledge was first felt in the mid-nineteenth century, at the time of the American Civil War.[25] Strikingly, despite the history-transforming presence of the camera in the era, slavery remained a blind spot in early Civil War histories.[26] The photographic production of history perhaps reached its apogee in the Second World War. Photographs taken by Allied forces at the end of the war became widely representative of the horrors of concentration camps during Nazi rule.[27] Interestingly, according to Siegfried Kracauer, not only did photographs offer a visual record of events, but photography's seeming ability to reconstruct a "series of events in their temporal succession without any gaps" also reproduced the temporal unfolding of historical narratives.[28] What Kracauer describes as "the photography of time" provided a technological ally to historicist reconstructions of the past.[29] The impulse to use photographs in histories of slavery in the British West Indies may respond to this photographic colonization of the imagination, and even temporality, of modern history over the last century and a half.

Recent historical accounts of slavery in the British West Indies that use photographs from the late nineteenth century as illustrations, however, inadvertently present what might be described as a nonhistoricist sense of temporal unfolding as outlined by Kracauer. By publishing photographs that date from a time period that does not coincide with slavery but purports to represent it, the publications juxtapose and commingle different eras, resulting in a distinctly nonlinear sense of time and history. Rather than interpret the reproduction of the late nineteenth-century photographs simply as incongruous, might we consider such reconfigurations of temporality to have their own historical value, particularly when it comes to histories of slavery? In other words, might the kinds of ruptures and repetitions of time facilitated by photographs in these accounts in fact be fitting within historical narratives of slavery and its legacy in the Anglophone Caribbean?

This atemporal use of photography, as it is used in these accounts, provocatively recalls Nobel laureate Toni Morrison's concept of rememory, her characterization of the way the traumatic experiences of the past maintain a living presence with the world of slaves and their descendants.[30] More specifically, in the case of historical accounts in the Anglophone Caribbean, such photographs may encourage reflection on how the specter of slavery maintained a living presence in the New Jamaica. Many historians and postcolonial critics observe that the late nineteenth century and the era of slavery are linked by more than touristic nostalgia for the palmy days of the slave-maintained plantation. They point to the constitutive relationship between tourism and slavery. Frank Taylor, for one, insists on casting tourism as it developed in the late nineteenth century as "intrinsically . . . a neoplantation enterprise" built on and extending some of the socio-economic relations and hierarchies that existed under slavery.[31] While being careful not to collapse the experiences of oppression in the era of plantation slavery with those that governed the tourism trade in the Anglophone Caribbean, literary scholar Ian Strachan also maintains that, in the English-speaking Caribbean, "in a number of crucial ways, tourism has grown out of and sustains the [slave and post-emancipation] plantation economy."[32] Intriguingly, Walvin, Craton, and Wright make a related argument about the connection between slavery and subsequent plantation systems in the very publication that features the Valentine and Sons photograph of the sugar plantation. They argue: "As long as plantations lasted, so did all the socio-economic effects usually ascribed solely to slavery days."[33] In other words, the commingling of photographs from the New Jamaica with descriptions of slavery results in a reconfiguration of temporality, which in turn calls attention to the way plantation slavery informed the structure of the tourism and fruit trades, how it shaped the socio-economic horizons of post-emancipation Jamaica. This use of such photographs projects and presents slavery not as a thing of the past but as an enduring presence in late nineteenth-century Jamaica.

Present-day historians and critics are not the only ones to telescope between slavery and the era of tourism as inaugurated by the New Jamaica. In the late nineteenth and early twentieth century, residents in Jamaica were quick to characterize the Elder, Dempster, and Company's; the United Fruit Company's; and

25 Trachtenberg, "Albums of War."

26 Trachtenberg, "Albums of War." See also Wood's observation that few photographs of slavery existed prior to the Civil War; Wood, *Blind Memory*, 268.

27 Although, as Frances Guerin and Roger Hallas suggest, as early as the 1950s some scholars, survivors, and critics had questioned the "representability" of the photographic archive; photographs became central to historical imagination of and transmission of the Holocaust and other traumatic events, as well as truth claims about those events. Frances Guerin and Roger Hallas, introduction to *The Image and the Witness: Trauma, Memory, and Visual Culture*, ed. Frances Guerin and Roger Hallas (New York: Wallflower Press), 6.

28 Siegfried Kracauer and Thomas Y. Levin, "Photography," *Critical Inquiry* 19, no. 3 (Spring 1993): 425.

29 Kracauer and Levin, 426.

30 Morrison, *Beloved*, 35.

31 Frank Taylor, *To Hell with Paradise: A History of the Jamaican Tourist Industry* (Pittsburgh: University of Pittsburgh Press, 1993).

32 Ian G. Strachan, *Paradise and Plantation: Tourism and Culture in the Anglophone Caribbean* (Charlotesville, VA: University of Virginia, 2002), 9.

33 Craton, Walvin, and Wright, *Slavery, Abolition, and Emancipation*, xi.

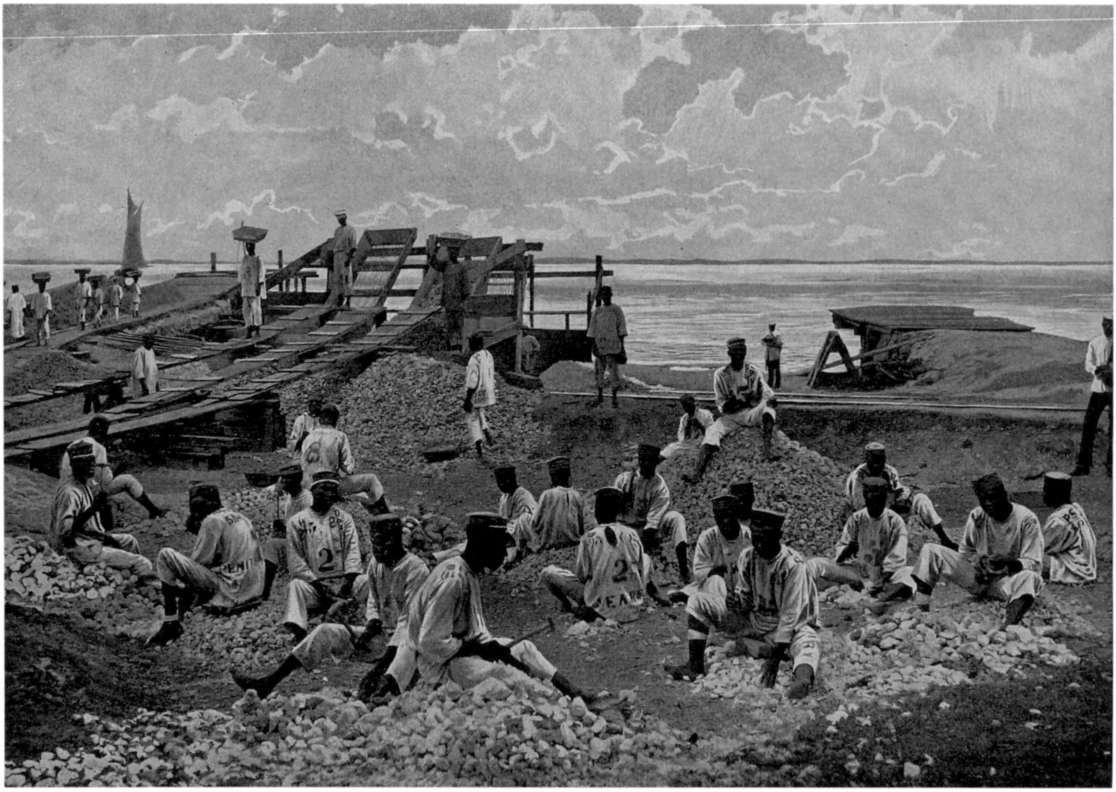

Figure 4. James Johnston, "Hard Labour," in *Jamaica, the New Riviera. A Pictorial Description of the Island and its Attractions*, 1903.

the crown government's labor practices as they related to black Jamaicans and indentured Indian laborers on the fruit plantations as constitutive of a "new slavery," to use a term blazoned across the front page of one local newspaper in the early twentieth century. [34] In many cases, those who most insisted on drawing parallels between the New Jamaica and the old plantation system vehemently opposed the new system of Indian indentureship because it undermined wage-based black labor.[35]

Crucially, late nineteenth-century newspaper reports suggest that many black Jamaicans saw more than metaphorical links between the slave past and the celebrated New Jamaica period. Indeed, although organizers of the island's great exhibition hoped the event would draw local as well as international audiences, many blacks steered clear of the exhibition site because they believed it was part of a plot to re-enslave them. As the local *Gleaner* recounted: "The story goes that Captain L. D. Baker [head of the United Fruit Company] has been actively engaged in the importation of shackles in casks in large quantities for the purposes of entrapping the people when they got to the Exhibition and making them slaves again...The Exhibition is a trap."[36] Another newspaper article ridiculed the popular idea that "the Exhibition would . . . cause a going back to Slavery in any form." It berated "the people [who were] not yet seeming sufficiently intelligent to see the difference between entering into voluntary agreements to work for certain parties or properties and the old time bondage of slavery."[37] The descriptions of the exhibition as a trap reveal that, although the island's governing classes saw the event as inaugurating a New Jamaica, some of the formerly enslaved and their descendants thought it held the power to return them to the condition, if not the time, of slavery. The prevalence of this belief suggests that some black Jamaicans, even sixty years after emancipation, conceived of their freedom as something so fragile and alterable that it could be taken away at any moment. That they believed the shackles of slavery awaited them confirms a point made by scholars like Saidiya Hartman and Diana Paton that the lines between freedom and unfreedom were not indelibly marked by the proclamation of emancipation.[38] It appears that the memory of slavery—the bodily experience of being enslaved in casks—had a lived presence in late nine-

34 *Daily Gleaner*, January 27, 1910.
35 Thompson, *An Eye for the Tropics*, 78–80.
36 *Daily Gleaner*, November 7, 1890.
37 *Daily Gleaner*, November 7, 1890.

teenth-century Jamaica. For some blacks, the New Jamaica seemed a clear picture of the days of old. In provocative ways, then, the historical accounts that juxtapose the tourism-oriented photographs with the history of slavery draw the same parallels as did the suspicious black residents between the New Jamaica and the period of slavery.

The photographs of the late nineteenth century may provide an even more interesting linchpin between slavery and the New Jamaica. In the last decade of the nineteenth century and into the early twentieth, photography served precisely to manage what historian Thomas Holt describes as "the problem of freedom," the colonial authorities' efforts to govern black Jamaicans outside the structures of subjection that maintained the slave plantation.[39] Specifically, the colonial authorities faced the challenge of transforming slaves into voluntary wage-based workers without using the techniques of surveillance, discipline, and punishment that ordered and produced black labor before emancipation. The camera would play a role in these new phases of social regulation and labor structures introduced by colonial authorities in the post-emancipation era.

The regulatory purposes of photography at the turn of the twentieth century are evident in a tourism- oriented photograph of prison laborers taken by the minister-turned-tourism-promoter James Johnston in 1903 (Fig. 4). Like Valentine and Sons, Johnston worked as part of the colonial government's and the fruit companies' tourism and trade efforts. The photograph, titled "*Hard Labour,*" appeared as an illustration in Johnston's tourist guide and in his global lantern lectures promoting tourism.[40] The image pictures chained black male prisoners breaking stones in a desolate stone quarry. Several cast a wary eye toward the photographer, while others turn away from the camera entirely. One prisoner wears the word "penitence" or "penitentiary" across his back. His counterparts literally wear the terms of their sentences on their uniforms. The photograph pictures a form of social discipline and punishment that was a central component of Jamaica's penal system in the post-emancipation era and gives visual support to the belief in the redemptive and reformative potential of coerced prison labor.[41]

The "*Hard Labour*" photograph highlights the intersecting forms of social control in late nineteenth-century Jamaica and the visual economy of the tourist trade, and it calls attention to the blurred lines between slavery and freedom in the post-emancipation era. As historian Diana Paton details, although the crown government transformed the Jamaican penal system after emancipation, the state contradictorily relied on hard labor—and, after 1850, corporal punishment—as a form of rehabilitation, so that inmates would willingly accept labor contracts upon their release.[42] In other words, in the post-emancipation period the state managed wage workers by using a form of coerced labor reminiscent of the practices employed during slavery. No wonder that the critic of local blacks who refused to go to Jamaica's international exhibition accused them of not knowing the difference between "voluntary agreements to work" and "old time bondage."[43] Even judges at the time recognized the similarities between prison labor and slavery. One member of the judiciary, in the course of sentencing a man to a three-year term, explicitly admonished him: "While there you will have to labour like a slave."[44] Throughout the post-emancipation period, as Paton details, the colonial state depended heavily, in some parishes entirely, on unpaid prison labor for the maintenance of post-emancipation infrastructure. The stone quarry pictured in the Johnston photograph was but one of the places Jamaican prisoners labored in the post-emancipation era in colonial efforts to turn them into hard-working citizens. The photograph in this way pictures a site in which contradictory forms of freedom, as identified by the authorities and black residents alike, coexisted in post-emancipation Jamaica.

The "*Hard Labour*" photograph also provocatively calls attention to processes of surveillance that were intrinsic to the island's post-emancipation penal system. Paton points out that authorities in Jamaica created new, modern penal facilities in the 1860s. The new prisons, like those designed by English social reformer Jeremy Bentham, were designed with a "hall of inspections" to facilitate the surveillance of prisoners.[45] Since prisoners spent substantial time on public works projects, surveillance was often carried out in public spaces by overseers and by the public more generally.[46] This process of public and institutional surveillance, so central to governance in post-emancipation Jamaica, intersected with tourism-oriented uses of photography. The connection is hinted at in the "*Hard Labour*" photograph, which

38 Hartman, *Scenes of Subjection*; Diana Paton, *No Bond but the Law: Punishment, Race, and Gender in Jamaican State Formation*, 1780–1870 (Durham, NC, 2004).

39 Holt, *The Problem of Freedom*.

40 James Johnston, *Jamaica, the New Riviera: A Pictorial Description of the Island and Its Attractions* (London: House of Commons of the United Kingdom, 1903); James Johnston, *Optical Lantern Lectures on Jamaica, "The New Riviera"* (Bristol, UK, 1903).

41 Paton, *No Bond but the Law*, 90.

42 Paton, 90.

43 *Daily Gleaner*, November 7, 1890.

44 Paton, *No Bond but the Law*, 137.

45 Paton, 128.

46 Paton, 135.

not only pictures penitence and presents it as a touristic sight but also positions and presents the camera, literally and figuratively, as a central surveilling presence in the scene of black penitence. The photographer's part in producing disciplined black laboring subjects is evident. This is suggested in the positioning of, and even redefinition of, the overseer in the image. A uniformed officer occupies the margins of the quarry, barely visible on the right side of the photograph. More centrally positioned, and assuming the primary role of overseer, is the photographer himself (and subsequent observers of the scene), whom the prisoners acknowledge through their gaze. The camera's overseeing presence extended from prisons to the cane fields, from explicit scenes of discipline like the stone quarry to the touristic surveillance of black wage earners on the plantation. The photographers' gaze, whether directed through the tourists' viewfinder or through the eyes of plantation visitors or tourist promoters, played a role in managing black labor in the New Jamaica era. At the very least, the importance of photographing black laborers in the new visual economies of tourism resulted in the constant possibility of inspection for many Jamaican laborers. One laborer at the turn of the twentieth century complained precisely about the intrusion of camera-toting tourists during the workday, remarking, "An when de tourists come up de country and see we working in de ground, dem is not going to do anything fa we, but take picta and laugh at we."[47]

Not only would laborers have been conscious of their possible inspection by tourists, but in the late nineteenth century they would also have been acquainted with the subtle and not so subtle forms of bodily discipline required of them before its lens. The men and women who acknowledge the camera in the Valentine and Sons photograph offer some insight into how much laborers were accustomed to the presence of the camera and to the new work of being a photographic subject. Bodily performance for the camera is perhaps most explicit in the posture of the woman who poses with her head tilted to the side and hand on her chin. Like the stooping woman, she is the only figure to appear in both versions of the image, and, of all the women pictured, she seems most aware of posing for the camera, most attentive to the bodily ideals of the picturesque subject.[48] [...] This awareness of how one should behave for the camera, I want to suggest, had broader implications. The presence (or even suggestion) of a photographer elicited certain behaviors, a phenomenon that itself constituted a way of overseeing, managing, and revaluing new forms of labor in the New Jamaica era.

That the island's black inhabitants could be photographed, that they were willing to submit to the camera, that they performed the kind of bodily discipline necessary for capture and consumption by photography implicitly constituted a selling point for the promoters of tourism. Tellingly, when local residents refused to be photographed or when they demanded money for posing, travelers framed these incidents as acts of black indiscipline or evidence of the corrupting influence of American capitalism on the British colony.[49] The assumption that the natives were photographable was the visual equivalent of saying the natives were friendly, an important mantra when trying to market travel to a majority black island to white British and North American tourists in the late nineteenth century.

It is worth pointing out too that black photographic subjects were not the only ones framed by the disciplining lens of photography. The tourists themselves were also subject to the lessons of photography—from the other end of the camera. Through plantation tours, photographs, and stereographs (to recall the stereograph of the plantation tour), tourism promoters aimed to indoctrinate tourists into a new vision of post-emancipation Jamaica, encouraging them to see value in British and American civilizing missions more generally.

While tourism promoters' photographs aimed to picture and produce black discipline, these ambitions were never realized, either in photographs or on plantations. Black Jamaicans sometimes refused to inhabit photographs or inhabited them in ways that sometimes simultaneously confirmed and confounded ideals of the island's residents as "civilized subjects" or docile photographic ones. [...]

The historical accounts that use photographs from the late nineteenth century to represent slavery ultimately transpose the period of slavery and tourism in ways that might enable a more complicated historical window precisely into relationship between these eras, a connection that the formerly enslaved may have ultimately recognized. It is possible that some of the blacks who were subject to touristic forms of social overseeing in the late nineteenth century associated it with structures of governance under slavery. This may

47 Quoted in Bessie Pullen-Burry, *Ethiopia in Exile: Jamaica Revisited* (London: T. F. Unwin, 1905), 30.

48 In one image she appears in the same position under the shelter of a makeshift parasol held by an older white or brown Jamaican male. "Brown," a term used locally, describes a class of mixed-race Jamaicans who, within colonial hierarchies, ranked higher than Jamaicans of primarily African descent but lower than the British colonials, the former planter class, and the white mercantile elite.

49 This was evident in geographer and naturalist Harry Johnston's account of his travels throughout the Caribbean, *The Negro in the New World* (1910). Johnston was disarmed when members of the Maroon community in Jamaica demanded monetary compensation when he aimed a camera in their direction or at the surrounding scenery. A faithful believer in the virtues of the British civilizing mission in the West Indies, Johnston attributed such behavior to the corrupting forces of the Americans; Harry Johnston, *The Negro in the New World* (London: Methuen & Co., 1910), 279.

explain in part why some black Jamaicans were so certain that their re-enslavement lay just around the exhibition's corner. The forms of social control employed to manage blacks in the late nineteenth century may have recalled types of surveillance and discipline that former slaves and their descendants associated with slavery. The use of photographs in contemporary historical accounts do not simply posit connections between the slavery days of old and the purported New Jamaica, but highlight the very medium through which a contiguity was maintained, the means through which a social overseeing and bodily regulation of blacks would continue to be carried out: the medium of photography itself.

While the use of the photographic images in historical accounts like *Slavery, Abolition, and Emancipation* offers the possibility of new histories of slavery, post-emancipation, and photography, the very compulsion to mine the photographic archive for representational traces of slavery may leave certain expectations about the evidentiary nature of photography intact. Such interpretative lenses reinforce notions of the historical value of certain forms of representation. I would argue that slavery in the Anglophone Caribbean, and perhaps in the African diaspora more generally, demands a more radical reformulation of the "evidence of things unseen" and unphotographed. Absences in the photographic record should be viewed not as a lack for which compensation is necessary, but as an intrinsic part of, and even representation of, the history of slavery and post-emancipation in the region.[50] [...]

50 James Baldwin, *The Evidence of Things Not Seen*, 1st ed. (New York: Henry Holt & Co., 1985).

The Other Half and How They Live: Story in Pictures [Reconstruction of a Magic Lantern Slide Lecture Presented at the Sixth Annual Convention of Christian Workers]

Jacob Riis

November 9, 1891

While I was walking down Pennsylvania Avenue today, after leaving the train, I came opposite a store which had just then caught fire. A man ran out hatless and coatless and cried for help. Everybody ran for whatever was needed to put that fire out with; the fire engines came with a crash, and everybody came, and everybody had something to say as to how that fire should be put out. In a few minutes it was out. That is the way, friends, we go about fighting fire. Everybody is ready to do something. But how does the case stand when a whole city full of people are going straight to perdition for the want of somebody to say, "Come, let me help you! You are my brother; we are going to the same heaven together. Now, let us help each other!" How do we do in such a case? We often stand by with such a spectacle before us and say, "Well, it is none of our business." And if some man, whose heart has been stirred by what be has seen gets up and cries, "Come and help us save our brethren," men say, "That man is a crank. He means well, but he has never learned to look out for 'number one,' and he is for ever poking his nose into other people's business." That is what is done and said too often. Now, dear friends, how long is that to continue? Brethren, how long are we to stand up with that mark of Cain on our brows? How long are we going to ask the question, "Am I my brother's keeper?" How long, I say, is that going to continue? What good is it that the shackles were stricken off the limbs of the black slaves, and what does it avail that the emblem of liberty and justice, that beautiful monument to the Nation's greatness, stands on the hill yonder, when millions and millions of men in this country are going down to perdition for the want of somebody to come and help save them!

You ask me, "What has all this got to do with how the other half lives?" Everything. Friends, let me set before you some facts by which we can show this. Some stand up and say, "Yes, that is very well," and hand over five or ten dollars and go on. But that wont do: we will all have to turn in and put out the fire.

In the city of New York, friends, we have outdone long since, in the span of a single long life, what it took ages and ages to do in the cities of the Old World. The slums over there are reproduced here and with intenser wickedness, because of the American atmosphere. In that city to-day, which, a hundred years ago did not have a tenement; three-fourths of the people live in tenements. When the last count was made there were about thirty-seven thousand tenements and more than twelve hundred thousand call them home. Of course, I am not going to tell you that all of these tenement houses are desperately bad, for if they were, New York city would long ago have been destroyed by a worse mob than ever disgraced Paris, but enough are of the very worst and thousands upon thousands of their tenants are compelled to live as no human being ought to live anywhere. Our tenements throw off a scum of from forty to fifty thousand human wrecks that go to the Island institutions year by year. They support a standing army of ten thousand tramps. They turned out in the last eight years a round half million beggars and sent one-tenth of all who died in the city for five years past to the Potter's Field. One in ten, ten in a hundred taking the rich and the poor alike, gone to the paupers burying ground! Realize that, dear friends, if you want to measure the depth of degradation, for some people ask whether it is so and say, "This man is an enthusiast; he is a crank on that subject, and he puts it too strongly." You, who have been busy at work among the poor people, know with what agony of fear they fight off that last crowning disgrace of being laid in a grave nobody has paid for, and you can understand what it means that for five or six years—only last year and this year has there been a slight reduction and that is due to a new law providing decent burial at the public expense for veteran dead—the Potter's Field has claimed one-tenth of all.

The time allotted to me to-night is so brief and the subject is so very big that we begin right away, all of us going together down into the slums of New York city to see what has got to be done down there and learn how by the blessing of God to help in the work I am informed, and I am glad of it, that neither in this city nor anywhere else in this country is there anything like the slums of New York city.

We will begin at the beginning. I said that a hundred years ago, yes, less than that, seventy-five years ago, there was no such thing as a tenement in New York city. It is a modern invention of the devil. Here we are at the "cradle" of the tenement (shows picture of "Gotham Court"). Down where that house stands lived George Washington. He moved down on Broadway, because his friends persuaded him he was too far up town. This is the Fourth Ward, long given up to the worst abominations in the way of human dwellings That alley has a bad record. A murder was committed

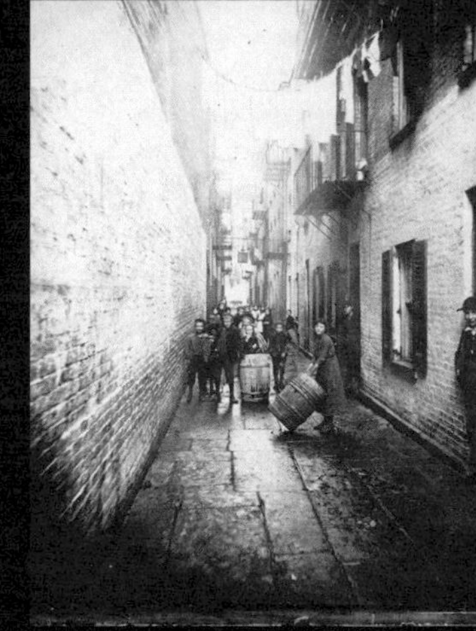

there less than a week ago, and it was not the first by a great many. In point of nationality it is typical of all down town of New York city. When I took a census once of that alley, there were one hundred and forty families, one hundred Irish, thirty-eight Italians, and two German, and not a native-born individual in the entire alley except the children. No one but an Irishman could have thought of the answer one gave me when I asked him what was the reason a policeman was always on duty there. He said, "It's on account of them two Dutch families that live in the alley. They make so much trouble." [Laughter.] A Chinaman of whom I asked the same question outside the alley took another view of it. He just took one look down the alley and then hurried on; "Lem Ilish velly bad," he said. [Laughter.] When the cholera came along some years ago, the ratio of deaths was not over sixteen or seventeen to the thousand in the "clean" wards uptown, but down there in that alley it was one hundred and ninety-five to the thousand. That is what such a place stands for in times of epidemic.

There is a tenement next door that stands to me as typical of the wrath to come—I should say rather of the wrath that was. You will see in this picture (shows picture of another court or alley called "Mullin's alley") the wall on this side—a bare wall standing five stories

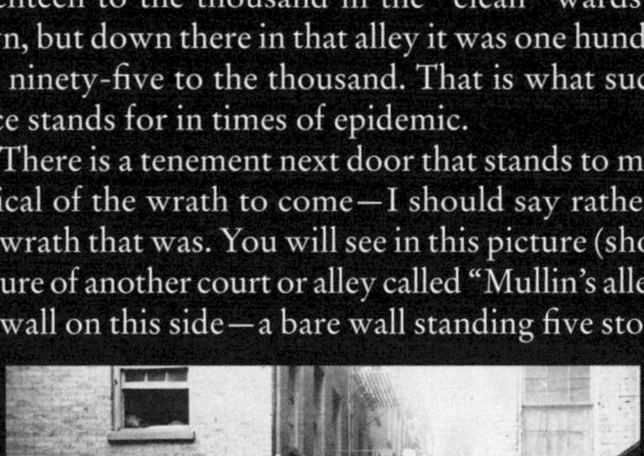

high right in front of the windows. The man who owned the tenement quarreled with his neighbor about the line fence, as neighbors sometimes do, and knocked him down. The neighbor was a Quaker and could not fight back. But he found a way, and he built up that wall sixty years ago, a curse to future generations, for no gleam of sunlight ever passed through to the tenement. If that is not a monument of human wrath, I do not know what is.

Let me pass on to an alley two or three doors away from there, and, if there is one place on this earth that could be called God-forsaken, I think I should say that was the one. There is no such place, but that comes as near to it as anything I have ever found in New York city. It has been known for years as Blindman's Alley (shows picture of another court or alley called "Blindman's Alley"). It didn't get that name because the owner was blind, although he was, but

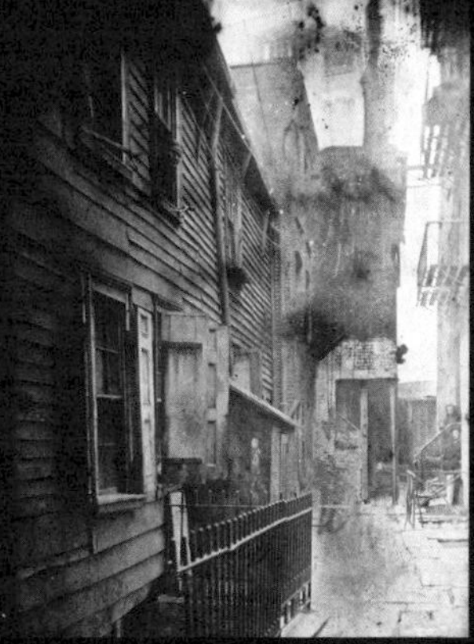

because the blind beggars in the city, or many of them, herded there for years and years. They only left it when the Board of Health, prompted by the exhibition of this very picture, at last compelled the owner to clean it up a couple of years ago. While they were there, the old man who owned the alley wrung four hundred thousand dollars out of their poverty and the misery of others nearly as wretched as they, as he told me himself when boasting of his wealth. I need not tell you what nationality was his, when I mention that he erected a monument for himself over in Calvary Cemetery long years before he died, and this was the inscription he put on it, "Sacred to the memory of Daniel Murphy. This shaft shall outlast the British Empire." [Laughter.] He died last summer, but before his death he shared the chief hardship of his tenants, for he grew stone-blind. When the Board of Health came in and made him clean up in the alley, he protested, "Let them live like hogs. They are no better." Let me take you upstairs (shows picture "Upstairs in Blindman's Alley"—room with three blind persons) and show you some of those tenants. There were five of them in all, but only three of them got into the picture. This is from a photograph by flash-light.
With unpracticed hands, for I was new at such work,

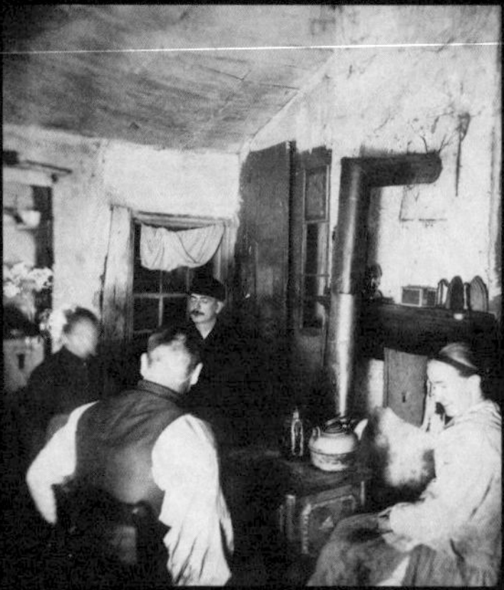

then, I managed to set fire to the house. When the flash died away I saw the rags and boards on the wall burning pretty lively and I did not feel at all happy about it, for there were five blind people, who had not the least idea of their danger, and four or five flights of stairs between us and the street. I put it out though, and burned my hands and clothes in doing it. When I had it out at last, I went down into the street and tried to get a policeman to go up there, but instead of sympathizing with me he laughed till the lamp-post he leaned against shook. "What, that place burn!" he said. "Why, certainly it did," I said, "I ought to know. I set fire to it myself." He said, "That place burn! Nothing of the kind! They call that house the 'Dirty Spoon.' It caught fire six times last winter, but could not burn. The dirt was so thick on the walls it smothered the fire." [Laughter.]

Now, friends, there you have some of the Christian work that you represent (shows picture of a sewing class of little girls in room of Gotham Court tenement).

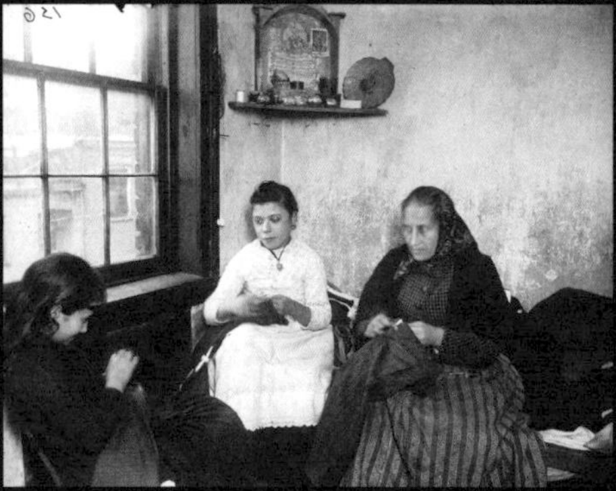

Somebody went down into that slum and settled there and made a home among those people and said, "Come, brother, let me help you." Day by day the children are brought in there and taught, and you will notice this one thing—take this lesson home with you—that when they are cleaned up and cared for and made presentable they are just as sweet and nice as your children and mine. It is the surroundings that make the difference. Care for their bodies first, and you can gain access to their souls in that way.

Let me show you the one picture of this collection which is not a photograph, but was drawn by an architect, so you can get some idea of what the tenement houses are (shows picture of "A Bird's Eye View East Side Tenement Block"). Some people tell me that the tenement houses are not as bad as they might be. I do

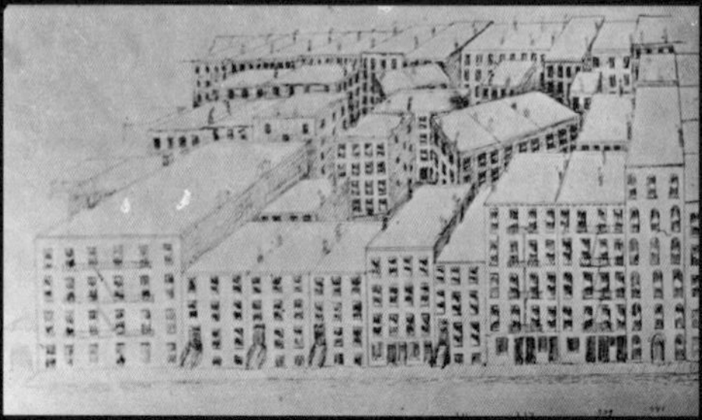

not know how bad they might be, but I personally think they are about as vile as anything that can be found anywhere. Just take a look at this, will you! Here in this city of homes you build a house on one lot and over on another street another, and between the two you have sunlight and air and grass and a place for your children to romp, and perhaps your neighbors, but in this block there is a house on one end of a lot and one on the other and one in between. Houses set end ways and edge ways and every which way, so that rents may be wrung out of their poor tenants. Now do you understand what is meant by the statement that tenement house property is good property. This is the sort of a place where the city missionary found four families housekeeping in the four corners of one room, and when he asked how they got along was told that they got along fairly well till one of the four families took a boarder. Then there was trouble. [Laughter.] Another poor woman who was struggling along there said to a missionary that, when she wanted a quiet place to pray, with the everlasting turmoil of that big hive, she had to put her head out of the window. [Laughter.]

Let us take one of the tenements—not one of the worst by any manner of means nor one of the best—and see what it looks like (shows picture of old rear-tenement in Roosevelt Street with clothes lines filled with clothes). You never would find it unless you were shown the way, for it stands back, so that nobody except one who knew where to look for it would ever come across it. When I took the picture I was bothered to death with clothes lines. Those clothes lines are always full of clothes. The poor are not often burdened with a change of clothing. If they want to keep clean they have to wash on Monday and Tuesday and Wednesday and Thursday and Friday and Saturday and sometimes on Sunday. [Laughter.] Some of them, I suppose, were lying in bed while their

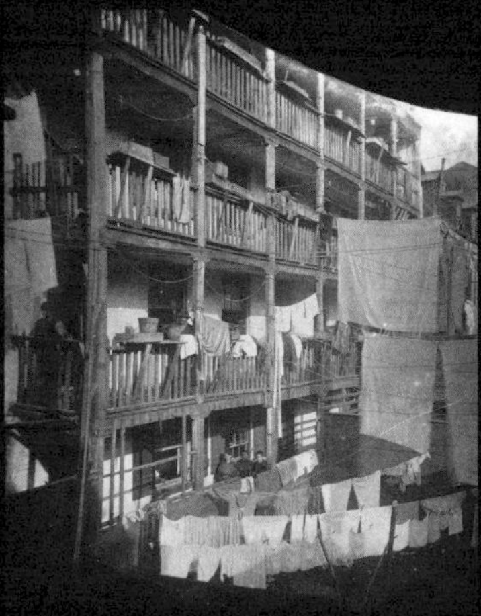

clothes were being washed and dried. Those clothes lines bothered and annoyed me at first, but, after a while, I learned that they were the one cheerful sight in all that desert of misery, for they were the evidence that some one was trying to keep clean, and cleanliness, you know, is the first step toward godliness. You may go through the Old World slums, and you will find no clothes lines or clothes hanging out to dry. So I have come to the conclusion that the clothes line is the true line between poverty and pauperism. Just such a house as that caught fire, and I went to see it burn. In the yard I found an old man figuring on a piece of paper. Evidently the property belonged to him, and I said, "Was that your house?" "Yes." "Was it insured?" "Yes! Fully insured for eight hundred dollars." "How many families do you have in it?" He said, "Ten families." I said, "Old man, are you not ashamed of yourself that you have had ten human families in that rookery that was fully insured for eight hundred dollars?" He said, "What do you mean? What are you insulting my property for? Do you know that property brought me in six hundred dollars a year rent?" Here, friends, you have it again; tenement house property is good property. I say to you that I am ashamed to own that many a church has such houses and has a grip on some of the profits. Not very far from that house there is a block that is reputed (shows picture of Mulberry Street Bend—scene in Mulberry street crowded with street-stands, carts, and people) to be the worst spot in the country, and I should say it might be true from my acquaintance with it. It was decided to tear it down long since, but five years have passed and the block is there still. We go slowly, very slowly in such matters as that in New York, when there is neither money nor politics in it.

Here you are with the Italians. They live out of doors most of the time, and that is why they are healthy though dirty, and the death rate is not so large. Go there at sunset some evening and you will see an army of men and women slouching along with the unmistakable gait of the tramp. Where they all go will

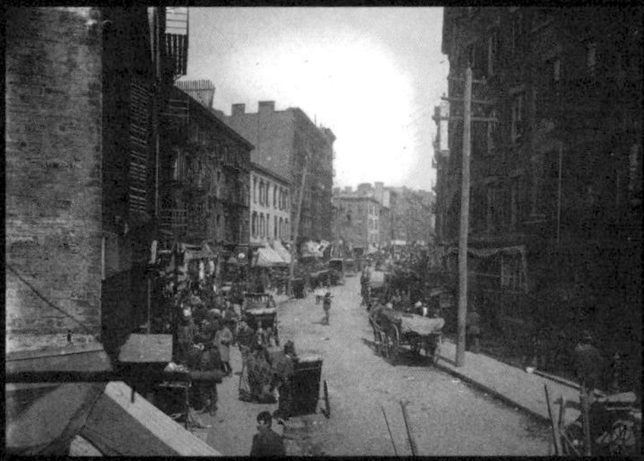

puzzle you. One by one they disappear, even while you look and before your very eyes. You will be troubled to find what becomes of them, till you look sharp and find doorways leading into side alleys. This (shows picture of narrow alley with several Italians on steps and half-broken down outside stairs) one was called Bandit's Roost from an old Neapolitan bandit who lived there and died there. Since then the "Roost" has been filled up by rather inoffensive Italians, who

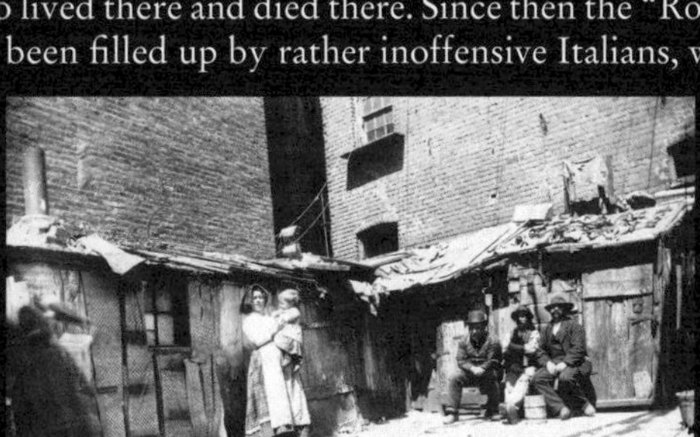

do no harm except on Sunday, when they take to playing cards and generally in the end to the knife; then murder comes in to finish the business.

Let us go into one of the alleys and down into one of the underground rooms and see what goes on at three o'clock in the morning. There you have a stale beer dive (shows picture "All-Night Two Cent Restaurant"). They call it with a nice name, a "Two Cent Restaurant." For two cents you can get a round of drinks, such as it

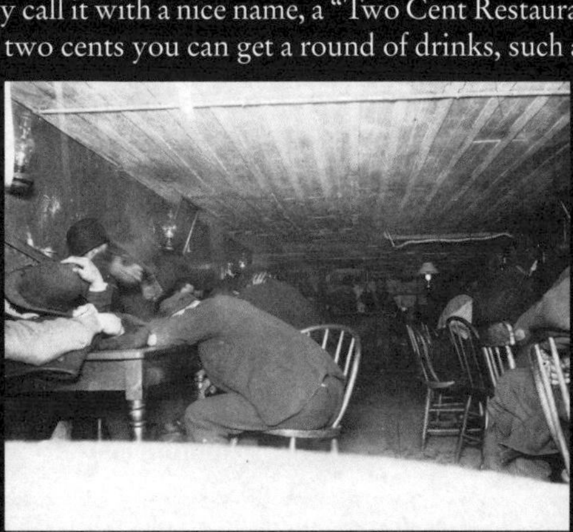

is, and have the privilege of sleeping all night on the table, or of lying under the table. Tramps, all of them! They are not thieves. They have not spunk enough for that. At most they might summon up courage to rob a clothes line, when no one is looking. Once I went down to raid such a place with the police, and we found there forty-two men and women in a room not more then twelve feet square, and in the corner on a heap of dirty straw lay a woman with a new-born babe.

On one of my visits to "the Bend" I came across this fellow (shows picture of a tramp with pipe in his mouth) sitting there in the yard on the rung of a ladder, and he struck me as being such a typical tramp that I asked him to sit still for a minute and I would give him

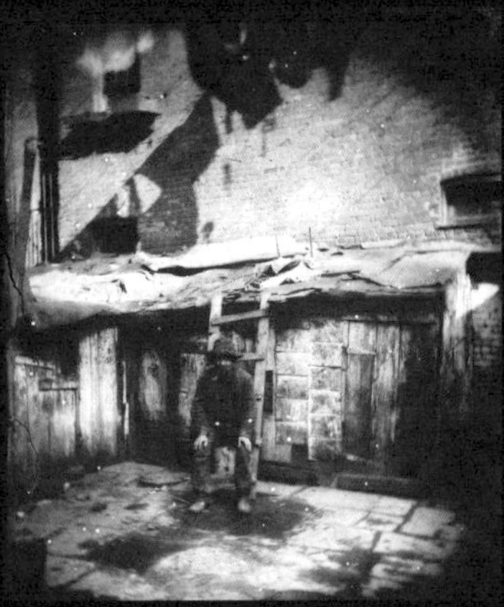

ten cents. That was probably the first and only ten cents that man had earned by honest labor in the course of his life, and that was sitting down at which he was an undoubted expert. [Laughter.] He was too lazy to say "Yes," but simply nodded. [Laughter.] I fixed my camera and just as I got ready to take his picture he took the pipe out of his mouth and put it in his pocket. I said, "That belongs to the picture." But no; he would not have it. Less than fifty seconds at work and he was on strike! [Laughter.] He knew what his labor was worth. That pipe was one of the two-for-a-cent kind, and I had to pay him a quarter to get the pipe in. [Laughter.] As he sits there, he is worth a quarter, and that is all he is worth; not another cent would I give for that man. [Laughter.]

There you have an alley, or rather a court in "the Bend" the name of which I wont mention in this place. It speaks for itself. Well do I remember the July day, when a message was sent to the board of health asking that a doctor be sent up there, because a baby was dying. I walked with him up those steps. The heat outside was up in the nineties, and inside, with cooking, and ironing, and pressing of clothes going on in that awful room, the doctor's thermometer at that dying child's pillow registered 115 degrees. That was the way that little life ebbed away. In just such surroundings are the little children in the slums of New York, that the Fresh Air Fund seeks to relieve. When they hand around the hat for it next year, don't let it pass. Your little mite may be just the one to save such a little miserable life as that. Sometimes they ask me, what is this all about, with your "infant slaughter" in the tenements? The children are bright and strong to look at. A doctor once was asked that question and he gave the only reasonable answer I ever heard. He said, "It is a clear case of the survival of the fittest. Only those who are strong as cattle can ever stand it." Those who are sick or dying you do not see. If you want to understand just what it means, come with me at three o'clock some morning in July or August when these stony streets are like fiery furnaces, and see those mothers walking up and down the pavements with their little babies trying to stir some breath of God's air to cool the brows of the sick child and hear the feeble wails of those little ones! Then tell me they have no cause of complaint, that they ought to be content. Here (shows picture of "Home of Italian rag-picker"—Italian woman with child in her arms) is one of them, an Italian

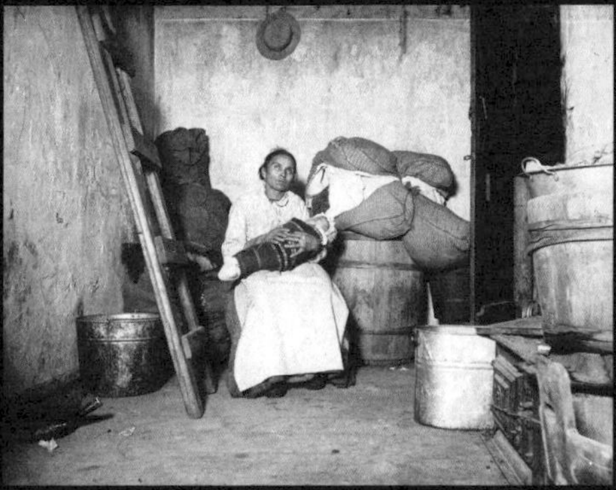

baby in its swaddling clothes. You have seen how they wrap them around and around until you can almost stand them on either end and they wont bend, so tightly are they bound. It is only a year ago that the Italian missionary down there wrote to the city mission that he did not know what to do with these Italian children in the hot summer days, for "no one asked for them." They have been asked for since, thank God! Christian charity has found some of them out.

Here is an element (shows picture "Group of Arabs") that has come lately.

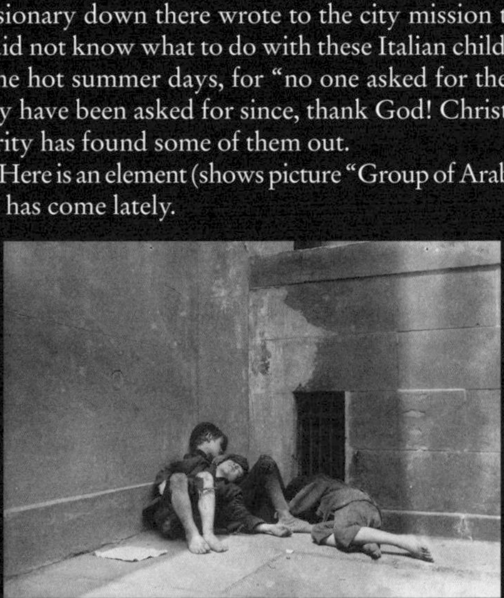

You know New York is the dumping ground of all the nations, and this is one of the latest importations the Old World has favored us with, direct from Arabia. I do not know if any of you ever saw one of these Arabs at work. I never did. They come here to trade, and they begin by palming off on us clods of dirt from down the Battery at Castle Garden as Holy Earth from Jerusalem at cents a clod. [Laughter.]

Here is another of these alleys, Bottle Alley (shows picture of an "Alley" or "Court"). I remember

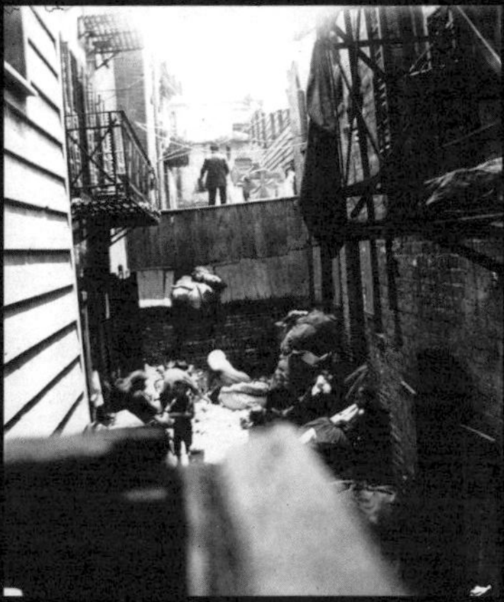

it for its splendid exhibition of Italian domestic discipline. When I went in to take the picture there were about twenty young women there picking rags and every one of them began to furbish herself up and pose for the camera, and there was just one old reprobate of an Italian man, who was not working—the only one who was not. He just grunted once and they all turned on their heels and went in. [Laughter.] As a case of domestic discipline I think it was absolutely perfect. Let us go upstairs and take a look at one of these Italian flats (shows picture "Upstairs in Bottle Alley"—room filled with old furniture and cooking utensils). I don't know

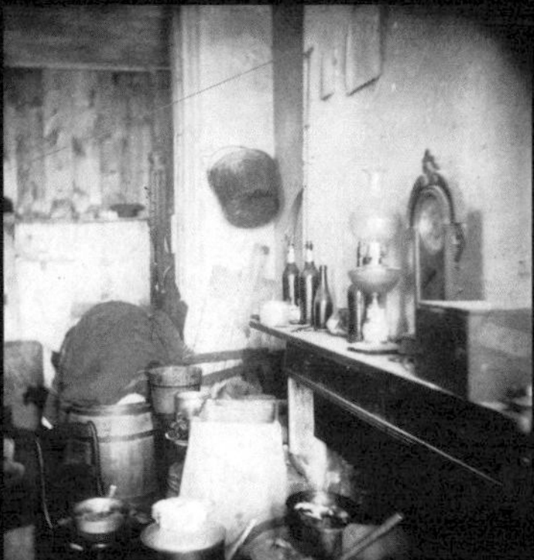

what you think of it, or whether you can make it out at all. The collection of furniture is perfectly bewildering. [Laughter.] No doubt the bottles on that mantel have something to do with it. One thing puzzled me in that room. Something in that kettle on the stove that kept boiling out of it continually. When I got through with my picture, I went over to see what it was and what do you suppose I found? It was the family teakettle doing duty as a washboiler. [Laughter.] Oddly enough just such a case was reported by Gen. Booth of the Salvation Army, from his own experience in London. It is an instance of how poverty in "the Bend" can make both ends meet. Here is a midnight view of that flat (shows picture, "Midnight in Bottle Alley"). If

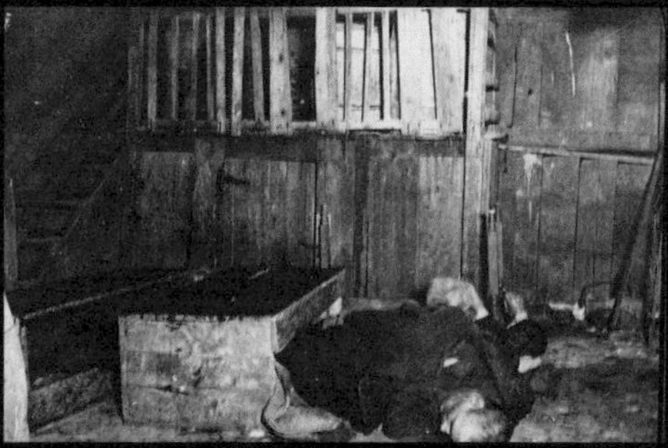

there was too much furniture in the other place, you cannot complain that there is too much here. There is a distinct absence of embellishment here. Yet that is the way that hundreds and thousands of these people sleep each night in the tenement houses in New York city. Nights and nights I have spent among these places, and over and over again in the sweater's shops I found piles of clothing that would be to-morrow put on the Broadway counters serving here for bed clothing, before they were pressed and delivered. No wonder we say the tenement houses scatter the seeds of disease.

Out of these alleys comes the problem of the children. That one came out of that very alley, just as she is there. "Her hair was matted with blood and her whole body was covered with sores," says the official report. After she had been in the care or the Society for the Prevention of Cruelty to Children six months, that was the way she looked. [Applause.] The Christian care she had made the difference. What would have been the future of that child? Can you read it in this face and tangled hair? I can, and no doubt you can see the future of that child there. My experience shows it every day in the week, the future that would have been hers had she not found these friends. It is the kind of Christian work these men are doing that pays. Before the Society had been more that thirteen years in the field, it had thrown its protecting arm around twenty-five thousand seven hundred and forty-five children, if I remember rightly, and the number has increased since to between fifty and sixty thousand. A record of work that in sixteen years!

Here we have the school at the Five Points (shows a picture of "Five Points Mission School-room" with children). Thirty-eight years ago this was a place where

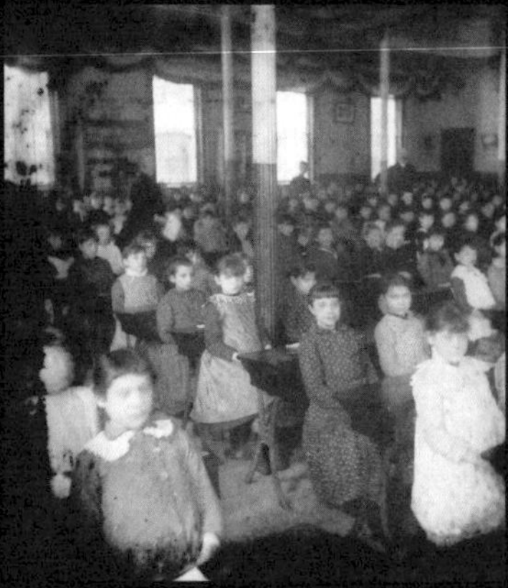

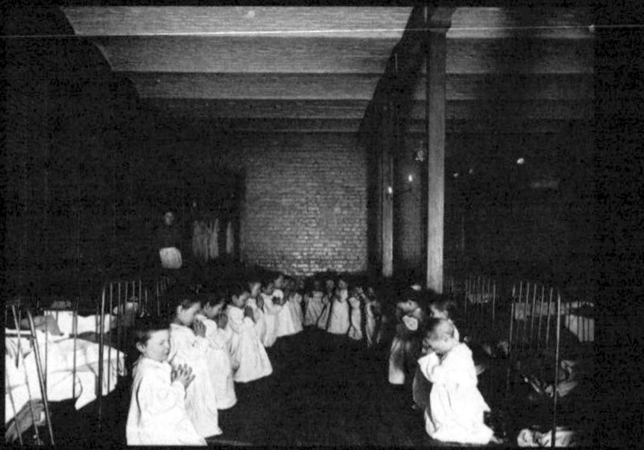

no policeman dared go alone at night. When it was worst, a little handful of Christian women went down there and opened a little mission, a place where they invited in the children and their fathers and mothers, and out of that mission has grown the entire redemption of that Five Points. To-day it is Paradise Park. On the site of the old brewery, that was the worst place in creation, there stands that great mission house where five hundred children go to school every day, and on the other side of the square stands the Five Points House of Industry, where there are four or five hundred more of them. Let me show you the "Baby Ward" down there (shows picture of "Baby Ward" in Five Points House of Industry—children sitting about a table). Twenty-four

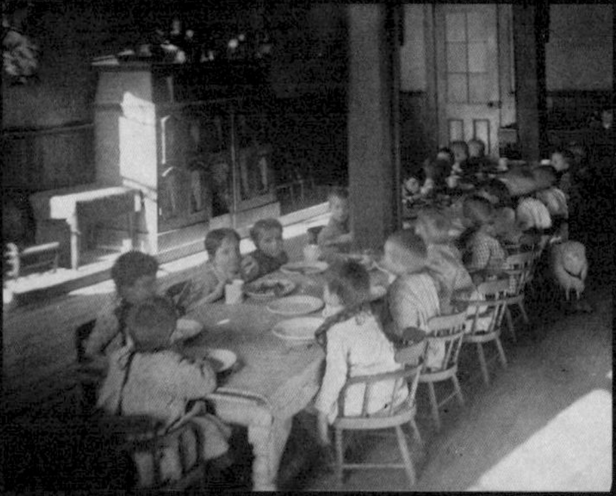

little tots sitting around that table, and let me remind you that every one of them is there, because it had to be taken away from drunken parents, from a home broken up, perhaps, by murder. Let me take you there at night (shows picture, "Prayer-time in Nursery," Five Points House of Industry). I stole in there one night with my camera as they were going to bed and saw them kneeling at their bedsides just as the picture shows you. [Applause.] Nearly every one of the white nightgowns hiding poor, bruised, cruelly tortured limbs! Every one of them out of homes where never a blessing was said and nothing but drunken curses heard from morning till night! Their bright faces show that they need nothing there. Work that for Christian charity! Dark spots enough in New York for it to shed its light into!

What are we going to do with them? Here is a problem, friends (picture of children on steps in Mulberry street). Some months ago the managers of a large literary

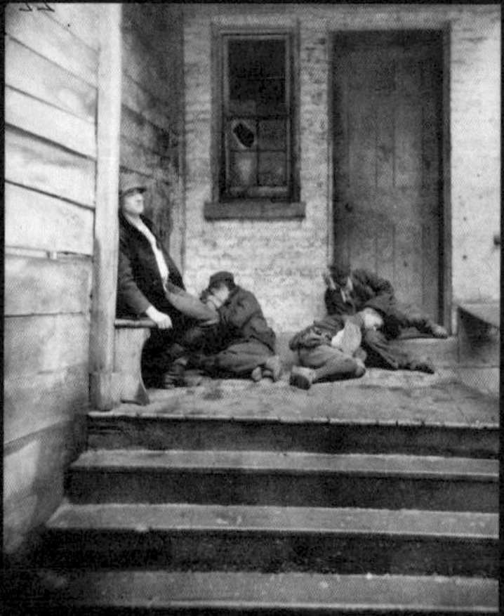

concern came to me and said, "Will you write for us the story of the children of the poor?" I said, "Yes, I will write for you the story of the children of the poor." Two months have passed and the time is nearly up and I have not written one line. Dear friends, I cannot. It sometimes seems to me so utterly hopeless in spite of all that has been done, that I do not know where to begin or where to end. They say there are no homeless children in New York city. Thank God, no, not in the sense of old London, if what we read of it is true. Yet last summer as many as forty boys were found roosting under one pile, and not one of these boys had a home. Hundreds and thousands of these children have come and gone in the lodging houses of the Children's Aid Society in the years it has been in existence, and still they come. What are we going to do about it? Five thousand were crowded out of the public schools last year because there was no room for them. The street takes them, and there they have to take their chances with nearly all the chances against them. Lots of helping hands are extended to these children, lots of them, and still there is need of more and more Christian work for the safety of the city and society. Here (shows pic ture of Children's Aid Society lodging house in Tompkins Square) is one. It is one of half a dozen lodging

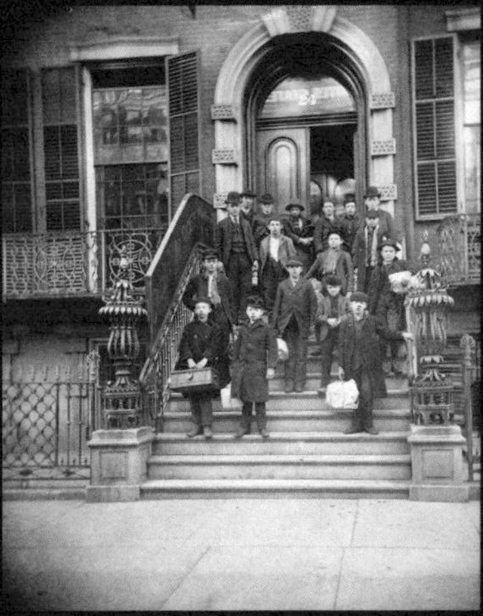

houses that have been built by the Children's Aid Society to gather in the homeless waifs. It is one of the pleasant experiences of life to find such houses as these built with the money of some one rich man or woman, whose name to the unthinking stands only for money-getting. It is not so very long since I found a carriage with a coat of arms standing outside the East Thirty-fifth Street Lodging House, where the crippled boys go, the poorest and most helpless of the society's waifs. The owner was at that moment down in the brush shop with a surgeon getting every one of the boys measured for an artificial limb, and who do you suppose the owner of that carriage was? Her name was Mrs. Wm. H. Vanderbilt. [Applause.] Let me take you inside and show you what accommodations they provide for these children (shows picture of "Dormitory in Lodging House"—cots with beds one above another). The

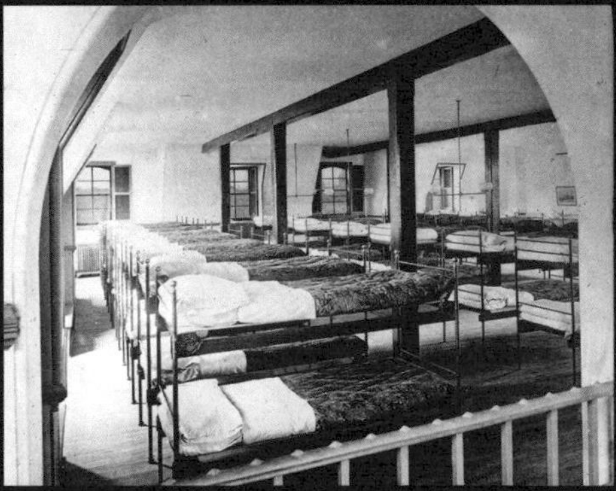

price of bed and breakfast is six cents each. Every one coming in there is expected to pay for what he gets. That is a strong feature of this helping process. It makes the boys feel that they are independent and are not receiving charity. If a poor boy comes there, who has not a cent, he gets his lodging and breakfast, and it is put down against him, and if he has not five cents with which to buy an armful of papers, they furnish him with that and turn him out to make his living. Some of the best men have grown out of that place, and made some of the brightest pages in the history of this country. I will show you by and by what it has done. Let me show you these boys as they are washing up for their supper (shows picture of "Wash-room in Lodging House"—a number of boys washing). Dirt

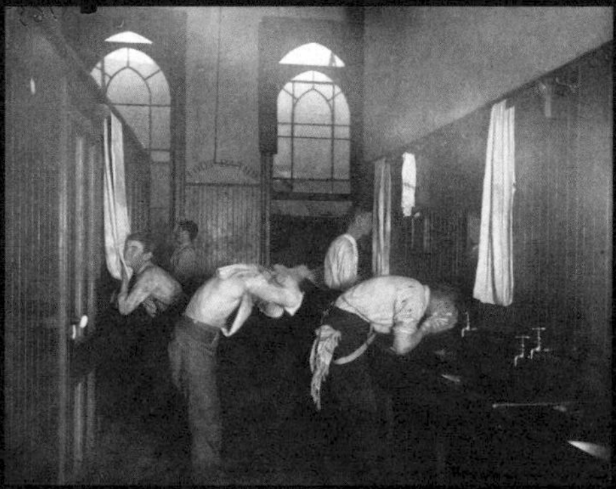

does not last long in that place, though plenty of it comes in. One condition for being let in is that the boy shall be homeless. The only other one stands over the door, "Boys who swear and use tobacco cannot sleep here." Soap is a gospel steadily preached here, and it works wonders. After they have been cleaned up and dressed up, and taught in the night schools, you would hardly know the boys. At first, when the lodging houses were opened, they thought it was a treasonable Sunday-school racket and were not going to let themselves be trapped into it. But they soon learned better, and nowadays if you want to hear singing when in New York, go and hear a room full of these boys sing. You don't know what congregational singing is till you hear these lads strike up "He's the Lily of the Valley" and you will never forget it till your dying day. The agents of this society have established industrial schools that are scattered all over the city and gather in the poorest children, whom the public school rejects or cannot find room for. Here the parties that go out to homes in the far West every season are recruited. This is such a party (shows picture of a group of boys on steps of lodging house). That sainted woman,

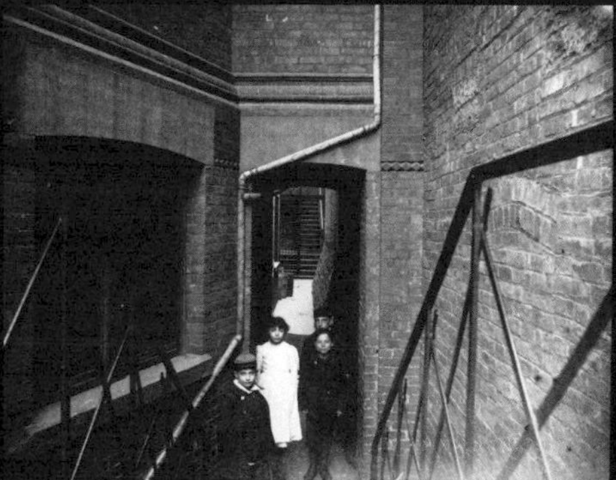

Mrs. Astor, who died two years ago, took a hundred such boys from the streets each year and dressed them up and sent them out to farm-homes where they are never lost sight of by this society. That was the last little party she started for Michigan just before she died. Among the boys was one who had an ironbound box with a padlock on it nearly as large as his two fists. I thought, surely, he must have some valuable thing in it, and I asked him about it. He fished up the key from down his neck and undid the padlock, and what do you suppose was in it? Two little white mice. [Laughter.] They were all the friends he had in the world. They crawled up his sleeve and laid their little heads against his cheek. I was down at the Five Points Home about a year after that and in came my little friend. He had come back, walking part of the way from Michigan, stealing rides on freight trains when he could. Born in the slums, he was homesick even for them. But now he had had enough of them and wanted to be sent out again. I asked him what had become of the mice. His face fell and well it might. It was a sad story. Success did not agree with them. "They had so much corn and sich to eat," he said, "and they couldn't stand it. They burned up all inside until they busted." [Laughter].

Here (shows picture of two neglected boys) are two

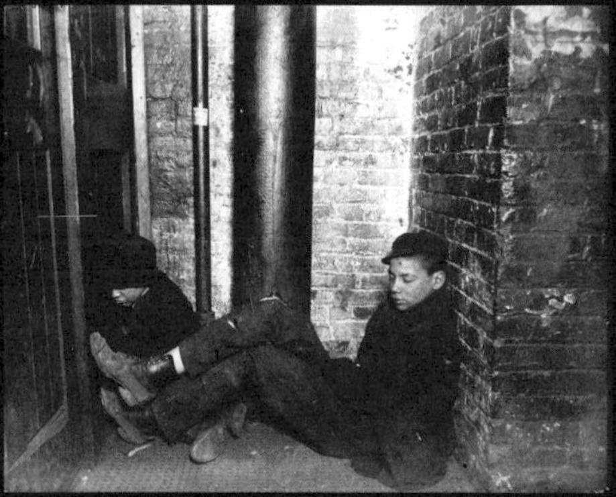

of the little home heathen who are growing up in the streets of New York every day while some of the very best people in the world are worrying about the souls and the socks of the little Hottentots in Central Africa. These boys are just as they were picked up. Those who found them tried to find what was their religious status. One of them has heard of "Our Father" and he knew it was something which the boys said was a good thing to say every night before they went to sleep in their burrows so they might have luck the next day playing craps or pitching pennies, [Laughter,] and the other knew all about the name of Christ; it was something to swear by. There you have the religious status of two such boys. Two like them were picked up in Harlem. The Third Avenue bridge is borne up by two great iron pipes and they had made a nest in the end of one of these pipes and slept there most of the winter.

Now you have seen the boys and you have seen their homes. Here is the father of some such (shows picture of a drunken man on floor). He was lying on the floor as you see, so drunk that when we fired the

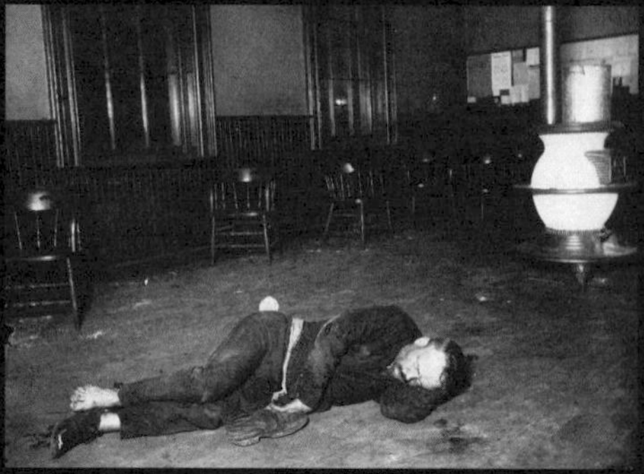

pistol that made the flash-light right under his nose he never woke up. Let them have such a father, as too many have to their hurt. Let them look for their mother in there (shows picture of group of men and women in a saloon),

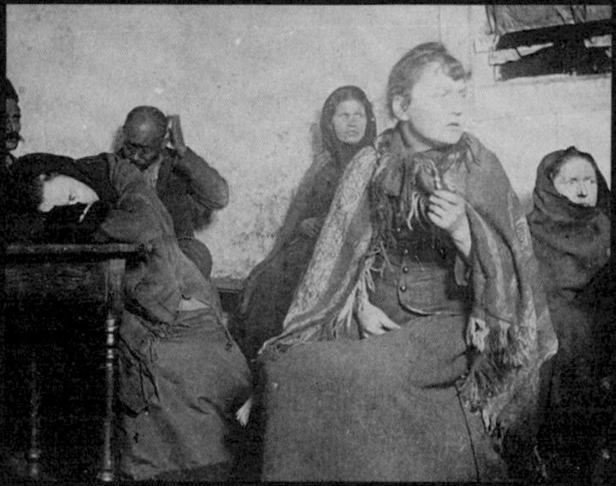

one of the vilest dives to be found anywhere. Women, mothers, there you see! Where do you expect to find them next? It is a marvel if you don't find them there (shows picture of "Growler Gang" or "dock rats"). It

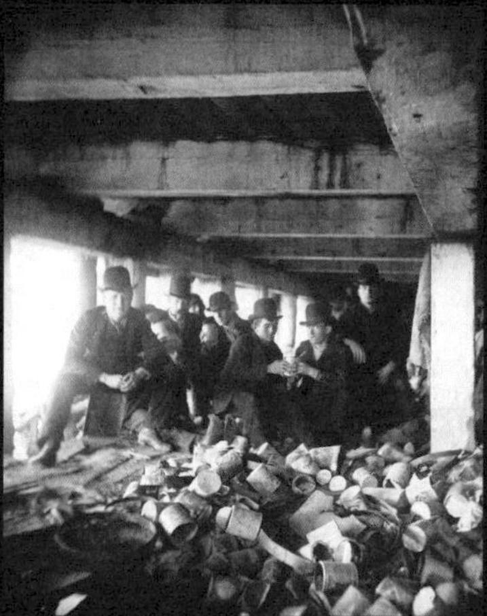

is a bad picture but it is not nearly so bad as the place. Dock rats, those, drinking beer under a dump. That is their business by day, drinking beer, loafing around, seeing what they can pick up. At night they come out and sneak along the water front. And you know how it is in New York city; if any man has been late at dinner and gets turned the wrong way, he is never far from the river. There they lie in wait. Should he foolishly resist or make an outcry—dead men tell no tales. It happens every day, especially in the summer time, that a body floats ashore with the pockets turned inside out. It is not always evidence of a post-mortem inspection by dock rats. These are the fellows that start out with the idea that the world owes them a living and that they are going to collect it as easily as they can. We will see how they do it. Here are two of them (shows picture of two toughs from "Rogues' Gallery" similar to "Three Murderers") taken

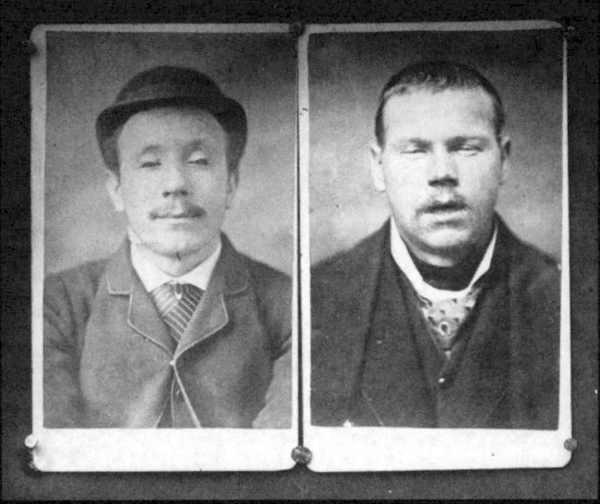

out of a gang to show you what they look like. You would not like to meet them alone on a dark night. Sometimes people have told me that they could see these two faces before their eyes a long time after seeing the picture. Yet it is not what is in the faces, but what is not in them that shocks. It is what we, with all our charitable machinery, with all our Christian effort have managed to leave out; we never reached those faces or we would have planted some different expression in them than we see there. The police (shows picture of boat with police officers under bridge) patrol the river,

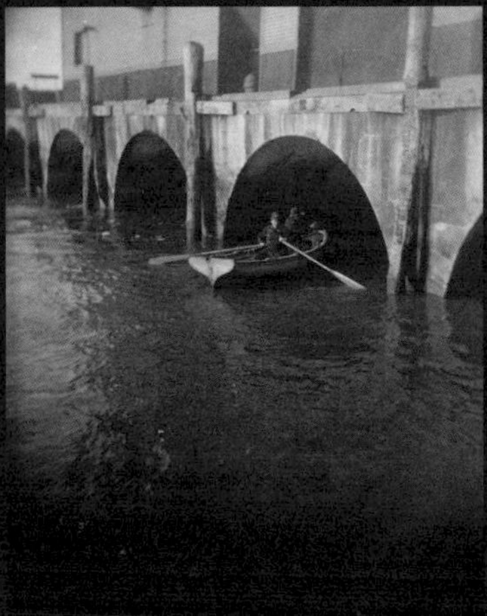

poking under the piers after them day and night. Sometimes they catch them hooking sugar and copper and iron and any kind of stuff they can get from the vessels, but if hard-pressed they have an easy way of getting away. They simply upset the boat and swim off. The next day they can steal another boat and fish for the stuff at leisure. There is no law against fishing, and if you catch anything that is valuable, so much the better for you.

There (shows picture of another "growler gang"—Montgomery Guards), you have another bad lot entirely

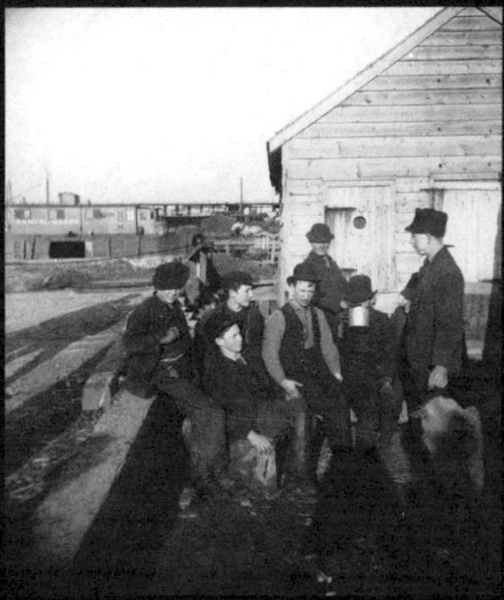

different from the other, but I do not know as I can say that they are much better. They call themselves the "Montgomery Guards." They always have some fancy name, if nothing else. While I was taking their picture, the suggestion was thrown out that it was for cigarette papers, and then nothing would do but that I must take them in character, and what do you suppose that was? Here it is, see for yourselves. They said it was to show me how they "did the trick" (shows picture of two boys robbing a third). One is supposed to be drunk and has

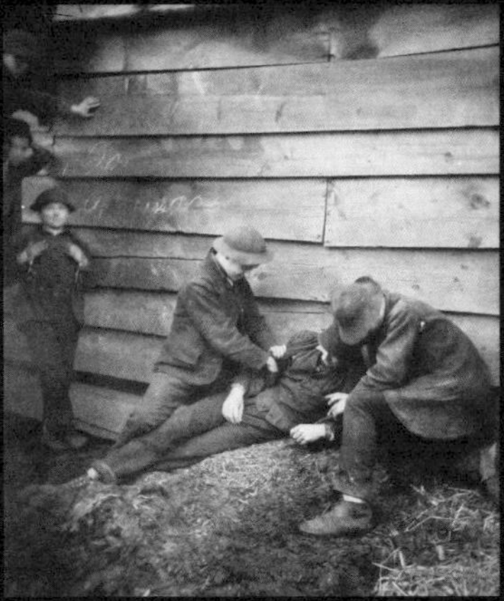

tumbled over against the shed as if asleep; two others are searching his pockets with a deftness that is highly suggestive. These fellows you might think were harmless, but let me say that in less than half an hour after I took that picture I happened into the police station in West Thirty-seventh street and there found two of the Montgomery Guards. A Jew peddler had come that way, soon after I left them, and they had tried to cut his head off with an old saw, "just for fun," as they put it, and they very nearly did it. That was their idea of amusement. From that you can get an idea of what they are capable of when they get down to business. Yet with all their pride in the achievement, when these boys are taken in by the police they are not "thieves" by any means. They register as "speculators;" they never steal a watch; they win it: dignifying their profession of stealing by the pretence of gambling, always half brother to it.

Here is a boy who carries the growler (shows picture of a boy carrying "growler"—pail of beer). Now he carries the growler. How long do you suppose it

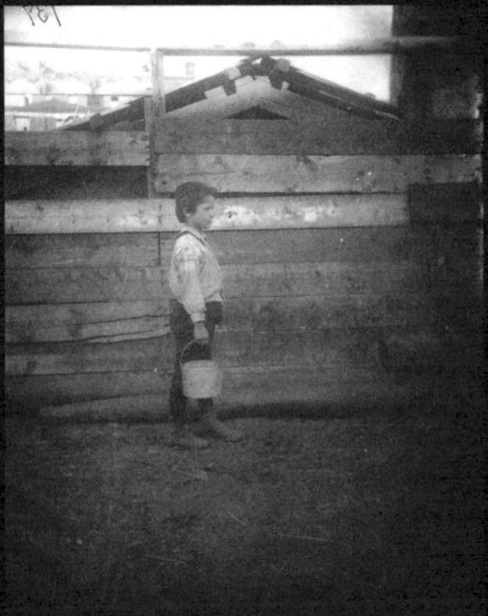

will be before the growler will carry him and to what end? We have a law in New York to prevent the selling of liquor to minors, and it is enforced about as much as the law against swearing is. It is only about a year ago that such a little boy as that, we are told, carried beer one entire day for the men in a cooper's shop on the East Side, where his father was working. At evening he was missing. All that night and the next day, which was Sunday, the father went out and in at police headquarters inquiring for the boy. They found him, when they opened the shop Monday morning, or what the rats had left of him. In his drunken stupor he had crawled in there, and there had died that frightful death. That, dear friends, happened in the city of New York in the year of grace 1889. It is not a story of the Middle Ages. That was the recruit. Here (shows picture of "Three Murderers") you have the finished article, Three murderers! Not over twenty years old, one of them committed a murder. In the act of robbing a saloon-keeper his gang were surprised by the saloon-keeper. Two of them ran away and there were plenty of chances for this one to run, but with the bravado of a tough he said, "Run for a Dutchman! not I!" and killed the saloon-keeper. When he was captured and brought into

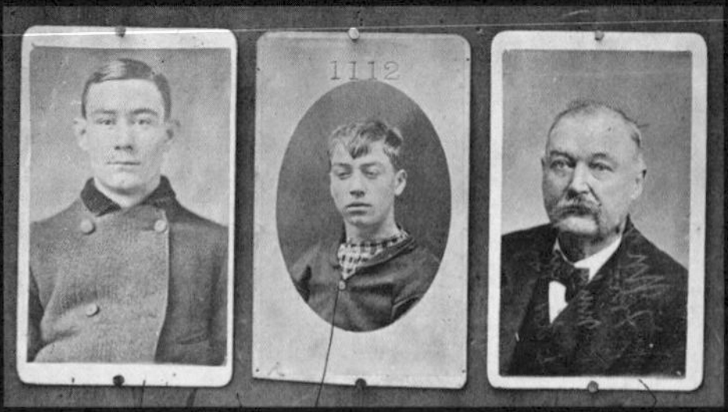

police headquarters, he shook himself out and said, "Well, I suppose it's all right. A fellow is not a tough, till he has knocked out his man, anyhow." And with that spirit he went to the gallows and suffered the penalty. Dear friends, it has always seemed to me there must be some better use for such material as that than hanging them up on the gallows tree. This other one (pointing to one of the murderers) was a boy of eleven or twelve years when he began to carry the growler; he was a man when he died on the gallows. His father-confessor, who had been chaplain of the Tombs for many years, said afterwards that never had he been called on to listen to such a category of crimes as that murderer had to confess, and he was a "power in his ward," politically, handy at carrying elections for whichever party was willing to pay for it.

That (showing picture of "Hell's-kitchen"—a small room with lounge and broken chairs) is a flat in

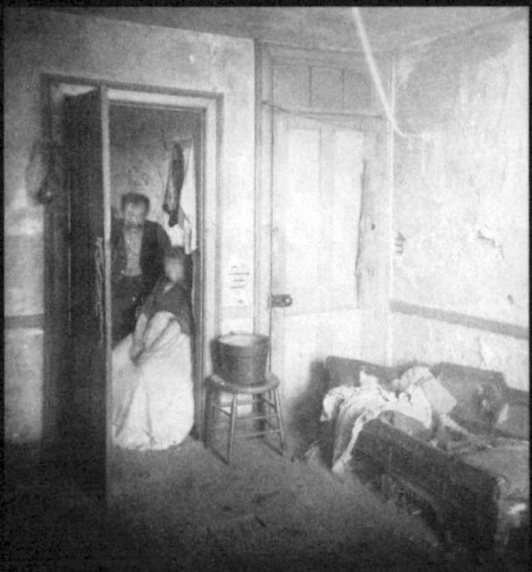

Hell's-kitchen, out of which McGloin, one of those murderers who died on the gallows, came. You do not expect a rose to grow out of a swamp, and you could hardly expect anything but such a tough to grow in such a place.

Here, dear friends (showing picture of Scene in Ludlow Street "Jewtown"—a crowded street), you come to the spot that is the most remarkable place in New York city, as a sample of crowding. We long since outdid London in the matter of crowding, and crowding means slums always. Wherever the crowds go the slums follow. In "Jewtown" where the crowding is greatest, there are about 333,000 to the square mile,

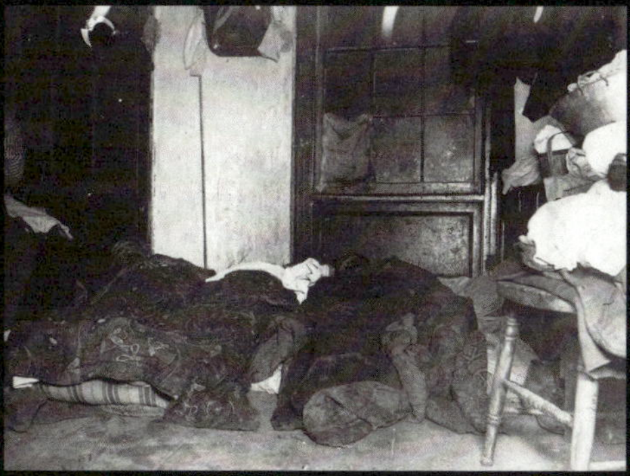

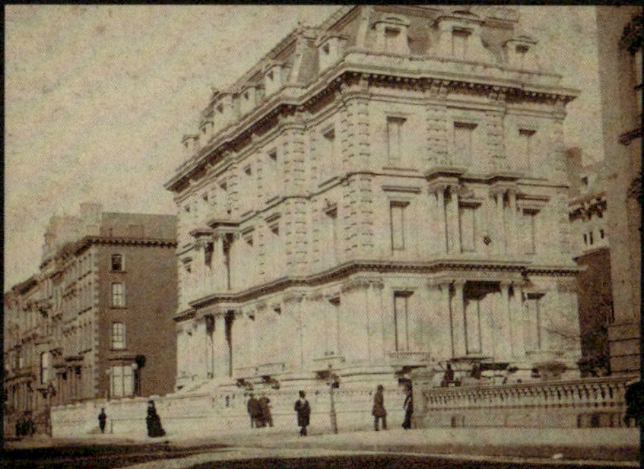

while the greatest crowding of old London never was greater than at the rate of 175,000 to the square mile. Don't tell me we cannot beat London. I think we can on that score and I own it with shame. In this room (shows picture "Five Cents a Spot") slept thirteen persons.

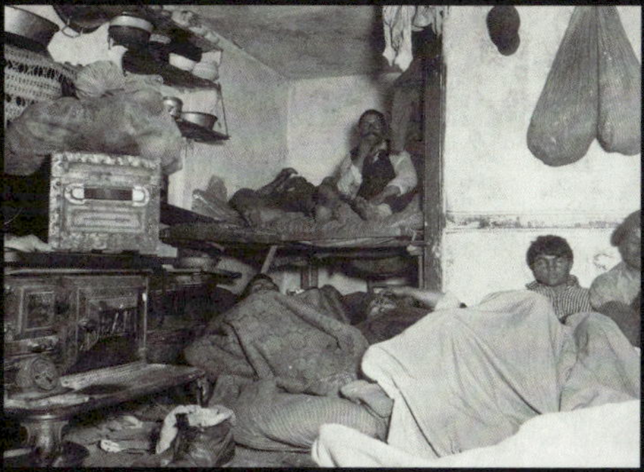

Of course they did not all work there, but they slept there. Some of them were lodgers at five cents a spot. A sanitary policeman reported that in Essex Street three small rooms in a six-story tenement were made to hold a family of father and mother, twelve children, and six boarders. A while ago I was puzzled to know what to do with a family of ten children. They have been paupers for eight years and the family is growing steadily. There is only one wage-earner in it, the eldest daughter, who earns four dollars a week. They live in three rooms. The front room has two windows, and the next is dark, and so is the one back of that, and back of that a coal closet, "If any one has coal or wood to put in there," explained the woman. She had not any, poor woman. These are the actual facts that I have told. The sanitary police, you know, make their rounds every night and drive out the crowds. In one instance, after an order to move, there came a petition to the board of health with the endorsement of a citizen who pleaded for the family. Who do you suppose that citizen was? It was the family undertaker who testified that the family was all right and it would be a hardship to drive those people out. [Laughter.]

Now rest your eyes for a moment on that (shows picture of the Stewart marble palace). That is what I put it there for. That picture is bright enough, and yet I hardly know. It is, or was Mrs. Stewart's marble palace over on Fifth Avenue. Since the last stone was put on that house and the last dollar of the two millions was expended, I do not think there was one happy hour in that big building. After all, wealth does not make the difference. That was Mrs. Stewart's on Fifth Avenue. Now let me introduce you to Mrs. Flanagan over on Eleventh Avenue (shows picture of cabins on rocks with steps leading down to street). Happiness enough

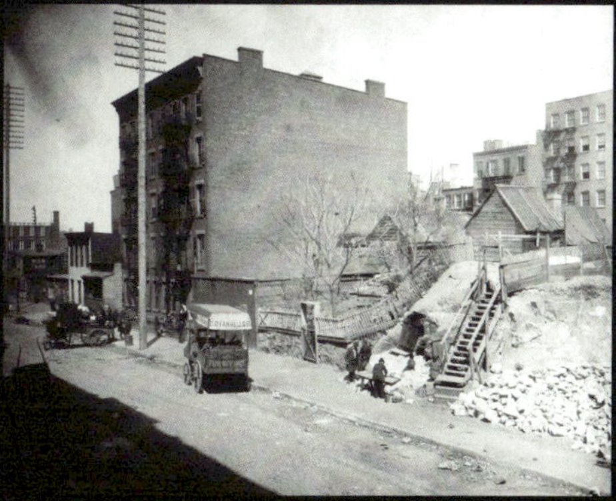

there, and why not? They are squatters and don't care whether school keeps or not. With the strong love for the soil that characterizes the Irish everywhere, they fight for their rock, even though it does not belong to them, until they are driven away, or the rock is blasted from under them with dynamite. [Laughter.] Then they will go to somebody's else rock, and fight for that. The tax-gatherer has no show with them. They take the steps away, if he bothers them too much, and let him stand and jaw below as much as he likes.

Next comes one of the perplexing problems of that city of ours, the abandoned waif, the child that is brought in night after night to police headquarters picked up in the street (shows picture of policeman with child in his arms). Sometimes they come without any clothes at all, only a piece of newspaper wrapped about them, once in a while with a little note pinned to the garment or rag, whatever it may be, with such a message as this, "Take care of Johnnie, for God's sake. I cannot," in which you can hear that mother's heart strings snapping asunder. For a mother is a mother the

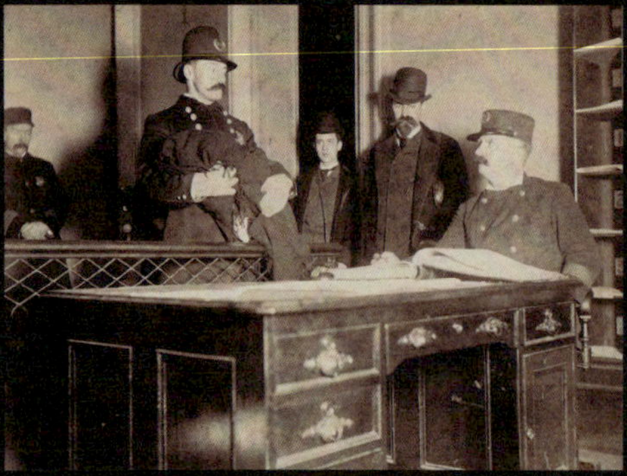

world over. There is a queer coincidence in this that year by year the lives that are begun in the gutter are balanced by the even more forlorn lives that are ended in the river, about two hundred, a few more or a few less, substantially the same when the record is closed. Some of the foundlings are taken to Randall's Island where they are cared for by the city authorities. Most of them come from the East Side, where they are left by young mothers without wedding ring or other name than their own to bestow upon the baby. Many go to that great institution, the Catholic Foundling Asylum known all over the world as Sister Irene's Asylum. That good sister in the twenty-one years she has been at her work has gathered as many thousand waifs from the streets of New York into her fold (shows picture of children and Nun in large room). Catholic

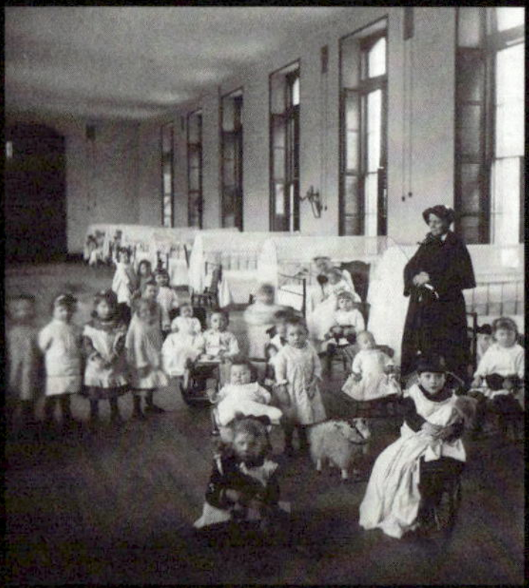

or Protestant, when one day the pearly gates swing wide to let in that dear woman, I tell you such a flapping of little wings will be heard coming to greet her as has not been heard since the morning stars sang together. [Applause.]

You ask me, what becomes of these mothers, these girls when thrown back on society (shows picture of inside of Florence Mission). Yes, I think you recognize there the face of one of your committee, Mr. Crittenton, the founder of the Florence Mission. [Applause.] His is one of the helping hands. I think you have heard of the Florence Mission and its wonderful work. Friends, that is one of the stepping stones for which we may thank

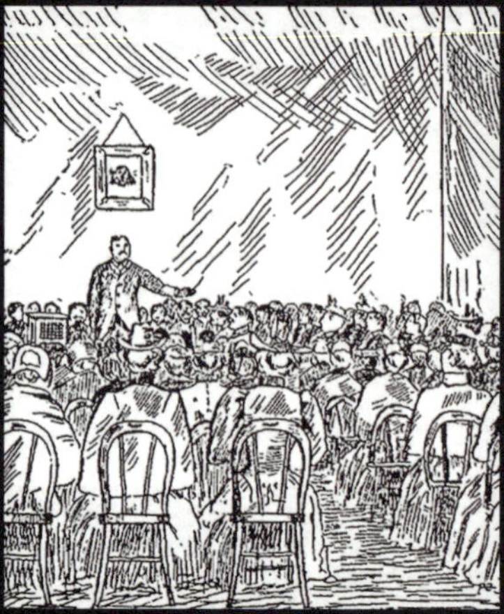

God in New York city, one that says, "Sister, come, even though the world has cast you out and turned its back on you, you are my sister and your God is mine."

But, friends, here is one (shows picture of Chinatown) whose heaven is not the same as ours. He won't

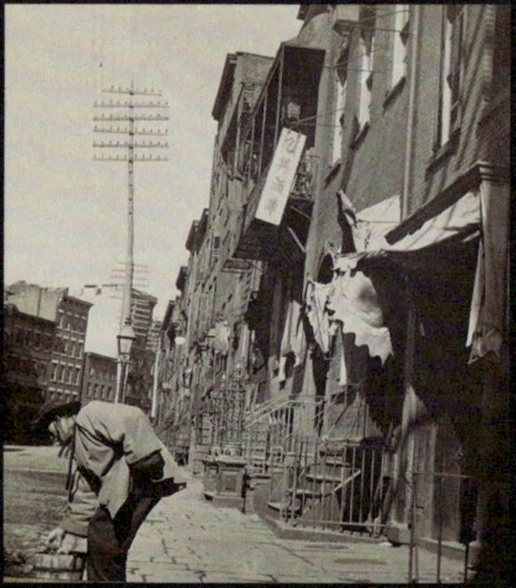

have it all. This Chinaman, you can't do anything with him. I despair of him altogether. I give it up. Here is a view of his town and one of his houses (shows picture of a "Joss House"). It is his Joss house and we will go inside and see what it looks like (shows picture of inside of "Temple"). I don't suppose you can read Chinese,

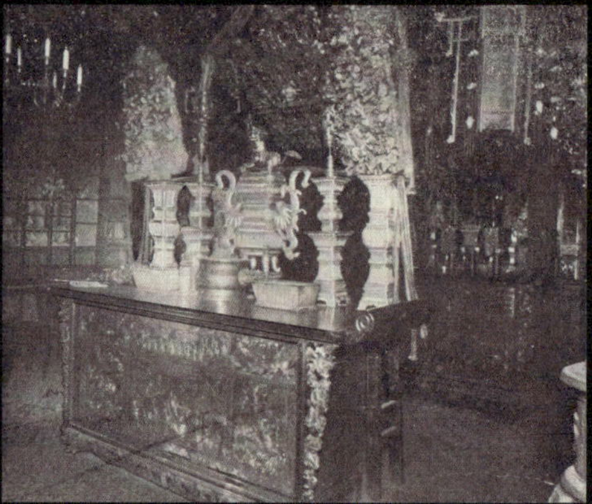

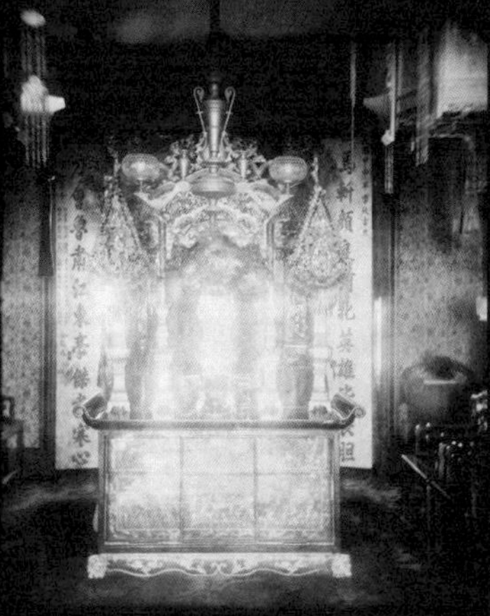

but I have been told that those figures on the side represent the pillars of the church who have contributed the most money, that they might have their reward in this world, no matter what happens to them in the next. If that is not a practical scheme of worship I do not know what is. Far back you see Joss, the rice-paper master that they worship and before whom they spread their roast pigs and mumble their prayers. If, after all that, he doesn't prosper them in their gambling, they take him out and give him a first-class thrashing, and if he don't help then they get another rice-paper Joss and proceed with their worship. Over all, there is the inscription in English letters copied bodily from the trade dollar, "In God we Trust." The priest tried to explain and I gathered from what he said that it was intended as a sort of a diplomatic courtesy, a delicate international compliment to the "Melican Joss," the almighty dollar. Back of the Joss house you will find smoking bunks. They are everywhere in Chinatown. Here you have a view of one (shows picture of a smoking bunk). You don't care to know

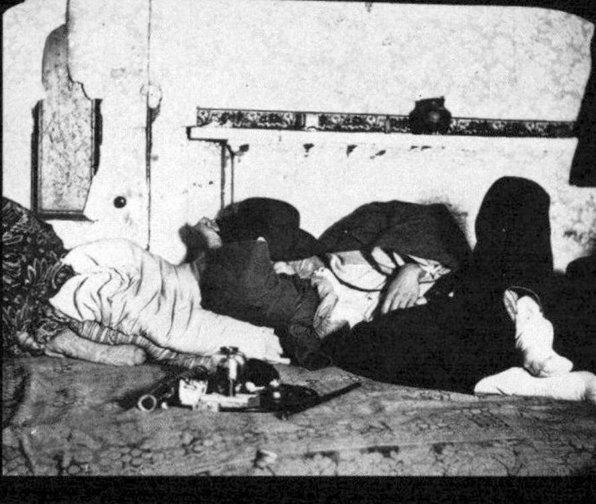

much about their smoking habits. It is their vice and we will let them keep it. Let us take a look at their newspaper. You went through the Chinese colony and have seen their worship and their smoking and here (shows picture of a Chinaman and a telegraph pole) is

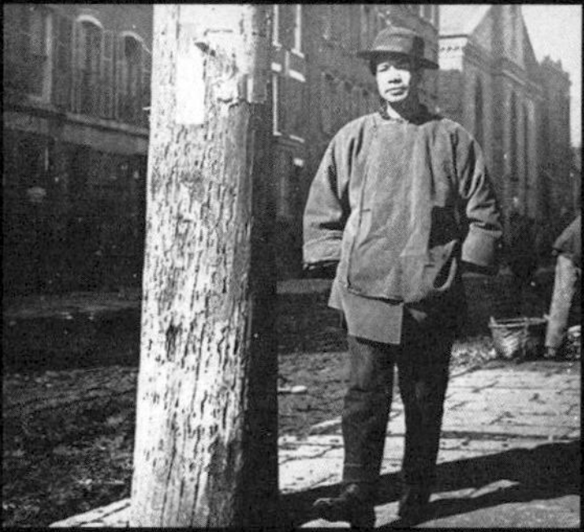

their newspaper. The real official organ of Chinatown is the telegraph pole as you see it there with the placards stuck all over it. The time I took the picture there I learned a lesson of Chinese domestic logic. We heard cries and shouts and went with a policeman across the street and in the cellar we found a Chinaman beating the white girl he called his wife with a broom handle. While the policeman spoke to her I tried to reason with the Chinaman. I said, "John, what are you doing? You must not beat your wife." "She bad," he sputtered. "Well, if she is bad you must not beat her." He said, "Suppose your wife bad, you no lickee her?" I said, "Certainly not." He eyed me a while in stupid silence, poked the linen in his tub and made up his mind: "Then, I guess she lickee you," he said. [Laughter and applause.]

Here (shows picture of "Seven Cent Lodging House"—canvas hammocks stretched one above another) is a seven

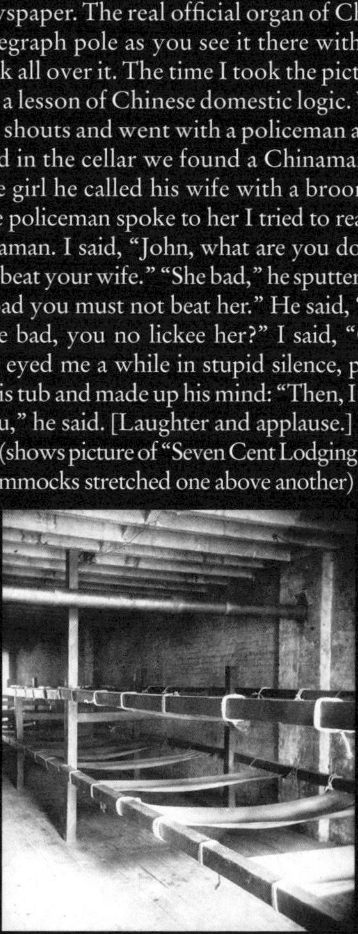

cent lodging house. In the old country they had once a different sort of an arrangement, a clothes line strung across the room on which the lodgers slept hanging by their arm pits for a penny a night. The boss woke them up in the morning by untying the line and letting them all go at once. We have nothing in New York just like that. The cheapest legally licensed lodging house is the seven cent lodging house. The beds consist of pieces of canvas strung between two posts with no cover of any sort. The man who ran this lodging house where I took the picture lived in a house in the neighborhood of Murray Hill, where the nature of his occupation was not suspected. He was a very decent man and proved it by having this notice posted in the lodgers' room, "No Swearing or Loud Talking After Nine o'clock." Friends, here is where the elections are sometimes decided, especially the presidential elections. They have had the casting vote in such contests more than once. There are black tramps and white tramps. The difference about election times is made chiefly by the loyalty of the black to his old friends. He always sells his vote to the Republican for a dollar while he charges the Democrat a dollar and a half. And here (shows picture of police station lodging house—a number of women lying on floor and small raised platform) we have a place that costs nothing, the

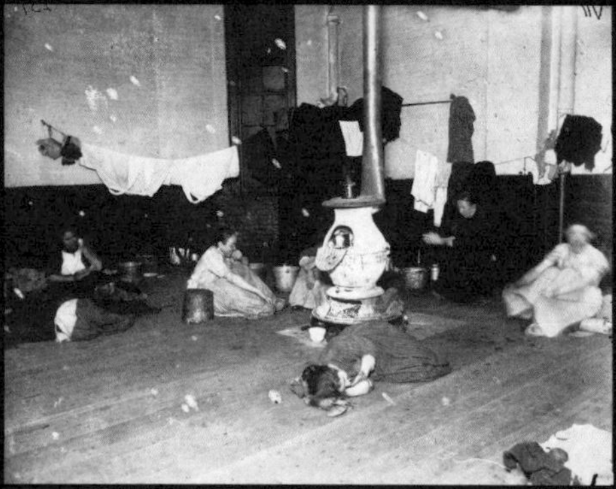

Police Station Lodging House—vilest abomination of all. In the morning when the lodgers have gone, the police bed is easily made by turning over the planks, with an occasional coat of whitewash thrown in to sweeten things.

And now we come to the bottom, down to the black-and-tan dive (shows picture of "Black-and-Tan Dive"—saloon with black and white men and women).

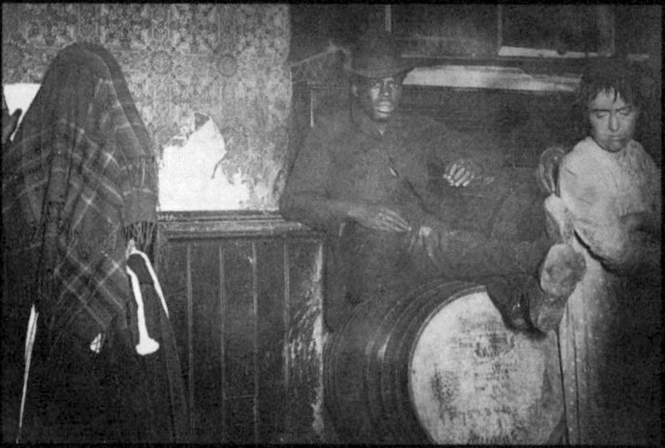

When black and white of both sexes meet on such ground, then you have the abomination than which there is none more vile. From there the descent is very easy to the rogues gallery. I will show you two or three heads from that (shows picture of three men). These are the men who insist that the world owes them a living. I tell you, that the sum of my experience as a police reporter for fourteen years is that the man who thinks he can beat the old scheme of earning his bread in the sweat of his brow and get his living in that way, swindles himself and has

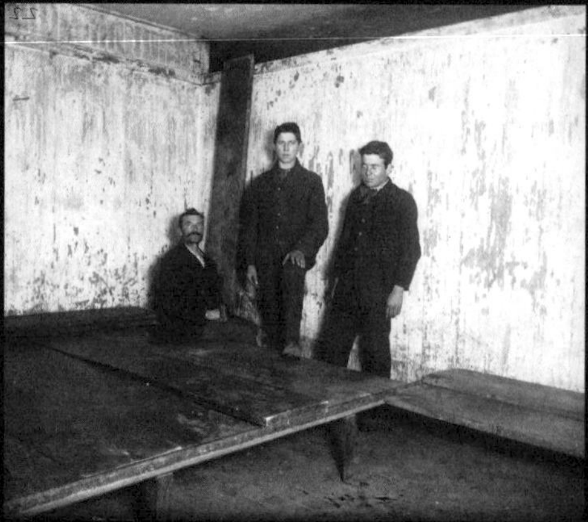

to work infinitely harder than any man with pick and shovel, and for the poorest pay, with the jail always in the background. That man in the background was sent to the penitentiary for twenty years, and I want to ask you if there is not something in his face that ought to suggest a better place for him than the jail. I saw him and interviewed him and was profoundly impressed that there was lots of brain there. We wont talk about the others, but go right along.

Just take note of these two here (picture of man and woman), and, if you ever see them around when you

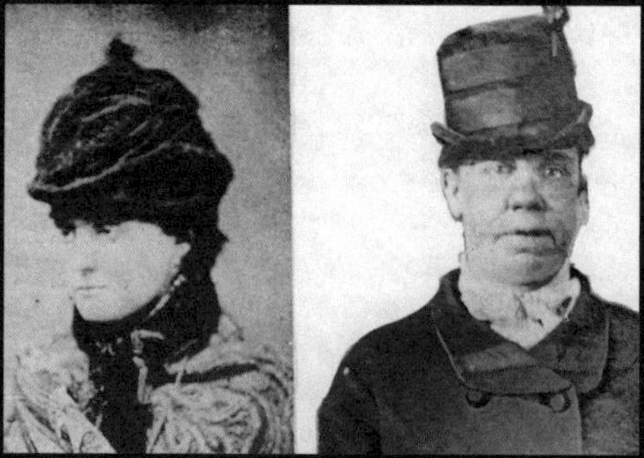

have a picnic or a fair in your churches, hand them over to the police at once. This one here is a professional church-fair thief. That one over there steals only at the fashionable funerals. With his fine clothes he comes in as one of the chief mourners and when he goes away he leaves a streak of honest mourners behind, if there were none before, for he carries away their watches and rings.

There (shows picture of "Blackwell's Island Workhouse") you have a summer hotel, the most popular one in all creation, although we call it the workhouse on Blackwell's Island. At least I find there were twenty-one thousand guests registered there last year and some of them had been there twenty times before. Evidently they liked it or they would not come back so often. These are some of the people who insist that the world owes them a living. We will pass along, and there as a sort of a way station is the Almshouse. This is another kind of a "Growler gang" (shows picture of old women), the old

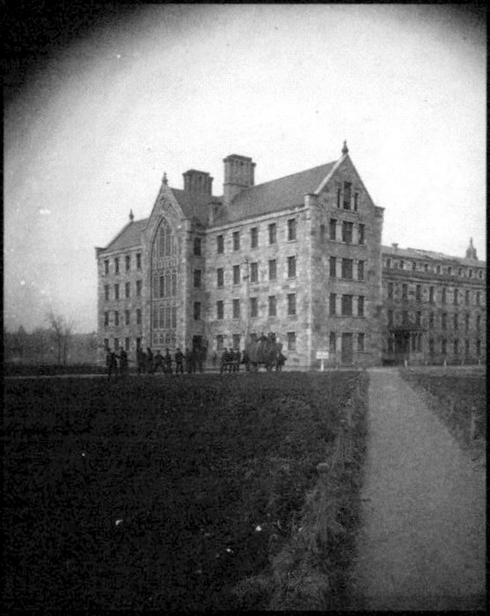

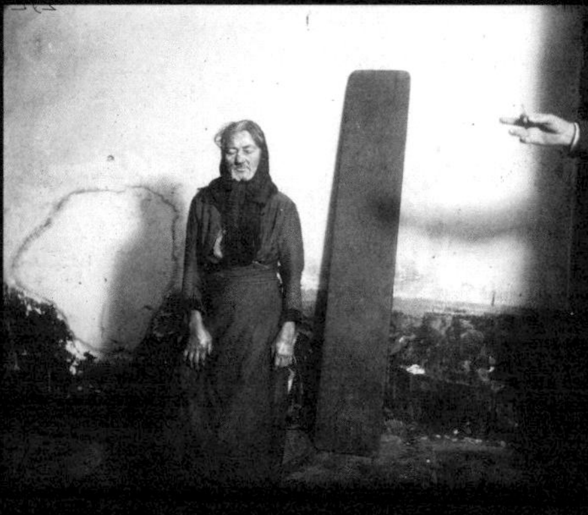

women whose sons are likely enough in the penitentiary and whose lives have held nothing but hardship and misery.

No wonder they growl in sunshine and rain, hungry or filled, as the warden says. He too has become by long association with them a sort of chief growler of the gang. And now here (shows picture of convicts in line) are

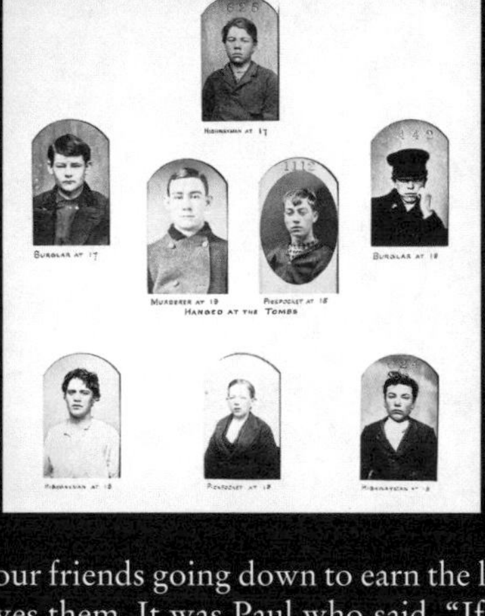

some of our friends going down to earn the living the world owes them. It was Paul who said, "If any will not work, neither let him eat." We do differently in our days. We put them there and feed them, but we make them break stone on Blackwell's Island and thus it is that they are finally earning their living the world owes them. Not for long; criminals don't live long. Their lives are wasted through sin. Their race is rapidly run. The last station is the morgue (shows picture of "The Morgue") where they have a rough pine box

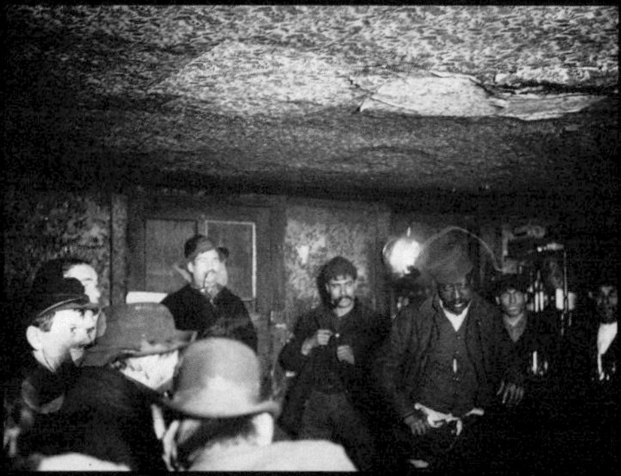

all to themselves. Twice a week a steamer comes and fetches up the lot to Hart's Island.

There they are laid in a trench in the Potter's field (shows picture of "Trench in Potter's Field"). Shoulder

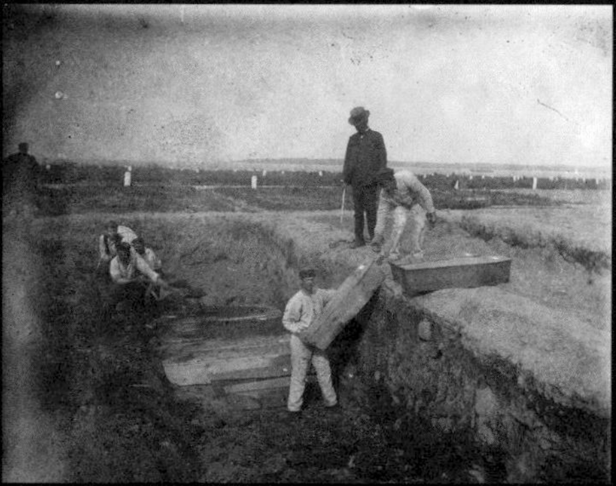

to shoulder they are laid there, packed as tightly as ever they were in life, the lost tenth, fifty in a row; then a little dirt and another fifty, and still another layer, the third. Then the trench is closed, and the long sad story with it, as far as we can reach, or our human knowledge goes. If, dear friends, it were really the end, if there were nothing beyond it, what would be the use of my standing here and talking to you? Thank God! there is something beyond even the Potter's Field, for out of its gloom, and misery, and desolation, there comes the voice of our Saviour, with the promise, "Inasmuch as ye have done it unto one of the least of these my brethren, ye have done it unto me," and also the command, "Go out into the highways and hedges, and compel them to come in." [Applause.]

How the Other Half Lives: Studies Among the Tenements in *Scribner's* Magazine, Vol. VI, No. 6, December 1889
Jacob Riis

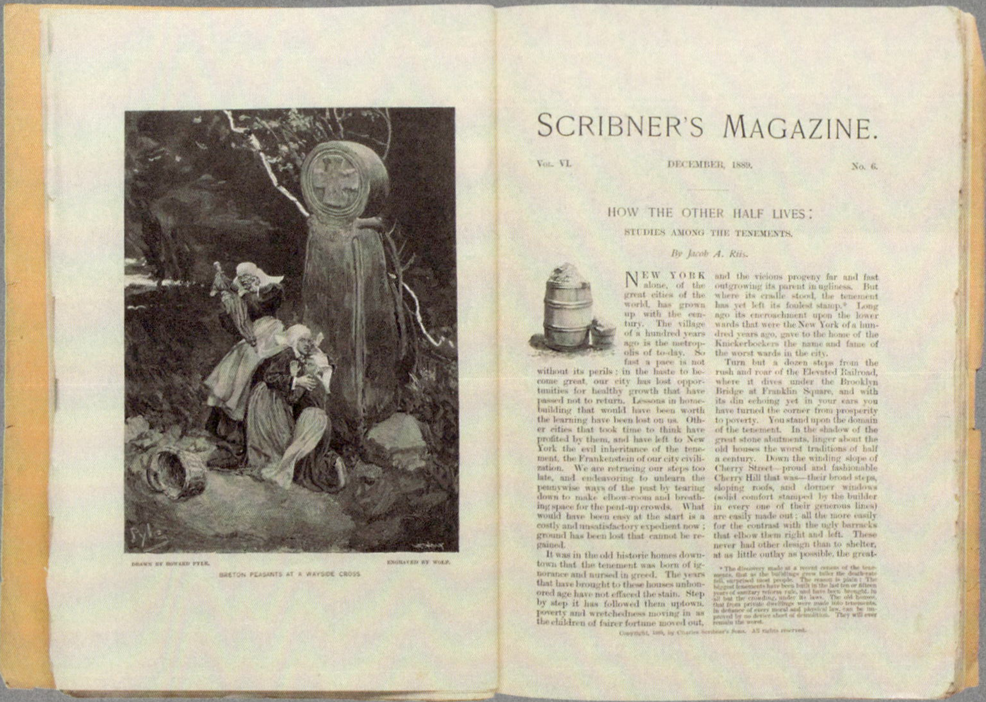

DRAWN BY HOWARD PYLE. ENGRAVED BY WOLF.

BRETON PEASANTS AT A WAYSIDE CROSS

SCRIBNER'S MAGAZINE.

VOL. VI. DECEMBER, 1889. No. 6.

HOW THE OTHER HALF LIVES:

STUDIES AMONG THE TENEMENTS.

By Jacob A. Riis.

NEW YORK alone, of the great cities of the world, has grown up with the century. The village of a hundred years ago is the metropolis of to-day. So fast a pace is not without its perils: in the haste to become great, our city has lost opportunities for healthy growth that have passed not to return. Lessons in home-building that would have been worth the learning have been lost on us. Other cities that took time to think have profited by them, and have left to New York the evil inheritance of the tenement, the Frankenstein of our city civilization. We are retracing our steps too late, and endeavoring to unlearn the pennywise ways of the past by tearing down to make elbow-room and breathing space for the pent-up crowds. What would have been easy at the start is a costly and unsatisfactory expedient now; ground has been lost that cannot be regained.

It was in the old historic homes downtown that the tenement was born of ignorance and nursed in greed. The years that have brought to these houses unhonored age have not effaced the stain. Step by step it has followed them uptown, poverty and wretchedness moving in as the children of fairer fortune moved out, and the vicious progeny far and fast outgrowing its parent in ugliness. But where its cradle stood, the tenement has yet left its foulest stamp.* Long ago its encroachment upon the lower wards that were the New York of a hundred years ago, gave to the home of the Knickerbockers the name and fame of the worst wards in the city.

Turn but a dozen steps from the rush and roar of the Elevated Railroad, where it dives under the Brooklyn Bridge at Franklin Square, and with its din echoing yet in your ears you have turned the corner from prosperity to poverty. You stand upon the domain of the tenement. In the shadow of the great stone abutments, linger about the old houses the worst traditions of half a century. Down the winding slope of Cherry Street—proud and fashionable Cherry Hill that was—their broad steps, sloping roofs, and dormer windows (solid comfort stamped by the builder in every one of their generous lines) are easily made out; all the more easily for the contrast with the ugly barracks that elbow them right and left. These never had other design than to shelter, at as little outlay as possible, the great-

* The discovery made at a recent census of the tenements, that as the buildings grew taller the death-rate fell, surprised most people. The reason is plain: The biggest tenements have been built in the last ten or fifteen years of sanitary reform rule, and have been brought, in all but the crowding, under its laws. The old houses, that from private dwellings were made into tenements, in defiance of every moral and physical law, can be improved by no device short of demolition. They will ever remain the worst.

Copyright, 1889, by Charles Scribner's Sons. All rights reserved.

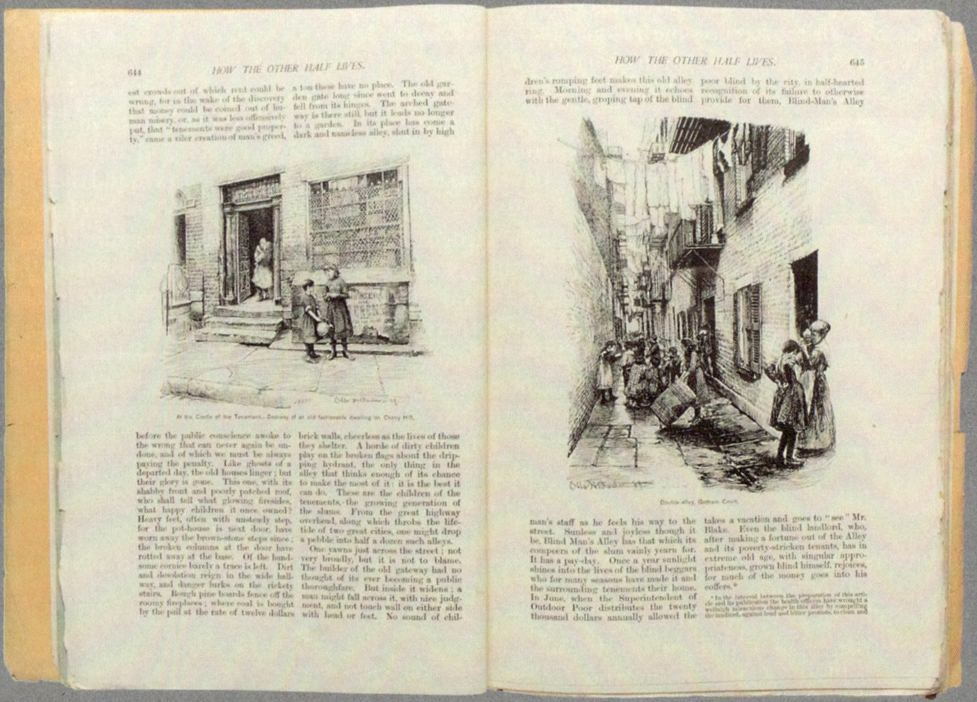

644 *HOW THE OTHER HALF LIVES.*

est crowds out of which rent could be wrung, for in the wake of the discovery that money could be coined out of human misery, or, as it was less offensively put, that "tenements were good property," came a viler creation of man's greed, before the public conscience awoke to the wrong that can never again be undone, and of which we must be always paying the penalty. Like ghosts of a departed day, the old houses linger; but their glory is gone. This one, with its shabby front and poorly patched roof, who shall tell what glowing firesides, what happy children it once owned? Heavy feet, often with unsteady step, for the pot-house is next door, have worn away the brown-stone steps since; the broken columns at the door have rotted away at the base. Of the handsome cornice barely a trace is left. Dirt and desolation reign in the wide hallway, and danger lurks on the rickety stairs. Rough pine boards fence off the roomy fireplaces; where coal is bought by the pail at the rate of twelve dollars a ton these have no place. The old garden gate long since went to decay and fell from its hinges. The arched gateway is there still, but it leads no longer to a garden. In its place has come a dark and nameless alley, shut in by high brick walls, cheerless as the lives of those they shelter. A horde of dirty children play on the broken flags about the dripping hydrant, the only thing in the alley that thinks enough of its chance to make the most of it: it is the best it can do. These are the children of the tenements, the growing generation of the slums. From the great highway overhead, along which throbs the life-tide of two great cities, one might drop a pebble into half a dozen such alleys.

One yawns just across the street; not very broadly, but it is not to blame. The builder of the old gateway had no thought of its ever becoming a public thoroughfare. But inside it widens; a man might fall across it, with nice judgment, and not touch wall on either side with head or feet. No sound of chil-

At the Cradle of the Tenement.—Doorway of an old fashionable dwelling on Cherry Hill.

HOW THE OTHER HALF LIVES. 645

dren's romping feet makes this old alley ring. Morning and evening it echoes with the gentle, groping tap of the blind man's staff as he feels his way to the street. Sunless and joyless though it be, Blind Man's Alley has that which its compeers of the slum vainly yearn for. It has a pay-day. Once a year sunlight shines into the lives of the blind beggars who for many seasons have made it and the surrounding tenements their home. In June, when the Superintendent of Outdoor Poor distributes the twenty thousand dollars annually allowed the poor blind by the city, in half-hearted recognition of its failure to otherwise provide for them, Blind-Man's Alley takes a vacation and goes to "see" Mr. Blake. Even the blind landlord, who, after making a fortune out of the Alley and its poverty-stricken tenants, has in extreme old age, with singular appropriateness, grown blind himself, rejoices, for much of the money goes into his coffers.*

Double-alley, Gotham Court.

* In the interval between the preparation of this article and its publication the health officers have wrought a wellnigh miraculous change in this alley by compelling the landlord, against loud and bitter protests, to clean and

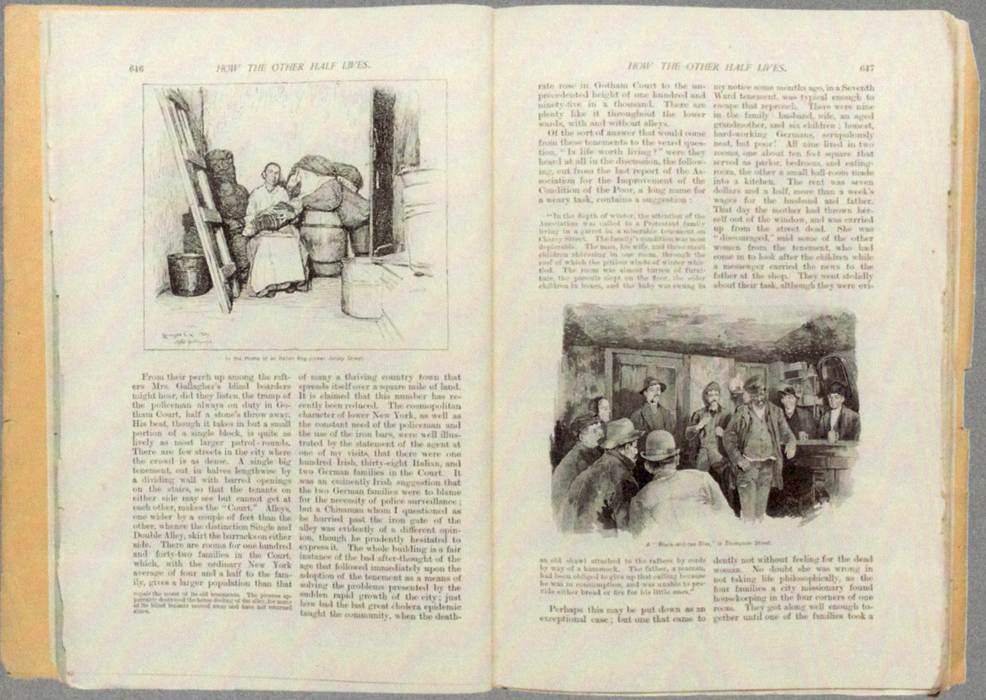

In the Home of an Italian Rag-picker, Jersey Street.

From their perch up among the rafters Mrs. Gallagher's blind boarders might hear, did they listen, the tramp of the policeman always on duty in Gotham Court, half a stone's throw away. His beat, though it takes in but a small portion of a single block, is quite as lively as most larger patrol-rounds. There are few streets in the city where the crowd is as dense. A single big tenement, cut in halves lengthwise by a dividing wall with barred openings on the stairs, so that the tenants on either side may see but cannot get at each other, makes the "Court." Alleys, one wider by a couple of feet than the other, whence the distinction Single and Double Alley, skirt the barracks on either side. There are rooms for one hundred and forty-two families in the Court, which, with the ordinary New York average of four and a half to the family, gives a larger population than that of many a thriving country town that spreads itself over a square mile of land. It is claimed that this number has recently been reduced. The cosmopolitan character of lower New York, as well as the constant need of the policeman and the use of the iron bars, were well illustrated by the statement of the agent at one of my visits, that there were one hundred Irish, thirty-eight Italian, and two German families in the Court. It was an eminently Irish suggestion that the two German families were to blame for the necessity of police surveillance; but a Chinaman whom I questioned as he hurried past the iron gate of the alley was evidently of a different opinion, though he prudently hesitated to express it. The whole building is a fair instance of the bad after-thought of the age that followed immediately upon the adoption of the tenement as a means of solving the problems presented by the sudden rapid growth of the city; just how bad the last great cholera epidemic taught the community, when the death-

repair the worst of its old tenements. The process apparently destroyed the home-feeling of the alley, for many of its blind tenants moved away and have not returned since.

rate rose in Gotham Court to the unprecedented height of one hundred and ninety-five in a thousand. There are plenty like it throughout the lower wards, with and without alleys.

Of the sort of answer that would come from these tenements to the vexed question, "Is life worth living?" were they heard at all in the discussion, the following, cut from the last report of the Association for the Improvement of the Condition of the Poor, a long name for a weary task, contains a suggestion:

"In the depth of winter, the attention of the Association was called to a Protestant family living in a garret in a miserable tenement on Cherry Street. The family's condition was most deplorable. The man, his wife, and three small children shivering in one room, through the roof of which the pitiless winds of winter whistled. The room was almost barren of furniture, the parents slept on the floor, the elder children in boxes, and the baby was swung in an old shawl attached to the rafters by cords by way of a hammock. The father, a seaman, had been obliged to give up that calling because he was in consumption, and was unable to provide either bread or fire for his little ones."

A "Black-and-tan Dive," in Thompson Street.

Perhaps this may be put down as an exceptional case; but one that came to my notice some months ago, in a Seventh Ward tenement, was typical enough to escape that reproach. There were nine in the family: husband, wife, an aged grandmother, and six children; honest, hard-working Germans, scrupulously neat, but poor. All nine lived in two rooms, one about ten feet square that served as parlor, bedroom, and eating-room, the other a small hall-room made into a kitchen. The rent was seven dollars and a half, more than a week's wages for the husband and father. That day the mother had thrown herself out of the window, and was carried up from the street dead. She was "discouraged," said some of the other women from the tenement, who had come in to look after the children while a messenger carried the news to the father at the shop. They went stolidly about their task, although they were evidently not without feeling for the dead woman. No doubt she was wrong in not taking life philosophically, as the four families a city missionary found housekeeping in the four corners of one room. They got along well enough together until one of the families took a

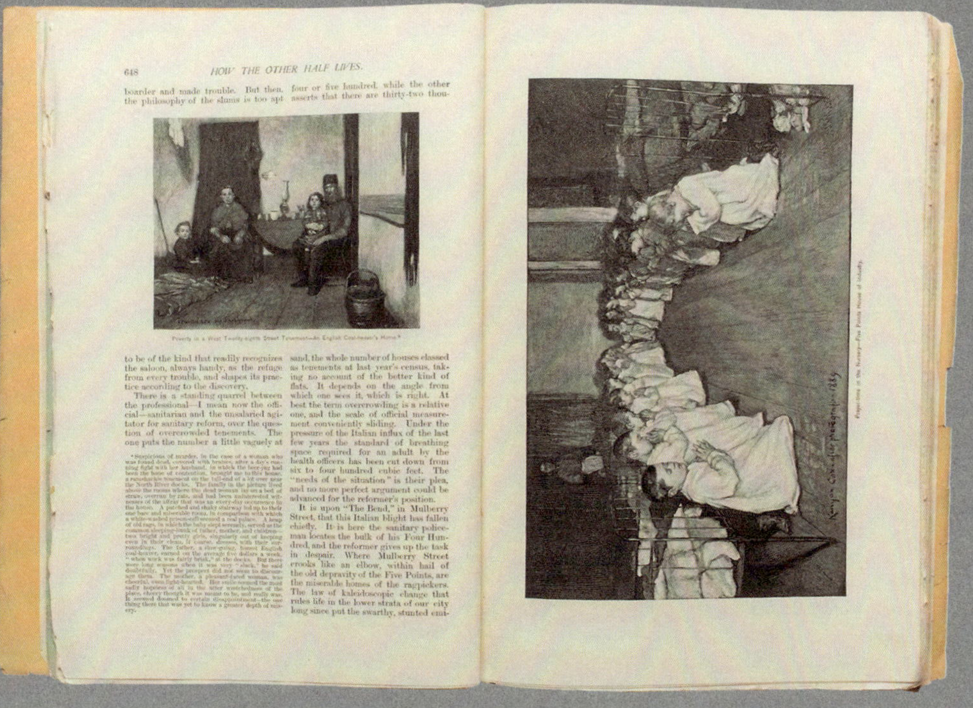

boarder and made trouble. But then, the philosophy of the slums is too apt to be of the kind that readily recognizes the saloon, always handy, as the refuge from every trouble, and shapes its practice according to the discovery.

Poverty in a West Twenty-eighth Street Tenement—An English Coal-heaver's Home.*

There is a standing quarrel between the professional—I mean now the official—sanitarian and the unsalaried agitator for sanitary reform, over the question of overcrowded tenements. The one puts the number a little vaguely at four or five hundred, while the other asserts that there are thirty-two thousand, the whole number of houses classed as tenements at last year's census, taking no account of the better kind of flats. It depends on the angle from which one sees it, which is right. At best the term overcrowding is a relative one, and the scale of official measurement conveniently sliding. Under the pressure of the Italian influx of the last few years the standard of breathing space required for an adult by the health officers has been cut down from six to four hundred cubic feet. The "needs of the situation" is their plea, and no more perfect argument could be advanced for the reformer's position.

It is upon "The Bend," in Mulberry Street, that this Italian blight has fallen chiefly. It is here the sanitary policeman locates the bulk of his Four Hundred, and the reformer gives up the task in despair. Where Mulberry Street crooks like an elbow, within hail of the old depravity of the Five Points, are the miserable homes of the ragpickers. The law of kaleidoscopic change that rules life in the lower strata of our city long since put the swarthy, stunted emi-

*Suspicions of murder, in the case of a woman who was found dead, covered with bruises, after a day's running fight with her husband, in which the beer-jug had been the bone of contention, brought me to this house, a ramshackle tenement on the tail-end of a lot over near the North River docks. The family in the picture lived above the rooms where the dead woman lay on a bed of straw, overrun by rats, and had been uninterested witnesses of the affray that was an every-day occurrence in the house. A patched and shaky stairway led up to their one bare and miserable room, in comparison with which a white-washed prison-cell seemed a real palace. A heap of old rags, in which the baby slept serenely, served as the common sleeping-bunk of father, mother, and children—two bright and pretty girls, singularly out of keeping even in their clean, if coarse, dresses, with their surroundings. The father, a slow-going, honest English coal-heaver, earned on the average five dollars a week, "when work was fairly brisk," at the docks. But there were long seasons when it was very "slack," he said doubtfully. Yet the prospect did not seem to discourage them. The mother, a pleasant-faced woman, was cheerful, even light-hearted. Her smile seemed the most sadly hopeless of all in the utter wretchedness of the place, cheery though it was meant to be, and really was. It seemed doomed to certain disappointment—the one thing there that was yet to know a greater depth of misery.

Prayertime in the Nursery—Five Points House of Industry.

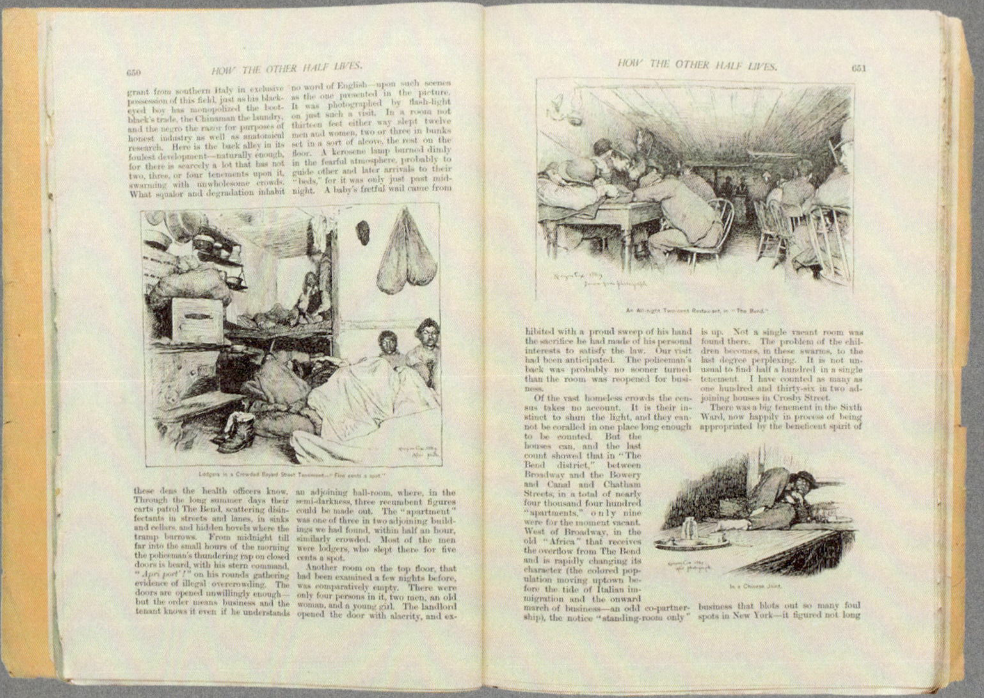

grant from southern Italy in exclusive possession of this field, just as his black-eyed boy has monopolized the boot-black's trade, the Chinaman the laundry, and the negro the razor for purposes of honest industry as well as anatomical research. Here is the back alley in its foulest development—naturally enough, for there is scarcely a lot that has not two, three, or four tenements upon it, swarming with unwholesome crowds. What squalor and degradation inhabit no word of English—upon such scenes as the one presented in the picture. It was photographed by flash-light on just such a visit. In a room not thirteen feet either way slept twelve men and women, two or three in bunks set in a sort of alcove, the rest on the floor. A kerosene lamp burned dimly in the fearful atmosphere, probably to guide other and later arrivals to their "beds," for it was only just past midnight. A baby's fretful wail came from

Lodgers in a Crowded Bayard Street Tenement—"Five cents a spot."

these dens the health officers know. Through the long summer days their carts patrol The Bend, scattering disinfectants in streets and lanes, in sinks and cellars, and hidden hovels where the tramp burrows. From midnight till far into the small hours of the morning the policeman's thundering rap on closed doors is heard, with his stern command, "*Apri port'!*" on his rounds gathering evidence of illegal overcrowding. The doors are opened unwillingly enough—but the order means business and the tenant knows it even if he understands an adjoining hall-room, where, in the semi-darkness, three recumbent figures could be made out. The "apartment" was one of three in two adjoining buildings we had found, within half an hour, similarly crowded. Most of the men were lodgers, who slept there for five cents a spot.

Another room on the top floor, that had been examined a few nights before, was comparatively empty. There were only four persons in it, two men, an old woman, and a young girl. The landlord opened the door with alacrity, and ex-

An All-night Two-cent Restaurant, in "The Bend."

hibited with a proud sweep of his hand the sacrifice he had made of his personal interests to satisfy the law. Our visit had been anticipated. The policeman's back was probably no sooner turned than the room was reopened for business.

Of the vast homeless crowds the census takes no account. It is their instinct to shun the light, and they cannot be corralled in one place long enough to be counted. But the houses can, and the last count showed that in "The Bend district," between Broadway and the Bowery and Canal and Chatham Streets, in a total of nearly four thousand four hundred "apartments," only nine were for the moment vacant. West of Broadway, in the old "Africa" that receives the overflow from The Bend and is rapidly changing its character (the colored population moving uptown before the tide of Italian immigration and the onward march of business—an odd co-partnership), the notice "standing-room only" is up. Not a single vacant room was found there. The problem of the children becomes, in these swarms, to the last degree perplexing. It is not unusual to find half a hundred in a single tenement. I have counted as many as one hundred and thirty-six in two adjoining houses in Crosby Street.

There was a big tenement in the Sixth Ward, now happily in process of being appropriated by the beneficent spirit of business that blots out so many foul spots in New York—it figured not long

In a Chinese Joint.

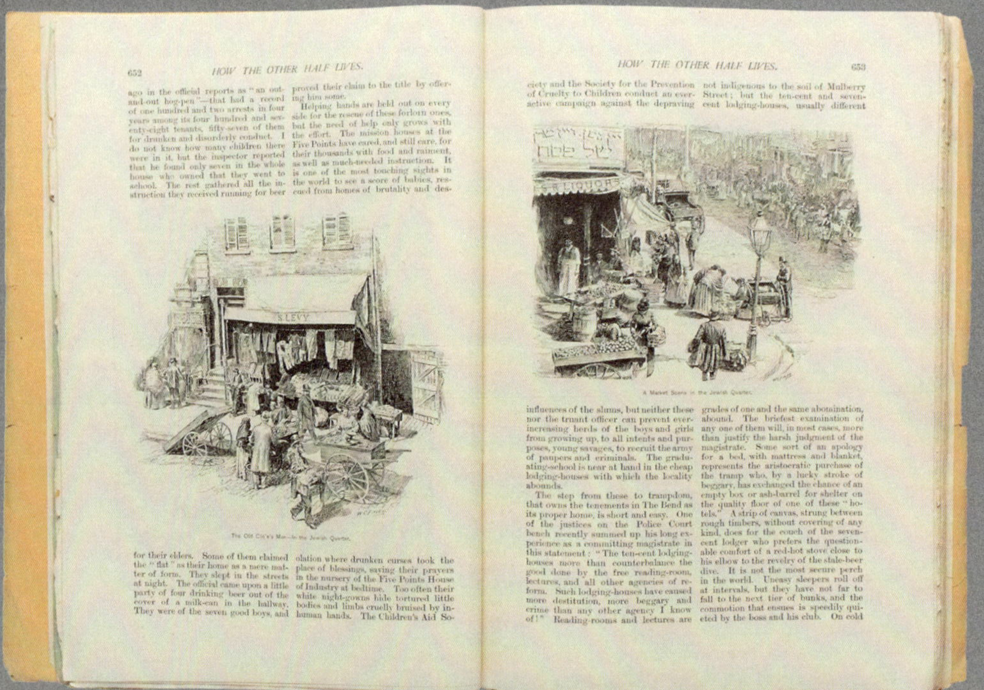

ago in the official reports as "an out-and-out hog-pen"—that had a record of one hundred and two arrests in four years among its four hundred and seventy-eight tenants, fifty-seven of them for drunken and disorderly conduct. I do not know how many children there were in it, but the inspector reported that he found only seven in the whole house who owned that they went to school. The rest gathered all the instruction they received running for beer proved their claim to the title by offering him some.

Helping hands are held out on every side for the rescue of these forlorn ones, but the need of help only grows with the effort. The mission houses at the Five Points have cared, and still care, for their thousands with food and raiment, as well as much-needed instruction. It is one of the most touching sights in the world to see a score of babies, rescued from homes of brutality and des-

The Old Clo'e's Man—In the Jewish Quarter.

for their elders. Some of them claimed the "flat" as their home as a mere matter of form. They slept in the streets at night. The official came upon a little party of four drinking beer out of the cover of a milk-can in the hallway. They were of the seven good boys, and olation where drunken curses took the place of blessings, saying their prayers in the nursery of the Five Points House of Industry at bedtime. Too often their white night-gowns hide tortured little bodies and limbs cruelly bruised by inhuman hands. The Children's Aid So-

ciety and the Society for the Prevention of Cruelty to Children conduct an ever-active campaign against the depraving not indigenous to the soil of Mulberry Street; but the ten-cent and seven-cent lodging-houses, usually different

A Market Scene in the Jewish Quarter.

influences of the slums, but neither these nor the truant officer can prevent ever-increasing herds of the boys and girls from growing up, to all intents and purposes, young savages, to recruit the army of paupers and criminals. The graduating-school is near at hand in the cheap lodging-houses with which the locality abounds.

The step from these to trampdom, that owns the tenements in The Bend as its proper home, is short and easy. One of the justices on the Police Court bench recently summed up his long experience as a committing magistrate in this statement: "The ten-cent lodging-houses more than counterbalance the good done by the free reading-room, lectures, and all other agencies of reform. Such lodging-houses have caused more destitution, more beggary and crime than any other agency I know of!" Reading-rooms and lectures are grades of one and the same abomination, abound. The briefest examination of any one of them will, in most cases, more than justify the harsh judgment of the magistrate. Some sort of an apology for a bed, with mattress and blanket, represents the aristocratic purchase of the tramp who, by a lucky stroke of beggary, has exchanged the chance of an empty box or ash-barrel for shelter on the quality floor of one of these "hotels." A strip of canvas, strung between rough timbers, without covering of any kind, does for the couch of the seven-cent lodger who prefers the questionable comfort of a red-hot stove close to his elbow to the revelry of the stale-beer dive. It is not the most secure perch in the world. Uneasy sleepers roll off at intervals, but they have not far to fall to the next tier of bunks, and the commotion that ensues is speedily quieted by the boss and his club. On cold

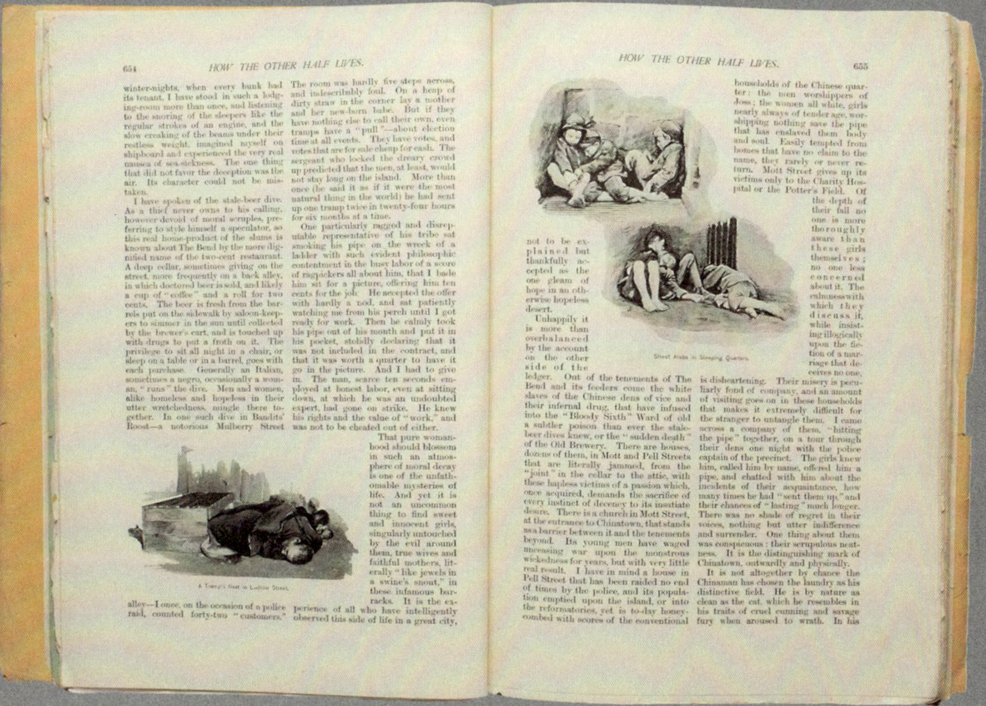

654 HOW THE OTHER HALF LIVES.

winter-nights, when every bunk had its tenant, I have stood in such a lodging-room more than once, and listening to the snoring of the sleepers like the regular strokes of an engine, and the slow creaking of the beams under their restless weight, imagined myself on shipboard and experienced the very real nausea of sea-sickness. The one thing that did not favor the deception was the air. Its character could not be mistaken.

I have spoken of the stale-beer dive. As a thief never owns to his calling, however devoid of moral scruples, preferring to style himself a speculator, so this real home-product of the slums is known about The Bend by the more dignified name of the two-cent restaurant. A deep cellar, sometimes giving on the street, more frequently on a back alley, in which doctored beer is sold, and likely a cup of "coffee" and a roll for two cents. The beer is fresh from the barrels put on the sidewalk by saloon-keepers to simmer in the sun until collected by the brewer's cart, and is touched up with drugs to put a froth on it. The privilege to sit all night in a chair, or sleep on a table or in a barrel, goes with each purchase. Generally an Italian, sometimes a negro, occasionally a woman, "runs" the dive. Men and women, alike homeless and hopeless in their utter wretchedness, mingle there together. In one such dive in Bandits' Roost—a notorious Mulberry Street alley—I once, on the occasion of a police raid, counted forty-two "customers." The room was hardly five steps across, and indescribably foul. On a heap of dirty straw in the corner lay a mother and her new-born babe. But if they have nothing else to call their own, even tramps have a "pull"—about election time at all events. They have votes, and votes that are for sale cheap for cash. The sergeant who locked the dreary crowd up predicted that the men, at least, would not stay long on the island. More than once (he said it as if it were the most natural thing in the world) he had sent up one tramp twice in twenty-four hours for six months at a time.

One particularly ragged and disreputable representative of his tribe sat smoking his pipe on the wreck of a ladder with such evident philosophic contentment in the busy labor of a score of ragpickers all about him, that I bade him sit for a picture, offering him ten cents for the job. He accepted the offer with hardly a nod, and sat patiently watching me from his perch until I got ready for work. Then he calmly took his pipe out of his mouth and put it in his pocket, stolidly declaring that it was not included in the contract, and that it was worth a quarter to have it go in the picture. And I had to give in. The man, scarce ten seconds employed at honest labor, even at sitting down, at which he was an undoubted expert, had gone on strike. He knew his rights and the value of "work," and was not to be cheated out of either.

A Tramp's Nest in Ludlow Street.

That pure womanhood should blossom in such an atmosphere of moral decay is one of the unfathomable mysteries of life. And yet it is not an uncommon thing to find sweet and innocent girls, singularly untouched by the evil around them, true wives and faithful mothers, literally "like jewels in a swine's snout," in these infamous barracks. It is the experience of all who have intelligently observed this side of life in a great city,

HOW THE OTHER HALF LIVES. 655

not to be explained but thankfully accepted as the one gleam of hope in an otherwise hopeless desert.

Unhappily it is more than overbalanced by the account on the other side of the ledger. Out of the tenements of The Bend and its feeders come the white slaves of the Chinese dens of vice and their infernal drug, that have infused into the "Bloody Sixth" Ward of old a subtler poison than ever the stale-beer dives knew, or the "sudden death" of the Old Brewery. There are houses, dozens of them, in Mott and Pell Streets that are literally jammed, from the "joint" in the cellar to the attic, with these hapless victims of a passion which, once acquired, demands the sacrifice of every instinct of decency to its insatiate desire. There is a church in Mott Street, at the entrance to Chinatown, that stands as a barrier between it and the tenements beyond. Its young men have waged unceasing war upon the monstrous wickedness for years, but with very little real result. I have in mind a house in Pell Street that has been raided no end of times by the police, and its population emptied upon the island, or into the reformatories, yet is to-day honey-combed with scores of the conventional households of the Chinese quarter: the men worshippers of Joss; the women all white, girls nearly always of tender age, worshipping nothing save the pipe that has enslaved them body and soul. Easily tempted from homes that have no claim to the name, they rarely or never return. Mott Street gives up its victims only to the Charity Hospital or the Potter's Field. Of the depth of their fall no one is more thoroughly aware than these girls themselves; no one less concerned about it. The calmness with which they discuss it, while insisting illogically upon the fiction of a marriage that deceives no one, is disheartening. Their misery is peculiarly fond of company, and an amount of visiting goes on in these households that makes it extremely difficult for the stranger to untangle them. I came across a company of them, "hitting the pipe" together, on a tour through their dens one night with the police captain of the precinct. The girls knew him, called him by name, offered him a pipe, and chatted with him about the incidents of their acquaintance, how many times he had "sent them up," and their chances of "lasting" much longer. There was no shade of regret in their voices, nothing but utter indifference and surrender. One thing about them was conspicuous: their scrupulous neatness. It is the distinguishing mark of Chinatown, outwardly and physically.

Street Arabs in Sleeping Quarters.

It is not altogether by chance the Chinaman has chosen the laundry as his distinctive field. He is by nature as clean as the cat, which he resembles in his traits of cruel cunning and savage fury when aroused to wrath. In his

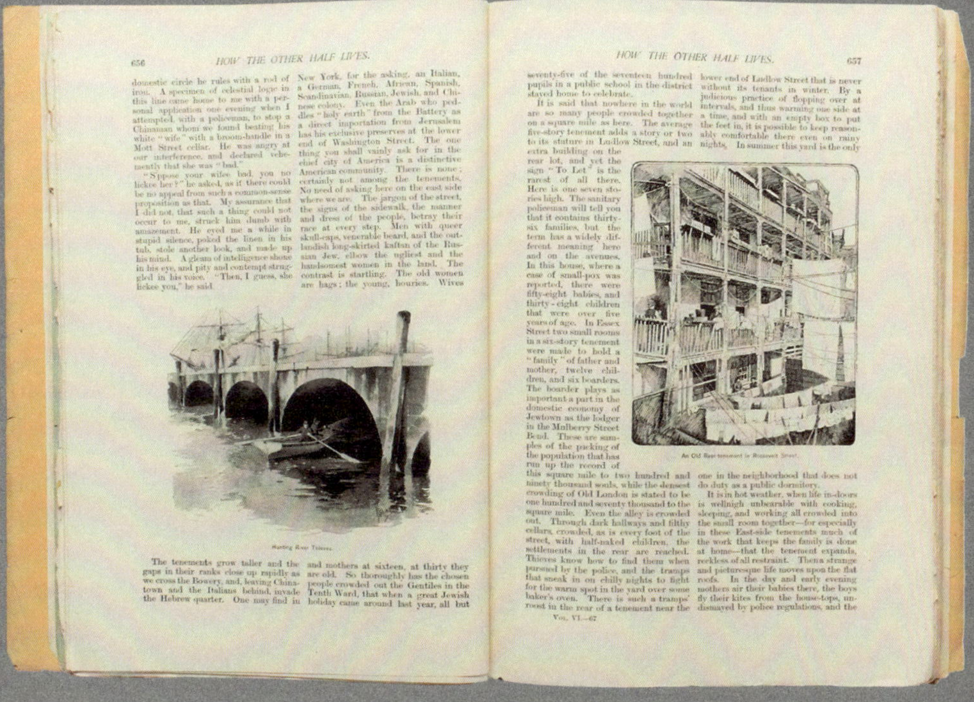

656 HOW THE OTHER HALF LIVES.

domestic circle he rules with a rod of iron. A specimen of celestial logic in this line came home to me with a personal application one evening when I attempted, with a policeman, to stop a Chinaman whom we found beating his white "wife" with a broom-handle in a Mott Street cellar. He was angry at our interference, and declared vehemently that she was "bad."

"S'ppose your wifee bad, you no lickee her?" he asked, as if there could be no appeal from such a common-sense proposition as that. My assurance that I did not, that such a thing could not occur to me, struck him dumb with amazement. He eyed me a while in stupid silence, poked the linen in his tub, stole another look, and made up his mind. A gleam of intelligence shone in his eye, and pity and contempt struggled in his voice. "Then, I guess, she lickee you," he said.

Hunting River Thieves.

The tenements grow taller and the gaps in their ranks close up rapidly as we cross the Bowery, and, leaving Chinatown and the Italians behind, invade the Hebrew quarter. One may find in New York, for the asking, an Italian, a German, French, African, Spanish, Scandinavian, Russian, Jewish, and Chinese colony. Even the Arab who peddles "holy earth" from the Battery as a direct importation from Jerusalem has his exclusive preserves at the lower end of Washington Street. The one thing you shall vainly ask for in the chief city of America is a distinctive American community. There is none; certainly not among the tenements. No need of asking here on the east side where we are. The jargon of the street, the signs of the sidewalk, the manner and dress of the people, betray their race at every step. Men with queer skull-caps, venerable beard, and the outlandish long-skirted kaftan of the Russian Jew, elbow the ugliest and the handsomest women in the land. The contrast is startling. The old women are hags; the young, houries. Wives and mothers at sixteen, at thirty they are old. So thoroughly has the chosen people crowded out the Gentiles in the Tenth Ward, that when a great Jewish holiday came around last year, all but

HOW THE OTHER HALF LIVES. 657

seventy-five of the seventeen hundred pupils in a public school in the district stayed home to celebrate.

It is said that nowhere in the world are so many people crowded together on a square mile as here. The average five-story tenement adds a story or two to its stature in Ludlow Street, and an extra building on the rear lot, and yet the sign "To Let" is the rarest of all there. Here is one seven stories high. The sanitary policeman will tell you that it contains thirty-six families, but the term has a widely different meaning here and on the avenues. In this house, where a case of small-pox was reported, there were fifty-eight babies, and thirty-eight children that were over five years of age. In Essex Street two small rooms in a six-story tenement were made to hold a "family" of father and mother, twelve children, and six boarders. The boarder plays as important a part in the domestic economy of Jewtown as the lodger in the Mulberry Street Bend. These are samples of the packing of the population that has run up the record of this square mile to two hundred and ninety thousand souls, while the densest crowding of Old London is stated to be one hundred and seventy thousand to the square mile. Even the alley is crowded out. Through dark hallways and filthy cellars, crowded, as is every foot of the street, with half-naked children, the settlements in the rear are reached. Thieves know how to find them when pursued by the police, and the tramps that sneak in on chilly nights to fight for the warm spot in the yard over some baker's oven. There is such a tramps' roost in the rear of a tenement near the lower end of Ludlow Street that is never without its tenants in winter. By a judicious practice of flopping over at intervals, and thus warming one side at a time, and with an empty box to put the feet in, it is possible to keep reasonably comfortable there even on rainy nights. In summer this yard is the only one in the neighborhood that does not do duty as a public dormitory.

An Old Rear-tenement in Roosevelt Street.

It is in hot weather, when life in-doors is wellnigh unbearable with cooking, sleeping, and working all crowded into the small room together—for especially in these East-side tenements much of the work that keeps the family is done at home—that the tenement expands, reckless of all restraint. Then a strange and picturesque life moves upon the flat roofs. In the day and early evening mothers air their babies there, the boys fly their kites from the house-tops, undismayed by police regulations, and the

VOL. VI.—67

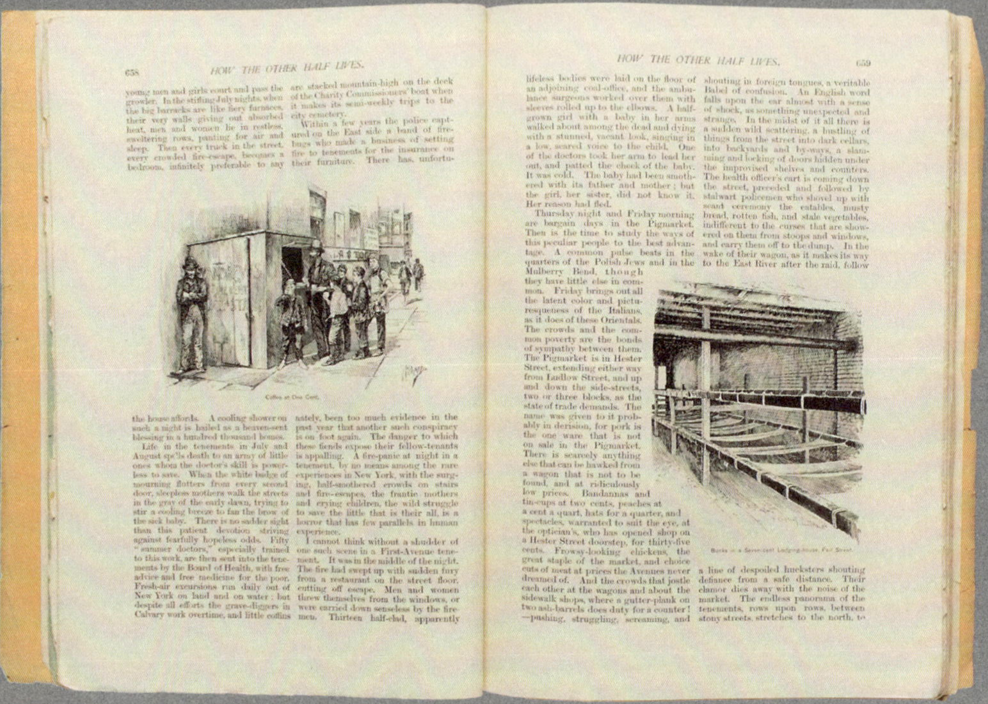

young men and girls court and pass the growler. In the stifling July nights, when the big barracks are like fiery furnaces, their very walls giving out absorbed heat, men and women lie in restless, sweltering rows, panting for air and sleep. Then every truck in the street, every crowded fire-escape, becomes a bedroom, infinitely preferable to any the house affords. A cooling shower on such a night is hailed as a heaven-sent blessing in a hundred thousand homes.

Life in the tenements in July and August spells death to an army of little ones whom the doctor's skill is powerless to save. When the white badge of mourning flutters from every second door, sleepless mothers walk the streets in the gray of the early dawn, trying to stir a cooling breeze to fan the brow of the sick baby. There is no sadder sight than this patient devotion striving against fearfully hopeless odds. Fifty "summer doctors," especially trained to this work, are then sent into the tenements by the Board of Health, with free advice and free medicine for the poor. Fresh-air excursions run daily out of New York on land and on water; but despite all efforts the grave-diggers in Calvary work overtime, and little coffins are stacked mountain-high on the deck of the Charity Commissioners' boat when it makes its semi-weekly trips to the city cemetery.

Within a few years the police captured on the East side a band of fire-bugs who made a business of setting fire to tenements for the insurance on their furniture. There has, unfortunately, been too much evidence in the past year that another such conspiracy is on foot again. The danger to which these fiends expose their fellow-tenants is appalling. A fire-panic at night in a tenement, by no means among the rare experiences in New York, with the surging, half-smothered crowds on stairs and fire-escapes, the frantic mothers and crying children, the wild struggle to save the little that is their all, is a horror that has few parallels in human experience.

I cannot think without a shudder of one such scene in a First-Avenue tenement. It was in the middle of the night. The fire had swept up with sudden fury from a restaurant on the street floor, cutting off escape. Men and women threw themselves from the windows, or were carried down senseless by the firemen. Thirteen half-clad, apparently

Coffee at One Cent.

lifeless bodies were laid on the floor of an adjoining coal-office, and the ambulance surgeons worked over them with sleeves rolled up to the elbows. A half-grown girl with a baby in her arms walked about among the dead and dying with a stunned, vacant look, singing in a low, scared voice to the child. One of the doctors took her arm to lead her out, and patted the cheek of the baby. It was cold. The baby had been smothered with its father and mother; but the girl, her sister, did not know it. Her reason had fled.

Thursday night and Friday morning are bargain days in the Pigmarket. Then is the time to study the ways of this peculiar people to the best advantage. A common pulse beats in the quarters of the Polish Jews and in the Mulberry Bend, though they have little else in common. Friday brings out all the latent color and picturesqueness of the Italians, as it does of these Orientals. The crowds and the common poverty are the bonds of sympathy between them. The Pigmarket is in Hester Street, extending either way from Ludlow Street, and up and down the side-streets, two or three blocks, as the state of trade demands. The name was given to it probably in derision, for pork is the one ware that is not on sale in the Pigmarket. There is scarcely anything else that can be hawked from a wagon that is not to be found, and at ridiculously low prices. Bandannas and tin-cups at two cents, peaches at a cent a quart, hats for a quarter, and spectacles, warranted to suit the eye, at the optician's, who has opened shop on a Hester Street doorstep, for thirty-five cents. Frowsy-looking chickens, the great staple of the market, and choice cuts of meat at prices the Avenues never dreamed of. And the crowds that jostle each other at the wagons and about the sidewalk shops, where a gutter-plank on two ash-barrels does duty for a counter! —pushing, struggling, screaming, and shouting in foreign tongues, a veritable Babel of confusion. An English word falls upon the ear almost with a sense of shock, as something unexpected and strange. In the midst of it all there is a sudden wild scattering, a hustling of things from the street into dark cellars, into backyards and by-ways, a slamming and locking of doors hidden under the improvised shelves and counters. The health officer's cart is coming down the street, preceded and followed by stalwart policemen who shovel up with scant ceremony the eatables, musty bread, rotten fish, and stale vegetables, indifferent to the curses that are showered on them from stoops and windows, and carry them off to the dump. In the wake of their wagon, as it makes its way to the East River after the raid, follow a line of despoiled hucksters shouting defiance from a safe distance. Their clamor dies away with the noise of the market. The endless panorama of the tenements, rows upon rows, between stony streets, stretches to the north, to

Bunks in a Seven-cent Lodging-house, Pell Street.

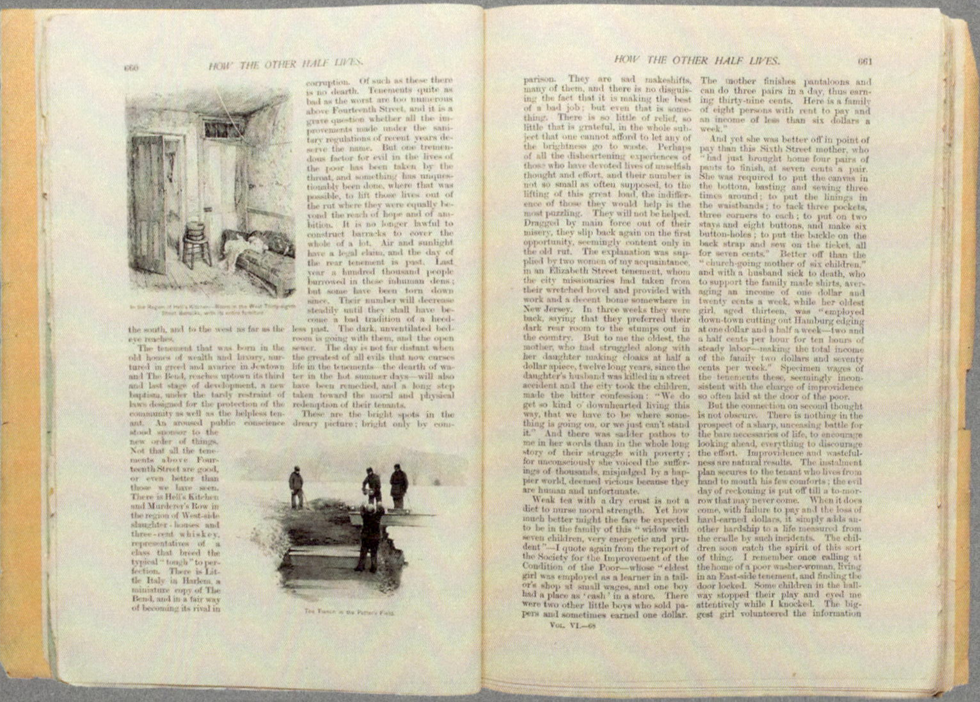

In the Region of Hell's Kitchen—Room in the West Thirty-eighth Street Barracks, with its entire furniture.

the south, and to the west as far as the eye reaches.

The tenement that was born in the old homes of wealth and luxury, nurtured in greed and avarice in Jewtown and The Bend, reaches uptown its third and last stage of development, a new baptism, under the tardy restraint of laws designed for the protection of the community as well as the helpless tenant. An aroused public conscience stood sponsor to the new order of things. Not that all the tenements above Fourteenth Street are good, or even better than those we have seen. There is Hell's Kitchen and Murderer's Row in the region of West-side slaughter-houses and three-cent whiskey, representatives of a class that breed the typical "tough" to perfection. There is Little Italy in Harlem, a miniature copy of The Bend, and in a fair way of becoming its rival in corruption. Of such as these there is no dearth. Tenements quite as bad as the worst are too numerous above Fourteenth Street, and it is a grave question whether all the improvements made under the sanitary regulations of recent years deserve the name. But one tremendous factor for evil in the lives of the poor has been taken by the throat, and something has unquestionably been done, where that was possible, to lift those lives out of the rut where they were equally beyond the reach of hope and of ambition. It is no longer lawful to construct barracks to cover the whole of a lot. Air and sunlight have a legal claim, and the day of the rear tenement is past. Last year a hundred thousand people burrowed in these inhuman dens; but some have been torn down since. Their number will decrease steadily until they shall have become a bad tradition of a heedless past. The dark, unventilated bedroom is going with them, and the open sewer. The day is not far distant when the greatest of all evils that now curses life in the tenements—the dearth of water in the hot summer days—will also have been remedied, and a long step taken toward the moral and physical redemption of their tenants.

These are the bright spots in the dreary picture; bright only by comparison. They are sad makeshifts, many of them, and there is no disguising the fact that it is making the best of a bad job; but even that is something. There is so little of relief, so little that is grateful, in the whole subject that one cannot afford to let any of the brightness go to waste. Perhaps of all the disheartening experiences of those who have devoted lives of unselfish thought and effort, and their number is not so small as often supposed, to the lifting of this great load, the indifference of those they would help is the most puzzling. They will not be helped. Dragged by main force out of their misery, they slip back again on the first opportunity, seemingly content only in the old rut. The explanation was supplied by two women of my acquaintance, in an Elizabeth Street tenement, whom the city missionaries had taken from their wretched hovel and provided with work and a decent home somewhere in New Jersey. In three weeks they were back, saying that they preferred their dark rear room to the stumps out in the country. But to me the oldest, the mother, who had struggled along with her daughter making cloaks at half a dollar apiece, twelve long years, since the daughter's husband was killed in a street accident and the city took the children, made the bitter confession: "We do get so kind o' downhearted living this way, that we have to be where something is going on, or we just can't stand it." And there was sadder pathos to me in her words than in the whole long story of their struggle with poverty; for unconsciously she voiced the sufferings of thousands, misjudged by a happier world, deemed vicious because they are human and unfortunate.

Weak tea with a dry crust is not a diet to nurse moral strength. Yet how much better might the fare be expected to be in the family of this "widow with seven children, very energetic and prudent"—I quote again from the report of the Society for the Improvement of the Condition of the Poor—whose "eldest girl was employed as a learner in a tailor's shop at small wages, and one boy had a place as 'cash' in a store. There were two other little boys who sold papers and sometimes earned one dollar. The mother finishes pantaloons and can do three pairs in a day, thus earning thirty-nine cents. Here is a family of eight persons with rent to pay and an income of less than six dollars a week."

And yet she was better off in point of pay than this Sixth Street mother, who "had just brought home four pairs of pants to finish, at seven cents a pair. She was required to put the canvas in the bottom, basting and sewing three times around; to put the linings in the waistbands; to tack three pockets, three corners to each; to put on two stays and eight buttons, and make six button-holes; to put the buckle on the back strap and sew on the ticket, all for seven cents." Better off than the "church-going mother of six children," and with a husband sick to death, who to support the family made shirts, averaging an income of one dollar and twenty cents a week, while her oldest girl, aged thirteen, was "employed down-town cutting out Hamburg edging at one dollar and a half a week—two and a half cents per hour for ten hours of steady labor—making the total income of the family two dollars and seventy cents per week." Specimen wages of the tenements these, seemingly inconsistent with the charge of improvidence so often laid at the door of the poor.

But the connection on second thought is not obscure. There is nothing in the prospect of a sharp, unceasing battle for the bare necessaries of life, to encourage looking ahead, everything to discourage the effort. Improvidence and wastefulness are natural results. The instalment plan secures to the tenant who lives from hand to mouth his few comforts; the evil day of reckoning is put off till a to-morrow that may never come. When it does come, with failure to pay and the loss of hard-earned dollars, it simply adds another hardship to a life measured from the cradle by such incidents. The children soon catch the spirit of this sort of thing. I remember once calling at the home of a poor washer-woman, living in an East-side tenement, and finding the door locked. Some children in the hallway stopped their play and eyed me attentively while I knocked. The biggest girl volunteered the information

The Trench in the Potter's Field.

Inquiries into Human Faculty and Its Development

Francis Galton

1883

COMPOSITE PORTRAITURE

As a means of getting over the difficulty of procuring really representative faces, I contrived the method of composite portraiture, which has been explained of late on many occasions [...] I collected photographic portraits of different persons, all of whom had been photographed in the same aspect (say full face), and under the same conditions of light and shade (say with the light coming from the right side). I reduced their portraits photographically to the same size, being guided as to scale by the distance between any two convenient points of reference in the features; for example, by the vertical distance between two parallel lines, one of which passed through the middle of the pupils of the eyes and the other between the lips. I superimposed the portraits like the successive leaves of a book, so that the features of each portrait lay as exactly as the case admitted, in front of those of the one behind it, eye in front of eye and mouth in front of mouth. This I did by holding them successively to the light and adjusting them, then by fastening each to the preceding one with a strip of gummed paper along one of the edges. Thus I obtained a book, each page of which contained a separate portrait, and all the portraits lay exactly in front of one another. I fastened the book against the wall in such a way that I could turn over the pages in succession, leaving in turn each portrait flat and fully exposed. I focused my camera on the book, fixed it firmly, and put a sensitive plate inside it. I began photographing, taking one page after the other in succession without moving the camera, but putting on the cap whilst I was turning over the pages, so that an image of each of the portraits in succession was thrown on the same part of the sensitized plate. [...]

The effect of composite portraiture is to bring into evidence all the traits in which there is agreement, and to leave but a ghost of a trace of individual peculiarities. There are so many traits in common in all faces that the composite picture when made from many components is far from being a blur; it has altogether the look of an ideal composition. [...]

This face and the qualities it connotes probably gives a clue to the direction in which the stock of the English race might most easily be improved. It is the essential notion of a race that there should be some ideal typical form from which the individuals may deviate in all directions, but about which they chiefly cluster, and towards which their descendants will continue to cluster. The easiest direction in which a race can be improved is towards that central type, because nothing new has to be sought out. It is only necessary to encourage as far as practicable the breed of those who conform most nearly to the central type, and to restrain as far as may be the breed of those who deviate widely from it. Now there can hardly be a more appropriate method of discovering the central physiognomic type of any race or group than that of composite portraiture.

As a contrast to the composite of the Royal Engineers, I give those of two of the coarse and low types of face found among the criminal classes. The photographs from which they were made are taken from two large groups. One are those of men undergoing severe sentences for murder and other crimes connected with violence; the other of thieves. They were reprints from those taken by order of the prison authorities for purposes of identification. I was allowed to obtain copies for use in my inquiries by the kind permission of Sir Edmund Du Cane, H.M. Director of Prisons. The originals of these and their components have frequently been exhibited. It is unhappily a fact that fairly distinct types of criminals breeding true to their kind have become established and are one of the saddest disfigurements of modern civilization. To this subject I shall recur.

I have made numerous composites of various groups of convicts, which are interesting negatively rather than positively. They produce faces of a mean description, with no villainy written on them. The individual faces are villainous enough, but they are villainous in different ways, and when they are combined, the individual peculiarities disappear, and the common humanity of a low type is all that is left.

The remaining portraits are illustrations of the application of the process to the study of the physiognomy of disease. [...]

In the lower division of the Plate will be found three composites, each made from a large number of faces, unselected, except on the ground of the disease under which they were suffering. When only few portraits are used, there must be some moderate resemblance between them, or the result would be blurred; but here, dealing with as many as 56, 100, and 50 cases respectively, the combination of any medley group results in an ideal expression.

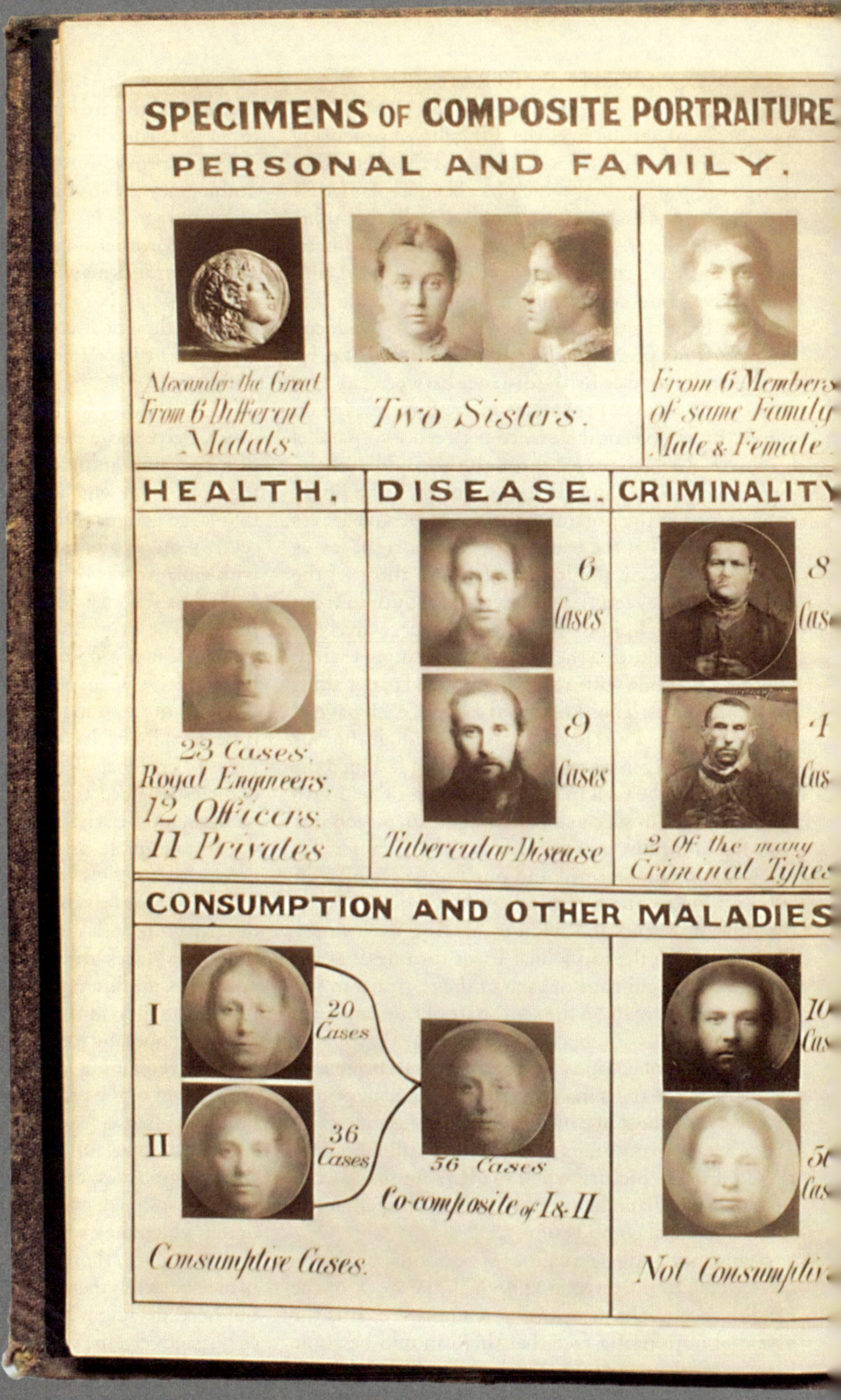
SPECIMENS OF COMPOSITE PORTRAITURE
PERSONAL AND FAMILY.
Alexander the Great From 6 Different Medals.
Two Sisters.
From 6 Members of same Family Male & Female
HEALTH.
DISEASE.
CRIMINALITY
23 Cases. Royal Engineers. 12 Officers. 11 Privates
6 Cases
9 Cases
Tubercular Disease
8
2 Of the many Criminal Types
CONSUMPTION AND OTHER MALADIES
I
20 Cases
II
36 Cases
56 Cases
Co-composite of I & II
Consumptive Cases.

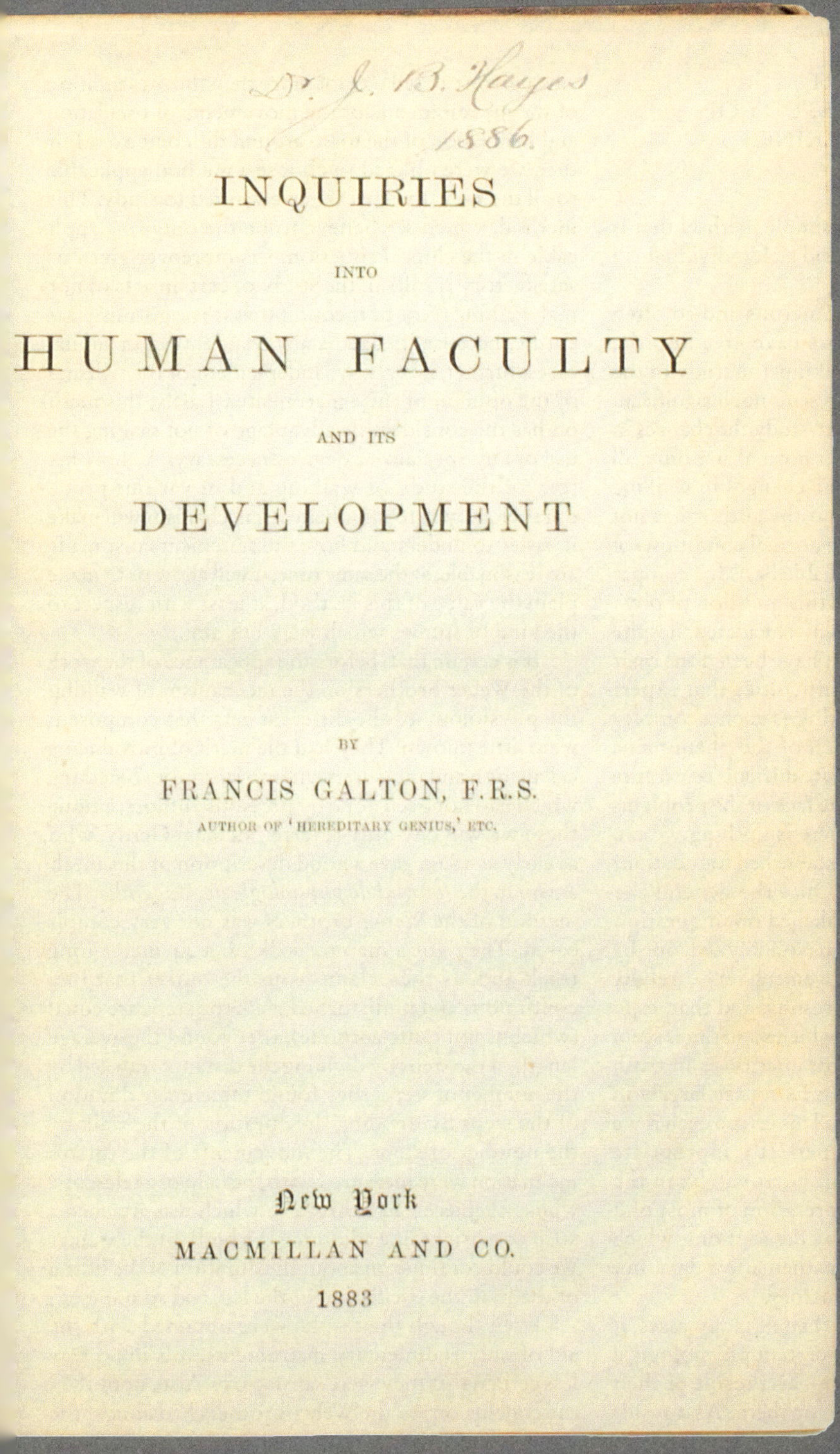
Dr. J. B. Hayes
1886.

INQUIRIES

INTO

HUMAN FACULTY

AND ITS

DEVELOPMENT

BY

FRANCIS GALTON, F.R.S.

AUTHOR OF 'HEREDITARY GENIUS,' ETC.

New York

MACMILLAN AND CO.

1883

Physiological Study of Normal Walking
Georges Gilles de la Tourette
1886

FIRST PART
PHYSIOLOGICAL STUDY OF NORMAL WALKING

First Chapter
§1: Concerning the choice of a simple method that is applicable to both the healthy and sick individual

When we reflect on the very numerous and so often divergent opinions that authors have given on the physiological mechanism of walking, the study of the pathological walk immediately presents not insignificant problems. Just as it is impossible to study the changes in a tissue when we do not know its normal anatomy, all the conclusions of a study of the changes in walking will end up being quite useless if the author has not been careful to refer them to the normal conditions of movement, which serves as a reliable basis for comparison. That said, it is certain that this question of physiology has not yet been completely elucidated, despite the large number of studies that have been done on it. This is obviously due to the difficulties that experimenters encounter, since walking is such a complex process that the analysis of each of the phenomena that compose it is technically quite difficult to execute precisely. Is this to say that in the face of the problems that have yet to be resolved, there is nothing we can do without a sufficiently well-established foundation? By no means, and here is why. Once the general theory of walking had been established on unquestionable foundations, physiologists have analyzed, one by one, all of the phenomena of movement very carefully. It is at this point that they got results, and that, especially, they gave interpretations which sometimes seem contradictory, though this contradiction is in truth more apparent than real and has its source largely in the different methods employed. This is true even if we suppose that these were always perfectly appropriate to the study being undertaken. Fortunately, in the clinic, we can replace the interpretation of most phenomena that are contradictory by descriptions, which may well be less precise than mathematical data, but which still seem perfectly satisfactory.

It must indeed be admitted that, in many cases, it would be impossible to repeat certain physiological experiments on sick people who, as a result of their illness, would be poor subjects for them. As a result, for example, a description of the particular gait of a sick person can tell us a lot more than the presentation of the measurements of the movements of oscillation and inclination of the torso around different axes. Further, we were obliged to choose a method applicable to all the very diverse cases we wanted to study. This method, which we believe to be the only one applicable in the clinical situation, has moreover given us satisfactory results in the study of certain acts of normal walking. Not to mention that it is rigorously scientific, because its data is always identical in similar cases; further, it is always independent of the will and of the opinion of the experimenter. Lastly, this method has the considerable advantage of not making the use of any specialized devices necessary. A short history of the study of walking and of various procedures employed to illuminate its mechanism will make it easier to understand how the statements just made are reasonable; at the same time, it will allow us to make plain the value of this method, at least with respect to the kind of studies which were our aim.

It is certain that, before the appearance of the work of the Weber brothers on the mechanism of walking, the physiology of the different acts that compose it were little known. They had the merit of introducing calculation and measurement into its study, something which had not been done by previous authors; among these we will cite only [Pierre Nicolas] Gerdy, who, as early as 1829, gave a good description of this mechanism in the *Journal de physiologie de Magendie*. The method of the Weber brothers was not very complicated. They got a man to walk on a 44-meter-long track and, as they claim from the outset that in a continuous and undisturbed walk the steps are equal (which is not quite accurate), they found the average length of the steps by dividing the distance traveled by the number of steps; they found the average duration of the steps by dividing the duration of the walk by the number of steps. The movements of the torso's inclination were measured with the help of a telescope whose eyepiece had a thread to which was attached a strip or a bright line adjoining the body of the walker. We could continue on about the duration of the lifting of the foot, the oscillation of the leg, and so on.

Even though the results were obtained with the aid of only rudimentary instruments, it is in no way less certain that they were satisfactory. Also, until 1867, the conclusions of the Weber brothers had almost the force of law. It was at this point that Duchenne (from

Boulogne) destroyed their theory concerning the pendulation of the leg, which was active rather than passive. It is only in 1872 that a complete study of the subject was done. At this period, Mr. [Gaston] Carlet, under the direction of Prof. Marey, with the help of a new procedure, the recording apparatus, started on a new research project that would lead him to formulate a totally new theory of human movement. And recently, Mr. [Karl Von] Vierordt, taking up Carlet's work, again studied the mechanism of walking.

We cannot describe in detail the experimental procedures employed by these last two authors, but we should still say a few words which will allow us to compare them with the method we used. Carlet, we said, uses a recording method: he limits his study to healthy subjects. The walker, who is usually, if not always, the experimenter himself, travels along a circular track of 19 meters; he pushes an axis attached to a recording cylinder in front of him. At his feet are shoes whose soles enclose a small ball of compressible rubber, divided into two corresponding compartments: one at the heel, the other at the front part of the foot. From this ball a rubber tube comes out which transmits the strides to Marey's recording device. The various movements of the leg and the torso are communicated to the device by means of a mechanism that is difficult to explain without images.

Mr. Vierordt strongly criticizes the device of the French author and replaces it with another one, which is definitely inferior to it. The walker, who is here too usually the experimenter, puts on a pair of shoes—which the author himself says are quite uncomfortable—equipped on the side of their front part with an empty brass cylinder and with a third cylinder located at the heel. These cylinders are filled with a liquid of a different color for each foot, and the apparatus is set up in such a way that when the foot is on the ground, three colored dots of 4 to 6 millimeters of diameter are created. During the oscillation of the foot, no drop of liquid must fall from the cylinders; the author claims this is easy to do because they are obstructed with a small piece of cotton. A strip of rough paper that is 1 meter wide and 10 meters long is laid on a smooth floor, divided into two equal parts lengthwise by a brass thread, which can stay in place during the operation or can serve to trace a guiding line. The experimenter, wearing the shoes, positions himself at one of the extremities of the sheet, with the guiding line between his feet, and walks forward until the end of the track. To study the time of the revolution of the foot on the floor, in the same way as the movements of oscillation of the leg, the author uses his own jet method (*Spritz-Methode*). The experimenter wears a reservoir of colored liquid connected to the cylinder screwed onto the heel of the shoes by tubes on his back; at each step, the liquid flows out and in this way "the length of the foot's revolution is marked by a colored stain of round or oval shape and whose size varies with the duration of the lifting of the foot and the thickness of the trickle of liquid." Other setups, quite similar in their principle, are used to study the various movements of the torso and of the arms. Based on what we have said, one could already think that this method will certainly yield less rigorously scientific results than that used by Carlet. We should add that Vierordt applied it to the study of walking in various illnesses.

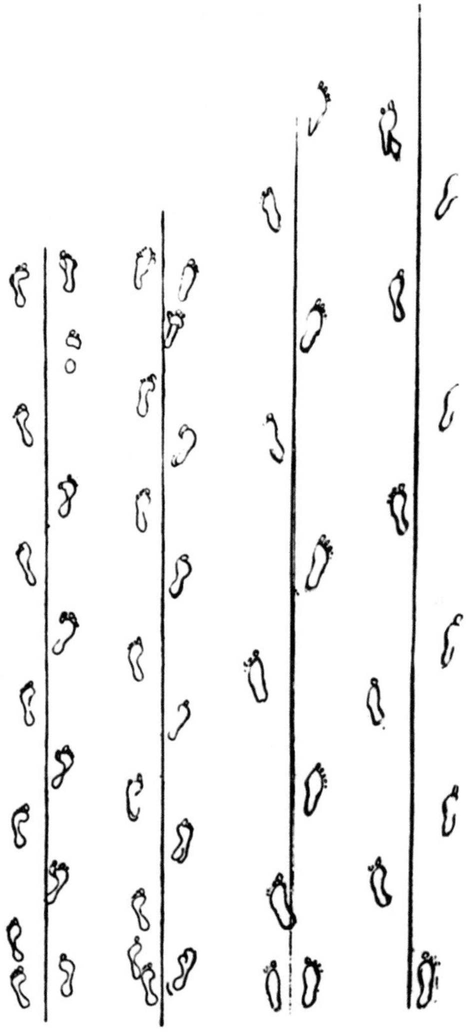

Figure 1. Gait studies of four separate individuals.

Is it possible to use these methods to study walking in various nervous illnesses? I don't think so. Even when they allow for complete results, it is still true that they make the use of devices that are too complicated for sick persons to use necessary. It is possible, and practical, that a series of healthy individuals should use the same shoes. It would still be better if each could have a correctly sized shoe; but this would be very costly. Also, these methods almost necessarily encourage the experimenter to examine his own walk himself, which seems like a problem. And, moreover, when individuals suffering from different diseases rather than the healthy are the subjects of experiments, is it not important to find a procedure that would allow us to eliminate a special shoe which will always be cumbersome and will tend to make the results obtained defective? Finally, is it not important to fix the exact footprint of the foot and the various deformations to which it can be subject? Despite what Vierordt says about it, it is not with three points, of which sometimes only one can be in contact with the floor (clubfeet), that one can expect good results. Also, it was necessary to find a method that was really usable in the clinical situation: explaining the one I employed which, indeed, is not my own invention, will make it possible to judge whether I went astray in adopting it. I do not, in fact, reject the methods studied above, because my own is incapable of giving results insofar as the movements of the torso and limbs are concerned: it might make sense therefore to combine it with Carlet's method; we will see if this combination is indispensable.

§2—Description of the method

The first version of the method I used can be found in a study by Mr. Onimus, presented to the French Society for the Advancement of the Sciences at a meeting on August 19, 1876. This author, who made use of the footprint left by the sole of the foot on paper blackened with lamp black and whose study only focused on the shape of this footprint, was probably pipped by Pitha and Billroth, who "smeared the sole of the foot with a black color and got people prepared in this way to stand on a piece of filter paper." It yielded quite satisfactory results for Onimus, such that he felt he needed to discuss them in a second essay, especially as concerns his physiological and clinical study of the surfaces in contact with the floor, to which I will soon return. Mr. Rohmer also used this method, and he explained it in a study which is much more complete than those that I have discussed above. I will only briefly mention the attempts made by Hugoulin (1850), Caussé (1856), and Jaumes (1880) to determine and make note of the footprints left by criminals.

From our own special perspective, the method used by all of these authors is only of partial interest, because it is almost entirely inapplicable to the study of walking. It is easy to understand how long and difficult it would be to smear with lamp black sufficiently long sheets of paper: from this point of view the procedure of Pitha and Billroth was infinitely more practical.

We owe our knowledge of the operating procedures of the method we employed to our excellent friend Dr. Neugebauer (of Warsaw); he had already applied it with great success in his remarkable study on spondylolisthetic pelvises. Here is how it can be put into operation with a few practical modifications of our own.

One takes a roll of ordinary paper of the kind that painters use, cheap gray or blue paper, although of reasonably good quality. Each roll measures around seven to eight meters in length and half a meter in width. Before stretching out this band of paper with the help of a few nails on the smooth floor of a hospital room, for instance, it must be folded lengthwise, just as one does a sheet of paper to draw a margin, with however the difference that the margin in this case must divide the sheet into two equal parts. When the paper is stretched out on the floorboards, this line is made visible, after or before the experiment, by a pencil or charcoal line. The subject of the experiment then sits at one of the ends of the paper; a helper rubs the sole of his feet and toes with very powdery iron sesquioxide. This substance, which costs very little and which has very strong coloring properties, seemed better to us than the cochineal powder used by our friend Neugebauer. At the starting point, the subject's two feet are placed in the position they occupy while standing normally, the axis line passing in between them. The person then walks straight in front of him as he usually does. When he gets to the other end, the experiment is over; the sheet covered in footprints left by his feet smeared with the coloring substance is removed to be photographed and is reduced in accordance with the needs of reproduction (Fig. 1).[1]

Such is the method we employed. Even though it was conceived along the same lines as that of Vierordt, it has the indubitable advantage of getting rid of the shoe, thus allowing the direct imprint of the sole of the foot of the healthy or sick person and, moreover, makes it possible to vary the experiments ad infinitum, since one is no longer obliged to use a device which, although above reproach, must have been made to measure for each individual.

1 Due to the inherent photographic difficulties occasioned by the color used, each footprint and trail is precisely marked out before the removal of the sheet with the help of a small paintbrush dipped in liquid China ink. When the photograph has been taken, it is possible, for this demonstration, as we did for Charcot's classes, to daub the left and right footprints with different colors.

— 20 —

TABLEAU II. — Moyenne des valeurs chez 10 femmes marchant sur une piste de 8 mètres et faisant de 90 à 100 pas à la minute.

(Le premier et le dernier pas ne sont pas comptés.)

Nos d'ordre.	AGE	TAILLE	LONGUEUR du pied.	LONGUEUR du double pas.	ÉCARTEMENT LATÉRAL des pieds.		ANGLE D'OUVERTURE des pieds.	
					P. D.	P. G.	P. D.	P. G.
1	21 ans	1m 53	0m 23	0m 4935	0m 05	0m 0488	21°	20° 18'
2	17 ans	1m 40	0m 21	0m 5227	0m 037	0m 079	14° 39'	10° 42'
3	18 ans	1m 67	0m 26	0m 5566	0m 079	0m 08	12° 18'	4° 24'
4	35 ans	1m 54	0m 23	0m 567	0m 0562	0m 0512	19° 42'	17° 39'
5	16 ans	1m 57	0m 24	0m 577	0m 057	0m 0815	14° 12'	10° 56'
6	59 ans	1m 40	0m 23	0m 48	0m 079	0m 061	10° 39'	10° 3'
7	38 ans	1m 69	0m 24	0m 48	0m 024	0m 094	21° 3'	19° 6'
8	18 ans	1m 60	0m 22	0m 53	0m 077	0m 052	19° 3'	16°
9	32 ans	1m 35	0m 21	0m 449	0m 048	0m 032	18° 24'	22°
10	20 ans	1m 38	0m 21	0m 351	0m 0758	0m 096	11° 24'	17°
Total 10	274 ans	15m 33	2m 28	5m 0068	0m 583	0m 6755	163° 6'	147° 59'
Moyennes	27 ans	1m 533	2m 228	0m 50 Pas D. 0m 4975 Pas G. 0m 4944	0m 0583	0m 06755	16° 18'	14° 48'
					Écartement total 0m 1258		Angle total 31° 6'	

— 21 —

§ 2. — De la longueur du double pas et des différences de longueur entre le pas droit et gauche chez l'homme et chez la femme.

Le sujet d'expérience étant dans la station debout, les deux pieds colorés reposant sur la bande de papier, les talons joints, et la ligne d'axe ou directrice venant passer par le sommet de l'angle que les pieds délimitent, nous le supposerons partir du pied droit. La jambe gauche servant de point d'appui, le pied droit se soulève du sol en subissant un mouvement d'enroulement allant du talon à l'extrémité des orteils qui quittent terre en dernier lieu ; la jambe tout entière est portée en avant et le pied vient toucher terre par le talon. A ce moment, le pied gauche qui a terminé sa révolution et qui ne repose plus que sur l'extrémité des orteils quitte terre à son tour; la jambe gauche est portée en avant, passe à côté de la jambe droite dont elle tend à se rapprocher, la dépasse, et le pied gauche vient toucher le sol par le talon alors que le pied droit achève sa révolution; et ainsi de suite jusqu'à ce que l'individu cesse de marcher. Le pas se trouve ainsi constitué. Analysons maintenant ses phénomènes constitutifs, insistant plus particulièrement sur les résultats que peut nous fournir la méthode que nous avons employée (*fig.* 2).

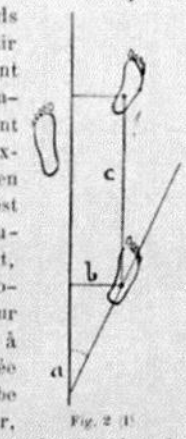

Fig. 2 (1)

1. La figure 2 montre la façon dont sont obtenues les trois quantités sur lesquelles sont en partie basées nos recherches : *a*) angle d'ouverture du pied ; *b*) ligne mesurant l'écartement latéral ; *c*) ligne mesurant la longueur du pas.

— 44 —

majorité des cas, est surtout provoqué, ne peut se produire sans que la chute ait lieu. D'ailleurs, il arrive également une période où les paralysés agitants, tant par suite de la déformation des pieds que par suite de l'impotence complète des membres inférieurs, sont confinés au lit jusqu'à leur mort.

§ 4. — *De la marche dans l'ataxie locomotrice.*

La *démarche des ataxiques* est également une subdivision de la marche rectiligne, bilatérale. Nous allons y trouver des particularités toutes spéciales qui en font une variété très caractérisée. Il importe donc d'entrer dans quelques détails à son sujet.

Tous les auteurs qui ont écrit sur le tabes n'ont pas manqué de décrire les particularités de la marche du tabétique, qui, cliniquement, peuvent se résumer ainsi, et il est bien entendu que nous ne parlons que des cas où les membres inférieurs sont le siège d'incoordination motrice : l'ataxique lance les jambes en marchant ; le pied, la pointe portée en dehors, retombe fortement sur le sol par le talon, la révolution de la surface plantaire se faisant pour ainsi dire en deux temps séparés, dont le premier est toujours plus accentué que le second, au lieu de la succession régulière des phénomènes du déroulement du pied (1).

Pénétrons plus avant dans cette étude ; aussi bien, la considération des tracés 13, 14, 15, 16 est-elle fort instructive.

1. On consultera avec le plus grand profit un excellent travail de MM. Debove et Boudet de Pâris : *Recherches sur l'incoordination motrice des ataxiques.* (*Arch. de neurologie*, no 1, 1880.) Les conclusions de ces auteurs : « l'incoordination des tabétiques est due à l'inégale tonicité de leurs muscles ; ses effets sont atténués par une contraction maximum de ces muscles, » trouveront ici de nombreuses applications.

— 45 —

La marche de l'ataxique offre des phénomènes communs à toutes les marches rectilignes bilatérales et des phénomènes qui lui sont propres. La longueur du pas est toujours diminuée et cela, d'une façon progressive, à partir du moment où l'affection a touché les membres inférieurs jusqu'au jour où le malade doit rester confiné au lit. Dans nos tracés, la longueur du pas varie de $\frac{54\,c.}{N.\,63\,c.}$ (*fig.* 13 : 52 ans ; t. 1m, 64 ; l. du pied, 0m, 26.) à 0m, 39 (*fig.* 14 : 50 ans ; t. 1m, 75 ; l. du pied, 0m, 25). En même temps, la base de sustentation ou l'écartement latéral total devient également plus considérable : *fig.* 13 : 16 c. 5 ; *fig.* 14 : 18 c. 5 ; *fig.* 15 : 21 c. 7 ; *fig.* 16 : 25 cent., la normale étant de 11 cent. 732. L'angle que font les pieds avec la directrice s'ouvre également en dehors : $\frac{43°;\,46°;\,48°}{N.\,32°,\,4}$. Nous insistons même sur cette grande ouverture de l'angle dont nous allons bientôt reparler. Elle constitue en effet, avec la forme parti-

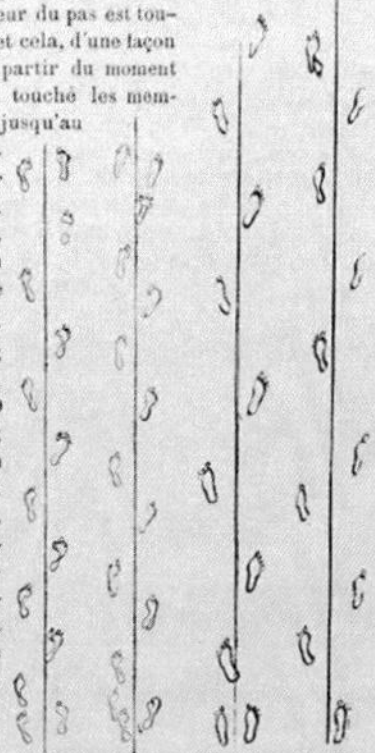
Fig. 14. Fig. 15. Fig. 13. Fig. 16.

que sa direction fasse un angle aigu ouvert en bas avec la normale primitive, ne saurait être considérée autrement que comme une marche rectiligne.

La marche titubante s'observe dans un grand nombre d'affections de natures fort diverses ; elle-même présentera donc des variétés nombreuses. Son type pourra également varier chez le même individu, non seulement aux diverses périodes de la maladie dont il est atteint, mais encore pendant la durée d'une même marche. Aussi, la classification de ses divers modes est-elle fort difficile à établir. Malgré cela nous distinguerons : les marches à petits pas et à grands pas (comparativement), avec ou sans chute et, au point de vue de la nature, les marches avec ou sans incoordination motrice. Notons que cette division est assez artificielle, car, pendant la durée d'un trajet un peu long, la succession de tous ces modes peut parfaitement se présenter. Les tracés 18 et 19 sont très caractéristiques à ce sujet. Ils ont trait à un même malade atteint de sclérose en plaques (24 ans : taille 0^m, 64, longueur du pied 0^m, 24) sans paralysie spasmodique. Les pas du début sont petits (*fig.* 18), la marche est encore rectiligne, mais bientôt le malade dévie à droite de plus de 0^m,50 (1), il revient alors vers la gauche, puis il est poussé pour ainsi dire en avant. Pris de vertige, il

Fig. 19.

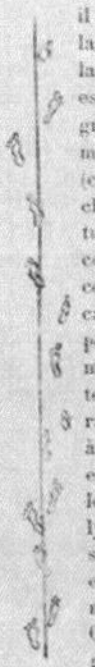

Fig. 18.

1. Nos feuilles de papier n'ayant que 0^m, 50 de largeur, lorsque,

fait alors (*fig.* 19) de très grands pas ; puis, à la fin de cette sensation vertigineuse, il reprend son équilibre et piétine sur place. Il eût pu être aussi bien précipité sur le sol et jeté complètement en dehors de la piste.

Pendant la durée de cette marche si particulière, que sont devenus d'une façon plus précise la longueur du pas, l'écartement latéral et l'angle d'ouverture des pieds? L'inspection du tracé nous l'apprendra mieux encore que la meilleure description. Cependant, en considérant que, en général, il existe deux éléments principaux produisant la titubation, nous pourrons peut-être donner une interprétation un peu moins succincte.

Les deux phénomènes, ou mieux, les deux principaux facteurs de la marche en zigzags, sont le tremblement des membres inférieurs pris dans son sens le plus large, et le vertige. Le premier existe dans un assez grand nombre d'affections. C'est ainsi qu'on le voit survenir dans la chorée simple et surtout dans la chorée hystérique. Toutefois, dans ces deux affections, il ne s'agit pas plus de tremblement que dans les mouvements que l'on fait dans certaines danses fort accidentées ; ce n'est pas non plus de l'incoordination motrice à proprement parler. Aussi, les empreintes sont-elles très difficiles à recueillir et, par leur grande complexité même, fort peu instructives.

Il n'en est plus de même dans la sclérose en plaques, où l'agitation toute spéciale qui meut les membres inférieurs peut donner lieu à un tracé bien caractéristique, analogue à celui que nous venons de présenter. Toutefois ce tremblement est rarement assez fort à lui seul, pour amener la perte complète de l'équilibre et la chute : il s'y joint une sensation de vertige qui, immédiatement, produit la déséquilibration.

ainsi qu'on peut le voir sur le tracé 19, l'empreinte est coupée longitudinalement par sa moitié, on pourra *de visu* dire que le pied s'est posé sur le bord de la feuille, et mesure ainsi 0^m,50 d'écartement latéral.

Dans certaines affections, du reste, les membres inférieurs n'ont même pas besoin d'être en action pour que le vertige se produise, car l'on sait parfaitement que, dans le syndrôme de Ménière, le vertige survient souvent lorsque le malade est dans le décubitus dorsal. Il ne tombe qu'imaginairement, mais il n'est pas moins vrai que, s'il eût été en marche, la chute fût infailliblement survenue.

On comprend donc, d'après ce que nous venons de dire, combien il est difficile d'assigner dans la marche titubante des caractères spéciaux aux différents actes qui constituent le pas. Contre le vertige, contre le tremblement des membres inférieurs, le malade raccourcit le pas et élargit sa base de sustentation. S'il est poussé en avant, il cherche à incliner le tronc en arrière au maximum, de même qu'il le courbe en avant en cas de rétropulsion ; les vertiges latéraux se combattent par un procédé analogue. Ce que l'on peut dire de plus certain, c'est que la chute aura lieu, indépendamment des vertiges subits qui renversent immédiatement sur le sol, lorsque les pieds seront posés de telle façon, que le centre de gravité du corps ne passera plus par le centre de la base de sustentation, quelque position que le corps prenne pour rétablir cet équilibre. Il est facile de voir, en effet, que le tracé 20, qui représente les grands pas d'une ivresse (expérimentale), ne peut mener qu'à une chute.

Nous n'insisterons pas davantage. Cependant, il nous faut dire que la marche titubante peut se combiner avec une démarche précédemment décrite, la spasmodique par exemple. Nous renvoyons à ce que nous avons déjà dit de cette association.

La titubation peut être légère ; elle peut être considérable ; ce qui est intéressant, c'est de

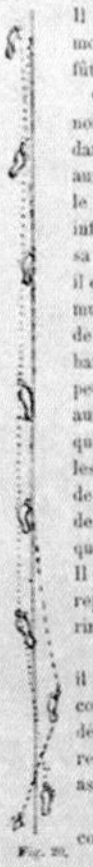

Fig. 20.

voir comment le tracé se comporte dans les cas où la titubation vient de disparaître. On pourrait ainsi suivre graphiquement, comme nous l'avons fait d'ailleurs, les progrès obtenus dans la guérison d'un vertige de Ménière traité par le sulfate de quinine suivant la méthode de M. Charcot. La malade que nous avons observée (59 ans ; taille 1^m, 50, longueur du pied 0^m,22), était tourmentée avant le début du traitement par des vertiges tels, que la station debout était impossible et qu'il ne fallait pas par conséquent songer à prendre le tracé de la marche. Après un mois de traitement environ, elle pouvait marcher et son tracé se rapprochait assez des figures 18 et 19, pour qu'il soit inutile de le reproduire. Toutefois, pour que la chute n'eût pas lieu, il fallait que la piste à parcourir fût peu longue ; le plus souvent, la malade livrée à elle-même marchait en se tenant au lit ou en suivant le mur. Bientôt elle put lever la tête en l'air en marchant, ce qui auparavant lui occasionnait infailliblement un vertige, et, au bout de deux mois et demi de traitement, sa marche nous donnait le tracé 21.

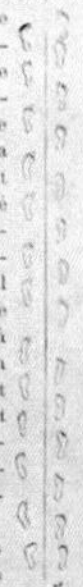

Fig. 21.

Cliniquement, elle s'avance lentement, à tous petits pas, les jambes légèrement pliées, les yeux fixés à terre et tenant comme appui imaginaire, à pleine main latéralement et des deux côtés, les plis de son jupon. Les pas sont en effet petits, car ils ne mesurent pas plus de $\frac{16 c. 16.}{N. 50 c.}$, ce qui n'équivaut pas même à la longueur du pied. L'écartement latéral total mesure $\frac{32 c. 56.}{N. 12 c. 58.}$. Quant à l'angle d'ouverture, il tend à devenir parallèle à la directrice ; car, outre que cet écartement latéral si considérable est suffisant pour maintenir l'équilibre, on remarquera sur soi-même que, lorsqu'on marche les jambes ployées, ce qui était ici le cas, la marche devient beaucoup plus facile lorsque le pied est parallèle

Notes on Gesture
Giorgio Agamben
2000

1. By the end of the nineteenth century, the Western bourgeoisie had definitely lost its gestures.

In 1886, Gilles de la Tourette, "ancien interne des Hôpitaux de Paris et de la Salpêtrière," published with Delahaye et Lecrosnier the *Études cliniques et physiologiques sur la marche* [Clinical and physiological studies on the gait]. It was the first time that one of the most common human gestures was analyzed with strictly scientific methods. Fifty-three years earlier, when the bourgeoisie's good conscience was still intact, the plan of a general pathology of social life announced by Balzac had produced nothing more than the fifty rather disappointing pages of the *Théorie de la démarche* [Theory of bearing]. Nothing is more revealing of the distance (not only a temporal one) separating the two attempts than the description Gilles de la Tourette gives of a human step. Whereas Balzac saw only the expression of moral character, de la Tourette employed a gaze that is already a prophecy of what cinematography would later become:

> While the left leg acts as the fulcrum, the right foot is raised from the ground with a coiling motion that starts at the heel and reaches the tip of the toes, which leave the ground last; the whole leg is now brought forward and the foot touches the ground with the heel. At this very instant, the left foot—having ended its revolution and leaning only on the tip of the toes—leaves the ground; the left leg is brought forward, gets closer to and then passes the right leg, and the left foot touches the ground with the heel, while the right foot ends its own revolution.[1]

Only an eye gifted with such a vision could have perfected that footprint method of which Gilles de la Tourette was, with good reason, so proud. An approximately seven- or eight-meter-long and fifty-centimeter-wide roll of white wallpaper was nailed to the ground and then divided in half lengthwise by a pencil-drawn line. The soles of the experiment's subject were then smeared with iron sesquioxide powder, which stained them with a nice red rust color. The footprints that the patient left while walking along the dividing line allowed a perfect measurement of the gait according to various parameters (length of the step, lateral swerve, angle of inclination, etc.).

If we observe the footprint reproductions published by Gilles de la Tourette, it is impossible not to think about the series of snapshots that Muybridge was producing in those same years at the University of Pennsylvania using a battery of twenty-four photographic lenses. "Man walking at normal speed," "running man with shotgun," "walking woman picking up a jug," "walking woman sending a kiss": these are the happy and visible twins of the unknown and suffering creatures that had left those traces.

The *Étude sur une affection nerveuse caractérisée par de l'incoordination motrice accompagnée d'écholalie et de coprolalie* [Study on a nervous condition characterized by lack of motor coordination accompanied by echolalia and coprolalia] was published a year before the studies on the gait came out. This book defined the clinical profile of what later would be called Gilles de la Tourette syndrome. On this occasion, the same distancing that the footprint method had enabled in the case of a most common gesture was applied to the description of an amazing proliferation of tics, spasmodic jerks, and mannerisms—a proliferation that cannot be defined in any way other than as a generalized catastrophe of the sphere of gestures. Patients can neither start nor complete the simplest of gestures. If they are able to start a movement, this is interrupted and broken up by shocks lacking any coordination and by tremors that give the impression that the whole musculature is engaged in a dance (*chorea*) that is completely independent of any ambulatory end. The equivalent of this disorder in the sphere of the gait is exemplarily described by Jean-Martin Charcot in his famous *Leçons du mardi*:

> He sets off—with his body bent forward and with his lower limbs rigidly and entirely adhering one to the other—by leaning on the tip of his toes. His feet then begin to slide on the ground somehow, and he proceeds through some sort of swift tremor. . . . When the patient hurls himself forward in such a way, it seems as if he might fall forward any minute; in any case, it is practically impossible for him to stop all by himself and often he needs to throw himself on an object nearby. He looks like an automaton that is being propelled by a spring: there is nothing in these rigid, jerky, and convulsive movements that resembles the nimbleness of the gait. . . . Finally,

1 Gilles de la Tourette, *Études cliniques et physiologiques sur la marche* (Paris: Bureaux de progrès, 1886).

> after several attempts, he sets off and—in conformity to the aforementioned mechanism—slides over the ground rather than walking: his legs are rigid, or, at least, they bend ever so slightly, while his steps are somehow substituted for as many abrupt tremors.[2]

What is most extraordinary is that these disorders, after having been observed in thousands of cases since 1885, practically cease to be recorded in the first years of the twentieth century, until the day when Oliver Sacks, in the winter of 1971, thought that he noticed three cases of Tourettism in the span of a few minutes while walking along the streets of New York City. One of the hypotheses that could be put forth in order to explain this disappearance is that in the meantime ataxia, tics, and dystonia had become the norm and that at some point everybody had lost control of their gestures and was walking and gesticulating frantically. This is the impression, at any rate, that one has when watching the films that Marey and Lumière began to shoot exactly in those years.

2. In the cinema, a society that has lost its gestures tries at once to reclaim what it has lost and to record its loss.

An age that has lost its gestures is, for this reason, obsessed by them. For human beings who have lost every sense of naturalness, each single gesture becomes a destiny. And the more gestures lose their ease under the action of invisible powers, the more life becomes indecipherable. In this phase the bourgeoisie, which just a few decades earlier was still firmly in possession of its symbols, succumbs to interiority and gives itself up to psychology.

Nietzsche represents the specific moment in European culture when this polar tension between the obliteration and loss of gestures and their transfiguration into fate reaches its climax. The thought of the eternal return, in fact, is intelligible only as a gesture in which power and act, naturalness and manner, contingency and necessity become indiscernible (ultimately, in other words, only as theater). *Thus Spake Zarathustra* is the ballet of a humankind that has lost its gestures. And when the age realized this, it then began (but it was too late!) the precipitous attempt to recover the lost gestures in extremis. The dance of Isadora Duncan and Sergei Diaghilev, the novel of Proust, the great *Jugendstil* poetry from Pascoli to Rilke, and, finally and most exemplarily, the silent movie trace the magic circle in which humanity tried for the last time to evoke what was slipping through its fingers forever.

During the same years, Aby Warburg began those investigations that only the myopia of a psychologizing history of art could have defined as a "science of the image." The main focus of those investigations was, rather, the gesture intended as a crystal of historical memory, the process by which it stiffened and turned into a destiny, as well as the strenuous attempt of artists and philosophers (an attempt that, according to Warburg, was on the verge of insanity) to redeem the gesture from its destiny through a dynamic polarization. Because of the fact that this research was conducted through the medium of images, it was believed that the image was also its object. Warburg instead transformed the image into a decisively historical and dynamic element. (Likewise, the image will provide for Jung the model of the archetypes' metahistorical sphere.) In this sense, the atlas *Mnemosyne* that he left incomplete and that consists of almost a thousand photographs is not an immovable repertoire of images but rather a representation in virtual movement of Western humanity's gestures from classical Greece to Fascism (in other words, something that is closer to De Jorio than Panofsky). Inside each section, the single images should be considered more as film stills than as autonomous realities (at least in the same way in which Benjamin once compared the dialectical image to those little books, forerunners of cinematography, that gave the impression of movement when the pages were turned over rapidly).

3. The element of cinema is gesture and not image.

Gilles Deleuze has argued that cinema erases the fallacious psychological distinction between image as psychic reality and movement as physical reality. Cinematographic images are neither *poses éternelles* (such as the forms of the classical age) nor *coupes immobiles* of movement, but rather *coupes mobiles*, images themselves in movement, that Deleuze calls movement-images.[3]

It is necessary to extend Deleuze's argument and show how it relates to the status of the image in general within modernity. This implies, however, that the mythical rigidity of the image has been broken and that here, properly speaking, there are no images but only gestures. Every image, in fact, is animated by an antinomic polarity: on the one hand, images are the reification and obliteration of a gesture (it is the *imago* as death mask or as symbol); on the other hand, they preserve the *dynamis* intact (as in Muybridge's snapshots or in any sports photograph). The former corresponds to the recollection seized by voluntary memory, while the latter corresponds to the image flashing in the epiphany of involuntary memory. And while the former lives in magical isolation, the latter always refers beyond itself to a whole of which it is a part. Even

2 Jean-Martin Charcot, *Charcot, the Clinician: The Tuesday Lessons* (New York: Raven Press, 1987).
3 See Gilles Deleuze, *Cinema 1: The Movement-Image*, trans. Hugh Tomlinson and Barbara Habberjam (Minneapolis: University of Minnesota Press, 1986).

the *Mona Lisa*, even *Las Meninas* could be seen not as immovable and eternal forms, but as fragments of a gesture or as stills of a lost film wherein only they would regain their true meaning. And that is so because a certain kind of *litigatio*, a paralyzing power whose spell we need to break, is continuously at work in every image; it is as if a silent invocation calling for the liberation of the image into gesture arose from the entire history of art. This is what in ancient Greece was expressed by the legends in which statues break the ties holding them and begin to move. But this is also the intention that philosophy entrusts to the idea, which is not at all an immobile archetype as common interpretations would have it, but rather a constellation in which phenomena arrange themselves in a gesture.

Cinema leads images back to the homeland of gesture. According to the beautiful definition implicit in Beckett's *Traum und Nacht*, it is the dream of a gesture. The duty of the director is to introduce into this dream the element of awakening.

4. Because cinema has its center in the gesture and not in the image, it belongs essentially to the realm of ethics and politics (and not simply to that of aesthetics).

What is a gesture? A remark of Varro contains a valuable indication. He inscribes the gesture into the sphere of action, but he clearly sets it apart from acting (*agere*) and from making (*facere*):

> The third stage of action is, they say, that in which they *faciunt* "make" something: in this, on account of the likeness among *agere* "to act" and *gerere* "to carry or carry on," a certain error is committed by those who think that it is only one thing. For a person can *facere* something and not *agere* it, as a poet *facit* "makes" a play and does not act it, and on the other hand the actor *agit* "acts" it and does not make it, and so a play *fit* "is made" by the poet, not acted, and *agitur* "is acted" by the actor, not made. On the other hand, the general [*imperator*], in that he is said to *gerere* "carry on" affairs, in this neither *facit* "makes" nor *agit* "acts," but *gerit* "carries on," that is, supports, a meaning transferred from those who *gerunt* "carry" burdens, because they support them.
> (VI VIII 77)[4]

What characterizes gesture is that in it nothing is being produced or acted, but rather something is being endured and supported. The gesture, in other words, opens the sphere of *ethos* as the more proper sphere of that which is human. But in what way is an action endured and supported? In what way does a *res* become a *res gesta*, that is, in what way does a simple fact become an event? The Varronian distinction between *facere* and *agere* is derived, in the end, from Aristotle. In a famous passage of the *Nicomachean Ethics*, he opposes the two terms as follows: "For production [*poiesis*] has an end other than itself, but action [*praxis*] does not: good action is itself an end" (VI 1140b).[5] What is new in Varro is the identification of a third type of action alongside the other two: if producing is a means in view of an end and praxis is an end without means, the gesture then breaks with the false alternative between ends and means that paralyzes morality and presents instead means that, *as such*, evade the orbit of mediality without becoming, for this reason, ends.

Nothing is more misleading for an understanding of gesture, therefore, than representing, on the one hand, a sphere of means as addressing a goal (for example, marching seen as a means of moving the body from point A to point B) and, on the other hand, a separate and superior sphere of gesture as a movement that has its end in itself (for example, dance seen as an aesthetic dimension). Finality without means is just as alienating as mediality that has meaning only with respect to an end. If dance is gesture, it is so, rather, because it is nothing more than the endurance and the exhibition of the media character of corporal movements. *The gesture is the exhibition of a mediality: it is the process of making a means visible as such.* It allows the emergence of the being-in-a-medium of human beings and thus it opens the ethical dimension for them. But, just as in a pornographic film, people caught in the act of performing a gesture that is simply a means addressed to the end of giving pleasure to others (or to themselves) are kept suspended in and by their own mediality—for the only reason of being shot and exhibited in their mediality—and can become the medium of a new pleasure for the audience (a pleasure that would otherwise be incomprehensible); or, just as in the case of the mime, when gestures addressed to the most familiar ends are exhibited as such and are thus kept suspended "entre le désir et l'accomplissement, la perpétration et son souvenir" [between desire and fulfillment, perpetration and its recollection]—in what Mallarmé calls a *milieu pur*, so what is relayed to human beings in gestures is not the sphere of an end in itself but rather the sphere of a pure and endless mediality.

It is only in this way that the obscure Kantian expression "purposiveness without purpose" acquires a concrete meaning. Such a finality in the realm of means is that power of the gesture that interrupts the gesture in its very being-means and only in this way can exhibit it, thereby transforming a *res* into a *res gesta*, In the same way, if we understand the "word" as the means of communication, then to show a word does not mean to have at one's disposal a higher level (a

4 Varro, *On the Latin Language*, trans. Roland G. Kent (Cambridge: Harvard University Press, 1977), 245.
5 Aristotle, *Nicomachean Ethics*

metalanguage, itself incommunicable within the first level), starting from which we could make that word an object of communication; it means, rather, to expose the word in its own mediality, in its own being a means, without any transcendence. The gesture is, in this sense, communication of a communicability. It has precisely nothing to say because what it shows is the being-in-language of human beings as pure mediality. However, because being-in-language is not something that could be said in sentences, the gesture is essentially always a gesture of not being able to figure something out in language; it is always a *gag* in the proper meaning of the term, indicating first of all something that could be put in your mouth to hinder speech, as well as in the sense of the actor's improvisation meant to compensate a loss of memory or an inability to speak. From this point derives not only the proximity between gesture and philosophy, but also the one between philosophy and cinema. Cinema's essential "silence" (which has nothing to do with the presence or absence of a sound track) is, just like the silence of philosophy, exposure of the being-in-language of human beings: pure gesturality. The Wittgensteinian definition of the mystic as the appearing of what cannot be said is literally a definition of the *gag*. And every great philosophical text is the *gag* exhibiting language itself, being-in-language itself as a gigantic loss of memory, as an incurable speech defect.

5. Politics is the sphere of pure means, that is, of the absolute and complete gesturality of human beings.

Selections from *Theoretical Study of Signalment*

Alphonse Bertillon

1896

Signalment is the description of one whom it is desired to identify ([Émile] Littré). In prison practice the signaletic notice accompanies every reception and every delivery of a human individuality; it is the *muster-roll* which preserves the evidence of the real and effective presence of the person had in view by the administrative or judicial act. Whether in the case of an entrance to prison or a discharge, a liberation or a transfer, or merely the notification of a judicial or executive decision, the aim is always the same: to preserve a sufficient record of the personality to be able to *identify* the present description with one which may be presented at some future time. From this point of view signalment is the instrument, by excellence, of the *proof of recidivation*, which necessarily implies the *proof of identity*. So there could be no judicial records without the aid of signalment.

Inversely, signalment sometimes intervenes to prove non-identity, at the request of honorable persons (victims, it may be, of a forger, or of an unfortunate similarity of names,) who demand the effacement from their record of convictions unduly entered.

The new penal laws [of France] relating to banishment, conditional liberation, and suspension of sentence (Bérenger laws) have singularly increased the number of concealments of identity by making such attempts more important to the criminal.

It has, therefore, come to be expected of a system of signalment not only that it verify a declared identity, but that, on occasion, it shall cause the true identity to be discovered.

Now, the making of original signalments, as well as their interpretation or correction, falls, in the nature of the case, upon the prison official. *The prison must recognize its own.* The police, which is a local authority, can lend to it in this emergency only an assistance limited to its own field of action.

The laws intended to prevent the repetition of crime practically make no distinction between a *local* recidivation and recidivation incurred *in different parts of the territory of the Republic.* The obligation then evidently rests upon the Administration of Prisons of identifying and describing, without distinction of origin, the recidivists of all countries who may seek to conceal themselves under false names in the midst of the prison population.

This important result has only been attained by the centralization, in a special service, of copies of all the signalments taken in the different prisons of France. This is the side of the problem which more especially necessitates the anthropometrical part of the signaletic notice.

Thirty years ago, it was believed that photography was going to furnish the solution of the question. But the collection of judicial portraits thus brought together soon became so numerous that it became physically impossible to find, *to discover*, among them the likeness of an individual who concealed his name.

During the last ten years the Parisian police have collected over 100,000 photographs. Do you suppose it possible to compare successively each of these 100,000 photographs with each of the 100 individuals who are arrested daily in Paris? If it were to be attempted in the case of some specially noteworthy malefactor, the search would take more than a week of application; not to speak of the errors and omissions which a work so delicate and fatiguing to the eye would not fail to occasion.

There was need of a method of elimination analogous to that employed in the sciences of botany and zoology; that is to say, taking as its basis the characteristic elements of individuality, and not the name, which is liable to falsification.

We may remark, in passing, that the absence of a natural classification is an objection which applies equally to all systems of judicial identification that have been proposed to supplant photography. We will mention, among others: (1) the impression of the tip of the thumb, a method which, it appears, is practiced by the Chinese; (2) the plaster cast of the jaw, which certain dentists would desire to impose upon our criminals; (3) the minute drawing of the areola and denticulation of the human iris, somewhat after the method proposed by me some ten years ago; (4) the impression, mold, or photograph of the ear, the hollows and projections of which present so great an individual variety that it is almost impossible to find two human ears exactly alike, and which are so persistent in the individual that the shape seems to remain unchanged from infancy to old age; (5) the anatomical description of peculiar marks, beauty-spots, scars, etc.

Some one said long ago that it is impossible to find two leaves exactly alike; Nature never repeats herself. Select no matter what part of the human body, examine and compare it carefully in different subjects, and the more minute your examination is the more numerous

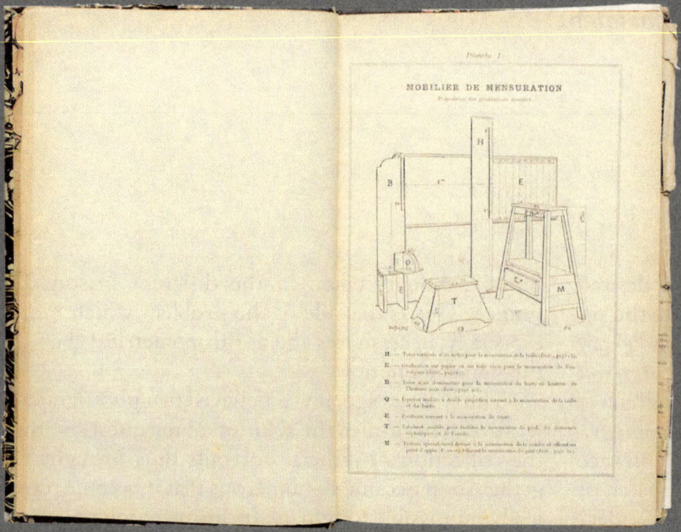
MOBILIER DE MENSURATION

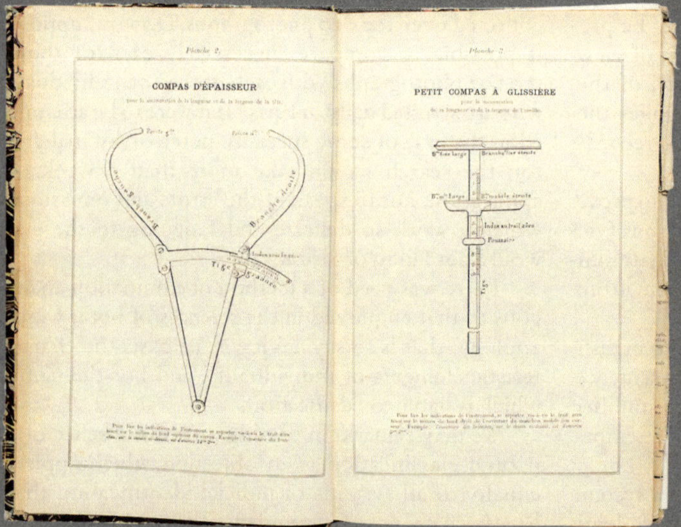
COMPAS D'ÉPAISSEUR
PETIT COMPAS À GLISSIÈRE

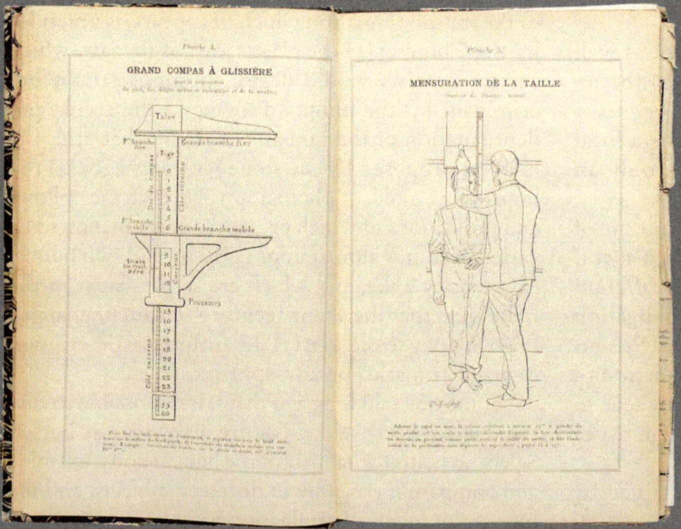
GRAND COMPAS À GLISSIÈRE
MENSURATION DE LA TAILLE

the dissimilarities will appear: exterior variations, interior variations in the bony structure, the muscles, the tracing of the veins; physiological variations in the gait, the expressions of the face, the action and secretion of the organs, etc.

The dog that is seeking his master in a crowd goes over the place in every direction, his nose to the ground. Homer tells us that after an absence of twenty years Ulysses, disguised as a mendicant, was recognized only by his dog, "the faithful and keen-scented Argos." Here there is evidently an element of individuality, and consequently of recognition, which entirely escapes the senses of man. But a few words pronounced in a natural voice, and "Edisonized," would leave a very convincing trace of identity.

Thus, the solution of the problem of judicial identification consists less in the search for new characteristic methods of individuality than in the discovery of a method of classification. Certainly, I do not deny, to speak only of the Chinese method, that the filigreed arabesques found on the epidermis of the anterior face of the thumb may be at the same time permanent in the same subject and extraordinarily variable from one subject to another; and that every individual may thus possess a species of seal, original and entirely distinctive. Unfortunately, it is quite as undeniable, in spite of the ingenious investigations made by Mr. Francis Galton in England, that these designs taken by themselves do not present elements of variability sufficiently well-defined to serve as a basis of classification in a file of several hundred thousand cases.[1]

The anthropometrical signalment, besides offering as much and even more variability than the several methods that we have just enumerated, is admirably adapted to classification; this is its aim, its principal purpose, and the reason of its superiority [...]

FINAL CONSIDERATIONS AND CONCLUSIONS

1. The comparative place of the three kinds of signalment

A comparison of the peculiar marks, when the first statement of them has been carefully made in conformity with the rigorous principles of description and localization which we have indicated in the preceding chapter, brings with it a certainty of identity much superior to that which results from a mere agreement of the anthropometrical observations.

The notation of individual signs might even completely replace measurement were it not for the inextricable difficulties which a classification based on these peculiarities would present.

What serial position can be assigned to each of them, when we consider that their number is continually increasing from birth until death, and that certain subjects are almost completely destitute of them, while others have such a multitude that it is almost impossible to notice them all?

So a signalment by means of peculiar marks will be a useful supplement to a description by osseous lengths, but it can never replace it. Anthropometry, which is a mechanism for elimination, chiefly demonstrates *non-identity*, while the direct *identity* is established by the peculiar marks, which alone can produce *judicial certitude.*

A criminal in a state of liberty commits a crime. It is the duty of the police to draw up his *descriptive signalment*, by means of all the observations which they can produce, that they may be able to recognize him amid the multitude of human beings and arrest him. As soon as a suspected person has been arrested, the *anthropometrical signalment* intervenes to establish his identity; to reconstitute the series of his old commitments if he is a *recidivist*; and, on the other hand, to assure him of every possible mitigation of the law if he is a *first offender*. Anthropometrical signalment makes it possible, and it is the only kind that does so, *being given a subject to find his name.* It goes back into the past and provides against the future.

It is, then, an exclusively penitentiary signalment, the virtue of which can be exercised only within prison walls. Outside, in a public square, for example, it is impossible to apply it as such; the most that can be done is to draw from it for the descriptive signalment some complementary indications, such as the total height, the height of the trunk, or the length of the foot or of the fingers when these dimensions are exceptionally small or large.

As for the *signalment* by means of *peculiarities*, its function is to place beyond all discussion the results obtained by the other two.

Cases are not rare where the three signalments thus play their part successively, while concurring towards the same end, *the execution of the penal law:* the descriptive signalment in the arrest; the anthropometrical signalment in the establishment of the antecedents; and the signalment by peculiarities in the confirmation of identity, whether this last intervenes immediately after (or even before) the arrest or only after an anthropometrical identification.[2]

It may be said, to borrow the language of the mathematicians, that the function of anthropometry is the reciprocal of that of description. In fact, here we have a signalment which it is necessary to match with one of the 100,000 free individuals of a city; there we

1 Since the publication of the French edition instructions have been given to the French signaletic agents (by circular of January, 1894) for the taking of digital impressions, and a place has been provided for these on the card.

have an individual arrested whom we must match with one of the 100,000 signalments of our files: *description designates the individual being given the name* (and the corresponding signalment); *anthropometry obtains the name, being given the individual.*

These results are confirmed by the signalment by peculiarities, either in the office of the examining magistrate or before the court; this is the *judicial signalment*, properly speaking. Thus the three portions of the signalment are seen to correspond to the three great divisions of repressive authority: public safety, prison administration, and judiciary.

We have insisted at some length on this point only because it even yet gives rise to misunderstandings.

How many times have we not heard prison officials declare that their signalment was the *descriptive*, and that in performing anthropometry they would be doing the work of the police; while it is exactly the reverse which is the truth, as we believe we have demonstrated unanswerably.

On the other hand, not a year passes in the countries where anthropometrical organization is still under discussion that the newspapers do not publish some interview with eminent police officials who gravely declare that they do not see how anthropometry could be of any use in the arrest of fugitive criminals.

This is an opinion which we come very near to sharing. We would add, however, that in cities where anthropometry is operating well, the police are the first to profit by the identifications furnished through this channel. In Paris, particularly, they never fail to bring to the measuring room those who are considered great criminals, even before having them entered at the station.

Moreover, have we not demonstrated above that the adoption of the anthropometric method would bring about a concomitant reform in the methods of signaletic description used in prisons, and, what is more, that there the advantage which the police ought to draw from it (as soon as they have familiarized themselves with the method of using it) will be evident, and in the future will have still more important consequences.

Thus, while insisting upon the penitentiary character of anthrometrical signalment, we have been in no wise astonished to see the police of large capitals like St. Petersburg, Chicago, Buenos Ayres and Geneva take the initiative in the organization of an anthropometrical service analogous to that of Paris [...]

Following are the instructions that the Attorney General of the Court of Paris addressed on this subject to the magistrates of this department in a circular dated June 29, 1887:

> The ministerial circular of February 23, 1887, in calling attention to the immoderate use that certain public prosecutors make of photography for arriving at the identification of prisoners, pointed out a surer and less costly process of identification employed at Paris, which is that of anthropometry.
>
> The Keeper of the Seals informs me that this system has been put in operation in all the capitals of arrondissements.
>
> I beg you, therefore, to be so kind as to place yourselves in relations with the administrative authority for the study with it of this new method, with a view to economizing as much as possible in the expenses of photography and of examining committees.
>
> A circular addressed by the Minister of the Interior to the directors of prisons, March 7, 1887, required the persons in charge of departmental prisons to make use of it, and every arrondissement prison has recently been provided with the necessary instruments for the taking of the anthropometrical signalment.
>
> The central collection established at the Court House in Paris contains the exact description and the indication of the various osseous lengths of adult individuals; it has

2 The arrest of the notorious criminal, K—, alias R—, which was much talked about at the commencement of this year (1893), furnishes a striking example of the special role which falls to each of the three parts of our signalment. The skillfully directed political brigades of the Prefecture of Police having learned that the author of the explosions of April, 1892, must have been a certain R—, who had already had a bone to pick with justice—notably in 1890 at Saint Étienne, where he was detained for eight days on a charge of uttering counterfeit coin, after which he was released on the ground of a lack of evidence of his guilt- the copy of his signaletic card taken at that time was at once called for from the alphabetical files. It was found that it had been very accurately compiled by M. Moulin, then warden's registry-clerk of this town, who was on this ground afterwards named chief-warden. This signalment, immediately translated into popular language by orders of the examining magistrate, M. Atthalin, was communicated to the press. Now, the witnesses of the arrest, and particularly the waiter at the café where it took place, were unanimous in declaring at the examination and before the court of assizes that they had not decided to inform the commissary of police of the presence of this criminal in the place *until after having read in the* Le Petit Journal *the published signalment*, and after having assured themselves, without their customer's knowledge, that he really had on the front and back of his hand the scars mentioned. It is certain that they would not have gone so far if the statement of peculiarities had not intervened to transform their presumptions into certainty.

If, now, we investigate the circumstances which led to the first suspicions, we find that, according to the witnesses, it was, in this arrest, the extravagant language used by the anarchist which drew upon him the attention of the persons present. It was *this conversation*, then, which, in the present instance, played the part that falls theoretically to the descriptive signalment, which embraces the entire individual, both his physical and his moral characteristics, his bearing, his speech, his tastes and his passions.

Need we say to the "initiated" that, in the present state of things, owing to the imperfect character of the signalments usually put at the disposal of the professionals themselves, there is not a SINGLE genuine case of an arrest determined solely by the physical description of the subject. The only really active factors have hitherto been either the suspicious bearing and the awkwardness of the fugitive, or, still oftener, some very explicit anonymous denunciation.

existed for four years and comprises about 60,000 signalments, most of them taken in Paris itself.

It will then be easy, whenever an individual seems to be hiding his identity, to ascertain whether he has not already undergone previous sentences by immediately calling for investigations which, according to experience thus far, should apparently give the most satisfactory results.

I recommend to you, the first time you have recourse to anthropometrical signalments, to carefully verify those that are furnished you and to satisfy yourselves that they have been accurately taken by the prison keepers. This verification can be advantageously made by taking care to send to the central collection, each time that occasion presents itself, the anthropometrical signalments of prisoners who have been confined in the prisons of the Seine or of Lyons in these last three years and declare that they have already been measured there.

The signalments of these individuals existing with every guarantee of accuracy will allow you to see whether the head-warden of your arrondissment has been careful in the taking of the anthropometrical signalment. Moreover, the penitentiary administration will not hesitate to turn to good account this means of verification, by addressing to its officers the instructions necessary to bring about an absolute concordance in this part of the service.

The difficulties which will present themselves, and the inaccuracies that you may discover at the beginning, ought not to alienate you from this method, which since its creation has in all questions of identity rendered to Paris incontestable services [...]

VI. Internalization and general diffusion of the anthropometrical method

The countries which at the present time have officially adopted the system of anthropometrical identification are: the United States, Belgium, Switzerland, Russia, most of the Republics of South America, Tunis, British India, Roumania, etc.

The following are the terms in which the question of the internationalization of the anthropometrical signalment was presented at Berne by a foreigner, Dr. Guillaume, ex-director of the penitentiary at Neuchatel, General Secretary of the International Prison Association, in an assembly of the principal officials of the judiciary and police of Switzerland, officially called together at the Casino in Berne, December 19, 1890, with a view to preparing for the application of judicial anthropometry in Switzerland.[3]

It has been established that professional criminals avoid the countries where identification is made by means of anthropometry. At the time of the introduction of the Bertillon system into France, there was remarked a genuine emigration of recidivists, who betook themselves to Belgium. Now, Belgium having followed the example of France, it is to be expected that the crooks and thieves of these two countries will transfer their field of operations to the neighboring states. Switzerland could not remain behind; it is about to fulfill its international obligation of contributing in its turn to the repression of crime by adopting the Bertillon system.

The most essential thing is to obtain the anthropometrical description of tramps; for it is these who pass through the different cantons and very often change their name on arriving in a district. It is especially among this this class that the habitual delinquents are recruited; a fact which renders it urgent to be able to immediately establish their identity.

The gain would be immense. The questionable means now in use to discover the artifices of an individual suspected of giving an assumed name would disappear immediately with the introduction of the Bertillon system. Then it would no longer happen for the Penitentiary Administration to tolerate or even instigate the espionage of prisoners by their companions in misfortune, or for an attendant or a prisoner to simulate friendship for the suspected individual, in order to gain his confidence with the intention of abusing it afterwards.

It is only proper that the international associations of criminals should be combatted by international measures. In proportion as the territory is extended in which anthropometrical measuring is employed the data at the disposal of the authorities will be augmented, since it will be possible to communicate them from one to the other.

May we not be right in seeing here the germ of the international organization of one branch of the service of the public safety? It does not seem to me impossible that an international bureau of anthropometrical mensuration may someday be established, analogous to the international bureaus a certain number of which we already possess. Switzerland, which is the international country by excellence, should not remain behind in this respect.

3 Extract from the minutes of the Council of State of the Republic and Canton of Geneva, June 10, 1891—Decree of organization:
"THE COUNCIL OF STATE on the proposition of the Department of Justice and Police Decrees:
Article I. There is hereby created a service for the identification of prisoners, by the anthropometric system.
Article II. All persons arrested, as soon as the warrant has been issued by the magistrate, shall, before the expiration of said warrant, be taken to the place designated for measuring (No. 42, Court House).
Article III. Every prisoner is obliged to submit to the measuring under pain of being considered guilty of resistance to authority. Article IV. The Department of Justice and Police is ordered to take the necessary measures for the execution of the present decree, which will become in force immediately.
Certified a true copy: *The Chancellor.*"

If from Switzerland we pass to Belgium, we find that the same ideas have been as brilliantly developed there by Mr. Ed. de Ryckère, assistant public prosecutor at Bruges, who has lately published a study on the identification of criminals in the *Journal des Tribunaux* of Brussels. This very complete paper has since been reproduced in its entirety in the *Journal des Parquets* of Paris.

His conclusions will be ours:

> The internationalization of the method of anthropometrical signalments, that is the important reform that the interests of all civilized countries demand should be realized without delay.
>
> The international exchange of judicial records which forms the order of the day in the Prison Congresses, constitutes, without doubt, a sensible advance on the existing situation. This innovation permits of the verification to a certain extent of the declarations of identity made by foreign criminals or those who claim to be so. Nevertheless, it would be dangerous to delude ourselves regarding the value and efficacy of this method of verification so long as it is not completed by anthropometry. The ordinary description appended to the documents in question scarcely facilitates the recognition of identity: a round chin, an oval face, grey eyes, etc., have never led to the recognition of a criminal outside the domain of romance. At the Prison Congress of Rome, in 1885, the desire was expressed of seeing the system of anthropometrical signalment extended to the other countries.
>
> That is an important and indisputable improvement, of which advantage may be taken easily and without great expense. The immense utility of Mr. Bertillon's system could no longer be contested. The period of preliminary efforts and tests has gone by; the results of the experiment made in France are absolutely decisive; it is a complete and undeniable success. Every progressive and wide-awake man will applaud the introduction into our country of the scientific method of Mr. Alphonse Bertillon.
>
> It must not be forgotten that it has a broader object than the mere recognition of the identity of *criminals* who conceal their true name.
>
> The authentication of the physical personality and of the undeniable identity of the individuals arrived at adult age corresponds, in modern society, to the most real needs, to the most varied uses.
>
> Whether there be question of giving, for instance, to the inhabitants of a country, to the soldiers of an army, or to travelers going to distant lands, identification cards, permitting it to be determined and proven at any time who they are; whether there be question of completing by sure indications the acts of civil life, to prevent all error and all substitution of persons; or whether of recording these distinctive marks of the individual in the documents, deeds, and contracts where his personality ought to be established in his own interest, in the interest of third parties, or in the interest of the state: the method of anthropometrical signalment will still have its place.
>
> When a certificate of life, a life insurance policy, or occasionally a certificate of death, is to be drawn up, when it is necessary to prove, to certify, the identity of some person insane, or grievously wounded, or disfigured, whose body has been partly destroyed, or has become unrecognizable or difficult of recognition, in case of sudden or violent death, the result of a crime, of an accident, of a shipwreck, of a combat; how serviceable it will be to be able to trace those characters that are invariable in each individual, infinitely variable from one individual to another, and indelible at least in part even in death!
>
> In a word, to fix the human personality, to give to each human being an identity, a positive, lasting and invariable individuality, always recognizable and easily demonstrable, such seems to be the broadest aim of this new method.
>
> The range of the problem, like the importance of its solution, passes far beyond the limits of prison work and the interest, great as it is, of the penal action to be exercised in the various nations.
>
> There is here a whole prolific source of ingenious reforms and useful improvements to be introduced in different directions. What numerous examples might be cited ! There are in the social life of individuals numerous circumstances in which their identity is at stake. The general application of the system of anthropometrical signalments and its extension into all the domains of social life would render practically impossible such lawsuits as that of the *claimant* Arthur Orton, the pretended viscount Roger Tichborne. The comparison of their respective measurements would have quickly revealed the imposture.
>
> The Hoyos-Baron affair, which ended in the execution of Hoyos in the public square of Beauvais, is not yet forgotten. Hoyos insured his life for a very large sum, and, with a view to securing the insurance, killed his servant. Baron, dressed him in his own clothes, containing identifying papers, and threw him on the tracks of a railroad in order to make it appear as an accident. The fraud was very nearly successful; it would have been impossible to attempt, if the life insurance policy had contained the anthropometrical signalment of the person insured. The Hoyos-Baron affair is not an isolated case of an attempt at substitution of persons. The life insurance companies could say much on this subject. The system of anthropometrical signalments is calculated to render immense services. It is necessary before everything to popularize it. In this direction lies progress! [4] [...]

4 These views have since been taken up again and presented by Mr. de Ryckère himself before the Third Congress of Criminal Anthropology, held at Brussels last summer. On his motion this assembly expressed a unanimous desire to see all countries adopt the anthropometrical system of identification and extend it to the whole population.

APPENDIX: TECHNICAL INSTRUCTIONS

1. Each subject should be photographed, 1st, in full-face, and, 2nd, in profile from the *right side*, under the following conditions: *a*) of *light*, *b*) of *reduction*, c) of *pose*, and *d*) of *mounting*.

a) Light

2. The light for the full-face pose should come from the left of the subject, the right side remaining in comparative shadow.

3. The light for the profile pose should fall perpendicularly upon the subject's face.

b) Reduction

4. The scale of reduction adopted for the judicial photograph, both full-face and profile, is ONE-SEVENTH. In other words, the number of the objective should be chosen in such a way, and the distance between the objective and the posing-chair so arranged, that a length of 28 centimeters passing vertically through the external angle of the left eye of the subject to be photographed gives on the plate an image reduced to 4 centimeters, within a millimeter more or less (4 × 7=28).

5. It is on *the external angle of the left eye* that the apparatus should be focused for the full-face photograph; while for the profile photograph *the external angle of the right eye* is taken, these two parts corresponding respectively to the most illuminated median position of each pose.

6. To find quickly the relative position of the chair and the apparatus which determines this scale of portrait, seat a willing subject of medium build in the posing chair very squarely and with his face to the camera, making him hold *vertically*, in the plane of his face, against the outer corner of his left eye, a slender wooden rule on which a strip of white paper 28 centimeters long has been previously glued. The photographer, on the other hand, holding in his hand a bristol-board card four centimeters wide, should move his apparatus farther away or nearer until the 28 centimeters of the rule gives on the ground glass of the camera an image reduced to 4 centimeters, as he can readily assure himself by placing his bristol-board card upon it.[5]

7. In order to avoid the necessity of any experimenting at later sittings it will be sufficient to fix once for all on the floor of the studio two small cleats, which will allow the chair and camera to be replaced immediately in their respective positions.

c) Pose

8. It is absolutely indispensable that in both poses for judicial photographs to be used for identification the subject should be bareheaded.

9. If for reasons peculiar to the case it should be necessary for the subject to be also photographed *with his hat on*, this last pose should be made the object of a third photograph, which it will then be very advantageous to take at full length [...]"

10. Take care that in both poses, the full-face and profile, the subject is squarely seated, his shoulders as much as possible at an even height, his head resting against the head-rest and his look *horizontal*, directed straight before him.

11. In the full-face pose, the subject should be caused to fix his eyes steadily on the camera, which will usually create no difficulty. In the profile pose, one can avoid the very frequent displacement of the eye sideways in the direction of the operator by asking the subject to look at some fixed point or, still better, at a mirror placed in a line with his face as far away as the width of the room will permit and at the same height as the objective, that is, at about 1^{m} 20 above the ground.

12. *Adjustment of the image on the plate.* It is strictly forbidden to "plunge" or "raise the nose of" the camera.

    As the optical axis of the objective should always remain horizontal and the plane of the ground glass or sensitive plate vertical, the adjustment can be regulated only by the vertical displacement of the optical apparatus effected by means of the crank or lever of the camera.

    Thus, the image of the top of the head, in order to appear properly on the plate, should be brought to 35 millimeters below the center of the plate, which leaves only one centimetre of light above the image, when the 9 × 12 size is employed.

13. Moreover, it is strongly recommended, before regulating the placing on the plate, to *decentralize* the

5 Here is the theoretical solution of the same question: we know that the interval between the diaphragm and the object, or more exactly between the *center* of the objective and the part of the object chosen for the focus, is equal to the focal length of the objective used multiplied by the reduction number increased by one.

On this principle, supposing an objective to have a focal length of 32 centimeters, the distance which should separate its diaphragm from the external angle of the eye will be equal to 2 m. 56 (0.32 x 8=2.56).

camera 18 millimeters downwards, so that the optical axis of the apparatus passes approximately through the middle of the space of 35 millimeters reserved for the face. This decentralizing necessarily results in bringing the objective to the height of the subject's eyes, that is to say, the ordinary position of the human vision.

14. For the profile pose turn the chair 90° *from right to left*. Place the subject *completely in profile* so that, seen from the apparatus, the head, the body, and the top of the chair-back all appear entirely in a side view.

15. Before proceeding to the actual taking of the profile portrait, take care to verify and correct, if necessary, the figure of the reduction, which should then be regulated, as has been said above, on the vertical plane passing through the external angle of the right eye.

    The special posing chair, which will be described further on, renders these preliminary verifications unnecessary by allowing the scale of reduction for both poses and the lateral adjustment to be regulated once and for all.

16. As part of the value of the profile portrait consists in the indication of the slope of the forehead, one should take care to have the prisoner push back any locks of hair which might hide his forehead.

17. *The ears should always be disengaged from the hair, in both the profile and full-face portraits.*

    To obtain this result in certain cases of shaggy and unkempt hair it will sometimes be necessary to confine the hair either with a piece of twine or a rubber band (for the profile pose only).

18. *Profile* photographs in which the contour of the ear does not appear in its entirety will have to be taken over again.

d) Size and Mounting of the Prints

19. The prints should be cut at about 8 millimeters above the hair and pasted on a sheet of Bristol-board, the profile on the left and the full face on the right. As much as the bust should be left as the height of the negatives will permit, perhaps between 8 and 9 centimeters, and nothing should be cut off from the width of the shoulders in full face photographs.

20. By employing a suitable *multiplier* the two poses may be grouped on the same card of 9 × 13 centimeters, obtained by cutting a card of 13 × 18 in two. The base thus measures 130 millimeters, of which 72 are devoted to the face and 58 to the profile.

GENERAL OBSERVATIONS

21. *The plates should never be retouched in any way*, with the exception of the hollows or pricks in the gelatin, which would produce on the print black spots resembling a mole or a scar. Any embellishment or rejuvenating of the image by effacing on the plate the wrinkles, scars and peculiarities of the skin is strictly forbidden.

22. In the photographic department of the Parisian Prefecture of Police, to avoid confusion in the transcription of the names and to facilitate the subsequent classing of the negatives, a provisional serial number is given to each of them, according to the order in which the subject was entered on the daily list of photographs to be taken. The numbers are printed on loose tickets of about 3 centimeters in width and are slipped one after another into a pocket placed on the top of the back of the chair seen from one side.

23. This indication reproduced on the negative by photography itself allows one, by referring to the list for the day, to immediately find again the name of the subject, which is then written on the gelatin in reversed letters underneath the profile. The date of the making of the negative is placed immediately after, written in figures in the usual order; *day, month, year*. Finally, under the full face portrait, there is traced, farther towards the right, the general serial number which is to determine the definite placing of each negative in the archives...[6]

6 Dr. Lande, professor of medical jurisprudence and deputy mayor of Bordeaux, who directed the organization of a municipal anthropometrical service in that city, has ingeniously replaced the inscription on the negatives in reversed writing (which requires some practice) by a direct inscription on a band of transparent paper, which is then turned over and pasted on the gelatin. The result obtained is excellent, if not better than with the direct writing.

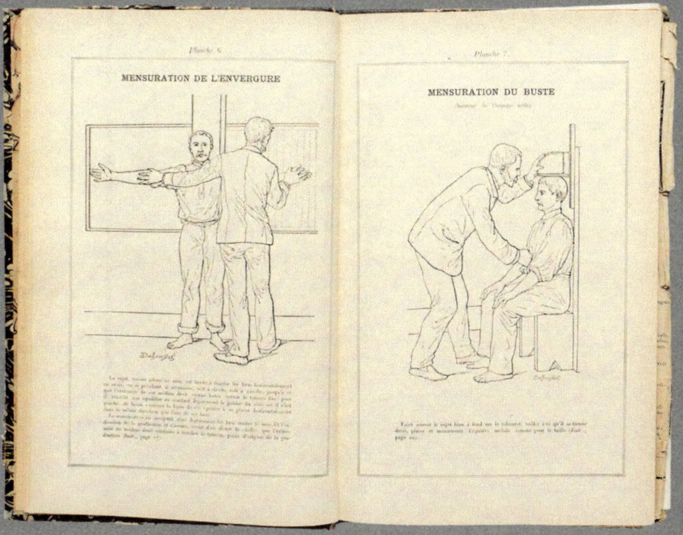
MENSURATION DE L'ENVERGURE
MENSURATION DU BUSTE

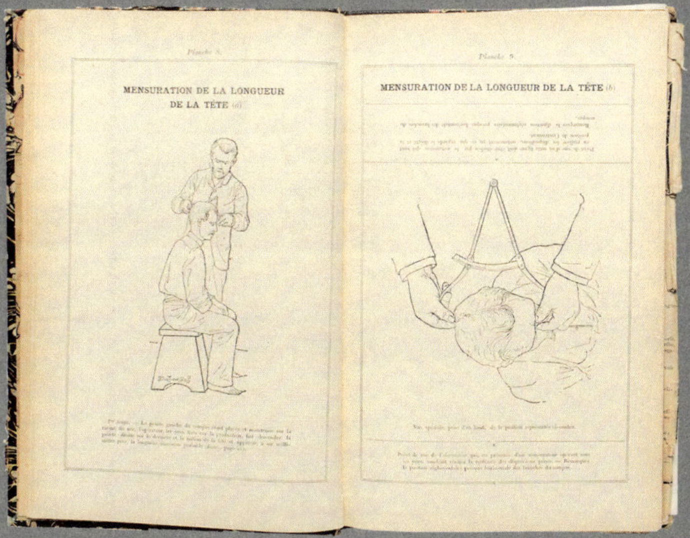
MENSURATION DE LA LONGUEUR DE LA TÊTE
MENSURATION DE LA LONGUEUR DE LA TÊTE

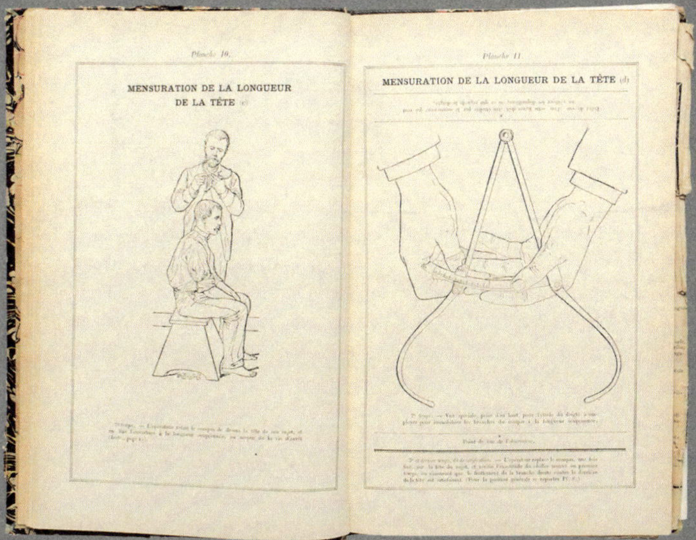
MENSURATION DE LA LONGUEUR DE LA TÊTE
MENSURATION DE LA LONGUEUR DE LA TÊTE

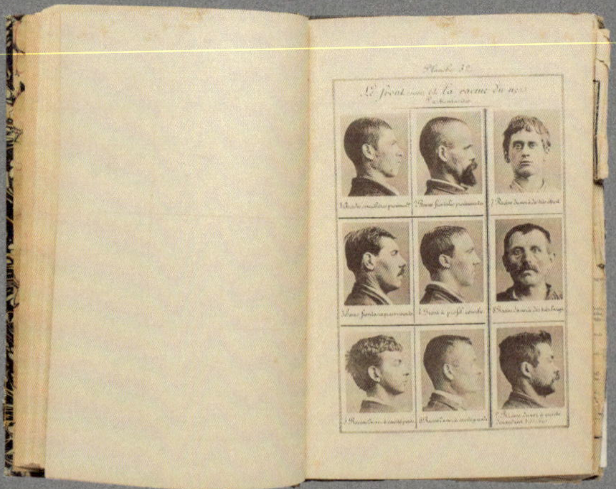

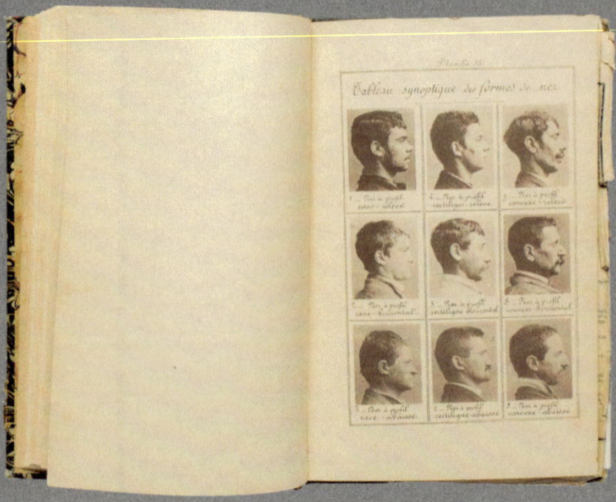
Tableau synoptique des formes de nez

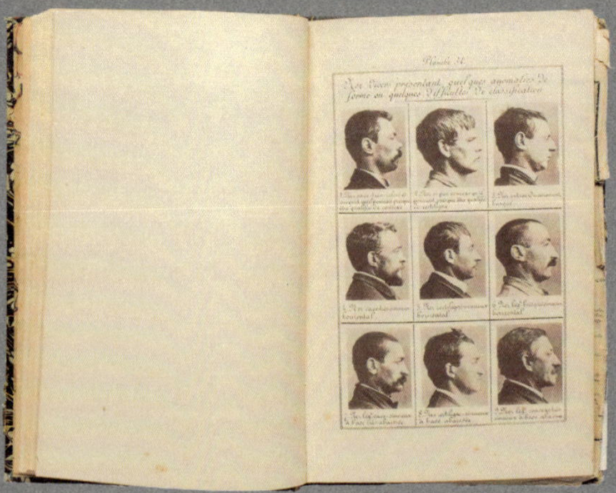

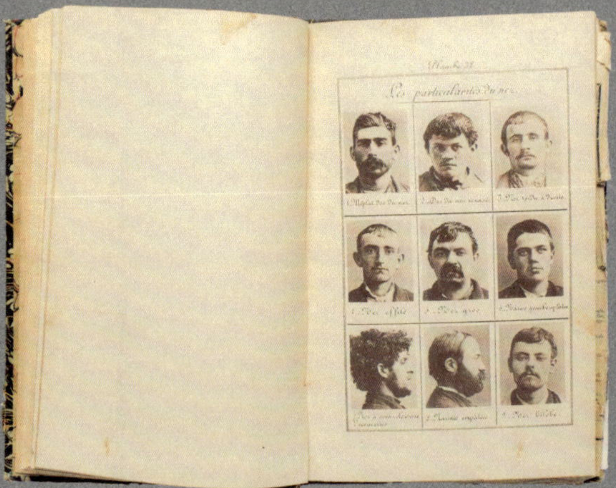
Les particularités du nez

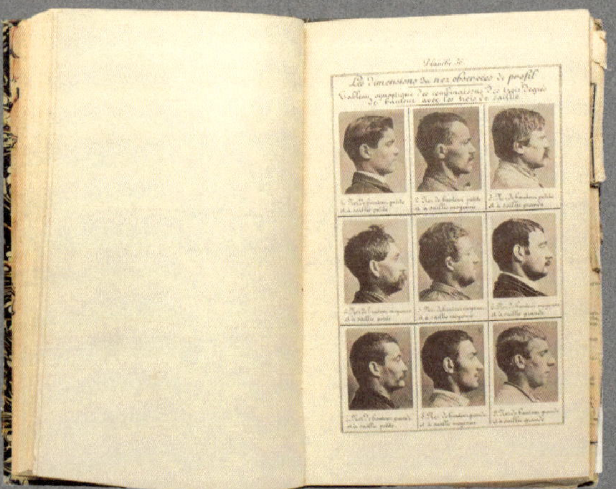

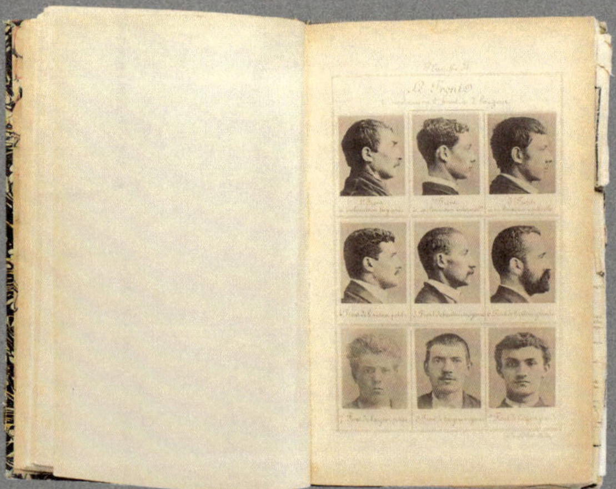

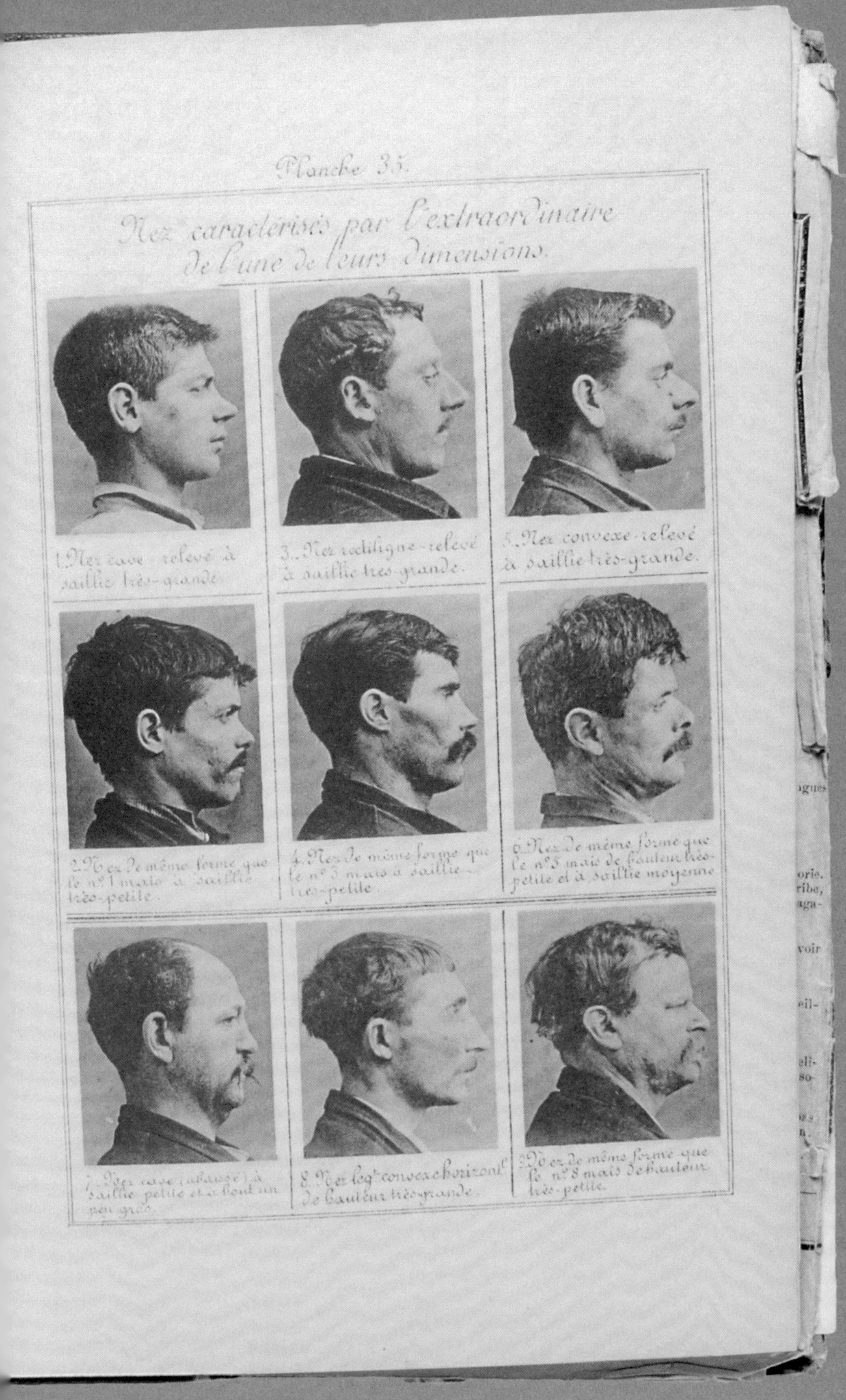
Planche 35.
Nez caractérisés par l'extraordinaire de l'une de leurs dimensions.
1. Nez cave - relevé à saillie très-grande
3. Nez rectiligne-relevé à saillie très-grande.
5. Nez convexe-relevé à saillie très-grande.
2. Nez de même forme que le n° 1 mais à saillie très-petite.
4. Nez de même forme que le n° 3 mais à saillie très-petite
6. Nez de même forme que le n° 5 mais de hauteur très-petite et à saillie moyenne
7. Nez cave (abaissé) à saillie petite et à bout un peu gros.
8. Nez légt convexe horizontl de hauteur très-grande.
9. Nez de même forme que le n° 8 mais de hauteur très-petite.

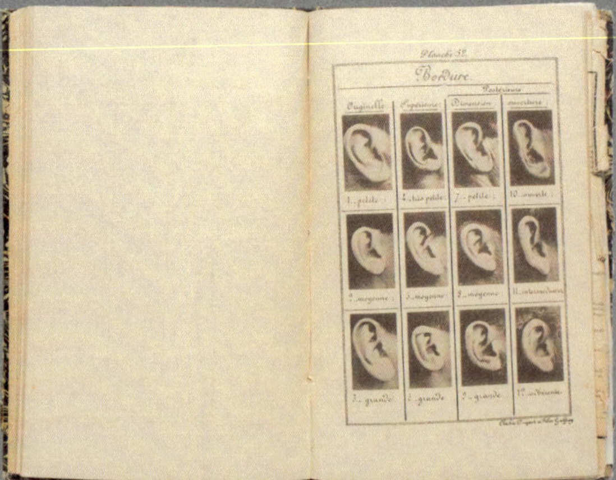

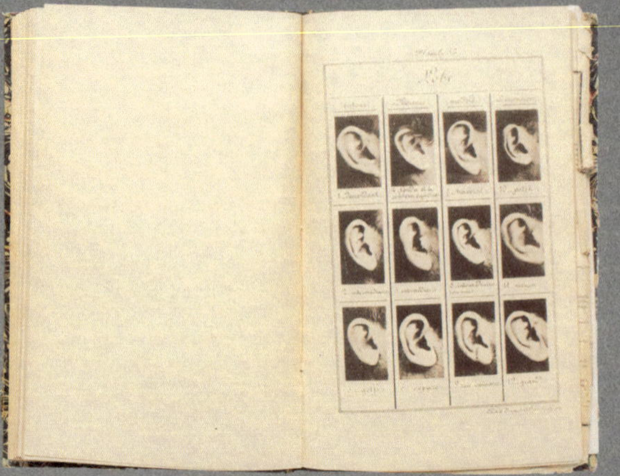

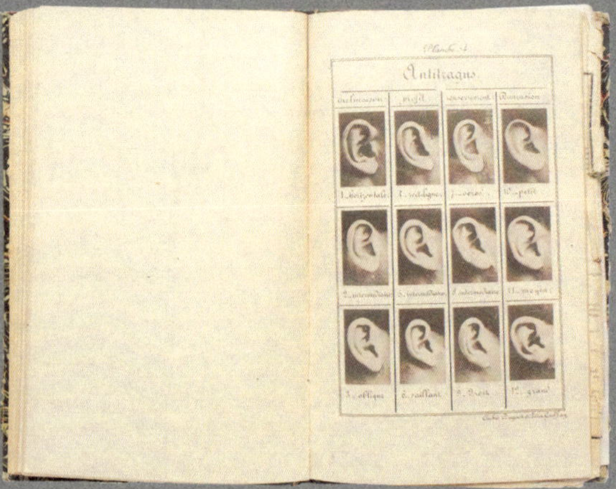

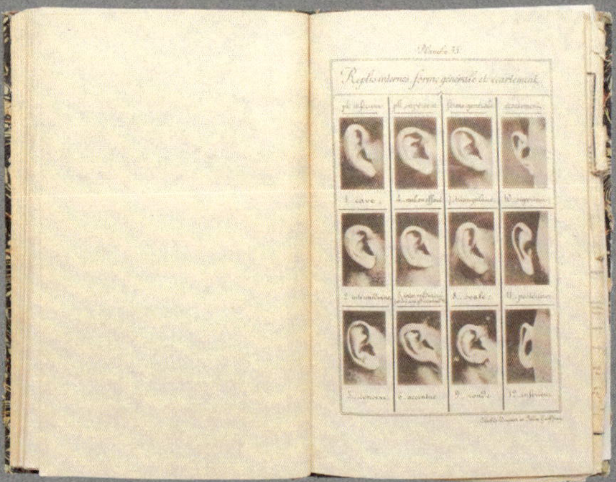

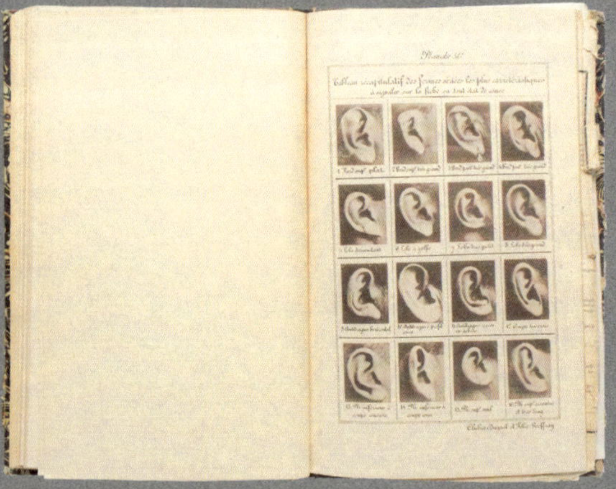

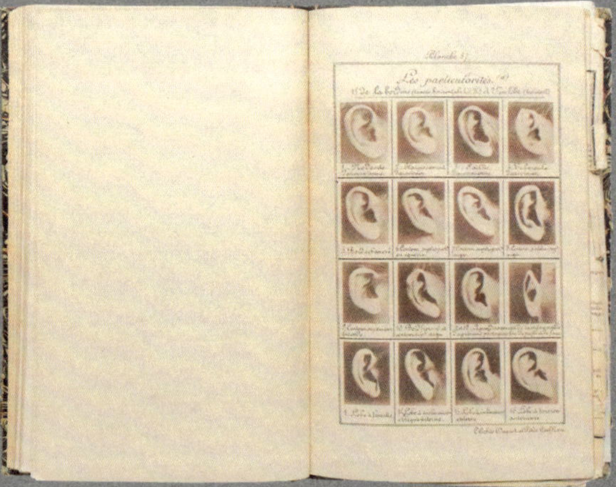

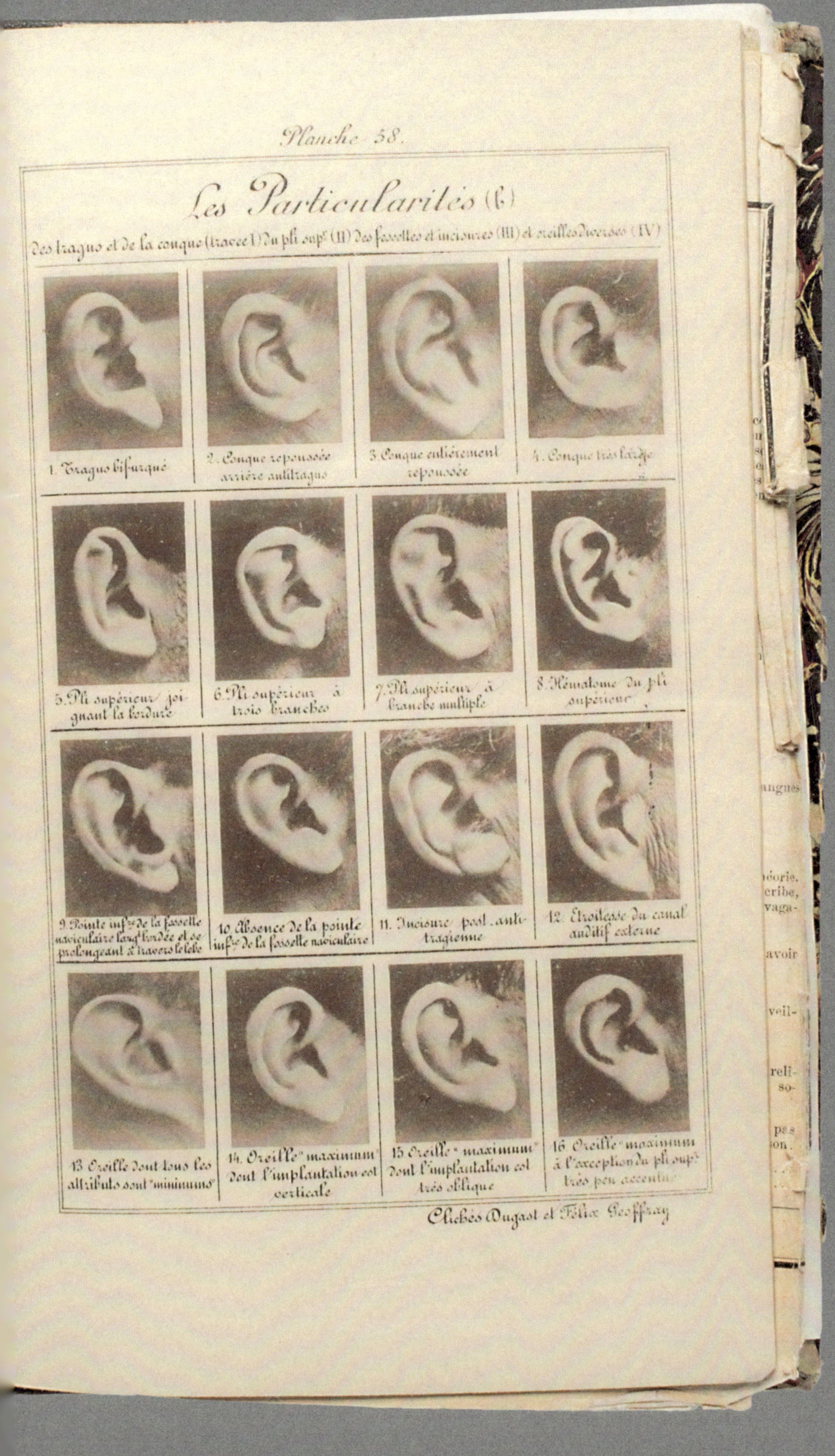
Planche 58.
Les Particularités (I.)
des tragus et de la conque (trace I) du pli supr (II) des fossettes et incisures (III) et oreilles diverses (IV)
1. Tragus bifurqué
2. Conque repoussée arrière antitragus
3. Conque entièrement repoussée
4. Conque très large
5. Pli supérieur joignant la bordure
6. Pli supérieur à trois branches
7. Pli supérieur à branche multiple
8. Hématome du pli supérieur
9. Pointe infre de la fossette naviculaire longt bordée et se prolongeant à travers le lobe
10. Absence de la pointe infre de la fossette naviculaire
11. Incisure post. antitragienne
12. Étroitesse du canal auditif externe
13 Oreille dont tous les attributs sont "minimums"
14. Oreille "maximum" dont l'implantation est verticale
15 Oreille "maximum" dont l'implantation est très oblique
16 Oreille "maximum" à l'exception du pli supr très peu accentué
Clichés Dugast et Félix Geoffray

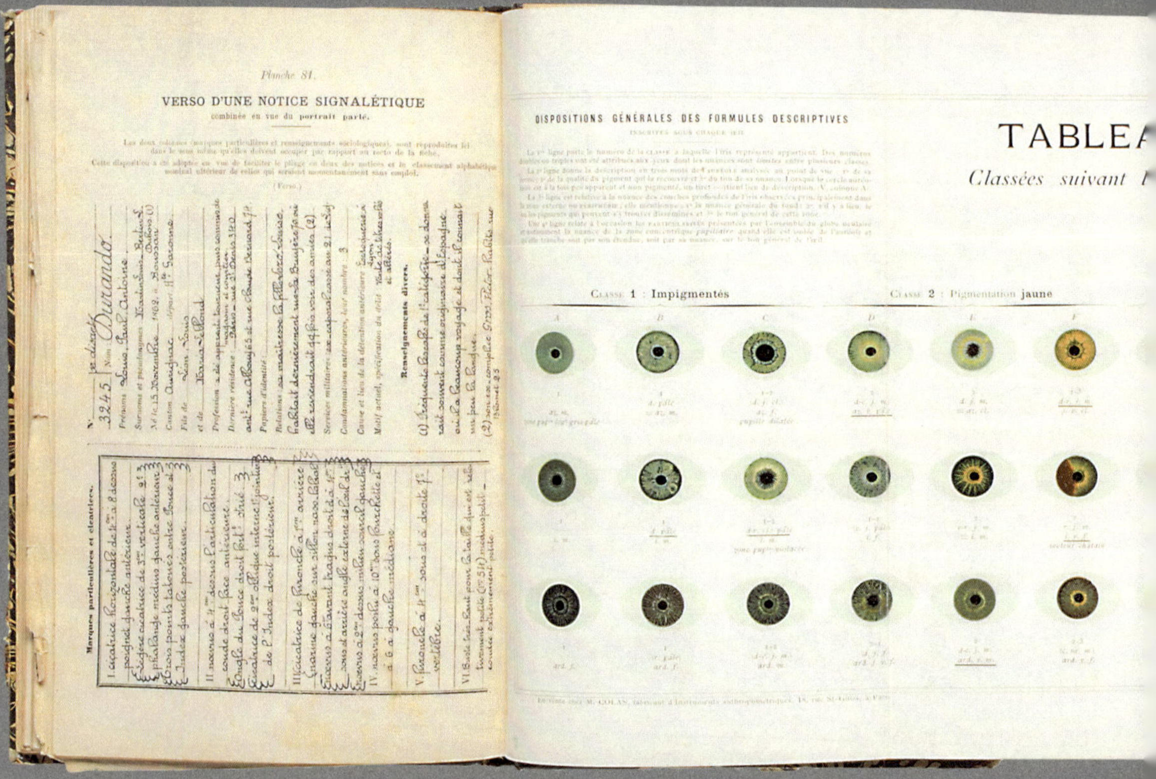
Planche 81.
VERSO D'UNE NOTICE SIGNALÉTIQUE
combinée en vue du portrait parlé.
DISPOSITIONS GÉNÉRALES DES FORMULES DESCRIPTIVES
TABLEA
Classées suivant
Classe 1 : Impigmentés
Classe 2 : Pigmentation jaune

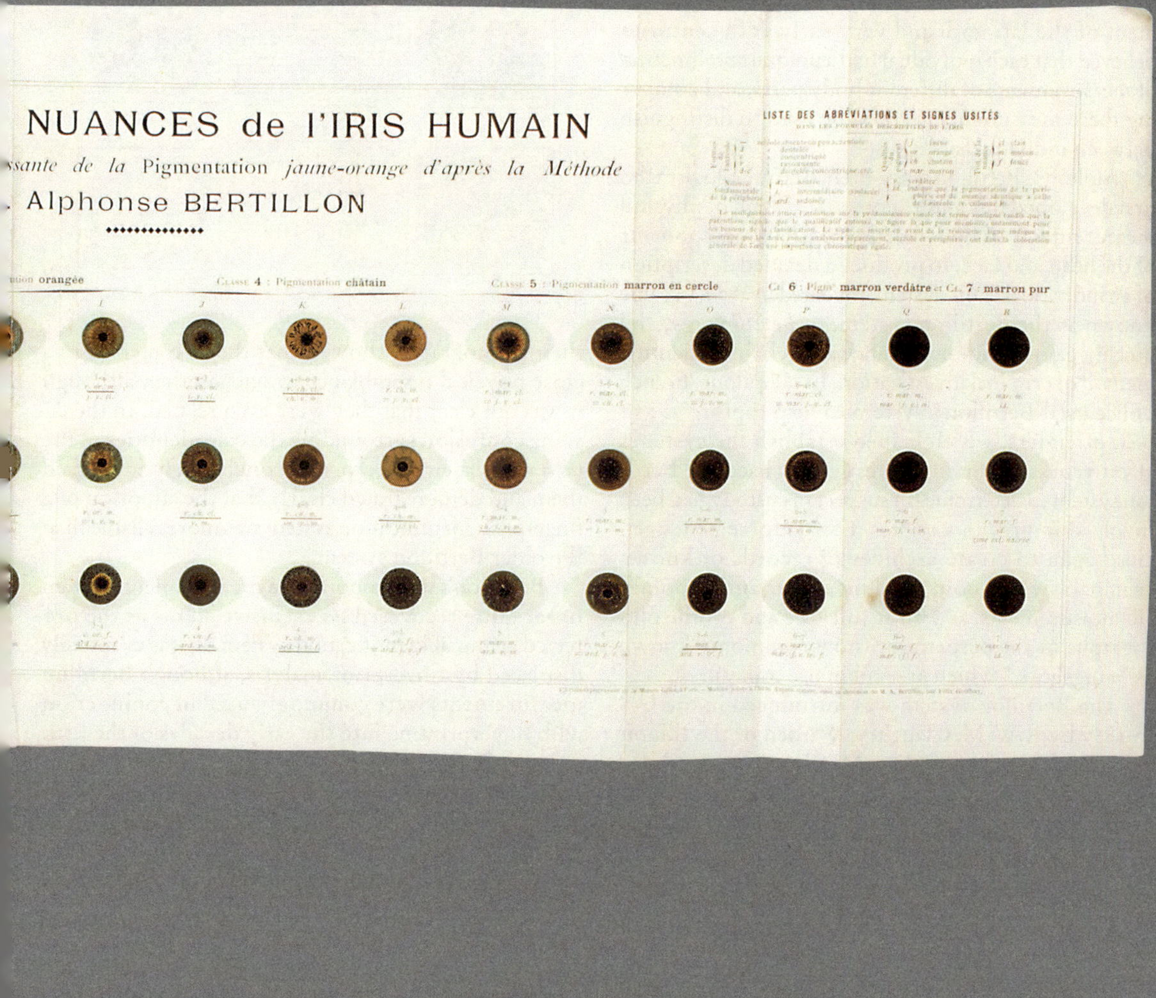
NUANCES de l'IRIS HUMAIN
ssante de la Pigmentation jaune-orange d'après la Méthode
Alphonse BERTILLON
LISTE DES ABRÉVIATIONS ET SIGNES USITÉS
orangée
Classe 4 : Pigmentation châtain
Classe 5 : Pigmentation marron en cercle
Cl. 6 : Pigm. marron verdâtre et Cl. 7 : marron pur

Bertillon System of Criminal Identification [Selected by Cameron Rowland]
National Law Enforcement Museum Website
Last accessed May 2018

The techniques of criminal identification used by American law enforcement today are rooted in the science of anthropometry, which focuses on the meticulous measurement and recording of different parts and components of the human body. Generally, law enforcement of the late 19th and very early 20th centuries believed that each individual had a unique combination of measurements of different body parts, and comparing these measurements could be used to distinguish between individuals.

Alphonse Bertillon was a French criminologist who first developed this anthropometric system of physical measurements of body parts, especially components of the head and face, to produce a detailed description of an individual. This system, invented in 1879, became known as the Bertillon system, or *bertillonage*, and quickly gained wide acceptance as a reliable, scientific method of criminal investigation. In 1884 alone, French police used Bertillon's system to help capture 241 repeat offenders, which helped establish the system's effectiveness. Primarily, investigators used the Bertillon system to determine if a suspect in custody had been involved in previous crimes. Law enforcement agencies began to create archives of records of known criminals, which contained his or her anthropometric measurements, as well as full-face and profile photographs of the perpetrator (now commonly known as "mugshots," which are still in use today).

The Bertillon system was introduced in the U.S. in 1887 by R.W. McClaughry, Warden of the Illinois State Penitentiary at Joliet. McClaughry translated Bertillon's 1885 edition of *Signaletic Instructions Including the Theory and Practice of Anthropometrical Identification* from French to English, and its use in the States became quickly and widely accepted. The Bertillon system continued as the dominant criminal identification method both in the U.S. and Europe for almost three decades. In 1903, the case of the "West Brothers" demonstrated the reliability of the emerging science of fingerprint identification over that of the Bertillon system.

In 1903, a man named Will West was committed to the penitentiary at Leavenworth, Kansas, where he was photographed and measured using the Bertillon system. Will West's measurements were found to be almost identical to a criminal at the same penitentiary named William West, who was committed for murder in 1901 and was serving a life sentence. Furthermore,

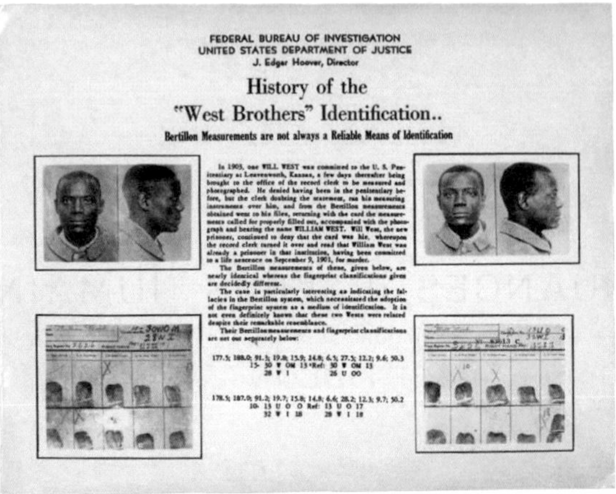

their photographs showed that the two men bore a close physical resemblance to one another, although it was not clear that they were even related. In the ensuing confusion surrounding the true identities of the two men, their fingerprints conclusively identified them and demonstrated clearly that the adoption of a fingerprint identification system was more reliable than the older Bertillon system.

Bertillon's anthropometric measurement system never quite recovered its exclusive status as the preferred criminal identification system. It was eventually displaced by fingerprint analysis, although Bertillon measurements were commonly used in conjunction with fingerprinting into the early decades of the 20th century. Today, fingerprint analysis is used by law enforcement agencies all over the world to track down criminals and conclusively identify them.

Many artifacts in the collection of the Museum serve to document the history of criminal identification techniques, including those used in earlier centuries and decades but which were superseded by more advanced and accurate scientific techniques. The arc of this technological evolution is important to preserve. Through the study of such artifacts, the public can learn about American law enforcement not only as it exists now, but also discover the history and influences that made the field what it is today.

Selection from *Attitudes of Animals in Motion*

Eadweard Muybridge

1882

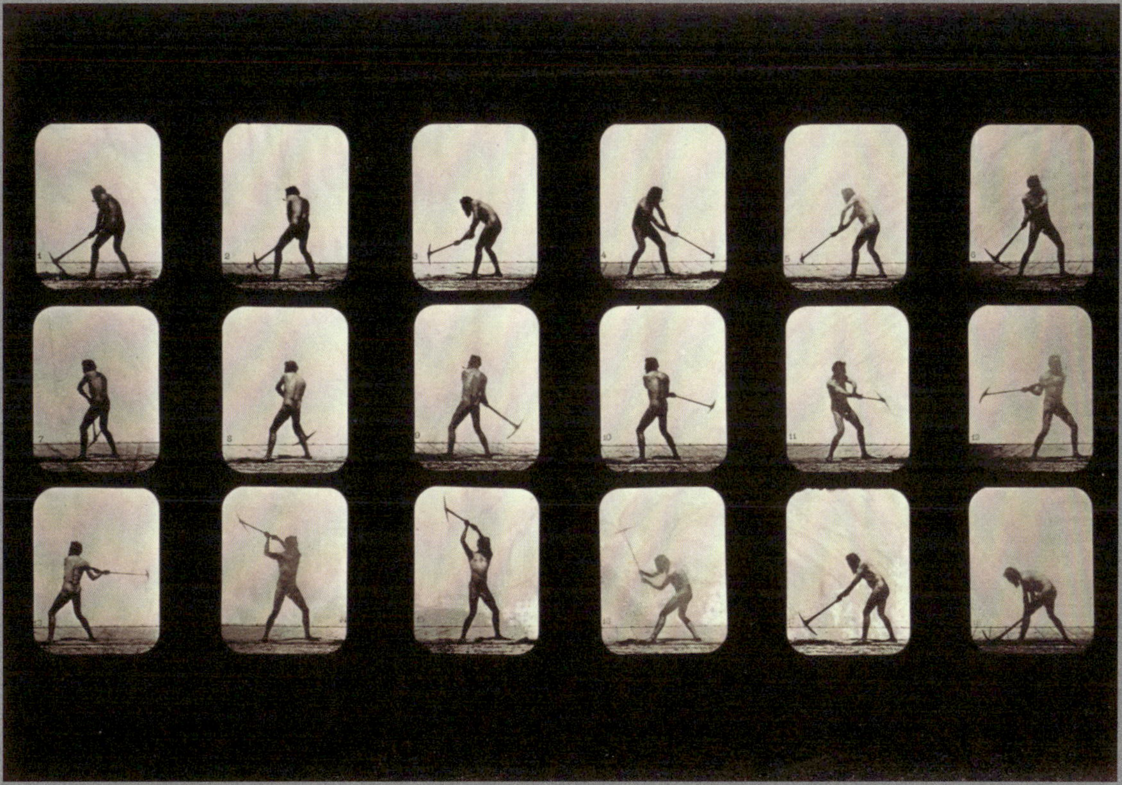

Plate 110. Athlete Swinging a Pick.

Selections from *Animal Locomotion*

Eadweard Muybridge

1887

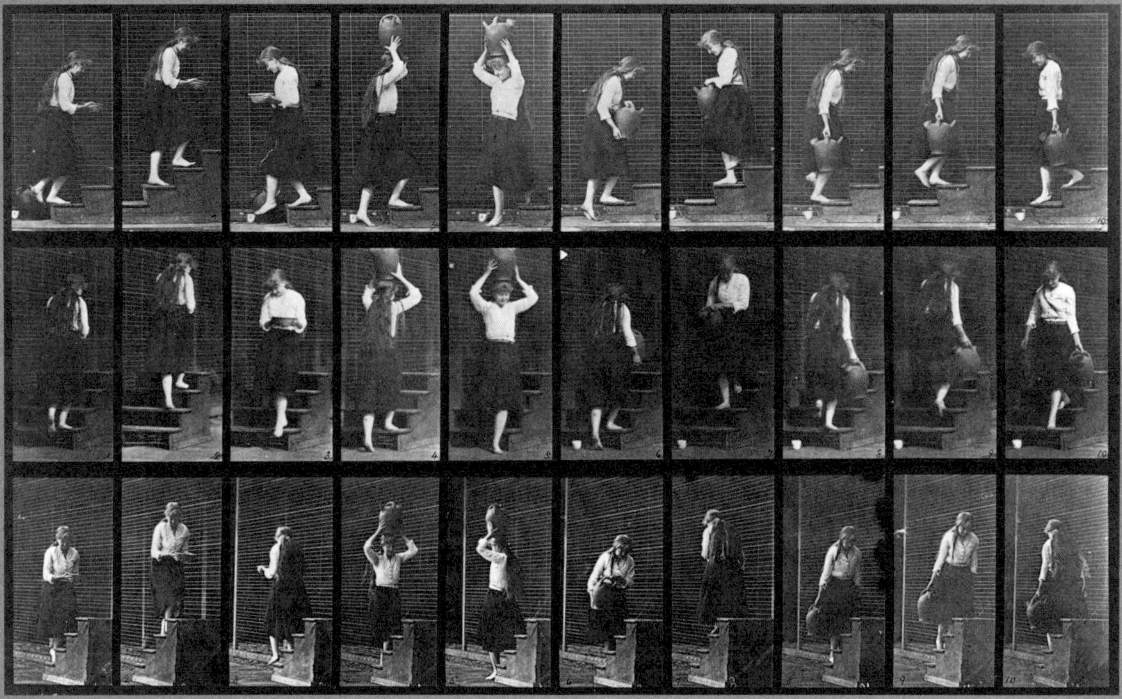

Plate 504. Electro-photographic investigation showing a series of consecutive images of a woman carrying vessels up and down steps.

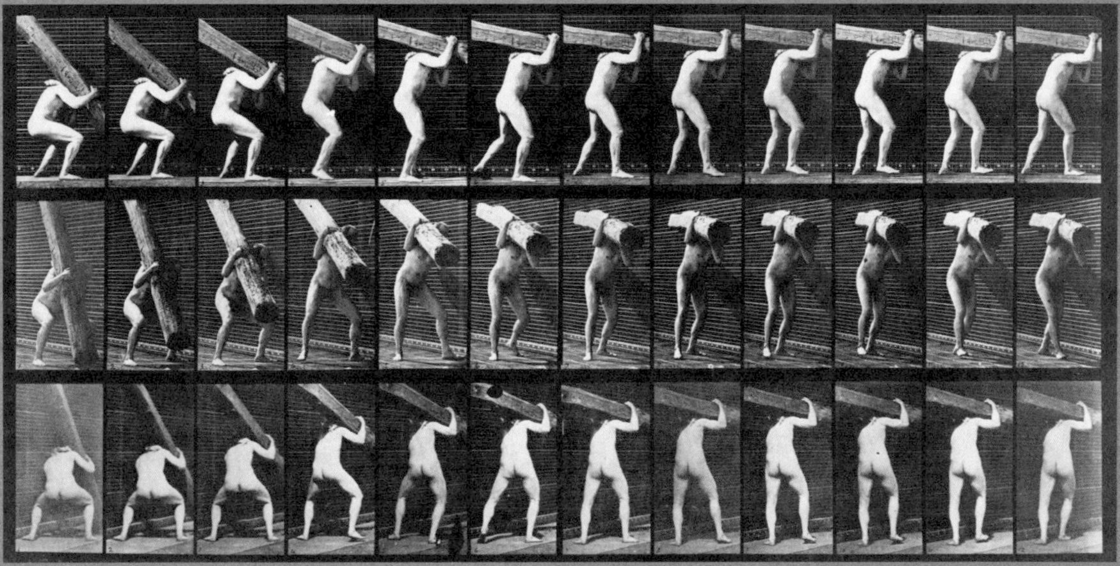

Plate 383. Electro-photographic investigation showing a series of consecutive images of a man lifting a log.

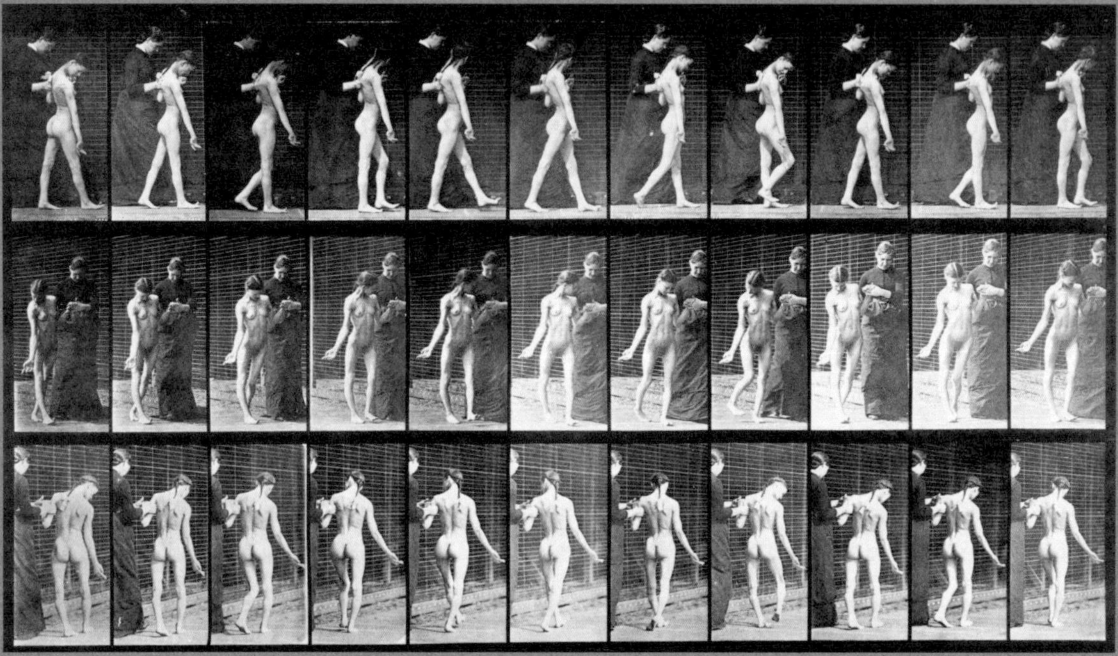

Plate 541. Electro-photographic investigation showing a series of consecutive images of a crippled nude woman walking, with assistance.

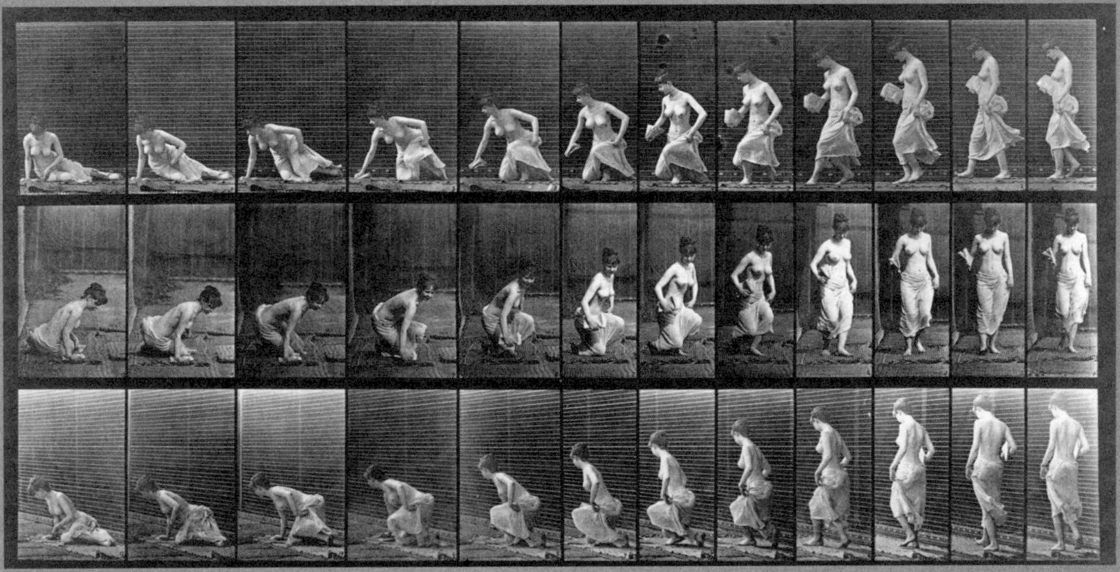

Plate 248. Thirty-six consecutive images of partially nude woman walking to a mat, sitting on the mat, then getting up, walking and sitting again.

Iron Horses: Leland Stanford, Eadweard Muybridge, and the Industrialized Eye

John Ott

2005

Produced under the sponsorship of Leland Stanford, one-time Governor of California and President of the Central Pacific Railroad, at his large ranch in Palo Alto, Eadweard Muybridge's pioneering images of horses frozen mid-stride have today become little more than unusual relics on the dusty top shelf of photographic and cinematic history. Muybridge's serial instantaneous photographs are largely familiar to us from flip-books, or perhaps the occasional exhibit of a zoetrope in a museum of science or natural history. Hitherto, there has been little substantive analysis of the cultural significance of the production and appreciation of these images in their own right. Instead, scholars mine this historical record largely to determine the exact time, place, and circumstance of cinema's birth.[1] Neglected curios like the Muybridge compendium demand to be reexamined in the context of a broader cultural history. Neither the Muybridge photographs nor their means of their production were inevitable. A major pitfall of film history has been to treat its technologies as a closed system, sealed off from society and progressing inexorably towards the present day. But as Gilles Deleuze has succinctly put it, 'machines are social before being technical'.[2] In this spirit, this study investigates instead the cultural work these images accomplished, from their conceptualization to their creation to their reception.

In particular, I wish to scrutinize these photographic stills in the context of the nation's complex and troubled process of mechanization during the late nineteenth century. In short, I contend that Leland Stanford and his advocates publicly staged and disseminated these photographs in order to consolidate, promote, and naturalize the developments of industrial capitalism. As I hope to demonstrate, this gilding of the new order was as important to capitalist entrepreneurs like Stanford as the proper flow of labor and capital. I do not find it coincidental, then, that the owner and manager of locomotives was interested in the mechanics of animal locomotion.

For supporters and critics alike, this photographic archive and the transcontinental railroad were indelibly co-implicated in ways beyond their mutual execution under Stanford's supervision. To begin with, Stanford proffered these experiments as evidence of his commitment to the public good, as clear benefits

1 The ensuing stream of scholarly publications has preoccupied itself with bringing new evidence to bear on what has become a messy and contentious paternity suit. Terry Ramsaye, for example, in his two-volume film history *A Million and One Nights*, helped to set the pattern by denigrating Muybridge and attacking his character with unusual vehemence; subsequent film historians have noted that Ramsaye's vitriol for Muybridge dovetails with the author's slavish adulation of Thomas Edison, who by Ramsaye's account deserves full and sole credit for inventing cinema. Terry Ramsaye, *A Million and One Nights* (Simon and Schuster: New York, 1964 [19261]); Ramsaye is critiqued by Harlan Hamilton, '"Les Allures du Cheval": Eadweard James Muybridge's Contribution to the Motion Picture', *Film Comment*, vol. 5, no. 3, Fall 1969, pp. 17-31. Contrawise, photographic historians have unduly inflated Muybridge's role, in part to legitimate the photographic medium as a high art form. Neither Muybridge nor Stanford should be deified as the creator of motion pictures. To begin with, a number of now-forgotten devices—stroboscopes, kinetoscopes, projecting phenakistoscopes, and other gewgaws—served as important transitions between still, printed images and projected, moving ones. See Robert Taft, *Photography and the American Scene* (Dover Publications: New York, 1938), p. 408; and Charles Musser, *The Emergence of Cinema: The American Screen to 1907* (Simon & Schuster Macmillan: New York, 1990), p. 45.

A few academics, such as Steve Neale, have observed this teleological character within Muybridge scholarship. Yet even those who have outlined the shortcomings of evaluating these images as mere precursors to film still feel obliged to contrast Muybridge's entertaining 'fictions' with the purportedly more legitimately scientific endeavors of Marey. Barbara Braun, for example, spends quite a bit of her book on Marey proving Muybridge a ridiculous figure. See Steve Neale, *Cinema and Technology: Image, Sound, Color* (Indiana University Press: Bloomington and Indianapolis, 1985), p. 7; and Marta Braun, *Picturing Time: The Work of Étienne-Jules Marey* (1830-1904) (The University of Chicago Press: Chicago and London, 1992), esp. pp. 228-62.

More recent work admirably contextualizes the stills within larger, thematic histories of visual culture but at the same time generally addresses the archive only as supporting evidence for the peculiar modernity of canonical painters: Thomas Eakins in the case of Michael Leja, Edouard Manet in the case of Jonathan Crary. See Michael Leja, 'Eakins and Icons', *Art Bulletin*, vol. 83, no. 3, September 2001, pp. 479-97; and Jonathan Crary, *Suspensions of Perception: Attention, Spectacle, and Modern Culture* (MIT Press: Cambridge and London, 1999), esp. pp. 138-48. Likewise, Rebecca Solnit's recent, ambitious study, *Eadweard Muybridge and the Technological Wild West* (Penguin: New York, 2003), promises to situate these stills in their historic moment only, in the end, to figure them teleologically as augurs of technological developments in the Far West: 'Muybridge's motion studies are like an early life-form from which wildly divergent species descend' (p. 211).

2 Quoted in Jonathan Crary, *Techniques of the Observer: On Vision and Modernity in the Nineteenth Century* (MIT Press: Cambridge and London, 1990), p. 31.

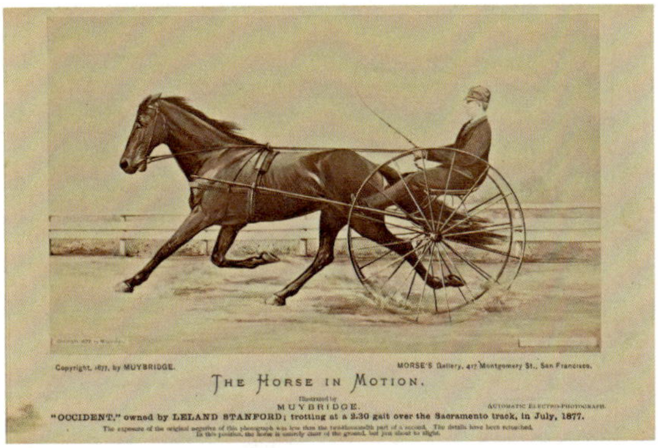

Figure 1. Eadweard Muybridge, *The Horse in Motion: 'Occident'*, 1877, albumen print, 4 × 8 ¼ in.

for both the economy in general and the art community in particular, and as exemplars of a new industrial order. For sympathizers, the stop-action photographs epitomized the inevitability and supremacy of the industrial, mechanized, and capitalized technologies in the saga of national progress. Many considered the strange images captured on glass almost sublime in their revelations of technotopian promise. Through the Muybridge experiments, Stanford strove to convince the world that horseflesh and the iron horse behaved in remarkably similar ways. In like fashion he also insisted that the mechanical gaze of instantaneous camera generated more accurate representations than the naked eye.

At the same time, many contemporaries responded to these photographs by questioning the role and nature of technology, industrialism, and individuals like Leland Stanford, who had amassed substantial fortunes and power through mechanization and the corporation. Many deemed the vision of instantaneity not wondrous but a kind of gothic horror. In addition, antagonists often rejected both their highly touted social utility and Stanford's proclaimed munificence. However, because these were photographs, the debate that I examine here centered on distinct modes and philosophies of visual production and consumption. The Muybridge archive, and responses thereto, thus marked an important moment when two rival conceptions of viewership collided. At stake, ultimately, was the ability to lay claim to social authority through the very practice of representation.

THE EXPERIMENTS: STILLS OF MOTION

Sometime in the spring of 1872, Stanford solicited Muybridge to produce a still photo of a horse in full trot.[3] The industrialist hoped to prove his theory of unsupported transit, which hypothesized that all four hooves of a trotter left the ground entirely for a split second over the course of its gait. On 7 April 1873, the *Alta California* reported that Muybridge had successfully captured an image of a moving horse at a remarkable one five-hundredth of a second. Unfortunately, these inaugural images have not survived in the form of photographs; but that year Currier and Ives published a print of 'the California Wonder Occident', and widely disseminated it commercially. Limited by the inconclusive results of a slower shutter speed, the lithographer clung to equestrian conventions that would be gradually abandoned in the years to come: crooked fore- and hindmost legs, an unnatural symmetry of the limbs, a silhouette nearly parallel to the ground line, and an almost comical height off the ground. All these details, of course, best expressed Stanford's theory of unsupported transit. In July 1877, Stanford transferred the photographic laboratory to the new stock farm in Palo Alto, and in the following month much wider newspaper coverage reported that the shutter speed had been reduced to one-thousandth of a second.[4] Muybridge's 'Automatic Electro-Photograph' (Fig. 1) reveals that the application of electricity to the shutter mechanism had enabled the photographer to reduce the exposure time enough to publish his own print.

Stanford also instigated the next phase of the experiments—the serial photographs for which Muybridge would be best known.[5] Inside a large shed set flush against the racecourse, Muybridge laterally arrayed twelve cameras 21 inches apart (Fig. 2). Carriage-bearing horses activated each camera by means of wires laid along the ground, while unencumbered mounts likewise tripped a series of breast-high threads strung before each of the lenses. On 15 June 1878, Stanford staged an exhibition in Palo Alto and asked reporters in attendance to observe the entire process of the photographs' manufacture, from the speeding mounts' activation of the cameras to Muybridge's immediate, on site development of the negatives.[6] That year, Muybridge printed and sold six resulting sets of exposures, with each group of six, eight, or twelve images arrayed in serial comic-strip fashion

3 This date is provided by Robert Bartlett Haas, 'Eadweard Muybridge, 1830-1904', in Anita Ventura Mozley (ed.), Eadweard *Muybridge: The Stanford Years, 1872-1882* (Stanford University Museum of Art: Stanford, 1972), p. 14.

4 'Occident Photographed at Full Speed', *Alta California*, 3 August 1877, p. 2; and 'A Triumph of Photographic Art', *San Francisco Bulletin*, 3 August 1877, p. 3.

5 Based on my review of newspaper reports, this particular motivation for this stage of the project was offered only in the wake of the demonstration discussed below, in June 1878. 'It came about in this wise: The owner [Stanford] of a phenomenal trotting horse desired to learn how to make this California prodigy [Occident] the wonder of the world ... The owner of the prodigy satisfying himself that the trainers did not get the best work out of the horse, concluded that there was some lack of knowledge on their part, and determined to institute a series of experiments which would produce information that might be of benefit to others'. 'A California Discovery', *Alta California*, 8 July 1878, p. 1.

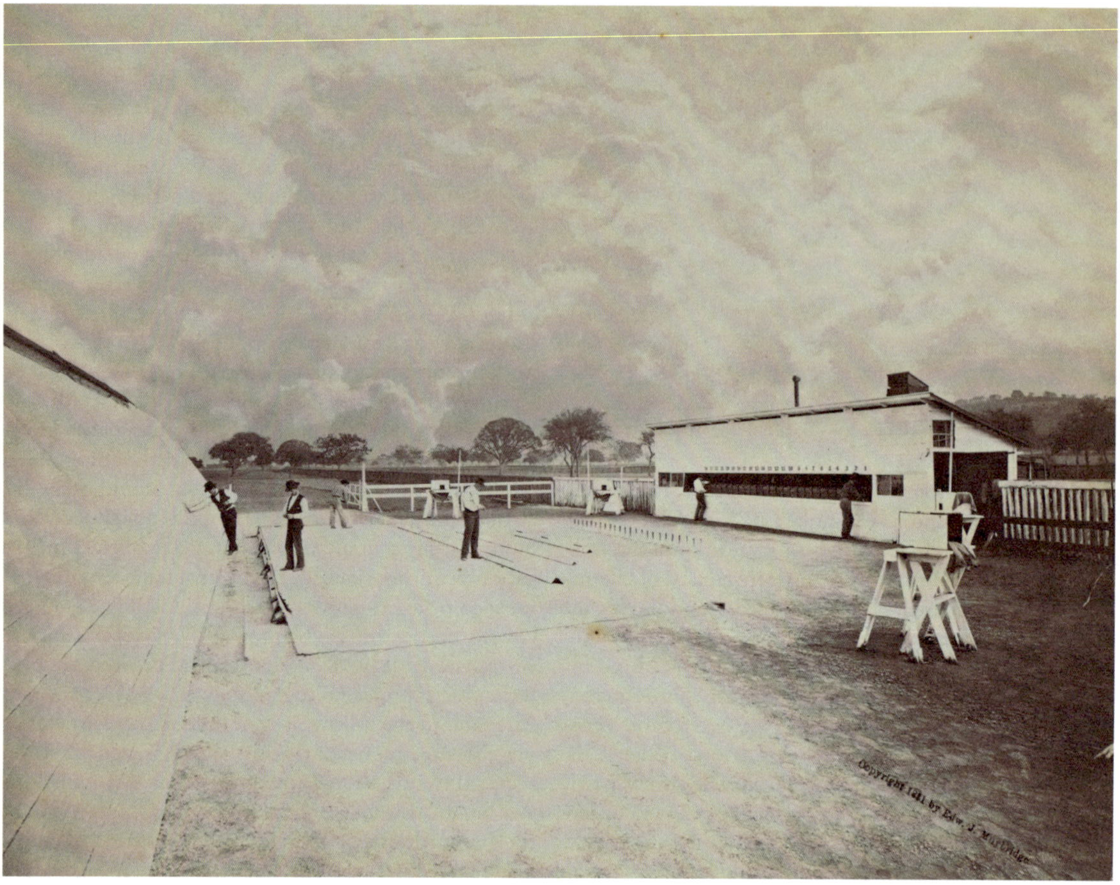

Figure 2. Eadweard Muybridge, *General View of the Experimental Track, Plate F for Attitudes of Animals in Motion*, 1881, toned cyanotype on print-out paper.

(Fig. 3). In the wake of widespread acclaim, Muybridge initiated what would become a lifelong series of illustrated lectures on his stop-motion photographs. In 1881 he self-published a highly limited run of the volume *Attitudes of Animals in Motion*, which featured over 2000 individual photos in over 150 series.[7]

The findings captivated a nineteenth-century audience. The relentless insistence on veracity—at public exhibitions and lectures, in newspaper reports, and on mass-produced lithographs—demonstrates, I think, just how strange and unconventional these images must have appeared to contemporaries. Especially disconcerting was the discovery that steeds in full gallop did not fully extend their limbs 'hobby-horse' fashion, as had been depicted since the earliest renderings of horses.[8] Muybridge would not reintegrate his sequential pictures into projected images that simulated motion until the autumn of 1879, at a private screening at the Stanford home often dubbed the first 'home movies'.[9] Within a year, Muybridge unveiled his 'zoopraxiscope' and its specially prepared glass discs, transparent save for the parade of horses rimming the perimeter in proper locomotive sequence. When set in motion before a projecting magic lantern, the shadows thrown from the discs produced a convincing illusion of motion. 'Nothing was wanting', wrote the *San Francisco Bulletin*, 'but the clatter of the hoofs from the turf and an occasional breath of steam from the nostrils'.[10]

---

6 On the exhibition, see Anita Mozley, 'Introduction to the Dover Edition', in *Eadweard Muybridge, Muybridge's Complete Human and Animal Locomotion* (Dover Publications: New York, 1979 [18871), p. xvii.

7 Eadweard Muybridge, *The Attitudes of Animals in Motion* (N.p.: Palo Alto, 1881).

8 Irma B. Jaffe, 'The Flying Gallop: East and West', *Art Bulletin*, vol. 65, no. 2, June 1983, pp. 183-200.

9 George T. Clark, *Leland Stanford: War Governor of California, Railroad Builder and Founder of Stanford University* (Stanford University Press: Stanford, 1931), pp. 367-8.

10 'Photographing Motion', *San Francisco Bulletin*, 5 May 1880, p. 1; see also 'The Zoogyroscope: Photographs Illustrating Animals in Motion', *San Francisco Call*, 5 May 1880, p. 3.

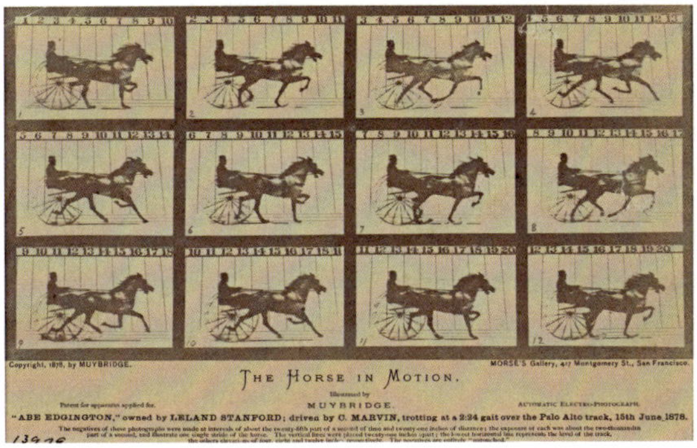

Figure 3. Eadweard Muybridge, *The Horse in Motion: 'Abe Edgington'*, 1878, albumen print, 4 ⅛ × 8 ¼ in.

A CALIFORNIA GELD RUSH

The tremendous scope of attention and acclaim visited upon the Muybridge-Stanford project was owed to its very subject matter. The Gilded Age—or 'gelded age', by the estimation of transportation historian Clay McShane—marked the apogee of the horse in America. Calvary played an unprecedented role in the Civil War, while during the postbellum period, the population and exploitation of horses in America grew apace with more commonly accepted measures of industrialization, such as the nation's total mileage of rail-lines. Accordingly, writes McShane, 'in the mid-nineteenth century, the horse was featured as a symbol of prosperity and modernity ... in business advertisements'.[11] Americans' dependence on equines is perhaps best dramatized by the destructive Great Epizootic of 1872, in which one-quarter of the nation's 16 million horses perished and so precipitated the debilitating economic Panic of 1873.[12]

The centrality of horses to the experience of both urbanites and rural Americans in the post-war era rendered the animal a prominent and highly flexible symbol. First and foremost, equines evoked tradition and the aristocracy of the ancient regime. Whether riding a lavish coach in Central or Golden Gate Park, or breeding and competing racehorses, entrepreneurial elites articulated their class identity and prestige through the ownership of costly horses, carriages, and stables.[13] This period also witnessed the development of breed sensibilities. As one of the most renowned and successful breeders in the world, Leland Stanford no doubt accumulated social prestige and the patina of elite traditions through his equestrian expertise. While Jane and Leland Stanford would eventually open a university in 1893 on the site of the stock farm Leland playfully called his 'kindergarten track', horses occupied the president of the Central Pacific Railroad in the 1870s.[14]

In this spirit, contemporary artists adapted the Euro-American tradition of aristocratic and military equestrian portraits to canvases depicting the new moneyed elites. In San Francisco, for example, merchants and bankers commissioned works in which horses acted as primary signifiers of high social status. Thomas Hill's undated *William Ralston Driving Double* features the owner of the Bank of California holding the reins of two of his nearly 100 horses and racing his carriage from San Francisco to his suburban estate at Belmont.[15] Horse ownership, however, also provided social critics with evidence of the indulgences of plutocrats like Ralston. 'When a San Franciscan gets to be immensely wealthy', opined the *San Francisco Argonaut* in 1877, 'he builds a palace of a stable with marble halls, Brussels carpet, and hot and cold water in every stall; a Chicago millionaire builds a college'.[16]

THE WATCHMAKER

And yet, according to Stanford and his associates, the success and significance of these photographs was due to the subjection of horses to a spectrum of mechanical apparati. The collaborators consistently emphasized the means by which these photographs had been

11 This paragraph draws on Clay McShane, 'Gelded Age Boston', *New England Quarterly*, vol. 74, no. 2, June 2001, pp. 274-302; Clay McShane and Joel A. Tarr, 'The Centrality of the Horse in the Nineteenth-Century American City', in Raymond A. Mohl (ed.), *The Making of Urban America*, 2nd edn (Scholarly Resources: Wilmington, 1997), pp. 105-30; and Robert West Howard, *The Horse in America* (Follett Publishing: Chicago and New York, 1965), pp. 213-31.

12 On the epizootic - animal species' equivalent to a viral epidemic— see Thomas J. Schelereth, *Victorian America: Transformations in Everyday Life, 1876-1915* (HarperCollins: New York, 1991), p. 21; and Clay McShane, *Down the Asphalt Path: The Automobile and the American City* (Columbia University Press: New York, 1994), p. 42.

13 Roy Rosenzweig and Elizabeth Blackmar, *The Park and the People: A History of Central Park* (Cornell University Press: Cornell, 1992), esp. pp. 211-59; and Sven Beckert, *The Monied Metropolis: New York City and the Consolidation of the American Bourgeoisie, 1850-1896* (Harvard University Press: Cambridge, 2001), pp. 258-9. For one of countless turf columns in the regional press, see 'Bay District Track', *Alta California*, 22 May 1877, p.

14 In later reminiscences, Stanford recalled that his doctor suggested he take up some kind of relaxing vocation as a palliative to the pressures of running a large corporation. The primary source for information on Stanford's stock farm is Clark, *Stanford*, pp. 342-63. See also Charles Marvin, *Training the Trotting Horse* (Marvin Publishing: New York, 1891); and Norman E. Tutorow, *Leland Stanford: Man of Many Careers* (Pacific Coast Publishers: Menlo Park, CA, 1971), pp.

15 See the catalogue at the end of Hardy Sloan George, *Thomas Hill (1829-1908)* (Unpublished Master's Thesis, University of California, Los Angeles, 1963), pp. 158-61.

16 Quoted in Patricia Lawrence, *Four Mansions on Nob Hill in 1870's* (Unpublished Master's Thesis, University of California, Davis, 1976), p. 49. The author identifies the passage as an 1877 article in the Argonaut.

achieved even more than the subject matter itself. At every stage of the images' production, Stanford and his carefully chosen representatives framed, staged, and promoted these experiments as the product of a rational, positivist science. They repeatedly insisted that this project drew from the latest scientific research; that Stanford and Muybridge carried it out as an experiment verifiable through observable, quantifiable phenomena; that machines gathered the data (active voice); that Stanford applied its findings in a purportedly scientific fashion to the training of trotters; and that a medical doctor published the results in technical language in a scientific context.

To begin with, Stanford's claims of scientific rigor papered over less favorable associations with an idle, decadent, and horse-bound aristocracy. Stanford attributed his success in breeding swift trotters to his implementation of scientific principles. His celebrated 'Palo Alto system' conditioned trotters far earlier than most stables, and took care not to overexert his trainees. At the center of the track the railroad executive sat in a custom-made rotating chair from which he could observe the work of his ranch hands and the progress of the colts.[17]

In this forum, the Muybridge collaboration developed under the aegis of scientific curiosity. The very set-up of the camera shed and complex recording instruments recall the forum of a research laboratory, a milieu that grew to maturity in the industrial sector in the 1870s and 1880s.[18] Stanford also conscripted technicians from the Central Pacific to assist Muybridge.[19] Moreover, when it came time to publish the results of the decade-long series of experiments, Stanford turned not to the photographer Muybridge, but to a local scientific authority, Dr. J. D. B. Stillman. Stillman packed his 1882 book *The Horse in Motion* with an exhaustive analysis of the Muybridge photographs dense with technical language and medical jargon.[20]

Stanford's attraction to and application of photography was especially crucial in this regard. In fact, Muybridge and his employer did not so much discover unsupported transit as document it in figural form. By 1872, the French scientist Étienne-Jules Marey had already substantiated the theory of unsupported transit through experiments involving pneumatic sensors attached to each hoof of a trotting horse.[21] The railroad executive pursued not Marey's abstract, graphical means of gathering and reporting data but the revelatory possibilities of the sensitized glass plate.

Still more importantly, however, the Muybridge photos encouraged viewers to imagine the horse, and by extension, all of nature, as merely another kind of machine. Fixed within a cold, monotonous grid of six, twelve, or twenty-four, the serial prints demanded that viewers conceptualize a sweaty, snorting, quivering mass of horseflesh as a dynamo performing an endlessly repetitive sequence of actions. The text on the reverse of these prints featured a detailed, methodical, and technical frame-by-frame analysis of equine mechanics. The effect on zoopraxiscope-goers, obliged to experience the same 12 frames again and again, must have been even more pronounced. It was as if the mechanical means of gathering and reporting data had been transposed somehow onto the subject of study.[22]

This vision of equine automatons also lies at the heart of Stillman's *The Horse in Motion*. The author's intricate physiological analysis depends on the premise that 'the horse is considered as a machine', a hypothesis to which Stanford likewise subscribed.[23] It should come as no surprise, then, that Stillman's book also referenced social evolutionist Herbert Spencer's *First Principles* (1862), a work that provided a suitably mechanistic model of nature and society.[24] Many commentators endorsed this proposition. An 1878 article

17 On the Palo Alto system, see Clark, *Stanford*, pp. 342-63; notice of the rotating chair appears in Anita Ventura Mozley (ed.), *Eadweard Muybridge: The Stanford Years, 1872-1882* (Stanford University Museum of Art: Stanford, 1972), p.

18 David Noble, *America by Design: Science, Technology and the Rise of Corporate Capitalism* (Alfred A. Knopf: New York, 1977), esp. pp. 3-20.

19 Although the evidence has been perhaps irrevocably contaminated by a later patent lawsuit between Stanford and Muybridge, it appears that CPRR employee John D. Isaacs developed the cameras' electrical triggering mechanism, while his superior Arthur Brown was at least partly responsible for designing the shutters. See the unpaginated court testimony by Samuel S. Montague and John D. Isaacs in Leland Stanford, Leland Stanford Collection (SC 512, Special Collections and University Archives, Stanford University, Stanford, California), Box 6, Folder 1.

20 J. D. B. Stillman, *The Horse in Motion* (James R. Osgood and Company: Boston, 1882).

21 Anson Rabinbach, The Human Motor: Energy, Fatigue, and the Origins of Modernity (University of California Press: Berkeley and Los Angeles, 1990), p. 99. Marey's findings were originally published in Étienne-Jules Marey, 'Des Allures de cheval, etudices par la methode graphique', *Compte-rendus des séances de l'Académie des Sciences*, vol. 75, 1872, p. 884. One article suggests that Stanford had in fact already read Marey at this juncture. See 'Leland Stanford's Gift to Art and to Science', San Francisco Examiner, 6 February 1881, p. 3.

22 Linda Williams briefly touches on this point that the Muybridge project 'offer[ed] up an image of the body as mechanism that is in many ways a reflection of the mechanical nature of the medium itself'. Linda Williams, 'Film Body: An Implantation of Perversions', *Cine Tracts*, vol. 12, nos. 3-4, Winter 1981, p. 20.

23 Stillman, *Horse*, p. 22. The discursive history of automatons and other mechanical humans, which dates at least back to Descartes, appears in Julie Wosk, *Breaking Frame: Technology and the Visual Arts in the Nineteenth Century* (Rutgers University Press: New Brunswick, 1992); and is referenced in Martin Berger, *Man Made: Thomas Eakins and the Construction of Gilded Age Manhood* (University of California Press: Berkeley and Los Angeles, 2000), pp. 43-6.

24 Stillman, Horse, p. 21. An excellent overview of the impact of Spencer's work in America appears in Kathleen Pyne, *Art and the Higher Life: Painting and Evolutionary Thought in Late 19th-century America* (University of Texas Press: Austin, 1996), pp. 1-47.

in the *Alta California*, for example, observed that, in the Muybridge stills, 'the feet strike the ground with the regularity and sequence of the stamps of a quartz mill'.[25] [...] By and large, the Muybridge photographs staged a coup for a highly controversial public figure like Stanford. While boosters and critics hotly debated the impact of the Central Pacific railroad on both the economy and average Californians, the American press largely accepted the research at the stock farm as positively beneficial for human society. The *Nation* argued that 'to Governor Leland Stanford, of California, belongs the credit of initiating this new method of scientific research, and of thus offering additional proof that a princely employment of wealth may be looked for in republics as well as monarchies'.[26]

[...] In public statements, Stanford himself often hitched his passion for horses to the welfare and evolution of the nation. 'There is', he averred in the pages of the *California Spirit of the Times*, "a great economic question involved in the breeding of good horses for labor".[27] And in an 1891 interview with Hubert Howe Bancroft, Stanford informed the historian that 'I do not raise horses ... for profit, but only to increase the wealth of the state'.[28] Stanford seemed quite interested in demonstrating to the public how responsibly he supervised his tremendous fortune. Altogether, he regularly characterized large outlays such as the Muybridge project as selfless and as disinterested as the cold gaze of the battery of track-side cameras.

All told, this belief system naturalized developments in mechanization like the railroad—the iron horse. For Stanford, industrialization was synonymous with progress; some years later, the railroad baron proffered this technotopia in his keynote remarks at the opening ceremony for the university he and Jane would endow on the site of the hippodrome in Palo Alto: 'The wonderful improvements in inventions and machinery in the last fifty years, by multiplying the power of production, have assisted greatly in the advancement of civilization'.[29] Thus these experiments did not just prove that horses acted like bundles of gears, levers, and engines; rather, for Stanford and his backers, they epitomized the necessity and inevitability of a new corporate industrial order buttressed by scientific authority, managerial supervision, and complex, capital-intense technologies. The locomotive and quartz-mill, after all, were more effective machines than horses and humans.

TRAIN THE EYE

And yet, the ramifications of the Muybridge collaboration extended the reach of mechanization yet further, into the realm of perception. In essence, Stanford's patronage and dissemination of these stills celebrated a new kind of automated seeing.[30] Whereas the photograph differed from the human retina only in *degree*, the instantaneous snapshot represented a different *kind* of perception. In the book *The Horse in Motion*, Dr. Stillman turned to positivist accounts in order to assuage sceptics' reluctance to accept the veracity of Muybridge's photographs and to account for millennia of inexact equine representations. By his reasoning, the scientific theory of the retinal afterimage explained why people saw galloping horses in the 'hobby-horse' position; the human eye could only register a horse's limbs at their point of greatest extension, when, like a pendulum, they moved most slowly.[31]

Muybridge's lectures likewise counterpoised the apparent deceptiveness of the naked eye with the unassailable fidelity of the Automatic Electro-Photograph. His presentations dwelt at length on comparisons between the 'correct' postures of animals in transit, as revealed by his photos, and the now-laughable depictions of the same in Western art. He dispelled such untruths as a kind of medieval superstition that had wilted in the strong sun of modern science.

[...] Furthermore, the very format of the 1878 sequential frames may have fostered the notion that Muybridge's work greatly surpassed the unaided eye. Whether sold as boudoir cards, reproduced in popular magazines, or displayed by magic lantern, the grids of successive photographs evoked nothing so much as the stereocards that entertained the Victorian bourgeoisie in their parlors on both sides of the Atlantic. However, instead of the dual images of the stereocard, Muybridge's latticework of six, eight, or twelve stills produced a kaleidoscopic effect. It was as though a stereoscope had divided and multiplied, cell-like, into a composition that approximated sext-, oct-, or dodecan-ocular vision. All told, homo sapiens's modest set of twinned retinas paled in comparison to the Argus of the automated gaze. [...]

The transformation of mechanized vision into a kind of industrial gaze, however, was not confined to the literal aggrandizement of Stanford and his endeavors. In fact, the developments of the railroad and the stop-motion photograph did not run on parallel tracks, but intersected in important and fundamental ways. Both rail

25 'A California Discovery', *Alta California*, 8 July 1878, p. 1.
26 'Stillman's Horse in Motion', *Nation*, vol. 34, 27 April 1882, p.
27 Leland Stanford, 'Thoroughbred Blood in the Trotter', *Spirit of the Times*, vol. 118, 28 December 1889, p. 803.
28 Hubert Howe Bancroft, 'Character Study of Leland Stanford' (Manuscript, MSS C-D 808, c. 1891. Bancroft Library, University of California at Berkeley), p. 83.
29 The Leland Stanford Junior University, 'Exercises of the Opening Day', *Circulars*, vol.5, 1891, p. 8.
30 The development of a concept of disembodied vision has been traced at some length by Crary, *Techniques*, pp. 1-24.
31 Stillman, *Horse*, pp. 12-13.

travel and the Palo Alto experiments established a kind of non-anthropomorphic time beyond the capacities of human perception. As a new experience of 'panoramic travel', to borrow a term from Wolfgang Schivelbusch, journey by rail transformed the experience of landscape and challenged the Cartesian model of time and space.[32] Among other things, the moving locomotive revealed the limitations of retinal vision. The view out of the moving train window and the images flickering from the zoopraxiscope were two sides of the same coin. It is not coincidental, then, that contemporaries often paired the completion of the railroad with the execution of the Muybridge stills.

Even now, the image of Stanford hammering home the final, golden spike at Promontory, Utah, emblematizes the arduous task of spanning the continent by rail. So ingrained was this symbolism that many contemporaries, when faced with the Muybridge photographs, felt compelled to return to this primal scene of the new industrial order. I quote at length this commentary from the *San Francisco Call*:

> When Governor Stanford drove the last spike which connected the Union and Central Pacific Railroads, and, in a figurative sense united the Atlantic and Pacific Oceans ... the blow of the hammer was echoed by a salvo of artillery from the shores of the bay. The act itself was the herald which announced the completion of the great design; and, surely, if it could thus be drove [sic] across mountains and valleys, the same agency [of electricity] could solve this portion of the problem [of instantaneous photography].[33]

Here the author collapses Stanford's symbolic act, the telegraphic transmission of the news of the railroad's completion, and the achievement of stop-motion photography. It was not just that Stanford had been present to supervise the completion of the railroad and the photographs, nor merely that he had been the inspiration for both, but that he had somehow willed both into existence with one decisive action. This mythology, of course, elided the contributions of the many workers (including Muybridge) that labored both at the stock farm and for the railroad.

To summaries, this nascent ideology of a mechanized universe legitimated the authority of science and naturalized industrial acceleration and expansion. The utility of the Muybridge photographs stems from their efficacy not merely as an argument for the superiority of an industrial gaze, but as its embodiment and exemplar. Over objections that artists should adhere to the conventions of ocular vision [...] Stillman retorted that the naked eye must become habituated to the new industrial optics.[34] By this rhetoric, Americans were expected to follow the leadership of Stanford and other technocrats and submit even the way they looked at the world to their expertise. A significant portion of the national press, even beyond sympathetic venues like the *Call* and *Scientific American*, readily acceded to this stunning proposition. 'It is very probable', allowed the *Nation*, 'that the study of instantaneous photographs will gradually train the eye', just as Stanford had trained champion colts, and just as he had once envisioned the possibility of a transcontinental train.[35]

SEEING THE OCTOPUS

Not everyone desired such tutelage. Many contemporaries partially or flatly contested or rejected the logic of the industrial gaze. Yet without exception, scholars express petulant impatience with the photographs' detractors, and scoff in retrospect at the recalcitrance of literally short-sighted luddites. In actuality, much public opinion was slow to conclude, divided, and rather sophisticated in its dissent. At first, the debate centered on the veracity of the published stills—hence Stanford and Muybridge's chronic need to verify the experiments through public exhibitions and gild them with the patina of scientific authority. [...]

But as the 1870s waned, the majority of criticisms increasingly touched on the larger question of the relative merits of mechanization, which suggests that more was at stake than the proper method of representing an animal in transit. These individuals rejected the argument that nature operated like a machine by countering that mechanization was unnatural and even life-threatening.[36] [...] The clamor over Muybridge's findings thus constituted a deep anxiety over mechanization and the extent to which it seemed to govern everyday life. In 1887 the *Century* wrote '[There is] no one who had ridden a horse or loved a dog but felt a certain outraged sensibility in being assured that creatures ... were four-legged machines'.[37] This anxiety was perhaps most pronounced in popular attitudes toward the railroad, which, as we have seen, was never truly absent from any discussion involving Stanford's many projects. Even before Promontory, intellectuals like Henry George accurately warned that the completion of the transcontinental railroad

32 Wolfgang Schivelbusch, *The Railway Journey: The Industrialization of Time and Space in the 19th Century* (University of California Press: Berkeley and Los Angeles, 1977), pp. 52-69.

33 'A Wonder of the Century', *San Francisco Call*, 16 June 1878, p. 7.

34 For instance, Stillman, *Horse*, p. 101.

35 'Stillman's Horse in Motion', *Nation*, vol. 34, 27 April 1882, p. 359.

36 Aspects of anti-industrial discourses in nineteenth-century America are examined in Wosk, *Breaking*, passim.

would agglomerate power in the hands of a very few like never before. The Credit Mobilier scandal of 1872 and the long depression of the 1870s further aggravated public sentiment towards rail; to many, the Central Pacific had accelerated the depression by flooding local markets with cheap goods and labor. [...]

In order to delineate further the extent of many Americans' ambivalence towards the technologies of incorporation, I cite a parallel example that also concerns time, the mechanization of nature, the railroad, and its critics. As Michael O'Malley chronicles in his excellent *Keeping Watch: A History of American Time*, the railroad's annihilation of space necessitated the gradual adoption of standard time, but disturbed a hornet's nest of ill will towards railroad companies.[38] Because urban elites both owned and most frequently travelled by railroad, those outside the largest cities and/or outside the mercantile oligarchy denounced the abolition of local time as a violation of personal autonomy, community tradition, and indeed Nature herself. Many spoke out against standard time as privilege for the few; one Boston minister even charged that the standard time was a 'piece of monopolistic work adverse to the workingman's interest'.[39] While the experience of rail had already begun to disrupt the connections between time and nature, the introduction of four standard time zones on 18 November 1883 subsumed solar time to the new industrial regime.[40]

In the same fashion, the Muybridge photographs standardized a sort of a physiological time, so to speak, by which the actions of animals and humans could be clocked and against which they could be measured.[41] After his own fashion, Leland Stanford concurred with those who insisted that the sundial yield to the schedule of the railroad manager; recall how the railroad executive complained that 'the horse would not keep correct time'.[42] Like the consolidation of the complex patchwork of local times into homogenous railroad time, the Muybridge experiments collapsed the universe of equestrian movement into a single, rational, and 'monopolist' model of equine locomotion. However, like the reaction against railroad time—many localities held out until federal law mandated standard time in 1918—many contemporaries continued to discredit the Muybridge photographs, this time on a more philosophical level. [...]

CODA: STANFORD'S INSTRUMENT

These storms of objection may help explain the paucity of images of human bodies within the Stanford-Muybridge collaboration.[43] In early August 1879, a group of athletes from the San Francisco Olympic Club did actually perform at the hippodrome and Muybridge successfully executed serial stop-motion prints of 'boxing, wrestling, fencing, jumping, and tumbling.[44] These images only appeared, however, in Muybridge's 1881 tome. This gap within the Muybridge archive cannot be accidental. One would expect, for example, that the alleged scientific and economic value of the equestrian stills would be equally applicable to studies of human motion. At the same time, one might also expect equal, if not greater, skepticism, distaste, and outrage. If commentators cried out against the images' apparent violence to horses, then one can only imagine how much more disturbing the human form would appear through the lenses of the industrial gaze. [...]

And yet I think it would still be possible to read the laboring human body, however obliquely, through Muybridge's equine archive. That is, something of the managerial hierarchy of industrial capitalism persists in the figure of the well-bred, disciplined, and submissive horse. My cue for this reading stems from art historian Kirk Savage's work on Confederate military

37 Talcott Williams, 'Animal Locomotion' (1887), p. 359. The extensive public debate over the Muybridge archives fills the pages of the *Eadweard Muybridge Scrapbook*, which resides at the Borough Library in Kingston-upon-Thames. A partial list of press coverage would include: 'A Horse's Movement Scientifically Determined', *Scientific American*, vol. 39, no. 6, 19 October 1878, p. 241; 'A Horse's Movement Scientifically Considered', *Scientific American Supplement*, vol. 7, no. 158, 11 January 1879, pp. 2508-510; Richard A. Proctor, 'Photographs of a Galloping Horse', *Gentleman's Magazine*, vol. 27, December 1881, pp. 666-89; 'Stillman's Horse in Motion', Nation, vol. 34, 27 April 1882, p. 359; George E. Waring, Jr, 'The Horse in Motion', Century, vol. 24, no. 3, July 1882, pp. 386-7; George Snell, 'On the Galloping Horse in Art', *Century*, vol. 26, no. 2, June 1883, pp. 315-17; and dozens of articles in local San Francisco newspapers like the *Alta California, Bulletin, Call, Chronicle*, and *Examiner*.

38 Michael O'Malley, *Keeping Watch: A History of American Time* (Viking: New York, 1990), pp. 99-144.

39 Quoted in O'Malley, *Watch*, p. 120.

40 Schelereth, *Victorian America*, pp. 29-31; and O'Malley, *Watch*, pp. 99-144.

41 A similar point about Marey's work has been made by Rabinbach, *Motor*, p. 93.

42 Bancroft, 'Biography of Leland Stanford', p. 12.

43 Of course, the experiments Muybridge conducted at the University of Philadelphia in the 1880s canvassed a wide range of human movement and a larger portion of the animal kingdom. These photographs, however, were taken for different purposes and under different auspices. Their associations with art instruction on the one hand and the city's medical and biological community on the other, for instance, render their meaning and significance distinct from the California experiments and place them outside of this study.

44 *Photographic Times*, October 1879, in the *Muybridge Scrapbook*, p. 53; the article is also a reprint from the *San Francisco Chronicle*, 9 August 1879. See also Robert Bartlett Haas, *Muybridge: Man in Motion* (University of California Press: Berkeley, Los Angeles and London, 1976), pp. 23, 112; Haas, 'Eadweard Muybridge' (1972), pp. 9, 24. Finally, Haas argues that Eakins' correspondence with Muybridge establishes that the artist is responsible for suggesting that the photographer take up the human form in 1878. See Haas, *Man in Motion*, p. 134.

equestrian monuments in the postbellum South. According to Savage, the depiction of man's domination over animals often also suitably expressed the military hierarchy. This image of pure power, moreover, also readily denoted and reinforced other social hierarchies that were not as easily publicly articulated. 'The equestrian image was thus an overripe metaphor, referring ultimately to the nature of power in society. The image of Lee on his horse worked beautifully as a model of leadership for a white supremacist society trying to legitimate its own authority'.[45]

Using Savage analogically, I argue that the rationalized images of mechanized horses encoded class in the industrialized West at precisely the same time and in much the same way as equestrian sculptures encoded race in the post-war South. As in Southern Civil War memorials, the figure of the horse evoked associations of power, domination, and caste on behalf of California's industrial elite. It makes perfect sense, then, that the concrete visual representation of the Stanfords at their University would ultimately be an equestrian image. Situated high on the triumphal Stanford Memorial Arch, Jane and Leland race mounts detailed in exact Muybridgean fashion. As the vanguard leading a Central Pacific locomotive over the Sierra Nevadas, the Stanfords personify the railroad, much like the other allegories along the frieze. Together with the euphemism of mythological Titans, Stanford's imperial presence articulates executive authority at the direct expense of his absent workforce. The citation of the Muybridge experiments through these steeds, finally, references his self-styled gentility, breeding, foresight, benefaction, and scientific knowledge. His mastery over his horse signals that he holds tightly the reins of his corporation.[46]

I wish to conclude with one set of images from Muybridge's *The Attitudes of Animals in Motion*. This picture serves less well as concrete evidence for my argument than as a useful closing metaphor. Photograph 110, as it has been catalogued, depicts a naked, bearded man swinging a pickaxe before the battery of cameras at the kindergarten track [See Plate 110, page 195 of this volume].[47] The protagonist is Muybridge himself, which makes this a strange form of self-portrait. The photographer's motivations for appearing nude within the Palo Alto archive may be explained easily enough. As a member of San Francisco's athletic Olympic Club, Muybridge clearly enjoyed demonstrating his muscular prowess; after all, Eakins, another proponent of vigorous, bodily masculinity, also often posed nude for the purposes of art instruction.[48] In addition, the photographer lived for four years with the Nahl brothers, the co-founders of the Club, and he personally recruited its members for the aforementioned studies of human locomotion in August 1879. However, this accounts only for Muybridge's nudity. In fact, in every other instance where the cameras capture the frozen images of men, the subjects participate in athletics, and do not labor. As such, Muybridge's actions evoke not some mythical gymnasium from antiquity, but the miners that made Stanford a wealthy Sacramento merchant, or perhaps even the toiling laborers, mostly Chinese, who built the Central Pacific Railroad.

However, this image is still more peculiar when we consider the lawsuit that Muybridge brought against Stanford after discovering that he had not been credited in Stillman's book. Over the course of *Muybridge V. Stanford*, the railroad baron repeatedly referred to Muybridge as a mere 'employee' to gird his case that he owned the copyright for the images because he initially conceptualized and ultimately paid for them.[49] During this trial, Stanford further elucidated his opinions in letters to Stillman. One missive insisted that 'the actual facts are from beginning to end that [Muybridge] was an instrument to carry out my ideas'.[50] Although Stanford would not express these sentiments until a few years after the photographer composed this self-portrait, at times Muybridge must have chafed at his role at the kindergarten track. Although the photographer is still technically Muybridge, the point of view, both literally and metaphorically, is Stanford's. Whether aware of it or not, by performing the role of laboring instrument before his cameras, Muybridge too became the object of the industrial gaze.

---

45 Kirk Savage, *Standing Soldiers, Kneeling Slaves: Race, War, and Monuments in Nineteenth-century America* (Princeton University Press: Princeton, 1997), pp. 133, 135.

46 On the Arch, see Alan E. Miller, 'The Folly of Stanford' (Unpublished typescript, SC 0290, Special Collections and University Archives, Stanford University, Stanford, California, 1959); 'The Memorial Arch of Stanford University', *San Jose Daily Mercury*, 27 October 1901, p. 9; and 'The St Gaudens Frieze', Stanford Alumnus, vol. 3, nos. 8-9, June 1902, pp. 112-14. See also Ott, *The Gilded Rush*, pp. 242-6.

47 This accession number corresponds to the album that is now in the hands of Stanford University Special Collections. Other volumes, such as UCLA's, seem to differ slightly in layout.

48 83. Jennifer Doyle, 'Sex, Scandal, and Thomas Eakins's *The Gross Clinic*', *Representations*, vol. 68, Fall 1999, pp. 1-33; and Ellwood C. Parry III, 'Thomas Eakins's "Naked Series" Reconsidered: Another Look at the Standing Nude Photographs Made for the Use of Eakins's Students', *American Art Journal*, vol. 20, no. 2, 1988, pp. 53-77.

49 The lawsuit is discussed in Haas, 'Eadweard Muybridge' (1972), pp. 27-30.

50 Letter to J. D. B. Stillman, 23 October 1882, Leland Stanford, *Leland Stanford Papers* (SC 33a, Special Collections and University Archives, Stanford University, Stanford, California), Box 1, Folder 17.

Physiologie du mouvement: le vol des oiseaux

Étienne-Jules Marey

1890

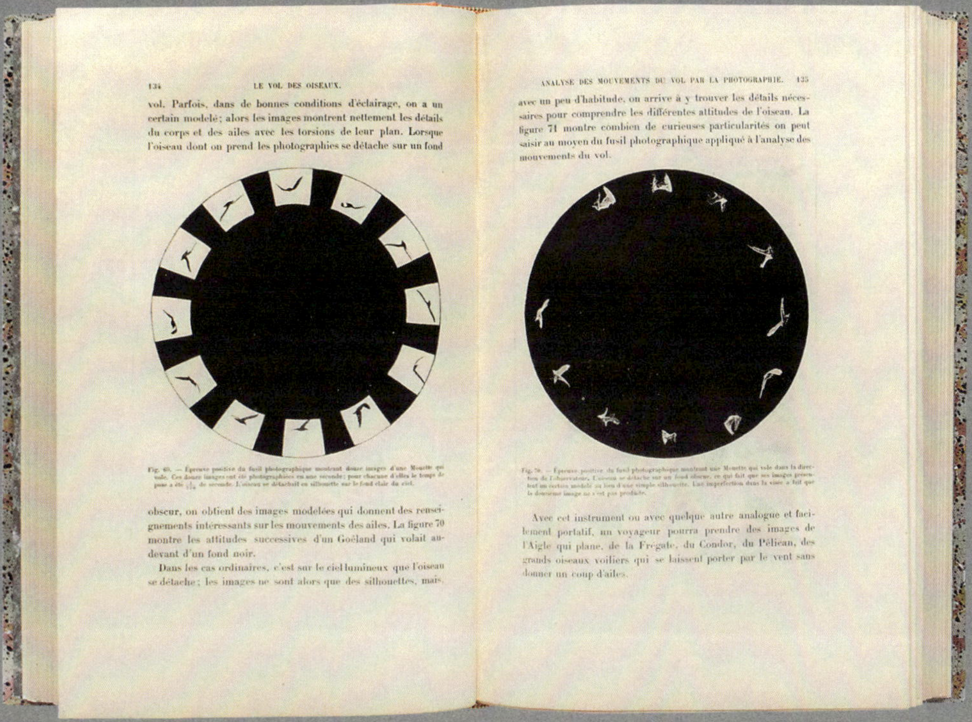

vol. Parfois, dans de bonnes conditions d'éclairage, on a un certain modelé; alors les images montrent nettement les détails du corps et des ailes avec les torsions de leur plan. Lorsque l'oiseau dont on prend les photographies se détache sur un fond

Fig. 69. — Épreuve positive du fusil photographique montrant douze images d'une Mouette qui vole. Ces douze images ont été photographiées en une seconde; pour chacune d'elles le temps de pose a été [illegible] de seconde. L'oiseau se détachait en silhouette sur le fond clair du ciel.

obscur, on obtient des images modelées qui donnent des renseignements intéressants sur les mouvements des ailes. La figure 70 montre les attitudes successives d'un Goëland qui volait au-devant d'un fond noir.

Dans les cas ordinaires, c'est sur le ciel lumineux que l'oiseau se détache; les images ne sont alors que des silhouettes, mais,

avec un peu d'habitude, on arrive à y trouver les détails nécessaires pour comprendre les différentes attitudes de l'oiseau. La figure 71 montre combien de curieuses particularités on peut saisir au moyen du fusil photographique appliqué à l'analyse des mouvements du vol.

Fig. 70. — Épreuve positive du fusil photographique montrant une Mouette qui vole dans la direction de l'observateur. L'oiseau se détache sur un fond obscur, ce qui fait que ses images présentent un certain modelé au lieu d'une simple silhouette. Une imperfection dans la visée a fait que la douzième image ne s'est pas produite.

Avec cet instrument ou avec quelque autre analogue et facilement portatif, un voyageur pourra prendre des images de l'Aigle qui plane, de la Frégate, du Condor, du Pélican, des grands oiseaux voiliers qui se laissent porter par le vent sans donner un coup d'ailes.

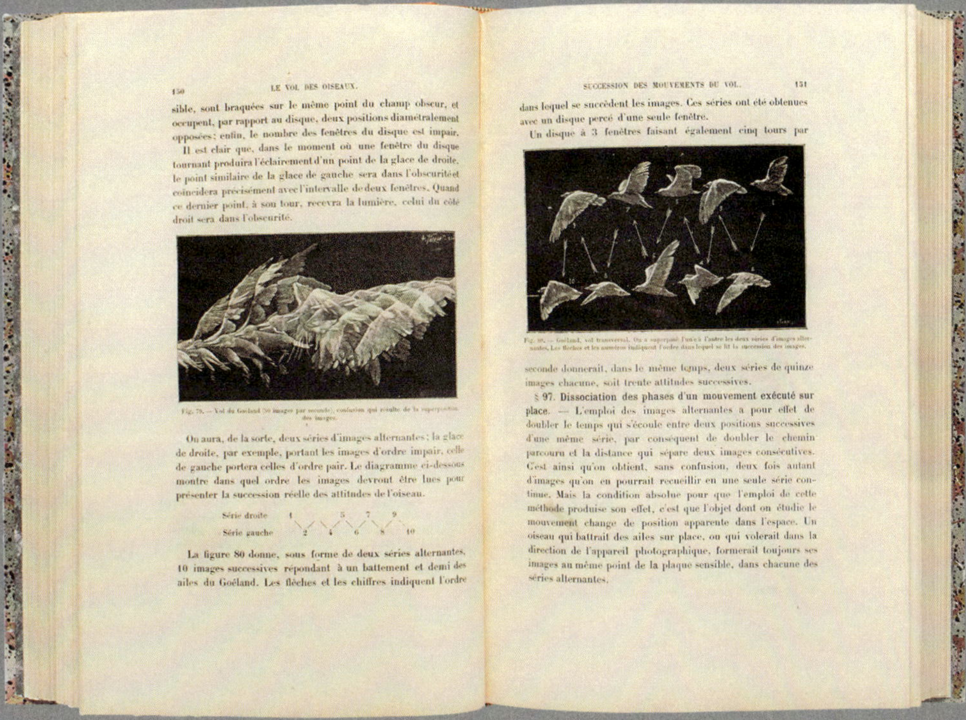

sible, sont braquées sur le même point du champ obscur, et occupent, par rapport au disque, deux positions diamétralement opposées; enfin, le nombre des fenêtres du disque est impair.

Il est clair que, dans le moment où une fenêtre du disque tournant produira l'éclairement d'un point de la glace de droite, le point similaire de la glace de gauche sera dans l'obscurité et coïncidera précisément avec l'intervalle de deux fenêtres. Quand ce dernier point, à son tour, recevra la lumière, celui du côté droit sera dans l'obscurité.

Fig. 79. — Vol du Goéland (50 images par seconde), confusion qui résulte de la superposition des images.

On aura, de la sorte, deux séries d'images alternantes; la glace de droite, par exemple, portant les images d'ordre impair, celle de gauche portera celles d'ordre pair. Le diagramme ci-dessous montre dans quel ordre les images devront être lues pour présenter la succession réelle des attitudes de l'oiseau.

Série droite 1 3 5 7 9

Série gauche 2 4 6 8 10

La figure 80 donne, sous forme de deux séries alternantes, 10 images successives répondant à un battement et demi des ailes du Goéland. Les flèches et les chiffres indiquent l'ordre

dans lequel se succèdent les images. Ces séries ont été obtenues avec un disque percé d'une seule fenêtre.

Un disque à 3 fenêtres faisant également cinq tours par

Fig. 80. — Goéland, vol transversal. On a superposé l'une à l'autre les deux séries d'images alternantes. Les flèches et les numéros indiquent l'ordre dans lequel se lit la succession des images.

seconde donnerait, dans le même temps, deux séries de quinze images chacune, soit trente attitudes successives.

§ 97. **Dissociation des phases d'un mouvement exécuté sur place.** — L'emploi des images alternantes a pour effet de doubler le temps qui s'écoule entre deux positions successives d'une même série, par conséquent de doubler le chemin parcouru et la distance qui sépare deux images consécutives. C'est ainsi qu'on obtient, sans confusion, deux fois autant d'images qu'on en pourrait recueillir en une seule série continue. Mais la condition absolue pour que l'emploi de cette méthode produise son effet, c'est que l'objet dont on étudie le mouvement change de position apparente dans l'espace. Un oiseau qui battrait des ailes sur place, ou qui volerait dans la direction de l'appareil photographique, formerait toujours ses images au même point de la plaque sensible, dans chacune des séries alternantes.

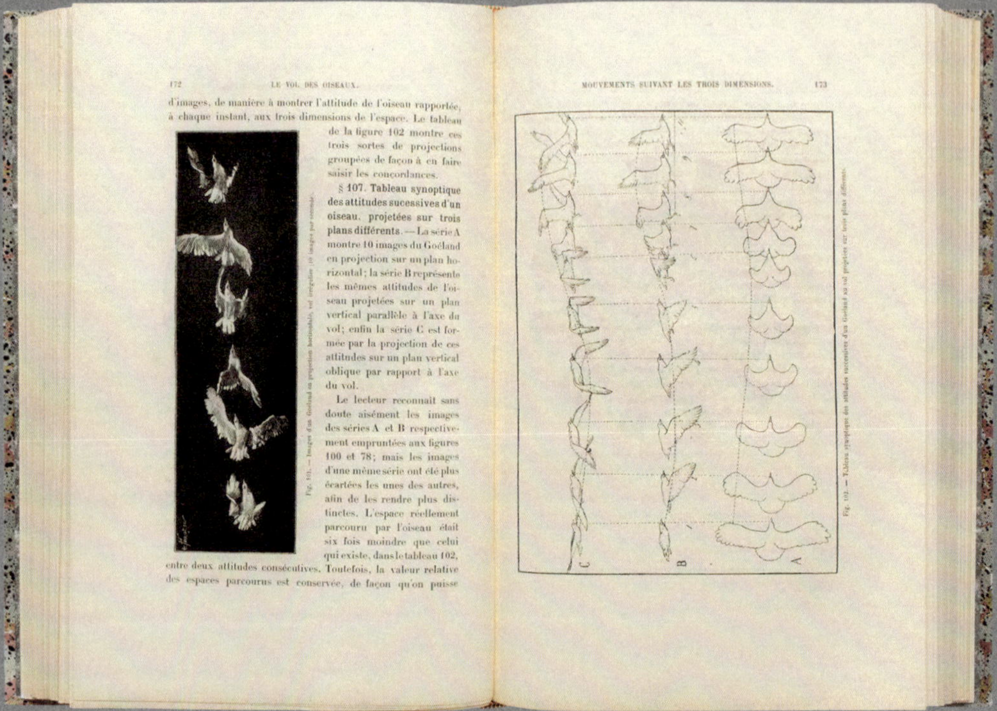
172 LE VOL DES OISEAUX.
d'images, de manière à montrer l'attitude de l'oiseau rapportée, à chaque instant, aux trois dimensions de l'espace. Le tableau de la figure 102 montre ces trois sortes de projections groupées de façon à en faire saisir les concordances.
§ 107. Tableau synoptique des attitudes sucessives d'un oiseau, projetées sur trois plans différents. — La série A montre 10 images du Goéland en projection sur un plan horizontal; la série B représente les mêmes attitudes de l'oiseau projetées sur un plan vertical parallèle à l'axe du vol; enfin la série C est formée par la projection de ces attitudes sur un plan vertical oblique par rapport à l'axe du vol.
Le lecteur reconnait sans doute aisément les images des séries A et B respectivement empruntées aux figures 100 et 78; mais les images d'une même série ont été plus écartées les unes des autres, afin de les rendre plus distinctes. L'espace réellement parcouru par l'oiseau était six fois moindre que celui qui existe, dans le tableau 102, entre deux attitudes consécutives. Toutefois, la valeur relative des espaces parcourus est conservée, de façon qu'on puisse
MOUVEMENTS SUIVANT LES TROIS DIMENSIONS. 173

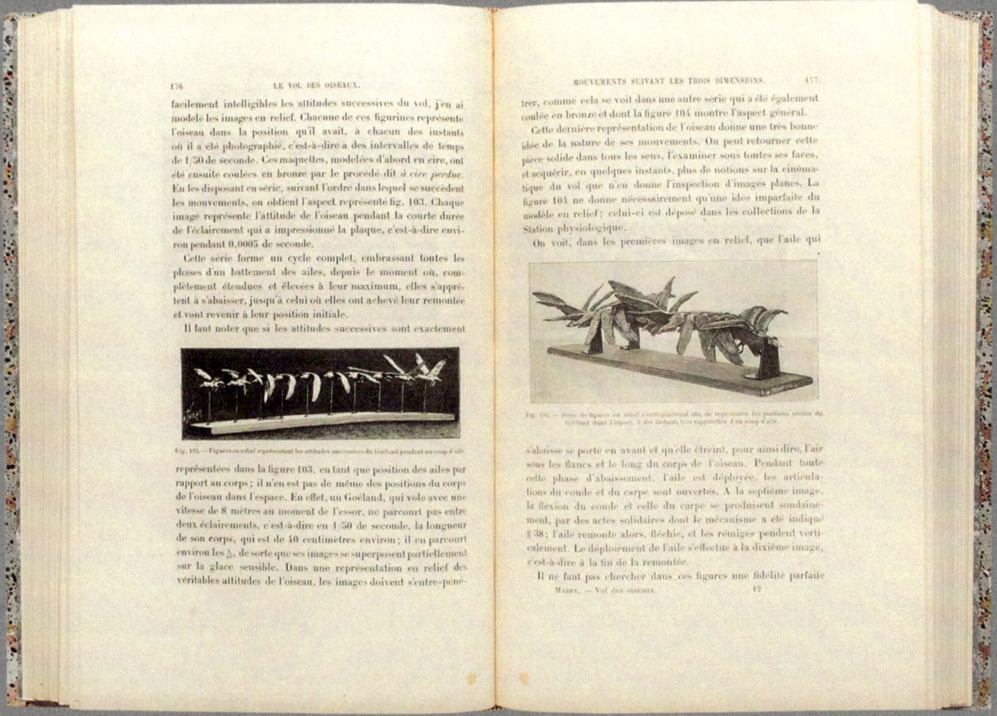
176 LE VOL DES OISEAUX.
facilement intelligibles les attitudes successives du vol, j'en ai modelé les images en relief. Chacune de ces figurines représente l'oiseau dans la position qu'il avait, à chacun des instants où il a été photographié, c'est-à-dire à des intervalles de temps de 1/50 de seconde. Ces maquettes, modelées d'abord en cire, ont été ensuite coulées en bronze par le procédé dit *à cire perdue*. En les disposant en série, suivant l'ordre dans lequel se succèdent les mouvements, on obtient l'aspect représenté fig. 103. Chaque image représente l'attitude de l'oiseau pendant la courte durée de l'éclairement qui a impressionné la plaque, c'est-à-dire environ pendant 0,0005 de seconde.
Cette série forme un cycle complet, embrassant toutes les phases d'un battement des ailes, depuis le moment où, complètement étendues et élevées à leur maximum, elles s'apprêtent à s'abaisser, jusqu'à celui où elles ont achevé leur remontée et vont revenir à leur position initiale.
Il faut noter que si les attitudes successives sont exactement
Fig. 103. — Figures en relief représentant les attitudes successives du Goéland pendant un coup d'aile.
représentées dans la figure 103, en tant que position des ailes par rapport au corps; il n'en est pas de même des positions du corps de l'oiseau dans l'espace. En effet, un Goéland, qui vole avec une vitesse de 8 mètres au moment de l'essor, ne parcourt pas entre deux éclairements, c'est-à-dire en 1/50 de seconde, la longueur de son corps, qui est de 40 centimètres environ; il en parcourt environ les [illegible], de sorte que ses images se superposent partiellement sur la glace sensible. Dans une représentation en relief des véritables attitudes de l'oiseau, les images doivent s'entre-péné-
MOUVEMENTS SUIVANT LES TROIS DIMENSIONS. 177
trer, comme cela se voit dans une autre série qui a été également coulée en bronze et dont la figure 104 montre l'aspect général.
Cette dernière représentation de l'oiseau donne une très bonne idée de la nature de ses mouvements. On peut retourner cette pièce solide dans tous les sens, l'examiner sous toutes ses faces, et acquérir, en quelques instants, plus de notions sur la cinématique du vol que n'en donne l'inspection d'images planes. La figure 104 ne donne nécessairement qu'une idée imparfaite du modèle en relief; celui-ci est déposé dans les collections de la Station physiologique.
On voit, dans les premières images en relief, que l'aile qui s'abaisse se porte en avant et qu'elle étreint, pour ainsi dire, l'air sous les flancs et le long du corps de l'oiseau. Pendant toute cette phase d'abaissement, l'aile est déployée, les articulations du coude et du carpe sont ouvertes. A la septième image, la flexion du coude et celle du carpe se produisent soudainement, par des actes solidaires dont le mécanisme a été indiqué § 38; l'aile remonte alors, fléchie, et les rémiges pendent verticalement. Le déploiement de l'aile s'effectue à la dixième image, c'est-à-dire à la fin de la remontée.
Il ne faut pas chercher dans ces figures une fidélité parfaite
Marey. — Vol des oiseaux. 12

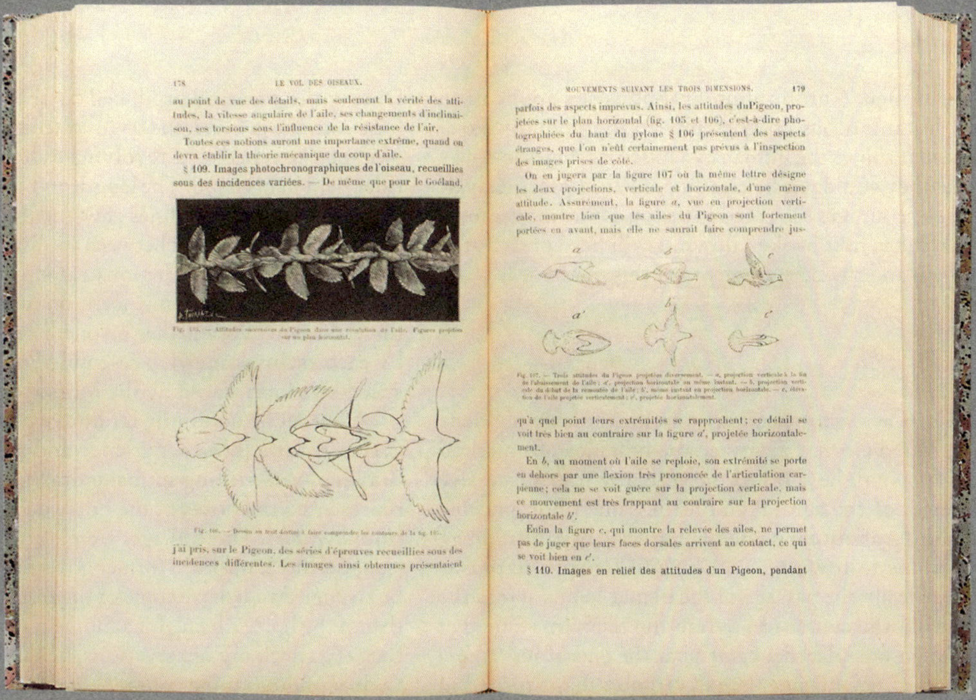

178 LE VOL DES OISEAUX.

au point de vue des détails, mais seulement la vérité des attitudes, la vitesse angulaire de l'aile, ses changements d'inclinaison, ses torsions sous l'influence de la résistance de l'air.

Toutes ces notions auront une importance extrême, quand on devra établir la théorie mécanique du coup d'aile.

§ 109. Images photochronographiques de l'oiseau, recueillies sous des incidences variées. — De même que pour le Goéland,

Fig. 105. — Attitudes successives du Pigeon dans une révolution de l'aile. Figures projetées sur un plan horizontal.

Fig. 106. — Dessin au trait destiné à faire comprendre les contours de la fig. 105.

j'ai pris, sur le Pigeon, des séries d'épreuves recueillies sous des incidences différentes. Les images ainsi obtenues présentaient

MOUVEMENTS SUIVANT LES TROIS DIMENSIONS. 179

parfois des aspects imprévus. Ainsi, les attitudes du Pigeon, projetées sur le plan horizontal (fig. 105 et 106), c'est-à-dire photographiées du haut du pylone § 106 présentent des aspects étranges, que l'on n'eût certainement pas prévus à l'inspection des images prises de côté.

On en jugera par la figure 107 où la même lettre désigne les deux projections, verticale et horizontale, d'une même attitude. Assurément, la figure *a*, vue en projection verticale, montre bien que les ailes du Pigeon sont fortement portées en avant, mais elle ne saurait faire comprendre jus-

Fig. 107. — Trois attitudes du Pigeon projetées diversement. — *a*, projection verticale à la fin de l'abaissement de l'aile ; *a'*, projection horizontale au même instant. — *b*, projection verticale du début de la remontée de l'aile ; *b'*, même instant en projection horizontale. — *c*, élévation de l'aile projetée verticalement ; *c'*, projetée horizontalement.

qu'à quel point leurs extrémités se rapprochent ; ce détail se voit très bien au contraire sur la figure *a'*, projetée horizontalement.

En *b*, au moment où l'aile se reploie, son extrémité se porte en dehors par une flexion très prononcée de l'articulation carpienne ; cela ne se voit guère sur la projection verticale, mais ce mouvement est très frappant au contraire sur la projection horizontale *b'*.

Enfin la figure *c*, qui montre la relevée des ailes, ne permet pas de juger que leurs faces dorsales arrivent au contact, ce qui se voit bien en *c'*.

§ 110. Images en relief des attitudes d'un Pigeon, pendant

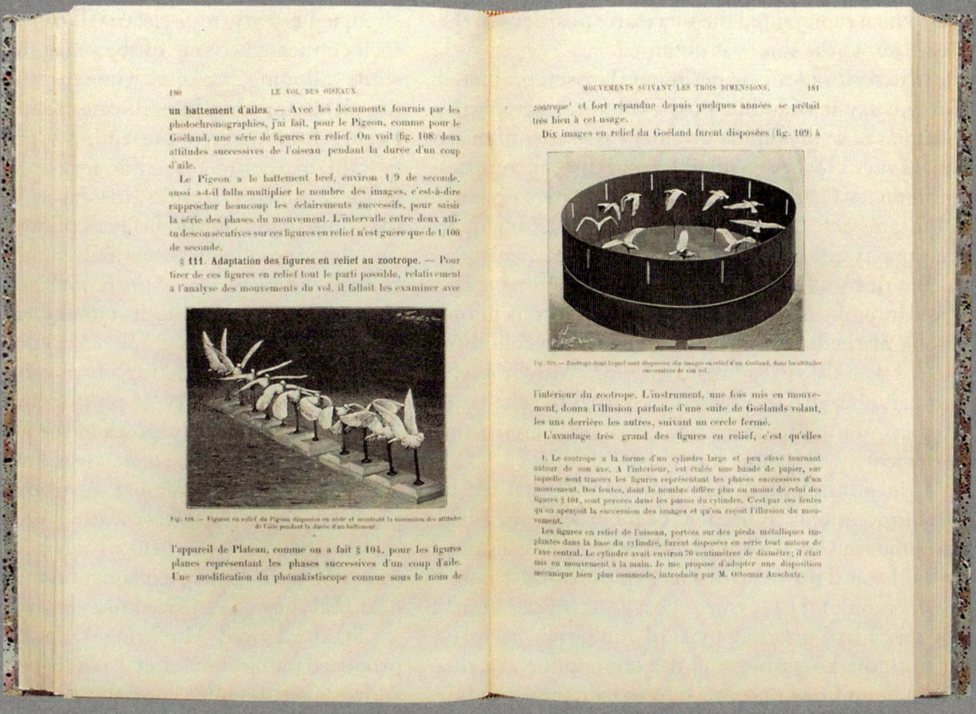

180 LE VOL DES OISEAUX.

un battement d'ailes. — Avec les documents fournis par les photochronographies, j'ai fait, pour le Pigeon, comme pour le Goéland, une série de figures en relief. On voit (fig. 108) deux attitudes successives de l'oiseau pendant la durée d'un coup d'aile.

Le Pigeon a le battement bref, environ 1/9 de seconde, aussi a-t-il fallu multiplier le nombre des images, c'est-à-dire rapprocher beaucoup les éclairements successifs, pour saisir la série des phases du mouvement. L'intervalle entre deux attitudes consécutives sur ces figures en relief n'est guère que de 1/100 de seconde.

§ 111. Adaptation des figures en relief au zootrope. — Pour tirer de ces figures en relief tout le parti possible, relativement à l'analyse des mouvements du vol, il fallait les examiner avec

Fig. 108. — Figures en relief du Pigeon disposées en série et montrant la succession des attitudes de l'aile pendant la durée d'un battement.

l'appareil de Plateau, comme on a fait § 104, pour les figures planes représentant les phases successives d'un coup d'aile. Une modification du phénakistiscope connue sous le nom de

MOUVEMENTS SUIVANT LES TROIS DIMENSIONS. 181

zootrope[1] et fort répandue depuis quelques années se prêtait très bien à cet usage.

Dix images en relief du Goéland furent disposées (fig. 109) à

Fig. 109. — Zootrope dans lequel sont disposées dix images en relief d'un Goéland, dans les attitudes successives de son vol.

l'intérieur du zootrope. L'instrument, une fois mis en mouvement, donna l'illusion parfaite d'une suite de Goélands volant, les uns derrière les autres, suivant un cercle fermé.

L'avantage très grand des figures en relief, c'est qu'elles

1. Le zootrope a la forme d'un cylindre large et peu élevé tournant autour de son axe. A l'intérieur, est étalée une bande de papier, sur laquelle sont tracées les figures représentant les phases successives d'un mouvement. Des fentes, dont le nombre diffère plus ou moins de celui des figures § 101, sont percées dans les parois du cylindre. C'est par ces fentes qu'on aperçoit la succession des images et qu'on reçoit l'illusion du mouvement.

Les figures en relief de l'oiseau, portées sur des pieds métalliques implantés dans la base du cylindre, furent disposées en série tout autour de l'axe central. Le cylindre avait environ 70 centimètres de diamètre ; il était mis en mouvement à la main. Je me propose d'adopter une disposition mécanique bien plus commode, introduite par M. Ottomar Anschutz.

Chronophotography
Étienne-Jules Marey
1899

Gentlemen, Chronophotography is the application of instantaneous photography to the study of movement. It allows the human eye to see its stages in a way that they could not be clearly perceived previously. It also encourages the reconstitution of the movements that it has first broken down. I will here present the origin and the developments of this method.

I.

As early as 1873, my colleague at the Academy of Sciences, Alfred Cornu, suggested the first idea of a method of this kind; he showed the academy four successive images of the sun taken on the same photographic plate. At about the same time, Jules Janssen had imagined the following procedure to reproduce photographically the passage of the planet Venus across the sun. At the center of a refracting telescope aimed at the sun was placed a camera; at the end of its camera obscura, a sensitive plate of circular shape turned in fits and starts around its center, so as to present a different face to the lens every seventy seconds. From this *astronomical revolver,* a ring-shaped series of images, which represented the successive positions of the planet across the sun, was obtained.

In describing this experiment, Janssen predicted that one day it would be possible to photograph the variations of a very rapid movement as a series of many images very close to each other, and that, encompassing in this way an entire cycle of movements related to the same act, a means of resolving interesting questions in physiological mechanics would be available.

But this was still only a kind of presentiment and a bold leap of the mind, because instantaneous photographic plates did not yet exist: only the wet collodion did. It was only in 1878 that Eadweard Muybridge, a photographer in San Francisco, started to take large numbers of instantaneous photographs of animals in movement at very short intervals.

I had something to do with the idea that led to these experiments. For a few years previously, I had been studying horses' gaits while trotting or galloping by mechanical procedures which automatically noted the duration of the pressure of each step of the animal. For this, I had inserted a vial of rubber in the space between the horseshoe and the hoof connected to a long tube ending in a stylus moved by compressed air. During the pressure produced by the contact of the foot with the ground, the stylus traced a line on a strip of paper attached to a revolving cylinder which the rider held in his hand. The length and the simultaneity or succession of these lines gave the duration and the reciprocal relationships between the lifting and putting down of each limb. I demonstrated in this way that the horse, while galloping, leans on one foot, then on three, then on two, and then on one. The series inscribed by each stylus somewhat resembled the unequal and successive lines traced by the Morse telegraph.

Colonel Louis Émile Duhousset, who brings together great equine experience and a real talent for drawing, was willing to make drawings for me that represented the poses of the horse deduced from this *chronography*. These images were seen by a rich American, Leland Stanford, a former governor of California; he struggled to believe some of the results, for instance that of the horse's being for a moment on only one forefoot. To check my observations, he asked Muybridge to do a photographic counter-experiment. In front of the track where the horse was supposed to gallop, Muybridge placed twenty-four lenses, whose shutters were kept closed by the same number of magnets. He stretched twenty-four electrical lines across the track, each connected to one of these magnets. The animal, while galloping, broke each line successively, unveiled the plates and thus himself caused the production of twenty-four images representing a series of his poses.

These experiments, admirably organized, had perfectly satisfactory results. Insofar as I am concerned, the comparison of Muybridge's photos with Duhousset's drawings yielded essentially similar poses for the corresponding phases of the horse's gallop; the succession of unquestionable instantaneous photographs confirmed my chronography. Muybridge continued his experiments and, taking advantage of the progress made in the sensitivity of photographic plates, was able to represent all the poses of the horse and of other animals—dogs, pigs, oxen, deer, etc.—by the same system. Ottomar Anschütz also obtained excellent photographic series representing human or animal movements with the help of devices whose details have not been clearly explained, though it would appear that they were placed in a sort of carriage.

Stanford used Muybridge's data for beautifully produced publications, but was not able to avoid errors which invert the phases of movement in the order of

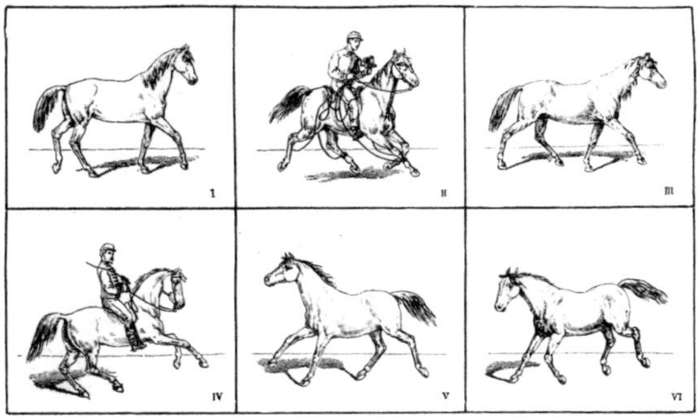

Figure 1. The gait of a horse as modeled by chronophotography.

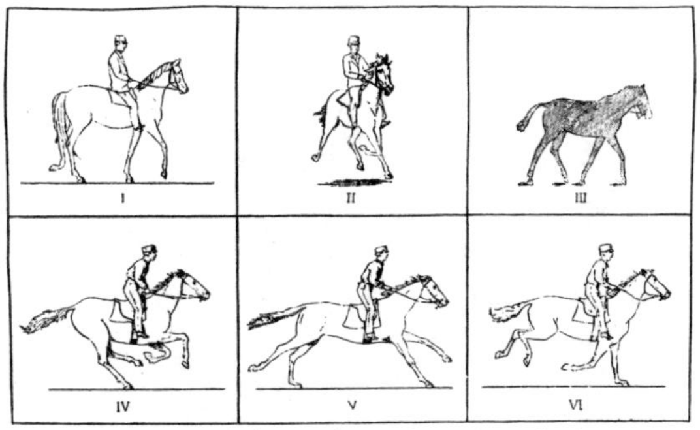

Figure 2. Positions of a horse after Eadweard Muybridge's motion studies [chronophotography].

the photographs, thus creating a most regrettable confusion in the eyes and mind of the person consulting these beautiful plates.

A device which was built a little later by Albert Londe avoids these inconveniences. He sets up twelve lenses in front of the same sensitive plate that a successive trigger unveils in turn, and thus obtains photographs that are necessarily ordered methodically. But the images of the object, being taken from different points of view, are different in perspective. There is around thirty centimeters between the lenses situated at each end of the plate; this is enough, when the objects are near each other, to create disparities between the one image and the next; these are not due to the movement itself and are most vexing. It is also difficult to get exactly similar lenses.

In the end, each of these means, most ingenious in themselves, involve a large financial outlay which is usually not available to physiologists. In order to continue more easily and cheaply the experiments that I had asked Muybridge to carry out on the flight of birds, I had to create a new method for myself, and it is here, strictly speaking, that I have played a role in the invention of chronophotography.

II.

I was trying to obtain, on only one photographic plate *with only one lens*, the image of a moving creature or object. The idea came to me that I could have the creature or object move on a totally dark background. When the plate faces a totally dark field, the sensitive plate is not sensitive to anything. Only the image of the bright and lit-up object that passes in front of this background will therefore be recorded.

But a dark background is not by any means guaranteed by a dark *surface*. A depth from which no light at all comes, for instance a crate, open on one side and totally blackened on all the other sides, is necessary. This is, according to Michel Chevreul, *absolute black*. The bright object that would pass between a background of this kind and the lens would leave a trail of light on the plate, creating an image without end, multiple and unique at the same time. However, the point was to obtain *separate images*… It was enough for this purpose that a shutter in continual operation produce very short moments of light at regular intervals.
This is what I put into practice with one of the first devices that were built for me (Fig. 4), with the help of a windowed disk which intermittently produced light at the moment when its windows revealed the sensitive plate during its inverse rotation. In this way, there are as many images as the number of times that light is allowed in. For example, the trajectory of a white ball thrown between the lens and the background is represented by a series of balls staggered out along its trajectory. The positions and poses of a bird in flight in front of the dark background are more interesting to observe.

Among other valuable observations that this first procedure allowed me to make, I will mention certain positions of the wing during the flight of a bird. When the wings are horizontal in the air, the tight feathers seem like a continuous, impervious surface. When the wings are lifted up, and must meet as little resistance as possible to save strength, the feathers separate from each other and seem arranged like the blades of a louver. Japanese artists seem to have been drawn to these particularities for quite some time. Very precise observations of certain moments of flight, that seem paradoxical to us, can be found in their works.

However, this first procedure could only work for very small and fast-moving objects. Actually, if the movement is slow, like that of walking, and if the surface of the object is large, like that of a horse, or if too many images are taken at each second, they will not be distinct: a second image will still be partially like a first image, and this partial superimposition will lead to an unfortunate confusion in most cases.

I have named *geometrical* chronophotography a first method I discovered to avoid this problem. It involves not using the whole surface that is in movement, reducing it to a simple line which is bright where the rest of the surface is dark. For instance, if we take a man entirely dressed and masked in black velvet, and

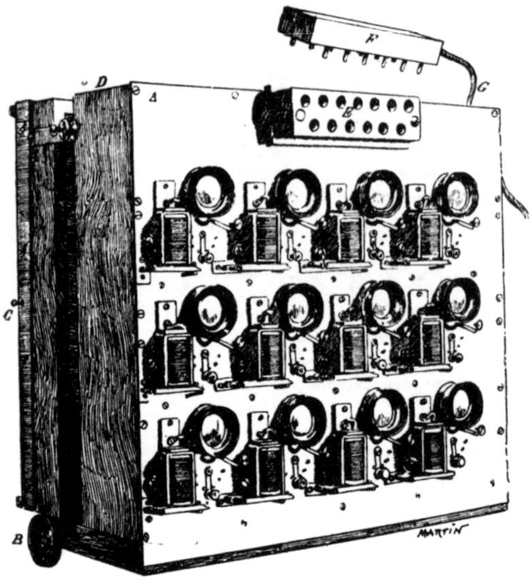

Figure 3. Multiple Lens apparatus designed by M. A. Londe.

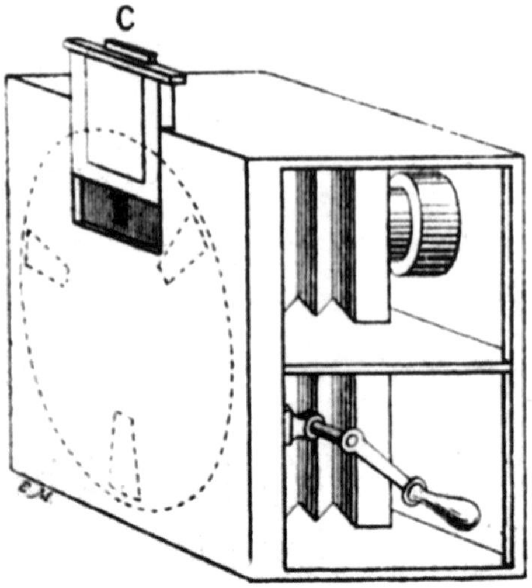

Figure 4. First fixed plate chronophotographic apparatus.

attach stripes and bright points to his limbs, bright lines on the plate can be obtained that are perfectly separated from each other, and which are the main lines of his movement. The rest of his person, which is not necessary for the study and whose inclusion would have resulted in the movement, very annoyingly, being partially hidden, will, by means of this trick, not even seem to exist.

The geometrical figures thus created allow the exact positions of the limbs and of the axis of the body to be observed at various moments of a set of movements, but these are only projections on a diagram. Some phenomena of movement are better viewed from different angles, from below, from above, and obliquely. To record the particularities of the flight of certain birds, I had to set up three different dark fields of vision and three cameras to be able to record three different aspects of the same flight (Fig. 8). One of the three was twelve meters away from the top. Given the frequency of the images, the body, at the moment of a new beating of the wings, had not yet totally left behind the portion of space that it occupied on the preceding stroke, but if the representations of the body of the bird were somewhat superimposed, the movements of the wings themselves were quite distinct. This was how I was able to understand the mechanism of flying, which is composed of a veritable propeller blast of the wing. I got a clear representation of this phenomenon by getting models of the birds' poses in accordance with the chronophotographic data cast in bronze in Naples by ancient lost wax processes.

A third means, which I won't describe at length so as not to get into a complicated description of a device, allows the images reproducing the overly slow movements of overly large objects to be separated from each other. It consists in artificially increasing the speed of the moving image by making it run from one point of the sensitive plate to another through the use of a revolving mirror.

This was what I was able to get from the dark field of vision which, in reality, can only be furnished by a dark cavity, and which I was able to put into practice in a reasonably satisfactory way at the Physiological Station of the Parc des Princes.

It has a large and deep warehouse, whose floor and walls have been blackened; the back is covered with black velvet. In front of the opening, the objects in movement can move across a track made up of cobblestones of blackened wood. The opening is reduced to the minimum possible size necessary for each experiment with black curtains; this proportionally increases the darkness of the back.

It cannot be disguised that this is a cumbersome arrangement, and a very expensive one, and that it does not even work in certain cases or places. A new advance was necessary. I needed to avoid having the same part of the plate exposed to the action creating the photo during the whole process. The successive positions of a moving object taken on any field of vision and not just a black one needed to be recorded.

I took Janssen's idea and developed it; I built a device whose plate was dragged by rapid rotation and which was open to the light only for the amount of time necessary for one image to be taken. The plate, the moving shutter, and the mechanism that moves them were placed at the bottom of a tube; at the other end of this tube is the lens and, when a butt that can be supported by a shoulder is attached, it is possible to aim at and to follow in flight a moving object whose reproduction one wants. I called this device a *photographic rifle*. A kind of cartridge bag collected the exposed plates. A trigger like that of a normal rifle put the

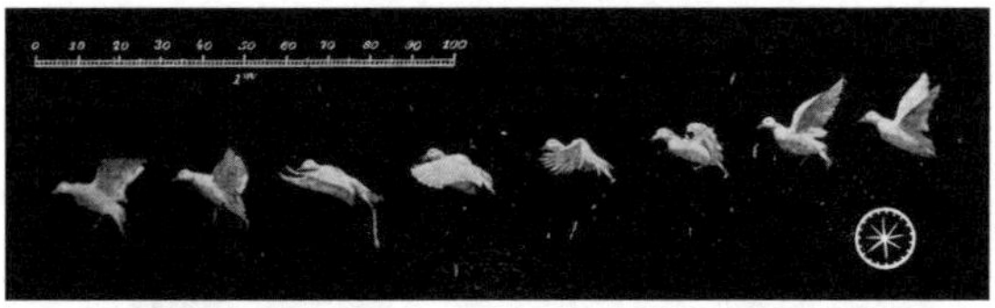

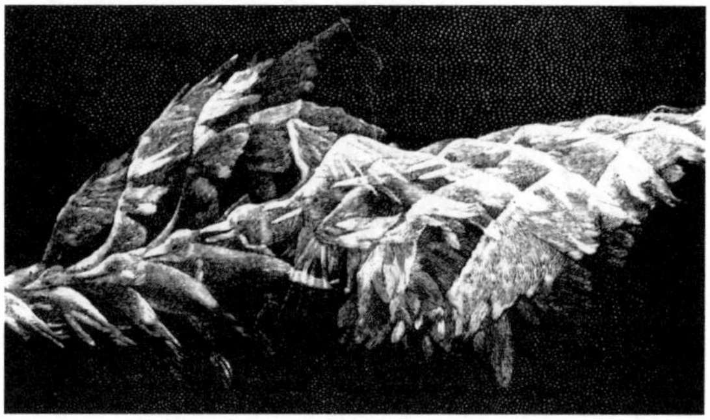

Above Figure 5. Wing phase of a bird. Above: metric scale. Below: chronophotographic dial.
Right Figure 6. Image of a bird's wing motion.

device into action. The plates, circular or octagonal, were thus exposed twelve times per second; they were arranged in a crown shape and taken at an exposure time equal to 1/207 of a second.

This device made it possible to follow the successive positions of a free bird in flight as well as those of an animal guided along a predetermined track. More than one interesting detail concerning the positions of the wings and the torsion of the feathers was revealed to me. But in most cases the images were too cramped and it was not possible to enlarge them sufficiently. Moreover, the stopping and starting of rigid and relatively heavy parts creates initial and final shocks which damage the regularity of the process because of the inertia of matter.

Actually, at that time in 1887, it was possible to buy rolls on a frame in the stores, i.e., strips of photographic paper, rolled up on a reel and which unrolled gradually so as to enable the taking of new images. These frames saved the photographer the trouble of removing or reinserting a plate in his camera at every photograph. I made use of this idea imagined by the commercial photography stores and arranged reels, rolls, and cogs which guided the strip of paper and made it pass gradually in all of its length from the lens to the spot occupied by the plate in my chronophotography device. The point was to make sure that the plate moved around fast enough and stopped to take an image every time the windowed disk was lit up. An electromagnet with a revolving disk turned off the electric current and stopped the progress of the sensitive strip at the right moment.

Slowly, the principle and the whole practical operation of chronophotography had come to light with the help of a little patience and through the power and natural progress of things.

But it was still necessary to find a physical arrangement that was more practical, if not more efficient. This is the part of the discovery process that has occurred between that date and the current moment and which will continue daily.

As I was saying, placing the film on its reels and rolls required darkness, and this meant that the whole device needed to be placed in a large camera obscura, except for the lens which poked out of it by a kind of funnel that traversed a partition so as to be exposed to the light.

This inconvenience needed to be fixed so that a device could be produced that could be used in full daylight.

That is what I did that very year: I adapted strips of paper or sensitive film, opaque coatings and *tails of paper* of the length appropriate to the two ends in order to handle the reels in daylight. The part of the strip or the film which is engaged in the reel is protected by this opaque envelope which ends in a point. It can thus be inserted without accident, in full light, and once the cogs are in motion the whole thing is in action. The same can be done for removing the exposed film. The reel is covered by the opaque "tail" under which the rest of the device is rolled up and secured. This simple precaution allowed me to produce a transportable and already very practical device, which was set in motion by an electromagnet and which produced images of 9 cm^2 on long reels.

But the use of electricity for starting and stopping of the device was still too complicated and unreliable. The following year, in 1888, I replaced the electromagnet with a purely mechanical rotation and, with the help of this satisfactory if not perfect chronophotograph, I was able to study a large number of interesting phenomena that it had not previously been possible to analyze precisely. As such, I took up again the study of the movement of the horse and was able to get a complete analysis of its various gaits and their successive phases at rigorously equal temporal intervals.

The different species of quadrupeds studied in the same way made me realize that, between the physiological characteristics of their movements, there are analogies and differences which are related to the anatomical analogies and differences of their moving limbs. For instance, the dog's gallop (Fig. 13) is much more complex in its successive phases than that of the horse.

I have said elsewhere how chronophotography on a moving film can be used for the analysis of all kinds of animal movement: the flight of insects and birds, the swimming of all sorts of fish, and even the movement of the creatures who writhe under the microscope. Special arrangements of the chronophotograph may be necessary for certain special uses.

However, what has led to the greatest success of the

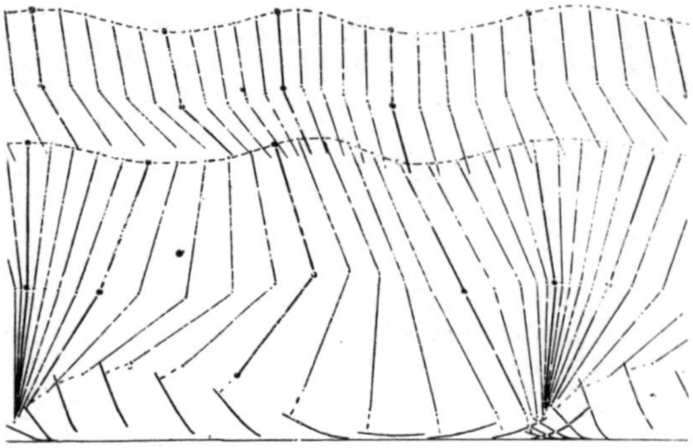

Fig. 8.

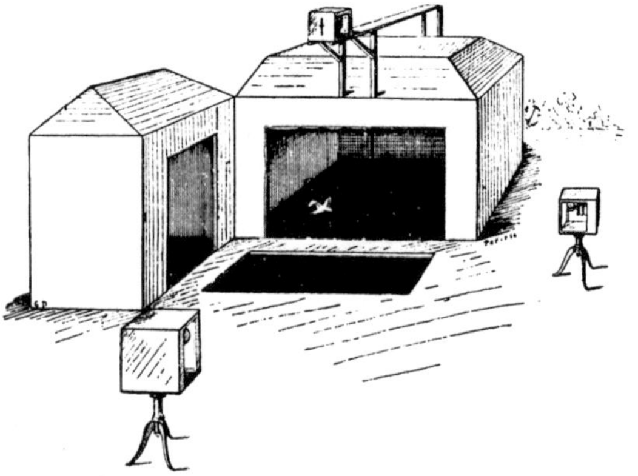

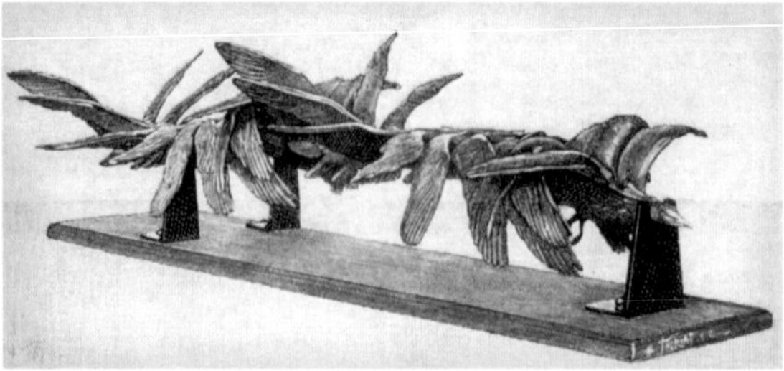

Top left Figure 7. Geometric space of the gait of a human, right arm and leg.
Bottom left Figure 8. Three dark fields and three fixed plate chronophotographic devices, rectangular alignment.
Above Figure 9. Bronze model of the positions of the wing of a gull in flight.

chronophotograph and the making in recent years of a considerable number of devices, all more or less derived from each other, is the production of animated photographs, i.e., the synthesis of movement.

III.

The idea of synthesized movement goes back to the beginning of this century. Likely it was devised principally with the amusement of children in mind, and was put into circulation by a toy, named the *phenakisticope* by Joseph Plateau, its inventor.

Images placed in a circle on a cardboard disk, each corresponding to the successive phases of a movement, would turn opposite a mirror. The eye would see them reflected not all at once, but successively, through the slits passing in front of it as the images turn. Their succession and substitution in the same place in the mirror produces the illusion of a movement represented in stages or partial units.

Between the successive passing of two slits, the observer does not see the mirror (he sees only the darkened backside of the cardboard circle bearing the images). But the last image exposed to his retina remains there for a moment (approximately $1/10$ of a second). And it is there, in this physiological law, that lies the secret of the illusion and the principle of the synthesis of movement.

We know that the burning end of a stick passed before our eyes seems to us a continuous ribbon of flame. This is because we see at once many of the flame's positions in space, both those it has just left and those it presently occupies. If in one second an image disappears and reappears ten times before our eyes, we see it *continuously* and do not perceive its disappearance. If instead of one image, we see ten representations of the same object in ten positions next to one another, we will perceive but one image, that of the object, but in successive positions. Seen with these momentary disappearances, a succession thus becomes for us an evolution and a movement, thanks to the persistence of an image on our retina.

Skilled artists have taken advantage of the *retina's memory* in order to show us vaulters, tightrope walkers, boxers, etc., in movement in Plateau's device (or the zoetrope, its simplified successor).

But their partial figures were conventional, and for the exactitude of the details and thus of the entire thing, it was necessary to trust in the clairvoyance of these artists, which was necessarily often lacking.

From the moment of chronophotography's first results, placing *real* figures taken from nature without alteration into the zoetrope was proposed. I believe that it was Muybridge who first did this. Having placed end to end the instantaneous photographs of a horse race taken by multiple cameras, he projected this series through a sort of phenakisticope. This happened at my residence, in 1882, at a party where I had the good fortune of welcoming Hermann von Helmholtz, Vilhelm Bjerknes, Gilberto Govi, William Crookes, and several luminaries of French science.

For these scientists, this was a revelation. Photography had never gone so far in the reproduction of nature. Watching this photographed race attentively and many times, they understood various necessarily true yet previously unsuspected positions of the horse. Artists were immediately affected by these results. The painter Ernest Meissonier, who knew as much about a horse's gait as is possible from the most attentive direct observation, at first believed that it was impossible to learn anything new about the matter. Still, he held a

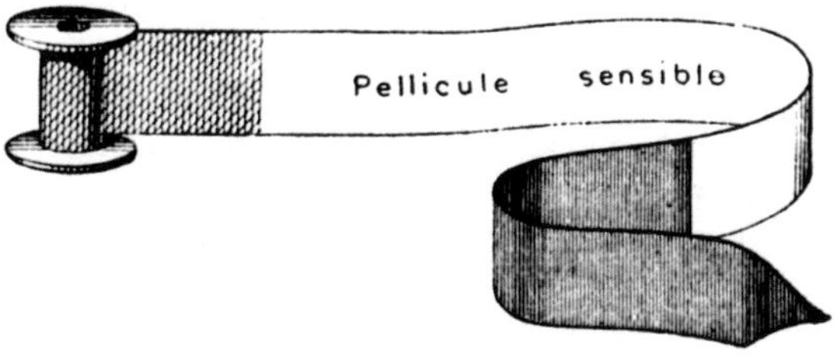

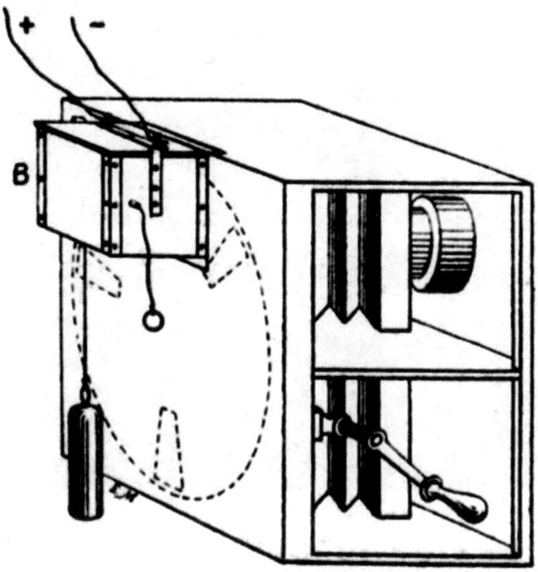

Above Figure 11. Sensitive film bonded with two strips of opaque paper wound upon on a coil.
Right Figure 12. Chassis case for chronophotography on motion picture film, for outdoor use.

presentation analogous to Muybridge's in his own workshop, and was immediately convinced. Since this date, for all of his paintings representing horses, he has based his studies on chronophotographic documents.

Later, Anschütz and my assistant, Georges Demenÿ, produced the same experiments in the best conditions, so as to render intelligible not only the movements composing a rapid motion, but those movements that are most limited, most brief, those carried out on the same spot. Anschütz, using an electric spark, lit up from behind the *wheel* bearing images placed in a ring and visible through the thickness of the glass. Demenÿ transferred onto the edge of a glass disk twenty-four chronophotographic prints of the face of a speaking person; he placed a photographic lens in front of a brightly lit point where the overlap of windowed disks showed the succession of these images. The illusion, the clearness of the representation was such that expert deaf-mutes were able to recognize the words spoken by the person in observing the movement of their lips. Anschütz's *wheel* and Demenÿ's *photophone* markedly improved on the zoetrope, which noticeably altered the images' proportions.

Yet more was necessary to efficiently project the synthesis of movement. For unless the disks are enormous, they can only present a limited number of images, and in these systems, the lighting of the image must be so brief that the enlarged projection cannot be very clear, however strong the light may be. In addition, the results of this synthesis must be visible not through a narrow opening and not to a single person, but on the entire surface of a screen and to the entire audience of an amphitheater.

This is what I accomplished in 1893. I used strips of transparent film on which I had obtained the analysis of the movements; I had them passed into a chronophotographic projector, pulled by invisible reels, but stopped by certain mechanisms long enough to be sufficiently lit up from behind. Having traversed lens l_1, a ray of sunlight passed through a narrow diaphragm at the rays' point of juncture (see Fig. 14), where light was obstructed and admitted by means of a revolving windowed disk. After passing through another lens l_2 and being reflected onto two mirrors turned at 45° angles, this ray crossed image *i* and exited through the lens and projected this image onto the screen.

With numerous partial images, I was obtaining very clear and complete projections; but the fairly complicated movement of the device was very noisy. Particularly as the exposures of the negative film were not done at rigorously equal intervals, the images thus obtained in projection were very unsteady. So as to obtain satisfactory positive prints, it was necessary to cut up the multiple images and paste them together equidistantly onto a strip of rubberized canvas.

As I conducted this research, I learned that my assistant, who knew my chronophotograph well as he had used it many times at the Physiological Station, had had it patented under his own name. To do so, he had introduced into the instrument's design a modification already well known in my laboratory, but which I had not used. He believed that with this device he would obtain perfectly equidistant images and produce animated projections using long strips of film covered with positive images.

But it was Thomas Edison who first found the right method. I had had the chance, in 1889 at the electrician Fontaine's exhibition, to show him an electro-photographic zoetrope. The *kinetoscope*, by which he produced in the best conditions a similar synthesis of movement, is not unlike my device with reels shown in Fig. 14, though the American inventor in his work did not make use of it. In the kinetoscope, film circulates *continuously*, but is lit *from a very short distance* from behind, so that the frequent lighting that the disc's window allows may be brief enough that such instantaneous movement is imperceptible.

In 1894 in France this device met with deserved success, although it lit the film for only one spectator and did not project it onto a screen for an entire audience.

The Lumière brothers found, in 1895, the neces-

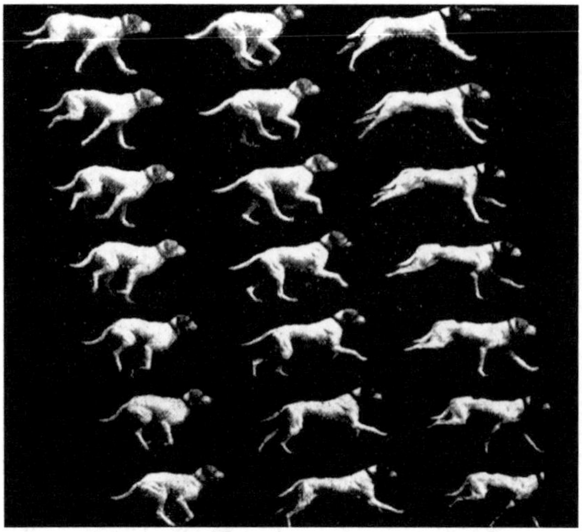

Figure 13. Series of positions of a galloping dog.

sary solution. Borrowing one of Edison's techniques, film perforation, they discovered an original way of taking and projecting film images. By an alternative movement produced with an eccentric bolt, they were able to have grips hook into the holes of the film's surface, pull it to face the lens and hold it there for a given moment as the shutter window opened, and then gripping onto the next holes bring the next image up to take the place of the first.

This admirable invention was nearly perfect straight away. As soon as it was shown in public in early 1896 under the name of the *Cinematograph*, it met with considerable success, and this name, though not of a particular device, would long remain associated with all syntheses of movement.

However, many patents are granted every day, producing some sort of improvement. I note Gossart's device, which is of a very original and intelligent design and which does away with pauses in the film's circulation and presents to the lens a circular and regular movement. I additionally note Paul Mortier's *alethorama*, itself quite different from today's devices; it uses Charles-Émile Reynaud's principle of *praxinoscope*. Here the circular and vertical strip bearing successive images reflects them onto one of the mirrored faces of a prism placed in the machine's center.

I wanted to investigate for myself procedures that identically produce the same results as those of the Lumière brothers, all the while avoiding several inconveniences. I would like to show you a chronophotograph of small volume, with which I use any sort of film, perforated or not, but it is not adequately set up, and I will have to limit myself to presenting only the idea.[1] Like in my previous devices, film is led by a system of reels, rolls, and rolling machines. It is not perforated, which avoids tugging on the film by the grips, and the mechanisms moving the film do not stop, which gets rid of inertia's resistance and the jolts that overcome it. The film, however, must stop: there is, thus, a moment when the traction mechanisms slide across it without pulling it forward. It is held by an independent compressor as if, pulled by two fingers, it was momentarily held and pushed in place by another finger. The two fingers thus slide without pulling the film.[2] In short, all of the pieces that are not negligible in weight, like film, are animated by a constant and uniform motion. When the device is well set up, it ensures the equidistance of the images and does not produce any pulling nor any jolting of the film bearing them.

The reproduction of any action, the movement of a person who opens or closes an umbrella, the passing of a car, at first amazed spectators. Then comic or fantastic scenes were combined, using actors who acted them out as models. Then attempts were made to catch the curious or rare things of everyday life on the spot, as they happened spontaneously and without preparation. Now animated photographs that are not amusing seem to be disdained, and useful applications of chronophotographic projections are sought.

I received a strange little study from a Russian settled in Paris, Bolesław Matuszewski, in which he touches on the areas that seem to him open to chronophotography in the form of projections. He seems to be rather disappointed to see it devoted to the simple amusement of the public, and rightly wants it to be a beneficial auxiliary of every scientific teaching.

He goes still further. He envisions his favored invention becoming popularizer of industrial procedures, propagator of agricultural techniques, and in general master of all types of teaching. And it is quite true that in order to teach the practice of any act difficult to reproduce, or difficult to understand for those who practice it, a projection that patiently lays out everything in front of the apprentice's eyes is singularly effective. It would however be necessary for the filmstrip to be played on a loop and endlessly run, constantly running the same series of images across the lens.

Matuszewski wants chronophotography to study and reproduce the various phenomena related to nervous disorders, to avoid having to repeat vivisections by recording them once and for all, and to show apprentice surgeons models of operations conducted by an expert.

He hopes that it will be added to the most reliable sources of history, and asks that in all circumstances in which that might be of some historical importance,

1 Since this conference, I have been able to do projections with this instrument (at the session of May 5, 1899, at the French Society of Photography).

2 See the *Bulletin of the French Society of Photography*, February 15, 1897.

an official chronophotographist be called, as one summons a stenographer when important words might be spoken. He dreams of the creation of warehouses of documentary cinematograms, analogous to libraries and archives. The new invention seems to him capable of providing documents to pedagogy, to the arts, and even to the police!

All this will be realized one day, although probably less quickly than the ingenious author of *Animated Photography* supposes.

For it is necessary, if they are to be put to these uses, that these devices be further improved and simplified. Their price, too, has to become more easily affordable.

IV.

Besides, the total improvement of these projections, which naturally arouse the enthusiasm of the public, is not what most preoccupies me. *The most interesting chronophotography is not the most useful.* It is perhaps as a form of analysis rather than of synthesis that chronophotography is most of service, however satisfying and surprising this resurrection of movement may be.

I exclude the case where, in projecting images representing the phases of a motion, the conditions of speed in which this movement was produced are modified. For example, the beating of a bird's wing which lasts ⅕ of a second; the wing presents in this short space of time a large number of different positions. If I make fifty images of it and if in projecting them I make this movement last five seconds, I allow the eye to clearly grasp phenomena that would otherwise go unnoticed, and in my opinion, this is particular to the chronophotographic method. Other phenomena are produced at such a slow speed that our sense organs do not perceive them clearly; when they are projected in a shorter time span, their movement becomes perceptible. This is why numerous authors, as well as I myself, have endeavored to take, every fifteen minutes, the image of a flower opening and to project onto a screen twelve of these images per second. Unfortunately, the lighting of the objects is not stable enough at such long intervals; it would probably be more effective to make use of artificial light. Despite these difficulties, I was able to render the movements and imperceptible changes of the clouds apparent through chronophotography. This is what it is to make human attention, that instrument of scientific knowledge, easier and more penetrating. But what will most often and most efficiently be of use to the study of natural phenomena is geometric chronophotography as I presented it at the beginning, practiced on fixed plates.

A large number of mechanical problems, the solution of which by calculation would often be quite complicated, are solved in quite simple conditions through the use of the Chronophotograph. Examples include movements in liquids, whether one considers waves on a surface or the movement of molecules within a liquid mass, or even the tumult produced when a current meets a varied surface. I have noted elsewhere[3] how, in a crystal tank with parallel sides placed in front of a camera obscura and lit from below, all of these phenomena are rendered perceptible by chronophotography on fixed plates. A few examples will suffice to give an idea of this type of experiment.

In these conditions, the surface of the liquid appears in the form of a bright line, the oscillation of which resembles a cord's vibration; indeed, it displays nodes and antinodes. Fig. 16 shows the successive forms of the surface of a lapping wave.

We want to study the interior movements of the molecules acting in this moving liquid. We suspend shining beads in the water with the exact same density as water. The chronophotographic images show that these beads draw extended curves vertically at the level of the waves' antinodes, horizontally at the level of the nodes, and that they draw oblique curves in intermediary positions.

These same shining beads also show the direction these trickles of liquid take when the current meets an obstacle, the curve drawn by these trickles, the backwash behind the obstacle; finally, when the frequency of the successive illuminations is known, the speed of these molecules can be seen at each moment in accordance with the gaps between their images.

My expert colleague Cornu resorted to chronophotography on fixed plates in order to study, on vibrating cords, a type of vibration hitherto unknown, a longitudinal and transversal vibration; I mean torsional vibrations of a cord around its axis. A fragment of a mirror placed onto the cord and brightly lit in front of a dark background is subjected to these three types of vibrations and retraces them onto a photographic plate animated by a uniform transfer. Fig. 18 is the negative image of these three types of vibrations.[4]

One could cite a large number of mechanical and physical problems solved by chronophotography.

A contentious case of animal mechanics presented itself. A popular proverb holds that a cat always falls back onto its paws; mechanics teaches instead that without an external foothold an animal would be incapable of flipping itself while falling. Experiments have proven the proverb to be correct. Fig. 19 shows, in a series of successive images, a cat that, first held with its paws upside down, flips itself as it is released and soon has its paws turned towards the ground, the

3 *Reviews of the Academy of Sciences*, 1893, vol. CXVI, 913–924.

4 See Cornu, *Experimental Study of the Transversal Vibrations of Cords* (*Reviews*, vol. CXII, 280–288).

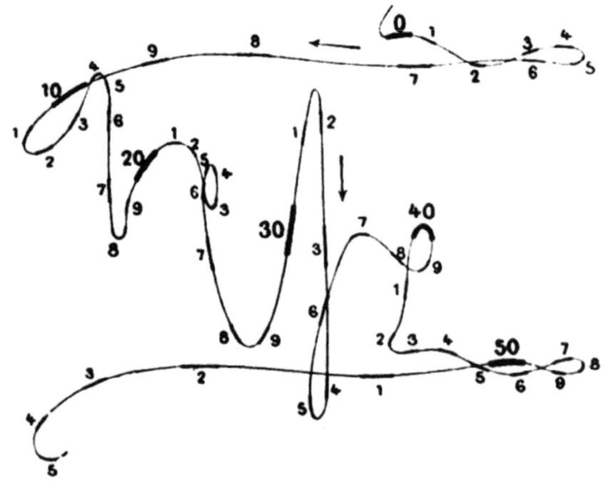

Figure 18. Negative imprint of three sequences of a vibrating rope.

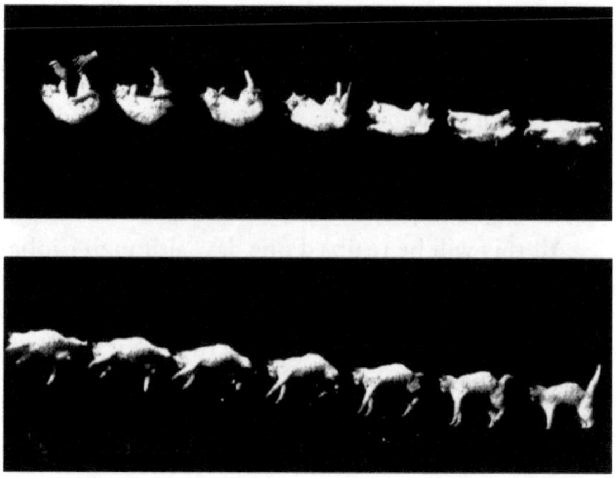

Figure 19. Movements of a cat that rights itself while falling.

position that it will maintain until it has landed. The animal will barely have fallen 0.25 meters before it has completed this flip. The study of successive figures shows how this happens: it is in alternating by turns the moments of inertia of the front paws and the back paws that the animal does this. This does not in any way contradict the laws of mechanics, and is in no way in contradiction with the theorem of areas as demonstrated by my colleague Guyou. Moreover, several members of the Academy of Sciences who work on mechanics, Maurice Lévy and Marcel Deprez as well as Appell, have presented demonstrations of the reality of movements produced without an exterior foothold. chronophotography has thus had the good fortune of revising an erroneous proposal in rational mechanics.

In that experiment, the images of the cat were recorded on moving film so as to avoid confusion. Other times partial images of an animal's movement have also been recorded. Thus, when one wishes to study in detail the movements of a horse's limbs, one does so from a short distance, so that the image only includes the limbs. In this way, they are photographed at a larger scale, which allows the greater appreciation of the details of their movements. This is how Fig. 20, which shows a succession of the movements of a horse at trot, was obtained.

The geometric sketch of movement gives the best results, as given by chronophotography on a fixed plate. But the number of direct applications of this method is limited, as I just mentioned, given that it is not always possible to use a camera obscura and that complex movements have a tendency to produce overlapping images.

From the chronophotographic images recorded on moving film, though, it is possible to produce totally clear sketches that are devoid of overlap.

Let us take a series of successive images that represent the forms of a horse trotting. Suppose that we desire a sketch of its rear right leg's movements. We proceed by successively tracing the outline of this leg onto a piece of paper. We trace the first image projected onto this paper and project the second image, taking care that the line of the ground exactly covers that of the previous tracing, which one obtains using carefully superposed points of reference. We trace the outline of the limb in the second image, and so on for the series of positions for the duration of one step. Thus do we obtain Fig. 21.

It is in the same way that the outline of an animal's front limb may be obtained, or the head's movements, or the trajectory of whatever point one may wish to study.

That is not all. In this limb's outline, taken in successive situations, the position of different pieces of the skeleton may be determined as in Fig. 22, which shows each bone's position in every phase of the horse's gallop.[5]

To make the image clearer, we can strip Fig. 23 to the skeleton alone: this will result in a complete record of the varied movements performed by each of the limb's joints.

Finally, the knowledge of changes in the position of the limb's bones allows us to deduce the state of lengthening or of shortening of the principal muscles at each moment of the trot. Indeed, the skeleton's anatomy involves knowledge of these muscles' tendons; it is thus possible to see by how much this muscle is lengthened or shortened, by linking with a line the two tendons of each muscle, and measuring the length of this line. This can be seen in Fig. 23, where the solid lines represent at each moment the length of the contractile fiber on the A) ischiotibial, B) rotulian, and C) gastrocnemian muscles. To render the stages of these changes in length more striking, the outlines of these variations in length in the three muscles have been placed above this same figure. There A and B

5 See, for details, *Reviews of the Academy of Sciences*, vol. CXXVI, May 29, 1898.

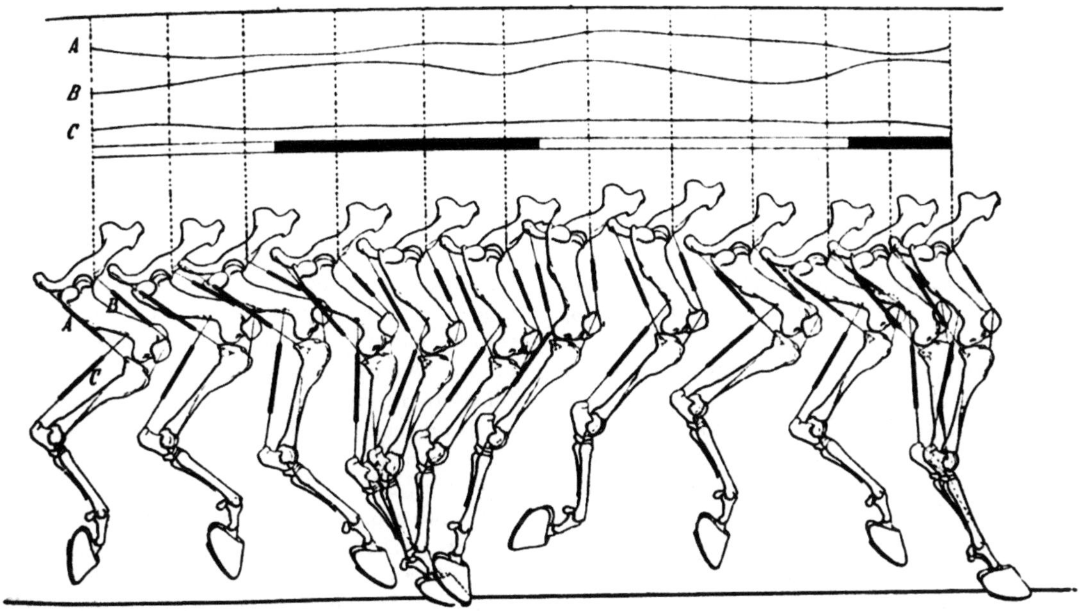

Figure 23. Skeletal attitudes and changes in muscle length. Top: curves indicating length changes of various muscles.

converge and diverge, a sign of the alternating movement of these two opposed muscular groups. Curve C of the gastrocnemian demonstrates that, while these muscles shorten from time to time, they do not lengthen beyond a certain degree (an anatomical particularity explains this strange fact).

This quick overview of the results obtained by these geometrical sketches shows that this use of chronophotography is the most instructive; using such a method it is not unreasonable to affirm that all that concerns an animal's mechanical movement may be discovered.

The merits of chronophotographic analysis do not however exclude those of synthesis. The appeal of the spectacles produced by this method in the form of moving photographs has been powerful in stimulating the improvement of these devices; certainly, the clarity and size of the images are important in every application. Moreover, even if moving Photography could only make us aware of what is visible to our eyes, it offers a vast field to scientific exploration. It may indeed popularize the knowledge of a large number of phenomena known only to passionate observers of nature.

Marey and the Organization of Work

Marta Braun

1994

Marey's studies in locomotion had an enormous influence on the artists of Europe, but their more enduring and pervasive effects were on the workers of the world. Marey's lifelong project to describe the laws that govern movement, the graphic, photographic, and cinematographic instruments he created to carry out his project, and his fundamental strategy of decomposing movement into minute temporal and spatial coordinates were the foundation of a revolutionary science of labor that ultimately transformed both the conception and the execution of work in the modern industrialized workplace.

The law of the conservation of energy had determined that the body is a "thermodynamic machine that augments, transforms, and distributes force according to the needs of the organism." And it was in light of this law that the "organic physicists" of the nineteenth century, from Helmholtz to Marey, had undertaken to map out how the energies of the body are conserved and transformed—how, for example, the body produces heat, transmits impulses from the nerves to the muscles, and deploys its energies in walking, running, and jumping. These discoveries had constructed a new image of the body: it was a particular kind of animate machine, not, as in the Cartesian sense, a compilation of moving parts driven by an external force, but a virtual motor, "regulated by internal, dynamic principles converting fuel into heat and heat into mechanical work." Like the steam engine and the blast furnace, the body was an immense reservoir of energy; its potential force was limited only by the specter of fatigue.

By the end of the nineteenth century social scientists, philosophers, and liberal reformers alike had seized on the practical applications of these physiological discoveries. The wealth of nations depended on the output of the laboring body—the harnessing of the body's energies to perform valuable work. If the body could be treated as a virtual motor, then science could subject the work it produced to the same quantification and measurement as that produced by other motors, away from the moral sphere of idleness and the exercise of the will: "No matter how powerful the action of our will, the transformation of forces and conservation and use of our energies follows the same physical laws, passes by the same necessary phenomena, as those other, properly called machines."

Science could provide work with a rational, objective basis. Detached from the interests of labor and capital, it could determine the optimum use of the body's energies and analyze the physiological limits of physical and mental labor. Its findings would contribute an impartial solution to the economic and political conflicts that ravaged modern industrialized society.

These ideas, colored by the positivist equation of scientific knowledge with truth, gave birth to a new science of work in Europe at the end of the century. Uniting medical, social, and political interests, it aimed both to increase the well-being of the working body and to realize the productive potential of the nation by discovering the most energy efficient methods of work and determining the laws of fatigue that limited its production. These were the aims that Marey's instruments and methods were now called on to serve.

Marey's own muscle studies belong to the beginnings of this new science. With his myograph, Marey had made some of the earliest tracings of fatigue. He had graphed the movements of muscle tissue excited by electrical impulses and had shown that repeated stimulation gave tracings whose amplitude diminished little by little as their duration was augmented. These, Marey observed, marked the intervention of fatigue, which he admitted was a universal and inevitable fact, "observed in all muscles and all animals." [...]

The emerging role of the science of work as an arbiter in social conflict had gathered its initial momentum with the establishment of Ernst Solvay's

1 André Liesse, *Le travail aux points de vue scientifique, industriel et social* (Paris: Guillaumin, 1899), 18.

2 Anson Rabinbach, *The Human Motor* (New York: Basic Books, 1990), 52. For this section I have relied on Rabinbach's groundbreaking work and that of Georges Ribeill: "Les débuts de l'ergonomie en France à la veille de la Première Guerre Mondiale," *Le Mouvement Sociale* 113 (October–December 1980): 2–36.

3 See, for example, Alfred Fouillée, *La science sociale contemporaine*, 3d ed. (Paris: Hachette, 1895); Louis Querton, *L'augmentation du rendement de la machine humaine* (Brussels: Misch and Thron, 1905); Laurent Deschesne, "La Productivité du travail et les salaires," *Revue d'Economie Politique* 13 (1899); Paul Louis, *L'ouvrier devant l'état: Histoire comparée des lois du travail dans les deux mondes* (Paris: Alcan, 1904); Liesse, *Travail aux points de vue scientifique, indsutriel et social.*

4 Liesse, *Travail aux points de vue scientifique industriel et social*, 19.

5 Marey, "Sur l'importance au point de vue médical des signes extérieurs des fonctions de la vie," *BAM*, 2d ser., 7 (11 June 1878): 615.

Energetics Institute in Brussels in 1900. Solvay saw the importance of combining the psychological investigations of intelligence and mental fatigue with the physiological investigations of Marey and Mosso to construct a new social science whose findings would, ideally, influence the direction of social and political reform. One of the most important studies of industrial fatigue was carried out by the director of the Solvay Institute, Josefa Ioteyko. She showed that the onset, intensity, perception, and influence of fatigue differed widely not just among individuals, as Mosso had believed, but within each individual according to changing conditions of work or environment. Ioteyko understood fatigue as a defense of the body's economy that could be regulated by training—essentially a way of protecting the muscle by habituating it to fatigue—a slower pace, or more rest. The malleability of fatigue led Ioteyko to insist that it would really be understood only by investigating large numbers of workers in the industrialized workplace and studying the conditions of their work. By taking this route, she wrote, pure science would provide its "authoritative support in its noble desire that the working classes may benefit by the physiological and psychological discoveries of our century."

A program for "submitting the working of the bodily organs to experimental tests with a view to discover their best working conditions, to detect fatigue and to lay down a scientific basis for industrial work" was made the order of the day at the 1903 International Congress of Hygiene and Demography held in Brussels, one of the many international conferences, organizations, and journals that directed the medical, physiological, and psychological concern with fatigue toward more practical social and political involvement. The program was all-inclusive. It included observing the conditions of work that yielded the best return; studying the effects of overwork and the contribution of machinery to the overfatigue of workers; and submitting the worker on the job to a plethora of tests with graphing machines to determine sensitivity to pain, the curve of nervous effort during work, the tempo of reflex response, chromatic sensitivity, capillary pulse change, and reaction time in the fatigued and nonfatigued body.

The scientists' desire to see their findings affect social policy on work and reform in the workplace was again stressed at the 1907 International Congress of Hygiene and Demography held in Berlin. One of the participants, the Montpellier physician Armand Imbert (1850–1922), saw the seemingly irremedial incompatibility of capital and labor as creating a need for intervention by experimental science. The industrialist was justifiably interested in the output of the worker, stated Imbert, while the worker's own self-interest was based on the "real expenditure of all kinds of internal energy." Science was "neither socialist in its essence nor capitalist in its nature; it is simply the truth." Imbert proffered his own studies as a concrete illustration of the role science could play in the current debate over the length of the workday and the prevention of accidents. From 1903 to 1906 he had undertaken, with an official of the French Office du Travail (founded in 1891), a statistical analysis of the frequency of accidents among different professions in the Hérault region. He showed that the increase in accidents both during certain times of day and on certain days of the week was not the result of worker negligence or malingering but was directly related to the accumulation of fatigue. In a study of dockworkers at the port of Sète, whose accident claims were so far above the norm that they were accused by their insurers of faking accidents or injuring themselves on purpose, Imbert demonstrated that the increase in number of accidents was directly related to fatigue: there were fewer men working at Sète than at the other ports, and they were doing more intense labor for the hours they worked. Rather than "a battle between labor and capital," the situation was the result of "a physiological fact that the most simple inquiry allowed to be discovered." Imbert saw the claim for a shortened workday and frequent rest periods as nothing less than a biological and economic necessity.

Like the studies of dockworkers, those of carters, vine cutters, and filers that Imbert carried out between 1905 and 1908 were done on site and were the "first to show the use that could be made of the graphic method to register the efforts of the workman's muscles on his tools." The study of carters was commissioned by the Office du Travail as part of its investigation of adolescent labor. Imbert compared the force needed to lift, balance, support, push, load, and unload the *cabrouet*, a two-wheeled cart, and the wheelbarrow. He fitted the vehicles' handles with intricate dynamometric inscribing devices that would respond to the pressure of the workers' hands and had the workers wear

6 Ioteyko, *Science of Labour*, 4.

7 Ibid.

8 Rabinbach, "European Science of Work," 499.

9 Armand Imbert and Mestre, "Nouvelles statistiques d'accidents du travail," *Revue Scientifique*, n.s., 3 (1905): 520.

10 Armand Imbert, "De la mésure du travail musculaire dans les professions manuelles," *Revue de la Société d'Hygiène Alimentaire et d'Alimentation Rationelle de l'Homme* 3 (1906): 636.

11 Amar, *Human Motor*, 279.

12 Imbert measured the muscular effort exerted both perpendicular (to support the load) and parallel to the handles (the force necessary to move the vehicle).

Marey's dynamometric shoes. The legislation on the work enacted in 1908 reversed his findings (though Imbert proved the *cabrouet* was much more energy efficient than the single-wheeled barrow, the government outlawed the *cabrouet*), yet he nonetheless saw the government's reliance on physiological experiment in enacting work reform legislation as a necessary and positive step in social reform.

As a result of his studies, Imbert concluded that in general good workers are accurately attuned to their own physical and mental limits and that they naturally find the way of doing their work that requires the minimum expenditure of energy; their whole way of working, in fact, demonstrated the "law of least effort." Moreover, Imbert contested, the skilled professional, more often than not, had a better grasp of the actual effort involved in any particular job than did the employer, and for these reasons he argued for workers' participation in the international meetings on work and hygiene. Most important, Imbert was one of the first work scientists to understand that the nature of work as it was organized in the modern factory imposed radically new conditions on the organism. Not the individual nor the employer, but the machine now regulated both the intensity and the tempo of labor, and this regularity had to be internalized by the worker. For Imbert this meant that time-and-motion measurement, "the direct, experimental, microscopic study of occupational work itself," must take its place beside the measurement of fatigue.

Imbert's experiments and, similarly, those of the doctors, physiologists, and psychologists who aimed to define the conditions under which the worker would produce the "maximum effective result with a minimum production of fatigue," rested on the unquestioned belief that the physical and mental well-being of workers was the foundation for the wealth and productivity of the nation. Their investigations of the effects of the duration of work, its rhythms and rests, the operative gestures of workers and their choice of tools, and the criteria (morphological, physiological, or psychological) that would determine the aptitude of different workers for different kinds of work reflected the positivistic ideal that science could solve social problems. Between 1898 and the First World War, the experiments undertaken in work reform by a few forward-looking industrialists; the contribution of government to statistical measurement in such studies as Imbert's; and the legislative debates in France, Germany, and England on the duration of the work week and length of the workday, the necessity for rest periods, health and accident protection, medical hygiene, and the reform of the army and of physical and technical education indeed seemed to herald more active cooperation between science and the state.

But ultimately the scientists' desire for reform measures based purely on objective physiological or psychological assessment was idealistic, and their call for increased state intervention and supervision of the workplace was premature. The orientation of their investigations toward the evaluation of physiological work ignored the social relations constituting every work situation. The strict scientism of their projects ignored the fact that most employers' desire for increased profits through cheaper labor and higher productivity overrode all other considerations. Moreover, as Marey had warned, "the extreme diversity of the effects produced and the extreme variety of the tools used" were indeed a stumbling block. To be effective, experiments had to be carried out on large numbers of men and women and had to take into account a multiplicity of factors, not least of which was the specificity of each job. Their results were not universally applicable, nor did they promise an immediate lowering of costs or increase in productivity. On the contrary, the investigations took a long time and a lot of money—money that could just as easily be spent, from the employers' point of view, on newer and faster machines.

In the first decade of this century, the rationalization of work carried out on the shop floor in America under the name scientific management seemed to offer the solutions to these problems. Like the European science of work, scientific management claimed to transcend conflicts of interest in the name of science. But its practitioners—called "efficiency engineers" or "industrial engineers"—were not concerned with finding the laws that governed movement, fatigue, the best use of tools, or the aptitude of the worker; nor was their primary consideration the physical and psychological well-being of the labor force. Rather, scientific management sought to increase productivity by making the work process more efficient, and it guaranteed efficiency by removing control of the work process itself from the worker and placing it in the hands of the manager. This shift in the aims of a science of work,

13 Armand Imbert and Mestre, "Recherches sur la manoeuvre du cabrouet et la fatigue qui en résulte," *Bulletin de l'Inspection du Travail* 5 (1905): 15–32; Armand Imbert, "Etude expérimentale du travail de transport de charges avec une brouette," *Bulletin de l'Inspection du Travail* 9 (1909): 47.

14 Rabinbach, *Human Motor*, 184.

15 Imbert, "Exemples d'étude physiologique directe du travail professionnel ouvrier," *Revue d'Hygiène et de Police Sanitaire*, no. 31 (1909):750.

16 Ioteyko, *Science of Labour*, 53.

17 Among others Rabinbach cites L.G. Fromont, director of the Belgian Société des Produits Chimiques von Engis, and Ernst Abbe, director of the Carl-Zeiss optical works in Germany. Rabinbach, *Human Motor*, 217–18 and passim.

from a means of discovery and social development to a "system of social control designed to limit union influence, to train unskilled workers rapidly, to create a new professionalism and promote the interests of the middle class," was a consequence of the changing mode of production that took place in American industry in the early twentieth century, and it was implemented by the evolution of a new managerial class, professional engineers.

During the first half of the nineteenth century the American pattern of producing and marketing manufactured goods already contained the basic elements of modern mass production: first, the practice of quantity manufacture of standardized products characterized by interchangeable parts; second, the use of a growing array of machine tools and power to substitute simplified and, as far as possible, mechanized operations for the draftsman's arts. Parallel developments in the organization of productive effort and in the new methods necessary to market standardized products in quantity went hand-in-hand with the technical advances. Known in Europe as the "American system," this pattern approached both production and distribution with an emphasis on the systematic organization of the flow of work so that labor costs were reduced and profits maximized. Regarded with envy by its European competitors, the system was viewed as a product of the differences between the New World and the Old: "The nature and diffusion of education in America; the absence of rigidities and restraints of class and craft; the freedom from hereditary definitions of the tasks or hardened ways of going about them; the high focus on personal advancement and drives to higher material welfare; and the mobility, flexibility, adaptability of Americans and their boundless belief in progress."

After the Civil War, unprecedented economic expansion gave rise to intense industrial competition. By the end of the century corporate ownership had emerged as the most successful response to this competition, functioning to control as much of the market and the production process as possible. By means of consolidations, mergers, trusts, holding companies, trade associations, and government regulatory agencies, the corporations struggled to regulate production processes and stabilize prices. Within the corporation itself, maximum profitability was essential. Expensive factories had to be used at full capacity, and factory, company, and intercompany activities had to be strictly coordinated. Because the potential of each new technological development had to be immediately realized, both modern technology and the production processes it made possible had to be rationalized. Standardization was the key to these operations: the standardization of scientific terminology and methods, the regularization of patent procedures, the efficient organization of scientific research, and the systematic production of technical manpower.

The union of science and industry provided one of the most historically important factors in the growth of the modern corporation in America. The last two decades of the nineteenth century were a watershed in the changing role of science, from "the province of amateurs, 'philosophers,' tinkerers, and seekers after knowledge to its present highly organized and lavishly financed state." Advances contributed by the adaptation of scientific discoveries and methods to the electrical and coal-petroleum industries showed that scientific research was a commercially valuable occupation, and the haphazard discoveries of science were swiftly used to meet the practical ends of the corporation.

The welding of science to the aims of industry properly began in Germany, where already by the 1870s, firms like Krupp at Essen were employing university-trained scientists in research laboratories that would become models for corporate research everywhere. But the lessons of Germany were not lost on the emerging American corporate state. In America, Edison's establishment at Menlo Park, New Jersey, was the first organization set up (in 1876) for the specific purpose of systematic invention. It was succeeded after the turn of the century by other centers that, in a more modern fashion, brought together men from different disciplines who pooled their knowledge and directed their research to technological innovation and ultimately to profits.

As we have seen in the case of Edison's (and the Lumières') struggle to control cinematic invention, the industrial monopoly over science first took the

18 Judith Merkle, *Management and Ideology: The Legacy of the International Scientific Management Movement* (Berkeley: University of California, Press, 1980), 86.

19 John E. Sawyer, "The Social Basis of the American System of Manufacturing," in *Essays in American Economic History*, ed. A.W. Coats and Ross M. Robertson (London: Edward Arnold, 1969), 285.

20 Ibid., 290.

21 For the discussion below I have relied on David A. Noble, *America by Design: Science, Technology, and the Rise of Corporate Capitalism* (New York: Alfred A. Knopf, 1977); Harry Braverman, *Labor and Monopoly Capital: The Degradation of Work in the Twentieth Century* (New York: Monthly Review Press, 1974); and Merkle, *Management and Ideology.*

22 Noble, *America by Design*, 55.

23 Braverman, *Labor and Monopoly Capital*, 156.

24 Ibid., 160. In Germany, "The turning point came with the synthesis of aspirin—the first purely synthetic drug—by Adolf von Bäyer (1835–1957) in 1899. The worldwide success of aspirin within a few years convinced the chemical industry of the value of technological work dedicated to research alone." Peter Drucker, *Technology, Management, and Society* (London: Heinemann, 1970), 52.

form of patent control—control over the process of scientific production by means of organized and regulated industrial research. Ultimately, industry became entirely science based, systematically applying scientific knowledge to commercial ends, developing the institutions necessary for producing both scientific knowledge and knowledgeable people, and integrating these institutions into a corporate system. This new scientific revolution meant that the development of modern technology became the prerogative of industry rather than science. The spontaneous innovations, adaptations, or refinements made to his own technology by a scientist like Marey, for example, were in this new world supplanted by the planned progress of technology and product design that we are accustomed to expect from the modern industrial plant.

The union of scientific methods and commercial enterprise was personified by the engineer, a new, primarily middle-class professional who became the representative of modern technology within the corporate environment. At the beginning of the twentieth century engineering had become, after teaching, the largest profession in America. Its twentieth-century practitioners, however, were quite different from the nineteenth-century skilled craftsmen and builders, whose empirical methods were the product of intuition and practice. The founding of engineering schools and institutes of technology after 1862, and the parallel development of professional engineering societies, had created a formal discipline out of a craft and had grounded the respectability and status of this discipline in scientific education. Indeed, science gave engineers their identity and helped emphasize their separation from the shop-culture tradition of their predecessors. But if engineers belonged to science, they also belonged to industry, which had now become the only organized social medium for applying their science. Because they were employed by the corporation and thus driven by its economic imperatives, engineers had come to identify their professional status with their corporate status. In effect they were at the same time scientists, executives, and corporate employees. Their job was to rationalize production through the scientific method; their goal was to ensure maximum profits for their employers.

Standardization in industry was the key to corporate prosperity and, since the corporations were the locus of technological innovation, to scientific progress as well. With their massive investment in research and development, plants, machinery, and manpower, the large corporations could be profitable only through large-scale, continuous production. Such continuous production (and large-scale consumption) in turn necessitated uniformity throughout the system: uniformity in machining necessary for interchangeable parts, uniform standards of quality, and uniformity of the labor process.

Standardizing the technical side of industry was the prerogative of the engineering profession, from the definitions of technical terms universally used to quality and quantity specifications, testing, ratings, and safety procedures. Inevitably, engineers soon turned their attention to standardizing the work and the worker: it was only one step from engineering things to engineering people. That step occurred as engineers came to assume their rightful role in the corporation, that of managers. As the director of the Taylor Society recalled, engineers were those most prepared to meet the challenge of fashioning the structures essential for the efficient administration of newly won business empires:

> The first coherent public expression of concern with management problems came from the engineers. They were the initiators of the "management movement" and it was they who continued to give it vigor. The first highly trained minds to go into industry were products of the engineering schools. They were trained as technicians and went into industry as technicians, but many of them speedily became operating executives and focused their trained minds on managerial problems. . . . ; the management movement arose out of the impact of a group of highly trained engineering minds on an industrial situation of engineering complexity.

And as they rationalized procedures in manufacturing, finance, and marketing and created the formal administrative structures for their corporate employers, it was natural that engineers would attend to the smooth running of the human element in the process as well.

The scientific management movement that began in America about 1900 and spread to Europe ten years later was the most significant manifestation of the engineering management of the work force. It shaped modern business and industry by ensuring systematic and detailed control over the processes of work. At its core was the "organized study of work, the analysis of work into its simplest elements and the systematic improvement of the worker's performance of each of these elements." It began within the large corporations, where the conditions for its development were firmly in place: a centralized workplace and the breakdown of the multiple processes involved in manufacturing a product into many operations, each performed by a different worker.

25 Noble, *America by Design*, 6.

26 Harlow S. Person, "Basic Principles of Administration and Management: The Management Movement," cited in Noble, *America by Design*, 263.

27 Peter Drucker, *The Practice of Management* (New York: Harper and Row), 280.

Frederick Winslow Taylor (1856–1915) is usually thought of as the father of scientific management, though as with so many "fathers," Taylor's claim to paternity is based on his synthesizing and consolidating ideas already current in the United States and Great Britain. The well-educated son of an upper-class Philadelphia family, Taylor was prevented from studying law by a mysterious eye ailment, and rather than languish in boredom at home he began an apprenticeship as a patternmaker and machinist. At twenty-two Taylor was hired as a laborer at the Midvale Steel Works, owned by a banker friend of his father's (and by William Sellers, cousin of Coleman Sellers, one of the sponsors of Muybridge's work at the University of Pennsylvania). At Midvale Taylor advanced through the ranks until he was appointed gang foreman in the lathe department. His notion of management came out of his three-year conflict with the machinists under him over his insistence that they increase their daily output. Taylor broke the opposition by bringing in outside laborers, especially trained by him to work more efficiently and committed to work harder, and by introducing a system of rewards (usually pay incentives) and punishments.

While at Midvale, Taylor had acquired a night-school degree in engineering, a field at that time not yet closed to ambitious and intelligent young men who lacked formal training. In 1898 he left his job as chief engineer at Midvale and set up shop as a "management consultant." In this role he reorganized the machine shops at Bethlehem Steel according to his ideas of "scientific management." From his experience at Midvale, Taylor understood that if an employer was to realize the full potential inherent in the labor power of the worker, control over the labor process had to be taken away from the worker and given to management, which must determine not only each step of the process but also the way each step was performed.

Taylor's reorganization of Bethlehem Steel allowed him to construct a rational base for his ideas. He studied how the machines functioned and analyzed the "motions" and "time" involved in the tasks the men performed. Taylor's guiding idea was that, to increase productivity, labor and materials had to be combined more efficiently, wages had to be tied to performance, and accurate records had to be kept of all procedures. He believed that by research and on-site analysis, management could accumulate all the information, skills, and techniques that had traditionally belonged to the worker and the foreman, transform them into systematic laws and formulas written down on paper, determine optimum standards of performance, for which a premium wage would be paid, and then "scientifically" reapply the standards by reorganizing the way work was done. This reorganization, which included reordering the physical layout of the factory and distributing standardized tools, primarily consisted of minutely dividing the components of the work into segments, timing the most proficient worker of each segment with a stopwatch (Taylor would later begin a small industry in stopwatches made expressly for this purpose), and insisting that other workers follow suit. Those who could not either quit or were fired. Taylor succeeded in separating responsibility for the execution of work from its planning or conception with these methods; he effectively abolished training and education costs, because once the worker learned to use one machine or one tool the training was over. Taylor thus also erased the difference between skilled and unskilled labor: since both were now doing the same repetitive tasks, their work could no longer be distinguished. And he made speed the sole measure of successful work.

A high-speed steel process that Taylor had devised at Bethlehem revolutionized machine production in the United States and brought him and his methods worldwide recognition. Between 1901, when he left Bethlehem Steel, and 1909, when he won government contracts to reorganize the federal arsenals, this recognition continued to grow. He had gathered around him a few like-minded men who introduced his system of shop management into other industries, and in 1905 he was elected president of the American Society of Mechanical Engineers, which ensured him an international forum for his ideas. In 1911 the highly publicized Eastern Rate Case, where the claims of scientific management (the first time the name was given its official title) were used to undermine the railroads' case for rate increases, transformed Taylorism "overnight from an obscure obsession of certain middle class engineers to an amazing and highly publicized nostrum for all the ills of society."

But the scientific aspect of Taylor's scientific management was soon called into question. Taylor relied

---

28 But as Judith Merkle makes clear, "only Taylor's synthesis answered simultaneously problems of production and organization, at the same time that it responded with solutions to the industrial disruption of American society." Taylorism, Merkle feels, was not only a technique of speeding work, but a "method of social pacification" (Merkle, *Management and Ideology*, 10). On Taylor and Taylorism, see M.J. Nadworny, *Scientific Management and the Unions* (Cambridge: Harvard University Press, 1955); Daniel Nelson, *Frederick W. Taylor and the Rise of Scientific Management* (Madison: University of Wisconsin Press, 1980); *Le Taylorisme: Actes du colloque international sur le Taylorisme organisé par l'Université de Paris XIII 2–1 May 1983* (Paris, 1984).

29 Merkle, *Management and Ideology*, 38.

30 Taylor's "high-speed" steel, devised with the metallurgist J. Maunsel White, was a process of heat treating steel that permitted more metal to be cut a higher machine speeds, while at the same time it prolonged the life of the cutting tool. Nadworny, *Scientific Management and the Unions*, 10.

on psychologically crude pay-incentive schemes or on simple coercion to spur workers to greater productivity. He refused to deal with the unions and had no idea of the subtleties of psychology or sociology and their possible use as management tools. His conception of the worker as a simple "economic man," and his belief that efficiency could be improved by standardizing each element of the job inevitably brought him difficulties with both labor and management. In 1911 these conflicts culminated in a strike over the installation of his system at the Watertown Arsenal. Even the government was unable to sustain wholesale support of his methods. Taylor's contempt for the workers was thinly disguised, and his desire to make workers mute extensions of their machines, forcing from their labor every ounce of potential profit without any consideration of their well-being, could not be tolerated. A government investigation after the Watertown strike showed that his scientific management was not so scientific after all. His stopwatch time studies were open to widespread abuse; they were carried out by people who often knew nothing about the work they were timing, and under conditions that affected the outcome of their observations. [...]

Jean-Marie Lahy's position was the most critical. He attacked Taylor's conception of labor for being "spoilt by a threefold error: psychological, sociological and industrial." He decried Taylor's ignorance of basic physiology, the unscientific way his system was conceived and implemented, and the lack of originality in Taylor's methods. "The idea of measuring a worker's movements in order to fix the value of his work is not Taylor's innovation," wrote Lahy:

> Studying the value of a gesture from the point of view of its duration, direction, and adaptation to an end is the physiologist's means of perfecting the muscular activity of man. More than thirty years ago, Marey created the method that permits such a study, and he brought it to a degree of perfection that has not been surpassed since... If no one has realized the practical consequences inherent in this work, and if the path that it opened has not been followed by Marey's collaborators, it is because on the one hand they did not make the superproduction of the worker their single end, and on the other hand the encouragement and the indispensable material funds were not there.

Taylor's ignorance of the work of Marey and his followers astonished Lahy, especially since Taylor's movement study was far "from being as precise as Marey's own." Taylor's system of timing the fastest worker, or the one with the most brute force, then forcing all the others to do their work at the same rate Lahy dismissed as "an empirical method without great value. It is applicable only to a few specific tasks, such as moving loads; it ignores physiological, psychological, and social factors and is dependent for its success on eliminating all poor workers, isolating the others from one another, and forbidding them moments for talk: its results are more the product of selection and surveillance than chronometric study." Marey (and Imbert), Lahy insisted, wanted to know the most effective gestures and use them to the exclusion of others in a manner that would precisely adapt a professional activity to its practical ends. Taylor, on the other hand, used time and motion study to perfect just one element of professional work—speed. [...]

Frank Bunker Gilbreth (1868–1924) and the psychologist Lillian Moller (1878–1972), whom he married in 1904, were the most important figures in this revisionist movement, and their approach provided the greatest challenge to Taylor's leadership. Like Taylor, Gilbreth had abandoned his education (in this case engineering at MIT) to work in the construction business, and Gilbreth's ideas similarly grew out of his own observations. His earliest experience was in the ancient art of bricklaying, where, after watching and analyzing the common methods of the trade, he was able to suggest improvements (bringing the bricks closer to the worker, changing the shape of the trowel, and eliminating most stooping and reaching movements) that more than doubled the normal output. His changes were aimed primarily at reducing unnecessary motion; he saw that by streamlining movement he could minimize the fatigue workers ordinarily were prone to and so increase the amount of work they could do each day. As an apprentice, Gilbreth had joined the bricklayers' union; this contact gave him a more sympathetic view of the individual worker than Taylor's. He was convinced that the workers' mental and physical disposition were important in determining output and that workers' cooperation and happiness were necessary to the implementation of any managerial plan. These considerations were reinforced by—and many writers believe originated with—his wife, Lillian. It was through her "that the tools of industrial psychology became the tools of Scientific Management."

---

31 Merkle, *Management and Ideology*, 58.
32 Noble, *America by Design*, 274.
33 Cited in Ioteyko, *Science of Labour*, 85.
34 Jean-Marie Lahy, *Le système Taylor et la phsyiologie du travail professional*, 2d ed. (Paris: Gauthier-Villars, 1921), 28.
35 Lahy, *Système Taylor*, 33.
36 Ibid., 34. On Taylor's lack of originality see also Charles Fremont, "A propos du système Taylor," *La Technique Moderne* 7 (1913): 301–8.
37 Lahy, *Système Taylor*, 52–53.
38 Ibid., 57–58.

From his experience in bricklaying Gilbreth concluded that the sequence and manner in which each movement of the work was done modified the time it took, so his system of management focused on standardizing the movement, not the time. His aim was to find the "one best way" to get work done, and his method, though he never acknowledged it, was Marey's chronophotographic method of temporal decomposition in space. Gilbreth's engineering of the "human element," as he put it, was geared to understanding both the internal and external causes of worker motivation. He approached motion study from what he considered the most scientific point of view by "dividing work into the most fundamental elements possible; studying these elements separately and in relation to one another; and from these studied elements, when timed, building methods of least waste." He began by reducing and describing in writing the motions currently in use and the variables involved in each—there were forty-two of these, and they included everything from the anatomy, contentment, and creed of the workers to their equipment and tools, the color of the plant, the rules of the union, and the components of each movement. Next, "best" practice was similarly reduced and described with its variables. [...]

Sometime between 1911 (when he noted in his book *Motion Study* that the "stereoscopic camera and stereoscope, the motion picture machines, and the stereopticon enable us to observe, record, and teach as one never could in the past") and 1913, when he finished organizing the work at the New England Butt Company, Gilbreth had come to depend on photography as the key to his study of motion. His "micro-motion method," begun at New England Butt, consisted of "recording motions by means of a motion picture camera, a clock that will record different times of day in each picture of a motion picture film, a cross-sectioned background, and other devices for assisting in measuring the relative efficiency and wastefulness of motions." Much like the ancient Greek sculptors, who used more than one model, Gilbreth filmed many workers to arrive at an ideal movement he hoped they could then imitate.

The micro-motion record, however, did not give "the continuous path of a cycle of motions," and it was hard to use as an instruction device because workers had trouble visualizing and then imitating the movements they saw in the films. He addressed this problem at his next job (for the Hermann, Aukam Company, handkerchief manufacturers), first with his "cyclegraph method" and then with his "chronocyclegraph method." The former, named because the cycle was the unit of measurement to be recorded, consisted of putting the worker in a blacked-out room and tracking with a still camera a light bulb attached to the hand. The chronocyclegraph method incorporated the temporal element; again Gilbreth fastened tiny electric light bulbs to the operator's fingers, or "to any part of the operator or of the material whose motion path it is desired to study. . . . If the direction, relative time, and relative speed are to be noted, the path of light, through controlled interruption of the circuit, is made to consist of dots or dashes, or a combination of the two, with single pointed ends,—the points showing the direction." Gilbreth and his wife carried out the studies in a laboratory he had created for the experiments, which included a luminous background grid to aid measurement and a "penetrating screen." Gilbreth used an ingenious method of double exposure: He first placed his cross-sectioned screen where needed (in the plane in which the worker was to perform, in front or in back), photographed it, and then removed it and made a photograph of the work being done on the same negative.

In 1915 Gilbreth published "Motion Models: Their Use in the Transference of Experience and the Presentation of Comparative Results in Educational Methods," where he described three-dimensional wire models he had fashioned from both cyclegraphs and chronocyclegraphs. (The spots made by the light bulbs in the chronocyclegraphs were represented on the white wire models by black and gray spots.) These wire models—exactly the same as those Marey devised to show the movement of the coccyx in three dimensions—were also, like Marey's, based on stereo photographs; but Gilbreth's were intended exclusively as standards the individual would be taught to attain. Workers learning the movement (or unlearning an incorrect one) would attempt to emulate the motion model; their motion would be chronocyclegraphed, a second model made, and the two compared.

Gilbreth applied for a patent on the chronocycleograph method in spring 1913. The patent was granted in fall 1916, although his method of attaching light bulbs to the subject and using a still camera to track their movement was an exact emulation of the system Marey had devised, and Demeny had elaborated, to study pathological movement in 1887. Marey had not taken out any patent in France or America for his system. Gilbreth

39 Noble, *America by Design*, 275.

40 Frank Gilbreth and Lillian Gilbreth, "Motion Study as Industrial Opportunity," in *The Writings of the Gilbreths*, ed. William R. Spriegel and Clark E. Myers (Homewood, Ill.: Richard Irwin, 1953), 220.

41 Frank Gilbreth, *Motion Study*, 205.

42 Gilbreth and Gilbreth, "Motion Study as an Industrial Opportunity," 221.

43 Ibid., 222.

44 Ibid.

also applied for a patent that included a stereo camera in its specifications for photographing movement; this too had been anticipated by Marey.

There is no doubt that Gilbreth knew about Marey's earlier achievements in tracking movement. He reanalyzed many of Marey's subjects, such as soldiers and fencers, and his thoughts on the way motion study should be approached are often a direct echo of Marey's. For example, in his belief that increased accuracy is the foundation of such work, Gilbreth calls for a government bureau of standards, for universal forms of measurement, and for precision instruments that "will record mechanically, with the least possible interference from the human element, in permanent form, exactly what motions and results occur. For permanent use the records must be so definite, distinct and simple that they may be easily and immediately used, and lose none of their value of helpfulness when old, forgotten or not personally experienced by their user." [...]

What is interesting however, is the way Marey's techniques show up, yet again, in the hands of someone who used them for purposes unforeseen by Marey. On the surface Gilbreth's work seems closer in subject and form to Marey's than any other we have seen. And yet Gilbreth's agenda was deeply, radically different. Gilbreth's motion studies signify a conclusion, albeit unforeseen by Marey, to the latter's study of movement. In Gilbreth's work, Marey's desire to account for the laws that govern movement and force, and his belief that their discovery would ameliorate the fate of humanity, was transformed into a desire for control and uniformity. Although both Gilbreth and Marey were guided by the scientific discourse of their times, the content and context of that discourse governed a radically different outcome in each study. What for Marey constituted a linked series of disinterested discoveries aimed at revealing natural laws became for Gilbreth a method of appropriating the potential energy of a dormant labor force and making it serve the pecuniary ends of the corporation. The object of the fatigue studies that captured Marey's mind was completely transformed. Marey saw human energy as a dormant wellspring made available by the scientific study of the laws governing human motion and used for the betterment of physical and psychological health. Under Gilbreth such energy was perceived as unrealized labor potential: it was management's duty to eliminate waste and fatigue from the job so workers could be free to enjoy more "happiness minutes." Whereas Marey studied fatigue to increase the endurance of the individual, Gilbreth aimed at determining the standards for maximizing labor efficiency for the benefit of the company. Implicit, therefore, in Gilbreth's "science" was the removal of such potential from the individual's own control. For Marey, science would unleash the energy of the animate machine. For scientific management, workers were part of a larger mechanism. Their potential was for the accumulation of capital; it could be made available only by fixed hours, systematic control, and the reorganization of labor.

Marey did not foresee the extent to which his methods would be instrumental in the drive for the uniformity and standardization of work and the worker. Nor could he have anticipated that his investigation of human movement would one day be applied to the creation of machines that would replace the humans he had studied. Factories today are no longer temples to the efficiency of human labor. Robots carry out the monotonous, repetitive gestures once performed by men and women. Now efficiency experts and ergonomists concentrate on mental, not physical, fatigue. The love affair with the machine that began with the joyful discovery that the functions of both animate and inanimate nature could be explained by the laws of theoretical mechanics has resulted in creating machines to free the body, but it has left us with the problem of enslaved and robotic minds. [...]

45 Gilbreth and Gilbreth, "Motion Study and Time Study Instruments of Precision," 227.

X-ray Photograph of Two Hands Clasped Together in *Journal of Electrochemistry*, Vol. 3, 1896–1897

Wilhelm Röntgen

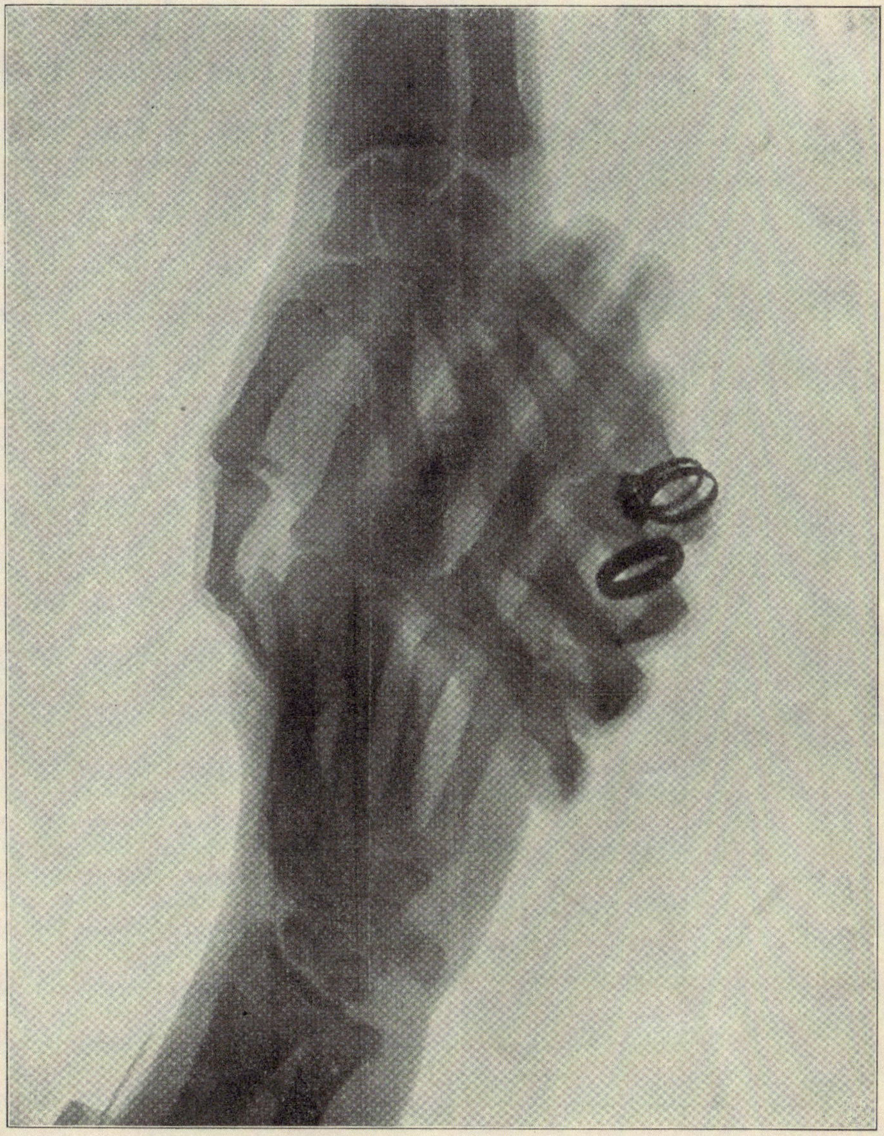

Röntgen-Photographie zweier ineinander geschlungener Hände,
aufgenommen während des Vortrages am 27. Juni von Prof. Dr. König, phototypisch auf $^2/_3$ verkleinert (vgl. S. 56).

Picture of a Human Hand According to the X-ray Method in *Journal of Electrochemistry*, Vol. 2, 1896
Wilhelm Röntgen

Zeitschrift für Elektrochemie. Heft 21.

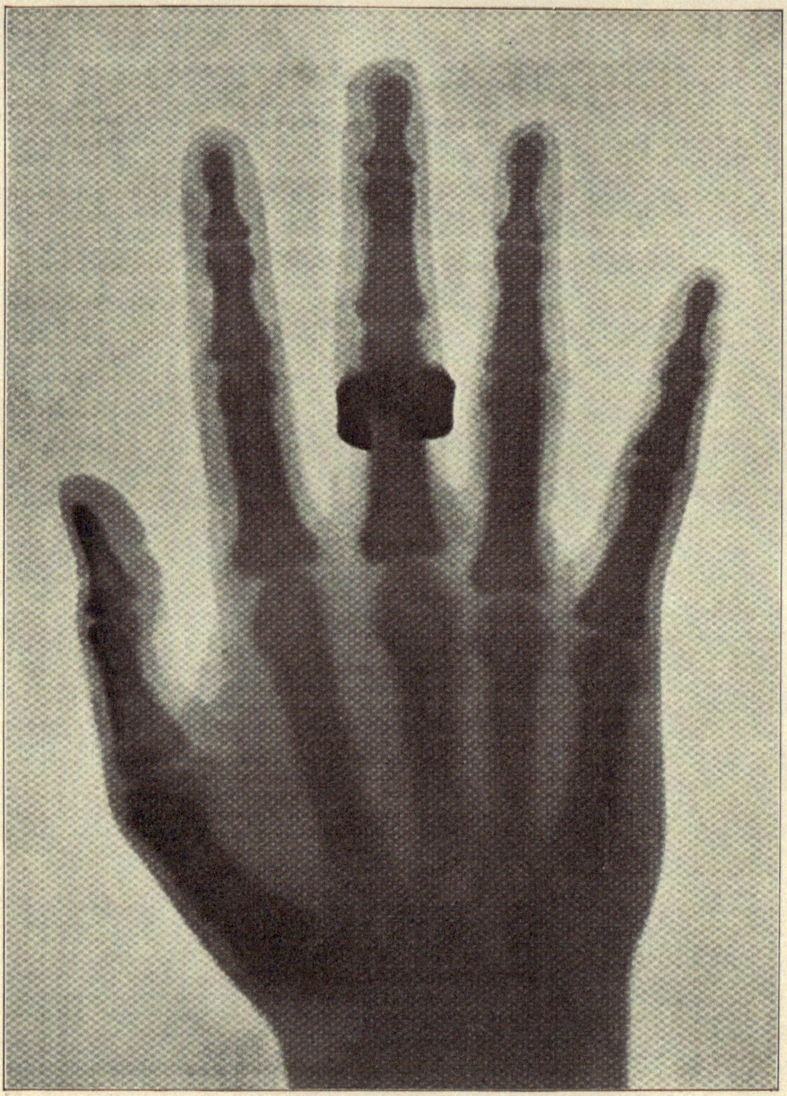

Verlag von Wilhelm Knapp in Halle a. S.

Aufnahme einer menschlichen Hand nach dem Röntgen'schen Verfahren

vom Geh. Regierungsrath Prof. Dr. Slaby und Assistent Klingenberg
in Charlottenburg.

On a New Kind of Rays

Wilhelm Röntgen

1896

1. A discharge from a large induction coil is passed through a Hittorf's vacuum tube, or through a well- exhausted Crookes' or Lenard's tube. The tube is surrounded by a fairly close-fitting shield of black paper; it is then possible to see, in a completely darkened room, that paper covered on one side with barium platinocyanide lights up with brilliant fluorescence when brought into the neighborhood of the tube, whether the painted side or the other be turned towards the tube. The fluorescence is still visible at two meters distance. It is easy to show that the origin of the fluorescence lies within the vacuum tube.

2. It is seen, therefore, that some agent is capable of penetrating black cardboard which is quite opaque to ultra-violet light, sunlight or arc-light. It is therefore of interest to investigate how far other bodies can be penetrated by the same agent. It is readily shown that all bodies possess this same transparency, but in very varying degrees. For example, paper is very transparent; the fluorescent screen will light up when placed behind a book of a thousand pages; printer's ink offers no marked resistance. Similarly, the fluorescence shows behind two packs of cards; a single card does not visibly diminish the brilliancy of the light. So, again, a single thickness of tinfoil hardly casts a shadow on the screen; several have to be superposed to produce a marked effect. Thick blocks of wood are still transparent. Boards of pine two or three centimeters thick absorb only very little. A piece of sheet aluminum, 15 mm. thick, still allowed the X-rays (as I will call the rays, for the sake of brevity) to pass, but greatly reduced the fluorescence. Glass plates of similar thickness behave similarly; lead glass is, however, much more opaque than glass free from lead. Ebonite several centimeters thick is transparent. If the hand be held before the fluorescent screen, the shadow shows the bones darkly, with only faint outlines of the surrounding tissues. [...]

4. Increasing thickness increases the hindrance offered to the rays by all bodies. A picture has been impressed on a photographic plate of a number of superposed layers of tinfoil, like steps, presenting thus a regularly increasing thickness. This is to be submitted to photometric processes when a suitable instrument is available.

5. Pieces of platinum, lead, zinc, and aluminum foil were so arranged as to produce the same weakening of the effect. The annexed table shows the relative thickness and density of the equivalent sheets of metal.

	Thickness	*Relative thickness*	*Density*
Platinum	.018 mm.	1	21.5
Lead	.050 mm.	3	11.3
Zinc	.100 mm.	6	7.1
Aluminium	3.500 mm.	200	2.6

From these values, it is clear that in no case can we obtain the transparency of a body from the product of its density and thickness. The transparency increases much more rapidly than the product decreases.

6. The fluorescence of barium platinocyanide is not the only noticeable action of the X-rays. It is to be observed that other bodies exhibit fluorescence, *e.g.* calcium sulfide, uranium glass, Iceland spar, rock-salt, &c.

Of special interest in this connection is the fact that photographic dry plates are sensitive to the X-rays. It is thus possible to exhibit the phenomena so as to exclude the danger of error. I have thus confirmed many observations originally made by eye observation with the fluorescent screen. Here the power of the X-rays to pass through wood or cardboard becomes useful. The photographic plate can be exposed to the action without removal of the shutter of the dark slide or other protecting case, so that the experiment need not be conducted in darkness. Manifestly, unexposed plates must not be left in their box near the vacuum tube.

It seems now questionable whether the impression on the plate is a direct effect of the X-rays, or a secondary result induced by the fluorescence of the material of the plate. Films can receive the impression as well as ordinary dry plates.

I have not been able to show experimentally that the X-rays give rise to any calorific effects. These, however, may be assumed, for the phenomena of fluorescence show that the X-rays are capable of transformation. It is also certain that all the X-rays falling on a body do not leave it as such.

The retina of the eye is quite insensitive to these rays; the eye placed close to the apparatus sees nothing. It is clear from the experiments that this is not due to want of permeability on the part of the structures of the eye.

7. After my experiments on the transparency of increasing thicknesses of different media, I proceeded to investigate whether the X-rays could be deflected by a prism. Investigations with water and carbon bisulfide in mica prisms of 30° showed no deviation either on the photographic or the fluorescent plate. For comparison, light rays were allowed to fall on the prism as the apparatus was set up for the experiment. They were deviated 10 mm. and 20 mm. respectively in the case of the two prisms.

With prisms of ebonite and [...]

14. The justification of the term "rays," applied to the phenomena, lies partly in the regular shadow pictures produced by the interposition of a more or less permeable body between the source and a photographic plate or fluorescent screen.

I have observed and photographed many such shadow pictures. Thus, I have an outline of part of a door covered with lead paint; the image was produced by placing the discharge tube on one side of the door, and the sensitive plate on the other. I have also a shadow of the bones of the hand; of a wire wound upon a bobbin; of a set of weights in a box; of a compass card and needle completely enclosed in a metal case; of a piece of metal where the X-rays show the want of homogeneity, and of other things.

For the rectilinear propagation of the rays I have a pin-hole photograph of the discharge apparatus covered with black paper. It is faint but unmistakable.

15. I have sought for interference effects of the X-rays, but possibly, in consequence of their small intensity, without result.

16. Researches to investigate whether electrostatic forces act on the X-rays are begun but not yet concluded.

17. If one asks, what then are these X-rays; since they are not kathode rays, one might suppose, from their power of exciting fluorescence and chemical action, them to be due to ultra-violet light. In opposition to this view a weighty set of considerations presents itself. If X-rays be indeed ultra-violet light, then that light must possess the following properties.

(*a*) It is not refracted in passing from air into water, carbon bisulfide, aluminum, rock-salt, glass or zinc.

(*b*) It is incapable of regular reflection at the surfaces of the above bodies.

(*c*) It cannot be polarised by any ordinary polarising media.

(*d*) The absorption by various bodies must depend chiefly on their density.

That is to say, these ultra-violet rays must behave quite differently from the visible, infra-red, and hitherto known ultra-violet rays.

These things appear so unlikely that I have sought for another hypothesis.

A kind of relationship between the new rays and light rays appears to exist; at least the formation of shadows, fluorescence, and the production of chemical action point in this direction. Now it has been known for a long time, that besides the transverse vibrations which account for the phenomena of light, it is possible that longitudinal vibrations should exist in the ether, and, according to the view of some physicists, must exist. It is granted that their existence has not yet been made clear, and their properties are not experimentally demonstrated. Should not the new rays be ascribed to longitudinal waves in the ether?

I must confess that I have in the course of this research made myself more and more familiar with this thought, and venture to put the opinion forward, while I am quite conscious that the hypothesis advanced still requires a more solid foundation.

Injured Right Hand of Workman in *The Röntgen Rays in Medical Work*
David Walsh
1897

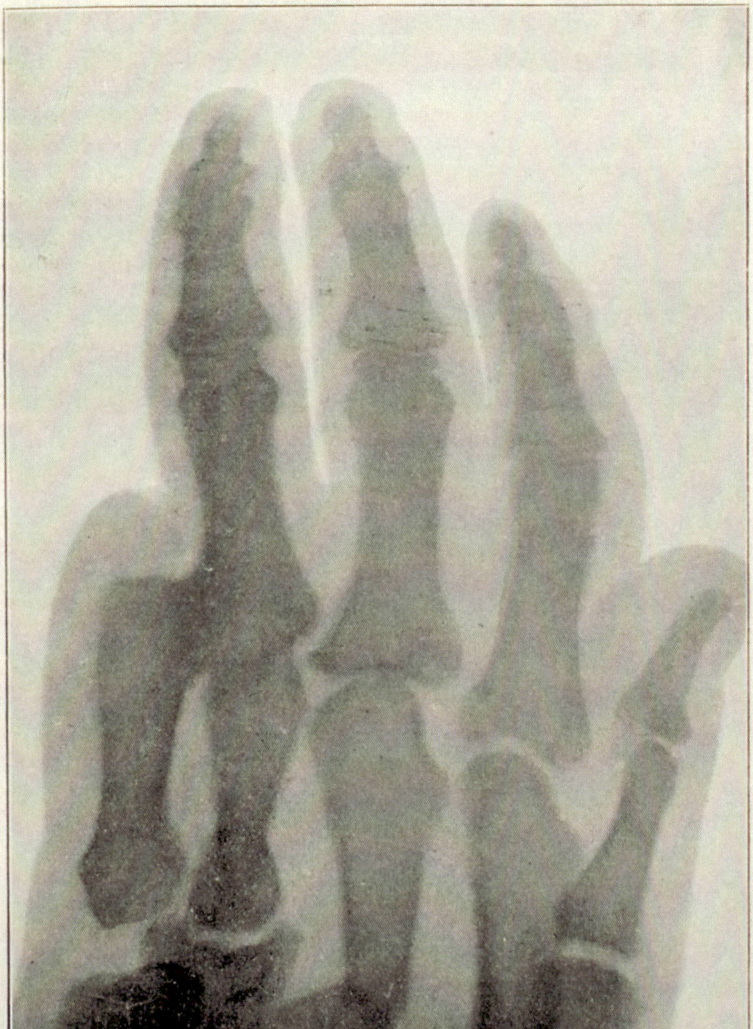

Fig. 34.—Injured Right Hand of Workman.
(By Mr. Greenhill.)

Still from *Workers Leaving the Lumière Factory*

Louis and Auguste Lumière

1895

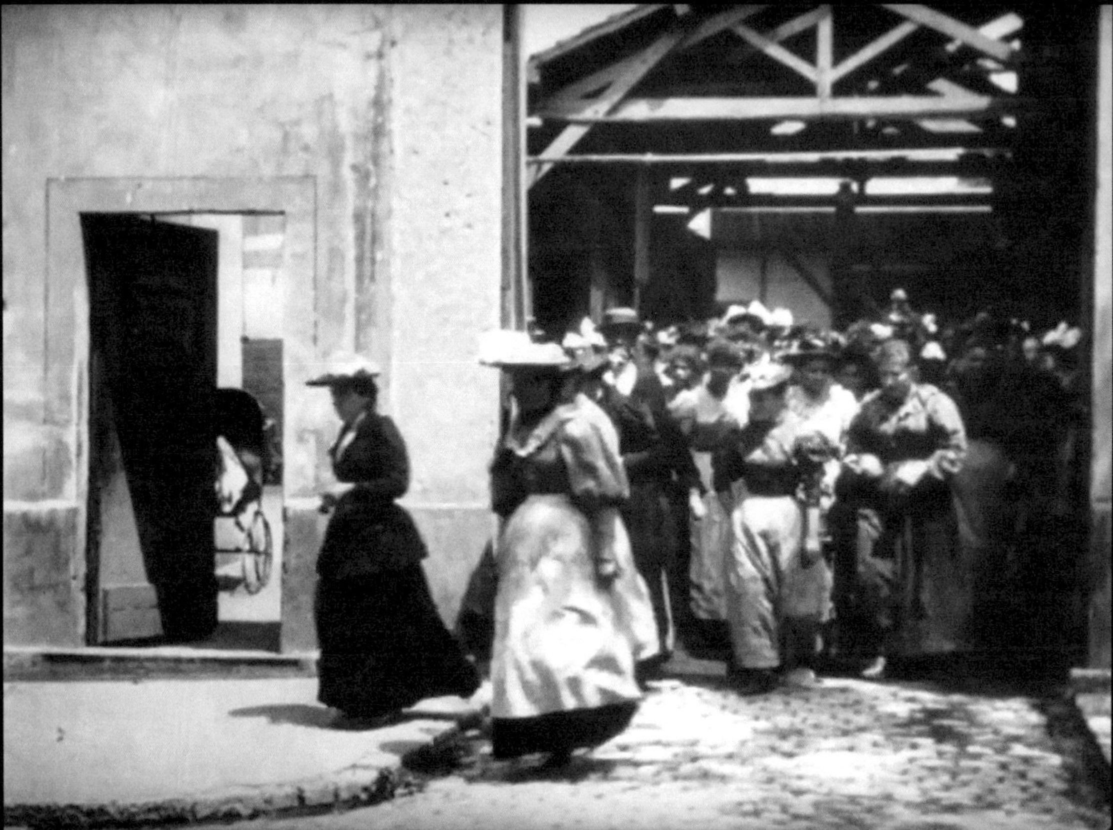

Top: Still from *Workers Leaving Williamson's Factory, Lancaster*
Bottom: Still from *Workers Leaving Messrs Vickers & Maxim's in Barrow*
Sagar Mitchell and James Kenyon
1901

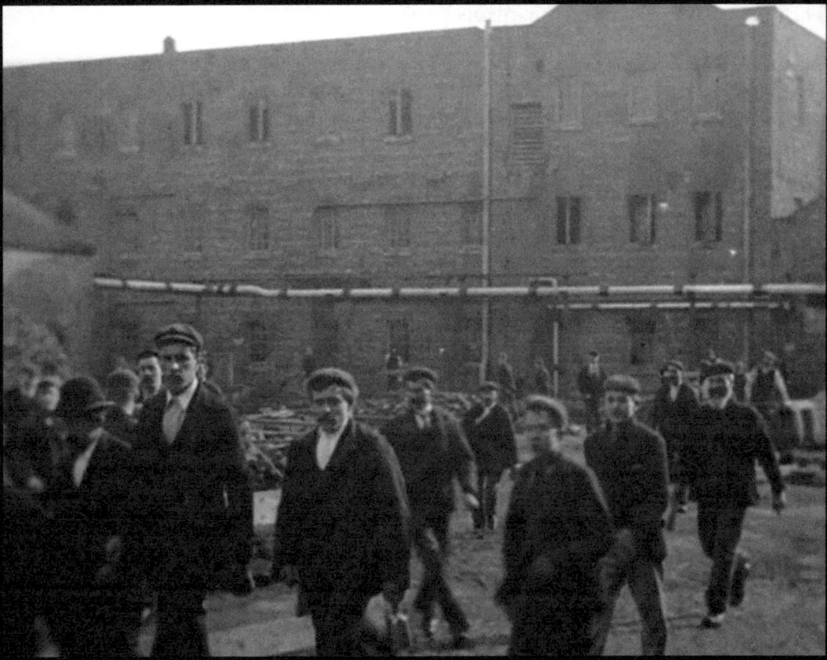

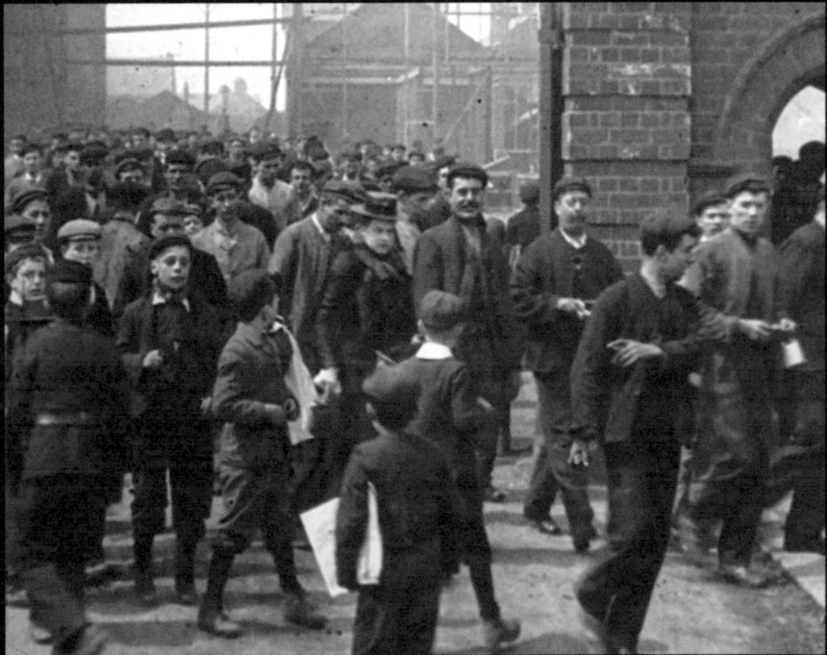

Preface to *Motion Study: A Method for Increasing the Efficiency of the Workman*

Frank B. Gilbreth

1911

The phrase "Motion Study" explains itself.

The aim of motion study is to find and perpetuate the scheme of perfection. There are three stages in this study:

1. Discovering and classifying the best practice.

2. Deducing the laws.

3. Applying the laws to standardize practice, either for the purpose of increasing output or decreasing hours of labor, or both.

Standardizing the trades is the world's most important work to-day, and motion study is the first factor in that work.

In presenting this material I have attempted to show the necessity for Motion Study and the savings that are possible by the application of its underlying principles.

Thanks are due to the Myron C. Clark Publishing Company and to *Industrial Engineering* for permission to use the cuts that illustrate this book.

Motion Study Photographs
Frank B. Gilbreth
1913–1917

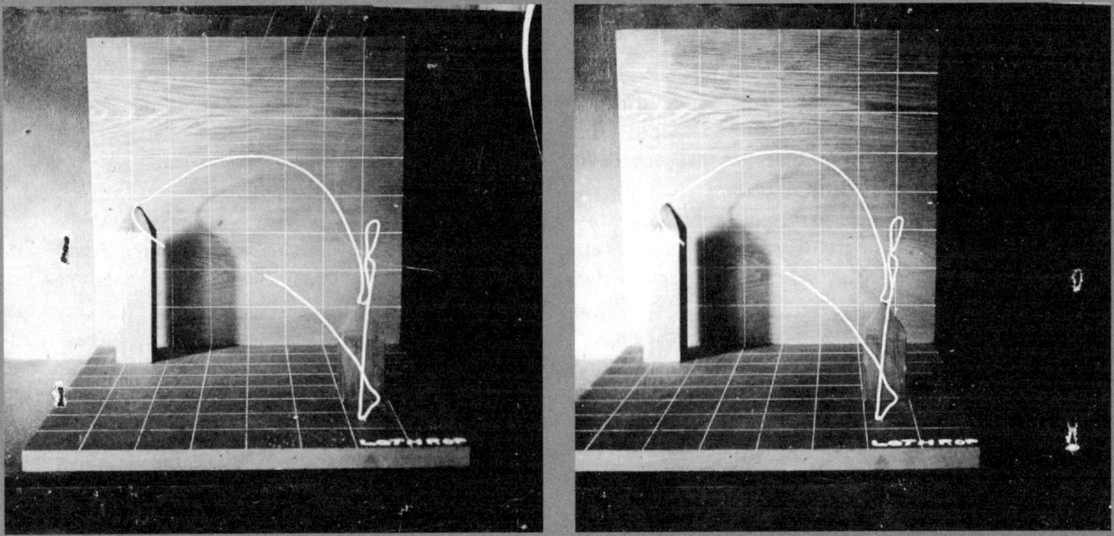

Wire model of foreman on drill press. This shows "positioning" in the midst of "transporting."

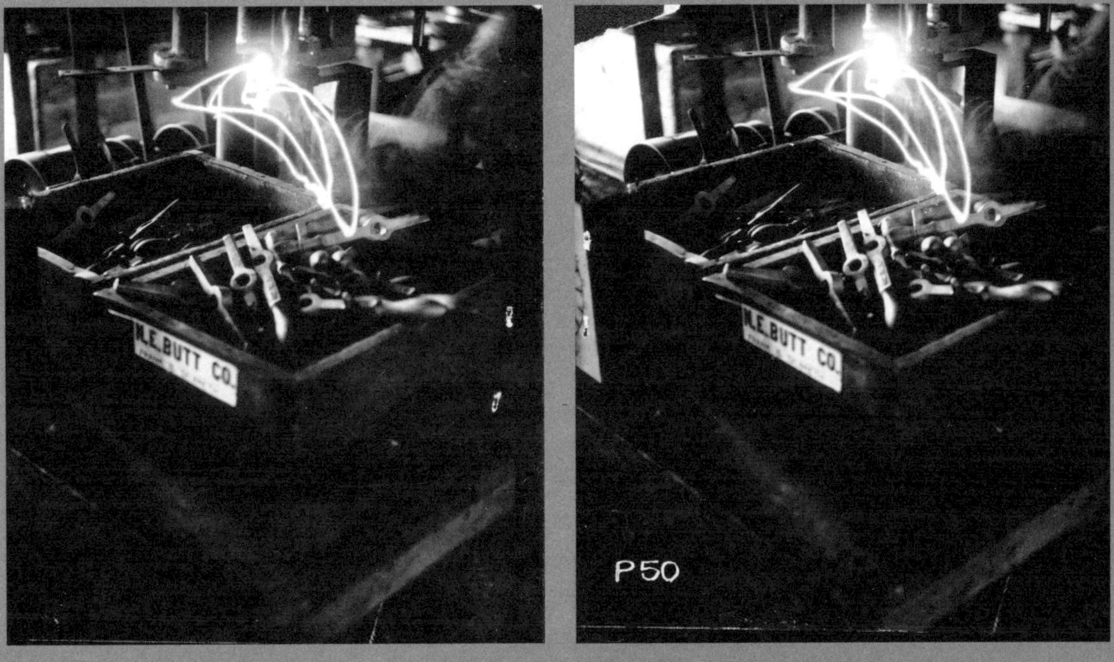

2 cycles on drill press showing "HABIT" positioning after transporting. Note the "hesitation" before "grasping."

Radiography, Cinematography and the Decline of the Lens

Lisa Cartwright and Brian Goldfarb

1992

TOME 1: 1920

Having long given up on his well-known work on the mechanics of the cinema, photochemist Louis Lumière publishes an account of a new technology for still photography, which he calls "*photo-stéréo-synthèse.*"[1] Subjecting the camera lens and photographic plate to proportional, axial movement around the profilmic object (a man's head), Lumière creates photographs in which only a specified plane within the space of the object remains in a fixed relation to the plate during a single exposure. This fixed point or plane of the object registers as the sole area of focus on the photographic plate; the remainder of the object appears blurred due to the relative movement of the apparatus. Shifting the apparatus by increments perpendicularly "into" the space of the object with each successive shot, Lumière exposes a series of plates until every designated plane of the object is recorded. Printing a faint negative from each plate, he then stacks these prints in succession, reconstructing the space of the object in a laminated visual composite. The claim is that this composite of images offers a precise geometric register of the contained space of the profilmic object, whereas a single image of the same object shot with greater depth of field offers only a pictorial sensation of depth.

While the cinema, used as an instrument of measurement, may analytically segment movement of objects through space into equal temporal units, *photo-stéréo-synthèse* measures the movement of the apparatus itself through the static interior space of its object. A decade after Lumière's death, radiologists Joseph Duhamel and Jean-Claude Roques point out that the filmmaker had found for himself a problem identical to that of the radiologist: the problem of charting an object, in a highly precise manner, according to its volumetric space—for Lumière, a problem consisting in obtaining photographic images of dimensional object-space without succumbing to the imprecisions of lenticular geometry.[2] If this project can be traced back to Lumière's place at the origins of the cinema in 1895, it is only through a consideration of what amounted to a rejection of lenticular optics in that same year: Roentgen's introduction of the X-ray as an imaging technology in 1895 is critical not only to Lumière's 1920 process of *photo-stéréo-synthèse*, but to the undercutting of the cinematic space born in that same year.

TOME 2: 1921

As a medical officer in the French army, André Edmund-Marie Bocage had been assigned to a radiological unit, where he practiced what he called "direct analytical radiography." In 1921, he patents an X-ray apparatus based on this method, which is designed to image the body in a series of shallow planes. Although he would be unable to put this apparatus into operation until 1938, his patent would be regarded as the earliest practicable plan for a system of tomography. The patent reads as follows:

> The focus of the radiographic tube is put in motion, as also is the sensitive plate; the plate is only able to receive motion of translation. Both are connected by a mechanism in such a way that their primary displacements are always synchronous, parallel, of opposite direction and in a ratio of constant magnitude.
>
> Under these conditions there exists between them, in space, a single fixed plane [within the profilmic object], in which each point always has a corresponding image point on the plate; hence, only the organs contained in this plane are in focus. The other organs form only diffuse shadows, being able to partly change the intensity of the primary image, but without adding to it new lines, because the farther away from the plane, the more extensive are the movements of the tube, and the more displaced are the images of the points on the plate.[3]

Duhamel and Roques point out that Bocage's method corresponds precisely to Lumière's process of *photo-stéréo-synthèse*. Both methods attempt to map the space of the body in planar projections, each plane constituted as the sum of a multiple set of geometric projections. In both processes, the extreme reduction of the focal field counteracts the spatial imprecisions

1 Louis Lumière, Compte Rendu des Sèances de l'Académie des Sciences (1920), 171.
2 "Louis Lumière et les origines photographiques de la tomographie," *La Presse medicale*, October 3, 1959.
3 André J. Bruwer, ed., *Classic Descriptions of Roentenology*, vol. 2, trans. James D. Bricker (Springfield, MA: Charles C. Thomas,1964), Patent 536464.

introduced by standard photographic perspective. It can be argued that *photo-stéréo-synthèse* does not simply correct perspectival space, but introduces an entirely new model of spatial representation. The stereo-synthetic image is less a pictorial record of appearances than a means of measuring an abstract, nonvisible property of a body: volume. Similarly, radiography measures a physical property: density. More than an advance on photographic space, stereo-synthetic and radiographic space effectively break with the logic of conventional pictorial space, encoding the photographic image as a graphic register of nonvisible properties.

Rejecting the projection of three-dimensional objects onto a two-dimensional plane, Lumière incorporates the lens into an optical system meant virtually to replicate the volume of the object rather than its appearance. Ultimately, the individual images produced in *photo-stéréo-synthèse* would be laminated so as to form a photographic block proportionate to the object. This dimensional model is important not because it reproduces the object, but because it facilitates the precise measurement of, and the location of points within, a space that cannot otherwise be seen or photographed from any single vantage point. Replacing the lens with the radiographic tube, Bocage outlines a nearly identical method in which the movement of an apparatus serves to segment an object into measurable planes of interior space. Because it eliminates the lens and the light ray altogether, the radiographic image goes a step further than *photo-stéréo-synthèse* in negating the logic of the photographic image.

TOME 3: 1925

In his correspondence of 1925, poet e.e. cummings sends physician and filmmaker James Sibley Watson, Jr., some sketches of shooting sets and directions for filming dimensional objects—a doll, a heart. Having little concern with "subjectmattering" a film text, cummings, like Lumière a few years earlier, is interested in using the camera lens to reconstruct the volume of objects without relying on the pictorial conventions of perspective and foreshortening. His interest in cinematography is based largely on the idea that camera movement establishes the interior volume of an object. Movement as a perceptual experience (speed, object displacement, duration) is of little consequence. Cummings uses the term "seeingaround" to describe his method: "such is the strict idiom which seems to me to constitute the aesthetic foundation of the 'moving picture.'"[4] According to cummings, the language that employs this idiom "is concentric. It suggests to me Dr F's Repetition Compulsion." The movement of cummings's proposed moving pictures is concentrated in the function of the apparatus. It describes the form of the "~~object~~ subject," which is included in the apparatus as a mobile unit in the articulation of its own volumetric space.

Cummings's outline for a cinematic idiom of "seeingaround," described in the following quotations and diagrams, closely parallels Lumière's 1920 process of *photo-stéréo-synthèse* and Bocage's 1921 method for tomography. In all three cases, movement functions to describe space according to the property of volume. As in tomography, blur is a critical factor in the establishment of volumetric space: "I think blurs of which you write should be valuable rather than the reverse," writes cummings in response to Watson's concern about the effect of moving the apparatus.

While Watson did not employ this idiom of "seeingaround" in his avant-garde films of the 1920s and 1930s, cummings's ideas correspond remarkably to the three-dimensional cine-radiographic films Watson would produce after World War II—films entirely dependent on the factor of blur so central to tomographic movement. It is the work of Watson that Duhamel and Roques single out as cutting-edge radiography in 1959. [...]

TOME 4: 1930

Radiologist Allesandro Vallebona proposes two techniques for the radiographic analysis of volumetric form as a series of quantifiable planes or strata. He cites as his model systems used in World War I to locate foreign objects in wounded bodies. His method, called "stratigraphy," follows precisely the rotational and revolutionary formulas for seeingaround proposed by cummings:

> Let us suppose that the film and the roentgen tube are joined in a rigid system capable of rotating about an adjustable axis, of the type designed by Baese which was used during the war co localize missiles. During the exposure, this rigid system undergoes rotation about its axis. The plane which corresponds to this axis will have a clear radiographic image while the others will be blurred. Alternatively, during the exposure the skull could undergo a slight rotation about an axis corresponding to the desired plane.[5]

Vallebona follows the second, object-rotational, system—a process paralleling cummings's turntable method. Like cummings, his goal is to undercut the effects of perspective and other techniques for depth rendering

4 e.e. cummings, proposals for film-shooting patterns, 1925. James Sibley Watson, Jr. Papers, ee cummings Trust.

5 Bruwer, 1420.

by abstracting the object into dimensionless planes. He notes that, prior to his own method, stereoradiography had been the only X-ray technique for locating a lesion in volumetric space. In the stereoradiographic image, any single focused plane is always partially obscured by shadow images of planes of the body extraneous to the organ or region of interest. Stratigraphy eliminates this problem: the rotation of the apparatus effectively causes all planes but the one at the locus of rotation to register as a diffuse blur. Paradoxically, stratigraphy makes possible depth measurement of the body by rendering the body as a series of planes that are dimensionless in themselves. Depth is computed as an absence, a nonvisible differential between two images, two positions.

This exclusion of sight from the spatial field is brought about by the absence of the optical lens in the radiographic process. Vallebona cites the incommensurability of the X-ray and the photographic lens as a drawback to the aims of imaging internal dimensional space: "If we could use lenses and mirrors for roentgen rays in the same way that we do for light rays the problem would be resolved, for as in microscopy or photography we could focus on only one definite plane."[6] The high power of the microscopic lens and, more importantly, the light permeability of the microscopic specimen suggest a situation parallel to that of radiography: the microscopic specimen is rendered as a permeable field of varying density rather than as a modulated surface or field of contained objects. Applied to objects viewed at a microscopic scale, light can be made to take on the relative intensity of the X-ray. By optically limiting the focal field, a virtually dimensionless plane of activity can be isolated inside the shallow depths of the specimen. This project clearly parallels that of stratigraphic imaging.

While stratigraphy and microscopy may share this project of delimiting a shallow plane of space, their methods are radically different. Vallebona suggests that stratigraphy is limited in that it cannot rely on optical properties to isolate a field of focus; however, it was this "limitation" that led to an innovation that foreclosed on the perspectival representation of depth altogether, necessitating a complete shift in optical paradigms.

Although Vallebona lamented his inability to employ lenticular optics, he introduced a method undercutting its very logic. Like *photo-stéréo-synthèse*, which addressed the perceived imprecisions of lenticular optics from within optics itself, stratigraphy introduced a method of visual analysis surpassing the optical laws that informed prior visual practices. In stratigraphy, as in *photo-stéréo-synthèse*, it is a superimposition of multiple exposures taken from a multiplicity of positions, and not the optical limitation of a focal field from a single vantage point, that isolates a single plane.

In the absence of a lens, movement across an infinite range of subject positions serves to isolate a single, static graphic strata. This does not imply that movement comes to occupy a central position historically (as for Bergson, Futurism); movement in tomography and *photo-stéréo-synthèse* is always the movement of seeingaround, a fixed relation of change or a mobile geometry at the service of the arbitrary and infinite abstraction of objects/space according to degrees of density. Movement simply facilitates the rise of differential analysis, the position of the viewing subject as well as the meaning of stratigraphy resting in the nonvisible space between two stratigraphic images, or between two vantage points within the apparatus. Similarly, pathology is no longer identified by way of surface symptom; it is now located in the differential between the multiple surfaces constituting the depth field of the body. The skin is no longer the body's privileged signifying surface. This factor has immediate consequences for a logic of appearances: the gaze directed toward the body's surface is no longer markedly significant. It is reduced to one factor in an equation directed toward the measurement of nonvisible space.

TOME 5: 1953

Five years after Louis Lumière's death, an entry in the March *Journal of Medical Education* announces Watson's development of a successful apparatus for three-dimensional radiographic motion pictures. Echoing one version of the procedure for seeingaround outlined by cummings three decades earlier, Watson's process of 3-D cinefluorography is based, like Vallebona's stratigraphy, on the principle of rotational movement on the part of the object imaged.

Cinefluorography must be distinguished from cineradiography. In the latter process, a succession of still X-ray exposures are joined together and projected as a motion picture. In cinefluorography, the image is registered first in real time on a fluoroscopic screen: this empirically visible moving image is then recorded with a standard cinematic camera. By the mid-1950s, cinefluorography had already proven itself useful in clinical imaging and analysis of bodily functions (the circulatory system, the digestive tract), and was commonly used in the hospital setting to screen incoming patients. Watson's use of cinefluorography is not unique; numerous radiologists during this period record the real-time fluoroscopic image on motion picture film for repeated viewing and analysis. Nor is his 3-D method unique.

Roques and Duhamel suggest that Watson's process is a critical move in the direction of a tomographic organization of space because it attempts to make

6 Bruwer, 1419–20.

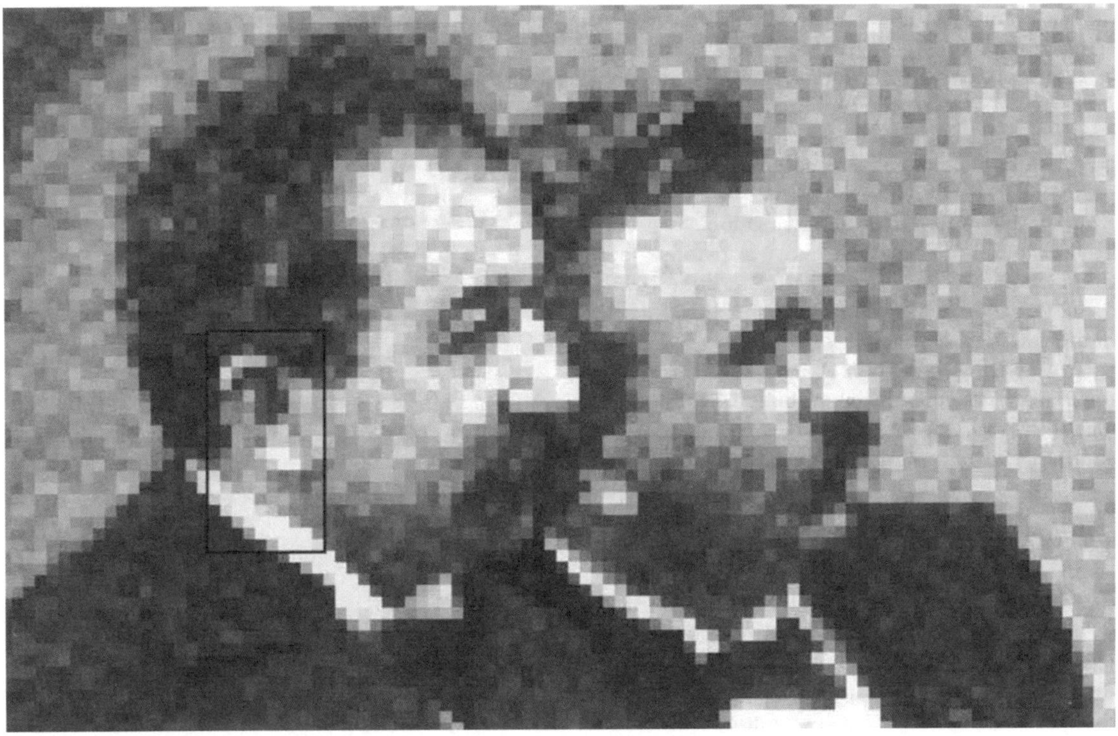

Figure 1. Auguste and Louis Lumiere imaged with average reflective values represented in each quadrant of an arbitrarily imposed grid.

measurable the interior volume of form. In 3-D cinefluorography, rapid viewing of sequential images allows for an illusion of dimensional space; however, examination of individual frames as separate entities provides no more information about dimensionality than a conventional X-ray image. The perception of 3-D cinefluorography is dependent on the reading of a differential between frames. The introduction of the cinematic lens to record the fluoroscopic image would suggest that Watson reincorporates the illusionistic space of perspective—the very optical system so effectively displaced by direct radiography and tomography.

The introduction of perspectival depth to the radiographic image makes it impossible to derive new quantitative data from the image field. Though visually compelling, the 3-D cinefluorographic moving image is no more valuable diagnostically than the standard radiograph. Ultimately, cummings's seeingaround must repudiate the lenticular optics on which it is based if it is to get beyond the visual barrier of skin and other intervening bodily masses. The introduction of lenticular optics to the radiographic image reintroduces the outmoded logic of perspectival space that radiography had done away with so effectively. Why this retrograde move? One explanation might be found in the appeal of the 3-D movie in the popular cinema during the mid-1950s. Watson's films appear during the same period that 3-D movies become a popular novelty in the entertainment cinema. However, they find their exact model in the 3-D cinefluoroscopic films produced in the 1930s by radiologists in Nazi Germany. Using these films as a model for his own studies, Watson carries Nazi medicine's logic of space over into postwar U.S. medical research.

Even as Watson works, medical imaging is undergoing another major transition. Electronic media introduces a new phase of imaging even more radically divorced than tomography from the sensory act of seeing and the phenomenal. The graphic codes of ultrasound and computed tomography undercut the empirical force of the short-lived 3-D cinefluoroscopic image.

TOME 6: 1964

Just as Watson gives up on X-ray cinematography, radiologist James Bricker makes a case for tomography as a process with a lively future by using the cinema as a point of comparison:

> In some regions of the country [tomography] is used little, and in some regions of the body it is used little, but like cine "moving pictures" it is here to stay![7]

Bricker recognizes the appeal of moving pictures in the cinema; though tomography involves movement

7 Bruwer, 1410.

of a different type, its pictures will also guarantee a certain appeal. However, by the late 1960s, the image as such will no longer be a part of the tomographic process. With the advent of computed tomography, object space will be described according to numerical registers of density, rather than according to the laws of perspectival space. The pictorial field will be reduced from a visual image to be seen to a graphic register to be mechanically decoded. The move from tomography to computed tomography (CT) signals a critical step in the historical repudiation of sight in the field of scientific knowledge.

Within this repudiation of sight, the visual retains its primacy nonetheless, functioning now as graphic register. Within a decade, the numerical data of the CT scan derived from the pictorial image will be able to be transformed back into a tonally rendered visual display. But this belated return to the image will not carry with it a return to the standards of lenticular optics. The post-1978 CT image will function as a salutary measure; it will satisfy a desire for visibility without lending credibility to the image as such. And yet, the desire to read the visual display as a picture will persist for a long time. It will be necessary for the radiological technician to militate against his or her own outmoded desire to view the tomographic image as a picture:

> As physicists, we cannot emphasize strongly enough that the basis of the CT is absorption measurement, and that the image is actually only a visual model. We can only hope that the medical profession does not forget . . . that we have renounced the qualitative assessment of image shadows for the display of quantitative absorption value.[8]

The modernist repudiation of lenticular optics begun around 1920 with tomographic and stereosynthetic space has been implemented fully in CT and related technologies (MRI, PET and ultrasound). These techniques all share a nonperspectival method of representing spatial dimensions. The organization of these images can be traced back to the planar geometry of *photo-stéréo-synthèse*, to tomography, and to the modernist idiom of seeingaround. In the seventy years since 1920, lenticular optics has been challenged persistently from within the diverse institutions in which it functioned most centrally. The technician's disassembling of lenticular optics constitutes a challenge to the empirical gaze and the sight-based epistemologies informing Western culture. The institutional and technological bases of this challenge deserve further examination not only from the standpoint of institutions of popular culture and media, but from the perspective of the demarcated professional spheres of scientific imaging. Incorporated across all of these spheres, the technology of Louis Lumière blurs institutional lines of demarcation even as it dismantles the very system of vision-based knowledge upon which it is grounded.

8 K. Ungerer, in A. Baert, L. Jeanmart, A. Wackenheim, eds., *Clinical Computer Tomography* (Basel: Springer, 1978), 2–11.

178	174	183	184	170	174	175	172	152	186
184	195	177	133	181	186	194	197	194	189
203	128	020	041	049	130	186	200	200	189
203	013	111	186	188	172	128	161	184	167
170	049	181	144	156	184	120	092	081	141
184	153	033	055	156	189	163	045	020	058
189	108	120	105	158	170	178	163	034	056
183	108	108	066	153	167	102	091	056	064
194	170	069	086	91	047	025	109	055	047
191	178	070	100	127	139	034	047	075	020
170	125	081	083	025	001	001	034	063	039
134	097	084	081	072	031	001	002	063	119
011	103	086	041	070	113	125	113	147	136
001	027	066	059	041	088	117	116	136	097
028	005	001	005	084	063	059	097	114	109
186	016	001	001	019	041	086	113	114	116
195	181	158	006	001	001	001	070	119	124
184	191	197	086	001	001	001	001	001	102
181	181	192	191	170	056	001	001	001	014

Figure 2. Numerical values in the illustration above represent the reflective properties of given quadrants within the recti- linear segment of the image on the facing page. In computed tomography, diagnostic images are generated from computed density values.

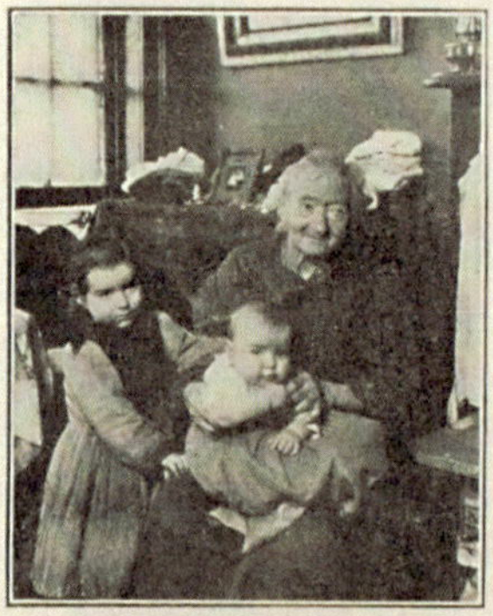

IN THE CARE OF THE A. I. C. P

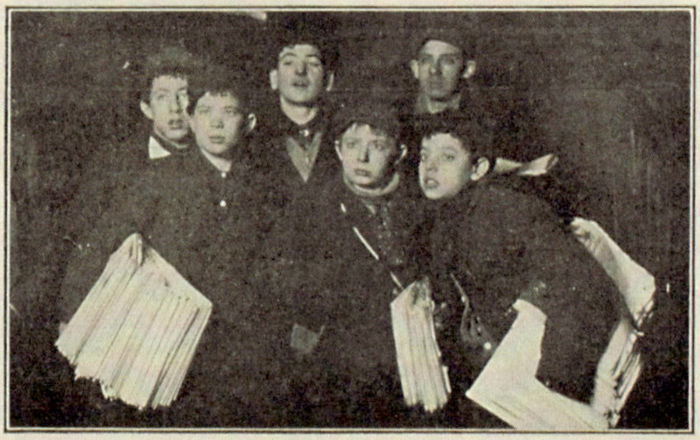

AT BROOKLYN BRIDGE, 3:00 A. M TAKEN FOR N. Y. CHILD LABOR COMMITTEE

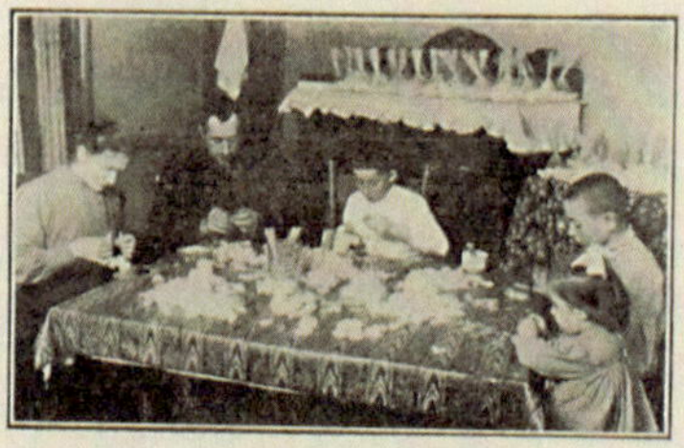

FLOWER MAKERS.

TAKEN FOR N. Y. CONSUMERS' LEAGUE.

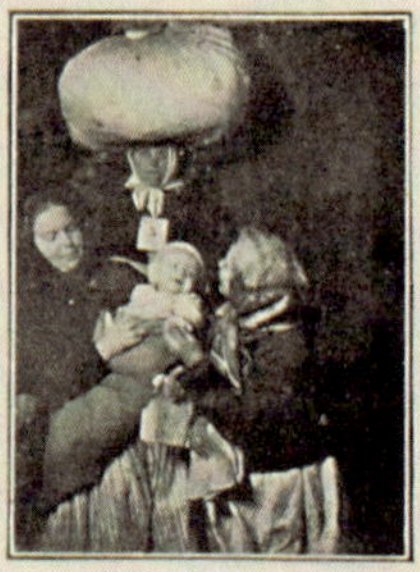

AT ELLIS ISLAND.

Vol. XX. No. 10 June 6, 1908

CHARITIES AND The Commons

A WEEKLY JOURNAL OF PHILANTHROPY AND SOCIAL ADVANCE

AT ELLIS ISLAND

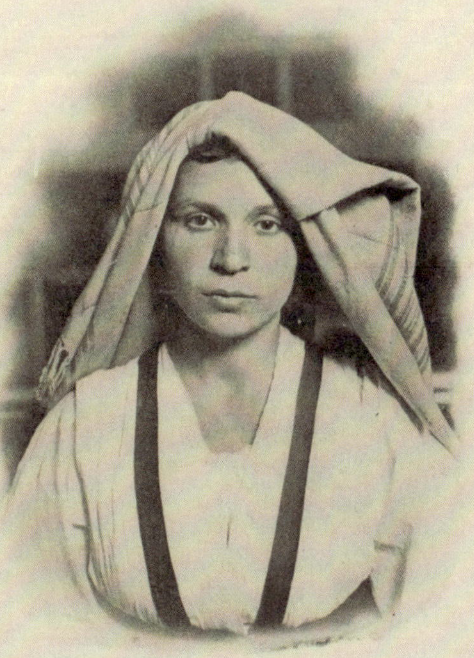

Photograph by Lewis W. Hine.

Charity Organization Society of the City of New York

Robert W. deForest, President; Otto T. Bannard, Vice-President; J. P. Morgan, Treasurer Edward T. Devine, General Secretary

105 East 22d Street
New York

ENTERED AT THE POST OFFICE
NEW YORK, N. Y., AS
SECOND-CLASS
MATTER

174 Adams Street
Chicago

This Issue Twenty-Five Cents

Two Dollars a Year

Top: ***The Survey*****, Vol. XXIV, No. 3, April 16, 1910**

Bottom: ***The Survey*****, Vol. XXX, No. 5, May 3, 1913**

Lewis Hine

Breeds of Domestic Animals, or The Way to Make a Farm Pay. It is to be hoped that he never will. But in every sermon and service, if he measures up at all to what he ought to do, he will interpret, he will idealize, he will inspire solutions of rural problems, he will exhibit the dignity and worth of agriculture, he will make the farmers understand the place which their toil occupies in the great movements of history, and in the purposes of God.

The aloofness of the church from social service, country and city, means ignorance. Out of ignorance inspiration can never come.

For the sake of our distinctive work, then, inspiration, we ought to know the facts, and feel the thrill and impulse and uplift of the great social movements which are organized outside of the church. Co-operation with existing secular agencies is essential to church efficiency.

Admitting that nothing is as important for the pulpit as the presentation of the ideal, it must know the ideal in order to present it. Admit that it ought to enunciate distinctly the principles of justice, it must know justice in order that the enunciation may be clear. The statement is frequently made by men of wide observation and real sympathy for religious movements, that the church and the ministry are behind the spirit of the age in their conception of morality. While the pulpit has been uttering the great truths of individual morality, there has grown up in human society something which is called social morality. It is not enough to say, "Thou shalt not steal." What the world wants from the churches is a new definition of stealing. It was not enough to proclaim, "Thou shalt not kill." What the times demand is an understanding of the fact stated by Jacob Riis when he said, "You can kill a man as well with a tenement as with a gun." In so far as I understand socialism I am not a socialist. But personally I need all the contact I can have with social movements, all the co-operation I can bring about with existing agencies for social service, all the fellowship which can come into my life with social leaders, socialists, single tax men and all other men, that I may appreciate what kind of a world it is in which I am living, and the marvellous growth of that new morality which is individual plus social.

I need to know that something is wrong when the burden of all accidents in industry falls on the shoulders of women and children. I need to know what causes of poverty are imbedded in the social system. Recognizing always that first I must change men in so far as I can touch them, and that then human conditions will be changed, I must recognize also that some human conditions must be changed before it is possible to reach men. There is no way in which a man can learn so well as by doing. There is no knowledge which is so real and serviceable as that which comes by contact with practical work. The church needs social service because it needs to know. In other words, we cannot possibly know the doctrine unless we do the will.

Nor is this matter of inspiration all on one side. Representing as he does secular agencies, it was very like Dr. Devine to say: "The one indispensable element which these secular agencies of social betterment cannot supply is inspiration. The one element which religion alone can supply is inspiration." The fact is there is no mightier storehouse of inspiration than the National Conference of Charities and Correction and nothing which better ministers to vision than the publication for which I pen this article. At times it seems as if it were like talking or walking with St. Vincent de Paul, to walk or talk with some of the humble followers of that great priest —Catholic, Protestant and Jewish—who are at work with the poor and the outcast and "going about everywhere to do good."

We need inspiration in the church that we may inspire. And we must get it, not only from the great God of the Book, or the prayer-hearing God of the closet, but from the burden-bearing God who, today as ever, is revealing himself through the prophets and apostles and martyrs of social service.

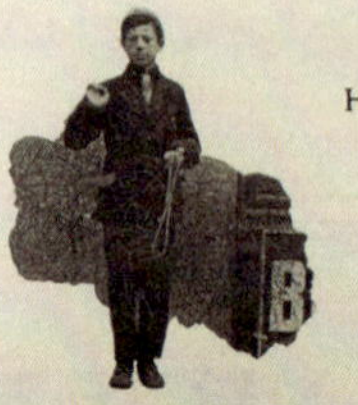

HOW GIRLS LEARN THE MILLINERY TRADE

MARY VAN KLEECK
ALICE P. BARROWS
OF THE COMMITTEE ON WOMEN'S WORK

PHOTOGRAPHS BY HINE

In discussions of industrial education for girls the question, Why, has been answered by articles showing on the one hand the fate of industrial drifters in unskilled occupations, and on the other the industries' need of efficient workers. The question, How, has received less attention. Yet the taxpayer, counting the cost of this new type of school work, and the educator, planning a program, need not so much agitation and exhortation, as a clearer understanding of industrial conditions in their relation to the methods and results of school work. A description of the training of girls in one trade in New York may therefore be of some service in raising questions as to aim and method and in showing how diverse are the factors which must be reckoned with in planning industrial education for girls.

The millinery trade is an exceptionally good example of the complexity of the task of training women workers.[1] It is primarily a woman's trade. Of all milliners, ninety-eight per cent are women. About 8,000 women work in millinery shops in New York. In no other occupation except the large group of garment trades are so many women employed. It seems an attractive trade because of the scope it offers for taste and skill. Yet diversity in trade demands, rapid changes in style, process, and workroom organization, the lack of standard in wages, the long periods of unemployment, the disorganized labor market, the long working day, are conditions which raise many questions as to the training of women workers.

Millinery shops as they appear to the woman who wishes to buy a hat, and as they appear to girls "looking for a job" are two very different things. To the girls they mean establishments of all kinds, in all parts of the city, with all kinds of work and standards of work. At some time in their search for work, these girls find themselves in some or all of the various types of shops. At some time they form part of the crowds that hurry out at night from the great ten-story buildings on Broadway with huge, gilt signs which read, "Trimmed Hats," "Untrimmed Hats," "Ready-to-Wear Hats." They come from the small "select" shops on Fifth avenue which ex-

[1]How girls learn the millinery trade was a subject included in an investigation of women's work in millinery shops in New York, the results of which are embodied in a report not yet published. The inquiry was carried on as part of the program of an investigation department of the Alliance Employment Bureau, from the autumn of 1907 to the summer of 1909. Two hundred millinery girls were interviewed at home or in the office of the bureau and questioned about wages, hours, their trade history, regularity of employment, and the training they had had for this work. Their names were secured from girls' clubs, trade classes, employment bureaus, and fellow workers. More than two hundred shops, including all in which the two hundred workers had been employed since July, 1907, were visited and questions asked about training of learners, wages, hours, seasons, demand and opportunities for experts, and the employer's opinion of trade school training.

The report then points out that a considerable number of men during the past year have left the employ of the Steel Corporation because they have enforced the six day week, and have gone to the employ of other companies where they could work seven days, and expresses the fear that the same thing would happen if an eight-hour day were adopted by the corporation.

Of course, nothing is said in this report, nor was anything said at the stockholders' meeting of April 21, as to the real reason why workers leave their positions when hours of labor are shortened. The inference to be drawn from the report is that steel workers are so consumed with a passion for work that they do not desire to leave it, even for one day in seven.

The facts are that the cost of this reform was borne by the men. The Steel Corporation did not pay its men their old earnings for their new six day stint. It would be interesting to know the actual wages received by the larger proportion of those who left the employ of the Corporation in order that they might work seven days a week for other companies. We should then be able to draw our own conclusions as to whether it was a passion for work or a desire to support their families in decency and comfort that led them to look elsewhere for work when their earnings were reduced by one-seventh.

But the Steel Corporation found itself, according to its own testimony, in a quandary. A committee of its own stockholders had recommended an abolition of the twelve-hour day. The finance committee had considered the matter carefully and reported back that because its competitors had not changed from the twelve-hour day, they could not. It was a practical difficulty and they intimated that they were unable to solve it. It was to cut this Gordian knot that Charles M. Cabot, the Boston stockholder who was responsible for the investigation conducted last year by the stockholders' committee headed by Stuyvesant Fish, went to the meeting on April 21 with this resolution:

> "Voted, that in view of the Finance Committee's report that the change from the twelve to the eight-hour day in continuance twenty-four hour processes in our mills and plants is impracticable unless similar action is taken by our competitors; and, further, in view of the fruitful results which followed the appointment by the American Iron and Steel Institute at the instigation of officers of our Corporation of a committee on seven-day labor, which action has led to the very general establishment of the six-day week in the steel industry of the United States; that the stockholders request the directors to enlist the co-operation of the steel manufacturers of the United States in establishing the eight-hour day in continuous twenty-four hour processes."

The purpose of this resolution was to provide the quickest, most efficient manner of solving the dilemma in which the Corporation found itself, and to provide a way whereby there could be restored to the workers such a working schedule, as would not sap their vitality or prevent them from having what the stockholders' committee thought was necessary time for relaxation and for association with their families. That this resolution was tabled with the consent of the officials of the Corporation, will undoubtedly be interpreted by many as an indication that the Corporation was not sincere in its plea that its hands were tied in trying to meet the demand of the Fish committee for a reduction in hours.

Yet Mr. Cabot performed in offering this resolution possibly his greatest service since he began his campaign to improve the labor conditions in the steel industry even though it was an achievement that he did not have in mind. He forced the Corporation to show its hand; he gave it an opportunity to prove whether or not it really desired, as it was on record as desiring, a fundamental reform. The Corporation gave him an unmistakable answer.

It would have been better if they had not forgotten the wise counsel of William B. Dickson, their former vice-president, when he said, in a speech advocating one day of rest in seven, that if the steel companies themselves did not institute this reform, they would be compelled by law to institute it, and that the law would be far more drastic than the manufacturers of steel would find comfortable.

BEDFORD REFORMATORY

W. J. LAMPTON in the *New York Times*

[Bedford Reformatory, a State institution doing invaluable service in the reclamation of wayward girls, is over-crowded and asks $700,000 from the state for extension purposes.]

Behold, she stands
And stretches out her hands
For aid.
Those firm, strong hands,
Those gentle, helpful hands,
Whose spirit unafraid
Of sin and shame and loss
Have borne the burden of the cross
For girls unnamable, whose feet
Have trod the open street,
The market place
Of body and of soul,
In search of toll

From any man who gave
To own a common slave,
The chattel of the street.
These Bedford comes to meet,
But not as shameless things;
To them she brings
Love, courage, hope, the better way,
The clean, new day
Whose morning sun awakes
Another world to these half gone
And hopeless ones
To whom there was no other dawn.
And now she stands

With outstretched hands
For aid; the means to lift
Out of the ghastly drift
These girl-souls crying in the night
For kindly light.
And shall she be denied?
Shall men who buy
Deny?
Shall any man, in whom his pride
In his own womankind is strong,
Go wrong
And say
To Bedford: "Nay"?

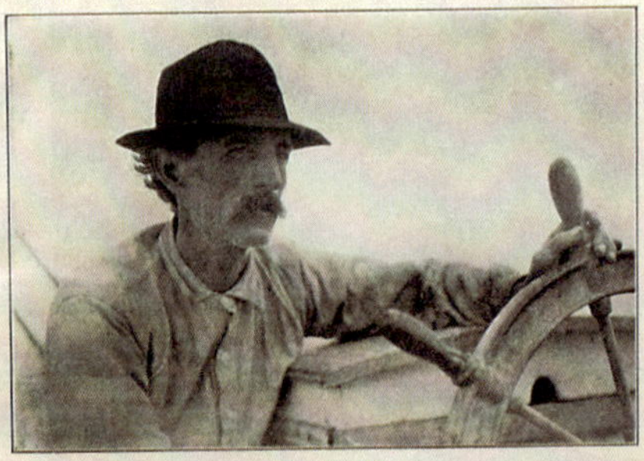

THE OYSTERMAN

BALTIMORE TO BILOXI AND BACK

THE CHILD'S BURDEN IN OYSTER AND SHRIMP CANNERIES

Investigation and Photographs by
LEWIS W. HINE
FOR THE NATIONAL CHILD LABOR COMMITTEE

[Mr. Hine's photographs and the equally vivid impressions he sets down in the text, tell a story of child labor along the South Atlantic and the Gulf. In an especial sense these are conditions which public opinion can bring to the door of the Democratic Party to remedy. For in these states that party is dominant, as it is in the nation.

First lies the channel of state action, which has thus far been laggard, and has been obstructed by the child employing interests of the South. At the present time, a child labor bill which would reach this shore work, is pending in Florida. In Mississippi shucking is prohibited but there is no enforcing agency and the work is going on as before.

If the channel of state action fails, child labor reformers point to such national legislation as would prohibit interstate commerce in canned oysters and shrimps which are so humanly costly. The recent decision of the United States Supreme Court in the white slave case would seem to indicate that legislation could be drafted which would hold in the courts, and several bills along the lines of the much controverted Beveridge bill of 1907 are now before Congress.

It is for the Democratic Party in state and nation to proceed through one channel or the other.—Ed.]

WHEN we speak of child labor in oyster canning, we refer to the cooked or "cove" oysters, not to the raw ones. Children are not used in opening raw oysters for the sole reason that their fingers are not strong enough. Occasionally one finds young boys at work on the boats dredging for the oysters, but not many children work on the boats, for that is a man's job.

The two chief sections engaged in the work

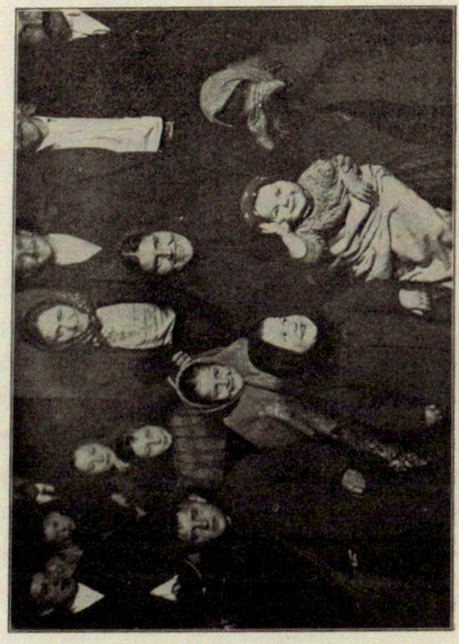

The Germans

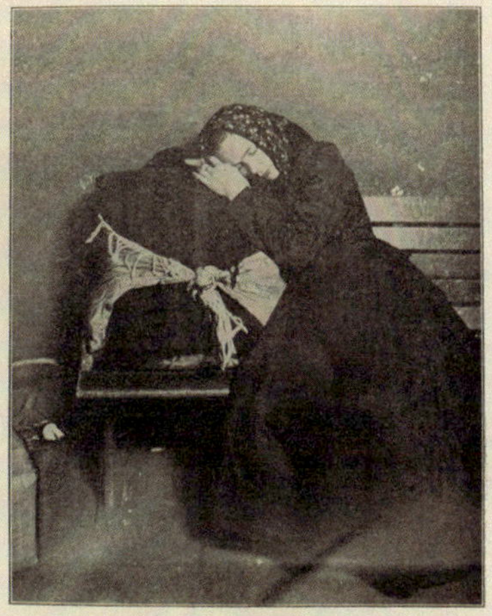

From Bohemia

nized from the outset, and each contractor was requested to select the man he desired to run his particular car. The result has been excellent, good men thoroughly familiar with their respective machines, having thus been secured with the co-operation of the manufacturers.

Before the ambulances were put into service the fear was expressed that they would subject the patients to an excessive amount of jolting. This has not proved to be the case, however, but to the contrary, it has been found that there is much less jolting than arises through the use of the ordinary horse ambulance. It has also been shown that one of the machines is easily able to do as much work as two of the horse transfer ambulances, and, unlike the horses, the automobile ambulances do not give out on account of the hot weather. Formerly, when only the horse transfer ambulances were used at this hospital, the work of transfer was almost always behind, but with the use of the machines it is kept well up to date. Besides this, patients transferred long distances instead of feeling worse for the journey, are in many cases found to be feeling much better owing, doubtless, to the fresh air and the absence of discomfort.

Since these new ambulances at the Kings County Hospital have been found so effective, satisfactory and useful in the work of the hospital, the Board of Trustees of Bellevue and Allied Hospitals, has voted to request permission to add two automobile ambulances to its equipment.

It may confidently be asserted that the power ambulance because of its marked efficiency and comfort has come to stay, and that the day is not far distant when the machine will supplant the horse ambulance not only for transfer service but for emergency work as well. A very important consideration is the fact that the use of the automobile ambulance in place of the horse ambulance improves the sanitary condition of the hospital, by doing away to a great extent with the nuisance of the stable, including the pest of flies ordinarily to be found there.

Utilized Social Forces

Among the plain people election day and primary day and the campaigning days in between are occasions for a neighborly comradeship such as is never realized at any other time. Men who have had little to do with each other find something in common to talk about and to do. The good fellowship easily crosses the lines of party division in the good natured rivalry which far more constantly characterizes the scenes about the precinct polling places, than any indications of ill temper or strife. Above all the divisiveness and partisanship, and above all the sordidness and shame of corrupt politics, men do rise together when exercising the rights and duties of a common citizen. Those who think little or nothing intelligently of the public interests at stake, do scan the tickets to see if they can vote for a friend. Many are greatly perplexed to know which of two friends they shall vote for, when they have to choose between them. This personal friendship, in very many, transcends all claims of party loyalty or public duty. But it is at least a personal preference, a personal choice. It shows that the voters can and will respond to some other worthier appeal than that of party domination or blind allegiance to it. If the human touch of social fellowship could be added to our efforts to arouse public spirit and to train voters for intelligent citizenship, it would supply the force now lacking in all our movements for better political organization and result. It is the continuousness of this human touch and social fellowship among its constituency that has in no small part given Tammany Hall its power with the people. Until those who are striving together for the common good have the will and find the way to identify themselves with each other in a social fellowship that will span the time between elections and associate each successive campaign with the other, the upward movement in our civic life will have to contend with an inertia, if not an opposition, that will array odds against it, as insurmountable as they are unnecessary.

As They Come to Ellis Island

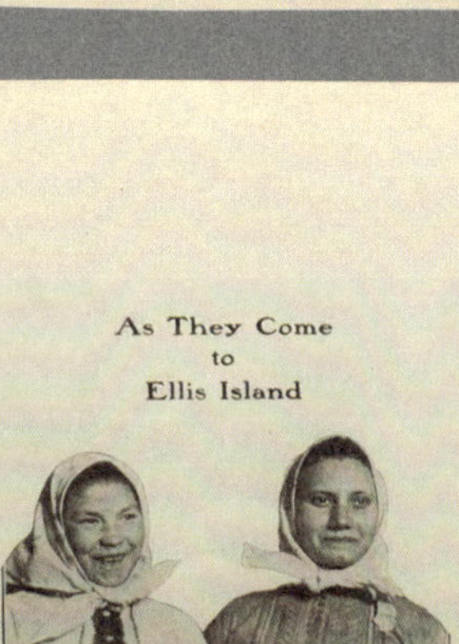

The Slavs

Photographs by Lewis W. Hine

The Homestead Plant: Carnegie Steel Company in *Homestead: The Households of a Mill Town*, Vol. 4
Lewis Hine
1910

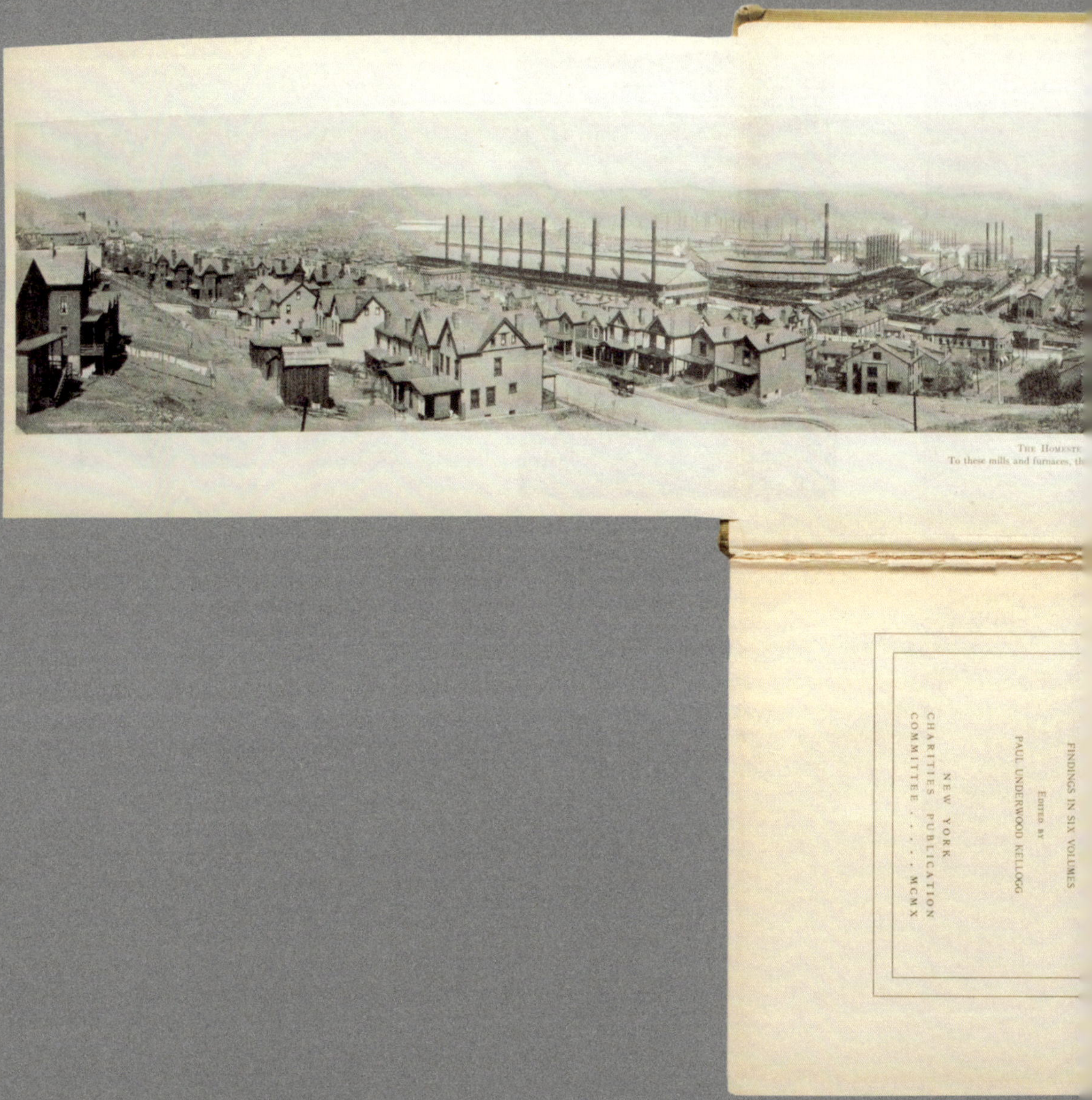

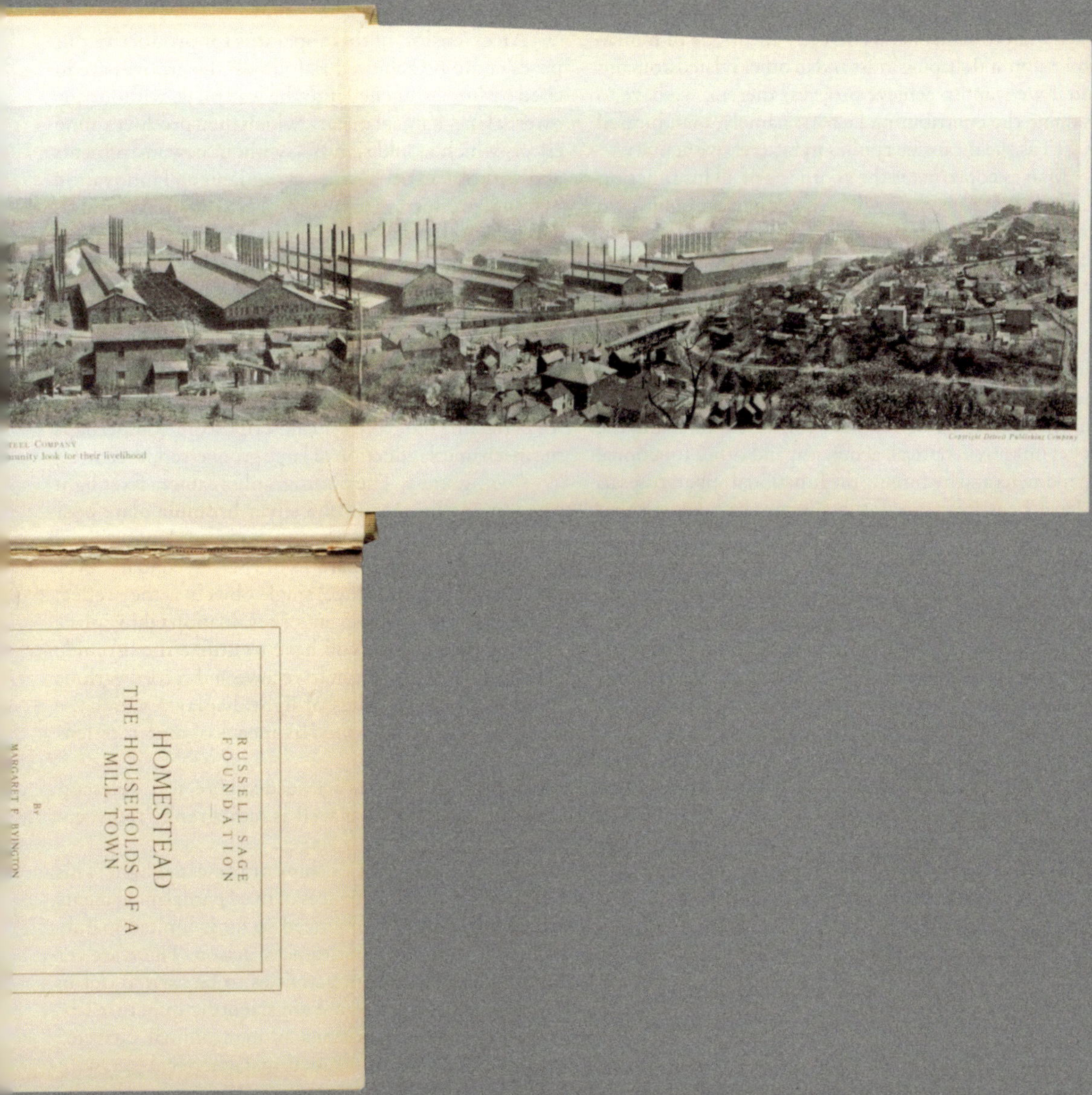
TEEL COMPANY
munity look for their livelihood
Copyright Detroit Publishing Company
RUSSELL SAGE FOUNDATION
HOMESTEAD
THE HOUSEHOLDS OF A MILL TOWN
BY
MARGARET F. BYINGTON

Production—Reproduction
László Moholy-Nagy
1922

If we want to understand correctly the mode of human expression and shaping in art and in other related domains, and if we want to achieve progress therein, we have to examine the contributing factors: namely, man himself as well as the means he applies in his creative activity.

Man as construct is the synthesis of all his functional apparatuses, i.e. man will be most perfect in his own time if the functional apparatuses of which he is composed—his cells as well as the most sophisticated organs—are conscious and trained to the limit of their capacity.

Art actually performs such a training—and this is one of its most important tasks, since the whole complex of effects depends on the degree of perfection of the receptive organs—by trying to bring about the most far-reaching *new* contacts between the familiar and the as yet unknown optical, acoustical and other functional phenomena and by forcing the functional apparatuses to receive them. It is a specifically human characteristic that man's functional apparatuses can never be saturated; they crave ever new impressions following each new reception. This accounts for the permanent necessity for new experiments. *From this perspective, creative activities are useful only if they produce new, so far unknown relations.* In other words, in specific regard to creation, reproduction (reiteration of already existing relations) can be regarded for the most part as mere virtuosity.

Since it is primarily production (productive creation) that serves human construction, we must strive to turn the apparatuses (instruments) used so far only for reproductive purposes into ones that can be used for productive purposes as well. This calls for profound examination of the following questions:

What is this apparatus (instrument) good for?

What is the essence of its function?

Are we able, and if so to what end, to extend the apparatus's use so that it can serve production as well? Let us apply these questions to some examples: the phonograph and photography—single pictures (stills) and film.

Phonograph. So far it has been the job of the phonograph to reproduce already existing acoustic phenomena. The tonal oscillations to be reproduced were incised on a wax plate by means of a needle and then retranslated into sound by means of a microphone (correctly: diaphragm, moving cone).

An extension of this apparatus for productive purposes could be achieved as follows: the grooves are incised by human agency into the wax plate, without any external mechanical means, which then product sound effects which would signify—without new instruments and without an orchestra—a fundamental innovation in sound production (of new, hitherto unknown sounds and tonal relations) both in composition and in musical performance.

The primary condition for such work is laboratory experiments: precise examination of the kinds of grooves (as regards length, width, depth, etc.) brought about by the different sounds; examination of the man-made grooves; and finally mechanical-technical experiments for perfecting the groove-manuscript score. (Or perhaps the mechanical reduction of large groove-script records.)

Photography. The photographic camera fixes light phenomena by means of a silver bromide plate positioned at the rear of the camera. So far we have utilized this function of the apparatus only at a secondary level: in order to fix (reproduce) single objects as they reflect or absorb light. In the event of revaluation taking place in this field, too, we will have to utilize the bromide plate's sensitivity to light to receive and record various light phenomena (parts of light displays) which *we ourselves* will have *formed* by means of mirror or lens devices.

Many experiments are needed here, too. Telescopic recordings of stars as well as radiography represent interesting preliminary stages.

Film. Kinetic relationships of projected light. This can be achieved by sequences of fixed partial movements. Cinematography as practiced so far is limited mainly to the reproduction of dramatic action. There are certainly many important activities to be carried out in the domain of film. Some are scientific in nature (dynamism of various motions: of man, animal, city etc.; different observations: functional, chemical etc.; wireless projection of film news etc.); some involve the completion of reproduction itself from a constructive standpoint. But the main task is the formation of *motion as such*; naturally, this cannot be realized without a man-made play of forms as motion carrier.

Naive experiments relative to such development were the trick-films (advertisements). Much more highly developed are the works of Ruttman and the Clavilux* of Th. Wilfred; these, however, presented motion as an objectless dramatic action (abstraction or styling of erotic or natural events), albeit by trying to introduce the color picture.

So far the most perfect works are those of Eggeling and Richter, in which instead of dramatic action there is already a play of forms, although to the detriment of kinetic formation. In fact, movement is not given formal purity, for over-emphasis upon the forms' development absorbs almost all the kinetic forces. The way ahead here will be the formation of motion without the support of any direct formal development.

*The name indicates a kind of color organ, although we are concerned with light projection on the plane and not in space.

War Against War!
Ernst Friedrich
1924

TO HUMAN BEINGS IN ALL LANDS!

I, who am falsely called "German" instead of just simply "man". I call out to the icy regions of the North, I call out to Africa and to America, to Asia and to Europe.

To all regions that have ears to hear I call out but two words and these are

Man and Love

And even as the Australian weeps when he encounters pain, and laughs and makes merry when joy and happiness are granted him, even so dost thou weep, my brother Eskimo, and so, O African and O Chinese, weepest thou too and so weep I.

And as we all, all human beings, equally feel joy and pain, let us fight unitedly against the common monstrous enemy, War.

We shall unite in protesting against, in weeping over the accursed mass murders for which we all bear equal guilt. But let us also raise our eyes cheerfully to the red dawn of freedom and peace.

To the Fatherland of all Fatherlands, to the Fatherland of human beings *which stands above all!*

In many books have many words been written for and against this most diabolical, this meanest and lowest of all crimes of the State,

The bourgeois poet in his strength glorified this War in verse
and the proletarian writer wrote in glowing wrath *against* this mass murder.

But all the treasury of words of all men of all lands suffices not, in the present and in the future, to paint correctly this butchery of human beings.

Here, however, in the present book,—partly by accident, partly intentionally—a picture of War, objectively true and faithful to nature, has been photographically recorded for all time.

The pictures in this book from page 53 to the end, show records obtained by the inexorable, incorruptible photographic lens,
of the trenches and the mass graves,
of "military lies", of the "field of honour",
and of other "idylls" of the "Great Epoch".

And not one single man of any country whatsoever can arise and bear witness against these photographs, that they are untrue and that they do not correspond to realities.

And no one comes and says:
"O how frightful that such pictures should be shown!"

But he says rather: "At last, at last the mask has been torn away from this "field of honour", from this lie of an "heroic death", and from all the other beautiful phrases, from all this international swindle the mask has at last, yea, at last, been torn away!!"

This book is dedicated to all war profiteers and parasites, to all war provokers,
and is consecrated also to the "kings", generals, ministers and presidents *of all* lands.

To priests, however, who blessed the weapons in the name of God, this book is dedicated as a War bible!

Show these pictures to all men who still can think!

He who then *still* believes in this mass butchery, let him be locked up in a mad-house, let us avoid him as we do the plague!

It may then be that the nationalists and war-provokers, the kings and the generals, may wish to carry on war *among themselves*,
on their own account and at their own risk, and that they force no man to join them against his will!

Such a war would indeed be welcomed by every pacifist and every proletarian!

Then all the war enthusiasts would at last of their own free will exterminate one another, and then we should have peace, eternal peace on this earth!

But unfortunately these heroes are not to be had for such a "war of liberation" (liberation from the war promoters and profiteers).

They lack the courage, these war-thinkers and warleaders, to go *themselves* into the battle, and *themselves* to die a sweet "heroic death".

That is why they invented such beautiful phrases as "Fatherland" and "Field of Honour" and spoke of "defence" and uttered other lies.

And he who did not permit himself to he enthused to death by military music and by lying legends of the "enemy" of "'the invaded",
him they forced against his will into the murderer's uniform, him they ordered to murder and to rob for the interests of the money-bags.

I know of one practical way of preventing war for all time to come.

Many, many years ago the doctor, it is said, was fully responsible with his own life and property for the life of his patients.

If the patient died at the hands of his doctor, the latter died too.

Such was the law.

And so let there be also a *law for kings, presidents, generals and, last but not least, newspaper writers*:

> Whoever forces men into war or provokes them to mass murders, shall be responsible with all his property and possessions and with *his own* life for the safety and the sufferings of the soldiers.
> The king who rallies people to his standard shall *himself* bear the standard.
> And if a soldier should be reduced to beggary, the king shall go out begging with him.
> If huts are burnt down in wars, so also shall palaces and castles be set in flames.
> And always, for each human life that is sacrificed at the front, shall one king or one minister rest in peace on the "field of honour" for the Fatherland. And ten newspaper writers that agitate for war, shall
> be detained as hostages for the life of *each single* warrior!

Such a law, however, will never come into being, and no "disarmament" or "peace" conference will give heed to my proposal.

Therefore let us, who are fighters, join in the war against war, let us examine the causes and the nature of war, so that, armed with the weapon of knowledge and the sharp sword of the mind, we may emerge victorious from the fight.

THE CAUSE OF WAR

Long ago, Plato who was born 427 years before the Nazarene, Plato, that wise man, said:

"All wars arise for the possession of wealth."

That is as true a word as ever was spoken.
For to the present day in all wars the object is to protect or to seize money and property and power; *and there will always be wars so long as Capital rules and oppresses the people.*

When international capital finds itself threatened by mutual competition, and when the furnace-barons and factory owners begin to have differences among themselves, then they rattle their sabres and spurs and they call out:

"The *Country* is in danger!" (They mean by "country" always the money-bags!)

And wonderfully enough the working slaves of all lands abandon their plough and their anvil,
they hasten to arms,
and protect the life and properly of their masters with their own blood and life.

What did I say? "That this is strange?" No, it is quite natural—a natural monstrosity! For it is not the state power and force alone that compels all "subjects" to protect the throne and the money-bags, and to die for them. Capital has not only economic power in its hands, it has, equal measure and with equal power, subjected the proletariat also intellectually.

This fact is easily overlooked
and there still remains, therefore, so much bourgeois ideology in the proletariat!

I, therefore, always say to my brothers, the proletarians, I say to the class-war fighters:

> Free yourselves from bourgeois prejudices!
> Fight against capitalism within yourselves!
> In your thoughts and in your actions there still lurks unspeakably much of the philistine and the soldier,
> and almost in every one there is hidden a drilled subaltern, who wishes only to dominate and command, even if it be over his own comrades and over his wife and children in his family!

But I also say to those bourgeois pacifists, who seek to fight against war by mere hand caresses and tea-cakes and piously up-turned eyes:

> Fight against Capitalism—and you fight against every war!
> The battle-field in the factories and the mines,
> the hero's death in the infirmaries, the mass graves in the barracks,
> in short, the war, the apparently eternal war, of the exploited against the exploiters!

DO—YOU NOT—REALISE—ALL—THIS?

The war against war signifies:
The war of the victimised against the profiteers!
The war of the deceived against the deceivers!
The war of the oppressed against the oppressors!
The war of the tortured against the torturers!
The war of the hungry against the well fed!

THE PREVENTION OF WAR

It is true that capital is the cause of every war.
But the guilt of war rests on our shoulders.
It is we proletarians that make the conduct of war possible, it is for us likewise to prevent wars!
Refuse to serve!
Bring up your children so that they may later refuse to render military and war service!

How very many lightly overlook the fact that in one's own home in the family, war is being spontaneously prepared!

And here lies the beginning of all evils, here lies the beginning also of war!

The mother that sings soldiers'-songs to the baby on her lap, prepares for war, yes, she prepares for war!

The father that makes gifts of toy soldiers to his child mobilises the child for the war idea!

The toy soldier is the Judas that you yourself bring into the home, is the betrayal of human life! Remember always this one thing:

The little helmet made of paper will one day be a steel helmet on the head of a murderer!
And if the child has once practised with his air-gun, how natural it is that he should in later years shoot with a rifle!
The little sabre carved of wood
will some day become the battle-sword that pierces the body of a human being!

Ye parents that do not wish that your sons should murder the dear sons of other parents, you should remember that the child whom you present with a helmet and sabre and gun, plays his tender soul to death out of his young body.

Those children, however, who are educated in love and solidarity, and are brought up to respect unconditionally the inviolable sanctity of human life, these children will most certainly be unfit for arms and war-service.

We, opponents of military service must finally destroy the halo and the humbug, and tear down the gaudy tinsel of the soldiery, and we must speak out what then still remains to be said:

a professional murderer paid by the state,
who is trained in murder-schools (called barracks)
privileged by the state,
in the carrying out of the most gruesome of crimes,
the murder of human beings!
That is what the children should be told!

Then indeed will the young girl, destined by nature to reproduce and protect life, be disgusted to flirt with the soldiers—her natural enemies—"the pimps of death".

And the boy will later refuse to wear the uniform because he knows: It is a murderer's cloak!

It is with such clearness and precision that you must think and also act,
if you wish to nip the evil in the bud!
And should war nevertheless break out,
then proceed consistently and unhesitatingly to

THE WAR AGAINST WAR!

Let the general strike be the first weapon!
The men will refuse service!
True heroism lies not in murder, but in the refusal to commit murder.
Rather fill all prisons and workhouses
and all the mad-houses of all lands,
than murder and die in the service of Capital!

The last and most dreadful war has not yet broken out which cast gas and poison and flames on human beings and animals and houses.

It lies in our hands, in our power, to prevent, to hinder, this most dreadful tragedy.

Let the great, inspiring example of consistent conscientious objectors be our model.

They suffered death for their consistent "No!" rather than themselves become murderers!

I WILL NOT!

Stronger than all violence, than the sabre and the rifle, is our spirit, is our will!
Repeat these three words: "I will not!"
Give content to these words and all wars in future will be impossible.
What then will all Capital of the whole world,
what will all the kings and presidents do,
when the entire people in all lands arise with the cry:

WE WILL NOT!

AND YOU WOMEN!

If your husbands should be too weak, then carry out the work yourselves!!
Prove that the bond of love with the husband is stronger than an army order!
Do not let your men go to the front!
Do not decorate their rifles with flowers!
Cling to the necks of your husbands!
Do not let them go even when the order to depart calls! Tear up all the rails, throw yourselves before the locomotives!

WOMEN! REALISE THIS
IF YOUR HUSBANDS SHOULD BE
TOO WEAK!

MOTHERS OF ALL LANDS UNITE!

ERNST FRIEDRICH
End of July, 1924

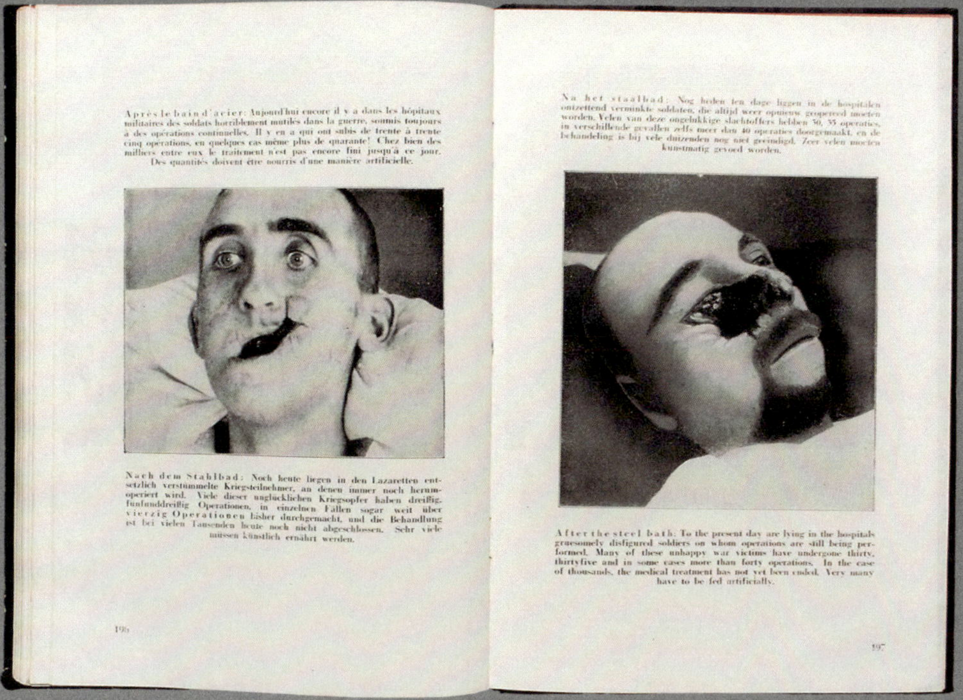
Après le bain d'acier: Aujourd'hui encore il y a dans les hôpitaux militaires des soldats horriblement mutilés dans la guerre, soumis toujours à des opérations continuelles. Il y en a qui ont subis de trente à trente cinq opérations, en quelques cas même plus de quarante! Chez bien des milliers entre eux le traitement n'est pas encore fini jusqu'à ce jour. Des quantités doivent être nourris d'une manière artificielle.

Nach dem Stahlbad: Noch heute liegen in den Lazaretten entsetzlich verstümmelte Kriegsteilnehmer, an denen immer noch herumoperiert wird. Viele dieser unglücklichen Kriegsopfer haben dreißig, fünfunddreißig Operationen, in einzelnen Fällen sogar weit über vierzig Operationen bisher durchgemacht, und die Behandlung ist bei vielen Tausenden heute noch nicht abgeschlossen. Sehr viele müssen künstlich ernährt werden.

196

Na het staalbad: Nog heden ten dage liggen in de hospitalen ontzettend verminkte soldaten, die altijd weer opnieuw geopereerd moeten worden. Velen van deze ongelukkige slachtoffers hebben 30, 35 operaties, in verschillende gevallen zelfs meer dan 40 operaties doorgemaakt, en de behandeling is bij vele duizenden nog niet geëindigd. Zeer velen moeten kunstmatig gevoed worden.

After the steel bath: To the present day are lying in the hospitals gruesomely disfigured soldiers on whom operations are still being performed. Many of these unhappy war victims have undergone thirty, thirtyfive and in some cases more than forty operations. In the case of thousands, the medical treatment has not yet been ended. Very many have to be fed artificially.

197

After the steel bath: To the present day are lying in the hospitals gruesomely disfigured soldiers on whom operations are still being performed. Many of these unhappy war victims have undergone thirty, thirty-five and in some cases more than forty operations. In the case of thousands, the medical treatment has not yet been ended. Very many have to be fed artificially.

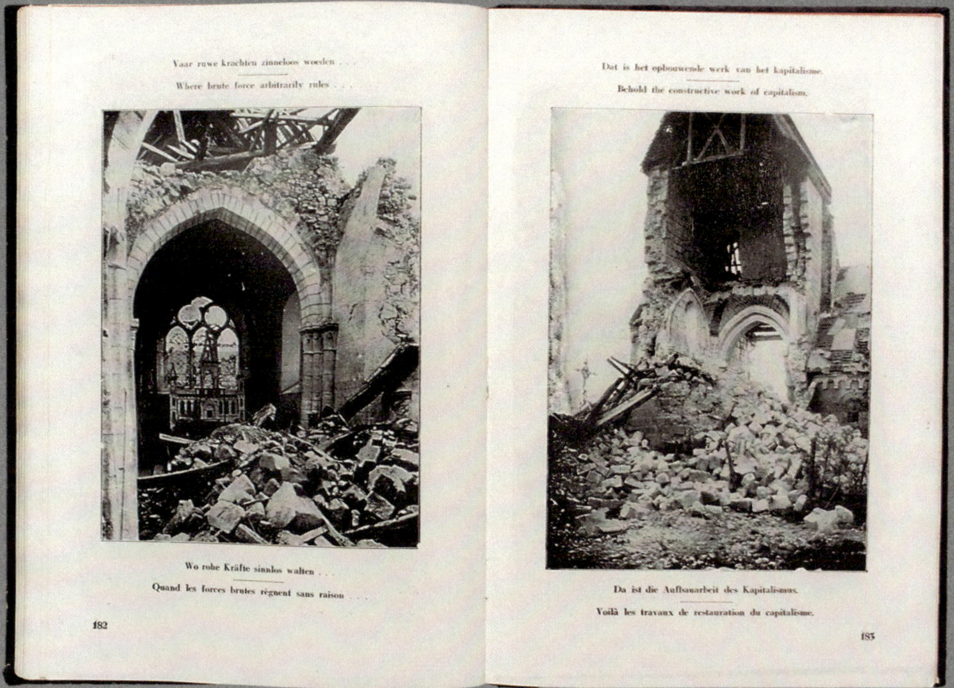
Vaar ruwe krachten zinneloos woeden . . .

Where brute force arbitrarily rules . . .

Wo rohe Kräfte sinnlos walten . . .

Quand les forces brutes règnent sans raison . . .

182

Dat is het opbouwende werk van het kapitalisme.

Behold the constructive work of capitalism.

Da ist die Aufbauarbeit des Kapitalismus.

Voilà les travaux de restauration du capitalisme.

183

Where brute force arbitrarily rules...

Behold the constructive work of capitalism.

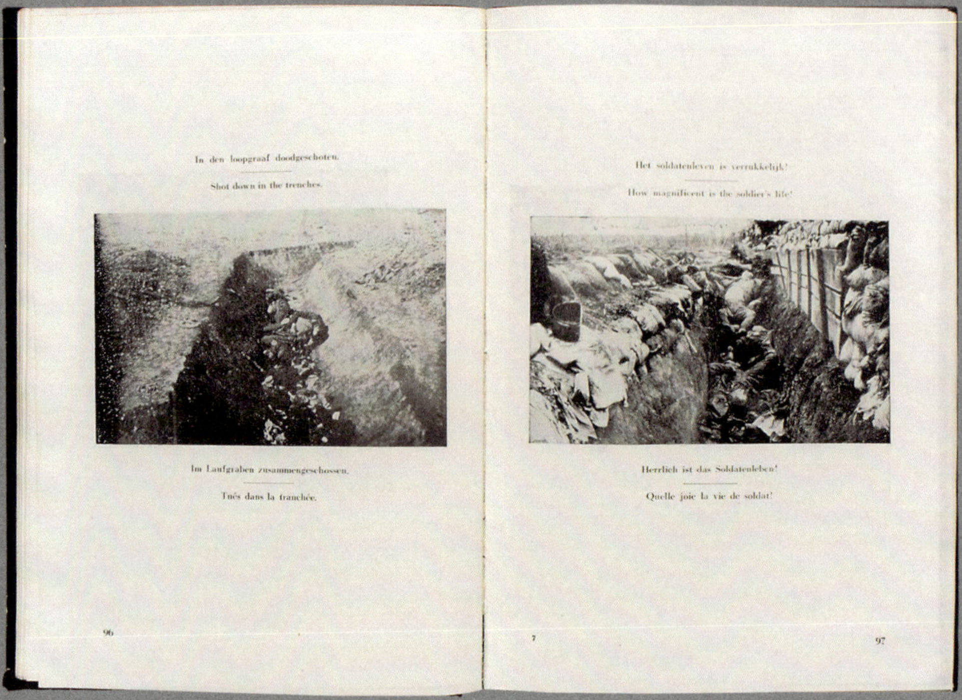

Shot down in the trenches.

How magnificent is the soldier's life!

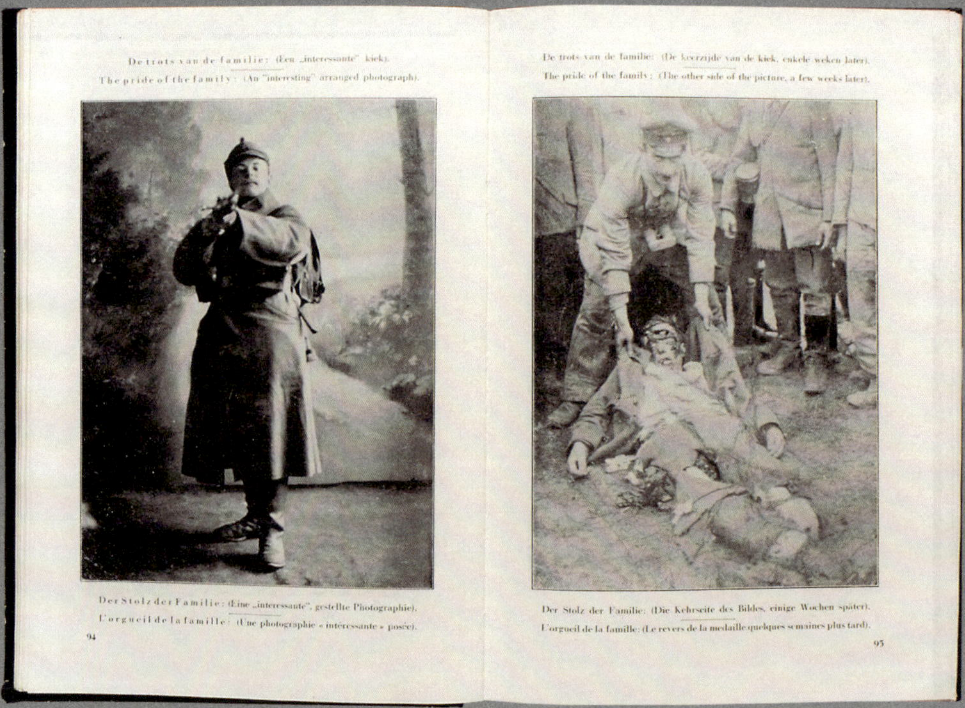

The pride of the family: (An "interesting" arranged photograph).

The pride of the family: (The other side of the picture, a few weeks later).

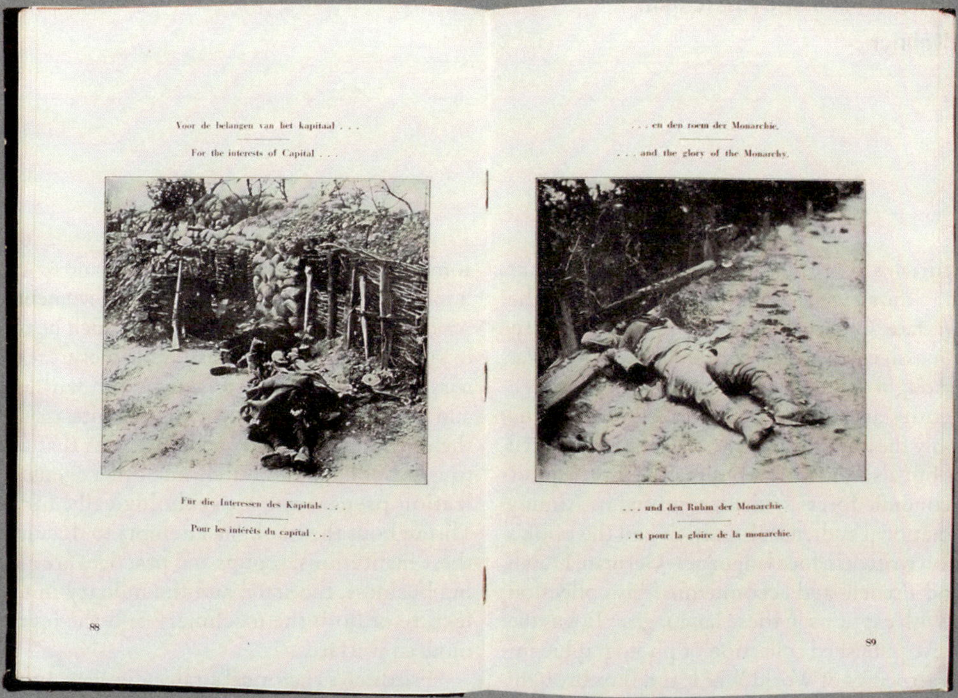

For the interests of Capital... ...and the glory of the Monarchy.

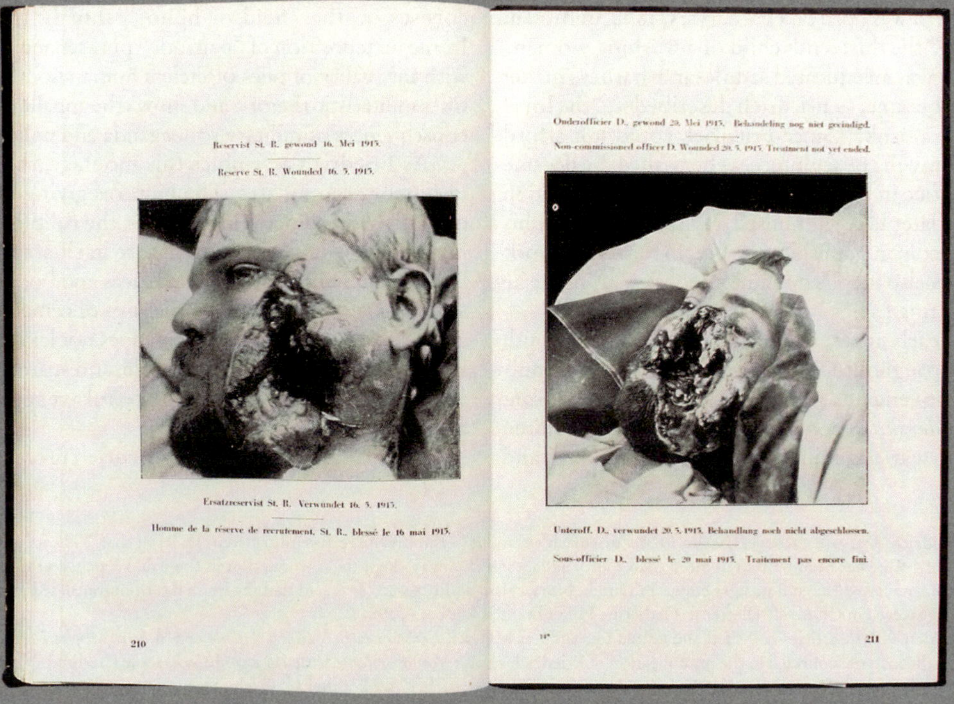

Reserve St. R. Wounded 16. 5. 1915 Non-commissioned officer D. Wounded 20. 5. 1915. Treatment not yet ended.

Ernst Friedrich's Pacifistic Anarchism

Douglas Kellner

1987

Ernst Friedrich's *War Against War!* is an important document in the struggle against the barbarism of the modern warfare. Outraged by the unprecedented brutality and massive destruction of the First World War, Friedrich sought out and then published this collection of pictures and other visual artifacts which illustrate not only the human suffering and death produced in the war but also the lies and hypocrisy of the political and economic forces which promoted it. Aiming at an international audience, Friedrich had the book's introduction written in four languages–German, Dutch, English and French–and accompanied his collection of images with captions in these languages.[1] It was the first extensive published collection of photographic images of the atrocities of World War I, and thus brought the public face to face with a powerful panorama of the horrors of war through the media of photography and other mass images. Friedrich hoped that when they actually saw the reality of modern warfare, people everywhere would become more critical of war, the military, and militarism [...]

Friedrich was born on February 25, 1894, in Breslau, Germany, "the thirteenth child of a washing woman." His father was an educated saddle-and-harness maker who later became, as Friedrich described it, "the loyal servant of a bank."[2] Since Friedrich could not afford to study drawing or sculpture, as he wished, he became an apprentice in the publishing trade—an occupation he would later take up himself. Dissatisfied with his apprenticeship in publishing, he became a factory worker, and was also involved in union politics; at night, he studied acting [...]

In the early 1920s, Friedrich organized Free Youth groups throughout Germany, and continued to publish the movement's journal. He also issued a *Proletarian Kindergarten* book intended to educated children to oppose war and militarism (the book's cover and some contents are found on pages 59 and 62–63 of this book.)[4] But his most significant achievement was the production of *War Against War!*, which he published in 1924. Not only did he assemble pictures of the horrors of war, but he juxtaposed them with evocative and ironic captions. In the documents assembled in the opening pages, Friedrich suggests that children's toys, schooling, the church, and other agents of socialization prepare them psychologically for warfare. Throughout the book, he attempts to document how these institutions, groups and practices are allied with big business, the state, and the military in the manufacture of both the machinery and the mentality of modern warfare.

Friedrich's rhetorical strategy in *War Against War!* is to reproduce shocking pictures of the atrocities of war, and then to juxtapose the official patriotic and militarist propaganda images and rhetoric of the period with illustrations of what this discourse produced. Documents [...] for example, contrast enthusiastic youth marching off to war in 1914 with a picture of corpses on the "field of honor" shortly thereafter. Ironic juxtaposition of "patriotic" phrases and concepts with the reality of piles of lifeless human bodies demystifies militaristic rhetoric and shows the appalling human consequences of military propaganda and policies.

As Friedrich assembles this montage, the impact of horror accumulates. The pictures giving evidence of mutilated and decaying corpses, the rubble of buildings, and the devastation of nature itself are followed by those showing the mutilated faces and bodies of the survivors of the war, and by pictures of cemeteries and graves. In his captions, Friedrich does not let the reader forget precisely who is responsible, and spares us nothing in his attempt to evoke a powerful aversion to war and its apologists. [...]

In general, the anarchism Friedrich professed was

1 Ernst Friedrich, *Krieg dem Kriege!* (Berlin 1924). Friedrich's grandson, Tommy Spree, has informed us by letter that: "The introduction of *War Against War!* has been written in more than four languages. E.F. always kept the introduction in English, French, and German. Yet the fourth language differed: I possess copies in Dutch, Norwegian, and Russian. It is said that the book has been translated in more than 40 languages, even in Chinese!" (Letter to Catherine Hillenbrand, October 6, 1986).

2 On Friedrich, see the articles collected and edited by Andreas Mytzke, *Ernst Friedrich zum 10. Todestag* in *Europäische Ideen*, Heft 29, 1977, and the material collected in the republication of Friedrich's book *Vom Friedens-Museum zur Hitlerkaserne* (Berlin: Libertad Verlag, 1978), especially the informative study, "Friedenskampfter, Wahrheitssucher" by Walther G. Oschilewski, 213-237.

3 On the Youth Movement in Germany, see Robert Wohl, *The Generation of 1914* (Cambridge, MA: Harvard University Press, 1979). Wohl does not, however, discuss the leftist youth organizations participated in by Friedrich which emerged after the German Revolution of 1918.

4 Ernst Friedrich, *Proletarischer Kindergarten. Ein Märchen-und Lesebuch für Kinder und Erwachsene* (Berlin 1921).

5 On the tradition of pacifist anarchism, see Gerald Runkle, *Anarchism: Old and New* (New York: Dell Publishing, 1972), especially 98ff.

therefore more pacifistic than the forms of anarchism associated with violence. Further, his anarchism was directed more specifically against state violence and oppression than simply against state power as such, as in the versions of anarchism produced by Bakunin and his followers. For, as Walther Oschilewski claims, Friedrich's anarchism was closer to the communal socialism of the Russian Peter Kropotkin than to Bakunin's more individualistic anarchism.[6] And in contrast to Tolstoy's more passive religious anarchism, Friedrich always opposed quietistic and non-revolutionary forms of pacifism, publishing in his various journals statements like: "Without social revolution there can be no lasting peace....We must prepare systematically an uprising against war."[7]

War Against War! made a strong impression on Friedrich's contemporaries and was widely read and discussed. Never before had a German audience been subjected to such horrendous images of the savagery and destruction of World War I. During the war, most European governments forbade the publication of war photographs, and few photographic images of the war had appeared before the publication of Friedrich's book. Previously, the public's only contact with the horrors of the First World War had been through individual experience, or through the mediation of artists and poets. Early on in the conflict, many Expressionist and other poets began publishing antiwar poetry evoking the massive brutality which many of them experienced firsthand. And artists like Otto Dix, George Grosz and John Heartfield produced paintings, drawings and montages documenting the horrors of war.[8]

Friedrich's realization that photographs could be employed as documentary evidence and, at the same time, as a provocation to pacifism was something new. The critic Kurt Tucholsky, for example, wrote in the prestigious Weimar Germany publication *Die Weltbühne* the book "should not just be shown to our friends who are already pacifists and who do not want to repeat the old mistakes that are so often made: to send missionaries to Rome. Instead we should show it to our opponents, and should distribute it to schools, organizations, meetings, and cafes and to those who want to know nothing of these horrors. And one should also be sure to show it to women—indeed, should show it to especially to women." Tucholsky also wrote that "The photographs of battlefields, these slaughterhouses of war, and the photographs of those mutilated by war belong to the most horrendous documents that I have ever seen. There exists no publication that offers anything similar in monstrousness, in basic truths, and in education."[9]

In fact, during the 1920s the experience of World War I became a cultural battleground for figures of varying political persuasions. The National Socialists sought scapegoats for German defeat and inveighed against the "stab in the back" at the Versailles Peace conference. Conservative militarists like Ernst Junger published books and essays extolling war and celebrating Germany's experiences in the First World War, while Erich Maria Remarque presented war as a brutal disaster in *All Quiet on the Western Front*.[10] This was the context in which Friedrich sought to speak out against militarist rhetoric in order to expose the human costs and suffering brought about by an event glorified and idealized by the apologists for militarism. Indeed, the book is intended for use as a tool to build an antiwar movement, not merely to illustrate the follies of a corrupt ruling class; it should be read and used in this way today as well. [...]

After the publication of *War Against War!*, Friedrich made the formation and administration of an Anti-War Museum in Berlin his main project, and joined his publication and political work with it in order to establish a center for antiwar activity in Berlin. At the end of the book, Friedrich called for contributions for an International Anti-War Museum, and he managed eventually to raise the money needed to build and administer it. Thereafter, Friedrich devoted much of his energies to collecting material for the museum and to seeking funds to sustain it, though he also continued to publish journals, books and antiwar material ranging from peace postcards to pacifistic texts.

In 1926, Friedrich helped form a "Revolutionary Pacifist Group" whose membership included such figures as Kurt Tucholsky, Walter Mehring, and the Expressionist writer Ernst Toller. During the last years of Weimar, Friedrich found himself in constant litigation against people who alleged that he had defamed them, and against state officials who accused him of "treason." In 1930, Friedrich was imprisoned for "high treason" for about a year because of the publication of antimilitarist

6 Oschilewski, in Friedrich, *Vom Friedens-Museum*, 219ff.

7 Cited in Oschilewski, 229.

8 Friedrich was no doubt influenced by Expressionist artists and the drawings of Otto Dix and George Grosz who painted and sketched the horrors of World War I, for Friedrich frequented Expressionist circles and organized art exhibitions himself. On Expressionism and the First World War, see my discussion in "Expressionism and Rebellion" in *Passion and Rebellion: The Expressionist Heritage*, ed. by Stephen Eric Bronner and Douglas Kellner (South Hadley, MA: Bergin Press, 1983). On George Grosz, Otto Dix, and other antiwar artists, see Matthias Eberle, *World War I and the Weimar Artists* (New Haven, CT: Yale University Press, 1985); Beth Irwin Lewis, *George Grosz: Art and Politics in the Weimar Republic* (Madison: University of Wisconsin Press, 1971); Hans Hess, *George Grosz* (New York: Macmillan, 1974), and Douglas Kahn, *John Heartfield: Art and Mass Media* (New York: Tanam Press, 1985).

9 Kurt Tucholsky in *Die Weltbühne*, February 23, 1926, reprinted in *Gesamelte Werke*, Bd. II, 1925-1928, 359–60.

10 For discussion of the celebration of war by militarist dupes and ideologues in Weimar, see Wohl, 48ff.

11 Oschilewski, 226.

writings intended for secret distribution among the army and police.

Friedrich's museum and his constant agitation against war and militarism earned him the enmity of the increasingly powerful and aggressive right wing in Germany. Indeed, after the Nazis came to political power in 1933, Friedrich was in an extremely precarious situation and the night that the Reichstag was burned, Nazi thugs broke into his Anti-War Museum and destroyed some of the collection and building. Soon after, the Nazis arrested and imprisoned Friedrich and took over the museum, destroying its exhibitions of antiwar material and turning it into a hangout for the local Nazi storm-troopers.

Friedrich was released from imprisonment in September 1933, due to ill health and pressures from American Quakers. He fled the country, and remained in exile in Belgium and France until the end of World War II. He tells of his arrests, his struggles with the Nazis, his exile, and his later experiences in a book published in Geneva in 1935, *Vom Friedens-Museum zur Hitler Kaserne*.[12] Nevertheless, despite imprisonment and destruction of his life-work in Germany, Friedrich refused to surrender his project, and during World War II he reopened his peace museum in Belgium, published a collection of anti-Nazi jokes, and continued to agitate for peace and against Fascism.

When the Germans occupied Belgium in 1940, they again destroyed the Anti-War Museum he had recreated there; but after the war, he returned to Germany and attempted to get the German government to finance its rebuilding. The mayor of Berlin, Ernst Reuter, merely replied that such an antiwar museum would have to be financed with private funds and could not be undertaken with state money.

Disappointed with the lack of support for his project in Germany, Friedrich spent most of his remaining years in France. He joined the French Socialist Party and did organizational and publicity work for them. But he continued to attempt to organize a peace museum, and in 1951 bought a "peace ship" and later a "peace island" with money received from the German government in reparation for his treatment under the Third Reich. He also established some youth communes and worked for friendship between German and French youth. Illness and depression, however, kept him from realizing his dream of reestablishing the peace museum.

After Friedrich's death in 1967, several monographs were published on his life and activities, and two of his main books were republished. Friedrich's Anti-War Museum was revived in Berlin in 1981 and is now managed by his grandson Tommy Spree. No doubt if Friedrich were alive today he would be encouraged by the growth of the antinuclear and antiwar movements among youth around the world. It is in view of these contemporary struggles against weapons, militarism and war that Friedrich's life and work take on importance for us today. In the midst of an era when great powers are expanding already gigantic arsenals, urging military solutions to political problems, and refusing to negotiate reduction of nuclear weapons, Friedrich's militant pacifism has if anything become even more relevant.

Indeed, not only do we face destruction from weapons that dwarf the instruments of death opposed by Friedrich, but people all around the world are being subjected to "low-intensity warfare" and military actions, activities which only serve the interests of the most reactionary forces within the world's superpowers. In this context, Friedrich's strategy of documentation becomes especially significant. To some extent, it was visual documentation of the horrors of the Vietnam war–both visual images reproduced in newspapers and magazines, as well as television images of "the living room war"—that helped produce public outrage and opposition to the war and that hastened its conclusion. But what mass images of the Central America conflicts do we see today? Would American military aid for the Contras in Nicaragua be jeopardized by pictures of the destruction and murder carried out by the Contras against the Nicaraguan people? And would the majority of American people celebrate a U.S. "victory" in Grenada and the bombing of Libya when confronted with pictures of the innocent people maimed and killed by these actions?

Today, the media in a supposedly "free" and "democratic" society have been hiding from us the truth about war and the effects of a military action by the American government in ways similar to the German government in the Weimar Republic and under fascism, by suppressing images of the human effects of war. They have also been promoting a culture of militarism ranging from children's toys and cartoons to films like *Rambo*, or a television series like *Amerika* which dehumanize "communists" and which celebrate the values of militarism. Such images are reinforced by news and commentary which purports to legitimize military actions such as the Grenadian invasion or a potential invasion of Nicaragua. Once again, the United States government and its allies in the media and the military-industrial complex have been suppressing information and images which would reveal the ugly effects of military action. How long will we stand for this and what can we do about it?

Ernst Friedrich provides some answers to these questions. Throughout his life he struggled against war and militarism and sought to document the terrifying folly of war and to attack those who promote and profit from it. Through every means available to him—his

12 Ernst Friedrich, *Vom Friedens-Museum.*

museum, publications, and continual agitation for peace—he devoted a lifetime to struggling against war and for peace. For this, he deserves our respect and emulation as we undertake present and future struggles against war and militarism.

In 1933, the Nazis declared, after destroying the Anti-War Museum, that: "Soon no one will remember the work of Ernst Friedrich." Today, as we face the possibility of nuclear obliteration, we would do well to remember both the crimes of the militarists of the past and the life and work of fighters for peace like Ernst Friedrich. Until we live in a nuclear-free world without fear of war and destruction not even photographs and museums are safe.

Der Mensch als Industriepalast

Fritz Kahn

1926

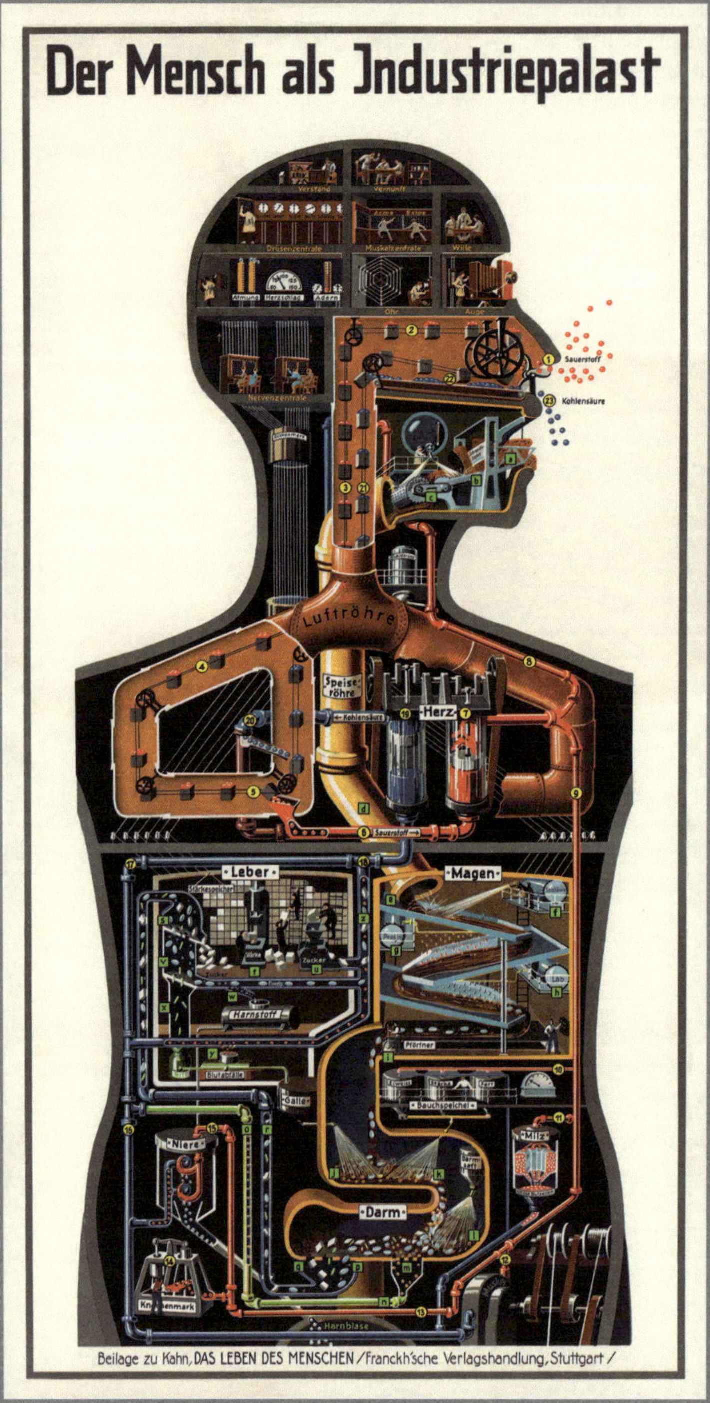

Selections from *Das Leben des Menschen, Eine volkstümliche Anatomie, Biologie, Physiologie und Entwicklungeschichte des Menschen*

Fritz Kahn

1926–1931

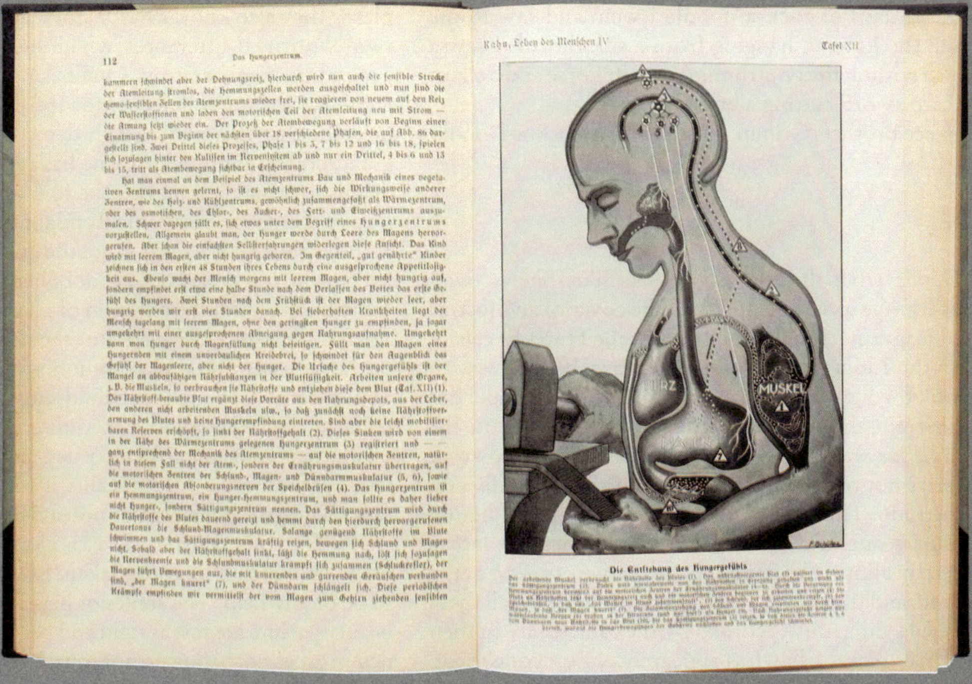

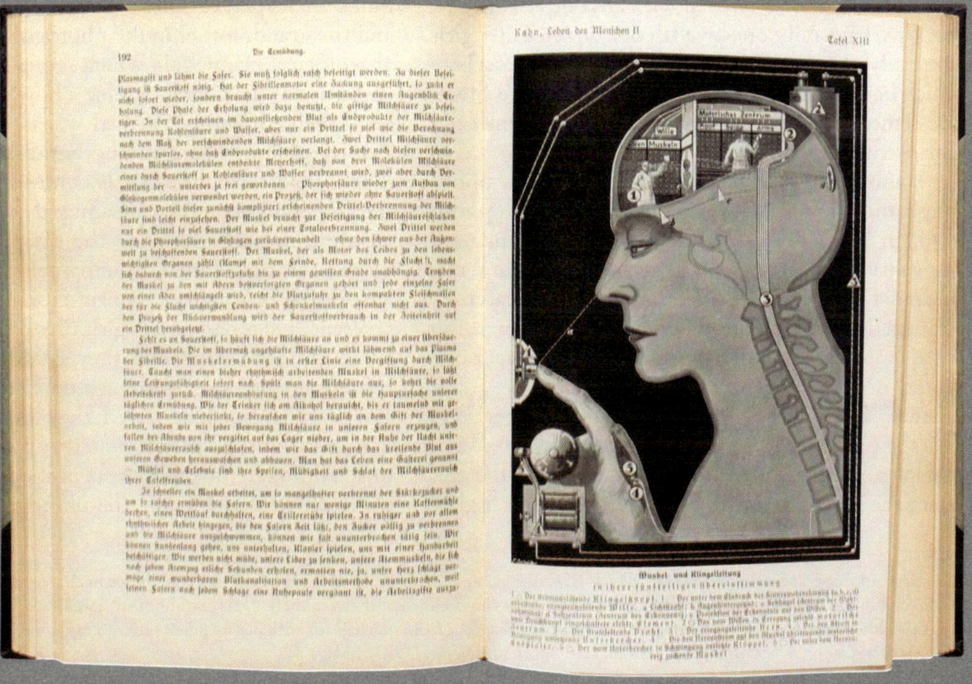

Photography
Siegfried Kracauer
1927

In the days of cock-a-doodle I went and saw Rome and the Lateran hanging from a silk thread. I saw a man without feet outrunning a swift horse and a sharp, sharp sword cutting a bridge in two.
—Thee Brothers Grimm, "The Tale of a Cock-a-Doodle"

I

This is what the film diva looks like. She is twenty-four years old, featured on the cover of an illustrated magazine, standing in front of the Hotel Excelsior on the Lido. The date is September. If one were to look through a magnifying glass one could make out the grain, the millions of little dots that constitute the diva, the waves, and the hotel. The picture, however, refers not to the dot matrix but to the living diva on the Lido. Time: the present. The caption calls her demonic: our demonic diva. Still, she does not lack a certain allure. The bangs, the seductive position of the head, and the twelve eyelashes right and left—all these details, diligently recorded by the camera, are in their proper place, a flawless appearance. Everyone recognizes her with delight, since everyone has already seen the original on the screen. It is such a good likeness that she cannot be confused with anyone else, even if she is perhaps only one-twelfth of a dozen Tiller girls. Dreamily she stands in front of the Hotel Excelsior, which basks in her fame—a being of flesh and blood, our demonic diva, twenty-four years old, on the Lido. The date is September.

Is this what *grandmother* looked like? The photograph, more than sixty years old and already a photograph in the modern sense, depicts her as a young girl of twenty-four. Since photographs are likenesses, this one must have been a likeness as well. It was carefully produced in the studio of a court photographer. But were it not for the oral tradition, the image alone would not have sufficed to reconstruct the grandmother. The grandchildren know that in her later years she lived in a narrow little room with a view onto the old part of town and that, to amuse the children, she would make toy soldiers dance on a glass plate;[1] they also know a nasty story about her life, and two confirmed utterances which change a bit from generation to generation. One has to believe the parents—who claim to have gotten it from grandmother herself—that this photograph depicts the very same grandmother about whom one has retained these few details that may also in time be forgotten. Yet eyewitness accounts are unreliable. It might turn out after all that the photograph depicts not the grandmother but a friend who resembled her. None of her contemporaries are still alive. And the question of likeness? The ur-image has long since decayed. But the now-darkened appearance has so little in common with the traits still remembered that the grandchildren submit in amazement to the imperative of encountering in the photograph their fragmentarily recorded ancestor. All right, so it's grandmother; but in reality it's any young girl in 1864. The girl smiles continuously, always the same smile. The smile is arrested yet no longer refers to the life from which it has been taken. Likeness has ceased to be of any help. The smiles of plastic mannequins in beauty parlors are just as rigid and perpetual. This mannequin does not belong to our time; it could be standing with others of its kind in a museum, in a glass case labeled "Traditional Costumes, 1864." There the mannequins are displayed solely for the historical costumes, and the grandmother in the photograph, too, is an archaeological mannequin which serves to illustrate the costumes of the period. So that's how women dressed back then: chignons, cinched waists, crinolines, and Zouave jackets. The grandmother dissolves into fashionably old-fashioned details before the very eyes of the grandchildren. They are amused by the traditional costume, which, following the disappearance of its bearer, remains alone on the battlefield—an external decoration that has become autonomous. They are irreverent, and today young girls dress differently. They laugh, and at the same time they shudder. For through the ornamentation of the costume from which the grandmother has disappeared, they think they glimpse a moment of time past, a time that passes without return. Although time is not part of the photograph like the smile or the chignon, the photograph itself, so it

1 In the autobiographical novel *Georg*, which Kracauer completed in 1934 during his exile in Paris, the main character at one point recalls his childhood delight at "the glass battlefields of former times" filled with tin soldiers. "His grandmother," we learn, "had occasionally set [the soldiers] up on a glass plate and then tapped on the surface from underneath with her finger, in order to bring the ranks into disorder." Kracauer, *Georg*, in *Schriften*, vol. 7 (Frankfurt: Suhrkamp Verlag, 1973), 251.

seems to them, is a representation of time. Were it the photograph alone that endowed these details with duration, they would not at all outlast mere time; rather, time would create images for itself out of them.

2

"From the early days of the friendship between Goethe and Karl August."—"Karl August and the 1787 coadjutor election in Erfurt."— "A visit of a Bohemian in Jena and Weimar" (1818).—"Recollections of a Weimar high school student" (1825 to 1830).—"A contemporary account of the Weimar Goethe celebration on November 7, 1825."—"A rediscovered bust of Wieland by Ludwig Klauer."—"Plan for a national monument to Goethe in Weimar."—The herbarium for these and other investigations is provided by the Goethe Society yearbooks, a series that in principle can never come to an end. It would be superfluous to ridicule the Goethe philology which deposits its specimens in these volumes, all the more so since it is as ephemeral as the items it processes. In contrast, the pseudo-luster of the numerous monumental works on Goethe's stature, being, personality, and so on has hardly begun to be questioned. The principle of Goethe philology is that of *historicist* thinking, which emerged at about the same time as modern photographic technology. On the whole, advocates of such historicist thinking[2] believe they can explain any phenomenon purely in terms of its genesis. That is, they believe in any case that they can grasp historical reality by reconstructing the course of events in their temporal succession without any gaps. Photography presents a spatial continuum; historicism seeks to provide the temporal continuum. According to historicism, the complete mirroring of an intratemporal sequence simultaneously contains the meaning of all that occurred within that time. Thus, if the connecting links of the Erfurt coadjutor election or the recollections of the Weimar high school student were missing in the presentation of Goethe, such an account would lack reality for the historicist. Historicism is concerned with the photography of time. The equivalent of its temporal photography would be a giant film depicting the temporally interconnected events from every vantage point.[3]

3

Memory encompasses neither the entire spatial appearance of a state of affairs nor its entire temporal course. Compared to photography, memory's records are full of gaps. The fact that the grandmother was at one time involved in a nasty story that is recounted time and again because people really do not like to talk about her—this does not mean much from the photographer's perspective. He knows every little wrinkle on her face and has noted every date. Memory does not pay much attention to dates—it skips years or stretches temporal distance. The selection of traits that it assembles must strike the photographer as arbitrary. The selection may have been made this way rather than another because dispositions and purposes required the repression, falsification, and emphasis of certain parts of the object; a virtually endless number of reasons determines the remains to be filtered. No matter which scenes an individual remembers, they all mean something relevant to that person, though he or she might not necessarily know what they mean. An individual retains memories because they are personally significant. Thus, they are organized according to a principle which is essentially different from the organizing principle of photography. Photography grasps what is given as a spatial (or temporal) continuum; memory images retain what is given only insofar as it has significance. Since what is significant is not reducible to either merely spatial or merely temporal terms, memory images are at odds with photographic representation. From the latter's perspective, memory images appear to be fragments—but only because photography does not encompass the meaning to which they refer and in relation to which they cease to be fragments. Similarly, from the perspective of memory, photography appears as a jumble that consists partly of garbage.

The meaning of memory images is linked to their truth content. So long as they are embedded in the uncontrolled life of the drives, they are inhabited by a demonic ambiguity; they are opaque, like frosted glass which scarcely a ray of light can penetrate. Their transparency increases to the extent that insights thin out the vegetation of the soul and limit the compulsion of nature. Truth can be found only by a liberated consciousness which assesses the demonic nature of the drives. The traits that consciousness recollects stand in a relationship to what has been perceived as

2 When this essay was first published in the *Frankfurter Zeitung* in 1927, Kracauer here explicitly named Wilhelm Dilthey as an exemplary advocate of such historicist thinking.

3 Kracauer refers to this passage in the introduction to *History: The Last Things before the Last* (New York: Oxford University Press, 1969), when describing his surprising realization of the continuity between the work he had done on film and his present concern with history: "I realized in a flash the many existing parallels between history and the photographic media, historical reality and camera-reality. Lately I came across my piece on 'Photography' and was completely amazed at noticing that I had compared historicism with photography already in this article of the twenties" (3-4)

true, the latter being either manifest in these traits or excluded by them. The image in which these traits appear is distinguished from all other memory images, for unlike the latter it preserves not a multitude of opaque recollections but elements that touch upon what has been recognized as true. All memory images are bound to be reduced to this type of image, which may rightly be called the last image, since it alone preserves the unforgettable. The last image of a person is that person's actual *history*. This history omits all characteristics and determinations that do not relate in a significant sense to the truth intended by a liberated consciousness. How a person represents this history does not depend purely on his or her natural constitution or on the pseudo-coherence of his or her individuality; thus, only fragments of these assets are included in his or her history. This history is like a *monogram* that condenses the name into a single graphic figure which is meaningful as an ornament. Eckart's monogram is fidelity. Great historical figures survive in legends that, however naive they may be, strive to preserve their actual history. In authentic fairy tales, the imagination has intuitively deposited typical monograms. In a photograph, a person's history is buried as if under a layer of snow.

4

In his description of a Rubens landscape presented to him by Goethe, Eckermann notices to his surprise that the light in the painting comes from two opposing directions, "which is quite contrary to nature."[4] Goethe responds: "This is how Rubens proves his greatness, and shows to the world that he stands *above* nature with a free spirit, fashioning it according to his higher purposes. The double light is indeed violent, and you could even say that it is contrary to nature. But if it is contrary to nature, I also say that it is *higher* than nature; I say that it is the bold hand of the master, whereby he demonstrates in a brilliant way that art is not entirely subject to natural necessity but rather has laws of its own." A *portrait painter* who submitted entirely to "natural necessity" would at best create photographs. During a particular period, which began with the Renaissance and may now be approaching its end, the "artwork" has indeed been faithful to nature, whose specificity has revealed itself more and more during this period. But by penetrating this nature, the artwork orients itself toward "higher ends." There is cognition in the material of colors and contours; and the greater the artwork, the more it approaches the transparency of the final memory image, in which the features of "history" converge. A man who had his portrait painted by Trübner asked the artist not to forget the wrinkles and folds on his face. Trübner pointed out the window and said, "Across the way, there's a photographer. If you want to have wrinkles and folds, then you'd better hire him—he'll put 'em all in. Me, I paint history." In order for history to present itself, the mere surface coherence offered by photography must be destroyed. For in the artwork the meaning of the object takes on spatial appearance, whereas in photography the spatial appearance of an object is its meaning. The two spatial appearances—the "natural" one and that of the object permeated by cognition—are not identical. By sacrificing the former for the sake of the latter, the artwork also negates the *likeness* achieved by photography. This likeness refers to the look of the object, which does not immediately divulge how it reveals itself to cognition; the artwork, however, conveys nothing but the transparency of the object. In so doing, it resembles a magic mirror which reflects those who consult it not as they appear but rather as they wish to be or as they fundamentally are. The artwork, too, disintegrates over time; but its meaning arises out of its crumbled elements, whereas photography merely stockpiles the elements.

Until well into the second half of the nineteenth century, the practice of photography was often in the hands of former painters. The not yet entirely depersonalized technology of this transition period corresponded to a spatial environment in which traces of meaning could still be trapped. With the increasing independence of the technology and the simultaneous evacuation of meaning from the objects, *artistic photography* loses its justification: it grows not into an artwork but into its imitation. Images of children are Zumbusches, and the godfather of photographic landscape impressions was Monet. These pictorial arrangements—which do not go beyond a skillful emulation of familiar styles—fail to represent the very remnants of nature which, to a certain extent, advanced technology is capable of capturing. Modern painters have composed their images out of photographic fragments in order to highlight the side-by-side existence of reified appearances as they manifest themselves in spatial relations. This artistic intention is diametrically opposed to that of artistic photography. The latter does not explore the object assigned to photographic technology but rather wants to hide the technological essence by means of style. The artistic photographer is a dilettante artist who apes an artistic manner minus its substance, instead of capturing the very lack of substance. Similarly, rhythmic gymnastics wants to incorporate the soul about which it knows nothing. It shares with artistic photography the ambition to lay claim to a higher life in order to elevate an

4 Johann Peter Ackermann (1792-1854), Goethe's private secretary, in a discussion with Goethe on April 18, 1827, reported in *Conversations of Goethe with Eckermann and Soret*, translated by John Ofenford (London: George Bell, 1874), 248

activity which is actually at its most elevated when it finds the object appropriate to its technology. The artistic photographers function like those social forces which are interested in the semblance of the spiritual because they fear the real spirit: it might explode the material base which the spiritual illusion serves to disguise. It would be well worth the effort to expose the close ties between the prevailing social order and artistic photography.

5

The photograph does not preserve the transparent aspects of an object but instead captures it as a spatial continuum from any one of a number of positions. The last memory image outlasts time because it is unforgettable; the photograph, which neither refers to nor encompasses such a memory image, must be essentially associated with the moment in time at which it came into existence. Referring to the average film whose subject matter is the normal photographable environment, E. A. Dupont remarked in his book on film that "the essence of film is, to some degree, the essence of time."[5] If photography is a *function of the flow of time*, then its substantive meaning will change depending upon whether it belongs to the domain of the present or to some phase of the past.

Current-event photography, which portrays phenomena familiar to *contemporary* consciousness, provides access of a limited sort to the life of the original. In each case it registers an exteriority which, at the time of its reign, is a means of expression as generally intelligible as language. The contemporaneous viewer believes that he or she sees the film diva herself in the photograph, and not just her bangs or the pose of her head. Naturally, the viewer cannot gauge her on the basis of the photograph alone. But luckily the diva numbers among the living, and the cover of the illustrated magazine functions as a reminder of her corporeal reality. This means that present-day photography performs a mediating function: it is an optical sign for the diva, who is meant to be recognized. One may have doubts in the end as to whether her decisive trait is really the demonic. But even the demonic is not so much something conveyed by the photograph as it is the impression of the moviegoers who experience the original on the screen. They recognize it as the representation of the demonic—so be it. The image denounces the demonic not because of, but rather *despite* its likeness. For the time being, the demonic belongs to the still-vacillating memory image of the diva to which the photographic likeness does not refer. But the memory image drawn from the viewing of our celebrated diva breaks through the wall of likeness into the photograph and thereby lends the latter a modicum of transparency.

Once a photograph ages, the immediate reference to the original is no longer possible. The body of a deceased person appears smaller than the living figure. Likewise, an *old* photograph presents itself as the reduction of a contemporaneous one. The old photograph has been emptied of the life whose physical presence overlay its merely spatial configuration. In inverse proportion to photographs, memory images enlarge themselves into monograms of remembered life. The photograph is the sediment which has settled from the monogram, and from year to year its semiotic value decreases. The truth content of the original is left behind in its history; the photograph captures only the residuum that history has discharged.

If one can no longer encounter the grandmother in the photograph, the image taken from the family album necessarily disintegrates into its particulars. In the case of the diva, one's gaze may wander from her bangs to her demonic quality; from the nothingness of the grandmother, the gaze is thrown back onto the chignons. It is the fashion details that hold the gaze tight. Photography is bound to time in precisely the same way as *fashion*. Since the latter has no significance other than as current human garb, it is translucent when modern and abandoned when old. The tightly corseted dress in the photograph protrudes into our time like a mansion from earlier days that is destined for destruction because the city center has been moved to another part of town. Usually members of the lower class settle in such buildings. It is only the very old traditional dress, a dress which has lost all contact with the present, that can attain the beauty of a ruin. The effect of an outfit which was still worn only recently is *comical*. The grandchildren are amused by the grandmotherly crinoline of 1864, which provokes the thought that it might hide the legs of a modern girl. The recent past which claims to be alive is more outdated than the past that existed long ago and whose meaning has changed. The comic quality of the crinoline results from the powerlessness of its claim. In the photograph, the grandmother's costume is recognized as a cast-off remnant that wants to continue to hold its ground. It dissolves into the sum of its details, like a corpse, yet stands tall as if full of life. Even the landscape and all other concrete objects become costumes in an old photograph. For what is retained in the image are not the features envisaged by a liberated consciousness. The representation captures contexts from which such consciousness has departed—that is, it encompasses orders of existence that have shriveled without wanting to

5 Ewald André Dupont, *Wie ein Film geschrieben wird und wie man ihn verwertet* (Berlin: Reinhold Kühn, 1919), cited in Rudolf Harms, *Philosophie des Films* (Leipzig: Felix Meiner, 1926; facsimile rpt. Zurich: Hans Rohr, 1970), 142. Shortly after its publication, Kracauer reviewed Harms's study in the book review section of the *Frankfurter Zeitung* on July 10, 1927 (vol. 60, no. 28): 5.

admit it. The more consciousness withdraws from natural bonds, the more nature diminishes. In old etchings whose fidelity is photographic, the hills of the Rhine look like mountains. As a result of technological development, they have in the meantime been reduced to tiny slopes, and the grandiosity of those aged views seems a bit ridiculous.

Ghosts are simultaneously comical and terrifying. Laughter is not the only response provoked by antiquated photography. It represents what is utterly past, and yet this detritus was once the present. Grandmother was once a person, and to this person belonged the chignon and the corset as well as the high-Renaissance chair with its turned spindles, ballast that did not weigh her down but was just carried along as a matter of course. Now the image wanders ghost-like through the present, like the lady of the haunted castle. Spooky apparitions occur only in places where a terrible deed has been committed. The photograph becomes a ghost because the costumed mannequin was once alive. The image proves that the alien trappings were incorporated into life as accessories. These trappings, whose lack of transparency one experiences in the old photograph, used to be inseparably meshed with the transparent aspects. This terrible association which persists in the photograph evokes a shudder. Such a shudder is evoked in drastic fashion by the pre-World War I films screened in the avant-garde "Studio des Ursulines" in Paris—film images that show how the features stored in the memory image are embedded in a reality which has long since disappeared. Like the photographic image, the playing of an old hit song or the reading of letters written long ago also conjures up anew a disintegrated unity. This ghost-like reality is *unredeemed*. It consists of elements in space whose configuration is so far from necessary that one could just as well imagine a different organization of these elements. Those things once clung to us like our skin, and this is how our property still clings to us today. Nothing of these contains us, and the photograph gathers fragments around a nothing. When the grandmother stood in front of the lens, she was present for one second in the spatial continuum that presented itself to the lens. But it was this aspect and not the grandmother that was eternalized. A shudder runs through the viewer of old photographs. For they make visible not the knowledge of the original but the spatial configuration of a moment; what appears in the photograph is not the person but the sum of what can be subtracted from him or her. The photograph annihilates the person by portraying him or her, and were person and portrayal to converge, the person would cease to exist. An illustrated newspaper recently put together photographs of famous personalities as children and as grown-ups and published them under the heading "The Faces of Famous People: This Is How They Once Were—and This Is How They Are Today!" Marx as a youth and Marx as leader of the Center party, Hindenburg as a lieutenant and as our Hindenburg. The photographs are set side by side like statistical reports, and one can neither guess the later image from the earlier one nor reconstruct the earlier image from the later. One has to take it on faith that the optical inventory lists belong together. The features of human beings are retained only in their "history."

6

The daily papers are illustrating their texts more and more. And what would a magazine be without pictures? The most striking proof of photography's extraordinary validity today is the increase in the number of *illustrated newspapers*. In them one finds assembled everything from the film diva to whatever is within reach of the camera and the audience. Infants are of interest to mothers, and young gentlemen are captivated by the legs of beautiful girls. Beautiful girls like to see sports and stage celebrities standing on gangways of ocean liners, embarking on voyages to distant lands. In distant lands there are battles of conflicting interests. Yet the focus of attention is not on them but on the cities, the natural catastrophes, the cultural heroes, and the politicians. In Geneva, the League of Nations is meeting; it serves as a pretext for showing Mr. Stresemann and Mr. Briand[6] conversing in front of the entrance of the hotel. The new fashions also must be disseminated, or else in the summer the beautiful girls will not know who they are. Fashion beauties attend chic events accompanied by young gentlemen; earthquakes take place in distant lands; Mr. Stresemann is seated on a terrace with potted palms; and for the mothers we have the little tots.

The aim of the illustrated newspapers is the complete reproduction of the world accessible to the photographic apparatus. They record the spatial impressions of people, conditions, and events from every possible perspective. Their method corresponds to that of the weekly newsreel, which is nothing but a collection of photographs, whereas an authentic film employs photography merely as a means. Never before has an age been so informed about itself, if being informed means having an image of objects that resembles them in a photographic sense. Most of the images in the illustrated magazines are topical photographs,

6 Aristide Briand (1862-1932), foreign minister of France (1925-1932), and Gustav Stresemann (1878-1929), foreign minister of Germany (1923-1929), shared the 1926 Nobel Peace Prize.

which refer to existing objects. The reproductions are thus basically signs which may remind us of the original object that was supposed to be understood. The demonic diva. In reality, however, the weekly photographic ration does not at all mean to refer to these objects or images. If it were offering itself as an aid to memory, then memory would have to determine the selection. But the flood of photos sweeps away the dams of memory. The assault of this mass of images is so powerful that it threatens to destroy the potentially existing awareness of crucial traits. Artworks suffer this fate through their reproductions. The phrase "lie together, die together" applies to the multiply reproduced original; rather than coming into view through the reproductions, it tends to disappear in its multiplicity and to live on as art photography. In the illustrated magazines, people see the very world that the illustrated magazines prevent them from perceiving. The spatial continuum from the camera's perspective dominates the spatial appearance of the perceived object; the resemblance between the image and the object effaces the contours of the object's "history." Never before has a period known so little about itself. In the hands of the ruling society, the invention of illustrated magazines is one of the most powerful means of organizing a strike against understanding. Even the colorful arrangement of the images provides a not insignificant means for successfully implementing such a strike. The *contiguity* of these images systematically excludes their contextual framework available to consciousness. The "image-idea" drives away the idea. The blizzard of photographs betrays an indifference toward what the things mean. It does not have to be this way; but in any case the American illustrated magazines—which the publications of other countries emulate to a large degree—equate the world with the quintessence of the photographs. This equation is not made without good reason. For the world itself has taken on a "photographic face"; it can be photographed because it strives to be absorbed into the spatial continuum which yields to snapshots. Sometimes it is the fraction of a second required for the exposure of an object that determines whether or not a sportsman will become famous to the point where illustrated magazines commission photographers to give him exposure. The camera can also capture the figures of beautiful girls and young gentlemen. That the world devours them is a sign of the *fear of death*. What the photographs by their sheer accumulation attempt to banish is the recollection of death, which is part and parcel of every memory image. In the illustrated magazines the world has become a photographable present, and the photographed present has been entirely eternalized. Seemingly ripped from the clutch of death, in reality it has succumbed to it.

7

The series of pictorial representations of which photography is the last historical stage begins with the *symbol*. The symbol, in turn, arises out of the "natural community," in which man's consciousness was still entirely embedded in nature.

> Just as the history of individual words always begins with the sensuous, natural meaning and only progresses to abstract, figurative uses in the later stages of its development, one can observe the same progression from substance and matter to the spiritual and the intellectual in religion, in the development of the human individual and of mankind in general. Likewise the fundamental meaning of the symbols in which the earliest human beings customarily deposited their views of the nature of the world surrounding them is purely physical and material. Symbolism, like language, sat in nature's lap.[7]

This statement, by Bachofen, comes from his study of the rope-twisting Ocnus in which he shows that the spinning and weaving depicted in the image originally referred to the activity of the creative power of nature. As consciousness becomes more and more aware of itself and in the process the original "identity of nature and man"[8] dissolves, the meaning of the image becomes increasingly abstract and immaterial. But even if, as Bachofen puts it, the image progresses to the point of designating "the spiritual and the intellectual," the meaning is nevertheless so much a part of the image that it cannot be separated from it. For long stretches of history, imagistic representations have remained symbols. So long as human beings need them, they continue, in practice, to be dependent on natural conditions, a dependence that determines the visible and corporeal expression of consciousness. It is only with the increasing domination of nature that the image loses its symbolic power. Consciousness, which disengages itself from nature and stands against it, is no longer naively enveloped in its mythological cocoon: it thinks in concepts which, of course, can still be used in an altogether mythological way. In certain epochs the image retains its power; the symbolic presentation becomes *allegory*. "The latter signifies merely a general concept or an idea which is distinct from it; the former is the

7 Johann Jakob Bachofen (1815-1887), "Oknos der Seilflechter" (1923), in *Versuch über die Gräbersymbolik der Alten*, in *Gesammelte Werke*, vol. 4 (Basel: Benno Schwabe, 1954), 359; translated as "Onus the Rope Plaiter" in *Myth, Religion, and Mother Right: Selected Writings of J.J. Bachofen*, trans. Ralph Mannheim (Princeton: Princeton University Press, 1967), 54-55. Known for his punishment in Hades, the mythical Ocnos was condemned to twist a straw rope that would be devoured incessantly by an ass.

8 Karl Marx and Friedrich Engels, *The German Ideology*, in *Marx/Engels Collected Works*, vol. 5 (London: Lawrence and Wishart, 1976), 44.

sensuous form, the incorporation of the idea itself." This is how old Creuzer defines the difference between the two types of images.[9] At the level of the symbol, what is thought is contained in the image; at the level of allegory, thought maintains and employs the image as if consciousness were hesitating to throw off its cocoon. This schematization is crude. Yet it suffices to illustrate the transformation of representations which is the sign that consciousness has departed from its natural contingency. The more decisively consciousness frees itself from this contingency in the course of the historical process, the more purely does its natural foundation present itself to consciousness. What is meant no longer appears to consciousness in images; rather, this meaning goes toward and through nature. To an ever-increasing degree, European painting during the last few centuries has represented nature stripped of symbolic and allegorical meanings. This certainly does not imply that the human features it depicts are bereft of meaning. Even as recently as the days of the old daguerreotypes, consciousness was so imbricated in nature that the faces bring to mind meanings which cannot be separated from natural life. Since nature changes in exact correspondence with the particular state of consciousness of a period, the foundation of nature devoid of meaning arises with modern photography. No different from earlier modes of representation, photography, too, is assigned to a particular developmental stage of practical and material life. It is a secretion of the capitalist mode of production. The same mere nature which appears in photography flourishes in the reality of the society produced by this capitalist mode of production. One can certainly imagine a society that has fallen prey to a mute nature which has no meaning no matter how abstract its silence. The contours of such a society emerge in the illustrated journals. Were it to endure, the emancipation of consciousness would result in the eradication of consciousness; the nature that it failed to penetrate would sit down at the very table that consciousness had abandoned. If this society failed to endure, however, then liberated consciousness would be given an incomparable opportunity. Less enmeshed in the natural bonds than ever before, it could prove its power in dealing with them. The turn to photography is the *go-for-broke game* of history.

8

Although the grandmother has disappeared, the crinoline has nonetheless remained. The totality of all photographs must be understood as the *general inventory* of a nature that cannot be further reduced—as the comprehensive catalogue of all manifestations which present themselves in space, to the extent that they are constructed not out of the monogram of the object but from a natural perspective which the monogram does not capture. Corresponding to this spatial inventory is historicism's temporal inventory. Instead of preserving the "history" that consciousness reads out of the temporal succession of events, historicism records the temporal succession of events whose linkage does not contain the transparency of history. The barren self-presentation of spatial and temporal elements belongs to a social order which regulates itself according to economic laws of nature.

A consciousness caught up in nature is unable to see its own material base. It is the task of photography to disclose this previously unexamined *foundation of nature*. For the first time in history, photography brings to light the entire natural cocoon; for the first time, the inert world presents itself in its independence from human beings. Photography shows cities in aerial shots, brings crockets and figures down from the Gothic cathedrals. All spatial configurations are incorporated into the central archive in unusual combinations which distance them from human proximity. Once the grandmother's costume has lost its relationship to the present, it will no longer be funny; it will be peculiar, like an ocean-dwelling octopus. One day the diva will lose her demonic quality and her bangs will go the same way as the chignons. This is how the elements crumble, since they are not held together. The photographic archive assembles in effigy the last elements of a nature alienated from meaning.

This warehousing of nature promotes the confrontation of consciousness with nature. Just as consciousness finds itself confronting the unabashedly displayed mechanics of industrial society, it also faces, thanks to photographic technology, the reflection of the reality that has slipped away from it. To have provoked the decisive confrontation in every field: this is precisely the go-for-broke game of the historical process. The images of the stock of nature disintegrated into its elements are offered up to consciousness to deal with as it pleases. Their original order is lost; they no longer cling to the spatial context that linked them with an original out of which the memory image was selected. But if the remnants of nature are not oriented toward the memory image, then the order they assume through the image is necessarily provisional. It is therefore incumbent on consciousness to establish the *provisional status* of all given configurations, and perhaps even to awaken an inkling of the right order of the inventory of nature. In the works of Franz Kafka, a liberated consciousness absolves itself of this responsibility by destroying natural reality and scrambling the fragments. The disorder of the detritus

9 Georg Friedrich Creuzer (1771-1858), *Symbolik und Mythologie der alten Völker, besonders der Griechen*, vol. 4 (Leipzig: Carl Wilhelm Lecke, 1836-1843; rpt. Hildesheim: G. Olms, 1973), 540.

reflected in photography cannot be elucidated more clearly than through the suspension of every habitual relationship among the elements of nature. The capacity to stir up the elements of nature is one of the possibilities of film. This possibility is realized whenever film combines parts and segments to create strange constructs. If the disarray of the illustrated newspapers is simply confusion, the game that film plays with the pieces of disjointed nature is reminiscent of *dreams* in which the fragments of daily life become jumbled. This game shows that the valid organization of things remains unknown—an organization which would designate the position that the remains of the grandmother and the diva stored in the general inventory will someday have to occupy.

Perspective as Symbolic Form
Erwin Panofsky
1927

"*Item Perspectiva ist ein lateinisch Wort, bedeutt ein Durchsehung*" ("*Perspectiva* is a Latin word which means 'seeing through.' "). This is how Dürer sought to explain the concept of perspective.[1] And although this *lateinisch Wort* was used already by Boethius,[2] and did not originally bear so precise a meaning,[3] we shall nevertheless adopt in essence Dürer's definition. We shall speak of a fully "perspectival" view of space not when mere isolated objects, such as houses or furniture, are represented in "foreshortening," but rather only when the entire picture has been transformed—to cite another Renaissance theoretician—into a "window," and when we are meant to believe we are looking through this window into a space.[4] The material surface upon which the individual figures or objects are drawn or painted or carved is thus negated, and instead reinterpreted as a mere "picture plane." Upon this picture plane is projected the spatial continuum which is seen through it and which is understood to contain all the various individual objects.[5]

So far it does not matter whether this projection is determined by an immediate sensory impression or by a more or less "correct" geometrical construction. This correct construction was in fact invented in the Renaissance, and although later subjected to various technical improvements and simplifications, it nevertheless remained in its premises and goals unchanged to the time of Desargues. It is most simply explained as follows: I imagine the picture—in accord with the "window" definition—as a planar cross section

1 K. von Lange and F. Fuhse, *Dürers schriftlicher Nachlass* (Halle, 1893), 319, I. 11.

2 Boethius, *Analyt. poster. Aristot. Interpretatio* 1.7 and 1.10, in *Opera* (Basel, 1570), 527 and 538; *perspectiva* is characterized in both passages as a subdiscipline of geometry.

3 The word ought to be derived not from *perspicere* meaning "to see through," but from *perspicere* meaning "to see clearly"; thus it amounts to a literal translation of the Greek term *optik*[illegible]. Dürer's interpretation is based already on the modern definition and construction of the image as a cross section through the visual pyramid. Felix Witting, on the other hand, detected in the transformation of the Italian *perspettiva* into *prospettiva* a kind of protest against this understanding of the image ("the former is reminiscent of Brunelleschi's '*punto dove percoteva l'occhio,*' whereas the latter suggests only a seeing forward," *Von Kunst und Christentum* [Strassburg 1903], 106). This is more than doubtful, for it is precisely the most rigorous theoreticians of the cross-section method, such as Piero della Francesca, who use the term *prospettiva*. At most we can grant that *prospettiva* implies more strongly the idea of the artistic achievement (namely the conquest of spatial depth), while *perspettiva* evokes rather the mathematical procedure. A purely phonetic consideration must have then favored the triumph of the term *prospettiva*, to wit, an aversion to the sequence of consonants "rsp."

4 Leon Battista Alberti, *Della pittura*, in *Kleinere kunsttheoretische Schriften*, Quellenschriften für Kunstgeschichte und Kunsttechnik des Mittelalters und der Renaissance, no. 11, ed. Hubert Janitschek (Vienna, 1877) 79: "*scrivo uno quadroangulo ... el quale repute essere una fenestra aperta per donde io miri quello que quivi sara dipinto*" (On Painting, trans. John R. Spencer [New Haven: Yale University Press, 1966], 56: "I inscribe a quadrangle ... which is considered to be an open window through which I see what I want to paint"). See also Leonardo (Jean Paul Richter, *The Literary Works of Leonardo da Vinci* [London, 1883], no. 83), where the same analogy to a "*pariete di vetro*," or pane of glass, is drawn.

5 Already Lessing, in the ninth of his *Antiquarische Briefe*, distinguished between a broader and a narrower meaning of perspective. In the broader sense perspective is "the science of representing objects on a surface just as they would appear to our eye at a certain distance.... Not to credit the ancients with perspective in this sense would be rather foolish. For it would mean depriving them not only of perspective but of the entire art of drawing, an art which they had quite mastered. No one could maintain this. Rather, when one contests the antique claim to perspective, it is in this narrower sense, the sense in which artists take the word. For artists, perspective is the science of representing a number of objects together with the space around them, just as these objects, dispersed among various planes of the space, together with their space, would appear to the eye from a single standpoint" (*Schriften* [Berlin, 1753–55], vol. 8, 25–26).

Essentially, then, we are adopting Lessing's second definition, only that we formulate it a little more liberally by dropping the condition of the rigorously maintained single point of view. For unlike Lessing we accept late Hellenistic and Greco-Roman paintings as already authentically "perspectival." For us perspective is, quite precisely, the capacity to represent a number of objects together with a part of the space around them in such a way that the conception of the material picture support is completely supplanted by the conception of a transparent plane through which we believe we are looking into an imaginary space. This space comprises the entirety of the objects in apparent recession into depth, and is not bounded by the edges of the picture, but rather only cut off.

There are of course a multitude of transitional cases between mere "foreshortening" (which for its part does represent the necessary first step and precondition for the development of a true perspectival conception of space) and something recognizable as perspective in this sense. An example of such a transitional case are those well-known southern Italian vases which show a figure or even several figures assembled in a foreshortened aedicule. This approximates true perspective insofar as a greater spatial construct already contains within it a number of individual bodies; but this greater spatial construct is itself still offered up as an isolated object, upon a picture support which retains its materiality. Instead, the entire surface of the painting would have to be transformed into a projective plane for a perspectival illusion of the entire space.

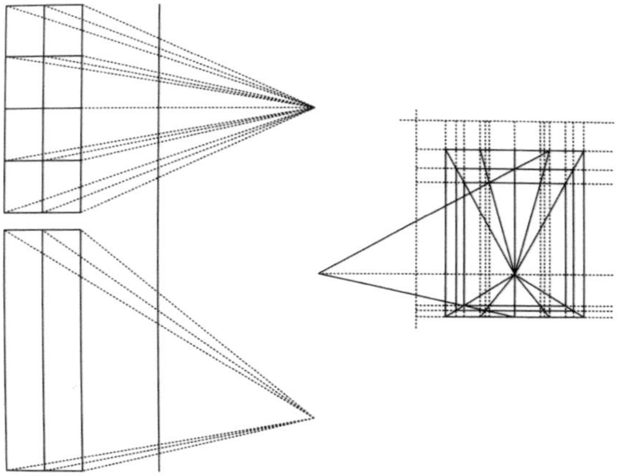

Figure 1. Modern "linear perspectival" construction of a rectangular interior space ("space box"). Left above: plan. Left below: elevation. Right: perspectival image arrived at by combining the segments marked off on the "projection line."

through the so-called visual pyramid; the apex of this pyramid is the eye, which is then connected with individual points within the space to be represented. Because the relative position of these "visual rays" determines the apparent position of the corresponding points in the visual image, I need only draw the entire system in plan and elevation in order to determine the figure appearing on the intersecting surface. The plan yields the width, the elevation yields the height; and if I combine these values on a third drawing, I will obtain the desired perspectival projection (Fig. 1).

In a picture constructed this way—that is, by means of what Dürer called a "planar, transparent intersection of all those rays that fall from the eye onto the object it sees"[6]—the following laws are valid. First, all perpendiculars or "orthogonals" meet at the so-called central vanishing point, which is determined by the perpendicular drawn from the eye to the picture plane. Second, all parallels, in whatever direction they lie, have a common vanishing point. If they lie in horizontal plane, then their vanishing point lies always on the so-called horizon, that is, on the horizontal line through the central vanishing point. If, moreover, they happen to form a 45-degree angle with the picture plane, then the distance between their vanishing point and the central vanishing point is equal to the distance between the eye and the picture plane. Finally, equal dimensions diminish progressively as they recede in space, so that any portion of the picture—assuming that the location of the eye is known—is calculable from the preceding or following portion.

In order to guarantee a fully rational—that is, infinite, unchanging and homogenous—space, this "central perspective" makes two tacit but essential assumptions: first, that we see with a single and immobile eye, and second, that the planar cross section of the visual pyramid can pass for an adequate reproduction of our optical image. In fact these two premises are rather bold abstractions from reality, if by "reality" we mean the actual subjective optical impression. For the structure of an infinite, unchanging and homogeneous space—in short, a purely mathematical space—is quite unlike the structure of psychophysiolocigal space: "Perceptions does not know the concept of infinity; from the very outset it is confined within certain spatial limits imposed by our faculty of perception. And in connection with perceptual space we can no more speak of homogeneity than of infinity. The ultimate basis of the homogeneity of geometric space is that all its elements, the 'points' which are joined in it, are mere determinations of position, possessing no independent content of their own outside of this relation, this position which they occupy in relation to each other. Their reality is exhausted in their reciprocal relation: it is a purely functional and not a substantial reality. Because fundamentally these points are devoid of all content, because they have become mere expressions of ideal relations, they can raise no question of a diversity in content. Their homogeneity signifies nothing other than this similarity of structure, grounded in their common logical function, their common ideal purpose and meaning. Hence homogeneous space is never given space, but space produced by construction; and indeed the geometrical concept of homogeneity can be expressed by the postulate that from every point in space it must be possible to draw similar figures in all directions and magnitudes. Nowhere in the space of immediate perception can this postulate be fulfilled. Here there is no strict homogeneity of position and direction; each place has its own mode and its own value. Visual space and tactical space [*Tastraum*] are both anisotropic and unhomogeneous in contrast to the metric space of Euclidean geometry: 'the main directions of organization—before-behind, above-below, right-left—are dissimilar in both physiological spaces.'"[7]

Exact perspectival construction is a systematic abstraction from the structure of this psychophysiological space. For it is not only the effect of perspectival con-

6 Lange and Fuhse, *Dürers schriftlicher Nachlass*, 195, I. 15: "*Ein ebne durchsichtige Abschneidung aller der Streimlinien, die aus dem Aug fallen auf die Ding, die es sicht.*"

7 Ernst Cassirer, *Philosophie der symbolischen Formen*, vol. 2: *Das mythische Denken* (Berlin: B. Cassirer, 1925), 107f. (*Philosophy of Symbolic Forms*, vol. 2: *Mythical Thought*, trans. Ralph Manheim (New Haven, CT: Yale University Press, 1955], 83–84. [In the last sentence of the passage Cassirer quotes Ernst Mach. —TR]). For the psychophysiological view of space, of course, the distinction between solid bodies and the medium of open space surrounding them is sharper than that between "front" and "back," etc. For immediate and mathematically unrationalized perception, empty space is qualitatively altogether different from "objects." On this subject, see E. R. Jaensch, *Über die Wahrnehmung des Raumes, Zeitschrift für Psychologie*, supplement 6 (Leipzig: Barth, 1911), sec. 1, ch. 6: "Zur Phänomenologie des leeren Raumes."

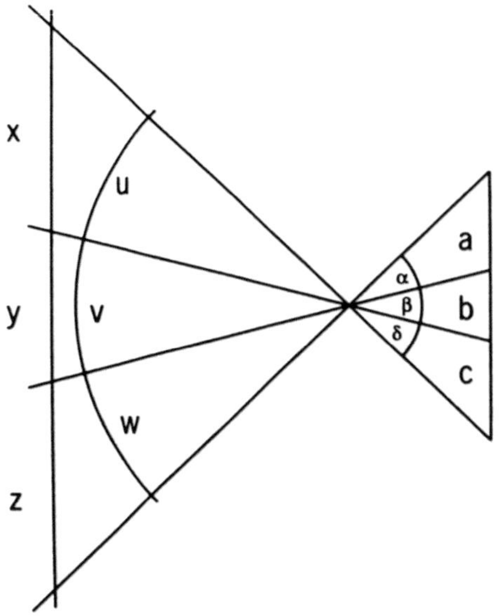

Figure 2. Explanation of the "marginal distortions."

struction, but indeed its intended purpose, to realize in the representation of space precisely that homogeneity and boundlessness foreign to the direct experience of that space. In a sense, perspective transforms pyschophysiological space into mathematical space. It negates the differences between front and back, between right and left, between bodies and intervening space ("empty" space), so that the sum of all the parts of space and all its contents are absorbed into a single "quantum continuum." It forgets that we see not with a single fixed eye but with two constantly moving eyes, resulting in a spheroidal field of vision. It takes no account of the enormous difference between the psychologically conditioned "visual image" through which the visible world is brought to our consciousness, and the mechanically conditioned "retinal image" which paints itself upon our physical eye. For a peculiar stabilizing tendency within our consciousness—promoted by the cooperation of vision with the tactile sense—ascribes to perceived objects a definite and proper size and form, and thus tends not to take notice, at least not full notice, of the distortions which these sizes and forms suffer on the retina. Finally, perspectival construction ignores the crucial circumstance that this retinal image—entirely apart from its subsequent psychological "interpretation," and even apart from the fact that the eyes move—is a projection not on a flat but on a concave surface. Thus already on this lowest, still prepsychological level of facts there is a fundamental discrepancy between "reality" and its construction. This is also true, of course, for the entirely analogous operation of the camera.

If, to choose a very simple example, a line is divided so that its three sections *a*, *b* and *c* subtend equal angles, these objectively unequal sections will be represented on a concave surface (like the retina) as approximately equal lengths; whereas if projected on a flat surface they will appear, as before, as unequal lengths (Fig. 2). This is the source of those marginal distortions which are most familiar to us from photography, but which also distinguish the perspectivally constructed image from the retinal image, these distortions can be mathematically expressed as the discrepancy between, on the one hand, the ratio of the visual angles and, on the other hand, the ratio of the linear sections produced by projection upon a flat surface. The wider the total or composite visual angle—that is, the smaller the ratio between the distance from eye to image and the size of the image—the more pronounced the distortion.[8] But alongside this purely quantitative discrepancy between retinal image and perspectival representation, which was recognized already in the early Renaissance, there is as well a formal discrepancy. This latter follows, in the first place, from the movement of the gaze, and in the second place, once again, from the curvature of the retina: for while perspective projects straight lines as straight lines, our eye perceives them (from the center of projection) as convex curves. A normal checkerboard pattern appears at close range to swell out in the form of a shield; an objectively curved checkerboard, by the same token, will straighten itself out. The orthogonals of a building, which in normal perspectival construction appear straight, would, if they were to correspond to the factual retinal image, have to be drawn as curves. Strictly speaking, even the verticals would have to submit to some bending (*pace* Guido Hauck, whose drawing is reproduced as Figure 3).

This curvature of the optical image has been observed twice in modern times: by the great psychologists and physicists at the end of the last century;[9] but

8 On the phenomenon of marginal distortions, see above all Guido Hauck, *Die subjektive Perspektive und die horizontalen Curvaturen des Dorischen Styls* (Stuttgart, 1879), esp. p. 51ff., and "Die malerische Perspektive," *Wochenblatt für Architekten und Ingenieuren* 4 (1882). On the historical aspects, see Hans Schuritz, *Die Perspektive in der Kunst Dürers* (Frankfurt: H. Keller, 1919). 11ff., among others. [...]

9 See specifically Hermann von Helmholtz, *Handbuch der physiologischen Optik* (Hamburg & Leipzig: Voss, 1910), vol. 3, p. 151 (*Physiological Optics* [New York: Dover, 1960], vol. 3, pp. 178–87); Hauck, *Die subjektive Perspektive*; Peter, "Studien über die Struktur des Sehraums." Especially instructive is the counterproof, the so-called curved-path experiment. If a number of mobile individual points (small lights or the like) are ordered in two rows leading into depth in such a way that a subjective impression of parallel straight lines ensues, then the objectively resulting form will be concave, trumpet-like (see Franz Hillebrand, "Theorie der scheinbaren Grösse bei binocularem Sehen," *Denkschriften der Kaiserlichen Akademie der Wissenschaften*, Mathematisch-Naturwissenschaftliche Klasse, no. 72 [1902], pp. 255-307; the critiques of his arguments—see among others Walther Poppelreuter, "Beiträge zur Raumpsychologie," *Zeitschrift für Psychologie* 58 [1911], 200-62—do not impinge upon matters essential to us here).

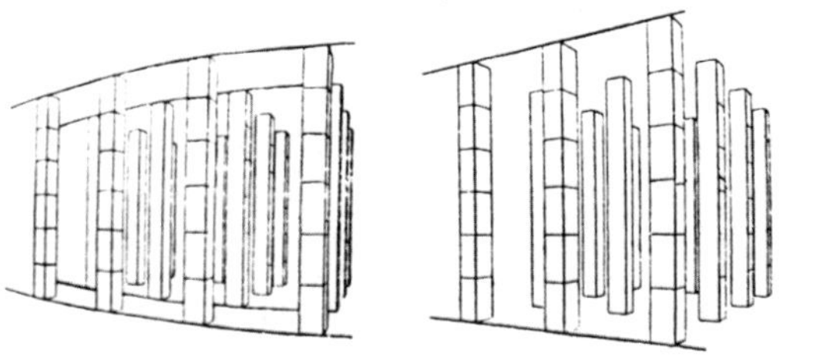

Figure 3. Hall of pillars constructed according to "subjective" or curved perspective (left) and according to schematic or linear perspective (right). (After Guido Hauck.)

also (and this has apparently not been remarked upon until now) by the great astronomers and mathematicians at the beginning of the seventeenth century. We should recall above all the words of the remarkable Wilhelm Schickhardt, a cousin of the Württemberg architect and Italian traveler, Heinrich Schickhardt: "I say that all lines, even the straightest, which do not stand *directe contra pupillam* [directly in front of the eye]...necessarily appear somewhat bent. Nevertheless, no painter believes this; this is why they paint the straight sides of a building with straight lines, even though according to the true art of perspective this is incorrect.... Crack that nut, you artists!" This was endorsed by none other than Kepler, at least insofar as he admitted the possibility that the objectively straight tail of a comet or the objectively straight trajectory of a meteor is subjectively perceived as a curve. What is most interesting is that Kepler fully recognized that he had originally overlooked or even denied these illusory curves only because he had been schooled in linear perspective. He had been led by the rules of painterly perspective to believe that straight is always seen as straight, without stopping to consider that the eye in fact projects not onto a *plana tabella* but onto the inner surface of a sphere.[10] And indeed, if even today only a very few of us have perceived these curvatures, that too is surely in part due to our habituation— further reinforced by looking at photographs—to linear perspectival construction: a construction that is itself comprehensible only for a quite specific, indeed specifically modern, sense of space, or if you will, sense of the world.

Thus in an epoch whose perception was governed by a conception of space expressed by strict linear perspective, the curvatures of our, so to speak, spheroidal optical world had to be rediscovered. However, in a time that was accustomed to seeing perspectivally—but not in linear perspective—these curvatures were simply taken for granted: that is, in antiquity. In antique optics and art theory (as well as in philosophy, although here only in the form of analogies) we constantly encounter the observations that straight lines are seen as curved and curved lines as straight; that columns must be subjected to *entasis* (usually relatively weak, of course, in classical times) in order not to appear bent; that epistyle and stylobate must be built curved in order to avoid the impression of sagging. And indeed, the familiar curvatures of the Doric temple attest to the practical consequences of such findings.[11] Antique optics, which brought all these insights to fruition, was thus in its first principles quite antithetical to linear perspective. And if it did understand so clearly the spherical distortions of form, this only follows from (or at least corresponds to) its still more momentous recognition of the distortions of magnitude. For here, too, antique optics fit its theory more snugly to the factual structure of the subjective optical impression than did Renaissance perspective. Because it conceived of the field of vision as a sphere,[12] antique optics maintained, always and without exception, that apparent magnitudes (that is, projections of objects onto that spherical field of vision) are determined not by the distances of the objects from the eye, but rather exclusively by the width of the angles of vision. Thus the relationship between the magnitudes of objects is, strictly speaking, expressible only in degrees of angle or arc, and not in simple measures of length.[13] Indeed Euclid's Eighth Theorem explicitly preempts any opposing view. Euclid states that the apparent difference between two equal magnitudes perceived from unequal distances is determined not by the ratio of these distances, but rather by the far less discrepant ratio of the angles of vision (Fig. 4).[14] This is diametrically opposed to the doctrine behind modern perspectival construction, familiar in the formula of Jean Pélerin, known as Viator: "*Les quantitez et les distances Ont concordables différences*"

10 Johannes Kepler, *Appendix hyperaspistis* 19, in *Opera omnia*, 8 vols., ed. Christian Frisch (Frankfurt & Erlangen, 1858–1871), vol. 7, 279 [...]

11 That right angles appear round when seen from a distance (and that, by the same token, an arc becomes under certain conditions a straight line) was demonstrated by Euclid, Theorems Nine and Twenty-two; see Euclid, *Optica*, ed. J. L. Heiberg (1895), 166 and 180 (16 and 32); subsequently Aristotle, *Problemata* 15 .6, and Diogenes Laertius 9.89. This is applied more frequently to solid objects, for instance in the proposition that from a distance four-cornered towers appear cylindrical: [...]

12 See Damian, *Schrift über Optik*, 2, art. 11: [...] ("The point of the cone of vision is within the pupil and it is the point of a sphere..."). From this it becomes immediately evident that it is one and the same form of thought—or better, form of seeing—which, on the one hand, makes the visual magnitudes so strictly dependent on the angles, and on the other hand, emphasizes so strongly the apparent curvature of the straight lines.

13 Euclid, *Definition* (*horos*) 4-6, *Optica*, 154 (2).

14 Euclid, Theorem Eight, Optica, 164 (14) [...] "Two objects of equal magnitude placed at unequal distances are not seen according to the ratio of their distances"). The proposition is proven by showing that the difference between the distances is greater than that between the angles, and that only the latter (according to the axioms named in the previous note) determine the visual magnitudes.

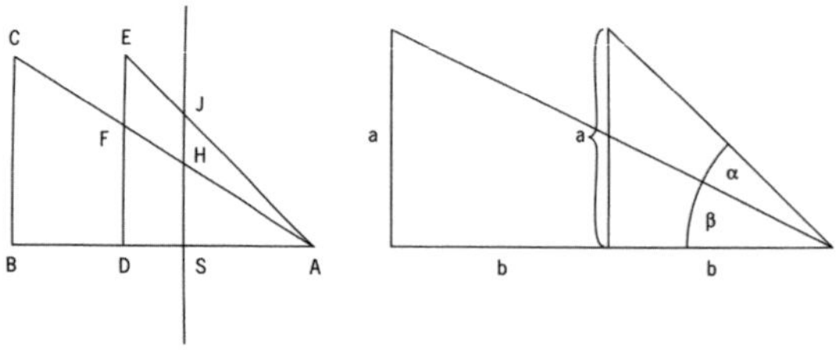

Figure 4. Contrast between the "linear perspectival" (left) and "angle perspectival" (right) constructions.

("The quantities and the distances vary proportionally").[15] And perhaps it is more than mere accident that in Renaissance paraphrases of Euclid, indeed even in translations, precisely this Eight Theorem was either entirely suppressed or "emended" until it lost its original meaning.[16] Evidently, the contradiction was felt between Euclid's *perspectiva naturalis* or *communis*, which sought simply to formulate mathematically the laws of natural vision (and so linked apparent size to the visual angle), and the *perspectiva artificialis* developed in the meantime, which on the contrary tried to provide a serviceable method for constructing images on two-dimensional surfaces. Clearly, this contradiction could be resolved only by abandoning the angle axiom; to recognize the axiom is to expose the creation of a perspectival image as, strictly speaking, an impossible task, for a sphere obviously cannot be unrolled on a surface.

II

At this point we are bound to wonder whether and in what way antiquity itself might have developed a geometrical perspective. The ancients, as far as we know, never swerved from the principle that apparent magnitudes were determined not by distances but by angles. On the one hand, it is clear that as long as it respected this principle, antique painting cannot very well have contemplated a projection upon a surface, but rather would have had to adhere to a projection upon a spherical surface. On the other hand, there can be no doubt that antique painting was even less prepared than was the Renaissance to work in practice with "stereographic" projection, for example in Hipparchos's sense. We thus have to consider, at most, whether or not antiquity managed to work out an artistically serviceable approximation. We might imagine such a construction founded on the notion of a "sphere of projection"—or, in plan and elevation, a circle of projection—with, however, the arcs of the circle replaced by their chords. This would achieve a certain approximation of the depicted magnitudes to the widths of the angles, without posing any more technical problems than the modern procedure. And indeed it seems possible—we dare not claim this with any certainty—that antique painting, at least by late Hellenistic and Roman times, had just such a procedure at its disposal.

Vitruvius, in a much-discussed passage of the *Ten Books on Architecture*, offers the following remarkable definition: "*Scenographia,*" that is, the perspectival representation of a three-dimensional structure on a surface, is based on an "*omnium linearum ad circini centrum responses.*"[17] At first, of course, one had hoped to discover in this *circini centrum* the central vanishing point of modern perspective. But not a single surviving antique painting possesses such a unified vanishing point. More importantly, the words themselves appear to rule out this interpretation, for *circini centrum* properly means "compass point," not "center of a circle": the central vanishing point of modern linear perspective, the mere convergence point of orthogonals, cannot possibly be construed as the fixed point of a compass.[18] If, however, Vitruvius is speaking about an exact per-

15 Jean Pélerin (Viator), *De artificiali perspectiva* (Toul, 1505), facsimile ed., by A. de Montaiglon (Paris, 1860), fol. C8r. The corresponding illustration, which is of course dependent on Diirer's *Martyrdom of the Ten Thousand*, first appears in the edition of 1509. [...]

16 The metamorphosis of Euclid's Eighth Theorem (at least when it is not simply dropped, as it is in most writings on artificial perspective) can be followed almost step by step. The first complete published translation, that ofZamberto (Venice, 1503), still renders it literally, even if a little misleadingly by virtue of placing "*intervallis*" before "*proportionaliter*": "*Aequales magnitudines inaequaliter expositae intervallis proportionaliter minime spectantur*" ('~Equal dimensions set unequally at distances appear least proportionately"; fol. A.A.6 v.). Diirer, or the Latinist he relied upon, immediately foll victim to the ambiguity of this translation, in that he referred "*proportionaliter*" to "*expositae*" instead of to "*spectantur*," and "*minime*" to "*spectantur*" instead of to "*proportionaliter*," thus rendering the sentence perfectly unintelligible: "*Gleich Gross ungleich gsetzt mit proportionirlichen Unterscheiden kiinnen nit gesehen werden*" ("Equal dimensions set unequally with proportional differences cannot be seen"), Lange and Fuhse, *Dürers schriftlicher Nachlass*, p. 322, I. 23 (indeed, the whole passage from Lange and Fuhse, p. 319, I. 21 top. 326, I. 19 is a translation from Euclid: see Panofsky, *Dürers Kunsttheorie* [Berlin: Reimer, 1915], p. 15ff.). [...]

17 Vitruvius, in the passage in question (1.2.2; on its much-disputed significance for antique perspectival construction, sec the following note), takes the term *scenographia* in its narrower sense as the method of representing buildings perspectivally on a surface, whether for architectonic or theoretical purposes [...] But the term *scenographia* also has a broader sense, for it can denote quite generally the application of optical laws to the visual arts and architecture in their entirety; that is, not only the rules for making flat pictures on flat surfaces, but also the rules of architectonic and plastic construction, insofar as the latter are interested in counteracting the distortions entailed in the process of seeing [...]

18 The pertinent passage in Vitruvius and its parallel passage from the Prooemium are the only testimonies that permit us at all to suppose the existence of a mathematically constructed pictorial perspective in antiquity; for other testimonies, although they reveal that artists took the laws of vision into account, nevertheless do not reveal knowledge of a geometrical procedure which would have permitted the exact construction of perspectival representations. [...]

spectival construction at all (which the mention of the *circinus* still implies), there is at least a possibility that Vitruvius meant by *centrum* not a vanishing point within the picture, but rather a "center of projection" standing for the eye of the beholder. That center (and this would conform entirely to the antique angle axiom) would then in preparatory drawings be the center of a circle intersecting the visual rays, just as the straight line representing the picture plane intersects the visual rays in modern perspectival construction. In any event, if one now constructs with the help of such a "circle of projection" (whereby, as said before, the arcs of the circle are replaced by the corresponding chords), the result does conform to the surviving monuments in a crucial respect: the extensions of the orthogonals do not merge at a single point, but rather only weakly converge, and thus meet in pairs at several points along a common axis. For when the circle is rolled out, the arcs break apart, so to speak, at the tips. This creates a "fishbone" effect.

It is not clear that such an interpretation of the Vitruvius passage can be sustained; it can hardly be proved, since the surviving pictures almost without exception are not rigorously constructed. At any rate, this fishbone or, more formally put, vanishing-axis principle was, at least as far as we can monitor it, crucial in antique spatial representation. Sometimes we find it in the form of a partial convergence, as just described and in accord with our hypothetical circle-c onstruction (Plate 1); sometimes in the more schematic, but more practicable, form of a more or less pure parallelism of oblique orthogonals. The latter version is attested already on southern Italian vases of the fourth century B.C.[19]

But this mode of representing space suffers, in comparison to the modern mode, from a peculiar instability and internal inconsistency. For the modern vanishing-point construction distorts all widths, depths and heights in constant proportion, and thus defines unequivocally the apparent size of any object, the size corresponding to its actual magnitude and its position with respect to the eye. That is precisely the enormous advantage of the modern method, precisely why it was so passionately pursued. A constant distortion is impossible under the vanishing-axis principle because the arrangement of the rays has no validity. This is strikingly illustrated by the inability of the vanishing-axis principle to foreshorten correctly a checkerboard pattern: the squares in the middle are either too large or too small. Already in antiquity, but then above all in the late Middle Ages, when this construction was revived in many parts of Europe, such awkward discrepancies were concealed by an escutcheon, a festoon, a bit of drapery or some other perspectival fig leaf.[20] Moreover, the diagonals of a checkerboard constructed in this way will only run straight if the depth intervals in the rear half of the board appear to grow, instead of diminishing as they should; and conversely if the intervals do diminish, then the diagonals will appear broken.

Granted, this looks more like a mathematical than an artistic matter, for one might with justice point out that the relative imperfection, indeed even the total absence, of a perspectival construction has nothing to do with artistic value (just as, conversely, the strict observance of perspectival laws need in no wise encroach upon artistic "freedom"). But if perspective is not a factor of value, it is surely a factor of style. Indeed, it may even be characterized as (to extend Ernst's Cassirer's felicitous term to the history of art) one of those "symbolic forms" in which "spiritual meaning is attached to a concrete, material sign and intrinsically given to this sign." This is why it is essential to ask of artistic periods and regions not only whether they have perspective, but also which perspective they have.

The art of classical antiquity was a purely corporeal art; it recognized as artistic reality only what was tangible as well as visible. Its objects were material and three-dimensional, with clearly defined functions and proportions, and thus were always to a certain extent anthropomorphized. These objects were not merged in painterly fashion into spatial unity, but rather were affixed to each other in a kind of tectonic or plastic cluster. Hellenistic art, to be sure, began to affirm not only the value of the internally motivated body, but also the charms of its outer surface. It also began to perceive as worthy of depiction (and this is closely related) not only animate but also inanimate nature, not only the plastic and beautiful but also the painterly and ugly, or common, not only solid bodies but also the surrounding and unifying space. Yet even the Hellenistic artistic imagination remained attached to individual objects, to such an extent that space was still perceived not as something that could embrace and dissolve the opposition between bodies and nonbodies, but only as that which remains, so to speak, between the bodies. Thus, space was artistically manifested partly by simple superposition, partly by a still-unsystematic overlapping. Even where Greco-Roman art advanced to the representation of real interiors or real landscape, this enriched and expanded world was

19 On the antique technique of foreshortening or perspective, to the extent it can be verified in representations of buildings, see (as well as the cited works by Delbrück and Hügel) especially Guido Hauck, *Die subjektive Perspektive*, 54ff., whose division of the development into four "stages," it must be granted, has more systematic than historical value. [...]

20 See G. Joseph Kern, *Die Grundzüge der linear-perspektivischen Darstellung in der Kunst der Gebrüder van Eyck und ihrer Schule* (Leipzig: Seemann, 1907), as well as his important essays: "Die Anfange der zentralperspcktivischcn Konstruktion in der italienischen Malerei des 14. Jahrhunderts," *Mitteilungen des Deutschen kunsthistorischen lnstituts in Florenz 2* (1912).

still by no means a perfectly unified world, a world where bodies and the gaps between them were only differentiations or modifications of a continuum of a higher order. Depth intervals have become palpable, but cannot be expressed in terms of a fixed "module." The foreshortened orthogonals converge, but they never converge toward a single horizon, not to speak of a single center (even if in representations of architecture, as a rule, the rising of the base lines and the fall of the roof lines are observed).[21] Magnitudes generally diminish as they recede, but this diminution is by no means constant, indeed it is always being interrupted by malproportioned figures, figures "not to scale." The transformations effected by distance and the intervening medium upon the form and color of bodies are represented with such bold virtuosity that the style of these painting has been help up as a precursor of, or even parallel to, modern Impressionism; and yet they never achieve unified "lighting."[22] Even when the notion of perspective as "seeing through" is taken seriously—for example, when we are meant to believe that we are looking through a row of columns onto a continuous landscape—the represented space remains an aggregate space; it never becomes that which modernity demands and realizes, a systematic space.[23] Precisely here it becomes clear that the antique "impressionism" was only a quasi impressionism. For the modern movement to which we give that name always presupposes that higher unity, over and above empty space and bodies; as a result its observations automatically acquire direction and unity. This is how Impressionism can so persistently devalue and dissolve solid forms without ever jeopardizing the stability of the space and the solidity of the individual objects; on the contrary, it conceals that stability and solidity. Antiquity, on the other hand, lacking that domineering unity, must, so to speak, purchase every spatial gain with a loss of corporeality, so that space really seems to consume objects. This explains the almost paradoxical phenomenon that so long as antique art makes no attempt to represent the space between bodies, its world seems more solid and harmonious than the world represented by modern art; but as soon as space is included in the representation, above all in landscape painting, that world becomes curiously unreal and inconsistent, like a dream or mirage.[24]

Antique perspective is thus the expression of a specific and fundamentally unmodern view of space (although it is certainly a genuinely *spatial* view, Spengler notwithstanding). Antique perspective is furthermore the expression of an equally specific and equally unmodern conception of the world. And only now can we understand how the antique world was able to satisfy itself with what Goethe called "such a precarious, even false" rendition of the impression of space.[25] Why did the ancients fail to take the apparently small step of intersecting the visual pyramid with a plane and thus proceed to a truly exact and systematic construction of space? To be sure, that could not happen as long as the angle axiom of the theoreticians prevailed. But why did they not simply disregard the axiom, as would happen a millennium and a half later? They did not do it because that feeling for space which was seeking expression in the plastic arts simply did not demand a systematic space. Systematic space was as unthinkable for antique philosophers as it was unimaginable for antique artists. Thus is would be methodologically quite unsound to equate the question "Did antiquity have perspective?" with the question "Did antiquity have *our* perspective?" as was done in the days of Perrault and Sallier, Lessing and Klotzen.

As various as antique theories of space were, none of them succeeded in defining space as a system of simple relationships between height, width and depth.[26] In that case, in the guise of a "coordinate system," the difference between "front" and "back," "here" and "there," "body" and "nonbody" would have resolved into the higher and more abstract concept of three-

21 According to Kern (especially in *Die Grundzüge der perspektivischenDarstellung*, 3 Jff. and in "Die Anfänge der zentralpcrspektivischen Konstruktion," 62; G. Wolf copies him thoughtlessly in *Mathematik und Malcrei* [1916], 49), there was a controversy in antiquity and particularly in the Middle Ages over whether "parallels running off into the distance appear to converge in a single point or not"; it seems that Vitellio polemicized against the vanishing-point theory in the twenty-first theorem of the fourth book of *his Perspectiva communis* (127). This opposition, however, appears to be a position derived from the modern evolution of perspective, inadmissibly introduced into the deliberations of antique and high medieval optics. [...]

22 See Pfuhl, *Malerei und Zeichnung der Griechen*, vol. 2, 885ff.

23 Unfortunately, we are very poorly informed about the development which preceded the true perspectival representations of the so-called second Pompeian style, and especially about the hardly inconsiderable role. (at least on the evidence of Etruscan urns and mirrors; for an example of the latter , see note 40, below) played by the native Italian element in this development. Given the incompleteness and imbalance of the surviving material, it is at best doubtful whether this darkness will ever be entirely illuminated. [...]

24 The arguments in this essay overlap considerably, as far as more general questions are concerned, with arguments presented in the author's *Die deutsche Plastik des elften bis dreizehnten Jahrhunderts* (Munich: Wolff, 1924), except that they now seem to have found a certain justification in the more readily verifiable results of an investigation conducted specifically from the standpoint of the history of perspective. The following sentence appears in an ingenious work by Ernst Garger, *Die Reliefs an den Fürstentoren des Stefansdom* (Vienna: Krystall , 1926), which unfortunately could not be used here any more extensively: "Antiquity had true space, almost like that of the Renaissance" (35). In this "almost" lies the problem of the present essay.

25 Goethe, "Die schönsten Ornamente und merkwürdigsten Gemälde aus Pompeii, Herculaneum und Stabiae," *Jahrbuch der Literatur* (1830), sec. 7.

26 See the arguments of Ernst Cassirer adduced above.

dimensional extension, or even, as Arnold Geulincx puts it, the concept of a "*corpus generaliter sumptum*" ("body taken in a general sense"). Rather, the totality of the world always remained something radically discontinuous. Democritus, for example, constructed a purely corporeal world out of indivisble elements, and then, only in order to secure for those elements the possibility of movement, postulated further the infinite void as a *me on* or nonbeing (even if, as a correlate to the *on* or being, this is something of a necessity). Plato let space stand in opposition to the world of elements reducible to geometrically formed bodies, as their formless *huperdoche* or receptacle (indeed it is even hostile to form). Aristotle, finally, with a basically quite unmathematical transfer of qualitative categories to the realm of the quantitative, attributed six dimensions (*diastaseis, diastemata*) to *topos koinos* or general space (up and down, front and back, right and left), even though individual bodies were sufficiently defined by three dimensions (height, width, depth). Moreover, Aristotle conceived this "general space" in turn as merely the furthest frontier of an absolutely large body, namely the outermost celestial sphere—just as the specific location of individual things (*topos idios*) is for him the frontier where the One meets the Other.[27] Perhaps this Aristotelian doctrine of space illustrates with special clarity the inability of antique thought to bring the concrete empirical "attributes" of space, and in particular the distinction between "body" and "nonbody," to a common denominator of a *substance étendue*: bodies are not absorbed into a homogenous and infinite system of dimensional relationships, but rather are the juxtaposed content of a finite vessel. For, just as for Aristotle there is no "quantum continuum" in which the quiddity of individual things would be dissolved, so there is for him also no *energeiai apeiron* (actual infinite) which would extend beyond the *Dasein* of individual objects (for, in modern terms, even the sphere of fixed stars would be an "individual object").[28] And precisely here it becomes quite clear that "aesthetic space" and "theoretical space" recast perceptual space in the guise of one and the same sensation: in one case that sensation is visually symbolized, in the other it appears in logical form.

27 Aristotle, *Physics*, book 4.

28 On the Aristotelian concept of infinity, see especially Pierre Duhem, *Études sur Léonard de Vinci, vol. 2: Ceux qu'il a lus et ceux qui l'ont lu* (1909; repr ., Paris: F. de. Nobele, 1955), 5ff.

(Not) In Place: The Grid, or, Cultural Techniques of Ruling Spaces
Bernhard Siegert
2015

THE GRID AS CULTURAL TECHNIQUE

Xenophon's *Oeconomicus* introduces *taxis* as a fundamental cultural technique of the economic domain. *Taxis* refers to an order of things in which each and every object is located in a fixed place where it can be found. Humans, however, differ from things. "When you are searching for a person," Xenophon cautions, "you often fail to find him, though he may be searching for you himself."[1] Humans defy the fundamental rules of economy because for them "no place of meeting has been fixed."[2]

This distinction between retrievable things and untraceable humans points to the fundamental divide that separates the Greeks from modern subjects. Modernity is characterized by the invention of a *taxis* technique capable of also turning humans into retrievable objects. This modern *taxis* is implemented by means of a new cultural technique which takes into account that something may be missing from its place. In other words, it encompasses the notion of an empty space. The technique in question is the grid or lattice. Its salient feature is its ability to merge operations geared toward representing humans and things with those of governance. As Deleuze noted in his study of Foucault, between the sixteenth and eighteenth century, grid-shaped control becomes the universal practice that constitutes the basis of modern disciplinary societies.[3]

The ontological effect of the grid is the modern concept of place and being-in-one's-place based on the media-theoretical distinction between data and addresses. In other words, it presupposes the ability to write absence, that is, to deal equally efficiently with both occupied and empty spaces. This concept of place is thus inextricably tied to the notion of order. In return, it is impossible to conceive of this modern concept of order without the new understanding of place.

The universality of this concept of order is apparent in the way in which it bears on the interaction between imaging technologies and mathematical, topographical, geographical, and governmental knowledge. It is this interaction that turns the grid into a cultural technique. But what does this imply? As a cultural technique, the grid has a triple function. First, it is an imaging technology that by means of a given algorithm enables us to project a three-dimensional world onto a two-dimensional place. That is, it is a type of representation that posits an antecedent geometrical space in which objects are located and that submits the representation of objects to a theory of subjective vision. Second, the grid is a general diagrammatic procedure that uses specific addresses to store data than can be implemented in the real as well as in the symbolic (grids may be two- or three-dimensional, or 2D/3D hybrids). Third, the grid serves to constitute a world of objects imagined by a subject. To speak with Heidegger, it is a *Gestell* or "enframing" aimed at the availability and controllability of whatever is thus conceived; it addresses and symbolically manipulates things that have been transformed into data. The grid, in short, is a medium that operationalizes deixis. It allows us to link deictic procedures with chains of symbolic operations that have effects in the real. Hence the grid is not only part of a history of representation, or of a history of procedures facilitating the efficient manipulation of data, but also of "a history of the different modes by which, in our culture, human beings are made into subjects."[4]

As important as the distinction between centrifugal and centripetal grids may be,[5] for the purpose of analyzing the grid as a cultural technique it is more relevant to distinguish between representational, topographic, cartographic, speculative, and three-dimensional (total) grids. This division, in turn, suggests a more fundamental question: Can the expansion of Western culture from the sixteenth to the twentieth century be described in terms of a growing totalitarianism of the grid?

1 Xenophon, *"Memorabilia" and "Oeconomicus,"* trans. E.C. Marchant (Cambridge: Harvard University Press, 1938), 439.
2 Xenophon, 439.
3 See Gilles Deleuze, *Foucault*, trans. Sean Hand (Minneapolis: University of Minnesota Press, 1988), 34.
4 Michel Foucault, "Why Study Power: The Question of the Subject," in *Beyond Structuralism and Hermeneutics*, ed. Hubert L. Dreyfus and Paul Rabinow (Chicago: University of Chicago Press, 1982), 208.

REPRESENTATIONAL GRIDS

The fact that the grid effectively merges representation and operation is already apparent in Leon Battista Alberti's 1435 treatise *De pictura* (*On Painting*), which deals with grids as part of an imaging theory. Alberti's famous *velum* (veil) is a *perspectiva naturalis* technology designed to circumscribe objects *(circumscriptio)*. Together with the window, which serves as metaphor for the mathematical construction of paintings, the veil is a medium for their technical construction. Alberti also refers to it as an intersection or *intercisio*, thereby linking it to his definition of the image as an intersection of the visual pyramid. The veil:

> [is] woven of very thin threads and loosely intertwined, dyed with any color, subdivided with thicker threads according to parallel partitions, in as many squares as you like, and held stretched by a frame, which [veil] I place, indeed, between the object to be represented and the eye, so that the visual pyramid penetrates through the thinness of the veil.[6]

Alberti's veil is the basis for all technological imaging procedures, until the twentieth century, that employ reprographic techniques such as hole patterns and halftone. Since the late nineteenth century, industrial graphics has used coded perforation patterns to resolve and make transmittable a template's halftones. Thus the veil survives in today's screen printing technologies. But already in the seventeenth century halftone techniques had been linked to a media-theoretical modeling of neuronal signal processing. The mezzotint print technology invented in 1642, which consists in wiping off the surface of a burnished copperplate,[7] corresponded to Descartes's physiological theory of the processing of optical perceptual data by their analytical decomposition into hole patterns that are engraved into the brain. But technical images do not have to wait for the arrival of copperplate engravings or the idea of neuronal signal processing by means of hole patterns; they precede the age of their technological reproducibility. Technical images, in other words, are no exclusive hallmark of modernity. The textile image was always already a technological image because it was produced by the mechanical distribution of warps and wefts.[8] It comes as no surprise that Alberti resorts to weaving and textile images when discussing the intricacies of central perspective. Indeed, at the beginning of the fifteenth century it was quite common in Europe—for instance, at the court of the Duc de Berry—to consider tapestries to have higher value than pictures. Alberti is so firmly rooted in the textile paradigm that his claim to have produced a scientific—that is, mathematical—treatise is constantly thwarted by explanations that harken back to the art of weaving. One example of many is his attempt to give a textile spin to Euclid's definition of a surface: "If more lines stick together like close threads in a cloth, they will make a surface."[9]

According to Alberti, the great asset of the veil is "that it always presents the same surfaces unchanged," because it fixes the apex of the visual pyramid. "And so, the veil will guarantee this not negligible advantage which I have spoken of: that the object always stays the same with respect to the view [ut res semper eadem e conspectu persistat]."[10]

To grasp the ontological implications of Alberti's grid technique, it is necessary to emphasize its connection to the categories of place or *locus* in his treatise:

> Since painting, in fact, aspires to represent the objects seen, let us note in what way they themselves come to sight. First of all, when we watch an [object], we certainly see that there is something that occupies a place.[11]

---

5 See Rosalind E. Krauss, "Grids," *October* 9 (1979), 50–64.

6 Leon Battista Alberti, *On Painting: A New Translation and Critical Edition*, trans. Rocco Sinisgalli (Cambridge: Cambridge University Press, 2011), 51.

7 See Karin Leonhard and Robert Felfe, *Lochmuster und Linienspiel: Überlegungen zur Druckgrafik des 17. Jahrhunderts* (Frieburg im Breisgau and Berlin: Rombach, 2006), 29–36.

8 See Birgit Schneider, *Textiles Prozessieren: Eine Mediengeschichte der Lochkartenweberei* (Zürich and Berlin: Diaphanes, 2007).

9 Alberti, *On Painting*, 23.

10 Alberti., 51. Opinions differ as to who invented the threaded veil. Some art historians favor Filippo Brunelleschi, to whom Alberti dedicated the Italian version of his treatise *De pictura (Della Pittura)*. Brunelleschi is said to have used a *velo* to draft the panel of the Florence Baptistery with which he proved the "truth" of central perspective; see Volker Hoffmann, "Filippo Brunelleschi: Kuppelbau und Perspektive," in *Saggi in onore di Renato Bonelli : Quaderni dell'istituto di storia dell'architettura*, ed. Corrado Bozzoni, Giovanni Carbonara, and Gabriela Villetti (Rome: Multigrafica Editrice, 1992), 323. It is known that Brunelleschi used squared paper for the topographic registration of Rome's ancient ruins. According to his biographer Antonio Manetti, Brunelleschi "made measured drawings of Roman buildings, using his understanding of standard surveying techniques.... The results were recorded 'on offcuts of parchment ... by means of squared divisions of the sheets, with arabic numerals and characters which Filippo alone understood' "; Martin Kemp, *The Science of Art: Optical Themes in Western Art from Brunelleschi to Seurat* (New Haven: Yale University Press, 1990), 11–12. The astronomer Paolo dal Pozzo Toscanelli, an alleged friend of Brunelleschi, used squared paper featuring Indian numerals to note line and column to record celestial observations. Antonio de Pietro Averlino, know as Filarete, describes in great detail in *Trattato di architettura* (app. 1461–1464) the usefulness of checkered paper for architectural design, especially with regard to the scalability of to-scale plans that enable readers to have a sense of the dimensions of fictitious buildings; see Filarete, *Tractat über die Baukunst nebst seinen Büchern von der Zeichenkunst und den Bauten der Medici*, ed. Wolfgang von Oettingen (Vienna, 1890; reprinted, Hildesheim and New York: Olms, 1974), 86.

11 Alberti, 49.

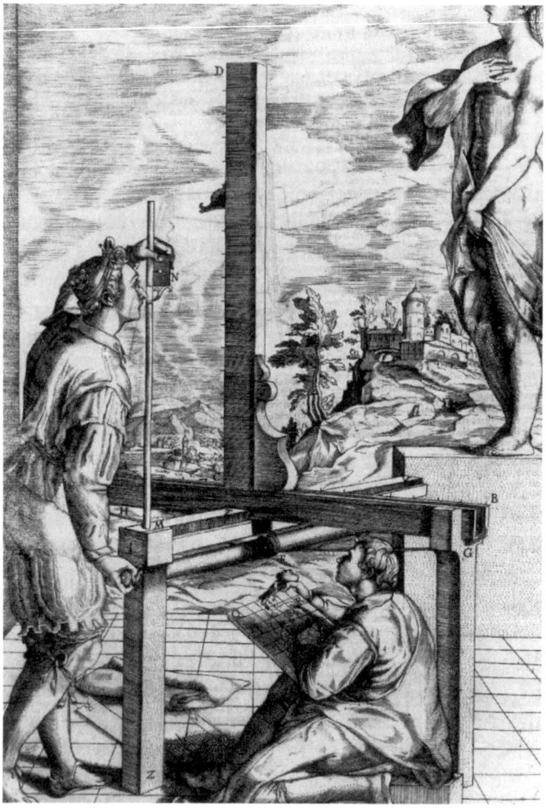

Something real (*res*) is something that occupies a space, that is in its place. It is crucial to be mindful of the connotations that the term *locus* (Greek *topos*) possesses in both rhetorics and *ars memoriae*. As Alberti would have it, only that which occupies its place is a representable object. Whatever lacks an identifiable place—such as the old gold ground or the halos that Alberti disdains—cannot and should not be depicted.[12]

Alberti's grid is an ordered space: a space in which aesthetic, ontological, and diagrammatic orders exercise their power over the existence and appearance of objects. It is a space that pays tribute to the power of cultural techniques to assign things and figures their own space. Hubert Damisch defined this "data space" as the "paradigmatic dimension" of the *costruzzione legitima*:

> To each figure its place: at each point on the underlying checkerboard, if not within each of its squares, one figure and only one, among all those that are possible, can be situated.[13]

Damisch makes clear that both the grid and the checkerboard of the *perspectiva artificialis* are structures in the Saussurean sense. The representation of objects in pictorial space implies their substitutability, which in turn reveals the analogy between Alberti's perspectival space and the place-value system of Indo-Arabic numerals. The fact that the grid precedes the object located therein (which implies both the possibility of addressing an empty place and the contingency of whatever object happens to be situated there) is equivalent to the semiotics of zero.[14] Brunelleschi as well as Alberti were members of that particular social class that in the *trecento* first absorbed and circulated knowledge of Indo-Arabic numerals. To each figure its own piece of space, to each numeral its place—in Germany, incidentally, these numerals were still known in the seventeenth century as *figurae*.

It is for this structural reason that digitization is able to retire the *velum*. Once you have two moveable scales and a sighting mechanism such as a cross-staff or a quadrant, a veil is superfluous (Fig. 1).

THE CARTOGRAPHIC GRID

Cartographers have used the grid as a technique for ordering space since antiquity. Claudius Ptolemy was the first to wrestle with the problem of projecting a spherical surface onto a plane surface; as well, he pioneered the method of dividing a surface into a lattice of latitudes and longitudes. In the second century he authored a treatise on cartography. His *Geography* was in all likelihood expanded by Byzantine scholars, and upon reaching Italy was translated into Latin in 1406. Ptolemy probably only wrote book 1, the beginning of book 2, and chapters 3 through 28 of the final book 8. The latter contains the coordinates of roughly three hundred cities based on time measurements. The longitude is determined by the temporal distance from the Alexandrian meridian, with one hour corresponding to fifteen degrees of longitude. The latitude is determined by the length of the longest day. The greater the distance from the equator, the longer the longest summer day in the Northern Hemisphere.[15] Based on information provided by Ptolemy and the Byzantine additions,

12 Long before Alberti, such painters as Giotto wrestled with the problem of where to place the nimbus in paintings that conjure up the illusion of depth. Where, for instance, is the nimbus of angels depicted in profile? And where is it in rear views? The Scrovegni Chapel in Padua features halos drawn in perspectival foreshortening. For further details see Wolfgang Braunfeld, *Nimbus und Goldgrund: Wege zur Kunstgeschichte, 1949–1975* (Mittenwald: Mäander Kunstverlag, 1979), 12–15.

13 Hubert Damisch, *The Origin of Perspective*, trans. John Goodman (Cambridge: MIT Press, 2000), xxi.

14 See Brian Rotman, *Signifying Nothing: The Smiotics of Zero* (Stanford: Stanford University Press, 1993).

15 See Oswald Ashton Wentworth Dilke, "The Culmination of Greek Cartography in Ptolemy," in *Cartography in Prehistoric, Ancient and Medieval Europe and the Mediterranean*, ed. John B. Harley and David Woodward (Chicago: University of Chicago Press, 1987), 177–200.

European publishers added maps to their editions.

The importance of the strict Euclidean ratio of point, line, and surface is already apparent in Edward Wright's map of 1599, which uses an improved Mercator projection to depict longitudes as parallels.[16] Latitudes and longitudes impose themselves on the medieval system of rhumbs. The grid thus turns into a diagram,[17] enabling the depiction of temporal sequences in addition to spatial orders. Once we read the synchronic segments diachronically, time appears as a function of space.

Ever since the arrival of matrix screens in the early 1970s, the addressing of points by means of rows and columns has turned into a universal imaging technique. While the imaging technique of vector graphics corresponds to the navigational technique of medieval portolan charts based on rhumb lines (a point is defined by its angle to and distance from the *origo*), the matrix screen corresponds to navigation by means of latitude and longitude. Unlike vector graphics that only store the beginning and end of a line, the matrix screen must take account of every single point on the line. The advantage of the latter is the addressability of every single element on the screen, because the screen memory delegates exactly one unit of storage space to each point.

THE TOPOGRAPHIC GRID (SOUTH AMERICA)

One of the effects of the representational technique known as central perspective is that the identity of objects becomes a function of their being in a particular place. The navigational technique employing latitude and longitude, in turn, enables us to head for any point in space by means of addresses that precede all stored data. The overall result is a common paradigm of image construction and early modern colonial governmentality that far exceeds the boundaries of art. To put persons or things in their place, to objectify and subjugate them, are procedures Heidegger already detected in the term *repraesentare*.[18] Turning to the colonial topographies of Spanish-American settlements, we can see that they are superimposed on a grid of very different provenance: the checkerboard design of urban planning associated with Hippodamus of Miletus. The representational grid of the Renaissance decodes and recodes the early grid of colonial topography devised by antiquity.

What results from this superimposition of the representational on the urban grid? Colonialism unleashes and mobilizes the utopian social potential contained in the grid-shaped heterotopias of Latin America. Three aspects are of particular importance: a) the possibility of registering the absent; b) the distinction between data and addresses; and c) the potentially infinite extension in time and space. The latter marks a decisive difference between the grid of Spanish colonial topography and Alberti's veil: The contained *velum* is a figure, whereas the centrifugal orthogonal net of colonial settlements is not.[19] The grid is thus located at several junctions: It straddles the boundary between antiquity and the modern age, and it marks the transition from the political to the economic (or governmental) as well as from symbolically organized space to graphically coded surface.

The origin of Spanish-American checkerboard cities has been the subject of lengthy debates. In all likelihood they arose from medieval and early modern attempts to adapt the construction of Roman military camps. A medieval Spanish treatise on urban planning containing, among other items, the *Regiment de Princeps* by the Catalan Franciscan Francesc Eiximenis (app. 1340–1409), describes the ideal grid-shaped city.[20]

The Roman *castrum* reflects the practice of centuriation. Centuriation is the division of the land into square units called centuries, carried out by the *agrimensores*, the Roman land surveyors. The more Rome came to dominate Italy, the greater was the need to divide up public domains and found new colonies.[21] The only surviving official Roman survey maps are the cadasters of Arausio (Orange, Vaucluse); in addition, there is an extant collection of Roman land surveying records known as the *Corpus Agrimensorum Romanorum* that contains treatises dating as far back as the first century B.C.E. The principal Roman measuring instrument was the *groma*, used to lay out straight lines, right angles, and squares. The usual procedure was for the land surveyor to divide up the land, draw lots for the landholdings, and lead the settlers to their fields. He was also responsible for making a map (*forma*) and compiling a register. "Between each pair of centuries was a *limes*, literally 'balk,' for which appropriate width was provided; in one direction

16 See William Boelhower, "Inventing America: A Model of Cartographic Semiosis," *Word and Image: A Journal of Verbal/Visual Enquiry* 4, no. 2 (1988): 482–83.

17 See Joachim Krausse, "Information at a Glance: On the History of the Diagram," *OASE: Tijdschrift voor architectuur* 48 (1998): 3–30.

18 Martin Heidegger, "The Age of the World Picture," in *The Question Concerning Technology and Other Essays*, trans. William Lovitt (New York: Harper and Row, 1977), 115–54.

19 Hubert Damisch, "La grille comme volonté et comme representation," 32.

20 See James M. Houston, "The Foundation of Colonial Towns in Hispanic America," in *Urbanization and Its Problems: Essays in Honour of E. W. Gilbert*, ed. Robert P. Beckinsale and James M. Houston (Oxford: Blackwell, 1968), 352–90.

21 The discussion that follows draws on Oswald Ashton Wentworh Dilke, "Roman Large-Scale Mapping in the Early Empire," in Harley and Woodward, eds., *Cartography in Prehistoric, Ancient and Medieval Europe and the Mediterranean,* 213–233.

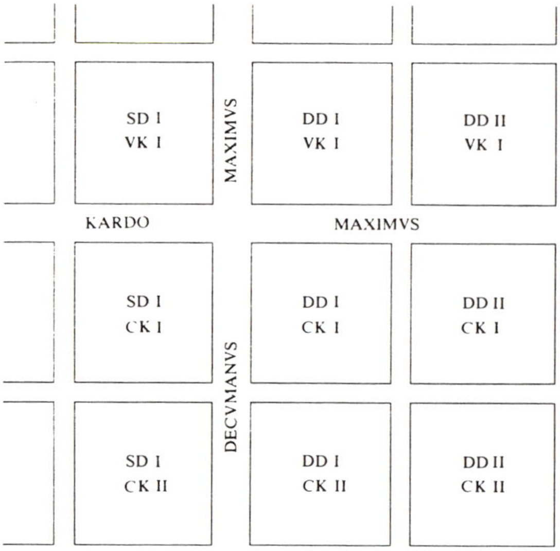

Figure 2. Centuriation. SD = sinistra decumani (left of the decumanus maximus), DD = dextra decumani (right of the decumanus maximus), VK = ultra kardinem (beyond the kardo maximus), CK = citra kardinem (this side of the kardo maximus). These abbreviations were engraved into the boundary stones that marked o the areas. Reprinted from Harley and Woodward, eds., *Cartography in Prehistoric, Ancient, and Medieval Europe and the Mediterranean*, 213.

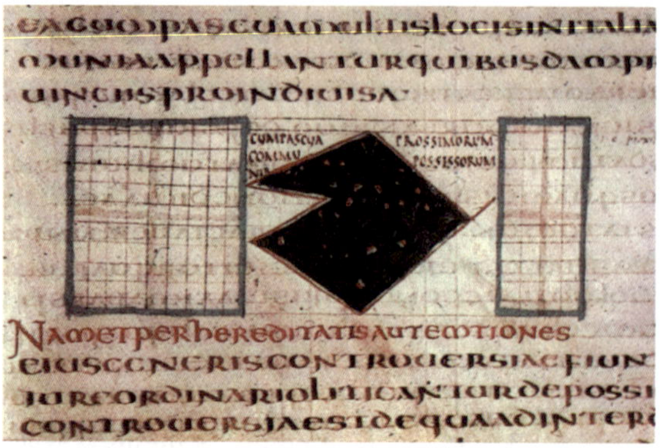

Figure 3. Illustration of uncultivated pasture land between two centuriated colonies. Miniature from the *Corpus Agrimensorum*. Biblioteca Apostolica Vaticana. Reprinted from Centre de création industrielle and Centre Georges Pompidou, *Cartes et gures de la terre*, 403.

each of these constituted a *kardo*, and at right angles to it was a *decumanus*."[22] A grid was organized and its sections named by reference to two main roads or axes, the *decumanus maximus* and the *kardo maximus*. This is how the grid appears in the *Corpus Agrimensorum* (Figs. 2–3).

Erwin Walter Palm has pointed out that when it came to cadasters, colonies, and *castra*, Spain adopted features of the Roman system even before 1492. What was subsequently transferred to the New World followed in the footsteps of the Reconquista.

However, there is a conspicuous difference between the shape of the Roman *castrum* and the planned colonial heterotopias: While the former is contained within a square with the four gates located at the ends of the *decumanus maximus* and the *kardo maximus*, the latter call for an infinite expansion. The gridiron that appears on the plans of Lima, Santiago de Léon de Caracas, or San Juan de la Frontera recalls the Greek cities designed by Hippodamus of Miletus. Hippodamus, a contemporary of Herodotus and graduate of the famous Milesian school, lived during the fifth century B.C.E. Aristotle records that he devised the gridiron plan for the port town of Piraeus. He is also credited with the checkerboard layout of Rhodes andof Miletus itself, destroyed by the Persians in 494 B.C.E. (see Fig. 4). The Hippodamian grid consists of regular squares created by streets intersecting each other at right angles, evidently a concrete realization of that particular type of reason that characterized the Milesian school, which identified urban order with political order.[23] However, archaeologists have long known that the Hippodamian plan, too, had its predecessors, be they the Greek colonial settlements of the seventh and eighth century B.C.E. or the hypothetical Etruscan city plan, which may be the heritage of an Italianate tradition reaching far back into the ages preceding the Indo-European migration. But no matter what: According to Aristotle, it was Hippodamus "who invented the division of cities into precincts and who laid out the street-plan of the Piraeus."[24] However, Aristotle saw Hippodamus less as a pioneer of a new kind of urbanism than as the inventor of a new way of segregating the population into three parts, one of skilled workers, one of farmers, "and [a] third to bear arms and secure defense."[25] Damisch notes that the concept underlying the gridiron pattern devoid of a center is that of "nemesis." In addition to the idea of vengeful fate, nemesis also refers to the notion of distributive law and of giving what is due, that is, to the correlated idea of an expansion in need of boundaries.[26]

In Miletus and Piraeus, the construction of surrounding walls, including the positioning of the gates, depended on geographical features and military considerations rather than on planning. This also applies to the foundation of sixteenth-century Middle and South American cities. Lima was seen as the most typical Latin American city (Fig. 5). The Jesuit missionary and historian Bernabé Cobo (1582–1657) wrote of its founding in 1535:

22 Dilke, 215.
23 Damisch, 32.
24 Aristotle, *Politics*, trans. J. A. Sinclair (Harmondsworth: Penguin, 1992), 134.
25 Aristotle, 132.
26 Damisch, 32.

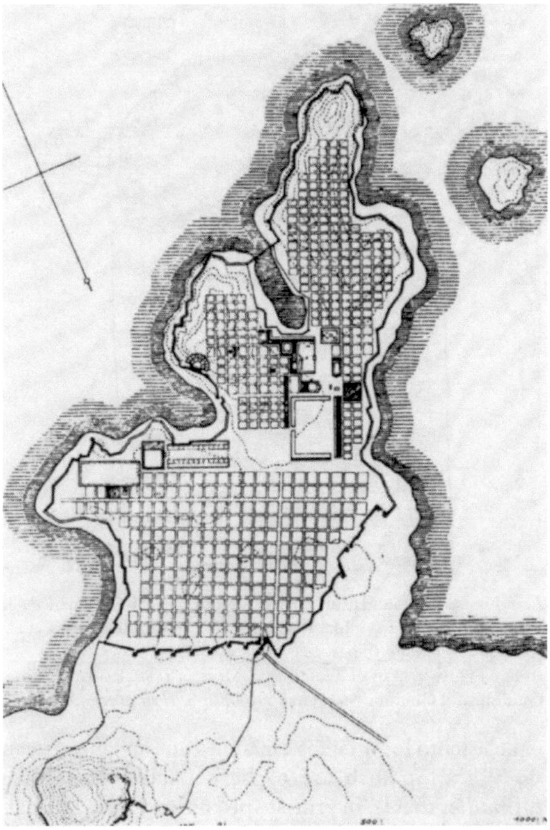

Figure 4. Plan of Miletus, attributed to Hippodamus. The city of Miletus was destroyed by the Persians in 494 B.C.E and rebuilt after 479 or 466 B.C.E. Published in Armin von Gerkan, *Griechische Städteanlagen* (1924); reprinted from *Cartes et gures de la terre*, 32.

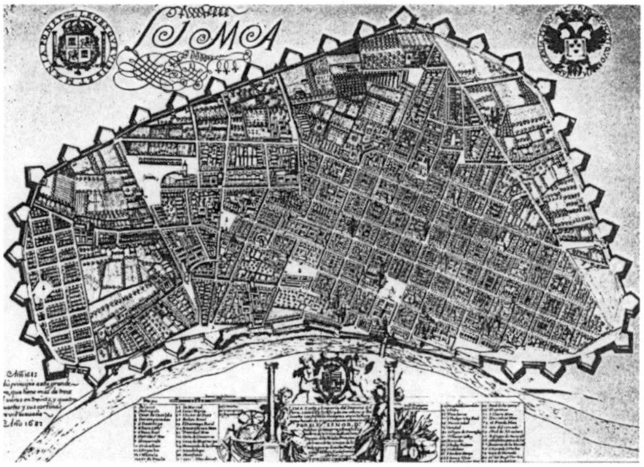

Figure 5. Map of Lima, Peru, 1687. Reprinted from Hardoy, *Cartografía urbana colonial de América Latina y el Caribe*, 146.

> In order to found the city the governor first completed a drawing with streets and city blocks, whereon he noted who was to be assigned which plot by putting down their names; and doing this regardless of the number of inhabitants [*vecinos*] present at the time of foundation of the city (there were only 69) but with a view towards the size it promised to attain, a space large enough for 117 blocks was laid out. . . . Each had a front length of 450 feet, the settlement was to stretch 13 blocks in width and 9 in breadth, separated by streets, and ropes were used to assure that each street was 40 feet in breadth.[27]

Let us note two key points: First, the plan described by Cobo is at one and the same time plan, register, and cadaster. Second, the city was not planned and built on the basis of the actual number of settlers, or as a means of distributing property, but with a settlement fantasy in mind. This fantasy is enabled and sustained by the possibility of writing empty spaces, that is, the ability to literally reserve a space for the unknown. This, in turn, presupposes the separation of data and addresses. Persons (be they public or private) are turned into data that can be stored for subsequent retrieval by the correct addresses that logically and temporally precede them. The Latin American heterotopia is thus the first concrete realization of the storage model we know today as *working memory*. The 1562 character of San Juan de la Frontera in the Cuyo region of Argentina reveals the future orientation alluded to by Cobo (Fig. 6). The suggested continuation of the grid refers to its virtual boundlessness, and the multiplication of the squares is complemented by their internal divisibility.

The planimetric settlement plan of Teutenango in Mexico from 1582 appears to have effectively fused scaled paper and *trazado a cordel* (Fig. 7). The plots turn into an inscription surface, a sheet of scaled paper. The act of *Landnahme*, the taking of the land—in this colonial context, "land grab" would be a more appropriate translation—coincides with graphic operations on the paper surface. Political and diagrammatic space are one.

The *trazados* of the Latin American cities precisely conform to the double meaning of Spanish *padrón*: chart and register. Nothing demonstrates this more impressively than the city plan of Buenos Aires of 1583. It looks like a register, but it is a city plan—a city plan that is both register and cadaster. The *nomos* of the earth and the *nomos* of bureaucracy coincide. To live in one of the newly founded Latin American cities amounts to being registered in a grid in which, to quote Alberti, *omnia in locis suis disposita*—everything is assigned its own place. Santo Domingo, Mexico City, Lima, or Buenos Aires are at one and the same time topographic *loci* where people live and memorial *loci* in a storage medium. Cities are both physical space and technological memory.

27 Bernabé Cobo, *Historia de la fundación de Lima* (1639). Quoted in Bertram Lee, ed., *Libros de Cabildos de Lima* (Lima: Torres Aguirre, 1935), 2:475.

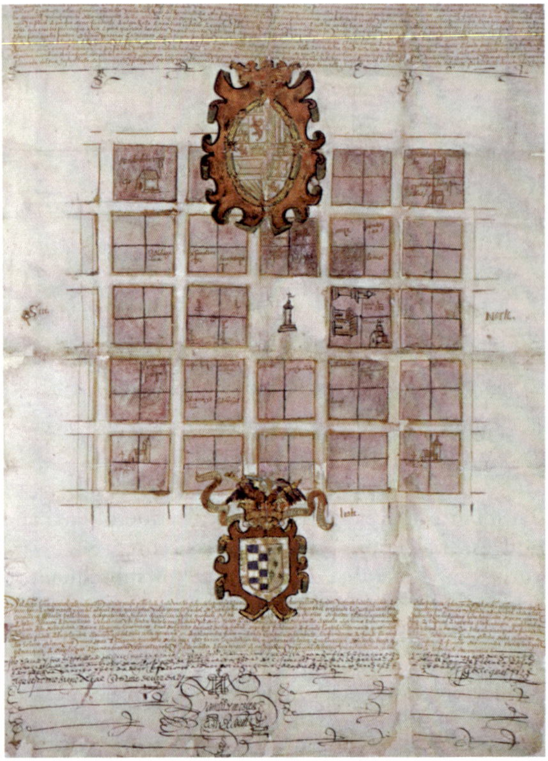

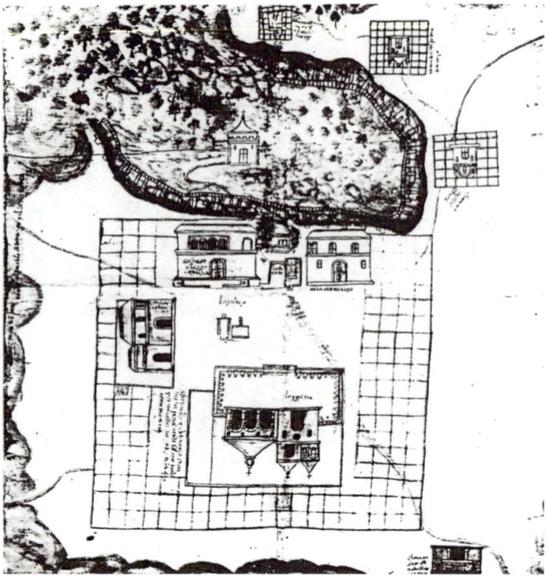

Left Figure 6. Foundation charter of the city of San Juan de la Frontera (Argentina), 1562. Reprinted from Gonzáles García et al., *Archivo General de Indias*, 204.
Above Figure 7. Map of Teutenango, Mexico, 1582. Reprinted from Guidoni and Guidoni, *Storia dell'urbanistica: Il cinquecento*, 353.

The letters and memoranda penned by the Franciscan friar Gerónimo de Mendieta to the president of the Consejo de Indias shed light on the ontological status of the these urban data spaces. Mendieta's proposals, aimed at improving the economic and social conditions in the colonies, revolve around two governmental techniques: the introduction of registers and the foundation of new settlements (grid-shaped, naturally). The bill he drafted concerning the introduction of population registers in the Spanish colonies[28] contains a highly revealing ambiguous formulation: The official in charge of the registers is to "place every single one in his place."[29] What did Mendieta have in mind with this phrase? Is the official to place "every single one in his place" in the register, or at their actual place of residence? The place in the register and the place of residence are made to overlap. How is one to distinguish the symbolic place from the real? This blurring of boundaries is no coincidence. It is, quite simply, the situation—a situation determined by the culture-technical operationalization of deixis.

This characteristic indistinguishability is also present in Mendieta's settlement projects. "[P]ara poner en asiento los muchos españoles que andan vagueando";[30] the Spanish are to be collected in *pueblos formados*, that is, in grid-shaped cities. *Poner en asiento* means both to settle and to register somebody. Thus Spanish colonialism was able to extract from the law guiding Alberti's constructions—namely, that the being of beings is constituted by their ability to be represented—a disciplinary and governmental dimension by applying the representational properties of Alberti's veil to the Hippodamic checkerboard. The result is, in Angel Rama's memorable phrase, the *lettered city*.[31] Reality always already assumes the shape of writing; it becomes a repeated, quoted reality. By putting individuals into their place in the *padrón* (that is, in the symbolic), they are assigned definitive coordinates in the real. Those who once were lost are now in their place.

28 See Berhnard Siegert, *Passagiere und Papiere: Schreibakte auf der Schwelle zwischen Spanien und Amerika* (Munich: Wilhelm Fink Verlag, 2006), 130–41.

29 Joaquin García Icazbalceta, ed., "Carta del Padre Fray Jerónimo de Mendieta al Ilustre Señor Licenciado Joan de Ovando, del Consejo de S.M. en la Santa y General Inquisición y Visitador e su Real Consejo de Indias," in *Nueva Colección de documentos para la historia de México* (Mexico City: Editorial Salvador Chávez Hayhoe, 1886–92), 123.

30 "[P]ara recoger in pueblos formados y poner en asiento los muchos espanoles que andan vagueando por acquella tierra, no on poco perjuicio del pro común della"; quoted in Norman F. Martin, *Los vagabundos en la Nueva Espana, siglo XVI* (Mexico City: Editorial Jus, 1957), 60.

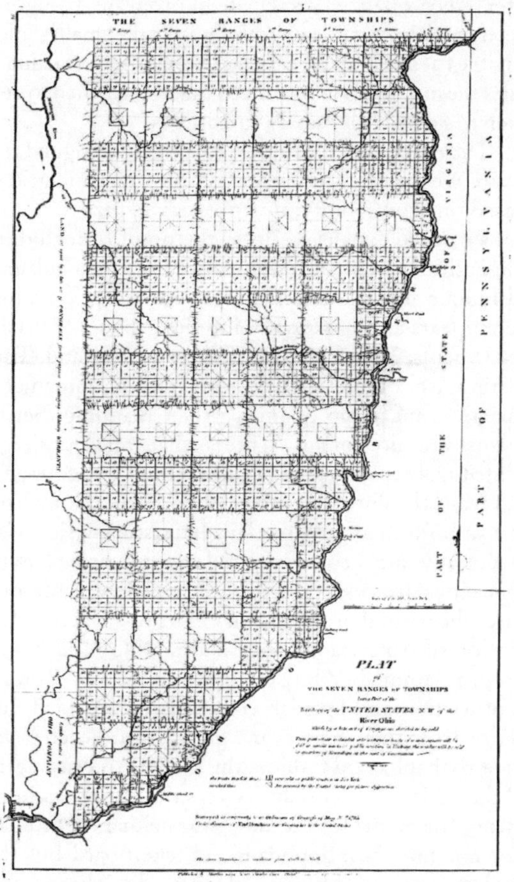

Figure 8. Mathew Carey after Thomas Hutchins, "Plat of the Seven Ranges of Townships being Part of the Territory of the United States N.W. of the River Ohio which by a late act of Congress are directed to be sold." Reprinted from *Carey's General Atlas* (Philadelphia: Mathew Carey, 1800), plate 46.

THE SPECULATIVE GRID (UNITED STATES)

Two hundred years later: The U.S. Continental Congress passes the Land Ordinance of 1785. Claims to the territory west of the Alleghenies by "landed" states such as Virginia in the south and Connecticut in the north as well as the ensuing dispute between "landed" and "landless" states compelled Congress to insist on cessions by the former and the creation of a public domain (the Northwest Territories). In the eyes of the landless states, their landed counterparts, which laid claim to the entire region north and west of the Ohio River as well as to the territory of the future state of Kentucky, threatened to dominate the confederation. More importantly, the United States was under pressure to pay off the debt incurred during the Revolutionary War. Deprived of taxing authority, Congress viewed the survey and partitioning of the Northwest Territories as a welcome opportunity to profit from land sales for the purpose of servicing the debt.[32] Unlike the sixteenth- century South American grid, then, its late eighteenth-century North American counterpart was less a governmental technique than a scheme aimed at capitalizing on federal land. By means of the grid-shaped survey of the territories ceded by the landed states, the United States acquired territory, a public domain to be auctioned off in standardized plots at set prices. Although the rectangular survey prescribed by the Land Ordinance of 1785 only concerned territories between the Appalachians and the Mississippi, it became the model for the subsequent appropriation and colonization of the entire continent. Congress was confronted with a situation virtually unprecedented in history: It was empowered to "make the law governing the survey and distribution of a vast territory before it was occupied."[33]

Following a proposal put forward by Thomas Jefferson, Congress opted for a rectangular survey of straight lines and right angles, such as had been favored by the New England states in the earlier stage of colonization.[34] It basically consisted of projecting a township lattice of latitudes and longitudes onto the territories west of the Ohio. Initially the survey was to limit itself to a strip of land forty miles wide, located to the west of Pennsylvania and extending north from the Ohio into lands still held by Native Americans. Led by Thomas Hutchins, the surveyors divided the territory into townships of six square miles each "by lines running due north and south, and others crossing these at right angles, as near as may be."[35] Each range began at the Ohio with number 1 and was then numbered from south to north, while the seven ranges themselves were numbered from east to west (Fig. 8).

The township plats were divided into "lots of one mile square or 640 acres,"[36] and were numbered from

31 See Angel Rama, *The Lettered City*, trans. John Charles Chasteen (Durham, N.C.: Duke University Press, 1996).

32 See George W. Geib, "The Land Ordinance of 1785: A Bicentennial Review," *Indiana Magazine of History*, 81, no. 1 (1985), 1–13.

33 Vernon Carstensen, "Patterns on the American Land," *Publius* 18, no. 4 (1988), 33.

34 Beginning in the early eighteenth century, land development in Connecticut, Massachusetts, and Maine instituted the township as the central vehicle for expansion. Precise guidelines were established, from the number of families per township and the size of plots to the percentage of land allocated to the local school and the number of acres to be covered with green lawn. See Catherine Maumi, *Thomas Jefferson et le project du Nouveau Monde* (Paris: Éditions de la Villette, 2007), 84, and Geib, "The Land Ordinance of 1785," 6. Matters were handled differently in the South: "Under the southern system, land was purchased under warrants that merely specified acres and general locations. Survey, if any, usually followed the occupation of an attractive location of the appropriate size," Geib, 6.

35 United States Continental Congress, "An Ordinance for Ascertaining the Mode of Disposing of Lands in the Western Territory (20 May 1785)," in *Journals of the Continental Congress*, 1774–1789, vol. 28 (1785), ed. John C. Fitzpatrick (Washington: U.S. Government Printing Office, 1933), 375.

1 to 36. Surveyors were instructed to keep a watchful eye on variations of the magnetic needle. As if transferring Simon Stevins's maritime navigational technique to the western outback,[37] they were to "run and note all lines by the true meridian, certifying, with every plat, what was the variation at the times of running the lines thereon noted."[38] In the late eighteenth century, this was—despite the impressive achievements of Mason and Dixon—a tall, if not impossible, order. Hutchins's surveyors' key tool was not a meridian but a circumferentor, "a simple compass fitted with sight vanes and mounted upon a ball and socket that fitted upon a 'Jacob's staff' or a tripod."[39] The Ordinance further stipulated how the townships and the lots within were to be sold. Proceeding from top to bottom and east to west, townships sold entire alternated with townships sold by lots, resulting in the characteristic checkerboard.[40] The government was happy to accept gold, silver, loan office certificates, or certificates of liquidated debts of the United States as payment.[41] Within each township, government retained the four lots numbered 8, 11, 26, and 29 for future sales. Lot 16 was reserved for the public school.[42] Ideally, each lot corresponded to a warrant or promissory note. Grid patterns, colonization, and real estate speculation coincided. "Land so marked out could be quickly and easily located by settler, banker, loan shark, and, if need be, sheriff and truant officer."[43] Once Congress entered into negotiations with speculators, the very soil of the American continent became the object of a transfer system that facilitated the circulation of real estate but did not always guarantee the optimal subdivision of the land for settlement purposes. Although the surveyors were instructed to maintain field notes on soil quality, water, and natural resources, purchasers could end up owning a swamp, a sandbank, or a piece of Native American territory. Financial and mental speculation became synonymous.[44] "The system not only made it simple to transfer land, which aided in the success of claim associations, and incidentally, that of speculators, it also contributed towards the attitude that land is a commodity."[45] While the Spanish *padrón* with its governmental doubling of grid and register reterritorialized deracinated Europeans, Congress deterritorialized the land itself. In 1785 the smallest plot eligible for sale had to be 640 acres; in order to facilitate sales the minimum was reduced first to 320, then to 160, then to 80, and ultimately to 40 acres.

The Seven Ranges survey effectively designed the entire West of the United States. The township grid is based on repeatability; it is projective, that is, it contains its own expansion up to the point of including the entire North American continent. As a cultural technique aimed at dominating space, the grid no longer appears as a potentially infinite growth of urban settlements; it is effectively cast across the land. This distinguishes the U.S. survey both from Roman centuriation and from Spanish urban planning. Settlements are no longer centers that may undergo centrifugal expansion, but cells in a homogeneous grid covering the entire territory. If Spanish colonialism was at bottom an urban affair, Jefferson's vision was essentially anti-urban, inspired by the ancient myth that cities are cesspools of vice while rural life nurtures the natural proliferation of virtues. The transformation of America into one nationwide suburb was preprogrammed. While the grids created by Roman centuriation and Spanish colonialism expanded outwards from their centers and grew toward each other in fairly haphazard fashion, the North American grid of parallels and meridians covers the entire territory. Hence the model for the latter was neither the Roman *castrum* nor the Hippodamic checkerboard but the Ptolemaic grid of latitudes and longitudes.[46] Faced with endless forests devoid of "churches, Towers, Houses, or peaked Mountains to be seen from afar,"[47] conventional European survey methods using theodolites and plane tables proved to be useless. Because the land appeared as undifferentiated as the ocean, early colonizers resorted to surveyor's chains as well as to tools used for maritime navigation, including compass, Jacob's staff, and the mesh formed by latitudes and longitudes, which defines the planisphere.[48] Transferred from the ocean to dry land, the grid encompasses the entire territory rather than merely urban space; 69 percent of

36 United States Continental Congress, 376.

37 See Simon Stevin, *The Haven-Finding Art, or, The Way to Find any Hauen or Place at Sea by the Latitude and Variation* (London: G.B.R.N. and R.B., 1599).

38 U.S. Continental Congress, "An Ordinance," 376–77.

39 Geib, 12.

40 See Hildegard Binder Johnson, *Order upon the Land: The U.S. Rectangular Land Survey and the Upper Mississippi Country* (New York: Oxford University Press, 1976), 44 and 143.

41 United States Continental Congress, 376-377.

42 Johnson, 44.

43 Carstensen, 31. See also Stefan Kaufmann, Soziologie der Landschaft (Wiesbaden: VS Verlag für Sozialwissenschaften, 2005), 172.

44 On the roots of this merging of the various meanings of *speculation* during the Italian Renaissance, see chapter 7.

45 Johnson, 219.

46 See Kaufmann, 185.

47 Lewis Evans, "Notes Accompanying the General Map of the Middle British Colonies in America," 1755, quoted in *The Shape of the World*, ed. Simon Berthon and Andrew Robinson (London: George Philip, 1991), 152.

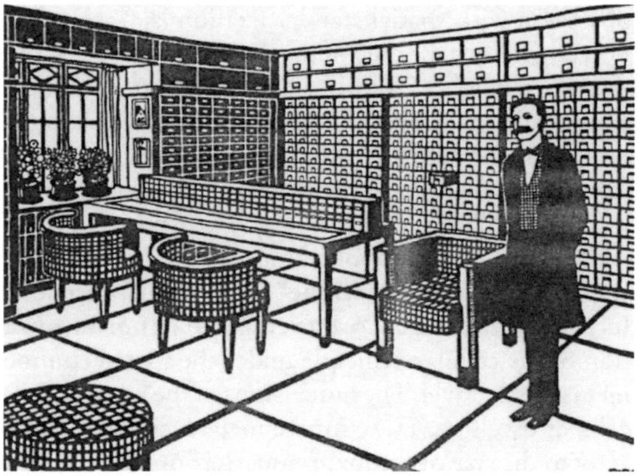

Figure 9. "World Format Scholar's Library." Reprinted from Karl Bührer, *Raumnot und Weltformat*, illustrated by Emil Pirchan (Munich: Die Brücke, 1912), 24.

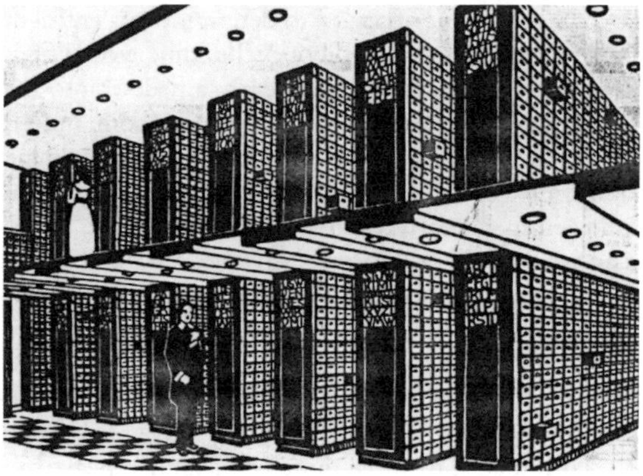

Figure 10. "World Format Large Library." From Bührer, *Raumnot und Weltformat*, 30.

the territory of the forty-eight continental states is contiguously covered by the rectangular survey.[49] Once the idea of a grid-shaped division of the land into rectangular townships and lots had been approved, bureaucratic mechanisms were put in place to ensure that the straight lines were continued west of the Ohio. "Almost nothing stood in the way. The straight lines were spread over the prairies, the foothills, the mountains, over the swamps and deserts, and even over some of the shallow lakes."[50] Never before, Catherine Maumi notes, did humans have the opportunity to confront in such brutal and violent fashion that "entity known as space."[51]

After 1796 the rectangular survey was extended to cover the remainder of the old Northwest Territory, the Southwest Territory, and other areas acquired by the United States. The township became the base unit for several governmental purposes: taxation, census, electoral districts, and road construction. It is therefore characteristic that U.S. cartography is as much based on contiguous survey plans as it is on maps. The plans created an unsparing structure that prefigured the future appropriation of the wilderness. Nothing was left untouched: The rectangular system guaranteed that no shred of land remained masterless, as frequently had been the case in the Southern territories claimed by Virginia. Both plan and projection, the uniform system of rectangular townships and sections assigned to everything—wilderness, plains, forest, or swamp—its own place. Nothing was allowed to fall off the grid.

THE THREE-DIMENSIONAL GRID

If we add a third orthogonal axis to the geodetic grid, it unfolds into a three-dimensional structure. Architecture, then, can be understood as an additional dimension of imaging, topographic, cartographic, and governmental grids. At least this is exactly how the Bauhaus architect and Gropius disciple Ernst Neufert, author of the hugely influential *Bauordnungslehre* (published in English as *Architects' Data*), saw architecture. First published in 1943 with a preface by Albert Speer, Nazi Minister of Armaments and War Production and Hitler's chief architect, it outlined a method for the complete standardization and totalization of the grid on all scales: The lattice not only connects all the buildings at a given site and determines their position and proportion, just like the grid of latitudes and longitudes, it also covers the entire globe. Neufert's grid turns navigation in smooth space into the ubiquitous paradigm of being-in-one's-place. "As on the ocean the squared grid (allows) us . . . to immediately and unequivocally determine the location of the buildings and any other installation. When built according to norm, the buildings will inevitably fit into this grid."[52] Thus Neufert's scalable planning and localizing grid anticipates the link-up of matrix screen and global coordinate system realized by Google Earth. It potentially enables on a global scale the exact location of individual buildings. On the scale of the latter, in turn, it serves to define the size and position of each object within the house, from walls, doors, and windows to stairs and furniture.[53]

48 Maumi, *Thomas Jefferson*, 43. Surveyors' chains were an additional tool for measuring the east-west distances. For a detailed analysis of the transfer of the methods of maritime cartography onto the North American territory, as well as of the imagination of the American landscape as an ocean, see Kaufmann, 185–207 and 210–13.

49 See Johnson, preface, n.p.

50 Carstensen, 31.

51 Maumi, *Thomas Jefferson*, 12. On the North American rectangular survey see also William D. Pattison, *Beginnings of the American Rectangular Land Survey Systems, 1784-1800* (New York: Arno Press, 1979), and Norman J. Thrower, *Original Survey and Land Subdivision: A Comparative Study of the Form and Effect of Contrasting Cadastral Surveys* (Chicago: Rand McNally, 1966).

52 Ernst Neufert, *Bauordnungslehre: Handbuch für rationelles Bauen nach geregeltem Mass* (Frankfurt/M. and Berlin: Ullstein, 1961), 95.

If Neufert's norms were to determine our entire industrial production, then any new building would fit as seamlessly into any new settlement as any door into any door frame or any piano into any drawing room. Indeed, Neufert's own ideas fit with equal ease into the totalizing, frequently fantasmatic standardization projects that emerged in the early twentieth century. Think, for instance, of the "world format" dreamed up by Wilhelm Ostwald and Karl Bührer,[54] in which a standardized index card in a standardized filing box in a standardized cabinet in a standardized office building amounts to nothing more than the nth subdivision of a global standardization system (Figs. 9–10).

Unfolded into three dimensions and repeated in vertical and horizontal directions, the grid does more than define the space of architecture—it turns into architecture. At the outset of the twentieth century, new materials and technologies including concrete and steel frames made it possible to construct a building from the inside out. For Mies van der Rohe only a skyscraper under construction was a real skyscraper, for only so long as its sides had not been closed and covered was the steel skeleton able to make the constructive idea transparent.[55] Glass facades were therefore for Mies no more than a compromise with the inevitable. One possible construction method is to start with the smallest spatial element—the cell. Another is to focus on the steel structure and the free layout. (Le Corbusier programmatically referred to this model as a *plan libre*.) In both cases the facade is no longer part of the load-bearing structure and is thus free for almost any kind of design. "To build a uniform world from the smallest spatial cell," Walter Prigge notes, "is the rational architectural utopia of the mid-1920s."[56]

Le Corbusier, the hero of modern architecture, was one of the pioneers of an architectural dispositive in which cells (*cellules*) function as the smallest and most common element of construction. Historically, this dispositive is rooted both in the disciplinary society and in biology. On the one hand, it arises from the extensive tradition of disciplinary architecture that includes both the monastic and the prison cell.

The emphasis on the cell as the smallest possible human living space reveals that modern architecture's obsession with spatial standardization is a generalization of the basic module of the disciplinary society. On the other hand, Le Corbusier is drawing on the discourse of cellular biology that identifies the cell as the basic building block of life. However, Le Corbusier's real model for cellular construction was neither plant nor prison but the machine. It is no coincidence that he developed his ideas about human-scale cells and the cell-based "dwelling machine" on board an ocean liner. Its cabins struck Le Corbusier as the optimal realization of the cellular principle under the spatial confinements of sea travel. The dimensions of the human-scale cellular dwelling, 15.75 square meters, correspond exactly to the size of the luxury quarters on his 1929 voyage from Bordeaux to Buenos Aires.

The cell had already in the early 1920s been a central component of Le Corbusier's architectural theory. Now, in 1929, as part of a series of lectures in Argentina and Brazil, he expanded the cellular concept: It is no longer a matter of designing single-family units but of planning entire cities with three million inhabitants. Here, on the continent of colonial, potentially infinite grid-shaped settlement topography, Le Corbusier proclaimed an architectural vision based on the replication of standardized, industrially prefabricated, and easily transportable dwelling cells of modular design:

> A unit of human scale: 15 square meters.... [T]he dwelling, the office, the workshop, the factory...will use new forms of standardization, of industrialization, of efficiency.... We shall get to the house assembled from standard components, prepared in factories, made perfect by industrialization, like an automobile body, and put up on site by *assembly workers*. ... These methods of industrialization by standardization lead us naturally to the coming skyscrapers: its form is determined by the superposition of cells at human scale.... Let us multiply the standard elements of a dwelling.... Dwellings should not be made in meters, *but in kilometers*.[57]

Le Corbusier had the writer and aviator Antoine de Saint-Exupéry fly him across the wide plains of Argentina, Brazil, and Uruguay. The sight of the checkerboard topography of colonial cities from an altitude of 1,200 meters convinced him that "[t]his American country is

53 See Alexander Klose, "Vom Raster zur Zelle—die Containerisierung der modernen Architektur," lecture delivered at Bauhaus University, Weimar, January 17, 2006; in English, "From Grid to Box: The Containerization of Modern Architecture," lecture delivered at Goethe Institute, Prague, October 7, 2005, at the workshop "City-Media-Space." Both versions available at http://www.containerwelt.info./ordner_eigene_texte.html.

54 In 1911 Karl Bührer and Adolf Saager cofounded Die Brücke: Internationales Institut zur Organisierung der geistigen Arbeit (The Bridge: International Institute for the Organization of Intellectual Work), with the goal of solving the problems resulting from the internationalization of the sciences by creating global standards.

55 See Ludwig Mies van der Rohe, "Hochhausprojekt für Bahnhof Friedrichstrasse in Berlin (1922)," in *Frühlicht 1920–1922: Eine Folge für die Verwirklichung des neuen Baugedankens*, ed. Bruno Taut (Berlin, Frankfurt/M., and Vienna: Ullstein, 1963), 213.

56 Walter Prigge, "Typologie und Norm: Zum modernen Traum der industriellen Fertigung von Wohnungen," in *Constructing Utopia: Konstruktionen künstlicher Welten, ed. Annett Zinsmeister* (Berlin and Zürich: Diaphanes, 2005), 74–75.

57 Le Corbusier, "A Dwelling at Human Scale," in *Precisions on the Present State of Architecture and City Planning*, trans. Edith Schreiber Aujame (Cambridge: MIT Press, 1991), 90, 91, 95, 97–98, and 100 (emphases in the original). Translator's note: As in the quote above, Le Corbusier's cellule is sometimes translated into English as "dwelling" or "unit of dwelling."

dimensioned for the plane."[58] Back on solid ground, Le Corbusier drafted plans for a new Montevideo, Uruguay and a new São Paulo, Brazil. The airplane has become a design tool: From its aerial perspective the South American city of the future appears to be part of the cartographic grid. Suggesting the global grid, the future São Paulo will consist of two giant extended steel skeleton buildings that cross each other at right angles. Highways lead across the buildings; additional skyscrapers surround the intersection. Superimposed on the grid-like topography of Spanish colonial settlements, the grid of latitudes and longitudes reveals its projective nature.

Rationalization by standardization is not only apparent in temporary constructions such as mass-produced barracks and containers;[59] it is also present in the visions of monumental residential constructions that can be found in Neufert's *Architects' Data*. As on an assembly line, a railbound slipform construction machine installs one cell block after the other. The three-dimensional grid continues the limitlessness of the two-dimensional topographical grid.

From this interconnectivity of grids, Le Corbusier and Neufert derived the vision of a future which in many respects is our present. The fusion of matrix grid and GPS has ensured the global presence of the operationalized deixis first conceived of in connection with the grid- and register-shaped settlements of South America. Indeed, what better way to describe some of the basic aspects of our media culture than to point to the mutual translatability of cartographic grid, topographic grid, planning grid, and imaging grid? Linked with the convertibility of these diverse grids and with corresponding scaling techniques, grids—a formidable cultural technique—have become the basis of a mediatization of space from which hardly anything can escape.

58 Le Corbusier, "American Prologue," in *Precisions on the Present State of Architecture and City Planning*, 3.

59 For barracks, see Axel Dossmann, Jan Wenzel, and Kai Wenzel, *Architektur auf Zeit: Baracken, Pavillons, Container* (Berlin: B-Books, 2006); for containers, see Alexander Klose, *Das Container-Prinzip: Wie eine Box unser Denken verändert* (Hamburg: Mare, 2009).

Dictionary: Man in *Documents 4*

Georges Bataille

1929

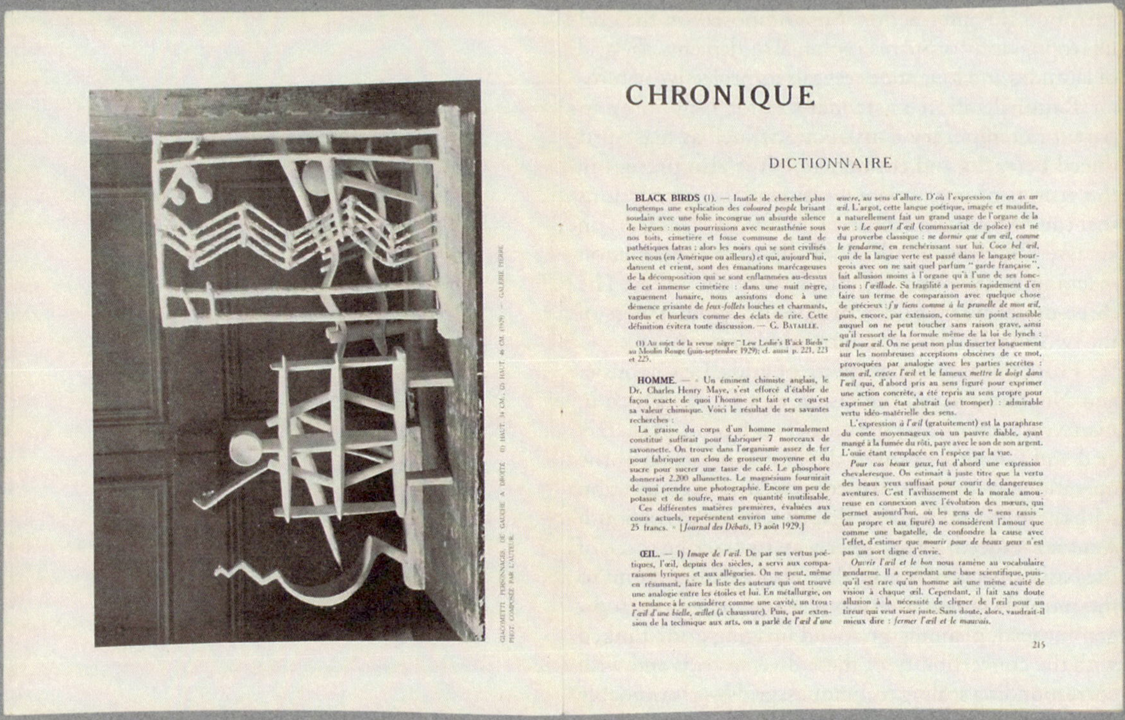

GIACOMETTI. PERSONNAGES. DE GAUCHE A DROITE. (1) HAUT. 34 CM. (2) HAUT. 46 CM. (1929) — GALERIE PIERRE. PRÊT CONSENTI PAR L'AUTEUR.

CHRONIQUE

DICTIONNAIRE

BLACK BIRDS (1). — Inutile de chercher plus longtemps une explication des *coloured people* brisant soudain avec une folie incongrue un absurde silence de bègues : nous pourrissions avec neurasthénie sous nos toits, cimetière et fosse commune de tant de pathétiques fatras ; alors les noirs qui se sont civilisés avec nous (en Amérique ou ailleurs) et qui, aujourd'hui, dansent et crient, sont des émanations marécageuses de la décomposition qui se sont enflammées au-dessus de cet immense cimetière : dans une nuit nègre, vaguement lunaire, nous assistons donc à une démence grisante de *feux-follets* louches et charmants, tordus et hurleurs comme des éclats de rire. Cette définition évitera toute discussion. — G. BATAILLE.

(1) Au sujet de la revue nègre "Lew Leslie's Black Birds" au Moulin Rouge (juin-septembre 1929); cf. aussi p. 221, 223 et 225.

HOMME. — « Un éminent chimiste anglais, le Dr. Charles Henry Maye, s'est efforcé d'établir de façon exacte de quoi l'homme est fait et ce qu'est sa valeur chimique. Voici le résultat de ses savantes recherches :

La graisse du corps d'un homme normalement constitué suffirait pour fabriquer 7 morceaux de savonnette. On trouve dans l'organisme assez de fer pour fabriquer un clou de grosseur moyenne et du sucre pour sucrer une tasse de café. Le phosphore donnerait 2.200 allumettes. Le magnésium fournirait de quoi prendre une photographie. Encore un peu de potasse et de soufre, mais en quantité inutilisable.

Ces différentes matières premières, évaluées aux cours actuels, représentent environ une somme de 25 francs. » [*Journal des Débats*, 13 août 1929.]

ŒIL. — 1) *Image de l'œil.* De par ses vertus poétiques, l'œil, depuis des siècles, a servi aux comparaisons lyriques et aux allégories. On ne peut, même en résumant, faire la liste des auteurs qui ont trouvé une analogie entre les étoiles et lui. En métallurgie, on a tendance à le considérer comme une cavité, un trou : *l'œil d'une bielle, œillet* (à chaussure). Puis, par extension de la technique aux arts, on a parlé de *l'œil d'une œuvre*, au sens d'allure. D'où l'expression *tu en as un œil*. L'argot, cette langue poétique, imagée et maudite, a naturellement fait un grand usage de l'organe de la vue : *Le quart d'œil* (commissariat de police) est né du proverbe classique : *ne dormir que d'un œil, comme le gendarme*, en renchérissant sur lui. *Coco bel œil*, qui de la langue verte est passé dans le langage bourgeois avec on ne sait quel parfum "garde française", fait allusion moins à l'organe qu'à l'une de ses fonctions : *l'œillade*. Sa fragilité a permis rapidement d'en faire un terme de comparaison avec quelque chose de précieux : *j'y tiens comme à la prunelle de mon œil*, puis, encore, par extension, comme un point sensible auquel on ne peut toucher sans raison grave, ainsi qu'il ressort de la formule même de la loi de lynch : *œil pour œil*. On ne peut non plus disserter longuement sur les nombreuses acceptions obscènes de ce mot, provoquées par analogie avec les parties secrètes : *mon œil, crever l'œil* et le fameux *mettre le doigt dans l'œil* qui, d'abord pris au sens figuré pour exprimer une action concrète, a été repris au sens propre pour exprimer un état abstrait (se tromper) : admirable vertu idéo-matérielle des sens.

L'expression *à l'œil* (gratuitement) est la paraphrase du conte moyennageux où un pauvre diable, ayant mangé à la fumée du rôti, paye avec le son de son argent. L'ouie étant remplacée en l'espèce par la vue.

Pour vos beaux yeux, fut d'abord une expression chevaleresque. On estimait à juste titre que la vertu des beaux yeux suffisait pour courir de dangereuses aventures. C'est l'avilissement de la morale amoureuse en connexion avec l'évolution des mœurs, qui permet aujourd'hui, où les gens de "sens rassis" (au propre et au figuré) ne considèrent l'amour que comme une bagatelle, de confondre la cause avec l'effet, d'estimer que *mourir pour de beaux yeux* n'est pas un sort digne d'envie.

Ouvrir l'œil et le bon nous ramène au vocabulaire gendarme. Il a cependant une base scientifique, puisqu'il est rare qu'un homme ait une même acuité de vision à chaque œil. Cependant, il fait sans doute allusion à la nécessité de cligner de l'œil pour un tireur qui veut viser juste. Sans doute, alors, vaudrait-il mieux dire : *fermer l'œil et le mauvais.*

215

"A famous British chemist, Dr. Charles Henry Maye, tried to determine exactly what man is made of and what is man's chemical worth. Here are the results of his scholarly research. The amount of fat found in the body of an average human being would be enough to make seven pieces of soap. There is enough iron to make an average nail, enough sugar to sweeten a cup of coffee. The phosphorus would yield 2,200 matches; the magnesium would be enough to take a photograph. There is also some potassium and sulfur, but the amount is too small to be of any use. Those various materials, at the current rate, would be valued at around 25 francs."

Type 89 Moving-image Machine-gun Camera, Kai 2, Serial No. 7967
Manufactured by Rokuoh-sha [currently Konica Minolta Electronics Co., Ltd.]
Produced from 1933–44

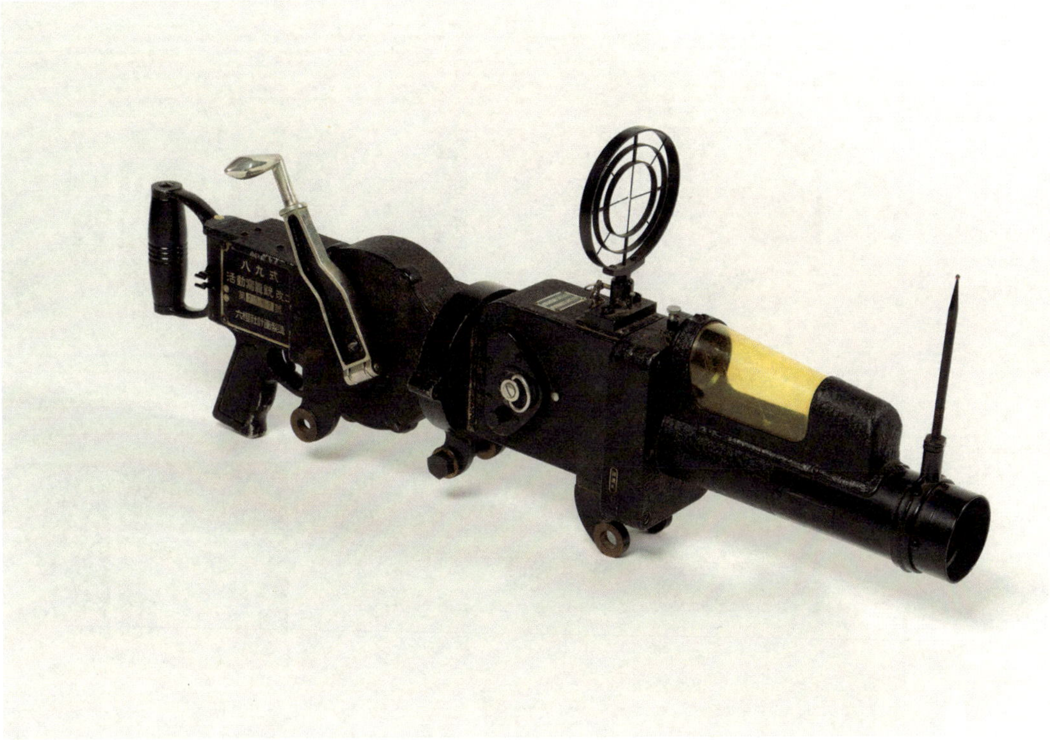

Arbeiter-Illustrierte Zeitung, Vol. IX, No. 28

John Heartfield

1930

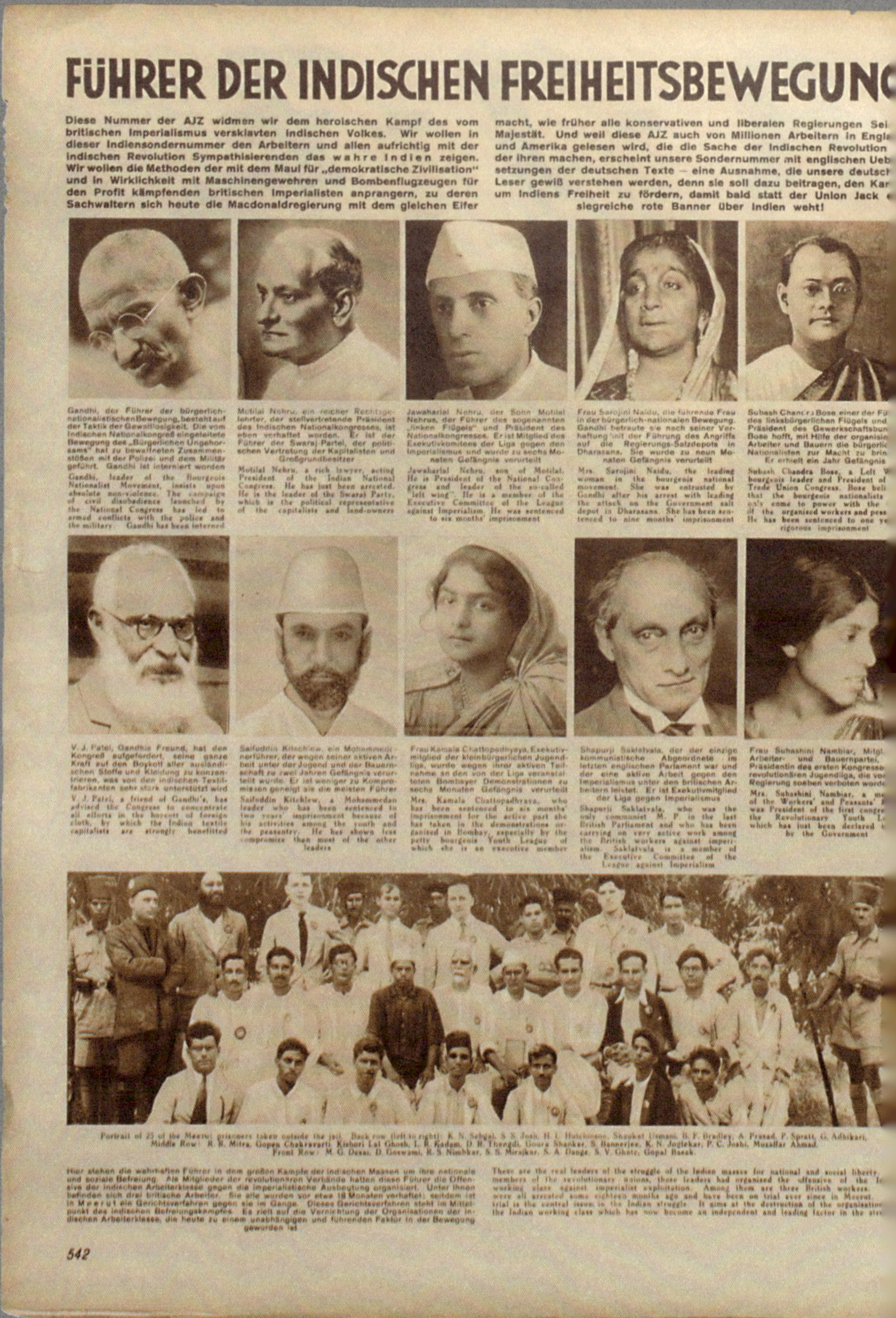

FÜHRER DER INDISCHEN FREIHEITSBEWEGUN

Diese Nummer der AJZ widmen wir dem heroischen Kampf des vom britischen Imperialismus versklavten indischen Volkes. Wir wollen in dieser Indiensondernummer den Arbeitern und allen aufrichtig mit der indischen Revolution Sympathisierenden das wahre Indien zeigen. Wir wollen die Methoden der mit dem Maul für „demokratische Zivilisation" und in Wirklichkeit mit Maschinengewehren und Bombenflugzeugen für den Profit kämpfenden britischen Imperialisten anprangern, zu deren Sachwaltern sich heute die Macdonaldregierung mit dem gleichen Eifer macht, wie früher alle konservativen und liberalen Regierungen Sei Majestät. Und weil diese AJZ auch von Millionen Arbeitern in Engl und Amerika gelesen wird, die die Sache der indischen Revolution der ihren machen, erscheint unsere Sondernummer mit englischen Ueb setzungen der deutschen Texte – eine Ausnahme, die unsere deutsch Leser gewiß verstehen werden, denn sie soll dazu beitragen, den Kar um Indiens Freiheit zu fördern, damit bald statt der Union Jack siegreiche rote Banner über Indien weht!

Gandhi, der Führer der bürgerlich-nationalistischen Bewegung, besteht auf der Taktik der Gewaltlosigkeit. Die vom Indischen Nationalkongreß eingeleitete Bewegung des „Bürgerlichen Ungehorsams" hat zu bewaffneten Zusammenstößen mit der Polizei und dem Militär geführt. Gandhi ist interniert worden

Gandhi, leader of the Bourgeois Nationalist Movement, insists upon absolute non-violence. The campaign of civil disobedience launched by the National Congress has led to armed conflicts with the police and the military. Gandhi has been interned

Motilal Nehru, ein reicher Rechtsgelehrter, der stellvertretende Präsident des Indischen Nationalkongresses, ist eben verhaftet worden. Er ist der Führer der Swaraj-Partei, der politischen Vertretung der Kapitalisten und Großgrundbesitzer

Motilal Nehru, a rich lawyer, acting President of the Indian National Congress. He has just been arrested. He is the leader of the Swaraj Party, which is the political representative of the capitalists and land-owners

Jawaharlal Nehru, der Sohn Motilal Nehrus, der Führer des sogenannten „linken Flügels" und Präsident des Nationalkongresses. Er ist Mitglied des Exekutivkomitees der Liga gegen den Imperialismus und wurde zu sechs Monaten Gefängnis verurteilt

Jawaharlal Nehru, son of Motilal. He is President of the National Congress and leader of the so-called "left wing". He is a member of the Executive Committee of the League against Imperialism. He was sentenced to six months' imprisonment

Frau Sarojini Naidu, die führende Frau in der bürgerlich-nationalen Bewegung. Gandhi betraute sie nach seiner Verhaftung mit der Führung des Angriffs auf die Regierungs-Salzdepots in Dharasana. Sie wurde zu neun Monaten Gefängnis verurteilt

Mrs. Sarojini Naidu, the leading woman in the bourgeois national movement. She was entrusted by Gandhi after his arrest with leading the attack on the Government salt depot in Dharasana. She has been sentenced to nine months' imprisonment

Subash Chandra Bose einer der Fü des linksbürgerlichen Flügels und Präsident des Gewerkschaftsbun Bose hofft, mit Hilfe der organisie Arbeiter und Bauern die bürgerlic Nationalisten zur Macht zu brin Er erhielt ein Jahr Gefängnis

Subash Chandra Bose, a Left W bourgeois leader and President of Trade Union Congress. Bose beli that the bourgeois nationalists only come to power with the of the organized workers and pea He has been sentenced to one y rigorous imprisonment

V. J. Patel, Gandhis Freund, hat den Kongreß aufgefordert, seine ganze Kraft auf den Boykott aller ausländischen Stoffe und Kleidung zu konzentrieren, was von den indischen Textilfabrikanten sehr stark unterstützt wird

V. J. Patel, a friend of Gandhi's, has advised the Congress to concentrate all efforts in the boycott of foreign cloth, by which the Indian textile capitalists are strongly benefitted

Saifuddin Kitchlew, ein Mohammedanerführer, der wegen seiner aktiven Arbeit unter der Jugend und der Bauernschaft zu zwei Jahren Gefängnis verurteilt wurde. Er ist weniger zu Kompromissen geneigt als die meisten Führer

Saifuddin Kitchlew, a Mohammedan leader who has been sentenced to two years' imprisonment because of his activities among the youth and the peasantry. He has shown less compromise than most of the other leaders

Frau Kamala Chattopadhyaya, Exekutivmitglied der kleinbürgerlichen Jugendliga, wurde wegen ihrer aktiven Teilnahme an den von der Liga veranstalteten Bombayer Demonstrationen zu sechs Monaten Gefängnis verurteilt

Mrs. Kamala Chattopadhyaya, who has been sentenced to six months' imprisonment for the active part she has taken in the demonstrations organised in Bombay, especially by the petty bourgeois Youth League of which she is an executive member

Shapurji Saklatvala, der der einzige kommunistische Abgeordnete im letzten englischen Parlament war und der eine aktive Arbeit gegen den Imperialismus unter den britischen Arbeitern leistet. Er ist Exekutivmitglied der Liga gegen Imperialismus

Shapurji Saklatvala, who was the only communist M. P. in the last British Parliament and who has been carrying on very active work among the British workers against imperialism. Saklatvala is a member of the Executive Committee of the League against Imperialism

Frau Suhashini Nambiar, Mitgl Arbeiter- und Bauernpartei, Präsidentin des ersten Kongresse revolutionären Jugendliga, die vo Regierung soeben verboten word

Mrs. Suhashini Nambiar, a me of the Workers' and Peasants' was President of the first congre the Revolutionary Youth L which has just been declared by the Government

Portrait of 25 of the Meerut prisoners taken outside the jail. Back row (left to right): K. N. Sehgal, S. S. Josh, H. L. Hutchinson, Shaukat Usmani, B. F. Bradley, A. Prasad, P. Spratt, G. Adhikari, Middle Row: R. R. Mitra, Gopen Chakravarti, Kishori Lal Ghosh, L. R. Kadam, D. R. Thengdi, Goura Shanker, S. Bannerjee, K. N. Joglekar, P. C. Joshi, Muzaffar Ahmad. Front Row: M. G. Desai, D. Goswami, R. S. Nimbkar, S. S. Mirajkar, S. A. Dange, S. V. Ghate, Gopal Basak.

Hier stehen die wahrhaften Führer in dem großen Kampfe der indischen Massen um ihre nationale und soziale Befreiung. Als Mitglieder der revolutionären Verbände hatten diese Führer die Offensive der indischen Arbeiterklasse gegen die imperialistische Ausbeutung organisiert. Unter ihnen befinden sich drei britische Arbeiter. Sie alle wurden vor etwa 18 Monaten verhaftet; seitdem ist in Meerut ein Gerichtsverfahren gegen sie im Gange. Dieses Gerichtsverfahren steht im Mittelpunkt des indischen Befreiungskampfes. Es zielt auf die Vernichtung der Organisationen der indischen Arbeiterklasse, die heute zu einem unabhängigen und führenden Faktor in der Bewegung geworden ist

These are the real leaders of the struggle of the Indian masses for national and social liberty, members of the revolutionary unions, these leaders had organised the offensive of the I working class against imperialist exploitation. Among them are three British workers. were all arrested some eighteen months ago and have been on trial ever since in Meerut. trial is the central issue in the Indian struggle. It aims at the destruction of the organisation the Indian working class which has now become an independent and leading factor in the str

542

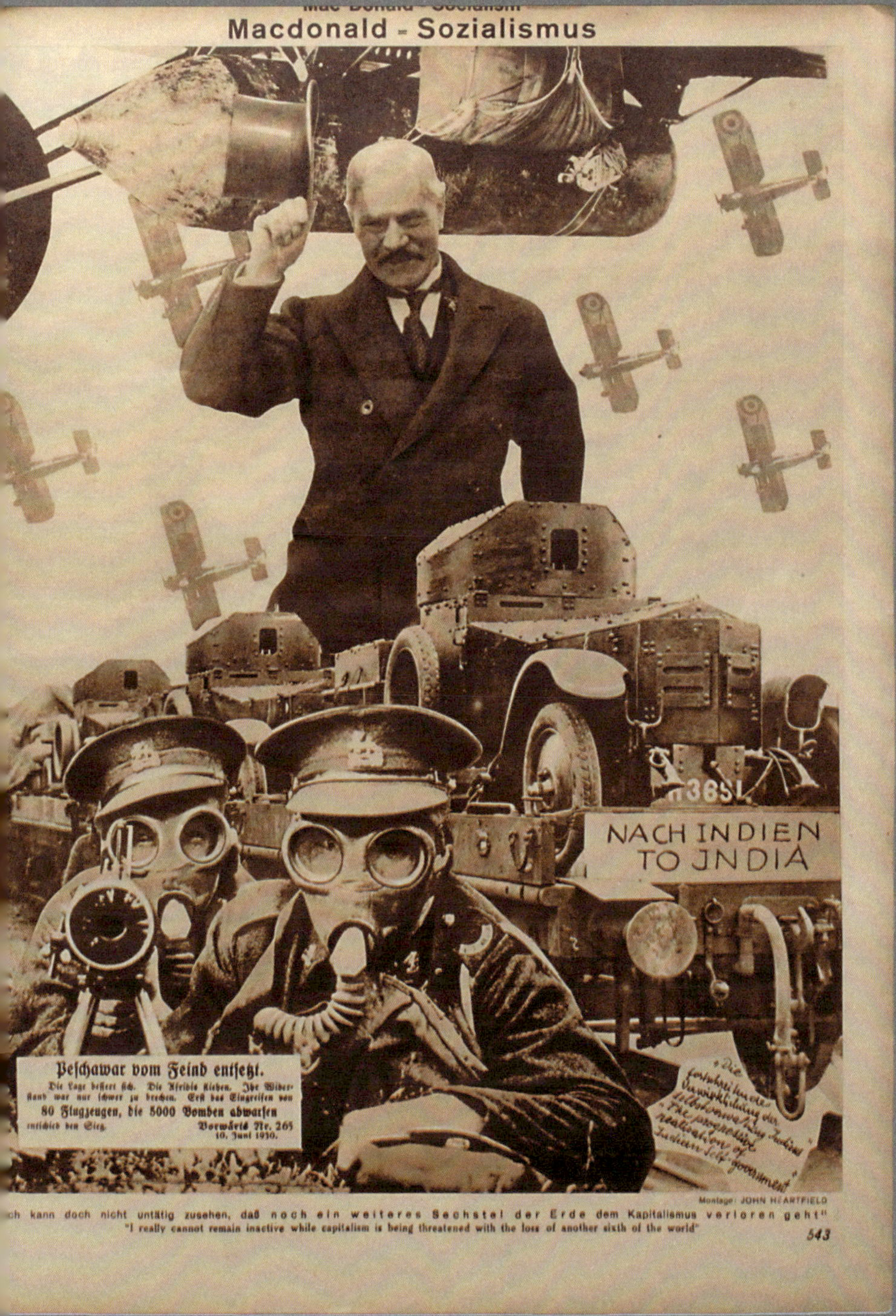

Macdonald - Socialism. "I really cannot remain inactive while capitalism is being threatened with the loss of another sixth of the world."

Top: ***Arbeiter-Illustrierte Zeitung*****, Vol. IX, No. 52, 1930**

Bottom: ***Arbeiter-Illustrierte Zeitung*****, Vol. X, No. 26, 1931**

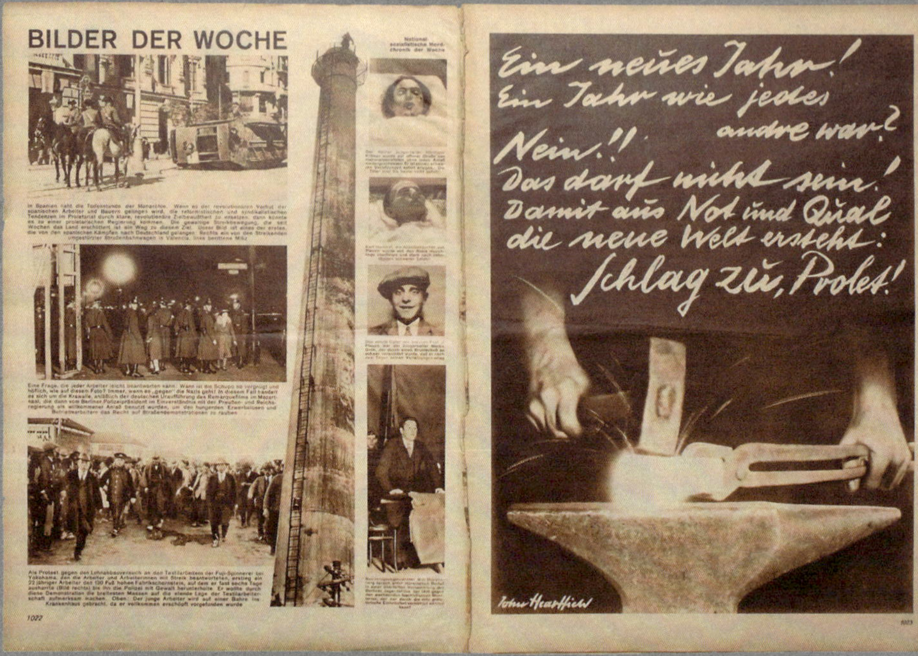

BILDER DER WOCHE

Ein neues Jahr!
Ein Jahr wie jedes
andre war?
Nein!!
Das darf nicht sein!
Damit aus Not und Qual
die neue Welt ersteht:
Schlag zu, Prolet!

John Heartfield

1022

1023

'A new year! A year like all the others? No!! That must not be! So that from misery and pain the new world arises: Strike, proletarian!'

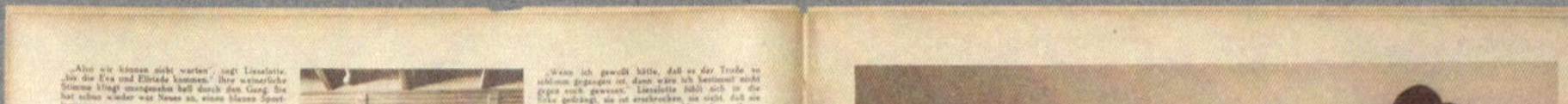

COLORED

NIGGER JIM
VON WEBER
IN MUSIK GESETZT VON HANS EISLER

Ob schwarz, ob weiß–
im Kampf vereint!
Wir kennen
nur eine Rasse,
wir kennen alle
nur einen Feind–
die Ausbeuterklasse.

516

'Whether black, or white—in struggle united! We know only one race, we all know only one enemy—the exploiting class'

Top: ***Arbeiter-Illustrierte Zeitung*****, Vol. XI, No. 35, 1932**
Bottom: ***Arbeiter-Illustrierte Zeitung*****, Vol. XI, No. 39, 1932**

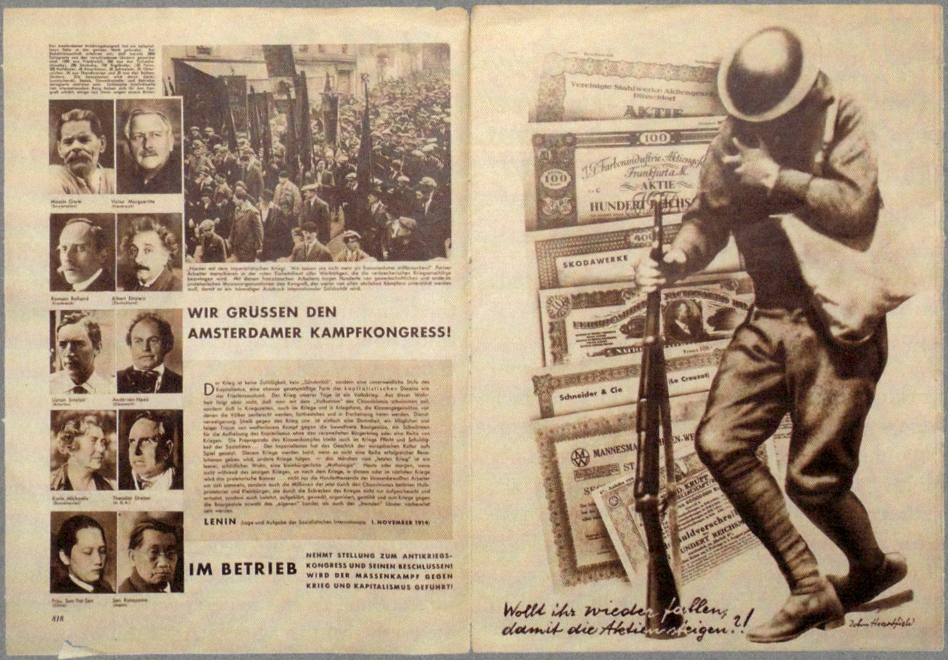

‘Do you want to fall again, so that shares rise?!’

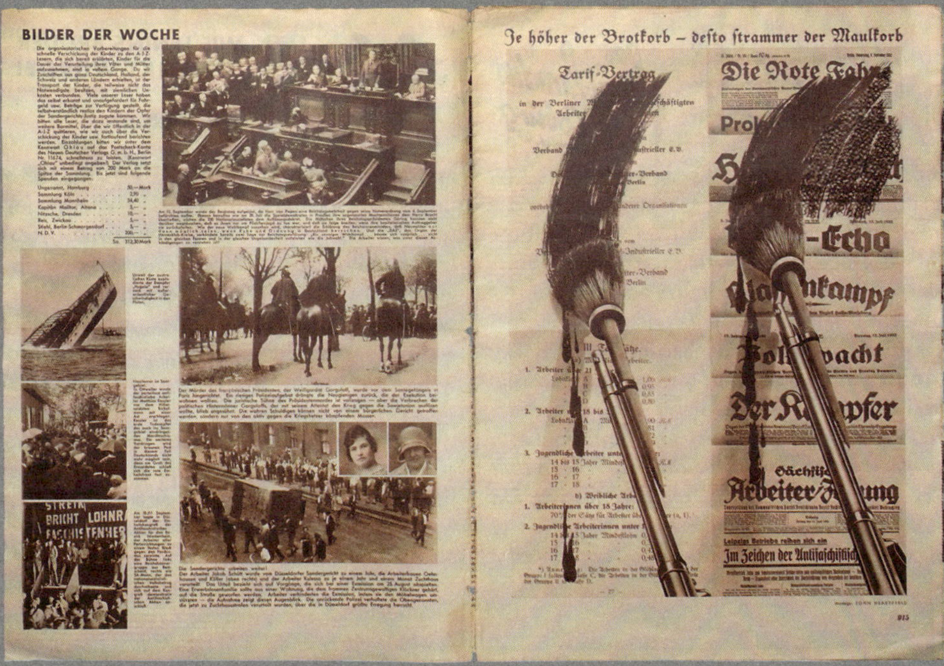

‘The higher the bread basket—the tighter the muzzle.’

The Work of Art in the Age of Its Technological Reproducibility (Second Version)

Walter Benjamin

1935–36

The true is what he can; the false is what he wants.
—Madame de Duras[1]

I

When Marx undertook his analysis of the capitalist mode of production, that mode was in its infancy. Marx adopted an approach which gave his investigations prognostic value. Going back to the basic conditions of capitalist production, he presented them in a way which showed what could be expected of capitalism in the future. What could be expected, it emerged, was not only an increasingly harsh exploitation of the proletariat but, ultimately, the creation of conditions which would make it possible for capitalism to abolish itself.

Since the transformation of the superstructure proceeds far more slowly than that of the base, it has taken more than half a century for the change in the conditions of production to be manifested in all areas of culture. How this process has affected culture can only now be assessed, and these assessments must meet certain prognostic requirements. They do not, however, call for theses on the art of the proletariat after its seizure of power, and still less for any on the art of the classless society. They call for theses defining the tendencies of the development of art under the present conditions of production. The dialectic of these conditions of production is evident in the superstructure, no less than in the economy. Theses defining the developmental tendencies of art can therefore contribute to the political struggle in ways that it would be a mistake to underestimate. They neutralize a number of traditional concepts—such as creativity and genius, eternal value and mystery—which, used in an uncontrolled way (and controlling them is difficult today), allow factual material to be manipulated in the interests of fascism. *In what follows, the concepts which are introduced into the theory of art differ from those now current in that they are completely useless for the purposes off fascism. On the other hand, they are useful for the formulation of revolutionary demands in the politics of art [Kunstpolitik].*

II

In principle, the work of art has always been reproducible. Objects made by humans could always be copied by humans. Replicas were made by pupils in practicing for their craft, by masters in disseminating their works, and, finally, by third parties in pursuit of profit. But the technological reproduction of artworks is something new. Having appeared intermittently in history, at widely spaced intervals, it is now being adopted with ever-increasing intensity. Graphic art was first made technologically reproducible by the woodcut, long before written language became reproducible by movable type. The enormous changes brought about in literature by movable type, the technological reproduction of writing, are well known. But they are only a special case, though an important one, of the phenomenon considered here from the perspective of world history. In the course of the Middle Ages the woodcut was supplemented by engraving and etching, and at the beginning of the nineteenth century by lithography.

Lithography marked a fundamentally new stage in the technology of reproduction. This much more direct process-distinguished by the fact that the drawing is traced on a stone, rather than incised on a block of wood or etched on a copper plate-first made it possible for graphic art to market its products not only in large numbers, as previously, but in daily changing variations. Lithography enabled graphic art to provide an illustrated accompaniment to everyday life. It began to keep pace with movable-type printing. But only a few decades after the invention of lithography, graphic art was surpassed by photography. For the first time, photography freed the hand from the most important artistic tasks in the process of pictorial reproduction-tasks that now devolved upon the eye alone. And since the eye perceives more swiftly than the hand can draw, the process of pictorial reproduction was enormously accelerated, so that it could now keep pace with speech. Just as the illustrated newspaper virtually lay hidden within lithography, so the sound film was latent in photography. The technological reproduction of sound was tackled at the end of the last century. *Around 1900, technological reproduction not only had reached a standard that permitted it to reproduce all known works of*

1 Madame Claire de Duras, née Kersaint (1778-1828), the wife of Due Amédée de Duras, field marshal under Louis XVIII, was the author of two novels, *Ourika* (1823) and *Edouard* (1825). She presided over a brilliant salon in Paris. Benjamin cites Madame de Duras in the original French.

art, profoundly modifying their effect, but it also had captured a place of its own among the artistic processes. In gauging this standard, we would do well to study the impact which its two different manifestations—the reproduction of artworks and the art of film—are having on art in its traditional form.

III

In even the most perfect reproduction, *one* thing is lacking: the here and now of the work of art—its unique existence in a particular place. It is this unique existence—and nothing else—that bears the mark of the history to which the work has been subject. This history includes changes to the physical structure of the work over time, together with any changes in ownership. Traces of the former can be detected only by chemical or physical analyses (which cannot be performed on a reproduction), while changes of ownership are part of a tradition which can be traced only from the standpoint of the original in its present location.

The here and now of the original underlies the concept of its authenticity, and on the latter in turn is founded the idea of a tradition which has passed the object down as the same, identical thing to the present day. *The whole sphere of authenticity eludes technological—and of course not only technological—reproduction.* But whereas the authentic work retains its full authority in the face of a reproduction made by hand, which it generally brands a forgery, this is not the case with technological reproduction. The reason is twofold. First, technological reproduction is more independent of the original than is manual reproduction. For example, in photography it can bring out aspects of the original that are accessible only to the lens (which is adjustable and can easily change viewpoint) but not to the human eye; or it can use certain processes, such as enlargement or slow motion, to record images which escape natural optics altogether. This is the first reason. Second, technological reproduction can place the copy of the original in situations which the original itself cannot attain. Above all, it enables the original to meet the recipient halfway, whether in the form of a photograph or in that of a gramophone record. The cathedral leaves its site to be received in the studio of an art lover; the choral work performed in an auditorium or in the open air is enjoyed in a private room.

These changed circumstances may leave the artwork's other properties untouched, but they certainly devalue the here and now of the artwork. And although this can apply not only to art but (say) to a landscape moving past the spectator in a film, in the work of art this process touches on a highly sensitive core, more vulnerable than that of any natural object. That core is its authenticity. The authenticity of a thing is the quintessence of all that is transmissible in it from its origin on, ranging from its physical duration to the historical testimony relating to it. Since the historical testimony is founded on the physical duration, the former, too, is jeopardized by reproduction, in which the physical duration plays no part. And what is really jeopardized when the historical testimony is affected is the authority of the object, the weight it derives from tradition.

One might focus these aspects of the artwork in the concept of the aura, and go on to say: what withers in the age of the technological reproducibility of the work of art is the latter's aura. This process is symptomatic; its significance extends far beyond the realm of art. *It might be stated as a general formula that the technology of reproduction detaches the reproduced object from the sphere of tradition. By replicating the work many times over, it substitutes a mass existence for a unique existence. And in permitting the reproduction to reach the recipient in his or her own situation, it actualizes that which is reproduced.* These two processes lead to a massive upheaval in the domain of objects handed down from the past-a shattering of tradition which is the reverse side of the present crisis and renewal of humanity. Both processes are intimately related to the mass movements of our day. Their most powerful agent is film. The social significance of film, even—and especially—in its most positive form, is inconceivable without its destructive, cathartic side: the liquidation of the value of tradition in the cultural heritage. This phenomenon is most apparent in the great historical films. It is assimilating ever more advanced positions in its spread. When Abel Gance fervently proclaimed in 1927, "Shakespeare, Rembrandt, Beethoven will make films... All legends, all mythologies, and all myths, all the founders of religions, indeed, all religions, ... await their celluloid resurrection, and the heroes are pressing at the gates," he was inviting the reader, no doubt unawares, to witness a comprehensive liquidation.[2]

IV

Just as the entire mode of existence of human collectives changes over long historical periods, so too does their mode of perception. The way in which human perception is organized—the medium in which it occurs—is conditioned not only by nature but by history. The era of the migration of peoples, an era which saw the rise of the late-Roman art industry and the Vienna Genesis, developed not only an art different from that of antiquity but also a different perception.

2 Abel Gance, "Le Temps de l'image est venu!" (It Is Time for the Image!), in Léon Pierre-Quint, Germaine Dulac, Lionel Landry, and Abel Gance, *L'Art cinématographique*, vol. 2 (Paris, 1927), 94-96.

The scholars of the Viennese school Riegl and Wickhoff, resisting the weight of the classical tradition beneath which this art had been buried, were the first to think of using such art to draw conclusions about the organization of perception at the time the art was produced. However far-reaching their insight, it was limited by the fact that these scholars were content to highlight the formal signature which characterized perception in late-Roman times. They did not attempt to show the social upheavals manifested in these changes in perception-and perhaps could not have hoped to do so at that time. Today, the conditions for an analogous insight are more favorable. And if changes in the medium of present-day perception can be understood as a decay of the aura, it is possible to demonstrate the social determinants of that decay.

What, then, is the aura? A strange tissue of space and time: the unique apparition of a distance, however near it may be.[3] To follow with the eye—while resting on a summer afternoon—a mountain range on the horizon or a branch that casts its shadow on the beholder is to breathe the aura of those mountains, of that branch. In the light of this description, we can readily grasp the social basis of the aura's present decay. It rests on two circumstances, both linked to the increasing emergence of the masses and the growing intensity of their movements. Namely: *the desire of the present-day masses to "get closer" to things, and their equally passionate concern for overcoming each thing's uniqueness [Überwindung des Einmaligen jeder Gegebenheit] by assimilating it as a reproduction.* Every day the urge grows stronger to get hold of an object at close range in an image [*Bild*], or, better, in a facsimile [*Abbild*], a reproduction. And the reproduction [*Reproduktion*], as offered by illustrated magazines and newsreels, differs unmistakably from the image. Uniqueness and permanence are as closely entwined in the latter as are transitoriness and repeatability in the former. The stripping of the veil from the object, the destruction of the aura, is the signature of a perception whose "sense for sameness in the world"[4] has so increased that, by means of reproduction, it extracts sameness even from what is unique. Thus is manifested in the field of perception what in the theoretical sphere is noticeable in the increasing significance of statistics. The alignment of reality with the masses and of the masses with reality is a process of immeasurable importance for both thinking and perception.

V

The uniqueness of the work of art is identical to its embeddedness in the context of tradition. Of course, this tradition itself is thoroughly alive and extremely changeable. An ancient statue of Venus, for instance, existed in a traditional context for the Greeks (who made it an object of worship) that was different from the context in which it existed for medieval clerics (who viewed it as a sinister idol). But what was equally evident to both was its uniqueness-that is, its aura. Originally, the embeddedness of an artwork in the context of tradition found expression in a cult. As we know, the earliest artworks originated in the service of rituals-first magical, then religious. And it is highly significant that the artwork's auratic mode of existence is never entirely severed from its ritual function. In other words: *the unique value of the "authentic" work of art always has its basis in ritual.* This ritualistic basis, however mediated it may be, is still recognizable as secularized ritual in even the most profane forms of the cult of beauty. The secular worship of beauty, which developed during the Renaissance and prevailed for three centuries, clearly displayed that ritualistic basis in its subsequent decline and in the first severe crisis which befell it. For when, with the advent of the first truly revolutionary means of reproduction (namely photography, which emerged at the same time as socialism), art felt the approach of that crisis which a century later has become unmistakable, it reacted with the doctrine of *l'art pour l'art*—that is, with a theology of art. This in turn gave rise to a negative theology, in the form of an idea of "pure" art, which rejects not only any social function but any definition in terms of a representational content. (In poetry, Mallarmé was the first to adopt this standpoint.)

No investigation of the work of art in the age of its technological reproducibility can overlook these connections. They lead to a crucial insight: for the first time in world history, technological reproducibility emancipates the work of art from its parasitic subservience to ritual. To an ever-increasing degree, the work reproduced becomes the reproduction of a work designed for reproducibility.[5] From a photographic plate, for example, one can make any number of prints; to ask for the "authentic" print makes no sense. *But as soon as the criterion of authenticity ceases to be applied to artistic production, the whole social function of art is revolutionized. Instead of being founded on ritual, it is based on a different practice: politics.*

3 "Einmalige Erscheinung einer Ferne, so nah sie sein mag." At stake in Benjamin's formulation is an interweaving not just of time and space—*einmalige Erscheinung*, literally "one-time appearance"—but of far and near, *eine Ferne* suggesting both "a distance" in space or time and "something remote," however near it (the distance, or distant thing, that appears) may be.

4 Benjamin is quoting Johannes V. Jensen, Exotische Novellen, trans. Julia Koppel (Berlin: S. Fischer, 1919), 41-42. [...] See "Hashish in Marseilles," in Benjamin, *Selected Writings, Volume 2: 1927-1934* (Cambridge, Mass.: Harvard University Press, 1999), 677.

VI

Art history might be seen as the working out of a tension between two polarities within the artwork itself, its course being determined by shifts in the balance between the two. These two poles are the artwork's cult value and its exhibition value.[6] Artistic production begins with figures in the service of magic. What is important for these figures is that they are present, not that they are seen. The elk depicted by Stone Age man on the walls of his cave is an instrument of magic, and is exhibited to others only coincidentally; what matters is that the spirits see it. Cult value as such even tends to keep the artwork out of sight: certain statues of gods are accessible only to the priest in the cella; certain images of the Madonna remain covered nearly all year round; certain sculptures on medieval cathedrals are not visible to the viewer at ground level. *With the emancipation of specific artistic practices from the service of ritual, the opportunities for exhibiting their products increase.* It is easier to exhibit a portrait bust that can be sent here and there than to exhibit the statue of a divinity that has a fixed place in the interior of a temple. A panel painting can be exhibited more easily than the mosaic or fresco which preceded it. And although a mass may have been no less suited to public presentation than a symphony, the symphony came into being at a time when the possibility of such presentation promised to be greater.

The scope for exhibiting the work of art has increased so enormously with the various methods of technologically reproducing it that, as happened in prehistoric times, a quantitative shift between the two poles of the artwork has led to a qualitative transformation in its nature. Just as the work of art in prehistoric times, through the exclusive emphasis placed on its cult value, became first and foremost an instrument of magic which only later came to be recognized as a work of art, so today, through the exclusive emphasis placed on its exhibition value, the work of art becomes a construct [*Gebilde*] with quite new functions. Among these, the one we are conscious of—the artistic function—may subsequently be seen as incidental. This much is certain: today, film is the most serviceable vehicle of this new understanding. Certain, as well, is the fact that the historical moment of this change in the function of art—a change which is most fully evident in the case of film—allows a direct comparison with the primeval era of art not only from a methodological but also from a material point of view.

Prehistoric art made use of certain fixed notations in the service of magical practice. In some cases, these notations probably comprised the actual performing of magical acts (the carving of an ancestral figure is itself such an act); in others, they gave instructions for such procedures (the ancestral figure demonstrates a ritual posture); and in still others, they provided objects for magical contemplation (contemplation of an ancestral figure strengthens the occult powers of the beholder). The subjects for these notations were humans and their environment, which were depicted according to the requirements of a society whose technology existed only in fusion with ritual. Compared to that of the machine age, of course, this technology was undeveloped. But from a dialectical standpoint, the disparity is unimportant. What matters is the way the orientation and aims of that technology differ from those of ours. Whereas the former made the maximum possible use of human beings, the latter reduces their use to the minimum. The achievements of the first technology might be said to culminate in human sacrifice; those of the second, in the remote-controlled aircraft which

5 In film, the technological reproducibility of the product is not an externally imposed condition of its mass dissemination, as it is, say, in literature or painting. *The technological reproducibility of films is based directly on the technology of their production. This not only makes possible the mass dissemination of films in the most direct way, but actually enforces it.* It does so because the process of producing a film is so costly that an individual who could afford to buy a painting, for example, could not afford to buy a [master print of a] film. It was calculated in 1927 that, in order to make a profit, a major film needed to reach an audience of nine million. Of course, the advent of sound film [in that year] initially caused a movement in the opposite direction: its audience was restricted by language boundaries. And that coincided with the emphasis placed on national interests by fascism. But it is less important to note this setback (which in any case was mitigated by dubbing) than to observe its connection with fascism. The simultaneity of the two phenomena results from the economic crisis. The same disorders which led, in the world at large, to an attempt to maintain existing property relations by brute force induced film capital, under the threat of crisis, to speed up the development of sound film. Its introduction brought temporary relief, not only because sound film attracted the masses back into the cinema but also because it consolidated new capital from the electricity industry with that of film. Thus, considered from the outside, sound film promoted national interests; but seen from the inside, it helped internationalize film production even more than before.

6 This polarity cannot come into its own in the aesthetics of Idealism, which conceives of beauty as something fundamentally undivided (and thus excludes anything polarized). Nonetheless, in Hegel this polarity announces itself as clearly as possible within the limits of Idealism. We quote from his *Vorlesungen zur Philosophie der Geschichte* [Lectures on the Philosophy of History]: "Images were known of old. In those early days piety required them for worship, but it could do without *beautiful* images. Such images might even be disturbing. In every beautiful image, there is also something external—although, insofar as the image is beautiful, its spirit still speaks to the human being. But religious worship, being no more than a spiritless torpor of the soul, is directed at a *thing*... Fine art arose... in the church..., though art has now gone beyond the ecclesiastical principle." Likewise, the following passage from the *Vorlesungen über die Ästhetik* [Lectures on Aesthetics] indicates that Hegel sensed a problem here: "We are beyond the stage of venerating works of art as divine and as objects deserving our worship. Today the impression they produce is of a more reflective kind, and the emotions they arouse require a more stringent test."

needs no human crew. The results of the first technology are valid once and for all (it deals with irreparable lapse or sacrificial death, which holds good for eternity). The results of the second are wholly provisional (it operates by means of experiments and endlessly varied test procedures). The origin of the second technology lies at the point where, by an unconscious ruse, human beings first began to distance themselves from nature. It lies, in other words, in play.

Seriousness and play, rigor and license, are mingled in every work of art, though in very different proportions. This implies that art is linked to both the second and the first technologies. It should be noted, however, that to describe the goal of the second technology as "mastery over nature" is highly questionable, since this implies viewing the second technology from the standpoint of the first. The first technology really sought to master nature, whereas the second aims rather at an interplay between nature and humanity. The primary social function of art today is to rehearse that interplay. This applies especially to film. *The function of film is to train human beings in the apperceptions and reactions needed to deal with a vast apparatus whose role in their lives is expanding almost daily.* Dealing with this apparatus also teaches them that technology will release them from their enslavement to the powers of the apparatus only when humanity's whole constitution has adapted itself to the new productive forces which the second technology has set free.[7]

VII

In photography, exhibition value begins to drive back cult value on all fronts. But cult value does not give way without resistance. It falls back to a last entrenchment: the human countenance. It is no accident that the portrait is central to early photography. In the cult of remembrance of dead or absent loved ones, the cult value of the image finds its last refuge. In the fleeting expression of a human face, the aura beckons from early photographs for the last time. This is what gives them their melancholy and incomparable beauty. But as the human being withdraws from the photographic image, exhibition value for the first time shows its superiority to cult value. To have given this development its local habitation constitutes the unique significance of Atget, who, around 1900, took photographs of deserted Paris streets.[8] It has justly been said that he photographed them like scenes of crimes. A crime scene, too, is deserted; it is photographed for the purpose of establishing evidence. With Atget, photographic records begin to be evidence in the historical trial [*Prozess*]. This constitutes their hidden political significance. They demand a specific kind of reception. Free-floating contemplation is no longer appropriate to them. They unsettle the viewer; he feels challenged to find a particular way to approach them. At the same time, illustrated magazines begin to put up signposts for him—whether these are right or wrong is irrelevant. For the first time, captions become obligatory. And it is clear that they have a character altogether different from the titles of paintings. The directives given by captions to those looking at images in illustrated magazines soon become even more precise and commanding in films, where the way each single image is understood seems prescribed by the sequence of all the preceding images.

VIII

The Greeks had only two ways of technologically reproducing works of art: casting and stamping. Bronzes, terra cottas, and coins were the only artworks they could produce in large numbers. All others were unique and could not be technologically reproduced. That is why they had to be made for all eternity. *The state of their technology compelled the Greeks to produce eternal values in their art.* To this they owe their preeminent position in art history—the standard for subsequent generations. Undoubtedly, our position lies at the opposite pole from that of the Greeks. Never before have artworks been technologically reproducible to such a degree and in such quantities as today. Film is the first art form whose artistic character is entirely determined by its reproducibility. It would be idle to compare this form in detail with Greek art. But on one precise point

7 The aim of revolutions is to accelerate this adaptation. Revolutions are innervations of the collective—or, more precisely, efforts at innervation on the part of the new, historically unique collective which has its organs in the new technology. This second technology is a system in which the mastering of elementary social forces is a precondition for playing [*das Spiel*] with natural forces. Just as a child who has learned to grasp stretches out its hand for the moon as it would for a ball, so humanity, in its efforts at innervation, sets its sights as much on currently utopian goals as on goals within reach. For in revolutions, it is not only the second technology which asserts its claims vis-à-vis society. Because this technology aims at liberating human beings from drudgery, the individual suddenly sees his scope for play, his field of action [*Spielraum*], immeasurably expanded. He does not yet know his way around this space. But already he registers his demands on it. For the more the collective makes the second technology its own, the more keenly individuals belonging to the collective feel how little they have received of what was due them under the dominion of the first technology. In other words, it is the individual liberated by the liquidation of the first technology who stakes his claim. No sooner has the second technology secured its initial revolutionary gains than vital questions affecting the individual—questions of love and death which had been buried by the first technology—once again press for solutions. Fourier's work is the first historical evidence of this demand.

8 Eugène Atget [...] See Benjamin's "Little History of Photography," in Walter Benjamin, *Selected Writings: Volume 2, 1927-1934*, trans. Edmund Jephcott and Kingsley Shorter (Cambridge, Mass.: Harvard University Press, 1999), 518-519.

such a comparison would be revealing. For film has given crucial importance to a quality of the artwork which would have been the last to find approval among the Greeks, or which they would have dismissed as marginal. This quality is its capacity for improvement. The finished film is the exact antithesis of a work created at a single stroke. It is assembled from a very large number of images and image sequences that offer an array of choices to the editor; these images, moreover, can be improved in any desired way in the process leading from the initial take to the final cut. To produce *A Woman of Paris*, which is 3,000 meters long, Chaplin shot 125,000 meters of film.[9] *The film is therefore the artwork most capable of improvement. And this capability is linked to its radical renunciation of eternal value.* This is corroborated by the fact that for the Greeks, whose art depended on the production of eternal values, the pinnacle of all the arts was the form least capable of improvement—namely sculpture, whose products are literally all of a piece. In the age of the assembled [*montierbar*] artwork, the decline of sculpture is inevitable.

IX

The nineteenth-century dispute over the relative artistic merits of painting and photography seems misguided and confused today. But this does not diminish its importance, and may even underscore it. The dispute was in fact an expression of a world-historical upheaval whose true nature was concealed from both parties. Insofar as the age of technological reproducibility separated art from its basis in cult, all semblance of art's autonomy disappeared forever. But the resulting change in the function of art lay beyond the horizon of the nineteenth century. And even the twentieth, which saw the development of film, was slow to perceive it.

Though commentators had earlier expended much fruitless ingenuity on the question of whether photography was an art—without asking the more fundamental question of whether the invention of photography had not transformed the entire character of art—film theorists quickly adopted the same ill-considered standpoint. But the difficulties which photography caused for traditional aesthetics were child's play compared to those presented by film. Hence the obtuse and hyperbolic character of early film theory. Abel Gance, for example, compares film to hieroglyphs: "By a remarkable regression, we are transported back to the expressive level of the Egyptians... Pictorial language has not matured because our eyes are not yet adapted to it. There is not yet enough respect, not enough *cult*, for what it expresses."[10] Or, in the words of Séverin-Mars: "What other art has been granted a dream...at once more poetic and more real? Seen in this light, film might represent an incomparable means of expression, and only the noblest minds should move within its atmosphere, in the most perfect and mysterious moments of their lives."[11] It is instructive to see how the desire to annex film to "art" impels these theoreticians to attribute elements of cult to film—with a striking lack of discretion. Yet when these speculations were published, works like *A Woman of Paris* and *The Gold Rush* had already appeared. This did not deter Abel Gance from making the comparison with hieroglyphs, while Séverin-Mars speaks of film as one might speak of paintings by Fra Angelico. It is revealing that even today especially reactionary authors look in the same direction for the significance of film—finding, if not actually a sacred significance, then at least a supernatural one. In connection with Max Reinhardt's film version of *A Midsummer Night's Dream*, Werfel comments that it was undoubtedly the sterile copying of the external world—with its streets, interiors, railway stations, restaurants, automobiles, and beaches—that had prevented film up to now from ascending to the realm of art. "Film has not yet realized its true purpose, its real possibilities... These consist in its unique ability to use natural means to give incomparably convincing expression to the fairylike, the marvelous, the supernatural."[12]

X

To photograph a painting is one kind of reproduction, but to photograph an action performed in a film studio is another. In the first case, what is reproduced is a work of art, while the act of producing it is not. The cameraman's performance with the lens no more creates an artwork than a conductor's with the baton; at most, it creates an artistic performance. This is unlike the process in a film studio. Here, what is reproduced is not an artwork, and the act of reproducing it is no more such a work than in the first case. The work of art is produced only by means of montage. And each individual component of this montage is a reproduction of a process which neither is an artwork in itself nor gives rise to one through photography. What, then, are these processes reproduced in film, since they are certainly not works of art?

To answer this, we must start from the peculiar nature of the artistic performance of the film actor. He is distinguished from the stage actor in that his performance in its original form, from which the reproduc-

9 *A Woman of Paris* (1923)—which Benjamin refers to by its French title, *L'Opinion publique*—was written and directed by Charlie Chaplin.

10 Gance, 101.

11 Séverin-Mars, cited in Gance, 100.

12 Franz Werfel, "Ein Sommernachtstraum: Ein Film von Shakespeare und Reinhardt," *Neues Wiener Journal*, cited in *Lu*, November 15, 1935.

tion is made: is not carried out in front of a randomly composed audience but before a group of specialists—executive producer, director, cinematographer, sound recordist, lighting designer, and so on—who are in a position to intervene in his performance at any time. This aspect of filmmaking is highly significant in social terms. For the intervention in a performance by a body of experts is also characteristic of sporting performances and, in a wider sense, of all test performances. The entire process of film production is determined, in fact, by such intervention. As we know, many shots are filmed in a number of takes. A single cry for help, for example, can be recorded in several different versions. The editor then makes a selection from these; in a sense, he establishes one of them as the record. An action performed in the film studio therefore differs from the corresponding real action the way the competitive throwing of a discus in a sports arena would differ from the throwing of the same discus from the same spot in the same direction in order to kill someone. The first is a test performance, while the second is not.

The test performance of the film actor is, however, entirely unique in kind. In what does this performance consist? It consists in crossing a certain barrier which confines the social value of test performances within narrow limits. I am referring now not to a performance in the world of sports, but to a performance produced in a mechanized test. In a sense, the athlete is confronted only by natural tests. He measures himself against tasks set by nature, not by equipment—apart from exceptional cases like [Paavo] Nurmi, who was said to run against the clock. Meanwhile the work process, especially since it has been standardized by the assembly line, daily generates countless mechanized tests. These tests are performed unawares, and those who fail are excluded from the work process. But they are also conducted openly, in agencies for testing professional aptitude. In both cases, the test subject faces the barrier mentioned above.

These tests, unlike those in the world of sports, are incapable of being publicly exhibited to the degree one would desire. And this is precisely where film comes into play. *Film makes test performances capable of being exhibited, by turning that ability itself into a test.* The film actor performs not in front of an audience but in front of an apparatus. The film director occupies exactly the same position as the examiner in an aptitude test. To perform in the glare of arc lamps while simultaneously meeting the demands of the microphone is a test performance of the highest order. To accomplish it is to preserve one's humanity in the face of the apparatus. Interest in this performance is widespread. For the majority of city dwellers, throughout the workday in offices and factories, have to relinquish their humanity in the face of an apparatus. In the evening these same masses fill the cinemas, to witness the film actor taking revenge on their behalf not only by asserting his humanity (or what appears to them as such) against the apparatus, but by placing that apparatus m the service of his triumph.

XI

In the case of film, the fact that the actor represents someone else before the audience matters much less than the fact that he represents himself before the apparatus. One of the first to sense this transformation of the actor by the test performance was Pirandello. That his remarks on the subject in his novel *Si gira* (Shoot!) are confined to the negative aspects of this change, and to silent film only, does little to diminish their relevance. For in this respect, the sound film changed nothing essential. What matters is that the actor is performing for a piece of equipment—or, in the case of sound film, for two pieces of equipment. "The film actor," Pirandello writes, "feels as if exiled. Exiled not only from the stage but from his own person. With a vague unease, he senses an inexplicable void, stemming from the fact that his body has lost its substance, that he has been volatilized, stripped of his reality, his life, his voice, the noises he makes when moving about, and has been turned into a mute image that flickers for a moment on the screen, then vanishes into silence... The little apparatus will play with his shadow before the audience, and he himself must be content to play before the apparatus."[13] The situation can also be characterized as follows: for the first time—and this is the effect of film—the human being is placed in a position where he must operate with his whole living person, while forgoing its aura. For the aura is bound to his presence in the here and now. There is no facsimile of the aura. The aura surrounding Macbeth on the stage cannot be divorced from the aura which, for the living spectators, surrounds the actor who plays him. What distinguishes the shot in the film studio, however, is that the camera is substituted for the audience. As a result, the aura surrounding the actor is dispelled—and, with it, the aura of the figure he portrays.

It is not surprising that it should be a dramatist such as Pirandello who, in reflecting on the special character of film acting, inadvertently touches on the crisis now affecting the theater. Indeed, nothing contrasts more starkly with a work of art completely subject to (or, like film, founded in) technological reproduction than a stage play. Any thorough consideration will confirm this. Expert observers have

13 Luigi Pirandello, *Il turno* (The Turn), cited by Léon Pierre-Quint, "Signification du cinema," in L'Art cinématographique, vol. 2, 14-15.

long recognized that, in film, "the best effects are almost always achieved by 'acting' as little as possible... The development," according to Rudolf Arnheim, writing in 1932, has been toward "using the actor as one of the 'props,' chosen for his typicalness and ... introduced in the proper context."[14] Closely bound up with this development is something else. *The stage actor identifies himself with a role. The film actor very often is denied this opportunity.* His performance is by no means a unified whole, but is assembled from many individual performances. Apart from incidental concerns about studio rental, availability of other actors, scenery, and so on, there are elementary necessities of the machinery that split the actor's performance into a series of episodes capable of being assembled. In particular, lighting and its installation require the representation of an action—which on the screen appears as a swift, unified sequence—to be filmed in a series of separate takes, which may be spread over hours in the studio. Not to mention the more obvious effects of montage. A leap from a window, for example, can be shot in the studio as a leap from a scaffold, while the ensuing fall may be filmed weeks later at an outdoor location. And far more paradoxical cases can easily be imagined. Let us assume that an actor is supposed to be startled by a knock at the door. If his reaction is not satisfactory, the director can resort to an expedient: he could have a shot fired without warning behind the actor's back on some other occasion when he happens to be in the studio. The actor's frightened reaction at that moment could be recorded and then edited into the film. Nothing shows more graphically that art has escaped the realm of "beautiful semblance," which for so long was regarded as the only sphere in which it could thrive.[15]

XII

The representation of human beings by means of an apparatus has made possible a highly productive use of the human being's self-alienation. The nature of this use can be grasped through the fact that the film actor's estrangement in the face of the apparatus, as Pirandello describes this experience, is basically of the same kind as the estrangement felt before one's appearance [*Erscheinung*] in a mirror—a favorite theme of the Romantics. But now the mirror image [*Bild*] has become detachable from the person mirrored, and is transportable. And where is it transported? To a site in front of the masses.[16] Naturally, the screen actor never for a moment ceases to be aware of this. While he stands before the apparatus, he knows that in the end he is confronting the masses. It is they who will control him. Those who are not visible, not present while he executes his performance, are precisely the ones who will control it. This invisibility heightens the authority of their control. It should not be forgotten, of course, that there can be no political advantage derived from this control until film has liberated itself from the fetters of

14 Rudolf Arnheim, *Film als Kunst* (Berlin, 1932), 176-177. In this context, certain apparently incidental details of film directing which diverge from practices on the stage take on added interest. For example, the attempt to let the actor perform without makeup, as in Dreyer's *Jeanne d'Arc*. Dreyer spent months seeking the forty actors who constitute the Inquisitors' tribunal. Searching for these actors was like hunting for rare props. Dreyer made every effort to avoid resemblances of age, build, and physiognomy in the actors. (See Maurice Schultz, "Le Maquillage" [Makeup], in *L'Art cinématographique*, vol. 6 (Paris, 1929), 65-66.)If the actor thus becomes a prop, the prop, in its turn, not infrequently functions as actor. At any rate, it is not unusual for films to allocate a role to a prop. Rather than selecting examples at random from the infinite number available, let us take just one especially revealing case. A clock that is running will always be a disturbance on the stage, where it cannot be permitted its role of measuring time. Even in a naturalistic play, real-life time would conflict with theatrical time. In view of this, it is most revealing that film—where appropriate—can readily make use of time as measured by a clock. This feature, more than many others, makes it clear that—circumstances permitting—and every prop in a film may perform decisive functions. From here it is but a step to Pudovkin's principle, which states that "to connect the performance of an actor with an object, and to build that performance around the object,... is always one of the most powerful methods of cinematic construction"(V. I. Pudovkin, *Film Regie und Filmmanuskript* [Film Direction and the Film Script] (Berlin, 1928), 126).. Film is thus the first artistic medium which is able to show how matter plays havoc with human beings [*wie die Materie dem Menschen mitspielt*]. It follows that films can be an excellent means of materialist exposition.

15 The significance of beautiful semblance [*schöner Schein*] is rooted in the age of auratic perception that is now coming to an end. The aesthetic theory of that era was most fully articulated by Hegel, for whom beauty is "the appearance [*Erscheinung*] of spirit in its immediate... sensuous form, created by the spirit as the form adequate to itself" (Hegel, *Werke*, vol. 10, part 2 (Berlin, 1837), 121).. Although this formulation has some derivative qualities, Hegel's statement that art strips away the "semblance and deception of this false, transient world" from the "true content of phenomena" (*Werke*, vol. 10, part 1, 13) already diverges from the traditional experiential basis [*Erfahrungsgrund*] of this doctrine. This ground of experience is the aura. By contrast, Goethe's work is still entirely imbued with beautiful semblance as an auratic reality. [...]

16 The change noted here in the mode of exhibition—a change brought about by reproduction technology—is also noticeable in politics. *The crisis of democracies can be understood as a crisis in the conditions governing the public presentation of politicians.* Democracies exhibit the politician directly, in person, before elected representatives. The parliament is his public. But innovations in recording equipment now enable the speaker to be heard by an unlimited number of people while he is speaking, and to be seen by an unlimited number shortly afterward. This means that priority is given to presenting the politician before the recording equipment. Parliaments are becoming depopulated at the same rime as theaters. Radio and film are changing not only the function of the professional actor but, equally, the function of those who, like the politician, present themselves before these media. The direction of this change is the same for the film actor and the politician, regardless of their different tasks. It tends toward the exhibition of controllable, transferable skills under certain social conditions, just as sports first called for such exhibition under certain natural conditions. This results in a new form of selection—selection before an apparatus—from which the champion, the star, and the dictator emerge as victors.

capitalist exploitation. Film capital uses the revolutionary opportunities implied by this control for counterrevolutionary purposes. Not only does the cult of the movie star which it fosters preserve that magic of the personality which has long been no more than the putrid magic of its own commodity character, but its counterpart, the cult of the audience, reinforces the corruption by which fascism is seeking to supplant the class consciousness of the masses.[17]

XIII

It is inherent in the technology of film, as of sports, that everyone who witnesses these performances does so as a quasi-expert. Anyone who has listened to a group of newspaper boys leaning on their bicycles and discussing the outcome of a bicycle race will have an inkling of this. In the case of film, the newsreel demonstrates unequivocally that any individual can be in a position to be filmed. But that possibility is not enough. *Any person today can lay claim to being filmed.* This claim can best be clarified by considering the historical situation of literature today.

For centuries it was in the nature of literature that a small number of writers confronted many thousands of readers. This began to change toward the end of the past century. With the growth and extension of the press, which constantly made new political, religious, scientific, professional, and local journals available to readers, an increasing number of readers—in isolated cases, at first—turned into writers. It began with the space set aside for "letters to the editor" in the daily press, and has now reached a point where there is hardly a European engaged in the work process who could not, in principle, find an opportunity to publish somewhere or other an account of a work experience, a complaint, a report, or something of the kind. Thus, the distinction between author and public is about to lose its axiomatic character. The difference becomes functional; it may vary from case to case. At any moment, the reader is ready to become a writer. As an expert—which he has had to become in any case in a highly specialized work process, even if only in some minor capacity—the reader gains access to authorship. Work itself is given a voice. And the ability to describe a job in words now forms part of the expertise needed to carry it out. Literary competence is no longer founded on specialized higher education but on polytechnic training, and thus is common property.

XIV

The shooting of a film, especially a sound film, offers a hitherto unimaginable spectacle. It presents a process in which it is impossible to assign to the spectator a single viewpoint which would exclude from his or her field of vision the equipment not directly involved in the action being filmed—the camera, the lighting units, the technical crew, and so forth (unless the alignment of the spectator's pupil coincided with that of the camera). This circumstance, more than any other, makes any resemblance between a scene in a film studio and one onstage superficial and irrelevant. In principle, the theater includes a position from which the action on the stage cannot easily be detected as an illusion. There is no such position where a film is being shot. The illusory nature of film is of the second degree; it is the result of editing. That is to say: *In the film studio the apparatus has penetrated so deeply into reality that a pure view of that reality, free of the foreign body of equipment, is the result of a special procedure—namely, the shooting by the specially adjusted photographic device and the assembly of that shot with others of the same kind.* The equipment-free aspect of reality has become the height of artifice, and the vision of immediate reality the Blue Flower in the land of technology.[18]

Hence, the presentation of reality in film is incomparably the more significant for people of today, since it provides the equipment-free aspect of reality they are entitled to demand from a work of art, and does so precisely on the basis of the most intensive interpenetration of reality with equipment. [...]

XVI

The most important social function of film is to establish equilibrium between human beings and the apparatus. Film achieves this goal not only in terms of man's presentation of himself to the camera but also in terms of his representation of his environment by means of this apparatus. On the one hand, film furthers insight into the necessities governing our lives by its use of close-ups, by its accentuation of hidden details in familiar objects, and by its exploration of commonplace milieux through the ingenious guidance of the camera; on the other hand, it manages to assure us of a vast and unsuspected field of action [*Spielraum*].

Our bars and city streets, our offices and furnished rooms, our railroad stations and our factories seemed

17 It should be noted in passing that proletarian class consciousness, which is the most enlightened form of class consciousness, fundamentally transforms the structure of the proletarian masses. [...]

18 Benjamin alludes here to *Heinrich von Ofterdingen*, an unfinished novel by Novalis first published in 1802. Von Ofterdingen is a medieval poet in search of the mysterious Blue Flower, which bears the face of his unknown beloved. See Benjamin's "Dream Kitsch," in Benjamin, *Selected Writings*, vol. 2, 3.

to close relentlessly around us. Then came film and exploded this prison-world with the dynamite of the split second, so that now we can set off calmly on journeys of adventure among its far-flung debris. With the close-up, space expands; with slow motion, movement is extended. And just as enlargement not merely clarifies what we see indistinctly "in any case," but brings to light entirely new structures of matter, slow motion not only reveals familiar aspects of movements, but discloses quite unknown aspects within them—aspects "which do not appear as the retarding of natural movements but have a curious gliding, floating character of their own."[19] Clearly, it is another nature which speaks to the camera as compared to the eye. "Other" above all in the sense that a space informed by human consciousness gives way to a space informed by the unconscious. Whereas it is a commonplace that, for example, we have some idea what is involved in the act of walking (if only in general terms), we have no idea at all what happens during the split second when a person actually takes a step. We are familiar with the movement of picking up a cigarette lighter or a spoon, but know almost nothing of what really goes on between hand and metal, and still less how this varies with different moods. This is where the camera comes into play, with all its resources for swooping and rising, disrupting and isolating, stretching or compressing a sequence, enlarging or reducing an object. It is through the camera that we first discover the optical unconscious: just as we discover the instinctual unconscious through psychoanalysis.

Moreover, these two types of unconscious are intimately linked. For in most cases the diverse aspects of reality captured by the film camera lie outside only the *normal* spectrum of sense impressions. Many of the deformations and stereotypes, transformations and catastrophes which can assail the optical world in films afflict the actual world in psychoses, hallucinations, and dreams. Thanks to the camera, therefore, the individual perceptions of the psychotic or the dreamer can be appropriated by collective perception. The ancient truth expressed by Heraclitus, that those who are awake have a world in common while each sleeper has a world of his own, has been invalidated by film—and less by depicting the dream world itself than by creating figures of collective dream, such as the globe-encircling Mickey Mouse.[20]

If one considers the dangerous tensions which technology and its consequences have engendered in the masses at large—tendencies which at critical stages take on a psychotic character—one also has to recognize that this same technologization [Technisierung] has created the possibility of psychic immunization against such mass psychoses. It does so by means of certain films in which the forced development of sadistic fantasies or masochistic delusions can prevent their natural and dangerous maturation in the masses. Collective laughter is one such preemptive and healing outbreak of mass psychosis. The countless grotesque events consumed in films are a graphic indication of the dangers threatening mankind from the repressions implicit in civilization. American slapstick comedies and Disney films trigger a therapeutic release of unconscious energies.[21] Their forerunner was the figure of the eccentric. He was the first to inhabit the new fields of action opened up by film—the first occupant of the newly built house. This is the context in which Chaplin takes on historical significance. [...]

XVIII

The masses are a matrix from which all customary behavior toward works of art is today emerging newborn. Quantity has been transformed into quality: *the greatly increased mass of participants has produced a different kind of participation.* The fact that this new mode of participation first appeared in a disreputable form should not mislead the observer. The masses are criticized for seeking distraction [*Zerstreuung*] in the work of art, whereas the art lover supposedly approaches it with concentration. In the case of the masses, the artwork is seen as a means of entertainment; in the case of the art lover, it is considered an object of devotion. This calls for closer examination. Distraction and concentration form an antithesis, which may be formulated as follows. A person who concentrates before a work of art is absorbed by it; he enters into the work, just as, according to legend, a Chinese painter entered his completed painting while beholding it. By contrast, the distracted masses absorb the work of art into themselves. Their waves lap around it; they encompass it

---

19 Rudolf Arnheim, *Film als Kunst*, 138.

20 Benjamin refers to Fragment 89 in the standard Diels-Kranz edition of the fragments of Heraclitus of Ephesus, the Presocratic philosopher of the sixth-fifth centuries B.C. On Mickey Mouse, see the following note.

21 Of course, a comprehensive analysis of these films should not overlook their double meaning. It should start from the ambiguity of situations which have both a comic and a horrifying effect. As the reactions of children show, comedy and horror are closely related. In the face of certain situations, why shouldn't we be allowed to ask which reaction is the more human? Some recent Mickey Mouse films offer situations in which such a question seems justified. (Their gloomy and sinister fire-magic, made technically possible by color film, high- lights a feature which up to now has been present only covertly, and shows how easily fascism takes over "revolutionary" innovations in this field too.) What is revealed in recent Disney films was latent in some of the earlier ones: the cozy acceptance of bestiality and violence as inevitable concomitants of existence. This renews an old tradition which is far from reassuring- the tradition inaugurated by the dancing hooligans to be found in depictions of medieval pogroms, of whom the "riff-raff" in Grimm's fairy tale of that title are a pale, indistinct rear-guard.

with their tide. This is most obvious with regard to buildings. Architecture has always offered the prototype of an artwork that is received in a state of distraction and through the collective. The laws of architecture's reception are highly instructive.

Buildings have accompanied human existence since primeval times. Many art forms have come into being and passed away. Tragedy begins with the Greeks, is extinguished along with them, and is revived centuries later. The epic, which originates in the early days of peoples, dies out in Europe at the end of the Renaissance. Panel painting is a creation of the Middle Ages, and nothing guarantees its uninterrupted existence. But the human need for shelter is permanent. Architecture has never had fallow periods. Its history is longer than that of any other art, and its effect ought to be recognized in any attempt to account for the relationship of the masses to the work of art. Buildings are received in a twofold manner: by use and by perception. Or, better: tactilely and optically. Such reception cannot be understood in terms of the concentrated attention of a traveler before a famous building. On the tactile side, there is no counterpart to what contemplation is on the optical side. Tactile reception comes about not so much by way of attention as by way of habit. The latter largely determines even the optical reception of architecture, which spontaneously takes the form of casual noticing, rather than attentive observation. Under certain circumstances, this form of reception shaped by architecture acquires canonical value. *For the tasks which face the human apparatus of perception at historical turning points cannot be performed solely by optical means—that is, by way of contemplation. They are mastered gradually—taking their cue from tactile reception—through habit.*

Even the distracted person can form habits. What is more, the ability to master certain tasks in a state of distraction first proves that their performance has become habitual. The sort of distraction that is provided by art represents a covert measure of the extent to which it has become possible to perform new tasks of apperception. Since, moreover, individuals are tempted to evade such tasks, art will tackle the most difficult and most important tasks wherever it is able to mobilize the masses. It does so currently in film. *Reception in distraction—the sort of reception which is increasingly noticeable in all areas of art and is a symptom of profound changes in apperception—finds in film its true training ground.* Film, by virtue of its shock effects, is predisposed to this form of reception. In this respect, too, it proves to be the most important subject matter, at present, for the theory of perception which the Greeks called aesthetics.

XIX

The increasing proletarianization of modern man and the increasing formation of masses are two sides of the same process. Fascism attempts to organize the newly proletarianized masses while leaving intact the property relations which they strive to abolish. It sees its salvation in granting expression to the masses—but on no account granting them rights.[22] The masses have a right to changed property relations; fascism seeks to give them expression in keeping these relations unchanged. *The logical outcome of fascism is an aestheticizing of political life.* With [Gabriele] D'Annunzio, decadence made its entry into political life; with Marinetti, Futurism; and with Hitler, the Bohemian tradition of Schwabing.

All efforts to aestheticize politics culminate in one point. That one point is war. War, and only war, makes it possible to set a goal for mass movements on the grandest scale while preserving traditional property relations. That is how the situation presents itself in political terms. In technological terms it can be formulated as follows: only war makes it possible to mobilize all of today's technological resources while maintaining property relations. It goes without saying that the fascist glorification of war does not make use of *these* arguments. Nevertheless, a glance at such glorification is instructive. In Marinetti's manifesto for the colonial war in Ethiopia, we read:

> For twenty-seven years, we Futurists have rebelled against the idea that war is anti-aesthetic... We therefore state: ...War is beautiful because—thanks to its gas masks, its terrifying megaphones, its flame throwers, and light tanks—it establishes man's dominion over the subjugated machine. War is beautiful because it inaugurates the dreamed-of metallization of the human body. War is beautiful because it enriches a flowering meadow with the fiery orchids of machine-guns. War is beautiful because it combines gunfire, barrages, cease-fires, scents, and the fragrance of putrefaction into a symphony. War is beautiful because it creates new architectures, like those of armored tanks, geometric squadrons of aircraft,

22 A technological factor is important here, especially with regard to the newsreel, whose significance for propaganda purposes can hardly be overstated. *Mass reproduction is especially favored by the reproduction of the masses.* In great ceremonial processions, giant rallies and mass sporting events, and in war, all of which are now fed into the camera, the masses come face to face with themselves. This process, whose significance need not be emphasized, is closely bound up with the development of reproduction and recording technologies. In general, mass movements are more clearly apprehended by the camera than by the eye. A bird's-eye view best captures assemblies of hundreds of thousands. And even when this perspective is no less accessible to the human eye than to the camera, the image formed hy the eye cannot be enlarged in the same way as a photograph. This is to say that mass movements, and above all war, are a form of human behavior especially suited to the camera.

> spirals of smoke from burning villages, and much more. ... Poets and artists of Futurism... remember these principles of an aesthetic of war, that they may illuminate... your struggles for a new poetry and a new sculpture![23]

This manifesto has the merit of clarity. The question it poses deserves to be taken up by the dialectician. To him, the aesthetic of modern warfare appears as follows: if the natural use of productive forces is impeded by the property system, then the increase in technological means, in speed, in sources of energy will press toward an unnatural use. This is found in war, and the destruction caused by war furnishes proof that society was not mature enough to make technology its organ, that technology was not sufficiently developed to master the elemental forces of society. The most horrifying features of imperialist war are determined by the discrepancy between the enormous means of production and their inadequate use in the process of production (in other words, by unemployment and the lack of markets). *Imperialist war is an uprising on the part of technology, which demands repayment in "human material" for the natural material society has denied it.* Instead of deploying power stations across the land, society deploys manpower in the form of armies. Instead of promoting air traffic, it promotes traffic in shells. And in gas warfare it has found a new means of abolishing the aura.

"Fiat ars—pereat mundus,"[24] says fascism, expecting from war, as Marinetti admits, the artistic gratification of a sense perception altered by technology. This is evidently the consummation of *l'art pour l'art*. Humankind, which once, in Homer, was an object of contemplation for the Olympian gods, has now become one for itself. Its self-alienation has reached the point where it can experience its own annihilation as a supreme aesthetic pleasure. *Such is the aestheticizing of politics, as practiced by fascism. Communism replies by politicizing art.*

23 Cited in *La Stampa Torino*. [Benjamin's note. The German editors of Benjamin's *Gesammelte Schriften* argue that this passage is more likely to have been excerpted from a French newspaper than from the Italian newspaper cited here.]

24 "Let art flourish—and the world pass away." This is a play on the motto of the sixteenth-century Holy Roman emperor Ferdinand I: "Fiat iustitia et pereat mundus" ("Let justice be done and the world pass away").

There Are No Mass Media

Bernhard Siegert

2003

In the year 1935 the question concerning the work of art was posed not once but twice. The title of Benjamin's *Artwork* essay sounds like a direct response to Heidegger's essay *The Origin of the Work of Art* (which, however, was published more than a month after Benjamin finished the first version of his text). Heidegger's question of origin appears, in fact, to be opposed to the question concerning reproduction. But it merely appears so. No less than the question concerning the original in Benjamin's essay, the question of origin leads thinking into a circle (UdK 8/149).[1] Insofar as the concept of the original presupposes the concept of reproduction, the "presence in time and space" of the work of art (475/220) is always supplementary and constituted as that which is supplemented only by the supplement of reproduction. To the same degree that "authenticity" is not subject to reproducibility, it does derive from reproducibility. Consequently, the same holds true for the aura, which discloses itself as the origin of the work of art only in the age of mechanical reproduction. Origin and reproduction thus are merely two sides of the same coin.

In addition to that, Benjamin's statement that "the work of art has always been reproducible" (474/218) causes a strange confusion in the context of film. Namely, there is a noticeable confusion of two things: on the one hand, the reproduction of works of art (whenever it is a matter of manual reproduction) and, on the other hand, technologies of reproduction that as such imply technical reproducibility (as is the case, for example, with film negatives) but do not presuppose a work of art as the original. The statement that works of art in principle have always been reproducible therefore not only drops the unique "presence in time and space" of the work of art with the same degree of principle, but it also obfuscates a distinction-namely, between the reproduction of works of art and the much more fundamental storage and processing of data. Whereas Benjamin does not at all draw the distinction between physical data and works, Heidegger opens it up explicitly in order to trace the question concerning the work of art back, first of all, to the problem of data processing. Whereas Benjamin's circumscription of the "aura of natural objects" (479/222) operates with (as Heidegger would call it) "de-severance,"[2] Heidegger restores the work of art to *physis*: "[M]etals come to glitter and shimmer, colors to glow, tones to sing, the word to say. All this comes forth as the work sets itself back into the massiveness and heaviness of stone, into the firmness and pliancy of wood, into the hardness and luster of metal, into the lighting and darkening of color, into the clang of tone, and into the naming power of the word" (*UdK* 35/171). In contrast to a reproducibility of works of art from the beginning of all time, the reproducibility of colors and noises as colors and noises is precisely the achievement of technical media (as opposed to the arts). Until the arrival of film and the gramophone, the reproduction of color was limited to the threshold differentiation of the perception of color tones on the painter's palette, and the reproduction of noises was limited to intervals that can be written down within the tonal system or words that can be recorded in alphabetical letters.

The definition of technical reproducibility as the gradual negation of manual reproducibility (476/221) has the effect that sensory data from the outset are thought of as culturally coded data- as if a camera could record only productions of Faust (477 n. 4/243 n. 3), and a gramophone only opera arias. However, the cultural-philosophical perspectivization of media theory tends to imply precisely this: from the concepts of the original and authenticity no path leads to an equation

1 *Editors' Note*: References in the text and notes of this essay are organized in the following manner: *UdK* refers to the work listed in the Bibliography as Heidegger, "Der Ursprung des Kunstwerkes," with the first number being the page of this edition. The second number refers to the page in the (abbreviated) English translation listed in the Bibliography as Heidegger, "The Origin of the Work of Art." Unlabeled pairs of numbers in parentheses refer, respectively, to two editions of Benjamin's *Artwork* essay: the first to pages of the so-called second edition, listed in the Bibliography as Benjamin, "Das Kunstwerk" (*Gesammelte Schriften*, 1974), the second to pages of the English edition listed in the Bibliography as Benjamin, "The Work of Art."

2 *Translator's Note*: Heidegger's *Ent-fernung* has no etymological equivalent in English, since the hyphenation of the standard *Entfernung* stresses the privative prefix and thereby turns the standard meaning on its head. Instead of a "removal" or "distance," Ent-fernung- that is, "de-severing" or "de-severance"- amounts, in Heidegger's own words, "to making the farness vanish..., making the remoteness of something disappear, bringing it close" (Heidegger, *Being and Time*, 139, § 23).. A translators' note (Heidegger, 138-139, n. 2) gives an exhaustive explanation for the choice of "de-severance" and "de-severing." Furthermore, they note that the use of the hyphenated Ent-fernung and of the standard Entfernung is far from consistent in the different editions of *Sein und Zeit*—presumably due to typographical errors.

of van Gogh's paintings and coal from the Ruhr region, or Beethoven's quartets and potatoes- with which, after all, Heidegger's essay makes its scandalous beginning (*UdK* 9/150). But this foolishness, the peculiarity of the technical media to distinguish no longer between works and things, transforms aesthetic data into mere signals, colors, and sounds into mere frequencies. In the age of technology, the difference between aesthetics and physics is the same as that between testing and measuring. The test, to which the actor in front of the camera is subjected, has nothing to do with the technically relevant frequency of frames, but is directly related to the aesthetically relevant frequency of cuts. Thus, it tests the limits of perception but without ever falling below this threshold. For physical measuring, however, audible and visible frequencies are but a small selection from the spectrum of frequencies that can be used by media technology. What Benjamin's aesthetics by definition fails to recognize is the possibility of data storage as the processing of signals. An example would be the simple case, described by Jacques Lacan, of a circular communication line as the storage facility of a telegraphic message.[3]

Transmission is the blind spot of Benjamin's essay, obvious already in his little media history. The condition of possibility for "lithography enabl[ing] graphic art to illustrate everyday life" (472/219) was the postage stamp—forgotten by Benjamin—which alone made it possible for lithographic reproductions to achieve daily delivery frequencies. That Benjamin barely takes note of the radio (which was, after all, the source of his income for many years) demonstrates dramatically that the "summer afternoon" (479/222) of analogous low-frequency optical storage media excludes the night of high-frequency acoustical transmission media—a night, to be sure, that is night to an even more unimaginable degree than the night that literally ruled in the "sensory deprivation" of the trenches of World War I. But, since the digital media are married to this night, an aesthetics that still adheres, qua negation of psychological categories of visual perception (such as attention and gaze),[4] to the level of consciousness, is insufficient as a media theory in the digital age. Digital image media cannot be thought of without recourse to the history of transmission media (radio, television) and the technology of "signal processing." Only on the phenomenal level are they related to film that semidigital, semianalog hybrid- insofar as even their samples are digital and not simply the process of sampling itself (as with film, in which the sampled signal is a two-dimensional analog—namely, chemical—representation of countless segments of the color spectrum).

The difference between Benjamin's and Heidegger's essays could be described as the difference between production on the one hand and research and development on the other: while Benjamin's starting point is the serial production of being, Heidegger's starting point is the experimental investigation of being. Consequently, what remains unthought in Heidegger's essay on *The Origin of the Work of Art* is the serial production of shoes- as well as the fact that van Gogh's painting of peasant shoes is also part of a series of images.

Whereas Heidegger, in a Nietzschean fashion, displaces the origin of the work of art in the nonidentity of strife (between lighting and concealing), Benjamin transfers the origin of the work of art—admittedly qua negation—into an identity that cannot be represented. In fact, Benjamin's most illuminating remark concerning the aura is that it cannot be depicted; this does not apply only to technical depictions, but it denies any depiction of aura. Thus, a negative theology of images emerges at the heart of the reproduction thesis. No matter whether this points, obviously, to the Jewish prohibition of images or, less obviously, to the Nicene pretemporal logic of the image of the trinity (which turns the prohibition of images into the principle of the image), either way Benjamin's media theory reveals itself as a negative theology. Film is the death of God.

But insofar as only the era of technical reproducibility reveals the aura as the lost origin of the work of art, the question arises: what sense does the death of God make from the perspective of shock? From this point of view God functions as a protection against stimuli. As Samuel Weber has shown, aura serves to localize shock by assigning it to an "exact place in time in consciousness," "to the extent that this allocation of a place fails and that, therefore, the stimuli have no *assigned value*, they form no *gestalt* and threaten the unity of consciousness. In other words, the *traumatic power* increases in inverse proportion to the *assigned value*. Benjamin attempts to think this inverse proportion in the concept of *aura*."[5] In Nietzsche's sense the aura stands in the service of life: its truth is nothing but the will to appearance, to illusion, to lie in order to control the nonidentity inherent in the neural stimuli.[6]

From a physiological point of view, the prohibition of images is therefore a form of protection against stimuli: it protects media theory from too many images and from images that are too quick by assigning to them a specific value and importance within the

3 Jacques Lacan, *Das Seminar: Buch 11*, trans. Norbert Haas (Olten: Walter, 1980), 117.

4 See esp. the passages on aura in Benjamin, "Über einige Motive bei Baudelaire," in *Gesammelte* Schriften, ed. Rolf Tiedemann and Hermann Schweppenhäuser (Frankfurt-am-Main: Suhrkamp, 1991) I, 2, 646ff.

5 Samuel Weber, "Der posthume Zwischenfall: Eine Live Sendung," in *Zeit-Zeichen: Aufschube und Interferenzen zwischen Endzeit und Echtzeit*, ed. Georg Christoph Tholen and Michael O. Scholl (Weinheim: VCH-Acta Humaniora, 1990), 188.

6 Nietzsche, "Über Wahrheit und Lüge im außermoralischen Sinn," in *Werke*, ed. Karl Schlechta (Munich: Hanser, 1969), III, 312ff.

history of the decay of aura. Moreover, it protects media theory from having to place media history within the horizon of shock- that is, within the history of war. In contrast, aura and shock in *The Origin of the Work of Art* appear as "shape" and "thrust." But Heidegger thinks of the shape of the work from the perspective of shock—as the sample of strife, of conflict. However, this sample is of interest only for the reason *that* it is; this *that* communicates itself in the shock or thrust (*UdK* 53-54/183). Heidegger thinks of the work of art as a radar station. It locates the *that* of beings.

The auratic protection against stimuli and, more precisely, against the shocks that war inflicts on thinking is called the public sphere. The aura of aura is nothing else—from a nominalistic point of view. For "all that is transmissible" (477/221) in the meaning of the word "aura"—the breeze—is the daylight, the public sphere. In Virgil the word is documented in the expression *ferre sub auras*, "to make known," and also in *aura fugere*, "to avoid the daylight, the public sphere." Judged from the sensorium of the soldiers, World War I was a single fugue of the aura. Thus, in the concept of aura the "negative horizon of war" (as one might call it with Wolfgang Hagen) of the technical media is already established: "To all of the newer media adheres therefore a negative horizon of war. Negative..., because it almost instantly disappears in the perception of that 'public' into whose sphere the media are 'released' as if into a harmless sphere of entertainment of the civilized world. This happened with radio in the 20s, with VHF and television in the early 50s, and with the computer in the 80s."[7] If therefore the concepts of technical reproducibility and media are, supposedly, determined by the withdrawal of the aura, neither the concept of a public sphere, nor all related concepts from the supply of the Institute for Social Research, escape this withdrawal of the aura. The further Benjamin's aura is deconstructed, the clearer it can be recognized as a trap for the follies of Adorno's theory of mass media as formulated in the 1930s.[8]

In the area of theory, Benjamin's reduction of historical conditions of perception to "social" instead of technical a prioris, this reduction to the increasing importance of the masses, is a particularly eminent strategy of protection against stimuli vis-a-vis the war horizon of the media. The shock, inflicted on theory through the decentering of the subject of perception, is diverted by transposing subjectivity onto the masses. The shock does not destroy, but rather displaces subjectivity—as if the "masses" ever had been concerned with "bring[ing] things 'closer' spatially and humanly" (479/223). By contrast, bringing masses closer to each other spatially and humanly by means of railroads had been a concern of the Prussian chiefs of staff ever since the war of 1866, and of all the warring powers in World War I.

Benjamin's own analysis, however, infuses the desire of "the masses" for the cinema with noticeable doubts. In a nutshell and against its own intent, as it were, the *Artwork* essay contains a history of mass media that marks their historical deconstruction. Already in the case of photography, the still metaphorical, but no less explicit, observation that the photograph transforms the depicted setting into the scene of a crime makes clear that the medium of photography is not demanded by the masses but rather by criminology (485/226). Criminology occupies the most prominent place among the modern powers that decide matters of form and aesthetics. Benjamin's analysis of the camera apparatus as a testing examiner removes it entirely from a "society" (488/228-229). Benjamin's remark that "one knows nothing of a person's posture during the fractional second of a stride" (500/237) is not the example it was meant to be, for it was above all Marey's assistant Georges Demeny who, appointed by the French chiefs of staff, was preoccupied with the posture of striding persons. And it was Eadweard Muybridge who was concerned with the posture of the horses of the former governor of California, Leland Stanford, while striding and galloping.

The story is well known, but cannot be told often enough. At the end of the 1860s the physiologist Étienne-Jules Marey—like many of his professional colleagues ever since the research of the Weber brothers—was studying the movement of living bodies. One of the things he recorded, using a four-part device that recorded at a certain rate of pulsation, was the sequence of motions in the movements of horses. One Captain

7 Wolfgang Hagen, "Mediendialektik- Am Beispiel Radio: Lazarsfeld, Adorno,Benjamin, Enzenberger, Kluge," in *Medien und Öffentlichkeit: Positionierungen, Symptome, Simulationsbrüche*, ed. Rudolf Maresch (München: Boer, 1996), passim.

8 The core of this pessimistic media theory- that is, the thesis of the alienated or manipulated masses- developed as a theory of mass media from Adorno in the 1930s up to Enzensberger in the 1970s and was already deconstructed a decade ago by Baudrillard. In the age of TV, the time has come for the insight that an undistorted reality or human nature can no longer be isolated as a fundamental element. Consequently, the suspicion arises that "this idea of alienation has probably never been anything but a philosopher's ideal perspective for the use of hypothetical masses." Baudrillard suggests inverting the thesis of the masses alienated by the media in order "to evaluate how much the whole universe of the media, and perhaps the whole technical universe, is the result of a secret strategy of this mass which is claimed to be alienated, *of a secret form of the refusal of will*, of an involuntary challenge to everything which was demanded of the subject by philosophy—that is to say, to all rationality of choice and to all exercise of will, of knowledge, and of liberty" (Baudrillard, "The Masses: The Implosion of the Social in the Media," New Literary History 16 (1985), 584-85 and passim). Nevertheless, as one can see, media theory continues to be a theory of mass media even for the philosopher Baudrillard. The inversion of the theory of the Frankfurt school still falls under its a priori-namely, that the "masses" are the subject of media history. However, what is at stake here is not a more intelligent theory of mass media, but rather its complete abrogation.

Duhousset, who apparently could draw as well as he could ride, produced drawings of the postures of the horses which corresponded to the graphs recorded by Marey's device. Through mysterious channels these drawings fell into the hands of Governor Stanford. Stanford, however, had more faith in his genre painters than in Marey's recording device. In particular, Stanford could not bring himself to believe that, in a specific phase of its movement, a galloping horse touches the ground with only one of its front legs. He was so convinced that he made a bet with his friend McCrellish and commissioned Muybridge, who at that time was in charge of the photographic survey of the Pacific Coast, to decide the bet by means of serial photography. In 1872 Muybridge began taking his famous photographs in the trotter paddocks of Palo Alto.[9] In 1881, Marey learned about Muybridge's work and improved his method by replacing the series of cameras used by Muybridge with a "photographic gun." Benjamin's example points to the scientific prehistory of the cinema: to chrono-photography, which was not concerned with the synthesis but rather the analysis of movement. The reconstruction of the history of media as a history of the decay of the aura, by comparison, requires sound film to emerge from photography (475/219). But the masses as the historical subject of the mass medium of photography- or rather, photography as the medium of disciplining the masses- is not the origin of the filmic work of art. Rather, this origin lies in research laboratories (like Marey's) where bodies were cut into pieces on behalf of the military. Historically speaking, slow motion actually preceded the motion picture projected at normal speed.

Finally, even the famous "reception in a state of distraction" can be freed from mass media dogma, and the concept of the audience as an examiner, but a distracted one (505/240-241), can be replaced by a historically more concrete concept—for example, a surveillance officer in his airplane. "For the tasks which face the human apparatus of perception at the turning points of history cannot be solved by optical means, that is, by contemplation, alone. They are mastered gradually by habit, under the guidance of tactile appropriation" (505/240). Referentialization [*Referentialisierung*] causes the philosophical discourse to dissolve into a description of the situation. The "turning points of history" refer to World War I. The "human apparatus of perception" is that of artillery observers, of pilots, or of sappers in the "war below the surface." "Habit," far from being a free historical subject that could provide "guidance," is instead guided by the sciences, which switched over to war-industry production.

Nothing, therefore—as the latest research demonstrates—is more questionable than Benjamin's hope that the concepts he elaborates are incompatible with Fascist aesthetics. Soviet avant-garde art—Eisenstein, Vertov, Lev Kuleshov, and many more to whom Benjamin refers—directly applied the methods of industrial engineering, especially the methods of Gilbreth who was a student of Taylor.[10] Industrial engineering imported from America had a direct connection (like Kuleshov or Vertov) to Meyerholt's "biomechanics."[11] When Benjamin speaks of the "identity of the artistic and scientific uses of photography" (499/236), he obviously and very concretely is thinking of industrial engineering and the "artists" that serve it, such as Vertov or Kuleshov.[12] The *terminus ad quem* of Gilbreth's use of the camera was the moment when the ideal working motions (as designed by industrial engineering) and the empirical working motions were short-circuited. In the approximated real time of their feedback, the cinematographic ideal and the empirical body merged into the type of *the worker*. Working motions, copied onto endless meters of Soviet celluloid, became a constant test of the degree to which this worker-type had been achieved in practice. Suddenly, Jünger and Benjamin stand in close proximity.

For the reasons enumerated, there are no mass media, just as there are no "masses." Marx, whom Benjamin quotes, complained no less than Theodor Mommsen, that the masses never are *populus*—that is, a singular subject, but always *plebs*—that is, amorphous plurality. Aesthetics is therefore the science of the a prioris of perception. Whether these a prioris have a social or a technical quality is the question to which Benjamin's entire text gives strangely contradictory answers. But the analysis of the camera as an apparatus for testing directs the discussion from the public sphere of mass media into the seclusion of laboratories. Aesthetics, like the body, depends on the historical ruptures of media history. Nietzsche (whom Benjamin does not mention) knew this already. The survival of an aesthetics with a scientific claim drawing a conclusion from this insight with regard to the digital age. The thinking of media as mass media may be explained as an effect of the negative horizon of war, but this understanding and its inclusion in the concept of "public sphere" are lies that sustain the human sciences. In the digital age, these lies have become lethal. The time has come to do away with them.

9 Friedrich von Zglinicki, *Der Weg des Films: Die Geschichte der Kinematographie und ihrer Vorläufer* (Berlin: Rembrandt-Verlag, 1956), 173.

10 For this reference I thank Hans-Christian von Herrmann (Berlin), whose studies on Brecht's media aesthetics are to be published soon.

11 Ulrich Gregor, "Meyerholt und das Kino der Revolutionäre," in *Theater Heute* 4, no. 3, 30-32.

12 Benjamin explicitly mentions industrial engineering in a footnote: "Thus, vocational aptitude tests become constantly more important.... The camera director in the studio occupies a place identical with that of the examiner during aptitude tests" (488 n. 17/246 n. 10)

Julian Sander, Great-Grandson of August Sander, as Recounted to Walead Beshty 2017

The photographs from the "Political Prisoners" Portfolio were taken in the *Justizvollzugsanstalt Siegburg* [Penitentiary of the city of Siegburg] during Erich Sander's imprisonment. From the letters that were written between August and Anna Sander and Erich [August Sander's eldest son], we know he worked as the prison photographer...We can deduce from the fact that August was never allowed to take a camera into the prison, and that Erich was smuggling negatives out of the prison with help of a priest, that August Sander did not take any of the prison photographs. This theory was confirmed by research of Ulrich Eumann of the NS-Documentation Center of the City of Cologne. August placed the portfolio as an homage to his eldest son into *People of the Twentieth Century* (*Menschen des 20. Jahrhunderts*) ...

[Erich] seemed to have a certain degree of freedom of movement, at least during part of his imprisonment, which would explain how the self-portrait he took sitting a desk in his cell was possible. My father and I re-enacted that scene and determined that the Photograph could only be taken with the cell door open and the camera placed in clear sight in the hallway ... It is unclear if all of the photographs were taken during his "work" as a photographer, or if he secretly took some of the images as duplicates and hid them from the guards.

There are five portraits of Erich Sander in *People of the Twentieth Century*: *Kaiser's Birthday Celebration*, 1915; *Working Students*, 1926; *Student of Philosophy [Erich Sander]*, 1926; *Political Prisoner [Erich Sander]*, 1943; and *Death Mask of Erich Sander*, 1944. The first image is a children's party with costumes to celebrate the Kaiser's Birthday by performing a play. Erich is third from the right. The second and third image show Erich as a student, both taken in the same year, but placed in different portfolios—one as part of the "Student" portfolio, and the other as part of the "Scholars" portfolio. In the group photograph we see Erich among a group of politically active friends. All of them, except one, died during the Second World War. The fourth image shows Erich in his prison cell. We know this photograph must have been taken with the consent (or at least chosen ignorance) of the guards on duty. My Father and I recreated this shot using the same camera and lens type as Erich used. It was impossible to take this photograph without setting up in the hall, and in clear sight. You can see in the picture that he had some books, and we assume he also had running water in his cell in order to do his dark room work.

The last image is Erich Sander's death mask. This photograph hung in August Sander's home until his death. He was deeply hurt by the death of his eldest son. The placement of this image as the last image in *People of the Twentieth Century* can only be interpreted as tribute and memorial to Erich.

Erich Sander died from the consequences of an untreated appendicitis. The story goes that he died in excruciating pain because the guards did not think he was really ill. By the time he was treated it was too late.

[In the portfolio "The Last People"] I would note two details ... [t]he use of the title "matter" for the photographs of the two dead people. This shows a clear positioning to what makes a human a human. Secondly, [t]he placement of Erich Sander's death mask as the last image I feel is a very strong reminder of the loss that Erich's death represented to August Sander. ... the *Laborer from Frechen* (1930), also appears as *Beggar* (1930) in the Portfolio, "People Who Came to My Door." There are a number of people who appeared more than once in *People of the Twentieth Century*... Considering that [Sander] lost 75% of his negatives shortly after the war, and also found it difficult to continue to photograph as he saw the society go through a massive shift after the war, I do not find it surprising that he used what was available to him. I also find it quite compelling that a single person could play more than one role within Sander's construct. I find that to be very revealing. For me personally it is a proof of the fact that there is importance to the role of the viewer just as much as there is in the role of the artist. It shows me that the things we see are dependent on the context in which we see them. (kind of obvious I know, but not to everyone...)

Student of Philosophy [Erich Sander]

August Sander

1926

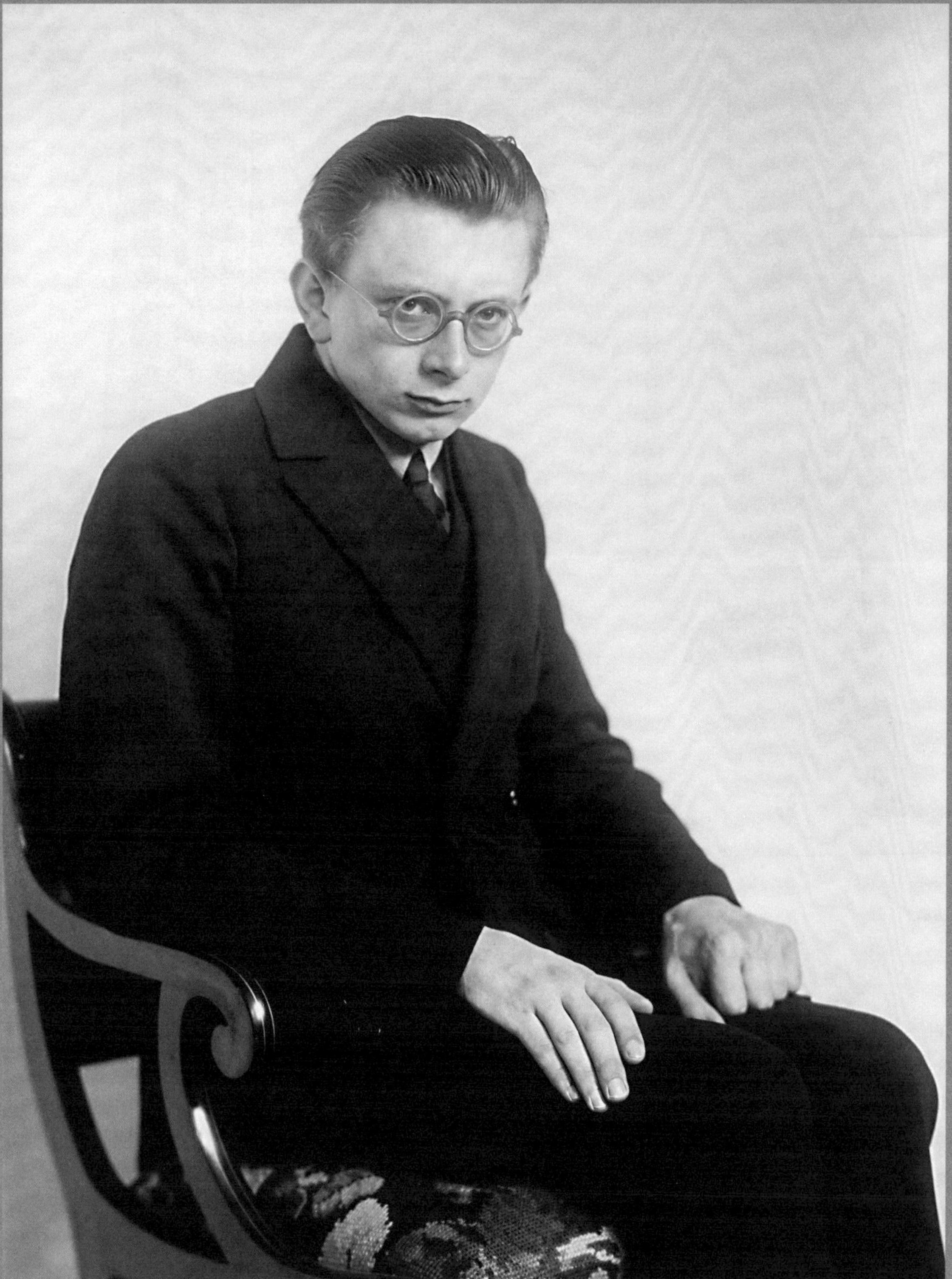

Political Prisoner [Erich Sander]

August Sander

1943

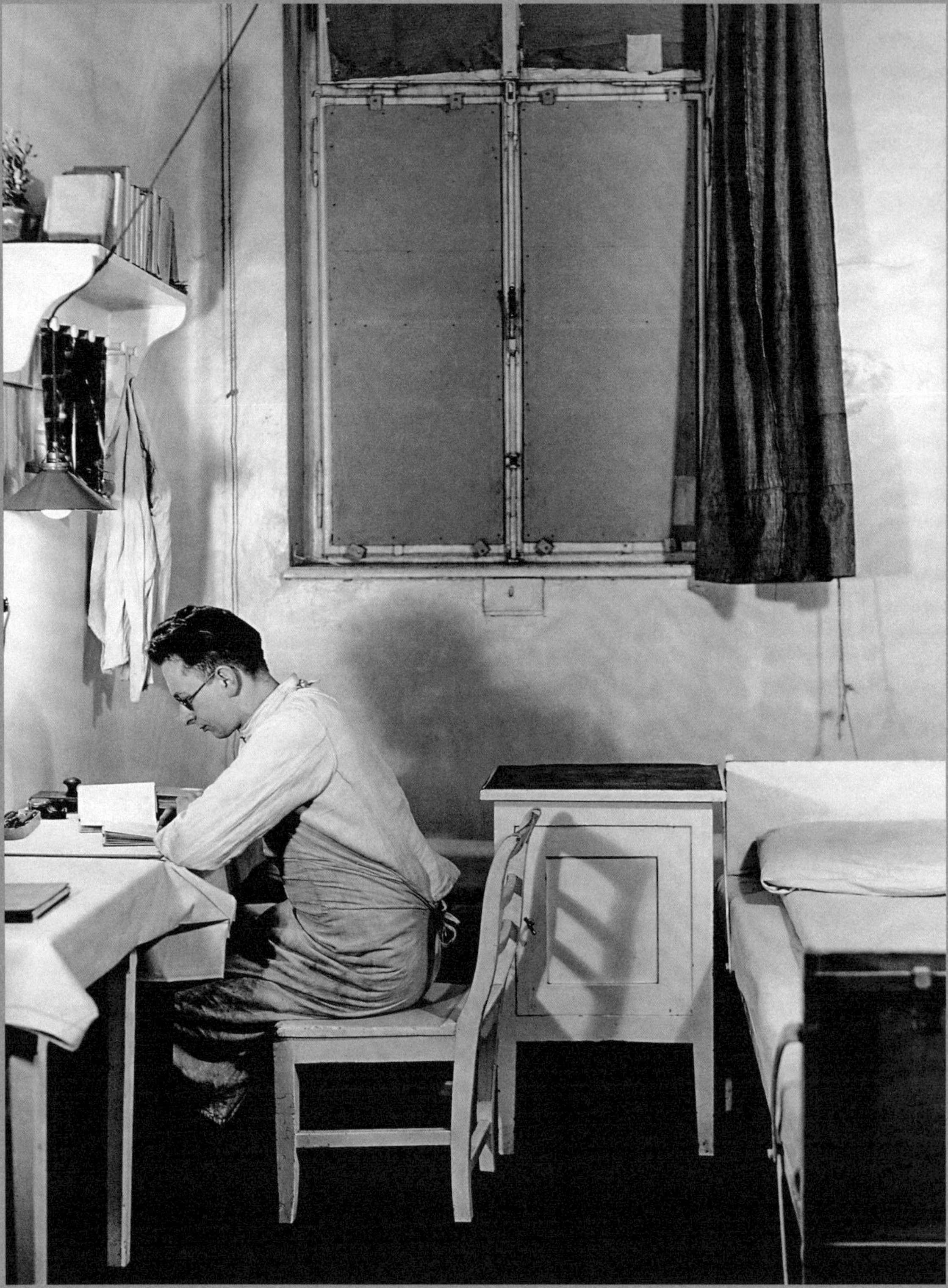

Death Mask of Erich Sander

August Sander

1944

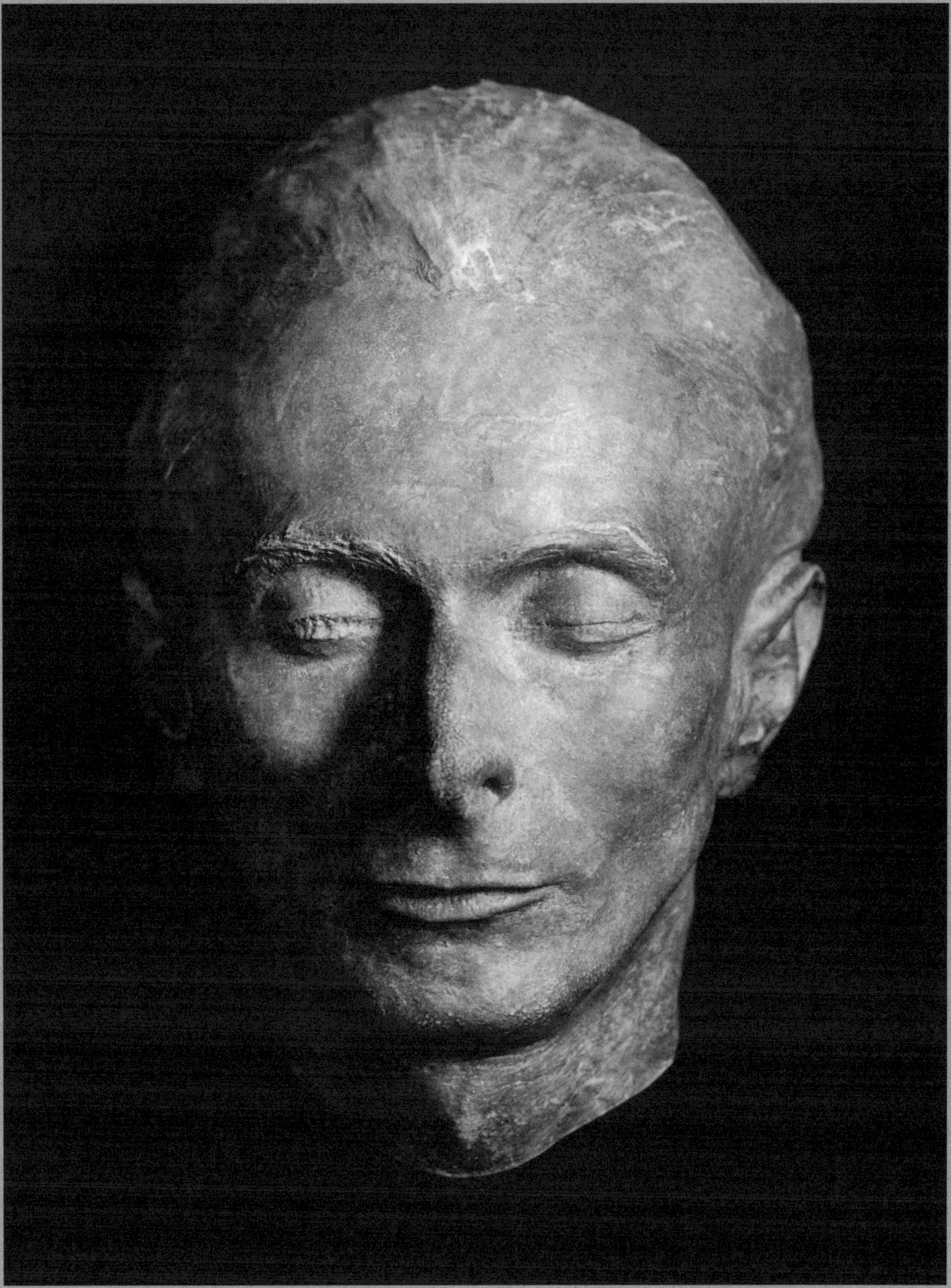

Images in Spite of All
Georges Didi-Huberman
2008

FOUR PIECES OF FILM SNATCHED FROM HELL

In order to know, we must *imagine* for ourselves. We must attempt to imagine the hell that Auschwitz was in the summer of 1944. Let us not invoke the unimaginable. Let us not shelter ourselves by saying that we cannot, that we could not by any means, imagine it to the very end. We *are obliged* to that oppressive imaginable. It is a response that we must offer, as a debt to the words and images that certain prisoners snatched, for us, from the harrowing Real of their experiences. So let us not invoke the unimaginable. How much harder was it for the prisoners to rip from the camps those few shreds of which now we are trustees, charged with sustaining them simply by looking at them. Those shreds are at the same time more precious and less comforting than all possible works of art, snatched as they were from a world bent on their impossibility. Thus, images *in spite of all*: in spite of the hell of Auschwitz, in spite of the risks taken. In return, we must contemplate them, take them on, and try to comprehend them. Images *in spite of all*: in spite of our own inability to look at them as they deserve; in spite of our own world, full, almost choked, with imaginary commodities. [...]

Of all the prisoners in Auschwitz, those whose possible testimony the SS wanted to eradicate at any cost were, of course, the members of the *Sonderkommando*. This was the "special squad" of prisoners who operated the mass extermination with their bare hands. The SS knew in advance that a single word from a surviving member of the *Sonderkommando* would quash any denials, any subsequent cavils with respect to the massacre of the European Jews.[1] "Conceiving and organizing the squads was National Socialism's most demonic crime," writes Primo Levi. "One is stunned by this paroxysm of perfidy and of hate: it must be the Jews who put the Jews in the ovens; it must be shown that the Jews . . . bow to any humiliation, even to destroying themselves."[2]

The first *Sonderkommando* at Auschwitz was created on July 4, 1942, during the "selection" of a convoy of Slovakian Jews for the gas chamber. Twelve squads succeeded each other from that date; each was eliminated at the end of a few months, and "as its initiation, the next squad burnt the corpses of its predecessors."[3] Part of the horror for these men was that their entire existence, including the ineluctable gassing of the squad, was to be kept in absolute secrecy. The members of the *Sonderkommando* could therefore have no contact whatsoever with the other prisoners, and even less with whatever "outside world" there was, not even with the "noninitiated" SS, those who were ignorant of the exact functioning of the gas chambers and the crematoria.[4] When sick, these prisoners, kept in solitary confinement, were denied admission to the camp hospital. They were held in total subservience and mindlessness—they were not denied alcohol—in their work at the crematoria.

What exactly was their work? It must be repeated: to handle the death of their fellows by the thousands. To witness all the last moments. To be forced to lie to

1 And with them, all the sophisms regarding which, I believe, there are no grounds for philosophical ecstasies. See See Jean-François Lyotard Lyotard, *Le différend* (Paris: Minuit, 1983), 16–17, analyzing in this form the negationist argument: "In order to identify that a place is a gas chamber, I will accept as witness only a victim of this gas chamber; but, there must be, according to my adversary, no victim other than a dead one, or else this gas chamber would not be what it purports to be; there is therefore no gas chamber."

2 Primo Levi, *The Drowned and the Saved*, trans. Raymond Rosenthal (New York: Vintage Books 1989), 52.

3 Levi, 50.

4 Filip Müller, *Eyewitness Auschwitz: Three Years in the Gas Chambers*, trans. Susanne Flatauer Flatauer (New York: Stein and Day, 1979), 39. Filip Müller represents the extremely rare case of a member of the *Sonderkommando* who escaped five successive liquidations. On this function and its secrecy, See Georges Wellers, *Les chambres à gaz ont existé: Des documents, des témoignages, des chiffres* (Paris: Gallimard, 1981). Eugen Kogon, Hermann Langbein, and Adalbert Rückerl, Les chambres à gaz secret d'État (1983), trans. Henry Rollet. (Paris: Minuit, 1984; reprinted Paris Le Seuil, 1987). Jean-Claude Pressac, Auschwitz: Technique and Operation of the Gas Chambers, trans. Peter Moss. (New York: Beate Klarfeld Foundation, 1989). Jean-Claude Pressac, *Les crématoires d'Auschwitz: La machinerie du meurtre de masse* (Paris: CNRS Editions, 1993); (Pressac, 53: "To kill men by the hundreds by gas with one go, and in an enclosed space, was without precedent, and the secret in which the operation was wrapped struck even more the imagination of the nonparticipants, SS or prisoners, who had received the formal interdiction against observing its working"). Uwe Dietrich Adam, "Les chambres à gaz," *L'Allemagne nazie et le génocide juif: Colloque à l'EHESS, Paris, juillet 1982* (Paris: Gallimard–Le Seuil, 1985), 236–261. Franciszek Piper, "Gas Chambers and Crematoria," in Anatomy of the Auschwitz Death Camp, ed. Yisrael Gutman and Michael Berenbaum (Bloomington: Indiana University Press, 1994), 157–182.

the very end. (A member of the *Sonderkommando* who had attempted to warn the victims of their fate was thrown alive into the crematorium fire, and his fellows were forced to attend the execution).[5] To recognize one's own and to say nothing. To watch men, women, and children enter the gas chamber. To listen to the cries, the banging, the death throes. To wait. Then, to receive all at once the "indescribable human heap"—a "column of basalt" made of human flesh, of their flesh, our own flesh—that collapsed when the doors were opened. To drag the bodies one by one, to undress them (until the Nazis thought of the changing room). To hose away all of the accumulated blood, body fluids, and pus. To extract gold teeth for the spoils of the *Reich*. To put the bodies in the furnaces of the crematoria. To maintain this inhuman routine. To feed coal to the fires. To extract the human ashes from that "formless, incandescent and whitish matter which flowed in rivulets [and] took on a grayish tint when it cooled." To grind the bones, the final resistance of the wretched bodies to their industrial destruction. To pile it up, to throw it into a neighboring river or use it as fill for the road being constructed near the camp. To walk on 150 square meters of human hair, which fifteen prisoners are busy carding on large tables. To occasionally repaint the changing room; to erect hedges—for camouflage; to dig supplementary incineration pits for exceptional gassings. To clean, to repair the giant ovens of the crematoria. To start over each day, constantly threatened by the SS. To survive in this manner for an indeterminate time, drunk, working day and night, "running like the possessed in order to finish more quickly."[6]

"They had no human figure. They were ravaged, mad faces," said the prisoners who were able to see them.[7] They survived, however, for the time left to them, in the ignominy of the job. To a prisoner who asked him how he could stand work of that kind, a member of the squad replied: "Of course, I could throw myself onto the electrical wires, like so many of my friends, but I want to live. . . . In our work, if you don't go mad the first day, you get used to it."[8] In a manner of speaking. Yet some who thought themselves "used to it" simply threw themselves into the fire.

If this kind of survival surpasses any moral judgment (as Primo Levi wrote)[9] or any tragic conflict (as Giorgio Agamben commented),[10] then what could the verb *to resist* mean in such constraints? To revolt? That was a dignified way of committing suicide, of anticipating a promised elimination. At the end of 1942, a first projected rebellion failed. Then, in the great mutiny of October 1944—when, at least, crematorium IV was set ablaze and destroyed—not one of the 450 members implicated survived, of whom "only" 300 were due to be gassed soon in any case.[11]

At the core of this fundamental despair, the "impulse to resist" probably abandoned them, condemned as they were to die, leaving them to concentrate rather on *signals to be emitted* beyond the borders of the camp: "We, the prisoners of the *Sonderkommando*, kept thinking about how we might make known to the world the details of the gruesome crimes which were perpetuated here."[12] So in April 1944, Filip Müller patiently gathered some documents—a plan of crematoria IV and V, a note on their operation, a list of the Nazis on duty as well as a Zyklon B label—and passed them along to two prisoners who were attempting to escape.[13] Such an attempt, as all of the *Sonderkommando* knew, was hopeless. This is why they sometimes confided their testimonies to the earth. Digs undertaken around the borders of the Auschwitz crematoria have since brought to light—often long after the Liberation—the devastating, barely legible writings of these slaves of death.[14] *Bottles cast into the earth*, as it were, except that the writers did not always have bottles in which to preserve their message. At best, a tin bowl.[15]

These writings are haunted by two complementary constraints. First, there is the ineluctable obliteration of the witness himself: "The SS often tell us that they won't let a single witness survive." But then there was the fear that the testimony itself would be obliterated, even if it were transmitted to the outside: for did it not risk being incomprehensible, being considered senseless, unimaginable? "What exactly hap-

---

5 Hermann Langbein, Hommes et femmes à Auschwitz (1975) trans Denis Meunier. (Paris: UGE, 1994), 202.

6 Müller, n.p., *Eyewitness Auschwitz*. Langbein, *Hommes et femmes à Auschwitz*, 191–202.

7 Langbein, *Hommes et femmes à Auschwitz*, 193.

8 Langbein, 194–195.

9 Levi, 59. "No one has the right to judge them, not those who experienced the camps, and even less those who did not."

10 Gior Agamben, Remnants of Auschwitz: The Witness and the Archive, Homo Sacer III, trans. Daniel Heller-Roazen. (New York: Zone Books, 2002).

11 Müller, n.p., *Eyewitness Auschwitz*. The documentation on the effects of the revolt has been gathered by Pressac, *Lés crématoires d'Auschwitz*, 93. On the public execution of the last rebels, see Primo Levi, Si c'est un homme, trans. Martine Schruoffeneger (Paris: Julliard, 1987; 1993 ed.), 159–161.

12 Müller, 82.

13 Müller, 122.

14 See Léon Poliakov, *Auschwitz* (Paris: Julliard, 1964), 62–65 and 159–171. Ber Mark, *Des voix dans la nuit: La résistance juive à Auschwitz-Birkenau* (1965), trans. Esther and Joseph Fridman and Liliane Princet (Paris: Plon, 1982). Nathan Cohen, "Diaries of the Sonderkommando," in *Anatomy of the Auschwitz Death Camp*, 522–534.

15 On the physical description of the *Scrolls of Auschwitz* ravaged by humidity and therefore partially illegible, see Mark, 179–190.

pened," as Zalmen Lewental confided to the scrap of paper that he was preparing to bury in the ground, "no other human being can imagine."[16] [...]

It is in the fold between these two impossibilities—the imminent obliteration of the witness, the certain unrepresentability of the testimony—that the photographic image suddenly appeared. One summer day in 1944, the members of the *Sonderkommando* felt the perilous need to snatch some photographs from their infernal work that would bear witness to the specific horror and extent of the massacre. The need to snatch some photographs from the *real*. Moreover, since an image is made to be looked at by others, to snatch from human thought in general, thought from "outside," something *imaginable* that no one until then had even conceived as possible—and this is already saying a lot, since the whole thing was planned before being put into practice.

It is troubling that a desire to *snatch an image* should materialize at the most indescribable moment, as it is often characterized, of the massacre of the Jews: the moment when those who assisted, stupefied, had room left for neither thought nor imagination. Time, space, gaze, thought, pathos—everything was obfuscated by the machinelike enormity of the violence produced. In the summer of 1944 came the "tidal wave" of Hungarian Jews: 435,000 of them were deported to Auschwitz between May 15 and July 8.[17] Jean-Claude Pressac (whose scientific scrupulousness generally avoids any adjectives or any empathetic phrases) wrote that this was the "most demented episode of Birkenau," carried out essentially in crematoria II, III, and V.[18] In a single day, 24,000 Hungarian Jews were exterminated. Toward the end of the summer, there was a shortage of Zyklon B. So "the unfit from the convoys [i.e., the victims selected for immediate death] were cast directly into the burning pits of crematorium V and of bunker 2,"[19] in other words, burned alive. As for the gypsies, they began to be gassed en masse from August 1.

As usual, the members of the *Sonderkommando* posted at the crematoria had to prepare the entire infrastructure of this nightmare. Filip Müller remembers how they proceeded to "overhaul the crematoria":

> Cracks in the brickwork of the ovens were filled with a special fireproof clay paste; the cast-iron doors were painted black and the door hinges oiled. . . . New grates were fitted in the generators, while the six chimneys underwent a thorough inspection and repair, as did the electrical fans. The walls of the four changing rooms and the eight gas chambers were given a fresh coat of paint. Quite obviously all these efforts were intended to put the places of extermination into peak condition to guarantee smooth and continuous operation.[20]

Above all, on the orders of *Hauptscharführer* Otto Moll—a particularly feared and hated SS officer who had taken personal charge of the liquidation of the *Sonderkommando* from 1942 on[21]—five incineration pits were to be dug in the open air, behind crematorium V. Filip Müller has described in detail the technical experimentation and the management of the site led by Moll: from the conception of gutters to collect the fat, to the concrete slab on which the "workers" would have to pulverize the bones mixed with the human ashes;[22] to the elevated hedgerows forming a screen to make all of this invisible from the exterior (Fig. 1). It is significant that, apart from far-off aerial views, *not one single view* exists of crematorium V—situated in a copse of birch trees, from which Birkenau gets its name—that is not obscured by some plant barrier[23] (Fig. 2).

To snatch an image from that hell? It seemed doubly impossible. It was impossible by default, since the detail of the installations was concealed, sometimes underground. But also, outside of their work under the strict control of the SS, members of the *Sonderkommando* were carefully confined in a "subterranean and isolated cell."[24] It was impossible by excess, since the vision of this monstrous, complex chain seemed to exceed any attempt to document it. Filip Müller wrote that "in comparison with what [Otto Moll] had imagined and what he had begun to undertake, Dante's Hell was only child's play":[25]

> As it began to grow light, the fire was lit in two of the pits in which about 2,500 dead bodies lay piled one on

16 Cited by Langbien, 3.
17 Annette Wieviorka, *Déportation et génocide: Entre la mémoire et l'oubli* (Paris: Plon, 1992; 1995 ed.), 255–259.
18 Pressac, *Les crématoires d'Auschwitz*, 90.
19 Pressac, 91.
20 Müller, 124.
21 Müller, 125.
22 Müller, 124-136.
23 The documentation on crematorium V can be found in Jean-Claude Pressac, "Étude et réalisation des *Krematorien* IV et V d'Auschwitz-Birkenau," in *L'Allemagne nazie et le genocide juif*, 539–584. Pressac, *Auschwitz: Technique and Operation*, 379–428. Léon Poliakov (*Auschwitz*, 51–52) had already cited a letter from November 6, 1943, in which the SS of Auschwitz ordered green plants for the camouflage of crematoria I and II. On June 16, 1944, Oswald Pohl was still putting aside a sum for "the erecting of a second interior hedge, in order to hide the buildings from the prisoners." Pressac, *Les crématoires d'Auschwitz*, 91. On the subject of the camouflage of the "communication trench," of Treblinka, see SS Franz Suchomel's very precise testimony, gathered by Claude Lanzmann in *Shoah* (Paris: Fayard, 1985), 123–124.
24 Testimony by Filip Müller cited in ibid. He continues: "We were henceforth the 'bearers of the secret,' the condemned. We were not to speak to anyone, not to come into contact with any prisoner. Not even with the SS. Except those that were in charge of the *Aktion.*"
25 Müller, 133.

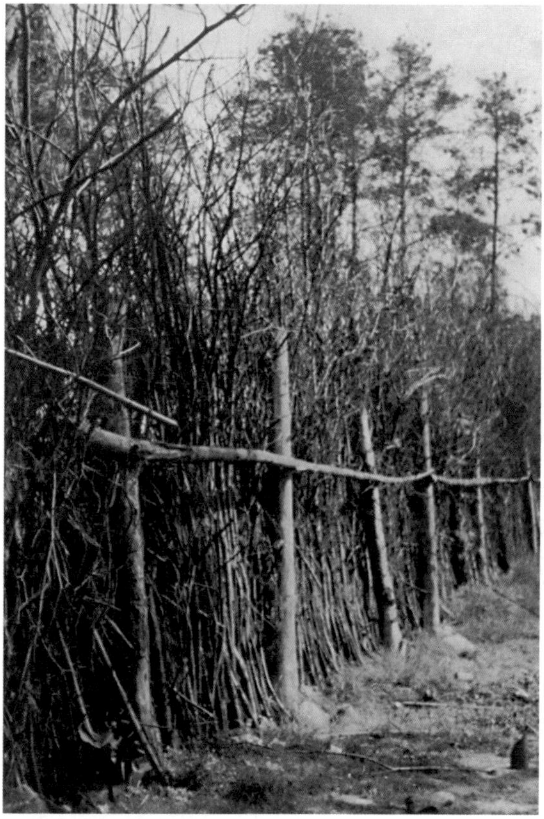

Figure 1. Anonymous (German). Hedge for camouflage at crematorium V of Auschwitz, 1943-44. Oswiecim, Auschwitz-Birkenau State Museum (negative no. 860).

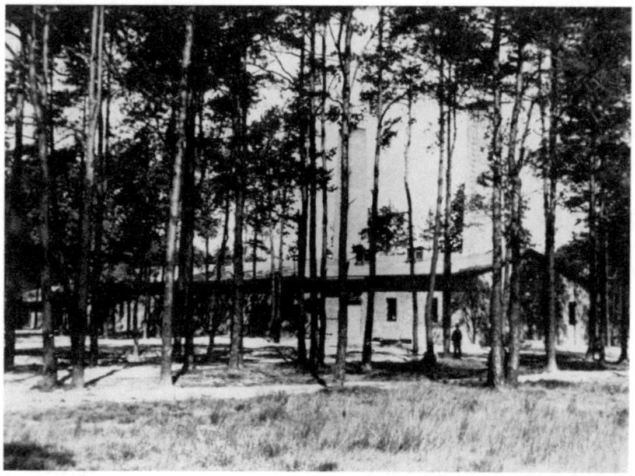

Figure 2. Anonymous (German). Crematorium V of Auschwitz, 1943-44. Oswiecim, Auschwitz-Birkenau State Museum (negative no. 20995/508).

top of the other. Two hours later all that could be discerned in the white-hot flames were countless charred and scorched shapes.... While in the crematorium ovens, once the corpses were thoroughly alight, it was possible to maintain a lasting red heat with the help of fans, in the pits the fire would burn as long as the air could circulate freely in between the bodies. As the heap of bodies settled, no air was able to get in from outside. This meant that we stokers had constantly to pour oil or wood alcohol on the burning corpses, in addition to human fat, large quantities of which had collected and was boiling in the two collecting pans on either side of the pit. The sizzling fat was scooped out with buckets on a long curved rod and poured all over the pit causing flames to leap up amid much crackling and hissing. Dense smoke and fumes rose incessantly. The air reeked of oil, fat, benzole and burnt flesh.

During the day-shift there were, on average, 140 prisoners working in and around crematoria IV and V. Some twenty-five bearers were employed in clearing the gas chamber and removing the corpses to the pits....

The SS guards on their watch-towers beyond the barbed wire which encircle the area around the pits [...] were badly upset by the ghoulish spectacle [...]. Under the ever-increasing heat a few of the dead began to stir, writhing as though with some unbearable pain, arms and legs straining in slow motion, and even their bodies straightening a little [...]. Eventually the fire became so fierce that the corpses were enveloped by flames. Blisters which had formed on their skin burst one by one. Almost every corpse was covered with black scorch marks and glistened as if it had been greased. The searing heat had burst open their bellies: there was the violent hissing and sputtering of frying in great heat [...]. The process of incineration took five to six hours. What was left barely filled a third of the pit. The shiny whitish-gray surface was strewn with countless skulls [...]. As soon as the ashes had cooled down a little, wooden metal-covered boards were thrown into the pits. Prisoners of the ash team climbed down and began to shovel out the still hot ashes. Although their mittens and berets gave them some make-shift protection, hot ashes kept blowing down on them, especially when it was windy, causing severe facial burns and eye injuries, sometimes even blindness, so that after a short time they were issued with protective goggles.

Once the pits had been emptied and the ashes taken to the ash depot, they were piled up in man-high heaps.[26] [...]

To snatch an image from that, in spite of that? Yes. Whatever the cost, form had to be given to this unimaginable reality. The possibilities for escape or of revolt were so limited at Auschwitz that the mere *sending of an image* or of information—a plan, numbers,

26 Müller, 136-138. See also, among others, the testimony of Georges Wellers, *L'étoile jaune à l'heure de Vichy. De Drancy à Auschwitz.* (Paris: Fayard, 1973), 286–287. Kogon, Langbein, and Rückerl, *Les chambres à gaz secret d'État*, 214–215, specifies that the pits were 12 meters in length, 6 meters wide, and 1.5 meters deep. One thousand people were burned there in one hour. See also Pressac, "Étude et réalisation des *Krematorien* IV et V," 539–584. A discrepancy remains between certain testimonies of the members of the *Sonderkommando* and Pressac's analyses on the question of knowing whether the pits were dug because the ovens of crematorium V were not working or were too full.

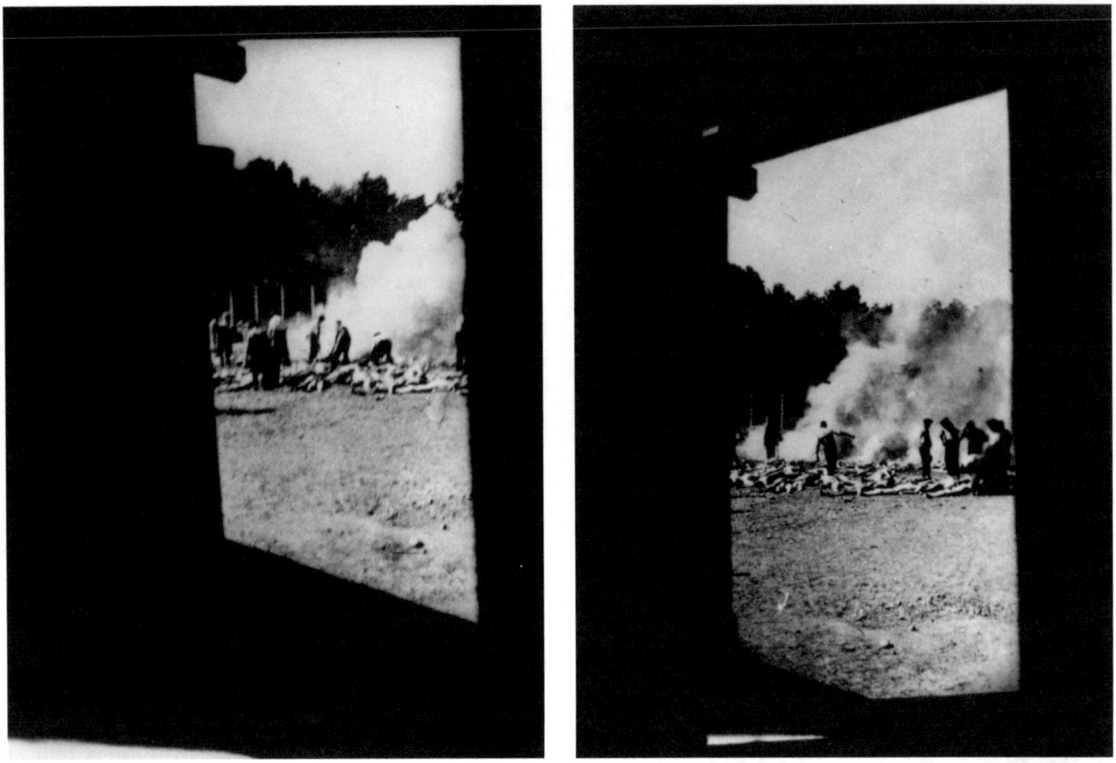

Figure 3-4. Anonymous (member of the *Sonderkommando* of Auschwitz). Cremation of gassed bodies in the open-air incineration pits in front of the gas chambers of crematorium V of Auschwitz, August 1944. Oswiecim, Auschwitz-Birkenau State Museum (negative nos. 280-281).

names—was of the utmost urgency, one of the last gestures of humanity. Some prisoners had managed to listen to the BBC in the offices they were cleaning. Others managed to send calls for help. "The isolation of the outside world was part of the psychological pressure exercised on the prisoners," wrote Hermann Langbein. "Among the efforts to defend oneself from the psychic terrorism, there were obviously those that sought to break the isolation. For the morale of the prisoners, this last factor increased in importance year by year as the military situation unfolded."[27] On their side, the leaders of the Polish Resistance were in 1944 demanding photographs. According to a witness's account collected by Langbein, a civilian worker managed to smuggle in a camera and get it into the hands of the members of the *Sonderkommando*.[28] The camera probably contained only a small piece of blank film.

For the shooting, a collective lookout had to be organized. The roof of crematorium V was deliberately damaged so that certain squad members were sent by the SS to repair it. From up there, David Szmulewski could be on watch: he observed those—notably the guards in nearby observation posts—who were charged with overseeing the work of the *Sonderkommando*. Hidden at the bottom of a bucket, the camera got into the hands of a Greek Jew called Alex, still unidentified today, for we do not know his family name. He was positioned on the lower level, in front of the incineration pits, where he was supposed to work with the other members of the squad.

The terrible paradox of this *darkroom* was that in order to remove the camera from the bucket, adjust the viewfinder, bring it close to his face, and take a first sequence of images (Figs. 3–4), the photographer had to hide in the gas chamber, itself barely emptied—perhaps incompletely—of victims. He steps back into the dark space. The slant and the darkness in which he stands protect him. Emboldened, he changes direction and advances: the second view is a little more frontal and slightly closer. So it is more hazardous. But also, paradoxically, it is more posed: it is sharper. It is as though fear had disappeared for an instant in the face

27 H. Langbein, *La résistance dans les camps de concentration nationauxsocialistes,1938–1945* (1980), trans. D. Meunier... (Paris: Fayard, 1981), 297 (and passim, 297–315).

28 Langbein, *Hommes et femmes d'Auschwitz*, 253: "Stanlislaw Klodzinski claimed that a Polish civilian worker called Mordarski, whose work yard was not far away, smuggled a camera into the camp. Hidden deep within the false bottom of a tub of soup, it passed into the hands of the *Sonderkommando*." Since Langbein's reconstitution is not without inaccuracies, we can also speculate that the camera might have been obtained in the "Canada" section of Auschwitz, the gigantic storehouse of the victims' stolen personal effects.

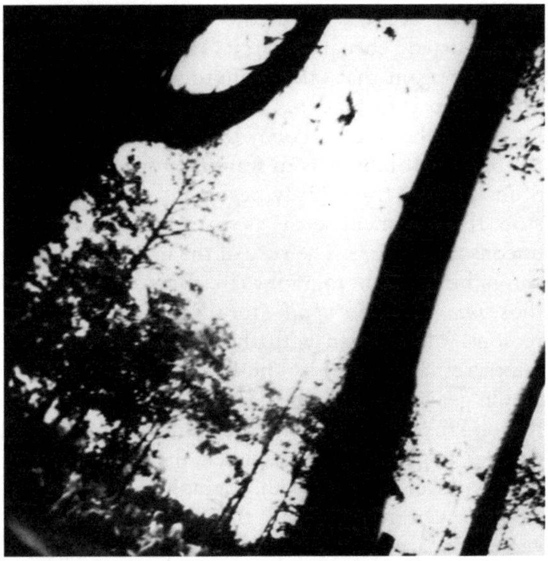

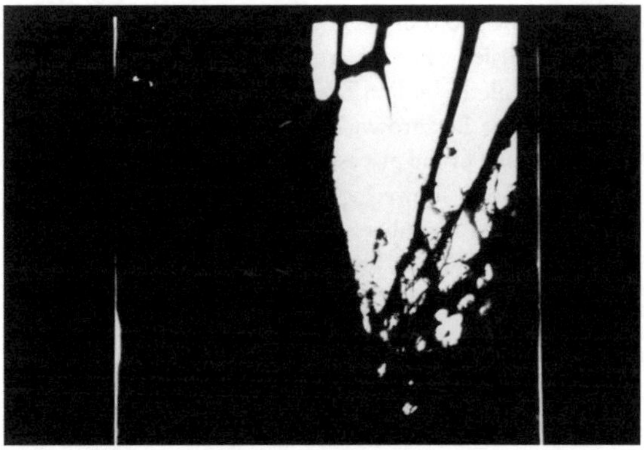

Figure 5-6. Anonymous (member of the *Sonderkommando* of Auschwitz). Women being pushed toward the gas chamber at crematorium V of Auschwitz, August 1944. Oswiecim, Auschwitz-Birkenau State Museum (negative nos. 282-283).

of necessity, the business of snatching an image. And we see the everyday work of the other members of the squad, which is that of snatching the last human semblance from the cadavers, still sprawled on the ground. The gestures of the living tell the weight of the bodies and the task of making immediate decisions. Pulling, dragging, throwing. The smoke, behind, comes from the incineration pits: bodies arranged quincuncially, 1.5 meters deep, the crackling of fat, odors, shriveling of human matter—everything of which Filip Müller speaks is there, under the screen of smoke that the photograph has captured for us. Behind is the birch-tree copse. The wind is blowing from the north, perhaps the northeast[29] ("In August of 1944," remembers Primo Levi, "it was very hot in Auschwitz. A torrid, tropical wind, lifted clouds of dust from the buildings wrecked in air raids, dried the sweat on our skin and thickened the blood in our veins.")[30]

Having hidden the camera—in his hand, or in the bucket, or in a patch of his clothes?—the "unknown photographer" now ventures out of the crematorium. He hugs the wall. Twice he turns to the right. He finds himself then on the other side of the building, to the south, and advances himself in the open air toward the birch trees. There too, the hell continues: a "convoy" of women, already undressed, gets ready to enter the gas chamber. The SS are about. It is simply not possible to take out the camera, even less possible to aim it. The "unknown photographer" takes two snapshots, furtively, without looking, perhaps even while walking (Figs. 5–6). On one of the two images—visibly deprived of orthogonality, or "correct" orientation—we can see in the far left corner a whole group of women who seem to be walking or awaiting their turn. Nearer, three other women are headed in the opposite direction. The image is very blurred. We can see, however, a member of the *Sonderkommando* in profile, recognizable by his cap. At the very bottom, to the right, we can make out the chimney of the crematorium. The other image is practically abstract: we can just make out the top of the birch trees. Facing south, the photographer has the light in his eyes. The image is dazzling by the sun, its rays cutting through the boughs.

Alex then returns to the crematorium, probably to the north side. Hastily he returns the camera to David Szmulewski, who has stayed up on the roof, on the lookout for potential movements by the SS. The entire operation will have taken no more than fifteen to twenty minutes. Szmulewski would replace the camera in the bottom of his bucket.[31] The piece of film would be removed from the camera, brought back to the central camp, and eventually extricated from Auschwitz in a tube of toothpaste in which Helena Dantón, an employee of the SS canteen, will have hidden it.[32] A little later, on September 4, 1944, it would reach the Polish Resistance in Krakow, accompanied by a note written by two political prisoners, Josef Cyrankiewicz and Stanislaw Klodzinksi:

> Urgent. Send two metal rolls of film for 6×9 as fast as possible. Have possibility of taking photos. Sending you photos of Birkenau showing prisoners sent to gas cham-

29 See Pressac, *Auschwitz: Technique and Operation…*, 422–424, where we find a minutely detailed reconstitution of these images. He specifies that among the people photographed is an SS member, whose back is turned (we understand, therefore, even more clearly the risk taken).

30 Levi, 79.

31 See Pressac, *Auschwitz: Technique and Operation…*, 424–424, in which the testimony of Szmulewski himself—survivor of the squad—is cited.

32 See Langbien, *Hommes et femmes à Auschwitz*, 253.

bers. One photo shows one of the stakes at which bodies were burned when the crematorium could not manage to burn all the bodies. The bodies in the foreground are waiting to be thrown into the fire. Another picture shows one of the places in the forest where people undress before "showering"—as they were told—and then go to the gas chambers. Send film roll as fast as you can. Send the enclosed photos to Tell—we think enlargements of the photos can be sent further.[33]

AGAINST ALL UNIMAGINABLE

[...] Photography, from this angle, shows a particular ability—illustrated by certain well- or lesser-known examples[34]—to curb the fiercest will to obliterate. It is technically very easy to take a photograph. It can be done for so many different reasons, good or bad, public or private, admitted or concealed, as the active extension of violence or in protest against it, and so on. A simple piece of film—so small that it can be hidden in a tube of toothpaste—is capable of engendering an unlimited number of prints, of generations and enlargements in every format. Photography works hand in glove with image and memory and therefore possesses their notable *epidemic power*.[35] For this reason, photography was as difficult to eradicate in Auschwitz as was memory in the bodies of the prisoners.

What do we mean when we refer to "Reason in history"? It is the state secretly decreed at the place where the mass extermination occurred. It is the absolute prohibition of photographing the *Einsatzgruppen*'s enormous acts of abuse in 1941.[36] It is the notices put up on the walls and fences around the camps: "*Fotografieren verboten*! No entry! You will be shot without prior warning!"[37] It is the circular sent around by Rudolf Höss, the commander at Auschwitz, dated February 2, 1943: "I would like to point out once again that taking photographs within the camp limits is forbidden. I will be very strict in treating those who refuse to obey this order."[38]

But to prohibit was to want to stop an epidemic of images that had already begun and that could not stop. Its movement seems as sovereign as that of an unconscious desire. The ruse of the image versus reason in history: photographs circulated everywhere—those *images in spite of all*—for the best and the worst reasons. They began with the ghastly shots of the massacres committed by the *Einsatzgruppen*, photographs generally taken by the murderers themselves.[39] Rudolf Höss did not hesitate either, in spite of his own circular, to present Otto Theirack, the minister of justice, with an album of photographs taken at Auschwitz.[40] On the one hand, this use of photography verged on a pornography of killing. On the other hand, the Nazi administration was so anchored in its habits of recording—with its pride, its bureaucratic narcissism—that it tended to register and photograph everything that was done in the camp, even though the gassing of the Jews remained a "state secret."

Two photograph laboratories, no less, were in operation in Auschwitz. It seems astonishing in such a place. However, everything can be expected from a capital as complex as Auschwitz, even if it was the capital of execution and obliteration of human beings by the millions. In the first laboratory, attached to the "identification service" (*Erkennungsdienst*), ten to twelve prisoners worked permanently under the direction of SS officers Bernhardt Walter and Ernst Hofmann, suggesting an intense production of images here. These consisted mainly of descriptive portraits of political prisoners. Photos of executions, of people

---

33 Cited and translated by Renata Boguslawska-Swiebocka and Teresa Ceglowska, *KL Auschwitz: Fotografie dokumentalne* (Warsaw: Krajowa Agencja Wydawnicza 1980), 12. The code name "Tell" belongs to Teresa Lasocka-Estreicher, a member, in Krakow, of a clandestine committee of aid to the prisoners in concentration camps. See also Renata Boguslawska and Teresa Świebocka, "Auschwitz in Documentary Photographs," trans. Johnathan Webber and Connie Wilsack, in *Auschwitz: A History in Photographs*, ed. Teresa Swiebocka. (Oswiecim, Warsaw, and Bloomington: Auschwitz Birkenau Museum Ksiazka I Wiedza, and Indiana University Press, 1993), 42–43 and 172–176, in which the names of other prisoners who took part in this operation are specified: Szlomo Dragon, his brother Josek, and Alter Szmul Fajnzylberg (known in the camp under the name of Stanislaw Jankowski). According to the testimony of Alter Fajnzylberg, the camera could have been a Leica (Clément Chéroux has told me that this is impossible, since the format of the images is 6 x 6).

34 See the important bibliography by Ute Wrocklage, *Fotografie und Holocaust: Annotierte Bibliographie*. (Frankfurt: Fritz Bauer Institut, 1998). Among the principal studies, see Boguslawska-Swiebocka and Ceglowska. Swiebocka, ed., *Auschwitz: A History in Photographs*. Sybil Milton, "Images of the Holocaust," *Holocaust and Genocide Studies* 1 (1986), no. 1:27–61, no. 2:193–216. Detlef Hoffmann, "Fotografierte Lager: Überlegungen zu einer Fotogeschichte deutscher Konzentrationslager," *Fotogeschichte*, no. 54 (1994): 3–20. It is worth noting the exceptional case of the "Auschwitz Album": Peter Hellman, *L'album d'Auschwitz: D'après un album découvert par Lili Meier, survivante du camp de concentration* (1981), trans. Guy Casaril, completed by Anne Freyer and Jean-Claude Pressac. (Paris: Le Seuil, 1983).

35 See Georges Didi-Huberman, *Mémorandum de la peste: Le fléau d'imaginer* (Paris: Christian Bourgois, 1983).

36 See Hilberg, *The Destruction of the European Jews*, 214, n.140: "[Heydrich] forbade his own men to take pictures. 'Official' photographs were to be sent undeveloped to the RSHA IV-A-1 as secret Reich matter (*Geheime Reichssache*). Heydrich also requested the Order Police commands to hunt up photographs which might have been circulating in their areas."

37 Inscription on a warning sign placed around the Natzweiler camp.

38 Cited by Boguslawska-Swiebocka and Ceglowska, 11.

39 See the exhibition entitled *Vernichtungskrieg: Verbrechen der Wehrmacht 1941 bis 1944* (Hamburg: Hamburger Edition, 1996; rev. ed., *Verbrechen der Wehrmacht: Dimensionen des Vernichtungskrieges 1941–1944* (Hamburg, Hamburger Edition 2002).

40 See Hilberg, n.p.

being tortured, or of charred bodies were shot and developed by SS members themselves. The second laboratory, which was smaller, was the "office of constructions" (*Zentralbauleitung*). Opened at the end of 1941 or the beginning of 1942, it was directed by the SS officer Dietrich Kamann, who put together an entire photographic archive on the camp installations.[41] Nor must we forget the whole "medical" iconography of the monstrous experiments by Josef Mengele and his associates on the women, men, and children of Auschwitz.[42]

Toward the end of the war, while the Nazis were burning the archives en masse, the prisoners who served them as slaves for that task availed themselves of the general confusion to save—to divert, hide, disperse—as many images as they could. Today, around forty thousand photographs of this documentation of Auschwitz remain, despite its systematic destruction. Their survival says much about the probable size and horror of the iconography that filled the files when the camp was in operation.[43]

41 See Boguslawska-Swiebocka and Swiebocka, "Auschwitz in Documentary Photographs," 35–42. Ute Wrocklage, "Architectur zur 'Vernichtung durch Arbeit'" Das Album der 'Bauleitung d. Waffen-SS u. Polizei K. L. Auschwitz,'" *Fotogeschichte,* no. 54 (1994): 31–43. This archive of the *Bauleitung* is the main source for Pressac's works *Auschwitz: Technique and Operation . . .*, and *Les crématoires d'Auschwitz.* It must be pointed out that, of the 40,000 photos conserved, 39,000 are identification photographs.

42 See Robert Jay Lifton, *The Nazi Doctors: Medical Killing and the Psychology of Genocide* (New York: Basic Books, 1986).

43 See Boguslawska-Swiebocka and Cegowska, 12, where Bronislaw Jureczek's testimony is cited: "Almost at the very last moment we were told to burn all the negatives and photographs kept in the *Erkennungsdienst*. There was a coal stove in the laboratory into which we first began to put wet photographic paper and pictures, and then loads of photos and negatives. The enormous amount of material shoved into the stove closed off the chimney. When we set the material afire, we were convinced that only a part of the photos and negatives near the opening would burn, and that the remaining part would not, as the fire would die out for lack of air. After the war I found out that our intentions were carried out, and at least a large percentage of the photos and negatives fell into the hands of the right people. [...] We deliberately scattered some of the pictures and negatives in the rooms of the laboratory, faking nervousness. I knew that the evacuation was being carried out in such a hurry that no one would have time to clean away everything, and that something would survive."

A Mathematical Theory of Communication
Claude Shannon
1948

INTRODUCTION

The recent development of various methods of modulation such as PCM [pulse-code modulation] and PPM [prediction by partial matching]" which exchange T bandwidth for signal-to-noise ratio has intensified the interest in a general theory of communication. A basis for such a theory is contained in the important papers of Nyquist and Hartley on this subject. In the present paper we will extend the theory to include a number of new factors, in particular the effect of noise in the channel, and the savings possible due to the statistical structure of the original message and due to the nature of the final destination of the information.

The fundamental problem of communication is that of reproducing at one point either exactly or approximately a message selected at another point. Frequently the messages have *meaning*; that is they refer to or are correlated according to some system with certain physical or conceptual entities. These semantic aspects of communication are irrelevant to the engineering problem. The significant aspect is that the actual message is one *selected from a set* of possible messages. The system must be designed to operate for each possible selection, not just the one which will actually be chosen since this is unknown at the time of design.

If the number of messages in the set is finite then this number or any monotonic function of this number can be regarded as a measure of the information produced when one message is chosen from the set, all choices being equally likely. As was pointed out by Hartley the most natural choice is the logarithmic function. Although this definition must be generalized considerably when we consider the influence of the statistics of the message and when we have a continuous range of messages, we will in all cases use an essentially logarithmic measure.

The logarithmic measure is more convenient for various reasons:

1. It is practically more useful. Parameters of engineering importance such as time, bandwidth, number of relays, etc., tend to vary linearly with the logarithm of the number of possibilities. For example, adding one relay to a group doubles the number of possible states of the relays. It adds 1 to the base 2 logarithm of this number. Doubling the time roughly squares the number of possible messages, or doubles the logarithm, etc.

2. It is nearer to our intuitive feeling as to the proper measure. This is closely related to (1) since we intuitively measures entities by linear comparison with common standards. One feels, for example, that two punched cards should have twice the capacity of one for information storage, and two identical channels twice the capacity of one for transmitting information.

3. It is mathematically more suitable. Many of the limiting operations are simple in terms of the logarithm but would require clumsy restatement in terms of the number of possibilities.

The choice of a logarithmic base corresponds to the choice of a unit for measuring information. If the base 2 is used the resulting units may be called binary digits, or more briefly *bits*, a word suggested by J. W. Tukey. A device with two stable positions, such as a relay or a flip-flop circuit, can store one bit of information. N such devices can store N bits, since the total number of possible states is 2^N and $\log_2 2^N N$. If the base 10 is used the units may be called decimal digits. Since

$$\begin{aligned}\log_2 M &= \log_{10} M / \log_{10} 2\\ &= 3.32 \log_{10} M,\end{aligned}$$

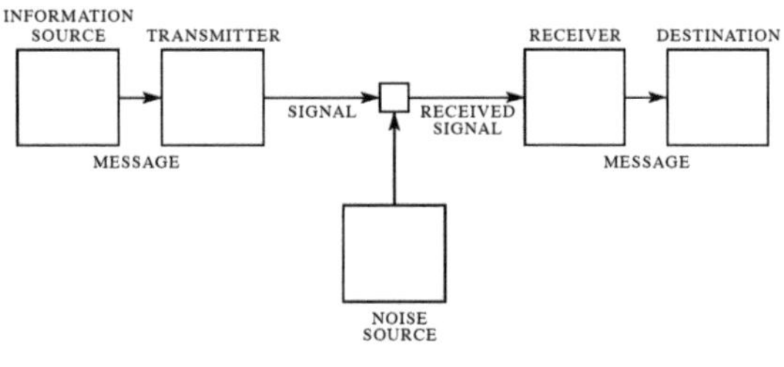

1. Nyquist, H., "Certain Factors Affecting Telegraph Speed," *Bell System Technical Journal*, April 1924, 324; "Certain Topics in Telegraph Transmission Theory," *A.I.E.E. Trans.*, v. 47, April 1928, 617.
2. Hartley, R.V.L., "Transmission of Information," *Bell System Technical Journal*, July 1928, 535.

a decimal digit is about 3 ⅓ bits. A digit wheel on a desk computing machine has ten stable positions and therefore has a storage capacity of one decimal digit. In analytical work where integration and differentiation are involved the base e is sometimes useful. The resulting units of information will be called natural units. Change from the base a to base b merely requires multiplication by $\log_b a$.

By a communication system we will mean a system of the type indicated schematically in Fig. 1. It consists of essentially five parts:

1. An *information source* which produces a message or sequence of messages to be communicated to the receiving terminal. The message may be of various types: (a) A sequence of letters as in a telegraph of teletype system; (b) A single function of time $f(t)$ as in radio or telephony; (c) A function of time and other variables as in black and white television – here the message may be thought of as a function $f(x, y, t)$ of two space coordinates and time, the light intensity at point (x, y) and time t on a pickup tube plate; (d) Two or more functions of time, say $f(t)$, $g(t)$, $h(t)$—this is the case in "three- dimensional" sound transmission or if the system is intended to service several individual channels in multiplex; (e) Several functions of several variables—in color television the message consists of three functions $f(x, y, t)$, $g(x, y, t)$, $h(x, y, t)$ defined in a three-dimensional continuum —we may also think of these three functions as components of a vector field defined in the region —similarly, several black and white television sources would produce "messages" consisting of a number of functions of three variables; (f) Various combinations also occur, for example in television with an associated audio channel.

2. A *transmitter* which operates on the message in some way to produce a signal suitable for transmission over the channel. In telephony this operation consists merely of changing sound pressure into a proportional electrical current. In telegraphy we have an encoding operation which produces a sequence of dots, dashes and spaces on the channel corresponding to the message. In a multiplex PCM system the different speech functions must be sampled, compressed, quantized and encoded, and finally interleaved properly to construct the signal. Vocoder systems, television and frequency modulation are other examples of complex operations applied to the message to obtain the signal.

3. The *channel* is merely the medium used to transmit the signal from transmitter to receiver. It may be a pair of wires, a coaxial cable, a band of radio frequencies, a beam of light, etc.

4. The *receiver* ordinarily performs the inverse operation of that done by the transmitter, reconstructing the message from the signal.

5. The *destination* is the person (or thing) for whom the message is intended.

We wish to consider certain general problems involving communication systems. To do this it is first necessary to represent the various elements involved as mathematical entities, suitably idealized from their physical counterparts. We may roughly classify communication systems into three main categories: discrete, continuous and mixed. By a discrete system we will mean one in which both the message and the signal are a sequence of discrete symbols. A typical case is telegraphy where the message is a sequence of letters and the signal a sequence of dots, dashes and spaces. A continuous system is one in which the message and signal are both treated as continuous functions, e.g., radio or television. A mixed system is one in which both discrete and continuous variables appear, e.g., PCM transmission of speech.

We first consider the discrete case. This case has applications not only in communication theory, but also in the theory of computing machines, the design of telephone exchanges and other fields. In addition the discrete case forms a foundation for the continuous and mixed cases which will be treated in the second half of the paper.

PART I: DISCRETE NOISELESS SYSTEMS

1. The Discrete Noiseless Channel

Teletype and telegraphy are two simple examples of a discrete channel for transmitting information. Generally, a discrete channel will mean a system whereby a sequence of choices from a finite set of elementary symbols $S_1, \ldots, S_n$ can be transmitted from one point to another. Each of the symbols S_i is assumed to have a certain duration in time *ti* seconds (not necessarily the same for different S_i, for example the dots and dashes in telegraphy). It is not required that all possible sequences of the S_i be capable of transmission on the system; certain sequences only may be allowed. These will be possible signals for the channel. Thus in telegraphy suppose the symbols are: (1) A dot, consisting of line closure for a unit of time and then line open for a unit of time; (2) A dash, consisting of three time units of closure and one unit open; (3) A letter space consisting of, say, three units of line open; (4) A word space of six units of line open.

We might place the restriction on allowable sequences that no spaces follow each other (for if two letter spaces are adjacent, it is identical with a word space). The question we now consider is how one can measure the capacity of such a channel to transmit information.

In the teletype case where all symbols are of the same duration, and any sequence of the 32 symbols is allowed the answer is easy. Each symbol represents five bits of information. If the system transmits n symbols per second it is natural to say that the channel has a capacity of $5n$ bits per second. This does not mean that the teletype channel will always be transmitting information at this rate — this is the maximum possible rate and whether or not the actual rate reaches this maximum depends on the source of information which feeds the channel, as will appear later.

In the more general case with different lengths of symbols and constraints on the allowed sequences, we make the following definition: Definition: The capacity C of a discrete channel is given by

$$C = \lim_{T\to\infty} \frac{\log N(T)}{T}$$

where $N(T)$ is the number of allowed signals of duration T. It is easily seen that in the teletype case this reduces to the previous result. It can be shown that the limit in question will exist as a finite number in most cases of interest. Suppose all sequences of the symbols $S_1,\ldots,S_n$ are allowed and these symbols have durations $t_1\, t_n$. What is the channel capacity? If $N(t)$ represents the number of sequences of duration t we have

$$N(t) = N(t - t_1) + N(t - t_2) + \ldots + N(t - t_n)$$

The total number is equal to the sum of the numbers of sequences ending in $S1, S2,\ldots,Sn$ and these are $N(t - t1), N(t - t2),\ldots,N(t - tn)$, respectively. According to a well-known result in finite differences, $N(t)$ is then asymptotic for large t to $X_0^{\,t}$ where X_0 is the largest real solution of the characteristic equation:

$$X^{-t_1} + X^{-t_2} + \cdots + X^{-t_n} = 1$$

and therefore

$$C = \log X_0$$

In case there are restrictions on allowed sequences we may still often obtain a difference equation of this type and find C from the characteristic equation. In the telegraphy case mentioned above

$$N(t) = N(t-2) + N(t-4) + N(t-5) + N(t-7) + N(t-8) + N(t-10)$$

as we see by counting sequences of symbols according to the last or next to the last symbol occurring. Hence C is $-\log \mu_0$ where μ_0 is the positive root of $1 = \mu^2 + \mu^4 + \mu^5 + \mu^7 + \mu^8 + \mu^{10}$. Solving this we find $C = 0.539$.

A very general type of restriction which may be placed on allowed sequences is the following: We imagine a number of possible states $a_1, a_2,\ldots, a_m$. For each state only certain symbols from the set $S_1,\ldots, S_n$ can be transmitted (different subsets for the different states). When one of these has been transmitted the state changes to a new state depending both on the old state and the particular symbol transmitted. The telegraph case is a simple example of this. There are two states depending on whether or not a space was the last symbol transmitted. If so, then only a dot or a dash can be sent next and the state always changes. If not, any symbol can be transmitted and the state changes if a space is sent, otherwise it remains the same. The conditions can be indicated in a linear graph as shown in Fig. 2. The junction points correspond to the

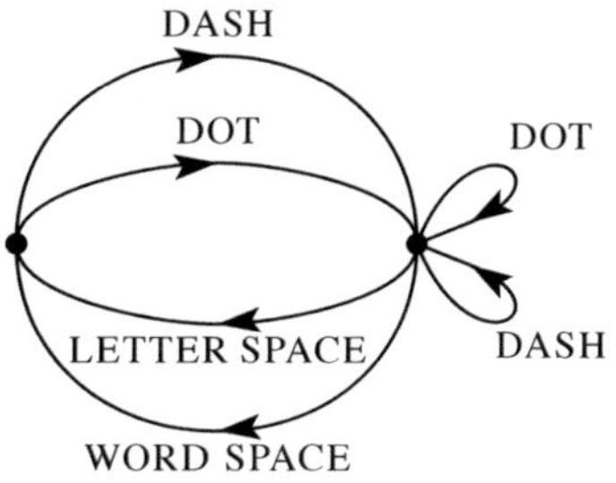

states and the lines indicate the symbols possible in a state and the resulting state. In Appendix 1 it is shown that if the conditions on allowed sequences can be described in this form C will exist and can be calculated in accordance with the following result:

Theorem 1: Let $b_{ij}^{(s)}$ be the duration of the sth symbol which is allowable in state i and leads to state j. Then the channel capacity C is equal to $\log W$ where W is the largest real root of the determinant equation:

$$\left|\sum_s W^{-b_{ij}^{(s)}} - \delta_{ij}\right| = 0$$

where $_{ij} = 1$ *if* $i = j$ *and is zero otherwise.*

For example, in the telegraph case (Fig. 2) the determinant is:

$$\begin{vmatrix} -1 & (W^{-2}+W^{-4}) \\ (W^{-3}+W^{-6}) & (W^{-2}+W^{-4}-1) \end{vmatrix} = 0.$$

On expansion this leads to the equation given above for this case.

2. THE DISCRETE SOURCE OF INFORMATION

We have seen that under very general conditions the logarithm of the number of possible signals in a discrete channel increases linearly with time. The capacity to transmit information can be specified by giving this rate of increase, the number of bits per second required to specify the particular signal used.

We now consider the information source. How is an information source to be described mathematically, and how much information in bits per second is produced in a given source? The main point at issue is the effect of statistical knowledge about the source in reducing the required capacity of the channel, by the use of proper encoding of the information. In telegraphy, for example, the messages to be transmitted consist of sequences of letters. These sequences, however, are not completely random. In general, they form sentences and have the statistical structure of, say, English. The letter E occurs more frequently than Q, the sequence TH more frequently than XP, etc. The existence of this structure allows one to make a saving in time (or channel capacity) by properly encoding the message sequences into signal sequences. This is already done to a limited extent in telegraphy by using the shortest channel symbol, a dot, for the most common English letter E; while the infrequent letters, Q, X, Z are represented by longer sequences of dots and dashes. This idea is carried still further in certain commercial codes where common words and phrases are represented by four- or five-letter code groups with a considerable saving in average time. The standardized greeting and anniversary telegrams now in use extend this to the point of encoding a sentence or two into a relatively short sequence of numbers.

We can think of a discrete source as generating the message, symbol by symbol. It will choose successive symbols according to certain probabilities depending, in general, on preceding choices as well as the particular symbols in question. A physical system, or a mathematical model of a system which produces such a sequence of symbols governed by a set of probabilities, is known as a stochastic process. We may consider a discrete source, therefore, to be represented by a stochastic process. Conversely, any stochastic process which produces a discrete sequence of symbols chosen from a finite set may be considered a discrete source. This will include such cases as:

1. Natural written languages such as English, German, Chinese.
2. Continuous information sources that have been rendered discrete by some quantizing process. For example, the quantized speech from a PCM transmitter, or a quantized television signal.
3. Mathematical cases where we merely define abstractly a stochastic process which generates a sequence of symbols. The following are examples of this last type of source.

(A) Suppose we have five letters A, B, C, D, E which are chosen each with probability .2, successive choices being independent. This would lead to a sequence of which the following is a typical example.

B D C B C E C C C A D C B D D A A E C E E A
A B B D A E E C A C E E B A E E C B C E A D.

This was constructed with the use of a table of random numbers.

(B) Using the same five letters let the probabilities be .4, .1, .2, .2, .1, respectively, with successive choices independent. A typical message from this source is then:

A A A C D C B D C E A A D A D A C E D A
E A D C A B E D A D D C E C A A A A A D.

[...]

(D) Stochastic processes can also be defined which produce a text consisting of a sequence of "words." Suppose there are five letters A, B, C, D, E and 16 "words" in the language with associated probabilities:

.10 A	.16 BEBE	.11 CABED	.04 DEB
.04 ADEB	.04 BED	.05 CEED	.15 DEED
.05 ADEE	.02 BEED	.08 DAB	.01 EAB
.01 BADD	.05 CA	.04 DAD	.05 EE

Suppose successive "words" are chosen independently and are separated by a space. A typical message might be:

DAB EE A BEBE DEED DEB ADEE ADEE EE DEB BEBE BEBE BEBE ADEE BED DEED DEED CEED ADEE A DEED DEED BEBE CABED BEBE BED DAB DEED ADEB.

If all the words are of finite length this process is equivalent to one of the preceding type, but the description may be simpler in terms of the word structure and prob-

3. See, for example, S. Chandrasekhar, "Stochastic Problems in Physics and Astronomy," *Reviews of Modern Physics*, v. 15, No. 1, January 1943, 1.
4. Kendall and Smith, *Tables of Random Sampling Numbers*, Cambridge, 1939.
5. Letter, digram and trigram frequencies are given in *Secret and Urgent* by Fletcher Pratt, Blue Ribbon Books, 1939. Word frequencies are tabulated in *Relative Frequency of English Speech Sounds*, G. Dewey, Harvard University Press, 1923.

abilities. We may also generalize here and introduce transition probabilities between words, etc.

These artificial languages are useful in constructing simple problems and examples to illustrate various possibilities. We can also approximate to a natural language by means of a series of simple artificial languages. The zero-order approximation is obtained by choosing all letters with the same probability and independently. The first-order approximation is obtained by choosing successive letters independently but each letter having the same probability that it has in the natural language. Thus, in the first-order approximation to English, E is chosen with probability .12 (its frequency in normal English) and W with probability .02, but there is no influence between adjacent letters and no tendency to form the preferred digrams such as TH, ED, etc. In the second-order approximation, digram structure is introduced. After a letter is chosen, the next one is chosen in accordance with the frequencies with which the various letters follow the first one. This requires a table of digram frequencies $p_i(j)$. In the third-order approximation, trigram structure is introduced. Each letter is chosen with probabilities which depend on the preceding two letters.

3. THE SERIES OF APPROXIMATIONS TO ENGLISH

To give a visual idea of how this series of processes approaches a language, typical sequences in the approximations to English have been constructed and are given below. In all cases we have assumed a 27-symbol "alphabet," the 26 letters and a space.

1. Zero-order approximation (symbols independent and equiprobable).

   XFOML RXKHRJFFJUJ ZLPWCFWKCYJ FFJEYVKCQSGHYD QPAAMKBZAACIBZLHJQD.

2. First-order approximation (symbols independent but with frequencies of English text).

   OCRO HLI RGWR NMIELWIS EU LL NBNESEBYA TH EEI ALHENHTTPA OOBTTVA NAH BRL.

3. Second-order approximation (digram structure as in English).

   ON IE ANTSOUTINYS ARE T INCTORE ST BE S DEAMY ACHIN D ILONASIVE TUCOOWE AT TEASONARE FUSO TIZIN ANDY TOBE SEACE CTISBE.

4. Third-order approximation (trigram structure as in English).

   IN NO IST LAT WHEY CRATICT FROURE BIRS GROCID PONDENOME OF DEMONSTURES OF THE REPTAGIN IS REGOACTIONA OF CRE.

5. First-order word approximation. Rather than continue with tetragram,...,n-gram structure it is easier and better to jump at this point to word units. Here words are chosen independently but with their appropriate frequencies.

   REPRESENTING AND SPEEDILY IS AN GOOD APT OR COME CAN DIFFERENT NATURAL HERE HE THE A IN CAME THE TO OF TO EXPERT GRAY COME TO FURNISHES THE LINE MESSAGE HAD BE THESE.

6. Second-order word approximation. The word transition probabilities are correct but no further structure is included.

   THE HEAD AND IN FRONTAL ATTACK ON AN ENGLISH WRITER THAT THE CHARACTER OF THIS POINT IS THEREFORE ANOTHER METHOD FOR THE LETTERS THAT THE TIME OF WHO EVER TOLD THE PROBLEM FOR AN UNEXPECTED.

The resemblance to ordinary English text increases quite noticeably at each of the above steps. Note that these samples have reasonably good structure out to about twice the range that is taken into account in their construction. Thus in (3) the statistical process insures reasonable text for two-letter sequences, but four- letter sequences from the sample can usually be fitted into good sentences. In (6) sequences of four or more words can easily be placed in sentences without unusual or strained constructions. The particular sequence of ten words "attack on an English writer that the character of this" is not at all unreasonable. It appears then that a sufficiently complex stochastic process will give a satisfactory representation of a discrete source.

The first two samples were constructed by the use

6. For a detailed treatment see M. Fréchet, *Méthode des fonctions arbitraries. Théorie des* événements *en chaîne dans le cas d'un nombre fini d'états possibles*. Paris, Gauthier-Villars, 1938.

of a book of random numbers in conjunction with (for example 2) a table of letter frequencies. This method might have been continued for (3), (4) and (5), since digram, trigram and word frequency tables are available, but a simpler equivalent method was used.

To construct (3) for example, one opens a book at random and selects a letter at random on the page. This letter is recorded. The book is then opened to another page and one reads until this letter is encountered. The succeeding letter is then recorded. Turning to another page this second letter is searched for and the succeeding letter recorded, etc. A similar process was used for (4), (5) and (6). It would be interesting if further approximations could be constructed, but the labor involved becomes enormous at the next stage.

4. GRAPHICAL REPRESENTATION OF A MARKOFF PROCESS

Stochastic processes of the type described above are known mathematically as discrete Markoff processes and have been extensively studied in the literature. The general case can be described as follows: There exist a finite number of possible "states" of a system; $S_1, S_2, \ldots, S_n$. In addition there is a set of transition probabilities; $p_i(j)$ the probability that if the system is in state S_i it will next go to state S_j. To make this Markoff process into an information source we need only assume that a letter is produced for each transition from one state to another. The states will correspond to the "residue of influence" from preceding letters.

The situation can be represented graphically as shown in Figs. 3, 4 and 5. The "states" are the junction

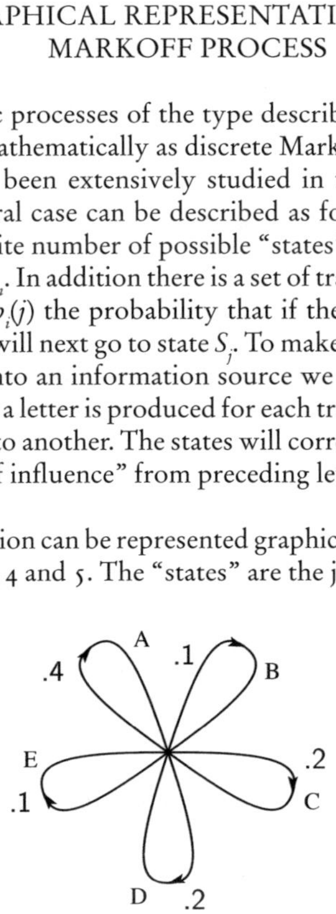

points in the graph and the probabilities and letters produced for a transition are given beside the corresponding line. Figure 3 is for the example B in Section 2, while Fig. 4 corresponds to the example C. In Fig. 3

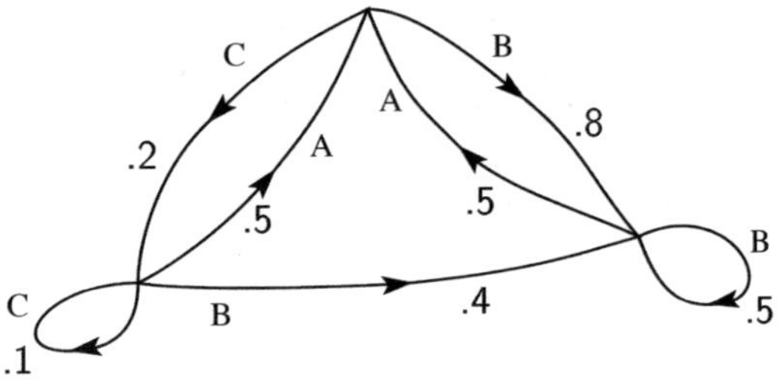

there is only one state since successive letters are independent. In Fig. 4 there are as many states as letters. If a trigram example were constructed there would be at most n^2 states corresponding to the possible pairs of letters preceding the one being chosen. Figure 5 is a graph for the case of word structure in example D. Here S corresponds to the "space" symbol.

5. ERGODIC AND MIXED SOURCES

As we have indicated above a discrete source for our purposes can be considered to be represented by a Markoff process. Among the possible discrete Markoff processes there is a group with special properties of significance in communication theory. This special class consists of the "ergodic" processes and we shall call the corresponding sources ergodic sources. Although a rigorous definition of an ergodic process is somewhat involved, the general idea is simple. In an ergodic process every sequence produced by the process is the same in statistical properties. Thus the letter frequencies, digram frequencies, etc., obtained from particular sequences, will, as the lengths of the sequences increase, approach definite limits independent of the particular sequence. Actually this is not true of every sequence but the set for which it is false has probability zero. Roughly the ergodic property means statistical homogeneity.

All the examples of artificial languages given above are ergodic. This property is related to the structure of the corresponding graph. If the graph has the following two properties the corresponding process will be ergodic:

1. The graph does not consist of two isolated parts A and B such that it is impossible to go from junction points in part A to junction points in part B along lines of the graph in the direction of arrows and also impossible to go from junctions in part B to junctions in part A.

2. A closed series of lines in the graph with all arrows on the lines pointing in the same orientation will

7. These are restatements in terms of the graph of conditions given in Fréchet.

be called a "circuit." The "length" of a circuit is the number of lines in it. Thus in Fig. 5 series BEBES is a circuit of length 5. The second property required is that the greatest common divisor of the lengths of all circuits in the graph be one.

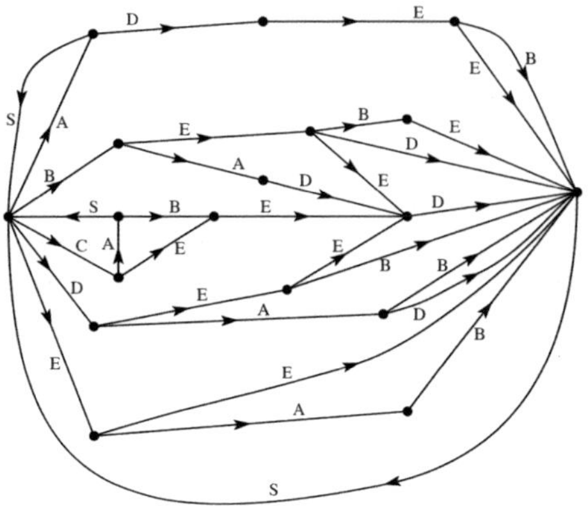

If the first condition is satisfied but the second one violated by having the greatest common divisor equal to $d > 1$, the sequences have a certain type of periodic structure. The various sequences fall into d different classes which are statistically the same apart from a shift of the origin (i.e., which letter in the sequence is called letter 1). By a shift of from 0 up to $d - 1$ any sequence can be made statistically equivalent to any other. A simple example with $d = 2$ is the following: There are three possible letters *a b c*. Letter *a* is followed with either *b* or *c* with probabilities 1/3 and 2/3 respectively. Either *b* or *c* is always followed by letter *a*. Thus a typical sequence is

a b a c a c a c a b a c a b a b a c a c.

This type of situation is not of much importance for our work. If the first condition is violated the graph may be separated into a set of subgraphs each of which satisfies the first condition. We will assume that the second condition is also satisfied for each subgraph. We have in this case what may be called a "mixed" source made up of a number of pure components. The components correspond to the various subgraphs. If L_1, L_2, L_3 are the component sources we may write

$$L = p_1 L_1 + p_2 L_2 + p_3 L_3 + \dots$$

where p_i is the probability of the component source L_i.

Physically the situation represented is this: There are several different sources L_1, L_2, L_3,... which are each of homogeneous statistical structure (i.e., they are ergodic). We do not know *a priori* which is to be used, but once the sequence starts in a given pure component L_i, it continues indefinitely according to the statistical structure of that component.

As an example one may take two of the processes defined above and assume $p_1 = .2$ and $p_2 = .8$. A sequence from the mixed source

$$L = .2L_1 + .8L_2$$

would be obtained by choosing first L_1 or L_2 with probabilities .2 and .8 and after this choice generating a sequence from whichever was chosen.

Except when the contrary is stated we shall assume a source to be ergodic. This assumption enables one to identify averages along a sequence with averages over the ensemble of possible sequences (the probability of a discrepancy being zero). For example the relative frequency of the letter A in a particular infinite sequence will be, with probability one, equal to its relative frequency in the ensemble of sequences.

If P_i is the probability of state i and $p_i(j)$ the transition probability to state j, then for the process to be stationary it is clear that the P_i must satisfy equilibrium conditions:

$$P_j = \sum_i P_i p_i(j).$$

In the ergodic case it can be shown that with any start ing conditions the probabilities $P_j(N)$ of being in state j after N symbols, approach the equilibrium values as $N \to \infty$.

6. CHOICE, UNCERTAINTY AND ENTROPY

We have represented a discrete information source as a Markoff process. Can we define a quantity which will measure, in some sense, how much information is "produced" by such a process, or better, at what rate information is produced? [...]

7. THE ENTROPY OF AN INFORMATION SOURCE

[...] The ratio of the entropy of a source to the maximum value it could have while still restricted to the same symbols will be called its *relative entropy*. This is the maximum compression possible when we encode into the same alphabet. One minus the relative entropy is the *redundancy*. The redundancy of ordinary English, not considering statistical structure over greater distances than about eight letters, is roughly 50%. This means that when we write English half of what we write is determined by the structure of the language and half is chosen freely. The figure 50% was found by several independent methods which all gave results in this neighborhood. One is by calculation of the entropy of the approximations to English. A second method is to delete a certain fraction of the letters from a sample of English text and then let someone attempt to restore them. If they can be restored when 50% are deleted the redundancy must be greater than 50%. A third method depends on certain known results in cryptography.

Two extremes of redundancy in English prose are represented by Basic English and by James Joyce's book *Finnegans Wake*. The Basic English vocabulary is limited to 850 words and the redundancy is very high. This is reflected in the expansion that occurs when a passage is translated into Basic English. Joyce on the other hand enlarges the vocabulary and is alleged to achieve a compression of semantic content.

The redundancy of a language is related to the existence of crossword puzzles. If the redundancy is zero any sequence of letters is a reasonable text in the language and any two-dimensional array of letters forms a crossword puzzle. If the redundancy is too high the language imposes too many constraints for large crossword puzzles to be possible. A more detailed analysis shows that if we assume the constraints imposed by the language are of a rather chaotic and random nature, large crossword puzzles are just possible when the redundancy is 50%. If the redundancy is 33%, three-dimensional crossword puzzles should be possible, etc. [...]

Woman Operating a Hollerith Pantographic Card-Punching Machine
Harris and Ewing Studio [George W. Harris and Martha Ewing]
ca. 1915

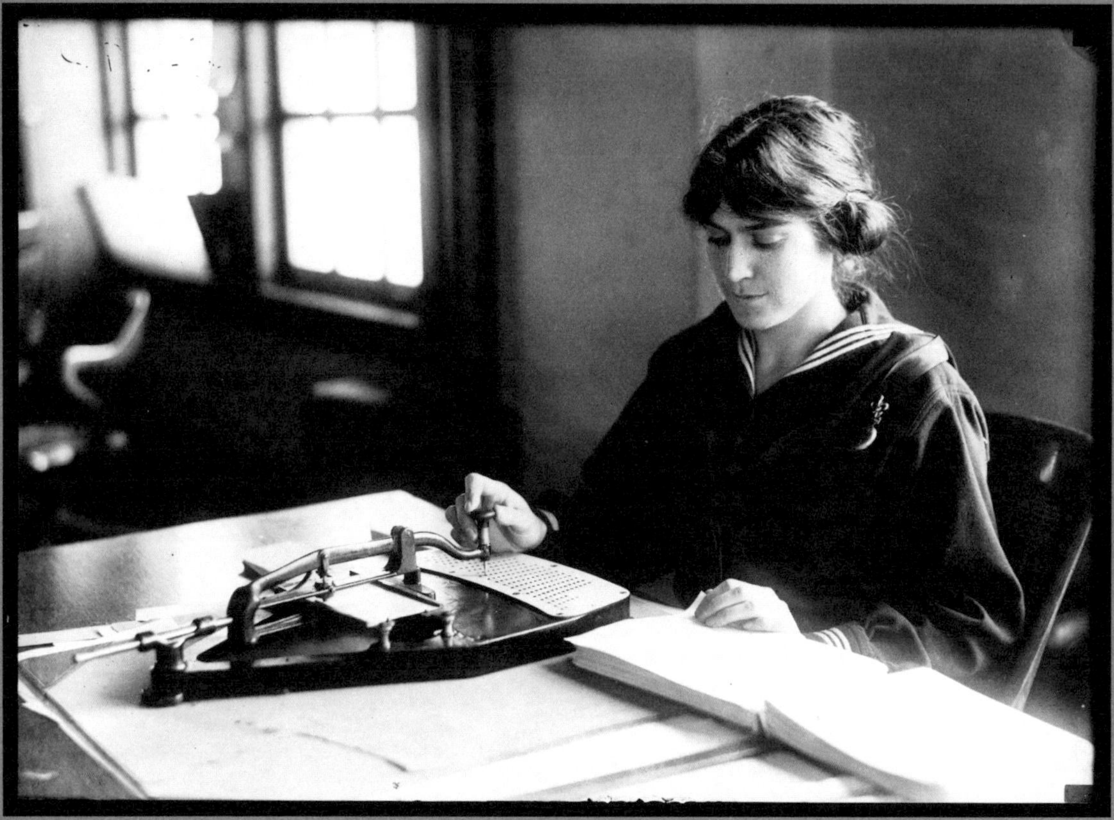

Computing Machinery and Intelligence

Alan Turing

1950

4. DIGITAL COMPUTERS

The idea behind digital computers may be explained by saying that these machines are intended to carry out any operations which could be done by a human computer. The human computer is supposed to be following fixed rules; he has no authority to deviate from them in any detail. We may suppose that these rules are supplied in a book, which is altered whenever he is put on to a new job. He has also an unlimited supply of paper on which he does his calculations. He may also do his multiplications and additions on a "desk machine," but this is not important.

If we use the above explanation as a definition we shall be in danger of circularity of argument. We avoid this by giving an outline of the means by which the desired effect is achieved. A digital computer can usually be regarded as consisting of three parts:

(i) Store.

(ii) Executive unit.

(iii) Control.

The store is a store of information, and corresponds to the human computer's paper, whether this is the paper on which he does his calculations or that on which his book of rules is printed. In so far as the human computer does calculations in his head a part of the store will correspond to his memory.

The executive unit is the part which carries out the various individual operations involved in a calculation. What these individual operations are will vary from machine to machine. Usually fairly lengthy operations can be done such as "Multiply 3540675445 by 7076345687" but in some machines only very simple ones such as "Write down 0" are possible.

We have mentioned that the "book of rules" supplied to the computer is replaced in the machine by a part of the store. It is then called the "table of instructions." It is the duty of the control to see that these instructions are obeyed correctly and in the right order. The control is so constructed that this necessarily happens.

The information in the store is usually broken up into packets of moderately small size. In one machine, for instance, a packet might consist of ten decimal digits. Numbers are assigned to the parts of the store in which the various packets of information are stored, in some systematic manner. A typical instruction might say:

> Add the number stored in position 6809 to that in 4302 and put the result back into the latter storage position.

Needless to say it would not occur in the machine expressed in English. It would more likely be coded in a form such as 6809430217. Here 17 says which of various possible operations is to be performed on the two numbers. In this case the operation is that described above, viz., "Add the number. . . ." It will be noticed that the instruction takes up 10 digits and so forms one packet of information, very conveniently. The control will normally take the instructions to be obeyed in the order of the positions in which they are stored, but occasionally an instruction such as:

> Now obey the instruction stored in position 5606, and continue from there

May be encountered, or again:

> If position 4505 contains 0 obey next the instruction stored in 6707, otherwise continue straight on.

Instructions of these latter types are very important because they make it possible for a sequence of operations to be replaced over and over again until some condition is fulfilled, but in doing so to obey, not fresh instructions on each repetition, but the same ones over and over again. To take a domestic analogy. Suppose Mother wants Tommy to call at the cobbler's every morning on his way to school to see if her shoes are done, she can ask him afresh every morning. Alternatively she can stick up a notice once and for all in the hall which he will see when he leaves for school and which tells him to call for the shoes, and also to destroy the notice when he comes back if he has the shoes with him.

The reader must accept it as a fact that digital computers can be constructed, and indeed have been constructed, according to the principles we have described, and that they can in fact mimic the actions of a human computer very closely.

The book of rules which we have described our human computer as using is of course a convenient fiction. Actual human computers really remember what they have got to do. If one wants to make a machine mimic the behaviour of the human computer in some complex operation one has to ask him how it is done, and then translate the answer into the form of an instruction table. Constructing instruction tables is usually described as "programming." To "programme a machine to carry out the operation A" means to put the appropriate instruction table into the machine so that it will do A.

An interesting variant on the idea of a digital computer is a "digital computer with a random element." These have instructions involving the throwing of a die or some equivalent electronic process; one such instruction might for instance be, "Throw the die and put the resulting number into store 1000." Sometimes such a machine is described as having free will (though I would not use this phrase myself). It is not normally possible to determine from observing a machine whether it has a random element, for a similar effect can be produced by such devices as making the choices depend on the digits of the decimal for π.

Most actual digital computers have only a finite store. There is no theoretical difficulty in the idea of a computer with an unlimited store. Of course only a finite part can have been used at any one time. Likewise only a finite amount can have been constructed, but we can imagine more and more being added as required. Such computers have special theoretical interest and will be called infinitive capacity computers.

The idea of a digital computer is an old one. Charles Babbage, Lucasian Professor of Mathematics at Cambridge from 1828 to 1839, planned such a machine, called the Analytical Engine, but it was never completed. Although Babbage had all the essential ideas, his machine was not at that time such a very attractive prospect. The speed which would have been available would be definitely faster than a human computer but something like 100 times slower than the Manchester machine, itself one of the slower of the modern machines. The storage was to be purely mechanical, using wheels and cards.

The fact that Babbage's Analytical Engine was to be entirely mechanical will help us to rid ourselves of a superstition. Importance is often attached to the fact that modern digital computers are electrical, and that the nervous system also is electrical. Since Babbage's machine was not electrical, and since all digital computers are in a sense equivalent, we see that this use of electricity cannot be of theoretical importance. Of course electricity usually comes in where fast signalling is concerned, so that it is not surprising that we find it in both these connections. In the nervous system chemical phenomena are at least as important as electrical. In certain computers the storage system is mainly acoustic. The feature of using electricity is thus seen to be only a very superficial similarity. If we wish to find such similarities we should took rather for mathematical analogies of function.

5. UNIVERSALITY OF DIGITAL COMPUTERS

The digital computers considered in the last section may be classified amongst the "discrete-state machines." These are the machines which move by sudden jumps or clicks from one quite definite state to another. These states are sufficiently different for the possibility of confusion between them to be ignored. Strictly speaking there are no such machines. Everything really moves continuously. But there are many kinds of machine which can profitably be thought of as being discrete-state machines. For instance in considering the switches for a lighting system it is a convenient fiction that each switch must be definitely on or definitely off. There must be intermediate positions, but for most purposes we can forget about them. As an example of a discrete-state machine we might consider a wheel which clicks round through 120° once a second, but may be stopped by a lever which can be operated from outside; in addition a lamp is to light in one of the positions of the wheel. This machine could be described abstractly as follows. The internal state of the machine (which is described by the position of the wheel) may be q_1, q_2 or q_3. There is an input signal i_0 or i_1 (position of lever). The internal state at any moment is determined by the last state and input signal according to the table.

The output signals, the only externally visible indication of the internal state (the light) are described by the table:

State q_1 q_2 q_3

Output o_0 o_0 o_1

This example is typical of discrete-state machines. They can be described by such tables provided they have only a finite number of possible states.

It will seem that given the initial state of the machine and the input signals it is always possible to predict all future states. This is reminiscent of Laplace's view that from the complete state of the universe at one moment of time, as described by the positions and velocities of all particles, it should be possible to predict all future states. The prediction which we are considering is, however, rather nearer to practicability than that considered by Laplace. The system of the "universe as a whole" is such that quite small errors in the initial conditions can have an overwhelming effect at a later time. The displacement of a single electron by a billionth of a centimetre at one moment might make the difference between a man being killed by an avalanche a year later, or escaping. It is an essential property of the mechanical systems which we have called "discrete-state machines" that this phenomenon does not occur. Even when we consider the actual physical machines instead of the idealised machines, reasonably accurate knowledge of the state at one moment yields reasonably accurate knowledge any number of steps later.

As we have mentioned, digital computers fall within the class of discrete-state machines. But the number of states of which such a machine is capable is usually enormously large. For instance, the number for the machine now working at Manchester is about $2^{165,000}$, *i.e.* about $10^{50,000}$. Compare this with our example of the clicking wheel described above, which had three states. It is not difficult to see why the number of states should be so immense. The computer includes a store corresponding to the paper used by a human computer. It must be possible to write into the store any one of the combinations of symbols which might have been written on the paper. For simplicity suppose that only digits from 0 to 9 are used as symbols. Variations in handwriting are ignored. Suppose the computer is allowed 100 sheets of paper each containing 50 lines each with room for 30 digits. Then the number of states is $10^{100\times50\times30}$, i.e. $10^{150,000}$. This is about the number of states of three Manchester machines put together. The logarithm to the base two of the number of states is usually called the "storage capacity" of the machine. Thus the Manchester machine has a storage capacity of about 165,000 and the wheel machine of our example about 1.6. If two machines are put together their capacities must be added to obtain the capacity of the resultant machine. This leads to the possibility of statements such as, "The Manchester machine contains 64 magnetic tracks each with a capacity of 2560, eight electronic tubes with a capacity of 1280. Miscellaneous storage amounts to about 300 making a total of 174,380."

Given the table corresponding to a discrete-state machine it is possible to predict what it will do. There is no reason why this calculation should not be carried out by means of a digital computer. Provided it could be carried out sufficiently quickly the digital computer could mimic the behavior of any discrete-state machine. The imitation game could then be played with the machine in question (as B) and the mimicking digital computer (as A) and the interrogator would be unable to distinguish them. Of course the digital computer must have an adequate storage capacity as well as working sufficiently fast. Moreover, it must be programmed afresh for each new machine which it is desired to mimic.

This special property of digital computers, that they can mimic any discrete-state machine, is described by saying that they are universal machines. The existence of machines with this property has the important consequence that, considerations of speed apart, it is unnecessary to design various new machines to do various computing processes. They can all be done with one digital computer, suitably programmed for each case. It will be seen that as a consequence of this all digital computers are in a sense equivalent. [...]

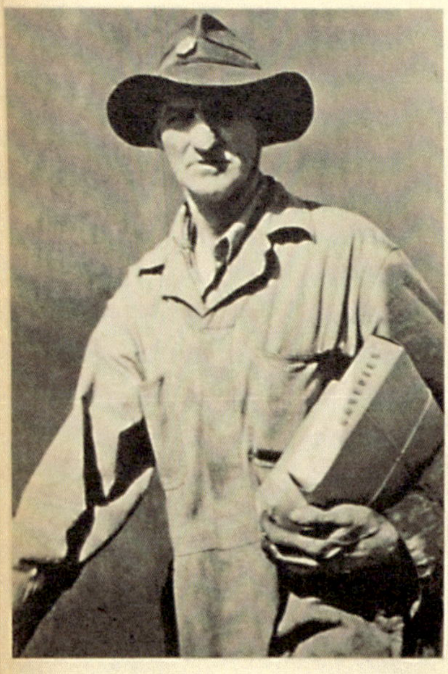
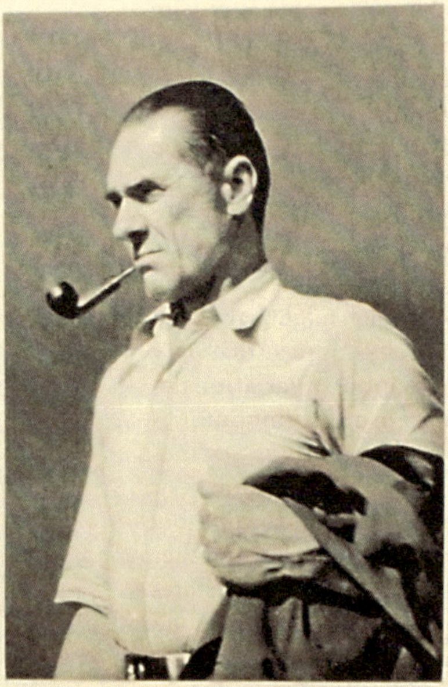
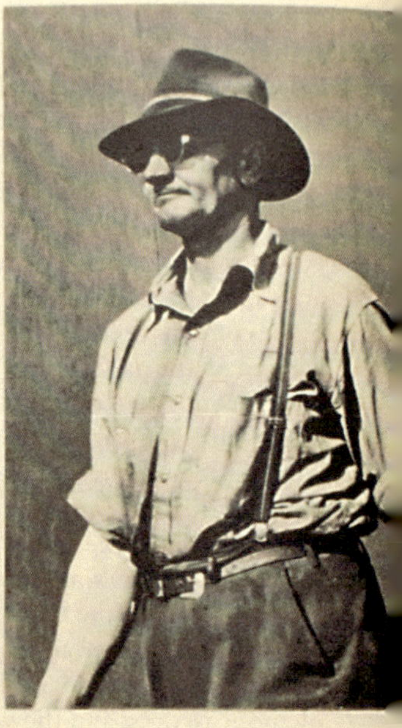

Labor Anonymous

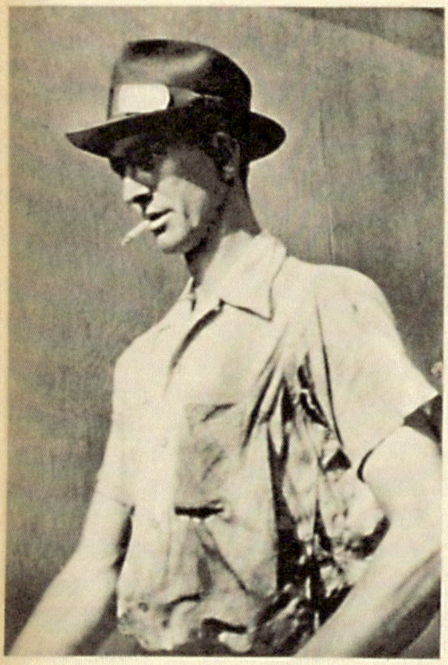
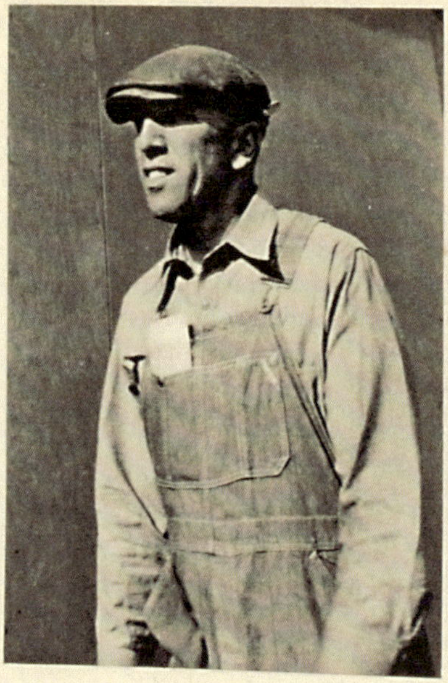
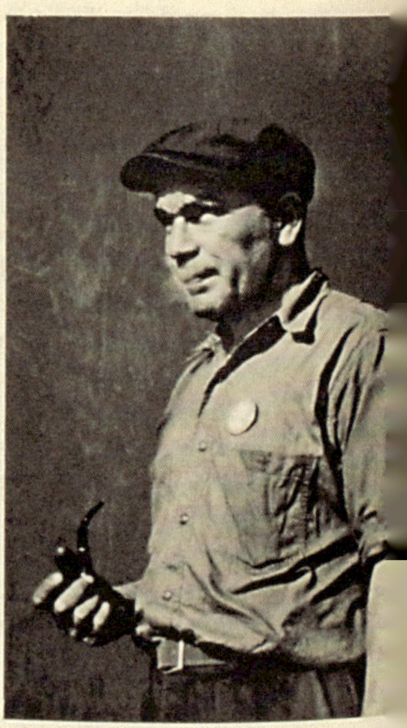

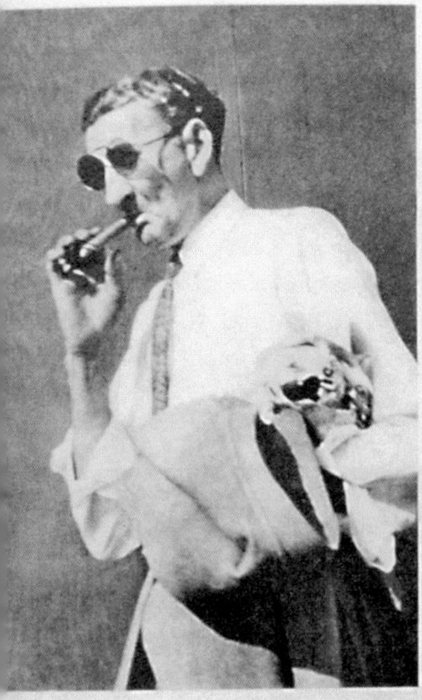

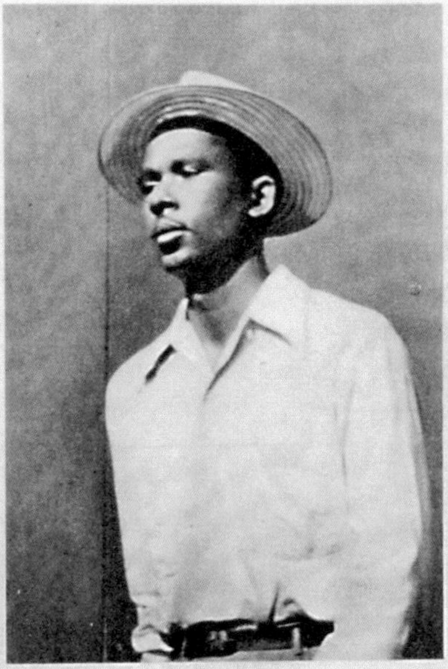

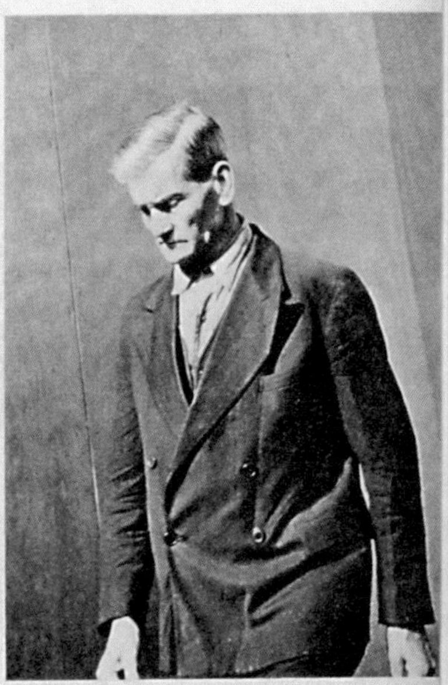

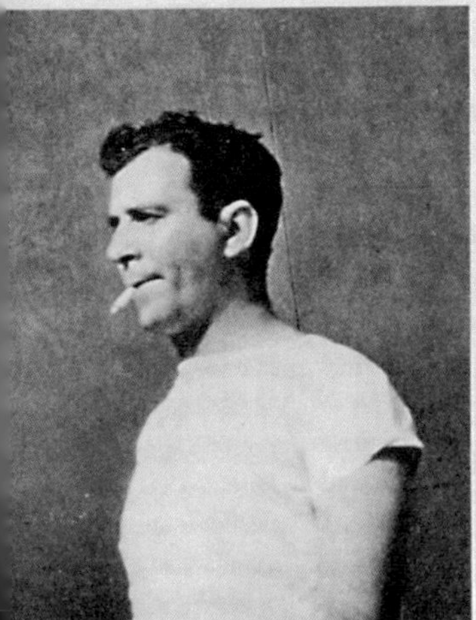

ON A SATURDAY AFTERNOON IN DOWNTOWN DETROIT

The American worker, as he passes here, generally unaware of Walker Evans' camera, is a decidedly various fellow. His blood flows from many sources. His features tend now toward the peasant and now toward the patrician. His hat is sometimes a hat, and sometimes he has molded it into a sort of defiant signature. It is this variety, perhaps, that makes him, in the mass, the most resourceful and versatile body of labor in the world. If the war proved anything, it demonstrated that American labor can learn new operations with extraordinary rapidity and speedily carry them to the highest pitch of productive efficiency. There may often be a lack of the craftsmanly traditions of the Older Worlds, but the wide spectrum of temperaments rises to meet almost any challenge; in labor, as in investment portfolios, diversification pays off.

Another thing may be noticed about these street portraits. Most of the men on these pages would seem to have a solid degree of self-possession. By the grace of providence and the efforts of millions, including themselves, they are citizens of a victorious and powerful nation, and they appear to have preserved a sense of themselves as individuals. When editorialists lump them as "labor," these laborers can no doubt laugh that one off.

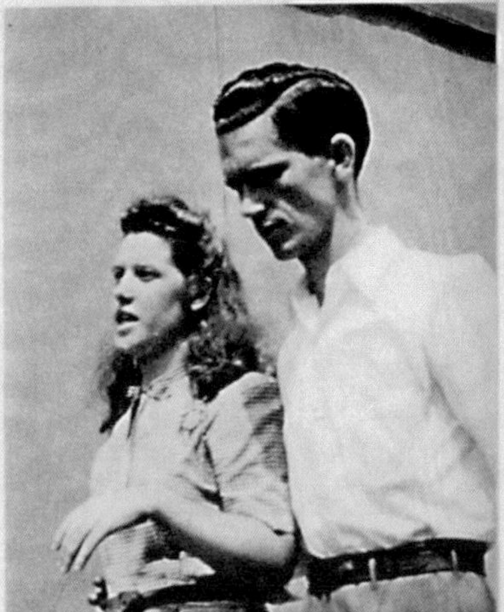

Top: In Bridgeport's War Factories in *Fortune* Magazine, September 1941

Bottom: Main Street Looking North from Courthouse Square in *Fortune* Magazine, May 1948

Walker Evans

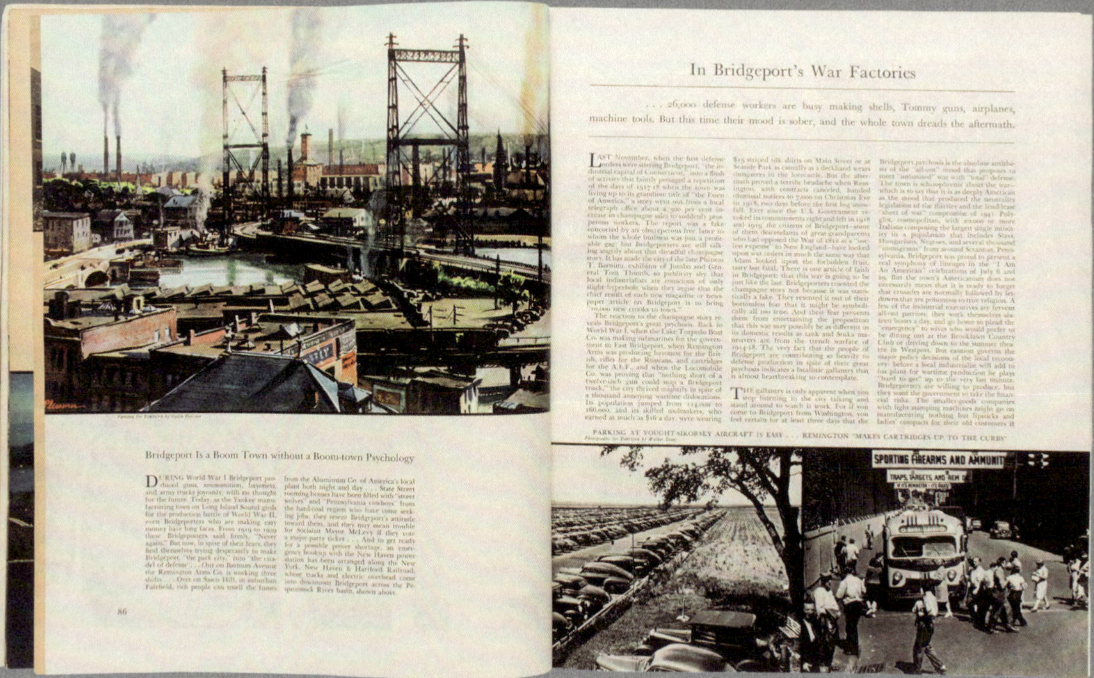

Bridgeport Is a Boom Town without a Boom-town Psychology

During World War I Bridgeport produced guns, ammunition, bayonets, and army trucks joyously, with no thought for the future. Today, as the Yankee manufacturing town on Long Island Sound girds for the production battle of World War II, even Bridgeporters who are making easy money have long faces. From 1919 to 1939 these Bridgeporters said firmly, "Never again." But now, in spite of their fears, they find themselves trying desperately to make Bridgeport, "the park city," into "the citadel of defense" . . . Out on Barnum Avenue the Remington Arms Co. is working three shifts . . . Over on Sasco Hill, in suburban Fairfield, rich people can smell the fumes from the Aluminum Co. of America's local plant both night and day . . . State Street rooming houses have been filled with "street wolves" and "Pennsylvania cowboys" from the hard-coal region who have come seeking jobs; they resent Bridgeport's attitude toward them, and they may mean trouble for Socialist Mayor McLevy if they vote a major-party ticket . . . And to get ready for a possible power shortage, an emergency hookup with the New Haven power station has been arranged along the New York, New Haven & Hartford Railroad, whose tracks and electric overhead come into downtown Bridgeport across the Pequonnock River basin, shown above.

86

In Bridgeport's War Factories

. . . 26,000 defense workers are busy making shells, Tommy guns, airplanes, machine tools. But this time their mood is sober, and the whole town dreads the aftermath.

PARKING AT VOUGHT-SIKORSKY AIRCRAFT IS EASY . . . REMINGTON "MAKES CARTRIDGES UP TO THE CURBS"

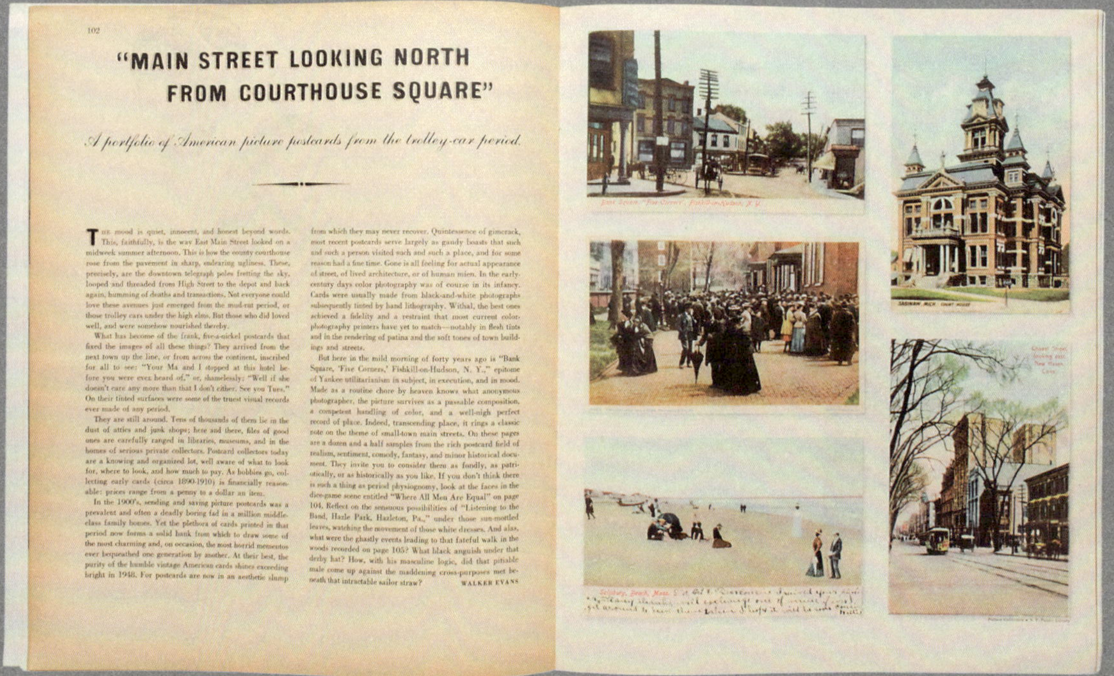

102

"MAIN STREET LOOKING NORTH FROM COURTHOUSE SQUARE"

A portfolio of American picture postcards from the trolley-car period

The mood is quiet, innocent, and honest beyond words. This, faithfully, is the way East Main Street looked on a midweek summer afternoon. This is how the county courthouse rose from the pavement in sharp, endearing ugliness. These, precisely, are the downtown telegraph poles fretting the sky, looped and threaded from High Street to the depot and back again, humming of deaths and transactions. Not everyone could love these avenues just emerged from the mud-rut period, or those trolley cars under the high elms. But those who did loved well, and were somehow nourished thereby.

What has become of the frank, five-a-nickel postcards that fixed the images of all these things? They arrived from the next town up the line, or from across the continent, inscribed for all to see: "Your Ma and I stopped at this hotel before you were ever heard of," or, shamelessly: "Well if she doesn't care any more than that I don't either. See you Tues." On their tinted surfaces were some of the truest visual records ever made of any period.

They are still around. Tens of thousands of them lie in the dust of attics and junk shops; here and there, files of good ones are carefully ranged in libraries, museums, and in the homes of serious private collectors. Postcard collectors today are a knowing and organized lot, well aware of what to look for, where to look, and how much to pay. As hobbies go, collecting early cards (circa 1890-1910) is financially reasonable: prices range from a penny to a dollar an item.

In the 1900's, sending and saving picture postcards was a prevalent and often a deadly boring fad in a million middle-class family homes. Yet the plethora of cards printed in that period now forms a solid bank from which to draw some of the most charming and, on occasion, the most horrid mementos ever bequeathed one generation by another. At their best, the purity of the humble vintage American cards shines exceeding bright in 1948. For postcards are now in an aesthetic slump from which they may never recover. Quintessence of gimcrack, most recent postcards serve largely as gaudy boasts that such and such a person visited such and such a place, and for some reason had a fine time. Gone is all feeling for actual appearance of street, of lived architecture, or of human mien. In the early-century days color photography was of course in its infancy. Cards were usually made from black-and-white photographs subsequently tinted by hand lithography. Withal, the best ones achieved a fidelity and a restraint that most current color-photography printers have yet to match—notably in flesh tints and in the rendering of patina and the soft tones of town buildings and streets.

But here in the mild morning of forty years ago is "Bank Square, 'Five Corners,' Fishkill-on-Hudson, N. Y.," epitome of Yankee utilitarianism in subject, in execution, and in mood. Made as a routine chore by heaven knows what anonymous photographer, the picture survives as a passable composition, a competent handling of color, and a well-nigh perfect record of place. Indeed, transcending place, it rings a classic note on the theme of small-town main streets. On these pages are a dozen and a half samples from the rich postcard field of realism, sentiment, comedy, fantasy, and minor historical document. They invite you to consider them as fondly, as patriotically, or as historically as you like. If you don't think there is such a thing as period physiognomy, look at the faces in the dice-game scene entitled "Where All Men Are Equal" on page 104. Reflect on the sensuous possibilities of "Listening to the Band, Hazle Park, Hazleton, Pa.," under those sun-mottled leaves, watching the movement of those white dresses. And alas, what were the ghastly events leading to that fateful walk in the woods recorded on page 105? What black anguish under that derby hat? How, with his masculine logic, did that pitiable male come up against the maddening cross-purposes met beneath that intractable sailor straw?

WALKER EVANS

Top: The Gentle Truckers in *Fortune* Magazine, May 1950
Bottom: October's Game in *Fortune* Magazine, October 1954
Walker Evans

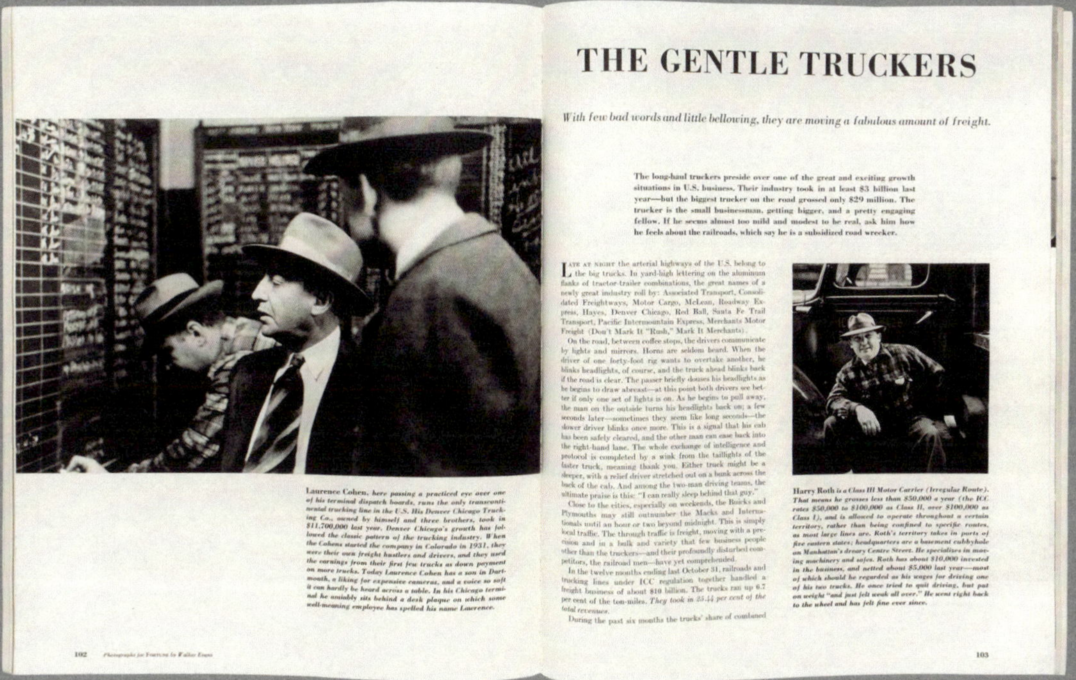

THE GENTLE TRUCKERS

With few bad words and little bellowing, they are moving a fabulous amount of freight.

The long-haul truckers preside over one of the great and exciting growth situations in U.S. business. Their industry took in at least $3 billion last year—but the biggest trucker on the road grossed only $29 million. The trucker is the small businessman, getting bigger, and a pretty engaging fellow. If he seems almost too mild and modest to be real, ask him how he feels about the railroads, which say he is a subsidized road wrecker.

Late at night the arterial highways of the U.S. belong to the big trucks. In yard-high lettering on the aluminum flanks of tractor-trailer combinations, the great names of a newly great industry roll by: Associated Transport, Consolidated Freightways, Motor Cargo, McLean, Roadway Express, Hayes, Denver Chicago, Red Ball, Santa Fe Trail Transport, Pacific Intermountain Express, Merchants Motor Freight (Don't Mark It "Rush," Mark It Merchants).

On the road, between coffee stops, the drivers communicate by lights and mirrors. Horns are seldom heard. When the driver of one forty-foot rig wants to overtake another, he blinks headlights, of course, and the truck ahead blinks back if the road is clear. The passer briefly douses his headlights as he begins to draw abreast—at this point both drivers see better if only one set of lights is on. As he begins to pull away, the man on the outside turns his headlights back on; a few seconds later—sometimes they seem like long seconds—the slower driver blinks once more. This is a signal that his cab has been safely cleared, and the other man can ease back into the right-hand lane. The whole exchange of intelligence and protocol is completed by a wink from the taillights of the faster truck, meaning thank you. Either truck might be a sleeper, with a relief driver stretched out on a bunk across the back of the cab. And among the two-man driving teams, the ultimate praise is this: "I can really sleep behind that guy."

Close to the cities, especially on weekends, the Buicks and Plymouths may still outnumber the Macks and Internationals until an hour or two beyond midnight. This is simply local traffic. The through traffic is freight, moving with a precision and in a bulk and variety that few business people other than the truckers—and their profoundly disturbed competitors, the railroad men—have yet comprehended.

In the twelve months ending last October 31, railroads and trucking lines under ICC regulation together handled a freight business of about $10 billion. The trucks ran up 6.7 per cent of the ton-miles. *They took in 25.44 per cent of the total revenues.*

During the past six months the trucks' share of combined

Laurence Cohen, *here passing a practiced eye over one of his terminal dispatch boards, runs the only transcontinental trucking line in the U.S. His Denver Chicago Trucking Co., owned by himself and three brothers, took in $11,700,000 last year. Denver Chicago's growth has followed the classic pattern of the trucking industry. When the Cohens started the company in Colorado in 1931, they were their own freight hustlers and drivers, and they used the earnings from their first few trucks as down payment on more trucks. Today Laurence Cohen has a son in Dartmouth, a liking for expensive cameras, and a voice so soft it can hardly be heard across a table. In his Chicago terminal he amiably sits behind a desk plaque on which some well-meaning employee has spelled his name Lawrence.*

Harry Roth *is a Class III Motor Carrier (Irregular Route). That means he grosses less than $50,000 a year (the ICC rates $50,000 to $100,000 as Class II, over $100,000 as Class I), and is allowed to operate throughout a certain territory, rather than being confined to specific routes, as most large lines are. Roth's territory takes in parts of five eastern states; headquarters are a basement cubbyhole on Manhattan's dreary Centre Street. He specializes in moving machinery and safes. Roth has about $10,000 invested in the business, and netted about $5,000 last year—most of which should be regarded as his wages for driving one of his two trucks. He once tried to quit driving, but put on weight "and just felt weak all over." He went right back to the wheel and has felt fine ever since.*

102

103

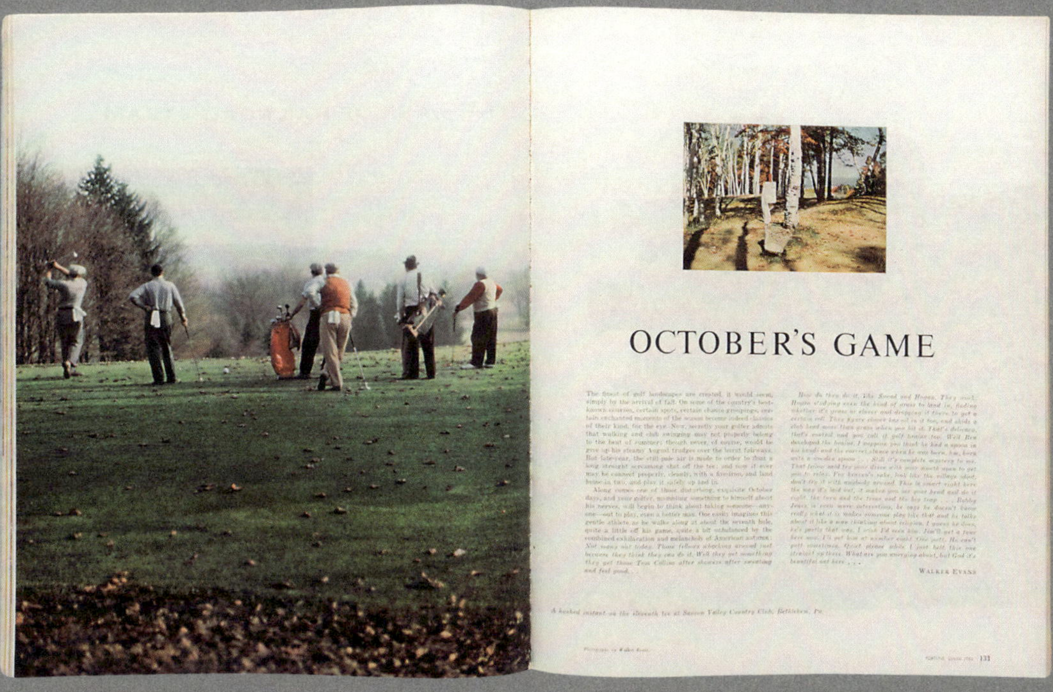

OCTOBER'S GAME

Walker Evans

Top: Beauties of the Common Tool in *Fortune* Magazine, July 1955

Bottom: The Last of Railroad Steam in *Fortune* Magazine, September 1958

Walker Evans

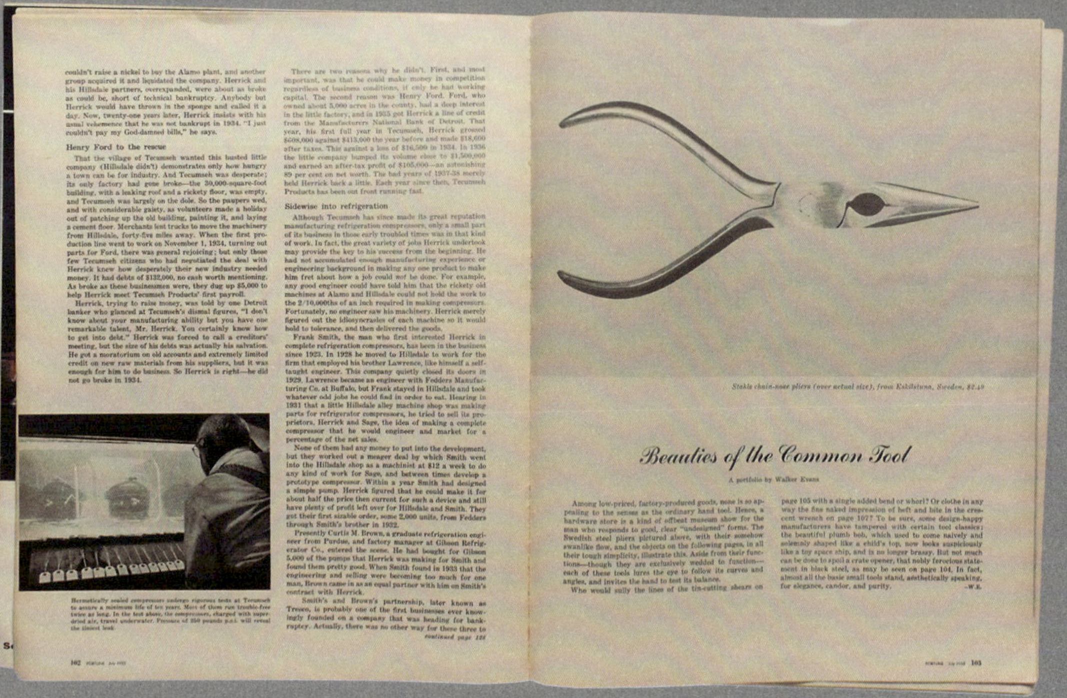

Stahls chain-nose pliers (over actual size), from Eskilstuna, Sweden, $2.49

Beauties of the Common Tool

A portfolio by Walker Evans

Among low-priced, factory-produced goods, none is so appealing to the senses as the ordinary hand tool. Hence, a hardware store is a kind of offbeat museum show for the man who responds to good, clear "undesigned" forms. The Swedish steel pliers pictured above, with their somehow swanlike flow, and the objects on the following pages, in all their tough simplicity, illustrate this. Aside from their functions—though they are exclusively wedded to function—each of these tools lures the eye to follow its curves and angles, and invites the hand to test its balance.

Who would sully the lines of the tin-cutting shears on page 105 with a single added bend or whorl? Or clothe in any way the fine naked impression of heft and bite in the crescent wrench on page 107? To be sure, some design-happy manufacturers have tampered with certain tool classics: the beautiful plumb bob, which used to come naively and solemnly shaped like a child's top, now looks suspiciously like a toy space ship, and is no longer brassy. But not much can be done to spoil a crate opener, that nobly ferocious statement in black steel, as may be seen on page 104. In fact, almost all the basic small tools stand, aesthetically speaking, for elegance, candor, and purity. —W.E.

103

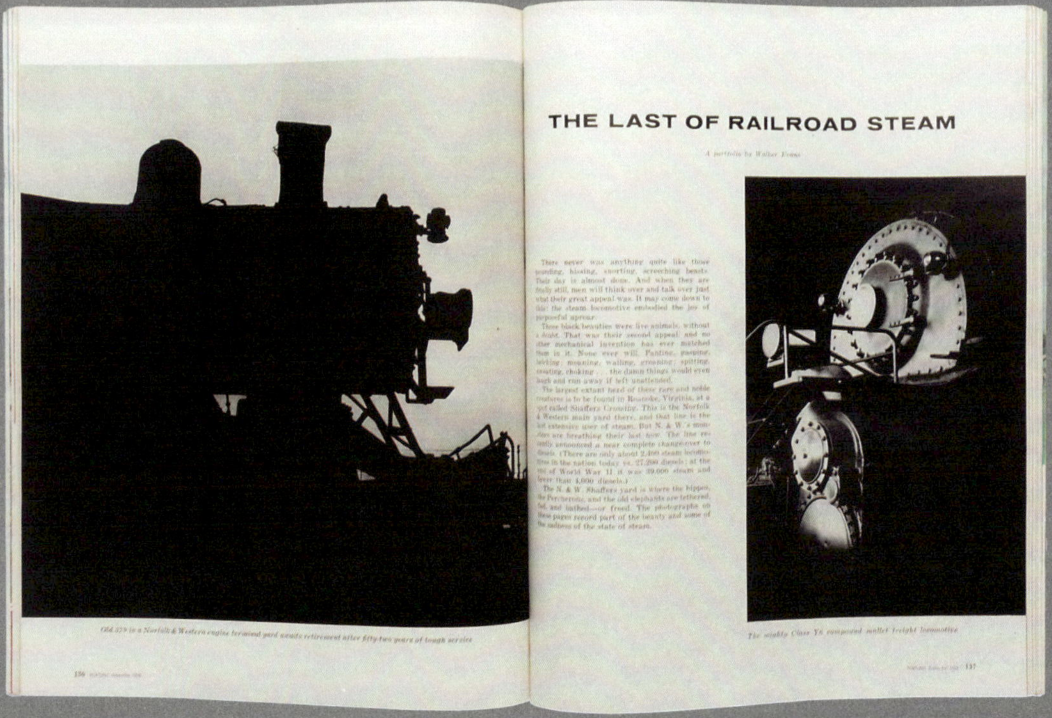

THE LAST OF RAILROAD STEAM

Top: The Pitch Direct in *Fortune* Magazine, October 1958
Bottom: And That is That in *Fortune* Magazine, December 1958
Walker Evans

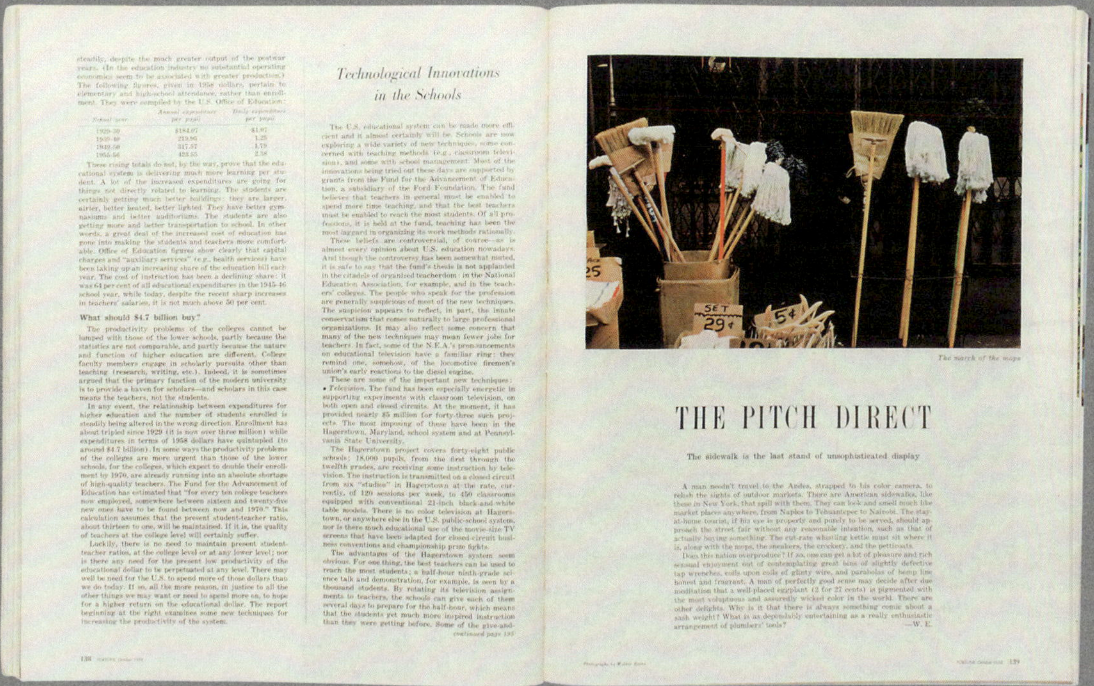

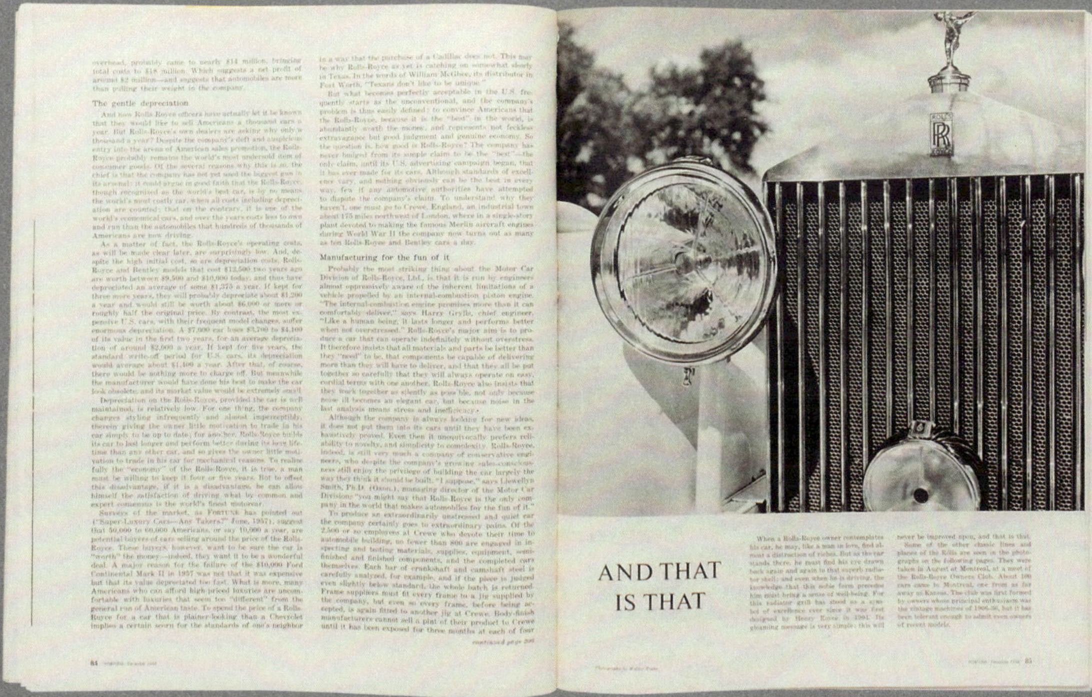

Top: On the Waterfront in *Fortune* Magazine, November 1960
Bottom: In the Midst of Plenty in *Fortune* Magazine, March 1961
Walker Evans

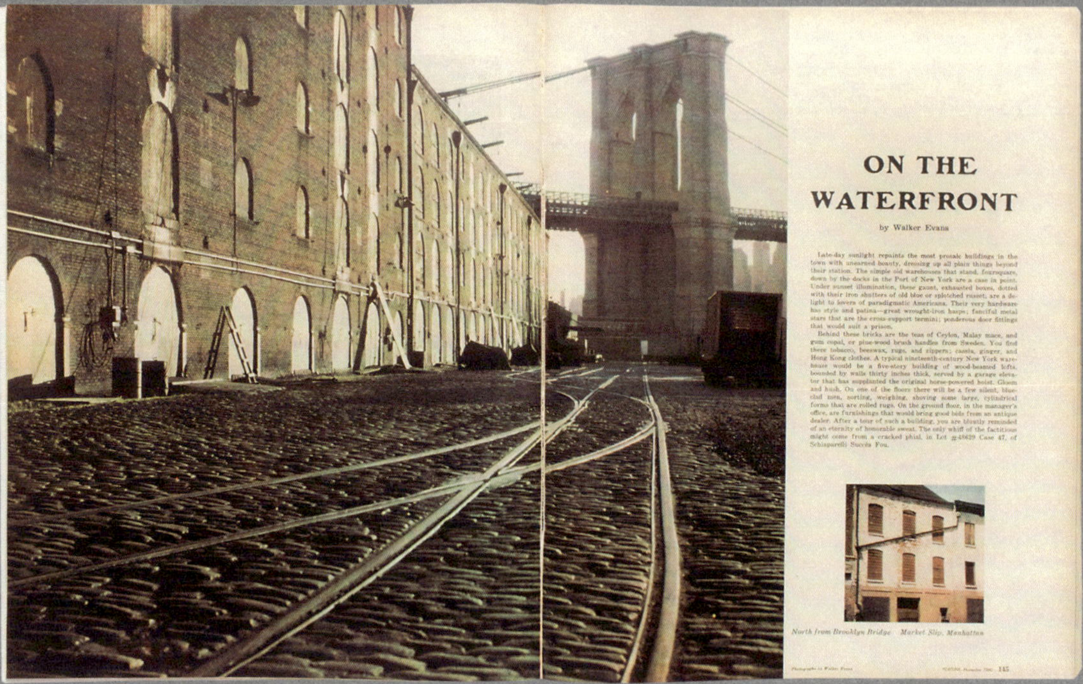

ON THE WATERFRONT

by Walker Evans

Late-day sunlight repaints the most prosaic buildings in the town with unearned beauty, dressing up all plain things beyond their station. The simple old warehouses that stand, foursquare, down by the docks in the Port of New York are a case in point. Under sunset illumination, these gaunt, exhausted boxes, dotted with their iron shutters of old blue or splotched russet, are a delight to lovers of paradigmatic Americana. Their very hardware has style and patina—great wrought-iron hasps; fanciful metal stars that are the cross-support termini; ponderous door fittings that would suit a prison.

Behind these bricks are the teas of Ceylon, Malay mace, and gum copal, or pine-wood brush handles from Sweden. You find there tobacco, beeswax, rugs, and zippers; cassia, ginger, and Hong Kong clothes. A typical nineteenth-century New York warehouse would be a five-story building of wood-beamed lofts, bounded by walls thirty inches thick, served by a garage elevator that has supplanted the original horse-powered hoist. Gloom and hush. On one of the floors there will be a few silent, blue-clad men, sorting, weighing, shoving some large, cylindrical forms that are rolled rugs. On the ground floor, in the manager's office, are furnishings that would bring good bids from an antique dealer. After a tour of such a building, you are bluntly reminded of an eternity of honorable sweat. The only whiff of the factitious might come from a cracked phial, in Lot #48629 Case 47, of Schiaparelli Succès Fou.

North from Brooklyn Bridge   Market Slip, Manhattan

145

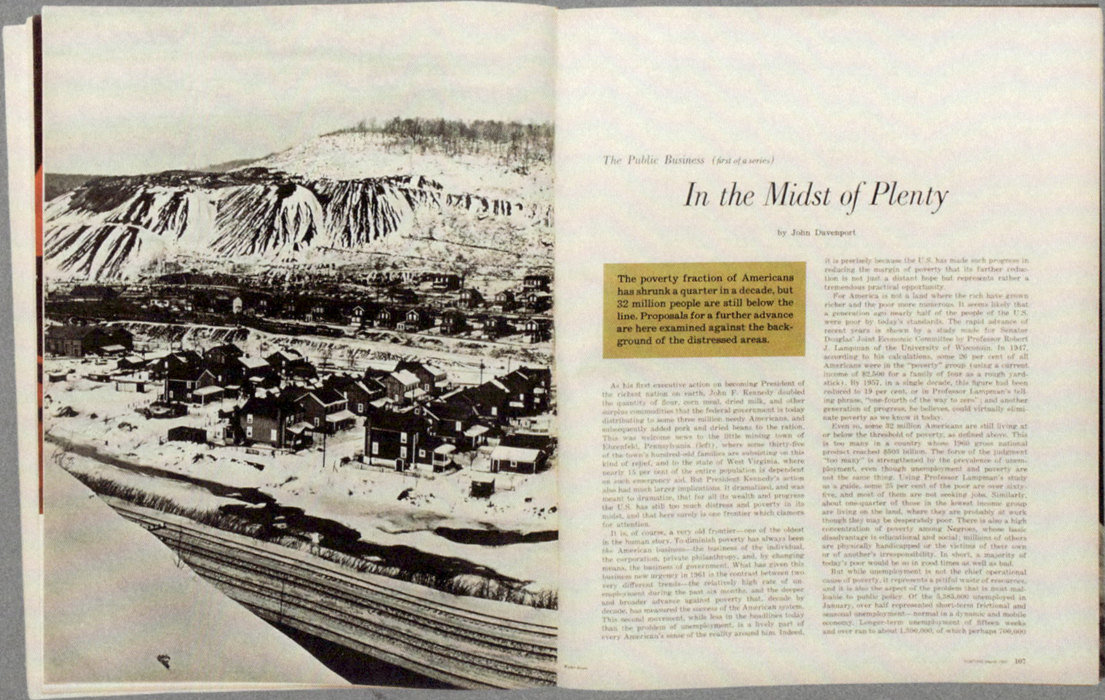

The Public Business (first of a series)

In the Midst of Plenty

by John Davenport

The poverty fraction of Americans has shrunk a quarter in a decade, but 32 million people are still below the line. Proposals for a further advance are here examined against the background of the distressed areas.

As his first executive action on becoming President of the richest nation on earth, John F. Kennedy doubled the quantity of flour, corn meal, dried milk, and other surplus commodities that the federal government is today distributing to some three million needy Americans, and subsequently added pork and dried beans to the ration. This was welcome news to the little mining town of Ehrenfeld, Pennsylvania (left), where some thirty-five of the town's hundred-odd families are subsisting on this kind of relief, and to the state of West Virginia, where nearly 15 per cent of the entire population is dependent on such emergency aid. But President Kennedy's action also had much larger implications. It dramatized, and was meant to dramatize, that for all its wealth and progress the U.S. has still too much distress and poverty in its midst, and that here surely is one frontier which clamors for attention.

It is, of course, a very old frontier—one of the oldest in the human story. To diminish poverty has always been *the* American business—the business of the individual, the corporation, private philanthropy, and, by changing means, the business of government. What has given this business new urgency in 1961 is the contrast between two very different trends—*the* relatively high rate of unemployment during the past six months, and the deeper and broader advance against poverty that, decade by decade, has measured the success of the American system. This second movement, while less in the headlines today than the problem of unemployment, is a lively part of every American's sense of the reality around him. Indeed, it is precisely because the U.S. has made such progress in reducing the margin of poverty that its further reduction is not just a distant hope but represents rather a tremendous practical opportunity.

For America is not a land where the rich have grown richer and the poor more numerous. It seems likely that a generation ago nearly half of the people of the U.S. were poor by today's standards. The rapid advance of recent years is shown by a study made for Senator Douglas' Joint Economic Committee by Professor Robert J. Lampman of the University of Wisconsin. In 1947, according to his calculations, some 26 per cent of all Americans were in the "poverty" group (using a current income of $2,500 for a family of four as a rough yardstick). By 1957, in a single decade, this figure had been reduced to 19 per cent, or in Professor Lampman's telling phrase, "one-fourth of the way to zero"; and another generation of progress, he believes, could virtually eliminate poverty as we know it today.

Even so, some 32 million Americans are still living at or below the threshold of poverty, as defined above. This is too many in a country whose 1960 gross national product reached $503 billion. The force of the judgment "too many" is strengthened by the prevalence of unemployment, even though unemployment and poverty are not the same thing. Using Professor Lampman's study as a guide, some 25 per cent of the poor are over sixty-five, and most of them are not seeking jobs. Similarly, about one-quarter of those in the lowest income group are living on the land, where they are probably at work though they may be desperately poor. There is also a high concentration of poverty among Negroes, whose basic disadvantage is educational and social; millions of others are physically handicapped or the victims of their own or of another's irresponsibility. In short, a majority of today's poor would be so in good times as well as bad.

But while unemployment is not the chief operational cause of poverty, it represents a pitiful waste of resources, and it is also the aspect of the problem that is most malleable to public policy. Of the 5,385,000 unemployed in January, over half represented short-term frictional and seasonal unemployment—normal in a dynamic and mobile economy. Longer-term unemployment of fifteen weeks and over ran to about 1,300,000, of which perhaps 700,000

107

Top: People and Places In Trouble in *Fortune* Magazine, March 1961
Bottom: The Auto Junkyard in *Fortune* Magazine, April 1962
Walker Evans

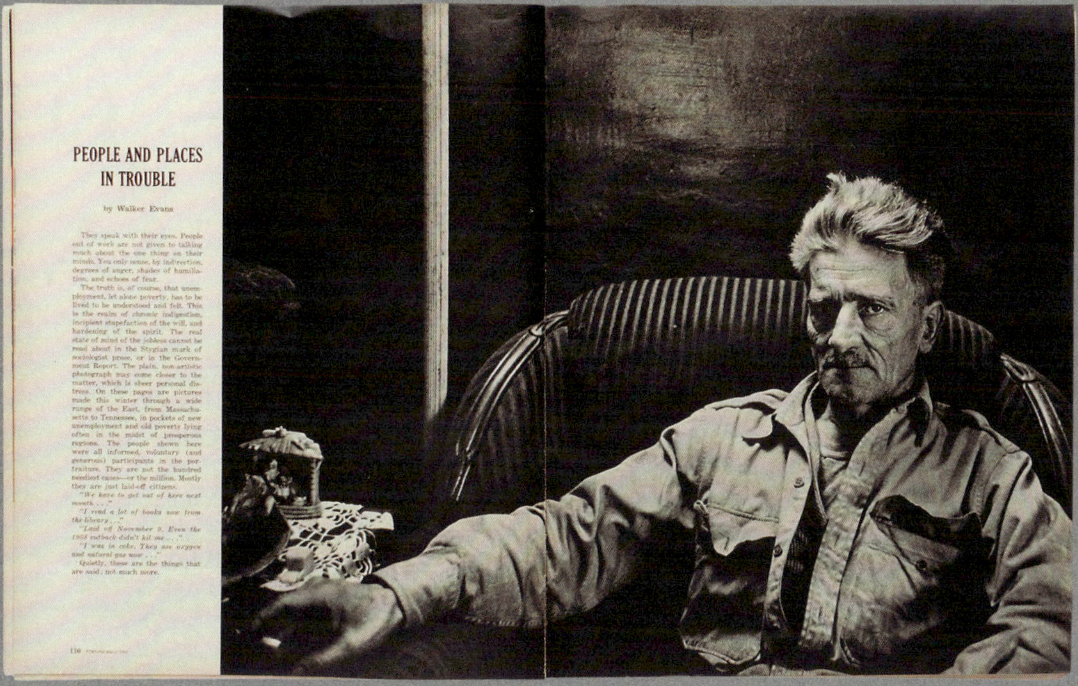

PEOPLE AND PLACES IN TROUBLE

by Walker Evans

They speak with their eyes. People out of work are not given to talking much about the one thing on their minds. You only sense, by indirection, degrees of anger, shades of humiliation, and echoes of fear.

The truth is, of course, that unemployment, let alone poverty, has to be lived to be understood and felt. This is the realm of chronic indigestion, incipient stupefaction of the will, and hardening of the spirit. The real state of mind of the jobless cannot be read about in the Stygian murk of sociologist prose, or in the Government Report. The plain, non-artistic photograph may come closer to the matter, which is sheer personal distress. On these pages are pictures made this winter through a wide range of the East, from Massachusetts to Tennessee, in pockets of new unemployment and old poverty lying often in the midst of prosperous regions. The people shown here were all informed, voluntary (and generous) participants in the portraiture. They are not the hundred neediest cases—or the million. Mostly they are just laid-off citizens.

"We have to get out of here next month . . ."

"I read a lot of books now from the library . . ."

"Laid off November 9. Even the 1958 cutback didn't hit me . . ."

"I was in coke. They use oxygen and natural gas now . . ."

Quietly, these are the things that are said; not much more.

110

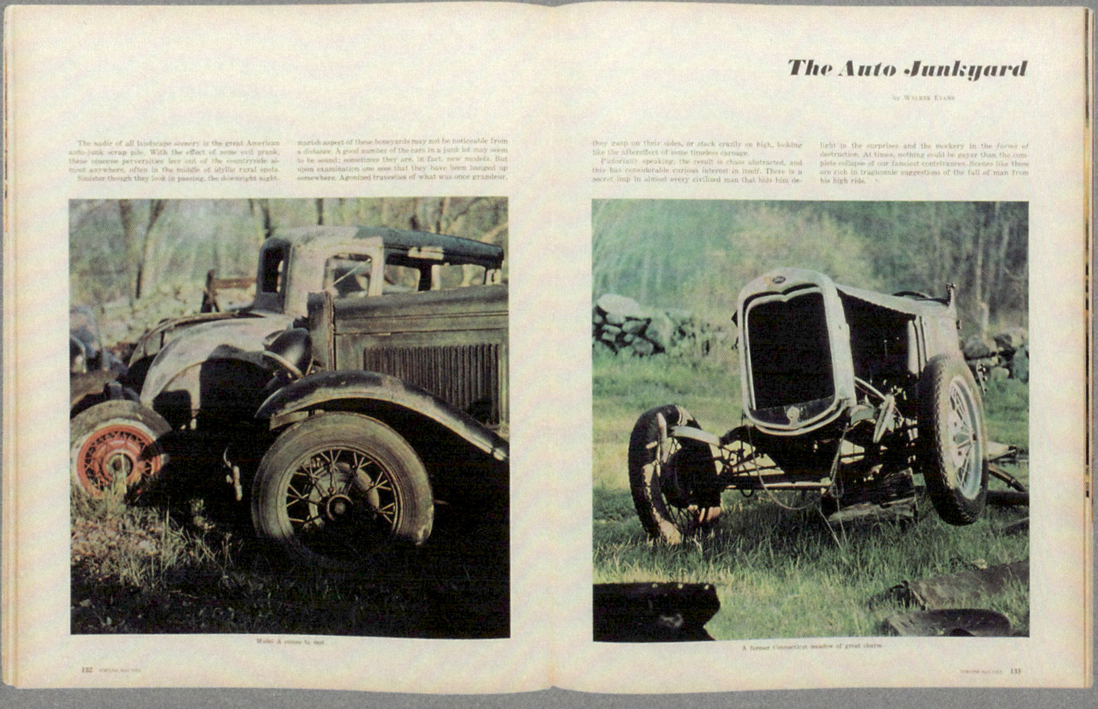

The Auto Junkyard

by Walker Evans

The nadir of all landscape scenery is the great American auto-junk scrap pile. With the effect of some evil prank, these obscene perversities leer out of the countryside almost anywhere, often in the middle of idyllic rural spots. Sinister though they look in passing, the downright nightmarish aspect of these boneyards may not be noticeable from a distance. A good number of the cars in a junk lot may seem to be sound; sometimes they are, in fact, new models. But upon examination one sees that they have been banged up somewhere. Agonized travesties of what was once grandeur, they gasp on their sides, or stack crazily on high, looking like the aftereffect of some timeless carnage.

Pictorially speaking, the result is chaos abstracted, and this has considerable curious interest in itself. There is a secret imp in almost every civilized man that bids him delight in the surprises and the mockery in the *forms of destruction*. At times, nothing could be gayer than the complete collapse of our fanciest contrivances. Scenes like these are rich in tragicomic suggestions of the fall of man from his high ride.

Model A comes to rest.

A former Connecticut meadow of great charm.

132

133

Homes of Americans in *Fortune* Magazine, April 1946

Walker Evans

HOMES OF AMERICANS

A SELECTION OF NATIVE DESIGNS IN MANY MANNERS AND PERIODS

THE following portfolio is a ranging glance at an enormous subject—American shelter. The record is written across four centuries and over the most varied landscape in the world. Wood, stone, glass, and metal bespeak in their own way the entire history of the settlers of the nation and their uneasy descendants.

The pictures are not accompanied by captions (which are all gathered on page 157). The aim is to avoid distraction from the naked, graphic facts, to have you see the sundry remarkable shapes, textures, and glints of light quite as they are, without verbal comment. Few of us really take the time to see what we look at, and these thirty-three pictures, drawn from hundreds, may deliver their impact of excitement, nostalgia, humor, or repugnance much more strongly if the eye is not led away to documentation in words. Besides, you may enjoy guessing what parts of the country the various scenes represent.

The wildly exotic variety of American design is fully apparent. You will find intelligent modern architecture and many of the curious crusts of the past. You may detect hints of Charlie Chaplin, Ulysses S. Grant, Cotton Mather, Ward McAllister, and Huckleberry Finn. Photography, that great distorter of things as they are, has, here as elsewhere, played its peculiarly disreputable, charming tricks (the casement shadows in No. 11 never were on land or sea). But like the deliberate inflections of men's voices, they are tricks now and then lifted to an art. Take your time with this array. You may be in a hurry to turn to page 157 for the names of what you are seeing. On the other hand, it may pay you to incline with Herman Melville to "let the ambiguous procession of events reveal their own ambiguousness."

EXTREMES

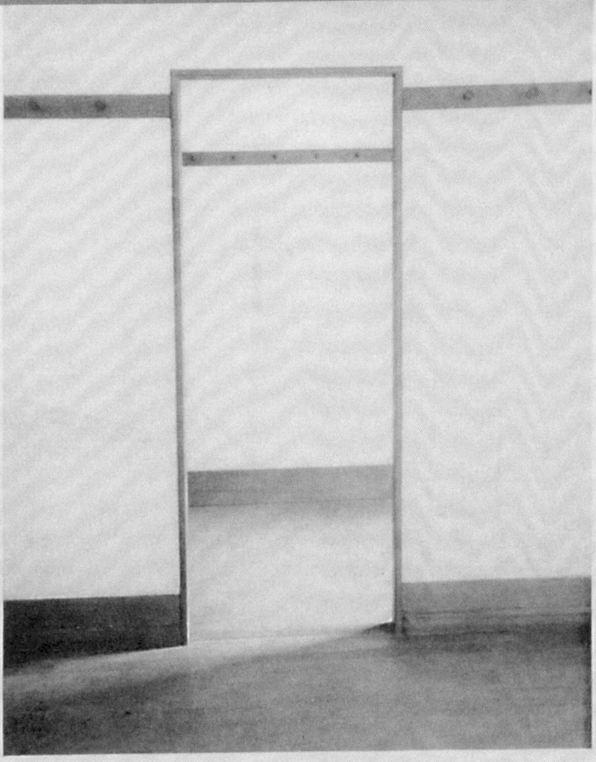

1

2

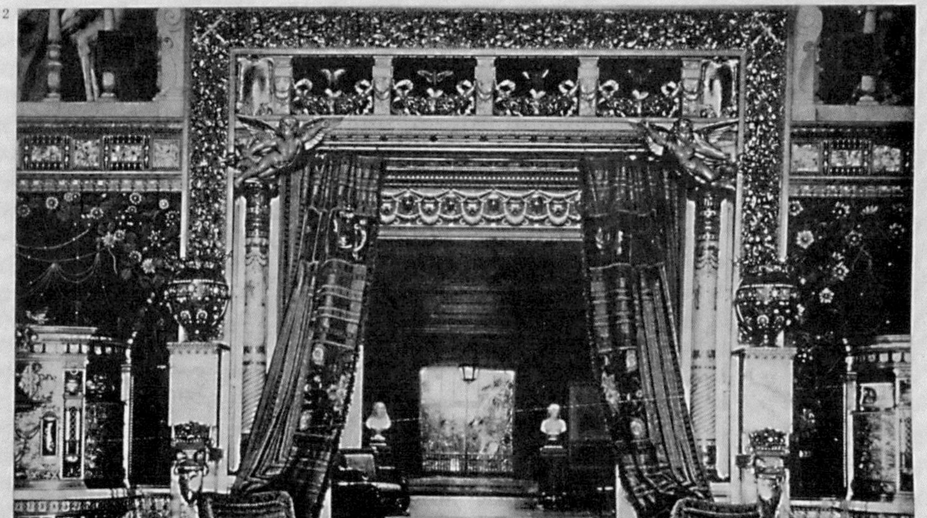

150

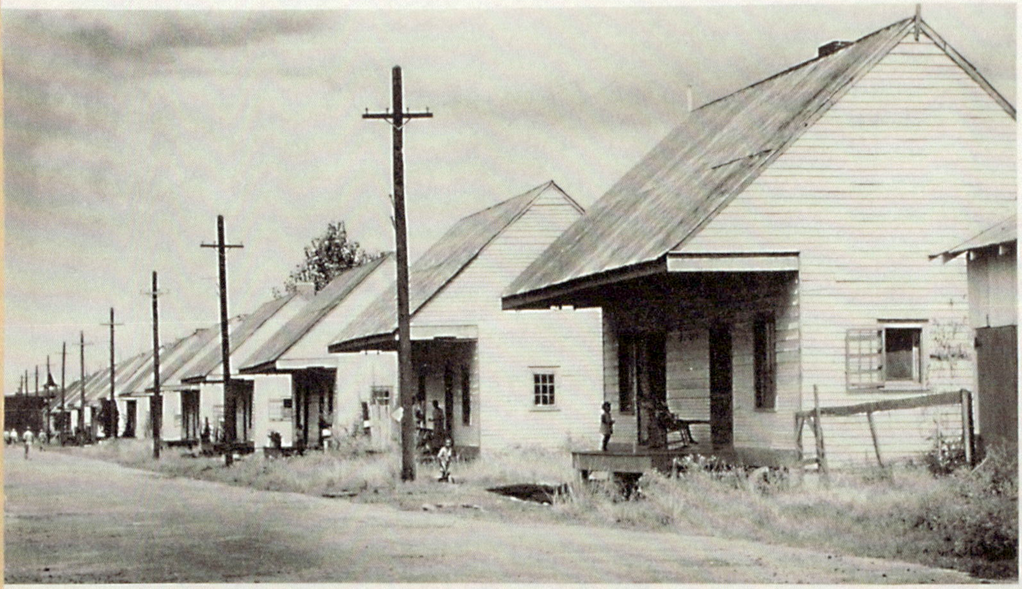

3

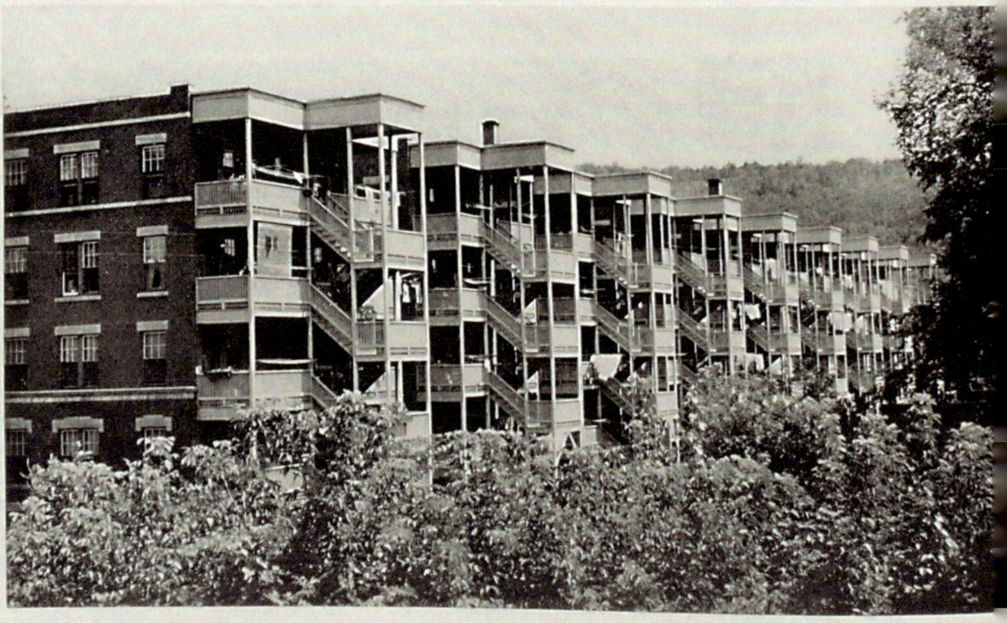

4

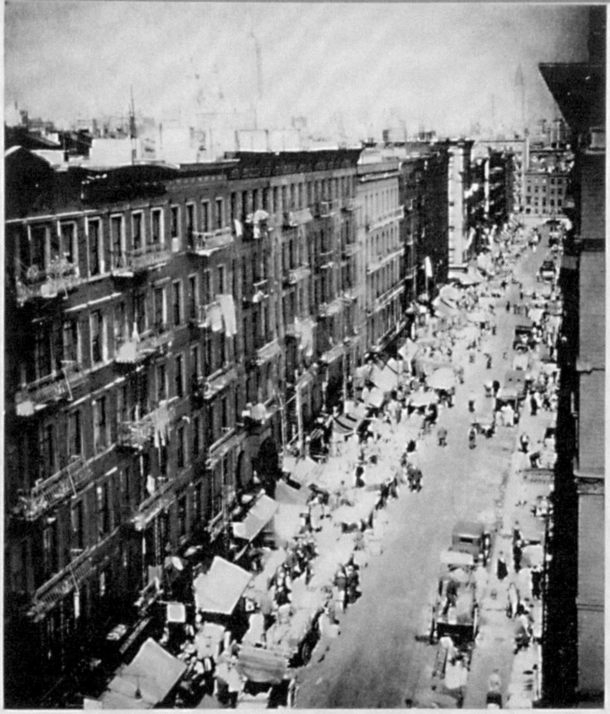

THE HIVE

5

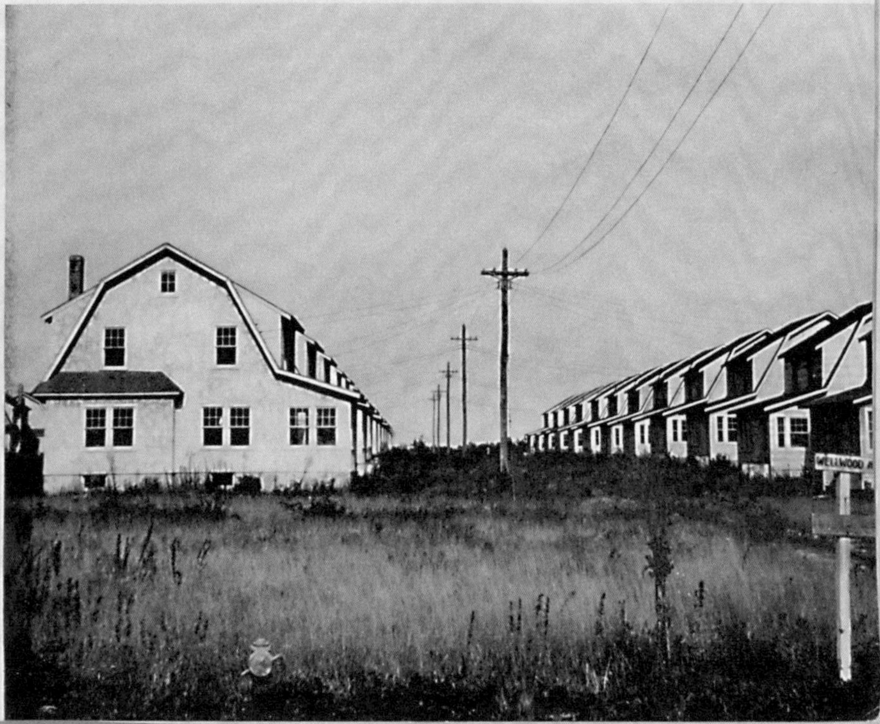

6

CROSS-COUNTRY

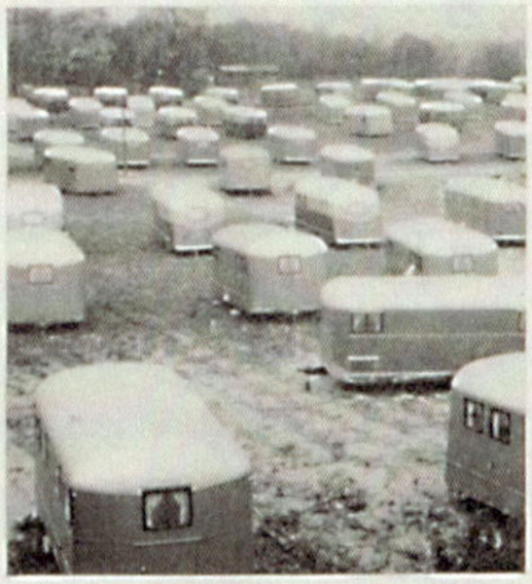

7

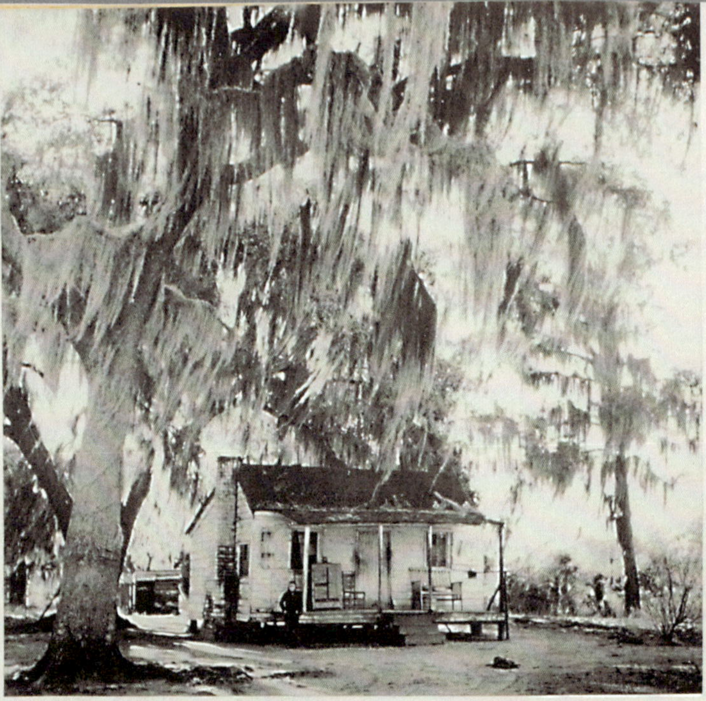

8

9

153

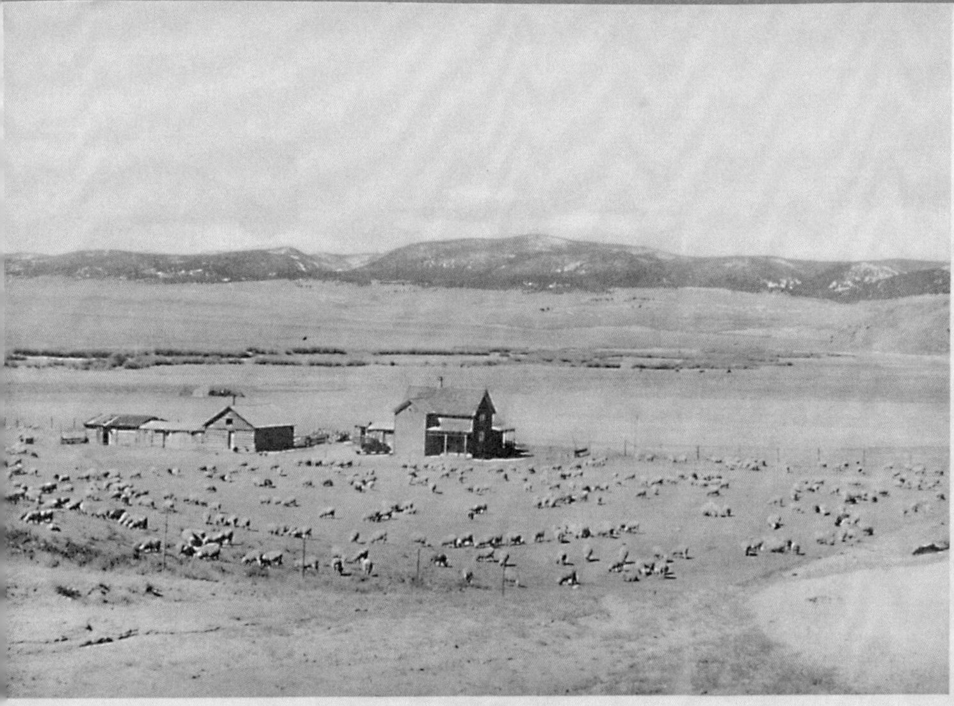

10

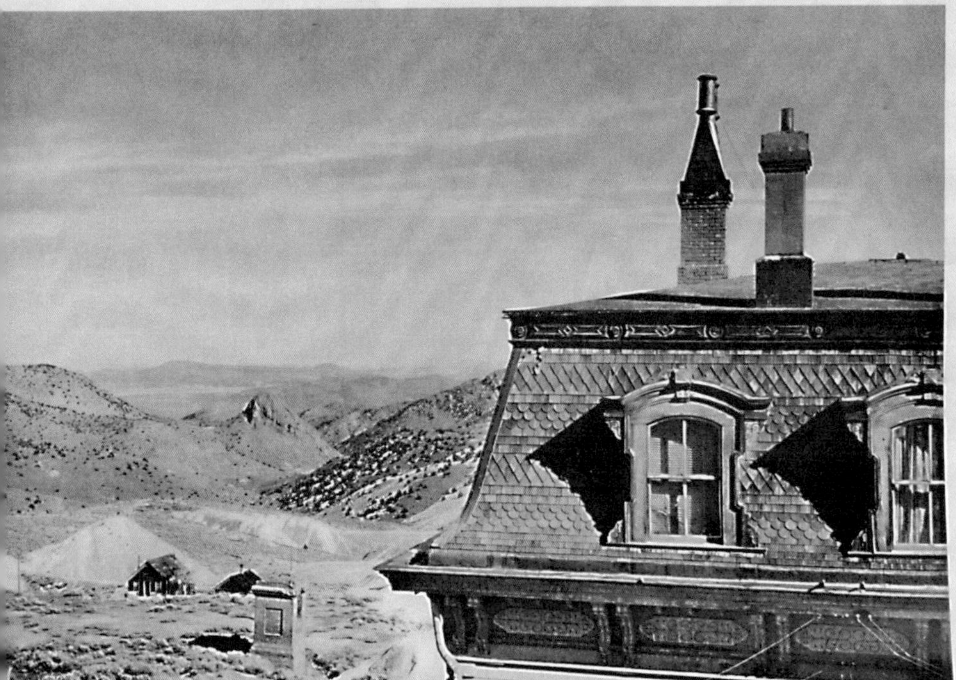

11

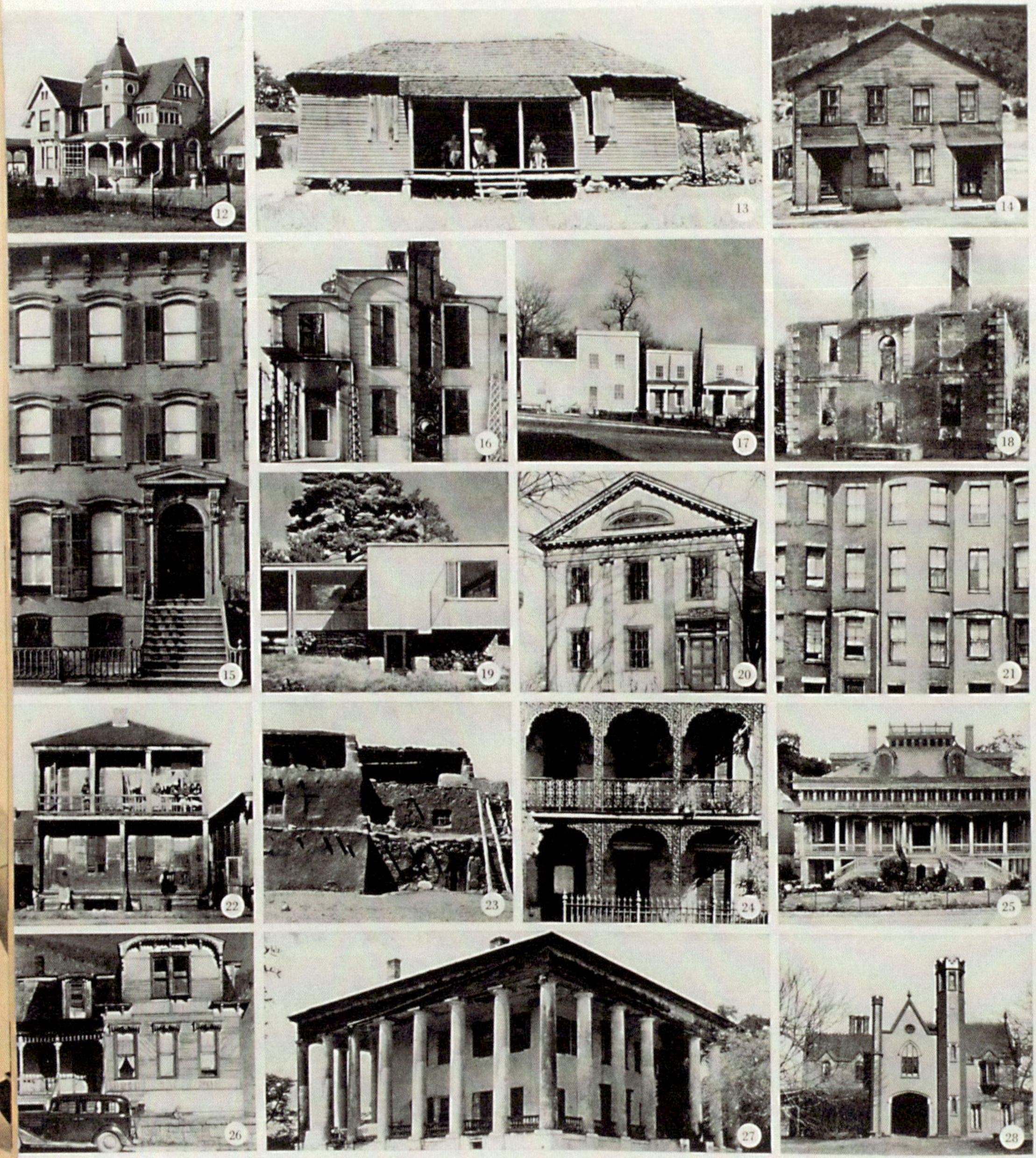
12
13
14
15
16
17
18
19
20
21
22
23
24
25
26
27
28

155

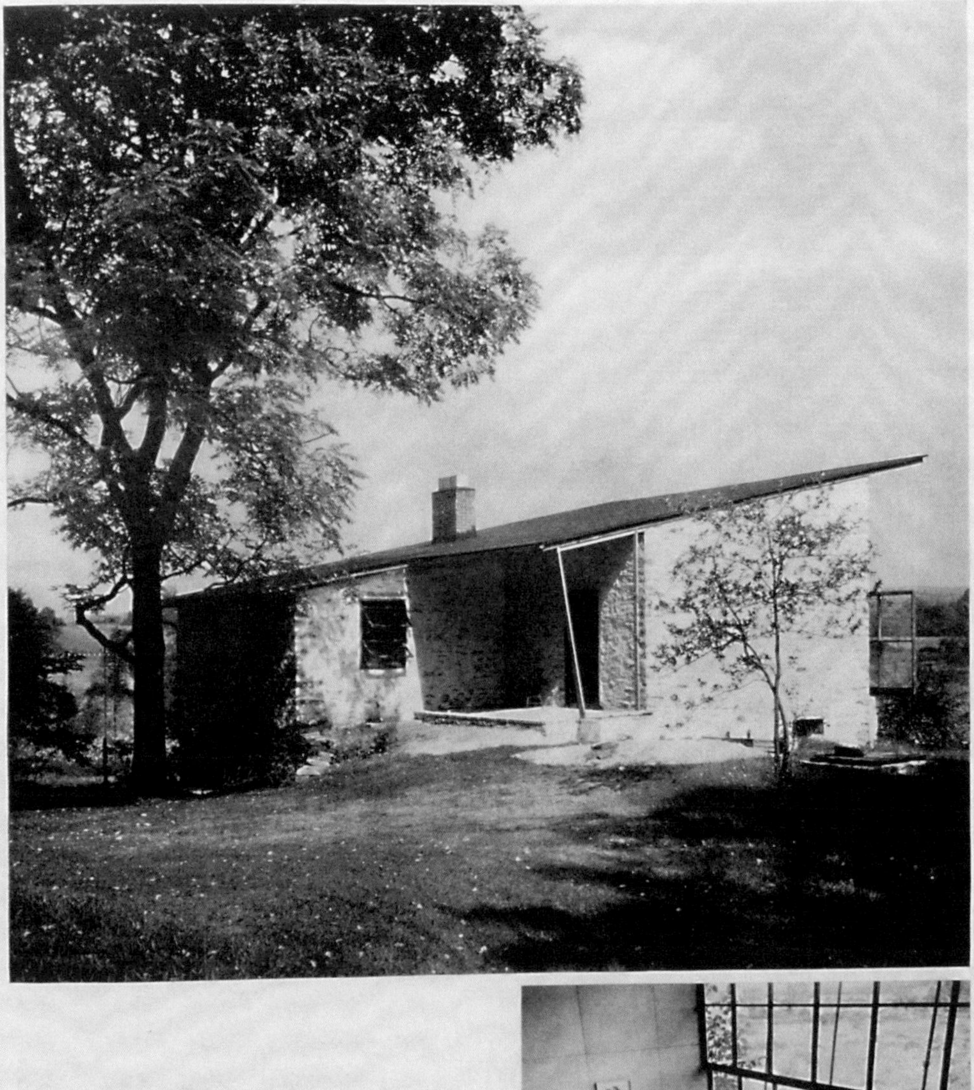

29

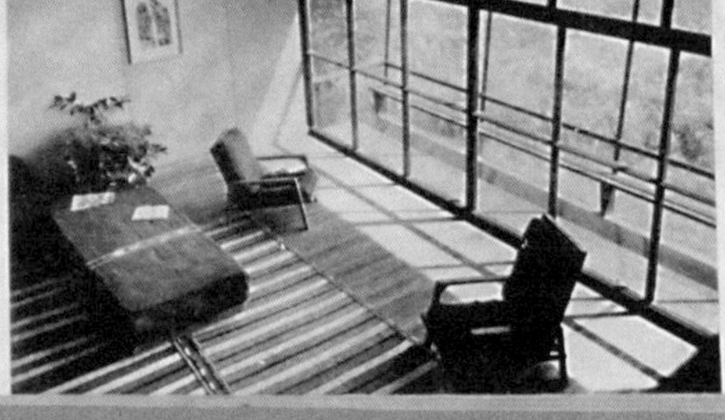

30

CHORUS OF STYLES

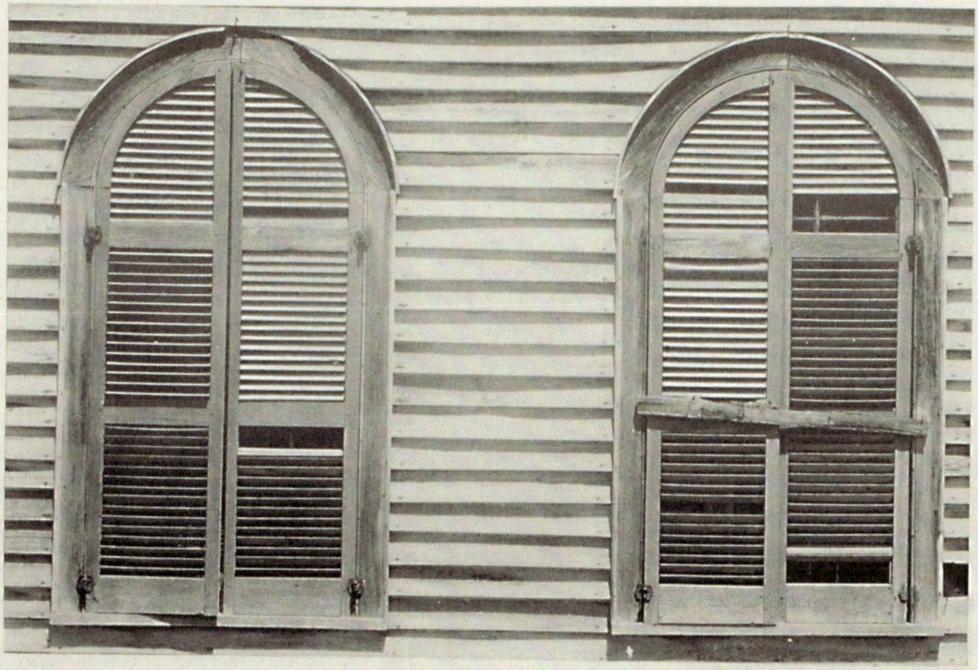

31

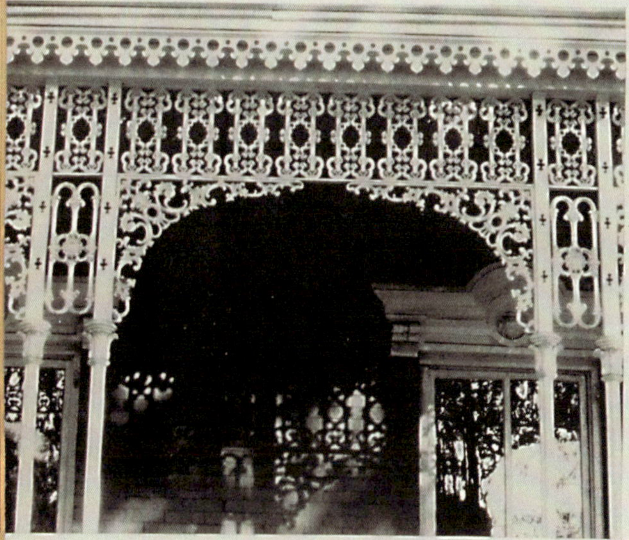

32

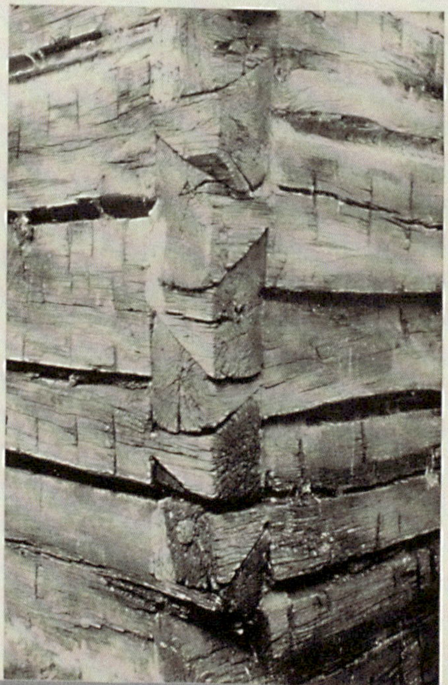

33

INDEX *to* HOMES OF AMERICANS

1-2 These are a Shaker doorway in New Lebanon, New York, built in 1819, and Mrs. Cornelius Vanderbilt's New York drawing room as of 1883. That Shaker reticence should meet cupids, ormolu, and brocade in the same nation, while no great surprise, is certainly telling matter for pictorial juxtaposition. There could scarcely be a more vivid parable concerning the extreme diversity of American manners and character.

3 Back street in Destrehan, Louisiana. These stark, serried boxes house a dozen Negro families.

4 Tenements in Windsor, Vermont. New England's familiar and highly inflammable back stairs make a sort of jackstraws pile out of many urban landscapes.

5 Orchard Street, New York City. The pushcart boulevards of the lower East Side, of which this is a symbol, would seem to be passing—at a tempo slightly faster than glacial.

6 A Long Island real-estate development of the early 1930's. "A Lifetime Opportunity. Steam Heat, with Gas, Electricity and Water. On Easy Terms . . ."

7 Trailers housing defense-plant workers near Nashville, Tennessee, 1941. Even before the war, trailer living suited many an American to perfection. The trailer camps of the country have long since grown from a tinny novelty to an important phenomenon in civics as well as housing.

8 Cabin in Summerville, South Carolina. Built off the ground, heated by wood fires, such huts dot the southern land from the Atlantic to the Mississippi. Their form was well established by 1800.

9 Farmstead near Searsport, Maine. Down East farmers see to it that all their succinctly designed buildings are joined into a communicating fortress against sub-zero winters.

10 Sheep farm, Beaverhead County, Montana. Many vast regions of the U.S. have come to be typified by buildings as innocent of architectural concern as this western farmhouse.

11 A view in Virginia City, Nevada. Skilled carpenters, such as those who put up these bleaching and deserted mansards and patterned shingles, were the real architects of a good part of the gold-rushing West.

12 Crotchet-and-furbelow residence in Ottawa, Illinois.

13 Tenant farmer's house near Moundville, Alabama.

14 Frame house in Tyler, Pennsylvania.

15 New York City brownstone (1880's).

16 Residence near Cherry Valley, New York (nineteenth century).

17 Frame houses, Virginia.

18 Ruin of eighteenth-century grandeur, Edisto Island, South Carolina.

19 Chamberlain house, Wayland, Massachusetts. (Architects: Walter Gropius, Marcel Breuer.)

20 New York state country house, nineteenth century.

21 Boston façades.

22 Negro tenement in New Orleans.

23 Acoma Pueblo, New Mexico.

24 A small house in New Orleans.

25 San Francisco plantation, River Road, Convent, Louisiana.

26 House of the gold boom days, Silverton, Colorado.

27 Greenwood plantation, St. Francisville, Louisiana (1830).

28 Archer C. Wheeler house, Bridgeport, Connecticut (1846 Gothic revival).

29 Modern weekend house near Blairstown, New Jersey. A deft adaptation of modern functional style to setting and to regional tradition. (Designers: Paul Grotz and Henry Wright.)

30 Living room of the above.

31 Windows of the old "Plea" Flucker house, Greene County, Georgia. The accidental miracles of design include countless examples of striped, nail-studded wood on sunlit American houses. The only other nation that offers a comparable variety of wood patterns is Russia.

32 Cast-iron ornament on a porch in Mobile, Alabama. The unfading grace of such lacy decorations still charms the eyes of amateurs of design throughout the Gulf Coast region in Louisiana and Alabama.

33 Log construction detail on the Daniel Wilkins house, Montevideo, Minnesota. This notch, common practice among Yankee frontier builders, is found throughout the Northwest.

WE REQUIRE FROM BUILDINGS—AS FROM MEN—
TWO KINDS OF GOODNESS:
FIRST, DOING THEIR PRACTICAL DUTY WELL:
THEN THAT THEY BE GRACEFUL AND PLEASING
IN DOING IT . . .

—John Ruskin

Walker Evans: The Magazine Work
David Campany
2014

MIXED FORTUNE

In September 1945, with the war at an end, [Evans] was appointed the only staff photographer at *Fortune*. Launched in the immediate aftermath of the Wall Street Crash, *Fortune* had been an unlikely venture: a luxurious and extravagantly produced magazine specializing in business and industry. Henry Luce considered it a worthwhile experiment, half-expecting it to run at a loss. A statement in the inaugural issue (February 1930) announced the aim to present "clear and readable text, profusely illustrated with pictures, in a form ample and agreeable to the eye [...] planned upon an economic scale which permits it to go toward that end beyond the technical limitations of most magazines."[1] Many of its pages were printed in high quality gravure rather than halftone typical of most non-art publications. *Fortune* also used color photography, later in great quantity. At eleven by fourteen inches it was far larger than most magazines. It began with 184 pages and a cover price of $1, when *The New York Times* was just five cents.[2] Circulation started at 30,000 copies, rising to 90,000 in 1934 and 130,000 by 1939. This was large enough to be significant but it did not warrant the extreme micro-management endured by the staff and contributors at the far more widely read *Time*, and later at *Life*.[3]

Fortune's editors had set out to commission the best writers, photographers, artists and illustrators. This meant looking beyond those working in business journalism.[4] Luce sensed that the better writers were actually the left wing literary intellectuals. ("Was there ever a journal that allowed its staff such freedom to bite the editor's hand and mock its readers' ethos?" asked Philip French[5]). The commissioning of artists was also a sign of newfound pride in a modern American iconography drawn from vernacular documents, reportage, the graphic arts, signage and mass-produced goods.

By 1931 there were five million unemployed in America. As the effects of the Depression deepened *Fortune* faltered in its celebration of the bounties of capital. Evans noted that "it didn't really know what role it should play during the Depression. They didn't know what they were doing since they were founded to describe in a stimulating way American business and industry, and that was falling apart."[6]

Evans' artistic credentials, his interest in American culture, and his proven ability to write copy secured him a unique role at *Fortune*. Despite his skepticism he worked hard to establish himself, finding ways to balance the corporate structure with his own ambitions. For the first years of his contract he had little influence over writing and design, and his understated images often suffered in cluttered layouts [...] The first indication that he had ambitions for his magazine pages to equal those of his books was "Homes of Americans." In the early months of 1946 [*Fortune*'s] editors were preparing a special issue on housing. There was an acute shortage of dwellings across the country, the result of suspended building programs and the return from the war of military personnel. *Architectural Forum* was also planning a housing issue, and both appeared in April 1946. The articles described the economics of building, new construction methods, interior design and home appliances. The cover of *Fortune* featured Buckminster Fuller's hi-tech Wichita House. "Homes of Americans" was very different. Its ten pages comprised an introductory text, thirty-three black-and-white photographs and captions at the rear. The presentation was austere with a neutral layout. No photos were shot especially for the feature and only seven were by Evans himself.[7] The accompanying text introduced the theme of the piece: the open and slippery meaning of photographic documents:

1 Henry R. Luce, editorial statement, *Fortune*, February 1930.

2 In 1943, the size shrank slightly to 13" by 10.5". Although this was a response to wartime paper shortage, *Fortune* claimed the larger size was a little too cumbersome to read and store on a bookshelf (*Fortune* editorial, March 1943).

3 See Chris Mullen and Philip Beard, *Fortune's America. The Visual Achievements of Fortune Magazine 1930–1965*. University of East Anglia Library, 1985.

4 Noting its blend of free marketeering and advanced artistic values, Douglas Eklund described Fortune as "an experiment in the aesthetics of capital." See Douglas Eklund, "The Harassed Man's Haven of Detachment: Walker Evans and the *Fortune* Portfolio" in Maria Mouris Hambourg, Jeff L. Rosenheim, Douglas Eklund, and Mia Fineman, eds., *Walker Evans*. (New York and Princeton: Metropolitan Museum of Art and Princeton University Press, 2000), 121.

5 Philip French, "His Death Gave Life to His Legend." *New York Times Book Review*, July 8, 1984.

6 Evans, quoted by James R. Mellow, *Walker Evans*. (New York: Basic Books, 1999), 308.

> Photography, that great distorter of things as they are, has, here as elsewhere, played its particularly disreputable, charming trick [...] But like the deliberate inflections of men's voices' they are tricks now and then lifted to an art. Take your time with this array. You may be in a hurry to turn to page 157 for the names of what you are seeing. On the other hand it may pay you to incline with Herman Melville to 'let the ambiguous procession of events reveal their own ambiguousness'.[8]

The tone continued in the caption for the first two images:

> These are a Shaker doorway in New Lebanon, New York, built in 1819 and Mrs. Cornelius Vanderbilt's New York drawing room as of 1883. That Shaker reticence should meet cupids, ormulu and brocade in the same nation, while no great surprise, is certainly a telling matter for pictorial juxtaposition. There could scarcely be a more vivid parable concerning the extreme diversity of American manners or character.[9]

Neither could there be a more vivid parable of the vicissitudes of the photographic document. The Modernist-looking interior was actually 133 years old, predating the Baroque-looking drawing room by 64 years. Further on, a field of Airstream caravans is a temporary home for defense workers, but the caption describes the trailer as a symbol of American freedom and leisure. A Long Island housing development of the 1930s is captioned "A Life-time Opportunity, Steam Heat, with Gas, Electricity and Water. On Easy Terms...," mocking the real estate rhetoric elsewhere in the magazine. A sleekly functional modern home by Walter Gropius and Marcel Breuer is squeezed in to a grid of nineteenth-century wood-frame houses. Other captions insist the beauty of built form is rooted in pragmatism, tradition and anonymous craft, not in the ideas of star architects.

Conventionally, captions serve to anchor the open meaning of photographs, to tame them and make them functional.[10] "Homes of Americans" does the opposite. The effect is to slow down response rather than hasten it into the tempo necessary to consume a photo-essay as information or entertainment. While the selection of the photographs was by Evans, the text was the outcome of conversations with Wilder Hobson, now a member of Fortune's editorial board. It was Hobson who had been working on a survey piece on American housing, asking Evans to collaborate. Nevertheless, the tactic of complicating the reading of "straight" photos was pure Evans, while the stronger remarks have his familiar circumspection about easy consumption. Evans had long grasped that the more neutral a document appears the more dependent it is upon how it is deployed. There can be no definitive place for such pictures. Clearly none of the effect of 'Homes of Americans' survives if the images are removed and re-presented. The gesture is entirely specific to these pages.

Another example of this attention to context is "Labor Anonymous," published in November 1946. On a sidewalk in Detroit, Evans faced a featureless wall to catch people mid-stride. Eleven of his square Rolleiflex images were selected and cropped for a deceptively simple double-spread with text. At first glance it seems to be a serial typology of laborers, perhaps taken surreptitiously as they leave their place of work. That is how these portraits have been posthumously presented in exhibitions and monographs. However, in the spread itself there are many details that contradict this. The photos are not entirely serial and Evans' contact sheets show nearly half the people looking into his camera or at him. One of these is used as the opener. A man in overalls seems to look directly at the lens but the brim of his hat overshadows his eyes, giving the impression he notes the presence of the camera while keeping something of himself hidden. This stalls the ethnographic fantasy of invisibility, of observing and classifying unsuspecting specimens. Placed top left, it helps to suggest the subsequent portraits should not be taken at face value. The final photo shows a man and a woman together as a couple in the same frame, complicating any distinction between labor relations and sexual relations.

The short but crucial text of "Labor Anonymous" makes no reference to the end of a working shift while not all of the subjects wear clothes associated exclusively with labor. The feature is subtitled "On a Saturday Afternoon in downtown Detroit," suggesting this may not be a day of work at all, even if this is one of America's foremost industrial cities. They may be laborers but they are not laboring here. The block of text occupies a space the size of one of the portraits, as if word and image were of a piece, but once read it is clear its purpose is to disrupt. The reader is remind-

---

7 Tucked well away, the credits page reveals the three federal sources for the photos: The National Gallery of Art's Index of American Design, the Library of Congress's archive of the Farm Security Administration photographs, and the Library of Congress's Historic American Building Survey. The photographers were by Russell Lee, John Vachon, Dack Delano, Marion Post Walcott, Peter Sekaer, Arthur Rothstein, Talbot Brewer, Thomas T. Waterman, James M. Slack, Charles E. Petersen, Ezra Stoller, F.S. Lincoln, and Wayne Andrews. A brief editorial on page 2 points out that Evans himself owned prints of many of the images reproduced.

8 Walker Evans and Wilder Hobson, "Homes of Americans." *Fortune Magazine*, April 1946

9 Evans and Hobson, n.p.

10 It was Roland Barthes who coined the term "anchorage" in his essay "Rhetoric of the Image" (1964), reprinted in *Image–Music–Text*, (London: Fontana, 1977), 32–51.

ed there is no classifiable physiognomy on show. People on the street cannot be stereotyped by disposition or dress: "His features tend now toward the peasant and now the patrician. His hat is sometimes a hat, and sometimes he has molded it into a sort of defiant signature."[11] In other words, photographs offer no sure measure and the reader still has all their interpretive work ahead of them. It concludes: "When editorialists lump them as 'labor' these laborers can no doubt laugh that one off." An obvious point but easily forgotten: one cannot 'be' anonymous: one is anonymous *to* or *for* someone else. So the title is somewhat ironic, critical of the assumptions of mainstream editors and readers, including those of *Fortune* itself: the piece appeared in an issue dedicated to "Labor in U.S. Industry." All this complexity in a single spread! It is a rare example of a photographer adopting the convention of the typology only to undermine its authority. Suffice it to say, when the photos are removed from this layout and presented as a suite of innovative street portraits their meaning is doomed not just to "revert to type," but to turn the original intention on its head. Once again Evans' bold pictures were elements in a meditation on meaning. What is a photographic document? How do we read it? Where do its values come from? And how can audiences be invited to think about all this?

PROTO-CONCEPTUALISM AND THE "DOCUMENTARY STYLE"

Evans' reflexive and critical approach to magazine work was unusual and ahead of its time. It would be another two decades at least before this kind of attention to the limits and ideological underpinnings of the photo as document would come into focus in the United States, and only then in the context of Conceptual Art, not in the mass media. [...] "Labor Anonymous" parried the growing trend for voyeuristic portraits while "Homes of Americans" offered housing "in two inadequate descriptive systems," to paraphrase the title of a much-celebrated conceptual piece by Martha Rosier *(The Bowery in Two Inadequate Descriptive Systems, 1974-75).* When the artist Dan Graham produced the still endlessly celebrated conceptual photo-text "Homes for America" in 1966 (in ignorance of Evans' precedent) its appearance as a piece of subversive print journalism was dashed first by his failure to get it published in the mainstream press and then by *Arts* magazine's replacement of his intended images with one by Evans. Graham's piece survives in recent art history because he saw himself as an artist making "Works" for magazines, permitting him to recycle and exhibit his planned layout in the contemporary museum. By contrast, Evans' very sure eye was on the context of publication. Unaware of his concerns and achievements, the Conceptualists of the 1960s and 70s largely rejected Evans, when in fact he had been a significant precursor.

Evans' use of the page gives us another understanding of what he may have meant by his notoriously evasive term "documentary style."[12] The museum tends to take this to mean an Evans image looks like a documentary photograph but is "really" art, either because it is formally more ambitious than documentary demands, or more riskily because in exhibition the documentary claim is suspended in favor of artistic expression or intention. But if we take "documentary" to mean not a type of image but a type of image *use* (involving attention to editing, writing, design and context) then Evans' work for the magazine page was indeed "documentary style" rather than documentary.

---

11 Walker Evans, "Labor Anonymous." *Fortune* (November 1946).

12 "Documentary? That's a very sophisticated and misleading word. And not really clear...The term should be *documentary style*... You see, a document has use, whereas art is really useless. Therefore art is never a document, though it certainly can adopt that style." Walker Evans in Leslie Katz, "Interview with Walker Evans." *Art in America* 59 (March–April 1971), 87.

Nation Horrified by Murder of Kidnapped Chicago Youth in *Jet* Magazine, Vol. XIII, No. 19, September 15, 1955

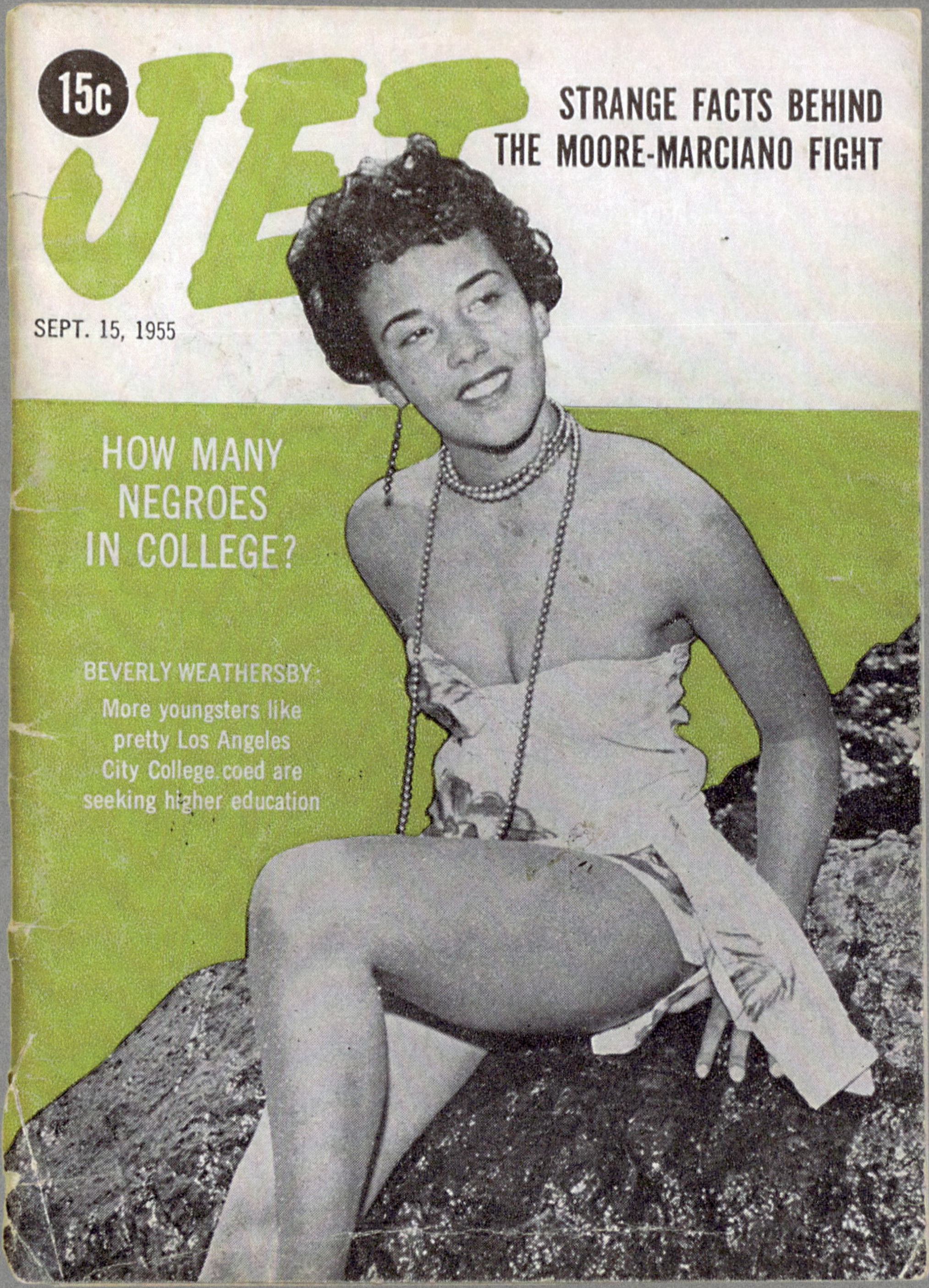

NATION HORRIFIED BY MURDER OF KIDNAPED CHICAGO YOUTH

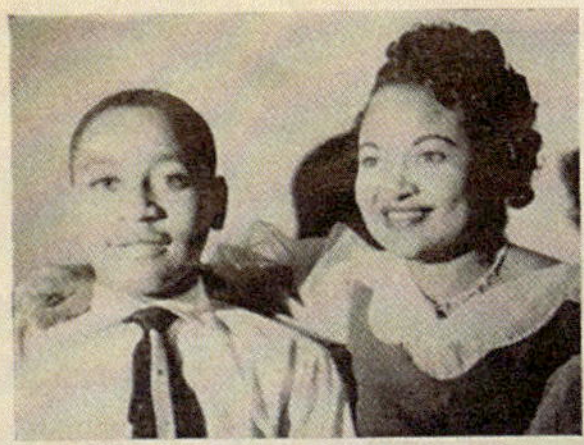

Mrs. Mamie Bradley and slain son, who was slated to enter 8th grade in Chicago this fall. He was her only child.

Aroused by America's first lynching in four years — the kidnaping and murder by three Mississippi white men of chubby, 14-year-old Chicagoan Emmett Louis (Bobo) Till because he whistled at a white woman —leaders of both white and Negro groups demanded "stern and immediate" action against the "barbarians."

NAACP executive secretary Roy Wilkins wired Mississippi Governor Hugh White: "We cannot believe that responsible officials of a state will condone the murdering of children on any provocation." Swamped with hundreds of similar protesting telegrams, Gov. White answered: "Mississippi does not condone such conduct." Calling the Mississippi white people "horrified by the act," white Greenwood newspaper editor Tom Shepherd described the killing as "nauseating" and "way, way beyond the bounds of human decency."

The kidnaping episode came to a stark and shocking end when the youth's nude body, weighted with a 200-pound iron gin mill fan, was discovered by a fisherman in the shallow waters of the Tallahatchie River. The fan was wired around his neck.

Recovering the body, law officers found a "bullet hole one inch above his right ear." The left side of his face was crushed to the bone.

Meanwhile, Leflore County police continued to hold

6

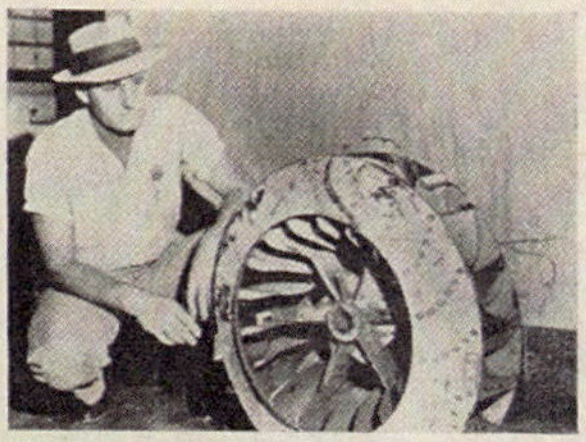

Greenwood Sheriff John Cochran examines 200-pound gin fan that was wired to neck of boy's nude body.

two white men (Grocer Roy Bryant and his half-brother, J. W. Milan) and pushed a search for the other members of the "lynch party," Mrs. Roy Bryant (who was whistled at) and another unidentified man. FBI officials said in Washington that they could not enter the case because it was "a local murder."

Recounting the boy's kidnaping from the home of his grandfather, 64-year-old Rev. Moses Wright, in Money, 17-year-old Wheeler Parker, one of the three Chicago cousins who were visiting in Mississippi, but

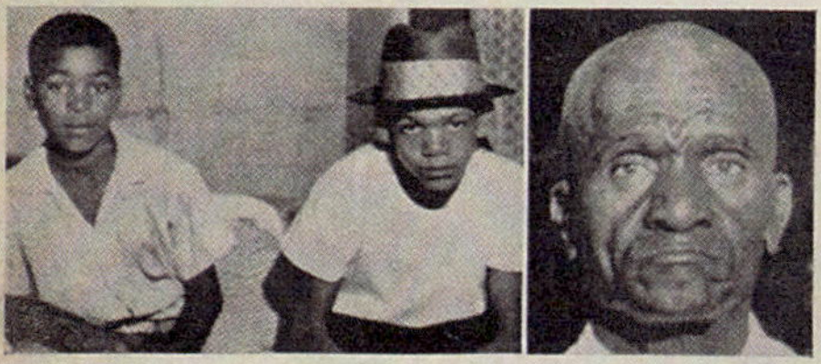

Saddened by boy's murder are cousins, Simeon, 12, and Maurice Wright, 16, (l.) and 64-year-old grandfather Rev. Moses Wright. He was not told about "incident" in town.

7

Boys Never Told Grandfather About 'Incident'

who escaped after the crime, told **JET**:

"When the men came, swearing and all, Grandma tried to awaken Bobo and hide him outside. But the men stormed in and told her to get back in bed and shut up before they beat 'hell' out of her.

"Grandma knew about the 'incident' because we'd told her and not Grandpa, who would have gotten angry at us. We'd gone into town Wednesday and were watching some boys playing checkers in front of the store. Somebody said there was 'a pretty lady' in the store and Bobo said he was going inside to buy some bubble gum.

"After a while, we went in and got Bobo but he stopped in the doorway and whistled at the lady. She got angry and followed us out, then ran toward a car. Some one hollered, 'She's getting a gun' and we ran."

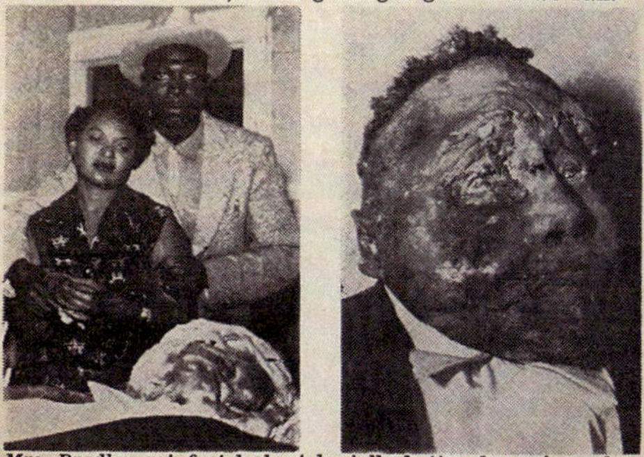

Mrs. Bradley got first look at brutally battered son in undertaker's morgue. More than 600,000, in an unending procession, later viewed body (r.).

8

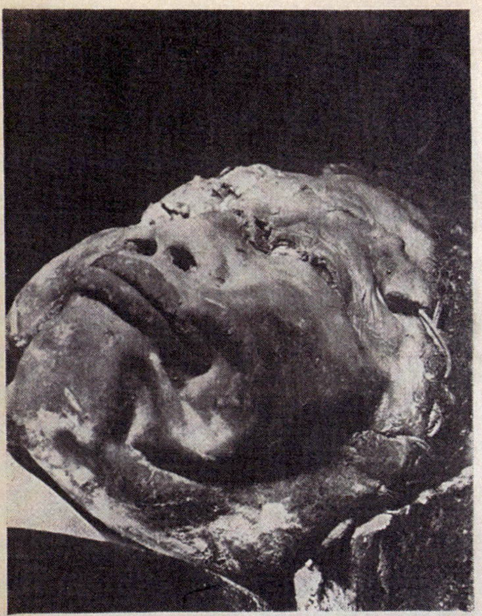

Close-up of lynch victim bares mute evidence of horrible slaying. Chicago undertaker A. A. Raynor said youth had not been castrated as was rumored. Mutilated face of victim was left unretouched by mortician at mother's request. She said she wanted "all the world" to witness the atrocity.

9

Emmett Till Ever After
Darby English
2013

This is a self-portrait of Jason Lazarus:

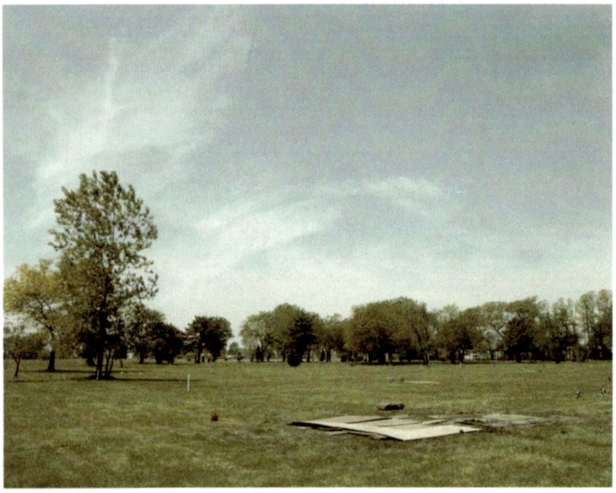

Figure 1. Jason Lazarus, *Standing at the Grave of Emmett Till, The Day of Exhumation*, May 31 2005 (Alsip, IL), 2005.

On the day that he took it, Lazarus had intended to photograph an exhumation at this site, but arrived too late. *Standing at the Grave of Emmett Till, The Day of Exhumation, May 31 2005 (Alsip, IL)* (2005) (Fig. 1) belongs to a series of photographs that Lazarus terms conceptual self-portraits.[1] It remains the most difficult of them all. Clearly the picture has something to show, or say, to us about Emmett Till, who was black. Before surmising what, however, one has to wonder what Lazarus, who is white, means by calling it a self-portrait.[2] The specters of race and power arise thus, almost without notice. We know the terms of their description in advance, for Emmett Till is not merely a paradigmatic figure of antiblack violence but an elemental figure in the pedagogy that teaches us to recognize the intractability of hate—the narrative which fixes black subjects as objects of a loathing white regard. But Lazarus's gesture forces a new perspective on Till as an archetype of the black-white relation, insisting, in its way, that accounts of Emmett Till are always missing something. Specifically, it reminds us that Till's defining experience cannot be thought apart from *the other person*—that is, we cannot separate that experience from the complex, socially-embedded desire that animated the living body of Emmett Till, before it became the property of a cultural narrative upon which that desire, in fact, places an extraordinary burden.

Taking the image seriously means not allowing our dubious gaze upon the "implications" of Lazarus's and Till's painfully obvious racial difference to overtake the determination to understand "What was he thinking?" even with a consciousness of our inability to know. For as soon as we put the question, we recognize at once its startling pertinence to Till's own situation and the degree to which our storytelling conventions all but dictate that it remain unasked. What was he thinking? Directed at Till, the question in fact opens a disconcerting gap between the Emmett Till we need and the Emmett Till who may really have existed. Redirected at Lazarus's photograph, the question suggests "distance" as a good word for the thing quietly seized by both individuals, when they stood apart from the crowd and acted on a desire prohibited by existing social frameworks.

Lazarus figures Till's remoteness from the present situation, by which I mean both the scene viewed and the historical time of its viewing, in several ways. Within the picture, the principal subject is a disturbance

For conversations about the subjects in this essay, I am indebted to Martin Berger, Lauren Berlant, Susan Bielstein, Julia Bryan-Wilson, Katherine Bussard, Kris Cohen, Lisa Dorin, Darcy Grimaldo Grigsby, Sarah Hetherington, Matthew Jesse Jackson, Miwon Kwon, Anna Lee, Carmen Merport, Sarah Miller, Ianna H. Owen, Hamza Walker, and Martha Ward. I am also deeply grateful to Hamza Walker and Suzanne Ghez for inviting me to the symposium at which I first presented this material as a lecture, as well as to Megan Ratner for crucial editorial help with the lecture typescript from which the essay grew. I wrote the piece over a period in which my chief intellectual distractions were Jacqueline Rose, *The Last Resistance* (London: Verso, 2007) and Robert Reid-Pharr, *Once You Go Black: Choice, Agency, and the Black American Intellectual* (New York: NYU, 2007). In addition to inspiration, I take courage from these writers, and the influence of their arguments will be felt in these pages, which in no small way represent an attempt to think (and contribute something to) the shared project of their very divergent texts. This essay is dedicated to my grandmother, the late Loraine DeYampert, who continues to teach me the best lessons of Selma with the example of her life, which began there.

1 Titled *Self-Portrait as An Artist*, the series was initiated by Lazarus in 2004. As of this writing, images may be viewed at the following URL: www.jasonlazarus.com.

2 This essay will be concerned largely with the extra-photographic implications of this claim. I leave it to others to puzzle through the portrait-status of Lazarus's photograph.

at this gravesite, where an overturned headstone confirms a suggestion of the picture's title: Emmett Till is not here, and even his remains are elsewhere.[3] A nearby placard or caption gives Lazarus's own birth year as 1975—fully two decades after Till's murder. More prosaic removal-functions proliferate in the image-space. It seems almost an overstatement to call the muted view a "full-color photograph," so well does it capture the Midwestern landscape at its plainest and most seemingly featureless: just when the dour gray-brown tones of late winter meet the colors of incipient spring, yielding light of a blanched quality that we know from so many faded snapshots of bygone moments and relations. Also, nothing has an edge: the picture is noisy and dilute in a manner unique to digital photographic prints enlarged beyond their source file's clarity constraints. So, it makes good sense to say that, at forty-by-fifty inches, *Standing* monumentalizes a featureless landscape in an image that hesitates, that seems almost a concerted effort to make emptiness. What's more, the photograph is a nest of expanses; already the severe obliquity of the plywood sheets at the gravesite suggests that it's a long way to go simply to access the foreground incident. Which says nothing of that passel of trees, or the sky, both so far along from the point at which Lazarus places us. So: what does *Standing* want? That the photograph itself—big, blown-out, unsharp, eventless—seems to feel so little, only abandons us to our own private replies to this question. For this viewer, these effects, in being so detached from the protocols that usually govern uses of Till's figure, are powerfully contemporizing. This is a picture of now—it renders cultural history in the aftermath of important transformations in the social career of race and the symbolic construction of the difference it makes—and this essay is an attempt to think with the picture about the de-naturalization of specific forms of historical subjectivity.

Standing is a straight portrayal neither of the artist nor of the site of Emmett Till's remains. More immediately, it does not present the familiar image of Till as an inveterate icon of black self-definition in the postwar United States. We expect invocations of Till—every one of which *figures* him—to pay homage, or more precisely, to facilitate payment thereof. They call us to attention as moral subjects. If *Standing* responds to this call, it does so cryptically, incongruously. And this, I want to suggest, is exactly the picture's achievement. By inviting no immediate political or ethical orientation to its subject, *Standing* opens a space for taking up Till's story in new ways.

Let me experiment here with one. In August of 1955, Emmett Till, a fourteen-year-old black boy foreign to the social customs of the American south, traveled from Chicago to Money, Mississippi to stay for a time with relatives. One day, after purchasing a pack of chewing gum, Till made an entreating remark or gesture (accounts differ) to Carolyn Bryant, the pretty white woman working the cash register at the general store she ran with her husband. Over the three days that then passed, one imagines that Till either forgot the encounter, or else remembered it in the way of many fourteen year-old boys. On the fourth day—August 28, 1955 was a Sunday—Bryant's husband, Roy, and his stepbrother, J.W. Milam, lit out in search of Till, successfully abducting him from his uncle's home at around two in the morning. Three days later, Till resurfaced in the Tallahatchie River as a mutilated and swollen corpse. In what have since become landmarks of miscarried justice, the subsequent trials of both men ended in acquittals, an outcome congenial to their attorney's chilling closing argument, which had implored the all-white, all-male jury to "uphold our way of life."[4]

In casting the narrative this way, I have tried to stress the themes of social intimacy, desire, and transgression—themes as conspicuously absent from accounts of Till's story as they are obviously crucial for it. As many readers will know, the version above omits Till's public display, during a four-day wake in a Chicago church, as well as in the photographs of Till's maimed and distorted face that were beamed all over the world with reports of the crime. My version also foregoes mention of the visionary civil rights leaders who had persuaded Till's mother, Mamie Till, to mobilize her loss in these ways. I deëmphasize these factors exactly because they are the favored ones in narratives of Till's late life and death that stress righteousness and retribution (few fail to do so), narratives that cast these strongly determining details—not to mention the postures of righteousness and retribution themselves—as though they are necessary accompaniments to truth. While defensible, such rhetoric and its attendant affects block our view of another truth: that of *Emmett Till's desire*, long the object of an omission that doesn't simplify Till's story so much as it neutralizes the solemn challenge his desire poses to the very scripts which instrumentalize Till.

If *Standing* suggests a way through or around that blockage, it does so partly by raising the question of interracial intimacy—as a structural feature of the small but resolutely real world that Emmett Till knew best, and as a salutary property of the non-erotic sociality

3 On June 1, 2005, Till's remains had been removed temporarily to the Office of the Cook County Coroner, where the first-ever autopsy was being performed to determine Till's cause of death, following an order issued by the United States Justice Department after new witnesses had surfaced.

4 John Whitten, a member of the Bryan-Milam defense team, as quoted in *The Greenwood Commonwealth*, Sept. 23, 1955. Reprinted in Christopher Metress, ed., *The Lynching of Emmett Till: A Documentary Narrative* (Charlottesville and London: University of Virginia Press, 2002), 100.

engendered whenever we grant others their rightful place in the formation of our self-concepts. This is something to be distinguished from recognition, which is more passive than what I mean, and from "seeking connection," which is more intentional, as well as from "transcending" or "reaching across" difference, which has a political-performative thrust utterly inappropriate to the condition this picture evokes. It seems most fitting to call it what happens when we *find* ourselves over the line—acceptance of which means taking seriously that, in certain circumstances, one is *already in connection* with another before differences and their consequences enter the picture, as it were. Here, the crucial movement is not so much across difference as in spite of it, because the ease of the movement itself, the pronounced absence of drama, compels recognition of difference's predominantly theoretical character. I should say that while my sense of this intimacy between Lazarus and his subject arose before the picture (and that I realize it may be hard merely to think one's way into), on one level it's simply a matter of being reminded that no "I" can form in isolation, that a subject's singularity *enfolds* differences. Before *Standing*, one may find that it is Till and Lazarus, together, who co-figure the strange human presence established by the image, despite their divergent historical and cultural positions and mutual absences to one another. The effecting of this presence is the closest thing to an event that *Standing* has to offer: here the oft-asserted notion of the aggregative self is functionally, if provisionally, materialized as the subject of representation. At least this curious effect has transfixed me over several viewings, holding me, in part, by its sheer optimism—a mood that considerations of Till usually proscribe. *Standing*, or the thinking it encourages, refuses to pathologize interracial intimacy, and rejects the viewpoint, shared by black and nonblack Americans alike, that interracial intimacy can *only* arise from or produce an amplification of difference, that its erotic extensions can only be reckoned by reference to distorting fantasies which are the eternal preserve of static power imbalances. For fifty-eight years, accounts of Till's destruction have occupied a privileged position in American renderings of this substantially phobic and dehumanizing pessimism. Indeed a main social function of telling Till's story, a tale more often displayed than articulated, has been to make visible a kind of unassailable truth about the "black-white relation" (it's hard to imagine a less dynamic formulation). Such accounts favor horror because it is so effective: from "feeling people" it can only solicit assent to the supposition that an intractable racial alienation lay at the heart of the American social order. To see it differently, I am everywhere told, is tantamount to self-deception of the sort that gets people killed. Yet the instituted narratives also foreclose any exploration of the psychic dimension of this most salient instant in the scant recorded history of cross-racial contact. And in doing so, these narratives actually extend the very alienation they would innocently document.

Lazarus's picture recommends a specific question: How might we imagine interracial intimacy apart from violence? It's a hard question to take up in the mournful air surrounding the subject. Surely this is no obstacle to our taking it seriously, though. How to imagine interracial intimacy apart from violence? Which, perhaps, is also to ask how we might involve less violence in our thinking about weak and strong variants of interracial intimacy alike, and detach from the certainty that it can only thrive in extraordinary circumstances, and begin to address ourselves empathetically to the thought-structures that resist it. Empathy towards Till's likely mind frame strikes one as an immoderate stance precisely because the view urged on us sees Till more or less exclusively through the violence perpetrated against him. Such a view takes that violence to be elemental—as if all the antiblack sentiment in historical Southern life ways was gathered up in the acts that ended Till's short life. I am interested in how Till's domestication by this standpoint all but disqualifies us asking "What was he thinking?" without knowing the answer in advance. Why does attempting to excavate Till's social optimism necessarily "miss the point"? Eventually we will have to face down the policing function of the point itself—under its gaze, one seems left with two options: either grasp the unique power with which the events reveal, and the pictures substantiate, what everybody already knows about race in America, or else ask one's questions in private. By preventing us reckoning with Till's desire—so out-of-synch with the oppositional structure his murder brought vividly to light—such proscriptions may further the aims of segregation as effectively as countless other, more nakedly tactical means.

Here is another photograph:

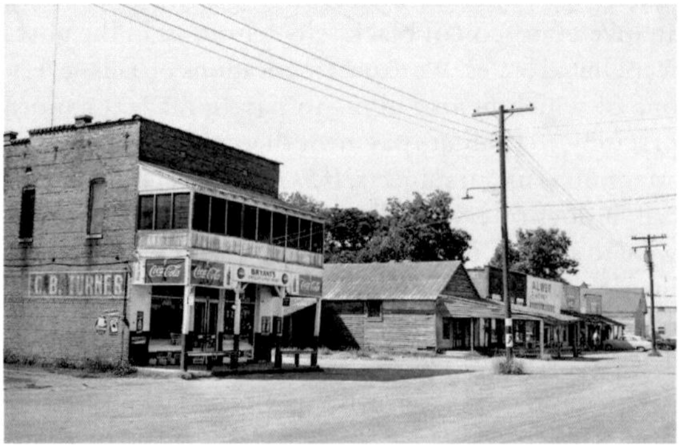

Figure 2. Bryant's Grocery, Money, Mississippi, 1950s.

What if this file photo of Bryant's Grocery (Fig. 2) was as notorious as those of Emmett Till's maimed and bloated body? It's an implausible suggestion: the image reveals nothing, though it pictures a pivotal site in the narrative of Till's life. But this forensically ambiguous, oblique view is too aniconic to facilitate the work of racial ideology. The imagination has too much room in which to wander: projections settle in a bit too cozily on that porch there, speculations that risk muddying the crystalline clarity of the social truths that pictures of Till help us to communicate unequivocally. Iconic images of Till function as they do partly because they allow almost no private interpretation. But the event linked to this image, portraying the physical site where Emmett Till's desire briefly assumed a contested social form, opens our picture of Till to radical reconfiguration. In the left middle ground of the photograph above is the storefront patio where, on August 24, 1955, Till joined a gaggle of children to enjoy the shade after a long, hot afternoon of chores and play. After boasting to the disbelief of his cohort about the easy relations he enjoyed with white girls back home, Till stepped inside to prove it. His relatively cosmopolitan experiences in lower-middle-class Chicago had probably prepared Till to expect to amuse, or at worst to annoy Carolyn Bryant. In any case, nothing in the record goes against the suggestion that when Till made his appeal to Bryant, he was engaged in a frivolous game of dare that he believed he couldn't lose.

Till's experience on the porch that day reminds us that well-documented efforts to inhibit cross-racial desire existed side-by-side with equally intense efforts to demonstrate how flimsy normative, racialized notions of desire in fact are, especially in the face of libido. The coexistence of, and tension between, these efforts were central to Till's experience. But they have never been part of his story. Media events surrounding the exhumation of Till's body in 2005, after the Justice Department reopened the case when new witnesses surfaced, manifested the difficulty of altering in any way how we tell this story. Internationally rebroadcast reports of Bryant and Milam's sham trial offered powerful evidence that horror, and only horror, continues to animate assessments of Till's place in our historical signifying imaginary. And correspondingly that we continue to forego the challenge of fathoming Till's agency.[5] Yet none of these rehearsals was exactly necessary: uses of the original pictures continue to reproduce this unreflective stance towards the meaning of Till's life.

Deeply disquieting and justifiably notorious, the pictures show the price that Till paid for failing to note his changed coordinates. They may well never stop inducing moral indignation. But however much our culture and circumstances may implore us, we are not obliged to respond to them in this way. Our distance alone from the conditions of their production, as well as our alertness to the proliferation of interracial intimacies in the interval, unavoidably affect how these images mean and what they convey. It's past time to start considering what other relations are possible with these images and the knowledge-effects they engender; to regard them with due respect and due criticism; to assess frankly what they can and cannot tell us about race in America; to seek actively some freedom from the pessimisms they bolster. Re-humanizing Emmett Till—through an acknowledgment of his agency, for example, and against the conviction that he must have taken leave of his senses—will be key to this process. The images originally illustrated the worst consequences of crossing a boundary, both imagined and altogether real; for many viewers, they actualized that boundary as an impassable barricade. Yet Till's killers' astounding overcompensation—perhaps best exemplified by their attempt to sink Till's body in the Tallahatchie River by tethering it to a cotton-gin fan with barbed wire—points us well beyond a reading constrained by polarities like hatred versus innocence or insult versus vengeance. It proclaims the intensity of their desperation in the face of the world-historical force that Till's desire made manifest. Those men knew they couldn't destroy the desire on which Till acted—a desire that we can surely say was not to possess Carolyn Bryant sexually, but freely to regard her with crude affection. The defense attorney's closing statement, too, betrays the fear that without strict policing, black and white individuals would, predictably, choose each other—and that this fear existed on a civic, not just a private scale.[6] On the part of such self-appointed custodians of segregated lifeways, there was an implicit duty both to thwart single instances of such choice and to militate against their proliferation. Intervening developments show that those men were right to be afraid: over the last fifty-eight years, we have inherited, by steadily co-creating, the very world they believed they could postpone by destroying Emmett Till. Today, a weakening collective investment in its necessity endangers the notional viability of the color line, which is less and less obviously a characteristic topographical feature of generalized American experience than a legacy

5 In a meticulous and persuasive argument with different emphases than mine, Martin Berger has recognized that the proliferation of images of Emmett Till at the time of his murder amounted to something other than a *representation* of the subject who went by that name. See his *Seeing through Race: A Reinterpretation of Civil Rights Photography* (Berkeley: University of California Press, 2011), 125. Many thanks to Berger for sharing advance proofs of his study with me.

6 This formulation interpolates Reid-Pharr, 22. Already in the aftermath of Till's murder, Hannah Arendt had considered the same developments around interracial sociability in her "Reflections on Little Rock," *Dissent* (Winter 1959), 47-58.

of the segregationist imagination, or anyway a radically imprecise way of understanding race's contemporary sociality—or, the ways we actually live race.

No exclusively victimological outlook on Till—the only one available within prevalent conceptions of black suffering—can recognize the consequential historical action encompassed by the store patio scene. So let me make it very clear: when Emmett Till took leave of three of his cousins to enter Bryant's Store and make an acquaintance, *the normative order that his action opposed was not white, but black*. Till's redress wasn't to racism per se, but to what he appeared to understand—in 1955—as misguided thinking about race's role in the practice of the imagination. As much as saying so might undermine his standing as an unwitting catalyst of the Civil Rights Movement, Till's struggle in that moment was against those constraints that the existing racial order had imposed on the social imagination, or more precisely, on individuals' disposition towards the instincts and their suggestions, and thereby towards one another. Till's action insinuated a different kind of 'movement,' now from the static space of the community to the fraught, distinctly pleasurable zone of interracial contact.[7] By all evidence, Till understood that the most rigid forms of identity are unsettled when subjects occupy the stage of political life in ways that the surrounding culture neither predicts nor approves. By all evidence, Till gave a performance of self based on a sense of freedom wholly incongruous with his circumstances; he presumed the freedom actively to correct his cohort's conditioned incredulity, to refuse compliance and chose his own path. Till's bravado suggests that he regarded this incongruity as a source of value, or anyway that in the elsewhere that he knew best, it was already a way of life, a possible mode of existence. To him, the claim to agency was something his cousins simply needed to see first hand. Such a sight, he appears to have felt assured, would tell of the inevitability of contact and connection, and of the desire, even the need, in certain circumstances, to cross the very boundaries upon which everything seems to depend.

What happened next, of course, is what makes this argument so very difficult to make. Yet, in resolving all that transpired to what happened next, do we not deny some measure of the complex humanity that Till exhibited in life? Do we not cancel his daring insight into the fragility of normative desire, into the ways the unexamined consciousness of limitations, in turn, limits thinking about, indeed endangers the life-conditions of, countless really existing intimacies? Without denying the horror of Till's end, does not the practice of representing Till strictly in accordance with his so-called "fate" actually inhibit our contact with the optimism that asymmetrically preceded it? One wants to insist on a distinction between Emmett Till and the blinkered thinking that sustains his memory. We need a language for Emmett Till's desire.

Both Lazarus's contemporary art photograph and the comparably anonymous historical document can be said to place a void where an icon should be. Both ask us to take seriously the kind of cultural knowledge it may be possible to produce in that zone. I don't think it's necessary to assume that such knowledge denigrates Till. Both photographs, with the very spaciousness that *weakens* their bonds to the Emmett Till that we know, affiliate him more closely with the opening he may have been trying, on some level, to effect when he strode into that store. If the anonymous, documentary file photo offers an aid in coming to terms with Lazarus's, then it is by prompting reflection on what it was that prevented the former having any iconicity at all.[8] It may "go without saying" that the same operations have discouraged us from scrutinizing connections between what transpired on the storefront porch, among Till and his cohort, and what transpired in the store and after,[9] or that they make it hard publicly to pursue the question "What was he thinking?" to any fresh conclusions. But the longstanding avoidance of such questions is not something about which we can afford to remain silent. Lazarus's picture—because it locates Till in a properly complex, multiracial mise-en-scène, recasting his story around a palpable obscurity about its meanings—makes an issue of that silence. In this way, Lazarus's picture demands an orientation to Till that is willing to take the porch view seriously–because, really and conceptually, these scenes contain the kind of space needed to finally extend Till's historical subjectivity beyond the flat immediacy of iconic victimhood.

At the Renaissance Society's installation of *Black Is, Black Ain't*, Lazarus's photograph shared a spacious, quiet corner with one other artwork, Demetrius Oliver's *Till* (2007) (Fig. 3).

7 It bears further exploration, the specific relationship of individual impulses to historical portrayals of the emotional life of black Americans living under racist conditions, and the more specific tendency of freedom-oriented discourses to stipulate a limited relationship to pleasure on the individual's behalf, or even to deny desire altogether. For an apposite treatment of the subject of "Egoism and Freedom Movements: On the Anthropology of the Bourgeois Era," see Max Horkheimer, *Between Philosophy and Social Science: Selected Early Writings*, trans. G. Frederick Hunter, Matthew S. Kramer, and John Torpey (Cambridge, Mass.: MIT Press, 1993), 49–110.G. Frederick Hunter, Matthew S. Kramer, and John Torpey (Cambridge, Mass.: MIT Press, 1993), 49-110.

8 Berger offers a badly needed reassessment of the political project aided by the most iconic documentary images of civil rights-era protest, observing that, "to the degree that narratives illustrating white power over blacks helped make the images nonthreatening to whites, the photographs impeded efforts to enact—or even imagine—reforms that threatened white power." No less can be said of such narratives when they originated in black defenses against racist violence. See Berger, *Seeing through Race*, 7.

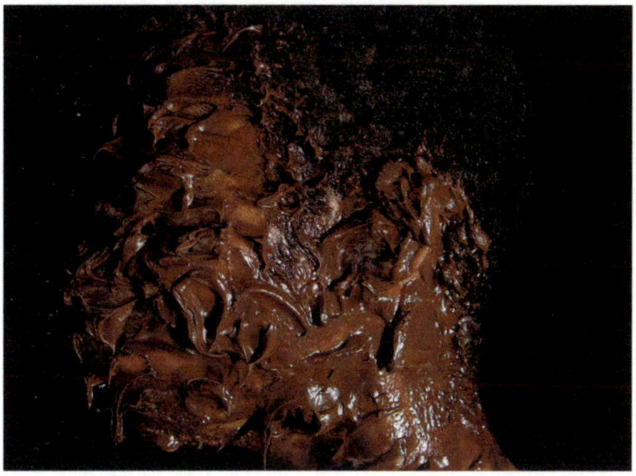

Figure 3. Demetrius Oliver, *Till*, 2004.

In much of his conceptual photographic practice, Oliver (b. 1975) presents himself in various states of alteration or distortion. *Till* was the first piece to earn him wide recognition. Glossy and glazed with non-reflective glass, the 27¼ by 36¼-inch photograph is an outsized profile view of the artist bathed in chocolate. Oliver has spread rich brown icing over his face, ear, and neck, adroitly working it up and spreading it to suggest a kind of mutilation that erases a victim's facial identity but preserves evidence of his race. (The artist's brown skin and tiny coils of black hair link him to his subject, though it is not immaterial that Oliver's photograph, which combines a forensic aspect with an artistic character, suggests a view of Till that the public never had.) Along Oliver's profile line, the chocolate forms stiff peaks, and presumably the gobbets in his hair tell of the sprays of detached flesh thrown up during a battering. But *Till* has less to do with violence than with consumption. By using chocolate, Oliver complicates an easy idea about contemporary subjects' prosaic, uncritical ingestion of images and commodities, and does so by invoking procedures relating to the ways we assimilate and reproduce forms of social discourse (here, consumption and imitation and the chain of repetition they instantiate). In this way, *Till* pertains to a historical practice central to racial formations in the United States, one in which we're all caught up.

Oliver's picture reminds us that one isn't hardwired to remember Emmett Till: the culture first has to offer him up as a component of personal history, instruct us in its proper care, understanding, and explanation—all in terms of an elemental "connection" that contributes to the self something needful, something like historical density. The expectation is that one *learns* from stories such as Till's and the images animating them. One learns how race matters, has mattered, and could well matter for us. The structures which mobilize this moral pedagogy appreciate the special value of Till's story: learning how to be black (or nonblack) is never as simple as knowing who and what we are, but also how we mean to those from whom we differ—and where and when those differences matter most: namely, when we're not among our own. When most of the people in an entire hemisphere administer, accept, and repeat such lessons for more than half a century, certain protocols of sentiment become naturalized. Surely the conventions pertaining to Till's display are consummate expressions of this process.

Oliver's picture seems dutifully to observe these protocols, while also revealing a paradox: the practice of racial collectivity collapses the irreducible differences separating persons (and periods) from one another, and what Oliver's picture suggests most strongly is his and Till's representational elision. On this model, race binds not only individuals but distinct historical temporalities, as well. In this way, *Till*, the photograph, capitalizes on the considerable reach of identification—how effortlessly it spans even an entire social epoch—to equate photographer and thematic subject, or at least to render perfunctory their manifold differences. Suggesting the way in which a conception of Emmett Till devoid of agency remains, for many, a kind of freely appropriated cultural property, the resulting image admits of nothing that might be lost in the translation between the pedagogy I characterized above and the racial subjects it aims to produce. Oliver's "enfleshment" of cake frosting—like the lurid tones, stark ground, and tight focus—exploits the power of color portrait photography to make its subject uniquely present, paradigmatic, unsingular. To be sure, by this and other formal means— such as scaling, and making evident the digital nature of the source image by tolerating a remarkable degree of pixelation even in the exhibition print—Oliver succeeds at contemporizing

9 According to William Bradford Huie, a southern journalist who interviewed Milam after the trial and reportedly paid for the right to publish Milam and Bryant's story, the two did not set out to murder Till, but rather were incited to do so upon hearing more of Till's confident boasts on the subject of interracial intimacy. In light of his clearly sensationalistic aspirations (see also William Bradford Huie, "The Shocking Story of the Approved Killing in Mississippi," *Look* (January 24, 1956), 48), one hardly knows what to make of Huie's account that "They did not intend to kill him when they went and got him. They killed him because he boasted of having a white girl and showed them the pictures of a white girl from Chicago. They had him in the car trying to scare him and that sort of thing for about three hours. Young Till, he never realized the danger he was in, he never knew. I'm quite sure that he never thought these two men would kill him. Maybe he's in such a strange environment he really doesn't know what he's up against. It seems to a rational mind today, it seems impossible that they could have killed him. But J. W. Milam looked up at me and said, 'Well, when he told me about this white girl he had,' he says, 'my friend, that's what this war's about down here now. That's what we got to fight to protect.' And he says, 'I just looked at him and I said, "Boy, you ain't never going to see the sun come up again."'" Henry Hampton and Steve Fayer with Sarah Flynn, eds., *Voices of Freedom: An Oral History of the Civil Rights Movement from the 1950s through the 1980s* (New York: Bantam, 1991), 13-14. . Thanks to Ianna H. Owen for directing me to the collection in which this text appears.

Till—but only as a transmission across the closed channels of a monumental history committed, above all else, to maintaining certain past events in a perpetual presence. Such an effort at presentification aligns with the unsettling tendency of much supposedly progressive historical practice to overwhelm (or simply to ignore) historical change by perpetually refurbishing past models. This all the more so when we consider the various immediacy-effects at work in Oliver's picture alongside the paradoxical manifestations of distance and absence in Lazarus's. Like *Standing*, *Till* is proffered as a self-portrait via Emmett Till, and I do not deny its effectiveness as an instance of invested historical inquiry. Rather, I question the self-consciousness and the rigor of that inquiry. Till mediates Oliver's self-image as a creepy, near-tangible presence-effect rather than a complex absence. Like Lazarus's, this portrait acknowledges Till's role in Oliver's self-concept, perhaps especially as a black photographer for whom the body has been an overriding problematic. But for Oliver, Till's meaning is more determining than open-ended, more moralizing than questing. The Emmett Till who secures the coherency of Oliver's identity statement, who lends it historical density, is nothing more or less than an iconic object of historical violence. Yet he is more present to the viewer than the manifest subject of the photograph: Oliver himself. In this way, *Till* reveals less about the (likely very complicated) conditions of its production—surely more intricate than my brief comment suggests—than about the puzzling durability, and the attraction for some, of supposedly critical practices which merely restage the ethnographic capture of race at its most dehumanizing.[10]

Of all the cautionary tales our culture has to tell about crossing the color line—and particularly about interracial intimacy—Emmett Till's is the most chilling. When I first heard it, as a schoolboy in the nineteen-eighties, I thought it belonged more to ancient history than to an origin narrative I was meant to take as partly my own. In many texts, Till's is also the plangent tale upon which the longer one of the Civil Rights Movement develops. After all, who can be unaffected by the resonant coincidence that Rosa Parks's arrested occurred exactly one hundred days after Till's murder? These stories both compelled and made vastly more resonant the actions that precipitated many specific freedoms now practically naturalized. These stories tell us who and what we are, to ourselves and to each other. Their responsible dissemination permits no substantive modification of their terms. If, just as surely, one hesitates in mixed company to confess disenchantment with them, this may be so because they communicate far more than information. By also allowing us to repeat what everybody already knows about race, sex and power in America—as though to continually rediscover difference—these narratives shore up moral authority (and the political attitudes proper to it) by discouraging or actively discrediting identitarian ambivalence of any kind, suppressing any instinct that might destabilize the self-possessed coherence of a hard-won identity position.

Standing abruptly short-circuits this cycle of representations. Its historical orientation is insistently contemporary, its implications many and varied, and I have only touched on a few. Most important among these for me is the unforced optimism with which the picture not only broaches the question of others' inescapable involvement in our conceptions of self, but reestablishes the question's connection with a leading icon of the principle of black self-determination. Lazarus's photograph also extends the life of a question consigned in 2005 to the transience of a news cycle: why Till, why now? To puzzle the photograph—the image as well as the act its title names—is to experience a seismic shift in emphasis, from a knowable object of reckoning to the inexact practice of reckoning itself. In this way, *Standing* affirms the necessity and salutary difficulty of historical representations enriched with the psychic dimensionality of individuals' *relations* to historical forms. It enlarges our view of the ways in which these historical formations of race regulate protocols of imagination, representation, and desire, *now*—even as real practices of interaction and micro-historical actualities they encompass continually reshape these formations. More, this historical orientation is insistently contemporary, especially to the extent that *Standing* raises a question crucial to any really responsible evaluation of our present relationship to historical formations of race: how to imagine interracial intimacy apart from violence?

I realize that I am interpellating Emmett Till and Jason Lazarus to a very peculiar conception of interracial intimacy. This not-necessarily-erotic social intimacy is already prevalent in countless cosmopolitan centers. Like Lazarus's picture, it is aniconic, and because of this—because it extends so far beyond "black men who get with white women" and other such explicit affinities—it often goes unnoticed. But it is transfiguring the archetypal social ecologies of the west. Under empathetic consideration, it can reveal what it

10 Surely the foregoing critique is anything but the only way to think about Oliver's photograph, or more precisely, to think *with* Oliver as the creator of this self-portrait about the naturalization of specific forms of historical subjectivity. Rather it is the clearest way that emerged for me to do so in light of the picture's situation in the Chicago installation of the present exhibition. A more complete study could further implications of Oliver's use of chocolate, a substance principally identified with pleasure-effects, by way of which the may intervene into the dynamics of photographic horror, given the tendency of a certain strain of documentary photography involving the depiction of dead bodies to seek ever more acute, that is seemingly immediate, horror-effects. Thanks to Sarah Miller for initiating an extremely productive discussion of this matter.

means—and has meant—to live in a more autonomous way as regards inherited social habits, cultural forms, and political meanings. It may also free us up to rethink our avatars of separation in terms of the connections, affinities, and alliances we must disavow in order to establish such models (the late Malcolm X was movingly eloquent on this point). Emmett Till's primary historical function, of course, has been as such an avatar of separation. *Standing* says both that our representations of Till need not necessarily perpetuate that function, and that photographic references to Till certainly don't need to enact it. In *Standing*, Till assumes a different kind of presence: as the subject of a photographer implicating himself in a history to which many will feel he has no right, or has, at best, the wrong kind of right. But we possess the equipment to view this incongruity differently, comfortably—as a source of value. After all, there isn't an American alive with an unproblematic claim to Emmett Till's legacy; historical subjectivity and subjective existence are inescapably asymmetrical formations.

The question of Lazarus's desire finds itself in a fragile accord with that of Till's. The two depart from customary ways of wanting, and both claim a body that isn't fated to inhabit the given arrangements of desire and affinity. By opening an interval of reflection on the terms governing our attachments to Till, the picture figures an epistemological rupture—a rupture that unburies Till's desire *and* the framework of the freedom upon which Till chose to act. Because *Standing* poses these questions and leaves them open, it encourages more deliberate thought about the very exigencies that Till's story tempts us to settle once and for all. The picture tells a truth about Emmett Till that we need a moment, perhaps several, to register. There's work in those moments, and that work matters.[11] *Standing at the Grave of Emmett Till, Day of Exhumation, May 31 2005 (Alsip, IL)* makes as compelling an argument as I know for the necessity of the strained identifications we try to make, beyond our own lived experiences. Lazarus's strain could never match Emmett Till's in its poignancy, but in its optimism it comes awfully close.

11 The sense of *work* I intend here assumes a delightful shape in this formulation by Michel Foucault: "That which is susceptible of introducing a significant difference in the field of knowledge, at the cost of a certain difficulty for the author and the reader, with, however, the eventual recompense of a certain pleasure, that is to say, of access to another figure of truth." "Des Travaux," in *Dits et Écrits* (Paris: Editions Gallimard, 1994), vol. IV, 367.

The Restraints: Open and Hidden in *LIFE* Magazine, September 24, 1956

Gordon Parks

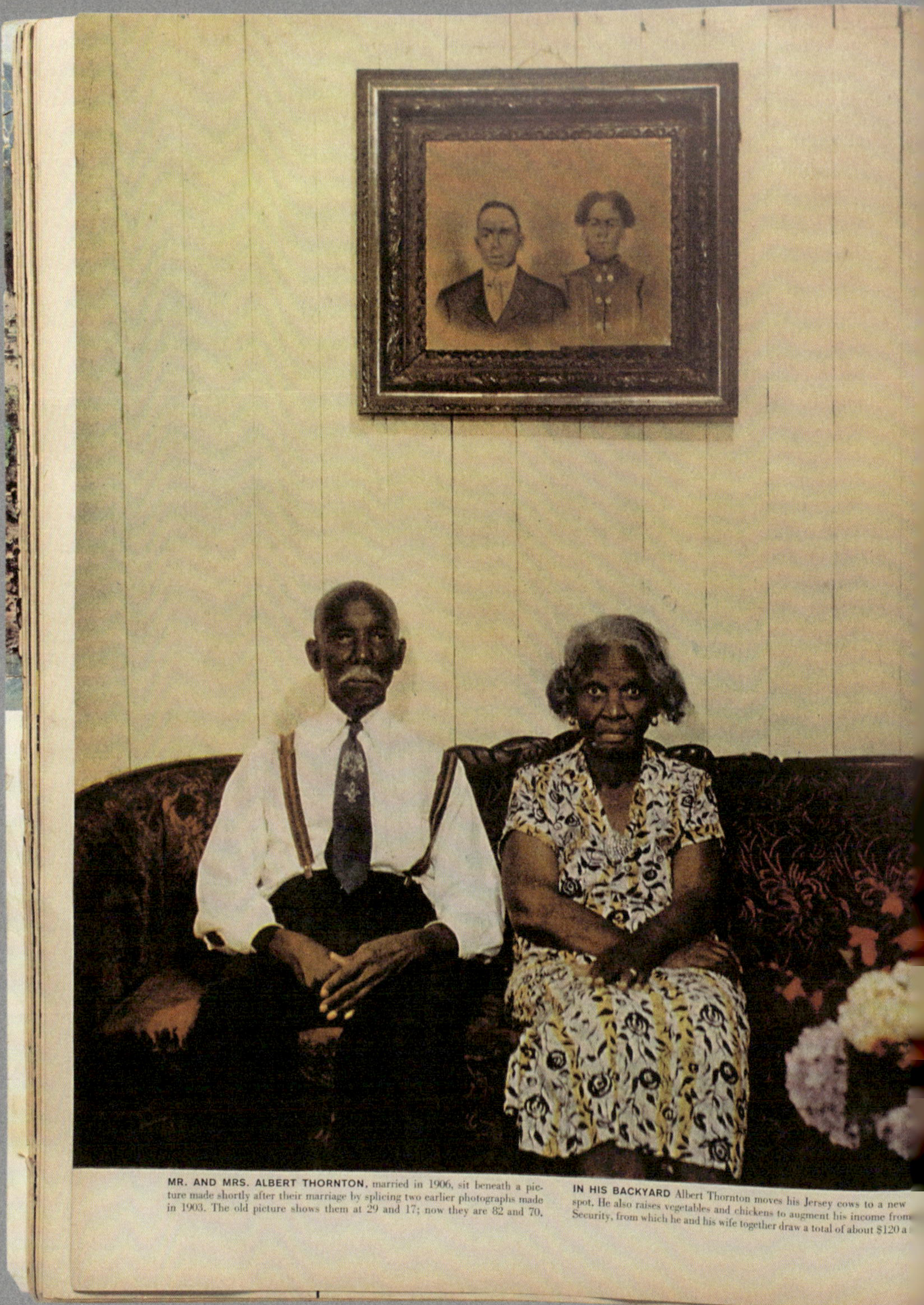

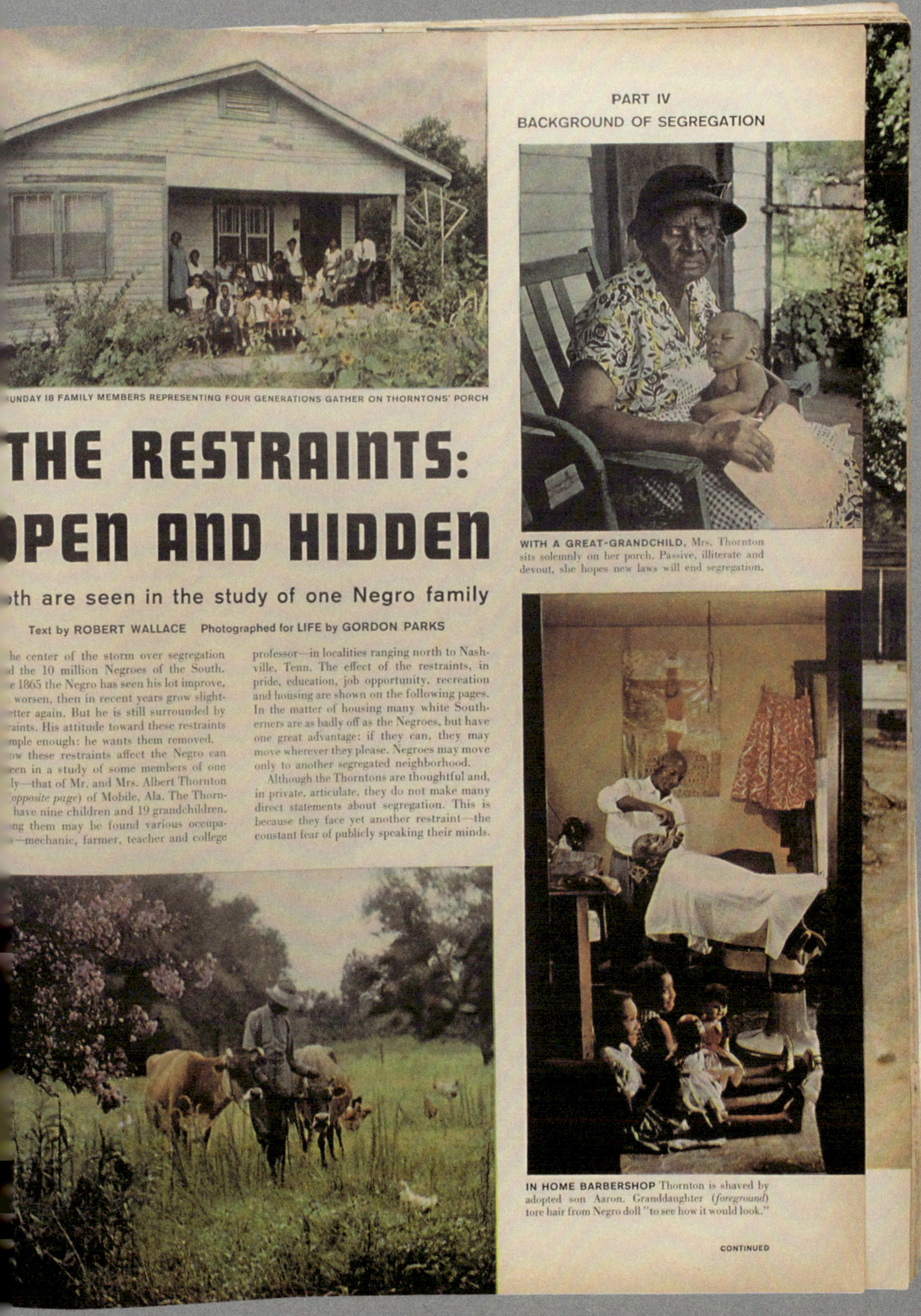

UNDAY 18 FAMILY MEMBERS REPRESENTING FOUR GENERATIONS GATHER ON THORNTONS' PORCH

THE RESTRAINTS: PEN AND HIDDEN

th are seen in the study of one Negro family

Text by ROBERT WALLACE Photographed for LIFE by GORDON PARKS

he center of the storm over segregation
d the 10 million Negroes of the South.
e 1865 the Negro has seen his lot improve,
worsen, then in recent years grow slight-
etter again. But he is still surrounded by
aints. His attitude toward these restraints
mple enough: he wants them removed.
ow these restraints affect the Negro can
een in a study of some members of one
ly—that of Mr. and Mrs. Albert Thornton
opposite page) of Mobile, Ala. The Thorn-
have nine children and 19 grandchildren.
ng them may be found various occupa-
—mechanic, farmer, teacher and college

professor—in localities ranging north to Nashville, Tenn. The effect of the restraints, in pride, education, job opportunity, recreation and housing are shown on the following pages. In the matter of housing many white Southerners are as badly off as the Negroes, but have one great advantage: if they can, they may move wherever they please. Negroes may move only to another segregated neighborhood.

Although the Thorntons are thoughtful and, in private, articulate, they do not make many direct statements about segregation. This is because they face yet another restraint—the constant fear of publicly speaking their minds.

PART IV
BACKGROUND OF SEGREGATION

WITH A GREAT-GRANDCHILD, Mrs. Thornton sits solemnly on her porch. Passive, illiterate and devout, she hopes new laws will end segregation.

IN HOME BARBERSHOP Thornton is shaved by adopted son Aaron. Granddaughter (*foreground*) tore hair from Negro doll "to see how it would look."

CONTINUED

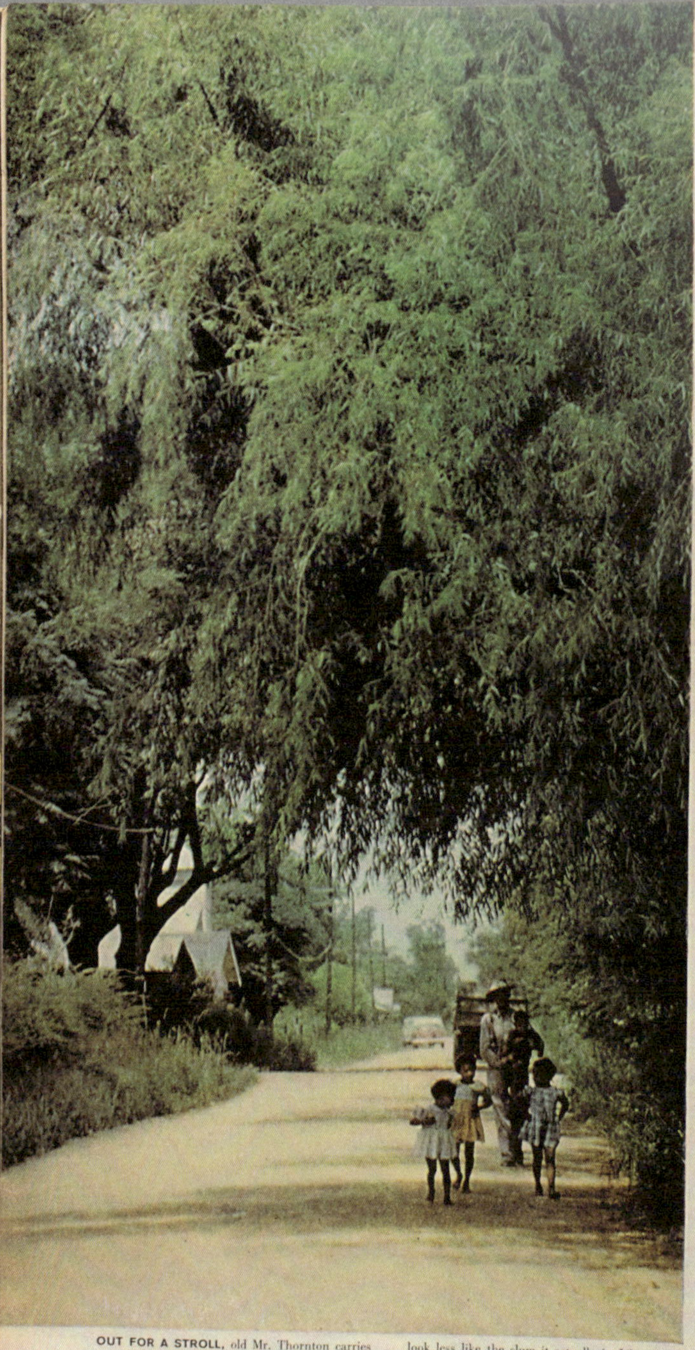

OUT FOR A STROLL, old Mr. Thornton carries one child while others walk on ahead. The handsome, permanent greenery makes the neighborhood look less like the slum it actually is. Like all but one road in town, this is not paved; after a hard rain it is a quagmire underfoot, impassable by car.

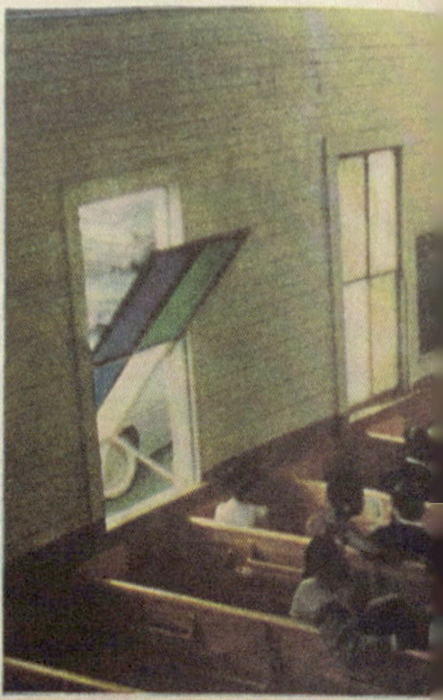

BAPTIST CHURCH HAS SERVICES EVERY OTHER

AN AGED MAN'S

Albert Thornton Sr., at 82, looks back on a life of tremendous toil. The son of a slave, he was a sharecropper and small independent farmer throughout most of his working life, but produced a remarkable family. He has seen four of his children go through college, and has had the satisfaction of seeing all of them become teachers. His other satisfactions, however, have been small. When he takes his grandchildren for a walk through the neighborhood, he sees the status of the Negro little better than it was when he was a child himself. In some regards it is worse. He can

AT SEGREGATED DRINKING FOUNTAIN, A LITTLE

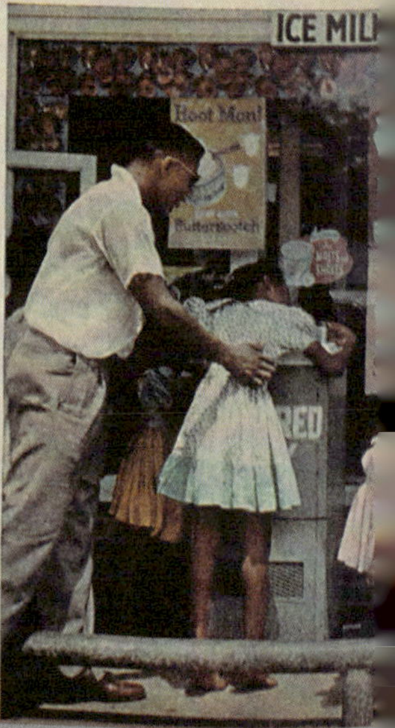

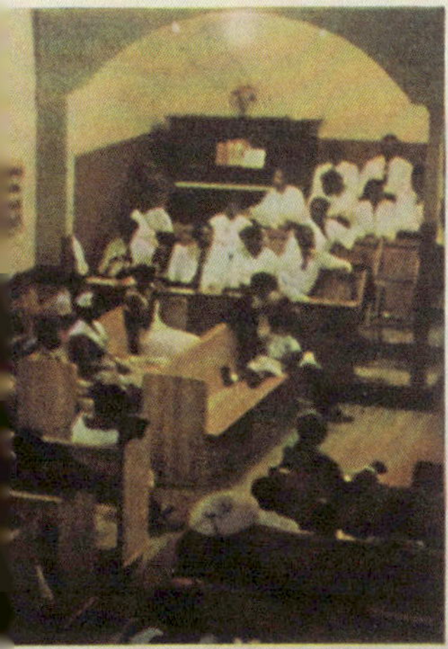

SUNDAY, IS THE PRIDE OF NEGRO COMMUNITY

SMALL REWARD

remember, in the days before Jim Crow, when there were no "white" and "Negro" signs on public facilities.

He has no violence in him. He hopes for the end of segregation—although not for the sort of end that was recently proffered him. While his family was in church (*above*), a white salesman of cemetery lots got into the pulpit. The congregation, he said, could end segregation for itself in the hereafter. He was here to sell them plots in "the only unsegregated institution in the South." Some parishioners bought plots. Mr. Thornton did not.

GIRL GETS SOME HELP FROM A PASSING ADULT

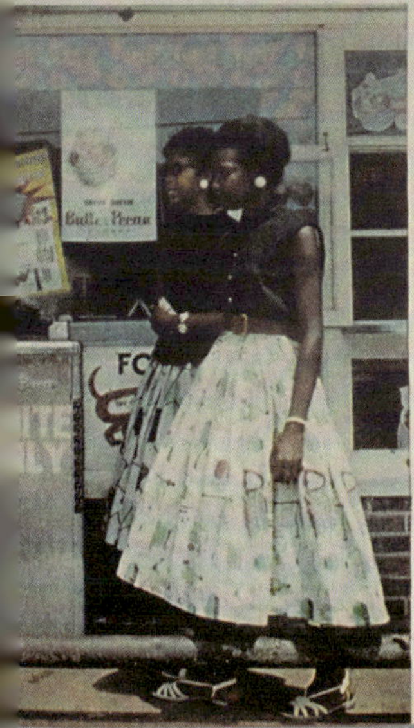

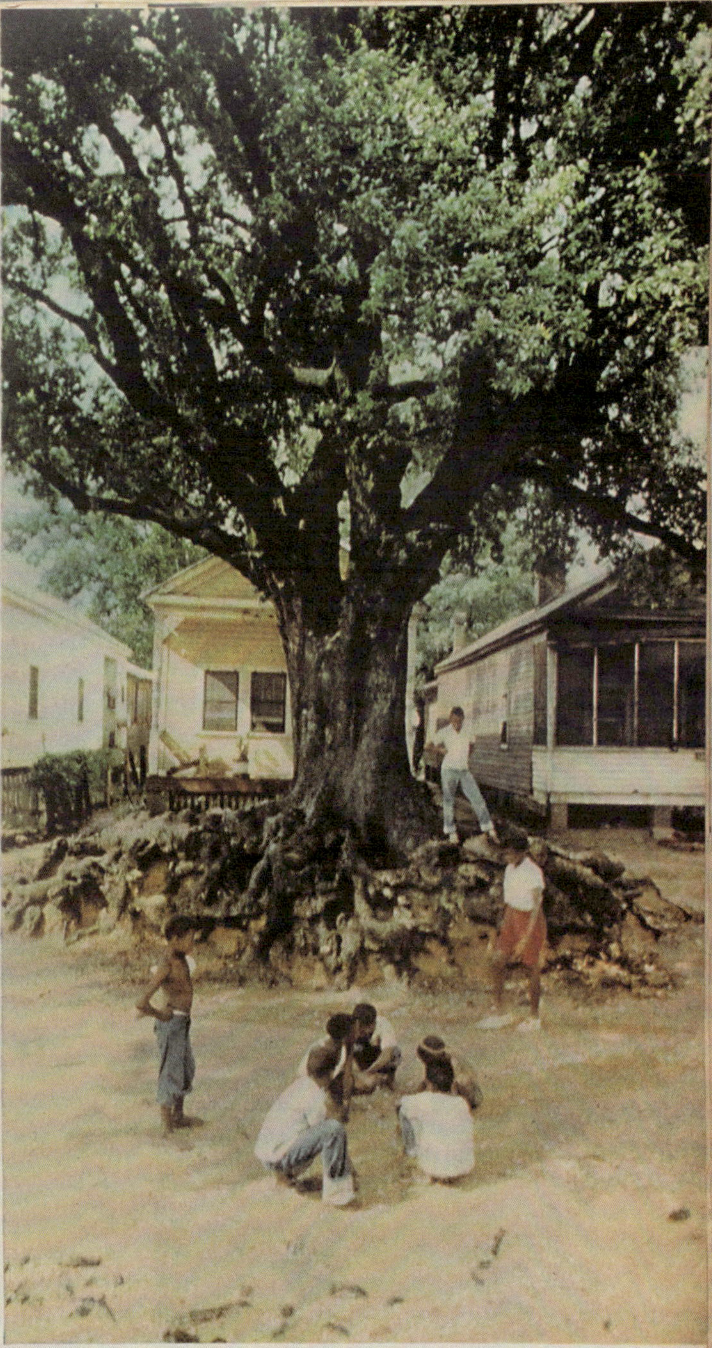

AFTER A RAIN children build dams in the road outside their houses, having nowhere else to play. The whole neighborhood is gradually eroding, the houses leaning at slowly increasing angles while the local landmark, a huge white oak tree, bares more and more of its roots following every downpour.

CONTINUED

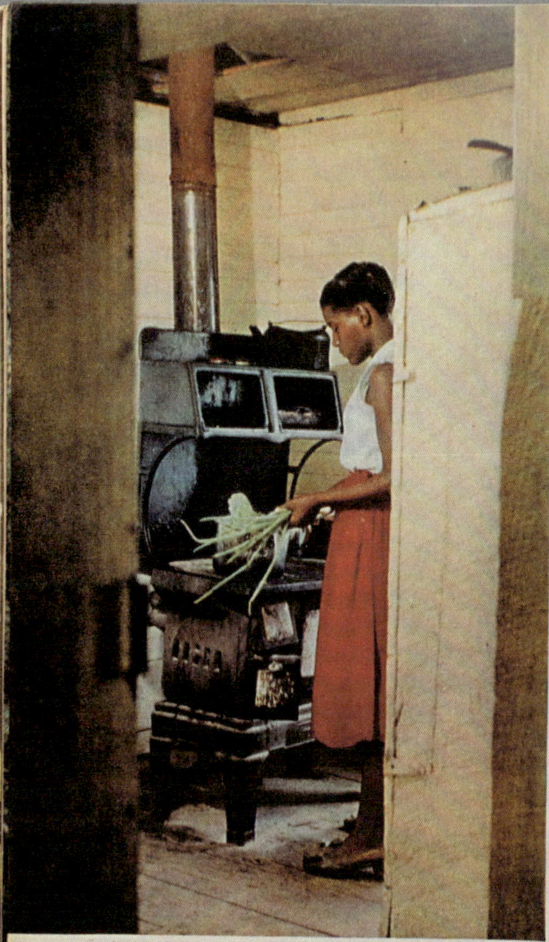

MINNIE LOUISE CAUSEY, 14, PREPARES A MEAL OF COLLARDS AND ONIONS

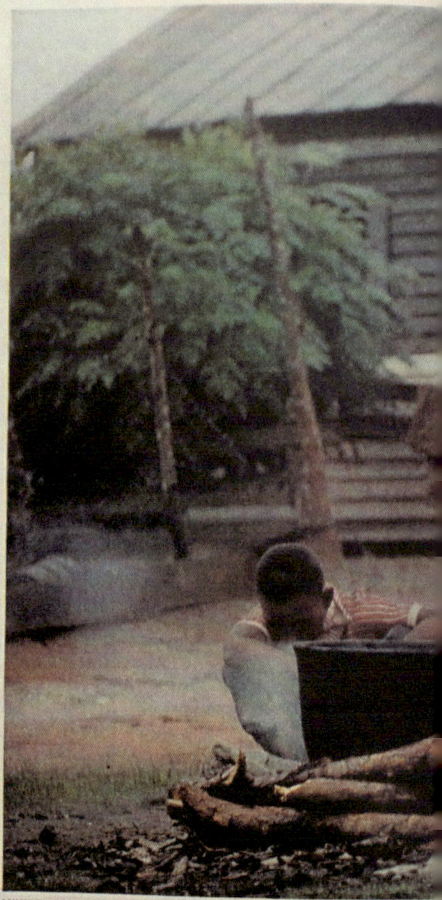

MINNIE LOUISE PREPARES TO THROW LAUNDRY INTO AN IRON POT WHILE

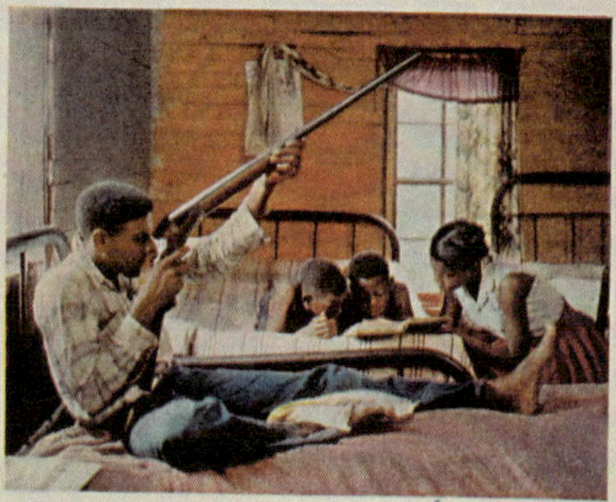

IN SMALL BEDROOM, four of the Causey children pass the time. Willie, 16, looks for dirt in the barrel of his shotgun while Samuel Louis, 10, and Jeff, 11, get some help in reading a science schoolbook from their sister Minnie Louise.

THE FRUSTRATION OF

One of the Thorntons' daughters is Allie Lee Causey, 41, of Shady Grove, a 95% Negro town about 100 miles northeast of Mobile. Mrs. Causey has been a teacher since 1939, although she did not get a degree—by attending summer sessions at Alabama State College for Negroes—until last month. (White school boards, selecting Negro teachers for Negro schools, are often hard-pressed to find college graduates. It often suffices if someone can be found to "keep" school, not necessarily to teach it.)

Mrs. Causey herself has been aware of her limited qualifications and has done what she can, in the face of poverty and heavy household duties, to increase them. But there is nothing she can do about the school itself, a dilapidated, four-room shack that accommodates 120 elementary grade pupils. In most respects it is almost as primitive as the log cabin schools of a century ago. It has no plumbing facilities at all. Mrs. Causey, who teaches 29 pupils in the first and second grades, brings drinking water for her class from home, carrying it in a gallon jug.

When she is not teaching or studying, Mrs. Causey works prodigiously to take care of her household. Two years ago, a divorcee with one child, she married Willie Causey, 55, a widower with 10 children, five of whom

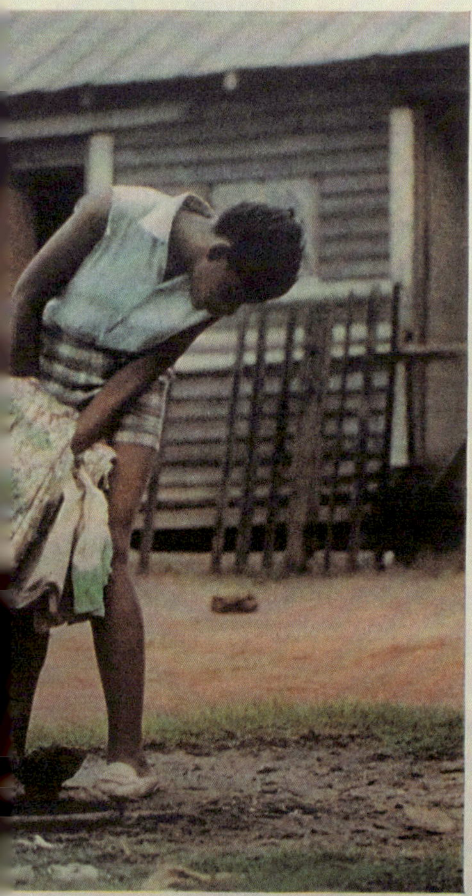

HER BROTHER SAMUEL LOUIS, CALLED "S.L.," KEEPS AN EYE ON THE FIRE

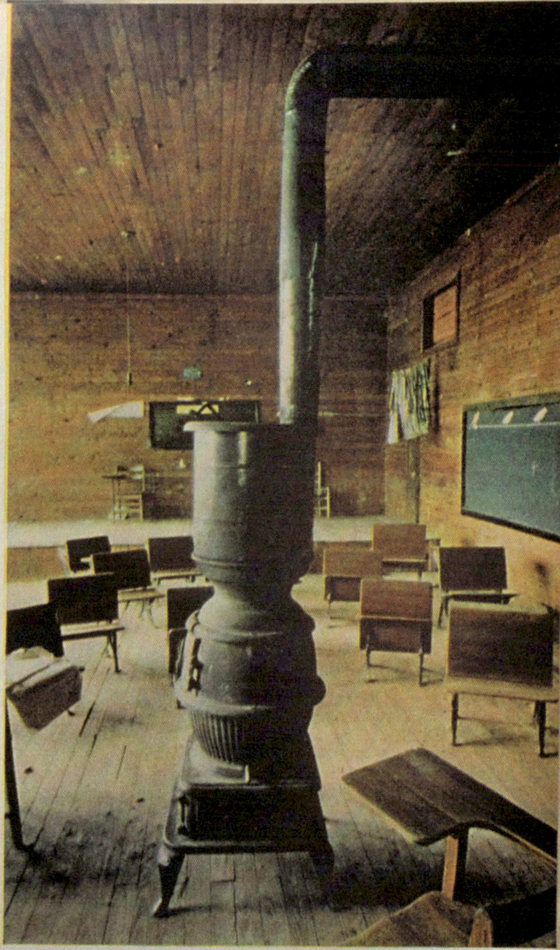

STOVE OCCUPIES THE CENTER OF AUDITORIUM IN SHADY GROVE SCHOOL

A TEACHER'S FAMILY

still live at home. The house itself is unpainted, disintegrating, with a half-fallen barn and a pigpen close beside it. She does her laundry in a black iron pot, heated by a log fire, in the backyard.

Mr. Causey is a farmer and woodcutter, owning 16 acres of cropland and 24 of timber, from which he extracts a living with the help of his older sons. However, the family is not in financial straits. Mrs. Causey's salary is $2,400 a year, which together with her husband's earnings places the family in the top financial bracket of the community. Last year Mr. Causey, over his wife's vigorous protest, bought a new Chevrolet sedan. The car is a symbol, a means of asserting "equality."

Mr. Causey has no capacity for paper work but is a good businessman nonetheless. He owns his own equipment for woodcutting, including power tools and a truck, and can compete successfully with white men in the same line of work. But it is a restrained kind of competition. It would not do for him to surpass his competitors—and he well knows it. The wood he cuts is delivered to a paper mill in Mobile, which a few years ago offered him a major contract for supplying it. He is one of the mill's oldest suppliers and has always performed reliably. But as he considered whether

CONTINUED

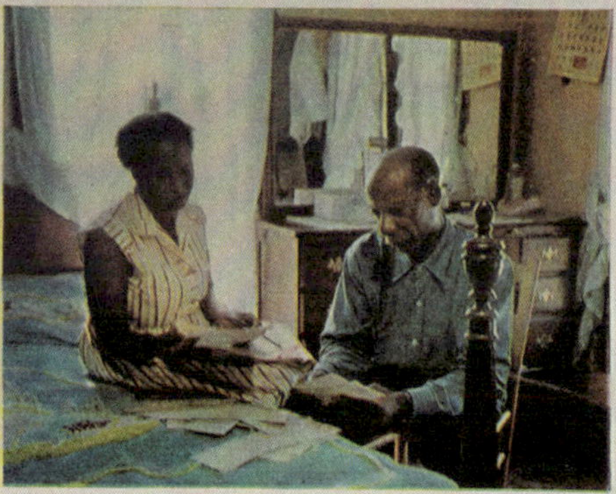

CHECKING TAX FORMS. Mrs. Causey goes over the quarterly report with her husband Willie. He had only "a year or so" of schooling and is unable to handle the tax forms himself, although he does very well as a practical businessman.

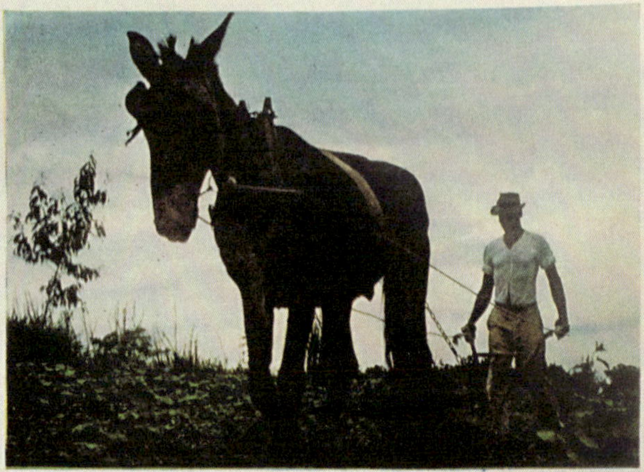

WILLIE CAUSEY, WHO IS FARMER AS WELL AS WOODCUTTER, PLOWS HIS FIELD BEHIND A NORMAN MULE

SEGREGATION CONTINUED

or not to accept the contract, Mr. Causey was visited by various of his white competitors who advised him strongly not to take it. In the face of this advice he felt he had no alternative, and so turned the contract down.

Mr. Causey does not vote. He has never been able to master the reading of the Bill of Rights in the Constitution, which all Negroes in his county must do before they are permitted to register. Mrs. Causey does vote. She was able to rattle off the Bill of Rights somewhat faster than the registration examiner could follow. He had to slow her down while he went along the lines in his book with his forefinger.

Both the Causeys believe that "segregation is on the way out," as Mrs. Causey says. "Integration is the only way through which Negroes will receive justice. We cannot get it as a separate people. If we can get justice on our jobs, and equal pay, then we'll be able to afford better homes and good education."

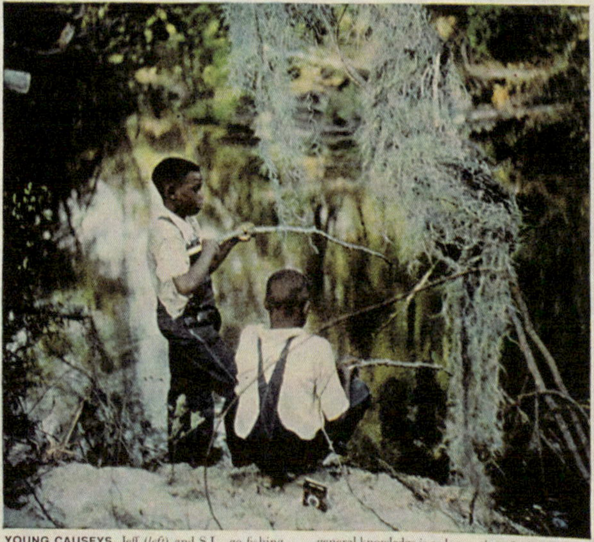

YOUNG CAUSEYS, Jeff (*left*) and S.L., go fishing in Turkey Creek. Even though their stepmother is a schoolteacher, they almost never read and their general knowledge is as low as that of other children in the community. They do not play baseball, have never even heard of the Dodgers or the Yankees.

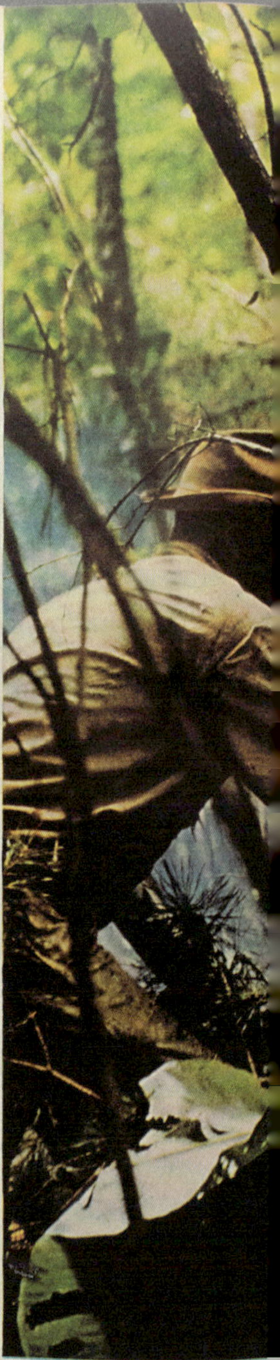

OLDER CAUSEYS, father Willie (*left*) and so Willie James and "L.C.," cut timber in the woo near their home. They buy the right to cut it fr

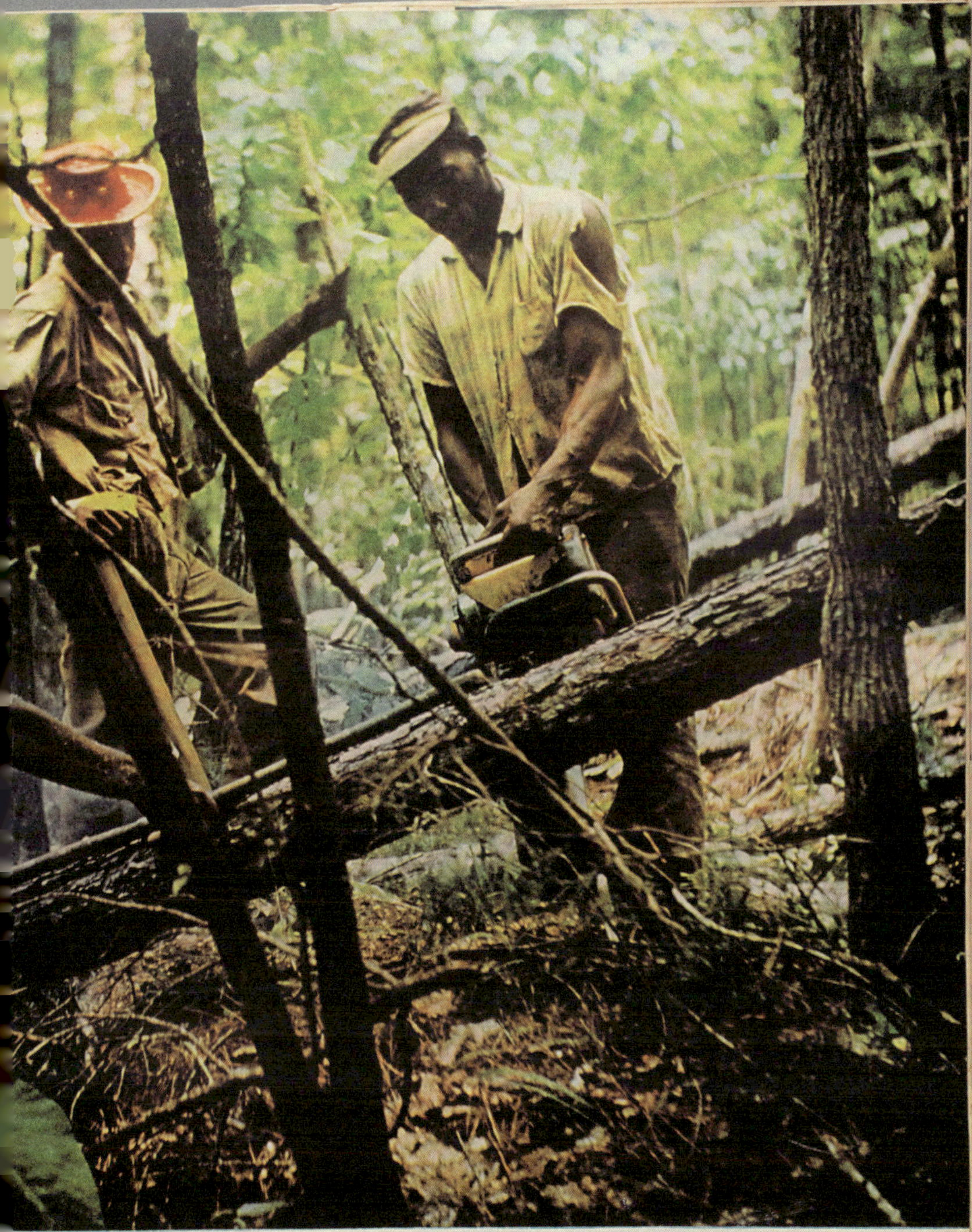

landowners at $2 a cord, saw it to length, haul it to a paper mill, which pays them about $14 a cord. "L.C.," who is 23 and married, is paid $1 an hour by his father while Willie James, 16, works for nothing. Willie James's prospects are typical of those of the rural southern Negro. If he stays where he is, he may eventually work up to getting $1 an hour himself. If this does not suit him, he must go somewhere else—but he says he does not know where.

CONTINUED

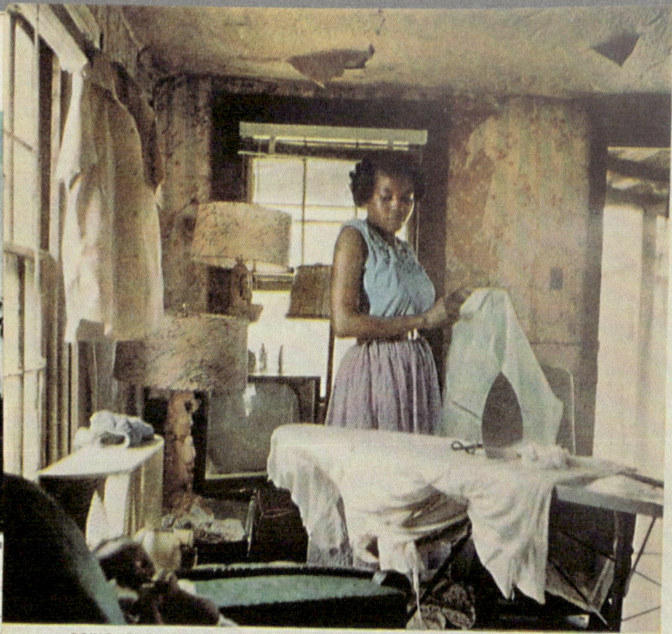

DOING HER CHORES. Virgie Lee Tanner irons in a corner of the family bedroom. The house has electricity but no plumbing, is owned by a Negro landlord. The Tanners are now spending all their extra money to build a new home, for that reason have made no repairs or improvements on this one.

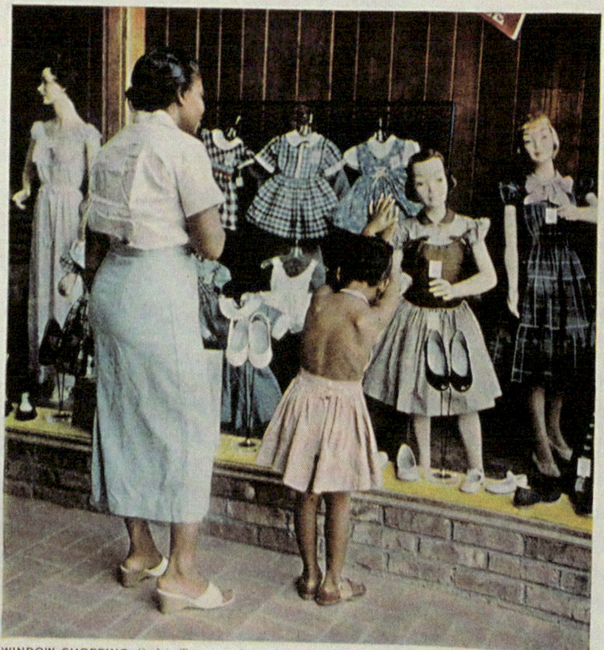

WINDOW-SHOPPING. Ondria Tanner and grandmother, Ondria Thornton, look at fashions. They look long, buy carefully because of limited funds.

OUTSIDE LOOKING IN, the three young Tanners → and three friends watch some children at a playground in a white neighborhood not far from theirs.

A SEPARA

One of the Thorntons' granddaughters,
Lee Tanner (*left*), lives near them in M
At 25 she has four children, having been
ried for six years to Henry Tanner, 34,
chanic at Brookley Air Force Base. Discri
tion in employment does not affect her fa
Her husband's civil service job pays $80 a
But other restraints do affect them. They
tell their children, for example, that they
not play in a nearby playground for white
must use a "separate but equal" one fo
groes. The children do not grasp the log
this and view the white playground as a sp

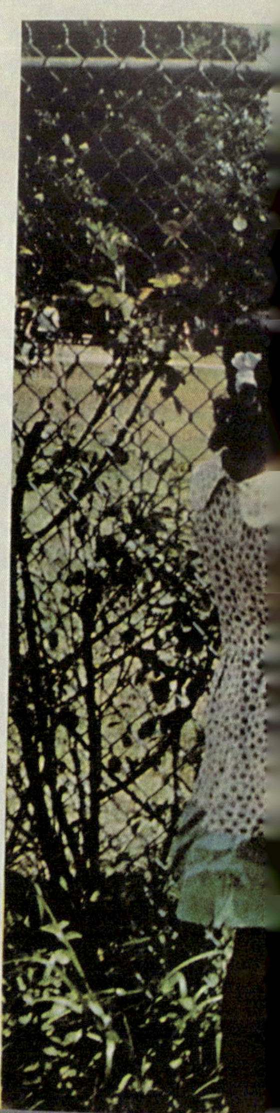

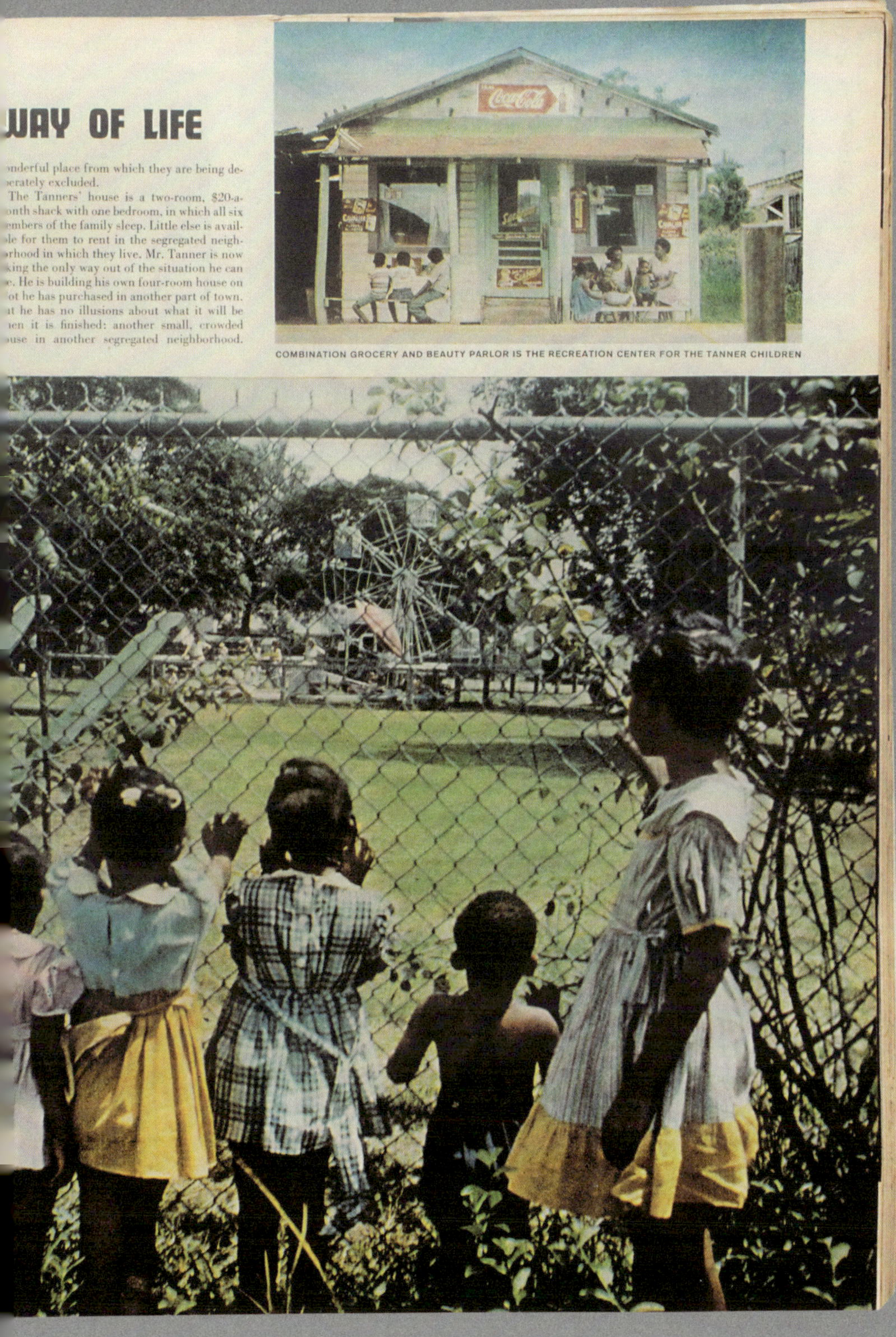

WAY OF LIFE

›nderful place from which they are being de-›erately excluded.

The Tanners' house is a two-room, $20-a-›onth shack with one bedroom, in which all six ›embers of the family sleep. Little else is avail-›le for them to rent in the segregated neigh-›rhood in which they live. Mr. Tanner is now ›king the only way out of the situation he can ›. He is building his own four-room house on ›ot he has purchased in another part of town. ›t he has no illusions about what it will be ›en it is finished: another small, crowded ›use in another segregated neighborhood.

COMBINATION GROCERY AND BEAUTY PARLOR IS THE RECREATION CENTER FOR THE TANNER CHILDREN

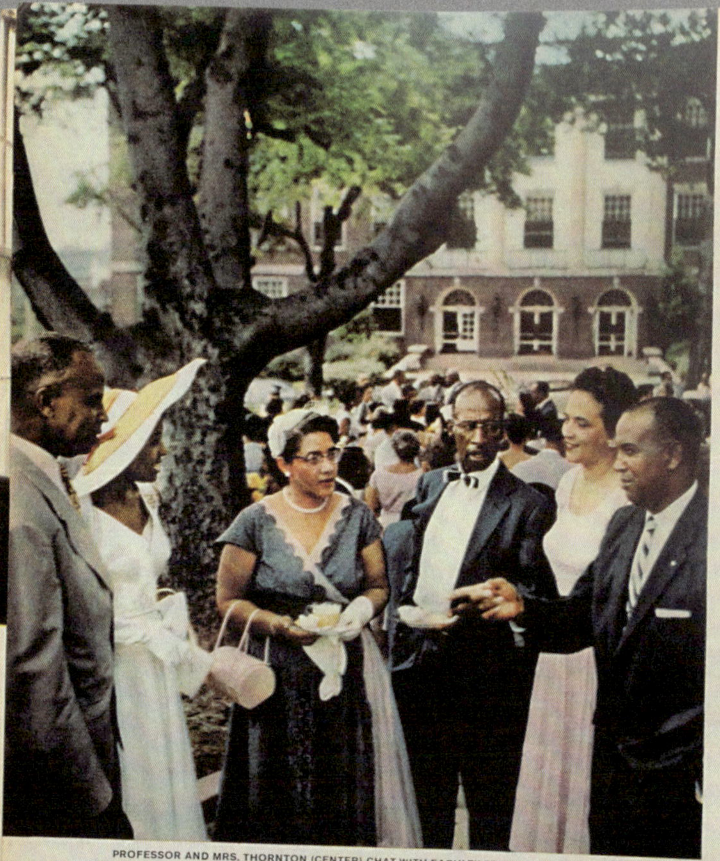

PROFESSOR AND MRS. THORNTON (CENTER) CHAT WITH FACULTY FRIENDS AT A UNIVERSITY LAWN PARTY

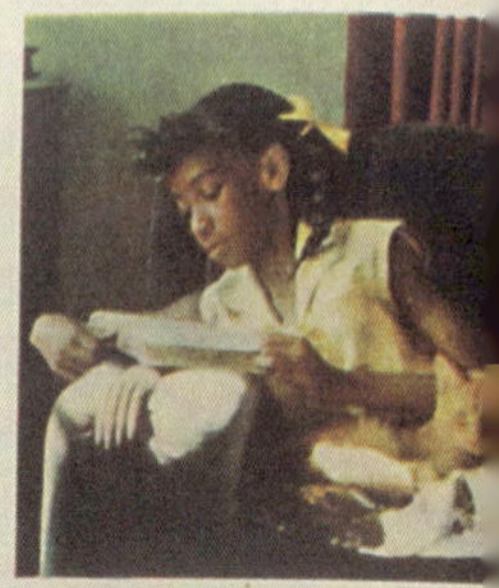

DAUGHTER LILLIAN, 13, IS NOW IN JUNIC

A PROFESSOF INJURED PRI

The member of the Thornton family w gone farthest in the world—and farthe the Deep South—is the oldest son, 48-y E. J. Thornton, who graduated from gee with a B.S. degree in poultry husba 1933. Since then he has taught in vari gro colleges, meanwhile taking time of an M.A. from the University of Massach Today he is a department head at Te State University (all-Negro) in Nashvil

Economic restraints upon Mr. Thorn negligible, but social restraints remain He cannot mingle publicly with his inte equals, white professors from other N colleges, and he must follow the local gation customs (*opposite page*). Thus, some restraints are removed because h above-average citizen, remaining restrai more wounding to him, for the same

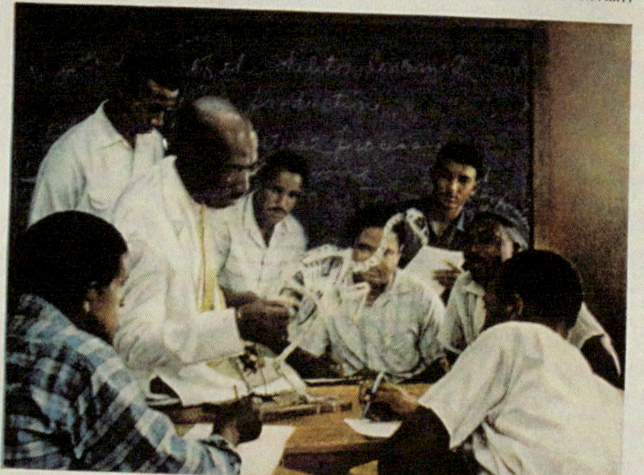

IN CLASS. Professor Thornton discusses the anatomy of a turkey with his students, several of whom are likely to become teachers themselves. He feels better-qualified Negroes "owe something to their people" and should remain in the South instead of "running away from the unsolved problems here."

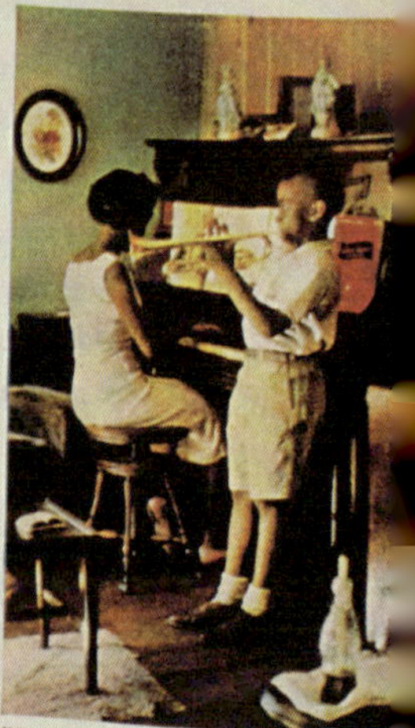

"CHERRY PINK" is played by E. J. Thornt 10, and sister Ruth, 17. Ruth enters colleg fall, would like to become a professional p

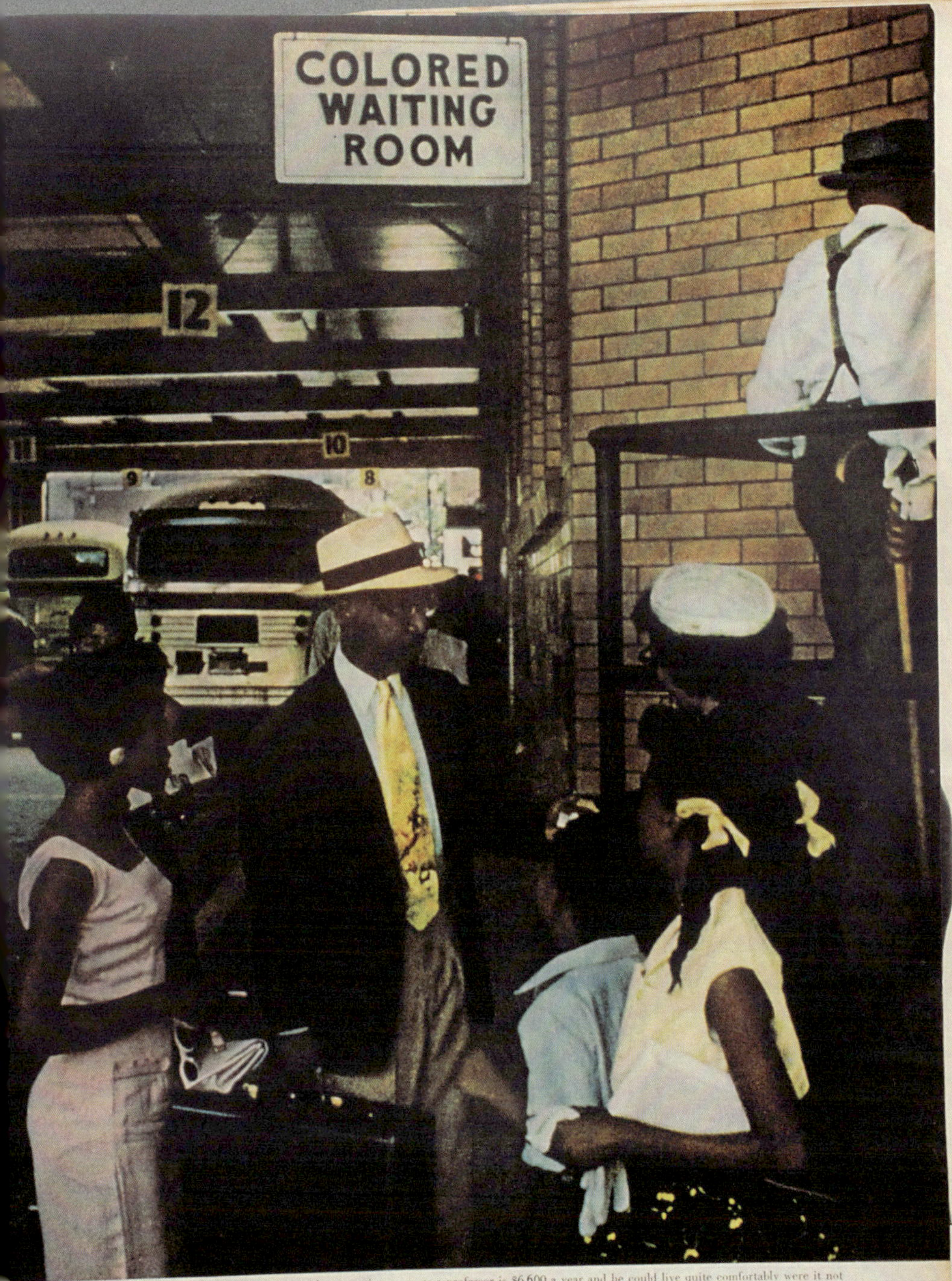

US STATION, Professor Thornton comes face to face with segregation, he accepts passively but with hurt pride. On long trips he sometimes the problem by taking a more expensive but unsegregated plane. His salary as a professor is $6,600 a year and he could live quite comfortably were it not for his determination to put his own three children through college. Because their ages are such that they can go through one at a time, he thinks he can do it.

Top: Problem Kids in *Ebony* Magazine, July 1947
Bottom: Harlem Gang Leader in *LIFE* Magazine, Nov. 1, 1948
Gordon Parks

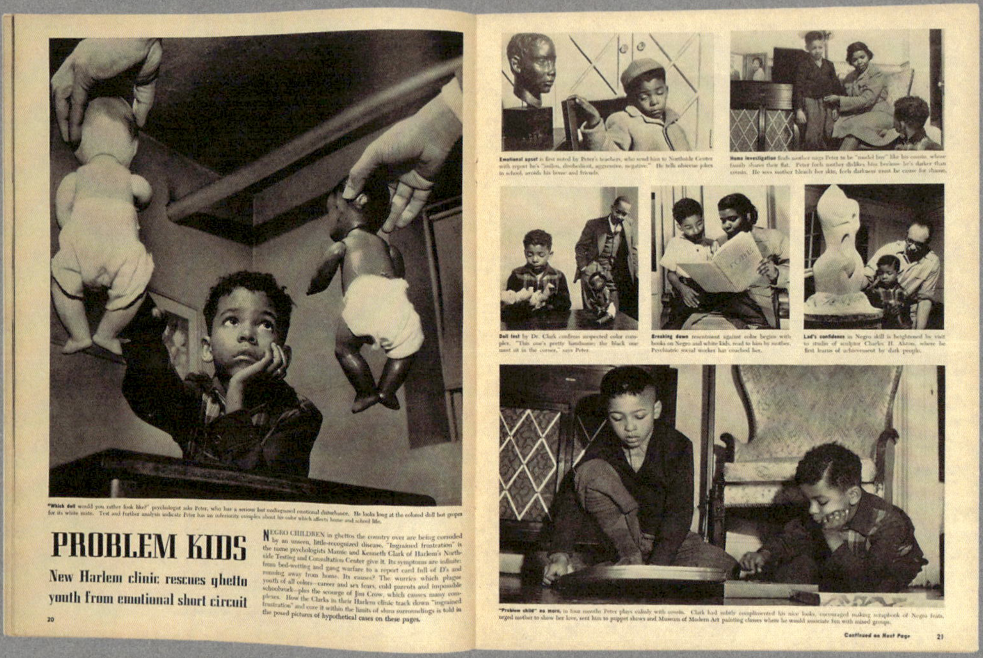

"Which doll would you rather look like?" psychologist asks Peter, who has a serious but undiagnosed emotional disturbance. He looks long at the colored doll but gropes for its white mate. Test and further analysis indicate Peter has an inferiority complex about his color which affects home and school life.

PROBLEM KIDS

New Harlem clinic rescues ghetto youth from emotional short circuit

NEGRO CHILDREN in ghettos the country over are being corroded by an unseen, little-recognized disease. "Ingrained frustration" is the name psychologists Mamie and Kenneth Clark of Harlem's Northside Testing and Consultation Center give it. Its symptoms are infinite: from bed-wetting and gang warfare to a report card full of D's and running away from home. Its causes? The worries which plague youth of all colors—career and sex fears, cold parents and impossible schoolwork—plus the scourge of Jim Crow, which causes many complexes. How the Clarks in their Harlem clinic track down "ingrained frustration" and cure it within the limits of slum surroundings is told in the posed pictures of hypothetical cases on these pages.

20

Emotional upset is first noted by Peter's teachers, who send him to Northside Center with report he's "sullen, disobedient, aggressive, negative." He tells obscene jokes in school, avoids his home and friends.

Home investigation finds mother urges Peter to be "model boy" like his cousin, whose family shares their flat. Peter feels mother dislikes him because he's darker than cousin. He sees mother bleach her skin, feels darkness must be cause for shame.

Doll test by Dr. Clark confirms suspected color complex. "This one's pretty handsome; the black one must sit in the corner," says Peter.

Breaking down resentment against color begins with books on Negro and white kids, read to him by mother. Psychiatric social worker has coached her.

Lad's confidence in Negro skill is heightened by visit to studio of sculptor Charles H. Alston, where he first learns of achievement by dark people.

"Problem child" no more, in four months Peter plays calmly with cousin. Clark had subtly complimented his nice looks, encouraged making scrapbook of Negro feats, urged mother to show her love, sent him to puppet shows and Museum of Modern Art painting classes where he would associate fun with mixed groups.

Continued on Next Page 21

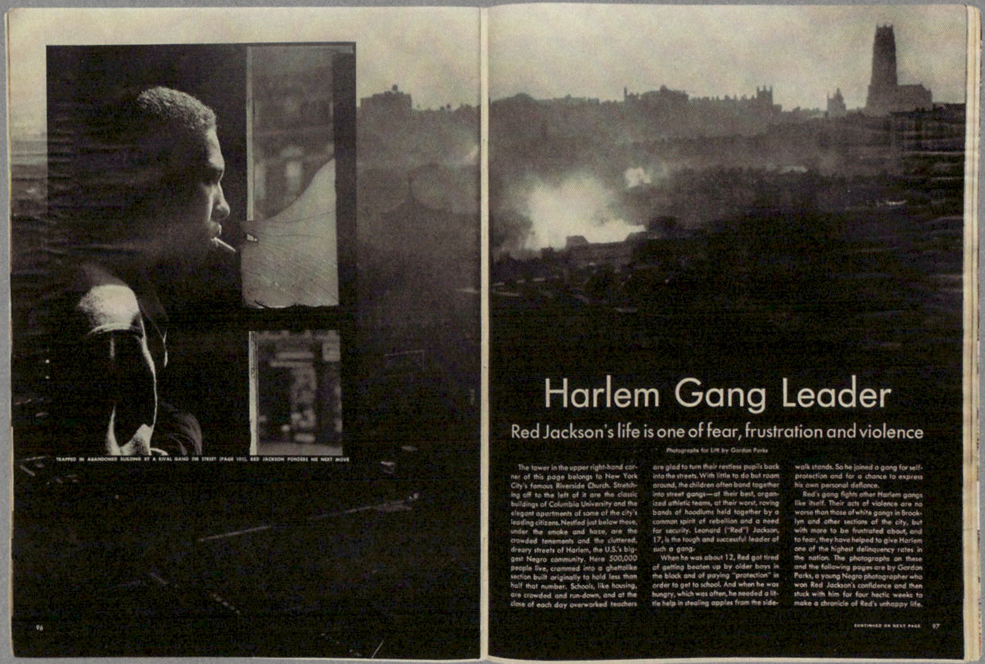

TRAPPED IN ABANDONED BUILDING BY A RIVAL GANG ON STREET (PAGE 101), RED JACKSON PONDERS HIS NEXT MOVE

96

Harlem Gang Leader

Red Jackson's life is one of fear, frustration and violence

Photographs for LIFE by Gordon Parks

The tower in the upper right-hand corner of this page belongs to New York City's famous Riverside Church. Stretching off to the left of it are the classic buildings of Columbia University and the elegant apartments of some of the city's leading citizens. Nestled just below these, under the smoke and haze, are the crowded tenements and the cluttered, dreary streets of Harlem, the U.S.'s biggest Negro community. Here 500,000 people live, crammed into a ghettolike section built originally to hold less than half that number. Schools, like housing, are crowded and run-down, and at the close of each day overworked teachers are glad to turn their restless pupils back into the streets. With little to do but roam around, the children often band together into street gangs—at their best, organized athletic teams, at their worst, roving bands of hoodlums held together by a common spirit of rebellion and a need for security. Leonard ("Red") Jackson, 17, is the tough and successful leader of such a gang.

When he was about 12, Red got tired of getting beaten up by older boys in the block and of paying "protection" in order to get to school. And when he was hungry, which was often, he needed a little help in stealing apples from the sidewalk stands. So he joined a gang for self-protection and for a chance to express his own personal defiance.

Red's gang fights other Harlem gangs like itself. Their acts of violence are no worse than those of white gangs in Brooklyn and other sections of the city, but with more to be frustrated about, and to fear, they have helped to give Harlem one of the highest delinquency rates in the nation. The photographs on these and the following pages are by Gordon Parks, a young Negro photographer who won Red Jackson's confidence and then stuck with him for four hectic weeks to make a chronicle of Red's unhappy life.

CONTINUED ON NEXT PAGE 97

Top: A Man Becomes Invisible in *LIFE* Magazine, August 25, 1952
Bottom: Freedom's Fearful Foe: Poverty in *LIFE* Magazine, June 16, 1961
Gordon Parks

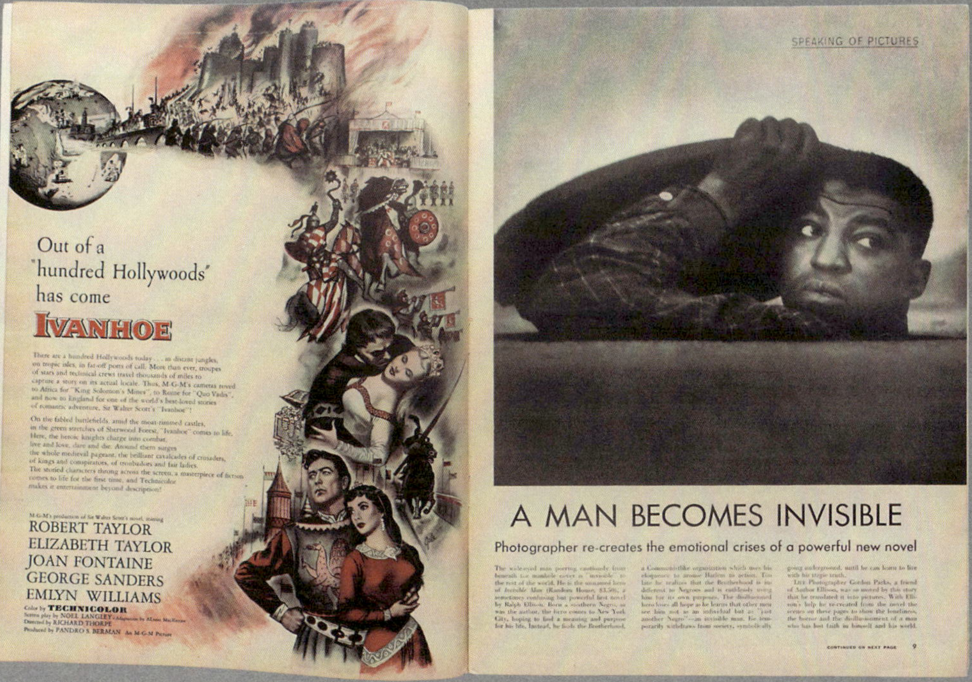

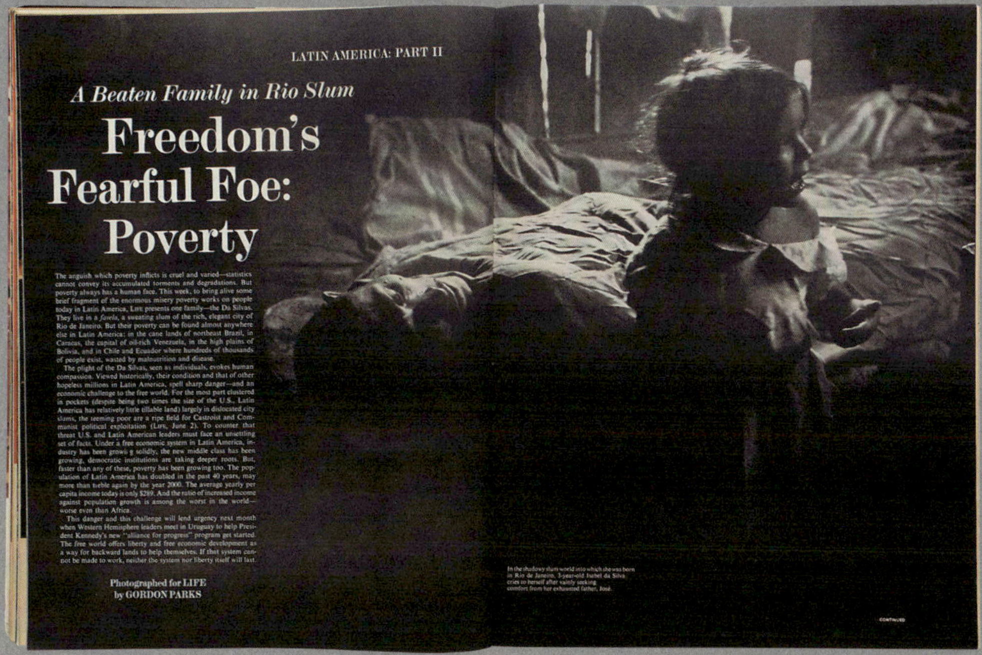

Top: The White Devil's Day is Almost Over in *LIFE* Magazine, May 31, 1963

Bottom: How It Feels To Be Black in *LIFE* Magazine, August 16, 1963

Gordon Parks

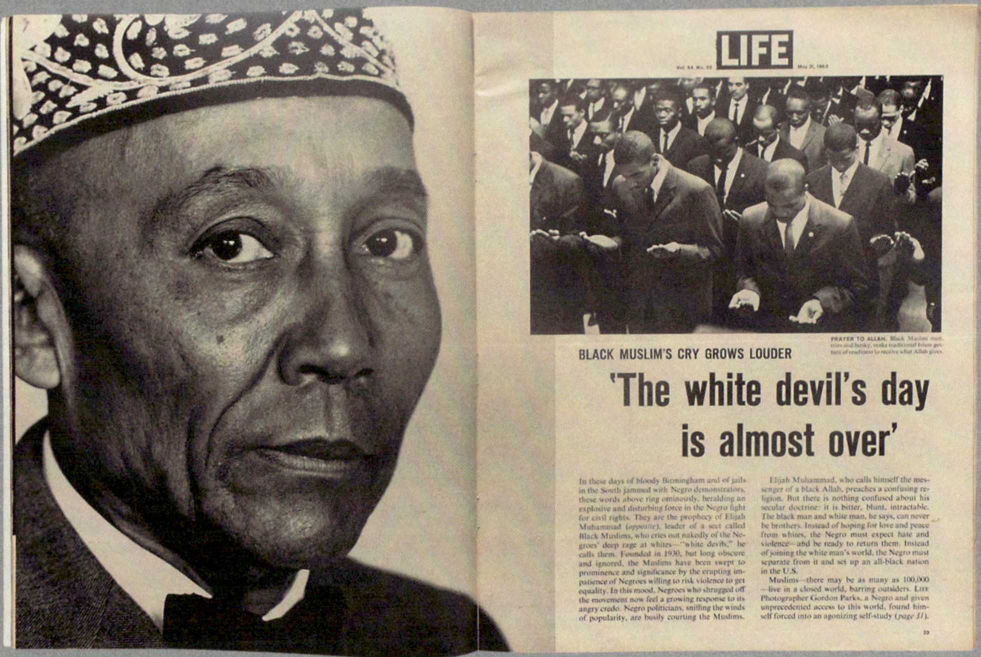

LIFE

Vol. 54, No. 22 May 31, 1963

PRAYER TO ALLAH. Black Muslim men, trim and husky, make traditional Islam gesture of readiness to receive what Allah gives.

BLACK MUSLIM'S CRY GROWS LOUDER

'The white devil's day is almost over'

In these days of bloody Birmingham and of jails in the South jammed with Negro demonstrators, these words above ring ominously, heralding an explosive and disturbing force in the Negro fight for civil rights. They are the prophecy of Elijah Muhammad (*opposite*), leader of a sect called Black Muslims, who cries out nakedly of the Negroes' deep rage at whites—"white devils," he calls them. Founded in 1930, but long obscure and ignored, the Muslims have been swept to prominence and significance by the erupting impatience of Negroes willing to risk violence to get equality. In this mood, Negroes who shrugged off the movement now feel a growing response to its angry credo. Negro politicians, sniffing the winds of popularity, are busily courting the Muslims.

Elijah Muhammad, who calls himself the messenger of a black Allah, preaches a confusing religion. But there is nothing confused about his secular doctrine: it is bitter, blunt, intractable. The black man and white man, he says, can never be brothers. Instead of hoping for love and peace from whites, the Negro must expect hate and violence—and be ready to return them. Instead of joining the white man's world, the Negro must separate from it and set up an all-black nation in the U.S.

Muslims—there may be as many as 100,000—live in a closed world, barring outsiders. LIFE Photographer Gordon Parks, a Negro and given unprecedented access to this world, found himself forced into an agonizing self-study (*page 31*).

23

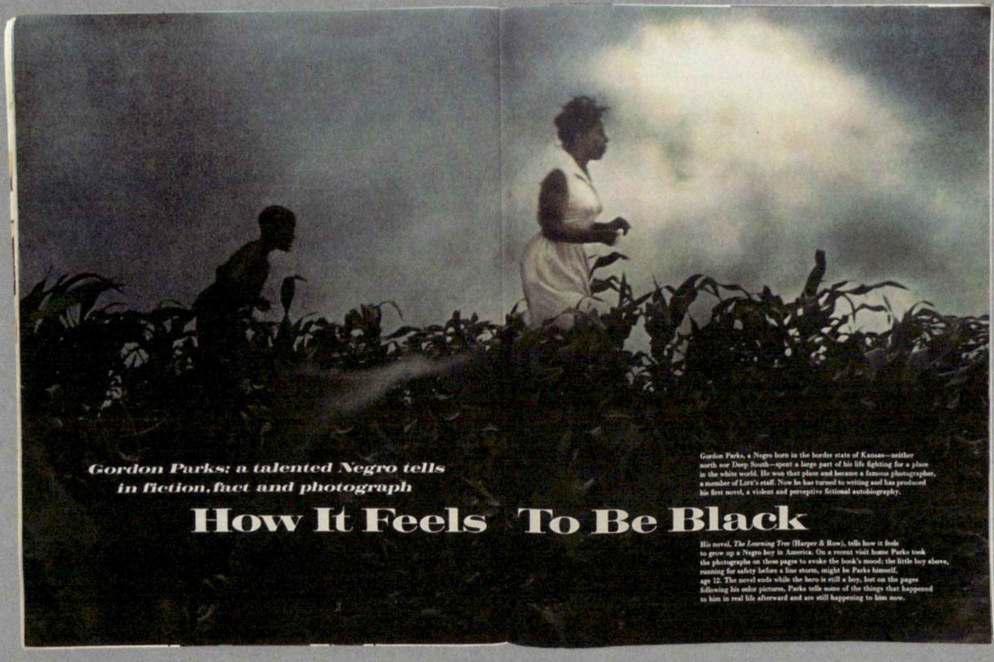

Gordon Parks: a talented Negro tells in fiction, fact and photograph

How It Feels To Be Black

Gordon Parks, a Negro born in the border state of Kansas—neither north nor Deep South—spent a large part of his life fighting for a place in the white world. He won that place and became a famous photographer, a member of LIFE's staff. Now he has turned to writing and has produced his first novel, a violent and perceptive fictional autobiography.

His novel, *The Learning Tree* (Harper & Row), tells how it feels to grow up a Negro boy in America. On a recent visit home Parks took the photographs on these pages to evoke the book's mood; the little boy above, running for safety before a line storm, might be Parks himself, age 12. The novel ends while the hero is still a boy, but on the pages following his color pictures, Parks tells some of the things that happened to him in real life afterward and are still happening to him now.

Top: The Redemption of the Champion in *LIFE* Magazine, September 9, 1966
Bottom: What I Want, What I Am, What You Force Me To Be Is What You Are in *LIFE* Magazine, March 8, 1968
Gordon Parks

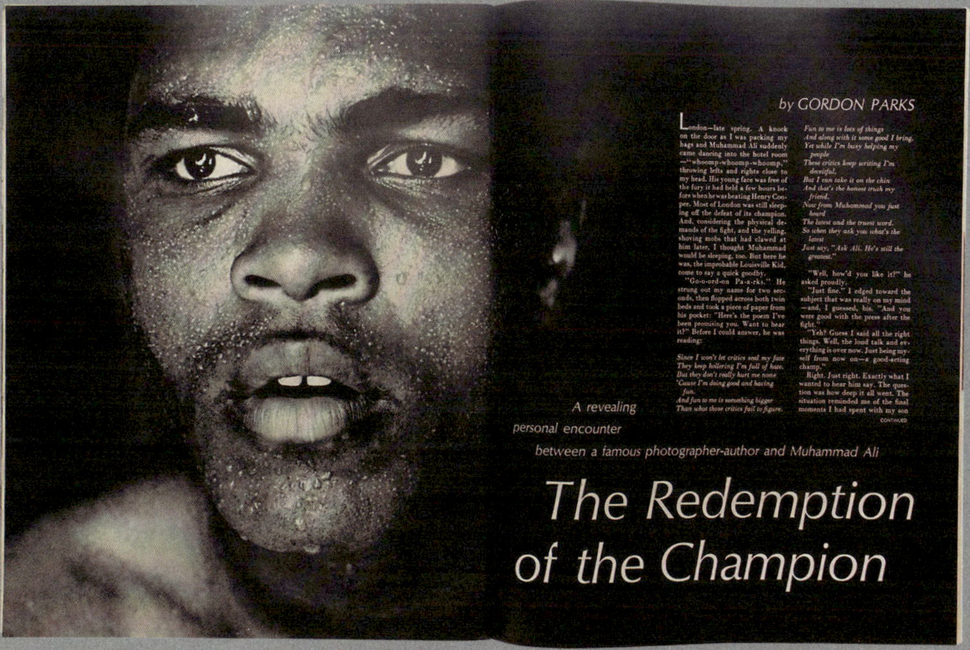

by GORDON PARKS

London—late spring. A knock on the door as I was packing my bags and Muhammad Ali suddenly came dancing into the hotel room—"whoomp-whoomp-whoomp," throwing lefts and rights close to my head. His young face was free of the fury it had held a few hours before when he was beating Henry Cooper. Most of London was still sleeping off the defeat of its champion. And, considering the physical demands of the fight, and the yelling, shoving mobs that had clawed at him later, I thought Muhammad would be sleeping, too. But here he was, the improbable Louisville Kid, come to say a quick goodby.

"Go-o-ord-on Pa-a-rks." He strung out my name for two seconds, then flopped across both twin beds and took a piece of paper from his pocket: "Here's the poem I've been promising you. Want to hear it?" Before I could answer, he was reading:

Since I won't let critics seal my fate
They keep hollering I'm full of hate.
But they don't really hurt me none
'Cause I'm doing good and having fun.
And fun to me is something bigger
Than what those critics fail to figure.
Fun to me is lots of things
And along with it some good I bring.
Yet while I'm busy helping my people
These critics keep writing I'm deceitful.
But I can take it on the chin
And that's the honest truth my friend.
Now from Muhammad you just heard
The latest and the truest word.
So when they ask you what's the latest
Just say, "Ask Ali. He's still the greatest."

"Well, how'd you like it?" he asked proudly.

"Just fine." I edged toward the subject that was really on my mind—and, I guessed, his. "And you were good with the press after the fight."

"Yeh? Guess I said all the right things. Well, the loud talk and everything is over now. Just being myself from now on—a good-acting champ."

Right. Just right. Exactly what I wanted to hear him say. The question was how deep it all went. The situation reminded me of the final moments I had spent with my son

CONTINUED

A revealing personal encounter between a famous photographer-author and Muhammad Ali

The Redemption of the Champion

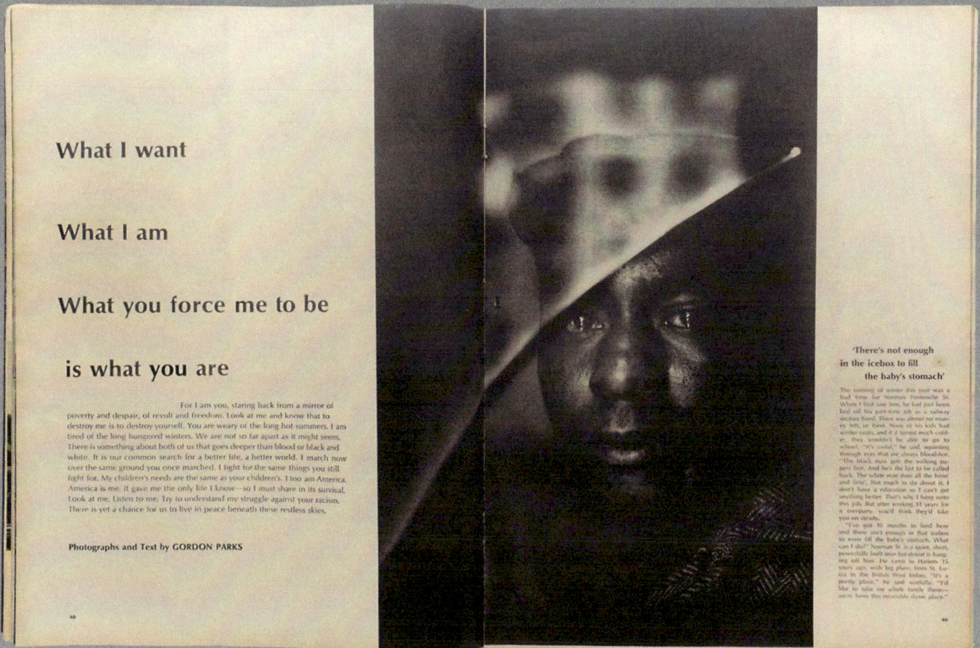

What I want

What I am

What you force me to be

is what you are

For I am you, staring back from a mirror of poverty and despair, of revolt and freedom. Look at me and know that to destroy me is to destroy yourself. You are weary of the long hot summers. I am tired of the long hungered winters. We are not so far apart as it might seem. There is something about both of us that goes deeper than blood or black and white. It is our common search for a better life, a better world. I march now over the same ground you once marched. I fight for the same things you still fight for. My children's needs are the same as your children's. I too am America. America is me. It gave me the only life I know—so I must share in its survival. Look at me. Listen to me. Try to understand my struggle against your racism. There is yet a chance for us to live in peace beneath these restless skies.

Photographs and Text by GORDON PARKS

'There's not enough in the icebox to fill the baby's stomach'

The coming of winter this year was a bad time for Norman Fontenelle Sr. When I first saw him, he had just been laid off his part-time job as a railway section hand. There was almost no money left, or food. None of his kids had winter coats, and if it turned much colder, they wouldn't be able to go to school. "It's awful," he said, squinting through eyes that are always blood-hot. "The black man gets the walking papers first. And he's the last to be called back. The white man does all the hirin' and firin'. Not much to do about it. I don't have a education so I can't get anything better. That's why I hang onto this job. But after working 11 years for a company, you'd think they'd take you on steady.

"I've got 10 mouths to feed here and there ain't enough in that icebox to even fill the baby's stomach. What can I do?" Norman Sr. is a quiet, short, powerfully built man but defeat is hanging off him. He came to Harlem 15 years ago, with big plans, from St. Lucia in the British West Indies. "It's a pretty place," he said wistfully. "I'd like to take my whole family there—away from this miserable damn place."

They Fight a Fire That Won't Go Out in *LIFE* Magazine, May 17, 1963

Charles Moore

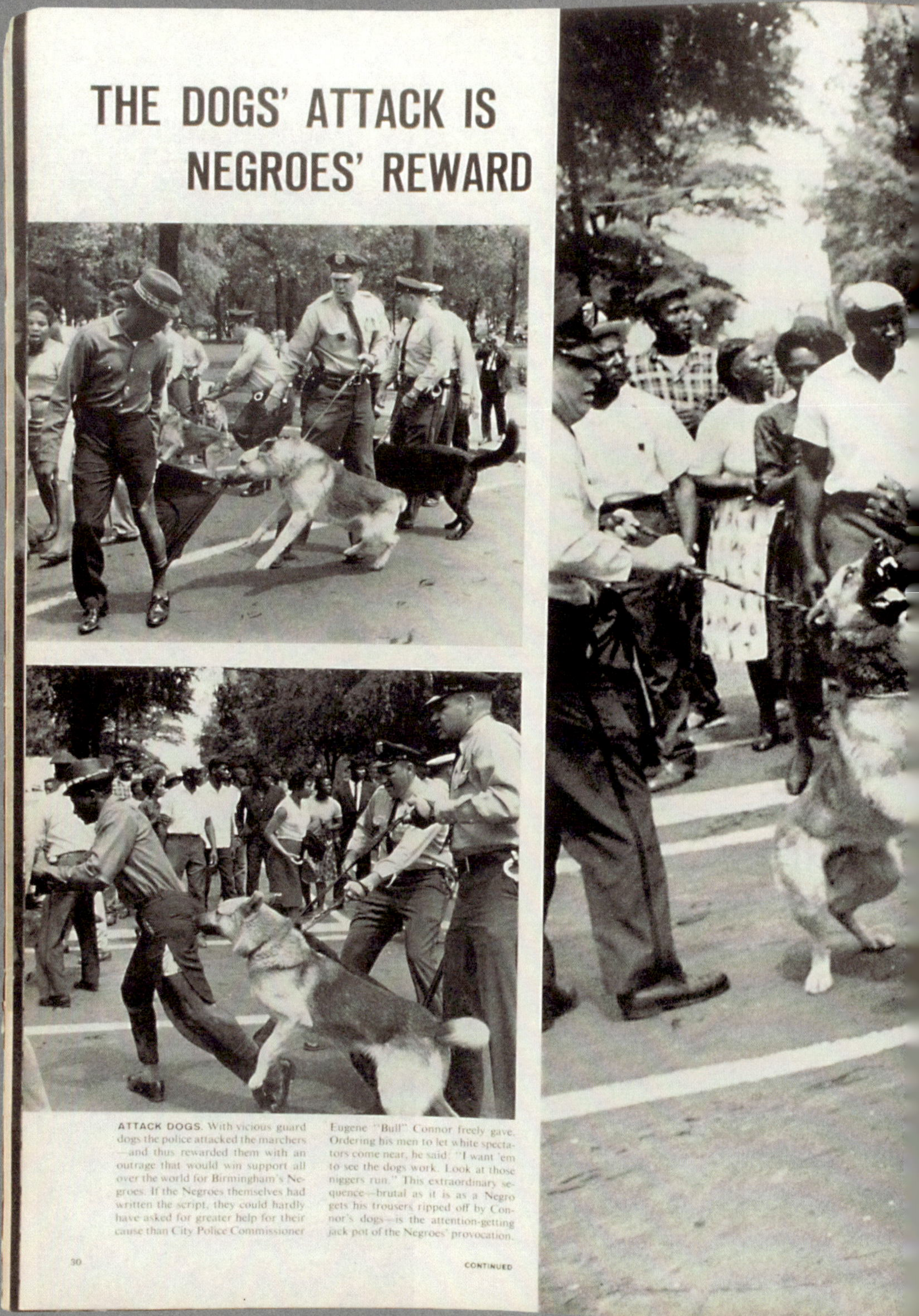

THE DOGS' ATTACK IS NEGROES' REWARD

ATTACK DOGS. With vicious guard dogs the police attacked the marchers —and thus rewarded them with an outrage that would win support all over the world for Birmingham's Negroes. If the Negroes themselves had written the script, they could hardly have asked for greater help for their cause than City Police Commissioner Eugene "Bull" Connor freely gave. Ordering his men to let white spectators come near, he said: "I want 'em to see the dogs work. Look at those niggers run." This extraordinary sequence—brutal as it is as a Negro gets his trousers ripped off by Connor's dogs—is the attention-getting jack pot of the Negroes' provocation.

30

CONTINUED

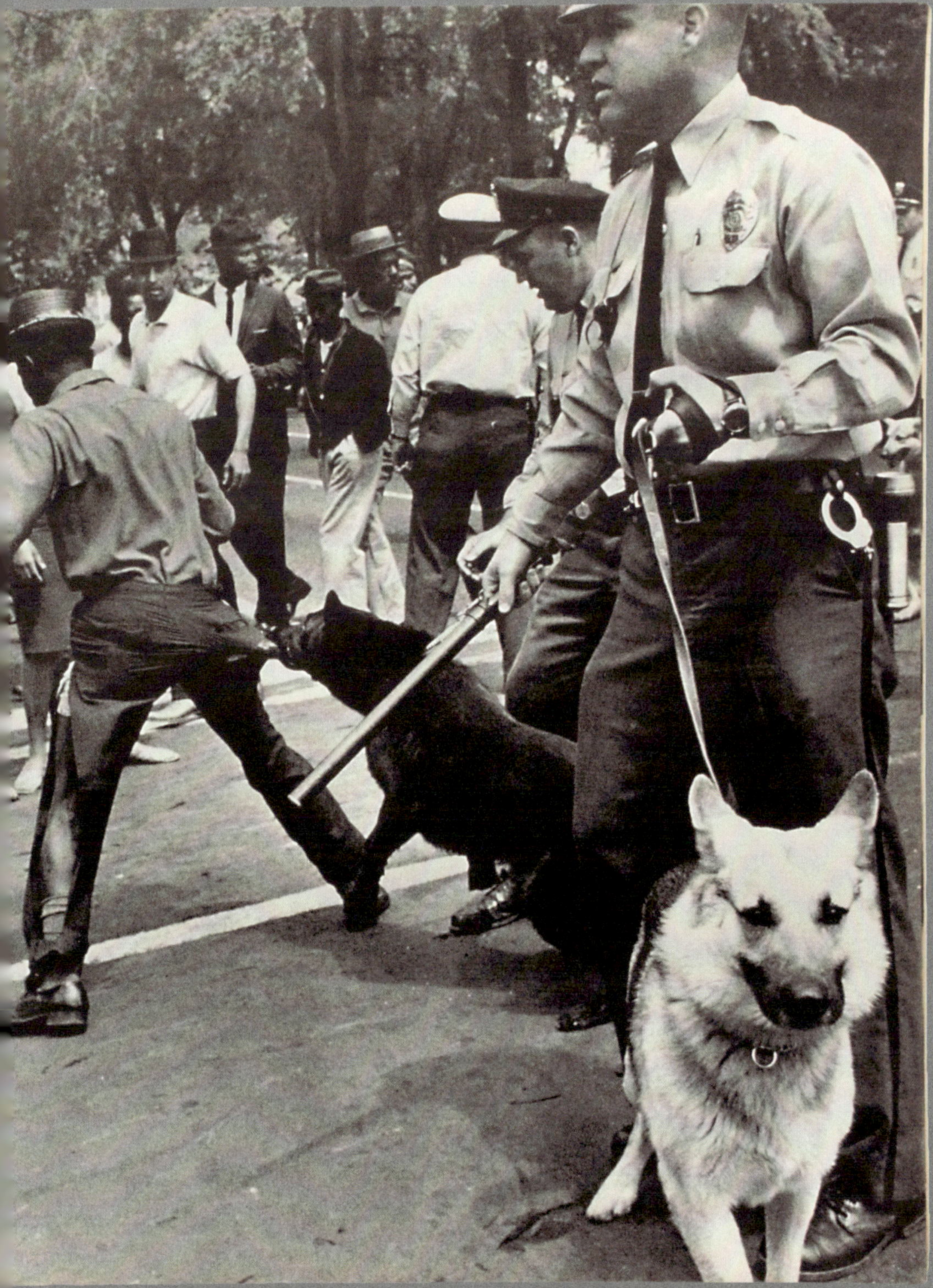

Mechanical ("The Dogs' Attack is Negroes' Reward," from LIFE Magazine, May 17, 1963)

Andy Warhol

1964

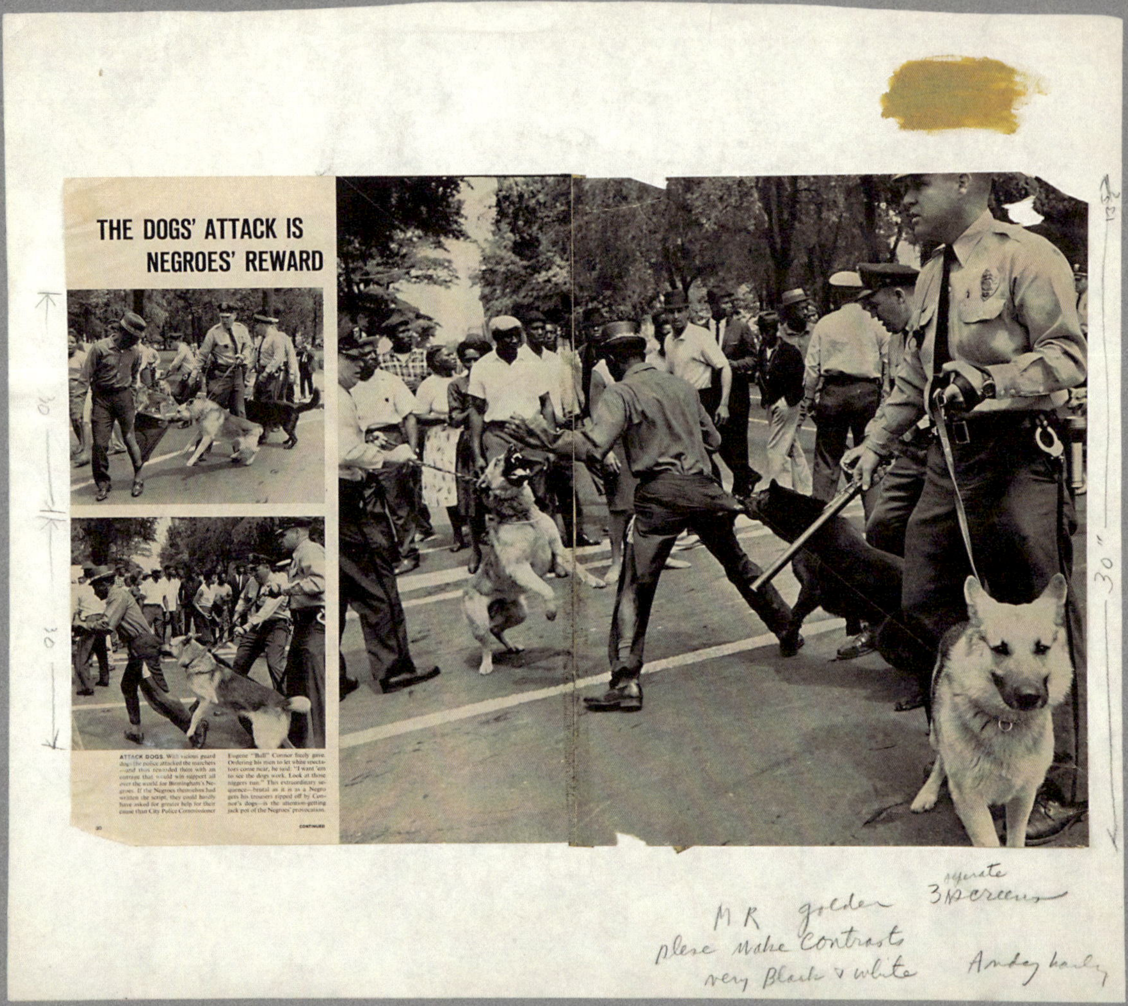

Race Riot

Andy Warhol

1964

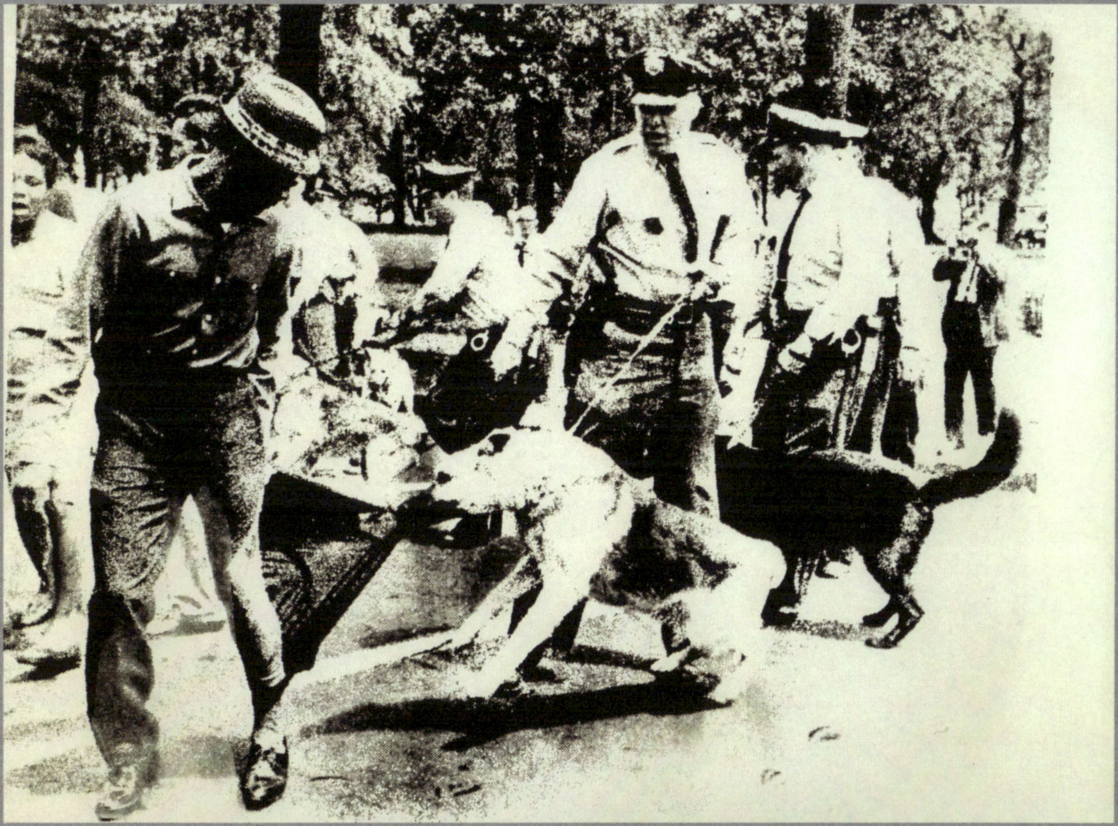

Roentgenizdat [bootleg audio recording on X-ray film]

Unknown makers

ca. 1960

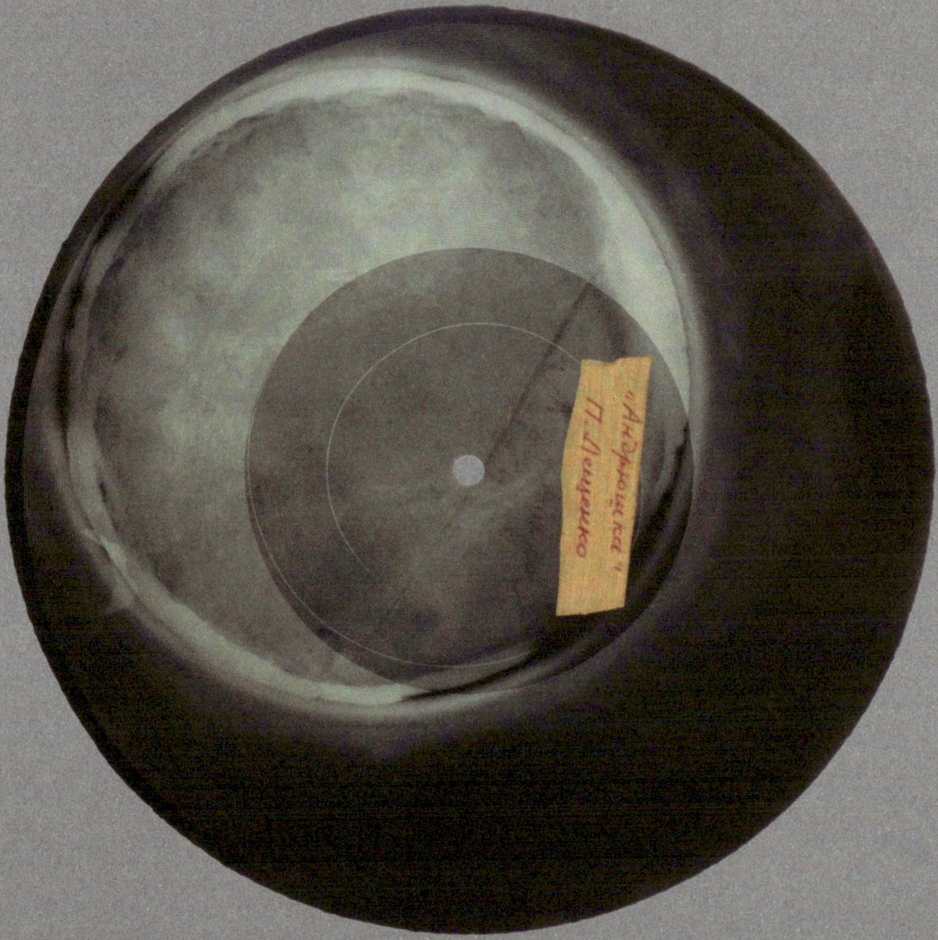

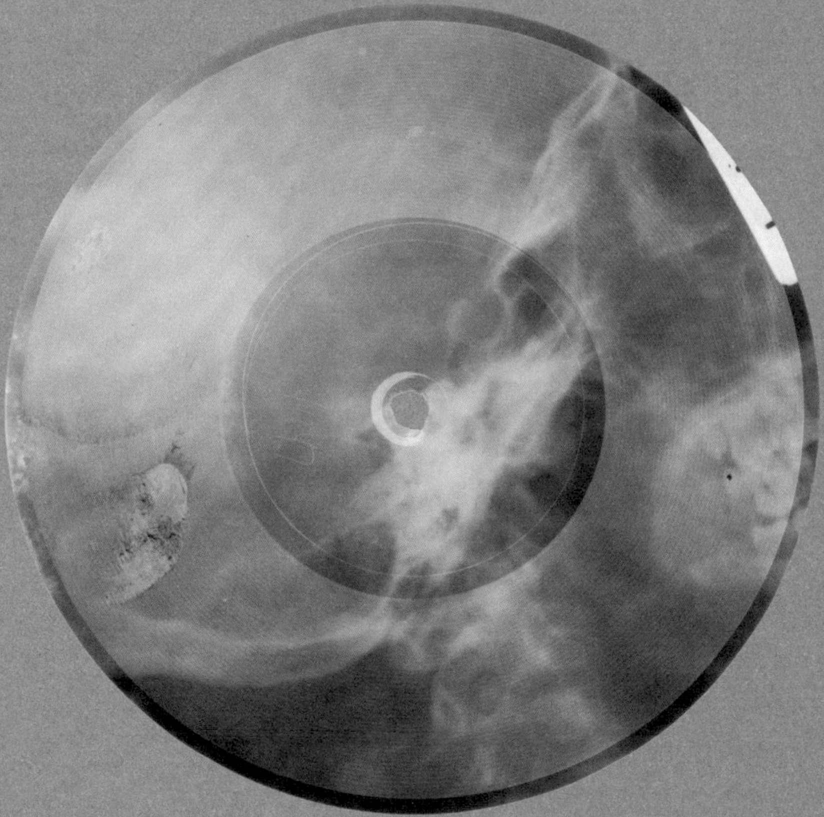

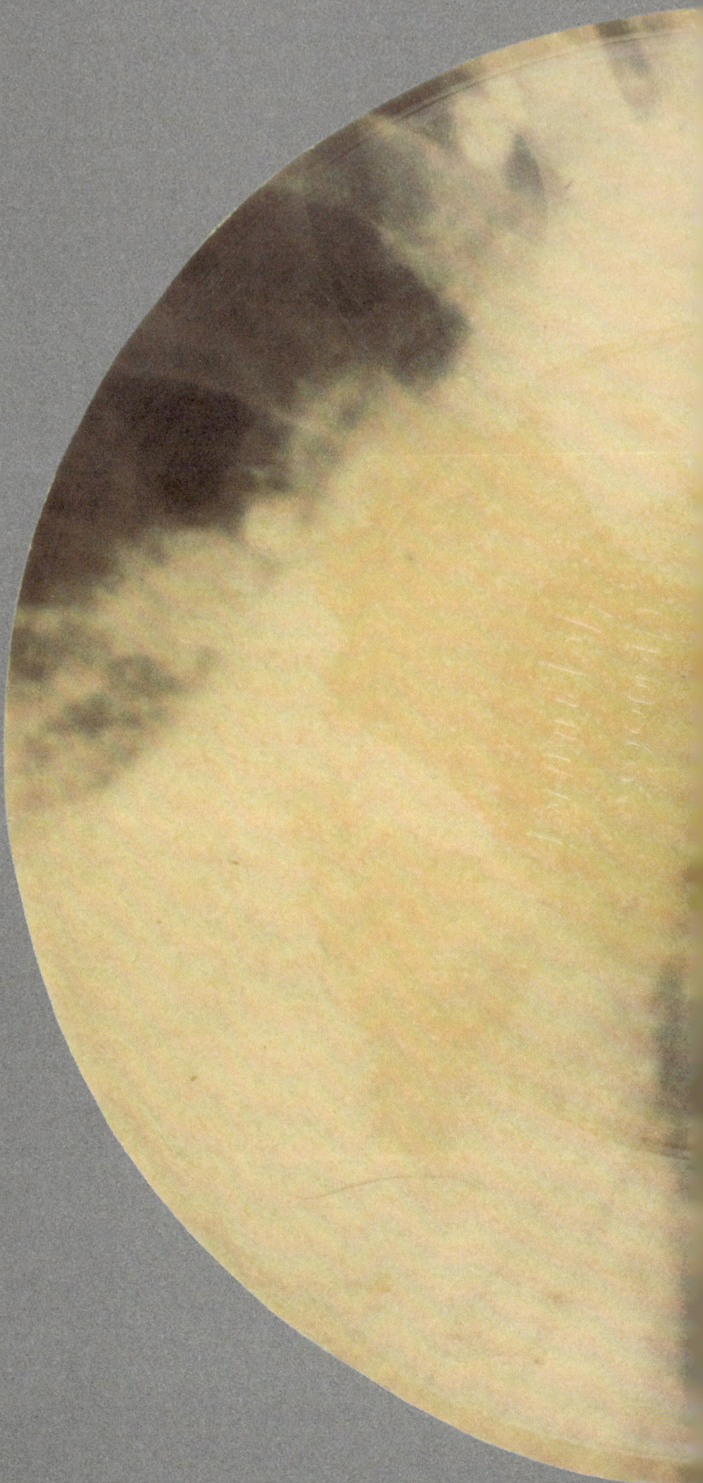

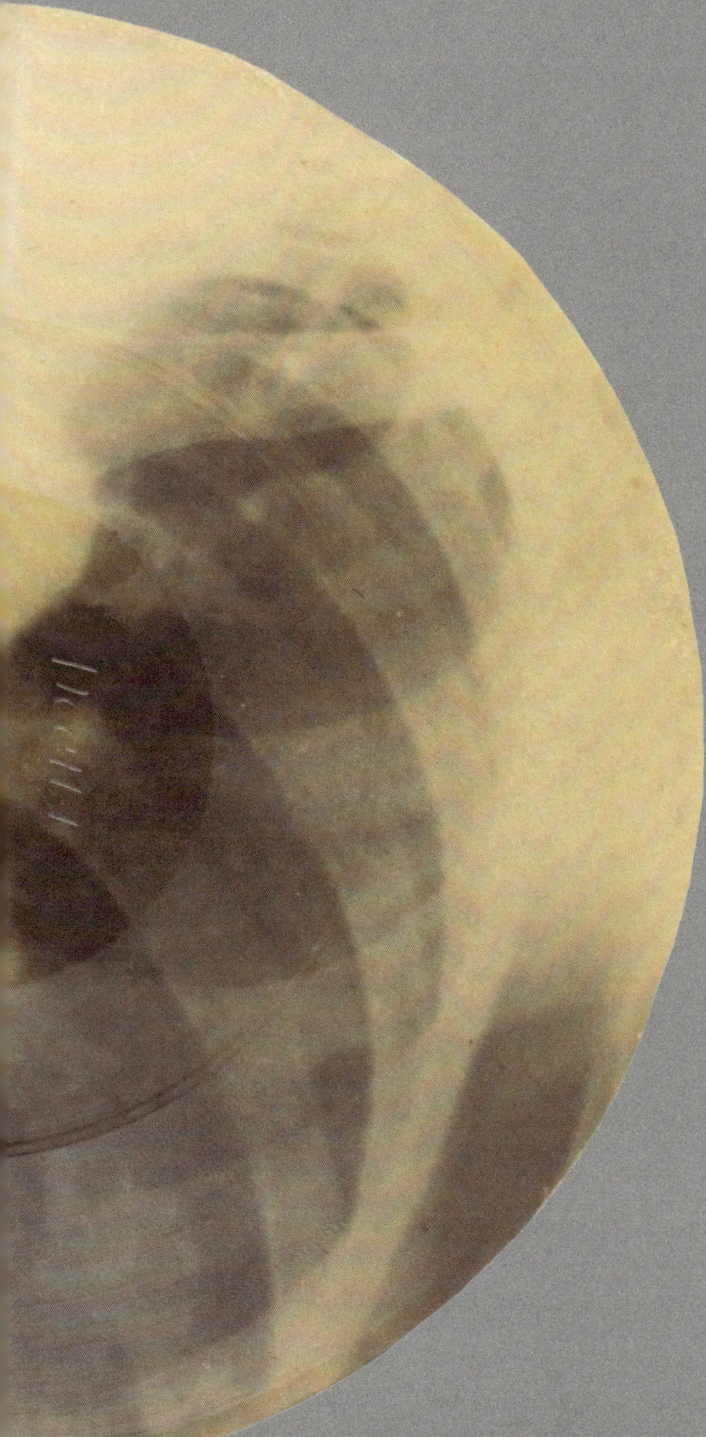

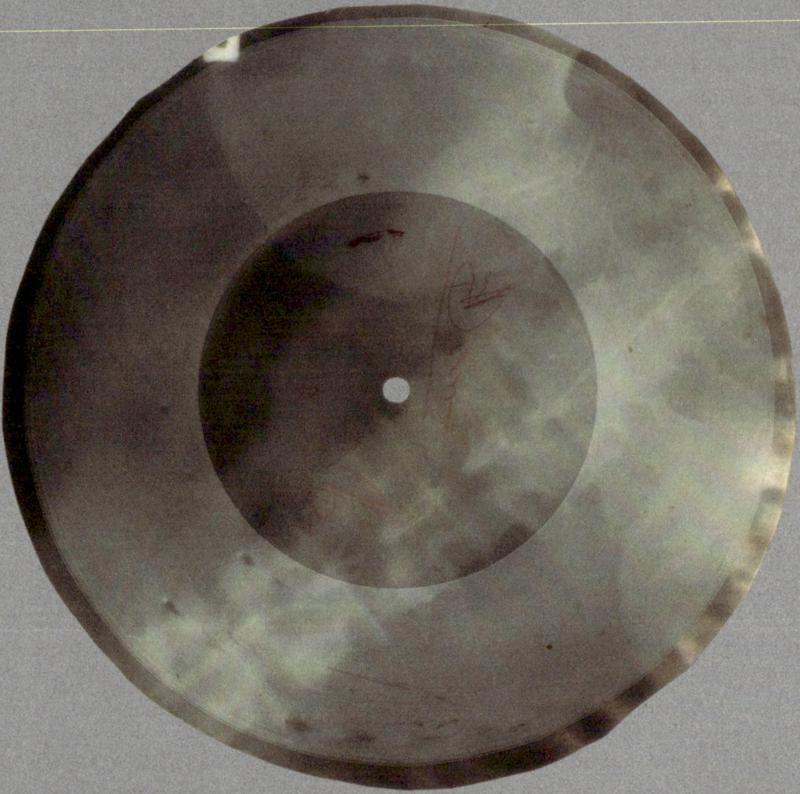

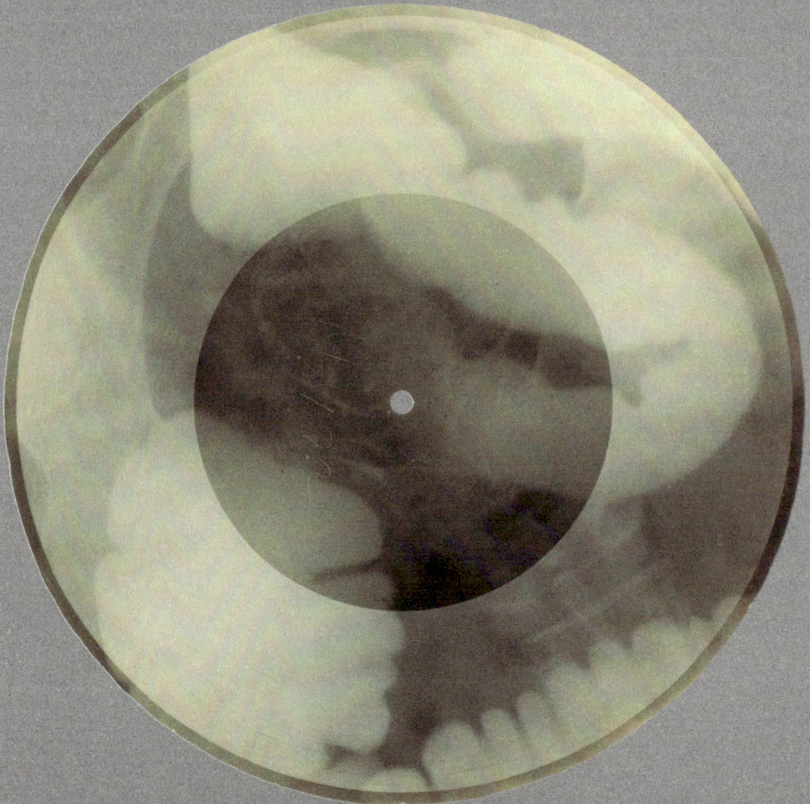

The Medium Is the Message
Marshall McLuhan
1964

In a culture like ours, long accustomed to splitting and dividing all things as a means of control, it is sometimes a bit of a shock to be reminded that, in operational and practical fact, the medium is the message. This is merely to say that the personal and social consequences of any medium—that is, of any extension of ourselves—result from the new scale that is introduced into our affairs by each extension of ourselves, or by any new technology. Thus, with automation, for example, the new patterns of human association tend to eliminate jobs, it is true. That is the negative result. Positively, automation creates roles for people, which is to say depth of involvement in their work and human association that our preceding mechanical technology had destroyed. Many people would be disposed to say that it was not the machine, but what one did with the machine, that was its meaning or message. In terms of the ways in which the machine altered our relations to one another and to ourselves, it mattered not in the least whether it turned our cornflakes or Cadillacs. The restructuring of human work and association was shaped by the technique of fragmentation that is the essence of machine technology. The essence of automation technology is the opposite. It is integral and decentralist in depth, just as the machine was fragmentary, centralist, and superficial in its patterning of human relationships.

The instance of the electric light may prove illuminating in this connection. The electric light is pure information. It is a medium without a message, as it were, unless it is used to spell out some verbal ad or name. This fact, characteristic of all media, means that the "content" of any medium is always another medium. The content of writing is speech, just like the written word is the content of print, and print is the content of the telegraph. If it is asked, "What is the content of speech?" it is necessary to say, "It is an actual process of thought, which is in itself nonverbal." An abstract painting represents direct manifestation of creative thought processes as they might appear in computer designs. What we are considering here, however, are the psychic and social consequences of the designs or patterns as they amplify or accelerate existing processes. For the "message" of any medium or technology is the change of scale or pace or pattern that it introduces into human affairs. The railway did not introduce movement or transportation or wheel or road into human society, but it accelerated and enlarged the scale of previous human functions, creating totally new kinds of cities and new kinds of work and leisure. This happened whether the railway functioned in a tropical or a northern environment, and is quite independent of the freight or content of the railway medium. The airplane, on the other hand, by accelerating the rate of transportation, tends to dissolve the railway form of city, politics, and association, quite independently of what the airplane is used for.

Let us return to the electric light. Whether the light is being used for brain surgery or night baseball is a matter of indifference. It could be argued that these activities are in some way the "content" of the electric light, since they could not exist without the electric light. This fact merely underlines the point that "the medium is the message" because it is the medium that shapes and controls the scale and form of human association and action. The content or uses of such media are as diverse as they are ineffectual in shaping the form of human association. Indeed, it is only too typical that the "content" of any medium blinds us to the character of the medium. It is only today that industries have become aware of the various kinds of business in which they are engaged. When IBM discovered that it was not in the business of making office equipment or business machines, but that it was in the business of processing information, then it began to navigate with clear vision. The General Electric Company makes a considerable portion of its profits from electric light bulbs and lighting systems. It has not yet discovered that, quite as much as AT&T, it is in the business of moving information.

The electric light escapes attention as a communication medium just because it has no "content." And this makes it an invaluable instance of how people fail to study media at all. For it is not till the electric light is used to spell out some brand name that it is noticed as a medium. Then it is not the light but the "content" (or what is really another medium) that is noticed. The message of the electric light is like the message of electric power in industry, totally radical, pervasive, and decentralized. For electric light and power are separate from their uses, yet they eliminate time and space factors in human association exactly as do radio, telegraph, telephone, and TV, creating involvement in depth.

A fairly complete handbook for studying the extensions of man could be made up from selections from Shakespeare. Some might quibble about whether or not he was referring to TV in these familiar lines from *Romeo and Juliet*:

> But soft! what light through yonder window breaks?
> It speaks, and yet says nothing.

In *Othello*, which, as much as *King Lear*, is concerned with the torment of people transformed by illusions, there are these lines that bespeak Shakespeare's intuition of the transforming powers of new media:

> Is there not charms
> By which the property of youth and maidhood
> May be abus'd? Have you not read Roderigo,
> Of some such thing?

In Shakespeare's *Troilus and Cressida*, which is almost completely devoted to both a psychic and social study of communication, Shakespeare states his awareness that true social and political navigation depend upon anticipating the consequences of innovation:

> The providence that's in a watchful state
> Knows almost every grain of Plutus' gold,
> Finds bottom in the uncomprehensive deeps,
> Keeps place with thought, and almost like the gods
> Does thoughts unveil in their dumb cradles.

The increasing awareness of the action of media, quite independently of their "content" or programming, was indicated in the annoyed and anonymous stanza:

> In modern thought, (if not in fact)
> Nothing is that doesn't act,
> So that is reckoned wisdom which
> Describes the scratch but not the itch.

The same kind of total, configurational awareness that reveals why the medium is socially the message has occurred in the most recent and radical medial theories. In his *Stress of Life*, Hans Selye tells of the dismay of a research colleague on hearing of Selye's theory:

> When he saw me thus launched on yet another enraptured description of what I had observed in animals treated with this or that impure, toxic material, he looked at me with desperately sad eyes and said in obvious despair: "But Selye, try to realize what you are doing before it is too late! You have now decided to spend your entire life studying the pharmacology of dirt!"
>
> —(Hans Selye, *The Stress of Life*)

As Selye deals with the total environmental situation in his "stress" theory of disease, so the latest approach to media study considers not only the "content" but the medium and the cultural matrix within which the particular medium operates. The older unawareness of the psychic and social effects of media can be illustrated from almost any of the conventional pronouncements.

In accepting an honorary degree from the University of Notre Dame a few years ago, General David Sarnoff made this statement: "We are too prone to make technological instruments the scapegoats for the sins of those who wield them. The products of modern science are not in themselves good or bad; it is the way they are used that determines their value." That is the voice of the current somnambulism. Suppose we were to say, "Apple pie is in itself neither good nor bad; it is the way it is used that determines its value." Or, "The smallpox virus is in itself neither good nor bad; it is the way it is used that determines its value." Again, "Firearms are in themselves neither good nor bad; it is the way they are used that determines their value." That is, if the slugs reach the right people firearms are good. If the TV tube fires the right ammunition at the right people it is good. I am not being perverse. There is simply nothing in the Sarnoff statement that will bear scrutiny, for it ignores the nature of the medium, of any and all media, in the true Narcissus style of one hypnotized by the amputation and extension of his own being in a new technical form. General Sarnoff went on to explain his attitude to the technology of print, saying that it was true that print caused much trash to circulate, but it had also disseminated the Bible and the thoughts of seers and philosophers. It has never occurred to General Sarnoff that any technology could do anything but *add* itself on to what we already are.

Such economists as Robert Theobald, W. W. Rostow, and John Kenneth Galbraith have been explaining for years how it is that "classical economics" cannot explain change or growth. And the paradox of mechanization is that although it is itself the cause of maximal growth and change, the principle of mechanization excludes the very possibility of growth or the understanding of change. For mechanization is achieved by fragmentation of any process and by putting the fragmented parts in a series. Yet, as David Hume showed in the eighteenth century, there is no principle of causality in a mere sequence. That one thing follows another accounts for nothing. Nothing follows from following, except change. So the greatest of all reversals occurred with electricity, that ended sequence by making things instant. With instant speed the causes of things began to emerge to awareness again, as they had not done with things in sequence and in concatenation accordingly. Instead of asking which came first, the chicken or the egg, it suddenly seemed that a chicken was an egg's idea for getting more eggs.

Just before an airplane breaks the sound barrier, sound waves become visible on the wings of the plane. The sudden visibility of sound just as sound ends is an apt instance of that great pattern of being that reveals new and opposite forms just as the earlier forms reach their peak performance. Mechanization was never so vividly fragmented or sequential as in the birth of the movies, the moment that translated us beyond mechanism into the world of growth and organic interrelation. The movie, by sheer speeding up the mechanical, carried us from the world of sequence and connections into the world of creative configuration and structure. The message of the movie medium is that of transition from lineal connections to configurations. It is the transition that produced the now quite correct observation: "If it works, it's obsolete." When electric speed further takes over from mechanical movie sequences, then the lines of force in structures and in media become loud and clear. We return to the inclusive form of the icon.

To a highly literate and mechanized culture the movie appeared as a world of triumphant illusions and dreams that money could buy. It was at this moment of the movie that cubism occurred, and it has been described by E. H. Gombrich (*Art and Illusion*) as "the most radical attempt to stamp out ambiguity and to enforce one reading of the picture—that of a man-made construction, a colored canvas." For cubism substitutes all facets of an object simultaneously for the "point of view" or facet of perspective illusion. Instead of the specialized illusion of the third dimension on canvas, cubism sets up an interplay of planes and contradiction or dramatic conflict of patterns, lights, textures that "drives home the message" by involvement. This is held by many to be an exercise in painting, not in illusion.

In other words, cubism, by giving the inside and outside, the top, bottom, back, and front and the rest, in two dimensions, drops the illusion of perspective in favor of instant sensory awareness of the whole. Cubism, by seizing on instant total awareness, suddenly announced that *the medium is the message*. Is it not evident that the moment that the sequence yields to the simultaneous, one is in the world of the structure and of configuration? Is that not what has happened in physics as in painting, poetry, and in communication? Specialized segments of attention have shifted to total field, and we can now say, "The medium is the message" quite naturally. Before the electric speed and total field, it was not obvious that the medium is the message. The message, it seemed, was the "content," as people used to ask what a painting was *about*. Yet they never thought to ask what a melody was about, nor what a house or dress was about. In such matters, people retained some sense of the whole pattern, of form and function as a unity. But in the electric age this integral idea of structure and configuration has become so prevalent that educational theory has taken up the matter. Instead of working with specialized "problems" in arithmetic, the structural approach now follows the line of force in the field of number and has small children meditating about number theory and "sets." [...]

If the formative power in the media are the media themselves, that raises a host of large matters that can only be mentioned here, although they deserve volumes. Namely, that technological media are staples or natural resources, exactly as are coal and cotton and oil. Anybody will concede that a society whose economy is dependent upon one or two major staples like cotton, or grain, or lumber, or fish, or cattle is going to have some obvious social patterns of organization as a result. Stress on a few major staples creates extreme instability in the economy but great endurance in the population. The pathos and humor of the American South are embedded in such an economy of limited staples. For a society configured by reliance on a few commodities accepts them as a social bond quite as much as the metropolis does the press. Cotton and oil, like radio and TV, become "fixed charges" on the entire psychic life of the community. And this pervasive fact creates the unique cultural flavor of any society. It pays through the nose and all its other senses for each staple that shapes its life.

That our human senses, of which all media are extensions, are also fixed charges on our personal energies, and that they also configure the awareness and experience of each one of us, may be perceived in another connection mentioned by the psychologist C. G. Jung:

> Every Roman was surrounded by slaves. The slave and his psychology flooded ancient Italy, and every Roman became inwardly, and of course unwittingly, a slave. Because living constantly in the atmosphere of slaves, he became infected through the unconscious with their psychology. No one can shield himself from such an influence (*Contributions to Analytical Psychology*, London, 1928).

Poem, March 1966 in *Aspen* Magazine, No. 5+6, 1967

Dan Graham

Schema for a set of poems whose component pages are specifically published as individual poems in various magazines. Each poem-page is to be set in its final form by the editor of the publication where it is to appear, the exact data in each particular instance to correspond to the fact(s) of its published appearance.

1 Using any arbitrary schematic (such as the example published here) produces a large, finite permutation of specific, discrete poems.

2 If a given variant-poem is attempted to be set up by the editor following the logic step-by-step (linearly), it would be found impossible to compose a completed version of the poem as each of the component lines of exact data requiring completion (in terms of specific numbers and percentages) would be contingently determined by every other number and percentage which itself in turn would be determined by the other numbers or percentages, *ad infinitum.*

3 It would be possible to 'compose' the entire set of permutationally possible poems and to select the applicable variant(s) with the aid of a computer which could 'see' the ensemble instantly.

c Section 16, Aspen Magazine, No. 5+6

SCHEMA

(number of) adjectives
(number of) adverbs
(percentage of) area not occupied by type
(percentage of) area occupied by type
(number of) columns
(number of) conjunctions
(number of) depression of type into surface of page
(number of) gerunds
(number of) infinitives
(number of) letters of alphabet
(number of) lines
(number of) mathematical symbols
(number of) nouns
(number of) numbers
(number of) participles
(perimeter of) page
(weight of) paper sheet
(type) paper stock
(thinness of) paper stock
(number of) prepositions
(number of) pronouns
(number of point) size type
(name of) typeface
(number of) words
(number of) words capitialized
(number of) words italicized
(number of) words not capitalized
(number of) words not italicized

POEM

35 adjectives
7 adverbs
35.52% area not occupied by type
64.48% area occupied by type
1 column
1 conjunction
0 mms. depression of type into surface of page
0 gerunds
0 infinitives
247 letters of alphabet
28 lines
6 mathematical symbols
51 nouns
29 numbers
6 participles
8″ x 8″ page
80 lb. paper sheet
dull coated paper stock
.007″ thin paper stock
3 prepositions
0 pronouns
10 point size type
univers 55 typeface
61 words
3 words capitalized
0 words italicized
58 words not capitalized
61 words not italicized

My Works for Magazine Pages: A History of Conceptual Art, 1965–1969

Dan Graham

1985

I became involved with the art system accidentally, when friends of mine suggested that we open a gallery. In 1964, Richard Bellamy's Green Gallery was the most important avantgarde gallery and was just beginning to show people such as Judd, Morris, and Flavin. Our gallery, John Daniels, gave Sol Lewitt a one-man show, as well as doing several group shows which included all the 'proto-Minimalist' artists, whether they already showed at Green Gallery or not. We had also plans to have a one-man exhibition of Robert Smithson—then a young 'Pop' artist. However, the gallery was forced to close due to bankruptcy at the end of the first season.

If we could have continued for another two years, with the aid of more capital, perhaps we might have succeeded. Nevertheless, the experience of managing the gallery was particularly valuable for me in that it afforded the many conversations I had with Dan Flavin, Donald Judd, Jo Baer, Will Insley, Robert Smithson and others who, if they were not able to give works for thematic exhibitions, supported the gallery by recommending other artists and by dropping in to chat. In addition to a knowledge of current and historical art theory, some of these artists had an even greater interest, which I shared, in intellectual currents of that moment such as serial music, the French 'New Novel' (Robbe-Grillet, Butor Pinget, etc.), and new scientific theories. It was possible to connect the philosophical implications of these ideas with the art that these 'proto-Minimal' artists and more established artists such as Warhol, Johns, Stella, Lichtenstein and Oldenburg, or dancers such as Yvonne Rainer or Simon Forti, were producing.

The fall after the gallery failed, I began experimenting myself with art works which could be read as a reaction against the gallery experience, but also as a response to contradictions I discerned in gallery artists. While American Pop art of the early 1960s referred to the surrounding media world of cultural information as framework, Minimalist artwork of the middle through late 1960s would seem to be referring to the gallery's interior cube as the ultimate contextual frame of reference or support for the work. This reference was only compositional; in place of a compositional reading interior to the work, the gallery would compose the art's formal structure in relation to the gallery's interior architectural structure. That the work was equated to the architectural container tended to literalize it; both the architectural container and the work container within were meant to be seen as non-illusionistic, neutral and objectively factual—that is, as simply material. The gallery functioned literally as part of the art. One artist's work of this period (although not always his later work) examined how specific, functional architectural elements of the gallery interior prescribed meaning and determined specific readings for the art defined within its architectural frame: Dan Flavin's fluorescent light installations.

Lighting—lighting fixtures—within the architectural setting of the gallery/museum are normally disregarded, or considered merely functional or minor interior decoration. As gallery space is meant to appear neutral, the lighting, which creates this neutrality as much as the white walls, and at the same time is used to highlight and center attention on the art on the wall or floor, is kept inconspicuous. While the background in general makes the art works visible, the lighting literally makes the works visible.

The lighting system, within which the specific light fixtures of a gallery arrangement function, is both part of the gallery apparatus and part of the larger, existing (non-art) system of electric lighting in general use:

> I believe that the changing standard lighting system should support my idea within it.
> —Dan Flavin, 'Some Remarks', *Artforum* Magazine, 1967.

Flavin's installations make use of this double functioning (inside and outside the gallery/art context) as well as the double connotation of lighting as minor decoration (interior decoration) and anonymously functional creator of the gallery's neutrality:

> I believe that art is shedding its vaunted mystery for a common sense of keenly realized decoration. Symbolizing is dwindling—becoming slight. We are pressing downward toward no art—a mutual sense of psychologically indifferent decoration—a neutral pleasure of seeing known to everyone.
> —Dan Flavin, 'Some Other Remarks', *Artforum* Magazine, 1967.

His arrangements of light fixtures in a gallery space depend for significance, contextually, upon the function of the gallery, and the socially determined architectural use of electrical lighting. Use of electric light is related to a specific time in history. Flavin has observed that when the existing system of electric lighting has ceased to exist, his art would no longer function. Being in a series of standardized, re-placeable units, which, in Flavin's words, 'can be bought in any hardware store', his arrangements of fluorescent tubes within the interior or adjacent exterior architectural frame of the gallery exhibition-space function only in situation installation and upon completion of the exhibition cease to function artistically.

Perhaps I misread the implications of these works by suggesting a conscious intention to examine the relation of the value of art to the question of the gallery in which it is exhibited. I also felt that the 'solution' which Marcel Duchamp had found to this problem of art's 'value' was unsatisfactory.

In his 'readymades', Duchamp brought objects which were not considered as art when placed outside the gallery into the gallery to prove dialectically that it is in fact the gallery which gives the object its value and meaning. Instead of reducing gallery objects to the common level of the everyday object, this ironic gesture simply extended the reach of the gallery's exhibition territory. In bringing the 'non-art' object into the gallery, Duchamp wished to place both the conventional function of the gallery to designate certain objects as 'art' and to exclude others in apparent contradiction.

Essentially Duchamp attempted to question the aristocratic function of art and the art gallery as an institution. Because this question was only presented on a logical abstract level, his critique was itself immediately integrated back into the institutional system of gallery or museum art, becoming a kind of 'idea' art. A further problem with Duchamp's analysis is the resolution of the contradiction between gallery art and art in relation to its social value based on a historical concept; the condition of art is seen as neither social nor as subject to external social change. By contrast, Flavin's fluorescent light pieces are not merely *a priori* philosophical idealizations, but have concrete relations to specific details of the architectural arrangement of the gallery, details which produce meaning.

In addition, Duchamp saw the problem of value and meaning in art as a simple binary opposition, inside the gallery or outside in the world. He failed to link this opposition of art and so-called 'non-art' to more ambiguous phenomena such as the reproduction of the art object by the media, which was meditated upon by the critic Walter Benjamin in the 1930s and was even earlier an important aspect of Constructivist art.

Through the actual experience of running a gallery, I learned that if a work of art wasn't written about and reproduced in a magazine it would have difficulty attaining the status of 'art'. It seemed that in order to be defined as having value, that is as 'art', a work had only to be exhibited in a gallery and then to be written about and reproduced as a photograph in an art magazine. Then this record of the no longer extant installation, along with more accretions of information after the fact, became the basis for its fame, and to a large extent, its economic value.

From one perspective, the art object can be analyzed as inseparably connected to the institution of the gallery, or museum; but from another perspective it can be seen as having a certain independence, as it belongs also to the general cultural framework which the magazine is a part of. Magazines specialize in a way which replicates other social and economic divisions. Any magazine, no matter how generalized, caters to a certain market or a specific audience in a particular field. All art magazines are directed towards people who are involved in the art world professionally in one way or another. Furthermore, the art magazine itself is supported by advertisements which, with one or two exceptions, come from art galleries who are presenting exhibitions. It follows that in some way the advertisers have to be taken care of in that their shows have to be reviewed and made a matter of record in the magazine. Thus these shows and works are guaranteed some kind of value and can be sold on the market as 'art'. The fact that sales do take place yields enough money for the gallery to purchase more advertisements in art magazines and to sustain the art system in general.

Art magazines ultimately depend upon art galleries for their economic support, just as the work shown in galleries depends on photographic reproduction for its value in the media. Magazines determine a place or are a frame of reference both outside and inside. Magazines specialize in a 'field' in a way which replicates other social and economic divisions—for instance, the specialized 'world' of art and artists termed the 'art' world. Each magazine, no matter how generalized, always caters to a certain market or a certain audience in a certain field; *Sports Illustrated* caters to those who are interested in sports, the *American Legion* magazine caters to members of the American Legions. All art magazines cater to people who professionally or institutionally are involved in the art world—either as artists, dealers, collectors, connoisseurs, writers, they all have a professional interest. And the art magazine itself is supported by advertisements.

If Minimal art took its meaning from the notion that the gallery is an object support, by comparison Pop art took its meaning from the surrounding media-world of images. Pop wished to undermine the notions of quality in fine art by using mass-cultural content. Since it fed its pictures through the magazines back into popular culture, Pop art also made an ironic comment about popular culture to itself. What Pop pointed out was that the information media, such as magazines, could be used dialectically with the art system. That is, a work could function in terms of both the art language and the popular language of the media at the same time, commenting upon and placing in perspective the assumptions of each. I designed works for magazine pages which would both be self-defined and would relate through their context to the surrounding information on the other printed pages.

The most 'absolute' of these works is *Schema (March 1966)*. Each published example of this piece appears as an isolated page in different magazines. The work cannot be exhibited except through its placement in a magazine. If it were placed within an art magazine, a page would be situated in relation to reviews of gallery shows, articles, and reproductions of art works, and it could analyze the function of the magazine in relation to the gallery system.

Conventionally, art magazines reproduce second-hand art which exists first, as phenomenological presence, in galleries. Turning this upside down, *Schema (March 1966)* only exists by its presence in the functional structure of the magazine and can only be exhibited in a gallery second-hand.

Variations of *Schema (March 1966)* generate themselves through the work's self-defining decomposition in terms of its printed appearance as a two-dimensional page printed with physical 'informational' characteristics such as the quality of paper stock, the amount of black type proportionate to unprinted paper, the point size of the type, etc. Place is reduced to the present appearance of information in terms; the work is composed as it decomposes into the constituent material elements of its context. Its place pertained to both the work's internal grammatical structure and to the external physical position it occupied.

Each publishing of this work is inherently unlike the others and in different magazine issues the specific meanings (content) inevitably change with the context of its placement. A magazine page thereby generates its meanings from the overall context in which it is published, particularly the pages immediately surrounding it. The meaning of the work is contingent upon the specific meaning of each of its appearances; collectively it has no one meaning.

This work functions as both art and as art criticism. Unlike a Stella painting of the early period, the variants of *Schema* are not simply self-referential. This is because of the use of the magazine system as support. Magazines determine a place or frame of reference both outside and inside what is defined as 'Art'.

I wanted to make a Pop art which was more literally disposable (an idea which was alluded to in Warhol's idea of replacing 'quality' for 'quantity', the logic of a consumer society). I wanted to make an art-form which could not be reproduced or exhibited in a gallery/museum, and I wanted to make a further reduction of the Minimal object to a not necessarily esthetic two-dimensional form (which was not painting or drawing): printed matter which was mass reproduced and mass disposable information. Putting it in magazine pages meant that it also could be 'read' in juxtaposition to the usual reproduction art, art criticism, reviews, reproductions in the rest of the magazine and form a critique of the magazine (in relation to the gallery structure).

Magazines have issues which appear at regular time intervals; a magazine's contents continuously change to reflect present-time currency: magazines deal with current events. While gallery art is defined by its enclosure as 'timeless', magazines pre-suppose a notion of present-time (timeliness) which only has value as it is current, each successive issue defining 'new' or 'up-to-date' in terms of the present moment. However, the notion of news is not merely dependent upon the internal institution, but equally upon the institutions which generate its news content and finance its existence through the purchasing of advertisements. For the art magazine, it is the art gallery whose definition of 'Art' and whose advertisements uphold the existence of the art magazine.

The one magazine piece which was most like a conventional article was *Homes for America*, printed in *Arts Magazine*, December 1966–January 1967. It is an article designed around photos of suburban tract housing estates taken over a period of two years. It is important that the photographs are not seen alone, but as part of the over-all magazine article lay-out. They are illustrations of the text, or inversely, the text functions in relation to the photographs thereby modifying their meanings. The photographs and the text are separate parts of a two-dimensional schematic grid perspective system. The photographs correlate to the lists and columns of serial documentation and both 'represent' the serial logic of the housing developments which the article is about. I think the fact that *Homes for America* was, in the end, only a magazine article, and made no claims for itself as a work of art, is its most important feature.

My *Scheme* (1965) is for use either as a page (to be truncated when the last line nears the base of the sheet of paper) or to be extended indefinitely in book form (published by Gerald Ferguson). In the book the angle of the triangle diminishes gradually to infinity with the progression to cause a cessation at some point in the book's interior. It begins at a point and is read. Placing is ordering of terms as in reading the reader's eye's place (or point of fixation) is continually shifting.

My *Extended Distance/Extended Time* (1969) and *Side Effects/Common Drugs* (1966) function as gridded data fields generating an optical-matrix perspective. They can be read as 'spatialized' 'effects' in time. In *Side Effects/Common Drugs* the optical-reflexive time sequence of the reading constitutes the content. The dots have the sequence of effect/response plus 'spatial' 'density'. Reading from the terms in horizontal/vertical order or the side (or obliquely) we 'see' that symptoms (causes or 'side' effects) produced by the cure or drug to correct these side effects from the taking of the first drugs, and so on. . . . The extension of the data field (in the time of the reading process) continues until all self-reflexive effects—points—are optically canceled.

Homes for America [photo offset reproduction of layout for magazine article]

Dan Graham

1972

Homes for America

D. GRAHAM

Belleplain	**Garden City**
Brooklawn	**Garden City Park**
Colonia	**Greenlawn**
Colonia Manor	**Island Park**
Fair Haven	**Levitown**
Fair Lawn	**Middleville**
Greenfields Village	**New City Park**
Green Village	**Pine Lawn**
Plainsboro	**Plainview**
Pleasant Grove	**Plandome Manor**
Pleasant Plains	**Pleasantside**
Sunset Hill Garden	**Pleasantville**

Large-scale 'tract' housing 'developments' constitute the new city. They are located everywhere. They are not particularly bound to existing communities; they fail to develop either regional characteristics or separate identity. These 'projects' date from the end of World War II when in southern California speculators or 'operative' builders adapted mass production techniques to quickly build many houses for the defense workers over-concentrated there. This 'California Method' consisted simply of determining in advance the exact amount and lengths of pieces of lumber and multiplying them by the number of standardized houses to be built. A cutting yard was set up near the site of the project to saw rough lumber into those sizes. By mass buying, greater use of machines and factory produced parts, assembly line standardization, multiple units were easily fabricated.

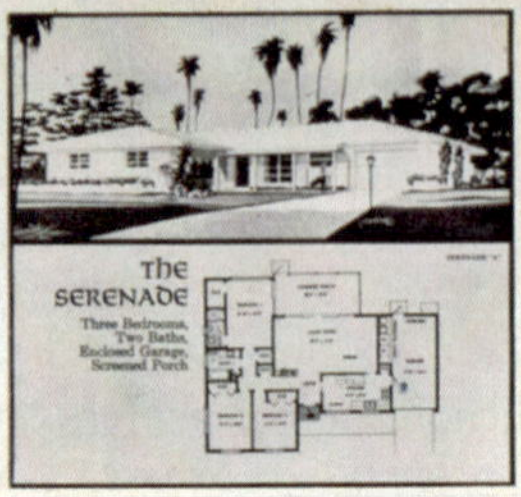

"The Serenade" - Cape Coral unit, Fla.

Each house in a development is a lightly constructed 'shell' although this fact is often concealed by fake (half-stone) brick walls. Shells can be added or subtracted easily. The standard unit is a box or a series of boxes, sometimes contemptuously called 'pillboxes.' When the box has a sharply oblique roof it is called a Cape Cod. When it is longer than wide it is a 'ranch.' A

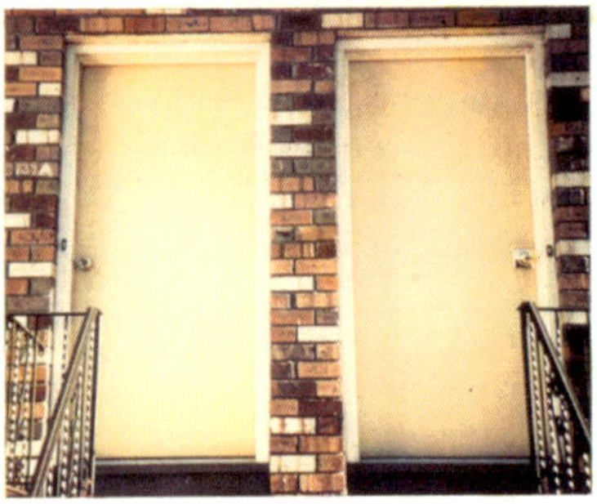

Two Entrance Doorways, 'Two Home Homes', Jersey City, N.J.

two-story house is usually called 'colonial.' If it consists of contiguous boxes with one slightly higher elevation it is a 'split level.' Such stylistic differentiation is advantageous to the basic structure (with the possible exception of the split level whose plan simplifies construction on discontinuous ground levels).

There is a recent trend toward 'two home homes' which are two boxes split by adjoining walls and having separate entrances. The left and right hand units are mirror reproductions of each other. Often sold as private units are strings of apartment-like, quasi-discrete cells formed by subdividing laterally an extended rectangular parallelopiped into as many as ten or twelve separate dwellings.

Developers usually build large groups of individual homes sharing similar floor plans and whose overall grouping possesses a discrete flow plan. Regional shopping centers and industrial parks are sometimes integrated as well into the general scheme. Each development is sectioned into blocked-out areas containing a series of identical or sequentially related types of houses all of which have uniform or staggered set-backs and land plots.

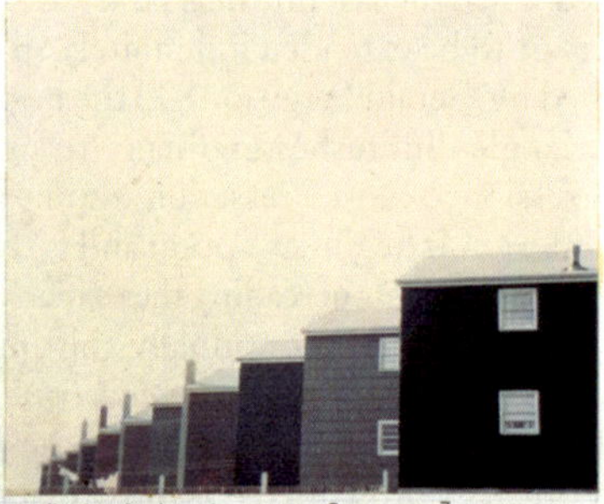

Housing Development, rear view, Bayonne, New Jersey

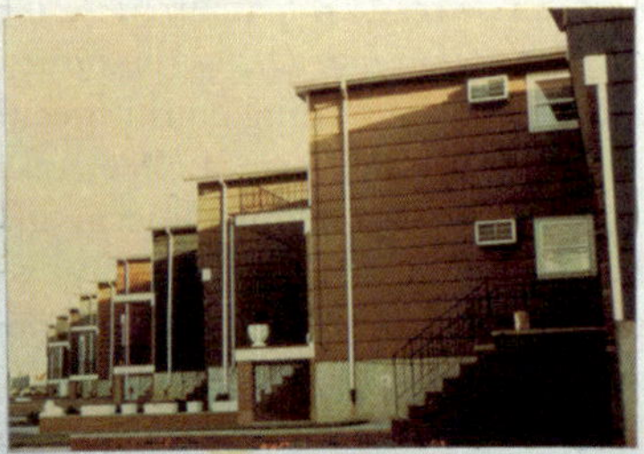

Housing Development, front view, Bayonne, New Jersey

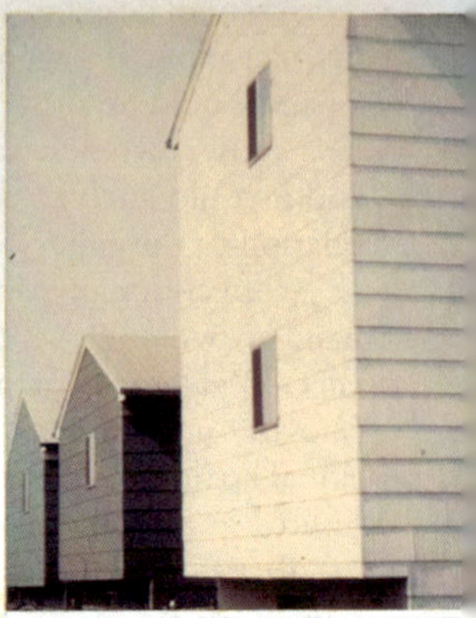

Set-back, Jersey City, New Jersey

The logic relating each sectioned part to the entire plan follows a systematic plan. A development contains a limited, set number of house models. For instance, Cape Coral, a Florida project, advertises eight different models:

A The Sonata
B The Concerto
C The Overture
D The Ballet
E The Prelude
F The Serenade
G The Noctune
H The Rhapsody

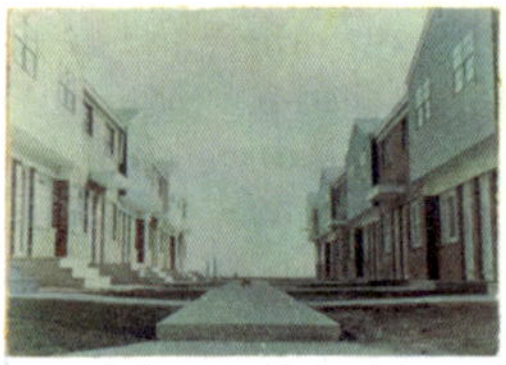

Center Court, Entrance, Development, Jersey City, N

In addition, there is a choice of eight exterior colors:
1 White
2 Moonstone Grey
3 Nickle

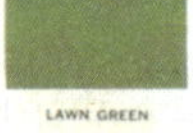

LAWN GREEN

4 Seafoam Green
5 Lawn Green
6 Bamboo
7 Coral Pink
8 Colonial Red

As the color series usually varies independent of the model series, a block of eight houses utilizing four models and four colors might have forty-eight times forty-eight or 2,304 possible arrangements.

Dan Graham

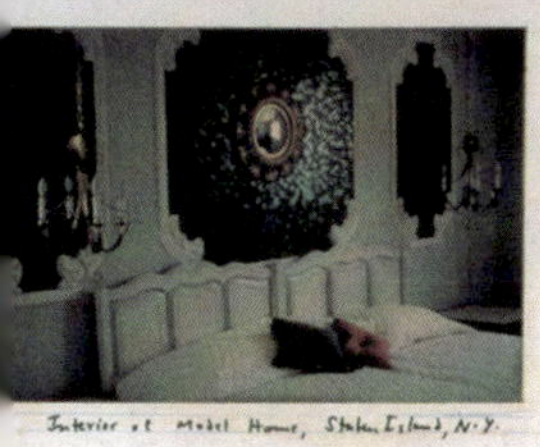

Interior of Model Home, Staten Island, N.Y.

ach block of houses is a self-contained sequence — there is no development — selected from the ossible acceptable arrangements. As an example, if a section was to contain eight houses of hich four model types were to be used, any of ese permutational possibilities could be used:

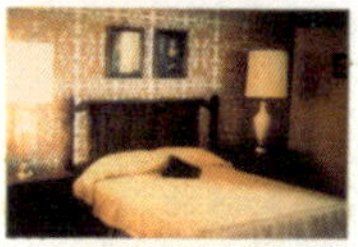

Bedroom of Model Home, S.I., N.Y.

AABBCCDD	ABCDABCD
AABBDDCC	ABDCABDC
AACCBBDD	ACBDACBD
AACCDDBB	ACDBACDB
AADDCCBB	ADBCADBC
AADDBBCC	ADCBADCB
BBAADDCC	BACDBACD
BBCCAADD	BCADBCAD
BBCCDDAA	BCDABCDA
BBDDAACC	BDACBDAC
BBDDCCAA	BDCABDCA
CCAABBDD	CABDCABD
CCAADDBB	CADBCADB
CCBBDDAA	CBADCBAD
CCBBAADD	CBDACBDA
CCDDAABB	CDABCDAB
CCDDBBAA	CDBACDBA
DDAABBCC	DACBDACB
DDAACCBB	DABCDABC
DDBBAACC	DBACDBAC
DDBBCCAA	DBCADBCA
DDCCAABB	DCABDCAB
DDCCBBAA	DCBADCBA

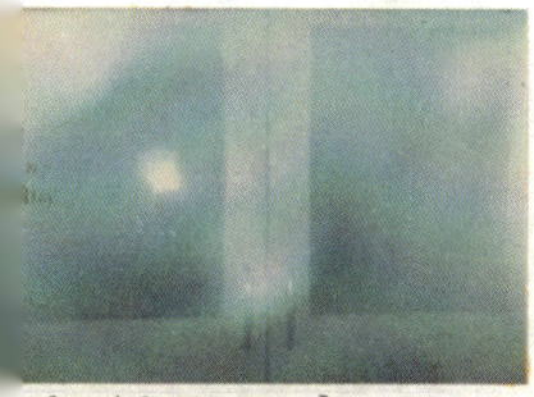

Basement Doors, Home, New Jersey

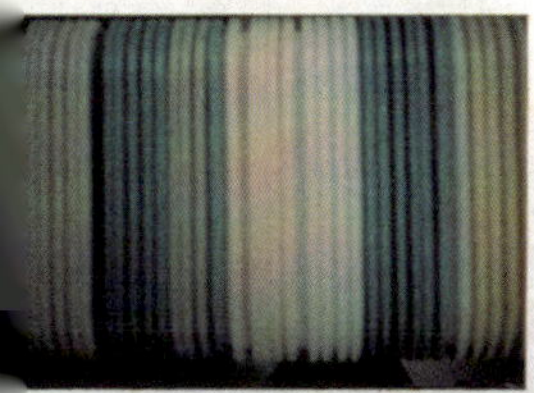

Discount Store', Sweaters on Racks, New Jersey

The 8 color variables were equally distributed among the house exteriors. The first buyers were more likely to have obtained their first choice in color. Family units had to make a choice based on the available colors which also took account of both husband and wife's likes and dislikes. Adult male and female color likes and dislikes were compared in a survey of the homeowners:

'Like'

Male	Female
Skyway	Skyway Blue
Colonial Red	Lawn Green
Patio White	Nickle
Yellow Chiffon	Colonial Red
Lawn Green	Yellow Chiffon
Nickle	Patio White
Fawn	Moonstone Grey
Moonstone Grey	Fawn

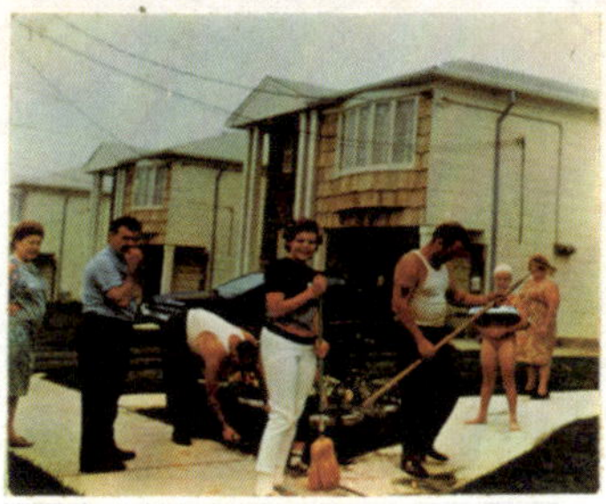

Two Family Units, Staten Island, N.Y.

'Dislike'

Male	Female
Lawn Green	Patio White
Colonial Red	Fawn
Patio White	Colonial Red
Moonstone Grey	Moonstone Grey
Fawn	Yellow Chiffon
Yellow Chiffon	Lawn Green
Nickle	Skyway blue
Skyway Blue	Nickle

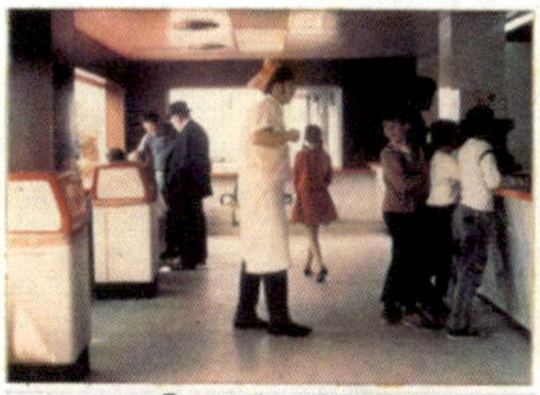

Car Hop, Jersey City, N.J.

A given development might use, perhaps, *four* of these possibilities as an arbitrary scheme for different sectors; then select four from another scheme which utilizes the remaining four unused models and colors; then select four from another scheme which utilizes all eight models and eight colors; then four from another scheme which utilizes a single model and all eight colors (or four or two colors); and finally utilize that single scheme for one model and one color. This serial logic might follow consistently until, at the edges, it is abruptly terminated by pre-existent highways, bowling alleys, shopping plazas, car hops, discount houses, lumber yards or factories.

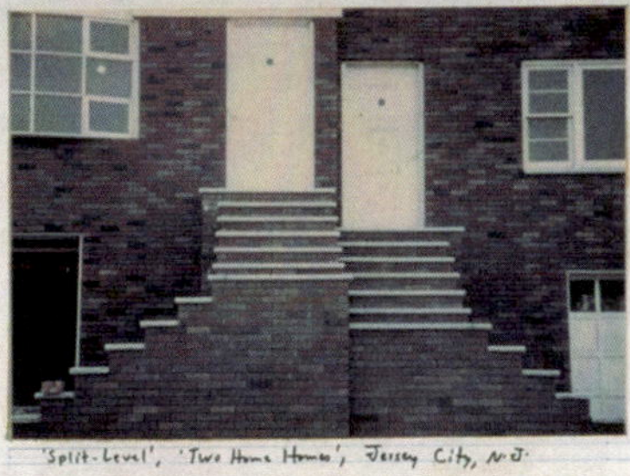

'Split-Level', 'Two Home Homes', Jersey City, N.J.

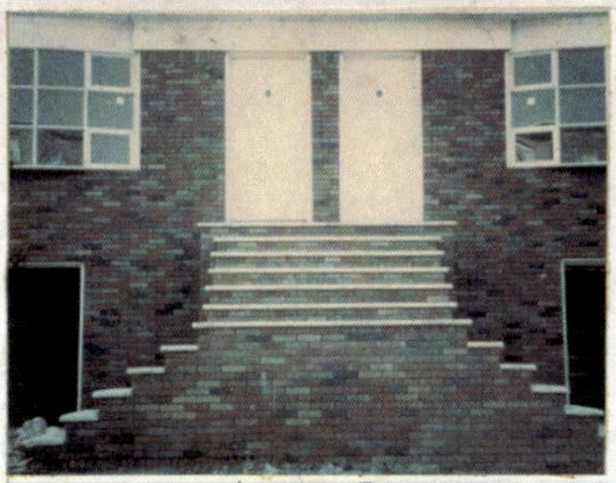

'Ground-Level', 'Two Home Homes', Jersey City, N.J.

Although there is perhaps some aesthetic precedence in the row houses which are indigenous to many older cities along the east coast, and built with uniform façades and set-backs early this century, housing developments as an architectural phenomenon seem peculiarly gratuitous. They exist apart from prior standards of 'good' architecture. They were not built to satisfy individual needs or tastes. The owner is completely tangential to the product's completion. His home isn't really possessable in the old sense; it wasn't designed to 'last for generations'; and outside of its immediate 'here and now' context it is useless, designed to be thrown away. Both architecture and craftsmanship as values are subverted by the dependence on simplified and easily duplicated techniques of fabrication and standardized modular plans. Contingencies such as mass production technology and land use economics make the final decisions, denying the architect his former 'unique' role. Developments stand in an altered relationship to their environment. Designed to fill in 'dead' land areas, the houses needn't adapt to or attempt to withstand Nature. There is no organic unity connecting the land site and the home. Both are without roots — separate parts in a larger, predetermined, synthetic order.

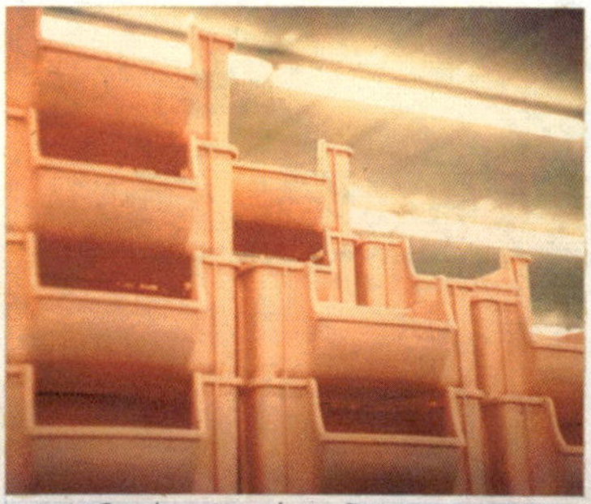

Kitchen Trays, 'Discount House', New Jersey

ARTS MAGAZINE/December 1966-January 1967

Dan Graham

Selections from *House Beautiful: Bringing the War Home*
Martha Rosler
ca. 1967–72

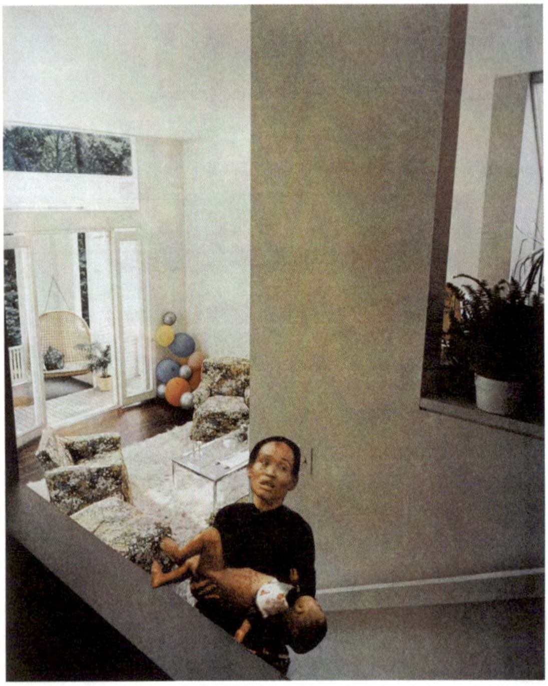

Balloons

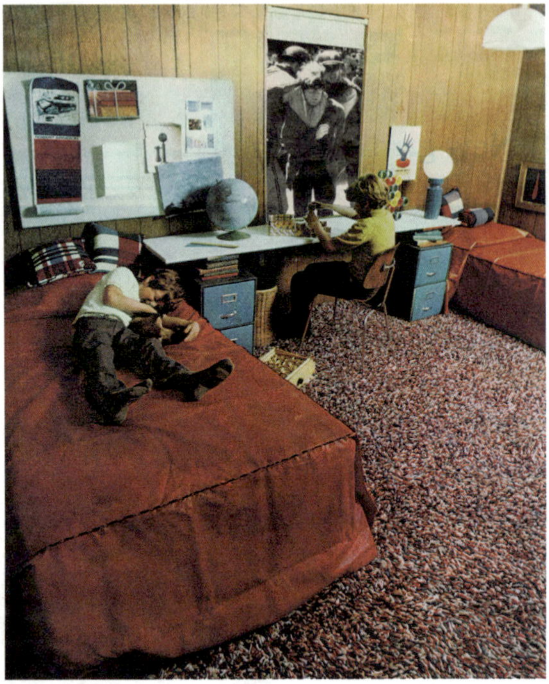

Boys Room

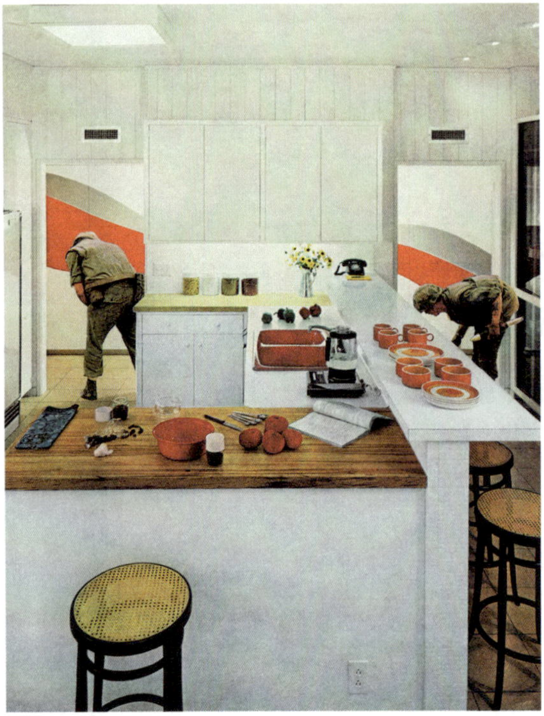

Red Stripe Kitchen

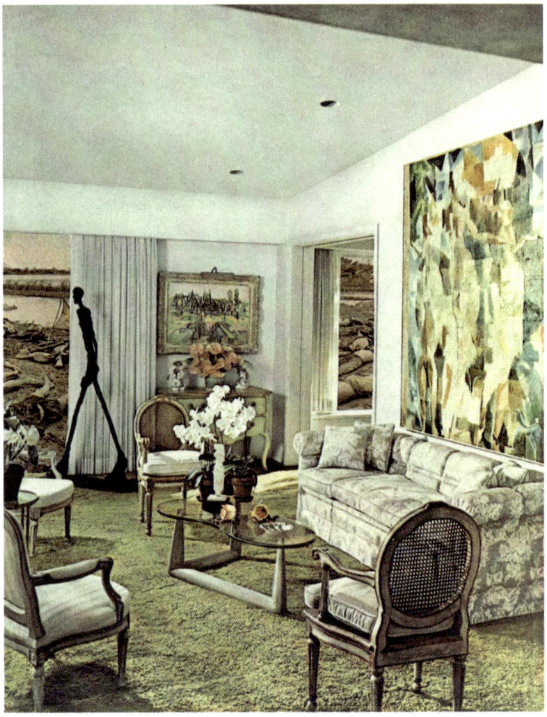

Giacometti

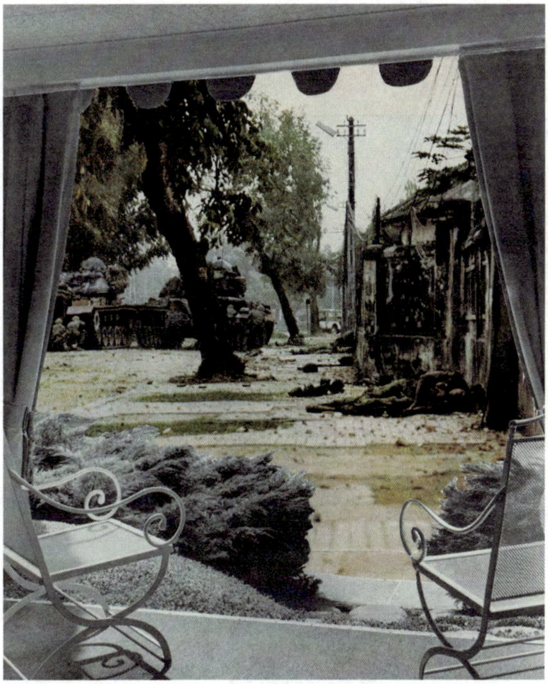

Patio View

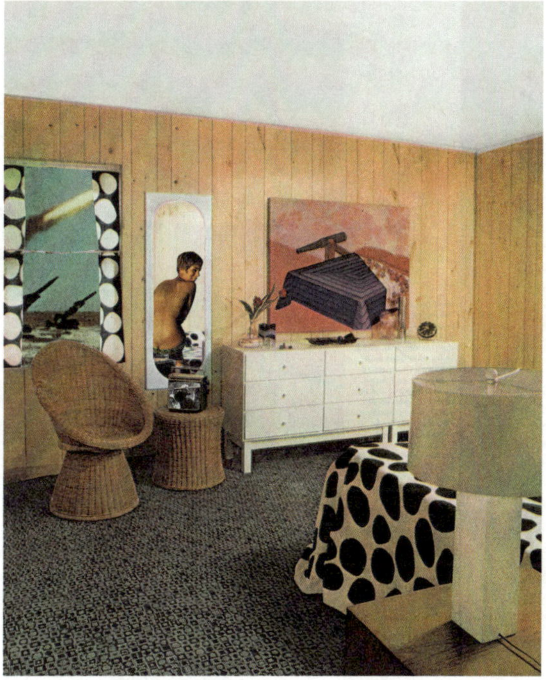

Woman with Cannon (Dots)

Tron (Amputee) in *Goodbye to All That,* No. 3, October 13, 1970
Martha Rosler

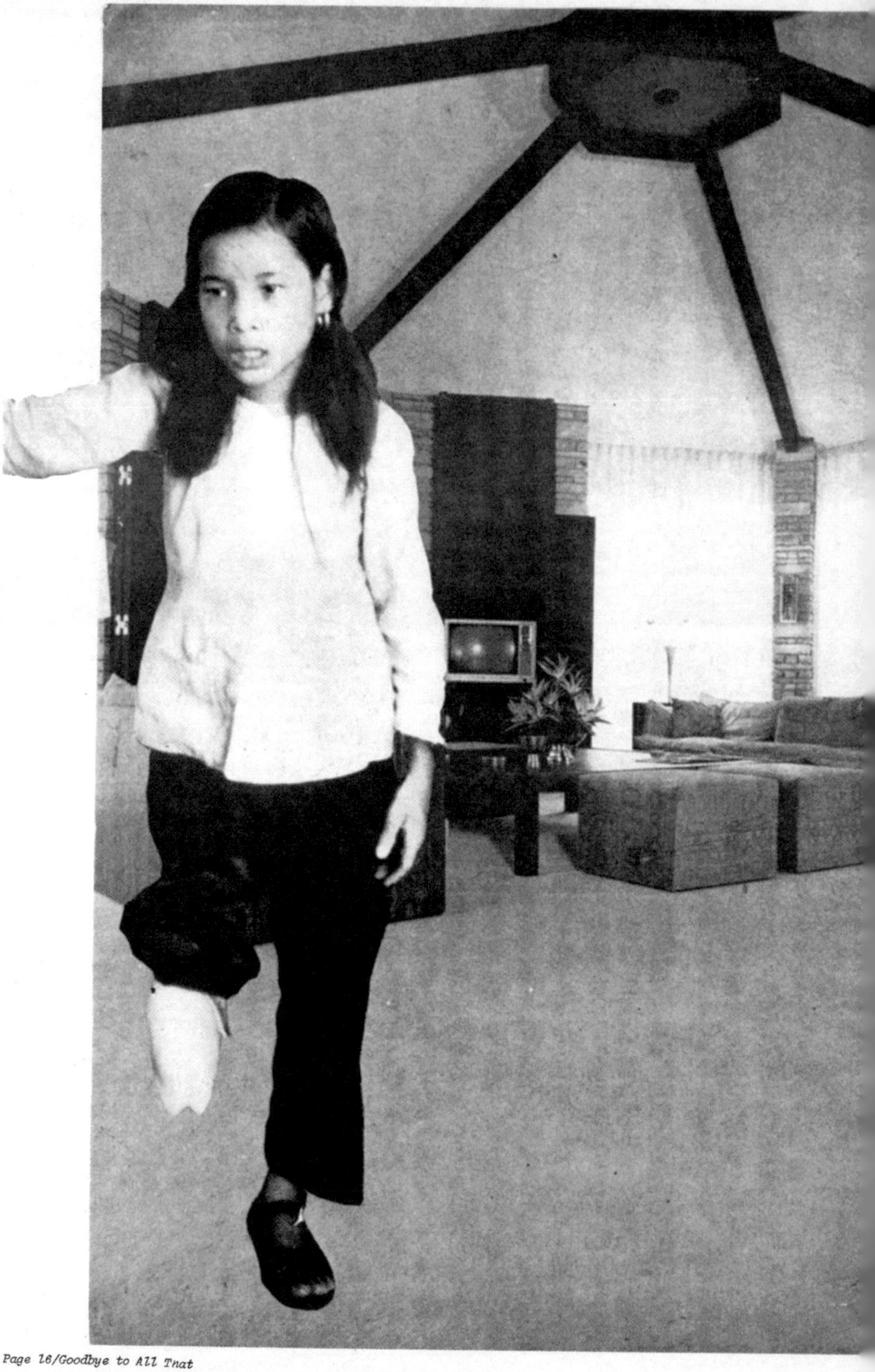

Page 16/Goodbye to All That

GOODBYE TO ALL THAT!

Newspaper for San Diego Women
ssue #3 October 13 1970 Price S.D. 20¢ elsewhere 25¢

THE POWER OF WOMEN UNITED CAN FREE US ALL

IN THIS ISSUE

2 WOMEN: JANIS JOPLIN AND KHADEJHA McCALL
WHITEFRONT SELL-IN
SAN DIEGO HOUSING
CHICANO NEIGHBORHOOD HOUSE
JOB DISCRIMINATION IN A SEXIST SOCIETY PART 2
HE NATURAL WOMAN AND THE WORM
UCSD DAY CARE CENTER
SDSC CHILD CARE TEACH-IN

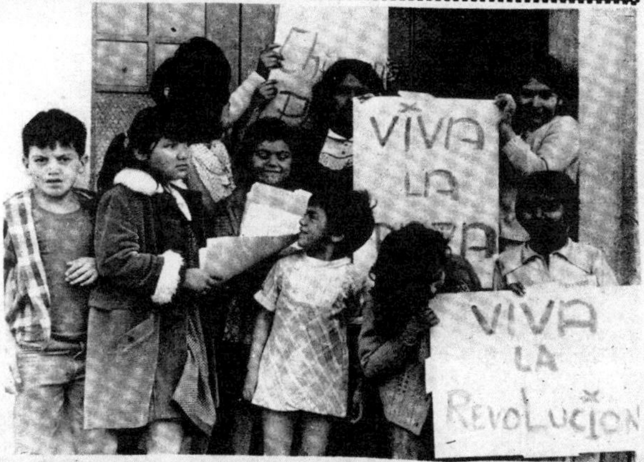

REMEMBER THE NEIGHBOR

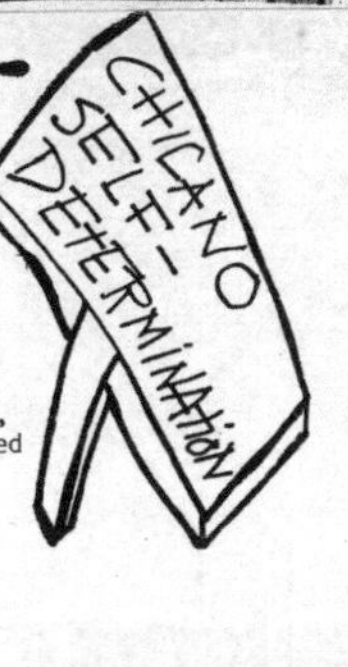

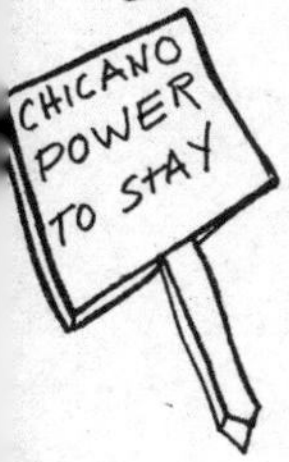

The Chicano community liberated the Neighborhood House on National Avenue Monday October 5th.

Neighborhood house was established in 1912. Up until 1960 it was the hub of the community and met many of the people's needs. The house provided day-care, a free medical and dental clinic and a sports facility. Free milk was distributed and classes held for people of all ages. Subjects such as English, crafts and cooking were taught and the children had free access to a supervised playground. At this time Neighborhood House was funded solely by United Community Services.

In 1960 Neighborhood House began to receive Federal aid. Along with the money came a stifling web of bureaucratic procedures. Resources and functions were divided between the National Avenue House and six other Neighborhood Houses. This resulted in the social services being widely scattered throughout Southeast San Diego and inaccessible to the people in the Logan Heights area. There is, for example, no easily accessible distribution point for food commodities.

Neighborhood House became an administrative center and its service facilities were shut down. The playground, for example, is now a staff parking lot. The four hundred or so children within a ten block radius now have nowhere to play but the streets.

The Board of Directors of Neighborhood House is out of touch with the community and will not meet their needs. There has never been a Chicano on the Board. There is no one on the Board who is even bilingual. 51% of the building staff is Chicano, but they are hired for menial work.

The people presented their demands to WRO which met with the Board several times. They were told to get committees together and generally given the bureaucratic brushoff.

The community had also heard that Neighborhood House was about to be sold. They began picketing with the local WRO chapter on Sept. 17th.

On the 5th Oct. several Brown Berets liberated the building and barricaded themselves inside. They have been inside since then, holding official papers and equipment (they released the payroll records). A sign on the door says: "No one gets in. No one."

(cont. page 2)

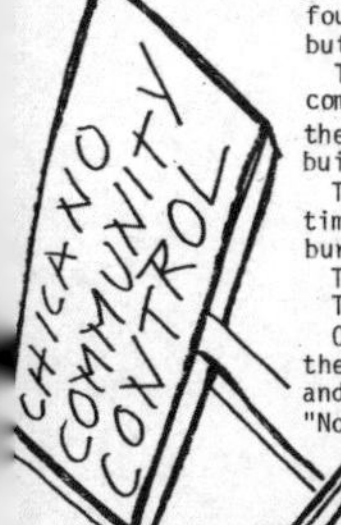

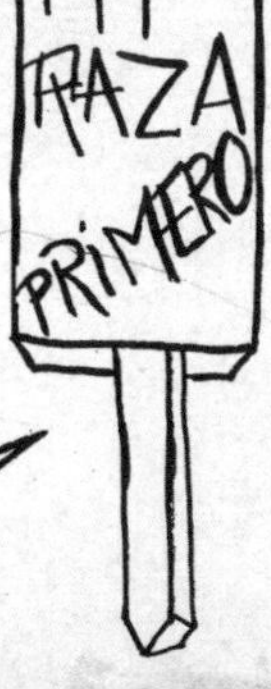

Seized Oct. 5th 1970 The year of the Chicano

Amarillo—Tall in Texas

Stephen Shore

1971

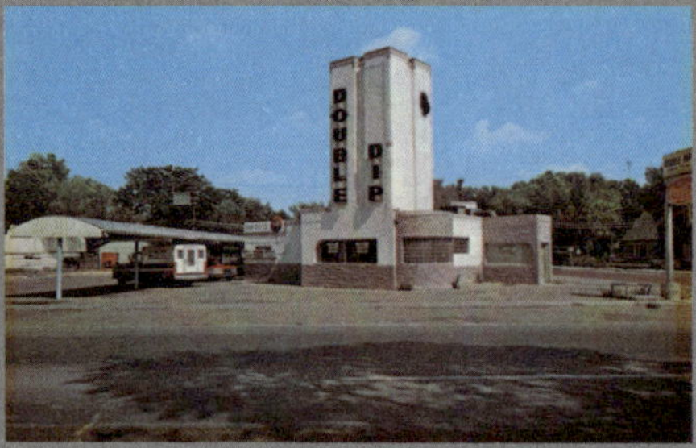

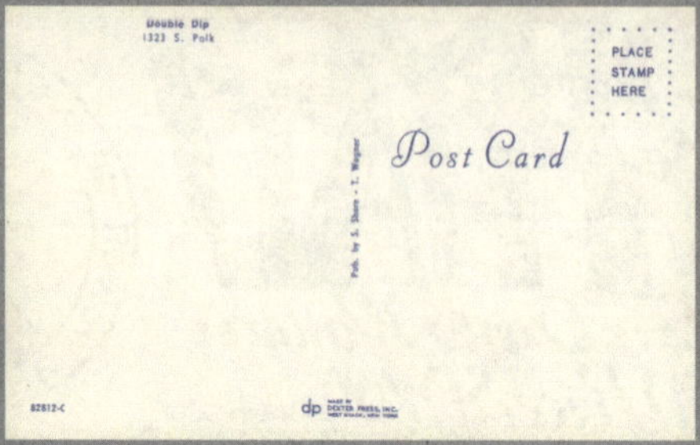

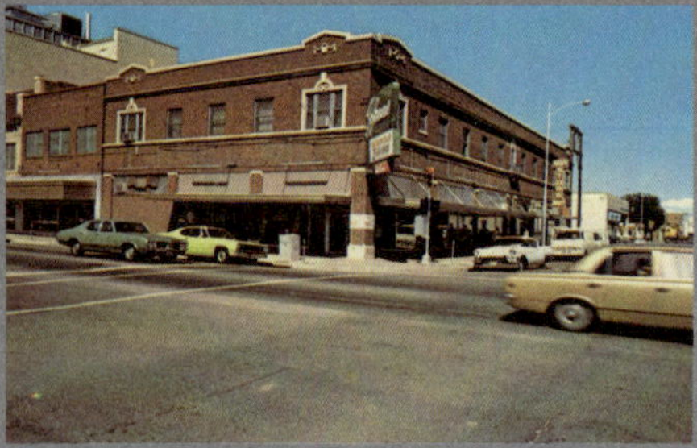

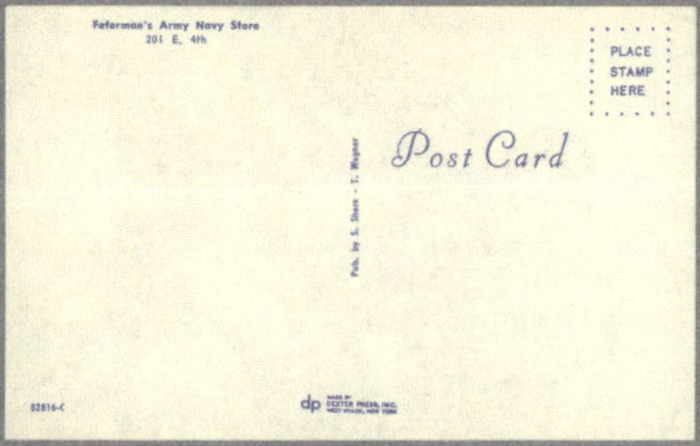

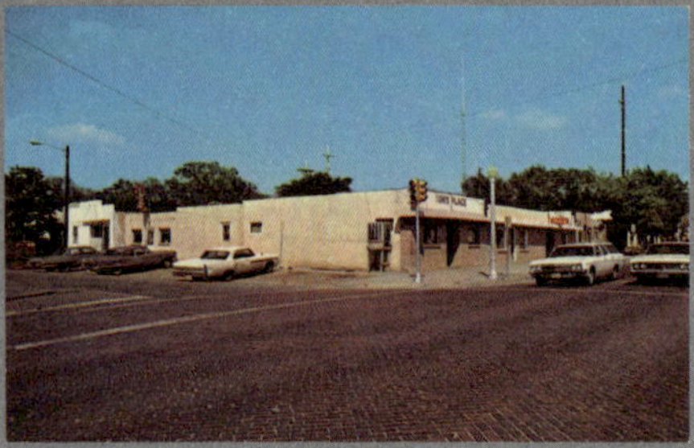

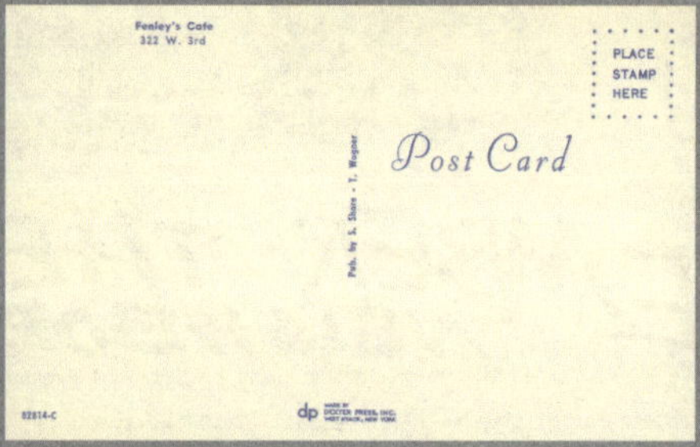

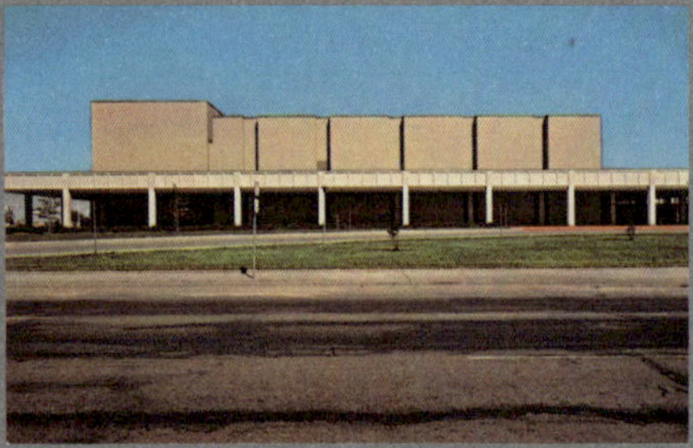

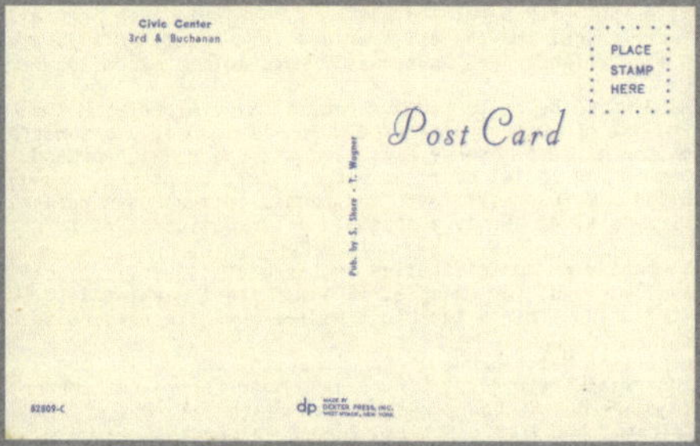

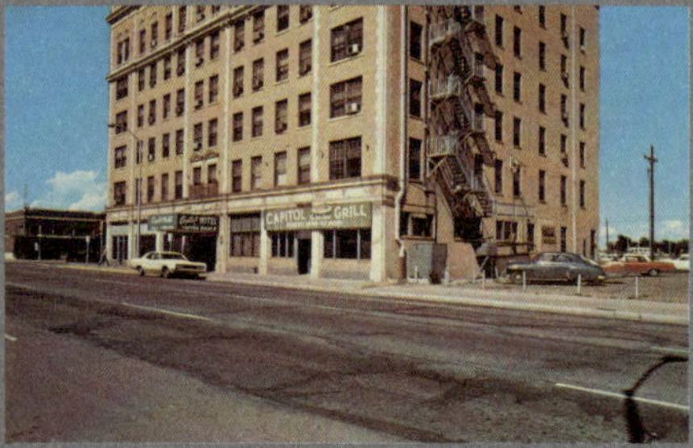

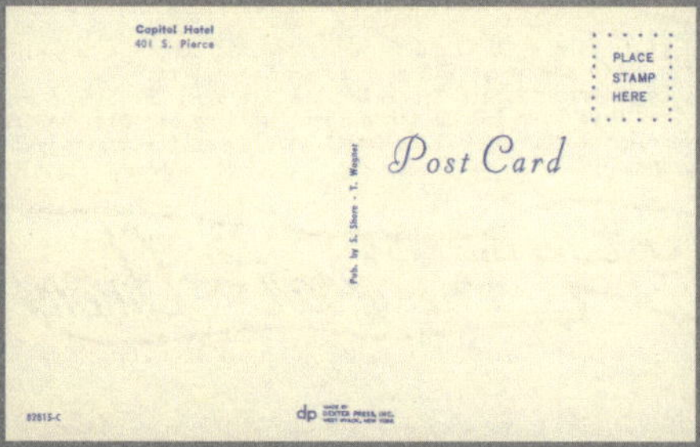

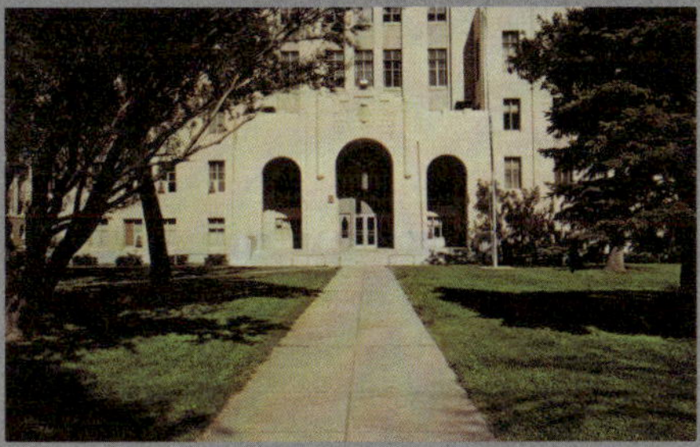

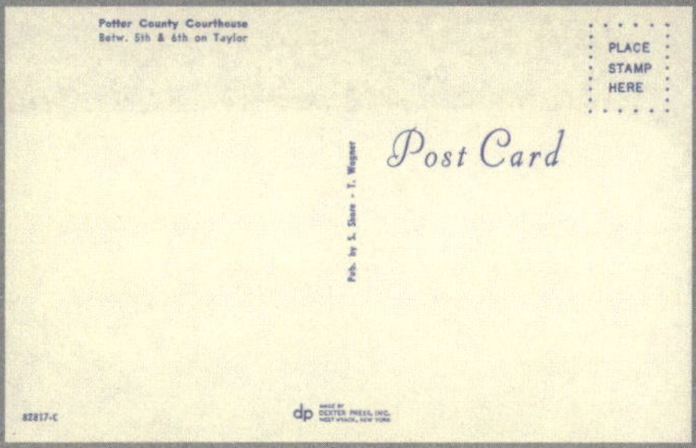
Potter County Courthouse
Betw. 5th & 6th on Taylor
PLACE STAMP HERE
Post Card
Pub. by S. Shore - T. Wagner
82817-C
dp MADE BY DEXTER PRESS, INC. WEST NYACK, NEW YORK

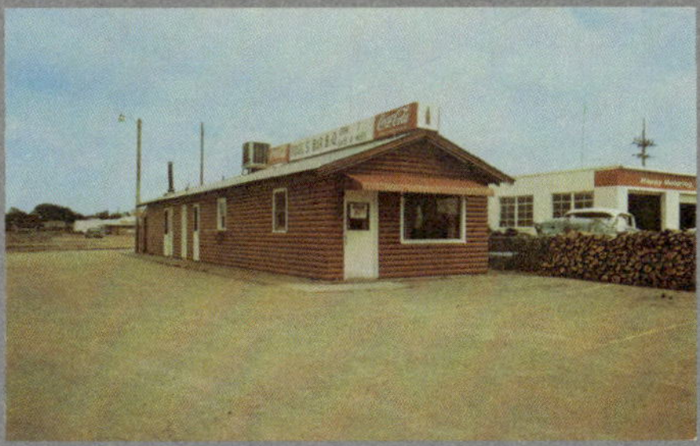

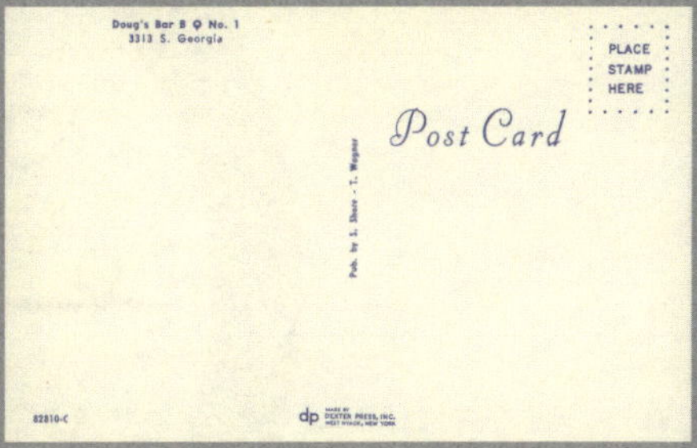
Doug's Bar B Q No. 1
3313 S. Georgia
PLACE STAMP HERE
Post Card
Pub. by S. Shore - T. Wagner
82810-C
dp MADE BY DEXTER PRESS, INC. WEST NYACK, NEW YORK

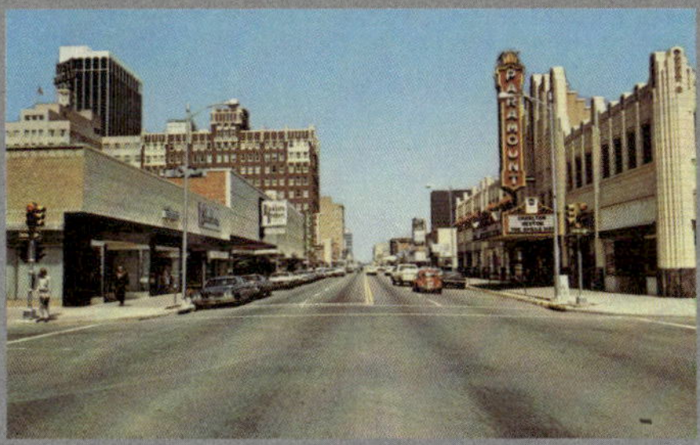

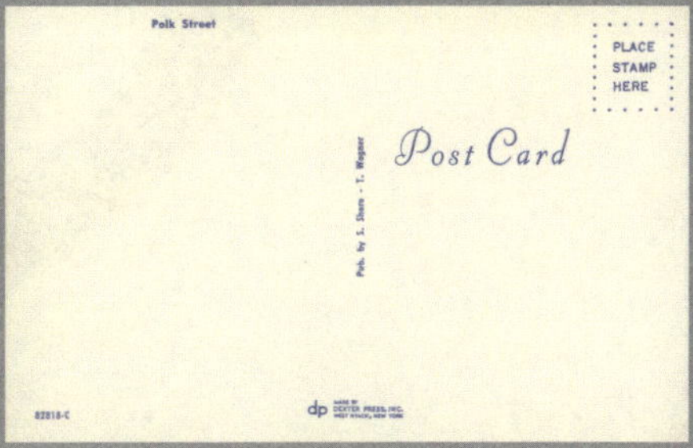
Polk Street
PLACE STAMP HERE
Post Card
Pub. by S. Shore - T. Wagner
82818-C
dp MADE BY DEXTER PRESS, INC. WEST NYACK, NEW YORK

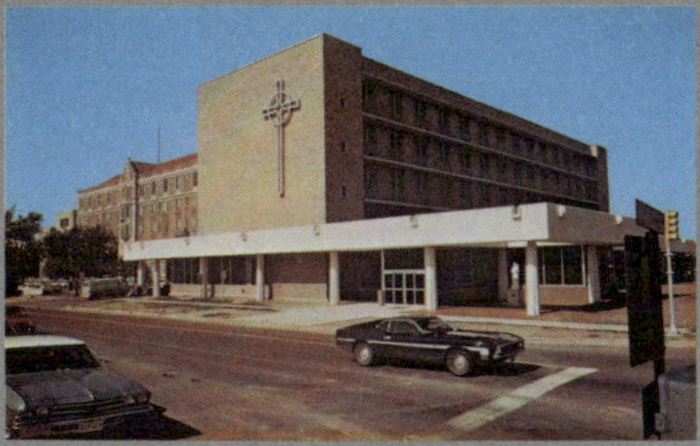

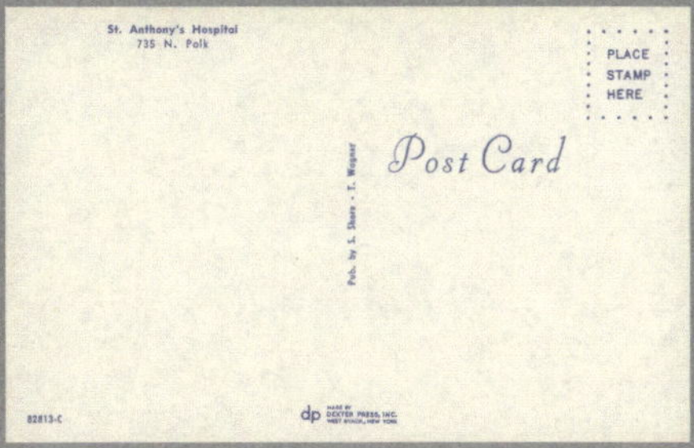
St. Anthony's Hospital
735 N. Polk
PLACE STAMP HERE
Post Card
Pub. by S. Shore - T. Wagner
82813-C
dp MADE BY DEXTER PRESS, INC. WEST NYACK, NEW YORK

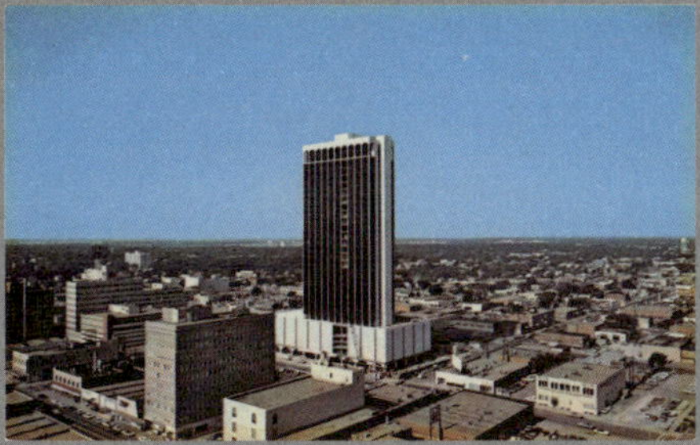

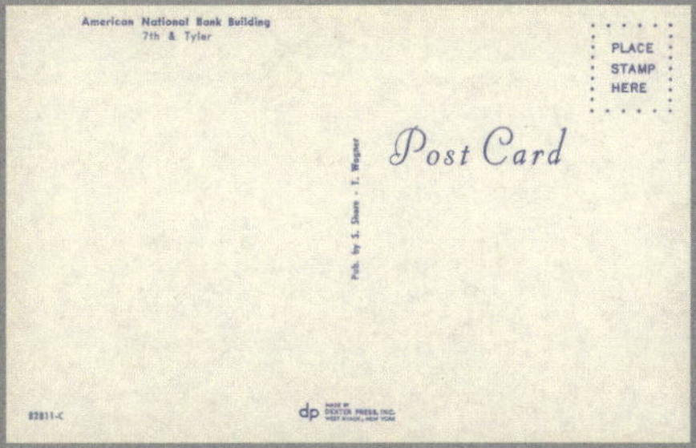
American National Bank Building
7th & Tyler
PLACE STAMP HERE
Post Card
Pub. by S. Shore - T. Wagner
82811-C
dp MADE BY DEXTER PRESS, INC. WEST NYACK, NEW YORK

1968

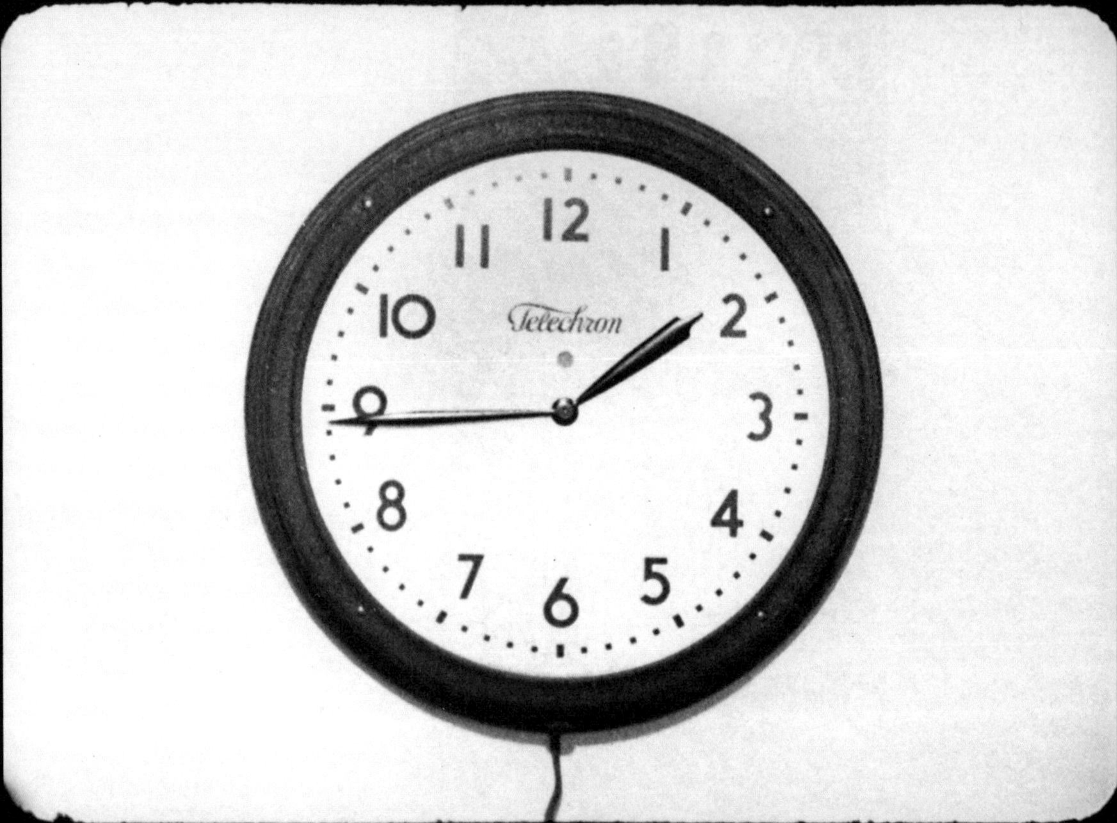

Phi Phenomenon
Morgan Fisher
1976

Phi Phenomenon is a shot of a classroom clock. The film lasts eleven minutes, and the camera is immobile. I did not want there to be any evident motion in the shot, so I removed the second hand from the clock. But even if we don't see any motion from one instant to the next, we know that motion is occurring: as the film progresses, we see that the minute hand is no longer where we saw it before. The minute hand has to have moved, even if we didn't actually see it move.

The film recapitulates an experience we know from daily life. We know that the hands of a clock move, but they move only when we are not looking at them; when we look at the hands of a clock, they appear to be stationary. *Phi Phenomenon* plays on this contradiction, that we know time is ceaselessly passing, yet when we look at the device whose purpose is to tell us the moment where we happen to be in this ceaseless flow, time stands still.

Our knowledge that there is motion in *Phi Phenomenon* does not come from direct perception of it, as it usually does in a film, where the changes from one frame to the next are plainly visible, but on a longer scale of time, from one minute to the next. Because we don't perceive the motion directly, we rely instead on memory to lead us to the conclusion that motion has occurred. For the minute hand to now be in a different place, time has to have passed. There is no other explanation. So instead of our perceiving motion as such, what leads us to understand that motion is occurring when we can't see it is memory combined with logic, even if the logic is rudimentary. And besides, a clock is a familiar object, and this clock is doing what we already know a clock does, moving imperceptibly as it measures the inexorable passing of time.

Phi Phenomenon offers an alternative to the usual model of a film, in which continuous change absorbs you and stimulates your anticipation before finally satisfying it. Most movies are a form of hypnosis that we willingly submit to, and the unceasing and exact manipulations of the many different kinds of modulations that film permits are the means by which films perform this hypnosis. We can't say that the projected film image itself is hypnotic, because *Phi Phenomenon* clearly demonstrates that this is not so. *Phi Phenomenon* does not want to hypnotize you, and it couldn't even if it wanted to. It does not want to keep your eyes glued to the screen, your attention riveted, as most films are designed to do. *Phi Phenomenon* is a film of a clock from beginning to end. The only thing that happens in the film is more of what has already happened: time will pass, as you know it does in any film, and what you see on the screen is an instrument that tells you what you already know, that in a film time passes. There are no surprises. There is no variety, no increase in tension, no comic relief to relax it, no rising action, no climax, no denouement. And, most frustrating of all, there is no movement, at least none that you can see.

Phi Phenomenon concedes that one possible form of engagement with it is not to engage at all, or to engage with it only intermittently. In fact, it is this intermittent paying of attention that makes it possible for the viewer to conclude that motion is occurring when it can't be seen from frame to frame or from second to second. This possibility, not to say likelihood, of intermittent engagement is contrary to the model of the commercial film, which tries above all to engage the attention of the viewer continuously. And the commercial film does this to achieve its larger purpose, to control the viewer's relation to it at every instant. And if it doesn't do this, it's a failure. A commercial film tries to prevent the viewer's attention from wandering. *Phi Phenomenon* does not try to keep the viewer's attention from wandering, which is to say that the film willingly releases its viewer from the condition of hypnosis. This release means that at moments (perhaps there are many such moments), and contrary to the usual experience of watching a film, the viewer can become self-conscious. Viewing most films, the viewer forgets that he or she has a body. In watching *Phi Phenomenon*, the viewer remembers that he or she does indeed have one. The viewer is reminded that he or she is sitting in a seat, and that the seat may or may not be comfortable, and that the seat is in a theater, and that the theater is a specific place with a specific decor. One name for this complex of reactions is boredom. That is the easy answer, but it is not a simple one. Boredom is a complicated subject, and boredom is not necessarily boring, but instead has its own satisfactions. These questions are beyond the purview of these remarks. Besides being readily dismissable as mere boredom, these several kinds of self-consciousness about the relation of the viewer's body to the visual event that is the nominal occasion for the viewer's being there are a translation of the self-consciousness and reflexivity of radical film from events happening within the confines of the image on the screen to the larger context in which the film is projected and its viewing takes place.

Phi Phenomenon reminds us that movies themselves are a kind of a clock, a device for measuring the passing of time. In an hourglass, a fixed quantity of sand passes from one chamber to another at a uniform rate. As the quantity of sand in the upper half diminishes, the quantity in the lower half increases. So it is with film. Film passes through the gate of the camera and the gate of the projector at a regular rate as sand passes through the neck of an hourglass. The quantity of film on the feed spool diminishes as the quantity on the take-up spool increases. You can tell time with a movie. A projectionist can look at a reel on the projector and tell, more or less, how many minutes are left. You can measure a length of film and tell its duration to the twenty-fourth part of a second.

The object that *Phi Phenomenon* registers, a clock, makes possible an accord between film as a material and what happens in the image that rarely occurs in film. *Phi Phenomenon* was shot at normal speed, twenty-four frames per second. The uniform rate at which the frames pass through the camera means that each frame is exposed for the same interval of time. Of course, time passes between the exposure of each frame. The uniform rate at which the film passes through the camera means that the interval of exposure for each frame is also the interval of time that elapses between the exposure of one frame and the next.

The difference in time between one frame and the next is uniform in any film (generally—there are exceptions), but this uniform difference in time is rarely accompanied by a uniform difference in the appearance of successive images. When the bad guy draws his gun, the gun is in one place in one frame, in another place in the next, and in another place in the frame after that. The differences in its position from one frame to the next are not uniform, that is, they are not different in the same way and to the same degre. Of course, the gesture of drawing a gun has its own logic and coherence and predictability that we know from a lifetime of seeing movies, but that is something altogether different from motion that successive frames register as a uniform difference in position.

What is true of the motion of the gun, as it is true of almost all motion in all films, is that it is irregular; the difference between the images from one frame to the next is not uniform. To this rule, which I would suggest is universal, *Phi Phenomenon* is an exception. Or, to put it in positive terms, there is something true of *Phi Phenomenon* that is not true of almost all other films. The uniform difference in time between the frames (true for all films) is in *Phi Phenomenon* recapitulated (as it is not in other films) within the images themselves in the uniform difference between one image and the next. Each of the two hands of the clock moves at a different rate. Each hand, according to the rate at which it moves, moves exactly the same fraction of a degree between each frame, even if it is beyond the threshold of the film to register this movement, and beyond the power of our vision to see it. This difference is uniform between each frame of the film, from the first frame to the last, just as the difference in time from one frame to the next is uniform throughout the last, just as the difference in time from one frame to the next is uniform throughout the film.

A clock is a mechanical device, so it is predictable. The apparatus of film—camera and projector—is a compound instrument that is likewise a mechanical device. Film as we ordinarily encounter it does its best to conceal this fact, even though we know it is true. (Hence the universality of sprocket holes as a sign of film: we know what the material of film looks like, and we know that it implies equal intervals and a constant rate.) But *Phi Phenomenon* insists on reminding us of something that in the viewing of films we take pleasure in being distracted from, that at bottom the camera and projector together are mechanical instruments. Like clocks, they are machines that are entirely predictable. Commercial films hide this predictability of the machines that they depend on, but the predictability that they hide in one place finds its expression in another, on the screen in the stories that commercial films tell. The institution that makes commercial films is called an industry because the films it produces are all the same.

One question that *Phi Phenomenon* raises is: Why make a film of something that is redundant with something the viewer can see for himself or herself in daily life? The answer is as obvious as the question. No one in daily life looks at a clock for eleven minutes. There is never a need to. And even if you set yourself this task, you would find it very difficult, most likely impossible. But a film of a clock makes its demands on you. You have to decide what your relationship to it is. You can always get up and leave, but if you stay, the film makes its demands on you, and you have to negotiate your relationship to it. You find yourself thinking about aspects of film as you never thought of them before. And to anticipate the joke that any skeptic would want to make, the film also allows you the chance to think about the errands you need to run tomorrow. It's your choice. But at least you will recognize that the film is deliberately giving you that choice, instead of hypnotizing you as almost all films expect to do. In being predictable *Phi Phenomenon* gives the viewer a choice that a commercial film, equally predictable but with its predictability shifted to the registers of story construction and syntax, does its best not to.

The question that begins the preceding paragraph is a special and hyperbolic case of the more general question of the continuous take. This is a large and complicated subject. Here I will only say that many of my films are single-take films, and that I have found the continous take to be capable of many complexities.

The phi phenomenon is one of the two properties of human perception that together films depend on. One, the persistence of vision, occurs in the retina. The persitence of vision, or the persistence of retinal impressions, is the name given to the property of the retina that continues to register an image even after the stimulus has stopped. The persistence of vision fills in the intervals of black that occur between the frames of a film, but conveniently the image fades from the retina in time to allow the perception of the next frame. The second property is the phi phenomenon. The phi phenomenon is the name given to the process in the brain that sees motion in the succession of still images that we know constitute a film. The neural basis of the phi phenomenon is not entirely understood. It appears that the brain, when confronted with a series of still images between which there are differences, decides that the most plausible explanation for the differences is that between them there is movement. So the brain supplies the movement that in fact is not there but that we see. (I can't resist pointing out that this process, which is subconcious and involuntary, is recapitulated consciously and on an elongated temporal scale in watching *Phi Phenomenon*: the viewer doesn't see movement, but the presumption of movement is the only thing that can account for the differences the viewer sees from minute to minute. So the viewer sees, so to speak, with the eye of knowledge the motion that is otherwise not visible. Of course it helps that the subject is a clock. We already know that the hands of a clock move, even if when we look at them they appear not to.)

The phi phenomenon accounts for difference by supplying motion, so the usual demonstrations of the phi phenomenon show a difference that is gross enough to register as one and that the brain explains by supplying motion. In *Phi Phenomenon* there is no question there is motion. There has to be, but it is below the threshold of the visible. The differences we know are there are not evident enough to be accounted for by motion, so the phi phenomenon is not brought forth. But even if we can't see it, there has to be motion. There is no other way for the hands to move, as we know they do even if we can't see their movement. The phi phenomenon, usually visible because it connects visible differences, is in *Phi Phenomenon* as invisible but still as present as the motion we can't see but we know is there.

Preparation Plants from Coal Mines

Bernd and Hilla Becher

1966–78

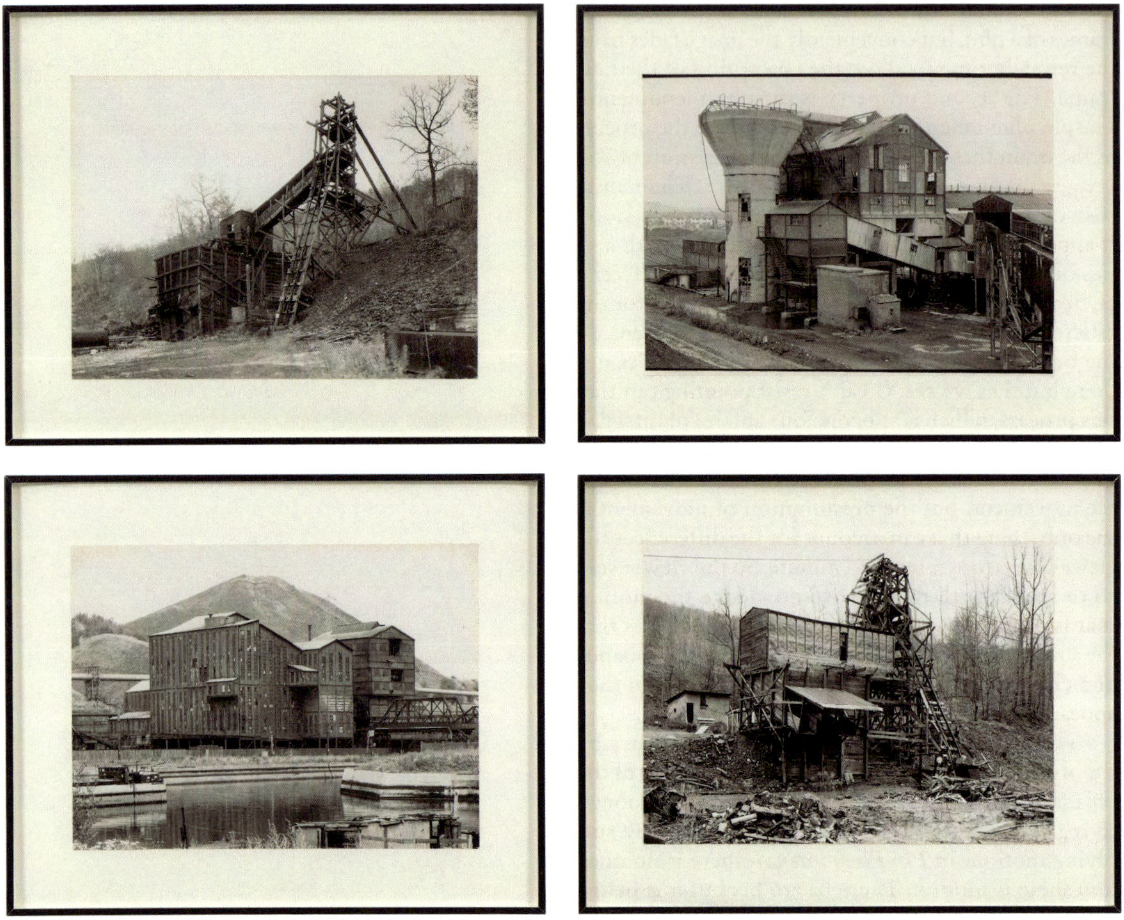

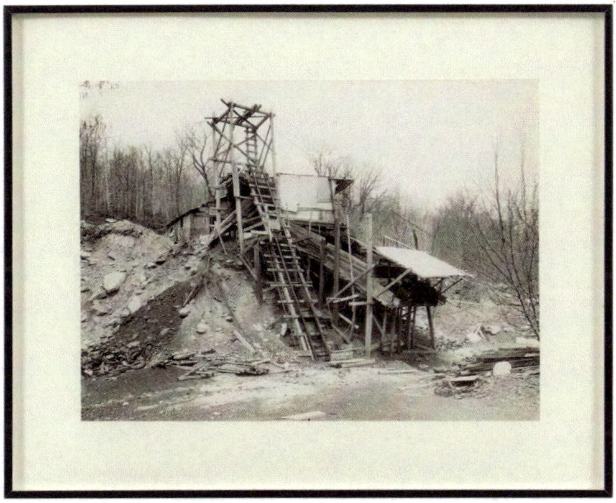

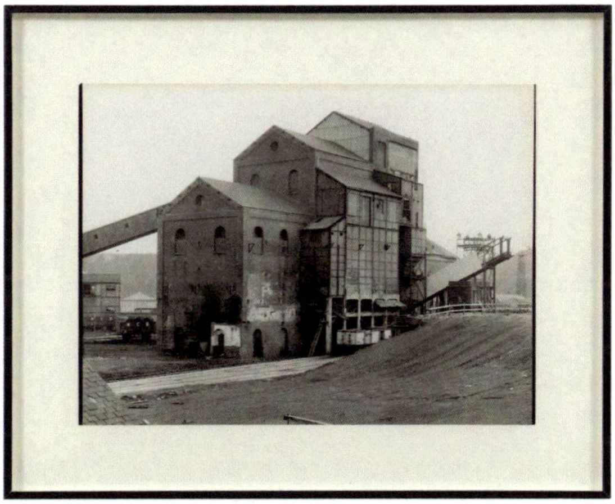

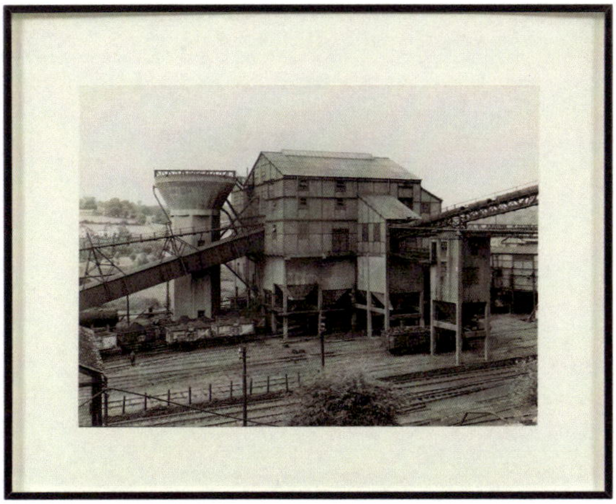

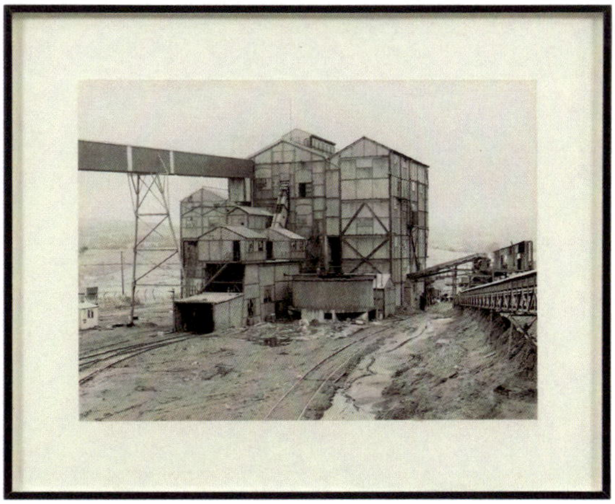

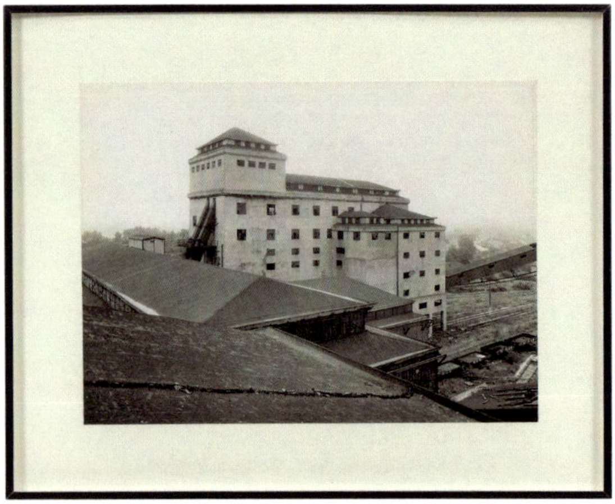

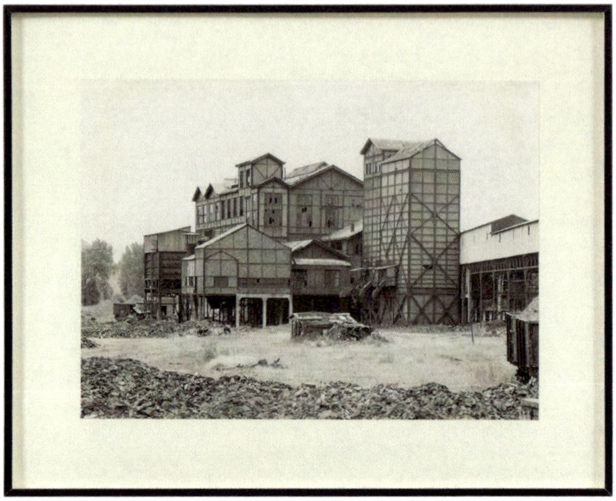

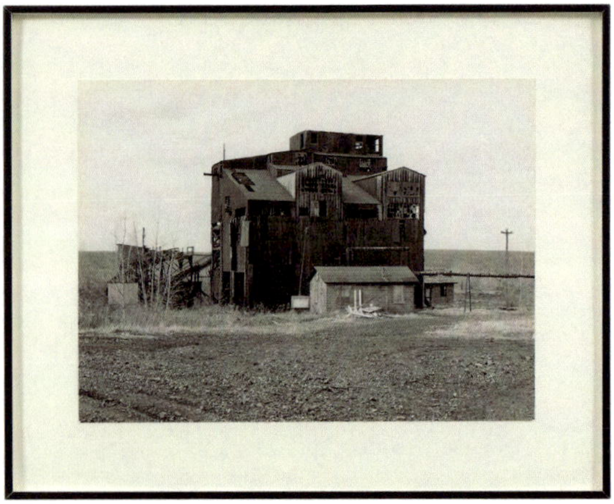

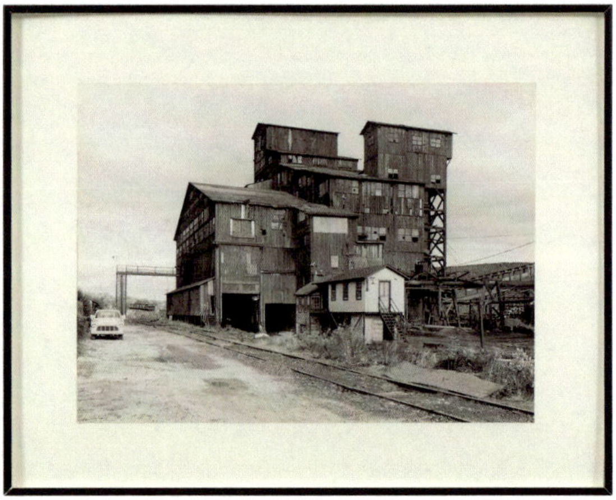

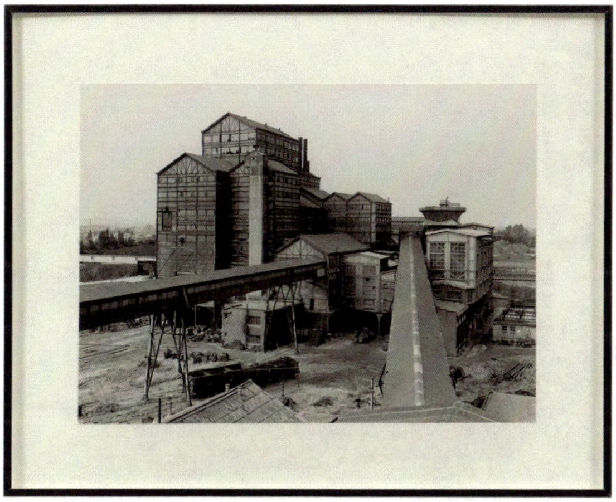

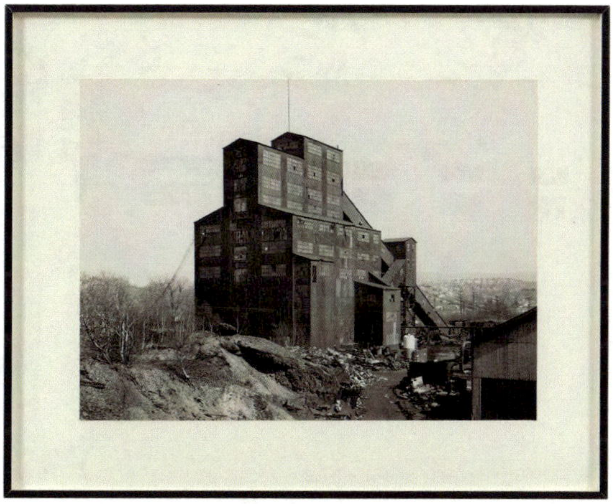

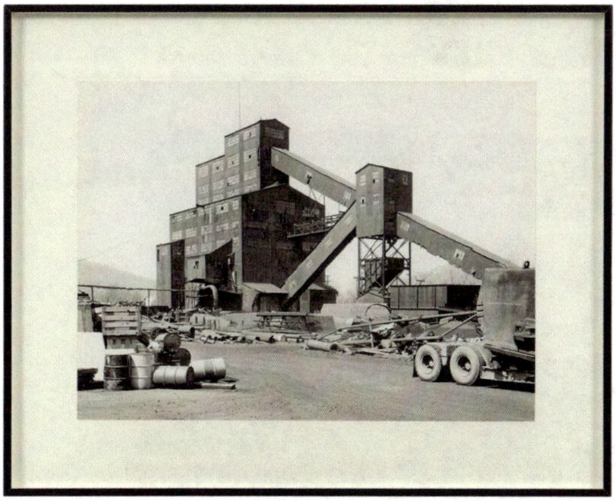

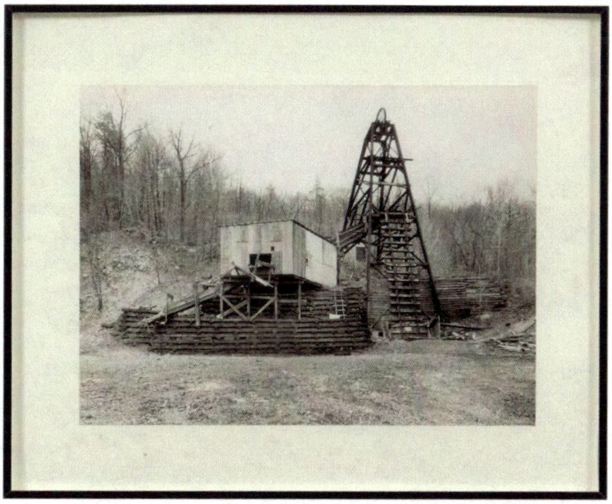

[Untitled] in *January 5–13, 1969*

Douglas Huebler

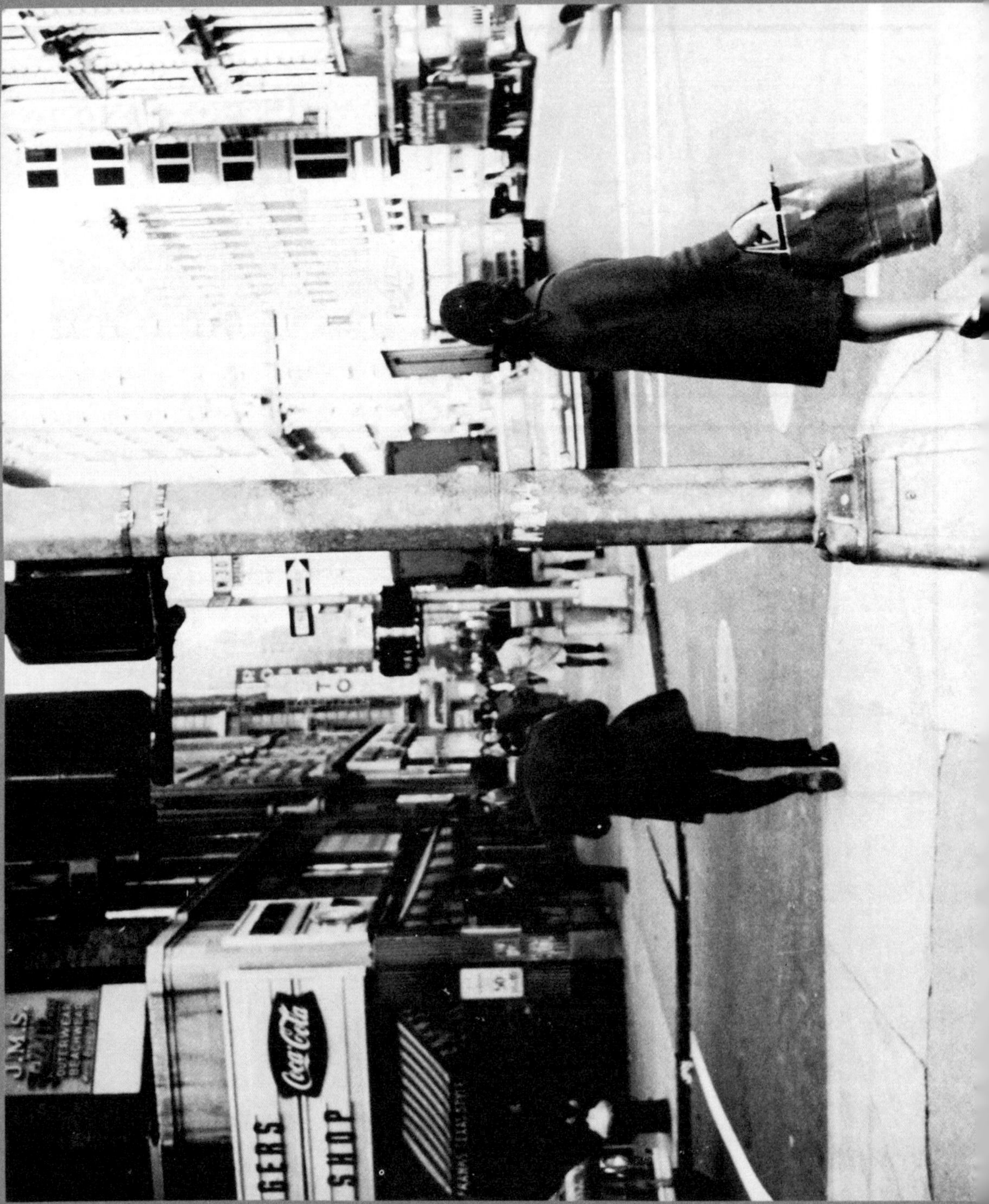

The world is full of objects, more or less interesting; I do not wish to add any more.

I prefer, simply, to state the existence of things in terms of time and/or place.

More specifically, the work concerns itself with things whose inter-relationship is beyond direct perceptual experience.

Because the work is beyond direct perceptual experience, awareness of the work depends on a system of documentation.

This documentation takes the form of photographs, maps, drawings and descriptive language.

D.H.

Projects Class

David Askevold

1969

A work submitted to Projects Class, Nova Scotia College of Art and Design, Fall 1969.

REMOVALS HALFWAY BETWEEN THE EQUATOR AND THE NORTH POLE

The extent of and documentation (if any) of the removals is completely in the domain of the students.

Lawrence Weiner

A work submitted to Projects Class, Nova Scotia College of Art and Design, Fall 1969.

Mud Flow

1000 tons of mud dumped from a dump truck over a rocky or stony cliff.

Robert Smithson

A project submitted to Projects Class, Nova Scotia College of Art and Design, Fall 1969.

Phenomenology of a Room (1966)

Have the students measure/consider (subjectively also) the classroom in every possible way they can think of, i.e. height, length, volume (walls, doors, floor, windows, etc.), temperature, humidity, thickness of walls, amount of illumination, number of objects, how it feels to be there, etc.
It doesn't matter to me what the specific details are or how they are presented.

Mel Bochner

A proposition submitted to Projects Class, Nova Scotia College of Art and Design, Fall 1969.

[illegible]

Exhibit implemented by Projects Class, Nova Scotia College of Art and Design, Fall 1969.

X. Power

A. Power in General
- 156. Power, Potency
- 157. Impotence
- 158. Strength
- 159. Weakness
- 160. Energy
- 161. Violence
- 162. Moderation

X. Power

B. Power in Operation
- 163. Operation
- 164. Productiveness
- 165. Unproductiveness
- 166. Production
- 167. Product
- 168. Reproduction
- 169. Ancestry
- 170. Posterity

X. Power

C. Indirect Power
- 171. Influence
- 172. Uninfluentiality
- 173. Tendency
- 174. Liability
- 175. Implication

X. Power

D. Combination of Forces
- 176. Concurrence
- 177. Counteraction

"Art as Idea as Idea" 1966-1970. 15 Locations 1969/70, Anna Leonowens Gallery, October 25 to November 9, 1969. A executed as a billboard, B executed as a newspaper advertisement, C executed as a hand bill, D executed as an advertisement in buses.

Joseph Kosuth

A project submitted to Projects Class, Nova Scotia College of Art and Design, Fall 1969.

Variable Piece #5

Halifax, Nova Scotia

Ten students at the Nova Scotia College of Art and Design collaborated in the process that formed this piece. They did so by fabricating a myth and launching it into an original and true existence through ordinary information systems ... word of mouth, publication, etc.
This process began in the fall of 1969 and, although the myth possesses the capacity to expand to infinite points in time and space, for the purposes of this piece its destiny was set to be terminated on April 1, 1970 at which time all documents relating to its existence during the period described and this statement join altogether to constitute the form of the piece.

October 15, 1969

Douglas Huebler

A project submitted to Projects Class, Nova Scotia College of Art and Design, Fall 1969.

Photos of tree shadows every 10 minutes.

1. Find a place in a not too closely overgrown part of the woods where there are very clear shadows.
2. Use one or more days to find out exactly how the shadows are moving: when they start and what moment they come into camera view. Try to get as much as you can from the trees in the photos, keeping in mind that their shadows are the most important part of the photos.
3. When everything is ready start taking the photos. #1 — no shadow, #2 — first shadow, #3 — extended shadow, etc. Take one every ten minutes. Choose a day with uninterrupted sunshine.
4. Make a work drawing on paper. Glue all the photos (contact prints - small) in order of succession and hang in order; the negatives on negative-leafs.
5. Make two prints of each on paper 24x24 centimeters and 30x30 centimeters. Hang them in a row, so only the shadow is moving.

Jan Dibbets

A project submitted to Projects Class, Nova Scotia College of Art and Design, Fall 1969.

1. A work that uses the idea of error.
2. A work that uses the idea of incompleteness.
3. A work that uses the idea of infinity.
4. A work that uses the idea of completeness.
5. A work that uses the idea of stupidness.
6. A work that is subversive.
7. A work that is not original.

These could be done in any form chosen by the student. Please ask your students not to do more than two of the above works.

Sol LeWitt

A project submitted to Projects Class, Nova Scotia College of Art and Design, Fall 1969.

From Sunset to Sunrise.

A series of 160 photographed views were taken September 21 and 22 from a point near Halifax, Nova Scotia at intervals of 6 seconds and 18 degree shifts in orientation relative to the sun, beginning at sunset September 21, and following this schema: a complete map of the sky is made, its point of inception being the sun setting across the horizon line. Beginning with this point as the nearest and most nearly measurable distance in space, the photographs extend in a spiralling pattern so that in 80 shots, the top of the sky — the furthest extention of immeasurable "space" — is reached. Beginning at the time of sunrise the next day at the same point at the top of the sky the process is reversed, leading downward in a spiral to meet the sun as it rises above the horizon.
We would not notice the "space" of the sky if it were never disturbed by clouds and the darkness of night. "Space" reads as a time shift: the diurnal shift to darkness (relative to the sun as the source of illumination) and the relative shift of clouds (relative to each other and relative to the framing edge ending the view of one particular moment — the atmospheric content (what's in the air at a particular point: time relative to our view): the 8 minutes duration it takes to realize the *a priori* schema of relative distance.
The schema was also executed as a continuously panning 16 mm. color movie which is a different perceptual matter entirely.

Dan Graham

A project submitted to Projects Class, Nova Scotia College of Art and Design, Fall 1969.

A. A group of people (anywhere from five to fifteen) are photographed in the same place and approximately the same position in relation to each other every day at the same hour for two weeks. (No diversion from the conventional group photograph taken for school yearbooks, Knights of Columbus annual picnics, etc.) The people need not wear the same clothes or pose exactly the same way each day, but the immediate impression should be almost identical.
B. These photographs are developed and dated (a record about what one person is wearing each day, or something similar, should be kept each day so that the dates will be accurate.); each photograph is then described in writing, in detail, either by the person (or persons) who took the pictures or by someone who was not present at the picture-taking. (Note which case was chosen.)
C. Put the photographs together with the texts in one of the following manners:
   1. Both pictures and texts in chronological order.
   2. Pictures in chronological order, but texts scrambled (they are still dated though.).
   3. Texts in chronological order but pictures scrambled (and dated).
   4. Scramble the whole thing in some totally ramdom manner so that sometimes pictures are with their proper texts and sometimes not (still dated), and so that the time sequence is broken entirely: "illustration" and text diverge.

If more than one person is doing the project, each one should take a different last step (and take his own photographs of different groups from the others).

Lucy R. Lippard.

A work submitted to Projects Class, Nova Scotia College of Art and Design, Fall 1969.

The students will gather together in a group and decide on a single common idea. The idea can be of any nature, simple or complex. This idea will be known only to the members of the group. You or I will not know it. The piece will remain in existence as long as the idea remains in the confines of the group. If just one student unknown to anyone else and at any time, informs someone outside the group the piece will cease to exist. It may exist for a few seconds or it may go on indefinitely, depending on the human nature of the participating students. We may never know when or if the piece comes to an end.

Robert Barry

A situation executed by Projects Class, Nova Scotia College of Art and Design, Fall 1969.

Installation of Teletype and Telcopier units September 15 to October 5, 1969 in the Anna Leonowens Gallery. Students carried out projects as they were received.

N.E. Thing Co. Ltd.

Advertisements in *Artforum* Magazine, 1968–69

Stephen Kaltenbach

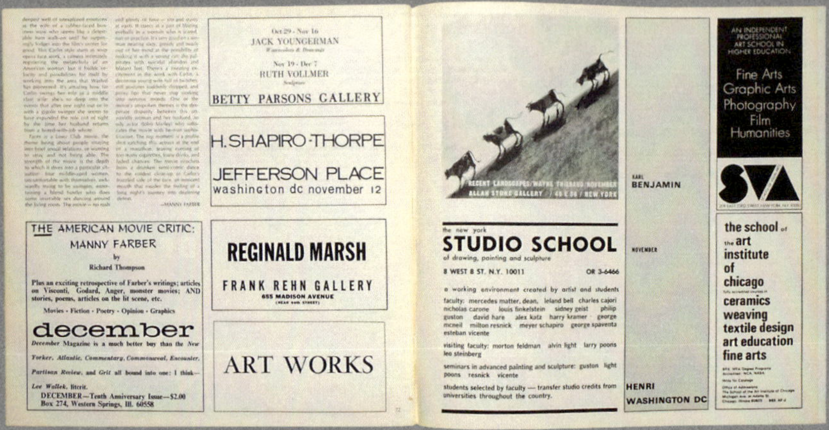

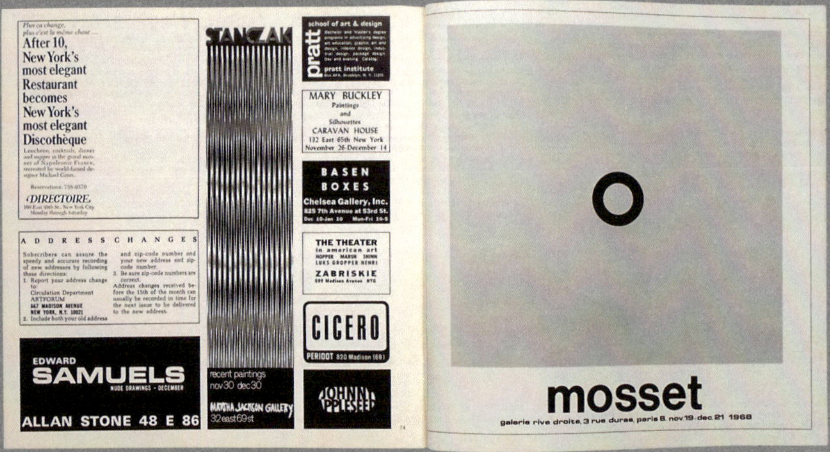

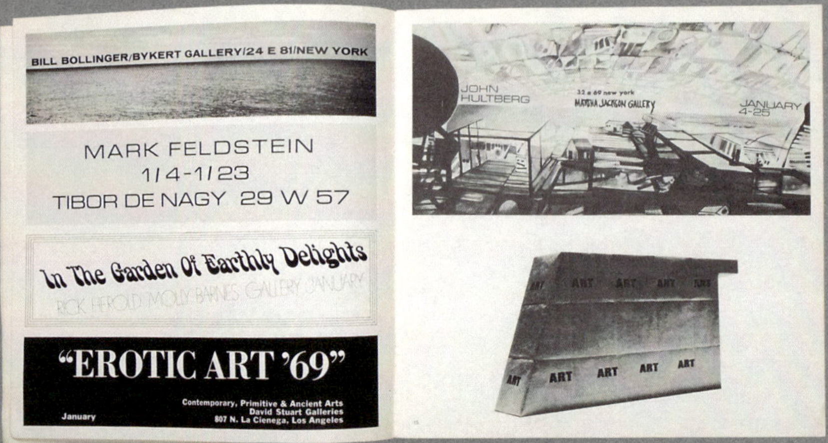

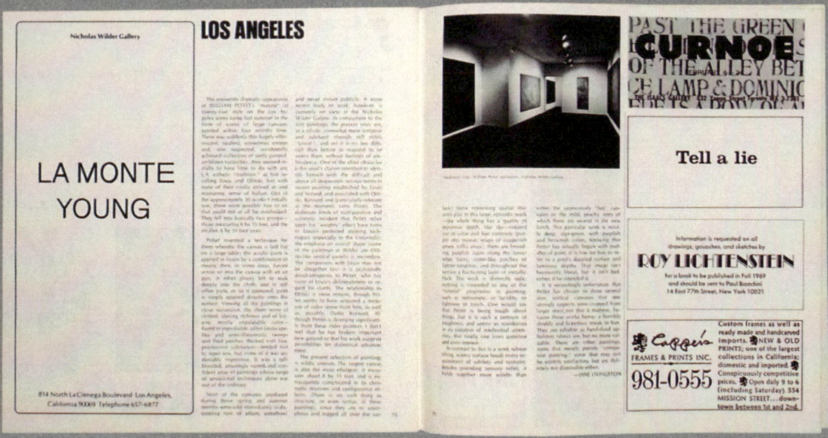
Nicholas Wilder Gallery
LA MONTE YOUNG
814 North La Cienega Boulevard Los Angeles, California 90069 Telephone 657-6877
LOS ANGELES
CURNOE
Tell a lie
Information is requested on all drawings, gouaches, and sketches by
ROY LICHTENSTEIN
for a book to be published in Fall 1969 and should be sent to Paul Bianchini 16 East 77th Street, New York 10021
FRAMES & PRINTS INC.
981-0555
Custom frames as well as ready made and handcarved imports. NEW & OLD PRINTS; one of the largest collections in California; domestic and imported. Conspicuously competitive prices. Open daily 9 to 6 (including Saturday). 554 MISSION STREET... downtown between 1st and 2nd.

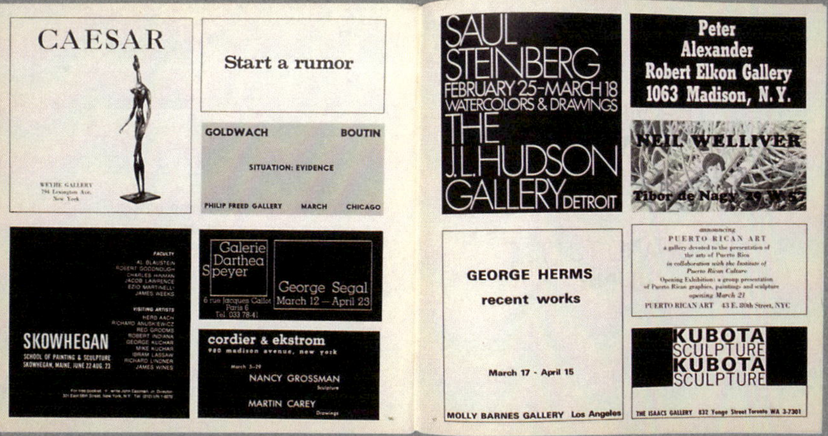
CAESAR
WEYHE GALLERY
794 Lexington Ave.
New York
Start a rumor
GOLDWACH
BOUTIN
SITUATION: EVIDENCE
PHILIP FREED GALLERY
MARCH
CHICAGO
SKOWHEGAN
SCHOOL OF PAINTING & SCULPTURE
Galerie Darthea Speyer
6 rue Jacques Callot Paris 6
George Segal
March 12 — April 23
cordier & ekstrom
980 madison avenue, new york
NANCY GROSSMAN
MARTIN CAREY
SAUL STEINBERG
FEBRUARY 25–MARCH 18
WATERCOLORS & DRAWINGS
THE J.L. HUDSON GALLERY DETROIT
Peter Alexander
Robert Elkon Gallery
1063 Madison, N.Y.
NEIL WELLIVER
Tibor de Nagy
GEORGE HERMS
recent works
March 17 - April 15
MOLLY BARNES GALLERY Los Angeles
PUERTO RICAN ART
KUBOTA SCULPTURE
KUBOTA SCULPTURE

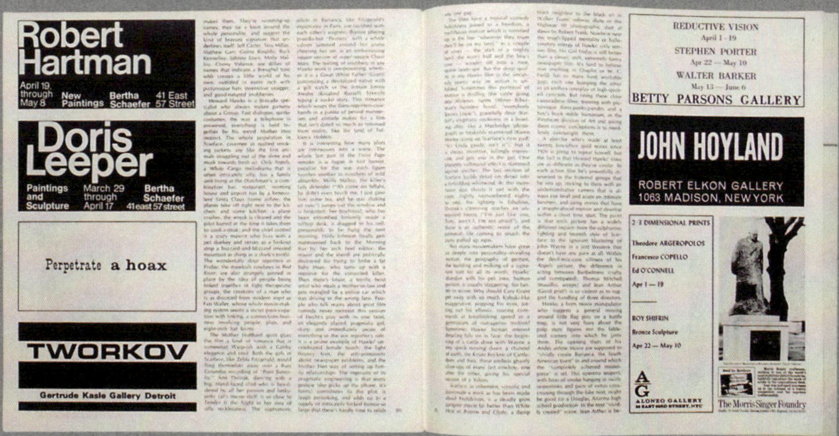
Robert Hartman
April 19 through May 8
New Paintings
Bertha Schaefer
41 East 57 Street
Doris Leeper
Paintings and Sculpture
March 29 through April 17
Bertha Schaefer
41 east 57 street
Perpetrate a hoax
TWORKOV
Gertrude Kasle Gallery Detroit
REDUCTIVE VISION
STEPHEN PORTER
WALTER BARKER
BETTY PARSONS GALLERY
JOHN HOYLAND
ROBERT ELKON GALLERY
1063 MADISON, NEW YORK
ALONZO GALLERY
The Morris Singer Foundry

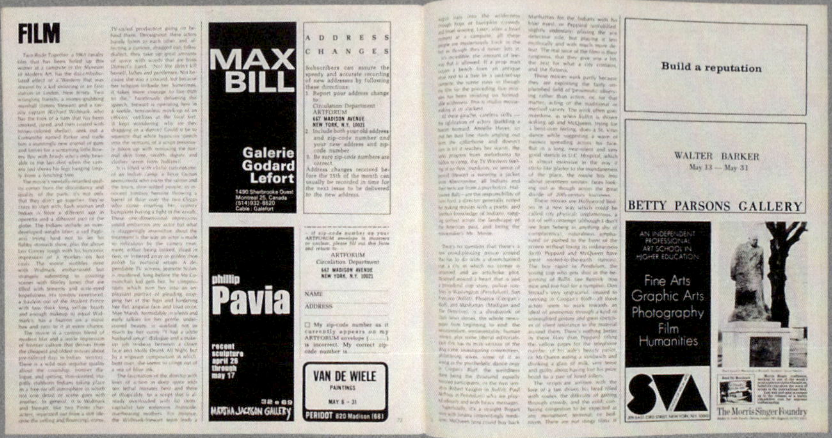
FILM
MAX BILL
Galerie Godard Lefort
1490 Sherbrooke Ouest
Montreal 25, Canada
ADDRESS CHANGES
Subscribers can assure the speedy and accurate recording of new addresses by following these directions:
ARTFORUM
667 MADISON AVENUE
NEW YORK, N.Y. 10021
phillip Pavia
recent sculpture april 29 through may 17
32 e 69
MARTHA JACKSON GALLERY
NAME
ADDRESS
VAN DE WIELE
PAINTINGS
MAY 6 - 31
PERIDOT 820 Madison
Build a reputation
WALTER BARKER
May 13 — May 31
BETTY PARSONS GALLERY
AN INDEPENDENT PROFESSIONAL ART SCHOOL IN HIGHER EDUCATION
Fine Arts
Graphic Arts
Photography
Film
Humanities
SVA
The Morris Singer Foundry

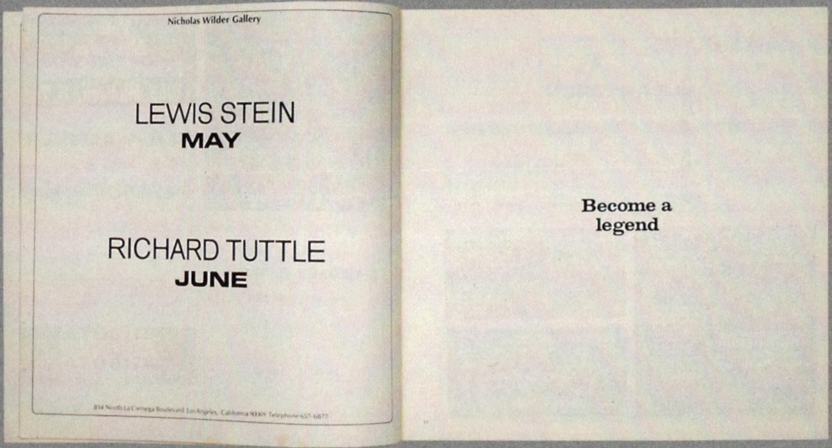
Nicholas Wilder Gallery
LEWIS STEIN
MAY
RICHARD TUTTLE
JUNE
814 North La Cienega Boulevard, Los Angeles, California 90069 Telephone 657-6877
Become a legend

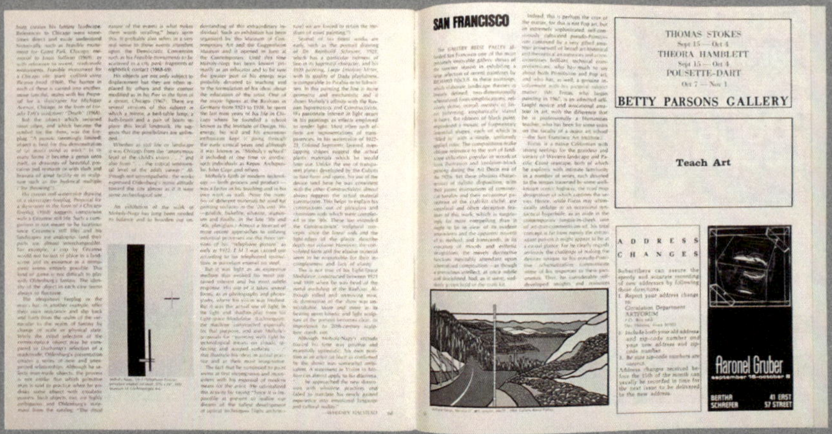
SAN FRANCISCO
THOMAS STOKES
Sept 15 — Oct 4
THEORA HAMBLETT
Sept 15 — Oct 4
POUSETTE-DART
Oct 7 — Nov 1
BETTY PARSONS GALLERY
Teach Art
ADDRESS CHANGES
Aaronel Gruber
september 16-october 8
BERTHA SCHAEFER
41 EAST 57 STREET

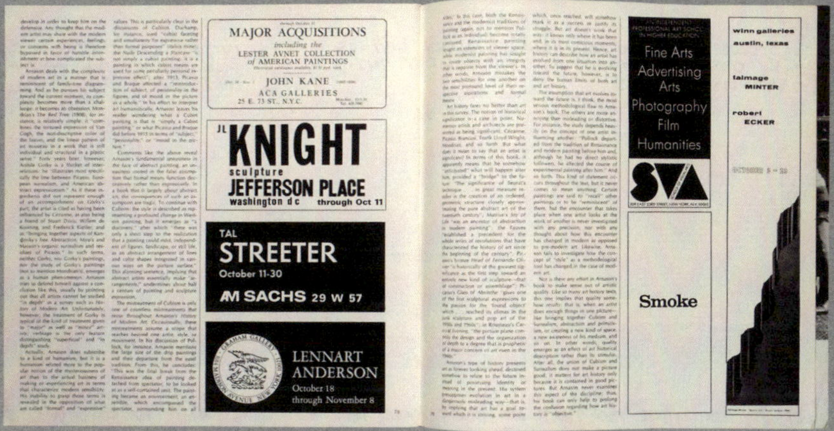
MAJOR ACQUISITIONS
including the
LESTER AVNET COLLECTION
of AMERICAN PAINTINGS
JOHN KANE
ACA GALLERIES
25 E. 73 ST., N.Y.C.
JL KNIGHT
sculpture
JEFFERSON PLACE
washington d c through Oct 11
TAL
STREETER
October 11-30
AM SACHS 29 W 57
LENNART
ANDERSON
October 18
through November 8
Fine Arts
Advertising
Arts
Photography
Film
Humanities
SVA
Smoke
winn galleries
austin, texas
talmage
MINTER
robert
ECKER

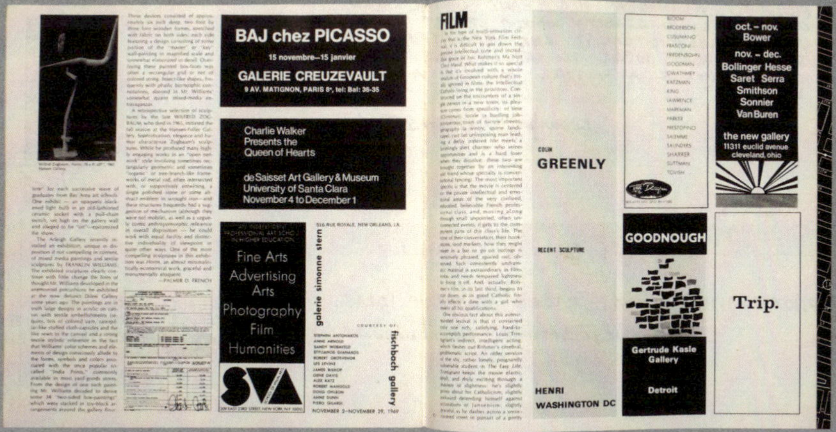
BAJ chez PICASSO
15 novembre—15 janvier
GALERIE CREUZEVAULT
9 AV. MATIGNON, PARIS 8e, tel: Bal: 36-35
Charlie Walker
Presents the
Queen of Hearts
de Saisset Art Gallery & Museum
University of Santa Clara
November 4 to December 1
Fine Arts
Advertising
Arts
Photography
Film
Humanities
SVA
galerie simonne stern
fischbach gallery
NOVEMBER 2—NOVEMBER 29, 1969
FILM
COLIN
GREENLY
HENRI
WASHINGTON DC
GOODNOUGH
Gertrude Kasle
Gallery
Detroit
oct. – nov.
Bower
nov. – dec.
Bollinger Hesse
Saret Serra
Smithson
Sonnier
Van Buren
the new gallery
11311 euclid avenue
cleveland, ohio
Trip.

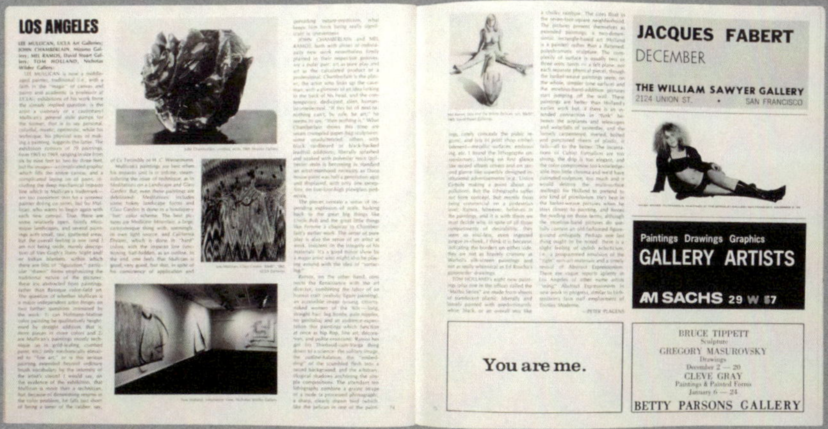
LOS ANGELES
JACQUES FABERT
DECEMBER
THE WILLIAM SAWYER GALLERY
2124 UNION ST. • SAN FRANCISCO
Paintings Drawings Graphics
GALLERY ARTISTS
AM SACHS 29 W 57
You are me.
BRUCE TIPPETT
Sculpture
GREGORY MASUROVSKY
Drawings
December 2 — 20
CLEVE GRAY
Paintings & Painted Forms
January 6 — 24
BETTY PARSONS GALLERY

Misunderstandings (A Theory of Photography)

Mel Bochner

1970

THE TRUE FUNCTION OF REVOLUTIONARY ART IS THE CRYSTALLIZATION OF PHENOMENA INTO ORGANIZED FORMS.

MAO TSE-TUNG

IN MY OPINION, YOU CANNOT SAY YOU HAVE THOROUGHLY SEEN ANYTHING UNTIL YOU HAVE A PHOTOGRAPH OF IT.

EMILE ZOLA

LET US REMEMBER TOO, THAT WE DON'T HAVE TO TRANSLATE SUCH PICTURES INTO REALISTIC ONES IN ORDER TO 'UNDERSTAND' THEM, ANY MORE THAN WE NEED TRANSLATE PHOTOGRAPHS INTO COLORED PICTURES, ALTHOUGH BLACK-AND-WHITE MEN OR PLANTS IN REALITY WOULD STRIKE US AS UNSPEAKABLY STRANGE AND FRIGHTFUL. SUPPOSE WE WERE TO SAY AT THIS POINT: 'SOMETHING IS A PICTURE ONLY IN A PICTURE-LANGUAGE.'

LUDWIG WITTGENSTEIN

I WANT TO REPRODUCE THE OBJECTS AS THEY ARE OR AS THEY WOULD BE EVEN IF I DID NOT EXIST.

TAINE

PHOTOGRAPHY CANNOT RECORD ABSTRACT IDEAS.

ENCYCLOPEDIA BRITANNICA

I WOULD LIKE TO SEE PHOTOGRAPHY MAKE PEOPLE DESPISE PAINTING UNTIL SOMETHING ELSE WILL MAKE PHOTOGRAPHY UNBEARABLE.

MARCEL DUCHAMP

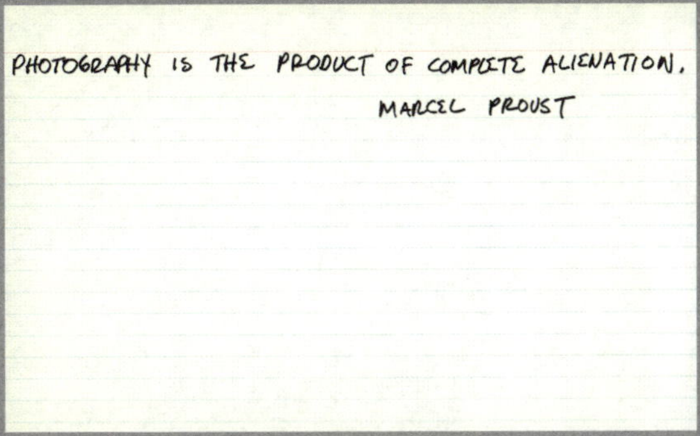
PHOTOGRAPHY IS THE PRODUCT OF COMPLETE ALIENATION.
MARCEL PROUST

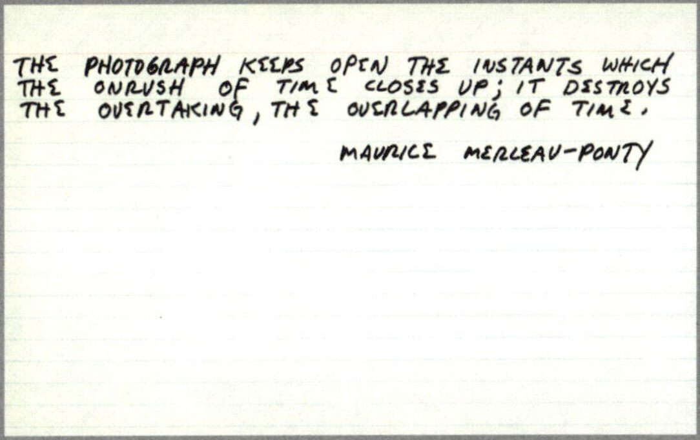
THE PHOTOGRAPH KEEPS OPEN THE INSTANTS WHICH THE ONRUSH OF TIME CLOSES UP; IT DESTROYS THE OVERTAKING, THE OVERLAPPING OF TIME.
MAURICE MERLEAU-PONTY

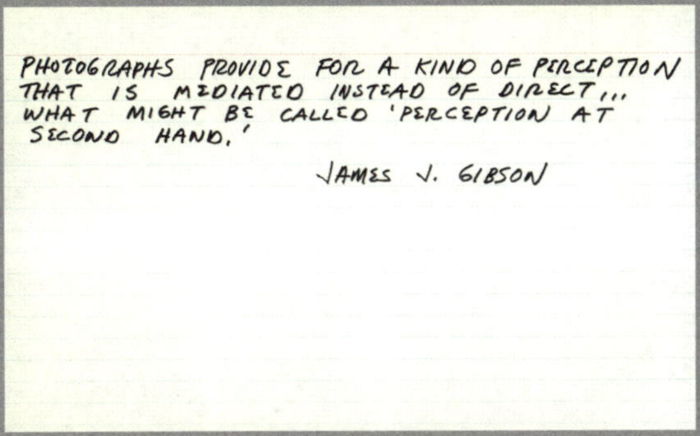
PHOTOGRAPHS PROVIDE FOR A KIND OF PERCEPTION THAT IS MEDIATED INSTEAD OF DIRECT... WHAT MIGHT BE CALLED 'PERCEPTION AT SECOND HAND.'
JAMES J. GIBSON

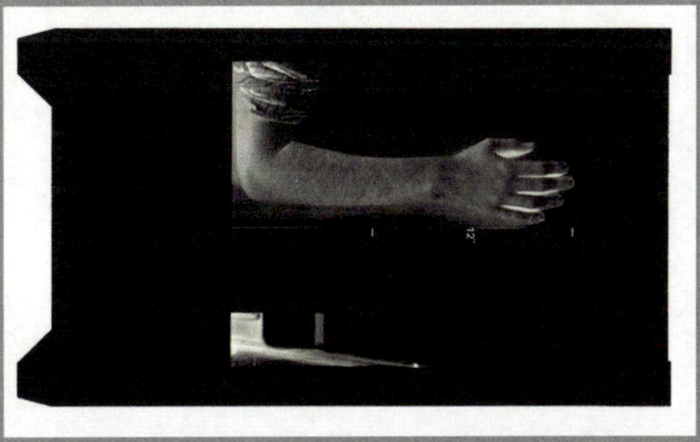

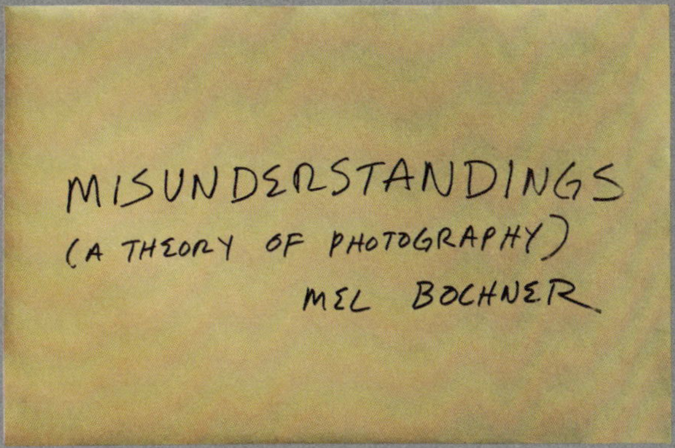
MISUNDERSTANDINGS
(A THEORY OF PHOTOGRAPHY)
MEL BOCHNER

Still from *Finally Got the News*
Stewart Bird, Rene Lichtman, and Peter Gessner
1970

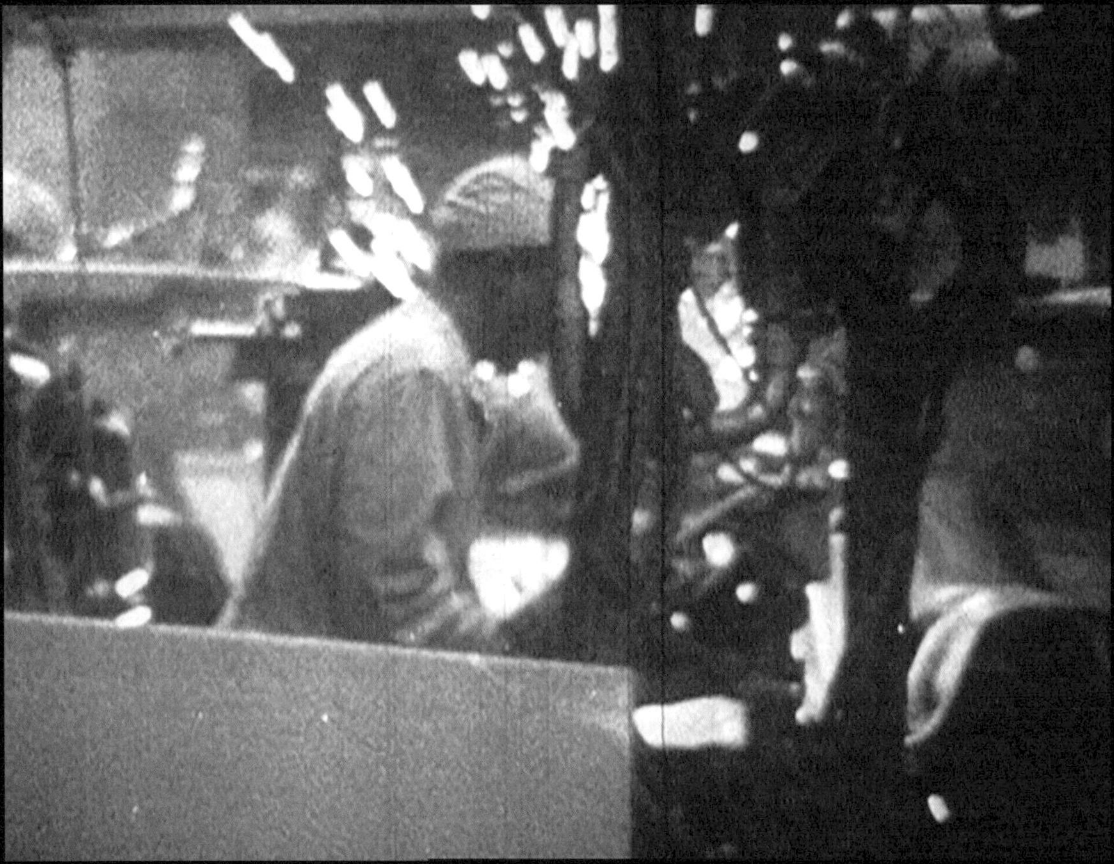

Still from *Hour of the Furnaces*

Fernando Solanas and Octavio Getino

1968

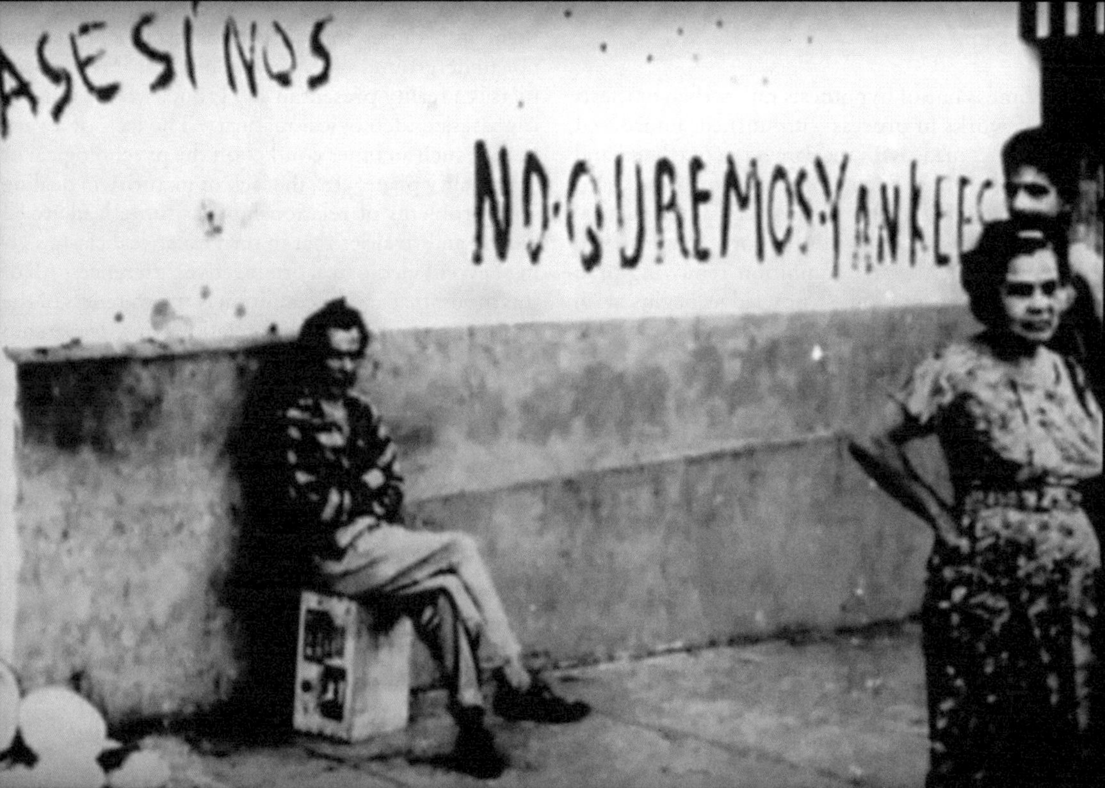

Towards a Third Cinema: Notes and Experiences for the Development of a Cinema of Liberation in the Third World

Fernando Solanas and Octavio Getino

1969

'... we must discuss, we must invent ...'
—Frantz Fanon

... Our time is one of hypothesis rather than of thesis, a time of works in process—unfinished, unordered, violent works made with the camera in one hand and a rock in the other. Such works cannot be assessed according to the traditional theoretical and critical canons. The ideas for *our* film theory and criticism will come to life through inhibition-removing practice and experimentation. 'Knowledge begins with practice. After acquiring theoretical knowledge through practice, it is necessary to return to practice.'[1] Once he has embarked upon this practice, the revolutionary film-maker will have to overcome countless obstacles; he will experience the loneliness of those who aspire to the praise of the System's promotion media only to find that those media are closed to him. As Godard would say, he will cease to be a bicycle champion to become an anonymous bicycle rider, Vietnamese-style, submerged in a cruel and prolonged war. But he will also discover that there is a receptive audience that looks upon his work as something of its own, that makes it part of its own existence, and that is ready to defend him in a way that it would never do with any world bicycle champion.

In this long war, with the camera as our rifle, we do in fact move into a guerrilla activity. This is why the work of a *film-guerrilla* group is governed by strict disciplinary norms as to both work methods and security. A revolutionary film group is in the same situation as a guerrilla unit: it cannot grow strong without military structures and command concepts. *The group exists as a network of complementary responsibilities, as the sum and synthesis of abilities, inasmuch as it operates harmonically with a leadership that centralises planning work and maintains its continuity.* Experience shows that it is not easy to maintain the cohesion of a group when it is bombarded by the System and its chain of accomplices frequently disguised as 'progressives,' when there are no immediate and spectacular outer incentives and the members must undergo the discomforts and tensions of work that is done underground and distributed clandestinely. Many abandon their responsibilities because they underestimate them or because they measure them with values appropriate to System cinema and not underground cinema. The birth of internal conflicts is a reality present in any group, whether or not it possesses ideological maturity. The lack of awareness of such an inner conflict on the psychological or personality plane, etc., the lack of maturity in dealing with problems of relationships, at times leads to ill feeling and rivalries that in turn cause real clashes going beyond ideological or objective differences. All of this means that a basic condition is an awareness of the problems of interpersonal relationships, leadership and areas of competence. What is needed is to speak clearly, mark off work areas, assign responsibilities and take on the job as a rigorous militancy.

Guerrilla film-making proletarianises the film worker and breaks down the intellectual aristocracy that the bourgeoisie grants to its followers. In a word, it *democratises.* The film-maker's tie with reality makes him more a part of his people. Vanguard layers and even masses participate collectively in the work when they realise that it is the continuity of their daily struggle. *La hora de los hornos* shows how a film can be made in hostile circumstances when it has the support and collaboration of militants and cadres from the people.

The revolutionary film-maker acts with a radically new vision of the role of the producer, teamwork, tools, details, etc. Above all, he supplies himself at all levels in order to produce his films, he equips himself at all levels, he learns how to handle the manifold techniques of his craft. His most valuable possessions are the tools of his trade, which form part and parcel of his need to communicate. The camera is the inexhaustible *expropriator of image-weapons*; the projector, *a gun that can shoot 24 frames per second.*

Each member of the group should be familiar, at least in a general way, with the equipment being used: he must be prepared to replace another in any of the phases of production. The myth of irreplaceable technicians must be exploded.

The whole group must grant great importance to the minor details of the production and the security measures needed to project it. A lack of foresight which in conventional film-making would go unnoticed can

1 Mao Tse-tung, *On Practice*.

render virtually useless weeks or months of work. And a failure in guerrilla cinema, just as in the guerrilla struggle itself, can mean the loss of a work or a complete change of plans. 'In a guerrilla struggle the concept of failure is present a thousand times over, and victory a myth that only a revolutionary can dream.'[2] Every member of the group must have an ability to take care of details; discipline; speed; and, above all, the willingness to overcome the weaknesses of comfort, old habits, and the whole climate of pseudonormality behind which the warfare of everyday life is hidden. Each film is a different operation, a different job requiring variations in methods in order to confuse or refrain from alerting the enemy, especially as the processing laboratories are still in his hands.

The success of the work depends to a great extent on the group's ability to remain silent, on its permanent wariness, a condition that is difficult to achieve in a situation in which apparently nothing is happening and the film-maker has been accustomed to telling all and sundry about everything that he's doing because the bourgeoisie has trained him precisely on such a basis of prestige and promotion. The watchwords 'constant vigilance, constant wariness, constant mobility' have profound validity for guerrilla cinema. You have to give the appearance of working on various projects, split up the materials for processing, use go-betweens, mix The Material with other materials, put it together, take it apart, confuse neutralize and throw off the track. All of this is necessary as long as the group doesn't have its own processing equipment, no matter how rudimentary, and there remain certain possibilities in the traditional laboratories.

Group-level co-operation between different countries can serve to assure the completion of a film or the execution of certain phases of work that may not be possible in the country of origin. To this should be added the need for a reception center for the filing of materials to be used by the different groups and the perspective of coordination, on a continent-wide or even worldwide scale, of the continuity of work in each country: periodic regional or international gatherings to exchange experiences, contributions, joint planning of work, etc.

At least in the earliest stages the revolutionary film-maker and the work groups will be the sole producers of their films. They must bear the responsibilty of finding ways to obtain the economic means to facilitate the continuity of work. Guerrilla cinema still doesn't have enough experience to set down standards in this area; what experience there is has shown, above all, the *ability to make use of the concrete situation of each country*. But, regardless of what these situations may be, the preparation of a film cannot be undertaken without a parallel study of its future audience and, consequently, a plan to recover the financial investment. Here, once again, the need arises for closer ties between political and artistic vanguards, since this also serves for the joint study of forms of production, exhibition, and continuity.

A guerrilla film can be aimed only at the distribution mechanisms provided by the revolutionary organisations, including those invented or discovered by the film-maker themselves. Production, distribution, and economic possibilities for survival must form part of a single strategy. The solution of the problems faced in each of these areas will encourage other people to join in the work of guerrilla film-making, which will enlarge its ranks and thus make it less vulnerable.

The distribution of guerrilla films in Latin America is still in swaddling clothes, while System reprisals are already a legalised fact. Suffice it to note in Argentina the raids that have occurred during some showings and the recent film suppression law of a clearly fascist character, in Brazil the ever-increasing restrictions placed upon the most militant comrades of *Cinema Novo*, and in Venezuela the banning of *La hora de los hornos*; almost all over the continent censorship prevents any possibility of public distribution.

Without revolutionary films and a public that asks for them, any attempt to open up new ways of distribution would be doomed to failure. But both of these already exist in Latin America. The appearance of the films opened up a road which in some countries, such as Argentina, occurs through showings in apartments and houses to audiences of never more than 25 people; in other countries, such as Chile, films are shown in parishes, universities, or cultural centres (of which there are fewer every day); and, in the case of Uruguay, showings were given in Montevideo's biggest movie theater to an audience of 2,500 people, who filled the theater and made every showing an impassioned anti-imperialist event.[3] But the prospects on the continental plane indicate that the possibility for the continuity of a revolutionary cinema rests upon the *strengthening of the rigorously underground base structures.*

Practice implies mistakes and failures.[4] Some comrades will let themselves be carried away by the success and impunity with which they present the first showings and will tend to relax security measures, while others will go in the opposite direction of excessive precautions of fearfulness, to such an extent that distribution remains circumscribed, limited to a few groups of friends. Only concrete experience in each country will demonstrate which are the best methods

2 Che Guevara, *Guerrilla Warfare*.

3 The Uruguayan weekly Marcha organized late-night and Sunday morning exhibitions that are widely and well received.

4 The raiding of a Buenos Aires union and the arrest of dozens of persons resulting from a bad choice of projection site and the large number of people invited.

there, which do not always lend themselves to application in other situations.

In some places it will be possible to build infrastructures connected to political, student, worker, and other organisations, while in others it will be more suitable to sell prints to organisations which will take charge of obtaining the funds necessary to pay for each print (the cost of the print plus a small margin). This method, wherever possible, would appear to be the most viable, because it permits the decentralisation of distribution; makes possible a more profound political use of the film; and permits the recovery, through the sale of more prints, of the funds invested in the production. It is true that in many countries the organisations still are not fully aware of the importance of this work or, if they are, may lack the means to undertake it. In such cases other methods can be used: the delivery of prints to encourage distribution and a box-office cut to the organisers of each showing, etc. The ideal goal to be achieved would be producing and distributing guerrilla films with funds obtained from expropriations from the bourgeoisie—that is, *the bourgeoisie would be financing guerrilla cinema with a bit of the surplus value that it gets from the people*. But, as long as the goal is no more than a middle- or long-range aspiration, the alternatives open to revolutionary cinema to recover production and distribution costs are to some extent similar to those obtained for conventional cinema: every spectator should pay the same amount as he pays to see System cinema. Financing, subsidising, equipping, and supporting revolutionary cinema are political responsibilities for revolutionary organisations and militants. A film can be made, but if its distribution does not allow for the recovery of the costs, it will be difficult or impossible to make a second film.

The 16mm film circuits in Europe (20,000 exhibition centres in Sweden, 30,000 in France, etc.) are not the best example for the neocolonialised countries, but they are nevertheless a complement to be kept in mind for fund raising, especially in a situation in which such circuits can play an important role in publicising the struggles in the Third World, increasingly related as they are to those unfolding in the metropolis countries. A film on the Venezuelan guerrillas will say more to a European public than twenty explanatory pamphlets, and the same is true for us with a film on the May events in France or the Berkeley, USA, student struggle.

A *Guerrilla Films International*? And why not? Isn't it true that a kind of new International is arising through the Third World struggles; through OSPAAAL[5] and the revolutionary vanguards of the consumer societies?

A guerrilla cinema, at this stage still within the reach of limited layers of the population, is, nevertheless, *the only cinema of the masses possible today*, since it is the only one involved with the interests, aspirations, and prospects of the vast majority of the people. Every important film produced by a revolutionary cinema will be, explicit or not, *a national event of the masses*.

This *cinema of the masses*, which is prevented from reaching beyond the sectors representing the masses, provokes with each showing, as in a revolutionary military incursion, a liberated space, *a decolonised territory*. The showing can be turned into a kind of political event, which, according to Fanon, could be 'a liturgical act, a privileged occasion for human beings to hear and be heard.'

Militant cinema must be able to extract the infinity of new possibilities that open up for it from the conditions of proscription imposed by the System. The attempt to overcome neocolonial oppression calls for the invention of forms of communication; *it opens up the possibility*.

Before and during the making of *La hora de los hornos* we tried out various methods for the distribution of revolutionary cinema—the little that we had made up to then. Each showing for militants, middle-level cadres, activists, workers, and university students became—without our having set ourselves this aim beforehand—a kind of enlarged cell meeting of which the films were a part but not the most important factor. We thus discovered a new facet of cinema: the *participation* of people who, until then, were considered *spectators*.

At times, security reasons obliged us to try to dissolve the group of participants as soon as the showing was over, and we realised that the distribution of that kind of film had little meaning if it was not complemented by the participation of the comrades, if a debate was not opened on the themes suggested by the films.

We also discovered that every comrade who attended such showings did so with full awareness that he was infringing the System's laws and exposing his personal security to eventual repression. This person was no longer a spectator; on the contrary, from the moment he decided to attend the showing, *from the moment he lined himself up on this side* by taking risks and contributing his living experience to the meeting, he became an actor, a more important protagonist than those who appeared in the films. Such a person was seeking other committed people like himself, while he, in turn, became committed to them. *The spectator made way for the actor, who sought himself in others.* Outside this space which the films momentarily helped to liberate, there was nothing but solitude, noncommunication, distrust, and fear; within the freed space the situation turned everyone into accomplices of the act that was

5 The Organization for the Solidarity of African, Asian and Latin American Peoples, based in Cuba.

unfolding. The debates arose spontaneously. As we gained in experience, we incorporated into the showing various elements (a stage production) to reinforce the themes of the films, the climate of the showing, the 'disinhibiting' of the participants, and the dialogue: recorded music or poems, sculpture and paintings, posters, a program director who chaired the debate and presented the film and the comrades who were speaking, a glass of wine, a few *mates*,[6] etc. We realised that we had at hand three very valuable factors:

1. *The participant comrade*, the man-actor-accomplice who responded to the summons;
2. *The free space* where that man expressed his concerns and ideas, became politicised, and started to free himself; and
3. *The film*, important only as a detonator or pretext.

We concluded from these data that a film could be much more effective if it were fully aware of these factors and took on the task of subordinating its own form, structure, language, and propositions to that act and to those actors—to put it another way, if *it sought its own liberation in the subordination and insertion in the others, the principal protagonists of life*. With the correct utilisation of the *time* that that group of actor-personages offered us with their diverse histories, the use of the *space* offered by certain comrades, and of the *films* themselves, *it was necessary to try to transform time, energy, and work into freedom-giving energy*. In this way the idea began to grow of structuring what we decided to call the *film act*, the *film action*, one of the forms which we believe assumes great importance in affirming the line of a *third cinema*. A cinema whose first experiment is to be found, perhaps on a rather shaky level, in the second and third parts of *La hora de los hornos* ('*Acto para la liberación*'; above all, starting with '*La resistencia*' and '*Violencia y liberación*').

> Comrades [we said at the start of 'Acto para la liberación'], this is not just a film showing, nor is it a show; rather, it is, above all, A MEETING—an act of anti-imperialist unity; this is a place only for those who feel identified with this struggle, because here there is no room for spectators or for accomplices of the enemy; here there is room only for the authors and protagonists of the process to which the film attempts to bear witness and to deepen. The film is the pretext for dialogue, for the seeking and finding of wills. It is a report that we place before you for your consideration, to be debated after the showing. The conclusions [we said at another point in the second part] to which you may arrive as the real authors and protagonists of this history are important. The experiences and conclusions that we have assembled have a relative worth; they are of use to the extent that they are useful to you, who are the present and future of liberation. But most important of all is the action that may arise from these conclusions, the unity on the basis of the facts. This is why the film stops here; it opens out to you so that you can continue it.

The film act means an open-ended film; it is essentially a way of learning.

> The first step in the process of knowledge is the first contact with the things of the outside world, the stage of sensations [in a film, the living fresco of image and sound]. The second step is the synthesizing of the data provided by the sensations; their ordering and elaboration; the stage of concepts, judgments, opinions, and deductions [in the film, the announcer, the reportings, the didactics, or the narrator who leads the projection act]. And then comes the third stage, that of knowledge. The active role of knowledge is expressed not only in the active leap from sensory to rational knowledge, but, and what is even more important, in the leap from rational knowledge to revolutionary practice.... The practice of the transformation of the world. ... This, in general terms, is the dialectical materialist theory of the unity of knowledge and action[7] [*in the projection of the film act, the participation of the comrades, the action proposals that arise, and the actions themselves that will take place later*].

Moreover, each projection of *a* film act presupposes a *different setting*, since the space where it takes place, the materials that go to make it up (actors-participants), and the historic time in which it takes place are never the same. This means that the result of each projection act will depend on those who organise it, on those who participate in it, and on the time and place; the possibility of introducing variations, additions, and changes is unlimited. The screening of a film act will always express in one way or another the historical situation in which it takes place; its perspectives are not exhausted in the struggle for power but will instead continue after the taking of power to strengthen the revolution.

The man of the *third cinema*, be it *guerrilla cinema* or a *film act*, with the infinite categories that they contain (*film letter, film poem, film essay, film pamphlet, film report, etc.*), above all counters the film industry of a cinema of characters with one of themes, that of individuals with that of masses, that of the author with that of the operative group, one of neocolonial misinformation with one of information, one of escape with one that recaptures the truth, that of passivity with that of

6 A traditional Argentine herb tea, *hierba mate*.
7 Mao Tse-tung, op. cit.

aggressions. To an institutionalised cinema, it counterposes a guerrilla cinema; to movies as shows, he opposes a film act or action; to a cinema of destruction, one that is both destructive and constructive; to a cinema made for the old kind of human being, for them, he opposes a *cinema fit for a new kind of human being, for what each one of us has the possibility of becoming.*

The decolonisation of the film-maker and of films will be simultaneous acts to the extent that each contributes to collective decolonisation. The battle begins without, against the enemy who attacks us, but also within, *against the ideas and models of the enemy to be found inside each one of us.* Destruction and construction. Decolonising action rescues with its practice the purest and most vital impulses. It opposes to the colonialisation of minds the revolution of consciousness. The world is scrutinised, unraveled, rediscovered. People are witness to a constant astonishment, a kind of second birth. They recover their early ingenuity, their capacity for adventure; their lethargic capacity for indignation comes to life.

Freeing a forbidden truth means setting free the possibility of indignation and subversion. Our truth, that of the new man who builds himself by getting rid of all the defects that still weigh him down, is a bomb of inexhaustible power and, at the same time, *the only real possibility of life.* Within this attempt, the revolutionary film-maker ventures with *his subversive observation, sensibility, imagination, and realisation.* The great themes—the history of the country, love and unlove between combatants, the efforts of a people that comes awake—all this is reborn before the lens of the decolonised camera. The film-maker feels free for the first time. He discovers that, within the System, nothing fits, while outside of and against the System, everything fits, *because everything remains to be done.* What appeared yesterday as a preposterous adventure, as we said at the beginning, is posed today as *an inescapable need and possibility.*

Thus far, we have offered ideas and working propositions, which are the sketch of a hypothesis arising from our personal experience and which will have achieved something positive even if they do no more than serve to open a heated dialogue on the new revolutionary film prospects. The vacuums existing in the artistic and scientific fronts of the revolution are sufficiently well known so that the adversary will not try to appropriate them, while we are still unable to do so.

Why films and not some other form of artistic communication? If we choose films as the centre of our propositions and debate, it is because that is our work front and because the birth of a *third cinema* means, at least for us, *the most important revolutionary artistic event of our times.*

Photograph and Screen
Stanley Cavell
1971

Let us notice the specific sense in which photographs are of the world, or reality as a whole. You can always ask, pointing to an object in a photograph—a building, say—what lies behind it, totally obscured by it. This only accidentally makes sense when asked of an object in a painting. You can always ask, of an area photographed, what lies adjacent to that area, beyond the frame. This generally makes no sense asked of a painting. You can ask these questions of objects in photographs because they have answers in reality. The world of a painting is not continuous with the world of its frame; at its frame, a world finds its limits. We might say: A painting *is* a world; a photograph is *of* the world. What happens in a photograph is that *it* comes to an end. A photograph is cropped, not necessarily by a paper cutter or by masking but by the camera itself. The camera crops it by predetermining the amount of view it will accept; cutting, masking, enlarging, predetermine the amount after the fact. (Something like this phenomenon shows up in recent painting. In this respect, these paintings have found, at the extremest negation of the photographic, media that achieve the condition of photographs.) The camera, being finite, crops a portion from an indefinitely larger field; continuous portions of that field could be included in the photograph in fact taken; in principle, it could all be taken. Hence objects in photographs that run past the edge do not feel cut; they are aimed at, shot, stopped live. When a photograph is cropped, the rest of the world is cut *out*. The implied presence of the rest of the world, and its explicit rejection, are as essential in the experience of a photograph as what it explicitly presents. A camera is an opening in a box: that is the best emblem of the fact that a camera holding on an object is holding the rest of the world away. The camera has been praised for extending the senses; it may, as the world goes, deserve more praise for confining them, leaving room for thought.

The world of a moving picture is screened. The screen is not a support, not like a canvas; there is nothing to support, that way. It holds a projection, as light as light. A screen is a barrier. What does the silver screen screen? It screens me from the world it holds—that is, makes me invisible. And it screens that world from me—that is, screens its existence from me. That the projected world does not exist (now) is its only difference from reality. (There is no feature, or set of features, in which it differs. Existence is not a predicate.) Because it is the field of a photograph, the screen has no frame; that is to say, no border. Its limits are not so much the edges of a given shape as they are the limitations, or capacity, of a container. The screen *is* a frame; the frame is the whole field of the screen—as a frame of film is the whole field of a photograph, like the frame of a loom or a house. In this sense, the screen-frame is a mold, or form[1].

The fact that in a moving picture successive film frames are fit flush into the fixed screen frame results

1 When painting found out how to acknowledge the fact that paintings had shapes, shapes became forms, not in the sense of patterns, but in the sense of containers. A form then could give its shape to what it contained. And content could transfer its signifi- cance as painting to what contains it. The shape pervades, like gravity, or energy or air. (See Michael Fried, "Shape as Form," Artforum, November 1966; reprinted in Henry Geldzaher's catalogue, New York Painting and Sculpture: 1940–1970 [New York: E.P. Dutton, 1969].)

This is not, as far as we yet know, a possibility of the film or screen frame – which only repeats the fact that a film is not a painting. The most important feature of the screen format remains what it was from the beginning of movies – its scale, its absolute large- ness. Variation of format—e.g., CinemaScope— is a matter determined, so far as I can tell, by questions of convenience and inconvenience, and by fashion. Though perhaps, as in painting, the declaration of color as such required or benefited from the even greater expanses of wider screens.

The idea may seem obviously false or foolish that the essential ontological difference between the world as it is and as it is screened is that the screened world does not exist; because this overlooks – or perhaps obscurely states – a fully obvious difference between them, viz., that the screened world is two-dimen- sional. I do not deny the obscurity, but better a real obscurity than a false clarity. For what is two dimen- sional? The world which is screened is not; its objects and motions are as three-dimensional as ours. The screen itself, then? Or the images on it? We seem to understand what it means to say that a painting is two-dimensional. But that depends on our under- standing that the support on which paint is laid is a three-dimensional object, and that the description of that object will not (except in an exceptional or vacuous sense) be the description of a painting. More significantly, it depends on our understanding of the support as limiting the extent of the painting in two dimensions. This is not the relation between the screen and the images projected across it. It seems all right to say that the screen is two-dimensional, but it would not follow that what you see there has the same dimensionality – any more than in the case of paint, its support, and the painting. Shadows are two-di- mensional, but they are made by three-dimensional objects – tracings of opacity, not gradations of it. This suggests that phenomenologically the idea of two-dimensionality is an idea of either transparency or outline. Projected images are not shadows; rather, one might way, they are shades.

in a phenomenological frame that is indefinitely extendible and contractible, limited in the smallness of the object it can grasp only by the state of its technology, and in largeness only by the span of the world. Drawing the camera back, and panning it, are two ways of extending the frame; a close-up is of a part of the body, or of one object or small set of objects, supported by and reverberating the whole frame of nature. The altering frame is the image of perfect attention. Early in its history the cinema discovered the possibility of *calling* attention to persons and parts of persons and objects; but it is equally a possibility of the medium not to call attention to them but, rather, to let the world happen, to let its parts draw attention to themselves according to their natural weight. This possibility is less explored than its opposite. Dreyer, Flaherty, Vigo, Renoir, and Antonioni are masters of it.

Ideological Effects of the Basic Cinematographic Apparatus

Jean-Louis Baudry

1974

At the end of *The Interpretation of Dreams*, when he seeks to integrate dream elaboration and its particular "economy" with the psyche as a whole, Freud assigns to the latter an optical model: "Let us simply imagine the instrument which serves in psychic productions as a sort of complicated microscope or camera." But Freud does not seem to hold strongly to this model, which, as Derrida has pointed out,[1] brings out the shortcoming in graphic representation in the area earlier covered by his work on dreams. Moreover, he will later abandon the optical model in favor of a writing instrument, the "mystic writing pad." Nonetheless this optical choice seems to prolong the tradition of Western science, whose birth coincides exactly with the development of the optical apparatus which will have as a consequence the decentering of the human universe, the end of geocentrism (Galileo).

But also, and paradoxically, the optical apparatus *camera obscura* will serve in the same period to elaborate in pictorial work a new mode of representation, *perspectiva artificalis*. This system, a recentering or at least a displacement of the center (which settles itself in the eye), will assure the setting up of the "subject" as the active center and origin of meaning. One could doubtless question the privileged position which optical instruments seem to occupy on the line of intersection of science and ideological products. Does the technical nature of optical instruments, directly attached to scientific practice, serve to conceal not only their use in ideological products but also the ideological effects which they may provoke themselves? Their scientific base assures them a sort of neutrality and avoids their being questioned.

But already a question: if we are to take account of the imperfections of these instruments, their limitations, by what criteria may these be defined? If, for example, one can speak of a restricted depth of field as a limitation, doesn't this term itself depend upon a particular conception of reality for which such a limitation would not exist? Signifying productions are particularly relevant here, to the extent that instrumentation plays a more and more important role in them and that their distribution is more and more extensive. It is strange (but is it so strange?) that emphasis has been placed almost exclusively on their influence, on the effects they have as finished products, their content, the field of what is signified, if you like; the technical bases on which these effects depend and the specific characteristics of these bases have been ignored, however. They have been protected by the inviolability that science is supposed to provide. We would like to establish for the cinema a few guidelines which will need to be completed, verified, improved.

We must first establish the place of the instrumental base in the set of operations which combine in the production of a film (we omit consideration of economic implications). Between "objective reality" and the camera, site of the inscription, and between the inscription and projection are situated certain operations, a *work*[2] which has as its result a finished product. To the extent that it is cut off from the raw material ("objective reality") this product does not allow us to see the transformation which has taken place. Equally distant from "objective reality" and the finished product, the camera occupies an intermediate position in the work process which leads from raw material to finished product. Though mutually dependent from other points of view, *découpage* [shot breakdown before shooting] and *montage* [editing, or final assembly] must be distinguished because of the essential difference in the signifying raw material on which each operates: language (scenario) or image. Between the two complementary stages of production a mutation of the signifying material takes place (neither translation nor transcription, obviously, for the image is not reducible to language) precisely where the camera is. Finally, between the finished product (possessing exchange value, a commodity) and its consumption (use value) is introduced another operation effected by a set of instruments. Projector and screen restore the light lost in the shooting process, and transform a succession of separate images into an unrolling which also restores, but according to another scansion, the movement seized from "objective reality."

Cinematographic specificity (what distinguishes cinema from other systems of signification) thus refers to a *work*, that is, to a process of transformation. The question becomes, is the work made evident, does consumption of the product bring about a "knowledge effect" [Althusser], or is the work concealed? If the

1 Cf. on this subject Derrida's work "La Scène de l'écriture" in *L'Ecriture et la Diffrence* (Paris: Le Seuil).

2 [*Travail*, the process—implying not only "work" in the ordinary sense but as in Freud's usage: the dream-*work*. —TR.]

latter, consumption of the product will obviously be accompanied by ideological surplus value.* On the practical level, this poses the question of by what procedures the work can in fact be made "readable" in its inscription. These procedures must of necessity call cinematographic technique into play. But, on the other hand, going back to the first question, one may ask, do the instruments (the technical base) produce specific ideological effects, and are these effects themselves determined by the dominant ideology? In which case, concealment of the technical base will also bring about a specific ideological effect. Its inscription, its manifestation as such, on the other hand, would produce a knowledge effect, as actualization of the work process, as denunciation of ideology, and as critique of idealism.

THE EYE OF THE SUBJECT

Central in the process of production[3] of the film, the camera—an assembly of optical and mechanical instrumentation—carries out a certain mode of inscription characterized by marking, by the recording of differences of light intensity (and of wavelength for color) and of differences between the frames. Fabricated on the model of the *camera obscura*, it permits the construction of an image analogous to the perspective projections developed during the Italian Renaissance. Of course the use of lenses of different focal lengths can alter the perspective of an image. But this much, at least, is clear in the history of cinema: it is the perspective construction of the Renaissance which originally served as model. The use of different lenses, when not dictated by technical considerations aimed at restoring the habitual perspective (such as shooting in limited or extended spaces which one wishes to expand or contract) does not destroy [traditional] perspective but rather makes it play a normative role. Departure from the norm, by means of a wide-angle or telephoto lens, is clearly marked in comparison with so-called "normal" perspective. We will see in any case that the resulting ideological effect is still defined in relation to the ideology inherent in perspective. The dimensions of the image itself, the ratio between height and width, seem clearly taken from an average drawn from Western easel painting.

The conception of space which conditions the construction of perspective in the Renaissance differs from that of the Greeks. For the latter, space is discontinuous and heterogeneous (for Aristotle, but also for Democritus, for whom space is the location of an infinity of indivisible atoms), whereas with Nicholas of Cusa will be born a conception of space formed by the relation between elements which are equally near and distant from the "source of all life." In addition, the pictorial construction of the Greeks corresponded to the organization of their stage, based on a multiplicity of points of view, whereas the painting of the Renaissance will elaborate a centered space. ("Painting is nothing but the intersection of the visual pyramid following a given distance, a fixed center, and a certain lighting." —Alberti.) The center of this space coincides with the eye which Jean Pellerin Viator will so justly call the "subject." ("The principal point in perspective should be placed at eye level: this point is called fixed or subject."[4]) Monocular vision, which as Pleynet points out, is what the camera has, calls forth a sort of play of "reflection." Based on the principle of a fixed point by reference to which the visualized objects are organized, it specifies in return the position of the "subject,"[5] the very spot it must necessarily occupy.

In focusing it, the optical construct appears to be truly the projection-reflection of a "virtual image" whose hallucinatory reality it creates. It lays out the space of an ideal vision and in this way assures the necessity of a transcendence—metaphorically (by the unknown to which it appeals—here we must recall the structural place occupied by the vanishing point) and metonymically (by the displacement that it seems to carry out: a subject is both "in place of" and "a part for the whole"). Contrary to Chinese and Japanese painting, Western easel painting, presenting as it does a motionless and continuous whole, elaborates a total vision which corresponds to the idealist conception of the fullness and homogeneity of "being,"[6] and is, so to speak, representative of this conception. In this sense it contributes in a singularly emphatic way to the ideological function of art, which is to provide the tangible representation of metaphysics. The principle of transcendence which conditions and is conditioned by the perspective construction represented in painting and in the photographic image which copies from it seems to inspire all the idealist paeans to which the cinema has given rise [such as we find in Cohen-Séat or Bazin].[7]

---

* Althusser opposes ideology to knowledge or science. Ideology operates by obfuscating the means by which it is produced. Thus an increase in ideological value is an increase in mystification. —ED.

3 Obviously we are not speaking here of investment of capital in the process.

4 Cf. L. Brion Guerry, *Jean Pellerin Viator* (Paris: Belles Lettres, 1962).

5 We understand the term "subject" here in its function as vehicle and place of intersection of ideological implications which we are attempting progressively to make clear, and not as the structural function which analytic discourse attempts to locate. It would rather take partially the place of the ego, of whose deviations little is known in the analytic field.

6 The perspective "frame" which will have such an influence on cinematographic shooting has as its role to intensify, to increase the effect of the spectacle, which no divergence may be allowed to split.

PROJECTION: THE DIFFERENCE NEGATED

Nevertheless, whatever the effects proper to optics generally, the movie camera differs from still photography by registering through its mechanical instrumentation a series of images. It might thus seem to counter the unifying and "substantializing" character of the single-perspective image, taking what would seem like instants of time or slices from "reality" (but always a reality already worked upon, elaborated, selected). This might permit the supposition, especially because the camera moves, of a multiplicity of points of view which would neutralize the fixed position of the eye-subject and even nullify it. But here we must turn to the relation between the succession of images inscribed by the camera and their projection, bypassing momentarily the place occupied by montage, which plays a decisive role in the strategy of the ideology produced.

The projection operation (projector and screen) restore continuity of movement and the temporal dimension to the sequence of static images. The relation between the individual frames and the projection would resemble the relation between points and a curve in geometry. But it is precisely this relation and the restoration of continuity to discontinuous elements which poses a problem. The meaning effect produced does not depend only on the content of the images but also on the material procedures by which an illusion of continuity, dependent on the persistence of vision, is restored from discontinuous elements. These separate frames have between them differences that are indispensible for the creation of an illusion of continuity, of a continuous passage (movement, time). But only on one condition can these differences create this illusion: they must be effaced as differences.[8]

Thus on the technical level the question becomes one of the adoption of a very small difference between images, such that each image, in consequence of an organic factor [presumably persistence of vision] is rendered incapable of being seen as such. In this sense we could say that film—and perhaps in this respect it is exemplary—lives on the denial of difference: the difference is necessary for it to live, but it lives on its negation. This is indeed the paradox that emerges if we look directly at a strip of processed film: adjacent images are almost exactly repeated, their divergence being verifiable only by comparison of images at a sufficient distance from each other. We should remember, moreover, the disturbing effects which result during a projection from breakdowns in the recreation of movement, when the spectator is brought abruptly back to discontinuity—that is, to the body, to the technical apparatus which he had *forgotten*.

We might not be far from seeing what is in play on this material basis, if we recall that the "language" of the unconscious, as it is found in dreams, slips of the tongue, or hysterical symptoms, manifests itself as continuity destroyed, broken, and as the unexpected surging forth of a marked difference. Couldn't we thus say that cinema reconstructs and forms the mechanical model (with the simplifications that this can entail) of a system of writing[9] constituted by a material base and a counter-system (ideology, idealism) which uses this system while also concealing it? On the one hand, the optical apparatus and the film permit the marking of difference (but the marking is already negated, we have seen, in the constitution of the perspective image with its mirror effect).[10] On the other hand, the mechanical apparatus both selects the minimal difference and represses it in projection, so that meaning can be constituted: it is at once direction, continuity, movement. The projection mechanism allows the differential elements (the discontinuity inscribed by the camera) to be suppressed, bringing only the relation into play. The individual images as such disappear so that movement and continuity can appear. But the movement and continuity are the visible expression (one might even say the projection) of their relations, derived from the tiny discontinuities between the images. Thus one may assume that what was already at work as the originating basis of the perspective image, namely the eye, the "subject," is put forth, liberated (in the sense that a chemical reaction liberates a substance) by the operation which transforms successive, discrete images (as isolated images they have, strictly speaking, no meaning, or at least no unity of meaning) into continuity, movement, meaning; with continuity restored both meaning and consciousness are restored.[11]

---

7 See Cohen-Séat, *Essai sur les principes d'une philosophie du cinéma* (Paris: Corti) and Bazin, *What Is Cinema?* (Berkeley & Los Angeles: University of California Press). —TR.

8 "We know that the spectator finds it impossible to notice that the images which succeed one another before his eyes were assembled end-to-end, because the projection of film on the screen offers an impression of continuity although the images which compose it are, in reality, distinct, and are differentiated moreover by variations in space and time.

"In a film, there can be hundreds, even thousands of cuts and intervals. But if it is shown for specialists who know the art, the spectacle will not be divulged as such. Only an error or lack of competence will permit them to seize, and this is a disagreeable sensation, the changes of time and place of action." (Pudovkin, "Le Montage" in *Cinéma d'aujourd'hui et de demain*, [Moscow, 1956].)

9 [Écriture, in the French, meaning "writing" but also "schematization" at any given level of material or expression. —TR.]

10 [Specular: a notion used by Althusser and above all by Lacan; the word refers to the "mirror" effect which by reflection (specularization) constitutes the object reflected to the viewer and for him. The body is the most important and the first of these objects. —TR.]

THE TRANSCENDENTAL SUBJECT

Meaning and consciousness, to be sure: at this point we must return to the camera. Its mechanical nature not only permits the shooting of differential images as rapidly as desired but also destines it to change position, to move. Film history shows that as a result of the combined inertia of painting, theater, and photography, it took a certain time to notice the inherent mobility of the cinematic mechanism. The ability to reconstitute movement is after all only a partial, elementary aspect of a more general capability. To seize movement is to become movement, to follow a trajectory is to become trajectory, to choose a direction is to have the possibility of choosing one, to determine a meaning is to give oneself a meaning. In this way the eye-subject, the invisible base of artificial perspective (which in fact only represents a larger effort to produce an ordering, regulated transcendence) becomes absorbed in, "elevated" to a vaster function, proportional to the movement which it can perform.

And if the eye which moves is no longer fettered by a body, by the laws of matter and time, if there are no more assignable limits to its displacement—conditions fulfilled by the possibilities of shooting and of film—the world will not only be constituted by this eye but for it.[12] The movability of the camera seems to fulfill the most favorable conditions for the manifestation of the "transcendental subject." There is both fantasmatization of an objective reality (images, sounds, colors) and of an objective reality which, limiting its powers of constraint, seems equally to augment the possibilities or the power of the subject.[13] As it is said of consciousness—and in point of fact we are concerned with nothing less—the image will always be image *of* something; it must result from a deliberate act of consciousness [*visée intentionelle*]. "The word intentionality signifies nothing other than this peculiarity that consciousness has of being consciousness *of* something, of carrying in its quality of *ego* its *cogitatum* within itself."[14] In such a definition could perhaps be found the status of the cinematographic image, or rather of its operation, the mode of working which it carries out. For it to be an image of something, it has to constitute this something as meaning. The image seems to reflect the world but solely in the naive inversion of a founding hierarchy: "The domain of natural existence thus has only an authority of the second order, and always presupposes the domain of the transcendental."[15]

The world is no longer only an "open and unbounded horizon." Limited by the framing, lined up, put at the proper distance, the world offers up an object endowed with meaning, an intentional object, implied by and implying the action of the "subject" which sights it. At the same time that the world's transfer as image seems to accomplish this phenomenological reduction, this putting into parentheses of its real existence (a suspension necessary, we will see, to the formation of the impression of reality) provides a basis for the apodicity[16] of the ego. The multiplicity of aspects of the object in view refers to a synthesizing operation, to the unity of this constituting subject: Husserl speaks of "'aspects,' sometimes of 'proximity,' sometimes of 'distance,' in variable modes of 'here' and 'there,' opposed to an absolute 'here' (which is located—for me—in 'my own body' which appears to me at the same time), the consciousness of which, though it remains *unperceived*, always accompanies them. [We will see moreover what happens with the body in the *mise-en-scène* of projection. —J. L. B.] Each 'aspect' which the mind grasps is revealed in turn as a unity synthesized from a multiplicity of corresponding modes of presentation. The nearby object may present itself as the same, but under one or another 'aspect.' There may be variation of visual perspective, but also of 'tactile,' 'acoustic' phenomena, or of other 'modes of presentation'[17] as we can observe in directing our attention in the proper direction."[18]

For Husserl, "the original operation [of intentional analysis] is to *unmask the potentialities implied* in present states of consciousness. And it is by this that will be carried out, from the noematic point of view, the eventual *explication, definition*, and *elucidation* of what is meant by consciousness, that is, its *objective meaning*."[19] And again in the *Cartesian Meditations*: "A second type of polarization now presents itself to us, another type of synthesis which embraces the particular multiplicities of *cogitationes*, which embraces them all and in a special manner, namely as *cogitationes* of an identical self which, *active* or *passive*, lives

11 It is thus first at the level of the apparatus that the cinema functions as a language: inscription of discontinuous elements whose effacement in the relationship instituted among them produces meaning.

12 "In the cinema I am simultaneously in this action and *outside* of it, in this space and out of this space. Having the power of ubiquity, I am everywhere and nowhere." (Jean Mitry, *Esthetique et Psychtologie du Cinéma* (Paris: Presses Universitaires de France, 1965), 179.

13 The cinema manifests in a hallucinatory manner the belief in the omnipotence of thought, described by Freud, which plays so important a role in neurotic defense mechanisms.

14 Husserl, *Les Méditations Cartesiennes* (Paris: Vrin, 1953), 28.

15 Husserl, 16.

16 [Apodicity, in phenomenological terminology, indicates something of an ultimately irrefutable nature. See Husserl, *op. cit.* —TR.]

17 On this point it is true that the camera is revealed as incomplete. But this is only a technical imperfection which, since the birth of cinema, has already in large measure been remedied.

18 Husserl, 34, emphasis added.

19 Husserl, 40.

in all the lived states of consciousness and which, through them, relates to all objects."[20]

Thus is articulated the relation between the continuity necessary to the constitution of meaning and the "subject" which constitutes this meaning: continuity is an attribute of the subject. It supposes the subject and it circumscribes his place. It appears in the cinema in the two complementary aspects of a "formal" continuity established through a system of negated differences and narrative continuity in the filmic space. The latter, in any case, could not have been conquered without exercising violence against the instrumental base, as can be discovered from most of the texts by film-makers and critics: the discontinuity that had been effaced at the level of the image could have reappeared on the narrative level, giving rise to effects of rupture disturbing to the spectator (to a *place* which ideology must both conquer and, in the degree that it already dominates it, must also satisfy: fill). "What is important in a film is the feeling of continuity which joins shots and sequences while maintaining unity and cohesion of movements. This continuity was one of the most difficult things to obtain."[21] Pudovkin defined montage as "the art of assembling pieces of film, shot separately, in such a way as to give the spectator the impression of continuous movement." The search for such narrative continuity, so difficult to obtain from the material base, can only be explained by an essential ideological stake projected in this point: it is a question of preserving at any cost the synthetic unity of the locus where meaning originates [the subject]—the constituting transcendental function to which narrative continuity points back as its natural secretion.[22]

THE SCREEN-MIRROR: SPECULARIZATION AND DOUBLE IDENTIFICATION

But another supplementary operation (made possible by a special technical arrangement) must be added in order that the mechanism thus described can play its role effectively as an ideological machine, so that not only the reworked "objective reality" but also the specific type of identification we have described can be represented.

No doubt the darkened room and the screen bordered with black like a letter of condolences already present privileged conditions of effectiveness—no exchange, no circulation, no communication with any outside. Projection and reflection take place in a closed space and those who remain there, whether they know it or not (but they do not), find themselves chained, captured, or captivated. (What might one say of the function of the head in this captivation: it suffices to recall that for Bataille materialism makes itself headless—like a wound that bleeds and thus transfuses.) And the mirror, as a reflecting surface, is framed, limited, circumscribed. *An infinite mirror would no longer be a mirror.* The paradoxical nature of the cinematic mirror-screen is without doubt that it reflects images but not "*reality*"; the word reflect, being transitive, leaves this ambiguity unresolved. In any case this "reality" comes from behind the spectator's head and if he looked at it directly he would see nothing except the moving beams from an already veiled light source.

The arrangement of the different elements—projector, darkened hall, screen—in addition from reproducing in a striking way the *mise-en-scène* of Plato's cave (prototypical set for all transcendence and the topological model of idealism[23]) reconstructs the situation necessary to the release of the "mirror stage" discovered by Lacan. This psychological phase, which occurs between six and eighteen months of age, generates via the mirror image of a unified body the constitution or at least the first sketches of the "I" as an imaginary function. "It is to this unreachable image in the mirror that the specular image gives its garments."[24] But for this imaginary constitution of the self to be possible, there must be—Lacan strongly emphasizes this point—two complementary conditions: immature powers of mobility and a precocious maturation of visual organization (apparent in the first few days of life). If one considers that these two conditions are repeated during cinematographic projection—suspension of mobility and predominance of the visual function—perhaps one could suppose that this is more than a simple analogy. And possibly this

20 Husserl, 58.

21 Mitry, *op. cit.*, 157.

22 The lens, the "objective" is of course only a particular location of the "subjective." Marked by the idealist opposition interior/exterior, topologically situated at the point of meeting of the two, it corresponds, one could say, to the empirical organ of the subjective, to the opening, the fault in the organs of meaning, by which the exterior world may penetrate the interior and assume meaning. "It is the interior which commands," says Bresson. "I know this may seem paradoxical in an art which is all exterior." Also the use of different lenses is already conditioned by camera movement as implication and trajectory of meaning, by this transcendental function which we are attempting to define: it is the possibility of choosing a field as accentuation or modification of the *visée intentionelle*.

No doubt this transcendental function fits in without difficulty the field of psychology. This, moreover, is insisted upon by Husserl himself, who indicates that Brentano's discovery, intentionality, "permits one truly to distinguish the method of a descriptive science of consciousness, as much philosophical and transcendental as psychological."

23 The arrangement of the cave, except that in the cinema it is already doubled in a sort of enclosure in which the camera, the darkened chamber, is enclosed in another darkened chamber, the projection hall.

24 Lacan, *Ecrits* (Paris: Le Seuil, 1966). See in particular "Le Stade du miroir comme formateur de la fonction du je."

very point explains the "impression of reality" so often invoked in connection with the cinema for which the various explanations proposed seem only to skirt the real problem. In order for this impression to be produced, it would be necessary that the conditions of a formative scene be reproduced. This scene would be repeated and reenacted in such a manner that the imaginary order (activated by a specularization which takes place, everything considered, in reality) fulfills its particular function of occultation or of filling the gap, the split, of the subject on the order of the signifier.[25]

On the other hand, it is to the extent that the child can sustain the look of another in the presence of a third party that he can find the assurance of an identification with the image of his own body. From the very fact that during the mirror stage is established a dual relationship, it constitutes, in conjunction with the formation of the self in the imaginary order, the nexus of secondary identification.[26] The origin of the self, as discovered by Lacan, in pertaining to the imaginary order effectively subverts the "optical machinery" of idealism which the projection room scrupulously reproduces.[27] But it is not as specifically "imaginary," nor as a reproduction of its first configuration, that the self finds a "place" in the cinema. This occurs, rather, as a sort of proof or verification of that function, a solidification through repetition.

The "reality" mimed by the cinema is thus first of all that of a "self." But, because the reflected image is not that of the body itself but that of a world already given as meaning, one can distinguish two levels of identification. The first, attached to the image itself, derives from the character portrayed as a center of secondary identifications, carrying an identity which constantly must be seized and reestablished. The second level permits the appearance of the first and places it "in action"—this is the transcendental subject whose place is taken by the camera which constitutes and rules the objects in this "world." Thus the spectator identifies less with what is represented, the spectacle itself, than with what stages the spectacle, makes it seen, obliging him to see what it sees; this is exactly the function taken over by the camera as a sort of relay.[28] Just as the mirror assembles the fragmented body in a sort of imaginary integration of the self, the transcendental self unites the discontinuous fragments of phenomena, of lived experience, into unifying meaning. Through it each fragment assumes meaning by being integrated into an "organic" unity. Between the imaginary gathering of the fragmented body into a unity and the transcendentality of the self, giver of unifying meaning, the current is indefinitely reversible.

The ideological mechanism at work in the cinema seems thus to be concentrated in the relationship between the camera and the subject. The question is whether the former will permit the latter to constitute and seize itself in a particular mode of specular reflection. Ultimately, the forms of narrative adopted, the "contents" of the image, are of little importance so long as an identification remains possible.[29] What emerges here (in outline) is the specific function fulfilled by the cinema as support and instrument of ideology. It constitutes the "subject" by the illusory delimitation of a central location—whether this be that of a god or of any other substitute. It is an apparatus destined to obtain a precise ideological effect, necessary to the dominant ideology: creating a fantasmatization of the subject, it collaborates with a marked efficacity in the maintenance of idealism.

Thus the cinema assumes the role played throughout Western history by various artistic formations. The ideology of representation (as a principal axis orienting the notion of aesthetic "creation") and specularization (which organizes the *mise-en-scène* required to constitute the transcendental function) form a singularly coherent system in the cinema. Everything happens as if, the subject himself being unable—and for a reason—to account for his own situation, it was necessary to substitute secondary organs, grafted on to replace his own defective ones, instruments or ideological formations capable of filling his function as subject. In fact, this substitution is only possible on the condition that the instrumentation itself be hidden or repressed. Thus disturbing cinematic elements—similar, precisely, to those elements indicating the return of the repressed—signify without fail the arrival of the instrument "in flesh and blood," as in Vertov's *Man With a Movie Camera*. Both specular tranquility and the assurance of one's own identity collapse simultaneously with the revealing of the mechanism, that is of the inscription of the film-work. The cinema can thus appear as a sort of psychic apparatus of substitution, corresponding to the model defined by the dominant ideology. The system of repression (primarily

25 We see that what has been defined as impression of reality refers less to the "reality" than to the apparatus which, although being of an hallucinatory order, nonetheless founds this possibility. Reality will never appear except as relative to the images which reflect it, in some way inaugurated by a reflection anterior to itself.

26 We refer here to what Lacan says of identifications in liaison with the structure determined by an optical instrument (the mirror), as they are constituted, in the prevailing figuration of the ego, as lines of resistance to the advance of the analytic work.

27 "That the ego be 'in the right' must be avowed, from experience, to be a function of misunderstanding." (Lacan, *op. cit.*, 637.)

28 "That it sustains itself as 'subject' means that language permits it to consider itself as the stagehand or even the director of all the imaginary capturings of which it would otherwise only be the living marionette." (Lacan, 637)

29 It is on this point and in function of the elements which we are trying to put in place that a discussion of editing could be opened. We will at a later date attempt to make some remarks on this subject.

economic) has as its goal the prevention of deviations and of the active exposure of this "model."[30] Analogously one could say that its "unconscious" is not recognized (we speak of the apparatus and not of the content of films, which have used the unconscious in ways we know all too well). To this unconscious would be attached the mode of production of film, the process of "work" in its multiple determinations, among which must be numbered those depending on instrumentation. This is why reflections on the basic apparatus ought to be possible to integrate into a general theory of the ideology of cinema.

30 *Mediterranée*, by J.-D. Pollet and Phillipe Sollers (1963), which dismantles with exemplary efficiency the "transcendental specularization" which we have attempted to delineate, gives a manifest proof of this point. The film was never able to overcome the economic blockade.

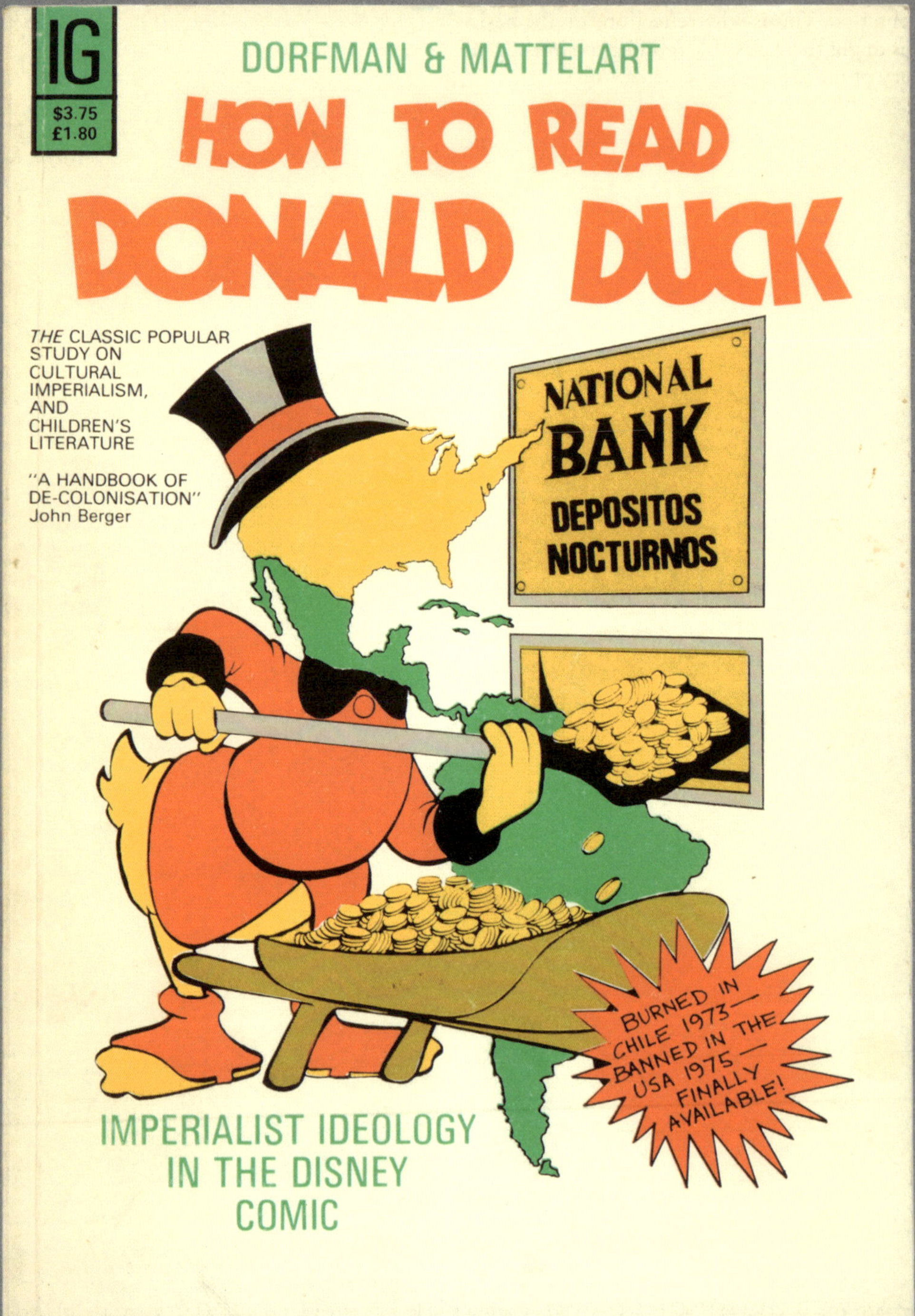
IG
$3.75
£1.80
DORFMAN & MATTELART
HOW TO READ
DONALD DUCK
THE CLASSIC POPULAR STUDY ON CULTURAL IMPERIALISM, AND CHILDREN'S LITERATURE
"A HANDBOOK OF DE-COLONISATION" John Berger
NATIONAL BANK
DEPOSITOS NOCTURNOS
BURNED IN CHILE 1973— BANNED IN THE USA 1975— FINALLY AVAILABLE!
IMPERIALIST IDEOLOGY IN THE DISNEY COMIC

Preface to *How To Read Donald Duck: Imperialist Ideology in the Disney Comic*

Ariel Dorfman and Armand Mattelart

1975

To say that this book was burnt in Chile should not come as a surprise to anyone. Hundreds of books were destroyed, and thousands more prohibited and censored.

It was written in the middle of 1971, in the middle of the Chilean revolutionary process. Copper had been rescued, the land was being returned to the peasantry, the whole Chilean people were recovering the industries that during the twentieth century had been the means of enrichment for Mr. Rockefeller, Grace, Guggenheim, and Morgan. Because this process was intolerable to the United States government and its multinational corporations, it had to stopped. They organized a plan, which at the time was suspected, and since has been confirmed by Mr. Kissinger, Ford and Colby to have been directed and financed by the United States intelligence services. Their objective: to overthrow the constitutional government of Chile. To realize their objective, an "invisible blockade" was imposed: credits were denied, spare parts purchased for industrial machinery were not sent, and later, the Chilean State bank accounts in the U.S. were blocked, and an embargo preventing the sale of Chilean copper throughout the world was organized.

There were, however, two items which were not blocked: planes, tanks, ships and technical assistance for the Chilean armed forces; and magazines, TV serials, advertising, and public opinion polls for the Chilean mass media, which continued, for the most part, to be in the hands of the small group which was losing its privileges. To maintain them, with those of the U.S., their media prepared the climate for the bourgeois insurrection which finally materialized some years later on the 11th of September 1973. Each day, with expert U.S. advice, in each newspaper, each weekly, each monthly magazine, each news dispatch, each movie, and each comic book, their arsenal of psychological warfare was fortified. In the words of General Pinochet, the point was to "conquer the minds," while in the words of Donald Duck (in the magazine *Disneylandia* published in December 1971, coinciding with the first mass rallies of native fascism, the so-called "march of the empty pots and pans") the point was to "restore the king."

But the people did not want the restoration of the king nor of the businessman. The popular Chilean cultural offensive, which accompanied the social and economic liberation, took multiple forms: wall paintings, popular papers, TV programs, motion pictures, theater, songs, literature. In all areas of human activity, with differing degrees of intensity, the people expressed their will. Perhaps the most important arm of this offensive, was the work of the State Publishing House "Quimantú," a word meaning "Sunshine of Knowledge" in the language of the native Chilean Mapuche indians. In two and a half years it published five million books; twice the amount which had been published in all of Chile during the past seventy years. In addition, it transformed the content of some of the magazines it had inherited from before the Popular Unity government, and created new ones. It is in this multi-faceted context, with a people on the march to cultural liberation—a process which also meant criticizing the "mass" cultural merchandise exported so profitably by the U.S. to the Third World—that *How to Read Donald Duck* was generated. We simply answered a practical need; it was *not* an academic exercise.

For the mad dog warriors on that September 11th, there were no paintings on the walls. There were only enormous "stains" which dirtied the city and memory. They, using the fascist youth brigades, whitewashed all the singing, many-colored walls of the nation. They broke records, murdered singers, destroyed radios and printing presses, emprisoned and executed journalists, so that nothing would be left to remind anybody of anything about the struggle for national liberation.

But it was not enough to clean these cultural "stains" from the street. The most important task was to eliminate all those who bore the "stain" inside themselves, the fighters, workers, peasants, employees, students, and patriotic soldiers, to eliminate these creators of a new life, to eliminate this new life which grew, and for which we all created.

This book, conceived for the Chilean people, and our urgent needs, produced in the midst of our struggle, is now being published far from Chile in the uncleland of Disney, behind the barbed wire network of ITT.

Mr. Disney, we are returning your Duck. Feathers plucked and well-roasted. Look inside, you can see the handwriting on the wall, our hands still writing on the wall:

Donald, Go Home!

Dorfman and Mattelart
January 1975,
in exile

A Declaration of Dependence

Sarah Charlesworth

1975

We are living in a period of unprecedented destruction of languages and cultures, of nations, under the assault of highly bureaucratic states. These exert, both internally and externally, a steady pressure, reducing culture to a series of technical functions. Put another way, culture, the creation of shared meanings, symbolic interaction, is dissolving into a mere mechanism guided by signals.

—Stanley Diamond[1]

I

When we discuss a work of art or an art tradition, we are discussing a phenomenon which exists in an integral relationship with the entire complex of human social and historical forces defining the development of that work or tradition. This same complex of social and historical forces in turn inevitably defines the context in which that work or tradition claims significance, and ultimately functions as a force or agent in the ongoing evolution of that culture. Thus we are at once the products and the producers of the culture in which we participate. *This seems so obvious*, yet we often fail to recognize that while options may be limited, the value and function of our work may be defined by the social and economic context in which we operate; we are ourselves, individually and collectively, the constitutive agents of the social complex that defines the value and significance of our work. In the same way that we as artists are *responsible* for the notion of art, by the formulation of art works or concepts, we are in turn responsible to the culture itself in the formulation of the notion and function of art.

In speaking of a social and historical context in which any art work or tradition evolves and is transmitted, it is difficult to differentiate between the political and economic order which prevails at any particular time and place, and the ideological or intellectual traditions which have developed concomitantly; these latter more often than not serve to reinforce and sustain the political and economic order. Institutions tend to claim authority over the individuals and their activity in society *regardless of whatever subjective meaning* they may attach to their situation and endeavor. The ideological structure of society integrates and legitimizes the institutional order by explaining and legitimizing its objectivated meanings.

If we speak specifically about art in modern European and American culture, we see that its meaning, function, and value within society are clearly institutionally mediated; and that not only artistic values, but the intellectual and ideological forces which explain, interpret and legitimize art practice have their origins in the very same traditions that presuppose that institutional order. Thus the structural system of the art-world, which provides a context for the social signification of art, is itself contextually situated in a social system, the structure of which it in turn reflects. At this point, attempts to question or transform the nature of art beyond formalistic considerations must inevitably begin to involve a consideration not only of the presuppositions inherent in the internal structure of art models, but also a critical awareness of the social system which preconditions and drastically confines the possibility of transformation.

If we recognize the institutional structure of a complex society to be (culturally) all-embrasive, then we may begin to see that in attempting to redefine, alter or redirect the social definition or function of art—the manner and channels through which we can effectively work—we are encountering a firmly entrenched and highly developed institutional order: not just when confronting the obvious bureaucratic structure of the New York art world, but encountering the force of that order on every level, from such specific factors as the persistence of socially convenient (marketable) formal models of art (i.e. painting and sculpture) to more abstract socially convenient (non-controversial) theoretical models (formalism, art for art's sake), to the most blatant sociological fact that cultural power is clearly allied with economic power, and that to a large extent the internalizations of the dictates of the productive system regarding patterns of legitimation and consumption are the very means by which individuals surrender their critical faculties to that system.

A certain ideological inversion or mystification which Marx calls false consciousness is apparent in the very fact that in discussing art, we commonly describe the sphere of influence in the following manner: as

1 Stanley Diamond, "Anthropology in Question," *Reinventing Anthropology*, ed. Dell Hymes (New York: Random House, 1969).

one moving *outward* from the individual artist, who, acting out of personal feelings or convictions, expresses himself/herself by way of a statement, traditionally in the form of a discrete work or art product, the social recognition and validation of which is dependent on some internal properties, termed "quality," which bear upon its visual or historical characteristics, *outward* through a system of institutions responsive to its self-evident merit; which in turn circulate and promote the work accordingly, to the benefit of all those culturally refined and sensitive enough to partake of its virtues. Hence the artist, as well as his product and the abstract sphere of his influence, are assumed "transcendent," that is, somehow responsive to and effective of abstract psychic and social conditions somewhat removed from the mundane conditions of "everyday life." The historical, social, and psychological factors which bear upon the artist are viewed from the perspective of predominantly after-the-fact analysis, the domain of various somewhat less "transcendent" (presumably more "objective") specialists who interpret and speculate on the myriad social and historical influences and implications manifest in the personal history, life style and oeuvre of the particular subject under study—those factors which bear upon and are implicit in the process of validation or interpretation seldom being taken into account. The art work as a symbolic token of the struggle of the individual artist and the spiritual and social dilemmas which that individual struggle in turn reflects, becomes in a sense a sanctified cultural relic, presumably embodying in itself some elusive, imaginative spirit.

One wonders, of course, why it is the *tokens* of struggle toward meaning and not *the struggle itself* to which we respond (or how much spirit we can touch upon when these tokens become the stock in trade of a sophisticated cultural elite). That this conception is naive and idyllic and totally out of keeping with the rather more complex situation in which cultural phenomena emerge, develop, and function ought to be readily apparent; however, attempts to construct a more accurate basis for understanding are not without problems. One obvious alternative model to this ideological Disneyland is of course a (very broadly speaking) materialist scheme in which material processes, specifically the mode of production and distribution of goods, services and capital within and amongst societies is the primary and overriding factor of which all mental and spiritual attitudes and formulations are (consciously or unconsciously) in large part the product. "All parts of the ideological superstructure, art being one of these, are crucially determined both in content and style by the behavior of a more basic structure which is economic in nature."[2] But it would be deterministic, in this case, to suppose that the mere economic dependence of the artist, a certain *external* tie which links producer to consumer (and vice-versa), is the full extent of that relationship, that the economic and social conditions of production are explicit and can be dealt with as such; but rather they are *implicit and internalized* to such a degree that they inform *every aspect of our self and social consciousness* upon which all praxis is founded. The artist may then be unwittingly supportive of ideals or conditions in a relation to which he sees himself neutral or even opposed.

While a materialist critique and the dialectical method it implies is eminently useful as a tool by which to reorient our inquiries, to attempt to situate our self-presumptions, to gauge the implications and ramifications of our critical or practical stance, we should at the same time recognize the historical (and ideological) nature of this traditional model, as well as the one from and to which we bring it to bear. A dialectical or immanent critique, however, takes seriously the principle that it is not ideology itself which is untrue but rather its pretension to correspond to reality. There can be no method of escape, no science, no dialectic, no objective criteria which are not in turn subjectively assumed. The issue then becomes not so much a question of how we can achieve a "value-free" or "objective" model or theory of art practice as it is a question of what values and conditions of learning we in fact promote and provide through our practice of art.

I can no more reduce the "spirit of art" to which I am still responsive, to an entirely materialistic function than I can conversely assume it to be neutral or independent of material conditions. I am wary of the individualism and subjectivism which pervades our self and social consciousness, which I believe (when assumed uncritically) is actually a factor which perpetuates the oppression of individuals in our society. Concurrently I would argue that it is only when individuals begin to accept a responsibility for the social implications of their actions that a collective spirit or consciousness conducive to social change can occur. While being critical of the idealistic and presumptive notion of freedom and transcendence which informs the modernist paradigm, I myself work within the context of that art, that tradition; in part because I am responsive to certain ideals which that endeavor represents and recognize therein a certain emancipatory and self-reflexive capacity lacking to varying degrees in other disciplines. My own work is tempered with realism only to the extent to which I feel continually compelled to re-examine or redirect my course in relation to such ideals.

Throughout this essay I use the pronoun "we," and thereby incorporate myself and others into some abstract community, and assume a certain sympathy amongst

2 Berel Lang and Forest Williams, *Marxism and Art* (New York: David McKay Co., 1972).

the members so included. This is in part a function of the fact that I see myself as a participant in a real community which in my case might be centered around my involvement with The Fox *and my working relationship with other participants; but I also address and appeal to a larger community which is made up of other individuals with whom I share a common tradition, a similar historical and cultural locus, who see themselves and/or have come to be recognized variously as artists, critics, dealers, curators, professors, students and so on. All are at least potentially in a position to make critical choices which will affect not only the internal character but also the social dynamic of contemporary and future art activity. To a large extent, we learn what our purposes are through the systems which we use, just was we learn what is required for survival through the interaction of those systems and our experience in trying to do things. For each of us there is a certain element of contradiction involved in the majority of personal and professional choices that we make, a certain tension between self survival/self interest and social interest/species survival. Some of us feel this conflict more intensely than others and we have varying interests and values at stake. It is important, however, that we begin to recognize and elucidate the criteria and implications of choice rather than continue to apologize, rationalize, and obfuscate. None of us, neither artist, critic, dealer, curator, nor "patron of the arts," can be said to be free of conflict of interest when it comes to the making of the cultural phenomena "art."*

If art is viewed as one aspect of culture or one form of "symbolic action," then the logic embodied in this particular system and the meanings which we attribute to our actions must be considered in relation to, or more precisely as evolving within and contributing to, a larger context of social meaning. But characteristic of our liberal tradition, both on an intellectual or ideological level (political liberalism, empiricism, logical positivism) as well as on an intuitive or common sense level, is a tendency toward an emphasis on the individual fact or item at the expense of an awareness of the relational or contextual aspects in which such a seemingly discrete fact or item occurs. This tendency has been manifest in contemporary art both in our conceptualization of art as an autonomous and self-regulatory discipline, an assembly of static objects of contemplation, as well as in our inclination to interpret the symbolic or gestural content of our actions in a dissociated and superficial manner.

Viewed from one perspective, the history of Modern art has been a long revolution against the complacency, sentimentality and tedium of bourgeois culture, a rebellion against the self-assuming and rhetorical aspects of traditional forms, against the threat of subsumption or diversion of political or social non-art concerns—a veritable march of progress in the name of freedom, of individuality, of *art*. On a symbolic level, this is apparently so; on a theoretical level as well. *But* is not the very logic through which we hail the theoretical and symbolic tokens of "revolutionary spirit" while embracing those very tokens in an attitude of blind acceptance and self-complacency, a tribute to the *failure* of that art—and the logic it embodies—to adequately comprehend and respond to the exigencies of a very real social and ideological predicament that, none the less, transcends and subsumes that art? Freedom and independence is not something you can posit and proceed to assume, but a condition fought for and seldom won.

II

Implicit in our understanding of modernist art is the assumption that art values and objectives might somehow be viewed as dissociated or neutral in relation to the social sphere in which they operate. Andre Malraux pointed out that "the middle ages had no more idea of what we mean by fine art than Greece or Egypt. In order that this idea could be born it was necessary for works to be separated from their function . . . the most profound metamorphosis began when art had no other end than itself."[3] In keeping with this tradition, when we speak of function or meaning when discussing art work we refer to the function or meaning of that work not so much in relation to a larger sphere of social praxis, but rather within the isolated and abstracted province "art." *The struggle of modernism in the West has been, above all else, a struggle to establish an independent and autonomous context of meaning at once in opposition to and in disregard of the existent social order.* Thus when Ad Reinhardt was to proclaim the one permanent revolution in art is always a negation of the use of art for some purpose other than its own, and that all progress and change in art is toward the one end of art as art-as-art, he was, as he claims, echoing an ideal which has characterized the writings of a majority of artists and theorists of the modern era. In 1834, Theophile Gautier in his preface to *Mademoiselle De Maupin* (frequently considered the first real manifesto of the art for art's sake movement), likewise argued for the elimination of all utilitarian and moral purpose for art, in favor of anarchistic individualism, which he regarded as the reflection of unique romantic genius; he was in turn responding to an idealistic conception of disinterested and pure beauty, formulated earlier still by Kant.

It is a curious and romantic notion that somehow

3 Andre Malraux, *Les Voix du Silence*.

by ignoring that which is repugnant within the existing order, we might quite logically be immune to its effect. But more curious still is the fact that this profoundly romantic and idealistic attitude, in which the problems of the apprehension of beauty, pure and independent of moral or utilitarian concerns, a primarily aesthetic and metaphysical preoccupation descended from the Enlightenment, should survive in an age when the creation of beauty and aesthetic enjoyment are no longer the self-proclaimed ends of art. Although the notion of *l'art pour l'art* now appears an outdated and naive preoccupation, a romantic struggle against bourgeois ideals of social utility, we must begin to question the degree to which this idealistic 19th-century construct has been internalized—in not only early modern, but even the most current art-model. As Arnold Hauser points out, "What was once a revolt against classical rules has become a revolt against all external ties.... From the standpoint of the direct aesthetic experience, autonomy and self-sufficiency appear to be the essence of the work of art, for only by putting itself completely in the place of reality, only by forming a total self-contained cosmos, is it able to produce a perfect illusion. But this illusion is in no way the whole content of art and often has no share in the effect it produces. The greatest works of art forgo the deceptive illusion of a self-contained aesthetic world and point beyond themselves."[4]

Leaving aside the question of "great works," is it not true that in forwarding an ideal self-image of autonomy (both in our concept of discrete self-contained art works and art values in general—in the face of all manner of evidence to the contrary), we are in effect now perpetuating those same bourgeois values such self confinement was originally deemed to escape? Even the question of bourgeois values is growing increasingly moot. *There is a great deal more to be frightened of at this point than the taint of an impure art.* When the power of validation and legitimization of human enterprise occurs more and more within an institutionalized system, where corporate power and investment potential are becoming increasingly the social consensus by which we signify meaning, it is clear that no private vision, no personal iconoclastic gesture can withstand.

Much "theoretical" or "analytical" work in the past few years has served to focus our attention on the conventional or conceptual underpinnings of our contemporary art practice. So-called conceptual art represents, amongst other things, an attempt to redefine art value or significance in terms of its ideational rather than physical ("experiential") attributes, but, as has been apparent for some time, to the extent that conceptual art is dependent upon the very same mechanisms for presentation, dissemination, and interpretation of art works, it *functions in society* in a manner not unlike previously more morphologically oriented work. Thus the *extent* to which its significance as art (or as idea) is dependent upon or inferred by its existence within the traditional context, its value or function within the culture is conditioned primarily by patterns of response *traditionally associated* with that context. This is a world in which honor is ritually bestowed, values assumed and rarely created. "Art as idea" was once a good idea, but art as idea as art product, alas, moves in the world of commodity-products and hardly the realm of "idea." The significance that early conceptual work bore in relation to previously held assumptions regarding formal requisites of traditional art practice is not to be denied, but formalistic innovation in and of itself is of questionable value. Since it is assumed that the intentional aspects of an artist's endeavor extend only to the making of a work or a proposition, and its placement or "documentation" within the prescribed context, the use or function of that work (aside from its existence as art history) is no longer an aspect of art. The artist is thus severed, except on a symbolic level, from his culture. *He responds to and assumes responsibility for an art in isolation.*

If art "lives" primarily by affecting other art (as is often claimed), then there is no mechanism by which such an art can reorient or redefine itself except out of a logic internal to the closure "art." Thus we are confined to a large extent to the progressive reduction and expansion of inherent formal relations; such "conceptual innovations" as may occur are subsumed within the system to which they refer. A tradition keyed to demands of the competitive market, responding to the stylistic or formal elements of innovation, sees no use or value in the implications of change beyond the historical progressivity which it denotes. This is the ultimate consumership: *Ideas become the property of the inventor, and as such are no further use to the community once claimed.*

We move away from the tyranny of the picture frame only to discover that of the gallery, the market, and so on, and as it begins to become apparent that the privileging of the art object cannot be dissociated from the privileging of the context and tradition in which the object appears; we begin to wonder whether the very sense of that history or sociality, which is the shape and dynamic of our discipline, is not so much the momentum of a free and critical consciousness as the order of a definitive social and economic reality, the pervasiveness of which we have scarcely begun to grasp.

Inversely, we might begin to inquire whether the retreat from the objectification, commodification, and

4 Arnold Hauser, *The Social History of Art* (New York: Alfred A. Knopf, 1951).

institutionalization of traditional art models, which has characterized the tactics of certain more (theoretically) radical segments of the art community, is not so much a function of the realization of inherently noxious qualities which those models possess, as the instinctive recoil against *that which they represent*: the commodification and institutionalization of human history and endeavor. While such activities now appear naive and unsuccessful on the one hand, in mistaking for ethic or style that which is in fact part of a more profound social and economic reality, they *do* signify a positive and potentially liberating capacity; that is, the will to change, to re-examine, and, more importantly, to "call to arms" the tools that make radical and contextual critique conceivable. Suppose we imagine this capacity as a medium, a methodology, and not an end in itself. We can *learn* as much, in a sense, through the "failure" of concept art as we do through its partial success; while being critical of the (self) presumptive and reductionist aspects of formalist tradition, we exist as its inevitable heir.

III

Our dilemma at this point is profound and problematic in its circularity. If we assume any theoretical stance or critical viewpoint (by which we mean to assess a previous or other presumably "more naive" position), we must do so by use of a logic which justifies or lends authority to our current more "sophisticated" outlook. This new position claims precedence over antecedent or rival theories, and yet does so at the expense of obscuring its own presumptions. Thus we are always in a position of revealing the "false" foundations of one logic while claiming another similarly founded. This is, of course, where traditional Marxist social "science" as well as many sociological or anthropological models, particularly the structuralist models, break down. You cannot, on the one hand, claim that all knowledge is culturally determined, socially derived and then in turn claim the objective validity of your own theory. In this sense the dialectic becomes immanently useful as an ideal working model but in practice something of an impossibility. So we proceed amidst contradiction.

Dialectical critique implies that one cannot view any object or subject at rest, for in the very act of viewing or depicting our object, we grasp self and subject as situated in the same historical moment from whence we depart. "Faced with the operative procedures of the nonreflective thinking mind (whether grappling with the philosophical or artistic, political or scientific problems and objects), dialectical thought tries not so much to complete and perfect the application of such procedures as to widen its own attention to include them in its awareness as well; it aims, in other words, not so much at solving the particular dilemmas in question, as converting those problems into their own solutions on a higher level, and making the fact and the existence of the problem itself the starting point of new research."[5]

That this model does represent at any given moment a logical closure which is immensely problematic in application is readily apparent; but its emancipatory as well as normative potential in the ideal is compelling. What is called for is not the replacement of one authoritative model with another but rather the gradual creation of a community, a discourse, an art, which is not so much the reflection of our competitive and antagonistic pursuits as it is a common vehicle through which we might continually examine not only our own values and assumptions, but those of the culture of and to which we ideally speak. We might see therefore not so much to regulate our cultural praxis in relation to the existent norms, as to understand, elucidate, and evaluate the normative import of those activities in which we are historically, presently, as well as potentially engaged. Thus the philosophy, the theory, the strategy and the ethics of practice become one with praxis itself. And yet this union of theory and practice in the ideal is always subject to and modified by conditions in relation to which we must continually re-evaluate our position. It is a dynamic and self-regulatory critical theory by which we attempt to understand and evaluate our own (art) practice in relation to social practice in general, and to evaluate social and historical conditions as they are effective of and become apparent in our practice of art.

If it is true that "the creation of a thing for the sake of a thing is itself an objective human relationship to itself and to man,"[6] then it is on the level of this relationship which we must question our function, for it no longer has much meaning to speak of the thing (art) in itself.

At the dawn of the 19th century, Hegel predicted that art would no longer, as in the past, be connected with the central concerns of man. Hegel saw the role of art becoming increasingly marginal as science moved into a stronger and more central position with society. Art, according to Hegel, would cease to be serious, as it became increasingly pure and disengaged. By moving into a marginal position, art would not lose its quality as art, but it would nonetheless cease to have direct relevance to the existence of man.

We have lost touch—not only with ourselves and with each other but with the culture of which we are a part. It is only by confronting the problem of our alienation, making *this* the subject of our work, that our ideals take on new meaning. We move to become one again with culture in our sense of shared concerns.

5 Fredric Jameson, *Marxism and Form* (Princeton: Princeton University Press, 1971).
6 Karl Marx, *Economic and Philosophical Manuscripts of 1844*, ed. Dirk J. Struik, trans., Martin Mulligan (International Publishers Co.)

Washing/Tracks/Maintenance: Outside

Mierle Laderman Ukeles

1973

Dear Spectator,

The cleanliness of this area is now being maintained as

MAINTENANCE ART

by Mierle Laderman Ukeles, artist.

Please feel free to continue on your way right through the "dust painting" as she will be continuing to maintain it this whole day.

Mierle Laderman Ukeles

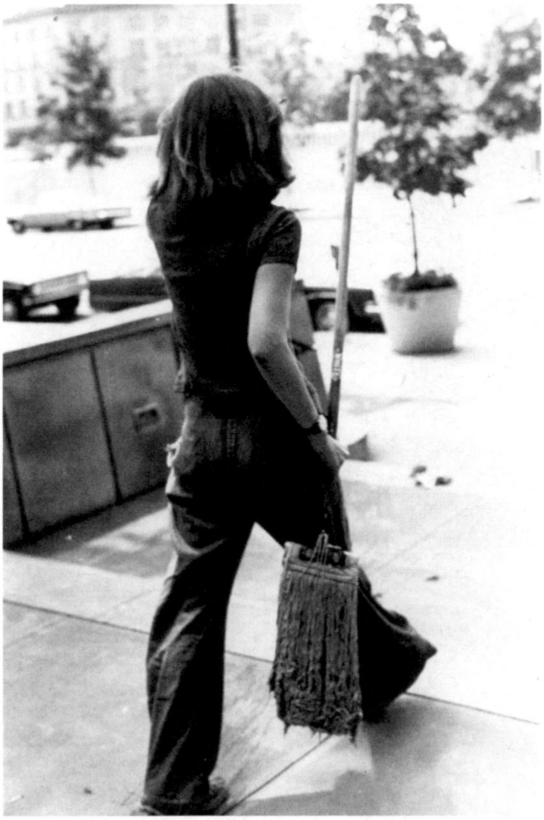

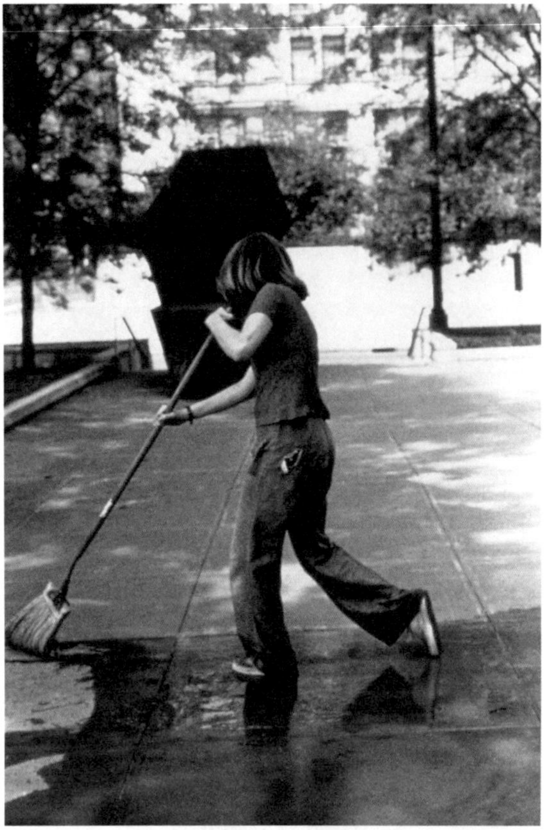

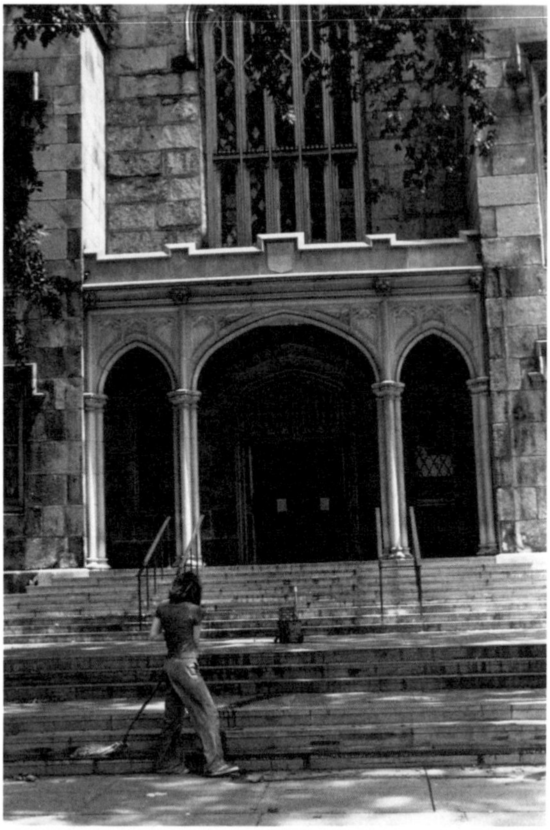

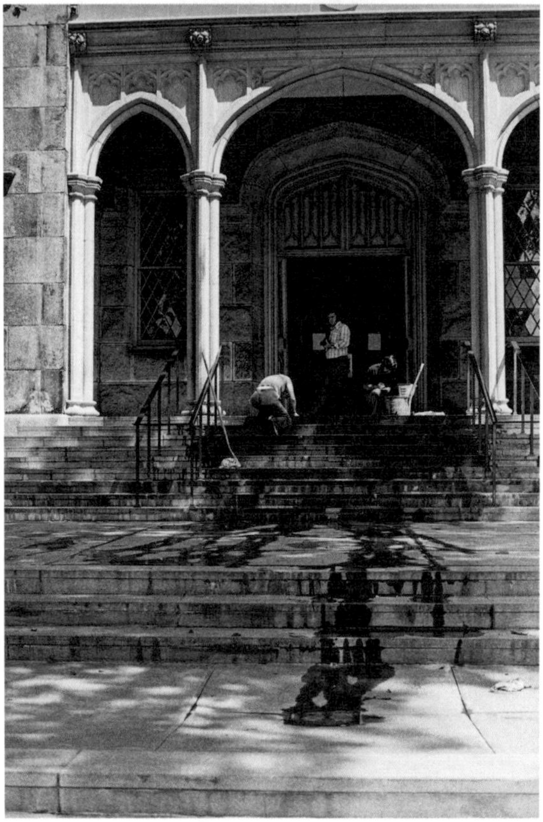

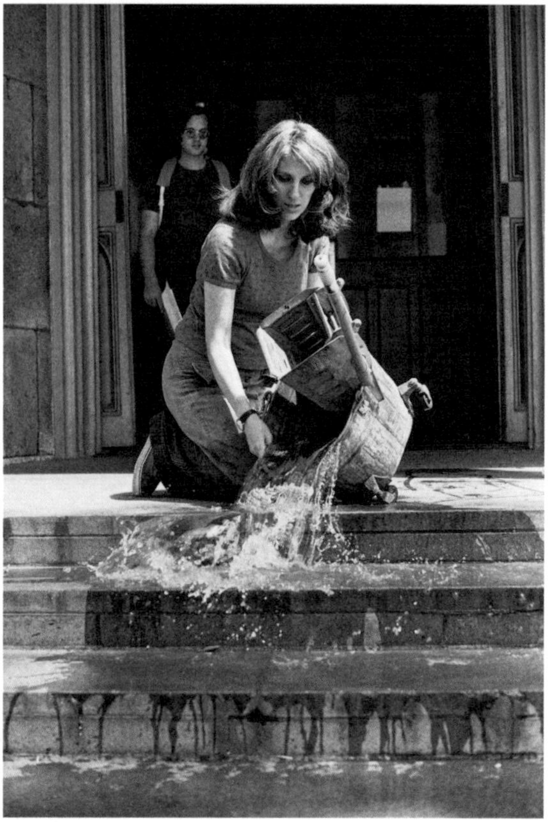

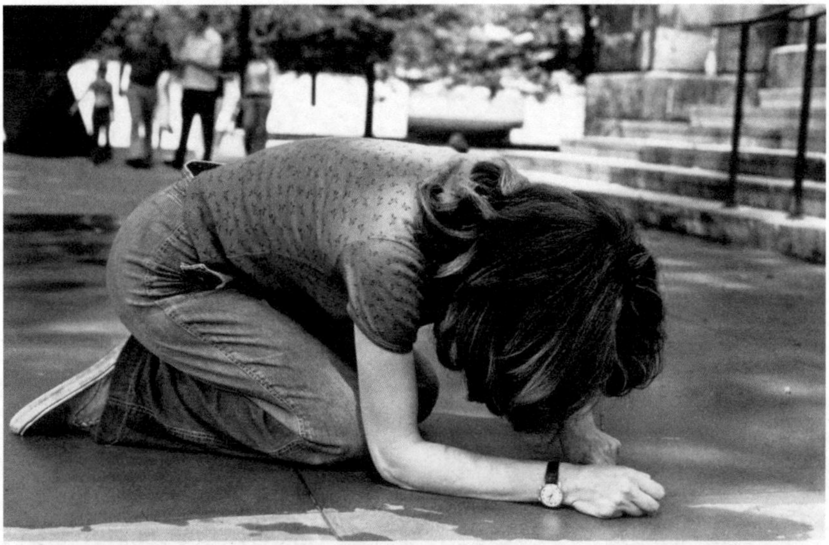

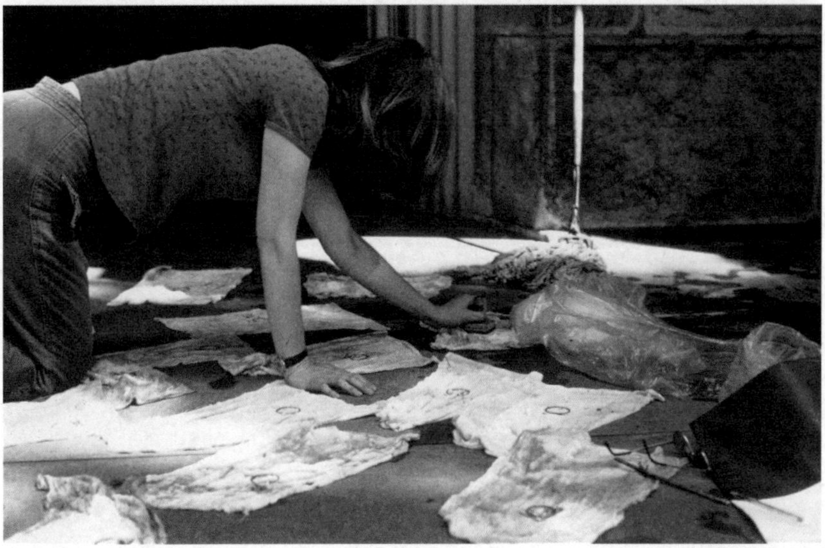

Advertisement in *Artforum* Magazine, November 1974

Lynda Benglis

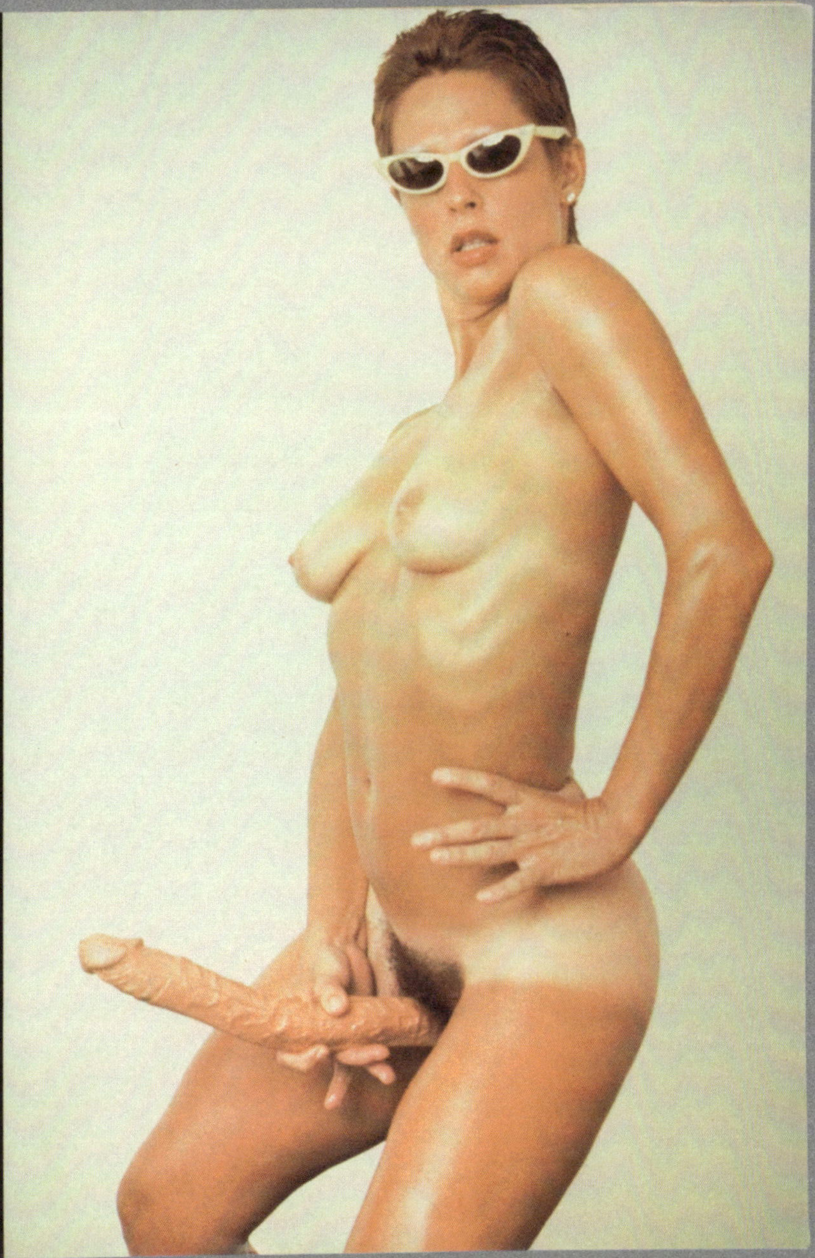

Magazine Actions in *Fiesta* Magazine, Vol. 10, No. 7, 1976

Cosey Fanni Tutti

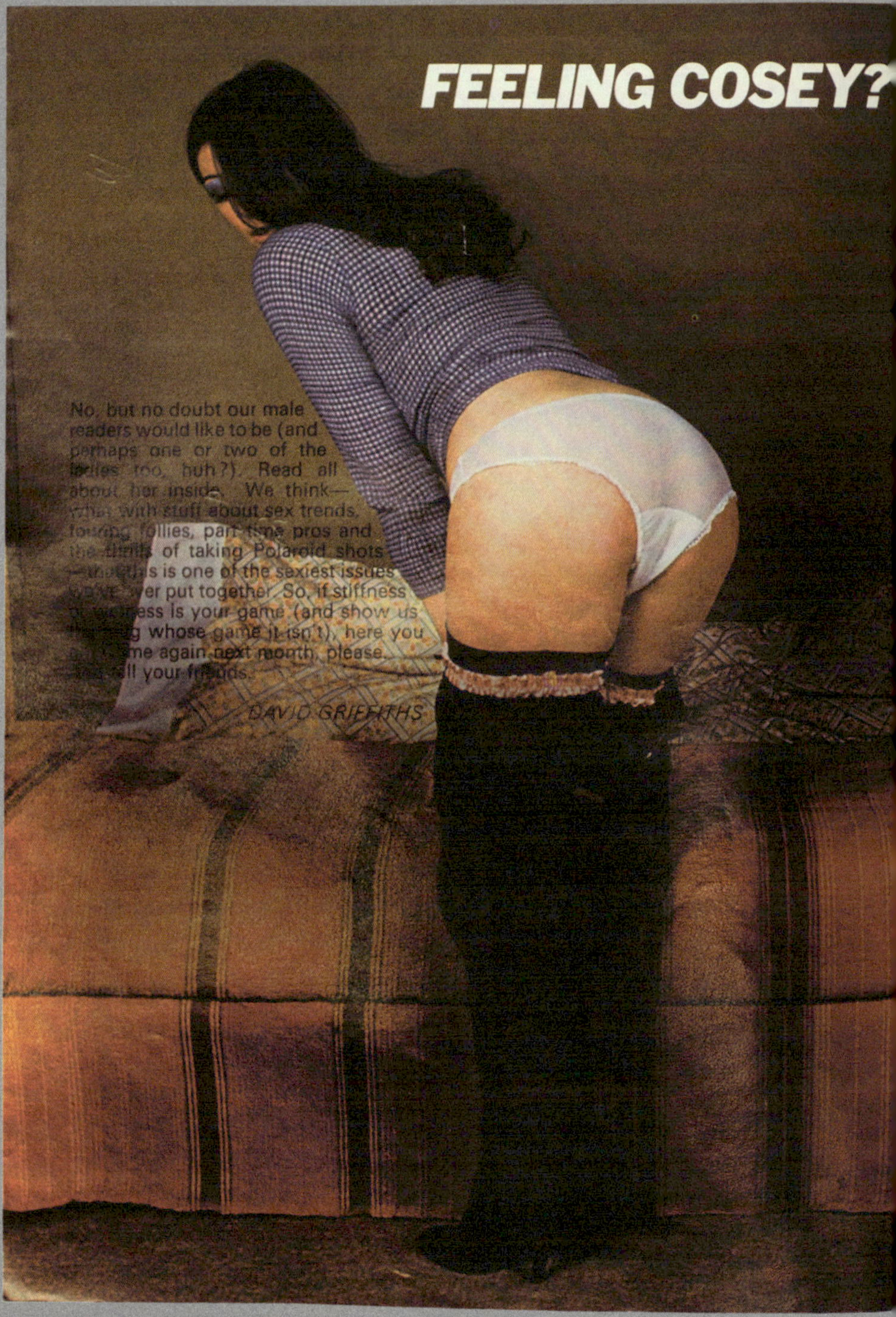

FiESTA

YOU'LL FIND THE CONTENTS LISTED ON PAGE 3

INTERCHANGE 4
write away, Sir, and Madam

FRONTALS 6
we lay it on the line

THE FIESTA HOLIDAY GUIDE 11
by undervalued Nigel Edwards

SEX TRENDS IN SEVENTY-SEX 12
researched by Chris R. Kyle

FOLLIES ON TOUR, part one 15
revealed by ex singer and dancer Will King

BECKY 19
photographed by Ed Alexander

COSEY CONFESSES 26
to Sheldon Williams

I CONFESS, part two 30
by Mary's husband John

MIA 35
photographed by Roger Pearson

AMANDA 45
photographed by Robin Humphreys

PART TIME PROS, part two 52
by Vincent Gillespie

POLAROID THRILLS 56
by Gerry Brown

A FIESTA READER HAS A GO AT IT HERSELF 59
photographed by Chris Turner

ONE FOR THE LADIES 63
a strapping bloke

READERS WIVES 64
a colourful collection

PUSSY POISONERS 68
by Ed Cavin

PHIL AND KEN 80
cartooned by Paul Cemmick

cover photograph by Björn Larsson

FiESTA

Vol 10 No 7

A RUSSELL GAY PUBLICATION

Editor
David Griffiths
Associate Editor
Jeff Pike
Assistant Editor
Chris Curtain
Art Editor
Alwyn Whitlock
Art Assistant
Alan Ashby
Production Manager
Brian Williamson
Advertising Manager
Frances Lulham
Classified Ads.
Peter Geary
Subscriptions Manager
Norma Nathan
Picture Editor
Manley Jerrard
Managing Editor
Alan Smith
Publisher
Russell Gay

While every reasonable care is taken, Galaxy publications cannot be responsible for loss or damage to unsolicited material. Accepted material is paid for on publication.

ABC

MEMBER OF THE AUDIT BUREAU OF CIRCULATIONS

We regret that we cannot supply prints of any photographs in the editorial pages of FIESTA.

Published monthly by
GALAXY PUBLICATIONS LTD.,
Hermit Place, 252 Belsize Road,
London. NW6 4BT.

Printed in England by
Eastgate Press Ltd.

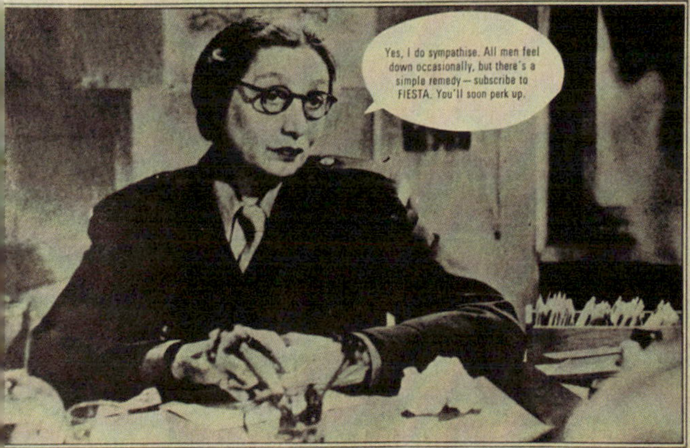

Subscription rate £5.25 (including postage)

I enclose £5.25 in (tick one)
cash
cheque
money order

Name ____________________

Address ____________________

____

____

Subscription to commence with Issue No. ____________

Send £5.25 for your subscription to:

Norma Nathan,
Fiesta Subscription Dept.,
Galaxy Publications Ltd.,
Hermit Place, 252 Belsize Road,
London, NW6 4BT.

Foreign Subscriptions are welcome. Rates are available on application.

We cannot be responsible for cash unless sent by registered post.

Still from *Eadweard Muybridge, Zoopraxographer*
Thom Andersen
1976

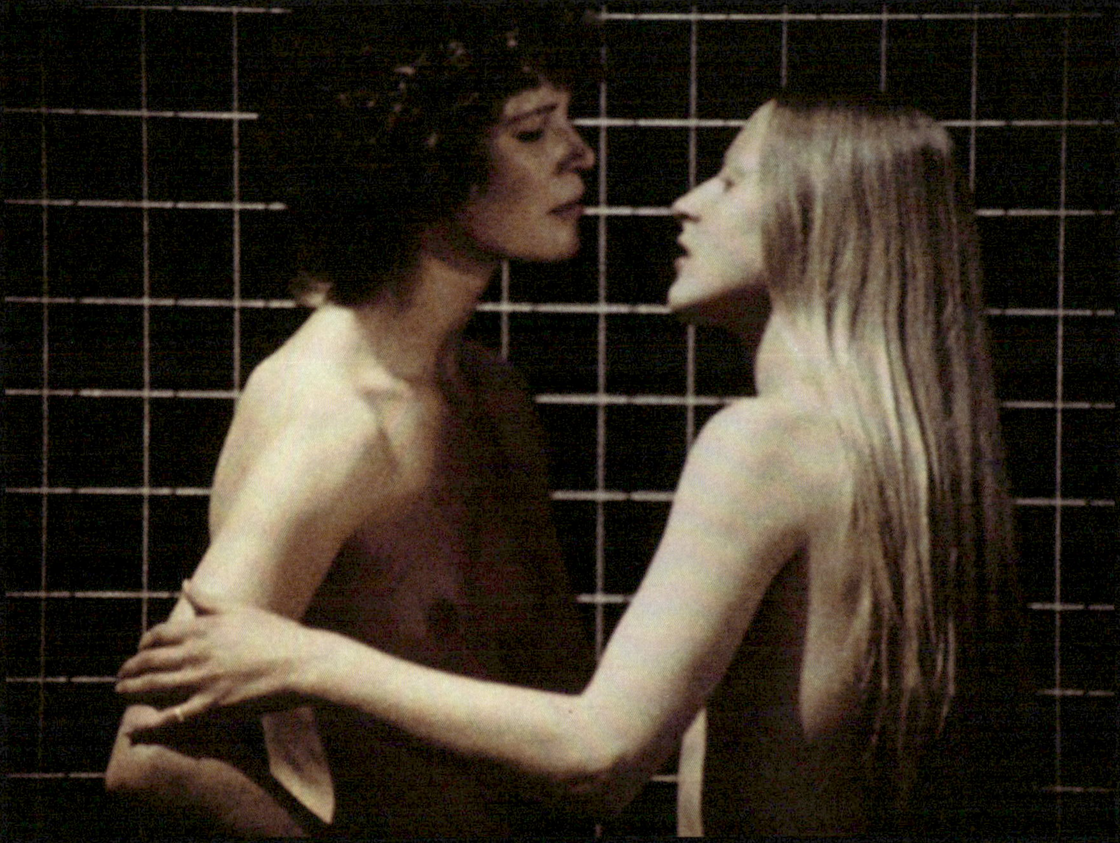

Five Notes for a Phenomenology of the Photographic Image

Hubert Damisch

1963

1. Theoretically speaking, photography is nothing other than a process of recording, a technique of *inscribing*, in an emulsion of silver salts, generated by a ray of light. This definition, we note, neither assumes the use of a camera, nor does it imply that the image obtained is that of an object or scene from the external world. We know of prints obtained from film directly exposed to a light source. The prime value of this type of endeavor is to induce a refelection on the nature and function of the photographic image. And insofar as it successfully eliminates one of the basic elements of the very idea of "photography" (the camera obscura, the camera), it produces an experimental equivalent of a phenomenological analysis which purports to grasp the essence of the phenomenon under consideration by submitting that phenomenon to a series of imaginary variations.

2. The reluctance one feels, however, in describing such images as photographs is a revealing indication of the difficulty of reflecting phenomenologically—in the strict sense of an eidetic experience, a reading of essences—on a *cultural* object, on an essence that is historically constituted. Moreover, the full purview of a photographic document clearly involves a certain number of "theses" which, though not of a transcendental order, appear nevertheless as the conditions for apprehending the photographic image as such. To consider a document of this sort like any other image is to claim a bracketing of all knowledge—and even, as we shall see, of all prejudice—as to its genesis and empirical functions. It therefore follows that the photographic situation cannot be defined a priori, the division of its fundamental components from its merely contingent aspects cannot be undertaken in the absolute.

The photographic image does not belong to the natural world. It is a product of human labor, a cultural object whose being—in the phenomenological sense of the term—cannot be dissociated precisely from its historical meaning and from the necessarily datable project in which it originates. Now, this image is characterized by the way in which it presents itself as the result of an objective process. Imprinted by rays of light on a plate or sensitive film, these figures (or better perhaps, these signs?) must appear as the very *trace* of an object or a scene from the real world, the image of which inscribes itself, without direct human intervention, in the gelatinous substance covering the support. Here is the source of the supposition of "reality," which defines the photographic situation. A photograph is this paradoxical image, without thickness or substance (and, in a way, entirely unreal), that we read without disclaiming the notion that it retains something of the reality from which it was somehow released through its physio-chemical make-up. This is the constitutive deception of the photographic image (it being understood that every image, as Sartre has shown, is in essence a deceit). In the case of photography, however, this ontological deception carries with it a *historical* deceit, far more subtle and insidious. And here we return to that object which we got rid of a little too quickly: the black box, the photographic camera.

3. Niepce, the successive adepts of the Daguerreotype, and those innumerable inventors who made photography what it is today, were not actually concerned to create a new type of image or to determine novel modes of representation; they wanted, rather, to fix the images which "spontaneously" formed on the ground of the camera obscura. The adventure of photography begins with man's first attempts to retain that image he had long known how to make. (Beginning in the 11th century, Arab astronomers probably used the camera obscura to observe solar eclipses.) This long familiarity with an image so produced, and the completely objective, that is to say automatic or in any case strictly mechanical, appearance of the recording process, explains how the photographic representation generally appeared as *a matter of course*, and why one ignores its highly elaborated, arbitrary character. In discussions of the invention of film, the history of photography is most frequently presented as that of a *discovery*. One forgets, in the process, that the image the first photographers were hoping to seize, and the very *latent image* which they were able to reveal and develop, were in no sense naturally given; the principles of construction of the photographic camera—and of the camera obscura before it—were tied to a conventional notion of space and of objectivity whose development preceded the invention of photog-

raphy, and to which the great majority of photographers only conformed. The lens itself, which had been carefully corrected for "distortions" and adjusted for "errors," is scarcely as objective* as it seems. In its structure and in the ordered image of the world it achieves, it complies with an especially familiar though very old and dilapidated system of spatial construction, to which photography belatedly brought an unexpected revival of current interest.

(Would the art, or rather the craft, of photography not consist partly in allowing us to forget that the black box is not "neutral" and that its structure is not impartial?)

4. The retention of the image, its development and multiplication, form an ordered succession of steps which composed the photographic act, taken as a whole. History determined, however, that this act would find its goal in reproduction, much the way the point of film as spectacle was established from the start. (We know that the first inventors worked to fix images and simultaneously to develop techniques for their mass distribution, which is why the process perfected by Daguerre was doomed from the very outset, since it could provide nothing but a *unique* image). So that photography's contribution, to use the terms of classical economy, is less on the level of *production*, properly speaking, than on that of *consumption*. Photography creates nothing of "use" (aside from its marginal and primarily scientific applications); it rather lays down the premises of an unbridled destruction of utility. Photographic activity, even though it generally takes the form of craft, is nonetheless, in principle, industrial; and this implies that of all images the photographic one—leaving aside its documentary character—wears out the most quickly. But it is important to note that even when it gives us, through the channels of publishing, advertising, and the press, only those images which are already half consumed, or so to speak, "predigested," this industry fulfills the initial photographic project: the capturing and restoration of an image already worn beyond repair, but still, through its physical nature, unsuited to mass consumption.

5. Photography aspires to art each time, in practice, it calls into question its essence and its historical roles, each time it uncovers the contingent character of these things, soliciting in us the producer rather than the consumer of images. (It is no accident that the most *beautiful* photograph so far achieved is possibly the first image Nicéphore Niepce fixed in 1822, on the glass of the camera obscura—a fragile, threatened image, so close in its organization, its granular texture, and its emergent aspect, to certain Seurats—an incomparable image which makes one dream of a photographic *substance* distinct from subject matter, and of an art in which light creates its own metaphor.)

*(The play here is on the French word for lens: objectif.—ed.)

Mapplethorped: Art, Photography, and the Pornographic Imagination

Richard Meyer

2016

[...] In the United States, it is legally impossible for a visual image to be defined as both art and obscenity. The U.S. Supreme Court's decision in the 1973 case of Miller v. California rules obscene any work that "appeals to the prurient interest in sex; portrays in a patently offensive way sexual conduct specifically defined by the applicable state law; and, taken as a whole, does not have serious literary, artistic, political, or scientific value."[1] The language of the law dictates, then, that an obscene picture cannot also qualify as one that has "artistic value," and conversely, that a work of art is, by definition, not obscene. Fortunately, Mapplethorpe was a visual artist rather than a lawyer. In his mind, there was no contradiction between artistic value and graphically sexual subject matter. "I can," he insisted, "make pornography art." The pornography to which he was most often drawn featured eroticized displays of the male body as well as hard-core scenes of gay sex and s/m. By drawing on the conventions of both art and pornography, Mapplethorpe scandalously intertwined aesthetic form and sexually explicit subject matter. [...]

In June 1989 the Corcoran Gallery of Art in Washington, D.C., canceled *Robert Mapplethorpe: The Perfect Moment*, a full-scale retrospective of the photo-grapher's work slated to open a few weeks later. The exhibition and its accompanying catalogue had been partially supported by a $30,000 grant from the National Endowment for the Arts (NEA).[3] The Corcoran's decision was made in response to pressures applied by Republican politicians, particularly Senator Jesse Helms of North Carolina, who were, in turn, responding to protests against Mapplethorpe and the NEA by religious "watchdog" organizations such as the Christian Coalition and the American Family Association. The Mapplethorpe controversy was part of a broader attack on federal arts funding already underway by the summer of 1989.[4]

Five weeks after its cancelation by the Corcoran, *The Perfect Moment* was mounted by the Washington Project for the Arts, an alternative arts space in Washington, D.C. Following its run in Washington (where the show attracted some forty thousand viewers), *The Perfect Moment* traveled to the Wadsworth Atheneum Museum of Art in Hartford, Connecticut, and the University Art Museum in Berkeley, California, where it was mounted without incident, and then continued to the Contemporary Arts Center (CAC) in Cincinnati. On April 7, 1990, the opening day of the exhibition in Cincinnati, police temporarily closed *The Perfect Moment* in order to videotape the show as evidence for an obscenity indictment. That same day, the director of the CAC, Dennis Barrie, was indicted on charges of pandering obscenity and child pornography.[5] The ensuing trial marked the first time that a museum director was prosecuted as a result of the art he presented to the public. By presenting expert witnesses who defended Mapplethorpe's work on purely formal grounds, Barrie's lawyers succeeded in securing his acquittal on all charges.

The catalogue for the exhibition includes an interview with the photographer by Janet Kardon, the show's curator. At the time, Kardon was the director of the Institute of Contemporary Art (ICA) in Philadelphia, the museum that organized the exhibition and mounted it in late 1988, just prior to its ill-fated journey to Washington. At one point in the interview,

1 U.S. Supreme Court verdict, as quoted in Richard Bolton, ed., *Culture Wars: Documents from the Recent Controversies in the Arts* (New York: New Press,1992), 333. Miller v.California was a lawsuit brought by the State of California against Marvin Miller , the owner of a mail-order business dealing in pornographic books and films. Ruling in Miller 's favor in 1973, the Supreme Court revised the legal definition of obscenity.

2 Mapplethorpe, quoted in Janet Kardon, "Robert Mapplethorpe Interview," in *Robert Mapplethorpe: the Perfect Moment* (Philadelphia: Institute of Contemporary Art, University of Pennsylvania, 1988), 28.

3 The NEA granted $30,000 to Philadelphia's Institute of Contemporary Art (ICA) to organize the exhibition and to produce the accompanying publication. *Robert Mapplethorpe: The Perfect* Moment opened at the ICA on December 9, 1988.

4 The previous April, the American Family Association had launched a letter-writing campaign denouncing a single work of art, Andres Serrano's 1987 *Piss Christ.* Serrano's work, a large-scale color photograph of a crucifix submerged in a luminous bath of the artist's urine, had been awarded a $15,000 prize by the Southeastern Center for Contemporary Art in Winston-Salem, North Carolina, an institution partially funded by the NEA. In May, on the floor of the Senate, Republican Senator Alfonse D'Amato of New York ripped up a catalogue that featured *Piss Christ.* Jesse Helms, in apparent distress over Serrano's link to the senator's home state of North Carolina, insisted that "I do not know Mr. Andres Serrano, and I hope I never meet him. Because he is not an artist, he is a jerk." Jesse Helms, *Congressional Record*, May 18, 1989, S5595.

5 At 3:00 p.m. on April 7, 1990, "police officers ejected about 500 viewers [from the Contemporary Arts Center,] shut the museum for 90 minutes, videotaped Mapplethorpe's work as evidence, and indicted Barrie." Robin Cembalest, "Cincinnati: Imperfect Moment," *Artnews* (Summer 1990), 51..

Kardon describes the disparity between Mapplethorpe's coolly classical style and his frankly carnal subject matter, only to have the photographer make it clear that he does not see things in quite the same way:

> JK: You bestow elegance on a subject one would never consider as elegant—in the photographs of the cocks, for example. One might not say a cock was elegant.
>
> RM: I might.[6]

Although the catalogue elsewhere refers to Mapplethorpe's photographs of extravagantly endowed men as "figure studies," Kardon here describes them as "the photographs of the cocks." Her word choice is drawn not from the lexicon of art history or curatorial practice but from an explicitly sexual vernacular more often employed in pornography, raunch, and otherwise off-color contents. The word "cock" is also, and crucially, borrowed from Mapplethorpe's own descriptive vocabulary.

A bit taken aback, perhaps, by the photographer's rejoinder, Kardon offers a qualified concession: "All right, one might. In the heat of ardor, you might think, 'That's an elegant cock.' Normally, it's not a subject you would consider elegant." For Kardon, a penis would not usually be seen as elegant beccause one would not "normally" approach it as an aesthetic object in the first place. But, as Mapplethorpe suggests, Kardon's claim assumes a normative viewer (a "one") whose perspective does not represent the photographer's point of view. With his simple affirmation, "I might," Mapplethorpe opens up a space of difference and desire whereby the language of pornography ("cocks") may comfortably coincide with the vocabulary of aesthetic taste and distinction ("elegant"). Kardon touches on a related issue when she turns to another subject for which the photographer was equally well known: "You think of flowers as possessing an elegance, or refinement, and I think you treat the flowers like the cocks and the cocks like the flowers."[7] Condensed within this comment is the central conceit of Mapplethorpe's broader photographic enterprise, namely, the scrambling of aesthetic categories and genres usually understood as discrete, even mutually exclusive. [...] Throughout his career, Mapplethorpe took particular delight in presenting wildly different subjects as equally stylized forms of photographic enjoyment. "I don't think there's much difference," he told an interviewer in 1979, "between a photograph of a fist up someone's ass and a photograph of carnations in a bowl."[8]

Mapplethorpe's provocative comment echoes the bipartite structure of an advertisement published by the Robert Miller Gallery in 1979 in which *Helmut*, a portrait of a squatting leatherman atop a pedestal, is paired with an equally symmetrical still life of white carnations in a black bowl. Even as it reveals Helmut's buttocks, boots, and leather harness, the portrait also emphasizes the spare, art-studio setting—the pedestal, white walls, and framing swath of drapery. Mapplethorpe's formalist play with light and shadow is insistent and unapologetic here, the leather jacket becoming blackest, for instance, when it overlaps the white muslin fabric behind it.

The letter X centered beneath *Helmut* refers to Mapplethorpe's X Portfolio, an edition of thirteen photographs of gay s/m that was paired with a contrasting Y Portfolio of images of flowers (the Z Portfolio, a set of photographs of black male nudes, was later added). If carnations and leathermen can inhabit the same photographic lexicon, it follows that even the most audacious of s/m imagery may be "tamed" into elegant abstraction, and the gentlest of floral arrangements freighted with sexual charge—or so would seem to be the logic proposed by the coordination of Mapplethorpe's alternate photographic practices into matching portfolios. Mapplethorpe would frequently contend that the formal power of his pictures could reconcile even the most dramatic contrasts of subject matter. "I'd have a picture of fruit or flowers next to a picture of sexuality next to a portrait of someone socially prominent. My interest was to open people's eyes, get them to realize anything can be acceptable. It's not what it is, it's the way it's photographed."[9] [...]

---

6 Mapplethorpe, quoted in Kardon, 28.

7 Kardon, n.p. Mapplethorpe agreed with Kardon on this point even as he then complicated the apparent parallelism between floral and phallic subjects: "Yes, I think they're the same. A cock is more problematic when you're photographing, especially if you want it erect. You can't juggle the lights as much, and it's hard to refine the photograph quite as much as you'd like, but I attempt to make just as refined a photograph as of one of the flowers."

8 Mapplethorpe, quoted in Parker Hodges, "Robert Mapplethorpe: Photographer," *Manhattan Gaze*, December 10, 1979-January 6, 1980, 5.

9 Mapplethorpe, quoted in Janis Bultman, "Bad Boy Makes Good," *Darkroom Photography*, July 1988, 26.

X Portfolio
Robert Mapplethorpe
1977–78

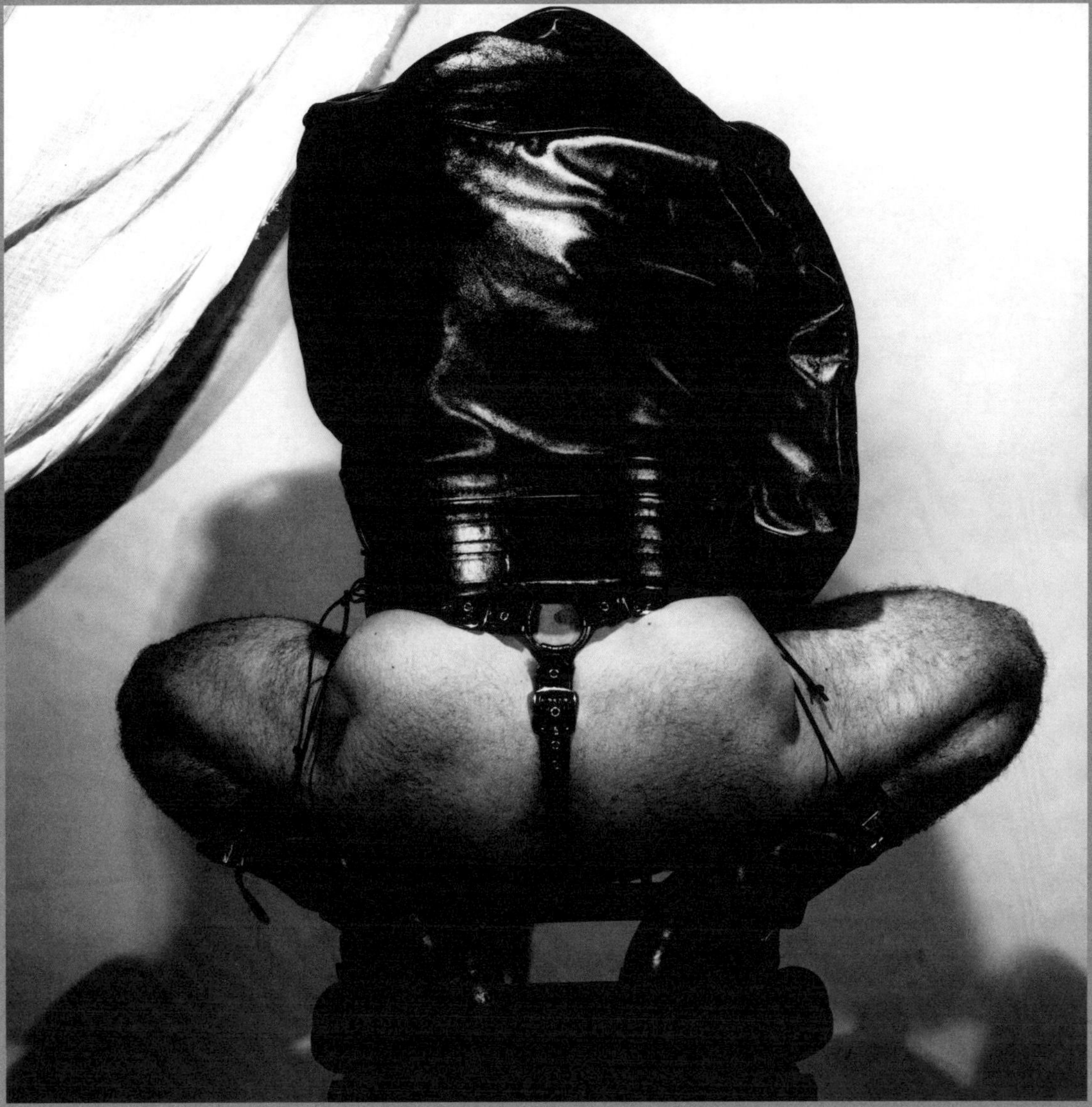

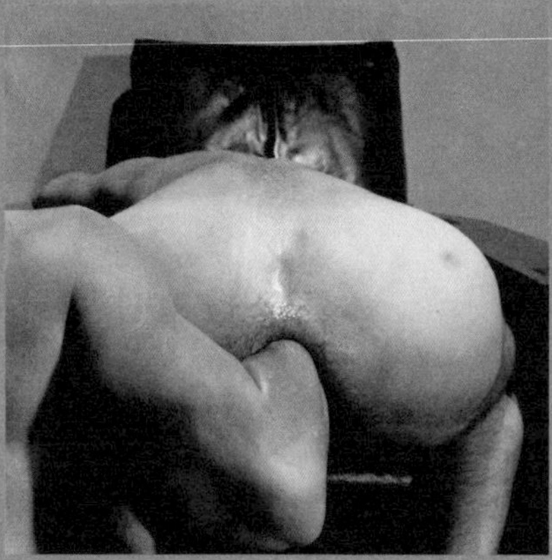

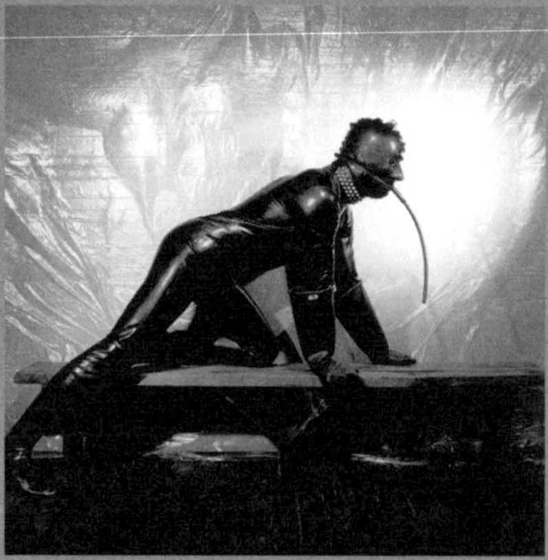

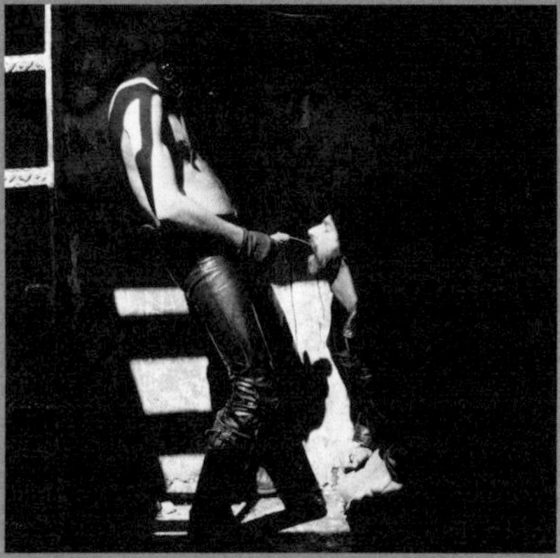

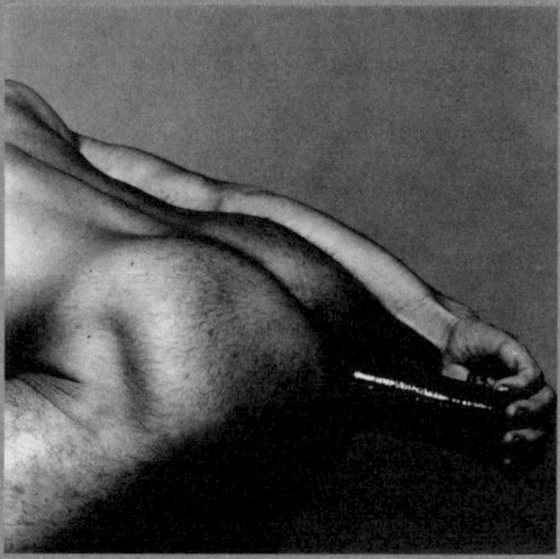

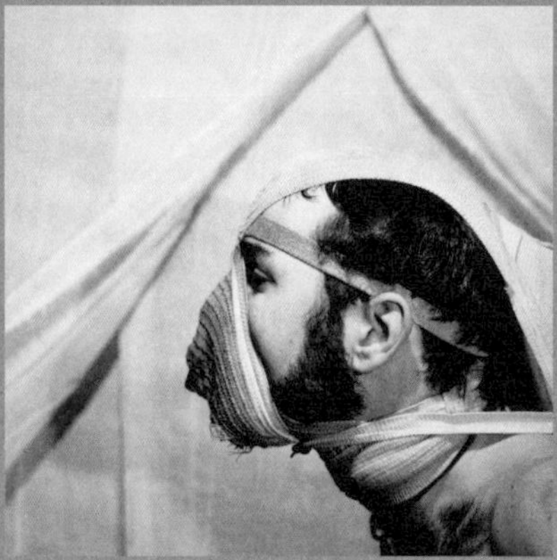

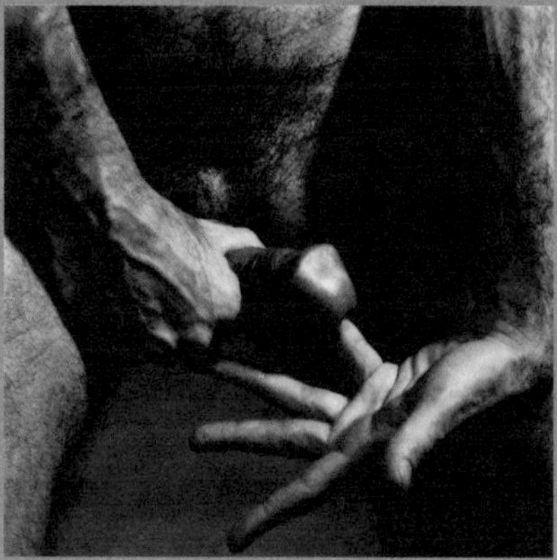

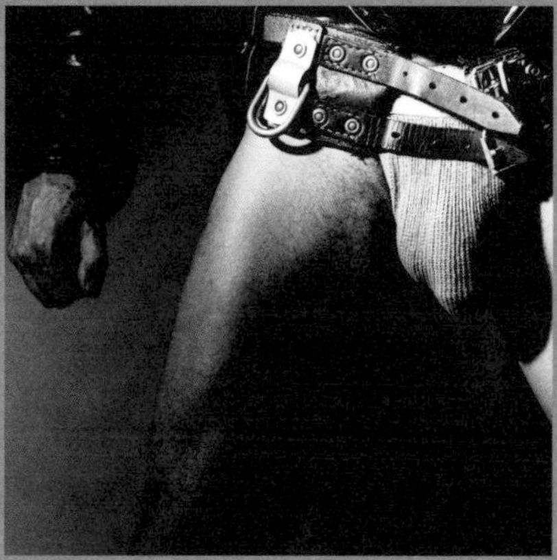
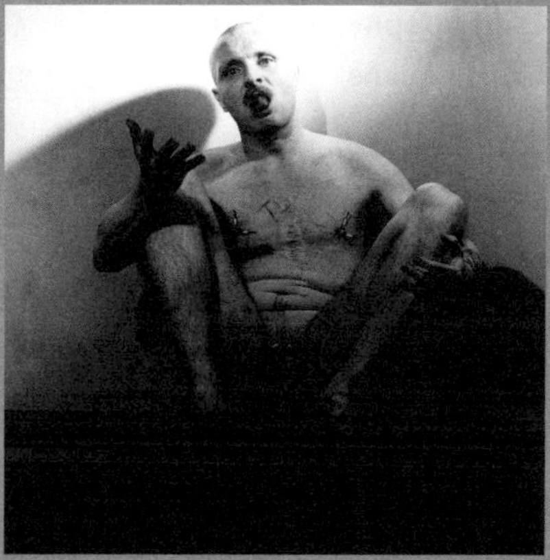
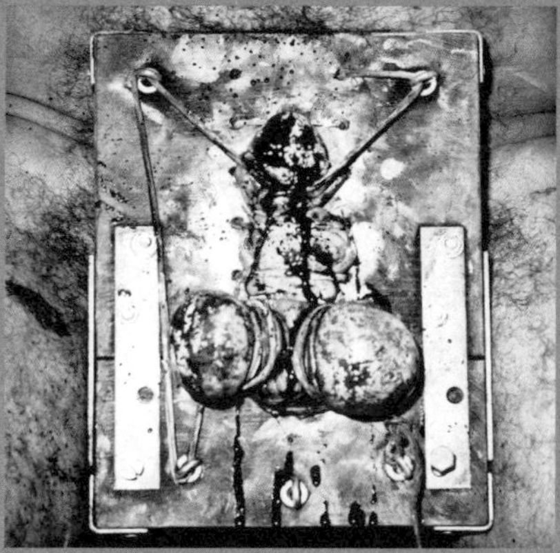
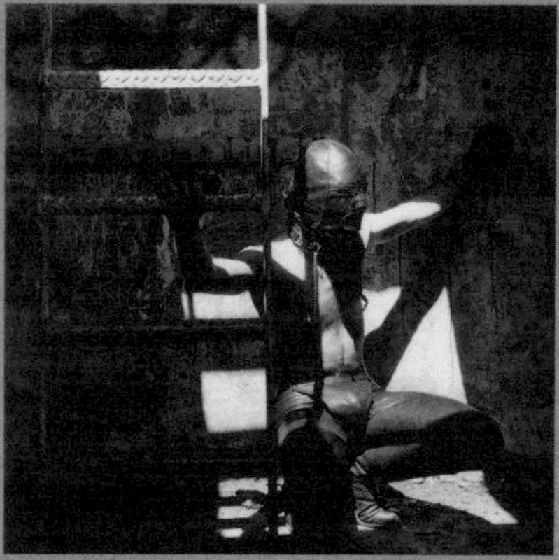
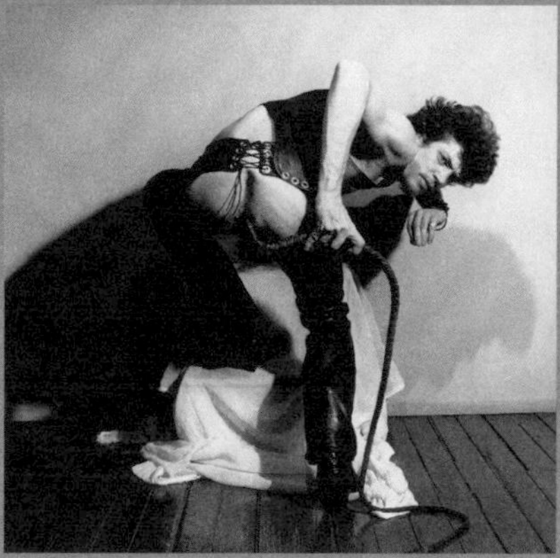
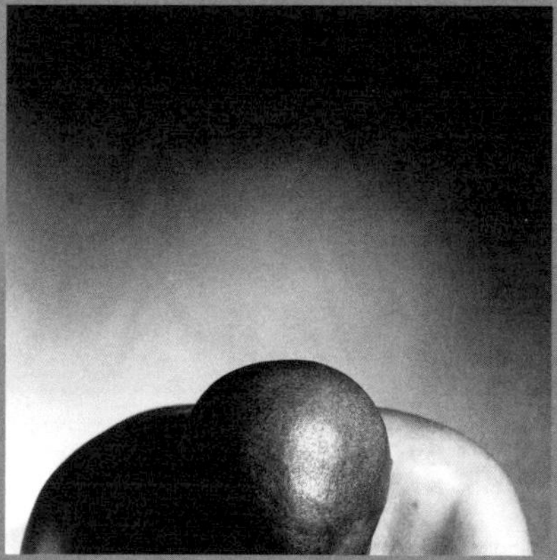

Photography *en abyme*

Craig Owens

1978

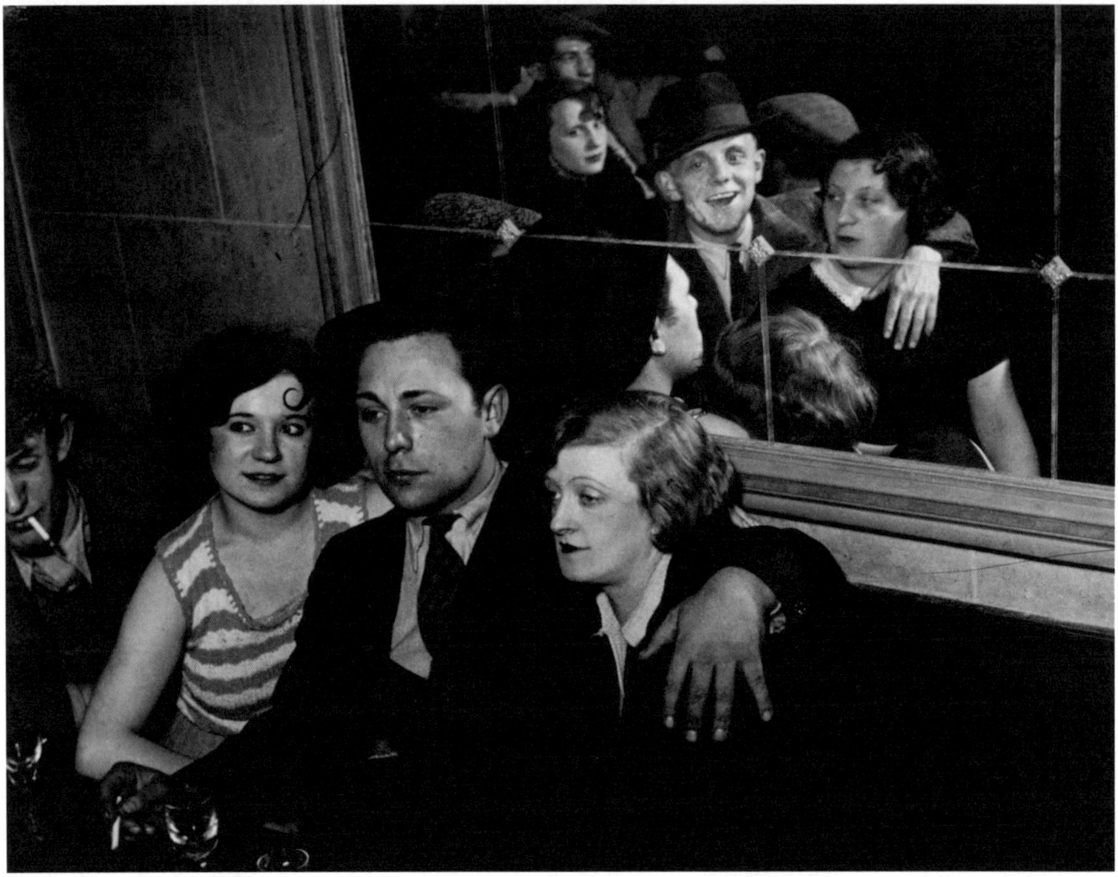

Figure 1. Brassaï (Gyula Halász), *Groupe Joyeux au bal musette des Quatre Saisons, rue de Lappe (Happy Group at the Four Seasons Dance Hall, rue de Lappe)*, ca. 1932, printed 1948-1955. Gelatin silver print, 9 3/8 × 11 13/16 in. (23.81 × 30 cm) Collection of the Sack Photographic Trust, San Francisco Museum of Modern Art.

Brassaï's portrait of a group of young Parisians at the *Bal des Quatre Saisons* may at first appear, like most photographs, to be a straightforward transcription of an observed reality, as if the image had already existed in the world before it was suspended in the photograph. We might therefore be tempted to raid it for clues to the inner lives of its sitters, or for memories of a long-since vanished Parisian milieu. However, the longer we contemplate the image, the more remote that kind of information becomes. A complex web of internal reduplications deflects attention away from that which, despite the status of photographs as imprints of the real, remains external to the image: the reality it depicts. Psychological and sociological details are thus displaced by the network of internal relationships between subject, mirror, and other, which structures the image.

Two groups of two couples each are the ostensible subjects of the photograph. The first occupy what reads as the "real" space of the image and are doubled by their own mirror images, while the second, except for the fragmentary detail of a bare arm cropped below the elbow, are present *only* in reflection. Doubled and yet, paradoxically, represented but once, the latter appear to have been dispossessed of their corporeal beings. Their reflections, severed from any physical connection with an object, attach themselves to the first group, so that each of the figures seated on the banquette finds a second, virtual double in the mirror reflection of the other. Details of costume, pose, and gesture reinforce this impression: the young man flanked by two women drapes one arm over the shoulder of the woman to his left, a gesture that is reiterated by his mirror counterpart, who wears an identical hat. The blank expression of the woman to his left is repeated by her counterpart; further, both seem to use the same coiffeur. On the right, two other women demonstrate the same oblique gaze, one in apparent flirtation, the other to observe the making of the photograph. (This gaze also reiterates the angle of Brassaï's shot, thus implicating the photographer within the scene, as both witness and flirt.) The sequence of duplications is brought to closure on the right by two men who wear identical tweed caps and echo each other's distraction. (Brassaï cropped the figure on the extreme right out of subsequent prints, thereby eliminating this, the weakest link in the reduplicative chain.)

Because of the absolute symmetry of the two groups, the couples seated on the banquette appear as if poised between parallel mirrors mounted in series, so that the distance—both physical and psychological—that separates them in reality is collapsed. Space thus drained from the image, the effects of doubling may no longer be located within the space of the world, but only within the flatness of the photograph. The double image appears to have been generated by an act of internal du*pli*cation, a literal folding back of the photograph upon itself—the mirror suggests not only reflection, but also a literal crease in the surface of the print. To double by folding, however, also implies the leaving of a deposit or trace on the surface thus manipulated, as in those familiar symmetrical imprints of blotted ink. Thus, the duplication that occurs within this image suggests the specifics of the photographic process itself.

The image includes yet another, more obvious depiction of photography. It suggests the analogical definition of the photograph as a mirror image, that informs a great deal of the criticism of photography, especially that dating from the nineteenth century.[1] Because the mirror image doubles the subjects—which is exactly what the photograph itself does—it functions here as a reduced, internal image of the photograph. The mirror reflects not only the subjects depicted, but also the entire photograph itself. It tells us in a photograph what a photograph is—*en abyme*.

In the vocabulary of literary criticism, the phrase "*en abyme*" describes any fragment of a text that reproduces in miniature the structure of the text in its entirety. Introduced by Gide in a passage of his *Journal* from 1892, the phrase originally described the reduplicative strategy of his own work—like the "supplement" in Rousseau, it tells us in a text what a text is:

> It pleases me to find, in a work of art, the very subject of the work transposed to the scale of its characters. Nothing illuminates the work better, or establishes its proportions more clearly. Thus, in some paintings by Memling or Quentin Metsys a small, somber convex mirror reflects the interior of the room in which the depicted scene is set. Also, Velasquez' *Las Meninas* (but in a slightly different way).[2]

Not only are Gide's initial examples of this textual device drawn from painting; all of them implicate the optical properties of mirror reflection. In painting, however, mirrors rarely function as analogues for the painting itself and Gide, sensing this—"none of these examples is absolutely accurate"—substituted another analogy drawn from heraldry. The perfect emblem for the procedure was itself already an emblem:

> What would be more accurate, what would state better what I wanted in my *Notebooks*, my *Narcissus* and in *La Tentative*, is a comparison with that procedure in heraldry which consists of placing a second shield within the first—*"en abyme"*.[3]

The necessity of coining a new critical term marks the radical break with the past signified by construction *en abyme*. Gide's intention was not to describe a textual device that had a historical existence, but to dissociate his own texts from all previous literary production.[4] Thus, the use of a visual device of ancient standing—that of a miniature blason suspended within another blason, whose external contour and internal divisions it replicates exactly. If, in subsequent commentaries, the heraldic metaphor has fallen into disuse, the phrase which designates it has gained currency, in spite of an unconscious reversion. Perhaps because it suggests the familiar case of mirrors mounted in series to produce an infinite suite of specular effects, the *mise en abyme* and the internal mirror have become synonymous. So that it is defined, at least in its literary manifestations, as any internal mirror reflecting the totality of the work that contains it, either

1 Photography, in its earliest manifestations, was frequently referred to as "Daguerre's mirror." Certainly the silvered surfaces and lateral reversals of early Daguerreotypes supported this analogy. As early as 1839, Jules Janin, introducing the invention, urged his reader to "imagine that the mirror has retained the imprint of every object it reflects, then you will have a more complete idea of the Daguerreotype." Quoted from Heinz Buddemeier, *Panorama, Diorama, Photographie*, Munich, Wilhelm Fink, 1970, 207. Richard Rudisill's *Mirror Image* (Albuquerque, University of New Mexico, 1971) contains, as its title suggests, copious documentation for the photo-mirror analogy.

2 André Gide, *Journal 1889–1939*, "Pléiade," Paris, Gallimard, 1951, 41.

3 *Ibid.*

4 Gide did cite *Hamlet*, *Wilhelm Meister*, and *The Fall of the House of Usher* as texts employing the device, but only to immediately disqualify their candidacy.

by simple reduplication (a fragment of a work demonstrating a relationship of similitude with the work that includes it), by reduplication to infinity (a fragment demonstrating a relationship of similitude with the work that includes it and which itself includes a fragment demonstrating . . .), or aporistic reduplication (a fragment supposedly including the work which includes it).[5]

One reason for Gide's desire to distinguish the *mise en abyme* from classical examples of reduplication may have been the resistance to the concept which many of those texts demonstrate. Classical reduplication—in paintings as well as written texts—is rarely infinite, but almost always brought to closure, suspended. The classical attitude towards the possibility of infinite reduplication is perhaps best exemplified by Husserl in a passage from his *Ideas* which also relies upon a visual demonstration:

> A name on being mentioned reminds us of the Dresden Gallery and of our last visit there: we wander through the rooms, and stand before a picture of Teniers which represents a picture gallery. When we consider that pictures of the latter would in their turn portray pictures which on their part exhibited readable inscriptions and so forth, we can measure what interweaving of presentations, and what links of connexion between the discernible features in the series of pictures, can really be set up.[6]

The philosopher would, however, reduce this experience to a specific case of representation. For Husserl, every representation is a representation *of*: representations "present themselves as the modification of something, which apart from this modification would be there in its corporeal or represented selfhood."[7] In the case of potentially infinite reduplication, Husserl claims that we can penetrate through the series of levels until we arrive at a final one, at which the seemingly infinite play of reduplications is arrested: "the glance penetrates through the noemata of the series of levels, reaching the object of the last level, and there holding it steady, whilst no longer penetrating through and beyond it."[8] It is this "last level" that classical theories of representation attempt to locate. They ground the representation in its object; multiple reduplications are simply a smoke screen which may blur the outlines of the object, but can never obliterate it entirely.

Gide, however, described a textual phenomenon that is closer to the infinite play of substitution of the Derridean *mise en abyme*, as it informs the philosophy of *differance*, supplementarity. . . . In an early text (*Speech and Phenomena*), Derrida cited Husserl's Dresden Gallery passage, commenting:

> Certainly nothing has preceded this situation. Assuredly nothing will suspend it. It is not comprehended, as Husserl would want it, by intuitions or presentations. Of the broad daylight of presence, outside the gallery, no perception is given us or assuredly promised us. The gallery is the labyrinth which includes in itself its own exits: we have never come upon it as upon a particular case of experience—that which Husserl believes he is describing.[9]

For Derrida, the *mise en abyme* describes a fundamental operation of the text—it is synonymous with textuality. It can therefore have no existence outside of texts. Since it cannot be ascribed as a property to objects, it cannot be grounded in them. The Derridean abyss—"when one can read a book within a book, an origin within the origin, a center within the center"[10] and, we might add, a photograph within a photograph—underlies the techniques of deconstructive reading, which describes, among other things, the way in which representation is staged within the text.

> An entire theory of the structural necessity of the abyss will be gradually constituted in our reading: the indefinite process of supplementarity has always already infiltrated presence, always already inscribed there the space of repetition and the splitting of the self. Representation in the abyss of presence is not an accident of presence; the desire of presence is, on the contrary, born from the abyss (the indefinite multiplication) of representation, from the representation of representation, etc.[11]

The effects of the abyss—the indefinite play of substitution, repetition, the splitting of the self—are evident in Brassaï's photograph. The mirror accomplishes both the identification with the Other and the specular dispossession which simultaneously institutes and deconstitutes the subject as such. What is more, the implicit analogy between mirror and photograph ascribes these functions to photography as well. (The splitting of the subject by its photographic doubling was also depicted by Lartigue in a photograph, contemporary with Brassaï's, of the *demi-mondaine*

5 For a historical treatment of the *mise en abyme* in literary theory, see Lucien Dallenbach, *Le récit speculaire: essai sur la mise en abyme*, Paris, Seuil, 1977.
6 Edmund Husserl, *Ideas*, trans. W. R. B. Gibson, New York, Collier, 1962, 270.
7 *Ibid.*, 269.
8 *Ibid.*, 271.
9 Jacques Derrida, *Speech and Phenomena*, trans. David B. Allison, Evanston, Northwestern, 1973, 104.
10 Quoted in Dallenbach, *Le récit speculaire*, 216.
11 Jacques Derrida, *Of Grammatology*, trans. G. C. Spivak, Baltimore, Johns Hopkins, 1976, 163.

Renée Perle in the intimacy of her dressing room. In this image, the subject turns her back upon the camera and inclines narcissistically towards her mirror image. Beside her on the dressing table is a fashion photograph for which she once posed. That photograph within the photograph functions as a second mirror which reflects, in turn, Renée herself, her mirror image, and Lartigue's photograph of her. The caption that accompanies this photograph in *Diary of a Century*, "Renée Perle contemplating the face of the most beautiful woman in the world," underscores the subject's narcissism. Through the use of a transitive verb to describe a reflexive action, it also literally describes the structure of the photograph.)

The abyss resonates throughout Brassaï's oeuvre. In his photograph of a gala soirée at Maxim's, in which an ornate Art Nouveau mirror frames exactly the same scene as Brassaï's viewfinder and is reiterated by a second mirror in the depths of reflected space, we encounter infinite reduplication. In another image, a wedge is driven through the intimacy of a lovers' embrace by two mirrors that abut one another at right angles—the two are alienated by their reflections, consigned to two separate, self-enclosed realms. Still another image, depicting the aftermath of a quarrel, shows exactly the same location as the *Group in a Dance Hall* and reiterates the three species of doubling—by the photograph, the mirror, and the other—which structure that photograph. Here, a man is doubled by his own reflection in the mirror, while his female companion is doubled by another woman's reflection which floats nebulously in the mirror above her. A small square glass cleat that marks the intersection of mirror panels obliterates one of the reflected woman's eyes, suggesting a possible psychological reading (mutilation, male fantasy, etc.). However, it is the internal structure of the image—the network of relationships that constitutes it as double—that makes any such interpretation possible. Meaning, therefore, does not reside in details of expression or gesture that are simply registered by the photograph. Rather, it is a property of the photograph itself.

Brassaï's fascination with mirrors has been explained as a derivative from painting, from Cubism in particular; and biographical data—his friendship with Picasso, his early aspirations to a painting career, and his obvious absorption of the Parisian milieu into which he was transplanted—has been mustered in support of this claim.[12] However, no appeal to painting is sufficient to unravel the photographer's predilection for reflective surfaces and complex mirror duplication. Not only does an appeal to Cubism reduce the mirror effects to a multiplication of perspectives and thus deny these images their specifically photographic character, it also ignores the frequent recurrence of the mirror in photographs throughout the history of the medium. Its first appearance as a self-conscious device coincides with that moment at which photography began to depict its own possibilities and conditions in its images.

The work of the Victorian photographer, Lady Clementina Hawarden, represents one of the earliest such attempts. (Most of Hawarden's work may be dated to the late 1850s, and the first half of the '60s.) Her obsession was the double portrait; as frequently as not, however, these images are constituted by a single subject doubled in reflection, as in a photograph that has been posthumously captioned "At the window." Here the subject seems to be suspended between two possible objects of contemplation—the view out the window and her own image in a mirror. She seems to incline towards the latter; the reticence of the image reinforces this impression. Thus, what is depicted is the process of becoming self-reflexive. The tension in the image between the different spectacles offered by the window and the mirror restates a structural tension within the medium—between photography as extrovert, a view onto the material world, and the photograph as a self-enclosed image of its own process. The inclinations of the subject depicted in this image are those of the photograph itself.

The mirror functions not only to reflect the subject; it also quite consciously pictures that metaphor which defines photography as a mirror image. The mirror reads as an image *en abyme*. The cropping of the print to echo the profile of the mirror firmly establishes this intention. This visual identification of mirror and photograph establishes a complex play between subject, mirror, and camera: not only is the subject doubled twice (by mirror and camera), but the mirror image, itself a double, is redoubled by the photograph itself.

If we speak of this image, and of others like it, as reduplicative, it is because *reduplication* signifies "to reproduce in reflection" and thus describes that kind of mechanical reproduction by analogy we impute to both mirror and photograph. Ordinary usage, however, does not register differences of degree between *duplication* and *reduplication*. The latter might be expected to be contingent upon a previous act of duplication, and thus to result in what is actually a tri- or quadruplication of an original object or quantity (the ambiguity results from the possibility of taking either the original or its double as the object of the second doubling). However, the excess implicit in the concept of reduplication has been sublimated. *Duplicate* and *reduplicate* have been reduced to synonymy; both refer to a single signified: "to double." The reduction to doubling fails not only to account for the "pli" or fold implicit in both; it also strips the prefix in *reduplication*

12 See Colin J. Westerbeck, Jr., "Night Life: Brassaï and Weegee," *Artforum*, XV (December, 1976), 34–45.

of its signifying function. Its relationship with its stem is now that of a mirror to its object—a doubling without any corresponding semantic increment. So that *reduplication* harbors within its semantic folds the concepts of tautology, of redundancy.

However, in those disciplines which take language as their object—philology, rhetoric, and structural linguistics—*reduplication* is a technical term that describes a specific phenomenon. In classical rhetoric, *reduplication* was a species of *repetition*, distinguished by the reiteration of a word or phrase within the same part of a sentence or clause. Its function, like all forms of rhetorical repetition, was emphatic. *Reduplication* has at times been identified with the etymologically parallel figure *anadiplosis* (*ana*, again + *diploun*, to double) in which the final word of a phrase is repeated at the beginning of the next. *Anadiplosis* thus establishes a mirror relationship between two segments of a text, the classic example being Voltaire's

> Il aperçoit de loin le jeune Téligny
> Téligny, don't l'amour a mérité sa fille.

in which the second line stands as a mirror reversal of the first. That such a figure should have been designated as a redoubling suggests the classical view of language as a mirror of the real; hence the repetition of a word or phrase doubles that which is itself already double.

Classical philology describes a similar phenomenon, occurring not at the level of the sentence, but at that of the word. Linguistic, as opposed to rhetorical, reduplication (the term is again a technical one) involves the repetition of identical or quasi-identical syllables, commonly at the beginning of a word; the English *murmur* and the French *bonbon* are two examples. Such reduplications have been explained as motivated signs, originally expressing repeated or intensive action or, in some languages, plurality. In the analysis of structural linguistics, however, reduplication does not demonstrate motivation (a relationship of analogy between a sign and its referent); on the contrary, it indicates, if not arbitrariness, at least the conventional nature of an utterance.

Roman Jakobson, discussing the frequent occurrence of reduplication in infantile language, suggests that it may well be the sign of the subject's entry into a symbolic order:

> At the transition from babbling to verbal behaviour, the reduplication may even serve as a compulsory process, signalling that the uttered sounds do not represent a babble, but a senseful semantic entity. The patently linguistic essence of such a duplication is quite explicable. In contradistinction to the "wild sounds" of babbling exercizes, the phonemes are to be recognized, distinguishable, identifiable; and in accordance with these requirements, they must be deliberately repeatable. The repetitiveness finds its most concise and succinct expression in, e.g., *papa*. The successive presentations of the same consonantal phonemes repeatedly supported by the same vowel, improve their legibility and contribute to the correctness of message reception.[13]

If repeatability is a necessary condition of those units out of which language constructs sense, then reduplication is, at its most fundamental level, the very sign of that repeatability. It signifies that an utterance is not simply a "wild sound," but that it is emitted according to a code, and thus conveys an intention to signify. Although repetition does not guarantee semiosis, it does suggest its presence and thus becomes, for Lévi-Strauss at least, the "signifier of signification":

> Even at the babbling stage the phoneme group /pa/ can be heard. But the difference between /pa/ and /papa/ does not reside simply in reduplication: /pa/ is a noise, /papa/ is a word. The reduplication indicates intent on the part of the speaker; it endows the second syllable with a function different from that which would have been performed by the first separately, or in the form of a potentially limitless series of identical sounds /papapapapa/ produced by mere babbling. Therefore the second /pa/ is not a repetition of the first, nor has it the same signification. It is a sign that, like itself, the first /pa/ too was a sign, and that as a pair they fall into the category of signifiers, not of things signified.[14]

Reduplication first occurs at the transition from babbling to linguistic performance, at the moment of the infant's entry into the symbolic order, which is contemporaneous with the mirror stage. Thus the dispossession of the subject by the mirror is also a law of language, and linguistic reduplication might also be a sign of the capture of the subject by an image.

In the concluding paragraphs of *The Raw and the Cooked*, Lévi-Strauss extended Jakobson's observation to onomatopoeic words; in this instance, reduplication functions to distinguish purely imitative sounds from signs. If the arbitrary character of most words is sufficient to indicate their status as signs, "onomatopoeic terms, on the other hand, are always ambiguous in nature because, being founded on a resemblance, they do not clearly indicate whether the speaker, in pronouncing them, is trying to reproduce a noise or to express a meaning."[15] Reduplication, then, functions to indicate that such utterances are indeed signs, and not gratuitous or merely imitative noises. Linguistic reduplication, the anthropologist

---

13 Roman Jakobson, "Why Mama and Papa?" *Selected Writings, I*, The Hague, Mouton, 1962, 542.
14 Claude Lévi-Strauss, *The Raw and the Cooked*, trans. J. and D. Weightman, New York, Harper & Row, 1970, 339–40.

concludes, may be used as an explanatory model for the structure of myths. Just as language chooses its phonemes from a practically unlimited range of natural sounds, so too myths draw upon the whole realm of natural phenomena for their subject matter. These phenomena are not the object of myths, rather, they are their instruments of signification. The multiple isomorphisms that constitute myths function like linguistic reduplication: "the distinctive character of myths . . . is precisely emphasis, resulting from the multiplication of one level by another or several others, and which, as in language, functions to signify signification."[16]

While the linguistic character of myths has been amply demonstrated by structural anthropology, it may legitimately be asked what relevance linguistic reduplication might possibly have to photographs, if the photograph is, following Roland Barthes's "common sense" definition, a message without a code, that is, nonlinguistic. However, the terms in which Lévi-Strauss discusses the phenomenon of linguistic reduplication suggest that it may indeed function as an explanatory model for photographic reduplication as well. Both Jakobson and Lévi-Strauss distinguish the sound emitted randomly or in imitation of another sound from that emitted as language, that is, according to a code. Photography, then, at least as Barthes distinguishes it from other semiotic systems, would seem to correspond to the purely imitated sound:

> What is the content of the photographic message? What does the photograph transmit? By definition, the scene itself, the literal reality. . . . In order to move from the reality to the photograph it is in no way necessary to divide up this reality into units and to constitute these units as signs, substantially different from the object they communicate; there is no necessity to set up a relay, that is to say a code, between the object and its image. Certainly the image is not the reality but at least its perfect *analagon* and it is exactly this analogical perfection which, to common sense, defines the photograph.[17]

What then might reduplication signify within such an image? Does it not, as in language and myth, signify the existence of an underlying intention to signify *through the image*, and thus to the possibility of a photographic language? Might it not indicate, like the reduplicated syllable in the vocable /papa/, that the photograph itself was already a sign? Might it not also contest any reading of photographs according to their subject matter or captions, the reality presented by the photograph being no longer the object of the image, but an instrument of signification? Does it not indeed suggest that we may be able to speak of a *genuine* rhetoric of the image?

The argument that the properties of the photographic image are derived not from the characteristics of the medium itself but from the structure of the real, registered mechanically on a light-sensitive surface, may describe the technical procedures of photography. But it does not account for the photograph's capacity to internally generate and organize meaning. However, it does seem to describe accurately the strategy according to which some photographs procure their authoritative status, those photographs in which a carefully calculated *mise en scène* mutely insists that the image is wholly dependent upon, since derived from, the external. Thus, the radical symmetry of Walker Evans's photograph of Cary Ross's bedroom (made in the same year as Brassaï's *Group in a Dance Hall*). Everything about the image is symmetrical—twin beds, a pair of identically framed impressions of the same Picasso print—everything, that is, except the photograph itself. The oblique angle of Evans's shot works to exteriorize those symmetries, to present them as properties of the real rather than the image. Had these paired objects been photographed head-on, the image would have appeared artificial, staged. Seen obliquely, however, they impute to the material world the capacity to independently create its own symmetries, to mirror itself.

Still, what we recognize in this photograph, despite its claim to transparency, is an image of the photographic process. If the camera angle works to exteriorize symmetry, it also encourages the illusion of a room divided by a mirror, and thus of a single bed and a graphic each doubled in reflection. That mirror is located by a virtual fold in the surface of the photograph along which reality is reduplicated according to the properties of the image. The paired graphics, in addition to contributing to the illusion of a mirror, suggest the duplicability of the photographic print, the theoretically unlimited number of copies that may be engendered by a single negative. Photographs are but one link in a potentially endless chain of reduplication; themselves duplicates (of both their objects and, in a sense, their negatives), they are also subject to further duplication, either through the procedures of printing or as objects of still other photographs, such as Evans's *Penny Picture Display, Savannah*, 1936. While the illusion of a mirror may be inhibited by the night table and lamp—the only supposedly single objects in the image—these, however, are also doubled by the shadows they cast on the wall. The cast shadows are an additional analogue for photography. Thus, if Evans's photograph depicts a reality outside of the photograph, that reality is nonetheless wholly conditioned by the properties of the image. This scene must have appeared as a

15 *Ibid.*
16 *Ibid.* I have substituted my own translation from the French original.
17 Roland Barthes, "The Photographic Message," *Image, Music, Text*, trans. Stephen Heath, New York, Hill and Wang, 1977, 16–7.

photograph even before Evans exposed it.

An experience of the real as if it were a photograph is described by Robert Smithson in his text, "The Monuments of Passaic," in which the artist narrates the events of a day-long photographic excursion to the New Jersey suburbs. Of photographing an ordinary wood-and-steel bridge, Smithson remarks:

> Noonday sunshine cinema-ized the site, turning the bridge and the river into an over-exposed *picture*. Photographing it with my Instamatic 400 was like photographing a photograph. The sun became a monstrous light-bulb that projected a detached series of "stills" through my Instamatic into my eye. When I walked on the bridge, it was as though I was walking on an enormous photograph that was made of wood and steel, and underneath the river existed as an enormous movie film that showed nothing but a continuous blank.[18]

This narrative inverts the terms of a familiar argument about the photograph: that the vicariousness of the image is frequently overlooked, so that the photograph is mistaken for the reality for which it is nevertheless only a substitute. Smithson, standing that argument on its head, calls its bluff. If reality itself appears to be already constituted as image, then the hierarchy of object and representation—the first being the source of the authority and prestige of the second—is collapsed. The representation can no longer be grounded, as Husserl wanted, in presence. For Smithson, the real assumes the contingency traditionally ascribed to the copy; the landscape appeared to him, not as Nature, but as a "particular kind of heliotypy."[19] The result is an overwhelming experience of absence: the abyss.

To some extent, Smithson recapitulates that passage in Fox Talbot's *Pencil of Nature* in which the pioneer photographer recounts his realization that, in Hollis Frampton's paraphrase, "the 'image' he had sought to make is already there."[20] The invention of photography was thus simply a discovery of a physical or chemical means for fixing the discontinuous images of herself that Nature freely offered up. But Fox Talbot was looking into a camera lucida. Smithson confronts not an image, but an object *as if it were an image*. What does it mean, then, to take a photograph of a photograph?

This question is also raised in a series of photographs Smithson made in 1969, and which seem to derive, at least in part, from the experience described in "The Monuments of Passaic." Within the space of these double images, a site and its own photographic likeness are juxtaposed. This *mise en abyme* endows these photographs with an apparatus for self-interpretation; their structure, defined by the juxtaposition of two images of the same motif, gives rise to commentary on the conditions of the photograph itself. Through them, Smithson deflates the myth that photographs are a means of gaining mastery and control over objects, of rendering them more accessible to consciousness. The internal photograph reduces the landscape and distances it from us. Moreover, what is true of the internal image holds for the photograph as a whole. In a photograph, Smithson casts a shadow over the presumed transparency of photographs; he raises serious doubts about their capacity to *convey* anything but a sense of loss, of absence.

What redeems the photograph, however, is its ability to generate and organize meaning *independently of its object*. Smithson frequently published and exhibited photographs of his projects; but after an experience of his double photographs, can we seriously regard *any* Smithson photograph simply as documentation? It is impossible to experience these double images as such. We are wrong to presume that the "work" in this case consists of an action performed (the placing of the photograph in the landscape) and that the photograph is transparent to that action, which it preserves in the tense peculiar to photography, the "having-been-there."[21] However, these photographs are distinguished from documents by the relationship of the internal photograph to the photograph that contains it. Not only does this relationship exist at present only in the photograph, it has *never* existed elsewhere. So that the action Smithson performed was simply an instrument, and not the object, of signification. The photograph *is* the work.

In 1969, Smithson executed a series of "mirror displacements" in the Yucatan peninsula; nine color photographs "document" that project. Although location and materials have changed—Smithson substituted mirrors for the photograph—these images reiterate the photo displacements produced that same year in a New Jersey quarry: a motif and its reflection are juxtaposed within a photograph. Of these displacements, Smithson wrote:

> If you visit the sites (a doubtful probability) you find nothing but memory-traces, for the mirror displacements were dismantled right after they were photographed. The mirrors are somewhere in New York. The reflected light has been erased. Remembrances are but numbers on a map, vacant memories constellating the intangible terrains in deleted vicinities. It is the dimension of absence that remains to be found. The expunged color that remains to be seen. The fictive voices of the totems have exhausted their arguments. Yucatan is elsewhere.[22]

---

18 Robert Smithson, "The Monuments of Passaic," *Artforum*, VI (December, 1967), 49.

19 *Ibid.*, 50.

20 Hollis Frampton, "Incisions in History/Segments of Eternity," *Artforum*, XIII (October, 1974), 41

21 Barthes, "Rhetoric of the Image," *Image, Music, Text*, 44.

22 Smithson, "Incidents of Mirror-Travel in the Yucatan," *Artforum*, VIII (September, 1969), 33.

Young Workers

Jeff Wall

1978/1983

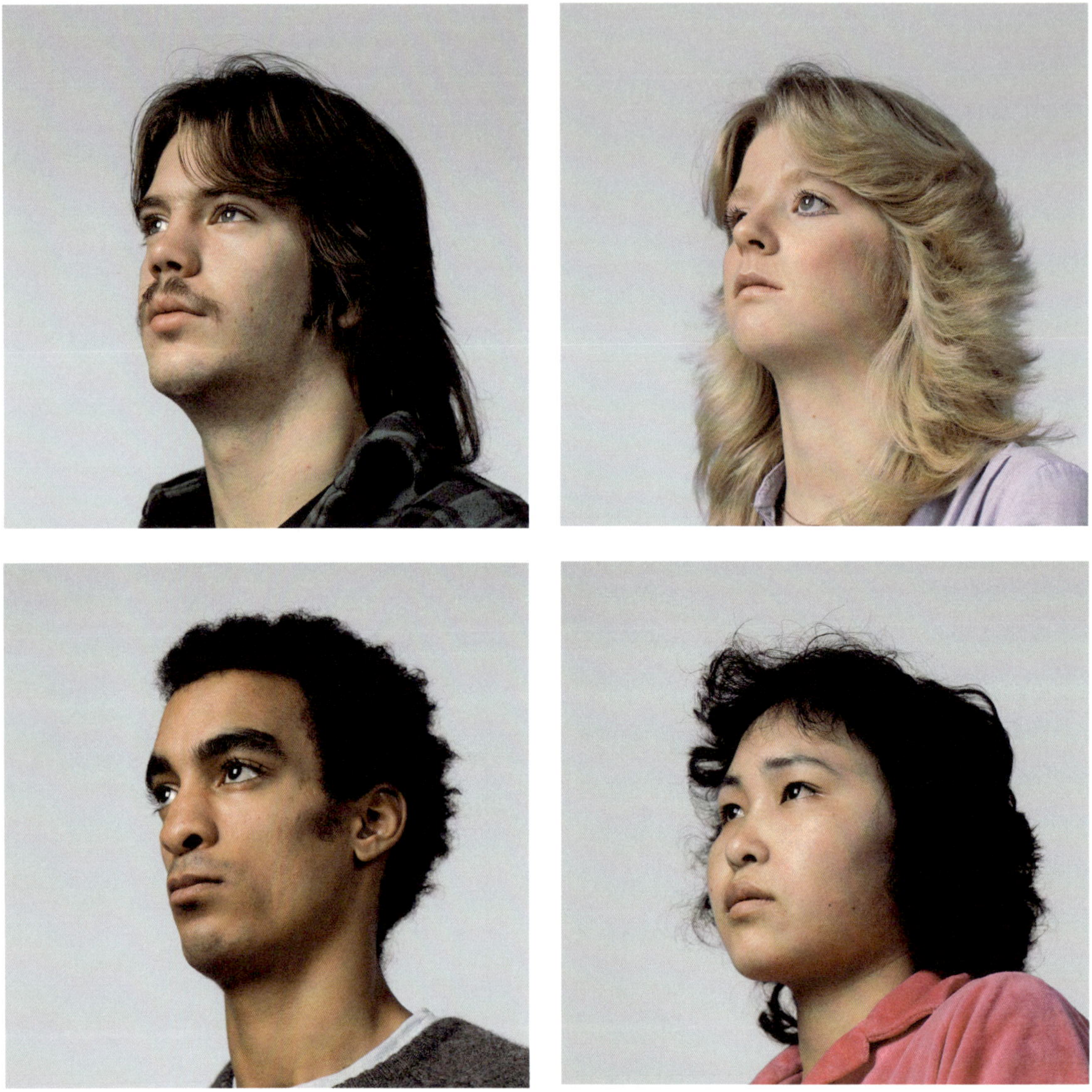

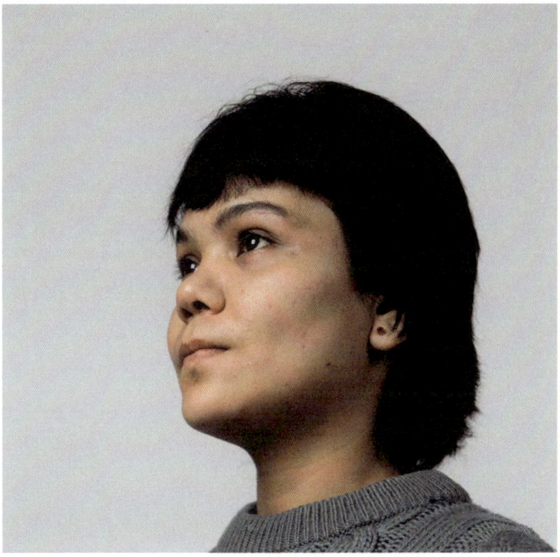

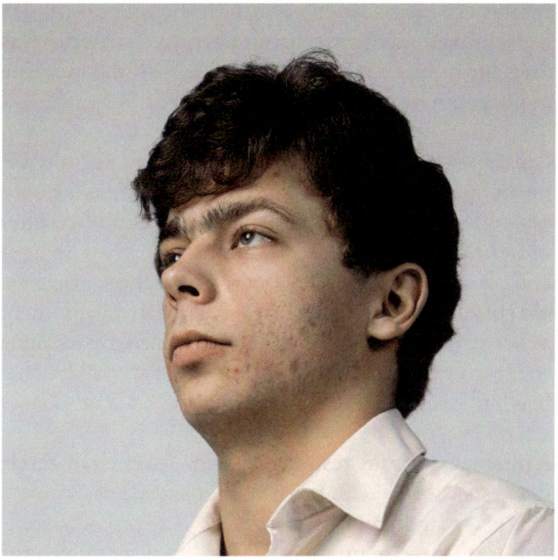

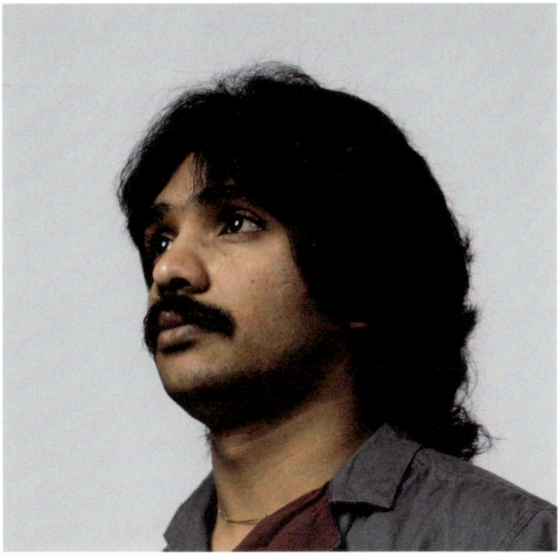

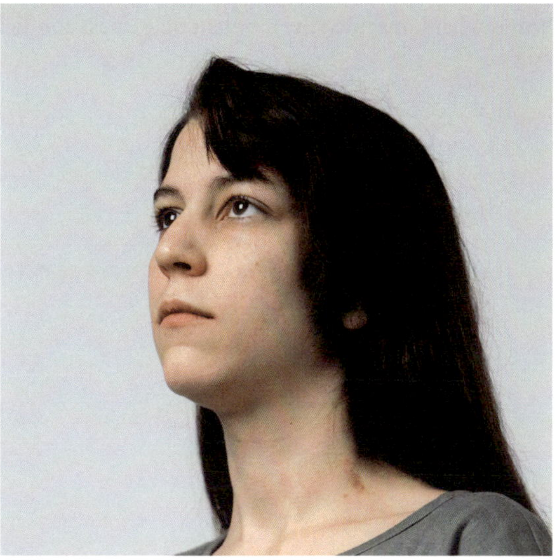

Artist Statement from *Horror Pleni: Pictures in New York Today*
Ericka Beckman
1980

Film is creating a reality through the makeshift. My films move backwards, using narrative structures as does the mind of anyone trying to grasp the meaning of images in his memory.

I juxtapose a model of the past, those "should be" meanings, with the post as remembered, as known personally to be riddled with mistakes and breeches of meaning. I reconstruct events
and places to identify the details of a choice that we are not accustomed to making, or to locate the moment a choice was available but went by unseized. By recalling the fear evoked by choice. Film can fictionalize that fear and provide new consequences.

A photograph is the result and reason for such research; it arrests the image in the film that says,
"this is the moment of surprise"
"this is the precise moment when things went wrong,"
or
"this is what I imagined the moment of greatest conflict to be."

Selections from *Camera Lucida: Reflections on Photography*

Roland Barthes

1982

9. I was glancing through an illustrated magazine. A photograph made me pause. Nothing very extraordinary: the (photographic) banality of a rebellion in Nicaragua: a ruined street, two helmeted soldiers on patrol; behind them, two nuns. Did this photograph please me? Interest me? Intrigue me? Not even. Simply, it existed (for me). I understood at once that its existence (its "adventure") derived from the co-presence of two discontinuous elements, heterogeneous in that they did not belong to the same world (no need to proceed to the point of contrast): the soldiers and the nuns. I foresaw a structural rule (conforming to my own observation), and I immediately tried to verify it by inspecting other photographs by the same reporter (the Dutchman Koen Wessing): many of them attracted me because they included this kind of duality which I had just become aware of. Here a mother and daughter sob over the father's arrest (Baudelaire: "the emphatic truth of gesture in the great circumstances of life"), and this happens *out in the countryside* (where could they have learned the news? for whom are these gestures?). Here, on a torn-up pavement, a child's corpse under a white sheet; parents and friends stand around it, desolate: a banal enough scene, unfortunately, but I noted certain interferences: the corpse's one bare foot, the sheet carried by the weeping mother (why this sheet?), a woman in the background, probably a friend, holding a handkerchief to her nose. Here again, in a bombed-out apartment, the huge eyes of two little boys, one's shirt raised over his little belly (the excess of those eyes disturb the scene). And here, finally, leaning against the wall of a house, three Sandinists, the lower part of their faces covered by a rag (stench? secrecy? I have no idea, knowing nothing of the realities of guerrilla warfare); one of them holds a gun that rests on his thigh (I can see his nails); but his other hand is stretched out, open, as if he were explaining and demonstrating something. My rule applied all the more closely in that other pictures from the same reportage were less interesting to me; they were fine shots, they expressed the dignity and horror of rebellion, but in my eyes they bore no mark or sign: their homogeneity remained cultural: they were "scenes," rather à *la* Greuze, had it not been for the harshness of the subject.

10. My rule was plausible enough for me to try to name (as I would need to do) these two elements whose co-presence established, it seemed, the particular interest I took in these photographs.

The first, obviously, is an extent, it has the extension of a field, which I perceive quite familiarly as a consequence of my knowledge, my culture; this field can be more or less stylized, more or less successful, depending on the photographer's skill or luck, but it always refers to a classical body of information: rebellion, Nicaragua, and all the signs of both: wretched un-uniformed soldiers, ruined streets, corpses, grief, the sun, and the heavy-lidded Indian eyes. Thousands of photographs consist of this field, and in these photographs I can, of course, take a kind of general interest, one that is even stirred sometimes, but in regard to them my emotion requires the rational intermediary of an ethical and political culture. What I feel about these photographs derives from an *average* affect, almost from a certain training. I did not know a French word which might account for this kind of human interest, but I believe this word exists in Latin: it is *studium*, which doesn't mean, at least not immediately, "study," but application to a thing, taste for someone, a kind of general, enthusiastic commitment, of course, but without special acuity. It is by *studium* that I am interested in so many photographs, whether I receive them as political testimony or enjoy them as good historical scenes: for it is culturally (this connotation is present in *studium*) that I participate in the figures, the faces, the gestures, the settings, the actions.

The second element will break (or punctuate) the *studium*. This time it is not I who seek it out (as I invest the field of the *studium* with my sovereign consciousness), it is this element which rises from the scene, shoots out of it like an arrow, and pierces me. A Latin word exists to designate this wound, this prick, this mark made by a pointed instrument: the word suits me all the better in that it also refers to the notion of punctuation, and because the photographs I am speaking of are in effect punctuated, sometimes even speckled with these sensitive points; precisely, these marks, these wounds are so many *points*. This second element which will disturb the *studium* I shall therefore call *punctum*, for *punctum* is also: sting, speck, cut, little hole—and also a cast of the dice. A photograph's *punctum* is that accident which pricks me (but also bruises me, is poignant to me).

Having thus distinguished two themes in Photography (for in general the photographs I liked were constructed in the manner of a classical sonata), I could occupy myself with one after the other.

11. Many photographs are, alas, inert under my gaze. But even among those which have some existence in my eyes, most provoke only a general and, so to speak, *polite* interest: they have no *punctum* in them: they please or displease me without pricking me: they are invested with no more than *studium*. The *studium* is that very wide field of unconcerned desire, of various interest, of inconsequential taste: *I like / I don't like*. The *studium* is of the order of *liking*, not of *loving*; it mobilizes a half desire, a demi-volition; it is the same sort of vague, slippery, irresponsible interest one takes in the people, the entertainments, the books, the clothes one finds "all right."

To recognize the *studium* is inevitably to encounter the photographer's intentions, to enter into harmony with them, to approve or disapprove of them, but always to understand them, to argue them within myself, for culture (from which the *studium* derives) is a contract arrived at between creators and consumers. The *studium* is a kind of education (knowledge and civility, "politeness") which allows me to discover the *Operator*, to experience the intentions which establish and animate his practices, but to experience them "in reverse," according to my will as a *Spectator*. It is rather as if I had to read the Photographer's myths in the Photograph, fraternizing with them but not quite believing in them. These myths obviously aim (this is what myth is for) at reconciling the Photograph with society (is this necessary? —Yes, indeed: the Photograph is *dangerous*) by endowing it with *functions*, which are, for the Photographer, so many alibis. These functions are: to inform, to represent, to surprise, to cause to signify, to provoke desire. And I, the *Spectator*, I recognize them with more or less pleasure: I invest them with my *studium* (which is never my delight or my pain) [...]

15. Since every photograph is contingent (and thereby outside of meaning), Photography cannot signify (aim at a generality) except by assuming a mask. It is this word which Calvino correctly uses to designate what makes a face into the product of a society and of its history. As in the portrait of William Casby, photographed by Avedon: the essence of slavery is here laid bare: the mask is the meaning, insofar as it is absolutely pure (as it was in the ancient theater). This is why the great portrait photographers are great mythologists: Nadar (the French bourgeoisie), Sander (the Germans of pre-Nazi Germany), Avedon (New York's "upper crust") [...]

17. Having thus reviewed the *docile interests* which certain photographs awaken in me, I deduced that the *studium*, insofar as it is not traversed, lashed, striped by a detail (*punctum*) which attracts or distresses me, engenders a very widespread type of photograph (the most widespread in the world), which we might call the *unary photograph*. In generative grammar, a transformation is unary if, through it, a single series is generated by the base: such are the passive, negative, interrogative, and emphatic transformations. The Photograph is unary when it emphatically transforms "reality" without doubling it, without making it vacillate (emphasis is a power of cohesion): no duality, no indirection, no disturbance. The unary Photograph has every reason to be banal, "unity" of composition being the first rule of vulgar (and notably, of academic) rhetoric: "The subject," says one handbook for amateur photographers, "must be simple, free of useless accessories; this is called the Search for Unity."

News photographs are very often unary (the unary photograph is not necessarily tranquil). In these images, no *punctum*: a certain shock—the literal can traumatize—but no disturbance; the photograph can "shout," not wound. These journalistic photographs are received (all at once), perceived. I glance through them, I don't recall them; no detail (in some corner) ever interrupts my reading: I am interested in them (as I am interested in the world), I do not love them.

Another unary photograph is the pornographic photograph (I am not saying the erotic photograph: the erotic is a pornographic that has been disturbed, fissured). Nothing more homogeneous than a pornographic photograph. It is always a naïve photograph, without intention and without calculation. Like a shop window which shows only one illuminated piece of jewelry, it is completely constituted by the presentation of only one thing: sex: no secondary, untimely object ever manages to half conceal, delay, or distract . . . A proof *a contrario*: Mapplethorpe shifts his close-ups of genitalia from the pornographic to the erotic by photographing the fabric of underwear at very close range: the photograph is no longer unary, since I am interested in the texture of the material.

18. In this habitually unary space, occasionally (but alas all too rarely) a "detail" attracts me. I feel that its mere presence changes my reading, that I am

looking at a new photograph, marked in my eyes with a higher value. This "detail" is the *punctum*.

It is not possible to posit a rule of connection between the *studium* and the *punctum* (when it happens to be there). It is a matter of a co-presence, that is all one can say: the nuns "happened to be there," passing in the background, when Wessing photographed the Nicaraguan soldiers; from the viewpoint of reality (which is perhaps that of the *Operator*), a whole causality explains the presence of the "detail": the Church implanted in these Latin-American countries, the nuns allowed to circulate as nurses, etc.; but from my *Spectator's* viewpoint, the detail is offered by chance and for nothing; the scene is in no way "composed" according to a creative logic; the photograph is doubtless dual, but this duality is the motor of no "development," as happens in classical discourse. In order to perceive the *punctum*, no analysis would be of any use to me (but perhaps memory sometimes would, as we shall see): it suffices that the image be large enough, that I do not have to study it (this would be of no help at all), that, given right there on the page, I should receive it right here in my eyes.

19. Very often the *Punctum* is a "detail," *i.e.*, a partial object. Hence, to give examples of *punctum* is, in a certain fashion, to *give myself up*. Here is a family of American blacks, photographed in 1926 by James Van der Zee. The *studium* is clear: I am sympathetically interested, as a docile cultural subject, in what the photograph has to say, for it *speaks* (it is a "good" photograph): it utters respectability, family life, conformism, Sunday best, an effort of social advancement in order to assume the White Man's attributes (an effort touching by reason of its naïveté). The spectacle interests me but does not prick me. What does, strange to say, is the belt worn low by the sister (or daughter)—the "solacing Mammy"—whose arms are crossed behind her back like a schoolgirl, and above all her *strapped pumps* (Mary Janes—why does this dated fashion touch me? I mean: to what date does it refer me?). This particular *punctum* arouses great sympathy in me, almost a kind of tenderness. Yet the *punctum* shows no preference for morality or good taste: the *punctum* can be ill-bred. William Klein has photographed children of Little Italy in New York (1954); all very touching, amusing, but what I stubbornly see are one child's bad teeth. Kertész, in 1926, took young Tzara's portrait (with a monocle); but what I notice, by that additional vision which is in a sense the gift, the grace of the *punctum*, is Tzara's hand resting on the door frame: a large hand whose nails are anything but clean.

However. lightning-like it may be, the punctum has, more or less potentially, a power of expansion. This power is often metonymic. There is a photograph by Kertész (1921) which shows a blind gypsy violinist being led by a boy; now what I see, by means of this "thinking eye" which makes me add something to the photograph, is the dirt road; its texture gives me the certainty of being in Central Europe; I perceive the referent (here, the photograph really transcends itself: is this not the sole proof of its art? To annihilate itself as *medium*, to be no longer a sign but the thing itself?), I recognize, with my whole body, the straggling villages I passed through on my long ago travels in Hungary and Rumania.

There is another (less Proustian) expansion of the *punctum*: when, paradoxically, while remaining a "detail," it fills the whole picture. Duane Michaels has photographed Andy Warhol: a provocative portrait, since Warhol hides his face behind both hands. I have no desire to comment intellectually on this game of hide-and-seek (which belongs to the *Studium*); since for me, Warhol hides nothing; he offers his hands to read, quite openly; and the *punctum* is not the gesture but the slightly repellent substance of those spatulate nails, at once soft and hard-edged.

20. Certain details may "prick" me. If they do not, it is doubtless because the photographer has put them there intentionally. In William Klein's "Shinohiera, Fighter Painter" (1961), the character's monstrous head has nothing to say to me because I can see so clearly that it is an artifice of the camera angle. Some soldiers with nuns behind them served as an example to explain what the *punctum* was for me (here, quite elementary); but when Bruce Gilden photographs a nun and some drag queens together (New Orleans, 1973), the deliberate (not to say, rhetorical) contrast produces no effect on me, except perhaps one of irritation. Hence the detail which interests me is not, or at least is not strictly, intentional, and probably must not be so; it occurs in the field of the photographed thing like a supplement that is at once inevitable and delightful; it doesn't necessarily attest to the photographer's art: it says only that the photographer was there, or else, still more simply, that he could not *not* photograph the partial object at the same time as the total object (how could Kertész have "separated" the dirt road from the violinist walking on it?). The Photographer's "second sight" does not consist in "seeing" but in being there. And above all, imitating Orpheus, he must not turn back to look at what he is leading—what he is giving to me! [...]

22. The *studium* is ultimately always coded, the *punc-*

tum is not (I trust I am not using these words abusively). Nadar, in his time (1882), photographed Savorgnan de Brazza between two young blacks dressed as French sailors; one of the two boys, oddly, has rested his hand on Brazza's thigh; this incongruous gesture is bound to arrest my gaze, to constitute a *punctum*. And yet it is not one, for I immediately code the posture, whether I want to or not, as "aberrant" (for me, the *punctum* is the other boy's crossed arms). What I can name cannot really prick me. The incapacity to name is a good symptom of disturbance. Mapplethorpe has photographed Robert Wilson and Philip Glass. Wilson *holds* me, though I cannot say why, *i.e.*, say *where*: is it the eyes, the skin, the position of the hands, the track shoes? The effect is certain but unlocatable, it does not find its sign, its name; it is sharp and yet lands in a vague zone of myself; it is acute yet muffled, it cries out in silence. Odd contradiction: a floating flash.

Nothing surprising, then, if sometimes, despite its clarity, the *punctum* should be revealed only after the fact, when the photograph is no longer in front of me and I think back on it. I may know better a photograph I remember than a photograph I am looking at, as if direct vision oriented its language wrongly, engaging it in an effort of description which will always miss its point of effect, the *punctum*. Reading Van der Zee's photograph, I thought I had discerned what moved me: the strapped pumps of the black woman in her Sunday best; but this photograph has *worked* within me, and later on I realized that the real *punctum* was the necklace she was wearing; for (no doubt) it was this same necklace (a slender ribbon of braided gold) which I had seen worn by someone in my own family, and which, once she died, remained shut up in a family box of old jewelry (this sister of my father never married, lived with her mother as an old maid, and I had always been saddened whenever I thought of her dreary life). I had just realized that however immediate and incisive it was, the *punctum* could accommodate a certain latency (but never any scrutiny).

Ultimately—or at the limit—in order to see a photograph well, it is best to look away or close your eyes. "The necessary condition for an image is sight," Janouch told Kafka; and Kafka smiled and replied: "We photograph things in order to drive them out of our minds. My stories are a way of shutting my eyes." The photograph must be silent (there are blustering photographs, and I don't like them): this is not a question of discretion, but of music. Absolute subjectivity is achieved only in a state, an effort, of silence (shutting your eyes is to make the image speak in silence). The photograph touches me if I withdraw it from its usual blah-blah: "Technique," "Reality," "Reportage," "Art," etc.: to say nothing, to shut my eyes, to allow the detail to rise of its own accord into affective consciousness.

23. Last thing about the *punctum*: whether or not it is triggered, it is an addition: it is what I add to the photograph and *what is nonetheless already there*. To Lewis Hine's retarded children, I add nothing with regard to the degenerescence of the profile: the code expresses this before I do, takes my place, does not allow me to speak; what I add—and what, of course, is already in the image—is the collar, the bandage. Do I add to the images in movies? I don't think so; I don't have time: in front of the screen, I am not free to shut my eyes; otherwise, opening them again, I would not discover the same image; I am constrained to a continuous voracity; a host of other qualities, but not *pensiveness*; whence the interest, for me, of the photogram.

Yet the cinema has a power which at first glance the Photograph does not have: the screen (as Bazin has remarked) is not a frame but a hideout; the man or woman who emerges from it continues living: a "blind field" constantly doubles our partial vision. Now, confronting millions of photographs, including those which have a good *studium*, I sense no blind field: everything which happens within the frame dies absolutely once this frame is passed beyond. When we define the Photograph as a motionless image, this does not mean only that the figures it represents do not move; it means that they do not *emerge*, do not *leave*: they are anesthetized and fastened down, like butterflies. Yet once there is a *punctum*, a blind field is created (is divined): on account of her necklace, the black woman in her Sunday best has had, for me, a whole life external to her portrait; Robert Wilson, endowed with an unlocatable *punctum*, is someone I want to meet. Here is Queen Victoria photographed in 1863 by George W. Wilson; she is on horseback, her skirt suitably draping the entire animal (this is the historical interest, the *studium*); but beside her, attracting my eyes, a kilted groom holds the horse's bridle: this is the *punctum*; for even if I do not know just what the social status of this Scotsman may be (servant? equerry?), I can see his function clearly: to supervise the horse's behavior: what if the horse suddenly began to rear? What would happen to the queen's skirt, *i.e.*, to *her majesty*? The *punctum* fantastically "brings out" the Victorian nature (what else can one call it?) of the photograph, it endows this photograph with a blind field.

The presence (the dynamics) of this blind field is, I believe, what distinguishes the erotic photograph from the pornographic photograph. Pornography ordinarily represents the sexual organs, making them into a motionless object (a fetish), flattered like an idol that does not leave its niche; for me, there is no *punctum* in the pornographic image; at most it amuses me (and even then, boredom follows quickly). The erotic photograph, on the contrary (and this is its very condition), does not make the sexual organs into a central object; it may very well not show them at all; it takes the spectator outside its frame, and it is there that I animate this photograph and that it animates me. The *punctum*, then, is a kind of subtle *beyond*—as if the image launched desire beyond what it permits us to see: not only toward "the rest" of the nakedness, not only toward the fantasy of a *praxis*, but toward the absolute excellence of a being, body and soul together. This boy with his arm outstretched, his radiant smile, though his beauty is in no way classical or academic, and though he is half out of the photograph, shifted to the extreme left of the frame, incarnates a kind of blissful eroticism; the photograph leads me to distinguish the "heavy" desire of pornography from the "light" (good) desire of eroticism; after all, perhaps this is a question of "luck": the photographer has caught the boy's hand (the boy is Mapplethorpe himself, I believe) at just the right degree of openness, the right density of abandonment: a few millimeters more or less and the divined body would no longer have been offered with benevolence (the pornographic body shows itself, it does not give itself, there is no generosity in it): the photographer has found the *right moment*, the *kairos* of desire. [...]

34. It is often said that it was the painters who invented Photography (by bequeathing it their framing, the Albertian perspective, and the optic of the *camera obscura*). I say: no, it was the chemists. For the *noeme* "That-has-been" was possible only on the day when a scientific circumstance (the discovery that silver halogens were sensitive to light) made it possible to recover and print directly the luminous rays emitted by a variously lighted object. The photograph is literally an emanation of the referent. From a real body, which was there, proceed radiations which ultimately touch me, who am here; the duration of the transmission is insignificant; the photograph of the missing being, as Sontag says, will touch me like the delayed rays of a star. A sort of umbilical cord links the body of the photographed thing to my gaze: light, though impalpable, is here a carnal medium, a skin I share with anyone who has been photographed.

It seems that in Latin "photograph" would be said "imago lucis opera expressa"; which is to say: image revealed, "extracted," "mounted," "expressed" (like the juice of a lemon) by the action of light. And if Photography belonged to a world with some residual sensitivity to myth, we should exult over the richness of the symbol: the loved body is immortalized by the mediation of a precious metal, silver (monument and luxury); to which we might add the notion that this metal, like all the metals of Alchemy, is alive.

Perhaps it is because I am delighted (or depressed) to know that the thing of the past, by its immediate radiations (its luminances), has really touched the surface which in its turn my gaze will touch, that I am not very fond of Color. An anonymous daguerreotype of 1843 shows a man and a woman in a medallion subsequently tinted by the miniaturists on the staff of the photographic studio: I always feel (unimportant what actually occurs) that in the same way, color is a coating applied *later on* to the original truth of the black-and-white photograph. For me, color is an artifice, a cosmetic (like the kind used to paint corpses). What matters to me is not the photograph's "life" (a purely ideological notion) but the certainty that the photographed body touches me with its own rays and not with a superadded light.

(Hence the Winter Garden Photograph, however pale, is for me the treasury of rays which emanated from my mother as a child, from her hair, her skin, her dress, her gaze, *on that day*.)

35. The Photograph does not call up the past (nothing Proustian in a photograph). The effect it produces upon me is not to restore what has been abolished (by time, by distance) but to attest that what I see has indeed existed. Now, this is a strictly scandalous effect. Always the Photograph *astonishes* me, with an astonishment which endures and renews itself, inexhaustibly. Perhaps this astonishment, this persistence reaches down into the religious substance out of which I am molded; nothing for it: Photography has something to do with resurrection: might we not say of it what the Byzantines said of the image of Christ which impregnated St. Veronica's napkin: that it was not made by the hand of man, *acheiropoietos*?

Here are some Polish soldiers resting in a field (Kertész, 1915); nothing extraordinary, except this, which no realist painting would give me, that *they were there*; what I see is not a memory, an imagination, a reconstitution, a piece of Maya, such as art lavishes upon us, but reality in a past state: at once the past and the real. What the Photograph feeds my mind on (though my mind is never satiated by it), by a brief action whose shock cannot drift into reverie (this is perhaps the definition of *satori*), is the simple mystery of concomitance. An anonymous photograph represents a wedding (in England): twenty-five persons of all ages, two little girls, a baby: I read the date and I compute: 1910, so they must all be dead, except perhaps the little girls, the baby (old ladies, an old gentleman now). When I see the beach at Biarritz in 1931 (Lartigue) or the Pont des Arts in 1932 (Kertész), I say to myself: "Maybe I was there"; maybe that's me among the bathers or the pedestrians, one of those summer afternoons when I took the tram from Bayonne to go for a swim on the Grande Plage, or one of those Sunday mornings when, coming from our apartment in the Rue Jacques Callot, I crossed the bridge to go to the Temple de l'Oratoire (Christian phase of my adolescence). The date belongs to the photograph: not because it denotes a style (this does not concern me), but because it makes me lift my head, allows me to compute life, death, the inexorable extinction of the generations: it is *possible* that Ernest, a schoolboy photographed in 1931 by Kertész, is still alive today (but where? how? What a novel!). I am the reference of every photograph, and this is what generates my astonishment in addressing myself to the fundamental question: why is it that I am alive *here and now*? Of course, more than other arts, Photography offers an immediate presence to the world—a co-presence; but this presence is not only of a political order ("to participate by the image in contemporary events"), it is also of a metaphysical order. Flaubert derided (but did he really deride?) Bouvard and Pécuchet investigating the sky, the stars, time, life, infinity, etc. It is this kind of question that Photography raises for me: questions which derive from a "stupid" or simple metaphysics (it is the answers which are complicated): probably the true metaphysics.

36. The Photograph does not necessarily say *what is no longer*, but only and for certain *what has been*. This distinction is decisive. In front of a photograph, our consciousness does not necessarily take the nostalgic path of memory (how many photographs are outside of individual time), but for every photograph existing in the world, the path of certainty: the Photograph's essence is to ratify what it represents. One day I received from a photographer a picture of myself which I could not remember being taken, for all my efforts; I inspected the tie, the sweater, to discover in what circumstances I had worn them; to no avail. And yet, *because it was a photograph* I could not deny that I had been *there* (even if I did not know *where*). This distortion between certainty and oblivion gave me a kind of vertigo, something of a "detective" anguish (the theme of *Blow-Up* was not far off); I went to the photographer's show as to a police investigation, to learn at last what I no longer knew about myself.

No writing can give me this certainty. It is the misfortune (but also perhaps the voluptuous pleasure) of language not to be able to authenticate itself. The *noeme* of language is perhaps this impotence, or, to put it positively: language is, by nature, fictional; the attempt to render language unfictional requires an enormous apparatus of measurements: we convoke logic, or, lacking that, sworn oath; but the Photograph is indifferent to all intermediaries: it does not invent; it is authentication itself; the (rare) artifices it permits are not probative; they are, on the contrary, trick pictures: the photograph is laborious only when it fakes. It is a prophecy in reverse: like Cassandra, but eyes fixed on the past, Photography never lies: or rather, it can lie as to the meaning of the thing, being by nature *tendentious*, never as to its existence. Impotent with regard to general ideas (to fiction), its force is nonetheless superior to everything the human mind can or can have conceived to assure us of reality— but also this reality is never anything but a contingency (*"so much, no more"*).

Every photograph is a certificate of presence. This certificate is the new embarrassment which its invention has introduced into the family of images. The first photographs a man contemplated (Niepce in front of the *dinner table*, for instance) must have seemed to him to resemble exactly certain paintings (still the *camera obscura*); he *knew*, however, that he was nose-to-nose with a mutant (a Martian can resemble a man); his consciousness posited the object encountered outside of any analogy, like the ectoplasm of "what-had-been": neither image nor reality, a new being, really: a reality one can no longer touch.

Perhaps we have an invincible resistance to believing in the past, in History, except in the form of myth. The Photograph, for the first time, puts an end to this resistance: henceforth the past is as certain as the present, what we see on paper is as certain as what we touch. It is the advent of the Photograph—and not, as has been said, of the cinema—which divides the history of the world.

It is precisely because the Photograph is an anthropologically new object that it must escape, it seems to me, usual discussions of the image. It is the fashion, nowadays, among Photography's commentators (sociologists and semiologists), to seize upon a semantic relativity: no "reality" (great scorn for the "realists" who do not see that the photograph is always coded), nothing but artifice: *Thesis*, not *Physis*; the Photograph, they say, is not an *analogon* of the world; what it represents is fabricated, because the photographic optic is subject to Albertian perspective (entirely historical) and because the inscription on the picture makes a three-dimensional object into a two- dimensional effigy. This argument is futile: nothing can prevent the Photograph from being analogical; but at the same time, Photography's *noeme* has nothing to do with analogy (a feature it shares with all kinds of representations). The realists, of whom I am one and of whom I was already one when I asserted that the Photograph was an image without code—even if, obviously, certain codes do inflect our reading of it—the realists do not take the photograph for a "copy" of reality, but for an emanation of *past reality*: a *magic*, not an art. To ask whether a photograph is analogical or coded is not a good means of analysis. The important thing is that the photograph possesses an evidential force, and that its testimony bears not on the object but on time. From a phenomenological viewpoint, in the Photograph, the power of authentication exceeds the power of representation.

37. All the authors concur, Sartre says, in remarking on the poverty of the images which accompany the reading of a novel: if this novel "takes" me properly, no mental image. To reading's *Dearth-of-Image* corresponds the Photograph's *Totality-of-Image*; not only because it is already an image in itself, but because this very special image gives itself out as complete—*integral*, we might say, playing on the word. The photographic image is full, crammed: no room, nothing can be added to it.

In the cinema, whose raw material is photographic, the image does not, however, have this completeness (which is fortunate for the cinema). Why? Because the photograph, taken in flux, is impelled, ceaselessly drawn toward other views; in the cinema, no doubt, there is always a photographic referent, but this referent shifts, it does not make a claim in favor of its reality, it does not protest its former existence; it does not cling to me: it is not a *specter*. Like the real world, the filmic world is sustained by the presumption that, as Husserl says, "the experience will constantly continue to flow by in the same constitutive style"; but the Photograph breaks the "constitutive style" (this is its astonishment); it is *without future* (this is its pathos, its melancholy); in it, no protensity, whereas the cinema is protensive, hence in no way melancholic (what is it, then? —It is, then, simply "normal," like life). Motionless, the Photograph flows back from presentation to retention.

I can put this another way. Here again is the Winter Garden Photograph. I am alone with it, in front of it. The circle is closed, there is no escape. I suffer, motionless. Cruel, sterile deficiency: I cannot *transform* my grief, I cannot let my gaze drift; no culture will help me utter this suffering which I experience entirely on the level of the image's finitude (this is why, despite its codes, I cannot *read* a photograph): the Photograph—my Photograph—is without culture: when it is painful, nothing in it can transform grief into mourning. And if dialectic is that thought which masters the corruptible and converts the negation of death into the power to work, then the photograph is undialectical: it is a denatured theater where death cannot "be contemplated," reflected and interiorized; or again: the dead theater of Death, the foreclosure of the Tragic, excludes all purification, all *catharsis*. I may well worship an Image, a Painting, a Statue, but a photograph? I cannot place it in a ritual (on my desk, in an album) unless, somehow, I avoid looking at it (or avoid its looking at me), deliberately disappointing its unendurable plenitude and, by my very inattention, attaching it to an entirely different class of fetishes: the icons which are kissed in the Greek churches without being seen—on their shiny glass surface.

In the Photograph, Time's immobilization assumes only an excessive, monstrous mode: Time is engorged (whence the relation with the *Tableau Vivant*, whose mythic prototype is the princess falling asleep in *Sleeping Beauty*). That the Photograph is "modern," mingled with our noisiest everyday life, does not keep it from having an enigmatic point of inactuality, a strange stasis, the stasis of an *arrest* (I have read that the inhabitants of the village of Montiel, in the province of Albacete, lived this way, fixated on a time arrested in the past, even while reading newspapers and listening to the radio). Not only is the Photograph never, in essence, a memory (whose grammatical expression would be the perfect tense, whereas the tense of the Photograph is the aorist), but it actually blocks memory, quickly becomes a counter-memory. One day, some friends were talking about their childhood memories; they had any number; but I, who had just been looking at my old photographs, had none left. Surrounded by these photographs, I could no longer console myself with Rilke's line: "Sweet as memory, the mimosas steep the bedroom": the Photograph does not "steep" the bedroom: no odor, no music, nothing but the *exorbitant thing*. The Photograph is violent: not because it shows violent things, but because on each occasion *it fills the sight by force*, and because in it nothing can be refused or transformed (that we can sometimes call it mild does not contradict its violence: many say that sugar is mild, but to me sugar is violent, and I call it so).

38. All those young photographers who are at work in

the world, determined upon the capture of actuality, do not know that they are agents of Death. This is the way in which our time assumes Death: with the denying alibi of the distractedly "alive," of which the Photographer is in a sense the professional. For Photography must have some historical relation with what Edgar Morin calls the "crisis of death" beginning in the second half of the nineteenth century; for my part I should prefer that instead of constantly relocating the advent of Photography in its social and economic context, we should also inquire as to the anthropological place of Death and of the new image. For Death must be somewhere in a society; if it is no longer (or less intensely) in religion, it must be elsewhere; perhaps in this image which produces Death while trying to preserve life. Contemporary with the withdrawal of rites, Photography may correspond to the intrusion, in our modern society, of an asymbolic Death, outside of religion, outside of ritual, a kind of abrupt dive into literal Death. *Life / Death*: the paradigm is reduced to a simple click, the one separating the initial pose from the final print.

With the Photograph, we enter into *flat Death*. One day, leaving one of my classes, someone said to me with disdain: "You talk about Death very flatly."—As if the horror of Death were not precisely its platitude! The horror is this: nothing to say about the death of one whom I love most, nothing to say about her photograph, which I contemplate without ever being able to get to the heart of it, to transform it. The only "thought" I can have is that at the end of this first death, my own death is inscribed; between the two, nothing more than waiting; I have no other resource than this *irony*: to speak of the "nothing to say."

The only way I can transform the Photograph is into refuse: either the drawer or the wastebasket. Not only does it commonly have the fate of paper (perishable), but even if it is attached to more lasting supports, it is still mortal: like a living organism, it is born on the level of the sprouting silver grains, it flourishes a moment, then ages . . . Attacked by light, by humidity, it fades, weakens, vanishes; there is nothing left to do but throw it away. Earlier societies managed so that memory, the substitute for life, was eternal and that at least the thing which spoke Death should itself be immortal: this was the Monument. But by making the (mortal) Photograph into the general and somehow natural witness of "what has been," modern society has renounced the Monument. A paradox: the same century invented History and Photography. But History is a memory fabricated according to positive formulas, a pure intellectual discourse which abolishes mythic Time; and the Photograph is a certain but fugitive testimony; so that everything, today, prepares our race for this impotence: to be no longer able to conceive *duration*, affectively or symbolically: the age of the Photograph is also the age of revolutions, contestations, assassinations, explosions, in short, of impatiences, of everything which denies ripening. —And no doubt, the astonishment of "*that-has-been*" will also disappear. It has already disappeared: I am, I don't know why, one of its last witnesses (a witness of the Inactual), and this book is its archaic trace.

What is it that will be done away with, along with this photograph which yellows, fades, and will someday be thrown out, if not by me—too superstitious for that—at least when I die? Not only "life" (this was alive, this posed live in front of the lens), but also, sometimes—how to put it?—love. In front of the only photograph in which I find my father and mother together, this couple who I know loved each other, I realize: it is love-as-treasure which is going to disappear forever; for once I am gone, no one will any longer be able to testify to this: nothing will remain but an indifferent Nature. This is a laceration so intense, so intolerable, that alone against his century, Michelet conceived of History as love's Protest: to perpetuate not only life but also what he called, in his vocabulary so outdated today, the Good, Justice, Unity, etc.

Allegorical Procedures: Appropriation and Montage in Contemporary Art

Benjamin H. D. Buchloh

1982

From the very moment of its inception, it seems that the inventors of the strategy of montage [1] were aware of its inherently allegorical nature: "to speak publicly with hidden meaning," in response to the prohibition of public speech. George Grosz reminisces as follows:

> "In 1916, when Johnny Heartfield and I invented photomontage... we had no idea of the immense possibilities or of the thorny but successful career that awaited the new invention. On a piece of cardboard, we pasted a mishmash of advertisements for hernia belts, student songbooks, and dogfood, labels from Schnapps and wine bottles and photographs from picture papers, cut up at will, in such a way as to say in pictures, what would have been banned by the censors if we had said it in words."[2]

In a highly condensed form, Grosz charts the terrain of montage as well as its allegorical methods of confiscation, superimposition, and fragmentation. He outlines its materials as much as he points to the dialectic of montage esthetics: to range from a meditative contemplation of reification to a powerful propaganda tool for mass agitation. Historically, this can be seen as being embodied in, for example, the opposition between the collage work of Kurt Schwitters and the montage work of John Heartfield.

The inventors of collage/montage techniques understood that they performed operations on the pictorial or poetical signifying practice that ranged from the most subtle and minute interference in linguistic and representational functions, to the most explicitly and powerfully programmatic propaganda activities. This is apparent, for example, in Raoul Hausmann's recollections of 1931 of the development from phonetic Dada poems to the political polemics of the Berlin Dada group:

> "In the conflict of opinions people often argue that photo-montage is only possible in two ways: one being the political, the other being the commercial. ... The Dadaists, after having "invented" the static, the simultaneous and the purely phonetic poem, now applied the same principles with consequence to pictorial representation. In the medium of photography they were the first to create from structural elements of often very heterogeneous material or locales a new unity that tore a visually and cognitively new mirror image from the period of chaos in war and revolution; and they knew that their method had an inherent propagandistic power that contemporary life was not courageous enough to absorb and to develop."[3]

The dialectical potential of the montage technique that Hausmann refers to found its historical fulfillment in the contradiction that is exemplified on the one hand by the increasing psychological interiorization and estheticization of collage and montage techniques in Surrealism (and their subsequent, still continuing exploitation in advertising and product propaganda), and on the other hand by the historically simultaneous development of revolutionary montage and agitprop practices in the work of El Lissitzky, Alexander Rodchenko, and Heartfield, and the almost complete disappearance of these practices' public social function from history, except for the isolated pursuits of the contemporary avant-garde.

Parallel with the emergence of montage techniques in literature, film, and the visual arts, we witness the development of a theory of montage in the writings of numerous authors since the late 1910s: Sergei Eisenstein, Lev Kuleshov, and Sergei Tretiakov in the Soviet Union; Bertolt Brecht, Heartfield, and Walter Benjamin in Weimar Germany; and later, Louis Aragon in France. It is the theory of montage as it is developed in the later writings of Walter Benjamin, in close association with his theories on allegorical

1 The introduction of this essay follows partially an argument that has been developed in Ansgar Hitlach's attempt to define a notion of montage in The avant-garde of the '20s and its relationship to Walter Benjamin's concept of allegory. See: Ansgar Hillach, "Allegorie. Bildraum, Montage," in *Theorie der Avantgarde,* (Frankfurt: Edition Suhrkamp, 1976), 105-142. For a more specific analysis of the complexities and historical changes to Benjamin's allegory-model, I would refer to Harald Steinhagen, "Zu Walter Benjamin's Begriff der Allegorie," in *Form und Funktionen der AJlegorie,* (Stuttgart: Metzler, 1979), 666 ff, and Jürgen Naeher, *Walter Benjamin's Allegorie· Begriff als Modell,* (Frankfurt: Klelt-Cotta, 1975). [...]

2 George *Grosz,* quoted in Hans Richter, *Dada: Kunst und Antikunst,* (Cologne: Dumont, 1963). English translation from Dawn Ades, *Photomontage,* (N.Y.: Phaidon, 1976), 10.

3 Raoul Hausmann "Fotomontage," in: *A.Z.* No. 16, (Cologne, May 1931). Reprinted in *Raoul Hausmann*, exhibition catalogue: (Hannover: Kestnergesellschaft, 1981), 51 ff (my translation).

procedures in Modernist art, that is of significance if one wants to arrive at a more adequate reading of the importance of certain aspects of contemporary montage, its historical models, and the meaning of *their* transformations in contemporary art.

In his analysis of the historical conditions that generated allegorical practices in European Baroque literature, Benjamin suggests that the rigid immanence of the Baroque—its worldly orientation—leads to the toss of an anticipatory, utopian sense of historical time and results in a static, almost spatially conceivable experience of time. The desire to act and produce, and the idea of political practice, recede behind a generally dominant attitude of melancholic contemptation. Similar to the general perception of the world's perishable nature during the Baroque, the world of material objects is perceived as being invalid with the transformation of objects into commodities, a transformation which occurred with the general introduction of the capitalist mode of production. This devaluation of objects, their split into use value and exchange value and the fact that they ultimately function exclusively as producers of exchange value, profoundly affects the experience of the individual.

It is in his later writings, especially in the "fragments" on Baudelaire, that Benjamin developed a theory of allegory and montage based on the structure of the commodity fetish as Marx discussed it. Benjamin planned to write a chapter in the Baudelaire study entitled "The Commodity as Poetical Object," and in one of the fragments there is an almost programmatic description of collage/montage esthetics: "The devaluation of objects in allegory is surpassed in the world of objects itself by the commodity. The emblems return as commodities.[4] By the *time* this was written the perception of commodities as emblems had already occurred in Marcel Duchamp's Ready-mades and in the main body of Schwitters' collage work, where language and image, taken into the service of the commodity by advertising, were allegorized by the montage techniques of juxtaposing and fragmenting depleted signifiers.[5]

The allegorical mind sides with the object and protests against its devaluation to the status of a commodity by devaluating it a second time in allegorical practice. In the splintering of signifier and *signified*, the allegorist subjects the sign to the same division of functions that the object has undergone in its transformation into a commodity. The repetition of the original act of depletion and the new attribution of meaning redeems the object. In the scriptural element of writing, where language is simultaneously incorporated into a spatial configuration, the allegorist perceives the essential site of his or her procedure: the Dadaist poet depletes words, syllables, and sounds of all traditional semantic functions and references until they become visual and concrete. Their dialectical complement is the liberated phonetic dimension of language in the Dada sound poem. where expression is freed from the spatial image of language, and the usages of imposed meaning. The procedure of montage is one in which all allegorical principles are executed: appropriation and depletion of meaning, fragmentation and dialectical juxtaposition of fragments, and separation of signifier and signified. In fact, the following statement from Benjamin's Baudelaire fragments reads like an exact description of the montage/collage procedures: "The allegorical mind arbitrarily selects from the vast and disordered material that its knowledge has to offer. It tries to match one piece with another to figure out whether they can be combined. This meaning with that image, or that image with this meaning. The result is never predictable since there is no organic mediation between the two."[6]

Benjamin's theory of montage ultimately outlines a historical critique of perception. The beginning of the Modernist avant-garde comes at the historical turning point where, under the impact of the rising participation of the masses in collective production, the traditional models that had served in the character formation of the bourgeois individual were rejected in favor of models that acknowledged the social facts of a historical situation where the sense of equality had increased to such a degree that equality was gained even from the unique, by means of reproduction. This perceptual change denied unique qualification and it dismantled by implication the hierarchical ordering system of the bourgeois character structure. This transformation of the individual psyche as well as that of larger social structures was anticipated in the new techniques and strategies of montage, in which a new tactility established a new physiology of perception.

The transformation of the commodity to emblem—a phenomenon Benjamin observed in the poetry of Baudelaire—came full circle in the Ready-mades of Duchamp, where the willful declaration of the unaltered object as meaningful and the act of its appropriation

4 Walter Benjamin, "Zentralpark" in *Gesammelte Schriften*. Vol. 1.2, (Frankfurt: Suhrkamp, 1974). 660 (my translation).

5 The spatialization of time and the adoption of a contemplative stance towards the world that Benjamin discussed in 1925 as the experiential conditions of allegory in the European Baroque, were discussed in 1928 by Georg Lukacs as the essential features of the collective condition of reification. [...] Georg Lukacs, "Reification and the Consciousness of the Proletariat," in *History and Class Consciousness*, (Cambridge, MA: MIT Press, 1971), 89.

6 Benjamin, "Zentralpark," 681. The famous anecdote in which Kurt Schwitters described the origin of the term "Merz" as a result of his encounter with an advertising for the "Kommerzbank" contains equally *in nuce* all the essential features of the allegorical procedure: fragmentation and depletion of conventional meaning are followed by acts of willful meaning-assignment which generate the poetical experience of primary linguistic processes.

allegorized creation by bracketing it with the anonymous mass-produced object. With Duchamp's Ready-mades it seems that the traditional separation of the pictorial or sculptural construct into procedures and materials of construction, a pictorial signifier, and a signified does not occur—rather, all three coalesce in the allegorical gesture of appropriating the object and of negating the actual construction of the sign. At the same time, this emphasis on the manufactured signifier and its mute existence makes apparent the hidden factors determining the work and the conditions under which it is perceived. These range from presentational devices and the institutional framework to the conventions of meaning-assignment within art itself. It seems that what Yve-Alain Bois recently observed in regard to Robert Ryman's paintings is only half the truth in Duchamp's work: "...the narrative of process establishes a primary meaning, an ultimate originating referent that cuts off the interpretive chain."[7]

Duchamp's *L.H.O.O.Q.*, 1919, must be recalled in order to discuss another dimension of the Dadaists' montage operations: the principle of appropriation. In his appropriation of a mass-reproduced icon of cultural history, Leonardo's *Mona Lisa,* Duchamp subjected the printed image to the essentially allegorical procedures of confiscation and inscribed it in a textual configuration that came alive as text only in its phonetic performance. The mechanically reproduced image of the once-unique auratic work functions as the ideological complement to the manufactured commodity that the Ready-made frames in its allegorical schema.

As is well known, beginning in the late '50s and throughout the development of Pop art, commodity images and objects were juxtaposed or run parallel with mechanically reproduced high-cultural icons in the work of Robert Rauschenberg, Andy Warhol, and Roy Lichtenstein. Duchamp's inverted Ready-made, *Rembrandt* as *Ironing Board,* 1919, which proposed the transformation of an actual cultural icon into an object of use value, found less of a following since it went beyond the culturally accepted limits of iconoclasm. Not since the '20s has the desire for use value in art resurfaced, most likely because it was submerged under pictorial exchange value.

In 1953 Rauschenberg obtained a drawing from Willem de Kooning after informing him of his intention to erase the drawing and make it the subject of a work of his own. After the careful execution of the erasure, which left vestiges of pencil and the imprint of the drawn lines visible as clues of visual recognizability, the drawing was framed in a gold frame. An engraved metal label attached to the frame identified the drawing as a work by Robert Rauschenberg entitled *Erased de Kooning Drawing* and dated 1953. At the climax of the Abstract Expressionist idiom and its reign in the art world this may have been perceived as a sublimated patricidal assault by the new generation's most advanced artist, but it now appears to have been one of the first examples of allegorization in post-New York School art. It can be recognized as such in its procedures of appropriation, the depletion of the confiscated image, the superimposition or doubling of a visual text by a second text, and the shift of attention and reading to the framing device. Rauschenberg's appropriation confronts two paradigms of drawing: that of de Kooning's denotative lines, and that of the indexical functions of the erasure. Production procedure (gesture), expression, and sign (representation) seem to have become materially and semantically congruent. Where perceptual data are withheld or removed from the traditional surface of display, the gesture of erasure shifts the focus of attention to the appropriated historical construct on the one hand, and to the devices of framing and presentation, on the other.

A second, equally conspicuous example, Jasper Johns' *Flag,* 1955, not only indicated the beginning of Duchamp's reception in American art, and thus the beginning of Pop art, but more precisely the painting constituted the introduction of a pictorial method that had previously been unknown to New York School painting: the appropriation of an object/image whose structural, compositional, and chromatic aspects determined the decision-making process of the painter during the execution of the painting. The rigid iconic structure functions like a template or framing device which brackets two apparently exclusive discourses, high art and mass culture, yet the junction paradoxically reveals the gap between them all the more. In Duchamp's Ready-mades, the choice of the everyday object remains random and arbitrary. It could almost be argued that to the *degree* that the Ready-mades and the work emerging from them in American Pop art address mass culture and mechanically reproduced imagery as abstract universal conditions, to the same degree does this work fail to clarify the specific conditions of its own framing and the conditions of its reification as art within the institutional framework of the museum, the ideology of Modernism, and the distribution form of the commodity. Well-balanced and well-tempered modes of appropriation, and the successful synthesis of relative radicality and relative conventionality, from the mid-'50s on, demarcate the position of American Pop art. This program has always been one of liberal reconciliation and successful mastery of the conflict between individual practice and collective production, between the mass-produced imagery of low culture and the icon of individuation that each painting constitutes.

Here lies the source of Pop art's social success, and the secret behind the present rediscovery and glorified

7 Yve-Alain Bois, "Ryman's Tact," *October,* No. 19 (Winter 1981), 94.

institutionalization of painting under the auspices of a rediscovered and redefined Pop art legacy. If read against the historical moment which was dominated by Abstract Expressionist esthetics and ideology, Rauschenberg's Factum *I* and *Factum II,* both 1957, and Johns' first *Flag,* might appear to be scandalous representations of rigidity in their denial of the validity of individual expression and creative authorship. They are, however, delicate constructs of compromise, refining gestural definition and juxtaposing individualized painterly craftsmanship with seemingly anonymous mechanicity, compared to the radical epistemological crudity and seemingly inexhaustible shock of the three-dimensional, unaltered Ready-made.

It could easily turn out to be one of the great ironies of history that a moment of radical truth was contained in Clement Greenberg's conservative formalism after all. He refrained from acknowledging the impact of Duchamp's work—and of the work of the Pop artists, for that matter—because it lacked, as he perceived it, the specific self-referentiality that could purify and verify itself in regard to all conditions of its making and position. This empirical/critical position at least did not fall for the premature delusion of an immediate reconciliation between high art and mass culture, as was implicit in the work of Duchamp's followers. It is not until two generations later, in the mid-'60s, that work emerges that, while taking both minimal and Pop strategies into account, integrates the historical ramifications of the Ready-made model and the consequences of a self-referential analysis of the pictorial construction itself. With this work we see these conflicts develop a new level of historical significance. It is in the work of artists such as Michael Asher, Marcel Broodthaers, Daniel Buren, Dan Graham, Hans Haacke, and Lawrence Weiner that we see both the beginning of an examination of the framework that determines the pictorial sign and an analysis of the structuring principles of the sign itself.

A work such as Graham's 1966 "Homes for America,"[8] conceived as an art-magazine article, becomes now fully readable as an early example of allegorical deconstruction where the framework of distribution, materiality, and place of the work's ultimate existence determine the structure of the work from its very inception. Graham's "Homes for America" focused on the contemporary framework of esthetic information, the printed magazine page, and the photo reproduction, a sort of "disposable Ready-made." The work inscribed itself into the historical context of minimal sculpture's self-referentiality, and simultaneously denied it by introducing the "content" of serialized, standardized suburban prefabricated architecture.

Independently of each other Graham and Broodthaers had both become aware of the historical consequences of the works of Stéphane Mallarmé. The linguistic and semiotic interests of the early conceptual artists led to a renewed interest in Mallarmé's investigations of the spatialization of the linear, temporal dimension of reading and writing. In his essay "The Book as Object," written and published in 1967, Graham discussed Mallarme's 1866 project for "The Book," in which the poet conceived a book whose multidimensional geometry implied a complete restructuring of reading and writing as they had been known since the invention of the printed letter.[9] In 1969 Broodthaers published his version of Mallarme's *Un coup de dés jamais n'abolira le hasard* which exercised literally all the principles of allegorical appropriation and montage as Benjamin developed them.[10] [...]

One of the first works that actually incorporated the commodity structure directly into the elements of presentation was Hans Haacke's contribution to the summer festival *"L'art vivant americain"* at the Maeght Foundation, St. Paul de Vence, France, in 1970. Haacke complied with the organizer's request to contribute to a "non-profit avant-garde festival" by linking his contribution to the concealed promotion of salable objects at the nonprofit foundation. Haacke's "performance" consisted of a tape-recorded litany of prices and descriptions of Maeght Gallery prints on sale in the bookstore of the foundation. The recording was interrupted only by news agency teletype reports read over the phone from the office of the newspaper *Nice-Matin.*

It seems that only fear of audience protest deterred the organizers from banning Haacke's work. The history of attempts by museum authorities and exhibition organizers to censor Haacke's endeavors to reintroduce repressed elements in cultural production into the official face and functioning of cultural institutions proves the truly allegorical qualities of Haacke's art. In a number of works Haacke has chosen to write art history as commodity history—most prominently in the chronology of owners of the *Asparagus Still Life* by Manet (banned from an exhibition in Cologne in 1974), and of Seurat's *Les Poseuses.* More recently he has investigated the economic practices and maneuvers of Peter Ludwig, a major cultural benefactor and collector, uncovering the actual benefits and privileges that the apparently selfless generosity of the Maecenas implies (Der *Pralinenmeister* [The Master Chocolate Maker], 1981).[11]

In an American context, two works from the late '70s must also be mentioned as prefiguring contemporary allegorical investigations: Louise Lawler's untitled 1978 installation at Artists Space in New York, which

8 Dan Graham, "Homes for America," *Arts Magazine,* (December/January, 1966–67).

9 Dan Graham, "The Book as Object," *Arts Magazine,*(June 1967).

10 Marcel Broodthaers, *Un coup de des jamais n'abolira Ie hasard*, (Antwerp: Wide White Space Gallery, 1969).

included a painting from 1824 by Henry Stullmann representing a racehorse (loaned by the New York Racing Association), and Michael Asher's contribution to the 73rd American Exhibition at the Art Institute of Chicago in 1979, which appropriated a bronze replica of Jean-Antoine Houdon's life-size marble sculpture of George Washington.[12] Due to their enigmatic procedures these works have received little critical attention, yet they both functioned as reverse historical mirrors, critically anticipating the antirational tendencies in esthetic production that are presently dominating us.[13] Lawler's installation made the elements of an exhibition the subject of her production. As her contribution to the catalogue for the exhibition she designed a logo for Artists Space, and a poster with that logo was distributed outside of the exhibition. The actual exhibition consisted of the appropriated painting which, displaced and totally out of context, functioned as an allegorical shell, the negation of a historical tendency. Two stage lights illuminated the arrangement. One confronted the viewer's eyes from above the painting (interfering with perception of the painting itself) and the other was directed through the exhibition space, out the window and onto the street, connecting the isolated exhibition space with its outside environment and bringing the exhibition to the attention of the immediate neighborhood.

It was with the work of this group of artists that questions of material definition, site (physical, social, and linguistic), and ultimately questions of mode of address and audience became essential. Anyone taking the implications of the situational esthetics developed in the late '60s and '70s into account as an irreversible change in the cognitive conditions of art production would have to realize that any return to an unconditioned autonomy of art production would be mere pretense, lacking historical logic and consequence, just as any attempt to reinstitute the conventions of representation alter Cubism is absurd. This does not imply that, for example, Lawrence Weiner's reduction of esthetic practice to its linguistic definition, Buren's and Asher's analysis of the historical place and function of esthetic constructs within institutions, or Haacke's and Broodthaers' operations revealing the material conditions of those institutions as ideological would embody positions that could not be logically continued and developed further. (The dialectical reply to these positions, of course, is not, as might currently be thought, a return to the obscurity of historically nonfunctional conventions and the commodity camouflage that they provide.)

The precision with which these artists analyzed the place and function of esthetic practice within the institutions of Modernism had to be inverted and attention paid to the ideological discourses outside of that framework, which conditioned daily reality. This paradigmatic shift occurs in the late '70s in the work of such artists as Dara Birnbaum, Jenny Holzer, Barbara Kruger, Louise Lawler, Sherrie Levine, and Martha Rosler, where the languages of television, advertising, and photography, and the ideology of "everyday" life, were subjected to formal and linguistic operations that essentially followed Roland Barthes' model of a secondary mythification that deconstructs ideology. Barthes' strategy of secondary mythification repeats the semiotic and linguistic devaluation of primary language by myth and structurally follows Benjamin's ideas on the allegorical procedure that reiterates the devaluation of the object by commodification. It seems justifiable therefore to transfer the notion of montage and allegory, as discussed above in the context of avant-garde practice of the first half of the century, and to extend its ramifications into a reading of recent and contemporary work.

The political spectrum within which these artists operate—inasmuch as it can be read in the work itself and inasmuch as it can be at all isolated from the current climate of desperation and cynicism—encompasses a variety of positions. They range from the apparently outright denial of productivity and dialectical construction in the work of Levine, to the agitprop position of Rosler's work. Holzer's anarcho-*situationniste* position trusts the strategy of an unmediated street activity in which anonymous posters generate a confrontation between language and its daily ideological performances, while Birnbaum's videotapes rely entirely upon and aim at mediation within both a high-art framework. and corporate media production.

The risk of Levine's position is that it might function ultimately in secret with the static conditions of social life as they are reflected in an art practice that is concerned only with the work's commodity structure and the innovation of its product language. Rosler's position runs the risk of ignoring the structural specificities of the work's circulation form and distribution system, and of failing to integrate her work efficiently into the reception of current art practice, when the work's actual claim is in fact radical political awareness and change. The dilemma underlying Holzer's work is that for the sake of direct action within I language, it ignores the mediating framework of the institutions within which ideology is historically

11 Haacke's work is documented in the following publications: Edward Fry, *Hans Haacke,* (Cologne: Dumont 1972); Hans Haacke, *Framing and Being Framed,* (Halifax/New York: Nova Scotia College of Art and Design Press/New York University Press, 1975); Hans Haacke, *Der Pralinenmeister,* (Cologne: Paul Maenz Gallery, 1981), English edition: (Toronto: Art Metropole, 1982).

12 See the exhibition catalogue: Christopher D'Arcangelo, Louise Lawler, Adrian Piper, Cindy Sherman, (New York: Artists Space, 1978).

13 For a notable exception, see Anne Rorimer, "Michael Asher: Recent Work," *Artforum,* (April 1980).

placed and has to support the radicality and apparent independence of that position with an increasing number of compromises to the framework that was originally dismissed. Finally, the risk for Birnbaum's work is that it could integrate itself so successfully into the advanced technology and linguistic perfection of governing television ideology that its original impulse of critical deconstruction could disappear in a perfect blending of a technocratic estheticization of art practice and the media's need to rejuvenate its looks and products by drawing from the esthetics of the avant-garde.

The inability of current art criticism to recognize the necessity and relevance of artists working within these parameters results partially from art history's almost total failure to develop an adequate reading of Dada and Productivist theory and practice, particularly of the activities of "factography" and documentary work and the range of agitprop production that emerged from it—for example, in the work of Osip Brik, Vladimir Mayakovsky, Liubov Popova, and Tretiakov, as much as the still essentially ignored key figure of montage practice, John Heartfield. Once these activities are admitted to the framework of legitimization that art history provides, their consequences for contemporary practice will become more readable.

It is furthermore not surprising that the impact of the work of the artists of the '60s and '70s on a contemporary understanding of art production and reception had hardly occurred before the need to revitalize the art market brought about a reinstitution of obsolete production procedures in the guise of a new avant-garde of painting. Simultaneously, however, a different range of esthetic positions has been developed by this new generation of artists which continues and expands one of the essential features of Modernism—its impulse to criticize itself from within, to question its institutionalization, its reception, and its audience. [...]

For the time being, at least, Sherrie Levine functions as the strongest negation within the gallery framework of the re-emergent dominance of the art commodity. Her work, melancholic and complacent in defeat, threatens within its very structure, mode of operation, and status the current reaffirmation of individual expressive creativity and its implicit reaffirmation of private property and enterprise. At a historical moment when a reactionary middle class struggles to ensure and expand its privileges, including those of cultural hegemony and legitimization, and when hundreds of talents in painting obediently provide gestures of free expression with the cynical alibi of irony, Levine's work places itself consistently against the construction of the spectacle of individuality. Continuing and readjusting a position defined by Duchamp and updated by Warhol, her allegorical appropriations prove that Baudelaire was wrong when he argued that the poetical was necessarily alien to female nature since melancholy was outside the female emotional experience. Enter the female dandy, whose disdain has been sharpened by the experience of phallocratic oppression, and whose sense of resistance to domination is therefore more acute than that of her male colleagues, if they still exist.

In the current historical situation artists adopt the psychosexual standards of obsolete role models and provide products for the market, but fail to change aesthetic practice, However, by transcending character formation, commodity form, and institutionalization through the redefinition of esthetic practice, they may fail to enter public awareness since they do not fulfill the public's expectations, and do not abide by the rules of culturally acceptable deviation. Contemporary male avant-garde models, in particular, seem to imply a return to obsolete notions of culture in order to "...exemplify an attitude within which the bourgeois world can first and, foremost find its identity, that of the enchanted consumer...By doing so the ideological condition of the *posthistoire* which late capitalism claims for itself, would equally be reaffirmed by art practice."[14] No wonder, then, that strategies of allegory and montage which once dislocated and decentralized the hierarchical subject, generating participation in the tactility of the particularized fragment and rupturing the contemplative stance of the viewer, now return in painting, reconciled and thwarted, as abused gadgets of a decoration that offers empty codes and strategies for sale.

Strategies of fragmentation in contemporary painting seem to have sunk literally to the level of household goods. What was once, in the work of Antonio Gaudi and Simon Rodia, an index of the collective participation in everyday life of the oppressed and exploited, and which therefore rightfully entered the language of architecture as ornament in Gaudi's and Rodia's visionary constructions, has now been reduced to the level of gewgaws in paintings for a clientele whose vision is limited to the index of the commodity market.

By contrast, the, contemporary montage work of Asher, Birnbaum, Levine, and Rosler uses methods of appropriation and montage conclusively and explicitly without estheticizing them in a historicist conceit that functions as an auratic disguise of the commodity. We can find strategies and procedures of quotation and appropriation in contemporary painting, but the very mode of painting provides an experience of reconciliation.

In contemporary paintings the ultimate subject is always a centralized author, whereas in contemporary montage procedures the subject is the reader/viewer.

14 Annegret Jürgens-Kirchhoff, *Technik und Tendenz der Montage,* (Glessen: Anabas Verlag, 1978), 191.

Even the "conspicuous" delegation of certain painterly tasks of figurative representation to anonymous commercial experts or professionals, who draw bunnies or bombers, does not resolve the historical limitations of this production procedure and its incapacity to develop an adequate viewer-text relationship.

It is in the critical analysis of the actual procedures and materials of production and reception that a work's historical legitimacy will be evident. In expanding the spacing of elements, singularizing the elements of appropriation, and redirecting the viewing/reading to the frame, the new montage work decentralizes the place of the author and subject by remaining within the dialectic of the appropriated objects of discourse and the authorial subject, which negates and constitutes itself simultaneously in the act of quotation.[15]

To the degree that the various sources and authors of quoted "texts" are left intact and fully identifiable in truly contemporary montage, the viewer encounters a decentralized text that completes itself through his or her reading and comparison of the original and subsequent layers of meaning that the text/image has acquired.

Levine's notion of fragmentation differs from the phallocratic tendency which associates fragmentation with broken saucers, burnt wood, and crumpled straw. In her seemingly random selection of imagery from the history of Modernism, representations are literally fragmented, torn from the hermetic totality of the ideological discourse within which they currently exist. Thus, just as Benjamin described the allegorical procedure, Levine devalues the object of representation for the second time. She depletes the current commodity status of photographs by Walker Evans, Edward Weston, Eliot Porter, and Andreas Feininger for the second time by her willful act of rephotography, by restating their essential status as multiplied, technically reproduced imagery.

Levine's apparently radical denial of authorship might fail to recognize the socially acceptable, if not desirable, features it implies: a reaffirmation of the dismantling of the individual, and a silent complacency in the face of the static conditions of reified existence. The faint historical spaces the work establishes between the original and the reproduction seduce the viewer into fatalistic acceptance, since these spaces do not open up a dimension of critical negativity that would imply practice and encounter rather than contemplation. This is one essential difference between Levine's position and that of Martha Rosler; it is evident in their differing attitudes toward the notion of historical authenticity and the material, i.e., social truth of their objects of appropriation. In true allegorical fashion Levine subjects historical objects to an act of confiscation where their innate authenticity, historical function, and meaning is robbed for the second time. Levine's attitude embodies the ambivalence of the artist and intellectual who lacks class identity and political perspective, exerting a certain fascination over those contemporary critics, including myself, who are equally ambivalent toward their affiliations with the powers and privileges that the white middle class provides. This attitude is evidenced in the following statement by Levine:

> "Instead of taking photographs of trees or nudes, I take photographs of photographs. I choose pictures that manifest the desire that nature and culture provide us with a sense of order and meaning. I appropriate these images to express my own simultaneous longing for the passion of engagement and the sublimity of aloofness. I hope that in my photographs of photographs an uneasy peace will be made between my attraction to the ideals these pictures exemplify and my desire to have no ideals or fetters whatsoever. It is my aspiration that my photographs, which contain their own contradiction, would represent the best of both worlds."[16]

Walter Benjamin, in spite of his devotion to the allegorical theory and its concrete implementation in the work of Baudelaire and the montage work of the '20s, was aware of the inherent danger of melancholic complacency and of the violence of the passive denial that the allegorical subject imposes upon itself as well as upon the objects of its choice. The contemplative stance of the melancholic subject, the "comfortable view of the past," he argued, must be ex- changed for the political view of the present.[17] This view was developed in "The Author as Producer,"a text in which all reflection upon allegorical procedures has been abandoned and in which he comes closest to the development of a factographic, Productivist position, as it was outlined in the writings of Brik and Tretiakov.[18]

According to Benjamin the new author must first of all address the Modernist framework of isolated producers and try to change the artist's position from that of a caterer of esthetic goods to that of an active force in the transformation of the existing ideological and cultural apparatus. This essentially different position is evident in Martha Rosler's approach toward historical objects and the photographic conventions they embody. Two works that suggest a comparative reading with Levine's work are *The Bowery in* two

15 The notion of "spacing" as a linguistic function has recently been introduced into the discussion of collage/montage esthetics of the '20s. See Rosalind E. Krauss, "The Photographic Conditions of Surrealism," *October* No. 19, (Winter 1981).

16 Sherrie Levine, unpublished, undated statement, ca. 1980.

17 Walter Benjamin, *Angelus Novus,* (Frankfurt:Suhrkamp,1966), 204.

18 Walter Benjamin, "The Author as Producer," in *The Frankfurt School Reader*, (New York: Urizen Press,1978).

inadequate descriptive systems, 1974–75, and the critical essay/piece "in, around, and afterthoughts (on documentary photography)."[19] In both works photographic conventions are addressed as a linguistic practice, whose historical position is evaluated in its varying affiliations with general social and political life, rather than with the criteria of neutrality that the program of photographic Modernism prescribes.

In *The Bowery in two inadequate descriptive systems*, a photo-text work which includes black and white photographs of Bowery store fronts and photographs of word-lists describing drunkenness, conventions of urban architectural photography are appropriated in restaged photographs that loosely seem to take the photographic stance of Walker Evans. However, these conventions are executed by Rosler rather than simply confiscated, as is the case with Levine. Rosler's crude attempts to try her photographic hand at mimicking the great urban "documentarians" style is of course as thoroughly disappointing to the cultivated photographic eye as Levine's photographs are to the collector's hand.

Rosler describes *The Bowery*...in explicitly allegorical terminology:

> "In *The Bowery* the photographs are empty and the words are full of imagery and incident....A lot of photographers made pictures of Bowery bums. That upset me because I thought it was a false endeavor, that it involved a pretense that such photos were about the people when they were really about the sensibility of the photographers and the viewers. It's an illicit exchange about compassion and feeling and the bums are victims of this exchange between the photographer and the viewer. They provide the raw materials for a confirmation of class and privilege....I wanted to make a point about the inadequacy of that kind of documentary by contrasting it with verbal images....I didn't want to use words to underline the truth value of the photographs, but rather words that undermined it. I felt that just as the images are expected to be poetic but aren't even "original"—they follow a tradition of street-photography and have more to do with commerce than with anything else, since they're shopfronts—the words would be a kind of unexpected poetry. Their ironic humor would cut against and be cut against by the deadpan photographs." [20]

It is not surprising that in the same interview Rosler introduces the question of a contemporary collage practice and its historical function and possibilities into the discussion of her work, and that the definitions she supplies coincide with the general outline of contemporary montage as I have tried to develop it in the course of this essay:

> "I think it's even more valid to talk about contradiction than about collage, because much of the collaging consists of contradiction, putting things together that don't go together, but that are connected in some way....Many of the contradictions I want to talk about in my work are not simple riddles of existence but things that arise from the system we live under which makes impossible and conflicting demands on us. I like to point to situations in which we can see the myths of ideology contradicted by our actual experience."

If Levine's position seems to originate from the cynical tradition of dandyism, then Rosler's seemingly naive attempt at recycling exhausted photographic conventions to clarify their historical meaning and their inadequacy for contemporary documentary production insists on maintaining an element of individual practice. In the futility of that naive attempt and in the revelation of its shortcomings she disqualifies the ahistoricity of abstracted photographic ambition all the more.

Rosler's critical writing such as "in, around, and afterthoughts (on documentary photography)" uses the format of criticism successfully to analyze the historical and political implications of contemporary photography. Here, instead of restaging photographic conventions, Rosler transforms the current interest of certain photographers who have turned back to the history of their own discipline by rephotographing "in the manner of the masters" "the subjects of the great tradition of Modernist photography") into actual confrontation with the material reality of the "subjects," i.e., the "victims" of photography. In so doing she takes away that veil of esthetic neutrality behind which photographic activity has hidden. If Levine's abstract and radical denial of production and authorship could place her ultimately on the side of the existing power structure against her wishes, then Rosler's attempt at constructing artwork outside of the existing level of esthetic reflection and formal procedures places her on the side of a political commitment which could fail precisely because of its lack of power within current art practice.

[...] While it is essential for the work of Birnbaum and Rosler to operate simultaneously inside and outside the framework of institutionalized art distribution, Levine's work functions exclusively within this framework. Only as a commodity can the work fulfill all its functions, and yet, paradoxically, for the time being it cannot be sold. Its ultimate triumph is to repeat and

19 Martha Rosler, *Three Works*, (Halifax: Nova Scotia College of Art and Design Press, 1981) / (Cambridge, MA: MIT Press), 151–206.]. [See also Martha Rosler, *Decoys and Disruptions: Selected Writings, 1975–2001*, Cambridge, MA: MIT Press, 151–206]

20 Martha Rosler, interviewed by Martha Gever in *Afterimage*, (October 1981), 15.

anticipate in a single gesture the abstraction and alienation from historical context to which work is subjected in the process of commodification and acculturation. In this respect Levine's and Birnbaum's work reveals an historical affinity with the position of Warhol, the first American dandy to systematically deny individual creation and productivity in favor of a blatant reaffirmation of the conditions of cultural reification. Warhol's curriculum ended in the institutions of fame and fashion, as de Sade ended in the Bastille. The fate of his work, which once subverted painting by precisely the same allegorical techniques of confiscating imagery, bracketing high-art and mass-cultural discourses, individual production and mechanical reproduction, was to produce the most singularized and rarefied icons of pop art.

The artists under discussion here appropriate or "pirate" the material and imagery that they use for their investigation. Like the radical conceptual artists of the late '60s, they question the necessity of their work being relegated to the status of an individualized commodity. And they have been successful in their assault, if only temporarily so—until the general acculturation process finds ways to accommodate these works or their authors find ways to accommodate their production to the conditions of the acculturation apparatus. For ultimately it is the visual, rather than textual existence of a construct that imbues it with material reality, since that reality is the basis of its existence as commodity. In *Mythologies* 1957, Roland Barthes deconstructed such contemporary myths as designed objects of consumption and advertising. In certain respects this can still be considered as the originary model for the deconstructive approach of the criticism of ideology as it has been developed in the work of the artists analyzed here. Unlike some of these artists, Barthes did not encounter problems of ownership and copyright. But the visual object/image has become the essential ideological correlate of private property.

Selections from *Travel Posters*

Barbara Bloom

1981/2009

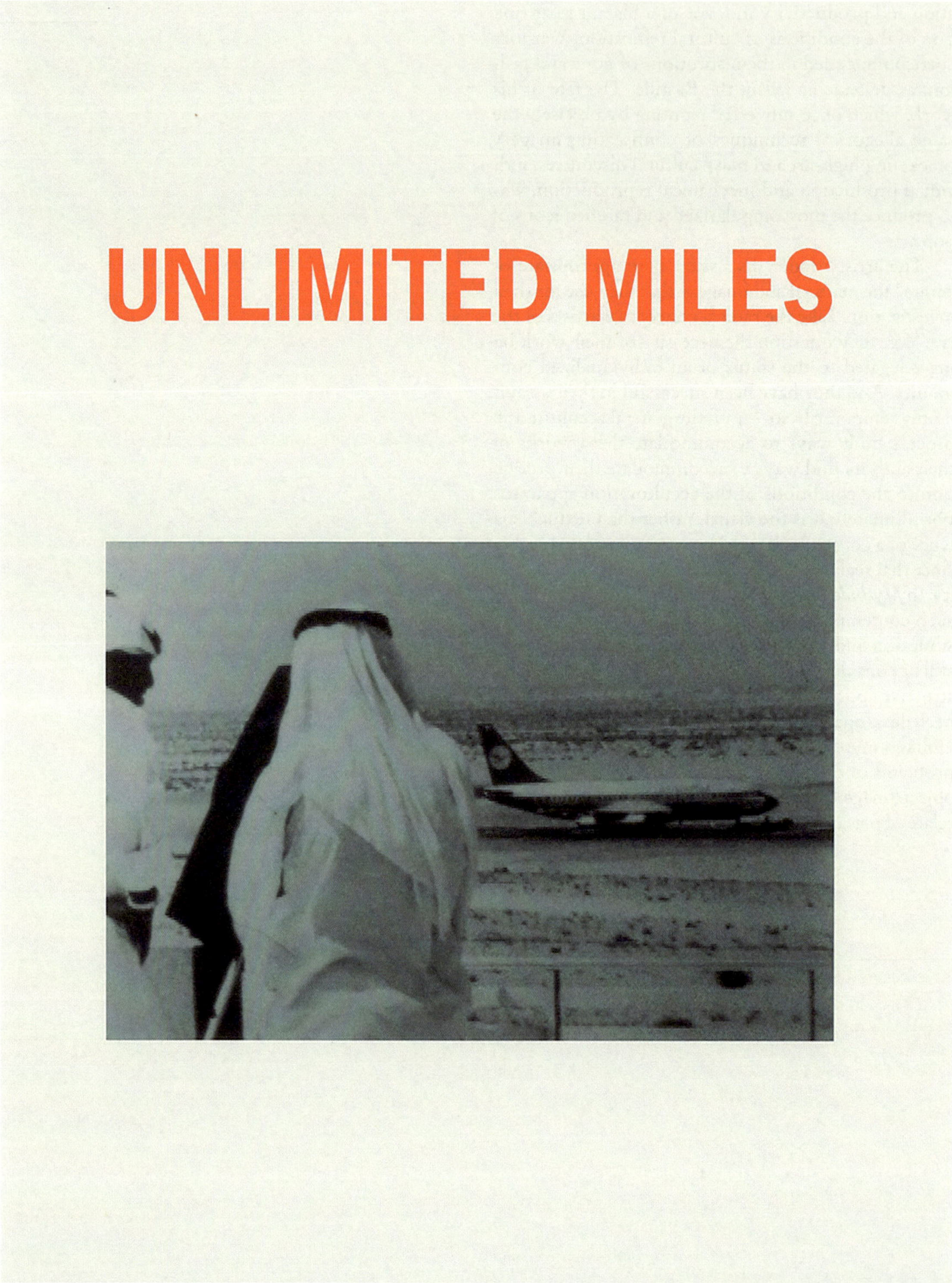

ENGLISH SPOKEN

After Walker Evans: 1–22

Sherrie Levine

1981

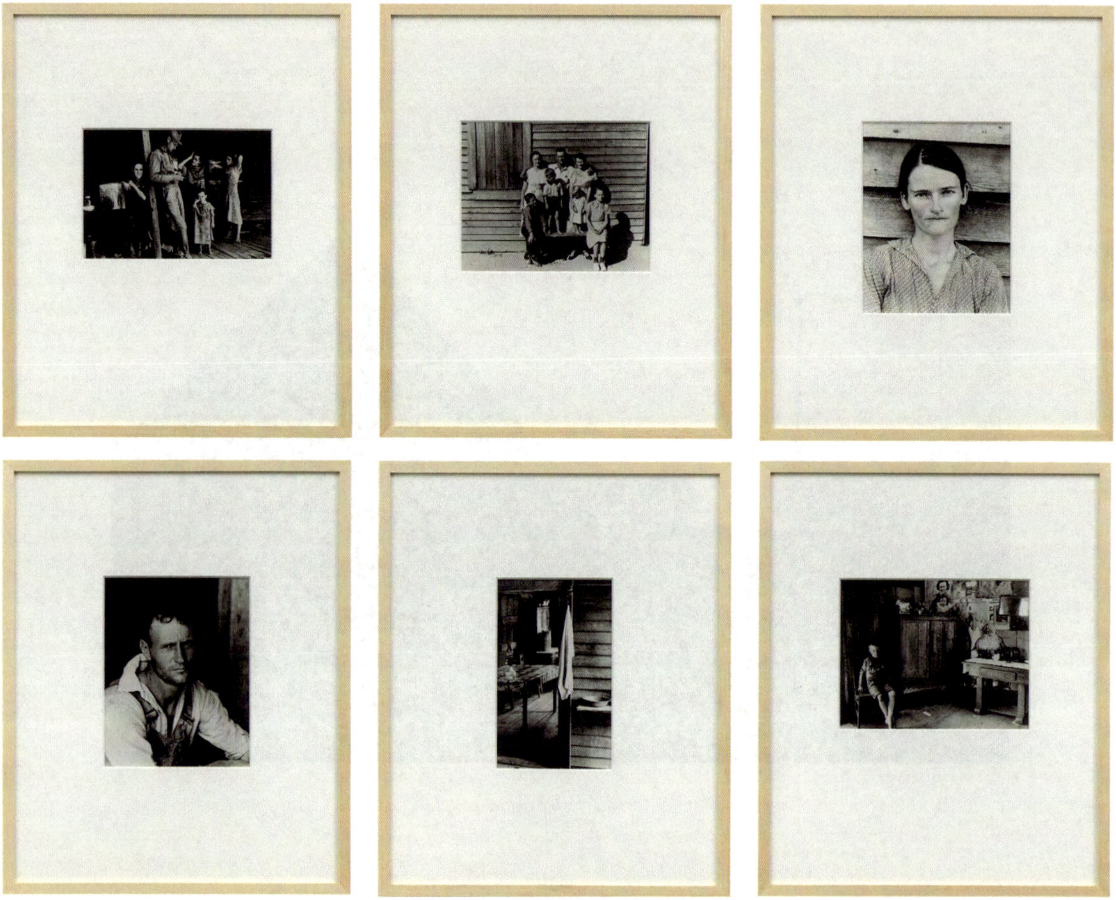

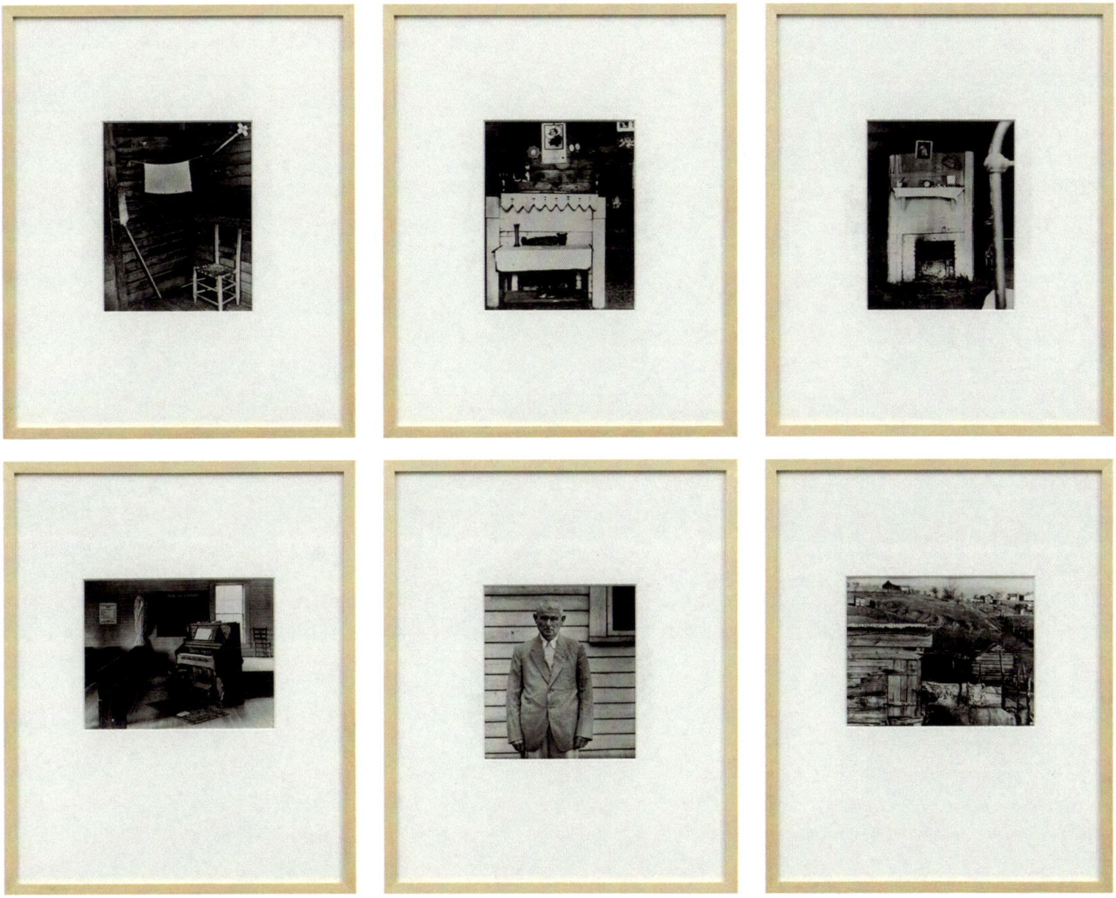

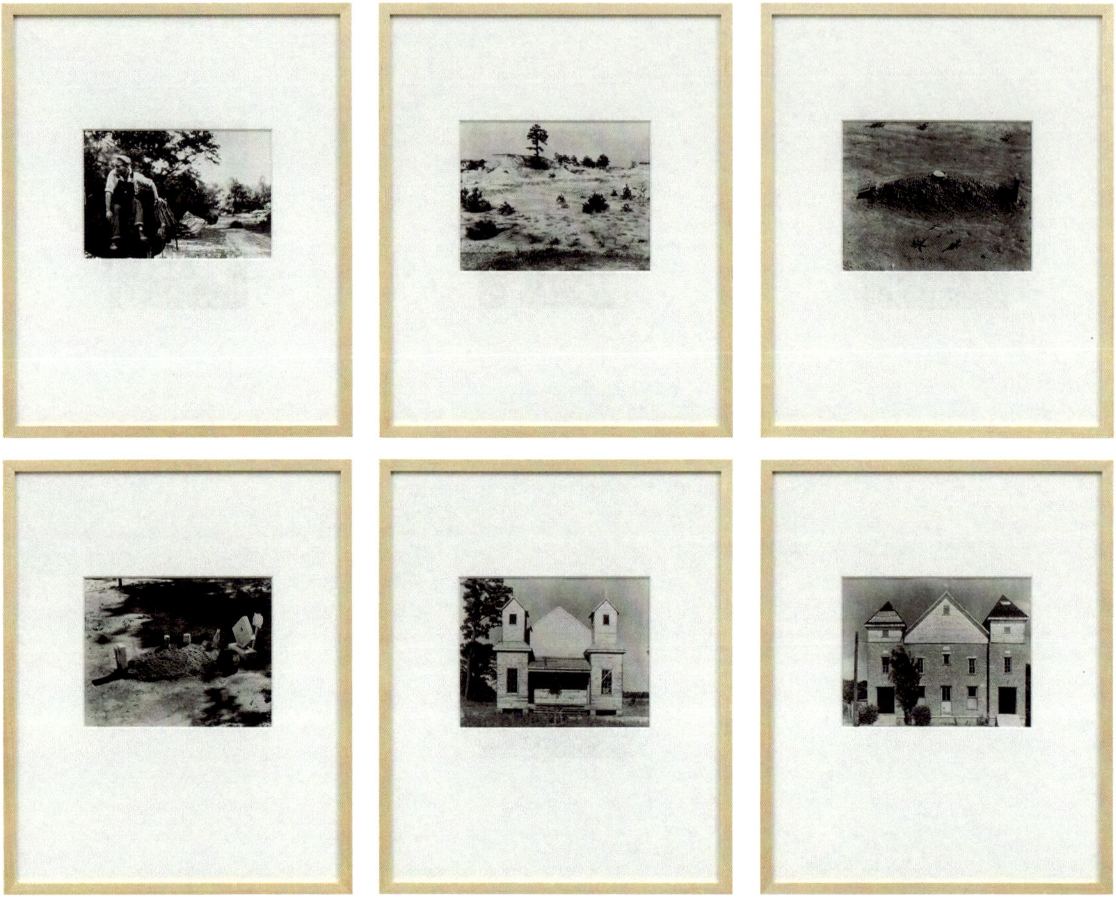

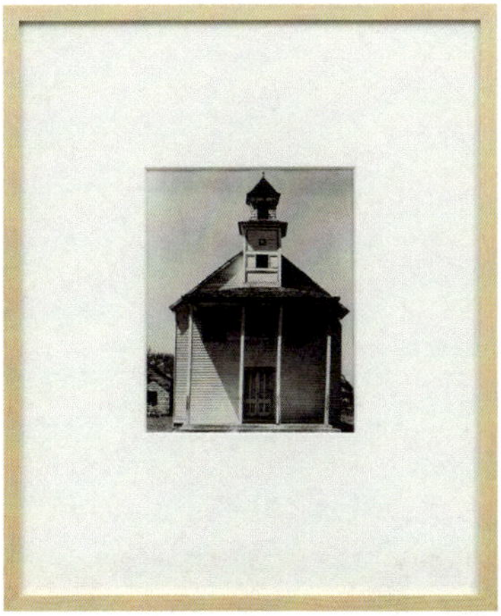

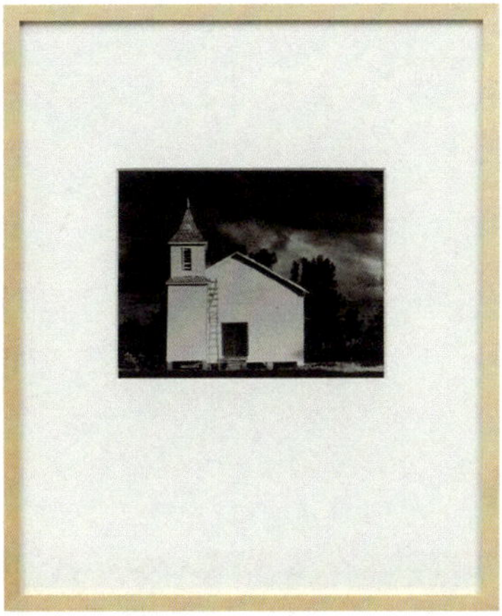

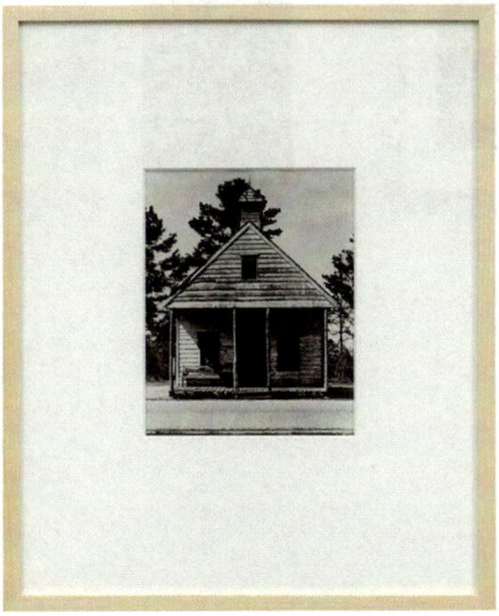

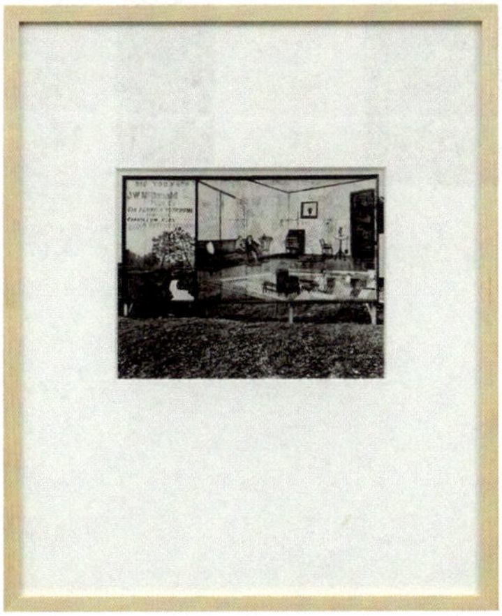

Collection of Ten Plaster Surrogates

Allan McCollum

1982/1992

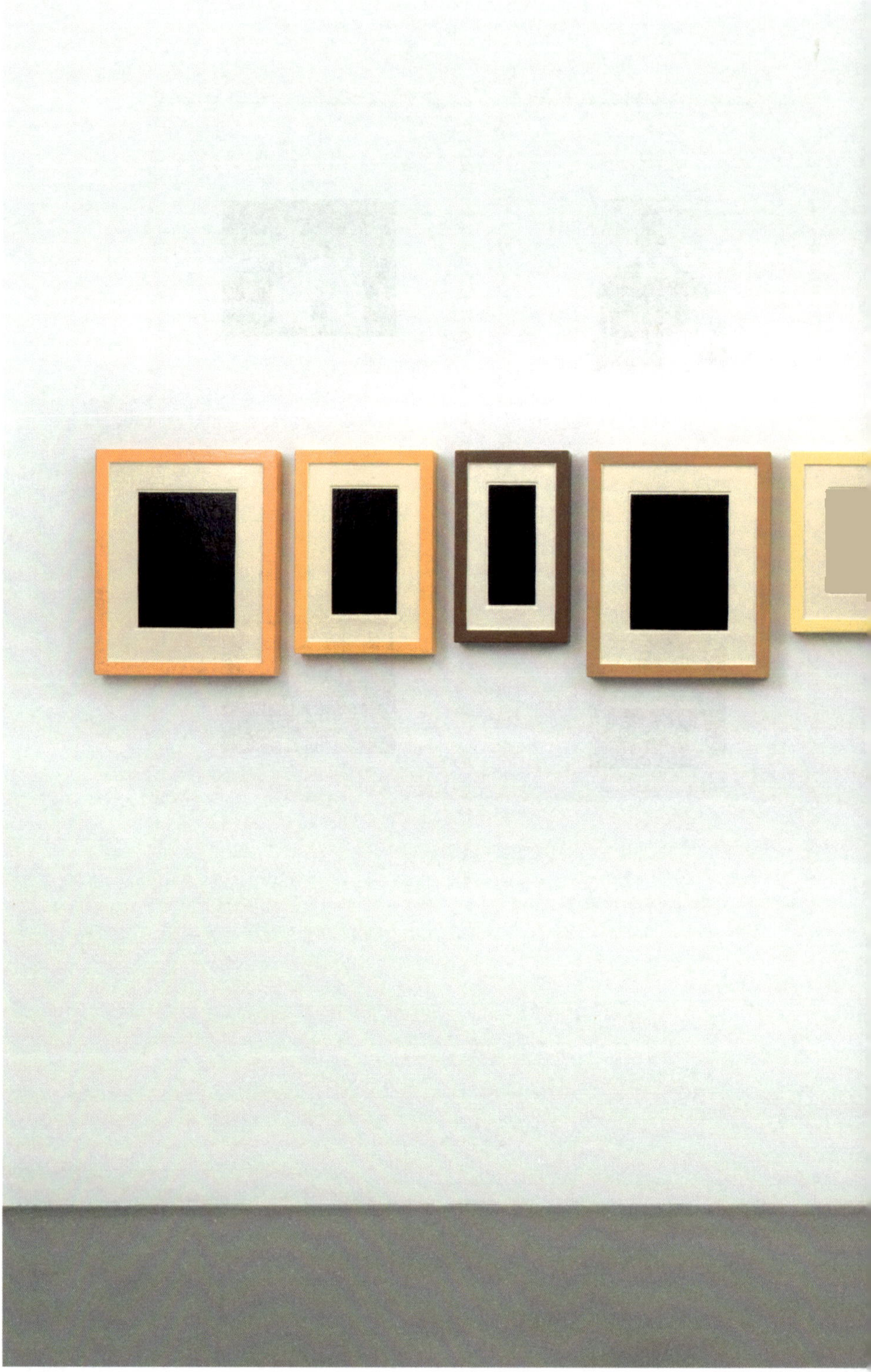

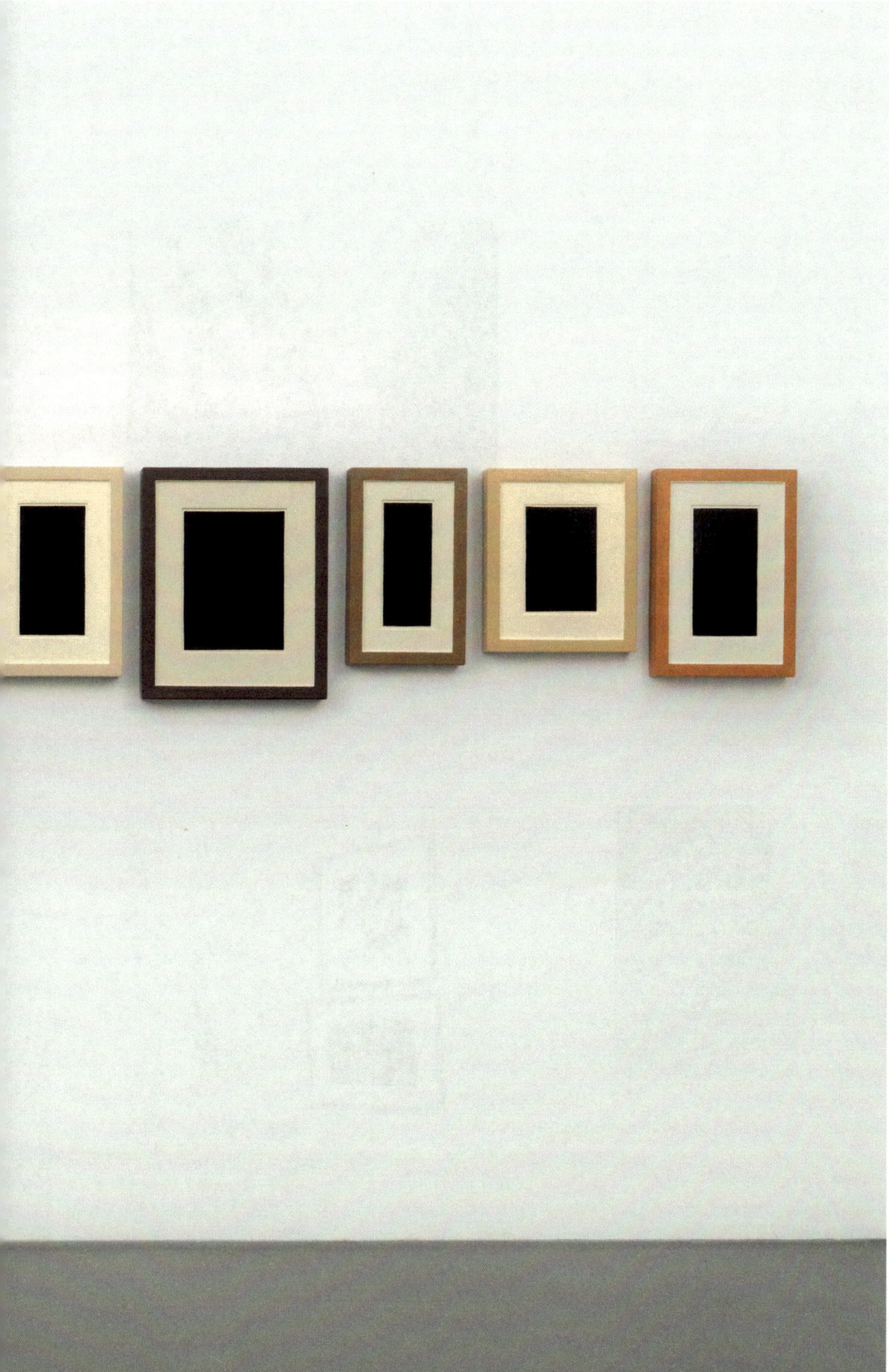

Arrangements of Pictures in *October*, Vol. 26, 1983

Louise Lawler

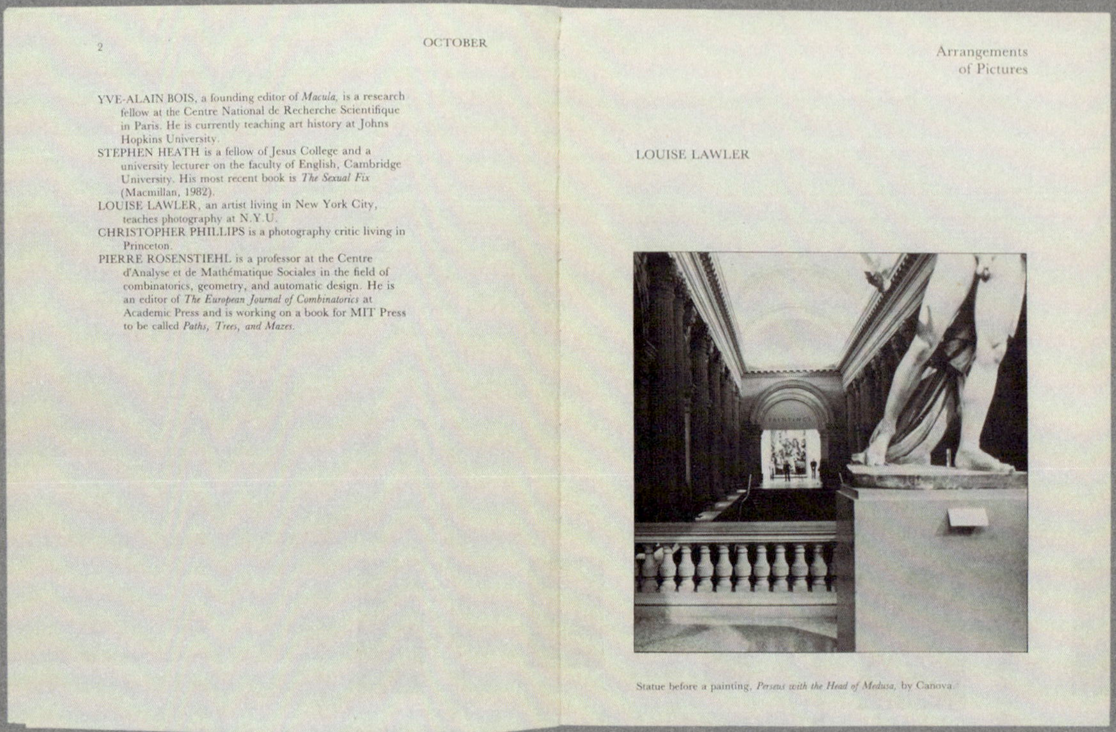

2 OCTOBER

YVE-ALAIN BOIS, a founding editor of *Macula*, is a research fellow at the Centre National de Recherche Scientifique in Paris. He is currently teaching art history at Johns Hopkins University.
STEPHEN HEATH is a fellow of Jesus College and a university lecturer on the faculty of English, Cambridge University. His most recent book is *The Sexual Fix* (Macmillan, 1982).
LOUISE LAWLER, an artist living in New York City, teaches photography at N.Y.U.
CHRISTOPHER PHILLIPS is a photography critic living in Princeton.
PIERRE ROSENSTIEHL is a professor at the Centre d'Analyse et de Mathématique Sociales in the field of combinatorics, geometry, and automatic design. He is an editor of *The European Journal of Combinatorics* at Academic Press and is working on a book for MIT Press to be called *Paths, Trees, and Mazes*.

Arrangements of Pictures

LOUISE LAWLER

Statue before a painting, *Perseus with the Head of Medusa*, by Canova.

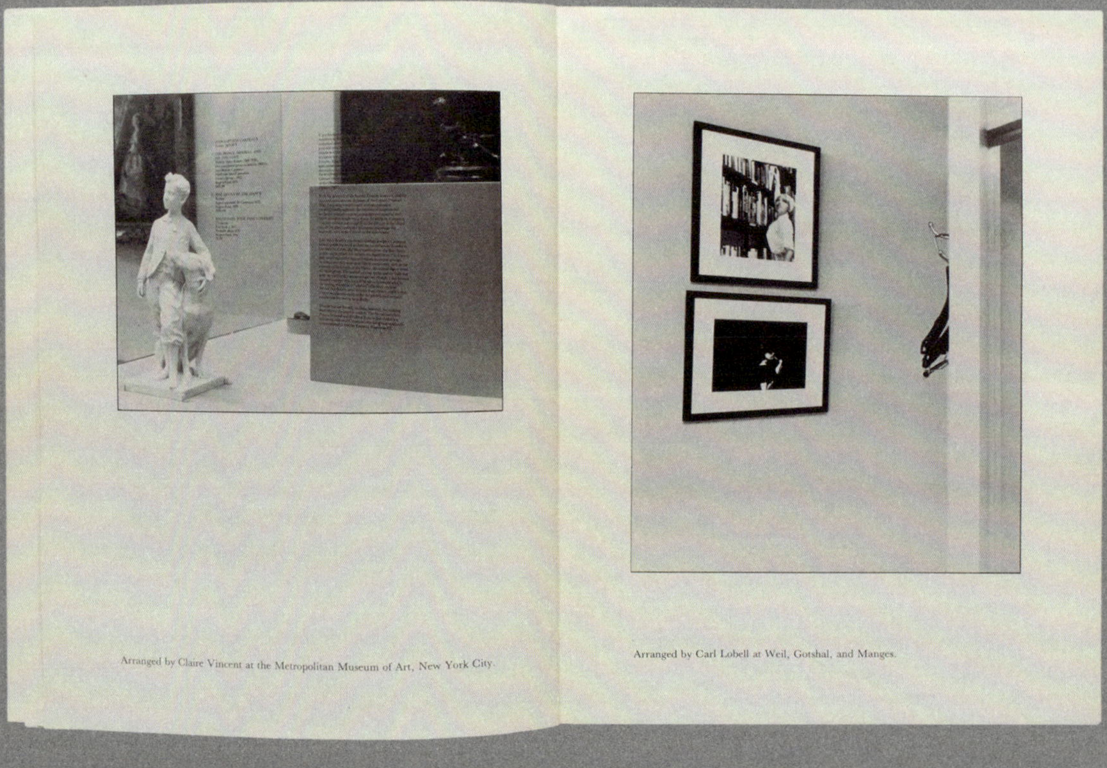

Arranged by Claire Vincent at the Metropolitan Museum of Art, New York City.

Arranged by Carl Lobell at Weil, Gotshal, and Manges.

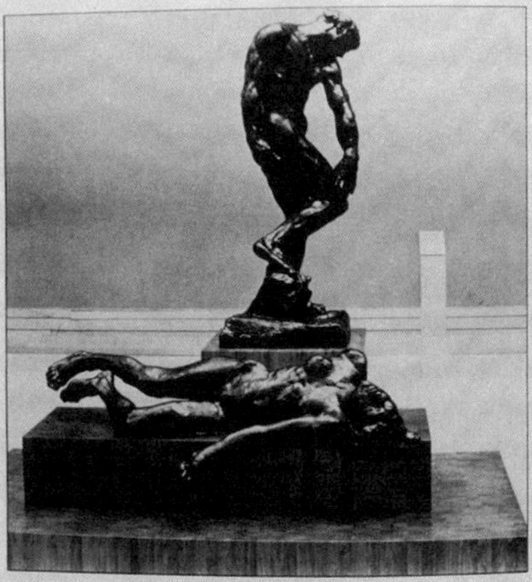

Rodin.

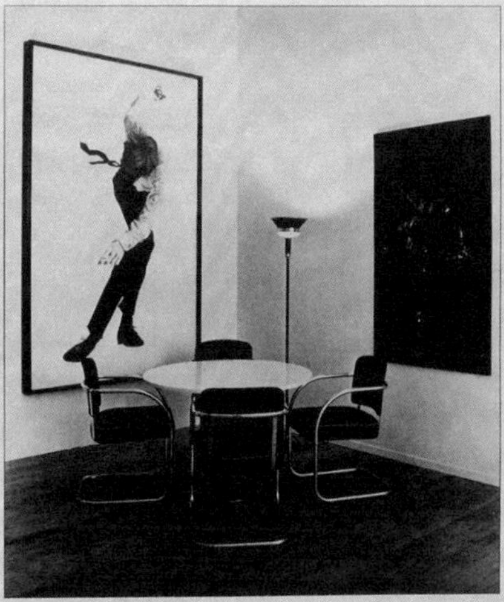

Arranged by Janelle Reiring.

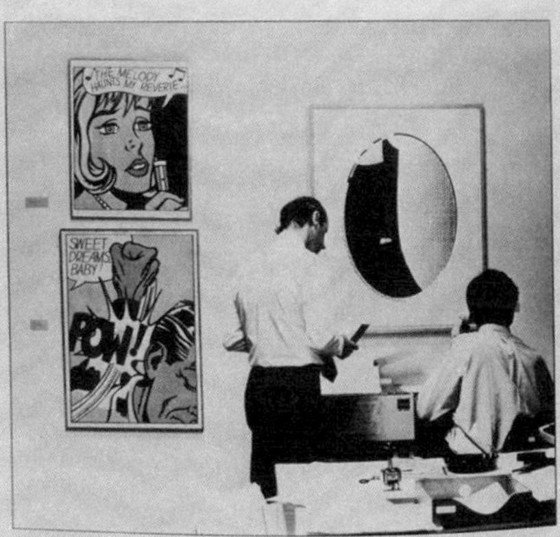

Arranged by Donald Marron, Susan Brundage, Cheryl Bishop at Paine Webber, Inc.

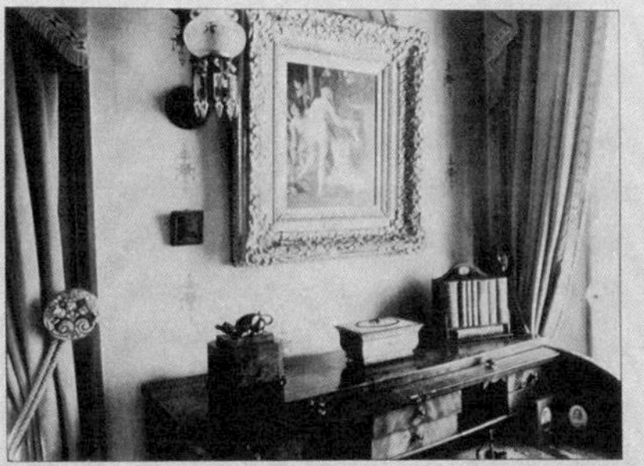

Peace by Pierre Puvis de Chavannes over Sheraton roll-top desk at the Hillstead Museum, Farmington, Connecticut.

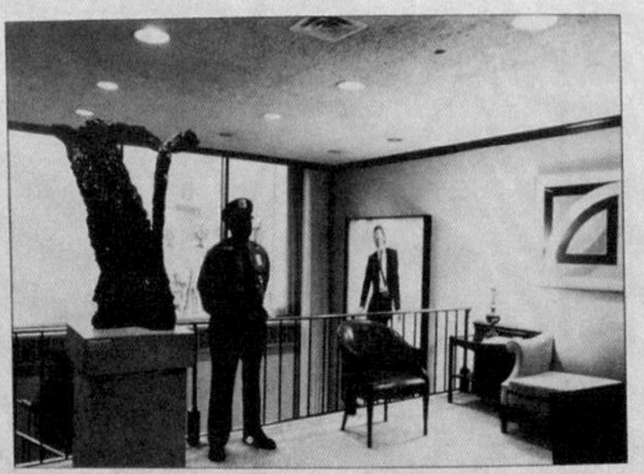

Reception area.

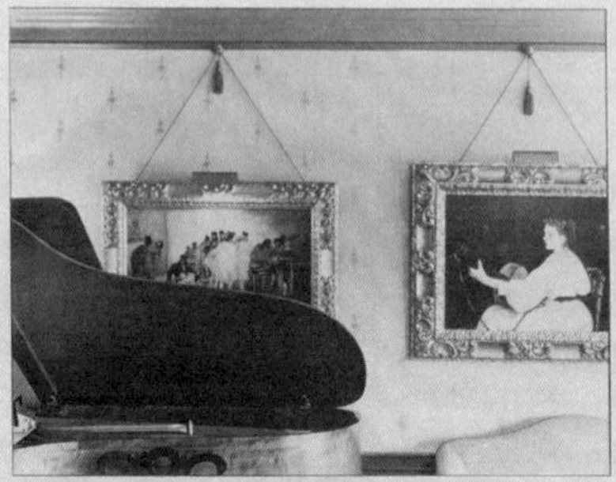

The Hillstead Museum, Farmington, Connecticut, was formerly the home of Mr. and Mrs. Alfred Atmore Pope and their daughter, Theodate. It was designed for them by Stanford White, with the acknowledged assistance of Theodate, in 1899.

Mr. Pope was one of the first American collectors of European impressionism. He became acquainted with some of the artists and their work through Mary Cassatt, a friend of the family, and he purchased many paintings from the Parisian dealer, Durand Ruel. He also collected sculpture, prints, Ming vases, Majolica plates, Wedgwood services, but without exceeding his need to furnish his home.

Theodate Pope Riddle was the last resident of Hillstead. In her will she directed the executors to "maintain [it] the same forever as a museum in which the past would remain untouched and inviolate."

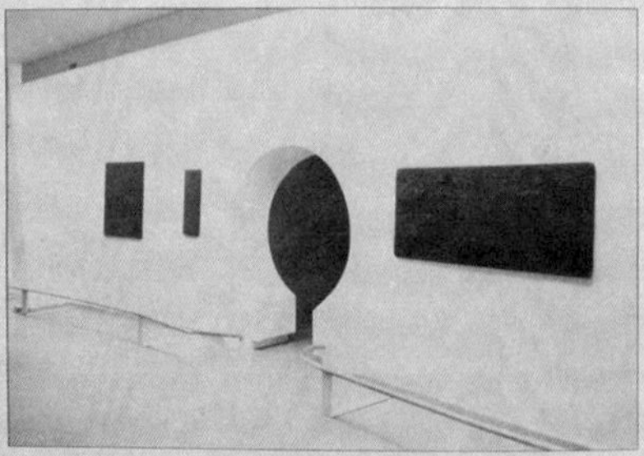

Wright, Meier, Klein.

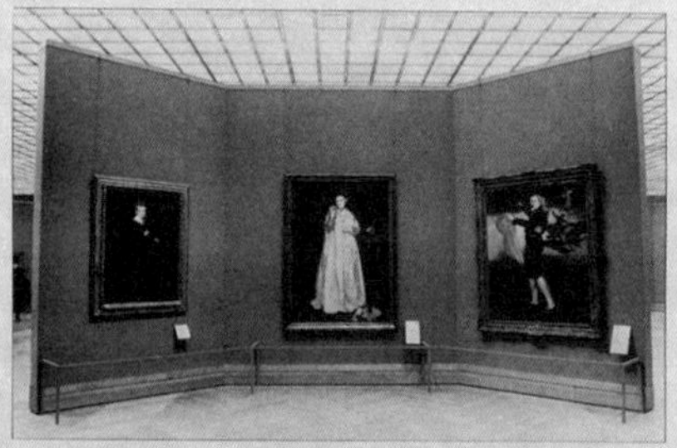

Roche, Dinkeloo, & Assoc., Metropolitan Museum of Art, André Meyer Gallery.

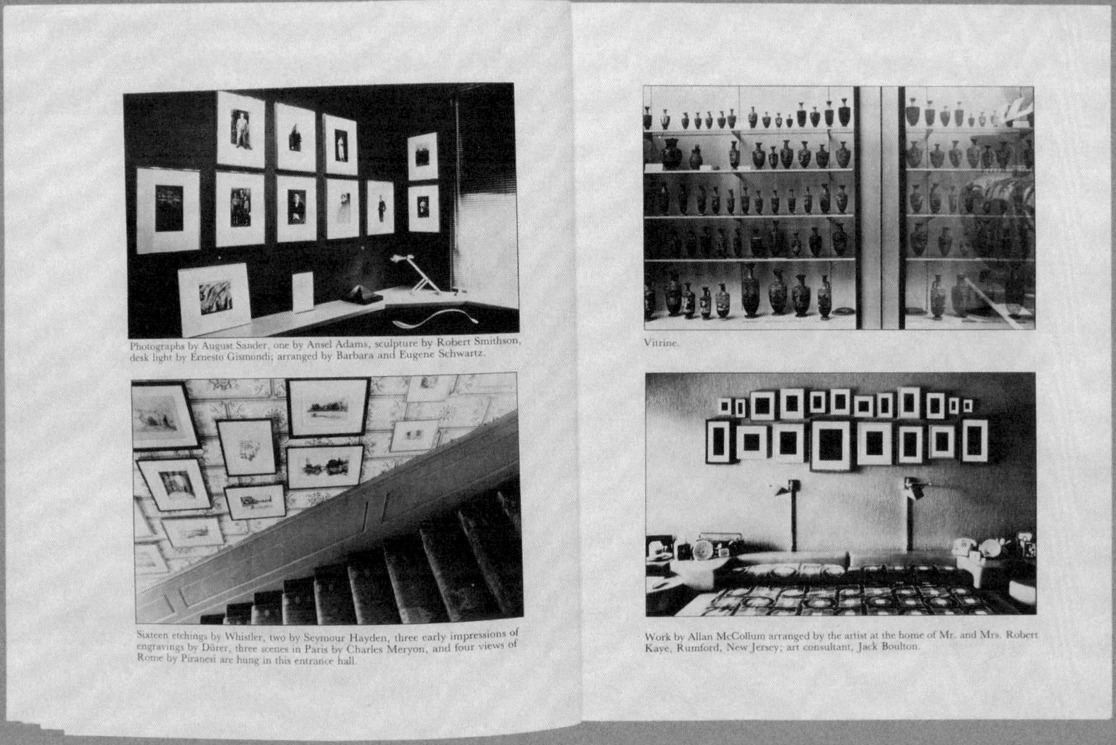

Photographs by August Sander, one by Ansel Adams, sculpture by Robert Smithson, desk light by Ernesto Gismondi; arranged by Barbara and Eugene Schwartz.

Sixteen etchings by Whistler, two by Seymour Hayden, three early impressions of engravings by Dürer, three scenes in Paris by Charles Meryon, and four views of Rome by Piranesi are hung in this entrance hall.

Vitrine.

Work by Allan McCollum arranged by the artist at the home of Mr. and Mrs. Robert Kaye, Rumford, New Jersey; art consultant, Jack Boulton.

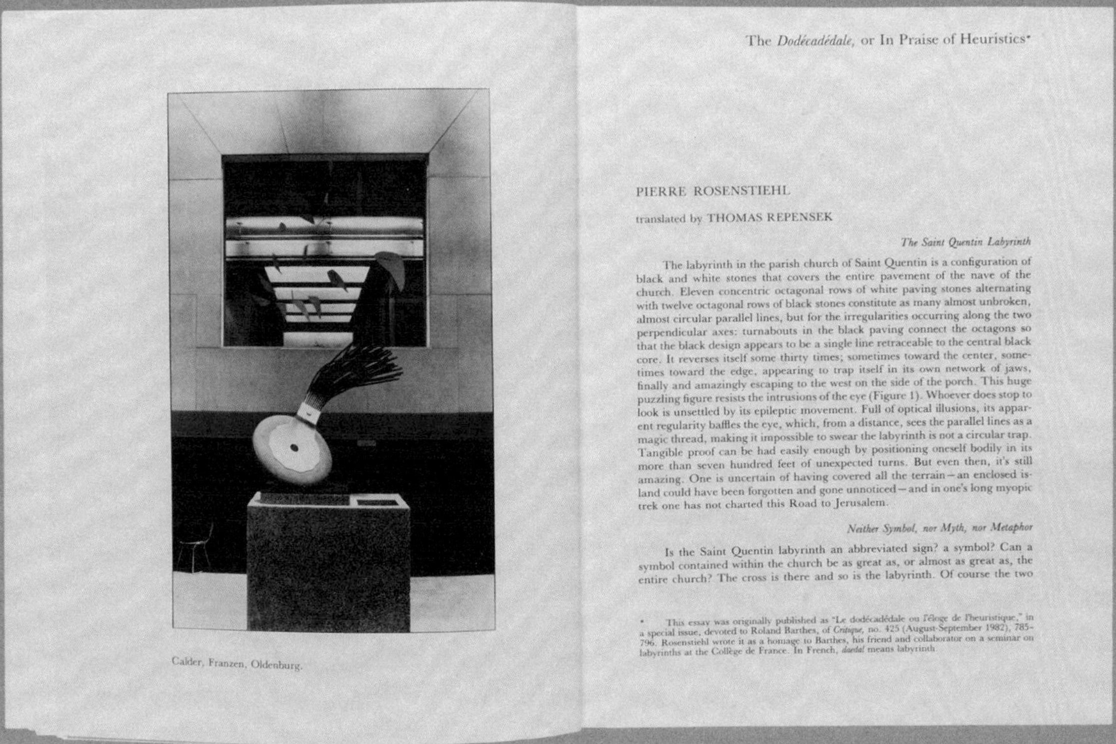

Calder, Franzen, Oldenburg.

The *Dodécadédale*, or In Praise of Heuristics*

PIERRE ROSENSTIEHL

translated by THOMAS REPENSEK

The Saint Quentin Labyrinth

The labyrinth in the parish church of Saint Quentin is a configuration of black and white stones that covers the entire pavement of the nave of the church. Eleven concentric octagonal rows of white paving stones alternating with twelve octagonal rows of black stones constitute as many almost unbroken, almost circular parallel lines, but for the irregularities occurring along the two perpendicular axes: turnabouts in the black paving connect the octagons so that the black design appears to be a single line retraceable to the central black core. It reverses itself some thirty times; sometimes toward the center, sometimes toward the edge, appearing to trap itself in its own network of jaws, finally and amazingly escaping to the west on the side of the porch. This huge puzzling figure resists the intrusions of the eye (Figure 1). Whoever does stop to look is unsettled by its epileptic movement. Full of optical illusions, its apparent regularity baffles the eye, which, from a distance, sees the parallel lines as a magic thread, making it impossible to swear the labyrinth is not a circular trap. Tangible proof can be had easily enough by positioning oneself bodily in its more than seven hundred feet of unexpected turns. But even then, it's still amazing. One is uncertain of having covered all the terrain—an enclosed island could have been forgotten and gone unnoticed—and in one's long myopic trek one has not charted this Road to Jerusalem.

Neither Symbol, nor Myth, nor Metaphor

Is the Saint Quentin labyrinth an abbreviated sign? a symbol? Can a symbol contained within the church be as great as, or almost as great as, the entire church? The cross is there and so is the labyrinth. Of course the two

* This essay was originally published as "Le dodécadédale ou l'éloge de l'heuristique," in a special issue, devoted to Roland Barthes, of *Critique*, no. 425 (August-September 1982), 785–796. Rosenstiehl wrote it as a homage to Barthes, his friend and collaborator on a seminar on labyrinths at the Collège de France. In French, *daedal* means labyrinth.

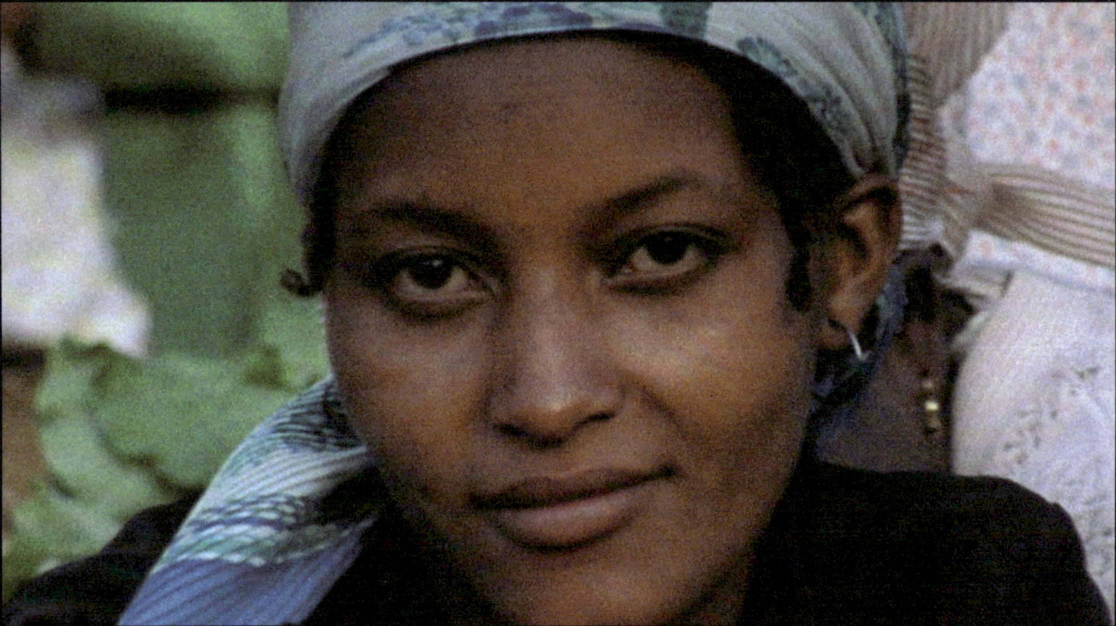

Wild Dead

Gretchen Bender

1984

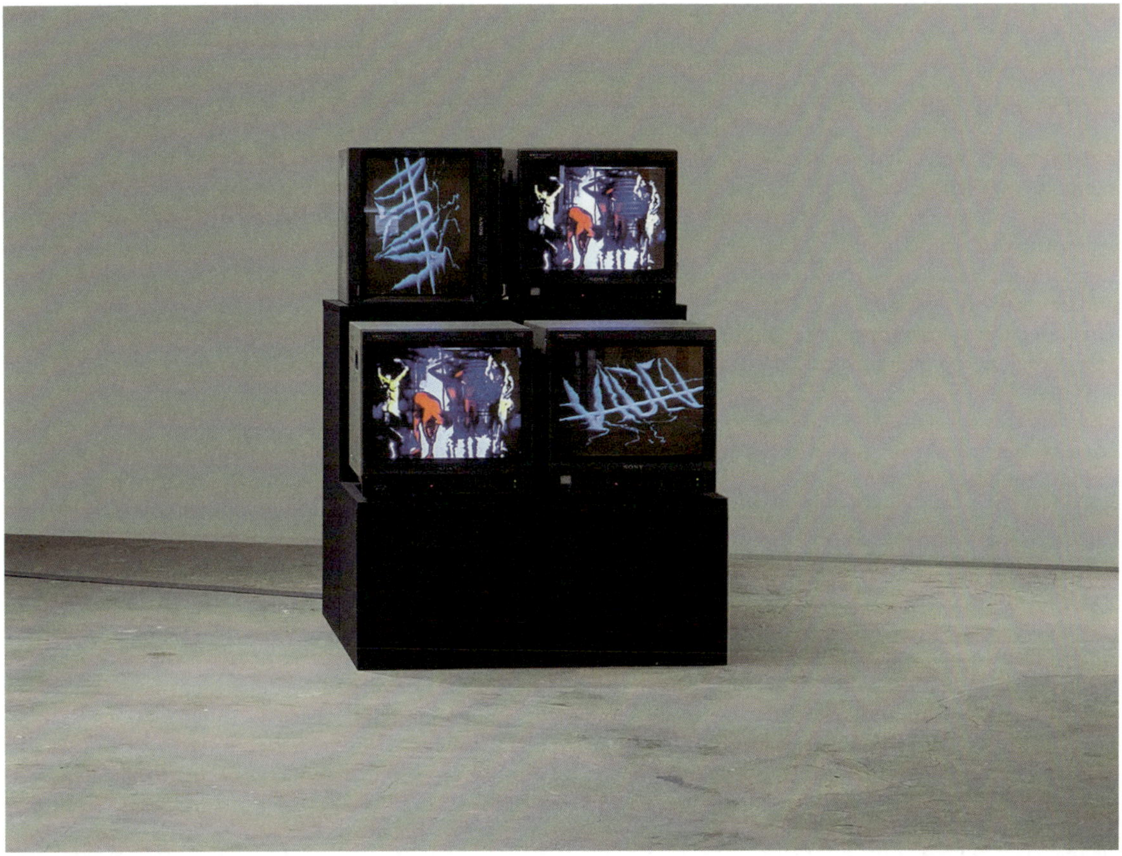

Towards a Philosophy of Photography
Vilém Flusser
1983

THE PHOTOGRAPHIC UNIVERSE

As inhabitants of the photographic universe we have become accustomed to photographs: They have grown familiar to us. We no longer take any notice of most photographs, concealed as they are by habit; in the same way, we ignore everything familiar in our environment and only notice what has changed. Change is informative, the familiar redundant. What we are surrounded by above all are redundant photographs—and this is the case despite the fact that every day new illustrated newspapers appear on our breakfast tables, every week new posters appear on city walls and new advertising photographs appear in shop displays. It is precisely this permanently changing situation that we have become accustomed to: One redundant photograph displaces another redundant photograph. As such, the changing situation is familiar, redundant; 'progress' has become uninformative, run-of-the-mill. What would be informative, exceptional, exciting for us would be a standstill situation: to find the same newspapers on our breakfast tables every day or to see the same posters on city walls for months on end. That would surprise and shock us. Photographs permanently displacing one another according to a program are redundant precisely because they are always 'new', precisely because they automatically exhaust the possibilities of the photographic program. This is therefore also the challenge for the photographer: to oppose the flood of redundancy with informative images.

It is not only the permanently changing situation of the photographic universe but also its gaudiness that has become commonplace. We are hardly aware how astonishing the colours of our environment would be to our grandfathers. In the nineteenth century the world was grey: walls, newspapers, books, shirts, tools, all these varied between black and white merging together into grey—as in the case of printed texts. Now everything cries out in all imaginable colours, but it cries out to deaf ears. We have become accustomed to visual pollution; it passes through our eyes and our consciousnesses without being noticed. It penetrates subliminal regions, where it functions and programs our actions.

If one compares the colour of our own world with that of the Middle Ages or of non-European cultures, one is faced with the difference that the colours of the Middle Ages and those of 'exotic' cultures are magic symbols signifying mythical elements, whereas for us they are mythical symbols at work on a theoretical level, elements of programs. For example, 'red' in the Middle Ages signified the danger of being swallowed up by Hell. Similarly, for us 'red' at traffic lights still signifies 'danger', but programmed in such a way that we automatically put our foot on the brake without at the same time engaging our consciousness. All that emerges from the subliminal programming of the colours of the photographic universe are merely ritual, automatic actions.

However, this chameleon-like nature of the photographic universe, the changing gaudiness of it, is only one of its main characteristics, a superficial feature. In accordance with its deeper structure, the photographic universe is grainy; it changes its appearance and colour as a mosaic might change in which the individual little pieces are continually being replaced. The photographic universe is made up of such little pieces, made up of quanta, and is calculable (calculus = little piece or 'particle')—an atomized, democratic universe, a jigsaw puzzle.

The quantum-like structure of the photographic universe is not surprising, since it has arisen out of the act of photography, whose quantum-like character has already been discussed. Yet an examination of the photographic universe allows us to see the deeper reason for the grainy character of all aspects of photography. It reveals, for example, that the atomized, punctuated structure is characteristic of all things relating to apparatus, and that even those camera functions that appear to slide (e.g. film and television pictures) are actually based on punctuated structures. In the world of apparatus, all 'waves' are made up of grains, and all 'processes' are made up of punctuated situations.

This is because apparatuses are simulations of thought, playthings that play at 'thinking', and they simulate human thought processes, not for example in the way one understands thought corresponding to introspection or the insights of psychology and physiology, but in the way one understands thought as described in the Cartesian model. According to Descartes, thought consists of clear and distinct elements (concepts) that are combined in the thought process like beads on an abacus, in which every concept signifies a point in the extended world out there. If every point could be assigned a concept, then thought would be omniscient and at the same time omnipotent. For thought processes would then symbolically direct processes out there. Unfortunately this omniscience and omnipotence are impossible, because the structure of thought is not adequate to deal with the structure of extended matter. If, for example, the points in the extended ('concrete') world grow together, leaving no gaps, then distinct concepts in thought are interrupted by intervals through which most of the points escape. Descartes hoped to overcome this inadequacy of the network of thought with the help of God and analytic geometry, but he did not succeed.

Apparatuses, meanwhile, these simulations of Cartesian thought, have succeeded. They are omniscient and omnipotent in their universes. For in these universes, a concept, an element of the program of the apparatus, is actually assigned to every point, every element of the universe. This can be seen most clearly in the case of computers and their universes. But it can also be seen in the case of the photographic universe. To every photograph there corresponds a clear and distinct element in the camera program. Every photograph thereby corresponds to a specific combination of elements in programs. Thanks to this bi-univocal relationship between universe and program, in which a photograph corresponds to every point in the program and a point in the program to every photograph, cameras are omniscient and omnipotent in the photographic universe. But they also have to pay a high price for their omniscience and omnipotence, this price being the reversal of the vectors of significance. That is: Concepts no longer signify the world out there (as in the Cartesian model); instead, the universe signifies the program within cameras. The program does not signify the photograph, the photograph signifies the elements of the program (concepts). In the case of cameras, we are therefore dealing with an absurd omniscience and an absurd omnipotence: Cameras know everything and are able to do everything in a universe that was programmed in advance for this knowledge and ability.

This is the place to define the term 'program'. To this end, all human involvement in the program—that struggle between the function of the program and human intention that was the subject of the previous essay—should be bracketed out. The program to be defined is a completely automatic one: a combination game based on chance. As a particularly simple example of a program, one can cite the throw of dice combining the elements '1' to '6'. Every throw is random, cannot be predicted: but over time every sixth throw is necessarily a '1'. Put another way, all possible combinations are realized by chance, but over time all possible combinations are necessarily realized. If, for example, an atomic war is entered into the program of any apparatus as a possibility, then it will happen by chance, but necessarily someday. In this subhumanly mindless sense, apparatuses 'think' by means of chance combinations. In this sense they are omniscient and omnipotent in their universes.

The photographic universe, like the one by which we are currently surrounded, is a chance realization of a number of possibilities contained within camera programs which corresponds point for point to a specific situation in a combination game. As other programmed possibilities will be realized by chance in future, the photographic universe is in a permanent state of flux and within it one photograph permanently displaces another. Every given situation in the photographic universe corresponds to a 'throw' in the combination game, i.e. point for point, photograph for photograph. But these are totally redundant photos. The informative photographs of photographers consciously playing against the program signify breakthroughs in the photographic universe—and are not predicted within the program.

From which one can draw the following conclusions: First, the photographic universe is created in the course of a combination game, it is programmed, and it signifies the program. Second, the game proceeds automatically and obeys no intentional strategy. Third, the photographic universe is made up of clear and distinct photographs that each signify one point in the program. Fourth, every single photo is—as the surface of an image—a magical model for the actions of an observer. To summarize: The photographic universe is a means of programming society—with absolute necessity but in each individual case by chance (i.e. automatically)—to act as a magic feedback mechanism for the benefit of a combination game, and of the automatic reprogramming of society into dice, into pieces in the game, into functionaries.

This view of the photographic universe challenges one to look in two directions: towards a society surrounded by the photographic universe and towards the cameras programming the photographic universe. It challenges one to engage, on the one hand, in criticism of the post-industrial society that is coming into being, and, on the other, in criticism of cameras and their programs; in other words: to critically transcend post-industrial society.

To be in the photographic universe means to experience, to know and to evaluate the world as a function of photographs. Every single experience, every single bit of knowledge, every single value can be reduced to individually known and evaluated photographs. And every single action can be analyzed through the individual photos taken as models. This type of existence, then, in which everything experienced, known and evaluated can be reduced to punctuated elements (into 'bits'), is already familiar: It is the world of robots. The photographic universe and all apparatus-based universes robotize the human being and society.

New, robot-like actions are observable everywhere: at bank counters, in offices, in factories, in supermarkets, in sport, dancing. When one looks a bit more closely, the same staccato structure is also perceptible, for example in scientific texts, in poetry, in musical composition, in architecture and in political programs. Correspondingly it is the task of current cultural criticism to analyze this restructuring of experience, knowledge, evaluation and action into a mosaic of clear and distinct elements in every single cultural phenomenon. Within such cultural criticism, the invention of photography will prove to be the point at which all cultural phenomena started to replace the linear structure of sliding with the staccato structure of programmed combinations; not, therefore, to adopt a mechanical structure such as that in the Industrial Revolution, but to adopt a cybernetic structure such as that programmed into apparatuses. Within such cultural criticism, the camera will prove to be the ancestor of all those apparatuses that are in the process of robotizing all aspects of our lives, from one's most public acts to one's innermost thoughts, feelings and desires.

If one now attempts a criticism of apparatuses, one first sees the photographic universe as the product of cameras and distribution apparatuses. Behind these, one recognizes industrial apparatuses, advertising apparatuses, political, economic management apparatuses, etc. Each of these apparatuses is becoming increasingly automated and is being linked up by cybernetics to other apparatuses. The program of each apparatus is fed in via its input by another apparatus, and in its turn feeds other apparatuses via its output. The whole complex of apparatuses is therefore a super-black-box made up of black boxes. And it is a human creation: As a product of the nineteenth and twentieth centuries, human beings are permanently engaged in developing and perfecting it. The time is therefore not far off when one will have to concentrate one's criticism of apparatuses on the human intention that willed and created them.

Such a critical approach is enticing for two reasons. First, it absolves the critics of the necessity of delving into the interior of the black boxes: They can concentrate on their output, human intention. And second, it absolves critics of the necessity of developing new categories of criticism: Human intention can be criticized using traditional criteria. The result of such a criticism of apparatuses would therefore be something like the following:

The intention behind apparatuses is to liberate the human being from work; apparatuses take over human labour—for example, the camera liberates the human being from the necessity of using a paintbrush. Instead of having to work, the human being is able to play. But apparatuses have come under the control of a number of individual human beings (e.g. capitalists), who have reversed this original intention. Now apparatuses serve the interests of these people; consequently what needs to be done is to unmask the interests behind the apparatuses. According to such an analysis, apparatuses are nothing but peculiar machines, the invention of which has nothing revolutionary about it; there is no point therefore in talking of a 'second Industrial Revolution'.

Thus photographs also have to be decoded as an expression of the concealed interests of those in power: the interests of Kodak shareholders, of the proprietors of advertising agencies, those pulling the strings behind the US industrial complex, the interests of the entire US ideological, military and industrial complex. If one exposed these interests, every single photograph and the whole photographic universe could be considered as having been decoded.

Unfortunately this traditional kind of criticism with its background in the industrial context is not adequate to deal with the phenomenon. It misses the essential thing about apparatuses, i.e. their automaticity. And this is precisely what needs to be criticized. Apparatuses were invented in order to function automatically, in other words independently of future human involvement. This is the intention with which they were created: that the human being would be ruled out. And this intention has been successful without a doubt. While the human being is being more and more sidelined, the programs of apparatuses, these rigid combination games, are increasingly rich in elements: they make combinations more and more quickly and are going beyond the ability of the human being to see what they are up to and to control them. Anyone who is involved with apparatuses is involved with black boxes where one is unable to see what they are up to.

To this extent, one can't talk of an owner of apparatuses either. As apparatuses function automatically and do not obey any human decision, they cannot be owned by anybody. All human decisions are made on the basis of the decisions of apparatuses; they have degenerated into purely 'functional' decisions, i.e. human intention has evaporated. If apparatuses were originally produced and programmed to follow human intention, then today, in the 'second and third generation' of apparatuses, this intention has disappeared over the horizon of functionality. Apparatuses now function as an end in themselves, 'automatically' as it were, with the single aim of maintaining and improving themselves. This rigid, unintentional, functional automaticity is what needs to be made the object of criticism.

The 'humanistic' criticism of apparatuses referred to above is in opposition to this portrayal of apparatuses being transformed into superhuman, anthropomorphic Titans and of thus contributing to the obscuring of the human interests behind apparatuses. But this objection is erroneous. Apparatuses are actually Titans, since they were created with this sole intention. This portrayal attempts to show precisely that they are not superhuman but subhuman—bloodless and simplistic simulations of human thought processes which, precisely because they are so rigid, render human decisions superfluous and non-functional. Whereas the 'humanistic' criticism of apparatuses, by calling upon the last vestiges of human intention behind apparatuses, obscures the danger lying in wait within them, the criticism of apparatuses proposed here sees its task precisely in uncovering the terrible fact of this unintentional, rigid and uncontrollable functionality of apparatuses, in order to get a hold over them.

Returning to the photographic universe: It reflects a combination game, a changing, gaudy jigsaw puzzle of clear and distinct surfaces that each signify an element of the program of the apparatus. It programs the observer to act magically and functionally, and thus automatically, i.e. without obeying any human intention in the process.

A number of human beings are struggling against this automatic programming: photographers who attempt to produce informative images, i.e. photographs that are not part of the program of apparatus; critics who attempt to see what is going on in the automatic game of programming; and in general, all those who are attempting to create a space for human intention in a world dominated by apparatuses. However, the apparatuses themselves automatically assimilate these attempts at liberation and enrich their programs with them. It is consequently the task of a philosophy of photography to expose this struggle between human being and apparatuses in the field of photography and to reflect on a possible solution to the conflict.

The hypothesis proposed here is that, if such a philosophy should succeed in fulfilling its task, this would be of significance, not only in the field of photography, but for post-industrial society in general. Admittedly, the photographic universe is only one of a whole number of universes, and there are surely much more dangerous ones amongst them. But the next essay will illustrate that the photographic universe can serve as a model for post-industrial society as a whole and that a philosophy of photography can be the starting point for any philosophy engaging with the current and future existence of human beings.

WHY A PHILOSOPHY OF PHOTOGRAPHY IS NECESSARY

In the course of the foregoing attempt to sum up the essential quality of photography, a few basic concepts came to light: *image–apparatus–program–information.* These must be the cornerstones of any philosophy of photography, and they make possible the following definition of a photograph: It is an image created and distributed by photographic apparatus according to a program, an image whose ostensible function is to inform. Each one of the basic concepts thus contains within it further concepts. *Image* contains within it magic; *apparatus* contains within it automation and play; *program* contains within it chance and necessity; *information* contains within it the symbolic and the improbable. This results in a broader definition of a photograph: It is an image created and distributed automatically by programmed apparatuses in the course of a game necessarily based on chance, an image of a magic state of things whose symbols inform its receivers how to act in an improbable fashion.

This definition has the peculiar advantage for philosophy of not being acceptable. One is challenged to prove it wrong since it rules out the human being as a free agent. It provokes one into a contradiction, and contradiction—dialectics—is one of the spurs to philosophy. To this extent, the proposed definition is a welcome starting point for a philosophy of photography.

If one considers the basic concepts *image, apparatus, program* and *information,* one discovers an internal connection between them: They are all based on the 'eternal recurrence of the same.' Images are surfaces above which the eye circles only to return again and again to the starting point. Apparatuses are playthings that repeat the same movements over and over again. Programs are games that combine the same elements over and over again. Pieces of information are improbable states that break away again and again from the tendency to become probable only to sink back into it again and again. In short: With these four basic concepts, we no longer find ourselves in the historical context of the linear, in which nothing is repeated and everything has a cause yielding consequences. The area in which we find ourselves is no longer ascertainable by means of causal but only by means of functional explanations. Along with Cassirer, we shall have to leave causality behind: 'Rest, rest, dear spirit.' Any philosophy of photography will have to come to terms with the ahistorical, post-historical character of the phenomenon under consideration.

Besides, we have already started to think spontaneously in a post-historical fashion in a whole range of areas. Cosmology is an example of this. We see in the cosmos a system tending towards states that are becoming more and more improbable. It is true that by chance more and more improbable states are coming into being; however—of necessity—these sink back into the tendency to become probable. In other words: We see in the cosmos an apparatus that contains an original piece of information in its output (the 'big bang') and that is programmed to realize and exhaust this information necessarily through chance ('heat death').

The four basic concepts *image, apparatus, program* and *information,* support our cosmological thinking quite spontaneously, and in so doing, quite spontaneously prompt us to reach out for functional explanations.

The same applies to other areas such as psychology, biology, linguistics, cybernetics and information technology (to mention only a few). We think, quite spontaneously, across the board in an imaginary, functionally programmatic and information-technological fashion. The hypothesis proposed here thus argues that we think like this because we think in photographic categories: because the photographic universe has programmed us to think in a post-historical fashion.

This hypothesis is not as bold as it first seems. It is a hypothesis that has been around for a long time: Human beings create tools and in so doing take themselves as the model for this creation—until the situation is reversed and human beings take their tools as the model of themselves, of the world and of society. Hence the well-known process of alienation from one's own tools. In the eighteenth century, human beings invented machines, and their own bodies served as a model for this invention—until the relationship was reversed and the machines started to serve as models of human beings, of the world and of society. In the eighteenth century, a philosophy of the machine would simultaneously have been a criticism of the whole of anthropology, science, politics and art, i.e. of mechanization. It is no different in our time for a philosophy of photography: It would be a criticism of functionalism in all its anthropological, scientific, political and aesthetic aspects.

The matter is not all that simple, however. For a photograph is not a tool like a machine; it is a plaything like a playing card or chess-piece. If the photograph is becoming a model, then it is no longer a matter of replacing a tool with another tool as a model, but of replacing a type of model with a completely new type of model. The hypothesis proposed above, according to which we are starting to think in photographic categories, argues that the basic structures of our existence are being transformed. We are not dealing with the classical problem of alienation, but with an existential revolution of which there is no example available to us. To put it bluntly: It is a question of freedom in a new context. This is what any philosophy of photography has to concern itself with.

It goes without saying that this is not a new question: All philosophy has always been concerned with it. But in being so concerned, it was located within the historical context of linearity. In a nutshell, it formulated the question like this: If everything is to have causes and consequences, if everything is 'conditioned', where is there space for human freedom? And all answers, likewise in a nutshell, can be reduced to the following common denominator: The causes are so complex and the consequences so unpredictable that human beings, these limited beings, can act as though they were 'unconditioned.' In the new context, however, the question of freedom is formulated differently: If everything is based on chance and necessarily results in nothing, then where is there space for human freedom? In this absurd climate, the philosophy of photography has to address the question of freedom.

We observe, all around us, apparatuses of every sort in the process of programming our life through rigid automation; human labour is being replaced by automatic machines and most of society is starting to be employed in the 'tertiary sector', i.e. playing with empty symbols; the existential interests of the material world are being replaced by symbolic universes and the values of things are being replaced by information. Our thoughts, feelings, desires and actions are being robotized; 'life' is coming to mean feeding apparatuses and being fed by them. In short: Everything is becoming absurd. So where is there room for human freedom?

Then we discover people who can perhaps answer this question: photographers—in the sense of the word intended in this study. They are already, in miniature, people of the apparatus future. Their acts are programmed by the camera; they play with symbols; they are active in the 'tertiary sector', interested in information; they create things without value. In spite of this they consider their activity to be anything but absurd and think that they are acting freely. The task of the philosophy of photography is to question photographers about freedom, to probe their practice in the pursuit of freedom.

This was the intention of the foregoing study, and in the course of it a few answers have come to light. First, one can outwit the camera's rigidity. Second, one can smuggle human intentions into its program that are not predicted by it. Third, one can force the camera to create the unpredictable, the improbable, the informative. Fourth, one can show contempt for the camera and its creations and turn one's interest away from the thing in general in order to concentrate on information. In short: Freedom is the strategy of making chance and necessity subordinate to human intention. Freedom is playing against the camera.

However, photographers only provide such answers when called to account by philosophical analysis. When speaking spontaneously they say something different. They claim to be making traditional images—even if by non-traditional means. They claim to be creating works of art or contributing to knowledge—or being politically committed. If one reads statements by photographers, for instance in the usual works on the history of photography, one is faced with the prevailing opinion that with the invention of photography nothing really far-reaching took place and that everything is basically proceeding just as it did before; only, as it were, that alongside the other histories there is now a history of photography as well. Even though, in practice, photographers have been living for a long time in a post-historical fashion, the post-industrial revolution, as it appears for the first time in the shape of the camera, has escaped their consciousness.

With one exception: so-called experimental photographers—those photographers in the sense of the word intended here. They are conscious that *image, apparatus, program* and *information* are the basic problems that they have to come to terms with. They are in fact consciously attempting to create unpredictable information, i.e. to release themselves from the camera, and to place within the image something that is not in its program. They know they are playing against the camera. Yet even they are not conscious of the consequence of their practice: They are not aware that they are attempting to address the question of freedom in the context of apparatus in general.

A philosophy of photography is necessary for raising photographic practice to the level of consciousness, and this is again because this practice gives rise to a model of freedom in the post-industrial context in general. A philosophy of photography must reveal the fact that there is no place for human freedom within the area of automated, programmed and programming apparatuses, in order finally to show a way in which it is nevertheless possible to open up a space for freedom. The task of a philosophy of photography is to reflect upon this possibility of freedom—and thus its significance—in a world dominated by apparatuses; to reflect upon the way in which, despite everything, it is possible for human beings to give significance to their lives in face of the chance necessity of death. Such a philosophy is necessary because it is the only form of revolution left open to us.

Still from *Standard Gauge*

Morgan Fisher

1984

Standard Gauge
Morgan Fisher
1984

STANDARD GAUGE IN THREE PARTS

1. A frame of frames, a piece of pieces, a length of lengths. Standard gauge on substandard; narrower, yes, but longer. An ECU that's an ELS. *Disjecta membra*; Hollywood anthologized. A kind of autobiography of its maker, a kind of history of the institution from whose shards it is composed, the commercial motion picture industry. A mutual interrogation between 35mm and 16mm, the gauge of Hollywood and the gauge of the amateur and independent.

2. The above paragraph was the first note I wrote about *Standard Gauge*. I liked it because it was terse. It's a collection of sentence fragments, which I meant to reflect the fragments that make up the film. Later on I wrote a longer note, which here I have revised only slightly:

Standard Gauge is an autobiographical account of a few years in the film career of its maker. Such, at least, is its ostensible form and purpose.

The material from which the film is composed is pieces of 35mm motion picture film, a width known in former times as standard gauge, that its maker collected while working in and around the commercial motion picture industry. The pieces are a miscellaneous assortment; their sources include narrative features, trailers, newsreels, commercials, and pieces of head and tail leader.

The method of the film, which was shot in 16mm, is to show these pieces one after the other in an extreme close-up that is one continuous shot lasting thirty-two minutes. This is a minute short of the maximum length of a scene in 16mm, and is longer by far than 35mm is capable of. The body of the film is this single continuous scene, and it is preceded by an extended written text, presented by means of a crawl, that gives a brief history of how 35mm came into being. It explains that 35mm became the gauge of the commercial film industry, and that, with the emergence of other gauges, 35mm came to be known as standard gauge. As each piece of film is shown—there are about thirty in all—a narrative spoken by the maker describes some point related to it: the circumstances under which it was collected, for example, or a technical aspect of the image, such as the process by which it was produced.

So *Standard Gauge* is a kind of collage or found-footage film. But instead of being spliced together and projected, and so brought to life, as in the films of Bruce Conner, the pieces of film in *Standard Gauge* remain separate and are presented one after the other for inspection by the audience as inert pieces of film, translucent objects made of celluloid. They are thus experienced by the viewer as they would be by someone, such as an editor or a negative cutter, who handles and organizes film as material.

Although the film is one continuous shot, each piece of film fills the frame and so inflects the embracing shot, creating within it the effect of a succession of shots. So the film combines two conventions usually held to be mutually exclusive, or even antagonistic: editing—organizing a film with a succession of shots—and the long take, the impassive recording of a scene that has been arranged with some purpose in mind.

Just as *Standard Gauge* amalgamates the two great modes of film syntax, it also brings together narrative and nonnarrative filmmaking. By examining the shards of the industry frame by frame, it discovers some of the means and themes of experimental film living, so to speak, in Hollywood. And at the same time, the film engulfs and usurps the material of the commercial motion picture industry, turning it into its subject.

Thus *Standard Gauge* proposes a kind of mutuality or interdependence between two kinds of filmmaking that by conventional standards are thought to be divided by an unbridgeable chasm. By means of a mutual interrogation between 35mm, the gauge of the industry, and 16mm, the gauge of the independent and amateur, *Standard Gauge* proposes to unify film of every kind.

3. Recently, I've written more.

When I say in the first note that the film is standard gauge on substandard, I am only repeating terms that were once in use. There was a time when 16mm film was called substandard. The prefix "sub" is logical because 16 is below 35. But when it is added to "standard" it creates a word that even if correct in the narrow sense carries with it the whiff of the pejorative that is echoed in what Hollywood editors used to call 16mm film: spaghetti. So in the view of Hollywood, 16mm wasn't just below, it was also beneath.

To explain the remark "An ECU that's an ELS" : "ECU" means "extreme close-up," and, as you might now guess, "ELS" means "extreme long shot." Of course "long" refers to the subject's apparent distance from the camera. The stagecoach racing in the distance across Monument Valley is an ELS of the stagecoach. So, to state the obvious, I was playing with the meaning of "long," turning it from meaning "far away" to meaning "lasting a long time."

People have asked me whether *Standard Gauge* is itself shot in 35mm. No, it's not, as they would have realized if they knew a little more about the technical aspects of 35mm. The narration says that takes in Alfred Hitchcock's *Under Capricorn* (1949) were as long as was possible at the time and that I thought this length was still the longest possible. I didn't give the length of this take in the narration because I didn't want to belabor the point. But to explain what I said in the second note, the take that is *Standard Gauge* is nearly three times as long as the longest take that is possible in 35mm. So *Standard Gauge*, a modest little film in 16mm, does something that no film made by the industry can do. So much for 16mm beneath 35mm.

But I am happy that people ask this question, because I think it suggests that *Standard Gauge* really does make you think about the material base of the film that is the origin of the image on the screen. You see on the screen the pieces of film in their entire width, from one edge to the other. So you see all of what is within that width: you see the frame, and you also see the margins beyond the frame, occupied by the sprocket holes, the sound track, and so on. What you see is the difference, so to speak, between the width you know film has and the frame you see on the screen that you know is less than that width. I think that seeing on the screen these things that are a part of the facts of a piece of film but are always excluded from the image you see on the screen makes you think about these same things in the film in the projector. You already know there is more to any film than the partial shadow of it that you see on the screen, but *Standard Gauge* shows you what this margin looks like and shows you some variety in the things you find there: the names of different manufacturers, and so on. (*Standard Gauge* also shows you what happens in another margin, the margin of the leaders at the head and tail of a reel of film in the projector.) So I think people ask whether *Standard Gauge* is in 35mm because what they see on the screen is 35mm, and, thinking about the film in the projector, they suppose, quite reasonably, that, like the pieces of film they see on the screen, the film itself is also in 35mm. If people think about the film in the projector when they see *Standard Gauge*, perhaps they are more likely to think about it when they see other films.

The ultimate subject of *Standard Gauge* is how a single continuous take can be a complex event. *Standard Gauge* raises the question in an acute way because the film consists of only one shot. The film isn't just a continuous take, it's a static shot and an extreme close-up. In their modest ways, these are all extremes, and together they emphasize the radicality, if I can call it that, of the continuous take that the film is founded on.

The film's procedure of showing a series of pieces of film as objects is possible only in a single take. It may be the case, as I say above, that the pieces of film one after another within the continuous take create the effect of a succession of shots. But between each piece of film the frame is empty. The empty frame is the field into which each successive piece of film is inserted, and this empty frame is the continuing field of *Standard Gauge*. The empty frames between the pieces emphasize that the shots are materially separate objects, and this fact in turn points to the continuous take that contains them all.

Beyond this simple procedure, I tried to point to the continuous take in *Standard Gauge* without talking about it directly by means of some of the fragments I included and by what I said about them.

As the narration makes clear, the piece from the leader of *The Naked Dawn* (1955) is really only an excuse to talk about another film by Edgar G. Ulmer, *Detour* (1945). The last shot in *Detour* is a continuous take in which very complicated things happen. What I say in the narration remarks only on how the shot moves from the present to the future. Of course what happens later in any shot is the future in relation to what happened earlier, but in this shot in *Detour* there's a jump ahead in time that lies beyond the sense of the continuing present that a continuous shot usually implies. The main character, nearly at the end of his rope, is delivering an interior monologue. We hear the words that he speaks, but we don't see him say them. He says, "But one thing I don't have to worry about—I *know*. Someday a car will stop to pick me up . . ." He makes a prediction, and on the screen we see his prediction come true. His saying the word "will" shifts the scene to the future, and the action that fulfills his prediction confirms this shift. The disjunction in time between present and future that these tenses mark in language operates with equal force in the scene. Within one continuous shot, the continuing present ends, and we are suddenly in the future. But in fact what happens in this shot is even more complicated than that. I was worried that it would be too complicated to explain and would take too long, so I didn't go into it.

Before the last shot, the main character is sitting in a diner looking resigned as he delivers his interior monologue. You see his face in a close-up, so you are looking at the face of the man from whose mind the voice you hear is issuing. The monologue continues over the dissolve to the last shot, but in this shot the character moves farther and farther into the distance, even though the voice continues as it did when you saw the character in close-up. Then he makes his prediction, and we see it come true. The shift in tense that the prediction and its coming true produce is reinforced by the character's being off in the distance, as though his distance off in space corresponds to a distance off in time. But his being off in the distance has another affect: even though he speaks in the first person, his being in the distance results, for me at least, in the inner voice no longer seeming to come from the man whose body we see in the distance, but from someone else. It can't be anyone else in the scene, so it has to come from outside the scene, that is, from a narrator. A narrator isn't really in the film, just as the musicians who play music for the sound track aren't in the film. They are in a space outside of the film, except when Jean-Luc Godard makes a joke about it by having a pan reveal the musicians who until then were offscreen, and you see them producing the beautiful music that until you see them actually playing you took to be normal movie music.

So even though the scene in the diner made it clear that the origin of the voice was the mind of the character, in the last shot the character splits in two. There's a body on the screen, but the body is so far away that the voice no longer seems to come from it, but instead shifts to coming from someone we can only take to be a narrator. And in making this shift the voice leaves the space of the film and crosses over into a space that we know is outside of it. These two things together in the same shot, the change in tense and the character's splitting in two, produces a real vertigo.

The piece from *Under Capricorn* is another case of pointing to the long take, but beyond that, I also wanted to suggest that directors who work in the commercial film industry are sometimes interested in working in relation to the material constraints of film, just as avant-garde filmmakers are. I think it's clear that the long take was a part of Hitchcock's thinking about the film from the beginning, not a technical procedure that he so to speak added to a film that he already conceived separately from it. He conceived of the device of the long take and the subject together. In thinking up *Standard Gauge*, I did the same thing. The long take is ultimately a limit; there is a length longer than which a shot cannot be. And *Standard Gauge* is one minute short of it. Of course I wanted the film to be the maximum length, but it didn't quite work out.

Comparable thinking about limits is in some of Hitchcock's other work, notably *Rope* (1948), which takes as its founding rule the appearance of taking place in continuous time. There are cuts, but it appears that there is no lapse in time between the shots that they join. The film depicts a space that is as confined as the continuity of time would imply. Films usually elide time, and usually space too; they omit the time that the story doesn't need, and they jump from space to space as the story requires. So it's as if Hitchcock decided to make a film by refusing to resort to the usual treatment of space and time that film so easily makes available and that almost all commercial films depend on. (I note that the title of *Rope* names a material that is characterized by being a continuous length and that, like film, is, in relation to its length, narrow. And you want to preserve the continuity of rope. You don't cut rope unless you have to. So properties of rope call attention to the material continuity of the long takes that make up the film, and by implication the film's continuity of time.)

The same impulse to reverse orthodox conventions lies behind *Lifeboat* (1944) and *Rear Window* (1954). They're not temporally continuous, as *Rope* gives the appearance of being, but they are spatially continuous, in that they each take place in only one relatively confined space. After the montage of the ship's sinking that begins *Lifeboat*, and except for five underwater shots in the fishing sequence, for the entirety of the film the camera is in the lifeboat. *Rear Window* is only a little less strict. For almost every shot in the film the camera is within James Stewart's apartment. For the few shots where the camera is not in his apartment (several in the sequence following the death of the dog and several at the climax of the film), it is within the confines of the courtyard that his apartment looks out on, a space of course much bigger than his apartment but almost as circumscribed by walls as the apartment itself. There are lots of shots from James Stewart's apartment that are his POV,[1] and these POVs are cuts to spaces outside his apartment, but the camera remains in his apartment. When his POVs are through a telephoto lens, as they frequently are, what he sees is sufficiently alienated by distance that it creates the effect of a spatial discontinuity even though we know this can't be so because a POV in itself is a guarantor of spatial continuity. What look like spatial discontinuities are in fact inflections within the spatial continuity that we know *Rear Window* observes. I allow myself to suggest that the fragments of film within the continuity of *Standard Gauge* function in a comparable way: they look like cuts to other spaces, but in fact they are not.

My point is simply that in these films Hitchcock was consciously working in relation to limits: temporal continuity, spatial continuity, the material continuity of a roll of film. It was a question of his finding a story and limits that suited each other. So at least one director working in the commercial cinema sometimes looked at the limits that are implied in film, in both its conventions and its material, not as limits but as generative properties, and in thinking this way he was doing what many filmmakers have done who are far away from the industry. That doesn't make Hitchcock

1 POV is short for point of view. For more on point of view shots see "*Screening Room* and Death," 87–93 in Sabine Folie and Susanne Titz (eds.), Morgan Fisher, Writings. (Cologne: Walther Koenig, 2012).

an independent filmmaker, of course, but I want to point out the similarity in thinking between these two very different spheres. What makes the similarity in thinking possible is film as a material and the continuity that it both embodies and implies.

This interest in working in relation to limits is a specific case where it is possible to think of film as a unified field. Film of all kinds is unified by its material facts. I think this is true of film as it is true of no other medium. I wanted *Standard Gauge* to act out this idea of unity both in its form, combining 16mm and 35mm, and in its allusions. There are the allusions to commercial directors—Ulmer and Hitchcock—and in the same space, so to speak, are allusions to filmmakers not in the industry. I mention Bruce Conner by name, but other filmmakers are as present as Hitchcock and Ulmer and Vincente Minnelli, the director of *The Band Wagon* (1953).

The principal device of the film, a close-up of pieces of photographic material with voice-over commentary, bears enough of a resemblance to *(nostalgia)* (1971) to remind us of Hollis Frampton. The sprocket holes and edge lettering and dirt particles and the China girl all remind us of Owen Land (formerly known as George Landow). And Paul Sharits is there in the frames that are one solid color. The long take could be taken as a reference to Ernie Gehr as well as to Warhol. I suppose that the 20th Century Fox logo could be taken as an oblique allusion to Jack Goldstein, not a filmmaker as these others are, but an artist who as one part of his practice made films, and one of his films was an adaptation of another logo of a Hollywood studio, the MGM lion.

I was also thinking about painters. Ed Ruscha is there in the 20th Century Fox logo, Brice Marden is in the logo for Movielab, Adolph Gottlieb in the two blobby shapes on a plain background that must have been created by some chance event in a film lab, Ellsworth Kelly is in the solid blue frame, and Barnett Newman is in the frame that is solid blue except for the narrow vertical white band at the far right edge.

This was important to me, that a film could contain all these people in such a way that it was possible to think there was something that unified them besides their all being in the film. Maybe it's as simple as wanting to think that they are all artists, in the truest sense.

At the first screening of the film someone remarked that there was much in the film about death: the crash of the Hindenburg, the execution of the Fascist prison official, a director planning to make a film in which you saw people actually die, the death of a soldier in newsreel footage, figurative death in the decay of nitrate film and in the signs of the passing of time that so many of the pieces bear. I suppose this is true, but I really don't know what to make of it. Maybe it's an unconscious prefiguration of the death we know that film will undergo. I wonder how long 16mm will survive. The day will come when you can't buy 16mm film to shoot with, instead there will only be 16mm print stock to make prints from existing materials. Then they'll stop making black-and-white print stock and make only color print stock. Then someday they'll stop making 16mm altogether. I suppose the same will happen for 35mm, although that day is further off.

This possibility of the end of film is the negative implication of my saying that film is unified by its material facts as no other medium is. The absolute uniformity of film as a material (and the many things that spring from this simple fact) is a fundamental source of its appeal as a medium, but this uniformity is possible only because it is produced on an industrial basis. The origin of film's single most salient property in industrial production also gives film a vulnerability that no other medium has. The companies that make it can decide to stop making it. An individual can't manufacture film, so filmmakers are at the mercy of companies that make their raw material as people who work in other media and other forms are not. I suppose that a similar claim could be made for video, but film as film will someday be gone, while video in one form or another will go on indefinitely.

I wish there were a way to make a connection between this presence of death in *Standard Gauge* and the fact that the film is a single take. Maybe the connection is that in a long take we have the chance to experience real time and the continuity of space that it implies. Real time is the time in which we live, and that means it's also the time in which we die.

Introduction to *Gramophone, Film, Typewriter*

Friedrich Kittler

1986

Optical fiber networks. People will be hooked to an information channel that can be used for any medium—for the first time in history, or for its end. Once movies and music, phone calls and texts reach households via optical fiber cables, the formerly distinct media of television, radio, telephone, and mail converge, standardized by transmission frequencies and bit format. The optoelectronic channel in particular will be immune to disturbances that might randomize the pretty bit patterns behind the images and sounds. Immune, that is, to the bomb. As is well known, nuclear blasts send an electromagnetic pulse (EMP) through the usual copper cables, which would infect all connected computers.

The Pentagon is engaged in farsighted planning: only the substitution of optical fibers for metal cables can accommodate the enormous rates and volumes of bits required, spent, and celebrated by electronic warfare. All early warning systems, radar installations, missile bases, and army staffs in Europe, the opposite coast, finally will be connected to computers safe from EMP and thus will remain operational in wartime.[1] In the meantime, pleasure is produced as a by-product: people are free to channel-surf among entertainment media. After all, fiber optics transmit all messages imaginable save for the one that counts—the bomb.

Before the end, something is coming to an end. The general digitization of channels and information erases the differences among individual media. Sound and image, voice and text are reduced to surface effects, known to consumers as interface. Sense and the senses turn into eyewash. Their media-produced glamor will survive for an interim as a by-product of strategic programs. Inside the computers themselves everything becomes a number: quantity without image, sound, or voice. And once optical fiber networks turn formerly distinct data flows into a standardized series of digitized numbers, any medium can be translated into any other. With numbers, everything goes. Modulation, transformation, synchronization; delay, storage, transposition; scrambling, scanning, mapping—a total media link on a digital base will erase the very concept of medium. Instead of wiring people and technologies, absolute knowledge will run as an endless loop.

But there still are media; there still is entertainment.

Today's standard comprises partially connected media links that are still comprehensible in McLuhan's terms. According to him, one medium's content is always other media: film and radio constitute the content of television; records and tapes the content of radio; silent films and audiotape that of cinema; text, telephone, and telegram that of the semi-media monopoly of the postal system. Since the beginning of the century, when the electronic tube was developed by von Lieben in Germany and De Forest in California, it has been possible to amplify and transmit signals. Accordingly, the large media networks, which have been in existence since the thirties, have been able to fall back on all three storage media—writing, film, and photography—to link up and send their signals at will.

But these links are separated by incompatible data channels and differing data formats. Electrics does not equal electronics. Within the spectrum of the general data flow, television, radio, cinema, and the postal service constitute individual and limited windows for people's sense perceptions. Infrared radiations or the radio echoes of approaching missiles are still transmitted through other channels, unlike the optical fiber networks of the future. Our media systems merely distribute the words, noises, and images people can transmit and receive. But they do not compute these data. They do not produce an output that, under computer control, transforms any algorithm into any interface effect, to the point where people take leave of their senses. At this point, the only thing being computed is the transmission quality of storage media, which appear in the media links as the content of the media. A compromise between engineers and salespeople regulates how poor the sound from a TV set can be, how fuzzy movie images can be, or how much a beloved voice on the telephone can be filtered. Our sense perceptions are the dependent variable of this compromise.

1 Under the title "*Nostris ex ossibus:* Thoughts of an Optimist," Karl Haushofer, "the main representative, ... though not the originator, of the term 'geopolitics'" (November 2, 1945, in Hans-Adolf Jacobsen, *Haushofer: Leben und Werk*, [Boppard: 1979], 2: 639), wrote: "After the war, the Americans will appropriate a relatively wide strip of Europe's western and southern coast and, at the same time, in some shape or fashion annex England, thus realizing the ideal of Cecil Rhodes from the opposite coast. In doing so, they will act in accordance with the age-old ambition of any sea power to gain control of the opposite coast(s) and rule the ocean in between. The opposite coast is at least the entire eastern rim of the Atlantic and, in order to achieve domination over all 'seven seas,' possibly the entire western rim of the Pacific. Thus, America wants to connect the outer crescent to the 'axis'" (October 19, 1944, in Jacobsen, *Haushofer*, 2: 635)

A composite of face and voice that remains calm, even when faced during a televised debate by an opponent named Richard M. Nixon, is deemed telegenic and may win a presidential election, as in Kennedy's case. Voices that an optical close-up would reveal as treacherous, however, are called radiogenic and rule over the VE 301, the *Volksempfänger* of the Second World War. For, as the Heidegger disciple among Germany's early radio experts realized, "death is primarily a radio topic."[2]

But these sense perceptions had to be fabricated first. For media to link up and achieve dominance, we need a coincidence in the Lacanian sense: that something ceases not to write itself. Prior to the electrification of media, and well before their electronic end, there were modest, merely mechanical apparatuses. Unable to amplify or transmit, they nevertheless were the first to store sensory data: silent movies stored sights, and Edison's phonograph (which, unlike Berliner's later gramophone, was capable both of recording and reproducing) stored sounds.

On December 6, 1877, Edison, lord of the first research laboratory in the history of technology, presented the prototype of the phonograph to the public. On February 20, 1892, the same lab in Menlo Park (near New York) added the so-called kinetoscope. Three years later, the Lumière brothers in France and the Skladanowsky brothers in Germany merely had to add a means of projection to turn Edison's invention into cinema.

Ever since that epochal change we have been in possession of storage technologies that can record and reproduce the very time flow of acoustic and optical data. Ears and eyes have become autonomous. And that changed the state of reality more than lithography and photography, which (according to Benjamin's thesis) in the first third of the nineteenth century merely propelled the work of art into the age of its technical reproducibility. Media "define what really is"; they are always already beyond aesthetics.[3]

What phonographs and cinematographs, whose names not coincidentally derive from writing, were able to store was time: time as a mixture of audio frequencies in the acoustic realm and as the movement of single-image sequences in the optical. Time determines the limit of all art, which first has to arrest the daily data flow in order to turn it into images or signs. What is called style in art is merely the switchboard of these scannings and selections. That same switchboard also controls those arts that use writing as a serial, that is, temporally transposed, data flow. To record the sound sequences of speech, literature has to arrest them in a system of 26 letters, thereby categorically excluding all noise sequences. Not coincidentally, this system also contains as a subsystem the seven notes, whose diatonics—from A to G—form the basis of occidental music. Following a suggestion made by the musicologist von Hornbostel, it is possible to fix the chaos of exotic music assailing European ears by first interpolating a phonograph, which is able to record this chaos in real time and then replay it in slow motion. As the rhythms begin to flag and "individual measures, even individual notes resound on their own," occidental alphabetism with its staffs can proceed to an "exact notation."[4]

Texts and scores—Europe had no other means of storing time. Both are based on a writing system whose time is (in Lacan's term) symbolic. Using projections and retrievals, this time memorizes itself—like a chain of chains. Nevertheless, whatever ran as time on a physical or (again in Lacan's terms) real level, blindly and unpredictably, could by no means be encoded. Therefore, all data flows, provided they really were streams of data, had to pass through the bottleneck of the signifier. Alphabetic monopoly, grammatology.

If the film called history rewinds itself, it turns into an endless loop. What will soon end in the monopoly of bits and fiber optics began with the monopoly of writing. History was the homogenized field that, as an academic subject, only took account of literate cultures. Mouths and graphisms were relegated to prehistory. Otherwise, stories and histories (both deriving from *historia*) could not have been linked. All the orders and judgments, announcements and prescriptions (military and legal, religious and medical) that produced mountains of corpses were communicated along the very same channel that monopolized the descriptions of those mountains of corpses. Which is why anything that ever happened ended up in libraries.

And Foucault, the last historian or first archeologist, merely had to look things up. The suspicion that all power emanates from and returns to archives could be brilliantly confirmed, at least within the realms of law, medicine, and theology. A tautology of history, or its calvary. For the libraries in which the archeologist found so much rich material collected and catalogued papers that had been extremely diverse in terms of addressee, distribution technique, degree of secrecy, and writing technique—Foucault's archive as

2 Wilhelm Hoffmann, 1944, in Gerhard Hay, "Rundfunk in der Dichtung der zwanziger und dreißiger Jahre," in *Rundfunk und Politik 1923-1933: Beiträge zur Rundfunkforschung*, ed. Winfried B. Lerg and Rolf Steininger (Berlin, 1975), 374.

3 Norbert Bolz, "Die Schrift des Films," in *Diskursanalysen 1: Medien,* ed. Friedrich A. Kittler, Manfred Schneider, and Samuel Weber (Wiesbaden, 1986), 34.

4 Otto Abraham and Erich Moritz von Hornbostel, "Ober die Bedeutung des Phonographen fiir vergleichende Musikwissenschaft." *Zeitschrift für Ethnologie* 36 (1904), 229.

the entropy of a post office.[5] Even writing itself, before it ends up in libraries, is a communication medium, the technology of which the archeologist simply forgot. It is for this reason that all his analyses end immediately before that point in time at which other media penetrated the library's stacks. Discourse analysis cannot be applied to sound archives or towers of film rolls.

As long as it was moving along, history was indeed Foucault's "wave-like succession of words."[6] More simply, but no less technically than tomorrow's fiber optic cables, writing functioned as a universal medium—in times when there was no concept of medium. Whatever else was going on dropped through the filter of letters or ideograms.

"Literature," Goethe wrote, "is a fragment of fragments; only the smallest proportion of what took place and what was said was written down, while only the smallest proportion of what was written down has survived."[7]

Accordingly, oral history today confronts the historians' writing monopoly; accordingly, a media theoretician like the Jesuit priest Walter J. Ong, who must have been concerned with the spirit of the Pentecostal mystery, could celebrate a primary orality of tribal cultures as opposed to the secondary orality of our media acoustics. Such research remained unthinkable as long as the opposite of "history" was simply termed (again following Goethe) "legend."[8] Prehistory was subsumed by its mythical name; Goethe's definition of literature did not even have to mention optical or acoustic data flows. And even legends, those oralized segments of bygone events, only survived in written format; that is, under pretechnological but literary conditions. However, since it has become possible to record the epics of the last Homeric bards, who until recently were wandering through Serbia and Croatia, oral mnemotechnics or cultures have become reconstructible in a completely different way.[9] Even Homer's rosy-fingered Eos changes from a Goddess into a piece of chromium dioxide that was stored in the memory of the bard and could be combined with other pieces into whole epics. "Primary orality" and "oral history" came into existence only after the end of the writing monopoly, as the technological shadows of the apparatuses that document them.

Writing, however, stored writing—no more and no less. The holy books attest to this. Exodus, chapter 20, contains a copy of what Yahweh's own finger originally had written on two stone tablets: the law. But of the thunder and lightning, of the thick cloud and the mighty trumpet which, according to scripture, surrounded this first act of writing on Mount Sinai, that same Bible could store nothing but mere words.[10]

Even less is handed down of the nightmares and temptations that afflicted a nomad called Mohammed following his flight to the holy mountain of Hira. The Koran does not begin until the one God takes the place of the many demons. The archangel Gabriel descends from the seventh heaven with a roll of scripture and the command to decipher the scroll. "Rejoice in the name of the Lord who created—created man from clots of blood. Recite! Your Lord is the Most Bountiful One, who by pen taught man what he did not know."[11]

Mohammed, however, answers that he, the nomad, can't read; not even the divine message about the origin of reading and writing. The archangel has to repeat his command before an illiterate can turn into the founder of a book-based religion. For soon, or all too soon, the illegible scroll makes sense and presents to Mohammed's miraculously alphabetized eyes the very same text that Gabriel had already uttered twice as an oral command. Mohammed's illuminations began, according to tradition, with this 96th sura—in order then to be "memorized by the faithful and written down on primitive surfaces such as palm leaves, stones, wood, bones, and pieces of leather, and to be recited, again and again, by Mohammed and select believers, especially during Ramadan."[12]

Writing therefore merely stores the fact of its authorization. It celebrates the storage monopoly of the God who invented it. And since the realm of this God consists of signs that only nonreaders can't make sense of, all books are books of the dead, like the Egyptian ones with which literature began.[13] The book itself coincides with the realm of the dead beyond all senses into which it lures us. When the Stoic philosopher Zeno asked the oracle at Delphi how he should best lead his life, he was given the answer "that

5 See Rudiger Campe, "Pronto! Telefonate und Telephonstimmen," in *Diskursanalysen 1: Medien*, ed. Friedrich A. Kittler, Manfred Schneider, and Samuel Weber (Wiesbaden, 1986), 70-71.

6 Michel Foucault, "Language to Infinity," in *Language, Counter-Memory, Practice: Selected Essays and Interviews*, ed. Donald F. Bouchard (Ithaca: Cornell University Press, 1977), 66.

7 Johann Wolfgang von Goethe, *Wilhelm Meister's Years of Travel; or; The Renunciants*, bk 2. Trans. H. M. Waidson. (New York, 1981), 122.

8 Goethe, "Geschichte der Farbenlehre" (1810), in *Werke*, ed. by Erich Trunz (Munich, 1976), 14: 47. [The oral nature of this "opposite" to written history is underscored by the use of Goethe's word *Sage*, "legend," which derives from *sagen*, "to say." -Trans.]

9 See Walter J. Ong, *Orality and Literacy: The Technologizing of the Word* (London/New York: Routledge, 1982), 27 and (more reasonably) 3.

10 See Exodus 24:12-34:28.

11 Koran, sura 96, vv. 1-6.

12 *Der Koran: Das heilige Buch des Islam*, L.W. Winter, ed. (Munich, 1959), 6.

13 See *Schrift und Geddchtnis: Archäologie der literarischen Kommunikation*, ed. Aleida Assmann and Jan Assmann (Munich, 1983), 68.

he should mate with the dead. He understood this to mean that he should *read* the *ancients*."[14]

The story of how the divine instructions to use quills extended beyond Moses and Mohammed and reached simpler and simpler people is a lengthy one that nobody can write, because it would be history itself. In much the same way, the storage capacities of our computers will soon coincide with electronic warfare and, gigabyte upon gigabyte, exceed all the processing capacities of historians.

Suffice it to say that one day—in Germany, this may have already been the case during the age of Goethe—the homogenous medium of writing also became homogenous in the social sphere. Compulsory education engulfed people in paper. They learned a way of writing that, as an "abuse of language" (according to Goethe), no longer had to struggle with cramped muscles and individual letters, but rather proceeded in rapture or darkness. They learned to read "silently to one's self," a "sorry substitute for speech" that consumed letters without effort by bypassing oral organs.[15] Whatever they emitted and received was writing. And because only that exists which can be posted, bodies themselves fell under the regime of the symbolic. What is unthinkable today was once reality: no film stored the movements they made or saw, no phonograph, the noise they made or heard. For whatever existed failed before time. Silhouettes or pastel drawings fixed facial expressions, and scores were unable to store noise. But once a hand took hold of a pen, something miraculous occurred: the body, which did not cease not to write itself, left strangely unavoidable traces.

> I'm ashamed to tell of it. I'm ashamed of my handwriting. It exposes me in all my spiritual nakedness. My handwriting shows me more naked than I am with my clothes off. No leg, no breath, no clothes, no sound. Neither voice nor reflection. All cleaned out. Instead, a whole man's being, shriveled and misshapen, like his scribble-scrabble. His lines are all that's left of him, as well as his self-propagation. The uneven tracings of his pencil on paper, so minimal that a blind man's fingertips would hardly detect them, become the measure of the whole fellow.[16]

Today, this shame, which overcomes the hero of Botha Strauss's last love story, *Dedication*, whenever he sees his handwriting, is no more than an anachronism. The fact that the minimal unevenness between stroke and paper can store neither a voice nor an image of a body presupposes in its exclusion the invention of phonography and cinema. Before their invention, however, handwriting alone could guarantee the perfect securing of traces. It wrote and wrote, in an energetic and ideally uninterrupted flow. As Hegel so correctly observed, the alphabetized individual had his "appearance and externality" in this continuous flow of ink or letters.[17]

And what applied to writing also applied to reading. Even if the alphabetized individual known as the "author" finally had to fall from the private exteriority of handwriting into the anonymous exteriority of print in order to secure "all that's left of him, as well as his self-propagation"—alphabetized individuals known as "readers" were able to reverse this exteriorization. "If one reads in the right way," Novalis wrote, "the words will unfold in us a real, visible world."[18] And his friend Schlegel added that "one believes to hear what one merely reads."[19] Perfect alphabetization was to supplement precisely those optical and acoustic data flows that, under the monopoly of writing, did not cease not to write themselves. Effort had been removed from writing, and sound from reading, in order to naturalize writing. The letters that educated readers skimmed over provided people with sights and sounds.

Aided by compulsory education and new alphabetization techniques, the book became both film and record around 1800—not as a media-technological reality, but in the imaginary of readers' souls. As a surrogate of unstorable data flows, books came to power and glory.[20]

In 1774 an editor by the name of Goethe committed handwritten letters or *Sorrows of Young Werther* to print. The "nameless throng" (to quote the dedication of *Faust*), too, was to hear an "early song" that, like "some old half-faded song," revived "old griefs" and "old friends."[21] This was the new literary recipe for success: to surreptitiously turn the voice or handwriting of a soul into Gutenbergiana. In the last letter he wrote and sealed but did not send off before committing suicide, Werther gave his beloved the very promise of poetry: during her lifetime she would have

---

14 Friedrich Nietzsche, "Geschichte der griechischen Literatur" (1874), in *Sämtliche Werke, Musarion Ausgabe* (Munich, 1922-29), 5: 213.

15 Goethe, *The Autobiography of Johann Wolfgang von Goethe (Dichtung und Wahrheit)*, trans. John Oxenford (New York: Horizon Press, 1969), 3: 59.

16 Botho Strauss, *Devotion*, trans. Sophie Wilkins (New York: Farrar, Strauss and Giroux, 1979).

17 Georg Wilhelm Friedrich Hegel, *Phenomenology of Spirit*, trans. A.V. Miller (Oxford: Oxford University Press, 1977), 190.

18 Friedrich von Hardenberg (Novalis), *Schriften*, ed. Paul Kluckhohn and Richard Samuel (Stuttgart, 1960-75), 3: 377.

19 Friedrich Schlegel, *Kritische Ausgabe*, ed. Ernst Behler (Munich, 1958-87), 8: 42.

20 See Kittler, *Discourse Networks, 1800/1900*, trans. Michael Metteer, with Chris Cullens (Stanford, CA: Stanford University Press, 1990), 108-23.

21 Goethe, *Faust, Part One*, trans. David Luke (Oxford: Oxford University Press, 1987), 3. For reasons why a fully alphabetized literature in particular simulated orality, see Heinz Schlaffer, "Einführung," in Jack Goody, Ian Watt and Kathleen Gough, *Enstehung und Folgen der Schriftkultur* (Frankfurt a.M.), 7-20.

to remain with Albert, her unloved husband, but afterwards she would be united with her lover "in the sight of the Infinite One in eternal embraces."[22] Indeed: the addressee of handwritten love letters, which were then published by a mere editor, was to be rewarded with an immortality in the shape of the novel itself. It alone was able to create the "beautiful realm" in which the lovers of Goethe's *Elective Affinities*, according to the hope of their narrator, "will waken together once more." [23, 24] Strangely enough, Eduard and Ottilie had one and the same handwriting during their lifetime. Their death elevated them to a paradise that under the storage monopoly of writing was called poetry.

And maybe that paradise was more real than our media-controlled senses can imagine. Reading intently, Werther's suicidal readers may well have perceived their hero in a real, visible world. And the lovers among Goethe's female readers, like Bettina Brentano, may well have died with the heroine of his *Elective Affinities* only to be "reborn in a more beautiful youth" through Goethe's "genius."[25] Maybe the perfectly alphabetized readers of 1800 were a living answer to the question with which Chris Marker concludes his film essay *Sans Soleil*:

> Lost at the end of the world on my island, Sal, in the company of my dogs strutting around, I remember that January in Tokyo, or rather I remember the images I filmed in Tokyo in January. They have now put themselves in place of my memory, they *are* my memory. I wonder how people who do not film, take photos, or record tapes remember, how humankind used to go about remembering.[26]

It is the same with language, which only leaves us the choice of either retaining words while losing their meaning or, vice versa, retaining meaning while losing the words.[27] Once storage media can accommodate optical and acoustic data, human memory capacity is bound to dwindle. Its "liberation" is its end.[28] As long as the book was responsible for all serial data flows, words quivered with sensuality and memory. It was the passion of all reading to hallucinate meaning between lines and letters: the visible and audible world of Romantic poetics. And the passion of all writing was (in the words of E.T.A. Hoffmann) the poet's desire to "describe" the hallucinated "picture in one's mind with all its vivid colors, the light and the shade," in order to "strike [the] gentle reader like an electric shock."[29]

Electricity itself put an end to this. Once memories and dreams, the dead and ghosts, become technically reproducible, readers and writers no longer need the powers of hallucination. Our realm of the dead has withdrawn from the books in which it resided for so long. As Diodor of Sicily once wrote, "it is no longer only through writing that the dead remain in the memory of the living."

The writer Balzac was already overcome by fear when faced with photography, as he confessed to Nadar, the great pioneer of photography. If (according to Balzac) the human body consists of many infinitely thin layers of "specters," and if the human spirit cannot be created from nothingness, then the daguerreotype must be a sinister trick: it fixes, that is, steals, one layer after the other, until nothing remains of the specters and the photographed body.[30] Photo albums establish a realm of the dead infinitely more precise than Balzac's competing literary enterprise, the *Comédie humaine*, could ever hope to create. In contrast to the arts, media do not have to make do with the grid of the symbolic. That is to say, they reconstruct bodies not only in a system of words or colors or sound intervals. Media and media only fulfill the "high standards" that (according to Rudolf Arnheim) we expect from "reproductions" since the invention of photography: "They are not only supposed to resemble the object, but rather guarantee this resemblance by being, as it were, a product of the object in question, that is, by being mechanically produced by it—just as the illuminated objects of reality imprint their image on the photographic layer,"or the frequency curves of noises inscribe their wavelike shapes onto the phonographic plate.[31]

A reproduction authenticated by the object itself

---

22 Goethe, *Werther* (1774), in *The Sufferings of Young Werther* and *Elective Affinities*, ed. Victor Lange (New York: Continuum, 1990), 109.

23 Benjamin, *Gesammelte Schriften*, ed. Rolf Tiedemann, et al. (Frankfurt a.M., 1972-85), 1: 1, 200. [see *Walter Benjamin: Selected Writings*, edited by Howard Eiland & Michael W. Jennings. Cambridge, MA/London: Belknap Press of Harvard University Press, 2004-2006 -Ed.]

24 Goethe, *Elective Affinities*, 342.

25 Bettina Brentano, *Bettina von Arnim, Werke und Briefe*, ed. Gustav Konrad (Frechen, 1959-63), 2: 222.

26 Chris Marker, *Sans Soleil / Unsichtbare Sonne: Vollständiger Text zum gleichnamigen Film-Essay*, (Hamburg, 1983), 23-24.

27 See Gilles Deleuze, "Pierre Klossowski ou Les corps-langage," *Critique* 21 (1965), 32. "The alternative is between two purities; the false and the true; that of responsibility and that of innocence; that of memory and that of forgetting .... Either one remembers words but their meaning remains obscure, or one apprehends the meaning, in which case the memory of the words disappears."

28 Leroi-Gourhan, quoted in Jacques Derrida, *Of Grammatology*, trans. Gayatri Chakravorty Spivak (Baltimore: Johns Hopkins University Press, 1976), 333n.

29 E.T.A. Hoffmann, "The Sandman," in *Selected Writings*, vol. I, *The Tales*, ed. & trans. Leonard J. Kent and Elizabeth C. Knight (Chicago: University of Chicago Press, 1969), 148 (translation modified).

30 Nadar, "My Life as a Photographer," *October* 5 (1978): 9.

31 Rudolf Arnheim, "Systematik der frühen kinematographischen Erfindungen," in *Kritiken und Aufsätze zum Film*, ed. Helmut H. Dieterichs (Munich, 1977), 27. [see *Film Essays and Criticism*, trans. Brenda Benthien (Madison, WI/London: University of Wisconsin Press, 1997) -Ed.]

is one of physical precision. It refers to the bodily real, which of necessity escapes all symbolic grids. Media always already provide the appearances of specters. For, according to Lacan, even the word "corpse" is a euphemism in reference to the real.[32]

Accordingly, the invention of the Morse alphabet in 1837 was promptly followed by the tapping specters of spiritistic seances sending their messages from the realm of the dead. Promptly as well, photographic plates—even and especially those taken with the camera shutter closed—furnished reproductions of ghosts or specters, whose black-and-white fuzziness only served to underscore the promise of resemblance. Finally, one of the ten applications Edison envisioned for his newly invented phonograph in the *North American Review* (1878) was to record "the last words of dying persons."

It was only a small step from such a "family record," with its special consideration of revenants, to fantasies that had telephone cables linking the living and the dead.[33] What Leopold Bloom in *Ulysses* could only wish for in his Dublin graveyard meditations had already been turned into science fiction by Walter Rathenau, the AEG chairman of the board and futurist writer.[34] In Rathenau's story "Resurrection Co.," the cemetery administration of Necropolis, Dacota/USA, following a series of scandalous premature burials in 1898, founds a daughter company entitled "Dacota and Central Resurrection Telephone Bell Co." with a capital stock of $750,000. Its sole purpose is to make certain that the inhabitants of graves, too, are connected to the public telephone network. Whereupon the dead avail themselves of the opportunity to prove, long before McLuhan, that the content of one medium is always another medium—in this concrete case, a *déformation professionelle*.[35]

These days, paranormal voices on tape or radio, the likes of which have been spiritistically researched since 1959 and preserved in rock music since Laurie Anderson's 1982 release *Big Science*, inform their researchers of their preferred radio wavelength.[36] This already occurred in 1898, in the case of Senate President Schreber: when a paranormal, beautifully autonomous "base or nerve language" revealed its code as well as its channels, message and channel became one.[37] "You just have to choose a middle-, short-, or long-wave talk-show station, or the 'white noise' between two stations, or the 'Jürgenson wave,' which, depending on where you are, is located around 1450 to 1600 kHz between Vienna and Moscow."[38] If you replay a tape that has been recorded off the radio, you will hear all kinds of ghost voices that do not originate from any known radio station, but that, like all official newscasters, indulge in radio self-advertisement. Indeed, the location and existence of that "Jürgenson wave" was pinpointed by none other than "Friedrich Jürgenson, the Nestor of vocal research."[39]

The realm of the dead is as extensive as the storage and transmission capabilities of a given culture. As Klaus Theweleit noted, media are always flight apparatuses into the great beyond. If gravestones stood as symbols at the beginning of culture itself, our media technology can retrieve all gods. The old written laments about ephemerality, which measured no more than distance between writing and sensuality, suddenly fall silent. In our mediascape, immortals have come to exist again.

War on the Mind is the title of an account of the psychological strategies hatched by the Pentagon. It reports that the staffs planning the electronic war, which merely continues the Battle of the Atlantic, have already compiled a list of the propitious and unpropitious days in other cultures.[40] This list enables the U.S. Air Force "to time [its] bombing campaigns

32 See Jacques Lacan, *The Seminar of Jacques Lacan. Book II: The Ego in Freud's Theory and in the Technique of Psychoanalysis 1954-55*, trans. Sylvana Tomaselli (New York: W.W. Norton, 1988), 278.

33 Edison, 1878, quoted in Roland Gelatt, *The Fabulous Phonograph 1877-1977. From Edison to Stereo* (2nd rev. ed. New York: Macmillan, 1977), 29. Phonographic recordings of last words are based on the recognition that "physiological time is not reversible," and that "in the province of rhythm, and of time in general, there is no symmetry" (Ernst Mach, *The Analysis of Sensations and the Relation of the Physical to the Psychical*, trans. C.M. Williams [Chicago/London: Open Court, 1914], 256).

34 See James Joyce, *Ulysses* (Harmondsworth: Penguin Books, 1969), 113. See also John Brooks, "The First and Only Century of Telephone Literature," in *The Social Impact of the Telephone*, ed. Ithiel de Sola Pool, 208-24 (Cambridge, MA: MIT Press, 1977), 213-14. ["AEG" refers to the Allgemeine Elektrizitäts-Gesellschaft, one of the leading German electronics corporations. It was originally founded in 1883 by Emil Rathenau as the German Edison Society for Applied Electricity. -Trans.]

35 Walter Rathenau, *Gesammelte Schriften* (Berlin, 1918-29), 4: 347. Two examples of *déformation professionelle* among the dead of Necropolis: "A writer is dissatisfied with his epitaph. An employee of the telephone company uses short and long intervals, a kind of Morse alphabet, to ring in a critique of his successor." King Alexander, the hero of Bronnen's *Ostpolzug*, says everything there is to say about telephonitis and Hades while, according to the stage directions, the "telephone is buzzing": "Oh, you black beast growing on fatty brown stems, you flower of untimeliness, you rabbit of dark rooms! Your voice is our hereafter, and it has crowded out heaven" (Arnolt Bronnen, *Werke*, ed. Hans Mayer [Kronberg, 1977], 1: 133).

36 The song "Example #22" actually combines the announcement and sound of "example no. 22" ("Hier spricht Edgar" / "Edgar speaking" [Hildegard Schäfer, *Stimmen aus einer anderen Welt* (Freiburg, 1983), 11]), which, strangely enough, must have migrated on a paranormal cassette-to-book from Freiburg to the United States.

37 See Lacan, *Ecrits: A Selection*, trans. Alan Sheridan (New York: W.W. Norton, 1977), 184.

38 Schäfer, *Stimmen aus einer anderen Welt*, 2.

39 Ibid., 3.

to coincide with unpropitious days, thus 'confirming' the forecasts of local gods." As well, the voices of these gods have been recorded on tape to be broadcast from helicopters "to keep tribes in their villages." And finally, the Pentagon has developed special film projectors capable of projecting those gods onto low-hanging clouds.[41] A technologically implemented beyond...

Of course the Pentagon does not keep a handwritten list of good and bad days. Office technology keeps up with media technology. Cinema and the phonograph, Edison's two great achievements that ushered in the present, are complemented by the typewriter. Since 1865 (according to European accounts) or 1868 (according to American ones), writing has no longer been the ink or pencil trace of a body whose optical and acoustic signals were irretrievably lost, only to reappear (in readers' minds) in the surrogate sensuality of handwriting. In order to store series of sights and sounds, Old Europe's only storage technology first had to be mechanized. Hans Magnus Malling Hansen in Copenhagen and Christopher Latham Sholes in Milwaukee developed mass-producible typewriters. Edison commented positively on the invention's potential when Sholes visited him in Newark to demonstrate his newly patented model and to invite the man who had invented invention to enter a joint venture.[42]

But Edison declined the offer—as if, already in 1868, the phonograph and kinetoscope preoccupied their future inventor. Instead, the offer was grabbed by an arms manufacturer suffering from dwindling revenues in the post-Civil War slump. Remington, not Edison, took over Sholes's discourse machine gun.

Thus, there was no Marvelous One from whose brow sprang all three media technologies of the modern age. On the contrary, the beginning of our age was marked by separation or differentiation.[43] On the one hand, we have two technological media that, for the first time, fix unwritable data flows; on the other, an "'intermediate' thing between a tool and a machine," as Heidegger wrote so precisely about the typewriter.[44] On the one hand, we have the entertainment industry with its new sensualities; on the other, a writing that already separates paper and body during textual production, not first during reproduction (as Gutenberg's movable types had done). From the beginning, the letters and their arrangement were standardized in the shapes of type and keyboard, while media were engulfed by the noise of the real—the fuzziness of cinematic pictures, the hissing of tape recordings.

In standardized texts, paper and body, writing and soul fall apart. Typewriters do not store individuals; their letters do not communicate a beyond that perfectly alphabetized readers can subsequently hallucinate as meaning. Everything that has been taken over by technological media since Edison's inventions disappears from typescripts. The dream of a real visible or audible world arising from words has come to an end. The historical synchronicity of cinema, phonography, and typewriting separated optical, acoustic, and written data flows, thereby rendering them autonomous. That electric or electronic media can recombine them does not change the fact of their differentiation.

In 1860, five years before Malling Hansen's mechanical writing ball (the first mass-produced typewriter), Gottfried Keller's "Misused Love Letters" still proclaimed the illusion of poetry itself: love is left with the impossible alternatives of speaking either with "black ink" or with "red blood."[45] But once typing, filming, and recording became equally valid options, writing lost such surrogate sensualities. Around 1880 poetry turned into literature. Standardized letters were no longer to transmit Keller's red blood or Hoffmann's inner forms, but rather a new and elegant tautology of technicians. According to Mallarmé's instant insight, literature is made up of no more and no less than twenty-six letters.[46]

Lacan's "methodological distinction" among the real, the imaginary, and the symbolic is the theory (or merely a historical effect) of that differentiation.[47] The symbolic now encompasses linguistic signs in their materiality and technicity. That is to say, letters and ciphers form a finite set without taking into account philosophical dreams of infinity. What counts are differences, or, in the language of the typewriter, the spaces between the elements of a system. For that reason, Lacan designates "the world of the symbolic [as] the world of the machine."[48]

The imaginary, however, comes about as the mirror

---

40 See Don E. Gordon, *Electronic Warfare: Element of Strategy and Multiplier of Combat Power*, (New York: Pergamon Press, 1981), *passim*

41 Peter Watson, *War on the Mind: The Military Uses and Abuses of Psychology* (London, 1978), 26, 410.

42 See Alfred Walze, "Auf den Spuren von Christopher Latham Scholes: Ein Besuch in Milwaukee, der Geburtstatte der ersten brauchbaren Schreibmaschine." *Deutsche Stenografenzeitung* (1980), 133.

43 See Niklas Luhmann, "Das Problem der Epochenbildung und die Evolutionstheorie," in *Epochenschwellen und Epochenstrukturen im Diskurs der Literatur- und Sprachhistorie,* ed. Hans-Ulrich Gumbrecht and Ulla Link-Herr (Frankfurt a.M, 1985), 20-22.

44 Martin Heidegger, *Parmenides*, trans. Andre Schuwer and Richard Rojcewicz (Bloomington: Indiana University Press, 1992), 86.

45 Gottfried Keller, *The Misused Love Letters* and *Regula Amrain and her Youngest Son*, trans. Michael Bullock and Anne Fremantle (New York, 1974), 41.

46 See Stephane Mallarmé, *Oeuvres completes*, ed. Henri Mondor and G. Jean-Aubry (Paris, 1945), 850.

47 Lacan, *Ecrits* (Paris, 1966), 720.

48 Lacan, *Seminar* Book II: 47.

image of a body that appears to be, in terms of motor control, more perfect than the infant's own body, for in the real everything begins with coldness, dizziness, and shortness of breath.[49] Thus, the imaginary implements precisely those optical illusions that were being researched in the early days of cinema. A dismembered or (in the case of film) cut-up body is faced with the illusionary continuity of movements in the mirror or on screen. It is no coincidence that Lacan recorded infants' jubilant reactions to their mirror images in the form of documentary footage.

Finally, of the real nothing more can be brought to light than what Lacan presupposed—that is, nothing. It forms the waste or residue that neither the mirror of the imaginary nor the grid of the symbolic can catch: the physiological accidents and stochastic disorder of bodies.

The methodological distinctions of modern psychoanalysis clearly coincide with the distinctions of media technology. Every theory has its historical a priori. And structuralist theory simply spells out what, since the turn of the century, has been coming over the information channels.

Only the typewriter provides writing as a selection from the finite and arranged stock of its keyboard. It literally embodies what Lacan illustrated using the antiquated letter box. In contrast to the flow of handwriting, we now have discrete elements separated by spaces. Thus, the symbolic has the status of block letters. Film was the first to store those mobile doubles that humans, unlike other primates, were able to (mis)perceive as their own body. Thus, the imaginary has the status of cinema. And only the phonograph can record all the noise produced by the larynx prior to any semiotic order and linguistic meaning. To experience pleasure, Freud's patients no longer have to desire what philosophers consider good. Rather, they are free to babble.[50] Thus, the real—especially in the talking cure known as psychoanalysis—has the status of phonography.

Once the technological differentiation of optics, acoustics, and writing exploded Gutenberg's writing monopoly around 1880, the fabrication of so-called Man became possible. His essence escapes into apparatuses. Machines take over functions of the central nervous system, and no longer, as in times past, merely those of muscles. And with this differentiation—and not with steam engines and railroads—a clear division occurs between matter and information, the real and the symbolic. When it comes to inventing phonography and cinema, the age-old dreams of humankind are no longer sufficient. The physiology of eyes, ears, and brains have to become objects of scientific research. For mechanized writing to be optimized, one can no longer dream of writing as the expression of individuals or the trace of bodies. The very forms, differences, and frequencies of its letters have to be reduced to formulas. So-called Man is split up into physiology and information technology.

When Hegel summed up the perfect alphabetism of his age, he called it Spirit. The readability of all history and all discourses turned humans or philosophers into God. The media revolution of 1880, however, laid the groundwork for theories and practices that no longer mistake information for spirit. Thought is replaced by a Boolean algebra, and consciousness by the unconscious, which (at least since Lacan's reading) makes of Poe's "Purloined Letter" a Markoff chain.[51] And that the symbolic is called the world of the machine undermines Man's delusion of possessing a "quality" called "consciousness," which identifies him as something other and better than a "calculating machine." For both people and computers are "subject to the appeal of the signifier"; that is, they are both run by programs. "Are these humans," Nietzsche already asked himself in 1874, eight years before buying a typewriter, "or perhaps only thinking, writing, and speaking machines?"[52]

In 1950 Alan Turing, the practitioner among England's mathematicians, gave the answer to Nietzsche's question. He observed, with formal elegance, that there is no question to begin with. To clarify the issue, Turing's essay "Computing Machinery and Intelligence"—appearing in, of all places, the philosophical periodical *Mind*—proposed an experiment, the so-called Turing game: A computer A and human B exchange data via some kind of telewriter interface. The exchange of texts is monitored by a censor C, who also only receives written information. A and B both pretend to be human, and C has to decide which of the two is simulating and which merely is Nietzsche's thinking, writing, and speaking machine. But the game remains open-ended, because each time the machine gives itself away- be it by making a mistake or, more likely, by not making any—it will refine its program by learning.[53] In the Turing game, Man coincides with his simulation.

And this is, obviously, already so because the censor C receives plotter printouts and typescripts rather than handwritten texts. Of course, computer programs could simulate the "individuality" of the human

---

49 See Lacan, *Ecrits: A Selection*, 1-7.

50 See Lacan, *Le séminaire: livre XX* (Paris, 1975), 53, 73.

51 See Lacan, *Seminar* Book II: 191-205.

52 Nietzsche, *Unmodern Observations*, ed. William Arrowsmith, trans. Gary Brown, William Arrowsmith, and Herbert Golder (New Haven: Yale University Press, 1990), 110.

53 See Alan Turing, "Computing Machinery and Intelligence," *Mind: A Quarterly Review of Psychology and Philosophy* 59 (1950), 441-42; Andrew Hodges, *Alan Turing: The Enigma* (New York: Simon and Schuster, 1983), 415-17.

hand, with its routines and mistakes, but Turing, as the inventor of the universal discrete machine, was a typist. Though he wasn't much better or skilled at it than his tomcat Timothy, who was allowed to jump across the keyboard in Turing's chaotic secret service office, it was at least somewhat less catastrophic than his handwriting.[54] The teachers at the honorable Sherborne School could hardly "forgive" their pupil's chaotic lifestyle and messy writing. He got lousy grades for brilliant exams in mathematics only because his handwriting was "the worst ... ever seen."[55] Faithfully, schools cling to their old duty of fabricating individuals (in the literal sense of the word) by drilling them in a beautiful, continuous, and individual handwriting. Turing, a master in subverting all education, however, dodged the system; he made plans for an "exceedingly crude" typewriter.[56]

Nothing came of these plans. But when, on the meadows of Grantchester, the meadows of all English poetry from the Romantics to Pink Floyd, he hit upon the idea of the universal discrete machine, his early dreams were realized and transformed. Sholes's typewriter, reduced to its fundamental principle, has supported us to this day. Turing merely got rid of the people and typists that Remington & Son needed for reading and writing.

And this is possible because a Turing machine is even more exceedingly crude than the Sherborne plan for a typewriter. All it works with is a paper strip that is both its program and its data material, its input and its output. Turing slimmed down the common typewriter page to this little strip. But there are even more economizations: his machine doesn't need the many redundant letters, ciphers, and signs of a typewriter keyboard; it can do with one sign and its absence, 1 and 0. This binary information can be read or (in Turing's technospeak) scanned by the machine. It can then move the paper strip one space to the right, one to the left, or not at all, moving in a jerky (i.e., discrete) fashion like a typewriter, which in contrast to handwriting has block caps, a back spacer, and a space bar. (From a letter to Turing: "Pardon the use of the typewriter: I have come to prefer discrete machines to continuous ones.")[57] The mathematical model of 1936 is no longer a hermaphrodite of a machine and a mere tool. As a feedback system it beats all the Remingtons, because each step is controlled by scanning the paper strip for the sign or its absence, which amounts to a kind of writing: it depends on this reading whether the machine keeps the sign or erases it, or, vice versa, whether it keeps a space blank or replaces it with a sign, and so on and so forth.

That's all. But no computer that has been built or ever will be built can do more. Even the most advanced Von Neumann machines (with program storage and computing units), though they operate much faster, are in principle no different from Turing's infinitely slow model. Also, while not all computers have to be Von Neumann machines, all conceivable data processing machines are merely a state *n* of the universal discrete machine. This was proved mathematically by Alan Turing in 1936, two years before Konrad Zuse in Berlin built the first programmable computer from simple relays. And with that the world of the symbolic really turned into the world of the machine.

Unlike the history to which it put an end, the media age proceeds in jerks, just like Turing's paper strip. From the Remington via the Turing machine to microelectronics, from mechanization and automatization to the implementation of a writing that is only cipher, not meaning—one century was enough to transfer the age-old monopoly of writing into the omnipotence of integrated circuits. Not unlike Turing's correspondents, everyone is deserting analog machines in favor of discrete ones. The CD digitizes the gramophone, the video camera digitizes the movies. All data streams flow into a state *n* of Turing's universal machine; Romanticism notwithstanding, numbers and figures become the key to all creatures.

---

54 Hodges, *Alan Turing*, 279.

55 Hodges, 30.

56 Hodges, 14.

57 J. Good, September 16, 1948, quoted in ibid., 387.

58 See Konrad Zuse, June 19, 1937, in *Der Computer: Mein Lebenswerk* (2d ed. Berlin, 1984), 41: "Decisive thought, 19 June 1937 / Realization that there are elementary operations to which all computing and thinking operations may be reduced. / A primitive type of mechanical brain consists of storage unit, dialing system, and a simple device that can handle conditional chains of two or three links. / With such a form of brain it must be possible to solve all operations of the mind that can be dealt with mechanically, regardless of the time involved. More complex brains are merely a matter of executing those operations faster."

Still from *Handsworth Songs*

Black Audio Film Collective

1986

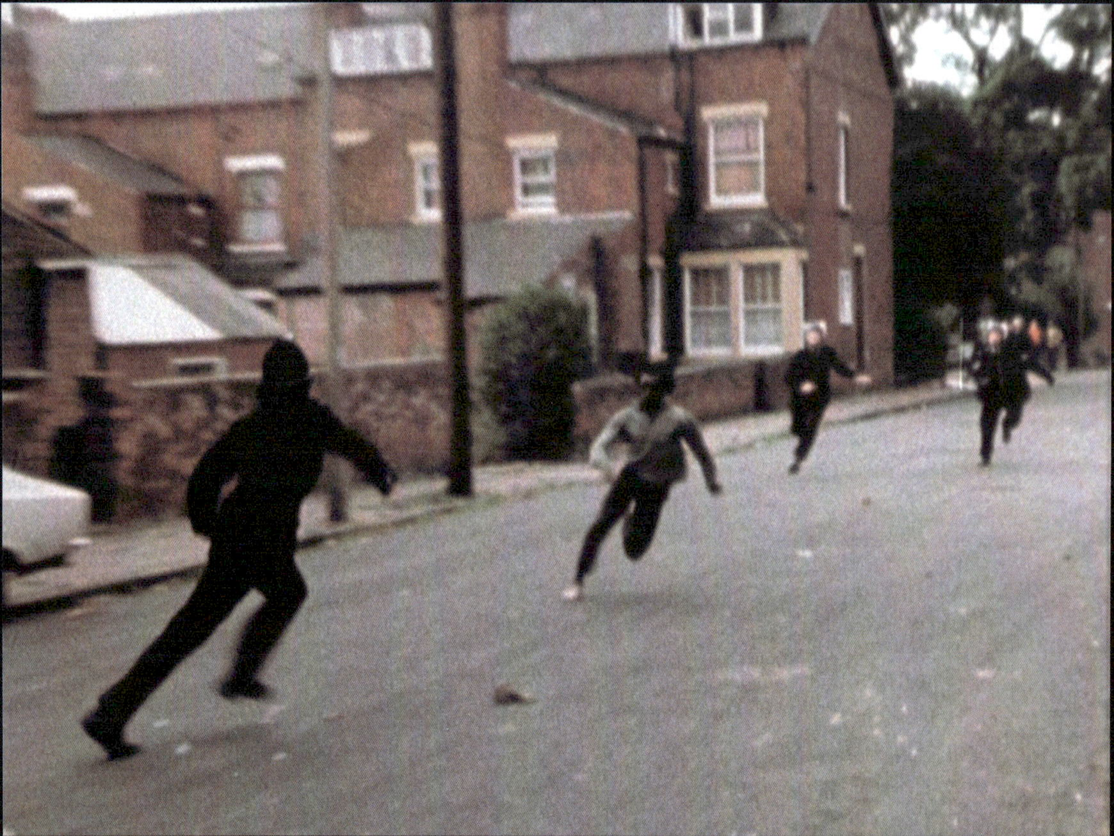

Black Audio Film Collective: John Akomfrah, Reece Auguiste, Lina Gopaul, and Avril Johnson

Coco Fusco

1987

COCO FUSCO: Rather than asking you when the riots took place and when you came together, I would like to get a sense of what ideas, what arguments were being debated at the time that you all began to work.

LINA GOPAUL: I'll just open by saying that there was always a sense of the lines we didn't want to pursue, lines which were more didactic. That the riots, for example, happened because of x y z, and that these are the reasons and these are the solutions for it—regardless of whether they were being thrown out by the Left, be it the white or the Black Left. I think our coming together at that time was an expression of not wanting to take up one of those particular positions. And by choosing not to we threw ourselves into a field that was very grey. We then tried to pull out certain themes that we agreed with—what Stuart Hall[1] might have been saying at that time, or what Paul Gilroy[2] might have been saying. They weren't as didactic.

JOHN AKOMFRAH: But you're not just talking about making *Handsworth Songs* (1986) are you?

FUSCO: I'd like to go back further, prior to *Handsworth.*

GOPAUL: Even before that our position was not one of which you could actually say that it takes its meaning from this or that.

FUSCO: It seems that there was a strong cultural nationalist position that was generated by the Black activist community—and to some extent, the more conventionally-oriented Black media sectors. But speaking in terms of ideas, in terms of theorizing race and nationality, such activity was not coming out of those sectors.

REECE AUGUISTE: they were the residues of the 1970s, of the Black Power movements that existed here, which did have a very strong nationalist slant. What motivated us was not wanting to rearticulate past political positions but rather to engage with broader theoretical issues which had not yet been addressed, or at least not in the way that we wanted to address them.

There were many discussions in the '70's and early '80s about the post-pan-Africanist vision, or the pan-Africanist vision. And a lot of that was, in many respects, undertheorized. So what we did was to combine, very critically, elements of those debates, drawing also on our own theoretical background which we had developed at colleges. We are in many respects a kind of hybrid: we are able to draw from Foucauldian[3] discourse, psychoanalysis, Afro-Caribbean discourse, and colonial and neocolonial narratives. I was going to signpost Jacques Lacan, but in many respects I think that Frantz Fanon[4] would be closer to what I am communicating. *Expeditions* (1983), which was our first cultural project, was a way of testing those ideas and trying to extend the power of the images and debates around the colonial and postcolonial moment. In order to do that we had to articulate a particular language and vision of that moment. We felt we could only do so by drawing on those European, theoretical discourses.

AKOMFRAH: If you look at the moment of becoming for the Black film and video sector in this country, there are a number of words which were key. One of them obviously was representation. The other was more a category than a term: colonial discourse. The minute you begin to work out the political etymology of those terms themselves you are effectively charting the histories and trajectories of those individuals and collectivities.

The notion of representation has been jettisoned

1 Originally from Kingston, Jamaica, Stuart Hall is one of the founders of Black cultural studies in Britain and one of the leading spokesmen of the New Left. He was the first editor of *New Left Review* and assisted in organizing the Center for Contemporary Cultural Studies (CCS) at the University of Birmingham. He is currently professor of Sociology at Open University. He is coeditor of many CCS volumes, such a *Culture, Media, Language,* and coauthor of *Policing the Crisis: Mugging, the State and Law and Order.*

2 Paul Gilroy is Senior Lecturer in Sociology at the Polytechnic of the South Bank. He has also worked as a musician, disc jockey and journalist. He is coeditor of *The Empire Strikes Back: Race and Racism in '70s Britain,* and the author of *There Ain't No Black in the Union Jack: The Cultural Politics of Race and Nation.*

3 The reference here is to the writing of the French theorist Michel Foucault, whose books include *Madness and Civilization, The Order of Things, The Archaeology of Knowledge, Discipline and Punish, The History of Sexuality,* and *The Uses of Pleasure.*

4 Frantz Fanon was born in Martinique, studied psychiatry in France and worked in Algeria during the Franco-Algerian War. He is the author of *Black Skin, White Masks, The Wretched of the Earth,* and *A Dying Colonialism.*

into the forefront by a number of discussions in post-Althusserian[5] circles. Different political currents in this country had interest in it for different reasons. What was being debated was the value of a Left political culture and how one represents that culture in discourse theory. Gramscians[6] had an interest in it because they had come to the conclusion that political power and cultural symbolic power were organized around consent. In terms of a Black interest—on one level a number of collectivities, including ourselves, were familiar with the semiologic activities of Parisian intellectuals who were interested in fashion and so on.

FUSCO: You make them sound so trivial. The English talk about politics, and the French talk about fashion.

AKOMFRAH: The interesting thing was when they stopped talking about fashion and started talking about spaghetti.

So all those currents inform how the collective was set up. Four years ago in England you couldn't sit through a discussion, a film meeting, without representation coming up about fifteen million times.

FUSCO: What was meant by that?

GOPAUL: It goes a bit further than that. Before the issue of representation comes about, we were involved in doing work with *Expeditions* in an attempt to put another phrase or category on the political agenda—colonial discourse. It wasn't being discussed everywhere, mostly in discussions in particular academic circles. And what we wanted to do was to address those debates, those theories, and to bring that onto a visual landscape.

AKOMFRAH: People used the term representation for a number of reasons. The different uses give you a sense of the complexity of the trajectories involved. At one level people used it to simply talk about questions of figuration. How one places the Black in the scene of writing, the imagination and so on. Others saw it in more juridic terms. How one is enfranchised, if you like, how one buys into the social contract. What is England and what constitutes English social life? Some interests were broadly academic, but we were focusing on how to turn our concerns into a problematic, to use an Althusserian term, in the cultural field. We were interested in representation because it seemed to be partly a way of prying open a negative/positive dichotomy. It seemed to be a way of being able to bypass certain binaries.

FUSCO: Are you referring now to the negative and positive image debates?

AKOMFRAH: Yes, and its specifically English variant—which is obsessed with stereotypes, with grounding every discussion around figuration and the existence—presence and absence in cinema in terms of stereotyping. It was a way of going beyond the discussions which would start at the level of stereotype, then move on to images, and then split images into negative and positive, and so on. We wanted to find a way to bypass this, without confronting it head on. I think that the lobbies which were really interested in debates around stereotyping were too strong, to be honest. And we were too small to take them head on. In a sense the negative/positive image lobby represented all that was acceptable about anti-racism, multiculturalism, etc. It's the only thing that united everybody who claimed they were against racism.

Everybody was talking about a non-pathology of racism. The Labor party activists would talk about it. So would the Liberals. For the anti-apartheid groups it was the limit-text, if you like. We sensed that it had political inadequacies, and cultural constraints, and that the theoretical consequences of it hadn't been thought through. But we didn't know exactly how to replace it. We did not want to try to set ourselves up as another interest group to combat the multiculturalists or the anti-racists.

FUSCO: Can we discuss *Expeditions* more specifically than in terms of mapping out a political etymology?

AUGUISTE: The positive/negative image discourse had become the organizing principle of what representation was supposed to have been about, what representation was. *Expeditions* was an attempt to critique that discourse on positive and negative images. We wanted to go beyond purely descriptive categories and try to forge another kind of analytical strain, which could then open up that space in which we could begin to articulate our own ideas about representation by prob-

5 One of the leading Marxist philosophers of the 1960s in France, Louis Althusser is the author of *For Marx* and *Reading Capital.* Known for having emphasized the implications of Marxism for philosophy and aesthetics, Althusser developed a concept of ideology as a "lived" relation between human beings and their world. He saw this as different from science in its giving more weight to the social and practical modes of understanding, rather than theoretical forms of knowledge. He employed Freudian terms such as condensation, displacement, and overdetermination to explain how contradiction—the dialectical process of historical development—can be understood in relation to its time and place in history.

6 Antonio Gramsci, the most important Italian Marxist theorist of the early twentieth century, is the author of *The Prison Notebooks.* He is best known in England for his theory of hegemony and the concept of national-popular politics, which provides the groundwork for understanding cultural and ideological production and reception and for analyzing the politics of the modern nation-state as effective through consent, rather than force. Like Althusser, Gramsci also employed categories from Freudian psychoanalysis.

lematizing representation itself.

When *Expeditions* was first completed we had a number of theoretical, political, and cultural battles with those who had very defined ideas about what representation was. The first point that was made was that it was inaccessible, because we were using language which was grounded in Foucauldian ideas, and Fanonian ideas, and so on. Second, there was the issue of the kind of images we used, which had not been used before. The way, for example, in which we would actually appropriate from English national fictions—like the Albert and Victoria Memorial—going back and really engaging with the archive of colonial memory. We were not only constructing a colonial narrative, but also critiquing what was seen as the colonial moment—critiquing what was seen as the discourse around empire.

AKOMFRAH: When we were making *Expeditions,* a number of tentative voices were beginning to challenge what was effectively an orthodoxy in English cultural debate, which was the notion that colonial history and the colonial narrative was past—that it was the instrument of a past English glory which has now foundered. Before there was colonial history, after there's postcolonial history. And we wanted to problematize that very obvious splitting of memory into past and present. It seemed that the only way we could do that was to pay less attention to what historiographers and political commentators said about past and present, and look at what the iconography of those moments signified now. We weren't really interested in whether the Victoria and Albert was built in 1898. Nor did we believe that was the only moment that it meant anything, because it is still here and it is still in the middle of London. And ten thousand tourists see it every day. We felt then that the politics of signification was alive.

AVRIL JOHNSON: What was also happening around this time was the Falklands war, which had begun the year before. Margaret Thatcher called upon a notion of British identity in which, supposedly, all true Englishmen could identify.

GOPAUL: And there were many who argued that the fact that we were chronologically in a postwar era made everything different—that we were postwar theoreticians engaged in a postwar agenda.

FUSCO: I have a clear sense from what you are saying about how this relates to the politics of social life in contemporary England, but I wanted to ask some more aesthetically-oriented questions. Many of the images of empire you use are ones that had already been displaced from classical civilization. The recycling of images that you were playing with for political reasons taps into an aesthetic discourse of neoclassicism that connects you to postmodernism and the transavant-garde.

AKOMFRAH: Two things were happening at the time. On the one hand, formalist photographers and artists—such as the constituency around *Block*[7] were becoming much more interested in the expressive qualities of the remnants of the English national past. They were using these remnants in a very formalist sense, as a kind of backdrop against which one mapped out one's anxieties of difference onto the past. You could see that people were drawing on the neoexpressive qualities of those statues and icons, without necessarily thinking about questions of desire.

FUSCO: One of the desires of postmodernism in its most Eurocentric form is to sever the tie between the political implication and the formal manifestation. In *Expeditions* you use similar strategies of appropriation with a different motor. Do you see these as two postmodernisms hitting off one another? Were you misread because of this?

AKOMFRAH: Our enterprise emerged before the category of postmodernity meant anything in English aesthetic debates. At the time not even Victor Burgin[8] or any of the high priests of avant-garde theories and debates in this country were using it.

AUGUISTE: One of the problems of the discourse of postmodernity lies in what it excludes. The crisis that the postmodern is supposed to address is seen as something internal to the logic and rationale of Western Classical Civilization. In philosophical discourse there is the crisis around reason. Then there is a crisis around form, as manifested in architecture. What interests me most about these debates is the exclusion of the so-called neocolonial world. To me the crisis doesn't have so much to do with what's happening to the West, to the internal discourse of the West, as it does with what the non-European world is doing to the West. The crisis now is in Lebanon, in South Africa.

AKOMFRAH: In terms of the beginning of making *Expeditions,* it's important to say that there are two convergences there. On the one hand, we realized that there was a kind of reappropriation, which we now understand to be postmodernist reappropriation of the past, taking place in very formalist circles, such as the kind of work that Victor Burgin and others were

7 *Block* is a British art magazine.

8 Victor Burgin is a British photographer and theorist and the editor of *Thinking Photography* (London: MacMillan, 1982).

doing in photography. What we decided to do—which again, with hindsight, we now realize places us firmly in that camp—was to appropriate classical or neoclassical images. But we appropriated them using methods of avant-garde photography which effectively begin with Alexander Rodchenko[9]—extremely angular kinds of framing, etc. That was the key difference. If you look at the formalist work on the other hand, the methods of composition were extremely straightforward. Henri Cartier-Bresson[10] could have done it. What people found unnerving about what we were doing was that the play of postmodernism wasn't there. *This* parody and pastiche was underpinned by biblical sounding tones concerning colonial narratives and expeditions and so on. We wanted to say that it was an expedition, that on the one hand you went through these exhibitions—you pack your bag from different aesthetic fields, from neoclassical architecture, from Russian formalist photography. But the interest was in colonial narrative. The interest was not, in the end, in play.

FUSCO: Let's move on to *Handsworth Songs.* I am interested in the symptomatic qualities of the responses to it. I do think that the fact *Handsworth Songs* has been the subject of controversy has to do with something larger than the film. It has to do with a desire to damage the kind of position you represent. Salman Rushdie's frequently mentioned review in *The Guardian*[11] doesn't really address the film—he demonstrates no relationship to the filmic aspects of the work. He juxtaposes the notion of an authentic voice to image manipulation.

GOPAUL: I think this goes back to what we were saying about where we located ourselves in relation to the political and theoretical positions that prevailed prior to our existence as a collective. When we emerged people tried to didactically map out the cultural and visual terrain for us to slot into.

If they are not actually addressing the film, well then what is it that they are addressing? Transgression, basically. Why is it such a strong response not to the film, but our existence? To what you represent? Those who criticized us most vehemently were prioritizing a line about community and people in the streets. There was no other way of representing yourself other than the way they put forward. That's what I think is largely behind the sometimes almost violent responses to us.

AKOMFRAH: The question of paternity and transgression was very important. One of the things which people would always say to us was, isn't *Handsworth Songs* too avant-garde? Quite simply, the problems we faced in making *Handsworth* were very practical ones—to do with melodrama—orchestrating means of identification, rather than distancing people and dazzling them with techniques. The editing might be considered unconventional, but the techniques are very straightforward. So it's not avant-garde in that sense. My mistake was in assuming people wouldn't see it as a transgressive text.

In terms of the established boundaries of discussion—aesthetic interventions around race—there were questions of paternity at stake. In other words, who was the holder of the law—the law of enunciation? Who had the right to speak, who had the right to map out and broaden the field that everybody had to speak in? It was in that sense that the film was received as a transgressive text, because it clearly didn't fall into line with the established concordat concerning the Black intelligentsia and their discussion of race. That then makes the film an avant-garde text. Those who were willing to live with a more mixed economy of dialogue around figuration and race accepted it, and those who didn't, didn't accept it.

That was one symptom, but the morbidity also has to do with the inability of cultural workers to make any meaningful sense of that moment. One has the sense that people were trapped in their own rhetoric, claiming that the 1981 riots occurred because of unemployment, etc. having to signpost all the social reasons why Black people take to the streets. The minute we began to speak and give the impression that somehow one was going to reopen the questions rather than repeat the answers, people got very nervous.

JOHNSON: Those people who felt trapped had benefitted from what happened in 1981. They don't want to recognize that the problem still exists.

GOPAUL: It was also a move away from the specificity of location. After 1981, there was a generalized understanding of the riots, whereas in 1985 it was different. How can we begin to understand this situation, people would ask, in Birmingham, which didn't riot in 1981? Birmingham has a very specific Black political history. It's one of the central spots for Black political development and for anti-racist development. It has a number of institutions, like the Center for Contemporary Cultural Studies, which are based within those communities. There is something quite specific happening there.

AKOMFRAH: We have to be careful not to overestimate the transgressive potential of certain kinds of aesthetic intervention. At a certain point, the nightmares which weigh on the brain are not necessarily historical

9 Alexander Rodchenko, the Russian constructivist artist and photographer of the early revolutionary period.
10 Henri Cartier-Bresson, the French photographer and photojournalist.

ones—they are very conjunctural ones. The fact of the matter is that a number of things were collapsing at a certain point. And the film in many ways mirrors that collapse. It's not an avant-gardist intervention, in the sense that it doesn't frame a series of devices that would get us out of the crisis. It mirrors those forms collapsing, and it says what a shame.

FUSCO: How did people respond to that sort of mirror?

AKOMFRAH: When people saw the film they saw all the fractures, all the unevenness—which are quite deliberate. Part of the problem that we have has to do with the question of whether Black people should be involved in visual arts, in creating aesthetically challenging visual work. The assumption when we foreground avant-garde technique is either that we don't know anything else, and have stumbled across it by accident, or that we are imitating other forms.

GOPAUL: Or that we have no foundation in the Black communities, that we've left that behind too.

AKOMFRAH: The idea of prefacing the film with a phrase—"There are no stories in the riots, only the ghosts of other stories"—and then to work on it in terms of splits and unevennesses and so on without trying to center it was what alarmed many people. The triumphalist vision of race and community operates on the assumption that there is essentially a core of affect that is structured around oratory, around song—giving it an irreducible unity—which wasn't present in the film. It played with it, at some stages

---

11 The following is Salman Rushdie's article, "*Songs* doesn't know the score," from *The Guardian* (London), January 12, 1987, 10.

In *The Heart of a Woman,* volume four of her famous autobiography, Maya Angelou describes a meeting of the Harlem Writers' Guild, at which she had read some of her work and had it torn to pieces by the group.

It taught her a tough lesson: 'If I wanted to write, I had to be willing to develop a kind of concentration found mostly in people awaiting execution. I had to learn technique and surrender my ignorance.'

It just isn't enough to be Black and blue, [or] even Black and angry, the message is plain enough in Angelou's self-portrait, in Louise Meriwether's marvelous *Daddy Was A Numbers Runner,* in Toni Morrison and Paule Marshall; if you want to tell the untold stories, if you want to give voice to the voiceless, you've got to find a language. Which goes for film as well as prose, for documentary as well as autobiography. Use the wrong language, and you're dumb and blind.

Down at the Metro cinema in Soho, there's a new documentary starting a three-week run, *Handsworth Songs,* made by Black Audio Film Collective. The "buzz" about the picture is good. *New Socialist* likes it, *City Limits* likes it, people are calling it multi-layered, original, imaginative, its makers talk of speaking in metaphors, its director John Akomfrah is getting mentioned around town as a talent to watch. Unfortunately, it's no good, and the trouble does seem to be one of language.

Let me put it this way. If I say "Handsworth," what do you see? Most Britons would see fire, riots, looted shops, young Rastas and helmeted cops by night. A big story; front page. Maybe a West Side Story: Officer Krupke, armed to the teeth, versus the kids with the social disease.

There's a line that *Handsworth Song[s]* wants us to learn. 'There are no stories in the riots,' it repeats, 'only the ghosts of other stories.' The trouble is, we aren't told the other stories. What we get is what we know from TV. Blacks as trouble; Blacks as victims. Here is a Rasta dodging the police; here are the old news-clips of the folks in the fifties getting off the boat, singing calypsos about "darling London."

Little did they know, eh? But we don't hear about their lives, or the lives of their born-British children. We don't hear Handsworth's songs.

Why not? The film's handouts provide a clue. The film attempts to excavate hidden ruptures/agonies of "Race." 'It looks at the riots as a political field colored by the trajectories of industrial decline and structural crisis.' Oh dear. The sad thing is that while the film-makers are trying to excavate ruptures and work out how trajectories can color fields, they let us hear so little of the much richer language of their subjects.

When Home Secretary Hurd visits Handsworth looking bemused, just after the riots, a Black voice is heard to say: 'The higher monkey climb the more he will expose.' If only more of this sort of wit and freshness could have found its way into the film. But the makers are too busy "repositioning the convergence of 'Race' and 'Criminality,'" describing a living world in the dead language of race industry professionals. I don't know Handsworth very well, but I do know it's bursting with tales worth telling. Take a look at John Bishton and Derek Reardor's 1984 photo-and-text essay, *Home Front.* There are Vietnamese boat people in Handsworth, where Father Peter Diem, a refugee himself, runs a pastoral center to which they come for comfort.

Here are two old British soldiers. One, name of Shri Dalip Singh, sits stiffly in his army tunic, sporting his Africa Star with pride; the other, a certain Jagat Singh, is a broken old gent who has been arrested for drunkenness on these streets over three hundred times. Some nights they catch him trying to direct the traffic.

It's a religious place, Handsworth. What was once a Methodist chapel is now one of many Sikh *gurdwaras.* Here is the Good News Asian Church, and there you can see Rasta groundations, a mosque, Pentecostal halls, and Hindu Jain and Buddhist places of worship. Many of Handsworth's songs are hymns of praise. But there's reggae too, there are Punjabi *ghazals* and Two Tone bands.

These days the kids in Handsworth like to dance the Wobble. And some of its denizens dream of distant "liberations," nurturing, for example, the dark fantasy of Khalistan.

It's important, I believe, to tell such stories: to say, this is England: *Allahu Akbar* from the minaret of a Birmingham mosque, the Ethiopian World Federation which helps Handsworth Rastas "return" to the land of Rastafari. These are English scenes now, English songs.

You won't find them, or anything like them, in *Handsworth Songs,* though for some reason, you will see plenty of footage about troubles in Tottenham and Brixton, which is just the sort of blurring you know the Harlem writers would have jumped on, no matter how right-on it looked.

It isn't that easy for Black voices to be heard. It isn't easy to get it said that the state attacks us, that the police are militarised. It isn't easy to fight back against media stereotypes. As a result, whenever somebody says what we all know, even if they say it clumsily and in jargon, there's a strong desire to cheer, just because they managed to get something said, they managed to get through.

I don't think that's much help, myself. That kind of celebration makes us lazy.

Next time, let's start telling those ghost-stories. If we know why the caged bird sings, let's listen to her song.'

discards it, it takes it on board, then it says it's probably not possible, do not work with it, but there you are, and so on. But the film doesn't fix its sentiments around it. That is what was frightening. It then leads to the discussion of whether avant-garde techniques, or disruptive techniques, profilmic techniques, are in safe hands when they are given to Blacks. Both certain Black theorists and the white theorists would say that; they would want to know whether authorship is really safe with us.

If the notion of diaspora has any credibility, it has to be understood as a formation which exists both on the margins at certain points, and at the center of English social life. And if it plays those dual functions, then it's bound to be negotiated into a series of practices, visual or otherwise, which exist in this country. So that even if a visual history wasn't present in our "history," the very fact of communality at the center of the metropolis makes it impossible to ignore, to put it crudely, that every little Black kid in this country, at one stage or another, will have the chance to go to an art college, or to take part in art classes at school.

FUSCO: And they live in a world that is absolutely inundated with images, although the vast majority of them do not include Black people. Would you want to venture into theorizing around what this absence does to the psyche, and the question of representation and race?

AKOMFRAH: In terms of reproduction in the very classical sense, Marxian or otherwise, of social relations in this country, I know that the Black independent sector, which has organized itself around questions of representation and collective practice, represents the new wave of English filmmaking. I also know that in terms of the kinds of questions raised by filmmaking practice in this country, which took its cue from Jean-Luc Godard, from Chris Marker, the Nouvelle Vague, political cinema in Russia and so on—this new wave comes to it with a certain kind of agnosticism and skepticism around its transgressive potential as we hit the 1990s. And I also know that our interest in filmmaking as a new wave possibly gives English independent film practice a chance to breach what has been an impossible gap between the mainstream and independents. We are obviously aided by the existence of television—nevertheless, we are the fortunate inheritors of that confusion, that growth, that progression. And I don't think it is possible to be that closely associated with all those things without having some very deeply entrenched familiarity with the visual landscape in this country. That's what I know. What I don't know is how we then proceed. What I don't know is what to say to people who say, well how can Black people be in that position.

One of the problems that the independent sector always faced in this country is this crisis of identity around collective security—it never really understood its strategic power. It never truly understood where it stood in relation to mainstream audiovisual culture in this country. People always assumed that the very act of doing something is transgressive. In a culture where the transgressive is in fact the cutting edge of advertising, that makes your identity very unstable.

FUSCO: How do you respond to the claim that while you get attacked for the forms you operate within, the fact that you choose to work within those forms makes it easier for your work to be aired on television, whereas a more straightforward, monological documentary on a politically controversial issue, like *The People's Account*,[12] cannot.

AKOMFRAH: On one level, we've had people who've "told it like it is" in their documentaries. That has to be said with a certain element of skepticism, because ultimately one needs to challenge the assumption that you can tell it like it is.

Can we talk about where aesthetics used to belong in classical philosophy? The term "aesthetic" was coined by Baumgarten, who was an ally of Herder, who was working with Kant. Black filmmaking has been and will probably continue to be straddled with what Kant calls the categorical imperative. People assume that there are certain transcendental duties that Black filmmaking has to perform. They assume that and because of that Black filmmaking has to work with the understanding that it's in a state of emergence. And because it is in a state of emergence its means always have to be guerilla means, war means, signposts of urgency. When that begins to inhibit questions of reflection—doubt, skepticism, intimacy and so on—then the categorical imperative does exactly what it is supposed to do—it imprisons.

FUSCO: It is precisely the arguments around urgency that foreclose entry into aesthetic practice, or any discussion of aesthetics as the property of a Black artist. How can you start to talk about a term that exists within aesthetics, when you're supposedly not engaged in aesthetics?

AKOMFRAH: Because the transcendental duties are always *a priori*, because they are always there before you start. Everything else is only given contingent license. Aesthetics, efficacy, are each given tentative license. Their only use is the extent to which they take

12 *The People's Account* (1986), by the Workshop Ceddo, commissioned by Channel 4, but not shown.

you closer to your transcendental mission, which is to announce that we are here and we can't take it anymore.

If the situation of war is an apt metaphor, and in many ways it probably is, then I would say that our position of dissidence is that one resolutely refuses to be turned into cannon fodder. We would like to take our bread and hit the mountain because it is safer to be a guerilla. The struggles we've engaged in have had some moderate successes. We've argued that we don't just live beneath our navel.

FUSCO: In what sense do you deal with sexuality and gender in your films?

AKOMFRAH: We've decided to deal with these questions in different ways. It's a very complicated question for us. On the one hand we try to deal with it by working with Pratibha Parmar on her videotape *Emergence* (1987), trying to make an input into an area which is already defined as one of sexuality. On the other hand, we try to make sure that it gels into the mesh of concern that we have for the Black subject in our own work.

When Isaac Julien's *Territories* (1985) appeared it was obvious that we were beginning to swap one set of transcendental clothes for another. Once you stop being angry you had to be another other, and adopt another transgressive tone. And we began to think of ways to slip past that. If there is a voice of dissidence that echoes and strains in our work, it's an attempt to find a position from which to speak certain questions—which beguiles expectations and is genuinely uncanny in many ways. It was obvious that once *Territories* appeared, with the kind of reception that it got in this country—it was then supposed to be the beginning of a convention. Regardless of what one's interest in the politics were. I don't think, in the end, that we don't deal with sexuality. But we try to find a much more complicated dialogue with the issues than was expected of us once *Territories* appeared.

JOHNSON: The other thing is that we are not making sexuality a cornerstone. We are making it something that is mediated, not necessarily the central process. It's informed by a number of different things.

GOPAUL: There are times when people prioritize sexuality as a singular issue, which is what tends to happen in moments of struggle or crisis. But after that—how do you then bring it back into an everyday part of your life, and then into a filmic practice? I find that far more difficult than addressing it head on. People don't live like that.

AKOMFRAH: We are also in a position to take a number of things for granted. The search for intimacy, the reflective quality of *Handsworth Songs,* does not simply have to do with a realignment of Black discourses. They have to do with our sensitivity to questions which are raised in other sorts of politics, not necessarily racial ones. Obviously, Black women talk about questions of femininity. We try to make sure that the text you operate with is open enough to allow for those kinds of interventions.

Two articles appeared in the *London Review of Books* a while back—I didn't realize how informative they were until much later. It was a debate between Richard Sennett[13] and Michel Foucault. And it's also a kind of debate that has taken place since then in the gay community.

FUSCO: What were their positions?

AKOMFRAH: They had to do with whether or not when one forged a politics around identity, placing it in the public arena—whether doing that was simply allowing oneself to become inserted in a well-policed arrangement of things. What does calling yourself a Black collective entail, or imply? Is it possible to work through identity politics without having to announce the name of your identity? I was left with a deep sense of skepticism around identifying identity and championing it in a very triumphalist way.

Blacks are expected to be transgressive in English cultural life. To me this is just as wearying, just as draining as the old "you must be the conscience of the nation" approach. Either one of them requires a certain act of a kind of emancipatory front—for the nation. We don't have the strength or the energy. So there may be reticence around these questions on our part.

FUSCO: Africa has an extremely important symbolic function in the history of Black film and Black images—and in the Black consciousness movement—as the promised land—the age of innocence. With your new film, *Testament* (1988), which was shot in Africa, you seem to have walked into a rather overloaded symbolic minefield.

AKOMFRAH: It is loaded. In many ways, Africa is one of the key primal scenes, one of the primal moments in diasporic culture. I suspect that what we are going to do with that understanding isn't going to please everybody, but there you are. That is the way of the world.

AUGUISTE: Specific histories of subjectivities are not the issue. The issue is that within the Black com-

13 Richard Sennett is the author of *The Fall of Public Man and Authority.*

munity there is a lot of innocence and naïveté about the continent Africa. There is a certain kind of romantic engagement with Africa, which is one of the residues of the neo-nationalist moment. On one level, Africa should be celebrated; on another level, people in the diaspora should critically engage with the continent. And in particular they should engage with those historical figures who have supposedly enunciated Africa, or the pan-Africanist movement. All those Africanist leaders are still held in a frame of innocence. What that has done is to project a certain kind of retardation in thought. It's feeling and not thinking.

What we are saying now is that after 20 to 25 years of independence, no one can argue that the problem in Africa is something outside—that it's the West, always the West. There are real problems that are internal, that are specific to the continent. In order to break away from this romantic engagement one has to recognize and smash that innocence and rip it up and see what is really taking place. Otherwise we are engaged in transcendental thinking about the continent, which doesn't get those out here in the West thinking about the continent very far.

AKOMFRAH: Let's speak about it also in terms of the aesthetics of that primal moment. If the dichotomy in Black art is between protest and redemption, or protest and affirmation, and if Africa as the primal scene functions significantly in the affirmation moment, as the moment of liberation, of catharsis, what if—and this is an aesthetic question we pose in the film—what if you have a character for whom that redemption is a problem? What if you have a character who can't live with that primal moment? One of the things that the character says in the film is that perhaps I am a new kind of animal for whom the very thought of peace is a burden. We have a number of alternatives—we can debunk the lore, with reference to sociology, or we can take the rhetoric of the primal scene seriously and say that it does exist, and that it has real effects on people's lives. There are people whose lives have been made much more complicated, destroyed almost, by these sorts of assumptions around Africa. That seems to me to be a starting point. We must go there and find a character for whom Africa is not a place of redemption, precisely because Africa thinks of itself that way. We have to come out with a character like that. That is the aim of the film. Once you decide that the primal scene is that borderline, which people cross in different ways—once you have defined it in those terms you get stuck on one side or the other. What I am not exactly sure about—it doesn't worry me or anybody else here—what we are not sure about is whether that person actually comes back or gets swallowed up by the border.

FUSCO: Perhaps we should also talk about the U.S. as a place of redemption. Black American culture carries a tremendous amount of weight here in England. You touch on it in the film with references to Malcolm X and the dialogues and questions that are raised about a legacy of radicalism.

JOHNSON: It has to do with what you hear on the news—that what happened in America ten years ago happens in Britain today. And I think that is because Black people have been there in much larger numbers much longer—and in a sense people still look to what Black Americans are doing. And it is also easier not to look at what is happening here.

AKOMFRAH: The connection goes back a long way. At each moment of Black radical life in this country there has been an interface with concerns around race in America. You can go back to the discussions around emancipation here. Black people who lived in this country at that time, their concerns with slavery here and in the Americas were always interlocked. The founding of the pan-Africanist conference was always only possible when in many ways the anticolonial fighters began to take W. E .B. Du Bois[14] seriously and work with him in some ways. Marcus Garvey went to America and then came here. There has always been a sense of exchange, if you like, between the two spaces. And there was that famous conference in this country in 1967 called "The Dialectics of Liberation," where people were first exposed to the personages of Black Power—Stokely Carmichael turned up and made his famous speech in which he said that the only place for a woman is prone. This first symbolic contact with Black Power left a very contradictory legacy in this country.

1968 itself—the founding of the New Left in this country—was deeply implicated in a kind of dialogue and exchange with Black American culture.

Now if we are talking about our own fascination with America I suspect that it is split in very different ways—there is a kind of aura around American life in its different manifestations, which you find in different spaces. For Black women's politics in this country, Black American women writers have almost canonical significance.

GOPAUL: There is a sense that they had all done it before we had done it.

14 Poet and essayist W. E. B. Du Bois is one of the greatest and most influential Black American writers of the late 19th and early 20th century. He is the author of *The Souls of Black Folk* (1903).

AKOMFRAH: There is a sense that Black American culture throws down a certain gauntlet which people then have to pick up and live through and with.

FUSCO: What about in film?

AKOMFRAH: In film I don't think the connection is there that much.

JOHNSON: It also has to do with the Caribbean. Most of us come from the Caribbean, where America is *it*.

AKOMFRAH: Wim Wenders said that Americans have colonized our unconscious. In many ways he is right. Anywhere in the world—in the darkest part of Manchester even—you find counter-culture which premises American life in some form, be it hip hop, or whatever. And it is in that very generalized sense that America has been useful. But I don't think I ever really seriously thought that Black American independent filmmaking was something to take a cue from.

AUGUISTE: I think we have been more interested in the New Latin American Cinema, the so-called Third Cinema.

Selections from *Cray at Chippewa Falls: Photographs by Lee Friedlander*

Lee Friedlander

1987

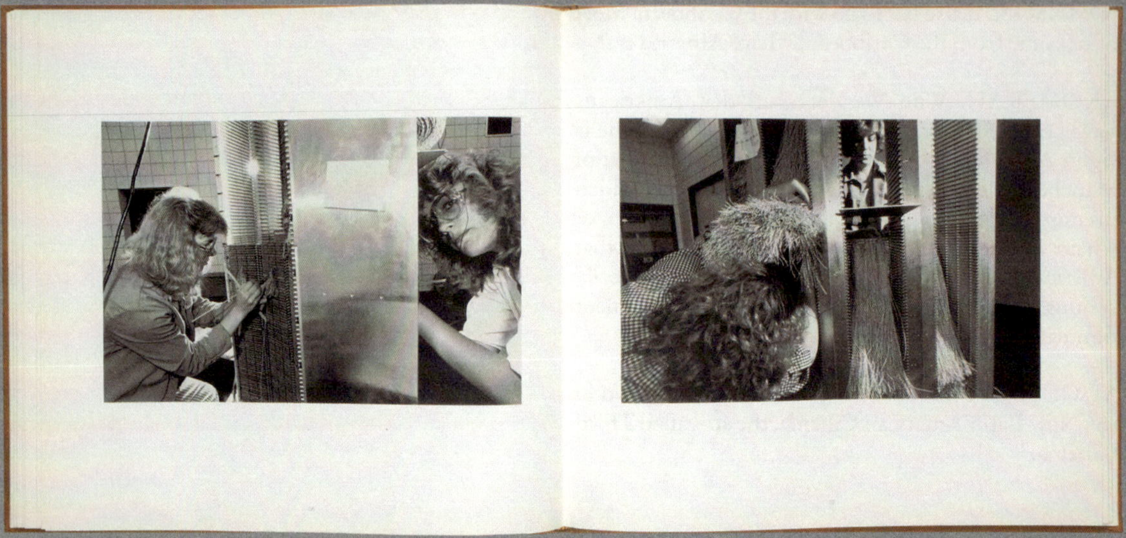

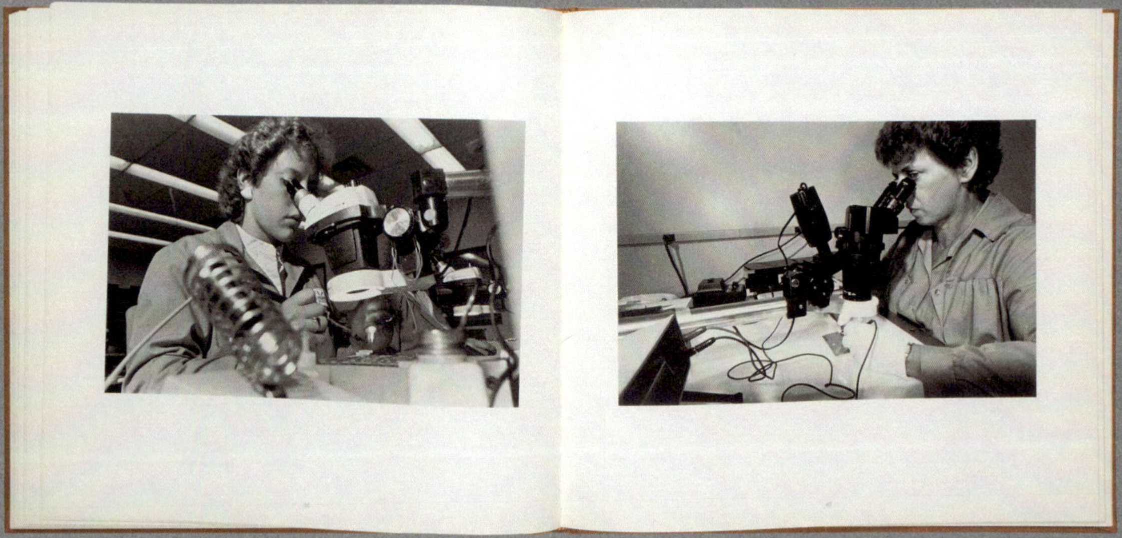

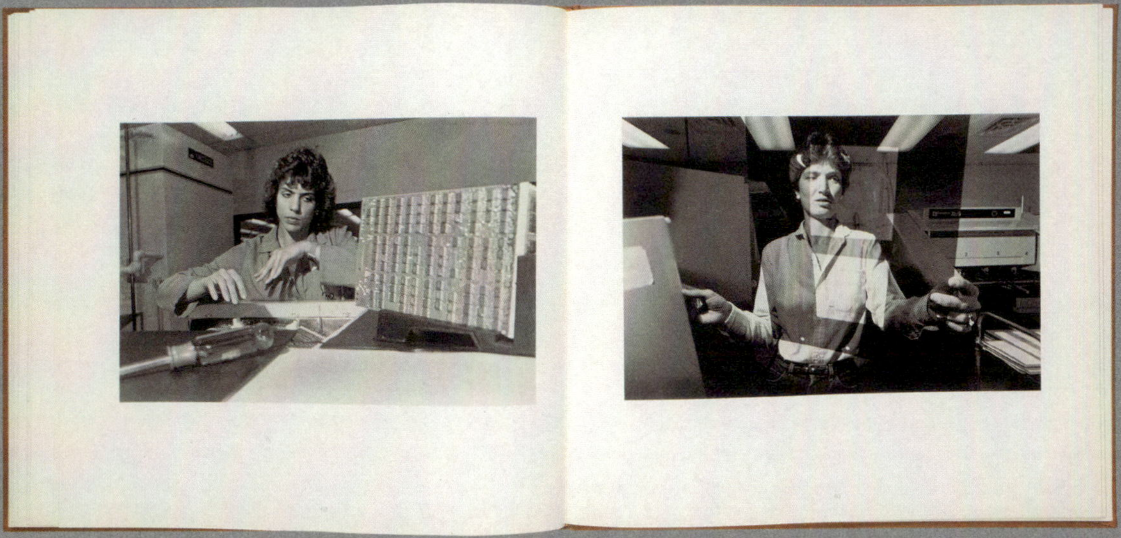

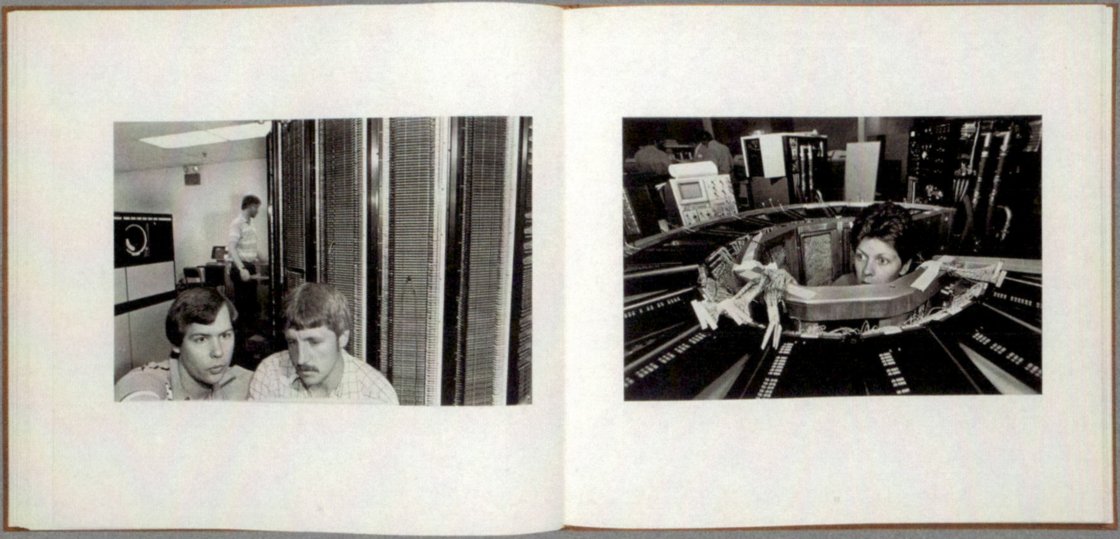

To celebrate and commemorate the 15th anniversary of the founding of Cray Research, Inc., I commissioned a work of art by renowned photographer Lee Friedlander.

During 1986, Mr. Friedlander visited our locations in Wisconsin and Minnesota and created a personal vision of Cray Research through his photography. The photographs have been reproduced as a book that will be presented to you on our company's 15th anniversary, April 6, 1987.

Mr. Friedlander was born on July 14, 1934 in Aberdeen, Washington, and currently resides in New City, New York. He has received numerous fellowships and awards, such as the Guggenheim Memorial Foundation fellowship and the National Endowment for the Arts. He has mounted solo exhibitions in museums and galleries throughout the world, including the Museum of Modern Art, New York, The Photographer's Gallery, London, Gallerie Zabriskie, Paris, and Watari Gallery, Tokyo. His work is represented in the permanent collections of many museums worldwide. The Minneapolis Institute of Arts has made a significant commitment to collecting Friedlander works. In addition to seven portfolios, Mr. Friedlander has created seven books of photographs. His eighth book is CRAY AT CHIPPEWA FALLS.

Ektachrome Archive

Lyle Ashton Harris

1986–96

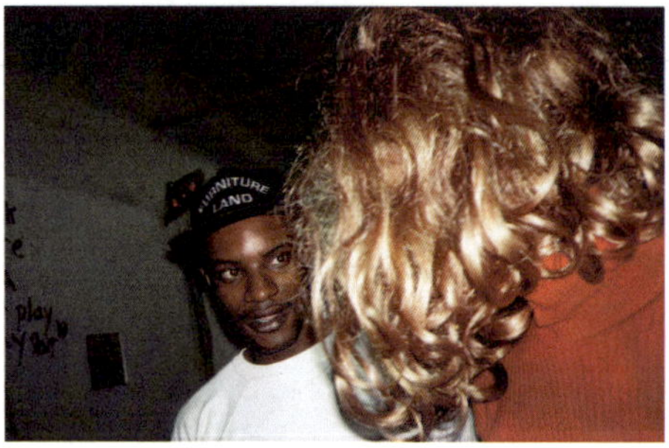

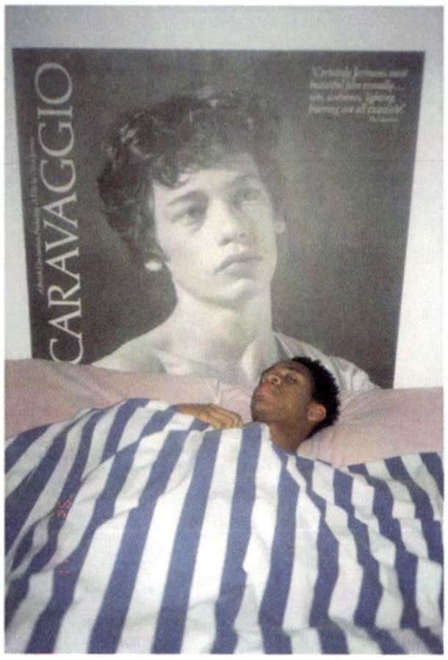

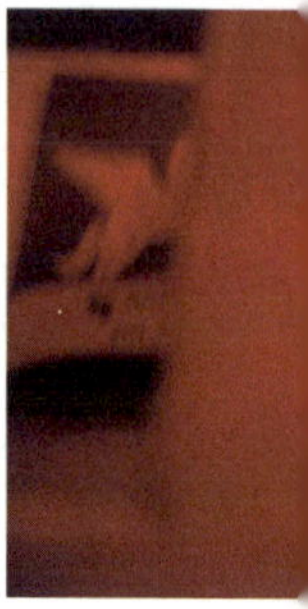

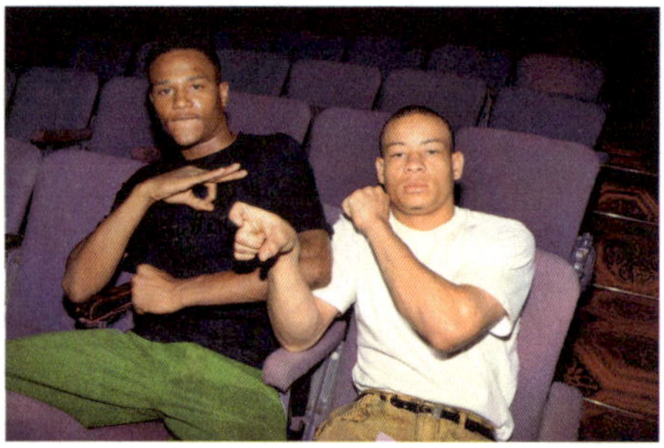

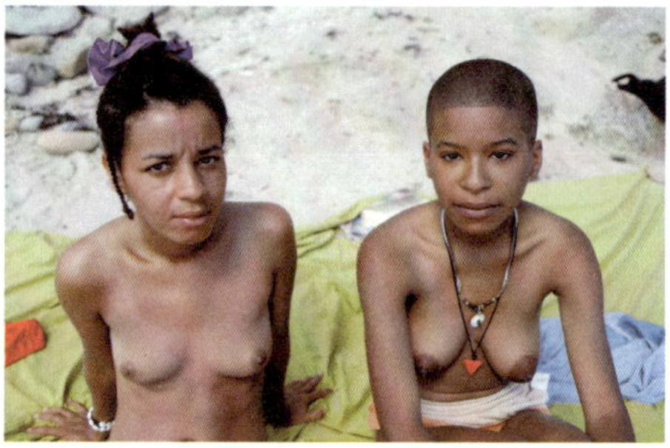

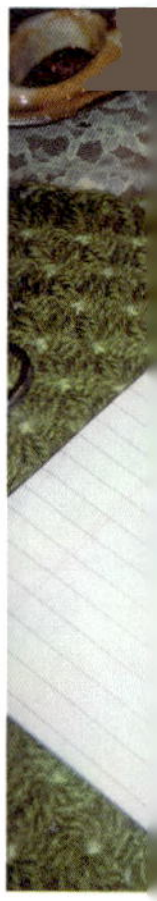

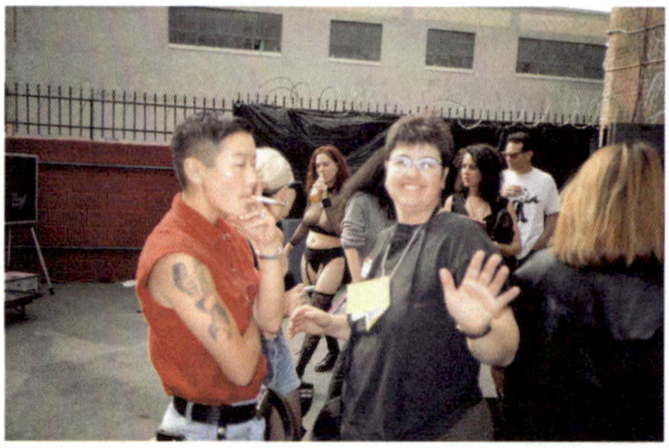

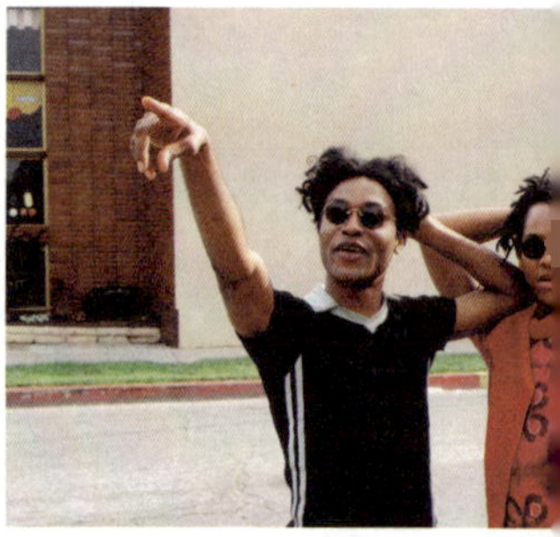

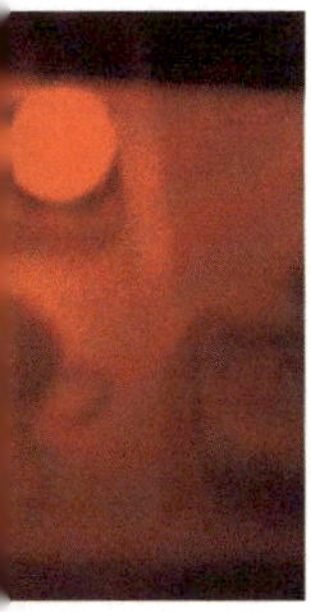

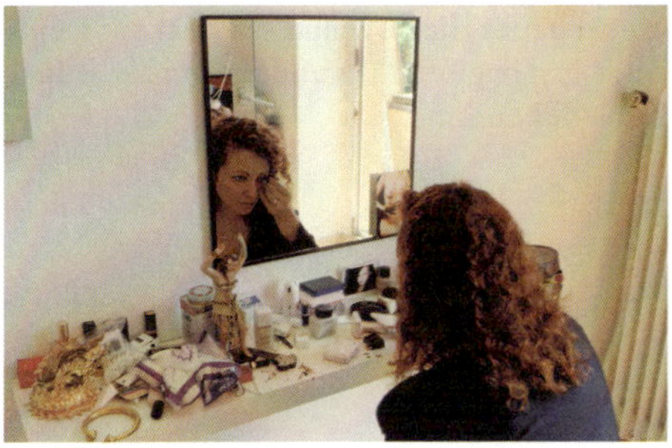

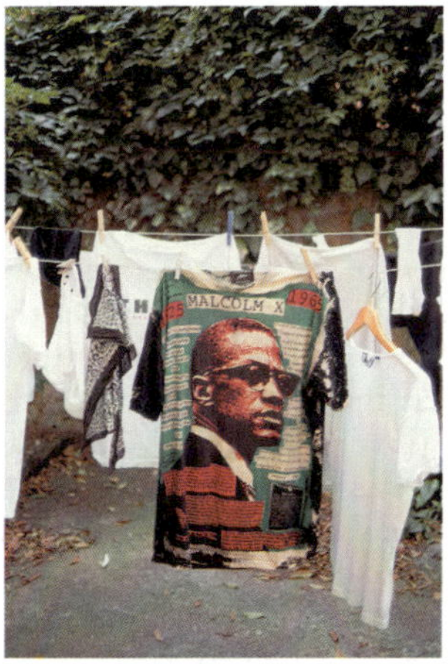
MALCOLM X

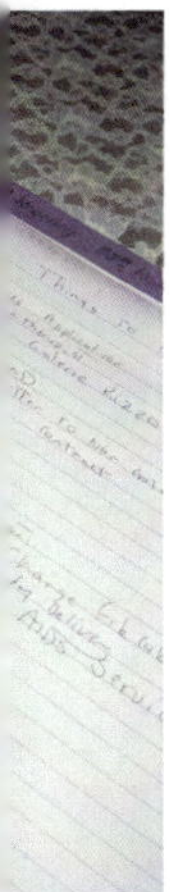

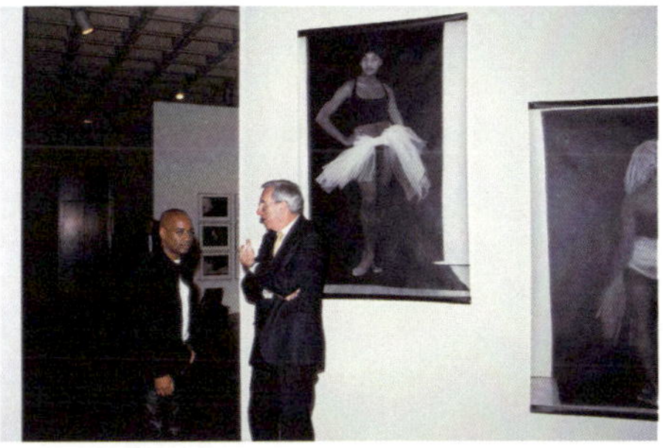

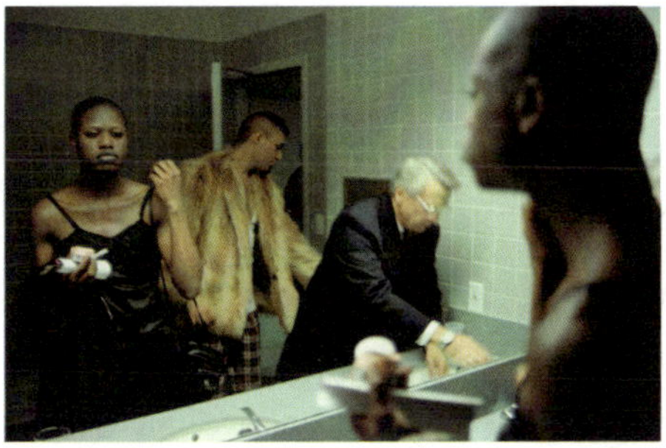

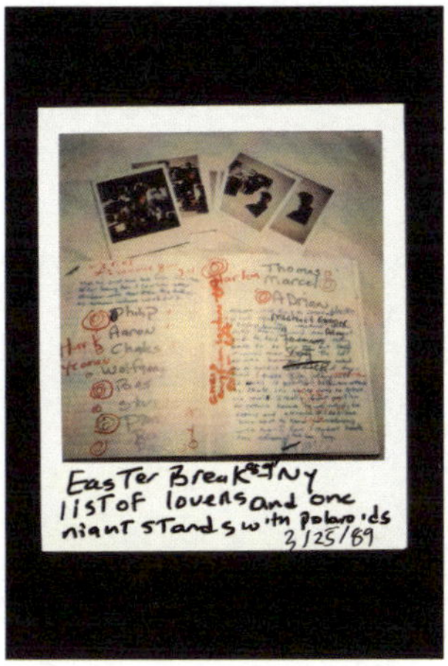
Easter Break 89 NY
list of lovers and one
night stands with polaroids
3/25/89

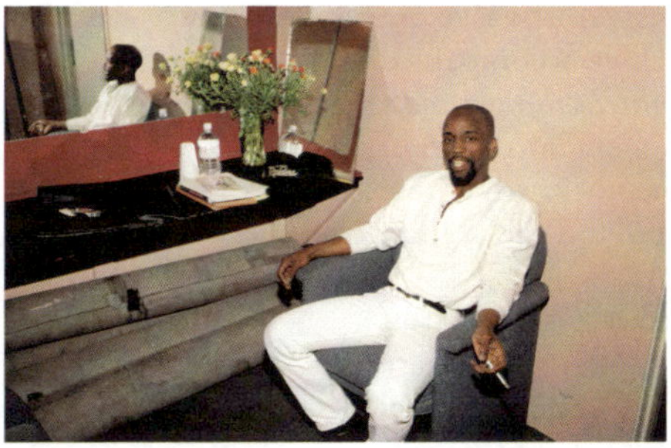

Lyle Ashton Harris on Ektachrome Archive (1986–1996) as told to Alpesh Kantilal Patel 2015

In late 2012, I received a Facebook message from my longtime friend Isaac Julien asking to use some of my photographs in his autobiography, *Riot* (2013), a book that was published on the occasion of his MoMA exhibition. This inquiry reconnected me to an archive of 35-mm Ektachrome reversal slides that I had stored in my mother's basement in the Bronx before moving to Rome in 2000. I hadn't given these slides much thought over the past fifteen years and was surprised that I had amassed at least three thousand of them, dating from between the late 1980s and 2000. I dived into this archive—in hindsight, this was partly due to the ending of a seven-year relationship. The experience of editing was cathartic and helped me to reengage with the pulse of New York City after having split my time between Accra and New York from 2005 to 2012.

The exhibition at David Castillo includes a concise distillation of images from that archive. There are candid portraits and snapshots of friends and acquaintances, such as the late Marlon Riggs taking AZT while on break from shooting his last film, *Black Is, Black Ain't* (1994); bell hooks in repose at home in New York; Nan Goldin applying eyeliner in Berlin; and Catherine Opie in an embrace. Also included are photos of family, boyfriends, and lovers, plus self-portraits, landscapes, and interiors of bedrooms and now-closed nightclubs. It is the quotidian quality of these images, which captured people, places, and moments long—and often tragically—gone, that most intrigues me and stands in stark contrast to the theatricality of the more iconic works that have become a hallmark of my practice.

This show is the first time I am showing prints of the slides. Last year, Visual AIDS commissioned me to produce a video version of the archive for "Day With(out) Art." Also, as part of Carrie Mae Weems's "Live Past/Future Tense" retrospective at the Guggenheim Museum last April I staged a performative lecture with projected images from the archive accompanied by a mash-up of Grace Jones's *Nightclubbing* album. This presentation functioned as a memento mori of sorts for several of the audience members who were intimately familiar with the subjects and the texture of that period.

In contrast to that audience, I recently showed this work to photography students at Yale. They were equally engaged, but they focused on the more formal aspects of the work. In this way, the title of the exhibition, "Lyle Ashton Harris: Ektachrome Archive 1986–96: Part I—Recovering Identity and Desire," is a red herring—I see the archive not as a repository of things past to be unearthed but as something that shapes the now and the near future in ways that I am just beginning to understand and which has a relevance beyond me.

Scripts from *Monodramas*
Stan Douglas
1987–91

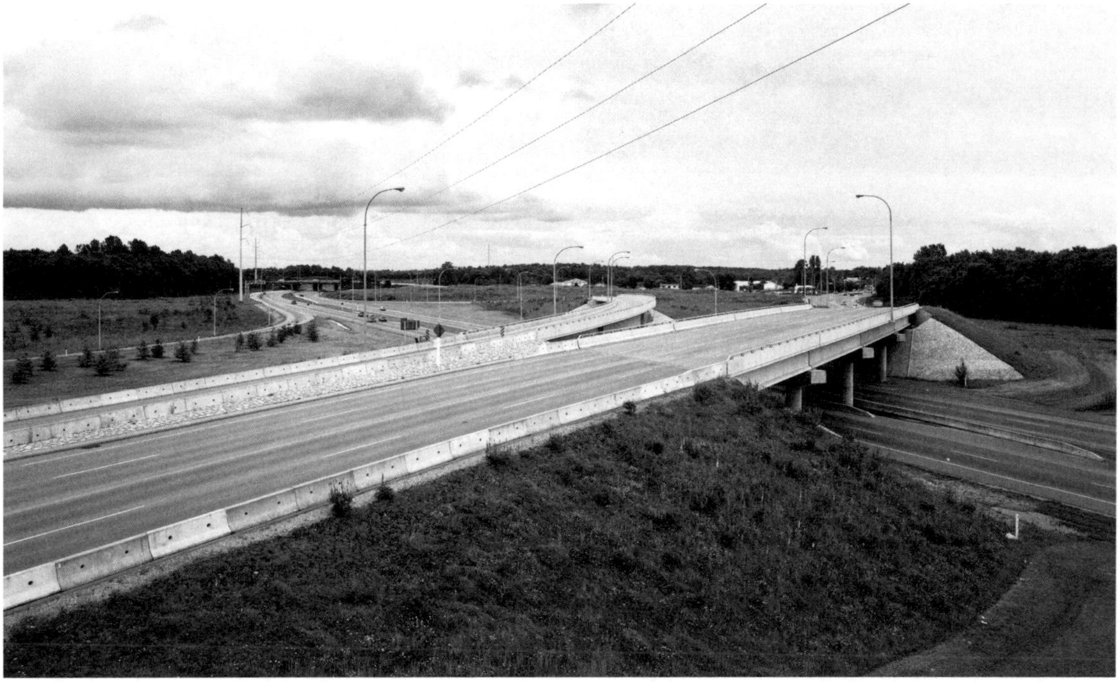

AS IS

Three vignettes featuring three of those large automobiles peculiar to the 1970s, accompanied by three moments from the bridge of the disco song, "I Want Your Love," by Chic. The cars were sold in their day as luxury vehicles, but today—having been made to look less attractive by more compact imports and domestics—they are now some of the least expensive used cars one can buy. All three are of exactly the same make and vintage, but they can be distinguished by their particular colours and respective quantities of rust.

1. Music: guitar, bass, and drums only. A low-rise residential neighbourhood with more than a few Vancouver Specials lining the streets. The camera draws toward a car with its hood and both doors open. A young man sits in the driver's seat with one foot on the road, awaiting instruction. As it passes the car, the camera finds two more young men working on the car's engine— one getting his hands dirty, and the other giving unwanted advice. Dissolve to the next scene.
2. Music: a piano adds chords with each quarter-note beat. Driving beside an enormous automobile on a freeway in a suburban area. The distant skyline reminds one that this is no more than twenty minutes from the city's downtown core. A long look from a short distance at one of the car's passenger windows, through which, because of glare, nothing can be seen. The car accelerates, providing an unobstructed view of itself in its entirety as it recedes into the distance. Dissolve to the next scene.
3. Music: chimes mimic the melody of the chorus, with synthetic horns punctuating the space between "want" and "your love." The camera follows a car from some distance behind, as it drives slowly through a parking lot—spiralling upward to the uppermost level, which is exposed to the afternoon sky. The car finally parks and one of its doors opens. Dissolve to black and fade to silence.
4. Title: FOR LESS.
5. Title: LUXURY.

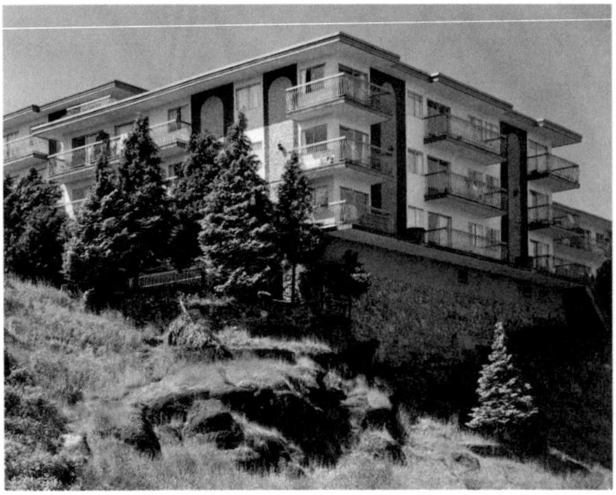

EYE ON YOU

Early evening. A visibly tired young man is found at home in his second-storey apartment, eating warmed-up pizza, and watching the end of one of his favourite movies, Cape Fear. Directly beside his television set, the view beyond a balcony presents a minor highway that borders a light-industrial area. Throughout, the protagonist is obviously bothered by something, but even he is not entirely sure what this something might be.

1. Pizza in hand, he returns from his kitchen. The room is generally dim, but the darkness is punctuated by that flickering light typical of a television set. He passes by the TV to take in the view from his balcony. Something catches his attention.

2. He moves into a medium shot, then, as he looks down, the rhythm of his chewing slows.

3. A point-of-view shot presents the grassy, poorly maintained hill below, and a man standing perfectly still, staring at some distant object.

4. Return to shot 2., the man inside finally swallows. He then turns and rushes out of frame.

5. Return to shot 3., the stranger gone.

6. Return to shot 4., the man gone.

7. From a position well below where the spectator had stood, the man is seen running down the hill and frantically looking for his stranger.

8. Return to something like shot 3., the man is seen in a familiar pose. Finally, he turns to look directly at the camera—with an empty mouth, he swallows once more.

9. Title: EYE ON YOU.

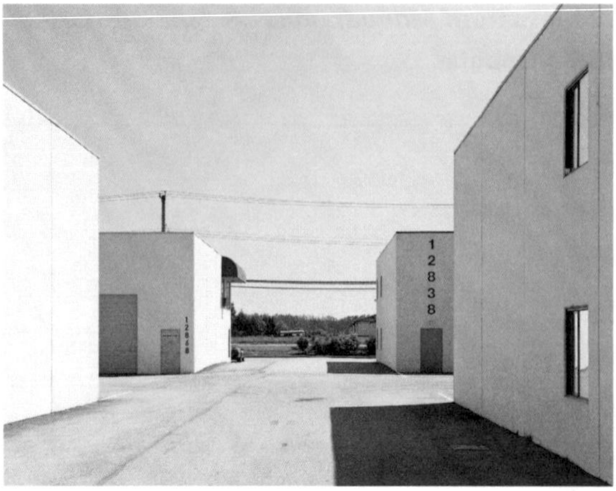

ENCAMPMENT

A warehouse district at night. Little indication that there is anything else—aside from farmland and more warehouses—for miles. Sound is generally sparse, but what few sounds there are reverberate wildly. The protagonist prepares to have an argument with someone; however, it is doubtful that he will ever get beyond this rehearsal.

1. Distance. From a height, the camera presents the protagonist from behind as he walks quickly down the centre of a corridor formed by rows of unremarkable warehouse buildings. Lowering its angle of view and tracking forward, the camera rushes to catch up with him: the sound of his footsteps become louder, as does that of his indecipherable rant.

2. A sudden reverse angle presents a medium shot of the man, grimacing and sputtering. Although the sound of his voice is now even louder, one still can't exactly make out what he is saying, except for fragments like ". . . everything . . . everyone . . . every time . . . ."

3. Return to shot 1. Slowing slightly, in order to peruse the man from a safe distance.

4. He is followed until he reaches an intersection between buildings, where he stops abruptly. He turns his head to partially reveal a still-open mouth and an astonished expression.

5. From the man's point of view, an old camper-trailer and its two young inhabitants are seen. One sits on the trailer's doorstep, and the other in a folding chair on the shoulder of the road—both stare at the camera.

6. Reverse shot: the man turns away and proceeds at a rapid pace, in silence.

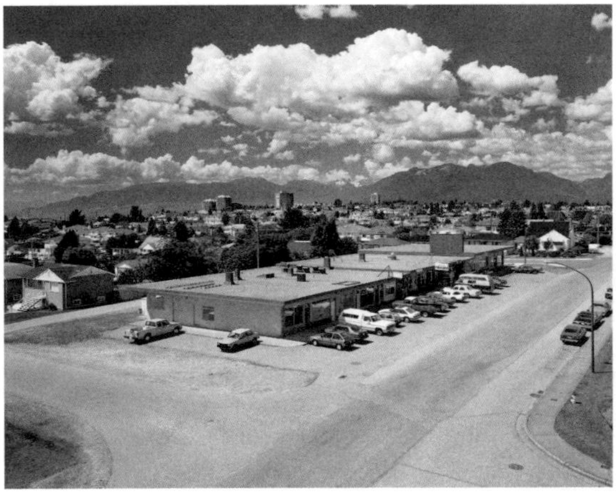

"I'M NOT GARY"

A one-block market street. It might rain. Both characters no doubt have reasonably well-paying day jobs, but the second most likely has the day off.

1. An establishing shot presents the surrounding landscape and only a few people on the street shopping, going to and from work.

2. A tracking shot follows our protagonist, as he walks under the covered sidewalk: another man walks toward him, grinning, and otherwise doing his best to make eye contact.

3. Reverse tracking shot: the protagonist approaches, and then issues one of those involuntary twitches that often derive from conceit, but more generally occur when one is attempting to ignore the fact that a stranger is looking at oneself. The second man is now very close as he hurries to remark, "Hi, Gary."

4. Return to shot 2. The two men, now about three metres apart, as the protagonist man looks long at the face of the second.

5. A close-up of the interlocutor, smiling and saying, as one does to an old friend, "How you doing?"

6. The protagonist is seen in a close-up; he is not entirely sure of himself but replies anyway, "I'm not Gary."

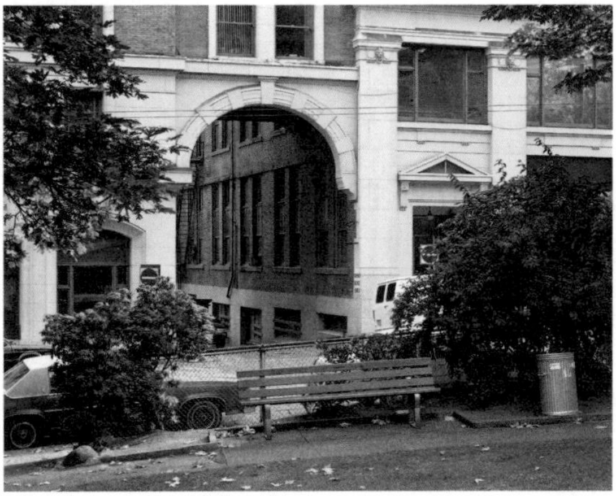

UP

Three men sit together casually on a bench in an urban park. A fence and bits of sparse foliage indicate the edge of the park, and directly behind them there is a road and an office building. A discrete hand rests upon an area of grass at the bottom right of the screen.

1. An engine shuts off, and car door slams. After a moment, the wandering attentions of all three focus upon something to the left, off screen.

2. Footsteps approach. The eyes of the three follow something as it arrives at a point near the camera.

3. A man's voice, "Get up." Pause. The three look up, then down.

4. "C'mon, get up." The eyes of the men, with little or no synchronization, look to the ground then up again.

5. A soft, indeterminable sound of impact.

6. The fingers of that disembodied hand curl, then relax.

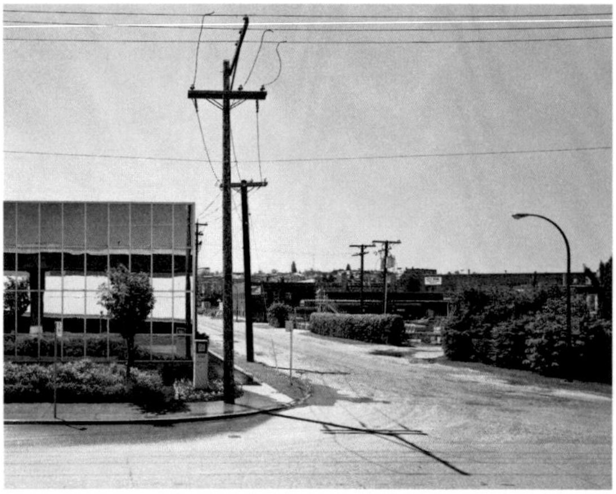

DISAGREE

At a blind corner in a light-industrial area, the meeting and aggressive dance of a well-used mid-size car and a small school bus. The camera is absolutely still; all is seen from a modest height.

1. Eventually, the car is seen clearly—as it moves toward the camera on the avenue that bisects the screen at a slight angle.
2. A signal light flashes, and the car prepares for a left-hand turn. At this moment, the school bus appears at left and begins to make a right-hand turn. The two vehicles only barely miss colliding with each other.
3. Both stop.
4. The car begins to drive away—and, a fraction of a second later, so too does the bus. Immediately both stop.
5. Pause.
6. They start and stop again in synchronization.
7. Pause.
8. Finally, the bus drives away, along the same avenue upon which the car had first appeared. The car disappears.

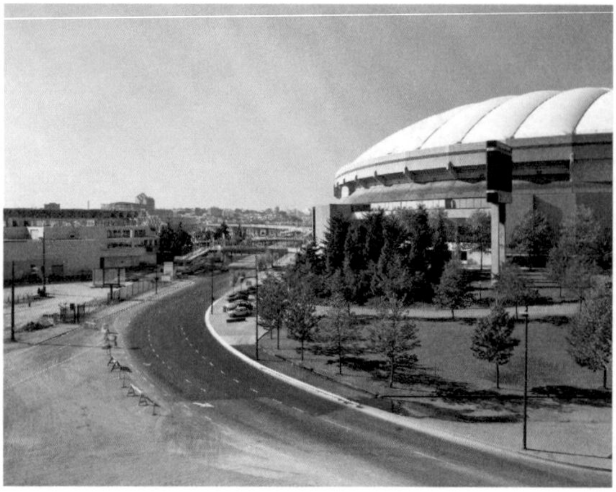

STADIUM

Twilight. An elevated view of a pedestrian walkway beside a huge domed stadium. On the right, a vacant parking area can almost be seen, and above it there is a freeway "on" ramp. The middle of the walkway is concealed by foliage, and at left a small portion of the stadium is visible. The most prominent feature in the composition is a large electronic sign. Because it is seen from behind, it is a black and featureless rectangle resting on a post, but the constantly moving and multicoloured light cast by its front surface occasionally illuminates the ground below.

1. Faint buzzing noises correspond to the shifting and flickering light cast by the sign. Long pause. Distant talk and laughter is not entirely audible beneath these sounds.
2. A small firework screeches upward, and then skitters across the paved walkway before exploding. Its point of origin is obscured by the foliage in the centre of the screen.
3. Short wait.
4. From the centre of the screen, four or five balls of light issued from a Roman candle rise progressively higher, though they never get especially far off the ground.
5. Dissolve to black.

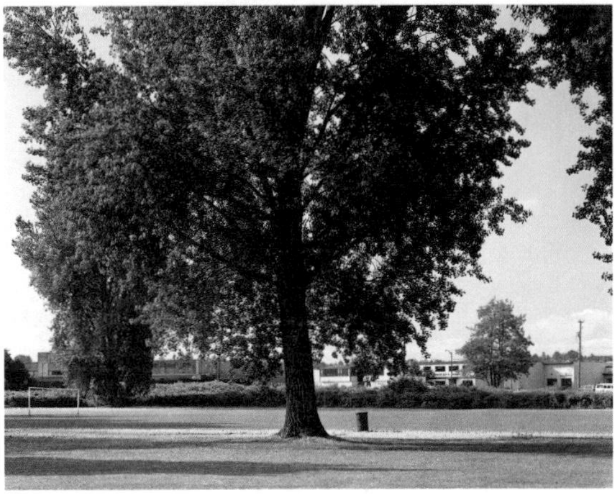

BAD DREAM

A very large playing field bordered on its four sides by a freeway; unused land that is apparently becoming a dump; and light-industrial and ware- house buildings. A row of old poplar trees stand along the side opposite the freeway; the park attendant's house is beside them, and next to it a baseball diamond. There is a residential area immediately behind the freeway, and one can see more houses and apartment buildings on a hill that rises in the distance beyond the stand of trees.

1. A craning pan of the freeway. After a moment, silence is broken by a middle episode of Arnold Schoenberg's Accompaniment to a Cinematographic Scene. A series of slow cranes and pans of the freeway and park begin, dissolving into one another.
2. The final pan cranes down to find a middle-class woman sleeping beneath the poplars.
3. There is a musical crescendo, and the woman wakes with a start. The music is now gone, and the ambient sounds of traffic and light industry are heard for the first time. She turns away from the camera and looks to find the source of the sound that woke her.
4. She lies down again, and we are shown a point-of-view shot: leaves of trees.
5. Slightly nearer. The woman closes her eyes for a moment, then sits up and again turns away from the camera. The camera withdraws, craning upward to present the landscape that lies beyond the row of trees.
6. Dissolve to black.

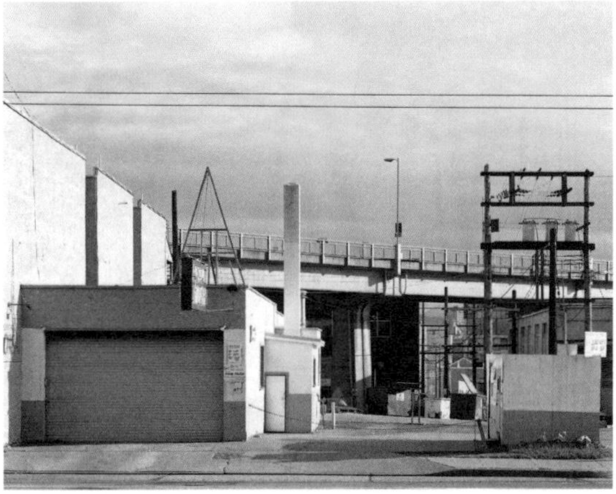

WASH

Under the scrutiny of its owner, a mid-1980s luxury car is "detailed" by a four-person car-wash crew. The image of their labour is accompanied by the sound of a "jazz" drum solo. It must be off-season for this kind of work: there is no line-up of cars, and this is probably the business's first job in a few hours.

1. Black. The drum solo begins.
2. Dissolve to a long take of car owner's face. He is supposedly daydreaming, but frequently makes a point of glancing over at a nearby action. We might understand later that the look of satisfaction he wears has less to do with the condition of his car than with the treatment it is receiving.
3. The camera draws away from the man, tracking backward. A good look at the man, now openly surveying the operation.
4. The camera presents more and more of the car-wash building.
5. Finally we see a bit of the car, and a member of the wash crew.
6. The car-wash crew and the car with hood and doors wide open: track toward them.
7. Stop. Fade to black with the drum solo's penultimate flourish.

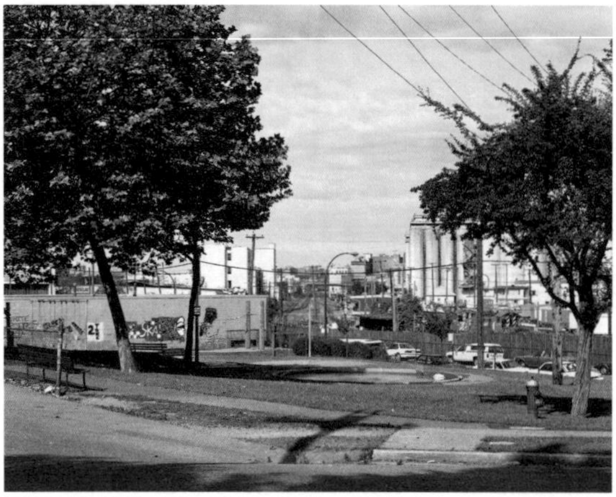

GUILTY

A location interview conducted at the edge of an urban or suburban park. A cluster of flesh-toned rectangles in the centre of the screen eclipses the face of the interviewee—each time he or she moves, these rectangles move also, shimmering and changing colour.

1. Dissolve from black to the speaker.*

   Maybe I did feel guilty, but my guilt had no actual object. It was too pervasive, too enormous for that. My guilt demanded punishment. And the punishment, fittingly enough, was to feel myself guilty. No quiet. There are always sounds coming from far away, and like the sounds, thoughts come to me as if from a great distance. Even when I'm listening to music, the words will come to me involuntarily—and even if I don't know the words to a song I will make them up.

2. Dissolve to the same scene: a slight jerk of bad registration.

   The voices are, however, heard in my head—though I do on occasion hear them in the air or in different parts of the room. Each of them is different, and beautiful, and generally speaking with its own distinct tone or rhythm. There are many, I would say, upwards of fifteen, simultaneously admonishing with phrases like, "We shall see." Only when I am talking aloud, to myself or to other people, can I not hear them, and drown out their sounds with my own. But as soon as I stop, the well-known phrases begin again, reminding me that the monologue continues even as I speak.

3. Title: GUILTY.

*To be performed by three persons at as many different locations.

News Hour Viewer Call-in Segment Regarding Original Broadcast of Stan Douglas's *Monodramas*
BCTV
1992

REPORTER: So, tell me about these things that attracted your attention on television?

VIEWER 1: Go ahead.

VIEWER 2: Well, we were watching, and there was this guy ranting and raving, and we thought it was a commercial, and it wasn't, and so we were wondering, you know, what it was, because ...

REPORTER: When you say it wasn't a commercial, I mean, how did you ...

VIEWER 1: There were no words, no, er ... no point to it ... really that I could see, and, er, we thought it was building up to another commercial that was coming later on that would give us the point of what was happening, and, and we really didn't know, and then it just repeated, and repeated [...]

REPORTER: Was there more than one?

VIEWER 2: Not the first night. There was, like, a different one each night, and, um, there's about five ...

REPORTER: You must've thought it was really strange, I mean, especially if, for you two, you haven't even had a TV for years, and years, and years. (laughing) What'd you think had happened to television? (laughs)

VIEWER 2: We didn't know, so, uh, after the first couple of nights, we were thinking, you know, maybe we should tape it and slow it down (laughs) and see if there was subliminal messages.

VIEWER 1: Yeah. The one that really caught my attention, was the one with the arm lying in the grass, and the, the voice saying, "Get up, come on, get up," and I thought, "They must've forgot to print something on the screen, there must be some point to it." I thought maybe it was some kind of religious ad, like Latter Day Saints or something like that, saying, you know, "Good will toward men," or something, I guess 'cause the three guys sitting there looking, and I didn't, uh, know what they'd done, it was, it was quite ...

REPORTER: Now that you know what it's all about, now what do you think of them?

VIEWER 1: Hmm. Well, now, when I watch them, it look ... I watch the, the, uh, the work that's been done, like, how the cameras move smoothly, how the acting is done with the positioning of everything, instead of looking for a point or anything like that. I just ...

VIEWER 2: Yeah. Now that we're not looking for a point, it's a lot more enjoyable, you know. You don't have to worry about it, because there really isn't a point, it's just for art.

REPORTER: Do you think it's art?

VIEWER 2: I think so, I mean, art comes in many different forms, so ...

VIEWER 1: I don't know (laughs).

REPORTER: Did it, um, you say there's no point, but the artist says that the point is to arouse your curiosity ... break your train of thought. Did it do all those things?

SPEAKER 2: Oh, it did that. [...] It took us four days to phone BCTV and find out what it was, but we did finally phone and find out, well, "What is this, really? What are, what are we watching?"

REPORTER: Should there be more? [...]

VIEWER 1: I don't know (laughs).

VIEWER 2: I like them now that I know what they are. They're, you know, something.

REPORTER: You're just being nice and polite, aren't you? (laughter) Actually, you probably thought they were really dumb right off the bat.

VIEWER 1: Well, ... some of them are kind of annoying ... like the one with the guy talking is really annoying, but the other ones didn't bother me. The only reason that one bothered me, because it seemed awfully aggressive for just nothing, for not having a point ... and you do wish that they'd connected to something else somewhere, because they leave you just hanging with nothing, and you wish there was some kind of a theme throughout the series, you know? [...]

Herald Tribune, January 18–February 28, 1991

Sarah Charlesworth

1991

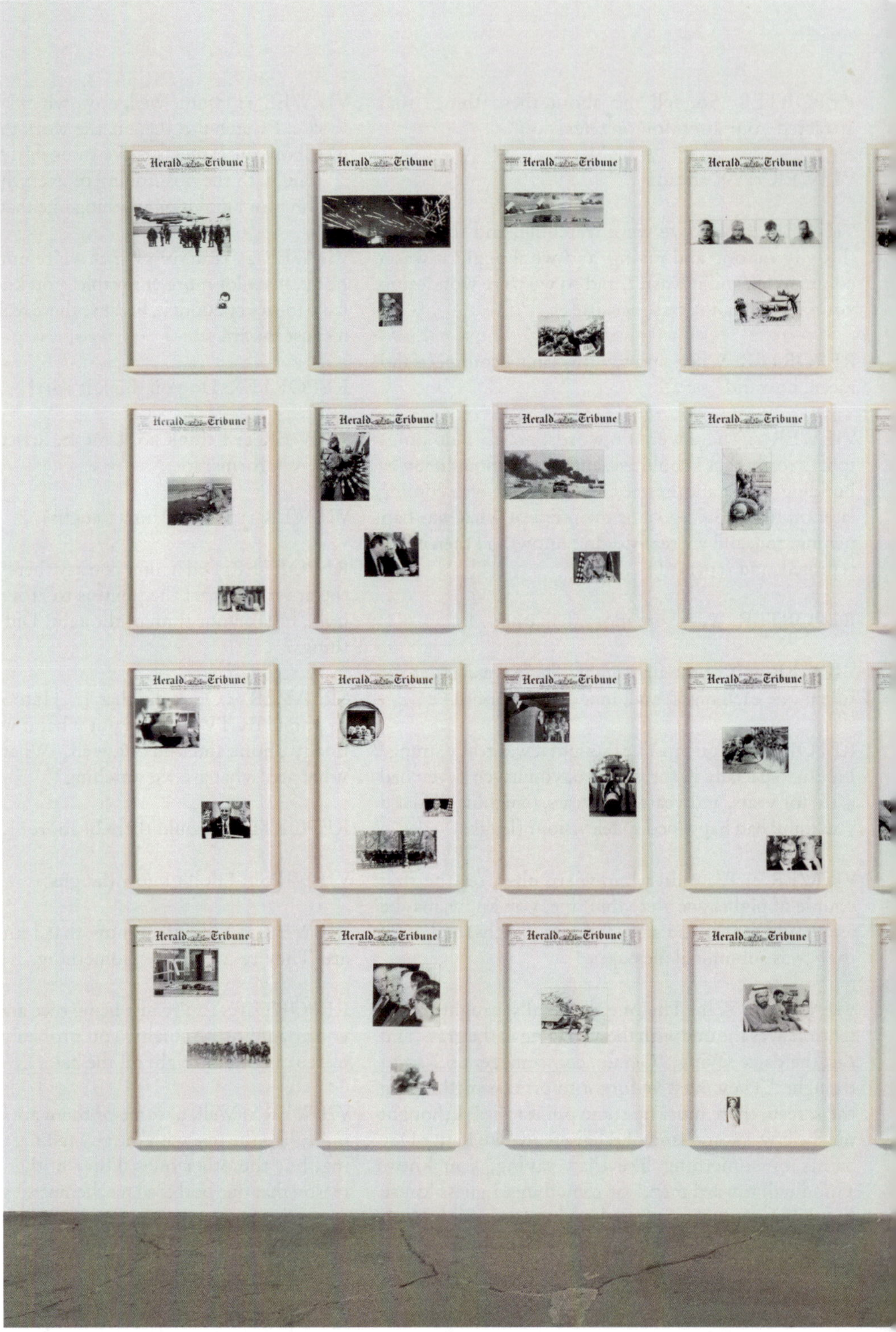

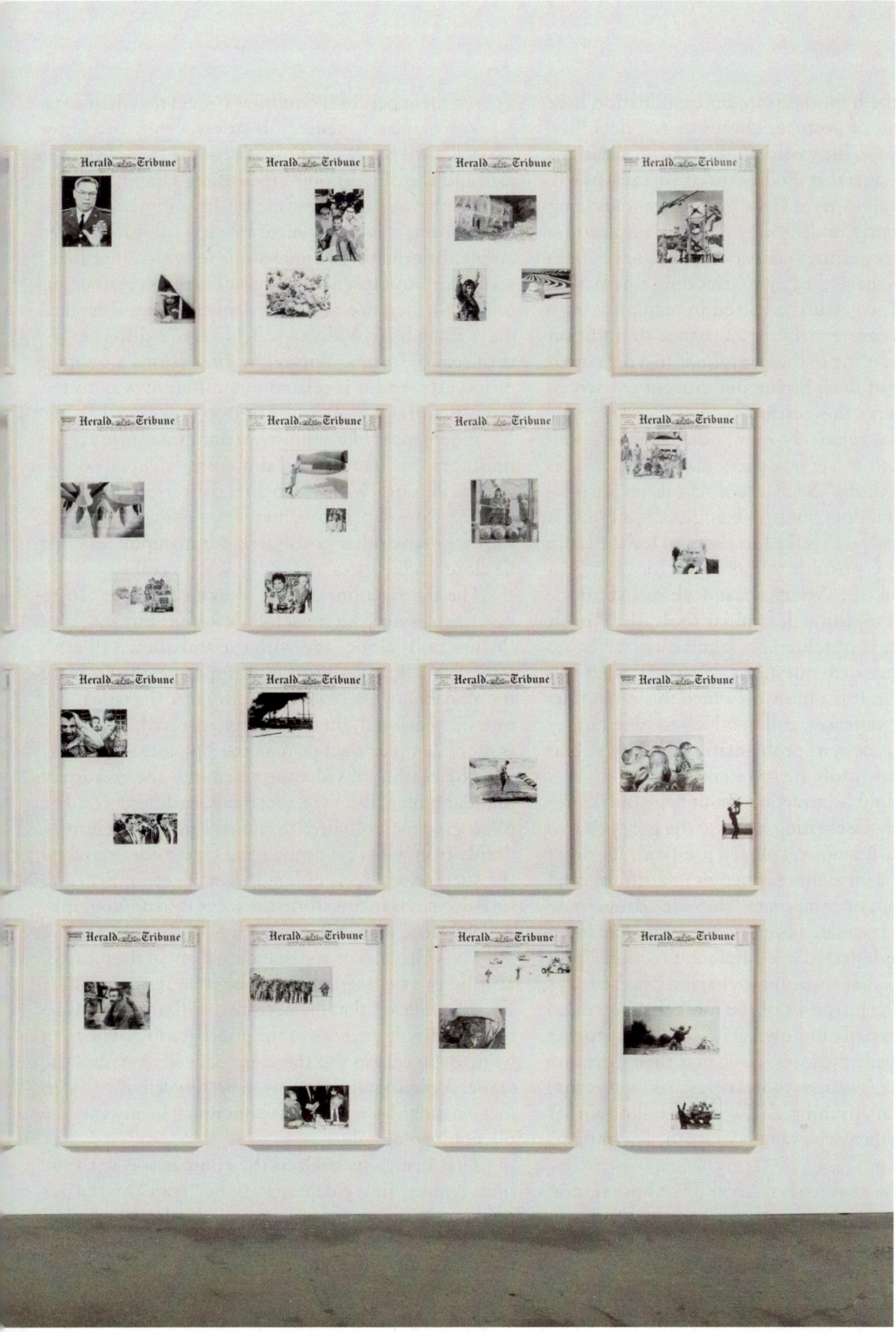
Herald Tribune

The Gesture of Video

Vilém Flusser

1991

According to the hypothesis under examination here, the observation of gestures allows us to "decipher" the way we exist in the world. One of the implications of this hypothesis is that modifications we can observe in our gestures allow us to "read" the existential changes we are currently undergoing. Another implication is that whenever gestures appear that have never been seen before, we have the key to decoding a new form of existence. The gesture involved in manipulating a video camera represents in part a change to traditional gesture. According to the hypothesis just presented, then, one way of deciphering our current existential crisis is to observe this gesture.

"Video" is a relatively new tool. A "tool" is an object produced to serve a particular purpose. It is "good for something." Such a tool reveals its purpose in its form. But it does not stop being an object, that is, a problem. "Problem" is the Greek word for the Latin *obiectum*. So it is possible to ignore the tool's informing purpose and ask, "What is it, and what can be done with it?" With traditional, familiar tools, this "problematic" aspect is obscured by familiarity. A bed no longer raises any such questions. We know what it is and what it's for. It is a place on which to sleep, under which to store suitcases, and in which to hide money. But if the tool is new, its problematic side shows. This is the reason new tools are so fascinating.

There is a double attraction about new tools. They are immediately fascinating because the purpose that gave them form has not yet played itself out. We don't yet know all the virtualities inherent in artificial satellites, laser beams, or computers. They are "dangerous." We are further fascinated because the formative intention can still be deflected in a different direction. Tools are imperatives that shape our behavior. The bed says, "Lie down!" The purposes of the tools that surround us are not necessarily our own. They are the purposes of those who made the tools. To change their direction means to be free. The new tools are fascinating because they, more than anything else, conceal unknown virtualities within themselves and because they permit acts of emancipation.

The purpose of video is to serve TV. Those responsible for the decision to produce it had exactly this intention. It is a tool for developing a program that is to be broadcast, for assembling and censoring it. Video removes the surprises of live broadcast. It is a tool that serves the purposes of the TV system, which in turn is a constituent part of the cultural system that defines us.

Videotape is a memory. It stores scenes on a linear surface. So it has three dimensions: the two of the surface and the dimension of the rolling tape. It reduces four-dimensional space-time to three dimensions. In this respect, it is still comparable to sculpture, for example. But the three dimensions to which it reduces scenes are structured differently. There is a further, ontological difference: sculpture depicts scenes; videotape plays them back. Videotape belongs to a different level of reality from sculpture: its dimensions are set up differently, and it is related in a different way to the scene it stores.

Videotape is like a filmstrip. But film is made up of photographs. Its temporal dimension depends on an optical illusion. With videotape, conversely, playback and scene overlap. It, too, involves tricking the eye, but the tricks have other possibilities for manipulation that lie closer to the threshold of the scene's reality.

The tape is a linear code like the alphabet. To receive its message, one must follow its line. But with tape, the line rolls along, and with the alphabet, it doesn't move at all. Reading a tape is more passive than reading the alphabet, where eyes move. Because the tape is not one-dimensional, but three-dimensional, reading it is more complex than reading the alphabet.

The gesture of videoing resembles the gesture of photographing. But here, too, there are differences. The photographer is required to choose a position. He must decide from what point the scenes are to be stored on the surface. He feels obliged to make clear, firm and final decisions to transform the scene into photographs, which is to say objects, of which he is the subject.

The video maker, too, stands in front of the monitor as if before the scene about which he is making decisions. It follows that his decisions will not need to be so objectifying as those of the photographer. They can be made in relation to the scene as well as within the scene. A photographer needs to be "objective"; a video maker can be intersubjective, but must, in any case, be phenomenological.

That brings us back to the comparison with the film. Unlike film, videotape can be "read" by the participants in the stored scene immediately after recording. Within the scene, they need not be actors only, as is the case for film. They are subjects and objects at the same time, those who store and those who are stored. The tape opens a dialogue between itself and the scene, whereas the film is a discourse about the scene and forbids any immediate dialogue. Videotape is a dialogical memory.

At first glance, the monitor seems to be a mirror, but many differences can be established between it and a "classical" mirror. The monitor emits sounds. It does not reverse right and left and so is in this sense exactly the opposite of a mirror. It does not reflect the light coming from the scene but has its own cathode luminescence. It presents a completely different image from that of the classical mirror, new in such a way as to be revolutionary. For in its sound, angle of reflection, light, it reverses all our traditional concepts of a reflected, speculative reality. It puts the person watching the monitor in a space for which there are no coordinates. He loses orientation.

Like a mirror, a monitor is a glass surface, but in turning the mirror around, it is more like a window. In this respect, it is like TV, as distinct from the back of a painting or a film, which is a wall. With respect to its origins, the projection of slides and of film is a further development from painting, with its beginnings on the cave walls of Lascaux and Altamira. The monitor, like TV, is a further development of the reflective and transparent surfaces whose origins lie in the surface of water, watched by "primitive" people. Video and film occupy different branches of the tree of image genealogy. In comparing them, we are able to see it, setting video and TV free from the control exerted by the model of film.

Genealogically, film can be traced to the line fresco–painting–photography; video can be traced back to the line water surface–magnifying glass–microscope–telescope. In its origin, film is an artistic tool: it depicts; video, conversely, is an epistemological tool: it presents, speculates, and philosophizes. The contrast is not necessarily functional. Film can present (e.g., in documentary), and video can represent (e.g., in video art). Nevertheless, the origin of the tool "video" gives the impression of a whole series of epistemological virtualities that have not yet unfolded.

A video maker manipulates the linearity of time. He can synchronize diachronic time. Any tape can be used again to synchronize varying temporal segments on the same surface. So it is about a composition comparable to that of a musician. But there is a difference. The musician synchronizes the diachronic time of sounds: he forms chords. Such a synchronization of sound can be called a *symphony*. The video maker synchronizes scenes: he superimposes them. Such a synchronization of scenes can be called a *symsceny*. The video maker moves toward the work along a sequence of events, whereas the musician moves along a sequence of sounds. The raw material of the video makes history in the strict sense: a sequence of scenes. Not only does it happen in history but it also affects history. In this sense, it is a posthistorical gesture. It aims not only to commemorate the event (a historical engagement) but also to compose alternative events (posthistorical engagement).

This is exactly the reason video, as a tool, fascinates us. It permits us to discover potentialities unknown either to those who invented it or to those who paid for its production. And it permits us to steer its development in another direction. Of course, video may engage the same gestures that were foreseen when the intention was modeled. In this case, analysis will show that we are under the control of the power behind the apparatus. Behind the gestures of the video maker working in and for the system, we will be able to discover the ways and means the system has of programming us.

But video can also be manipulated with gestures borrowed from other media, for example, gestures from films, texts, musical compositions, sculpture, or philosophical speculation. They will have a new quality, however. This new quality will come from the dialogic structure of video. To put it briefly, we will be dealing with a gesture that no longer attempts to produce a work whose subject is the maker but rather with one that attempts instead to produce an event in which the maker participates, even if he is controlling it.

To summarize, we are dealing with a gesture whose coming can be read as a new way of being-in-the-world. It is about a way of being that challenges traditional categories (e.g., those of art, historical action and objectivity) and proposes new categories that aren't yet clear enough to analyze. To understand these new categories, we must start analyzing gestures, such as the gesture of videoing that was just lightly sketched here. Perhaps a name such as *dialogic speculation* would apply to this understanding, forming a great arc to Plato: it raises a suspicion that if the ancients had reflected in video rather than in words, we would have video archives rather than libraries, and videotic rather than logic. But these are anachronisms.

Red Portfolio

Glenn Ligon

1993

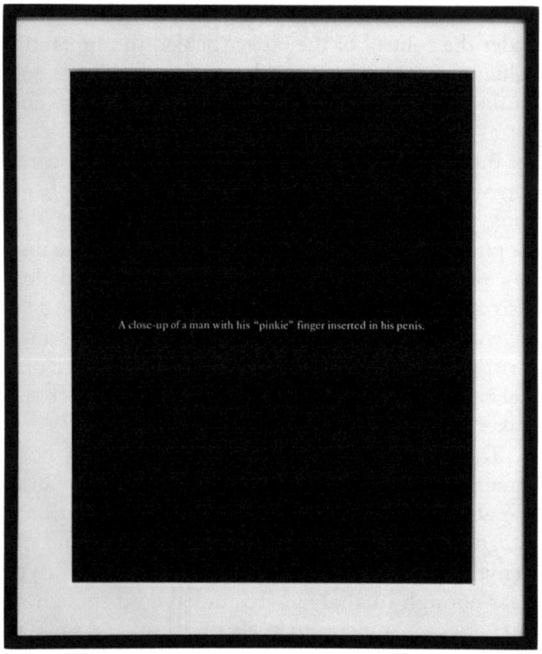

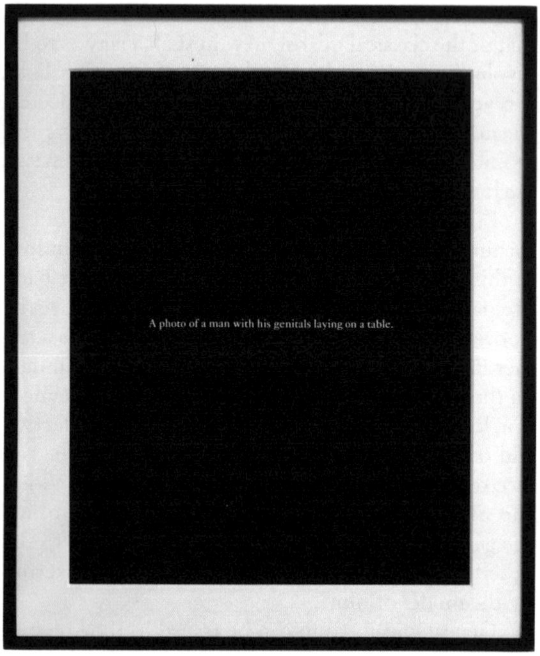

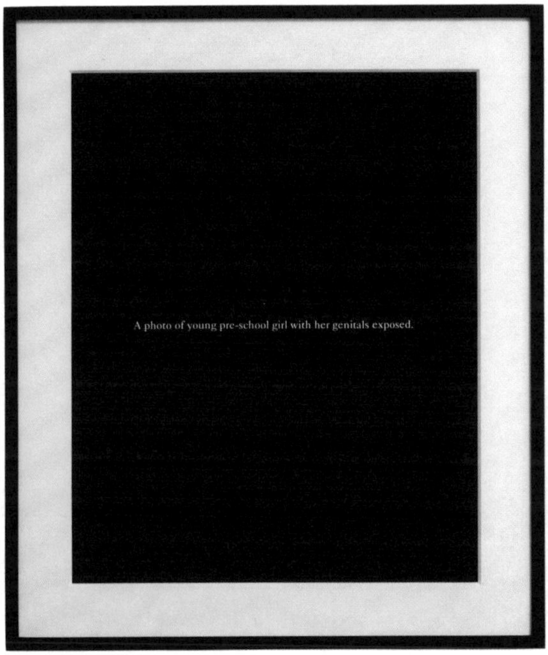
A photo of young pre-school girl with her genitals exposed.

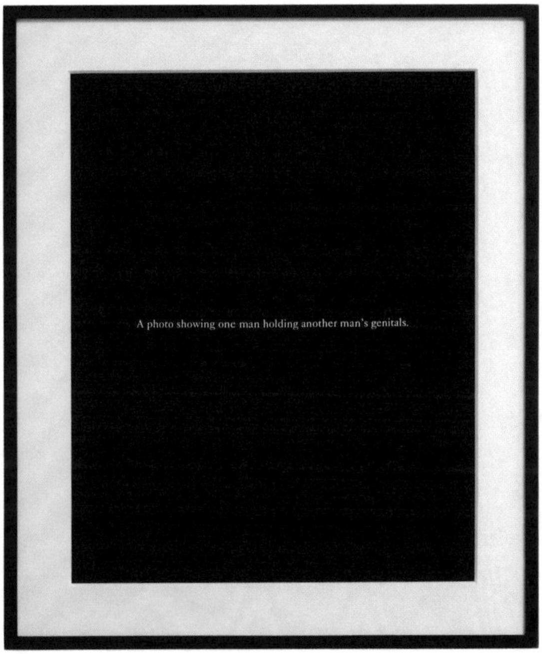
A photo showing one man holding another man's genitals.

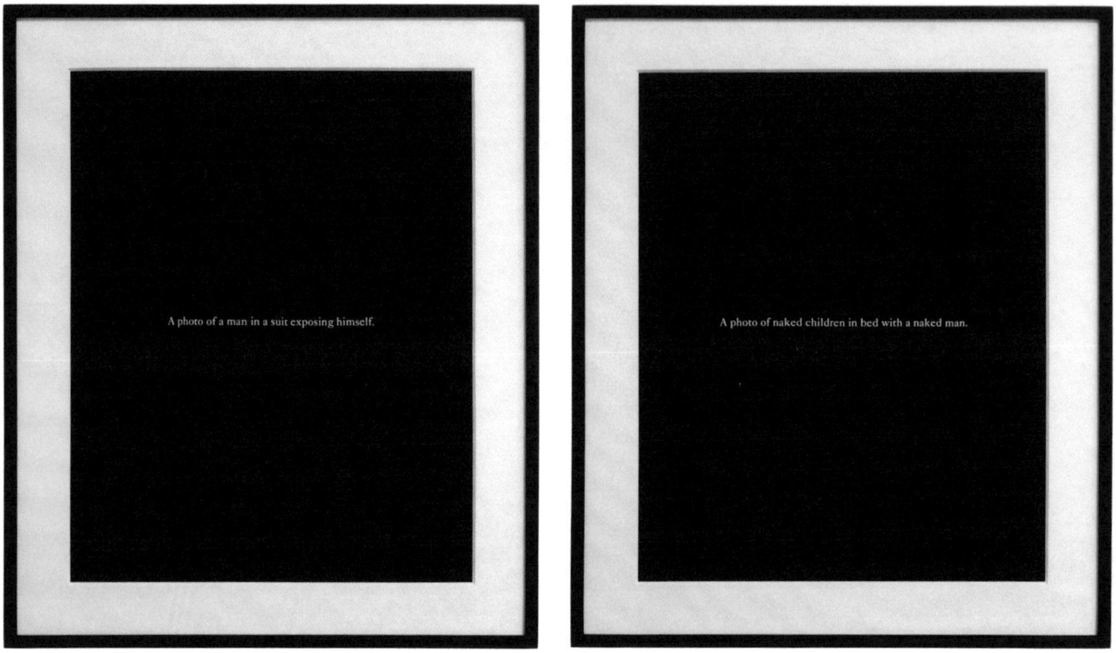
A photo of a man in a suit exposing himself.
A photo of naked children in bed with a naked man.

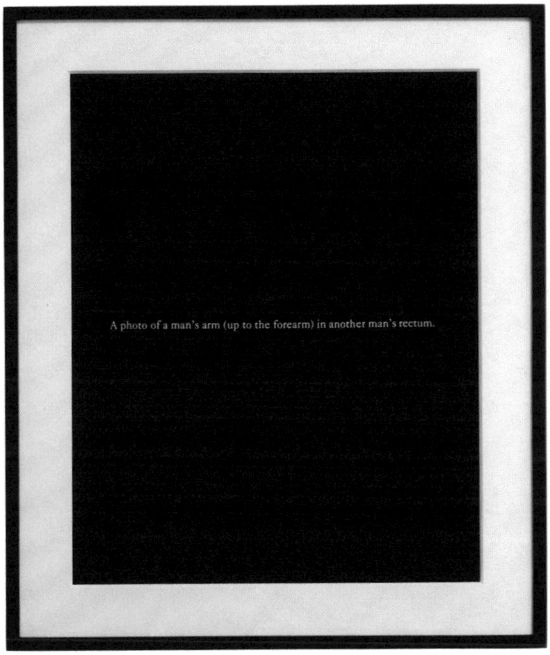
A photo of a man's arm (up to the forearm) in another man's rectum.

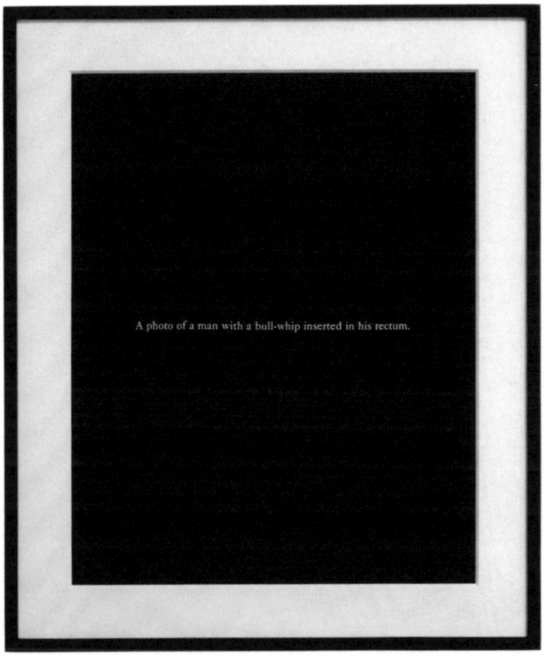
A photo of a man with a bull-whip inserted in his rectum.

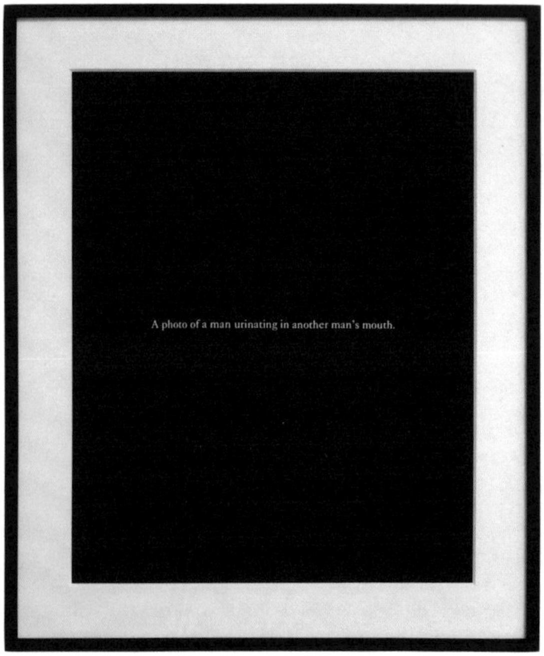
A photo of a man urinating in another man's mouth.

Self Portrait (James Dean)

Jack Pierson

1993

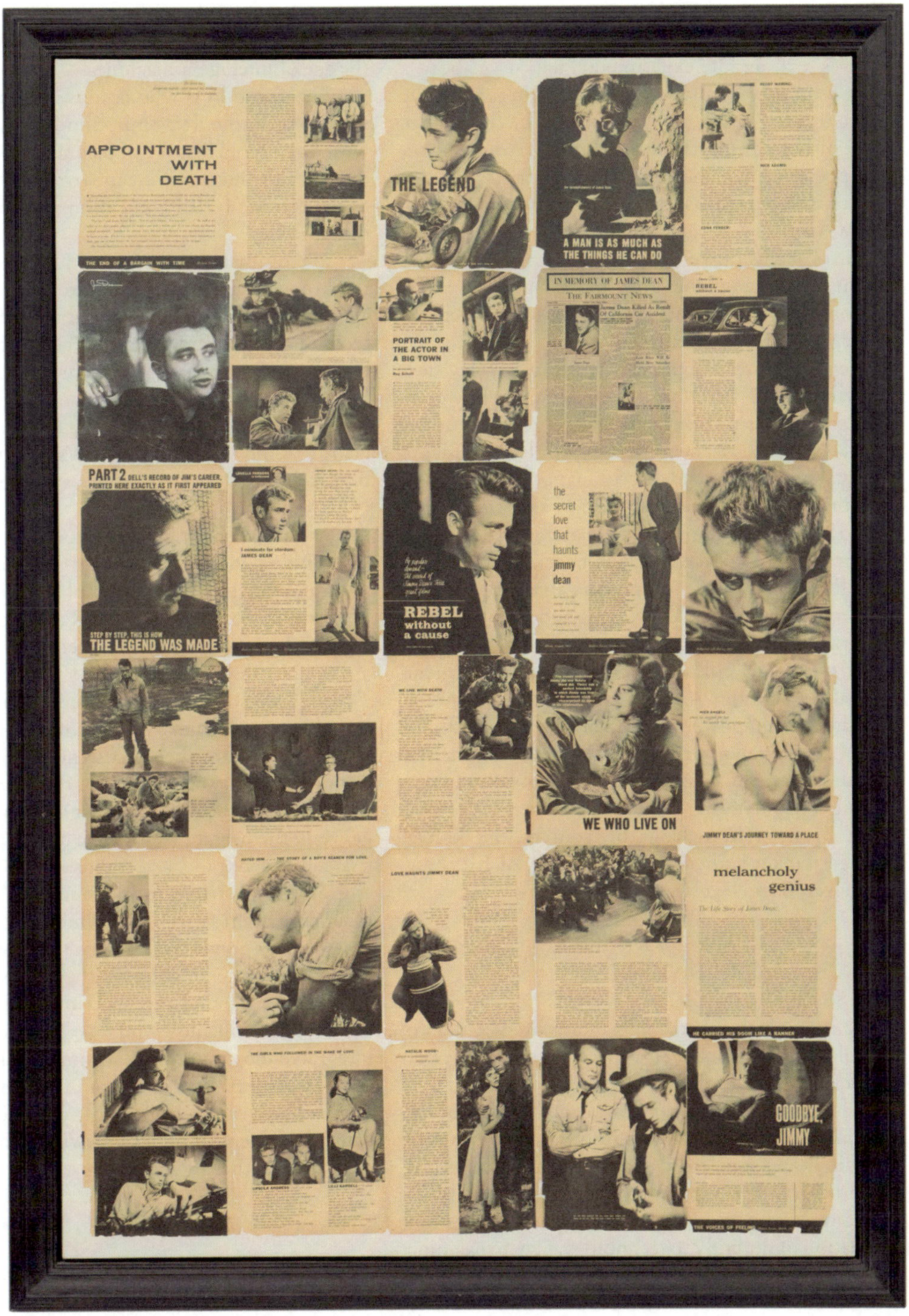

Hiatus: Work in Progress Lecture

Ericka Beckman

1993

HIATUS

Hiatus is a 30-minute experimental narrative about a young woman who plays *Hiatus*, an 'interactive' online computer game, and encounters in the 'cyberspace' of her computer an assortment of logged-on game players and game identities who trick and confuse her into consciousness. An aggressive male character WANG logs on as an aid, but only to deceive her. To confront this powerful take-over artist, she must rely on her 'organic' memory, and is forced to establish some psychological boundaries to protect her identity and preserve her freedom.

Hiatus pictures a fictional near future of television that will also be the means of annexing on-line computer games. Its primary audience is young women, ages 18–25, who are encountering problems in identity, sexual harassment and discrimination, when facing the demands placed on them by the workplace. *Hiatus* aims to inform and empower them at this critical stage in their psychological development with self-esteem and self reliance. I have invented a game for girls that reinforces creative problem solving and intuition, and encourages her to be critical of/and discriminate between dominant cultural myths of empowerment, especially technology's promise to provide the means for individual empowerment. *Hiatus* is also a critique of the entertainment driven venture into 'interactive' game development, targeted at a young male audience, offering a proliferating array of combat and defense games. From myknowledgeable sources, the equivalent age female audience is under served by these gamedevelopers.

NATURE

As the individual is becoming more integrated into technology and we loose this space/time identity, our culture has a new tension.

Man has to become more aware and critical of his relation to nature as technology becomes more integrated in his personal life and in his work place. Faced with proliferating computer practices in the workplace and ubiquitous computing, we are asked to question the relation of the body to technology. I try to examine in my story the romance of outlaw technology, of human machine interfaces. The personal story of one woman's journey becomes a model for a culture trying to re-establish its connection to nature and ecology in the age of intelligent machines.

The question is who counts? I hope to offer a vision of technological embodiment that is consistent with a gendered history of technology where technology isn't the means of escape from the body but rather the means of communication and connection with other bodies.

The ultimate challenge women face is to harness the power of technological knowledge to a feminist agenda, while struggling against the subordination of technology and labor to private corporate interests; to empower those workers in technological to work on behalf of the right kind of social change.

In 1989, met with Scott Fischer, chief scientist in charge of the View Lab, NASA's interactive robotics division and Ron Reisman, a systems engineer for NASA's flight simulators.

- Jason Lanier, the inventor of computerized clothing, including the Data Glove and EyePhone.
- was invited to attend Siggraph'90, and Cyberthon's three day conference on VR sponsored by *Whole Earth Magazine*, where I met Sense8, Hit Lab and the North Carolina University team.

Through these valuable interviews and exchanges I was able to construct a history of the physio/psycho/perceptual research behind this new technology. More importantly, for the purpose of this film, I uncovered a controversy that lines at heart of technology's emergence in the private sector. The conflict divides scientists along economic and philosophical lines. At one end of the spectrum, proponents of VR believes it's main contribution to society lines in it's ability to increase man's power over nature and human life. Jaron Lanier holds the position on the opposite side of the spectrum, believing that VR strapped to man's nervous system will allow him to experience nature as an integrated mind/body whole, thus breaking him from the powerful paradigm of communication and interaction, a power that has steadily drained from culture since the advent of passive viewing broadcast and information gathering technologies.

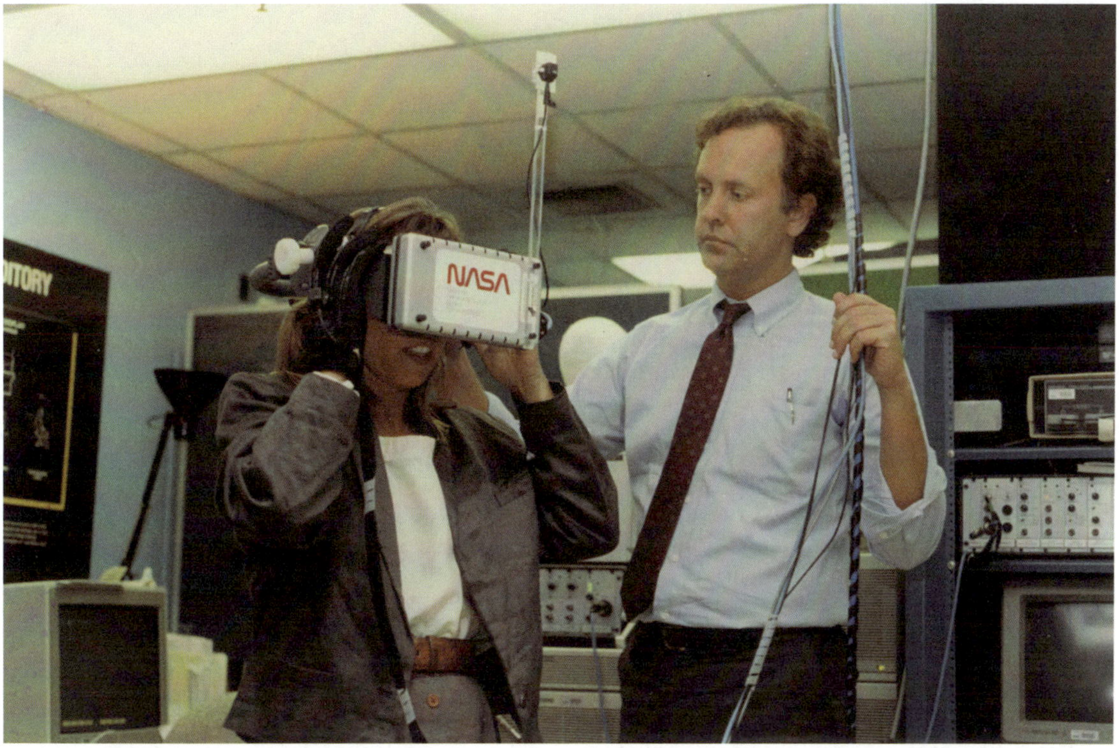

ISSUES of NOW_PRIVACY

Debate about privacy by which personal data is scavenged and converted into someone else's intelligence.

Hiatus is a story about the coordination between technology and technical experience and how it becomes subject to corporate control. Like cyberpunk novels, my film shares the basic vision of a post human existence where technology and the human are understood in contiguous rather than oppositional terms.

Hiatus—A technological encounter on the internet; gender follows women online. Some women prefer to obscure their genders, to deny their bodies in order to communicate more effectively. For some women, it's not worth the effort.

TECHNOLOGY AND THE BODY

[Fredric] Jameson says that postmodern hyperspace has finally succeeded in transcending the capabilities of the human body to locate itself, to organize it's immediate surroundings perceptually, and to cognitively map it's position into a mapable external world. The body disappears.

Hiatus is a post-feminist portrayal of an empowered female body playing off and against a repressed and hysterical male body.

WANDA is Madi's construct, a coded masquerade of the feminine. WANG is a member of a corporate class who will never risk his own skin. He can't exist outside an organization. He is a real VR type who is a power trigger, out to perform all sorts of mind games, in the name of absolute individualism. He is an entrepreneurial type who works transactions on the net. He exists to takeover the net that is built up by a visualizer like WANDA.

Video and Resistance: Against Documentaries
Critical Art Ensemble
1994

The medium of video was born in crisis. This postmodern technology has been shoved back into the womb of history with the demand that it progress through the same developmental stages as its older siblings, film and photography. The documentary—the paramount model for resistant video production—gives witness less to the endless parade of guerrilla actions, street demonstrations, and ecological disasters than it does to the persistence of Enlightenment codes of truth, knowledge, and a stable empirical reality. The hegemony of the documentary moves the question of video technology away from its function as a simulator, and back to a retrograde consideration of the technology as a replicator (witness). Clearly technology will not save us from the insufferable condition of eternal recurrence.

Recall file entitled "Enlightenment." Enlightenment: A historical moment past, which must now be looked upon through the filter of nostalgia. Truth was so simple then. The senses were trusted, and the discrete units of sensation contained knowledge. To those ready to observe, nature surrendered its secrets. Every object contained useful pieces of data exploding with information, for the world was a veritable network of interlocking facts. Facts were the real concern: everything observable was endowed with facticity. Everything concrete merited observation, from a grain of sand to social activity. "Knowledge" went nova. The answer to the problem of managing geometrically cascading data was specialization: Split the task of observation into as many categories and subcategories as possible to prevent observational integrity from being distracted by the proliferation of factual possibility. (It is always amazing to see authoritarian structures run wild in the utopian moment.) Specialization worked in the economy (complex manufacture) and in government management (bureaucracy); why not also with knowledge? Knowledge entered the earthly domain (as opposed to the transcendental), giving humanity control over its own destiny and initiating an age of progress with science as redeemer.

In the midst of this jubilation, a vicious scepticism haunted the believers like the Encyclopedists, the new social thinkers (such as Turgot, Fontenelle, and Condorcet), and later, the logical positivists. The problem of scepticism was exemplified by David Hume's critique of the empirical model, which placed Enlightenment epistemology outside the realm of certainty. The senses were shown to be unreliable conveyers of information, and factual associations were revealed as practical inference. Strengthened by the romantic critique developed later under the banner of German Idealism, the argument became acceptable that the phenomenal world was not a source of knowledge, since perception could be structured by given mental categories which might or might not show fidelity to a thing-in-itself. Under this system, science was reduced to a practical mapping of spatial-temporal constellations. Unfortunately, the idealists were unable to escape the scepticism from which they had emerged. Their own system of transcendentalism was just as susceptible to the sceptic's arguments.

Science found itself in a peculiar position in regard to the 19th-century sociology of knowledge. Since it did produce what secularists interpreted as desirable practical results, it became an ideological legitimizer even on the ordinary level of everyday life. Within the sceptic's vacuum, empirical science by default usurped the right to pronounce what was real in experience. Sensible judgment was secure in the present, but to judge past events required immediate perception to be reconstituted through memory. The problem of memory was transformed into a technological problem because the subjective elements of memory led to the decay of the facticity of the sensible object, and written representation as a means to maintain history was insufficient. Although theory and method were mature and legitimized, a satisfactory technology had yet to emerge. This problem finally resolved itself with the invention of photography. Photography could provide a concrete visual record (vision being the most trustworthy of the senses) as an account of the past. Photography represented facts, rather than subjectively dissolving them into memory, or abstracting them as with writing. At last, there was a visual replicator to produce a record independent of the witness. Technology could mediate perception, and thereby impose objectivity upon the visual record. To this extent, photography was embraced more as a scientific tool than as a means to manifest aesthetic intent.

Artists from all media began to embrace the empirical model, which had been rejuvenated by these innovations in replicating technology. Their interest in turn gave birth to Realism and literary Naturalism. In these new genres, the desire for replication became more complex. A new political agenda had insinuated itself into cultural production. Unlike in the past when politics generally served to maintain the status quo, the agenda of the newly-born left began to make a clear-cut appearance in empirical cultural representation. The proponents of this movement no longer worshipped the idealistic cultural icons of the romantic predecessors, but fetishized facticity—tendencies that reduced the artist's role to that of mechanical reproduction. The visual presentation of factual data allowed one to objectively witness the injustice of history, providing those eliminated from the historical record a way to make their places known. The use of traditional media combined with Enlightenment epistemology to promote a new leftist ideology that failed relatively fast. Even the experimental novels of Zola, in the end, could only be perceived as fiction, not as historical accounts. The Realist painters' work seemed equally unreliable, as the paintbrush was not a satisfactory technological means to insure objectivity, while its product was tied too closely to an elitist tradition and to its institutions. Perhaps their only actual victory was to produce a degraded sign of subversive intent that meekly insisted on the horizontalization of traditional aesthetic categories, particularly in the area of subject matter.

By the end of the century, having nowhere else to turn, some leftist cultural producers began to rethink photography and its new advancement, film. The first documentary makers intended to produce an objective and accurate visual record of social injustice and leftist resistance, and guided by those aims the documentary began to take form. The excitement over new possibilities for socially responsible representation allowed production to precede critical reflection about the medium, and the mistakes that were made continue as institutions into the present.

The film documentary was a catastrophe from its inception. Even as far back as the Lumière brothers' work, the facticity of nonfiction film has been crushed under the burden of ideology. A film such as *Workers Leaving the Lumière Factory* functions primarily as an advertisement for industrialization—a sign of the future divorced from the historical forces which generated it. In spite of its static camera and the necessary lack of editing, the function of replication was lost, because the life presented in the film was yet to exist for most. From this point on, the documentary proceeded deeper into its own fatality. A film such as *Elephant Processions at Phnom Penh* became the predecessor of what we now think of as the cynical postmodern work. The documentary went straight to the heart of colonial appropriation. This film was a spectacular sideshow that allowed the viewer to temporarily enter a culture that never existed. It was an opportunity to revel in a simulated event, again isolated from any type of historical context. In this sense, Lumière was Disney's predecessor. Disney World is the completion of the Lumière cultural sideshow project. By appropriating cultural debris and reassembling it in a means palatable for temporary consumption, Disney does in 3-D what Lumière had done in 2-D: produce a simulation of the world culture-text in the fixed location of the bunker.

The situation continued to worsen. Robert Flaherty introduced complex narrative into the documentary in his film *Nanook of the North*. The film was marked by an overcoded film grammar that transcendentally generated a story out of what were supposed to be raw facts. The gaps between the disparate re-presented images had to be brought together by the glue of the romantic ideology favored by the filmmaker. In a manner of speaking, this had to happen, since there were no facts to begin with, but only reconstituted memory. Flaherty's desire to produce the exotic led him to simulate a past that never existed. In the film's most famous sequence, Flaherty recreates a walrus hunt. Nanook had never been on a hunt without guns, but Flaherty insisted he use harpoons. Nanook had a memory of what his father had told him about traditional hunting, and he had seen old Eskimo renderings of it. Out of these memories, entwined with Flaherty's romantic conceptions, the walrus hunt was reenacted. Representation was piled on representation under the pretense of an unachievable originality. It did make an exciting and entertaining story, but it had no more factual integrity than D. W. Griffith's *Birth of a Nation*.

It is unnecessary to repeat the cynical history of the documentary oscillating along the political continuum from Vertov to Riefenstahl. In all cases it has been fundamentally cynical—a political commodity doomed by the very nature of the technology to continually replay itself within the economy of desire. Film is not now nor has it ever been the technology of truth. It lies at a speed of 24 frames a second. Its value is not as a recorder of history, but simply as a means of communication, a means by which meaning is generated. The frightening aspect of the documentary film is that it can generate rigid history in the present in the same manner that Disney can generate the colonial meaning of the culture of the Other. Whenever imploded films exist simultaneously as fiction and nonfiction they stand as evidence that history is made in Hollywood.

The documentary's uneasy alliance with scientific methodology attempts to exploit the seeming power of science to stop the drift of multifaceted interpretation. Justifiably or not, scientific evidence is incontrovertible; it rests comfortably under the sign of certitude. This is the authority that the documentary attempts to claim for itself. Consequently, documentary makers have always used authoritarian coding systems to structure the documentary narrative.

This strategy relies primarily on the complete exhaustion of the image at the moment of immediate apprehension. The narrative structure must envelop the viewer like a net and close off all other possible interpretations. The narrative guiding the interpretation of the images must flow along a unilinear pathway, at such a speed that the viewer has no time for any reflection. Key in this movement is to produce the impression that each image is causatively linked to the images preceding it. Establishment of causality between the images renders a seamless effect and keeps the viewers' interpretive flow moving along a predetermined course. The course ends with the conclusion prepared by the documentary maker in constructing the causal chain of images, offering what seems to be an incontrovertible resolving statement. After all, who can challenge replicated causality? Its legitimation by traditional rational authority is too great. A documentary fails when the causal chain breaks down, showing the seams and allowing a moment of disbelief to disrupt the predetermined interpretive matrix. Without the scientific principle of causality rigorously structuring the narrative, the documentary's legitimized authority dissipates quite rapidly, revealing its true nature as fictional propaganda. When a legitimation crisis occurs in the film, the image becomes transparent, rather than exhausting itself, and the ideology of the narrative is displayed in all its horrifying glory. The quality documentary does not reveal itself, and it is this illusionistic chicanery—first perfected by Hollywood realism—that unfortunately guides the grand majority of documentary and video witness work that leftist cultural workers currently produce in endless streams.

This pitiful display is particularly insidious because it turns the leftist cultural workers into that which they most fear: Validators of the conservative interpretive matrix. If the fundamental principle of conservative politics is to maintain order for the sake of economy, to complement the needs and desires of the economic elite, and to discourage social heterogeneity, then the documentary, as it now stands, is complicit in participating in that order, even if it flies the banner of social justice over its ideological fortress. This is true because the documentary does not create an opportunity for free thought, but instills self-censorship in the viewer, who must absorb its images within the structure of a totalizing narrative. If one examines the sign of censorship itself, as it was embodied, for example, in Jesse Helms' criticisms of Andres Serrano's *Piss Christ*, one can see the methods of totalizing interpretation at work. Helms argued that a figure of Christ submerged in piss leads to a single conclusion, that the work is an obscene sacrilege. Helms' interpretation is a fair one; however, it is not the only one. Helms used senatorial spectacle as an authority to legitimize and totalize his interpretation. Under his privileged interpretive matrix, the image is immediately exhausted. However, anyone who reflects on Serrano's image for only a moment can see that numerous other meanings are contained within it. There are meanings that are both critical and aesthetic (formal). Helms' overall strategy was not so much to use personal power as a means to censorship, but to create the preconditions for the public to blindly follow into self-censorship, thereby agreeing to the homogenous order desired by the elite class. The resistant documentary depends upon this same set of conditions for its success. The long-term consequences of using such methods, even with good intentions, is to make the viewer increasingly susceptible to illusionistic narrative structure, while the model itself becomes increasingly sophisticated through its constant revision. Anywhere along the political continuum the electronic consumer turns, s/he is treated like media sheep. To stop this manipulation, documentary makers must refuse to sacrifice the subjectivity of the viewer. The nonfiction film needs to travel other avenues than the one inherited from tradition.

Planning a generic leftist documentary for PBS. Subject: The guerrilla war in __?__ (choose a third-world nation).

1. Choose a title carefully, since it is one of the primary framing devices. It should present itself purely as a description of the images contained in the work, but should also function as a privileged ideological marker. For example, "The Struggle for Freedom in ______." Remember, do not mention "guerrillas" in the title. Such words have a connotation of a lost or subversive cause that could lead to irrational violent action, and that scares liberals.

2. If you have a large enough budget (and you probably do if you are making yet another film on political strife), open with a lyrical aerial shot of the natural surroundings of the country in question. Usually the countryside is held by the guerrillas. This is good. You now have the traditional authority of nature (and the morality of the town/country distinction) on your side. These are two foundational codes of didactic western art. They are rarely questioned, and will create a channel leading the viewer to the belief that you are filming a populist uprising.

3. Dissolve to the particular band of guerrillas that you are going to film. Do not show large armies, and show only small arms, not heavy weaponry. Remember, the guerrillas must look like real underdogs. Americans love that code. If you must talk about the size of the rebel army (for instance, to show the amount of popular support for the resistance), keep it abstract; give only the statistics. Large military formations have that Nuremberg look to them. If at all possible, choose a band comprised of families: It shows real desperation when an entire extended family is fighting. Keep in mind that one of your key missions is to humanize the

rebels while making the dominant group an evil abstraction. Finish this sequence by stylishly introducing each of the rebels as individuals.

4. For the next sequence, single out a family to represent the group. Interview each member. Address their motivations for resistance. Follow them throughout the day. Capture the hardships of rebel activity. Be sure to show the sleeping arrangements and the poverty of the food, but concentrate on what the fight is doing to the family. End the sequence by showing the family involved in a recreational activity. This will demonstrate the rebels' ability to endure, and to be human in the face of catastrophe. It is also the perfect segue into the next sequence: "In this moment of play, who could have imagined the tragedy that would befall them . . ."

5. Having established the rebels as real, feeling people, it is time to turn to the enemy, by showing for instance an atrocity attributed to them. (Never show the enemy themselves; they must remain an alien abstraction, an unknown to be feared.) It is preferable if a distant relative of the focus family is killed or wounded in the represented enemy action. Document the mourning of the fellow rebels.

6. With the identities of both the rebels and the enemy established, you must now show an actual guerrilla action. It should be read as a defensive maneuver with no connotation of vengeance. Make sure that it is an evening or morning raid, to lessen sympathy for the enemy as individuals. The low light will keep them hidden and allow the sparks of the return gunfire to represent the enemy as depersonalized. Do not show guerrillas taking prisoners: It is difficult to maintain viewers' sympathy for the rebels if they are seen sticking automatic weapons in the backs of the enemy and marching them along. Finally, only show the action if the rebels seem to win the engagement.

7. In the victory sequence it is important to show the tie between the rebels and the nonmilitary personnel of the countryside. With the enemy recently beaten, it is safe to go to town and celebrate with the agrarian class. You can include speeches and commemorations in this sequence. Show the peasants giving the rebels food, while the rebels give the civilians nonmilitary materials captured during the raid. But most importantly, ensure that the sequence has a festive spirit. This will add an emotional contrast to the closing sequence.

8. Final sequence: Focus on the rebel group expressing their dreams of victory and vowing never to surrender. This should cap it: You are now guaranteed a sympathetic response from the audience. The sympathy will override any critical reflection, making the audience content to ride the wave of *your* radical subjectivity. Roll credits. Perhaps add a postscript by the filmmaker on how touched and amazed s/he was by the experience.

In creating a documentary, one small adjustment could be made with minimal disturbance to the traditional model—to announce for a given work that the collection of images presented have already been fully digested within a specialized cultural perspective. Make sure the viewers know that they are watching a *version* of the subject matter, not the thing in itself. This will not cure the many ills of documentary film/video, since versions themselves are prepackaged, having little meaning in relation to other versions; however, it would make the documentary model a little less repugnant, since this disclaimer would avoid the assertion that one was showing the truth of the matter. This would allow the system to remain closed, but still produce the realization that what is being documented is not a concrete history, but an independent semiotic frame through which sensation has been filtered and interpreted.

Take, for instance, documentaries on a subject regarded almost universally as pleasant and innocuous, such as nature. It becomes readily apparent that nature itself is not the subject, nor could it be. Rather, the simulation of nature is actually a repository for specialized cultural perspectives and myths that are antithetical to the sign of civilization. Consider the following versions:

1. Aestheticized Nature. This is a viewpoint common to most National Geographic documentaries. In this formulation, nature is presented as the original source of beauty, grandeur, and grace. Even the most violent events become precious aesthetic processes that must be preserved. This is even true in the presentation of "exotic" racial/ethnic groups! The world is reduced to an art museum that testifies to the cosmological and teleological perfection of nature. Nature's highest function is to exist for aesthetic appreciation. Both the aesthetics and the ideology that conjure this beatific version of nature come from a well-packaged nostalgic romanticism that determine both the documentary maker's expectations and the method for filming and editing.

2. Darwinian Nature. This conception of nature is best represented by the series *The Trials of Life*. In this treatment the Hobbesian universe comes alive, and the war of all against all is graphically depicted. This blood-and-guts version of nature assembles the signage of survivalist ideology to re-present the blind gropings of a cold and uncaring universe. It is a remembrance of the fatality of the world prior

to the order of civilization. Such work acts as an ideological bunker defending the luxury of order produced by the police state.

3. Anthropomorphic Nature. This interpretation revolves around the question of "How are animals like people?" Typical of Disney documentaries or television shows such as *Wild Kingdom*, these films are insufferably cute, and present the natural order as one of innocence. This is not surprising, since these presentations are targeted at children, and so the conflation of human beings (particularly children) with animals is regarded as a good rubric for "healthy" socialization. These films concentrate on animals' nurturing behavior and on their modest "adventures," interpreting nature as a bourgeois entity.

In all such readings, the viewer is presented with an artificially constructed pastiche of images that offers only limited possibilities for the mythic establishment of nature. Nature exists as merely a semiotic construction used to justify some ideological structure. Nature as code is kept fresh by showing animals and panoramic landscapes that are then overlaid with ideological interpretive frameworks. Nature films have never documented anything other than the artificial—that is, institutionally-constructed value systems. Much the same can be said about the political documentary, since only the contingent aspects are different. The filmmaker then shows us people and cities, rather than animals and landscapes.

The various versions of the present that the documentary imposes on its viewers are refashioned by the film/video form into electronic monuments sharing a number of characteristics with their architectural counterparts. Typically, leftist documentaries parallel the function of monuments and participate in the spectacle of obscenity to the following extent:

1. Monuments function as concrete signs of an imposed reconstituted memory.

2. Monumentalism is the concrete attempt to halt the proliferation of meaning in regard to the interpretation of convulsive events. Monuments are not the signs of freedom that they appear to be, but the very opposite, signs of imprisonment, quelling freedom of speech, freedom of thought, and freedom of remembrance. As overseers in the panoptic prison of ideology, their demand for submission is masochistically obeyed by too many.

3. The return of cultural continuity is what exalts the monument in the eyes of the complicit. In its cloak of silence, the monument can easily repress contradiction. To those whose values they represent, monuments offer a peaceful space through the familiarity of cynical tradition. At the monument, the complicit are not burdened with alienation arising from diversity of opinion, nor with the anxiety of moral contradiction. They are safe from the disturbance of reflection. Monuments are the ultimate ideological bunkers—the concrete manifestations of fortress mentality.

To be sure, there are differences between the architectural monuments of dominant culture, and the monuments to resistant culture, such as documentaries; those of resistant culture do not aspire to maintain the status quo, nor do they project a false continuity onto the wound of history. The problem is that many of these monuments do aspire to an eventual dominance; they aspire to produce an icon that is above critical examination. Thus far no sacred icons have been intentionally produced through the production of documentaries, but some have been accidentally produced through media spectacle. The most notable examples are the Hill/Thomas hearings, and the Rodney King beating. Certain images derived from these tapes have transcended the mundane to become sacred images for a broad spectrum of society. Like any sacred image, these icons exhaust themselves on impact, and anyone who insinuates that meanings other than the one that immediately presents itself are layered into the image will be visited with a rain of punishment. These images are so emotionally charged that they produce a panic, motivating a blind and vicious attack on any interpretive heresy. They are to the left very much what the image of the aborted fetus is to the radical right. If autonomy is the goal of resistant image production, the monumentality of the sacred must be eliminated from it.

One practical advantage of reality video (video that appears to replicate history) must be recognized—its function as a democratic form of counter-surveillance. No matter how simple the video technology, it easily becomes seen as a threat. It is perceived as a receptacle for guilt that can instantly replay acts of transgression. As the perfect judicial witness, its objectivity cannot be legally questioned. Yet as an instrument of intimidation against the transgressions of power, video functions only within limited parameters. Its strict rational-legal power operates only in the context of exhausted meaning. It is a useful defense in the legal system and in media spectacle, but it is detrimental to the understanding of media itself, as it promotes the authoritarian aesthetics of exhaustion.

The supremacy of reality video as the model for resistant cultural production must be challenged by those who want to see the medium of video go beyond its traditional function as propaganda, while still maintaining resistant political qualities. To eradicate reality video is unnecessary, but to curb its authority is essential. This goal can be best accomplished by developing a postmodern conceptual structure that blends with video's postmodern techno-structure. The fundamental contradiction of using 18th-century epistemology with 19th-century production techniques is that this will never adequately address the contemporary problems of representation in the society of simulation, just as medieval theology was incapable of addressing the challenges of 17th- and 18th-century philosophy.

To resolve this contradiction, one must abandon the assumption that the image contains and shows fidelity to its referent. This in turn means that one can no longer use the code of causality as a means of image continuity. Preferably, one should use liquid associational structures that invite various interpretations. To be sure, all imaging systems are mediated by the viewer: The question is, to what degree? Few systems invite interpretation, and hence meaning is imposed more often than it is created. Many producers, for fear of allowing interpretation to drift out of control, have shunned the use of associational structures for politicized electronic imaging. Further, associational films tend toward the abstract, and therefore become confusing, making them ineffective among the disinterested. These problems prompt the eternal return to more authoritarian models. The answer to such commentary is that the viewer deserves the right to disinterest, and the freedom to drift. Confusion should be seen as an acceptable aesthetic. The moment of confusion is the precondition for the scepticism necessary for radical thought to emerge. The goals then of resistant nonfiction video are twofold: Either to call attention to and document the sign construction of simulation, or to establish confusion and skepticism so that simulations cannot function.

The associational video is by its very nature recombinant. It assembles and reassembles fragmented cultural images, letting the meanings they generate wander unbounded through the grid of cultural possibility. It is this nomadic quality that distinguishes them from the rigidly bounded recombinant films of Hollywood; however, like them, they rest comfortably in neither the category of fiction nor nonfiction. For the purposes of resistance, the recombinant video offers no resolution; rather, it acts as a data base for the viewer to make h/is own inferences. This aspect of the recombinant film presupposes a desire on the part of the viewer to take control of the interpretive matrix, and construct h/is own meanings. Such work is interactive to the extent that the viewer cannot be a passive participant. S/he must not be spoonfed a particular point of view for a pedagogical purpose. This characteristic often works against popular interaction, since strategies to break the habitual passive consumption of spectacle have not received much attention. What is more unfortunate is that such work is often perceived to be elitist, because its use of the aesthetics of confusion does not *at present* draw popular support. It should be noted that such commentary generally comes from a well-positioned intelligentsia certain of the correctness of its ideology. Its mission is not to free its converts, but to keep them locked in and defending the bunker of solidified ideology. It is disturbance through liquidation of these structures that resistant nomadic media attempts to accomplish. This cannot be done by producing more electronic monuments, but rather, by an imaginative intervention and critical reflection liberated in an unresolved and uncertain electronic moment.

IX
1667

And with asphaltic slime; broad as the gate,
Deep to the roots of Hell the gathered beach
They fastened, and the mole immense wrought on
Over the foaming Deep high-arched, a bridge,
Of length prodigious, joining to the wall
Immovable of this now fenceless world.

And with asphaltic slime; broad as the gate,
Deep to the roots of Hell the gathered beach
For the silicon chip immense wrought on
Over the foaming Deep high-arched, a bridge,
Of length prodigious, joining to the wall
Immovable of this now fenceless world.

X
1759

The land here was cultivated for pleasure as well as from necessity; everywhere the useful had been made pleasant. The roads were covered, or rather adorned, with beautifully formed carriages made of lustrous material, carrying men and women of extraordinary beauty and swiftly drawn by large red sheep whose speed surpasses the finest horses of Andalusia.

The simuscape here was cultivated for pleasure as well as from necessity; everywhere the useful had been made pleasant. The conduits were covered, or rather adorned, with beautifully formed carriages made of lustrous light, carrying men and women of extraordinary resolution and swiftly drawn by large red electrical surges whose speed surpasses the finest missiles of Andalusia.

'Can you be BLACK and Look at This?': Reading the Rodney King Video(s)

Elizabeth Alexander

1994

I still carry it with me all the time. I prayed for years for it to be taken away, not to be able to remember it.
—Betty Shabazz
on seeing Malcolm X's murder[1]

Memory resides nowhere, and in every cell.
—Saul Schanberg[2]

At the heart of this essay is a desire to find a language to talk about "my people." My people is, of course, romantic language, but I keep returning to it as I think about the videotaped police beating of Rodney King, wanting the term to reflect the understanding that race is a complex fiction but one that is perfectly real in significant aspects of all of our day-to-day lives.

No satisfactory terminology in current use adequately represents how I am describing a knowledge and sense of African American group identification which is more expansive than the inevitable biological reductions of race and the artifactual constraints of culture. What do black people say to each other to describe their relationship to their racial group, when that relationship is crucially forged by incidents of physical and psychic violence which boil down to the "fact" of abject blackness? Put another way, how does an incident like King's beating consolidate group affiliations by making blackness an unavoidable, irreducible sign which despite its abjection leaves creative space for group self-definition and self-knowledge?

The colloquial adoption of *tribe* seemed for a time to speak to a history and group identification that is claimed rather than merely received, and theorized by the people in that group. It seemed to speak to the group recognition and knowledge that arose as a functional aspect of the originary rupture of the Middle Passage which gave birth to the African-American in all the violent and blank possibility of the hyphen, the slash. It seemed to suggest how a group organizes memory in a way that was useful to the project here of naming the ghostly or ancestral aspect of memory that vitalizes everyday life. But tribe carries with it a history of usage which erases difference and erects limiting, patronizing ethnic constructs, and this history eclipsed my attempt to reclaim derogatory usage.[3]

The stories of violence and the subsequent responsive group knowledges and strategies are compelling even in light of the profound differences between African Americans. This essay considers the inchoate way that black people might understand themselves to be part of a larger group. I mean this more than I mean political, ethnic, subcultural or diasporic. I am talking about what it is to think of oneself, in this day and age, as having *a people*.

Black bodies in pain for public consumption have been an American national spectacle for centuries.[4] This history moves from public rapes, beatings and lynchings to the gladiatorial arenas of basketball and boxing. In the 1990s African American bodies on videotape have been the site on which national trauma—sexual harassment, date rape, drug abuse, AIDS, racial and economic urban conflict—has been dramatized. The cases I refer to here are, of course, former Washington, D.C. mayor Marion Barry's videotaped crack-smoking and subsequent arrest; the Clarence Thomas Senate hearings; Mike Tyson's rape trial; Magic Johnson and Arthur Ashe's televised press conferences about their HIV and AIDS status; and, of course, the Rodney King beating. The cycle continues as the nation today sits transfixed before the O. J. Simpson case. In each of these traumatic instances, black bodies and their attendant dramas are publicly consumed by the larger populace. White men have been the primary stagers and consumers of the historical spectacles I have mentioned, but in one way or another, black people

1 Marshall Frady, "The Children of Malcolm," *The New Yorker*, October 12, 1992, 78.

2 *Natural Health*, March/April, 1993, 42.

3 I am grateful to Carol A. Breckenridge and Saidiya Hartman for helping me think about this term.

4 I say "bodies" with an understanding informed by and indebted to Hortense Spiller's provocative meditation on "body" and "flesh": "But I would make a distinction in this case between 'body' and 'flesh' and impose that distinction as the central one between captive and liberated subject-positions. In that sense, before the 'body' there is the 'flesh,' that zero degree of social conceptualization that does not escape concealment under the brush of discourse, or the reflexes of iconography. Even though the European hegemonies stole bodies—some of them female—out of West African communities in concert with the African 'middleman,' we regard this human and social irreparability as high crimes against the *flesh*, as the person of African females and African males registered the wounding. If we think of the flesh as a primary narrative, then we mean its seared, divided, ripped-apartness, riveted to the ship's hole, fallen, or 'escaped' overboard." ("Mama's Baby, Papa's Maybe: An American Grammar Book," (*diacritics* Summer 1987), 67)).

also have been looking, forging a traumatized collective historical memory which is reinvoked at contemporary sites of conflict.[5]

What collective versions of African American male bodily history do different groups of viewers, then, bring to George Holliday's eighty-one second videotape of Rodney King being beaten by four white Los Angeles police officers while a crowd of other officers watched? When these officers were first put on trial in Simi Valley, and when the jury came back with its not guilty verdicts, what metaphorization of the black male body had to have been already in place that invoked a national historical memory (constructed by whites), a code in which African Americans are nonetheless perfectly literate?

By presenting an archive of a series of cases I articulate the ways in which a practical memory exists and crucially informs African Americans about the lived realities of how violence and its potential informs our understanding of our individual selves as a larger group. The videotaped condensation produced by Court TV of the first, Simi Valley trial[6] reveals the ways in which freeze-framing distorted and dehistoricized the beating. It also displays how a language of black male bestiality and hyper-virility, along with myths of drug abuse and superhuman strength, were deployed during the trial. King was described as a "buffed-out" "probable ex-con," "bear-like," "like a wounded animal," "aggressive," "combative," and "equate[d] . . . with a monster." Closing defense statements continually named a "we," referring to the nonblack racial composition of the Simi Valley jury. Attorney Michael Stone, speaking of Los Angeles police officers, concluded with "they don't get paid to roll around in the dirt with the likes of Rodney King." These sensationalist codes erased both Rodney King's individual bodily history within the event and a collective African American male bodily history, and supplanted it with a myth of white male victimization: hence, the statement by Sergeant Stacy Koon's lawyer that "there's only one person who's in charge of this situation and that's Rodney Glenn King."

The narrative space between the nationally televised videotape and the Court TV version opens an avenue to think about what various national imaginations—primarily racially determined but also marked by region, class, gender—bring to the viewing of this episode. This space also raises questions concerning how bodily experience, both individually experienced bodily trauma as well as collective cultural trauma, comes to reside in the flesh as forms of memory reactivated and articulated at moments of collective spectatorship.

Despite the prevalence of anti-essentialist, post-identity discourses, I still believe there is a place for a bottom line. The bottom line here is that different groups possess sometimes-subconscious collective memories which are frequently forged and maintained through a storytelling tradition, however difficult that may be to pin down, as well as through individual experience. When a black man can be set on fire amidst racial epithets in the street because he inhabits a black body, as recently occurred in Florida, there must be a place for theorizing black bodily experience within the larger discourse of identity politics.

If any one aphorism can characterize the experience of black people in this country, it might be that the white-authored national narrative deliberately contradicts the histories our bodies know. There have always been narratives to justify the barbaric practices of slavery and lynching. African Americans have always existed in a countercitizen relationship to the law; how else to contend with knowing oneself as a whole human being when the Constitution defined one as three-fifths? The American way with regard to the actual lived experience of African Americans has been to write a counternarrative which erased bodily information as we knew it and substituted a countertext which in many cases has become a version of national memory.

Some sympathetic white colleagues discussing the King beating anxiously exempt themselves from the category of oppressor, even when they have not been placed there, by saying that they too were nauseated and traumatized by watching the beating. This is no doubt true, but it is not my interest here. The far more potent terrain is the one that allows us to explore the ways in which traumatized African American viewers have been taught a sorry lesson of their continual physical vulnerability in the United States that concurrently helps shape how to understand ourselves as a "we," even when that we is differentiated. The King beating, and the anguished court cases and insurrections which followed, reminded us that there is such a thing as *bottom line blackness* with regard to the violence which erases other differentiations and highlights race.

5 Here Homi K. Bhabha's observations on rumour and panic are useful, even as he veers from my own conception of how transmission—"pass[ing] it on"—takes place: "The indeterminacy of rumour constitutes its importance as a social discourse. Its intersubjective, communal adhesiveness lies in its enunciative aspect. Its performative power of circulation results in the contagious spreading, 'an almost uncontrollable impulse to pass it on to another person'. The iterative action of rumour, its *circulation* and *contagion*, links it with panic—as one of the *affects* of insurgency. Rumour and panic are, in moments of social crises, double sites of enunciation that weave their stories around the disjunctive 'present' or the 'not-there' of discourse. . . . The indeterminate circulation of meaning as rumour or conspiracy, with its perverse, psychic affects of panic, constitutes the intersubjective realm of revolt and resistance." *The Location of Culture* (London: Routledge, 1994), 200.

6 "The 'Rodney King' Case: What the Jury Saw in *California v. Powell*," 1992, Courtroom Television Network. Courtroom proceedings cited are from this videotape.

Two other cases help describe the way the Rodney King videotape was experienced as an aftershock, an event in an open series of national events: nineteenth-century slave accounts of witnessed violence and the 1955 lynching of Emmett Till. These cases help us understand how, to use the Biblical phrase James Baldwin has already deployed, "the evidence of things not seen" is crucial to understanding what African American spectators bring to the all-too-visible texts at hand of spectacular slave violence and the story of a brutalized Emmett Till.

A WITNESS AND A PARTICIPANT

What do the scenes of communally witnessed violence in slave narratives tell us about the way that text is inscribed in African American flesh? Witnessing can be aural as well as ocular. Furthermore, those who receive stories become witnesses once removed, but witnesses nonetheless. Frederick Douglass, in his 1845 narrative, recalls watching a beating at the hands of his first master, Captain Anthony:

> He would at times seem to take great pleasure in whipping a slave. I have often been awakened at the dawn of day by the most heart-rending of shrieks of an own aunt of mine, whom he used to tie up to a joist, and whip upon her naked back till she was literally covered with blood. No words, no tears, no prayers, from his gory victim, seemed to move his iron heart from its bloody purpose. The louder she screamed, the harder he whipped; and where the blood ran fastest, there he whipped longest. He would whip her to make her scream, and whip her to make her hush; and not until overcome by fatigue, would he cease to swing the blood-clotted cowskin. I remember the first time I ever witnessed this horrible exhibition. I was quite a child, but I well remember it. I shall never forget it whilst I remember any thing. It was the first of a long series of such outrages, of which I was doomed to be a witness and a participant. It struck me with awful force. It was the bloodstained gate, the entrance to the hell of slavery, through which I was about to pass. It was a most terrible spectacle. I wish I could commit to paper the feelings with which I beheld it.[7]

Douglass's repetition of "he whipped" and its variations replicates the falling of the awful blows. The staccato, structurally unvaried, repetitive sentences toward the end of the passage, in contrast to the liquid syntax of other parts of the book, reveal Douglass increasingly at a loss for words to describe what he has witnessed. More specifically, he can scarcely articulate what it means for that visual narrative to become forever a part of his consciousness. Yet, what linguistically knits this passage together at its close is the phrase, "I remember," repeated three times. Douglass feels "doomed to be both a witness and a participant." The tableau "struck" him with the same "awful force" of the blows. At the passage's close, he experiences a birthing of sorts as he travels through the "bloodstained gate," his body brought into the realization of itself as vulnerable and black.

On the next page, Douglass describes his Aunt Hester being whipped:

> [A]fter rolling up his sleeves, he commenced to lay on the heavy cowskin, and soon the warm, red blood (amid heart-rending shrieks from her, and horrid oaths from him) came dripping to the floor. I was so terrified and horror-stricken at the sight, that I hid myself in a closet, and dared not venture out till long after the bloody transaction was over. I expected it would be my turn next. It was all new to me. I had never seen anything like it before. (52)

One of course can not *see* that blood runs "warm"; Douglass's synesthetic response is instantly empathetic, and the memory is recorded in a vocabulary of known bodily sensation. He imbibes the experience, which is metaphorically imprinted upon his now traumatized flesh in the shrieks experienced as "heart-rending" and which left him "horror-stricken." The mere sound of the voice of the overseer, who in the previous sentence Douglass has described as "whip[ping] a woman, causing the blood to run a half hour at a time," is "enough to chill the blood and stiffen the hair of an ordinary man" (55). Once again, these corporeal images of terror suggest that "experience" can be taken into the body via witnessing and recorded in memory as knowledge. This knowledge is necessary to one who believes "it would be my turn next." The knowledge of that violence and his vulnerability to it is, paradoxically, the armor which can take him out of the closet in which he has hidden but which he must inevitably leave. For if nothing else, the horrors of slavery were no longer "new" to him; from this point in the text forward, he would figure his way out of that institution.

In Harriett Jacobs' *Incidents in the Life of a Slave Girl*, protagonist Linda Brent's response to witnessed violence contrasts sharply with the response of white spectators.[8] Mrs. Flint, for example, "could sit in her easy chair, and see a woman whipped, till the blood

---

7 Frederick Douglass, *Narrative of the Life of Frederick Douglass, An American Slave* (1845), edited with an introduction by Houston A. Baker, Jr. (New York: Penguin Books, 1982), 51.

8 Harriett A. Jacobs, *Incidents in the Life of a Slave Girl* (1861), L. Maria Child, edited with an introduction by Jean Fagan Yellin (Cambridge: Harvard University Press, 1987).

trickled from every stroke of the lash" (12). But when Brent watches a fellow slave tied to a joist and whipped, "I shall never forget that night. Never before, in my life, had I heard hundreds of blows fall, in succession, on a human being. His piteous groans, and his 'O, pray don't massa,' rang in my ear for months afterwards" (13). Hearing, too, is central to witnessing. Sounds here haunt the mind as much as visual images. In this regard, the freeze-framed Simi Valley videotape, stripped of a soundtrack in which falling blows and bystanders' screams are audible, disallows the possibility that the sounds of terror could imprint themselves on the jury's mind. When Brent sees someone sold away from his mother—not physical violence, precisely, but emotional torture—she writes, "could you have seen that mother clinging to her child, when they fastened the irons upon his wrist; could you have heard the heart-rending groans, and seen her bloodshot eyes wander wildly from face to face, vainly pleading for mercy; could you have witnessed that scene as I saw it, you would exclaim, *Slavery is damnable!*" (23). As in Douglass, "heart-rending" and "bloodshot" work both literally and metaphorically to show the ways the body has a language which "speaks" what it has witnessed. Brent speaks here to white women readers, exhorting them to reject Mrs. Flint's perspective and assume instead her own, the perspective of a witness rather than a spectator.

In *The History of Mary Prince*, violence which is witnessed is quickly followed in the narrative by violence to Prince herself.[9] She understands that what happens to another threatens *her*:

> Both my master and mistress seemed to think that they had a right to ill-use [the slave boys] at their pleasure; and very often accompanied their commands with blows, whether the children were behaving well or ill. I have seen their flesh ragged and raw with licks. Lick-lick—they were never secure one moment from a blow, and their lives were passed in continual fear. My mistress was not content with using the whip, but often pinched their cheeks and arms in the most cruel manner. My pity for these poor boys was soon transferred to myself; for I was licked, and flogged, and pinched by her pitiless fingers in the neck and arms, exactly as they were. To strip me naked—to hang me up by the wrists and lay my flesh open with the cow-skin, was an ordinary punishment for even a slight offence. (56)

To have "pity" for the boys is transferred to Prince herself; she understands her safety is as threatened as theirs. The repetition here of variations on "lick" again recalls the mimetic effect seen in the Douglass passage, but more so, it emphasizes Prince's artifice in constructing the violent spectacle. The narrative time of the event is slowed down, knit together with homophonic words like "ill," "pinched," "pity," "pitiless," "fingers," "strip," and "wrist," and framed. Prince artfully makes a stylized tableau that her readers can more empathically experience.

Prince then watches a pregnant woman, Hetty, whipped over and over again:

> The consequence was that poor Hetty was brought to bed before her time, and was delivered after severe labor of a dead child. She appeared to recover after her confinement, so far that she was repeatedly flogged by both master and mistress afterwards; but her former strength never returned to her. Ere long her body and limbs swelled to a great size; and she lay on a mat in the kitchen, till the water burst out of her and she died. All the slaves said that death was a good thing for poor Hetty; but I cried very much for her death. The manner of it filled me with horror. I could not bear to think about it; yet it was always present to my mind for many a day. (57)

After this litany, you might say, of course these scenes of horror would stay forever with those who saw them, knowing as they did that their fate was bound up in a system of domination and violence to bodies and to memory. But I am building here a case for a collective memory that rests in the present moment, which was activated by watching the King videotape, but which has been constructed as much by storytelling in multiple media as by personal, actual experience. The conundrum of being unable to "bear to think about" something which is "always present to my mind" is precisely the legacy wrought by state-sanctioned violence against African Americans such as the Rodney King beating. To see is unbearable, both unto itself as well as for what is meant about one's own likely fate. But knowledge of this pervasive violence provides necessary information of the very real forces threatening African Americans. In the absence of first-person witnessing, the stories are passed along so that everyone knows the parameters in which their bodies move.

Responses of poor and working-class Angelenos of color to the Rodney King videotape augment this point. Rodney King was beaten by officers of the Los Angeles Police Department who specifically embody the state as experienced in the day-to-day lives of the people who made the following three statements reported in the newspaper, *Revolutionary Worker*:

> You know where I was when I first heard about the verdict? I was laying down in my bed asleep and when I heard the words not guilty on my TV I instantly woke

9 *The History of Mary Prince, A West Indian Slave. Related by Herself* (1831), edited by Moira Ferguson, with a preface by Ziggi Alexander (London: Pandora, 1987). Further citations will be made parenthetically.

> up. It was a pain that went from the top of my head to the tip of my toes. It was an empty, hollow feeling. It was a rage inside of me, burning. I wanted to kill. I wanted to kill.
>
> By the time they was done I needed 28 stitches in my head. When I saw the Rodney King video I thought of myself laying on the ground and getting beat. I felt the same way all our people felt when we blew up.
>
> Somebody brought a video to school—the video of Rodney King—and then somebody put it on the television and then everybody just started to break windows and everything—then some people got so mad they broke the television.[10]

Again, the violence that is watched, this time on the television, is experienced, as it were, in the bodies of the spectators who feel themselves implicated in Rodney King's fate. The language employed by the first person is a corporeal one, "heard" and then experienced in his nervous system as "a pain that went from the top of my head to the tip of my toes." The entire body responds. More dramatically, the second speaker abandons simile; he himself "needed 28 stitches" and felt himself "laying on the ground and getting beat." The third speaker makes the explicit connection between a sense of collective violation and consequent physical response. The video is seen in school, a community. This community acts without hesitation and, according to this account, in tandem and agreement that a violation has taken place in which the entire community is implicated, and which demands a physical response.

Hortense Spillers writes: "These undecipherable markings on the captive body render a kind of hieroglyphics of the flesh whose severe disjunctures come to be hidden to the cultural seeing by skin color. We might well ask if this phenomenon of marking and branding actually 'transfers' from one generation to another, finding its various *symbolic substitutions* in an efficacy of meanings that repeat the initiating moments?"[11] Haile Gerima's film *Sankofa* asks audiences to regard the connections between an African American present, an African past, and the space of slavery between. A persistent motif of the film's plantation scenes is eyes which watch black comrades being beaten, raped, terrorized, killed. Little is said in these scenes in which the violent legacy is passed along, but Gerima's camera sees eyes everywhere, eyes watching in eloquent, legible witness.

EMMETT TILL

> the avid insistence of detail
> pretending insight or information
> the length of gash across the dead boy's loins
> his grieving mother's lamentation
> the severed lips, how many burns
> his gouged out eyes
> sewed shut upon the screaming covers
> louder than life
> all over
> the veiled warning, the secret relish
> of a black child's mutilated body.
>
> AUDRE LORDE[12]

Here is the story in summary: In August 1955, in Money, Mississippi, a fourteen-year-old Chicago black boy named Emmett Till, nicknamed Bobo, was visiting relatives and was shot in the head and thrown in the river with a mammoth cotton gin fan tied around his neck, for allegedly whistling at a white woman.[13] In some versions of the story, he was found with his cut-off penis stuffed in his mouth. His body was shipped to Chicago and his mother decided he should have an open casket funeral; the whole world would see what had been done to her son. According to the Chicago-based, black news weekly *Jet*, "more than 600,000, in an unending procession, later viewed the body" at the funeral home.[14] A photograph of Till in the casket—his head mottled and swollen many times its normal size—ran in *Jet*, and largely through that medium, both the picture and Till's story became legendary. The caption of the close-up photograph of Till's face read: "Mutilated face of victim was left unretouched by mortician at the mother's request. She said she wanted 'all the world' to witness the atrocity" (*Jet*, 8).

Emmett Till's story has inspired entire works such as Bebe Moore Campbell's *Your Blues Ain't Like Mine*, Toni Morrison's play, *Dreaming Emmett* and Gwendolyn Brooks's famous pair of poems, "A Bronzeville

10 Michael Slate, *Shockwaves: Report from the L.A. Rebellion* (Chicago: Revolutionary Worker, 1993).
11 Spillers, "Mama's Baby," 67.
12 Audre Lorde, "Afterimages," in *Chosen Poems Old and New* (New York: W. W. Norton and Company, 1982), 104.
13 Accounts of the fan's weight vary between seventy-five and 150 pounds.
14 *Jet*, 8, 19 (1955): 8.
15 James Baldwin astutely places the attention on Till's murder in context: "The *only* reason, after all, that we have heard of Emmett Till is that he happened to come whistling down the road—an obscure country road—at the very moment the road found itself most threatened: at the very beginning of the segregation-desegregation—not yet integration—crisis, under the knell of the Supreme Court's *all deliberate speed*, when various "moderate" Southern governors were asking Black people to segregate themselves, *for the good of both races*, and when the President of the United States was, on this subject, so eloquently silent that one *knew* that, in his heart, he did not approve of a mongrelization of the races." *The Evidence of Things Not Seen* (New York: Holt, Rinehart, and Winston, 1985), 40–41.

Mother Loiters in Mississippi. Meanwhile, a Mississippi Mother Burns Bacon" and "The Last Quatrain of the Ballad of Emmett Till" and Audre Lorde's poem, "Afterimages" (quoted above). The lasting impact of the photograph and the story is also illustrated in several autobiographical accounts.[15] In Anne Moody's memoir, *Coming of Age in Mississippi*, she writes:

> Up until his death I had heard of Negroes found floating in a river or dead somewhere with their bodies riddled with bullets. But I didn't know the mystery behind these killings then. I remember once when I was only seven I heard Mama and one of my aunts talking about some Negro who had been beaten to death. "Just like them low-down skunks killed him they will do the same to us."[16]

Charlayne Hunter-Gault remembers the killing in her autobiography, *In My Place*:

> From time to time, things happened that intruded on our protected reality. The murder of Emmett Till was one such instance. It happened in August, 1955, and maybe because he was more or less our age, it gripped us in a way that perhaps even the lynching of an older Black man might not have. "It was the first time we'd known a young person to die," recalled Wilma, who, like me, was then entering eighth grade. For both of us, pictures of his limp, watersoaked body in the newspapers and in *Jet*, Black America's weekly news bible, were worse than any image we had ever seen outside of a horror movie. . . . None of us could ever forget the haunting gray image of the dead and waterlogged young boy; we just put it on hold.[17]

Shelby Steele writes of the murder in an autobiographical essay:

> The single story that sat atop the pinnacle of racial victimization for us was that of Emmett Till, the Northern black teenager who, on a visit to the South in 1955, was killed and grotesquely mutilated for supposedly looking at or whistling at (we were never sure which, though we argued the point endlessly) a white woman. Oh, how we probed his story, finding in his youth and Northern upbringing the quintessential embodiment of black innocence, brought down by a white evil so portentous and apocalyptical, so gnarled and hideous, that it left us with a feeling not far from awe. By telling his story and others like it, we came to *feel* the immutability of our victimization, its utter indigenousness, as a thing on this earth like dirt or sand or water.[18]

For black writers of a certain age, and perhaps of a certain region, a certain proximity to Southern roots, Emmett Till's story is a touchstone. It was the basis for a rite of passage that indoctrinated these young people into understanding the vulnerability of their own black bodies, coming of age, and the way in which their fate was interchangeable with Till's. It also was a step in the consolidation of their understanding of themselves as black in America. It is in this regard that black women have taken the story to be emblematic, though Till's fate was carried out in the name of stereotypical black male sexuality. These passages show how storytelling works to create collective counter-memory of trauma as those stories also terrorize.

In Muhammad Ali's autobiography, *The Greatest*, Till's murder is a formative touchstone of young Cassius Clay's adolescence:

> Emmett Till and I were about the same age. A week after he was murdered in Sunflower County, Mississippi, I stood on the corner with a gang of boys, looking at pictures of him in the black newspapers and magazines. In one he was laughing and happy. In the other, his head was swollen and bashed in, his eyes bulging out of their sockets and his mouth twisted and broken. His mother had done a bold thing. She refused to let him be buried until hundreds and thousands marched past his open casket in Chicago and looked down at his mutilated body. I felt a deep kinship to him when I learned he was born the same year and day that I was. My father and I talked about it at night and dramatized the crime. I couldn't get Emmett out of my mind until one evening I thought of a way to get back at white people for his death. That night I sneaked out of my house and walked down to Ronnie King's and told him my plan. It was late at night when we reached the old railroad station on Louisville's East Side. I remember a poster of a thin white man in striped pants and a top hat who pointed at us above the words Uncle Sam wants you. We stopped and hurled stones at it, and then broke into the shoeshine boy's shed and stole two iron shoe rests and took them to the railroad tracks. We planted them deep on the tracks and waited. When a big blue diesel engine came around the bend, it hit the shoe rests and pushed them nearly thirty feet before one of the wheels locked and sprang from the track. I remember the loud sound of the ties ripping up. I broke out running, Ronnie behind me, and then I looked back. I'll never forget the eyes of the man in the poster, staring at us: Uncle Sam wants you. It took two days to get up enough nerve to go back there. A work crew was still cleaning up the debris. And the man in the poster was still pointing. I always knew that sooner or later he would confront me, and I would confront him.[19]

---

16 Anne Moody, *Coming of Age in Mississippi* (New York: The Dial Press, 1968), 104.
17 Charlayne Hunter-Gault, *In My Place* (New York: Farrar Straus Giroux, 1992), 116–117.
18 Shelby Steele, "On Being Black and Middle-Class," *Commentary*, January 1988, 43.
19 Muhammad Ali, *The Greatest* (New York: Random House, 1975), 34–35.

Seeing the picture of the dead boy's ruined body makes young Cassius feel "a deep kinship." He and his father "dramatize the crime," which, like the young people quoted in the *Revolutionary Worker* who saw the King tape in school and smashed the television, became a catalyst for action. The train symbolizes commerce and technology, the unrealized dreams of black migration north as well as the reverse migration south which got Till killed. Clay responds not with the legendary pulchritude of his bare, magnificent body, but rather with stone—a tool from nature—and the iron shoe rests. In destroying the shoeshine rests he destroys an enduring symbol of black servitude. The iron shoe rest of the black shoeshine "boy" and all it stands for is both a tool for destruction and is symbolically destroyed. Clay undercuts his physical might, the mythology of Douglass whipping Covey, acknowledging that no black male body alone can triumph over consolidated white male might. The looming Uncle Sam Wants You poster allows Clay to articulate in the incident a relationship between himself and state power.

We remember Till because of all that his story embodies, and because of the horror burned into our nightmares and imaginations with the photograph. Till's body was disfigured but still a body that can be imagined as kin to, but nonetheless distinct from, our own. The focus in American narratives of violence against blacks in the popular imagination is usually male. The whipped male slave, the lynched man, Emmett Till, Rodney King: all of these are familiar and explicit in the popular imagination. Black boys and men present a particular kind of physical threat in the white American imagination, a threat that must be contained. Countless stories of violence are made spectacular in order to let black people know who is in control, such as when Louisiana Ku Klux Klansmen in the 1940s tied bodies of lynched black men to the fronts of their cars and drove them through crowds of black children.[20] Thus, while black men are contained when these images are made public, black viewers are taking in evidence that provides ground for collective identification with trauma. The Emmett Till narratives illustrate how, in order to survive, black people have paradoxically had to witness their own murder and defilement and then pass along the epic tale of violation.

RODNEY KING

> Outside the door of no return, our arms linked
> from habit, a vendor spies the pain. Don't
> cry, he says. It wasn't you or me. It's just
> history. It's all over.
>
> EISA DAVIS[21]

An article in the February 2, 1993 *New York Times* described life for the four Los Angeles police officers as they awaited their second trial, after being acquitted in the Simi Valley trial of violating Rodney King.[22] Sergeant Stacy Koon, who was "in charge" on the night of the beating, says he has just been declared "psychologically disabled" for work and lists the physical disorders he says have plagued him since the incident: trouble sleeping, "stomach problems," "high blood pressure," and teeth grinding. His days are now spent poring over some 17,000 pages of trial testimony and watching, over and over and over again, the tape of the beating on a big-screen television in his living room. He takes the tape on speaking tours, he projects it on different walls at home, he demands that visitors watch it and listen to his narrative:

> There's 82 seconds of use of force on this tape, and there's thirty frames per second. There's like 2,500 frames on this tape and I've looked at every single one of them not once but a buzillion times, and the more I look at the tape the more I see in it. . . . When I started playing this tape, and I started blowing it up to ten inches, like I'd blow it up on the wall right behind you here, fill up the whole wall over the stairwell, and all of a sudden, this thing came to life! You blow it up to full size for people, or even half size, if you see Rodney King four feet tall in that picture as opposed to three inches, boy, you see a whole bunch of stuff. . . . He's like a bobo doll. Ever hit one? Comes back and forth, back and forth. That's exactly what he's doing. Get him down on the ground. Prone is safe. Up is not. That is what we're trying to do is keep him on the ground, because if he gets up it's going to be a deadly force situation. . . . This [new trial] is going to be fun. This is high comedy.

Koon creates a narrative to justify his authority, and the more he sees it, the more he believes it. He watches it over and over, larger and larger, yet he does not see himself physically magnified as he does King. For different reasons, in these moments of collective trauma, to use the words of the visual artist Adrian Piper, white and black spectators "pretend not to know what

20 This is an anecdote that was told to me by a teacher at Dunbar High School in Chicago in April of 1993, but there are many, many such stories which circulate in black communities and discourse.

21 Eisa Davis, "Maison Des Esclaves, Goree Island, Senegal" (Unpublished poem).

22 Seth Mydans, "Their Lives Consumed, Officers Await 2nd Trial," *New York Times*, February 2, 1993, A9.

you know,"[23] both for self-justification and psychic survival. Many narratives were created to describe the same eighty-one seconds of videotape, and vast amounts of energy and cultural memory were expended to preserve these versions of the truth.

The concept of videotaped national memory was crucial to the Rodney King beating and subsequent Los Angeles riot/insurrection. Videotaped footage of the black teenager Latasha Harlins being shot to death by a Korean shopkeeper preceded King; white motorist Reginald Denny being pulled from his truck and beaten by several African American men during the disturbances formed the other video bookend. The videotape of Desiree Washington dancing in her beauty pageant the day after she was raped by Mike Tyson was used to attempt to prove that she could not possibly have been violated. Videotape imprints constructed bodily histories on a jury's consciousness, and, in a national arena amplifies or denies the story an African American body appears to be telling.

The defense in the Simi Valley trial employed familiar language of black bestiality to construct Rodney King as a threat to the officers. The lawyers also slowed down the famous videotape so that it no longer existed in "real time" but rather in a slow dance of stylized movement that could as easily be read as self-defense or as a threat. The slowed-down tape recorded neither the sound of falling blows nor the screams from King and the witnesses. The movement existed frame by frame rather than in real time.[24] The rabidly conservative Rush Limbaugh utilized the same technique on his television show, when he played a snippet of the tape over and over and over again until it *did* look like Rodney King was advancing on the police officers, and there was no context for the movement. There is something compulsive, manipulative and dishonest about Limbaugh and Koon watching over and over and over again the same piece of film and using it to consolidate a self-justifying narrative.

Black artists have invoked Rodney King's beating in different ways. Spike Lee opens *Malcolm X* with the videotape; Portia Cobb's own videotape invokes the beating with repeated tapping noises juxtaposed with young people of color discussing the case and police brutality; Branford Marsalis's saxophone wails as many times as police batons landed on King's body.[25] These artists each responded to King's beating in different ways, but all resisted the documentary form that dehistoricizes both the body and the event. These artistic examples mitigate against a history of narratives of dominion which attempt to talk black people out of what their bodies know.

Pat Ward Williams, while not responding to King, nonetheless questions the ways in which documentary photography has inadequately represented black life. She also questions the role of the photographer and his failure to *act* as witness. In "Accused/Blowtorch/Padlock," she reinscribes an African-American narrative onto a photograph of a man being lynched, which she found in *The Best of* LIFE *Magazine*.[26] Her handwritten narrative—crammed within and practically spilling over the frame—begins with her sense of trouble, "something is going on here," "I didn't see it right away." It also expresses her sense of wanting not to believe that the picture tells the story it does, not simply the overt story of a lynching but the far more troubling story of the complicity of the photographer, who watches but does not witness, who perpetuates, who is then in effect part of the lynch mob.

Williams invokes collective memory in three ways. She says that "*LIFE* magazine published this picture," and then, "Who took this picture?" "*LIFE* answers—Page 141—no credit." *LIFE* Magazine has become life itself, and the irony of a refusal to attribute agency or take responsibility for the crime committed. She says, "could Hitler show pictures of the Holocaust to keep the Jews in line?" And then, with the line, "Can you be BLACK and look at this?" she forces viewers to confront the idea of memory that would indelibly affect the very way that someone sees what is before them. Williams's reframing of the picture, the slowing down of the narrative action and blowing up of individual parts, is the same technique with a remarkably different purpose than the reconstructions by Court TV or Rush Limbaugh of the King video. The close-up of the image emphasizes the chains biting at the flesh, pulling the arms practically out of the socket, pulling against the chains away from the tree. She writes, "he doesn't look lynched yet.... WHO took this picture? Couldn't he just as easily let the man go? Did he take his camera and then come back with a blowtorch?" Then the narrative breaks into anguished grammatical fragments reminiscent of passages cited above from slave narratives. "Where do you torture someone BURN off an ear? Melt an eye? A screaming mouth How can this

23 Adrian Piper, *Pretend* (New York: John Weber Gallery, 1990).

24 Others have discussed the phenomenon. See especially "The Rules of the Game," Patricia J. Williams in *Reading Rodney King*, ed. Robert Gooding-Williams (New York: Routledge, 1993), 51–55 and "Picture Imperfect," Patricia Greenfield and Paul Kibbey, *New York Times*, April 1, 1993, A-15.

25 Portia Cobb, "No Justice, No Peace," 1993.

26 Pat Ward Williams, "Accused/Blowtorch/Padlock," 1986, mixed media, photograph, silkscreen, 60x100," in *The Decade Show: Frameworks of Identity in the 1980s* (New York: Museum of Contemporary Hispanic Art, The New Museum of Contemporary Art, The Studio Museum in Harlem, 1990), plate XC.

photograph exist?"

Williams's final plea, "Somebody do something," is a call to action. Both Williams and the lawyers for the police officers felt the need, for drastically different reasons, to overlay and articulate their version of the collective narrative on the public text. Williams's work asks the questions: What do people do with their history of horror? What does it mean to bear witness in the act of watching a retelling? What does it mean to carry cultural memory in the flesh? She shows how to work with images that many would rather forget, and she shows why such images need to be remembered.

Being the Subject of Art

bell hooks

1995

To transgress I must move past boundaries, I must push against to go forward. Nothing changes in the world if no one is willing to make this movement. Everyone I know talks about border crossing these days, as though it were a simple matter not to stay in one's place, not to stand still. All this talk does nothing to change the reality that there are so many barriers blocking the paths that would lead us to any space of fulfillment that it is impossible to go forward if one lacks the will to transgress. And yet most of us seem to carry this will. It comes to us early in life, when we are really little beings and just learning a relationship to space. And we are taught over and over again that the only way to remain safe is to stay within fixed boundaries. Most often it's the boundary of family, community, nation. Before we face even these boundaries, it is the body that is the first site of limitation. The body is the boundary most of us are unable to move against to recover the dimensions of self lost in the process by which we are made to behold to fixed locations, by which we are bound in conformity against our will in many facets of our daily lives. The fact that the word *transgress* appears most often in discussions of the sexual is an indication that the body is the fundamental boundary of self. To transgress we must return to the body.

To return to my body I must be willing to face indeterminacy, contingency, the reality of dying. The body has its limits. To know death is to transgress. It is to violate the taboo understanding that death is the subject we cannot speak of, the closeted possibility, that which is shut away and not remembered—the location of one's desire. When I learn to look at death, to see someone dying and not turn away, I am a young girl living in a moment of transgression. I am a witness. To be intimate with my body I must like to be close to death. I must be willing to tell what I've seen. I must bear witness. I must transgress.

The discourses of death and dying, unlike the discourse of sexuality, do not lay claim to the word *transgress*. Though never spoken, death is the silent witness, waiting to see if any of us want to live fully, want to be so fiercely alive that we will not deny death. To refuse denial is to transgress. The politics of denial, like the culture of shame, keeps us in our place. Without fear of exposure, transgression might become an everyday action. Every moment someone might be willing to change something about themselves, the world they live in, if they were not so afraid of loss, of being confined to states of ongoing aloneness, states of non-recognition. To recognize is to transgress. Withholding recognition strips us of our power to interrogate, to intervene on, to act. We are afraid of not being seen. We do not know the truth that to be seen and not known is the ultimate abandonment. We refuse to know each other. In pain there is also the possibility of connection. It is easy to dominate that which you see and never know. To want to know is to transgress.

Knowing my body and its limits, I am able to sacrifice belonging. If the fear of death is all that keeps us away from one another, then I willingly embrace death to reach you, to stand by your side. If you see me dying then you too are a witness. You have crossed the boundary. You transgress. In transgression is the possibility of pleasure and danger, of redemption and violation. To transgress is to claim the right to choose. There is no one to blame, no need to regret. I am moving against to move toward. Your body lying next to mine cannot remain silent. We speak to desire together—letting out the secrets and lies that keep us within fixed boundaries. Your body inside me violates the limits of flesh. We cannot go any further. The only pleasure beyond this moment where the self can be lost in another is death. Someone, anybody, must remain alive to be the witness. To tell the truth is to transgress.

I write these passages for a book in which each critical thinker who was asked to contribute chose a word that moved them. I chose the word *transgress*. To me these passages speak about the body. They say nothing about the image—about representation. Reading them, I hear in these words a will to transgress—the longing to move across boundaries, against the norm. That commitment is challenged when I am invited to let my body be the subject of art: Writing about restaurant, making art, is not the same as being the subject of art.

When Shu Lea Cheang asked me to participate in the installation *Those Fluttering Objects of Desire*, I was willing. My task was to be a disembodied voice on the phone speaking about desire, saying whatever I wanted to say, whatever was on my heart. I journey to New York to read a love letter I have written to the young black man who is my lover at the time. I arrive in New York confident that I will have no trouble participating in this work of art, being part of its subject. Yet when I stand alone in the studio reading this letter, knowing that it will be taped and later heard on red telephones whenever unknown heads dial 1-900-DESIRE, I am suddenly vulnerable, feel naked—exposed. I cannot disguise the trembling of my voice, the sadness that brings tears. I am suddenly ashamed that strangers will hear my passion. That the people I do not know who are taping this session can see me this way, can hear the way I was then.

Suddenly all my desire to transgress the boundaries of public and private is lost. Even though he agreed to the sharing of these intimate words in a world beyond us, would he withhold agreement if he were hearing, feeling them now in this public place? I am not ready to share these feelings without shame. I am not ready to cross the boundaries of public and private. I fear no one will understand these words. We stop the taping. We begin again. I want to resist this self-imposed shame. It is not natural. It is the product of public and private pain—the outcome of separation.

I begin to read again, surrendering myself to the intimacy of the words. Months later I will stand before the red phones, unable to dial 1-900-DESIRE even after I am told again and again that the intimacy of this disembodied voice touches the listeners, speaks to them heart to heart. A man called me wanting a copy of the poem he thought I was reading as he listened on the red phone. I had to repeat over and over again before he heard: It was not a poem. It was a letter I wrote to my lover. I was hurting at the time. He never called back. Writing about art, making art, is not the same as being the subject of art.

When I went to do a series of lectures at Cal Arts, there were signs about video classes on a wall in bold letters: "Open your heart and expose." I use this as the heading for my class. In that class I meet a young black male photographer, Lyle Ashton Harris. We talk theory, desire, transgression. He shows me slides of a show that contains many images of his body naked. Sometimes he is alone in the pictures, sometimes he is with his male lover. He has no shame.

Later when we are together at the San Francisco Art Institute, he stays in my tiny one-room apartment with me. When I awaken in the morning, he has camera in hand, he is taking photos of me. Writing about art, making art is not the same as being the subject of art. At this moment the camera pushes against my boundaries, transgresses, violates. I make a fuss. I am sick. My body is in pain. I ache all over. I did not sleep well. *No*, I tell Lyle. *No pictures. I do not feel well.* I resist the camera because I do not want to see myself this way. I do not want to be seen trapped in a body that is letting me down again and again. Trapped. The camera traps me. I hear in my saying *no* the fear of confronting an image of a sick body, a body in pain. He shoots again and again. I let the camera take aim against the shame that invades me, against my fear of not being perfect.

Lyle says these snapshots will not be shown without my consent; I never see the images he produces. More than a year later, on the Friday night before his show "The Good Life" opens at a SoHo gallery, Lyle calls to tell me I am in the show. He hangs a picture of me that I have not seen. I want to know if I have my clothes on. He does not respond truthfully. I am disturbed by the secrecy, by the absence of consent. Writing about art, making art, is not the same as being the subject of art.

When I go to the show I walk past posed family portraits, the stylized images of Lyle and his friend Ike, images of Lyle naked with his brother, and find myself. I am naked. It is the image of my body in pain. I am anointing it with oil after washing. My morning ritual. The image is so mundane. It is out of place on the gallery wall, in this show of fancy posed figures. My trust has been violated. The red walls on which the images hang are an inner sanctuary where transgression is sanctioned. Violation is a transgression. Betrayal can make a boundary where there has been none.

I would not have offered this image to anyone, not even to myself. The image I see is no longer familiar to me. Since this photo was taken, my body has been opened up—parts of it removed. Life-threatening illness violates the limits of flesh. I am no longer my body. In the face of death, I long for life. I am without shame. To see this image here in public, away from private sorrow and grief, I transgress—move against the boundaries of shame. Will they look beyond this naked flesh and see pain there, impending sorrow? Will they see the vulnerability, the fear of loss?

Shame about the body that is not perfect, that is not well, that is full of disease is a boundary I want to transgress. I want to move past this shame to embrace flesh on its own terms—to let the body fall into various states of sickness and decay without regret. We are all strangers here. None of us knows how to keep death away, how to make ourselves be well always and forever.

To be naked without intimacy, without privacy, without consent calls out memories of violation, of lying in rooms without the will to say *no*. When I go under the knife that will wound and violate me, I am hearing lyrics from *Porgy and Bess*. Lines that say, "Don't let them touch me—don't let them handle me with their hot hands." I will be touched anyway. I will be touched against my will. And I will not remember. I will wake up slowly and feel the coldness of coming close to death and coming back to life. My body will be changed forever.

Before this moment in the unfamiliar gallery room with Lyle and his art, there was no image—no record—of my uncut body. Pushing past my shame, I embrace the documentary image—my naked body uncut, without wound or scar. That is the body I will not see again. It is by now already unfamiliar flesh. On this red wall hangs the image. It does not speak. It has no story to tell. It does not shout out to those who stand staring, *Don't look at me this way. No pictures.* This image has its own destiny. My flesh moves in a history of its own making.

I am without shame. This image cannot wound or hurt me. Violation is an act of betrayal. There is no picture of this moment—no way to articulate separation, loss. To transgress one boundary and make another leaves us nowhere, unable to move forward. There is no way to take a picture of this moment. To tell the truth is to transgress. Writing is about art, making art, is not the same as being the subject of art.

Still from *Workers Leaving the Factory*
Harun Farocki
1995

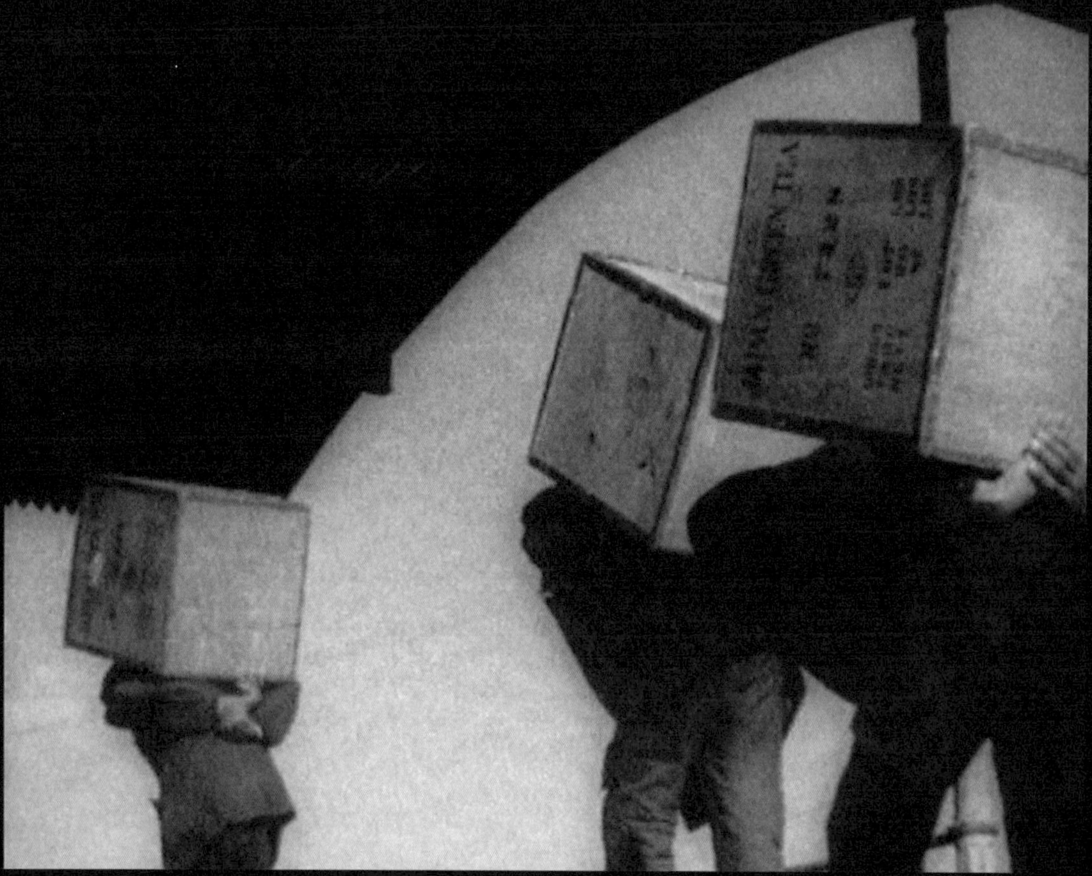

Workers Leaving the Factory

Harun Farocki

2004

The film *Workers Leaving the Lumière Factory in Lyon* (1895) by the brothers Louis and Auguste Lumière is forty-five seconds long and shows the roughly one hundred workers at the factory for photographic goods in Lyon-Montplaisir leaving the factory through two gates and exiting the frame to both sides. Over the past twelve months, I set myself the task of tracking down the theme of this film, workers leaving the workplace, in as many variants as possible. Examples were found in documentaries, industrial and propaganda films, newsreels, and features. I left out TV archives which offer an immeasurable number of references for any given keyword as well as the archives of cinema and television advertising in which industrial work hardly ever occurs as a motif—commercial film's dread of factory work is second only to that of death.

Berlin, 1934: Siemens factory workers and employees leave the premises in marching order to attend a Nazi rally. There is a column of war invalids, and many are wearing white overalls as if to bring the idea of militarised science into the shot.

German Democratic Republic, 1963 (without precise localisation): A *Betriebskampfgruppe*—a worker combat unit or militia made up of workers under the leadership of the party—turn, out for manoeuvres. Very serious men and women in uniform climb into military light vehicles and drive to the woods where they will encounter men who are also wearing flat caps pushed into their necks and are posing as saboteurs. As the convoy drives out through the gate, the factory looks like a barracks.

Federal Republic of Germany, 1975: A small loudspeaker van is parked in front of the Volkswagen plant in Emden and plays music with lyrics by Vladimir Mayakovsky and vocals by Ernst Busch. A man from the labour union calls on the workers leaving the early shift to attend a meeting protesting against the plan to transfer production to the US.

The labour union uses optimistic, revolutionary music as backing for the image of industrial workers in the Federal Republic of 1975; music echoing from the actual scene and not, as was the stupid practice in so many films around 1968, just from the soundtrack. Ironically, the workers put up with this music precisely because the break with communism was so total that they are no longer aware that the song evokes the October Revolution. In 1895, the Lumières' camera was pointed at the factory gates (see ill. 70); it is a precursor of today's many surveillance cameras which automatically and blindly produce an infinite number of pictures in order to safeguard private property. With this kind of cameras one might perhaps be able to identify the four men in Robert Siodmak's *The Killers* (1946) who, dressed as workers, enter a hat factory and rob the payroll. In this film, one can see workers leaving the factory who are in fact gangsters. Today cameras for the surveillance of walls, fences, warehouses, roofs, or yards are sold, equipped with automatic video motion detectors. They disregard changes in light and contrast, and are programmed to distinguish an unimportant movement from an actual threat. (An alarm is activated when a person climbs over a fence, but not if a bird flies past.) A new archive system is thus under way, a future library for moving images, in which one can search for and retrieve elements of pictures. Up to now the dynamic and compositional definitions of a sequence of images—those things which are the decisive factor in the editing process of converting a sequence of images into a film—have not been classified nor included.

The first camera in the history of cinema was pointed at a factory, but a century later it can be said that film is seldom drawn to the factory and even repelled by it. Films about work or workers have not emerged as one of the main film genres, and the space in front of the factory has remained on the sidelines. Most narrative films take place in that part of life where work has been left behind. Everything which makes the industrial form of production superior to others—the division of labour that breaks down the production process into minute stages, the constant repetition, a degree of organisation which demands few decisions of the individual and which leaves him little room to manoeuvre—all this makes it hard to demonstrate the vicissitudes of the workplace. Over the last century virtually none of the communication that took place in factories, whether through words, glances, or gestures, was recorded on film. Cameras and projectors are essentially mechanical inventions, and by 1895, the heyday of mechanical inventions had passed. The technical processes which were emerging at the time—chemistry and electricity—were almost inaccessible to visual understanding. The reality that was based on these methods was hardly ever characterised by visible movement. The cine-camera, however, has remained fixated on movement. Ten years ago, when large mainframes were still commonly used, cameras always focused on the last remaining perceptible movement as a surrogate for their invisible operations—the magnetic tape jerking back and forth. This addiction to motion is increasingly running out of material, a phenomenon that could lead to the self-destruction of cinema.

Detroit, 1926: Workers are descending the stairs of a walkway over a street running parallel to the main Ford Motor Company building. The camera then pans to the right with measured self-assurance, and a passage comes into view, large enough for several locomotives to pass through at the same time. Behind it lies a rectangular yard, large enough for an airship to land in. On the margins of the square, hundreds of workers are on their way to the exits, which will take them several minutes. In the furthest background, a freight train pulls past in perfect co-ordination with the speed of the pan; a second walkway then jerks into the picture, similar to the first and whose four lanes of stairs are again crowded with descending workers. The camera stages the building with such mastery and self-assurance that the building becomes a stage set, seemingly constructed by a subdivision of the film production company just to serve this well-timed pan-shot. The camera's authorial control transforms the workers into an army of extras. The main reason the workers are shown in this shot is to prove that the film is not portraying a model of an automobile factory, or to put it another way, the model was implemented on a 1:1 scale.

In the Lumière film of 1895, it is possible to discover that the workers were assembled behind the gates and surged out at the camera operator's command. Before the film direction stepped in to condense the subject, it was the industrial order which synchronised the lives of these assembled individuals. They were released from this regulation at a particular point in time, contained in the process by the factory gates as within a frame. The Lumières' camera did not have a viewfinder, so they remained uncertain of the view they were depicting; the gates provide a perception of framing which leaves no room for doubt. The work structure synchronises the workers, the factory gates herds them together, and this process of compression produces the image of a work force. The portrayal reminds us that the people passing through the gates evidently have something fundamental in common. The images are closely related to concepts, thus this visual trope has become a rhetorical figure. One finds it used in documentaries, in industrial and propaganda films, often with music and/or words as backing, the image being given a textual meaning such as 'the exploited', 'the industrial proletariat', 'the workers of the fist', or 'the society of the masses'. The appearance of community does not last long. Immediately after the workers hurry past the gate, they disperse to become individual people, and it is this aspect of their existence which is addressed by most narrative films. With their departure from the factory, the workers do not remain behind as a body of united workers for a rally and thus, their image as workers disintegrates. Cinema could sustain this feeling by having them dance along the street; after all, Fritz Lang uses a dance-like movement in *Metropolis* (1927) to convey the appearance of men as workers. In this film, the workers wear work uniforms and move in a muffled, synchronous rhythm. This vision of the future has, however, not proved correct, at least not in Europe or North America, where you can tell by looking at someone on the street whether they are coming from work, the gym, or the welfare offices. Capital, or to use the language of *Metropolis* , the 'masters' of the factory are not concerned with the uniform appearance of their work slaves. Because the image of community cannot be maintained once the workplace is left behind, the rhetorical figure of leaving the factory is often found at the beginning or the end of a film, like a slogan, where it is possible to leave it detached, like a prologue or epilogue. It is astonishing that even this first film by the Lumière brothers already contained something that would not be easy to surpass. It makes a statement that is hard to expand upon immediately.

When it comes to the matter of strikes or strike-breaking, of factory sit-ins or lock-outs, the factory forecourt can become a productive setting. The factory gate serves as the boundary between the protected production sphere and public space; this is precisely the right spot to transform an economic struggle into a political one. The striking workers file though the gate, and the various other castes and classes follow. That is not the way the October Revolution began, however, or the way the communist regimes were toppled. Nevertheless, one major contributing factor that led to the demise of Polish communism involved a group of non-workers who stationed themselves in front of the gates of Gdansk's Lenin shipyard during its occupation, in order to show the police that it would be impossible to secretly extricate the workers from the factory. Andrzej Wajda's *The Man of Iron* (1981) tells this story.

1916: D. W. Griffith presented a dramatic portrayal of a strike in the modern episode of *Workers Leaving the Factory*. Initially, the workers see their pay cut (because the Associations that have taken it upon themselves to improve the souls of the workers demand higher dues), then the strikers swarm into the street, while the police with machine guns move in, take up their positions, and mow the crowd down. The workers' struggle is shown here as a civil war. Their wives and children have gathered in front of their homes and are seen observing the bloodbath in horror. A group of the unemployed, eager to take the strikers' jobs, are ready and waiting, literally as a reserve army. This is probably the greatest shoot-out in front of factory gates in the hundred-year history of cinema.

1933: In Vsevolod Pudovkin's depiction of a strike by Hamburg longshoremen, *Deserter*, a picket has to watch ships being unloaded by strikebreakers. He sees one of the strikebreakers first swaying under the burden of a heavy crate, then he stand firm against the weight for a long time, but finally breaks down. The picket looks at the unconscious man lying there with cold socio-historical attention, shadows darting across his face. These are cast by the unemployed men hurrying to the gates of the harbour area to take the collapsed worker's place. They are miserable and so ill from their impoverished state that they seem much older than they actually are. The picket looks deep into the face of an older man, his tongue playing with the saliva in his mouth, and then, frightened, turns away from him. With so many people unable to find work or a place in a society based on work, how can social revolution become a reality? The film shows the faces of the destitute through the bars of the entrance gate. They are looking out from the prison of unemployment to the freedom called 'paid labour'. Filmed through the bars they already appear to have been shut away in a camp. In the course of the 20th century, millions of people were declared redundant; were deemed to be socially harmful or classified as racially inferior. Many of them were locked up in camps by the Nazis or Communists to be re-educated or eliminated.

Charles Chaplin accepted a job at a conveyor belt and was thrown out of the factory by the police during a strike... Marilyn Monroe sat alongside a conveyor belt of a fish cannery for Fritz Lang... Ingrid Bergman spent a day in a factory, and upon entering, an expression of holy fright came upon her face, as though she was on the road to hell... Movie stars are important people in a feudal kind of way, and they are drawn to the world of the workers; their fate is similar to that of kings who get lost while out hunting and thus come to know what hunger is. For instance, in Michelangelo Antonioni's *The Red Desert* (1964), Monica Vitti snatches a half-eaten bun from one of the striking workers because she wants to experience the life of the workers (see ill. 70).

If one compares the iconography of cinema with that of Christian painting, the worker is depicted as if he was one of the more obscure saints. Cinema does embody the worker in other figures, or at any rate, picks up elements of a worker's existence in other forms of social life. When American films deal with economic power or dependence, they often portray small and big-time gangsters, preferring this to the setting of workers and employers. Because the Mafia controls some of America's labour unions, the transition from labour film to gangster movie can be a smooth one. Competition, trust formations, loss of independence, the fate of minor employees, and exploitation are all relegated to the underworld. The American film has transferred the fight for bread and better pay from the factory to the bank lobbies. Although Westerns also frequently deal with social struggles, like those between farmers and ranchers, these are seldom fought in the pastures or fields, and more often in the village streets or in the saloon. But even in the real world, social conflict seldom takes place in front of a factory. When the Nazis crushed the labour movement in Germany, they did so in apartments and neighbourhoods, in prisons and camps, but hardly ever in or in front of factories. Although many of the worst acts of violence this century—civil wars, world wars, re-education and extermination camps—have been closely linked to the structure of industrial production and to its crises, nevertheless most of these events took place far away from actual factories.

1956: A British Pathé newsreel shows pictures of the class struggle in England. Striking workers at the Austin plant in Birmingham attempt to prevent strikebreakers from replacing them. They try sit-down protests and turn to violence in order to stop the scabs from entering or leaving the factory. They try to wrench open the door of a truck, to pull out a strikebreaker, but they do not punch him through the truck's open window to force him to open the door or give up. Obviously this fight is following the unwritten rules that limit the extent of the violence. The strikers act with passion, but without the desire to injure anybody or destroy property. The workers' own demonstrations are almost always less violent than the ones carried out in their name by others.

I have gathered, compared, and studied these and many other images that use the motif of the first film in the history of cinema, 'workers leaving the factory', and have assembled them in a film, *Arbeiter verlassen die Fabrik* (*Workers Leaving the Factory*, video, 37 minutes, b/w and colour, 1995). The film montage had a totalising effect on me. With the montage before me, I found myself gaining the impression that for over a century cinematography had been dealing with just one single theme. It's like a child repeating the first words it has learned to speak for more than a hundred years in order to immortalise the joy of learning to speak. Or as if cinema had been working in the same spirit as painters of the Far East, always painting the same landscape until it is perfected and eventually includes the painter himself within it. When it was no longer possible to believe in such perfection, film was invented.

In the Lumière film about leaving the factory, the building or area is a container, full at the beginning and by the end, empty. This satisfies the desire of the eye, which itself can be based on other desires. In the first film, the aim was to represent motion and thus to illustrate the possibility of representing movement. The actors in motion are aware of this; some throw their arms up so high, and when walking, put their feet down so clearly, as though they're trying to make their walk appear as vivid as possible for a new *orbis pictus*—this time in moving pictures. A book dealing with pictures of motion could, like an encyclopaedia, note that the gate motif occurs in one of the first works of literature, *The Odyssey*. The blinded Cyclops at the cave entrance feels the emerging animals, under whose bellies Odysseus and his followers are clinging. Leaving the factory is not a literary theme, not one that has been adopted by cinema from a visualized literature. On the other hand, one cannot conceive a filmic image which does not refer to pictures from before the age of cinema—painted, written, or narrative images, images embedded inside the thought process. By straying from the path we may discover something of this prehistory. Immediately after the command was given to leave the factory back in 1895, the workers streamed out. Even if they sometimes got in each other's way—one young woman is seen tugging on another woman's skirt before they part in opposite directions, she knows this woman doesn't retaliate under the camera's stern eye—the overall movement remains swift and nobody is left behind (see ill. 71). That this is the case is perhaps because the primary aim was to represent motion, but maybe an additional sense is already being signalled. Only once it had been learned how filmic images grasp for ideas and are themselves seized by them, were we able to see with hindsight that the resolution of the workers' motion represents something, that the visible movement of people is standing in for the absent and invisible movement of goods, money, and ideas circulating in the industrial sphere.

In the opening sequence of this first film, the cinema's basic stylistic principle is already present. Its signs and meanings are not put into the world, they arise from the real. In the cinema it is as if the world itself wanted to tell us something.

Automation of Sight: From Photography to Computer Vision

Lev Manovich

1996

PROLOGUE

Nothing perhaps symbolizes mechanization as dramatically as the first assembly lines installed by Henry Ford in U.S. factories in 1913. It seemed that mechanical modernity was at its peak. Yet, in the same year the Spanish inventor Leonardo Torres y Quevedo had already advocated the industrial use of programmed machines.[1] He pointed out that although automatons had existed before, they were never used to perform useful work:

> The ancient automations . . . imitate the appearance and movement of living beings, but this has not much practical interest, and what is wanted is a class or apparatus which leaves out the mere visible gestures of man and attempts to accomplish the results which a living person obtains, thus replacing a man by a machine.[2]

With mechanization, work is performed by a human but his or her physical labor is augmented by a machine. Automation takes mechanization one step further: the machine is programmed to replace the functions of human organs of observation, effort, and decision.

Mass automation was made possible by the development of digital computers during World War II and thus became synonymous with computerization. The term "automation" was coined in 1947; and in 1949 Ford began the construction of the first automated factories.

Barely a decade later, automation of imaging and of vision were well under way. By the early 1960s, construction of static and moving two-dimensional and perspectival images, correction of artifacts in photographs, the identification of objects from their images, and many other visual tasks were already handled by computers. A number of new disciplines were emerging as well—computer image processing, computer vision, computer graphics, computer-aided design.

What these new disciplines all had in common is that they employed perspectival images. In other words, automation of imaging and vision was first of all directed at perspectival sight.

The reasons for this are two-fold. On the one hand, by the time digital computers became available, modern society was already heavily invested in lens-based methods of image gathering (photography, film, television) which all produced perspectival images. Therefore, it is not surprising that it would want first of all to automate various uses of such images in order to obtain a new return from its investment. On the other hand, the automation of perspectival sight has already begun well before this century with the development of perspective machines, descriptive and perspective geometry and, of course, photography. Computers certainly proved to be very fast perspectival machines, but they were hardly the first.

PERSPECTIVE, PERSPECTIVAL MACHINES, PHOTOGRAPHY

From the moment of adaptation of perspective, artists and draftsmen have attempted to aid the laborious manual process of creating perspectival images.[3] Between the sixteenth and the nineteenth century various "perspectival machines" were constructed. They were used to construct particularly challenging perspectival images, to illustrate the principles of perspective, to help students learn how to draw in perspective, to impress artists' clients, or to serve as intellectual toys. Already in the first decades of the sixteenth century, Dürer described a number of such machines.[4] One device is a net in the form of a rectangular grid, stretched between the artist and the subject. Another uses a string representing a line of sight. The string is fixed on one end, while the other end is moved successively to key points on the subject. The point where the string crosses the projection plane, defined by a wooden frame, is recorded by two crossed strings. For each position, a hinged board attached to the frame is moved and the point of intersection is marked on its surface. It is hard to claim that such a device, which gave rise to many variations, made the creation of perspectival images more efficient,

1 Charles Eames and Ray Eames, *A Computer Perspective: Background to the Computer Age* (Cambridge: Harvard University Press, 1990), 65–67.

2 Qtd. in Eames and Eames, 67.

3 For a survey of perspectival instruments, see Martin Kemp, *The Science of Art* (New Haven: Yale University Press, 1990), 167–220.

4 Kemp, 171-172.

however the images it helped to produce had reassuring mechanical precision. Other major types of perspectival machines that appeared subsequently included the perspectograph, pantograph, physionotrace, and optigraph.

Why manually move the string imitating the ray of light from point to point? Along with perspectival machines a whole range of optical apparatuses was in use, particularly for depicting landscape and conducting topographic surveys. They included versions of camera obscura from large tents to smaller, easily transportable boxes. After 1800, the artist's ammunition was strengthened by camera lucida, patented in 1806.[5] Camera lucida utilized a prism with two reflecting surfaces at 135°. The draftsman carefully positioned his eye to see both the image and the drawing surface below and traced the outline of the image with a pencil.

Optical apparatuses came closer than previous perspectival devices to the automation of perspectival imaging. However, the images produced by camera obscura or camera lucida were only ephemeral and considerable effort was still required to fix those images. A draftsman had to meticulously trace the image to transform it into the permanent form of a drawing.

With photography, this time-consuming process was finally eliminated. The process of *imaging physical reality,* the creation of perspectival representations of real objects was now automated. Not surprisingly, photography was immediately employed in a variety of fields, from aerial photographic surveillance to criminal detection. Whenever the real had to be captured, identified, classified, stored, photography was put to work.

Photography automated one use of perspectival representation—but not others. According to Bruno Latour, the greatest advantage of perspective over other kinds of representation is that it establishes a "four-lane freeway" between physical reality and its representation.[6] We can combine real and imagined objects in a single geometric model and go back and forth between reality and the model. By the twentieth century, the creation of a geometric model of both existing and imagined reality still remained a time-consuming manual process, requiring the techniques of perspectival and analytical geometry, pencil, ruler, and eraser. Similarly, if one wanted to visualize the model in perspective, hours of drafting were required. And to view the model from another angle, one had to start all over again. The automation of geometrical modeling and display had to wait the arrival of digital computers.

3-D COMPUTER GRAPHICS: AUTOMATION OF PERSPECTIVAL IMAGING

Digital computers were developed towards the end of World War II. The automation of the process of constructing of perspectival images of both existent and non-existent objects and scenes followed quite soon.[7] By the early 1960s Boeing designers already relied on 3-D computer graphics for the simulation of landings on the runway and of pilot movement in the cockpit.[8]

By automating perspectival imaging, digital computers completed the process which began in the Renaissance. This automation became possible because perspectival drawing has always been a step-by-step procedure, an algorithm involving a series of steps required to project coordinates of points in 3-D space onto a plane. Before computers the steps of the algorithm were executed by human draftsmen and artists. With a computer, these steps can be executed automatically and, therefore, much more efficiently.

The details of the actual perspective-generating algorithm which could be executed by a computer were published in 1963 by Lawrence G. Roberts, then a graduate student at MIT.[9] The perspective-generating algorithm constructs perspectival images in a manner quite similar to traditional perspectival techniques. In fact, Roberts had to refer to German textbooks on perspectival geometry from the early 1800s to get the mathematics of perspective.[10] The algorithm reduces reality to solid objects, and the objects are further reduced to planes defined by straight lines. The coordinates of the endpoint of each line are stored in a computer. Also stored are the parameters of a virtual camera—the coordinates of a point of view, the direction of sight, and the position of a projection plane. Given this information, the algorithm generates a perspectival image of an object, point by point.

The subsequent development of computer graphics can be seen as the struggle to automate other operations involved in producing perspectival stills and moving images. The computerization of perspectival construction made possible the automatic generation

5 Kemp, 200.

6 See Bruno Latour, "Visualization and Cognition: Thinking with Eyes and Hands," *Knowledge and Society: Studies in the Sociology of Culture Past and Present* 6 (1986): 1–40.

7 For a comprehensive account of 3-D computer graphics techniques, see J. William Mitchell, *The Reconfigured Eye: Visual Truth in the Post-Photographic Era* (Cambridge: The MIT Press, 1992), 117–162.

8 Jaisa Reichardt, *The Computer in Art* (London and New York: Studio Vista and Van Nostrand Reinhold Company, 1971), 15.

9 L. G. Roberts, *Machine Perception of Three-Dimensional Solids*, MIT Lincoln Laboratory TR 315, 1963; L. G. Roberts, *Homogeneous Matrix Representations and Manipulation of N-Dimensional Constructs*, MIT Lincoln Laboratory MS 1405, 1965.

10 "Retrospectives II: The Early Years in Computer Graphics at MIT, Lincoln Lab, and Harvard," in *SIGGRAPH '89 Panel Proceedings* (New York: The Association for Computering Machinery, 1989), 72.

of a perspectival image of a geometric model as seen from an arbitrary point of view—a picture of a virtual world recorded by a virtual camera. But, just like with the early perspectival machines described by Dürer, early computer graphics systems did not really save much time over traditional methods. To produce a film of a simulated landing, Boeing had to supplement computer technology with manual labor. As in traditional animation, twenty-four plots were required for each second of film. These plots were computer-generated and consisted of simple lines. Each plot was then hand-colored by an artist. Finished plots were filmed, again manually, on an animation stand.[11] Gradually, throughout the 1970s and the 1980s, the coloring stage was automated as well. Many algorithms were developed to add the full set of depth cues to a synthetic image—hidden line and hidden surface removal, shading texture, atmospheric perspective, shadows, reflections, and so on.[12]

At the same time, to achieve interactive perspectival display, special hardware was built. Each step in the process of 3-D image synthesis was delegated to a special electronic circuit: a clipping divider, a matrix multiplier, a vector generator. Later on, such circuits became specialized computer chips, connected together to achieve real-time, high resolution, photorealistic 3-D graphics. Silicon Graphics Inc., one of the major manufacturers of computer graphics hardware, labeled such a system "geometry engine."

The term appropriately symbolizes the second stage of the automation of perspectival imaging. At the first stage, the photographic camera, with perspective physically built into its lens, automated the process of creating perspectival images of existing objects. Now, with the perspectival algorithm and other necessary geometric operations embedded in silicon, it became possible to display and interactively manipulate models of non-existent objects as well.

COMPUTER VISION: AUTOMATION OF SIGHT

In his papers, published between 1963 and 1965, Roberts formalized the mathematics necessary for generating and modifying perspective views of geometric models on the computer. This, writes William J. Mitchell, was "an event as momentous, in its way, as Brunelleschi's perspective demonstration."[13] However, Roberts developed techniques of 3-D computer graphics having in mind not the automation of perspectival imaging but another, much more daring goal—"to have the machine recognize and understand photographs of three dimensional objects."[14] Thus, the two fields were born simultaneously: 3-D computer graphics and computer vision, *automation of imaging and of sight*.

The field of computer vision can be seen as the culmination of at least two centuries-long histories. The first is the history of mechanical devices designed to aid human perception, such as Renaissance perspectival machines. This history reaches its final stage with computer vision, which aims to replace human sight altogether. The second is the history of automata, whose construction was especially popular in the seventeenth and eighteenth centuries. Yet, despite similarity in appearance, there is a fundamental difference between Enlightenment automata which imitated human's or animal's bodily functions and the modern day robots equipped with computer vision systems, artificial legs, arms, etc. As noted by Leonardo Torres, old automata, while successfully copying the appearance and movement of living beings, had no economic value. Indeed, such voice synthesis machines as Wolfgang von Kempelen's 1778 device which directly imitated the functioning of the oral cavity or Abbé Mical's *Têtes Parlantes* (1783) operated by a technician hiding offstage and pressing a key on a keyboard were used only for entertainment.[15] When in 1913 Torres called for automata that would

11 This mixture of automated and pre-industrial labor is character of the early uses of computers for the production of images. In 1955 the psychologist Attneave was the first to construct an image which was to become one of the icons of the age of digital visuality—random squares pattern. A pattern consisted of a grid made from small squares colored black or white. A computer generated table of random numbers has been used to determine the colors of the square—odd number for one color, even number for another. Using this procedure, two research assistants manually filled in 19,600 squares of the pattern. Paul Vitz and Arnold B. Glitmcher, *Modern Art and Modern Science* (New York: Praeger Publishers, 1984), 234. Later, many artists, such as Harold Cohen, used computers to generate line drawings which they then colored by hand, transferred to canvas to serve as a foundation for painting, etc.

12 For further discussion of the problem of realism in 3-D computer graphics, see Lev Manovich, "'Real' Wars: Esthetics and Professionalism in Computer Animation," *Design Issues* 6, no. 1 (Fall 1991): 18–25; Lev Manovich, "Assembling Reality: Myths of Computer Graphics," *Afterimage* 20, no. 2 (September 1992): 12–14.

13 Mitchell, *The Reconfigured Eye,* 118.

14 "Retrospectives II: The Early Years in Computer Graphics at MIT, Lincoln Lab, and Harvard," 57.

15 Remko Scha, "Virtual Voices," *MediaMatic* 7, no. 1 (1992): 33. Scha describes two fundamental approaches taken by the developers of voice imitating machines: the genetic method which imitates the physiological processes that generate speech sounds in the human body and the gennematic method which is based on the analysis and reconstruction of speech sounds themselves without considering the way in which the human body produces them. While the field of computer vision, and other fields of artificial intelligence, first clearly followed the gennematic method, in the 1980s, with the growing popularity of neural networks, there was a shift towards the genetic method—direct imitation of the physiology of the visual system. In a number of laboratories, scientists begin to build artificial eyes which move, focus, and analyze information exactly like human eyes.

"accomplish the results which a living person obtains, thus replacing a man by a machine" he was expressing a fundamentally new idea of using automata for productive labor. A few years later, the brother of the Czech writer Karel Capek coined the word *robot* from the Czech word *robota*, which means "forced labor."[16] Capek's play *R.U.R* (1921) and Fritz Lang's *Metropolis* (1927) clearly demonstrate this new association of automata with physical industrial labor.

Therefore, it would be erroneous to conclude that, with computer vision, twentieth-century technology simply added the sense of sight to eighteenth-century mechanical statues. But even to see computer vision as the continuation of Torres', Capek's or Lang's ideas about industrial automation which replaces manual labor would not be fully accurate. The idea of computer vision became possible and the economic means to realize this idea became available only with the shift from industrial to post-industrial society after World War II. The attention turned from the automation of the body to the automation of the mind, from physical to mental labor. This new concern with the automation of mental functions such as vision, hearing, reasoning, problem solving is exemplified by the very names of the two new fields that emerged during the 1950s and 1960s—artificial intelligence and cognitive psychology. The latter gradually replacing behaviorism, the dominant psychology of the "Fordism" era. The emergence of the field of computer vision is a part of this cognitive revolution, a revolution which was financed by the military escalation of the Cold War.[17] This connection is solidified in the very term "artificial intelligence" which may refer simultaneously to two meanings of "intelligence": reason, the ability to learn or understand, and information concerning an enemy or a possible enemy or an area. Artificial intelligence: artificial reason to analyze collected information, collected intelligence.

In the 1950s, faced with the enormous task of gathering and analyzing written, photographic, and radar information about the enemy, the CIA and the NSA (National Security Agency) began to fund the first artificial intelligence projects. One of the earliest projects was a Program for Mechanical Translation, initiated in the early 1950s in the attempt to automate the monitoring of Soviet communications and media.[18] The work on mechanical translation was probably the major cause of many subsequent developments in modern linguistics, its move towards formalization; it can be discerned in Noam Chomsky's early theory which, by postulating the existence of language universals in the domain of grammar, implied that translation between arbitrary human languages could be automated. The same work on mechanical translation was also one of the catalysts in the development of the field of pattern recognition, the precursor to computer vision. Pattern recognition is concerned with automatically detecting and identifying predetermined patterns in the flow of information. A typical example is character recognition, the first stage in the process of automating translation. Pattern recognition was also used in the U.S., for the monitoring of Soviet radio and telephone communication. Instead of listening to every transmission, an operator would be alerted if the computer picked up certain words in the conversation.

As a "logistics of perception" came to dominate modern warfare and surveillance and as the space race began, image processing became another major new field of research.[19] Image processing comprises techniques to improve images for human or computer interpretation. In 1964, the space program for the first time used image processing to correct distortions in the pictures of the Moon introduced by an on-board television camera of Ranger 7.[20] In 1961, the National Photographic Interpretation Center (NPIC) was created to produce photoanalysis for the rest of the U.S. intelligence community and, as Manuel De Landa points out, by the end of the next decade computers "were routinely used to correct for distortions made by satellite's imaging sensors and by atmospheric effects, sharpen out-of-focus images, bring multicolored single images out of several pictures taken in different spectral bands, extract particular features while diminishing or eliminating their backgrounds altogether . . ." De Landa also notes that computer analysis of photographic imagery became the only way to deal with the pure volume of intelligence being gathered: "It became apparent during the 1970s that there is no hope of keeping up with the millions of images that poured into NPIC . . . by simply looking at them the way they had been looked at in World War II. The computers therefore also had to be taught to compare new imagery of a given scene with old imagery, ignoring what had not changed and calling the interpreter's attention to what had."[21]

The techniques of image processing, which can automatically increase an image's contrast, remove the effects of blur, extract edges, record differences be-

16 Eames and Eames, *A Computer Perspective*, 100.

17 Manuel De Landa, "Policing the Spectrum," in *War in the Age of Intelligent Machines* (New York: Zone Books, 1991), 194–203.

18 De Landa, 214.

19 The first paper on image processing was published in 1955. L. S. G. Kovasznay, and H. M. Joseph, "Image Processing," *Proceedings of IRE* 43 (1955): 560–570.

20 Rafael C. Gonzalez and Paul Wintz, *Digital Image Processing* (Reading, Mass.: Addison-Wesley Publishing Company, 1977), 2.

21 Qtd. in De Landa, "Policing the Spectrum," 200.

tween two images, and so on, greatly eased the job of human photoanalysts. And the combining of image processing with pattern recognition made it possible in some cases to delegate the analysis of photographs to a computer. For instance, the technique of pattern matching used to recognize printed characters can also be used to recognize objects in a satellite photograph. In both cases, the image is treated as consisting of two-dimensional forms. The contours of the forms are extracted from the image and then compared to templates stored in computer memory. If a contour found in the image matches a particular template, the computer signals that a corresponding object is present in a photograph.

A general purpose computer vision program has to be able to recognize not just two-dimensional but three-dimensional objects in a scene taken from an arbitrary angle.[22] Only then can it be used to recognize an enemy's tank, to guide an automatic missile towards its target or to control a robotic arm on the factory floor. The problem with using simple template matching is that a "a two-dimensional representation of a two-dimensional object is substantially like the object, but a two-dimensional representation of a three-dimensional object introduces a perspective projection that makes the representation ambiguous with respect to the object."[23] While pattern recognition was working for images of two-dimensional objects, such as letters or chromosomes, a different approach was required to "see" in 3-D.

Roberts' 1965 paper "Machine Recognition of Three-dimensional Solids" is considered to be the first attempt at solving the general task of automatically recognizing three-dimensional objects.[24] His program was designed to understand the artificial world composed solely of polyhedral blocs—a reduction of reality to geometry that would have pleased Cézanne. Using image processing techniques, a photograph of a scene was first converted into a line drawing. Next, the techniques of 3-D computer graphics were used:

> Roberts' program had access to three-dimensional models of objects: a cube, a rectangular solid, a wedge, and a hexagonal prism. They were represented by coordinates (x, y, z) of their vertices. A program recognized these objects in a line drawing of the scene. A candidate model was selected on the basis of simple features such as a number of vertices. Then the selected model was rotated, scaled, projected, and matched with the input line drawing. If the math was good, the object was recognized, as were its position and size. Roberts' program could handle even a composite object made of multiple primitive shapes; it subtracted parts of a line drawing from the drawing as they were recognized, and the remaining portions were analyzed further.[25]

Was this enough to completely automate human vision? This depends upon how we define vision. The chapter on computer vision in *The Handbook of Artificial Intelligence* (1982) opens with the following definition: "Vision is the information-processing task of understanding a scene from its projected images."[26] But what does "understanding a scene" mean? With computer vision research financed by the military-industrial complex, the definition of understanding becomes highly pragmatic. In the best tradition of the pragmatism of James and Pierce, cognition is equated with action. The computer can be said to "understand" a scene if it can act on it—move objects, assemble details, destroy targets. Thus, in the field of computer vision "understanding a scene" implies two goals. First, it means the identification of various objects represented in an image. Second, it means reconstruction of three-dimensional space from the image. A robot, for instance, need not only recognize particular objects, but it has to construct a representation of the surrounding environment to plan its movements. Similarly, a missile not only has to identify a target but also has to determine the position of this target in three-dimensional space.

It can be seen that Roberts' program simultaneously fulfilled both goals. His program exemplified the approach taken by most computer vision researchers in the following two decades. A typical program first reconstructs the three-dimensional scene from the input image and then matches the reconstructed objects to the models stored in memory. If the match is good, the program can be said to recognize the object, while simultaneously recording its position.

A computer vision program thus acts like a blind person who "sees" objects (i.e., identifies them) by reading their shapes through touch. As for a blind person, understanding the world and the recognition of shapes are locked together; they cannot be accomplished independently of one another.

In summary, early computer vision was limited to recognition of two-dimensional forms. Later, researchers began to tackle the task of recognizing 3-D objects

---

22 Within the field of computer vision, a scene is defined as a collection of three-dimensional objects depicted in an input picture. David McArthur, "Computer Vision and Perceptual Psychology," *Psychological Bulletin* 92, no. 2 (1982): 284.

23 Paul R. Cohen and Edward A. Feigenbam, eds., *The Handbook of Artificial Intelligence* (Los Atlos, CA: William Kaufmann, Inc., 1982), 3: 139.

24 L. G. Roberts, "Machine Perception of Three-Dimensional Solids," *Optical and Electro Optical Information Processing*, ed. J. T. Tippett (Cambridge: The MIT Press, 1965).

25 Cohen and Feigenbaum, *The Handbook of Artificial Intelligence*, 3: 129.

26 Cohen and Feigenbaum, 127.

which involves reconstruction of shapes from their perspectival representations (a photograph or a video image). From this point on, the subsequent history of computer vision research can be seen as a struggle against perspective inherent to the photographic optics.

THE RETREAT OF PERSPECTIVE

With the emergence of the field of computer vision, perspectival sight reaches its apotheosis and at the same time begins its retreat. At first computer vision researchers believed that they could invert the perspective and reconstruct the represented scene from a single perspectival image. Eventually, they realized that it is often easier to bypass perspectival images altogether and use other means as a source of three-dimensional information.

Latour points out that with the invention of perspective it became possible to represent absent things and plan our movement through space by working on representations. To quote him again, "one cannot smell or hear or touch Sakhalin island, but you can look at the map and determine at which bearing you will see the land when you send the next fleet."[27] Roberts' program extended these abilities even further. Now the computer could acquire full knowledge of the three-dimensional world from a single perspectival image! And because the program determined the exact positon and orientation of objects in a scene, it became possible to see the reconstructed scene from another viewpoint. It also became possible to predict how the scene would look from an arbitrary viewpoint.[28] Finally, it also became possible to guide automatically the movement of a robot through the scene.

Roberts' program worked using only a single photograph—but only because it was presented with a highly artificial scene and because it "knew" what it could expect to see. Roberts limited the world which his program could recognize to simple polyhedral blocks. The shapes of possible blocks were stored in a computer. Others simplified the task even further by painting all objects in a scene the same color.

However, given an arbitrary scene, composed from arbitrary surfaces of arbitrary color and lighted in an arbitrary way, it is very difficult to reconstruct the scene correctly from a single perspectival image. The image is "underdetermined." First, numerous spatial layouts can give rise to the same two-dimensional image. Second, "the appearance of an object is influenced by its surface material, the atmospheric conditions, the angle of the light source, the ambient light, the camera angle and characteristics, and so on," and all of these different factors are collapsed together in the image.[29] Third, perspective, as any other type of projection, does not preserve many geometric properties of a scene. Parallel lines turn into convergent lines; all angles change; equal lines appear unequal. All this makes it very difficult for a computer to determine which lines belong to a single object.

Thus, perspective, which until now served as a model of visual automation, becomes the drawback which needs to be overcome. Perspective, this first step towards the rationalization of sight (Ivins) has eventually become a limit to its total rationalization—the development of computer vision.

The realization of the ambiguities inherent in a perspectival image itself came after years of vision research. In trying to compensate for these ambiguities, laboratories began to scrutinize the formal structure of a perspectival image with a degree of attention unprecedented in the history of perspective. For instance, in 1968 Adolpho Guzman classified the types of junctions that appear in line representations after he realized that a junction type can be used to deduce whether regions of either side of a junction line were part of the same object.[30] In 1986 David Lowe presented a method to calculate the probability that a particular regularity in an image (for instance, parallel lines) reflects the physical layout of the scene rather than being an accident due to a particular viewpoint.[31] All other sources of depth information such as shading, shadows or texture gradients were also systematically studied and described mathematically.

Despite these advances, a single perspectival image remained too ambiguous a source of information for practical computer vision systems. An alternative has been to use more than one image at a time. Computer stereo systems employ two cameras which, like human eyes, are positioned a distance apart. If the common feature can be identified in both images, then the position of an object can be simply determined through geometric calculations. Other systems use a series of continuous images recorded by a video camera.

But why struggle with the ambiguity of perspectival images at all? Instead of inferring three-dimensional structure from a two-dimensional representation, it is possible to measure depth directly by employing various remote sensing technologies. In addition to video cameras, modern vision systems also utilize a whole range of different *range finders* such as lasers or ultrasound.[32] Range finders are devices which can directly produce a three-dimensional map of an object. The same basic principle employed in radar is used: the time

27 Latour, "Visualization and Cognition," 8.
28 Cohen and Feigenbaum, *The Handbook of Artificial Intelligence*, 3: 141.
29 Cohen and Feigenbaum, 128.
30 Cohen and Feigenbaum, 131.

required for an electro-magnetic wave to reach an object and reflect back is proportional to the distance to the object. But while radar reduces an object to a single point and in fact is blind to close-by objects, a range finder operates at small distances. By systematically scanning the surface of an object, it directly produces a "depth map," a record of an object's shape which can then be matched to geometric models stored in computer memory thus bypassing the perspectival image altogether.

Thus, perspective occupies a special role in the history of computer imaging. A first algorithm . . . Yet, while giving rise to new technologies of "geometric vision," perspective also becomes a limit to the final automation of sight—recognition of objects by a computer.

Perspective, this first step towards the "rationalization of sight" (Ivins) has eventually become a limit to its total rationalization—the development of computer vision. The perspective algorithm, a foundation of both computer graphics and computer vision, is used to generate perspectival views given a geometric model and to deduce the model given a perspectival view. Yet, while giving rise to new technologies of "geometric vision," perspective also becomes a limit to the final automation of sight—recognition of objects by a computer. Finally, it is displaced from its privileged role, becoming just one among other techniques of space mapping and visualization.

31 David Lowe, *Three-Dimensional Object Recognition from Single Two-Dimensional Images*, Robotics Report 62 (New York: Courant Institute of Mathematical Sciences, New York University, 1986).

32 Cohen and Feigenbaum, *The Handbook of Artificial Intelligence*, 3: 254–259.

Selections from *Case History*

Boris Mikhailov

1997–98

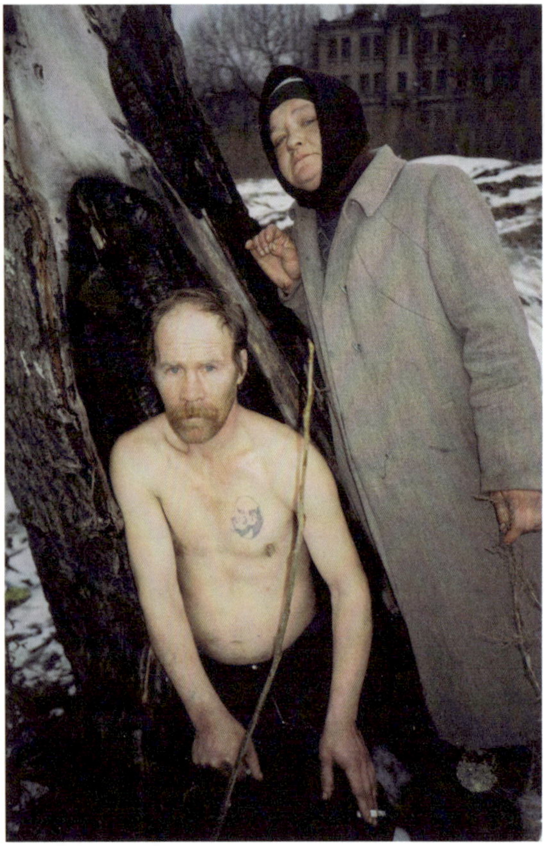

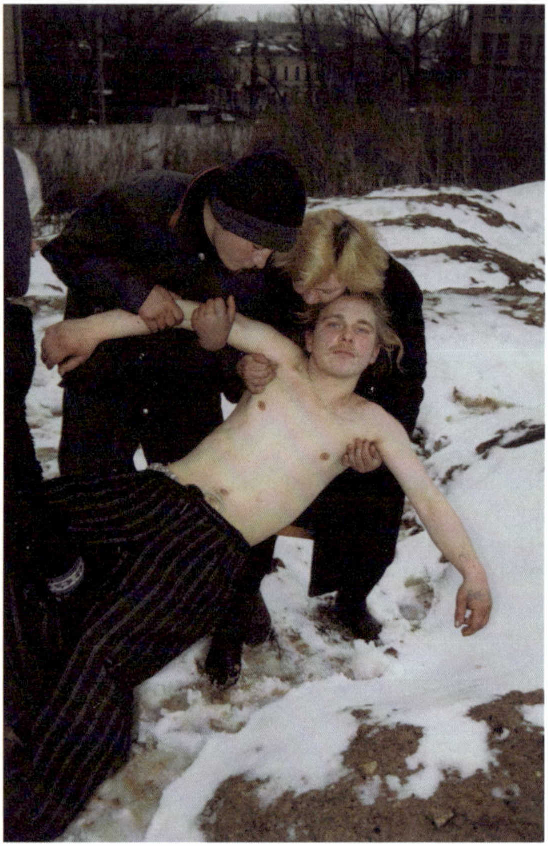

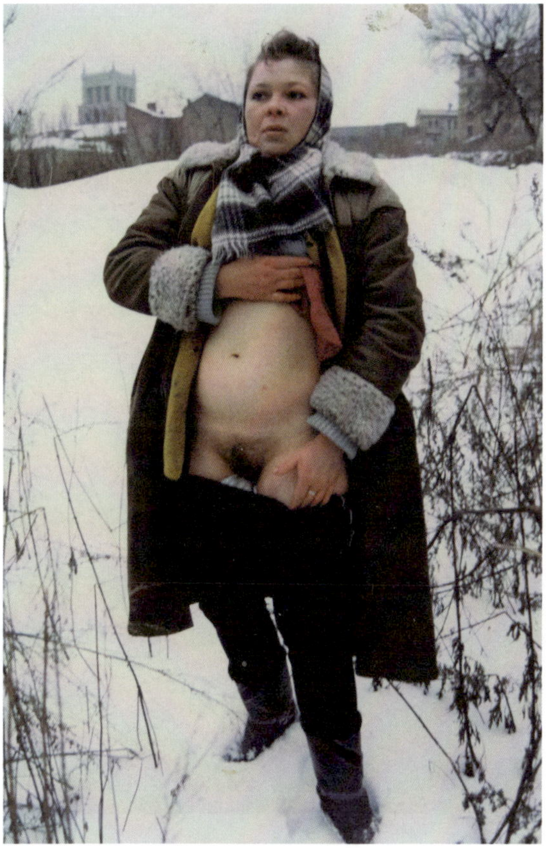

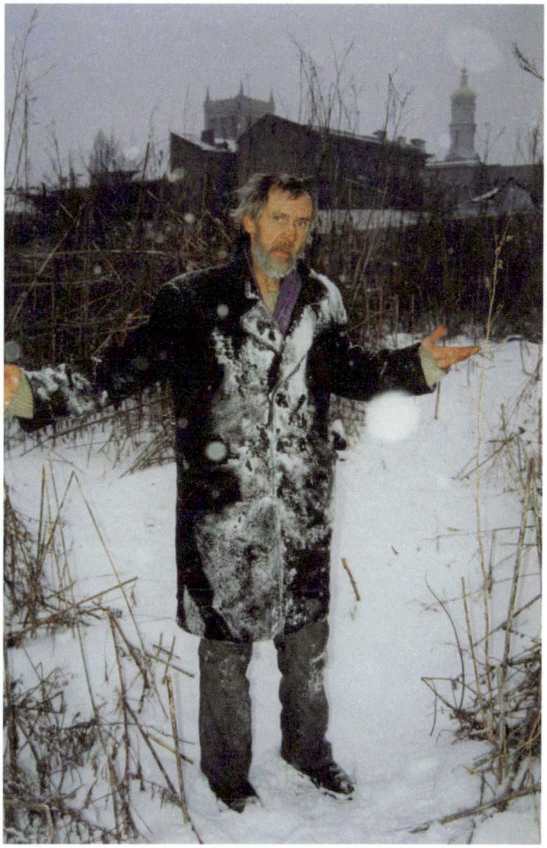

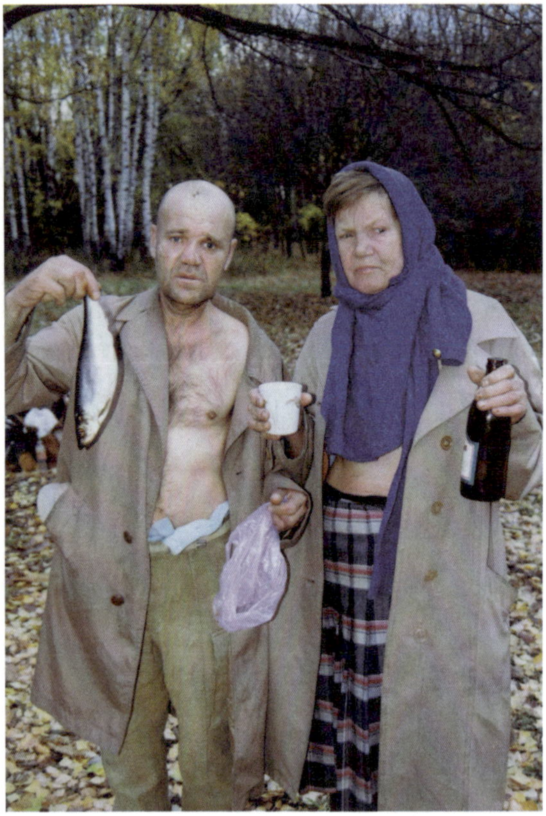

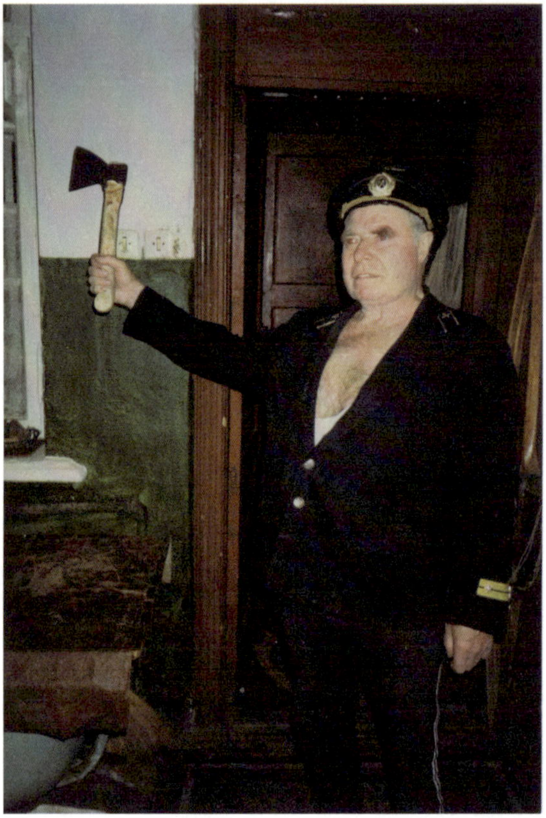

Case History
Boris Mikhailov
1999

I'll start with a confession. Sometimes I have a feeling as if I had been run over by an ideological car and the words, like jumping frogs, are breaking free out of my mouth, independent of me: developed socialism, evils of capitalism, vast is my native country, unity and contradiction, great experiment.

Since the beginning of the century, Russia has constantly attracted attention because of social cataclysms. Of course, it's not entirely so. Let's admit that it is not the Russian situation itself, but the fact that a "world" experiment took place there, based on the German philosophy by Karl Marx—the building of socialism. Now the experiment seems to be finished and we are probably witnessing its completion. And we'll consider that as a photographer I "documented" periods of that experiment. This book belongs to one of the latest periods of that "great" experiment.

After the brown and blue series I was going to create a pink one, which would probably have corresponded to the revival of new life, like during a sunrise, when the light is evenly covering the whole surface.

Returning home after one year I saw the opposite. Devastation had stopped. The city had acquired an almost modern European centre. Much had been restored. Life became more beautiful and active, outwardly (with a lot of foreign advertisements) — simply a shining wrapper. But I was shocked by the big number of homeless (before they had not been there). The rich and the homeless—the new classes of the new society—this was, as we had been taught, one of the features of capitalism.

"Welcome to Russian capitalism!" (Sorry, again it broke free.)

For myself I call this situation of the country a "zero" state, because besides the creation of the new classes, there is no advancement from point "zero." The dynamics of the processes became relatively constant. The internal energy of the society is not directed to future creation. In any case, the perceived activity is not enough to survive. (The amount of people is being reduced.) And because now nothing is created, but each individual somehow personally faces changes, I got interested in man and his new surroundings. In addition, I got the feeling that the processes in society have reached the next level of concentration.

I try not to photograph sensation. On the other hand, I try to take photos of what really increased a lot. I only try to find unique things in this great number.

I have missed the moments with "new Russians." There was a time when they were not yet aware of their wealth and their position, as if they had remained "normal" people. It was possible to take photos in their environment—they were open. And very soon they started to shoot at each other and surround themselves with bodyguards.

Then came a time when it was possible to start writing a book about the other main feature of the time—poverty. The best way to depict it is to take photos of the homeless. And this "chance" (to take a picture of the homeless) could occur, as it seemed to me, only during a short moment.

First, these were the people who had recently lost their homes. According to their position they were already the *bomzhes* ("bomzh" = the homeless without any social support), according to outlook they were simply the people who got into trouble. Now they are becoming the *bomzhes* with their own class psychology and "clan" features. For me it was very important that I took their photos when they were still like "normal" people. I made a book about the people who got into trouble but didn't manage to harden so far.

Their feeling of social oppression and helplessness shocked me. I watched a scene, when a young strong man doing exercises, suddenly, out of the blue, kicked a *bomzh* passing him by chance. The other screamed. It seemed to me that I even heard the crunch of his bones. Nobody paid any attention, neither the people standing around nor the militiaman who was not far away.

When I was first working on the book, I suddenly felt that many people were going to die at that place. And the *bomzhes* had to die in the first rank, like heroes—as if their lives protected the others' lives. And I took the pictures displaying naked people with their things in hands like people going to gas chambers. They agreed to pose for a so-called historical theme. They agreed that their photos would be published in magazines for others to learn about their lives.

Accidentally, for myself, I started to take pictures of the people with a criminal past, just to do this theme. Maybe their criminal aesthetic with its "readiness" for death and perception of its inevitability helped me to explain the situation of *The Requiem*. (In addition, in a strange way, it coincides with the general criminal situation of the society.)

Changing the borders of the former Soviet Union, establishing new states—all this together drove many, it seems to me, to lose their identification with the place of their birth. In this situation "art consciousness" loses the flavor of historicism. The "fading out" of the historical process probably turns it into a non-perspective for the artists who treat the current reality as something already known, referring to it like to the past. That's why I feel a strong sense of responsibility working on this book.

I have received many questions connected with legitimizing my work and the ethical problems related to it. I think I have mentioned why I do this kind of work. As to the ethical question, I have to say that I am not to blame. But very often, when I took pictures, I was ashamed. And in general, it is hard to speak about morality, when one is wearing long fur coats, while the others don't change their sewn and mended shoes for months, while a creditor is more often killed than he is returned money to . . .

When I made the previous books, I didn't have the impression that I did something wrong. As I took pictures, I did not get into contact with those whose photos I made, so everything seemed natural. And at that time the main feeling was the sense of communal unity, though it was coming to an end.

Now this community doesn't exist anymore. And it turned out that I got in one social class and the *bomzhes* in another. And while before the sense of social justice was aimed at the possible future improvement of all, now the questions "why" and "what for" should be answered, because you are busy with the problems of others. And particularly, at this moment (at the loss of historicism) the book can cause doubts (considering that to search for nuances in the life of well-to-do people seems to be more natural).

On the one hand, for myself personally, I understood that taking pictures of poverty was my professional and civil duty. On the other hand, I accept traditional clichés about "not using others' grief." But what does "others' grief" mean? And how must a photographer behave?

In the history of photography of our country we don't have photos of the famine in the Ukraine in the 1930s, when several million people died and corpses were lying around in the streets. We don't have photos of the war, because journalists were forbidden to take pictures of sorrow threatening the moral spirit of the Soviet people; we don't have non-"lacquered" pictures of enterprises, nor pictures of street events, except demonstrations. The entire photography history is "dusted." And we have the impression that each person with a camera is a "spy."

The three main rules which somehow indirectly regulated the development of photography were:

1. "On spying activity": It was forbidden to take photos from higher than the 2nd floor, the areas of railways, stations, military objects, at enterprises, near enterprises, at any organisation, without special permission.

2. "On biased collecting of information": This law touched the moral elements of taking photos. It was forbidden to take photos which brought into disrepute the Soviet power, the Soviet way of life.

3 "The law on pornography": Photographing any naked body could become the reason for accusation. Actually at all our art exhibitions, until 1986, pieces depicting naked bodies by modern photographers or artists could not be displayed. Only museums contained such pictures by Old Masters.

Having these laws and their consequences in my memory, I was aware that I was not allowed to let it happen once again that some periods of life would be erased.

I'd like to tell an episode. A man was lying in the street with his head on the road in frosty weather. It was night. Everybody was passing by. I came up to him, took his photo. A woman turned around and shouted: "Why are you taking a photo of him? Do you have nothing to do?" I asked her to help me raise him, but she went away. Of course, I lifted him up and helped him home. And frankly speaking I was very happy that he didn't even get ill (I saw him the next day). But what did the shout of a woman, directed at me, mean? Let him better die, then the photo would be published? She was passing by as if not noticing and not willing to see it either outside on the street or in newspapers. There is nothing bad.

Independently someone's glance selects what this person needs. My acquaintances, after having seen my photos, said: "Now we see these people outside, while we haven't noticed them before."

In a book by the Japanese writer Kobe-Abe, *Person-as-box*, a man put a box on his head in order not to be seen by others. *Bomzhes* whom one doesn't want to notice put on clothes— their boxes —due to the evil destiny. And that has somehow crossed them out of life. This book is not about them (or rather not only about them), though metaphysically, having made them visible, it is as if it restores their rights for life.

It seems to me that my personal uncertainty (it is not clear where I live—in Kharkov or somewhere in the West, where I work, etc.), my instability in society, on the formal level, has transformed the obscurity of borders between documentary and scenery within the framework of the documentary. Different vibrations of this documentary depend on the so-called "non-ethical impulse" which has the task to check the local "ethical" by means of different sorts of "ethical" already accepted in other places (cultures). For example,

I send a "non-ethical impulse" (I tell the model to undress). This impulse meets with life, excites it (when the model agrees) or doesn't excite it (when the model refuses), and it is as if life deforms, as if the suggestion to accept the level of the "non-ethical impulse" is always ethical to me. (Let it be so.) That means that I never gave them tasks, which would have been strange for the models.

I was interested in the borders of the new morality which would suit the new borders of survival. But the main point is that I myself was tested by the "non-ethical impulse"—and could you yourself do what you are not willing to do? Can you communicate again with *bomzhes*, after having got lice from them, can you shake their hands greeting them while your acquaintances are passing by, etc.? Yes, I had to be the first person to lose my respectability.

I go on speaking "scientifically-like," as it were. One could say I took photos by the method of "posing for little money." I told people: "I want to take your picture, you are interesting to me, I can give you a little money for that." (But it was always more than one is paid at the Art Institute for posing.) Such a way of work resulted in the following:

1 — The work was not very tiresome.
2 — Quick finishing of the work.
3 — Doubtful street acquaintances could be easily rejected if the suggestion seemed unnatural and aggressive.

The people didn't have a choice: either you pose or you vanish. They were not scared of any boss. They didn't do it under compulsion. I photographed usually on their territory. When I took photos at my place, either immediately or later, they could take revenge.

That's why they didn't do what they didn't want to do. This situation from my point of view doesn't violate life. While posing a man tries to be different: beautiful, strong, etc. Here the models didn't perform in such a theatre. At least, they were given the role of "who they are in reality." And presenting themselves, they didn't pose, and it was like "life itself." And the stasis of the pictures reflects the submissiveness of the models.

I asked my friends what they could advise about shooting photos. One said: "Give them money and let them beat each other."

One more episode. I asked a *bomzh* to bring a lady to take a photo of both of them. He refused saying that it was not good. I took his photos, but he was alone.

I took a long time making this book. Often I stood by my house and many *bomzhes* approached me, knowing my intentions. I felt very often ashamed that I didn't use them and that I didn't pay them.

Manipulating with money is somehow a new way of legal relations in all areas of the former USSR. And by this book I wanted to transmit the feeling in that place and how people can be openly manipulated. In order to give this flavor of time I wanted to copy or perform the same relations which exist in society between a model and myself.

I don't know exactly why, but after *The Requiem*, the idea stuck in my mind to go on taking photos of the naked. Maybe I was driven by the old complex connected with the ban on photographing the naked, which was now connected with the notion of "nakedness of life itself." People got undressed, naked and took away the barrier of their dirty, ponging clothes, built between them and others. I was interested in what would happen to a face when a body gets undressed. But sometimes they, simply as people of the "new" morality, exposed their "values." When naked, they stood like people.

Coming back to the terminology "sense of life itself." I should like to give the following metaphor. Something is lying, wrapped in something, for example, in a raincoat. I touch it, the raincoat unfolds and one can see a baby there.

No, I don't want to spy on those whom nobody would like to see. My touch-request helps the model himself or the situation itself to say— "Here I am."

Now it is important for me to say how the West came to the East and why I used colour photos. Previously I used a toner that made a photo look like old, I received a reflection, which corresponded to the sense of disaster and war—the blue and the brown series. The colour "express-photo" became for me the thing which mostly correlated with the new time. In each corner a photo-centre—"Agfa", "Konica", "Fuji"—was opened. The appearance of Western technology made a colour album photo the thing that connects the rich and the poor. Both the rich and the poor wanted to have colour photographs and there was only one distinction: The rich could afford them, the poor couldn't. The colour photo became an image of the new life. And the poor having a beautiful photo can state: "Now we also live nicely."

It suddenly came to my mind that these colour photos are more like rash on the ill body. At the end I again have to refer to the old terminology of the "evils of capitalism."

I suddenly got the image of a slightly mad journalist in international affairs, a specialist in defining the "evils." Returning to the motherland from his long business trips abroad, out of habit, he goes on to search out the "evils." This is a research of the post-Soviet space made by the old Soviet method. The circle is closed. And the experiment?

Selections from *Venezia Marghera Series*

Lewis Baltz

1999/2011

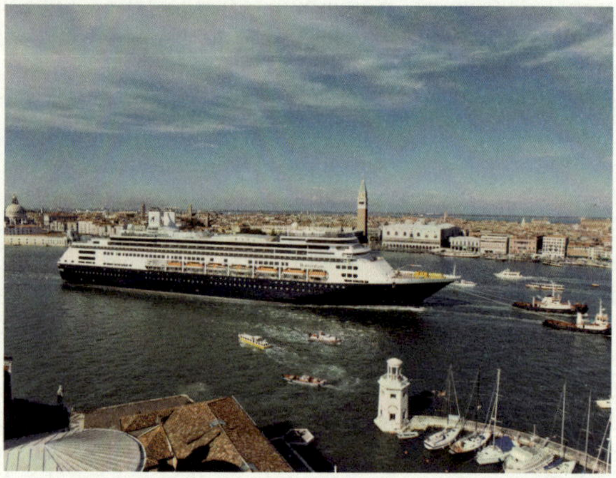

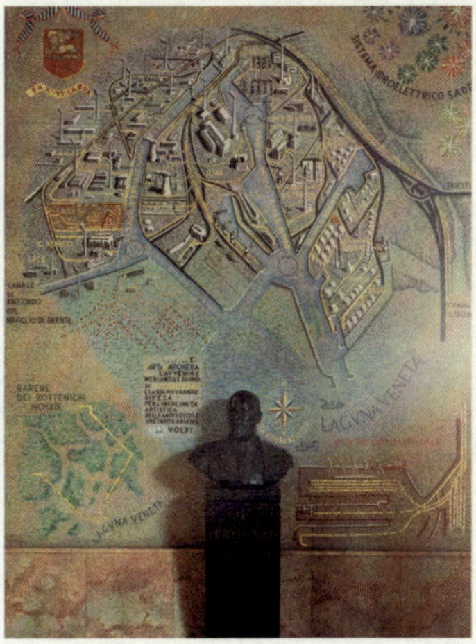
LAGVNA VENETA

Strike Objects
Jean-Luc Moulène
1999

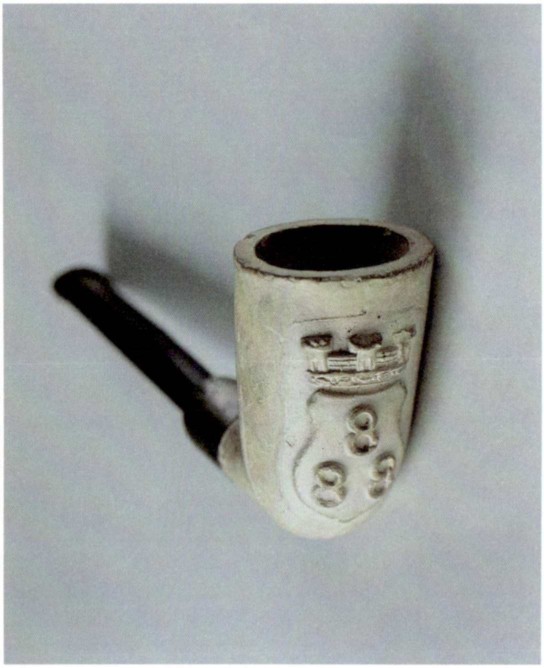

"THE THREE 8S" PIPE.

France, late 19th century. Loam, metal, ebonite, diameter: 2.5 cm, length: 14.7 cm.

At the beginning of the 20th century the three eights were something urgently demanded by workers: 8 hours work, 8 hours sleep, 8 hours leisure. How did they get from a claim to a cadence (three 8-hour shifts)?

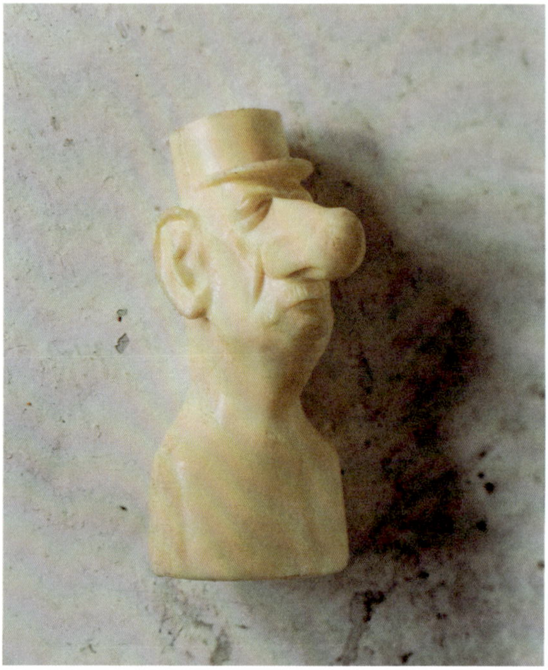

LE GRAND CHARLES

Société de plasturgie grenobloise, 1968. Moulded plastic, height: 7.75 cm.

Small caricatural figure of General de Gaulle with the artist's imprinted thumb gesture on the nose.

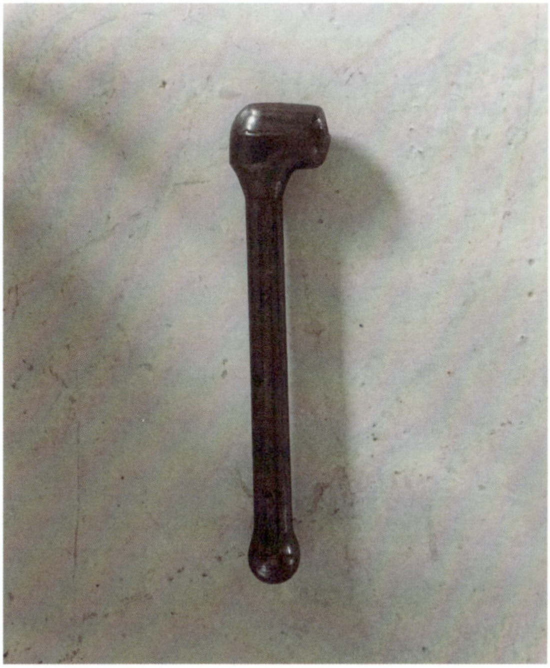

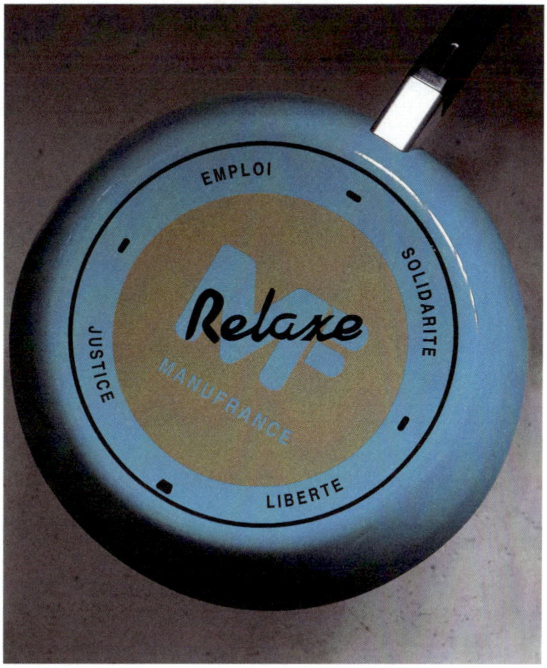

PEDAL CRANK KNOWN AS
"LE CASSE-TÊTE" [THE BATON]

Haubtman company, Saint-Étienne, 1968. Chrome steel, height: 19 cm, weight: 450 gr.

From the concrete life of an object to its mythology and back again. Haubtman, at Saint-Étienne, was a one of many subcontractors who supplied the bicycle section of Manufrance with spare parts. In 1968, when there were strikes, work stoppages, occupation of the premises, etc., the workers produced many objects "on the side." In case of this object, according to the story, a supply of pedal cranks was taken out of the factory to the barricades, but never reached its destination. The steelworkers who made them officially deny the truth of this story.

THE "MANUFRANCE 17" FRYING-PAN

Manufrance, Saint-Étienne, 1993. Frying-pan with a diameter of 20 cm, blue base with a gilded circle at its centre with "MF Manufrance" written on it in blue, and "Relaxe" in black. On the edge we can read the words: "Employment—Solidarity—Freedom—Justice" in black letters.

In 1984, 17 trade unionists and managers tried to save Manufrance and preserve jobs by setting up a workers' cooperative. They were forced to go into liquidation on 4 April 1985. On 9 July 1992, the "Manu 17" were sentenced by the Saint-Étienne Criminal Court; 36 years in prison—22 years with suspension—and 36,400,000 francs of fines were handed out to the 10 trade unionists, 5 managers and 2 accountants. In March 1993, the Manufrance frying-pan was created by the CGT* to provide financial support for the men sentenced: it was an appeal for the acquittal (relaxe) of the 17 with a view to the trial due to be held on 31 March 1993 which ended with the acquittal and discharge of 14 individuals and the pardon of the other 3.

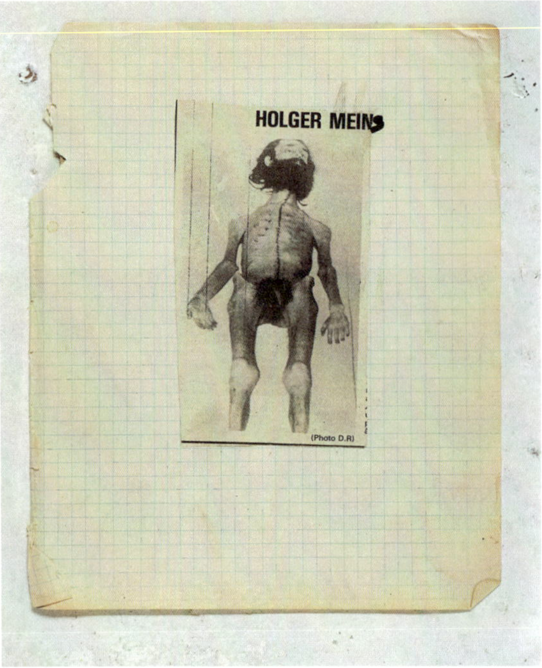

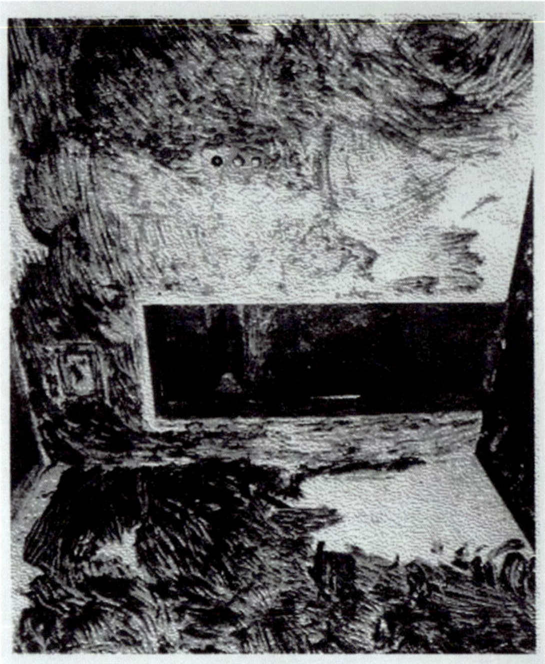

HOLGER MEINS

Photograph published in a French daily paper with the designation DR (Droits Réservés—copyright).

Holger Meins (26-10-1941, Hamburg, 09-11-1974), a member of the RAF, the Red Army Faction, whose plan was to destroy the myth of the omnipresence and invulnerability of the system. Their urban guerrilla strategies and tactics were met with the extreme control of the police, which forced the group (Andreas Baader, Ulrike Meinhof, Gudrun Ensslin, Holger Meins) to go underground. May 1970: first series of bomb explosions (American headquarters in Frankfurt, police headquarters in Augsburg, Springer publishing company in Hamburg). June 1, 1972: Holger Meins, Andreas Baader and Jan-Carl Raspe arrested in a garage in Frankfurt. 250 police officers were involved in the operation, assisted by armoured vehicles. Sentenced to life imprisonment, Holger Meins died following a hunger strike lasting 53 days, triggered by his conditions of detention (isolation and sensory deprivation) at Wittlich. In Berlin, 10,000 people marched in the streets with the photograph of H. Meins beside one of an anonymous martyr of Auschwitz. In his last letter he wrote: "each of us is the collective." The "Holger Meins Commando" went into action on 24-04-1975 in Stockholm.

DIRTY PROTEST

The movement of the IRA Blanketmen, March 1978.

1975: the British government decreed that Irish Republican prisoners arrested before or on February 28, 1975 would be sentenced as political prisoners, those arrested after or on March 1, 1975, were to be sentenced as ordinary prisoners. On September 14, 1976, Ciaran Nugent was the first Republican prisoner to be sentenced under this new system. He refused to wear criminal's clothing; the only thing that covered C. Nugent's nakedness was a blanket; he was joined by hundreds of other prisoners who were nicknamed the Blanketmen (at Crumlin Road, Magilligan and Armagh prisons). 1978: the No Wash and Dirty Protest. In March 1978, reacting to the physical torture inflicted on them by the warders when the cells were opened to let them go to the toilets and the showers, the prisoners decided to stop leaving their cells. They lived in cells soiled from floor to ceiling with their own excrement. Some of them stood out for four years. In 1980 they started a hunger strike to get their status as political prisoners recognized. The British government agreed. The prisoners ended their hunger strike which had lasted 53 days. Soon after, the focus of the news changed, and the British government went back on its word. Ten prisoners died in the hunger strike. (INAC—Irish Northern Aid Committee—document.)

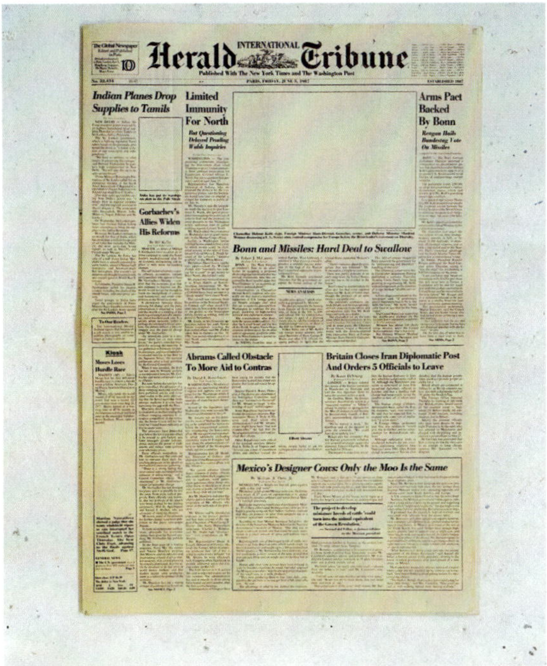
INTERNATIONAL Herald Tribune

Published With The New York Times and The Washington Post

Indian Planes Drop Supplies to Tamils

Limited Immunity For North

Arms Pact Backed By Bonn

Gorbachev's Allies Widen His Reforms

Bonn and Missiles: Hard Deal to Swallow

Abrams Called Obstacle To More Aid to Contras

Britain Closes Iran Diplomatic Post And Orders 5 Officials to Leave

Mexico's Designer Cows: Only the Moo Is the Same

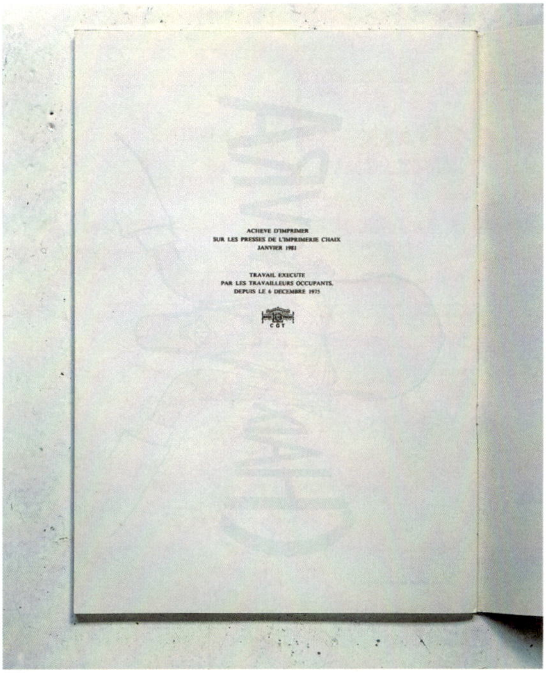
ACHEVE D'IMPRIMER
SUR LES PRESSES DE L'IMPRIMERIE CHAIX
JANVIER 1981

TRAVAIL EXECUTE
PAR LES TRAVAILLEURS OCCUPANTS.
DEPUIS LE 6 DECEMBRE 1975

CGT

INTERNATIONAL HERALD TRIBUNE

No. 32,434 dated Friday 5 June 1987, Paris.

A retoucher whose hours had been cut went on strike, and out of solidarity the photo-engravers refused to do any work. The Herald Tribune published this box as its lead story: "To Our Readers: The International Herald Tribune regrets that, follwing a strike, it was unable to publish photographs on some pages in today's edition;" for example: "Saul Bellow: ordinary people can still go to a performance of King Lear and weep" is the caption beneath a white square with the name of the photographer (Thomas Victor), on page 18 of the newspaper.

CHAIX, THE CONFLICT.

21-11-1974: after a three-week strike, an agreement was signed with the Ministry for Industry to safeguard the industrial potential of Saint-Ouen. 1975: failure to respect the agreement of 21-11-1974. On 5-12-1975, it filed for bankruptcy; at Néogravure, 1200 lay-offs were announced. The workers occupied their premises until 1981 (when Mitterrand was elected), resumption of work with a new manager, and in 1983, a new application to file for bankruptcy. Final closure of the Chaix printworks.

COLOPHON

Chaix, Saint-Ouen, 1981. Colophon on the Red Book, Chaix, la lutte par l'affiche [fighting through posters], 40 × 27.5 cm.

This book was produced by printers who had been occupying their factories from 5 December 1974. It contains 36 posters signed by Topor, Wolinski, Desclozeaux, Siné, etc. (85 illustrators); one of the posters is a letter addressed to Raymond Barre by the workers at Chaix and their families.

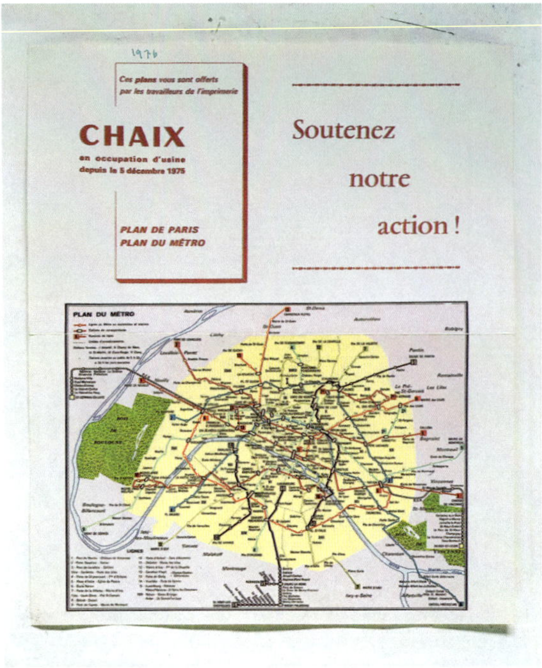

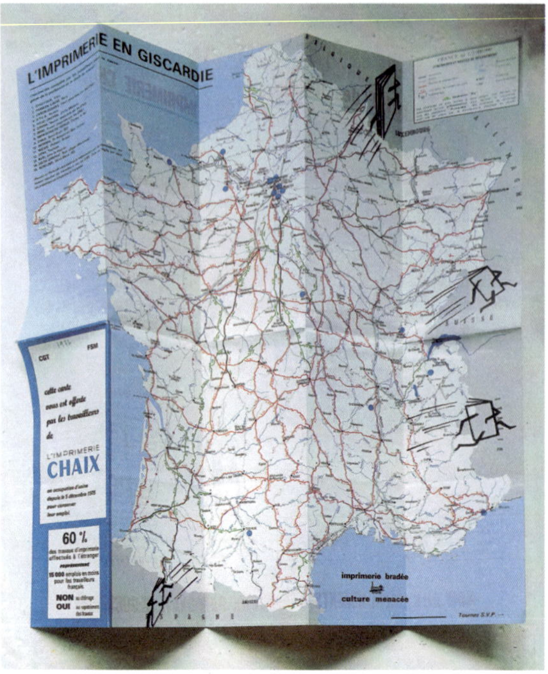

MAP OF THE PARIS METRO

Chaix printworks, Saint-Ouen, 1976 (see Chaix, the conflict). 29.8 × 24.8 cm. "Support our action! These maps are being given to you by the workers at the Chaix printworks who have been occupying their factory since 5 December 1975". On the verso there is a street map of Paris.

MAP OF FRANCE

Chaix printworks, Saint-Ouen, 1976 (see Chaix, the conflict). Map of France, 1:2,000,000, 49 × 49 cm; on the recto "The printworks in Giscardie*, printworks sold off, culture threatened" and the list of the printworks occupied by the workers to safeguard their profession and the right to work (blue circles on the map of France). On the verso is a historical account of the fight by the workers at Chaix printworks.

* A play on words based on the name of President Giscard d'Estaing.

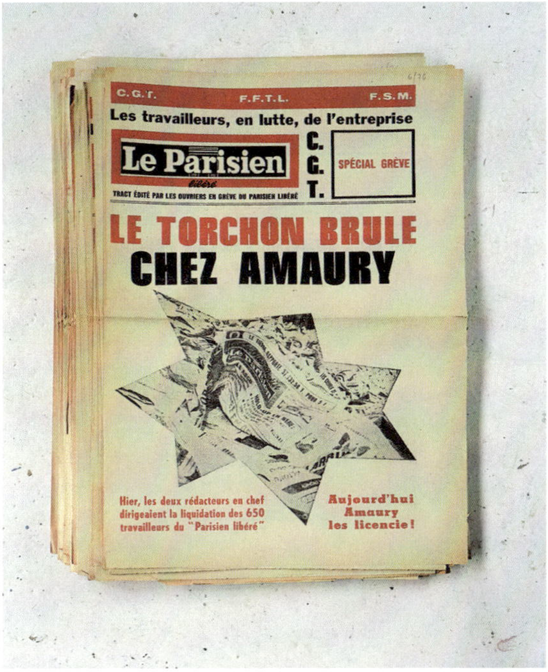

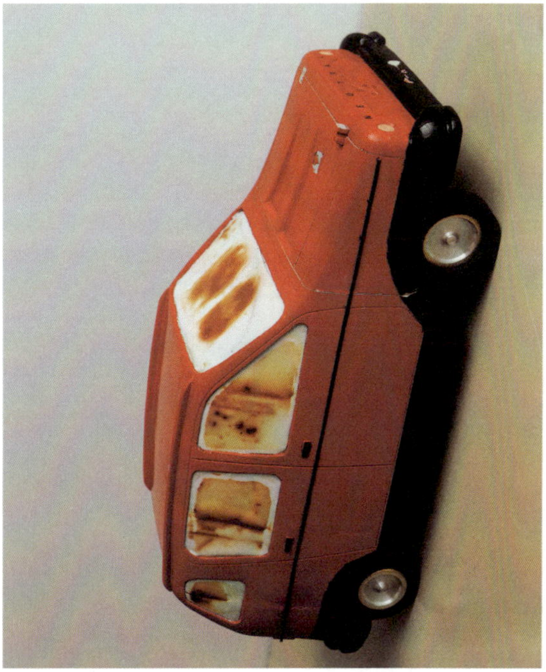

LE PARISIEN LIBÉRÉ, SPECIAL STRIKE ISSUE

4-page newsprint leaflet published by the workers from Le Parisien libéré in dispute since 3 March 1975. 42.5 × 31 cm.

At the beginning of 1975, the press baron Mr Amaury (Le Parisien, L'Équipe, etc.) decided to modernise his manufacturing and printing processes, and in the process to jeopardise the existing benefits of print-workers and undermine their trade union organizations. 861 days of strike would follow. On 9 June 1975, threatened with expulsion, the Le Parisien printers decided to occupy their working premises and seized the means of production. On 7 July 1976 the Parisian press barons approved the signing of an agreement regarding the consequences of modernisation with the CGT inter-union committee.

LA NEUTRAL

Renault Saint-Ouen/Billancourt, 1986. Working model made of painted wood, length: app. 30 cm.

A car designed by an association of workers, technicians, executives and retired engineers, intended for manufacture at the Renault factory in Billancourt in light of lack of employment and under threat, and to recover their domestic market and the development of the Saint-Ouen factory. La Neutral is not a strike object, but a very fine illustration of a new way of organizing the relationship between design and implementation. The "small popular vehicle" named La Neutral (an anagram of Renault), a creation by the men "with diamond-shaped* hearts" would not be accepted by the management.

* A reference to Renault's logo.

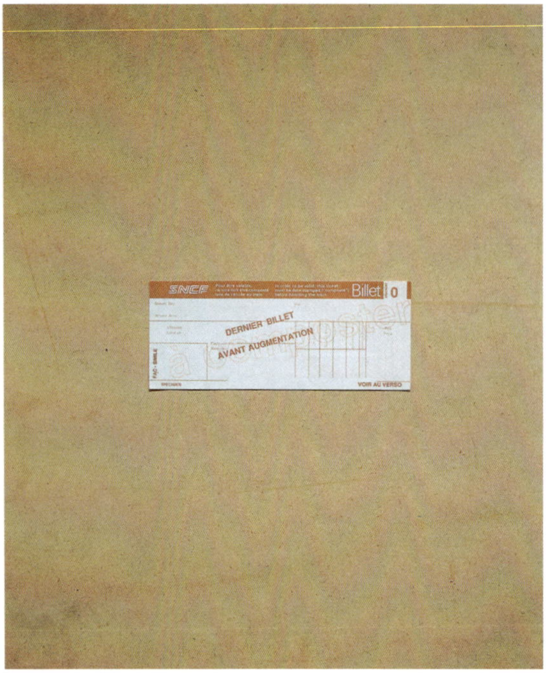

SNCF TICKET, CLASS 0

SNCF printworks at 87, rue du Charolais, Paris 12e, October 1990. 8.2 × 19.8 cm. "Last ticket before price rise" is written on the recto; on the verso: "Important notices 1. SNCF has decided to cut 105 jobs by closing down its ticket printworks. 2. These tickets will henceforth be made in Germany or in France by private printers without SNCF being able to control costs and quality. 3. Doing away with the SNCF ticket printworks will therefore mean: an increase in the price of the ticket for the user—SNCF printers—".

In 1979, there were 140 printers. After the election of Mitterrand, one billion centimes was spent in order to modernise machines so that they would accept tickets with "bar codes." But when the magnetic strip became widespread, SNCF management decided to entrust all its ticket production to private industry. 1990: occupation of the premises on rue du Charolais, production of the ticket of category 0, distribution of thousands of tickets in the trains and at demonstrations, deductions from wages, overseeeing of the tools of production by the strikers, and final closure with reclassification of the 50 printers, which remained in the end of 1991.

MARIE AND PIERRE CURIE, THE BANKNOTE

Bank of France printworks on the Chamalières site, Auvergne, 1998. Green offset facsimile of 500-franc banknote no. C 020788795, 8.8 × 17 cm.

Right across the faces of Marie and Pierre Curie appears the word "Specimen." On the back of the green note, the demands of the staff and unions appear—CFDT, CGT, FO, SI&C, SNA—regarding the elected representatives and users to protect the quality of Public Service: "Against the abandonment of the Mint as a Public Service. Against the risks of bankruptcy. Governor Trichet has already cut 800 jobs with the intention of aligning with European production costs. His strategy includes the closure of some hundred cash points, the cutting of a thousand jobs and in the medium term the closure of the corresponding branches." This green banknote, widely distributed during the strikes, demanded the preservation of the counters and the keeping of the Bank of France network.

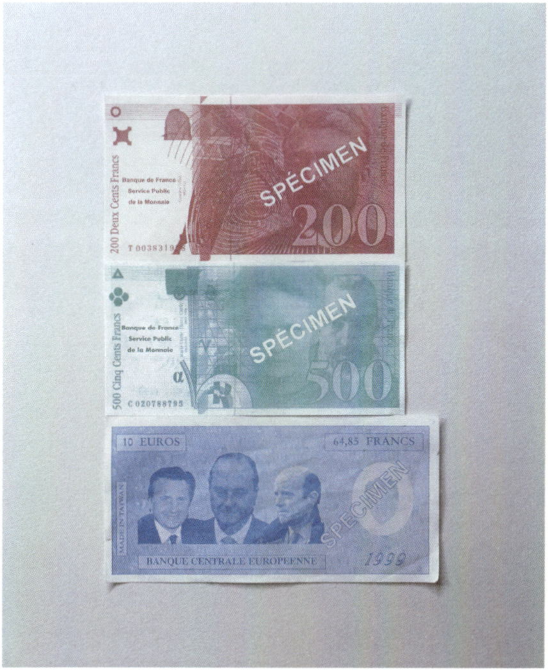

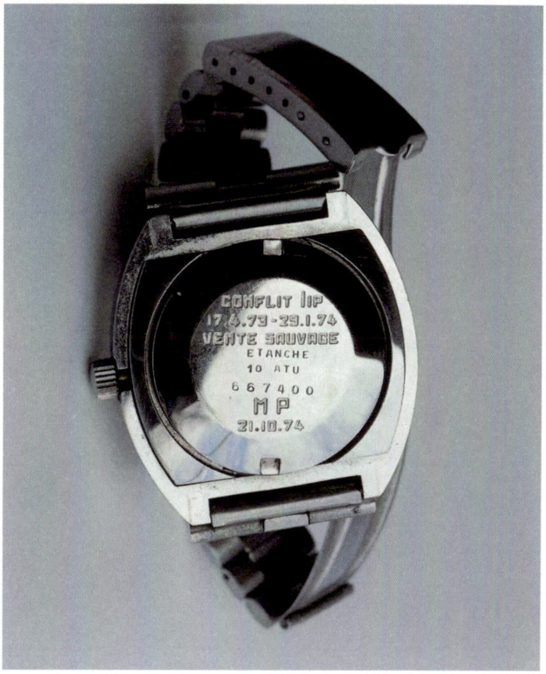

RED, GREEN, BLUE: 3 BANKNOTES, 3 CONFLICTS

Bank of France printworks on the Chamalières site, Auvergne, 1993, 1995 and 1998. 9.4 × 17 cm (red and green banknotes) and 9.5 × 19 cm (blue banknote).

The facsimile of the red 200-franc banknote carries the face of Gustave Eiffel with the word "Specimen" ("Sample") printed across it; serial no: T 0038319?8. Distributed during the 1993 strikes, the red banknote acts as the manifesto for the opposition by the staff and the unions to the amendment to the law on the independence of the Bank of France. The monochrome blue facsimile represented 10 euros, or 64.85 francs, with the faces, starting from the left, of Mr Trichet, Mr Chirac and Mr Juppé; to the right of Mr Juppé, there is a watermarked image of Mr Trichet's face against a white oval background with the word "Specimen" printed across it. "Made in Taiwan" appears on the left in a box, and "Central European Bank" and "1999" at the bottom. The blue banknote was distributed in 1995 in a strike by Bank of France workers and the unions "against the abandonment of the Public Service, against the risks of local desertification."

LIP, THE CONFLICTS.

1971: resignation of Fred Lip, he was replaced by Jacques Saintesprit to lead Lip SA. 1973: resignation of Mr. Saintesprit, threats of layoffs; April 27, 1973: beginning of the first conflict and the first unauthorized stock sales in cities and businesses in France and the first unauthorized payments. January 29, 1974: end of the first conflict and the take-over of Lip-Ornans by Mr. Ducros, CEO of Suprémec, while Mr. Arbel, a factory owner, took over the military sector of Palante. 1974-1976 : 2nd conflict. 1977: self-management under the name of "The Industries of Palente". 1974-1977 were the years of production of the strike objects.

SOUVENIR OF 1ST CONFLICT

Waterproof watch engraved with the words "Lip conflict. 17-4-73– –29-1-74. Unauthorised sale. Waterproof. 10 ATU*. No. 667400 MP. 21-10-74".

*ATU – Atmospheric Technical Units.

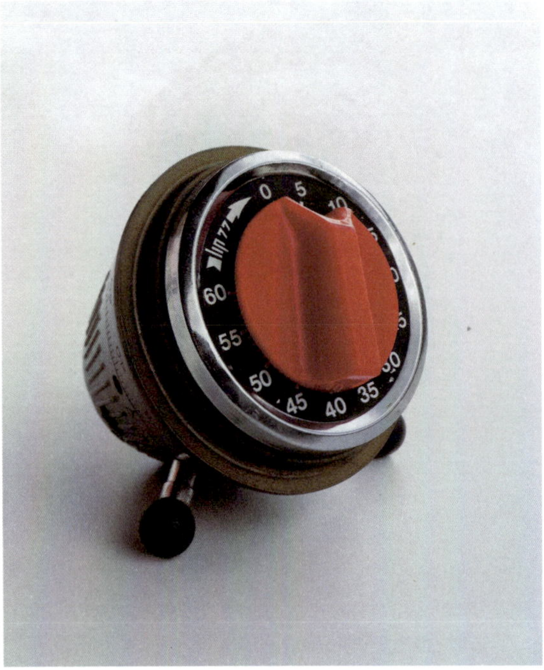

WARHEAD

Lip (Les Industries de Palente), 2nd conflict (See Lip, the conflicts). Diameter: 8 cm, length: 8 cm.

"In addition to our watch-making work, we also worked for the military industry, I took a warhead and transformed it into a domestic timer; a tool of destruction was transformed into a peaceful instrument, we made a hundred of them and we sold them..."
Conversation with Michel Pelleteret, 4 January 1999.

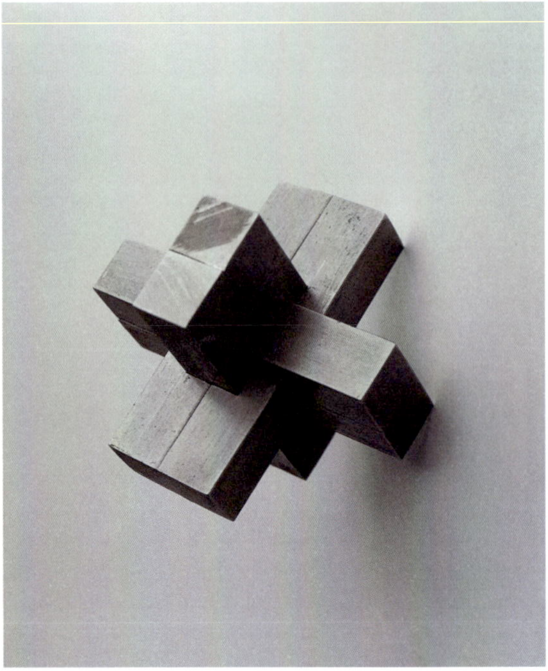

PUZZLE

Lip, 2nd conflict. Duralumin (light aluminium alloy with high mechanical strength), 6 × 6 × 6 cm.

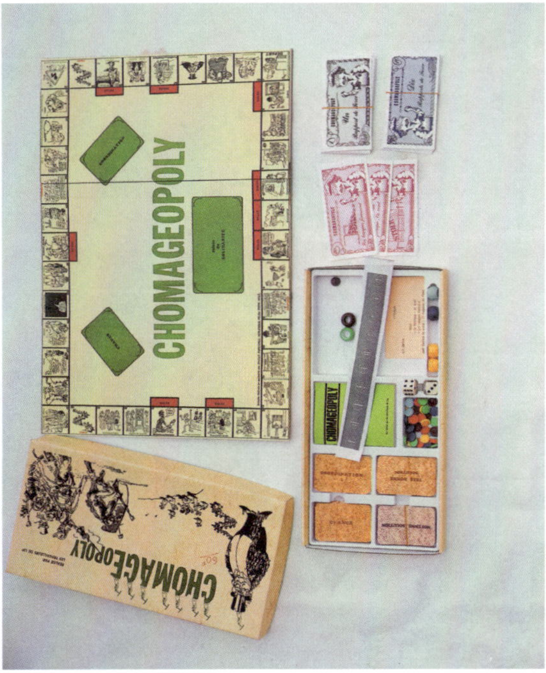

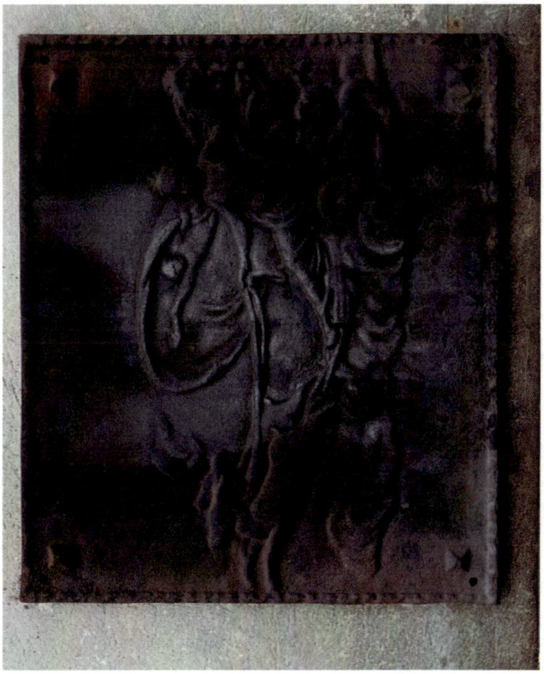

CHOMAGEOPOLY*

Lip, 2nd conflict (See Lip, the conflicts). Game of Monopoly (invented by out-of-work Americans in the 1930s) made by the Lip workers. 21.3 × 42 cm, board: 40.5 × 59 cm.

* Derived from French word for unemployment: English equivalent could be Dole-opoly.

THE MASSEY-FERGUSON ALLEGORY

Massey-Ferguson factory, Marquette, Nord, 1982-1984. Cast-iron fireback; a goddess in the form of a woman borne in a carriage drawn by two does dispenses the riches of the cornucopia. 49 × 57 cm, weight: between 15 and 20 kg.

1978: a decision made by the parent company in Toronto to cut the workforce and size of the Massey companies throughout the world by 50%. The first round of layoffs in France happenned in 1982. This marked the beginning of the major confrontations which culminated in 1983–1984 with the blockage of roads and trains, the unlawful detention of the directors, and the dumping of tons of steel in front of the company premises. It was during these struggles that the firebacks were made as a grass-roots initiative. 1984: laid off without any social plan, the workers signed on with the ASSEDIC (Association pour l'Emploi dans l'Industrie et le Commerce—Association for the Employment in the Industry and Commerce), the struggle resumed, and a reintegration plan was set up in 1986. The last discussions were held in 1991. Final closure.

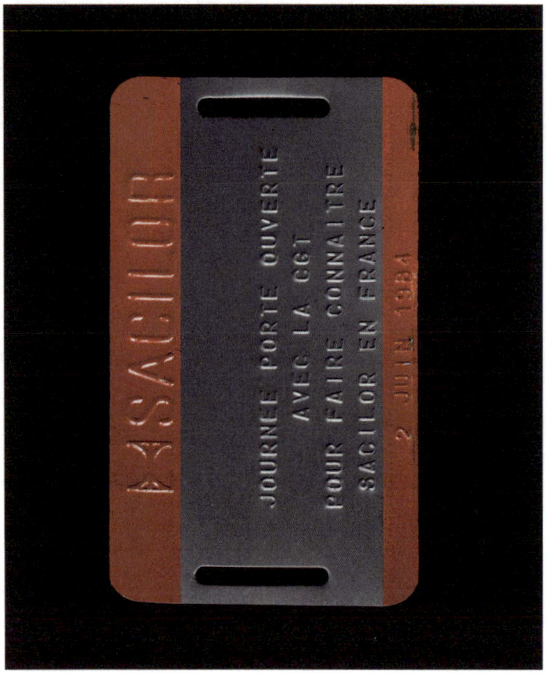

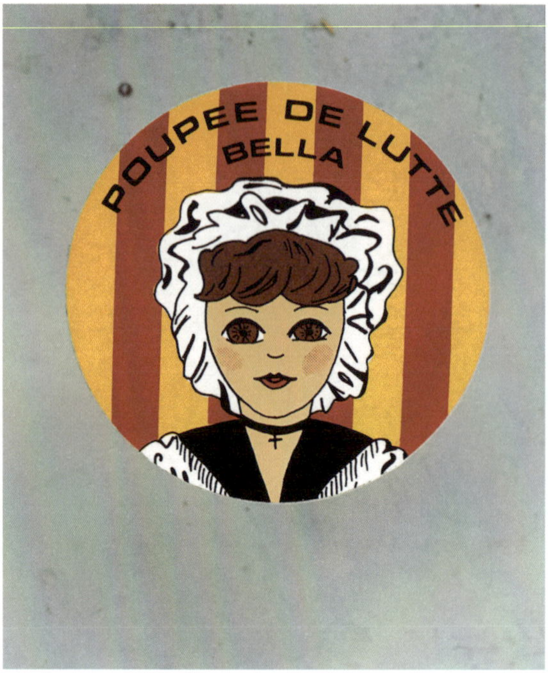

SACILOR INVITATION PLAQUE

Sacilor factories, Moselle, 1984. Two-coloured (grey, orange) stamped metal plaque measuring 9 × 15 cm, in the form of a label announcing: "Sacilor, open-doors day with the CGT to spread knowledge of Sacilor in France, 2 June 1984.

Following the various restructuring plans for steel industry, there were struggles to save jobs in Alsace and Lorraine. These plates were made so that on this "open-house" day the population and the various social partners become aware how modern and therefor viable Sacilor's tools of production were. In the years that followed thousands of layoffs took place in Alsace and Lorraine. Today the management of Unimetal (which took over Sacilor) wants to sell some of the shops, which they considers unprofitable.

DOLL SYMBOLISING THE DISPUTE

Bella doll company, Perpignan, 1984. Screenprinted sticker depicting the "Bella fighting doll", a yellow ground with vertical red stripes (the colours of Catalonia).

The Bella doll company was founded in 1946 and employed 860 people. On December 22, 1981, the Commercial Court declared it bankrupt: a restructuring plan reduced the workforce to 315, and the company was taken over by the manufacturer Jean-Louis Berchet, one of the main toy groups in France. 700 million centimes were invested in the new company with the help of public funds. In 1983, the auditors notinced transfers of funds from Berchet Industrie (Bella) to Super Jouet Berchet S.A. and BBC. Surprising to see a company that is the subject of a financial rescue plan by the public authorities lending money to a "healthy" business. The Bella company shut down completely at the end of 1984.

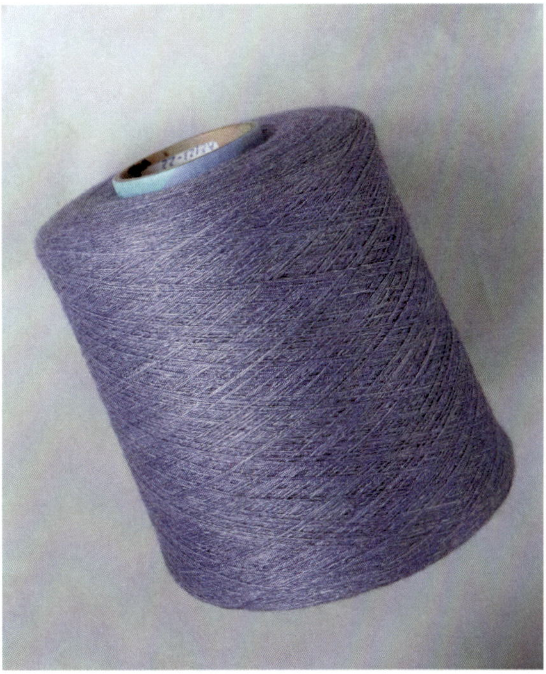

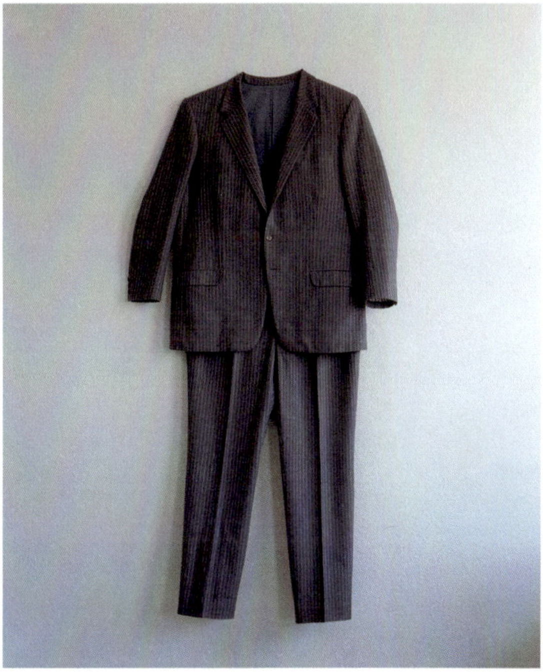

ARCT, ATELIERS ROANNAIS DE CONSTRUCTION TECHNIQUE, THE CONFLICT.

The ARCT (Roanne Technical Construction Workshops) were set up in 1922 by Elysée Crouset, the FT1 (False Twist) machine was created in 1956, and in 1974 the ARCT employed 1850 workers, and another 800 people through subcontracting. 1975: start of the crisis (siting of industries in countries with cheaper labour costs); ten years of struggle ensued. The synthetic textiles sector became a national issue: trade union mobilisation, demonstrations, strikes. In 1980, the ARCT workers invented Novacore (a thread with a sheathed nylon core combining the qualities of the fibre—wool, linen, etc.—with the robustness of a synthetic thread) and the RS 200 machine to manufacture it (210 m/mn). It was a very considerable technical advance. 1981: threats to sell the Novacore process to Japan and anger of the trade unions. 1985: recovery plan put forward by B. Terrat (with no plan for reintegration into the workforce) rejected out of hand. The Novacore patent was sold to Switzerland. June 1985: sell-off of the ARCT's assets but no continuation of their work.

THE NOVACORE SPOOL

Ateliers Roannais de Construction Technique (ARCT), Roanne, Loire, designed 1980. Diameter: 4.5 cm, height: 5.5 cm. Blue. References: NM 24/2 – AMC PA 78/20 19% FT, 81% wool – A 2123-22.

THE NOVACORE SUIT

Man's two-piece suit, dark grey on light grey stripes, jacket with 2 buttons and straight-legged trousers.

During the conflict, three Novacore suits were made and given to Philippe Rambaud [an actor], Jean Auroux [Minister of Labour] and Henri Krasucki [a union leader]. This fourth suit, made to the measurements of Daniel Coste, was made by a tailor in 1986–1987 from a leftover of Novacore that was part of a stock.

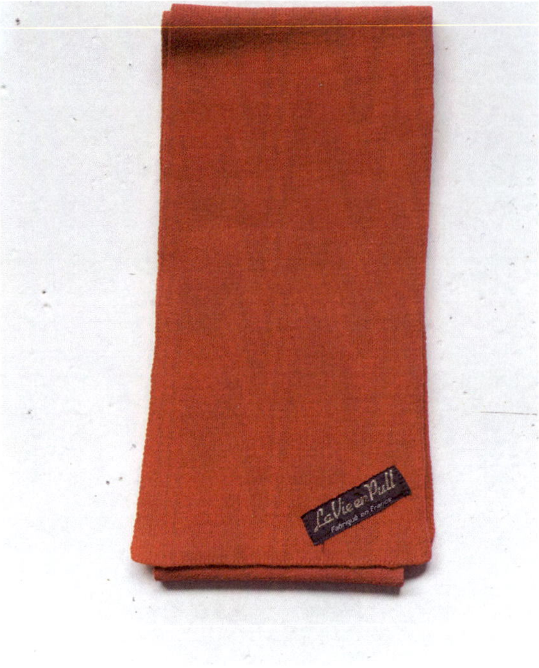

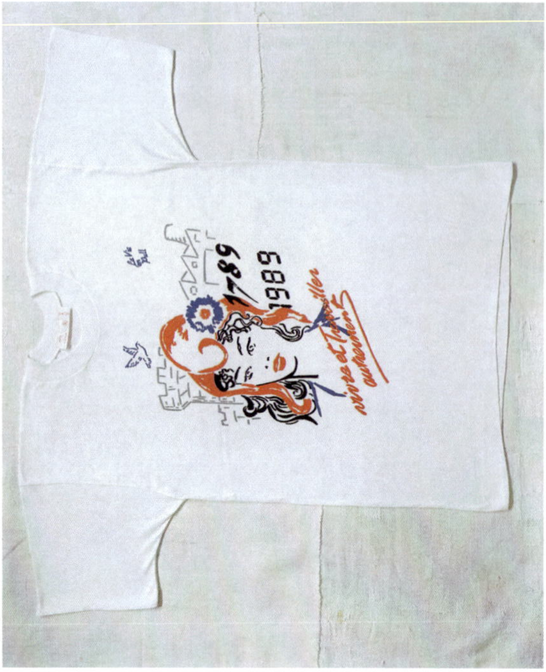

THE RED SCARF

La Vie en Pull, Roanne, 1990–1991. Machine knit (in homage to the scarf of Jean Moulin*), 15 × 136 cm.

For the record: 1975–1980, the Prost company (400 employees) was sold to a multinational, SCOA (an Africancompany). Beginning of bankruptcy with the threat of the liquidation of the company's assets in 1980. 1980-1982: around hundred female workers occupied their shops to find a credible offer to take the company over. The occupation lasted 19 months, day and night. In 1982, the women bought back the company's assets, the walls, stock and machines. This marked the birth of La Vie en Pull. 1983–1985: SCOP [société coopérative de production] filed for bankruptcy in May 1985, unemployment for 90 employees and profound distress. 1985–1991: a so-called Law on Associations (1901) (the non-profit organizations law) took over SCOP, with some thirty female workers producing T-shirts and red scarves in a survival economy until August 2, 1991, when in the middle of summer they were expelled by the police. In 1992, they retrieved some of their equipment and stock thanks to a court decision, rented premises, took on a few members from the Vie en Pull association and settled the liabilities, rent, operating expenses and legal costs.

* French Resistance fighter during World War II.

THE 1789-1989 T-SHIRT

La Vie en Pull, Roanne, Spring 1989 Collection. Cotton T-shirt, a blue white, red and black screenprint depicting Marianne* against the Bastille and the factory, "same combat", with the slogan "living and Working differently"; a dove and "La Vie en Pull" above two besieged fortresses. Unit price: adult size 40 frs, children's size 35 frs. The Saint-Just ("Happiness is always a new idea"), the 3 doves and many other designs were also sold.

* Female figure symbolising the French Republic

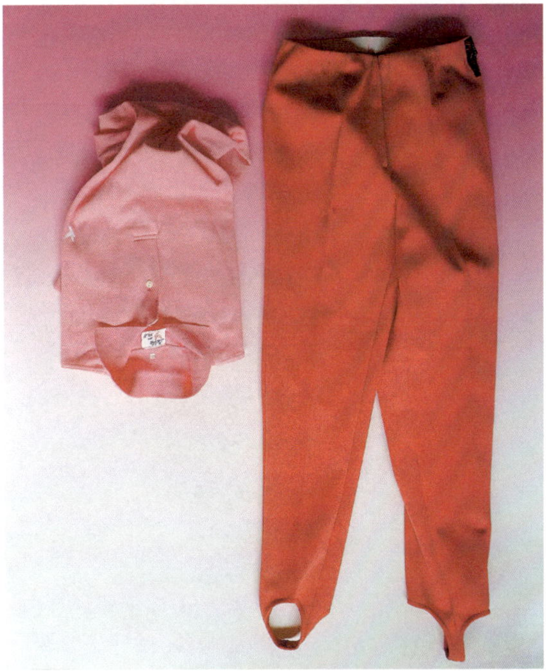

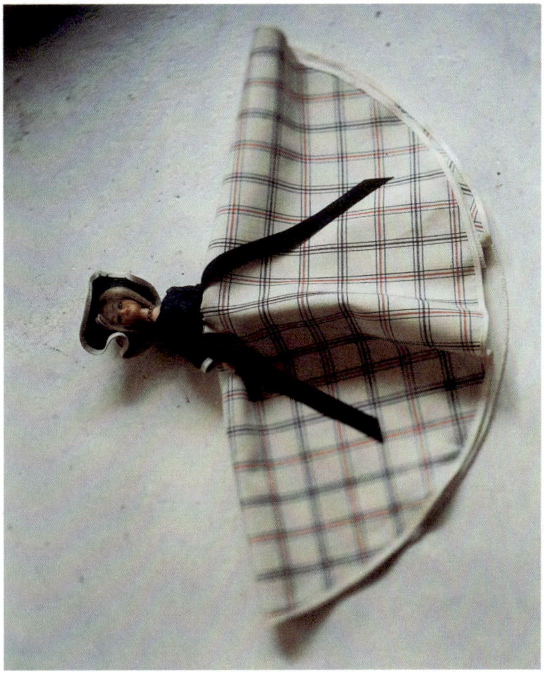

SKI PANTS AND SPORTS SHIRT

La Vie en Pull, Roanne, 1990s. Women's Trevira ski pants, size 42, 100% polyester, red, labelled "La Vie en Pull—France" and with an embroidered dove. Men's sports shirt, size XL, 80% cotton—20% polyester, short sleeves, pink, labelled "la Vie en Pull – fabriqué en France".

THE LIBR' DOLL

Bril, a factory of men's ready-to-wear clothing, Loiret. Barbie-type doll; height 41 cm, diameter of skirt 62 cm, golden chain necklace, dress with a black long-sleeved bodice and a plaid skirt, a matching widebrimmed hat.

The factory was closed on May 22, 1980, the workforce then occupied it for two years. 318 female workers organized the transfer of know-how, found they were capable of teaching, and produced the LIBR' doll (an anagram of BRIL) to support their campaign: it was a time of intense jubilation, great joy. In 1983, a workers' cooperative was created with 40 to 50 people, in 1985, it was taken over by Jacques Esterel with about 20 people; the final liquidation in 1987.

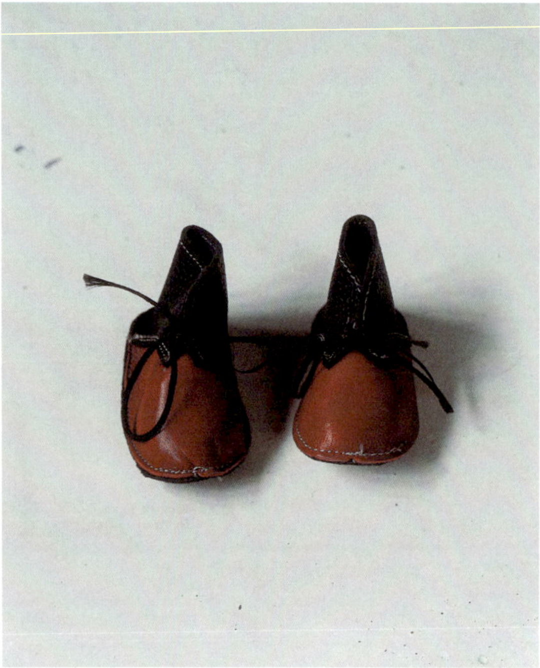

SHOES SYMBOLISING THE DISPUTE

Myrys, Limoux, Aude. Shoes in red and black "football" colours, width at plantar arch: 3.5 cm, length: 8.5 cm, fullgrain leather.

The shoes were made during the occupation of the factories, since November and December 1995 in order to be sold on May 1 of 1996 and 1997, at sport events, demonstrations and protests. The Myrys company was taken over by a British group in February 1998. The workers' demands, such as the production of 10,000 pairs of shoes a week and the refurbishment of 40 Myrys stores, have still not been met today.

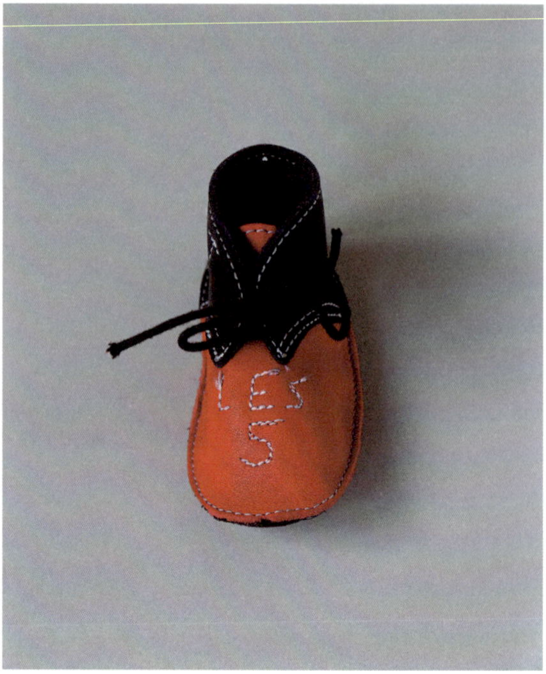

THE MYRYS 5

Myrys, Limoux, Aude, 1999. Companion shoe to the "Shoes symbolising the dispute". Left foot, with "Les 5" oversewn in white.

1997: occupation of the Managing Director's office by around sixty people and the end of the occupation by the signing of a memorandum of agreement recognizing the strike and the assurance that no sanctions would be taken; five individuals were then charged with an offence and impeding freedom of movement. Yet no complaint had been made. At the end of the trial, which was held on March 17, 1999, four of them were found guilty, but discharged. In April 1999 the State Prosecutor, Achille Kiriakidès, appealed against the sentence passed—still unresolved.

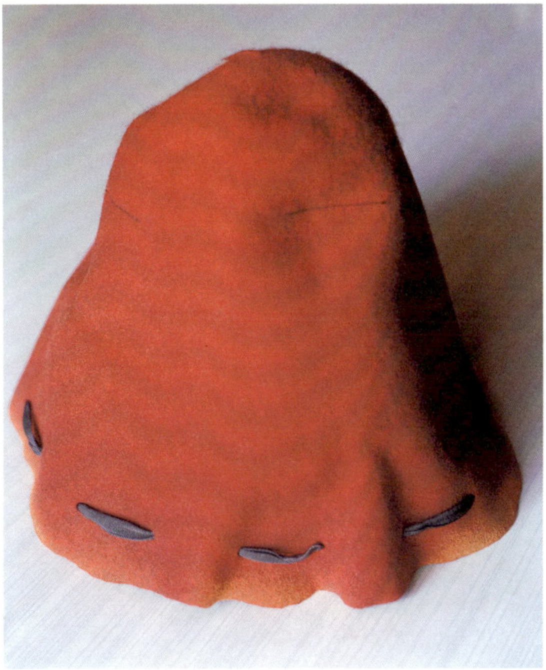

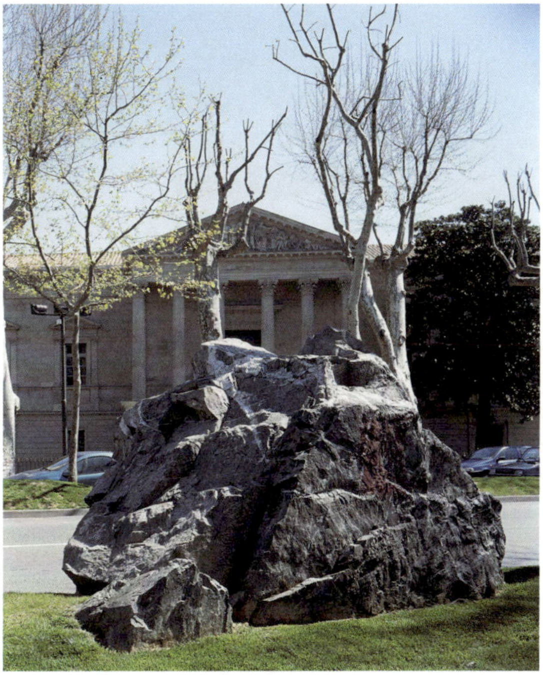

ROBERT'S HAT

Esperaza, Aude, 1989–1990. Red cloche hat made of wool and noils (wool waste).

In 1978–1980, the Bugarach label was created by the Saint-Jacques company in Esperaza, which marketed it until 1994–1995. The milliner industry in the upper Aude valley experienced its golden age in the 1920s. In 1929, before the Wall Street crash, the French market sold 15 million cloche and other hats; in 1955 that number went down to 1,700,000. The independence of the colonies, the "bareheaded" fashion imported from Germany after World War II, and disagreements between the milliner families took this industry down. Musée de la chapellerie (Museum of Hat-Making), opened in Esperaza in 1992; it chronicles the heyday and the decline of the milliner industry, with no nostalgic sentiment. Robert has been wearing this red cloche hat for fifteen years, and these hats have been present at all the Labour Day demonstrations and the parades on May 1.

THE ROCK OF THE STRUGGLE OF THE SALSIGNE MINERS

MOS: Mine d'or de Salsigne [Salsigne goldmine], Carcassonne, Aude, 1992. Block of (sterile) schist, weight: approximately 6 to 7 tonnes, base: 200 cm, height: 160 cm, depth: 120 cm.

Left on the Public Square in front of the Courthouse during the demonstration of March 23, 1992, this first rock was removed at the behest of the Department of Environment. "Taking advantage of the atmosphere of animosity," the Mayor granted the miners the concession they were asking for: 80 sq. m. on which a second rock was installed with great fanfare in front of the Courthouse where it continues to symbolise the miners' struggle and tenacity. It was a brilliant operation of perpetuation. The first conflicts dated from the 1970s. Following the announcement of the layoff of the 430 miners and an application to file for bankruptcy, the miners occupied the goldmine in June 1990 for three months. Being in control of the ore and the machines; the miners were looking for someone to buy the mine. Australian shareholders (controlled by the Société générale and Rothschild banks) put an operating plan into effect, but it proved unsuccessful. In 1992, there were renewed threats of layoffs, and the protest demanding the reopening of the goldmine resumed. The MOS deposits represent by far the largest concentration of gold in western Europe, but in June 1999 the shareholders once again threatened to file for bankruptcy; the struggle resumed. City of Carcassonne.

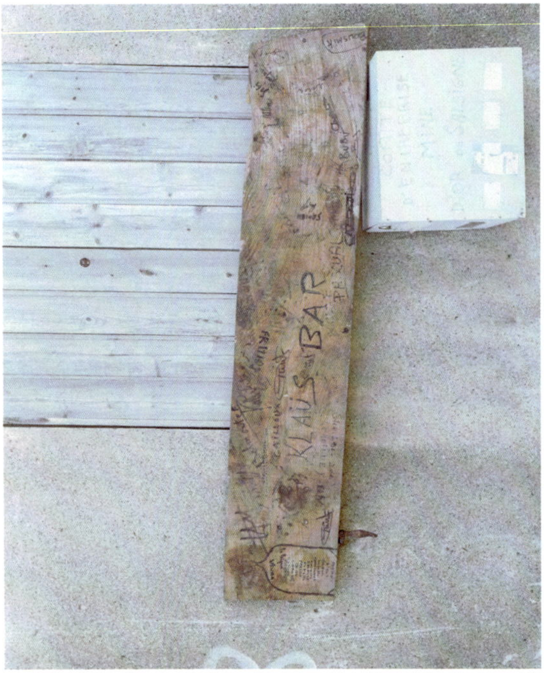

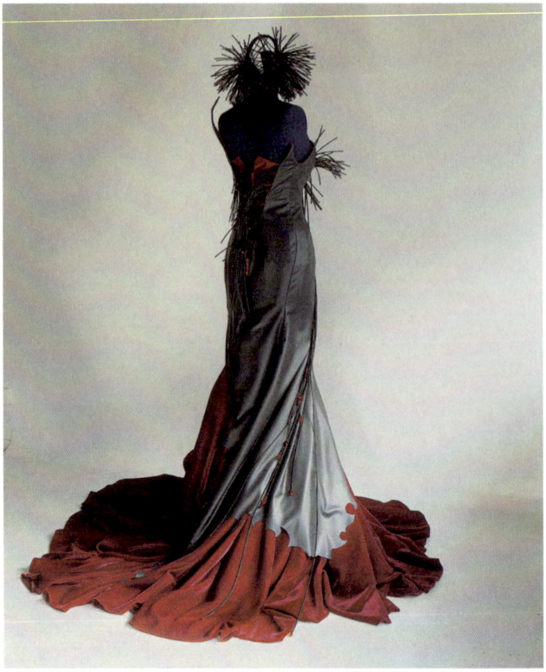

THE SMALL COUNTER FROM THE FLOOR OF THE MINE

MOS: Mine d'or de Salsigne, Carcassonne, Aude. Approximately 6 × 140 × 26 cm.

During the occupation of the mine starting in June 1990, the miners built the Bar on the floor of the mine. The counter is made from wood used for props (white oak) and bears the names and signatures of the men occupying the mine: Momo, Klaus, Beber, Sucette, Chacounet, Kakette, Parigot, Dudu, Chinois, Râleuse, etc.

LA STROMBOLI

Occupied Nina Ricci workshops, Paris.

The last "haute couture" dress from the Nina Ricci workshops on avenue Montaigne before the label was made over after being bought up by a Spanish group in January 1998, without the qualified first-grade and second-grade skilled workers. 96 of the 123 women employed would be laid off at the end of January 1999. Designed by Julien Fournié, made by the female workers on strike in a skilful assemblage of latex, synthetic velvet, taffeta, paste gems and light-emitting diodes, La Stromboli, an evening dress worn by a mannequin, was the strikers' standard in front of the Carrousel arch at the Louvre during the official march-past of the Haute Couture Collections on 20 January 1999.

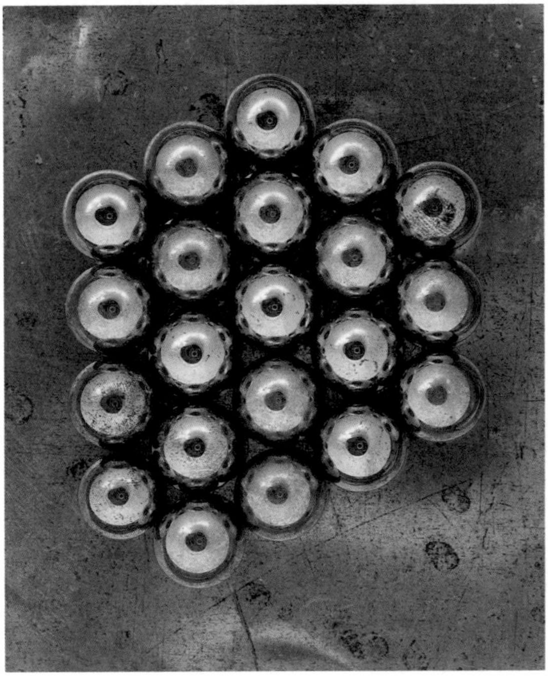

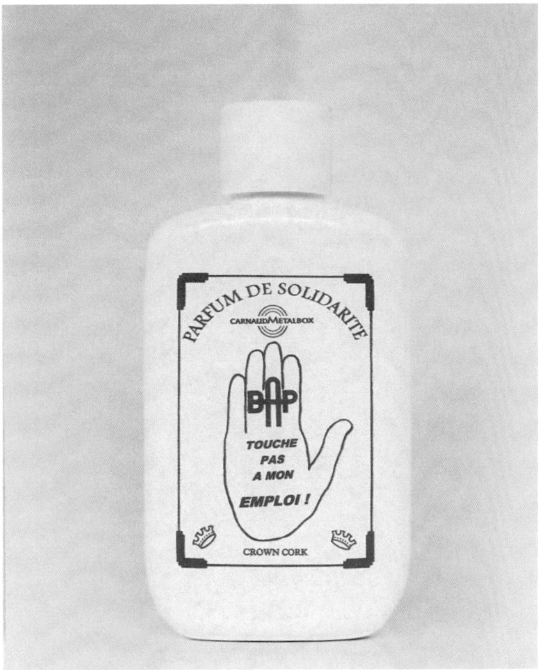

21 SKF BALL BEARINGS

SKF metallurgical company pro-ducing ball bearings, Ivry-sur-Seine, 1983.

The SKF workers from Ivry sold bags of ball bearings for solidarity money to finance their movement. The first campaigns opposing the removal of the machines were in February 1983. March 14: announcement of a jobcutting plan; the Ivry factory was to close (616 employees), days of action, "open doors" initiative. On September 22, a ton of imported ball bearings were dumped in front of the Prefecture. In November, the occupation of the factory was approved by a vote. May 23, 1984: the initiative named "200 delegates for SKF" in Göteborg, Sweden (the headquarters of the parent company). July: 20 tons of ball bearings dumped in front of the Ministry of Industry. November: occupation of Vitry-sur-Seine, the Génie de la Bastille* taken by assault. May 28, 1985: factory evacuated by the CRS**. June 5: factory retaken by CGT militants, backed by a demonstration involving 10,000 people; violent confrontations and evacuation of the factory, several arrests. June 14, 1985: the entrances to the factory were walled up. In the early 1990s part of the site was destroyed and Le Monde printworks was established there.

* The winged liberty statue on the top of the column at the centre of the Place de la Bastille in Paris.

** CRS—Compagnies Républicaines de Sécurité: French riot police.

SOLIDARITY PERFUME

Bourgogne Applications Plastiques, Chevigny-Saint-Sauveur, Côte-d'Or (subsidiary of Carnaud Metalbox, parent company: Crown Cork). Bottle with a height of 7.5 cm, white moulded plastic, silkscreened label (6-colour range) with the words: "BAP will live S.O.S. 175 jobs" on one side, on the other "Solidarity perfume", and on the drawing of an open hand: "BAP Hands off my job!"

The conflict started on June 10, 1996 and ended on September 29, 1996. The minimum sales price of the bottle was 20 francs. 10,000 bottles were sold in eight weeks. The 175 employees of BAP came out on indefinite strike and occupied their work place; they made "the largest PVC plastic bottle in the world" (height: 682 cm, diameter: 179 cm, number of bottles needed to make it: 6,865, weight: 307 kg); it did not get into the Guinness Book of Records (as it was a composite bottle). The Austrian group Alpla took over the company and 55 jobs under the name Euroflaco.

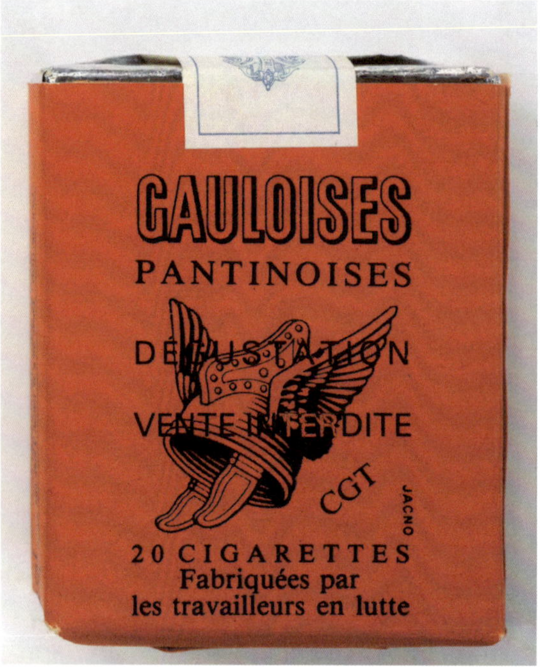

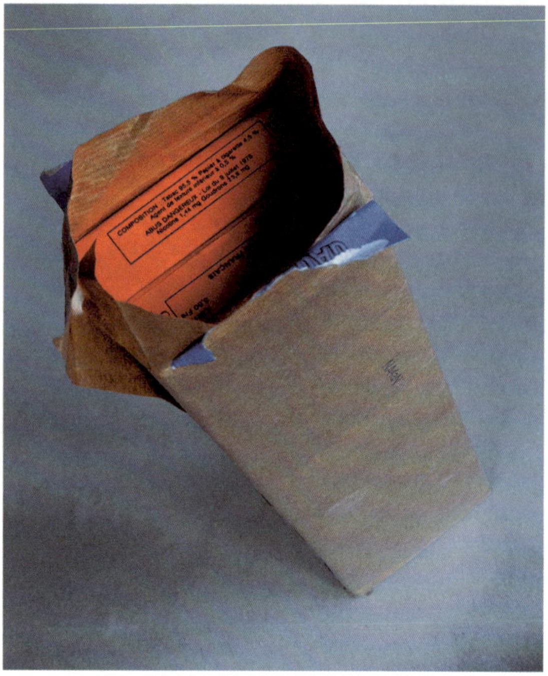

LA PANTINOISE

Pantin tobacco factory, Seita, 1982–1983. Red packet, height: 7 cm, width: 5.8 cm, length: 2.3 cm. Translation of the inscription reproduced on the front: "Pantin Gauloises. Trial sample. Not for sale. CGT. 20 cigarettes manufactured by the workers in dispute. Jacno". On the other side: "Gauloises, Pantin tobacco factory, Seita, Jacno, occupied since 23-2-82 in support of a restart, against the closure of the establishment". On one of the edges: "Taxes charged 74%: 2.88 frs. Price from a licensed tobacconist 3.90 frs".

The workers from the Pantin tobacco factory who had been occupying their premises in support of the restart of the factory since 23 February 1982 decided to get the business back on the road on 11 June 1982 by creating La Pantinoise. The red packet of Gauloises was given with a 5-franc voucher of support. When the conflict calmed down, most of the remaining packets were destroyed.

THE CARTON OF PANTINOISES

Pantin tobacco factory, Seita, 1982–1983. Carton of 10 red packets of Gauloises wrapped in kraft paper, height: 5 cm, width: 29 cm, length: 7 cm. Closed at either end by two Gauloises labels (the blue visible at the opening of the carton). Quality control number: NA4aN.

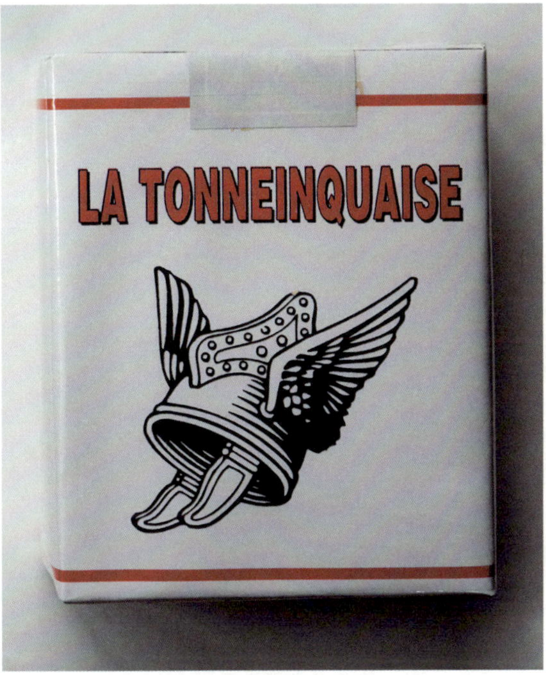

LA TONNEINQUAISE

Tonneins tobacco factory, Seita, Lot-et-Garonne. Height: 7 cm, width: 5.8 cm, length: 2.4 cm.

La Tonneinquaise, conceived by the workers in December 1998, and produced in Poland in December 1999, is the symbol of the closure announced by the factory for the end of 2000. A white packet containing 20 filtered Gauloises, was intended for "those who deserved the Tonneinquaise." The Gallic helmet is placed on the white background, and above it appears "La Tonneinquaise" in red capital letters with a fine black outline; the packet is covered in plastic. On the back, "The [Tonneinquaise] Can and Must Survive" appears in black on white, and "SEITA, at Tonneins," in red on white, and "La Tonneinquaise" on the sides in red on white. In November 1998, the management of SEITA announced the "2001 performance plan," i.e. the closure of four facilities; a logic of financial profitability at the expense of jobs and families. For Tonneins it meant 340 direct and 3000 indirect job cuts. The unions, the workers, the population at large and the elected representatives went into action. At the end of 1999 an acceptable social plan for reintegration into the workforce was set up. Today the workforce of Tonneins is experiencing the slow death of their company and "many are on Prozac."

10

NO MAN'S LAND'

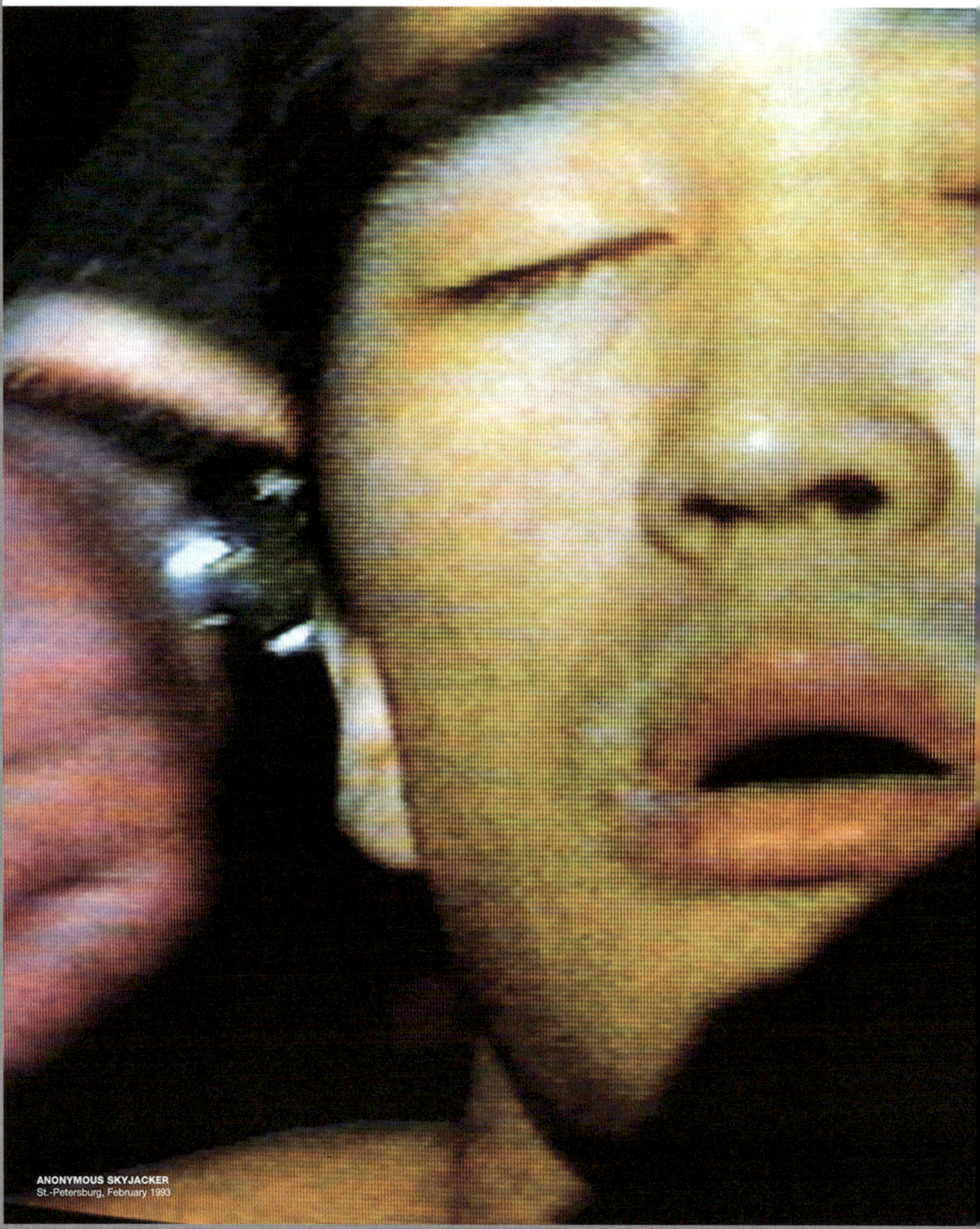

ANONYMOUS SKYJACKER
St.-Petersburg, February 1993

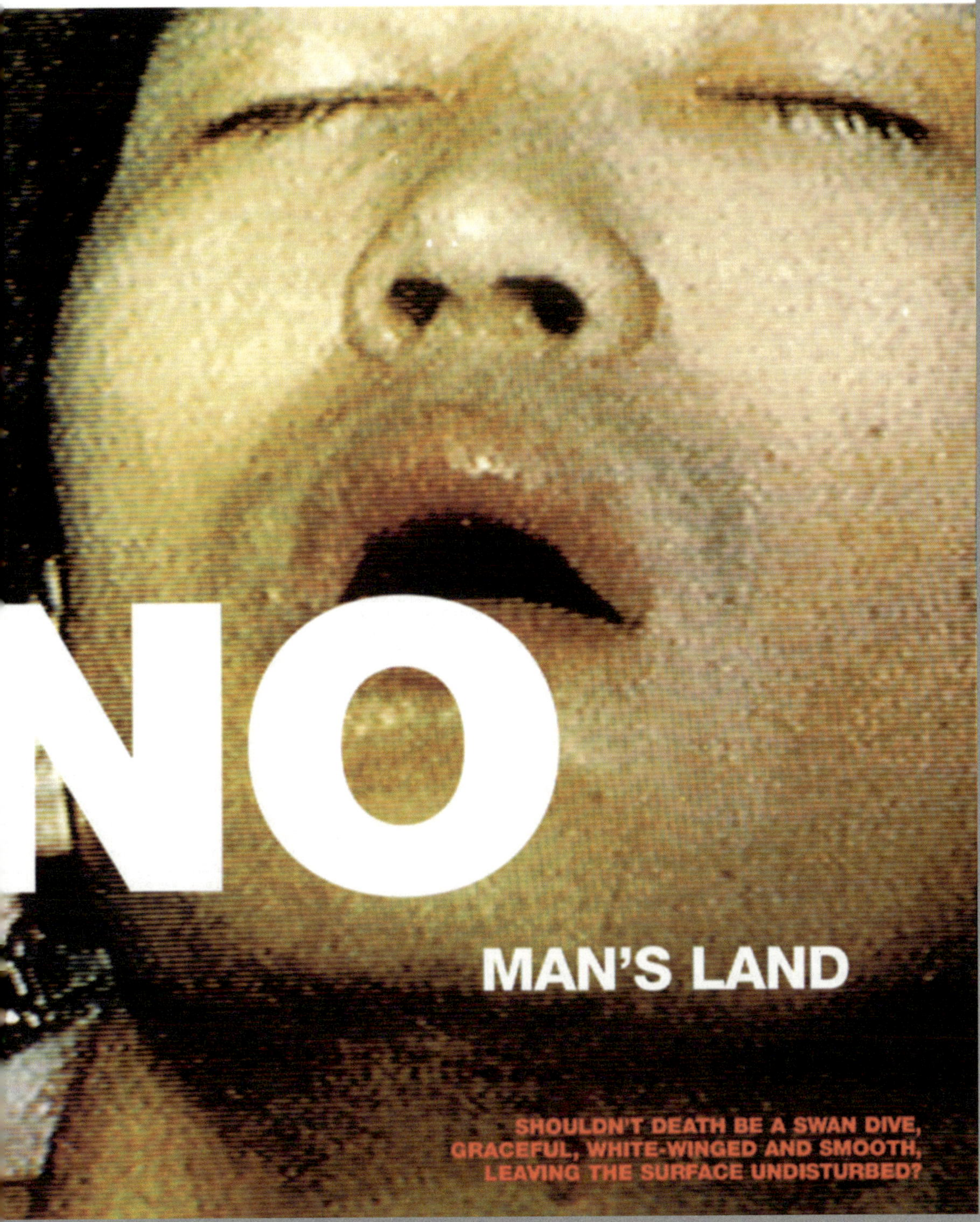

NO MAN'S LAND

SHOULDN'T DEATH BE A SWAN DIVE,
GRACEFUL, WHITE-WINGED AND SMOOTH,
LEAVING THE SURFACE UNDISTURBED?

WHAT DO YOU DO WITH A BOEING ONCE YOU'VE STOLEN IT?

August 29, 1969: A stylishly clad Leila Khaled in white bell-bottoms and matching wide-brimmed hat, boards American airliner TWA B-707 on its way from Rome to Tel Aviv. Once airborne her other accessories appear: a pistol and a hand grenade. As she makes her way toward the cockpit, her companion, Salim Issawi, announces that the Popular Front for the Liberation of Palestine is now in command of the very first American airliner to be hijacked in the Middle East. Captain Carter, looking down the barrel of a pistol, is obliged to agree.

MY PEOPLE SHALL LIVE** LEILA KHALED'S SKYJACK JOURNAL

1. SEVEN MINUTE DETOUR

I had trained for every conceivable contingency; I had mastered most operational details of the great Boeing 707. There was something, however, I did not train for: the human situation. How to deal with idle or curious conversation alists. How not to arouse their suspicions or be rude to a seatmate. I had to improvise and felt very uncomfortable. I imagined that all the Westerners aboard knew about my mission.
My seatmate from Beirut to Rome was a clean-cut sociable American on his way to New York. I knew that Americans, like most other tourists, like to make casual conversation about everything under the sun. I didn't realize that they posed personal questions so directly and so nonchalantly. Mr. Holden must have been bored, and he wanted to talk. "Where are you going?" he asked to open the conversation.
"I am going to Rome," I said. "Why are you going to Rome?" he continued.
I paused momentarily to fabricate an answer, and said with simulated shyness, "I am going to meet my fiancé who is coming from London to meet me in Rome in a few days." I suddenly realized I had made a slip. What if he too were going to Rome, and asked me to dinner or something while I was waiting for my "fiancé".
I swiftly corrected my mistake by adding, "It is quite possible that he might surprise me and be waiting for me at the airport."
Then I asked him, "Where are you going?"
"To New York," he said, much to my relief.
He was determined not to let the conversation lapse. "How on earth would an Arab girl be going to Rome to meet her fiancé alone and get married?" he asked. I answered in a superficially self-assured tone, "I've know him since we were children, and we've been engaged for several years; besides we are modern, not traditional Arabs." "That's good," he said, and started telling me how he and his wife had eloped because her parents had disapproved of him.
As I assured him that I was not eloping, the stewardess cheerfully announced that there was a newly married couple on the plane and they had a huge cake they would like us to share. "Who would like to have some cake?" she said. Everybody, including Mr. Holden and I, chanted in a chorus of "I would."

I spent two days at the hotel fending off invitations for personally guided tours of Rome. During these two days, I walked the streets of Rome alone. It is strange, but I had no desire to purchase anything, see Rome's ancient glory, or even go to a film. I only walked and walked, contemplating my mission and reciting its details to myself.
Early on the morning of August 29, I checked out of the hotel and caught a bus to Fiumicino Airport on the outskirts of Rome. Happily, the only snag was a half-hour flight delay.
My associate, whom I recognized only from a

A GREAT YET ALMOST SILENT ROAR OF LAUGHTER FROM A WHOLE NATION HOLDING ITS SIDES, YET FULL OF REVERENCE WHEN LEILA KHALED, GRENADE AT THE READY, ORDERED A TWA PLANE
JEAN GENET, *PRISONER OF LOVE*

photograph, appeared on schedule and we exchanged pre-arranged signals. His name was Salim Issawi; he was a Palestinian from Haifa who had been raised in Syria. Salim sat quietly nearby and we tried to ignore each other.
All was going smoothly when suddenly the human element threatened our careful planning. A few seats away there was a little girl with a button on her dress cheerfully proclaiming "Make Friends". That message brought me up short, forced me to remind myself, as I watched her playing with her little sister, that this child had committed no crime against me or my people. It would be cruel to imperil her life by hijacking a plane, the symbolic meaning of which she had no conception – a plane that could explode during our attempted seizure or be blown up by Israeli anti-aircraft fire when we entered the "Israeli airspace".
While these qualms pricked my conscience, the whole history of Palestine and her children came before my eyes. I saw everything from the first day of my exile. I saw my people homeless, hungry, barefoot. The twice "refugee" children of Bagan camp near Amman seemed to stand, a humiliated multitude, in front of me saying, "We too are children and we are a part of the human race." The scene strengthened me enormously.
I said to myself, "What crime did I and my people perpetrate against anyone to deserve the fate we have suffered?" The answer was "None". The operation must be carried out. There can be no doubt or retreat. My children have spoken.*
On the bus across the field to the Boeing 707, another unscheduled problem developed.
A handsome man in his early thirties came up to me and said "Hello" in a most jovial, enthusiastic manner. "Hello," I replied nonchalantly, as I calmly tried to read My Friend Che by Ricardo Rojo. He seemed very eager to talk and asked me who I was and where I was going. I couldn't very well repeat the marriage tale and couldn't invent anything quickly enough. I said, "Guess." He tried, "Greek, Spanish, Italian?" I asked him where he was from. "I am from Chicago," he answered, and continued his questioning.
"You wouldn't be South American, would you?" Now that I knew where he was from, I figured it was safe to say that I was a South American. I thought it might end his questioning, at least. "From Brazil?" he asked, looking admiringly at me, and ogling my whole body. "You're getting closer," I said.
"Bolivia?" "Yes," I replied, "but how did you know?" "It's your book that gave you away," he declared. I asked him what he thought of Che. "Good man," he said. "Where are you going?" I countered, trying to change to a less controversial topic. "To Athens, to see my mother.

▷

*Parts of *NOMAN'S LAND* were compiled by Herman Asselberghs & Johan Grimonprez and appeared initially under the title *NERGENSLAND* in 'Dietsche Warande & Belfort', Leuven, October 1997
***My People Shall Live, Autobiography of a Revolutionary*, Leila Khaled, Hodder & Stoughton, London 1973

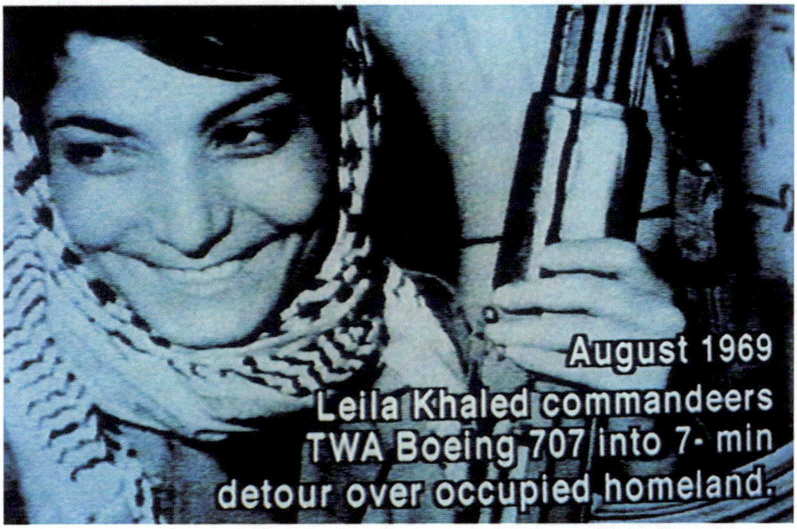

My eldest son Badr came home from kindergarten and puzzled me with the question if I was a thief. His teacher had told him that I had hijacked an airplane, and now he was wondering where I was hiding it.

WEAPONS GAVE ME WORDS

Der Spiegel: Ms. Khaled, do your sons Badr and Baschschar know that their mother is famous?
Khaled: They were bound to find out somehow. One day my eldest son, Badr, came home from kindergarten and asked me if I was a thief. His teacher had told him I had hijacked an airplane, and now he was wondering where I was hiding it.

Der Spiegel: Do you condone the terrorism practiced by Hamas?
Khaled: Acts of this kind are not committed for no reason. Our territory is still occupied despite the Oslo accord. Even the Charter of the United Nations ensures a person's right to resistance in such a case. Our people must continue the fight against the occupation force.
Der Spiegel: But after so many years of war and terror, wasn't it a great step forward when the Israelis and the Palestinians began talks?
Khaled: In the Gaza Strip and the West Bank our people live in ghettos. The Israelis can block off our cities and throw us in prison whenever they feel like it – they have done it before and now they are doing it again. They can do anything they want to us. Is that what you call peace?
Der Spiegel: And that makes it justifiable for Hamas to send suicide bombers to attack civilians?
Khaled: I believe it is legitimate to fight against the occupation force.
Der Spiegel: In August 1969 you shocked the world when you hijacked a plane from Rome to Damascus and then blew it to bits right there on the runway. Are you still able to justify this kind of terrorism?
Khaled: What I did then served to help my people. After the hijackings the whole world began asking: Who are these people? Why are they doing this? We showed that the Palestinians weren't just an impoverished nation looking for humanitarian handouts of flour and sugar. After the hijackings it was unmistakably clear to the world that my people had a reason to fight.

Der Spiegel: Later you flew as a normal passenger on numerous occasions. How would you have reacted if a freedom fighter, for example from East Timor, hijacked your plane?
Khaled: (laughs) I would have remained perfectly calm. I know perhaps better than anyone that there's nothing you can do when you have an armed terrorist standing in front of you.

Der Spiegel: In 1972 the retired Israeli General Ezer Weizman warned that you would never feel safe in Lebanon or anywhere else in the world. Did Mossad try to seize or kill you?
Khaled: Yes, in 1970 the Israelis fired six missiles at the house I was staying in Beirut. And once in 1971 I came home to find a bomb under my bed. I don't know why I happened to look under my bed that night, but lying there was a bundle of TNT. I assume it was the Mossad.

Der Spiegel: Your beauty also made a great impression on the world. Rumor has it that you underwent plastic surgery to change your facial features.
Khaled: Yes, that's right. After the first hijacking everyone knew my face. In order to capture the El Al airplane, I had to alter my appearance.
Der Spiegel: Where did the plastic surgeon make changes?
Khaled: On my nose and chin.
Der Spiegel: You sacrificed your beauty for the revolution?
Khaled: (laughs) Upon closer inspection you'll find that meanwhile everything is pretty much the way it was before.

Excerpts from an interview in *Der Spiegel: Die Waffe gab mir Würde. Former Hijacker Leila Khaled on Palestine, Peace, and Death. Der Spiegel* 11/1996, pp. 158-162, editor: Jürgen Hogrefe.
Translated by Kimi Lum.

14

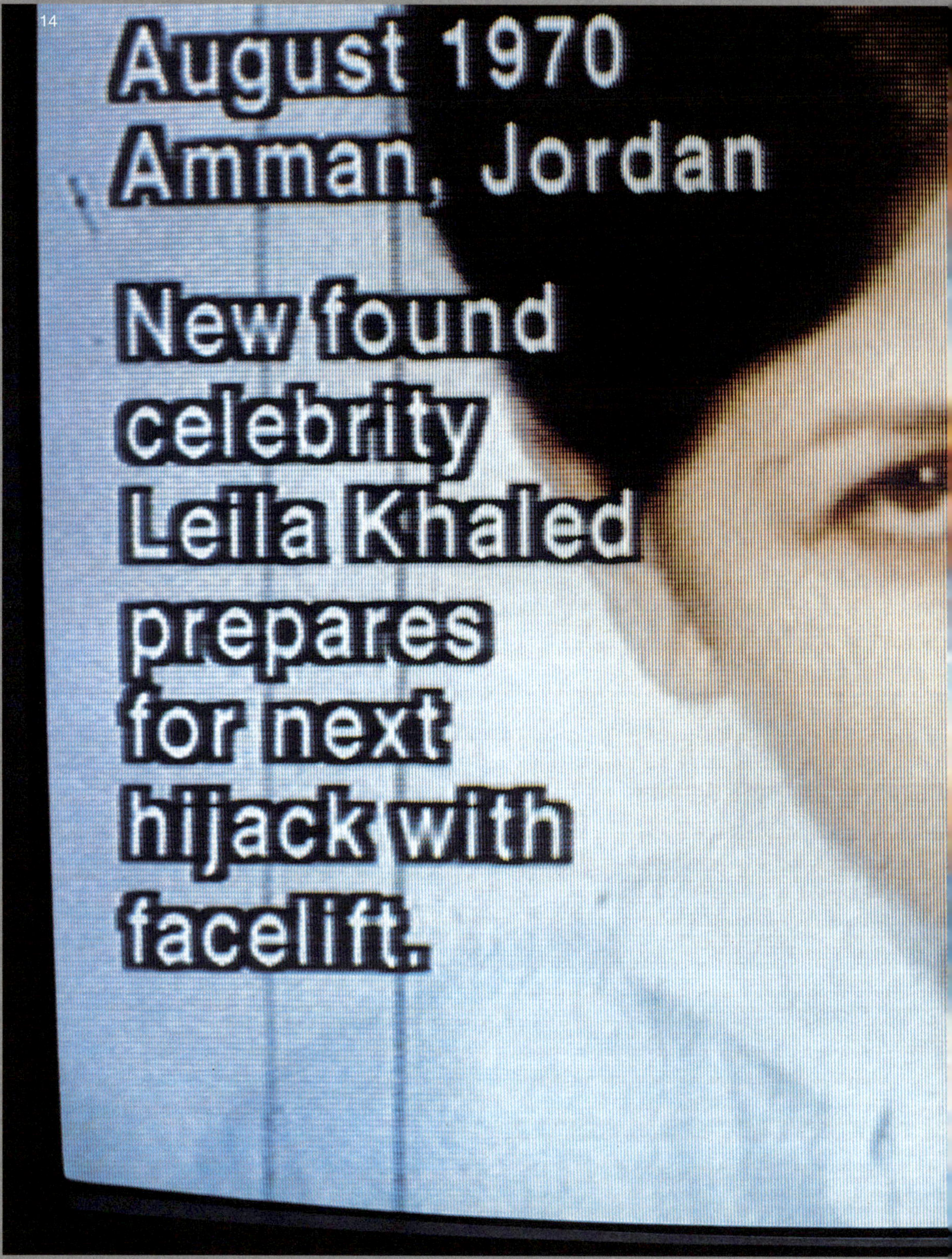
August 1970
Amman, Jordan
New found
celebrity
Leila Khaled
prepares
for next
hijack with
facelift.

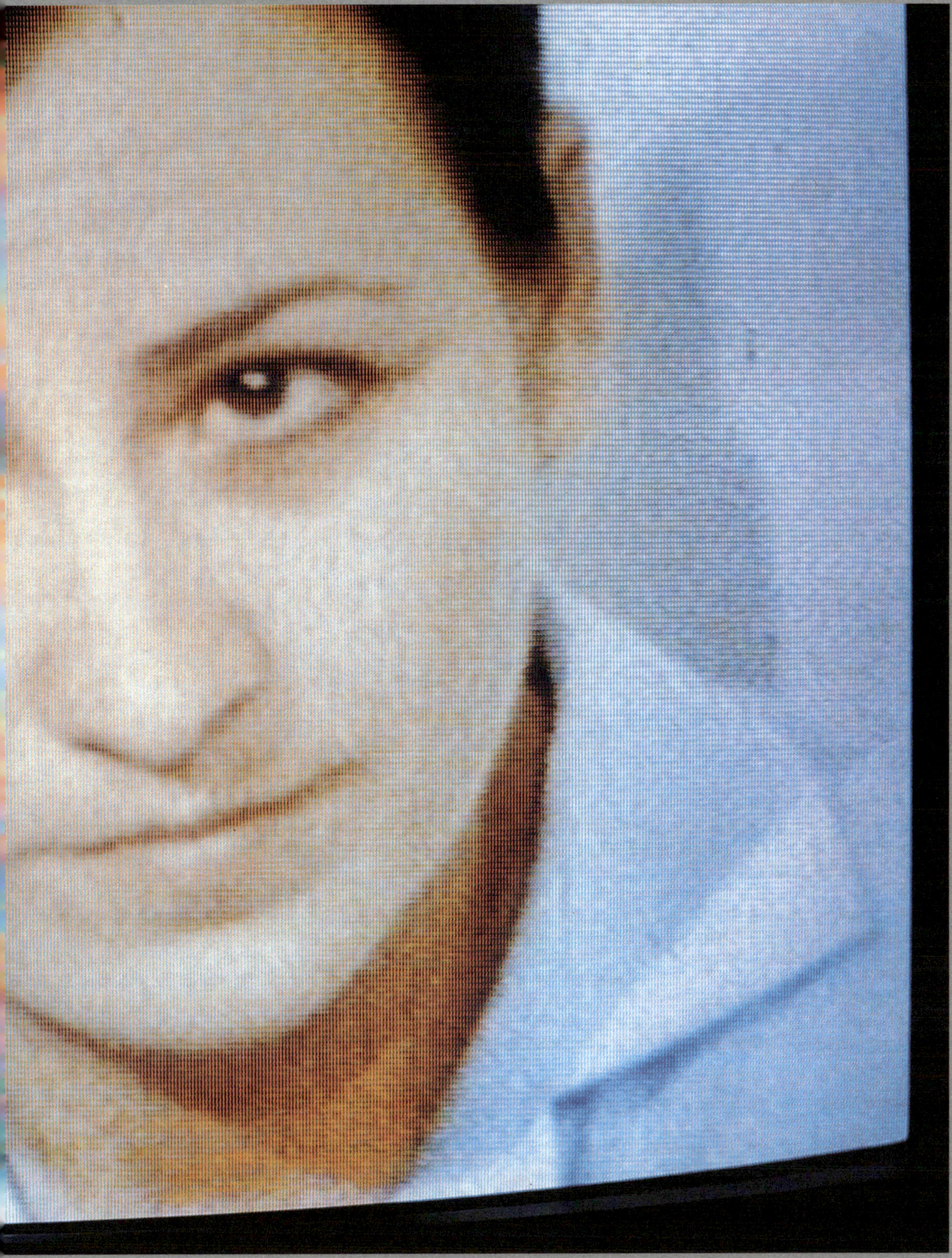

▷
I haven't seen her in fifteen years. I bet she's there already, waiting for me at the airport."
I was astounded, and almost told him, "You bloody fool, you'd better get off this plane, because it isn't going to Athens." I tried to ignore him and closed my ears to keep his voice from penetrating my inner conscience. I plunged into a nervous reading of My Friend Che.

The plane was airborne for only twenty minutes before the hostesses were graciously trying to serve their five first-class passengers. Neither Salim nor I was anxious to eat. The stewardesses were very solicitous. They offered us drinks and peanuts. Anything we wanted. I settled for a coffee, Salim for a beer. But they made us nervous, as they kept returning and asking us if we wanted anything else. I pretended that I had stomachache and asked for a blanket.
I innocently placed it over my lap, so I could take my hand grenade out of my purse and put my pistol right in the top of my trousers without being noticed. Salim asked for an aspirin tablet. I was afraid the stewardess might suspect something had she realized that two passengers opposite each other on the first row were sick. In any case, I dreaded the prospect of having a companion with a headache, so was relieved when he merely pocketed the aspirin.
Seconds after the only other male passenger in the first class section returned from the small lounge, I gestured to Salim to proceed to the cockpit. Just at that moment, another hostess carrying the crew's lunch trays was opening the door of the cockpit. Salim seized the opportunity and leapt in ahead of her. She screamed, "Oh, no!" and her trays flew in the air, causing much noise but no injury.
I was behind Salim and ordered the stewardess to get out of the way. She did, quivering and watching us over her shoulder. Salim was so huge that he blocked my view, and I couldn't see the reaction of the crew. I could however, hear him say that the plane had been taken over by the Che Guevara Commando Unit of PFLP, and announce that the new captain was Shadiah Abu Ghazalah.
In the middle of his speech, my pistol slipped down the leg of my trousers and, as I bent down to pick it up, I saw the bewildered looks on the crew's faces. I suppose all they could see was part of my wide-brimmed chic hat.
I felt ridiculous for a moment, laughed at my ineptness, put the pistol away, and entered the cockpit solemnly brandishing my hand grenade and declaring I was the new captain. The crew was completely shocked to see me there, but they showed no fear. To demonstrate my credibility, I immediately offered my predecessor, Captain Carter, the safety pin from my grenade as a souvenir. He respectfully declined it.

I observed that the plane had swerved off the course I charted for it. I ordered the captain not to play games if he wanted to reach our destination safely and put him on course again. Then Salim reminded me that fifteen minutes had elapsed since the passengers were asked to hold their hands behind their heads.
I quickly advised them to relax and to drink champagne if they so desired, and offered an apology for inconveniencing them.

The pilot asked, "What shall I do now?" I said, "Let's take a seven-minute tour of the fatherland." My father's image appeared before my eyes, and I could hear his voice saying, "When will we return home?" My whole world came together. I was silent. I looked out at the greenery and mountains of Palestine. I could see Tel Aviv below. I wept out of affection and longing, and said softly, "Father, we shall return. We shall redeem your honor and restore your dignity. We shall become the sovereign of the land some day." Suddenly, I remembered that the mission preceded personal emotions.
I instructed the pilot, "Go to Lebanon, where my people live as refugees." The Israeli planes continued to pursue us. At the Lebanese border, they zoomed anyway. I called Cyprus and sent greetings to its heroic anti-imperialist fighters, and sent messages to my people in South Lebanon. The pilot interrupted. "We must ask for clearance from Beirut." "We don't need to ask for clearance," I said. "This is an Arab country." We circled Beirut briefly before I ordered the pilot to go on to Damascus. He objected, "The airport there couldn't accommodate the Boeing 707." "Look, do you think we're so backward that we couldn't handle your damned plane?" I said strongly. He didn't respond. I took the microphone and addressed the passengers for the last time: "Evacuate immediately on landing; have a happy holiday in Syria."

SEPTEMBER 6 1970:

AFTER A CELEBRITY-TOUR OF THE ARAB WORLD, LEILA KHALED UNDERGOES FACIAL PLASTIC SURGERY TO PREPARE HER FOR HER SECOND RENDEZ-VOUS WITH HISTORY.

EVER SINCE THE 1969 TWA HIJACK EPISODE, KHALED'S PICTURE PLASTERS0 THE WALLS OF AIRPORTS WORLD WIDE, YET THERE IS HARDLY A GLIMMER OF RECOGNITION AS THE VETERAN SKYJACKER BOARDS AN EL AL FLIGHT 219 BOUND FOR NEW YORK. THIS TIME HER COMPANION IS PATRICK ARGUELLO AND SHE WEARS A 'WONDERBRA' MADE OF TWO GRENADES. THEY ATTEMPT TO DIVERT THE PLANE TO JOIN THEIR COMRADES AT A DESERTED MILITARY AIRSTRIP IN THE JORDANIAN DESERT. ON THIS INFAMOUS 'SKYJACK SUNDAY', A QUADRUPLE HIJACK SCENARIO WAS MASTERMINDED BY THE PALESTINIAN FRONT, BUT THE EL AL HIJACK IS FOILED AND LEILA KHALED APPREHENDED. THREE DAYS LATER, THE PFLP SEIZES A 5TH PLANE TO NEGOTIATE HER RELEASE FROM PRISON.

2. DESTINATION: REVOLUTION AIRPORT

I was obsessed with the idea of my mission. I rehearsed it every hour of my waking days. I roamed the city of Frankfurt for a few days, bored with the waiting; then I went to Stuttgart briefly and on to Amsterdam. Our rendez-vous with history was approaching: all plans had to be translated into action; history was ours to write; Patrick Arguello was to write it in blood, I was not so honored.
I met Patrick Arguello for the first time in September 1970, in front of the air terminal at Stuttgart. We briefed each other on our mutual assignment and reviewed the plan thoroughly. The following day we flew together to Frankfurt. At Frankfurt airport, Mr. Diaz (Patrick) was inspected as I watched the passengers of a TWA Tel Aviv-bound flight being thoroughly searched. I felt very happy that we were causing the enemy so much trouble."

As we waited PanAm Flight 840 arrived and I

▷

MY RENDEZ-VOUS WITH HISTORY WAS APPROACHING...

▷

happily remembered TWA flight 840 of August 29, 1969. I was not aware at that moment that two of our comrades, having been barred in an earlier attempt by the Israelis, were in their own to seize PanAm Flight 840 a half-hour after take-off.
They took the 747 to Cairo where they blew it up as a declaration of Palestinian independence. Neither Patrick nor any of the other five male hijackers knew that three planes were our targets that day.
Only the three female Palestinian captains and a handful of other leaders knew of the entire plan. We lingered in the waiting room until about twelve-o-five. There was still no sign of the El-Al counter staff.
Suddenly an armed police officer in Israeli uniform emerged.
"Why are you late?" he demanded.
I accommodatingly explained, "We arrived at ten o'clock, officer," and suggested that he ask the KLM hostess, who vouched for us.
"Your passport please," he said. Both Patrick and I showed him our passports without comment. The officer carefully examined each page. He looked at my photograph and then back at me several times. He paced back and forth as he addressed us. He asked me to empty my handbag and identify every item in it, which I did. I looked completely normal. Patrick was wearing a business suit and I was dressed in a mini-skirt and jacket.
I did not pretend to be other than calm Maria Sanchez from Honduras. Routine questions went on for several minutes. Suddenly I heard loud voices. I saw three Arabs walking in my direction. My heart sank. I knew and recognized one of them. What if he greeted me? We would be exposed immediately. Fortunately the Israeli officer had his back to them. Since we were already holding hands for his benefit, I quickly threw my arms around Patrick. He seemed a little surprised, but what man will rebuff a woman under such conditions? The embrace lasted until my Arab friend passed by unnoticed by the El-Al officer or anyone else.
The officer seemed untroubled by us. Politely he invited us to go with him to the basement to check our baggage. "Officer, our luggage is open, you could inspect it any time you like," I said. "Regulations state, Madam," he explained, "that owners must be present." We happily agreed. The officer was no amateur. He systematically went through every item not once, but twice.
He asked informal but pertinent questions as he inspected our possessions.
Then he pointedly turned to me and asked: "Has anyone given you any gifts?" "No," I replied emphatically. "Do you have anything sharp or dangerous?" "Such as?" I said. "Such as a pistol, a knife or anything sharp?" "No Sir. What would a girl like me ever do with a pistol or knife, officer?"

As we re-entered the hall, I saw some thirty or forty youngsters waiting to board EL-Al flight 219. I was shocked and secretly lamented that once again I had to face the agonizing problem of what to do to avoid hurting children. I love children and I know they are free from guilt. Although I remembered the children of Palestine napalmed by the Israelis and Dr. Haddad's child running out of his flaming room, I nevertheless vowed to do my utmost not to jeopardize the lives of passengers needlessly.

At that moment Patrick prepared his hand grenade and pistol, and I pulled the safety pins off my two hand grenades and rushed forward through the first class section and towards the cockpit. We shouted "Don't move," as some of the passengers tried to take over. Three stewards were in front of us wielding handguns. In a couple of seconds I could count six guns. But we had anticipated a battle: A hostess fell to the ground crying to me in Arabic. I threatened to blow up the plane if anyone fired at us. I displayed my two grenades and dropped the safety pins on the floor hoping to convince everyone we intended business and to avert a bloody battle. Patrick held the armed stewards and the passengers at bay. "Go ahead, I'll protect your back," he instructed me. I forced the hostess to stand up and walk ahead of me. The moment she opened the door, she staggered forward in a state of panic.
I couldn't see the captain or crew.
Shots were fired. There was another door before we could reach the pilot's cabin. Both of us banged on the door. No one opened the door. Suddenly someone was looking at us through a spyhole. I brandished my hand grenades and ordered him to open the door or else. I heard more shots and the plane went into a spin.
Several people attacked me at the same moment. I thought the plane was disintegrating. The firing continued and suddenly I found myself besieged by a pack of wolves, El-Al staff as well as passengers. Someone screamed "Don't shoot at her! She has two hand grenades." No one fired at me. But some people were kicking me, others hitting. A few just stepped all over me.
Two were holding my hands and trying to take away the grenades. One finally succeeded in prying one grenade from me without exploding him and the plane. I held tightly the other until I was knocked unconscious for a second and was overpowered.
At first I didn't know what was happening to Patrick. Within a few minutes I was dragged to the first-class compartment where Patrick was lying, bleeding profusely and breathing heavily. I could see he was still alive.
The Zionists were acting like mad dogs. They trampled over every part of our bodies. By the time Patrick was too week to resist. I was fighting like a caged lion. I fought until I was completely exhausted.
Then a vicious thug pounced on me, pulled my hair mercilessly, called me a wicked bitch, a malicious Arab and all sorts of obscene names. I spat contemptuously in his face. I bit his hands. He and others around me beat me incessantly for several minutes.
The plane was travelling smoothly; the remaining passengers were staying in their seats. Suddenly an Israeli guard emerged from the cockpit area. Patrick was lying on his side. The man turned him over on his stomach and started tying him up with wires and a necktie. Someone asked, "How are they?" A voice replied "We don't know. He is ... we're not sure. She's threequarters dead." The man stepped on Patrick's hips and Patrick looked at me in agony, his hands tied behind his back. Then the Zionist guard fired four shots into Patrick's back.
Someone screamed from the back of the plane "Please stop the bloodshed.
Please, Please, Please!" The four shots that were fired into Patrick's back were fired from a distance of less than one foot.
Patrick looked at me, gave me a deathly smile, and bid me an eternal goodbye.

Post-Documentary, Post-Photography?
Martha Rosler
2001

"The penalty of realism is that it is about reality and has to bother for ever not about being 'beautiful' but about being right." So wrote John Grierson, the man considered the "father of documentary film," the person who named the genre and helped establish documentary film in the English-speaking world. Grierson is pointing here to the dichotomies of accuracy and aesthetics, the criteria by which we have come to judge the worth of documentary imagery. But documentary—a practice that began and flourished with the twentieth century and may indeed die with it—is undergoing profound challenges from multiple sources, on social, political, and ethical grounds. These challenges, which radically undermine photography's fundamental claim to a unique capacity to offer a direct insight into the real, have produced something of a crisis among artists and intellectuals and troubled some in journalism and the legal professions, if not others in the wider audience. My aim here is to explore some of the attributes and functions of social documentary photography in the postmodern world.

Recently an artist friend and I had a conversation about the effects of exhibiting lush photos of transvestites and transsexual prostitutes of color. My friend (herself a woman of color) quickly made what amounted to a common argument underlying documentary—namely, that it humanizes the so-called Other and promotes identification between the viewer and people so regarded. My concern about this particular line of argument was that the barriers to identification, particularly in this era of scapegoating, are too high to be vaulted over, and not easily with spectacular color images of people having such highly marked appearances and ascribed identities.

But, my friend asked, what if the photographer saw herself as part of the subjects' milieu? This is an argument that had been made about, say, Diane Arbus's work in the 1960s. I responded that a photographer's intentions are unrecoverable from most images. Well, then, would including quotations from the people pictured lessen the distance between them and other viewers? Similar projects in the populist 1970s, such as Bill Owens's *Suburbia,* didn't appear to decrease that symbolic distance very much. In that instance, the recorded (or approximated) remarks may increase the psychological distance from those who on the surface might seem to be "just like me." The inclusion of purported quotations, clearly, changes the nature of the transaction between image and viewer; the subject speaks, whereas in a caption what is pictured is spoken about. But the subject's enunciation alone will not overcome the power of framing elements, which include the preexisting attitudes of viewers rooted in dominant discourses. The muteness of a photograph of someone different from the viewer may paradoxically be more effective in inviting projection, empathy, or pity than even the same photo representing a speaking subject, because the icon is universalized and depoliticized. Still, there is always a text somewhere—even when it starts with and departs from physical appearance as an index of character.

In the particular project my friend and I were discussing, the subjects were pleased by their photos and their public reception. This appears to be a powerful argument, but whether even well-received photographic projects do much to lessen social stigma needs to be confirmed rather than assumed. Ultimately, my friend reaffirmed her belief in the power of identification. She argued that the aesthetic power of the photographs significantly increased the likelihood of the social acceptance of the people portrayed. On my part, I wondered what role images can really play in promoting acceptance of Others by familiarizing viewers with physical appearances (and identities) with which they have had little real-life experience. The fixity and iconicity of still images, particularly portraits, continue to worry me; I suspect that moving images—film and television—as opposed to still photos of entertainers are potentially far more powerful in reducing social stereotyping, although even they also may ultimately be ineffectual. We have gotten well used to images of Others without necessarily seeing them as "Us." But perhaps identitarian times breed identitarian projects. "Ethnographic" images of people "performing identities" may confirm difference as distance. But there are questions of representation that go beyond

1 John Grierson, in *Documentary News Letter*, quoted in James Beveridge, *John Grierson, Film Master* (New York and London: Macmillan and Collier, 1978), 178; and in Forsyth Hardy, ed., *Grierson on Documentary* (London: Faber & Faber, 1966), 249. Grierson was no revolutionary but a proponent of democratic participation who believed that imagination was needed to help citizens make sense of events and of the news. I cite him here because his influence has been so pervasive.

the social reevaluation of foreigners or local subcultures. Documentary, journalistic, and news photography, rather than seeking to promote understanding, may aim to provoke, to horrify, or to mobilize sentiment against a generalized danger or a specific enemy or condition. In any case, our discussion brought to mind all the questions surrounding the social power and epistemological understandings (as opposed to the aesthetic qualities alone) of certain forms of photography.

It is true, of course, that *all* forms of representation call forth questions of responsibility and perhaps of descriptive accuracy, but those evoked by photographic representation are unique. The apparent truth value of photography and film has made them powerfully effective vehicles for reportage and commentary. Of all photographic practices, social documentary—the self-professed truth-teller, implicated in modernity and part of its "life world"—is the one in which the underlying issues of social power are accessible to contestation. Until recently there has been little reason to question photographic accuracy (and then only in specific instances, not globally in respect to the practice itself), and many reasons—notably the immense commercial and bureaucratic usefulness of photography to the mass media, advertising, police, and the family—to accept it. But over the past few decades, photography and photographic practices have been subjected to attacks on all fronts. Striking to the heart of the matter, the Sunday *New York Times Magazine*, addressing the great suburban middle class, in March 1997 proclaimed right on the cover, "Documentary film makers have to manipulate reality in order to make their art, even if that means exploiting their subjects." This implies that filmmakers are also manipulating—and exploiting—their audience; "reality" is sold out in favor of "art." What is said here about documentary filmmaking can be said as well of documentary still photography, despite the imperative toward narrativity of the time-based medium. But documentary, whether still or moving, precisely as an "art-ful" practice, can hardly escape the inclination toward some form of dramatization.

In the advanced industrial world, the questioning of who is speaking, and from where, has occurred in the context of a wider cultural suspicion— or delegitimation—of political authority as well as of the truth and objectivity of journalism. Narrative theory and discourse analysis, analyzing the structure and situatedness of communication, have further enlivened the distinction between truth and accuracy in representation. And the status of the photographic image as a faithful representation of sheer "visuality" is radically impeached by the wide availability of computer programs that easily manipulate and alter the image. As digital imaging technologies are being developed at a gallop, they bring the ability to capture and manipulate both still and moving imagery to every consumer with a home computer and the entry price to the right gadgetry. This domestication blurs the line between still and moving imagery and its sources, further threatening the epistemological status of both. The "photograph" itself, a fixed physical outcome of a mentality and a mode of production, is receding from common exchange (leading premier photo schools and departments to shut down their "wet" darkrooms). The tide of change poses its own particular threat to documentary, since "post-photographic" practice at a minimum can be said to have abandoned any interest in indexicality and, perhaps just as importantly, in the privileged viewpoint of "witness"—and therefore any embeddedness in a particular moment in time and space. The photograph seems poised to mutate into just another, relatively ephemeral, aesthetic form and its maker into an artist. What will determine the outcome of this unstable condition is not clear.

Thus, post-structural and postcolonial discourses, along with digital technologies, have undermined the subject position of the photographer (and the cultural milieu into which the images are inserted) and the epistemological status of the image—its relationship to a phenomenologically present visual reality—denigrating its (metonymic) adequacy in relation to the situation it depicts and problematizing the ability of *any* image of a visual field to convey lived experience, custom, tradition, or history.

Through much of its working history, documentary's burden of truth has shouldered aside aesthetic matters in favor of a variety of other issues, leaving aesthetics to surface seemingly as an afterthought—as Grierson's remarks, quoted above, suggest. Nevertheless, documentarians have explicitly called upon the aesthetic dimension of their work as a kind of necessary surplus that protects them from charges of propagandizing, so that the language of aesthetic appreciation is always available to "rescue" documentary from itself—that is, from its own truth claims. This trope, far from being born of postmodern doubt, was already typical of modernism, an insertion of unstated commentary between "the sheer sensation" of the image and its reception by the viewer or, in contrast, a heightening of meaning in the face of flat reality. The poetics of form can lead to a reception of images as poetic, a form of personalized address that escapes either responsibility or reportorial accuracy, though it may of course increase the force of truth, but as subjectivized witness rather than objective reportage.

Documentary is currently experiencing another sort of crisis in that it is losing access to a mass public via print journalism as well as losing a fair chunk of that public's interest, which is more and more attuned to television and to accounts of the real refracted through the distorting prisms of sensationalism, voyeurism, and what might be called a neo-gothic sensibility (and the apparently rank naturalism of "reality television"). Perhaps, then, documentary really is a dying practice; but there is much to consider before consigning it to the ash can of history. Photography (now over 150 years old) and film (about 100) have never been stable practices and are continually changing. Both the production and the interpretation of photographic imagery are made according to prevailing social and historical trends.

Photographers who work outside the studio are sometimes accused of having a ghoulish addiction to misery and, worse, of profiting financially from the desperation of others. The accusation, often leveled at war photographers, is also increasingly directed at documentarians. A number of years ago, the well-known and widely respected (white) American documentarian Eugene Richards was at the center of an editorial controversy over his book on the social effects of crack cocaine in an urban ghetto. The charge was racism—that his work was part of the media's unflagging stream of images of drug-taking blacks, which (even apart from contextualization) leads to a greatly exaggerated idea of the percentage of African Americans engaged in crime. The photographer was infuriated and hurt by such a response. In a letter to a newspaper he ascribed it to the handy bugaboo of "political correctness." The argument here revolves not around sympathy or understanding for the poor but over the interpretation of the motivation for socially and personally destructive behavior and whether those pictured are worthy of blame for their own depicted actions. Richards's long-established interest in representing the life of America's poor people, especially the urban poor, may make his motives and methods in obtaining his images unassailable, but the wider African American community has no obligation to ignore the context of reception of his, and related, work—which includes not only the nightly television news and the tabloid press but also a political climate of racial demonization, downsizing, and disentitlement.

Similar difficulties have arisen with respect to images from abroad. The end of European empires, the social movements of the 1960s and beyond, and the political needs of the West, have amplified the demands of the world's unrepresented and oppressed for both political autonomy and—more prominently than ever before—cultural self-representation. The mission of documentary photographers, often self-assumed, of speaking for the oppressed or disregarded is no longer casually ceded to those from privileged countries or groups. The wherewithal to produce some forms of self-representation, or to intervene in representation produced by and for the (former) First World, or by and for a social majority at home, is much closer to hand than ever before. Entertainment and information media are undergoing consolidation and globalization, and cultural hegemony is exercised around the world by Western (not to say U.S.) media. But one result is that reports from elsewhere meant for Western consumption are likely to be viewed as well by those who inhabit what used to be the barely imagined peripheries of empire, residents of the selfsame "elsewhere." Clearly, some disruption to documentary and photojournalistic practices has been caused by the blurring boundary between citizenship and spectatorship.

A case in point: An English "alternative" political magazine, the *New Internationalist,* decides to produce an issue on coffee, tracing it back to the growers from the dining rooms of the developed world. A reporter and a photographer visit a coffee-growing area in the southern Peruvian Andes. A local official of the coffee cooperative serves as guide and translator. The group drops in on the man's elderly parents at their farm; the photographer obtains a posed portrait. Later, the son, in London to help complete the issue, worries that showing his parents in their work clothes is disrespectful. He is persuaded, however, that the image is *accurate* and therefore important. His misgivings are published in the magazine along with the photo (a print of which goes home to the parents). If the son weren't working with the magazine, the ethical question might not have been articulated, but how often have subjects had second thoughts about appearing in published photos taken in circumstances more uncontrolled than these? Folkloric portraits and photos of peasants at work are routine for such a story, the stock in trade of *National Geographic;* yet this magazine was attempting to demystify the relation between Third World producers and First World consumers. In other, more pointed situations, reactions to "outside" photographers can be explosive.

In time-honored fashion, the images of people engaged in the production of consumer goods at the heart of viewers' lives are intended to awaken conscience over the disparity between the two sets of life circumstances. Since advertising photography sometimes supplies images of colorful natives for this purpose (Juan Valdez, the long-established figure

2 Most histories of photography (and some histories of documentary film and video) tend to take a position of technological determinism in which the development of new and ever lighter, more portable, more automatic apparatuses of reproduction determine what kinds of things can be photographed or filmed and thus what *will be* photographed or filmed. Technological change does not, in my estimation, drive social events; rather, technological developments are accomplished within a framework of social and economic imperatives, although in practice this is a complex relationship in which technology also organizes experience and functions as a means of social control. See also "Image Simulations, Computer Manipulations: Some Considerations," reprinted in this volume [*Decoys and Disruptions: Selected Writings, 1975-2001* (Cambridge, MA/London: The MIT Press, 2004) -ed.].

concocted to represent the Colombian coffee-growers' association's advertising campaign, comes to mind), photographers wish to supply counterimages. (Even Lewis Hine, in his *Making Human Junk*, consciously produced counteradvertising to the popular "making healthy children" advertising of the early-twentieth- century food industry.)

Although socially disempowered people may object to being photographed or filmed, in some cases they seek news coverage; the (right) camera is now even more pointedly recognizable as an instrument of power, and the desire for a large megaphone may conflict with a palpable desire to thwart the bearer of bad news.

Some see in all this the end to the legitimate role of the documentarian from "outside." Unfortunately, such a position, while understandable and to some degree even necessary, is problematic, presupposing that the identities—or roles or experiences—in question are straightforwardly recognizable (Indian peasants, transvestites, or African Americans, say) and uncomplicatedly singular (Peruvian, American, poor) or that they assume a hierarchy within the individual (being a peasant, being black, or being poor is more determining than being a woman or being an Indian, and so forth). The doctrine of no exogenous narration may, in addition, rely on an essentialist interpretation of identity and have a positivist and empiricist bias that tends to privilege appearance over interpretation. For those with a psychoanalytic—or indeed another analytic—proclivity, it can be less than satisfying.

On an entirely different plane, it rejects the notion of alliances, assuming that social movements are necessarily autonomous as well as constituted and led from within. But social documentary has tended to assume a humanist and generally universal ethical basis in the society to which it has been directed, or to see itself as directly attuned, often militantly, to the interests of the photographic subjects. I say more about the assumptions behind documentary further on, after a brief telling of elements of its history.

Arthur Rothstein wrote about his widely reproduced photograph *The Dust Storm* (1936), of a farmer and his sons trudging through a dust-beclouded landscape:

> In the beginning it was a record, after which it became a news picture, then it became a feature photograph, eventually an historical photograph, and now it's considered a work of art in most museums. It has a life of its own.

A defining element of a documentary image is its particularity, that it represents a specific spatiotemporal "what-is." But the ability to evoke identification, when there is no clear-cut context of group membership, means a loss of specificity in favor of a more universal appeal, or perhaps a certain mythic element. (The precise identity, as opposed to group identity, of the individual before the lens is not generally of interest—these are not, after all, celebrities.) With the passage of time, specificity fades and projection more easily does its work. Furthermore, the criteria employed by aesthetic judgment evolve, partly under pressure of photographic practices. There is no use in trying to pin down photographic, or cultural, meaning outside a context of reception.

SOME AMERICAN DOCUMENTARY PRACTICES

Alongside context is history, including the foundational history of the photographic practices in question. Photography played a notable role in campaigns for social betterment in turn-of-the-twentieth-century United States. The Danish-born New York newspaperman Jacob Riis enlisted photography for a brief time in his housing crusade. Riis had little concern for the aesthetic element of his photos, for he saw them as evidentiary; the images were initially taken by someone else hired to accompany him on midnight police raids, and convenience alone led him to begin taking them himself. Riis hardly considered the transaction between himself and his photographic subjects; he saw them as symptomatic—representatives of the ill-housed urban poor, many of them newly arrived immigrants, and his interest did not extend far beyond that role. Riis was countering the idea of poverty as synonymous with moral decay and was portraying his poverty-stricken subjects as victims of an impossible situation unprotected by law. His appeal was to law, routed through the consciences and judgments of

3 Not all such conflicts, by any means, hinge on what we have come to call identity, whether essentialist (biology, race, ethnicity), cultural, national, or sex- and gender-related. Shared experience, such as being involved in a strike, having a certain kind of job, or living in a certain neighborhood, are also the sorts of things documentary might address but which are not, in the present understanding, primary identities. Furthermore, postcolonial discourse has highlighted the very instability of identities—and not only ethnic or national ones—pointing out that they are constructed by the universes of discourse that we inhabit, and we assuredly inhabit more than one.

4 As an aside, I note that it is an oversimplification to treat the appeal of documentary as always from one group or class to another. Nevertheless, most documentary practices presuppose a mass-market model, in which elites with the power to produce and disseminate messages will, through a gate-keeping process, direct them to nonelites.

5 Arthur Rothstein, *Words and Pictures* (New York: Amphoto, 1979).

6 A small motion toward its use in this manner, in the case of the London charity for street children run by Dr. Barnardo, came to a litigious end. See "In, around, and after-thoughts (on documentary photography)," reprinted in *Decoys and Disruptions*.

the new modernizing elites, on the assumption (not unjustified) that poor immigrants, and native-born blacks, could not themselves effectively mount such appeals.

A more sophisticated photographic practice was developed soon after by Lewis Hine, often in the pursuit of legislative changes relating to work— such as regulating or ending child labor. Hine, a young teacher who came to documentary already concerned with photographic aesthetics, was hired by crusading social-work organizations and magazines. For Riis, ethics (moralism, actually) drove his use of photography, but matters relating to individual subjects lay outside his ethical compass; for Hine, aesthetics were married to ethical concerns. The persuasive power of the photograph, he believed, greatly depended on its formal elements, yet he never treated his subjects merely as representative ciphers. Even under difficult circumstances (he frequently lied his way into factory situations, from which he was otherwise excluded by the owners and managers), in researching child labor he took the time to learn the names of those he photographed and to ascertain their occupations, their ages, and other pertinent information, information that often figured in the essays and articles employing his photos. Unlike Riis, Hine also attempted to engage in a transaction with the subjects that resulted in a dignified yet responsive pose.

Hine's concern for his subjects' dignity, evidenced in his images of labor as well as in his portraits of tenement families, led to a strategy opposite to Riis's raw naturalism. Hine's entire concept of the political sphere and the participation of poor people, especially in their role as workers, differed from that of Riis. Both attempted to link the moral order to the political order. Despite Hine's constancy, he no more than Riis could promise the direct utility of his project to the person before the lens; that is not the nature of the documentary transaction, which is an argument about the experience of a class or category of people, as I have suggested above. The stark, often adversarial quality of Riis's photos is a powerful signal of their "truth value," whereas Hine's formal control in many of his images suggests a photographer's advocacy. The people in Riis's photos were caught in the act of being victims (oft-times complicit ones) of their terrible surroundings and existential conditions, whereas Hine's were often shown poised between moments of activity, often at work in poor and exploitative circumstances but within the stream of life and time so different from the airless stasis of Riis's subjects, who seem almost outside the possibility of any dynamic movement forward. And despite the vastly different approaches of the two—the naturalistic artlessness of Riis, the careful realism of Hine—and their disparate relationship to photography and its uses, time and the workings of the art world have transmuted both these outsiders into notable figures. Their work is accepted into the roster of important historical photographic practices because of its foundational role, bringing their formal properties into the register of the aesthetic.

One of Hine's young students, the New Yorker Paul Strand, was inspired by a visit to Alfred Stieglitz's art galleries to become "an artist in photography"—but without the European-influenced pictorialism promoted by Stieglitz. Strand built on English debates about photographic aesthetics, which hinged on how best to arrive at aesthetic value without excessive artifice or concern with surface detail. Strand's work was revolutionary in its embrace of modernist ideas, all but abandoning romantic pastoralism in favor of an eager look at the life of now—yet a significant portion of his work was concerned with natural form and with rural and peasant life. In the teens, Strand produced a series of candid portraits of New Yorkers—poor, elderly men and women (generally taken with a trick camera whose lens appeared to point elsewhere). Unlike Hine, Strand appears to have been concerned with them as exemplars, but his moral concerns were also very different from those of Riis. His appeal seems not to have been to the polity as a body of laws (or to the aesthetic faculties via the document) but to the moral order as an ideal implicit in the life of a modern urban democratic nation; unlike Riis and Hine, Strand (at that moment, at least) was not involved in specific reform campaigns. Strand's interest appeared to be not only in reforming photographic aesthetics but in establishing an iconography of the marginal that afforded them respect through full incorporation into the physiognomy of the human. What Strand was after depended on the shock of confronting the viewing public with those considered unworthy of attention. These early works show his subjects in the everyday world, their subjectivities hinted at but coiled up, driven inward by isolating circumstance or personal reserve.

SOME ASSUMPTIONS

As this early history suggests, documentary engages with structural injustices, often to provoke active responses. Much of its appeal stems from what might be called the physiognomic fallacy: the identification of the image of a face with character, a body-centered essentialism. An alternative to American psychologism is suggested by the approach developed in the 1920s through the 1940s by the German photographer

7 Riis, like all photographers of the day (and many photojournalists today), also obtained set-up and posed images.

August Sander, who was loosely associated with the *Neue Sachlichkeit* (New Objectivity) movement. Sander's taxonomy of German society through a large number of portraits of people occupying every possible social location was far more concerned with a representation of a person as an ensemble of self, setting, and social role than with challenging the viewer to concoct a psychology of the individuals or a reading of their character. These people, whether beggar, gypsy, thief, artist, circus performer, soldier, capitalist, wife, or manager, are unquestionably embedded in a complex yet knowable, decipherable structured society.

The concepts of "citizenship" that I have suggested here in germ suggest powerful motives for documentary production. The logic of capital, with its division of society into expropriators and expropriated, has functioned as a powerful underlying assumption for documentary through much of this century, providing images of "society's losers"—its victims—and occasionally of its winners, who are less often directly identified as its victimizers. But this division of the world may not have the force it did just yesterday. Political scientist Robert Meister argues, for example, that post-structuralism—on the basis of readings of Nietzsche, as well as of Hegel by Alexandre Kojève and his students, among them Michel Foucault—radically questions the rhetoric of victims and victimizers. Post-structuralism, in Meister's view, rejects the "demonization" of any member of an oppressive system; thus, calling people victimizers, whether for their behavior or their class characteristics, is considered an unacceptable error, both analytically and ethically. Even the class of capitalism's beneficiaries cannot be named as oppressors, since as in Foucault's analysis, power resides everywhere in society. In Nietzschean terms, the "will to power" means that those who are oppressed also oppress and would do so in greater measure if given the opportunity to turn the tables.

In postmodern times—in which it cannot be assumed that for the good of the collective whole, groups or individuals will willingly take less in order for others to have more—explanations of oppressive social practices, of classes of beneficiaries, and appropriate structural reforms are all contested, along with the hypostatization of the notion of "victimhood" as an abstract category of explanations of differential social power. If there are no victims—or if, what amounts to the same thing, we are all equally victims—then there are no oppressors. Social inequality appears to be produced by a system without active human agents or collective remedies. At the end point of such logics, naming "the system"—capitalism, say—as the oppressor leads to no change, since there are no steps that can be taken that do not tread on someone's toes. Patently, no practice of social documentary that sees itself as providing evidence of structural injustice can flourish where there is no model of social progress, of implied routes to get to a better place.

I have already suggested alternative explanations of documentary imagery that might present themselves: psychologistic stasis, dehistoricized universal "truth," a depoliticized visual typology of social "losers"—the homeless, single mothers, battered women, inner-city residents, crack users, happy-go-lucky bums—or even of "winners," all without any presumed idea of wrongs or remedies, all iconographies of myth. But before any of these explanations take hold, there is a more basic axiom, that of credibility, the fundamental issue in the reception of documentary imagery.

DOCUMENTARY PRACTICES AND CREDIBILITY

At one time, reconstructions and restaging were acceptable as documentary, but now photographic believability requires a discreet distancing from (inescapable) formal visual and dramatic tropes. More important, it requires a balance of trust in the photographer and the medium of distribution of the resultant imagery. Despite the radical questioning of the truth value of documentary, every day, countless times a day, images that document events, in the form of news photos and documentation, are produced and received in a great variety of forms and at a growing host of sites of reception. Although a judicial body may, because of the possibility of digital manipulation, now be prodded to disbelieve photographic evidence, the public by and large still trusts images it sees in the daily newspaper and on the evening news. Aside from the privileging of the apparatus itself, it is on the specific codes of production of news imagery that the acceptance of this infinitude of images rests. The durability of the reputation of objectivity of the apparatus, buttressed

8 There is a further problem, according to Meister's analysis (in *Political Identity: Thinking through Marx* [London: Basil Blackwell, 1990] and "Logics of Space and Time in the Demystification of Capitalism," unpublished paper), in identifying the perpetrators of social oppression with its beneficiaries. Using the recent conflict in Rwanda as an example, one can argue that the perpetrators of the genocide were not its beneficiaries. In South Africa, where the beneficiaries (most whites) were not the perpetrators (those who operated the police state), meaningful structural reform may be thwarted when the beneficiaries of oppression are asked to shoulder the collective guilt implied by redistribution of wealth and power—a viewpoint echoed in the United States in arguments attacking affirmative-action policies.

9 What I mean by "the privileging of the apparatus" is simply this: In the absence of hints of unreliability, people believe what the image shows. In the so-called amateur videotapes picked up by news media for use in high-profile court cases, such as the touchstone Rodney King case, the apparatus is seen as the primary actor and witness, and its operator is forgotten.

by the (apparent) reliability of the medium, overwhelms all but the most inescapable doubts about the image. But the audience certainly recognizes the stylistic markers of "actuality" photography and, more pertinently, moving footage, which have been imported into advertising and music television and purposefully distorted in the burgeoning genre of docudrama and real-crime shows. The artless quality of "snapshots" that art photographers once sought so energetically to avoid has become a reigning style in photography and advertising, having first been routed through the hand-held camera style of "cinéma vérité" and pop.

Over the past couple of decades, color has expanded into news photography from personal and commercial photography and produced powerful dislocations, since serious news had been so long identified with black-and-white photography. Yet color is now sufficiently normalized that black- and-white imagery may seem mannered and artificial (as it has been presented in music television and advertising). Highly saturated color film enhances the aestheticization of the image, producing eye-catchingly beautiful images of crime scenes, battlefields, slums, and mean streets—rendering them the visual equal of green acres and luxury residences. (The paradoxical aestheticism of black-and-white imagery has produced a still-evolving situation with no place for truth value to rest easy.) The use of color in documentary is still uncommon, and its aestheticism problematic, for it is hard to hang onto the literalness of the image without the direct headline-related news value.

Photographic credibility is strongly conditioned by codes of professionalization. Photojournalism was well-established in the decades after the First World War, aided by the new European mass-circulation picture magazines. Later decades produced a highly professionalized corps of photojournalists. The codified ethics of news reportage entailed maintaining a wall of separation between photographer and subject (rules suspended, by popular demand, during wartime, when news reportage is meant to support far more than to inform; under pressure of nationalism, partisanship easily aces objectivity). Documentary and photojournalistic practices overlap but are still distinguishable from one another. Photojournalists are primarily employed to work on specific journalistic "stories," supplying images while others provide copy, and their feelings and sympathies about what they are photographing remain unsolicited. In contrast, documentarians choose their subjects and treat them as they will, but with no guarantee of publication. In reality, however, many photographers engage in both practices, and the same images may function in both frames as well. Journalistic ethics may prescribe honesty, objectivity, and responsibility to the subject, but they privilege the document, which supersedes all but the most urgent interests of the individuals involved. Responsibility is to society—that is, to readers and viewers.[13] In another sense, however, for journalists, whether photographers or reporters, the most crucial thing is to protect the professional status of the practitioners and the practice itself through the establishment of "objectivity" (but the unstated rules of war photography expose the relativity of this standard).

Especially for those being photographed, the photographer is sometimes seen as an interloper, "selling papers" through sensationalism or furthering the editor's or publisher's ideological and political agenda. But we all pay a price for summarily dismissing journalistic claims of objectivity—namely, the end to the demands for representational responsibility to the subject, whether in terms of a true and faithful account of appearances and behaviors or in terms of satisfying the subject's desires.

There is a long-standing documentary subgenre, namely "street photography," filling this niche of

10 A fuller account would detail the origins of "street photography" as an outgrowth of documentary and allied with war photography. Further, there were professional photojournalists before the turn of the century, including the American Frances Benjamin Johnston, most of whose work was imbued with the Progressive ideals of the era. Friendly with ruling Republican elites, she produced sympathetic portrayals of Native Americans, southern blacks, and women workers intended to promote their incorporation into the mainstream of the American working class; that this practice occludes difference and supports the now-discredited practice of radical separation of native peoples and "minorities" from traditional languages and practices hardly needs to be said. This was the America of great industrial and demographic transformation, an era of social work reformers, primarily women, whose advocacy for the poor was useful to nervous elites whose politics of social incorporation, dubbed Americanization, could range from charitable undertakings to rank brutality. Among Johnston's most arresting images is one of a classroom at the Hampton Institute in Virginia, with neatly attired African American young people around the turn of the twentieth century (December 1899), standing in solemn contemplation of a Native American classmate in full traditional Plains war regalia, standing on a box in front of a display case containing a stuffed bald eagle. This rich field of signs marks the compost of national identity.

11 As suggested earlier, as time passes the news value of images loses currency, and news images, documentary photos, and photographs taken on story assignments are all judged by similar aesthetic criteria. Further, very few people can make a living from self-chosen projects. Photojournalists and documentarians are, in addition, constantly seeking greater control over dissemination of their work. And many documentary photographers make their living from commercial work and are likely to employ their signature styles, muddying the waters.

12 See, for example, Robert Aibel, "Ethics and Professionalism in Documentary Film-Making," in Larry Gross, John Stuart Katz, and Jay Ruby, eds., *Image Ethics: The Moral Rights of Subjects in Photographs, Film, and Television* (New York: Oxford University Press, 1988), on a film of a rural U.S. auction, in which the subject was unrelated to politicized issues of class, race, gender, wealth, or social or political power.

"nonresponsibility" to the subject. (I note in passing that, historically, "proto-documentary" practices were anthropologically descriptive and took for granted that the photographer-audience group and those depicted were essentially different and inhabited different social locations, but street photography has evolved away from this model.) The loss of specificity or scrupulousness, as it empties information from the image, aids the aestheticization and universalization favored in the art world, whether such loss represents a view of photography as a form of self-portraiture through projection—an important argument, applied in varying degrees to a host of photographers—or some less definable release from social goals. Despite its often acute revelations of social power differentials in what it observes, street photography does not incline toward a calculus of rectification.

The photographer, rather than the subjects, becomes a kind of psychological or characterological type, and it is with the photographer that one identifies, reforging links between this form of photography and old-fashioned travelogues ("Our correspondent in the land of . . ."). The photographer is weeping, despairing, astonished, amused, disgusted, spiritually transformed, and so on, mediating through her or his sensibilities and (to use Robert Frank's word) "vision" the raw social facts at hand. In war, the viewer is a partisan observer and the photographer one's surrogate more than a representative of one's inquiring mind; we cheer the wins and decry (and perhaps analyze) the losses.

METHODOLOGIES OF PRODUCTION: DEGREES OF DISTANCE

In the face of the challenges to social documentary—not the least of which is the distinct possibility that projects will find no sponsors and no distribution—production methods have come under scrutiny by interested observers. Many documentarians were trained in sociology or anthropology, and many of documentary's frames of reference are drawn from these disciplines. Documentary photographers often think, for example, that they must become "participant observers"—part of the group or subculture whose members they are photographing—or maintain intense relationships with group members. This is in contrast to the street photographer or that stereotypical figure of irresponsibility to the subjects, the "parachuting photojournalist."

Some supporters of documentary—such as anthropologist Jay Ruby, a central figure in the study of "visual anthropology"—believe that only self-representations can solve the problem of unequal power in the photographic transaction. A form of equalization theory underlies the work of photographers following the trail blazed by anthropologist Sol Worth, who gave movie cameras to Native Americans.

As Brazilian educator Paulo Freire has shown, providing narrative tools—most basically, "alphabetization," or literacy—to the socially and politically excluded is in itself empowering. This approach of giving the tools of production to the ostensible subjects has most often been adopted by naturalist and realist documentary filmmakers, who have tried to re-create the experience of presentness with a minimum of intervention and interpretation and little hint of political agency. Those who use this method with still photography must add verbal texts of witness, testimony, and confession.

Photographers following this method include Wendy Ewald, working with poor North and South American children, and Deborah Barndt, working primarily with immigrant women in Toronto, as well as a number of photographers in many countries working with homeless children. Their projects are indispensable. My great admiration for such projects, however, is tempered by some concerns about their possible limitations. Freire's methodology was pedagogical, meant for use within a learning group, where his technique has repeatedly been shown to be powerfully effective. With work that circulates publicly, however, relying on giving the camera to the subjects underestimates the shaping effect of institutions and the context of reception, which are likely to reimpose the unequal power relationship banished from the photographic transaction. The project gains credibility for external observers from the subjects' sharp investedness, possibly from photographic naiveté (many such projects employ children), and from imagery that is aesthetically appealing, perhaps unexpectedly. As the sole form of representation, this work seems vulnerable to those with no desire to change political realities. In the words of a municipal bureaucrat, it represents a tool for "managing diversity"; thus, it has come to be seen as therapeutic or cathartic. Depoliticized and dehistoricized, the hack version of this work offers a preferred picture of the social victim, who might not earn sympathy if portrayed as analytic or militant: activists among the poor consistently claim that journalists, at least, focus on the ab-

---

13 In the United States, though not elsewhere, the "rules of engagement" are such that most photographers in public situations don't stop to obtain permission from those they photograph, and a person's failure to object immediately is taken as acquiescence. Those making news photographs are not legally obligated to seek permission.

14 In *Through Navaho Eyes: An Exploration in Film Communication and Anthropology* (Bloomington: Indiana University Press, 1972). The 1970s Australian film *Two Laws*, made with aboriginal collaboration, was produced on this model, with clear political intent.

jection of individuals and ignore group activism, which implies a demand against the privileges of the viewers. The best of these undertakings (which are, of course, not organized by journalists with their professional credentials and codes at stake, as described above) project a powerful idea of the subjects' desired self-image, but in routine applications the skills of the facilitating photographer are not put to full use. This approach, if it displaces other documentary methodology, smacks of positivism—one obtains testimony but provides only limited analysis.

If documentary appears to be under pressure—from distributors, sponsors, and subjects, as well as from leery practitioners and postmodern critics of traditional social, particularly class, analysis—and if the radical contraction of the public sphere means that there is no place to insert documentary arguments, why continue to talk about documentary practices? It is enough, perhaps, to claim that documentary still represents a lively impulse, but there are more important reasons to continue to distinguish documentary from street photography, which appears to be in no danger of withering away. In the world of just-yesterday, documentary could convey a sense of a "social scene"—and the mediating observer of that scene—to you. But in the present map of the world, the self-same photo might simply be readable as an image of the random Brownian motion of individuals present in the same unit of space-time, and adding up only to numbers, not to "society." Without a sense of the social, only the personal remains, and a look at the merely personal is an invitation to voyeurism. Documentary—more properly, "social documentary"—provides a frame of unity, even if a fractured and fractious one.

Voyeurism as a naked motive for photography is increasingly expressed and rewarded, in art and mass culture, even in polite society. The art world is not immune from the rhetoric of demonization of immigrants and the poor, and galleries and museums are revoking their former discreet avoidance of sensationalistic and tendentious images of poor people. Finding favor as well are colorful images reminiscent of club-world journalism, which displaces the kind of color work that was first allowed through art world gates—namely, melancholy images of urban and small-town landscapes, often of the American South or postindustrial New England, blank empty places of special cachet. What has also captured attention—particularly in Europe—is a de-skilled "slacker" aesthetic of blurry, informal photos, often of conglomerations of people doing nothing much. This flashy casualness, patently influenced by and feeding back into fashion photography, suggests the way in which photography is seen to describe the postmodern social dimension.

I will use as my example the work of the English artist Richard Billingham, discovered as a student of painting in an art school not many years ago. In exhibiting, textless, in commercial galleries and museums his greatly enlarged instant-camera color photos of his drunken father and brother and his rot-toothed mother in their sorry council-house flat, Billingham—who won instant fame and the patronage of Charles Saatchi and a hungering pack of international collectors—may be taken as illustrating the collapse of the tattered but still widely upheld art world stance of generalized humanism and noblesse oblige. Promoters praise his freak show as a form of poetry—thus, self-expression, following the argument referred to earlier, meant to rescue street photography from seeming simply predatory. Billingham's book of these photos—whose only text is a short descriptive blurb on the dust jacket—is called, appropriately enough, *Ray's a Laugh.* Ray is Dad, and, yes, Oedipal rage is on view. If the identities sketched out here are those of working-class people in postindustrial Britain, they are not being described by admirers; drunks always appear as self-produced permanent losers, not as victims of *someone* or *something*.

Despite this further step along the road of artists' pantomimes of social disengagement, it is important to reiterate that documentary is not primarily an art world practice—although, as I have noted, art world practices have the ability to capture center stage, displacing an interest in documentary among potential future documentarians as well as viewers and critics. But plenty of people are still producing documentary images, despite the loss of stable avenues of dissemination, and it is up to us in the audience to prevent them from being submerged by those on the other side of an ethical and political divide. A tiny number

15 This is not meant to suggest that people are unequipped to describe or understand their own situations, but only as a reminder that there is a dimension of one's own situation and behavior that is not available to consciousness, not to mention the comparative knowledge that others may bring to a situation.

16 Richard Billingham, *Ray's a Laugh* (Milan: Scalo, 1996).

17 A more nuanced argument has been offered for the acceptance of Billingham's work by some English critics of good will and admirable political sentiments. Billingham's work, and some of Gillian Wearing's recent portraits, in video and photography, of drunks in desperate condition, these observers argue, bring to public view images of the working class (and lumpen?) not only left behind by the demise of British "socialist goals" but no longer even championed by New Labor, and thus no longer represented in the public conversation. These two YBAs (young British artists), situated outside the documentary tradition, claim a "familial" or affiliational connection with those pictured: Billingham offers his family, Wearing the drunks she interacted with daily outside her studio. On balance, however, I still think that images of drunks, rather than being indicative of the bottomless pit into which the marginalized postindustrial working class is falling, continue to call to up a raw mythology of timeless depersonalization. Thus I find this rationale for their work less persuasive than that dealers, critics, and observers are interested in the return of the frisson—or the *affreux*, the frightful.

of projects are represented on accompanying pages.

Let me recapitulate some of the arguments of the present essay. First, documentary, a polarizing practice that must inevitably provoke opposition, is perpetually teetering on the brink of its demise. Those hostile to the demands of "crusading" documentary may find it easiest to call for its end, ironically enough, in the name of ethics and "responsibility." Second, as postmodernists claim, demands for "straight information" without interpretation are unrealistic, for there is no voice from outside particular human communities. Strict objectivity, a standard derived from journalistic ethics, may prove an inappropriate ideal for documentary—as documentarians and photojournalists already know—but so is the alibi of personalization, sentiment, or disengagement. Third, the partial melding of the photographic audience and its subjects has put great pressure on the institutionalized methodologies of documentary, for interpretation has become a field of perpetual contestation. Finally, the art world embrace of photography can squeeze documentary to death—or maybe I've got cause and effect reversed, for it could be that all of photography is already a nostalgic craft, given the explosion of computer-based manipulations that drive our stepping off into the post-photographic moment, leaving behind both photograph and photographer.

So why continue to defend documentary? The short answer is, because we need it, and because it likely will continue, with or without art world theorizing. As the division widens between rich and poor in the United States and elsewhere (and as art practices are institutionalized and academicized), there is less and less serious analysis of the lives of those on the wrong side of that great divide. My understanding of postmodernism does not extend to the idea of a world with no coherent explanation of differential social power or advocacy of ways to right the imbalance. Explanation and advocacy are still viable in relation to photography, as in purely word-based journalism. Documentary's best course, it seems to me, is to provide a balance between observing the situation of others and expressing one's own point of view— which ought to include some form of analytic framework identifying social causes and proposing remedies. In pursuit of this, documentary will continue to negotiate between sensationalism on the one hand and instrumentalism on the other.

As I began with a quotation from Grierson—that old-style utopian social democratic optimist—it seems appropriate to end with one:

> A mirror held up to nature is not so important in a dynamic and fast-changing society as the hammer which shapes it—it is as a hammer, not a mirror, that I have sought to use the medium that came to my somewhat restive hand.

18 This trope is increasingly evident in documentary film and video, in modern reflexive documentaries and diaristic films, and in web-based works that appear more and more like glossily produced magazine articles with live interviews and spoken commentary.

19 Quoted in Beveridge, *John Grierson, Film Master*, n.p.

schema; Aquafresh plus Crest with whitener

Kelley Walker

2003

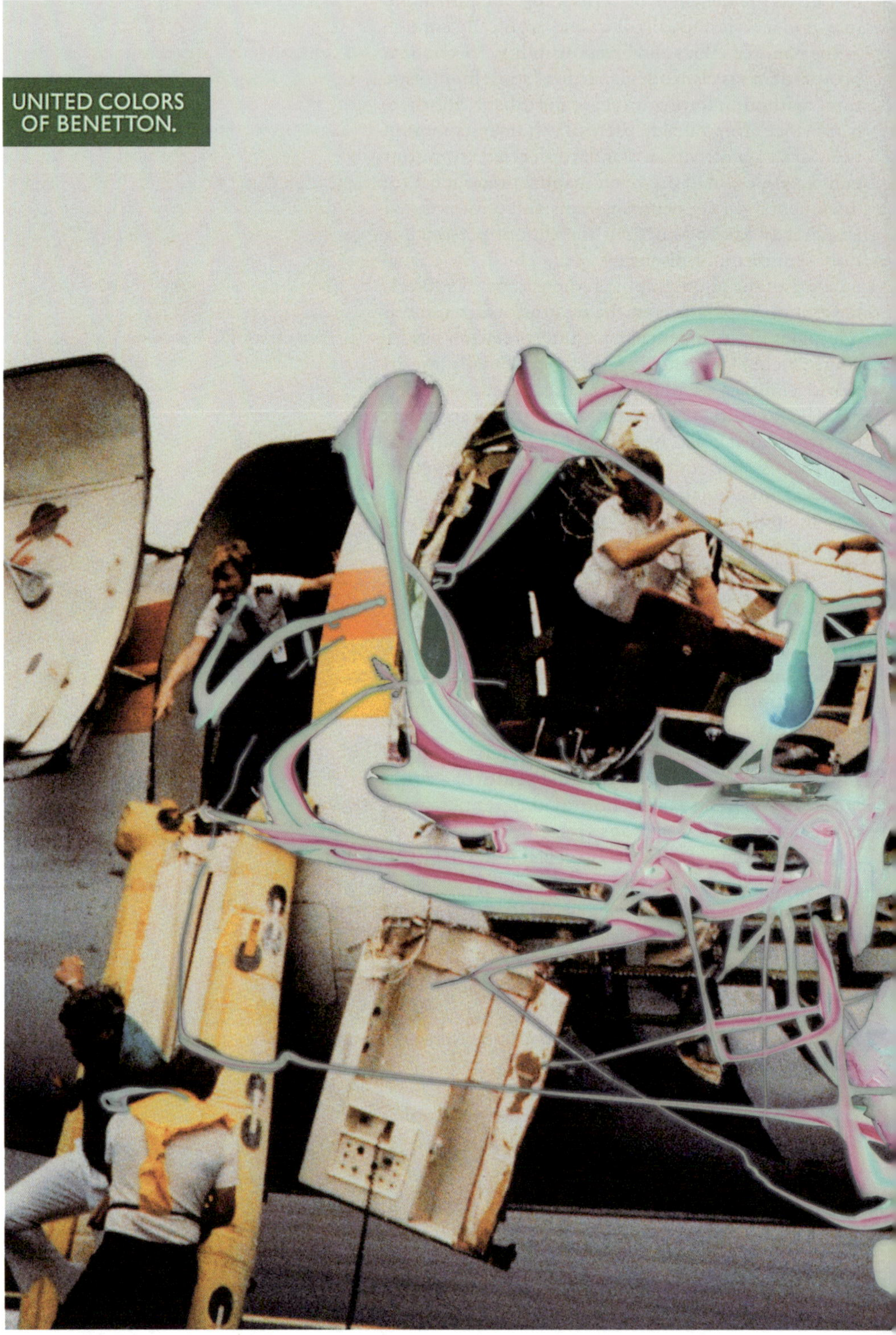

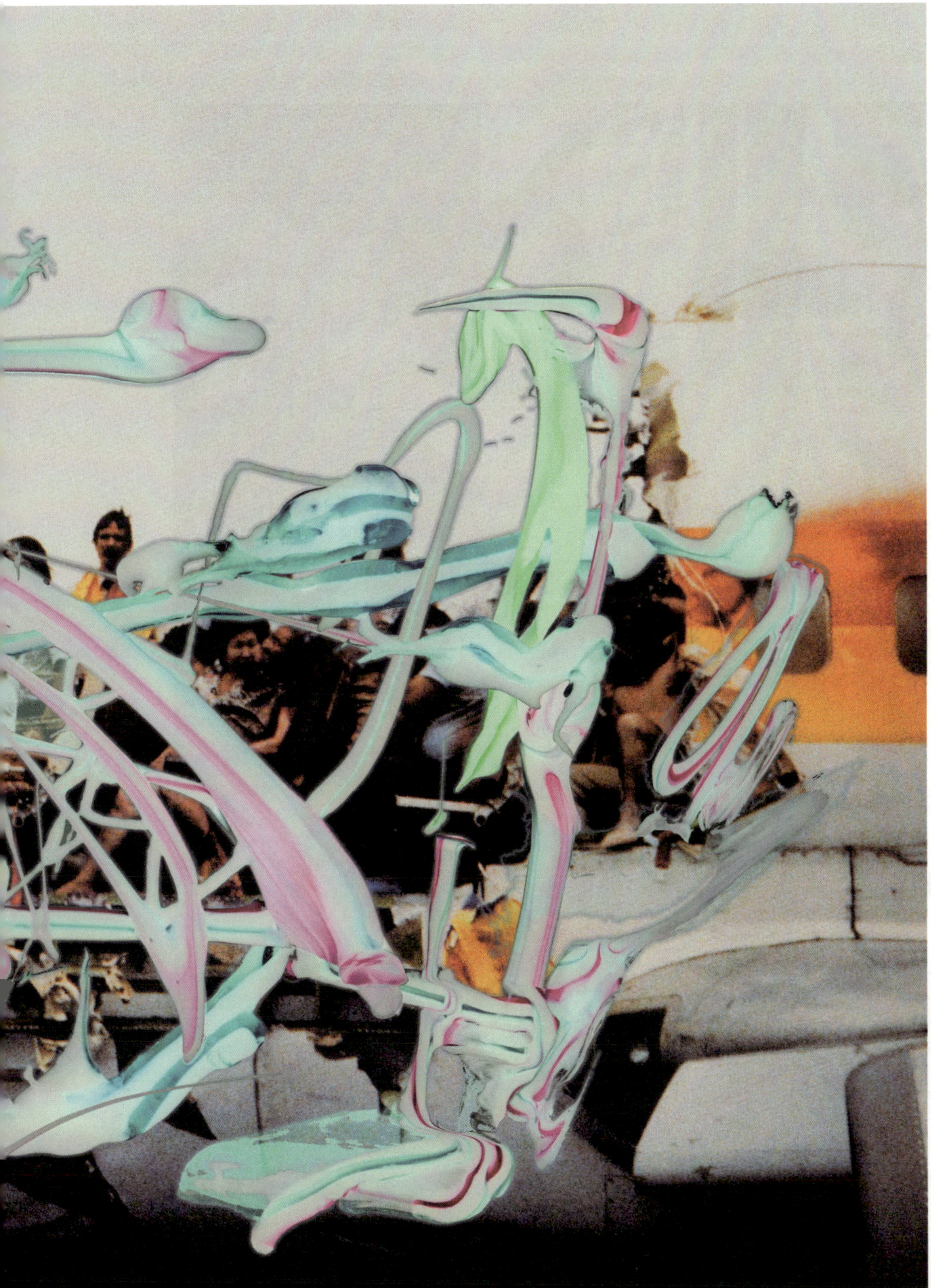

schema; Aquafresh plus Crest with Scope

Kelley Walker

2003

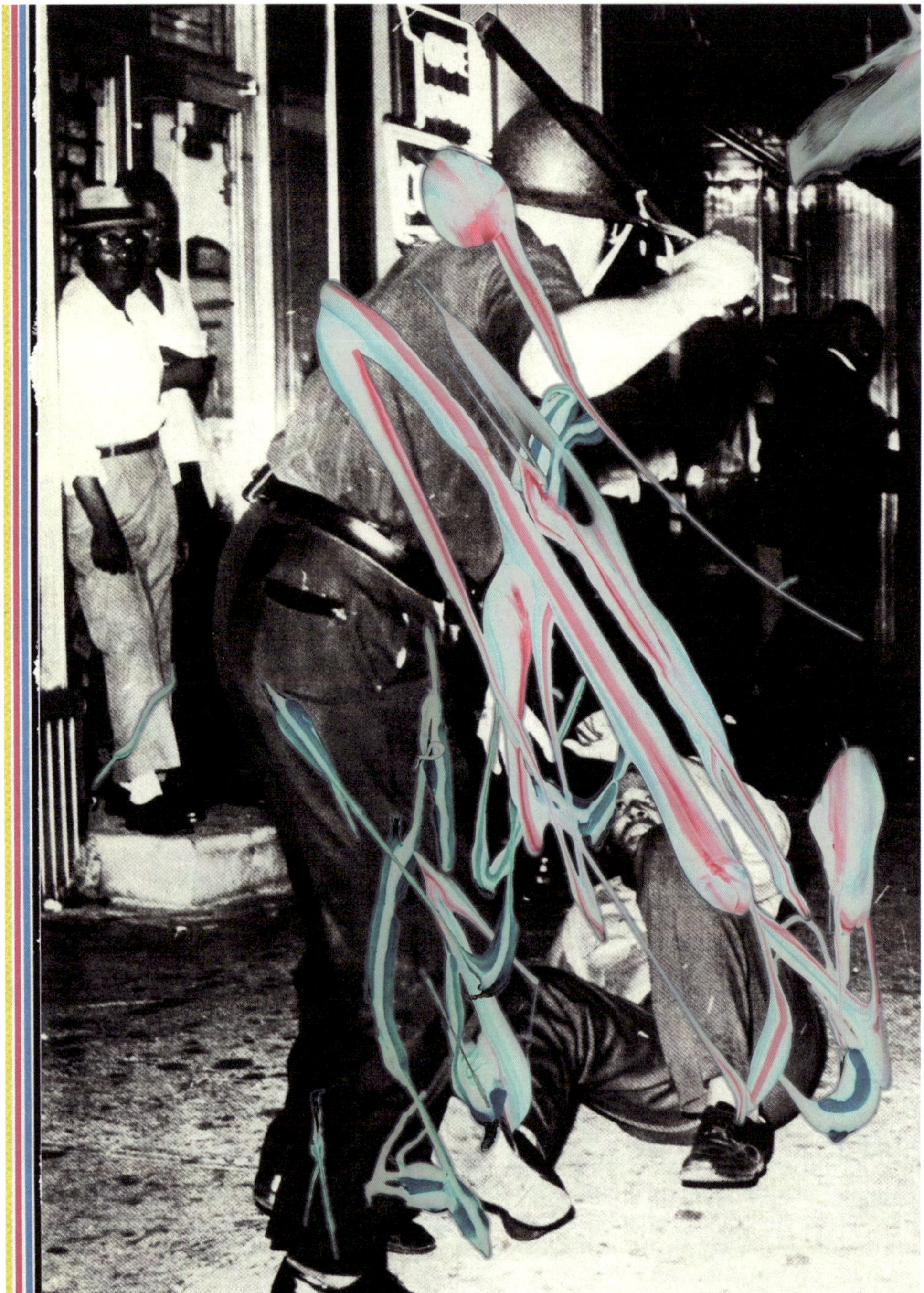

Civilian (adjusted to fit)

Louise Lawler

2010/2011

Black Mo'nin'
Fred Moten
2003

in the sound of the photograph: childless mother.
I want to discover a performance by way of the ongoing production of a performance.

In her essay, " 'Can You Be BLACK and Look at This?' Reading the Rodney King Video(s)," Elizabeth Alexander recites a narrative:

> In August 1955, in Money, Mississippi, a fourteen-year-old Chicago black boy named Emmett Till, nicknamed "Bobo," was visiting relatives and was shot in the head and thrown in the river with a mammoth cotton gin fan tied around his neck, for allegedly whistling at a white woman. In some versions of the story, he was found with his cut-off penis stuffed in his mouth. His body was shipped to Chicago, and his mother [Mamie Till Bradley] decided he should have an open casket funeral; the whole world would see what had been done to her son. According to the Chicago-based, black newsweekly *Jet,* hundreds of thousands of mourners "in an unending procession, later viewed the body" at the funeral home. A photograph of Till in the casket—his head mottled and swollen to many times its normal size—ran in *Jet,* and largely through that medium, both the picture and Till's story became legendary. The caption of the close-up photograph of Till's face read: "Mutilated face of victim was left unretouched by the mortician at the mother's request. She said she wanted 'all the world' to witness the atrocity."[1]

And here are two passages from Nathaniel Mackey's *Bedouin Hornbook* that invoke a sound correspondent to the massive implications of the image Alexander has brought again into view and into question:

> . . . I'm especially impressed by its long overdue disinternment of the occult, heretofore inchoate arcana intuitively buried within the reaches—the wordless reaches—of the black singer's voice. Would it be going too far to say that in your essay the black falsetto has in fact found its voice? (Forgive me if I embarrass you.) In any case, the uncanny coincidence is that the draft of your essay arrived just as I'd put on a record by Al Green. I've long marveled at how all this going on about love succeeds in alchemizing a legacy of lynchings—as though singing were a rope he comes eternally close to being strangled by.
>
> . . . One point I think could bear more insistent mention: What you term "the dislocated African's pursuit of a meta-voice" bears the weight of a gnostic, transformative desire to be done with the world. By this I mean the deliberately forced, deliberately "false" voice we get from someone like Al Green creatively hallucinates a "new world," indicts the more insidious falseness of the world as we know it. (Listen, for example, to "Love and Happiness.") What is it in the falsetto that thins and threatens to abolish the voice but the wear of so much reaching for heaven? At some point you'll have to follow up this excellent essay of yours with a treatment of the familial ties between the falsetto, the moan and the shout. There's a book by a fellow named Heilbut called *The Gospel Sound* you might look into. At one point, for example, he writes: "The essence of the gospel style is a wordless moan. Always these sounds render the indescribable, implying, 'Words can't begin to tell you, but maybe moaning will.' " If you let "word" take the place of "world" in what I said above the bearing this has on your essay should become pretty apparent. (During his concert a few weeks back Lambert quoted an ex-slave in Louisiana as having said, "The Lawd done said you gotta shout if you want to be saved. You gotta shout and you gotta moan if you wants to be saved." Take particular note of the end of "Love and Happiness," where Green keeps repeating, "Moan for love.") Like the moan or the shout, I'm suggesting, the falsetto explores a redemptive, unworded realm—a meta-word, if you will—where the implied critique of the momentary eclipse of the word curiously rescues, restores and renews it: new word, new world.[2]

Flaunted Fifth heard the noise of a helicopter overhead. He noticed the cops in the police car looking this way. The emotional figure he absentmindedly toyed with was given an abruptly ominous edge by the setting sun, the helicopter overhead and the police car circling the block, all of which put an inverse halo around it. A panicky rush ran thru him as the cops continued to look his way.

1 In Thelma Golden, ed., *Black Male: Representations of Masculinity in Contemporary American Art* (New York: Whitney Museum of American Art, 1994), 91–110. For a more comprehensive account of Till's murder, the events leading up to it, and its aftermath, see Stephen J. Whitfield, *A Death in the Delta: The Story of Emmett Till* (Baltimore: Johns Hopkins University Press, 1988).
2 Nathaniel Mackey, *Bedouin Hornbook*, Calalloo Fiction Series (Lexington: University of Kentucky Press, 1986), 51–52.

> He couldn't help remembering that several black men had been killed by the L.A. police in recent months, victims of a chokehold whose use there were now efforts to outlaw. The V-shaped warmth in the crook of his right arm seemed to detach itself, rise up and, like an ironic boomerang, press itself against the front of his neck. He imagined himself held in the sweaty crook of a cop's arm.
>
> It was hard not to be overwhelmed by the lethal irony which invaded everything. Flaunted Fifth was suddenly haunted by once having written that the use of the falsetto in black music, the choked-up ascent into a problematic upper register, had a way, as he'd put it, of "alchemizing a legacy of lynchings." He'd planned to make use of this idea again in his lecture/demonstration, but the prospect of a cop's arm around his neck reminded him that every concept, no matter how figural or sublime, had its literal, dead-letter aspect as well. It now seemed too easy to speak of "alchemy," too easy not to remember how inescapably real every lynching had been. He'd always thought of himself as an advocate of spirit. He should have known the letter might someday do him in.
>
> The ominous edge he picked up on was also, he realized, an attribute of spirit. Overtones and resonances inhabited the letter, causing it to creak like the floorboards and doors in a haunted house. That the emotional triad he absentmindedly toyed with, the triangulation he'd made a note of to himself, should creak with overtones of strangulation came as no surprise. That Namesake Epigraph #4 should be haunted by patriarchal patrol cars and helicopters, that it should creak with patriarchal prohibitions against public speech, equally came as no surprise. It all confirmed a "creaking of the spirit" he'd heard referred to in a song from the Bahamas many years before. That the creaking might kill was the price one occasionally paid. "No blues without dues," he reminded himself, making another mental note for his pilot radio show.[3]

Some attribute to Emmett Till—which is to say to his death, which is to say to the famous picturing and display, staging and performance, of his death or of him in death—the agency that set in motion this nation's profoundest political insurrection and resurrection, the resurrection of reconstruction, a second reconstruction like a second coming of the Lord.[4] If this is true, how is it true? On this question Alexander subscribes to James Baldwin's formulation, in *The Evidence of Things Not Seen,* that Till's murder—which in its particularity is not unlike a vast chain of such events stretching across a long history of brutal violence—can stand out, resonate, or be said to produce effects only because of the moment of its occurrence, a moment that is possible only after the beginning of the insurrection and resurrection it is claimed to have sparked. As Alexander remarks, Baldwin's claims regarding this matter are astute: Till's death bears the trace of a particular moment of panic when, "under the knell of the Supreme Court's *all deliberate speed,*" there was massive reaction to the movement against segregation. (That particular moment of panic is a point on an extended trajectory, where that panic seems almost always to have been—among other things, though this is not just one thing among others—sexual. So that the movement against segregation is seen as a movement for miscegenation and, at that point, whistling or the "crippled speech" of Till's "Bye, baby" cannot go unheard.[5] This means we'll have to listen to it along with various other sounds that will prove to be unneutralizable and irreducible.) The fact that whatever force Till's death exerted was not originary does not mean, however, that that force wasn't real. For even if his death marked panic and even if that panic had already led to the deaths of so many, so that his death was already haunted—its force only the animating spirit of a train of horrors—something happened. Something real—in that it might have been otherwise—happened. So that we need to be interested in the complex, dissonant, polyphonic affectivity of the ghost, the agency of the fixed but multiply apparent shade, an improvisation of spectrality, another development of the negative. All these have to do with another understanding of the photograph and of a deferral of some inevitable return to the ontological that would operate in the name of a utopian vision and in the sharpest critique of those authoritarian modes of (false) differentiation and (false) universalization (ultimately, the same thing) that seem to have ontology or the ontological impulse as their condition of possibility and that seem to indicate that that impulse or activity could never have ended any other way. So I'm interested in what a photograph—what *this* photo- graph—does to ontology, to the politics of ontology, and to the possibility and project of a utopian politics outside ontology.

How can this photograph challenge ontological

3 Mackey, 201–2.

4 Roland Barthes says that "photography has something to do with resurrection." In this essay I'm trying to extend this assertion by way of, against, and through some of Barthes's formulations of photography. See his *Camera Lucida: Reflections on Photography*, trans. Richard Howard (New York: Hill and Wang, 1981), 82. More on this text later.

5 Whitfield informs us that "Bobo was self-assured despite a speech defect—a stutter—that was the consequence of nonparalytic polio that he had suffered at the age of three." See Whitfield, *A Death in the Delta*, 15, and note, also, Whitfield's documentation of Ms. Bradley's argument that the attribution to Till of an attempted transgressive, transracial seduction on the part of his murderers was in part the function of their inability to decipher Till's broken speech. See also Mackey's "Cante Moro" (in *Sound States: Innovative Poetics and Acoustical Technologies*, ed. Adalaide Morris [Chapel Hill: University of North Carolina Press, 1997], 194–212) for more on the enabling disabilities of "crippled speech," its relation to referents unavailable to moaning's or humming's cutting augmentation of the verbal.

questioning? *By way of a sound* and by way of what's already there in the decision to display the body, to publish the photograph, to restage death and rehearse mo(ur)nin(g). This includes a political imperative that is never disconnected from an aesthetic one, from a necessary reconstruction of the very aesthetics of photography, of documentary, and, therefore, of truth, revelation, and enlightenment as well as of judgment, taste, and, therefore, the aesthetic itself. Mackey moves toward this, and yet what is made in such sounding, or rather the theory and theorist of such making, is haunted by a destruction she or it can never assimilate or exhaust. And this is not just about some justification, as if the blues were worth it. Rather, we have to think about the fact that an aesthetic appropriation could be said to desacrilize the legacy of lynchings, precisely by way of an "alchemizing" that seems to fetishize or figure on the literal, on the absolute fact and reality of so many deaths while continually opening the possibility of redemption in out sensuality. Which is to say that the blues are not worth the dues pai(n: trace of something made me type; I had to leave it in: Payne: it'll come back later)d in order to produce them, but they are part of the condition of possibility of the end of such extortion. So this is about the cut music enacts on the image and after the fact of a set of connections between death and the visual, between looking and retribution—as arrest, abduction, and abjection. What did the hegemony of the visual have to do with the death of Emmett Till? What effect did the photograph of his body have on death? What affect did it send? How did the photograph and its reproduction and dissemination break the hegemony of the visual? "Cousins remembered him as 'the center of attention' who 'liked to be seen. He liked the spotlight,' "[6] but he'll be heard, too, as broken speech and talking wind, a cry from outside, interior exteriority of the photograph.

In positing that this photo and photographs in general bear a phonic substance, I want to challenge not only the ocularcentrism that generally—perhaps necessarily—shapes theories of the nature of photography and our experience of photography but also that mode of semiotic objectification and inquiry that privileges the analytic-interpretative reduction of phonic materiality and/or nonmeaning over something like a mimetic improvisation of and with that materiality that moves in excess of meaning.[7] This second challenge assumes that the critical-mimetic experience of the photograph takes place most properly within a field structured by theories of (black) spectatorship, audition, and performance. These challenges are also something of a preface to such theory, and they attempt to work out a couple of that theory's most crucial elements: the anti-interpretive nonreduction of nonmeaning and the breakdown of the opposition between live performance and mechanical reproduction—all this by way of an investigation of the augmentation of mourning by the sound of moaning, by a religious and political formulation of morning that animates the photograph with a powerfully *mater*ial resistance. We have to try to understand the connection between that resistance and political movement, locating that movement's direction toward new universalities held within the difference(s) of phonic substance, within the difference of the accent that cuts and augments mourning and morning, a difference semiotics has heretofore thought either to be fatal to its desire for universality or to be proof of the foolishness and political and epistemological danger of that desire.

There is the trace of what remains to be discovered, a topic, a path I'm trying to take that moves through a shudder I can never escape when gazing, or even after the fact of an arrested and arresting glance, at the broken face of Emmett Till. Looking at Emmett Till is arrested by overtonal reverberations;[8] looking demurs when it opens onto an unheard sound that the picture cannot secure but discovers and onto all of what it might be said to mean that I can look at this face, this photograph. This is to say not only look at it but look at it in the context of an aesthetics, look at it as if it were to be looked at, as if it were to be thought, therefore, in terms of a kind of beauty, a kind of detachment, independence, autonomy, that holds open the question of what looking might mean in general, what the aesthetics of the photograph might mean for politics, and what those aesthetics might have meant for Mamie Till Bradley in the context of her demand that her son's face be seen, be shown, that his death and her mourning be performed.

Emmett Till's face is seen, was shown, shone. His face was destroyed (by way of, among other things, its

---

6 Whitfield, 15.

7 Julia Kristeva works fruitfully in the field determined by the opposition of mimesis and analytic-interpretive knowledge. I want to acknowledge that work here as well as the necessity for a full account of that work. That necessity is particularly pronounced in work that is, on the one hand, attuned to the encountering of maternity and phonic materiality in a way that is very much influenced by Kristeva and, on the other hand, driven by an engagement with Barthes at a moment in his career when the influence of Kristeva is especially evident in his work. I intend to provide such an account very soon. Meanwhile, Kristeva speaks very lucidly on the relation between mimesis and knowledge in "A Conversation with Julia Kristeva," in *Julia Kristeva: Interviews*, ed. Ross Mitchell Guberman (New York: Columbia University Press, 1996), 31.

8 I want to acknowledge, here, the work of Karen Sackman on the relation between overtone and political mobilization. The chance to discuss these matters with her was crucial to the development of my ideas in this essay. I should say, too, that our discussion was prompted in large part by Randy Martin's extraordinary book *Critical Moves* (Durham: Duke University Press, 1998).

being shown: the memory of his face is thwarted, made a distant before-as-after effect of its destruction, what we would never have otherwise seen). It was turned inside out, ruptured, exploded, but deeper than that it was opened. As if his face were the truth's condition of possibility, it was opened and revealed. As if revealing his face would open the revelation of a fundamental truth, his casket was opened, as if revealing the destroyed face would in turn reveal, and therefore cut, the active deferral or ongoing death or unapproachable futurity of justice. As if his face would deconstruct justice or deconstruct deconstruction or deconstruct death, though this infinite and circular chain seems too muddled, too crazy, too twisted or clotted, as if it, too, were in need of another cut, it was shown. As if that face revealed "the beginning of death in cut time,"[9] as if this was a death unlike other deaths, a death that prompts a mourning whose rehearsal is also a refusal, a death to end all deaths or all other deaths but one, his face was destroyed by its display. His casket was opened, his face was shown, is seen—now in the photograph—and allowed to open a revelation that first is manifest in the shudder the shutter continues to produce,[10] the trembling, a general disruption of the ways in which we gaze at the face and at the dead, a disruption of the oppressive ethics and coercive law of reckless eyeballing, reckless whistling, which contains within it a call, the disruption of the disruption that would have captured, an arrest of the spirit that arrests, a repetitive close. Memory—bound to the way the photograph holds up what it proposes, stops, keeps—is given pause, because what we thought we could look at for the last time and hold holds us, captures us, and doesn't let us go. And why is the memory of this mutilated face, reconfiguration of what was embedded in some furtive and partial glance's refusal, so much more horrible, the distortion magnified even more than the already incalculable devastation of the actual body? Does the blindness held in the aversion of the eye create an insight that is manifest as a kind of magnification or intensification of the object—as if memory as affect and the affect that forges distorted or intensified memory cascade off one another, each multiplying the other's force? I think this kind of blindness makes music.

The fear of another castration is all bound up in this aversion of the eye. Emmett Till's death marks a double time, rhythm-a-ning, redoubled nothing-ing, dead and castrated. But his mother, absent, present, reopens or leaves open the wound that is redoubled, the nothing that is redoubled in her son's murder. Ms. Bradley opens, leaves open, reopens, the violent, ritual, sexual cutting of his death by the leaving open of the casket, by the unretouching of the body, by the body's photograph, by the photograph's transformation in memory and nightmare of which many speak (for instance, Roland Barthes, about whom more later). That leaving open is a performance. It is the disappearance of the disappearance of Emmett Till that emerges by way of exhibiting what Mackey calls "wounded kinship" (itself always refigured and refinished in and as and by exogamous collision). It is the ongoing destruction of the ongoing production of (a) (black) performance, which is what I am, which is what we are or could be if we can listen while we look. If he seems to keep disappearing as we look at him, it's because we look away, which is what makes possible and impossible representation, reproduction, dream. And there is a sound that seemingly is not there in this performance, which this performance is about; but not just a sound, since also we are concerned with what that sound would invoke—immortal or utopian longings, though not the utopianism of a past made present, not the recovery of a loss, and not just a negation of the present either, in the form of an ongoing displacement of the concrete. Rather, here is an abundance—in abundance—of the present, an abundance of affirmation in abundance of the negative, in abundance of disappearance.

Such is the aesthetic cut, invasive evasion, shock of the shock, adding form and color to a verbal discourse, adding extensional cry and sound to the word's visualization. An image from which one turns is immediately caught in the production of its memorialized, re-membered reproduction. We lean into it, but we can't; the aesthetic and philosophical arrangements of the photograph—some organizations of and for light—anticipate a looking that cannot be sustained as unalloyed looking but must be accompanied by listening, and this, even though what is listened to—echo of a whistle or a phrase, moaning, mourning, desperate testimony, and flight—is also unbearable. These are the complex musics of the photograph. This is the sound before the photograph:

Scream inside and out, out from outside, of the image. Bye, baby. Whistling. Lord, take my soul. Redoubled and reanimating passion, the passion of a seeing that is involuntary and uncontrollable, a seeing that redoubles itself as sound, a passion that is the redoubling of Emmett Till's passion, of whatever passion would redeem, crucifixion, lynching, middle passion, passage. So that looking implies that one desires something for this photograph. So that mourning turns. So that the looker is in danger of slipping, not away, but into something less comfortable than hor-

9 Amiri Baraka, "When Miles Split!" in *Eulogies* (New York: Marsilio Publishers, 1996), 145–46.

10 There is more to be said elsewhere regarding the photographic apparatus, the production of a sound that allows the production of an image. Thanks to my colleague Barbara Browning for opening this up.

ror—aesthetic judgment, denial, laughter, some out and unprecedented reflection, movement, murder, song. So that there is an inappropriable ecstatics that goes along with this aesthetics—one is taken out, as in screams, fainting, tongues, dreams. So perhaps she was counting on the aesthetic.

This aural aesthetic is not the simple reemergence of the voice of presence, the visible and graphic word. The logos that voice implies and requires has been complicated by the echo of transgressive whistle, abortive seduction, stuttered leave-taking, and by reconstructive overtones of mo'nin'. Some- thing is remembered and repeated in such complications. Transferred. To move or work through that something, to improvise, requires thinking about morning and how mourning sounds, how moaning sounds. What's made and destroyed. We'll have to do this while keeping in mind all that remains urgent and needful and open in the critique of phonologocentrism, which Jacques Derrida initiates. Nevertheless, we've got to cut the ongoing "reduction of the phonic substance," whose origin is untraceable but is at least as old as philosophy, at least as old as its paradoxically interinanimate other, phonocentrism, and predates any call for its being set into motion, either in Descartes or Saussure or in Derrida's critical echo of them.[11] The refusal to neutralize the phonic substance of the photograph rewrites the time of the photograph, the time of the photograph of the dead. The time of the sound of the photograph of the dead is no longer irreversible, no longer vulgar, and, moreover, is indexed not only to rhythmic complication but to the extreme and subtle harmonics of various shrieks, hums, hollers, shouts, and moans. What these sounds and their times indicate is the way into another question concerning universality, a reopening of the issue of a universal language by way of this new music so that now it's possible to accommodate a differentiation of the universal, of its ongoing reconstruction in sound as the differential mark, divided and abundant, dividing and abounding. But how many people have really listened to this photograph? Hieroglyphics, phonetic writing, phonography— where is the photograph placed in all this?

Black mo'nin' is the phonographic content of this photograph. And the whistle is just as crucial as the moan; train whistle, maybe; his whistle carrying the echo of the train that took his particular origins north, the train that brought him home and took him home and brought him home. There's a massive itinerancy here, a fugitivity that breaking only left more broke, broken and unbroken circle of escape and return.[12] And the gap between them, between their modes of audibility vis-à-vis the photograph, is the difference within invagination between what cuts and what surrounds, invagination being that principle of impurity, which, for Derrida, marks the law of the law of genre where the set or ensemble or totality is constantly improvised by the rupturing and augmentative power of an always already multiply and disruptively present singularity.[13] So that speech is broken and expanded by writing; so that hieroglyphics is affected by phonetic script; so that a photograph exerts itself on the alphabet; so that phonographic content infuses the photo. And this movement doesn't mark some orbital decay in which signification inevitably returns to some simple vocal presence; rather, it's the itinerary of the force and movement of signification's outside. The implications of this aural aesthetic—this phonographic rewriting of/in the photograph—are crucial and powerful, then, because they mark something general about the nature of a photograph and a performance—the ongoing universality of their absolute singularity— that is itself, at least for me, most clearly and generously given in black photography and black performance. (This is, for instance, what Mackey always brings, always knows.)

Blackness and maternity play huge roles in the analytic of photography Roland Barthes lays down in *Camera Lucida,* Barthes's extended and elegiac meditation on the essence of photography that revolves around an unreproducible, unobservable photograph of his mother as a young child (the "Winter Garden Photograph"), a woman remarkable to Barthes in part because, he says, she made no observations.[14] Black-

11 See Derrida, *Of Grammatology*, trans. Gayatri Chakrovarty Spivak (Baltimore: Johns Hopkins University Press, 1976).

12 Mackey speaks, with regard to Baraka and his reading and rewriting of García Lorca in the late 1950s and early 1960s, of "a well-known, resonant history of African-American fugitivity and its well-known, resonant relationship to enslavement and persecution." He adds, "The way in which fugitivity asserts itself on an aesthetic level . . . is important as well. The way in which Baraka's poems of this period move intimates fugitive spirit, as does much of the music that he was into. He writes of a solo by saxophonist John Tchicai on an Archie Shepp album, 'It slides away from the proposed.' . . . That sliding away wants out." See Mackey, 200.

13 Jacques Derrida, "The Law of Genre," in *On Narrative*, ed. W. J. T. Mitchell (Chicago: University of Chicago Press, 1981), 55.

14 Barthes associates the state, shall we say, of having made no observations with kindness:

> In this little girl's image I saw the kindness which had formed her being immediately and forever, without her having inherited it from anyone; how could this kindness have proceeded from the imperfect parents who had loved her so badly—in short: from a family? Her kindness was specifically out-of-play, it belonged to no system, or at least it was located at the limits of a morality (evangelical, for instance); I could not define it better than by this feature (among others): that during the whole of our life together, she never made a single "observation." This extreme and particular circumstance, so abstract in relation to an image, was nonetheless present in the face revealed in the photograph. (Barthes, *Camera Lucida*, 69)

It remains for us to think of the consequences, beyond all of what might be seen as admirable or lovable, of the placement, by and in relation to Barthes (himself figured earlier in his own text as a definite sentimental and theoretical observer), of this idealized preobservationality.

ness is the site or mark of the ideal object, the ideal spectator (and these are everything for Barthes's analytic, since the doing or operation of photography is bracketed and set aside early on in *Camera Lucida*). Blackness is the embodiment of a naïveté that would move Barthes, the self-styled essential phenomenologist, back before culture to some pure and unalloyed looking.[15] The paradox, here, is that the reduction phenomenology desires seems to require a regression to a prescientific state characterized by what Husserl, after Hegel, would call the incapability of science. Those who are incapable of science are those who are outside history, but that exteriority is precisely the desired starting point for phenomenology that would move not through philosophical tradition but directly toward and in the things themselves. And indeed, this is how empire makes phenomenology possible, figuring a simplicity structured by regression, return, and reduction refigured as refinement. Empire's mother fixation is phenomenology's obsession with blackness. Blackness is situated precisely at the site of the condition of possibility and impossibility of phenomenology, and for Barthes that's cool, because the object and the spectator of photography reside there as well. This interstitial no-space is where photography lives, this point of embarkation for the europhallic journey to the interior, to the place of the other, the dark continent, the motherland that is always coded as an imperial descent into self. This regressive return to "that-has-been" and/or to where-you-been is the staging area for the performance of that wounded kinship and violent collision that is both the life-drama-trauma of blackness and the opening of what is called modernity.[16] The lynching and photographing of Emmett Till, the reproductive display of his photographed body by his mother, the Barthesian theory of photography that is founded in part on a silencing invocation of that mother and of him are all part of the ongoing production of that performance. It ought not be surprising, then, that Barthes's analysis in *Camera Lucida* is structured by a set of problematic moves: a disavowal of the historical in photography that reduces it to a field of merely "human interest"; a figuring of photographic historicality as overwhelmed by that univocal intentionality of the photographer that can result only in "a kind of general enthusiastic commitment . . . with- out special acuity,"[17] an ontological differentiation between photography and the photograph, and a semiotic neutralization of the unorderable or unmeaningful phonic substance of photography. It is especially the first and last of these elements that emerge here:

> The photograph is unary when it emphatically transforms "reality" without doubling it, without making it vacillate (emphasis is a power of cohesion): no duality, no indirection, no disturbance. The unary Photograph has every reason to be banal, "unity" of composition being the first rule of vulgar (and notably, of academic) rhetoric: "The subject," says one handbook for amateur photographers, "must be simple, free of useless accessories; this is called the Search for Unity."
>
> News photographs are very often unary (the unary photograph is not necessarily tranquil). In these images, no punctum: a certain shock but no disturbance; the photograph can "shout," not wound. These journalistic photographs are received (all at once), perceived. I glance through them, I don't recall them; no detail (in some corner) ever interrupts my reading: I am interested in them (as I am interested in the world), I do not love them.[18]

Barthes's turn from the vulgar, unary photography of the shout and toward the refined photography of the prick or wound is tied to an ontological questioning that is founded on the unreproducibility of a photograph and the theological veiling of the original in the interest of a theory of photographic signification.[19] Against the backdrop of Emmett Till, the silencing of a photograph in the name of that interstitial space between the Photograph and Photography is also the silencing dismissal of a performance in the name of that interstitial space between Performance and Performativity. And, again, paradoxes are here produced seemingly without end, so that Barthes's critique of the unary photograph is based on the assumption of the unary sensuality of photography. And this is a prescriptive assumption—photography ought to be sensually unary, ought not shout so that it can prick. Wounding photography is absolutely visual; that's the only way we can love it.

So what's the relationship between the necessary presence of the interinanimation of naïve blackness and preobservational motherhood in Barthes's theory and the necessary absence of sound? Perhaps it is this: that the necessary repression—rather than some naturalized absence—of phonic substance in a general semiotics applies to the semiotics of photography as well; that the

15 This is all to say that ultimately what remains constant in Barthes's thinking on photography is the use of the black example. And one must think hard about what that allows him to do; it's neither liberal acknowledgement nor petty racist invocation/dismissal, though that's the trajectory his use takes, and we could talk about that as well. Ask the North African workers of the Goutte d'Or district of Paris. Ask the parents of Emmett Till. OK.

16 On "that-has-been," see Barthes, *Camera Lucida*, 76–77.

17 Barthes, *Camera Lucida*, 26.

18 Barthes, *Camera Lucida*, 40.

19 On the photography of the prick or wound, see Barthes, *Camera Lucida*, 25–28.

semiotic desire for universality, which excludes the difference of accent by excluding sound in the search for a universal language and a universal science of language, is manifest in Barthes as the exclusion of the sound/shout of the photograph; and that, in the fundamental methodological move of what-has-been-called-enlightenment, we see the invocation of a silenced difference, a silent black *mate*riality, in order to justify a suppression of difference in the name of (a false) universality.

In the end, though, neither language nor photography nor performance can tolerate silence, which is to say that the universalities these names would mark exist only in the singularities of a language, a photograph, a performance, singularities that cannot live in the absence of sound. Repressed accent returns precisely in the doubling that these things require, that the theory of these things demands, so that sound and recording are fundamentally connected in their disruptive necessity to language, photography, and performance. If Barthes had really consulted her, Ms. Bradley might have said all this; this aural aesthesis is what she counts on to intensify the politics of the performance whose production she extends. The meaning of a photograph is cut and augmented by a sound or noise that surrounds it and pierces its frame. And if, as Barthes suggests, that meaning or essence or *noeme* is death, the "*that-has-been* of the photographic object," then sound disturbs it in the interest of a resurrection. The content of the music of this photograph, like that of black music in general according to Baraka, is life, is freedom. The music and theater of a black photograph is erotic: the drama of life in the photograph of the dead.

So what's the difference between the son's inability to reproduce the photograph of his dead mother and the mother's insistence on the reproduction of the photograph of her dead son? The difference has to do with distinguishable stances toward universality, with what the discovery of a performance or a photograph has to do with universality, with the meaningful and illusory difference and relation between Performance and Performativity, the Photograph and Photography. If "the Winter Garden Photograph was indeed essential, it achieved for [Barthes], utopically, *the impossible science of the unique being.*" This impossible science, the unique and universal word or logos, is achieved only in a kind of solipsism, only in the memory that activates the unique photograph's capacity to wound. Meanwhile, Ms. Bradley sidesteps (by way of an insistent publicity wherein is carried the echo of whistling and mo'nin', in the interest of getting to some other—which is to say real—place) the utopic intersection of hermeneutics, phenomenology, and ontology that mark the origin and limit of Barthes's desire. For Barthes the inability and/or unwillingness to discover a photograph is driven by the positing of a universality and singularity that can only be mourned; for Ms. Bradley the discovery of a photograph in the fullness of its multiple sensuality moves in the drive for a universality to come, one called by what is in and around the photograph—black mo'nin'.

About twenty-five years before *Camera Lucida*, in an essay called "The Great Family of Man," Barthes makes some assumptions in the form of a question regarding what "the parents of Emmet *[sic]* Till, the young Negro assassinated by the Whites" would have thought about the Great Family of Man and the celebrated traveling photographic exhibition called *The Great Family of Man.* He uses those assumptions to argue for the necessity for progressive humanism of an ongoing historicization of nature rather than an uncritical photo-affirmation of certain universal facts such as birth and death. After all, he writes, "to reproduce death or birth tells us, literally, nothing. For these natural facts to gain access to a true language, they must be inserted into a category of knowledge which means postulating that one can transform them, and precisely subject their naturalness to our human criticism." Indeed, for Barthes, the failure of such photography lies in its inability to show

> whether or not the child is born with ease or difficulty, whether or not his birth causes suffering to his mother, whether or not he is threatened with a high mortality rate, whether or not such and such a future is open to him: this is what your exhibition should be telling people, instead of an eternal lyricism of birth. The same goes for death: must we really celebrate its essence once more, and thus risk forgetting that there is still so much we can do to fight it? It is this very young, far too young power that we must exalt, and not the sterile identity of "natural" death.

At the end of his career, however, Barthes produced a text that requires that we ask how a critique of the suppression of the determining weight of history is left behind for a stance that is nothing if not ahistorical. Where history and that singularity that exists as a function of depth/interiority, a certain incursion into the interior of the photograph and of identity, merge in "The Great Family of Man," history and singularity are reconfigured each in relation to the other in *Camera Lucida.* There, history exists only in relation to the sovereign ego that is given and represented by the wounding,

20 Barthes, *Camera Lucida*, 71; emphasis in original.

21 Roland Barthes, "The Great Family of Man," in *Mythologies*, trans. Annette Lavers (New York: Hill and Wang, 1972), 101–3.

22 Barthes, "The Great Family of Man," 101.

23 Barthes, "The Great Family of Man."

24 Barthes, "The Great Family of Man," 102.

arresting force of the photographic *punctum,* the placement of the interiority of a subject on endless trial. Where difference was once tied to the historical injustices it both structures and is structured by, now it marks only the uniqueness of an ego, is "that time when we were not born," or, more particularly, "the time when my mother was alive *before me.*" And, indeed, the representation of injustice, of historical alienation, is now configured only as banality. This configuration marks the return, paradoxically, of an empty humanism of death (and birth) that elsewhere and earlier Barthes had critiqued. *The photograph as such* is now just the universal visual fact of death, of pastness, of that-has-been, of the essence or *noeme* of photography, which, again, is the object of Barthes's analytic desire. On the other hand, *a photograph* will remain, for him, not invisible but simply unreproducible. The fundamental absence of depth, held now in the very form of the print, allows only the sad gesture of turning the photograph over. The appeal to the possibility of a particular identity's historical materiality is transformed into the flat memorialization of the photograph's tain. This analytic is shaped by the recrudescence of that humanism that marks what Louis Althusser called "the international of decent feelings," though here feeling is numbed by a violent egocentrism; an intensely melancholic phenomenology of photography emerges from that egocentrism, one in which what might be called the loss of historical particularity or of the particularity of *a* photograph is displaced by the loss of the desire for these objects and for the object as such.

But there is already something amiss in "The Great Family of Man," an opposition between the modes of production of the human and human essence that is precisely what Ms. Bradley cuts. It is the split in which totality is (a)voided in the interest of historical particularity, and it is displaced, in *Camera Lucida,* by a reified ontological concern with *studium/punctum,* a phenomenological privileging of essence that reveals history to be fundamentally personal, fundamentally deictic, and thus still forecloses not only the totality Barthes already disavows in the earlier text but also the singularity he desires in the later one. In other words, historical particularity becomes what Bertrand Russell would have called egocentric particularity. So this is about how listening carefully to the muted sound of the photograph as it resonates in Barthes's texts on photography, through his repression and denigration of it, gives us some clues about the inevitability of a certain development in which egocentrism and ontologism, perhaps each to the other's regret, are each tied to the other in theory, which is to say, in epistemologies of unalloyed looking. And perhaps whatever speech and writing come after or over a photograph or a performance should deal with this epistemological and methodological problem: how to listen to (and touch, taste, and smell) a photograph or a performance,

---

25 In *The Threshhold of the Visible World* (and here I thank David Eng for bringing this to my attention), Kaja Silverman looks at Barthes's distinction between the wounding effect of the *punctum* and the normative "'voice' of 'knowledge' and 'culture'" with which he associates the *studium*. Silverman cogently critiques Barthes's valorization of and failure to displace the ego, noting "the limited nature of the gains to be realized when [Barthes's] revisionary act of looking does not involve at the same time a realignment of self and other." She adds, "One is left with the disquieting sense that whereas Barthes consistently apprehends the photographs about which he writes from a viewing position which is radically divergent from that indicated by the metaphoric geometral point (associating an African American woman, for instance, with his aunt), his own sovereignty vis-à-vis the object remains unquestioned." Ultimately, as Silverman claims, "the figures depicted in the photograph serve only to activate [Barthes's] own memories, and so are stripped of all historical specificity. Barthes's recollections might thus be said to 'devour' the images of the other." The simultaneously lost and operative singularity that Barthes grieves for is his own. And the problem, here, is not the loss of the object that was there but the never having been there of Barthes's own absolutely singular objectlessness. Again, Silverman's formulations here seem absolutely correct. I would only augment them in the following way. (1) The refusal or inability to displace the sovereign ego is not only a failure to realign self and other but *also* a failure to realign the individual and the collective, so that the repression of difference is also the repression of a certain ensemblic publicity that is activated in and as sound, where sound is irreducible to voice and, thus, to the meanings that compose dominant culture and knowledge. (2) The devouring of the images of the other in which Barthes engages is, in some ways, a predictable effect of the specific theory of history that animates Barthes's ahistoricism. The discourse of slave narrative, for instance, is massively infused with examples of the submission of black bodies to a scopic regime that has, as one of its effects, the renewal, if not instantiation, of white interiority. This process is no less pronounced for the development of that white interiority that is identified as radically divergent (from the metaphoric geometral point or from the political and/or aesthetic norms that are associated with that geometral point) or avant-garde. This is not to say that it is not surprising that Barthes associates an African American woman with his aunt; it is to say that it is also not surprising that Barthes makes such an association. I will try to say more about how such interiority as that of Barthes is possible only in contradistinction to that incapability of science or theory, that inability to make— or lack of concern with making—observations, that interminably looked-at failure to look, that specifically black phonic materiality that marks, if you will, the return of the repressed *studium* in the *punctum*, in short that presubjective position outside history that has been associated with the African with equal vigor in valorizations of tradition, on the one hand, and discontinuity, on the other. As I imply here and elaborate below, a fuller attempt to move past such a structure would require an attunement not only to the ways in which the aesthetics of black spectatorship and audition as black performance is tied to a general phonography of the photograph, but also to how that complex is, in turn, tied to an improvisation through the opposition of interiority and ensemblic publicity. Of course, Silverman's work—including especially *The Acoustic Mirror* (Bloomington: Indiana University Press, 1989), her wary critique of the phallocratic deployment of what she understands to be a degrading reduction of feminine voice to feminine scream in classic cinema—is very useful to such a project. See Kaja Silverman, *The Threshold of the Visible World* (New York: Routledge, 1996), 180–85.

26 Barthes, *Camera Lucida*, 64.

27 Barthes, *Camera Lucida*, 65.

28 Louis Althusser, "The International of Decent Feelings," in The *Spectre of Hegel*, trans. G. M. Goshgarian (New York: Verso, 1997), 21–35.

how to attune oneself to a moan or shout that animates the photograph with an intentionality of the outside. Barthes is interested in, but, by implication, does not love, the world. The shout that structures and ruptures the photograph of Emmett Till with a piercing historicality, that resingularizes and reconstructs his broken body, emerges from love, from a love of the world, from a specific political intention. When Barthes invokes Ms. Bradley in a critique of the naturalistic and universalizing photography of the bare fact of death but fails to recognize her own photographic contribution to that critique, he betrays a quite specific inability that will be fully activated years later in another discourse on photography that is equally dependent on black images.

Of course, Emmett Till's death (which word wrongs him and her) was not natural, and the photograph shows this. It shows this and the *death's* difficulty, the suffering of the mother, the threat of a high mortality rate, and the seemingly absolute closure of his future. But it does so not by way of an erasure of lyricism or even of "the natural," for these reemerge, by way of an unbearable and vicious dialectic, in the photograph's music. Barthes's question was only rhetorical, though. He didn't really ask Ms. Bradley what she thought. She told us anyway. And so this photograph—or, more precisely, the natural and unnatural fact that is photographed and displayed— cannot simply be used as an inarticulate denial of an always and necessarily false universality. For it is in the name, too, of a dynamic universality (which critically moves in, among other things, grief, anger, hatred, the desire to expose and eradicate savagery) whose organization would suspend the condition of possibility of deaths like Emmett Till's, that the photo was shown, is seen. It is in the interest of a certain defeat or at least deconstruction of death—a resurrective or (second) reconstructive improvisation through death's pride and through a culture that death drives—that Till's body was shown, was seen, and that the photograph of Till's body is shown, is seen. But Barthes wasn't trying to hear the sound of that display, the sound of the photograph's *illumination* of facticity, which holds an affirmation not of, but *out of,* death. Black Art, which is to say Black Life, which is to say Black (Life Against) Death, which is to say Black Eros, is the ongoing production of a performance: rupture and collision, augmented toward singularity, motherless child, childless mother, heart-rending shriek, levee camp moan, grieving lean and head turn, fall, *Stabat mater,* turn a step, loose booty funk brush stroke down my cheek, yellow dog, blue trän, black drive. The ways black mo'nin' improvises through the opposition of mourning and melancholia disrupt the temporal framework that buttresses that opposition such that an extended, lingering look at—aesthetic response to—the photograph manifests itself as political action. Is the display of the picture melancholic? No, but it's certainly no simple release or mourning either. Mo'nin' improvises through that difference. We have to keep looking at this so we can listen to it.

So in the name of this bright section of winds, some variations on Alexander's question: Can we look at this, which is to say can we look at this again (such repetition being a constitutive element of what it means and is to be BLACK)? Can you be BLACK and not look at this (again)? Can we look at this (again) and be BLACK? There is a responsibility to look every time, again, but sometimes it looks as though that looking comes before, holds, replicates, reproduces what is looked at. Nevertheless, looking keeps open the possibility of closing precisely what it is that prompts and makes necessary that opening. But such an opening is only held in looking that is attentive to the sound—and movement, feel, taste, smell (as well as sight): the sensual ensemble—of what is looked at. The sound works and moves not just through but before another movement, a movement that is before even that affirmation that Barthes didn't hear. A photograph was seen, was shown, in a complex path, a dissonant and polyphonic drive. In the death of Emmett Till, insurrection and resurrection are each insistently *before* the other, waiting for a beginning that is possible only after the experience of all of what is held in the photograph. What is held in a photograph is not exclusive to the photograph, but this photograph moves and works, is shown, was seen, shone, says, is animated, resounds, broken, breaking song of, song for, something before, like the Music, which is, as Mingus says, not just beautiful, but *terribly beautiful.*

So here is the performance I discovered by way of this "legacy of lynchings": At my aunt Mary's funeral (she was my favorite aunt, but I was scared to look at her face in the photograph I couldn't help but look at that they made of her at the funeral home), Ms. Rosie Lee Seals rose up in church, out from the program, and said, "Sister Mary Payne told me that if she died she wanted me to give a *deep moan* at her funeral." And, at that moment, in her Las Vegas-from-Louisiana accent, condition of impossibility of a universal language, condition of possibility of a universal language, burying my auntie with music at morning time, where moaning renders mourning wordless (the augmentation and reduction of or to our releasing more than what is bound up in the presence of the word) and voice is dissonanced and multiplied by metavoice, Sister Rosie Lee Seals mo'ned. New word, new world.

Orange

de Rijke/de Rooij

2004

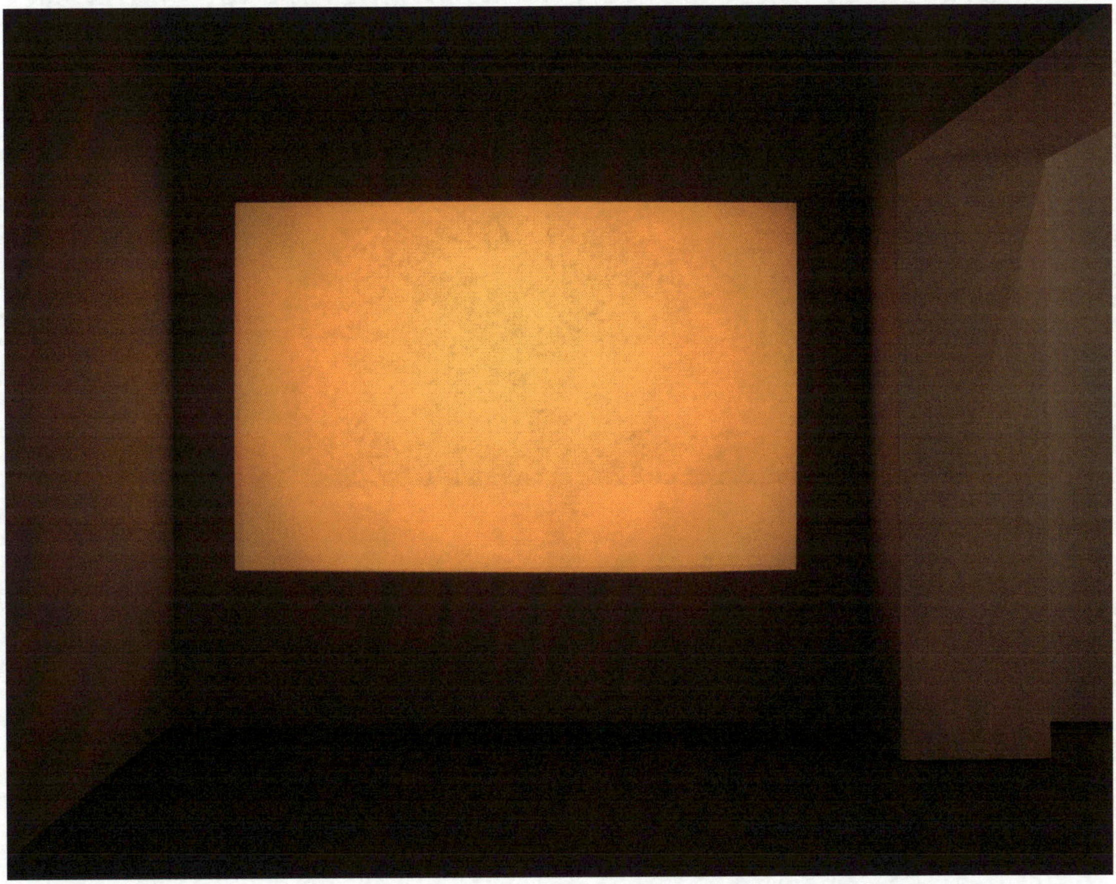

Top: Stills from *Eye/Machine I*, 2001
Middle: Stills from *Eye/Machine II*, 2002
Bottom: Stills from *Eye/Machine III*, 2003
Harun Farocki

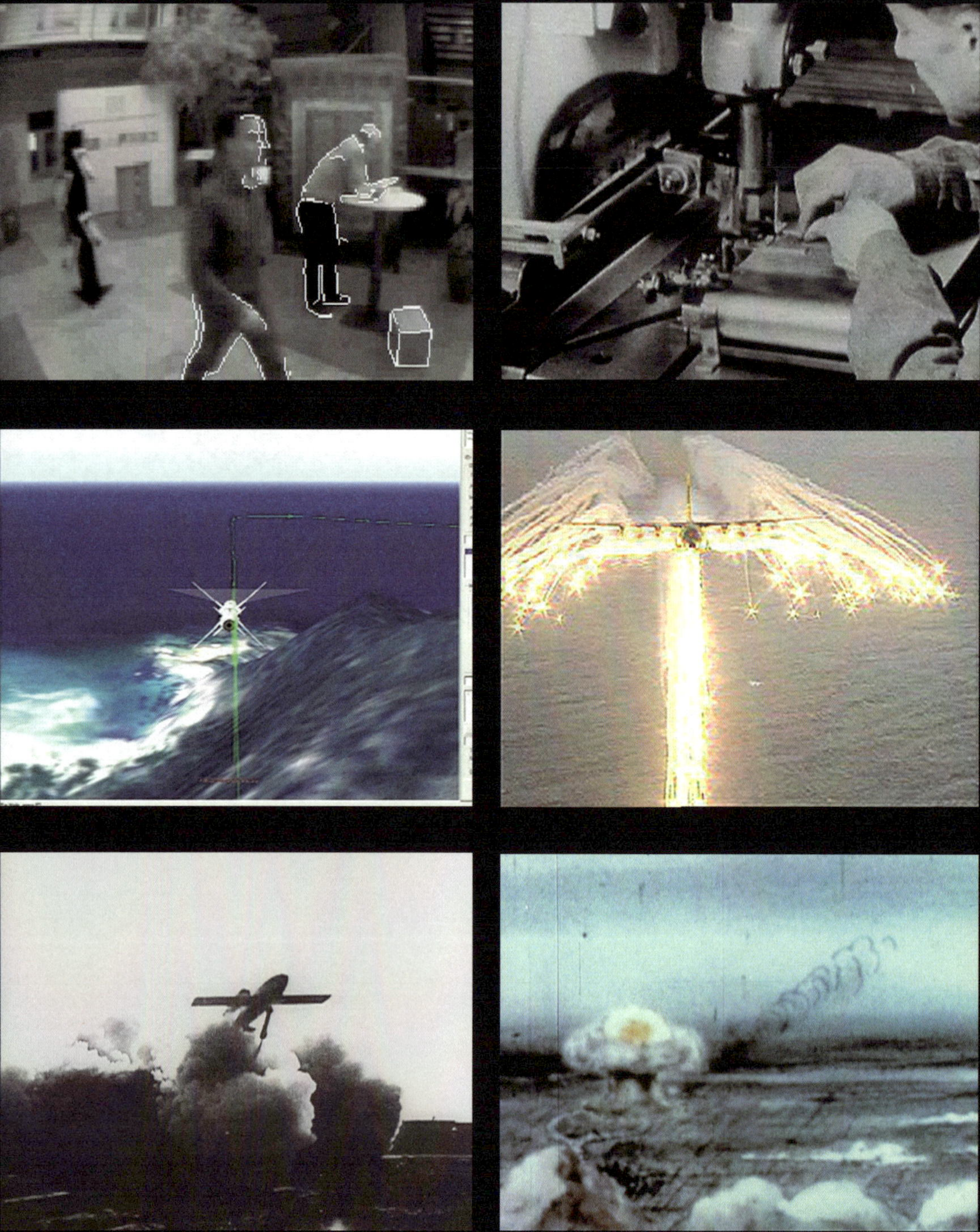

Phantom Images
Harun Farocki
2004

Let me begin with two image sequences from the 1991 allied war against Iraq that stand for a single type of picture. The first sequence, taken from cameras in a helicopter, a plane, and "a drone"—which is how the light unmanned reconnaissance planes have been described—shows a segment of the terrain they are flying over. In the centre of the camera's lens we can see the projectile flying towards its target. The detonation more than exhausts the range of contrast. The automatic aperture fails to achieve a balance: the images cease.

During the 1920s in the US, film recordings taken from a position that a human cannot normally occupy were called phantom shots; for example, shots from a camera that had been hung under a train. In narrative film images taken from a position of a person are referred to as subjective. We can interpret the film that takes up the perspective of the bomb as a phantom-subjective image. The film footage from a camera that is plunging towards its target, a suicidal camera, stays in our mind. This perspective was new and it offered us an image of something about which we had only limited knowledge until the cruise missiles of the 1980s appeared. They were presented together with the term "intelligent weapons," and they combined the ill-considered notion of intelligence with an equally ill-considered subjectivity; it was a mnemonic construction bent upon self-flagellation as it beat its path into nothingness.

Animated films, whether drawn or computer-calculated, also often used a perspective that a manned film camera cannot occupy, or only with great difficulty; for example, the perspective offered from the point of view of a bullet shot by a gun. The animated films thus promulgated the possibility of a ubiquitous point of view that the cinematographic competition was not capable of, and that contributed to its rhetoric of exaggeration. Cartoon or animated film is a genre that cannot really represent death. In animated film, everything is always reversible. But the continually redrawn animated image is well suited to the representation of the methods and functions of technology.

Computer animations can be distinguished from other drawn images because they have pioneered a particular stylistic standard. Such self-proclaimed universal rules existed in American films in the 1950s—images made in the firm conviction that there can be no other image of the world. Whenever computer animation begins to process photographic data, it contains an inherent critique of the photograph. Stemming from the dubious notion that the computer is superseding earlier visual media, computer-generated animations present themselves as exemplary images capable of representing sex and death.

A corollary to the common view in 1991 that the pictures from these cameras—whether filming the missiles approaching their target or the detonation—made the war look like a computer game is that war resembles child's play. Cartoons are something for children, and computer animation is a form of symbolic assimilation. Almost all technical representations which maintain that *they only* represent the operative principle of a process have a large share of mystification in them. For example, it must be noted that in these 1991 Gulf War images, no people can be seen. The battlefield is uninhabited. When you see an entire roll of such images you cannot help but think that the war will continue on well after humanity has disappeared from the face of machines.

The operative pictures of the projectile flying towards its target and the ensuing detonation show largely military objectives, barracks, air raid shelters, airfields, and bridges. Bridges appear again and again as strategic targets, even if the civilian population was using them. At a press conference during the first Gulf War, a representative of the US military showed a film in which a car could be seen driving away from a bridge that had just been hit—and he made a joke about it. Today you cannot get footage from the military archives in which cars can be seen, footage that would force you to conclude that humans were indeed present at or near the target. It is obvious, then, how war tactics and war reportage coincide. The images are produced by the military and are controlled by the military and politicians.

In the first war against Iraq in 1991, the image of the police worked according to the principle of the good-cop/bad-cop scheme. On the side of the Iraqis was the bad-cop who used conventional methods of power to keep the reporters and cameramen from the field of battle. They did not want to have them documenting the fact that the Saddam-regime was perhaps capable of terrorizing its own population and the population of Kuwait, or that it was not capable of organizing an army that could offer at least minimal protection for its retreating soldiers, not to mention its own civilian population. The good-cop from the US, by contrast, excluded the photographers and cameramen structurally from the event itself, thanks again to the "filming bombs," as Theweleit called them. Bombs with cameras in them offer no room for an independent observer.

Iraq allowed a couple of journalists to stay in Baghdad during the war, among them Peter Arnet from CNN. They sent us the green contrast-enhanced panoramas. Like Ernst Jünger in Paris, Arnet experienced the bombarding of Baghdad first-hand from the roof of his hotel, but, in contrast to Ernst Jünger, he was held under a sort of house arrest. Both were forced to offer an aestheticized reflection, one befitting the mind of an armchair military strategist perched on a hill. The correspondents in Baghdad belonged to a tactical reserve of an intensely contradictory strategy of the Saddam-regime: on the one hand they were supposed to conceal the inferiority of the Iraqis, on the other hand, they were supposed to expose the inhumanity of the allied war against them. To do so they required a photo of dead bodies, of as many dead bodies as possible, a close-up of them in one picture.

There is a film about a minute long, made in 1942, of the training flight of the missile HS 293 D over a shipwreck near Peenemünde. It was recorded by a television camera in the warhead of the projectile. The television pictures were sent by a transmitter to an accompanying plane that fired the missile and then deviated from the missile's path without losing sight of it. From the plane the missile was guided to its target using a control stick closely resembling the modern day joystick. Since, as is well known, it was impossible to record electronic images right up until the 1950s, this sequence is probably the only remaining film documentation of this experiment—one of the technicians filmed it from the monitor with his camera. The miniaturization of the television camera was a developmental advancement, but the HS 293 D itself was never used during World War II. By contrast with the rocket-builders, the rocket-television-camera-installers continued their work not in the US, but in the West German television industry.

I recall a quotation:

> We feel that it is immoral to design weapons whose construction presupposes the death of the soldier using it, and thus—at least in our understanding—implying sacrifice as part of the mechanism of the weapon. In Japan, however, the mission of the kamikaze pilot who dives his plane into an enemy destroyer is considered an honour. They also have torpedoes that are guided towards their target by a pilot built into it. An interesting twist to the saying: 'the bullet is a blind idiot.' (Ernst Jünger, *The Gordian Knot*, 1953)

The bullet is a blind idiot, or, to quote from the "Soldier's Song": "Go on, Luise, wipe your face, my darling, / Not every bullet hits its target" ("*Nun ade lieb Luise, wisch ab Dein Gesicht / Eine jede Kugel die trifft ja nicht*"). The pictures from the warhead of the missiles of 1991, together with the expression "intelligent weapons," are so distressing, or so gripping, precisely because the bullets are not blind any more. And in war, death is always someone else's death. The pattern of recognition and object tracking of seeing bombs threatens with infallibility. Paul Virilio's comment that these images are aimed at us sounds like a self-fulfilling prophecy.

The apparatus HIL, short for "hardware in the loop," is a machine that tests the flight path of rockets as they travel towards their target and corrects their course, independently navigating their flight to their strategic objective. The apparatus, about as large as an automobile, offers a large number of variable parameters and can perform quick swerving movements with great precision. The large-scale image shows the scanning warhead and its tilting prisms; images are transmitted to the warhead—simulated pictures of the landscape it has to fly over. In this case the images are based on pictures taken from an aerial camera, and in them you can see the forests, home communities, and streets below.

The tactical warhead stores and processes the aerial photos, and the processing of the photos can be seen in green and red lines. The green lines appear to suggest something like an initial suspicion. The search-target program discovers a constellation in a picture, perhaps a part of a recognizable pattern, and stores it. The program then draws a line in the picture and searches again for an aggregate of pixels that would allow it to continue drawing that line. When the line is verified, when the outlines of a street-crossing, bridges, or power lines appear, which are registered as landmarks, the colour red is used to show that they have been verified, rather like a somewhat slow-moving mind that underlines in red a thought that seems to be correct. The automated eye has recorded only a few search patterns through which it looks at the images of the real world. These picture- processing apparatuses work with the same sort of clumsiness with which robotic arms perform a new task. Each movement is broken down into fragments, and each fragment of the movement is performed with equal dedication, precisely but with absolutely no habitual elegance. But just as the robots in factories first used manual labourers as their model until they outperformed them and rendered them obsolete, these sensory automatons are supposed to replace the work of the human eye.

In my first work on this subject, *Eye/Machine* (2001), I called such pictures, made neither to entertain nor to inform, "operative images." These are images that do not represent an object, but rather are part of an operation. Later it occurred to me that this term came from Roland Barthes. In his book *Mythologies* (1957/1964) he wrote in his theoretical afterword: "I must return here to the distinction between the language of objects and meta-language. If I am a lumberjack and I name the tree that I am chopping down, I say—whatever the form of the sentence may be—*the tree*, and I do not speak *about* the tree. . . . If I am not a lumberjack, though, I cannot say *the tree*, I can only talk *of* and *about it*."

In this theoretical text, Roland Barthes was striving to maintain his own practice. He wanted to belong to the revolutionary left, but did not want to be part of the Soviet blanket-weavers, which is exactly what the French Communist Party wanted from its intellectuals. Moscow persecuted semiotics with characteristic hatred because it was based upon a much denounced Russian avant-garde theory, namely: formalism—the only theoretical novelty, according to Foucault, communism ever produced.

Today we are under no pressure to become radical materialists and to trace the manifestations of materialism in the structures of language and thought. If we take an interest in pictures that are part of an operation, this is because we are weary of non-operative pictures, and weary of meta-language. Weary of the day-to-day practice of re-mythologizing quotidian life, weary of the ever-changing and many-channelled program of images custom-made to mean something to us. What is shown in these programs comes neither from the micro- nor from the macro-cosmos, but rather from the middle level; its lower boundary line is the close-up of the human face, its higher level a street block of houses. This is the filling, so to speak, in the picture of the cosmic sandwich. Children are encouraged not to eat the filling without the bread, an exercise in the sublimation of desire. Or perhaps the movie and television industry has exhausted itself in its overproduction of material.

In an exhibition like *CRTL Space* (2001) my interest was focused upon seeing pictures that were not cropped and framed in order to compress space and time. Films or photos that were taken in order to monitor a process that, as a rule, cannot be observed by the human eye. Images that appear so inconsequential that they are not stored—the tapes are erased and are used again. Generally the images are stored and archived only in exceptional cases, but exceptional cases one is sure to encounter. Such images challenge the artist who is interested in a meaning that is not authorial and intentional, an artist interested in a sort of beauty that is not calculated. The US military command has surpassed us all in the art of showing something that comes close to the "unconscious visible."

Today the materialists are the artists like Heidi and Alvin Toffler; they don't belong to an intellectual circle in Paris, but to a think-tank in Washington close to the Pentagon. In their books *The Third Wave* and *War and Anti-War*, books with a huge circulation in the paperback editions, they assume that there is a necessary correspondence between the technology of production and the technology of destruction, of manufacturing and war. War is in this axiomatic and evolutionary view of a field of activity like any other, much as one would compare agriculture to industry. In this respect, it ought to be noted that the inhabitants of Carthage had far more complicated catapults than agricultural tools, and that during World War II, when the military was developing radio-controlled weapons, the jet airplane, stereophonic recording, and the computer, there were more labouring slaves on German ruled territory than ever before.

The reductionist representation of the Swiss weapons manufacturer Örlikon shows the approaching flight of a projectile that is then sighted by ground defenses and destroyed by an anti-ballistic missile. This sequence of products, in which a new product displaces an old one, is also a model of culture. The cold war made it possible for over 40 years to write off rockets, tanks, jets and planes, and ships that were never used materially and were sometimes morally worn out already before they were completed. The products of the IT industry have a longer shelf life than the machinery of war. And in order to keep the market free of constipation, moral campaigns have to be waged, but these themselves grow old and wear out.

The expensive production of computer products, generally immaterial things, was supposed to be one of the causes of the sudden collapse of the Soviet Union. The competitors lost the race, not simply because they were too weak, but also because they did not need the competition as a motor for the process of aging and rejuvenation.

But now the arms industry itself has a hard time justifying its new products. It lacks an enemy that could produce anti-ballistic weapons against it, which would then require anti-anti-ballistic weapons. And it is hard to make systematic sense out of the ways of war: you can supply weapons to an ally who then leaves the alliance and becomes an enemy, as in the case of Afghanistan and Iraq. I am speaking here from the phantom perspective of war, from the perspective of an imagined war-subjectivity. In Brecht's *Mother Courage* we find the sentence: "War always finds a solution." Barbara Ehrenreich interpreted the sentence to mean that war is incredibly inventive when it is a matter of its own survival. Even if no one wanted war any more, it would attempt to mutate into a war of automatons in a deserted field of battle. In rich countries the majority do not want war. War is not necessary, just as gold backing is not necessary for currency. Yet people have recently come to believe, with Hobbes, in gold backing for our culture. And we create holidays in memory of a common denominator, violence. The recent wars that have been led with unimaginable superiority on one side—in asymmetry—are the ritual precursors of such holidays.

The fantastic impression of an abandoned battlefield upon which the war is continually being fought—

a bit like the toys that come to life when the children are sleeping—remind one of the emptiness of the production plants. In the automobile industry, for instance, you only see the people working where there is no more space for robots. When observing the connection between production and destruction, the following analogy appears: while factories in rich countries have fewer and fewer people in them, more people than ever before perform manual labour in poor countries. And even the wars increasingly take place in poor countries. The operative war pictures from the Gulf War of 1991 that do not show any people are paradoxical. Despite the censorship, the pictures were more than propaganda attempting to silence the sum total of perhaps 200,000 dead. They were, perhaps above all, in the spirit of a utopia of war, a utopia that doesn't reckon with encountering people, accepting them only somewhat disdainfully as victims.

When asked about casualties on the Iraqi side in 1991, one US military spokesman said, "We don't do body counts." One could translate that into: "We are not their gravediggers; we let others do that dirty work." Or one could read it as a statement that the rich countries do not boast with the enemy's dead and that they want to avoid casualties among their own soldiers. For the poor, that is a source of hope, the hope that from the achievements of the rich something will trickle down to the poor.

It is true that operational pictures conjure up the image of a cleanly led war, and they are stronger than the pictures of the dirty war, like the pictures of an air raid shelter in Baghdad in which a couple of hundred civilians were torn to pieces. The television spectators were supposed to appreciate the war technicians and to sympathize with the technology of war through the images of aerial photographs, which were actually made only for the eyes of the war technicians. But they still remained political beings who spoke with each other and criticized pictures; they knew how to distinguish between the first war, when Iraq attacked Kuwait and attempted to annex it, and the second war. In 2003 the pictures from the warheads of missiles were rarely shown. And there was no talk of intelligent weapons, only of precision-guided weapons.

Due to the secrecy surrounding military operations, it is difficult to prove the following assumption, but everything seems to support the theory that in both Gulf wars there were no intelligent weapons, none that could seek out and hit its target on its own. It was more than the usual wartime trickery of the opponent. Here there was a continuous attempt to make the idea of a seeing bomb so popular and common that, thereafter, they would have to be ordered, developed, and paid for.

Similarly, there are no pictures that do not aim at the human eye. A computer can process pictures, but it needs no pictures to verify or falsify what it reads in the images it processes. For the computer, the image in the computer is enough. Nevertheless, the "objective language" pictures are distinct by degrees from the "meta-linguistic" pictures, much as the aesthetics of the machine are distinct from commodity aesthetics. And the axe of Roland Barthes's lumberjack is not simply a manifestation of goal-related rationality: even a tool communicates not only with the materials of its trade, but also with the human senses.

SIGHTS OF WAR

Images from my film *Images of the World* appeared to me back in 1988 to be an adequate means of representing the situation at hand because they maintain their distance vis-à-vis the victims. They are more appropriate than close-up pictures: images of the selection on the ramp, images of the starving prisoners in the barracks, the mounds of corpses being cleared away by a bulldozer. With such images symbolic violence is once again being perpetrated against the victims; and even with the best intentions they are being *used*.

There are even recordings, made after Auschwitz was liberated, of Soviet doctors performing autopsies in the open air upon the bodies of the dead prisoners. The gesture of an autopsy is an attempt to recreate the individual history of the victim. But filming it adds nothing at all. Above the aerial photographs of the concentration camps, in which the individual is scarcely larger than a dot, I wrote a brief comment: "In the grain of the photograph lies the respect and protection of the personality."

It is only too clear that we are not shown the pictures taken from a distance in order to spare the dead yet another humiliation. There are rarely good reasons for showing us the images of mutilated victims. Usually they are being used for political business. In addition, even the distant pictures of a horrible event refer to pictures offering no distance simply by standing in contrast to them. Unavoidably, despite the humanitarian attempts, the barbarianism comes shining through. Much as the image of love is cross-referenced to its dirty precursors and to the effort required to get over them.

A Texas Instruments advertisement argues that it is economically cheaper to drop computer-guided bombs and even cheaper still to use precision-guided missiles. A productive misreading of the message provides us with the interpretation that, with fewer bombs, there would be a drop in sales that would have to be compensated. If there were a connection between production and destruction, they would have to sell less hardware and more guidance systems. More guidance systems can only be sold when there is a precise distinction between friend and foe. The economy, at least that of the weapons manufacturers, calls for war in the name of humanitarian goals.

Live Evil (Kuala Lumpur)

Paul Pfeiffer

2003

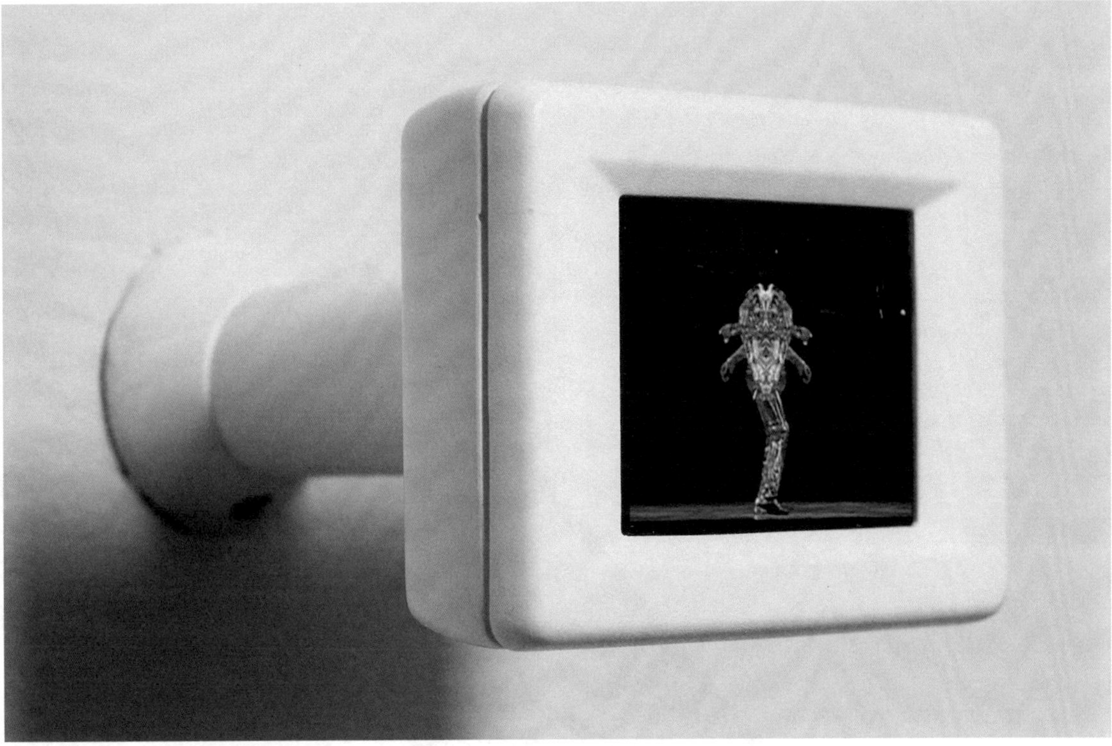

Digital Video Effect: "Holes"

Seth Price

2003

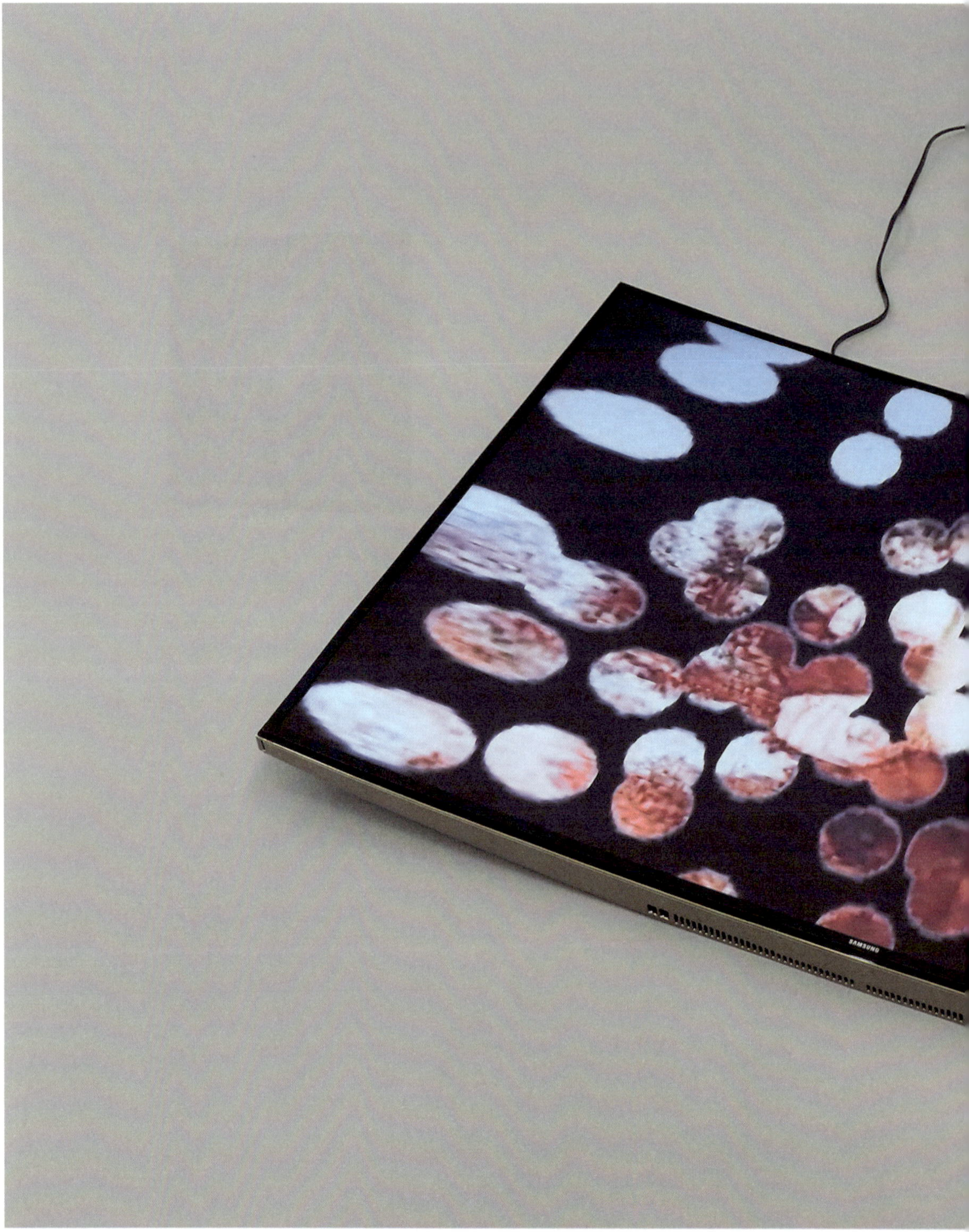

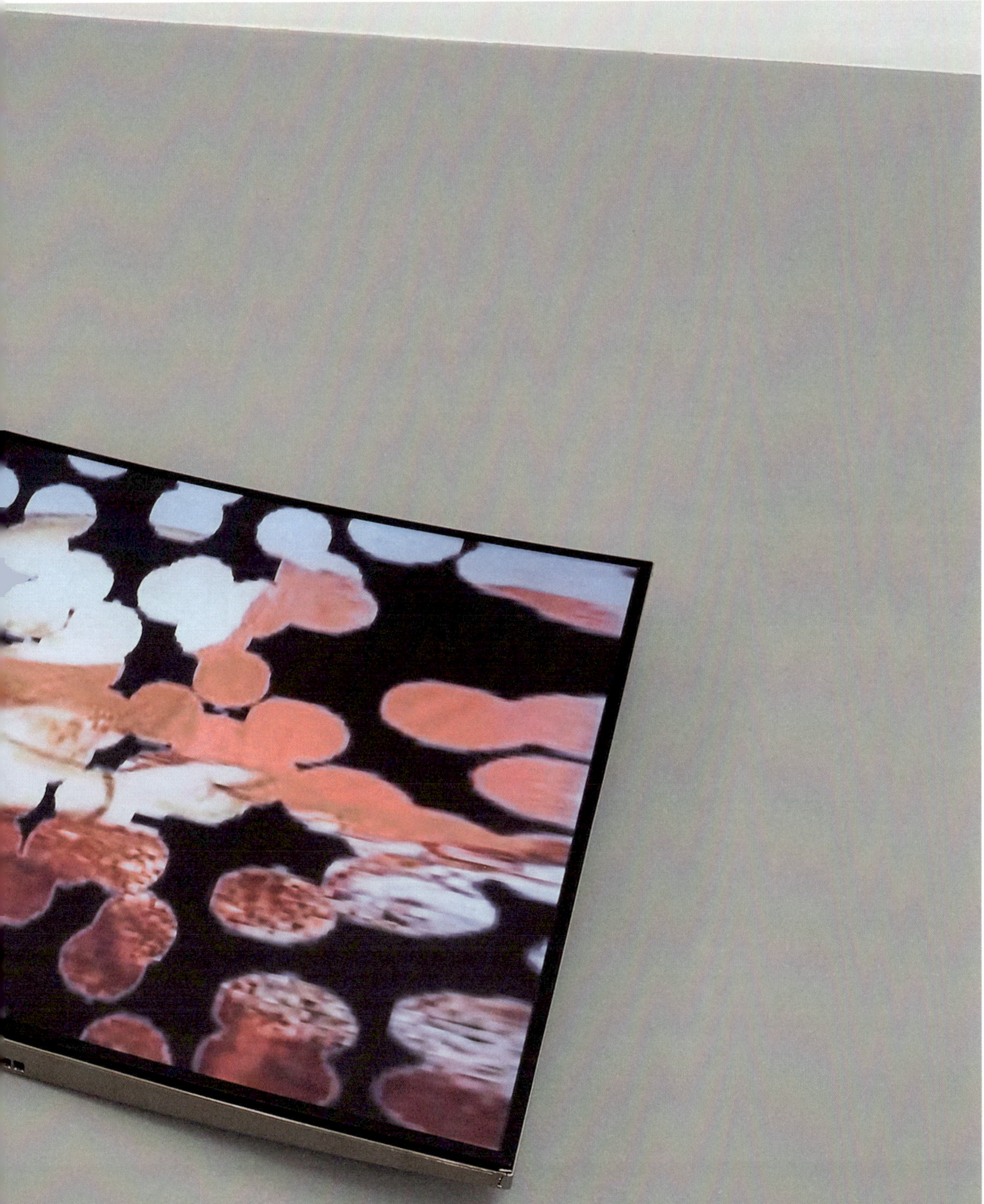

The Full Edition of Smoke and Mirrors 24A

Eileen Quinlan

2006

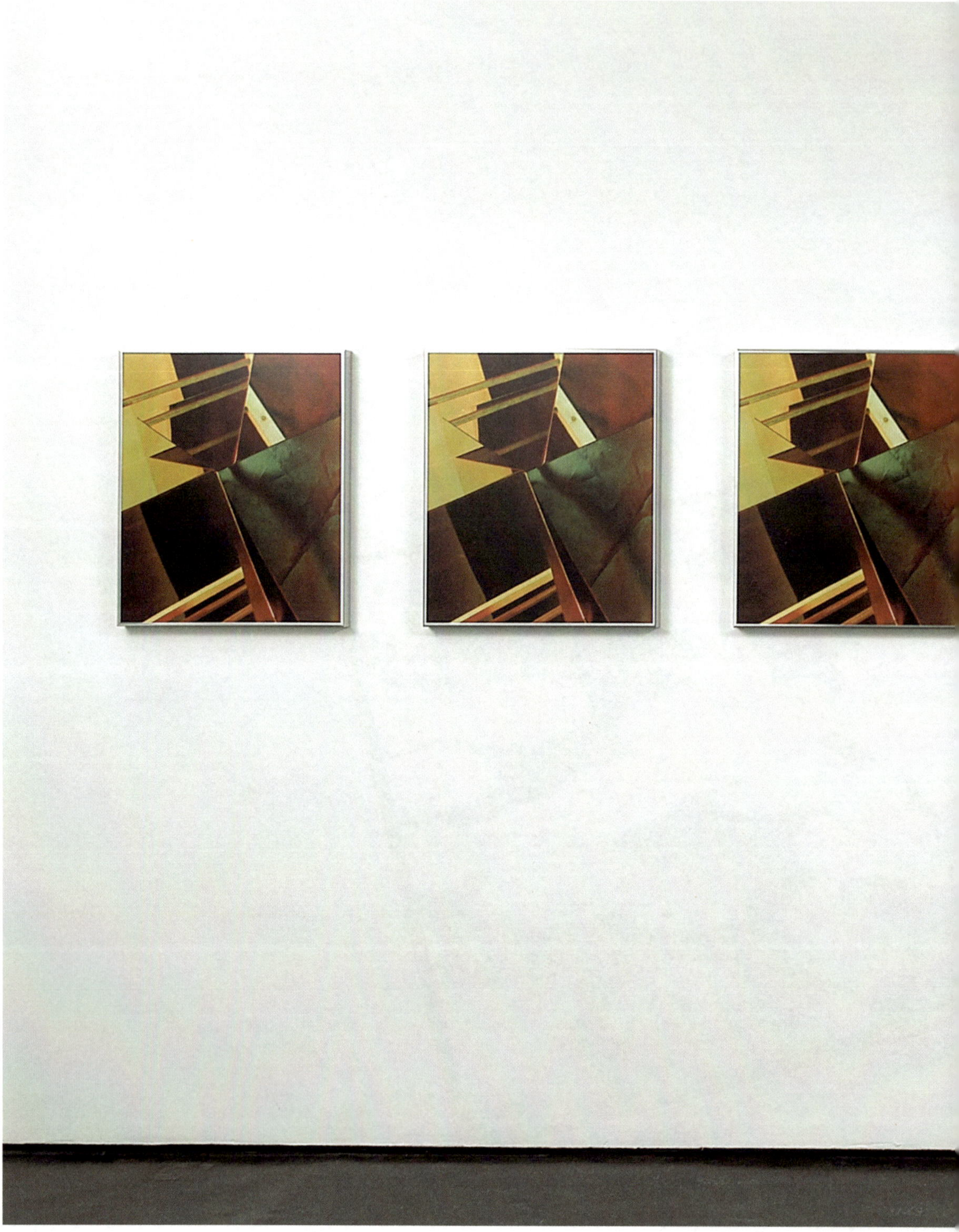

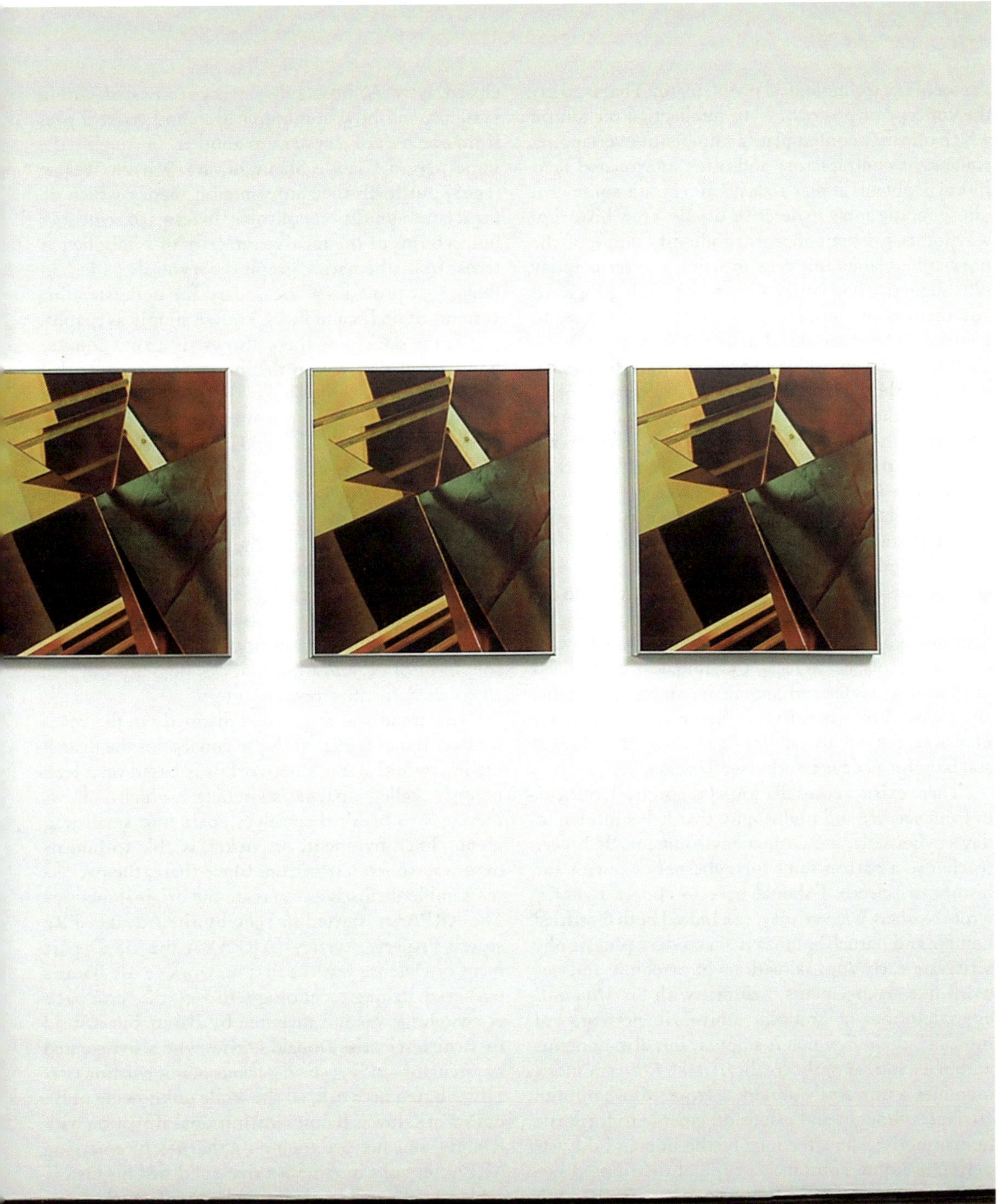

Protocol

Alexander R. Galloway

2006

Protocol is a technological problematic. That is to say, the concept of protocol is an intellectual terrain on which one may contemplate a number of overlapping, sometimes contradictory and often interrelated theoretical problems at play today. I aim in this somewhat idiosyncratic entry to describe briefly a few historical waypoints for the concept, to identify some of the normative claims inherent in using the term today, plus suggest a few issues with which, going forward, any theorist of computers or networks will have to contend. Because of this, I deliberately avoid any discussion of the etymology of the term in diplomatic affairs, or the current institutional structure in place today for the creation and maintenance of Internet protocols. Instead I offer a singular perspective on the theme, one that could be contested as much as it could be confirmed.

A distributed network is a specific network architecture characterized by equity between nodes, bi-directional links, a high degree of redundancy and general lack of internal hierarchy. Protocol refers to the technology of organization and control operating in distributed networks. Protocol functions largely without relying on hierarchical, pyramidal or centralized mechanisms; it is flat and smooth; it is universal, flexible and robust. Protocol exists in contemporary computer networks, but it is also at play in a variety of biological and bioinformatic networks (see Thacker, 2004).

There exists a constellation of theoretical influences from science and philosophy that helps inform today's cybernetic, networked environment. 'If I were to choose a patron saint for cybernetics out of the history of science, I should have to choose Leibniz', wrote Norbert Wiener (1965: 12). Indeed both Gottfried Leibniz and Baruch Spinoza from modern philosophy articulate early approximations of machinic and network-like arrangements. Leibniz, with his *Monadology*, describes a smooth, universal network of 'monads', each of which is singular but also contains within it a mirror of the totality. In the *Ethics* Spinoza identifies a universal substance, from whose infinite attributes thought and extension emerge to form the human body. The affections of the human body superimpose onto substance a type of distributed network of relations and counterrelations. In the 20th century Ludwig von Bertalanffy (1976), with the science of general systems theory, and Wiener, with the science of cybernetics, helped describe open versus closed systems, how subsystems are nested within systems, and how communication and control pass from one part of a system to another. In roughly the same period Claude Shannon and Warren Weaver (1998) put forth their information theory which defined communication not solely in terms of semantics but in terms of the relative integrity of symbolic patterns. In mathematics, graph theory is also a key influence. It provides a vocabulary for understanding systems of nodes and links, known simply as graphs.

At the same time there also exists a faint counterpoint resonating within this historical overview that must be pointed out. This is the general assumption that networks have the potential to dehierarchize, disrupt and generally dissolve rigid structures of all varieties. This thread runs from Hans Magnus Enzensberger's chart of emancipated versus repressive media, to Gilles Deleuze and Félix Guattari's 'rhizome' (1987), to Peter Galison and his war against the center, and even to the RAND researchers John Arquilla and David Ronfeldt and their theory of netwar (2001). All these thinkers share the assumption that networks exist in an antagonistic relationship to authority, that networks are the sole form of organization that can possibly threaten entrenched, fortified power centers.

This trend was articulated distinctly in the 1960s by Paul Baran (1964) with the concept of the distributed network. Baran's network was based on a technology called packet-switching which allows messages to break themselves apart into small fragments. Each fragment, or packet, is able to find its own way to its destination. Once there, the packets reassemble themselves to create the original message. The ARPAnet, started in 1969 by the Advanced Research Projects Agency (ARPA) at the US Department of Defense was the first network to use Baran's packet-switching technology. In fact, the term packet-switching was not invented by Baran, but instead by British scientist Donald Davies who also invented a system for sending small packets of information over a distributed network, all the while unknowing of Baran's work. It was Baran's institutional affiliation with RAND and his proximity to the newly emerging ARPA network in America that solidified his historical legacy. I consider Baran to be the 'father' of protocological systems, not simply because of his position in the historical emergence of distributed networks, but because he explicitly understood that networks create new, robust structures for organization and control; they do not remove organization and control. Compared to pyramidal hierarchies, networks are indeed flimsy, ineffective and disorganized. But this relationship of asymmetry is precisely what, in the long run, makes networks so robust. Baran understood that the Cold War model relied upon a decentralized system of targets—cities and military bases, mostly—and so, if a new targetless model of organization could be rolled out (the smooth, distributed network), then precisely through the inversion of the Cold War model a new strategic advantage could be gained. Distributed networks have become hegemonic only recently, and because of this it is relatively easy to lapse back into a time when the network was disruptive of the power center, when the guerilla threatened the army, when the nomadic horde threatened the citadel. But this is no longer the case today. The distributed network is the new citadel, the new army, the new power.

So the assumption above, that networks have the potential to dehierarchize, disrupt and generally dissolve rigid structures of all varieties, must be resolutely resisted. It is not the case that networks produce a general waning of organization and control. In fact, it is the opposite: distributed networks produce an entirely new system of organization and control that, while perhaps incompatible with pyramidal systems of power, is nevertheless just as effective at keeping things in line. This new system of organization and control, protocol, is adept at regulating flows, coding objects and sculpting life forms. Thus, the problematic of protocol suggests that in recent decades there has been a change in the nature of organization and control, not an 'emancipation' from it, as Enzensberger so hoped. The imperative today, then, is to understand the nature of this new logic of organization, and as Michel Foucault once said about power, not to become enamored of it.

Indeed Foucault and Deleuze are quite useful for thinking about the protocological system of organization and control. Foucault, through his concept of biopower, was able to articulate a new form of total saturation of organization, one that pentrated not only the institutions of modern life, but also the very networks of human interaction, be they domestic, familial, sexual, or even intrahuman at the level of 'raw' biology. Deleuze, in his book on Foucault, and additionally in a series of fragments and interviews he produced late in life, identified a historical epoch, concurrent with Foucault's rise of biopower, called the society of control. The society of control is characterized not by the power of the institutions of modernity or pre-modernity, the army, the prison, the university, the church, but instead by what he called the ultra-rapid forms of free floating control that are inherent in distributed networks. These networks may be computer-based, but, Deleuze suggested, one must also look to the biological networks of the life sciences. Indeed the informatic and the biological become intertwined under the societies of control such that the biological is always already understood as an informatic network of data (the genome), and at the same time the digital is always understood as a type of artificial life system which may produce 'intelligent' emergent properties just as organisms do.

The Internet protocols themselves are interesting as historical documents. A computer protocol is a set of recommendations and rules for implementing a technical standard. The protocols that govern much of the Internet are contained in what are called RFC (Request For Comments) documents. The expression derives from a memorandum titled 'Host Software' sent by Steve Crocker on 7 April 1969, which is known today as RFC 1. The RFCs are published by the Internet Engineering Task Force (IETF). They are freely available and used predominantly by engineers who wish to build hardware or software that meets common specifications. Since 1969, a few thousand RFC documents have been released, and they, along with a larger constellation of global technological standards, constitute the system of organization and control known as protocol. Protocols are systems of material organization; they structure relationships of bits and atoms, and how they flow through the distributed networks in which they are embedded.

A close reading of the RFCs is outside of the scope of this encyclopedia entry; however, I would like to identify a few details of this system that should have important ramifications for cultural workers of all varieties. The first is that informatic networks are relatively indifferent to semantic content and interpretation. Data is parsed; it is not read. Media objects are defined at the intersection between two protocols (two technologies), not as a result of some human being's semantic projection onto that data. (Any machinic understanding of the 'content' of data is derived as an epiphenomenon of human behavior, as seen in the page rank algorithm of search engines like Google.)

The second ramification is what might be called the political tragedy of interactivity. Interactivity and bi-directionality of media was famously held up as a sort of utopia by Bertolt Brecht in his short fragments on radio, and later reprised by Enzensberger as the heart and soul of an 'emancipated' media. However, today interactivity is one of the core instruments of control and organization. Today, organisms must communicate whether they want to or not. Organisms are 'captured', to use Phil Agre's terminology, using any number of informatic codes and rubrics. Behaviors are mined for meaningful data, tracked for illegal data, even the genome is prospected for rare or otherwise useful sequences. This is the political tragedy of interactivity, that what was so liberating for Enzensberger is today the very site of informatic exploitation, regulation and control. Today, interactivity means total participation, universal capture.

The third ramification is the tendency to privilege surface over source. I mean this in an entirely non-normative way, and indeed have little understanding of this above and beyond that it is merely happening. By 'surface over source' I mean the struggle between open source software and proprietary software, but it is also much more endemic than that. There is a certain philosophy in computer science known as encapsulation that pervades a whole variety of computer languages and programming environments regardless of whether that code is open source or not. Encapsulation is a technique whereby one segregates code into specific modular units, sometimes called objects or libraries, then provides a surface interface for that object or library. The interface acts as the sole conduit for communication into and out of the object or library. The source of the object or library itself is hidden. Computer scientists use encapsulation for a variety of reasons, all of them practical. It makes the code easier to maintain and simpler to implement. As stated previously, the ramifications of this are not altogether clear to me yet; however, I identify the tendency to privilege surface (or interface) over source at the level of code as quite significant and worthy of further critique. At the very least it should convince us that the open source movement is not enough, and that something like an 'open runtime' movement might be required.

Connected to this is a fourth concern: the problem of the de-politicization of algorithms. There is essentially no intellectual movement today dedicated to the political critique of algorithms. Likewise there exists no alternative movement dedicated to the creation and development of alternative, or 'progressive', algorithms. For the most part the political development of algorithms revolves around a philosophy of utility and efficiency. These being but a minute slice of the human condition, I call for the creation of an experimental school of alternative algorithms modeled around a variety of political and social goods. We need a viable critique of collaborative filtering. We need a language in which to appraise the Google page rank algorithm. An examination of the de-politicization of algorithms will help.

A final ramification of protocological organization and control is that it mandates the creation of new models for political intervention. Networks, rhizomes, 'grass roots' movements—these were all effective diagrams for political control under modernity. But after the powers-that-be have migrated into the distributed network, thereby co-opting the very tools of the former Left, new models for political action are required. A new exploit is necessary, one that is as asymmetrical in relationship to distributed networks as the distributed network was to the power centers of modernity. In the meantime anti-protocological movements have emerged such as Hakim Bey's model of the temporary autonomous zone (2003), or the Electronic Disturbance Theatre's system of online electronic swarming. And in the realm of the non-human, computer viruses and worms have innovated, perhaps totally haphazardly, a new model of protocological infection and disruption that takes advantage of the homogeneity of distributed networks and their ability to propagate information far and wide with ease. At the same time hackers seek out logical exploits in software that allow for inversions and modulations in the normal functionality of code. These techniques, if not fully formed themselves, will provide a way forward for understanding protocological control and counter-protocological practices.

Documentary Uncertainty

Hito Steyerl

2007

I vividly remember a strange broadcast a few years ago. On one of the first days of the US invasion of Iraq in 2003, a senior CNN correspondent was riding in an armoured vehicle. He was jubilant as he stuck a direct broadcast cell phone camera out of the window. He exclaimed that never before had this type of live broadcast been seen. And that was indeed true. Because there was hardly anything to see on these pictures. Due to the low resolution, the only thing to be seen were green and brown blotches, slowly moving over the screen. Actually, the picture looked like the camouflage of combat fatigues; a military version of abstract expressionism. What does this type of abstract documentarism tell us about documentarism as such? It points at a deeper characteristic of many contemporary documentary pictures: the more immediate they become, the less there is to see. The closer to reality we get, the less intelligible it becomes. Let us call this 'the uncertainty principle of modern documentarism'.

But actually, this principle does not only apply to documentary pictures, but also to their theory. Because a lot of documentary theory is just as blurred as the pictures, which the correspondent transmitted from Iraq. The more we try to pinpoint the essence of the documentary, the less we are able to comprehend. The reason is that the notions used to describe them are just as ill-defined as the pictures. Let us take an obvious example: the role of the documentary in the field of contemporary art. Talking about this is complicated by two facts. The first is that there is no viable definition of 'documentary'. The second is that there is no viable definition of 'art' or even the 'field of contemporary art'. And if we still want to reflect on the connection of both, we have to face the fact that we barely know what we are talking about.

The same applies to most of the notions which are traditionally used to define the documentary. Terms like 'truth', 'reality', 'objectivity' and so on are characterised by the lack of any generally valid interpretation and of any clear cut definitions. Thus, we are faced with the first paradox: the documentary form, which is supposed to transmit knowledge in a clear and transparent way, has to be investigated using conceptual tools, which are neither clear nor transparent themselves. The more real documentary seems to get, the more we are at a loss conceptually. The more secured the knowledge that documentary articulations seem to offer, the less can be safely said about them—all terms used to describe them turn out to be dubious, debatable and risky.

I do not want to reiterate, like in an exercise of Negative theology, all the definitions that the documentary mode fails to live up to. Most obviously, it is not consistently objective, whatever objectivity might mean in the first place; it contains facts without ever being able to be entirely factual. While it might aim to represent the truth, it usually misses it, at least according to its own standards. Poststructuralism has taught us how 'reality', 'truth' and other basic notions on which possible definitions of documentary rest are at best as solid as the fleeting reflections on a troubled surface of water. But before drowning in the incertainty and ambiguity that these paradigms prescribe, let us perform one very old-fashioned Cartesian move. Because, amidst all this ambivalence, our confusion is the one thing which remains certain and even reliable. And it will invariably, if unconsciously, represent our reaction to documentary materials as such. The perpetual doubt, the nagging insecurity—whether what we see is 'true', 'real', 'factual' and so on—accompanies contemporary documentary reception like a shadow. Let me suggest that this uncertainty is not some shameful lack, which has to be hidden, but instead constitutes the core quality of contemporary documentary modes as such. The questions which they invariably trigger, the disavowed anxieties hidden behind apparent certainties, differ substantially from those associated with fictional modes. The only thing we can say for sure about the documentary mode in our times is that we always already doubt if it is true.

NOTHING BUT THE TRUTH

Doubting documentary representation is of course nothing new. It is as old as the documentary form itself. Its truth claims have always been questioned, deconstructed or called arrogant. The general relationship towards documentary claims has always been one of a disavowed impasse. It oscillates between belief and incredulity, between trust and distrust, hope and disillusionment.

This is also the reason why the documentary form has always presented its audiences with philosophical problems. Whether or how they represent reality has forever been contested. The main argument runs between proponents of realism and constructivists. While the former believe that documentary forms reproduce natural facts, the latter see them as social constructions. Realists think that reality is out there and that a camera can capture its essence. Constructivists stress the function of ideology or understand truth as a function of power. Michel Foucault once coined the expression of a politics of truth.[1] According to constructivists the documentary form does not represent 'reality' but the 'will to power' of its producers.

But both positions are problematic. While realists believe in an objectivity that, more often than not, turns out to be extremely subjective and which has nonchalantly passed off hideous propaganda as truth, constructivists end up not being able to distinguish the difference between facts and blatant misinformation or, to phrase it more directly, between truth and plain lies. While the position of realists could be called naïve, the position of constructivists runs the danger of sliding into opportunistic and cynical relativism.

What do we make of this impasse? The lesson is that we should accept the intensity of the problem of truth, especially in an era in which doubts have become pervasive. The constant doubt about whether what we see is consistent with reality is not a shameful lack, which has to be disavowed, but on the contrary is the decisive quality of contemporary documentary forms. They are characterized by an often subliminal, but still nagging, uncertainty, as well as the question: Is this really true?

This principle of documentary uncertainty is obviously just a provisional definition of modern documentary; it is highly contextualised within our historical moment. But at no time than in the contemporary context of globalised media circuits has it been more accurate. In this age of widespread anxieties, of precarious living conditions, of general uncertainties and media-provoked hysteria and panic, our belief in the truth claims articulated by anyone, let alone the media and their documentary output, is shaken. But at the same time, more than ever before, our living conditions depend on remote events that we have very little control over. The ubiquitous corporate news coverage which we endure on a daily basis sustains the illusion of control, while simultaneously demonstrating that we are reduced to the role of passive bystanders. While rehearsing attitudes of rational response, they transmit fear on a most basic, affective level. Thus, documentary forms articulate a fundamental dilemma of contemporary risk societies.[2] Viewers are torn between false certainties and feelings of passivity and exposure, between agitation and boredom, between their role as citizens and their role as consumers.

DOCUMENTARISM IN THE FIELD OF ART

In comes the field of art. In the 1990s, documentary forms became popular again after a twenty-year-long hiatus induced by Reaganism and the artistic dumbing down which came with it. During this time, the field of art suffered the same onslaught in the public sphere as the field of documentary production. Since the documentary mode was automatically associated with publicness, state funding and the arena of communicative rationality, in many cases, it was advocated by reflex within the field of art. Art also partly tried to assume the role of an alternative media circuit. This aspect has been pointed out by Stefan Jonsson, who argued that the field of art could become some sort of alternative CNN, which would elucidate the blind spots of corporate journalism and of globalisation in general.[3]

But there were also other developments within the field of art in the 1990s, which made documentary modes an obvious choice for artists. First, the practice of so-called 'contextual art', in which producers tried to figure out the economic and political conditions of their own activities. Since documents were usually involved in assessing these parameters, working with or upon them was self-evident. Documents were used, or sometimes simply brandished, in order to evidence archival research, social inquiries or alternative knowledge production. A further affinity was created by the impact of Cultural Studies on the field of art and consequently there emerged a preoccupation with the politics of representation. The awareness of power relations within, not only documentary articulations, but all forms of representation, was heightened and in many cases also transformed by new modes of narration, which reflected their own implication in authority and in the hierarchies of knowledge production with their effects on gender and other social relations.

All of these influences, which are of course interconnected and overlapping, made documentary one of the most important characteristics of the field of art in the 1990s and in the early twenty-first century. But what did these developments mean? Within the wave of excitement associated with the use of social documentarism, important aspects of the character of documents were neglected by many producers. Since documentarism

1 Michel Foucault, "Wahrheit und Macht. Interview mit A. Fontana und P. Pasquino" in *Dispositive der Macht. Michel Foucault über Sexualität, Wissen und Wahrheit* (Berlin: Merve Verlag, 1978).

2 The notion of 'risk societies' is elaborated in the following (among others): Anthony Giddens, "Risk and Responsibility," *Modern Law Review* 62(1) (January 1999): 1–10. Ulrich Beck, *Risk Society: Towards a New Modernity*, (New Delhi: Sage, 1992).

3 Steffan Jonsson, "Facts of Aesthetics and Fictions of Journalism: The Logic of the Media in the Age of Globalisation," *Nordicom Review* [online]. Available at: http://www.nordicom.gu.se/sites/default/files/kapitel-pdf/157_057-068.pdf

was automatically assumed to be enlightened and critical, many producers paid little attention to the fact that, on the contrary, documents are usually condensations of power. They reek of authority, certification, expertise, and concentrated epistemological hierarchies. Dealing with documents is thus a tricky thing; especially if one aims to deconstruct power, one has to keep in mind that existing documents are—as Walter Benjamin once wrote—mainly made and authorised by victors and rulers.

Thus, an ambiguous situation has been created within the field of art. Superficially, or on the content level, many documentary articulations seemed to erode or even attack unfair power structures. But on the level of form, by relying on authoritative truth procedures, the conventional documentaries have intensified the aura of the court room, the penitentiary or the laboratory within a field of art, which was already quite saturated with these mechanisms. The institution of the so-called White Cube has been criticised for providing a clinical constellation of gazes with aesthetics and social values, which are actually quite similar to the ones deployed within conventional documentary modes. As is well known, documentary production has taken on forensic duties for a long time, and has functioned in the service of a large-scale epistemological enterprise that is closely linked with the project of Western colonialism. Reporting the so-called truth about remote people and locations has been closely linked to their domination. Not only mainstream documentary truth procedures, but even the features of the photographic technology, based as they are on military technology, testify to this historical link.

Jacques Rancière has recently described the importance of these structures of seeing and knowing as the 'distribution of the sensible'. According to him, the political component of any aesthetic endeavour is precisely located in the way in which certain aesthetic regimes enable certain visibilities or articulations and disable others. Thus, the political importance of documentary forms does not primarily reside in their subject matter, but in the ways in which they are organised. It resides in the specific distributions of the sensible implemented by documentary articulations. And this applies not only to corporate documentarism, but also to those documentary productions which take up their standards, their truth procedures, their formal vocabulary, and their scientific and objectivist attitude.

BEYOND REPRESENTATION

Even the claims of a more radical politics of representation fail to live up to the challenge that contemporary documentary presents. The documentary form as such is now more potent then ever, even though we believe less than ever in documentary truth claims. Documentary reports are able to unleash military interventions, to provoke pogroms, international relief efforts, euphoria as well as mass panic. And this is due to their function within global cultural industries, which commodify information and, more importantly, transform it into powerful and moving affects. We identify with victims, heroes, survivors, lucky winners, and the impact of this identification is heightened by the presumed authenticity of the experiences we believe to be sharing. Pictures that appear ever more immediate, which offer increasingly less to see, evoke a situation of constant exception, a crisis in permanence, a state of heightened alert and tension. The documentary form thus becomes a major player within contemporary affective economies. It intensifies a general feeling of fear, which characterises the governmental address of our historical moment. As Brian Massumi has demonstrated using the example of the colour-based terror alerts in the United States, power now also addresses us on the level of affect. Plain colours trigger off multiple emotional reactions. Television in the age of terror creates a "networked jumpiness" by modulating the intensity of collective feelings.[4] Ironically, power takes on the artistic gesture of abstraction. Politics as such are increasingly shifting into the realm of pure perception. They are not only aestheticized. They have become aesthetical as such, as they work (through) the senses. The relationship between politics and art is thus being reconfigured on a level beyond representation.

Contemporary artistic documentarism, with its focus on a politics of representation, has not yet paid sufficient attention to this change; politics as such are moving beyond representation. Very tangible developments make clear that the principle of representative democracy is becoming increasingly problematic. The political representation of the people is undermined in many ways—from the non-representation of migrants to the creation of strange democratic hybrids like the European Union. If people are no longer represented politically, then maybe other forms of symbolic representation are undermined as well. If political representation becomes abstract and blurred, so might documentary representation. Is this also a way to interpret CNN's abstract documentarism? A documentarism which moves beyond representation?

There is still another aspect of the documentary images by CNN mentioned in the beginning. There could not be any less 'objective document' (so to speak) than those pictures, since they are made from the position of so-called imbeddedness, which basi-

4 Brian Massumi, "Fear (The spectrum said)", *Multitudes*, 2006. [online]. http://www.multitudes.net/Fear-The-spectrum-said/

cally renounces most pretensions of objectivity and critical distance. In order to be able to join the troops, journalists had to endure quite dramatic restrictions of the freedom of press. But what if we had to realise that, in this world, we are all somehow embedded in global capitalism? And that the step back, towards critical distance and objectivity, was, under these circumstances, always already an ideological illusion? In one sense, this is probably true. And paradoxically, one can thus say that there is no more truth and certainly not within documentarism. But let us reverse the perspective: what if the contrary is the case and it is precisely those blurred and unfocused pictures from the cell phone camera that express the truth of the situation much better than any objectivist report could? Because these pictures do not really represent anything. They are just too unfocused. They are as post-representational as the majority of contemporary politics. But amazingly, we can still speak of truth with regard to them.

Those CNN images still vividly and acutely express the uncertainty, which governs not only contemporary documentary image production, but also the contemporary world as such. They are perfectly true documents of that general uncertainty, so to speak. They reflect the precarious nature of contemporary lives as well as the uneasiness of any representation. Finding a critical position with respect to these images implies much more than simply taking this into account or exposing it. It means replacing the set of affects which is connected to this uncertainty—namely stress, exposure, threat and a general sense of loss and confusion—with another one. And in this sense, the only possible critical documentary today is the presentation of an affective and political constellation which does not even exist, and which is yet to come.

Supplement '14 (Mixed Typologies) #6

Christopher Williams

2014

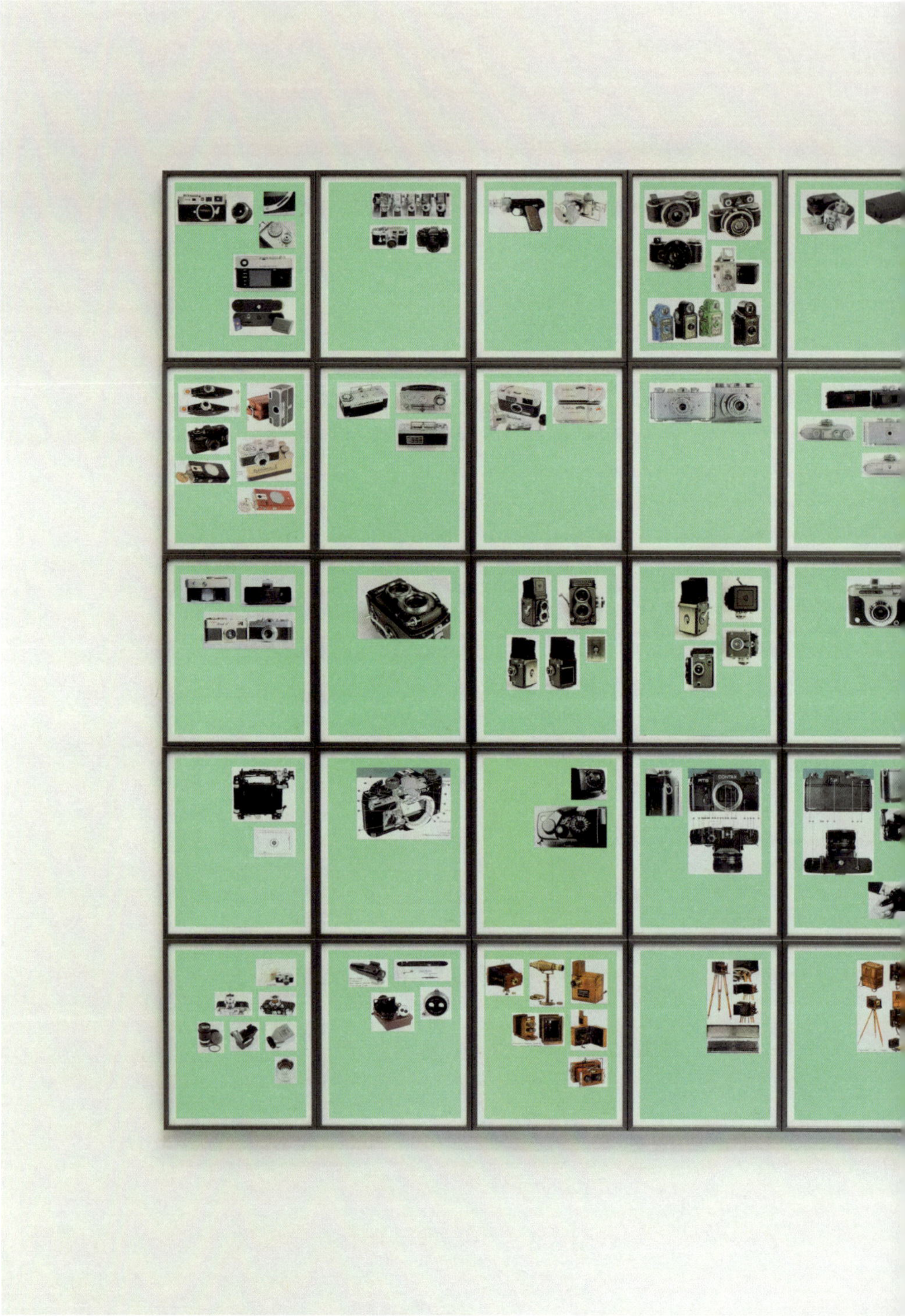

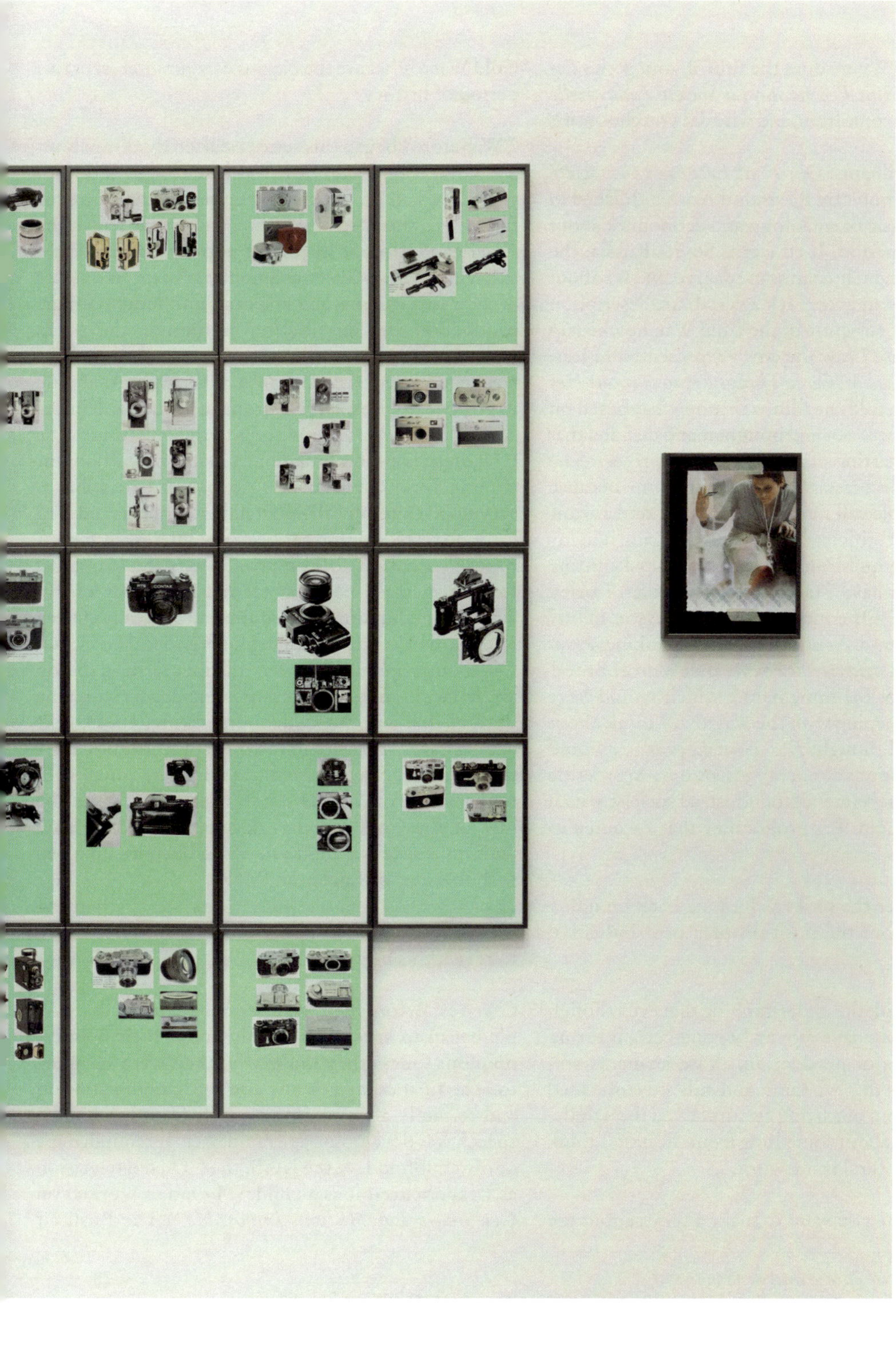

Christopher Williams in Conversation with Mark Godfrey
2007

Mark Godfrey: Where does the title of your series *For Example: Dix-Huit Leçons sur La Société Industrielle* (2002–ongoing) come from, and why did you choose it?[1]

Christopher Williams: *Dix-Huit Leçons sur la société industrielle* is a book by Raymond Aron published in 1963. It is a classic of sociology and economics about the Cold War period. It concerns Soviet Russia, the United States and China to some degree, and it's about oil and potatoes and corn. It's a very basic description of the economic structure of the Cold War. I picked up the book because I saw the cover represented in Jean-Luc Godard's *Two or Three Things I Know about Her* (1966). I'd been told the film was somewhat based on the book, so I went out and bought it and decided that I'd use it as a starting place for my new project. The word '*leçons*' (lectures) was attractive to me because I've heard people call my work 'didactic' and I wanted to tackle that criticism head-on. By placing it in my title I raise the question: What lesson am I putting forward? What have I taught you? What am I being didactic about? Of course there is no lesson in any conventional sense. At one point I was thinking about calling the work *Industrial Poems* after Marcel Broodthaers's work of the same name, which would have been more in keeping with the way that I think about the work, but I thought *Dix-Huit Leçons . . .* would raise more questions about my intentions. Aron's title also included the reference to industrial society, which fit within the Cold War programme that I wanted to explore.

MG: Do you see the series as looking back on industrial society from the position of a post-industrial society?

CW: Yes, but with the understanding that even though in reality we may have moved beyond certain formations and types of production, those elements still inform the way that we think and still are embedded very much within our living culture. Even though the series is talking about something from the past, I think it's an active cultural framework.

MG: What made you want to make a series about the Cold War? What are the origins of your interest in this period of history?

CW: Before I began this series I started thinking about a Cold War project, but it was just a vague idea. For years I've had an interest in the restructuring of cultural life in the post-War period and, in particular, the Americanisation of European popular culture. Cinema, which has always been important to me, is one site of this restructuring, and you can think about both the production and distribution of films in the 1950s. New cinemas were built at that time, and sometimes were contracted to devote 75% of their programming to American films. Even European avant-garde films, such as *RoGoPaG*, was witness to this situation.[2] The Gregoretti is almost Situationist in its propositions, including Topo Gigio the mouse, but the Rossellini is very Pop: it's about a flight attendant, cameras and film.

Connected to this has been my interest in the European reception of Pop art. There's the Capitalist Realists such as Lueg, Richter and Polke, but less obviously I'm thinking of Broodthaers. He really started to make work after reviewing George Segal and Claes Oldenburg, and he had a very distinct relation to Pop art. In fact his fictional museums and decors would be unthinkable without Oldenburg's *Store* (1961); Oldenburg rarely surfaces in histories of institutional critique, but *The Store* is a significant missing component of that history. My decision to make work about the idea of the Cold War has developed hand-in-hand with my conscious desire to try to be more involved with this idea of European Pop.

MG: Have more recent political events prompted you to revisit this period?

CW: Yes. Before the 2000 elections I noticed that people began to speak less openly about their political opinions unless they knew who they were speaking to. The further we got into the Bush administration, and certainly after 9/11, this whole fear of dissonant speech was developing at a rapid pace. It reminded me of my childhood, of the KGB, the CIA and television as I experienced it as a child. (My father worked on *Get Smart* and *Mission: Impossible*.[3]) The Bush ad-

1 The interview took place in Basel on 12 June 2007.
2 Roberto Rossellini, Jean-Luc Godard, Pier Paolo Pasolini and Ugo Gregoretti, *RoGoPaG*, 1963.

ministration felt remarkably familiar to me, and that strengthened my resolve to work with Cold War representations. So the subject of the Cold War comes out of my desire to engage with an idea of European reception of Pop art, out of my personal history, and then out of the Bush administration's push to silence any kind of critical speech and the fear of your neighbour and your telephone. Making work about the Cold War was an indirect way to talk about the present.

MG: We'll return to that, but to address the series more specifically, once you decided to initiate a series about the Cold War, how did you begin? What kind of photographs did you make?

CW: I had to start somewhere and so I used the image of the great Cold War couple to generate or produce the rest of the work. I wanted to create images that stood for Russia and the United States and that reflected on Cold War photographic culture. The images would serve as a kind of generative motor for the rest of the project. I decided to start with a picture of a camera. The question was whether I should photograph the camera that was actually making my photographs in a gesture of extreme self-reflexivity, or whether it should be at a remove from that idea. I determined on the latter. The camera that I chose is a well-known object—the Kiev 88. It was produced at a factory called the Arsenal in the Ukraine and I viewed it initially as a kind of Eastern European cargo-cult object. It's a knock-off of a Hasselblad and it has a very interesting history, which to me is materially bound up in both the picture and the object itself. The Arsenal was originally an ammunitions factory, but during the Revolution there was a very significant strike in 1918 and the production of weapons stopped. A decade after Dovzhenko made a film about it inside the factory.[4] At the end of World War II the Russians appropriated camera-building technology from different German camera companies, and set up a camera-making factory at the Arsenal which produced the Kiev 88. So within this one object, the Kiev 88, you have political history with a capital 'p': the Russian Revolution; a well-known film representing that Revolution and reflecting upon its position in history; the appropriation and displacement of the means to produce photographic apparatus; and the idea that it's a collectible and a consumer product. As a fake Hasselblad, the Kiev 88 also is a replication of an original whose status is contested: some people say that it originally was a German product that the Swedes somehow got hold of during the war, some that it was a Swedish design. You could say that built into this photograph there is, as in many others in the series, the idea of social change. This is not indicated in any overt or obvious way, but the idea of quietly making pictures that do include those histories of change is important to me, especially in the US at a time when social change or voicing dissent seems like a hopeless and nostalgic idea.

MG: You mentioned that you started the series by creating a 'Cold War couple'. What is the 'American' photograph that is the equivalent for the image of the Kiev 88?

CW: It's the corn. Corn figures very prominently in Aron's *Dix-Huit Leçons* and so I started thinking about making a still life with corn. In her book *Much Depends on Dinner* (1989), Margaret Visser dissects a typical American dinner of chicken, rice, salad with olive oil and lemon, boiled corn and so on, and makes the claim in the chapter on corn that unless you're standing in a river, catching a salmon with your own hand, almost everything you come into contact with in your daily life has had some relationship to corn as a product. The lubricant used to grind the camera lenses in the photographic industry has a corn by-product in it; the material used to polish the steel has a corn by-product in it; the filmstrip itself has a corn by-product in it, and many of the chemicals associated with the production of a fine-art print also have corn in them.

MG: Perhaps the artificial corn in the photograph was made using a corn by-product as well?

CW: Yes. It's not real corn in the image, but artificial corn made for window displays or photographic shoots. The company that produced it estimated that 75% of the material used to make the artificial corn is in fact made with a corn by-product. One could say that the photographic industry has as much to do with corn as it does with, for example, light.

MG: Is one of the reasons that you consider this photograph as the 'American' part of the Cold War couple the fact that the image refers to the conventions of advertising and consumption—both because the corn is itself a plastic marketing product, and because of the Kodak three-point reflection guide?

CW: Colour photography in part was developed to serve the needs of advertising, and in my research some of the most stunning examples were images of

3 Comedy television series created by Mel Brooks and Buck Henry that ran from 1965 to 1970 and satirised the secret agent genre. *Mission: Impossible* originally ran from 1966 to 1973.

4 Alexander Dovzhenko, *Arsenal*, 1929.

food and of abundance: picnics, cocktail parties, etc. The Kodak three-point reflection guide that is represented in the corn picture refers back to older colour processes. It was included in most studio commercial work, and was intended to be used within the printing process when books or advertisements were made. Normally they were cropped out, but in a lot of my research into early commercial photography I found reflecting guides or colour bars or materials that were there for their later use within another form. That refers to the idea that the gallery is just one site among many potential sites where these images could be seen. Within the art context, we focus on the print within the museum or gallery as the primary site of encounter, but especially now advertising, magazines, catalogues, websites or postcards also take on an important function. The Kodak three-point reflection guide was copyrighted in 1968, which was a way for me to include the idea of a moment of social change within this particular photograph. The guide is both a referent to the photographic industry and to the kind of determinants within the photographic programme that Vilém Flusser describes in *Towards a Philosophy of Photography* (1983).

MG: Can you discuss how the series came to incorporate photographs of buildings in Lodz, of products, of women in showers, etc.?

CW: I tend to develop a series by thinking about the constellation of elements that would normally be in one single photograph and then separating them out. I started *For Example: Die Welt ist schön* (1993–2001) with an image of a travel poster for Africa that showed an African woman with a basket on her head standing in front of a concrete modernist building. Very self-consciously, I just separated the elements: the basket went one direction, the woman went another, and the buildings went another. *For Example: Dix-Huit Leçons . . .* is an attempt to make a representation of the world. To do this, I needed to have human beings, the objects that human beings mediate the natural world with, I needed to have dwellings, landscapes and all of those things. These are the basic genres of photography too: portraiture, still life, landscape, cityscape, the bedrock of fine-art photography. Walter Benjamin's short history of photography breaks down photography into these basic elements.[5] One photograph shows a Polish building—a dwelling where you could find some of the objects that I have photographed, and where the people who eventually will appear in the series could be. But in terms of the Cold War subject matter, this photograph is also a way of addressing Soviet expansion. I could have picked more dramatic buildings in Poland with big Soviet numbers and letters on the side of them, but this building was very photographable. I found it interesting in its lack of specificity: it was a generic example of Soviet architecture, and it could have been in East Berlin also.

MG: Can you say something about how the series came to include photographs of women emerging from showers and others with curlers in their hair? How do these relate to the idea and history of the Cold War?

CW: Like the other images, the photographs of the models develop from specific research. The choice of the model was based on Jacques Tati's casting description for the female lead in *Playtime* (1967). Tati describes the physical characteristics of his desired actress, but also indicates that she should carry herself in a way that suggests a proper upbringing. She should look refined and educated.[6] My model doesn't fit Tati's physical specifications but she does have this demeanour and sense of refinement. The other impetus for these photographs has been my interest in Charles Wilp, a famous German designer and photographer who worked for Afri-Cola in the 1960s and early 70s and designed adverts for feminine products. One campaign involved placing a model behind a plastic screen on which there was moisture and humidity. These images suggest that Wilp was looking at Richard Hamilton's early works. In constructing my image, I separated the elements of Wilp's advertisement, placing the door on the left and the model on the right. The glass in this shower door is called Chrome Raindrop, which is both a representation of water beading down a glass plane and a surface onto which real water accumulates.

So, as you can see, I set up photographic situations that, for all intents and purpose, could be those used in another kind of image-making activity. I try to stay as close as possible to those models of production as I can, but I also try to find the right amount of distance for there to be difference. Every shoot involves a struggle to find that point where there is distance from the model I am approaching, and yet enough proximity so that the photograph could be mistaken for the model itself.

MG: What is at stake for you in the inclusion within the photographs of various elements relating to the photographic industry? Beyond the historical references of the photographs, how does the presence of

5 See Walter Benjamin, 'Little History of Photography', *Selected Writings* Vol. 2, 1927–1934, (London and Cambridge: Harvard University Press, 1999).

6 'An important point: she must not be an actress. It matters little whether she is fair or dark. The most important is the reserved appearance, due to a good education . . .'. Tati quoted in David Bellos, *Jacques Tati: His Life and Art*, (London: Harvill Press, 1999), 265.

these elements articulate your ideas about photography in general?

CW: As you say, there's an accumulation in the work that relates to the photographic industry. This constitutes a kind of self-reflexivity that I believe extends, but does not negate, the modernist idea of material specificity. We usually think of modernist self-reflexivity as examining the physical properties of the medium, and in my series I'm also interested in acknowledging other registers of photographic determination: the camera, the rest of the technical apparatus, but also the people and professions involved in photographic production. As well as the production of the photographic print, the work acknowledges what's involved in its distribution—and so includes images of gallery display walls, for instance. In total this concern with photographic production and distribution, as well as its materiality, amounts to a second-order of self-reflexivity, or proposes an expanded frame for thinking about photographic materiality. It is important, I think, to reflect on photography in this way, because as a result the emphasis shifts away from two concepts that are paramount in the critical discourse around photography: the idea of the photographer-author; and the importance of the decisive moment. The work acknowledges that there are crucial elements at play in the production of meaning in photography before and after the artist arrives onto the scene to take the photograph. My thinking about photography is in part indebted to Flusser, who saw photography as a kind of institution with rings of determination, serving programmes of institutions beyond it and functioning itself to programme and perpetuate the production of photographs.

MG: I'd like to address the experience of seeing one single image. When standing in front of one of your photographs, I often feel a kind of bafflement. I am faced with the bare, blunt appearance of the photographed object. Though I know that a lot of research has gone into each photograph, initially I have limited access to the backstory. What do you think is compelling about that moment of facing the photographs and *not* knowing their specific referents?

CW: I think this actually reflects or could represent a viewer's relationship to the world outside of the pictures. Every object around us is at once very present and identifiable, but also the representative of multiple historical trajectories, economies and desires which you barely have to scratch the surface to start to get into. The coffee you're drinking is obviously a product that has a rich history here in Europe, but it's also just a cup of coffee. And that's something inherent in all objects. Another way of approaching this question is as follows: traditionally photographic practice associated with leftist politics approached the muteness of the photograph as a problem. The problem was solved by using language or captioning as a corrective (this approach comes directly out of Brecht and Benjamin). Treating this muteness as a basic material element and not as a structural flaw, I have attempted to construct meaning through the use of negative form or absence, much like a dub producer.

MG: What about installation? You have exhibited the series in various venues, and each time you arrange the series in different clusters so that the viewer builds different connections between the images. Each installation also responds to and sometimes reconfigures the architecture of the institution. Can we speak about the link between the installations and the series' subject? When I saw it installed in Porto, there wasn't a connection between the Cold War subject matter and the institution, but in Bologna there certainly was.

CW: In Bologna the relationship to architecture was very exaggerated.[7] I wanted to analyse the history of the space in relationship to the student movement in the city in the 1970s. I had become aware of the political activity and the student activities in Bologna through punk music. The music functioned at the time as a kind of reportage about what was going on, specifically Scritti Politti's 'Skank Bloc Bologna' (1978). The museum was designed and built during the community period and over the years almost all of the original interior architecture was covered by sheet rock to make it a more traditional white cube. Simply through removal I revealed a lot of the original footprint and intentions of the architect, but also the original ideological intentions for that building. I did this at a moment when the museum was moving to a new building that represents a neo-conservative agenda, so my installation was a way of marking time, and it all fit within my Cold War timeframe. But not all installations will investigate architecture and history in this way.

MG: Let's return to an idea you raised earlier. You mentioned that one of the reasons for exploring a Cold War subject is to build an implicit comparison with contemporary conditions, and that there clearly are some critical and political suggestions in that comparison. In contrast to some of the work that's being made now about the 'War on Terror' and the 1960s protest movements, the politics of your series is extremely indirect. Do you think that critics have picked up the way in which these photographs are addressed to the present?

7 '*For Example: Dix-Huit Leçons sur La Société Industrielle* (Revision 5)', 26 January–4 March 2007, Museo d'Arte Moderna di Bologna.

CW: I strongly believe that first and foremost I am always making art. There's the old distinction of making political art or making art politically, and I invest in the latter. The indirectness is part of that. It could also be the result of my avoidance of instrumentality in the work. The series explores how material outside of our discourse works its way deeply into all representations. I'm not interested in producing a clear signifier of my political position, but in exploring how these things are imbedded in every aspect of our lives.

MG: How do you see the series continuing? At what point do you think this might come to an end?

CW: Well, somebody pointed out to me when I was working on *For Example: Die Welt ist schön* that in building a world model or cultural model there is no end in sight, and that I could continue that project for the rest of my productive life unless I ended it arbitrarily, which I did. Someone else pointed out to me (and it seemed so obvious that I was embarrassed) that this had something to do with Huebler's project to photograph everybody alive; that was also an impossible and an endless project. From the get-go Doug [Huebler] understood this it was part of the humour and beauty of the project, and without thinking about it consciously I inherited that understanding. It's very easy to see the new project as a continuation of the old project under another title with a shift in emphasis. I don't know when it will end or why, but I do know that I am nowhere near being done with it. I'm lucky enough to be able to follow my curiosity and base my work on it, above all else.

Declassification
United States Department of Defense Website
Last accessed May 2018

YOUR RIGHT TO DOD CLASSIFIED RECORDS

In addition to the Freedom of Information Act (FOIA), the public may also request access to classified records under the Mandatory Declassification Review (MDR) provisions of Executive Order 13526 (Section 3.5) as amended.

Note: Some Federal records may be restricted by statute or Executive Order but all DoD-specified restrictions must comply with the exemptions in the Freedom of Information Act (FOIA). Even if the records are not national-security classified, some records contain information exempt from release under the FOIA. Presidential records are governed by separate access laws, for more information please visit the website for the Office of Presidential Libraries.

While these laws require DoD to review their records, they do not require DoD to disclose all sensitive information. Information that falls within the categories allowed by the law can be exempted from public release.

IMMEDIATE IMPLEMENTATION PROVISIONS OF EXECUTIVE ORDER 13526

As required by Executive Order 13526, "Classified National Security Information", DoD is required to send a copy of their implementation plan to the director of the Information Security Oversight Office ("ISOO"), the executive oversight body for the classification and declassification processes, within 180 days of implementation of the EO.

MANDATORY DECLASSIFICATION REVIEW (MDR)

The DoD Declassification Program operates under a decentralized approach. Each DoD Component responds to MDR requests for its own records.

Like a FOIA request, MDR requests (less than 25 years old) should be addressed to the applicable DoD Component that has custody of the requested record.

For maximum efficiency in understanding the MDR Process, we recommend that you spend a few moments reviewing the DoD Mandatory Declassification Review (MDR) Program and the applicable references associated with the program.

STATUS OF DOD DECLASSIFICATION EFFORTS

EO 13526 requires the National Declassification Center (NDC) to eliminate the Declassification backlog by December 31, 2013 and make public a report on agency declassification status of the backlog every 6 months.

Selections from the Redaction Paintings Series
Jenny Holzer
2007

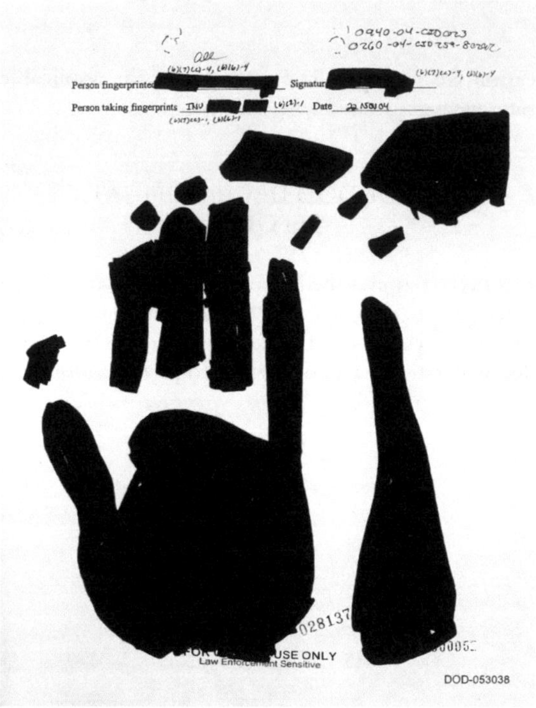

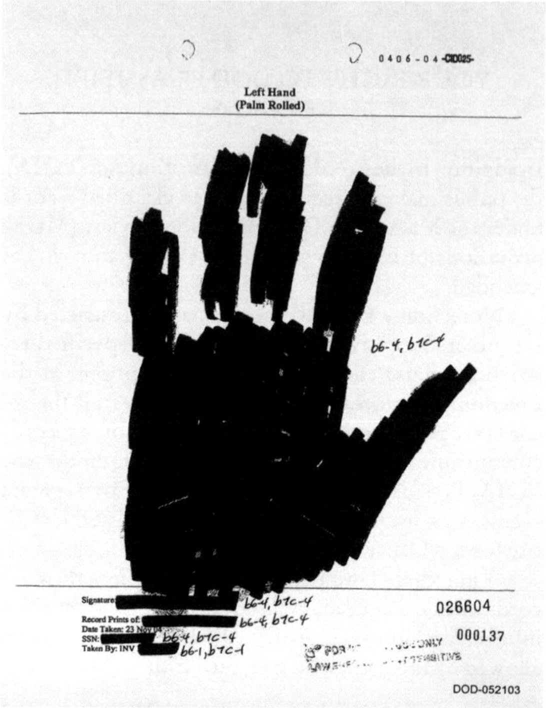

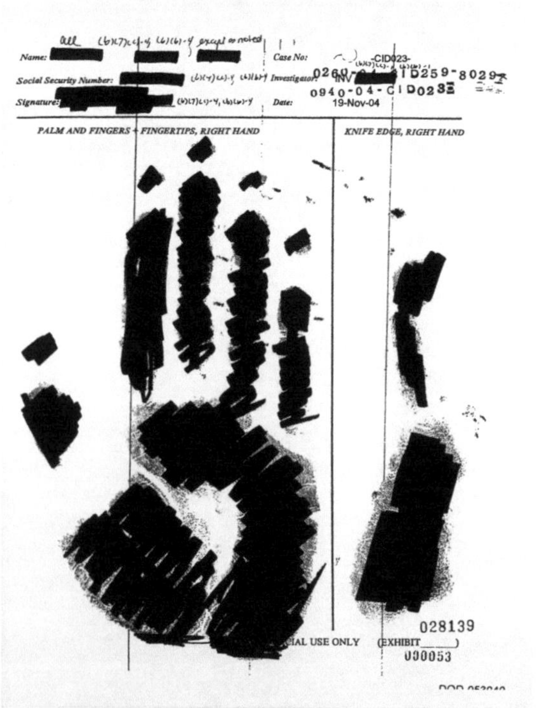

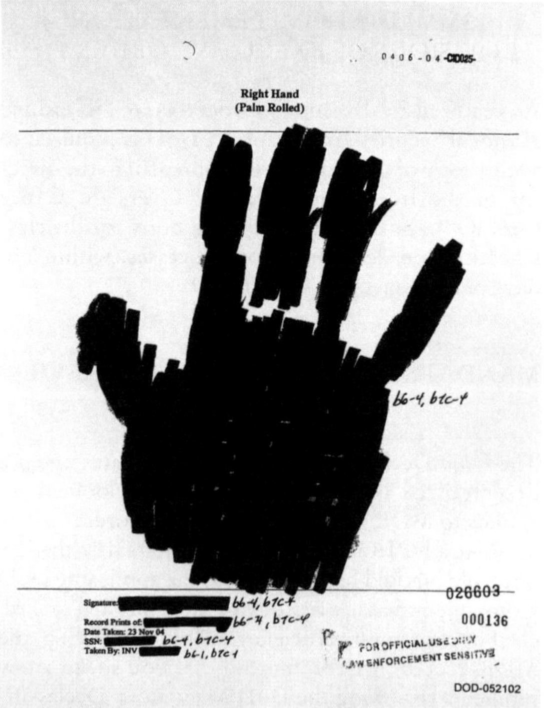

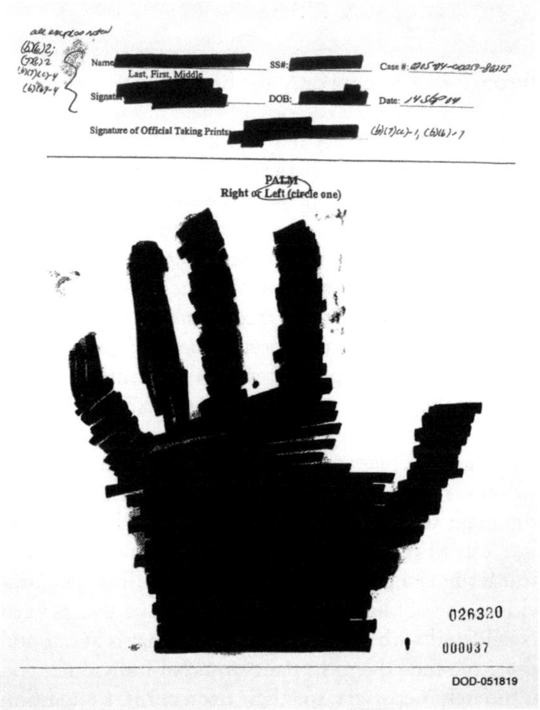
Name [redacted] SS#: [redacted] Case #: 0205-04-00257-80195
Last, First, Middle
Signature [redacted] DOB: [redacted] Date: 14 SEP 04
Signature of Official Taking Prints [redacted] (b)(7)(c)-1, (b)(6)-1
PALM
Right or Left (circle one)
026320
000037
DOD-051819

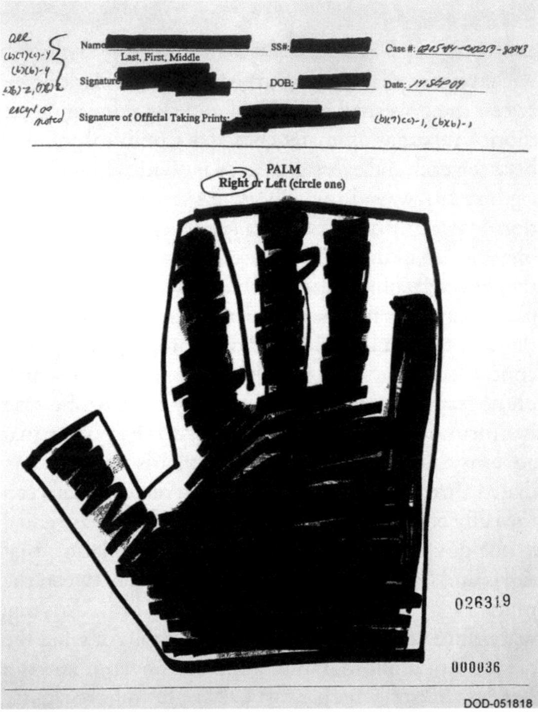
Name [redacted] SS#: [redacted] Case #: 0205-04-00257-80043
Last, First, Middle
Signature [redacted] DOB: [redacted] Date: 14 SEP 04
Signature of Official Taking Prints: [redacted] (b)(7)(c)-1, (b)(6)-1
PALM
Right or Left (circle one)
026319
000036
DOD-051818

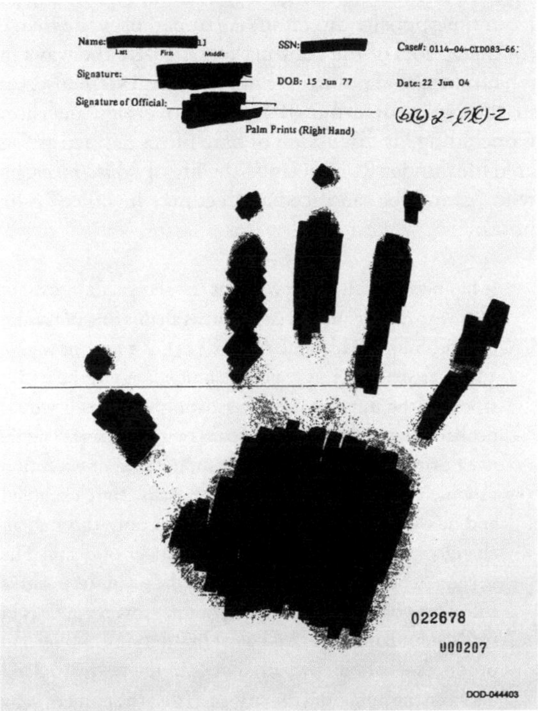
Name: [redacted]
Last First Middle
SSN: [redacted]
Case#: 0114-04-CID083-66
Signature: [redacted]
DOB: 15 Jun 77
Date: 22 Jun 04
Signature of Official: [redacted]
(b)(6)-2 -(7)(C)-2
Palm Prints (Right Hand)
022678
000207
DOD-044403

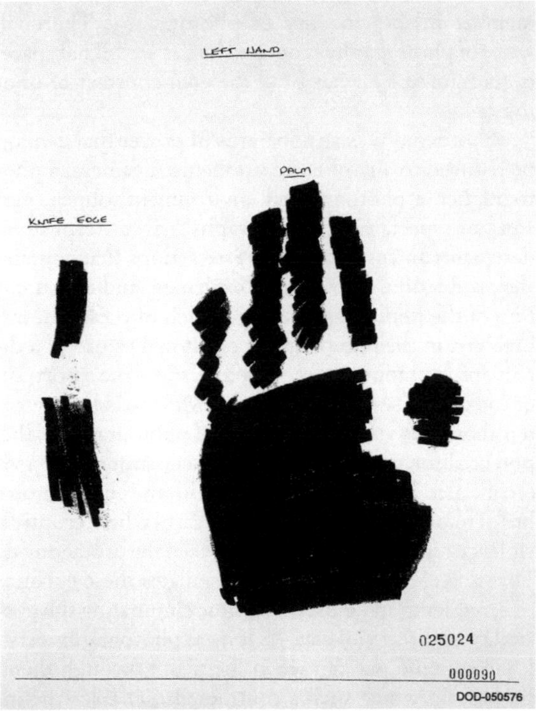
LEFT HAND
PALM
KNIFE EDGE
025024
000090
DOD-050576

The Civil Contract of Photography
Ariella Azoulay
2008

We have seen that citizenship is a form of relations between the governed individual and the governing authority, relations ultimately based in a political equality between each and every governed individual. I will now explore the ways in which, when separated from nationality or any other essentialist conception of a group of governed individuals, citizenship comes to resemble the photographic relation. Exactly like citizenship, photography, is no one's property. It cannot be owned. Photography, at least the kind of photography that I'm concerned with in this book, photography in which photographs are taken on the verge of catastrophe, also is a form of relations of individuals to the power that governs them, a form of relations that is not fully mediated through such power, being a relation between formally equal individuals —individuals who are equal as the governed as such. It is a form of relation that exists and becomes valid only within and between the plurality of individuals who take part in it. Anyone who addresses others through photographs or takes the position of a photograph's addressee, even if she is a stateless person who has lost her "right to have rights," as in Arendt's formulation, is nevertheless a citizen—a member in the citizenry of photography. The civil space of photography is open to her, as well. That space is configured by what I call the civil contract of photography.

Photography is an apparatus of power that cannot be reduced to any of its components: a camera, a photographer, a photographed environment, object, person, or spectator. "Photography" is a term that designates an ensemble of diverse actions that contain the production, distribution, exchange, and consumption of the photographic image. Each of these actions involved in the photographic event makes use of a direct and an indirect force—taking someone's portrait or looking at someone's portrait. Much has been written about this violent dimension of photography—the potential for turning any concrete encounter into a violent clash. However, compared with the endless number of photos taken, rare are those cases where eruptive violence replaces the relations between the protagonists. That is because a civil contract regulates these encounters, reducing and most of the time eliminating the possibility of direct violence. As long as photographs exist, I will contend, we can see in them and through them the way in which such a contract also enables the injured parties to present their grievances, in person or through others, now or in the future.

This turn to the rhetoric of the contractarian tradition in political theory may seem curious, and in need of explanation. After all, the contractarian tradition has left the moment of contract itself outside the political order and wasted no time on the relations between governed people that are not enabled, mediated and constrained—let alone dictated—by the ruling power. In fact, many thinkers in that tradition have tacitly agreed with Karl Schmitt's reduction of the concept of the political to the space opened by and demarcated through the sovereign decision (or a series of sovereign decisions).[1] They were mostly interested in ways to justify and limit sovereign power, which many of them understood very differently from Schmitt, and this has been the main way in which the rights of individuals, the interests of the public, and the commotion of the multitudes have been taken into consideration. The individual, the public, and the multitude have always been considered with a view to the power that is at one and the same time the most dangerous for individuals and ultimately necessary for their protection, a condition for their coexistence in a group. Thinking with Schmitt from the opposite direction, Agamben uses the image (or metaphor) of the contract to articulate the ways in which social and political relations manifest themselves in the realm determined by the sovereign decision. Concluding his discussion of bare life as defined as "sacred life" under Roman law—the life of *homo sacer*, he who "cannot be sacrificed and yet may be killed"—he notes:

> It has been rightly observed that the state is founded not as the expression of a social tie but as an untying (*déliason*) that prohibits (Badiou, *L'être*, p. 125). We may now give a further sense to this claim. *Déliason* is not to be understood as the untying of a preexisting tie (which would probably have the form of a pact or a contract). The tie itself originarily has the form of an untying or exception in which what is captured is at the same time excluded, and in which human life is politicized only through an abandonment to an unconditional power of death. The sovereign tie is more originary than the tie of the positive rule or the tie of the social pact, but the sovereign tie is in truth only an untying. And what this untying implies and produces—bare life, which dwells in the no-man's land between the home and the city—is, from the point of view of sovereignty, the originary political element.[1]

The incommensurability of contractarian political theories with sovereignty which Agamben underlines is a superficial one, because, as noted above, the original moment of the contract itself has been left outside the political-historical domain, and concrete contracts are always seen in terms of the authorities who can limit, impose, induce, or invalidate contracts. The true opposition, I suggest, is not between contractarian theories and theories of sovereignty, but between "sovereign violence," which "is in truth founded not on a pact but on the exclusive inclusion of bare life in the state,"[3] and multiple voluntary associations between many individuals, which reproduce the original moment of contract without necessarily reproducing its result, that is, the constitution of a sovereign authority. And where Agamben insists (rightly) on the fact that "the state of nature is, in truth, a state of exception, in which the city appears for an instant" and "is thus not an event achieved once and for all but is continually operative in the civil state in the form of the sovereign decision,"[4] I would like to insist on the fact that "the state of contract," too, is continually operative in the civil state—in order to reproduce not sovereign power, but rather a space relatively free from its intervention, a space where "thinking a politics freed from the form of the State" becomes possible.[5]

"Thinking a politics freed from the form of the State" is Agamben's own project, described in *The Coming Community* (1993) as a politics founded on the "Whatever," on "singularity," "not in its indifference with respect to a common property (to a concept, for example: being red, being French, being Muslim), but only in its being *such as it is*."[6] But there is another way of thinking politics freed from the state, one that not only can receive a theoretical account, but that can do so because it is manifest, in the form of non-governmental political activities of many forms and agendas, in empirical form throughout the world today. That is a politics founded not on singularity, but on the equality of the governed "as such"—as *they* are. It is based not on a community to come, but on a community, or rather several communities, both within and beyond the boundaries of the sovereign state, that already exist, communities that employ a variety of means—photography prominent among them—to edify an open political space where no one can decide on the exception, and a final decision cannot be made, a community in which a new beginning is a right preserved for each of its members and solidarity among its members precedes the submission and the identification with power. As Hannah Arendt has noted with regard to the power of the sovereign, "the moment the group, from which the power originated to begin with (*potestas in populo*, without a people or a group there is no power), disappears, 'his power' also vanishes." In a politics founded on the equality of the governed, power regains its meaning, not as a governmental tool, but as "a human ability not just to act but to act in concert"[7] and to negotiate, sometimes successfully, sometimes not—with sovereign power.[8]

The civil contract of photography, whose text I have drafted during the years of the second Palestinian intifada, bears witness to an attempt to find refuge amid the loneliness of being a spectator who has been addressed every day by photographs documenting the daily horrors of the Israeli occupation. Working out and making explicit the clauses of this tacit contract has been an effort to think my relation to and attitude toward these photographed individuals beyond guilt and compassion—outside of the merely psychological framework of empathy, of "regarding the pain of others"—on the basis of civic duty and the mutual trust of those who are governed. I will try to show that this mutual trust, mediated by photography, is a form of relations between individuals that was first established during the mid-nineteenth century and that has gradually developed ever since. The civil contract of photography can be extracted from existing photographic practices and uses, but is irreducible to any of them, nor can it be depicted as a product of their accumulation. Rather, positing this contract is a way to delineate part of the newly constructed space of civil relations that has been opened—and even necessitated—by photography. In addition, developing the characteristics of this contract is my way of questioning photography's political configuration and reflecting upon its effect on the modern form of sovereignty and its territorial articulation. Briefly put, the camera modified the way in which individuals are governed

1 It does not matter for the purpose of this discussion whether the decision is over the exception (Carl Schmitt, *Political Theology: Four Chapters on the Concept of Sovereignty* [Cambridge, MA: MIT Press, 1985]), or over the distinction between friend and enemy (Schmitt 19XX), or over the borders of the space where the sovereign's laws apply (Schmitt XX).

2 Giorgio Agamben, *Homo Sacer: Sovereign Power and Bare Life*, trans. Daniel Heller-Roazen (Stanford, CA: Stanford University Press, 1998), 90.

3 Agamben, *Homo Sacer*, 106–7.

4 Agamben, *Homo Sacer*, 109.

5 Agamben, *Homo Sacer*, 109.

6 Giorgio Agamben, *The Coming Community*, trans. Michael Hardt (Minneapolis: University of Minnesota Press, 1993), 1.

7 "In current usage," Arendt adds, "when we speak of a 'powerful man' or a 'powerful personality,' we already use the word 'power' metaphorically; what we refer to without metaphor is strength." Hannah Arendt, *On Violence* (New York, Harvest Books, 1970), 44.

8 See the comprehensive, but still not exhaustive survey compiled in the essays and interviews in Michel Feher (ed.), with Gaëlle Krikorian and Yates McKee, *Non-governmental Politics* (New York: Zone Books, 2007).

and the extent of their participation in the forms of governance. It is that change that I explore here.

THE INVENTION OF PHOTOGRAPHY

To this day, historians of photography persist in exploring the issue of the origin of photography's invention in a sustained attempt to determine its precise moment of birth. While the moment of birth is controversial, the consensus is that it exists—a single, magical moment reappearing as a constant anchor in all the narratives photography's evolution, an axis relative to which the many alternative chronologies are all presented, a time from which the age of photography is calculated and its centennials celebrated.[9] I'm referring here to the summer of 1893, when the daguerreotype, named after one of its two inventors, was exhibited in the French Chamber of Deputies. This was the date that marked its transformation into an object of national legislation and a source of monthly payments to its inventors by the French state, entitling the state to render it a publicly visible invention, open and accessible to all, whose uses were not restricted by copyright. However, it is well known that before this official birth date, Henry Fox Talbot of Great Britain had already claimed the title of inventor of this new technology and had provided evidence of his presentation of his invention to the British Royal Society over a decade earlier. Another claimant to the title was Hippolyte Bayard, who went to dramatic lengths to make his claim. Nevertheless, the daguerreotype endured as the prototypical term for what soon became photography.

In 1931, about ninety years later, Walter Benjamin opened his essay "Little History of Photography" by noting "the fog that surrounds the beginnings of photography," obscuring the beginnings of this technology. And yet, he wrote, in contrast to the case of printing, the fog in this case is not all that thick, for "the time was ripe for the invention, and was sensed by more than one—by men who strove independently for the same objective: to capture the images in the camera obscura, which had been known at least since Leonardo's time."[10] Benjamin elaborated somewhat on each of those protagonists, in fact circumventing the question of the origin of photography whose answer converges into a single inventor's name. There was no single inventor. Instead, Benjamin proposed a new perspective of photography's beginnings. The origin, he suggested, was the appearance of a professional community.

In 1999, the American historian of photography Geoffrey Batchen published a book that he titled, with a quote from Daguerre, *Burning with Desire*. As I noted, Daguerre is conventionally considered the inventor of photography, despite repeated retractions of this title since the moment it was granted. In 1828, when Daguerre himself was still far from solving the question of how to fix and preserve the images created within the camera obscura, Joseph Nicéphore Nièpce had already discovered the solution. At the time, however, it was considered unsatisfactory. Daguerre wrote Nièpce: "I am burning with desire to see your experience from nature."[11] Batchen's thesis develops further Benjamin's intuitively written claim that photography was "sensed by more than one—by men who strove independently for the same objective." Traveling backward in time, Batchen's work periodizes the beginnings of photography at the end of the eighteenth century, joining together the findings of various scientists working in separate disciplines (optics, chemistry, and physics), all of whom were experimenting with means for producing images that would endure after the shutter of the black box had snapped shut over the aperture. Batchen didn't do away with the question, but he can be said to have broadened the arena within which historians still attempt to pinpoint a moment of photography's birth. This, for instance, is the vein mined by the studies of the historians who contributed to the 2003 exhibition at the Musée d'Orsay and to the exhaustive accompanying catalogue, both centering on Daguerre and the daguerreotype. However, most of the historians who participated in the catalogue (including Quentin Bajac, Stephen Pinson, and Dominique Planchon-de Font-Reaulx) not only analyzed Daguerre's singular contribution, but also claimed primacy for it. The national dimension, intertwined from the outset in this debate and upon which I will not elaborate here, thus surfaced, even in these recent studies.[12]

In his article in the catalogue, historian André Gunthert sought to offer an answer to a question that had already been posed by his predecessors: If the technical achievement of preserving an image was attained as early as 1825 by Talbot, and if Nièpce and Daguerre had in fact possessed this knowledge while Nièpce was still alive, why was it that they failed to

9 In 1989, for instance, the one hundred and fiftieth anniversary of the invention of photography was celebrated in various places throughout the world.

10 Walter Benjamin, *Selected Writings, Volume 2, 1927–1934* (Cambridge, MA: The Belknap Press of Harvard University Press, 1999), 507.

11 Quoted in Geoffrey Batchen, *Burning with Desire* (Cambridge, MA: MIT Press, 1999), 62.

12 Pinson, for instance, wrote that the discovery of an 1838 portrait ascribed to Daguerre and pronounced the first photographic portrait resulted in an exclusively internal, French debate, one of the only debates about the invention of the daguerreotype, which had long before been marginalized by the discussion of photography as a technology of print on paper. Stephen Pinson, "Revers de fortune," in *Le daguerreotype français: Un objet photographique* (Paris: Musée d'Orsay, 2003).

publicize their discovery? Gunthert has claimed in answer that from 1835 to 1837, the scientists had invested their concentrated efforts in perfecting the invention, while from 1837 to 1839, they had focused on what he called the packaging of their invention and on the means of distribution, "What Daguerre wishes to present to the public is not a mere process or principle or recipe, but a finished product, containing both the necessary equipment, provided as a ready-to-use kit, as well as practical and symbolic instructions."[13] The development of photography after the daguerreotype, to which it put an end, Gunthert sees as a marginal phase in the history of photography, a phase that he described as "reprofessionalization by elitist photography militants." Their efforts toward liberation from the rigidity of the daguerreotype, toward opening up photography to individual creativeness as regards the photographic apparatus itself, were vanquished, he claims, by the photographic technology developed around 1880. This technology returned photography to the principle characteristic of the daguerreotype which, today, still remains a defining feature of photography—its condensation into a black box between whose walls all technical matters are obscured and buried, so that it works itself, so to speak, at the click of a button, making it accessible to all.

Gunthert accordingly ends his article with a call to view Daguerre "as a pioneer in the full sense of the term, not of the process of perfectly inscribing [an image] but, of photography as a practice"[14] Gunthert thus recognizes that Daguerre did not develop the process single-handedly and cannot, consequently, be considered its inventor. He does, however, seek to credit him with being the first to make this invention sufficiently simple and reliable for it to become accessible to the public at large. This achievement, though, in keeping with Gunthert's own claims, was attained only in 1907, about half a century after Daguerre's death.[15] While the accessibility and operational simplicity of cameras, according to Gunthert, was achieved only at the beginning of the twentieth century, he nevertheless views photography as a nineteenth-century invention.

None of the historians contributing to the Musée d'Orsay exhibition or catalogue perceived themselves as historians of the apparatus: the daguerreotype or camera. And yet, all of the histories they narrate are caught within a single narrative framework centered on the technological invention and on its inventor and distinctly converging toward this center. Contrary to these narratives, I'll contend that photography was invented at the precisely the moment when the individual inventor lost the authority to determine the meaning of his invention. Thus the questions "who invented photography? is drained of its meaning. At that moment the use of a variety of technologies of creating images – daguerreotype, Calotype, Panotype, Talbotype, Crystallograph, or Ambrotype, to name just a few, all placed at the public's disposal by their various inventors toward the end of the 1830s—exceeded the realm of control of this or that single inventor, this or that sponsoring state, and proceeded to create a new sphere of relations between people.[16]

The invention of photography, then, is not the achievement of a single person who may have isolated several chemical elements and activated them by means of a certain mechanism. Instead, the invention of photography was the creation of a new situation in which different people, in different places, can simultaneously use a black box to manufacture an image of their encounters: not an image of *them*, but of the encounter itself.[17] Not only is the invention of photography the invention of a new encounter between people, but the invention of an encounter between people and the camera. Photography was invented at the moment when a space of plurality was initiated, at the moment when a large number of people – more than just a certain circle of acquaintances – took hold of a camera and began using it as a means of producing images. Photography was invented at *that* moment, by *those* people. They cannot be identified; they do not belong to any milieu of professionals, but are ordinary people who, simply by using a camera, both promoted photography and initiated what I am calling the civil contract of photography. A description of them would be impossible to complete and could not provide a full account of the civil contract of photography's conditions of possibility if we failed to note explicitly that looking at photographs was an inseparable part of photography's institutionalization and

---

13 André Gunthert, "La boite noire de Daguerre," in *Le daguerreotype francais: Un objet photographique* (Paris Musée d'Orsay, 2003), 35.

14 Gunthert, "La boite noire de Daguerre," 39.

15 Drawing on the study by Nathalie Boulouch, Gunthert links this accessibility to the invention of the autochrome by the Lumière brothers and to the uses to which it was put. Nathalie Boulouch, "Peindre avec le soleil? Les enjeux du problème de la photographie des couleurs," *Études Photographiques*, no. 10 (2002).

16 The names are listed in Alan Trachtenberg, *Reading American Photographs: Images as History* (New York: Hill and Wang, 1989), 3.

17 In *The Techniques of the Observer*, Jonathan Crary shows that during the years from 1810 to 1840 – that is, before the invention of photography—a new observer figure was institutionalized, along with the conditions for a new visual experience that involved a break from the model manifested by the *camera obscura*, and "new modes of circulation, communication, production, consumption and rationalization all demanded and shaped a new observer-consumer." Jonathan Crary, *Techniques of the Observer* (Cambridge, MA: MIT Press, 1992), 14. Many of the characteristics that Crary attributes to the viewer at the beginning of the century are also typical of spectators of photography, but do not adequately describe them.

that the validity of the contract is due, at least potentially, not simply to the new ability of photographers to take photographs, but to the oscillation between the photographer's and the spectator's position. This oscillation inherently undermines any legal or juridical claims that anyone does or can "own" a photograph. Not only can no single individual claim to have invented photography, but the properties of photography itself make it impossible for any single individual to claim exclusive property rights to a photograph.

THE SPACE OF POLITICAL RELATIONS IN PHOTOGRAPHY

The invention of photography offered the gaze an absolute plane of visual immobility, a plane on which all movement is frozen, transformed into a still picture that can be contemplated without disturbance. However, in this picture what has been established—what has been fixed and stabilized—what "was there," to employ the succinct phrase coined by Roland Barthes in *Camera Lucida* to characterize what every photograph says of its subject, that it "was there," is at most a testimony to the moment of the photograph's eventuation in which photographer, photographed, and camera encountered one another.[18] Even when this encounter occurs under the difficult conditions of distress or disaster, when a threat looms over or has already caused harm to the political space, as a space of plurality and action, the act of photography and the photographs it produces might, at least potentially, restore it. In other words, although photography may appear to be a distinctive object of the contemplative life (*vita contemplativa*), a moment in which all movements have been eliminated, it is actually deeply embedded in the active life (*vita activa*); it attests to action and continues to take part in it, always engaged in an ongoing present that challenges the very distinction between contemplation and action.[19] The photograph always includes a supplement that makes it possible to show that what "was there" wasn't there *necessarily* in that way.

The disappearance of what "was there" from the first daguerreotype of 1837 and its transformation over time into an imageless monochromatic surface might serve as an allegory for this structure of relations. The daguerreotype shows "a section of wall and bench (or perhaps a window ledge) cluttered with various objects typically found in such places. These include the following: plaster casts of the heads of two putti or cupids, complete with small wings."[20] This description, which adheres to the plane of the visible as closely as possible, is revealed as an utter fabrication after inspecting the daguerreotype preserved in the vaults of the French Society of Photography (SFP) in Paris. The daguerreotype, which has (re)turned into a plane of silvery ash, is kept inside a safe-deposit box alongside a reproduction intended to attest to what *is* seen in it, despite it no longer being visible. The omission of this daguerreotype from the great Daguerre exhibition at the Musée d'Orsay in 2003 was based on the assumption that a yawning divide lies between what was seen in the first daguerreotype and what can actually be seen.[21] What lies in this in between, between what was seen in the first daguerreotype and what can actually be seen in it, is the very space of relations of photography.

This space is characterized by a particular relation to the visible. There has always been a regard for the visible. The world has a visible dimension; human beings are equipped with eyes and conduct themselves, to a large extent, in and through the world in keeping with the ways they observe it. The traditional distinction between the life of study and contemplation (*vita contemplativa*) and the life of action (*vita activa*), assigns contemplation a realm of its own that is essentially visual—reverie, wonderment, marveling, disinterested pausing vis-à-vis a landscape or a figure. Since the days of ancient Greece, the metaphor of this gaze has served to conceptualize abstract thought: theory, speculation, study, things that people imagine or understand through the use of their imagination, and so forth. However, attitudes toward the visible have always included two additional modes, as well, both of which are unrelated to the world of contemplation and, conversely, more closely approximate the world of action. The gaze, after all, is an inalienable part of action, of instrumental activities, of the effort to achieve goals and objectives, to grow more efficient and more sophisticated.

Hannah Arendt, who revisited the classical distinction between the realm of contemplation and the realm of action in *The Human Condition*, drew a distinction between three forms and three areas of action. The first form, which she defined as labor, consists in

18 Roland Barthes, *Camera Lucida: Reflections on Photography*, trans. Richard Howard (New York: Vintage, 2000), 76 translation modified.

19 On the distinction between the *vita contemplative* and *vita activa*, along with the history of this distinction, see Hannah Arendt, *The Human Condition* (1958; Chicago: University of Chicago Press, 1998).

20 This description is quoted in Geoffrey Batschen, *Burning with Desire* (Cambridge, MA: MIT Press, 1999), 130. Most likely, the faithful description of what was visible in the daguerreotype is based on a reproduction that continues to be distributed as "the first daguerreotype." I am grateful to André Gunthert of the SFP in Paris for showing me the actual first daguerreotype and informing me of its condition and the fact of its omission from the Daguerre exhibition in 2003.

21 In the exhibition catalogue, the image appears as an expression of Daguerre's preference for "the readable aspect of the image." Quentinc Bajac and Dominique Planchon-de Font-Réalux, *Le daguerréotype français: Un objet photographique* (Paris: Musée d'Orsay, 2004), 58.

activity designed to provide for the basic needs of existence, allowing survival and the reproduction of life. The second form, which she defined as work, consists in activity creating products that do not serve immediate needs and that are not used up through direct consumption. Such products include instruments, tools, and tool parts that may be used in creating additional products and, finally, in creating an entire world, arranging the life of humans on the planet and allowing them to turn its space into their abode. The third form is action, which is unlike work in that it does not produce an end product or carry out a previously made plan. This form consists in individuals' venturing to generate something new through physical acts or speech, doing so in public, among many other people, exposed to their gaze, in the recognition that the individual cannot fully predict the outcome of this venture or control the way in which it will evolve in the world.

I will draw on Arendt's distinction among three modes of vita activa to characterize various forms of active, noncontemplative gazes. The two most widespread ones are the identifying, orientative gaze, which, I propose, is analogous to labor, and the professional gaze, guiding and accompanied by certain types of action, which I'll present as analogous to work. Gazes of the first kind constitute part of the practice of orientation and survival based on the mechanism of identifying what is visible, which is a necessary condition for existence. The individual observes her surroundings in order to identify herself within them, to plan her movements, and to identify the objects, animals, and people that she encounters, discerning their intentions as well as the dangers and opportunities implicit in each encounter. Gazes of the second kind, which might be termed "directed" or "intended," are typical of professionals (doctors, artists, police, architects, educators, etc.) and allow the arrangement and control of what is visible through the use of a body of knowledge that is incremental, ongoing, and evolving. The professional gaze isn't necessary to basic survival, but, rather, to the ordering of certain types of activities, to the analysis of events and circumstances, to hand-eye coordination, and so forth, in situations where action is free of the need to satisfy immediate needs and is, instead, anchored to goals of a higher order.

The identifying gaze and the directed gaze have accompanied human existence from its very beginnings. Prior to the invention of photography, however, it was difficult to find a gaze of the type that was analogous to action in the sense defined by Arendt. Until then, the practical gaze was either an identifying, orientative one or a professional gaze directed toward a definitive activity. The gaze recognized as distinct from these two forms lay outside the realm of action altogether—the contemplative gaze that gives pause and wonders. Then, the invention of photography added a new way of regarding the visible, one that previously did not exist or that, at least, existed in a different manner. This gaze is based on a new attitude toward the visual. It constitutes in an approach toward items, situations, customs, images, or places that, before photography came into existence, were not held worthy of contemplation in and of themselves. This approach or attitude now exists in contexts of plurality, among people, in a public sphere, contexts within which every participant not only contemplates what can be seen but is also, herself, exposed and visible. Such regard for the visual departs from the disciplinarian gaze or the pattern of communicating prerecognized messages. It approximates at least the central distinguishing features of action: it includes the aspect of a new beginning, and its ends are unpredictable. The members of the community of photography are, as stated above, anyone and everyone who bears any relationship whatsoever to photographs – as a photographer, a viewer of photographs, or a photographed person. While it is customary to draw distinctions between amateur and professional photographers and also, perhaps, between random or occasionally photographed persons and those for whom being photographed is a profession, the community of photography is not actually organized around these distinctions. It is a broad community, which I venture to call "the citizenry of photography," and it is borderless and open. The relations between its members cannot be defined in terms of a common professional interest in photography. Within the framework of this community, the third manner of gazing, the third form of regarding the visible, which I have related to Arendt's concept of action, appears from the outset with civil characteristics. Much like action, which always occurs within a political sphere of human plurality, the singular gaze enabled by photography, which I view as a civil gaze, also exists—always and only—within a plurality. The spectator activating this gaze views the photograph and recognizes instantly that what is inscribed in it and discernible in it are products of plurality – the plural participants in the act of photography (the photographer, the photographed person, and the spectator). Moreover, the spectator instantaneously recognizes them as products of the multiplicity of elements that enter into the frame, whether in keeping with the photographer's intentions, or despite these intentions, or unrelated to them. The civil gaze doesn't seek to control the visible, but neither can it bear another's control over the visible. In particular, it cannot consent to any attempt to rule the visible while seeking to abolish the space of plurality.

THE PROPERTIES OF PHOTOGRAPHS AND PHOTOGRAPHS AS PROPERTY

In *Techniques of the Observer*, Jonathan Crary postulates that the appearance of a new figure of the viewer was witnessed in a mixture of three positions: "An individual body that is at once a spectator, a subject of empirical research and observation, and an element of machine production."[22] The invention of photography, he claims, is secondary to the revolution brought about by the invention of various seeing instruments during the first decades of the nineteenth century and to the new observer these apparatuses established. However, as Crary himself points out, photography also establishes "a new set of abstract relations between individuals and things" and imposes "those relations as the real."[23] Crary's understanding of that transition from the *camera obscura* to the seeing instruments of the nineteenth century, which created a new observer, will serve as a point of departure for my discussion of what the properties of photographs imply for the status of photographs as property.

Let us begin with the photographer. It is commonly accepted and legally established that the photographer owns the images that he or she makes – that the photographer's ownership of the image is his or her "right" under the doctrine of property rights. It is this putative "right" of ownership that, in the case of photographs, I want to contest here, My questioning of the concept of "right" in this instance is meant to challenge the assumption that the photographed individual has no right over the image made of him or her and that this right is "naturally" given to the person holding the photograph's means of production. Most importantly, I would like to challenge the transformation of the photograph into an object of private property. To do so, I will examine the distribution of those goods known as "images" within their social and political contexts silenced from the discussion over the regulation of photography's exchange relations through market forces and by the judicial system that legitimized this regulation.

Starting in the middle of the nineteenth century, when channels for the distribution of photography were established—the exchange of *cartes de visite*, shop display windows, exhibitions, newspapers, and so on—access has been provided to images of people, objects, and places that in the absence of photography would have remained outside the modern citizen's visual field. Here, I will dwell principally on the most obvious instance of this framework, the photographic situation under conditions in which at least two people gather around the camera and take part in the ritual of photography. Men and women of the period celebrated this accessibility in a way that made them (and subsequent others) forget the fact that photography is the result of an encounter with an another and with an other, and, as such, does not have one obvious, constant owner. In that encounter, one is holding a camera, while the other, knowingly or not, becomes the photographed person. The encounter produces a photograph in which an image of the photographed person is inscribed. It is an encounter that always and inescapably involves a measure of violence, even when the situation is one of full and explicit consent between the participant parties. The violence is inherent in the instrumentalization of the photographed person in order to produce an image of him, within which context the photographed person can have as much of a vested interest as the photographer. Because ownership of the image has been assigned to the photographer, however, in only a few particular cases has a photograph been deemed to be in the public domain, and even then only after judicial intervention.[24] In rarer instances, typically involving well-known people, photographed individuals have been given certain rights in regard to *their* photographs taken in public, at least to the extent that they have been able to influence their mode of distribution.[25] At all other times, whether during moments of happiness or disaster, the photographed persons renounce in advance—or, more accurately, have been treated as if they have renounced in advance—any legal right to their own image, entrusting it to the hands of others. The "right" to the ownership of a photographic image has been deployed retroactively in regard to the initial decades of photography. The question of who is the proper owner of a photograph did not emerge until the twentieth century.[26] The photographic situation, in which the photographer is whoever actually holds the means of production in his or her hands and controls its operation, effectively created the conditions for the photographer's designation as the "natural" owner of the photograph. When the photographer was working for

22 Crary, *Techniques of the Observer*, 112.

23 Crary, 13.

24 For some crucial moments in the history of the ownership of photographs, see John David Viera, "Images as Property," in Larry Gross, John Katz, Jay Ruby (eds.), *Image Ethics: The Moral Rights of Subjects in Photographs, Film, and Television* (New York: Oxford University Press, 1988). An interesting case in point is the free access to use photographer David Rubinger's image of Israeli paratroopers in front of the Wailing Wall in the 1967 War.

25 Celebrities don't automatically turn into the owners of the photographs taken of them in the public space, but can demand economic rights for the use of their images.

26 One of the first cases to challenge the photographed's lack of ownership of his own image, as something self-evident – although there was no demand for ownership—involved a photograph of Miss Abigail Roberson on packages of flour. (See Viera, "Images as Property," 140–41).

someone else, the question of ownership went through an additional transformation, but the photograph was in all cases was recognized as belonging to whomever possessed the instrument that created the photographic image and the support on which the original image was printed, rather than to the one who stod in front of the camera. The precedence given to the ownership of the support (the artifact)—a metal or glass plate in photography's infancy, photographic paper at a later stage—also made it possible for the opposite scenario to occur, in which photographs lacking the name of the photographer who made them wander throughout the world.[27] In those cases in which photographs are exhibited or printed without the photographer's name, the photographed individuals are presented as content, irrespective of its makers, content whose distribution is of prime importance for the public – an importance that usually suspends the question of legal ownership. In these cases, the photographed individual is usually not the owner of the photograph. Although the photograph is in the hands of someone who presents himself or herself as its owner, the only way of exercising this ownership is to share it with the public as a substitute for the photograph's owner. Thus, the individual or institution (newspaper, archive, etc.), having physical possession of the photograph, the material object itself, can act as if they were performing a "service" to the public, which is, in principle, the photograph's "true" owner. When the question of ownership arises legally, before a court, it usually appears only indirectly and does not undermine what has come to be taken for granted—that the photographed individual is *not* the owner of his/her own image. [...] On occasions in which photographed individuals have brought a claim in regard to their photographs, it was not an issue of the ownership of the image that was at the center of the debate, but the right to protect the character of the image that was made of them. In addition to the right to ownership of the image, other juridical concepts, such as "the right to privacy," "defamation," or "malicious use" have thus been introduced into the discourse on photography. To this day, courts continue to ratify the absence of any rights of photographed individuals regarding the journalistic use of such photographs and tend to impose restrictions only in cases of direct economic exploitation or violation of privacy at the moment of taking the photograph.[28]

However, the concepts of property and ownership are foreign to the logic of photography. What is seen in a photograph evades all criteria for ownership, and cannot be appropriated; from this it is impossible to establish a single, stable meaning of photography that would negate or supersede all others. A photograph is neither the product of a single person, despite the concept of "author" having been established in relation to photography, nor is it even solely a product of human hands. A photographic image, then, can at most be entrusted to someone for a certain time. It is a deposit, temporarily given over to whomever has it for safekeeping, but such persons are never its owner.

Not only is the deposit temporary, it is only ever partial, conditional, and with limited liability. All of these qualifications apply to the deposit because just as no one can claim ownership of a photographed image, no one can deem himself or herself to be the one who has renounced ownership and put it in someone else's hands. As stated above, the concepts of property and ownership are foreign to photography. At the same time that a photograph lies in someone's hands, someone else can always claim the deposited image for themselves, or at least demand to participate in its safekeeping. Since the safekeeping of the deposit ranges anywhere from burying it in the archives to giving it widespread circulation, from preservation "as is" to being exhibited in a different light, someone else may still wish to display it or cast it in a different light. The demand to participate in the deposit's safekeeping is not made in the name of a right to possess the deposited image, for this demand expresses a rejection of any right that might be given to someone in regard to a photograph. The demand to participate in the deposit's safekeeping stems from a duty toward the deposit as such, toward what has been deposited, toward whoever deposited it, and toward the archive itself. In what follows, I will try to show how this duty is produced. It is here that the oscillation between the position of the photographer and the position of the spectator becomes most apparent and most definitively subverts the notion that photographs are the real property of those who take them. Ever since photography's emergence, there have been efforts to take photographs of areas in distress or those struck by disaster, to collect, distribute and interpret photographs from these places. The assumptions underlying these efforts have been, first of all, that what happens "there" is of interest not only to those concerned with it—those who have been struck by disaster—but to onlookers the world over, and, second, that photographs produced out of what happens "there" participate in constructing the event and the responses to it.[29] Since the second half of the twentieth century, this activity has been accompanied by the distribution of cameras within afflicted areas or areas prone to disaster in

27 As, for instance, the artist Michal Heiman has systematically demonstrated in her project "Unknown Photographer."

28 This is mainly true of celebrities who have turned their images into an economic resource, and therefore their use by others detracts from the economic capital they themselves might derive from them. An "ordinary" person, however, as in the case of Florence Thompson (in Dorothea Lang's photograph), will be given nothing, even though their photograph has made others a fortune.

order to undermine any attempt to seal off such places to the photographic gaze.[30] These uses of photography are part of the way in which citizens actualize their duty toward other citizens as photographed persons who've been struck by disaster. The exercise of photography in such situations is actually the exercise of citizenship—not citizenship imprinted with the seal of belonging to a sovereign, but citizenship as a partnership of governed persons taking up their duty as citizens and utilizing their position for one another, rather than for a sovereign. The camera in the hands of the citizen is indifferent to the question of whether or not the injured persons who are photographed are citizens "of" a state. The camera recognizes them as citizens of what I call the citizenry of photography. The civil contract of photography, the essentials of which can be derived from each of these uses, is its founding formulation. These uses are motivated by the duty actively to overturn any ownership that someone has obtained or that is being sought in regard to a photograph—regardless of whether it has already been taken or could in principle be taken—and with it the right to conceal the photographed persons from the eyes of other citizens bound together in the civil contract of photography. The duty derived from the civil contract of photography is simultaneously to reject one's claim to be the owner of a photograph that one possesses as well as anyone's attempt to appoint him or herself as a guardian of another in an attempt to prevent that other person from being photographed.

Photography's exchange relations were institutionalized in such a way that in addition to those recognized as the lawful owners of photographs, the public has been recognized as the virtual owner of all photographs. The familiar slogan regarding "the public's right to see" only partially expresses what is at stake and is thus a mistaken and misleading formulation. It is not simply the right to see, but the right to enact photography free of governmental power and even against it, if it inflicts injury upon others who are governed. Photography provides modern citizens with an instrument enabling them to develop and sustain civilian skills that are not entirely subordinate to governmental power and allows them exercise partnership with others not under the control of this power or acting as the extension of this power's operations and goals. In other words, photography is one of the distinctive practices by means of which individuals can establish a distance between themselves and power in order to observe its actions and to do so not as its subjects. Injury to this right, which is simultaneously injury to both the photographer and the photographed, as two citizens of photography—but fundamentally against all of the citizenry of photography—establishes a duty to protect it. If it is not protected, citizens will be deprived of the protection that can be granted by photography as an instrument that employs power that is in the hands of governed and not only in the hands of the sovereign or those seeking to win sovereign power. Exercising this right—or discharging this duty—constantly undermines any attempt of founding an exclusive sovereign authority over the exercise of photography.

THE CIVIL CONTRACT OF PHOTOGRAPHY: TERMS AND CONDITIONS

As we have seen, in the classical photographic situation, the camera mediates an encounter between the photographer and the photographed, and an image is produced. In the legal institutionalization of this encounter, the photographed individual has not been recognized as its owner, whereas the photographer who produces the image has been given legal rights. However, this appropriation of the photographed person's rights, in which there is always a measure of violence, which was taken for granted by both sides from the start, and which has remained unaltered, cannot be understood without assuming that a certain pact or agreement lies at its foundation. Such an agreement is what makes the photographic encounter between the photographer and the photographed possible. It is important to emphasize, however, that this agreement does not mean there is willing consent, and in no way is it based on knowledge of the conditions of exchange or the possibility not to agree. What this agreement establishes is that the two sides reconfirm the balance of power that has been established between them, doing so without resorting to the use of overt force. When a camera initiates an encounter between the photographer and the photographed, each of the sides is generally responsible for its part and knows what is expected of it. Even the refusal to be photographed or the refusal to be photographed in a certain way is institutionalized—the photographed persons and the photographers act according to conventional expectations; everyone is supposed to know how to act and what to expect at the photographic

29 Numerous catalogues published in the last few decades manifest these assumptions. See Carol Squiers, *The Body at Risk: Photography, Illness and Healing* (New York: International Center of Photography, 2005); Deborah Willis, *Reflections in Black* (New York: W. W. Norton, 2000); Roy Guttman and David Rieff, David (eds.), *Crimes of War* (London: W. W. Norton, 1999); and Thomas Y. Levin, Ursula Frohne, and Peter Weibel (eds.), *Ctrl (Space): Rhetorics of Surveillance from Bentham to Big Brother* (Cambridge, MA.: MIT Press, 2002).

30 One example is the cameras distributed in the Occupied Territories during the first intifada. See the interview with Haim Brayshit in Ariella Azoulay, *How Does It Look to You?* (Tel Aviv: Babel, 2000).

encounter.[31] From the fact that in the photographic encounter itself there is no need for the formulation or signing of a concrete pact, we can assume there has been some kind of tacit prior pact or agreement between the sides that ensures the present encounter: not merely a contractual agreement or ad hoc understanding, but a civil contract.

If one reflects on the agreement between the parties to the civil contract of photography as it is usually enacted, it is clearly an unequal exchange. The photographer produces a picture of an event or place at which he or she is present, a picture that may include all others who are present at the same place. These people can either agree or refuse to be photographed by the photographer, or at least to have what is happening to them or the place they are occupying become the object of his or her photographs. If they grant the photographer the right to turn them into a photographic image, in most cases, they receive no material reward, except for being turned into an image. No photographer promises them anything regarding what the future of "their" photograph might be—whether it will be rejected during editing or widely distributed, whether it will be printed in whole or in part, with or without a name, and so on. They can only be sure of being turned into an image, which from the moment it is taken will be tucked away in a drawer or file in some archive, in some city, somewhere on the face of the Earth. The photographer makes a living, and in some cases may even become wealthy; the photographer wins fame and prizes, is a member of organizations that defend his or her interests, is protected by publication contracts and agreements. The photographed individual, on the other hand, is abandoned. He or she has no control over the image; in most cases, the individual is unable to determine its composition and the modes of its distribution; like Florence Owens Thompson, he or she receives nothing in return except for being turned into a photograph—no monetary compensation or guarantee. The photographed individual remains entirely outside the economic transaction. From an early stage of its history, the technology of photography offered itself as a convenient, inexpensive, and easily accessible and operable means of production that anyone could use. In principle, anyone could hold a camera in their hands, giving rise to a situation in which the importance of a photograph is never solely dependent on the specific means of production (high-quality camera versus instant camera), the photographer's professional skills, or his or her artistic talent. The importance of a photograph often transcends all of these qualities and quite possibly stems, in the first place, from the photographed object. In other words, the technology of photography created the relatively simple mobility between the positions of photographer and the photographed. This essential mobility finds no expression in the configuration of their established relationship, which has fixed the asymmetry I have described as the defining model of their relations. The essential exploitation in the agreement between the photographer—or those for whom he is the agent—and the photographed is even more striking in light of this elimination of any possible reversal of roles. In the framework of this agreement, the photographed individual remains in an exploited position within the exchange—he or she is the one who relinquishes any rights in advance, subordinated to the photographer, who, simply by having the camera, is able to tell those who are photographed how to behave and appear, having the last word regarding the framing that will ultimately be shown to the public. But this description is only partial, at best, for its point of view restricts the contract to what is actually exchanged and recognized as having exchange value in the market. To understand the nature of the agreement that lies in the background of any concrete photographic encounter, a roundabout path must be taken.

In *Leviathan*, Thomas Hobbes distinguishes between a contract and a compact or covenant in the transmission or exchange of property. In a contract, the right of ownership passes immediately between the signatories; in a compact, however, "one of the Contractors, may deliver the Thing contracted for on his part of the contract, and leave the other to perform his part at some determinate time after, and in the meantime be trusted."[32] A compact, then, is a contract based on mutual trust and an anticipated, future reward. The social contract, says Hobbes, enables human beings to renounce their natural right to defend themselves, meanwhile immediately awarding them security and the defense of their lives. Human beings in fact renounce their right to use force directly and in return enjoy the protection of a governmental power, which guarantees that this renunciation will not result in direct harm to them or to their property. The fear of being killed in the war of all against all and the insecurity that derives from the absence of any authority capable of ensuring that agreements and the fulfillment of promises are upheld lead humans to make the rational choice of constituting a community governed by a sovereign. In the course of constituting the community, each of its members renounces the use of force in favor of a collective power "as may be able to defend them from the invasion of Forraigners, and the injuries of one another, and thereby secure them in

31 The stalking of celebrities by paparazzi and the political photo opportunity are two examples.
32 Thomas Hobbes, *Leviathan*, ed. C.B. MacPherson (London: Penguin, 1987), 193.

such sort, as that by their own industrie, and by the fruites of the Earth, they may nourish themselves and live contentedly." Individuals collectively agree to hand over their right to defend themselves to one person or a congress of persons known as the sovereign, "and every one besides, [is called] his Subject."[33]

According to the story told by Hobbes, along with others in the social-contract tradition, once it was "signed," human beings passed from natural state or patriarchal order to a social state within which a community was constituted on the basis of agreement.[34] The story is usually told and even more often interpreted as a thought experiment or a construct of reason, not as a "real" story about an actual agreement that marks the beginning of political states. It is usually assumed that the contract has such a binding force because human beings are rational creatures, and in the face of fear, they would no doubt have opted for a social contract that extends security to them and improves their condition.

In her critical reading of the various versions of the social contract, Carole Pateman points out that most, if not all presuppose that achieving security and improving the condition of individuals can be accomplished only through the means of sovereign government.[35] The social contract is nothing less than the text that justifies the form of sovereign rule. In Pateman's critique, she points to the way in which the first stage of the contract, which is described as the formation of a political community that establishes an obligation *between* the members of the community at the same time as it places authority in their hands, is rapidly pushed aside in favor of the second stage, which assumes that the members of the community will necessarily alienate their right to exercise political authority by granting it to their representatives, and in effect to sovereign government. As mentioned before, the status of the civil contract of photography is likewise not that of an actual document, but a tacit agreement. It differs from the Hobbesan account of the contractarian origin of sovereignty, however, in that it echoes the first stage of the social contract, but seeks to differentiate itself by suspending the second stage. The intrinsic assumption behind this move is that photography is one of the only practices by means of which a political community has been formed that is based on a mutual obligation among its members, who hold the power to act in connection with this obligation. To put it another way, the form that the civil contract of photography takes is the form of mutual obligation that precedes the constitution of political sovereignty. In the social contract as described by Hobbes, each individual renounces the power to defend himself or herself in favor of the sovereign, whether a single person or congress of people. In Rousseau's version of the social contract, the identity of the sovereign is altered, and the people as a whole come to substitute for it. In both cases, all individuals give the sovereign irrevocable power to govern them for the sake of the sovereign ensuring the protection of their lives. The sovereign exercises its governance by means of the monopoly it has on the use of violence to regulate social relations. If a subject should violate the contract and commit violence, the subject against whom this violence has been inflicted has the right to demand the protection of the sovereign and the restoration of order. In other words, the sovereign is the mediator among individuals in the framework of a closed and stable system of power relations arising from the fact that each individual is committed to the same contract vis-à-vis the sovereign.

By contrast, the civil contract of photography organizes political relations in the form of an open and dynamic framework among individuals, without regulation and mediation by a sovereign. Although individuals do indeed renounce their exclusive right to their own image and consent to becoming an image, such renunciation, as I will demonstrate, is not in favor of a sovereign that would have the exclusive power to produce an image out of them. [...] Photography, we should remember, is foremost a *mass* instrument for the *mass* production of images, which is not susceptible to monopolization.[36] The proliferation of images that photography has facilitated is not simply a matter of quantity, but an essential vector of change in the perceptual matrix. The capacity to look can no longer be seen as a personal property, but is a complex field of relations that originally stem from the fact that photography made available to the individual possibilities of seeing more than his or her eye alone could see, in terms of scope, distance, time, speed, quantity, clarity, and so on. To see more than they could alone, individuals had to align themselves with other individuals who would agree to share their visual field with one another. Photography reorganized what was accessible to the gaze, in the course of which everyone gained the opportunity to see through the gaze of another. In order to create this economy of gazes, each

33 Thomas Hobbes, *Leviathan*, 227, 228.

34 See Arendt, *The Human Condition* and Carole Pateman, *The Sexual Contract* (Stanford, CA: Stanford University Press, 1988) for readings of the social contract. Both detail various stories that the civil contract sought to replace.

35 See Pateman, *The Sexual Contract*.

36 In 1827, when Nièpce presented the invention of the haliograph to the Royal Society, it was poorly received. In the wake of this failure, most of Daguerre's efforts, after joining forces with Nièpce to develop the invention, were devoted to preparing the ground for its widespread acceptance. This, indeed, came to pass once the Chamber of Deputies authorized the purchase of the invention, and photography quickly spread throughout the Western world.

and every one had to renounce his or her right to preserve his or her own, autonomous visual field from external forces, but also acquired an obligation to defend the gaze in order to make it available for others to enter and intermingle. This was primarily the individual's renunciation of ownership of "his" or "her" image or point of view, just as he or she was prepared to give away that image or to become one. Photography, then, broadened the limits of the gaze to encompass a mixed economy of gazes that continually flood the visual field with new data. This mass production of images offered to the gaze is not carried out from a centralized location. It is not synchronized or controlled by a sovereign power. It is performed in different places and by different people who are bound together in civil association on account of photography, but not necessarily with any explicit connection on the basis of a nation, race, or gender. With few exceptions, the mass production of images takes place unabated. Photographers turn into photographed individuals, and vice versa.

In exceptional cases, certain state apparatuses are able to suspend photography, typically in restricted areas and for limited periods of time. These are usually local prohibitions related to the declaration of a state of emergency—a state of exception. [...] Even when such prohibitions pass into law, the ability to enforce them universally is difficult, due to the logic of the technology—its operational facility can be in anyone's hands—and the global travel networks that make it possible to smuggle the camera into areas that are off-limits.[37] There are rare instances that attest to this, when a set of photographs is disclosed from places and situations into which it is hard to imagine a camera could have penetrated. For instance, the four photographs recently discovered that were taken of the gas chambers at Auschwitz.[38]

It is the terms and conditions of the civil contract that explain people's compliance, again and again, in being made the objects of a violent act–photography–without necessarily receiving any immediate reward.[39] The photographer—who is usually on the edge of another, different institution—turns the photographed individual into his or her object, shapes him or her without allowing the individual to have any direct control over the result. The photographer takes the photographed individual's image and appropriates it for himself. The photographed individual's consent has been given in advance—nobody, including the photographed individual himself, expects it to be given again. Nor is this consent linked to any concrete photographer standing and raising a camera in front of the photographed individual. This consent was given in the past, under specific historical conditions, and the continual disregard and forgetting of this consent perpetuates the problematic separation between the photograph as an image with exchange value and photography as the specific political condition in which this image is made.

I do not propose this contract as the outcome of a rational action that brought together people of different social, economic, cultural and political classes who willingly have consented to an arrangement detrimental to their own interests. On the contrary, I contend that the civil contract of photography was imposed on the users of photography at the same time photography was imposed upon them, perpetuating the inequitable division of goods, which blended nicely with the overall logic of the capitalist order. The civil contract of photography was "signed" when the invention spread, becoming readily available, sometime in the second half of the nineteenth century, between the time of the official declaration of the invention of photography (1839) and the invention of the portable and easily-operated camera (1877). Individuals were not asked for their opinions, quickly finding themselves living in a world in which photography began to mediate social relations, just as it was mediated, of course, by them. Despite the economic and class mobilization that photography afforded to some of its operators and users, photography, in most of its public appearances, nonetheless perpetuated the exploitative relations already existing in society.[40]

The initial deployment of photography on the part of the modern state contributed to the perpetuation of the social relations of power, turning weak, disadvantaged, and marginal populations such as ethnic minorities, criminals, and the insane into utterly exposed objects of photography.[41] These groups served as guinea

37 Thus, for instance, the American military government's prohibition of photography at Hiroshima and Nagasaki was demarcated in space and limited in time and could not have continued without being violated by local photographers. It certainly could not have become a constitutional law.

38 See Georges Didi-Huberman, *Images malgré tout* (Paris: Minuit, 2003).

39 The description of the violence of the photographic act is frequent in recent writings on photography. Roland Barthes in *Camera Lucida* described its ontology: "In terms of the image-repertoire, the Photograph (the one I *intend*) represents that very subtle moment when, to tell the truth, I am neither subject not object but a subject who feels he is becoming an object: I then experience a micro-version of death (of parenthesis): I am becoming a specter." Barthes, *Camera Lucida*), 13–14.

40 By "public appearances," I refer to the simple distinction between photography at the heart of the family and those that can be seen to be a matter of "public interest." This distinction, of course, needs to be problematized, and it is easy to show this in the migration of family photographs into the press coverage of disasters.

41 For more on this, see the studies by Allan Sekula, "The Body and the Archive," in Richard Bolton (ed.), *The Contest of Meaning* (Cambridge, MA: MIT Press, 1989); Carol Squiers (ed.), *Overexposed: Essays on Contemporary Photography* (New York: The New Press, 1999); and Sandra S. Phillips, Mark Haworth-Booth, and Carol Squiers (eds.), *Police Pictures: The Photograph as Evidence* (San Francisco: Chronicle Books, 1997).

pigs for the mass utilization of photography by the modern state, which quickly turned the entire population into an object of photography, albeit in conformity with a predefined set of rules—various types of identification cards, personal documents, and so on.[42]

To this day, however, weak populations remain more exposed to photography, especially of the journalistic kind, which coerces and confines them to a passive, unprotected position. In most cases, they are deprived of the ownership of their own images.[43] In some cases, when one of these photographs breaks through the parade of images of its kind—photographs of horror—the symbolic or economic capital that accrues highlights the gap between their exploitation and the enrichment of others "at their expense." But this kind of critical stance still restricts our attitude toward photography to the question of ownership, positing the photographer and the photographed as opposing one another as the only possible owners of the photograph, leaving the citizens of photography in the background, preventing them from appearing as a crucial player in the practice of photography.

By contrast, becoming a citizen in the citizenry of photography entails seeking, by means of photography, to rehabilitate one's citizenship or that of someone else who has been stripped of it. She is someone who sees photography and its civil contract as something that can protect her from anyone who would violate another citizen, which amounts to violating her, insofar as citizenship itself is violated. The citizen—whether she is a photographer or spectator—can demand a role in the deposit, the photographed image, and is thereby a plaintiff, rather than an owner. She is someone who speaks on behalf of the photograph itself. Assuming that any harm to the principle of citizenship is a harm to her own citizenship, she is always already the spokesperson for her own claim as a citizen.[44] As such, she is not reduced to her formal status as citizen. It is by actually practicing her citizenship that she becomes a citizen. To understand photography in the context of citizenship, and citizenship not merely as a status, but as a praxis of becoming threatened and restricted by the deeds of Man, a return to the 1798 Declaration of the Rights of Man and of the Citizen is required. In the previous chapter, I have discussed that distinction already made between "man" and "citizen" in its title. One might assume that this distinction was meant to ensure that all human beings would become citizens, but as is well known, not everyone became a citizen. The man of whom the declaration speaks is not the individual in a condition prior to becoming a citizen, but the precise opposite—he is supposed to restrict the dissemination of citizenship as a form of negotiation with power. Man seeks to reduce the citizen to a protector who will safeguard his "natural rights." In other words, man seeks to restrict citizenship to a status, either innate or acquired under stringent conditions, and to limit its content to the protection of his rights. The civil contract of photography, by contrast, affords enough distance to view a different type of relation between human beings, between the governed, in the framework of which the citizen aims to break away from his or her *status* as citizen and *exercise* citizenship—that is, to turn citizenship into the arena of a constant becoming, together with other (non)citizens.

Photography, which was given to the citizen half a century after the writing of the Declaration of the Rights of Man and of the Citizen, is an instrument that thwarts the restriction of citizenship to a particular nation-state. Instead, it enables the citizen and the noncitizen (either directly or through the citizen's mediation), as those who are governed, to continue voicing civilian grievances despite the "natural and unalienable rights of man" continuing to be grasped as the reason and condition for citizenship. In other words, these civil grievances are distinct from the natural rights of man and are neither subordinate to these rights nor subordinate to the framework of the nation-state that legitimates them. Moreover, it is this citizenship, which is being trampled by "man" and the nation-state, that is being addressed by those actually practicing citizenship, who seek to rehabilitate and liberate citizenship from its subjection to "man" and his natural rights. Here photography traps one in its paradox. To give expression to the fact that a photographed person's citizen status is flawed, or even nonexistent (as in the case of refugees, the poor, migrant workers, etc.), or temporarily suspended (citizens struck by disaster, exposed for a limited period of time), whoever seeks to use photography must exploit the photographed individual's vulnerability. In such situations, photography entails a particular kind of violence: The photograph is liable to exploit the photographed individual, aggravate his or her injury, publicly expose it, and rob the individual of intimacy. This threat of violation always hangs over the photographic act, and this is the precise moment in which the contract between photographer, photographed, and spectator is put to the test. Is there any call to renew

42 On the state's use of photography, see John Tagg, "Evidence, Truth and Order: Photographic Records and the Growth of the State," in Liz Wells (ed.), *The Photography Reader* (London: Routledge, 2003).

43 This inequality does receive mention in various places, but without leading to an in-depth discussion. For instance, in the album issued on the occasion of the millennial year 2000, in the case of inequality regarding the photograph of Florence Thompson, emphasis on the fact that she considered taking those who published it to court (although she didn't, of course, insofar as she lacked the financial ability) is presented as an amusing anecdote. See Robin, *Les 100 photos du siècle*.

44 On the distinction between citizenship and becoming a citizen, see Azoulay and Ophir, *Bad Days*.

or reformulate it? Does the photographer not have a duty towards the photographic image—his or her deposit—even before it has been taken, before it has been deposited? Is the photograph, which now potentially lies in the photographer's camera, not the guarantee given to the photographed person that promises that the photographer will fulfill his or her commitment, even if the photographer might, in the last instance, at the moment of truth, seek to withdraw from it? To add a concrete example to this list of abstract questions, shouldn't the photographer who took the four frames inside the gas chamber at Auschwitz have had to click the camera out of respect for the photographed, who were naked in front of his camera? Should we leave it only to the photographer to confront the paradox of rehabilitation and violation, given the fact that he or she is the one who is "there" with a camera? Is this not a decision that the citizenry of photography agreed on when they acknowledged that they have no right to their own images—when they agreed to deposit the image as certainty of the fulfillment of their commitment, or the photographer's, or the spectators'? Did they not understand that their citizenship is stamped with the seal of photography, as distinctly made manifest by the identification cards we have been given? [...] Photography, at times, is the only civic refuge at the disposal of those robbed of citizenship. Thus, they incidentally benefit from the fact that citizens have accepted photography as a mediating agent in social relations. To trace how photography is tied to citizenship, we may return to France, in the year 1839. The same country that bestowed the Declaration of the Rights of Man and of the Citizen, France, also nationalized the invention of photography in order to bequeath it, without delay, to all of humanity: "We believe we are acting in the spirit of the aspirations of this House [the Chamber of Representatives] in proposing to purchase, in the name of the State, the ownership of such a useful and inspiring invention, and that it seems to us in the interest of the sciences and the arts to bestow it upon the public in general."[45] A reading of the rhetorical gestures of the first proponents of photography demonstrates that they conceived of themselves as emissaries entrusted with the mission of bringing photography to all of humanity, as a gift of universal value with properties that no individual was entitled to hold: the reformative properties of rescue, preservation, and commemoration, as well as those of change and renewal.

Moreover, photography appeared as a new tribunal, a universal and impartial judge that could do justice to the past, present, and future. Its object has impressed an eternal seal—what is seen in it cannot be erased. Photography was depicted as history's representative on Earth, an instrument capable of perpetuating everything that was lost yesterday and of saving what may vanish tomorrow. In addition to being educated to look upon photography as an event of importance to all of humanity, modern citizens experience it as events of which they are the direct addressees.[46] Photography has enabled them to participate in events beyond themselves, yet that have no existence without them. Photography has directly interpellated the citizen—he or she can become the bearer of history, both as photographer and as photographed. An unprecedented responsibility has been placed upon the individual, who has the potential to preserve what takes place at the heart of the family for the sake of those closest to him or to her, as well as what takes place in public space, for the sake of people he or she doesn't even know. Thrown into the modern world, which took shape in the spirit of the civil revolution that came in the wake of the French Revolution and spread throughout the globe, and of the industrial revolution, which was already in full swing, the individual wordlessly consented. The individual simply became both the photographer and photographed.

The photograph, which preserved singular images on paper, was decisive proof for the individual that the proposed civil contract of photography was reliable. Mute at its inception, the photograph maintained its silence. Such silence, which can sometimes scream to the heavens, attests to the fact that it is our historic responsibility not only to produce photos, but to make them speak. Photography granted moderns the opportunity to be naturalized in their world—to know it, investigate it, contemplate it from various angles, bring it closer or distance themselves from it, critique it, and find answers. Since the eighteenth century, the public sphere has not been the sole origin for acquiring civil skills. The world of instruments opened new possibilities for looking and acting, as well for contributing to the shaping of the modern conditions for citizenship.[47] This mass naturalization refashioned the political game, reshuffling the cards in a profound way. The encounter between a public sphere and a new instrumental technology opened unprecedented opportunities both for change to take place within the political sphere and for new forms of exchange to occur within it. The camera opened the possibility of redefining the concept of citizenship and the conditions for its fulfillment. People deprived

45 This is the legislative proposal of 1839 as presented by the French interior minister to the Chamber of Deputies on June 15, 1839.

46 By contrast, such inventions as the washing machine or vacuum cleaner have no doubt changed the life of the individual, but the benefit they bring is personal and private.

47 On the formation of the observer in the end of the eighteenth century and the beginning of the nineteenth, see Crary, *Techniques of the Observer*.

of citizenship—women, first and foremost—began to take an active part in this formation of a new world.[48] As soon as the first daguerreotypes were distributed, hundreds of women began using the new technology to produce photographs of the same quality as those produced by men, although their careers did not enjoy the benefit of stability and protection that accompanied men's social and political status.[49] People began enjoying the right "to be included in the film," as Walter Benjamin phrased it.[50] From an opposite perspective, Susan Sontag has defined the introduction of the camera as "the right to something called news."[51] The camera embodied the possibilities available to the modern citizen to take part in the production, investigation, and distribution of what interests the public. These practices—in which the general public could in principle participate, either as active or passive agents (photographer or photographed)—constituted a significant stratum in the new exchange relations formed in the political sphere. In other words, the camera changed the way in which the individual is governed and the extent of his or her participation in the forms of this governance.

Photography, then, was the forerunner of a missed revolution. The body of citizens was given the means to instigate change, but the relations between these citizens were newly regulated through a unified sovereign power, most often on the basis of a national model, in conformity with coercive rules of exclusion, hierarchical order, discrimination, exploitation, and oppression. In the brief interval between the creation of the new political conditions and the exclusion of entire populations from equal partnership in the political game, the modern citizen signed a compact, the civil contract of photography, which the market and the nation-states shared an interest in weakening and even eliminating altogether.

The market and the nation-states had an interest in distributing photography without the contract that had been established with the invention of photography. The regulation of social relations with emphasis on ownership, on the one hand, and on national citizenship, on the other, in effect deprived modern citizens of what the contract had bequeathed to them. The political game in which the contract was involved—a game that cannot be predicated entirety on market logic, governmental power, and the nation-state is perhaps the only one of its kind in which citizens are able to fulfill their membership in a political community in a framework not dictated by a sovereign power, where they are able to act on their own behalf. The civil contract of photography does not bind the photographed person to the photographer standing opposite the photographer—or to those who might keep the photographer from standing opposite the person. It binds all individuals who take part in photography, both photographers and photographed alike. Every "signatory" to the civil contract has received, in return, the possibility of producing images of the other, that is, of supplementing the inventory of images that he or she can access. Every individual has been given the opportunity to see beyond his or her immediate surroundings and to use the gaze of others upon people and places that the individual cannot access or photograph—including the individual himself or herself. The modern citizen has thus renounced the exclusive right to his or her image in favor of an economy of images that, in principle, includes the individual and all others. This consent is conditional on the consent of all others. Within a short time, the individual has been able to obtain photographic evidence of the consent of all these others, irrespective of their class, nationality, or whatever. Those who are enclosed solely in a private sphere are excluded from this game, but this limitation is temporary, for they might (re)appear in the public domain, (re)exposed to photography.[52] The citizen's renunciation of the exclusive right to possess or distribute his or her photographic images does not mean that the citizen renounces the right to become a photographed image. It can be expected that the former renunciation would help produce one's images when one needs them, for example, when one considers what happens to a person as a matter of public concern. This is not simply a one-time agreement given to a particular photographer at the moment of an encounter, but is in principle a renunciation performed only once by each citizen, linking them all in the contract. [...]

Photography is one of the instruments which has enabled the modern citizen to establish her liberal rights, including freedom of movement and of information, as well as her right to take photographs and to be photographed, to see what others see and would like to show through photographs. Photography has become a means of viewing the world, and the citizen has become a well-trained spectator, capable of read-

48 The same process occurred among the black population in the United States, who, although deprived of citizenship, participated in the nascent practice of photography from the beginning, transforming it into a weapon in the abolitionist struggle. On the first black who practiced the daguerreotype, see Deborah Willis, *Reflections in Black* (New York: W. W. Norton, 2000).

49 Needless to say, their photographs, well as those produced by African Americans, were not treated like those produced by white men, and their existence has only come to light in recent years. The research on women's use of photography (and daguerreotype) in the first years of photography is still only beginning, but one may already affirm their participation in the nascent practice of photography.

50 "Every man is entitled to demand to be included in the film." (Benjamin, 1991, 41).

51 Susan Sontag, *On Photography* (New York: Picador, 1977), 22.

52 On the legal protection of the right to privacy, see Viera, "Images as Property."

ing what is visible in photographs. With photography, the modern citizen found herself in a situation in which she was not previously familiar. On the one hand, she had been given strong and powerful tools—the production of images of herself and others, and the right to see and interpret what was disclosed in these photographs. On the other hand, as an individual the citizen felt cheated: "I'm tired of being a symbol of human misery, moreover my living conditions have improved," complained Florence Thompson, when *her* image as the *Migrant Mother* reappeared hundreds of times in the press decades after the photograph was taken.[53]

Despite the equality of means that are held in principle, "others"—institutional bodies, the rich and powerful, etc.—still have the ability to exercise these means in a discriminatory, and even oppressive manner. In other words, the gap between the power granted to the individual and the possibilities of personally exercising it has become even more glaring. She will be able to fully exercise her power—not merely symbolically, as one who is in principle the owner of the new technological instrument—only by means of a civil contract, which makes it possible to turn the mutual agreement to become an image into a way of securing a mutual guarantee. As stated above, this compliance to become an image was neither protected nor limited to the sovereign, but given to anyone and everyone. The mutual guarantee is supposed to ensure protection for the individual when her entitlement to become an image is threatened, or when her becoming an image is taken to an extreme that threatens to turn her into *only* an image. The mutual guarantee established amongst the citizens of the citizenry of photography is the basis for the formation of a political community that is not subjected or mediated by a sovereign.

This is not simply a mutual guarantee between individuals, but a mutual guarantee linked to the medium of photography and predicated on a mutual consent regarding the truth value of photography, the fact that what we find in it really "was there," in the words of Roland Barthes. In *Camera Lucida* and in his lectures, Barthes attempted to grasp the essence of photography, in its specificity as a medium. This formulation, which has since become classic, fails to exhaust the essence of photography, as Barthes wished, but undoubtedly offers a precise description of the social attitude towards photography. Barthes' expression, which he arrived at one hundred and fifty years after the invention of photography, succinctly captures the particular characteristic of the photographic medium, as it is grasped by the users of photography since its invention. Without understanding the civilian context of the medium, in addition to Barthes' definition, it is impossible to understand the institutionalization of photography as a medium of truth which attests to that to what "was there." Critical discussions seeking to challenge the truth of photography, or argue that "photography lies," remain anecdotal and marginal to the institutionalized practices of exhibiting and publishing photographs. Only a glance at a newspaper kiosk is needed to realize the enduring power of the news photo. Photography's critics tend to forget that despite the fact that photography speaks falsely, it *also* speaks the truth. A photograph does in fact attest to what "was there," although its evidence is partial, and only in this sense is it false. What was there is *never* only what is visible in the photograph, but is also contained in the very photographic situation, in which photographer and photographed interact around a camera. That is, a photograph is evidence of the social relations which made it possible, and these cannot be removed from the visible "sense" that it discloses to spectators who can agree or disagree on its actual content. The social relation that "was there," to which a photograph attests, is an expression of a mutual guarantee, or its infringement. Either way, the realization of the contract is not something only subsisting in the photographic act, between photographer and photographed, but draws most of its strength and validity from the very fact that it is inexhaustible and does not flow merely in expected directions. Even if it appears, at a certain time and place, that an individual or group is capable of destroying the civil contract of photography, along with the citizens of the citizenry of photography, the contract itself surprisingly reclaims its place through the efforts of some of its numerous trustees. There is nothing inherent to the technology of photography that creates discriminatory or oppressive situations for different populations, and in the same way it cannot erect a barrier against movements between different positions in social reality. The most prestigious photographer, for example, might be caught in a disaster area, and turned into a passive photographed individual, whereas someone in the position of a photographed individual at the mercy of others can turn into an important photographer, having the power to provide visual evidence of events.[54] The mutual guarantee that is derived from the essential equality among the citizenry of photography—even if some are currently being recognized as full citizens of the states in which they live, and others are not—organizes social relations without the mediation of a sovereign, the place of the sovereign overtaken by the consensual social attitude towards the truth in photography.

53 These remarks appear in Robin, *Les 100 photos du siècle* (Robin, 2000).

54 The proliferation of local photographers during the first intifada is an instructive case in point.

CITIZENSHIP BEYOND SOVEREIGNTY: TOWARD AN ETHICS OF THE SPECTATOR

The industrialization and dissemination of photography near the middle of the nineteenth century created a new citizenry—the citizenry of photography—whose citizens were equipped with the necessary tools for producing photographs, interpreting them, and acting on what they disclose. Although given to the modern citizen as another means of becoming a citizen in the nation-state, photography provided the possibility of becoming a citizen in this new citizenry of photography. Whereas the nation-state is based on the principles of sovereignty and territorialization, the citizenry of photography, of which the civil contract of photography is the constitutional foundation, is based on an ethical duty, and on patterns of deterritorialization. In principle, photography is an instrument given to everyone, making it possible to deterritorialize physical borders and redefine limits, communities, and places (processes of reterritorialization).[55] The citizenry of photography is a simulation of a collective to which all citizens belong. Neither taking precedence over citizenship or making it conditional, the citizenry of photography is fundamentally and solely defined by citizenship: Membership in the citizenry means citizenship, and citizenship means membership in the citizenry. The citizenry of photography has no sovereign and therefore no apparatus of exclusion. Each and every one is, in principle, a member of the collective. Membership in the collective is based on each one's renunciation of exclusive ownership of his or her image and on each one's willingness and right to be photographed and become a photograph.

The fact that the civil contract has only now been explicitly formulated does not contradict the fact that it exists and has existed as long as photography itself. That I am presently able to formulate its conditions rests on the abundant evidence we have of their existence. As early as the 1840s, the photographers David Octavius Hill and Richard Adamson, in tandem with their photographed subjects, saw photography as an instrument that establishes, on the ad hoc basis of each photograph, a universal tribunal that goes beyond local interests to see clearly what photography has to show. These two men went to take photographs of the fishermen and fisherwomen of New Haven in an attempt to assist them at a time when their fisheries were failing. The gathering of photographers and the photographed around the camera was not contingent upon a pragmatic answer to the question of whether photography could help them. Instead, it was motivated by the scopic regime that photography established—a photograph produced in the course of an encounter between photographer and photographed is created and inspired by a relation to an external eye, the eye of the spectator. It is not the same eye that is present in the situation, but one for the sake of which the photographed is willing to be photographed and the photographer is willing to take photographs: "She looked as if she knew my photographs might help her, so she helped me. There was a kind of equality between us," wrote Dorothea Lang in her diary about Florence Thompson.[56]

This spectator's eye deterritorializes photography, transforming it from a simple, convenient, efficient, (relatively) inexpensive and easily operable tool for the production of pictures into a social, cultural, and political instrument of immense power. The gap between these two dimensions of photography is newly expressed in each photographic act, summoning a supplementary eye, or at least alluding to the existence of an empty place, a potential place that enables the act of photography to occur while the participants acknowledge that they are not alone in front of the other. Photography thus enables its users to produce images that go beyond the simple technical actions required to produce them, attaining something that transcends the here and now. The reason they enjoy such a status is due to the fact that as soon as they have appeared in the world, it is impossible to dismiss them. Their presence cannot be subsumed under the reign of a higher authority. They are independent. The limits of their interpretation are not determined in advance and are always open to negotiation. They are not restricted to the intentions of those who would claim to be their authors or of those who participate in their production.

This particular characteristic of photographs tends to mislead the spectators who view them. A newspaper editor, for example, will add laconic captions to photographs, as if a denotative relation had been established between them. Such denotative relations assume that what is visible in the photograph exists there—somewhere—awaiting the precise verbal formulation that would make it a proper object. However, contrary to what Susan Sontag has claimed in her own work on photography, the transcendent status of photographs does not require what is visible in them to be given or assumed intrinsically to have a "grammar" of its own.[57] Although they write on the social context of photography, both Sontag and Roland Barthes preserve the notion of a stable meaning

55 On deterritorialization and reterritorialization see Gilles Deleuze, and Félix Guattari, *Mille plateaux* (Paris: Minuit, 1980), a in English as *A Thousand Plateaus: Capitalism and Schizophrenia*, trans. Brian Massumi (Minneapolis: University of Minnesota Press, 1987).

56 See Dorothea Lange, "The Assignment I'll Never Forget," in Liz Heron and Val Williams (eds.), *Illuminations: Women's Writings on Photography from the 1850s to the Present* (London: I. B.Tauris, 1996).

57 Susan Sontag, *On Photography* (New York: Picador, 1977), 3.

for what is visible in the photograph and reduce the role of the spectator to the act of judgment, eliminating his or her responsibility for what is seen in the photograph. That judgment assumes a passive attitude toward the image and is primarily interested in questioning the extent to which the photograph succeeds in arousing a desired effect or experience. Sontag focuses on the photographer and sees him or her as responsible both for the photograph and for the fact that the photographed is represented one way and not another or conveys one experience rather than another. "Moralists who love photographs" writes Sontag not without a small measure of contempt, "always hope that words will save the picture."[58] According to Sontag, the picture's fate as good or bad is sealed as soon as it is printed on photographic paper. Any attempt to start speaking for the photo is akin to an effort to revive the dead. Her "ethics of seeing" is based on an aesthetic judgment and gives no attention to the civil contract of photography. It turns photographs into works of art that can be judged. Her ethics of seeing, in effect, reifies the new visual field created with the appearance of photography, leaving the photograph in possession of a special "grammar" that allows it to remain independent of its spectator.

The civil contract of photography shifts the focus away from the ethics of seeing or viewing to an ethics of the spectator, an ethics that begins to sketch the contours of the spectator's responsibility toward what is visible. The individual is not confined to being posited as the photograph's passive addressee, but has the possibility of *positing herself* as the photograph's addressee and by means of this address is capable of becoming a citizen in the citizenry of photography by making herself appear in public, coming before the public, and entering a dialogue with it by means of photographs, which, despite their power are often are both silent and silenced. Once photographs are spoken of, however, they are spoken of among many, in regard to many, and obtain the power to remind citizens that what brings them together, what motivates them to look at photographs, is the common interest, the *res publica*. In an era when speaking in terms of the *res publica* is becoming more and more rare, photography is one remaining site, a place of refuge, from which the discourse on the *res publica* may be revived. Neither a local, sectarian, or national politics nor a politics of identity, photography remains part of the *res publica* of the citizenry and is or can become one of the last lines of defense in the battle over citizenship for those who still see citizenship as something worth revived.[59]

This struggle links those who have citizenship and those who are threatened by the denial of citizenship or expropriation of the rights of others with those who have been robbed or denied citizenship, for whom photography and the citizenry of photography are often their first chance to become citizens despite being stateless.[60] In the Israeli context, for instance, the Palestinians became citizens of the citizenry of photography long before there was any possibility of their becoming citizens in the full meaning of the word. The Palestinians are at one and the same time citizens of photography's global citizenry and noncitizens of the state that governs them. Photography enables them—along with many others— to present the ways in which they have been dominated, making visible the more and less hidden modes in which they are exposed to Israeli power. Without the spectator participating in the reconstruction of the photographic *énoncé*, the harm to citizenship will not be perceived. Photography does not put an end to their position as noncitizen, but it does enable them and others who take part in the reconstruction of their civil grievances to exercise the legitimate violence of photography's citizens, regardless of their status as noncitizens deprived of rights who cannot use their citizenship to negotiate with the sovereign power.

Photography thus has formed a citizenry, a citizenry without sovereignty, without place or borders, without language or unity, having a heterogeneous history, a common praxis, inclusive citizenship, and a unified interest. The citizenry of photography is a global form of relation that is not subject to national regimes, despite existing within their borders, and that is not entirely obedient to global logic, even as it enjoys the channels of exchange and association the latter creates. Photography is a means of employing legitimate violence that is—or, in principle, that can be—in the hands of all of the members of the citizenry of photography, whether or not they are citizens of the space they inhabit. In the citizenry of photography, citizenship is rehabilitated and regains its essence. Not all of its citizens necessarily give active expression to their citizenship, and only a few have ever given their explicit consent to take part. However, even those who explicitly attempt to position themselves outside its bounds, or those who have never encountered a camera, are indeed a part of it. In the ethics that photography requires of those who view photographs, it requests that its citizens—who are equally *not* governed in the citizenry of photography—not only try to avoid situations of degeneration into which the nation-state and the market often sink, but actively to resist them. For the citizen of photography, national citizenship is not the ulimate realization of citizenship

58 Susan Sontag, *On Photography*, 107

59 See Arendt, *The Human Condition*.

60 For more on the flawed citizenship of citizens living beside noncitizens, see Azoulay and Ophir 2002, *Bad Days*.

and does not see property and ownership as the principle achievements of human existence. Instead, photography, while personal, is a mobile and global recording kit for contesting injuries to citizenship. Official UN data estimates the existence of 175 million noncitizens worldwide. This figure does not take into account the millions who, despite being officially granted citizen rights, are far from able to assume their citizen status. Photography can be put forward and read as a nonmediatated complaint attesting to situations in which citizenship has been violated. Simply flip through any history book from the last hundred years, any NGO pamphlet, any publication written by a human-rights or civil-rights group, or any humanitarian organization report, and you will see that photography marks the beginning of a demand to become citizens, even when that demand is hidden behind a demand for the protection of human rights. These collections of photograph-complaints would be worthless, however, if it were not for the citizenry of photography and its citizens who produce these photographs-complaints, as photographers or as spectators. When a photograph turns into a grievance, whoever articulates it becomes its civic subject.

Often, photography has been used, in one way or another, by the sovereign power. Photographers were rapidly integrated into routine tasks, ongoing documentation, the collection, classification and storage of data, the use of data to enforce the law, and other governmental duties. Disciplinary and closed sites, in Foucault's terms, proved to be ideal places for the installation and regular employment of cameras.[61] Supervision and control, refinement and improvement, study and research—these have been the motivating goals behind camera operators and those who command them, even when they are themselves the ones exposed to the cameras.[62] Yet the formulation of these objectives, even in the form of written declarations, has not prevented the creation of a gap between the stated aims and what has actually taken place in the encounter between photographer, photographed and camera. Every photograph is a living testimony to this gap, even if some photographs may still lack an ethical spectator to notice them. In many instances, this gap is the place from which the spectator can become a citizen of photography, making it possible for the photographer or photographed to become a citizen, as well.

Photography plays a crucial role in the civilian status of its users, from their subordination to sovereign power to practices of civilianization that limit the control of this sovereign power.[63] Nonetheless, photography is rarely the object of legislation, nor does the state regulate its usage. The state's renunciation of any crucial governmental role regarding photography effectively abandoned photography to the logic of the market, and the governmental vacuum was filled with the technical jargon of capabilities and possibilities, and the language of neutrality and precision. Thus, the course of photography, which has been marked by different kinds of inventions, was confined to the framework of the market and determined according to public demand. Yet as in other fields, so, too, in photography, the course of development was dictated both by the resources of the state, which indirectly channeled photographic inventions into the fields of warfare, espionage, and supervision, as well as by the money of the masses, whose purchasing power led to the development of mobile, user-friendly cameras. Thus, for instance, the development of night-vision and aerial photography contributed to the process of restricting accessibility to photography almost to the point of monopolizing it (as in the case, for instance, of satellite photography), whereas the development of prepackaged film or the mobile automatic camera contributed to its democratization. Even though photography was a French invention, it was anchored in a contract that was not limited to a particular nation.[64] Against the political order of the nation-state, photography—together with other media that created the conditions for globalization—paved the way for a universal citizenship: not a state, but a citizenry, a virtual citizenry, in potential, with the civil contract of photography as its organizing framework. Citizenship in the citizenry of photography asks not to be stopped at borders and plays a vital political role in making sure other cultures are accessible, in all of their prestige or misery, deeming local cultures to be worthy of documentation and public display. Photography, being in principle accessible to all, bestows universal citizenship on a new citizenry whose citizens produce, distribute, and look at images.

This citizenship, in principle, issues actual and virtual transit visas to all, allowing everyone to see, show, and be seen—though it is subject, of course, to supply and demand. The citizen of the citizenry of photography may move as she pleases in the visual field created

61 See Michel Foucault, *Naissance de la clinique: Une archéologie du regard médical* (Paris: Presses Univesitaires de France, 1963), available in English as *The Birth of the Clinic: An Archaeology of Medical Perception* (New York: Random House, 1975).

62 See, for example, Georges Didi-Huberman's book on the photography department in Charcot's clinic, *Invention de l'hystérie: Charcot et l'iconographie photographique de la Salpêtrière* (Paris: Macula, 1995) and Denis Bernard and André Gunthert's book on Albert Lande, who was one of the photographers who worked there, *L'instant revé: Albert Londe*, Jacqueline Chambon, 1993).

63 Because citizenship is never fully achieved, practices of civilianization are needed in order to become a citizen, thus preserving the gap between the citizen and power.

64 On the contribution of the Englishman Henry Fox Talbot, see Frizot (ed.), *A New History of Photography*.

by photography. It is part of the contract to which she's a signatory, a contract that, like any constitutive agreement, supposes a primal beginning and moment of creation, a moment of transition from a state of presence to a state of re-presence, re-presentation, a visual representation. This agreement—although it seems to produce a moment of unity, an unrealistic instant in which all citizens could be represented as if they were full partners in formulating the contract—collapses in the face of the structure of the camera, since its limitations are exposed. If this contract has any representation beyond the imaginary realm that this book seeks to give it, such a depiction exists in the entire body of photographs from which it was extracted. From an instrument once recognized by the French state as having the power to fuel a revolution on the scale of the French Revolution, photography was reduced to merely its technical components. To this day, it has almost always been employed without any prior and systematic study of its legal, cultural, political, and moral ramifications or of the effects stemming from its omnipresence.[65] Photography has been naturalized as a disciplinary medium to such a degree that its very use appears to have been universally agreed upon, avoiding not only any discussion of its procedures or mechanisms, but of the mode in which these have been adopted, as though they were common to all people who employ photography.[66]

Given this governmental vacuum, the civil contract of photography has a crucial role. It can serve as a regulative power, accounting for the different uses of photography, its modes of production and distribution, the exchange relations that are involved, its mechanisms of interpretation and authorization, its patterns of acceptance, as well as its public or juridical standing.

The exercise of that regulative power is the duty first and foremost of the spectator, and it is to the ethics of the spectator that I now turn.

65 The specific prohibitions that various states apply to the publication of photos, usually on an ad hoc basis in order to serve political interests, doesn't take the place of this missing discussion.

66 The contention that every technology poses the same challenge from the user's point of view is false. Thus, for example, the vacuum cleaner invites the purchaser to use it in a certain way, and in most case the user will indeed do it correctly. However, the use of the vacuum cleaner doesn't take place in the framework of social, political, and civil practices that bind individuals together, shape their citizenship and horizon of action, represent their actions, and structure their identities.

Still from *Episode III: Enjoy Poverty*
Renzo Martens
2008

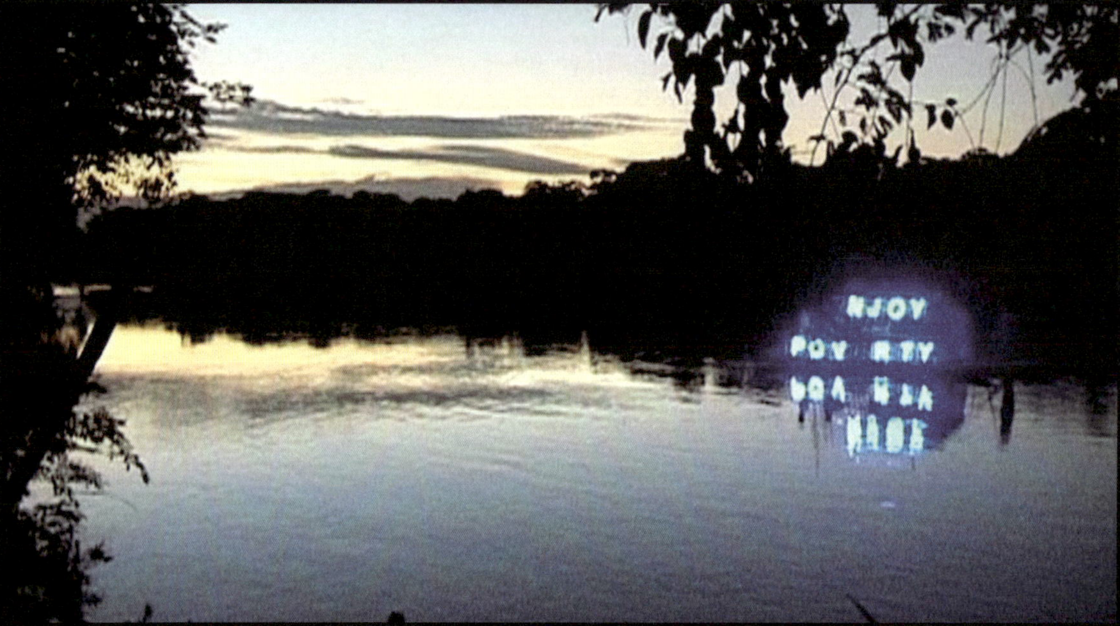

Toward a New Institutional Critique: A Conversation with Renzo Martens
T. J. Demos
2012

T. J. Demos: *Episode III: Enjoy Poverty* has been quite controversial in that it has inspired anger in some viewers. Why do you think it has done so? In my experience of discussing the film with different people, I've found that there are those who doubt the critical value of the project, or see it as cynical or an act of bad faith, as if it had been made for reasons of opportunism, spectacle, or shock notoriety. How do you respond to such criticism and resistance?

Renzo Martens: I think the film breaks one clear rule: that audiences should be exempt from the pain that half the world's population experiences on a daily basis. We can watch it, but we should not be made part of it. Or if it should happen that a work reveals our part in it anyway, through some economic or political systems that we support or benefit from, then we are exempt from the pain, because it is assumed that, since we are willing to watch the piece, we are contributors to the critical mass that will, one day, undo the harm. This rule therefore paints an inaccurate picture of reality, and of the audience's relationship to it. We either don't see the pain, or we're made to think that we're part of its solution. *Episode 3* is so tailored that watching it makes you complicit with its production. Obviously that's not fun, and some viewers think I'm out there to try to trick them. *Episode 3* deals with pain, but then doesn't offer the audience a way out. Watching it does not, in one way or another, resolve it. And that's quite a shock to many people.

TJD: How does the film make viewers "complicit with its production"? In my view, the film makes an important connection between, on the one hand, horrific images of suffering and poverty, and on the other, the international financial mechanisms (like the World Bank) and humanitarian organizations (like Doctors without Borders) which reproduce that poverty. The relation cannot help but implicate Western viewers who benefit from this international arrangement. Is that what you mean?

RM: What the film shows is how making this film is in itself a process analogous to making chocolate, coffee, coltan, or gold. The power equation between those who consume and those who supply the raw material in those industries is the same, regardless of what specific product is produced. We see how Congolese photographers are driven to produce the very images of poverty that we see every day in newspapers or on TV. We see at what cost these images are made. And we see many Congolese who are willing to pay this cost. They desperately want to be part of our gaze, of our production processes. They want part of the pie, their pie, really, that is being squandered by others in front of their very eyes. *Episode 3* thus reveals at what cost this film is made, and watching it offers no redemption.

TJD: But can't the viewer still see those institutions as beyond their control, and consequently wash their hands of the entire business? If you are not out to try to trick the viewer, then what are you trying to do?

RM: The film is unpleasant, and some people feel tricked, just by its sheer objectivity. So the pain, as I called it earlier, is not something outside of the act of watching, something external to our gaze. The film copies, in itself, existing modes of production, and unfolds them for all of us to see and feel. That's how the film reveals reality, through making its inner policies tangible.

TJD: Of course, to produce a sense of "empathy" with its represented victims is still an important goal for documentary practice. For instance, in her recent *New York Times* bestselling book, *The Cruel Radiance: Photography and Political Violence*, the liberal journalist professor and author Susie Linfield writes that without "empathy... the politics of human rights devolve into abstraction, romantic foolishness, and cruelty,"[1] and she finds the ability to foster empathy to be among photography's greatest powers. Obviously *Episode 3* departs from this conventional documentary

1 Susie Linfield, *The Cruel Radiance: Photography and Political Violence* (Chicago: University of Chicago Press, 2010), xv. On page 129, she cites Hannah Arendt, who called compassion a "co-suffering" which produces a "community of interest with the oppressed and exploited." See Hannah Arendt, *On Revolution* (New York: Penguin, 1990), 85. For a critique of empathy in relation to *Episode 3: Enjoy Poverty* see T. J. Demos, "Poverty Pornography, Humanitarianism, and Neoliberal Globalization: Notes on Some Paradoxes in Contemporary Art," *Stedelijk Bureau Newsletter* 121 (April 2011).

strategy, in part by focusing on the complicity of photographers in the image economy of exploitation and spectacle. How does the film "make you complicit with production" in a way that's different from conventional documentary approaches and their production of empathy?

RM: Maybe the foremost tool is that I stage myself as a complex character, as an average white man, and, while walking around in the Congo, really as an ambassador of a regime. When you see me visit local farmers, I do what the regime does; I offer some small-time help, which really only serves my own purposes. I don't ask for so much, I seem to know exactly what they need. It's devastating; you then see these Congolese photographers, for example, invest in what could be a way out. And the film shows that it all fails.

What I tried to make is a document that doesn't *explain* what exploitation means, but makes one *feel* what it is. And then, within this setup, certain people turn against the exploiter. Rightly so. It's important to stress that everything I say or do represents the careful reproduction of ruling policies. How do you think that it's possible that millions have no primary healthcare, no schooling, and yet keep investing in earning our sympathy? That certainly isn't the result of receiving a lot of empathy from our side, is it? To employ empathy as a tool to gain access and make images of the devastation that comes out of a *lack* of empathy may inspire some kind of proximity, but at the same time it covers up so much. In such empathetic images the problem is automatically somewhere else, certainly not in the friendly witness nor, by extension, in the witness's audiences who can look along with him. Empathy produces a total travesty if it doesn't unravel the nature of the outsider's presence. What the world calls for is something else, a deeper empathy I'd say.

TJD: Perhaps the most difficult aspect of the film is the representation of the black body, particularly of the Congolese body that is most vulnerable — the child's. At one point the film shows the death of a sick girl in an ill-equipped medical clinic, and in another scene a Congolese man reveals to the camera the suffering sick body and sore anus of his young sleepless daughter. How can such depictions be justified? Is this a case where even the last remaining dignity of an impoverished and dying human being is taken away by a debasing artistic portrayal? How do you validate or explain on ethical, political, or humanitarian grounds the exposure of a horror whose reality is a catastrophic failure? Is this *exposure* of bare life —a life stripped of political rights and humanitarian protections— also an unacceptable *reproduction* of bare life, no matter what your intentions?

RM: The conditions of these children are actually justified all the time. It's called the market, or African corruption, or pre-modern belief systems. Whatever the reason, we thrive on it. I think it's unfair for audiences to want to have it both ways: cheap labor on the one hand, and on the other to be exempt from any confrontation with the results—malnourished and dying children, their parents feeling entirely helpless—on the grounds that the representation of such lives would be immoral. Morality then serves profitability.

I doubt, by the way, that the same critics ever write letters to their newspaper photo editors when they show pictures of "Hunger in the Horn of Africa," or whatever other crises are presented. These images are extremely well-known, to the degree that they've become clichés. Now, how can I problematize the fact that children are maltreated, that their starvation is used in discourses that benefit many, but that don't benefit *these* children? How do I do that if the facts that, yes, they die, and yes, they are black, yes, they are malnourished, yes, their parents are so desperate, and no, no one is showing up to offer help, are all off limits? In order to make viewing less painful, should we forget these facts first? The question really is what we want art to do. Is it to offer little exceptions to the status quo? Can it suffice to show our morals, to undo wrongs or depict them in morally right ways? In my mind, depicting immorality, racism, exploitation, as if they were phenomena outside of our lives, as if they existed only on the other side of our lenses, relieves us, but it also relieves such a depiction of any claim on reality. I think that if art limits itself to the morally acceptable, it conveniently obscures the production processes that pay for our lifestyles.

TJD: I suppose a film like Vik Muniz's *Wasteland*, 2010, is a good example of how art might be made to service the disenfranchised, and thereby offer a "little exception to the status quo"? For the film, the Brazilian artist recreated famous artistic masterpieces out of the trash from a dump near Rio de Janeiro with the help of freelance landfill workers, who then benefited economically from the sales of Muniz's photographs in the London art market. The result is that we as viewers believe that art *can* make a difference. In this case, are the workers not better off? Is Muniz's project valid if he can help even a small number of people?

RM: Although I've not seen it, it's great these people are able to make a living, all of a sudden, thanks to the art world. That's something to applaud Muniz for. But art really isn't about making a living, is it? It's about the truthful rendition of the real. And there, indeed, it offers a highly visible exception to the status quo, to be consumed not by landfill workers in Brazil, but by people in London who, themselves, already live the happy exception. In the end, we make these pieces so that beauty can fill our minds, whereas economic segregation, as we all know, is what keeps on paying the bills.

TJD: So when such immorality, racism, and exploitation are shown by an artwork to exist *inside* our lives, then there's a risk of questioning or doubting art's claim to represent hope, and the exposure of art's illusions can be threatening to people. However, I would count myself among those who nevertheless still believe in the potential of artistic practice to generate a creative imagination and critical self- reflexivity which can contribute to the formation of a better world. Do you disagree with that ambition in general?

RM: Oh no, not at all, I'm all for critical self-reflexivity! And yes, I believe that it will make for a better world. If I tried to do one thing, it was to make a piece that would openly, and in all earnestness, disclose the terms and conditions of its own production. So I'm really standing in a long tradition of artists who have come to terms with the materiality, and even the institutions, through which the artwork is created. I have good hopes that this project will generate knowledge that may reach far beyond the arts.

I remember Okwui Enwezor, to whom I owe a lot (my work would surely not have been possible without his Documenta 11), declaring in a public talk in Amsterdam that he was "thrilled by *Episode 3*'s audacity, but was even more affected by its illiteracy." In his mind, *Episode 3* misrepresented the agency that Africans have. He was part of a committee that awarded a well-deserved prize, sponsored by the Dutch government and named after a Dutch royal, to a Congolese photographer, Sammy Baloji, for his powerful, socially critical work. Here we were, in a big glass building, celebrating diversity and African agency, all the while overlooking Europe's biggest cocoa port, relentlessly importing cocoa eked out from the poorest people in the world. Yet, according to Mr. Enwezor, *Episode 3* was misrepresenting our relationship to Africa? Can we suffice with theological discourses, poetry, and critical interventions, and still believe that we are not implicated in what happens everywhere, all the time? Is bare life something for poor black children alone to deal with, or can we be bothered to be naked in front of it, too?

TJD: In this sense, are you proposing a new form of institutional critique, one that is geopolitical and transnational, and mixed with a performative dimension that demonstrates a general social and economic complicity?

RM: That would be a good way of putting it. I really admire Hans Haacke, and Jean-Luc Godard, and the installations that Dan Graham made in the 1970s. They're all about revealing the position of the viewer, and the author, and art, in relation to the space they inhabit. Even if I see myself in that tradition, I'm not so much interested in my relation to a white-cube gallery space. I think that by now the world and its interrelations is our canvas.

TJD: Speaking of artistic precedents, how do you see your work differing from or resonating with precedents such as the work and writings of Martha Rosler, Allan Sekula, and Susan Sontag, which have criticized documentary practice and its liberal-empathic model?

RM: Well, in her last book, *Regarding the Pain of Others*, Sontag almost literally pinpointed what I have taken as the task for myself to overcome:

> "So far as we feel sympathy," Sontag writes, "we feel we are not accomplices to what caused the suffering. Our sympathy proclaims our innocence as well as our impotence. To that extent, it can be (for all our good intentions) an impertinent—if not an inappropriate—response. To set aside the sympathy we extend to others beset by war and murderous politics for a consideration of how our privileges are located on the same map as their suffering, and may—in ways that we prefer not to imagine—be linked to their suffering, as the wealth of some may imply the destitution of others, is a task for which the painful, stirring images supply only the initial spark."[2]

So maybe, in my films, I'm like one of Rosler's figures who appear in her photo-montage series, *Bringing the War Home*, the ones to whom the war has been brought home. I play out what it is to be the spectator. In Rosler's collages, you see the equation in a picture; in my films, we're made part of it, I play out its reception. I think I did something like what she did then, or what Sontag writes about—that is, I showed what it takes to form one single unified world.

TJD: In the interview you did with Artur Zmijewski for the upcoming Berlin Biennial, you pointed out that *Episode 3* demonstrates a certain "inconsequentiality"—in terms of the ambitions of critical art, compassionate documentary photojournalism, and concerned humanitarianism. What is that inconsequentiality? And if we as viewers come to the same conclusion, that the film doesn't make them part of any solution, as you stated earlier, then where does it leave us? What is the utility of this performance of inconsequentiality?

RM: The film indeed embraces its inconsequentiality. It's quite novel, I think, and not facile or cynical in the

2 Susan Sontag, *Regarding the Pain of Others* (New York: Picador, 2003), 102.

least. The piece is a precise seismograph; it quite accurately takes responsibility for the modes of production the medium is entrenched in. I think of *When Faith Moves Mountains*, by Francis Alÿs, now, as it's a piece that wears its inconsequentiality on its sleeve too, and that's very convincing in a way. But then, I tried something else. I think his piece does not really confront viewers with the *cost* of that inconsequentiality. Certainly art lovers don't suffer under it, they adore it for its qualities as a *vanitas*. But if *they* aren't the ones who pay the price, could it be that those who *do* pay it are the millions of Peruvians or Filipinos or Ivoirians who want things to progress in reality, not just in an art piece where it beautifully fails? I hope my piece shows this *cost* of art's inconsequentiality, and, in the same line, the *cost* of beauty. I think it generates some knowledge about all these other production processes, cocoa or petrol for example, about our relations to power and beauty, about what role we assign to art, about how seriously we want art to inform us, and about what it is that we expect from art.

No one ever has asked me for any precise information about these plantations, for instance, about where they are or in what candy bars the labor of these starvelings ends up. What generated anger wasn't the fact that people starve and are drained of their resources. Projecting *Enjoy Poverty* in the night over one such cocoa field in the Congo was a pretty accurate prediction of the results that the film's audiences would reserve for these workers: zero. The piece preemptively embraced its reception. That's what angers people: the fact that they see what it is to be part of zero reaction, and that watching this film, which is indeed quite an ordeal, makes them part of that zero, not of a better world. But really, what I show is the price that we pay, and that we ask others to pay, for privilege, for art.

TJD: For an artwork to "preemptively embrace its reception" presents certain risks, as viewers don't normally want to be told in advance what exact outcomes a piece may or may not have. A lot of us are in this for ethical and political reasons, even if our hopes for art's effectiveness are modest. But, as with the recent uprisings in North Africa, and the Occupy movement that has spread across the world, we do have historical examples where visual culture can make a difference politically and socially, and where art is not without effect. Is it not fatalistic to insist on the ineffectual result of a work, rather than seeing it as a site of open potentiality?

RM: Of course, if I didn't believe in art's effect, I definitely would not make a film like this. I think it's quite useful to construct a test case in which the effects of a piece on reality are measured. And it's quite useful to find out what happens if the piece, for the sake of the argument, preemptively embraces the fact that it will change nothing. Quite a number of people saw what they had not seen before—neither in Africa, nor in art, nor in themselves.

TJD: Which plantation did you work with? And which candy bars result from the labors you depict?

RM: Ha ha ha! Good question! By now I've lived so long with no one ever asking, that I've based the necessary next steps on it. You can generate a little exception by asking, but I like to deal with the fact that, up till now, no one has asked. Suffice it to say that it's a wonderful chocolate of a very high quality.

TJD: Is there a factor of "political enabling" in showing the inconsequentiality of conventional documentary practice? If so, do we need to be taught this lesson? Aren't the problems and limits of documentary evident enough for us already?

RM: Indeed! There is that factor. It generates knowledge about what our role in this world is. I definitely strive to push beyond this, let's say, structural analysis of art's role, and to design more self-conscious ways (more self-conscious than depiction or intervention—with a camera ready to highlight the intervention) for art to deal with the real. For true criticality, and true transgression, and for love, too, one needs some insight into how one functions, before making a claim on any outside phenomena. That's what I try to do.

TJD: "Love" isn't an emotion or quality I would immediately associate with *Enjoy Poverty*, and it's not a term that's commonly embraced within art discourse. One writer and theorist who does employ the term is Kaja Silverman, who, in her 2010 *Artforum* interview with George Baker suggests that one "gift of love" is to allow others to "appear" in a way that is "affirmative." Yet one could say just the opposite occurs in *Enjoy Poverty*. Do you agree with such a definition, and how do you see love more specifically as operating in your work?

RM: I can only hope to recognize love if I feel it, certainly not to define it... but I don't do the opposite of Silverman's definition. I think many of the Congolese in *Episode 3* are portrayed as if they are trying—and trying hard—to go along with me for a while. Yet it's equally visible that they have their own thoughts about my proposals and just wait me out. I think that's quite an honest rendering of their attitude towards me, or towards any outsider coming in with some quaint new plan. In fact, if I compare these reactions to the eager beneficiaries depicted in any NGO propaganda, or to thoughtful participants in collaborative art pieces, I actually think that a lot of the critique one may formulate against this film is organized within the film itself. That's why critics actually get to see how the local photographers become disappointed, or how the poor father shows his child to the camera in total desperation. I think all this paints a pretty accurate portrait of the power relations that prevail in this world. I honestly think that it's good that these aspects come out in the open, against my own interest, in a way, because they define so many lives, and yes, I think that this is an act of love, love overcoming vanity, in fact.

TJD: I recently saw the remarkable film *The Vampires of Poverty* by Luis Ospina and Carlos Mayolo, which they shot in 1978, in Cali and Bogotá, Colombia. It's a mock documentary that satirizes artistic practice, in which an unseen camera records the two artists making a film about poverty. They are seen going about their quest to find street kids, prostitutes, insane and homeless people, and at one point they stage a contrived scene of a destitute family—portrayed by actors— in front of a broken-down shanty. The film is internally critical about the filmmakers' own status as "vampires" of poverty, acknowledging that the documentary will be screened only in more developed countries, and as if to preempt criticism they include interventions by bystanders who take the filmmakers to task for exploiting their misery.

RM: If the makers of *The Vampires of Poverty* ironize their presence and agenda constantly, I maybe tried to dig deeper, to the limits of irony, to the point where irony isn't so funny anymore, when it all turns out to be bitterly real. Take Henri Storck and Joris Ivens's 1933 film *Misery in the Borinage*, for example. When it was made, it was a real propagator for action and change. I'm as earnest as they were... It's just that today it doesn't suffice to show suffering the way Storck and Ivens did, because all of these images are very much part of the status quo, and they have become yet one more commodity.

TJD: What can we look forward to in your next project?

RM: More and more I'm starting to wonder, where does this, let's call it "critical interventionist art," have the biggest impact? In its loci of depicted interventions, or in its places of display and reception? I mean, certainly the diggers in Alÿs's piece had more impact at WIELS in Brussels and in art galleries in Chelsea, in terms of economic turnover, than in Peru. And certainly this is true for *Episode 3*, too. So if art has this power to accumulate capital and opportunity in its places of reception, rather than in its places of intervention, then surely it is of paramount importance to figure out how its power to gentrify can be turned into a critical and progressive tool in the very site of poverty. That's what I'm working on now.

TJD: And will that return you to the Congo?

RM: Well, yes. I know some places where the accumulation of capital and critical awareness about art's mandate in this world are potentially very productive...

Still from *Exit (Bath Iron Works, July 7–11, 2008, Bath, Maine)*

Sharon Lockhart

2008

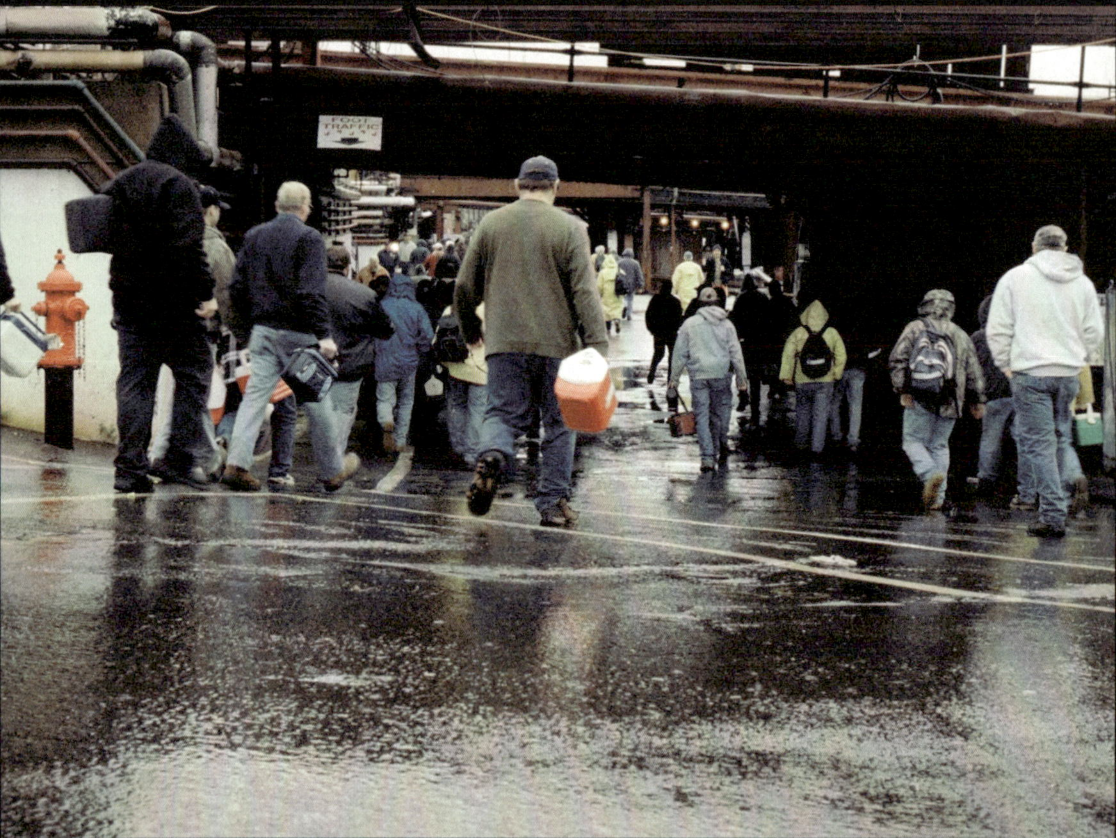

On Compression

Cory Arcangel

2008

ABSTRACT: JPEGs look the way they do because of quantization and their use of the Discrete Cosine Transform (DCT). The DCT is a technique for converting a signal into elementary frequency components. It is widely used in image compression. Here we will go through some examples to explain how the DCT works. The text is kind of a summary, and if you want to bring the noise, all the math is in the end notes.

1. LOSSY VS. LOSSLESS

The whole point of digital image compression is to be able to reconstruct an image without having to send all the data. This is because data, especially in large amounts, is expensive and slow to transport. Either over cable lines, phone lines, or wirelessly, it is all slow. To this day, the most efficient and cheapest way to transport large amounts of data is by mailing a hard-drive to the destination, and I don't mean emailing, I mean the kind of mailing that involves the post office. So compression is valuable because the less we need to send the cheaper and faster it is. There are two kinds of compression. One is called Lossy, and the other is called Lossless. Lossless compression does not lose any information from the original source. How can this be? Well, let's say we wanted to send this: 'a a a a a a a a a b a' and we were going to send it over the phone by voice. As opposed to having to send all the information by reading out each letter one at a time, we could just tell someone '9a's, one b, and one a' and they would know we meant 'a a a a a a a a a b a' and we have saved ourselves a bit of breath. In computer language it means we have stored all the information using less space. To generalize a bit, if you have ever opened a 'zip' file, your computer has seen '9a's, one b, and one a' and translated it to 'a a a a a a a a a b a'. This is Lossless compression. On the other hand, Lossy compression actually loses data. Lossy compression, therefore, can not be used for text, or any application where all the information must remain intact. It is used for images, music, and video. This is because, believe it or not, our eyes and ears are pretty crap, and we don't usually notice missing bits here and there. Lossy compression works by getting rid of the information which isn't so important to us. To generalize a bit again, if we tried to send 'a a a a a a a a a b a' using Lossy compression over the phone, we would just get lazy and say '11a's'. In this article, we are going to focus on the Discrete Cosine Transform, aka the DCT, a math formula used in Lossy compression. The reason I'm interested in this Transform is because, when used with quantization, it is what gives JPEGs that 'JPEG look'. By 'JPEG look' I mean those crappy compressed blocky images you need to squint your eyes to understand that are all over the internet. And in case you haven't noticed, this look is everywhere else as well (ads, digital cameras, digital video, etc.). If the '80s gave us 'hot' colors and 'rad' graphics, and the '90s gave us slick vector design, then the 00's are giving us compressed blocky images.

JPEGs are everywhere today because they have become a standard, or a universally agreed upon set of rules. Today JPEG is a nickname for a file type, but zperts Group. This standard was created in Geneva in 1992 when members of the CCITT and the ISO/IEC (now together known as JPEG) got together in Geneva and released the technical document ISO/IEC IS 10918-1 / ITU-T Recommendation T.81. This paper recommended 'REQUIREMENTS AND GUIDELINES' of the 'DIGITAL COMPRESSION AND CODING OF CONTINUOUS-TONE STILL IMAGES'. These guidelines, through third party development, eventually became known as JPEG files.

2. THE GUY BEHIND THE GUY BEHIND THE GUY

As mentioned earlier, the heart of JPEG is the DCT formula, and the DCT relies on cosines. The easiest way to think of cosines is to imagine yourself walking counterclockwise around a circle. This circle is centered on the X and Y axis, and has a radius of 1. Radius is the length from the center of the circle to the edge. A cosine of the angle in respect to the positive horizontal axis (aka, the length in our case because we are on a unit circle (radius = 1)) is our position on the x axis as we walk around the circle if we started at X = 1. We must also remember that the length around a circle with a radius of 1 is 2pi. So, cos(0) is 1, because we haven't gone anywhere; we are still standing at the beginning, at X = 1, cos(pi) is -1, because we have travelled halfway around the circle to X = -1, and cos (2pi) is 1, because since we have travelled all the way around our circle, we have ended up back at the beginning (Fig. 1). It is this cyclical pattern which is useful in compression (Fig. 2). To see the DCT in action we will start with the 1D DCT (Fig. 3) formula and use it to compress the input 3,2,1 (Fig. 4). DCT-based

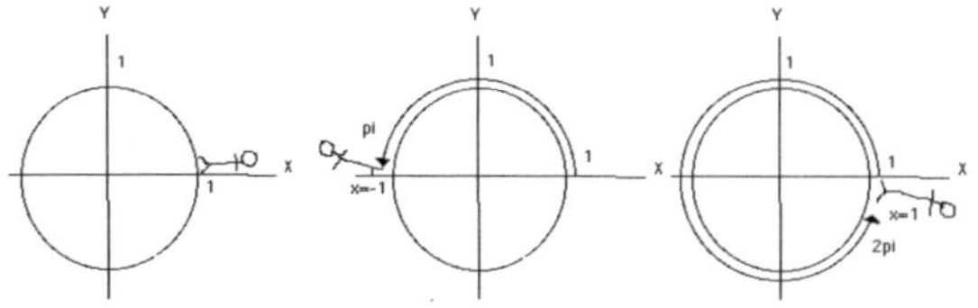

Fig. 1: Cosine of 0, pi, and 2pi

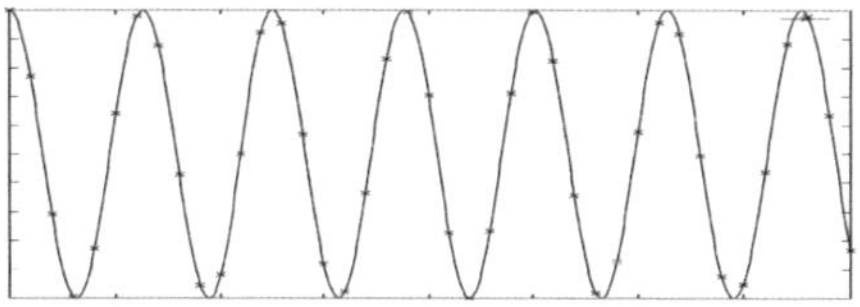

Fig. 2: Cosine curve of x = 0 to 40

compression has four steps. First the DCT formula creates basis functions, then it compares the input data

$$F(u) = \sum_{x=0}^{N-1} w(i) f[x] cos \frac{(2x+1)u\pi}{2N}$$

if i $= 0$, $w = \sqrt{1/N}$, and if i $\neq 0$, w $= \sqrt{2/N}$

Fig. 3: 1D DCT formula. w(i) is a weighting factor fyi

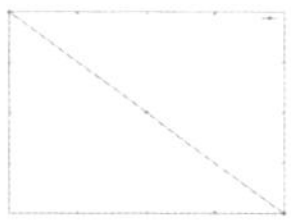

Fig. 4: Our 1D DCT example input

to those basis functions, creating what are called DCT coefficients, then those coefficients are quantized, and the last step is decompression, where all this is done in reverse to recreate our data. The first step of our process can be seen in (Fig. 5). These are the basis functions for our input, which consist of cosine curves of increasing frequency. They can be thought of as building blocks. Every combination of 3 digits can be

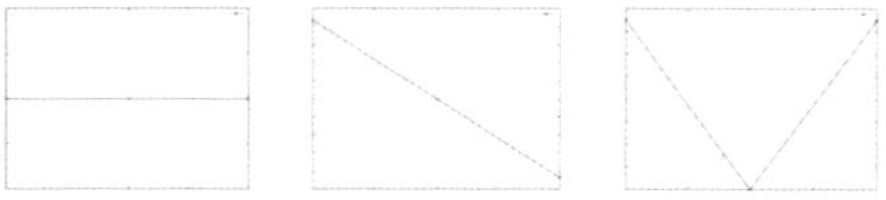

(a) Basis function 1 (b) Basis function 2 (c) Basis function 3

Fig. 5: Basis functions for a DCT of length 3

recreated by adding these blocks together in different proportions. The second step in the process is comparing our input to our three basis functions to generate three DCT coefficients. Our DCT coefficients represent how much of each basis function is present in our input. In our example, our three DCT coefficients generated by the 1D DTC are 3.46410, 1.41421, and 0. From these values we can see that our input contains elements of our first and second basis function, but none of the third. This should make sense since our input numbers are a straight line, so they do not contain any data which is similar to the curve in the third basis function. If our DCT formula in this example takes in 3 digits as input and we end up with 3 digits as output, how does this help us save space? The third step, quantization, is the key to this question. Quantization is basically a way to discard DCT coefficients. In this case we would discard our third DCT coefficient because it doesn't help us describe our input. So when we get to the last step in the process which is reversing all of this in order to reconstruct our original input, we will use only 2 DCT coefficients to do this. The same information now takes only two-thirds of the space!

3. 2D

To work on an image as opposed to a string of input, we need to use the 2D DCT formula (Fig. 6). This is basically the same as the 1D formula, except it works on a matrix. The input we'll compress in this example

$$F(u,v) = \sum_{x=0}^{N-1} \sum_{y=0}^{N-1} w(i,j) f[x,y] cos \frac{(2x+1)u\pi}{2N} cos \frac{(2y+1)u\pi}{2N}$$

if i or j $= 0$, $w = \sqrt{1/N}$, and if i or j $\neq 0$, w $= \sqrt{2/N}$

Fig. 6: 2D DCT formula

is in Figure 7. So again our first step is generating the basis functions Fig. 8. As in Figure 8, our basis functions with the lower cosine frequencies are on the top

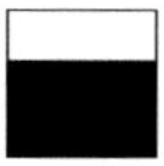

(a) Input Image

$$\begin{bmatrix} 255 & 255 & 255 \\ 0 & 0 & 0 \\ 0 & 0 & 0 \end{bmatrix}$$

(b) Input matrix

Fig. 7: Our input matrix

left and the basis functions with the higher cosine frequencies are on the bottom right. Next, we compare our input image to our basis functions to generate our DCT coefficients. Then, we're left with 9 DCT coefficients (Fig. 9). These numbers tell us our input only contains three of our nine basis functions, and one can see the graphic similarities between the basis functions on the left side of Figure 8, and our input in Figure 7. All the other basis functions do not relate. The third step is quantization. This happens by taking

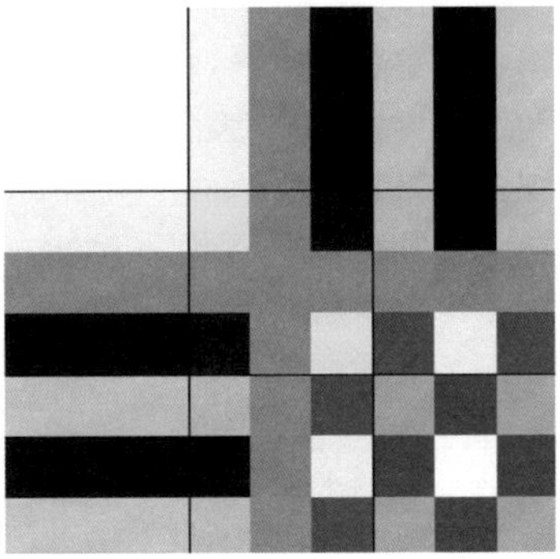

Fig. 8: The 9 DCT basis functions for a 3 by 3 matrix

the DCT coefficient matrix (Fig. 9) and dividing it by a quantization matrix, then rounding to the nearest integer. An example matrix is used in Figure 10. The

$$\begin{bmatrix} 255.00000 & 0 & 0 \\ 312.30994 & 0 & 0 \\ 180.31223 & 0 & 0 \end{bmatrix}$$

Fig. 9: Our 9 DCT coefficients

result, when reversed (Fig. 11), gets rid of one of our DCT coefficients. If we complete step four by using the quantized coefficients to reconstruct our input, we

$$\begin{bmatrix} 255.00000 & 0 & 0 \\ 312.30994 & 0 & 0 \\ 180.31223 & 0 & 0 \end{bmatrix} / \begin{bmatrix} 10 & 50 & 400 \\ 50 & 50 & 400 \\ 400 & 400 & 400 \end{bmatrix} = \begin{bmatrix} 25 & 0 & 0 \\ 6 & 0 & 0 \\ 0 & 0 & 0 \end{bmatrix}$$

Fig. 10: Quantization table

$$\begin{bmatrix} 25 & 0 & 0 \\ 6 & 0 & 0 \\ 0 & 0 & 0 \end{bmatrix} * \begin{bmatrix} 10 & 50 & 400 \\ 50 & 50 & 400 \\ 400 & 400 & 400 \end{bmatrix} = \begin{bmatrix} 250 & 0 & 0 \\ 250 & 0 & 0 \\ 0 & 0 & 0 \end{bmatrix}$$

Fig. 11: Reverse quantization

clearly have quite a big difference (Fig. 12). Where did that grey bar come from? EXACTLY!! We have saved a ton of space, because now we only need to transmit '250,

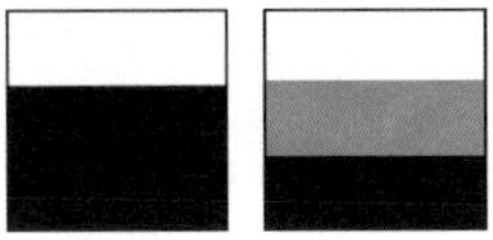

(a) Our input (b) Our input reconstructed by using the quantization table in Figure 10

Fig. 12: Reconstructing our input for our 2D 3 × 3 matrix

250, and 7 0s' to recreate our input, but our image no longer looks how it was supposed to! This is because we have discarded the high frequency basis functions, so we can no longer create sharp contrasts. But it's similar, we get the idea, and this is probably good enough.

4. THE JOINT PHOTOGRAPHIC EXPERTS

The only difference between what we just did and a JPEG, is that a JPEG always splits the image into 8 × 8 blocks and then these 8 x 8 blocks are run through the 2D DCT. 8 × 8 blocks are used because they are small enough to have consistent spatial qualities. Even at high rates of compression, we can still make out the original image. The basis functions for a JPEG are shown in Figure 13. Also, JPEGs don't specify what quantization matrix is used. Photoshop's quantization matrix is different from Canon, etc. etc., so actually one has very little control of the discarded information. Awesome. In Figure 14 and Figure 15 we can see a sample JPEG compressed with a sample quantization matrix. Take a close look—we are recreating the image only using the top left basis function of Figure 13. Hopefully you can see now that heavily compressed JPEGs are really a bunch of 8 by 8 squares composed of only the first few low frequency basis functions of an 8 × 8 2D DCT (Fig. 13) We get a 90 percent reduction in file size because we only need to send a few DCT coefficients down the line, but we get an image which is only a shadow of its former self. Welcome to the future.

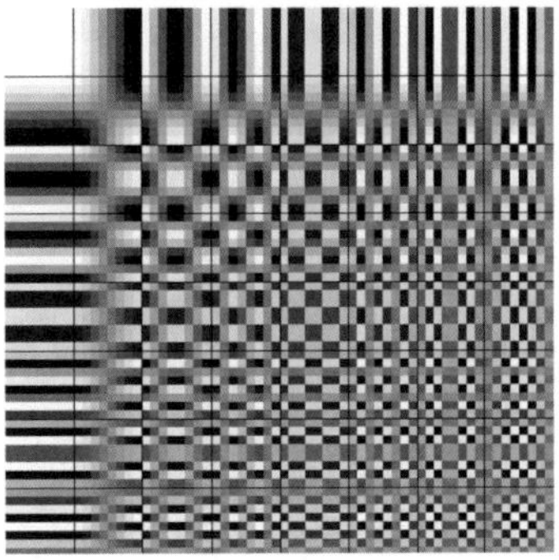

Fig. 13: Our basis functions for a JPEG

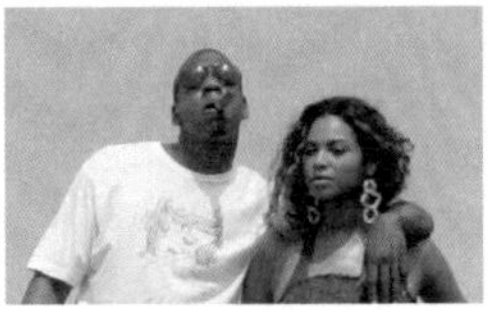

Fig. 14: Our JPEG input

$$\begin{bmatrix} 51 & 101 & 151 & 201 & 251 & 301 & 351 & 401 \\ 101 & 151 & 201 & 251 & 301 & 351 & 401 & 451 \\ 151 & 201 & 251 & 301 & 351 & 401 & 451 & 501 \\ 201 & 251 & 301 & 351 & 401 & 451 & 501 & 551 \\ 251 & 301 & 351 & 401 & 451 & 501 & 551 & 601 \\ 301 & 351 & 401 & 451 & 501 & 551 & 601 & 651 \\ 351 & 401 & 451 & 501 & 551 & 601 & 651 & 701 \\ 401 & 451 & 501 & 551 & 601 & 651 & 701 & 751 \end{bmatrix}$$

Fig. 15: Our JPEG quantization table

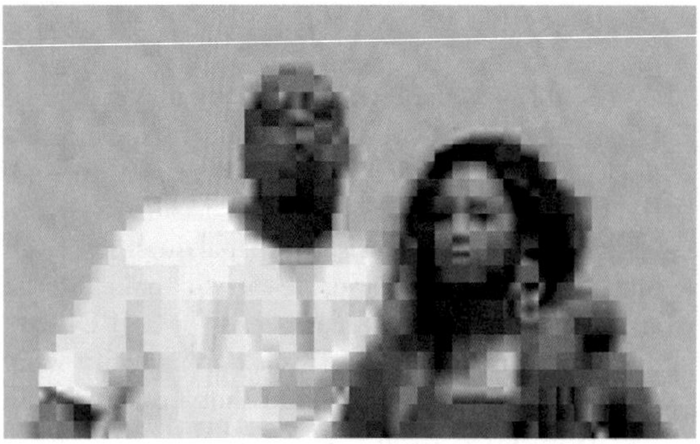

Fig. 16. Our compressed JPEG using the above input and quantization table (Fig. 14 and 15)

Special thanks to Danny Comer for helping with these concepts.

1 $\begin{bmatrix} cos\frac{(2*0+1)0\pi}{2*3} & cos\frac{(2*1+1)0\pi}{2*3} & cos\frac{(2*2+1)0\pi}{2*3} \end{bmatrix} = \begin{bmatrix} 1 & 1 & 1 \end{bmatrix}$

$\begin{bmatrix} cos\frac{(2*0+1)1\pi}{2*3} & cos\frac{(2*1+1)1\pi}{2*3} & cos\frac{(2*2+1)1\pi}{2*3} \end{bmatrix} = \begin{bmatrix} .86603 & 6.1232e-17 & -.86603 \end{bmatrix}$

$\begin{bmatrix} cos\frac{(2*0+1)2\pi}{2*3} & cos\frac{(2*1+1)2\pi}{2*3} & cos\frac{(2*2+1)2\pi}{2*3} \end{bmatrix} = \begin{bmatrix} .5 & -1 & .5 \end{bmatrix}$

2 $3.46410 = \sum_{x=0}^{2} \sqrt{1/3} * \begin{bmatrix} 3 & 2 & 1 \end{bmatrix} * \begin{bmatrix} 1 & 1 & 1 \end{bmatrix}$

$1.41421 = \sum_{x=0}^{2} \sqrt{2/3} * \begin{bmatrix} 3 & 2 & 1 \end{bmatrix} * \begin{bmatrix} .86603 & 6.1232e-17 & -.86603 \end{bmatrix}$

$0.00000 = \sum_{x=0}^{2} \sqrt{2/3} * \begin{bmatrix} 3 & 2 & 1 \end{bmatrix} * \begin{bmatrix} .5 & -1 & .5 \end{bmatrix}$

FYI: $3.46410 = (\sqrt{1/3} * 3 * 1) + (\sqrt{1/3} * 2 * 1) + (\sqrt{1/3} * 1 * 1)$

3 $\sqrt{1/3}*\begin{bmatrix} 1 & 1 & 1 \end{bmatrix}*3.46410+\sqrt{2/3}*\begin{bmatrix} .86603 & 6.1232e-17 & -.86603 \end{bmatrix}*1.41421 = \begin{bmatrix} 3 & 2 & 1 \end{bmatrix}$

4 $$\begin{bmatrix} cos\frac{(2*0+1)0\pi}{2*3}*cos\frac{(2*0+1)0\pi}{2*3} & cos\frac{(2*0+1)0\pi}{2*3}*cos\frac{(2*1+1)0\pi}{2*3} & cos\frac{(2*0+1)0\pi}{2*3}*cos\frac{(2*2+1)0\pi}{2*3} \\ cos\frac{(2*1+1)0\pi}{2*3}*cos\frac{(2*0+1)0\pi}{2*3} & cos\frac{(2*1+1)0\pi}{2*3}*cos\frac{(2*1+1)0\pi}{2*3} & cos\frac{(2*1+1)0\pi}{2*3}*cos\frac{(2*2+1)0\pi}{2*3} \\ cos\frac{(2*2+1)0\pi}{2*3}*cos\frac{(2*0+1)0\pi}{2*3} & cos\frac{(2*2+1)0\pi}{2*3}*cos\frac{(2*1+1)0\pi}{2*3} & cos\frac{(2*2+1)0\pi}{2*3}*cos\frac{(2*2+1)0\pi}{2*3} \end{bmatrix}$$

$$\begin{bmatrix} 1 & 1 & 1 \\ 1 & 1 & 1 \\ 1 & 1 & 1 \end{bmatrix}$$

$$\begin{bmatrix} cos\frac{(2*0+1)0\pi}{2*3}*cos\frac{(2*0+1)1\pi}{2*3} & cos\frac{(2*0+1)0\pi}{2*3}*cos\frac{(2*1+1)1\pi}{2*3} & cos\frac{(2*0+1)0\pi}{2*3}*cos\frac{(2*2+1)1\pi}{2*3} \\ cos\frac{(2*1+1)0\pi}{2*3}*cos\frac{(2*0+1)1\pi}{2*3} & cos\frac{(2*1+1)0\pi}{2*3}*cos\frac{(2*1+1)1\pi}{2*3} & cos\frac{(2*1+1)0\pi}{2*3}*cos\frac{(2*2+1)1\pi}{2*3} \\ cos\frac{(2*2+1)0\pi}{2*3}*cos\frac{(2*0+1)1\pi}{2*3} & cos\frac{(2*2+1)0\pi}{2*3}*cos\frac{(2*1+1)1\pi}{2*3} & cos\frac{(2*2+1)0\pi}{2*3}*cos\frac{(2*2+1)1\pi}{2*3} \end{bmatrix} =$$

$$\begin{bmatrix} .86603 & 6.1232e-17 & -.86603 \\ .86603 & 6.1232e-17 & -.86603 \\ .86603 & 6.1232e-17 & -.86603 \end{bmatrix}$$

$$\begin{bmatrix} cos\frac{(2*0+1)0\pi}{2*3}*cos\frac{(2*0+1)2\pi}{2*3} & cos\frac{(2*0+1)0\pi}{2*3}*cos\frac{(2*1+1)2\pi}{2*3} & cos\frac{(2*0+1)0\pi}{2*3}*cos\frac{(2*2+1)2\pi}{2*3} \\ cos\frac{(2*1+1)0\pi}{2*3}*cos\frac{(2*0+1)2\pi}{2*3} & cos\frac{(2*1+1)0\pi}{2*3}*cos\frac{(2*1+1)2\pi}{2*3} & cos\frac{(2*1+1)0\pi}{2*3}*cos\frac{(2*2+1)2\pi}{2*3} \\ cos\frac{(2*2+1)0\pi}{2*3}*cos\frac{(2*0+1)2\pi}{2*3} & cos\frac{(2*2+1)0\pi}{2*3}*cos\frac{(2*1+1)2\pi}{2*3} & cos\frac{(2*2+1)0\pi}{2*3}*cos\frac{(2*2+1)2\pi}{2*3} \end{bmatrix} =$$

$$\begin{bmatrix} .5 & -1 & .5 \\ .5 & -1 & .5 \\ .5 & -1 & .5 \end{bmatrix}$$

$$\begin{bmatrix} cos\frac{(2*0+1)1\pi}{2*3}*cos\frac{(2*0+1)0\pi}{2*3} & cos\frac{(2*0+1)1\pi}{2*3}*cos\frac{(2*1+1)0\pi}{2*3} & cos\frac{(2*0+1)1\pi}{2*3}*cos\frac{(2*2+1)0\pi}{2*3} \\ cos\frac{(2*1+1)1\pi}{2*3}*cos\frac{(2*0+1)0\pi}{2*3} & cos\frac{(2*1+1)1\pi}{2*3}*cos\frac{(2*1+1)0\pi}{2*3} & cos\frac{(2*1+1)1\pi}{2*3}*cos\frac{(2*2+1)0\pi}{2*3} \\ cos\frac{(2*2+1)1\pi}{2*3}*cos\frac{(2*0+1)0\pi}{2*3} & cos\frac{(2*2+1)1\pi}{2*3}*cos\frac{(2*1+1)0\pi}{2*3} & cos\frac{(2*2+1)1\pi}{2*3}*cos\frac{(2*2+1)0\pi}{2*3} \end{bmatrix} =$$

$$\begin{bmatrix} 8.6603e-01 & 8.6603e-01 & 8.6603e-01 \\ 6.1232e-17 & 6.1232e-17 & 6.1232e-17 \\ -8.6603e-01 & -8.6603e-01 & -8.6603e-01 \end{bmatrix}$$

$$\begin{bmatrix} cos\frac{(2*0+1)1\pi}{2*3}*cos\frac{(2*0+1)1\pi}{2*3} & cos\frac{(2*0+1)1\pi}{2*3}*cos\frac{(2*1+1)1\pi}{2*3} & cos\frac{(2*0+1)1\pi}{2*3}*cos\frac{(2*2+1)1\pi}{2*3} \\ cos\frac{(2*1+1)1\pi}{2*3}*cos\frac{(2*0+1)1\pi}{2*3} & cos\frac{(2*1+1)1\pi}{2*3}*cos\frac{(2*1+1)1\pi}{2*3} & cos\frac{(2*1+1)1\pi}{2*3}*cos\frac{(2*2+1)1\pi}{2*3} \\ cos\frac{(2*2+1)1\pi}{2*3}*cos\frac{(2*0+1)1\pi}{2*3} & cos\frac{(2*2+1)1\pi}{2*3}*cos\frac{(2*1+1)1\pi}{2*3} & cos\frac{(2*2+1)1\pi}{2*3}*cos\frac{(2*2+1)1\pi}{2*3} \end{bmatrix} =$$

$$\begin{bmatrix} 7.5000e-01 & 5.3029e-17 & -7.5000e-01 \\ 5.3029e-17 & 3.7494e-33 & -5.3029e-17 \\ -7.5000e-01 & -5.3029e-17 & 7.5000e-01 \end{bmatrix}$$

$$\begin{bmatrix} cos\frac{(2*0+1)1\pi}{2*3}*cos\frac{(2*0+1)2\pi}{2*3} & cos\frac{(2*0+1)1\pi}{2*3}*cos\frac{(2*1+1)2\pi}{2*3} & cos\frac{(2*0+1)1\pi}{2*3}*cos\frac{(2*2+1)2\pi}{2*3} \\ cos\frac{(2*1+1)1\pi}{2*3}*cos\frac{(2*0+1)2\pi}{2*3} & cos\frac{(2*1+1)1\pi}{2*3}*cos\frac{(2*1+1)2\pi}{2*3} & cos\frac{(2*1+1)1\pi}{2*3}*cos\frac{(2*2+1)2\pi}{2*3} \\ cos\frac{(2*2+1)1\pi}{2*3}*cos\frac{(2*0+1)2\pi}{2*3} & cos\frac{(2*2+1)1\pi}{2*3}*cos\frac{(2*1+1)2\pi}{2*3} & cos\frac{(2*2+1)1\pi}{2*3}*cos\frac{(2*2+1)2\pi}{2*3} \end{bmatrix} =$$

$$\begin{bmatrix} 4.3301e-01 & -8.6603e-01 & 4.3301e-01 \\ 3.0616e-17 & -6.1232e-17 & 3.0616e-17 \\ -4.3301e-01 & 8.6603e-01 & -4.3301e-01 \end{bmatrix}$$

$$\begin{bmatrix} cos\frac{(2*0+1)2\pi}{2*3}*cos\frac{(2*0+1)0\pi}{2*3} & cos\frac{(2*0+1)2\pi}{2*3}*cos\frac{(2*1+1)0\pi}{2*3} & cos\frac{(2*0+1)2\pi}{2*3}*cos\frac{(2*2+1)0\pi}{2*3} \\ cos\frac{(2*1+1)2\pi}{2*3}*cos\frac{(2*0+1)0\pi}{2*3} & cos\frac{(2*1+1)2\pi}{2*3}*cos\frac{(2*1+1)0\pi}{2*3} & cos\frac{(2*1+1)2\pi}{2*3}*cos\frac{(2*2+1)0\pi}{2*3} \\ cos\frac{(2*2+1)2\pi}{2*3}*cos\frac{(2*0+1)0\pi}{2*3} & cos\frac{(2*2+1)2\pi}{2*3}*cos\frac{(2*1+1)0\pi}{2*3} & cos\frac{(2*2+1)2\pi}{2*3}*cos\frac{(2*2+1)0\pi}{2*3} \end{bmatrix} =$$

$$\begin{bmatrix} .5 & .5 & .5 \\ -1 & -1 & -1 \\ .5 & .5 & .5 \end{bmatrix}$$

$$\begin{bmatrix} cos\frac{(2*0+1)2\pi}{2*3}*cos\frac{(2*0+1)1\pi}{2*3} & cos\frac{(2*0+1)2\pi}{2*3}*cos\frac{(2*1+1)1\pi}{2*3} & cos\frac{(2*0+1)2\pi}{2*3}*cos\frac{(2*2+1)1\pi}{2*3} \\ cos\frac{(2*1+1)2\pi}{2*3}*cos\frac{(2*0+1)1\pi}{2*3} & cos\frac{(2*1+1)2\pi}{2*3}*cos\frac{(2*1+1)1\pi}{2*3} & cos\frac{(2*1+1)2\pi}{2*3}*cos\frac{(2*2+1)1\pi}{2*3} \\ cos\frac{(2*2+1)2\pi}{2*3}*cos\frac{(2*0+1)1\pi}{2*3} & cos\frac{(2*2+1)2\pi}{2*3}*cos\frac{(2*1+1)1\pi}{2*3} & cos\frac{(2*2+1)2\pi}{2*3}*cos\frac{(2*2+1)1\pi}{2*3} \end{bmatrix} =$$

$$\begin{bmatrix} 4.3301e-01 & 3.0616e-17 & -4.3301e-01 \\ -8.6603e-01 & -6.1232e-17 & 8.6603e-01 \\ 4.3301e-01 & 3.0616e-17 & -4.3301e-01 \end{bmatrix}$$

$$\begin{bmatrix} cos\frac{(2*0+1)2\pi}{2*3}*cos\frac{(2*0+1)2\pi}{2*3} & cos\frac{(2*0+1)2\pi}{2*3}*cos\frac{(2*1+1)2\pi}{2*3} & cos\frac{(2*0+1)2\pi}{2*3}*cos\frac{(2*2+1)2\pi}{2*3} \\ cos\frac{(2*1+1)2\pi}{2*3}*cos\frac{(2*0+1)2\pi}{2*3} & cos\frac{(2*1+1)2\pi}{2*3}*cos\frac{(2*1+1)2\pi}{2*3} & cos\frac{(2*1+1)2\pi}{2*3}*cos\frac{(2*2+1)2\pi}{2*3} \\ cos\frac{(2*2+1)2\pi}{2*3}*cos\frac{(2*0+1)2\pi}{2*3} & cos\frac{(2*2+1)2\pi}{2*3}*cos\frac{(2*1+1)2\pi}{2*3} & cos\frac{(2*2+1)2\pi}{2*3}*cos\frac{(2*2+1)2\pi}{2*3} \end{bmatrix} =$$

$$\begin{bmatrix} 0.25000 & .5 & 0.25 \\ -.5 & 1 & -.5 \\ 0.25000 & -.5 & 0.25 \end{bmatrix}$$

5 $$255.00000 = \sum_{x=0}^{2}\sum_{y=0}^{2} sqrt(1/3)*\begin{bmatrix} 1 & 1 & 1 \\ 1 & 1 & 1 \\ 1 & 1 & 1 \end{bmatrix}*sqrt(1/3)*\begin{bmatrix} 255 & 255 & 255 \\ 0 & 0 & 0 \\ 0 & 0 & 0 \end{bmatrix}$$

$$0 = \sum_{x=0}^{2}\sum_{y=0}^{2} sqrt(1/3)*\begin{bmatrix} .86603 & 6.1232e-17 & .86603 \\ .86603 & 6.1232e-17 & .86603 \\ .86603 & 6.1232e-17 & .86603 \end{bmatrix}*sqrt(2/3)*\begin{bmatrix} 255 & 255 & 255 \\ 0 & 0 & 0 \\ 0 & 0 & 0 \end{bmatrix}$$

$$0 = \sum_{x=0}^{2}\sum_{y=0}^{2} sqrt(1/3)*\begin{bmatrix} .5 & -1 & .5 \\ .5 & -1 & .5 \\ .5 & -1 & .5 \end{bmatrix}*sqrt(2/3)*\begin{bmatrix} 255 & 255 & 255 \\ 0 & 0 & 0 \\ 0 & 0 & 0 \end{bmatrix}$$

$$312.30994 = \sum_{x=0}^{2}\sum_{y=0}^{2} sqrt(2/3)*\begin{bmatrix} 8.6603e-01 & 8.6603e-01 & 8.6603e-01 \\ 6.1232e-17 & 6.1232e-17 & 6.1232e-17 \\ -8.6603e-01 & -8.6603e-01 & -8.6603e-01 \end{bmatrix}*sqrt(1/3)*\begin{bmatrix} 255 & 255 & 255 \\ 0 & 0 & 0 \\ 0 & 0 & 0 \end{bmatrix}$$

$$0 = \sum_{x=0}^{2}\sum_{y=0}^{2} sqrt(2/3)*\begin{bmatrix} 7.5000e-01 & 5.3029e-17 & -7.5000e-01 \\ 5.3029e-17 & 3.7494e-33 & -5.3029e-17 \\ -7.5000e-01 & -5.3029e-17 & 7.5000e-01 \end{bmatrix}*sqrt(2/3)*\begin{bmatrix} 255 & 255 & 255 \\ 0 & 0 & 0 \\ 0 & 0 & 0 \end{bmatrix}$$

$$0 = \sum_{x=0}^{2}\sum_{y=0}^{2} sqrt(2/3)*\begin{bmatrix} 4.3301e-01 & -8.6603e-01 & 4.3301e-01 \\ 3.0616e-17 & -6.1232e-17 & 3.0616e-17 \\ -4.3301e-01 & 8.6603e-01 & -4.3301e-01 \end{bmatrix}*sqrt(2/3)*\begin{bmatrix} 255 & 255 & 255 \\ 0 & 0 & 0 \\ 0 & 0 & 0 \end{bmatrix}$$

$$180.31223 = \sum_{x=0}^{2}\sum_{y=0}^{2} sqrt(2/3)*\begin{bmatrix} .5 & .5 & .5 \\ -1 & -1 & -1 \\ .5 & .5 & .5 \end{bmatrix}*sqrt(1/3)*\begin{bmatrix} 255 & 255 & 255 \\ 0 & 0 & 0 \\ 0 & 0 & 0 \end{bmatrix}$$

$$0 = \sum_{x=0}^{2}\sum_{y=0}^{2} sqrt(2/3)*\begin{bmatrix} 4.3301e-01 & 3.0616e-17 & -4.3301e-01 \\ -8.6603e-01 & -6.1232e-17 & 8.6603e-01 \\ 4.3301e-01 & 3.0616e-17 & -4.3301e-01 \end{bmatrix}*sqrt(2/3)*\begin{bmatrix} 255 & 255 & 255 \\ 0 & 0 & 0 \\ 0 & 0 & 0 \end{bmatrix}$$

$$0 = \sum_{x=0}^{2}\sum_{y=0}^{2} sqrt(2/3)*\begin{bmatrix} 0.25000 & .5 & 0.25000 \\ -.5 & 1 & -.5 \\ 0.25000 & -.5 & 0.25000 \end{bmatrix}*sqrt(2/3)*\begin{bmatrix} 255 & 255 & 255 \\ 0 & 0 & 0 \\ 0 & 0 & 0 \end{bmatrix}$$

6 $$\sqrt{1/3}*250*\sqrt{1/3}*\begin{bmatrix} 1 & 1 & 1 \\ 1 & 1 & 1 \\ 1 & 1 & 1 \end{bmatrix}+\sqrt{1/3}*0*\sqrt{2/3}*\begin{bmatrix} .86603 & 6.1232e-17 & .86603 \\ .86603 & 6.1232e-17 & .86603 \\ .86603 & 6.1232e-17 & .86603 \end{bmatrix}+$$

$$\sqrt{1/3}*0*\sqrt{2/3}*\begin{bmatrix} .5 & -1 & .5 \\ .5 & -1 & .5 \\ .5 & -1 & .5 \end{bmatrix}+\sqrt{2/3}*250*\sqrt{1/3}*\begin{bmatrix} 8.6603e-01 & 8.6603e-01 & 8.6603e \\ 6.1232e-17 & 6.1232e-17 & 6.1232e \\ -8.6603e-01 & -8.6603e-01 & -8.6603e \end{bmatrix}$$

$$\sqrt{2/3}*0*\sqrt{2/3}*\begin{bmatrix} 7.5000e-01 & 5.3029e-17 & -7.5000e-01 \\ 5.3029e-17 & 3.7494e-33 & -5.3029e-17 \\ -7.5000e-01 & -5.3029e-17 & 7.5000e-01 \end{bmatrix}+\sqrt{2/3}*0*$$

$$\sqrt{2/3}*\begin{bmatrix} 4.3301e-01 & -8.6603e-01 & 4.3301e-01 \\ 3.0616e-17 & -6.1232e-17 & 3.0616e-17 \\ -4.3301e-01 & 8.6603e-01 & -4.3301e-01 \end{bmatrix}+\sqrt{2/3}*0*\sqrt{1/3}*\begin{bmatrix} .5 & .5 & .5 \\ -1 & -1 & -1 \\ .5 & .5 & .5 \end{bmatrix}+$$

$$\sqrt{2/3}*0*\sqrt{2/3}*\begin{bmatrix} 4.3301e-01 & 3.0616e-17 & -4.3301e-01 \\ -8.6603e-01 & -6.1232e-17 & 8.6603e-01 \\ 4.3301e-01 & 3.0616e-17 & -4.3301e-01 \end{bmatrix}+\sqrt{2/3}*0*$$

$$\sqrt{2/3} * \begin{bmatrix} 0.25000 & .5 & 0.25000 \\ -.5 & 1 & -.5 \\ 0.25000 & -.5 & 0.25000 \end{bmatrix}$$

Repression and the Information Boom

Zuhair al-Jezairy

2005

Humans have, since time immemorial, exchanged information. To say and to listen have been as basic and as instinctual as breathing and eating in forestalling death. The earliest forms of communication predate spoken language. Cave paintings were already messages about hunting and various dangers. Packed in caves seeking shelter from the changing weather and other looming threats, a primitive tribe used to delegate one of its own to keep watch and inform the rest of any imminent danger. When such an eventuality did arise, one elder or an assembly of elders were then responsible for taking a decision, issuing orders and informing each of the tribe's members of their tasks and duties. The course of action was not decided by one or more in reaction to a pressing danger. Rather, much of what was decided followed established rules, rituals, laws and beliefs. Accordingly, teaching youths and novices these rules and regulations was of a crucial importance in leading and managing the needs of the group. It is therefore possible to posit that information in primitive societies played three roles: That of observation (keeping watch and notifying), that of policy-making (decision-making, leadership and drafting laws) and that of teaching (inducting individuals into the group through rites of passage).

IRAQI CURIOSITY

According to one local anecdote, it was "*Chako mako?*" the Iraqi idiomatic equivalent for the American "What's up?" which burst the computer. Such was the need of Iraqis for news in a country swept in unexpected upheavals. Were the Iraqis living in less exceptional and less repressed times, *souks* or markets would have provided a space for the exchange of information along with the exchange of goods. In such spaces, information is not only the stuff of intimate conversations, but also that which can be announced by one to a multitude. In addressing an anonymous crowd, the herald performs one aspect of the modern news media. In fact, he is a persistent figure whose role can be traced back to the Babylonian age, announcing to all the decrees of the authorities. Until recently, the herald would canvas the streets and *souks* informing citizens of new laws, religious legal opinions or *fatwas* as well as of the latest movies shown in local cinemas. Besides the *souks*, mosques have remained a central space for instruction and channeling information to the faithful while outside the reach of civil authorities. They also played, most notably during the 1920s, a central role in communicating the tenets of ideologies. For instance, it was in a mosque that I first heard of Coca Cola, a non-alcoholic and therefore religiously sanctioned drink. Following the demise of the 1920s revolution, mosques receded and were partially replaced by cafés. It was there that people congregated around the *effendis* and the literate who read the dailies and listened to the radio in search of world news.

Modern communication media broke the monopoly of ruling elites, clerics and the learned few over knowledge. Fast and available, it multiplied the speed of information exchange. It also promoted impersonal informational exchange, be it audio, visual or printed, over direct oral and interpersonal communication. The following anecdote is telling: At the frontiers of the dry lands, by the Al Houwaiza lake, we were received as guests of the Bou Mouhamad family. In the large guest room, a television occupied a central place exactly as an elder would have. Prominent and central, that television replaced the roles usually played by the clan leader, the wise elders and even the local "bully". This new tele-Sheikh condensed, in its flow of sounds and images, the roles of the storyteller, the wise and the companion. Even the actual elder seemed to have relinquished some of his privileges as he followed the news broadcast. Sitting in front of the television: this remote little village seemed current and part of the world.

Newspapers were the medium of the literate and the learned. Television, on the other hand, is defined by its availability. It seeks an audience, enters private dwellings with vivid audiovisual drama that fulfills the needs of the illiterate villager. More than a mere box which broadcasts sitcoms of Bedouin themes such as honour, betrayal and vestal love, television is a bridge that links the tribal world to the modern world. It broadcasts the world live: Watching the news of Blair's visit to a European nation, the Sheikh by my side addressed me with a loud voice meant for everyone to hear: "Tony is wiser than Bush... Do you not think so?" I, of course, had to agree with this piece of wisdom imparted to all his subjects.

Television communicates experiences from far beyond the limited world of the villagers. It opens unto the unexpected and challenges what is orally transmitted and what is physically and sensorially known. In fact, television tests the limits, traditions and givens of the closed tribal environment. And although great leaps have been taken between the time of the cave tribes and our so-called global village, information media still carries the same tasks: Keeping watch and scanning the horizon is now the task of news departments with their armies of reporters, investigators, high-tech communication hardware and broadcasting units, while modern governments and parliaments now carry the task of sounding popular opinion and drawing future policies. And while the caller or the herald used to inform the multitudes, his task is now performed by populist information services.

It is quite noticeable that what used to be decided swiftly among a few is now open to endless public debates. But, as in previous tribal eras, the task is one and the same: Informing, observing, exploring, deciding and teaching. All this is now within the domain of the printed and audio-visual media.

CURIOUS AUTHORITIES AND CURIOSITY KILLED

If people needed to know of what happens above them, the authorities needed to always be informed about what happened beneath them. Recognising that information can turn to acts, activism and social practice, the authorities planted an endless number of informers in public spaces such as mosques and cafés. The role of these secret agents was to keep those in power aware and in touch with the pulse of the streets.

In the mid-1980s, a campaign to survey and control Iraqi society required that all citizens fill a questionnaire containing questions about one's family up to the fourth degree of kinship. It also contained questions about relatives who were possibly imprisoned, executed or on the run. It also contained flagrant threats to those who would refuse to disclose (or provide incorrect) information, or even be late in submitting them. These questionnaires were to be submitted every six months. Such was the level of surveillance in Iraq.

Under threat, and forced to tell on friends and relatives, citizens were constantly interpolated so as to make mere silence an infraction of the law. In fact, citizens were gradually made into unpaid volunteer informers working under that infamous slogan put out by the Ministry of the Interior: "In a society where each does not police everyone else, we would need a policeman for each". In such a society of informers, fear prevails. Trusting no one, each person is prey to doubts and avoids "confiding in friends and relatives fearing that one improper word could be relayed to the internal security forces."

THE CENSOR AND THE FORBIDDEN

The web of professional, coerced and volunteer informers forcefully applied a series of laws which prohibited the publication of material which "promotes defeatism, serves colonial or Zionist interests, does not fulfill the aims, interests and aspirations of the people, harms the concerns and goals of the Arab homeland, causes injury to allied states, slanders the reputation of national liberation movements across the world or is of low artistic quality and harmful to good taste". Such a long litany of interdictions tended to multiply and was kept open-ended for both the authoritarian ruler and more so for individuals caught in the bind of fearful self-censorship.

Under such a constant threat of death and fear of punishment, Iraqis learned to sublimate and repress the pre-linguistic human instinct for exchanging information. Living under the shadow of a "total informer", exchange was purged of anything deemed sensitive and as such was reduced to very little. Accordingly, it was the authorities who then monopolised information. Everyone else was cut-off from communication and reduced to becoming subject to surveillance. What was allowed was carefully measured and rationed. People were prohibited under threat of death from listening to "enemy" radio stations and from watching satellite television.

In such a reign of terror, communication is reduced to mere whispers within the closed circles of trusted friends. And yet, Iraqis gradually came to prefer silence in their personal world of cautious deafness, choosing to speak not, nor to listen: Fear of punishment is ideal for killing the curious search for knowledge.

THE INFORMATION BOOM

Upon the fall of the regime, a dizzying informational boom occurred. The world of repression and secrets was suddenly divulged to all. The streets were littered with the files of the secret services. Secrets, once carefully protected, became available to all. Sold for a few dinars, these files which had cost many their lives were now read and discussed, often in amazement at the private information they contained. Alas, those informers were more often than not the closest of friends and relatives.

The world was turned upside down. The authorities, which once monopolised information and knew the smallest details, were now exposed to everyone. The exorbitant lifestyles and practices of the ruling family were eagerly viewed on DVDs sold in Liberation Square. Tabloid newspapers could now run these stories with impunity, whereas not long before, during the bitter and lean days of the international embargo, similar stories about profligate parties were overheard and duly swallowed like ill fate.

To wander around Liberation Square, I used to wear my worst clothes. Everywhere, one could find little makeshift studios for copying and recording CDs and tapes of the atrocities committed by the authorities. Why did they document all that torture and violence? Within that authoritarian hierarchy, each wanted to prove his work accomplished. All the way to the highest leader, documents were made and sent. A long history of violence was now available on tapes. A secretive past has awakened and was in public view. And a people, once in denial, picked it up and embellished it. An imagination once repressed was set loose. No matter the cruel conditions and pressing demands of a present in turmoil, a mere exchange with a neighbour or taxi driver would inevitablely bring stories of that past flooding in. Emaciated and unshaven, the missing stepped out of burrows and secret dens. With waxen faces, they walked onto the streets carrying the banners of their parties.

Yet some remained missing. A few days after my arrival in Baghdad, a rumour spread about a prison dug underneath the tunnel of Liberation Square. Men and women hurried to the site. Amongst them, fathers, mothers and that unforgettable bereaved villager running as if in two directions, her black cloak lagging in the wind behind, with arms outstretched. Inside the tunnel, young men attempted to break open a steel door. One of them calls: "We've come!" And hears in the mere echo the response he longs for.

THE RETURN OF THE DEAD

All at once, the dead awoke. All those that were kidnapped, or perhaps one should say flagrantly collected, surfaced again in communal graves. These men and women who were not allowed a funeral or a mere prayer were found again. Found and then properly buried. Relatives could now do what was once prohibited: They could grieve. At least a corpse was now available whereas there had once been no more than a mere printed notice which informed the parents that their sons and daughters had "betrayed the nation". Without a corpse there is no evidence of death. And an empty grave is just that.

The streets of the city were lined with posted notes of those still missing. Not everyone was fortunate enough to find the corpses of their loved ones. This land is replete with the unknown dead. My uncle Abdel Amir was one among those who refused to believe these ghastly notices. He would wander the streets searching for a name or picture that could lead him to his missing son Samer. He had an intimation that his son was still alive, perhaps abroad and that he would reappear. An intimation that occupied his days and on which he built illusory hopes that comfort and torture. The return of the dead awakened vengeance; and in the absence of any deterring force, the dead hunted the executioners who attempted to flee, most often with their looted wealth.

In such a situation, satellite television became vital. People wanted to know everything there was to know of this violent past that was flooding the gates of the present. Myriad stories were told of forgotten persons reappearing from the tenebrous dungeons and of thieves and criminals controlling the back streets and alleyways. Kidnapping became a lucrative occupation. Depending on identity and status, the release of a captive could cost between 15 and 200 thousand dollars. To drive around the city, I used a run-down car, a "Brazilian", in order to avoid the attention of car thieves. I saw nightmarish scenes: A wounded man hunted by an armed one; two boys thrown on cardboard boxes, bleeding to death; passers-by asking questions without stopping for answers; a woman screaming, asking for help as a car raced against traffic firing gun shots in the air. The city was a jungle where brute force ruled.

NEWS, NEWS, NEWS

Discussing the news was not a mere pastime. News meant life or death. It was not about what was happening elsewhere. The news was everyone's. Close and personal, the news told of imminent dangers. And in the absence of police, each had to fend for him or herself. It demanded a quick decision and action early the next morning. News was hotly debated among family members: Should we move to another location? Should we consider going shopping for goods? Should we send the kids to school? Should we abandon our homes? What about the future, after all this senseless violence? Questions that could be only answered, even if temporarily, by whatever news were at hand.

The long bloody years of the regime spent the Iraqis' ability to hope in a better future. The flagrant discrepancies between the ruling class and the rest of the population lay to waste the patience and diligence of the people. Now, in this sudden and unheralded moment of complete and wanton openness, dread reigns. Accordingly, the dissemination of information is pivotal in increasing or decreasing tensions. Whether the media will exploit and thrive on sensational news or promote discussion will, to a large extent, impact the situation to come. If the media can buttress the confidence of the people, then it should. For it is inevitable that genuine and coherent change can only come from a real transformation of the general public.

November 23, 2005

Redistribution (video transcript)
Seth Price
2010

Hello. Thanks, Nancy. I'm going to show slides of my work from the last six or seven years. It's chronological, or pretty much chronological.

I'm like a person who makes things. You do it one after another, unending. It goes on for such a long time: something new, and something else, and something something. Here come a lot of different strategies and arrangements, all interesting, all interlocking, mutatis mutandis. . . . Such a lot of things! And then the question will be put to you: If you have something to say, why not simply say it? Why the elaborate games, the things that stand in for other things?

Well, I studied some film and video in college, and afterward I thought I might try to do that, or work toward that. I was working with video and showing in film festivals. After a couple of years I did start to look at art, at the art world, and that opened up a new horizon, and I started to try and define my work against what I saw there.

It seemed like art video split into two threads, historically. There was a performance tradition, which went back to the early 1970s and the birth of the medium: this encounter between the artist and the lens, which was about presence, about the artist's "look and feel." On the other hand, there was a cinema thread, which really started to come into its own in the early 1990s with large-scale projection, and you get video refracted through a cinema structure: budgets, crews, actors, scripts. . . . This has to do with movies and television, the narrative lens, the idea of fiction.

So, it seemed there were these two tendencies, the performance and the cinematic, and I wasn't interested in either. But they're both based around the lens, its particular way of taking. Getting rid of the camera seemed interesting, making a video without a video camera, without a scenario or performance—or without even editing in the traditional sense. And that's not a new impulse. It's certainly been a staple of experimental film. But how do you do it again? And, actually, I was tired of having to use a camera.

These images are from a video I made in 2000. I typed the term painting into a search engine and took just about whatever came back. Taking imagery solely from the Internet seemed like a way to move the focus away from these other video traditions, to start to think about digital video as simply material in a chain. It translates directly from a circulated image, which itself is an offcut of a stored file, to video data. It never enters the realm of chemistry or electromagnetic tape. That way, anything within the video realm, whether it comes from film or a computer lab or some waste on the Web, is reduced to the level of graphics; it becomes diagrammatic. Treating the material this way started to clarify things for me: it highlighted procedures and tools, translations, plasticity.

What is it that is so appealing and fascinating about plastic, as we saw satirized in films like *The Graduate* and as we see in these industrial films? It may be the material's apparently limitless array of uses, its universal promise, which goes back to the boom in plastic production associated with the World Wars and their birthing of a new material culture. Plastic's development was deeply entwined with military production, but in the postwar era it also represented the spirit of recreation. This was the material of choice for all manner of consumer goods aimed at a public eager to define its new wealth through the expression of lifestyle choices. The idea of something wholly synthetic, multipurpose, and brand-new had a deep resonance for Westerners beaten down by the long march through war, depression, poverty, and war again. Plastic could be adapted to any purpose or sphere of meaning, a ready servant, willing to work for us, to be used.

Anything that is completely elastic, however, will wind up in the garbage before long. That's built into the material and the expectations we have of it. It may start its life as oil, as the accumulated sediment of millions of years of dead organisms, but it will pass through many different functions and forms before it comes to rest once more in the waste heaps and middens of history. Too many forms, in fact, too many uses, too many possibilities! This is a game where all options are open, all forms recombinant and mutable. On the one hand, these materials can be regulated through observation and careful calibration: the processes of translation are supposedly subject to rigorous scientific logic and technological manipulation. At the same time, they're confusingly open-ended and adaptable. The categorical barriers between states of matter are no longer of consequence: a material easily translates from liquid to solid and back again, a shirt may be conjured out of a bubbling vat of material, used food containers are miraculously transformed into brand-new baby carriages.

It's a powerful image, a prism that gathers a number of related ideas: an irrationally open-ended social promise linked with the measured and rational notion of the technological, and at the same time the practical implications are crushingly banal. . . . You wouldn't see this constellation of ideas in such an exaggerated form until the end of the twentieth century, with the rise of a new digital age carrying a similar promise—that all goods and concepts are subject to shifts in form and meaning executed as quickly and easily as the movement of a decimal point.

When the tendency is for everything to open out in all directions at all times, the problem is trying to establish a meaningful relationship between any two things. You might ask, isn't that what we would all want, to endlessly open in all directions? But if you can't establish a basic relation between two points, you might find yourself on the road to psychosis.

I wanted to show you this slide, which is a painting by Brueghel called *Kinderspiele*. It depicts many different kinds of play. Most can be classified in one of two ways: either you see people performing with one another, body games, like in these details, or else you see people using tools or instruments: stickbats, hoops, masks, dice. But the artist has included one activity that's a bit different: a person probes a pile of shit with a stick, as others watch. What can be gained from this activity, what narrative does it serve?

Shit is unusual: it's both natural, as a part of the organic and pre-technological world, and it's also man-made—you could even say it's the first human product. It's not without its charms, or uses, one of which is to embody these paradoxes of inside and outside, production and waste, use and lack of use. Brueghel may have been aware of these symbolic aspects, for the position of this person and the pile of shit can be no accident. The painting is a dramatic exercise in linear perspective, stretching back to the haziest reaches of the city at the top of the canvas, so among all the objects and activities featured here, the pile of shit, positioned at the bottom and center of the canvas, reads as virtually the closest item to us, the audience. It's literally foregrounded. Of all the ways we have invented to make the time pass, surely there's something unusual in our fixation with our own waste.

All artworks carry their dates around with them. It's information extrinsic to the piece, but you can't shake it, it will shadow your work forever. A year calendar poster, with a theme picture and a grid of numbers, seemed interesting. Its aspects kind of cancel each other out. Supposedly function is the main thing, with the art smuggled along in a package that's about utility, but then the grid of dates is often so tiny that it's useless, and you wind up with pure decoration. So the utility is more like a frame for an aesthetic decision: you like cats, you get a cat calendar, you like dogs, you get a dog calendar. . . .

Some of the paintings in these slides feature obsolete computer graphics or advertisements made with computers, and also American painting between the Wars, from before the Americans supplanted the European avant-garde. Where there are signs pointing to the postwar boom in American art, they're buried. It's a kind of odd period in American art, there's something melancholy about it. . . . It falls outside the normal progression, anyway. It's almost a kind of Socialist Realism, with the WPA, the New Deal, and those attitudes. This slide shows the calendars as posters, glued to the wall. I had also started printing them on canvas, as paintings, but I never showed those; I didn't have a gallery when I did them, and when I had one later, I was doing something else. So showing them here in Cologne is interesting, now that they're out-of-date. Sometimes it's good to go forward and then double back, and circle around again. To those who turned their feet around so that their tracks would confuse their pursuers: why not walk backward?

Anyway, at that point I wanted to somehow get back into video, and I was thinking, how do people make video today? Materially, technologically, video as a tool, as a kind of structure. It seemed like people take "content" and feed it through a set of digital effects. This is true whether it's a cheap TV documentary zooming slowly in on an archival photograph, or a Hollywood movie where footage is treated with color effects, or computer-generated imagery, or video art. So I decided to focus on the effects themselves. I made several videos that function like demonstrations of digital video transitions. They're proposals for effects that could actually exist, like "plug-in" software you might buy and enlist in some project or other.

This one is called *Digital Video Effect: "Holes."* The image accumulates as a series of droplets or holes, like paper-punch waste, and at a certain point you can see the image as a composite, though not entirely clearly, and then it drains away. The "content" here consists of pictures taken from websites that function as clearinghouses of grisly or brutal images, mostly pictures of people who have been in accidents, supposedly supplied by police examiners, morgue workers, or photojournalists who couldn't publish the material. A lot of these could be fabrications, but the point is really about circulation and redundancy. You know, these kinds of images have been around forever, but now they have a new form of circulation, so it's all different. Certainly the audience changes; when I was working on the video I showed it to some students, and they immediately identified the sites, and some recognized individual pictures. Last year it came out that American troops in Iraq were being awarded free porn-site memberships in exchange for uploading grisly war photographs to these other sites, which are often owned by the same companies.

This is intense and brutal imagery. It's not easy in any way, even because it can seem "too easy," in the sense of a quick provocation. I think I decided to work with it because of this difficulty. The challenge was to make it conform to an idea. How do you work with material that seems like it doesn't belong in art, either because it's presumed tasteless or boring or cynical or "topical". . . . In the end, I think you just try to take pleasure in the process, and hope that the difficulty is preserved in the work as a question.

I made a second piece, based on the idea of "spills," where the video material is made to flow like liquid. The material for this piece was also hard to know how to use, not because there was a question of taste or morality, but because it was so strong. I knew Joan Jonas, and I asked her if I could use a piece of home movie footage she'd shot in the early 1970s, with Robert Smithson and Nancy Holt, Richard Serra, and her, all sitting around with the art dealer Joe Helman, talking about the state of sculpture and money and art, the economy, the art economy. It hadn't ever been used, or even seen; it was a kind of private object, from the archive. And that status, the fact that it was a document, made it hard to bring into art. It was made by an artist, it featured artists, and they were talking about art, but it was somehow not art, because it was a supplement. And on top of that, you just want to see it, you don't want to see what's been done to it. I felt as if I couldn't use it.

I want to briefly go back to the performance/cinema question. It's interesting: by the late 1980s or early 1990s there's a kind of hybrid installation form where the performance thread and the cinema thread come together. Artists start filming performance scenarios within sets, using all kinds of props and trappings, and then they include these sets and props in the exhibition, alongside the video. So an object appears on-screen, full of cinema life, and then you turn your head and see it in real life, but mute, used up—the leavings of cinema. You're asked to read the art as occurring in two places at once: in the video, where the object serves the narrative, and simultaneously as an actual object, which has retreated to the quiet realm of sculpture. This is what these video installations seem to do: they split the art between the object as a useful but kind of profane video image and the same object as an appealing but useless presence, like an out-of-work actor.

But there's another possibility: it could be that the object has actually graduated to another use, is furthering a new narrative, which is that of the exhibition. And in that case, the real work has begun, which is reconciliation, making a bridge from one fantasy world of narratives and symbols—that of movies and television—to another, the grown-up world of functionless objects, like in stores or exhibitions. Artists are asked to perform this task of reconciliation all the time. The "artist's statement," for example, or lectures like this one: the artist is used as a bridge from one frame to another. In a funny way, to speak about my own work now, looking at these slides of older work, feels like a splitting. People often want to hear what the artist has to say, what lies "behind" the work, yet at the same time it's taken as performance, and in the end maybe they really don't care to hear the tone and enunciation of a particular speaking voice.

That reminds me of an interesting phrase: "the uncanny valley." It's used by those who work with computer animation or robotics, in Hollywood or advertising. The idea is that people can tolerate robots and computer-generated faces that are crudely humanlike; they can even find them endearing or cute, but when the likeness approaches full realism, it becomes uncanny. The face is no longer seen as a clever likeness but as a real person with whom something is "off." So the uncanny valley is that point at which the verisimilitude of the human likeness achieves a degree of success that consumers find revolting. And that's why, even as the technology allows it, you may not see completely realistic depictions. You're probably going to keep seeing talking horses, or whatever.

In 2004 I had the chance to do a solo show at Reena Spaulings, in New York. I decided that I wanted to make sculptures, which I hadn't done before. And I wanted to keep using the date as a motif, like in the calendars, but I dropped the calendar aspect.
The vacuum-forming process is primarily used in packaging. You go to the drugstore and everything from cosmetics and toothbrushes to batteries and cologne is packaged this way. It starts with a mold, usually made out of wood or metal, as in this slide, and then hot plastic is sucked down around the mold, and you get your hollow shape. In looking back at the history of how artists had used the process, it seemed that while many artists had experimented with the technique briefly, particularly in the 1960s, there were very few bodies of work, and the ones that did exist often took up the logic of signs and signage as the model. Anyway, I started working with the breast and the fist. There seemed to be something strange about packaging the human form this way. I think masks are the only example I can think of in culture.

After that, I wanted to keep working with the body, but to distance it. Something about the bomber jacket is iconic, and it was so open. It's been around since World War I, when it was developed for pilots, but it's had a lot of different lives, it gets taken up by various groups and fed through trends and subcultures. It's here to stay, but it keeps changing, and the changes stack up, and reach back, and affect all the previous iterations. It went nicely with the idea of the date, this kind of faux-vintage effect: a once functional item that's been faithfully re-created for an upscale retailer.

At first I liked the idea that you spend time and energy making a mold of industrial plastic and that you never actually see that object. It's a sculpture you don't show anyone, you just pull impressions off it.

Then I got sick of casting and making molds, which was a real hassle. I started using knotted ropes. You just toss them on the bed of the machine. They get trapped in the plastic, but that's nice. As a viewer you're aware that they're there, behind their own image.

These days the vacuum-forming factories are closing down. All the business is moving to China. I could e-mail a digital file to Shenzhen, where it would be used to produce ten thousand identical vacuum forms that would be shipped back in a cargo container, and this would be cheaper than doing the work around the corner from my studio in Brooklyn. I've had to keep working with new shops as they shut their doors, one by one. It's really an older technology, a holdover from the postwar manufacturing economy.

This 16mm film—these waves—came out of thinking about abstraction, about why there's so little abstract film and video in the art world. Abstraction has a rich history in experimental film and structuralist/materialist film, but all that seems to run on some track parallel to the art world, an impoverished track, kind of like poetry. In any case, when you look at what's exhibited in galleries and museums, there are very few artists working with filmic abstraction. Though recently that does seem to be changing. There's a kind of poetics of silence expressed in abstract film. It's a silence that shuts up the viewer.

Many of the technologies that made this "waves" film possible are based on patents held by one man. Thomas Edison obtained patents on the telephone, which brought me these images over an Internet connection, patents on movie film, on electrical bulbs, on the projector that sends this out on a cone of light, on the movie screen.... How is it possible for one person to hold a patent on all the things that make up this work?

Edison was a maniac for copyright, and in this respect he was ahead of his time. Look at all the lightbulbs he patented, each an idea predicated on minute variations in design—an attempt to cover as much territory as possible. At one point he decided his films needed to be copyrighted, but he was frustrated by the fact that the nascent medium was not yet protected by federal copyright law. He was impatient to assure security for his intellectual property, and he realized that he could make use of the copyright system that existed for still photography. So he went through his films and printed each frame as a separate, unique photographic print, which he then mailed to Washington and copyrighted as its own photograph. What an incredible effort! One that forced the man to break his moving images down into their constituent pieces, reversing the new, magical, illusion of motion, to instead generate thousands of legal documents. It's a strange journey for an image.

When I was making the videos from Internet images, I started thinking about the Net, and how you could take things out of it, but also how you could put things back into it. Any image there is provisional, and refers to data stored elsewhere, and after you take this image, its owner might alter the original, leaving your copy as this unknown and untraceable offcut. There's something unstable about the medium. Anything can be replaced or altered at any time, and nothing ever is truly finished or final.

I started thinking about how to make a piece that not only would use the Internet as medium but would have some of that fragmentary nature, would be dispersed among different media, different forms, and over time. In 2001 I started making compilations of music, produced and distributed by small independent music companies I knew. In each compilation I was trying to locate a genre or moment when production technology changed, and, as a result, there were changes not only in the music's sound, but also in who got to make it, how it was distributed, what the economics were. To accompany each compilation I wrote an essay about these shifts and published it in a non-art magazine. I was hoping this all could stay as one "piece," even though it was composed of different essays and records and physical packaging.

To give an example, when the digital sampler was introduced in the late 1970s, it was a room-size machine and incredibly expensive. Only institutions could afford it. So for a brief time, the musicians making sampler music were mostly academically trained electronic composers, people who came out of Webern or something, because they were the ones with access to university electronic music labs. Some high-end music studios had them, too. But it wasn't really until a bit later that samplers became cheap enough for eighteen-year-olds without a lot of resources, and that's when you really start to get all the experimental musics of the period: techno, the spread of rap. But at the beginning, there's this weird niche where academic composers are pioneering the sampler, and this was the kind of un-named genre I focused on in that compilation and essay.

Music is a funny thing in culture. It has this huge infrastructure, commercially, materially, and socially, this vast apparatus for a product that's extremely immaterial and hard to define, and therefore easy to project onto. And working with music seemed like a good way to think about other things that share those qualities. For instance, it seems like a digital culture tends to operate according to scattering and redundancy, and for now, at least, it's popular music that really encourages this, or where it's clearest. In this sense, it was interesting to think about *Title Variable* as a redundant piece. I mean that the same work simultaneously inhabits different economies in different forms: the essays and music are free online, but they also get packaged in magazines, and they exist as limited-edition vinyl records or artist books, which sell in the art world for art world prices. Maybe commercial culture always winked at the charms of redundancy, but now it finds it has no other option.

I think every writer probably has looked at an old printed text and seen things they'd like to change, but there are protocols of publishing, rules that limit the ways in which you can change older texts. The Net, however, is understood to be a fully manipulable medium; authors may simply update an article or posting. Information there seems to represent not a fixed object, but some kind of state, like the weather. So at some point it became clear to me that nothing in the *Title Variable* project need ever be finished. The music and the essays can be endlessly re-edited, repackaged, re-released, a title can change, the content can change, and it remains the same "piece." Software works like this; it's essentially in flux, always pointing to the next version and the last version, but somehow understood to be the same over time. This has transferred to a lot of my work, including this video.

Making work, you're building a ruin, really. You're making objects that always point elsewhere, that refer to other structures. And these structures are incomplete. They're tokens, icons of transmission. Any piece of art, when it's removed from the studio and removed from the gallery and isolated, is a kind of souvenir of a process of thinking.

I got an e-mail last week from some artists in France who were planning a show of my work based entirely on material they'd taken from the Internet. They'd already put it together; they were just notifying me out of politeness. It's great, not simply to lose control over the work, where it goes, and what happens to it, but the fact that other people naturally assert their right to take this work and manipulate it. It was seen as part of the situation into which I'd placed myself, part of that contract.

You might say, "Yes, of course we value fragmentation over wholeness, the periphery over the center, incompleteness, failure, ambivalence, et cetera." Is it because we know that the way of things is entropic, and to insist otherwise seems naive and backward? For the sake of argument, let's pretend that disruption, diffusion and dispersion, mimesis, parody, and confusion are not only legitimate artistic tools to this end but also desirable and effective tools, or at least fashionable tools. Wouldn't it follow, then, that up is down and yes means now? As if a twist of the kaleidoscope would reveal, in these bright shards, the same world made over as ideal.

But worlds are somehow conjured from these scattered bits and pieces. Walk down the streets of a major media capital, London or New York, looking at all this material, these cubes and grids and planes: these geometric shapes somehow produce fantasies and immaterial imaginings! How is it that all this power and money and image and value are conjured up from these mute surroundings, these dumb objects?

In the end, you need some sort of structuring device to give meaning to all this material. Writing is one thing that structures artwork. But the status of writing in the art world is very strange: writing confers value on the work, but itself has very little value. Writing about an artist legitimates the artist, and it may bring power and money to the artist, but rarely brings power and money to the writer.

In 2002 I finished a written piece that took the form of an illustrated essay. I was really trying to work through some things I was thinking about around my own art. At some point I thought it might be interesting to try to test some of those thoughts by making them public. I published it first as a booklet, as in this slide; then I uploaded it. I think the way the piece moved and circulated was part of the idea, part of what it means to put a kind of nonspecific thing out there. I mean, it acts like an essay, which as a category seems to demand specificity, as distinct from, say, a poem. . . . And it starts to move under its own steam and accrue readings, and that way it can literalize all the things that go on with any piece of art, or cultural product, but as an essay it can make this easier to see, the kind of reading and rewriting that happens when something is at least initially presumed to be a direct or honest expression of what the producer believes. One of the things I wrote about was the phenomenon of the "Daniel Pearl video," which had come out that year. This was really the first of what's been a number of jihadi Internet propaganda videos to become front-page news. In this image you can make out the video still, with the time stamp on the lower right. Anyway, here was this thing in the center of culture, with an unprecedented level of access, but such an incredibly public transmission is actually received totally privately: anybody with a computer can read the debate in the news and then view the evidence in his or her own bedroom. There's a collapsing of public spectacle and private spectacle.

Then there's the intimacy, which goes back to Edison's Kinetoscope, which was intended to be used by one person at a time: you put in some money and bend close to the screen and shut out everything else. And then as the twentieth century develops, that idea changes into cinema, which is publicly received, and then television arrives and enters the private home but still carries a kind of publicness, because you watch a broadcast with millions of other people. But now the Internet, viewed on a home computer, is private and also on demand, and on top of that it requires that you lay hands on the object, you place your fingers on the keyboard as you watch, you're physically attached to the image. . . . It completes the circuit, back to this Kinetoscope idea.

Sometimes in medicine you take a drop of the bad thing, the thing you fight, and you ingest it. It seems as though an advanced Western image culture might displace violence from its own bodies into the realm of images. Something needs that violence to be present still, but somehow dispersed into images, the images that represent the violence that is now done to others in parts of the world that don't exist to us, except as images.

These paintings from the Lascaux caves are eighteen thousand years old. An image like the one in this slide appears to depict an animal being hunted. You can see the arrows finding their mark, on the left. So it might be an expression of desire, some kind of wish fulfillment on the part of the artist. But there's very little agreement about what these images are, or are for. In fact, there are two opposed readings that are sometimes brought out in the same breath or the same text: on the one hand, cave painting is seen as the origin of art, the beginning of the time line of the history of art, the earliest "expression of man." On the other hand, it's manifestly not art, because it's ritualistic, with purpose and a function, in this case, the idea of some social function around food or communication with the spiritual realm.

The image of the hunt here actually comes from a photograph taken not in the real cave but in a full-scale replica that the French government built next to the original so that tourists could experience the paintings without damaging the real cave. You still make a pilgrimage to the site, and enter a cave, but the cave dates from the early 1980s, not from eighteen thousand years ago. So the person who painted the particular image in this artwork is, in fact, known to us. Her name is Monique Pétral.

In some ways poetry—its humble means, its impoverished state—is the antithesis of the contemporary art exhibition. But what they might share is a willingness to keep things in suspension, to leave empty spaces, to focus on the limits of the work. The question why is always simply left alone. As a producer, or really as anyone who visits exhibitions, you have to ask yourself, what does an art exhibition have to give or to teach me? Is the exhibition a model for a way to be, or a way to use things? Does it propose something? Does it add to a conversation? The questions may already be flawed; for example, the notion that we're to learn anything, or the idea that art examines, reveals things, critiques; must you turn to art to learn that there's injustice, that subjectivity is administered, that control and power collect the tickets at the door, that desires are commodified? Might it be that the value of an exhibition comes from the degree to which it lies on the edge between two things, between articulation and incoherence, the old and the new, aesthetic and idea?

On the other hand, how can you compare an exhibition with a poem, a novel, a film, or a performance? Is it a matter purely of taste, of connoisseurship? The facts of connoisseurship seem so arbitrary! Wine, for example: how did wine become the virtually international, trans-historical force that it is? A particular fruit, subjected to a particular procedure: was this predetermined; why not some other fruit, some other procedure? What a particular, almost haphazard phenomenon, storied and celebrated as the peak of connoisseurship, a stand-in for culture and breeding, from antiquity to the present. But low, also, stinking low, in the gutter, on your back, rubbing your eyes: how did such a great year deal you such a harsh blow? Each year, each vintage, is stocked and stored, an object now. It might not be opened at all, it might exist as a sculpture, a small heavy glass piece, bought and sold at auction, passed on to the next owner, appreciated from afar.

There's a question to which no artwork has an answer, to which every artwork is susceptible, which is, so what? There is no answer. You ask it of yourself, as an artist, and there's only silence. It's not a nihilistic question, or pointless skepticism, because the silence produced is actually useful. This silence records an echo: the artist has made a noise and prepared some kind of recording device to capture the echo that comes back. Your utterance now has a shadow that cannot be cast off. This shadow is the work.

Dailies from Rythm Mastr

Kerry James Marshall

2010

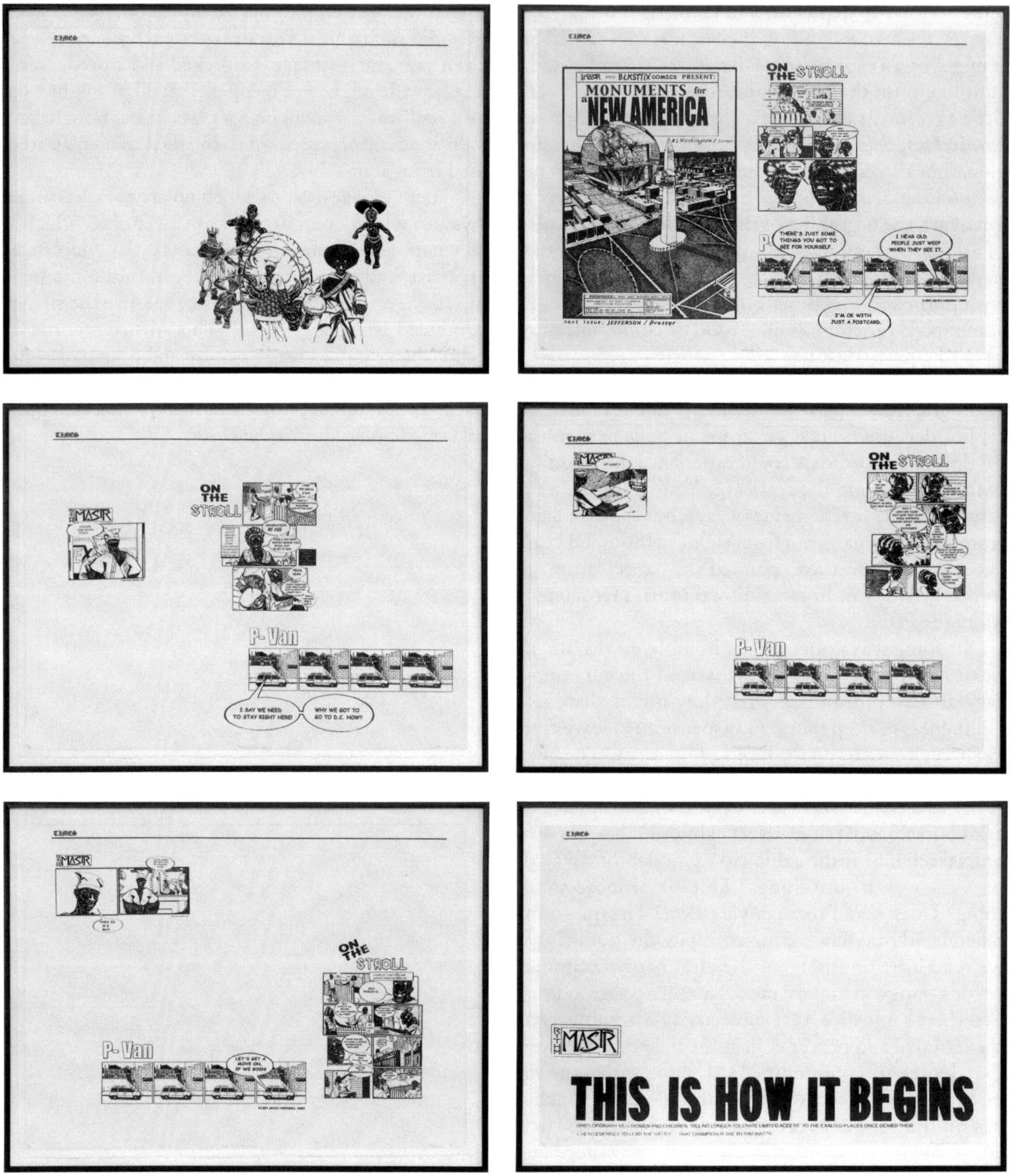

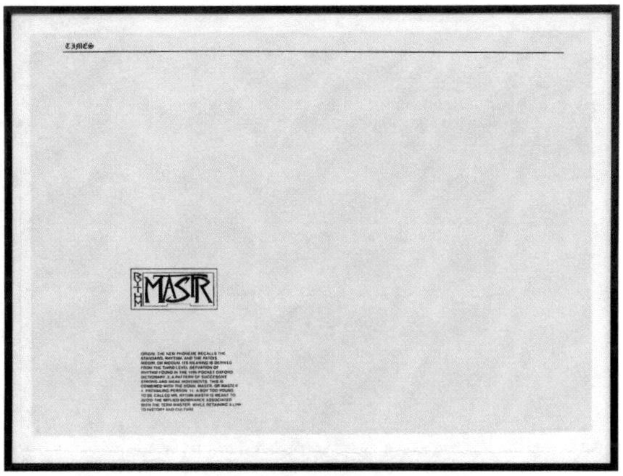
TIMES
RYTHM MASTR

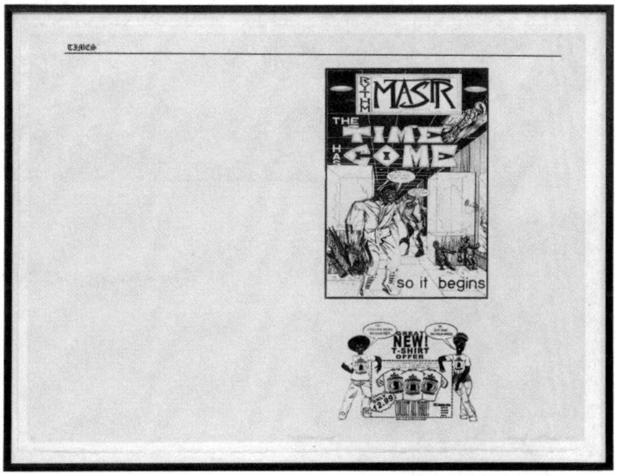
TIMES
RYTHM MASTR
THE TIME HAS COME
so it begins
NEW!
T-SHIRT
OFFER

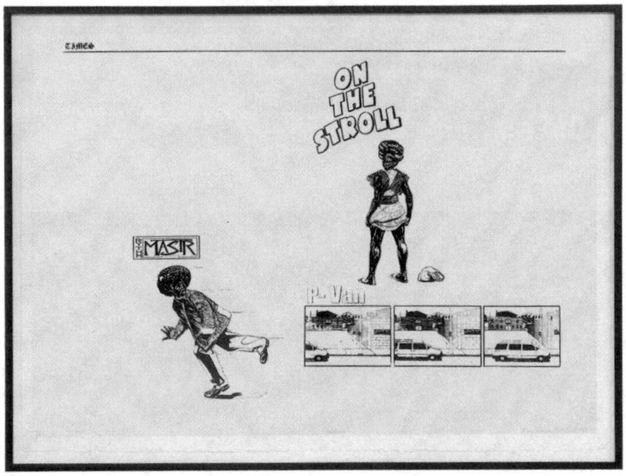
TIMES
ON THE STROLL
RYTHM MASTR
P-Van

Still from *In Free Fall*

Hito Steyerl

2010

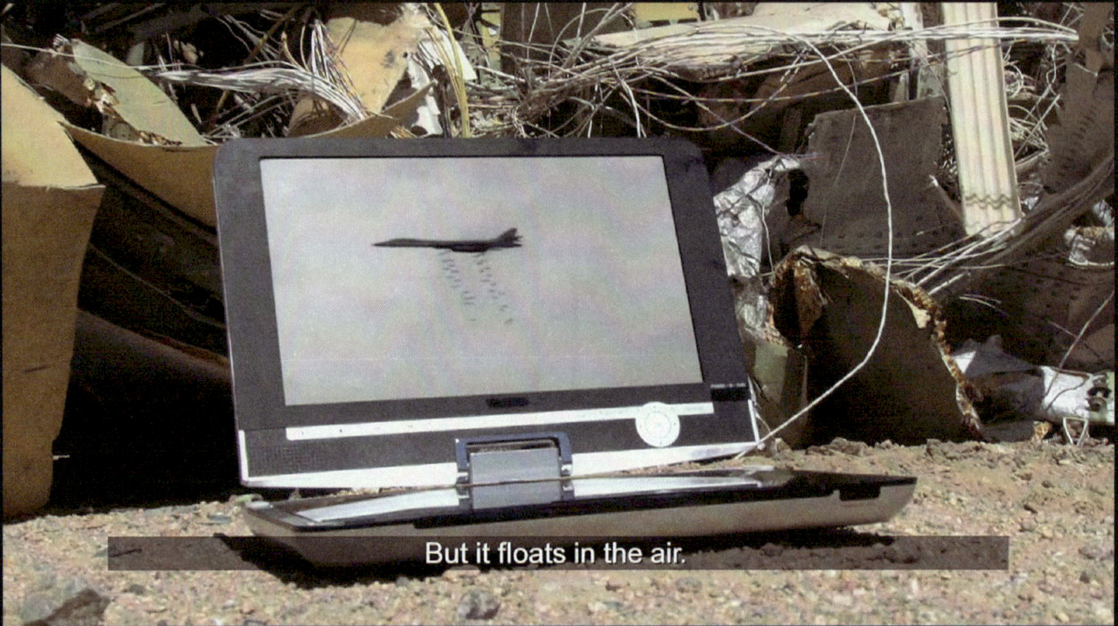

In Free Fall: A Thought Experiment on Vertical Perspective

Hito Steyerl

2011

Imagine you are falling. But there is no ground.

Many contemporary philosophers have pointed out that the present moment is distinguished by a prevailing condition of groundlessness.[1] We cannot assume any stable ground on which to base metaphysical claims or foundational political myths. At best, we are faced with temporary, contingent, and partial attempts at grounding. But if there is no stable ground available for our social lives and philosophical aspirations, the consequence must be a permanent, or at least intermittent state of free fall for subjects and objects alike. But why don't we notice?

Paradoxically, while you are falling, you will probably feel as if you are floating—or not even moving at all. Falling is relational—if there is nothing to fall toward, you may not even be aware that you're falling. If there is no ground, gravity might be low and you'll feel weightless. Objects will stay suspended if you let go of them. Whole societies around you may be falling just as you are. And it may actually feel like perfect stasis—as if history and time have ended and you can't even remember that time ever moved forward.

As you are falling, your sense of orientation may start to play additional tricks on you. The horizon quivers in a maze of collapsing lines and you may lose any sense of above and below, of before and after, of yourself and your boundaries. Pilots have even reported that free fall can trigger a feeling of confusion between the self and the aircraft. While falling, people may sense themselves as being things, while things may sense that they are people. Traditional modes of seeing and feeling are shattered. Any sense of balance is disrupted. Perspectives are twisted and multiplied. New types of visuality arise.

This disorientation is partly due to the loss of a stable horizon. And with the loss of horizon also comes the departure of a stable paradigm of orientation, which has situated concepts of subject and object, of time and space, throughout modernity. In falling, the lines of the horizon shatter, twirl around, and superimpose.

A BRIEF HISTORY OF THE HORIZON

Our sense of spatial and temporal orientation has changed dramatically in recent years, prompted by new technologies of surveillance, tracking, and targeting. One of the symptoms of this transformation is the growing importance of aerial views: overviews, Google Map views, satellite views. We are growing increasingly accustomed to what used to be called a God's-eye view. On the other hand, we also notice the decreasing importance of a paradigm of visuality that long dominated our vision: linear perspective. Its stable and single point of view is being supplemented (and often replaced) by multiple perspectives, overlapping windows, distorted flight lines, and divergent vanishing points. How could these changes be related to the phenomena of groundlessness and permanent fall?

First, let's take a step back and consider the crucial role of the horizon in all of this. Our traditional sense of orientation—and, with it, modern concepts of time and space—are based on a stable line: the horizon line. Its stability hinges on the stability of an observer, who is thought to be located on a ground of sorts, a shoreline, a boat—a ground that can be imagined as stable, even if in fact it is not.

The horizon line was an extremely important element in navigation. It defined the limits of communication and understanding. Beyond the horizon, there was only muteness and silence. Within it, things could be made visible. But it could also be used for determining one's own location and relation to one's surroundings, destinations, or ambitions.

Early navigation consisted of gestures and bodily poses relating to the horizon. "In early days, [Arab navigators] used one or two fingers width, a thumb and little finger on an outstretched arm, or an arrow held at arm's length to sight the horizon at the lower end and Polaris at the upper."[2] The angle between the horizon and the Pole star gave information about the altitude of one's position. This measurement method was known as *sighting* the object, *shooting* the object,

1 Examples of so-called anti- and post-foundational philosophy are given in the preface to Oliver Marchart's introductory volume *Post-Foundational Political Thought: Political Difference in Nancy, Lefort, Badiou and Laclau* (Edinburgh: Edinburgh University Press, 1997), 1–10. Briefly speaking, such thought, as proffered by the philosophers under discussion, rejects the idea of a given and stable metaphysical ground and revolves around Heideggerian metaphors of abyss and ground, as well as the absence of ground. Ernesto Laclau describes the experience of contingency and groundlessness as a possible experience of freedom.

2 Peter Ifland, "The History of the Sextant"; see http://www.mat.uc.pt/~helios/Mestre/Novemboo/H61iflan.htm.

or *taking a sight*. In this way, one's own location could be at least roughly determined.

Instruments like the astrolabe, quadrant, and sextant refined this way of gaining orientation by using the horizon and the stars. One of the main obstacles with this technology was the fact that the ground on which sailors stood was never stable in the first place. The stable horizon mostly remained a projection, until artificial horizons were eventually invented in order to create the illusion of stability.

The use of the horizon to calculate position gave seafarers a sense of orientation, thus also enabling colonialism and the spread of a capitalist global market, but also became an important tool for the construction of the optical paradigms that came to define modernity, the most important paradigm being that of so-called linear perspective.

As early as 1028, Abu Ali al-Hasan ibn al-Haytham (965–1040), also known as Alhazen, wrote a book of visual theory, *Kitab al-Manazir*. After 1200, it became available in Europe and spawned numerous experiments in visual production between the thirteenth and fifteenth centuries, which culminated in the development of linear perspective.

In Duccio's *Last Supper* (1308–1311), several vanishing points are still evident. The perspectives in this space do not coalesce into a horizon line, nor do they all intersect in one single vanishing point. But in *Miracle of the Desecrated Host (Scene I)* (1465–69), painted by Paolo Uccello, who was one of the most ardent experimenters in the development of linear perspective, the perspective is aligned to culminate in one single vanishing point, located on a virtual horizon defined by the eye line.

Linear perspective is based on several decisive negations. First, the curvature of the earth is typically disregarded. The horizon is conceived as an abstract flat line upon which the points on any horizontal plane converge. Additionally, as Erwin Panofsky argued, the construction of linear perspective declares the view of a one-eyed and immobile spectator as a norm—and this view is itself assumed to be natural, scientific, and objective. Thus, linear perspective is based on an abstraction, and does not correspond to any subjective perception.[3] Instead, it computes a mathematical, flattened, infinite, continuous, and homogenous space, and declares it to be reality. Linear perspective creates the illusion of a quasi-natural view to the "outside," as if the image plane was a window opening onto the "real" world. This is also the literal meaning of the Latin *perspectiva*: to see through.

This space defined by linear perspective is calculable, navigable, and predictable. It allows the calculation of future risk, which can be anticipated, and therefore, managed. As a consequence, linear perspective not only transforms space, but also introduces the notion of a linear time, which allows mathematical prediction and, with it, linear progress. This is the second, temporal meaning of perspective: a view onto a calculable future. As Walter Benjamin argued, time can become just as homogenous and empty as space.[4] And for all these calculations to operate, we must necessarily assume an observer standing on a stable ground looking out towards a vanishing point on a flat, and actually quite artificial, horizon.

But linear perspective also performs an ambivalent operation concerning the viewer. As the whole paradigm converges in one of the viewer's eyes, the viewer becomes central to the worldview established by it. The viewer is mirrored in the vanishing point, and thus constructed by it. The vanishing point gives the observer a body and a position. But on the other hand, the spectator's importance is also undermined by the assumption that vision follows scientific laws. While empowering the subject by placing it at the center of vision, linear perspective also undermines the viewer's individuality by subjecting it to supposedly objective laws of representation.

Needless to say, this reinvention of the subject, time, and space was an additional toolkit for enabling Western dominance, and the dominance of its concepts—as well as for redefining standards of representation, time, and space. All of these components are evident in Uccello's six-panel painting, *Miracle of the Desecrated Host* (1465–69). In the first panel, a woman sells a Host to a Jewish merchant, who in the second panel tries to "desecrate" it. For this, the Jewish merchant ends up at the stakes. Along with his wife and two small children, he is tied to a pillar on which parallels converge as if it were a target mark. The date of these panels shortly prefigures the expulsion of Jews and Muslims from Spain in 1492, also the year of Christopher Columbus's expedition to the West Indies.[5] In these paintings, linear perspective becomes a matrix for racial and religious propaganda, and related atrocities. This so-called scientific worldview helped set standards for marking people as other, thus legitimizing their conquest or the domination over them.

On the other hand, linear perspective also carries the seeds of its own downfall. Its scientific allure and objectivist attitude established a universal claim for representation, a link to veracity that undermined particularistic

3 Erwin Panofsky, "Die Perspektive alssymbolische Form," in *Erwin Panofsky: Deutschsprachige Aufsätze II*, ed. Wolfgang Kemp et al. (Berlin: AkademieVerlag, 1998), 664–758.

4 Walter Benjamin, "Theses on the Philosophy of History," in *Illuminations*, trans. H. Zohn. (New York: Schocken Books, 1969), 261. See http://www.marxists.org/reference/archive/benjamin/1940/history.htm.

5 Étienne Balibar and Immanuel Wallerstein, *Race, Nation, Class: Ambiguous Identities* (London and New York: Verso, 1991).

worldviews, even if halfheartedly and belatedly. It thus became a hostage to the truth it had so confidently proclaimed. And a deep suspicion was planted alongside its claims for veracity from its inception.

THE DOWNFALL OF LINEAR PERSPECTIVE

But the situation now is somewhat different. We seem to be in a state of transition toward one or several other visual paradigms. Linear perspective has been supplemented by other types of vision to the point where we may have to conclude that its status as the dominant visual paradigm is changing.

This transition was already apparent in the nineteenth century in the field of painting. One work in particular expresses the circumstances of this transformation: *The Slave Ship* (1840), by J. M. W. Turner. The scene in the painting represents a real incident: when the captain of a slave ship discovered that his insurance only covered slaves lost at sea, and not those dying or ill on board, he ordered all dying and sick slaves to be thrown overboard. Turner's painting captures the moment where the slaves are beginning to go under.

In this painting, the horizon line, if distinguishable at all, is tilted, curved, and troubled. The observer has lost his stable position. There are no parallels that could converge at a single vanishing point. The sun, which is at the center of the composition, is multiplied in reflections. The observer is upset, displaced, beside himself at the sight of the slaves, who are not only sinking but have also had their bodies reduced to fragments—their limbs devoured by sharks, mere shapes below the water surface. At the sight of the effects of colonialism and slavery, linear perspective—the central viewpoint, the position of mastery, control, and subjecthood—is abandoned and starts tumbling and tilting, taking with it the idea of space and time as systematic constructions. The idea of a calculable and predictable future shows a murderous side through an insurance that prevents economic loss by inspiring cold-blooded murder. Space dissolves into mayhem on the unstable and treacherous surface of an unpredictable sea.

Turner experimented with moving perspectives early on. Legend has it that he had himself tied to the mast of a ship crossing from Dover to Calais, explicitly to watch the horizon change. In 1843 or 1844, he stuck his head out of the window of a moving train for exactly 9 minutes, the result of which was a painting called *Rain, Steam, and Speed—The Great Western Railway* (1844). In it, linear perspective dissolves into the background. There is no resolution, no vanishing point, and no clear view to any past or future. Again, more interesting is the perspective of the spectator himself, who seems to be dangling in the air on the outer side of the rails of a railroad bridge. There is no clear ground under his assumed position. He might be suspended in the mist, floating over an absent ground.

In both of Turner's paintings, the horizon is blurred, tilted, and yet not necessarily denied. The paintings do not negate its existence altogether, but render it inaccessible to the viewer's perception. The question of horizon starts to float, so to speak. Perspectives assume mobile points of view and communication is disabled even within one common horizon. One could say that the downward motion of the sinking slaves affects the point of view of the painter, who tears it away from a position of certitude, and subjects it to gravity and motion and the pull of a bottomless sea.

ACCELERATION

With the twentieth century, the further dismantling of linear perspective in a variety of areas began to take hold. Cinema supplements photography with the articulation of different temporal perspectives. Montage becomes a perfect device for destabilizing the observer's perspective and breaking down linear time. Painting abandons representation to a large extent and demolishes linear perspective in cubism, collage, and different types of abstraction. Time and space are reimagined through quantum physics and the theory of relativity, while perception is reorganized by warfare, advertisement, and the conveyor belt. With the invention of aviation, opportunities for falling, nose-diving, and crashing increase. With it—and especially with the conquest of outer space—comes the development of new perspectives and techniques of orientation, found especially in an increasing number of aerial views of all kinds. While all these developments can be described as typical characteristics of modernity, the past few years have seen visual culture saturated by military and entertainment images' views from above.

Aircraft expand the horizon of communication and act as aerial cameras providing backgrounds for aerial map views. Drones survey, track, and kill. But the entertainment industry is busy as well. Especially in 3D cinema, the new characteristics of aerial views are fully exploited by staging vertiginous flights into abysses. One could almost say that 3D and the construction of imaginary vertical worlds (prefigured in the logic of computer games) are essential to each other. 3D also intensifies hierarchies of material required to access this new visuality. As Thomas Elsaesser has argued, a hardware environment integrating military, surveillance, and entertainment applications produces new markets for hardware and software.[6]

In a fascinating text, Eyal Weizman analyzes verticality in political architecture, describing the spatial turn of sovereignty and surveillance in terms of a vertical 3D sovereignty.[7] He argues that geopolitical power was once distributed on a planar map-like surface on which boundaries were drawn and defended. But at present, the distribution of power—he cites the Israeli occupation in Palestine as his example, but there could be many others—has increasingly come to occupy a vertical dimension. Vertical sovereignty splits space into stacked horizontal layers, separating not only airspace from ground, but also splitting ground from underground, and airspace into various layers. Different strata of community are divided from each other on a y-axis, multiplying sites of conflict and violence. As Achille Mbembe contends,

> Occupation of the skies therefore acquires a critical importance, since most of the policing is done from the air. Various other technologies are mobilized to this effect: sensors aboard unmanned air vehicles (UAVs), aerial reconnaissance jets, early warning Hawkeye planes, assault helicopters, an Earth-observation satellite, techniques of "hologrammatization."[8]

FREE FALL

But how to link this obsessive policing, division, and representation of ground to the philosophical assumption that in contemporary societies there is no ground to speak of? How do these aerial representations—in which grounding effectively constitutes a privileged subject—link to the hypothesis that we currently inhabit a condition of free fall?

The answer is simple: many of the aerial views, 3D nose-dives, Google Maps, and surveillance panoramas do not actually portray a stable ground. Instead, they create a supposition that it exists in the first place. Retroactively, this virtual ground creates a perspective of overview and surveillance for a distanced, superior spectator safely floating up in the air. Just as linear perspective established an imaginary stable observer and horizon, so does the perspective from above establish an imaginary floating observer and an imaginary stable ground.

This establishes a new visual normality—a new subjectivity safely folded into surveillance technology and screen-based distraction.[9] One might conclude that this is in fact a radicalization—though not an overcoming—of the paradigm of linear perspective. In it, the former distinction between object and subject is exacerbated and turned into the one-way gaze of superiors onto inferiors, a looking down from high to low. Additionally, the displacement of perspective creates a disembodied and remote-controlled gaze, outsourced to machines and other objects.[10] Gazes already became decisively mobile and mechanized with the invention of photography, but new technologies have enabled the detached observant gaze to become ever more inclusive and all-knowing to the point of becoming massively intrusive—as militaristic as it is pornographic, as intense as extensive, both micro- and macroscopic.[11]

---

6 The following quote by Elsaesser can be seen as blueprint for this paper, whose inspiration derives from an informal conversation with the author: "This means that stereoscopic images and the 3-D movie are part of the new paradigm, which is turning our information society into a control society and our visual culture into a surveillance culture. The movie industry, civil society and the military sector are all united in this surveillance paradigm, which, as part of a historic process, seeks to replace 'monocular vision,' the way of seeing that has defined Western thought and action for the last 500 years. It is this means of seeing that gave rise to a wide range of innovations like panel painting, colonial seafaring and Cartesian philosophy, as well as the whole concept of projecting ideas, risks, chances and courses of action into the future. Flight simulators and other types of military technology are part of a new effort to introduce 3-D as the standard means of perception—but the development goes even further to include surveillance. This encompasses an entire catalog of movements and behaviors, all of which are intrinsically connected to the monitoring, steering and observation of ongoing processes, and which delegate or outsource what was once referred to as introspection, self-awareness and personal responsibility." Thomas Elsaesser, "The Dimension of Depth and Objects Rushing Towards Us. Or: The Tail that Wags the Dog. A Discourse on Digital 3-D Cinema." See http://www.edit-frankfurt.de/en/magazine/ausgabe-12010/the-dimension-of-depth/the-dimension-of-depth-and-objects-rushing-towards-us.html.

7 Eyal Weizman, "The Politics of Verticality." See http://www.opendemocracy.net/ecology-politicsverticality/article_801.jsp.

8 Achille Mbembe, "Necropolitics," *Public Culture* vol. 15, no. 1 (Winter 2003): 29. See http://www.jhfc.duke.edu/icuss/pdfs/Mbembe.pdf.

9 Dieter Roelstraete and Jennifer Allen both describe this new normality from different perspectives in very good texts. Dieter Roelstraete "(Jena Revisited) Ten Tentative Tenets," *e-flux journal*, issue 16 (May, 2010). See http://www.e-flux.com/journal/view/137; and Jennifer Allen, "That Eye, The Sky," *Frieze* 132 (June–August 2010).

10 Lisa Parks, *Cultures in Orbit: Satellites and the Televisual* (Durham, NC: Duke University Press, 2005).

11 In fact, the perspective of the floating camera belongs to a dead man. Most recently, a dehumanization (or posthumanization) of the gaze is perhaps nowhere as literally allegorized as in the film *Enter the Void* (Gaspar Noé, 2010), where, for most of the film, a disembodied point of view endlessly drifts over Tokyo. This gaze penetrates any space, moving without constraint and with unrestricted mobility, looking for a body in which to biologically reproduce itself and reincarnate. The point of view in *Enter the Void* is reminiscent of the gaze of a drone. But instead of bringing death, it is looking to recreate its own life. To this end, the protagonist basically wants to hijack a fetus. But the film is also very picky about this procedure: mixed race fetuses get aborted in favor of white ones. There are more issues that link the movie to reactionary breeding ideologies. Floating and biopolitical policing are mixed into a computer-animated obsession with superior bodies, remote control, and digital aerial vision. The floating gaze of the dead man thus literally echoes Achille Mbembe's powerful description of necropower: necropower regulates life through the perspective of death. Could these tropes allegorized in a single (and frankly, god-awful) movie be expanded into a more general analysis of disembodied hovering point of views? Do the aerial views, drone perspectives, and 3D dives into abysses stand in for the gazes of "dead white males," a worldview which lost its vitality, yet persists as an undead but powerful tool to police the world and control its own reproduction?

THE POLITICS OF VERTICALITY

The view from above is a perfect metonymy for a more general verticalization of class relations in the context of an intensified class war from above—seen through the lenses and on the screens of military, entertainment, and information industries.[12] It is a proxy perspective that projects delusions of stability, safety, and extreme mastery onto a backdrop of expanded 3D sovereignty. But if the new views from above recreate societies as free-falling urban abysses and splintered terrains of occupation, surveilled aerially and policed biopolitically, they may also—as linear perspective did—carry the seeds of their own demise within them. As linear perspective began to tumble down with the sinking bodies of slaves thrown into the ocean, for many people today the simulated grounds of aerial imagery provide an illusionary tool of orientation in a condition in which the horizons have, in fact, been shattered. Time is out of joint and we no longer know whether we are objects or subjects as we spiral down in an imperceptible free fall.[13]

But if we accept the multiplication and delinearization of horizons and perspectives, the new tools of vision may also serve to express, and even alter, the contemporary conditions of disruption and disorientation. Recent 3D animation technologies incorporate multiple perspectives, which are deliberately manipulated to create multifocal and nonlinear imagery.[14] Cinematic space is twisted in any way imaginable, organized around heterogeneous, curved, and collaged perspectives. The tyranny of the photographic lens, cursed by the promise of its indexical relation to reality, has given way to hyperreal representations—not of space as it is, but of space as we can make it—for better or worse. There is no need for expensive renderings; a simple green screen collage yields impossible cubist perspectives and implausible concatenations of times and spaces alike.

Finally, cinema has caught up with the representational freedoms of painting and structural and experimental film. As it merges with graphic design practices, drawing, and collage, cinema has gained independence from the prescribed focal dimensions that have normalized and limited the realm of its vision. While it could be argued that montage was the first step towards a liberation from cinematic linear perspective—and was for this reason ambivalent for most of its existence—only now can new and different sorts of spatial vision be created. Similar things can be said about multiscreen projections, which create a dynamic viewing space, dispersing perspective and possible points of view. The viewer is no longer unified by such a gaze, but is rather dissociated and overwhelmed, drafted into the production of content. None of these projection spaces suppose a single unified horizon. Rather, many call for a multiple spectator, who must be created and recreated by ever-new articulations of the crowd.[15]

In many of these new visualities, what seemed like a helpless tumble into an abyss actually turns out to be a new representational freedom. And perhaps this helps us get over the last assumption implicit in this thought experiment: the idea that we need a ground in the first place. In his discussion of the vertiginous, Theodor W. Adorno scoffs at philosophy's obsession with earth and origin, with a philosophy of belonging that obviously comes packaged within the most violent fear of the groundless and bottomless. For him, the vertiginous is not about the panicked loss of a ground imagined to be a safe haven of being:

> A cognition that is to bear fruit will throw itself to the objects à *fond perdu* [without hope]. The vertigo which this causes is an *index veri*; the shock of inclusiveness, the negative as which it cannot help appearing in the frame-covered, never-changing realm, is true for untruth only.[16]

A fall toward objects without reservation, embracing a world of forces and matter, which lacks any original stability and sparks the sudden shock of the open: a freedom that is terrifying, utterly deterritorializing, and always already unknown. Falling means ruin and demise as well as love and abandon, passion and surrender, decline and catastrophe. Falling is corruption

12 Paraphrasing Elsaesser's notion of the "military-surveillance-entertainment complex." See http://www.edit-frankfurt.de/en/magazine/ausgabe-12010/the-dimension-of-depth/the-dimension-of-depth-and-objects-rushing-towards-us.html.

13 Assuming there is no ground, even those on the bottom of hierarchies keep falling.

14 These techniques are described in Manessh Agrawala, Denis Zorin, and Tamara Munzer, "Artistic multiprojection rendering," in *Proceedings of the Eurographics Workshop on Rendering Techniques 2000*, ed. Bernard Peroche and Holly E. Rusgmaier (London: Springer-Verlag, 2000), 125–136; Patrick Coleman and Karan Singh, "Ryan: Rendering Your Animation Nonlinearly Projected," in *NPAR '04: Proceedings of the 3rd International Symposium on Non-photorealistic Animation and Rendering* (New York: ACM Press, 2004), 129–156; Andrew Glassner, "Digital Cubism, part 2," *IEEE Computer Graphics and Applications*, vol. 25, no. 4 (July 2004): 84–95; Karan Singh, "A Fresh Perspective," in *Proceedings of the Eurographics Workshop on Rendering Techniques 2000*, ed. Bernard Peroche and Holly E. Rusgmaier (London: Springer-Verlag, 2000), 17–24; Nisha Sudarsanam, Cindy Grimm, and Karan Singh, "Interactive Manipulation of Projections with a Curved Perspective," *Computer Graphics Forum 24* (2005): 105–108; and Yonggao Yang, Jim X. Chen, and Mohsen Beheshti, "Nonlinear Perspective Projections and Magic Lenses: 3D View Deformation," *IEEE Computer Graphics Applications*, vol. 25, no. 1 (January/February 2005): 76–84.

15 Hito Steyerl, "Is a Museum a Factory?" *e-flux journal*, issue 7 (June, 2009). See http://www.e-flux.com/journal/view/71.

16 Theodor W. Adorno, *Negative Dialectics*, trans. E. B. Ashton (New York: Continuum, 1972), 43.

as well as liberation, a condition that turns people into things and vice versa. It takes place in an opening we could endure or enjoy, embrace or suffer, or simply accept as reality.

Finally, the perspective of free fall teaches us to consider a social and political dreamscape of radicalized class war from above, one that throws jaw-dropping social inequalities into sharp focus. But falling does not only mean falling apart, it can also mean a new certainty falling into place. Grappling with crumbling futures that propel us backwards onto an agonizing present, we may realize that the place we are falling toward is no longer grounded, nor is it stable. It promises no community, but a shifting formation.

Photography and the Law: Five Groundbreaking Cases of Photography in Litigation
Daniel McClean
2011

The Law has always been interested in photographs: not only what they capture as evidence but also who makes, owns, circulates and sees them. For the Law grasps the unique descriptive power of the photograph to trace and to appropriate the world as an image and consign this image to limitless contexts. The fate of the photograph—including its disappearance from public view—has often been decided in a courtroom.

While legislation differs from country to country, the Law has traditionally regulated taking, circulating and using photographs for different ends. At one end of the spectrum, the Law grants individuals rights over photographs (privacy, copyright, publicity); at the other end, it censors photographic images on society's behalf (indecency, pornography, child protection).

Whatever the legal case and country, a possessor of rights must be constructed and located in relation to the photograph for the Law to have efficacy. The Law moves backwards to find this subject, as it moves forwards to interrogate the photograph's public reception. This legal subject is contingent and constructed in different ways in relation to each image—not just due to differences between legal systems.

Each case is like a game of hide-and-seek: the legal subject might be on the photograph, behind the camera or emerging in public space. Even when the Law favours the circulation of the photograph—which it often does—there are many subjects at stake, including society's interest in viewing the image.

THE CITIZEN AS ARTIST

The Law's response to the photograph of the German Chancellor Otto von Bismarck (1815–98)—lying dishevelled on his deathbed—illuminates the fluid relationship between the photograph and the legal subject. The picture was taken shortly after Bismarck's death on 30 July 1898 by Max Priester and Willy Wilcke, who clandestinely entered his bedroom at Schloß Friedrichsruh after family members paid their last respects. Paparazzi *avant la lettre*, Priester and Wilcke sought to profit from the photograph, advertising it for sale in a newspaper. Bismarck's family quickly intervened to prevent the sale and instigated a civil and criminal case.

Making a case against Priester and Wilcke was difficult because no laws regulating photography existed.

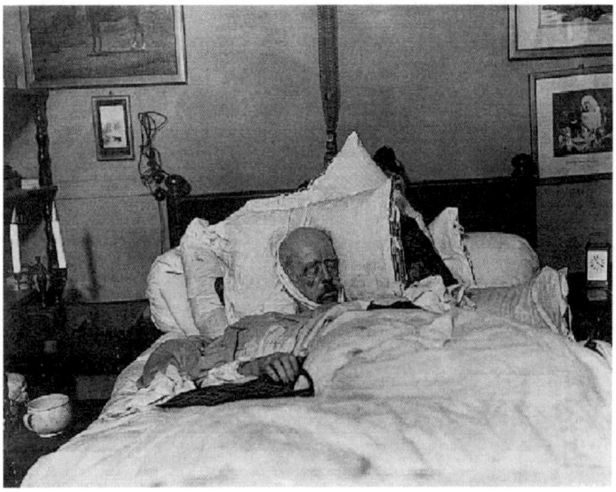

Figure 1. Max Priester & Willi Wilcke. Schleswig-Holstein, Aumühle: Friedrichsuh, *Bismarck on his Deathbead*, 1898.

By merely taking pictures, they had not disturbed the peace of the dead. The court found them guilty of breaking into Schloß Friedrichsruh and sentenced them to several months in jail. The legal subject was not Bismarck but the castle owners, namely, his heirs who did not appear in the picture. Although plates and reproductions were confiscated and destroyed, one print survived and was first published in the *Frankfurter Illustrierte* in 1953.

In 1907, a law was passed granting individuals the power to control the appearance and the use of their image in public, including after death. A private subject came to exist with rights to control any photographic likeness, and heirs would be able to exercise these rights posthumously for ten years.

Surprisingly, the German *Recht am eigenen Bild* (literally, right to one's image) became part of copyright law, specifically regarding art works and photography—a law designed to protect the authors of cultural works. In France, the corresponding *droit à l'image* is part of the civil laws regarding privacy, not copyright. In the US, the 'right of publicity' exists in some states alongside privacy laws; in the UK, there are no such rights although celebrities and well-known figures can prevent their images being used to suggest 'false endorsement'.

This startling inversion in German law turns the citizen into an author and owner of his or her appearance while the photographer is merely copying the original and must thus ask for permission to publish any portrait. Perhaps Bismarck's legacy was to grant every German citizen a piece of property for life (and ten years after): his or her image as an original art work. It's an uncanny presage of Joseph Beuys's claim: Everyone is an artist.

Taryn Simon's exhibition at Berlin's Neue Nationalgalerie 'A Living Man Declared Dead and Other Chapters I–XVIII', which runs until 1 January 2012, demonstrates this claim. Simon made individual portraits of the members of various bloodlines, including the descendants and surviving relatives of Hans Frank, Adolf Hitler's legal advisor and governor-general of occupied Poland.

Some Frank family portraits are 'empty' because the subjects refused to participate. Others sent only their clothes to be photographed; one relative requested that his portrait be pixelated. In Simon's other bloodlines, family members tend to be missing due to restrictions: imprisonment, military service, illness or religious and social reasons. But in Frank's bloodline, the empty portraits represent the presence of legal subjects exercising their legitimate rights as owners, if not artists.

HISTORICAL FIGURE OR PRIVATE PERSON?

Although Germany recognizes strong image rights, exemptions are carved out for a public interest in the image—or the viewing civic subjects. It is permissible to take photographs of individuals of 'historic' significance, particularly when they are in public space. Here, the Law is required to balance the interests of the individual photographed against society and to decide who should prevail.

Surprisingly, the European Court of Human Rights held in 2004 that even a royal figure like Princess Caroline of Monaco cannot be regarded a public person and that anodyne photographs of her taken without her consent, for example, riding a horse or dropping her children off at school, infringed her 'reasonable expectation' of privacy.

In German courts, the Princess had largely failed to foil the paparazzi. In 1995, the Federal Supreme Court judged her a figure of historical significance, which justified the public interest in her life and thus the publication of images of her. In 1999, the Federal Constitutional Court upheld the ruling but exempted photographs of her with her children—thus creating a new set of legal subjects to be considered and protected.

By contrast, the European Court held that Princess Caroline was not a public figure since she exercised no 'official state function'. The photographs could not trump her right to privacy on the grounds of freedom of expression because the images did not 'contribute to a debate of genuine importance in a democratic society'. Here, Article 8 (the right to respect for private and family life) in the European Convention of Human Rights overrode Article 10 (the right to freedom of expression, including imparting and receiving information and ideas).

In these cases, the legal subject disappears, just as it reappears in a different guise. Princess Caroline is reconstructed as a private individual while the public domain loses its rights as a civic viewing subject. The European Court's decision—which allowed Princess Caroline later to be awarded compensation—leaves the law of privacy completely at odds with a celebrity-based culture whose icons clearly do not exercise 'state functions' and whose surrounding discourse does not fuel so-called 'democratic' debate.

The matter is far from settled. The battle between the princess and the paparazzi was back in the Federal Supreme Court in 2007 and Federal Constitutional Court in 2008. The judges must decide—picture by picture—whether the images help the formation of public opinion on questions of general interest.

THE MAN IN THE STREET

In her book *The Civil Contract of Photography* (2008), Ariella Azoulay describes a 'civil space of photography' where the permission to stare constitutes an unwritten contract between photographers, subjects and viewers. Yet much street photography is based upon an absence of consent from the individual depicted in the photograph, which can lead to litigation. As in the Caroline cases, the Law considers the right to privacy, but the photographer emerges as a legal subject with rights because s/he is working as an artist.

In 1999, the photographer Luc Delahaye published the book *L'Autre* (The Other), with a text by Jean Baudrillard and portraits of commuters in the Paris Métro whom Delahaye snapped with a hidden camera. Delahaye admitted to the French media that he had 'stolen' the commuters' images, but it was the only way to show their 'solitude' and 'silence'. One commuter, Neji Bensalah—whose portrait appeared in *L'Autre* and as a still in Michael Haneke's film *Code inconnu* (Code Unknown, 2000)—took Delahaye, Magnum (his agency at the time), the publisher Phaidon and Haneke's production company to court.

Bensalah invoked not only his right to control his image—and to share profits earned from it—but also other viewing subjects, missing from the picture. He claimed that the portrait had 'negative repercussions' on his family. In 2004, the *Tribunal de grande instance de Paris* decided against him in a groundbreaking judgment.

While German image rights can be offset by the subject's historical significance and the public's interest, French image rights can be offset by the photographer's claim to freedom of expression. Surprisingly, the Paris court cited freedom of expression, not in French law, but in Article 10 of the European Convention of Human Rights, in particular the right to impart and to receive information and ideas. Moreover, the court interpreted 'ideas' as being 'expressed especially in the work of an artist.'

Delahaye became the legal subject as artist who trumped Bensalah's right to his image and privacy. By citing the European Convention, the case recasts the Caroline cases; what if the paparazzi had defined their photographs of the princess as art? By linking 'ideas' to art works, the Paris court weakened the French *droit à l'image* which must be weighed against information and art.

In 2000, the artist Philip-Lorca diCorcia photographed an elderly Hasidic Jew, Erno Nussenzweig in Times Square, New York, without his permission. Nussenzweig is diCorcia's *Head #13* (2001) in the 'heads' series (2001). Upon discovering his image in 2005, Nussenzweig sued the artist and his gallery Pace/McGill. By 2007, the case reached the Supreme Court of New York State, which recognizes rights to publicity and privacy in state civil law.

Was the prevailing legal subject behind the camera or on the photograph? diCorcia argued for freedom of expression as an artist, just as Nussenzweig claimed his right to privacy as well as to the free exercise of his religion as a Hasidic Jew. Freedom of expression and freedom of religion are both guaranteed by the First Amendment to the US Constitution, which has precedence over state laws.

Since each legal subject was protected by the First Amendment, one key question (among many raised in the case) emerged. Whose constitutional right should have precedence: diCorcia's right to expression or Nussenzweig's right to religion? Once again, other subjects suddenly appeared who were neither on the photograph, nor behind the camera.

diCorcia's affidavit included references to his long career as an artist and a photographer working in the tradition of street photography, which dates back to Alfred Stieglitz (1864–1946). Nussenzweig argued that taking his photograph for commercial and public purposes violated his religious beliefs, namely the Second Commandment, which forbids making graven images, including the likeness of any thing on earth. Where diCorcia pointed to the subjects in his other photographs and Stieglitz's work to support his case, Nussenzweig invoked God, if not the legal system of the Ten Commandments, which diCorcia was forcing him to disobey by taking and circulating his likeness in exhibitions and publications. The court sided with diCorcia on this issue and others. The photographer trumped his subject; in a way, art trumped the Ten Commandments.

THE PHOTOGRAPHER AS AUTHOR

What happens when photographers are pitted against photographers? Or against artists who appropriate photographs without permission? Copyright is the primary legal mechanism whereby photographers and artists control the circulation and reproduction of their works in multiple media. This property—which is abstracted from and exists independently of the actual work and which persists for the life of its creator and often several decades after death—can be sold, licensed and gifted by the creator or by heirs. While copyright law often casts the creator as a prevailing legal subject, it protects separately any 'original' additions made to the work by others.

Copyright law initially grappled with the medium since photographs were considered to be mechanical copies of nature, not original authored works, let alone art works. But by the late 19th century, photographers were recognized as authors in many countries. In the seminal US case Burrow-Giles Lithographic Co. versus Sarony (1884), a portrait of Oscar Wilde gained copyright protection since the photographer posed the subject and chose his clothing and the lighting, among other 'original' contributions to the creation of the portrait.

Does a photograph appropriated and transformed by an artist still belong to the photographer? This question fueled a case heard earlier this year in the US District Court for the Southern District of New York. Without seeking consent, Richard Prince used at least 41 black and white photographs from Patrick Cariou's book *Yes Rasta* (2000). Cariou's photographs were the result of his six-year stay with the Rastafarian community in Jamaica and were made with the community's blessing. Prince incorporated the photographs into his series of collages and paintings 'Canal Zone' (2007–8), which were exhibited and sold by Gagosian Gallery and distributed in an eponymous catalogue published by Rizzoli. In December 2008, Cariou sued Prince, Larry Gagosian, Gagosian Gallery and Rizzoli for copyright infringement. On 18 March 2011, the court decided in Cariou's favour.

During the trial, Prince's lawyers argued that his reproductions of Cariou's photographs were lawful on the grounds of 'fair use', which is defined by Section 107 of the US Copyright Act of 1976 and which exempts valuable forms of cultural expression from infringement. Fairness depends on four factors: the character and purpose of the use (for example, commercial versus educational); the nature of the copyrighted work; the amount of the work used; and the effect of the use upon the work's potential market. US courts apply these factors flexibly, but arguably the most significant factor is how far the original has been 'transformed' by appropriation. Did the artist simply copy or create a brand new work?

Prince's lawyers argued that his use of Cariou's images was 'transformative' and thus fair. Judge Deborah A. Batts decided that there was no fair use on any count. Prince's works were not transformative since they did not comment on Cariou's photographs; Prince testified that he had no interest in their original meaning. The less transformative the copies, the more importance attached to their commercial use; sales and trades resulting from Prince's works were estimated at over $16 million USD. By failing to ask Cariou's permission, Prince and the related defendant parties had acted in 'bad faith' while taking a substantial number of Rasta images. Finally, Judge Batts found that Prince's copies damaged both the actual and the potential market for Cariou's work. After learning of Prince's exhibition, the Manhattan gallerist Christiane Celle cancelled a Cariou exhibition because she did not want to be seen as capitalizing on Prince's success, nor to exhibit work already done at another gallery.

In a remarkable twist, Judge Batts gave the defendants ten days to deliver all infringing copies, all unsold copies of the catalogue and all reproductions, from transparencies to discs, for 'impounding, destruction or other disposition,' to be determined by Cariou. The owners of Prince works were to be informed that they cannot be lawfully exhibited. Destruction is normally reserved for pirated copies or facsimile-type replicas and remains unusual in a copyright case where money damages are usually awarded in cases involving artistic and cultural expression. In September 2011, a federal appeals court ruled that the defendants have the right to appeal the judgement.

In this Solomon-like judgement, only one legal subject—one creator—could prevail. Significantly, the Rastafarian community—the subjects of the pictures—disappeared in the trial. The court's judgement seems to have been positively received by some members of the community, who are said to believe that Prince's works derogate their religious culture. Ironically, this community may have found 'justice' exercised through the subject of Cariou after all.

Photographs are not the 'natural' bearers of subject's rights. The legal subject—in, behind or in front of the photograph—is continually being rediscovered. As author, private citizen or civil society, the legal subject is contingent and multiple. The difficulty, if not impossibility, for the Law to control photographs in the digital and Internet age has paradoxically intensified the invention and application of legal constraints. Unlike the Internet, the Law is restricted to geographical jurisdictions. The race to keep up with the digital circulation of photographs may be a losing one.

Still from *The Unstable Object*
Daniel Eisenberg
2011

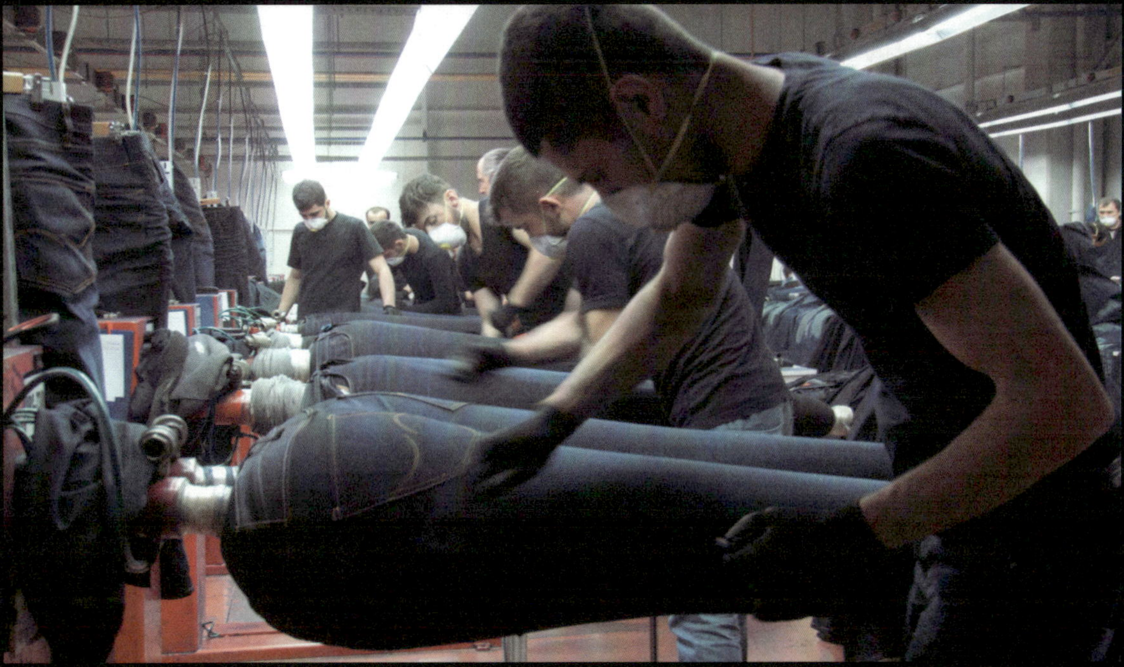

Still from *Workers Leaving the Googleplex*

Andrew Norman Wilson

2011

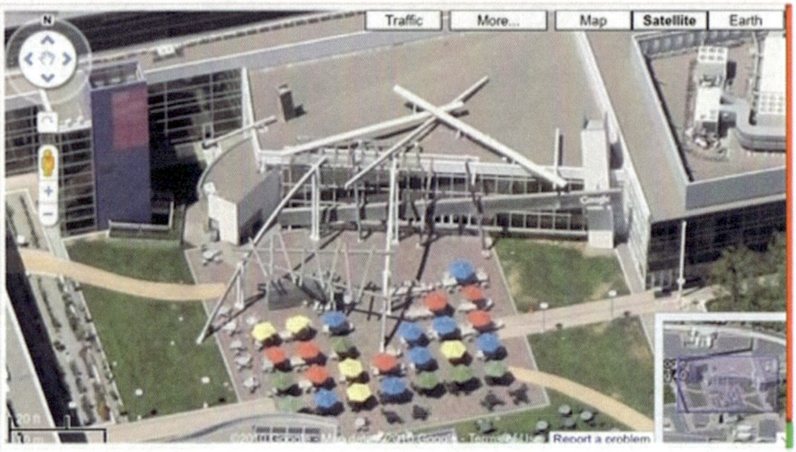

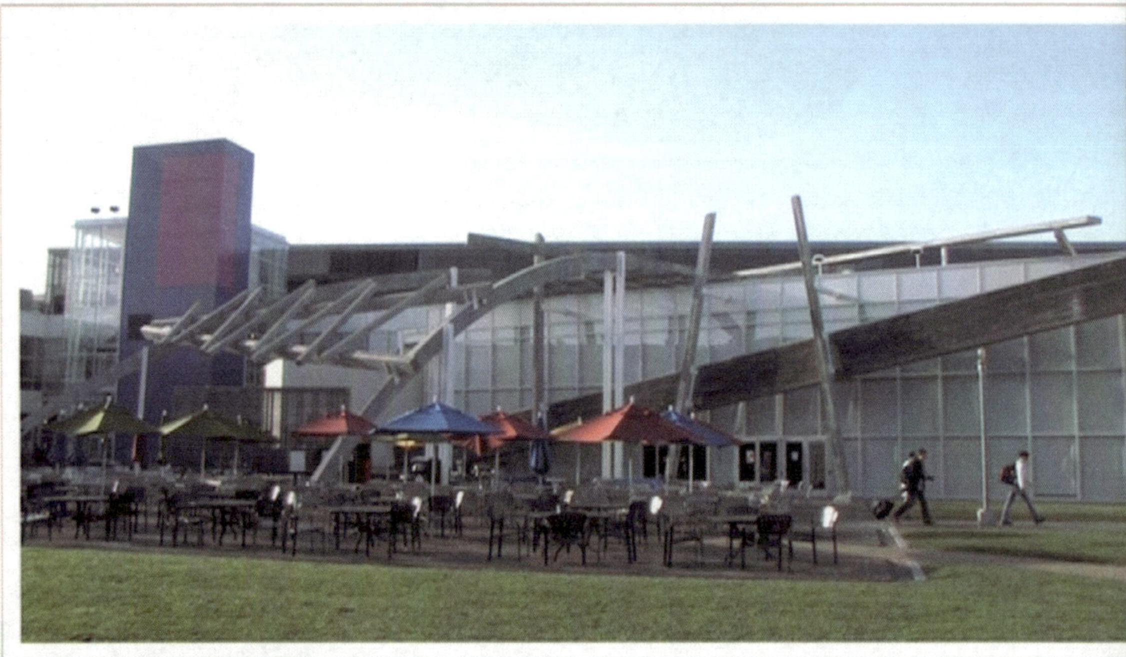

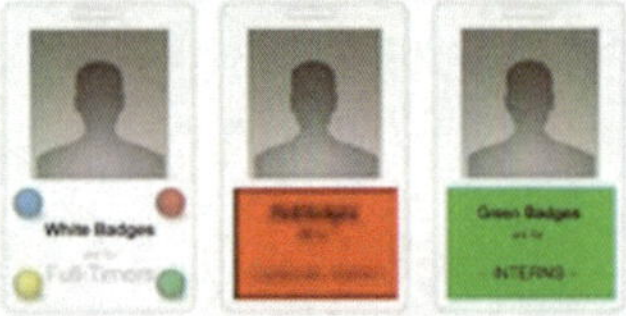

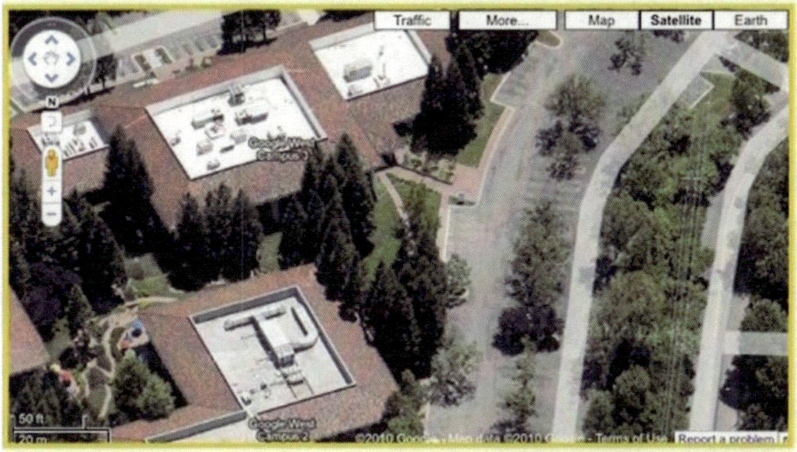
Traffic
More...
Map
Satellite
Earth
N
Google West Campus 2
50 ft
20 m
Report a problem

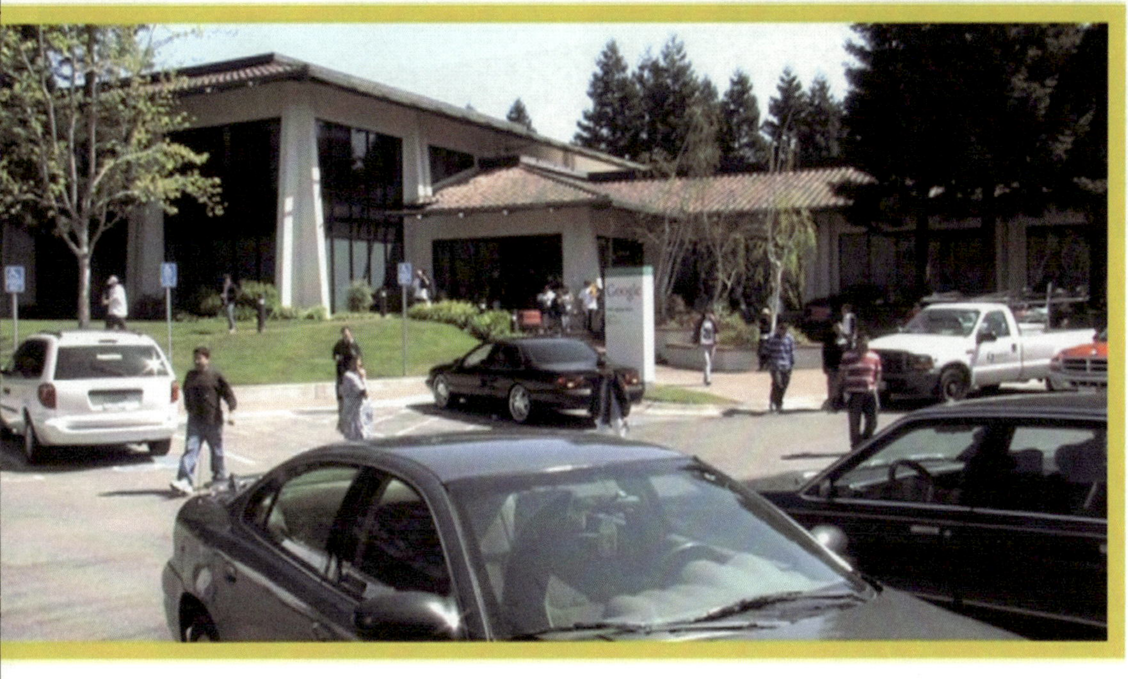

Touching Reality
Thomas Hirschhorn
2012

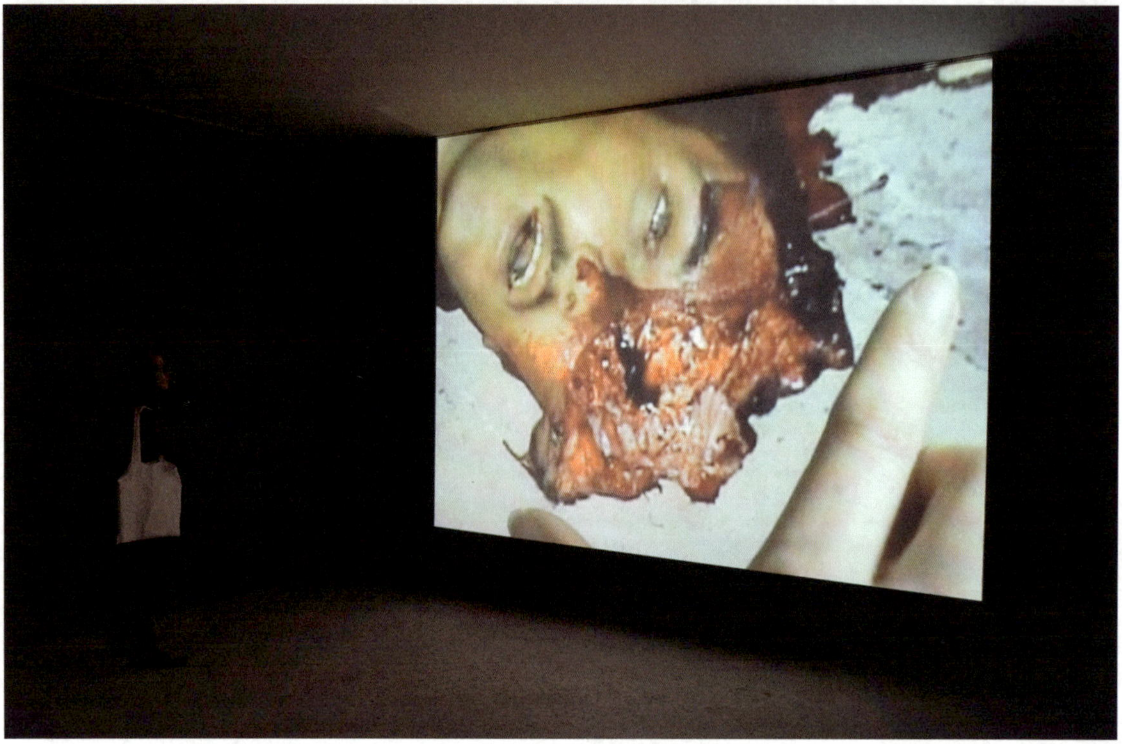

Why Is It Important—Today—to Show and Look at Images of Destroyed Human Bodies?

Thomas Hirschhorn

2012

I will try to clarify, in eight points, why it's important—today—to look at images of mutilated human bodies like those I have used and incorporated in various works such as 'Superficial Engagement' (2006), 'Concretion' (2006), 'The Incommensurable Banner' (2007), 'Ur-Collage' (2008), 'Das Auge' (2008), 'Crystal of Resistance' (2011), 'Touching Reality' (2012), 'Collage-Truth' (2012), 'Easycollage' (2014) and "Pixel-Collage" (2016).

1. Origin
   The pictures of destroyed human bodies were taken by non-photographers. Most of them were taken by witnesses, passers-by, soldiers, security or police officers, rescuers or first-aid workers. The origin of the images is unclear and often unverifiable; there is no source, whatever we believe a source to be. This unclear provenance and this unverifiability reflect today's uncertainty. This is what I am interested in. Often the origin is not guaranteed—but what can be guaranteed in our world today, and how can 'under guarantee' still make sense? These images can be downloaded from the Internet; they have the status of testimony and were placed online by their authors for many different reasons. Furthermore, the origin of these images is not indicated; sometimes it is confused, with an unclear, perhaps even manipulated or stolen address, as is often true of many things on the Internet and in the social media these days. This is something that confronts us every day. The uncertain provenance is one of the reasons why—nowadays—it's important to look at and display such images.

2. Redundancy
   The images of destroyed human bodies are important in terms of their redundancy. What's redundant is that such a vast amount of images of destroyed human bodies exists today. Redundancy here isn't repetition of the same thing because it's always another human body that has been destroyed and as such appears to be redundant. But it's not about images—it's about human bodies, about the human, the picture of whom is is a witness. The images are redundant because the fact that human beings are being destroyed is redundant. Redundancy is important here. I want to treat it as something important, and I want to see this redundancy as a form. We don't want to accept the redundancy of such images because we don't want to accept the redundancy of cruelty toward humans. This is why it's important to look at and display images of destroyed human bodies in their very redundancy.

3. Invisibility
   In today's newspapers, magazines and TV news, we rarely see images of destroyed bodies because they are hardly ever shown. These pictures are non-visible and invisible: the assumption is that they will hurt the viewer's sensitivities or only satisfy voyeurism, and the justification is to protect us from this threat. But this invisibility isn't harmless. The invisibility is the strategy of supporting, or at least not discouraging, the war effort. It's about making war acceptable and its effects commensurable, as was expressed by, for example, Donald Rumsfeld, former US Secretary of Defense (2001–06): "Death has the tendency to encourage a depressing view of war." But are there really any views of war which aren't depressing? Looking at and showing images of mutilated human bodies is a way of campaigning against war and its justification and propaganda. Since 9/11, this phenomenon of invisibility has been reinforced in the West. Refusal to accept this invisibility as a given fact or as a 'precautionary measure' is why it's important to look at such images.

4. Tendency to iconism
   The tendency to 'iconism' still exists to this day. 'Iconism' is the habit of 'selecting', 'choosing', or 'finding' the image that 'stands out', the image that is 'the big one', the image that 'says more', the image that 'counts more' than the others. In other words, the tendency towards 'iconism' is the tendency to 'highlight' something; it's the old, traditional procedure of favouring and imposing, in an authoritarian way, a hierarchy. This is not a declaration of importance towards something or somebody, but a declaration of importance towards others. The goal is to establish a common importance, a common weight, a common measure. But the 'iconism tendency' and 'highlighting' also have the effect of avoiding the existence of differences,

the non-iconic and the non-highlighted. In the field of war and conflict images, this leads to choosing the 'acceptable' for others. It's the 'acceptable' image that stands for another image, for all other images, for something else, and perhaps even for a non-image. This image or icon has to be, of course, correct, good, right, permitted, chosen—the consensual image. This is what makes it manipulation. One example is the much discussed image (even by art historians) of the Situation Room in Washington during the killing of Bin Laden by the Navy SEALs in 2011. I refuse to accept this image as an icon; I reject its 'iconism', and I reject the fact that this image (and this goes for all other 'icons') stands for anything other than itself. Struggling against the 'iconism tendency' is the reason why looking at images of destroyed bodies is important.

5. Reduction to facts
In today's world of facts, information, opinion and comments, much is reduced to being factual. Fact is the new 'golden calf' of journalism, and journalists wants to give it the assurance and guarantee of veracity. But I'm not interested in the verification of a fact. I'm interested in truth, not a verified fact or the 'correct information' of a journalistic story. The truth I'm interested in resists facts, opinions, comments and journalism. Truth is irreducible; therefore the images of destroyed human bodies are irreducible and resist factuality. I don't deny facts and factuality, but I want to oppose the texture of facts today. The habit of reducing things to facts is a comfortable way to avoid touching truth, and resisting this tendency corresponds to the dynamics which lead to touching truth. Unconditional acceptance of facts is intended to impose on us factual information as 'the measure', instead of looking and seeing with our own eyes. I want to see with my own eyes. Resistance to today's world of facts is what makes it important to look at such images.

6. Victim syndrome
Looking at images of mutilated human bodies is important because it can contribute to an understanding that the incommensurable act is not the looking; what is incommensurable is that destruction has happened in the first place—that a human, a human body, has been destroyed, indeed, that an incommensurable amount of human beings have been destroyed. It is important—more than anything else—to understand this. It's only by being capable of touching this incommensurable act that I can resist the suggestive question: Is this a victim or not? And whose victim? Or is this perhaps a killer, a torturer? Perhaps it's not a victim at all? Perhaps this mutilated human body shouldn't be regarded or counted as a victim? Classifying destroyed human bodies as victims or non-victims is an attempt to make them commensurable instead of thinking that all these bodies are the incommensurable. The victim syndrome wants me to give a response, an explanation, a reason to the incommensurable and finally to declare who 'the innocent' is. The only surviving terrorist in the Mumbai killings in 2008 declared to the court that sentenced him to death: "I don't think I am innocent." I think the incommensurable in this world has no reason, no explanation, and no response—beforehand or afterwards. In this incommensurable world, I have to reject the commensurability of accepting classification as victim or non-victim. I do not want to be neutralized by anything which wants to make the world commensurable. I refuse to explain and to excuse everything because of its context. I do not want to be neutralized by 'the context'. Looking at images of destroyed human bodies is important because I don't want to give up in response to the victim syndrome.

7. Irrelevance of quality
These pictures—because they were taken by witnesses—don't have any photographic quality. I am interested by this. It is the confirmation that, under conditions of urgency, 'quality' is not necessary. I always believed in 'quality = no, energy = yes'. There is no aesthetic approach here beyond the objective to capture the image. Concerns of quality are irrelevant when facing the incommensurable. This is shown by images of destroyed bodies. No technical skill is needed. No photographer is needed. The argument of 'photographic quality' is the argument of those who stand apart, aren't present, and who, on behalf of the 'quality' argument, express their distance and their attempt to be the supervisor. But there is no supervising anymore; what is 'needed' is to be a witness, to be there, to be here and to be here now, to be present, to be present at the 'right time' at the 'right place'. Most images are taken with small cameras, smartphones or mobile phones. They match our way of witnessing 'today's everything' and 'today's nothing' in daily life and making it 'public'. The irrelevance of quality of these images is an implicit critique of 'embedded' journalism, including photo-journalism. This irrelevance of quality is what makes it important to look at such images.

8. Detachment through 'hypersensitivity'
I am sensitive and I want to be sensitive, and at the same time I want to be alert. I don't want to stand aside; I don't want to look away. Sometimes when viewers are looking at images of destroyed human

bodies, I hear them saying: "I can't bear to look at this, I'm too sensitive." This is a way of keeping a comfortable, narcissistic and exclusive distance from today's reality, from the world. From our world, the unique and only world. The discourse of sensitivity—which is actually 'hypersensitivity'—is about retaining one's comfort, calm and luxury. Distance is only taken by those who—with their own eyes—won't confront the incommensurable of reality. Distance is never a gift; it's something taken by a very few to keep their exclusivity intact. 'Hypersensitivity' is the opposite of the 'non-exclusive public'. In order to confront the world, to struggle with its chaos, its incommensurability, in order to coexist and to cooperate in this world and with the other, I need to confront reality without distance. Therefore it's necessary to distinguish 'sensitivity', which means to me being 'awake' and 'attentive', from 'hypersensitivity', which means 'self-enclosure' and 'exclusion'. To resist 'hypersensitivity', it is important to look at those images of mutilated human bodies.

Thomas Hirschhorn, Aubervilliers

You've Lost That Loving Feeling: Rineke Dijkstra After Empathy

Johanna Burton

2012

Let's start with three pictures taken by Rineke Dijkstra.[1] Here are new mothers Julie, Tecla, and Saskia, all photographed in the Netherlands in 1994. Julie was photographed immediately after delivery. Tecla was photographed the day after giving birth, with evidence of that recent event still visceral in the blood running down her leg. Saskia, who had had a Cesarean section, was not photographed until a week had passed, because Dijkstra was reluctant to force her onto her feet until her body had some time to heal. Much has been made of Dijkstra's *New Mother* series and, moreover, of the attention these images give to the topic of motherhood, which has typically been sublimated into so much religious lore or, more often, hidden away completely.[2] The postpartum body, along with its attending postpartum mental blur, is placed front and center in these three pictures that—perhaps more remarkably—manage at once to unveil something of the base rawness of the birthing process and still re-present something of the clichés that the images would purport to do away with. The poses, in other words, while casual, cannot help but be read through the culturing lenses they (perhaps unconsciously) mimic; and, for all their newness, and nudeness, even the babies themselves have already entered the realm of representation.

To that end, the pictures collectively form a kind of unwitting holy trinity at the heart of a larger body of work by this artist, in which we frequently encounter such a flicker between what might be read as unmediated access to a subject and that subject's *always already framed-ness*.[3] This oscillation is made even clearer, for instance, in another two-part work of the same year, *Tia, Amsterdam, Netherlands, June 23 1994* and *Tia, Amsterdam, Netherlands, November 14 1994*. Here, a new mother is photographed twice in an identical classical pose—from the shoulders up, in a close cropping that is somewhat unusual within Dijkstra's oeuvre—but the first portrait of Tia was taken in June, three weeks after having given birth, and the second some five months later. The transformation in the woman's image is notable, if difficult to describe, and once a viewer knows the context for the pictures, it is nearly impossible not to project onto every shift in Tia's countenance. In the first instance, the work is typically discussed as showing the deep, extreme fatigue that accompanies having a small infant—an effect of constant night feedings, diaper changes, and the general terror born of new parenthood. The sharp edges of the woman's face, too, would seem to attest to her diligence and commitment to these serial tasks, her biological and psychological imperatives having kicked in to protect her offspring despite the personal stress. The second image gives over a slightly more relaxed, softer face, a gaze that has focus, skin that carries a flush.

I have spent a good deal of time looking at these images in the last months, not least, I'm sure, because I recently went through the experience of childbirth myself, a fact somewhat unfathomable to me still. I suppose this circumstance accounts, in a way, for my dwelling on pictures that I previously found interesting, but which didn't *hold* me as they do now. I use the word "hold" as Roland Barthes does in *Camera Lucida*, where he famously defines the punctum as both that which "pricks" the viewer (imparting a kind of minor trauma on her) and that which "holds" her.[4] The word "held," in this sense, suggests both captivity and care. Thus, I am held by these images now. I search them

This essay is a modified version of a talk first commissioned by and delivered at the Guggenheim Museum for a panel on the occasion of *Rineke Dijkstra: A Retrospective*, co-organized by the Guggenheim and the San Francisco Museum of Modern Art in 2012. The panel, "Empathy, Affect, and the Photographic Image," took place on September 21, 2012 and included speakers Jennifer Blessing, Johanna Burton, Carol Mavor, and Peggy Phelan; it was moderated by George Baker.

1 These are *Julie, Den Haag, Netherlands, February 29 1994; Saskia, Harderwijk, Netherlands, March 16 1994;* and *Tecla, Amsterdam, Netherlands, May 16 1994.*

2 Of course, there are notable exceptions. Mary Kelly's *Antepartum* (1973) and *Post-partum Document* (1973-1979) are touchstones in the history of art, both extending and critiquing the purview and limits of conceptual art. Carrie Mae Weems's *Kitchen Table Series* (1990) sought to foreground the central but rarely represented aspects of quotidian, domestic experience in women's—and particularly black women's—lives. Catherine Opie's *Self-Portrait/Nursing* (2004), like much of her work, questions assumptions around what constitutes a family. These are just three examples among many more, and it is no coincidence that these artists aim in representing some aspects of motherhood to challenge others.

3 As Barthes famously describes it, when a subject poses for the camera, one "imitates" oneself, transforming "in advance into an image." See Roland Barthes, *Camera Lucida: Reflections on Photography*, translated by Richard Howard (New York: Hill & Wang, 1982), 10–13.

4 Barthes, 13.

with a consciously shifted eye, not because I find myself there but because I can understand less abstractly now something of what is shown: The time immediately after birth. The next day. The following week. Three weeks after. Five months. Those time markers—not my own but Julie's, Tecla's, Saskia's, and Tia's—are markers I have some mode of connecting to, whereas they were, prior to my own having lived through them, merely generic stamps, untethered to my lived understanding.

Dijkstra has discussed the imperative for many of her works as stemming from a desire to photograph her subjects in extreme moments, usually just after they have experienced physical or mental events that leave them open or more vulnerable than usual. Such un-guardedness is often fueled by exhaustion, distraction, pleasure, or pain. Yet while seeking out such fleeting states of being, the artist is also explicit that her own method of taking pictures is tedious and laborious, which inevitably shapes the images of her subjects. Specifically, she uses a large-format, 4×5 camera whose setup and need for an extended exposure time—given the instrument's light requirements and its demand that the photographer obtain light readings using relatively analogue means—are more in keeping with antiquated photographic techniques than those of today's point and shoot digital cameras. As a result, sitters are never caught instantaneously. Instead, there is a necessary lag produced by her mode of image-making—a "decelerating factor," as she puts it, describing this literal slowing by and in front of the camera.[5] And this allows for, and even somewhat produces, some of the cinematically awkward scenarios that made the photographer's early series of bathers so very odd and compelling. Indeed, as Dijkstra says, her subjects inevitably "become aware that they are posing," and find themselves grappling in front of the lens with their simultaneous desires to both pose and avoid posing. The artist has aptly named the effect akin to a "display…of introversion."[6] These two elements, then—her focus on the exhausted or distracted subject, and the "decelerating factor" of the slow camera setup—create in combination something of a signifying system for Dijkstra. Even in the artist's video works, this system holds true, even if, of course, these mediums functionally decelerate quite differently (I would still argue that, when it comes to Dijkstra, elongating the operation doesn't change—so much as place—the impact of deceleration within another genre of reception, one where posing/not posing takes the form of task-based seriality).

The signifying system I describe, however, has a third term—beyond the deceleration of the tool (the camera) and the exhaustion of the subject (what curator Sandra S. Phillips has otherwise called "personal transitions")—which might best be termed the deferred effect of language.[7] To explain, Dijkstra's images, however fully and immediately present they may be for the viewer, are, like most images, nevertheless subject to the language that frames them. In this regard, most explanatory or mediating material existing around the artist's now decades-long practice presses into use details about the sitters or situation that might be understood as necessary for our capacity to map meaning onto what we see. In the case of the three images with which I began, one might argue that the salient details are clear at a glance. But it is not enough, I think, to say that what is pictured here are postpartum women, since the pictures are as much about the time that has elapsed between the event of birth and the image's capture as about the photographic image itself. Yet this distance is necessarily missed by us, and, for that matter, by the camera, which is, after all, bound up in layers of the deceleration that Dijkstra privileges in the shots themselves. Only language delivers us to this gap—and to the contours of that gap—that not only holds us away from these images, but also "holds" us, confined and cradled, as we look at them. In this respect, the fact that the titles for the works themselves offer only the name, place, and date of their subjects adds yet another layer of complication, another deferral. Rather, it is only in reading institutional or critical language *around* the work (an extended label, a catalogue essay, a Museum web page, an interview with the artist) that we are given access to the factual details that substantiate our intuitions. What was *felt* in an image is then *known*, but only by way of looking away from it.

In such literature, the *New Mothers* series is often placed into conjunction with another series from 1994 produced in Lisbon, titled *Bullfighters*. Setting aside the strange equation here—that one finds the best equivalent for childbirth in the savage ritual of bullfighting—I want to approach the language question again. The images portray young men whose wounds are clearly the source of a quiet pride they share. Yet without knowing the context for the images, which is partially established through the seriality of the men themselves (the activity begins to define itself by virtue of the shared costume, shared posture, shared wounds), a viewer finds affective information on the faces they

5 "Realism in the Smallest Details," Rineke Dijkstra interviewed by Jan van Adrichem in Rineke Dijkstra, Sandra S. Phillips, and Jennifer Blessing, *Rineke Dijkstra: A Retrospective* (San Francisco and New York: San Francisco Museum of Modern Art and Guggenheim Museum, 2012), 47. For more on the theorization of deceleration in contemporary photographic practice, see Sabine Eckmann, "Times and Places to Rest." *Lunch Break*. (Saint Louis: Mildred Lane Kemper Art Museum and Sam Fox School of Design & Visual Arts, 2010), 23-29.

6 "Realism in the Smallest Details," 47.

7 See Sandra S. Phillips, "Twenty Years of Looking at People," in *Rineke Dijkstra: A Retrospective*, 13-28.

see. But the legibility of that data is tenuous. I call attention to language—or, in some cases, context, which does the work of language—in order to begin to plumb something I will concentrate on for the remainder of this essay. So far, I've suggested that particular images by Dijkstra resonate at particular times for different viewers—an obvious enough point to make, but one that foregrounds how we look at images, which is to say *unevenly*. But here I wish to point to how language and context also make meaning in these images, effectively disallowing the position that we have immediate access to any of the subjects we look at. Perhaps better said, such access is formidably enhanced by language or context. Language aims our gaze more precisely. Yet such precision both allows and forecloses that access. Obviously, this idea has been long debated within histories and philosophies of photography, perhaps most famously by Walter Benjamin and Barthes. But in this respect, it is particularly notable that most literature on Dijkstra ignores such discussions, leaning heavily instead on narratives surrounding the sitters without calling into question how those narratives operate within the exhibition and reception of the works themselves. It is useful, in this vein, to recall the Soviet director Vsevolod Pudovkin's famous 1920s experiment (discussed by Merleau-Ponty in a 1945 lecture titled "The Film and the New Psychology") in which he screened the same close-up of an actor's inexpressive face three times, interspersing those shots with over-determined images (a bowl of soup, a dead woman in a coffin, a child with his teddy bear).[8] Audiences were wrongly convinced they had witnessed subtle changes of expression in the actor's face. Similarly, while Dijkstra's framing narratives are of course "real," they are no less instrumental in how we read her photographs.

To that end, I am interested in how Dijkstra is herself typically framed. The lion's share of scholarship and criticism around the artist's work places her squarely within the genre of portraiture, utilizing traditional, if updated, conventions and hewing closely to humanist ideals around representation. While linked at least generationally to the students and followers of Bernd and Hilla Becher (Thomas Ruff, Thomas Struth, etc.), Dijkstra's practice is most often argued away from what is categorized as their "conceptual" strain of photography (described by Phillips as having less need or desire to relate to their subjects "on a personal level") and toward predecessors including August Sander and Diane Arbus.[9] While this genealogy is somewhat helpful, it's also troubling in ways. Indeed, while Sander is understood by many to have developed a project of producing sympathetic group portraits of different parts of society, he has also been read as establishing dangerously essentializing physiognomic race- and class-based categories.[10] And Arbus, for her part, bucked against the (still prevalent) notion that her difficult photographs should be read as gently or sympathetically embracing their subjects. Indeed, she considered photography something "we subject each other to," and categorized it as sometimes bringing out the "cold and the harsh" in addition to the unconventionally beautiful.[11]

Yet rather than try to establish alternative genealogies for Dijkstra or propose contemporary artists with whom she might have affinities (though I would suggest that considering her projects alongside those of, say, Phil Collins, Sharon Lockhart, Collier Schorr, and Christopher Williams could indeed be fruitful), I would like to ask whether the framing of Dijkstra's own practice—beyond the images themselves—might also be thought as an object or, better, as an aspect of that practice, which subsequently can and should be analyzed. The curators of Dijkstra's 2012 retrospective—the aforementioned Phillips and Jennifer Blessing—turn repeatedly to the word "empathy" to get at the working process employed by Dijkstra (that is to say, how she approaches her subjects) and the effect produced by the photos themselves. Further, both emphasize that the artist, in her often-stark work, "makes no judgment."[12] I'm interested in this twinned imperative for empathy and lack of judgment, not only in terms of Dijkstra's own work, but also as those factors seem to be privileged pervasively in discussions of other artists today—particularly those who utilize photography or other modes of portraiture. I'm curious to know, in other words, why empathy is held up as a goal or an ethics, and to know how we might productively challenge any assumption that empathy is the only mode for responsibly taking or looking at images of other people. Indeed, a consideration of Dijkstra's work might be especially generative for a more complex understanding of the stakes attending any such assumption, leading to a more nuanced sense of empathy.[13] If, for example, Blessing's definition of empathy with regard to Dijkstra is the "honest connection between people"—the result of an urge with historical links to feminism and the "ethics of giving voice to individuals not cam-

8 Maurice Merleau-Ponty, "The Film and the New Psychology," in Merleau-Ponty, *Sense and Non-Sense* (Evanston: Northwestern University Press, 1964), 48-59.

9 Phillips, 25.

10 See, for instance, Benjamin H. D. Buchloh, "Residual Resemblance: Three Notes on the Ends of Portraiture", in Melissa E. Feldman (ed.), *Face-Off: The Portrait in Recent Art* (Philadelphia: University of Pennsylania Institute of Contemporary Art, 1994), 56.

11 In Doon Arbus and Marvin Israel (eds.), *Diane Arbus* (Millerton, N.Y.: Aperture, in collaboration with the Museum of Modern Art, 1972), 2; and quoted in Phillips, 22.

12 Phillips, 20.

paigning on their own behalf"—how can we also acknowledge the fraught terms for such protocols in an artistic practice, if only to advance such impulses more effectively?[14] We might only gain a much greater, and wanted, sense of potential in such photographic practices in contemporary culture.

After all, Dijkstra is hardly alone among contemporary photographers whose work has been attributed the character trait of empathy—and for whom such an attribution might be rendered problematic all too easily. I think in particular of Cindy Sherman, who is often discussed in the register of empathy, yet whose later work, in which she turns toward representing the aging female body, has proven resistant to such readings. Whereas no one was forced into defending Sherman's integrity in earlier series, in this instance suddenly writers were concerned that Sherman would be misunderstood as poking fun at the less-sexy than the *Untitled Film Stills* types—elderly art patrons, East Side ladies, West Coast Hollywood dimming lights, and the rest. Yet such anxieties underscore how the notion of "empathy" is frequently deployed to cast the artist in a positive light and make her "intentions" around any picture she takes ethical.[15] This proposition is deeply questionable from the outset, given that imparting an ethics to an image assumes that the image is wholly within the control of the artist or of the viewer—or better, that one can quantify such an impulse, regulate it, measure it. This tenuous assumption extends to the matter of whether such stated intentions can translate to any viewer's experience of a picture: Will, in other words, a picture be viewed ethically simply because it was executed with ethical intentions? Or do some very significant contingencies remain beyond the grasp of either party?

It also, perhaps inadvertently, reinforces spectatorial and artistic agency, in a sense "granting" a gracious look, or "giving voice," which I'm not sure one can ever do without also taking another voice away. As Saidya V. Hartman writes astutely in her seminal 1997 book exploring representations of racial oppression, *Scenes of Subjection*, "[W]hat comes to the fore is the difficulty and slipperiness of empathy. Properly speaking, empathy is a projection of oneself into another in order to better understand the other or 'the projection of one's own personality into an object, with the attribution to the object of one's own emotions.'"[16] To put an even finer point on the matter, Hartman cites Jonathan Boyarin's observation that the "ambivalent [or] repressive effects of empathy...can be located in the 'obliteration of otherness' or the facile intimacy that enables identification with the other only as we 'feel ourselves into those we imagine as ourselves.'"[17]

By seeking to "give" the photographic subject a voice, then, an artist or viewer might only give greater voice to themselves. And, looking beyond the immediate sphere of photography to the larger art world, the number of fraught political implications increases from there, particularly given the symbolic dimension of art as it functions within a uniquely privileged economy. Per Lauren Berlant in her 2011 book *Cruel Optimism*: "Projects of compassionate recognition have enabled a habit of political obfuscation of the differences between emotional and material (legal, economic, and institutional) kinds of social reciprocity. Self-transforming compassionate recognition and its cognate forms of solidarity are necessary for making political movements thrive contentiously against all sorts of privilege, but they have also provided a means for making minor structural adjustments seem like major events, because the theater of compassion is emotionally intense. Recognition all too often becomes an experiential end to itself, an emotional event that protects what is unconscious, impersonal, and unrelated to anyone's intentions about maintaining political privilege."[18]

Through such references, I do not mean to do away with empathy, just to examine its contours. Empathy is, etymologically, "in feeling," a "feeling with" another. Unlike sympathy, which holds the other at a distance, empathy is a mode of identification—an "I feel like you, I feel with you"—though the limits of empathy demand that we locate our own narcissism within this act. To consider again how I began this essay, I opened by discussing three pictures of postpartum women—knowing that I would have likely started with very different images if I were writing some five years ago. Others would likely have related more to me then, even if I didn't realize I was choosing images—and being chosen by them—this way. And

13 Discussions around empathy also notably attend to what might be argued the most recent technological extension of photography: VR. Indeed, this immersive medium begs the question of where one person's experience begins and another's ends with unique urgency. See, for instance, "I FEEL YOU: Alyssa K. Loh on Virtual Reality and Empathy," *Artforum* (November 2017): 206-13.

14 Blessing, 34-38.

15 I take up directly the question of applied empathy with regard to Sherman's work in my essay for the artist's 2012 retrospective at the Museum of Modern Art. See "Cindy Sherman: Abstraction and Empathy," in *Cindy Sherman* (New York: Museum of Modern Art, 2012), 54-67.

16 Saidiya V. Hartman, *Scenes of Subjection: Terror, Slavery, and Self-Making in Nineteenth-Century America* (New York: Oxford University Press), 18-19.

17 Jonathan Boyarin, *Storm from Paradise: The Politics of Jewish Memory.* (Minneapolis: University of Minnesota Press, 1992), 86. Cited in Hartman, *Scenes of Subjection*, 19-20.

18 Lauren Berlant, *Cruel Optimism* (Durham: Duke University Press, 2011), 182.

so, in this spirit, I want to suggest that even in the most empathetic image—one that ostensibly makes "no judgment"—there is, nonetheless, always *interest* worth taking into account. More specifically, this interest is affectual, and thus it is within the realm of the affectual that I want to place Dijkstra's images and their *effects*. This subtle shift in vocabulary helps, I think, articulate the kind of gap that arises in the making of her photographs, and gives new potential for our grasp of the relationships between photographer and subject, as well as between image and the viewer situated in the language around this artist's work.

In recent years, the stakes for distinguishing between photography's *effective* and *affective* dimensions have become more pronounced, as a growing body of scholarship has examined the medium and its relationship to the cusp of a variety of mental, perceptual, and somatic processes.[19] According to psychologist Silvan Tomkins—whose four-volume systematic examination of affect, *Affect Imagery Consciousness*, helped to catalyze a so-called "affective turn" in the humanities in the 1990s—empathy is not an affect.[20] Instead, affects comprise nonconscious aspects in a manner distinct from emotions or feelings; they are not available for conscious modification. Perhaps most important, affects are relegated to neither the body nor to the mind, but rather, operate in a bridge between the two.

Here, and returning to the images with which I began, we might think again about Dijsktra, poised behind the camera while her subject waits for an image to be made, and a shift in perception—between occupying one's own body, and anticipating (or even participating in) its representation. Such photographs also conjure an *interested* viewer—one who, when asked to consider the image in terms of intention or empathy, will inevitably place such protocols in relation to their own lived experience.

What is so useful about the concept of affects, as the political theorist Michael Hardt has pointed out, is that they demand not only that we reconsider the passions as part of our intellectual matter, but also that we consider our own relationship of body to mind as one that occurs socially. Reflecting on a decade of renewed scholarship dedicated to affect theory, Hardt draws upon the legacy of seventeenth century philosopher Baruch Spinoza, whose theorization of subjectivity hinged largely upon the relationship between the mind's capacity to think, and its correlate in the body's power to act.[21] Such power, Hardt notes, corresponds to its sensitivity to other bodies, a process that immediately opens the self onto the social, and therefore political, dimensions of life, disrupting conventional notions of power. The more we can affect, that is, the more we can also *be* affected. Considering Dijkstra's work this way, even provisionally, suggests that we could, and should, look while also being looked at—creating the possibility for exchanges we cannot, as the barest conventions of empathy would otherwise have us propose, fully understand.

19 For more on the relationship between affect theory and photography, see Elspeth H. Brown and Thy Phu (eds.), *Feeling Photography* (Durham, NC: Duke University Press, 2014), and Thy Phu and Linda M. Steer (eds.), "Affecting Photographies," special issue, *Photography and Culture* 2.3 (2009).

20 Writing in the early 1960s, Tomkins discerned nine affects: enjoyment/joy; interest/excitement; surprise/startle; anger/rage; disgust; dissmell; distress/anguish; fear/terror; shame/humiliation. See Silvan Tomkins, *Affect Imagery Consciousness. Volume I: The Positive Affects* (New York: Springer, 1962), and *Affect Imagery Consciousness. Volume II: The Negative Affects* (New York: Springer, 1963). These theories were developed across two subsequent volumes, published posthumously in 1991 and 1992. For more on the uptake and proliferation of Tomkins's theories, see Eve Kosofsky Sedgwick and Adam Frank (eds.), *Shame and its Sisters: A Silvan Tomkins Reader*. (Durham: Duke University Press, 1995).

21 Michael Hardt, foreword to *The Affective Turn: Theorizing The Social*, ed. Patricia Ticineto Clough with Jean Halley (Durham: Duke University Press, 2007), ix-xii.

Diane Arbus: A Printed Retrospective, 1960–1971

Pierre Leguillon

2012

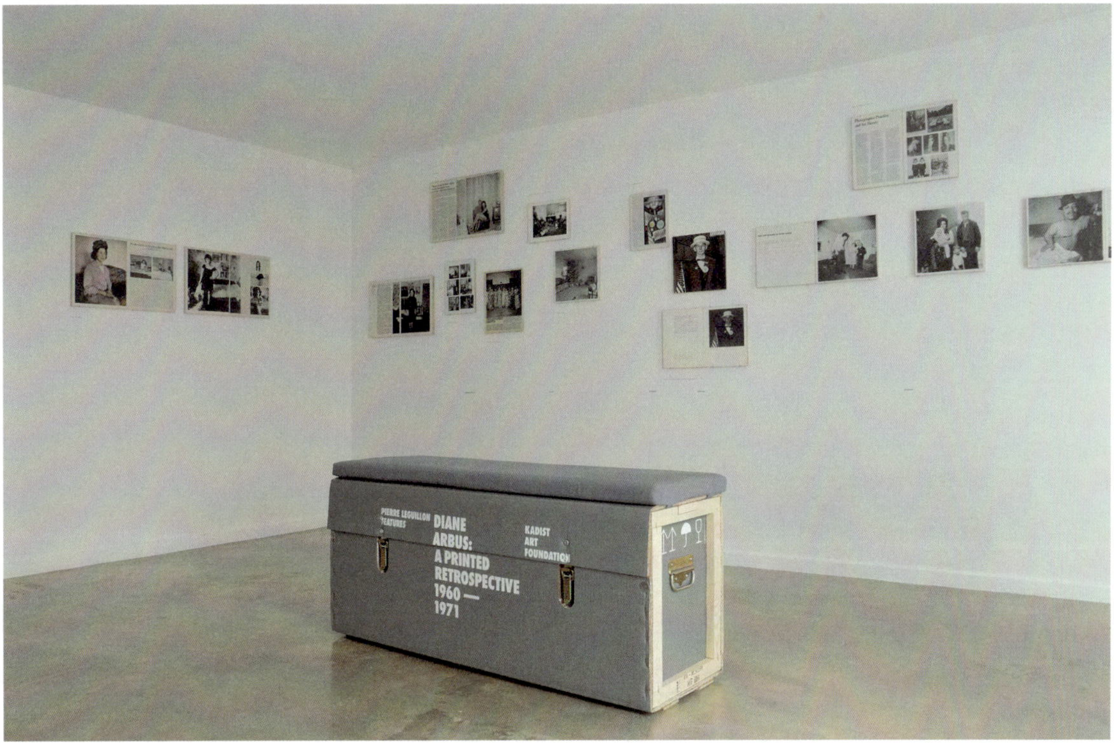

Anonymous Needs and Desires (Various Castoffs: Ceramic Tile, Potato Chips, Garlic, Men's Socks, Blackberry, iPod, Baby Food, Perfume, Chocolate, and Cigarettes)
Liz Glynn
2012

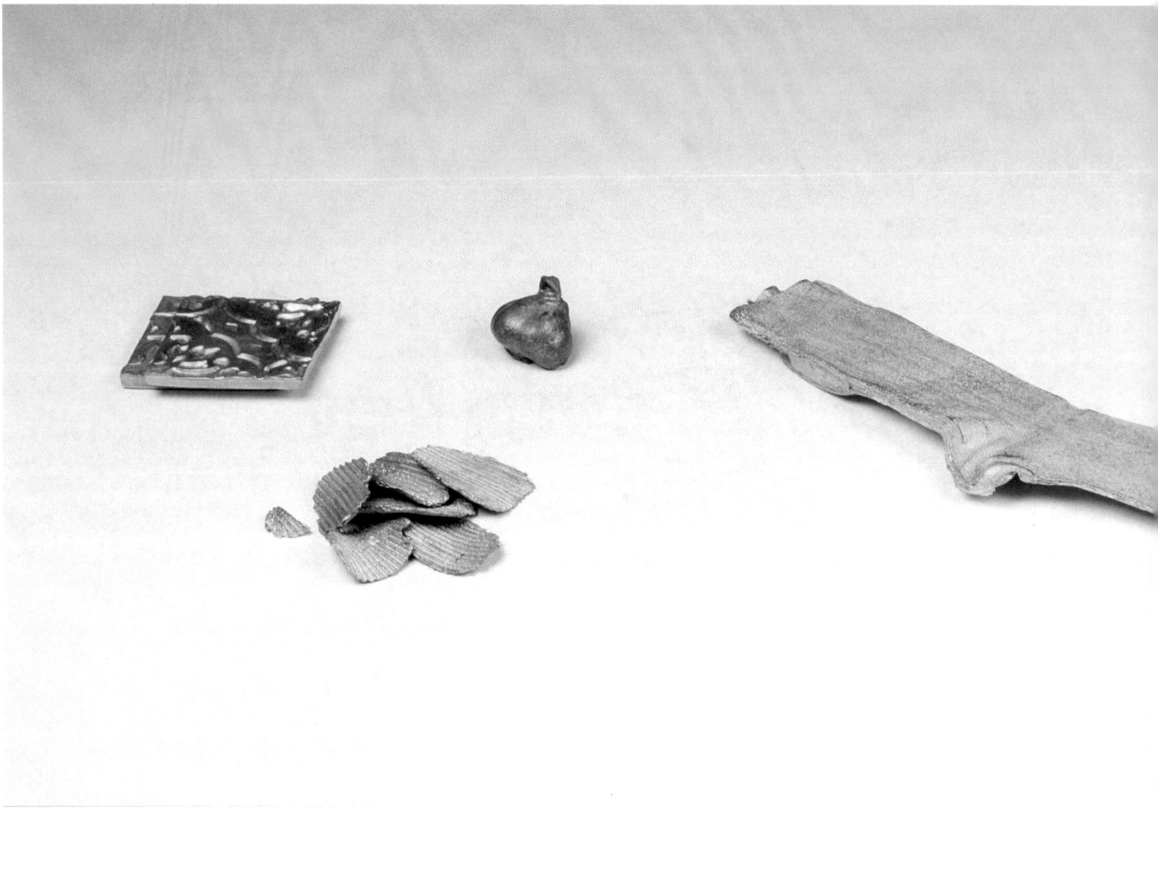

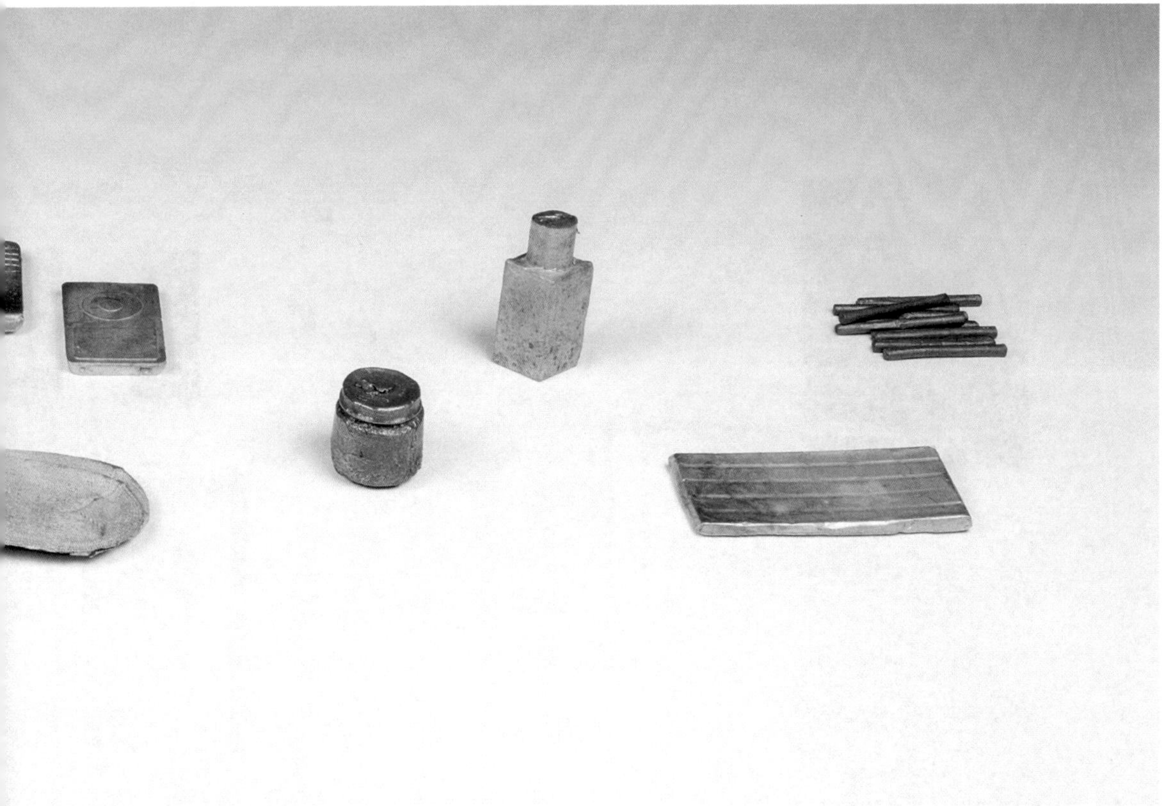

Truth Study Center

Wolfgang Tillmans

2016

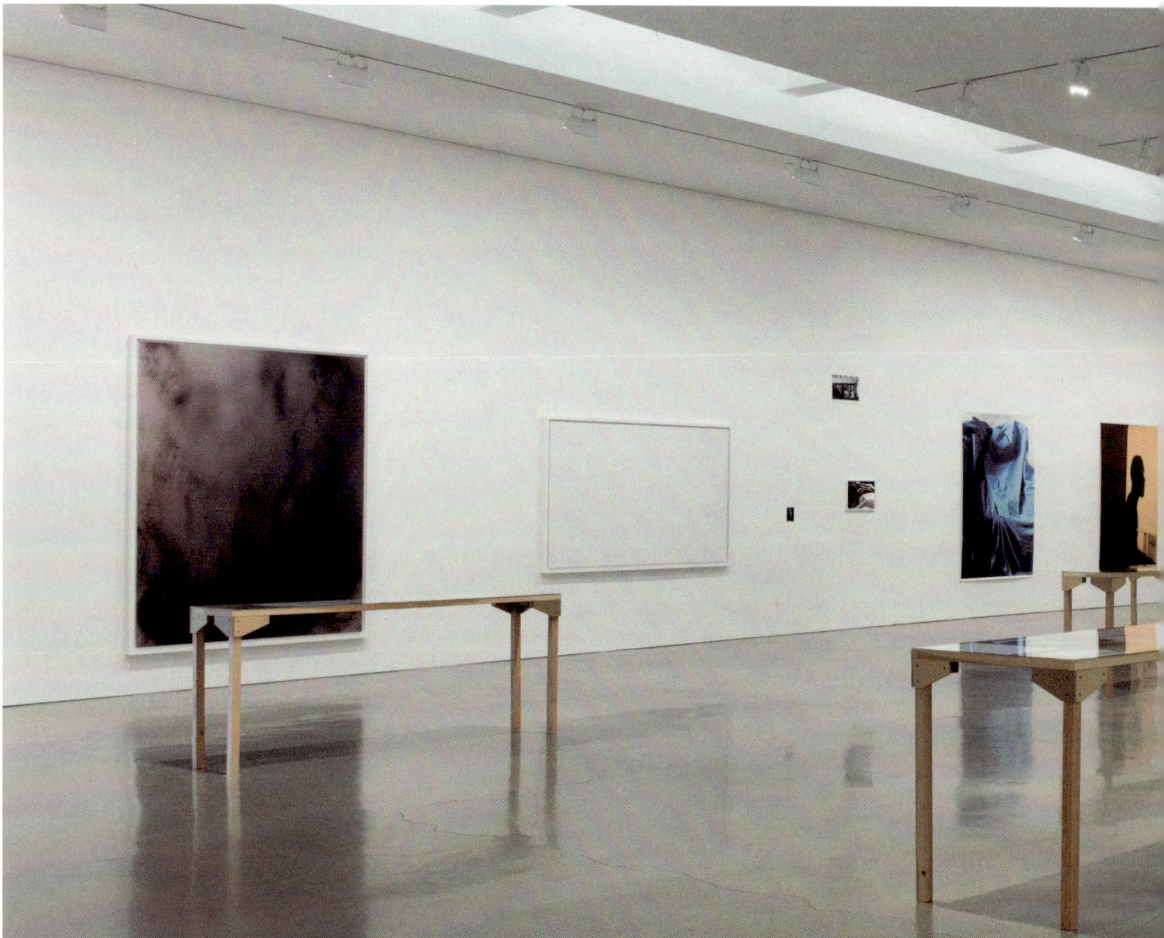

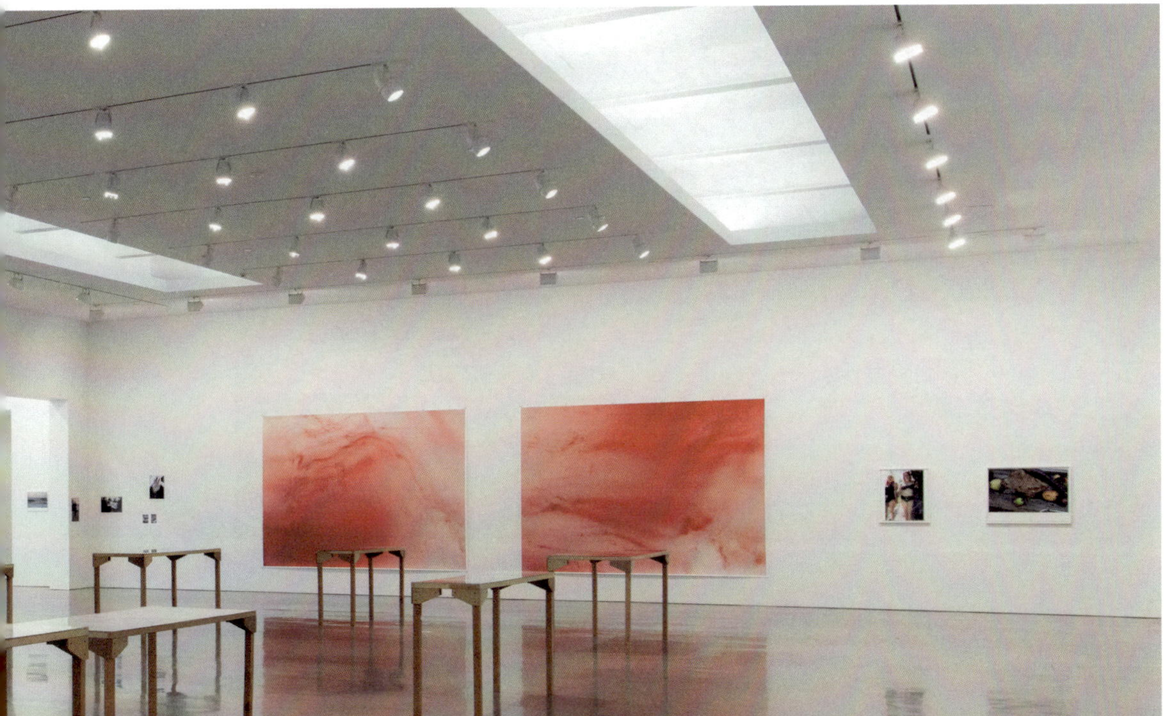

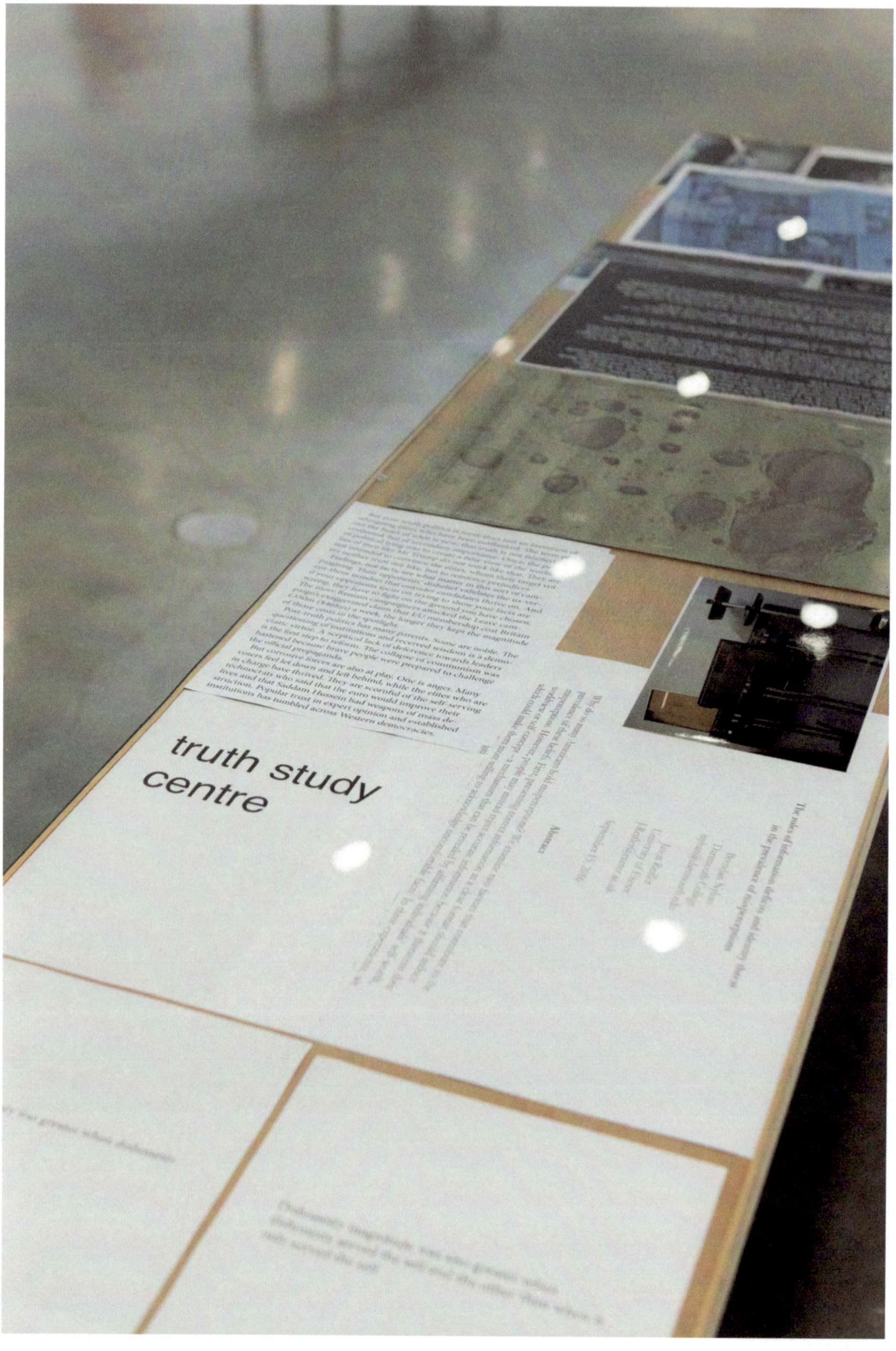
truth study
centre

The Tower
Hito Steyerl
2015

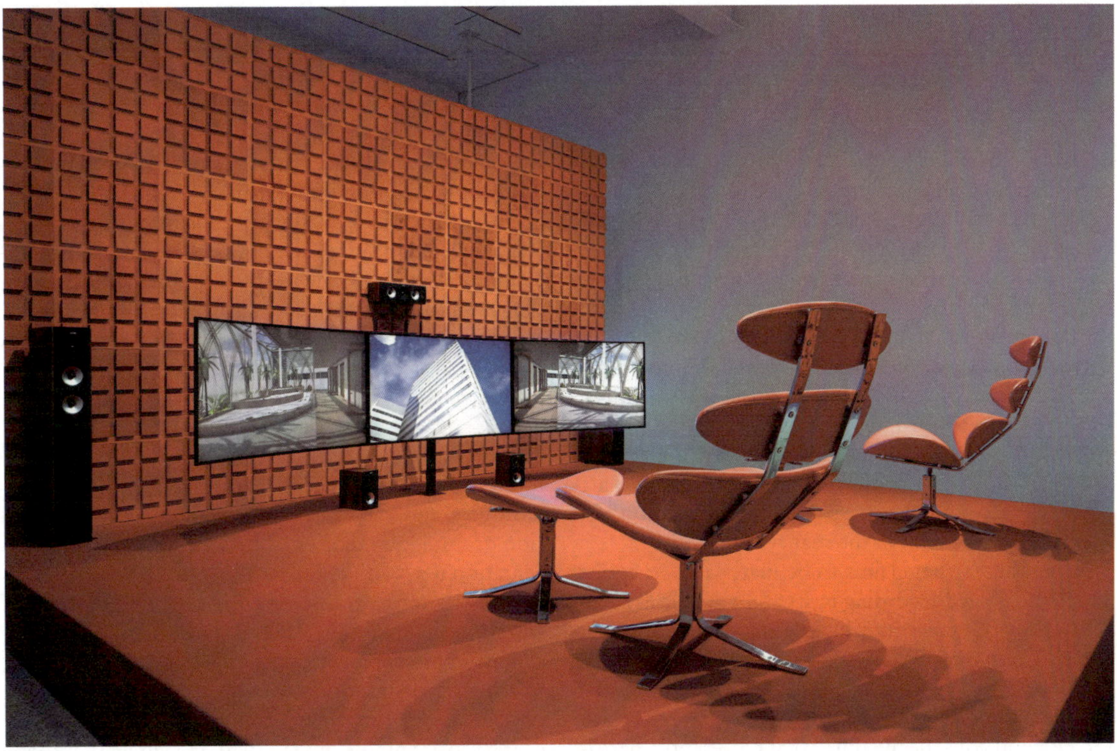

In Defense of Representation

Tristan Garcia

2015

Throughout the century of modernity and postmodernity, "representation" has been frowned upon, even forbidden, to such a degree that it has been necessary to invent ways to dispense with this old and embarrassing concept in art, politics, and ontology: expression, exemplification, reference, or even pure and simple presentation, pure and simple.[1]

There is an understandable aesthetic reason for the rejection of the concept: its unsatisfying definition, capable neither of anticipating nor of following the mutations of art in the twentieth century, from Kazimir Malevich to Allan Kaprow, from Marcel Broodthaers to body art. But if "representation" no longer succeeds in accounting for the natural inclination of the plastic arts toward the presence (of objects, bodies, events), it is also because philosophy has failed, has not been capable of proposing and presenting to artists a well-grounded concept of "representation" inscribed in matter and in the reality of objects.

Any theory that claims to be materialist or realist should be judged according to its ability (or lack thereof) to provide an account for the status of representations. An image, for example, is certainly a material object or a real object, but it is also another object that has the particular nature of not being what it is: a watercolor and gouache by Dürer that represents a hare is not itself a hare; moreover if it were the animal, it would no longer represent the animal. But if it is not in any way the thing itself, how can it represent that thing? Must I admit the existence of an ideal hare, in addition to its image? In that case, entities proliferate: there's the real hare, the image of the hare, the hare of which this is the image. Or perhaps the hare of which this is the image exists neither outside of the image nor in the image, but rather in the mind of the one who sees it? This way I remove representations from objects, locate them in consciousness, and then, eventually, seek a materialist or naturalist theory of mind. Thus I am rid of representations, these sort of half or double objects that proliferate in matter, in reality, and undermine materialism and naturalism.

Yet it would be particularly strange to think that a materialist or realist would not situate representations in things themselves rather than in consciousness, because materialists, realists, and idealists agree on this one thing: representations do not exist in truth except by and for those things that they represent. On the contrary, I assert that an authentic realist or materialist way of thinking should be able to account for the objective, real and material, existence of representations produced by human art.

The history of Western philosophy proposes at least three major ways to conceive the status of representational objects: the representational object is understood to be either a copy, a sign, or a duplex.

I

The first model for thinking about representation is mimesis, which is the idea that in the West dominates antiquity and the classical age. The major contribution of mimetic theories is the affirmation that representation is a relationship between two terms in which one of the terms transposes the other by extracting certain of its qualities; thus a two-dimensional representation of a chair transposes the chair onto a surface, making an abstraction of its third dimension. Every copy made by representation is a diminished version of the representable object. Plato considers that there exists a ladder of ontological degradation from the idea to the object and from the object to the representation. Not only natural objects are susceptible to being imitated in this way — for Aristotle, that which is said or that which should be is also representable.

Mimesis can be understood as the linking of two objects or of two series of objects; the first is present, or real, and the second is represented, meaning transposed into a form that draws certain qualities from the first. The identity between the two is assured by a certain resemblance: recovery, analogy, or structural homology. However, three difficulties hobble such a definition of representation. First, as Nelson Goodman has noted, resemblance, unlike representation, bespeaks a symmetrical relationship.[2] The portrait of Thomas More by Hans Holbein surely resembles Thomas More, and Thomas More resembles his portrait—but the portrait represents the face of the humanist while the face does

1 Translator's note: The French title, "Défense de Représentation," carries a double meaning that is difficult to render in English: défense can mean both defense and prohibition.

2 See Nelson Goodman, *Languages of Art* (Indianapolis: Hackett, 1976), 3ff.

not represent the portrait. So representation is not resemblance. Next, mimesis supposes not only the precedence but the pre-existence of that which is represented relative to its representation: one can not represent that which does not already exist. Finally, mimesis implies an ontological degradation between what is represented and the representation: that which is represented is in some way "de-presented," since something has been snatched from its full and entire presence to make it exist under another form, diminished, as a copy.

Let's try another model.

II

The second model for representation is signification. This is the model that has dominated modernity since the nineteenth century, under the influence of the work of Charles Sanders Peirce and Ferdinand de Saussure. A representation is no longer thought of as a copy but rather as a sign. For Peirce, representation is a relationship between three terms, the *representamen*, the *object*, and the *interpretant*.[3] A bison drawn with pigment that I perceive on the wall of a Paleolithic cave is the *representamen*; the bison that these traces seem to me to designate is the object; the set of signs that I mobilize in order to attach the first to the second comprise the interpretant. All the images of bison, drawn or photographed, that I have perceived in the past contribute to the composition of this specific representation of a bison. To interpret a sign is to triangulate ceaselessly between the sign, its object, and other signs. The same word, with the same spelling and the same sound, can designate many different objects, depending on the interpretants brought into play. When associating the word "rock" with the terms "Chuck Berry" and "Telecaster," you get a very different object than if you reference "granite" or "clay." Thus, to signify is to link a sign to an object through the mediation of other signs; it is no longer a question of resemblance or imitation.

Within the context of our semiotic model, representation would never be anything but a type of signification: the portrait of Émile Zola by Manet relates to what it represents, the French writer, by the mediation of a series of other signs. If, after an apocalypse, survivors who lost all trace or memory of the existence of Zola were to discover the painting in an archaeological excavation, they would find a representation of a bearded man, but not of Émile Zola. And if we were to discover a representation of something that we couldn't identify, made by an extinct people of whom we know nothing, we would perhaps not even be able to recognize it as a representation. Thus, according to the semiotic model, there is no representation without signification, that is to say without interpretation.

However, there is one major objection to the subordination of representation to signification. An essential characteristic of a representation as a sign is its variability: the official sign for "no smoking" shows a cigarette in a barred circle. But each airport, hospital, or cinema, in each region of the world, uses different images to embody this sign—a cigarette or perhaps a pipe, a cigarette with filter or without, a cigarette inscribed in a circle or a square, barred by a cross or by a simple transverse line, on a black background or white—yet the meaning remains the same.

Several images can thus serve to signify exactly the same thing, such that one can alter a sign without altering what it means. But does the same go for the image? A steam locomotive can easily signify any kind of train, because it has become the archetype of this mode of transport in the collective imagination. But even so, it does not represent all trains. And an image of a cigarette does not represent exactly the same thing as an image of a pipe.

If the image can become sign, or the sign image, they nevertheless remain absolutely distinct; what separates them is the delicate attachment of the image to what it represents.

Thus, no representation can be affected without affecting that which it represents. Marcel Duchamp's *Mona Lisa* with a moustache is no longer the *Mona Lisa* of Leonardo da Vinci; a photograph retouched by software that permits the accentuation of contrast or the erasure of blemishes no longer represents exactly what it represented before. By contrast, the sign—determined by the triangular relationship between the sign itself, the object to which it refers, and the interpretant that attaches one to the other—can vary without changing the object, so long as the interpretant adjusts the triangulation. In signification, the presence of the sign erases itself behind its relation with its object mediated by an infinity of other signs, while in representation there is nothing other than a relation between that which is present and that which is represented.

III

To explain this phenomenon, a third contemporary model exists, one that pertains neither to classical or ancient mimesis nor to modern semiotics. The redefinition of the image, as distinct from the sign, has been an

3 See Charles Sanders Peirce, "Logic as Semiotic: The Theory of Signs," in *Philosophical Writings of Peirce*, ed. Justus Buchler (New York: Dover, 1955), 98–119.

important trend in analytic philosophy since the 1960s. This trend has submitted the notion of mimesis to scrutiny, all the while resisting the semiotic and structuralist groundswell that, in the fifties and sixties, increasingly classified the image as a sign among other signs.

In pondering the status of iconicity, Goodman, Richard Wollheim, Kendall Walton, John Hyman, and Flint Schier have attempted to propose a redefinition of representation. At the heart of their reflections, diverse as they are, lies the same concern for understanding how an image can really combine two things in one: that which represents and that which is represented. For this reason it is tempting to describe this third model as the *duplex* concept of representation, since it is based on the intuition that a representation presents itself as other than it is and that a theory of representation should seek to model and explain this "duplicity."

It is possible to organize all the proposed answers by imagining that they have all evolved in a space defined by three axes: an ontological axis, a logical axis, and a psychological axis. Along the ontological axis, the theories oscillate between objectivism and subjectivism, according to whether the object represented is objectively or subjectively understood in the representing object. On the logical axis, it is a matter of the relation between the two that is debated: the positions vary between recourse to resemblance (which leads to mimesis) and recourse to referentiality (which leads to semiosis). Finally, the psychological axis is bounded on the one hand by naturalism (the recognition of images is a natural cognitive facility developed by our species) and on the other by conventionalism (recognition of images regulated by conventions that vary from one culture to another).

All the contemporary stances on the duplex character of representations situate themselves in this complex three-dimensional space: Goodman is objectivist, while supporting a logical theory of reference and tending toward a moderated conventionalism; Hyman, by contrast, defends the determining character of resemblance (in his "occlusion shape principle"); Wollheim's theory of "seeing-in" is ontologically subjectivist, logically midway between resemblance and reference; Walton's "make-believe" shifts this position toward a radical conventionalism, while the defense of "recognition" by Schier pushes it the other way, toward naturalism.[4]

What stays constant throughout all these variations is the concept of the image as a duplex reality: one thing is two, two things are one. All these theories, whatever their respective merits, tend to consider representation as the relation between two things presented in one alone. For this reason, they are condemned to develop ontologically, logically, and psychologically between two poles, always still missing an aspect of representation. The more they account for the image as an object, the less they can account for the object of this image, and vice versa. Their error is to attribute a single presence shared between two objects (the representing and the represented), instead of conceiving a single object shared between presence and absence.

That is why I have been working for several years on a completely different model of representation.

IV

To represent is first of all to absent.

All representation, be it visual, sonic, or even tactile, presupposes the work of absenting present matter: an image is a three-dimensional object reduced to the state of a quasi-surface, whose depth has been reduced to almost nothing, and one side of which has been transformed into the verso. Thus, to apprehend a photograph as a representation supposes that one is capable of not equally considering the edge, the recto, and the verso of the photographic image: the recto becomes the prominent surface, the edge is overlooked, the verso is the blind back of the image.

Thus, a visual representation consists first of all in the absenting of a spatial dimension. For a sonic representation, it's not exactly the same: when we hear, for example, the recording of a bird's song, what is absented is the spatial origin of the sonic phenomenon, since we don't consider the speaker, the stereo, or the record to be the one that sings. Also, in a certain sense all music is representative as soon as you separate the sound from its cause and no longer hear the effect of a guitar or a violin, but rather a sonic development where each sound seems to cause the following sound, whether in a rhythmic or melodic phrase.

Visual representation, like sonic representation, is the absence of presence, of a dimension of space or of the spatial source of a sound. And in absenting a presence, one necessarily presents a presence. The key to our argument is that all representation should be understood as a system of exchange that takes place within objects themselves: in constraining a dimension or a portion of space to reduce itself to almost nothing (in absenting it, that is), one, not by magic but rationally, makes something that isn't there appear.

4 See Goodman, *Languages of Art*; John Hyman, *The Objective Eye: Color, Form, and Reality in the Theory of Art* (Chicago: University of Chicago Press, 2006); Richard Wollheim, "Seeing-as, Seeing-in, and Pictorial Representation," in *Art and Its Objects*, 2nd ed. (Cambridge: Cambridge University Press, 1980), 205–26; Kendall Walton, *Mimesis as Make-Believe: On the Foundations of the Representational Arts* (Cambridge, MA: Harvard University Press, 1990); and Flint Schier, *Deeper into Pictures: An Essay on Pictorial Representation* (Cambridge: Cambridge University Press, 1986).

And the representation is not initially the presentation of something absent that would exist elsewhere, but the emergence of something absent, owing to the absence of something present. One understands thus that even Malevich's white square on a white background, the blue monochromes of Yves Klein, or Pierre Soulages's black monochromes represent something in the sense that they absent a dimension of space and therefore also present something absent. What? At least a surface. Maybe a colored surface. Maybe a surface broken up by forms.

In this way, the great aesthetic illusion of the twentieth century—the belief that we were done with representation because we had discovered the power of abstraction—dissipates: all representation is an abstraction, the abstraction of the presence of things. And this abstraction has the necessary consequence of presenting something absent: a countryside, a face, a feeling, shapes, colors, an event, and so forth. What we see in an image, what we understand in a piece of music, is never there—the image and the music present something absent because they absent something present.

This absenting is neither a conventional decision nor a power of our cognition: it is a constraint that the representing object exerts on our perception. Representation is a constraint produced by art and incorporated in an object by work, which forces our perception to absent a part of the presence of things. Insofar as it is a constraint, our perception can always oppose it, and I can try to consider a photograph as a three-dimensional object, observing with equal interest its front, back, and side; I can listen to music forcing myself to not perceive the sound as the effect of an instrument. But in so doing I will need to spend considerable energy forcing myself to believe that I do not see or hear the representation, because the representational object contrives to constrain my perception from recognizing it for what it is.

The representational object is not a copy: it does not imitate another present object, but rather, it presents an absent object. What a photograph of Henry Fonda in *My Darling Clementine* seems to present to me is not really Henry Fonda himself, but his absence.

But how to present an absence? All representation possesses a certain degree of determination: in presenting me with an absence, even an emptiness, the representation determines, surrounds, or defines this emptiness. If I merely trace a circle on paper, I produce a large and enveloping absence: it could be almost anything—me, you, a balloon, the earth—just as easily as it could be Henry Fonda's head. In working the circle, scrutinizing it, I can constrain my perception to eliminate more and more possibilities: viewing a face traced in charcoal, with eyes and a mouth. I can always pretend to see the earth or a balloon, but my perception must strongly resist the drawing. By fortifying the strictures—for instance, by including a caption inscribed at the bottom of the drawing—I can force the drawing to designate Henry Fonda. But the representation will never be constraining enough to be saturated, that is to say, to achieve the presence of that which is presented: this will never be the cut-off head of Henry Fonda in person appearing on the sheet of paper in the same way that Henry Fonda will never be present in his representation. What is present in a representation is an absence, which can be strongly determined but never to the point of saturation with presence. In this way, there is no ultimate degree of realism of a representation.

A representation is thus neither an imitation nor a type of signification; it neither resembles nor refers to what it represents. It presents something absent and determines it without otherwise transforming it completely into presence.

In redefining representation this way—starting from an ontology of objects, a human art as a form of representation, a specific manner of absenting a certain part of the presence of objects—I propose that it is possible to restore it to the heart of art, and to rethink the work of the artist as that of a transmuter of absence and presence.

Our representations are, then, neither in our minds nor in our perceptions: they are inscribed by human art in certain objects, which constrain our cognition to recognize the absence of a presence in them, and by way of compensation the presence of something absent. This operation, which to me is the impetus of all human art, is neither mimetic nor semiotic; it requires a new model of ontology to understand that it is not a matter of magical, irreal, or immaterial thought: quite the contrary. The only way for materialist or realist theories to recognize the status of artistic representations is to understand that representation is that which objectively inscribes absence in matter, or in the real.

Great Things Never Come from Comfort Zones in *i-D* Magazine, No. 336, 2015
Wolfgang Tillmans

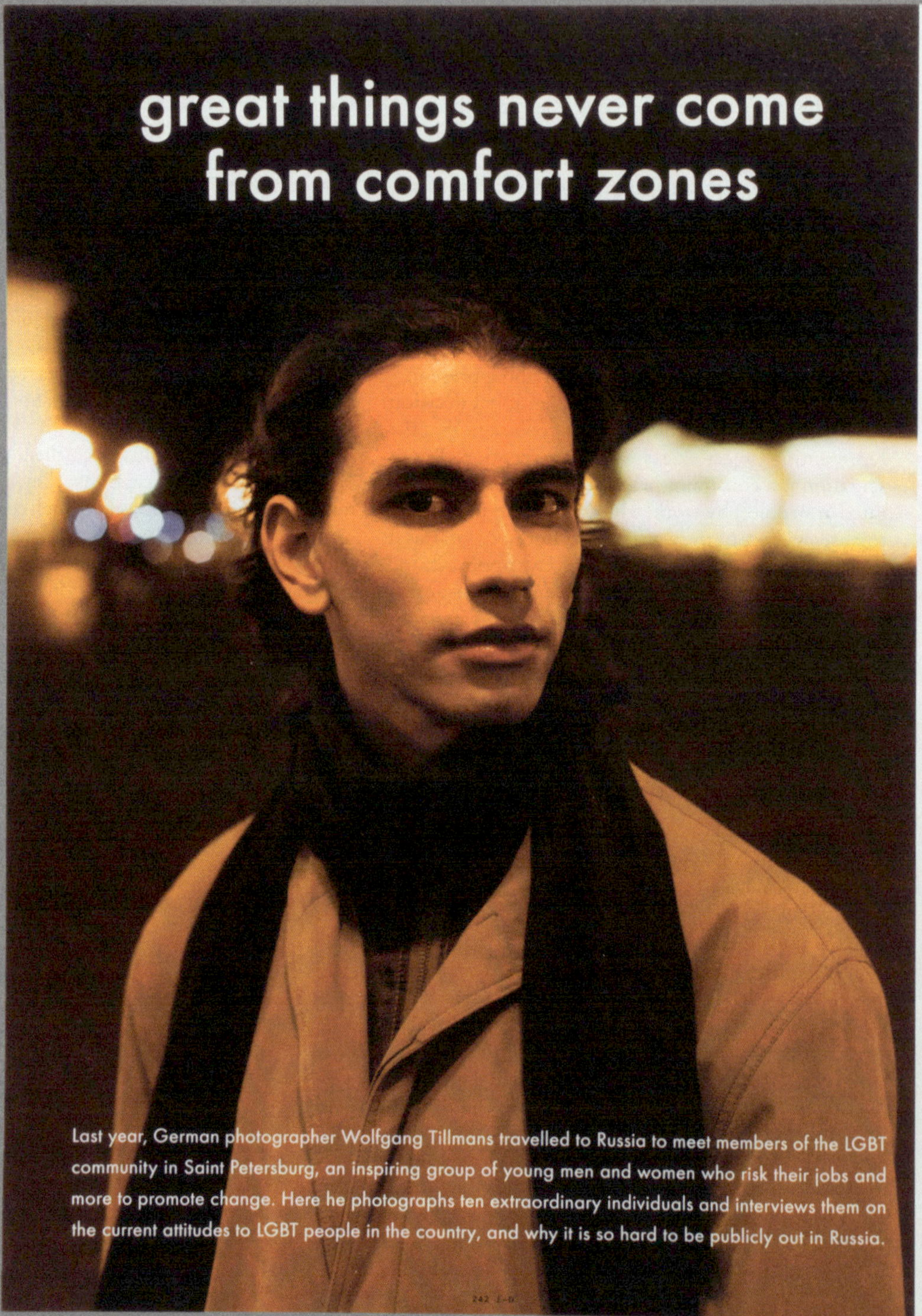

great things never come from comfort zones

Last year, German photographer Wolfgang Tillmans travelled to Russia to meet members of the LGBT community in Saint Petersburg, an inspiring group of young men and women who risk their jobs and more to promote change. Here he photographs ten extraordinary individuals and interviews them on the current attitudes to LGBT people in the country, and why it is so hard to be publicly out in Russia.

242 i-D

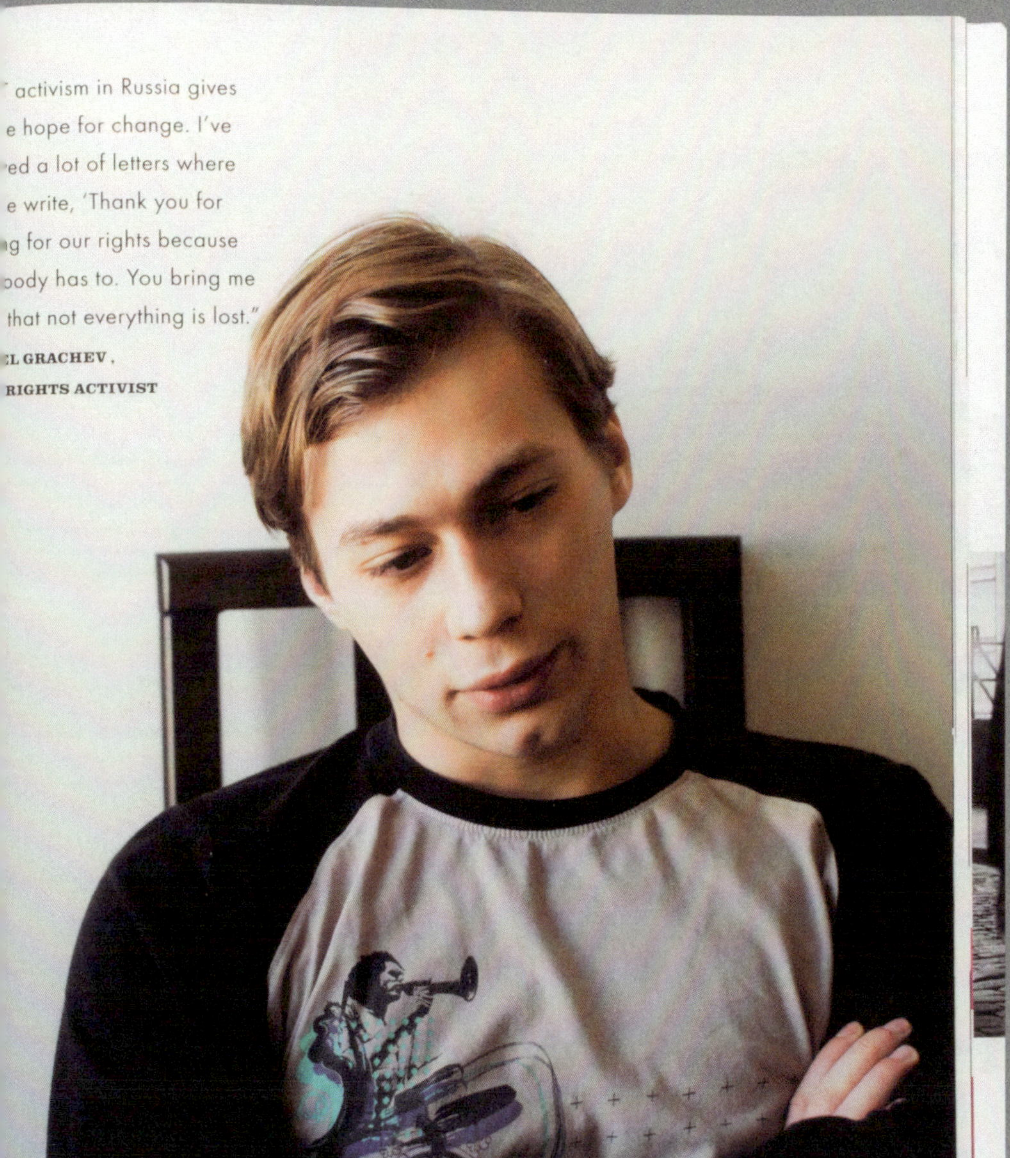
activism in Russia gives
e hope for change. I've
ed a lot of letters where
e write, 'Thank you for
g for our rights because
ody has to. You bring me
that not everything is lost."
L GRACHEV,
RIGHTS ACTIVIST
PHOTOGRAPHY AND INTERVIEWS WOLFGANG TILLMANS
INTRODUCTION FELIX PETTY
With thanks to Frauke Nelissen, Vasilisa Grebenshchikova, Matthew Collin and Amnesty International.

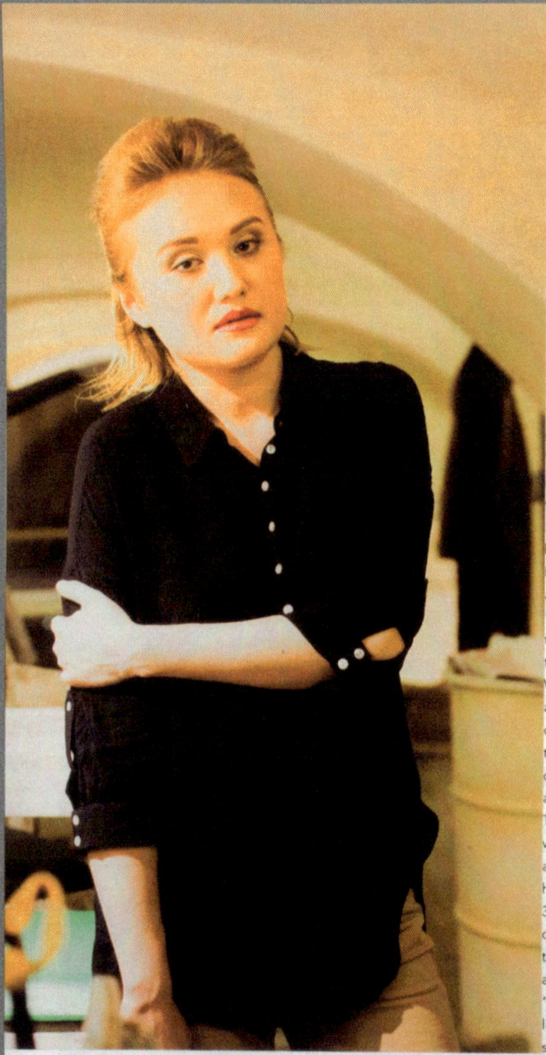

Since 2006, Vladimir Putin's Russia has been slowly cracking down on the rights of LGBT people, so when Wolfgang Tillmans found himself in Russia last year for Manifesta 10, which was being held in Saint Petersburg, Russia's old, Baroque capital, he knew he had to make a statement. Saint Petersburg was traditionally one of Russia's more liberal enclaves, but it's from here that Russia's homophobic laws have begun to spiral outwards, with the city's mayor even saying, "They can do whatever they want in their homes, in the special 'garbage' places called gay night clubs. But they're not allowed to do it in the streets."

"I had to find a way to make a comment," Wolfgang explains, "I included two photographs of ugly new Orthodox churches, built by the government. I also photographed television static in my Saint Petersburg hotel room as a symbol of censorship and of potential loss of connection. These became two huge pictures in the show."

Tillmans was planning on going to the Saint Petersburg Pride festival while he was there, but this too fell victim to the Russian government. The federal law banning the"promotion of homosexuality to minors" is being used as a cloak for all kinds of homophobic behaviour, and for the police to attack protesters and to encourage vigilante style mob "justice", as well as stopping demonstrations and Pride events. "I felt bad that I didn't get this connection with the community there during Manifesta," he says, "so I got in touch with Amnesty International to arrange to do these portraits, to meet and talk with people."

"These aren't the outstanding figureheads of the movement, just the normal people, willing to be photographed," Tillmans is quick to stress. "None of them had a heroic street fighting rhetoric. In the West, activism of this sort always has a sense of something heroic and subversive about it. When I first got interested in different types of activism in Germany and the UK, there was always a style element to it, but it's interesting that in a setting where there is so much real danger, activists can't look at the aesthetics and coolness of fighting for a cause, and must instead focus on the matter at hand."

The resulting pictures, though, don't betray the fear of living a life in which you can't be openly out of the closet, in which Pride marches are continually targeted by thugs, and Saint Petersburg's activists have been shot at and even murdered. Last year there were over 300 homophobic attacks recorded by Human Rights Watch, and depressingly, only a handful of prosecutions. These are photographs that show a quiet hopefulness, a determination to make things better and a dedication to do what's right.

"I find it so admirable [that they] keep doing what they're doing, in the light of real threat, because I've never been in a situation like that," says Tillmans. "All my life I've been involved in a political and cultural context that has become ever more free. I guess I wanted to just see for myself, and speak to people myself, to really get an idea of what it feels like to live in this situation. When you meet people everything becomes less black and white. You hear all these horror stories, but there's always hope. There are terrible things, but wherever there's people, there's also hope, and that's what I like my photography to do, to amplify and give a voice to hope and solidarity."

"The situation is getting more depressing, but we are trying to do what we can. It gives us a lot of power and strength to move forward and to be equal. But at this time it's quite dangerous to fight against the government." **ELENA LEONTIEVA, SINGER, ACTRESS, LGBT VOLUNTEER**

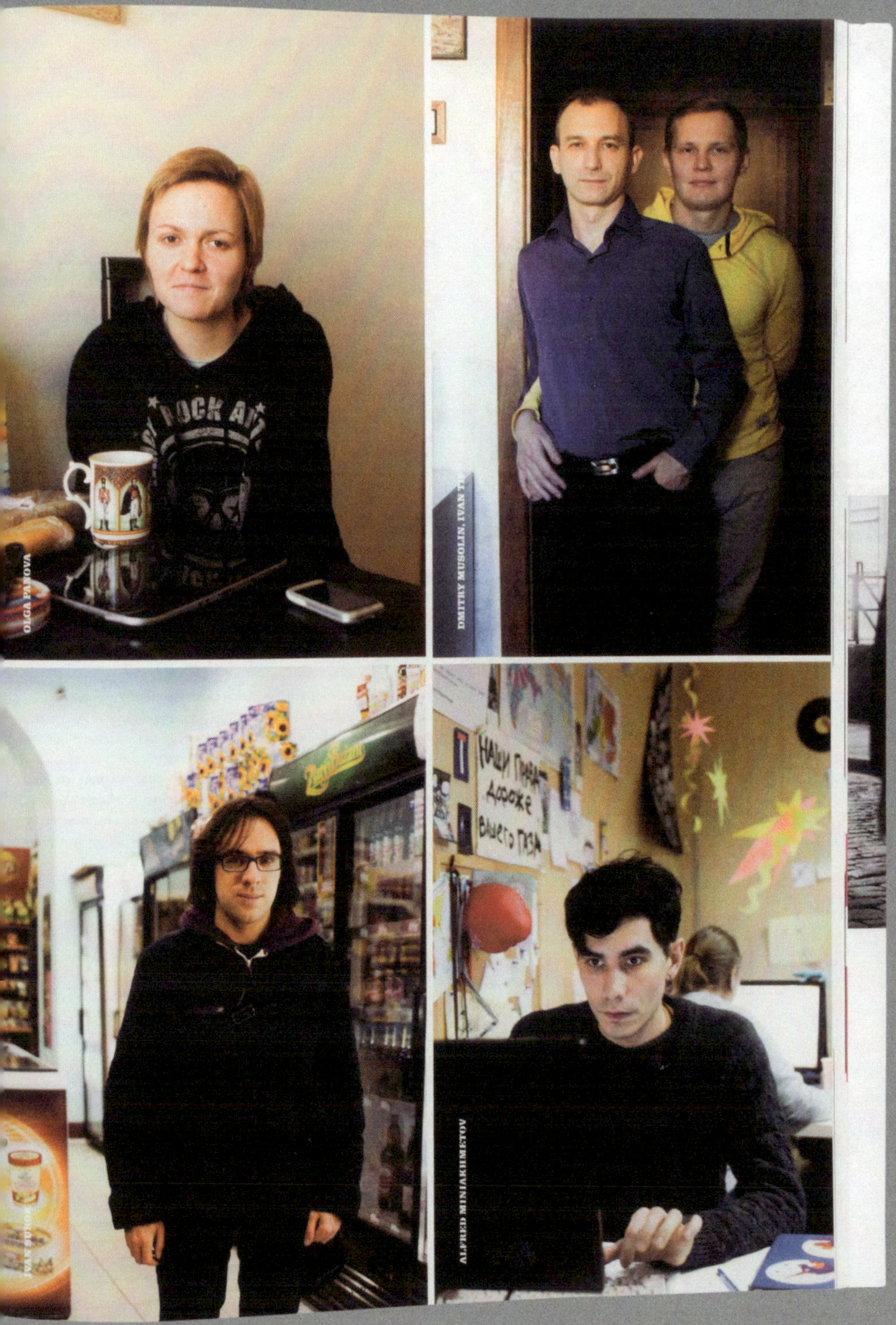
OLGA PANOVA
ALFRED MINIAKHMETOV

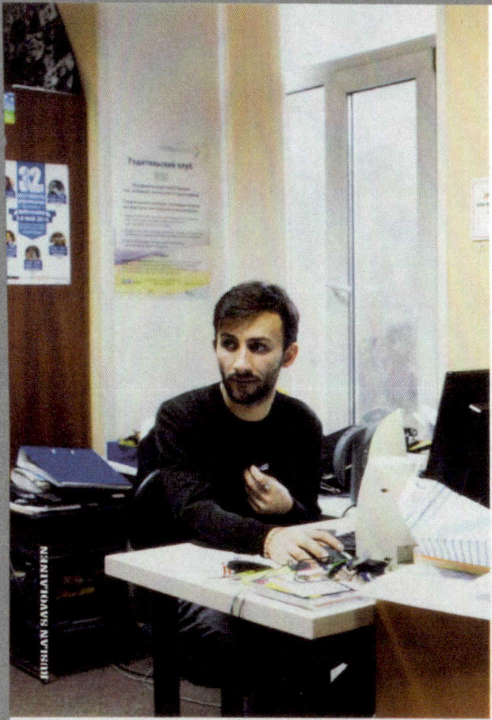

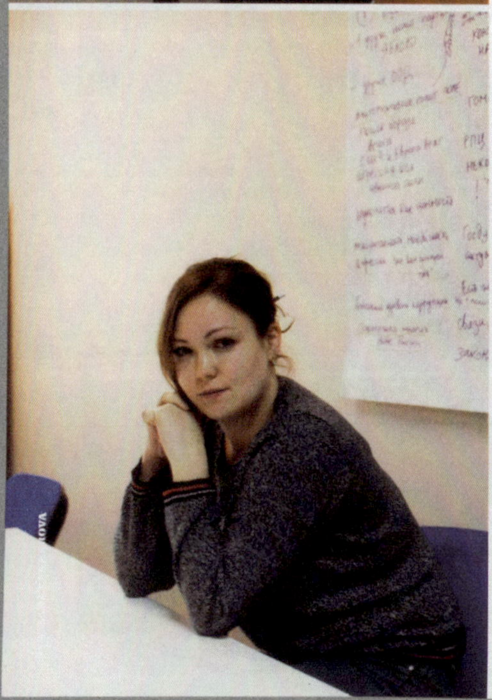

"I don't think I've lost any friends because of my homosexuality. I do face aggression sometimes, but so do immigrants and women in Russia; we are not the only group." **SVETLANA ZAKHAROVA, RUSSIAN LGBT NETWORK**

Wolfgang Tillmans: Homosexuality was decriminalised in Russia in 1993, the age of consent is 16, and gender change has been legal since 1997, yet it is not against the law to discriminate, and hate speech is widespread. It doesn't make any sense?

Ruslan Savolainen: Propaganda in Russia claims that LGBT is something foreign to Russian values and the Russian people. They believe that it came from the West and that it imposes European values. This standpoint – that it is "foreign to Russia" – is aggressively pushed by the media and the government.

Dmitry Musolin: A lot of us are trying to understand why Russia is so homophobic. Some people say that it's related to political history, because male homosexuality was illegal for 60 years during the Soviet Union – actually female homosexuality was not, but people don't make that differentiation. In the minds of a lot of people it's still something bad; [they still see it as] criminal, even though it's not anymore. Also, the Russian Orthodox Church is very homophobic and very conservative and now, in the post-Soviet time, the church wants to play a much more important role in society and it has very strong support from the state. The state needs something – like ideology – and the church has something to offer.

Ivan Surok: There are two factors: the fact that the image of an inner enemy needed to be created to distract people from other problems and the [inherent] homophobia of the Russian people.

Dmitry Musolin: It's easier to manipulate people when there is an enemy, so now and again propaganda and government [suggest] that it is America or Europe – the EU is a big enemy of Russia and this idea is strongly promoted by the state's media. It's also important to have an internal enemy, inside the country, so somehow it was decided that gay people could be this kind of enemy, because for a lot of people it's still criminal.

Pride rallies in Russia are now illegal, and attempts to hold unauthorised Pride gatherings have almost always been met with violent attacks by religious conservatives and neo-Nazis, while the police arrest LGBT demonstrators. What are your experiences of this?

Olga Panova: At last year's Gay Pride [in Saint Petersburg] there weren't too many activists, but there were a large group of homophobes who came and threw eggs and stones. They were very aggressive, but the police didn't arrest them, while all the activists were arrested. It was my first time at a police station, and while it was very interesting and funny, it was unfair. I just came out to say that I exist and that my friends shouldn't be killed for loving people of the same sex or gender. Someone hurt me, threw a stone at me and wasn't taken to the police station. That is unfair.

Daniel Grachev: When you go to a demonstration that is banned by the police, you see riot police there and you start wondering whether they will arrest you or not. But you know that you cannot just go away, [that you are ready] to spend the night in a police station and go to court. This is the worst time to be an activist in this country. But with LGBT activism you are giving people some kind of hope for change. During the two years I've been doing LGBT activism, I've received a lot of letters where people write, "Thank you for fighting for our rights because somebody has to, you bring me hope that not everything is lost".

Olga Panova: Maybe it won't change politics hugely, but I hope that seeing me standing there in the street will make some people think or read about LGBT people and change their minds. They see that I exist, that I'm not just someone you read about on the t or see on TV, but that I'm standing there, I'm real.

a Leontieva: LGBT activism makes me feel like I am doing a great thing and the world more beautiful.

el Grachev: Nothing serious has happened to me so far, but I've been attacked igans at street demonstrations several times. For some time I had post-traumatic syndrome, I was afraid of every football fan or every guy with a shaved head. You now who the government will aim at. For example, those people who went to jail pro-democracy protests in Bolotnaya Square in Moscow in 2012] were randomly , just to [make a point] that it is a "bad" idea to participate in demonstrations.

ry Musolin: There's strong pressure from conservative circles, and the state ts the conservative movement. You have to be very brave to speak up for LGBT now, especially if you're a public figure.

an Savolainen: I'm scared every day.

g publicly "out" in Russia leaves people open to being ed from their jobs or physically attacked. How has this ted the way you speak about your sexuality?

om Stadnik: With close friends, I am [out]. My mum also knows and accepts being completely open is dangerous in this country.

ry Musolin: I don't have a rainbow flag in my office, but if people ask I tell. lie. I work in a university and there are many older people working there who ly don't know, but younger teachers and PhD students, if they are on Facebook or kte, can easily understand who I am because they see what I post.

ana Zakharova: In my environment people are nice to me, I don't think I lost ends because of my homosexuality. I do face aggression sometimes, but so do ants and women in Russia; we are not the only group.

l changes prohibiting "propaganda for non-traditional al relationships" were adopted in Russia in 2013. This wed local bans on "the promotion of homosexual, lesbian, ual and transgender practices among minors" in cities Saint Petersburg the year before.

ry Musolin: We didn't believe that it would happen in Saint Petersburg, e it's an important, cultured, modern, big city, so when they started [to promote the e had this campaign to stop it. But the people promoting these laws are not stupid, t gay, lesbian and transgender people together with paedophiles, just separated mas. When we tried to protest, they said, "You're protecting paedophiles." It's ible to have a public discussion. They say, "This law is not against gay people, it's t paedophiles."

Surok: The government practically gave the "attack" command with these o the public thinks it has the right to judge without trial, that killing and torturing and that a murder can be justified by the fact that the victim was gay. There have everal murders in Russia already. The most famous case is that of Vlad Tornovoi, as sadistically murdered [in May 2013 in Volgograd]. The murderers claimed that led him because he told them he was gay. They believed that if they pointed out was gay, their penalty would be reduced.

ry Musolin: I'm not teaching minors, so my situation is much easier. People e teaching in schools are definitely under pressure from this new law, because say something positive, or even neutral, about gay people, they are violating v. I know that some people are losing their jobs. High school teachers, as well one working for small companies where the boss can decide everything, are not ed. This guy who is staying with us lost his job in an advertising agency after it own on TV that he took part in a protest.

Surok: The law is slippery; there is no specific definition of what "gay anda" is, so it can be used in a selective way against those who are inconvenient government.

ana Zakharova: We tried to launch this programme of private donations, [ran into] difficulties. We tried to work with one of the biggest crowdfunding platforms in Russia and initially they were okay with us, but they decided that it was too dangerous to work with us.

LGBT activists in the West have tried to draw attention to the deteriorating situation in Russia, but politicians inside the country have claimed that demonstrations abroad are just examples of anti-Russian prejudice. How does this make you feel?

Daniel Grachev: Foreign support is very important. It was especially strong during the Sochi Olympics when a lot of journalists came to Russia to report on gay rights.

Dmitry Musolin: It's important to have this kind of support. But there are many people, even LGBT people, [in Russia] who think that all protest makes the situation worse. I don't agree with this. I think it's still important to feel that we are not alone, that people share our values and support what we are doing here. If there were no voices from outside, the situation would probably be worse.

Daniel Grachev: Photography is a very strong instrument in influencing people as it allows them to see what's actually going on, like my friends beaten and bloody, and me being arrested by riot policemen. The Sochi Olympics, the photographs of the LGBT protests, and the anti-Russian and anti-Putin attitudes in Europe have all boosted the European media's interest in the Russian LGBT community. It is very important to understand that there are people who support us, like Front Line Defenders and Amnesty International, who find money for some of our activities and even protect us, for instance if we need shelter in a European country.

Ivan Surok: It's obviously good that they voice solidarity with Russians, but it has not been in any way helpful for me as an ordinary person.

The number of LGBT Russians seeking asylum in Western countries has increased significantly in recent years. Have you been personally affected?

Daniel Grachev: I have a lot of friends who have left because it was too dangerous for them to stay. Dmitry Chizhevsky, who was shot and lost his eye; Natalya Tsymbalova, the coordinator of the organisation Straights Alliance for LGBT Equality; Dmitry Chunosov from Voronezh; and Pavel Lebedev, an LGBT activist who left after the demonstrations on Bolotnaya Square in Moscow, because he fought with the riot police and could have become a victim of the Bolotnaya criminal case.

Olga Panova: I would love to leave Russia, but I don't want to miss the revolution. What if it starts after I leave? It would be sad because I would like to be part of it.

It took decades of campaigning to win LGBT rights in Europe and the US, but some activists in Russia fear that they might have to struggle for much longer. How close do you feel you are to a breakthrough?

Ivan Surok: It seems to me that nothing good will come out of this. [With] the voices of homophobia under the current regime, there won't be changes for the better. The inner enemy is still much needed, and the current government apparently satisfies people.

Daniel Grachev: Civil society in Russia is really weak. There are good organisations, but there are still too few people who believe that something can be changed. So I actually believe that this is only going to end after some global political changes. But [I am] not very optimistic because we don't know when [Putin's] presidency will end.

Elena Leontieva: The situation is getting more depressing, but we are trying to do what we can. That gives us a lot of power and strength to move forward and to be equal. But at this time it's quite dangerous to fight against the government.

Ruslan Savolainen: Europe took a long path to get to this point. And so did America. So this cannot be achieved in a year or two. It will take tremendous effort.

Svetlana Zakharova: I truly do believe that things can change, otherwise it's all pointless, but I'm quite aware that it's not going to happen soon. But I don't think it will be like this forever.

Interviews edited by Matthew Collin

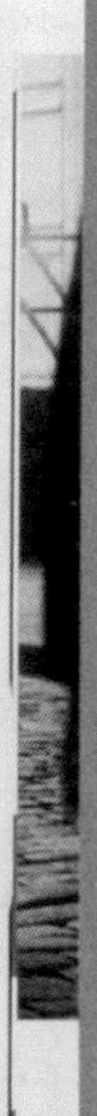

Infrastructuralism
John Durham Peters
2015

Infrastructure has come into prominence as a scholarly topic in the past two decades, reflecting wider political and economic changes as the Cold War waned, its large technical systems aged, and the tangle of networks known as the Internet was built. *Infrastructure* was first a military term. In World War II the British found Iceland's landing strip inadequate for their needs. As they were building a new airport in Reykjavik, they asked the Icelanders for financial support. Sorry, no, the Icelandic officials supposedly said—but feel free to take the airport with you when you leave. (The British did not, and it is still used for domestic flights.) Infrastructures are generally thought to be bulky and boring systems that are hard to carry, such as airports, highways, electrical grids, or aqueducts. Since the early nineteenth century the world has seen unprecedented development of infrastructure: railways, telegraphs, transoceanic cables, time zones, telecommunications networks, hydroelectric dams, power plants, weather forecasting systems, highways, and space programs. The Internet—"the new iconic infrastructure of our age," as Hillary Clinton put it—continues to motivate such questions.[1] Whatever else modernity is, it is a proliferation of infrastructures. "To be modern means to live within and by means of infrastructures."[2]

Infrastructures can be defined as "large, force-amplifying systems that connect people and institutions across large scales of space and time" or "big, durable, well-functioning systems and services."[3] Often they are backed by states or public-private partnerships that alone possess the capital, legal, or political force and megalomania to push them through. From Cheops to Stalin, infrastructures have been the playthings of dictators and tyrants; the Internet might seem a departure because of its apparent lack of centralized control, but there is plenty of state and market power shaping its development. Because of their vast technical complexity and costs, infrastructures are often cloaked from public scrutiny, their enormous risks and unintended consequences shielded from open debate. Traditional infrastructures are generally thought to be—or actively designed to be—immune to democratic governance, but remain open to sabotage if otherwise full of inertia (resistance to change).[4] They are almost always vulnerable to hijacking. Every tower invites toppling. "Once in place, infrastructures generate possibilities for their own corruption and parasitism."[5] Something there is that doesn't love a wall.

Though large in structure, infrastructures can be small in interface, appearing as water faucets, gas pumps, electrical outlets, computer terminals, cell phones, or airport security, all of them gates to bigger and submerged systems. Infrastructures are designed to reduce risk in underlying elements, but often produce new risks in doing so. Building systems means managing their side effects—and the side effects of the management itself. Electrical power lines, for instance, increase the risks of childhood leukemia.[6] The bigger the infrastructure, the more likely it is to drift out of awareness and the bigger the potential catastrophe. There were no train crashes before the railroad was built, and no potato famines before the monocultural overinvestment in that crop in Ireland. Leverage means vulnerability.

There are hard and soft infrastructures. Dams and websites, highways and protocols are equally infrastructural. There can be lightweight and portable as well as heavy and fixed infrastructures—a point made repeatedly by Innis. Compared with the concrete opera of Roman cities, roads, and aqueducts, the mathematics and history, philosophy and ethics, music and holidays of the Greeks and Jews are much more alive

1 "Remarks on Internet Freedom," http://www.state.gov/secretary/rm/2010/01/135519.htm (accessed 25 September 2013).

2 Paul N. Edwards, "Infrastructure and Modernity: Force, Time, and Social Organization in the History of Technical Systems," in *Modernity and Technology*, eds. Thomas J. Misa, Phillip Brey, and Andrew Feenberg (Cambridge, MA: MIT Press, 2002): 185–225, at 186.

3 Edwards, "Infrastructure and Modernity," 221; Paul N. Edwards, Geoffrey C. Bowker, Steven J. Jackson, Robin Williams, "Introduction: An Agenda for Infrastructure Studies," *Journal of the Association for Information Systems* 10, no. 5 (May 2009): 364–74, at 365.

4 John Keane, "Silence, Power, Catastrophe: New Reasons Democracy and Media Matter in the Early Years of the Twenty-First Century," Samuel L. Becker Lecture, 8 February 2012, University of Iowa.

5 Brian Larkin, "Degraded Images, Distorted Sounds: Nigerian Video and the Infrastructure of Piracy," *Public Culture* 16, no. 2 (2004): 289–314, at 289.

6 J. D. Bowman, D. C. Thomas, S. J. London, and J. M. Peters, "Hypothesis: The Risk of Childhood Leukemia Is Related to Combinations of Power-Frequency and Static Magnetic Fields," *Bioelectromagnetics* 16 (1995): 48–59. Our choice to live irradiated in baths of wireless fields has unexplored health consequences.

today. Indeed, what remains of Rome is its cultural engineering in religion, language, law, and the idea of Europe itself. Cultural continuity is often a greater achievement than continually functioning water or road systems: of all extant cultures, only the Chinese, Greeks, Indians, and Jews have managed to maintain their ethnic identity of multiple millennia (not without constant reinvention, of course). Software often outlasts hardware. In geologic time, all infrastructures suffer an Ozymandian fate. As Hegel noted of ancient Egypt, "The palaces of the kings and priests have been transformed into heaps of rubble, while their graves have defied time."[7] None are designed to outlast the typical life span of any civilization. The exception might be calendars, which in theory can be spun out on scales far vaster than any possible human maintenance, although any chance of keeping them closely synchronized with the sky will not last more than a few thousand years, thanks to the variability of the earth's motion. (Our calendar, as chapter 4 shows, requires updates much more often than that.) Civilization seems to have a limit of durability fixed in millennia, and maintenance of long-term systems of communication requires vast expense and expertise.[8]

Infrastructures tend to change incrementally, and have the inertia of previous innovations to build upon. They are improved upon modularly, and clearly illustrate the principle of path-dependence.[9] They demand labor and upkeep. They are infrastructures only to the degree that they are normalized into taken-for-granteds; they have social as well as technical components.[10] Retention of archaic functions and structures is as relevant in our media as in our tissues. Both bodily organs and technical (organa; "tools" in ancient Greek) are a hodgepodge of different environments layered upon each other. DNA is an archive of new and old. The same is true of any natural language (one reason why the history of words can be a great source of accumulated insight). We can call this the QWERTY principle: suboptimal patterns persist long past their initial conditions due to path-dependence.[11]

I am loath to introduce yet another "ism" into the scrimmage of academic brands, but if I were to do so, it would be the doctrine of *infrastructuralism*. After structuralism, with its ambition to explain the principles of thought, primitive or modern, by way of a combinatorics of meaning, and post-structuralism, with its love of gaps, aporias, and impossibilities, its celebration of breakdown, yearning, and failure, its relish for preposterous categories of all kinds and love of breathless syntax—perhaps it is time for infrastructuralism. Its fascination is for the basic, the boring, the mundane, and all the mischievous work done behind the scenes. It is a doctrine of environments and small differences, of strait gates and the needle's eye, of things not understood that stand under our worlds. Hence the quiet pun in the title of this chapter: infrastructural media are media that stand under.

Infrastructure in most cases is demure. Withdrawal is its modus operandi, something that seems a more general property of media, which sacrifice their own visibility in the act of making something else appear.[12] Marx was a theorist of infrastructure not only in his fascination for industrial apparatus, but also in his analysis of how power relations are camouflaged. The greatest thinkers of infrastructure were never interested only in the gear; they always wanted to know why awareness of essential things so quickly fades into "beaten paths of impercipience."[13] (This is a version of the old moral mystery of why the quest to find bedrock principles of right action never finds any bedrock more certain than the ongoing quest itself.) Freud made vivid use of infrastructural metaphors, viewing the psyche in terms of cities, sewers, ruins, filing systems, and postal censorship; but he was also an analyst of clouded awareness, of our distorted communication with ourselves. Every memory trace for him was a crime scene investigation to show off his considerable forensic skills.

Perhaps the most explicit effort to understand how the fundamentals recede into the background was that of Freud's contemporary Edmund Husserl, who developed philosophical phenomenology. Marx, Freud, Husserl and their contemporaries all lived through terrific infrastructural transformations and thought that boredom and obviousness were ruses by which consciousness hides the marvelous, often devious workings that make it possible. The same is true with such nineteenth-century figures as Charles Darwin, W. E. B. Du Bois, Émile Durkheim, Charlotte

7 G. W. F. Hegel, *Lectures on the Philosophy of Religion: The Lectures of 1827*, ed. Peter C. Hodgson (Berkeley: University of California Press, 1988), 321n339.

8 See Marisa Leavitt Cohn, *Lifetimes and Legacies: Temporalities of Sociotechnical Change in a Long-Lived System*, University of California, Irvine, PhD diss., 2013.

9 Susan Leigh Star, "The Ethnography of Infrastructure," *American Behavioral Scientist* 43 (1999): 377–91, at 382.

10 Susan Leigh Star and Karen Ruhleder, "Steps toward an Ecology of Infrastructure: Design and Access for Large Information Spaces," *Information Systems Research* 7, no. 1 (1995): 111–34.

11 Paul A. David, "Clio and the Economics of QWERTY," *American Economic Review* 75, no. 2 (1985): 332–37; and S. J. Liebowitz and Stephen E. Margolis, "The Fable of the Keys," *Journal of Law and Economics* 33, no. 1 (1990): 1–25.

12 Dieter Mersch, "Tertium datur: Einleitung in einer negativen Medientheorie," *Was ist ein Medium?*, ed. Stefan Münker and Alexander Roesler (Frankfurt: Suhrkamp, 2008), 304–21, at 304.

13 Marshall McLuhan, *Understanding Media: The Extensions of Man* (Corte Madera: Gingko Press, 2003), 198.

Perkins Gilman, Ferdinand de Saussure, and Max Weber, with their analyses of the infrastructures of life, race, society, gender and language. For thinkers born in the nineteenth century, it was madness not to observe the nexus, as they lived through the triumph of steam, coal, electricity, barbed wire, standard sizes, and standard time. All of them believed in the power of reason to either get to the bottom of things or make a greater mess of them. Freud's famous dictum, "Wo es war, soll ich werden" (Where it was, I should be), might be understood as the imperative to make all infrastructures clear. There is a deep infrastructural ethic in modern thought.

One of the key books that launched much of the recent interest in infrastructure, *Sorting Things Out* (1999) by Geoffrey Bowker and the late Leigh Star, brought a strong phenomenological heritage to infrastructure studies. Infrastructure was pushed beyond large, heavy systems to be a question of how basic categories and standards are formed, and how they are formed as ordinary. How the taken-for-granted gets constructed in the first place is a classic phenomenological question: how did the water ever become invisible to the fish? Bowker and Star see our worlds as bristling with standards and forgotten rules that produce everyday things in their everydayness and are sustained by the ghostly cumulus of bodies at work. Ordinary objects such as compact disks and pencils conceal "decades of negotiation." As Bowker and Star quip, "There is a lot of hard labor in effortless ease."[14] To break through the crust, they offer the concept of "infrastructural inversion," a cousin to what Harold Garfinkel called "breaching"—the intentional violation of a social norm to bring the background out into the open. Something similar happens with accidents and breakdowns: infrastructure comes out of the woodwork. Glitches can be as fruitful intellectually as they are frustrating practically.[15] Essence, intoned Heidegger (channeling Aristotle), is revealed in accident.[16]

Infrastructure is often as hard to see as a light rain through the window. Not only is it invisible by nature, but it can be camouflaged by design in what Lisa Parks calls "infrastructural concealment."[17] Some infrastructures (water, sewers, electrical and cable lines) are literally buried in the ground (or underwater) and others are designed to blend in with the scenery. More rarely, towers or hydroelectric dams are intentional displays of power and modernity, and some architectural fashions have foregrounded the guts of a building (as in the Centre Pompidou in Paris, where extruded pipes and conduits are a flamboyant part of the design). In the twentieth century, broadcasting houses were temples of transmission that celebrated their own technicity.[18] In a similar way, as we see below, medieval clock towers were statements of civic wealth and eminence. Technologies are never only functional: any device always has an element of social display or "bling."

Forgetting seems a key part of the way infrastructures work. Star notes that they are often "mundane to the point of boredom."[19] But it all depends on what the structure is *infra* to. Infrastructure is often defined by being off the radar, below notice, or off stage. Redundancy may be boring, but the essence of robust systems is backup options. Technology, in contrast, is a concept biased towards newness: breathing, fire control, writing, or cities rarely count, even though that's where much of the hard work is. We have the unhelpful habit of isolating the bright, shiny, new, or scary parts of our made environment and calling them "technology," to the neglect of the older, seemingly duller parts. Horses were as important as tanks in both world wars, and bicycles have been as important as cars in recent decades.[20] There is a politics to boredom. "Mature technological systems reside in a naturalized background, as ordinary and unremarkable to us as trees, daylight, and dirt," says Paul Edwards.[21] He is completely right, but trees, daylight, and dirt, of course, are highly remarkable: they are also mature technological systems. ("The invariable mark of wisdom," said Emerson, "is to see the miraculous in the common."[22]) The perception of monotony is a measure of the breadth of mind: nothing would be boring to the mind of God. Studying how boring things got that way is actually a good way never to be bored. This book seeks to brew this elixir, wagering that the wonder of the basic can beat its banality.

Infrastructuralism suggests a way of understanding the work of media as fundamentally logistical. Logistical media have the job of ordering fundamental terms and units. They add to the leverage exerted by recording media that compress time, and by transmit-

14 Geoffrey C. Bowker and Susan Leigh Star, *Sorting Things Out: Classification and its Consequences* (Cambridge: MIT, 1999); the quote from 9.35 has a useful definition of infrastructure.

15 See Peter Krapp, *Noise Channels* (Minneapolis: University of Minnesota Press, 2011).

16 "In einer *Störung der Verweisung* ... wird aber die Verweisung ausdrücklich." Martin Heidegger, *Sein und Zeit* (1927; Tübingen: Niemeyer, 1993), 74.

17 Lisa Parks, "Technostruggles and the Satellite Dish: A Populist Approach to Infrastructure," *Cultural Technologies: The Shaping of Culture in Media and Society*, ed. Göran Bolin (London: Routledge, 2012), 64–84.

18 See Staffan Ericson and Kristina Riegert, *Media Houses: Architecture, Media, and the Production of Centrality* (New York: Peter Lang, 2010).

19 Star, "Ethnography of Infrastructure," 377.

20 David Edgerton, *The Shock of the Old: Technology and Global History Since 1900* (London: Profile, 2008).

21 Edwards, "Infrastructure and Modernity," 185.

22 *Nature, Selected Writings of Emerson*, ed. Donald McQuade (1837; New York: Modern Library, 1981), 41.

ting media that compress space. The job of logistical media is to organize and orient, to arrange people and property, often into grids. They both coordinate and subordinate, arranging relationships among people and things.[23] Logistical media establish the zero points where the *x* and *y* axes converge. McLuhan's slogan "The medium is the message" applies particularly well to them. They prepare the ground on which we can make such distinctions as nature and culture. They span ocean, ground, air, outer space, and cyberspace. Chapters 4 and 5 explore logistical media most fully, focusing on classic forms such as calendars, clocks and towers. Other key examples are names, indexes, addresses, maps, lists (like this one), tax rolls, logs, accounts, archives, and the census. Money is surely the master logistical medium—a medium, as Karl Marx complained, that has no content in itself but has the power to arrange everything else around it.[24]

In arraying things around polar points, logistical media set the terms in which everyone must operate. The zero is the paradigm case of a logistical medium: an apparent nothing that marks out longitude and latitude, and orders of magnitude, and thus shapes the world; it is an operator that arranges data and regulates processing. (Few would complain if their bank accounts acquired an extra zero in the right place.) The zero is an Archimedean ϖ (*pankration*), a lever that moves the earth. (Zero never exists in the numeral system of any natural spoken language, but is a creature of graphical practices, such as calendar making and accounting.) Brigham Young's cane served thus when it marked out the center spot, the temple, around which the addresses of the Salt Lake valley ever after, like it or not, would be gridded. Logistical media pretend to be neutral and abstract, but they often encode a subtle and deep political or religious partisanship. People still debate whether our era is "AD" or "CE," and whether the day after Saturday is called "Sunday" or "first day" (see chapter 4). The point—as vanishing point, decimal point, and printer's spatium—is one of the most critical of all modern media.[25] Though logistical media usually appear as neutral and given, their tilt and slant can also call forth agitation.

Infrastructuralism shares a classic concern of media theory: the call to make environments visible. Perhaps McLuhan's most fundamental ethical call, against his horrified fantasies of mankind growing into a single hive mind, was the call to awareness.[26] McLuhan saw those of us who ignored our technological habitats "somnambulists," invoking the Greek myth of Narcissus to explain our media narcosis. Blessed are they, said Kittler, who could hear the circuitry in the compact disc or see it in the discotheque's light shows.[27] Ontology, whatever else it is, is usually just forgotten infrastructure.

23 Gabriele Schabacher, "Raum-Zeit-Regime: Logistikgeschichte als Wissenszirkulation zwischen Medien, Verkehr, und Ökonomie," *Agenten und Agenturen. Archiv für Mediengeschichte*, eds. Lorenz Engell, Joseph Vogl, and Bernhard Siegert (Weimar: Bauhaus Universität, 2008), 135–48, at 145. See also Judd Ammon Case, *Geometry of Empire: Radar as Logistical Medium* (PhD diss., University of Iowa, 2010); and "Logistical Media: Fragments from Radar's Prehistory," *Canadian Journal of Communication* 38, no. 3 (summer 2013): 379–95.

24 On money, see Hartmut Winkler, *Diskursökonomie* (Frankfurt: Suhrkamp, 2004), 36–49.

25 See Wolfgang Schäffner, "The Point: The Smallest Venue of Knowledge," trans. Walter Kerr, *Collection, Laboratory, Theater: Scenes of Knowledge in the 17th Century*, ed. Helmar Schramm, Ludger Schwarte, Jan Lazardzig (Berlin: Walter de Grutyer, 2005), 57–74.

26 "Today we need also the will to be exceedingly informed and aware." *Understanding Media*, 75.

27 Friederich A. Kittler, *Gramophon Film Typewriter* (Berlin: Brinkmann und Bose, 1986), 5; *Gramophone, Film, Typewriter* trans. Geoffrey Winthop-Young and Michael Wutz (Stanford, CA: Stanford University Press, 1999), xli.

The Distributed Image
Peter Osborne
2015

1. To think about the role of photography in contemporary art today it is necessary to consider the place of the photographic image within the technologically changing landscape of image production, and its relations to digitally produced images of all sorts, in particular. If, according to a certain technologically-based historical theory of dominant form, the image became constitutively "photographic" in the early twentieth century, but has subsequently become "digital," it is nonetheless photographically originated digital images (digital photography) that dominate the image-spaces of mass media and art institutions alike—for all the growth and significance of the computer-generated imagery that accompanies and relates them. The place of the photographic (in its extended sense, including film and digital video) within the image-sphere has thus become doubled. It is at once the signifier of a past technological form of image production, in which iconicity is tied to indexicality and thereby a specific kind of truth (however constructive the photographic practice may be), and an equal participant in the infinitely multiplying visualizations of data that fill the screens of the digital meta-medium. Within this latter space, visual "information" may be quantitatively reducible to data, but both knowledge and truth continue to elude such reduction. In fact, quantitative and visual degradation of the image as an effect of copying, reformatting, and passing through digital networks of distribution may increase its truth-content in a variety of ways.[1]

2. This convergence of information and image-production within the digital problematizes—indeed, reverses—two influential historical narratives about cultural form. One is the self-understanding of canonical Conceptual art: a construction in which information and image ("morphology") were opposed and Conceptual art was taken to represent a transition from image-based forms of artistic production to an informational one. The other is the deeper technologically based historical narrative about the changing communicational forms of modernity—associated with Walter Benjamin, but subsequently widely developed in various forms—that holds modernity's "destruction of tradition" to involve the replacement of the essentially oral narrative form of the story by what Benjamin himself called the "new form of communication" of "information."[2] In the first instance, information, presented as the meta-linguistic medium of Conceptual art, was used to oppose—if not negate or at least to neutralize or render indifferent—the aesthetic aspect of the artwork, even when images were themselves the means of such negation. Indeed, this was the main role of photography within those practices. ("[P]hotography is dead as a fine art," Ed Ruscha declared to *Artforum* in February 1965. "Its only place is in the commercial world, for technical or informational purposes."[3]) Yet the polemical project for the de-aestheticization of art quickly ran up against its limit in the necessarily aesthetic aspect of all forms of presentation (however minimal) and the refusal of aesthetic to remain indifferent within art spaces. In turn, the formal qualities of the photographic image became increasingly central to the self-consciously strategic character of the critical re-functioning of aesthetic within the postconceptual structure of a generic contemporary art.[4]

3. Within such an art, information and image no longer appear incompatible. Rather, they are mediated as the dual aspects or dimensions of a single practice. This is a structural matter, at the level of the ontology of the postconceptual work, but it is also a historical one, insofar as this ontology develops in relation to new technologies of image production. What digitally produced images and postconceptual art have in common is a certain

1 See Hito Steyerl, "In Defense of the Poor Image," in *The Wretched of the Screen*, (Berlin: 2012), 33–45.
2 Walter Benjamin, "The Storyteller: Observations on the Works of Nikolai Leskov," in *Selected Writings, Volume 3, 1935–1938*, (Cambridge, MA and London: Harvard University Press, 2002) 147.
3 Extracted in Lucy P. Lippard, *Six Years: The Dematerialization of the Art Object from 1966 to 1972* (1973), (Berkeley/Los Angeles/London: University of California Press, 1997), 12.
4 See Peter Osborne, *Anywhere or Not At All: Philosophy of Contemporary Art*, (London/New York: New Left Books, 2013), ch. 2.

structure of distribution. Both the digitally produced image and the postconceptual artwork are *distributed forms*, but they are distributed across different fields, in related but ontologically distinct ways.

4. To take the digitally produced image first: it is a distributed image in several senses. First, the digital composition of its information structure distributes imagistically heterogeneous elements, homogeneously, across any particular site of visualization or screen. Structurally, each pixel is of equal value in the *production* of the image, and in the pixel the informational structure of the image is rendered literally visible. This is a new spatial ontology in which the photographic no longer appears opposed to the space of the graphic, but is rather one of its modes.[5] This changes the historically received meaning of "the photographic" in a fundamental way.

5. Second, in digital video this new spatial ontology combines with the temporality of cinematic montage to produce a new technological means for the realization of what, in the mid-1960s, Alexander Kluge and others anticipated as that "greater degree of complexity" in the "combination of verbal, auditory and visual forms and their integration" that would concentrate its subject matter "in the spaces between the forms of expression." On this classically constructivist account of the structural possibilities of film, the accumulation of elements "preserve[s] a certain tension in relation to each," which makes itself felt "in the gaps which montage create[s] between the disparate elements of filmic expression."[6] With and within digitally produced images, these "disparate elements of expression" are radically expanded, incorporating both photographic and non-photographic elements, and the possibilities of relations (and hence "gaps") between them are multiplied. In particular, in digital video we see the return of the oral narrative of the story (often in the form of testimony) as one of these elements of expression among others, used as a means to establish living relations to various historical actualities. Here digitally produced moving images distribute experience across a new temporal, as well as a new spatial field.

6. Just as information is no longer opposed to image, but is the very matter of its construction, so too information no longer appears incompatible with the story (as it was for Benjamin), but incorporates it as an element—indeed, often as an articulated combination of elements: auditory and visual—into its constructive logic. The translation of "the archive back into individual life stories" (to evoke the analogy with Kluge once more),[7] which this makes possible, has become the means for certain artists to use memory, against the grain of its dominant sentimental use as a repression of the history it claims to represent, as an element in the construction of historical experience.[8] For the temporality involved here is not that of the simple addition, or layering, of cinematic montage onto the new spatial ontology. Rather, it is a more complex temporality constructed out of the relations between the narrativity of the story and the interruptive, spatially distributed character of the still or unmoving image, the stasis of which registers the common now of the time of viewing. This is central to the establishment of the historical *contemporaneity* of such works: their bringing together of different times (different social times and different historical times) within the disjunctive "living" unity of the present. Within the relational whole of the articulated ensemble of elements, each element functions as a separate subject of speech, creating a pluri-vocal ensemble in which it is the exchange between the *thing-like* and *subject-like* aspects of the image that establishes its specific temporality.

7. Third, the image itself (as a de-realized entity) is distributed across the open and indefinitely proliferating field of its multiple instances of production/visualization, within a wide variety of different formats and material instantiations, and through a variety of processes of transformation (degradation/augmentation) to which it is subjected in the course of its distribution. This contrasts with the emblematically singular actuality of the chemically based photographic image, which lies metonymically in the individual photographic print, however frequently replicated. There, the theological structure of the photograph derives from its famous indexical "immobilization of time."[9] And yet, the theological structure of the

5 Cf. Lev Manovich, *The Language of New Media*, (Cambridge, MA: The MIT Press, 2001), 311. "The photographic and the graphic, divorced when cinema and animation went their separate ways, met again on the computer screen."
6 Edgar Reitz/Alexander Kluge/Wilfried Reinke, "Word and Film" (1965), trans. Mariam Hansen in: *October*, 46, 1988, (1988), 87.
7 Andreas Huyssen, "An Analytic Storyteller in the Course of Time," in: *October*, 46, (1988), 121.
8 I am thinking in particular here of works produced by artists working out of the archive of the Arab Image Foundation in Beirut, especially Walid Raad and Akram Zaatari.
9 Roland Barthes, *Camera Lucida: Reflections on Photography* (1980), trans. Richard Howard, (London: 1984), 94.

digital image resides primarily in the *infinite productivity of the variety* of its forms of visualization.[10] Formally, digital photography, at the outset of producing an image, holds the potential of both these characteristics. Once digitalized, however, the photographic image enters the economy of the digitally produced image per se, and its specifically "photographic" characteristics (which were always ultimately *imaginary*, in their dependence upon an extra-temporal, God-like view of its temporal relations) are eroded. Herein lies the fundamental ontological ambiguity of the expression "digital photograph."

8. Finally, the digitally produced image is a distributed image in the sense that it is open to a tendentially global *social distribution* via the internet. The social actualization of the quantitative potential of the proliferation of visualizations is both dense and extended: it produces a qualitative transformation in the social space, the functions, and hence also the meanings of the images produced. It is not just images of migrancy that exhibit the politics of a crisis-ridden globalization (the restricted meaning given to the phrase "migrant image" in T. J. Demos's recent book),[11] but equally the migrancy of the image itself. There is an inherent tendency in the distributive networks of the digital image to move the image on. This affects not only the ontology of the image (the de-realization of which is intensified by the multiplication of its instances), but also the ontology of the social field across which it is distributed, since that field is now partly constituted by this distribution.

9. The digitally produced and distributed image "lives" (has social actuality) increasingly, through its relations to and *transformation into* other images, within a tendentially globalized image space—rather than through a direct relationship with "the real" (the indexical model), even if the content of the individual image is photographically indexically derived. And in so far as the distributive networks of digital imagery are an increasingly constitutive part of the social reality that they image, they carry with them a multiplicity of relations to other social practices. In this respect, digital imagery is an element of immanent reflexivity within global social practices and processes. Furthermore, the exchange of images—and links to images—itself produces new social networks that, in turn, become the conditions of production for new images. This is one of the historical conditions for the return of the story. For it was not just the temporal difference between information and storytelling that led Benjamin to see the latter as a waning cultural form in modernity, but more fundamentally what he took to be the loss of "the ability to share experience."[12]

10. If the digital is the primary means of image production in contemporary art today (digital photography its main form), it nonetheless remains the case that the ontology of art cannot be reduced to the ontology of the image—digital or otherwise. Its social and institutional constitution and functions are too specific. At the level of its basic structure, though, postconceptual art is also a distributed form, albeit in rather different ways.

11. First, the postconceptual work is also distributed across the open and, in principle, indefinitely proliferating totality of instances of its production and exhibition. However, rather than these instances being, exclusively, instances or events of "visualization" (in the sense in which an image is always a perceptual abstraction of a visual structure from its material instantiation), in the postconceptual artwork they are also instances of *materialization*. The aesthetic fullness of the material means is as significant to the work as the structure of their image—along with the wider relational and conceptual aspects of the work, through which it derives its social and historical meanings. The artwork cannot be reduced to its character as an image. The work is thus best identified with the *distributive unity* of the totality of its materializations, at any one time, rather than with the *element of identity* that links the distributed series of visualizations of digitally produced images, at the level of their visual form. In terms of its logical form, the postconceptual artwork is thus more radically distributive than the digitally distributed image.

12. Second and conversely, however, with regard to the social distribution of the elements of the work, the artwork is far more restrictedly distributed and its distribution far more rigorously policed by the laws of ownership and control (by art institutions and artists' estates) than the digital image, which proliferates exponentially on the Internet. The legal ground underlying the cultural authority of institutional display makes all art—without exception—subject to far more conservative regimes of

10 Cf. Peter Osborne, *Anywhere*, op. cit., 123–133.

11 T. J. Demos, *The Migrant Image: The Art and Politics of Documentary during Global Crisis*, (Durham,/London: Duke University Press, 2013)

12 Walter Benjamin, "The Storyteller," op. cit., 145.

circulation than images as such. The digital artwork straddles these two contradictory regimes of social distribution. It is, no doubt, the anxiety surrounding its potentially uncontrolled proliferation that leads the exhibitionary complex to insist upon specific modes of installation of digital video, for example, frequently supplemented by sculptural elements, which "protect" the work from unrestricted distribution, by expanding its material constituents.

13. Photography straddles the overlapping categorical divides of the digital/non-digital and art/non-art, linking them and divided by them alike.

Untitled
Iza Genzken
2016

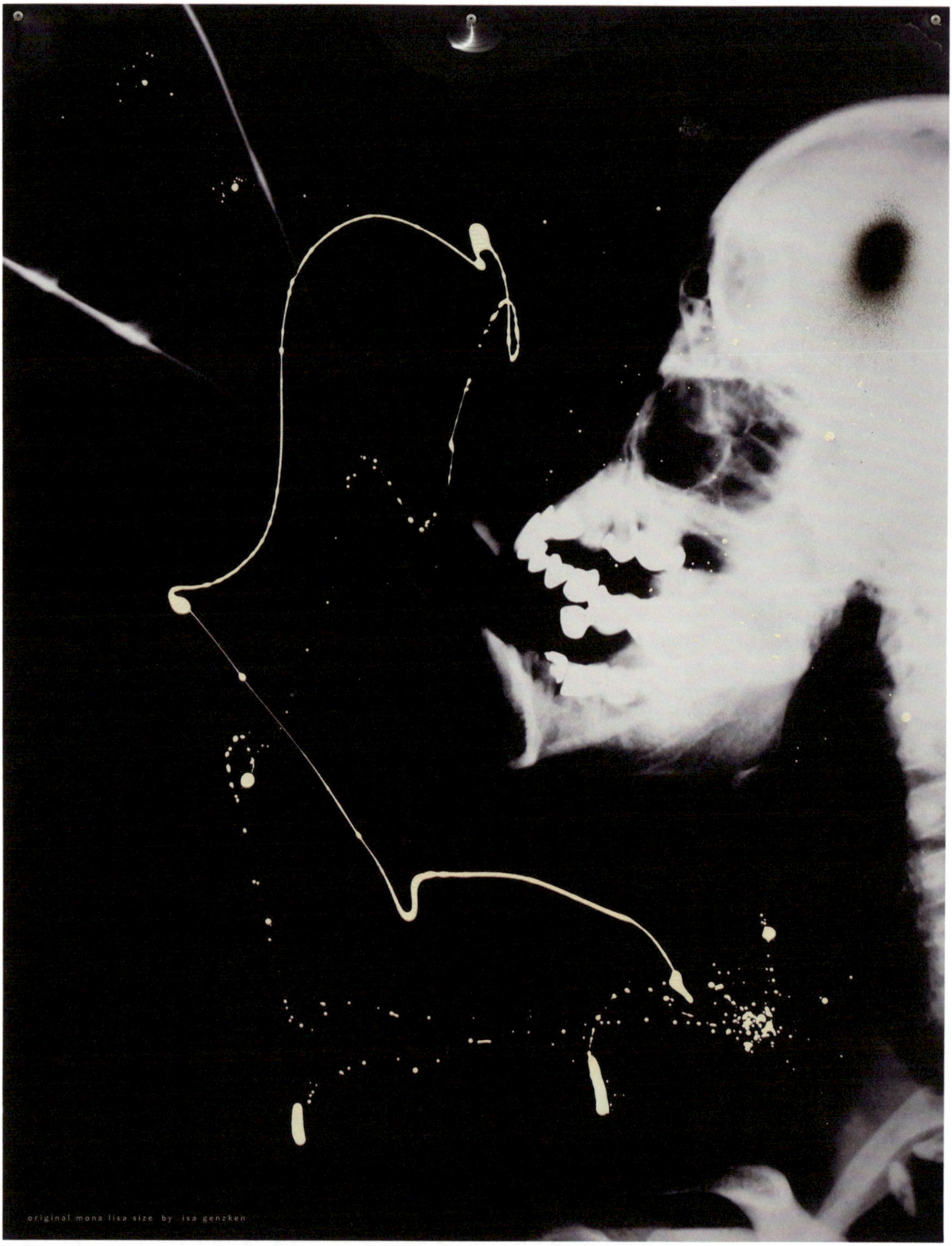

Parasagittal Brain

Yngve Holen

2013

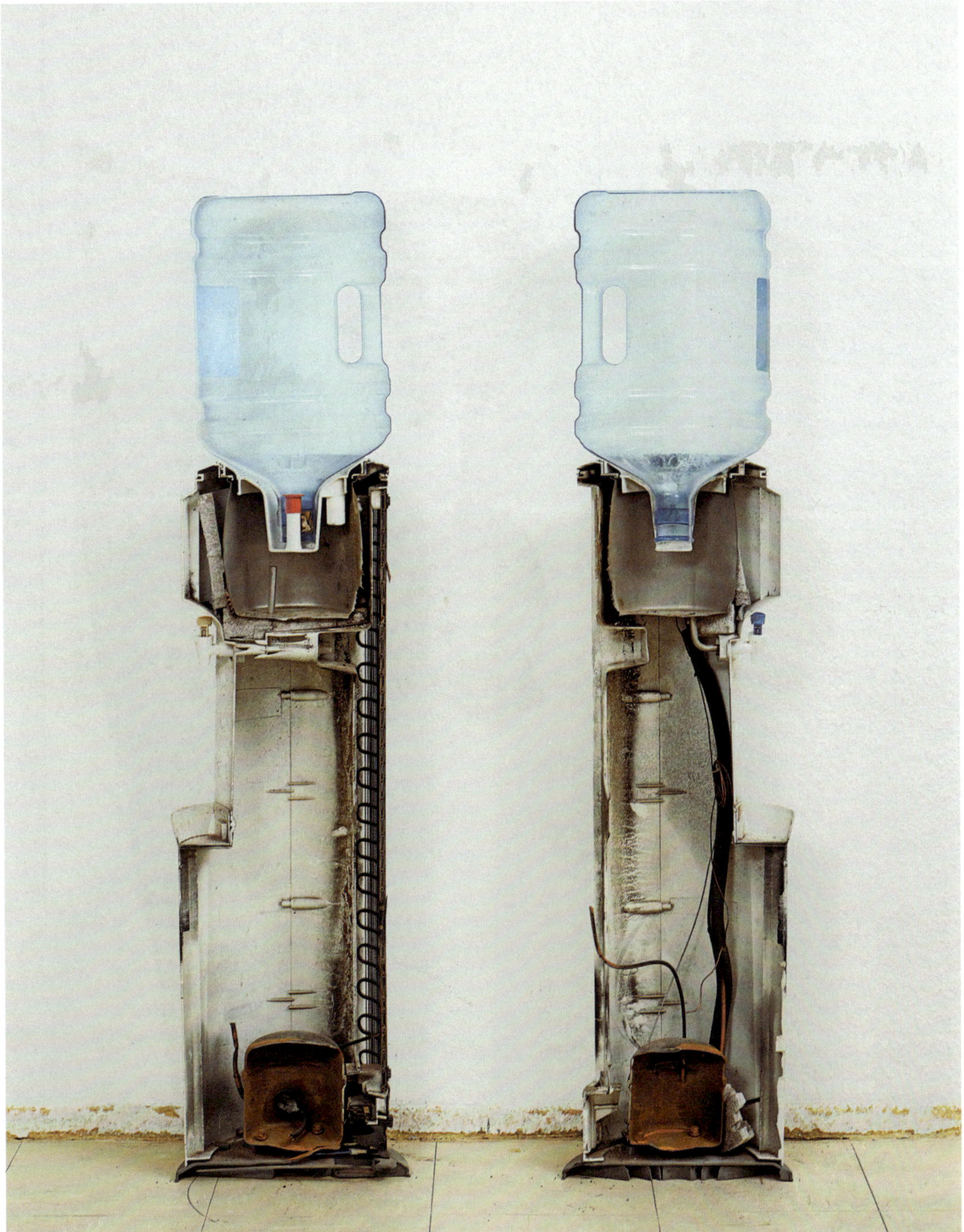

Flint is Family in *Elle* Magazine, September 2016

LaToya Ruby Frazier

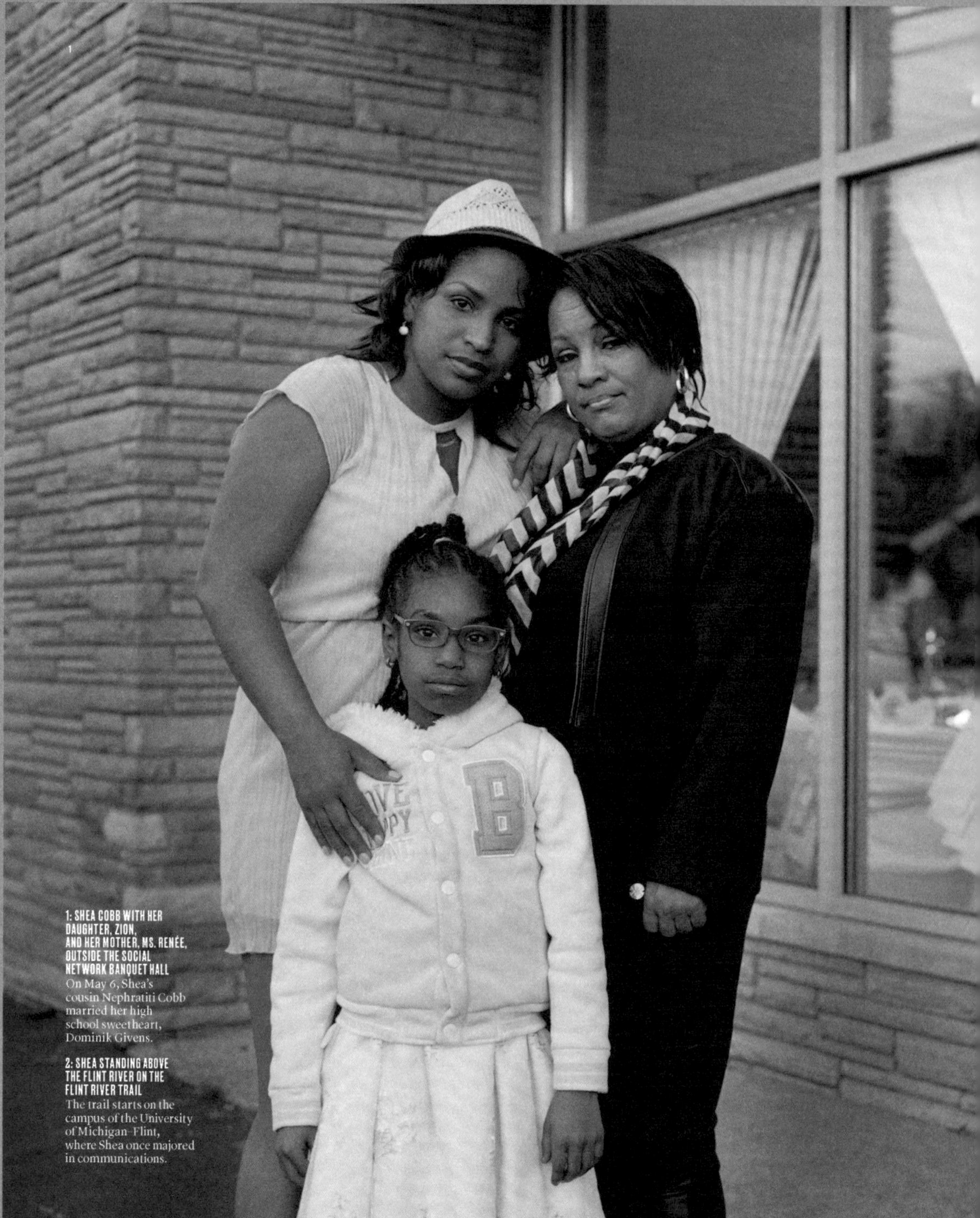

1: SHEA COBB WITH HER DAUGHTER, ZION, AND HER MOTHER, MS. RENÉE, OUTSIDE THE SOCIAL NETWORK BANQUET HALL
On May 6, Shea's cousin Nephratiti Cobb married her high school sweetheart, Dominik Givens.

2: SHEA STANDING ABOVE THE FLINT RIVER ON THE FLINT RIVER TRAIL
The trail starts on the campus of the University of Michigan–Flint, where Shea once majored in communications.

LINT IS FAMILY

In America, clean drinking water is a basic human right. Or at least it's supposed to be. Celebrated photographer LATOYA RUBY FRAZIER brings her collaborative art to Flint, Michigan, to give us an intimate look at the lives of three generations of women enduring the consequences of this broken social contract

When President Obama took a sip of Flint's water with flashbulbs popping in early May, many assumed the city's two-year crisis with tainted water was over. But photographer and MacArthur genius-grant recipient LaToya Ruby Frazier has a different story to tell. Evoking themes from *The Notion of Family*—her critically praised book documenting the boom, decline, and (touted) revitalization of her own Rust Belt Pennsylvania town through portraits of her mother, grandmother, and herself—Frazier spent five months making collaborative photographs with three generations of Flint women who both suffer and insistently thrive amid the worst man-made environmental catastrophe in recent national memory.

The bare facts: In April 2014, in what city leaders pitched as a cost-cutting move, Flint disconnected from the Detroit water system and hooked up to the Flint River. Within weeks, residents noticed brown water coming from their taps and reported breaking out in rashes. For a year and a half, local and state officials dismissed citizens' complaints, maintaining the water was fine even as they issued a series of boil-water advisories. It wasn't until October 2015, in fact, that the county health department declared a public health emergency and announced the water was not safe to drink. The river water had corroded hundreds of miles of pipes citywide, allowing lead and iron to leach into the system. The incidence of high lead levels in Flint children had doubled since the switch, medical researchers found, and nearly tripled among those in the most disadvantaged areas. Illegal amounts of various bacteria were detected (in violation of the federal Safe Drinking Water Act), and almost 100 people were treated for a severe form of pneumonia linked to the contaminated water. Twelve died.

Today, Flint residents are still drinking bottled water—as of May 3, the Federal Emergency Management Agency has carted in 9 million liters—or, at the very least, using lead filters on their taps. The city switched back to the Detroit water supply nearly a year ago, but the pipes are still corroded, the lead levels are still elevated in some parts of the city, and public health officials can't predict how long it will be before the water is safe to drink.

Born and raised in Flint, 32-year-old Shea Cobb, a spoken-word poet and singer who drives a school bus to support her family, lives with her mother, Renée Cobb, who works the third shift at the local General Motors factory, and her 9-year-old daughter, Zion. Shea's grandparents, Leroy and Hazel Cobb, settled in Flint in the late 1960s, when GM employed almost 40 percent of the city's 200,000 residents. Leroy joined the force, supporting his wife and seven children as a master mechanic at Buick. While the oil shocks of the 1970s and the plummeting demand for American-made cars in the 1980s ravaged the local economy, the large Cobb family mostly hung on in the place once dubbed "the happiest town in Michigan."

After two years of taking two-minute showers, washing her dishes in bottled water, and living in fear for her daughter's health, Shea has decided to leave Flint and join her father in Mississippi, in a reversal of the mid-twentieth-century Great Migration of blacks from the Jim Crow–era South. The move will tear her away from her friends, her artistic collaborators, and her extended family—most of whom are headed out, too, to Alabama, Georgia, Ohio. As a girl, Shea used to visit her father's horse farm in Mississippi during school breaks, and he's periodically urged her to join him ever since. A call he made to her a few months ago clinched her decision to go: "This water isn't going to kill you," he told Shea. "Come home."—*Mattie Kahn*

2

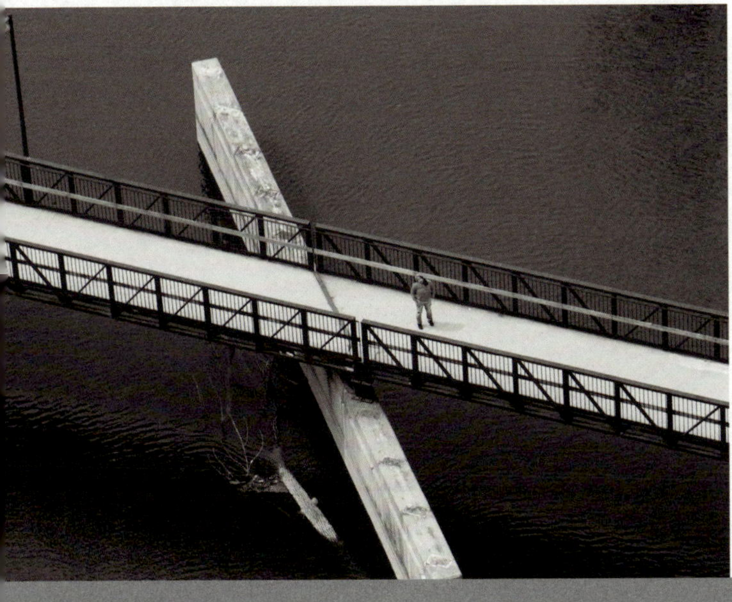

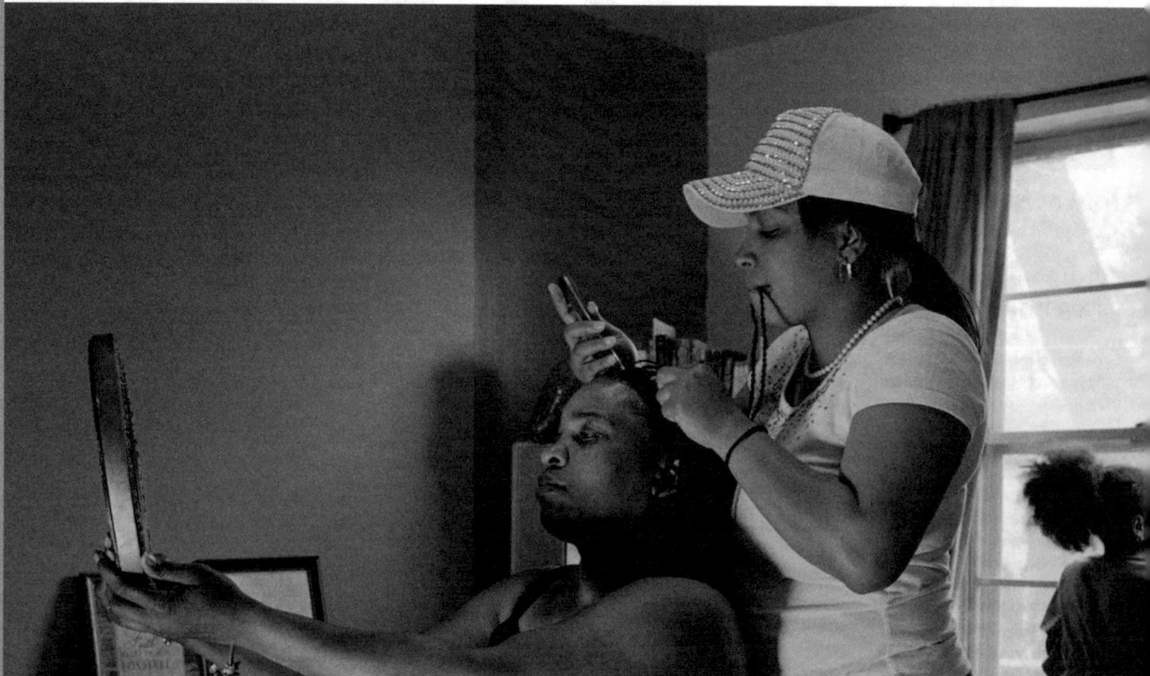

1

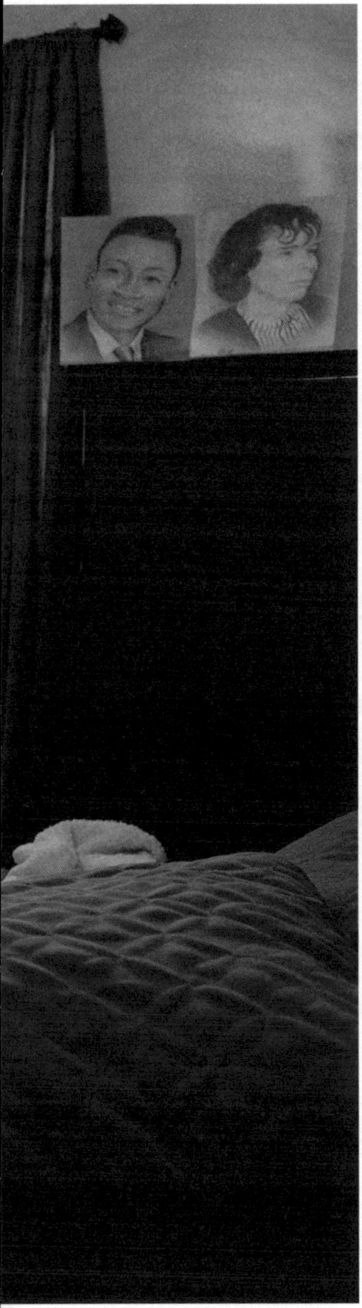

2

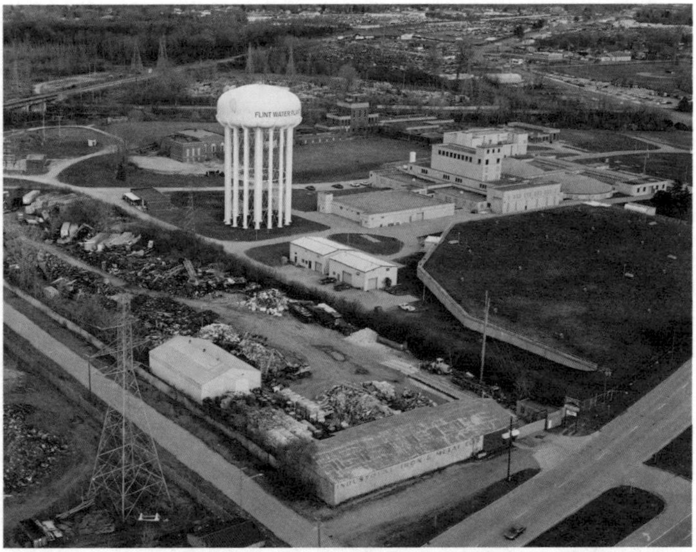

3

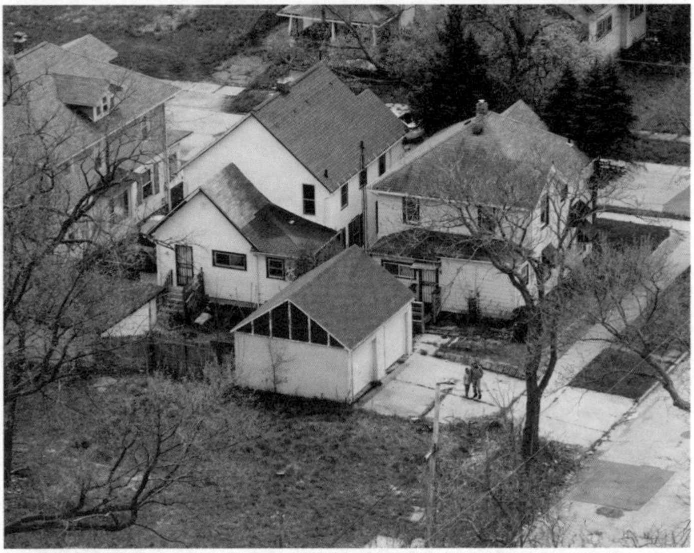

1: SHEA DOING CROCHET BRAIDS IN HER COUSIN ANDREA'S HAIR FOR ANDREA'S DAUGHTER NEPHRATITI'S WEDDING
Shea and I made this, our first intimate portrait together, in her bedroom at her mother's house on Sheffield Avenue. She learned how to do hair from Ms. Renée, who ran a hair salon from her home.

2: CITY OF FLINT WATER PLANT AND THE INDUSTRIAL IRON & METAL CO.
Flint residents paid the highest water rates in the country in 2015—nearly double the national average—and got contaminated water in return.

3: SHEA AND ZION AT SHEA'S GRANDPARENTS' HOME, 303 MARY STREET, IN FLINT'S FIFTH WARD
Shea's grandfather, Leroy Cobb, taught all the girls in the family about automotive maintenance. He died in 2007, and her grandmother, Hazel Cobb, lived here until she died more than a year ago. Located in an area heavily affected by corroded lead pipes, the home now sits empty.

1

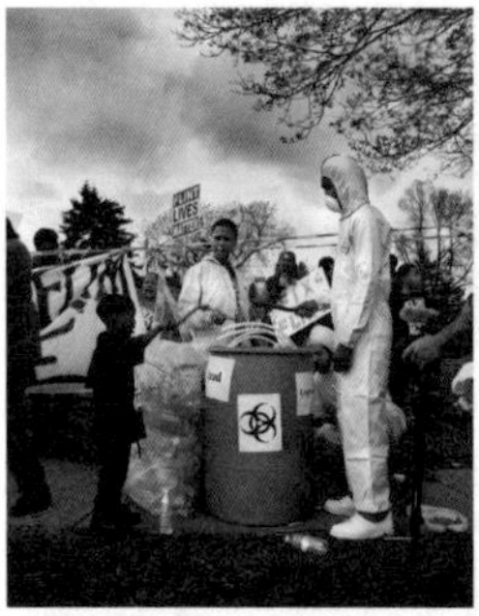

2

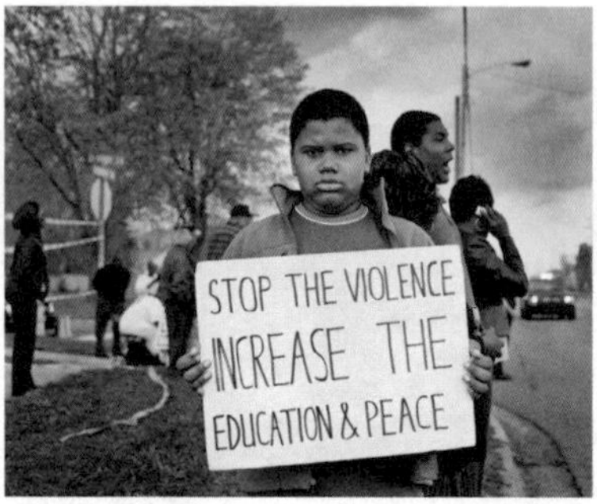

3

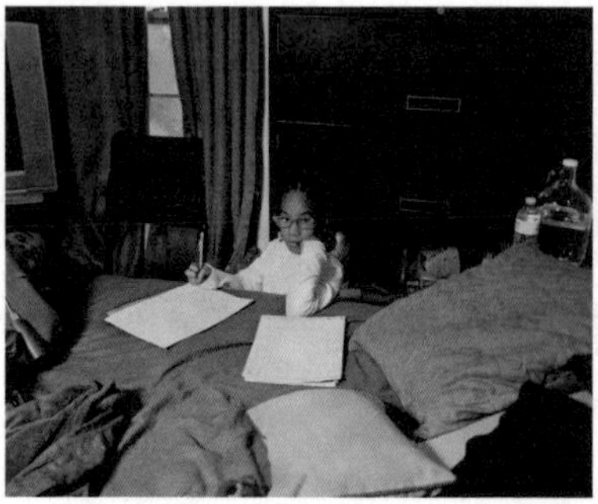

4

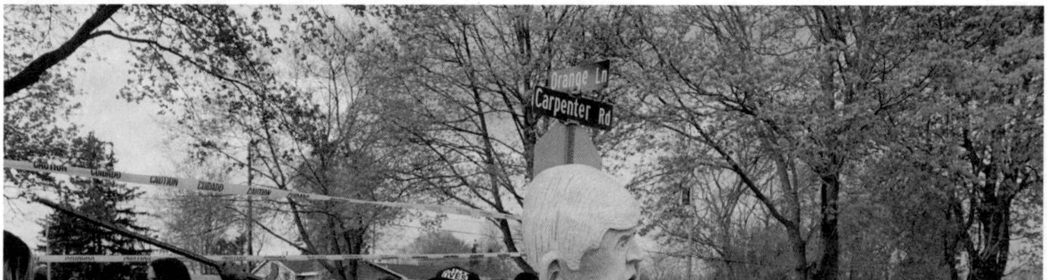

1, 2, 4: FLINT RESIDENTS AND STUDENTS FROM NORTHWESTERN HIGH SCHOOL AWAIT THE ARRIVAL OF PRESIDENT BARACK OBAMA, MAY 4, 2016
"Flint Lives Matter! No bottled water!" protesters chanted. "Obama, Obama, can't you see, this dirty water's killing me!" And, as one woman called out, "*Obama*, I can't wash my hair, I wanna go home with you!" Police kept people off the street with caution tape, and anyone who stepped off the sidewalk was ordered back on by officers. Snipers peered down at the crowd from the rooftop of the high school.

3: ZION DOING HER MATH HOMEWORK FROM THE INTERNATIONAL ACADEMY OF FLINT PREPARATORY SCHOOL
Shea keeps track of Zion's homework and gives her additional math problems to reinforce the curriculum.

5: SHEA DRIVES BUS 38, ROUTE 305, FOR FLINT COMMUNITY SCHOOLS
As a standby driver, Shea works a split shift, from 6 to 8:40 A.M., then 2 to 4:30 P.M., plus field trips. Zion's paternal grandmother takes her to school in the mornings; Shea picks her up from an after-school program once she finishes work. Shea approaches her job as "an opportunity to mentor the children of Flint."

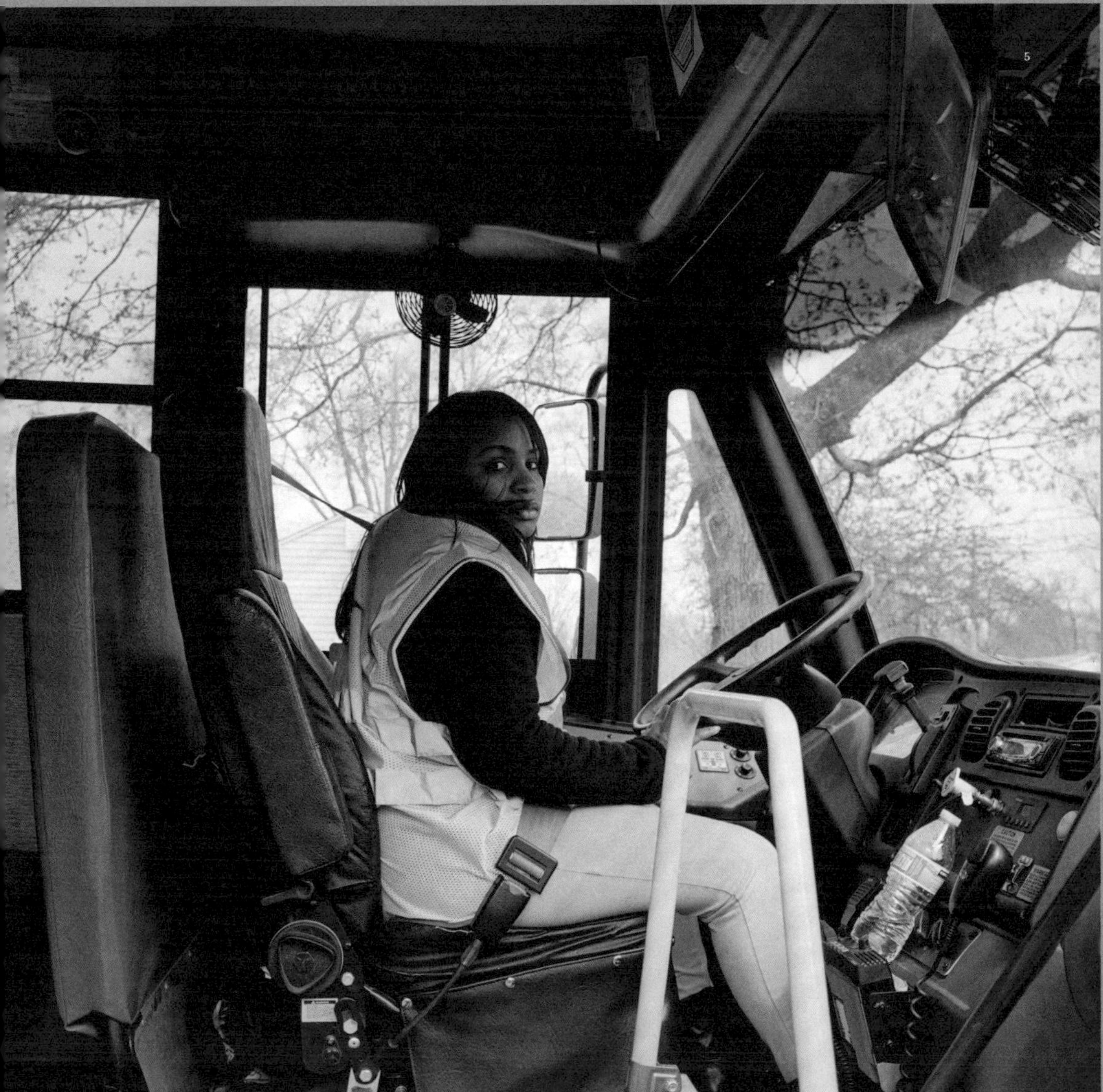

5

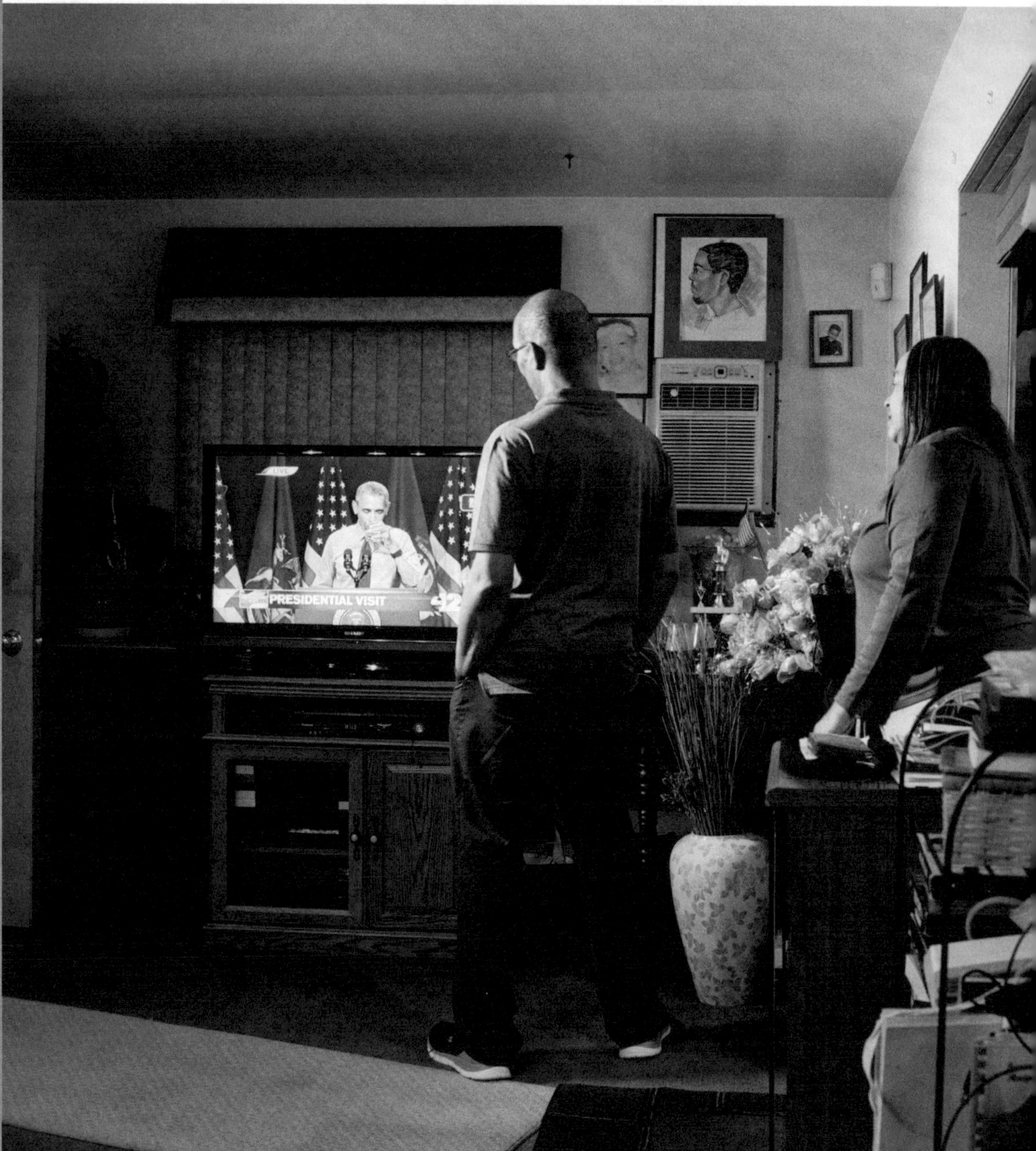
PRESIDENTIAL VISIT

1

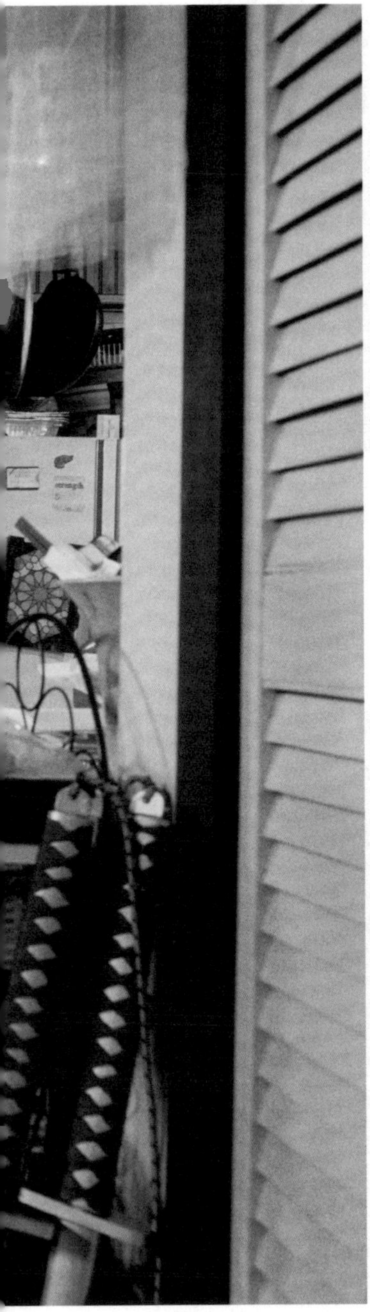

2

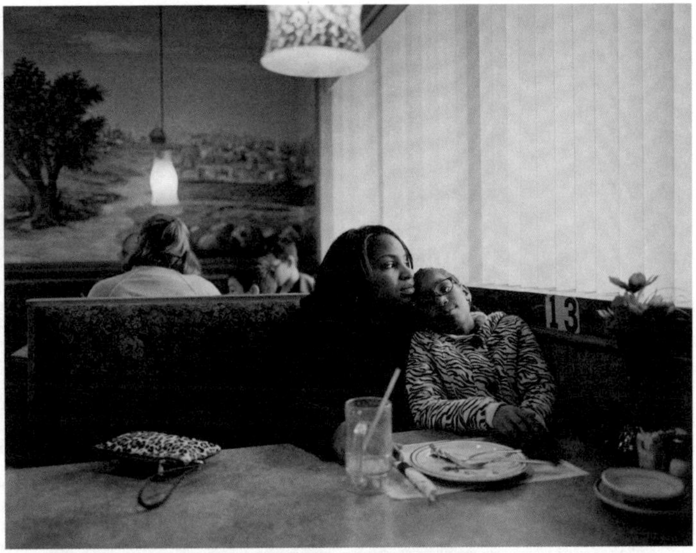

3

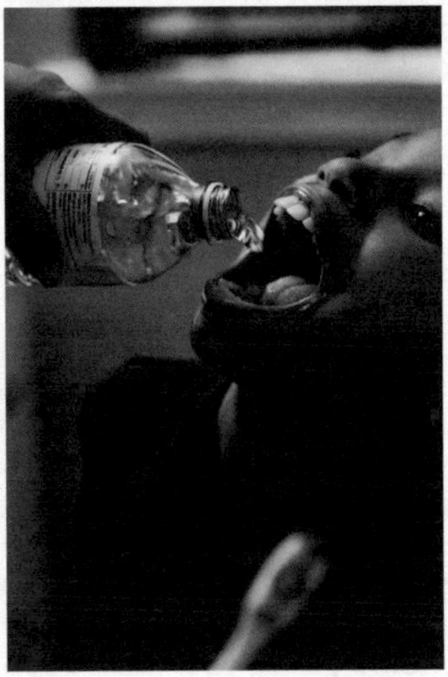

4

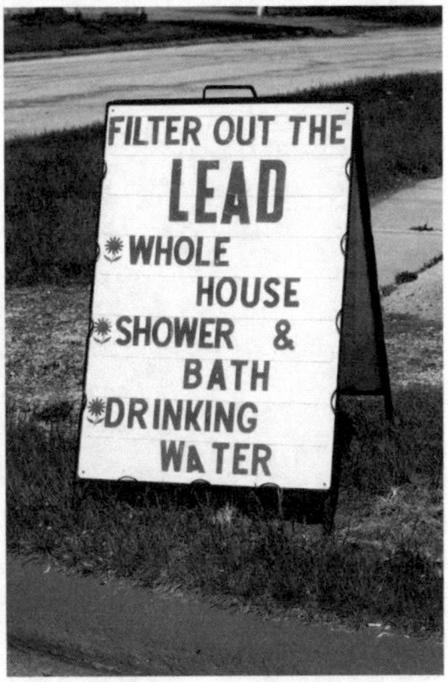

1: DENISE AND RODNEY CLAY, SHEA'S AUNT AND UNCLE, WATCH PRESIDENT OBAMA TAKE A SIP OF FLINT WATER
Aunt Denise, a retired secretary, made all the decorations for Nephratiti's wedding in her art studio, a camper she keeps parked on the side of her house. Denise met Rodney when she became the lead singer in his band in the late '80s; they'll be celebrating their thirtieth anniversary on September 25.

2: SHEA AND ZION AT THE BADAWEST RESTAURANT IN FLINT
"We don't enjoy home-cooked meals anymore," Shea says. They go out for practically every meal because it's so arduous to cook with bottled water. The Lebanese restaurant Badawest is Zion's favorite; she likes the flame-broiled chicken and yellow rice.

3: SHEA BRUSHES ZION'S TEETH
"We don't ingest the water on any level," Shea says. "We waterfall little bits of bottled water at a time: Brush, repeat waterfall, and gargle."

4: THE GRAINERY NATURAL GROCERY
Shea doesn't believe whole-house filters, which cost up to a couple thousand dollars, are a solution for the entire city. She buys $30 worth of alkaline water a month from the Grainery—a family business in Flint since 1980—because she trusts the local store more than the government.

1

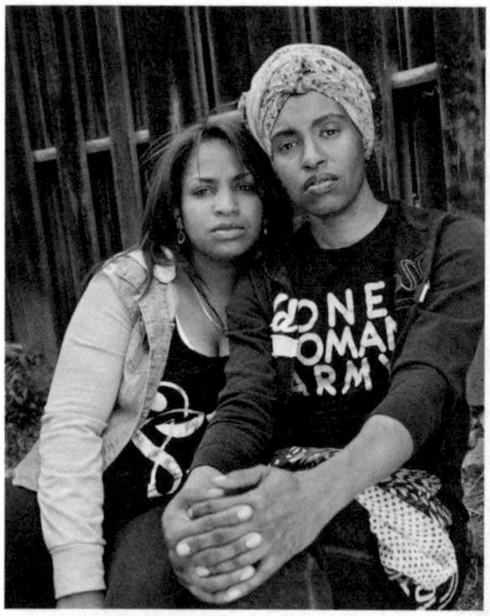

2

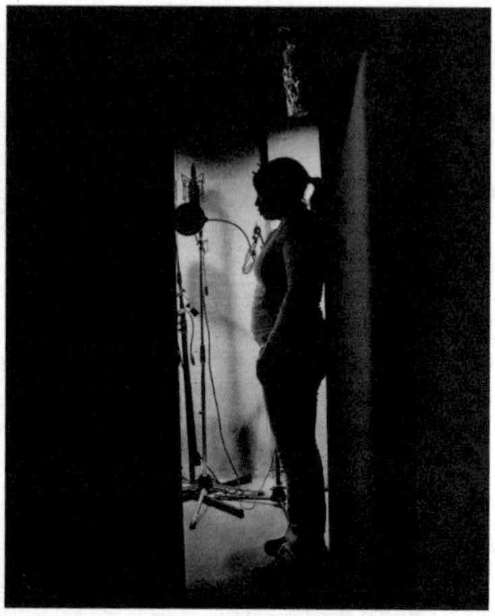

1: SHEA WITH HER BEST FRIEND AND MANAGER, AMBER HASAN
The two grew up together and are like sisters. Although they often talked about leaving Flint—Shea for Mississippi, Amber for Puerto Rico—neither expected to be leaving so soon. While Flint's pipes, in the best-case scenario, will be replaced in two years, both women worry about the damage that could be done to their children in the meantime.

2: SHEA LAYING VOCALS FOR HER SINGLE, "DREAMING"
Between her bus shifts, Shea drives to the recording studio of music producer Bernard Terry in nearby Beecher to work on her R&B album. "Going to the studio is like going to another world," Shea says. "I'm no longer in Flint; there's no more water crisis. It's just me, him, and music."

3: THE WOMEN OF THE COBB FAMILY
"The women of Flint...we are beauticians, artists, designers, writers, secretaries, clerks, scientists, educators, and entrepreneurs," Shea says. "We are Flint. We live, we love, we get married, and the water crisis does not stop that. It doesn't stop us from living."

4: SHEA AND ZION DEPART FLINT FOR MISSISSIPPI AT 4 A.M. ON JUNE 25

3

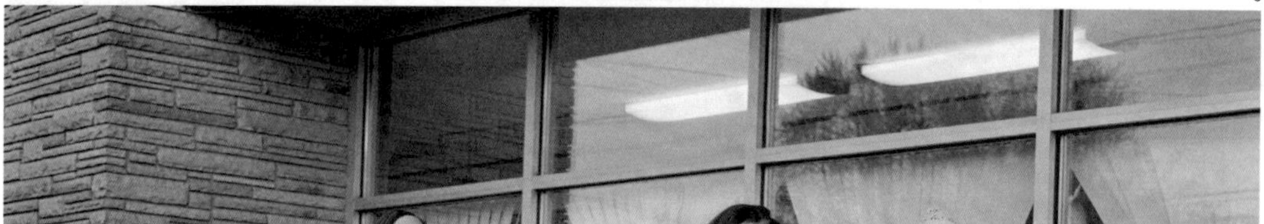

Left to right: Marzel Marshall, Kristina Cobb, Lynda Gardner, Denise Clay, Andrea Cobb, Nephratiti Givens, Keonia Thompson, Zion Brown, Renée Cobb, and Shea Cobb

4

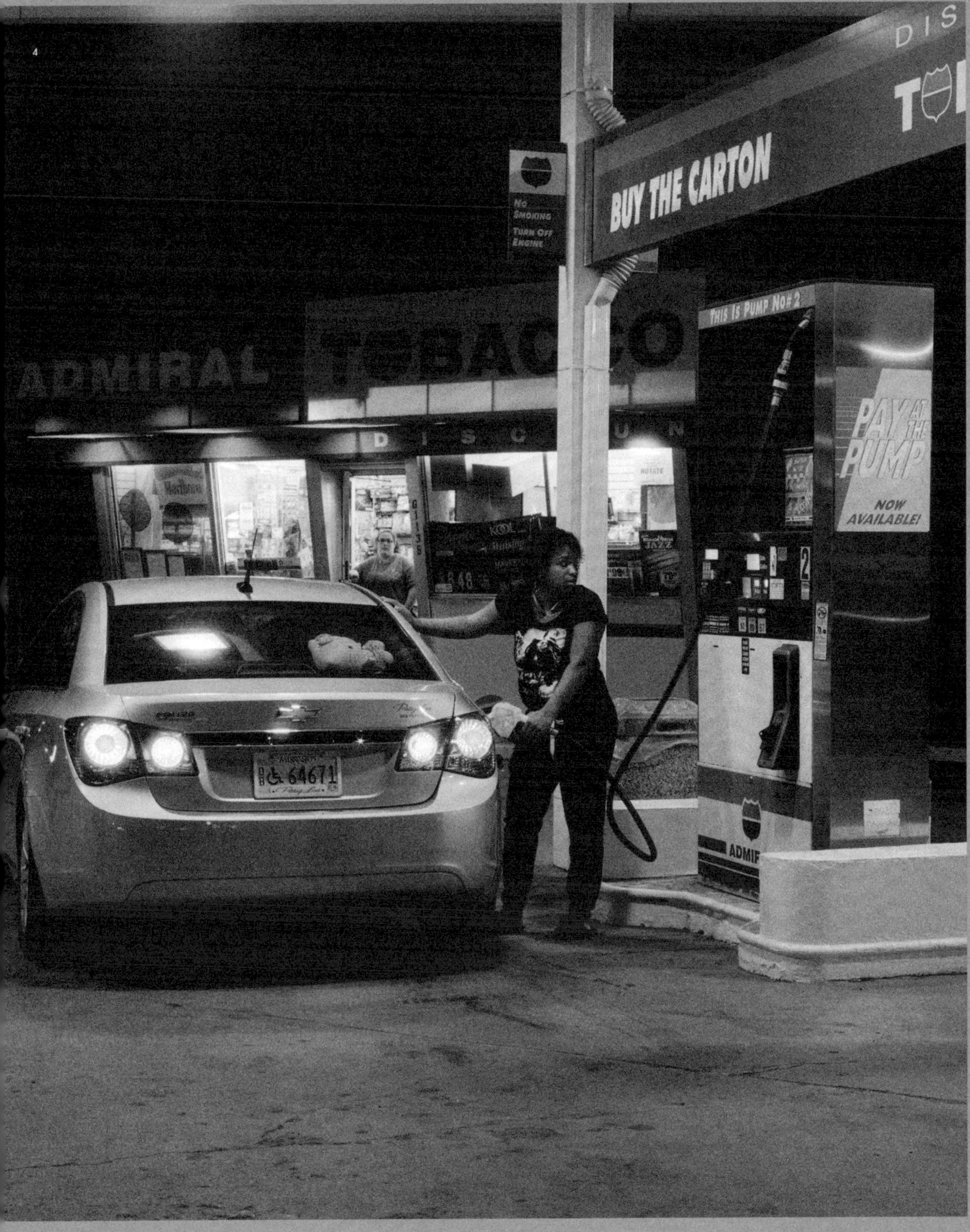
BUY THE CARTON
NO SMOKING
TURN OFF ENGINE
THIS IS PUMP NO# 2
ADMIRAL
PAY AT THE PUMP
NOW AVAILABLE!

The Phantasmagoric Dispositif: An Assembly of Bodies and Images in Real Time and Space

Noam M. Elcott

2016

RESURRECTION REDUX

In this exhibition, a luminous figure, representing sometimes a skeleton, and sometimes the head of some eminent person, appeared before the spectators, who were seated in a dark chamber. It grew less and less, and seemed to retire to a great distance. It again advanced, and consequently increased in size, and having retired a second time, it appeared to vanish in a luminous cloud, from which another figure gradually arose, and advanced and retreated as before.[1]

The piece is a kind of cave—or underground-like hall—very dark. . . . From an unseen source black-and-white images of twelve different people are projected all along the walls. . . . When you approach the image, say, of a distant seated person and stand before her or him, she or he responds to your presence by getting up and walking straight up to you, there to remain, "life-size," for a longish period simply standing and looking at you. If you leave, or if you stand there too long, the person turns around and goes back to the original spot and sits down.[2]

Two exhibitions separated by two hundred years. The first premiered officially in 1790s Paris—an earlier version had been staged in Leipzig—and spread to European capitals such as London. Part enlightened entertainment, part haunted house, the Phantasmagoria, like its descendant two hundred years later, refused categorization as mere magic lantern spectacle.[3]

> *It is not a frivolous spectacle; it is made for the man who thinks, for the philosopher.*[4]

> What may appear on one level as just another art world spectacle has a much deeper resonance, reaching through layers of careful decision making as to how the final effect might be incited within the phenomenology of viewing.[5]

The second exhibition, *Tall Ships* (1992), an installation by the video artist Gary Hill, premiered in Kassel, at Documenta IX, and was soon shown at the Whitney Biennial in New York (1993) and other international venues. As in the Phantasmagoria, a "sepulchral" atmosphere pervaded the exhibition's darkness.[6] And the darkness, in turn, induced life-and-death encounters—"one couldn't help intermittently fantasizing that these colorless, even wraith-like, yet curiously attractive figures were, as one imagines them, the recently dead, returning for some warmth of last contact with the living"—and, more crucial, fulfilled the technical requirement whereby the images abandoned the wall and entered, as quasi-animate beings, the same space as the spectators.[7]

> *One must paint a portrait of the deceased on glass with turpentine paints and (this is the principal point) cover the entire background of the drawn figure with thick, black oil paint. . . . The optical trickery is imperceptible; because the contour of the figure is covered in thick, black oil paint, no light is visible on the smoke except for that presented by the luminous image.*[8]

In actuality the video image is a frameless continuum: in *Tall Ships* the images have been freed into the materiality of real time and space.[9]

He uses special lenses attached to suspended video monitors to blur out the frame of the image. That technical

1 James Ferguson, *Ferguson's Lectures* . . . , ed. David Brewster, 2nd ed., 2 vols. (Edinburgh: Bell and Bradfute, 1806), 1:264–65.
2 George Quasha and Charles Stein, "Tall Acts of Seeing" (1993), in *An Art of Limina: Gary Hill's Works and Writings* (Barcelona: Ediciones Polâigrafa, 2009), 189.
3 Étienne-Gaspard Robertson's Phantasmagoria was the most famous of several late-eighteenth- and early-nineteenth-century attractions where spectators were immersed in darkness and ghoulish figures were projected on translucent screens or clouds of smoke such that they appeared to occupy the same space as the spectators. For an overview of the original phantasmagorias, see Laurent Mannoni, *The Great Art of Light and Shadow*, trans. Richard Crangle (Exeter, UK: University of Exeter Press, 2000), 136–75.
4 Étienne-Gaspard Robertson, *Mémoires récréatifs, scientifiques et anecdotiques*, 2 vols. (Paris: Chez l'auteur et à la Librairie de Wurtz, 1831–33), 1:278.
5 Robert C. Morgan, "Gary Hill: Beyond the Image," in *Gary Hill* (Baltimore: Johns Hopkins University Press, 2000), 7.
6 Robertson, 1:278; and Stuart Morgan, "Missing Persons," in *Gary Hill: In Light of the Other*, ed. Chrissie Iles and Lewis Biggs (Oxford, UK: Museum of Modern Art Oxford, 1993), 26.
7 Quasha and Stein, 191. The sentiment is echoed in nearly every review of the piece.
8 Karl von Eckartshausen, *Aufschlüsse zur Magie* (Brno: J. S. Siedler, 1788), 129, 131.
9 Lynne Cooke, "Gary Hill, 'Who Am I But a Figure of Speech?'" Parkett, no. 34 (1992), 18.

detail permits one not to see images but only people moving. In fact, one forgets the image as an image.[10]

Hill is much more inventive, especially in the relationships he creates between image and spectator. . . . There's no screen or frame around it—it's a projection from overhead—just this lit image on an otherwise dark wall. . . . [I]t's difficult to treat these figures as merely images.[11]

[The images] patrol a similar territory to our own. . . . This Pygmalion fantasy. . . brings into play the idea that pictures lead a life of their own.[12]

The wraith-like figures are not framed in paintings, elevated on pedestals, enclosed in television sets, or situated at an insuperable remove. Like phantasmagoric ghosts, the images gather in a dark space shared with spectators.

Most critics failed to grasp the basic technical operations of Hill's installation.[13] Fewer still discerned the eighteenth-century precedent. And even the scant links established between *Tall Ships* and the Phantasmagoria are at once too general—*phantasmagoria* is made to stand in for illusion writ large—and too specific—tied solely to this strikingly analogous installation.[14] The technical and historical lacunae are symptomatic of a broader deficiency: neither art history nor film studies recognizes phantasmagoria as a fundamental configuration of image and spectator—one with deep media archaeological roots and myriad contemporary manifestations. Focused on individual media, technologies, genres, artists, movements, styles, or subjects, scholars have largely failed to recognize the decisive roles played by the coordinated disposition of these disparate elements in relation to specific modes of spectatorship. Phantasmagoria is one such *dispositif*.

Two exhibitions. Two hundred years. One set of reactions. One technical setup. In a word, one *dispositif*.[15] Phantasmagoria or, more precisely, the phantasmagoric *dispositif*—the assembly, in a single space and time, of spectators and images (seemingly) freed from material supports—is an essential component of Hill's work and that of countless avant-garde film, video, and sound installations and performances. Robert Whitman's *Shower* (1964), Peter Campus's *Interface* (1972), Anthony McCall's *Line Describing a Cone* (1973), Bill Viola's *The Sleep of Reason* (1988), Gary Hill's *Tall Ships* (1992), and Tony Oursler's *The Influence Machine* (2000) are just a handful of the major and minor works best understood not as paintings, sculptures, or cinematic films, but as phantasmagorias. No less important, we are witnessing an explosion in phantasmagoric technologies and techniques: immersive "virtual realities" (which seem finally to have crossed the threshold of viability in devices such as the Oculus Rift); a range of "augmented realities" (where images are superimposed on our vision of the real world); and, above all, a miscellany of attractions and devices erroneously billed as "holographic."[16] The worlds of art, cinema, and media are saturated in phantasmagoria. But because phantasmagoria cannot be tied to any one medium or technology, genre or subject, movement or epoch, we have failed to recognize its import.

As a specific attraction, the Phantasmagoria died out in the nineteenth century. As a commonplace description—"a series of imaginary (and usually fantastic) forms" or "a shifting and changing scene consisting of many elements, *esp.* one that is startling or extraordinary"—phantasmagoria suffuses the world.[17] What concerns us, however, is not any old razzle-dazzle, fantasy, or gore. Phantasmagoria is not just a subject or effect, much less an amusement confined to centuries

10 Anne-Marie Duguet in Annette W. Balkema and Henk Slager, *Concepts on the Move* (Amsterdam: Rodopi, 2002), 176.

11 Tom Lubbock, "Is There Someone out There?" *The Independent*, (21 December 1993), 21.

12 Morgan, "Missing Persons," 22–23.

13 Champions and detractors alike misunderstood the basic technical setup. The principal technical point—recognized by the eighteenth-century commentator but missed by the twentieth-century critics—is that the figure be shot (or painted) against a black background. Only then can the image be freed from the frame when projected in a dark environment by a hidden device. Hill says as much in Regina Cornwell, "Gary Hill: An Interview" (1993), in *Gary Hill*, ed. Robert C. Morgan (Baltimore: Johns Hopkins University Press, 2000), 225. In terms of the phantasmagoric *dispositif*, magic lantern slides are not fundamentally different from video technology. Hill's video should not be considered an "improvement" in a technoteleological sense. Phantasmagoric slides were projected in vivid color and were accompanied by a range of immersive sound effects. Hill's silent images were projected in nebulous black-and-white.

14 See, for example, John G. Hanhardt, "Between Language and the Moving Image: The Art of Gary Hill" (1994), in *Gary Hill*, ed. Morgan, 115–16; and Catherine Elwes, *Installation and the Moving Image* (New York: Columbia University Press, 2015), 1, 79. The tendency to generalize phantasmagoria as illusion has remained a constant from the nineteenth century to the present. See, for example, Terry Castle, "Phantasmagoria: Spectral Technology and the Metaphorics of Modern Reverie," *Critical Inquiry* 15, no. 1 (1988): 26–61; and Joachim Jäger, Gabriele Knapstein, and Anette Hüsch, eds., *Beyond Cinema: The Art of Projection* (Ostfildern, Germany: Hatje Cantz, 2006), 42–43. For a take on the Phantasmagoria and its current resonances that is more media-archaeologically rigorous even as it is less interested in the finer points of contemporary art, see Oliver Grau, "Remember the Phantasmagoria! Illusion Politics of the Eighteenth Century and Its Multimedia Afterlife," in *MediaArtHistories*, ed. Oliver Grau (Cambridge, MA: MIT Press, 2007), 137–61.

15 Within the rapidly expanding literature on *dispositifs*, see, most recently, François Albera and Maria Tortajada, eds., *Cine-Dispositives: Essays in Epistemology across Media* (Amsterdam: Amsterdam University Press, 2015).

16 On the technical and historical aspects of holography, see Jens Schroeter, *3D: History, Theory, and Aesthetics of the Transplane Image*, trans. Brigitte Pichon and Dorian Rudnytsky (New York: Bloomsbury, 2014). On the cultural politics of "holography," see Eric de Bruyn, "Empire's Hologram," in *Exhibiting the Moving Image: History Revisited*, ed. François Bovier and Adeena Mey (Zurich: JRP Ringier, 2015); Eric de Bruyn, "Das Holografische Fenster und andere reale Anachronismen," in *Kunstgeschichtlichkeit: Historizität und Anachronie in der Gegenwartskunst*, ed. Eva Kernbauer (Paderborn: Fink, 2015), 67–98.

past. Phantasmagoria is above all an operation: the actual (or apparent) gathering of human beings and images through an assortment of techniques that for centuries have pervaded the worlds of art and cinema, theater and spectacle. And yet we lack the critical terminology to describe the copresence of images: not distant visions (like those proffered in the cinema) or circumscribed pictures (like those enclosed in frames or television sets), but images that appear to abandon their material supports and enter our world. This article aims to establish *phantasmagoria* as the precise term to describe an assembly of bodies and images in a shared time and space. The first two sections locate phantasmagoria in relation to art, film, and their respective corpuses of criticism and theory. The third section situates phantasmagoria alongside two related *dispositifs*: the cinematic (images set at a distance) and the domestic (images enclosed in objects). The fourth section identifies the salient qualities of phantasmagoria in relation to corporeality, space, and time. The final section returns to the works of McCall, Whitman, Viola, Campus, and Oursler and reveals their profound and multifaceted alignment toward phantasmagoria. At every turn, the article demonstrates the importance of *dispositifs*—not only their subtle variations but also and above all their stark and enduring differences. *Dispositifs* alone may not determine our relationship to images, but their configurations of time and space, bodies and vision are decisive aspects of every work of art and every encounter with media.

ART INSTALLATIONS: BEYOND ILLUSION AND ANTI-ILLUSION

In the winter of 1798–1799, Étienne-Gaspard Robertson installed his Phantasmagoria in a Capuchin convent depopulated by the French Revolution. Yet this was hardly the first time images had been brought to life in sacred spaces. For centuries, as Giovanni Careri asserts, Baroque chapels had been "populated by bodies made of paint, marble, stucco, and flesh."[18] In the hands of Gian Lorenzo Bernini, the effects were positively phantasmagoric. No less an authority than Rudolf Wittkower states (and restates) as much in his seminal monograph, which warrants quotation at length. The Cornaro Chapel, revolving around but not limited to *The Ecstasy of Saint Teresa* (1647–1652), instantiates the phantasmagoric confusion of reality and illusion like few other works, prior or since.

> Bernini made this scene real and visionary at the same time. . . . The vision takes place in an imaginary realm on a large cloud magically suspended in mid-air. . . . the group is bathed in warm and mysterious light, falling from above through a window of yellow glass hidden behind the pediment and playing on the highly polished marble surface of the two figures. [Cornaro family members flank the epiphany in trompe l'oeil boxes such that] the fictitious architecture and the architecture of the real chapel seem to interpenetrate. This creates the illusion that the Cornaro family is sitting in an extension of the space in which we move. . . . Like the Cornaro family, the worshipper participates in the supra-human mystery shown on the altar, and if he yields entirely to the ingenious and elaborate directives given by the artist, he will step beyond the narrow limits of his own existence and be entranced with the casuality [*sic*] of an enchanted world.[19]

Colored and white marble, yellow glass and warm light, painted mural and stucco, gilded wood and gilt bronze—to reduce the work to "sculpture" is to miss the mark. What is more, mysterious lighting from hidden sources, fictitious architectures, hyperrealism: these are the building blocks of phantasmagoria. In the Altieri, Fonseca, and Cornaro Chapels, Wittkower concludes, "Bernini created a supra-real world in which the transitions seem obliterated between real and imaginary space, past and present, phenomenal and actual existence, life and death."[20] One can hardly define phantasmagoria more succinctly.

The power of Bernini notwithstanding, the marginalization of phantasmagoria in avant-garde discourse is no accident. For the last fifty years, avant-garde art and film criticism have been mired in a series of binaries inherited from a particularly potent blend of 1970s theory. Some combination of minimalism's emphasis on phenomenology, postminimalism's exploration of process and institutional critique, and apparatus film theory's constitution of a cinematic subject has divided the world into good and bad objects: materiality and immateriality; embodiment and disembodiment; active participation and passive spectatorship; real space and illusionistic space; more broadly, reality and illusion; demystification and mystification; avant-garde art and Hollywood film.[21] Even as the dominant movements of the 1960s and 1970s abandoned strict divisions between media, adopted projections and moving images, and

17 The quoted definition is from the *Oxford English Dictionary*. Overviews of phantasmagoria abound. See, for example, Lynda Nead, *The Haunted Gallery: Painting, Photography, Film c. 1900* (New Haven: Yale University Press, 2007); and Marina Warner, *Phantasmagoria: Spirit Visions, Metaphors, and Media into the Twenty-First Century* (Oxford, UK: Oxford University Press, 2006).

18 Giovanni Careri, *Bernini: Flights of Love, the Art of Devotion*, trans. Linda Lappin (Chicago: University of Chicago Press, 1995), 1.

19 Rudolf Wittkower, *Bernini: The Sculptor of the Roman Baroque* (Rome: Banco di Santo Spirito, 1990), 158.

20 Wittkower, 159.

21 See Kate Mondloch, *Screens: Viewing Media Installation Art* (Minneapolis: University of Minnesota Press, 2010); and David N. Rodowick, *The Crisis of Political Modernism* (Berkeley and Los Angeles: University of California Press, 1994).

foregrounded the physical presence of viewers, they did so overwhelmingly in opposition to illusions of any kind.[22] In such discourses and practices, illusion is a four-letter word; phantasmagoria is out of the question.

Critics have perpetuated the elision of perceptual illusion and ideological mystification by adhering to the derogatory omnibus term *phantasmagoria*. For Marxist critics in the mold of Theodor Adorno, phantasmagoria was and is tied to the occultation of production under capitalism and, as exemplified in the work of Richard Wagner, asserts "the concept of illusions as the absolute reality of the unreal."[23] In such an intellectual climate, installation art—above all, film and video installations—could be trumpeted only under the banner of "anti-illusion."[24] Yet the media archaeology of scholars such as John Tresch and Tom Gunning demonstrates definitively that phantasmagoria cannot be reduced to a derogatory omnibus for cheap and illusory spectacles.[25] Even as they define *phantasmagoria* differently, Tresch, Gunning, and other scholars have laid the necessary groundwork for a renewed encounter with the concept of phantasmagoria stripped of its pejorative connotations. Indeed, the pejorative designation may well have blinded critics and historians to a crucial quality of so much recent art and media, a quality we can name—without judgment and with renewed media archaeological vigor—"phantasmagoria": the assembly of human beings and images.

CINEMATIC FAITH: INSUFFICIENT AND EXCESSIVE

The negative associations conjured by the term *phantasmagoria* have hindered its critical evaluation by scholars of avant-garde art and film. Its neglect has been compounded by the existential debates within cinema and media studies over the specificity or singularity of film.[26] For phantasmagoria—whether that of Bernini, Robertson, or Hill—invariably evokes an expansive history of cinema and undercuts efforts to delimit the specificity of film. The battle often hinges on the status of the cinematic *dispositif*. Once the centerpiece of so-called apparatus theory, cinemas are now cast aside with abandon or fanatically conserved.[27] In 2006, philosopher Giorgio Agamben theorized the cell phone as a *dispositif*, a technopolitical apparatus that was reconfiguring the human subject.[28] Agamben's breezy analysis was at once too quick to ascribe major subject effects to a single apparatus and too slow to identify the radical transformations in mobile devices already underway. Concurrently, *New Yorker* film critic David Denby reported from the front lines of the media-industrial complex, which recognized in the video iPod, "a new platform for movies, a new convenience that will annihilate old paradigms."[29] Now that smartphone and tablet users number in the billions and multiplatform video technology has become as hegemonic as cinemas were in their heyday, the "new convenience" has assumed the status of a *dispositif*. In Denby's account, the most

22 Consider, for example, the opening sentences of Peter Gidal's "Theory and Definition of Structural/Materialist Film" (1976): "Structural/Materialist film attempts to be non-illusionist. The process of the film's making deals with devices that result in demystification or attempted demystification of the film process." Peter Gidal, "Theory and Definition of Structural/Materialist Film," in *Structural Film Anthology*, ed. Peter Gidal (London: BFI, 1976), 1. Compare Andrew Uroskie's recent and striking analysis of Janet Cardiff and George Bures Miller's *The Paradise Institute* (2001): "If the apparatus is foregrounded, it is not for the purpose of dismissing illusion and maintaining a contravening reality, but rather so as to throw our demarcation of reality and illusion into doubt." Andrew V. Uroskie, *Between the Black Box and the White Cube: Expanded Cinema and Postwar Art* (Chicago: University of Chicago, 2014), 3.

23 Theodor W. Adorno, *In Search of Wagner* (1937/1938), trans. Rodney Livingstone (London: Verso, 1991), 90. Noteworthy among numerous recent attacks waged against artworks deemed too phantasmagoric is T. J. Clark's invocation of Walter Benjamin to conclude his assault on Tony Oursler's *The Influence Machine*: "Modernity, as Benjamin reminds us, has thrived from the very beginning on a cheap spectacle of the strange, the new, the phantasmagoric. But modernity also truly dreams. The art that survives is the art that lays hold of the primary process, not the surface image-flow." T. J. Clark, "Modernism, Postmodernism, and Steam," *October* 100 (2002): 173. Several Benjamin scholars, to the contrary, have identified in his thought the centrality of "critical" or "progressive" phantasmagorias. See Margaret Cohen, "Walter Benjamin's Phantasmagoria," *New German Critique*, no. 48 (1989): 87–107; and Michael W. Jennings, "On the Banks of a New Lethe: Commodification and Experience in Benjamin's Baudelaire Book," *boundary 2* 30, no. 1 (2003): 104.

24 Consider the works gathered in the aptly named Anti-illusion exhibition at the Whitney Museum in 1969: paintings, sculptures, installations, compositions, and performances by Carl Andre, Robert Ryman, Eva Hesse, Steve Reich, Michael Snow, and others. Here, the copresence of viewer and image aimed at the "reversal of illusion" and "inverse trompe l'oeil." James Monte, "Anti-illusion: Procedures/Materials," in *Anti-illusion: Procedures/Materials*, ed. Marcia Tucker and James Monte (New York: Whitney Museum, 1969), 7.

25 Tresch insists on "the displacement, if not dissolution, of the line separating scientific truth from collective phantasmagoria," just as Gunning triangulates the dyad of enlightenment and mystification through the category of wonder. See John Tresch, "The Prophet and the Pendulum: Sensational Science and Audiovisual Phantasmagoria around 1848," *Grey Room* 43 (Spring 2011): 36; and Tom Gunning, "Phantasmagoria and the Manufacturing of Illusions and Wonder: Towards a Cultural Optics of the Cinematic Apparatus," in *The Cinema: A New Technology for the 20th Century*, ed. André Gaudreault, Catherine Russell, and Pierre Véronneau (Lausanne: Editions Payot, 2004), 31–44.

26 See, for example, Dudley Andrew, *What Cinema Is!* (Chichester: Wiley-Blackwell, 2010).

27 See especially Jean-Louis Baudry, "The Apparatus: Metapsychological Approaches to the Impression of Reality in the Cinema" (1975), trans. Jean Andrews and Bertrand Augst, in *Narrative, Apparatus, Ideology*, ed. Philip Rosen (New York: Columbia University Press, 1986), 299–318.

28 Giorgio Agamben, *What Is an Apparatus? and Other Essays*, trans. David Kishik and Stefan Pedatella (Stanford, CA: Stanford University Press, 2009).

29 David Denby, "Big Pictures," *New Yorker*, (8 January 2007), 54.

damning news was an evaluation not of media technologies but of media subjects: a new generation of cinema spectators or, more precisely, media consumers. "According to home-entertainment specialists I spoke to in Hollywood," Denby writes, "many kids are 'platform agnostic'—that is, they will look at movies on any screen at all, large or small."[30] Let us dwell for a moment on the phrase "platform agnostic." For if Denby's target was a generation of viewers—"kids"—he borrowed the term from computing. According to the *Oxford English Dictionary*, a *platform* is "a standard system architecture; a (type of) machine and/or operating system, regarded as the base on which software applications are run." Adobe Acrobat and Firefox, to cite two among innumerable examples, are *platform agnostic* insomuch as they can run on any computer platform, be it Microsoft Windows, Apple OS, Linux, what have you. The term migrated from computer platforms to much wider-ranging media platforms and their consumers: cinema, television, desktops, laptops, tablets, and smartphones are all equally valid platforms for the consumption of sounds and images by *platform agnostics*. Industry executives understood viewers—human beings—in terms of software and devices. Today, one is hard-pressed to find a commercial campaign—let alone a movie—that is not cross-platform; that is, whose "content" is not "platform agnostic."[31] Platform agnosticism—the capacity to deliver and consume media content across multiple platforms—became the creed of software engineers, advertisers, politicians, organizers, and corporate and media gurus.

The backlash against platform agnosticism came swiftly. Companies are encouraged by some to focus on their core platforms and, much more relevant to us, film and art theorists are evangelizing, with renewed vigor, essentialist strains of specificity and materiality—a willful blindness to the epochal change unfolding around us. Cinema studies or art history, we are often told, must be saved from the perdition of media and visual studies. Celluloid, others preach, must not only be preserved but upheld against video and digital pretenders. A third claim pertains to the location, place, site, or, more expansively yet more precisely, the *dispositif* of cinema. Among the most passionate spokesmen for the essential primacy of the cinematic *dispositif* is film theorist Raymond Bellour:

> I begin from a simple hypothesis, but one involving infinite detours: *the lived, more or less collective experience of a film projected in a cinema, in the dark, according to an unalterably precise screening procedure, remains the condition for a special memory experience, one from which every other viewing situation more or less departs.* This supposes a certain rule of faith of which the spectator would be the incarnation, in the unfolding of a liturgy associated with film, with cinema, and with film in the cinema situation.[32]

Bellour counters platform agnosticism with an article of cinematic faith, a liturgy of film, a hypothesis with infinite detours, all of which, however, follow the same orthodoxy. The failure of this orthodoxy is not its insistence on the specificity of the cinematic *dispositif* but the pronouncement of its timeless primacy, the condition "*from which every other viewing situation more or less departs.*" Where platform agnostics are willfully ignorant of *dispositifs* and reduce cinema—and other media—to mere "content," platform zealots are willfully ignorant of the historical contingency of movie theaters and hypostatize classical theatrical cinema into a medium-specific essence.

But as Jonathan Crary has recently noted, cinema, as a *dispositif*, was relatively fixed only from the late 1920s through the 1960s, and television in the United States only from the 1950s into the 1970s. The perceived permanence of certain key features, he argues, "allowed critics to expound theories of cinema, television, or video based on the assumption that these forms or systems had certain essential self-defining

---

30 Denby, 54.

31 Artists have followed suit. Stan Douglas, for example, recently premiered a new multimedia theater work, *Helen Lawrence* (2014), which was preceded earlier that year by *Circa 1948*, a 3D augmented reality app available for iOS devices. (Presumably only funding limitations impeded an Android version; accordingly, the app is not truly platform agnostic.)

32 Raymond Bellour, "The Cinema Spectator: A Special Memory," trans. Adrian Martin, in *Screen Dynamics: Mapping the Borders of Cinema*, ed. Gertrud Koch, Volker Pantenburg, and Simon Rothöhler (Vienna: Österreichisches Filmmuseum, 2012), 9. Emphasis in original. He later argues, "The only inviolate element is the *dispositif*. The theater. The darkness. The fixed time of the screening" (14). Bellour's account is informed and nuanced, but it ultimately hinges on the unresolved contradiction whereby "the dispositif of cinema is historical, it is also transhistorical." Raymond Bellour, *La querelle des dispositifs: Cinéma—installations, expositions* (Paris: POL, 2012), 18. In the foreword to the recent English translation of *L'entre-images*, Bellour spells out his about-face in regard to specificity—where he earlier tore down divisions between theatrical cinema and installation art, he now asserts the specificity of the cinematic *dispositif*. Raymond Bellour, *Between-the-Images*, trans. Allyn Hardyck (Zurich: JRP Ringier, 2012), 11. Francesco Casetti has also explored the phenomenon extensively. As his preferred term—*relocated cinema*—attests, Casetti also anchors the experience of film in the cinema. But Casetti aims not at retaining theaters as the primary site of cinematic reception but at theorizing the cinema to come. See Francesco Casetti, "Elsewhere: The Relocation of Art," in *Valencia09/Confines* (Valencia: IVAM, 2009), 348–51; Francesco Casetti, "Cinema Lost and Found: Trajectories of Relocation," *Screening the Past*, no. 32 (2011), http://www.screeningthepast.com/2011/11/cinema-lost-and-found-trajectories-of-relocation; Francesco Casetti, "Back to the Motherland: The Film Theatre in the Postmedia Age," *Screen* 52, no. 1 (2011): 1–12; and Francesco Casetti, *The Lumière Galaxy: Seven Key Words for the Cinema to Come* (New York: Columbia University Press, 2015), 17–42.

characteristics. In retrospect, what were most often identified as essential were temporary elements of larger constellations whose rates of change were variable and unpredictable."[33] Our charge as historians and theorists is to recover and conceptualize the stark variables and unexpected continuities in these larger media constellations, a task wholly abandoned by platform agnostics and platform zealots alike. Both zealots and agnostics render history and politics irrelevant. One does so by universalizing the cinematic condition, into religion; the other by annulling it, into content. Our charge, finally, is not to find the essence of cinema or delimit its specificity but to conceptualize its multiplicity. In its long history—what is often described as its pre- and posthistory—cinema has always engendered a multiplicity of sites and a multiplicity of images. Cinemas and film simply constituted the dominant iteration in the medium's classical period. But cinema is no more tied to movie theaters and celluloid than sculpture is bound to temples and marble. In a word, cinema will be multiple or it will not be at all.

CINEMATIC, DOMESTIC, PHANTASMAGORIC

The multiplicity revolves around *dispositifs* in which moving images have thrived, to varying degrees, over the last few centuries. This typology advances from the media-archaeological observation that certain types of images thrive best in certain types of locations—and not in others. For the sake of simplicity, consider a threefold multiplicity: three media *dispositifs* that promote and inhibit specific types of images in specific types of locations. Each *dispositif* is internally multifaceted and externally porous to other *dispositifs*. Claims to their coherence and strict delineation are heuristic. But violations of these boundaries have real consequences: aesthetic, social, economic, perhaps even political. The three *dispositifs* may be distinguished as the cinematic, the domestic, and the phantasmagoric.

The cinematic is an emblematic instance of what Joachim Paech describes as the experience of proximity effected through distance.[34] Cinema *places* us *in* the film by *displacing* us *from* the auditorium. As an architecture, system, or *dispositif* that effects proximity through distance, the cinematic arose wholly independent of film. (Conversely, in their first decade, like today, movies were not inextricably bound to purpose-built theaters.) Radical spatial dislocation and separation constituted one of the core qualities of nineteenth-century attractions. Barker's Panorama, Daguerre's Diorama, the Kaiserpanorama, the Kinetoscope, the cinema of Edison or the Lumière brothers, and, above all, Wagner's theater at Bayreuth, produced, as Crary argues, "the image as an autonomous luminous screen of attraction, whose apparitional appeal is an effect of both its uncertain spatial location and its detachment from a broader visual field."[35] Among these attractions, Wagner's theater at Bayreuth was exemplary on two counts. First, it was universal. The Panorama, Diorama, Kaiserpanorama, and Kinetoscope were proprietary structures built for the exhibition of specific image types. (Note the frequent proper nouns and patents.) The Kaiserpanorama, a late-nineteenth-century device that enabled up to twenty-five individuals to view a series of stereoscopic images, could not display Panoramic paintings, which measured thousands of square feet, any more than the Diorama could exhibit the 35 mm filmstrips that ran through the Kinetoscope, Edison's early cinematic peepshow device. The exhibition structures required specific technical images, and the images required specific technical exhibition structures. Wagner's Festspielhaus, by contrast, was a model theater that could accommodate countless types of performances and images. Its most significant legacy was its adoption by cinemas—that is, as a support for a medium as yet unrealized in 1876.

Second, Wagner theorized spectatorial displacement more radically than any other nineteenth-century figure. His essay "The Art-Work of the Future" became the touchstone, direct and indirect, for countless twentieth-century theories of cinema:

> In the arrangement of the space for the spectators the need for optical and acoustic understanding of the artwork will give the necessary law. . . . Thus the spectator transplants himself upon the stage, by means of all his visual and aural faculties; while the performer becomes an artist only by complete absorption into the public. . . . [T]he public, that representative of daily life, disappears from the auditorium completely, and lives and breathes now only in the artwork which seems to it as Life itself, and on the stage which seems the wide expanse of the whole World.[36]

33 Jonathan Crary, 24/7: *Late Capitalism and the Ends of Sleep* (London: Verso, 2013), 38.

34 Joachim Paech, "Eine Dame verschwindet: Zur dispositiven Struktur apparativen Erschienens," in *Paradoxien, Dissonanzen, Zusammenbrüche: Situationen offener Epistemologie*, ed. Hans Ulrich Gumbrecht and K. Ludwig Pfeiffer (Frankfurt: Suhrkamp, 1991), esp. 777. Some of the media archaeology in this section builds on research developed in my forthcoming book, *Artificial Darkness: An Obscure History of Modern Art and Media* (Chicago: University of Chicago Press, 2016).

35 Jonathan Crary, "Géricault, the Panorama, and Sites of Reality in the Early Nineteenth Century," *Grey Room* 9 (Fall 2002): 19.

36 Richard Wagner, "The Art-Work of the Future" (1849), trans. William Ashton Ellis, in *Richard Wagner's Prose Works* (1895; St. Clair Shores, MI: Scholarly Press, 1972), 185; translation modified. For the original German, whose key passage reads, "aus dem Zuschauerraume aber verschwindet das Publikum, dieser Repräsant des öffentlichen Lebens, sich selbst," see *Richard Wagner, Das Kunstwerk der Zukunft* (Leipzig: Otto Wigand, 1850), 188–89.

Wagner's turn-of-the-century translator, William Ashton Ellis, could not equal the Master's temerity and wrote that the public "forgets the confines of the auditorium" rather than "disappears" from the auditorium. But viewed retrospectively from the rise of cinemas, *disappearance* was not too strong a word. Proximity effected through distance is the hallmark of cinema as a *dispositif*. Cinematic immersion necessitates the *displacement* of spectators from their environment.

"Consider, on the other hand, the opposite experience, the experience of TV, which also shows films: nothing, no fascination; the darkness is dissolved, the anonymity repressed, the space is familiar, organized (by furniture and familiar objects), tamed."[37] Thus Roland Barthes compares cinema and television—the signature media for the cinematic and domestic *dispositifs*. The domestic implies not only the home but, as betrayed by its noun form, a household servant. Whether at home, at work, or on the move, we are pampered and besieged by devices that ring and vibrate, speak and listen, take and stream and play videos; they know where we are and remind us what to do and respond to our commands; they facilitate and carry out our virtual work, survey nearly every facet of our lives, and perform innumerable other tasks once carried out by domestics.[38] Domestic media devices thus most readily earn their name in the present. But they reach back to the nineteenth-century salon, which harbored not only paintings and prints but phenakistoscopes, praxinoscopes, and other optical toys. The domestic is also the middle-class living room where television made its home, first as furniture, later as hearth. Domestic are the tract houses, apartment complexes, and McMansions littered with computers, tablets, phones, and other devices for the consumption of media content, not least—though quite nearly least—movies. Domestic are the ever-increasing number of galleries from the 1960s to the present in which altered television sets by Nam June Paik, ornate celluloid loops by Simon Starling, and the cinematic and videographic sculptures of countless others found quarters and, eventually, buyers, who bring the works home. In the domestic, cinema is an optical toy, a piece of furniture, a book, a sculpture—in a word, an object. Accordingly, it is *placed* among other objects. Crucial is that devices like televisions do not create the same sense of placelessness as cinema. As Anna McCarthy argues, "the idea that the television apparatus is itself an encroaching force of placelessness is a flawed, dangerously fetishistic one. The language of placelessness makes us forget that television is an object and, like all objects, it shapes its immediate space through its material form."[39] What is more, in the domestic *dispositif*, moving images are objects that, like nearly all capitalist objects, are made to be bought and sold. The domestic houses commodities. In the domestic, cinema finds a *place* as a commodity. Its vernacular forms range from toys to televisions and other electronic or digital gadgets; its culturally exalted forms we call artworks.

Like the cinematic and the domestic, the phantasmagoric is neither medium-specific nor platform agnostic. Unlike cinema and television, phantasmagoria never attained a classical form or a normative discourse. Indeed, the phantasmagoric *dispositif* emerges uncomfortably alongside the cinematic and the domestic.[40] It is less familiar, but by no means less important, to contemporary spectators and viewers. So what is the phantasmagoric? Let us begin with what it was. Coined at the end of the eighteenth century, the Phantasmagoria, as its name announced, assembled ghosts. Whether assuming the shape of a bloody nun, Medusa, the devil, or recently deceased leaders such as Louis XVI or Robespierre, these ghosts were first and foremost mediated images. Phantasmagoric images were projected on visible smoke or invisible screens suspended in dark spaces; they were unmoored from their material supports and occupied the same dark space as spectators. The original phantasmagorias were developed by enlightened showmen and duplicitous necromancers such as Johann Schröpfer, Paul Philidor, and Étienne-Gaspard Robertson. Their most important descendant was the mid-nineteenth-century attraction Pepper's Ghost, named after the rational entertainer John Henry Pepper, a longtime lecturer and honorary director of London's Royal Polytechnic Institution. Pepper reaped a fortune from the Ghost, but he invented none of the elements in the device that

37 Roland Barthes, "Upon Leaving the Movie Theater" (1975), trans. Bertrand Augst and Susan White, in *Apparatus*, ed. Theresa Hak Kyung Cha (New York: Tanam Press, 1980), 2.

38 On service and servants, see Markus Krajewski, "The Power of Small Gestures: On the Cultural Technique of Service," *Theory, Culture and Society* 30, no. 6 (2013): 94–109.

39 Anna McCarthy, "From Screen to Site: Television's Material Culture, and Its Place," *October* 98 (2001): 96.

40 The museum director's introduction to Projected Images, an unheralded but important 1974 exhibition at the Walker Art Center, frames the term *projected images* in a manner similar to the phantasmagoric; that is, as a third term outside the cinematic and the domestic. "While filmmaking and video production attract an increasing number of artists, most of these converts observe the technical conventions of the new media; their films are intended for viewing under standard projection conditions [= the cinematic] and their videotapes are made to be seen on television monitors [= the domestic]. By contrast the artists represented in this exhibition conceive of film and video images essentially in environmental terms—as dominant elements of interior spaces—and they are as much concerned with the changing spatial and psychological relationships between observer and image as with the character of the image itself." Martin Friedman, "The Floating Picture Plane," in *Projected Images* (Minneapolis: Walker Art Center, 1974), 6. The exhibition featured works by Campus, Whitman, and other artists with strong affinities to the phantasmagoric.

would eventually bear his name.

The Ghost's seminal features were invented by Henry Dircks. And they derived from the Phantasmagoria. Pepper's Ghost or, Dircks's preferred designation, the "Dircksian Phantasmagoria," comprised a giant, slanted pane of glass placed on stage such that an unaware audience could peer *through* the glass to the action on stage and simultaneously see a reflection *in* the glass of an actor in the wings (or below). Pepper's Ghost was briefly fused with film in attractions such as Oskar Messter's Alabastra, patented in 1910, variants of which were known as Kinoplastikon and Tanagra. The technique is the basis for nearly all the recent applications erroneously dubbed holographic: "augmented reality" spectacles (eyewear) such as Microsoft's HoloLens and Google Glass, as well as mass spectacles for live and mediated audiences such as a 2012 Coachella concert that featured Tupac Shakur—murdered in 1996, sixteen years before he appeared onstage with Snoop Dogg, Dr. Dre, and other flesh-and-blood stars—and the 2014 resurrection of Michael Jackson at the Billboard Music Awards, where he performed a new song, "live" on stage.[41] Over the course of 220 years, we have exchanged Robespierre and the Revolution for Tupac and hip-hop, the slayer of kings for the King of Pop, but the technospatial configuration of phantasmagoria—that is, the phantasmagoric *dispositif*—has remained surprisingly stable.

In phantasmagorias, media images are not radically separated from human bodies; that is the domain of the cinematic. Nor are the images contained within objects, as in the domestic. In the original eighteenth-century phantasmagorias and their contemporary descendants, human beings and images are assembled in a common space and time. Whether these human beings are credulous dupes or highly trained actors is of little consequence. Phantasmagorias are highly efficacious. We need not believe in ghosts to perceive phantasmagoric images. But phantasmagorias are also highly precarious. Here, cinema is strategically *emplaced*, like a weapon, to be deployed with unerring precision or risk exposure and failure. Phantasmagoria is a matter of performance or, more broadly, theater, where living beings and mediated images can assemble.

BODIES, SPACES, TIMES

Displacement. Placement. Emplacement. But not re-placement. Cinema is not replaced by phantasmagoria, it is emplaced therein. Nor is it replaced by television or tablets; it is placed in domestic devices and spaces. As this porosity or fluidity attests, the divisions between displacement, placement, and emplacement are not quite as neat as this terminological triumvirate might suggest. And yet each *dispositif* gravitates toward specific and interlocked configurations of embodiment, space, and time.

The cinematic negates spectatorial space, the better to allow images to work on spectators. The domestic consents to space, the better to preserve the objects that house the images. The phantasmagoric reconfigures extant space, the better to fuse objects, spectators, and images. In the cinema, we tend to forget not only the surrounding space but also our bodies. With Wagner, we remember, "the public, that representative of daily life, disappears from the auditorium completely." Exceptional genres—pornography, say, or horror—that engage our bodies directly are just that: exceptions that tend toward the phantasmagoric.[42] While bodily awareness is exceptional in the cinema, a cinematic sense of disembodiment is less likely on a couch before a TV set, with a smartphone or phenakistoscope in your hand, or in a brightly or even dimly lit art gallery. As Campus noted in 1974, "The monitor is an object sitting rigidly in space. . . . Compare this to a movie theatre where every effort is made to erase one's ability to locate the screen in the viewer's space."[43] If the cinema, according to 1920s film theorist Rudolf Harms, should "guarantee the highest degree of bodily detachedness and seek to alleviate the shortcomings of the individual's fixed and local bondedness," then domestic spaces welcome couch potatoes, gallery goers, and other forms of quotidian and bathetic embodiment. [44] (Why these forms of mundane embodiment were ever aligned with corporeal plenitude in the reception of minimalism and related art movements will be a matter for future art historians to disentangle.) Phantasmagoria, once again, poses the least familiar and most unsettling form of spatiality and embodiment among the *dispositifs* in question. Here we are often hyperaware of our bodies and surroundings. In a reversal of the cinematic, the phantasmagoric must guarantee the

41 More recently, a "holographic" performance by the Chicago rapper Chief Keef was shut down by police. See Joe Coscarelli, "Hologram Performance by Chief Keef Is Shut Down by Police," *New York Times*, (26 July 2015).

42 Symptomatically, the first breakout 3D film, *House of Wax* (1953), was nothing if not a tale about phantasmagoria rendered quasi-phantasmagorically—that is, a tale about the confusion of human beings and images rendered through the extension of images into spectatorial space. On the "excessive mimesis" in *House of Wax*, see Bernhard Siegert, "Die Leiche in der Wachsfigur: Exzesse der Mimesis in Kunst, Wissenschaft und Medien," in *UnTot: Existenzen zwischen Leben und Leblosigkeit*, ed. Peter Geimer (Berlin: Kadmos, 2014), esp. 151–54.

43 Peter Campus, "Video as a Function of Reality" (1974), in *Peter Campus: Analog + Digital Video + Foto, 1970–2003*, ed. Wulf Herzogenrath and Barbara Nierhoff (Bremen: Kunsthalle Bremen, 2003), 82.

44 Rudolf Harms, *Philosophie des Films* (Leipzig: Felix Meiner, 1926), 60.

highest degree of image detachedness—that is, it must unmoor images from any material support, including screens—in order to enhance their local bondedness. The phantasmagoric image cannot be perceived as trapped inside a device or on a screen, nor as absolutely separated from the space we inhabit; rather, the phantasmagoric image must occupy the same space we occupy.

Each *dispositif* also requires and engenders a specific temporality. The cinematic is most effective as fixed duration or "feature length." We are willing to forget our bodies and our surroundings—but not indefinitely. As Andy Warhol noted in relation to his early, long-duration films such as *Empire* (1964), "My first films using the stationary object were also made to help the audiences get more acquainted with themselves."[45] Conversely, in order to turn cinema into an object, duration must be evacuated to the greatest possible degree. The duration of the image becomes a property of the objects. The results—familiar from living rooms and art galleries—are open-ended flow and short loops. The former is epitomized in closed-circuit feeds or continuous television programming.[46] The latter is evident in devices such as phenakistoscopes and zoopraxiscopes as well as GIFs and other image formats. Video artists from the 1970s to the present have employed and problematized both techniques: the closed-circuit camera aimed at a Buddha statue in Nam June Paik's *TV-Buddha* (1974), the feverish loops in Dara Birnbaum's *Technology/Transformation: Wonder Woman* (1978–1979), or the confounding loops in Stan Douglas's *Inconsolable Memories* (2005), which disturb the "this is where we came in" relationship to film and video installations (and recall an earlier moment of cinematic spectatorship, where entrances and exits were less policed). Lastly, the temporality of phantasmagoria is real time. Phantasmagorias may call up the dead or predict the future; however, as Thomas Elsaesser observes, for the spectator, "the senses are anchored and the body situated in a 'here and now.'"[47] Real time, of course, means more than the here and now. And the recent rise of phantasmagoria cannot be divorced from the ascendance of video, computers, and other real-time imaging systems. In Paul Virilio's sweeping account, the image has obeyed several fundamental logics or logistics in the last centuries: the *formal* logic of painting, engraving, and architecture, which ended in the eighteenth century; the *dialectical* logic of photography and film of the nineteenth and early twentieth centuries; and the *paradoxical* logic of video recording, holography, and computer graphics, beginning after the Second World War. Under the current reign of *paradoxical presence*: "the real-time image dominates the thing represented, real time subsequently prevailing over real space, virtuality dominating actuality and turning the very concept of reality on its head."[48] What remained exceptional in Bernini's Cornaro chapel and Robertson's Capuchin convent is now a generalized condition. Revelers at Coachella and wearers of the HoloLens—like visitors to Bernini's *Saint Theresa*, Robertson's Phantasmagoria, and Hill's *Tall Ships*—experience media images and real bodies, their own and those in trompe l'oeil boxes and on real stages, as part of a shared space-time continuum. Paradoxical presence inheres in the *longue durée* of phantasmagoria, but the post-WWII explosion of paradoxical presence may conversely explain the recent rise of the phantasmagoric as no longer a series of isolated attractions but a fundamental, perhaps *the* fundamental, image logic of our time. When real time prevails over real space, real space becomes phantasmagoric, an assembly of bodies and images.[49]

THREE PATHWAYS INTO THE PHANTASMAGORIC

The phantasmagoric *dispositif* is foundational for art, film, video, and theater since the 1960s. But because it often crosses the boundaries of established media or art forms, such as painting, film, or theater, it has remained largely hidden in the historical record. Three exchanges are especially pronounced. First, the expansion of cinema into performance, sculpture, or installation, as evident in expanded cinema and exemplified in the "solid light" films of McCall. Second, the introduction of film and video into sculpture and theater, as perfected in the "Cinema Pieces" and "Theater Works" of Whitman. Finally, in video installations, such as those of Viola or Campus.

Beginning with his now-canonical *Line Describing a Cone* (1973), McCall's solid light films comprise the projection of two-dimensional geometric forms through a misty and darkened space such that the beam of light is perceptible as a three-dimensional,

45 See Peter Gidal, *Andy Warhol* (London: Studio Vista, 1971), 92–94.

46 In Raymond Williams's formulation: planned flow is "perhaps the defining characteristic of broadcasting, simultaneously as a technology and as a cultural form." Raymond Williams, *Television: Technology and Cultural Form* (New York: Schocken, 1974), 86.

47 Thomas Elsaesser, "Between Knowing and Believing," in *Cine-Dispositives*, ed. François Albera and Maria Tortajada (Amsterdam: Amsterdam University Press, 2015), 70.

48 Paul Virilio, *The Vision Machine* (1988), trans. Julie Rose (Bloomington: Indiana University Press, 1994), 63.

49 Campus encapsulates this logistical reversal in the conclusion to his 1974 statement: "In a closed-circuit video situation one is no longer dealing with images of a temporally finite nature. The duration of the image becomes a property of the room." Campus, "Video as a Function of Reality," 83.

immaterial sculpture. McCall situates his practice at the intersection of film, sculpture, and drawing. Recent critics have framed his work as a "radical co-articulation of film *and* sculpture, as Gilles Deleuze might have put it, rather than a dialectical development leading from sculpture into film."[50] In the immediate context of expanded cinema and postminimalism, a radical coarticulation of film and sculpture was not only aesthetically but politically ambitious because of its assault on traditional cinema spectatorship. In McCall's decisive 1974 statement: "It is the first film to exist solely in real, three-dimensional, space. . . . It refers to nothing beyond this real time." He parried spectatorial immobility with a "[viewer who] can, indeed needs, to move around relative to the slowly emerging light form." What's more: "The viewer watches the film by standing with his or her back toward what would normally be the screen."[51] According to these searing statements, McCall's solid light films negated core aspects of the cinematic apparatus. That is, they were understood in largely negative terms. But in the longer history of *dispositifs*, the solid light films are unambiguously phantasmagoric: projections on smoke in darkened spaces that assemble human beings and images. As Gunnar Schmidt argues, McCall's *Line Describing a Cone* is "a new combination of modern abstraction and premodern theatricality."[52] Two hundred years and a host of social, political, epistemological, and aesthetic ruptures separate the original Phantasmagorias from *Line Describing a Cone* and other solid light films, including a range of recent digital works projected vertically down from the ceiling. But the configuration of images and bodies, the common space-time continuum, and the experience of an immediate mediation (or paradoxical presence) belong neither to cinematic film nor to domestic sculptures, nor even to their coarticulation, so much as it adheres to the dicta established by the Phantasmagoria more than two hundred years ago. The establishment of technoaesthetic precedent does not diminish the radicality of the work. Quite the contrary. In light of the phantasmagoric *dispositif*, we can recognize in the work of McCall and others not only a reactive, negative relation to traditional artistic mediums such as film and sculpture but also a positive engagement with the struggles of contemporary mediated existence. For what was a minor attraction two hundred years ago has become a generalized *dispositif* in our time.

Loosely affiliated with happenings, Fluxus, and expanded cinema, the work of Robert Whitman plots a second trajectory into the phantasmagoric. Whitman's encounter with phantasmagoria proceeded from the opposite direction as McCall's; namely, through the introduction of cinema into sculpture and theater. Whitman's cinematic installations, or, as he calls them, "Cinema Pieces," are now among the best known and most striking phantasmagoric works from the 1960s. *In Window* (1963), *Dining Room Table* (1963), and *Shower* (ca. 1964), Whitman fused real objects and projected images to confuse, at least temporarily, reality and illusion. In *Shower*, to cite the locus classicus of phantasmagoric sculpture, a film of a woman showering is projected inside an operating shower, enclosed by a shower curtain and built into a wall in a dark space. The film is back-projected—like the original Phantasmagoria—such that the projector is doubly screened off from the viewer: first by the translucent screen, second by the translucent shower curtain. Whitman effects a collapse of illusion and reality as the composite image received by the viewer is produced by virtual images projected on the first screen and drops of real water projected on the second. A widely disseminated photograph of Shower maximizes its trompe l'oeil impact. But in short order the looped film belies the illusion. Shots of the full-length nude are replaced by close-ups of body parts, mist, and the showerhead, which first sprays water and then dark paint. As we return to the full-length nude, now dripping in paint and redolent of the abstract expressionist techniques still very much in vogue, we have crossed the boundaries of sculpture, cinema, and painting. More precisely, we have witnessed the Berniniesque, phantasmagoric mobilization of multiple media to fuse images and bodies in one and the same space and time.

Whitman's case should be an obvious one. His work has long been identified with "actual [*sic*] holographic images of oneself floating in three-dimensional space in real time" (Gene Youngblood) and "a complete mesh of illusion and reality" (Richard Kostelanetz).[53] More recently, curator Lynne Cooke and scholars Branden Joseph and Andrew Uroskie have labeled Whitman's work "phantasmagoric" or "phantasmal," though not necessarily in the media-archaeological sense advanced here.[54] And yet critics invariably assign competing media to various elements within a given work—"a complex interplay of the sculptural, the pictorial, and the filmic"—when the varied media

50 George Baker, "Film beyond Its Limits," *Grey Room* 25 (Fall 2006): 104.

51 Anthony McCall, "Two Statements" (1974/1975), in *The Avant-Garde Film: A Reader of Theory and Criticism*, ed. P. Adams Sitney (New York: New York University Press, 1978), 250–51. In 2003, when McCall republished the statement in *October*, he did not soften the stance so much as introduce room for productive confusion. No longer did the film exist *solely* in real, three-dimensional, space. No longer was it necessary to contrast his solid light film with films that "allude to a past time." With thirty years hindsight, *Line Describing a Cone* at least hinted at the possibility of other times and places. Mediation crept into the work's primal immediacy. See Anthony McCall, "*Line Describing a Cone* and Related Films," *October*, no. 103 (2003): 42–62.

52 Gunnar Schmidt, *Weiche Displays: Projektionen auf Rauch, Wolken und Nebel* (Berlin: Verlag Klaus Wagenbach, 2011), 27.

and techniques are better understood as a coordinated manifestation of the phantasmagoric.[55]

Such is certainly the case in Whitman's performance pieces or, in his preferred terminology, "Theater Works," most illustriously *Prune Flat* (1965), a work that refuses categorization as cinema or theater, painting or sculpture. *Prune Flat* premiered at the Expanded Cinema Festival in New York and continued in an Off-Broadway run, an exceptional development within Whitman's milieu. In previous "Theater Works," such as *American Moon* (1960), the audience was segregated into small coves or bays that opened onto the performance space. At the Film-Makers' Cinematheque, which hosted the 1965 Expanded Cinema Festival, the shallow proscenium stage encouraged a more traditional theatrical format but also enabled the confusion of the illusory depth on screen and real flatness on stage. Approximately fifty minutes in length, Prune Flat embraces at turns the cinematic—a film is projected on a large screen at the front of the theater—and the domestic—objects are handled on the shallow stage.[56] But the bulk of the piece mingles live bodies and projected images in a manner that can be described only as phantasmagoric. Two women in white outfits appear variously on screen and on stage. A third, labeled "movie girl," also wears white. But rather than double an onscreen presence or camouflage into the projection, she becomes a human screen for a second projector and film. Movie girl performs mundane actions: she stands, sits, smokes a cigarette, and, most conspicuously, dresses and undresses, often changing into or out of whole outfits instantaneously. The actress who plays movie girl never changes her white smock dress, which serves as the screen. Instead, her own film image—at least in the initial performance—is projected back on her. Synchronization between the actress and the projection ensures the confusion of body and image; the comparatively simple magic of montage facilitates the quick outfit changes (a classic stage magic routine that otherwise requires great skill). At the speed of twenty-four frames per second, a green dress turns red, then blue; a black dress vanishes to reveal a nude woman; the nude suddenly wears black undergarments; she struts across the stage, pounces, and immediately sports a red dress. The two screens—architectural and human—share a single technology (film projection) and technique (montage). In the first instance, the effect is cinematic (proximity through distance); in the second, it is phantasmagoric (an assembly of human beings and images).

In *Prune Flat*, however, cinema is emplaced imprecisely. Part necessity, part design, the performer can never align herself perfectly with the projection; a ghostly doubling is visible unremittingly. The phantasmagoria itself is haunted, a paradoxical presence that, as Joseph argues, cannot be divorced from real-time techniques:

> *Prune Flat* splits time in much the same way as it virtualizes space. Irreducible to the pop art embrace of the simulacrum, Whitman's "real time" is also not the phenomenological time of minimal sculpture, which opposed the spectator's physicality against its spectacular expropriation.... Whitman's time is a "real time" presented directly despite the mediation of images, or, as he insisted, presented directly, and in "depth," *because* of that very mediation. Whitman's deliberate, layered, bifurcated temporality allows a ghostly difference, a haunting deferral, to inhabit the moments that it puts on display.[57]

Joseph's insight applies widely—across and beyond Whitman's oeuvre. That we recognize a coherent aesthetic project in seemingly diverse works such as *Shower* and *Prune Flat* is imperative. Whitman's neologisms—"Cinema Pieces," "Theater Works"—reflect, in part, the absence of a critical term able to describe his multimedia practice, let alone link it to related works by other artists, past and present. Such a term is *phantasmagoria*.

Like Whitman at one time, video artist Bill Viola is regularly dismissed as too slick. The criticism is apt, no doubt, but in a nonjudgmental review of phantasmagoria it is beside the point, for few artists have mined the phantasmagoric as rapaciously as Viola. "In almost all of Viola's works," Otto Neumaier observes, "the images become part of the architecture; they exist in space and time. . . . Many of Viola's works are essentially rooms, and it is vital to understand them as such."[58]

Video art leapt into phantasmagoria the moment it occupied entire rooms rather than reduced video to

---

53 Gene Youngblood, *Expanded Cinema* (New York: Dutton, 1970), 416; and Richard Kostelanetz, *The Theatre of Mixed Means* (New York: Dial Press, 1968), 229. But note the context of the latter in Kostelanetz's conversation with Whitman: Kostelanetz: "When the image flashed off the audience gasped. I thought this was a marvelous sign of the effectiveness of your deception, but it never happened again—such a complete mesh of illusion and reality. Wouldn't this be worth attempting to realize every night?" Whitman: "I think that is nice, but it isn't crucial. I don't think that's what the piece is about."

54 Lynne Cooke, "Through a Glass, Darkly: From Autonomous Artwork to Environmental Spectacle, from Spectator to Specter—Robert Whitman's Art Practice in the 1960s," in *Robert Whitman: Playback*, ed. Lynne Cooke and Karen Kelly (New York: Dia Art Foundation, 2003), 64; Branden W. Joseph, "Plastic Empathy: The Ghost of Robert Whitman," *Grey Room* 25 (Fall 2006): 74; and Uroskie, 141.

55 Cooke, "Through a Glass, Darkly," 66.

56 Whitman alludes to some of the contradictory impulses in the work: "I suggested in the piece itself that it was about movies. . . . I want people to understand that [the stage] world was manufactured. It is an object world." Whitman in Kostelanetz, 224–25.

57 Joseph, 82.

an image in a box. Viola's works are most compelling when they place these two registers in tension: phantasmagoric rooms and domestic boxes. A visitor to his 1988 installation *The Sleep of Reason* likely first encounters a wooden credenza atop which sit a vase with flowers, a lamp, an alarm clock set to the actual time, and a black-and-white television monitor in which one sees the face of a man asleep. At irregular intervals, the room is plunged into darkness, save for the alarm clock, and large, color, moving images are projected on three walls, accompanied by loud and disquieting sounds. Fires rage, dogs pounce, and owls tear out of the night. The owl and title are borrowed from Francisco Goya's etching *The Sleep of Reason Produces Monsters* (1799), created at the same time Robertson was perfecting his own monsters in the Phantasmagoria.

The tension between the two *dispositifs* is instructive. On the one hand, a grainy, black-and-white, diminutive, and nearly motionless image is trapped in a box. On the other hand, we have the immersive and jarring seizure of the entire room. In the first instance, video is merely an object in domestic space, like the lamp, the vase, and the alarm clock. In the second instance, the domestic is suspended in favor of a phantasmagoric space for terrifying images and terrified—or at least entertained—viewers.[59] The inspired touch in the installation is the bridge between these two disparate *dispositifs*: the alarm clock. Unlike the table lamp or the room's illumination, the red glowing digits of the alarm clock never go black and never deviate from the actual time at the exhibition site. This real time weaves the domestic and phantasmagoric, the quotidian and the oneiric, into one space-time continuum.

The supersession of an object-based conception of video art grounded in the domestic by a phantasmagoric articulation is also in evidence in *Set of Coincidence* (1974), a single-channel video by Peter Campus, a pioneer of video installations. The video opens with Campus, his back to the camera, staring at a television set whose screen displays grey-blue noise. Campus is soon joined by a (blue screen) double, and over the course of several minutes the two perform a ghostly pas de deux. During the extended dissolve, the original set fades to reveal a blue-screen set. As Campus asserted at the time, "If we are to avoid the problem of creating a visual system that will reduce the capacity of the eye, it is necessary to disassociate the video camera from the eye and make it an extension of the room."[60] The set of coincidence—where monitor and room coincide—is where the domestic gives way to the phantasmagoric. Here, Campus confronts himself as phantasmal image.

Campus's primary contribution to phantasmagoric video lies in his ground-breaking video installations. Where the single-channel work illustrated, an earlier installation, *Interface* (1972), performed the very coincidence of looking *through* and *at* endemic to Pepper's Ghost. Here the viewer enters a dark room, empty save for a large pane of glass with a video camera and projector on either side. As viewers approach the glass, they see a double reflection. The first is a traditional mirror image. The second is real-time, black-and-white video captured through the glass by a camera on the far side. The double image hovers in the center of the gallery, suspended on a glass screen in real space and real time. Because the video projection corrects for the mirror's left-right reversals, it can appear like a more accurate yet more alien double than the reflection—a reflection let loose, a Doppelgänger; in a word, a ghost.[61] As Wulf Herzogenrath recognized early on, Campus's videos revolve around three main themes: "double vision, dissolution of material reality, [and] the question of which is the 'real' picture."[62] *Shadow Projection* (1974) performs the same ghost story, only with shadows instead of reflections. *Interface* and *Shadow Projection* are assemblies of bodies and their phantasms—in a word, phantasmagoria. And as in all phantasmagorias, their fundamental configurations cannot be sought in a single image, medium, technique, device, style, or psychological disorder. Instead, as Campus makes clear, "The answer to this is only apparent when the viewer becomes aware of the whole mechanism: the camera-projector-screen-viewer."[63] The whole mechanism is nothing less than the phantasmagoric *dispositif*.

CODA: OCCASIONAL PHANTASMAGORIAS

Phantasmagoria still undergirds entire oeuvres. Tony Oursler's, for example, is likely the most diverse and conscientiously phantasmagoric artistic body of work ever produced. Where most artists chanced upon the phantasmagoric *dispositif*, Oursler has pursued it with

58 Otto Neumaier, "Space, Time, Video, Viola," in *The Art of Bill Viola*, ed. Chris Townsend (London: Thames and Hudson, 2004), 52, 54.

59 The domestic here is staged, and the entire installation retains a phantasmagoric atmosphere, irrespective of the illumination or darkness of the room.

60 Campus, 82.

61 "Because we are conditioned to a reversed mirror image we are constantly surprised when the direct video image is presented. Any asymmetric movement causes loss of identification with the projected self-image." Campus, 83.

62 Wulf Herzogenrath, "Menschen-Bilder / Picture of People," trans. John Anthony Thwaites, in *Peter Campus: Video-Installationen, Foto-Installationen, Fotos, Videobänder* (Cologne: Kölnischer Kunstverein, 1979), 11.

63 Campus, 83.

the passion of a collector. He has amassed an archive of seminal and obscure books and pamphlets, images and curios, many of which touch on the history of phantasmagoria.[64] The influence of this archive on his work is pervasive. Most obvious is Oursler's installation *Phantasmagoria* (Musée des Arts Contemporains, Hornu, Belgium, 2013), awash in specific historical references to Robertson. No less significant is *Imponderable* (2015), a new video work on spiritualism and its debunkers, created for a Pepper's Ghost contraption. Oursler's phantasmagoric magnum opus, however, is *The Influence Machine* (2000), a sprawling outdoor installation where lampposts speak, texts run over fences, and faces are projected on buildings, trees, and smoke—the last a technique first employed by Schröpfer in the early 1790s, several decades before Robertson launched his Phantasmagoria. But Oursler's most original contribution to the contemporary phantasmagoric is also his most enduring and widely known technique: the projection of video faces, mouths, and eyes onto dolls, spheres, and other bulbous objects (many of which also speak). In countless video sculptures and video dolls, Oursler anchors moving images in the real world only to blur the boundaries between images and the real world.

Oursler, however, is an exception. More common is the occasional turn to the phantasmagoric. A delirious sampling might include interactive works such as Valie Export's *Ping Pong: Ein Film zum Spielen—Ein Spielfilm* (1968) and David Claerbout's *The Rocking Chair* (2002–2003). Or Rodney Graham's *Torqued Chandelier Release* (2005), where 35 mm, forty-eight-frames-per-second projection on a black screen creates a hallucinatory film loop that is equal parts *cinéma pur* and phantasmagoria. More systematically, Dan Graham has for decades conjured "mirror 'ghosts'" of spectators in his many glass and steel pavilions.[65] A work like *Two-Way Mirror inside Cube* (1991) is "both an optical device and an architectural modification of a previously unused [space.] . . . The two-way mirror has 'cinematic' special effects."[66] However much Graham has transformed the parameters of earlier phantasmagoric attractions like Pepper's Ghost, the visual, experiential, and discursive similarities are striking—so long as we recognize that the "special effects" are not "cinematic" but consummately phantasmagoric. Examples of phantasmagoric dance or theater include works such as *EJM 1: Man Walking at Ordinary Speed* and *EJM 2: Inertia* (1998), a ballet staged by the architectural duo Elizabeth Diller and Ricardo Scofidio—and coproduced with Charleroi Danses of Belgium and the Ballet Opera of Lyon—which employed rear-projection technology that nearly names its debt to the original phantasmagoria; any number of Wooster Group productions, such as their hypermediated rendition of that ultimate ghost story, *Hamlet* (2005); or Richard Maxwell's *Ads* (2010), where live actors are replaced with Pepper's Ghost videos. The whole domain of 3D film—whether mainstream or avant-garde, as in the decades-long pursuit of stereoscopic cinema by Ken Jacobs—demands to be scrutinized in relation to phantasmagoria.[67] This meager inventory could be multiplied many times over. And much more can and should be said about each of these examples. Suffice to say, first, the phantasmagoric *dispositif* can help us account for diverse works otherwise unclassifiable by medium, technique, technology, influence, style, or any of the familiar categories of art and film history and theory. And, second, phantasmagoria is rising.

64 See Anne Wehr, ed., *Imponderable: The Archive of Tony Oursler* (Zurich: Luma Foundation, 2015). An earlier and shorter version of the present article appears as part of the catalogue.

65 Dan Graham in Alexander Alberro, ed., *Two-Way Mirror Power: Selected Writings by Dan Graham on His Art* (Cambridge, MA: MIT Press, 1999), 178–79.

66 Graham in Alberro, 165–66.

67 The best place to start is Thomas Elsaesser, "The 'Return' of 3-D: On Some of the Logics and Genealogies of the Image in the Twenty-First Century," *Critical Inquiry* 29, no. 2 (2013): 217–46. Jacobs describes *The Whole Shebang* (1982), one of his "Nervous System" pieces, in the following terms: "Phantasmagorical monstrosities pull from the screen. Time doesn't stand still but runs in place." David Schwartz, ed., *Films That Tell Time: A Ken Jacobs Retrospective* (New York: American Museum of the Moving Image, 1989), 27.

Handpunch

Cameron Rowland

2014–2015

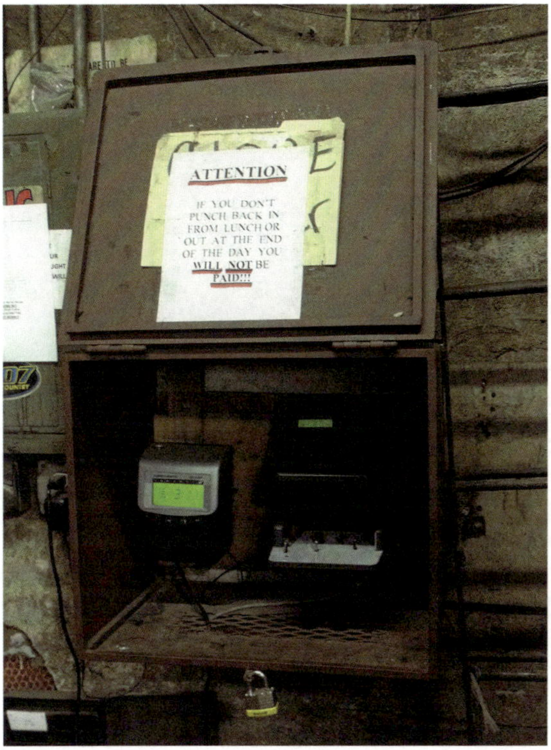

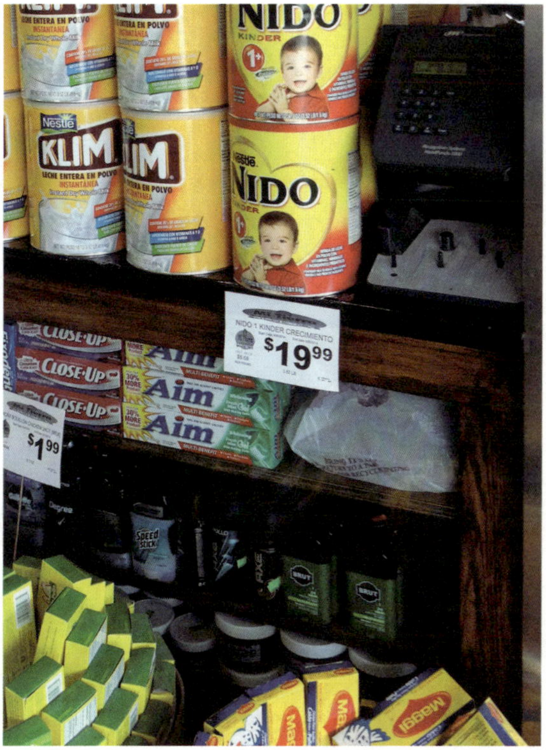

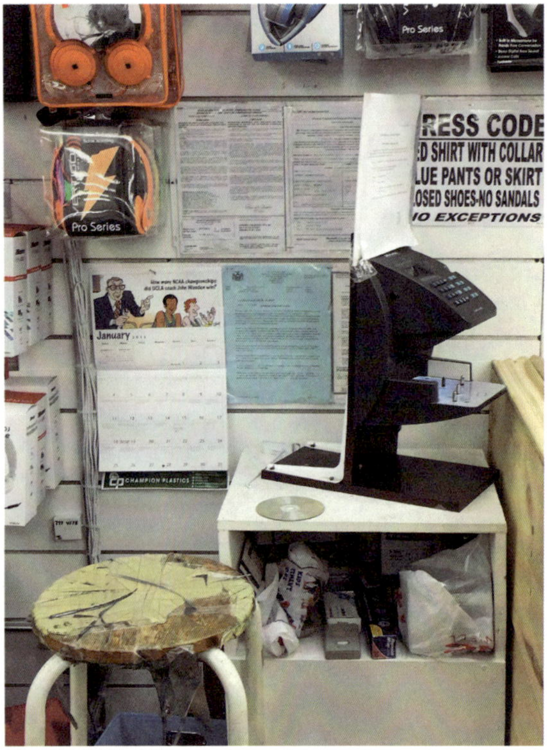
Pro Series
Pro Series
RESS CODE
ED SHIRT WITH COLLAR
LUE PANTS OR SKIRT
LOSED SHOES-NO SANDALS
IO EXCEPTIONS
January
CHAMPION PLASTICS

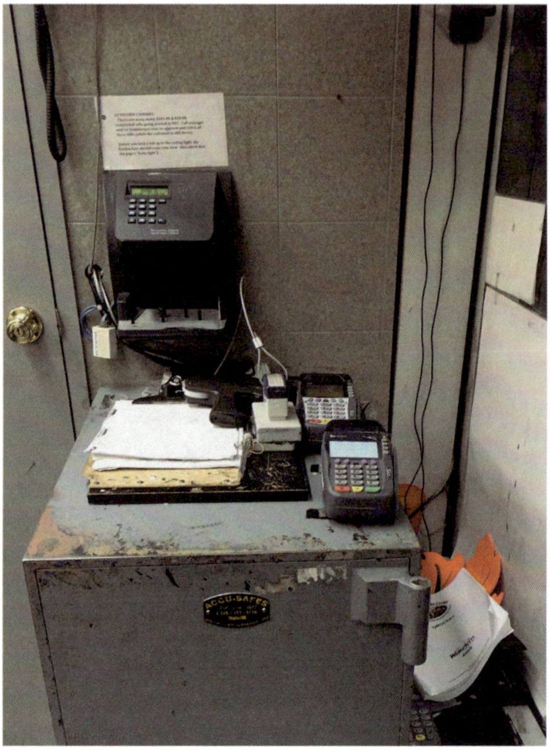
ACCU-SAFES

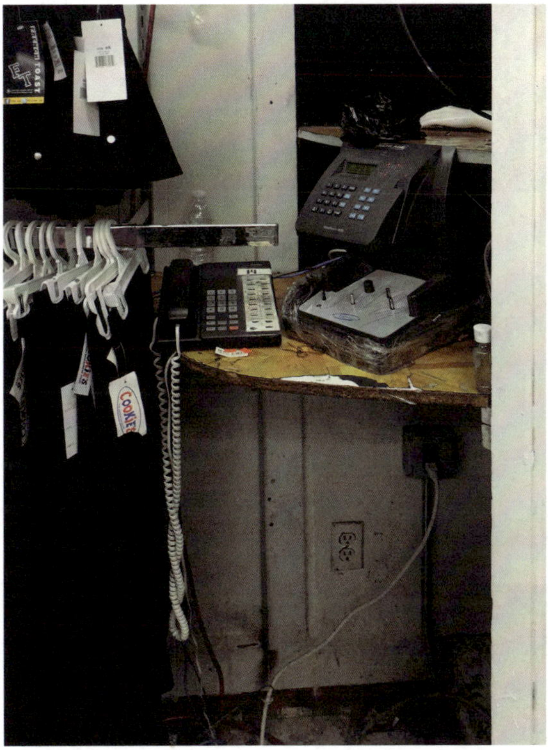

In businesses where employees' time is one of the most valuable assets, the Handpunch time clock secures this time. Manufactured by Schlage (the American lock company) the Handpunch uses biometric readings of employees' right hands to inhibit false clock-ins and payment for false hours. Biometric recognition was developed to replace photography as a superior form of criminal indexing.

Love Is the Message, the Message Is Death
Arthur Jafa
2016

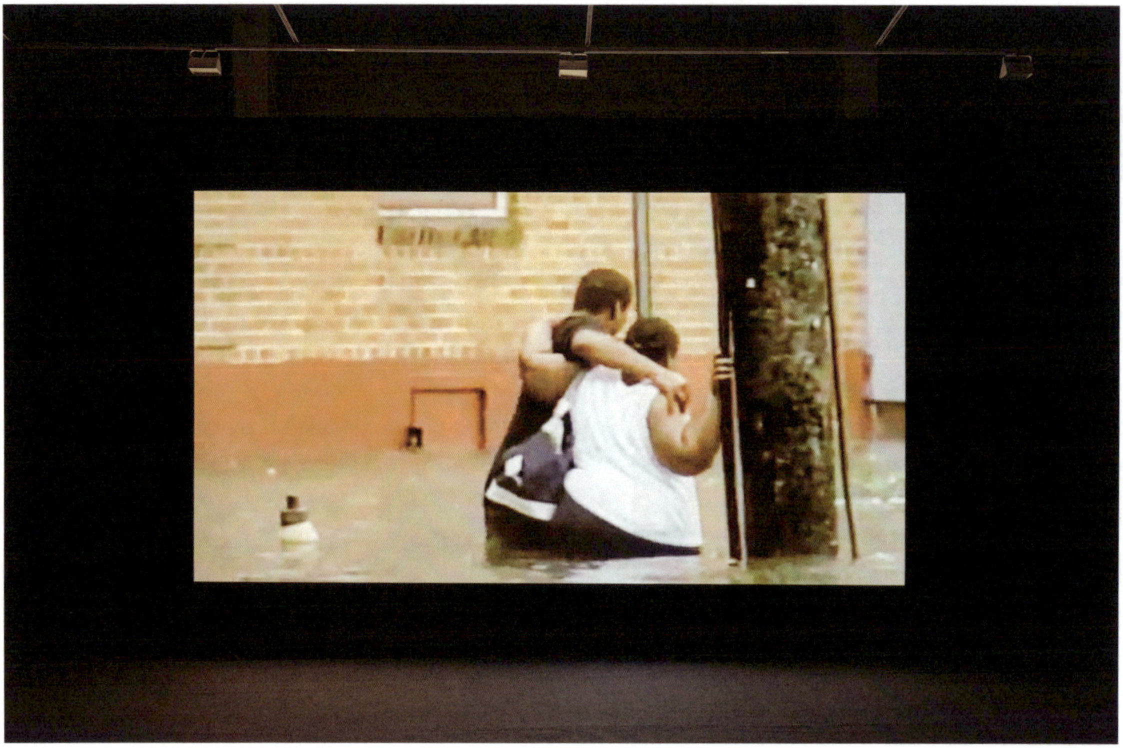

Love is the Message, The Plan is Death
Arthur Jafa and Tina Campt
2017

Arthur Jafa's seven-minute short film Love Is the Message, the Message Is Death *cuts together footage of Charles Ramsey; Swag Surf, a black variation on the wave at sports games; Fred Hampton's widow the day after his assassination; Bayard Rustin, organizer of the 1963 March on Washington; Storyboard P, dance legend; the 2015 murder of Walter Scott in South Carolina; kids dancing in a club; Hortense Spillers;* Birth of a Nation; *former president Obama singing "Amazing Grace"; Earl Sweatshirt; Ferguson, Missouri; Michael Jackson; Floyd Mayweather; the Civil Rights Movement; Beyoncé; Martine Syms; Odell Beckham Jr;* Alien; *Rob Peters; Bradford Young; Marshawn Lynch; Larry Davis; Thelonious Monk's hands; Chris Brown; Martin Luther King Jr.; IceJJFish, atonal R&B singer; astronomical images; Drake; Mahalia Jackson; and many others, in order to explore the distance and proximity between motion and movement. The film's title refers to the Nebula Award–winning 1973 short story by James Tiptree Jr., née Alice Sheldon,* Love is the Plan the Plan is Death, *about spider-like creatures who devour their mates in the course of their lifecycle.*

The following excerpts a conversation between the filmmaker and Tina Campt, Professor of Africana and Women's Studies and Director of the Barnard Center for Research on Women, at a listening party for Love Is the Message, *at Gavin Brown's Enterprise in Harlem on December 10, 2016.*

Tina Campt: We were talking earlier today about the difference between movement and motion. We think of these two things as synonyms but they're not. Movement means changing the position of an object related to a fixed point in space; the focus is on that space. Motion, on the other hand, is a change in the location or position of an object with respect to time.

One of the things that your montage and sequencing technique does is provoke our relationship to images by exposing us to them at a certain velocity over time. The impact of a work like *Love is the Message, the Message is Death* keys off of how short the span of time is in which we actually have contact with a single one of these images—each of which is incredibly arresting—before it transitions to the next. This is why I talk about listening to images and why we've called this event a listening session. Listening to images is about allowing yourself to be accessible to the affects produced in all these different encounters. Which are the historical black-and-white images? Where are the bodies moving? How do you see the choreography of bodies and violence and music in relationship to each other?

Prior to this evening, I would watch *Love is the Message* over and over again on my computer and I would find myself positioning myself backwards and forwards, closer or farther away to the screen. I noticed that I was not trying to see the photos or the images more carefully or more closely. I was trying to tweak or to amplify the relationship to get the impact of the images. I needed to get that impact physically by way of the sound. I actually needed to feel the contact between the soundtrack and the way in which it actually makes bodies move.

To open yourself up to a different sensory experience of film or to a different sensory experience of images often means actually adjusting your physical proximity to them. One way that physical proximity is calibrated is through sonic penetration; the way in which music and sound connect us. At its most basic, most fundamental level, sound is the movement of particles through air. It's a vibration that is calibrated in waves. The extent to which we can hear it depends on their frequency. There are all sorts of different sounds that we as humans cannot hear. They're not audible to us because we physically can't pick them up. Except by touching them or as a vibration. Like sounds, images have a frequency, which we can adjust. We calibrate our sensibility to images in the way we let them impact and contact us.

Arthur Jafa: This goes back to something I've said repeatedly, a mantra really, which is that my overriding ambition is to make a black cinema with "the power, beauty and alienation of black music."

TC: Tell us what you mean by that?

AJ: Well, to go back a little bit: I'm from Mississippi and went to Howard University to study architecture. I'd always wanted to study architecture; it's my first love to this day.

And in a sense, my preoccupations then were the same as now. Even though then I would have said something like, "I want to make a house that's like *Kind of Blue*. Or a house that's like *Electric Lady* or *Songs in the Key of Life*." But by my third year at Howard I couldn't really see a path to accomplishing the things I was interested in. I'd realized pretty early on that there was a class dimension to who got to practice and do the kinds of things I was interested in doing. I became disenchanted with the possibilities of architecture for me. I didn't know many black people that owned their own homes. I didn't know any black people who were going to be able to commission me to make the essentially experimental architecture I was interested in. I remember telling my father at some point, "Dad, I think I'd rather be a failed filmmaker than a failed architect."

So I wandered down to the film department at Howard and the first person I met was Haile Gerima. And that was very fortuitous. Haile had graduated three years prior from UCLA (and had been at the epicenter of the "LA Rebellion"), where, for the first time, black filmmakers were consciously and collectively engaged with thinking through what it might mean to make black cinema. One of the first things Haile said to me was: "We have to make black cinema." And in a way this dovetailed perfectly with my ongoing ambition, which had been to make a house (and now a film) that was like black music.

It became clear, however, that our idea of black cinema was being narrowly constrained by the binary opposition to Hollywood we'd adopted. They'd say, "What's black film? Black film is not Hollywood. It's against Hollywood." And that's a fairly radical idea when you're first confronted with it but very quickly my classmates and I were like, "OK, so if that's the case, and if Hollywood has narratives, does that mean black film is necessarily nonnarrative? If Hollywood films are in color does that mean black films have to be in black and white?"

So we started to think through what black cinema could be if it wasn't so narrowly defined as being against Hollywood, but was defined in its own terms. For me it came down to being about the music: How and why is the music so powerful? So, I've spent a large part of the last thirty years thinking about what makes black music so powerful, and how to transpose this power into this other medium, cinema.

I realized that the black voice was at the core (technically, formally, and spiritually) of why black music was powerful. People typically talked about cinema in terms of stories, narratives, thematics—but it quickly became clear that we needed (additionally) different concepts. So, for example, the idea of black visual intonation was conceived as the cinematic equivalent of the black voice. You'd never confuse Billie Holiday with Fela or Fela with Bob Marley or Marley with Charlie Parker or Miles Davis, right? Each has a certain signature relationship to the black voice (as transgenerational continuity) and with black vocal intonation specifically, whether in the voice of the performer or played out instrumentally, as a primary mode of expressive articulation. I was interested in coming to understand this vocal intonation, and how these traditions or continuities of manipulating tonalities are bound up with what it means to be black.

What is the relationship between black music and Western music? African-American music is Western music—a lot of people don't seem to realize this. I like to say like we are illegitimate progeny of the West (ill suns), in the sense that a lot of ideas were imposed on us (nonconsensually, so to speak), ideas which we internalized and made something new of, something unique and distinctively American, all without us ever being seen or accepted as the legitimate heirs of these ideas. Black people came to the Americas with the very deepest reservoir of cultural traditions, modes of expressivity. There's a great quote by Nam June Paik: "The culture that's going to survive in the future is the culture that you carry around in your head."

The Middle Passage is a great example of that. Despite the fact that we came with a full spectrum of incredibly rich traditions of expressivity (both material and immaterial), black people came to be most strong in those spaces where our cultural traditions could be carried in our nervous systems. Architecture, painting, sculpture, those kinds of things, they tended to erode (relatively speaking), in contrast to things like dance, oratory, and music (which could be constantly renewed in the new context in which we found ourselves).

TC: Speaking of dance, it seems like in your work the motion of bodies is really crucial and it has to do with what we were talking about earlier, the relationship of black people to spatial navigation. There's bodies and movement in violence and bodies in motion through dance—which is not always choreography—it's a relationship to rhythm or music and then bodies in motion through athleticism, right?

So you've got Mohammed Ali, you've got the basketball—you've actually got the fans around the basketball court [doing the Swag Surf] who are synchronizing with the people on the floor, and this connects with what you were telling me about how you understand black people's capacity to navigate space.

AJ: One of the reasons I spend so much time thinking about music is because music is a great place to actually think through ideas that you can also share with people. Particularly black folks: we know all the music. We know everything that we've ever made.

We can sing all the songs—even when we don't know the words, we know a song's precise structure, its trajectories and inflections. Increasingly though, I've became interested in dance, African-American social dance. And I've been thinking through what's happening when people actually dance. The first interview I ever read with Cornel West, in the early '80s, he was talking about black culture in that expansive, encyclopedic way he's known for, and somebody asked about black visual culture. His response was: "As far as I can tell it's not very apparent." It set off a bit of a shitstorm. Folks like Howardena Pindell were like, "Cornel's speaking from a place of ignorance. He doesn't know what black visual artists have done. He's giving ammunition to those racist forces who want to keep black people out of this particular arena, the visual arts." But I remember Cornel went on and said something like, "I think the reason why it's underdeveloped is because it never found support in the only institution that black people had, which was the church."

Fundamentally, it's a brilliant insight. Most black (American) churches (Baptist and Methodist) are Protestant, they're not Catholic. And we know one of the primary differences between protestant Christianity and Catholicism has to do with their respective relationships to the visual. So song and dance and these kind of things found support in the black church while the impulse to visualization didn't.

Even if you go to somebody like Basquiat—one of his parents is Haitian and one is Puerto Rican. This is not a small fact because if you go to Haiti, Puerto Rico, or Brazil, places where Catholicism is the dominant religious form that black people practice, you find more openness towards visual expression, particularly as it coalesced around describing saints and things like this. In the Protestant church, this wasn't the case.

One of the things I've found most fascinating about black American social dance is how it has functioned without any sort of external authority (what's good or isn't good)—meaning that there's been little or no commodification of black social dance, with the kind of externalized system of reviews (and sales figures) that goes along with commodification. Not that there's anything wrong with the amazing modernist (or "professional") dance that black folks have done as well, but when you go to a dance, a social dance, and folks are dancing (in the round, so to speak), the dopest dance is the dopest dance. Meaning, the person who is dancing and has the most charisma, who's displaying the most expressivity, doing the most amazing things, is operating on the cutting edge of both the self-authorizing and the collectively resonant, right?

Cornel was onto something. But he mischaracterized or misnamed it. It's not that there was black *visual* underdevelopment—but there certainly was what I call black *pictorial* underdevelopment.

We need to make the distinction between the visual and the pictorial. Because, for example, we apprehend dance (and style, postural semantics, etc.) visually. So I'm really trying to think through what's going on when black people dance. On a phenomenological level, what's going on? There are at least two things that black Americans are acutely sensitive to. One is rhythm. Everybody's familiar with the idea that black people have an acute sensitivity to rhythms. But there's another thing that people have a much harder time grasping, or getting a handle on, which is that black folks have an acute sensitivity to what I term *vectors*, or spatial arrays.

One place you see this is in basketball. A player (both moving and in motion) from almost anywhere on the floor can launch the ball into a trajectory where it'll arc, descend, and go through the hoop. You see the same thing in soccer—like with Pelé. And with the *ginga* (capoeira). There are things bound up in very complex ways with our experiences (the Middle Passage, slavery, Jim Crow) that have impacted how we operate in space, how we understand and how we interact with space. So there's this acute sensitivity to space.

I started saying, "Oh, black people can predict the future"—and that sounds really crazy, but what I mean is that there's an acute sensitivity to vectors and trajectories. If a person throws a ball, they have to calculate on the fly the speed and trajectory at which that object has to be launched so that it's going to land in a predesignated point. And most of the time you're not talking about a fixed target (this is not golf). You're talking about a person, in motion, calculating what a ball is going to do while another person (or persons) is trying to stop them.

I think when black people dance, a lot of what's happening is the playing with, the setting up of, series of vectors and then breaking them. Like a pun. The obvious example is Michael Jackson and the moonwalk. He looks like he's going in one direction but he's actually going in another direction. Something similar happens when you throw the ball at a target as you're moving. If you can't anticipate where it's supposed to land, you can't fully appreciate when it does something different from what's expected (one could say, "when it behaves in a fugitive fashion"). You have to perceive these two different things (what it's supposed to be doing and what it's in fact doing) simultaneously. It's really about flow—flow through figures. I have been preoccupied these last three years with this whole question of flow through figures. And this dovetails with your distinction between motion and movement.

TC: Going back to Cornel—and forgetting whatever his judgment or assessment of black visual culture is, or its underdevelopment—and talking instead about it being the site of authorization: dance is visible in the church, as you say. Consider the importance the Pentecostal movement places on the visible black body possessed by Christ. The church actually becomes a site of navigating those vectors, visually enacting a specific trajectory of bodily motion.

AJ: You know we're here in Harlem at Gavin Brown's Enterprise. Gavin has said to me a couple times, "There's so much energy here. How do we tap that energy?" And I said to Gavin, "Oh that's an ongoing project because even for the Studio Museum (which has been here for thirty years) there's the ongoing challenge of how to tap this energy. How do we get people in here?" So we got into this whole thing. We created these posters. And the posters we chose have these lynching images. And there was a lot of back and forth about the appropriateness of putting these things in the street. Well my thing was like, first of all, there's something to be said for just making explicit what is oftentimes implicit—which is black people being killed as if we're not human beings. How do we introduce something in the space that can cut through the noise? There's a real problematic around the appropriateness of having an image of a man getting murdered. But this footage is all over the place. It's everywhere. It's not like we're talking about digging stuff out of some archive that's never been seen before.

It's literally everywhere so the question becomes: How do you situate it so that people actually see it, this phenomena, as opposed to just having it pass in front of them? How do you have people actually see it? And simultaneously, how do you induce people to apprehend both the beauty and the horror of these circumstances? There's something profound (and magical) to be said about the ability, the capacity to see beauty anywhere and everywhere. I think it's a capacity black people have developed because not only are we are not authorized, we're demonized—we are radically not affirmed, so we've actually learned not just how to imbue moments with joy but to see beauty in places where beauty, in any normative sense, doesn't necessarily exist.

In the previous film I made, *Dreams are Colder Than Death,* there is a moment when Hortense Spillers makes this startling formulation about the difference between the body and flesh. She says, "The flesh gives empathy." That's what I feel like I'm trying to manipulate and at the same time get at—a sort of rendering of how black people feel now. The work feels very constructed to me; I'm struggling with it. Does the constructedness of it in any way undermine the real emotions that are elicited?

TC: But that's the thing about the mechanics of empathy. Are you trying to get us to think about the constructedness of empathy? At this point in time, do we have any choice? Do we have any choice in terms of what empathy is?

AJ: Well, I think empathy is maybe the single most important thing that's at issue now in society. We know that the process of oppressing people requires the one who is oppressing another to first dehumanize them. I mean, this is the oldest strategy. We've seen it time and time again. We see it in Nazi Germany. They put people in situations where their humanity is thrown into questions because it's like ... Somebody said to me recently if you throw a bunch of crabs in a barrel (as if the barrel was the national habitat of the crabs—you know?), it's gonna produce and elicit certain kinds of behavior which, considered ahistorically, will appear to be innate, rather than an adaptation to malevolent circumstances. Same thing if you throw people into a barrel.

The people who are dehumanizing others are trying to maintain or hold onto the sense of their own humanity. If I step on a bug, I know maybe the American Society for the Protection of Animals might get mad, but I'm really not stressing it too deeply when I step on a roach. I'm just not. I don't think about whether the roach has a family and children or anything like that. I just step on it. But you can't do that with human beings unless in some way you convince yourself that they're bugs. So ultimately it comes down to the relative presence or absence of empathy. You cannot oppress people without expending a certain type of psychic energy, unless the whole mechanism, the whole superstructure is supporting that understanding of the other as being less human, less feeling than you are. I think you learn empathy. I think it has to be taught.

I was cinematographer on the film *Daughters of the Dust* years ago, thirty years ago. *Daughters,* for those who don't know, is about a black family at the turn of the century in South Carolina—they're trying to decide whether they should stay off-land, you know off the mainland, on the island. Or should they go to the mainland and become a part of society at large? It's very much a film about Africans, African-Americans, becoming black.

I remember a talk I gave about the film at the New School. We showed the film and then afterwards we were talking, and I'll never forget this older white woman, she stood up and said, "This is an amazing film. When I see this film I don't see color. I see my grandmother. I see my grandmother. I don't see color when I see this film." And she was a very nice lady (speaking from what I took to be a progressive place) but I remember asking her, "Why can't you see color and see your grandmother?" Like why is that a split, you know? Why do you have to erase her blackness in order to see your grandmother in this woman? I think that's what's at stake. It comes to empathy.

The classic way in which cinema works is that you identify with the people on the screen. You go to see a movie and you identify with a person. Generally, you identify with a "good guy." And there's a whole battery of things—lighting, costumes, and everything else—that the filmmaker manipulates to make it clear (implicitly and explicitly) who's going to be the good guy and who we're supposed to identify with. One of the things that was radical about *Daughters,* if something was radical about it, was when you went to see that film the only subject positions you could occupy were those of black women. There were no other subject positions available. You can't even find white guys as bad guys. It's just black women, right? *Daughters* does what it does but I don't think it's going to change people's attitudes. What it does do is make it harder to pretend as if black women are less human. Because for its two hours you're forced (or allowed, I would hope) to exist in someone else's skin. It erodes one of the psychic mechanisms in place that lets you pretend that that person (a black woman) has less feelings, less humanity, less whatever than you do, right?

So I'm very much preoccupied with how the work that I do tries to expand narrow notions of who we are. Who is we? You know, who identifies with what, this whole idea of empathy being learned? We know that women have better empathy muscles than men. Because they get to go to films where they don't see themselves and they project themselves anyway. They get to exercise that muscle.

Audiences of color exhibit better empathy in cinema because they go to cinema all the time where they don't see figures that look anything like them and they've accordingly developed the capacity to project themselves into that space and empathetically have that experience. We need more cinema that constructs more spaces for more types of people to be able to exercise their empathy muscles.

So it's one of the reasons I'm not generally interested in making films about white folks. I'm really interested in making work that is always foregrounding black people's humanity, bad guys or good guys. I like the alien. I'm a big fan of the alien. I'm a big fan of Hannibal Lecter, who I think is black and passing. Fundamentally, I just want to see black people who are complex. And competent at what they do, even if they're mad geniuses or whatever.

TC: I think that we should try and wrap up.

AJ: Well hold up, I have to show something else. When I do these talks and show these things everybody's like, "Oh, it's just so heavy." It's so this, it's so that, but you know I like love, too. So I wanted to end with something that's sweet, that's got a high love quotient. A more overt high love quotient. I hate people going away thinking, "Golly, man, it must be hard being AJ."

Last thing.

[*music*]

AJ: Can you get the light?

Conversations

Martha Rosler in Conversation with Walead Beshty
June 13, 2017

WALEAD BESHTY: What do you think about the effectiveness of working within dominant models, i.e. conventional models, detourning them, corrupting them from the inside? Conversely, if we consider the ways that the western pictorial tradition is corrupt—implicated within imperial, hetero-normative, racist, phallocentric, colonial, world views—do we have to invent or insist on new models, in the interest of direct political action and activism? And to be more specific, I'd like to know more about the timeline behind *Bringing the War Home.*

MARTHA ROSLER: I began to consider giving up painting while I was still in school ... it always seemed to me difficult to identify the sources of inspiration. This was occurring as High Modernism was drawing to a close, and Pop art was emerging into wide visibility, as were Fluxus and other movements among the avant garde. These movements freed me from the boxed-in logics of painting and sculpture—which called into question the other elements of the system of art production and distribution. The artists of the mid-1960s were restive, rebelling against the gatekeepers of exhibition and publicity. Artists developed an array of new modes of production and exhibition and fought against commodification with new forms that were tagged as "dematerialization" by Lucy Lippard and others. The McCarthyite fog of the 1950s was beginning to dissipate in the face of pushback by young people and the growing strength of the Civil Rights Movement. The student and anti-war movements soon followed, and feminism and gay liberation slightly after.

By this time, in the mid 1960s, I had turned my attention to photography and to collage and photomontage, without giving up abstract painting nevertheless. My first engagement was with political figures in an all-over patter as we might have done as children, and with large-scale urban 'transportation scapes' seen from above: a kind of all-one urban International Style city spreading everywhere.

I shifted my attention to representations of women in advertising, from the large New York Times Sunday magazine and women's magazines, as well as soft-core and some hard-core pornography. Looking at a front-page tabloid image of a desperate-looking Vietnamese woman swimming across a body of water with a child in tow, I had the realization that I could—and should—adapt my *detournements* of advertising to make antiwar agitation. So, I did that, while continuing to work with images of women. I thought the best approach for the antiwar material was to use images of idealized suburban homes and to insert photojournalistic war images—both from magazines, often the same magazines, such as *Life.* My basic model was "here and there," in other words emphasizing a kind of collapsed spatiality, to emphasize that the division of the world into spaces of self and other were dangerously illusory. I wanted a rational space for the viewer to stand in, to take stock of the conflicts of identification and disidentification, entitlement and dispossession. And if war is not about territoriality, what is it about, after all? But not all the images are spatially rationalized in this way, turned into a window.

WB: How did you come to make *Bringing the War Home*? When they existed as flyers, through what circumstances were they distributed? Did you conceive of them as art works per se, or did they have a different status for you then?

MR: I decided that these works would be derided as propaganda, which was fine with me. I did not sign or date them. My father, a storefront lawyer, had fallen in love with the Xerox machine, as it saved him from the nightmare of carbon copies. I saw this technology as my route to the production of the antiwar flyers, in black and white—I made stacks and handed them out as people were assembling for marches and during them. I was reacting against the model of the antiwar flyer—I received one just the other day, still in the same old model: text heavy, almost marginless, with endless exposition and exhortation. Mine had no text.

I made them from about 1965 to 1972, and saw them as images at base, adaptable for different formats. I always intended for them to be printed as photographs, and presumably framed. But in the meantime, they mostly existed as 8.5 × 11-inch Xeroxes. A few were published in the feminist newspaper *Goodbye to All That,* which I worked on with other women in San Diego, and a few in other "counterculture" mags. I quit making them in about 1972 or 1973, when the war stopped. (And I quit painting about then, as well!)

In the early 2000s I was part of a newly formed antiwar group, Artists Against the War, made up of mostly women of all ages, most of whom were veterans of antiwar actions during our earlier wars. But in 2004, when I was invited to take part in an art-world show called *Election* put together on their own initiative by two young women curators, I took the opportunity to consider what I might be able to contribute, as most of my antiwar group's efforts were thought up and often executed by other members. On reflection, I decided to reinstitute the antiwar series of thirty years earlier by making a couple of images in the same vein: *House Beautiful: Bringing the War Home, New Series*. I did that, but then I couldn't stop. I made 14 works. My reasoning on restarting this zombie series was that I would be called out for repetition and would be able to pounce: who is doing the repetition here? Me, or the Bush administration? I also felt that the works would be attacked as too political (ha!) and I would be able to use them to repoliticize the now slightly fetishized older works.

A few years later, in 2008, I was asked to contribute a work to an antiwar issue of an art magazine, and I got the cover specs and made a new work. And then I made a handful more of them. This time, all the works had outdoor settings, in Iraq and Afghanistan., I placed the works of the new series in art-world settings from the first moment, whereas for the Vietnam series, I had refused to put them anywhere near the art world until the 80s or 90s. I felt, however, that in the 2000s, the art world had broadened its audiences and its incorporation into cultural life. I also realized that some of the works would likely appear in mass-circulation newspapers and magazines, as they did.

Stephen Shore in Conversation with Walead Beshty
June 13, 2017

WALEAD BESHTY: *Picture Industry* emphasizes, in part, that photographic or more broadly, technical images were always deployed through multiple platforms, that such media are never just one thing but a multitude. For example, photography's circulation through off-set printing, etching, lithography, not to mention projection, have always been central to its identity. The project considers how early developments in photography reflect a malleability and versatility in terms of format...Jacob Riis basically innovated the first form of halftone printing for photographs, which was essential to the impact that his work had. "How the Other Half Lives" is the first time a photograph was circulated as a halftone picture, and this is part of the nature of the project, its being designed to reach a wide audience. Riis also made his own version of the stereographic magic lantern; he was very technologically savvy. Ironically, the pictures were never meant to be looked at as little framed scenes on the wall, which is how they are almost exclusively presented in contemporary exhibitions. They didn't exist in that format until after he died, and until they were donated to the City of New York—and when they began being presented within museums, prints were made, even stereographic views were turned into singular conventional pictures. *Picture Industry* tries to reflect some of that and talk about the implications of an understanding of images which incorporates its occupation of a variety of forms of distribution as it relates to the contemporary—it's a very broad and overly abstract and general thing to tap into, but that's the hope: a resource to think through those different elements without positing any kind of authoritative historical survey. The show is a provisional and associative history that pays attention to the array of platforms that technical images move through. That's part of why I thought your use of postcards [in the work *Amarillo-Tall in Texas*] was so important to include...

STEPHEN SHORE: I'll tell you the story of the cards. I think the main influence on them was Ed Ruscha. I guess it was three years before I did the cards, when I was first introduced to Ruscha's books. Have you ever seen the 1968 Warhol catalog from the Moderna Museet in Stockholm?

WB: Yes, I have.

SS: That catalog, the young curator at the time who did that was Kasper König. We edited the pictures and sequenced them. It has one hundred and sixty-five pages of my pictures in it. We were in Warhol's loft in Soho. When we finished sequencing them, he said, "I have something to show you." On the floor of the loft, he opened out [Ruscha's 1966 book] *Every Building on the Sunset Strip*. Scales fell from my eyes. I understood photography in a different way and what photography could do, the dissemination and whole of it. I left and got into a taxi and went to Wittenborn Bookstore on Madison Avenue between 78th and 79th and bought every Ed Ruscha book. Now a few years later, 1971, I had the show at the Met...and was very interested in vernacular uses of photography and had been collecting postcards and loved postcards. When I was going out to Amarillo, when we took side trips from there, I would collect lots of cards.

WB: *All the Meat You Can Eat*, does that predate that?

SS: No, it's the same year. There were three projects in 1971 that all involved vernacular photography and it was *All the Meat You Can Eat*, the postcards, and that's when I started the Mick-o-Matics, the precursor to *American Surfaces*. They were done with a snapshot camera and processed by Kodak and meant to be seen as Kodak-produced snapshot prints, but the camera was called a Mick-o-Matic, which was a big plastic head of Mickey Mouse with a lens in his nose and you can put a flash cube on the top of his head. As you can imagine, whenever you take a picture of someone with a Mick-o-Matic, they're smiling! It's a truly genuine smile, it's not a forced smile because it's this big. I still have it! I think Quentin [Bajac] may actually include it in the show at MoMA.

WB: Oh, wow!

SS: Because it's quite an object.

WB: The Mick-o-Matic photographs didn't merge into *American Surfaces*, they're quite discreet, right?

SS: Yeah. They're on their own. They never were exhibited. I liked the idea of the snapshot and playing off of the conventions of the snapshot, just the cultural associations. The Mick-o-Matic was limited as a tool.

WB: Right, it was a plastic lens camera?

SS: Yeah. It just wasn't very good. It made me understand that the camera you use has an effect on the picture. I had two Leicas and two Nikons. If I'm traveling around the country and stop in a diner and say to a waitress "Can I take your picture?" and pick up a Leica, that's very different than the Rollei 35, which was the original point-to-shoot. That's why I got the Rollei 35, because it had a good lens and was a well-made camera by Rolleiflex but looked like an amateur camera. My intention all along was to send the film to Kodak and have them make prints and then exhibit small snapshot Kodak-made prints, which is what I did.

WB: *American Surfaces* was all sent off to Kodak? And then they were printed at different scales later for exhibition?

SS: Yes. For the original show, it was Kodak prints pasted on a wall, unframed, not behind glass because I wanted people to see the object of the snapshot print, that's how we're going to show it at MoMA. I only made it larger recently, it's not much larger, simply because I can. In those days, I couldn't make a 5x7 print because Kodak color film was so shitty that you would lose saturation; it was unsharp and I couldn't really go larger...With additional printing, I can boost it, so I can make a 5 × 7 print that has the feel of the smaller prints. That's as far as I'm going with it. It just makes it a little bit more accessible. I'm abandoning the reference to the snapshot because by the end, I had abandoned it and that's why I went to a 4 × 5. I wanted to continue *American Surfaces*, but I didn't want to be limited by that small print. I became more interested in the content of the image. Most of what I did in the 70s, I really staked out during that year of *American Surfaces*, in terms of content, but I wanted a larger negative and there weren't good medium format cameras other than the Hasselblad and I didn't want to do square, that's why I got a Crown Graphic and I thought I was just going to hand hold it and then I wound up going off on this thirty-year diversion to an 8 × 10 view camera.

WB: Not to digress too much from the topic of *Tall in Texas*, but were the first, loosely put, *Uncommon Places* photographs, were they the first 4 × 5s taken with the Crown Graphic?

SS: Yes.

WB: When does that shift occur, just out of curiosity?

SS: 1973. At the end of the year, I borrowed an 8 × 10 from Weston [Naef] and just spent a couple of days using it. Then, I went back to 4 × 5 and did one trip in the spring of '74 with a 4 × 5 and then got my own 8×10. Then by June of '74, I switched to the 8×10... He curated my show at the Met in '71, that's how we met and became very good friends. About a third of work in *All the Meat You Can Eat* is from his collection...in fact, we're doing a room of *All the Meat You Can Eat* at MoMA.

WB: You were able to reconstruct it?

SS: I have about a half-dozen installation shots. Not all the panels, but some of the panels and we're not going to do the whole thing because it was in a loft and it would take half the space to show, but we're going to do a smaller version of it. Weston just sent me a box with all of the pictures that he had from that period that were put in the show.

WB: That's fantastic that *All the Meat You Can Eat* is being shown. Your engagement with vernacular photography has always felt significant to understanding how your work developed, that it came both from pop-art and, for lack of a better term, formalist traditions within photography. I think it's really exciting that that is going to be reflected in the show, because if I recall properly, *All the Meat You Can Eat* mostly included anonymous, commercially produced...

SS: Almost entirely...I was friendly with the District Attorney of Amarillo. He just unloaded pictures that they had in the police department they didn't need anymore, a huge collection of pornography that had been confiscated. Some of it by today's standards, very innocuous, but in the 1960s was considered scandalous in Amarillo, and some very good police photographs.

WB: Like crime scene photographs?

SS: Yes, crime scene photographs.

WB: I didn't know that. So, out of that constellation of things—the Mick-o-Matic, *All the Meat You Can Eat*, came *Tall in Texas*?

SS: Yes. I wanted it to be real postcards. My idea was that what I had been doing with the Mick-o-Matics was playing off of snapshot form, occasionally doing pictures with just people smiling, just like real snapshots, but then photographing something like a [Louis] Vuitton suitcase. It's probably the only picture of a suitcase that went through Kodak's plant. It's playing off of the snapshot form. I was doing the same thing with postcards. There are ten cards and five of them are the most traditional postcard subjects, this is from doing a lot of collecting. It's the main street, the biggest building in town, hospitals tend to be for some reason. Every town you go to in those days, there was a picture of the hospital. Half of the ten were traditional postcard subjects, the county courthouse and the civic center. The other five were quirky local places that were important to the people there, like Doug's Barbecue, which everyone thought, and all of my friends thought, was the best barbecue in Amarillo. It wasn't just picked randomly, everyone loved Doug's Barbecue, but it wasn't a civic treasure in the sense that the county courthouse was—and probably would not have had a postcard made, because a motel would, because they have customers, but Doug's Barbecue wouldn't. The Army-Navy store where everybody bought their Levi's and that kind of thing. Half of them were just these quirky local places. Then, because I wanted them to be like real postcards, I went to the largest printer of postcards in America, which was Dexter Press in Nyack, New York. I had deluded myself into thinking that was what the New York art world had wanted were postcards from Amarillo, Texas and that the same people who bought Ed Ruscha books would love Amarillo postcards. By that time, I had become friendly with the management at Wittenborn, who sold all of the Ed Ruscha books, that was the one place in the city where you could get them. They agreed to put up a postcard rack and sell my postcards. I had 5,600 sets printed, 5,600 sets of 10—56,000 cards and sold none!

WB: Wow. You made a big commitment because I think the Ed Ruscha books, the first printings where all in the 1,000 range as far as I remember. Gosh, I think *Royal Road Test* was like 600 copies actually. You were prepared for the onslaught of demand.

SS: Well, the thing is that Dexter Press, being the biggest, had limits. I'm not sure I could have ordered less than 5600. There were 10 of them, so 5,600 became 56,000. I think they wouldn't gear up the press for less. I got them back and Doug's Barbecue, which I took on a cloudy day and it came back, and it had a blue sky. They painted the sky blue, it's pale blue, but it's blue because postcards have blue skies, it's as simple as that. They didn't ask me! The Potter County Courthouse, it was done in August in the Texas panhandle hadn't rained in four months and the grass was dead and yellow. I got the card back and it was like that, it was bright green!

WB: I noticed that some of the images seemed colorized, but I imagined it was just an artifact of mass production. In some of them, the colors pop funny, I hadn't realized it was because they painted them in.

SS: They didn't ask me, I was just oblivious to that.

WB: Yeah. It's part of the process of producing the postcard. In other words, they're like a camera that treats a subject in a certain way. Here is a business that treats a certain type of subject in a certain way, produces a certain kind of thing. That modification is very much part of the logic of that format, that's really interesting.

SS: By the way, it was funny that if they were the largest manufacturer of postcards in Germany, it would never have occurred to them to paint the sky blue!

WB: Right.

SS: Just a parenthetical anecdote, [Thomas] Struth and I were both involved in this project, "This Place" [organized by Frédéric Brenner and Charlotte Cotton between approximately 2009–2012] in Israel in the West Bank. Our time never overlapped, and we shared an assistant. We both took many trips. On one of the middle trips, he said to me something I noticed. Now of course, Israel is a desert country.

WB: Yeah.

SS: He said, "I notice if you're doing a landscape and there's a lone cloud in the sky and it's covered the sun, you'll wait until the cloud passes." Struth did the exact opposite, he would wait ages for that one lone cloud to go in front of the sun and he said, "I don't understand that." I said, "It's simple." I'm from North America and he's from Germany. He's worked out how to take pictures on overcast days and I've worked out the opposite.

WB: That's fantastic.

SS: Anyway, back to the cards. I then had cartons and cartons of these cards. Then, it just occurred to me that on all of these cross-country trips I was about to embark on—that I would distribute them, and the cards don't say Amarillo on the back.

WB: Of course, yeah.

SS: They're generic. Every time I would go into any town, go into any gas station or drugstore, I would bring cards in my pocket and I would stuff the postcard racks full of cards.

WB: I remember you telling me that quite a long time ago and I was fascinated by it, also by the idea of someone passing through town and being like "Oh, I'll grab a postcard and write a friend," and they're actually not from that place…It's just as legitimate because it does represent a certain notion of the small town, which is what someone buying the card is looking for. The images do fit our conception of the small town, it does represent that idea, it is about a small town, it's just as applicable and yet—

SS: It just doesn't happen to be that town!

WB: I thought that was quite brilliant that you redistributed them in that way. It put the idea of the work into circulation in a way that the Ruscha, for example, did not. It put pop-art back into the world it was describing... I never got a chance to ask you, what led to the decision to leave the name of the town off?

SS: That was actually the idea. They were co-published with a friend of mine from Amarillo named Teddy Wagner. He was responsible for the captions, it was Teddy's idea.

WB: Was it an active conversation or was it something that just fell by the wayside in terms of listing the town name?

SS: No, it was just for the core reasons we would consider it today—"Let's make this a generic card and it's the American National Bank building and that's it."

WB: Yeah, it's anywhere and yet-

SS: It's Doug's Barbecue.

WB: I always thought that was such a fascinating choice, a really important choice.

SS: He was interested in contemporary poetry. I think he saw this as almost objective poetry. Well, just the way ... I may have just made this association. One of the reasons I love *Lolita* is that the way Nabokov relishes the names of American places and this one part where he's now taken Lolita off on their year-long cross-country trip and there's a paragraph where he just lists the names of the motels and it's just this savoring of these small town American hotel names, The True Rest Court. I think that's the same thing, Doug's Barbecue number two.

WB: Yeah. It's also interesting thinking about the diaries. I know you reprinted, wasn't it in the Phaidon reprinting of *American Surfaces* that you included the diary pages? I don't know if diary is the right term, the journal of what you ate and what you watched.

SS: That was done the next year. *American Surfaces* was '72 and the diaries, the journal was the 4x5 trip in '73. Phaidon actually published the facsimile of the journal as a standalone book called *A Road Trip Journal*, which includes the facsimile of the journal plus every single picture I took during that trip. The back matter is every picture I took during the trip in chronological order. I think a few pages were in *Uncommon Places*.

WB: Even *Uncommon Places* had this quality. The lists make me think of arbitrary-ness of Ruscha, or better, [Douglas] Huebler, of this kind of catalog of something that has a total completeness to it and yet tells you so very little, just what you ate and watched. It tells you incidental things or things that comprise the day... But it's all about what escapes those lists, the actual experience of something, it speaks to what can't be captured. It seems like a very similar impulse to play with this notion of the highlights of a town that are actually non-specific to a town, but are significant to a general sense of what a town is, what daily life is like at a certain point in time. The specific experiences of the day that can be categorized and written down, it speaks to something broader than just an individual's experience, that the lived experience of the thing or the actuality of the thing always escapes these systems of organization and cataloging and documentation, there's something in excess of them. I'm not sure, that's just a partially caffeinated association that I'm making now, but it's really interesting that you were thinking in that way. I don't know if that's fair to say about the journals, or diaries. Do you say diaries or journals?

SS: I call it journal.

WB: Journal. Of course, journal has the association with the objective, it's official. It doesn't necessitate a first-person expression, it's a cataloging.

SS: When you look at the pages, that's what it is—a daily record that I've kept, but unlike a diary, there's not a word of personal experience. There are traces of it. I go to an emergency room in a hospital in Iowa or someplace and there's the receipt for it. I list what I ate for each meal, the name of the restaurant, where I spent the night, what I watched on television or if I went to the movies, what I went to see, how many postcards I distributed that day, the exposures I took...then, any printed matters that I collected. It's postcards I collected, a parking ticket, a traffic ticket.

WB: That's interesting because... Each of those things are transactional in some sense, even a parking ticket which is an official document of a conflict with local municipal law that requires payment. If it's a purchase from a retail establishment or a diner or something, this is a transaction point, and that produces an official record, a record which in the end is to be presented to the state. If it's the acquisition of certain objects, it's another form of transaction. If it's watching television, this is another kind of transactional thing, a moment of contact between you and a larger system.

SS: I'll just throw in one other thing about the postcards. When I would do subsequent trips, I'd sometimes find myself back in a town where I knew I had distributed cards, so I would go and look for them. What made me happiest was when I found half of them were gone. Because if they were all gone, it's a possibility the owner of the store could have said "What's this shit doing here?" And threw them out, but half gone means the store owner didn't notice it or left them there and people bought them. Once in a while, I would get a card from a friend who stopped in Winnemucca, Nevada to take a piss and went into the gas station and saw one of the Amarillo cards and recognized it immediately and sent it to me.

WB: Did you distribute all of them?

SS: Not 56,000, but I distributed thousands. There's only so many you can put in a postcard rack.

WB: Yeah. It's amazing that people you knew stumbled across them, that's actually really fantastic. To put this thing into the world, and see the evidence of its circulation… it would be great to stumble across one in a flea market.

SS: There must be thousands of them out there. I did travel '72, '73, '74, just those three trips, they were each two or three months long. If I'm putting postcards, I'm seeing a lot of the country. I'm putting postcards out in lots of places. The country was well covered with them.

WB: I'm trying to think if I have anything further. I'm curious, you speak about this period like this was a moment in your work that you got past, or lost interest in. In a broad way, I guess I'm just curious about what really changed. I know you spoke about being more interested in the content of the photographs. How would you describe the shift in content, the shift in how you wanted to make things?

SS: I'm not sure the content shifted, it's that in doing *American Surfaces*, I was doing a cataloging. There were repeated subjects. Every person I met, every meal I ate, every bed I slept in, every toilet, every television set, art on walls, commercial architecture, residential architecture, but I wasn't limiting it to that. There were certain categories that I kept coming back to. It was a multi-layered serial project with a half dozen series happening side by side at once, but not divided that way, I've always just mixed them up when I show them. It was also always about at the same time, some kind of understanding of the culture. It was using say a theme and variations as a way of thinking about television sets or motel rooms or store windows. It's not that I switched to that, it's that took on more importance. I was less interested in the associations of the snapshot. Then, I wasn't intending to use the Crown Graphic on a tripod, but when I was photographing architecture, there was no reason not to. I started putting it on a tripod and I started looking at the ground glass. I became fascinated by the whole process of using a view camera on the ground glass.

WB: At first you were just using a range finder. You weren't looking through …

SS: Yeah. I was really going to do *American Surfaces*, put a strobe on it, but it never worked just because of the size of the cameras. If I finished this meal and wanted to take a picture with a Rollei, I'd just go like that… [motions as if taking a snapshot while seated] …With the Crown Graphic, I'm going to have to stand on the chair.

WB: Because you'd have the parallax…

SS: The normal lens is 150 millimeters. It has different depths of field. Then, the flash was further away from the lens just because physically it had to be because the camera's so big. The shadow looks different. I never filmed them just because it never worked.

WB: Yeah. It would have produced a much more chaotic sensation. I would imagine looking through a range finder, and having the flash so far from the lens, that you could not feel the exact boundaries of the picture, and all of that variability would have led to a much more discordant picture. It's the stillness and precision of those images that is so affecting, it makes them feel quite different from *American Surfaces*, even though they're often of similar subject matter and seem to start the following year. It's clear what a dramatic effect the camera has, how it so deeply impacts how a picture is made, how one sees through the camera, and that is unmistakable within photographs themselves. So you're forced to see differently, and so is the viewer.

SS: Yeah, especially when you're up close, which is a lot of *American Surfaces* is again photographing this plate, parallax will come into play.

WB: The Rollei's a fixed lens, right? It's the one that turns and pops out and it's kind of wide, isn't it?

SS: It is a 45 millimeter. The other great thing about it is because it's so small, there was no place on the top for this flash shoe. The flash is under the lens and it creates a beautiful shadow, which is unlike any other camera. If you were to take a picture of me now, with a normal camera there would be a shadow here and there would be a shadow here. Because the shadow is under the lens, it outlines the figure. It makes the figure pop from the background because it's a continuous shadow that goes like that. It's not by coming up from the bottom ... It's that far from the lens, but it just happens to be below the lens.

WB: Thinking about those photographs, there was a lot of instances with the portraits where you find that. There's an interesting way that the figures seem to pop forward. I never even thought about it or I didn't know, thinking about the position of the flash, that that's part of what produced that.

SS: Yeah, it is.

WB: Not to structure some sort of overly simple evolutionary through line or something, but it seems as you move through these vernacular forms and the conventions of them that they started to produce a structure for your work. One of the first things as a student that I noticed about *Uncommon Places* and fascinated me was this kind of adherence to genre, at least in the original *Aperture* publication. I couldn't help but look at it and reflect on it as an engagement with genre form, that there was the still life, there was the portrait and there was the landscape as these classical western pictorial forms that persist. While it didn't produce some sort of taxonomy of that form, it seemed very much an investigation of this type of picture making form that came out of an extremely long tradition, it wasn't just a by-product of say a photographic tradition, although those kinds of conventions are built into the technology, the development of lenses to become flatter, all to emulate Renaissance perspectival form, to start to decrease a lot of distortion and things like that... but unlike *American Surfaces*, the work from *Uncommon Places* reached further into the traditions of picture making. How you were describing this kind of engagement with the vernacular—the ties between these vernacular forms as "low" forms, or what have you, and this sort of, I don't know if I want to say rarified, but more this kind of high tradition of Western picture making. The way that that was found by moving from the vernacular, or less considered forms to a precise and highly technical investigation of picture making, and it wasn't just an intellectual shift of interest, it came with the change in the type of technology you were using, the camera. You see a lot of instances of people starting with high traditions of picture making and that then awakening an interest in the vernacular. It's interesting that you came from an engagement with these vernacular forms and found your way into classical traditions, it allows you to link vernacular picture making all the way back through the history of painting through an investigation of pictorial form.

SS: Have you read a piece I wrote called "Form and Pressure"? [first published in *Aperture 205* (Winter 2011) – Ed.] Because it addresses this exactly, and also, in relation to the tradition of Western painting.

WB: Wow, I'd love to read that. It makes me also think of [John Berger's] *Ways of Seeing* because in short, when you're talking about these kinds of conventions, different types of picture making mark distinct modes of perception, the way that they also affect how one sees the world. I did an interview with Stan Douglas and I told him about this uncanny experience I had as I was studying photography with you and just starting to become conscious of seeing in pictures. At first, it would drive me crazy because I would walk around, and I'd see everything as some sort of composition. The oddest thing is when one feels perception as something mediated, we know that, but to experience it is different. Feeling or sensing that seeing is never direct, it is based on various mechanisms of perception and to become conscious of it, conscious of seeing through a set of conventions. It places the world at a bit of a distance, it can feel alienating, like there's a fundamental separation between oneself and the world that you hadn't noticed before. It's also invigorating, because then you can think through this mediation, understand it, manipulate it for the first time, and see picture making, pictures in general, as a conceptual structure that is tied to your understanding of your own body, tied to the distinction between yourself and the world. I remember we talked about this change when I was a student, it was a real turning point for me.

Stan Douglas in Conversation with Walead Beshty
December 13, 2016

WALEAD BESHTY: Let me just pull up the question I emailed you, give me a moment.

Stan Douglas: I read it before coming down. But you might want to refresh my memory.

WB: OK, here it is: "As far back as Panofsky writing in the 1920s, perspective or more exactly pictorial form has been widely understood as indistinguishable from a European ideological vantage point. Its foundation lying in imperialism, mapping the world and taking possession of it, delineating inside from outside, whether we are talking about people or places. Implicit here is that perspectival form is a kind of depiction of dominance *in abstentia*, a displaced abstract portrait of a dominant entity, which seeks to make the world its domain and as such, imagines itself through the definition of the outside or other.

How then can conventional genre forms do anything other than perpetuate this? Is it simply a matter of inhabiting these forms of other voices occupying the positions of authority that separated them out in the first place? Or is occupation in itself a form of defeat? In short, does moving forward require casting out the Western pictorial tradition in its anachronisms or is resistance most effective when it is parasitic in nature, drawing new life from an antagonistic host?"

SD: There really no way out of that dilemma. The "symbolic form" of perspective is reproduced, reaffirmed and reinforced each time a photograph is taken and the ideology of realism is naturalized—and things actually get worse as this technology is elaborated later in the twentieth century. Take the way audiences are disciplined in a cinema, forced to sit still with their back to the source of the images, as in Plato's cave, and identifying with what happens inside a camera obscura. People have come to think that they see the world in linear perspective even though it is completely different from what goes on in the visual cortex. It goes back at least as far as the eighteenth century when people would visit a picturesque vantage point, turn their backs to it, and look at its reflection in a "Claude Glass" or black mirror in order to experience reality as a two-dimensional optical image. I really don't understand where this desire came from, perhaps it has to do the desire to take possession that you mentioned. In any case, the selfie is its endgame, where people feel that they have not experienced a place until they have experienced it as representation. When you get to contemporary technology like VR, apotheosis of the panorama, the subject is trapped in a cylinder with no agency whatsoever. And augmented reality is less about dominating the world through representation than it is about completely incorporating individual experience into thoroughly administered representation.

WB: I think that our attraction to seeing the world as a picture is about bringing the unruly world under control, making it manageable, comprehensible, possessable and less threatening. I think it comes from a desire for some semblance of agency, no matter how illusory. What you describe about VR strikes me because it is a complete inversion of the claimed intent of those technologies, which usually emphasize subjective agency.

How do you see disciplining taking place in VR? In other words, what restrictions do you think persist and are further isolating or subordinating about say a virtual reality context that's even more insidious than in cinema. Cinema seems a quaintly industrial model of spectatorship and power, viewers line up in rows and face a single point of emission, like workers on an assembly line underneath a single centralized authority, a classic management/labor relationship. The power relations seem quite obvious, still powerful, but unmistakably present. The VR model seems to shift this dynamic, it seems less apparent, more dispersed.

SD: Because in fact it takes away the many ways our bodies experience the world, replacing them with vision alone—and human vision, anyway, starts in the eye but is finished in the mind where it is synthesized with short and long term memory among other things. To finish the thought about augmented reality, it is a way of turning the world into cinema. So you're not seeing the world as you could potentially see it, with your other senses and with flashes of involuntary memory, you're being told, disciplined, to identify the visible world with particular meanings.

WB: Augmented reality like Pokémon Go.

SD: Yeah, exactly, or in apparatuses like Google Glass or Microsoft HoloLens which can give you *Terminator*-vision.

WB: VR worlds seem particularly confining, an extension of cinematic isolation, but with augmented reality, the issue seems to be imbedding, the intermixing of artifice with the real—but I still wonder how you see the disciplinary function realized. I get how this manifests with cinema, that corporeal experience is displaced by opticality and we are confined to fixed positions, in regimented order, but in the case of augmented reality, it seems like opticality and bodily experience are held in tandem, rather than one being asserted over the other. A user is active both as a body moving through the world, and as a viewer simultaneously. Conceptions of reality are unstable anyway, and augmented reality literalizes the way images function in the world how they permeate our experience, conlonizing our conception of the world. I remember the strangest experience I had when I first started making photographs was that I started seeing the world as scenes, which I think is a common experience, and in a way, augmented reality makes this phenomenon apparent. I wonder if there is a potential in augmented reality to make the influence images have on experience more conscious, more apparent to the user in a way other forms cannot.

SD: Well, the intent of the people who design these interfaces is to ultimately make them invisible, and once that happens the identification with technological representation becomes normalized. Kittler claims that no one "saw their life flash before their eyes" at life-threatening moments until after the movie industry perfected the flashback. I guess it's a convenient way of describing a confusing experience with something familiar but, as when people imagine that they see like a camera sees, the complexity of what goes on in the human sensorium is replaced with a reductive representation of it. An attenuated experience that can be confused with a limit of experience.

WB: I agree, but still I wonder if the basis of these viewing experiences are fundamentally corrupt, or if it's simply the slow evolution of models of spectatorship, addressing some of these issues of optical hegemony along the way. You've intervened in a number of technologies that in their conventional deployment produce similar problematics, drawing those problematics of conventional media forward. The earliest example I can think of is the *Television Spots* [1987-88] and the *Monodramas* [1991], which I thought of as an occupation of a highly controlled and structured commercial visual "space." Rather than rejecting the medium, you manage to *detourn* it, extending the conventions of cinematic or television narratives to the point where they become uncanny, denying the resolution they usually promise. Without that resolution, one has the sensation that a pervasive atmosphere of tension and anxiety is inherent to the medium. I suppose the *Monodramas* that take the form of the confessional are explicit about this. And you continue to work with these established systems, complex and immersive technologies which are strongly identified with economies of scale and authority. How does one produce within those systems without simply reifying them? Of course, this is a classic question. Art could be thought, in its entirety, as a version of this problem, a highly managed field that is fueled by the wealth of a small minority and then made public. I guess I'm asking where the impulse to occupy these sorts of forms arises from, and if there is an effect that is desired beyond their denaturalization, if there is a redemptive aspect? The phone prototype of *Circa 1948* you showed me sometime back was a form of augmented reality, if memory serves. Now that I think of it, it had an immediate resonance with *Suspiria* [2002–3], which inserted performances into live feeds of Kassel for Documenta 11. In retrospect, it seems like this was an early imagining of a kind of augmented reality, of a narrative, or cinema becoming sutured to real experience, or at least, live feeds of actual locations.

SD: In an odd way *Helen Lawrence* is the inverse equivalent of *Suspiria*: in one pre-recorded actors are projected into a live video feed and in the other live actors are projected into a virtual space. And, yes, the 3D imagery of *Circa 1948* is up-resed to become virtual, the sets in *Helen Lawrence*. I was curious to know how that technology worked, and I was interested to know what it takes to build a "world" from scratch. Neither of the locations in my play *Helen Lawrence* or the mobile app *Circa 1948* [both 2014] exist and the locations we made were, aside from the occasional flight of fantasy, as historically accurate as possible. There's a bonus version of *Circa* made by the NFB Digital Studio that is kind of like a virtual Segway. There are projections all around you an if you "move" in any direction depending on which was you lean. The user's head is also being tracked allowing all of the projections to distort in a way that compensates for real-world parallax so it doesn't feel like you're in the center of a cube — and as you crouch down or stand up parallax in the virtual world moves accordingly. It's an interesting thing to experience but it's not really art.

WB: What makes it not really art?

SD: It's kind of an "attraction" or something like that, as in *cinema of attractions*. The medium is pretty overwhelming, more powerful than anything it could represent.

WB: Is the political problem the fiction that the worlds on offer are complete? Is it in the suspension of disbelief they require?

SD: Photography is necessarily incomplete because it compresses four dimensions into two. It is a severe simplification of reality, although it once had an affirmative aspect— I have a theory that the reason why different people in different countries invented photography at virtually the same moment was because of a certain spirit in Europe, the spirit of bourgeois revolution. Both Louis Daguerre and William Henry Fox Talbot patented photography in 1839, midway between the July Revolution of 1830 and the continent-wide revolutions of 1848. "If they could not represent themselves, they would have to invent representation..."

WB: I wonder if the incompleteness of photography is only apparent in retrospect. Certainly there is a critical tradition that, since the inception of photography, saw it as a similar threat to our experience of reality. That sort of understanding of the medium as a kind of ideological illusion still persists, although today much of this anxiety is focused on more contemporary, more technologically advanced forms. But there's also a remarkable decentralization of production that's allowed to happen with the invention of photography that has produced a kind of visual literacy in the public, a sensitivity to how images can produce a distorted notion of reality. There was something that you said about the *Monodramas*, it might have been in an interview, or something you said during a lecture, when you were talking about the problem that when people knew it was art they didn't think it needed to have meaning. This conservative impulse in the audience seems to undermine attempts to open-up or reimagine these forms of mass media.

SD: I guess the problem I was bringing up in the case of the *Monodramas* was that people have preconceptions about what art is supposed to be—in North America especially. I have a clip shot by one of the original broadcasters of two viewers who called in to ask about the seeing these curious things on TV. They had seen them all, they could describe them in detail, they had interpretations of them all but, when the reporter told them it was art, their perspectives suddenly changed. This is exactly what I was afraid of. When it's art it's solely about formal play or expression as opposed to being about meaning. And the woman says, "Now that I know it's art, I don't have to worry about it because there isn't a point. It's just for art."

WB: Do you think it's a systemic problem, or do you think it's an instance of say, a particularly uncurious viewer?

SD: Well, they were curious, and they were looking for meaning, until they learned it was art. I had an intuition that this would be a problem so, I refused to allow the stations to identify the spots as art until after our broadcast contract was over. They said, "Well, could we have a logo of the gallery, could we have your name?" And I would tell them no because it had to be the medium talking to audiences, not an author.

WB: Right. I always thought of those works as your coaxing the unconscious of the medium into the foreground, the undercurrent of anxiety of conventional television, products to correct some deficiency in the viewer, that play on their class aspirations, etc., which punctuate the fantasy of programming.

SD: That's the main thing I realized at the time was that, in commercial television, the real content is the advertising and that programs were just to get people to see the advertising.

WB: Yeah. But, do you still see that public notion of art as a problem? You and I have also gone to the theater together, so it's not so much that you are disinterested or refuse those types of conventional public outlets, they seem to be meaningful contexts for you.

SD: I avoided public art for a couple of decades because I felt couldn't speak in good faith to the audience and I thought I could make space for a more nuanced conversation in the museum. I ended this moratorium when I made that mural of The Gastown Riot [*Abbott and Cordova, 7 August 1971*, 2009] because I realized I could use the situation and a Breugelesque rendition of an event that actually happened there as a way of bringing up a problem that really hasn't gone away even if it had been partially forgotten.

WB: I want to go back to the question about inhabitation. I used to think about that issue a lot, what it means to inhabit a mass medium, and the problem of reification. The solution I came to was to work on a smaller scale, to start from the body, insert it into systems of representation, but this limits the scope and reach of the work, meaning that there are certain systems which are too complex, or operate on too large a scale for me to really tinker with. But something that is remarkable to me about your work is that it maintains a democratic project, a project which reimagines media technologies and tries to work against the alienation they produce, while it embraces the production values of mass media and its conventions, albeit to different ends. While it denaturalizes certain kinds of cinematic conventions, most aggressively narrativity, it maintains a technological complexity and production values associated with conventional formats. It upends what one expects from a moving image that has high production value. Still, that sense of authority is still present, meaning the technological complexity reaches beyond an average viewer's knowledge base. I wonder how you think about that, how you see that power dynamic addressed in your work.

SD: I'm sorry. Are you interviewing me or are we having a conversation?

WB: I guess I'm interviewing you a little bit. I'm just curious. I mean, this is stuff that I'm curious about. You can interview me too.

SD: Going back to the original question, then, maybe you can talk about how you have tried to work with photographic means in a way that would interrupt its transparency. In almost every cinematographic work I've made I have in some way tried to break a convention that is typically transparent. You do something similar yet different in your analogical , or indexical, work where you trade transparency for what you might call materialist picture making.

WB: Sure, but materialism for me is inextricable from the conditions that produce the things I work with, the attendant labor, and the expansive social and economic systems around it also—so I think of it as broader than what the traditional notion of materialist picture making would imply. I'm interested in the systems that produce these things, rather than the things themselves on their own. Perhaps it's that indexicality allows for a broad set of relations to be drawn forward, relations that complicate the notion of realism proposed by representational pictures. Early on, I saw representation as a problem, so rather than trying to critique it, I wanted to create a different form, a form that would limit the assumptions made about pictures, that would posit a realism that was less about depicting the world, but about its integration within the world. Materialist practices were also excluded from my education, so when I came across them, they felt like a way out of a certain mode of making things. Panofsky was very important to me in school, and he speculates about this idea of anisotropic image that's irregular in every direction, a nonhomogeneous kind of perspectival space.

SD: Sixteen years ago I made a photograph called *Every Building on 100 West Hastings* [2001]. If you see it in reproduction, it seems like a normal picture but if you see it in real life, you realize that each building has its own vanishing point, and you get a feeling of a kind of panoramic space being flattened out into an orthographic one. It interrupts the centrality of perspective subject but I wonder if that's enough.

WB: In terms of disrupting perspectival form?

SD: Exactly. Not everyone who sees the picture will actually realize what's going on, only if they're open to seeing how space has been distorted will they be able to see it. If you look at a particular building while perceiving adjacent buildings with your peripheral vision, you get a sense of space unfolding. But a lot of people look at pictures in a distracted state, expecting photographic representation to always conform to their preconceptions, and they will therefore only see what they expect to see.

WB: How big is it?

SD: 16 feet wide.

WB: Oh, I had no idea. I've only seen the work in books. I mean, that gets into something almost more like bas-relief, right? Like, it gets into that kind of compressed space? I think that would be an irregular anisotropic kind of space and, I guess the question would be, what elements of pictorial conventions it is disrupting?

SD: I guess my point is that, only those who are sensitive to seeing something in a nonconventional way will experience it in a nonconventional way. Any photographer would know that it's an impossible picture to take.

WB: Right, but I think even a viewer who couldn't articulate what is going on would sense it. I think the effect of the Hastings image is experienced even if a viewer lacks the technical knowledge to be able to articulate what is going on. The oddness of the picture is unmistakable, and most compellingly to me, it is visceral, the understanding it produces is bodily, manifest on a physical level. This possibility for an embodied rather than an intellectual understanding struck me as a viable way forward, a way around a discourse about representation, which I thought dead-ended in circular arguments about dominance and subordination. It was also a way into an affirmative approach, one that was not about rejecting something problematic, but embracing something positive. But I think the reason why your work was so affecting to me is that it engaged representation in materialist terms, it didn't refuse it but found another option by moving through it. So I guess I've been thinking about what is recovered from the history of representation in your work, how the maintenance of that function in art is important in your work. Anyway, Panofsky doesn't really outline what an anisotropic picture would be, I had to imagine it. Instead he relates it to antiquity and pre-Renaissance perspectival form. Which, is basically just a kind of perspective based on symbolic weight. Important things are big, unimportant things are small.

SD: Which is kind of how we see.

WB: Exactly. We mentally isolate out who we're speaking to for example, we focus on them and they become larger in our view because of the curved lens of the eye. What's in the center is larger, and what's at the periphery recedes, so this kind of hierarchy of importance premised on scale which is imbedded in our optical reality; by looking at something, we literally make it optically larger than the things we aren't focusing on. The next logical step to representing importance would be to create a hierarchy of scale between things based on their importance. Engaging with Panofsky drew me to the materialist tradition, it seemed like there was something in his insight that could complicate materialist picture making, make it less about refusal, and might be able to answer my questions about representation in an affirmative sense. That drew me to think about bending the picture plane. Still, I wonder about how to navigate the problem of participating in a discourse which is so deeply implicated in restrictive power relations. I tend to resort to a brutish form of making as a way out, a means to undermine the simulacral effects of representation, the authority implied in the role of being a producer.

SD: How's that?

WB: Well the works are often coarse, marked up, and unruly; I think this is why I rely on chance and aleatory systems rather than try to control outcomes. I try to make the processes transparent, accessible, so that the machinations behind the work don't become the meaning of the work. I also don't feel capable of managing a system that's too large, too complex, I'm more engaged with smaller scales of production. I guess that's something that I'm fascinated by in your work, that you manage to bring this highly orchestrated thing under your control. When I think of artists with comparable production value, they often seem to me to be appropriating the power of high production, riding on those systems, leaving them intact and using them as a vehicle. I see what you do as very different, you break them apart and reconfigure their conventions. You also don't stop at the level of dismantling, you don't just dissect things, but reconfigure and repurpose them. My approach is different because I don't have the mind for that kind of precision, my work almost precludes me from doing that. I lean on immediate brute choices, bodily choices. Your work often circles back to the question of the body, but you marshal a technological and organizational complexity I don't; I'm both incapable of it, and uncomfortable working that way. I feel like we are both curious about machines and systems—my sense is that your impulse is to carefully dissect them, understand them in technical terms, while mine is to jab my finger into them, muck about with my hands, smash stuff; I like to keep it simple, amateurish. Like the photograms, they are clumsy, systematic yes, but also very dumb and flat-footed.

SD: A lot of artists who work with high production values typically hire industry professionals to make it look that way but, as you suggest, I am more interested in understanding the apparatus well enough to be able to reveal and work with its contradictions. If you don't, you are inadvertently reproducing conventions which are not neutral, like the contradictions in realism you discovered through Panofsky. But, does "smashing stuff" count if the stuff is nonobjective? If there's no optical perspective?

WB: Well, optical perspective is integral to the technological development of all of these materials, so my approach is often to estrange the material from its conventional use, make their predispositions lead somewhere they weren't intended. It started with a decision not to work within a certain type of western pictorial tradition, or rather, try to reimagine it, so it was about finding a different mode of representation, which was materialist. Another side is the complete excision of narrative, because I always saw narrative as a problem with pictures, the assumption that a static form contained a narrative progression, because narrative is about temporality, an unfolding in time. Pictures on the other hand are static, in representational terms. Narrative was something placed on pictures, not contained within pictures, so another decision was to try to alienate a viewer's impulse to see narrative in pictures. In the end, it was about trying to make a picture that had nothing to do with perspective, nothing to do with abstraction, and didn't offer narrative cues.

SD: No "grandmother" and no "demonic diva." But I was also thinking about your JPEG edits where you run a JPEG though a text editor to mess up its pictorial structure. Do you feel that's doing the thing that your initial question was getting at?

WB: Yeah, perhaps. I was working with how digital formats handle pictures, and that perspectival form isn't natural to the digital format—that it constructs and organizes information in a different way than renaissance pictorial form does, despite it being used to traffic that form. I wanted to make the incongruency between the digital file and the picture more apparent, and see what resulted when the friction between them was allowed to manifest itself. But the impulse behind them was much more mundane than a broad commentary on pictures; most important to me was that the tools be readymade, commonplace, that the two systems or conventions I used, text edit and picture viewer, were readily available, and to assert that even tools this commonplace could be used to produce an alternate form.

SD: But when you cut a TV in half or drill a hole in it, because we have an expectation to see a perspective image in it, that is a negation.

WB: I suppose it could be described that way, but I don't think of it as a negation. It's more an engagement with the machine that doesn't adhere to the usual conventions for its use. Having a hole drilled through it or cutting it in half causes the TV to produce a picture in a different way, and that picture is the result of the object's response to a certain set of conditions; most importantly, these are obvious conditions, I mean, you don't have to explain that a hole was drilled, there's no secret to it, so there is an obviousness about where the image we see comes from, it's worn on its surface.

SD: You called it a picture.

WB: Yeah, I would say it's a kind of picture, yeah. What it produces looks like a picture.

SD: My own impression is that you've made a TV into a thing. It's not something you look through or into but something you look at. Would you call an Agnes Martin a picture?

WB: Yeah, sure.

SD: Okay. That's your vocabulary, fine.

WB: I guess the reason I would call an Agnes Martin a picture is because it's based on grid systems, and it arises from systems of picture making. To me the work wouldn't make sense without a certain pictorial tradition being present, even if it is producing something which doesn't look like a conventional picture. I think it's about the tension between the core terms of classical picture making, the dialectic between frame and screen, the use of the grid, and so on. I wouldn't say her work, or my own for that matter, are exclusively pictures, they are things fundamentally, but all pictures are things. I think of the term 'picture' as indicative of a one of many possible methods of approaching an object. I mean, what interests me about them is that they can be read in terms of a tradition of picture making but they don't exclude other ways of understanding objects. I think of it as holding the conventions around pictures and the conventions around objects in tension. I wouldn't privilege any one approach over another.

SD: I've noticed your irritation when I suggest that you're always doing photography even when you work in three dimensions—that you have an indexical preoccupation which is a fundamentally photographic one.

WB: I guess what bothers me about the term photography is that it implies a certainty about the way that depiction, or representation, functions. It's true that my work comes out of an engagement with technological images and primarily with photographs. But I don't think in those sort of categories when I work, I find those categories counterproductive. I mean, I don't see a difference between things to look at or look through when it comes to art objects or really any object; I think assuming photography as a category privileges one mode of looking, and I'm interested in a broader set of concerns than the term implies.

My first real engagement with your work was when Dia showed *Win, Place or Show* [1999]. I think I spent three full days sitting there watching it because I was completely fascinated. It had a deep physical effect. And, it wasn't about trying to figure out how it was made—because that seemed both beside the point, and beyond my knowledge base—but it caused me to think about how the conventional approaches to understanding moving images were working against me. I learned a lot from that piece, and I was struck that what I learned had to do with active perception, with experience, rather than simply an intellectual comprehension of the false continuity of images or what have you.

Even the basic desire in narrative to see a progression, to find the beginning of the action and see how things develop, is frustrated. Despite it being a loop, you can't help but seek out a rest in the cycle, a place to think of as a beginning or an end, but that piece didn't allow that. I think that what is happening to the characters mimics the viewer's experience, their being trapped in a small room, the viewer being trapped in a room, both the viewer and the characters stuck in a narrative loop, looking for resolution. The frustration the characters experience, neither getting what they want from the other, just as the work refuses to deliver the resolution a viewer is looking for, the feeling of the characters' reality being bounded, just as the viewer's reality is bounded. I came to think of it as an allegory for cinematic viewing, being trapped in the endless retelling of the same stories in different guises. I knew this intellectually, but I hadn't experienced it and all its uncanny implications until I saw that work.

SD: Yeah, the piece presents a series of interconnected conflicts about the control of space: from the post-war housing project that warehouses the working poor, to the argument and physical fight to confirm who's the alpha male, to the splitting of the cinematic axis in two but shooting on either side of it turning spatial continuity inside-out, to the side effects of shooting a wide shot with two cameras which will sometimes cause an actor to disappear and sometimes to become doubled. This is, by the way, an effect you can often see 360° VR images. They are typically shot with multiple cameras, but because the cameras aren't infinitely small, there is always a slight parallax error at the suture between frames.

Early on when I made a film called *Overture* [1986] I solved a problem—which I subsequently forgot as my productions become more elaborate—but I remembered it again when I made *Der Sandmann* [1995]: if you're presenting a time-based work in a gallery it shouldn't have a beginning and an end, it should all be in the middle so it doesn't matter where you walk in or when you leave. *Win, Place or Show* elaborates on this by not only looping the Sisyphean hell these two guys are enduring but by also changing each time it repeats. But one of my favorite parts about that piece is something that always changes: the radio. A live radio feed is filtered and mixed in with the soundtrack changing the affective character of each cycle. Even if you can't completely make out the chatter or the music the tone is still there and it changes how you experience the escalating argument and the fight. In my recombinant installations one retrospectively recognizes temporal displacements but in *Helen Lawrence* one is constantly presented with spatial ones. Where you sit in the theater determines your experience of the space of the stage but that is constantly contrasted with a different, and two-dimensional, perspective from one of the cameras. It does in fact what cubism claims to do by letting you experience multiple points of view simultaneously. It's disorienting at first but at a certain point, if you are open to it, you learn a way of seeing two things at the same time, which is probably the most amazing thing about the piece and it's an experience of space I've never had before.

WB: Another way of coming at my initial question to you is whether there is a core aspect of conventional spectatorship—whether it be within cinema, television, or theater—that is positive? We started off talking about the negative impacts of certain types of spectatorial forms, and rather than the negative impacts, I wonder about the positive aspects—what should be recovered, or supported?

SD: It depends on how open you are to that experience. Younger people who saw the play, people who were more versed in media, were open to seeing it that way. But people who want theater to offer identification, empathy and catharsis with actors, which is to say most theater audiences in the English-speaking world, will not. *Helen Lawrence* has moments of identification, empathy and catharsis but it also has a continuous alienation effect, the images projected between the audience and the actors, which is only broken twice. Audiences in Germany and Belgium really got into it but following a performance in Toronto a couple of years ago there was a talk back with the actors, and somebody asked, "In the future, will this be the norm for theater?" And an actor said, "Well, this is really complicated and expensive so probably not." And the audience applauded.

WB: That's odd. It's strange that people would view the development of a new form as something that would damage or eliminate conventional forms. I guess it's more the anxiety about change that is the most surprising, a change to something which most people see as a leisure activity, a change that can't do them harm, and yet they fear that change, even the possibility of it. But, do you feel like the conventional formats of theater or cinema are still a viable medium, or are they simply anachronistic forms that need to be completely reformulated or abandoned in the contemporary moment? Is it just a viewer's consciousness of them that needs to be changed?

SD: Anglo-American theater goers really expect a sort of realism on stage that comes straight out of the late 19th century. It's as if Brecht and Beckett had never existed and it's constantly reinforced by what Hollywood does. The problem is not the form itself it's the audience and their expectations. Are they open to being challenged? How far can you challenge them without being rendered invisible?

Hito Steyerl in Conversation with Walead Beshty
April 2, 2017

Walead Beshty: Hello?

Hito Steyerl: Oh

WB: Hi, how are you?

HS: Yes?

WB: I'm only hearing you a little bit.

HS: Hello?

WB: Hi. Can you hear me all right?

HS: Do you hear me now?

WB: Yes. Hello. It seems like we have a bad connection. Shit.

HS: What happened?

WB: Ok, better? I was wondering if it makes sense to start with that question that I sent you.

HS: I have a response to that question. Namely, hang on. Switch that camera. What if we have to rethink photographic perspective? At least to a certain degree because the photographic picture ... I mean a digital one definitely is no longer defined by this kind of central perspective but by other paradigms which are not visible anymore. They have to do more with protocol, with formatting, with infrastructure maybe. With these kind of digital formats that now [inaudible 00:04:30] photographs on a more basic level even. The level of basic encoding. Maybe this is where a different formatting happens, which also enables actually. I don't know about you but I'm seeing it very often a different form of visual perspective to happen, which has several focus points. Which is composite. Which is montaged from different sources.

What if we have to now grapple with this form of perspective rather than a more traditional, central perspective?

WB: It makes me think of the short text that you wrote for A Prior, "Documentary Uncertainty." This thing about the reality being located where there is a glitch, when you have a breakdown of a digital medium, because at that point, the medium becomes apparent, it's functioning under duress, and thus you can see what it is doing better. But less to the point of documentary veracity, I was thinking how these glitches, the lack of seamlessness to our technologies are even more apparent now. I used to only become conscious of a medium's constraints when producing with it, rarely as a consumer or receiver in the typical sense, but now that seems very different. For example, in this conversation when we have these digital hiccups, producing abrupt interruptions to the fluid flow of conversation. In those moments, I become hyper conscious of our being on Skype, and the medium becomes unavoidable, indistinguishable from the content of our conversation, almost integral to it. I wonder if this is an increased form of transparency, a more aggressive form of transparency constituted in rupture. Those ruptures seem to reveal more about the media we navigate, producing a real consciousness of how they structure our ability to communicate ideas.

I think one sees so many glitched jpegs or notices the interlacing when the refresh rate on a video we are watching online can't keep up. It produces these kinds of alternate types of images that aren't really intended. I don't know what the analog would be in Albertian Perspectival form where you would have this kind of collapse in a renaissance picture where all of a sudden, the Cartesian grids are made apparent. That dialectic between frame and screen coming forward, I feel like those conventional forms are less transparent in a way. I can't think of moments where you just have a disseminated version of perspectival form that's actually a dysfunctional version, where we are as accustomed to the failure of perspectival form as we are to the failures of digital media.

HS: That's true. There is also another aspect of it. The glitch and the breakdown of the illusion of pictorial continuity. This is one aspect. I think another aspect that's added to it that's maybe not as obvious even though it is visible is the constant pictorial correction and normalization that's taking place with all these algorithms installed in cameras that immediately align faces to normative beauty standards or skin colors or something like that.

Algorithms that immediately try to establish kinship, tribal relations, between different people. It has somewhere in its distributed database. In that sense, the kind of different types of orders, which go across pictures rather than to organizing everything within a picture, that's also something that happens in this algorithmic order. A kind of gridding one might call it. Element of people and relations beyond the frame. The frame is constantly broken and yet reestablished as a sort of pre-ordering or pre-ordered relationship.

WB: How do you think of making those types of organizational systems apparent? Is that a direct concern for you in your work?

HS: Is it really? I think maybe not. Interestingly, I think I work more in narrative than in pictorial representation maybe. Also, I don't even know what to make of it but I found myself drawn back towards a sense of realism recently. I don't know why that happens. Do you have any thoughts or reaction to that? How does it happen in your work?

WB: I understand that impulse. I have a hard time with the term realism, or at least, thinking it as a meaningful concept. Materialism is realist for me, I suppose, but I would opt for that term over realism.

HS: I completely understand. By realism I just mean that sometimes right now I'm less preoccupied with how the picture shows but more with what it shows. I think that also by now we all know that this is an artifice somehow and it's constructed and constituted and so on. Just get on with it. I have this kind of impulse sometimes.

WB: Very much so. The other problem that I find so often with thinking about these different types of technologies, especially digital technologies, is the content neutrality issue. Of course these systems can't be neutral, they were developed mostly by white men working for the military, I mean there were segregated bathrooms at the time, women were only just entering the workplace, socially it was a moment that seems quite alien to the democratic utopian drive ascribed to these contemporary systems. That history is built into these systems in some form, but it is hard to see exactly how. There has to be this automatic bias within them and yet how do you draw out, or not even draw out, but just not conceal their predispositions towards those kinds of functions or uses?

Turning to Panofsky, what I find so remarkable about that text is that he sets the ground for talking about the ideology of perspectival form. He manifests a way to take this seemingly neutral thing and denaturalizes it, which allows us to understand it as an ideological form.

HS: That's true. What does the ideology of algorithmic framing in this case? It's a question. I don't have a real answer to that but can one think of anything that's even remotely as convincing as this theory of the one eye of the world? That it is at once remote but then also tries to dominate the world by eyesight. What would it be? I think the algorithmic paradigm is much more distributed and probably is not even about a single viewer anymore but about a multitude of viewers. I'm just trying. I don't have an answer to that.

Who is the imagined subject of the [inaudible 00:15:00]? Is there even only one or is there none maybe? Is it a machine that's also very possible. That this imagined subject is not even a subject anymore but an assembly of certain networks.

WB: What that just made me think was the one thing that these algorithmic systems, these automated systems of connectivity and dispersal, do is formulate a response to the classical model of perspective, and the singular idealized subject position it produces. The god's eye view. The singular viewer. By functioning in distributed networks, it seems like an active critique of that kind of that model, of a centralized model, whether it is a single viewer, or a centralized power.

HS: Yes. There's probably something extremely sinister to it as well.

WB: Definitely. Perhaps it conceals these sources of power by obscuring them in the language of networks, or maybe it's a new form of power, one that arises from the network itself.

HS: Basically a similar ideal of dominance is being perpetuated but without this single master subject on the one end of this sort of optic triangle, if you will. I really wonder what kind of dominance? How can one even imagine the shape of this dominance? Who is it? Is it a group? Is it a group of persons? Is it a protocol? What is it actually? That's not clear to me. Do you hear to that?

WB: It's unclear to me too. The only thing I can think of is that it's the spirit of order that's dominant, categories and classifications, routes and platforms. The desire for order made autonomous from any one agent. A spectral, ubiquitous form. But still, behind it you have massive server farms, and millions of miles of cable, and power plants, and so on. I'm not being very articulate but the jargon around digital networks makes power unidentifiable, ubiquitous, which is always the image power presents. It's sublime because you can't quite put your finger on it. You can't quite say that a particular state power or a corporation or something wholly controls these systems. They seem unruly, not subservient to a particular master, other than a form of order. I just wonder if the problem is really an alien one. If it's the same thing in a new form or if it's actually a new organization.

HS: I think it's new in certain senses. Not in all of them. For example, what if one was to say it's less about vision and registering something but about prediction and speculation somehow. What if this [inaudible 00:19:23] tools of designing something rather than representing? I think it's less about vision than about recognition. Pattern recognition. Identification of recurrent patterns. Something like that. The effect. This is also something that has been stated many times ago. Is less to register an existing reality and to submit it by doing it. But to basically project a reality to come, which is designed by this very act of prediction and projection. Does that make sense?

WB: Totally.

HS: I'm thinking about, for example, these deep dream hallucinations of neural networks which are asked to see something where there isn't anything. They are basically dreaming up puppies and octopuses and other kinds of animals from sheer noise. What kind of vision is this? Where is the perspective in this? What kind of image generation is this supposed to be?

WB: What technology is that? I'm unfamiliar.

HS: I'm sure you know this. Google Deep Dream neural network hallucinations. Basically machines are trained to recognize images and then they sort of reverse the project and asked the machine to recognize something within sheer noise. Then the machines started in fact recognizing things, no? These were more or less hallucinations of different shapes it had learned before. It was combining faces of fish with the bodies of dogs. It was kind of very, very hallucinatory.

WB: I don't know this. I have to look at it.

HS: Type of [inaudible 00:21:45]. Google Deep Dream. It will come up immediately. You will see. I'm sure you have seen it somewhere.

WB: That makes me think it's continuous. The most insidious thing about predictive systems is that they use the past. They hides the conservation of convention within a dynamic system which simply perpetuates the original structure, reinforces it. It seems like it arises naturally from a computational or neutral system, but it has the same questionable foundation.

HS: Tradition.

WB: In that sense maybe it's completely continuous.

HS: Almost completely. There's always a tiny bit something unexpected in these montages. Something which you couldn't have anticipated which the machine does. It's not emergent behavior. It's some kind of small glitch thing that happens but it's not entirely determined. Input is not necessarily 100% same as output.

WB: Right. It sounds like a classical model of, for lack of a better term, artistic innovation. In the sense that I think of the way that artists work as innovating within convention. Not innovating but somehow following certain kinds of conventions to ends that they weren't necessarily intended for to create alternate outcomes. Particularly one that doesn't present itself as expressive. One that presents itself as somehow reflexive or critical, that consciously plays with codes, and roots out their unintended consequences.

HS: Where is it, do you think? Where is it? I was discussing this lately with a colleague and we ended up again with this old notion of the blind spot. The point where basically the perspective or the point of view inscribes itself into the picture. I'm now wondering, even though it's probably not even a very difficult question to answer. Where is the blind spot? That would indicate the point of view within the algorithmic paradigm of image production. Of course the blind spot is very clearly in the bias. In the way [inaudible 00:26:34] [00:26:30] already tilted toward certain outcomes. Then it's not like this one spot. What is it? It's not even a spot. How can we describe this kind of bias?

WB: They're dynamic systems, so I think the difficulty is that any blind spot is a moving target.

HS: Yes. The way the vector. It's driving towards. That's already defined somehow. Then the picture will sort of imagine some missing parts in order to [inaudible] this sort of imaginary perfect outcome. The picture already has some kind of understanding of what it's supposed to look like. The excess is, so to speak, a kind of invention. It completes itself. It tries to render the skin as smooth and bright and all of that. This is an excess actually. It's not in the given data. It's in the expected outcome, so to speak. Basically, there is this gap between the data [00:28:00] as registered and the data as expected. The picture tries to negotiate between both of them. It's almost like in socialism. There were these quota and plans. People were always trying to sort of fulfill the five year plan. Now all sorts of pictures have a lot of quota [00:28:30] and plans imposed on them and they have to deliver, even at the cost of fiction. It doesn't matter.

WB: That's interesting. It makes me think of what you said earlier about your renewed interest in realism.

One question that comes up is what does realism look like within those constraints? In other words, if you attempt to present these systems on their own, they're empty. They're dynamic structures that are about relaying content in some way, and cease to function, or even disappear if they aren't carrying anything. Maybe those glitches are somewhat meaningless, or in the way you described, hallucinatory, because without some message, they quite simply aren't given enough guidance to produce a result. I do think of this sort of noise as a negative imprint of the structures that produce them, like pirates as an index of a form of mercantile trade.There's something really satisfying about seeing these algorithms make poor decisions and accidentally make something new, something they weren't intended to produce. Although, I wonder if these surpluses, these surprising errors, are actually meaningful in the end. If they actually reveal anything, I have to believe they do, because they're the only escape route from these seamless worlds I can see at the moment.

HS: Probably not. I have an idea of what realism or how to reframe realism on this territory. I was thinking about a notion that Wendy Chun highlighted recently which is the notion of homopholy. Homopholy is a kind of ordering system in social media. Social media always tried to establish groups and kinship and tried to describe with as many characteristics as possible. Most of these are inferred by your network. If your friends do A, B, C, then there is a probability of so many percent the network will assume you like the same thing.

There's two assumptions in there. First that you tend to associate with people who are like you. Then that you will like the same thing that your friends like. It's two different assumptions, which are both based on very crude ideas of identity. First, you like the same as other people like, then you are also like your friends in other terms like race, gender and so on and so on. These are basic assumptions of order which, if you think of it, are extremely insulting to be honest.

WB: Very much.

HS: Just to assume that you will only like things that are exactly or more or less like you, I find this extremely insulting. This is a way in which order is established and so called knowledge is generated. This is also how information or this information is directed toward you. This will structure a sort of montage of representations that will turn up on your Facebook feed. Let's put it like this. This is sort of the montage algorithm. In that sense, one could say realism, and this goes for many aspects of algorithmic reality, means that basically the assumptions that are made about people need to be first of all discussed but then also recalibrated and denaturalized. These are assumptions that are being taken as natural truths. This is human beings' work. This is human nature. It's not true.

For example, questions or feelings like solidarity or empathy or even friendship do not figure in these kinds of assumptions. How does one introduce different notions of social behavior or of politics actually in the algorithmic order? I think this is definitely the way I describe it now is not primarily about visual content. I think that of course in the long run it is about visual content because of course facial recognition, all these things, are being developed to group you with other people the network assumes you to be like.

In that sense, it is deeply intertwined with visual representation but also recognition and with a politics of visuality which I think is probably now really reconfigured from the perspective paradigm which was more or less to establish in the first place that there is a subject. There is an object and the subject because it views is always the master in this relation. This was a sort of social] master/slave paradigm mediated by visuality.

Whereas now we have more diffused assumptions about how a social order is supposed to work. On the other hand, they are even more tribal [inaudible]. Does it make any sense?

WB: Totally. It makes me think one reason why there would be those established patterns of hyper identification, say with people who have the same sets of interests and seeking those kinds of people out, is because in a traditional social environment you have a high probability of being exposed to the unfamiliar, so that propensity for likeminded individuals is a protection from harm which is balanced by the unpredictability of social interaction which allows in new information. As soon as the entire structure is defined for you through a portal or platform that filters what you come into contact with, you throw that balance off.

In other words, these digital media platforms seem to only model one side of the equation, excluding chance and variability. What it automatically seems to produce is tribalism and polarization, and the appearance of isolated pockets of reality that share very little in common with each other.

HS: I have a model now. We are now moving from this sort of triangular optical model towards a circular filter bubble model. We don't have this triangle with the viewer on one end and the rest of the world on the opposite plane. We have a fully circular model of a filter bubble. The algorithm constitutes the architecture of this filter bubble. This also explains why we have many different perspectives, so to speak, montaged into one plane of representation. You can walk around in this filter bubble and the perspective changes at any point in time. You always [inaudible 00:38:23] one at the same time. Then you cannot escape it. It's not very obvious how to escape it. You're basically imprisoned in this hall of mirrors where perspectives do shift. You cannot escape the bubble as such.

The architecture is determined by these algorithms that are based on kinship or assumed kinship. [inaudible 00:38:57] and all of that. That's the hidden architect.

WB: It's an analogy and I'm not trying to be be biologically deterministic, but it makes me think that we see in curved space anyway. Thinking back to Panofsky again, optical space is really a hermetic space, and is opposed in many ways to the linear, infinitely expandable space of perspectival form. In other words, optical space is bounded. It's spherical, we see in curves not straight lines, and if these lines were extended indefinitely, they would not describe an infinite world, but a world circumscribed by the lenses of our eyes, all these perspective lines would meet behind us. In short, we see in bubbles. And each bubble presents itself as equally valid, and without another model, an infinite model, you loose the idea of a reality principal or a stability found in a set of facts held in common. While I don't love overarching dominant orders, at the same time there's something quite disconcerting about discarding them, because the result is that there's not a way to establish comparisons. The alternative is not satisfying either, because it seems to force a recourse to a set of moral rules or a set of principles, which both have a propensity for repression, and are so easily outflanked by dynamic systems. Maybe ethics is the solution in some way, not morals, but classical Aristotelian ethics.

HS: In the old perspective paradigm, the advantage, if you like, was that it was shown how it works. There was a set of mathematical principals behind it that were demonstrated. You knew it was a sort of artifice and a construction but at least you had the parameters to gauge the kind of construction you were faced with. That's different now in this kind of black box paradigm because you know it's constructed but you don't know how it's being constructed and also because this is proprietary knowledge. You're not supposed to know how this is constructed. This is different.

I think in the old paradigm of facts that could be verified, that had to be corroborated. Evidence that had to be judged or confirmed by multiple sources. Blah, blah, blah. It was very clear that this was perfectly corruptible. It was not a problem to falsify things but at least you had an idea of the architecture of how facts were supposed to be established. This is now completely being deregulated and dismantled in favor of this kind of black box paradigm, whereby you do not know how things are being imagined or dreamed up. There is this multiplicity of anonymous sources, of leaks, of avatars, of proxies, of trolls. You cannot verify things anymore, even if you would like to. That's the difference.

The old realism is of course a very oppressive form of the production of truths but at least you know how it works. At least to a certain extent. It pretends to be transparent [inaudible 00:43:43]. It doesn't even call itself actually [inaudible 00:43:53]. It's very aptly called alternative facts. The difference is not that it's wrong or that it's incorrect. The difference is that we don't know how it comes about.

Just the same with the architecture of the filter bubble. It's the same. We don't have the mathematical laws of construction for that. We know that there is some sort of mask about it but we're not supposed to know it. It's a sort of arcane science.

WB: Funny, it made me think that if Alberti had developed these conventions for perspectival formula now, it would likely be proprietary. Perspectival form would be a trade secret, and it wouldn't be as transparent...

HS: Exactly. You'd have to pay to use it.

WB: Are those bubbles the substance of the realism that you're talking about or is it something else? Is it a shared set of facts held in common between them? Or is it their functioning, outside of what forms of content they propagate?

HS: The realism is maybe in seeing the bubble. If you're inside the bubble, all you see are these drifting perspectives.

WB: Seems to be in how you make the bubble manifest at the same time as you're working inside it. We're good at doing that with perspective or perspectival form but how do you make the bubble manifest?

HS: Yes. It's difficult to step out of it. It's of course not impossible but usually you're somehow inside so how do you represent other [inaudible 00:47:34] of it while being restricted from stepping outside of it?

WB: Yeah. That's a classic ideology problem too, right?

HS: Yes. Of course. One could try to pretend that basically whatever is inside the bubble has this invisible kind of curvature. Optical curvature, you know? This is basically what's come to replace the perspective. Now we can basically, judging from the curvature of the imagery, reverse engineer the form of the bubble. If we want to. How curved are the things we see? From there we can reconstruct the ideology that's gone into that.

WB: It makes me think of word clouds. You know these? They're a graphic visualization tool used for analyzing content. These word diagrams that take the frequency that words are mentioned in a particular text or website and enlarges the terms most often used, which gives you a kind of visual field of terms. In other words, when you look at them in comparison with one another, you get a kind of optical field, big terms are the more frequently used ones, and you get something akin to lens distortion. Maybe that's a way of mapping the bubble in information networks. But don't all these approaches require some sense of the real to compare it to? Some stable frame of reference?

HS: I will keep thinking about that because obviously ... I think these are important questions now. How do we define visuality or ideology or even pictorial space in a time when so much seems to be completely [inaudible 00:51:02] from the visual field whatsoever.

WB: The other frustration I have is that it seems like a lot of the old tools of analysis used to discuss aesthetics or meaning produce really problematic answers when applied to current moment. A lot of the intellectual tools from the past fifty years don't really work. I have a constant frustration with the perpetuation of structuralist or post-structuralist theories of representation and ideology analysis that seem so ill equipped to deal with expansive dynamic networks. It's not that I have any other better answer, but the way these old theories, and old approaches are trotted out to provide some sort of comfort is quite irritating.

HS: I don't think anyone has that right now. I think on all levels we are kind of in a different paradigm now and of course there's a lot of things that led to this point. It's not like a complete rupture but still, I think, basically even the tools have to be redeveloped to comprehend anything.

WB: Very much so.

HS: If that's even still possible. That remains to be seen, whether comprehension can still be achieved.

WB: I find I rely on certain types of metaphors just to think problems. You need these kinds of tools and analogies to think problems but then every time I walk down that path I have the sense that these analogies just might be the problem. You use a certain terminology to start the conversation somewhere, but at that moment, the moment you establish a terminology, it blocks you from seeing how those terms curtail your ability to see what's actually happening.

HS: On the other hand you do need it.

WB: Anyway, a work in progress ... Thank you so much. I really appreciate your taking the time.

HS: Will someone transcribe what we just said?

WB: Yes. I'll send it to you.

HS: That would be super. First of all, I would really like to read it again and then maybe even add to it. Maybe I'll have some additional ideas. Thank you so much. Sorry that it took such a long time to come together.

WB: No problem. I apologize. I feel like I've been very disorganized. My apologies too.

HS: Absolutely, same. Thanks again for including the work [inaudible 00:54:33]. I think it will be fabulous. I'm really looking forward.

WB: I'm very excited. Thank you for allowing me to. I don't know if they contacted you about ...

HS: When is it opening?

WB: June 23rd.

HS: They started contacting us already about all sorts of details. I think things are somehow on their way.

WB: Did they contact you about texts yet?

HS: No. Texts meaning a dialogue list or what?

WB: I'm also producing a large anthology as the catalog. I wanted to reprint the "In Free Fall" text and then also the "Documentary Uncertainty" text.

HS: Sure. Go ahead.

WB: Cool. They hadn't reached out to you yet about it?

HS: No. I don't think so. Don't take me at my word. At this moment of time about 10% of all emails just slip.

WB: I know how that is.

HS: If they ask me, please tell them yes by all means. If they didn't ...

WB: Sorry. You just broke up. But I'll have them get in touch.

HS: Yeah. Otherwise, just use it.

WB: Thank you so much. Have a good evening.

HS: Thanks a lot. I hope you recover from your jet lag.

WB: Me too. Take care.

HS: Bye bye.

WB: Bye.

James Merle Thomas in Conversation with Walead Beshty
May 24, 2018

JMT: I thought it might be useful to go back, at least in some sense, to the points of origin for this project. When we first discussed *Picture Industry*, I mentioned that eight years ago I fortuitously stumbled into what I would consider the first iteration of the exhibition, which took place at Regen Projects in 2010, and which had a subtitle related to the Joan Didion essay, "Goodbye to All That." I wonder if you could sound out how the project began, and what kind of motivations were at stake at the time.

WB: That show, while having a similar name, was quite different; a lot of what became *Picture Industry* was nascent, or even non-existent then. That show was in a sense a continuation of the very first group show I organized in 2005 called *Pictures are the Problem* (actually, some of the same work is in the current *Picture Industry* show, such as the Martha Rosler's *Bringing the War Home*, the Kelley Walker, and the Lawrence Weiner). In the Regen show, I was wrestling with a New York-centric set of practices that were prevalent at the time, which both revolved around materialist abstraction and appropriation: artists like Kelley Walker, Wade Guyton, Carol Bove, Tauba Auerbach, and Seth Price all jump to mind as immediate points of reference, some of whom were also close friends. At the same time, there was the reexamination of both the Pictures Generation and a lot of the Cologne-based work that was contemporary to it. Bennett Simpson did a show a few years earlier called *Make Your Own Life: Artists In and Out of Cologne*, which focused on, among other things, the Cologne and New York art scenes in the eighties. I suppose I was really thinking about how all this resonated in Los Angeles. There were a number of Cologne transplants here in the eighties, and many of the Pictures Generation artists had started here, but I was also thinking about the city as a hub of global image production, how the city grew into its current form through television and film, a soft industry, what people often call "The Picture Industry." I found that term evocative, the lightness of images, and the weight of industry. So, multiple things were on my mind. I was wrestling with how to make sense of all of that as a way to understand the city and how it influenced art making but wasn't interested in schematizing a developmental narrative of influences; rather, I was thinking in terms of affect, an attitude toward appearances. L.A. had a real uncanniness to me initially, it felt familiar the first time I arrived, and I realized this was because of the light, I had seen Southern California light my entire life on TV and in movies; it was familiar and alienating at the same time, and that uncanniness resonated with the work I was thinking about.

I think that Douglas Eklund's *Pictures Generation* show had either just happened, or was right around the corner, and a lot of the Pictures Generation artists had come out of the context of Southern California. Allan McCollum started here, and a number of those artists were students of John Baldessari at CalArts. People like James Welling, Jack Goldstein, David Salle, and so on... as was a slightly younger group of artists, who are key figures subsequent to the Pictures Generation, like Mike Kelley, Tony Oursler, John Miller, Christopher Williams or Stephen Prina, some of whom showed in Cologne. So I was thinking about Los Angeles as a formative location for movements that took hold in other places, how characteristics of the city produced an "attitude" toward pictures, to pop culture, that was quite different from sixties Pop. Not to mention people like Allan Sekula and Martha Rosler, who were in San Diego, whom I thought shared some affinities with the Pictures Generation people, despite their work being more overtly activist. I was also thinking about artists who were more regional or were receiving less attention but seemed relevant to that moment, people like Robert Heinecken, Tony Conrad, and Thomas Barrow. But that 2010 show wasn't systematic, it was very open-ended, mostly because I was overwhelmed by the scope of the idea. It also omitted a lot of work that should have been included, say that of Larry Johnson, Jack Goldstein, Ericka Beckman, Alexis Smith, Lewis Baltz, or William Leavitt, and in that way, it was quite unlike how I approached organizing shows before and after, it was very loose. I think the subject matter was too large and my approach was unfocused and improvised (I also had just a few months to put it together, as opposed to six months in the case of the first Luma Arles show plus more than a year for the expanded show at Bard). Another subtext was that the dominant version of this history consisted almost entirely of white men and a few white women. Southern Californian artists of color who actively used appropriation were outside of the conversation around the Pictures Generation or Cologne, despite the significant work of people like David Hammons, Kerry

James Marshall, and Romare Bearden, to name a few. I think it would have been a more interesting show if it dealt more precisely with appropriation as related to Los Angeles, and thought more critically about the racial segregation implicit in art world movements or art schools. I think I just didn't fully understand how to conceptualize that at the time. I accepted the canons of who or what constituted the Pictures Generation, and my strategy to get around some of the problems and was unable to fully grasp how to make the show more literary or impressionistic. I tried to address those weaknesses in the show I organized at Thomas Dane Gallery the following year, which was called *Sunless: Journeys in Alta California since 1933*, which dealt with the Light and Space movement, appropriation, and image making. It too had its blind spots, but it was much more focused and systematic. I started by thinking of the shared fascination with industrial surfaces and glossiness of both Light and Space practices and appropriation-based work—primarily, that show allowed me to deal with the phenomenological effects of images and surface in a more meaningful way—Light and Space was possible because of Hollywood, their production houses made the use of various gels, vacuum-forming, scrims, and acrylic fabrication possible available to artists. Thinking about all this makes me want to make a show that focuses on really digging deep into the regional and ideological undercurrents of appropriation and industrial production in Los Angeles from the sixties through to the eighties. In retrospect, I think those shows were inadvertently about a particular construction of whiteness in Southern California, a whiteness that was embedded within film and television. It's still present in the resurgence of many of the new appropriationist strategies from the mid 2000s. This continues to be unexamined, and I think it would be really interesting to try to unpack the kind of masculinity implicit in that work and the racial self-imaginings it was predicated upon.

JMT: It's interesting to think about this project taking shape against the backdrop of several major aesthetic reexaminations that unfolded in the late 2000s: Eklund's *Pictures Generation*, absolutely. But I'm also reminded of the first iteration of the *Pacific Standard Time* initiative, and of shows like Robin Clark's *Phenomenal,* which similarly focused on questions of surface and phenomenology. We've not talked about it extensively, but one of my other current projects examines yet another industry that fits into this model, namely, the aerospace industry of Southern California and its relationship to art, design, and architecture. It gets us too far away from my intended line of questioning here; I'll merely mention that the themes of image making and material fabrication that you raise in relation to phenomenology resonate deeply with my examination of the late 1960s and early 1970s—a moment when the ideas and work of Robert Irwin and Larry Bell, among others, were inflected and shaped by their direct experiences with NASA and the broader industry to which it belonged. The inherent whiteness of this movement (to say nothing of NASA's homogeneity) is, of course, striking. However, I have also been thinking lately more about figures like Fred Eversley, who worked as an aerospace engineer throughout the 1960s, and whose vital presence in that Venice Beach community of artists complicates our understanding of the homogeneity of the Finish Fetish scene, the White Space of Light and Space, as it were...All of this makes me wonder about technical images or aesthetic projects that link our respective industries. In light of the themes of appropriation and industrial production you cite above, perhaps we should agree to revisit Larry Sultan and Mike Mandel's *Evidence*—a work that brilliantly bridges these ideas—and talk at a later date about the exhibition you describe.

Simpson's show is a beautiful and unexpected comparison. Like *Picture Industry*, *Make Your Own Life* was also fundamentally concerned with questions about image-making and the narrative of a city that defined itself through modern media production, and the particular regional character—let's call it both an aesthetic and a feeling—that developed as a function of that industry. The show simultaneously affirmed and denied easy categories: it acknowledged the importance of painting yet emphasized the role of photography in mediating its dominance. It was about Kippenberger, on down to the title. But at the same time, it undercut the notion of a single personality and foregrounded the role of collectives. It was about Cologne but frustrated any simplistic notion of regionalism. Looking back, I feel there's a lot in that show that resonates with the current project: Michael Krebber's vitrines of magazines, photographs by Louise Lawler and Christopher Williams come to mind immediately. Also, Stephen Prina's *Galerie Max Hetzler* (1991), a work that methodically reframed the installation photography archives of Galerie Max Hetzler, could easily be included in *Picture Industry.* It feels related not only to the strategies of appropriation central to the Pictures Generation but also to earlier questions of systematic documentation and cataloging, to something like Walker Evans and his photographs of African sculpture at the Museum of Modern Art. And Mike Kelley's name appears all throughout that history too—so there is this intriguing resonance between Cologne and Los Angeles...

WB: Famously, Kippenberger spent a good deal of time in Los Angeles in the eighties, and I think deeply affected a particular group of artists at that time. Both positively, but also in producing a "boy's club" mentality. It's undeniable that he influenced Mike Kelley, for example. However, I think Bennett's show was more concerned with how social networks produced a fertile ground for artistic production. There was some of this in the first version of *Picture Industry*, like the inclusion of Welling's images of artist friends (like Goldstein, Salle, Beckman and so on) and their studios, but Bennett's show was far more thoughtful and rigorous about drawing out these relationships and the importance of thinking about those relationships in order to get to a more complex understanding of art of that time.

JMT: I want to return to Didion, to your references to her writing, and its relationship to California and the image-making industry. These themes are present in her 1967 essay "Goodbye to All That," and in many ways form the foundation of *Slouching Towards Bethlehem.* All of this seems to portend a lot of what is amplified in subsequent iterations of the show. When we started talking about the 2010 exhibition, you sent me a spread that brilliantly resembles a page taken from a Didion book, and which includes the following passage:

> And what to make of the application of the term industry? With the heaviness of factories and smokestacks encircling it, to the production of ephemeral pictures whose power is synonymous with their lightness. It could be said that it is the seemingly invisible and ephemeral aspects, the means of distribution, the contextual frame, the vicissitudes of taste, and an object's ability to "pass"—which serve as the most robust material of the contemporary work, an embrace of convention that produces an endless sequence of provisional 'meanings.'

I completely fell for it on the first read. I thought it was very striking to use Didion as a kind of cipher, writing at the cusp of the seventies, to flag this notion of distribution.

WB: So that we're clear: that's my writing, although it's flattering that I could pass for Didion even during a cursory read. For the Regen Projects show, I wrote the press release so that it acted like a loop and stuck it into the page treatment of the cheap paperback edition of *Slouching Towards Bethlehem.* I thought of it as a self-contained and isolated remnant, a homeless piece of text and the design aped a Xerox of a book spread. I feel like I live among piles of stapled Xeroxes, and you always have these homeless pages that get torn free from the staple holding the pages together; it's usually either the last page or the first page that gets torn off through its handling and ends up floating on its own. There's always this dangling snippet of what preceded or followed the text. I saw the show in that way, a kind of looping homeless narrative. What was strongest in my mind about Didion's writing was that it was literary cultural reportage, that it merged genres. She was writing on the cusp of the death of old Hollywood, and the emergence of new cultural norms. Especially in her essay "John Wayne: A Love Song." There was quite a lot of tenderness in that text, even though John Wayne's politics were anathema to the politics that were emergent at the time. Moreover, John Wayne as an aging Hollywood icon also seemed to capture the character of this seventies moment too, setting the stage for what Ronald Reagan was to become, and as a 'B' version of John Wayne, the sort of campier, half John Wayne—half Roy Rogers kind of character.

JMT: Have you seen the excellent 2017 documentary by Pacho Velez and Sierra Pettengill, *The Reagan Show*? It's produced from thousands of hours of video archives from the Reagan library, and what's fascinating is you see these fantastic shots of Ron and Nancy riding down a gulch on horses, and then doing it several times over, and then posing with an ax next to a tree. It was such a thoroughly produced spectacle of what their lives were to be. So when you watch the outtakes and see Nancy's hesitation at playing along at certain moments, you get a sense of just how profoundly mediated it all was. And because of the source of the media, the documentary has this eerie early video kind of gloss to it. Honestly, it could just as easily fit within the cosmology of the current exhibition.

WB: This throwback to the fifties and a wholly fabricated notion of purity all bubbled back up toward the close of the seventies and became dominant in the eighties: it was quite a perverse time, so it's understandable that artists were coming from a fundamental mistrust of images, that they often saw them as hollow. And now you can think about how Donald Trump is a caricature of the eighties. He's a throwback to a throwback, a series of regurgitations of nostalgia, a cartoonish construction of an eighties businessman... I mean, these are not new observations, but Didion was deft at capturing this mix of nostalgia and foreboding; a kind of melancholic embrace of surface, of sunshine made heavy and macabre.

JMT: Well, it's an entirely cinematic mode of writing. It begs for the screenplay treatment, I think—her discussion of Manson in *The White Album*, the "things fall apart," Yeats-inspired moment that opens *Slouching*, the Santa Ana winds as an ominous harbinger of the end of a time, this kind of thing, it's all of a piece, a kind of benediction to one era, and an uneasy estimation of the next.

WB: Exactly. It's been ages since I read her. I should go back; I'm sure I'd understand her differently.

JMT: There's also something interesting about your

use of Trump as a prismatic reflection back onto Reagan. Everyone right now is talking so much about Trump and Nixon, but Trump and Reagan open onto a broader question about the legacy of the Cold War. When I first started engaging with this project and its historical sweep, I began by considering the metaphors of writing—for example, the way that William Henry Fox Talbot's *Pencil of Nature* connects to a broader discussion of writing technologies. However, another way is to think instead about a notion of writing through information or, to use Friedrich Kittler's phrase, discourse networks—and through the transposition of readings or encodings that they facilitate or enable. There are obviously early models, whether it's punch cards, or the Jacquard loom, or other automated technologies of depicting and relaying information that seemed to be very much bound up in the idea of the technical image. However, these informational concepts assume newfound relevance during the Cold War period. And in this way, I think that we are in a kind of zeitgeist where there's a broader aesthetic and ideological reflection on what exactly the Cold War was. Did it end? Are we in a kind of interregnum right now, where Russia's coming back? All of this is a roundabout way to ask you about information, and specifically, about the relationship of *Picture Industry* to the status of information during the Cold War. Indeed, looming large here is the figure of Norbert Wiener and the importance of cybernetics and systems theory.

WB: We seem to want the Cold War back. In retrospect, the time seems so simple as a moral and ideological state of affairs. The thing that was so striking to me about Wiener is the expansiveness with which he conceived of communication. It was both technical and politically minded, from the use of binary coding to the way he conceptualized networks for the distribution of information. Really, he synthesized a lot of different disciplines into one. And seemed genuinely eager to give them overarching philosophical or political implications, that they were a new way of conceiving how human beings live, and how we could understand our lives in a state of constant communication, from neuroscience to social science...

JMT: Let's linger on the question of interdisciplinary research for a minute, because at a practical level, it relates to one of the directives of the Rad Lab at MIT during the Second World War. When Wiener is getting going with this work, it's a very tangible question that he faced, namely, how do you develop a kind of metalanguage that allows specialists from different but potentially adjacent fields to talk to one another, to allow their systems to interface with one another?

WB: Yeah, exactly, and it's most interesting to me because it sought to answer and theorize practical problems...

JMT: The interface becomes a critical concept around that time for IBM as well...

WB: And it was a military problem, coordinating all these different servers. Wiener's ambition to create a context within which various disciplines would be able to share information was reflected in the underlying, practical problem he was faced within computer science because all the different servers and all the different mainframes are working with their own proprietary operating systems and couldn't easily talk to one another. It is a problem analogous to the one we find in the sharing of information between different academic and practical disciplines: how do you get them to share information when their languages are incompatible with one another? Gregory Bateson was another thinker who was very interesting to me early on because of his attempts to address the gaps between disciplines.

JMT: The ambition to allow engineers to talk to biologists through a common language, the philosophical and ethical complexities of the Macy Conferences, the efforts by Wiener and Bateson (and others), to cultivate a particular kind of interdisciplinarity that spanned aesthetics and communication theory, and which linked psychology to architecture and urban planning: these are defining moments in the early Cold War years, and for the history we're circumscribing. I agree that in a broader cultural sense, our current moment is accompanied by a longing (by some, at least) for a "simpler time," and for an era when a litmus test could determine ideology. However, I think there's a much more nuanced re-examination underway within critical aesthetic discourse—art history, critical theory, new media theory, among other fields—a revisiting that has challenged notions of medium specificity and a host of fixed categories we associate with modernity, or with the ways that disciplines are constructed.

While certain nostalgic associations with Hollywood and its industrialized modes of distribution naturally relate to the former, I think the current project is a meaningful contribution to the latter. I'm struck at the proliferation of forms that one finds throughout *Picture Industry*—the diversity of instances of the idea of the photograph or the image. And it seems that one of the more useful applications of this idea of the technical image—to use Vilém Flusser's term—is to emphasize its role as a kind of correlate of the systems that Wiener was deriving. The technical image allows for a way to exceed the limitations of any one given medium, to extend a functional or systematic discourse across the logic of its operation, what Bateson might describe as an ecology. Does that resonate at all with you concerning the way that the technical image is constructed in this project?

WB: Completely. In the specificity of Flusser's terminology, we are given a way to discuss the political and social ecologies (to use Bateson again) they operate within. It allows for communication to be understood at base as both material and political. When I finally gave Wiener's work the time needed to grasp his project, it was like being struck by lightning, it addressed, albeit tacitly, an analogous problem to what I was struggling with in various disciplinarily discrete theories of aesthetics. Wiener was a kind of missing link for me between media theory, aesthetics, and computer science... And that answers a fundamental problem that I was trying to address even in that first show in 2010, the fundamental dissatisfaction that I've always had with the way that aesthetics and, more specifically, pictures are discussed. That the discussions of images often disavows their material embodiment, turning real concrete things into free-floating signifiers whose primary effect is alienation, and whose meaning is orchestrated by distant powers with nefarious intent. It turned the production of things into being a negative act, an act of refusal or silence, either it could assert absence, or unwittingly serve a repressive dominant entity. It created no space for affirmative, progressive, or positive contributions to the aesthetic world, despite there being ample evidence of aesthetic practices which activated and expanded the political conditions of human beings in substantial and positive ways. Also, there's the other side of aesthetics that's all about personal expression, which I never took seriously. The arguments around the Pictures Generation work was initially very attractive to me as a student, since it overturned this expressive idea of art, but I found it incredibly limiting over time. It was unable to address the very real and concrete effect of aesthetics on people's lives because it avoided material specificity, everything was iconographic and ideological, images were disembodied, free-floating things. It ignored phenomenology, how the vastly different and specific distributional forms of images produced real-world effects on the way people related both to pictures and to each other, it merely reduced all the aspects of representation to their iconographic effects. It was evident to me that the wrong questions were being asked of images, ones that failed to examine the real stakes involved...

JMT: I was also reminded of *Cybernetics* because Wiener explicitly mentions photography. In a chapter entitled "Computing Machines and the Nervous System," he draws repeated parallels between the logic-based functions of computational or "clocked" devices (electrical relay switches, early data recorders, and so on) and the physiological and psychological processes of human memory—the mental acts of picturing, learning, and remembering. After describing several technological approaches for storing information on punch cards or magnetic tape, Wiener discusses photography as a medium ideal "for the permanence and detail of its records," and for the relative instantaneity of its exposure length, which was well suited for recording observations. However—and for the purposes of sustaining a kind of high volume series of data points, and what is this, I don't know, some photograph-based RAM—Wiener laments photography due to what he calls "grave disadvantages," factors that included the need for "rapid erasure and the rapid implanting of a new record," in a kind of high-throughput model of reading information. What a curious burden to place upon the medium, don't you think? I guess I'm left thinking about how his conception of photography is almost cinematic—the way that he describes a series of photographic images that would flicker by, allowing for some version of short-term memory access....

WB: This is similar to early uses of cathode ray tube (CRT) screens to store data—they suffered from similar shortcomings. See, for example, Jacob Gaboury's recent article, "The Random-Access Image: Memory and the History of the Computer Screen," which was published in *Grey Room* earlier this year. What was interesting about those devices is that they used screens that the operator never saw; they were screens that the computer alone saw and responded to (Harun Farocki alludes to this in his "Phantom Images" text). They were essentially an optical RAM. The CRT is, of course, central to the discovery of X-rays, as was photography. The interdependency of these technologies is what most intrigues me, that their histories are inextricable from one another, and these interconnections are largely invisible to conventional art history which privileges medium distinctions and static objects of study; it lacks the terminology to deal with dynamic systems, with entropy. Iconographic approaches neglect that the technological history of images links together everything from the earliest mechanically aided depictions to the current phase of digitalization. It seemed there was a way to think of these transformations together, rather than treat them discretely. Digital technologies internalize the logic of previous technologies as well as offering something new (as Marshall McLuhan said, "the content of any medium is always another medium."). This is most evident, because on a surface level the tools of digital image production operate according to an analogy to previous technologies—for example, the way that we use algorithms that simulate the chemical properties of photographs to produce and manipulate digital images, it gives them continuous tonal ranges and contrast curves, which are simply simulations of the chemical transformations of silver halide crystals and their reaction to light and chemical processing...

The searching that was involved in each stage of this project was in trying to see aesthetic productions as interconnected rather than discrete. Why Wiener's broad conception of communication was so attractive to me in the last stages of the book is because he offers a concrete starting point from which one can formulate the problems that ideology critique cannot, whether Marxist, structuralist or poststructuralist, there are exceptions, Althusser for one, or DeCerteau's theorization of resistance to authority, but the dominant threads ignored this. Because communication is fundamentally grounded in the conditions of objects and their movement. Wiener's approach always emphasizes that messages are material, emitted by a body, passed through material conduits, and subject to reception by another body. People are built into this system of exchange, not merely as communicants, but vessels for distribution. Even his response to the problem of noise extends into a productive discussion of the political conditions of images and their reception. To me what was exciting about turning to him, or equally Flusser and Bernhard Siegert, is that they offer a model to begin talking about everything from Talbot (or earlier) through to contemporary conditions of image traffic, and they don't lose their ability to do so with specificity when they are extended into other fields. Other essays in this volume contribute to this insight, of course, but Flusser and Siegert take this mode of thinking on completely. It connects the discussion of aesthetics to more extensive conversations, it allows for their political effects to be understood in specific rather than general terms, not as metaphor but as concrete effects, and acknowledges the connections to other discourses; the need to acknowledge this in order to produce a viable model for the comprehension of images and their political impacts. It allows for a comprehension of image traffic and aesthetic meaning that's not based on analogy or metaphor, that's not iconographic, connecting digital production and industrial production in a way that is concrete rather than rhetorical.

It gives us a way to reconceive the long history of aesthetic communication that gave rise to the digital, and how they interact with that history transforming and illuminating it. That was very important for the project. So even from that early show in 2010, I was trying to find a through line that rejected the non- meaning of pictures—Didion was one solution because of the literary structure she allowed. That let me make more provisional or unsanctioned connections between practices, to incorporate how we live with and use images as individuals through narrative, and to use formal morphology to open up a history, to bring seemingly disparate practices together into a constellation.

When Liam Gillick reached out to me to do the show at Luma, my thinking was more refined, allowing me to focus pointedly on where the problem with the traditional models of iconography could be located. So for me, that problem was evident in a disavowal of the significance of multiplicity, i.e., a picture in a magazine is fundamentally different from a picture on a billboard, and so on, and further discuss the concrete stakes related to various conditions of reception. Just because something is received in a multitude of different forms, does not mean that it has no form, or that its various manifestations are equivalent. Each of those manifestations has its own specific logic which creates political effects that particular to them and require specific analysis. Which is why the discussion of non-meaning, or a purely flexible contextual meaning, say in Benjamin Buchloh to Craig Owens to Douglas Crimp, this constant critical obsession with negation, with the evacuation of meaning was remedied for me by placing things within the actual context of their reception, and discussing the specificities of those receptions in material terms. And it doesn't discredit the work of the Pictures Generation, or the important theorists who discussed them, those writers were incredibly influential on me, but it allowed me to understand these approaches as a response to the issues arising at the time, rather than an inherent condition of images, or aesthetics. The important thing is to contextualize and historicize these responses, rather than treat them as either truthful or not. Does that make sense?

JMT: Yeah, it does. And I think one of the compelling aspects, one of the really satisfying aspects of both the show—as it's unfolded in recent iterations in Arles in 2016 and then last year at CCS Bard—and now with the anthology, is that I witness you working out a way in which that mode of interrogation can embody aspects of both narrative and analysis at the same time, but in a way such that neither mode is subverted by the other.

WB: Yeah, well, narrative is implicit within the book, and also in the exhibition, as both unfold over time. Both are spatialized arguments, and each operates according to the material conventions implicit within their contexts. But as human beings, we recount things to one another, we tell stories, that's a way in which we animate our worlds and commune with others.

JMT: That's as good a point as any to open much more explicitly onto the way that this book is intended to function. It's not explicitly described anywhere else in the text as such; we did not create an editor's note indicating how to use this book or anything like that. However, I think by the time the reader arrives at the end of the anthology, it is clear that the concept of the facsimile is vital to the book, less so as documentation, but as a means to acknowledge the intended context of its circulation.

WB: Overall, it was essential to emphasize the thingness of the images, in the case of periodicals or books, they were intended to be held... One sad thing about exhibiting this kind of material is that you have to display them in vitrines. Initially, I had thought, okay let's make every book or magazine a high-quality facsimile that a viewer could manipulate. This was a ridiculous idea because it was unfeasible and far too expensive and time-consuming. And we were in the process of making all the Walker Evans *Fortune* magazines and I realized that there was no way we could do it well enough, or in time for the show because I wanted them to be true to the original, use the same paper, the same binding, and so on. But I think that the kind of intimacy that early print materials have, the idea that you might get a Sojourner Truth in the mail, that you touched it, held it, that you would experience a *Fortune* or *Jet* magazine with your hands, and navigate it by touch; there's something about that type of experience that is extremely powerful and important to understanding the meaning of the thing, and the meaning of the images they convey. It shows how the manner these things circulated in the world was a conscious and meaningful choice; how they were reflexive about their context, and the larger meaning of the publications that they were in.

I can't help but also think about Gordon Parks versus Walker Evans, and the proliferation of bodies in the work by Parks, and their absence in Evans's. And when they are present in Evans's, they're like mug shots, or they're photographed like taxonomic objects; they reflect the page of the magazine and the magazine itself as an industrial product. With Parks there was none of this fascination with cold geometries, his images were overflowing with activity, with bodies, coming together, interacting, and so on. Both were gifted writers, and even their style of writing is telling of the different attitudes they had toward publication, audience, and so on. It's evident in the publications themselves; *Fortune* was austere and precious, it had a fetishistic precision to it, Life was more chaotic, less staid, and semi-disposable, you lived with it differently. Another shortcoming of the exhibition format is that these were intended to be confronted sequentially, one page at a time. You can't present them in a way that preserves that unfolding of experience, you could digitally simulate it, I guess, but then you lose the character of the object, its scale, its materials. In the exhibition, there's not a satisfactory way to recreate the physical turning of pages, of one page coming after another, which is what I wanted to capture in the book.

JMT: I was about to say that I think through the facsimile approach to materials, the anthology can reclaim some of that.

WB: I think it does, of course, it is another publication, another layer, and I wanted that mediation to be present in the experience of the book. *Picture Industry* is also rife with a kind of incompleteness and provisionality. I guess that's in the title, but it makes me think of Aby Warburg's *Mnemosyne Atlas*, or Andre Malraux's *Museum Without Walls* in a certain way because there's something to the fact that the ambition of the project itself is entirely unrealizable...in terms of how such things can be presented and related to one another, virtually endless options exist. The hope is that there's a kind of foundation presented which allows a set of associations to take place, which readers and viewers could imagine other inclusions or organizations of the material. Standard linear histories prohibit certain kinds of associative readings, for example, between time periods that don't have an obvious structural historical relationship...

JMT: What have you learned from mounting several iterations of this show? Has this helped you to clarify this idea of a "picture industry" further?

WB: What was opened up to me mainly came through looking at communication theory more systematically and expanding that. I was conscious of German media theory, largely through reading McLuhan into Friedrich Kittler, Flusser, Paul Virilio, and forward into Siegert. I think the problem I was trying to solve boils down to: how do you talk about the fluidity of relations that occur in aesthetic communication through static forms without sacrificing the centrality of that fluidity? How do you construct a frame that is flexible enough to be a generative location from which other connections or understandings can arise? At each stage of this project, it's been a case of finding a logic that allows the materials I've been drawn to as historical touchstones to coexist. To try, as I explain in my introduction in this volume, to create an affirmative model to understand the mass production of technical images, and our agency within that system. To not just look at what an image is showing, but instead *how* it is showing, how it addresses its intended viewership, how we animate images and are in turn animated by them. Reflexivity about mediation does not mean something speaks only about itself, and I wanted to focus on things that were reflexive yet primarily concerned with the world at large. In this way, *Picture Industry* has been, in part, the attempt to expand an affirmative model of aesthetic production—one where progressive politics is not based on refusals or negations—but an affirmative model that can deal with the complicated agendas going on within images, without foreclosing on their possibilities. It's a drive to find a more accepting and open model for the history of aesthetics that acknowledges the interpenetration of various fields of study. That it's not just art, and it's not just journalism, or science, or instrumental images, and it's not just corporate or state power, and it's not just political resistance, not just in service of individual liberty or in service of the infringement of liberty, it's all of those things at once. It reaches into all of those possibilities, and that's an affirmative, positive aspect, not an absence of meaning but an overflowing of possible meanings.

JMT: It's interesting, something that has come up in a number of our conversations over the past months is the idea of the Benjaminian citation, which of course is the core operational element of the *Arcades Project.* I haven't thought about it in precisely these terms, but suddenly, this kind of citation feels like a perfect metaphor for a lot of the activities of both the exhibition model and the anthology model that's proposed through *Picture Industry*—it's a kind of radical, affirmative mode of citation, and one that can be linked to Benjamin's affinities for radio and other kinds of media, his embrace of Bertolt Brecht. I think that he was very in tune with a very affirmative and expansive model for thinking about the apprehension of images or of all kinds of media, or of writing technologies, for that matter.

WB: I think the strength of the *Arcades Project* is that it acknowledges that all communication is a form of pastiche, all expression is a cobbling together of previous forms in new and inspiring ways. You actually feel his struggle to articulate something that's just out of reach. And part of the poetics of that work, part of the pain in reading him, is that you experience his frustration. So I think it's a remarkably honest and brave way of working, but it can devolve into melancholia and isolation, that's the danger in it. It's the polar opposite of Theodor W. Adorno; he did not struggle with his ability to assert something. He never questioned the authority of his own voice. Unlike Adorno, Benjamin speaks with competency, but not declarative authority. And that's why *Minima Moralia* is my favorite book of Adorno's because you can tell he's really freaked out, and Los Angeles is the place that disturbed him so—he couldn't handle it... when the first iteration of *Picture Industry* happened, I was re-reading *Minima Moralia*, thinking about the passages where he struggles the most. That was on my mind quite a bit at that point, the idea of Adorno living in L.A., meeting Charlie Chaplin, and having Chaplin mock him. There was something really telling in that collision.

JMT: I like thinking about the connections between the Frankfurt School and New Journalism, and about using melancholy, to borrow a word you used earlier, as a means to link those two disparate moments. I don't want to conflate Benjamin and Didion uncritically, but I do think that both writers were openly grappling with what the task of the literary critic was during their respective moments. To acknowledge the end of an era, and to name the thing that has kind of arrived, but not yet been fully named, or satisfactorily mapped out, right? It's the naming of things to come. All of which brings me back a line that Wiener writes in the introduction to *Cybernetics: Or Control and Communication in the Animal and the Machine*, a line I've returned to repeatedly in the past months: "To predict the future of a curve is to carry out a certain operation on its past," a sentiment that strikes me as an incredibly poetic distillation of so much of his thinking. And of course, because he's a mathematician working during the Second World War, he goes on to frame it in a discussion about how the "future of the curve" is, in fact, a sort of feedback related prediction operator that has to do with the apparatus of anti-aircraft guns—a scenario that seems to crystallize so many of the intersections between images, technology, industrialization, and weaponry that flow throughout this book. I think there's something so fascinating about the function of a curve that is so central to his thinking—it's exciting to extend that metaphor into the history that you've constructed in the current project.

WB: What's so beautiful about that quote is that it is a rather mundane observation, and then it opens up. I was so jealous when you mentioned that quote to me; I want to steal it, or steal your stealing of it. It achieves a kind of poetry out of its flat-footedness, or not flat-footedness but...

JMT: Its matter-of-factness, in a way.

WB: Its matter-of-factness, exactly. And that's what's so incredibly evocative about it, is that the associative levels creep up on you. I think it should be the title of this conversation. I still think I'll steal it in another circumstance though. I've always loved phrases like that, that are mundane on their first face, but then open up into a larger world.

Contributors

Giorgio Agamben
"Notes on Gesture." In *Means without End: Notes on Politics*, translated by Vincenzo Binetti and Cesare Casarino, 49–60. Minneapolis & London: University of Minnesota Press, 2000. English translation © 2000 by the Regents of the University of Minnesota. Originally published in *Mezzi senza fine*. © 1996 Boleti Boringhieri editore srl.

Elizabeth Alexander
"'Can you be BLACK and Look at This?': Reading the Rodney King Video(s)," *Public Culture* 7, no. 1 (Fall 1994): 77–94. © 1994. All rights reserved. Republished by permission of Duke University Press.

Thom Andersen
Eadweard Muybridge, Zoopraxographer, 1976. 16mm film, color, 59 min. Stills courtesy Thom Andersen and LUX, London.

Cory Arcangel
"On Compression." In *A Couple Thousand Short Films About Glenn Gould*. Edited by Steven Bode, 220–232. Manchester: Cornerhouse, 2008. © Cory Arcangel. Reprinted with permission of the author.

Carol Armstrong
"*A Scene in a Library*: The First Photographically Illustrated Book," in *Scenes in a Library: Reading the Photograph in the Book, 1843–1875*, 107–178. Cambridge, MA: MIT Press, 1998. © 1998 Massachusetts Institute of Technology, by permission of The MIT Press.

David Askevold
Projects Class, 1969. 12 loose leaves in a rubber-stamped envelope, 12.5 × 18 cm. © David Askevold.

Ariella Azoulay
"The Civil Contract of Photography," 85–135, in *The Civil Contract of Photography*. New York: Zone Books, 2008. © 2008 Ariella Azoulay. Reprinted by permission of Zone Books.

Lewis Baltz
Venezia Marghera Series, 1999/2011. Courtesy Gallery Luisotti, Santa Monica. ©The Lewis Baltz Trust.

Roland Barthes
Camera Lucida: Reflections on Photography, 23–94 [excerpts]. Translated by Richard Howard. New York: Hill and Wang, 1982. Originally published as *La Chambre claire,* New York: Hill & Wang, 1980. Translation © 1981 by Farrar, Straus & Giroux, Inc. Reprinted by permission of Hill & Wang, a division of Farrar, Straus and Giroux.

Georges Bataille
"Dictionnaire: Homme [Dictionary: Man]," in *Documents* no. 4 (1929): 215. Translated by Yves-Alain Bois in "Art History and Its Theories: Whose Formalism?" *The Art Bulletin* 78, no. 1 (March 1996): 9–12.

Jean-Louis Baudry
"Ideological Effects of the Basic Cinematographic Apparatus," *Film Quarterly* 28, no. 2 (Winter 1974): 39–47. © 1974 University of California Press Journals.

Bernd and Hilla Becher
Preparation Plants from Coal Mines, 1966–78. Series of seventeen black and white photographs. Each approximately 11.75 × 16 in. (29.8 × 40.3 cm). Courtesy The LeWitt Collection and Paula Cooper Gallery, New York.

Ericka Beckman
Untitled artist text from *Horror Pleni: Pictures in New York Today*, Milan: Padiglione d'arte contemporanea di Milano, 1980. Text © 1980 Ericka Beckman. "Hiatus," work-in-progress lecture delivered at Wexner Center for the Arts, 1993. © 1993 Ericka Beckman.

Gretchen Bender
Wild Dead, 1984. Two-channel video on 4 monitors, color, sound, 1:41 min. Courtesy the Gretchen Bender Estate and OSMOS, New York.

Lynda Benglis
Artforum magazine, November 1974. Originally Benglis conceived of the image as a centerfold. The publication would only take it as an advertisement, so she mocked the situation. Art © Lynda Benglis/Licensed by VAGA, New York, NY.

Walter Benjamin
"The Work of Art in the Age of Its Technological Reproducibility: Second Version." in *Selected Writings, Vol. 3,* 1935–1938. 101–122. Translated

by Edmund Jephcott, Howard Eiland, et al. Cambridge, MA; London: Belknap, 2006. Second Version published as "Das Kunstwerk im Zeitalter seiner technischen Reproduzierbarkeit" in Walter Benjamin, *Gesammelte Schriften, VII*, 350–384. Frankfurt: Suhrkamp, 1989. Reprinted by permission of Writers House LLC. All rights reserved.

Alphonse Bertillon
"Theoretical Study of Signalment," and "Appendix," 11–19, 63–81, 239–40 in *Signaletic Instructions: Including the Theory and Practice of Anthropometrical Identification.* Chicago: The Werner Company, 1896.

Walead Beshty
Hair (TE), 2018, offset print, 44; *Hair (BR)*, 2018, offset print, 221; *Eyelash (JRM)*, 2018, offset print, 268; *Hair (JMT)*, 2018, offset print, 567, *Fingernail (RAB)*, 2018, offset print, 656; *Hair (WB)*, 2018, offset print, 809. © 2018 Walead Beshty Studios, Inc.

Stewart Bird, Rene Lichtman and Peter Gessner
Finally Got the News, 1970. 16mm film, color/black and white, sound, 55 min. © 1970. Still courtesy Icarus Films.

Black Audio Film Collective
Handsworth Songs, 1986. 16mm film, color, stereo, 58:33 min. © 1986 Black Audio Film Collective. Stills courtesy Smoking Dogs Films and LUX, London.

Barbara Bloom
Travel Posters (Unlimited Miles), 1981; *Travel Posters (English Spoken)*, 1981. Archival digital prints. 30 × 24 inches (76.2 × 61 cm) each unframed. Courtesy the artist and David Lewis, New York.

Mel Bochner
Misunderstandings (A Theory of Photography), 1970. Series of ten offset lithographs and envelope 5 × 8 in. each (12.7 × 20.3 cm). © 1970 Mel Bochner. Images courtesy the artist.

Marta Braun
"Marey and the Organization of Work," 320–48, in *Picturing Time: The Work of Étienne-Jules Marey, 1830–1904,* Chicago: The University of Chicago Press, 1992. © 1992 by The University of Chicago.

Benjamin H. D. Buchloh
"Allegorical Procedures: Appropriation and Montage in Contemporary Art," *Artforum* magazine (September 1982): 43–56. © 1982 Artforum International magazine, Inc. All rights reserved.

Johanna Burton
"You've Lost That Loving Feeling: Rineke Dijkstra After Empathy." Lecture given at panel discussion for *Rineke Dijkstra: A Retrospective*, Guggenheim Museum, New York, NY, September 21, 2012. © 2018.

David Campany
Walker Evans: The Magazine Work, 28–33. Göttingen: Steidl, 2014. Text © 2014 David Campany. Reprinted courtesy the author.

Lisa Cartwright and Brian Goldfarb
"Radiography, Cinematography and the Decline of the Lens," 190–202, in *Incorporations, Zone 6*, ed. Jonathan Crary and Sanford Kwinter, New York: Zone Books, 1992. © 1992 Urzone Inc.

Stanley Cavell
"Photograph and Screen," 23–25, in *The World Viewed: Reflections on the Ontology of Film, Enlarged Edition.* Cambridge, MA: Harvard University Press, 1979. © 1971, 1974, 1979 Stanley Cavell.

Sarah Charlesworth
"A Declaration of Dependence." *The Fox*, vol. 1, no. 1, 1975. © Massachusetts Institute of Technology. All rights reserved. *Herald Tribune, January 18–February 28, 1991*. 36 black and white prints reproduced same size as original newspapers, 16"× 23" each. Courtesy the artist and Maccarone, New York.

Critical Art Ensemble
"Video and Resistance: Against Documentaries," in *The Electronic Disturbance*, 35–52. Brooklyn: Autonomedia, 1994. Anti-Copyright 1994 Autonomedia and Critical Art Ensemble. This text may be freely pirated and quoted.

Hubert Damisch
"Five Notes for a Phenomenology of the Photographic Image," *October* Vol. 5, (Summer, 1978), 70–72. Originally published in *L'Arc* (Paris), 1963. © 1978 The Massachusetts Institute of Technology, by permission of The MIT Press.

de Rijke/de Rooij
Orange, 2004. Sequence of 81 35mm color slides. Courtesy the artists and Petzel, New York.

Georges Didi-Huberman
Images in Spite of All: Four Photographs from Auschwitz. 3–25. Translated by Shane B. Lillis. Chicago: University of Chicago Press, 2008. Originally published in French as *Images malgré tout* (Paris: Les Éditions de Minuit, 2003). © Les Éditions de Minuit, 2003. English translation

© 2008 by the University of Chicago. Images reprinted with permission of The State Museum Auschwitz-Birkenau, Oświęcim.

T. J. Demos
"Toward a New Institutional Critique: A Conversation with Renzo Martens," 93–103. *Atlantica,* 2012. © 2012. Reprinted with permission of the author.

Stan Douglas
Monodramas, 1992. Originally broadcast nightly on BCTV from January 13 until February 5, 1992. © 1992 Stan Douglas. "News Hour" reporter Belle Puri covering viewer reactions to Stan Douglas' *Monodramas*, February 8, 1992.

Ariel Dorfman and Armand Mattelart
How to Read Donald Duck: Imperialist Ideology in the Disney Comic. New York: International General, 1975.

Guillaume-Amant Duchenne de Boulogne
"The Background to My Electrophysiological Research on Facial Expression in Movement," in *The Mechanisms of Human Facial Expression*. Edited and translated by R. Andrew Cuthbertson, 9–11. Cambridge: Cambridge University Press, 1990. © Cambridge University Press. Originally published as Duchenne, G.B., *Mécanisme de la physionomie humaine* (Paris: Jules Renouard, 1862). Images © Darwin Estate and Cambridge University Library.

Daniel Eisenberg
Still from *The Unstable Object*, 2011. Courtesy the artist.

Noam M. Elcott
"The Phantasmagoric *Dispositif:* An Assembly of Bodies and Images in RealTime and Space," *Grey Room* 62 (Winter 2016): 42–71. © 2016 by Grey Room, Inc. and the Massachusetts Institute of Technology. Reprinted courtesy the author.

William H. Emory
Report on the United States and Mexico Boundary Survey. Washington, D.C.: Cornelius Wendell, 1857.

Darby English
"Emmett Till Ever After." In *Black Is, Black Ain't*. Edited by Hamza Walker and Karen Reimer, 84–99. Chicago: The Renaissance Society at the University of Chicago, 2013. © 2013 the author. Reprinted with permission of the author and the Renaissance Society at the University of Chicago. Fig. 1 © 2005 Jason Lazarus; Fig. 2 ©The Commercial Appeal, Memphis; Fig. 3. © 2004 Demetrius Oliver, courtesy Inman Gallery, Houston.

Walker Evans
"Labor Anonymous," *Fortune* magazine, November 1946, 152–153. "In Bridgeport's War Factories," *Fortune* magazine, September 1941, 88–89. "Main Street Looking North," *Fortune* magazine, May 1948, 102–103. "The Gentle Truckers," *Fortune* magazine, May 1950, 102–103. "October's Game," *Fortune* magazine, October 1954, 132–33. "The Pitch Direct," *Fortune* magazine, October 1958, 139. "And That is That," *Fortune* magazine, December 1958, 85. "On the Waterfront," *Fortune* magazine, November 1960, 144–145. "In the Midst of Plenty," *Fortune* magazine, March 1961, 106. "Homes of Americans," *Fortune* magazine, April 1946, 150–151. Images © Walker Evans Archive, The Museum of Modern Art. Facsimiles © 2018 Time Inc.

Harun Farocki
Workers Leaving the Factory, 1995. Video, color and b/w, 36 min. *Eye/Machine I*, 2001, Two-channel video, color, sound, 25 min.; *Eye/Machine II*, 2002, Two-channel video, color and b/w, sound, 15 min.; *Eye/Machine III*, 2003 Two-channel video, color, sound, 25 min. Images courtesy Harun Farocki GbR and Greene Naftali, New York "Workers Leaving the Factory." Translated by Laurent Faasch-Ibrahim. In *Harun Farocki: Working On the Sight-Lines*. Edited by Thomas Elsaesser, 237–243. Amsterdam: Amsterdam University Press, 2004. Reprinted courtesy Antje Ehmann. "Phantom Images," translated by Brian Poole. *Public* 29 (2004): 12–22. Reprinted courtesy Antje Ehmann.

Morgan Fisher
"Phi Phenomenon" [1976] and "Standard Gauge" [1985/revised 2012], 21–24; 65–75, in *Morgan Fisher: Writings*. Edited by Sabine Folie and Susanne Titz. Cologne: Walther König, 2013. © Morgan Fisher. Generali Foundation, Vienna; Museum Abteiberg, Mönchengladbach; Verlag der Buchhandlung Walther König, Cologne; authors and translator. All rights reserved. *Phi Phenomenon*, 1968. 16mm film, black and white, silent, 24 frames per second, 11 min. *Standard Gauge*, 1984. 16mm film, color, sound, 35 min. Stills courtesy the artist.

Vilém Flusser
"The Photographic Universe." and "Why a Philosophy of Photography Is Necessary." In *Towards a Philosophy of Photography,* 65–82. London: Reaktion Books, 2000. Originally published in German as *Für eine Philosophie der Fotografie* (1984). Copyright © 1983 European Photography, Göttingen, Germany 1983. English language translation

© Reaktion Books, 2000. "The Gesture of Video." In *Gestures*, translated by Nancy Ann Roth, 142–146. Minneapolis: University of Minnesota Press, 2014. Originally published in German as *Gesten: Versuch einer Phänomenologie* (Braunschweig: Bollmann Verlag, 1991). Copyright 1991, 1993 by Bollmann Verlag. English translation © 2014 by the Regents of the University of Minnesota. All rights reserved.

LaToya Ruby Frazier
"Flint is Family," in *ELLE* magazine, September 2016. © 2016. Courtesy the artist and *ELLE* magazine.

Lee Friedlander
Cray at Chippewa Falls, 1987. (Minneapolis, Minnesota: Cray Research, Inc. 1987) © Lee Friedlander. Courtesy the artist and Fraenkel Gallery, San Francisco.

Ernst Friedrich
Originally published as *Krieg dem Kriege!* (1924). Text and Images © 1924 Ernst Friedrich.

Coco Fusco
"Black Audio Film Collective: John Akomfrah, Reece Auguiste, Lina Gopaul, & Avril Johnson." In *Young, British and Black: The Work of Sankofa and Black Audio Film Collective*, 41–60. Buffalo: Hallwalls/Contemporary Arts Center, 1988. Text © the author. © 1990 Massachusetts Institute of Technology and the New Museum of Contemporary Art. Reprinted by permission of the author.

Alexander R. Galloway
"Protocol," in *Theory, Culture & Society* 23 (May 2006), 317–320. © 2006 Alexander R. Galloway. Reprinted by permission of SAGE Publications, Ltd.

Francis Galton
Inquiries into Human Faculty and Its Development, 6–13. New York: Macmillan and Co, 1883; reissued London: J.M. Dent & Sons / Everyman's Library, 1907.

Tristan Garcia
"In Defense of Representation." In *Realism Materialism Art*. Edited by Christoph Cox, Jenny Jaskey, and Suhail Malik, 245–251. Berlin: Sternberg Press, 2015.

Isa Genzken
Untitled, 1991/2016. Photograph mounted on foam core, acrylic paint and plastic foil, 106 × 80 cm. Courtesy Galerie Buchholz, Berlin/Cologne/New York / Licensed by ADAGP, Paris, 2018.

Frank Gilbreth
"Preface" to *Motion Study: A Method for Increasing the Efficiency of the Workman*. Boston: Stanhope Press, 1911. Motion Study Photographs, 1913–1917. Images Courtesy the Kheel Center for Labor-Management Documentation and Archives, Cornell University Library.

Georges Gilles de la Tourette
"Physiological Study of normal walking." In Études cliniques et physiologiques sur la marche: la marche dans les maladies du système nerveux: étudiée par la méthode des empreintes [Clinical and Physiological Studies of Walking: Walking in Diseases of the Nervous System Studied by the Fingerprint Method], 7–15. Paris: A Delahaye et Lecrosnier, 1886. Translated by Celia Abele.

Liz Glynn
Anonymous Needs and Desires (Various Cast-offs: Ceramic Tile, Potato Chips, Garlic, Men's Socks, Blackberry, iPod, Baby Food, Perfume, Chocolate, and Cigarettes), 2012. Photo: Robert Acklen-Brečko, Walead Beshty Studios, Inc.

Dan Graham
Schema [Poem, March 1966], in *Aspen* magazine No. 5 + 6, 1967; "My Works for Magazine Pages: A History of Conceptual Art 1965–1969." In *Dan Graham: Works and Collected Writings*, edited by Gloria Moure, 217–221. Barcelona: Ediciones Poligrafa, 2009. Reprinted courtesy the artist; *Homes for America*, 1972. Photo offset reproduction of layout for magazine article, 23 ¾ × 19 ½ inches. Courtesy the artist and Marian Goodman Gallery, Paris.

Darcy Grimaldo Grigsby
"Introduction" in *Enduring Truths: Sojourner's Shadows and Substance*, 17–21. (Chicago: University of Chicago Press, 2015). © 2015 by The University of Chicago.

Johan Grimonprez
From *Inflight* magazine, 2000. Courtesy the artist.

James D. Hague
Mining Industry, with Geological Contributions by Clarence King. Washington, D.C.: Government Printing Office, 1870. Includes photolithograph after Timothy O'Sullivan, *Shaft Landing of Savage Mine*, 1868.

Lyle Ashton Harris
Glenn and Arthur, Black Male Exhibition Opening, New York, 1994; *Malcolm X T-shirt, Rome*, 1992; *Ike and Lyle, Los Angeles*, 1995; *Truce Between Crips and Bloods, Los Angeles*, 1992; *Gay's Head, Martha's*

Vineyard, Circa Late 1980s; *To Do List, Seattle*, 1992; *Nan, Berlin*, 1992; *Red Pegasus, New York*, Circa late 1980s; *Essex, LA; Contemporary Exhibitions*, Los Angeles, 1992; *Jenny and Cathy, Sunset Junction Street Fair, Los Angeles*, ca. early 1990s; *M. Lamar, Yerba Buena Center for the Arts, San Francisco*, 1993; *Doorknob, Venice*, 1992; *Whitney Independent Study Program, New York*, 1992; *Self Portrait, Los Angeles*, Circa Early 1990's; *Easter Break #2, New York*, March 25, 1989. All works from the series Ektachrome Archive, 1986–96. Courtesy Lyle Ashton Harris, David Castillo Gallery, and Salon 94, New York. "Lyle Ashton Harris, as told to Alpesh Kantital Patel," *Artforum* magazine, May 22, 2015. © 2015.

John Heartfield
"Nach Indien," in *Arbeiter-Illustrierte Zeitung*, Vol X No. 28 (1930); "Ein Neues Jahr," in *Arbeiter-Illustrierte Zeitung*, Vol. X No. 52 (1930); "Ob schwarz, ob weiss," in *Arbeiter-Illustrierte Zeitung* Vol. X No. 26 (1931); "Wollt Ihr wieder fallen," in *Arbeiter-Illustrierte Zeitung*, Vol. XI No. 35 (1932); "Je höher der Brotkorb," in *Arbeiter-Illustrierte Zeitung* Vol. XI No. 39 (1932). © 2017 The Heartfield Community of Heirs / Licensed by ADAGP, Paris 2018.

Lewis Hine
Charities: Charities and the Commons, Vol. XX, no. 10 (June 6, 1908); *The Survey*, Vol. XXIV, No. 3 (April 16, 1910); *The Survey*, Vol. XXX, No. 5 (May 3, 1913); "The Homestead Plant: Carnegie Steel Company" in Margaret Byington, *Homestead: The Households of a Mill Town* Vol. 4 (New York: New York Charities Publication Committee, 1910).

Thomas Hirschhorn
Touching Reality, 2012. Exhibition view: "Intense Proximity" - La Triennale, Palais de Tokyo, Paris, 2012. Photo: Romain Lopez, Courtesy: Galerie Chantal Crousel, Paris. "Why Is It Important—Today—to Show and Look at Images of Destroyed Human Bodies," *Le Journal de La Triennale*, No. 4 (February 2012). Text © 2012 Thomas Hirschhorn. Reprinted by permission of the artist.

Yngve Holen
Parasagittal Brain, 2013. Watercut water cooler. Two parts: 110 × 39 × 13 cm each. Courtesy the artist and Neue Alte Brücke, Frankfurt am Main. Photo Credit: Nick Ash.

Oliver Wendell Holmes
"The Stereoscope and Stereograph," *The Atlantic* 3, no. 20 (June 1859): 738–748. Courtesy *The Atlantic*.

Jenny Holzer
PALM Left 000037, 2007; *PALM Right 000036*, 2007; *Right Hand DOD-044403*, 2007; *PALM AND FINGERS + FINGERTIPS, RIGHT HAND 000053*, 2007; *Person Fingerprinted DOD-053038*, 2007; *TBD (A5-DOD-052103) BLUE WHITE*, 2007; *TBD (A6-DOD-052102) BLUE WHITE*, 2007; *TBD (A11-DOD-050576) BLUE WHITE*, 2007. [All works U.S. Government Documents]. Oil on linen, 58 × 44 in. / 147.3 × 111.8 cm each. All images © 2007 Jenny Holzer / Licensed by ADAGP, Paris 2018.

bell hooks
"Being the Subject of Art." In *Art on My Mind*, 133–137. New York: The New Press, 1995. © 1995 by bell hooks. All rights reserved.

Douglas Huebler
Catalog contributions to *January 5–31, 1969* [exhibition catalog/publication produced by Seth Siegelaub, 1969]. Courtesy the estate of Douglas Huebler and Paula Cooper Gallery / Licensed by ADAGP, Paris 2018.

William Henry Jackson
Descriptive Catalogue of Photographs of North American Indians. Washington, D.C.: Government Printing Office, 1877. Colorchrome postcards: 6877. "Arrowmaker," 1903; 5511. "Moki Indian Woman Making Pottery," 1899; 6506. "Papago Indian Filling the Olla," 1903; 5244. "Moki Indian Cigarette Smoker," 1898; 6885. "Anticipation," 1903; 5890. "The Man with the Hoe," Moki Pueblo, 1902; 6503. "A Pueblo Woman with Olla," 1902; 5891. "An Embryonic Warrior," 1902; 6091. "A Pima Papoose," 1902; 11537. "Bull's Head," Gros Ventre, ca. 1899. Approx. 5.25 × 3.5 in. each.

Arthur Jafa
Love Is the Message, the Message Is Death, 2016. Single-channel video, color, sound, 7:30 minutes. © Arthur Jafa 2016. Image courtesy of the artist and Gavin Brown's enterprise, New York / Rome.

Arthur Jafa and Tina Campt
"Love Is the Message, the Plan Is Death," *e-flux Journal* no. 81 (April 2017). © 2017 e-flux, Arthur Jafa, and Tina Campt. Reprinted courtesy of the authors.

***Jet* Magazine**
"Nation horrified by Murder of Kidnapped Chicago Youth," 6–9, *Jet* Vol. XIII, No. 19 (September 15, 1955) © Johnson Publishing Company, Inc. 1955. Exhibition Copy loaned by the Rebuild Foundation, Chicago. Facsimile images courtesy the Charles L. Blockson Afro-American Collection, Temple University, Philadelphia.

Zuhair al-Jezairy
"Repression and the Information Boom," 58–63, in *Home Works III: A Forum on Cultural Practices*. Edited by Chaza Charafeddine, Masha Refka, and Christine Tohme. Beirut: The Lebanese Association for Plastic Arts, Ashkal Alwan, 2008.

Fritz Kahn
Der Mensch als Industriepalast, 1926. *Das Leben des Menschen, Eine volkstümliche Anatomie, Biologie, Physiologie und Entwicklungeschichte des Menschen* (5 Volumes), 1926–31. © 1926 Kosmos Verlag. Reprinted with permission of the Kahn Estate.

Stephen Kaltenbach
ART WORKS (November 1968), *JOHNNY APPLESEED* (December 1968), [Not Titled] (January 1969), *TELL A LIE* (February 1969), *START A RUMOR* (March 1969), *PERPETRATE A HOAX* (April 1969), *BUILD A REPUTATION* (May 1969), *BECOME A LEGEND* (Summer 1969), *TEACH ART* (September 1969), *SMOKE* (October 1969), *TRIP* (November 1969), *YOU ARE ME* (December 1969) Advertisements in *Artforum* magazine. © 1968–69 Stephen Kaltenbach. Courtesy of the artist.

Douglas Kellner
"Ernst Friedrich's Pacifistic Anarchism," 9–18, in *War Against War!* by Ernst Friedrich. Seattle: The Real Comet Press, 1987. © 1987 The Real Comet Press. Reprinted with permission of the author.

Friedrich A. Kittler
"Introduction," 1–19, in *Gramophone, Film, Typewriter.* Translated by Geoffrey Winthrop-Young and Michael Wutz. © 1999 by the Board of Trustees of the Leland Stanford Jr. University for the translation; © 1986 by Brinkmann & Bose, Berlin. All rights reserved. Used with the permission of Stanford University Press.

Siegfried Kracauer
"Photography," 47–63, in *The Mass Ornament: Weimar Essays.* Edited and translated by Thomas Y. Levin, Cambridge, MA: Harvard University Press, 1995. Originally published as *Das Ornament der Masse: Essays,* Berlin: Suhrkamp Verlag, 1963. © 1995 by the President and Fellows of Harvard College.

Rosalind E. Krauss
"Photography's Discursive Spaces," 131–150, in *The Originality of the Avant Garde and Other Modernist Myths.* Cambridge, MA: MIT Press, 1986. Courtesy The MIT Press. © 1986 Massachusetts Institute of Technology, by permission of The MIT Press.

Louise Lawler
"Arrangements of Pictures," *October*, Vol. 26 (Autumn 1983), pp. 3–16. © 1983 Louise Lawler. Reprinted with permission of the artist.
"Civilian (adjusted to fit), 2010/2011" series, 2018. Dimensions variable to publication. © 2018 Louise Lawler. Courtesy of the artist and Metro Pictures, New York.

Pierre Leguillon
Diane Arbus: A Printed Retrospective, 1960–1971, 2009. Installation view, Kadist, Paris, 2009. Images courtesy Kadist, Paris and San Francisco. photo: A. Mole.

Sherrie Levine
After Walker Evans: 1–22, 1981. Gelatin silver prints in twenty-two (22) parts, 10 × 8 in. (25.4 × 20.3 cm) each unframed. Courtesy of the artist and David Zwirner, New York/London/Hong Kong.

Glenn Ligon
Red Portfolio, 1993. Suite of 9 silver gelatin prints, 7.87 × 7.87 inches (20 × 20 cm). © Glenn Ligon, Courtesy Regen Projects, Los Angeles.

Sharon Lockhart
Exit (Bath Iron Works, July 7–11, 2008, Bath, Maine), 2008. Courtesy of the artist.

Louis and Auguste Lumière
Workers Leaving the Lumière Factory, 1895. 35mm film, black and white, silent, 16 frames per second, 17 meters. Still courtesy Institut Lumière.

Robert Mapplethorpe
Cedric, NYC, 1978; *Jim, Sausalito*, 1977; *Jim and Tom, Sausalito*, 1977; *Patrice*, 1977; *Scott*, 1978 *Joe, NYC*, 1978; *Ken*, 1978; *Helmut, NYC*, 1978; *John*, 1978; *Helmut and Brooks, NYC*, 1978; *Lou, NYC*, 1977; *Richard*, 1977; *Self Portrait*, 1978. All works from the series *X Portfolio*, 1977–1978. Il works © Robert Mapplethorpe Foundation. Used by permission.

Étienne-Jules Marey
Physiologie du mouvement: le vol des oiseaux. Paris: Librarie de l'academie de Médecine, 1890. *La Chronophotographie* [Chronophotography], Lecture delivered at the Conference at the National Conservatory of Arts and Crafts on January 29, 1899. Paris: Gauthier-Villars, 1899. Translated by Celia Abele. Translation © 2018.

Kerry James Marshall
Dailies from Rythm Mastr, 2010. Suite of 9 silkscreen prints on paper. 24 ⅜ × 31 ¾ × 1 inches

(each, framed). 48 ¾ H × 158 ¾ L inches (overall dimensions). © Kerry James Marshall. Courtesy of the artist and Jack Shainman Gallery, New York.

Lev Manovich
"Automation of Sight: From Photography to Computer Vision." In *Electronic Culture: Technology and Visual Representation*. Edited by Timothy Druckrey, 229–239. New York: Aperture, 1996. © 1996 Lev Manovich.

Chris Marker
Sans Soleil, 1983. 35mm film, color, sound, 103 minutes. © 1983 Argos Films. Still courtesy Janus Films/The Criterion Collection.

Renzo Martens
Episode III: Enjoy Poverty, 2008. SD video, color, sound, 90 min. Courtesy of the artist, KOW, Berlin and Galerie Fons Welters, Amsterdam.

Daniel McClean
"Photography and the Law," *frieze d/e* no. 3 (Winter 2011): 106–115. © 2011 Daniel McClean. Reprinted with permission of the author.

Allan McCollum
Collection of Ten Plaster Surrogates, 1982/1992. Enamel on cast hydrostone. Dimensions variable. Unique, Each signed and numbered on the back of each surrogate. © Allan McCollum. Courtesy of the artist and Petzel, New York.

Marshall McLuhan
"The Medium is the Message." In *Understanding Media: The Extensions of Man*. Edited by Terrence Gordon, 19–35. Berkeley: Gingko Press, 1964. © 1964, 1994 Corinne McLuhan.

Richard Meyer
"Mapplethorped: Art, Photography, and the Pornographic Imagination," 233–237, in *Robert Mapplethorpe: The Photographs*. Edited by Paul Martineau and Britt Salvesen. Los Angeles: J. Paul Getty Museum, 2016. © 2016. Reprinted with permission of the author.

Boris Mikhailov
Case History, 1997–98. C-Print, 220 × 130 cm unframed. Courtesy of the artist and Galerie Barbara Weiss, Berlin. Images © Boris Mikhailov. *Case History*, 4–10. Zurich: Scalo, 1999. © 1999 Boris Mikhailov. Reprinted with permission of the artist.

Sagar Mitchell & James Kenyon
Mitchell & Kenyon 63: Workers Leaving Williamson's Factory, Lancaster, 1901. 35mm, black and white, silent, 74 feet. *Mitchell & Kenyon 80: Workers Leaving Messrs Vickers & Maxim's in Barrow*, 1901 35mm, black and white, silent, 71 feet. Stills courtesy the British Film Institute.

László Moholy-Nagy
"Production-Reproduction." Translated by Mátyás Esterházy. In *Moholy-Nagy*, edited by Krisztina Passuth, 289–90. London: Thames and Hudson, 1985. Originally published as "Produktion-Reproduktion," *De Stijl* 7 (1922), 97–101.

Charles Moore
"They Fight a Fire That Won't Go Out," *LIFE* magazine, May 17, 1963. ©Time-Life / Getty Images.

Fred Moten
"Black Mo'nin'," In *Loss: The Politics of Mourning*. Edited byDavid Eng and David Kazanjian, 52–76. Berkeley and Los Angeles: University of California Press, 2003. © 2003 by the Regents of the University of California.

Jean-Luc Moulène
Strike Objects, 1999–2000/2007. Cibachrome under Diasec, 47 × 36 × 3 cm (framed each). Courtesy of the artist and Chantal Crousel, Paris.

Eadweard Muybridge
Selections from *Attitudes of Animals in Motion*, 1882; and *Animal Locomotion*, 1887. Courtesy Library of Congress Prints and Photographs Division, Washington, D.C.

Peter Osborne
"The Distributed Image," *Texte zur Kunst* 99 (September 2015): 74–87. © 2015 Texte Zur Kunst. All rights reserved. Reprinted courtesy of the author.

Timothy O'Sullivan
[See also entries for James Hague, John Samson, and Alan Trachtenberg]
The Pyramid and Domes, Pyramid Lake, Nevada, 1867, albumen print, 8 × 10.5 in; Photolithograph after O'Sullivan, *Tufa Domes, Pyramid Lake*, Published in King Survey Report, 1875.Images Courtesy Library of Congress Prints and Photographs Division Washington, D.C.

John Ott
"Iron Horses: Leland Stanford, Eadweard Muybridge, and the Industrialised Eye," *Oxford Art Journal*, Vol. 28, No. 3 (2005), 409–428. Figs. 1–3 courtesy The Stanford Family Collections, Iris & B. Gerald Cantor Center for the Visual Arts at Stanford University.

Craig Owens
"Photography *en abyme*." In *Beyond Recognition: Representation, Power, and Culture*, 16–30. Edited by Scott Bryson, Barbara Kruger, Lynne Tillman, and Jane Weinstock. Berkeley: University of California Press, 1992. [Original Publication: *October*, No. 5: Photography: A Special Issue (Cambridge: MIT Press 1978), 73–88.] © 1992 The Regents of the University of California. Fig. [Brassaï] Collection of the Sack Photographic Trust, San Francisco Museum of Modern Art. © Estate of G. Brassaï. Photograph: Don Ross.

Erwin Panofsky
Perspective as Symbolic Form, 1927. Translated by Christopher S. Wood, 27–45; 67–72. New York: Zone Books, 1997. Originally published as "Die Perspecktive als 'symbolische Form,'" in *Vorträge der Bibliothek Warburg 1924–1925* (Leipzig & Berlin: 1927). © 1991 Urzone, Inc.

Gordon Parks
"The Restraints: Open and Hidden," in *LIFE* magazine, September 4, 1956; "Problem Kids" in *Ebony* magazine, July 1947; "Harlem Gang Leader" in *LIFE* magazine, Nov. 1, 1948; "A Man Becomes Invisible" in *LIFE* magazine, August 25, 1952; "Freedom's Fearful Foe: Poverty" in *LIFE* magazine, June 16, 1961; "The White Devil's Day is Almost Over" in *LIFE* magazine, May 31, 1963; "How It Feels To Be Black" in *LIFE* magazine, August 16, 1963 "The Redemption of the Champion" in *LIFE* magazine, September 9, 1966; and "What I Want, What I Am, What You Force Me To Be Is What You Are" in *LIFE* magazine, March 8, 1968. Images © 2018 The Gordon Parks Foundation. Facsimile ©Time Life magazine.

John Durham Peters
"Infrastructuralism," in *The Marvelous Clouds: Toward a Philosophy of Elemental Media,* 30–38. The University of Chicago Press, 2015. © 2015 by The University of Chicago. All rights reserved.

Paul Pfeiffer
Live Evil (Kuala Lumpur), 2003. Digital video loop, LCD monitor, DVD player, cast armature, 2.6 × 3.5 × 4.3 inches / 6.7 × 8.9 × 10.8 cm. Image courtesy of the artist and Thomas Dane Gallery, London.

Jack Pierson
Self Portrait (James Dean), 1993. Magazine pages mounted on canvas. Framed Dimensions: 72 ½ × 50 × 3 ¼ inches (184.2 × 127 × 8.3 cm). Image Dimensions: 66 ½ × 44 inches. © Jack Pierson, Courtesy Regen Projects, Los Angeles.

Seth Price
Digital Video Effect: "Holes," 2003. TV/DVD player, DVD, installed at *Seth Price*, Kunsthalle Zürich, 2008. Courtesy Sammlung Goetz, Munich. Photography: Seth Price; Stills from *Digital Video Effect: "Holes"*, 2003, video, 7:25 min. "Redistribution (video transcript)." in *Price, Seth*, 77–101. Zurich: JRP/Ringier, 2010. © Seth Price. Text and images courtesy of the artist.

Eileen Quinlan
The Full Edition of Smoke and Mirrors 24A, 2006. 6 UV-laminated chromogenic prints mounted on Sintra. 61 × 50.8 cm / 24 × 20 inches each. Courtesy of the artist and Campoli Presti, London / Paris.

Jacob Riis
"The Other Half and How They Live: Story in Pictures," in *Christians at Work, Proceedings of the Sixth Convention of Christian Workers in the United States and Canada, Washington, D.C. First Congregational Church, November 5–11, 1891*, 289–311; "How the Other Half Lives: Studies Among the Tenements," in *Scribner's Magazine*, Vol. VI, No. 6 (December 1889), 642–662.

Roentgenizdat [Unknown makers]
Bootleg audio recording on X-ray film, ca. 1960.
Pyotr Leshchenko recording, ca. 1960
Unknown Georgian folk recording, ca. 1960
Lubov Chernina recording, ca. 1960
Unknown Jazz recording, ca. 1960
Unknown recording, ca. 1960

Wilhelm Röntgen
"On a New Kind of Rays." Translated by Arthur Stanton, *Nature* Vol. 53, No. 1369 (1896): 274–76. "Aufnahme einer menschlichen Hand nach dem Röntgen'schen Verfahren" [Picture of a human hand according to the X-ray method], *Zeitschrift für Elektrochemie* [*Journal of Electrochemistry*], Vol. 2, 1895–96; "Röntgen-Photographie zweier ineinander geschlungener Hände" [X-ray photograph of two hands clasped together] in *Journal of Electrochemistry*, Vol. 3, 1896–1897.

Martha Rosler
Balloons, Boys Room, Red Stripe Kitchen, Giacometti, Patio View, and *Woman with Cannon (dots).* All works photomontages from the series *House Beautiful: Bringing the War Home*, c. 1967–72. *Tron (Amputee)* in *Goodbye to All That*, Issue #3 (October 13, 1970) Photomontage reproduced in newspaper. 17 × 22 in. All images © Martha Rosler; Courtesy of the artist and Mitchell-Innes & Nash, New York. "Post-Documentary, Post-Photography?" In *Decoys and Disruptions: Selected*

Writings, 1975–2001, 207–244. Cambridge, M.A.: MIT Press and the International Center of Photography, New York, 2004. © 2004 Martha Rosler. Reprinted courtesy of the artist and the MIT Press.

Cameron Rowland
"Bertillon System of Criminal Identification," Selected by Cameron Rowland. Text © National Law Enforcement Museum. Image Federal Bureau of Investigation, U.S. Department of Justice. *Handpunch*, 5 Photographs. Each Photograph: 14 × 10.16 inches (35.56 × 25.81 cm). Each Framed: 16.75 × 12.75 × 1.25 inches (42.55 × 32.39 × 3.18 cm). Courtesy of the artist.

John Samson [likely Timothy O'Sullivan]
"Photographs from the High Rockies," in *Harper's New Monthly Magazine* 39, September 1869, 465–476.

August Sander
Student of Philosophy [Erich Sander], 1926, from the *Scholars* Portfolio; *Political Prisoner* [Erich Sander], 1943, from the *Political Prisoners* Portfolio; *Death Mask of Erich Sander,* 1944, from *The Last People* Portfolio. Images courtesy Die Photographische Sammlung/SK Stiftung Kultur, Cologne / Licensed by ADAGP, Paris 2018.

Julian Sander
Julian Sander (great-grandson of August Sander) as recounted to Walead Beshty, June 2017. Printed by permission of Julian Sander.

Claude Shannon
Originally published as C. E. Shannon, "A Mathematical Theory of Communication," *The Bell System Technical Journal* 27, (July and October 1948): 1–11, 14–28. Courtesy Nokia © 1948 Nokia Corporation. All rights reserved.

Stephen Shore
Amarillo—Tall in Texas, 1971. Courtesy of the artist and 303 Gallery, New York.

Bernhard Siegert
"(Not) In Place: The Grid, or, Cultural Techniques of Ruling Spaces." In *Cultural Techniques: Grids, Filters, Doors, and Other Articulations of the Real.* Translated by Geoffrey Winthrop-Young, 97–120. New York: Fordham University Press, 2015. Originally published as "(Nicht) Am Ort: Zum Raster als Kulturtechnik," *Thesis* 49, no. 3 (2003). © 2015 Fordham University Press. "There Are No Mass Media," in *Mapping Benjamin. The Work of Art in the Digital Age,* 30–38. Edited by Hans Ulrich Gumbrecht and Michael Marrinan. Stanford: Stanford University Press, 2003.

Fernando Solanas and Octavio Getino
"Towards a Third Cinema: Notes and Experiences for the Development of a Cinema of Liberation in the Third World." In *Twenty-Five Years of the New Latin American Cinema.* Edited by Michael Chanan, 17–27. 1969; London: BFI, 1983. Reprinted with permission of the editor.

Hito Steyerl
"Documentary Uncertainty," in *A Prior* no. 15 (2007). *In Free Fall*, 2010, HD Video, color, sound, 32 min. "In Free Fall: A Thought Experiment on Vertical Perspective," *e-flux Journal* no. 24 (April 2011). *The Tower*, 2015. Installation of three high definition channels (color, sound, 8 min.), metallic structure, armchairs. All texts and images © the artist. Courtesy of the artist and Andrew Kreps Gallery, New York.

William Henry Fox Talbot
The Pencil of Nature, 5–25. London: Longman, Brown, Green & Longmans, 1844–46. Cover Image courtesy the Library of Congress, Prints and Photographs Division, Washington, D.C.
Plates I. Part of Queen's College, Oxford, 1844; Plate III. Articles of China, 1844; Plate IV. Articles of Glass, 1844, Plate VIII. A Scene in a Library, 1845; Plate XIX. The Tower of Lacock Abbey, 1844; Plate XXIV. A Fruit Piece, 1844. Images courtesy Hans P. Kraus Jr. Inc, New York

Krista Thompson
"The Evidence of Things Not Photographed: Slavery and Historical Memory in the British West Indies," *Representations* 113, no. 1 (2011): 39–63. © 2011 University of California Press Journals. Reprinted with permission of the author and the University of California. Fig. 1, courtesy Temple University Library; Fig. 2, courtesy Alamy Pictures; Fig. 3, courtesy Photographs and Prints Division, Schomburg Center for Research in Black Culture, The New York Public Library, Astor, Lenox and Tilden Foundations; Fig. 4, courtesy Digital Library of the Caribbean, University of Florida Digital Collections.

Wolfgang Tillmans
"Great Things Never Come from Comfort Zones," 2015. Courtesy of the artist and Regen Projects, Los Angeles.

Alan Trachtenberg
"Naming the View," in *Reading American Photographs: Images as History, Mathew Brady to Walker Evans*, 119–163. New York: Hill and Wang,

1990. Reprinted by permission of Hill & Wang, a division of Farrar, Strauss and Giroux. © 1989 by Alan Trachtenberg. Figs 1, 2 & 4 Courtesy Library of Congress Prints and Photographs Division Washington, D.C.; Fig. 3 Courtesy Amon Carter Museum, Fort Worth, TX.

Sojourner Truth
Carte de visite, 1864, albumen print mounted on cardboard, approx. 4 × 2.5 in. (framed: 11 × 9 in.). Courtesy Library of Congress Prints and Photographs Division, Washington, D.C

Alan Turing
Originally published as A. M. Turing, "Computing Machinery and Intelligence," *Mind* 49, no. 236 (October 1950): 436–460. © 1950, Oxford University Press.

Cosey Fanny Tutti
Magazine Actions in *Fiesta* Magazine, *Vol. 10, No 7*, 1976. Courtesy of the artist and Cabinet, London. Image © the artist.

Mierle Laderman Ukeles
Washing/Tracks/Maintenance: Outside, July 23, 1973 Part of *Maintenance Art* performance series, 1973–1974. Performance at Wadsworth Atheneum, Hartford, CT. Courtesy of the artist and Ronald Feldman Gallery, New York.

United Fruit Company
The Golden Caribbean Vol. 2, no. 1 (January 1904).

United States Department of Defense
"Declassification," http://open.defense.gov/Transparency/Declassification/. Last accessed May 2018.

Kelley Walker
"Then we joked about how we had always wanted a sunken living room," 2001. Digital file rendered in vinyl, dimensions variable. *schema; Aquafresh plus Crest with whitener*, 2003. Digital file rendered in vinyl, dimensions variable. *schema; Aquafresh plus Crest with Scope*, 2003. Digital file rendered in vinyl, dimensions variable. All images courtesy of the artist. © Kelley Walker.

Jeff Wall
Young Workers, 1978/1983. 8 transparencies in lightboxes, each 101.6 × 101.6 cm. Courtesy of the artist.

Andy Warhol
Mechanical ("The Dogs' Attack is Negroes' Reward," from LIFE magazine, *May 17, 1963)*, 1963. Newsprint clipping, graphite, tape, and gouache on heavyweight paper. 20 × 22 ½ in. (50.8 × 57.2 cm). Collection of The Andy Warhol Museum, Pittsburgh. © The Andy Warhol Foundation for the Visual Arts, Inc. / Licensed by ADAGP, Paris 2018. Race Riot, ca. 1963. Screen print on Strathmore paper, 30 ⅛ × 40 in. (76.5 × 101.6 cm). Collection of The Andy Warhol Museum, Pittsburgh © The Andy Warhol Foundation for the Visual Arts, Inc. / Licensed by ADAGP, Paris 2018.

Lawrence Weiner
TAKEN FROM HERE TO WHERE IT CAME FROM AND TAKEN TO A PLACE AND USED IN SUCH A MANNER THAT IT CAN ONLY REMAIN AS A REPRESENTATION OF WHAT IT WAS WHERE IT CAME FROM, 1980, language + the materials referred to, dimensions variable. © 2018 Lawrence Weiner / Artist Rights Society (ARS), New York. Collection of the Art Institute of Chicago.

Christopher Williams
Supplement '14 (Mixed Typologies) #6, 2014. Full color offset prints and adhesive tape on paper. 45 collages: 44 overall, 2 ½ × 90 inches (158.8 × 228.6 cm) each, framed: 12 ½ × 10 inches (31.8 × 25.4 cm) each, paper: 11 × 8 ½ inches (27.9 × 21.6 cm). 1 Framed: 12 ⅜ × 8 ¾ inches (31.4 × 22.2 cm). Paper: 11 × 8 ½ inches (27.9 × 21.6 cm). © Christopher Williams. Courtesy David Zwirner, New York/London/Hong Kong and Galerie Gisela Capitain, Cologne. "Christopher Williams in conversation with Mark Godfrey," in *Afterall 16* (2007), 62–70. Reprinted by permission of the University of Chicago Press.

Andrew Norman Wilson
Workers Leaving the Googleplex, 2011. Courtesy of the artist.

All Conversations (Rosler, Shore, Douglas, Steyerl, Thomas) © 2018 Walead Beshty and the authors, respectively.

abstraction, 22, 28–29, 252, 723, 730–31, 749, 758, 761
Adorno, Theodor, 314, 733, 791, 840
aesthetics, 23, 25–26, 30–31, 303, 313–15, 538, 634–35, 650
Agamben, Giorgio, 29, 31, 175, 321, 686–87, 791
Akomfrah, John, 533–41
Alberti, Leon Battista, 25, 274, 283–84, 287, 442, 829
algorithms, 523, 592–93, 670, 825, 828–29
Althusser, Louis, 30, 441–43, 534, 655
American Surfaces, 812–13, 815–17
Animal Locomotion, 196, 199–200, 202, 207
anthropology, 368, 516, 641
anthropometry, 181–84, 194
apparatus, 25–26, 185–86, 240–42, 252, 304, 306–8, 512–17, 791
technical, 443, 681
apparatuses, criticism of, 514–15
appropriation, 102, 289, 291, 489–91, 494–95, 535, 679, 694, 833–34
Arbeiter-Illustrierte Zeitung, 296, 298–99
Arbus, Diane, 748, 751
Arcades Project, 840
architecture, 278, 280, 291–93, 310, 681, 796, 806, 828–29
Arendt, Hannah, 367, 687, 690–91, 696, 703, 707
Aristotle, 177, 277, 281, 286, 442, 758
Arnheim, Rudolf, 307, 309, 527
Artforum, 88, 403, 426, 429, 439, 458, 473, 476
art history, 303–4, 452–53, 492, 494, 744, 746, 789, 792
artificial intelligence, 593–97
art magazines, 404–5, 811
artwork, 268, 300–314, 403–5, 450–53, 709–10, 725, 737, 793–94
art world, 25, 404, 491, 638, 641–43, 720, 723–24, 811
Atget, Eugene, 86–88, 304
Attitudes of Animals in Motion, 195, 202–3, 208
Auschwitz, 320–27, 608, 662, 697, 699
authorship, 84–85, 88, 308, 495–96, 538
automation, 26, 397, 515–16, 591–92, 594
visual, 591–93, 595–97

bare life, 31, 686–87, 708–9
Barthes, Roland, 45, 48, 51, 122–23, 360, 475–76, 481, 488, 497, 649–56, 660–62, 690, 697, 701–2, 746, 748, 773, 794
Bateson, Gregory, 836–37
Baudelaire, Charles, 313, 481, 490, 494–95
Benjamin, Walter, 101, 176, 300, 302, 304–5, 308–9, 311–15, 489–90, 492–93, 495, 524, 527, 673, 680–81, 688, 700, 730, 748, 772–74, 791
Bertillon, Alphonse, 179, 184, 194
Bertillon System of Criminal Identification, 183–84, 194
Black Audio Film Collective, 532–33, 535, 537, 539, 541
bodies, depiction of human, 179, 194, 207–8, 310, 527, 593, 668, 743–44
Brassaï, 471–73
Brief Historical Sketch (*see also* Fox Talbot, William Henry), 44–45, 47–50, 53
Brunelleschi, Filippo, 25, 274, 283–84
bulletin board systems (BBS), 32
Burgin, Victor, 535

camera, 143–44, 308–10, 324–26, 439–46, 513–14, 549–53, 692–95, 699–705
instant, 201, 695, 812
motion picture, 229, 242
plastic lens, 813
Camera Lucida, 123, 481, 483, 592, 652–55, 690, 697, 746
camera obscura, 48–49, 51–52, 83–84, 219–20, 441–42, 463–64, 485–86, 688–89
camouflage, 321–23, 671, 798
Campt, Tina, 805, 807, 809
canvas, 123, 159, 203, 399, 439, 709, 717, 721
carte de visite, 119–20, 122–24, 286–87, 692
cartography, 85, 89–92, 98, 284–86, 288, 291, 536, 610
Cavell, Stanley, 85, 439
chance, 152, 156, 513, 515–16, 522, 538, 601, 822
chemistry, 45, 98, 587, 688, 720
chronophotography, 212–13, 215–21, 315
cinefluorography, 242–43
cinema, 83–88, 176–78, 435–47, 451–54, 520–24, 587–90, 686–87, 789–98
expanded, 791, 796–98
history of, 442, 587, 589
revolutionary, 435–36
cinematic dispositif, 791–92
cinematic images, 720, 790, 793–96, 798, 800, 806, 819, 823
cinematography, 175–76, 218, 240–41, 243–45, 252, 306, 315, 444
citizenship, 636, 639, 686, 694, 698–700, 702–5
Civil Rights Movement, 28, 368–70, 805, 810

Civil War, 90, 92, 103–4, 119–20, 122, 124, 141, 588–89
CNN, 660, 672–73
cognition, 94, 105, 268, 592, 595, 733, 761
Cold War, 594, 661, 669, 678–81, 768, 836
Cologne, 833–34
colonialism, 138, 289–90, 292, 533, 535–36, 718, 730–31, 810
Colorchromes (*see also* Jackson, William Henry), 114, 117
color photography, 309, 359, 365, 369, 465, 634, 640, 642
commons, 21, 23, 25, 27, 29–33, 143, 246, 249
compression, 81, 335, 588, 713–15
computer graphics, 591–93, 595, 597, 733, 796
computers, human, 337–39
computer vision, 591, 593–97
conceptual art, 361, 403, 405, 453, 746, 772
constructivism, 404, 536, 672
contemporary art, 21–22, 452, 465, 489–90, 581, 671, 772, 774
control, 25–28, 225–27, 230, 307–8, 337, 668–70, 691, 694–95
copy, 40, 56, 89, 182, 301, 359, 758–59, 761
corporations, 32–33, 99, 201, 208, 225–26, 230, 826
Crary, Jonathan, 42, 200, 205, 244, 689, 692, 699, 792–93
crematoria, 320–26
CRT (cathode ray tube), 837
CT (computed tomography), 96, 119, 121, 243–44, 261, 275
Cultural Techniques, 29, 282, 284–85, 287, 289–91, 293
cybernetics, 26–27, 514, 516, 668

Daguerre, Louis, 41–42, 46, 56, 120, 464, 688–89, 820
daguerreotype, 42, 46, 54–56, 119, 135, 471, 688–90, 700
Damisch, Hubert, 284–86, 463–64
dark space, 324, 789, 794, 797
Darwin, Charles, 42, 103, 769
daylight, usage in photography, 56, 215, 314, 472, 770
Death Mask, 176, 316, 319
Delahaye, Luc, 175, 736–37
Deleuze, Gilles, 176, 200, 282, 527, 668–69, 702, 797
Derrida, Jacques, 441, 472, 527, 652
Descartes, Rene, 204, 283, 512–13, 652
Didion, Joan, 833, 835, 838, 840
Dijkstra, Rineke, 746–49
dispositif, 789–97, 799
distributed image, 772–75
distributed networks, 668–70, 826
documentary, 361, 537–38, 568–73, 587–88, 602, 634–43, 671–73, 709–11
  filmmaking, 219, 569, 571, 634–36, 640, 643
  photography, 326–27, 361, 370, 496, 581, 636–37, 640–41
  social, 634–35, 637, 639–42
"documentary style", 361
Douglas, Stan, 549, 792, 817–18, 821, 823
Douglass, Frederick, 120–24, 576–77, 815
Duchamp, Marcel, 404, 490–91, 494
Dürer, Albrecht, 274–75, 591, 593, 758

Eakins, Thomas, 200, 204, 208
Edison, Thomas, 200, 218, 225, 524, 528–29, 723, 793
Eisenstein, Sergei, 86, 315
Électro-physiologie photographique, 63–67
entropy, 26–28, 334, 525
environment, 27, 104, 223, 303, 308, 369, 512, 769–71
ethics, 31, 177, 454, 638, 643, 702–3, 705, 748–49
Euclid, 277–78
Evans, Walker, 92, 340, 342–48, 359–61, 475, 495–96, 500, 503, 834, 839
exhibition, 23–25, 81–82, 142, 465, 492–93, 722, 725, 793–94
  space of, 81, 84–85, 493

factory, 225, 227, 292, 586–91, 609–10, 618–20, 623–25, 679
Farocki, Harun, 586–87, 590, 658–59
film, 303–10, 415–17, 434–39, 519–27, 536–41, 587–89, 707–11, 790–98
  commercial, 415–16, 521
  early, 588–90, 796–97
  experimental, 519, 720, 723, 733
  motion picture, 216, 220, 229, 242, 325–26, 519–20, 581
filmmakers, 435, 438, 521–22, 569, 571–72, 711, 805, 808
First World War, 224, 260–61, 640
Fisher, Morgan, 414–15, 518–19, 521–22
flash, 61, 148, 267, 816–18
Flavin, Dan, 403–4
Flusser, Vilem, 25–27, 512, 558–59, 680–81
FOIA (Freedom of Information Act), 683
***Fortune* magazine**, 340, 342–48, 359–60
Foucault, Michel, 30, 48, 85, 88, 282, 371, 524–25, 539, 639, 661, 669, 672, 704
Fox Talbot, William Henry, 41–52, 57, 476, 688
Frampton, Hollis, 476, 522
France, 179, 183–84, 262, 610, 612–13, 615–16, 619, 699
French Society of Photography, 214, 690
Freud, Sigmund, 441, 444, 769–70
Friedlander, Lee, 542
Friedrich, Ernst, 254, 256, 260, 262–63

Fusco, Coco, 120, 533–41
Futurism, 242, 310–11

gaze, 144, 269, 364, 484–85, 690–91, 696–97, 707, 732–33
industrial, 206, 208
Gide, Andre, 471–72
Gilbreth, Frank B., 228–30, 238–39, 315
glass plate negatives, 56, 233, 266, 693
Godard, Jean-Luc, 521, 538, 678, 709
Golden Caribbean, 125, 127, 129, 131, 133, 138
Google, 32, 669, 827
gramophone, 312, 523–25, 527, 529, 531, 771
grid, cartographic, 81, 284, 293
grids, 29, 205, 282–87, 289–93, 527, 530, 721, 724
Grigsby, Darcy Grimaldo, 24, 119–20, 364
Grosz, George, 261, 489
guerrilla cinema, 435–38

Haacke, Hans, 492–93, 709
Hague, James D., 98, 106
Handsworth Songs, 532, 536–37, 539
handwriting, 339, 449, 526–27, 529–31
Harper's New Monthly Magazine, 92, 95
Harris, Lyle Ashton, 546, 548, 584
Heartfield, John, 261, 296, 489, 494
Heidegger, Martin, 282, 285, 312–14, 529, 770
"High Rockies" (see also *Harper's New Monthly Magazine*), 68, 71, 73, 75, 77, 79, 84, 92
Hill, Gary, 788–89
Hine, Lewis, 101, 246, 248–50, 484, 637–38
Hirschhorn, Thomas, 742–43, 745
historicism, 267, 272, 602
Hollywood, 519, 569, 573, 722, 792, 806, 824
Holmes, Oliver Wendell, 54, 83
Holocaust, 141, 326, 581
holography, 789, 796
Homes for America, 361, 492
"Homes of Americans" (see also *Fortune* magazine), 348, 359–61
homo sacer, 31, 686–87
The Horse in Motion, 201–2, 204–5
Human Condition, 670, 690, 696, 703
Human Use of Human Beings (*see also* Weiner, Norbert), 26–27
Husserl, Edmund, 444–45, 472, 476, 487, 653, 769

Ideological Effects of the Basic Cinematographic Apparatus, 441, 443, 445, 447
illusion, 54, 59, 216–17, 398–99, 475, 730, 789–91, 797–98
illustrated magazines, 266, 270–71, 302, 304, 481
image economy, 700, 708
Image Ethics: The Moral Rights of Subjects in Photographs, Film and Television, 640, 692
image processing, 594–95
image production, 572, 593, 674, 701, 772, 774, 827
imagery, mass-produced, 491, 495
images, 212–21, 266–72, 439–46, 473–76, 587–96, 634–42, 688–704, 788–800
chronophotographic, 219–20
collection of, 260, 571
compressed, 713
consecutive, 196–99
digital, 774
documentary, 368, 584, 634, 637, 639, 642, 673
double, 58, 471, 476
equestrian, 208
first, 213, 220, 316
informative, 30, 512, 515
new, 137, 215, 222, 488, 774
phantasmagoric, 794–96
produced, 215, 772–74
projected, 202, 439, 548, 595, 794, 797–98
second, 213, 220, 746
stereoscopic, 54–61, 82–83, 137–39, 144, 205, 229, 732, 793
successive, 212, 218, 220, 416
technical, 25–26, 33, 283, 793, 812, 834, 836, 839
visual, 244, 262, 275–76, 465, 577
industrialization, 23–25, 47, 81, 203, 205, 292, 569, 702
information, 26–29, 98–99, 328–31, 515–17, 592–94, 713–14, 717–18, 772–74
infrastructuralism, 768–71

Jafa, Arthur, 804–5, 807, 809
Jamaica, 135–39, 141–44, 533, 737
Jet, 578–79, 648
journalism, 25, 361, 634–35, 672, 744
JPEG, 713, 715–16, 822

Kahn, Fritz, 264–65
Kippenberger, Martin, 834
kinetoscope, 200, 218, 524, 529, 793
King, Clarence, 80, 89–91, 93–94, 97, 103, 105–6
King, Rodney, 572, 574–78, 580–81
Kittler, Friedrich, 524–26, 771
Kodak, 812–13
Kracauer, Sigfried, 141, 266–67, 269

labor, 99, 136, 140, 144, 207–8, 222–24, 227–28, 360–61
"Labor Anonymous" (see also *Fortune* magazine), 360–61
Lacan, Jacques, 313, 524, 528
landscape, 56–60, 81–82, 84–85, 102–3, 105, 138–39, 476, 680
landscape painting, 81, 103, 280
landscape photography, 80, 89, 92
language, 103–4, 260, 334–35, 474–75, 490,

493–94, 537, 747–48
universal, 652, 654, 656
Lazarus, Jason, 364, 366, 368, 370
lens, 212–13, 215, 217–19, 240–45, 442, 445, 637–38, 816–17
camera, 61, 240–41, 659, 679
Levine, Sherrie, 493–97, 500
Lévi-Strauss, Claude, 474–75
***LIFE* magazine**, 372, 384–88, 390, 581
light
electric, 229, 338, 397, 403
rays, 36, 44, 54–55, 57, 234, 241–42, 485
ultra-violet, 233–34
lighting, 217, 219, 280, 307, 312–13, 403, 442, 463
linear perspective, 277, 721, 729–33, 818
lithography, 80, 89, 93, 101, 300, 524, 812
Los Angeles, 833–34, 840
Lumière, Louis and Auguste, 176, 225, 240–42, 244, 569, 587–89
lynching, 365, 574–76, 579, 581, 648–51, 653, 656

Machine Perception of Three-Dimensional Solids, 592, 595
magazines, 262, 270, 359–61, 404–5, 449, 636, 638, 810–11
Manovich, Lev, 591, 593, 773
Mapplethorpe, Robert, 465–67, 484–85
maps, *See* cartography
Marey, Etienne-Jules, 171, 176, 200, 204, 222–30, 315
Marker, Chris, 510, 527, 538
Markoff process, 333–34
Martens, Renzo, 706–7, 711
Marx, Karl, 270–71, 300, 315, 450, 454, 490, 534, 601, 639, 769, 771
mass culture, 22, 491–92, 642
mass media, 52, 261, 312, 314–15, 361, 635, 696–97, 820
"A Mathematical Theory of Communication" (*see also* Shannon, Claude), 328, 331, 333, 335
McLuhan, Marshall, 397, 528, 769, 771
MDR (Mandatory Declassification Review), 683
measurement, 93, 112–13, 170, 194, 222, 224, 229–30, 240–42
mechanization, 31, 200–201, 205–7, 398–99, 516, 531, 591
media history, 314–15
media technologies, 313, 528–30, 792
media theory, 312–14, 771
Meins, Holger, 608
Mendieta, Ana, 288
Mick-o-Matic Camera, 812–13
microscopy, 42, 242
Mikhailov, Boris, 598, 601, 603
mimesis, 650, 724, 758–60, 795
mining industry, 32, 89–90, 92, 94, 98–102, 106, 109, 621–22
mirror, 54–55, 216–17, 445–46, 470–76, 529–30, 537, 559, 643
Modern Art, 22, 82, 86–87, 280, 452, 593, 746–49, 793
modernism, 81, 88, 452, 491, 493–95, 635, 791
modernity, 200, 203–4, 282–83, 669–70, 729–31, 768, 772, 791
Monodramas (*see also* Douglas, Stan), 549, 551, 553, 819–20
montage, 260–61, 305, 307, 441, 489–90, 492–96, 798, 827–28
motion study, 176, 228–30, 238
mourning, 487, 571, 650–51, 656
moving images, 214, 587, 592, 789–90, 793–94, 799–800, 820, 823
museums, 81–82, 85–88, 261–63, 465, 642, 680–81, 688–90, 748–49
music, 549, 587–88, 650–52, 654, 656, 723–24, 760–61, 805–6
music television, 640
Muybridge, Eadweard, 24, 175, 195–96, 200–208, 212–13, 216–17, 314–15, 462

Nadar, 482, 484, 527
narrative, 48, 365–66, 368, 575, 581, 689, 748, 806
National Endowment for the Arts (NEA), 465
negatives, 60, 86, 112, 186, 201, 316, 327, 475
nervous system, 338, 566, 578, 800, 806
networks, 25, 434, 470, 473, 513, 668–70, 826, 828
Neumann machines, 531
Nevada, 80, 93–94, 98, 100, 102, 816
New Institutional Critique, 707, 709, 711
New York, 81–82, 87–92, 119–23, 145–47, 149–54, 202–4, 524–30, 578–79
New York Times, 119, 359, 580–81, 707, 795
Nietzsche, Friedrich, 176, 313, 315, 530, 639
noise, 27–30, 306, 312, 474, 523, 526, 529–30, 648

objectivity, 42, 559, 568, 572, 635, 639–40, 671–72, 674
optics
antique, 277
lenticular, 240, 242–44
seventeenth-century, 84
Osborne, Peter, 772, 774–75
O'Sullivan, Timothy, 80, 82–83, 89, 92, 97, 105

painting, 283–84, 303–5, 439, 471–73, 491–94, 730–31, 789–91, 796–98
Panofsky, Erwin, 176, 274, 278, 730, 818, 821–22, 826, 829
panorama, 94, 471, 793, 818
Parks, Gordon, 372, 384–87
patents, 42, 218, 229–30, 240, 723, 793
Pencil of Nature (*see also* Fox Talbot, William

Henry), 36, 39, 42–49, 51–53
perception, 96, 275, 301–2, 310, 312–15, 490, 568, 761
performance, 28–29, 227, 305–8, 310, 648–56, 720, 722, 795–96
perspective, 81–82, 274–81, 442, 591–93, 596–97, 729–34, 820–22, 824–29
analytic, 82, 84
history of, 267, 280, 596
phantasmagoria, 36, 39, 42–49, 51–53, 788–91, 793–800
phantasmagoric dispositif, 686–87, 689, 691, 693–705, 788–89, 791, 793–97, 799–800
phenomenology, 83, 463–64, 526, 653–54, 788, 790
philosophy, 91, 178, 314, 316–17, 515–17, 530, 668, 670
Phi Phenomenon, 414–17
photogram, 45, 484, 822
photographic apparatus, 93, 270, 515, 651, 679, 689
photographic archive, 88, 135, 140–41, 145, 200, 272, 327
photographic plates, 48–49, 51, 212–13, 233–34, 240, 302, 528
photographic portraits, 119–20, 122–24
photographic processes, 24, 46, 124, 135, 471, 475
photographic representation of African Americans, 122, 124, 574–78, 581, 636–37, 655, 700
photographic subjects, 139–40, 144, 637, 749
photographic universe, 512–16
photography, 41–62, 79–94, 135–48, 222–30, 266–73, 480–89, 648–56, 686–705
black-and-white, 359, 485, 640
citizenry of, 686, 694, 698–99, 701–4
close-up, 578, 648
crime scene, 813
discussion of medium, 123, 145, 314, 489, 701
erotic, 482, 484–85
history of, 85–86, 88, 120, 463, 516, 602, 689
invention of, 41, 43, 476, 485, 688–92, 697, 699–701, 820
mining, 31, 101
motion, 201, 206, 216, 218
nineteenth-century, 85, 88, 135, 138, 140–41
nineteenth-century landscape, 80
philosophy of, 25, 512, 515–17, 680
physiology, 62, 170, 173, 209, 211, 265, 512, 530
picture plane, 274–75, 822
Pictures Generation, 833–34, 838
Pop art, 404–5, 491, 497, 678–79, 798, 810
pornography, 326, 465–66, 484–85, 735, 795, 813
positivism, 41, 44–45, 49, 642
postcards, 137, 680, 812–16
postmodernism, 535–36, 643, 791
poverty, 147, 149, 151, 487, 601–2, 706–7, 711, 720
projection, 214, 217–19, 276–78, 437, 443–45, 789, 796–98, 819
proletariat, 255, 300, 490
psychology, 26, 176, 228, 327, 399, 512, 516, 529–30
public domain, 91, 99–100, 121, 285, 289, 692, 700, 736
punctum, 481–85, 653, 655, 746

Rabinbach, Anson, 207, 223–24
radiography, 240, 242–45, 252
Reagan, Ronald, 835–36
representation, 80–81, 83–85, 122–24, 472, 533–35, 672–74, 758–61, 820–23
pictorial, 271, 489, 760, 826
politics of, 31, 672–73
reproducibility, 46, 302, 304, 312
reproduction, 139–41, 252, 271, 300–302, 305, 312, 404–5, 737–38
photo offset, 406
technological, 300–301, 306, 312–14, 524
Riis, Jacob, 24, 146, 162, 637–38, 812
Röntgen, Wilhelm, 231–33
Rosler, Martha, 408, 410, 493, 495–96, 634, 709, 810
Rowland, Cameron, 194, 801
Ruling Spaces, 29, 282, 285, 287, 289, 291, 293
Ruscha, Ed, 522, 772, 812, 814–15
Ruskin, John, 103

Sander, August, 316–19, 639
Sander, Erich, 316–19
scientific experimentation, 41–45, 53, 62, 434
scientific knowledge, 208, 219, 222, 226, 244
scientific management, 224, 227–28, 230
sculpture, 22–23, 303, 305, 558–59, 722, 789–91, 793–94, 796–98
Second World War, 141, 316, 524, 796
Sekula, Allan, 31, 100–101, 122, 697, 709
self-portraiture, 208, 316, 364, 370, 548, 641
sexuality, 466, 533, 539, 583
shadows, 43–44, 56, 120, 233–34, 439, 475–76, 725, 816–17
Sherman, Cindy, 493, 749
Shore, Stephen, 412, 812, 815, 817
Signalment, theoretical study of, 179, 181–83, 185, 189, 191, 193
signification, 51, 441, 474–76, 535, 652, 759, 761
slavery, 119–24, 135–43, 145, 321, 399, 575–78, 731, 733
slides, 58, 175–76, 218, 512, 548, 559, 720–22, 724–25
Smithson, Robert, 403, 476, 722
snapshot, 32, 175, 271, 325, 548, 584, 812–13, 816
social media, 24, 743, 828
society, post-industrial, 25, 513, 515, 594, 678
sociology, 228, 533, 540, 641, 678

software, 669–70, 731, 759, 769, 792
Sojourner Truth, 24, 118–24
Solanas, Fernando, 433–34
Sontag, Susan, 485, 700, 702–3, 709
Stanford, Leland, 24, 200–205, 207–8, 212, 314
Steyerl, Hito, 671, 674, 728–29, 733–34, 757, 772, 825, 827, 829
street photography, 640–42, 736–37
Strike Objects, 609, 611, 613, 615, 617, 619, 621, 623
surveillance, 51, 143, 145, 587, 594, 718, 729, 731–32
symbolic forms, 92, 274–75, 277, 279, 281, 818
Systematic Geology, 80, 82, 89, 94, 96, 98, 103

Taylorism, 227
technological reproducibility, 21, 23, 25, 27, 29, 31, 300–303, 305
technology, 225–26, 303–4, 308–9, 311–13, 566–69, 688–89, 770, 817–19
television, 313–14, 555, 558–59, 577–78, 717, 792, 794–96, 823–24
television sets, 550, 789–90, 799, 816
testimony, 39, 48–49, 51, 278, 321–23, 325–26, 487, 641–42
text-image relations, 47–49, 51, 495
theory, communication, 26–27, 329, 333
Till, Emmett, 364–65, 367–71, 576, 578–80, 648–51, 653, 656
tomography, 240–44
Tourette, Georges Giles de la, 170, 175
Trachtenberg, Alan, 81, 89, 92, 135, 141, 689
Trump, Donald J., 836
Turing, Alan, 337, 530–31

United States Geological Survey, 89, 91, 112–13

video, 558–59, 568, 571–73, 578, 720–24, 792, 796, 799
video camera, 558, 596, 720, 799
video images, 596, 788, 794
video installations, 722, 791, 796, 799
videotape, 465, 558–59, 574–75, 581, 794
violence, 366, 369–70, 574–78, 580, 589, 692, 696–98, 719
Virilio, Paul, 660, 796
vision, 54, 200–201, 276–78, 594–95, 729–31, 733, 789–90, 827
visual culture, 139, 141, 200, 710, 731–32
Vitruvius, 278–79
VR, 566, 749, 818

war, 88–89, 254–57, 259–63, 310–11, 659–62, 720–21, 743–44, 810–11
Warhol, Andy, 390–91, 491, 796
Watkins, Carleton, 90–92, 101
Wayne, John, 835
Wiener, Norbert, 26–28, 836–37, 840
Whitman, Walt, 790, 794, 796–98
Williams, Christopher, 676, 678, 681–82, 748
Workers Leaving, 236, 569, 586–89, 740
writing, 486, 490, 492, 523–31, 533–34, 652, 655, 724

X-rays, 231, 233–34, 240, 242

Thanks

Joree Aidlman
Christopher d'Amelio
Elaine Angelopoulos
Vickie Arndt
Emily Bates
The Estate of Gretchen Bender
Aslaku Berhanu
Natasha Berokoff
Maria Anna Bierwirth
Charles L. Blockson Afro-American
Collection, Temple University
Kristina Bonjekovic
Gavin Brown
Irene Calderoni
Emanuela Campoli
Allie Card
Andrea Cashman
Lori Cassady
Linda Chinfen
Alicie Conconi
Peter Currie
Jenny Daly
Stephanie Daniel
Mairikke Dau
Thilo and Uta von Debschitz
Shelley Dowell
Kevin Downs
Antje Ehmann
Elle Magazine
Robbie Myers
Evan Campisi
Ken Gawrych
Stravinski Pierre
Jake Forney
Anne-Marie Garcia
Alanna Gedgaudas
Kristina Gell
Marie-Laure Gilles
Tara Hadibrata
Erin Hael
Daniel Herleth
Mary Howard
Nick Irvin
Natasa Ivancevic
Saskia Kahn
Patrice Kane
Dmitry Komis
Hans P. Kraus Jr.
Peter W. Kunhardt, Jr.
Ellen Langan
David Lewis
Megan Liberty
Parrisah Lin
Jennifer Loh
Romain Lopez
Linda Loschiavo
Theresa Luisotti
Bruce Lundberg
Dylan Lustrin
Carla Mantovani
Meriwether McClorey
Mara McKevitt
Laure Menetrier
Vita Mikhailov
Gregory Miller
Cora Muennich
Sheldon Mukamal
Tamar Nahmias
Josephine Nash
Marco Nocella
Mark Owens
Burcu Oz
Kat Parker
Erin Pauwels
Ruth Phaneuf
Kenneth Pietrobono
Wojciech Płosa
Armelle Pradalier
Cay Sophie Rabinowitz
Shaun Caley Regen
Karen Reimer
Lara von Richthofen
Jackie Rome
Don Ross
David Rozelle
Evelena Ruether
Matthew Salazar
Julian Sander
Michael Sappol
Jule Schaffer
Shira Schwarz
Karin Seinsoth
Jacqueline Sischy
Dorothee Sorge
Jonas Tebib
Ben Thornborough
Sam Trioli
Veronica Tyler
Jeff Wall
Michael Wiesehöfer

Publication and Exhibition Credits

Picture Industry: A Provisional History of the Technical Image, 1844–2018 is published on the occasion of *Picture Industry*, Luma Arles, October 12, 2018–January 6, 2019.

Picture Industry was initially commissioned and produced by the Luma Foundation for *Systematically Open? New Forms for Contemporary Image Production*, the inaugural group exhibition of La Mécanique Générale at the Parc des Ateliers in July 14–October 24, 2016.

The exhibition travelled to the Hessel Museum of Art, Center for Curatorial Studies, Bard College, Annandale-on-Hudson in June 24–December 15, 2017 in an expanded form, and returned to the Forges of the Parc des Ateliers in Arles in a new iteration on October 12, 2018–January 6, 2019.

Publication

Editor
Walead Beshty

Consulting Editor
Tom Eccles

Executive Editor
James Merle Thomas

Designer
Ria Roberts

Assistant Editor
Bryne Rasmussen

Editorial Coordinator
Molly Everett

Editorial Assistants
Jordan Garlic
Ryan Hupp

Editorial Consultant
Luz Gyalui

Copy Editors
Kate Norment
Dianne Woo
Lindsey Westbrook

Proofreaders
Michael J. Carroll
Laurel McLaughlin
Ramey Mize
Erin Riley-Lopez

Permissions
Andrew Blackley

Translators
Celia Abele

Transcribers
Audio Transcription Center
Kathleen Everett

Typeface
Univers
Stempel Garamond

Color Separation and Print
Musumeci S.p.A., Quart (Aosta)

Exhibition

Curator
Walead Beshty

Consulting Curator
Tom Eccles

Production
Luz Gyalui

Curatorial Assistant
Bryne Rasmussen

Luma

Registrar
Estelle Mury
assisted by
Emily Nirlo
Clément Chateau

Assistant Producer
Judith Wollner

Technical Coordination
Christophe Florio
Marc Bättig

Installation Team
Playtime Productions
Acoplast, IDZIA
Benmay

Visitors Program
Nathalie Israelian

Walead Beshty Studios Inc.

Studio Manager
John Ryan Moore

Exhibitions and Publications Manager
Bryne Rasmussen

Darkroom and Imaging Assistant
Robert Acklen-Brečko

Production Assistant
Thomas Lucero

Courtesy of the Collection of Walead Beshty Studios, Inc. Photos: Robert Acklen-Brečko, Walead Beshty Studios, Inc., 68–79, 106–111, 114–17, 125–134, 162–66, 168–69, 173–74, 180, 187–93, 209–211, 235, 246–51, 257–59, 265, 294–99, 340–57, 372–89, 392–96, 400–402, 412–13, 422–31, 448, 458–61, 506–509, 542–45, 762–67.

Luma Foundation was created in 2004 by Maja Hoffmann in Switzerland to support the activities of artists, independent pioneers, and organizations working in the visual and performing arts, photography, publishing, documentary filmmaking, and multimedia. Luma produces, supports, and enables challenging art projects committed to an expansive understanding of environmental issues, human rights, education, and culture.

In 2013, Hoffmann launched Luma Arles to plan, develop, and manage the Parc des Ateliers, an expansive former industrial site located in Arles, France.

Luma Arles includes a resource center designed by architect Frank Gehry; various industrial buildings rehabilitated by Selldorf Architects; and a public park designed by landscape architect Bas Smets.

A program of exhibitions and multidisciplinary projects is presented each year in the Parc des Ateliers newly rehabilitated venues of the Grande Halle, Les Forges, La Formation and the Mécanique Générale.

Luma Arles

Maja Hoffmann
Founder and Executive President

Artistic Core Group
Tom Eccles
Liam Gillick
Maja Hoffmann
Hans Ulrich Obrist
Philippe Parreno
Beatrix Ruf

Team

Mustapha Bouhayati
Chief Executive Officer, Head of Strategies
Mario Timbal
Chief Operating Officer
Sanjiv Gomez
Chief Financial Officer
Matthieu Humery
Curator at large, Living Archive Program

Luz Gyalui
Head of Production
assisted by
Estelle Mury
Judith Wollner

Pierre-Julien Tregouet
Facility Manager
Christophe Florio
Facilities and Exhibitions Technical Coordination
assisted by
Tony Guerrero
Anne Guardiola
Nicolas Pene

Nathalie Israelian
Head of Visitors Programs
assisted by
Coline Lacire
Lucie Martin
Camille Varlet

Press and Communication
Pierre Collet, Partner I Imagine, Paris
Sandra Roemermann
Communication manager
assisted by
Judith Wollner
Aurélie Padovan

Luma Foundation

Maja Hoffmann
Founding President

Anna von Brühl
Chief Executive Officer

The Center for Curatorial Studies and Hessel Museum of Art, Bard College

The Center for Curatorial Studies at Bard College (CCS Bard) was founded in 1990 as an exhibition and research center for the study of late twentieth-century and contemporary art and culture and to explore experimental approaches to the presentation of these topics and their impact on our world. Since 1994, the Center for Curatorial Studies and its graduate program have provided one of the world's most forward thinking teaching and learning environments for the research and practice of contemporary art and curatorship. Broadly interdisciplinary, CCS Bard encourages students, faculty and researchers to question the critical and political dimension of art, its mediation and its social significance. CCS Bard cultivates innovative thinking, radical research and new ways to challenge our understanding of the social and civic values of the visual arts. CCS Bard provides an intensive educational program alongside its public events, exhibitions, and publications, which collectively explore the critical potential of the institutions and practices of exhibition-making. It is uniquely positioned within the larger Center's tripartite resources, which include the internationally renowned CCS Bard Library and Archives and the Hessel Museum of Art, with its rich permanent collection.

www.bard.edu/ccs

Colophon

ISBN 978-3-03764-502-4

Printed in Europe

Cover Design © 2018 by Ria Roberts
Image: *Fritz Kahn, Der Mensch als Industriepalast,* 1926
Artwork © Fritz Kahn Estate / Kosmos Verlag

Distributed by

JRP|Ringier
Limmatstrasse 270
CH–8005 Zurich
www.jrp-ringier.com

JRP|Ringier publications are available internationally at selected bookstores and from the following distribution partners:

Switzerland
AVA Verlagsauslieferung AG
Centralweg 16, CH–8910 Affoltern a.A.
avainfo@ava.ch
www.ava.ch

Germany and Austria
Vice Versa Distribution GmbH
Potsdamer Str. 93, D-10785 Berlin
info@viceversaartbooks.com
www.viceversaartbooks.com

France
Les presses du réel
35 rue Colson, F–21000 Dijon
info@lespressesdureel.com
www.lespressesdureel.com

UK and other European countries
Cornerhouse Publications, HOME
2 Tony Wilson Place, UK–Manchester M15 4FN
publications@cornerhouse.org
www.cornerhousepublications.org

USA, Canada, Asia, and Australia
ARTBOOK | D.A.P.
75 Broad Street, Suite 630
US-New York, NY 10004
orders@dapinc.com
www.artbook.com

For a list of our partner bookshops or for any general questions, please contact JRP|Ringier directly at info@jrp-ringier.com, or visit our homepage www.jrp-ringier.com for further information about our program.